# DICTIONARY
## OF
# INTERNATIONAL
# TRADE
## 7th Edition

Handbook of the Global Trade Community
Includes 26 Key Appendices

This book is dedicated to the memory of my father
**Allen Joseph Hinkelman**
who taught me the meaning of many words.

# DICTIONARY
## OF
# INTERNATIONAL
# TRADE
## 7th Edition

Handbook of the Global Trade Community
Includes 26 Key Appendices

## Edward G. Hinkelman

with contributions by:
Sibylla Putzi • Paul Denegri • Myron Manley • C.H. Wooley
Karla Shippey, J.D. • Philip Auerbach • Jonathan Clark
Greenbrier Companies • Zisser Customs Law Group • William "Jerry" Peck
U.S. Customs and Border Protection
John O'Conner • U.S. Department of Commerce • BNSF
International Chamber of Commerce (ICC) • Sea Land Shipping
IATA (International Air Transport Association)
Air Transport Association (of the U.S.) • CIGNA Worldwide
Insurance Company of North America • World Bank
Swiss Bank Corporation • Wells Fargo HSBC Trade Bank

**WORLD TRADE PRESS**®
*Books • E-Content • Databases • Maps • Software*

**World Trade Press**
800 Lindberg Lane, Suite 190
Petaluma, California 94952 USA
Tel: [1] (707) 778-1124; Fax: [1] (707) 778-1329
U.S. Order Line: [1] (800) 833-8586 x 203
E-mail: sales@worldtradepress.com
www.WorldTradePress.com
www.WorldTradeREF.com
www.BestCountryReports.com
www.GiantMapArt.com
www.GlobalRoadWarrior.com
www.HowToConnect.com
www.AtlasCartographic.com
Edward G. Hinkelman E-mail: ed@worldtradepress.com

**Disclaimer**

This publication is designed to provide information concerning the terminology used in international trade and the businesses that support international trade. It is sold with the understanding that the publisher is not engaged in rendering legal or any other professional service. If legal advice or other expert assistance is required, the services of a competent professional should be sought.

## Library of Congress Cataloging-in-Publication Data:

Hinkelman, Edward G., 1947–
      Dictionary of international trade : handbook of the global trade community, includes 21 key
appendices / Edward G. Hinkelman ; with contributions by Sibylla Putzi ... [et al.]. -- 7th ed.
        p. cm.
    Includes bibliographical references.
    ISBN 1-885073-73-9
    1. International trade--Dictionaries. 2. United States--Commerce Dictionaries.
I. Sibylla Putzi - II Title.
HF1373.H55 2006
382'.03--dc22                         2006054964

**Printed in the United States of America**

# Table of Contents

Dictionary of International Trade ............................................................... 7 – 182
Appendices
Acronyms and Abbreviations ................................................................... 183
Country Codes (ISO 3166) ..................................................................... 197
International Dialing Guide ...................................................................... 203
International Dialing Codes ...................................................................... 206
Currencies of the World .......................................................................... 220
Business Entities Worldwide .................................................................... 228
Weights and Measures ............................................................................ 236
Guide to INCOTERMS 2000 .................................................................. 247
Guide to Letters of Credit ....................................................................... 276
Computer Terms ..................................................................................... 293
Resources for International Trade ............................................................ 304
Web Resources ....................................................................................... 318
Guide to Trade Documents ..................................................................... 335
Ship Illustrations ..................................................................................... 361
Guide to Ocean Freight Containers ........................................................ 373
Seaports of the World ............................................................................. 401
Airplane Illustrations ............................................................................... 436
Guide to ULDs (Unit Load Devices/ Air Freight Containers) .................... 444
World Airports by IATA Code ................................................................. 453
World Airports by Airport ....................................................................... 494
Guide to Truck Trailers ........................................................................... 535
Guide to Railcars .................................................................................... 547
Guide to International Sourcing (Outsourcing) ......................................... 559
Global Supply Chain Security .................................................................. 583
    Security and the Supply Chain ............................................................. 584
    Customs-Trade Partnership Against Terrorism (C-TPAT) .................... 586
    Free and Secure Trade (FAST) ............................................................ 618
    C-TPAT Seal Requirements ................................................................. 623
    Container Security Initiative (CSI) ........................................................ 625
    U.S. FDA Food Facility Registration .................................................... 628
    International Ship and Port Facility Security (ISPS) Code ..................... 630
    Data Security ...................................................................................... 632
    Industrial Espionage ............................................................................ 634
    Glossary of Security Terms .................................................................. 637
    ACE (Automated Commercial Environment) ....................................... 649
    Pre-Arrival Processing System (PAPS) ................................................. 650
    Pre-Arrival Review System (PARS) ...................................................... 650
    Automated Manifest System ............................................................... 651
    Advance Manifest Regulations (1/2-, 1-, 2-, 24-Hour Rules, etc.) ........ 652
Key Words in 8 Languages ...................................................................... 662
Selected Quotations ................................................................................ 704
Regional Maps of the World .................................................................... 705

# A

### (a)(1)(A) List
(U.S. Customs) A list issued by U.S. Customs and Border Protection (CBP) of documents and records that U.S. importers and others must keep, retain, and, if the CBP demands, produce, or be subject to administrative penalties.

### abandonment
(shipping/insurance) (a) The act of refusing delivery of a shipment so badly damaged in transit that it is worthless. (b) Damage to a vessel that is so severe that it is considered a constructive total loss. *See* constructive total loss.

### abatement
(shipping) A deduction or discount given as a result of damage to a shipment or an overcharge in the payment of a bill.

### abbrochment
(law) The purchase at wholesale of all merchandise that is intended to be sold in a particular retail market for the purpose of controlling that market.

### Able-Bodied Seaman
(shipping) An experienced seaman in the merchant marine able to perform all routine duties on board a ship. Depending upon the vessel, these duties can include: standing watch, standing lookout, acting as helmsman, steering, handling rigging, operating a launch, operating cranes and gantries and other ship equipment. Able bodied seaman is the second level job of six towards becoming a capitan (ordinary seaman, able-bodied seaman, third mate, secon d mate, chief mate, captain).

### aboard
(shipping/logistics) (a) The placement or lading of cargo on any conveyance. (b) Cargo that has been placed or laden on any means of conveyance.

### about
(banking) In connection with letters of credit, "about" means a tolerance of plus/minus 10% regarding the letter of credit value, unit price or the quantity of the goods, depending on the context in which the tolerance is mentioned.

### above deck
(shipping) Location on or above the highest deck of a ship. Cargo or containers shipped above deck are subject to wind, rain and fluctuations in temperature. Some cargo, as a result of its size, must be shipped above deck. Some letters of credit and purchase contracts specifically forbid placement of cargo above deck.

### absolute advantage
(economics) The advantage of one nation or geographic region over another in the costs of manufacturing an item in terms of used resources.

### absorption
(economics) Investment and consumption purchases by households, businesses and governments, both domestic and imported. When absorption exceeds production, the excess is the country's current account deficit. *See* current account.

(shipping) The assumption by one carrier of the special charges of another carrier generally without increasing charges to the shipper.

### Accelerated Commercial Release Operation Support System (ACROSS)
(Canada Customs) A Canada Border Services Agency (CBSA) electronic data interchange (EDI) system that allows traders and brokers to file documents and transfer data to the CCRA 24 hours a day, 7 days a week. The system increases efficiency, decreases paperwork and speeds the release of shipments from Canada Customs. Shipment release information is provided to the CBSA through a computer to computer transmission rather than being submitted in a hard copy format on paper.

Under ACROSS, releases may be submitted in one of two methods, pre-arrival (PARS) or post-arrival and in any one of three following formats: The two most common cargo and release services, Release on Minimum Documentation (RMD) and Appraisal Quality Release (AQ) are available through ACROSS. The Frequent Importer Release System (FIRST), however, is not currently supported by the system.

- **R.M.D. Data** R.M.D. data describes basic shipment information such as who the goods were purchased by, to whom are they going, who are they from, when they shipped, the number of pieces, a general description of the goods imported (often times for enforcement purposes Customs will reject the release and ask for a better description) and a total value. Other basic information is also required.
- **Appraisal Quality** "Appraisal quality" release data requires the transmission of the complete Canada Customs Invoice along with other basic data elements such as the transaction number, etc.
- **Appraisal Quality with H.S.** The third type of release is appraisal quality with the Harmonized System tariff number attached. This is beneficial, when the importer, exporter and carrier of the goods all have good compliance records and have been approved by Customs for machine release.

For more information, go to: www.cbsa-asfc.gc.ca.

### accelerated tariff elimination
(customs) The gradual reduction of import duties over time. Accelerated tariff elimination is often a feature of free trade agreements. The North American Free Trade Agreement (NAFTA) is an example of a trade agreement with accelerated tariff elimination.

### acceptance
(law) (a) An unconditional assent to an offer. (b) An assent to an offer conditioned on only minor changes that do not affect any material terms of the offer. See counteroffer; offer.

(shipping) Receipt by the consignee of a shipment thus terminating the common carrier liability.

(banking) A time draft (bill of exchange) on the face of which the drawee has written "accepted" over his signature. The date and place payable are also indicated. The person accepting the draft is known as the acceptor. Note: The drawee's signature alone is a valid acceptance and is usually made across the left margin of the bill of exchange. *See* bank acceptance, bill of exchange.

### acceptance letter of credit
(banking) A letter of credit which, in addition to other required documents, requires presentation of a term draft drawn on the bank nominated as the accepting bank under the letter of credit. *See* acceptance; bank acceptance; letter of credit.

### accepted draft
(banking) A bill of exchange accepted by the drawee (acceptor) by putting his signature (acceptance) on its face. In doing so, he commits himself to pay the bill upon presentation at maturity. *See* acceptance; bank acceptance; bill of exchange.

**A**

### accepting bank
(banking) A bank who by signing a time draft accepts responsibility to pay when the draft becomes due. In this case the bank is the drawee (party asked to pay the draft), but only becomes the acceptor (party accepting responsibility to pay) upon acceptance (signing the draft). *See* acceptance; bill of exchange.

### acceptor
(banking) The party that signs a draft or obligation, thereby agreeing to pay the stated sum at maturity. *See* acceptance; bill of exchange.

### accession
The process by which a country becomes a member of an international agreement, such as the World Trade Organization (WTO), the GATT or the European Community (EC). Accession to the WTO involves negotiations to determine the specific obligations a nonmember country must undertake before it will be entitled to membership benefits. *See* accessions.

### accessions
(law) (a) Goods that are affixed to and become part of other goods. Examples include semiconductors that are inserted into computers, parts that are added onto vehicles and dials that are used in watches. (b) A nation's acceptance of a treaty already made between other countries. See accession.

### accessorial charges
(shipping) Charges made for additional, special, or supplemental services, normally over and above the line haul services.

### accessorial services
(shipping) Services performed by a shipping line or airline in addition to the normal transportation service. Common accessorial services include advancement of charges, pickup, delivery, C.O.D. service, signature service and storage.

### accommodation
(law) An action by one individual or legal entity (the accommodation party) that is taken as a favor, without any consideration, for another individual or legal entity (the accommodated party). An accommodation note or paper is a commercial instrument of debt that is issued by or for an accommodated party (who is expected to pay the debt) and that contains the name of the accommodation party. A person may make an accommodation, for example, to help another party raise money or obtain credit. An accommodation party is usually treated like a surety, who is responsible for the performance of the accommodated party. The distinction between an accommodation and a surety is that an accommodation is made without consideration, that is, it is freely given. *See* surety.

### accord and satisfaction
(law) A means of discharging a contract or cause of action by which the parties agree (the accord) to alter their obligations and then perform (the satisfaction) the new obligations. A seller who cannot, for example, obtain red fabric dye according to contract specifications and threatens to breach the contract may enter into an accord and satisfaction with the buyer to provide blue-dyed fabric for a slightly lower price.

### account number
(shipping) An identifying number issued by a carrier's accounting office to identify a shipper and/or consignee. The number helps ensure accurate invoicing procedures and customer traffic activity.

### account party
(banking) The party that instructs a bank (issuing bank) to open a letter of credit. The account party is usually the buyer or importer. *See* letter of credit.

### accounts payable
(accounting) A current liability representing the amount owed by an individual or a business to a creditor(s) for merchandise or services purchased on an open account or short-term credit. *See* accounts receivable.

### accounts receivable
(accounting) Money owed a business enterprise for merchandise or services bought on open account. *See* accounts payable.

### accrual of obligation
(law) The time at which an obligation matures or vests, requiring the obligor to perform. In a contract between a buyer and seller, for example, the seller's obligation to deliver goods may accrue when the buyer tenders payment in full. Alternatively, if the contract specifies a date for delivery of the goods, the seller's obligation accrues at that date, even if the buyer tenders payment before or after that date.

### ACE Stair Step
(Historic - U.S. Customs) The U.S. Customs and Border Protection (CBP) initial five-year plan for development of the Automated Commercial Environment (ACE), which l modernized CBP import processes. For more information, go to: www.cbp.gov.

### acquisition
The purchase of complete or majority ownership in a business enterprise, usually by another business enterprise.

### ACROSS
(Canada Customs) *See* Accelerated Commercial Release Operations Support System.

### Act of God
An act of nature beyond man's control such as lightning, flood, earthquake or hurricane. Many shipping and other performance contracts include a "force majeure" clause which excuses a party who breaches the contract due to Acts of God. *See* force majeure.

### action ex contractu
(law) A legal action for breach of a promise stated in an express or implied contract.

### action ex delicto
(law) (a) A legal action for a breach of a duty that is not stated in a contract but arises from the contract. A seller of goods, for example, who represents that the goods can be used for a certain purpose has a duty to furnish goods that can be so used, even if that duty is not stated in the contract. If the seller fails to provide such goods, the seller breaches that duty and the buyer has an action ex delicto based on the seller's fraudulent representation. (b) A legal action that arises from a wrongful act, such as fraud.

### activity-based costing (ABC)
(logistics) An accounting methodology that measures all the costs associated with a specific business activity regardless of organizational structure. The business activity can be the production, delivery or maintenance of a product or service.

### added-value tax
*See* value-added tax.

### address of record
(law) The official or primary location for an individual, company, or other organization.

### adhesion contract
(law) Contract with standard, often printed, terms for sale of goods and services offered to consumers who usually cannot negotiate any of the terms and cannot acquire the product unless they agree to the terms.

**adjustment**
(general) The refund or replacement of lost or damaged goods by either the seller or by an insurance carrier.
(insurance) The settlement of an insurance claim.
(U.S. government) The negative impact of increased import competition to U.S. businesses. See adjustment assistance.

**adjustment assistance**
(U.S. law) Financial, training and reemployment technical assistance to workers and technical assistance to firms and industries, to help them cope with adjustment difficulties arising from increased import competition. The objective of the assistance is usually to help an industry become more competitive in the same line of production, or to move into other economic activities. The aid to workers can take the form of training (to qualify the affected individuals for employment in new or expanding industries), relocation allowances (to help them move from areas characterized by high unemployment to areas where employment may be available) or unemployment compensation (to tide them over while they are searching for new jobs). The aid to firms can take the form of technical assistance through Trade Adjustment Assistance Centers located throughout the United States. Industry-wide technical assistance also is available through the Trade Adjustment Assistance program. The benefits of increased trade to an importing country generally exceed the costs of adjustment, but the benefits are widely shared and the adjustment costs are sometimes narrowly—and some would say unfairly—concentrated on a few domestic producers and communities. Adjustment assistance can also be designed to facilitate structural shifts of resources from less productive to more productive industries, contributing further to greater economic efficiency and improved standards of living. Trade Adjustment Assistance Centers: E-mail: info@taacenters.org; Web: www.taacenters.org. *See* Trade Adjustment Assistance Centers.

**Administrative Protective Order (APO)**
(U.S. law) An Administrative Protective Order, APO, is used to protect proprietary data that is obtained during an administrative proceeding. Within the U.S. Department of Commerce, APO is most frequently used in connection with antidumping and countervailing duty investigations to prohibit opposing counsel from releasing data. The term is also applied in connection with civil enforcement of export control laws to protect against the disclosure of information provided by companies being investigated for violations. A sample APO is available at http://ia.ita.doc.gov/apo/367-598.htm. *See* dumping; countervailing duties.

**admiralty**
(law/shipping) Any civil or criminal issue having to do with maritime law.

**admiralty court**
(law/shipping) A court of law that has jurisdiction over maritime legal issues. These generally include ocean shipping, collisions of vessels, charters, contracts and damage to cargo.

**admission temporaire**
(customs) The free entry of goods normally dutiable. *See* ATA Carnet.

**Admission Temporaire/ Temporary Admission Carnet**
*See* ATA Carnet.

**ad valorem**
Literally: according to value.
(general) Any charge, tax, or duty that is applied as a percentage of value.

(taxation) A tax calculated on the value of the property subject to the tax.
(shipping) A freight rate set at a certain percentage of the declared value of an article.
(U.S. Customs) Ad valorem duty. A duty assessed as a percentage rate or value of the imported merchandise. For example 5% ad valorem. *See* compound rate of duty; specific rate of duty; tariff.

**advance against collection**
(banking) A short term loan or credit extended to the seller (usually the exporter) by the seller's bank once a draft has been accepted by the buyer (generally the importer) of the seller's goods. Once the buyer pays, the loan is paid off. If the buyer does not pay the draft, the seller must still make good on the loan. *See* bill of exchange.

**advance arrangements**
(shipping) The shipment of certain classes of commodities—examples: gold, precious gems, furs, live animals, human remains and oversized shipments—require arrangements in advance with carriers.

**Advance Fee Fraud (AFF)**
(law) See 419 scam.

**advance shipment notice (ASN)**
(logistics) A document transmitted (by courier, fax or e-mail) to a consignee in advance of delivery detailing the contents and particulars of a shipment. The particulars may include such items as shipment date, method of transport, carrier, expected date and time of arrival and a full listing of contents.

**Advanced Technology Products (ATP)**
(U.S. trade law) About 500 of some 22,000 commodity classification codes used in reporting U.S. merchandise trade are identified as "advanced technology" codes and they meet the following criteria: (1) The code contains products whose technology is from a recognized high technology field (e.g., biotechnology); (2) These products represent leading edge technology in that field; and (3) Such products constitute a significant part of all items covered in the selected classification code.

**advancement of charges**
(shipping) A service under which a shipping line or airline, in some instances, pays incidental charges arising before or after a shipment or airhaul. Examples include cartage and warehousing costs. These charges can be in advance for the convenience of either the shipper or the receiver.

**advice**
(banking) The term "advice" connotes several types of forms used on the banking field. Generally speaking, an advice is a form of letter that relates or acknowledges a certain activity or result with regard to a customer's relations with a bank. Examples include credit advice, debit advice, advice of payment and advice of execution. In commercial transactions, information on a business transaction such as shipment of goods.
(banking/letters of credit) The forwarding of a letter of credit, or an amendment to a letter of credit to the seller, or beneficiary of the credit, by the advising bank (seller's bank). *See* issuance; letter of credit; amendment.

**advice of fate**
(banking) A bank's notification of the status of a collection which is still outstanding.

**advised credit**
(banking) A letter of credit whose terms and conditions have been confirmed by a bank. *See* letter of credit; confirmed letter of credit.

**advising bank**
(banking) The bank (also referred to as the seller's or exporter's bank) which receives a letter of credit or amend-

ment to a letter of credit from the issuing bank (the buyer's bank) and forwards it to the beneficiary (seller/exporter) of the credit. *See* letter of credit; confirming bank; issuing bank.

### Advisory Committee on Export Policy
(U.S. government) The ACEP is an interagency dispute resolution body that operates at the Assistant Secretary level. ACEP is chaired by the U.S. Department of Commerce; membership includes the Departments of Defense, Energy and State, the Arms Control and Disarmament Agency and the intelligence community. Disputes not resolved by the ACEP must be addressed by the cabinet-level Export Administration Review Board within specific time frames set forth under National Security Directive #53. *See* National Security Directive #53; Export Administration Review Board.

### Advisory Committee on Trade Policy and Negotiations (ACTPN)
(U.S. government) The ACTPN is a group (membership of 45; two-year terms) appointed by the president to provide advice on matters of trade policy and related issues, including trade agreements. The 1974 Trade Act requires the ACTPN's establishment and broad representation of key economic sectors affected by trade. Below the ACTPN are seven policy committees: SPAC (Services Policy Advisory Committee), INPAC (Investment Policy Advisory Committee), IGPAC (Intergovernmental Policy Advisory Committee), IPAC (Industry Policy Advisory Committee), APAC (Agriculture Policy Advisory Committee), LPAC (Labor Policy Advisory Committee) and DPAC (Defense Policy Advisory Committee). Below the policy committees are sectoral, technical and functional advisory committees. Information available at the Office of the U.S. Trade Representative on the web at: www.ustr.gov.
*See* Industry Consultations Program.

### AESDirect
(United States) The U.S. Census Bureau's free, Internet-based system for filing Shipper's Export Declaration (SED) information to the Automated Export System (AES). It can be used by U.S. Principal Parties in Interest (USPPIs), forwarders, or anyone else responsible for export reporting. Note that the SED now must be filed electronically. Paper filing is no longer allowed. For information go to www.aes-direct.gov.

### affiliate
A business enterprise located in one country which is directly or indirectly owned or controlled by a person of another country.
(U.S.) A business enterprise located in one country which is directly or indirectly owned or controlled by a person of another country to the extent of 10 percent or more of its voting securities for an incorporated business enterprise, or an equivalent interest for an unincorporated business enterprise, including a branch. For outward investment, the affiliate is referred to as a "foreign affiliate"; for inward investment, it is referred to as a "U.S. affiliate." *See* direct foreign investment; foreign direct investment in the United States; affiliated foreign group.

### affiliated foreign group
(U.S.) An affiliated foreign group means (a) the foreign parent, (b) any foreign person, proceeding up the foreign parent's ownership chain, which owns more than 50 percent of the person below it up to and including that person which is not owned more than 50 percent by another foreign person and (c) any foreign person, proceeding down the ownership chain(s) of each of these members, which is owned more than 50 percent by the person above it. *See* di-

rect foreign investment; foreign direct investment in the United States; affiliate; foreign-owned affiliate in the U.S.

### affreightment
(shipping) The hiring or chartering of all or part of a vessel for the transport of goods.

### affreightment contract
(shipping/law) A contract with a shipowner to hire all or part of a ship for transporting goods.

### afghani
The currency of Afghanistan. 1 Af = 100 puls.

### afloat
(shipping) Refers to a shipment of cargo which is currently onboard a vessel between ports (as opposed to on land).

### AFRA
(shipping) *See* Average Freight Rate Assessment.

### Aframax
(shipping) An ocean-going crude oil tanker vessel of standard size between 80,000 and 119,000 dwt that is the largest crude oil tanker size in the AFRA (Average Freight Rate Assessment) tanker rate system.

### African, Caribbean and Pacific Countries (ACP)
Developing countries which are designated beneficiaries under the Lome Convention. *See* Lome Convention.

### African Development Bank (AfDB)
The AfDB, established in 1963, provides financing through direct loans to African member states to cover the foreign exchange costs incurred in Bank-approved development projects in those countries. Fifty-one African countries are members and ordinarily receive loans. The Republic of South Africa is currently the only African country not a member. Contact: African Development Bank, Rue Joseph Anoma, 01 BP 1387, Abidjan 01, Cote d'Ivoire; Tel: [225] 20-20-44-44; Fax: [225] 20-20-49-59; E-mail: afdb@afdb.org; Web: www.afdb.org.

### African Development Foundation
An independent, nonprofit U.S. government corporation established to provide financial assistance to grassroots organizations in Africa. ADF became operational in 1984. Contact: African Development Foundation, 1400 Eye Street NW, 10th Floor, Washington, DC 20005-2248 USA; Tel: [1] (202) 673-3916; Fax: [1] (202) 673-3810; E-mail: info@adf.gov; Web: www.adf.gov.

### African Union (AU)
(Formerly, the Organization of African Unity - OAU) The OAU was founded in May 1963 with 32 African countries as original members; it had 51 members in 1990. The Organization's aim was to further African unity and solidarity, to coordinate political, economic, cultural, scientific, and defense policies; and to eliminate colonialism in Africa. The OAU, after a series of initiatives in the late 1990's, launched the African Union through the Durban Summit of 2002. Contact: The African Union, PO Box 3243, Addis Ababa, Ethiopia; Tel: [251] 11 551 77 00; Fax: [251] 11 551 78 44; Web: www.africa-union.org.

### aft
(shipping) Direction toward the stern of the vessel (ship or aircraft).

### after date
(banking) A notation used on financial instruments (such as drafts or bills of exchange) to fix the maturity date as a fixed number of days past the date of drawing of the draft. For example, if a draft stipulates "60 days after date," it means that the draft is due (payable) 60 days after the date it was drawn. This has the effect of fixing the date of maturity of the draft, independent of the date of acceptance of the draft. *See* acceptance; drawee; bill of exchange.

### aftermarket
(commerce) (a) The market for replacement parts, accessories and consumable supplies used in the repair, enhancement or maintenance of a product after its original sale. (b) The secondary or resale market for a product after sales of new products has ceased.

(securities) Trading activity in a security after its initial public offering (IPO).

### after sight
(banking) A notation on a draft that indicates that payment is due a fixed number of days after the draft has been presented to the drawee. For example, "30 days after sight" means that the drawee has 30 days from the date of presentation of the draft to make payment. *See* acceptance; drawee; bill of exchange.

### agency
(law) A relationship between one individual or legal entity (the agent) who represents, acts on behalf of, and binds another individual or legal entity (the principal) in accordance with the principal's request or instruction. In some countries, agency is more narrowly defined as a relationship created only by a written agreement or a power of attorney, entered into by a principal and a person who is designated to act for the principal within the limits of the written document creating the agency. See agent; principal; power of attorney.

(a) An **express agency** is established by a written or oral agreement between the parties. An express agency is created, for example, when a seller orally contracts with a sales representative to sell products or when a company makes a written power of attorney to authorize a person to act on its behalf.

(b) An **implied agency** arises as a result of the conduct of the parties. If a seller's assistant, for example, sometimes deals with customers, a court may determine from that conduct that an implied agency exists between the seller and the assistant.

(c) An **agency by estoppel** is imposed by law when an agent acts without authority, but the principal leads a third person to conclude reasonably that the agent had authority and to rely on that conclusion. If a seller, for example, informs a buyer that the seller's representative is authorized to negotiate any contract terms for the seller, a court may decide that an agency by estoppel existed, that the contract should be enforced and that the seller cannot avoid performing the contract by claiming that the representative in fact had no authority.

(d) An **agency del credere** arises when a principal entrusts goods, documents, or securities to an agent who has broad authority to collect from a buyer and who may be liable for ensuring that the buyer is solvent. A sales representative, for example, who is given goods and who is authorized to receive payment from buyers is an agent del credere.

(e) An **exclusive agency** is an arrangement with an agent under which the principal agrees not to sell property to a purchaser found by another agent. If a seller of green and red shoes, for example, gives a sales representative an exclusive agency to sell the green shoes in a particular country, the seller is not permitted to sell those shoes through any other representative in the same country. The seller may, however, authorize other agents to sell red shoes in that country.

(f) A **universal agency** authorizes the agent to do every transaction that a principal can legally delegate. A principal who will be traveling for some time may, for example, give an agent authority to deal with all business and personal transactions for the principal during that absence.

(g) A **general agency** authorizes an agent to do all acts related to the principal's business, which may include negotiating contracts, establishing credit, advertising, arranging for shipping and setting up overseas offices and outlets.

(h) A **special agency** gives an agent limited powers to conduct one transaction or a specific series of transactions. A contract with a representative to secure the sale of certain components to a particular factory creates a special agency. *See* agent; principal; power of attorney.

### agency by estoppel
*See* agency.

### agency del credere
*See* agency.

### Agency for International Development
(U.S. government) Formerly a unit of the now defunct United States International Development Cooperation Agency, in 1999 the AID was transferred to the Department of State and reports directly to the Secretary of State. AID administers U.S. foreign economic and humanitarian assistance programs in the developing world, Central and Eastern Europe and the Commonwealth of Independent States. Among the economic programs are those that foster employment growth and that promote use of clean and efficient energy and environmental technologies. Maintains economic, social and demographic statistics for many developing countries. AID has field missions and representatives in approximately 70 developing countries in Africa, Latin America, the Caribbean and the Near East. Contact: Agency for International Development, Ronald Reagan Building, Washington, DC 20523-1000 USA; Tel: [1] (202) 712-4320; Fax: [1] (202) 216-3524; Web: www.us-aid.gov. *See* Center for Trade and Investment Services.

### agent
(law) An individual or legal entity authorized to act on behalf of another individual or legal entity (the principal). An agent's authorized actions will bind the principal. A sales representative, for example, is an agent of the seller. *See* agency; principal; power of attorney.

### agent ad litem
(shipping/law) An agent who acts on behalf of a principal in prosecuting or defending a lawsuit.

### agent bank
(banking) (a) Bank acting for a foreign bank. (b) Bank handling administration of a loan in a syndicated credit.

### aggregate tender rate
(shipping) A reduced rate given to a shipper who tenders two or more shipments of the same or similar class at the same time and place. *See* class or kind (of merchandise); tender.

### aggregated shipments
(shipping) Numerous shipments from different shippers to one consignee that are consolidated and treated as a single consignment.

### agreed valuation
(shipping) The value of a shipment agreed upon by the shipper and carrier to secure a specific rate and/or liability.

### agriculture export connections
(U.S. government) The U.S. Foreign Agriculture Service through AgExport Connections (formerly Agriculture Information and Marketing Services) provides services designed to help U.S. exporters of agricultural products make direct contact with foreign buyers. Services include: Buyer Alerts, Trade Leads, Foreign Buyer List, U.S. Suppliers List and others. Contact: AgExport Connections, Foreign Agriculture Service, 1400 Independence Avenue, Ag Box 1052, Washington, DC 20250-1052 USA; Tel: [1] (202) 690-3421; Fax: [1] (202) 690-4374; Web: www.fas.usda.gov. Search for "agriculture export connections."

## airbill
*See* air waybill.

## air cargo
(shipping) Any property (freight, mail, express) carried or to be carried in an aircraft. Does not include passenger baggage.

## aircraft pallet
(shipping) A platform or pallet (in air freight usually from 3/4" to 2" thick) upon which a unitized shipment rests or on which goods are assembled and secured before being loaded as a unit onto an aircraft. Most carriers offer container discounts for palletized loads.

Palletization results in more efficient use of space aboard freighter aircraft and better cargo handling, particularly when used as part of mechanized systems employing such other advances as pallet loaders and pallet transporters. The **pallet loader** is a device employing one or more vertical lift platforms for the mechanical loading or unloading of palletized freight at planeside.

The **pallet transporter** is a vehicle for the movement of loaded pallets between the aircraft and the freight terminal or truck dock. Sometimes the functions of both the pallet loader and pallet transporter are combined into a single vehicle. *See* pallet.

## air express
(shipping) A term used to describe expedited handling of air freight service. *See* priority air freight; air freight.

## air freight
(shipping) A service providing for the air transport of goods. The volume of air freight has been increasing significantly due to: (1) decreased shipping time, (2) greater inventory control for just-in-time manufacturing and stocking, (3) generally superior condition of goods upon arrival, and (4) for certain commodities, lower shipping costs.

## air freight forwarder
(shipping) A freight forwarder for shipments by air. Air freight forwarders serve a dual role. The air freight forwarders are, to the shipper, an indirect carrier because they receive freight from various shippers under one tariff, usually consolidating the goods into a larger unit, which is then tendered to an airline. To the airlines, the air freight forwarder is a shipper. An air freight forwarder is ordinarily classed as an indirect air carrier; however, many air freight forwarders operate their own aircraft. *See* freight forwarder.

## airmail
(shipping) The term "airmail" as a class of mail is used only in international postal service. Within the United States, the U.S. Postal Service moves all first class mail, priority mail and express mail by air where doing so will expedite delivery.

## air parcel post
(shipping) A term commonly used for priority mail which consists of first class mail weighing more than 13 ounces. Priority mail is another economical and expedited service for the shipping of parcels by air.

## airport mail facility (AMF)
(shipping) A U.S. Postal Service facility located on or adjacent to an airport. AMFs are primarily engaged in the dispatch, receipt and transfer of mail directly with air carriers.

## Air Pre-Arrival Review System (AirPARS)
(Canada Customs) *See* Pre-Arrival Review System (PARS).

## air waybill (airbill)
(shipping) A shipping document used by the airlines for air freight. It is a contract for carriage that includes carrier conditions of carriage including such items as limits of liability and claims procedures. The air waybill also contains shipping instructions to airlines, a description of the commodity and applicable transportation charges. Air waybills are used by many truckers as through documents for coordinated air/truck service.

Air waybills are not negotiable. The airline industry has adopted a standard formatted air waybill that accommodates both domestic and international traffic. The standard document was designed to enhance the application of modern computerized systems to air freight processing for both the carrier and the shipper. *See* bill of lading; negotiable.

## airworthiness certification
(shipping) Documentation to show that an aircraft or components comply with all the airworthiness requirements related to its use as laid down by the regulatory authorities for the country in which the aircraft is registered.

## Aksjeselskap (A/S)
(Norway) Designation for a joint stock company with limited personal liability to shareholders. *See* Business Entities Appendix.

## Aktiebolag (AB)
(Finland, Sweden) Designation for a joint stock company with limited personal liability to shareholders. *See* Business Entities Appendix.

## Aktiengesellschaft (AG)
(Austria, Germany, Switzerland, Liechtenstein) Designation for a joint stock company with limited personal liability to shareholders. *See* Business Entities Appendix.

## Aktieselskab (A/S)
(Denmark) Designation for a joint stock company with limited personal liability to shareholders.

## Alcohol, Tobacco and Firearms (ATF)
*See* Bureau of Alcohol, Tobacco and Firearms.

## alienable
(law) The capacity to be transferred or conveyed. Interests in real or personal property, for example, are alienable.

## aliquot
(law) A fractional share. A court, for example, may award damages aliquot against several parties who breached a contract, meaning that each must pay a proportionate share of the damages. Aliquot liability differs from joint and several liability, in that the latter refers to whether the breaching parties may be sued and held liable together or individually. *See* joint and several liability.

## all-cargo aircraft
(shipping) An aircraft for the carriage of cargo only, rather than the combination of passengers and cargo. The all-cargo aircraft will carry cargo in bulk or container in the main deck as well as in the lower deck of the aircraft. It may include a scheduled and/or nonscheduled service.

## all risk
(insurance) Extensive insurance coverage of cargo, including coverage due to external causes such as fire, collision, pilferage etc., but usually excluding "special" risks such as those resulting from acts of war, labor strikes, the perishing of goods, and from internal damage due to faulty packaging, decay or loss of market.

All risk insurance covers only physical loss or damage from external cause(s) and specifically affirms the exclusion of war risks and strikes and riots unless covered by endorsement. These losses are excluded, either by expressed exclusions, conditions or warranties written into the policy or by implied conditions or warranties that are read into every marine policy by legal interpretation.

An "all risks" policy may expressly exclude certain types of damage such as marring and scratching of unboxed automobiles or bending and twisting entirely or unless amounting to a specified percentage or amount.

Also, certain perils such as war and strikes, riots and civil commotions are commonly excluded, but these perils can be and usually are reinstated, at least in part, by special endorsement or by a separate policy.

The "all risk" clause is a logical extension of the broader forms of "with average" coverage. The all risk clause generally reads:

"To cover against all risks of physical loss or damage from any external cause irrespective of percentage, but excluding, nevertheless, the risk of war, strikes, riots, seizure, detention and other risks excluded by the F.C.&S. (Free of Capture and Seizure) Warranty and the S.R.&C.C. (Strikes, Riots and Civil Commotion) Warranty in this policy, excepting to the extent that such risks are specifically covered by endorsement."

(air shipments) All risk insurance of air shipments usually excludes loss due to cold or changes in atmospheric pressure. *See* average; with average; free of particular average; inherent vice, war risk; strikes, riots and civil commotion.

### allowance
An amount paid or credited by a seller as a refund or reimbursement due to any one of a number of causes including: faulty packaging, shipment of goods which do not meet buyer's specifications, a late shipment, etc.

### alongside
(shipping) A phrase referring to the side of a ship. (a) Goods to be delivered "alongside" are to be placed on the dock or lighter within reach of the transport ship's tackle so that they can be loaded aboard the ship. (b) Goods delivered to the port of embarkation, but without loading fees.

### Alternative Marine Power (AMP)
See cold ironing.

### alternative tariff
(shipping) A tariff containing two or more rates from and to the same points, on the same goods, with authority to use the one which produces the lowest charge.

### amendment
(law/general) An addition, deletion, or change in a legal document.

(banking/letters of credit) A change in the terms and conditions of a letter of credit (e.g., extension of the letter of credit's validity period, shipping deadline, etc.), usually to meet the needs of the seller. The seller requests an amendment of the buyer who, if he agrees, instructs his bank (the issuing bank) to issue the amendment. The issuing bank informs the seller's bank (the advising bank) who then notifies the seller of the amendment. In the case of irrevocable letters of credit, amendments may only be made with the agreement of all parties to the transaction. *See* letter of credit.

### American Arbitration Association
A private not-for-profit organization formed in 1926 to encourage the use of arbitration in the settlement of disputes. Contact: American Arbitration Association, 335 Madison Avenue, Floor 10, New York, New York 10017-4605; Tel: (212) 716-5800; Fax: (212) 716-5905; E-mail: Websitemail@adr.org; Web: www.adr.org. *See* arbitration.

### American Association of Exporters and Importers
(U.S.) A trade association which advises members of legislation regarding importing and exporting, and fights against protectionism. Also hosts seminars and conferences for importers and exporters. Contact: American Association of Exporters and Importers, 1050 17th Street, NW, Suite 810, Washington, DC 20036; Tel: [1] (202) 857-8009; Fax: [1] (202) 857-7843; E-mail: hq@aaei.org; Web: www.aaei.org.

### American Institute in Taiwan
A nonprofit corporation that represents U.S. interests in Taiwan in lieu of an embassy. In 1979, the United States terminated formal diplomatic relations with Taiwan when it recognized the People's Republic of China as the sole legal government of Taiwan. The AIT was authorized to continue commercial, cultural and other relations between the U.S. and Taiwan. Contact: American Institute in Taiwan, 7, Section 3, Lane 134, Hsin Yi Road, Taipei, 10659, Taiwan; Tel: [886] (2) 2720-1550; Fax: [886] (2) 2757-7162; E-mail: aitarc@mail.ait.org.tw; Web: http://ait.org.tw.

### American National Standards
A set of product standards established by the American National Standards Institute (ANSI). *See* American National Standards Institute. *See* International Standards Organization.

### American National Standards Institute (ANSI)
An organization that develops and publishes a set of voluntary product standards called the American National Standards. In addition to product standards, ANSI publishes a guide to unit-load and transportation package sizes for containers. ANSI is also an influential member of the ISO (International Standards Organization). American National Standards Institute, 25 West 43rd Street, New York, NY 10036 USA; Tel: [1] (212) 642-4900; Fax: [1] (212) 398-0023; E-mail: info@ansi.org; Web: www.ansi.org. *See* International Standards Organization.

### American option
(banking/foreign exchange) A foreign exchange option containing a provision to the effect that it can be exercised at any time between the date of writing and the expiration date. *See* European option.

### American Traders Index (ATI)
A compilation of individual U.S. & Foreign Commercial Service (US&FCS) domestic client files, for use by overseas posts to generate mailing lists. *See* United States and Foreign Commercial Service.

### Americas Counter Smuggling Initiative (ACSI)
(United States) A U.S. Customs and Border Protection (CBP) program established in 1998 to build upon the success of the Carrier Initiative Program (CIP) and the Business Anti-Smuggling Coalition (BASC) by strengthening and expanding anti-narcotics and anti-terrorism security programs with industry and government. ACSI is made up of teams of CBP inspectors and agents detailed to assist businesses in developing security programs and initiatives that safeguard legitimate shipments from being used as vehicles for drug smuggling or terrorist actions. The target countries are the same as those where BASC chapters exist. The ACSI teams travel to each target country approximately four times a year to provide hands-on training and site surveys to BASC members in the trade industry. For information about the CBP Industry Partnership Programs, go to: www.cbp.gov.

### amidships
(shipping) At or in the middle of a vessel. Because a ship's movement is less in the middle of the vessel, shippers will sometimes specify that fragile freight be placed amidships.

### amortization
(banking) (a) The gradual extinguishment of any amount over a period of time (e.g., the retirement of a debt). (b) A reduction of the book value of a fixed asset.

### analysis certificate
*See* certificate of analysis.

### ancillary
(logistics) Supplemental or additional. For example, an ancillary charge.

### ancillary equipment
(shipping) Equipment used to build up a palletized load or to convey a unit load device outside an aircraft. *See* aircraft pallet.

**A**

**Andean Group**
An alliance of Latin American countries formed in 1969 to promote regional economic integration among medium-sized countries. Members include Bolivia, Colombia, Ecuador, Peru and Venezuela. Contact: Andean Group, Avenida Paseo de la Republica 3895, Casilla Postal 18-1177, Lima 27, Peru; Tel: [51] (14) 11-1400; Fax: [51] (12) 21-3329; E-mail: contacto@comunidadandina.org; Web: www.comunidadandina.org.

**Andean Trade Initiative (ATI)**
(obsolete) A former U.S. government initiative providing for assistance for alternative economic development to the drug producing countries of Bolivia, Colombia, Ecuador and Peru. The program provided ten years of duty-free treatment for most goods produced in one or a combination of these four countries.

**Animal and Plant Health Inspection Service (APHIS)**
(U.S. government) A U.S. government agency attached to the U.S. Department of Agriculture which has the responsibility of inspecting and certifying animals, plants and related products for import to or export from the United States. APHIS is also responsible for the inspection of animal and plant product processing facilities both in the United States and in countries that export to the United States. Contact: U.S. Department of Agriculture, Animal and Plant Health Inspection Service; 4700 River Road; Riverdale, MD 20737 USA; Tel: [1] (301) 734-7799; Fax: [1] (301) 734-5221; E-mail: aphis.web@aphis.usda.gov; Web: www.aphis.usda.gov. *See* phytosanitary inspection certificate.

**animal containers**
(shipping) The use of air freight as a means of transporting household pets led to the development of special containers designed to provide adequate protection and air circulation. Such containers may be purchased or rented from many air carriers.

**annual basis**
(accounting) Statistical shifting of data that are for a period less than 12 months in order to estimate the full results for an entire year. To be accurate the processing should consider the effect of the seasonal variation.

**ANSI**
*See* American National Standards Institute.

**ANSI 12**
(logistics/data interchange) The most widely accepted standards for EDI (Electronic Data Interchange) in the United States. *See* American National Standards Institute, EDI, UN/EDIFACT.

**antidumping**
(customs) Antidumping, as a reference to the system of laws to remedy dumping, is defined as the converse of dumping. *See* dumping; antidumping duties; General Agreement on Tariffs and Trade; Antidumping Act of 1974.

**Antidumping Act of 1974**
(U.S. law) Legislation designed to prevent the sales of goods at a lower price than exists in the goods' country or origin. The U.S. Treasury Department determines whether imported products are being sold at a "less than fair value" in the United States. Should it be determined that the domestic industry is harmed by the imports, extra duties can be imposed. *See* countervailing duties; dumping.

**Antidumping/Countervailing Duty System**
(U.S. Customs) A part of the U.S. Customs' Automated Commercial System, containing a case reference database and a statistical reporting system to capture data for International Trade Commission reports on antidumping and countervailing duties assessed and paid. *See* dumping; countervailing duties.

**antidumping duty**
(customs) Duty assessed on imported merchandise of a class or kind that is sold at a price less than the fair market value. Fair market value of merchandise is defined as the price at which it is normally sold in the manufacturer's home market. *See* dumping; countervailing duties.

**antidumping duty deposit**
(U.S. Customs) A cash deposit of estimated antidumping duties collected by U.S. Customs and Border Protection (CBP) at the time new customs entries are made for imports of products from countries for which the U.S. International Trade Administration (ITA) has issued an antidumping duty order. The actual amount of duty paid is determined at liquidation.
*See* antidumping duty, liquidation.

**antidumping petition**
(customs) A claim filed on behalf of a U.S. industry alleging that imported merchandise is being sold in the United States at "less than fair value," and that sales of such merchandise is causing or threatening injury to, or retarding the establishment of a U.S. industry. *See* dumping; countervailing duties.

**any quantity**
(shipping) A cargo rating that applies to an article regardless of weight (i.e., in any quantity).

**apparent good order and condition**
(shipping) A statement, on a bill of lading or other shipping document, indicating that the shipment is available for shipment or delivery with no apparent damage.

**appraiser, customs**
(U.S. Customs) An individual authorized by U.S. Customs & Border Protection (Department of Homeland Security) to examine and determine the value of imported merchandise.

**appreciation**
(foreign exchange) An increase in the value of the currency of one nation in relation to the currency of another nation.

**approval basis**
(banking/letters of credit) If documents containing discrepancies are presented to the nominated bank under a letter of credit, the bank can forward the documents to the issuing bank for approval, with the beneficiary's agreement. Because of the risk of loss in transit and delays resulting in interest loss, however, it is recommended that the beneficiary first try to correct the documents; but, if that is not possible, the beneficiary asks the nominated bank to contact the issuing bank for authorization to accept the discrepancies.

**approximately**
*See* about.

**appurtenance**
(law) An accessory that is connected to primary property, that is adapted to be used with that property and that generally is intended to be permanently affixed to that property. Appurtenances to a ship, for example, may include cranes attached to the ship for loading and unloading cargo. An easement for access to land is considered an appurtenance to that land. Industrial machinery that is affixed to a factory facility is an appurtenance to the building.

**apron**
(shipping) The area of an airport where aircraft are parked for loading and unloading of cargo or passengers.

**Arab League (League of Arab States)**
A regional alliance established in March 1945 which aims to improve relations among Arab nations. Headquarters are located in Cairo, Egypt. Members include: Algeria, Bahrain, Djibouti, Egypt, Iraq, Jordan, Kuwait, Lebanon, Libya,

Mauritania, Morocco, Oman, Qatar, Saudi Arabia, Somalia, Sudan, Syria, Tunisia, United Arab Emirates and Yemen. Contact: Arab League; P.O. Box 11642; Tahrir Square; Cairo, Egypt; Tel: [20] (2) 575-0511; Fax: [20] (2) 574-0331; Web: www.arableagueonline.org.

### Arab Maghreb Union (AMU)
A regional alliance established in February 1989 with the goal of joining the Gulf Cooperation Council and other states in a common market. AMU members include: Algeria, Morocco, Tunisia, Libya and Mauritania. Contact: Union du Maghreb Arabe, 14 Rue Zalagh Agdal, Rabat, Morocco; Tel: [212] (37) 671 274; Fax: [212] (37) 671 253; E-mail: sg.uma@maghrebarabe.org; Web: www.maghrebarabe.org.

### arbiter
*See* arbitration.

### arbitrage
(banking/finance/foreign exchange) The simultaneous buying and selling (or borrowing and lending) of identical securities, currencies, or commodities in two or more markets in order to take advantage of price differentials. *See* hedging.

### arbitrage, space
(banking/finance/foreign exchange) The simultaneous buying and selling (or borrowing and lending) of identical securities, currencies, or commodities in two or more locations in order to take advantage of price differentials.

### arbitrage, time
(banking/finance/foreign exchange) The simultaneous buying and selling (or borrowing and lending) of identical securities, currencies, or options at different maturity dates in order to take advantage of price differentials.

### arbitrageur
(finance) A person systematically engaged in arbitrage dealing.

### arbitration
(law) The resolution of a dispute between two parties through a voluntary or contractually required hearing and determination by an impartial third party. The impartial third party is called the arbiter or arbitrator and is chosen by a higher or disinterested body, or by the two parties in dispute. In the United States, the main arbitration body is the American Arbitration Association, 335 Madison Avenue, Floor 10, New York, New York 10017-4605; Tel: (212) 716-5800; Fax: (212) 716-5905; E-mail: Websitemail@adr.org; Web: www.adr.org. Internationally, the main arbitration body is the International Chamber of Commerce (ICC), 38 Cours Albert 1er, 75008 Paris, France; Tel: [33] 49-53-28-28; Fax: [33] 49-53-28-59; Web: www.iccwbo.org. For the U.S. representative of the ICC, contact: U.S. Council for International Business, 1212 Avenue of the Americas, New York, NY 10036 USA; Tel: [1] (212) 354-4480; Fax: [1] (212) 575-0327; E-mail: info@uscib.org; Web: www.uscib.org. *See* arbitration clause; American Arbitration Association; International Chamber of Commerce.

### arbitration clause
(law) A contract clause included in many international contracts stating for example:
"Any controversy or claim arising out of or relating to this contract, or the breach thereof, shall be settled by arbitration in accordance with the Commercial Arbitration Rules of the American Arbitration Association and judgment upon the award rendered by the arbitrator(s) may be entered in any court having jurisdiction thereof." *See* arbitration; American Arbitration Association; International Chamber of Commerce.

### area code
(shipping) A one-digit code that specifies the location of an ocean cargo container. The ten codes are:
**0 – Unreported**
Unreported
**1 – Great Lakes/U.S. East Coast**
Great Lakes/USEC
**2 – U.S. Gulf/North Coast South America**
US Gulf/NCSA
**3 – North Pacific/West Coast South America**
North Pacific/WCSA
**4 – East Coast South America/West Africa**
ECSA/WAfrica
**5 – UK/Continent/Scandanavia**
UK/Cont/Scandanavia
**6 – Mediterranean/Black Sea**
Med/Black Sea
**7 - Arabian Gulf/South Africa/India**
(Including Middle East Gulf)
AG/South Africa/India
**8 – Indonesia/Australasia**
Indonesia/Australasia
**9 – Far East**
Far East

### Arms Control and Disarmament Agency
(U.S.) An independent agency within the U.S. State Department which reviews dual-use license applications from a nonproliferation perspective—anything that could impact on the proliferation of missiles, chemical and biological weapons, and nuclear weapons. The agency was created in 1961, has about 200 to 250 staff and has a fairly substantial and growing technology transfer and export control function. The director is the principal arms control adviser to the secretary of state, the president and the NSC on: conventional arms transfer; commercial sales of munitions; nuclear, missile, chemical and biological warfare; East-West military munitions issues; and negotiating Memorandums of Understanding (MOUs) with the Third World on strategic trade. Contact at: U.S. Arms Control & Disarmament Agency, 320 21st St. N.W., Washington, D.C. 20451; Tel: [1] (800) 581-ACDA; Fax: (202) 647-6928; Web: http://dosfan.lib.uic.edu/acda/. *See* United States Department of State.

### arrival notice
(shipping) A notice furnished to consignee and shipping broker alerting them to the projected arrival of freight and availability of freight for pickup.

### arrivals
(customs) Imported goods which have been placed in a bonded warehouse for which duty has not been paid.

### articles of extraordinary value (AEV)
(shipping) Commodities identified as high value items, requiring special care in shipping.

### articulated lorry
(UK) British term for a truck with trailer or semi-trailer.

### as is
(law) A term indicating that goods offered for sale are without warranty or guarantee. The purchaser has no recourse to the vendor for quality or condition of the goods.

### Asia Pacific Economic Cooperation (APEC)
An informal grouping of Asia Pacific countries that provides a forum for ministerial level discussion of a broad range of economic issues. APEC includes the six ASEAN countries (Brunei, Indonesia, Malaysia, Philippines, Singapore and Thailand), plus: Australia, Canada, China, Hong Kong, Japan, South Korea, Taiwan and the United States. The Secretariat is located in Singapore. Contact at: APEC Secretariat, 35 Heng Mui Keng Terrace, Singapore

119616; Tel: (65) 6775 6012; Fax: (65) 6775 6013; E-mail: info@apec.org; Web: www.apec.org.

**Asian Development Bank (ADB)**
The ADB was formed in 1966 to foster economic growth and cooperation in Asia and to help accelerate economic development of members. Contact: Asian Development Bank, PO Box 789, Manila Central Post Office, 0980 Manila, Philippines; Tel: [63] (2) 632-4444; Fax: [63] (2) 636-2444; Web: www.adb.org.

**ask(ed) price; market price**
(finance) The price at which a security or commodity is quoted or offered for sale.

**assailing thieves**
(insurance) A reference to an insurance policy clause covering the forcible taking rather than the clandestine theft or mere pilferage of goods.

**assembly service**
(shipping) A service under which an airline assembles shipments from many shippers and transports them as one shipment to one receiver.

**assessment**
(customs) The imposition of antidumping duties on imported merchandise. *See* dumping; antidumping duties; countervailing duties.

**assign**
(law) To transfer or make over to another party.

**assignee**
(law) One to whom a right or property is transferred. *See* assignor; assignment.

**assignment**
(law/shipping/banking) The transfer of rights, title, interest and benefits of a contract or financial instrument to a third party.
(banking/letters of credit) The beneficiary of a letter of credit is entitled to assign his/her claims to any of the proceeds that he/she may be entitled to, or portions thereof, to a third party. Usually the beneficiary informs the issuing or advising bank that his/her claims or particle claims under the letter of credit were assigned and asks the bank to advise the assignee (third party) that it has acknowledged the assignment. The validity of the assignment is not dependent on bank approval. In contrast, the transfer requires the agreement of the nominated bank. An assignment is possible regardless of whether the letter of credit is transferable. *See* letter of credit.

**assignment of proceeds**
*See* assignment.

**assignor**
(law) One by whom a right or property is transferred. *See* assignee; assignment.

**assist**
(U.S. Customs) Any of a number of items that an importer provides directly or indirectly, free of charge, or at a reduced cost, for use in the production or sale of merchandise for export to the United States.
Assists are computed as part of the transaction value upon which duty is charged, when the duty rate is a percentage of the value of the merchandise.
Examples of assists are: materials, components, parts and similar items incorporated in the imported merchandise; tools, dies, molds and similar items used in producing the imported merchandise; engineering, development, artwork, design work and plans and sketches that are undertaken outside the United States. Engineering is not treated as an assist if the service or work is: (1) performed by a person domiciled within the United States, (2) performed while that person is acting as an employee or agent of the buyer of the imported merchandise, and (3) incidental to other en-

gineering, development, artwork, design work, or plans or sketches undertaken within the United States. *See* valuation; transaction value; deductive value; computed value.

**Association of Southeast Asian Nations (ASEAN)**
ASEAN was established in 1967 to promote political, economic and social cooperation among its six member countries: Indonesia, Malaysia, Philippines, Singapore, Thailand and Brunei. Contact: Association of Southeast Asian Nations, 70A Jalan Sisingamangaraja, Jakarta-12110, Indonesia; Tel: [62] (21) 726-2991; Fax: [62] (21) 739-8234; E-mail: public@aseansec.org; Web: www.aseansec.org.

**assumpsit**
(law) An assumption or undertaking by one person (the promisor) to perform an act for, or to pay a sum to, another person (the promisee), often without express agreement from the promisee to perform an act or remit consideration in return. An assumpsit is created, for example, when one person employs another without any written agreement as to compensation. In such an arrangement, the law will imply a duty to pay reasonable wages. An assumpsit also arises when one person receives money that belongs to another, in which event the law implies a duty to remit the sum to the owner.
(a) An **express assumpsit** is one in which the promisor states the assumption in distinct and definite language. A person who agrees to work for another on certain tasks for a specified time has made an express assumpsit.
(b) An **implied assumpsit** is one in which a promise is inferred by law from the conduct of a party or the circumstances of the case. If, without any express statement, a person begins working for another who knows and does not object to that work, a court may find that an implied assumpsit has arisen.
(c) An **action in assumpsit** is a court action to recover damages for breach of an oral or other informal contract. A seller who delivers goods to a buyer based on an oral contract and who does not receive payment may recover the proceeds in an action in assumpsit.

**assurance**
(insurance) British term for insurance.

**assurance of performance**
(law) A declaration intended to induce one contracting party to have full confidence in the other's performance. Pledges and sureties are forms of assurances.

**assured**
(insurance) The individual, company or entity which is insured.

**astern**
(shipping) (a) Behind a ship or aircraft, (b) Toward the back of a ship or aircraft, (c) Backward, as in the movement of a ship.

**at sight**
(banking) Terms of a financial instrument which is payable upon presentation or demand. A bill of exchange may be made payable, for example, at sight or after sight, which (respectively) means it is payable upon presentation or demand, or within a particular period after demand is made. *See* bill of exchange.

**ATA Carnet**
(customs) ATA is the acronym for the combined French and English words "Admission Temporaire/Temporary Admission." An ATA Carnet is an international customs document which may be used for the temporary admission of certain goods into 92 participating countries and territories worldwide in lieu of the usual customs documents and without having to pay duties or value-added taxes. The carnet serves as a guarantee against the payment of customs

duties and taxes (including VAT) which may become due on goods temporarily imported and not reexported. Carnets also simplify customs clearance and ensure re-entry into the originating country by acting as a "Certificate of Registration." While a Carnet acts as a "Merchandise Passport" and replaces the usual customs documents required, export licenses, quotas and visa are enforced where applicable.

This international customs document was established by the World Customs Organization (WCO) in 1961 and replaced the ECS (Echantillons Commerciaux/Commercial Samples") Carnet that was created by a 1956 convention sponsored by the Customs Cooperation Council.

The ATA program is administered by national chambers of commerce of participating countries that are affiliated with the Paris-based International Chamber of Commerce (ICC). The United States Council for International Business (USCIB) is the national guaranteeing association for carnets in the United States. Address: U.S. Council for International Business; 1212 Avenue of the Americas; New York, NY 10036 USA; Tel: [1] (212) 354-4480; www.uscib.org.

Roanoke Trade Services, Inc. has been an ATA Carnet issuing office and service provider for the USCIB since 1978. For information, call 1 (800)-CARNETS or visit www.carnetsonline.com. *See* International Chamber of Commerce, carnet, TECRO/AIT Carnet.

**athwartships**
(shipping) Across a vessel from side to side.

**attachment**
(law) Legal process for seizing property before a judgment to secure the payment of damages if awarded. A party who sues for damages for breach of contract may request, for example, that the court issue an order freezing all transfers of specific property owned by the breaching party pending resolution of the dispute.

**attendant accompanying shipments**
(shipping) Sometimes attendants accompany cargo shipments as when grooms or veterinarians accompany race horses or other live animals. This service requires advance arrangements with a shipping company or airline.

**at-the-money**
(foreign exchange/finance) A call or put option is at-the-money when the price of the underlying instrument is equivalent or very near to the strike price. *See* option; call option; put option.

**attorn**
(law) To agree to turn over or transfer money or goods to an individual or legal entity other than the party who was to originally receive them. A company that has bought out another legal entity may seek an attornment from a supplier who had an outstanding contract with the former entity, and if the supplier attorns, the company can obtain goods on the same terms as were agreed to with the former entity.

**attorney-in-fact**
(law) A person authorized to transact business generally or to perform a designated task of a nonlegal nature on behalf of another individual or legal entity. An attorney-in-fact is a type of agent. In many countries, this authority must be conferred by a written power of attorney. If a company buys goods from a foreign firm, for example, and agrees to place sufficient funds for the purchase in an escrow account, the buyer may authorize an attorney-in-fact in that foreign country to disburse the escrow funds on receiving verification from the buyer that the goods are satisfactory. A business enterprise may also authorize an attorney-in-fact to testify to facts on the company's behalf in arbitration or legal proceedings held in a foreign country. *See* agent; agency; power of attorney.

**audit**
(general) A formal examination of records or documents—usually financial documents.
(shipping) The formal examination of freight bills to determine their accuracy.

**austral**
The former currency of Argentina. 1A=100 centavos.

**Australia Group (AG)**
An informal forum through which 20 industrialized nations cooperate to curb proliferation of chemical and biological weapons through a supply approach. The AG's first meeting, held at the Australian Embassy in Paris in June 1986, was attended by Australia, Canada, Japan, New Zealand, the United States, and the ten member nations of the European Community. Membership has expanded to include the following: Argentina, Australia, Austria, Belgium, Bulgaria, Canada, Cyprus, Czech Republic, Denmark, Estonia, European Commission, Finland, France, Germany, Greece, Hungary, Iceland, Ireland, Italy, Japan, Latvia, Lithuania, Luxembourg, Malta, Netherlands, New Zealand, Norway, Poland, Portugal, Romania, Slovak Republic, Slovenia, South Korea, Spain, Sweden, Switzerland, Turkey, U.K., Ukraine, United States. Web: www.australiagroup.net.

**authentication**
(law) The act of certifying that a written document is genuine, credible, and reliable. An authentication is performed by an authorized person who attests that the document is in proper legal form and is executed by a person identified as having authority to do so. In many countries, persons authorized to authenticate documents include consulate officials, notaries public, and judicial officers.
(computers) To verify the identity of a user, device, or other entity in a computer system. Authentication is typically a prerequisite to access resources in a system.

**Automated Broker Interface (ABI)**
(U.S. Customs) ABI, a part of U.S. Customs' Automated Commercial System, permits transmission of data pertaining to merchandise being imported into the U.S. directly to U.S. Customs. Qualified participants include customs brokers, importers, carriers, port authorities, and independent data processing companies referred to as service centers. To use ABI, send a letter of intent to the District Director of Customs or to your nearest district Customs Office. *See* Automated Commercial System.

**Automated Clearinghouse (ACH)**
(U.S. Customs) ACH is a feature of the Automated Broker Interface which is a part of Customs' Automated Commercial System. The ACH combines elements of bank lock box arrangements with electronic funds transfer services to replace cash or check for payment of estimated duties, taxes, and fees on imported merchandise. *See* Automated Commercial System.

**Automated Commercial Environment (ACE)**
(U.S. Customs) A U.S. Customs and Border Protection (CBP) modernization replacement of its Automated Commercial System (ACS). ACE provides CBP and other participating government agencies the capability to access data throughout the international supply chain to anticipate, identify, track and intercept high-risk shipments.
ACE also revolutionizes how CBP processes goods imported into the United States by providing an integrated, fully automated information system to enable the efficient collection, processing and analysis of commercial import and export data. ACE also simplifies dealings between CBP and the trade community by automating time-consuming and labor-intensive transactions and moving goods through the ports and onto markets faster and at lower cost. It provides national processing as the CBP moves away

from port by port processing. By providing the right information, tools, and foresight, ACE will also serve as a critical element for trade enforcement and in preventing cargo from becoming an instrument of terrorism.

ACE benefits include:

- Enhanced border security
- Increased access to data
- Reduced paper handling
- Over 60 downloadable reports
- Increased flow of trade
- Simplified and expedited cargo release
- Periodic monthly statements
- On-line access to data

ACE is fully compatible with Windows and accessible via the Internet. It supplants the CBP's 18-year-old Automated Commercial System (ACS), a COBOL-based import-filing system. ACS suffers frequent "brownouts" (slowdowns) because its 80s-vintage technology is swamped by the demands of today's global marketplace.

Rather than being built on a mainframe computer like ACS is, ACE enjoys a modular structure that makes overhauling and modernization much easier.

In addition, ACE allows customs transactions using the International Trade Data System (ITDS), a new data-collection setup that will feed into various federal agencies and is designed to eliminate redundant paperwork requirements.

Also, thanks to ITDS, carriers will be able to file electronic manifests for the first time. That means trucks will cross the border faster -- because the information needed for their cargoes to clear customs will arrive electronically before they do. For more information, go to the CBP Web site at: www.cbp.gov.

### Automated Commercial System (ACS)

(U.S. Customs) The ACS is a joint public-private sector computerized data processing and telecommunications system linking customhouses, members of the import trade community, and other government agencies with the Customs computer.

Trade users file import data electronically, receive needed information on cargo status, and query Customs files to prepare submissions. Duties, taxes, and fees may be paid by electronic statement, through a Treasury-approved clearinghouse bank. ACS contains the import data used by Census to prepare U.S. foreign trade statistics. ACS began operating in February 1984 and includes: (1) the Automated Broker Interface, (2) the Census Interface System, (3) the Automated Manifest Systems, (4) the Bond System, (5) the In-Bond System, (6) the Cargo Selectivity System, (7) the Line Release System, (8) the Collections System, (9) the Security System, (10) the Quota System, (11) the Entry Summary Selectivity System, (12) the Entry Summary System, (13) the Automated Information Exchange, (14) the Antidumping/Countervailing Duty System, (15) the Firms System, (16) the Liquidation System, (17) the Drawback System, (18) the Fines, Penalties, and Forfeitures System, and (19) the Protest System. For more information go to the U.S. Customs and Border Protection website at www.cbp.gov.

### Automated Export System (AES)

(U.S. Customs) The U.S. Customs and Border Protection (CBP) system for electronic filing Shipper's Export Declarations (SED) and ocean manifest information directly to CBP. For complete information on how to participate, software options and more, go to: www.cbp.gov/xp/cgov/export/aes/easy_steps.xml. For information about AESDirect, the free internet application supported by the U.S. Census Bureau, go to: www.aesdirect.gov. *See* AESDirect.

### automated guided vehicle system (AGVS)

(logistics) A materials handling system that utilizes computer-controlled, battery-powered, driverless vehicles that move along guided paths. These systems are utilized in manufacturing plants and warehouses, may be automatically or manually loaded and unloaded and are designed for applications with load capacities ranging from 20 to 120,000 kilograms (10-55,000 pounds). For example, a manufacturing plant might utilize an AGVS with an automated storage and retrieval system (ASRS) to automatically retrieve component parts from a warehouse just as they are needed for assembly on the shop floor. *See* automated storage and retrieval system (ASRS).

### Automated Information Exchange (AIES)

(U.S. Customs) AIES, a part of Customs' Automated Commercial System, allows for exchange of classification and value information between field units and headquarters. *See* Automated Commercial System.

### Automated Manifest Systems (AMS)

(U.S. Customs) AMS, a part of Customs' Automated Commercial System (ACS), controls imported merchandise from the time a carrier's cargo manifest is electronically transmitted to Customs until control is relinquished to another segment of the ACS. *See* Automated Commercial System.

### automated storage and retrieval system (ASRS or AS/RS)

(logistics) A computer-controlled robotic storage, retrieval and shipment system used in manufacturing plants and warehouses for materials, component parts and finished products. These systems utilize specially designed automated guided vehicles, computer-controlled guideways and storage bin and rack systems. Advanced systems are capable of delivering materials and component parts to the shop floor, loading robotic manufacturing equipment, taking finished or partially finished goods to storage and delivering goods to a loading dock.

### Automated Targeting System

(United States) A U.S. Customs and Border Protection program designed to assist Customs officers in identifying imports which pose a high risk of containing narcotics or other contraband. The system standardizes bill-of-lading, entry, and entry summary data received from the Automated Commercial System (ACS) and creates integrated records called "shipments". These shipments are evaluated and scored through the use of over 300 weighted rules derived from targeting methods used by experienced Customs personnel. The higher the score, the more the shipment warrants attention. For information go to: www.cbp.gov.

### Automotive Parts Advisory Committee (APAC)

(U.S.) A working committee established by an amendment to the Trade Act to set up an advisory committee to the U.S. Department of Commerce for dealing with U.S.-Japan trade issues involving the auto parts industry. Contact: Office of Aerospace and Automotive Industries, Automotive Industries Team, Room 4036, U.S. Department of Commerce, Washington, DC 20230-0001; Tel: [1] (202) 482-0554; Web: www.ita.doc.gov/td/auto/staff/index.html.

### availability

(banking/letters of credit) In letters of credit, refers to the availability of documents in exchange for payment of the amount stated in the letter of credit. Availability options are:

(1) By **sight payment**: payment on receipt of the documents by the issuing bank or the bank nominated in the letter of credit.

(2) By **deferred payment**: payment after a period specified in the letter of credit, often calculated as number of

days after the date of presentation of the documents or after the shipping date.
(3) By **acceptance**: acceptance of a draft (to be presented together with other documents) by the issuing bank or by the bank nominated in the letter of credit, and the payment thereof at maturity.
(4) By **negotiation**: meaning the giving of value by the nominated bank to the beneficiary for the documents presented, subject to receipt of cover from the issuing bank. *See* letter of credit; bill of exchange; negotiation.

*aval*
(banking) Payment of a bill of exchange, which is the responsibility of the drawee, can be either completely or partially guaranteed via an aval (joint and several guarantee), where the guarantor places his/her signature on the draft either alone or with corresponding explanation "per aval" or "as guarantor." If other information is lacking, the guarantor commits him/herself on behalf of the issuer. *See* bill of exchange.

*average*
(insurance) A loss to a shipment of goods that is less than a total loss. It comes from the French word avarie, which means "damage to ship or cargo," (and ultimately from the Arabic word awarijah, which means "merchandise damaged by sea water").
(a) A **particular average** is an insurance loss that affects specific interests only.
(b) A **general average** is an insurance loss that affects all cargo interests on board the vessel as well as the ship herself. *See* particular average; general average; with average; free of particular average; deductible average.

**Average Freight Rate Assessment (AFRA)**
(shipping) The average transportation cost per ton for a given month for vessels in different size categories as established by the London Tanker Brokers' Panel. AFRA and its Terms of Reference were originally created by Shell Oil Company and then BP (British Petroleum) as a means of establishing internal rates for charging affiliates for the transport of crude oil and petroleum products. Shell and BP ceased their sponsorship of AFRA in 1982. Since that time the London Tanker Brokers' Panel has compiled the AFRA based upon known transportation agreements concluded on the open market. AFRA is recognized by the tax authorities of many countries for pricing of intra-company oil movements.
The six AFRA Rate Categories are:
General Purpose 16,500-24,999 dwt,
Medium Range 25,000-44,900 dwt,
Large Range 1 45,000-79,999 dwt,
Large Range 2 80,000-159,999 dwt,
VLCC 160,000-319,999 dwt, and
VLCC 320,000-549,999 dwt.

*average inventory*
(logistics) (a) The average quantity or volume of an inventory item held over a specified period of time (e.g., monthly, annually). (b) The average value of an inventory item held over a specified period of time.

*avoidance of contract*
(law) The legal cancellation of a contract because an event occurs that makes performance of the contract terms impossible or inequitable and that releases the parties from their obligations. *See* commercial frustration; commercial impracticability; force majeure.

*avoirdupois*
(measure) (a) French for "having weight." (b) A system of weight measurement based on the pound of 16 ounces and the ounce of 16 drams. Refer to Weights and Measures in the Appendix.

# B

*back haul*
(logistics) (a) The return movement of a transport vehicle from its original destination to its original point of departure. (b) The load carried by a transport vehicle all or part of the way from its original destination to its original point of departure.

*back order*
(logistics/commerce) A customer order for a material, component part or finished good that cannot be filled from current inventory.

*Background Notes*
A series of publications by the U.S. State Department providing an overview of a country's history, people, political conditions, economy, and foreign relations. Also includes map of country and travel notes. Available from: Superintendent of Documents, U.S. Government Printing Office, Mail Stop: IDCC, 732 N. Capitol Street, NW, Washington, DC 20401; Tel: [1] (866) 512-1800, [1] (202) 512-1800; Fax: [1] (202) 512-2104; Web: www.gpoaccess.gov. To receive catalog, contact U.S. Fax Watch: [1] (202) 512-1716.

*back-to-back borrowing*
(banking) The process whereby a bank brings together a borrower and a lender so that they agree on a loan contract.

*back-to-back letter of credit*
(banking) A new letter of credit opened in favor of another beneficiary on the basis of an already existing, nontransferable letter of credit. For example, a British merchant agrees to buy cotton in Egypt for sale to a Belgian shirtmaker. The Belgian establishes a nontransferable letter of credit for payment to the British merchant who then uses the strength of the letter of credit as a security with his bank for opening a letter of credit to finance payment to the Egyptian. *See* letter of credit.

*back-to-back loan*
(banking) Operations whereby a loan is made in one currency in one country against a loan in another currency in another country (e.g., a U.S. dollar loan in the U.S. against a pounds sterling loan in the U.K.).

*bad faith*
(law) The intent to mislead or deceive (mala fides). It does not include misleading by an honest, inadvertent or uncalled-for misstatement.

*bagged cargo*
(shipping) Goods shipped in sacks.

*baht*
The currency of Thailand. 1B=100 satangs.

*baksheesh*
Arabic for "gift." The term has a number of meanings including charitable giving (as to a beggar in the streets), a tip (as to a waiter in a restaurant), a facilitation payment (as to a bureaucrat to process paperwork that would have eventually been processed anyway) and a bribe (as paid to a corrupt official to influence a decision). The term is widely used in the Middle East and Southwest Asia.

*bailment*
(law) A delivery of goods or personal property by one person (the bailor) to another (the bailee) on an express or implied contract and for a particular purpose related to the goods while in possession of the bailee, who has a duty to redeliver them to the bailor or otherwise dispose of them in accordance with the bailor's instructions once the purpose has been accomplished. A bailment arises, for example, when a seller delivers goods to a shipping company with instructions to transport them to a buyer at a certain destination.

(a) A **bailment for hire** is a bailment contract in which the bailor agrees to compensate the bailee. A shipping contract is usually a bailment for hire because the shipper transports the goods for a fee. (b) A **special bailment** is one in which the law imposes greater duties and liabilities on the bailee than are ordinarily imposed on other bailees. Common carriers, for example, are special bailees, because the law imposes extra duties of due care with regard to the property and persons transported than are required of private carriers. *See* carrier.

### balance of payments
(economics) A statement identifying all the economic and financial transactions between companies, banks, private households and public authorities of one nation with those of other nations of the world over a specific time period. A transaction is defined as the transfer of ownership of something that has an economic value measurable in monetary terms from residents of one country to residents of another. The transfer may involve: (1) goods, which consist of tangible and visible commodities or products; (2) services, which consist of intangible economic outputs, which usually must be produced, transferred, and consumed at the same time and in the same place; (3) income on investments; and (4) financial claims on, and liabilities to, the rest of the world, including changes in a country's reserve assets held by the central monetary authorities. A transaction may also involve a gift, which is the provision by one party of something of economic value to another party without something of economic value being received in return.

International transactions are recorded in the balance of payments on the basis of the double-entry principle used in business accounting, in which each transaction gives rise to two offsetting entries of equal value so that, in principle, the resulting credit and debit entries always balance. Transactions are generally valued at market prices and are, to the extent possible, recorded when a change of ownership occurs.

These transactions are divided into two broad groups: current account and capital account. The **current account** includes exports and imports of goods, services (including investment income) and unilateral transfers. The **capital account** includes financial flows related to international direct investment, investment in government and private securities, international bank transactions and changes in official gold holdings and foreign exchange reserves.

(IMF) The International Monetary Fund (IMF), which strives for international comparability, defines the balance of payments as "a statistical statement for a given period showing (1) transactions in goods, services and income between an economy and the rest of the world, (2) changes of ownership and other changes in that economy's monetary gold, special drawing rights (SDRs) and claims on and liabilities to the rest of the world, and (3) unrequited transfers and counterpart entries that are needed to balance, in the accounting sense, any entries for the foregoing transactions and changes which are not mutually offsetting."

(U.S.) The six balances that are currently published quarterly concerning the U.S. balance of payments are:

(1) The **balance on merchandise trade**, which measures the net transfer of merchandise exports and imports (which differs in some ways from the trade balance published monthly by the Bureau of the Census);

(2) The **balance on services**, which measures the net transfer of services, such as travel, other transportation, and business, professional, and other technical services (this balance was redefined in 1990 to exclude investment income);

(3) The **balance on investment income**, which measures the net transfer income on direct and portfolio investments;

(4) The **balance on goods, services and income**, which measures the net transfer of merchandise plus services and income on direct and portfolio investment (this balance is equivalent to the pre-1990 balance on goods and services; it is also conceptually comparable to net exports of goods and services included in GNP);

(5) The **balance on unilateral transfers** (net), which measures the net value of gifts, contributions, government grants to foreign countries and other unrequited transfers;

(6) The **balance on current account** (widely used for analysis and forecasting), which measures transactions in goods, services, income and unilateral transfers between residents and nonresidents.

### balance of trade
(economics) The difference between a country's imports and exports over a set period. (a) A **balance of trade deficit** is when a country imports more than it exports. (b) A **balance of trade surplus** is when a country exports more than it imports.

### balance on ...
*See* balance of payments.

### balanced economy
(economics) A condition of national finances in which imports and exports are equal.

### balboa
The currency of Panama. 1B=100 centesimos.

### bale
(shipping) A large bundle of compressed, bound and usually wrapped goods, such as cotton.

### bale cargo
(shipping) Bulky cargo shipped in bales, usually of burlap.

### ballast
(shipping) Heavy material strategically placed on a ship to improve its trim or stability. In most vessels water is used as ballast.

### bandwidth
(computers/Internet) The data transmission capacity of an electric communications channel or connection. The more bandwidth, the more data can be transferred in a given period of time. Bandwidth is measured in bits per second (bps). The technical definition of bandwidth refers to the difference between the highest and lowest frequency that a connection can transmit and is measured in hertz (Hz) or cycles per second. The greater the difference between these two values the more data can be sent in a given period of time. Bandwidth differs greatly depending upon a number of factors. LANs (local area networks) as used in many office environments are much faster than WANs (wide area networks) such as dial-up modems, DSL and T1-3 lines as used in most Internet connections. The following chart gives a sampling of bandwidth for the most common network configurations.

**WAN Connections    Bandwidth**
**Switched Services**
Dial-up modems 9.6, 14.4, 28.8, 33.6 and 56 Kbps
ISDN   BRI      64-128 Kbps
       PRI      1.544 Mbps
**Unswitched Private Lines**
T1       1.5 Mbps
T3       44.7 Mbps
DSL      144 Kbps to 52 Mbps

| LAN Connections | Bandwidth |
| --- | --- |
| Ethernet (10 BaseT) | 10 Mbps |
| Fast Ethernet (100 BaseT) | 100 Mbps |
| Gigabit Ethernet | 1,000 Mbps |
| Token Ring | 4, 16 Mbps |
| ATM | 25, 45, 155, 622, and 2,488 Mbps+ |

**bank acceptance**
(banking) A bill of exchange drawn on or accepted by a bank to pay specific bills for one of its customers when the bill become due. Depending on the bank's creditworthiness, the acceptance becomes a financial instrument which can be discounted for immediate payment. *See* bill of exchange.

**bank affiliate export trading company**
(U.S.) An export trading company partially or wholly owned by a banking institution as provided under the U.S. Export Trading Company Act. *See* export trading company; Export Trading Company Act.

**bank draft**
(banking) A check drawn by one bank against funds deposited to its account in another bank.

**bank holiday**
(UK) British term for a legal holiday where banks and government offices are closed.

**Bank for International Settlements (BIS)**
(banking) Established in 1930, this organization was designed to foster cooperation among world central banks, to seek opportunities for development of financial activity among governments and to serve as an agent involving the transfer of payments. Contact: Bank for International Settlements, Centralbahnplatz 2, CH-4002 Basel, Switzerland; Tel: [41] (61) 280-8080; Fax: [41] (61) 280-9100; E-mail: email@bis.org; Web: www.bis.org.

**bank guarantee**
(banking) Unilateral contract between a bank as guarantor and a beneficiary as warrantee in which the bank commits itself to pay a certain sum if a third party fails to perform or if any other specified event resulting in a default fails to take place. *See* letter of credit.

**bank holding company**
(banking) Any company which directly or indirectly owns or controls, with power to vote, more than five percent of voting shares of each of one or more other banks.

**bank holiday**
(banking) A day on which banks are closed.

**bank note**
(banking) Paper issued by the central bank, redeemable as money and considered to be full legal tender.

**bank note rate**
(banking/foreign exchange) Exchange rate used in bank note dealing.

**bank release**
(banking) A document issued by a bank, after it has been paid or given an acceptance, giving authority to a person to take delivery of goods.

**bankruptcy**
(law) (a) The status of an individual or legal entity who does not have the financial resources needed to pay debts as they come due. (b) The legal proceedings for declaring bankruptcy and discharging or restructuring debts. Laws related to these proceedings vary greatly among different countries. In the United States, bankruptcy proceedings are brought before bankruptcy courts. In some countries, a bankruptcy is dealt with through administrative agencies and a bankrupt person must first attempt to make a composition with creditors. *See* composition with creditors.

**Bank Wire Service**
(banking) A private wire service linking over 250 banks through the facilities of Western Union. This service serves as a message system for transfer of funds and information for the member banks.

**banker's bank**
(banking) A bank that is established by mutual consent by independent and unaffiliated banks to provide a clearinghouse for financial transactions.

**banker's draft**
(banking) A draft payable on demand and drawn by, or on behalf of, a bank upon itself. A banker's draft is considered cash and cannot be returned unpaid.

**banque d'affaires**
(banking) A French bank involved in long-term financing and in the ownership of companies, usually industrial firms. Synonymous with merchant bank.

**bar code**
(logistics) A series of precisely printed parallel lines and spaces of varying widths used to represent data when "read" by a bar code scanner. Bar codes are used in many applications in industry to identify products, shipping units, assets, locations and services at every stage in the logistics chain. The most commonly seen are the EAN barcodes printed on virtually every commercially distributed product in the world from books to packaged food. If you have a World Trade Press edition of this book (all are published by World Trade Press, but thousands are sold in bulk with custom covers), you will see two bar codes on the lower right corner of the back cover. The one on the left identifies the ISBN (International Standard Book Number) while the one on the right identifies the price. *See* bar code character, bar code scanner, European Article Number Association International (EAN).

**bar code character**
(logistics) Within a bar code, a series of bars and spaces that identify a specific letter, number or other data. A series of bar code characters makes up the entire bar code. *See* bar code, bar code scanner.

**bar code scanner**
(logistics) A computer data input device designed to optically "read" the bars and spaces of a printed bar code and send the data to a computing device. Bar code scanners are used extensively in the entire logistics chain and can be stationary (as at most supermarket cash registers), or portable (as used by the major courier services at package pick-up). *See* bar code, bar code character.

**bareboat charter**
(shipping) A charter of a vessel where the charter party has the right to use his own master and crew on the vessel.

**barge**
(shipping) (a) A flatbottom marine vessel with or without propulsion, designed to carry dry or liquid bulk cargoes or heavy loads, especially on inland waterways. (b) A marine vessel without propulsion, designed to carry equipment, supplies, cranes and support and accommodation bases in offshore drilling, or as submarine pipe-laying vessels. (c) A narrow, shallow draft vessel, with or without propulsion, designed to carry cargo on canals and inland waterways. The width of the vessel was designed to fit within existing canal locks. The earliest barges were horse drawn. Note: small vessels with propulsion that transport cargo between ship and shore are known as lighters.

**barratry**
(shipping) The willful misconduct of ship's master or crew including theft, intentional casting away of vessel, or any breach of trust with dishonest intent.

**barter**
The direct exchange of goods for other goods without the use of money as a medium of exchange and without the involvement of a third party. *See* countertrade.

**B**

### Basel Convention
The Basel Convention restricts trade in hazardous waste, some nonhazardous wastes, solid wastes and incinerator ash. It was adopted in 1989 by a United Nations-sponsored conference of 116 nations in Basel, Switzerland. Twenty nations must ratify the treaty before it goes into effect. Contact at: Secretariat of the Basel Convention (SBC), International Environment House; 13-15 Chemin des Anémones, Building D; 1219 Châtelaine; Geneva Switzerland; Tel: [41] (22) 917-8218; Fax: [41] (22) 797-3454; E-mail: sbc@unep.ch; Web: www.basel.int.

### basing point
(shipping) A point (location) which is used in constructing through rates between other points.

### basing rate
(shipping) A rate used only for the purpose of constructing other rates.

### basket of currencies
(banking/foreign exchange) A means of establishing value for a composite unit consisting of the currencies of designated nations. Each currency is represented in proportion to its value in relation to the total. The European Currency Unit (now obsolete due to introduction of the Euro), for example, was a weighted average of the currencies of the European Community member nations, used as a unit of value in transactions among businesses in the member countries. *See* European Currency Unit.

### battens
(shipping) The protruding fixtures of the inside walls of a vessel's hold which keep cargo away from the walls of the vessel, or to fasten the cargo to the walls of the vessel.

### baud
(Internet) The measurement of the transmission speed of a computer modem expressed in bits per second.

### bearer
(general) The person in possession.
(banking/finance/law/shipping) A person who possesses a bearer document and who is entitled to payment of funds or transfer of title to property on presentation of the document to the payee or transferor. A buyer, for example, who presents bearer documents of title (such as a bill of lading) to a shipper that transported the goods is entitled to receive the shipment. A seller who presents to a bank a negotiable instrument, such as a check, that is payable to the bearer is entitled to payment of the funds. *See* bearer document; endorsement.

### bearer document
(banking/finance/law/shipping) A negotiable instrument, commercial paper, document of title, or security that is issued payable or transferable on demand to the individual who holds the instrument, or one that is endorsed in blank. A bearer document authorizes the payment of funds or the transfer of property to the bearer when the bearer presents the document to the person, such as a bank or a shipper, that is holding the funds or property. *See* bearer; endorsement.

### bearer instrument
*See* bearer document.

### beggar-thy-neighbor policy
(economics) A course of action through which a country tries to reduce unemployment and increase domestic output by raising tariffs and instituting non-tariff barriers that impede imports, or by accomplishing the same objective through competitive devaluation. Countries that pursued such policies in the early 1930s found that other countries retaliated by raising their own barriers against imports, which, by reducing export markets, tended to worsen the economic difficulties that precipitated the initial protection-

ist action. The Smoot-Hawley Tariff Act of 1930 is often cited as a conspicuous example of this approach.

### Belgium, Netherlands, Luxembourg Economic Union (BENELUX)
A cooperative organization formed by Belgium, The Netherlands and Luxembourg to encourage economic activity among the three nations. It has eight committees addressing such areas as economic relations, agriculture, commerce, industry, customs and social affairs. Contact: BENELUX, 39 rue de la Régence, 1000 Brussels, Belgium; Tel: [32] (2) 519-38-11; Fax: [32] (2) 513-42-06; E-mail: info@benelux.be; Web: www.benelux.be.

### bell
A unit of time measurement traditionally used on sailing ships and equal to one-half hour. A "watch" is the standard period of time a sailor is on duty and is divided into 8 bells or 4 hours. During a watch each half hour is marked by the sounding of the bell.

| SHIP'S BELLS | | | |
|---|---|---|---|
| Bells | Hour (AM or PM) | | |
| 1 | 12:30 | 4:30 | 8:30 |
| 2 | 1:00 | 5:00 | 9:00 |
| 3 | 1:30 | 5:30 | 9:30 |
| 4 | 2:00 | 6:00 | 10:00 |
| 5 | 2:30 | 6:30 | 10:30 |
| 6 | 3:00 | 7:00 | 11:00 |
| 7 | 3:30 | 7:30 | 11:30 |
| 8 | 4:00 | 8:00 | 12:00 |

### belly pits or holds
(shipping) Compartments located beneath the cabin of an aircraft and used for the carriage of cargo and passenger baggage.

### below deck
(shipping) Location below the highest deck of a ship. Cargo or containers shipped below deck are not subject to wind or rain and less susceptable to fluctuation in temperature than cargo shipped above deck. Some letters of credit and purchase contracts specifically forbid placement of cargo above deck.

### benchmarking
(a) A structured approach for identifying the best practices from industry and government and comparing and adapting them to an organization's operations. Such an approach is aimed at identifying more efficient and effective processes for achieving intended results and suggesting ambitious goals for program output, product and service quality, and process improvement. (b) Performance comparison of organizational business processes against an internal or external standard of recognized leaders. Most often the comparison is made against a similar process in another organization that is considered "world class."

### beneficiary
(banking/letter of credit) The individual or company in whose favor a letter of credit is opened.
(insurance) The person or legal entity named to receive the proceeds or benefits of an insurance policy.

### BENELUX
*See* Belgium, Netherlands, Luxembourg Economic Union.

### Berne Convention
### for the Protection of Literary and Artistic Works
Formal name: The International Union for the Protection of Literary and Artistic Works. Also called the Berne Union. A part of the World Intellectual Property Organization. An

international agreement that was concluded in Berne, Switzerland, by representatives of participating countries which provides copyright, patent, trademark and other intellectual property protection to countries that are signatories to the convention. *See* World Intellectual Property Organization; copyright; patent; trademark; service mark.

### berth
(shipping/logistics) (a) The place where a ship lies secured to a wharf, pier or quay and can be loaded or unloaded of its cargo. (b) The distance or space required to safely maneuver a ship. (c) The place where a truck or motor vehicle is loaded or unloaded.

### Besloten Vennootschap met Beperkte Aansprakelijkheid (B.V.B.A.)
(Belgium/Netherlands) Designation for a private limited liability corporation with limited liability to shareholders.

### best practices
(management) The processes, practices, and systems acknowledged as producing the best results in an industry, organization, process or sub-process. Best practices are widely recognized as improving an organization's overall performance and efficiency.

### bid bond
Guarantee established in connection with international tenders. Guarantees fulfillment of the offer, i.e. that the contract will be signed if awarded. *See* bond; tender.

### bilateral investment treaty (BIT)
(foreign investment) A treaty between two countries with the goals of ensuring investments abroad of national or most favored nation treatment; prohibiting the imposition of performance requirements; and allowing the investor to engage top management in a foreign country without regard to nationality. BITs ensure the right to make investment-related transfers and guarantee that expropriation takes place only in accordance with accepted international law. BITs also guarantee access by an investing party to impartial and binding international arbitration for dispute settlement.

### bilateral steel agreements
(trade agreement) Agreements between governments to reduce or eliminate state intervention—that is, domestic subsidies and market barriers, in the production and sale of steel. The U.S. has negotiated ten BSAs with major steel trading partners.

### bilateral trade
(economics) The commerce between two countries.

### bilateral trade agreement
A formal or informal agreement involving commerce between two countries. Such agreements sometimes list the quantities of specific goods that may be exchanged between participating countries within a given period.

### bill
(law) (a) A written statement of contract terms. (b) A listing of items in a transaction or demand. (c) A promissory obligation for the payment of money. (d) An account for goods sold, services, rendered, or work completed. *See* bill of . . .; bill of lading.

### bill of adventure
(law) A written certificate used if goods are shipped under the name of a merchant, shipmaster, or shipowner. It certifies that the property and risk in the goods belong to a person other than the shipper and that the shipper is accountable to that other person for only the proceeds.

### bill of credit
(law) A written statement, commonly used by business travelers, given by one individual or legal entity to another, to authorize the recipient to receive or collect money from a foreign correspondent, such as a bank in the recipient's country. *See* letter of credit.

### bill of exchange
(banking) An unconditional order in writing, signed by a person (drawer) such as a buyer, and addressed to another person (drawee), typically a bank, ordering the drawee to pay a stated sum of money to yet another person (payee), often a seller, on demand or at a fixed or determinable future time. The most common versions of a bill of exchange are:
(a) A **draft**, wherein the drawer instructs the drawee to pay a certain amount to a named person, usually in payment for the transfer of goods or services. **Sight drafts** are payable when presented. **Time drafts** (also called usance drafts) are payable at a future fixed (specific) date or determinable (30, 60, 90 days etc.) date. Time drafts are used as a financing tool (as with Documents against Acceptance, D/A terms) to give the buyer time to pay for his purchase.
(b) A **promissory note**, wherein the issuer promises to pay a certain amount.

### bill of health
(general) A certificate issued by port or customs authorities attesting to the health of the crew and passengers of a vessel or airplane upon arrival or departure from the port.
(a) A **clean bill of health** is issued by authorities when no contagious disease(s) has been found,
(b) A **suspected bill of health** is issued when no contagious disease(s) has been found, but authorities fear that one may develop, and
(c) A **foul bill of health** is issued when a contagious disease has been found.
In the cases of issuance of a suspected bill of health or a foul bill of health, the vessel, airplane, or its passengers must enter a quarantine. *See* quarantine.

### bill of lading
(shipping) A document issued by a carrier to a shipper, signed by the captain, agent, or owner of a vessel, furnishing written evidence regarding receipt of the goods (cargo), the conditions on which transportation is made (contract of carriage), and the engagement to deliver goods at the prescribed port of destination to the lawful holder of the bill of lading. A bill of lading is, therefore, both a receipt for merchandise and a contract to deliver it as freight. There are a number of different types of bills of lading.
(a) A **straight bill of lading** indicates that the shipper will deliver the goods to the consignee. The document itself does not give title to the goods (nonnegotiable). The consignee need only identify himself to claim the goods. A straight bill of lading is often used when payment for the goods has been made in advance.
(b) A **shipper's order bill of lading** is a title document to the goods, issued "to the order of" a party, usually the shipper, whose endorsement is required to effect its negotiation. Because it is negotiable, a shipper's order bill of lading can be bought, sold, or traded while goods are in transit and is commonly used for letter-of-credit transactions. The buyer usually needs the original or a copy as proof of ownership to take possession of the goods.
(c) An **air waybill** is a form of bill of lading used for the air transport of goods and is not negotiable. *See* air waybill for a fuller explanation.
(d) A **clean bill of lading** is a bill of lading where the carrier has noted that the merchandise has been received in apparent good condition (no apparent damage, loss, etc.) and which does not bear such notations as "Shipper's Load and Count," etc.
(e) A **claused bill of lading** is a bill of lading which contains notations which specify deficient condition(s) of the goods and/or packaging.

**B**

**bill of material (BOM)**
(a) A structured list of all the components required to produce a product. (b) A structured list of all the raw materials, ingredients, parts, sub-assemblies, intermediates and components that go into making a parent assembly or finished product.
A BOM will also include the quantities, qualities, source, and stock, reference or model numbers of each component required. A BOM is typically used in conjunction with a master production schedule to plan the acquisition of all required components. In specialized industries the BOM may also be called the formula, recipe or list of ingredients.

**bill of parcels**
(law) A statement that lists the descriptions and prices of goods in a parcel and that is sent to the buyer with the goods. This bill is often referred to as a packing slip.

**bill of sale**
(law) A written document by which an individual or legal entity assigns or transfers title to goods to another.

**bill of sight**
(U.S. Customs) A document used by U.S. Customs that permits a consignee of goods to see them before paying duties.

**billed weight**
(shipping) The weight shown in a waybill or freight bill.

**billing third party**
(shipping) The invoicing of transportation charges to other than shipper or consignee.

**bill-to party**
(shipping) Refers to the party designated on a bill of lading as the one responsible for payment of the freight charges; this can be the shipper, freight forwarder, consignee, or another person.

**bimodal trailer**
(trucking/railroads) A semi-trailer able to function as an on-road truck trailer with pneumatic tires, or, on railroad tracks with the deployment of a steel wheel rail assembly. In some cases the road tires retract to allow the trailer chassis (container) to mount on a pair of rail bogies. Also called a road-rail trailer.

**binder**
(insurance) A document certifying temporary insurance coverage. A binder is issued by an insurance company or its agent pending the issuance of an insurance policy.

**binding decisions**
(U.S. Customs) A binding tariff classification ruling (decision), which can be relied upon for placing or accepting orders or for making other business determinations. May be obtained by writing to a local Customs district director. The rulings will be binding at all ports of entry unless revoked by the Customs Service's Office of Regulations and Rulings. Note that while the port and district offices of Customs are, for many purposes, your best sources of information, informal information obtained on tariff classification is not binding.

**biological agents**
A biologically active material. Several classes of biological agents have been identified according to their degree of pathogenic hazard, and are unilaterally controlled by various governments. In the United States applications to export certain biological agents are referred to the Department of State and the intelligence community on a case-by-case basis.

**biomedical materials**
(shipping) Items that can cause human disease (infectious/etiological agent). (UN CLASS 6) Examples are live virus vaccines and etiologic agents. Hazards/precautions are: may be ignited if carrier is flammable; contact may cause infection/disease; and damage to outer container may not affect inner container.

**birr**
The currency of Ethiopia. 1Br (or 1E$)=100 cents.

**black market**
Buying or selling of products and commodities, or engaging in exchange of foreign currencies in violation of government restrictions.

**blank back**
(documentation) A form that does not have the terms and conditions printed on the reverse (back) of the form. For example, a blank back bill of lading, also called a short form bill of lading, does not have the terms and conditions of carriage printed on the reverse. Instead, they are listed in another document. Unless otherwise stipulated in a letter of credit, a blank back bill of lading is acceptable in most transactions. Note that the more common term is short form.

**blank endorsement**
(law/banking/shipping) The signature or endorsement of a person or firm on any negotiable instrument (such as a check, draft or bill of lading), usually on the reverse of the document, without designating another person to whom the endorsement is made. The document therefore becomes bearer paper. In shipping, for example, the holder of a blank endorsed bill of lading can take possession of the merchandise. *See* endorsement; bearer document.

**blanket rate**
(shipping) (a) A rate applicable from and/or to a group of points; (b) A special single rate applicable to different articles in a single shipment.

**blockade**
The act of preventing commercial exchange with a country or port, usually during wartime, by physically preventing carriers from entering a specific port or nation. *See* embargo.

**blocking or bracing**
(shipping) Wood or metal supports to keep shipments in place in or on containers.

**blood diamond**
*See* conflict diamond.

**board foot (fbm, BF, bd ft)**
(measurement) A unit of measurement used for lumber. One board foot is 12 inches by 12 inches by 1 inch, or one square foot of lumber one inch thick.

**bogey**
*See* bogie.

**bogie (bogey)**
(trucking) An assembly of two or more axles, usually a pair in tandem, with one or two wheels attached to the end of each axle that swivel to help a truck or its trailer(s) turn on curvy roads.
(rail transport) An assembly of two or more axles, that swivel to help a rail car turn on curvy track.

**bolivar**
The currency of Venezuela. 1B=100 centimos.

**boliviano**
The currency of Bolivia. 1$b=100 centavos.

**bona fide**
(law) In or with good faith, honesty and sincerity. A bona fide purchaser, for example, is one who buys goods for value and without knowledge of fraud or unfair dealing in the transaction. Knowledge of fraud or unfair dealing may be implied if the facts are such that the purchaser should have reasonably known that the transaction involved deceit, such as when goods that are susceptible to copyright piracy are provided without product documentation as to their origin.

## bond
(general) An interest-bearing certificate of debt, usually issued in series, by which the issuer obligates itself to pay the principal amount at a specified time and to pay interest periodically.

(banking) An instrument used as proof of a debt.

(finance) The obligation to answer for the debt of another person.

(insurance) A contract between a principal and a surety (insurance company or their agent) which is obtained to insure performance of an obligation (often imposed by law or regulation).

(U.S. Customs) A bond required by the federal government in connection with the payment of duties or to produce documentation. U.S. Customs entries must be accompanied by evidence that a surety bond is posted with Customs to cover any potential duties, taxes and penalties which may accrue. Bonds may be secured through a resident U.S. surety company, but may also be posted in the form of United States money or certain United States government obligations. In the event that a customs broker is employed for the purpose of making entry, the broker may permit the use of his or her bond to provide the required coverage. *See* bond system; surety; in bond.

## bonded
(U.S. Customs) Goods stored under supervision of customs until the import duties are paid or the goods are exported.

## bonded carrier
(a) A carrier licensed to transport goods in bond. (b) A carrier, licensed by the customs authority of a country to transport imported goods past the customs border of the country to another customs office in the same country where duties and taxes are then paid by the importer.

## bonded exchange
(foreign exchange) Foreign exchange which cannot be freely converted into other currencies. *See* foreign exchange.

## bonded stores
(customs) A place (usually a secured storeroom) on a vessel or airplane where non-customs-entered goods are placed under seal until the vessel leaves the port or country.

## bonded terminal
(customs) An airline terminal approved by the U.S. Treasury Department for storage of goods until Customs duties are paid or the goods are otherwise properly released.

## bonded warehouse
(U.S. Customs) A warehouse owned by persons approved by the Treasury Department, and under bond or guarantee for the strict observance of the revenue laws of the United States; utilized for storing goods until duties are paid or goods are otherwise properly released. Payment of customs duties is deferred until the goods enter the Customs Territory of the United States. The goods are not subject to duties if reshipped to foreign points. *See* bond; in bond.

## bond of indemnity
(shipping) An agreement made with a carrier relieving it from liability for any action on its part for which it would otherwise be liable.

## bond system
(U.S. Customs) A part of the U.S. Customs' Automated Commercial System, provides information on bond coverage. A Customs bond is a contract between a principal, usually an importer, and a surety which is obtained to insure performance of an obligation imposed by law or regulation. The bond covers potential loss of duties, taxes, and penalties for specific types of transactions. Customs is the contract beneficiary. *See* Automated Commercial System.

## booking
(shipping) The act of recording arrangements for the movement of goods by vessel.

## Border Cargo Selectivity
(United States) A program of the U.S. Customs and Border Protection (CBP) Automated Commercial System (ACS) that determines risk assessment and examination requirements for high-volume borders. The system uses the same editing process as the Cargo Selectivity system. For more information go to: www.cbp.gov.

## bordereau
(insurance) (a) A method of reporting shipments to an insurance company under an open insurance policy. (b) An insurance form, similar to a declaration, which provides for insurance coverage of multiple shipments within a prescribed reporting period, usually a month.

This form calls for the name of the vessel and sailing date, points of shipment and destination, nature of commodity, the amount of insurance desired, and the number of the open policy under which the shipment is made. The bordereau form is prepared by the assured and is forwarded within a prescribed reporting period, usually monthly. The forms are forwarded to the insurance agent or broker for transmission to the insurance company. The premium is billed monthly in accordance with the schedule of rates provided by the policy.

The bordereau is generally not used in cases where evidence of insurance must be supplied to a customer, to banks or to other third parties in order to permit collection of claims abroad. This calls for a special marine policy, occasionally referred to as a certificate. The bordereau, therefore, is mainly used for import shipments, not export shipments.

*See* special marine policy. *See* declaration.

## Bosun
(shipping) A petty officer on a merchant ship who controls or supervises the work of other seamen.

## bounties or grants
Payments by governments to producers of goods, often to strengthen their competitive position.

## bow
(shipping) The front of a vessel.

## box
(shipping) Colloquial term referring to a trailer, semi-trailer or container.

## box car
(shipping) A closed freight car.

## boycott
A refusal to deal commercially or otherwise with a person, firm or country.

## break bulk cargo
Conventional, uncontainerized cargo that is shipped in units of one (such as uncontainerized machinery or trucks) or shipped in units or packages (such as palletized or boxed cargo).

(U.S. Customs) Cargo that is not containerized and that cannot be classified as "bulk" cargo under the U.S. Customs and Border Protection definition. For example, new and used vehicles are considered break bulk cargo. Although uniform in nature, vehicles have identifying marks (such as a Vehicle Identification Number, or VIN). One necessary aspect of *bulk* cargo is fungibility (goods that are identical with others of the same nature). The presence of a VIN removes that component from the shipment of new or used vehicles.

It is important to note that the difference between bulk and break bulk is based not only on the type of cargo, but also on the way in which the cargo is stowed or loaded. For example, bananas stowed loosely in a hold (not in boxes or containers) is considered bulk. Palletized boxes of bananas loaded directly into a hold (but not loose or containerized) is considered break bulk. *See* bulk cargo.

**breakage**
(a) A monetary allowance or credit that a manufacturer agrees to give a buyer to compensate for damage caused to goods during transit or storage. (b) A fractional amount due as part of a payment to a party, such as pennies that result from a computation of interest on a loan or deposit.

**breakbulk**
(shipping) To unload and distribute a portion or all of the contents of a consolidated shipment for delivery or reconsignment.

**breakbulk vessel**
(shipping) A general cargo vessel designed to efficiently handle breakbulk loads. Breakbulk cargo vessels are usually self-sustaining in that they have their own loading and unloading machinery.

**break-even point**
(banking/foreign exchange) The price of a financial instrument at which the option buyer recovers the premium, meaning that he makes neither a loss nor a gain. In the case of a call option, the break-even point is the exercise price plus the premium, and in the case of a put option, the exercise price minus the premium. *See* option; call option; put option.

**Bretton-Woods Agreement of 1944**
(banking/foreign exchange) Articles of agreement adopted by the international monetary conference of 44 nations which met at Bretton Woods, New Hampshire in 1944. The International Monetary Fund and the International Bank for Reconstruction and Development were created as a result of this agreement. The Fund's major responsibility was to maintain orderly currency practices in international trade, while the Bank's function was to facilitate extension of long-term investments for productive purposes.
*See* Bretton-Woods System; International Monetary Fund; International Bank for Reconstruction and Development.

**Bretton-Woods System**
(banking/foreign exchange) The system of fixed exchange rates with fluctuation grids, in which every member of the International Monetary Fund (IMF) set a specific parity for its currency relative to gold or the dollar, and undertook to keep fluctuations within ±1% of parity by central bank market interventions. This system was in operation from the end of WWII through the early 1970s. *See* Bretton-Woods Agreement of 1944; International Monetary Fund; International Bank for Reconstruction and Development.

**bribe**
A payment resulting in the payer's receiving some right, benefit, or preference to which he has no legal right and which he would not have obtained except with the payment of the money. A bribe is a criminal offense in most countries, but may not be a criminal offense in a home country if committed in a foreign country. *See* Foreign Corrupt Practices Act.

**British High Commission (BHC)**
(diplomacy) The term British High Commission (BHC, or High Commission, HC, or Her Majesty's High Commission, HMHC) is used in lieu of "embassy" in Commonwealth countries.

**broken cross rates; triangular arbitrage**
(banking/foreign exchange) A forward foreign exchange arrangement which is not for a standard maturity period. Standard periods are: 1 week; 2 weeks; 1, 2, 3, 6 and 12 months.
(banking/foreign exchange) In foreign exchange, disparity among three or more rates; e.g., if DM 1=30 cents and FF 1.5 while FF 1=22 cents, a deutsch mark will bring 30

cents if converted directly but 33 cents if converted first into francs and then into dollars.

**broker**
An individual or firm that acts as an intermediary, often between a buyer and seller, usually for a commission. Often an agent.
(a) **Customs broker**—An individual or firm licensed to enter and clear goods through Customs for another individual or firm. *See* customs broker.
(b) **Insurance broker**—An individual or firm which acts as an intermediary between an insurance company and the insured. *See* insurance broker.

**brokerage license, domestic**
(U.S.) Authority granted by the U.S. Interstate Commerce Commission to persons to engage in the business of arranging for transportation of persons or property in interstate commerce.

**browser**
(Internet) A computer program used to access and search the Internet (World Wide Web).

**Brussels Tariff Nomenclature**
(customs) A once widely used international tariff classification system which preceded the Customs Cooperation Council Nomenclature (CCCN) and the Harmonized System Nomenclature (HS). *See* Harmonized Tariff Schedule; Customs Cooperation Council Nomenclature.

**buffer stock**
(logistics) Raw materials, component parts or finished goods maintained in inventory specifically in anticipation of unforeseen shortages of materials or component parts or unusual demand for finished goods. The volume of buffer stock held in inventory is typically determined by such factors as order fulfillment time from the supplier, delivery time from its point of origin, the potential for problems with supply and the potential for unusual increases in demand for finished products.

**building society**
(UK) British term for a savings and loan banking institution.

**bulk cargo**
Homogenous cargo that is stowed loose in the hold of a ship and is not enclosed in a shipping container or box, bale, bag, cask, or the like. Bulk cargo consists entirely of one commodity and is usually shipped without packaging. Specifically, bulk cargo is composed of either: 1) free flowing articles such as oil, grain, coal, ore, and the like which can be pumped or run through a chute or handled by dumping; or 2) uniform cargo that stows as solidly and requires mechanical handling for lading and discharging." This includes such items as coils, rails, rods, ingots, bars, plates, billets, slabs, pipes and sheets of steel or other metals; timber, lumber and paper products as a commodity; and certain perishable goods, not in boxes, bags or containerized, and not frozen, but laden and stowed in a way similar to other types of bulk cargo (includes seafood and produce). One necessary aspect of bulk cargo is fungibility (goods that are identical with others of the same nature).
It is important to note that the difference between bulk and break bulk is based not only on the type of cargo, but also on the way in which the cargo is stowed or loaded. For example, bananas stowed loosely in a hold (not in boxes or containers) is considered bulk. Palletized boxes of bananas loaded directly into a hold (but not loose or containerized) is considered break bulk. *See* break bulk cargo.

**bulk carrier**
(shipping) A vessel specifically designed to transport bulk cargo. There are two types of bulk carriers: those designed to transport dry bulk cargo such as grain or ore, and those designed to transport liquid bulk cargo such as oil.

**bulk container**
(shipping) An ocean or air freight container designed to ship dry bulk cargo such as malt. Bulk fluid cargo such as chemicals and fruit juices are shipped in tank containers. Bulk cargo such as ore, grain, and crude oil are generally shipped in specialized bulk cargo ships rather than in containers.

**bulk freight**
(shipping) Freight not in packages or containers. For example: grain, ore, timber.

**bulk liquids**
(shipping) Liquid cargo shipped in intermodal tank containers.

**bulk sale or transfer**
(law) A transfer of substantially all of the inventory or property of an enterprise to one individual or legal entity in a single transaction not in the ordinary course of the business of the enterprise. In some countries, bulk sales and transfers are regulated by law in an effort to reduce the potential for defrauding creditors through this type of transaction.

**bulk solids**
(shipping) Dry cargo shipped loose in containers.

**bulkhead**
(shipping) (a) A partition separating one part of a ship between decks from another. (b) A structure to resist the pressure of earth or water.

**Bundesbank**
(banking) Established in 1875, the central bank of Germany, located in Frankfurt.

**bundling**
(commerce/logistics) The combining of two or more usually related products or services for sale at the same time for a single price. For example, the bundling of a computer scanner and image-manipulation software for one price.

**bunker**
(shipping) A compartment on a ship for storage of fuel.

**bunker adjustment factor (BAF)**
(shipping) An adjustment in shipping charges to offset price fluctuations in the cost of bunker fuel.

**bunker charge**
*See* bunker adjustment factor.

**bunker fuel**
(shipping) The fuel used to power a ship.

**Bureau of Alcohol, Tobacco and Firearms (ATF)**
(U.S. government) An agency of the U.S. Department of Treasury, the ATF regulates the alcohol, firearms and explosives industry, ensures the collection of federal taxes imposed on alcohol and tobacco, investigates violations of federal firearms, explosives and tobacco laws. Contact: Bureau of Alcohol, Tobacco and Firearms, Department of the Treasury, 650 Massachusetts Ave. NW, Washington, DC 20226 USA; Tel: [1] (202) 927-8500; Fax: [1] (202) 927-8868; E-mail: ATFMail@atf.gov; Web: www.atf.gov.

**Bureau of Customs**
*See* United States Customs and Border Protection.

**Bureau of Export Administration**
(U.S. government) As of April 18, 2002 the Bureau of Export Administration is now called the Bureau of Industry and Security. *See* Bureau of Industry and Security.

**Bureau of Industry and Security**
(U.S. government) Formerly, the Bureau of Export Administration. Part of the U.S. Department of Commerce. Responsible for control of exports for reasons of national security, foreign policy and short supply. Licenses on controlled exports are issued and seminars on U.S. export regulations are held domestically and overseas. The Bureau of Industry and Security provides an Internet-based export license application program free of charge called the Simplified Network Application Process (SNAP) at Web: http://snap.bis.doc.gov. Telephone support for SNAP is also available at [1] (202) 482-4811. Contact: Bureau of Industry and Security; 14th Street and Constitution Avenue, N.W.; U.S. Department of Commerce; Washington, DC 20230 USA. Web: www.bis.doc.gov.

**Bureau International des Expositions**
(international organization) International Bureau of Expositions. An international organization established by the Paris Convention of 1928 to regulate the conduct and scheduling of international expositions in which foreign nations are officially invited to participate. The BIE divides international expositions into different categories and types and requires each member nation to observe specified minimum time intervals in scheduling each of these categories and types of operations. Under BIE rules, member nations may not ordinarily participate in an international exposition unless the exposition has been approved by the BIE. The U.S. became a member of the BIE in April 1968. Federal participation in a recognized international exposition requires specific authorization by the Congress, based on the president's finding that participation is in the national interest. Contact at Bureau; 34, Avenue d'Iéna 75116 Paris; Tel: [33] (45) 00 38 63; Fax: [33] (45) 00 96 15; Web: www.bie-paris.org.

**Business Anti-Smuggling Coalition (BASC)**
(United States) A U.S. Customs and Border Protection (CBP) program initiated in March 1996, as a business-led, CBP-supported alliance created to combat the smuggling of contraband via commercial trade. BASC was designed to complement and enhance the CIP program. The ultimate objective of BASC is to eliminate the contamination of legitimate business shipments by criminal hands. The program also provides businesses with heightened security awareness about the smuggling of contraband and other terrorist tools in the import and export communities. BASC is one of the CBP Industry Partnership Programs (IPP). For more information contact the CBP Industry Partnership Programs at [1] (202) 927-0520 or go to: www.cbp.gov.

**Business Executive Enforcement Team**
(U.S. government) A channel for private sector U.S. business executives to discuss export control enforcement matters with the Bureau of Export Administration. *See* Bureau of Export Administration. Contact: Export Enforcement -- BEET Conferences, Bureau of Industry and Security, Room 3727, U.S. Department of Commerce, Washington, DC 20230 USA; Tel: [1] (202) 482-2252; Web: www.bis.doc.gov/Enforcement/.

**Buy American acts**
U.S. federal and state government statutes that give a preference to U.S. produced goods in government contracts. These statutes are designed to protect domestic industry and labor, but tend to increase the price paid for goods and services government agencies buy. *See* non-tariff barriers or measures; trade barriers.

**buyback**
(economics) A form of countertrade that involves the exportation of technological know-how, specialized machinery and the construction of an entire factory in exchange for a set percentage of the factory's production over a five to twenty-five year period. Buyback is also known as compensation trading. *See* countertrade.

**buying rate (bid rate)**
(banking/foreign exchange) Rate at which a bank is prepared to buy foreign exchange or to accept deposits. The opposite of selling (or asked) rate.

# C

### cabotage
(shipping) Coast-wide water transportation, navigation or trade between ports of a nation. Many nations, like the U.S., have cabotage laws which require domestic owned vessels to perform domestic interport water transportation service.

### CADEX
(Canada) An electronic data interchange (EDI) system offered by the Canada Revenue Agency (CRA) allowing importers and brokers to file customs accounting documents (B3) form electronically. Information at:
Web: www.ccra-adrc.gc.ca.

### Cairns Group
An informal association of agricultural exporting countries established in August 1986. Members include Argentina, Australia, Bolivia, Brazil, Canada, Chile, Colombia, Costa Rica, Guatemala, Indonesia, Malaysia, New Zealand, Pakistan, Paraguay, the Philippines, South Africa, Thailand and Uruguay. Web: www.cairnsgroup.org.

### call
(banking) A demand of payment on a loan, often as a result of noncompliance on the part of the borrower to the terms and conditions of the loan.

### call in a contract
(law) (a) Demanding payment on a contract. A seller, for example, may be entitled under the contract terms to demand payment at the time the goods are ready to ship. (b) Submitting a formal, usually written, notice to collect payment on a contract. A seller who has not received payment, for example, may send a written letter to the buyer demanding remittance of the funds owed—that is calling in the contract.

### call money
(banking/finance/foreign exchange) Currency lent by banks on a very short-term basis, which can be called the same day, at one day's notice or at two days' notice. Called overnight money in Great Britain and Federal funds in the United States.

### call option
(banking/finance/foreign exchange) The right (but not the obligation) to buy a fixed amount of a commodity, security or currency from the option writer (option seller) at a predetermined rate and/or exercise price within a specified time limit. *See* option; put option; American Option; European Option.

### Calvo Doctrine
(foreign investment) The Calvo Doctrine (or principle) holds that jurisdiction in international investment disputes lies with the country in which the investment is located; thus, the investor has no recourse but to use the local courts. The principle, named after an Argentinian jurist, has been applied throughout Latin America and other areas of the world.

### Canada Border Services Agency (CBSA)
(Canada Customs) The CBSA was created on December 12, 2003 as part of the new portfolio of Public Safety and Emergency Preparedness, which includes emergency preparedness, crisis management, national security, corrections, policing, oversight, crime prevention, as well as border services.

The CBSA brings together all the major players involved in facilitating legitimate cross-border traffic and supporting economic development while stopping people and goods that pose a potential risk to Canada. It integrates several key functions previously spread among three organizations: the Customs program from the Canada Customs and Revenue Agency; the Intelligence, Interdiction and Enforcement program from Citizenship and Immigration Canada; and the Import Inspection at Ports of Entry program from the Canadian Food Inspection Agency.

The CBSA's role is to manage the nation's borders by administering and enforcing about 75 domestic laws that govern trade and travel, as well as international agreements and conventions.

The work of the CBSA includes: processing commercial goods, travellers, and conveyances, and identifying and interdicting high-risk individuals and goods; conducting secondary inspections of food and agricultural products imported by travellers at airports; conducting intelligence, such as screening visitors and immigrants and working with law enforcement agencies to maintain border integrity and ensure national security; engaging in enforcement activities, including investigations, detentions, hearings, and removals; supporting free trade negotiations; and conducting compliance audit reviews and dumping and subsidy investigations.

The CBSA operates at about 1,370 service points across Canada and nearly 40 locations abroad. It employs 10,000 public servants who serve some 170,000 commercial importers and more than 98 million travellers each year.

You can find more information about the creation of the CBSA at: www.pm.gc.ca
For information about CBSA, go to:
www.cbsa-asfc.gc.ca

### Canadian Commercial Corporation
(Canada) The prime contractor in government-to-government sales transactions, facilitating exports of a wide range of goods and services from Canadian sources. In response to requests from foreign governments and international agencies for individual products or services, CCC identifies Canadian firms capable of meeting the customer's requirements, executes prime as well as back-to-back contracts, and follows through with contract management, inspection, acceptance, and payment. Contact: Canadian Commercial Corporation (CCC), 50 O'Connor Street, 11th floor, Ottawa, ON K1A 0S6, Canada; Tel: [1] (613) 996-0034, or toll-free at [1] (800) 748-8191; Fax: [1] (613) 995-2121; Web: www.ccc.ca.

### cap
(banking/finance/foreign exchange) On borrowed funds with an interest rate which is tied to the market rate, an upside limit or cap can be agreed upon, i.e. against payment of a premium, an upper interest rate limit is agreed upon, which will not be exceeded even if the market rate rises above the stated level.

### capacity to contract
(law) Legal competency to make a contract. A party has capacity to contract if he or she has attained the age required by law and has the mental ability to understand the nature of contract obligations.

### Capesize
(shipping) An ocean-going cargo vessel that is physically too large to fit through the locks of either the Panama or Suez Canals and therefore must voyage via Cape Horn at the southernmost tip of South America to get to or from the Atlantic and Pacific Oceans, or the Cape of Good Hope at the southernmost tip of South Africa to get to or from the Indian and Atlantic Oceans. Capesize vessels generally serve deepwater terminals handling raw materials, such as iron ore and coal.

**capital account**
(economics) Juxtaposition of the long- and short-term capital imports and exports of a country. *See* balance of payments.

**capital flight**
(economics) The transfer of money or other financial resources from one country to another as a hedge against inflation or poor economic or political conditions.

**capital goods**
(economics) Manufactured goods that are for productive industrial use. For example: machine tools. *See* consumer goods.

**capital market**
(finance) The market for buying and selling long-term loanable funds, in the form of bonds, mortgages and the like. Unlike the money market, where short-term funds are traded, the capital market tends to center on well-organized institutions such as the stock exchange. However, there is no clear-cut distinction between the two other than that capital market loans are generally used by businesses, financial institutions and governments to buy capital goods whereas money-market loans generally fill a temporary need for working capital.

**capital movements**
(economics) (a) The international payments of a nation. (b) A nation's short- and long-term claims and liabilities, which are entered into vis-a-vis foreign countries, including repayment of foreign debt, direct investments, portfolio investments and purchase of private real estate.

**captain's protest**
(shipping) A document prepared by the captain of a vessel on arrival at port, showing unusual conditions encountered during voyage. Generally, a captain's protest is prepared to relieve the ship owner of any liability for any loss to cargo, thus requiring cargo owners to look to insurance companies for reimbursement.

**Captain, Ship's**
(shipping) The officer in command of a ship. Master of a ship. The captain leads, supervises and is responsible for the entire crew. Responsibilities include: all aspects of the running of a ship, customs and immigration issues and cargo manifests. Deals directly with the three department heads: Chief Engineer, Chief Steward and Chief Mate.

**cargo**
(shipping) Merchandise hauled by transportation lines.

**cargo agent**
(shipping) An agent appointed by an airline or shipping line to solicit and process international air and ocean freight for shipments. Cargo agents are paid commissions by the airline or shipping line.

**cargo aircraft**
*See* all-cargo aircraft.

**cargo manifest**
(shipping) A list of a ship's cargo or passengers, but without a listing of charges.

**cargo, N.O.S.**
(shipping) Articles not otherwise specifically provided for. In determining the freight rate, a general category of articles for shipment.

**cargo selectivity system**
(U.S. Customs) A part of U.S. Customs' Automated Commercial System, specifies the type of examination (intensive or general) to be conducted for imported merchandise. The type of examination is based on database selectivity criteria such as assessments of risk by filer, consignee, tariff number, country of origin, and manufacturer/shipper. A first time consignee is always selected for an intensive examination. An alert is also generated in cargo selectivity

the first time a consignee files an entry in a port with a particular tariff number, country of origin, or manufacturer/shipper. *See* Automated Commercial System.

**cargo tonnage**
(shipping) The weight of a shipment or of a ship's total cargo expressed in tons.

**Caribbean Basin Economic Recovery Act (CBERA)**
(U.S.) The CBERA affords nonreciprocal tariff preferences by the United States to developing countries in the Caribbean Basin area to aid their economic development and to diversify and expand their production and exports. The CBERA applies to merchandise entered, or withdrawn from warehouse for consumption, on or after January 1, 1984. This tariff preference program has no expiration date. *See* Caribbean Basin Initiative.

**Caribbean Basin Initiative (CBI)**
(U.S.) A program providing for the duty-free entry into the United States of merchandise from designated beneficiary countries or territories in the Caribbean Basin.

This program was enacted by the United States as the Caribbean Basin Economic Recovery Act and became effective January 1, 1984.

The purpose of the program is to increase economic aid and trade preferences for twenty-eight states of the Caribbean region. The Caribbean Basin Economic Recovery Act provided for twelve years of duty-free treatment of most goods produced in the Caribbean region. The Initiative was extended permanently (CBI II), by the Customs and Trade Act of August 1990. The 23 countries include Antigua and Barbuda, the Bahamas, Barbados, Belize, the British Virgin Islands, Costa Rica, Dominica, the Dominican Republic, El Salvador, Grenada, Guatemala, Guyana, Honduras, Jamaica, Montserrat, the Netherlands Antilles, Nicaragua, Panama, St. Christopher-Nevis, St. Lucia, St. Vincent and the Grenadines, Trinidad and Tobago. The following countries may be eligible for CBI benefits but have not formally requested designation: Anguilla, Cayman Islands, Suriname, and the Turks and Caicos Islands. Web: www.mac.doc.gov/CBI/webmain/intro.htm.

**Caribbean Common Market (CARICOM)**
A regional trade alliance composed of 13 English speaking Caribbean nations. Its purpose is to further economic development and increase social and cultural cooperation among member nations. Members include Antigua and Barbuda, the Bahamas, Barbados, Belize, Dominica, Grenada, Guyana, Jamaica, Montserrat, St. Kitts-Nevis, St. Lucia, St. Vincent and the Grenadines, and Trinidad and Tobago. Contact: Caribbean Common Market, Bank of Guyana Building, PO Box 10827, Georgetown, Guyana; Tel: (592) 222-0001-75; Fax: (592) 222-0171; E-mail: info@caricom.org; Web: www.caricom.org.

**carnet**
(customs) A customs document permitting the holder to carry or send merchandise temporarily into participating foreign countries (for display, demonstration, or similar purposes) without paying duties, value-added taxes or posting bonds. *See* ATA Carnet, TECRO/AIT Carnet.

**Carriage and Insurance Paid To (...named place of destination) (CIP)**
(Incoterms 2000) An international trade term of sale in which, for the quoted price, the seller/exporter clears the goods for export, delivers them to the carrier, and is responsible for paying for carriage and insurance to the named place of destination. However, once the goods are delivered to the carrier, the buyer is responsible for all additional costs.

In Incoterms 2000 the seller is also responsible for the costs of unloading, customs clearance, duties, and other costs if such costs are included in the cost of carriage such as in small package courier delivery.

The seller is responsible for procuring and paying for insurance cover.

The CIP term is valid for any form of transport including multimodal.

The "named place of destination" in CIP and all "C" Incoterms 2000 is domestic to the buyer, but is not necessarily the final delivery point.

The Carriage and Insurance Paid To term is often used in sales where the shipment is by air freight, containerized ocean freight, courier shipments of small parcels, and in "ro-ro" (roll-on, roll-off) shipments of motor vehicles.

A "carrier" can be a shipping line, airline, trucking firm, railway or also an individual or firm who undertakes to procure carriage by any of the above methods of transport including multimodal. Therefore, a person, such as a freight forwarder, can act as a "carrier" under this term.

If subsequent carriers are used for the carriage to the agreed destination, the risk passes when the goods have been delivered to the first carrier.

*See* Guide to Incoterms 2000 Appendix.

### Carriage of Goods by Sea Act of 1936

(U.S. shipping law) A U.S. law which, among other provisions, establishes statutory responsibility for the carrier's liability for certain types of damage. Where the COGSA applies, generally speaking, the vessel or carrier is responsible for damage resulting from negligence in the loading, stowing and discharge of cargo. It is not responsible for damage resulting from errors of navigation or management of the ship, from unseaworthiness of the vessel (unless caused by lack of due diligence to make it seaworthy), or from perils of the sea, fire, and a number of other listed causes. The burden of proof in establishing fault will rest at times upon the shipper and at times upon the carrier.

The degree to which a steamship company can be held responsible for damage sustained by a specific shipment is frequently difficult to determine. COGSA applies to import and export shipments and, by agreement, to much U.S. coast-wise and intercoastal business as well.

### Carriage Paid To
### (...named place of destination) (CPT)

(Incoterms 2000) An international trade term of sale in which, for the quoted price, the seller/exporter/manufacturer clears the goods for export, delivers them to the carrier, and is responsible for paying for carriage to the named place of destination. However, once the seller delivers the goods to the carrier, the buyer becomes responsible for all additional costs.

In Incoterms 2000 the seller is also responsible for the costs of unloading, customs clearance, duties, and other costs if such costs are included in the cost of carriage such as in small package courier delivery.

The seller is not responsible for procuring and paying for insurance cover.

The CPT term is valid for any form of transport including multimodal.

The "named place of destination" in CPT and all "C" Incoterms 2000 is domestic to the buyer, but is not necessarily the final delivery point.

The Carriage Paid To term is often used in sales where the shipment is by air freight, containerized ocean freight, courier shipments of small parcels, and in "ro-ro" (roll-on, roll-off) shipments of motor vehicles.

A "carrier" can be a shipping line, airline, trucking firm, railway or also an individual or firm who undertakes to procure carriage by any of the above methods of transport

including multimodal. Therefore, a person, such as a freight forwarder, can act as a "carrier" under this term.

If subsequent carriers are used for the carriage to the agreed destination, the risk passes when the goods have been delivered to the first carrier.

*See* Guide to Incoterms 2000 Appendix.

### carrier

(law/shipping) An individual or legal entity that is in the business of transporting passengers or goods for hire. Shipping lines, airlines, trucking companies, and railroad companies are all carriers.

Note: The worldwide acceptance of Incoterms 1990 (and now Incoterms 2000) has resulted in an expanded definition of "carrier." In the older and more limited definition, only shipping lines, airlines, trucking companies and railroad companies are carriers. However, the significant increase in multimodal transport and integrated logistics has placed freight forwarders into the position of "carrier." In the definition above, a freight forwarder is a "legal entity that is in the business of transporting goods."

The ICC (International Chamber of Commerce) has established the following definition:

(ICC definition) "Carrier means any person who, in a contract of carriage, undertakes to perform or to procure the performance of transport by rail, road, air, sea, inland waterway or by combination of such modes." Within the context of this definition, when a buyer nominates a freight forwarder to receive the goods, such as in the FCA (Free Carrier) Incoterm, the seller fulfills his obligation to deliver the goods by delivering to that person.

(a) A **common carrier** is one that by law must convey passengers or goods without refusal, provided the party requesting conveyance has paid the charge for transport.

(b) A **private or contract carrier** is one that transports only those persons or goods that it selects.

(U.S. shipping) By U.S. government regulation a common carrier publishes stated rates for carriage and must accept any passengers or goods for transport so long as space is available and the published rate is paid.

### Carrier Initiative Program (CIP)

(United States) A U.S. Customs and Border Protection (CBP) program established in 1984, as a joint effort among air, sea, land and rail carriers and CBP to address the problem of drug smuggling and terrorism in the United States on board commercial conveyances. By signing the CIP agreement with CBP, carriers agree to enhance their security at foreign and domestic terminals as well as on board their conveyances. Additionally, they agree to cooperate closely with CBP in identifying and reporting attempted or suspected smuggling attempts or other criminal activity. In return, the Customs Service agrees to conduct both domestic and foreign security site surveys, post-seizure analysis, and provide training to identify security weaknesses within their company and suggests improvements to better their security systems and measures. The CIP is one of the CBP Industry Partnership Programs (IPP). For more information contact the CBP Industry Partnership Programs at [1] (202) 927-0520 or go to: www.cbp.gov.

### carrier's certificate

(U.S. Customs) A document issued by a shipping company, addressed to a District Director of Customs, which certifies that a named individual is the owner or consignee of the articles listed in the certificate. This document is often the "evidence of right to make entry" required by U.S. Customs for an individual to clear goods through Customs.

*See* evidence of right to make entry.

**cartage**
(logistics) (a) The movement of goods for short distances, usually by truck. (b) The charge to pick up, move and deliver goods short distances.

**cartage agent**
(shipping) A ground service operator who provides pickup and delivery of freight in areas not served directly by an air or ocean carrier.

**cartage/drayage**
(shipping) (a) The local transport of goods. (b) The charge(s) made for hauling freight on carts, drays or trucks.

**cartel**
An organization of independent producers formed to regulate the production, pricing, or marketing practices of its members in order to limit competition and maximize their market power.

**casco**
(insurance) Marine insurance coverage on the hull of a ship.

**cash against documents (CAD)**
(commerce/banking) A method of payment where a seller, or an intermediary for a seller, delivers title documents for a shipment to the purchaser/buyer/consignee only upon payment for the shipment. This payment method holds less risk for the seller as title to the shipment does not pass until payment has been made. This is also called documents against payment. *See* documentary collection.

**cash in advance (CIA)**
(commerce) A method of payment where the seller requires payment for a shipment from the buyer prior to shipment or delivery. This method is advantageous to the seller, but disadvantageous to the buyer, who is subject to the risk that the seller may not ship or deliver as promised. *See* cash against documents, documentary collection.

**cash with order (CWO)**
(commerce) A method of payment where the buyer makes payment at the time the order is placed. This payment method is common for small orders (such as ordering a clothing item from a catalog company), where the buyer is unknown to an established seller or where the seller is known to the buyer and needs funds to produce the order. It is the same as the cash in advance payment method. *See* cash in advance.

**casus major**
(law/shipping) A major casualty that is usually accidental, such as a flood or shipwreck.

**catalog & video; catalog exhibitions**
(U.S.) A U.S. International Trade Administration program promoting low-cost exhibits of U.S. firms' catalogs and videos, offering small, less-experienced companies an opportunity to test overseas markets for their products without travel. The International Trade Administration promotes exhibitions, provides staff fluent in the local language to answer questions, and forwards all trade leads to participating firms. Contact: Trade Information Center; Tel: [1] (800) USA-TRADE. *See* International Trade Administration.

**category groups**
Groupings of controlled products. *See* export control classification number.

**cause of action**
(law) Facts that give a party a right to seek a judicial remedy against another individual or legal entity.

**caveat emptor**
(law) Latin for "Let the buyer beware." The purchaser buys at his own risk.

**CCC Mark**
(China) Acronym for China Compulsory Certification mark. A symbol printed on a product or product label by its manufacturer or importer declaring compliance with the requirements of various Chinese government laws for manufactured products related to human life and health, animals, plants, environmental protection and national security.
Products in 19 groups divided into 132 categories must acquire the mark before they can be marketed, imported or used for any commercial purpose in China. The CCC Mark law went into effect on August 1, 2003.
Various private organizations assist manufacturers and importers in acquiring the CCC mark. Search for "CCC mark" in your computer browser to find organizations to assist in acquiring the CCC mark for your products.
CCC mark directives are published by China's State General Administration of Quality Supervision and Inspection and Quarantine (AQSIQ) and the Certification and Accreditation Administration (CNCA), on its Web site at: www.cnca.gov.cn For additional information go to: www.mac.doc.gov/China/Docs/BusinessGuides/cccguide.htm.

**CE (mark or marking)**
(European Union) CE is the acronym for the French words "Conformité Européene" (European Conformity).
The "CE mark" is a symbol printed on a product or product label by its manufacturer or importer declaring compliance with the requirements of approximately 22 European Union "CE Marking Directives" related to health, safety and environmental protection.

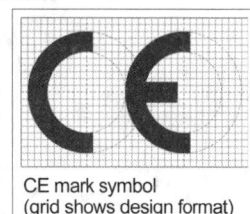
CE mark symbol (grid shows design format)

Individual Product Directives contain the "essential requirements," "performance levels" and/or "Harmonized Standards" to which the products must conform.
Harmonized Standards are technical specifications established by various European standards organizations such as the European Committee for Standardization (CEN) and the European Committee for Electrotechnical Standardization (CENELEC).
CE marking on a product is a legal requirement for its introduction, sale and free movement within the European Union. Therefore, the CE mark is important for manufacturers and importers wishing to place products in the European market.
The term "CE mark" was originally "EC mark" but was changed in 1993 to CE mark. "CE Mark" is still in use, but it is no longer the official term.
Search under "CE Mark" on your computer browser for the names of organizations that assist in acquiring CE marking for products.

**cedi**
The currency of Ghana. 1¢=100 pesewas.

**cell**
(shipping) The on board stowage space for one shipping container on a ship.

**cells**
(shipping) The modular construction system on board a cellular shipping vessel designed to allow containers to be stowed securely one on top of another with vertical bracing at the four corners.

**cellular vessel**
(shipping) A special use shipping vessel designed for the efficient stowage of ocean containers one on top of the other with vertical bracing at the four corners.

**C**

### Census Interface System
(U.S. Customs) A part of U.S. Customs' Automated Commercial System, which includes edits and validations provided by the Bureau of the Census to allow for the accurate and timely collection and submission of entry summary data. Census Interface is accomplished through Automated Broker Interface entry summary transmissions. *See* Automated Commercial System.

### Center for Trade and Investment Services
(U.S.) CTIS is the focal point in the Agency for International Development (AID) for the collection and dissemination of information on the agency's programs and activities that support international private enterprise in the developing countries where AID operates. CTIS is a full service, comprehensive "one-stop-shop" for information about AID's trade and investment programs and business opportunities in countries served by AID. The center's objective is to further economic development abroad by facilitating increased business activity between the private sectors of AID-assisted countries and the U.S. Contact: Global Technology Network, 1301 Pennsylvania Ave., NW, Suite 925, Washington, DC 20004 USA; Tel: [1] (202) 628-9750; Fax: [1] (202) 628-9740; general AID information: Web: www.usaid.gov.

### Central American Common Market
A regional trade alliance established in July 1991 comprised of Honduras, Guatemala, El Salvador, Nicaragua and Costa Rica. The common market covers all products traded within the region as of 1992. A second step toward regional integration will be the establishment of a common external tariff. Panama is becoming progressively more involved in the regional integration discussions. Contact: Central American Common Market, 4A Avda 10-25, Zona 14, Apdo Postal 1237, 01901, Guatemala City, Guatemala; Tel: [502] (3) 682-151; Fax: [502] (3) 681-071; E-mail: info@sieca.org.gt; Web: www.sieca.org.gt.

### Central and Eastern Europe Business Information Center (CEEBIC)
(Historic - U.S. government) A Department of Commerce facility that was opened in January 1990 to provide information on trade and investment opportunities in Eastern Europe. CEEBIC closed down operations on September 30, 2005.

### central bank
(banking) The only institution which has the right to issue banknotes and which constitutes the monetary and credit policy authority of a currency zone. Apart from this, it supplies the economy with money and credit, regulates domestic and foreign payments transactions and maintains internal and external monetary stability.

### certificate of analysis
A document issued by a recognized organization or governmental authority confirming the quality and composition of goods listed in the certificate. Certificates of analysis are often required by authorities in importing countries for animal and plant products for consumption and for pharmaceuticals. *See* certificate of inspection; phytosanitary inspection certificate.

### certificate of free sale (CFS)
A document issued by a government entity on behalf of an exporter stating that specified goods comply with the laws of the exporting country for distribution in that country's commerce. A certificate of free sale provides assurance to the country of import that the imported goods meet country of export state, provincial and national requirements for sale. Certificates of free sale are typically issued for food products, dietary supplements, drugs, cosmetics, and medical devices.

### certificate of inspection
A document certifying that merchandise (such as perishable goods) was in good condition at the time of inspection, usually immediately prior to shipment. Pre-shipment inspection is a requirement for importation of goods into many developing countries. Often used interchangeably with certificate of analysis. *See* phytosanitary inspection certificate; certificate of analysis.

### certificate of insurance
*See* insurance certificate.

### certificate of manufacture
A document (often notarized) in which a producer of goods certifies that the manufacturing has been completed and the goods are now at the disposal of the buyer.

### certificate of origin
(customs) A document attesting to the country of origin of goods. A certificate of origin is often required by the customs authorities of a country as part of the entry process. Such certificates are usually obtained through an official or quasi-official organization in the country of origin such as a consular office or local chamber of commerce. A certificate of origin may be required even though the commercial invoice contains the information.
**Certificate of Origin Form A.** A document required by customs in the United States and other developed countries to prove eligibility of merchandise under duty-free import programs such as the Generalized System of Preferences and the Caribbean Basin Initiative.

### certificate of weight
(shipping) A document stating the weight of a shipment.

### certification; legalization
Official certification of the authenticity of signatures or documents in connection with letter of credits, such as certificates of origin, commercial invoices, etc. by chambers of commerce, consulates and similar recognized government authorities.

### Certified Trade Fair Program
(trade event) The U.S. Department of Commerce Certified Trade Fair Program is designed to encourage private organizations to recruit new-to-market and new-to-export U.S. firms to exhibit in trade fairs overseas. To receive certification, the organization must demonstrate: (1) the fair is a leading international trade event for an industry and (2) the fair organizer is capable of recruiting U.S. exhibitors and assisting them with freight forwarding, customs clearance, exhibit design and setup, public relations, and overall show promotion. The show organizer must agree to assist new-to-export exhibitors as well as small businesses interested in exporting.
In addition to the services the organizer provides, the Department of Commerce will:
(1) Assign a Washington coordinator.
(2) Operate a business information office, which provides meeting space, translators, hospitality, and assistance from U.S. exhibitors and foreign customers.
(3) Help contact buyers, agents, distributors, and other business leads and provide marketing assistance.
(4) Provide a press release on certification.
Contact the U.S. Department of Commerce, 1401 Constitution Ave., NW, Washington, DC 20230 USA; Tel: [1] (202) 482-2000; Web: http://www.export.gov/comm_svc/trade_fair_certification.html; E-mail: tic@ita.doc.gov. *See* new-to-market; new-to-export.

### Certified Trade Missions Program
(U.S.) Former name: state/industry organized, government approved (S/IOGA). The U.S. Department of Commerce, through its Certified Trade Missions Program, offers guidance and assistance to federal, state and local development

agencies, chambers of commerce, industry trade associations, and other export-oriented groups that are interested in becoming more actively involved in export promotion. Certified Trade Missions open doors to government and business leaders in promising export markets around the world.

Once the sponsoring organization has selected the countries to be considered, proposed an itinerary, and outlined its mission goals and objectives, the Department of Commerce coordinates the mission itinerary with its commercial staff at U.S. embassies and consulates overseas. These posts help to arrange the mission's activities to make the most productive use of each member's time at each stop on the itinerary. Some missions also include informational or technical seminars specifically designed to exhibit and promote sales of sophisticated products, technology, or services in targeted markets. Contact: Certified Trade Missions, U.S. Department of Commerce, 1401 Constitution Ave., NW, Washington, DC 20230 USA; Web: www.export.gov; Tel: [1] (202) 482-2000; E-mail: tic@ita.doc.gov.

### cession of goods
(law) A surrender of goods. A relinquishment of a debtor's property to creditors when the debtor cannot pay his or her debts.

### C&F
*See* Cost and Freight; Incoterms.

### chaebol
(Korea) Korean conglomerates which are characterized by strong family control, authoritarian management, and centralized decision making. Chaebol dominate the Korean economy, growing out of the takeover of the Japanese monopoly of the Korean economy following World War II. Korean government tax breaks and financial incentives emphasizing industrial reconstruction and exports provided continuing support to the growth of Chaebols during the 1970s and 1980s. In 1988, the output of the 30 largest chaebol represented almost 95% of Korea's gross national product.

### chandlery
*See* ship chandlery.

### chargeable weight
(shipping) The weight of a shipment used in determining air or ocean freight charges. The chargeable weight may be the dimensional weight or on container shipments the gross weight of the shipment less the tare weight of the container.

### chargé d'affaires
(diplomacy) A subordinate diplomat who takes charge in the absence of the ambassador.

### charges advanced
*See* advancement of charges.

### charges collect
(shipping) The total transportation charges which may include pickup and/or delivery charges which are entered on the ocean or air waybill to be collected from the consignee. Equivalent terms are "freight collect" or "charges forward."

### charter
(law) (a) An instrument issued by a government to the governed people, a specific part of the people, a corporation, a colony, or a dependency confirming or conferring described rights, liberties, or powers. (b) A legislative act that creates a business corporation or that creates and defines a corporate franchise.
(shipping) (a) A **charter party** or **charter agreement** is a lease or agreement to hire an airplane, vessel, or other means of conveyance to transport goods on a designated voyage to one or more locations. (b) A **gross charter** is a

charter agreement by which the shipowner furnishes personnel and equipment and incurs other expenses, such as port costs. (c) A **bareboat charter** is a charter agreement under which an individual or legal entity charters a vessel without a crew, assumes full possession and control of the vessel, and is generally invested with temporary ownership powers.

### charter party bill of lading
(shipping) A bill of lading issued by a charter party. Charter party bills of lading are not acceptable by banks under letters of credit unless they are specifically authorized in the credit. *See* bill of lading.

### charter party contract
(shipping) Contract according to which the precisely designated freight room of a ship or the whole ship is leased by the owner to a charterer for a specific period, specific voyage or voyages. If a ship is chartered without crew this is a bareboat charter. The freight documents issued by the current charterer or his authorized party are called charter party bills of lading.

### charter service
(shipping) The temporary hiring of an aircraft, usually on a trip basis, for the movement of cargo or passengers.

### chartered bank
(Canada) Financial institution licensed by the Canadian Parliament under the Bank Act to operate as a bank.

### chartered ship
(shipping) A ship leased by its owner or agent for a stated time, voyage or voyages.

### chassis
(shipping) A special trailer or undercarriage on which containers are moved over the road. Chassis comes in skeletal types, parallel frame, perimeter frame and goose neck types, among others.

### chattel
(law) An item of personal property.

### chattel lien
(law) A lien on chattel in favor of a person who has expended labor, skill, or materials on the chattel or has furnished storage for it at the request of the owner, an agent, or a party who legally possesses it.

### chattel paper
(law) A writing or a group of writings that constitute a security interest in, or a lease of, specific goods for a monetary obligation.

### check digit
(logistics) A one-digit number added to the end of a data field (e.g., container serial number, air waybill number) for added security. A check digit is calculated from the preceding values in the data field using a mathematical formula.

### chemical/biological weapons
(U.S.) The Department of Commerce maintains foreign policy export controls on certain chemical precursors useful in chemical warfare. Through the Australia Group (AG), the United States cooperates with other nations in controlling chemical weapons proliferation. The AG has developed a Core List of nine chemicals considered essential to the development of chemical weapons. The AG also developed a Warning List which identifies 41 precursors which are useful for chemical weapons development. The AG also provides the forum in which the member countries share information concerning the activities of nonmember countries where the proliferation of these weapons is of concern, including entities that are seeking chemical precursors and related items.

The United States controls all 50 chemical precursors designated by the AG as useful in chemical weapons production. The nine core list chemicals are controlled worldwide,

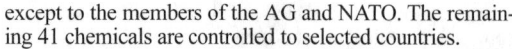

**C**

except to the members of the AG and NATO. The remaining 41 chemicals are controlled to selected countries.

The U.S. also maintains unilateral controls on certain biological organisms and requires an individual validated license to all destinations except Canada. U.S. Department of Commerce regulations are designed in the form of a "negative" list. The list identifies those organisms that have been determined to be of no or minimal level of hazard. Any organism that is not included on the list is controlled. The U.S. Department of Commerce requires individual validated licenses for the export of Class 2, 3, and 4 organisms to all destinations except Canada. (The higher the class, the greater the toxicity.) License applications are referred to the U.S. State Department for review and recommendation. Approval or denial is determined by analysis of the application and intelligence input. *See* Australia Group.

**Chief Mate**
(shipping) The second in command officer of a ship. Responsibilities include: the stability of the ship, loading the ship and all seamen and mates on board. Chief mate is the fifth level job of six towards becoming a capitan (ordinary seaman, able-bodied seaman, third mate, second mate, chief mate, captain).

**chill a sale**
(law) Combining or conspiring (of buyers or bidders) to suppress competition at a sale, in order to acquire property at less than fair value.

**chose in action**
*See* thing in action.

**CIF**
*See* Cost, Insurance, Freight; Incoterms.

**CIFCI**
*See* Cost, Insurance, Freight, Commission and Interest; Incoterms.

**CIM**
(shipping) An internationally standardized freight document issued in rail transport. CIM stands for "Convention Internationale concernant le transport des Marchandises par chemin de fer." The agreement has been in force since January 1, 1965, and constitutes the legal basis for the conclusion of freight contracts in international rail goods transport using one freight document.

**CISG**
*See* United Nations Convention on Contracts for the International Sale of Goods.

**city bank**
(Japan) A major Japanese commercial bank, located in a city, dealing with corporations and major accounts (as compared to a local bank).

**city terminal service**
(shipping) A service provided by some airlines to accept shipments at the terminals of their cartage agents or other designated in-town terminals or to deliver shipments to these terminals at lower rates than those charged for the door-to-door pickup and delivery service.

**Civil Aeronautics Board (CAB)**
(Historic - U.S.) A U.S. federal agency created by Congress in 1938 to promote the development of the U.S. air transport system, to award air routes, and to regulate passenger fares and cargo rates. Legislation passed by the U.S. Congress in 1978 terminated the CAB, effective January 1, 1985. Many of the CAB functions such as certificates, air carrier fitness, consumer protection, international rates and services were transferred to the U.S. Department of Transportation (DOT). *See* U.S. Department of Transportation.

**civil law**
(law) A body of law created by statutes and other enactments of legislatures and by rules and regulations adopted to give effect to those statutes and enactments. *See* common law.

**claim**
(shipping) A demand made upon a transportation line for payment on account of a loss sustained through its negligence.
(insurance) A demand made upon an insurance company for payment on account of an insured loss.

**claim tracer**
(shipping) A request for an advice concerning the status of a claim.

**class or kind (of merchandise)**
(customs) A term used in defining the scope of an antidumping investigation. Included in the "class or kind" of merchandise is merchandise sold in the home market which is "such or similar" to the petitioned product. "Such or similar" merchandise is that merchandise which is identical to or like the petitioned product in physical characteristics. *See* dumping.

**class rates**
(shipping) Shipping rates that apply to cargo covered in a single class of goods as defined in a cargo classification table. Cargo classification tables and rates are usually based on criteria such as weight, bulk, value, perishability, hazard/danger and method of packing. *See* class or kind (of merchandise).

**classification**
(general) The categorization of merchandise.
(shipping) The assignment of a category to a specific cargo for the purpose of applying class rates, together with governing rules and regulations.
(U.S. Customs) The categorization of merchandise according to the Harmonized Tariff Schedule of the United States (HTS or HTSUS). Classification affects the duty status of imported merchandise.
Classification and valuation of imported merchandise must be provided by commercial importers when an entry is filed. In addition, classification under the statistical suffixes of the tariff schedules must also be furnished even though this information is not pertinent to duitable status. Accordingly, classification is initially the responsibility of an importer, customs broker or other person preparing the entry papers. *See* Harmonized Tariff Schedule of the United States. *See* valuation.

**classification societies**
(shipping) Classification societies are organizations that survey and classify ships, both during their construction and operation. They are the principal means by which standards of construction and maintenance are enforced, and ship certificates can be issued by Flag States.
In order to be registered a ship must be certified to be of a particular type and size and to be maintained to certain minimum standards. Classification societies are licensed by states (national governments) to undertake this work on their behalf. Most states do not insist that ships be "classed." However, without a "class" there would be considerable difficulties in operating a ship, as "class" is generally a requirement of most insurance companies and shippers using the vessel.
The principal classification societies are:
• **American Bureau of Shipping (U.S.) (ABS)**
  www.eagle.org
• **Bureau Veritas (France) (BV)**
  www.bureauveritas.com

- **China Classification Society (CCS)**
  www.ccs.org.cn
- **Det Norske Veritas (Norway) (DNV)**
  www.dnv.com
- **Germanischer Lloyd (Germany) (GL)**
  www.glc.de
- **Hellenic Register of Shipping (Greece) (HRS)**
  www.hrs.gr
- **Indian Register of Shipping (India) (IRS)**
  www.irclass.org
- **Korean Register of Shipping (Korea) (KRS)**
  www.krs.co.kr
- **Lloyd's Register of Shipping (UK) (LR)**
  www.lr.org
- **Nippon Kaiji Kyokai (Japan) Class NK**
  www.classnk.or.jp
- **Polski Rejestr Statkow (Poland) (PRS)**
  www.prs.gda.pl
- **Registro Italiano Navale (Italy) (RINA)**
  www.rina.it

*claused bill of lading*
(shipping) Notations on bills of lading which specify deficient condition(s) of the goods and/or the packaging. *See* bill of lading.

*clean bill of exchange*
(banking) A bill of exchange having no other documents, such as a bill of lading affixed to it.

*clean bill of lading*
(shipping) A bill of lading receipted by the carrier for goods received in "apparent good order and condition," without damages or other irregularities, and without the notation "Shippers Load and Count."

*clean collection*
(banking) A collection in which the demand for payment (such as a draft) is presented without additional documents. *See* bill of exchange.

*clean draft*
(banking) A sight or time draft which has no other documents attached to it. This is to be distinguished from documentary draft. *See* bill of exchange.

*clean letter of credit*
(banking) A letter of credit against which the beneficiary of the credit may draw a bill of exchange without presentation of documents. *See* letter of credit.

*clean on board bill of lading*
(shipping) A document evidencing cargo laden aboard a vessel with no exceptions as to cargo condition or quantity.

*clearance*
(customs) The completion of customs entry formalities resulting in the release of goods from customs custody to the importer.

*close corporation*
*See* closely held corporation.

*closed conference*
(shipping) A shipping conference that reserves the right to refuse membership to applying carriers. *See* conference. *See* carrier.

*closed-end transaction*
(finance) A credit transaction that has a fixed amount and time for repayment.

*closely held corporation*
(law) A corporation with a small number of shareholders, who usually directly operate the corporation and have limited liability. A maximum number of shareholders is usually fixed by law. The minimum capitalization for a closely held corporation is less than that for a public corporation, and fewer formalities are required for managing it. The re-

quirements for closely held corporations vary among jurisdictions. *See* corporation.

*coastal trade*
(shipping) Trade between ports of one nation.

*Code of Federal Regulations (CFR)*
(U.S. law) A compilation of the administrative rules adopted and followed by departments and agencies of the United States federal government. Copies of the CFR are available at major public libraries in the United States and for purchase from the Superintendent of Documents, U.S. U.S. Government Printing Office, Mail Stop: IDCC, 732 N. Capitol Street, NW, Washington, DC 20401; Tel: [1] (866) 512-1800, [1] (202) 512-1800; Fax: [1] (202) 512-2104; Web: www.gpoaccess.gov. To receive catalog, contact U.S. FAX Watch: [1] (202) 512-1716.

*codes of conduct*
International instruments that indicate standards of behavior by nation states or multi-national corporations deemed desirable by the international community. Several codes of conduct were negotiated during the Tokyo Round of the General Agreement on Tariffs and Trade (GATT) that liberalized and harmonized domestic measures that might impede trade.
The United Nations has also encouraged the negotiation of several "voluntary" codes of conduct, including one that seeks to specify the rights and obligations of transnational corporations and of governments.

*coin silver*
Coin or "German" silver is an alloy of silver that is 800/1000 pure. An article of coin or German silver is often marked "800."

*cold ironing*
Providing shore-based electrical power to a ship while in port. The power is used to run the ship's electrical systems including lights, heating, air conditioning and hot water for the ship's crew. In practice, a heavy flexible wire encased in rubber or plastic, resembling an extension cord, is extended from the pier, plugged into the ship's receptacle and power is supplied to the ship. This allows the ship to shut down the diesel engines that normally drive its electrical generators and thereby greatly reduce diesel emissions. The Ports of Los Angeles/Long Beach among others have spearheaded the technique. Also called Alternative Marine Power (AMP).

*collar*
(banking) An agreement to put upper and lower (cap and floor) limits on an interest rate which will be adhered to even if the market rate lies outside this range.

*collect charges*
(shipping) The transportation practice under which the receiver of the goods pays charges.

*collect on delivery (COD)*
(shipping) A transportation service under which the purchase price of goods is collected by the carrier from the receiver at the time of delivery, and subsequently, payment is transmitted by the carrier to the shipper. Carriers charge a nominal fee for this service. As the term COD implies payment is due upon delivery. There are no credit provisions in COD service. Also called Cash On Delivery.

*collecting bank*
(banking) The bank that acts as agent for the seller and seller's bank in collecting payment or a time draft from the buyer to be forwarded to the remitting bank (usually the seller's bank).

*collection*
(general) The presentation for payment of an obligation and the payment thereof.

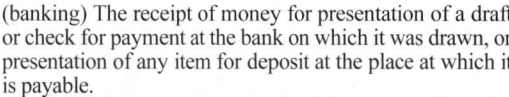

(banking) The receipt of money for presentation of a draft or check for payment at the bank on which it was drawn, or presentation of any item for deposit at the place at which it is payable.

### collection endorsement
*See* endorsement.

### collection papers
(banking) All documents (invoices, bills of lading, etc.) submitted to a buyer for the purpose of receiving payment for a shipment.
*See* documents against payment; documents against acceptance.

### collections system
(U.S. Customs) A part of U.S. Customs' Automated Commercial System, controls and accounts for the billions of dollars in payments collected by Customs each year and the millions in refunds processed each year. Daily statements are prepared for the automated brokers who select this service. The Collections System permits electronic payments of the related duties and taxes through the Automated Clearinghouse capability. Automated collections also meets the needs of the importing community through acceptance of electronic funds transfers for deferred tax bills and receipt of electronic payments from lockbox operations for Customs bills and fees. *See* Automated Commercial System.

### collective mark
(law) A trademark or service mark that a cooperative, association, or other collective group uses in commerce. A mark used to indicate membership in a union, association, or other organization.

### colón
The currency of:
Costa Rica, 1¢=100 centimos;
El Salvador, 1¢=100 centavos.

### colorable imitation
(law) A mark that is so similar to another registered trademark or service mark that it may be considered as calculated to deceive an ordinary person.

### colorable transaction
(law) A transaction that in appearance does not correspond to the actual transaction and that is usually intended to conceal or deceive.

### column 1 rates
(U.S. Customs) The Harmonized Tariff Schedules of the United States (HTS) is an organized listing of goods and their import duty rates which is used as the basis of classifying products for entry to the United States. Column 1 duty rates in the HTS are low and apply to imports from countries that have achieved Most Favored Nation (MFN) trading status with the United States. *See* Harmonized Tariff Schedule of the United States; column 2 rates.

### column 2 rates
(U.S. Customs) The Harmonized Tariff Schedules of the United States (HTS) is an organized listing of goods and their import duty rates which is used as the basis of classifying products for entry to the United States. Column 2 duty rates in the HTS apply to imports from countries that do not have Most Favored Nation (MFN) trading status with the United States. *See* Harmonized Tariff Schedule of the United States; column 1 rates.

### combi aircraft
*See* combination aircraft.

### combination aircraft
(shipping) An aircraft capable of transporting both passengers and cargo on the same flight. Such a plane will generally carry unitized cargo loads on the upper deck of the aircraft forward of the passenger compartment. Some cargo is carried on virtually all scheduled passenger flights in the belly pits below the passenger cabin.

### combination in restraint of trade
(law) An understanding or agreement between two or more individuals or legal entities to do the following: (1) restrict competition; (2) monopolize trade; (3) control production, distribution, and price; and (4) otherwise interfere with freedom of trade.

### combined bill of lading
(shipping) A bill of lading covering a shipment of goods by more than one mode of transportation. *See* bill of lading.

### combined transport
(shipping) Consignment sent by means of various modes of transport, such as by rail and by ocean.

### combined transport bill of lading
(shipping) A bill of lading covering a shipment of goods by more than one mode of transportation. *See* bill of lading.

### comity
(law) Courtesy, respect, and goodwill. Government agencies or courts in one jurisdiction, for example, may agree out of comity to give effect to court judgments or arbitration awards of other jurisdictions.

### command economy
(economics) An economic system where resources and decisions about production are controlled by a central government authority.

### Commanditaire Vennootschap (C.V.)
(Netherlands) Designation for a limited partnership in which at least one of the partners has general personal liability and at least one of the other partners has limited liability.

### Commerce Business Daily
(publication) A daily newspaper published by the U.S. Department of Commerce which lists government procurement invitations and contract awards, including foreign business opportunities and foreign government procurements. Available from: U.S. Department of Commerce, 1401 Constitution Ave., NW, Washington, DC 20230 USA; Tel: [1] (202) 482-2000; Web: www.commerce.gov.

### Commerce Control List (CCL)
(U.S.) A list of all items—commodities, software, and technical data—subject to U.S. Bureau of Industry and Security (formerly the Bureau of Export Administration) export controls. Incorporates items controlled for foreign policy and other reasons. The list adopts a totally new method of categorizing commodities and is divided into 10 general categories: (1) materials, (2) materials processing, (3) electronics, (4) computers, (5) telecommunications and cryptography, (6) sensors, (7) avionics and navigation, (8) marine technology, (9) propulsion systems and transportation equipment, and (10) miscellaneous. Replaced the former Commodity Control List as of September 1, 1991. Contact: Bureau of Industry and Security, Office of Public Affairs, Room 3895, 1401 Constitution Avenue NW, Washington, DC 20230 USA; Tel: [1] (202) 482-4811; Fax: [1] (202) 482-3617; Web: www.bis.doc.gov; *See* export control classification number.

### commercial bank
(banking) A bank that specializes in accepting demand deposits (deposits that can be withdrawn on demand by the depositor) and granting loans.

### commercial bill of exchange
*See* bill of exchange.

### Commercial Cash Entry Processing System (CCEPS)
(Canada Customs) A Canada Border Services Agency (CBSA) self-serve automated system designed to facilitate the document preparation process required for the clear-

C

ance of commercial importations. Personal computers are located at counters in designated customs offices. Based on importation information that the importer inputs for goods, CCEPS calculates the applicable duties and taxes. It then generates a completed hard copy of Canadian Import Form B3. A Canadian customs officer enters the data from Form B3 into the Accelerated Commercial Release Operation Support System (ACROSS) system and forwards the form to the cashier. Once the importer has accounted for the goods, he or she receives a copy of the form stamped "duty paid" and can take delivery of goods.

For more information, go to: http://www.cra-arc.gc.ca.

### commercial credit
(banking) A letter of credit used to facilitate a sale of goods by insuring that the seller will be paid once the seller has complied with the terms of credit that the buyer obtains. A letter of credit is usually issued by a bank (the issuer) on the request of its client (the buyer) to assure the seller that the buyer will pay for the goods sold. *See* letter of credit.

### commercial frustration
(law) A legal theory that implies a condition or term into a contract, if no express provision was made, to excuse the parties when performance becomes impossible because an event occurs that the contracting parties could not have reasonably foreseen or controlled. Commercial frustration may arise, for example, if a seller's shipment is lost in a shipwreck or if a manufacturer cannot obtain raw materials because war has broken out in the country supplying them. *See* force majeure.

### commercial impracticability
(law) A legal theory that implies a condition or term into a contract, if no express provision was made, to excuse either party when performance becomes impossible in practice because of the occurrence of a contingency, the nonoccurrence of which was a basic assumption for making the contract. A manufacturer, for example, who contracts to sell goods at a specific price in reliance on a subcontractor's bid to provide certain components at a low price may claim commercial impracticability if the subcontractor defaults and the manufacturer can only procure comparable components at a much higher price.

### Commercial Information Management System (CIMS)
(U.S.) CIMS is a trade-related application using National Trade Data Bank CD-ROMs to disseminate market research and international economic data to U.S. & Foreign Commercial Service (US&FCS) domestic offices and overseas posts. The system includes data on U.S. and foreign traders and supports local collection and update of information on business contacts. Not available to the public.

### commercial invoice
(general) A document identifying the seller and buyer of goods or services, identifying numbers such as invoice number, date, shipping date, mode of transport, delivery and payment terms, and a complete listing and description of the goods or services being sold including prices, discounts and quantities.

(customs) A commercial invoice is often used by governments to determine the true (transaction) value of goods for the assessment of customs duties and also to prepare consular documentation. Governments using the commercial invoice to control imports often specify its form, content, number of copies, language to be used, and other characteristics.

(U.S. Customs) U.S. Customs requires that a commercial invoice provide the following information: (1) The port of entry, (2) If merchandise is sold or agreed to be sold, the time, place and names of buyer and seller; if consigned, the time and origin of shipment, and names of shipper and receiver, (3) Detailed description of the merchandise, including the name by which each item is known, the grade or quality, and the marks, numbers, and symbols under which sold by the seller or manufacturer to the trade in the country of exportation, together with the marks and numbers of the packages in which the merchandise is packed, (4) The quantities in weights and measures, (5) If sold or agreed to be sold, the purchase price of each item in the currency of the sale, (6) If consigned, the value for each item, in the currency in which the transactions are usually made or, in the absence of such value, the price in such currency that the manufacturer, seller, shipper, or owner would have received, or was willing to receive, for such merchandise if sold in the ordinary course of trade and in the usual wholesale quantities in the country of exportation, (7) The kind of currency, (8) All charges upon the merchandise, itemized by name and amount including freight, insurance, commission, cases, containers, coverings, and cost of packing; and, if not included above, all charges, costs, and expenses incurred in bringing the merchandise from alongside the carrier at the first U.S. port of entry. The cost of packing, cases, containers, and inland freight to the port of exportation need not be itemized by amount if included in the invoice price and so identified. Where the required information does not appear on the invoice as originally prepared, it shall be shown on an attachment to the invoice, (9) All rebates, drawbacks, and bounties, separately itemized, allowed upon the exportation of the merchandise, (10) The country of origin, and (11) All goods or services furnished for the production of the merchandise not included in the invoice price. The invoice and all attachments must be in the English language.

### commercial letter of credit
(banking) An instrument by which a bank lends its credit to a customer to enable him to finance the purchase of goods. Addressed to the seller, it authorizes him to draw drafts on the bank under the terms stated in the letter. *See* letter of credit.

### commercial officers
(diplomacy) Embassy officials who assist businesses through arranging appointments with local business and government officials, providing counsel on local trade regulations, laws, and customs; identifying importers, buyers, agents, distributors, and joint venture partners; and other business assistance. *See* economic officers.

### commercial paper
(banking/law) Negotiable instruments used in commerce. Examples of commercial paper are bills of exchange, promissory notes, and bank checks. *See* negotiable instrument; bill of exchange.

### commercial risk
(economics) Economic risk resulting from the normal course of operating a business. Commercial risk includes financial risk, legal risk, production risk, market risk and even the risk of failure to adapt to changing markets and technology. *See* political risk.

### commercial set
(law) The primary documents for a shipment of goods. A commercial set usually includes, for example, an invoice, bill of lading, bill of exchange, and certificate of insurance.

### commercial treaty
An agreement between two or more countries setting forth the conditions under which business between the countries may be transacted. May outline tariff privileges, terms on which property may be owned, the manner in which claims may be settled, etc.

**C**

### commercial zone
(shipping/logistics) The area immediately surrounding a town or city that is subject to the same shipping rates as the city itself. *See* rate basis point.

### commingling
The packing or mingling of various articles subject to different rates of duty in such a way that the quantity or value of each class of articles cannot readily be ascertained by Customs without the physical segregation of the shipment or the contents of any package thereof. Commingled articles are subject to the highest rate of duty applicable to any part of the commingled lot, unless the consignee or his agent segregates the articles under Customs supervision.

### commission
(general) The amount paid to an agent, which may be an individual, a broker, or a financial institution, for consummating a transaction involving sale or purchase of assets or services.
(banking) Agents and brokers are usually compensated by being allowed to retain a certain percentage of the premiums they produce, known as a commission.

### Commission on Security and Cooperation in Europe
An economic and defense alliance whose members include all recognized countries of Europe, Canada, the USA, and the former republics of the USSR. Included are: Albania, Armenia, Austria, Azerbaijan, Belgium, Bulgaria, Belarus, Canada, Cyprus, Czech Republic, Denmark, Estonia, Finland, France, Germany, Greece, the Holy *See*, Hungary, Iceland, Ireland, Italy, Kazakhstan, Kyrgyzstan, Latvia, Liechtenstein, Lithuania, Luxembourg, Malta, Moldova, Monaco, Netherlands, Norway, Poland, Portugal, Romania, Russia, San Marino, Slovakia, Spain, Sweden, Switzerland, Tajikistan, Turkey, Turkmenistan, Ukraine, the United Kingdom, the United States, Uzbekistan and Yugoslavia. Note: The Federal Republic of Yugoslavia (Serbia & Montenegro) was suspended in July 1992. Contact: Commission on Security and Cooperation in Europe, 234 Ford House Office Building, 3rd and D Streets, SW, Washington, DC 20515 USA; Tel: [1] (202) 225-1901; Fax: [1] (202) 226-4199; E-mail: info@csce.gov; Web: www.csce.gov.

### Committee on Foreign Investment in the United States (CFIUS)
(U.S.) Created in 1975 to provide guidance on arrangements with foreign governments for advance consultations on prospective major foreign governmental investments in the United States, and to consider proposals for new legislation or regulation relating to foreign investment.
The authority of the Committee was amended by Section 5021 (the Exon-Florio provision) of the Omnibus Trade and Competitiveness Act of 1988 (Section 721 of the Defense Production Act), which gives the president authority to review mergers, acquisitions, and takeovers of U.S. companies by foreign interests and to prohibit, suspend, or seek divestiture in the courts of investments that may lead to actions that threaten to impair the national security.
By Executive Order in December 1988, the U.S. Treasury has authority to implement the Exon-Florio provision. CFIUS has eight members: Treasury (the chair), State, Defense, Commerce, the Council of Economic Advisors, the U.S. Trade Representative, the Attorney General, and the Office of Management and Budget.
The Office of Strategic Industries and Economic Security serves as Commerce's representative to CFIUS. Contact: Committee on Foreign Investment in the United States, Office of International Investment, Department of Treasury, 1500 Pennsylvania Avenue, N.W., Washington, DC 20220

USA; Tel: (202) 622-2000; Web: www.ustreas.gov/offices/international-affairs/exon-florio.

### commodity
Broadly defined, any article exchanged in trade, but most commonly used to refer to raw materials, including such minerals as tin, copper and manganese, and bulk-produced agricultural products such as coffee, tea and rubber.

### commodity code
(shipping) A system for identifying a given commodity by a number in order to establish its commodity rate in freight transport. *See* Harmonized System.

### commodity control list
*See* Commerce Control List.

### Commodity Credit Corporation
(U.S.) A U.S. government corporation controlled by the Department of Agriculture that provides financing and stability to the marketing and exporting of agricultural commodities. Contact: Commodity Credit Corporation, USDA, 1400 Independence Avenue, SW, Stop 0581, Washington, DC 20250-0581 USA; Tel: [1] (703) 305-1386; Web: www.fsa.usda.gov/ccc.

### commodity rate
(shipping) The rate (charges) applicable to shipping a specific commodity between certain specified points.

### common agricultural policy (CAP)
(European Union) A set of regulations by which member states of the European Union (EU) seek to merge their individual agricultural programs into a unified effort to promote regional agricultural development, raise standards of living for the farm population, stabilize agricultural markets, increase agricultural productivity, and establish methods of dealing with food supply security. Two of the principal elements of the CAP are the variable levy (an import duty amounting to the difference between EU target farm prices and the lowest available market prices of imported agricultural commodities) and export restitutions, or subsidies, to promote exports of farm goods that cannot be sold within the EU at the target prices.

### common carrier
*See* carrier.

### common external tariff (CXT)
(customs) A uniform tariff rate adopted by a customs union or common market such as the European Community, to imports from countries outside the union. For example, the European Common Market is based on the principle of a free internal trade area with a common external tariff (sometimes referred to in French as the Tarif Exterieur Commun—TEC) applied to products imported from non-member countries. "Free trade areas" do not necessarily have common external tariffs.

### common law
(law) The body of law derived from usages, customs, and judicial decisions, as distinguished from statutes. *See* civil law; stare decisis.

### common market
(economics) A common market (as opposed to a free trade area) has a common external tariff and may allow for labor mobility and common economic policies among the participating nations. The European Community is the most notable example of a common market.

### Common Market for Eastern and Southern Africa (COMESA)
(Formerly, the Preferential Trade Agreement for Eastern and Southern Africa - PTA). PTA was founded in 1981 in order to improve commercial and economic cooperation in Eastern and Southern Africa; transform the structure of national economies in the region; promote regional trade; support inter-country cooperation, cooperation in agricul-

tural development, and improvement of transport links. Accomplishments include: tariff reductions, multilateral trade, common travellers checks, a federation of chambers of commerce, a federation of commercial banks, and a commercial Arbitration board.

The Common Market for Eastern and Southern Africa (COMESA) was formed by members of the PTA in 1995. COMESA has established a customs union that aims to abolish all tariff and non-tariff barriers among member states.

COMESA's members are: Angola, Burundi, Comoros, Democratic Republic of The Congo, Djibouti, Egypt, Eritrea, Ethiopia, Kenya, Madagascar, Malawi, Mauritius, Namibia, Rwanda, Seychelles, Sudan, Swaziland, Tanzania, Uganda, Zambia, Zimbabwe,. Contact: COMESA, PO Box 30051, Lotti House, Cairo Rd., Lusaka 10101, Zambia; Tel: [260] (1) 229726; Fax: [260] (1) 225107; Web: www.mbendi.co.za/orgs/co4s.htm.

### Common Monetary Agreement
A regional economic alliance of South Africa, Lesotho, and Swaziland under which member states apply uniform exchange control regulations to ensure monetary order in the region. Funds are freely transferable among the three countries, and Lesotho and Swaziland have free access to South African capital markets. Lesotho also uses the South African currency, the rand. The CMA was formed in 1986 as a result of the renegotiation of the Rand Monetary Agreement (RMA), which was originally formed in 1974 by the same member countries.

### common point
(shipping) A point (location) serviced by two or more transportation lines.

### common tariff
(shipping) A tariff published by or for the account of two or more transportation lines as issuing carriers. *See* tariff.

### commonwealth
A free association of sovereign independent states that has no charter, treaty, or constitution. The association promotes cooperation, consultation, and mutual assistance among members. The British Commonwealth, the most notable example, included 54 states at the beginning of 2002.

### Commonwealth of Independent States (CIS)
An association of 11 republics of the former Soviet Union established in December 1991. The members include: Russia, Ukraine, Belarus (formerly Byelorussia), Moldova (formerly Moldavia), Armenia, Azerbaijan, Uzbekistan, Turkmenistan, Tajikistan, Kazakhstan, and Kyrgystan (formerly Kirghiziya). Georgia is presently an "observer"; the Baltic states did not join.

### Communications Satellite Corporation
(U.S.) COMSAT was established in 1963 under provision of the Communications Satellite Act of 1962. The legislation directed that COMSAT establish the world's first commercial international satellite communications system. The Act also stipulated that the company operate as a shareholder-owned "for-profit" corporation. COMSAT represents the U.S. in the International Telecommunications Satellite Organization (Intelsat). Contact: www.comsat.com.ar.

### commuter airline
(shipping/logistics) An air carrier with a prescribed time schedule for a specific route. A commuter airline generally operates over short distances and serves remote locations and small airports.

### Compagnie (Cie.)
(France, Luxembourg) General designation for a business organization.

### company (Co.)
(law) (a) An organization established to conduct business. (b) A legal entity established under the laws of a country, state, province or other administrative unit for the purpose of conducting business. (c) A generic and comprehensive term which may include sole proprietorships, individuals, partnerships, corporations, societies, associations, and organizations established and operating to prosecute a commercial, industrial or other legitimate business, enterprise or undertaking.

### comparative advantage
(economics) A central concept in international trade theory which holds that a country or a region should specialize in the production and export of those goods and services that it can produce relatively more efficiently than other goods and services, and import those goods and services in which it has a comparative disadvantage. This theory was first propounded by David Ricardo in 1817 as a basis for increasing the economic welfare of a population through international trade. The comparative advantage theory normally favors specialized production in a country based on intensive utilization of those factors of production in which the country is relatively well endowed (such as raw materials, fertile land or skilled labor); and perhaps also the accumulation of physical capital and the pace of research.

### compensatory trade
(economics) A form of countertrade where any combination of goods and services are bartered. *See* countertrade.

### competitive rate
(shipping) Rate established by a transportation line to meet competition of another transportation line.

### complementary imports
(economics) Imports of raw materials or products which a country itself does not possess or produce.

### compliance
Conformity in satisfying official requirements. *See* informed compliance.

### composition with creditors
(law) An agreement between an insolvent debtor and one or more creditors under which the creditors consent to accept less than the total amount of their claims in order to secure immediate payment. Creditors will usually prefer a composition if a debtor threatens to declare bankruptcy, because otherwise the creditors are likely to incur costs in making a legal claim against the debtor in a bankruptcy proceeding, payment of debts will be delayed during the proceeding, and the amount paid to each creditor will depend on the judicial decision in that proceeding.

### compound rate of duty
(customs) A combination of both a specific rate of duty and an ad valorem rate of duty. For example: 0.7 cents per pound plus 10 per cent ad valorem. *See* duty; ad valorem; specific rate of duty.

### compradore
An intermediary, agent or advisor in a foreign country employed by a domestic individual or company to facilitate transactions with local individuals or businesses in the foreign country.

### compressed gases
(shipping) Items requiring storage and handling under pressure in compressed gas cylinders. (UN CLASS 2.) Examples are acetylene and chlorine. Hazards/precautions are container may explode in heat or fire; contact with liquid may cause frostbite; may be flammable, poisonous, explosive, irritating, corrosive or suffocating; may be EXTREMELY HAZARDOUS.

**C**

## COMPRO
(information system) An on-line trade data retrieval system maintained by the International Trade Administration within the U.S. Department of Commerce. The system is exclusively for use within the federal government trade community (ITA, USTR, ITC, and other executive branch agencies). COMPRO includes:
(1) U.S. foreign trade data (detailed U.S. merchandise trade statistics compiled by Census);
(2) UN trade data (trade statistics of 170 countries;
(3) International Monetary Fund and World Bank databases (international finance, direction of trade, and developing country debt). COMPRO also maintains gateways to LABSTAT, a product of the Bureau of Labor Statistics.

## computed value
(U.S. Customs) Generally, the Customs value of all merchandise exported to the United States is the transaction value for the goods. If the transaction value cannot be used, then certain secondary bases are considered. The secondary bases of value, listed in order of precedence for use, are:
(1) Transaction value of identical merchandise, (2) Transaction value of similar merchandise, (3) Deductive value, and (4) Computed value. The order of precedence of the last two values can be reversed if the importer so requests. Computed value consists of the sum of the following items:
(1) Materials, fabrication, and other processing used in producing the imported merchandise, (2) Profit and general expenses, (3) Any assist, if not included in items 1 and 2, (4) Packaging costs.
See valuation; transaction value; identical merchandise; similar merchandise; assist; deductive value.

## concealed damage
(shipping) Damage to the contents of a package which is in good order externally. See inherent vice.

## concealed loss
(shipping) Loss from a package bearing concealed damage. See inherent vice.

## concord
(law) An agreement between two parties that states the terms of a settlement of a right of action for a breach or wrongdoing that one of the parties has against the other. A buyer who has paid for goods but has not received them, for example, may agree to forgo the right to sue the seller for breach if the seller agrees to return the money paid. See accord and satisfaction.

## conditional endorsement
See endorsement.

## conditions of carriage
See contract of carriage.

## conference
(shipping) A group of ocean freight carriers banding together, voluntarily, for the purpose of limiting and regulating competition among themselves. It may establish uniform tariff freight charges and terms and conditions of service. Conference establishment in the United States requires Federal Maritime Commission approval. Conferences in the United States are exempt from antitrust regulation. See open conference; closed conference.

## conference carrier
(shipping) A member of an association of ocean cargo carriers that has agreed to standardize services, practices, rates and tariffs. See carrier, conference.

## conference line
(shipping) Ocean shipping companies whose ships travel according to firmly established schedules along fixed routes. Uniform transport rates are established between the shipping lines. Such agreements are usually called conferences. The conference lines are therefore the shipping routes agreed by the conferences. See conference; open conference; closed conference.

## conference rate
(shipping) Rates arrived at by conference of carriers applicable to transportation—generally water transportation. See conference.

## confirmation
(law) A contract or written memorandum that ratifies, renders valid, and makes binding an agreement that was difficult to prove, invalid, or otherwise unenforceable. Parties who orally agree to a sale of goods, for example, may formalize that agreement by signing a written confirmation that contains all of the oral terms. See contract.

## confirmed letter of credit
(banking) A letter of credit which contains a guarantee on the part of both the issuing and advising banks of payment to the seller so long as the seller's documentation is in order and the terms of the letter of credit are met.
Confirmation is only added to irrevocable letters of credit, usually available with the advising bank. If confirmation of the letter of credit is desired, the applicant must state this expressly in his/her letter of credit application. The confirming bank assumes the credit risk of the issuing bank as well as the political and transfer risks of the purchaser's country.
If a letter of credit does not contain a confirmation request by the issuing bank, in certain circumstances the possibility exists of confirming the letter of credit "by silent confirmation," i.e. without the issuing bank's knowledge. Without confirmation of the letter of credit, the advising bank will forward the letter of credit to the beneficiary without taking on its own commitment. See letter of credit.

## confirming
A financial service in which an independent company confirms an export order in the seller's country and makes payment for the goods in the currency of that country. Among the items eligible for confirmation are the goods; inland, air, and ocean transportation costs; forwarding fees; custom brokerage fees; and duties. Confirming permits the entire export transaction from plant to end user to be fully coordinated and paid for.

## confirming bank
(banking) In letter of credit transactions, the bank that assumes responsibility to the seller (usually exporter) for payment from the issuing bank (buyer's bank) so long as the terms and conditions of the letter of credit have been met by the seller/exporter. See letter of credit.

## conflict diamond / blood diamond
A diamond mined in a war zone and sold for the purpose of financing an armed conflict, insurgency, invasion, war or terrorism. The trade in conflict diamonds has become an ethical issue in some countries and has produced calls for regulation and control of the industry. In 2002, representatives of various governments and the diamond industry met in Kimberly, South Africa and established the Kimberly Process Certification Scheme, which provided for industry self regulation, an internationally recognized certification scheme for rough diamonds and import/export standards. Many believe that the whole process was simply a public relations event as it has done little to control trade in conflict diamonds. Given that a great deal of the "value" of most diamonds used in the jewelry trade is related to marketing, not source, it is no wonder that conflict diamonds find their way into international markets.

## conflict of laws
(law) Differences between the laws of different countries or other jurisdictions that become significant in determining which law will apply when individuals or legal entities

have acquired rights, incurred obligations, suffered injuries or damages, or made contracts in two or more jurisdictions. The rules that courts apply to resolve conflicts of laws vary among countries. In addition, different rules apply depending on the subject matter of a controversy—that is, whether a controversy involves property or personal rights. *See* governing law clause; lex loci actus; lex loci solutionis.

**connecting carrier**
(shipping) A carrier which has a direct physical connection with another carrier or forms a connecting link between two or more carriers.

**consideration**
(law) The price or other motivation that induces a party to make a contract. A buyer may agree, for example, to pay a sum of money or to furnish certain products as consideration for receiving the seller's goods. A contracting party may also promise to forgo a legal right, such as a right to sue for breach of contract, as consideration for the other party's promise to pay damages that resulted from the breach.

**consignee**
(shipping) The person or firm named in a freight contract to whom goods have been shipped or turned over for care. *See* consignor.

**consignee marks**
(shipping) A symbol placed on packages for export, generally consisting of a square, triangle, diamond, circle, cross, etc., with designed letters and/or numbers for the purpose of identification.

**consignment**
(shipping) Shipment of one or more pieces of property, accepted by a carrier for one shipper at one time, receipted for in one lot, and moving on one bill of lading.
(commerce) Delivery of merchandise from an exporter (the consignor) to an agent (the consignee) under agreement that the agent sell the merchandise for the account of the exporter. The consignor retains title to the goods until sold. The consignee sells the goods for commission and remits the net proceeds to the consignor.

**consignment contract**
(law) An agreement by a seller (consignor) to deliver goods to an individual or legal entity (consignee) who will pay the seller for any goods sold, less a commission, and will return goods not sold. *See* consignment.

**consignor**
(shipping) The individual, company or entity that ships goods, or gives goods to another for care. The consignor is usually the exporter or his agent. *See* consignee; consignment.

**consolidated container**
(shipping) A shipping container containing cargo from a number of shippers for delivery to a number of different consignees.

**consolidation**
(shipping) The combining of less than truckload (LTL) shipments of cargo from a number of shippers at a centrally located point of origin by a freight consolidator, and transporting them as a single shipment to a destination point. Consolidation of cargo often results in reduced shipping rates.

**consolidation point**
(logistics) A terminal, container yard, loading dock or other physical location where the consolidation of freight takes place.

**consolidator**
(shipping) A company that provides consolidation services. Freight forwarders perform the functions of a consolidator. *See* consolidation.

**consolidator's bill of lading**
(shipping) A bill of lading issued by a consolidating freight forwarder to a shipper. *See* bill of lading; house air waybill.

**constructed value**
(U.S. Customs) In customs valuation, a means of determining fair or foreign market value when sales of such or similar merchandise do not exist or, for various reasons, cannot be used for comparison purposes. The "constructed value" consists of the cost of materials and fabrication or other processing employed in producing the merchandise, general expenses of not less than 10 percent of material and fabrication costs, and profit of not less than 8 percent of the sum of the production costs and general expenses. To this amount is added the cost of packing for exportation. *See* valuation; transaction value.

**constructive total loss**
(insurance) An insurance loss where the expense of recovering or repairing the insured goods would exceed their value after this expenditure had been incurred.
In the adjustment of constructive total losses, the value of any remaining salvage abandoned to underwriters may, by agreement, be taken into consideration, with payment to the assured upon a net basis. Otherwise, underwriters pay full insured value and may then dispose of the salvage for their own account, provided they have elected to accept abandonment.
If the loss was due to sea peril, a "master's protest" (also called "captain's protest) will usually be required. This certifies the fact that unusually heavy weather or other exceptional circumstance was encountered during the voyage and is extended to confirm the loss of the shipment in question. In claims for total loss, it is especially necessary that a full set of insurance certificates and bills of lading be submitted to the insurance company representative. *See* abandonment; captain's protest.

**consular declaration**
A formal statement, made in a country of export by the consul of an importing country, describing goods to be shipped to the importing country. *See* consular invoice.

**consular invoice**
(customs) An invoice covering a shipment of goods certified (usually in triplicate) by the consul of the country for which the merchandise is destined. This invoice is used by customs officials of the country of entry to verify the value, quantity, and nature of the merchandise imported. *See* commercial invoice.

**consular officers**
(diplomacy) Embassy officials who extend the protection of their home government to their country's citizens and property abroad. They maintain lists of local attorneys, act as liaison with police and other officials and have the authority to notarize documents.

**consular visa**
(travel/customs) Any one of several official endorsements by a consul of a country. A consular visa can be issued for travel, consular invoices, certificates of origin, shipping documents and other legal documents.

**consulate**
(diplomacy) The offices representing the commercial interests of the citizens of one country in another country.

**consumer goods**
(economics) Any goods produced to satisfy the needs of individuals rather than those produced for the manufacturing or production of other goods. Examples of consumer goods are food, clothing and entertainment products. *See* capital goods.

## consumption entry
(general) (a) A customs entry where the importer pays applicable duty and merchandise is released from customs custody at a port, foreign trade zone or from a customs bonded warehouse. (b) The formal process for entering commercial shipments of goods into the customs territory of a country. A "formal entry."
(U.S. Customs) (a) A U.S. Customs entry where the importer pays applicable duty and merchandise is released from customs custody at a U.S. port, foreign trade zone or from a customs bonded warehouse. (b) The formal U.S. Customs process for entering commercial shipments of goods into the Customs territory of the United States. A "formal entry."
The entry of goods is a two-part process consisting of (1) filing the documents necessary to determine whether merchandise may be released from Customs custody, and (2) filing the documents which contain information for duty assessment and statistical purposes. In certain instances, such as the entry of merchandise subject to quotas, all documents must be filed and accepted by Customs prior to the release of goods. *See* entry.

## container
(shipping/logistics) A single rigid, sealed, reusable metal box in which merchandise is shipped by vessel, truck or rail.
(ISO definition) An item of equipment defined for transport purposes. It must

20' ocean shipping container

be: a) of permanent character and accordingly strong enough to be suitable for repeated use. b) specially designed to facilitate the carriage of goods, by one or more modes of transport without intermediate reloading. c) fitted with devices permitting its ready handling, particularly from one mode of transport to another. d) so designed as to be easy to fill and empty. e) having an internal volume of 1m³ or more. The term container includes neither vehicles nor conventional packing.
All containers have construction fittings, or fastenings able to withstand, without permanent distortion, all stresses that may be applied in normal service use of continuous transportation.
Ocean shipping containers are generally 10, 20, 30 or 40 feet (3.029, 6.058, 9.087 or 12.192m) long and 8 or 8.5 feet (2.423 or 2.575m) tall, and conform to International Standards Organization (ISO) standards. (40-foot containers are generally able to hold about 40,000 pounds or 18,000 kilos.) Ocean freight container types include: standard, high cube, hardtop, open top, flat, platform, ventilated, insulated, refrigerated and bulk (dry or wet).
Air freight containers (ULDs or unit load devices) come in a multitude of sizes and shapes to fit the unique requirements of airplane holds and conform to standards established by the International Airline Transport Association (IATA).
*See* International Standards Organization; International Air Transport Association; unit load device (ULD); and appendices for Ocean Freight Containers and Air Freight Containers.

## container depot (CD)
(logistics) A storage area, other than a container yard, where shippers and consignees may pick up or drop off empty containers. A container depot may not be owned or

controlled by a shipper or its agent and may not receive loaded containers. *See* container yard.

## container freight charge
(shipping) Charge made for the packing or unpacking of cargo into or from ocean freight containers.

## container freight station (CFS)
(logistics) A carrier-designated facility at which (export) LCL (less than container load) cargo is received from consignors for consolidation and loading into containers or at which (import) LCL cargo is unloaded from containers and delivered to consignees.

## container load
(shipping) A shipment of cargo that fills a given container either by bulk or maximum weight.

## container load plan
(logistics) (a) A list of items loaded in an individual shipping container. (b) A list of the sequence in which items are to be loaded into a shipping container. (c) A plan for the physical placement of items in a shipping container. (d) A comprehensive list of items loaded into a shipping container including their weight, measurements, markings, consignors, consignees, countries of origin, countries of destination, and the physical location of items within the container.

## container number
(logistics) The unique identification number of an individual shipping container consisting of a four-letter owner's code, a six-digit container serial number and a check digit. For example, in the container number ABCD-123456-7, ABCD is the container prefix (owner's code), 123456 is the serial number, and 7 is the check digit.

## container on flat car
(shipping/rail shipping) A shipping container without chassis, bogies or wheels that is transported on a rail flat car.

## container part load
(shipping) A shipment of cargo that in either volume or weight is not sufficient to fill any one of many standard containers.

## container platform
(logistics) A flat rigid container floor without side or end walls, usually 20 or 40 feet in length, fitted with devices permitting ready handling and used for intermodal operations.

## container prefix
(logistics) A four-letter code that identifies the owner of a container and is the prefix of a container number. For example, in the container number ABCD-123456-7, ABCD is the container prefix (owner's code), 123456 is the serial number, and 7 is the check digit.

## Container Security Initiative (CSI)
(U.S. Customs) A U.S. Customs and Border Protection (CBP) initiative that serves to protect the global trading system and the trade lanes between CSI ports and the U.S. Under the CSI program, a team of CBP officers is deployed to work with host nation counterparts to identify and examine all U.S.-bound containers that pose a potential threat for terrorism before they are shipped to the United States. The concept is to prevent terrorist threats from being carried out and to make U.S. borders the last line of defense, not the first.
The CSI is founded on four core elements:
1. Using intelligence and automated information to identify and target containers that pose a risk for terrorism;
2. Pre-screening those containers that pose a risk at the port of departure before they arrive at U.S. ports;
3. Using detection technology to quickly pre-screen containers that pose a risk; and

4. Using smarter, tamper-evident containers.
*See* the CSI section in the Security appendix.

**container serial number**
(logistics) A unique six-digit number that identifies a container owner's specific container. Forms the second part of a complete container number. For example, in the container number ABCD-123456-7, ABCD is the container prefix (owner's code), 123456 is the serial number, and 7 is the check digit.

**container ship**
(shipping) An ocean going or inland waterway vessel designed to carry standardized shipping containers. A large container ship can accommodate as many as eight layers of containers stacked in wells in its hold and as many as four layers on deck.

**container terminal**
(shipping/logistics) An area at the end of a rail, ship, air or truck line which serves as a loading, unloading and transfer point for cargo and containers. Container terminals often include loading equipment, storage facilities, repair facilities and management offices.

**container vessel**
(shipping) An oceangoing vessel designed specifically to easily handle the loading, stowage and off-loading of ocean freight containers. Containers may be stowed either below deck or on deck.

**container yard (CY)**
(logistics) A facility at which FCL (full container load) and empty containers are received from or delivered to consignors and consignees by or on behalf of a carrier. Container yards are also used as a facility to receive merchandise from consignors for packing into containers. Synonym: marshalling yard. *See* container depot.

**containerization**
(shipping) The practice or technique of using a boxlike device (container) in which a number of packages are stored, protected, and handled as a single unit in transit. Advantages of containerization include: less handling of cargo, more protection against pilferage, less exposure to the elements, and reduced cost of shipping.
(air freight) Container descriptions have been broadened to include a unitized load on a carrier-owned pallet, loaded by shippers, and unloaded by receivers at places other than on airline premises, and restrained and contoured so as to permit proper positioning and tiedown aboard the aircraft.

**contango**
(banking/finance/foreign exchange) The amount (generally a percentage) a buyer pays a seller to delay transfer of a stock, security or foreign exchange to the next or any future day. The opposite of backwardation.

**contingency insurance**
(insurance) Also called difference in conditions insurance. Insurance which protects the interests of the insured in the event another party's insurance fails or falls short. Commonly used in both import and export situations:
Example 1: Exporting
There are several countries whose laws require that marine insurance on shipments to those countries be placed with local insurance companies. This has the effect of requiring the importer to furnish the insurance. The quality and extent of coverage of this insurance, however, may be in question. If the exporter feels that he has insurable interest he can still protect himself by the purchase of contingency or difference in conditions insurance which protects his own interests in the event the importer's insurance fails or falls short. While the cost of this is naturally less than the cost of primary insurance, it must be borne by the exporter.
Example 2: Importing

A domestic buyer on CIF (Cost, Insurance, Freight) terms must rely upon foreign underwriters, since the insurance will have been placed by the seller in the country of origin. Once again, the quality and extent of coverage of this insurance may be in question. If the importer feels that he has insurable interest he can still protect himself by the purchase of "contingency" or "difference in conditions" insurance which protects his own interests in the event the exporter's insurance fails or falls short. Note: By purchasing on FOB, C & F or similar terms, the domestic importer can control his own insurance. He will then be able to deal with his own underwriters in case of loss or in case of demand for general average security. *See* insurable interest.

**continuous replenishment planning (CRP)**
(logistics) A supply management system of regular or automatic shipments of raw materials, component parts or finished goods based upon a user's determined or projected needs over specific units of time. For example, a hospital might have an automated inventory system that feeds into a vendor's order system on a real-time basis via a computer link. If the current inventory of an item falls below a specified minimum based upon mutually defined stock level indicators, the vendor may either automatically send a set volume of the required item or automatically send a request for a purchase order to the hospital for the required item. Such systems are based upon formal supply contracts and enable purchasers to both negotiate a lower price as well as maintain smaller average inventories at their place of business.

**contra; contra account**
(banking) An account with an offsetting credit or debit entry. In accounting, a contra account is generally the right-hand or credit side of a balance sheet in which the liabilities appear.

**contraband**
(customs) Any product which a nation has deemed to be unsuitable to produce, possess or transport. Any product that a country has deemed to be unsuitable for entry into that country. Contraband is subject to interdiction, possible forfeiture and possible destruction by customs authorities. Examples of contraband are narcotic drugs (most countries), alcohol (certain Islamic countries), seditious literature (many countries), sexually oriented goods and literature (many countries).

**contract**
(law) An agreement made between two or more parties who promise to perform or not to perform specified acts, which agreement creates for each party a legal duty and the right to seek a remedy for breach of that duty.
(a) A **constructive or implied contract** is an agreement that is implied by law from the circumstances of a business dealing and in accordance with the common understanding between reasonable persons in order to carry out the intent of the parties and do justice between them. (b) An **express contract** is an oral or written agreement the terms of which are explicitly declared when the contract is made. (c) An **executory contract** is one that has not been performed.

**contract carrier**
(shipping) Any person not a common carrier who under special and individual contracts or agreements, transports passengers or property for compensation. *See* carrier.

**contract manufacturing**
(a) An agreement whereby a company agrees to manufacture a product to the specifications of another company or individual. This can be on an exclusive or nonexclusive sales basis. (b) An agreement by two companies to manufacture separate components of a product and jointly manu-

facture and sell the finished product in their respective markets.

### contract of carriage

(shipping) The contract between the shipper (consignor) and carrier (shipping firm) for the transport of freight, including the terms and conditions of carriage and costs to the shipper. These conditions are printed on the bill of lading or air waybill and include such items as limits of liability, claims limitations, indemnity and dimensional weight rules. *See* bill of lading.

### contracting parties

(law) Two or more individuals, companies or groups who are signatories to an agreement or contract.

### Convention on Contracts for the International Sale of Goods

(law) A United Nations convention which establishes uniform legal rules governing formation of international sales contracts and the rights and obligations of the buyer and seller. The CISG applies automatically to all contracts for the sale of goods between traders from two different countries that have both ratified the CISG, unless the parties to the contract expressly exclude all or part of the CISG or expressly stipulate a law other than the CISG. The CISG became the law of the United States in January 1988.

### Convention on International Trade in Endangered Species of Wild Fauna and Flora (CITES)

An international convention that controls and/or prohibits trade in endangered and threatened species of fauna and flora. Over 100 nations participate in the treaty that took effect in May 1977. The United States is a signatory to the treaty.

### conventional arms transfer

The transfer of nonnuclear weapons, aircraft, equipment, and military services from supplier states to recipient states. (U.S.) U.S. arms are transferred by grants as in the U.S. Military Assistance Program (MAP); by private commercial sales; and by government-to-government sales under Foreign Military Sales (FMS). MAP provides defense articles and defense services to eligible foreign governments on a grant basis.

FMS provides credits and loan repayment guarantees to enable eligible foreign governments to purchase defense articles and defense services.

### convertibility

(banking/foreign exchange) Ease of exchanging one currency for that of another nation or for gold.

### convertible currency

(foreign exchange) Currency that can be easily exchanged, bought and sold for other currencies.

### conveyance

(law) A document effecting the transfer of property title from one entity to another.

(shipping/logistics) A means of transportation of people or goods.

### conveyancing

(UK) British term for buying and selling properties.

### coordinated movement

(shipping) The extending of freight transportation systems to intermediate and smaller size communities through the use of interline agreements and the use of combined services of truck/air, helicopters, regional, and commuter airlines. In many cases such traffic moves under a joint freight rate. The success of such combined service hinges on preplanning on the part of the carriers, and often on the part of shippers, with regard to production and distribution schedules.

### Coordinating Committee on Multilateral Export Controls (CoCom)

(obsolete) CoCom was an informal organization established in 1951 by NATO member countries to cooperatively restrict strategic exports (products and technical data) to controlled countries.

CoCom has been replaced with the Wassenaar Arrangement. *See* Wassenaar Arrangement.

### copyleft

A play on the legal term "copyright" and essentially a "Public License" for computer software. Public license notices carried by GNU EMACS and other Free Software Foundation software grant a series of rights to use, access source code, adapt, improve and distribute the software for free. For information go to www.gnu.org and www.fsf.org.

### copyright

(law) An intangible right granted by law to the creator of a literary, musical, or artistic production to prevent any other person from copying, publishing, and selling those works. A copyright owner holds the sole and exclusive privilege to copy, publish, and sell the copyrighted work for the period specified by law. In general, copyright protection is available only after the work is fixed in a tangible medium, such as on paper, tape, canvas, or other materials, from which the work can be seen, reproduced, or otherwise communicated. It is not available to protect an idea, concept, procedure, process, system, operation method, principle, or discovery, but only the work as presented in a tangible medium. The works that can be copyrighted, the requirements for claiming a copyright, the extent of enforcement, and the time during which a copyright is effective varies from country to country. In the United States, for example, a copyright remains effective until 50 years after the death of the creator. In an effort to standardize copyright protection worldwide, many countries have become members of several international conventions on copyrights, including the Berne Convention for the Protection of Literary and Artistic Works, the Universal Copyright Convention, the UNESCO Treaty, the Convention for Protection of Producers of Phonograms against Unauthorized Duplication of Their Phonograms, and the International Convention for the Protection of Performers, Producers of Phonograms and Broadcasting Organizations. *See* Berne Convention for the Protection of Literary and Artistic Works; Universal Copyright Convention.

### córdoba

The currency of Nicaragua. 1C$=100 centavos.

### core inflation

(economics) The basic level of inflation over a period of time (e.g., a decade) as opposed to temporary fluctuations in the rate.

### corporate dumping

The practice of exporting banned or out-of-date products from a domestic market to another national market where they are not banned or where regulations are more lax than in the domestic market. Out-of-date pharmaceuticals, for example, might be shipped from the U.S. to an Asian country that does not impose the same restrictions on the product.

### corporation

(law) An association or entity created by persons under the authority of the laws of a particular jurisdiction. A corporation is treated as distinct from the persons (referred to as shareholders) who created it, and therefore the shareholders enjoy limited liability and the corporation has certain legal rights, such as the right to own property, enter contracts, and bring suit, similar to those given to individuals. *See* person.

**correspondent bank**
(banking) A bank that acts as a depository for another bank, accepting deposits and collecting items (such as drafts) on a reciprocal basis. Correspondent banks are often in different countries.

**corrosives**
(shipping) Items include materials that cause destruction to human tissue and corrode metal (i.e. steel) upon contact. (UN CLASS 8.) Examples are sodium hydroxide, hydrochloric acid, alkaline liquid. Hazards/precautions are contact causes burns to skin and eyes; may be harmful if breathed; fire may produce poisonous fumes; may react violently with water; may ignite combustibles; and explosive gasses may accumulate.

**Cost and Freight**
**(...named port of destination) (CFR)**
(Incoterms 2000) An international trade term of sale in which, for the quoted price, the seller/exporter/manufacturer clears the goods for export and is responsible for delivering the goods past the ship's rail at the port of shipment (not destination).
The seller is also responsible for paying for the costs associated with transport of the goods to the named port of destination. However, once the goods pass the ship's rail at the port of shipment, the buyer assumes responsibility for risk of loss or damage as well as any additional transport costs.
The Cost and Freight term is used only for ocean or inland waterway transport.
The "named port of destination" in Cost and Freight and all "C" Incoterms 2000 is domestic to the buyer.
The Cost and Freight term is commonly used in the sale of oversize and overweight cargo that will not fit into an ocean freight container or exceeds weight limitations of such containers. The term is also used for LCL (less than container load) cargo and for the shipment of goods by rail in boxcars to the ocean carrier.
*See* Guide to Incoterms 2000 Appendix.

**Cost, Insurance and Freight**
**(...named port of destination) (CIF)**
(Incoterms 2000) An international trade term of sale in which, for the quoted price, the seller/exporter/manufacturer clears the goods for export and is responsible for delivering the goods past the ship's rail at the port of shipment (not destination).
The seller is responsible for paying for the costs associated with transport of the goods to the named port of destination. However, once the goods pass the ship's rail at the port of shipment, the buyer assumes responsibility for risk of loss or damage as well as any additional transport costs. The seller is also responsible for procuring and paying for marine insurance in the buyer's name for the shipment.
The Cost, Insurance and Freight term is used only for ocean or inland waterway transport.
The "named port of destination" in Cost, Insurance and Freight and all "C" Incoterms 2000 is domestic to the buyer.
*See* Guide to Incoterms 2000 Appendix.

**Cost, Insurance, Freight, Commission, and Interest (CIFCI)**
(trade term) The same as CIF (cost, insurance and freight), plus commission and interest.

**cost of goods sold**
(economics/accounting) The purchase price of goods sold during a specified period, including transportation costs.

**cost of production**
(economics) The sum of the cost of materials, fabrication and/or other processing employed in producing the merchandise sold in a home market or to another country to-

gether with appropriate allocations of general administrative and selling expenses. COP is based on the producer's actual experience and does not include any mandatory minimum general expense or profit as in "constructed value." *See* valuation; constructed value.

**cost plus**
A pricing method whereby the purchaser agrees to pay the vendor an amount determined by the costs incurred by the vendor to produce the goods or services purchased, plus a fixed percentage of that cost for profit.

**costs of manufacture (COM)**
(U.S. Customs) In the context of dumping investigations, the costs of manufacture, COM, is equal to the sum of the materials, labor and both direct and indirect factory overhead expenses required to produce the merchandise under investigation. *See* dumping.

**cottage industry**
(economics) An industry dependent upon a labor force that works out of their own homes and often with their own equipment.

**Council of Economic Advisers**
(U.S. government) A three-member executive office of the president which analyzes the U.S. economy, advises the president on economic developments, appraises programs and policies, and recommends policies for economic growth to the president. Contact: Council of Economic Advisers, Old Executive Office Building, 17th St. & Pennsylvania Ave. NW, Washington, DC 20502 USA; Web: www.whitehouse.gov/cea.

**Council of Europe**
A regional alliance established in May 1949 to encourage unity and social and economic growth among members, which currently include: Austria, Belgium, Bulgaria, Cyprus, Denmark, Finland, France, Germany, Greece, Hungary, Iceland, Ireland, Italy, Liechtenstein, Luxembourg, Malta, the Netherlands, Norway, Poland, Portugal, San Marino, Spain, Sweden, Switzerland, Turkey, and the United Kingdom. Contact: The Council of Europe, Avenue de l'Europe, 67075 Strasbourg Cedex, France. Tel: [33] (3) 88-41-20-00; Fax: [33] (3) 88-41-27-45; E-mail: infopoint@coe.int; Web: www.coe.int.

**Council of Supply Chain Management Professionals (CSCMP)**
(logistics; until 2005, the Council of Logistics Management (CLM)) A not-for-profit organization of logistics professionals dedicated to the improvement of logistics management skills. The CSCMP works in cooperation with industry and other NGOs (nongovernmental organizations) to further the understanding and development of the logistics concept. The organization focuses on three main areas: 1) improving communication between members of the logistics profession, 2) conducting research into logistics and 3) building awareness of the importance of logistics in the world economy. The CLM promotes various activities and seminars throughout the year. Membership is open to any individual and its 15,000 members hail from countries all around the world. Contact: Council of Supply Chain Management Professionals; 2805 Butterfield Road, Suite 200; Oak Brook, IL 60523 USA; Tel: [1] (630) 574-0985; Fax: [1] (630) 574-0989; E-mail: cscmpadmin@cscmp.org; Web: www.cscmp.org.

**counteroffer**
(law) A reply to an offer that adds to, limits, or modifies materially the terms of the offer. A seller, for example, who accepts a buyer's offer, but informs the buyer that the goods will be of a different color has made a counteroffer. *See* acceptance; offer.

**C**

### counterpurchase

*See* countertrade.

### countertrade

An umbrella term for several sorts of trade in which the seller is required to accept goods or other instruments or trade, in partial or whole payment for its products.
Countertrade transactions include barter, buy-back or compensation, counterpurchase, offset requirements, swap, switch, or triangular trade, evidence or clearing accounts. The main types are:

(a) **Counterpurchase** (one of the most common forms of countertrade), where an exporter agrees to purchase a quantity of unrelated goods or services from a country in exchange for and in approximate value to the goods he or she has sold.

(b) **Offset**, where the exporter agrees to use goods and services from the buyer's country in the product being sold. Offsets may be direct or indirect, depending on whether the goods and services are integral parts of the product. In a **direct offset**, a U.S. manufacturer selling a product in a country uses a component that is made in the purchasing country. In an **indirect offset**, the exporter would buy products made in the purchasing country that are peripheral to the manufacture of its product.

(c) **Compensation** or **buy-back**, where exporters of heavy equipment, technology, or even entire facilities agree to purchase a certain percentage of the output of the new facility once it is in production.

(d) **Barter**, which is a simple swap of one good for another. Two parties directly exchange goods deemed to be of approximately equivalent value without any flow of money taking place.

(e) **Switch** trading is a more complicated form of barter that involves a chain of buyers and sellers in different markets. A switch arrangement permits the sale of unpaid balances in a **clearing account** to be sold to a third party, usually at a discount, that may be used for producing goods in the country holding the balance.

(f) **Swap**, where products from different locations are traded to save transportation costs. For example, Russian oil may be "swapped" for oil from a Latin American producer, so the Russian oil can be shipped to a country in South Asia, while the Latin American oil is shipped to Cuba.

(g) **Reverse countertrade,** where an importer (a U.S. buyer of machine tools from Poland, for example) is required to export goods equivalent in value to a specified percentage of the value of the imported goods—an obligation that can be sold to an exporter in a third country.

(h) **Clearing** agreements between two countries, which is an agreement to purchase specific amounts of each other's products over a specified period of time, using a designated "clearing currency" in the transactions.

### countervailing duties

(customs) Special duties imposed on imports to offset the benefits of subsidies to producers or exporters in the exporting country.

(WTO) The World Trade Organization (WTO) "Agreement on Subsidies and Countervailing Measures" permits the use of such duties if the importing country can prove that the subsidy would cause injury to domestic industry.

(U.S.) The Executive Branch of the U.S. government has been legally empowered since the 1890s to impose countervailing duties in amounts equal to any "bounties" or "grants" reflected in products imported into the United States. Under U.S. law and WTO rules a wide range of practices are recognized as constituting subsidies that may be offset through the imposition of countervailing duties.

The Trade Agreements Act of 1979, through amendments to the Tariff Act of 1930 (both U.S. laws) established rigorous procedures and deadlines for determining the existence of subsidies in response to petitions filed by interested parties such as domestic producers of competitive products and their workers. In all cases involving subsidized products from countries recognized by the United States as signatories to the Agreement on Subsidies and Countervailing Duties, or countries which have assumed obligations substantially equivalent to those under the Agreement, U.S. law requires that countervailing duties may be imposed only after the U.S. International Trade Commission has determined that the imports are causing or threatening to cause material injury to an industry in the United States.

Countervailing duties in the U.S. can only be imposed after the International Trade Commission has determined that the imports are causing or threatening to cause material injury to a U.S. industry.

*See* dumping; General Agreement on Tariffs and Trade; International Trade Commission.

### countervailing duty deposit

(U.S. Customs) A cash deposit of estimated countervailing duties collected by U.S. Customs and Border Protection (CBP) at the time new customs entries are made for imports of products from countries for which the U.S. International Trade Administration (ITA) has issued a countervailing duty order. The actual amount of duty to be paid is determined at liquidation. *See* countervailing duty, liquidation.

### country desk officers

(U.S. government) Country-specific export trade specialists working at the U.S. Department of Commerce in Washington, DC. Country desk officers provide assistance to U.S. exporters on a country-specific, rather than commodity-specific basis. Their responsibility is to remain current on any issues that would affect U.S. exporters and travelers in the specific country. For information call the United States Department of Commerce, Tel: [1] (202) 482-2000, or the Trade Information Center, Tel: [1] (800) USA-TRADE. *See* U.S. Department of Commerce.

### country marketing plan

(U.S.) An analysis of a country's business and economic climate, giving emphasis to marketing and trade issues. Usually prepared by the U.S. embassy in the subject country and published by the U.S. Department of Commerce, International Trade Administration. Also available on CD-ROM in the National Trade Data Bank, and available from the U.S. Department of Commerce, 1401 Constitution Ave., Washington, DC 20230 USA; Tel: [1] (202) 482-2000.

### country of departure

(shipping) The country from which a ship or shipment has or is scheduled to depart.

### country of destination

(shipping) The country that is the ultimate destination for a ship or shipment of goods.

### country of dispatch

(shipping) The country from which cargo was shipped.

### country of exportation

(shipping) Usually, but not necessarily, the country in which merchandise was manufactured or produced and from which it was first exported. For example, merchandise made in Switzerland and shipped to the United States through Frankfurt, Germany, has as the country of exportation Switzerland.

### country of export destination

The country where the goods are to be consumed, further processed, or manufactured, as known to the shipper at the time of exportation. If the shipper does not know the country of ultimate destination, the shipment is credited for statistical purposes to the last country to which the shipper knows that the merchandise will be shipped in the same form as when exported.

**country of origin**
(shipping/logistics/customs) (a) The country in which a shipment of goods was wholly grown, mined or manufactured. (b) The country which, for purposes of a country's import duty, quotas and other restrictions or prohibitions, a shipment of goods was grown, mined or manufactured.
For purposes of definition (b), one country's import regimen may state that the country of origin of a product is the last country in which it underwent a substantial transformation, while another country may state that the country of origin is the country which added the greatest value.
(U.S. Customs) In instances where the country of origin cannot be determined, transactions are credited to the country of shipment.

**country risk**
(economics) The financial risks of a transaction which relate to the political, economic or social instability of a country.

**courier**
(shipping) (a) An attendant who accompanies a shipment (generally of documents). (b) A company that provides full transportation service, without an accompanying attendant, offering door-to-door air service for time-sensitive documents or small packages on a same-day or next-day basis. Examples are DHL, FedEx (Federal Express) and UPS (United Parcel Service).

**courtage**
(banking) A European term for brokerage fee.

**cover; coverage**
*See* insurance coverage.

**cover note**
(insurance) Often also called "broker's cover note." Document issued by insurance companies or insurance brokers in lieu of insurance policies or insurance certificates which serves as proof of usual insurance notification and represents cover approval. Cover notes may be accepted under letters of credit only when they are expressly permitted.

**credit arrangements**
A series of programs under which service providers (such as ocean and air carriers, trucking companies, customs brokers and freight forwarders) extend credit to shippers and consignees for the payment of charges.

**credit risk insurance**
(insurance) Insurance designed to cover risks of nonpayment for delivered goods.

**creditor nation**
(economics) A nation that is owed more foreign currency obligations than it owes other nations. *See* debtor nation.

**creeping nationalization**
(economics/law) A continuing sequence of small but material changes to a firm's status that leads to nationalization. *See* nationalization.

**crewman**
(shipping/air transport) (a) A member of a ship's crew. (b) A member of a flight (airplane) crew.

**critical circumstances**
(U.S. Customs) A determination made by the Assistant Secretary for Import Administration as to whether there is a reasonable basis to believe or suspect that there is a history of dumping in the United States or elsewhere of the merchandise under consideration, or that the importer knew or should have known that the exporter was selling this merchandise at less than fair value, and there have been mas-

sive imports of this merchandise over a relatively short period. This determination is made if an allegation of critical circumstances is received from the petitioner. *See* dumping.

**cross rate**
(foreign exchange) Exchange rate parities which are not quoted against the dollar.

**cross-currency exchange risk**
(banking/foreign exchange) The exchange risk inherent in carrying out foreign exchange transactions in two or more currencies.

**cross-docking**
(logistics) The immediate transfer of cargo from one transport vehicle to another eliminating the intervening steps of receiving and shipping, thus facilitating the flow of product and reducing costs.

**crossed check**
(banking) A check that bears on its face two parallel transverse lines and that cannot be presented for cash. A bank that accepts the check may pay the proceeds only to another bank, which will credit the money to the account of the payee of the check. A crossed check may also include the words "and company." A specially crossed check contains in the crossing lines the name of the bank that will honor the check.

**cruzeiro real**
The currency of Brazil. 1Cr$=100 centavos.

**cube out**
(shipping/logistics) When a shipping container has been filled by volume but has not reached its maximum weight limit.

**cubic capacity**
(shipping) The carrying capacity of a container according to measurement in cubic feet, cubic centimeters or cubic meters.

**cubic foot**
(measurement) A unit of volume measurement equal to 1,728 cubic inches.

**currency**
(banking/foreign exchange) Name given to the material form of a country's payment medium, for example, "Swiss francs, divided into 100 centimes."

**currency adjustment factor (CAF)**
(logistics) A freight surcharge or adjustment factor imposed by an international carrier to offset foreign currency fluctuations. In some cases an emergency currency adjustment factor (ECAF) may be applied when a charge or rate has been originally published in a currency that is experiencing sustained or rapid decline. The CAF is charged as a percentage of the published rate. *See* emergency currency adjustment factor.

**currency area**
*See* currency zone.

**currency basket**
(banking/foreign exchange) A means of establishing value for a composite unit consisting of the currencies of designated nations. Each currency is represented in proportion to its value in relation to the total. The European Currency Unit (ecu) which is now obsolete, for example, was a weighted average of the currencies of the European Union member nations, used as a unit of value in transactions among businesses in the member countries. The ecu has been replaced by the European Union Euro.

**currency of the contract**
(commerce/law/banking) The required currency of payment as stated in a sales contract. The currency of a contract is generally a hard currency such as the U.S. dollar, Japanese yen, British pound or EU Euro. (Note that as of

**C**

January 1, 2002, the Euro replaced the Austrian schilling, Belgium franc, Dutch guilder, Finnish markka, French franc, German mark, Irish punt, Italian lira, Luxembourg franc, Portuguese escudo and Spanish peseta.) Choosing the currency of the contract is a point of negotiation and can be a significant economic factor, especially if the time from contract to delivery (or billing) is great, or if fluctuations in the currencies of the buyer and seller are anticipated over the course of the contract.

### currency snake
*See* snake system.

### currency swap
(banking/foreign exchange) System whereby an institution with funds in one currency converts them into another and enters into a forward exchange contract to recover the currency borrowed.

### currency (term) of insurance
(insurance) A statement of insurance coverage expressed either in time, or for transit from two physical points. For example: one year commencing on a specific date and time, or, from point a to point b.

Formerly, the marine insurance policy covered only from the time goods were actually loaded on board an ocean vessel at the port of shipment until they were "discharged and safely landed" at the port of destination. This was later extended by adding the words "including transit by craft, raft and/or lighter to and from the vessel."

More recently, insurance coverage has included risks to a shipment of goods from the time the goods leave the warehouse for commencement of transit and continue during ordinary course of transit until delivered to final warehouse (warehouse-to-warehouse coverage) at destination, or until the expiration of 15 days (30 if destination is outside the limits of the port), whichever shall first occur. In the case of delay in excess of the time limit specified, if it arises from circumstances beyond his control, the assured is "held covered" if he gives prompt notice and pays additional premium. *See* all risk; Marine Extension Clause 1943 & 1952.

### Currency Transaction Report (CTR)
(United States) A form (U.S. Treasury Form 4789) filed with the U.S. Internal Revenue Service (IRS) by all "financial institutions" detailing "transactions in currency" (deposit, withdrawal, exchange of currency, or other payment or transfer received or effected) of $10,000 or more. U.S. law explicitly defines "persons involved in real estate closing and settlements" as financial institutions. The regulations also contain elaborate rules designed to compel reporting when the financial institution knows or should know that payers of cash are structuring their payments to evade the $10,000 reporting trigger by making a series of smaller payments.

### currency translation
(accounting/foreign exchange) The recording in accounts of assets (or liabilities) in one currency when they are actually in another. No actual exchange of funds takes place. The World Bank, for example, translates all their assets and liabilities into U.S. dollar amounts, regardless of the actual currency in which they are denominated.

### currency zone
(banking/foreign exchange) A geographic area where one currency is valid. A currency zone normally, but not always coincides with the national frontiers of a country. A **supranational currency zone** arises when different currencies are connected either through convertibility or fixed exchange rates. An example is the Sterling zone.

### current account
(economics) That portion of a country's balance of payments that records current (as opposed to capital) transactions, including visible trade (exports and imports),

invisible trade (income and expenditures for services), profits earned from foreign operations, interest and transfer payments.
(UK) British term for a bank checking account.
*See* balance of payments.

### current balance
(economics) The value of all exports (goods plus services) less all imports of a country over a specific period of time, equal to the sum of the trade (visible) and invisible balances plus net receipts of interest, profits and dividends from abroad. *See* balance of payments.

### custody bill of lading
(shipping) A bill of lading issued by U.S. warehouses as a receipt for goods stored. *See* bill of lading.

### Custom House Guide
*See* United States Custom House Guide.

### customer automation
(shipping) The use of carrier automation equipment on the customer's premises that aids in the processing of shipments, i.e., airbill preparations, invoicing, weighing, and tracing.

### customhouse
The government building or the office where customs duties and other charges are paid, and the central place where most of the customs work and transactions are performed, and where all moneys, of every nature and wherever collected, are accounted for. (Note: "customshouse" with an "s" after the "m" is an incorrect spelling.)

### customhouse broker
*See* customs broker.

### Customized Market Analysis
(U.S.) A fee-based International Trade Administration service that provides firms with key marketing, pricing, and foreign representation information about their specific products. Overseas staff conduct on-site interviews to provide data in nine marketing areas about the product, such as sales potential in the market, comparable products, distribution channels, going price, competitive factors, and qualified purchasers. Information on pricing and on contacting a trade specialist near you can be found at: Web: www.export.gov/comm_svc (click "Contact Us").

### customs
(a) A government authority designated to regulate flow of goods to/from a country and to collect duties levied by a country on imports and exports. The term also applies to the procedures involved in such collection. (b) The United States Customs Service. *See* United States Customs Service. (c) Taxes imposed by a government on the import or export of products or services. *See* tariff.

### Customs Automated Data Exchange (CADEX)
(Canada Customs) A Canada Border Services Agency (CBSA) alternative to presenting paper copies of Form B3, the Canada Customs Coding Form. CBSA process 96% of all the B3 forms it receives using the CADEX system. This system also provides importers with access to reports and files to assist in the electronic preparation of Form B3. Importers who receive authorization to use CADEX can electronically transmit their Form B3 information directly to the CBSA computer system. For more information, go to: www.cbsa-asfc.gc.ca/import/servicesintro-e.html.

### customs bond
*See* bond; surety.

### customs bonded warehouse
(customs) A federal warehouse where goods remain until duty has been collected from the importer. Goods under bond are also kept here. *See* surety; bond; in bond; bonded warehouse.

### customs broker
(U.S. Customs) An individual or firm licensed by U.S. Customs & Border Protection to act for importers in handling the sequence of custom formalities and other details critical to the legal and speedy exporting and importing of goods.

### customs classification
(customs) The particular category in a tariff nomenclature in which a product is classified for tariff purposes; or, the procedure for determining the appropriate tariff category in a country's nomenclature system used for the classification, coding and description of internationally traded goods. *See* Harmonized System; Harmonized Tariff Schedule of the United States.

### Customs Cooperation Council (CCC)
An intergovernmental organization created in 1953 and headquartered in Brussels, through which customs officials of participating countries seek to simplify, standardize, and conciliate customs procedures. The Council has sponsored a standardized product classification, a set of definitions of commodities for customs purposes, a standardized definition of value and a number of recommendations designed to facilitate customs procedures. *See* Harmonized System.

### Customs Cooperation Council Nomenclature
A customs tariff system formerly used by many countries, including most European nations but not the United States. It has been superseded by the Harmonized System Nomenclature to which most major trading nations, including the U.S., adhere. *See* Harmonized System; Harmonized Tariff Schedule of the United States.

### customs court
(U.S. Customs) A U.S. Customs & Border Protection court based in New York, NY, consisting of three 3-party divisions to which importers may appeal or protest classification and valuation decisions and certain other actions taken by U.S. Customs & Border Protection.

### customs declaration
(U.S. Customs) An oral or written statement attesting to the correctness of description, quantity, value, etc., of merchandise offered for importation into the United States. *See* entry.

### customs duty
(customs) A tax levied and collected by custom officials in discharging the tariff regulations on imports. *See* tariff.

### customs harmonization
(customs) International efforts to increase the uniformity of customs nomenclatures and procedures in cooperating countries. The Customs Cooperation Council has developed an up-to-date and internationally accepted "Harmonized Commodity Coding and Description System" for classifying goods for customs, statistical, and other purposes. *See* Customs Cooperation Council; Harmonized System; Harmonized Tariff Schedule of the United States.

### customs import value
(U.S. Customs) U.S. Customs & Border Protection appraisal value of merchandise. Methodologically, the Customs value is similar to Free Alongside Ship (FAS) value since it is based on the value of the product in the foreign country of origin, and excludes charges incurred in bringing the merchandise to the United States (import duties, ocean freight, insurance, and so forth); but it differs in that U.S. Customs & Border Protection, not the importer or exporter, has the final authority to determine the value of the good. *See* valuation.

### Customs Information Exchange
(United States) A clearinghouse of information for U.S. Customs and Border Protection officers. *See* United States Customs and Border Protection.

### Customs Internet Gateway (CIG)
(Canada Customs) The CIG is a Canada Border Services Agency (CBSA) methodology for transmitting customs data to the CBSA. Clients can apply to transmit their CADEX B3 accounting data, ACROSS release data, send arrival messages and receive their RNS release messages over the Internet. The Customs Internet Gateway went into production on July 31, 2000. For more information, contact the Electronic Commerce Unit at 1-888-957-7224 or visit the Web site at: https://reg-pki-ext.ccra-adrc.gc.ca/cig/index-e.jsp

### customs invoice
(customs) An invoice made out on a special form prescribed by the customs authorities of the importing country. Used only in a few countries. *See* commercial invoice.

### Customs Rulings
(U.S. Customs) Rulings by U.S. Customs and Border Protection (CBP) regarding such issues as classification, drawback claims and country of origin. The Customs Rulings Online Search System (CROSS) is a searchable database of CBP rulings that can be retrieved based on simple or complex search characteristics using keywords and Boolean operators. For more information go to: http://rulings.cbp.gov/index.asp?sc=HQ&vw=results.

### Customs Self Assessment (CSA) Program
(Canada Customs) A Canada Border Services Agency (CSRA) certification program that gives approved importers the benefits of a streamlined accounting and payment process for all imported goods. This ends the need for importers to maintain separate and costly customs processes, allowing them to use their own business systems to fully self assess and meet their customs obligations.
The CSA program also gives approved importers, approved carriers, and registered drivers the benefits of a streamlined clearance option for CSA eligible goods. The streamlined clearance process ends the need for transactional transmissions of data related to eligible goods. This allows for the clearance of goods based on the identification of the approved importer, approved carrier, and registered driver.
To qualify for CSA-expedited shipping, the carrier, driver and Canadian importer all must be CSA-certified. The CSA program will allow the importer to submit payments once a month compared to numerous single transactions. All entities in the clearance process, i.e. importer, carrier, driver, must be accepted into the program and be approved in order to participate. For complete information, go to: www.cbsa-asfc.gc.ca/import/csa/assessment-e.html

### customs tariff
(customs) A schedule of charges assessed by government on imported or exported goods. *See* Harmonized System; Harmonized Tariff Schedule of the United States.

### customs territory
The geographic territory upon which a sovereign nation imposes its import and export regulations and duties. Certain territorial possessions and special economic zones (such as foreign trade zones) are often considered outside the customs territory of a nation.
(U.S. Customs) The customs territory of the United States consists of the 50 states, the District of Columbia, and Puerto Rico. Foreign trade zones are not considered customs territory of the United States. *See* United States Customs Service; foreign trade zone.

### Customs-Trade Partnership Against Terrorism (C-TPAT)
(U.S. Customs) A voluntary United States Customs and Border Protection (CBP) business initiative designed to encourage importers, carriers, brokers, warehouse operators and manufacturers to ensure the integrity of the supply chain by strengthening their security practices and commu-

nicating their security guidelines to their business partners within the supply chain.

Individual businesses must apply to CBP to participate. Accepted participants must sign an agreement that commits them to the following actions: 1) Conduct a comprehensive self-assessment of their supply chain security using C-TPAT security guidelines. 2) Submit a supply chain security profile questionnaire to CBP. 3) Develop and implement a program to enhance security throughout their supply chain in accordance with C-TPAT guidelines. 4) Communicate C-TPAT guidelines to other companies in their supply chain and work toward building the guidelines into relationships with these companies.

C-TPAT offers businesses an opportunity to play an active role in the war against terrorism. By participating in this first worldwide supply chain security initiative, companies will ensure a more secure supply chain for their employees, suppliers and customers. Beyond these essential security benefits, CBP will offer other potential benefits to C-TPAT members, including:

- Expedited release of cargo
- A reduced number of inspections (reduced border times)
- Eligibility for account-based processes (e.g., bimonthly/monthly payments)
- An emphasis on self-policing, not CBP verifications

For ongoing information and updates on the C-TPAT program, go to the U.S. Customs and Border Protection Web site at www.cbp.gov.

*See* the C-TPAT section in the Security Appendix.

### customs union

(customs) An agreement by two or more trading countries to dissolve trade restrictions such as tariffs and quotas among themselves, and to develop a common external policy or trade (e.g., trade agreement).

### customs value

The value of an import shipment of goods according to the customs authority of the country of import. The customs value of a shipment is used as the key component in assessing import duties and taxes, and the reporting of statistical data on that shipment. The customs value is calculated differently from country to country. Some examples of customs value include: 1) the transaction value of the goods in the country of origin, 2) the FAS (Free Alongside Ship) value of the goods at the country of export, and 3) the CIF (Cost Insurance and Freight) value of the goods delivered to the country of destination. *See* customs import value.

### cycle inventory

(logistics) An inventory-taking methodology where the counting of items occurs continuously but at different intervals for different items. Thus, some items may be inventoried monthly, quarterly, biannually or yearly. In some cases a cycle inventory eliminates the need for an annual inventory. *See* inventory.

### cycle time

(general) The interval of time required to complete an activity or a succession of related events.

(sales) The time it takes to make a sale, measured from the identification of the opportunity or prospect to the receipt of a purchase order.

(logistics) (a) The time required to fill an order, measured from the receipt of the order to the delivery of the product to the customer. Once measured in weeks and months, cycle time is now measured in days and even hours. (b) The time required to replenish stock of a raw material, component part or finished product, expressed as the sum of the time required to secure a purchase order plus the time required to obtain delivery from the supplier.

### D/A

*See* documentary collection.

### dalasi

The currency of Gambia. 1D=100 butut.

### damages

(law) (a) A loss or harm to a person or his or her property. (b) An award given to a person (usually as a result of a court action) as compensation for a loss.

### dangerous goods

(air transport) Articles or substances which are capable of posing a significant risk to health, safety, or property when transported by air and which are classified according to the most current editions of the International Civil Aviation Organization (ICAO) Technical Instructions for the Safe Transport of Dangerous Goods by Air and the IATA (International Air Transport Association) Dangerous Goods Regulations. Dangerous goods may be transported domestically and internationally by air. *See* hazardous materials.

### dangerous when wet

(shipping) These items include flammable solids that are reactive with water. (UN CLASS 4.) Examples: magnesium; aluminum phosphide; lithium hydride; calcium carbide. Hazards: may ignite in presence of moisture; contact with water produces flammable gas; may reignite after fire is extinguished; contact may cause burns to skin and eyes; skin contact may be poisonous; inhalation or vapors may be harmful. Precautions: prohibit flames or smoking in area.

### Data Interchange Standards Association (DISA)

(e-commerce) An international organization dedicated to the development of cross-industry electronic data interchange standards that provide the foundation to enable individuals, companies and organizations to participate in global e-business. The organization provides technical and administrative support for e-commerce and conducts training and seminars on XML and EDI. DISA publishes standards such as ASC X12, UN/EDIFACT, ANSI and offers EC/EDI publications. Contact: Data Interchange Standards Association; 7600 Leesburg Pike, Suite 430, Falls Church, VA 22043 USA; Tel: (703) 970-4480; Fax: (703) 970-4488; E-mail: info@disa.org; Web: www.disa.org.

### Data Universal Numbering System (DUNS or D-U-N-S) Number

(commerce) A company numbering and identification system developed and maintained by Dunn & Bradstreet Corporation (Web: www.dnb.com). The standard DUNS nine-digit universal identification number is particular to a specific listed company. The DUNS+4 number uniquely identifies an affiliate, subsidiary or division of a listed company.

DUNS number company identifiers are recognized, recommended or required by more than 50 global, industry and trade associations, including the United Nations, the U.S. Federal Government, the Australian Government and the European Commission. For more information, go to www.dnb.com/US/duns_update/index.html.

### date draft

(banking) A draft which matures a specified number of days after the date it is issued, without regard to the date of acceptance.

*See* acceptance; bill of exchange.

**dating**
The practice of granting extended credit terms by the seller to induce buyers to receive goods in advance of required delivery dates.

**dead heading**
(trucking) Operating a motor vehicle or vessel without a load of cargo. The term most commonly applies to the trucking industry and refers to either the return trip from delivering a cargo, or driving empty to a location in order to pick up cargo. Dead heading is considered a waste of resources and avoided whenever possible.

**deadweight**
(shipping) The maximum carrying capacity of a ship, expressed in tons, of cargo, stores, provisions and bunker fuel. Deadweight is used interchangeably with deadweight tonnage and deadweight carrying capacity. A vessel's capacity for cargo is less than its total deadweight tonnage.

**deadweight cargo**
(shipping) Cargo of such weight and volume that a long ton (2,240 pounds) is stowed in an area of less than 70 cubic feet.

**deadweight ton (DWT)**
(shipping) A unit of mass (weight) equal to 2,240 pounds.

**dealer**
An individual or firm who acts as a principal in the sale of merchandise.

**debt-for-export swap; debt-for-products swap**
(banking/trade) Swap whereby a bank arranges to export a variety of domestic products and commodities to offset part of its outstanding claims in the country.

**debt-for-nature swap**
(banking/trade) Swap arranged by private conservation group to use the proceeds of debt conversions to finance conservation projects relating to parkland or tropical forests.

**debtor nation**
(economics) A nation that is owed less foreign currency obligations than it owes other nations. *See* creditor nation.

**deck cargo**
(shipping) Cargo shipped on the deck of a vessel rather than in holds below deck. Cargo shipped on deck is more likely to be adversely affected by heat, cold, rain, seawater and movement of the ship. Some shippers require that their cargo not be shipped on deck. On the other hand, certain dangerous cargo, such as explosives are required to be shipped on deck.

**declaration**
(insurance) A method of reporting shipments to an insurance company under an open insurance policy. This "short form" calls for the name of the vessel and sailing date, points of shipment and destination, nature of commodity, description of units comprising the shipment, the amount of insurance desired and the number of the open policy under which the declaration is made. The declaration forms are prepared by the assured and are forwarded daily, weekly, or as shipments are made. The forms are forwarded to the insurance agent or broker for transmission to the insurance company. When full information is not available at the time a declaration is made, a provisional report may be sent in. The "provisional" is closed when value is finally known. The premium is billed monthly in accordance with the schedule of rates provided by the policy. The declaration is generally not used in cases where evidence of insurance must be supplied to a customer, to banks or to other third parties in order to permit collection of claims abroad. This calls for a special marine policy, occasionally referred to as a certificate. Declarations, therefore, are usually used for import shipments, not export shipments. *See* open policy; special marine policy; bordereau.

**declared value for carriage**
(shipping/insurance) The value of goods declared to the carrier by the shipper for the purposes of determining charges, or of establishing the limit of the carrier's liability for loss, damage, or delay. *See* valuation charges.

**declared value for customs**
(U.S. Customs) The selling price of a shipment or the replacement cost if the shipment is not for resale. The amount must be equal to or greater than the declared value. *See* valuation.

**deductible average**
(insurance) The deductible amount that is subtracted from each covered average loss whereby the assured always bears part of the loss. *See* average; particular average; general average; with average; free of particular average.

**deductive value**
(U.S. Customs) In valuation of merchandise for customs purposes, deductive value is the resale price of imported merchandise in the United States with deductions for certain items. Generally, the deductive value is calculated by starting with a unit price and making certain additions to and deductions from that price.
**Unit Price**: One of three prices constitutes the unit price in deductive value. The price used depends on *when* and in *what condition* the merchandise concerned is sold in the United States.
(1) *Time and Condition*: The merchandise is sold in the condition as imported at or about the date of importation of the merchandise being appraised. *Price*: The price used is the unit price at which the greatest aggregate quantity of the merchandise concerned is sold at or about the date of importation.
(2) *Time and Condition*: The merchandise concerned is sold in the condition as imported but not sold at or about the date of importation of the merchandise being appraised. *Price*: The price used is the unit price at which the greatest aggregate quantity of the merchandise concerned is sold after the date of importation of the merchandise being appraised, but before the close of the 90th day after the date of importation.
(3) *Time and Condition*: The merchandise concerned is not sold in the condition as imported and not sold before the close of the 90th day after the date of importation of the merchandise being appraised. *Price*: The price used is the unit price at which the greatest aggregate quantity of the merchandise being appraised, after further processing, is sold before the 180th day after the date of the importation. The third price is also known as the "further processing price" or "superdeductive."
**Additions**: Packing costs for the merchandise concerned are added to the price used for deductive value, provided these costs have not otherwise been included. These costs are added regardless of whether the importer or the buyer incurs the cost.
**Deductions**: Certain items are not part of the deductive value and must be deducted from the unit price. These items include:
(1) Commissions or profits and general expense,
(2) Transportation and insurance costs,
(3) Customs duties and federal taxes,
(4) Value of further processing.
If an assist is involved in a sale, that sale cannot be used in determining deductive value.
*See* valuation; transaction value; identical merchandise; similar merchandise; computed value.

**D**

### defective goods inventory (DGI)
(commerce/logistics) Inventory of damaged or defective goods. Specifically, goods that were damaged during handling in the warehouse, damaged during delivery and returned or damaged during delivery where a credit was issued to the buyer and that have an outstanding freight claim. *See* inventory.

### defense memoranda of understanding (MOU)
(U.S.) Defense cooperation agreements between the U.S. and allied nations. MOUs are signed by the U.S. Department of Defense (DOD) with allied nations and are related to research, development, or production of defense equipment or reciprocal procurement of defense items.

### Defense Threat Reduction Agency
(U.S. government) DTRA is the Department of Defense (DOD) organization which reviews applications for the export of items that are subject to the dual-use license controls of the U.S. Commerce Department. DTRA is located in the Office of the Secretary of Defense, and administers DOD technology security policy so that the U.S. is not technologically surprised on the battlefield. Contact: Defense Threat Reduction Agency, 8725 John J. Kingman Road, MSC 6201, Fort Belvoir, Virginia 22060-6201 USA; Tel: [1] (800) 701-5096; Fax: [1] (703) 767-4450; E-mail: dtra.publicaffairs@dtra.mil; Web: www.dtra.mil.

### Defense Trade Controls (DTC)
(U.S.) DTC (formerly the Office of Munitions Control, OMC) at the U.S. Department of State administers licenses for the export of items that are exclusively, or primarily, of munitions significance. These items are listed in the International Traffic in Arms Regulations (ITAR) and the U.S. Munitions List. In circumstances in which an item may be considered either dual-use or subject to the ITAR, the State Department has the option to assert jurisdiction. In some cases, decisions about jurisdiction are made after an item has been subject to a dual-use license application sent to the Commerce Department. Commerce is never involved in State's process, unless there are matters involving dual-use or issues involving jurisdiction. Contact: PM/DTC, SA-1, 12th Floor, Directorate of Defense Trade Controls, Bureau of Political and Military Affairs, U.S. Department of State, Washington, DC 20522-0112 USA; Tel: [1] (202) 663-2980; Fax: [1] (202) 261-8199; E-mail: DDTCResponseTeam@state.gov; Web: www.pmdtc.org.

### Defense Trade Working Group
(U.S.) A committee of officials from the U.S. Departments of Commerce, Defense, State and the United States Trade Representative (USTR) was established in 1990 to coordinate agency policies and resources in areas concerned with defense expenditures. The group works with industry to identify ways to target industry needs and increase the success of industry export efforts by minimizing government impediments, streamlining procedures, and improving the availability of market information. The DTWG includes three subgroups: (1) The **Defense Export Market Opportunity Subgroup**, chaired by the U.S. Department of Commerce, which helps implement Administration defense export policy and enhances U.S. government support for U.S. defense exporters; (2) The **European Defense Cooperation Subgroup**, chaired by the U.S. Department of State, which coordinates interagency input to U.S.-NATO International Staff for the NATO Council on National Armaments Directors (CNAD) study on defense trade; and (3) The **Technology Transfer/Third Country Reexport Subgroup**, chaired by the U.S. Department of Defense, which works with industry to define a more proactive technology transfer regime that could be implemented within

the limits of U.S. national security and industrial competitiveness interests.

### deferred air freight
(shipping) Air freight of a less time sensitive nature, with delivery provided over a period of days.

### deferred payment letter of credit
(banking) A letter of credit which enables the buyer to take possession of the title documents and the goods by agreeing to pay the issuing bank at a fixed time in the future. *See* letter of credit.

### del credere risk
(law) Risk that a counterparty is either unable or unwilling to fulfill his payment obligations.

### delay clause
(insurance) An insurance policy clause which excludes claims for loss of market and for loss, damage or deterioration arising from delay. This exclusion appears in almost every marine cargo insurance policy.
Insurance underwriters are exceedingly reluctant to assume any liability for loss of market, which is generally considered a "trade loss" and uninsurable. A market loss, furthermore, is an indirect or consequential damage. It is not a "physical loss or damage." *See* special marine policy.

### Delivered At Frontier (...named place) (DAF)
(Incoterms 2000) An international trade term of sale in which, for the quoted price, the seller/exporter/manufacturer clears the goods for export and is responsible for making them available to the buyer at the named point and place at the frontier, not unloaded, and not cleared for import.
In the DAF term, naming the precise point, place, and time of availability at the frontier is very important as the buyer must make arrangements to unload and secure the goods in a timely manner.
Frontier can mean any frontier including the frontier of export.
The DAF term is valid for any mode of shipment, so long as the final shipment to the named place at the frontier is by land.
The seller is not responsible for procuring and paying for insurance cover.
*See* Guide to Incoterms 2000 Appendix.

### Delivered Duty Paid (...named place of destination) (DDP)
(Incoterms 2000) An international trade term of sale in which, for the quoted price, the seller/exporter/manufacturer clears the goods for export and is responsible for making them available to the buyer at the named place of destination, cleared for import, but not unloaded from the transport vehicle.
The seller, therefore, assumes all responsibilities for delivering the goods to the named place of destination, including all responsibility for import clearance, duties, and other costs payable upon import. The DDP term can be used for any mode of transport.
The DDP term is used when the named place of destination (point of delivery) is other than the seaport or airport.
*See* Guide to Incoterms 2000 Appendix.

### Delivered Duty Unpaid (...named place of destination) (DDU)
(Incoterms 2000) An international trade term of sale in which, for the quoted price, the seller/exporter/manufacturer clears the goods for export and is responsible for making them available to the buyer at the named place of destination, not cleared for import.
The seller, therefore, assumes all responsibilities for delivering the goods to the named place of destination, but the buyer assumes all responsibility for import clearance, du-

ties, administrative costs, and any other costs upon import as well as transport to the final destination.

The DDU term can be used for any mode of transport. However, if the seller and buyer desire that delivery should take place on board a sea vessel or on a quay (wharf), the DES or DEQ terms are recommended.

The DDU term is used when the named place of destination (point of delivery) is other than the seaport or airport. *See* Guide to Incoterms 2000 Appendix.

### Delivered Ex Quay (...named port of destination) (DEQ)

(Incoterms 2000) An international trade term of sale in which, for the quoted price, the seller/exporter/manufacturer clears the goods for export and is responsible for making them available to the buyer on the quay (wharf) at the named port of destination, not cleared for import.

The buyer, therefore, assumes all responsibilities for import clearance, duties, and other costs upon import as well as transport to the final destination. (This is new for Incoterms 2000.)

The DEQ term is used only for shipments of goods arriving at the port of destination by ocean or by inland waterway. *See* Guide to Incoterms 2000 Appendix.

### Delivered Ex Ship (...named port of destination) (DES)

(Incoterms 2000) An international trade term of sale in which, for the quoted price, the seller/exporter/manufacturer clears the goods for export and is responsible for making them available to the buyer on board the ship at the named port of destination, not cleared for import.

The seller is thus responsible for all costs of getting the goods to the named port of destination prior to unloading.

The DES term is used only for shipments of goods by ocean or inland waterway or by multimodal transport where the final delivery is made on a vessel at the named port of destination. *See* Guide to Incoterms 2000 Appendix.

### delivery

(shipping/law) The act of transferring physical possession, such as the transfer of property from consignor to carrier, one carrier to another, or carrier to consignee.

### delivery carrier

(shipping) The carrier (transport company) whose responsibility is to place a shipment at the disposal of the consignee at the address stated on the bill of lading. *See* carrier; bill of lading.

### delivery instructions

(shipping) Specific delivery instructions for the freight forwarder or carrier (transport company) stating exactly where the goods are to be delivered, the deadline, and the name, address, and telephone number of the person to contact if delivery problems are encountered. *See* delivery order.

### delivery order

(shipping) (a) A document from the consignee, shipper, or owner of freight ordering a terminal operator, carrier, or warehouseman to deliver freight to another party. (b) An order from a steamship company to the terminal superintendent for the release of goods to a consignee following payment of freight charges. (c) Order to deliver specified packages out of a combined consignment covered by one single bill of lading.

### delta

(general/statistics) An increment of a variable.

(finance/foreign exchange) Measure of the relationship between an option price and the underlying futures contract or stock price.

The delta ratio indicates by how many units the premium on an option changes for a one unit change in the value of the underlying instrument. An at-the-money option has a delta of about 0.5. The deeper the option is in-the-money, the closer the delta gets to 1 and the deeper the option is out-of-the-money, the more the delta approaches 0.

### delta hedging

(banking/foreign exchange) A method used by options writers to hedge risk exposure of written options by purchase or sale of the underlying instrument in proportion to the delta. Example: the writer of a call option with a delta of 0.5 would have to buy half the amount of the instrument underlying the option (e.g., US$), which he might eventually be forced to deliver upon expiry of the option.

### Delta Nu Alpha (DNA)

(logistics) An international nonprofit organization of logistics professionals that encourages education in the field of transportation and logistics. The organization provides mentoring and financial assistance for students, continuing education for professionals in the field, and vigilance in communicating changes in regulations that affect the industry. Contact at: Delta Nu Alpha, 1451 Elm Hill Pike, Suite 205, Nashville, TN 37210 USA; Tel: [1] (615) 360-6863; Fax: [1] (615) 360-1891; E-mail: carolh24@msn.com; Web: www.deltanualpha.org.

### demand

(banking/law) (a) A request for the payment of a debt or other amount due. (b) A demand clause is a term in a note by which the note holder can compel full payment if the maker of the note fails to meet an installment.

### demand chain

(logistics) The concept that consumer demand can "pull" products through the logistics chain. Demand chain logistics is a counterpoint to supply chain logistics where products are "pushed" through the logistics system to the ultimate consumer by the actions of the producer and marketing and logistics professionals.

In demand chain logistics, however, it is the producers who are responding to the demands of customers in the marketplace. In demand chain logistics producers and logistics professionals must have a thorough understanding of their customers, an unimpeded flow of information and the ability to respond quickly to changing demand. *See* supply chain.

### de minimis

(law, taxation, customs) Latin expression meaning "about minimum things." Specifically, a shortened form of *de minimis non curat lex*, meaning "the law does not bother (concern) itself with trifles," or *de minimis non curat praetor*, meaning "magistrates do not bother (concern) themselves with trifles." In general, *de minimis* describes "minimal things" that do not interest the courts.

(law) In law, *de minimis* refers to a minimal or trifling injury to a person, property or rights that does not justify the time and trouble of a court's time (unworthy of the law's attention).

(insurance, risk assessment) In risk assessment, *de minimis* refers to a risk that is so small as to be considered insignificant.

(copyright law) In copyright law, *de minimis* refers to changes that are so small as to be insignificant. For example, attempting to claim copyright to a public domain work merely by correcting spelling errors or making very minor changes.

(customs) In customs law, *de minimis* rules figure prominently in classification of goods, rules of origin and payments of duties and taxes.

Example 1: Ingredients which are significant in terms of quantity or function must be considered in determining classification, whereas ingredients that are insignificant in quantity or function may be ignored.

Example 2: "Chapter 405: De Minimis" of the NAFTA Rules of Origin cover certain rules of origin. These rules (in short), establish that in determining the country of origin, a component value of seven percent or less of non-originating material(s) is *de minimis*, or may be ignored.

Example 3: In certain circumstances, the customs authority of a country may not require payment of a duty or tax if the amount due is less than what they consider to be worthwhile collecting.

### demise
(law) A lease of property. A demise charter is a bareboat charter. *See* bareboat charter.

### demurrage
(shipping) (a) The detention of a freight car or ship by the shipper beyond time permitted (grace period) for loading or unloading, (b) The extra charges a shipper pays for detaining a freight car or ship beyond time permitted for loading or unloading. Used interchangeably with detention. Detention applies to equipment. Demurrage applies to cargo. *See* detention.

### denar
The currency of Macedonia. 1 denar=100 deni.

### Denied Parties List
(U.S. export) The former title of the Denied Persons List. *See* Denied Persons List.

### Denied Persons List (DPL)
(U.S. trade law) (Formerly the Denied Parties List) A set of lists maintained by the U.S. Bureau of Industry and Security (formerly the U.S. Bureau of Export Administration) (Web: www.bis.doc.gov/DPL/Default.shtm) of individuals and firms denied export privileges, specifically for strategic and controlled materials, components and products.

### density
(shipping) (a) The weight of an article or container per cubic foot. (b) The ratio of mass to bulk or volume.

### Department of Agriculture (DOA)
*See* United States Department of Agriculture.

### Department of Commerce (DOC)
*See* United States Department of Commerce.

### Department of Defense (DOD)
*See* United States Department of Defense.

### Department of Energy (DOE)
*See* United States Department of Energy.

### Department of Labor (DOL)
*See* United States Department of Labor.

### Department of State
*See* United States Department of State.

### Department of the Interior (DOI)
*See* United States Department of the Interior.

### Department of the Treasury
*See* United States Department of the Treasury.

### Department of Transportation (DOT)
*See* United States Department of Transportation.

### deposit dealings
(banking) Money market operations.

### deposit money
(banking) Also known as bank or giro money. Bank, giro and postal giro account credit balances which can be converted at any time into notes and coinage, but which are normally used for cash-less payment transactions.

### deposit of estimated duties
(U.S. Customs) This refers to antidumping duties which must be deposited upon entry of merchandise into the United States which is the subject of an antidumping duty order for each manufacturer, producer or exporter equal to the amount by which the foreign market value exceeds the United States price of the merchandise. *See* antidumping duties; dumping.

### depreciation
(economics/accounting) (a) The charges against earnings to write-off the purchase price of an asset over its useful life. (b) The decline in the value of a property or asset.
(foreign exchange) The decline in value of one currency in relation to another currency.

### deputy chief of mission (DCM)
(diplomacy) Position second-in-command to ambassador in an embassy. The DCM is responsible for managing the daily operations of all departments in an embassy. Also serves as acting ambassador during the absence of the ambassador.

### destination
(shipping) The place to which a shipment is consigned.

### detention
(shipping) (a) Holding a carrier's driver and/or trailer beyond a certain stated period of "free time," often resulting in the assessment of detention charges. (b) The delay in clearing goods through customs resulting in storage and other charges. *See* demurrage.

### detention charges
(shipping) Charges assessed by a carrier against the consignor or consignee as compensation for holding a carrier's driver and/or trailer beyond a certain stated period of "free time." Detention is an accessorial service and charge. *See* demurrage.

### detention insurance
(insurance) Insurance coverage to pay for the costs resulting in the storage or maintenance of goods delayed in the clearance of customs at a foreign port.

### devaluation
(economics) The lowering of the value of a national currency in terms of the currency of another nation. Devaluation tends to reduce domestic demand for imports in a country by raising their prices in terms of the devalued currency and to raise foreign demand for the country's exports by reducing their prices in terms of foreign currencies. Devaluation can therefore help to correct a balance of payments deficit and sometimes provide a short-term basis for economic adjustment of a national economy.

In a fixed exchange rate situation, devaluation occurs as the result of an administrative action taken by a government to reduce the value of its domestic currency in terms of gold or foreign monies.

In a free exchange rate situation, devaluation occurs as a result of the action of the foreign exchange market where the value of the domestic currency drops by market forces against a specific unit of foreign currency.

### devanning
(shipping) The unloading of cargo from a container. Also called stripping.

### developed countries
(economics) A term used to distinguish the more industrialized nations—including all Organization for Economic Co-operation and Development (OECD) member countries as well as the Soviet Union and most of the socialist countries of Eastern Europe—from "developing"—or less developed countries. The developed countries are sometimes collectively designated as the "North," because most of them are in the Northern Hemisphere. *See* developing countries.

### developing countries
(economics) A broad range of countries that generally lack a high degree of industrialization, infrastructure and other capital investment, sophisticated technology, widespread literacy, and advanced living standards among their popu-

lations as a whole. The developing countries are sometimes collectively designated as the "South," because a large number of them are in the Southern Hemisphere. All of the countries of Africa (except South Africa), Asia and Oceania (except Australia, Japan and New Zealand), Latin America, and the Middle East are generally considered "developing countries" as are a few European countries (Cyprus, Malta, Turkey and countries of the former Yugoslavia, for example). Some experts differentiate four sub-categories of developing countries as having different economic needs and interests: (1) A few relatively wealthy Organization of Petroleum Exporting Countries (OPEC) countries— sometimes referred to as oil exporting developing countries—share a particular interest in a financially sound international economy and open capital markets; (2) Newly Industrializing Countries (NICs) have a growing stake in an open international trading system; (3) A number of middle income countries—principally commodity exporters—have shown a particular interest in commodity stabilization schemes; and (4) More than 30 very poor countries ("least developed countries") are predominantly agricultural, have sharply limited development prospects during the near future, and tend to be heavily dependent on official development assistance.

### difference in conditions insurance
*See* contingency insurance.

### differential
(shipping) An amount added to or deducted from a shipping base rate between two established points to make a rate to or from some other points or via another route.

### dimensional weight
(shipping) Dimensional weight refers to density, i.e., weight per cubic foot of a shipment of cargo. The weight of a shipment per cubic foot is one of its most important transportation characteristics. Some commodities, such as machinery, have a relatively high density. Others, like hats, have a relatively low density. Hence, the **dimensional weight rule** was developed as a practice applicable to low density shipments under which the transportation charges are based on a cubic dimensional weight rather than upon actual weight. Examples: one pound for each 194 cubic inches of the shipment in the case of most domestic air freight, one pound for each 266 cubic inches of cut flowers or nursery stock shipments, and one pound for each 194 cubic inches of most international shipments.

### dinar
The currency of:
Algeria, 1DA=100 centimes;
Bahrain, 1BD=1,000 fils;
Bosnia-Herzegovina, (no symbol available, no subcurrency);
Croatia, HrD (no subcurrency in use);
Iraq, 1ID=1,000 fils;
Jordan, 1JD=1,000 fils;
Kuwait, 1 KD=1,000 fils;
Libya, 1LD=100 dirhams;
Tunisia, 1D=1,000 fils;
Yugoslavia, Yun (no subcurrency in use).

### direct foreign investment (DFI)
(economics) Investment that is made to acquire a lasting interest in an enterprise operating in an economy other than that of the investor.
(U.S.) In the United States, direct investment is defined for statistical purposes as the ownership or control, directly or indirectly, by one person of 10 percent of more of the voting securities of an incorporated business enterprise, or an equivalent interest in an unincorporated business enterprise. Direct investment transactions are not limited to transactions in voting securities. The percentage ownership of voting securities is used to determine if direct investment exists, but once it is determined that it does, all parent-affiliate transactions, including those not involving voting securities, are recorded under direct investment. *See* affiliate; affiliated foreign group; foreign direct investment in the United States.

### direct store delivery (DSD)
(logistics) A logistics strategy where products sold in large volume on a regular basis are shipped directly from the producer or manufacturer to a store, eliminating the store's need to warehouse and handle the product in its own facilities. When store stocks fall below a prescribed level, orders are placed electronically either through an automated inventory system or manually and then are delivered directly to the store location. In DSD the producer or manufacturer handles both warehousing and delivery on a just-in-time delivery basis. Large volume products like beer or bread that are bulky and/or heavy are best candidates for DSD.

### dirham
The currency of:
Morocco, 1DH=100 centimes;
United Arab Emirates, 1Dh (or 1UD)=1,000 fils.

### dirty floating
*See* floating.

### discharge
(shipping) The unloading of passengers or cargo from a vessel, vehicle or aircraft.

### disclosure meeting
(U.S.) An informal meeting at which the International Trade Administration (ITA) discloses to parties the proceeding methodology used in determining the results of an antidumping investigation or administrative review. *See* dumping.

### discounting
(general) The sale at less than original price value of a commodity or monetary instrument, often for immediate payment.
(banking/letters of credit) The beneficiary under a usance/term letter of credit has the possibility of discounting his claim for immediate payment. The bank credits the beneficiary with the value of the documents, less the discount, but on an unconfirmed credit, reserves the right of recourse. (*See* recourse.) In the case of a confirmed letter of credit the discount would be without recourse.

### discount/markdown
(foreign exchange) In foreign exchange, refers to a situation where currency can be bought more cheaply at a future date than for immediate delivery. For example, if US$1 buys £1.55 for delivery now, while it buys £1.6 for delivery twelve months hence, then the pound sterling is said to be at a discount against the U.S. dollar.

### discount rate
(banking) (a) Annualized rate of discount applied to debt securities issued below par (e.g., U.S. Treasury bills). (b) Rate at which a central bank (Federal Reserve System in the U.S.) (re)discounts certain bills for financial institutions.

### discrepancies
(banking/letters of credit) The noncompliance of documents with the terms and conditions of a letter of credit. Information (or missing information or missing documents/ papers, etc.) in the documents submitted under a letter of credit, which: (1) is not consistent with its terms and conditions; (2) is inconsistent with other documents submitted; (3) does not meet the requirements of the Uniform Customs and Practice for Documentary Credits (UCPDC).

**D**

If the documents show discrepancies of any kind, the issuing bank is no longer obliged to pay and, in the case of a confirmed letter of credit, neither is the confirming bank (strict documentary compliance). *See* letter of credit; Uniform Customs and Practice.

### discrimination
(shipping) The granting of preferential rates or other privileges to some shippers or receivers which are not accorded to others under practically the same conditions. In the U.S., laws regulating common carriers prohibit discrimination.

### dishonor
(banking) The refusal of the maker of a promissory note to pay upon presentation of the note.

### dismissal of petition
(U.S.) A determination made by the U.S. Office of Administration that an antidumping petition does not properly allege the basis on which antidumping duties may be imposed, does not contain information deemed reasonably available to the petitioner supporting the allegations, or is not filed by an appropriate interested party. *See* dumping.

### dispatch
(shipping) (a) An amount paid by a vessel's operator to a charter if loading or unloading is completed in less time than stipulated in the charter agreement. (b) The release of a container to an interline carrier.

### displacement of vessel
(shipping) The weight of the quantity of water displaced by a vessel without stores, bunker fuel or cargo. Displacement "loaded" is the weight of the vessel, plus cargo and stores.

### disposable income
(economics) Personal income minus income taxes and other taxes paid by an individual, the balance being available for consumption or savings.

### dispute settlement
(general) Resolution of a conflict, usually through a compromise between opposing claims, sometimes facilitated through the efforts of an intermediary such as an arbiter.

### distrain
(law) The detention or seizure of the property of an individual or legal entity to secure that party's performance of a particular act. A court may order that property be distrained, for example, to ensure that an individual or legal entity will appear or be represented before the court at a hearing.

### distribution license
(U.S.) A license that allows the holder to make multiple exports of authorized commodities to foreign consignees who are approved in advance by the U.S. Bureau of Industry and Security (formerly the U.S. Bureau of Export Administration). The procedure also authorizes approved foreign consignees to reexport among themselves and to certain approved countries. *See* Bureau of Industry and Security.

### distribution requirements planning (DRP)
(logistics) A logistics strategy designed to manage a distribution network and link it with manufacturing. DRP involves planning for future stock requirements at various distribution points and determining the process by which these requirements will be met. DRP systems are based on manufacturing resources planning (MRP) technology and can span a whole logistics chain from remote warehouses to the factory floor. *See* MRP (manufacturing resources planning).

### distribution service
(shipping) A service under which an airline accepts one shipment from one shipper and, after transporting it as a single shipment, separates it into a number of parts at destination and distributes them to many receivers. *See* assembly service.

### distributor
An agent who sells directly for a supplier and maintains an inventory of the supplier's products.

### District Export Councils
(U.S.) A voluntary auxiliary of the United States and Foreign Commercial Service (US&FCS) district offices to support export expansion activities. There are 51 DECs with 1,800 members which help with workshops and also provide counseling to less experienced exporters. *See* United States and Foreign Commercial Service.

### diversion
(shipping) (a) Any change in the billing of a shipment after it has been received by the carrier at point of origin and prior to delivery at destination. (b) The diverting of a shipment of goods from the original port of destination to another port due to circumstances such as a storm at sea, breakdown of the vessel or other factors generally out of the control of the shipping line. *See* reconsignment.

### diversionary dumping
(customs) The sale of foreign products to a third country market at less than fair value where the product is further processed and shipped to another country. *See* dumping.

### dobra
The currency of Sao Tomé and Principe. 1Db=100 centimos.

### dock
(shipping) (a) Loading or unloading platform at an industrial location or carrier terminal. (b) The space or waterway between two piers or wharves for receiving a ship.

### dock examination
(U.S. Customs) A U.S. Customs examination during which a container is opened for a thorough inspection, as opposed to a tailgate examination, which requires only a visual inspection at the exit gate. It may be necessary to devan the container in order for customs to make its inspection.

### dock receipt
(shipping) A receipt issued by a warehouse supervisor or port officer certifying that goods have been received by the shipping company. The dock receipt is used to transfer accountability when an export item is moved by the domestic carrier to the port of embarkation and left with the international carrier for movement to its final destination.

### document
(law/banking/shipping) (a) An original or official paper that serves as proof, evidence or support of something. (b) Any recorded information, regardless of its physical form or characteristics, including, without limitation, written or printed matter, tapes, charts, maps, paintings, drawings, engravings, sketches, working notes and papers; reproductions of such things by any means or process; and sound, voice, magnetic, or electronic recordings in any form.
(computers) Any computer file created within an application program. A document can contain text, audio, and/or video. Examples include a letter written in a word processing application, a digital photograph, a digitized audio recording or an e-mail message.
The most common documents in international trade are the commercial invoice and bill of lading. Each type of document in international trade follows a particular format and requires specific types of information.
In international trade, and especially in documentary letters of credit and documentary collections, the term document has legally come to include an electronic document or electronic record of a document.

### documentary collection
(banking) A method of effecting payment for goods whereby the seller/exporter ships goods to the buyer, but instructs his bank to collect a certain sum from the buyer/

**D**

importer in exchange for the transfer of title, shipping and other documentation enabling the buyer/importer to take possession of the goods. The two types of documentary collection are:
(a) **Documents against Payment (D/P)** where the bank releases the documents to the buyer/importer only against a cash payment in a prescribed currency; and
(b) **Documents against Acceptance (D/A)** where the bank releases the documents to the buyer/importer against acceptance of a bill of exchange (draft) guaranteeing payment at a later date.
In documentary collections, banks act in a fiduciary capacity and make every effort to ensure that payment is received, but are liable only for the correct execution of the collection instructions, and do not make any commitment to pay the seller/exporter themselves.
Documentary collections are subject to the Uniform Rules of Collections, Brochure No. 322, revised 1978, of the International Chamber of Commerce (ICC) in Paris.
*See* Uniform Rules for Collections; International Chamber of Commerce.

*documentary credit*
*documentary letter of credit*
(banking) The formal terminology for letter of credit. *See* letter of credit.

*documentary instructions*
(banking) The formal list and description of documents (primarily shipping documents) a buyer requires of the seller, especially in a documentary letter of credit. *See* documentation; letter of credit.

*documentation*
(general) All or any of the financial and commercial documents relating to a transaction.
Documents in an international trade transaction may include commercial invoice, consular invoice, customs invoice, certificate of origin, bill of lading, inspection certificates, bills of exchange and others.
(banking) The documents required for a letter of credit or documentary collection (documents against payment or documents against acceptance) transaction. *See* letter of credit; documentary collection.
(customs) The documents required by the customs authority of a country to effect entry of merchandise into the country. *See* entry.
(shipping) The function of receiving, matching, reviewing, and preparing all the paperwork necessary to effect the shipment of cargo. This includes bills of lading, dock receipts, export declarations, manifests, etc.

*documents against acceptance (D/A)*
*See* documentary collection.

*documents against payment (D/P)*
*See* documentary collection.

*dog watch*
*See* watch.

*dollar*
The currency of:
American Samoa (uses U.S. dollar)
Anguilla, 1EC$=100 cents;
Antigua and Barbuda, 1EC$=100 cents;
Australia, 1$A=100 cents;
Bahamas, 1B$=100 cents;
Barbados, 1Bds$=100 cents;
Belize, 1Bz$=100 cents;
Bermuda, 1Ber$=100 cents;
British Virgin Islands (uses U.S. dollar);
Brunei, 1B$=100 cents;
Canada, 1Can$=100 cents;
Cayman Islands, 1CI$=100 cents;

Dominica, 1EC$-100 cents;
Fiji, 1F$=100 cents;
Grenada, 1EC$=100 cents;
Guam (uses U.S. dollar);
Guyana, 1G$=100 cents;
Hong Kong, 1HK$=100 cents;
Jamaica, 1J$=100 cents;
Kiribati (uses Australian dollar);
Liberia, 1$=100 cents;
Montserrat, 1EC$=100 cents;
Nauru (uses Australian dollar);
New Zealand, 1$NZ=100 cents;
Puerto Rico (uses U.S. dollar);
St. Christopher, 1EC$=100 cents;
St. Kitts-Nevis, 1EC$=100 cents;
St. Lucia, 1EC$=100 cents;
St. Vincent and the Grenadines, 1EC$=100 cents;
Singapore, 1S$=100 cents;
Solomon Islands, 1SI$=100 cents;
Taiwan, 1NT$=100 cents;
Trinidad and Tobago, 1TT$=100 cents;
Turks and Caicos Islands (uses U.S. dollar);
Tuvalu (uses Australian dollar);
United States, 1US$=100 cents;
Virgin Islands, U.S. & British (use U.S. dollar);
Zimbabwe, 1Z$=100 cents.

*dolly*
(shipping) A piece of equipment with wheels used to move containers, pallets or freight with or without the aid of a tractor.

*domestic exports*
(U.S.) Exports of commodities which are grown, produced, or manufactured in the United States, and commodities of foreign origin which have been changed in the United States, including U.S. foreign trade zones, from the form in which they were imported, or which have been enhanced in value by further manufacture in the United States.

*domestic international sales corporation (DISC)*
(U.S.) A special U.S. corporation authorized by the U.S. Revenue Act of 1971, as amended by the Tax Reform Act of 1984, to borrow from the U.S. Treasury at the average one-year Treasury bill interest rate to the extent of income tax liable on 94 percent of its annual corporate income. To qualify, the corporation must derive 95 percent of its income from U.S. exports; also, at least 95 percent of its gross assets, such as working capital, inventories, building and equipment, must be export-related. Such a corporation can buy and sell independently, or can operate as a subsidiary of another corporation. It can maintain sales and service facilities outside the United States to promote and market its goods. DISCs can now provide a tax deferral on up to $10 million of exports so long as the funds remain in export-related investments.

*domestic trunk line carrier*
(U.S. logistics) The now obsolete designation for air carriers that operate between major population centers. The new classification term is major carriers.

*domicile*
(banking) The place where a draft or acceptance is made payable. *See* bill of exchange.

*dong*
The currency of Vietnam. 1D=100 xu.

*door-to-door*
(shipping) Shipping service from shipper's door to consignee's door. Originating carrier spots (places) empty container at shipper's facility at carrier's expense for loading by and at expense of shipper. The delivering carrier spots

the loaded container at consignee's facility at carrier's expense for unloading by and at expense of consignee.

## double bottoms

(trucking) The combination of a tractor pulling two trailers, in tandem connected by a converter dolly. *See* tractor, trailer.

## double-column tariff

(customs) An import tariff schedule listing two rates. The rates in one column are for products imported from preferred trading partner countries, while the rates in the second column are for products imported from non-preferred trading countries. *See* column 1 rates; column 2 rates; Harmonized Tariff Schedules of the United States.

## downstream dumping

(customs) The sale of products by a manufacturer below cost to a secondary producer in its domestic market where the product is then further processed and shipped to another country. *See* dumping.

## D/P

*See* documentary collection.

## drachma

The currency of Greece. 1Dr=100 lepta.

## draft; draft bill of exchange

*See* bill of exchange.

## draft or draught

(shipping) The vertical distance between the waterline and the bottom of the keel of a vessel. The draft of a vessel determines the minimum depth of water in a channel or waterway required for the vessel to travel safely. *See* plimsoll mark.

## drawback—refund of duties

(U.S. Customs) The refund of all or part of customs duties, or domestic tax paid on imported merchandise which was subsequently either manufactured into a different article or reexported.

The purpose of drawback is to enable a domestic manufacturer to compete in foreign markets without the handicap of including in his costs, and consequently in his sales price, the duty paid on imported raw materials or merchandise used in the subsequent manufacture of the exported goods. There are several types of drawback:

(a) **Direct identification drawback** provides a refund of duties paid on imported merchandise that is partially or totally used in the manufacture of an exported article. Identification of the imported merchandise from import to export is required by proper record-keeping procedures. The imported merchandise must be used in the manufacturing process and exported within 5 years from date of importation of merchandise.

(b) **Substitution drawback** provides for a refund of duties paid on designated imported merchandise upon exportation of articles manufactured or produced with use of substituted domestic or imported merchandise that is of the same kind or quality as the designated imported merchandise. Same kind and quality means merchandise that is interchangeable in a specific manufacturing process. The imported materials must be used in a manufacturing process within 3 years after receipt by manufacturer, the domestic material of same kind and quality as imported materials must be used in manufacturing process within 3 years of receipt of the imported material and the exported products must be manufactured within 3 years after receipt of imported material by manufacturer, and exported within 5 years of date of importation of designated material.

(c) **Rejected merchandise drawback** is a 99 percent refund of duties paid on imported merchandise found not to conform to sample or specification, or shipped without the consent of the consignee, if returned to Customs custody within 90 days of its original Customs release (unless an extension is granted) for examination and exportation under Customs supervision.

Questions regarding the legal aspects of drawback should be addressed to: Chief, Entry Procedures and Carriers Branch, Office of Regulations and Rulings, U.S. Customs Service, 1300 Pennsylvania Avenue, NW, Washington, DC 20229; Tel: [1] (202) 927-2320; Web: www.cbp.gov.

## drawback system

(U.S. Customs) A part of U.S. Customs' Automated Commercial System, provides the means for processing and tracking of drawback claims. *See* Automated Commercial System; drawback.

## drawee

(banking) The individual or firm on whom a draft is drawn and who owes the indicated amount. In a documentary collection, the drawee is the buyer. *See* drawer; bill of exchange.

## drawer

(banking) The individual or firm that issues or signs a draft and thus stands to receive payment of the indicated amount from the drawee. In a documentary collection, the drawer is the seller. *See* drawee; bill of exchange.

## dray

(shipping) A vehicle used to haul cargo or goods.

## drayage

(shipping) The charge made for hauling freight or carts, drays or trucks.

## driving-time regulations

(U.S. trucking) U.S. Department of Transportation (U.S. DOT) rules that limit the number of consecutive daily and weekly hours that a driver can operate a motor vehicle in interstate commerce. Details of other regulations can be found at the Federal Motor Carrier Safety Administration Web site at Web: http://www.fmcsa.dot.gov. Contact: Federal Motor Carrier Safety Administration, 400 7 th Street, SW, Washington, D.C. 20590 USA; Tel: 1-800-832-5660.

## droit moral

(law) Moral right doctrine, which is a European legal theory that gives artists certain rights with respect to their works, including to create, disclose, and publish a work; to withdraw it from publication; to be identified as its creator; and to prevent alteration of it without permission.

## drop

(logistics) To place an unloaded or full trailer, boxcar or container at a client facility where it can be loaded or unloaded by the client.

(marketing) To deliver a bulk mailing to the postal services (or courier) for mailing. *See* drop date.

## drop date

(marketing) The date a bulk mailing is handed over to the postal services (or courier). *See* drop.

## drop shipment

(shipping) A shipment of goods from a manufacturer directly to a dealer or consumer, avoiding shipment to the wholesaler (drop shipper). The wholesaler, however, is compensated for taking the order.

## dropoff

(shipping) The delivery of a shipment by a shipper to a carrier for transportation.

## dropoff charge

(shipping) A charge made by a transportation company for delivery of a container.

## dry-bulk container

(shipping) A container designed to carry any of a number of free-flowing dry solids such as grain or sand.

**dry-cargo container**
(shipping) Any shipping container designed to transport goods other than liquids.

**dry cargo/freight**
(shipping) Cargo which does not require temperature control.

**dual exchange rate**
(foreign exchange) The existence of two or more exchange rates for a single currency.

**dual operation**
(logistics/trucking) A motor carrier that is registered to operate as both a common carrier and contract carrier.

**dual pricing**
The selling of identical products in different markets for different prices. This often reflects dumping practices. *See* dumping.

**dual-rate system**
(shipping) A conference carrier pricing system that allows ocean shippers who sign exclusive shipping agreements to receive discounted services.

**due diligence**
The systematic investigation, verification and evaluation of information in order to facilitate a decision regarding a proposed transaction. Performing a due diligence investigation is a standard operating procedure prior to: purchasing a business, investing in a business, awarding an important contract, investing venture capital, loaning money or offering securities. Due diligence can include checking financial references, background checks on key individuals, interviewing current and past clients, checking the legal status of a company and on-site evaluations.

**dumping**
(customs) The sale of a commodity in a foreign market at less than fair value, usually considered to be a price lower than that at which it is sold within the exporting country or to third countries.

"Fair value" can also be the constructed value of the merchandise, which includes cost of production plus a mandatory 8 percent profit margin.

Dumping is generally recognized as an unfair trade practice because it can disrupt markets and injure producers of competitive products in an importing country.

(a) With **price-price dumping**, the foreign producer can use its sales in the high-priced market (usually the home market) to subsidize its sales in the low-priced export market. The price difference is often due to protection in the high-priced market.

(b) **Price-cost dumping** indicates that the foreign supplier has a special advantage. Sustained sales below cost are normally possible only if the sales are somehow subsidized.

(c) **Diversionary dumping** is the sale of foreign products to a third country at less than fair value where the product is further processed and shipped to another country.

(d) **Downstream dumping** is the sale of products below cost to a secondary producer in the original producer's domestic market who then further processes the product and ships it to a foreign country.

(U.S.) The U.S. Antidumping Law of 1921, as amended, considered dumping as constituting "sales at less than fair value," combined with injury, the likelihood of injury, or the prevention of the establishment of a competitive industry in the United States. The Trade Act of 1974 added a "cost of production" provision, which required that dumping determinations ignore sales in the home market of the exporting country or in third country markets at prices that are too low to "permit recovery of all costs within a reasonable period of time in the normal course of trade." The Trade Agreements Act of 1979 repealed the 1921 act, but reenacted most of its substance in Title VII of the Tariff Act of 1930.

*See* countervailing duties; antidumping duties; constructed value; dumping margin; fair value.

**dumping margin**
(customs) The amount by which imported merchandise is sold in a country below the home market or third country price or the constructed value (that is, at less than its "fair value"). For example, if the U.S. "purchase price" of an imported article is $200 and the fair value is $220, the dumping margin is $20. This margin is expressed as a percentage of the import country price. In this example, the margin is 10 percent. *See* dumping; fair value.

**dunnage**
(shipping) Material placed around cargo to prevent damage or breakage by preventing movement. The material is normally furnished by the shipper and its weight is charged for in the rating of the shipment.

**durable goods**
(economics) Any product which is not consumed through use. Examples are automobiles, furniture, computers and machinery.

**dutiable list**
(customs) Items listed in a country's tariff schedule for which it charges import duty.
*See* Harmonized System; Harmonized Tariff Schedule of the United States.

**duty**
(customs) A tax levied by a government on the import, export or consumption of goods. Usually a tax imposed on imports by the customs authority of a country. Duties are generally based on the value of the goods (ad valorem duties), some other factors such as weight or quantity (specific duties), or a combination of value and other factors (compound duties).
*See* ad valorem; specific rate of duty; compound rate of duty.

(U.S. Customs) All goods imported into the United States are subject to duty or duty-free entry in accordance with their classification under the applicable items in the Harmonized Tariff Schedule of the United States (HTS or HTSUS). An annotated, loose-leaf edition of the HTS may be purchased from the Superintendent of Documents, U.S. Government Printing Office, Mail Stop: IDCC, 732 N. Capitol Street, NW, Washington, DC 20401; Tel: [1] (866) 512-1800, [1] (202) 512-1800; Fax: [1] (202) 512-2104; Web: www.gpoaccess.gov.

Note that duty rates are subject to the classification of goods by Customs. Articles that appear to be similar may have significantly different rates of duty. *See* classification. Note also that the actual duty paid is also determined by how Customs values the merchandise. *See* Harmonized Tariff Schedule; valuation.

**duty drawback**
*See* drawback.

# E

**e-**
(computers) Acronym for electronic, such as e-document, e-trade, e-bill of lading, e-commerce, etc.

**EAN**
Acronym for European Article Number, now also called IAN (International Article Numbering). An international standard numbering and bar coding system used primarily in retail applications developed by EAN International and which is compatible with the U.S. UPC (Universal Product Code). For information go to: www.ean-int.org.

**easement**
(law) A right to use another person's property. A property owner who, to enter and exit the property, is given a right to cross another person's adjoining property holds an easement. The right to use an easement is a servitude against the property burdened. *See* servitude.

**East-South trade**
(economics) Trade between developing countries (South) with non-market economies (East).

**East-West trade**
(economics) Trade between countries with developed market economies (West) and countries with nonmarket economies (East).

**ECB**
*See* European Central Bank.

**Economic Bulletin Board (EBB)**
(U.S.) The EBB, which was a personal computer-based economic bulletin board operated by the U.S. Department of Commerce, has been replaced by services available through the Department's fee-based STAT-USA/Internet service at Web: www.stat-usa.gov or at [1] (800) STAT-USA. *See* STAT-USA.

**Economic Community of West African States (ECOWAS)**
ECOWAS (CEDEAO in French and Portuguese) is a regional alliance, created in 1974, that includes: Benin, Burkina Faso, Cote d'Ivoire, Mali, Mauritania, Niger, and Senegal. (Togo has observer status). The ECOWAS operates as a free trade area for agricultural products and raw materials and as a preferential trading area for approved industrial products, with a regional cooperation tax (TCR) replacing import duties and encouraging trade among member states. In order to ensure that benefits of the regional grouping flow to all members, especially the least developed ones (Mali, Mauritania, Niger, and Burkina Faso), the ECOWAS has established a fund to provide financial services and guarantees to development lenders in both public and private sectors for projects in member states. In addition, ECOWAS has the long-term objective of creating a customs union with extensive harmonization of fiscal policies between member states, though no concrete achievements in this direction have been recorded. Contact: ECOWAS, 60 Yakubu Gowon Crescent, Asokoro District P.M.B. 401 Abuja, Nigeria; Tel: (234) (9) 314-7647; Fax : (234) (9) 314-3005; E-mail: info@ecowas-mail.net; Web: www.ecowas.int/.

**economic officers**
(U.S.) Embassy officials who analyze and report on macroeconomic trends and trade policies and their implications for U.S. policies and programs. Economic officers represent U.S. interests and arrange and participate in economic and commercial negotiations. *See* commercial officers; Foreign Service.

**economic order quantity (EOQ)**
(logistics) The optimum order size that achieves the best possible balance between meeting customer needs and minimizing ordering and inventory holding costs.

**economy of scale**
(economics) The decrease in unit cost as a result of increasing production so that fixed costs may be spread out over a greater number of units produced.

**ecotourism**
Personal travel to places of unique natural or ecological beauty that minimizes ecological impact to the land and wildlife while contributing to its preservation. Ecotourism is seen as a combination of appreciation of nature, adventure travel and cultural exploration. Also the provision of services to facilitate such travel. Ecotourism has become a booming subcategory of the worldwide travel industry and has been an important factor in the preservation of certain ecosystems.

**ecu or ECU**
*See* European Currency Unit.

**Edge Act corporations**
(banking) Banks that are subsidiaries either to bank holding companies or other banks established to engage in foreign business transactions.

**EDI**
(logistics/computers) Acronym for Electronic Data Interchange. (a) The transfer of structured data, by agreed message standards, from one computer application to another by electronic means and with a minimum of human intervention. (b) The electronic exchange of documents between businesses and organizations, or between businesses and government agencies.
Documents routinely sent by EDI include purchase orders, commercial invoices, inquiries, price sheets, shipping documents, test results, payment documents and compliance documents for government agencies. The trend is for more and more documentation to be sent by EDI. For example, a number of government agencies worldwide, including import and export authorities, now require that compliance documents be sent exclusively by EDI. The key issue in EDI today relates to establishing international and industry-specific standards for document transmittal. *See* UN/EDIFACT, American National Standards Organization; International Standards Organization.

**EDIFACT**
*See* UN/EDIFACT.

**effective exchange rate**
(banking/foreign exchange) Any spot exchange rate actually paid or received by the public, including any taxes or subsidies on the exchange transaction as well as any applicable banking commissions.

**efficient consumer response (ECR)**
(logistics) A demand-driven stock replenishment system that links point-of-sale data with all points in the logistics chain for the purpose of satisfying customer demand quickly, efficiently and at least cost.

**Electronic Data Interchange**
*See* EDI.

**Electronic Data Interchange for Administration, Commerce and Transportation**
*See* UN/EDIFACT.

**Electronic Data Interchange (EDI) Release**
(Canada Customs) EDI Release is a Canada Border Services Agency (CBSA) import shipment release program that allows importers to electronically transmit release data, including invoice information, to the Accelerated Commer-

cial Release Operations Support System (ACROSS). A customs officer reviews the information and transmits the release decision back to the importer via the RNS/CADEX Release Notification Report. For more information on EDI release, contact the Electronic Commerce Unit in Ottawa, Canada at 1-888-957-7224 or go to: www.cbsa-asfc.gc.ca/import/servicesintro-e.html

### electronic entry
The electronic transmission to the customs service of a country of 1) entry information required for the entry of merchandise, and 2) entry summary information required for the classification and appraisement of the merchandise, the verification of statistical information and the determination of compliance with applicable law.

### electronic funds transfer (EFT)
(banking) System of transferring funds from one account to another by electronic impulses rather than transfer of paper (such as a check).

### electronic transmission
The transfer of import or export data or information through an authorized electronic data interchange (EDI) system consisting of, but not limited to, computer modems and computer networks.

### embargo
A prohibition upon exports or imports, either with respect to specific products or specific countries. Historically, embargoes have been ordered most frequently in time of war, but they may also be applied for political, economic or sanitary purposes. Embargoes imposed against an individual country by the United Nations—or a group of nations—in an effort to influence its conduct or its policies are sometimes called "sanctions." *See* sanction.

### emergency currency adjustment factor (ECAF)
(logistics) A freight surcharge or adjustment factor imposed by an international carrier to compensate for sustained or rapid fluctuations in foreign currency exchange rates. The ECAF is charged as a percentage of the published rate. *See* currency adjustment factor.

### emphyteusis
(law) A tenant's right to enjoy property owned by another individual or legal entity for a lengthy time and for rent as if the tenant owned it. The tenant may, and is usually expected to, improve the property. The tenant may also demise, assign, or otherwise transfer his or her interest in the property, but the tenant must preserve the property from destruction.

### en route
(shipping) In transit (referring to goods, passengers or vessel).

### enabling clause
(WTO) A part of the World Trade Organization (WTO) framework which permits developed country members to give more favorable treatment to developing countries and special treatment to the least developed countries, notwithstanding most-favored-nation provisions.

### endorsement
(banking/law) (In U.K., indorsement) The act of a person who is the holder of a negotiable instrument in signing his or her name on the back of that instrument, thereby transferring title or ownership. An endorsement may be made in favor of another individual or legal entity, resulting in a transfer of the property to that other individual or legal entity.
(a) An **endorsement in blank** is the writing of only the endorser's name on the negotiable instrument without designating another person to whom the endorsement is made, and with the implied understanding that the instrument is payable to the bearer.

(b) A **collection endorsement** is one that restricts payment of the endorsed instrument to purposes of deposit or collection.
(c) A **conditional endorsement** is one that limits the time at which the instrument can be paid or further transferred or that requires the occurrence of an event before the instrument is payable.
(d) A **restrictive endorsement** is one that directs a specific payment of the instrument, such as for deposit or collection only, and that precludes any other transfer of it.

### Enhanced Proliferation Control Initiative (EPCI)
(U.S.) A series of measures to tighten export controls on goods and technologies useful in the production of chemical and missile weapons systems. EPCI allows the U.S. Department of Commerce greater authority to deny exports of low-level goods and technologies to nations of proliferation concern. *See* U.S. Department of Commerce.

### Enterprise for the Americas Initiative (EAI)
The EAI, which was launched in June 1990, is intended to develop a new economic relationship of the U.S. with Latin America. The EAI has trade investment, debt, and environment aspects. With regard to trade, the EAI involves an effort to move toward free trade agreements with markets in Latin America and the Caribbean, particularly with groups of countries that have associated for purposes of trade liberalization.
To begin the process of creating a hemispheric free trade system, the U.S. seeks to enter into "framework" agreements on trade and investment with interested countries or groups of countries. These agreements set up intergovernmental councils to discuss and, where appropriate, to negotiate the removal of trade and investment barriers.

### enterprise resource planning
*See* ERP.

### entity, legal
(law) An individual or organization (proprietorship, partnership or corporation) that can legally enter into an agreement or contract and can sue or be sued in a court of law. For example, a minor is not a legal entity and therefore cannot sue or be sued.

### entrepôt
(shipping) An intermediary storage facility where goods are kept temporarily for distribution within a country or for reexport.

### entrepôt trade
The import and export of goods without the further processing of the goods. Usually refers to a country, locale or business that buys and sells (imports and exports) as a middleman.

### entry
(customs) A statement of the kinds, quantities and values of goods imported together with duties due, if any, and declared before a customs officer or other designated officer.
(U.S. Customs) The process of, and documentation required for securing the release of imported merchandise from Customs.
*See* entry for consumption; entry for warehouse; mail entry; entry documents.

### entry documents
(customs) The documents required to secure the release of imported merchandise.
(U.S Customs) Within five working days of the date of arrival of a shipment at a U.S. port of entry, entry documents must be filed at a location specified by the district/area director, unless an extension is granted. These documents consist of:
(1) Entry Manifest, Customs Form 7533; or Application and Special Permit for Immediate Delivery, Customs Form

3461, or other form of merchandise release required by the district director.

(2) Evidence of right to make entry.

(3) Commercial invoice or a pro-forma invoice when the commercial invoice cannot be produced.

(4) Packing lists if appropriate.

(5) Other documents necessary to determine merchandise admissibility.

If the goods are to be released from Customs custody on entry documents, an entry summary for consumption must be filed and estimated duties deposited at the port of entry within 10 working days of the time the goods are entered and released. *See* entry.

### entry for consumption

(U.S. Customs) The process of effecting entry of goods into the United States for use in the United States. The entry of merchandise is a two-part process consisting of: (1) filing the documents necessary to determine whether merchandise may be released from Customs custody and (2) filing the documents which contain information for duty assessment and statistical purposes. In certain instances, such as the entry of merchandise subject to quotas, all documents must be filed and accepted by Customs prior to the release of the goods. *See* entry; entry documents.

### entry for warehouse

(U.S. Customs) A type of U.S. Customs entry where the release of goods (and payment of duty) is postponed by having them placed in a Customs bonded warehouse, where they may remain for up to five years from the date of importation. At any time during that period the goods may be reexported without the payment of duty, or they may be withdrawn for consumption upon the payment of duty at the rate of duty in effect on the date of withdrawal. If the goods are destroyed under Customs' supervision, no duty is payable. *See* entry; customs bonded warehouse; entry for consumption.

### entry number

(U.S. Customs) A unique 11-position alphanumeric identifier assigned by an entry filer to each entry transaction. The first 3 positions identify the filer. The next 7 positions are the number assigned to the entry by the filer. The last position is a check digit.

### entry summary selectivity system

(U.S. Customs) A part of U.S. Customs' Automated Commercial System, provides an automated review of entry data to determine whether team or routine review of entry is required. Selectivity criteria include an assessment of risk by importer, tariff number, country of origin, manufacturer, and value. Summaries with Census warnings, as well as quota, antidumping and countervailing duty entry summaries are selected for team review. A random sample of routine review summaries is also automatically selected for team review. *See* Automated Commercial System.

### Environmental Protection Agency (EPA)

(U.S. government) An independent agency in the executive branch whose mandate is to control and abate pollution in the areas of air, water, solid waste, pesticides, radiation, and toxic substances. This is achieved through a combination of research, monitoring, standard setting and enforcement activities. Contact: Environmental Protection Agency, Ariel Rios Building, 1200 Pennsylvania Avenue, N.W. Washington, DC 20460 USA; Tel: [1] (202) 272-0167; E-mail: Public-Access@epa.gov; Web: www.epa.gov.

### equalization

(shipping) A monetary allowance to the customer for picking up or delivering cargo to/from a point which is not the origin/destination shown on the bill of lading. Example, when the bill of lading destination indicates "San Fran-cisco" and cargo is discharged in "Oakland," if the customer picks up the cargo in Oakland, he is allowed the difference in cost between the Oakland pickup to the customer's place of business and the projected actual cost if pickup had been made in San Francisco and drayed to the customer's place of business in San Francisco. This provision is covered by tariff publication.

### equitable assignment

(law) An assignment that does not meet statutory requirements but that a court may nevertheless recognize and enforce in equity, that is, to do justice between the parties. If parties make an oral assignment that by statute must be in writing to be enforced, for example, a court may still enforce it as an equitable assignment, particularly if one party has acted in reliance on the assignment and would be harmed if it were not enforced. *See* assignment.

### ERP

(logistics) Acronym for Enterprise Resource Planning. A resource planning methodology (and application software) that integrates all aspects of forecasting, distribution and manufacturing for the purpose of efficiently allocating resources. It is the next generation of MRP II (Manufacturing Resources Planning) and includes additional functionality such as quality process operations management and regulatory reporting. *See* MRP (Manufacturing Resources Planning).

### errors & omissions excepted (E&OE)

(shipping) A notation adjacent to a signature on a document signifying that the signor is disclaiming responsibility for typographical errors or unintentional omissions.

### escape clause

A provision in a bilateral or multilateral commercial agreement permitting a signatory nation to suspend tariff or other concessions (temporarily violate their obligations) when imports threaten serious harm to the producers of competitive domestic goods.

(U.S.) Section 201 of the U.S. Trade Act of 1974 requires the U.S. International Trade Commission to investigate complaints formally known as "petitions" filed by domestic industries or workers claiming that they have been injured or are threatened with injury as a consequence of rapidly rising imports, and to complete any such investigation within six months. Section 203 of the Act provides that if the Commission finds that a domestic industry has been seriously injured or threatened with serious injury, it may recommend that the president grant relief to the industry in the form of adjustment assistance or temporary import restrictions in the form of tariffs, quotas, or tariff quotas. The president must then take action pursuant to the Commission's recommendations within 60 days, but he may accept, modify or reject them, according to his assessment of the national interest. The Congress can, through majority vote in both the Senate and the House of Representatives within 90 legislative days, override a presidential decision not to implement the Commission's recommendations. The law permits the president to impose import restrictions for an initial period of five years and to extend them for a maximum additional period of three years. *See* adjustment assistance.

### escudo

The currency of:

Cape Verde, 1C.V.Esc=100 centavos;

The former currency of Portugal, 1Esc=100 centavos. The new currency of Portugal is the European Union Euro (€ 1 = 100 cents).

### estate agent

(UK) British term for real estate agent.

**E**

### estimated time of arrival (ETA)
(shipping) The expected date and time of arrival of a shipment, passenger or vessel at a port, airport or terminal.

### estimated time of departure (ETD)
(shipping) The estimated date and time of departure of a shipment, passenger or vessel from a port, airport or terminal.

### ETA
Acronym for Estimated Time of Arrival. The term is used extensively in military and civilian air, ocean, truck and rail logistics.

### eUCP
(banking) Acronym for "Electronic Supplement to the Uniform Customs and Practice for Documentary Credits." The eUCP provides a framework of general principles for the electronic presentation of documents in documentary (letter of) credit operations. Documentary credits are not automatically subject to the rules of the eUCP. Individual credits must contain language stating that they are subject to the eUCP and the applicable version of the eUCP. The eUCP (as well as the UCP) were developed by the International Chamber of Commerce (ICC), which publishes both the rules and guidebooks for their use. *See* International Chamber of Commerce.

### EUR 1
(shipping) Goods transport certificate and proof of preference for export in countries and regions associated with the European Union (EU) and European Economic Area (EEA) through free trade agreements, association or preferential agreements, as long as the goods concerned are included in the tariffs preferences.

### Euro (euro)
The currency of the European Union. €1 = 100 cents. As of January 1, 2002, the Euro became the official currency of Austria, Belgium, Finland, France, Germany, Ireland, Italy, Luxembourg, Netherlands, Portugal and Spain.

### Eurobond
(finance) A bond issued in a currency other than that of the market or markets in which it is sold. The issue is handled by an international syndicate.

### Eurobond market
(finance) Euromarket for international long-term bonds (Eurobonds).

### Eurocard
(banking) A European credit card developed by the West German banking system that is accepted in most western European countries.

### Eurocheque
(banking) A credit card (in the form of a check) for purchasing goods in several western European countries.

### Eurocredit market
(finance) Euromarket for medium-term credits.

### Eurocurrency
(banking) A currency deposit held outside the country which issued the currency.

### Eurodollars
(banking) U.S. dollar-denominated deposits in banks and other financial institutions outside of the United States. Originating from, but not limited to, the large quantity of U.S. dollar deposits held in western Europe.

### Euromarket
(finance) An international capital market on which deposits and claims are traded in currencies outside the sovereign territory of the states in question. Euromoney markets exist in the major financial hubs of western Europe but are focused on London and Luxembourg. Exists alongside the national money markets.

### European Article Number Association International (EAN)
(international standards) A not-for-profit international organization whose mission is to develop a set of standards enabling the efficient management of global, multi-industry supply chains by uniquely identifying products, shipping units, assets, locations and services. Individuals worldwide see EAN bar codes on virtually all consumer products. Worldwide consistency in identification practices enables the sharing of electronic data and streamlines the supply chain. Founded in 1977 to form a Universal Product Code (UPC), EAN aimed to facilitate the development of such standards. It seized a lead role in encouraging and propagating standards and achieved worldwide acceptance. Today 97 member organizations from 99 countries support its activities and disseminate information to about 850,000 member companies who benefit from using the EAN-UPC system. The main activities of member organizations include the allocation of unique numbers, distribution of specialized publications, training on EDI and bar coding and supplying information on the continued development of EAN standards. Contact: EAN International, 145 rue Royale, B - 1000 Brussels, BELGIUM; Tel: [32] (2) 227-1020; Fax: [32] (2) 227-1021; E-mail: info@ean-int.org; Web: www.ean-int.org.

### European Bank for Reconstruction and Development (EBRD)
(banking) The EBRD provides assistance through direct loans. The loans are designed to facilitate the development of market-oriented economies and to promote private and entrepreneurial initiatives. EBRD began financing operations in June 1991. Contact: European Bank for Reconstruction and Development, One Exchange Square, London EC2A 2JN, UK; Tel: [44] (20) 7338-6000; Fax: [44] (20) 7338-6100; Web: www.ebrd.com.

### European Central Bank (ECB)
(banking) The central bank of the European Union (EU), which, along with the ESCB (European System of Central Banks), sets monetary policy for EU countries in the single currency (the Euro or €). Contact: Kaiserstrasse 29, D-60311 Frankfurt am Main, Germany; Tel: [49] 69 1344 0; Fax: [49] (69) 1344 6000; E-mail: info@ecb.int; Web: www.ecb.int.

### European Coal and Steel Community
*See* European Community.

### European Commission
One of the five major institutions of the European Union (EU), the Commission is responsible for ensuring the implementation of the Treaty of Rome and EU rules and obligations; submission of proposals to the Council of Ministers; execution of the Council's decisions; reconciliation of disagreements among Council members; administration of EC policies, such as the Common Agricultural Policy and coal and steel policies; taking necessary legal action against firms or member governments; and representing the EU in trade negotiations with nonmember countries. Contact: European Commission, 200 rue de la Loi, 1049 Brussels, Belgium; Web: http://europa.eu. *See* European Community; European Union; Treaty of Rome; common agricultural policy.

### European Committee for Electrotechnical Standardization (CENELEC)
CENELEC is a nonprofit international organization under Belgian law. CENELEC seeks to harmonize electrotechnical standards published by the national member organizations and to remove technical barriers to trade that may be caused by differences in standards. CENELEC members include Austria, Belgium, Denmark, Finland, France, Ger-

many, Greece, Iceland, Ireland, Italy, Luxembourg, Netherlands, Norway, Portugal, Spain, Sweden, Switzerland, and the United Kingdom. Contact: CENELEC (Comite European Normalization Electrotechnical), rue de Stassart 35, B-1050 Brussels, Belgium; Tel: [32] (2) 519-68-71; Fax: [32] (2) 519-6919; E-mail: info@cenelec.org; Web: www.cenelec.org.

The National Institute of Standards and Technology of the United States Department of Commerce operates an EC Hotline, which provides information on directives and draft CEN and CENELEC standards. Tel: [1] (301) 921-4164.

### European Committee for Standardization (CEN)

The CEN (Comité European de Normalisation) is an association of the national standards organizations of 18 countries of the European Community (EC) and of the European Free Trade Association (EFTA). CEN membership is open to the national standards organization of any European country which is, or is capable of becoming, a member of the EC or EFTA. CEN develops voluntary standards in building, machine tools, information technology, and in all sectors excluding the electrical ones covered by the European Committee for Electrotechnical Standardization. CEN is involved in accreditation of laboratories and certification bodies as well as quality assurance. Contact: CEN (Comité European de Normalisation), rue de Stassart 36, B-1050 Brussels, Belgium; Tel: [32] (2) 550-0811; Fax: [32] (2) 550-0819; Email: infodesk@cenorm.be; Web: www.cenorm.be.

The National Institute of Standards and Technology of the United States Department of Commerce operates an EU Hotline, which provides information on directives and draft CEN and CENELEC standards. Tel: [1] (301) 921-4164.

### European Community (EC)

A popular term for the European Communities that resulted from the 1967 "Treaty of Fusion" that merged the secretariat (the "Commission") and the intergovernmental executive body (the "Council") of the older European Economic Community (EEC) with those of the European Coal and Steel Community (ECSC) and the European Atomic Energy Community EURATOM, which was established to develop nuclear fuel and power for civilian purposes. The European Community has since been renamed the European Union (EU). *See* European Union.

### European Conference of Postal and Telecommunications Administrations (CEPT)

Founded in 1959 to strengthen relations between postal and telecommunications administrations and to improve their technical services. Contact: The CEPT Presidency, Federal Ministry of Economics and Labour, Scharnhorststr. 34-37, 10115 Berlin Germany; E-mail: cept.secretariat@ibpt.be; Web: www.cept.org.

### European Currency Unit (ecu or ECU)

(banking/foreign exchange-obsolete) The ecu was a "basket" of specified amounts of each European Union (EU) member state currency used as an internal accounting unit. Amounts were determined according to the economic size of each EU member. The ecu was conceived by the European Economic Community (EEC), the predecessor of the European Union. The ecu has been replaced by the European Union Euro (€). *See* currency basket.

### European Economic Community

*See* European Union.

### European Free Trade Association (EFTA)

A regional trade organization established in 1960 by the Stockholm Convention, as an alternative to the Common Market. EFTA was designed to provide a free trade area for industrial products among member countries. Unlike the European Community (now the European Union), however, EFTA members did not set up a common external tariff and did not include agricultural trade.

The EFTA is headquartered in Geneva, and comprises Austria, Iceland, Norway, Sweden, and Switzerland. Finland is an Associate Member. Denmark and the United Kingdom were formerly members, but they withdrew from EFTA when they joined the European Community in 1973. Portugal, also a former member, withdrew from EFTA in 1986 when it joined the EC (now the EU).

EFTA member countries have gradually eliminated tariffs on manufactured goods originating and traded within EFTA. Agricultural products, for the most part, are not included on the EFTA schedule for internal tariff reductions. Each member country maintains its own external tariff schedule and each has concluded a trade agreement with the European Community that provides for the mutual elimination of tariffs for most manufactured goods except for a few sensitive products. As a result, the European Community and EFTA form a de facto free trade area. Contact: EFTA; 9-11, rue de Varembé; CH-1211 Geneva 20, Switzerland; Tel: [41] (22) 332-2626; Fax: [41] (22) 332-2677; Email: mail.gva@efta.int; Web: www.efta.int. *See* European Union.

### European Investment Bank (EIB)

(banking) The EIB is an independent public institution set up by the Treaty of Rome to contribute to balanced and steady development in the European Community. The EIB provides loans and guarantees to companies and public institutions to finance regional development, structural development, and achieve cross-border objectives. The EIB has emphasized regional development and energy, with Italy, Greece, and Ireland receiving major support. Contact: European Investment Bank, 100 blvd. Konrad Adenauer, L-2950 Luxembourg; Tel: [352] 43 79 31 22; Fax: [352] 79 31 91; E-mail: info@eib.org; Web: www.eib.org.

### European Monetary System (EMS)

(banking/foreign exchange-obsolete) The former monetary system of the European Community (EC) member states (now the European Union-EU) which led to the creation of a zone of currency stability as the forerunner of the single European currency (the Euro or €).

The goal of the EMS was to move Europe toward closer economic integration and avoid the disruptions in trade that resulted from fluctuations in currency exchange rates. The EMS member countries deposited gold and dollar reserves with the European Monetary Cooperation Fund in exchange for the issuance of European Currency Units (ecu). Established in 1979; all EC (now EU) members except Greece and the United Kingdom participated in the exchange rate mechanism of the EMS. Note that as of January 1, 2002, the ecu has been replaced by the Euro (€).

*See* European Currency Unit; European Monetary Union; European Community, Euro.

### European option

(banking/foreign exchange) An option containing a provision to the effect that it can only be exercised on the expiry or maturity date. *See* American option; option.

### European Organization for Conformity Assessment (EOTC)

The EOTC (the organization has retained its old acronym for European Organization for Testing and Certification) was created in October 1990 by the European Community Commission under a memorandum of agreement with the European Committee for Standardization/European Committee for Electrotechnical Standardization (CEN/CENELEC) and the European Free Trade Association countries. The EOTC promotes mutual recognition of tests, test and certification procedures, and quality systems within the European private sector for product areas or characteristics not covered by European Community legislative requirements. Contact: EOTC; European Organization for Conformity Assessment; Avenue de Tervuren 363, B-1150 Brussels, Belgium ; Tel: [32] (2) 502-41-41; Fax: [32] (2) 502-42-39; E-mail: helpdesk@eotc.be; Web: www.eotc.be.

### European Patent Convention (EPC)
An agreement between European nations to centralize and standardize patent law and procedure. The EPC, which took effect in 1977, established a single "European patent" through application to the European Patent Office in Munich. Once granted, the patent matures into a bundle of individual patents—one in each member country. Contact: European Patent Office, D-80298, Munich, Germany; Tel: [49] (89) 2399-4636; Fax: [49] (89) 2399-4560; Web: www.european-patent-office.org.

### European Patent Office
*See* European Patent Convention.

### European (style) option
*See* European option.

### European Telecommunications Standards Institute (ETSI)
ETSI was established in March 1988 in response to the inability of the Council of European Post and Telecommunications Administration (CEPT) to keep up with the schedule of work on common European standards and specifications agreed to in the 1984 Memorandum of Understanding between CEPT and the European Community (EC). ETSI has a contractual relationship with the EC to pursue standards development for telecommunications equipment and services, and it cooperates with other European standards bodies such as the European Committee for Standardization/European Committee for Electrotechnical Standardization (CEN/CENELEC). ETSI membership includes the telecommunications administrations that constitute the CEPT as well as manufacturers, service providers, and users. Contact: European Telecommunications Standards Institute (ETSI), 650 route des Lucioles, 06291 Sophia-Antipolis Cedex, France; Tel: [33] (4) 92 94 42 00; Fax: [33] (4) 93 65 47 16; E-mail: helpdesk@etsi.org; Web: www.etsi.org.

### European Union (EU)
A regional economic, monetary, social and political association of European states founded for the purpose of the elimination of intraregional customs duties and other internal trade barriers, the establishment of a common external tariff against other countries, the establishment of a common monetary policy and common currency, the gradual adoption of other integrating measures, including a Common Agricultural Policy and guarantees of free movement of labor and capital.

The EU was originally established by the Maastricht Treaty in 1993. The Treaty extended the previous Treaties establishing the three European Communities, i.e., the European Coal and Steel Community (ECSC), the European Atomic Energy Community (Euratom), and the European Economic Community.

The EU is the result of a process of cooperation and integration which began in 1951 between six countries (Belgium, Germany, France, Italy, Luxembourg and the Netherlands). After nearly 50 years, with four waves of accessions (1973: Denmark, Ireland and the United Kingdom; 1981: Greece; 1986: Spain and Portugal; 1995: Austria, Finland and Sweden), the EU today has fifteen Member States and is preparing for its fifth enlargement, this time toward eastern and southern Europe.

**Objectives**

The European Union's mission is to organize relations between the Member States and between their peoples in a coherent manner and on the basis of solidarity.

The main objectives are:

1) to promote economic and social progress (the single market was established in 1993; the single currency was launched in 1999);

2) to assert the identity of the European Union on the international scene (through European humanitarian aid to non-EU countries, common foreign and security policy, action in international crises; common positions within international organizations);

3) to introduce European citizenship (which does not replace national citizenship but complements it and confers a number of civil and politic rights on European citizens);

4) to develop an area of freedom, security and justice (linked to the operation of the internal market and more particularly the freedom of movement of persons);

5) to maintain and build on established EU law (all the legislation adopted by the European institutions, together with the founding treaties).

**Institutions**

There are five institutions involved in running the European Union: the European Parliament (elected by the peoples of the Member States), the Council (representing the governments of the Member States), the Commission (the executive and the body having the right to initiate legislation), the Court of Justice (ensuring compliance with the law), and the Court of Auditors (responsible for auditing the accounts). These institutions are supported by other bodies: the Economic and Social Committee and the Committee of the Regions (advisory bodies which help to ensure that the positions of the EU's various economic and social categories and regions respectively are taken into account), the European Ombudsman (dealing with complaints from citizens concerning maladministration at European level), the European Investment Bank (EU financial institution) and the European Central Bank (responsible for monetary policy in the Euro-area).

European Union, 62 rue Belliard; 1040 Brussels, Belgium; Tel: [32] (2) 233-21-11; Fax: [32] (2) 231-10-75; E-mail: public.info@consilium.eu.int; Web: www.europa.eu.int.

### evidence of right to make entry
(U.S. Customs) Goods may be entered into the Customs territory of the United States only by the owner, purchaser, or a licensed customs broker acting on behalf of the owner or purchaser. Customs requires evidence of right to make entry as part of the entry documentation.

When the goods are consigned "to order," the bill of lading properly endorsed by the consignor may serve as evidence of the right to make entry. An air waybill may be used for merchandise arriving by air.

In most instances, entry is made by a person or firm certified by the carrier bringing the goods to the port of entry and is considered the "owner" of the goods for customs purposes. For example, a customs broker with a valid power of attorney signed by the owner of a shipment may present documents to customs as evidence of right to make entry. The document issued by the carrier is known as a "carrier's certificate." In certain circumstances, entry may be made by means of a duplicate bill of lading or a shipping receipt. *See* entry.

### ex ... (named point of origin)
(trade term) A term of sale where the price quoted applies only at the point of origin and the seller agrees to place the goods at the disposal of the buyer at the specified place on the date or within the period fixed. All other charges are for

**E**

the account of the buyer. For a more complete definition, *see* Ex Works. *See* Incoterms.

### ex dock
(trade term) A term of sale where the buyer takes title to the goods only when they are unloaded on his/her dock. *See* Ex Works; Incoterms.

### ex factory
(trade term) A term of sale where the buyer takes title to the goods when they leave the vendor's dock. *See* Ex Works; Incoterms.

### ex parte
(law) By one party or side only. An application ex parte, for example, is a request that is made by only one of the parties involved in a legal action. A hearing ex parte is a court proceeding at which the persons present represent only one side of the controversy. *See* letter of credit.

### ex quay
*See* Delivered Ex Quay; Incoterms.

### ex ship
*See* Delivered Ex Ship; Incoterms.

### ex warehouse
*See* Ex Works; Incoterms.

### Ex Works (...named place) (EXW)
(Incoterms 2000) An international trade term of sale in which, for the quoted price, the seller/exporter/manufacturer merely makes the goods available to the buyer at the seller's "named place" of business. This trade term places the greatest responsibility on the buyer and minimum obligations on the seller.

The seller does not clear the goods for export and does not load the goods onto a truck or other transport vehicle at the named place of departure. The parties to the transaction, however, may stipulate that the seller be responsible for the costs and risks of loading the goods onto a transport vehicle. Such a stipulation must be made within the contract of sale.

If the buyer cannot handle export formalities the Ex Works term should not be used. In such a case Free Carrier (FCA) is recommended.

The Ex Works term is often used when making an initial quotation for the sale of goods. It represents the cost of the goods without any other costs included. *See* Guide to Incoterms 2000 Appendix.

### exaction
(law) A fee or contribution demanded or levied by a government entity or by an individual or group in a position of power. Examples of exactions can include illegal "tolls" on public roads by outlaw police and army units in Third World countries, to harbor maintenance fees and antidumping fees collected by government authorities in First World industrialized countries.

### exception rate
(logistics/shipping) A deviation or exception to the published class rate for a shipment of cargo. Exception rates are often applied to unusual cargo that is difficult to transport, extremely heavy and/or bulky or that requires special handling, such as live animals, human remains, or motor vehicles. *See* class or kind (of merchandise).

### excess valuation
*See* declared value.

### exchange control(s)
(foreign exchange) The rationing of foreign currencies, bank drafts, and other monetary instruments for settling international financial obligations by countries seeking to ameliorate acute balance of payments difficulties. When such measures are imposed, importers must apply for prior authorization from the government to obtain the foreign currency required to bring in designated amounts and types of goods. Since such measures have the effect of restricting imports, they are considered nontariff barriers to trade. *See* balance of trade.

### exchange rate
(foreign exchange) The price of one currency expressed in terms of another, i.e., the number of units of one currency that may be exchanged for one unit of another currency. For example, $/SFr = 1.50, means that one U.S. dollar costs 1.50 Swiss francs.

(a) In a system of **free exchange rates**, the actual exchange rate is determined by supply and demand on the foreign exchange market.

(b) In a system of **fixed exchange rates**, the exchange rate is tied to a reference (e.g., gold, US$, etc.).

Influences on exchange rates include differences between interest rates and other asset yields between countries; investor expectations about future changes in a currency's value; investors' views on the overall quantity of assets in circulation; arbitrage; and central bank exchange rate support. *See* floating.

### excise tax
A selective tax—sometimes called a consumption tax—on certain goods produced within or imported into a country. An example is a tax on the import of crude oil, or a tax on certain luxury goods.

### exclusive agency
*See* agency.

### exclusive economic zone (EEZ)
(international law) EEZ refers to the rights of coastal states to control the living and nonliving resources of the sea for 200 miles off their coasts while allowing freedom of navigation to other states beyond 12 miles, as agreed at the sixth session of the Third UN Conference on the Law of the Sea (UNCLOS). The EEZ also gives the coastal states the responsibility for managing the conservation of all natural resources within the 200-mile limit.

### exclusive patronage agreements
(logistics/shipping) An agreement whereby a company agrees to ship cargo exclusively with a particular carrier and in return receives a preferred rate.

### exclusive use
(logistics) Vehicles assigned by a carrier to serve the exclusive needs of a particular shipper.

### exculpatory clause
(law) A contract clause by which a party is released from liability for wrongful acts committed by the other party. A seller may agree to release a buyer, for example, from liability for all or specified defects in the design, packaging, or manufacture of a product.

### execution
(law) (a) A signature on a document. (b) A legal process for enforcing a judgment for damages, usually by seizure and sale of the debtor's personal property. If a court awards damages in a breach of contract action, for example, but the breaching party has failed to remit such sum, the party awarded damages may request the court to order seizure and sale of the breaching party's inventory or property to the extent necessary to satisfy the award.

### exempt carrier
(U.S. logistics) A for-hire carrier that operates with an exemption from economic regulations.

### exercise price
*See* strike price.

### exhibit
(law) (a) A document or object given or produced as evidence, often in a court of law. (b) A document attached to a contract or proposal that serves as an addendum to or in ev-

idence of statements made in the body of the contract or proposal.

**EXIM Bank**
*See* Export-Import Bank of the United States.

**expiration date**
(banking) In letter of credit transaction, the final date the seller (beneficiary of the credit) may present documents and draw a draft under the terms of the letter of credit. Also called expiry date. *See* letter of credit.

**expiry day**
(banking/foreign exchange) In foreign exchange options business, the last day on which an option can be exercised.

**explosives**
(shipping) (UN CLASS 1.) EXPLOSIVE A: Items are capable of exploding with a small spark, shock, or flame and spreading the explosion hazard to other packages. EXPLOSIVE B: Items are very rapidly combustible. EXPLOSIVE C: Items are a low hazard but may explode under high heat when many are tightly packed together. Examples: A—dynamite; B—propellants or flares; C—common fireworks. Hazards/precautions: no flares, smoking, flames, or sparks in the hazard area; may explode if dropped, heated or sparked.

**export**
To ship an item away from a country for sale to another country.

**Export Administration Act (EAA)**
(U.S. law) Authorizes the president to control exports of U.S. goods and technology to all foreign destinations, as necessary for the purpose of national security, foreign policy, and short supply.
As the basic export administration statute, the EAA is the first big revision of export control law since enactment of the Export Control Act of 1949. The EAA is not permanent legislation; it must be reauthorized—usually every three years. There have been reauthorizations of the EAA in 1982, 1985 (the Export Administration Amendments Act), and 1988 (Omnibus Amendments of 1988) which have changed provisions of the basic Act. The Export Administration Act of 1990 was pocket vetoed by the president, charging that provisions involved micromanagement.

**Export Administration Regulations (EAR)**
(U.S. law) Provides specific instructions on the use and types of export licenses required and the types of commodities and technical data under export control. The text of the regulations, as well as other government documents pertaining to the regulations, are available from the U.S. Government Printing Office's Web site at http://www.access.gpo.gov/bis.

**Export Administration Review Board (EARB)**
(U.S. government) A U.S. cabinet-level export licensing dispute resolution group. The EARB was originally established in June 1970 under Executive Order 11533. Under Executive Order 12755 of March 1991, EARB membership includes the Departments of Commerce (as chair), State, Defense, and Energy, the Arms Control and Disarmament Agency and, as nonvoting members, the Joint Chiefs of Staff and the Central Intelligence Agency. The EARB is the final review body to resolve differences among agency views on the granting of an export license. Preceding EARB review are: (1) Operating Committees, and (2) the Advisory Committee on Export Policy. National Security Directive #53 requires escalation of disputes regarding an export license to the Advisory Committee on Export Policy (ACEP) not later than 100 days from the filing date of the applicant's application. Any cases not resolved at the ACEP level must be escalated to the EARB within 35 days of the date of the ACEP meeting.

Cases not resolved by the EARB must be escalated to the president for resolution. Contact: Export Administration Review Board, 14th and Constitution Avenue NW, Herbert Hoover Building, Room 2639, Washington, DC 20230 USA; Tel: [1] (202) 482-5863.

**export broker**
An individual or firm that brings together buyers and sellers for a fee but does not take part in actual sales transactions.

**export commodity classification number**
*See* export control classification number.

**export control**
(U.S. Customs) To exercise control over exports for statistical and strategic purposes, Customs enforces export control laws for the U.S. Department of Commerce and other federal agencies. *See* United States Customs Service.

**Export Control Automated Support System (ECASS)**
(U.S.) ECASS was implemented by the U.S. Department of Commerce in 1985 to automate a paper-based system. The system currently provides:
(1) electronic submission of export application forms directly by exporters;
(2) optical character recognition of applications submitted on paper;
(3) paperless workstations for all licensing officers to review the application, route it to other officers, branches, or external agencies, and to enter their final action along with riders and conditions;
(4) automated audit of all export licenses issued; and
(5) real-time management reporting on Licensing Officer workloads, average processing times, counts and times by license type, destination country, commodity code, and other data. The U.S. Department of Commerce's Bureau of Industry and Security (formerly the Bureau of Export Administration) is expanding ECASS to include export enforcement activities.
*See* United States Department of Commerce; Bureau of Industry and Security.

**export control classification number (ECCN)**
(U.S.) Every product has an export control classification number (formerly export commodity classification number) within the Commerce Control List. The ECCN consists of a five-character number that identifies categories, product groups, strategic level of control, and country groups. *See* Commerce Control List.

**export credit agencies (ECAs)**
Government agencies or programs providing government loans, guarantees or insurance to finance exports. In the U.S., the Export/Import Bank is the government's general purpose credit agency, while the Commodity Credit Corporation is the export credit agency for agricultural exports. *See* Export-Import Bank of the United States; Commodity Credit Corporation.

**Export Credit Enhanced Leverage Program (EXCEL)**
The EXCEL program was developed in 1990 by the World Bank in conjunction with a working group of the International Union of Credit and Investment Insurers (the Berne Union). The objective of EXCEL is to provide export credits at consensus rates for private sector borrowers in highly indebted countries, which would previously have been too great a risk for most agencies to cover.

**export credit insurance**
(insurance) Special insurance coverage for exporters to protect against commercial and political risks of making an international sale. Export credit insurance is available from

**E**

insurance underwriters as well as from government agencies. *See* export credit agencies.

### export declaration
(trade documentation) A document required of the exporter by the export authority of a country identifying the particulars of a specific export shipment, including the seller, buyer, goods shipped, quantities and description of the goods and other details.

(U.S. trade documentation) A document required by the U.S. Department of Treasury for the export of goods from the United States. Also known as the Shipper's Export Declaration (SED), this form includes complete particulars on an individual export shipment and is required by the U.S. Department of Commerce to control exports and act as a source document for export statistics. *See* shipper's export declaration.

### Export Development Corporation (EDC)
(Canada) Canada's official export credit agency, responsible for providing export credit insurance, loans, guarantees, and other financial services to promote Canadian export trade. Contact: Export Development Corporation, 151 O'Connor Street, Ottawa, ON K1A 1K3, Canada; Tel: [1] (613) 598-2500; Fax: [1] (613) 237-2690; Web: www.edc.ca.

### Export Development Office (EDO)
(U.S. government) Export Development Offices (EDOs) in seven cities (Tokyo, Sydney, Seoul, Milan, London, Mexico City, and São Paulo) provide services to U.S. exporters, including market research to identify specific marketing opportunities and products with the greatest sales potential; and to organize export promotion events. EDOs are staffed by U.S. and Foreign Commercial Service officers. When not in use for trade exhibitions, EDOs with exhibit and conference facilities are made available to individual firms or associations. *See* U.S. and Foreign Commercial Service.

### export draft
(banking) An unconditional order that is drawn by an exporting seller and that directs an importing buyer to pay the amount stated on the order to the seller or the seller's bank. (a) A **sight export draft** is one that is payable when presented. (b) A **time export draft or usance** is one that is payable at a specified future date. *See* bill of exchange.

### export duty
(customs) A tax imposed on exports of some nations. *See* duty; tariff.

### Export Enhancement Program (EEP)
(U.S.). A U.S. Department of Agriculture program that assists exporters who are shipping U.S. agricultural products to countries that subsidize agricultural products. Contact: Operations Division, Export Credits, Foreign Agricultural Service, USDA, 1400 Independence Ave., SW, Washington, DC 20250-1035 USA; Tel: [1] (202) 720-6211; Fax: [1] (202) 720-2495; Web: www.fas.usda.gov/info/factsheets/eep.asp.

### Export-Import Bank of the United States (Eximbank)
(U.S.) A public corporation created by executive order of the president in 1934 and given a statutory basis in 1945. The Bank makes guarantees and insures loans to help finance U.S. exports, particularly for equipment to be used in capital improvement projects. The Bank also provides short-term insurance for both commercial and political risks, either directly or in cooperation with U.S. commercial banks.

Eximbank offers four major export finance support programs: loans, guarantees, working capital guarantees, and insurance. Eximbank undertakes some of the risk associated with financing the production and sale of U.S.-made goods; provides financing to overseas customers for U.S.

goods when lenders are not prepared to finance the transactions; and enhances a U.S. exporter's ability to match foreign government subsidies by helping lenders meet lower rates, or by giving financing incentives directly to foreign buyers. The Export-Import Bank will consider aiding in the export financing of U.S. goods and services when there is a reasonable assurance of repayment. Eximbank is not to compete with private financing, but to supplement it when adequate funds are not available in the private sector. Contact: Export-Import Bank of the United States, 811 Vermont Avenue NW, Washington, DC 20571 USA; Tel: [1] (800) 565-3946; Fax: [1] (202) 565-3931; E-mail: E-mail: info@exim.gov; Web: www.exim.gov.

### Export Legal Assistance Network (ELAN)
(U.S.) A nationwide group of attorneys with experience in international trade who provide free initial consultations to small businesses on export-related matters. This service is available through the U.S. Small Business Administration (SBA). For the address and phone number of your nearest Small Business Administration District Office, call [1] (800) U-ASK-SBA. Contact: National Coordinator Judd Kessler, Porter, Wright, Morris, & Arthur, 1919 Pennsylvania Avenue, N.W., Suite 500, Washington, DC 20006-3434 USA; Tel: [1] (202) 778-3080; Fax: [1] (202) 778-3063; Web: www.export-legal-assistance.org.

### export license
A document prepared by a government authority, granting the right to export a specified quantity of a commodity to a specified country. This document may be required in some countries for most or all exports and in other countries only under special circumstances.

(U.S.) A document issued by the U.S. government authorizing the export of commodities for which written export authorization is required by law. For more information on export licensing in general, call Exporter Assistance at [1] (202) 482-4811. Contact: Bureau of Industry and Security (formerly the Bureau of Export Administration), U.S. Department of Commerce, 1401 Constitution Ave. NW, Washington, DC 20230 USA; Tel: [1] (202) 482-4811; Fax: [1] (202) 482-3617; Web: www.bis.doc.gov.

### Export License Application and Information Network (ELAIN)
(U.S.) ELAIN is a Bureau of Industry and Security (formerly the Bureau of Export Administration) 24-hour online service which allows exporters to submit license applications. Contact: Bureau of Industry and Security, 1401 Constitution Ave. NW, Washington, DC 20230; Tel: [1] (202) 482-4811; Fax: [1] (202) 482-3617; Web: www.bis.doc.gov.

### export management company
A private firm that serves as the export department for several manufacturers, soliciting and transacting export business on behalf of its clients in return for a commission, salary, or retainer plus commission.

### export merchant
A company that buys products directly from manufacturers, then packages and marks the merchandise for resale under its own name.

### export processing zone (EPZ)
Industrial parks designated by a government to provide tax and other incentives to export firms.

### export quotas
Specific restrictions or ceilings imposed by an exporting country on the value or volume of certain exports, designed to protect domestic producers and consumers from temporary shortages of the materials or goods affected, or to bolster their prices in world markets. Some International Commodity Agreements explicitly indicate when produc-

ers should apply such restraints. Export quotas are also often applied in orderly marketing agreements and voluntary restraint agreements, and to promote domestic processing of raw materials in countries that produce them. *See* international commodity agreement; orderly marketing agreements; voluntary restraint agreements.

**export restraint agreements**
*See* voluntary restraint agreements.

**export restraints**
Quantitative restrictions imposed by exporting countries to limit exports to specified foreign markets, usually pursuant to a formal or informal agreement concluded at the request of the importing countries. *See* voluntary restraint agreements.

**export revolving line of credit (ERLC)**
(U.S.) Financial assistance provided by the U.S. Small Business Administration (SBA) to exporters of U.S. products. The ERLC guarantees loans to U.S. firms to help bridge the working capital gap between the time inventory and production costs are disbursed until payment is received from a foreign buyer. SBA guarantees 85 percent of the ERLC subject to a $750,000 guarantee limit. The ERLC is granted on the likelihood of a company satisfactorily completing its export transaction. The guarantee covers default by the exporter, but does not cover default by a foreign buyer; failure on the buyer's side is expected to be covered by letters of credit or export credit insurance.
Under the SBA's ERLC program, any number of withdrawals and repayments can be made as long as the dollar limit on the line of credit is not exceeded and disbursements are made within the stated maturity period (not more than 18 months). Proceeds can be used only to finance labor and materials needed for manufacturing, to purchase inventory to meet an export order, and to penetrate or develop foreign markets. Examples of eligible expenses for developing foreign markets include professional export marketing advice or services, foreign business travel, and trade show participation. Under the ERLC program, funds may not be used to purchase fixed assets. Contact: SBA Answer Desk, 6302 Fairview Road, Suite 300, Charlotte, North Carolina 28210 USA; Tel: [1] (800) U-ASK-SBA (1-800-827-5722); E-mail: answerdesk@sba.gov; Web: www.sba.gov. *See* letter of credit.

**export service**
(shipping) Shipping lines, airlines and freight forwarders perform, at the request of shippers, many services relating to the transfer, storage, and documentation of freight destined for export. The same is true of imports. Some carriers have a tariff on such traffic, which sets forth a rate covering the air transportation from airport of origin to seaport and all relevant transfer and documentation procedures. On freight arriving in the United States, via an ocean vessel and having a subsequent movement by air, some airlines have a similar tariff program known as "Import Service."

**export statistics**
(U.S.) Export statistics measure the total physical quantity or value of merchandise (except for shipments to U.S. military forces overseas) moving out of the United States to foreign countries, whether such merchandise is exported from within the U.S. Customs territory or from a U.S. Customs bonded warehouse or a U.S. Foreign Trade Zone.

**export subsidies**
Government payments, economic inducements or other financially quantifiable benefits provided to domestic producers or exporters contingent on the export of their goods or services.
(WTO) The World Trade Organization (WTO) recognizes that subsidies in general, and especially export subsidies, distort normal commercial activities and hinder the achievement of WTO objectives. An Agreement on Subsidies and Countervailing Measures rules on export subsidies and provides for an outright prohibition of export subsidies by developed countries for manufactured and semi-manufactured products. Under certain conditions, the Agreement allows developing countries to use export subsidies on manufactured and semi-manufactured products, and on primary products as well, provided that the subsidies do not result in more than an equitable share of world exports of the product for the country. *See* subsidy.

**export trading company**
A corporation or other business unit organized and operated principally for the purpose of exporting goods and services, or of providing export related services to other companies. An ETC can be owned by foreigners and can import, barter, and arrange sales between third countries, as well as export.
(U.S.) The Export Trading Company Act of 1982 exempts authorized trading companies from certain provisions of U.S. antitrust laws. *See* Export Trading Company Act.

**Export Trading Company Act**
(U.S. law) The Export Trading Company Act of 1982 initiates the Export Trade Certificate of Review program that provides antitrust preclearance for export activities; permits bankers' banks and bank holding companies to invest in Export Trading Companies; and establishes a Contact Facilitation Service within the U.S. Department of Commerce designed to facilitate contact between firms that produce exportable goods and services and firms that provide export trade services.

**exporter**
An individual or company that transports goods or merchandise from one country to another in the course of trade.

**exporter identification number (EIN)**
(U.S.) An identification number required on the Shipper's Export Declaration for all export shipments. U.S. corporations may use their federal Employer Identification Number issued by the IRS. Individuals and companies that are not incorporated may use the Social Security number of the exporter. *See* shipper's export declaration.

**exporters sales price (ESP)**
(U.S.) A statutory term used to refer to the United States sales prices of merchandise which is sold or likely to be sold in the United States, before or after the time of importation, by or for the account of the exporter. Certain statutory adjustments are made to permit a meaningful comparison with the foreign market value of such or similar merchandise, e.g., import duties, United States selling and administrative expenses, and freight are deducted from the United States price.

**express agency**
*See* agency.

**expropriation**
(economics/law) The forcible acquisition, usually for compensation, of private property by a sovereign government. For example, a national government might expropriate real estate from private owners in order to construct a highway or government building. *See* nationalization.

**external value**
(economics/foreign exchange) The purchasing power of a currency abroad, converted using the exchange rate.

**extradition**
The surrender by one country of an alleged criminal to the authorities of the country that has jurisdiction to try the charge. Extradition usually occurs under the provisions of a treaty between the two countries.

# F

### 419 scam

(law) An Advance Fee Fraud (AFF) originating in Nigeria, but also from other African countries, most notably Western African nations including Cote d'Ivoire, Ghana, Liberia, Sierra Leone and Togo. "419" refers to the section of the Nigerian criminal code having to do with financial fraud schemes.

"419" scams can be very creative and have endless variations. Typical scams include offers to split revenues from: 1) illegal (overinvoiced or double invoiced) oil or arms deals, 2) dormant bank accounts, 3) bank accounts in the name of deceased individuals without heirs, and 4) lottery winnings. Prior to the late 1990s, "offers" from scammers used to arrive by mail and were written on elaborately printed and foil stamped bogus letterheads. Now, scammers are cluttering the e-mail inboxes of millions of people worldwide on a daily basis.

Commercial variations include such scams as ordering commercial merchandise and overpaying with a counterfeit certified check and then asking for the difference to be refunded by bank wire before the seller realizes that the original check is no good. A "person-to-person" variation includes such scams as befriending people on the Internet and asking them to send cash (via bank wire) in exchange for bogus money orders or travelers checks.

In advance fee fraud cases the scammer asks for personal and company information in order to "facilitate payment to your account." Scammers start by asking for telephone and fax numbers and then ask for bank account numbers.

The scammer also asks their victim for money in order to insure the transaction. Reasons offered for such payments include: 1) a "good faith" payment to show that you are serious about following through with the plan, 2) money required to bribe an official to make the transaction happen, 3) money required to pay for the chemical treatment of currency before it can be used, and endless variations.

In some cases the victim advances small or large sums of money that are never recovered. In other cases the scammer has found a way to deduct funds from personal or business bank accounts.

As a result of significant pressure from nations most affected by these scams, the Nigerian government appears to be making a effort to curb the practice. Some argue that the Nigerian government isn't doing enough. Others go so far as to argue that the Nigerian government has a history of implicit approval, as such scams are said to be the third to fifth largest source of foreign income for the country.

For an listing of web sites that detail and report on Nigerian 419 scams go to http://home.rica.net/alphae/419coal/fighters.htm. For other information on Nigerian AFF schemes go to http://abuja.usembassy.gov/eeeho419.html.

For an exceptional (entertaining and disturbing) *New Yorker* magazine article on Nigerian 419 scams refer to "The Perfect Mark" at: www.newyorker.com/fact/content/articles/060515fa_fact.

### facilitation

Any of a number of programs designed to expedite the flow of international commerce through modernizing and simplifying customs procedures, duty collection, and other procedures to which international cargo and passengers are subject. Examples of progress in facilitation include the elimination of certain export declaration requirements,
more expeditious release of cargo from customs, and clearance of cargo at point of origin.

### facsimile (fax)

(a) An office machine used to transmit a copy of a document (including graphic images) via telephone lines. (b) The physical paper output of a fax machine which is a copy of the document transmitted. Facsimile use has grown significantly in the past few years. Note that in some countries some facsimile documents are not considered legal documents.

### factor

(a) An agent who receives merchandise under a consignment or bailment contract, who sells it for the principal or in the factor's own name, and who is paid a commission for each sale. (b) A firm, such as a finance company, that purchases another company's receivables at a discount and processes and collects the remaining account balances.

### factorage

The commission or other compensation paid to a factor.

### factoring

The discounting of an account receivable in order to receive immediate payment. In international trade factoring is the discounting of a foreign account receivable that does not involve a draft. The exporter transfers title to its foreign accounts receivable to a factoring house (an organization that specializes in the financing of accounts receivable) for cash at a discount from the face value. Factoring is often done without recourse to the exporter. Factoring of foreign accounts receivable is less common than with domestic receivables.

### factoring houses

Certain companies which purchase domestic or foreign accounts receivables (e.g., the as yet unpaid invoices to domestic and foreign buyers) at a discounted price, usually about 2 to 4 percent less than their face value. *See* factor; factoring.

### factor's lien

The right of a factor to retain the principal's merchandise until the factor receives full compensation from the principal.

### fair trade

The social, economic and political theory that individuals and societies in producer nations should 1) gain a greater share of the final market value of the raw materials and products they produce, 2) enjoy better working conditions and 3) benefit from better environmental polices. Fair trade advocates seek to establish a more direct link between producers and consumers. For information go to: www.transfairusa.org.

### fair value

(U.S. Customs) The reference against which U.S. purchase prices of imported merchandise are compared during an antidumping investigation. Generally expressed as the weighted average of the exporter's domestic market prices, or prices of exports to third countries during the period of investigation.

In some cases fair value is the constructed value. Constructed value is used if there are no, or virtually no, home market or third country sales, or if the number of such sales made at prices below the cost of production is so great that remaining sales above the cost of production provide an inadequate basis for comparison. *See* dumping; constructed value.

### FAK

(shipping) Freight all kinds. Usually refers to consolidated cargo.

### family corporation

*See* closely held corporation.

### FAS

*See* Free Alongside Ship; Incoterms.

**F**

*FAST*
(United States/Canada/Mexico) Acronym for Free And Secure Trade. The first completely paperless cargo release mechanism put into place by U.S. Customs and Border Protection. This paperless processing is achieved through electronic data transmissions and transponder technology. FAST is highly automated and allows for the expedited release of highly compliant cargo from major importers, reducing congestion at U.S. land borders with Canada and Mexico. For more information refer to FAST in the Security section of this dictionary or contact U.S. Customs and Border Protection at: www.cbp.gov.

*fast track*
(U.S.) Fast track procedures for approval of trade agreements were included by the U.S. Congress in trade legislation in 1974, in 1979, and again in the 1988 Trade Act. Fast track provides two guarantees essential to the successful negotiation of trade agreements: (1) a vote on implementing legislation within a fixed period of time, and (2) a vote, yes or no, with no amendments to that legislation.
Provisions in the Omnibus Trade and Competitiveness Act of 1988 include that the foreign country request negotiation of a Free Trade Agreement (FTA) and that the president give the Congress a 60-legislative-day notice of intent to negotiate an FTA. During the 60-legislative-day period, either committee can disapprove fast track authority by a majority vote. Disapproval would likely end the possibility of FTA negotiations. The 60-legislative-days can translate into five to ten months of calendar time, depending on the congressional schedule. Formal negotiations would begin following this 60-day congressional consideration period.

*fathom*
(measurement) A unit of length equal to six feet. Used primarily to measure the depth of water.

*fax*
*See* facsimile.

*Federal Aviation Administration (FAA)*
(U.S.) Created under the Federal Aviation Act of 1958 as the Federal Aviation Agency and charged with the responsibility of promulgating operational standards and procedures for all classes of aviation in the United States. With the creation of the cabinet level Department of Transportation in 1966, FAA became a unit within the new Department and received the new designation Federal Aviation Administration. The FAA Administrator, however, continues to be a presidential appointee and the FAA remains a separate entity with most of its former functions. In the field of air cargo FAA promulgates certain stress standards which must be met in the tiedown of cargo in flight. For information: Federal Aviation Administration, 800 Independence Avenue, SW, Washington, DC 20591 USA; Tel: [1] (202) 267-3883; Toll-free: [1] (866) 835-5322; Web: www.faa.gov.

*Federal Maritime Commission (FMC)*
(U.S.) The U.S. federal agency responsible for overseeing rates and practices of ocean carriers who handle cargo to or from U.S. ports. Contact: Federal Maritime Commission, 800 North Capitol St. NW, Washington, DC 20573-0001 USA; E-mail: Inquiries@fmc.gov; Web: www.fmc.gov.

*Federal Reserve System*
(U.S. banking) The central banking system of the U.S. It has twelve Federal Reserve Banks divided up by geographical regions. The Board of Governors supervises the operations of the regional banks and coordinates monetary policy through its Federal Open Market Committee.

*Federal Trade Commission (FTC)*
(U.S.) Plays a key role in ensuring that consumers are protected against unfair methods of competition in the market-place. Contact: Federal Trade Commission, 600 Pennsylvania Avenue, NW, Washington, DC 20580 USA; Tel: [1] (202) 326-2222; Web: www.ftc.gov.

*federally chartered bank*
(U.S. banking) In the United States, a bank that has been chartered by the comptroller of currency, that belongs to the Federal Reserve System and meets the requirements for a national bank as defined under the National Bank Act. In the U.S. only federally and state chartered banks and other authorized institutions may receive deposits.

*feeder vessel*
(shipping) A vessel used to connect with a line vessel to service a port which is not served directly by the line vessel. *See* line haul vessel.

*FEU*
(shipping) Forty foot equivalent units. Two 20 ft. containers equal one FEU.

*fiat*
A legally binding command or decision, generally issued by a government.

*fiat money / fiat currency*
Coinage or currency that is accepted as a medium of exchange by virtue of government decree (fiat). Fiat money is not backed by a commodity such as gold or silver and only retains value so long as holders of the currency feel that they can find an exchange partner for it at some later time.

*field warehouse*
(logistics/finance) A warehouse operated by a third-party warehouse firm, but located on the property or premises of the owner of the goods. Field warehouses are used in special financing agreements where inventory pledged as collateral is physically separated from a company's other inventories and placed under the custody, control and supervision of a third-party warehouse firm.

*fieri facias writ*
(law) A judicial order issued to "cause to be done," which generally orders an officer of law or another authorized person to satisfy a judgment by seizure and sale of a debtor's property. *See* execution.

*fill rate*
(logistics) The percentage of order items that are picked and readied for shipment in a specified amount of time.

*final determination*
(U.S.) In antidumping investigations a final determination is made after the investigation of sales at "less than fair value" and the receipt of comments from interested parties. This determination usually is made within 75 days after the date a preliminary determination is made. However, if the preliminary determination was affirmative, the exporters who account for a significant proportion of the merchandise under consideration may request, in writing, a postponement of this determination. If the preliminary determination was negative, the petitioner may likewise request a postponement. In neither case can this postponement be more than 135 days after the date of the preliminary determination. If the final determination is affirmative and follows a negative preliminary determination, the matter is referred to the International Trade Commission (ITC) for a determination of the injury caused or threatened by the sales at less than fair value. (Had the preliminary determination been affirmative, the ITC would have begun its investigation at that time.) Not later than 45 days after the date the International Trade Administration makes an affirmative final determination, in a case where the preliminary determination also was affirmative, the International Trade Commission must render its decision on injury. Where the preliminary determination was negative, the ITC must render a decision not later than 75 days after

the affirmative final determination. A negative final determination by the Assistant Secretary for Import Administration terminates an antidumping investigation. *See* dumping; International Trade Commission.

**financial instrument**
(banking/finance) A document which has monetary value, or is evidence of a financial transaction. Examples of financial instruments are: checks, bonds, stock certificates, bills of exchange, promissory notes and bills of lading.

**financial market**
(banking/finance) Market for the exchange of capital and credit in an economy. It is divided into money markets, and capital market(s).

**Financial Times (of London)**
(publication) Considered by professionals as one of the best English-language newspapers for business and financial news. E-mail: help@ft.com; Web: www.ft.com.

**Fines, Penalties, and Forfeitures System (FPFS)**
(U.S. Customs) A part of the U.S. Customs' Automated Commercial System, is used to assess, control, and process penalties resulting from violations of law or Customs regulations. FPFS provides retrieval of case information for monitoring case status. *See* Automated Commercial System.

**finished goods inventory (FGI)**
(logistics) Inventory of products that have been manufactured, packed and stored and are ready for distribution.

**fire insurance**
(insurance) Marine insurance coverage that includes both direct fire damage and also consequential damage, as by smoke or steam, and loss resulting from efforts to extinguish a fire. Includes explosion caused by fire.

**firm planned order**
(logistics) In distribution requirements planning (DRP) or manufacturing resources planning (MRP) systems, an order whose status has been fixed in the computer system with regard to quantity and time. This is an issue in DRP and MRP systems as the software program, under certain circumstances, has the ability to change a planned order's status with regard to quantities and time. Firm planned orders are an aid in establishing a master production schedule. *See* planned order.

**FIRST**
(Canada) Frequent Importers Release System. A system operated by the Canada Border Security Agency (CBSA) that allows pre-authorized quick release of repetitive low-risk shipments for frequent importers. Information at Web: www.cbsa-asfc.gc.ca/E/pub/cm/d17-1-5/d17-1-5-03-e.html#P426_35932.

**first in, first out (FIFO)**
(a) An inventory management methodology whereby the oldest inventory (presumably the first in) is the first to be used, consumed, delivered or sold (first out). (b) A job production management methodology whereby the first job recorded (first in) is the first job to be completed (first out). (c) An inventory valuation methodology that assumes that the oldest inventory of a particular item (first in) is the first to be sold (first out).

**first party logistics (1PL)**
Logistics handled internally by a company. For example, a manufacturer that owns warehouses for storage and trucks that deliver products to customers. *See also*: second-party logistics, third-party logistics, fourth-party logistics.

**First World Countries**
(economics) Western, industrialized, noncommunist countries.

**five dragons**
*See* five tigers; five dragons.

**five tigers; five dragons**
Terms used to describe the emerging economies of Hong Kong, Singapore, South Korea, Taiwan and Thailand.

**fix**
(contracts/shipping) To establish all the terms for the chartering of a ship for a voyage or period of service.

**fixture**
(contracts/shipping) A specific contract of voyage between a shipowner and a charterer.

**fixed charges**
(general) Charges which do not vary with an increase in production or sales volume.
(shipping) Charges which do not vary with an increase or decrease in traffic.

**fixed exchange**
(foreign exchange) An administratively fixed exchange rate. With rate fixed exchange rates, no rate fluctuations are possible.

**fixed exchange rate**
*See* exchange rate; fixed exchange.

**fixed quantity inventory model**
(logistics) An inventory control, maintenance and reorder system that specifies that a fixed quantity of a product be reordered whenever inventory of that item falls below a preestablished minimum.

**fixing**
(foreign exchange) Establishing of the official exchange rate of a domestic currency against other negotiable currencies.

**flag**
(shipping) A reference to the country of registry of a vessel. A vessel flying the flag of the country of its registry.

**flag of convenience**
(shipping) The national flag flown by a ship that is registered in a country other than that of its owners (e.g., to escape taxes and high domestic wages).

**flag state**
(shipping) The country of registry of a sea-going vessel. A vessel is subject to the maritime regulations of its country (state) of registry, including safety standards, manning scales and consular representation.

**flammable**
(shipping) Any substance capable of catching fire. *See* flammable liquid; flammable solid.

**flammable liquid**
(shipping) Liquids with a flash point less than 100°F. (UN CLASS 3) Examples are ether, acetone, gasoline, toluene and pentane. Hazards/precautions are no flares, smoking, flames, or sparks in the hazard area; vapors are an explosion hazard; can be poisonous; check labels; if it is poisonous, it can cause death when inhaled, swallowed or touched.

**flammable solid**
(shipping) Any solid material which, under certain conditions, might cause fires or which can be ignited readily and burns vigorously. (UN CLASS 4) Examples are calcium resinate; potassium, sodium amide. Hazards/precautions are may ignite when exposed to air or moisture, may reignite after extinguishing; fires may produce irritation or poisonous gases; contact may cause burns to skin or eyes.

**flat**
(shipping) An ocean shipping "container" with end walls but without side walls. Used especially for heavy loads with overwidth cargo.

**flexible-path equipment**
(logistics) Non automated materials handling equipment used to move goods around a warehouse (e.g., pallet jacks, forklifts and hand trucks).

### flight number
(air transport) A five- to six-digit alpha-numeric code referencing a particular air carrier and flight. The code consists of two letters designating an airline, and three or four digits designating a particular voyage.

### flight of capital
(banking/finance) The movement of capital, which has usually been converted into a liquid asset, from one place to another to avoid loss or to increase gain.

### floating
(foreign exchange) (a) **Clean floating**: Free determination of exchange rates without intervention on the part of the central bank. Correspondingly, exchange rates are determined by supply and demand on the foreign exchange market. (b) **Dirty floating**: Monetary policy which in principle recognizes floating exchange rates, but which tries to influence the exchange rate level through more or less frequent interventions. *See* floating currency.

### floating currency
(banking/foreign exchange) One whose value in terms of foreign currency is not kept stable (on the basis of the par value or a fixed relationship to some other currency) but instead is allowed, without a multiplicity of exchange rates, to be determined (entirely or to some degree) by market forces. Even where a currency is floating, the authorities may influence its movements by official intervention; if such intervention is absent or minor, the expression "clean float" is sometimes used. *See* floating.

### floor
(banking/finance) With cash investments, where the rate of interest is subject to adjustment to the market rate, a so-called floor can be agreed upon, i.e., for a premium, a minimum interest rate is stipulated and remains valid even if the market interest rate is lower.

### floor load
(shipping containers) The weight carried by a shipping container expressed in pounds per square foot (lbs/f$^3$), tons per square foot (t/f$^3$), or kilograms per square meter (k/m$^3$). It is important to evenly distribute loads throughout a container and not to exceed the maximum floor load of a given container.

### florin
The currency of Aruba. 1F=100 cents.

### flotsam
(shipping) Floating debris or wreckage of a ship or a ship's cargo. *See* jetsam.

### flow rack
(logistics) A point-of-use storage and picking system where parts or products are loaded at one end of a gravity flow rack and picked for use or distribution from the other.

### FOB
(trade term) *See* Free On Board, Guide to Incoterms 2000 Appendix.

### FOB Airport
(trade term) An incorrect use of the trade term Free On Board. *See* Free on Board, Guide to Incoterms 2000 Appendix.

### FOB Destination, Freight Collect
(trade term) An incorrect use of the trade term Free On Board. *See* Free on Board, Guide to Incoterms 2000 Appendix.

### FOB Destination, Freight Prepaid
(trade term) An incorrect use of the trade term Free On Board. *See* Free on Board, Guide to Incoterms 2000 Appendix.

### FOB Origin, Freight Collect
(trade term) An incorrect use of the trade term Free On Board. *See* Free on Board, Guide to Incoterms 2000 Appendix.

### FOB Origin, Freight Prepaid and Charged
(trade term) An incorrect use of the trade term Free On Board. *See* Free on Board, Guide to Incoterms 2000 Appendix.

### Food and Agricultural Organization (FAO)
A specialized agency of the United Nations established in 1945 to combat hunger and malnutrition. The FAO serves as a coordinating body between government representatives, scientific groups, and non-governmental organizations to carry out development programs relating to food and agriculture. Contact: Food and Agriculture Organization, Viale delle Terme di Caracalla, 00100 Rome, Italy; Tel: [39] 065-7051; Telex: 610181; Fax: [39] 065-705-3152; E-mail: FAO-HQ@fao.org; Web: www.fao.org.

### Food and Drug Administration (FDA)
U.S. governmental agency which enforces the Federal Food Drug and Cosmetic Act, the Fair Packaging and Labeling Act, and sections of the Public Health Service Act. Contact: Food and Drug Administration, Public Relations, 5600 Fishers Lane, Rockwell, MD 20857; Tel: [1] (888) INFO-FDA (463-6332); Web: www.fda.gov.

### FOR
(trade term) Acronym for "free on rail" used in connection with transportation by rail, indicating that the price covers the goods loaded on the railcar. *See* Free On Board; Guide to Incoterms 2000 Appendix.

### force majeure
(shipping) Any condition or set of circumstances, such as earthquakes, floods, or war, beyond the carrier's control that prevents the carrier from performing fulfillment of their obligations.

### force majeure clause
(law/insurance/shipping) A contract clause, which usually excuses a party who breaches the contract because that party's performance is prevented by the occurrence of an event that is beyond the party's reasonable control. A force majeure clause may excuse performance on the occurrence of such events as natural disasters, labor strikes, bankruptcy, or failure of subcontractors to perform. If a force majeure clause is not expressly included in a contract, a legal action may be brought on the basis that such a clause should be implied under the doctrine of commercial frustration or commercial impracticability. *See* commercial frustration; commercial impracticability.

### Foreign Affairs/Customs Automated Permit System (EXCAPS)
(Canada Customs) EXCAPS is a Canada Border Services Agency (CBSA) program that gives Canadian importers and brokers the ability to apply for a permit with the Department of Foreign Affairs and International Trade (DFAIT) to electronically transmit import permit information to the ACROSS system. The importer/broker transmits the release information and ACROSS matches the release data to the EXCAPS permit. A customs inspector then processes the release and permit information, and once the goods are released, a notice is returned to DFAIT informing them that the permit has been used. For information, go to the DFAIT Web site at: www.fac-aec.gc.ca.

### foreign affiliate
*See* affiliate.

### foreign affiliate of a foreign parent
(U.S.) Any member of an affiliated foreign group owning a U.S. affiliate that is not a foreign parent of the U.S. affiliate. *See* affiliate.

### Foreign Agricultural Service (FAS)
(U.S.) An agency of the U.S. Department of Agriculture (USDA). FAS maintains a global network of agricultural officers as well as a Washington-based staff to analyze and disseminate information on world agriculture and trade, develop and expand export markets, and represent the agricultural trade policy interests of U.S. producers in multilateral forums. FAS also administers USDA's export credit and concessional sales programs. Contact: Information Staff, Foreign Agriculture Service, Department of Agriculture, 1400 Independence Avenue, S.W., Washington, DC 20250 USA; Tel: [1] (202) 720-7115; E-mail: info@fas.usda.gov; Web: www.fas.usda.gov.

### Foreign Assets Control (FAC)
(U.S.) An agency of the U.S. Treasury Department that administers sanctions programs involving specific countries and restricts the involvement of U.S. persons in third country strategic exports. Contact: Office of Foreign Assets Control, Department of Treasury, 1500 Pennsylvania Avenue NW, Washington, DC 20220 USA; Tel: [1] (202) 622-2480; Fax-on-demand: [1] (202) 622-0077; E-mail: ofac_feedback@do.treas.gov; Web: www.treas.gov/ofac.

### Foreign Assistance Act of 1991
(U.S.) This Act replaced the Support for East European Democracy (SEED) Act. The Foreign Assistance Act allows support to 26 countries, including all eastern European nations and most of the former Soviet republics.

### foreign availability
(U.S.) The U.S. Bureau of Industry and Security (formerly the Bureau of Export Administration) conducts reviews to determine the foreign availability of selected commodities or technology subject to U.S. export control. The reviews use four criteria to determine foreign availability: comparable quality, availability-in-fact, foreign source, and adequacy of available quantities that would render continuation of the U.S. control ineffective in meeting its intended purpose. A positive determination of foreign availability means that a non-U.S. origin item of comparable quality may be obtained by one or more proscribed countries in quantities sufficient to satisfy their needs so that U.S. exports of such item would not make a significant contribution to the military potential of such countries. A positive determination may result in the decontrol of a U.S. product that has been under export control, or the approval of an export license. However, the control may be maintained if the president invokes the national security override provision.

Beginning with the 1977 amendments to the Export Administration Act, the Congress directed that products with foreign availability be identified and decontrolled unless essential to national security. In January 1983, a program to assess the foreign availability of specific products was established within the Bureau of Export Administration, now the Bureau of Industry and Security. Further, 1985 amendments to the Act directed that an Office of Foreign Availability be created. *See* Bureau of Industry and Security.

### foreign bills
(banking) Bills of exchange or drafts drawn on a foreign party and denominated in foreign currency. *See* bill of exchange.

### foreign bond
(banking/finance) An international bond denominated in the currency of the country where it is issued.

### foreign bottom
(shipping) (a) An ocean vessel built in a foreign country. (b) An ocean vessel registered in a foreign country. Bottom refers to the part of the ship's hull below the water line.

### Foreign Buyer Program
*See* International Buyer Program.

### foreign commerce
(trade) Trade between individuals or legal entities in different countries.

### Foreign Corrupt Practices Act (FCPA)
(U.S. law) The FCPA makes it unlawful for any United States citizen or firm (or any person who acts on behalf of a U.S. citizen or firm) to offer, pay, transfer, promise to pay or transfer, or authorize a payment, transfer, or promise of money or anything of value to any foreign appointed or elected government official, foreign political party, or candidate for a foreign political office for a corrupt purpose, (that is, to influence a discretionary act or decision of the official) and for the purpose of obtaining or retaining business.

It is also unlawful for a U.S. business owner to make such an offer, promise, payment, or transfer to any person if the U.S. business owner knows, or has reason to know, that the person will offer, give, or promise directly or indirectly all or any part of the payment to a foreign government official, political party, or candidate. For purposes of the FCPA, the term knowledge means actual knowledge—the business owner in fact knew that the offer, payment, or transfer was included in the transaction—and implied knowledge—the business owner should have known from the facts and circumstances of a transaction that the agent paid a bribe, but failed to carry out a reasonable investigation into the transaction.

The provisions of the FCPA do not prohibit payments made to facilitate a routine government action. A facilitating payment is one made in connection with an action that a foreign official must perform as part of the job. In comparison, a corrupt payment is made to influence an official's discretionary decision. For example, payments are not generally considered corrupt if made to cover an official's overtime required to expedite the processing of export documentation for a legal shipment of merchandise, or to cover the expense of additional crew to handle a shipment.

Any person may request the Department of Justice to issue a statement of opinion on whether specific proposed business conduct would be considered a violation of the FCPA. The opinion procedure is detailed in 28 C.F.R. Part 77. If the Department of Justice issues an opinion stating that certain conduct conforms with current enforcement policy, conduct in accordance with that opinion is presumed to comply with FCPA provisions. Contact: United States Department of Justice, Washington, DC.

### Foreign Credit Insurance Association
(U.S.) An agency established in 1961 to offer insurance covering political and commercial risks on U.S. export receivables in partnership with the Export-Import Bank (Eximbank) of the United States.

The FCIA was founded in 1961 as a partnership of the Eximbank and a group of private insurance companies. Eximbank is responsible for the political risk and may underwrite or reinsure the commercial risk. The FCIA acts as an agent responsible for the marketing and daily administration of the program. Tel: [1] (212) 885-1500; Fax: [1] (212) 885-1535; E-mail: service@fcia.com; Web: www.fcia.com. *See* Export-Import Bank of the United States.

### foreign currency
(banking) The currency of any foreign country which is the authorized medium of circulation and the basis for record keeping in that country. Foreign currency is traded in by banks either by the actual handling of currency or checks,

or by establishing balances in foreign currency with banks in those countries.

### foreign currency account
(banking) An account maintained in a foreign bank in the currency of the country in which the bank is located. Foreign currency accounts are also maintained by banks in the United States for depositors. When such accounts are kept, they usually represent that portion of the carrying bank's foreign currency account that is in excess of its contractual requirements.

### foreign direct investment in the U.S. (FDIUS)
(foreign investment) Foreign direct investment in the United States is the ownership or control, directly or indirectly, by a single foreign person (an individual, or related group of individuals, company, or government) of 10 percent or more of the voting securities of an incorporated U.S. business enterprise or an equivalent interest in an unincorporated U.S. business enterprise, including real property. Such a business is referred to as a U.S. affiliate of a foreign direct investor. *See* Committee on Foreign Investment in the United States; foreign person; portfolio investment; affiliate; United States Affiliate.

### foreign draft
(banking) A draft drawn by an individual (drawer) or bank in one country on another individual (drawee) or bank in another country. *See* bill of exchange.

### Foreign Economic Trends
(publication) Reports prepared by U.S. embassies abroad to describe foreign country economic and commercial trends and trade and investment climates. The reports describe current economic conditions; provide updates on the principal factors influencing development and the possible impacts on U.S. exports; review newly announced foreign government policies as well as consumption, investment, and foreign debt trends. Available from: Superintendent of Documents, U.S. Government Printing Office, Mail Stop: IDCC, 732 N. Capitol Street, NW, Washington, DC 20401; Tel: [1] (866) 512-1800, [1] (202) 512-1800; Fax: [1] (202) 512-2104; Web: www.gpoaccess.gov.

### foreign exchange
(banking/foreign exchange) Current or liquid claims payable in foreign currency and in a foreign country (bank balances, checks, bills of exchange). Not to be confused with foreign bank notes and coin, which are not included in this definition. *See* bank notes.

### foreign exchange auctions
(foreign exchange) Auctions of foreign currency, as used in some developing countries, whereby the price obtained for the foreign currency at the auction is the rate of exchange applied till the next auction.

### foreign exchange contract
(foreign exchange) A contract for the sale or purchase of foreign exchange specifying an exchange rate and delivery date.

### foreign exchange control
(foreign exchange) Governmental control and supervision of: transactions within the country involving its currency, foreign exchange for imports and exports, capital movements of any currency or monetary instruments into and out of the country, and expenditures of currency by its own citizens traveling abroad.

### foreign exchange desk
(Federal Reserve Bank) The foreign exchange trading desk at the New York Federal Reserve Bank. The desk undertakes operations in the exchange markets for the account of the Federal Open Market Committee, as agent for the U.S. Treasury and as agent for foreign central banks.

### foreign exchange holdings
(foreign exchange) Holdings of current or liquid foreign exchange claims denominated in the currency of another country.

### foreign exchange market
(foreign exchange) (a) The worldwide system of contacts, either by telephone, teleprinter or in writing, which take place between nonbank foreign exchange dealers and foreign exchange traders at banks as well as foreign exchange traders amongst themselves, where the monies of different countries are bought and sold. (b) Wherever foreign exchange rates are determined.

### foreign exchange rate
(foreign exchange) The price of one currency in terms of another.

### foreign exchange trader
(foreign exchange) An individual engaged in the business of buying and selling foreign exchange on his own account or as an employee of a bank or other business authorized to deal in foreign exchange.

### foreign exchange trading
(foreign exchange) Buying and selling of foreign exchange, holding of currency positions, foreign exchange arbitrage, and foreign exchange speculation on the foreign exchange market.

### foreign exchange transactions
(foreign exchange) The purchase or sale of one currency with another. Foreign exchange rates refer to the number of units of one currency needed to purchase one unit of another, or the value of one currency in terms of another.

### foreign exports
(U.S.) The U.S. export of foreign merchandise (re-exports), consisting of commodities of foreign origin which have entered the United States for consumption or into Customs bonded warehouses or U.S. Foreign Trade Zones, and which, at the time of exportation, are in substantially the same condition as when imported. *See* re-export.

### foreign flag
(shipping) An ocean vessel flying the flag of a foreign nation. An ocean vessel legally registered in another country. Typically, an ocean vessel flies the flag of its country of registry. The term applies to both air and sea transportation.

### foreign freight forwarder
*See* freight forwarder.

### foreign income
(economics) Income earned from work performed in another country.

(U.S.) Income earned by U.S. citizens from work performed in another country. Under the Tax Reform Act of 1976, the amount of annual income that can be excluded from taxable income by U.S. citizens working abroad was reduced from $20,000 (in some cases from $25,000) to $15,000. Foreign employees of U.S. charitable organizations are able to exclude $20,000 each year.

### foreign investment
(banking) The purchase of assets from abroad.

### foreign investments
(economics) The flow of foreign capital into U.S. business enterprises in which foreign residents have significant control.

### Foreign Labor Trends
(publication) Published by U.S. Department of Labor, provides an overview of the labor sector of a country's economy. Includes information on labor standards, conditions of employment, human resource development and labor relations. Can be purchased from: Superintendent of Documents, U.S. Government Printing Office, Mail Stop: IDCC, 732 N. Capitol Street, NW, Washington, DC 20401; Tel:

[1] (866) 512-1800, [1] (202) 512-1800; Fax: [1] (202) 512-2104; Web: www.gpoaccess.gov.

### foreign market value

The price at which merchandise is sold, or offered for sale, in the principal markets of the country from which it is exported.

(U.S.) In U.S. dumping investigations, if information on foreign home market sales is not available, the foreign market value is based on prices of exports to third countries or constructed value. Adjustments for quantities sold, circumstances of sales, and differences in the merchandise can be made to those prices to ensure a proper comparison with the prices of goods exported to the United States. *See* dumping; constructive value.

### foreign military sales (FMS)

*See* conventional arms transfer.

### foreign-owned affiliate in the U.S.

(U.S.) A business in the United States in which there is sufficient foreign investment to be classified as direct foreign investment. To determine fully the foreign owners of a U.S. affiliate, three entities must be identified: the foreign parent, the ultimate beneficial owner, and the foreign parent group. All these entities are "persons" in the broad sense: thus, they may be individuals; business enterprises; governments; religious, charitable, and other nonprofit organizations; estates and trusts; or associated groups.

A U.S. affiliate may have an ultimate beneficial owner (UBO) that is not the immediate foreign parent; moreover, the affiliate may have several ownership chains above it, if it is owned at least 10 percent by more than one foreign person. In such cases, the affiliate may have more than one foreign parent, UBO, and/or foreign parent group.

*See* United States Affiliate; foreign parent group; person; ultimate beneficial owner; affiliate; foreign parent.

### foreign parent

(U.S.) The first foreign person or entity outside the United States in an affiliate's ownership chain that has direct investment in the affiliate. The foreign parent consists only of the first person or entity outside the United States in the affiliate's ownership chain; all other affiliated foreign persons are excluded.

### foreign parent group (FPG)

(U.S.) Consists of: (a) the foreign parent, (b) any foreign person or entity, proceeding up the foreign parent's ownership chain, that owns more than 50 percent of the party below it, up to and including the ultimate beneficial owner (UBO), and (c) any foreign person or entity, proceeding down the ownership chain(s) of each of these members, that is owned more than 50 percent by the party above it. A particular U.S. affiliate may have several ownership chains above it, if it is owned at least 10 percent by more than one foreign party. In such cases, the affiliate may have more than one foreign parent, UBO, and/or foreign parent group.

*See* United States Affiliate; affiliate; ultimate beneficial owner.

### foreign person

A person who is resident outside a particular country or subject to the jurisdiction of another country.

(U.S. law) Any person resident outside the United States or subject to the jurisdiction of a country other than the United States. "Person" is any individual, branch, partnership, association, associated group, estate, trust, corporation, or other organization (whether or not organized under the laws of any state), and any government (including a foreign government, the U.S. government, a state or local government, and any agency, corporation, financial institution, or other entity or instrumentality thereof, including a government sponsored agency.)

### foreign policy controls

(U.S.) U.S. export controls that are distinct from national security controls (such as the Coordinating Committee in Multilateral Export Controls or other international agreements) and are imposed to further U.S. foreign policy. The controls are typically imposed in response to developments in a country or countries—such as considerations regarding terrorism and human rights—or to developments involving a type or types of commodities and their related technical data. Foreign policy controls expire annually, unless extended.

### Foreign Remaining on Board (FROB)

(United States) Cargo that is loaded in a foreign port and which is to be unloaded in another foreign port with an intervening vessel stop in one or more ports in the United States. U.S. Customs and Border Protection considers "FROB" cargo a security concern because although the cargo does not have a final destination in the U.S., the cargo is transiting the U.S. Currently, carriers must correctly report FROB cargo upon arrival in the United States. Under the new regulations, FROB cargo must be reported 24 hours in advance of loading at the foreign port.

### foreign remittances

(banking) The transfer of any monetary instrument across national boundaries.

### foreign sales agent

An individual or firm that serves as the foreign representative of a domestic supplier and seeks sales abroad for the supplier.

### Foreign Service (U.S.)

(U.S. diplomacy) The Foreign Service supports the president of the United States and the secretary of state in pursuing U.S. foreign policy objectives. Foreign service functions include: representing U.S. interests; operating U.S. overseas missions; assisting U.S. citizens abroad; public diplomacy and reporting; and communicating and negotiating political, economic, consular, administrative, cultural, and commercial affairs. The Foreign Service comprises officers from the Departments of State, Commerce, and Agriculture and the United States Information Service. *See* commercial officers; economic officers.

### Foreign Service Institute

(U.S. government) The FSI was founded in 1946 to train U.S. foreign and civil service officials. Training courses cover administrative, consular, economic, commercial, and political work; foreign languages; and diplomatic life overseas. Contact: Foreign Service Institute, National Foreign Affairs Training Center, 4000 Arlington Blvd., Arlington, VA 22204-1500 USA; Tel: [1] (703) 302-6729; Web: www.state.gov/m/fsi.

### foreign status merchandise

(U.S. foreign trade zones) Imported merchandise which has not been released from U.S. Customs custody. Also refers to domestically produced merchandise which has been exported and later reimported into the U.S.

*See* foreign trade zone; Foreign Trade Zones Board; Foreign Trade Zone Act; grantee; operator; zone user; subzone.

### foreign trade zone (FTZ)

FTZs (or free zones, free ports, or bonded warehouses) are special commercial and industrial areas in or near ports of entry where foreign and domestic merchandise, including raw materials, components, and finished goods, may be brought in without being subject to payment of customs duties. Merchandise brought into these zones may be stored, sold, exhibited, repacked, assembled, sorted, graded, cleaned, or otherwise manipulated prior to reexport or entry into the national customs territory.

(U.S.) FTZs are restricted-access sites in or near ports of entry, which are licensed by the Foreign-Trade Zones Board and operated under the supervision of U.S. Customs and Border Protection. Zones are operated under public utility principles to create and maintain employment by encouraging operations in the U.S. which might otherwise have been carried on abroad.

**Subzones** are a special-purpose type of ancillary zone authorized by the Board for companies unable to operate effectively at public zone sites. Subzones may be approved when it can be demonstrated that the activity to be performed there will result in significant public benefit and is in the public interest.

A **Foreign Trade Zones Board**, created by the Foreign Trade Zones Act of 1934, reviews and approves applications to establish, operate, and maintain foreign trade zones.

*See* free trade area; grantee; operator; zone user; subzones; free trade agreement.

Location of and general information on U.S. Foreign Trade Zones may be obtained from Foreign Trade Zones Board, Department of Commerce, Washington, DC 20230 USA; Tel: [1] (202) 482-2862; Fax: [1] (202) 482-0002.

Questions relating to operational aspects of such responsibilities should be addressed to the appropriate district/area director of U.S. Customs.

The Foreign Trade Zones Manual, for grantees, operators, users, Customs brokers, may be purchased from the Superintendent of Documents, U.S. Government Printing Office, Mail Stop: IDCC, 732 N. Capitol Street, NW, Washington, DC 20401; Tel: [1] (866) 512-1800, [1] (202) 512-1800; Fax: [1] (202) 512-2104; Web: www.gpoaccess.gov.

Additional information may be obtained from the National Association of Foreign Trade Zones, 1000 Connecticut Ave. NW, Suite 350, Washington, DC 20036; Tel: [1] (202) 331-1950; Fax: [1] (202) 331-1994; E-mail: info@naftz.org; Web: www.naftz.org.

### Foreign Trade Zone Act (FTZA)
(U.S. law) The principal statute governing foreign trade zones is the Foreign Trade Zones Act of 1934 (FTZA), which has been codified in the United States Code as Title 19, Sections 81a through 81u. The FTZA has been periodically amended. The FTZA generally covers how and where zones are established, how they are administered and what may and may not be done in them. *See* foreign trade zone; Foreign Trade Zones Board.

### foreign trade zone entry
(U.S. Customs) The transfer of goods into a foreign trade zone. *See* foreign trade zone; entry.

### Foreign Trade Zones Board
(U.S. Customs) The administrative group responsible for the establishment, maintenance and administration of foreign trade zones in the United States under the Foreign Trade Zone Act. The Foreign Trade Zones Board consists of the U.S. Secretary of Commerce who is chairman and executive officer of the Board, the Secretary of the Treasury, and the Secretary of the Army. Contact: Foreign-Trade Zones Board, U.S. Department of Commerce, 1401 Constitution Ave., NW, Room 1115, Washington, DC 20230; Tel: [1] (202) 482-2862; Fax: [1] (202) 482-0002; Web: http://ia.ita.doc.gov/ftzpage. *See* foreign trade zone.

### Foreign Traders Index (FTI)
(publication) The Foreign Traders Index, which is part of the National Trade Data Bank (NTDB), identifies foreign firms that are interested in importing U.S. products. The FTI includes background information on foreign companies, address, contact person, sales figures, size of company, and products by SIC code. Information in the NTDB

is available from the Department of Commerce's STAT-USA/Internet service at Web: www.stat-usa.gov or at [1] (800) STAT-USA. Contact: U.S. Department of Commerce, HCHB Room 4885, Washington, DC 20230 USA; Tel: [1] (202) 482-1986; Fax: [1] (202) 482-2164; E-mail: statmail@esa.doc.gov; Web: www.stat-usa.gov.

### forex
Abbreviation for foreign exchange. *See* foreign exchange.

### forfaiting
(trade/finance) The selling, at a discount, of medium to longer term accounts receivable or promissory notes of a foreign buyer (including those arising out of a letter of credit transaction) for immediate payment. These instruments may also carry the guarantee of the foreign government. Forfaiting emerged after the Second World War to expedite finance transactions between Eastern and Western European countries. More recently, it has become popular in Asian and Third World countries. Both U.S. and European forfaiting houses, which purchase the instruments at a discount from the exporters, are active in the U.S. market. *See* factoring.

### forint
The currency of Hungary. 1Ft=100 fillér.

### forklift truck
(logistics) A highly maneuverable utility vehicle designed to move loaded pallets or skids in warehouses and manufacturing plants. Forklift trucks feature two long prongs (forks) that extend from the front of the vehicle and fit under or into openings at the bottom of a pallet or skid. These prongs can be raised, lowered or tilted to secure, move, raise, lower and position the loaded pallet in warehouse racks, containers, trucks or other vehicles. Special forklifts can handle very heavy weights and access high shelving. *See* pallet; skid.

### Form A
*See* Certificate of Origin Form A.

### forty foot equivalent unit (FEU)
Unit of measurement equivalent to one standard forty foot ocean cargo container.

### forward contract
(trade/finance) Purchase or sale of a specific quantity of a commodity, security, currency or other financial instrument at a predetermined rate with delivery and settlement at a specified future date.

### forward foreign exchange
(foreign exchange) An agreement to purchase foreign exchange (currency) at a future date at a predetermined rate of exchange. Forward foreign exchange contracts are often purchased by international buyers of goods who wish to hedge against foreign exchange fluctuations between the time the contract is negotiated and the time payment is to be made.

### forward market
(foreign exchange) The market for the purchase and sale of forward foreign exchange. Forward dates are usually one, three, six or twelve months in the future. *See* forward foreign exchange.

### forward operations
(foreign exchange) Foreign exchange transactions, on which the fulfillment of the mutual delivery obligations is made on a date later than the second business day after the transaction was concluded.

### forward rate
(foreign exchange) A contractually agreed upon exchange rate for a forward foreign exchange contract.

### forward rate agreements (FRA)
(banking) With forward rate agreements (also known as future rate agreements) two counterparties can hedge them-

**F**

selves against future interest rate changes. They agree upon an interest rate for a future period within a specific currency segment, which is valid for a predetermined amount. In contrast to futures, FRA's are not standardized and are not traded on exchanges but are used in interbank trading.

### forwarder
*See* freight forwarder.

### forwarder's bill of lading
(shipping) A bill of lading issued by a forwarding agent. *See* bill of lading.

### forwarding agent's bill of lading
(shipping) A bill of lading issued by a forwarding agent. *See* bill of lading.

### forwarding agent's receipt
(shipping) Receipt issued by a forwarding agent for goods received.

### FOT
*See* free on rail; free on truck; Incoterms.

### foul bill of lading
(shipping) A receipt for goods issued by a carrier with an indication that the goods were damaged or short in quantity when received. *See* bill of lading.

### four tigers, four dragons
A term used to describe the emerging economies of Hong Kong, Singapore, South Korea and Taiwan.

### fourth party logistics (4PL)
A logistics term coined and trademarked by Anderson Consulting (now Accenture) in 1996. There is controversy in the logistics industry regarding this term. According to Accenture, 4PL is "an integrator that assembles the resources, capabilities and technology of its own organization and other organizations to design, build and run comprehensive supply chain solutions." For some, 4PL is simply 3PL with a trademark attached. *See also*: first-party logistics, second-party logistics, third-party logistics.

### fractional currency
(banking) Any currency that is smaller than a standard money unit (e.g., any coin worth less than $1).

### framework agreement
(a) (GATT/WTO): The Tokyo Round of the GATT called for consideration to be given "to improvements in the international framework for the conduct of world trade." Four separate agreements make up what is known as the "framework agreement." They concern: (1) differential and more favorable treatment for, and reciprocity and fuller participation by, developing countries in the international framework for trade; (2) trade measures taken for balance of payments purposes; (3) safeguard actions for development purposes; and (4) an understanding on notification, consultation, dispute settlement, and surveillance in the GATT.
(b) Under the umbrella of the Enterprise for the Americas Initiative the United States and interested Western Hemisphere countries are negotiating bilateral "framework agreements" which establish agreed upon stages for eliminating counterproductive barriers to trade and investment. They also provide a forum for bilateral dispute settlement. Generally, bilateral framework agreements contain similar objectives. They are based on a statement of agreed principles regarding the benefits of open trade and investment, increased importance of services to economies, the need for adequate intellectual property rights protection, the importance of observing and promoting internationally recognized worker rights, and the desirability of resolving trade and investment problems expeditiously. The parties establish a Council on Trade and Investment to monitor trade and investment relations, hold consultations on specific trade and investment matters of interest to both sides, and work toward removing impediments to trade and invest-

ment flows. Framework agreements do not bind signatories to implement specific trade liberalization measures. *See* General Agreement on Tariffs and Trade.

### franc
The currency for:
Benin, CFAF;
Burkina Faso, 1CFAF=100 centimes;
Burundi, 1 FBu=100 centimes;
Cameroon, 1 CFAF=100 centimes;
Central African Republic, 1CFAF=100 centimes;
Chad, CFAF (centime eliminated);
Comoros, CFAF (centime eliminated);
Congo, CFAF (centime eliminated);
Djibouti, 1DF=100 centimes;
Equatorial Guinea, CFAF (centime eliminated);
French Pacific Islands, 1CFPF=100 centimes;
Gabon, CFAF (centime eliminated);
Guadeloupe, 1F=100 centimes;
Guinea, 1GFr=100 centimes;
Ivory Coast, CFAF (centime eliminated);
Liechtenstein (uses Swiss franc);
Madagascar, 1FMG=100 centimes;
Mali, CFAF (centime eliminated);
Niger, CFAF (centime eliminated);
Rwanda, 1RF=100 centimes;
St. Pierre, 1F=100 centimes;
Senegal, CFAF (centime eliminated);
Switzerland, 1SwF=100 centimes;
Togo, CFAF (centime eliminated).
The former currencies of: Andorra, Belgium, France, French Guiana, Guadeloupe, Luxembourg, Martinique, Monaco, Reunion Island and St. Pierre. The new currency of these countries is the European Union Euro. €1 = 100 cents.

### franco
(trade term) Free from duties, transportation charges and other levies. Used also as delivery condition, e.g., franco ... (named place of delivery), which means that the seller must bear all transportation charges and duties up to the named place. *See* Incoterms.

### fraud
(law) An intentional deception or false representation made to induce another person to act in reliance on that representation with the result that the person incurs damages. A buyer acts fraudulently, for example, by promising to pay for goods on delivery even though the buyer does not have the funds needed, accepting the goods as satisfactory, but not paying for them.

### Free Alongside Ship (...named port of shipment) (FAS)
(Incoterms 2000) An international trade term of sale in which, for the quoted price, the seller/exporter/manufacturer clears the goods for export and then places them alongside the vessel at the "named port of shipment." (The seller's clearing the goods for export is new to Incoterms 2000.)
The parties to the transaction, however, may stipulate in their contract of sale that the buyer will clear the goods for export.
The Free Alongside Ship term is used only for ocean or inland waterway transport.
The "named place" in Free Alongside Ship and all "F" Incoterms 2000 is domestic to the seller.
The Free Alongside Ship term is commonly used in the sale of bulk commodity cargo such as oil, grains, and ore.
*See* Guide to Incoterms 2000 Appendix.

### Free and Secure Trade (FAST)

(U.S./Canada, U.S./Mexico) A United States Customs and Border Protection (CBP) initiative designed to harmonize the commercial processes for clearance of commercial shipments at the U.S./Canada and U.S./Mexico borders. The FAST program is designed to:

1. Increase the integrity of supply chain security by offering expedited clearance to carriers and importers enrolled in the Customs-Trade Partnership Against Terrorism (C-TPAT) program.
2. Streamline and integrate registration processes for drivers, carriers and importers, minimizing paperwork and ensuring only low-risk participants are enrolled as members.
3. Expedite the clearance of transborder shipments of compliant low-risk partners by: reducing CBP information requirements, dedicating lanes at major crossings to FAST participants, using common technology, and minimal physical cargo examinations.
4. Serve as a catalyst for the Customs' administrations of the three countries to participate in enhanced technologies by using transponders, which will make it easier to clear low-risk shipments and will mitigate the cost of program participation for FAST partners.

FAST approved highway carriers will benefit from:

1. Dedicated lanes for greater speed and efficiency in the clearance of FAST transborder shipments.
2. Reduced number of examinations for continued compliance with CBP's FAST requirements.
3. A strong and ongoing partnership with the Canadian Partners in Protection (PIP), CBP's Customs-Trade Partnership Against Terrorism (C-TPAT) and Mexican Customs administrations.
4. Enhanced supply chain security and safety while protecting the economic prosperity of each country.
5. The knowledge that they are carrying shipments for a C-TPAT-approved importer.
6. A head start for the upcoming modifications to FAST that will expand eligible electronic cargo release methods.

*See* the FAST section in the Security Appendix.

### free astray

(shipping) A shipment miscarried or unloaded at the wrong station is billed and forwarded to the correct station, free of charges, on account of being astray, hence the term free astray.

### Free Carrier (...named place) (FCA)

(Incoterms 2000) An international trade term of sale in which, for the quoted price, the seller/exporter/manufacturer clears the goods for export and then delivers them to the carrier specified by the buyer at the named place.

If the named place is the seller's place of business, the seller is responsible for loading the goods onto the transport vehicle. If the named place is any other location, such as the loading dock of the carrier, the seller is not responsible for loading the goods onto the transport vehicle.

The Free Carrier term may be used for any mode of transport, including multimodal.

The "named place" in Free Carrier and all "F" Incoterms 2000 is domestic to the seller.

"Carrier" has a specific and somewhat expanded meaning. A carrier can be a shipping line, an airline, a trucking firm, or a railway. The carrier can also be an individual or firm who undertakes to procure carriage by any of the above methods of transport including multimodal. Therefore, a person, such as a freight forwarder, can act as a "carrier" under this term. In such a case, the buyer names the carrier or the individual who is to receive the goods.

The Free Carrier term is often used when making an initial quotation for the sale of goods.

*See* Guide to Incoterms 2000 Appendix.

### free domicile (door to door)

(trade term/logistics) A trade term that specifies that the shipper is responsible for all costs of delivery of a shipment, including customs clearance fees, directly to the door of the consignee. *See* Incoterms.

### free exchange rate

*See* exchange rate; floating.

### free in

(shipping) A pricing term indicating that the loading charges are for the account of the supplier.

### free in and out (FIO)

(shipping) A pricing term indicating that the charterer of a vessel is responsible for the cost of loading and unloading goods from the vessel.

### free list

(customs) A statement, prepared by the customs department of a country, of items that are not liable to the payment of duties.

### free market

(economics) Describes the unrestricted movement of items in and out from the market, unhampered by the existence of tariffs or other trade barriers.

### free of capture and seizure (F.C.&S.)

(insurance) An insurance policy provision stating that the policy does not cover warlike operations or its consequences, whether before or after the actual declaration of war. Currently, most open policies omit war perils from its insuring conditions and in all cases will include a F.C.&S. clause. War coverage is customarily furnished in conjunction with an open cargo policy and is written under a separate, distinct policy—the War Risk Only Policy. *See* war risk; all risk; special marine policy.

### free of particular average (FPA)

(insurance) A clause in an insurance policy that provides that in addition to total losses, partial losses resulting from perils of the sea are recoverable, but only in the event that the carrying vessel has stranded, sunk, burnt, been on fire or been in collision. *See* average; particular average; general average; with average; deductible average.

### Free On Board
### (...named port of shipment) (FOB)

(Incoterms 2000) An international trade term of sale in which, for the quoted price, the seller/exporter/manufacturer clears the goods for export and is responsible for the costs and risks of delivering the goods past the ship's rail at the named port of shipment.

The Free On Board term is used only for ocean or inland waterway transport.

The "named place" in Free On Board and all "F" Incoterms 2000 is domestic to the seller.

The Free On Board term is commonly used in the sale of bulk commodity cargo such as oil, grains, and ore where passing the ship's rail is important. However, it is also commonly used in shipping container loads of other goods.

The key document in FOB transactions is the "On Board Bill of Lading."

Sellers and buyers often confuse the Free On Board term with Free Carrier. Free On Board (FOB) does not mean loading the goods onto a truck at the seller's place of business. Free On Board is used only in reference to delivering the goods past a ship's rail in ocean or inland waterway transport. Free Carrier, on the other hand, is applicable to all modes of transport.

*See* Guide to Incoterms 2000 Appendix.

F

**free on rail; free on truck (FOR/FOT)**
(trade terms) These terms are synonymous, since the word "truck" relates to the railway wagons. The terms should only be used when the goods are to be carried by rail. *See* Free Carrier; Incoterms.

**free out**
(shipping) A pricing term indicating that unloading charges are for the account of the receiver.

**free port**
An area, such as a port city, into which imported merchandise may legally be moved without payment of duties. *See* foreign trade zone.

**free time**
(shipping) The time allowed shippers or receivers to load or unload cars before demurrage, detention, or storage charges accrue. *See* demurrage; detention.

**free trade**
(economics) A theoretical concept that assumes international trade unhampered by government measures such as tariffs or nontariff barriers. The objective of trade liberalization is to achieve "freer trade" rather than "free trade," it being generally recognized among trade policy officials that some restrictions on trade are likely to remain in effect for the foreseeable future.

**free trade agreement (FTA)**
An FTA is an arrangement which establishes unimpeded exchange and flow of goods and services between trading partners regardless of national borders. An FTA does not (as opposed to a common market) address labor mobility across borders or other common policies such as taxes. Member countries of a free trade area apply their individual tariff rates to countries outside the free trade area.

**free trade area**
A group of two or more countries that have eliminated tariff and most nontariff barriers affecting trade among themselves, while each participating country applies its own independent schedule of tariffs to imports from countries that are not members. A free trade area allows member countries to maintain individually separate tariff schedules for external countries; members of a customs union employ a common external tariff. The best known example is the European Free Trade Association (EFTA) and the free trade area for manufactured goods that has been created through the trade agreements that have been concluded between the European Community and the individual EFTA countries. The World Trade Organization (WTO) spells out the meaning of a free trade area and specifies the applicability of other WTO provisions to free trade areas. *See* European Community; European Free Trade Association; common market.

**free trade zone**
*See* foreign trade zone; free zone.

**free zone**
An area within a country (a seaport, airport, warehouse or any designated area) regarded as being outside its customs territory. Importers may therefore bring goods of foreign origin into such an area without paying customs duties and taxes, pending their eventual processing, transshipment or reexportation. Free zones are also known as "free ports," "free warehouses," and "foreign trade zones."

**freeboard**
(general) The vertical distance between the level of water in a channel, reservoir, canal or tank and the top of the sides of a levee, dam, tank or other structure that holds or confines the water.
(shipping) The vertical distance between the surface of water and a ship's gunwale. The more heavily laden a vessel becomes, the less freeboard. *See* Plimsoll mark.

**Freedoms of the Air**
Commercial aviation rights codified by the International Civil Aviation Organization (ICAO) granting airline(s) from one country various privileges to enter and land in another country's airspace. The text is part of the ICAO "Manual on the Regulation of International Air Transport." Contact ICAO; External Relations and Public Information Office (EPO); 999 University Street, Montreal, Quebec H3C 5H7, Canada; Tel: + 1 (514) 954-8219; Fax: + 1 (514) 954-6077; web: www.icao.int .

**First Freedom of the Air** - the right or privilege, in respect of scheduled international air services, granted by one State to another State or States to fly across its territory without landing (also known as a First Freedom Right).

**Second Freedom of the Air** - the right or privilege, in respect of scheduled international air services, granted by one State to another State or States to land in its territory for non-traffic purposes (also known as a Second Freedom Right).

**Third Freedom of The Air** - the right or privilege, in respect of scheduled international air services, granted by one State to another State to put down, in the territory of the first State, traffic coming from the home State of the carrier (also known as a Third Freedom Right).

**Fourth Freedom of The Air** - the right or privilege, in respect of scheduled international air services, granted by one State to another State to take on, in the territory of the first State, traffic destined for the home State of the carrier (also known as a Fourth Freedom Right).

**Fifth Freedom of The Air** - the right or privilege, in respect of scheduled international air services, granted by one State to another State to put down and to take on, in the territory of the first State, traffic coming from or destined to a third State (also known as a Fifth Freedom Right).

**Note**: ICAO characterizes all "freedoms" beyond the Fifth as "so-called" because only the first five "freedoms" have been officially recognized as such by international treaty.

**Sixth Freedom of The Air** - the right or privilege, in respect of scheduled international air services, of transporting, via the home State of the carrier, traffic moving between two other States (also known as a Sixth Freedom Right). The so-called Sixth Freedom of the Air, unlike the first five freedoms, is not incorporated as such into any widely recognized air service agreements such as the "Five Freedoms Agreement".

**Seventh Freedom of The Air** - the right or privilege, in respect of scheduled international air services, granted by one State to another State, of transporting traffic between the territory of the granting State and any third State with no requirement to include on such operation any point in the territory of the recipient State, i.e the service need not connect to or be an extension of any service to/from the home State of the carrier.

**Eighth Freedom of The Air** - the right or privilege, in respect of scheduled international air services, of transporting cabotage traffic between two points in the territory of the granting State on a service which originates or terminates in the home country of the foreign carrier or (in connection with the so-called Seventh Freedom of the Air) outside the territory of the granting State (also known as a Eighth Freedom Right or "consecutive cabotage").

**Ninth Freedom of The Air** - the right or privilege of transporting cabotage traffic of the granting State on a service performed entirely within the territory of the granting State (also known as a Ninth Freedom Right or "stand alone" cabotage).

Source: Manual on the Regulation of International Air Transport (Doc 9626, Part 4).

### freehold
(law) Fee simple, fee tail or life estate tenure in real property. (a) Fee simple means that an individual has tenure without limitation or restriction on transfer of ownership by sale or inheritance. (b) Fee tail means that only a specified individual or group of heirs is granted tenure. (c) Life estate means that tenure is granted to a specific individual during his or her lifetime or to an individual during the lifetime of the person in whose name the life estate is granted.

### freely negotiable
(banking) When a letter of credit is stated as "freely negotiable," the beneficiary of the letter of credit has the right to present his documents at a bank of his choice for negotiation. *See* letter of credit.

### freight
(shipping) All merchandise, goods, products, or commodities shipped by rail, air, road, or water, other than baggage, express mail, or regular mail.

### freight all kinds (FAK)
(shipping/logistics) A carrier's rate classification that usually refers to a consolidated cargo shipment where items of different classes (weight, bulk or value) are shipped in a single container, but charged at a single rate. This rate classification is used only for establishing shipping rates and is not acceptable on customs documents, which must detail the specific contents of a shipment. *See* class or kind (of merchandise).

### freight bill
(shipping) (a) **Destination freight bill**—A bill rendered by a transportation line to consignee, giving a description of the freight, the name of shipper, point or origin, weight and amount of charges (if not prepaid).
(b) **Prepaid freight bill**—A bill rendered by a transportation line to shipper, giving a description of the freight, the names of consignee and destination, weight and amount of charges.

### freight broker
(logistics) An individual or company who sells transportation services without actually providing the services. Freight brokers typically match small shippers with carriers.

### freight carriage ... and insurance paid to
*See* Cost, Insurance, Freight; Incoterms.

### freight carriage ... paid to
*See* Carriage Paid To; Incoterms 2000.

### freight charge
(shipping) The charge assessed for transporting freight.

### freight claim
(shipping) A demand upon a carrier for the payment of overcharge or loss or damage sustained by shipper or consignee.

### freight forwarder
(shipping) A person engaged in the business of assembling, collection, consolidating, shipping and distributing less-than-carload or less-than-truckload freight. Also, a person acting as agent in the transshipping of freight to or from foreign countries and the clearing of freight through customs, including full preparation of documents, arranging for shipping, warehousing, delivery and export clearance.

### freighter
(shipping) (a) A marine vessel designed to carry freight. Freighter is a general term used to refer to all vessels that carry freight, but more specifically applies to non-container vessels. (b) An airplane designed to carry freight. A cargo aircraft.

### Frequent Importer Release System (FIRST)
(Canada Customs) A Canada Border Services Agency (CBSA) Line Release System (LRS) import program that allows for the quick clearance of low-risk, low-revenue commercial shipments made on a regular basis into Canada. Frequent Canadian importers who have established a sound compliance record can apply for FIRST privileges.

For those accepted into the program, CBSA gives authorization numbers which appear on pre-approved import documents that identify FIRST shipments. When the goods arrive at the border, the carrier presents the import document with the bar-coded authorization and transaction number, a description of the goods and related invoices. CBSA inputs the bar code into a computer system to confirm that the importer has FIRST privileges for the goods on hand. The customs officer then decides whether to release the shipment or refer it for examination.

For information about CBSA and FIRST, go to: www.cbsa-asfc.gc.ca.

### fulfillment
(logistics) The processing of an order. Fulfillment includes warehousing, order receiving, invoice processing, packing and shipping. The term is typical in the publishing business. For example, a publishing company might have one fulfillment "house" or "service" in its domestic market and others in key markets around the world.

### full container load (FCL)
(logistics) A shipment of cargo that fills a given container either by bulk or maximum weight.

### full set
All the originals of a particular document (usually the bill of lading). The number of originals is usually indicated on the document itself.

### full truck load (FTL)
(logistics) A shipment of cargo that fills a given truck either by bulk or maximum weight.

### fundamental analysis
(economics) Analysis of basic economic data in a market (supply and demand), in order to be able to make assertions as to the future price trend of a traded commodity. Fundamental exchange rate analysis is based on the economic and business cycle data of the country in question and leads to longer-term exchange rate forecasts.

### fungibles
(law) Goods that are identical with other goods of the same nature. A merchant who is unable to deliver a specific load of grain, for example, may negotiate to replace that grain with fungibles, that is another load of grain of the same nature and quality.

### future exchange contract
*See* futures contract.

### future trading
The sale or purchase of a commodity, currency or security for future delivery.

### futures contract
(finance/foreign exchange) A contract for the future delivery of a specified commodity, currency or security on a specific date at a rate determined in the present. Standardized forward contracts are officially traded on an exchange such as the Chicago Board of Trade (CBOT), London International Financial Futures Exchange (LIFFE), Commodity Exchange Inc. (COMEX), or New York Mercantile Exchange (NYMEX). The contract is valid for a specific amount of a commodity or a fixed amount of a financial instrument.

# G

### G7 Import One Step Release on Full Documentation (RFD)

(Canada Customs) RDFD is a Canada Border Services Agency (CBSA) import shipment service option that allows Canadian importers or their agents to obtain the release of a shipment by submitting release and accounting information in a single EDI (Electronic Data Interchange) transmission, while deferring the payment of duties and taxes to a later date (usually on a monthly basis).

Importers or agents can transmit the information either before, or when, the shipment arrives. If they have an established relationship with a known supplier, they can submit the release and accounting information to customs officials before the release of the goods. These importers or agents may be interested in the RFD process.

Although the RFD process is a G7 Initiative, it is not restricted to shipments from G7 countries.

For information go to:
www.cbsa-asfc.gc.ca/eservices/g7/importing-e.html

### gamma
(statistics/banking/foreign exchange) The rate of change of an option's delta with respect to a marginal change in the price of the underlying instrument.

### gang
(shipping) A group of usually four to six stevedores with a supervisor who are assigned to the loading or unloading of a portion of a vessel.

### gangway
(shipping) (a) The opening through which a ship is boarded, (b) Either of the sides of the upper deck of a ship.

### gantry crane
(shipping) A specialized machine for the raising or lowering of cargo mounted on a structure spanning an open space on a ship. The hoisting device travels back and forth along the spanning structure from port to starboard, while the spanning structure itself is often mounted on a set of rails which enables it to move from fore to aft.

### gateway
(general) A major airport or seaport.

(customs) The port where customs clearance takes place.

(shipping) A point at which freight moving from one territory to another is interchanged between transportation lines.

### GATT
*See* General Agreement on Tariffs and Trade.

### geisha bond
(finance/banking) Bond issued on the Japanese market in currencies other than yen. Yen-denominated bonds are known as Samurai bonds.

### general agency
*See* agency.

### General Agreement on Tariffs and Trade (GATT)

*[The General Agreement on Tariffs and Trade has been superseded by the World Trade Organization (WTO). The following entry remains for historical purposes. See World Trade Organization (WTO).]*

Both a multilateral trade agreement aimed at expanding international trade and the organization which oversees the agreement. The main goals of GATT are to liberalize world trade and place it on a secure basis thereby contributing to economic growth and development and the welfare of the world's people. GATT is the only multilateral instrument that lays down agreed rules for international trade, and the organization is the principal international body concerned with negotiating the reduction of trade barriers and with international trade relations.

One hundred and seventeen countries accounting for approximately 90 percent of world trade are Contracting Parties to GATT, while some other countries apply GATT rules on a de facto basis. Approximately 2/3 of GATT's membership consists of developing countries.

The GATT was signed in 1948 by 23 nations as a response to the trade conflicts which contributed to the outbreak of World War II. Originally looked upon as an interim agreement, it has become recognized as the key institution concerned with international trade negotiations. An important element which contributed to GATT's importance early on came with the United States' refusal to ratify the Havana Charter of 1948, which would have created an International Trade Organization (ITO) as a Specialized Agency of the United Nations system, similar to the International Monetary Fund and the World Bank. The Interim Commission of the ITO (ICITO), which was established to facilitate the creation of the ITO, subsequently became the GATT Secretariat. One result of the recent Uruguay Round was the decision to replace the GATT Secretariat with a Multilateral Trading Organization (MTO), which will have more authority to enforce free trade rules, as through the assessment of trade penalties. In December, 1993, agreements were reached at the conclusion of the Uruguay Round to revise the framework of GATT. Member nations will sign the agreement in April, 1994, and it will go into effect July 1, 1995.

The purpose of the GATT organization, headquartered in Geneva, is to provide a forum for discussion of world trade issues that allows for the disciplined resolution of trade disputes, based on the founding principles of GATT which include nondiscrimination, national treatment, transparency, and most-favored-nations (MFN) treatment. International negotiations known as "Rounds" are conducted to lower tariffs and other barriers to trade, and a consultative mechanism that may be invoked by governments seeking to protect their trade interests.

A few of the fundamental principles and aims of GATT:

(1) **Trade without discrimination**—The first principle embodied in the famous "most-favored nation" clause is that trade must be conducted on the basis of non-discrimination. No country is to give special trading advantages to another or to discriminate against it; all are on an equal basis and all share the benefits of any moves towards lower trade barriers.

(2) **Protection through tariffs**—Ensures that if protection to a domestic industry is given, it should be extended through the customs tariff, and not through other commercial measures.

(3) **A stable basis for trade**—Provided partly by the binding of the tariff levels negotiated among contracting parties. These bound items are listed, for each country, in tariff schedules which form an integral part of the General Agreement.

(4) **Promoting fair competition**—Concerns over dumping and subsidies are addressed by the "Anti-dumping Code" which provides rules under which governments may respond to dumping in their domestic market by overseas competitors, and rules for the application of "countervailing" duties which can be imposed to negate the effects of export subsidies.

(5) **Quantitative restrictions on imports**—A basic provision of GATT is a general prohibition of quantitative re-

strictions (import quotas). The main exception to the general rule against these restrictions allows their use in balance-of-payments difficulties under Article XII.

**(6) The "waiver" and the possible emergency action**—Waiver procedures allow a country to seek release from particular GATT obligations, when its economic or trade circumstances so warrant. The "safeguards" rule of GATT (Article XIX) permits members, under carefully defined circumstances, to impose import restrictions or suspend tariff concessions on products which are being imported in such increased quantities and under such conditions that they cause serious injury to competing domestic producers.

**(7) Regional trading arrangements**—Regional trade groupings, as an exception to the general most-favored-nations treatment, are permitted in the form of a customs union or free trade area. Article XXIV recognizes the value of such agreements, which foster free trade by abolishing or reducing barriers against imports from countries in a particular region.

**(8) Settling trade disputes**—Consultation, conciliation, and dispute settlement are fundamental aspects of GATT's work. Countries can petition GATT for a fair settlement of cases in which they feel their rights under the General Agreement are being withheld or compromised by other members. Bilateral consultations are emphasized, but if necessary, unresolved cases go before a GATT panel of experts.

(U.S.) For the United States, the GATT came into existence as an executive agreement, which, under the U.S. Constitution does not require Senate ratification.

*See* rounds; Tokyo Round; Uruguay Round; multilateral trade negotiations; rollback; standstill; safeguards; special and different treatment.

*See* World Trade Organization (WTO).

### general average
(shipping) A loss that affects all cargo interests on board a vessel as well as the ship herself. These include the owner of the hull and the owners of all the cargoes aboard for their respective values plus the owner or charterer who stands to earn a specific income from freight charges for the voyage.

A general average loss may occur whether goods are insured or not. It is one that results from an intentional sacrifice (or expenditure) incurred by the master of a vessel in time of danger for the benefit of both ship and cargo. The classic example of this is jettison to lighten a stranded vessel. From the most ancient times, the maritime laws of all trading nations have held that such a sacrifice shall be borne by all for whose benefit the sacrifice was made, and not alone by the owner of the cargo thrown overboard.

The principles of general average have been refined over the years, and they have inevitably come to reflect the increasing complexity of present day commerce. A vessel owner may and does declare his vessel under general average whenever, for the common good in time of danger an intentional sacrifice of ship or cargo has been made, or an extraordinary expenditure has been incurred. In actual practice, general averages result mainly from strandings, fires, collisions and from engaging salvage assistance or putting into a port of refuge following a machinery breakdown or other peril.

As the name implies, general average claims affect all the interests which stand to suffer a financial loss if a particular voyage is not successfully completed.

(insurance) Insurance coverage for a general average loss.

*See* average; particular average; with average; free of particular average; deductible average.

### general cargo rate
(shipping) The rate a carrier charges for the shipment of cargo which does not have a special class rate or commodity rate.

### general cargo vessels
(shipping) A vessel designed to handle break-bulk cargo such as bags, cartons, cases, crates and drums, either individually or in unitized or palletized loads. *See* breakbulk vessel.

### general commodity rate
(shipping) A freight rate applicable to all commodities except those for which specific rates have been filed. Such rates are based on weight and distance and are published for each pair of ports or cities a carrier serves.

### general imports
(U.S. Customs) The total physical arrivals of merchandise from foreign countries, whether such merchandise enters consumption channels immediately or is entered into bonded warehouses or Foreign Trade Zones under U.S. Customs custody.

### general liability
(law) Unlimited responsibility for an obligation, such as payment of the debts of a business. *See* joint and several liability; limited liability.

### general license (GL)
(U.S.) [*Obsolete as of January 1997; information provided for historical reference only.*] Licenses, authorized in the past by the U.S. Bureau of Export Administration (now the Bureau of Industry and Security), that permitted the export of non-strategic goods to specified countries without the need for a validated license. No prior written authorization was required and no individual license was issued for these categories

There were over twenty different types of general licenses, each represented by a symbol. These licenses included:
(a) General license BAGGAGE
(b) General license CREW
(c) General license GATS
(d) General license GCG
(e) General license G-COCOM
(f) General license GCT
(g) General license G-DEST
(h) General license GFW
(i) General license GIFT
(j) General license GIT
(k) General license GLR
(l) General license GLV
(m) General license G-NNR
(n) General license GTDA
(o) General license GTDR
(p) General license G-TEMP
(q) General license GTF-U.S.
(r) General license GUS
(s) General license PLANE STORES
(t) General license RCS
(u) General license SAFEGUARDS
(v) General license SHIP STORES
Former contact: Bureau of Industry and Security, Office of Public Affairs, Room 3895, Fourteenth Street and Constitution Avenue NW, Washington, DC 20230 USA; Tel: [1] (202) 482-2721; Web: www.bis.doc.gov.

### general order (GO)
(U.S. Customs/shipping) Merchandise not entered within 5 working days after arrival of the carrier and then stored at the risk and expense of the importer. *See* general order warehouse.

**G**

### general order warehouse
(U.S. Customs) A customs bonded warehouse to which customs sends goods (at the owner's expense and risk) which have not been claimed within five days of arrival.

### general partnership
(law) A partnership in which all of the partners have joint and several liability for the partnership obligations. *See* joint and several liability.

### general tariff
A tariff that applies to countries that do not enjoy either preferential or most-favored-nation tariff treatment. Where the general tariff rate differs from the most-favored-nation rate, the general tariff rate is usually the higher rate.

### Generalized System of Preferences (GSP)
A program providing for free rates of duty for merchandise from beneficiary developing independent countries and territories to encourage their economic growth.

GSP is one element of a coordinated effort by the industrial trading nations to bring developing countries more fully into the international trading system.

The GSP reflects international agreement, negotiated at the United Nations Conference on Trade and Development II (UNCTAD-II) in New Delhi in 1968, that a temporary and non-reciprocal grant of preferences by developed countries to developing countries would be equitable and, in the long term, mutually beneficial.

(U.S.) The U.S. GSP scheme is a system of nonreciprocal tariff preferences for the benefit of these countries. The U.S. conducts annual GSP reviews to consider petitions requesting modification of product coverage and/or country eligibility. United States GSP law requires that a beneficiary country's laws and practices relating to market access, intellectual property rights protection, investment, export practices, and workers rights be considered in all GSP decisions.

The GSP eligibility list includes a wide range of products classifiable under approximately 3,000 different subheadings in the Harmonized Tariff Schedule of the United States (HTS or HTSUS). These items are identified either by an "A" or "A*" in the "Special" column 1 of the tariff schedule. Note that the eligible countries and eligible items change from time-to-time over the life of the program.

Eligible merchandise will be entitled to duty-free treatment provided the following conditions are met: (1) The merchandise must be destined for the United States without contingency for diversion at the time of exportation from the beneficiary developing country. (2) The UNCTAD (United Nations Conference on Trade and Development) Certificate of Origin Form A must be properly prepared, signed by the exporter and either be filed with the customs entry or furnished before liquidation or other final action on the entry if requested to do so by Customs. (3) The merchandise must be imported directly into the United States from the beneficiary country. (4) The cost or value of materials produced in the beneficiary developing country and/or the direct cost of processing performed there must represent at least 35 percent of the appraised value of the goods. *See* Certificate of Origin Form A; Harmonized Tariff Schedule of the United States.

### "German" silver
A silver-white alloy of copper, zinc and nickel that is more corrosion resistant than brass. Developed in the early 19th century and attributed to the German chemist E.A. Geitner. Now called nickel silver.

### Gesellschaft mit beschrankter Haftung (GmbH)
(Austria, Germany, Switzerland) Designation for a private limited liability corporation with limited liability to shareholders.

### giro
*See* deposit money.

### global bond
(banking/finance) A bond that can be traded immediately in any United States capital market and in the Euromarket.

### Global Public Goods
"Goods" that are in the public domain; goods that are there for all to consume. Goods may be in the public domain because:

- They cannot be made excludable (that is, their benefits cannot be withheld from the public), because doing so would be too expensive or technically impossible (e.g., the warming rays of the sun).
- They have been made public by design (e.g., a country's justice system, street signs, and basic education for all).
- They are public by default, due to policy neglect (e.g., air pollution, crime and violence, and communicable diseases) or due to lack of relevant information (e.g., food items or gases that one day science may recognize as being harmful to human health).

For more information, refer to *Providing Global Public Goods*, published by Oxford University Press in 2002, or contact: Office of Development Studies; United Nations Development Programme; 336 East 45 Street; Uganda House ; New York NY 10017 USA; Email: info@gpg-net.net; Web: www.undp.org/ods, or the Global Policy Forum at www.globalpolicy.org.

### global quota
(customs) A quota on the total imports of a product from all countries.

### globalization
(economics) The internationalization of business, communications and culture. The term has come to refer to the interdependence of the world economy and the fact that activities or events in one country can have far-reaching effects across the globe.

### gnomes of Zurich
(banking) Those financial and banking people of Zurich, Switzerland, involved in foreign exchange speculation. The term was coined by Great Britain's Labor ministers during the 1964 sterling crisis.

### godown
(Chinese) A warehouse where goods are stored.

### gold exchange standard
(banking/foreign exchange) An international monetary agreement according to which fiat national currencies can be converted into gold at established price ratios.

### gold fixing
(banking/commodity markets) In London, Paris and Zurich, at 10:30 a.m. and again at 3:30 p.m., gold specialists or bank officials specializing in gold bullion activity determine the price for the metal.

### Gold Key Service
(U.S.) An International Trade Administration, U.S. Department of Commerce service that provides customized information for U.S. firms visiting a country—market orientation briefings, market research, introductions to potential business partners, an interpreter for meetings, assistance in developing a market strategy, and help in putting together a follow-up plan. Trade specialists design an agenda of meetings, screen and select the right companies, arrange meetings with key people, and go with U.S. representatives to ensure that no unforeseen difficulties occur.

For further information, in the U.S. call [1] (800) USA-TRADE or on the Web at http://www.export.gov/comm_svc/goldkey.html.

### gold reserves
(banking/foreign exchange) Gold, retained by a nation's monetary agency, forming the backing of currency that the nation has issued.

### gold standard
(economics) A monetary agreement whereby all national currencies are backed 100 percent by gold and the gold is utilized for payments of foreign activity.

### gold tranche position in International Monetary Fund
(banking) Represents the amount that a member country can draw in foreign currencies virtually automatically from the International Monetary fund if such borrowings are needed to finance a balance-of-payments deficit.
(U.S.) In the case of the U.S., the gold tranche itself is determined by the U.S. quota paid in gold minus the holdings of dollars by the fund in excess of the dollar portion of the U.S. quota. Transactions of the fund in a member country's currency are transactions in monetary reserves. When the fund sells dollars to other countries to enable them to finance their international payments, the net position of the United States in the fund is improved. An improvement in the net position in the gold tranche is similar to an increase in the reserve assets of the United States. On the other hand, when the United States buys other currencies from the fund, or when other countries use dollars to meet obligations to the fund, the net position of the United States in the fund is reduced.

### Golden Share
(finance/economics/politics) (a) The right of a government to exercise veto power over a company's wishes to materially change its articles of association. This term came into use in the 1980s to refer to France's and Spain's continued control of companies they had privatized.
(b) A holding of voting stock in a company sufficient to exercise control of the company. Usually, this means 51% of the voting stock. However, if the balance of the voting stock is evenly divided over an issue, control of as little as 10 percent of the voting stock can control a company.

### gondola car
(shipping) An open railway car with sides and ends, used principally for hauling coal, sand, etc.

### goods
(law) (a) Merchandise, supplies, raw materials, and completed products. (b) All things that are movable and are designated as sold to a particular buyer.
(c) **Durable goods** are ones that last a relatively long time and that are not dissipated or depleted when used generally, such as machinery and tools. (d) **Consumer goods** are ones that are purchased primarily for the buyer's personal, family, or household use. (e) **Hard goods** are consumer durable goods, such as appliances. (f) **Soft goods** are consumer goods that are not durable, such as clothing.

### gourde
The currency of Haiti. 1G=100 centimes.

### governing law clause
(law) A contract clause by which the parties agree that their contract should be interpreted in accordance with the law of a designated jurisdiction. A court may decide not to follow the choice made by the parties, because the parties cannot deprive a court of jurisdiction, but courts will often agree to apply the law that the parties have specified.

### government bill of lading (GB/L)
(U.S. logistics) A special bill of lading used for shipments made by the U.S. government. The U.S. Government Bill

of Lading (GB/L) and the U.S. Government Bill of Lading - Privately Owned Personal Property (PPGBL) are the primary documents used by the U.S. government to procure freight, express transportation and other related services from commercial carriers.

### Government Printing Office
*See* Superintendent of Documents.

### government procurement policies and practices
The means and mechanisms through which official government agencies purchase goods and services. Government procurement policies and practices may be considered to be non-tariff barriers to trade, involving the discriminatory purchase by official government agencies of goods and services from domestic suppliers, despite their higher prices or inferior quality as compared with competitive goods that could be imported.
(U.S.) The United States pressed for an international agreement during the Tokyo Round (of the General Agreement on Tariffs and Trade, GATT) to ensure that government purchase of goods entering into international trade should be based on specific published regulations that prescribe open procedures for submitting bids, as had been the traditional practice in the United States. Most governments had traditionally awarded such contracts on the basis of bids solicited from selected domestic suppliers, or through private negotiations with suppliers that involved little, if any, competition. Other countries, including the United States, gave domestic suppliers a specified preferential margin, as compared with foreign suppliers. The Government Procurement Code negotiated during the Tokyo Round sought to reduce, if not eliminate, the "Buy National" bias underlying such practices by improving transparency and equity in national procurement practices and by ensuring effective recourse to dispute settlement procedures. The Code became effective Jan. l, 1981.
*See* General Agreement on Tariffs and Trade; Tokyo Round, World Trade Organization (WTO).

### graduation
The presumption that individual developing countries are capable of assuming greater responsibilities and obligations in the international community—within the WTO or the World Bank, for example—as their economies advance, as through industrialization, export development, and rising living standards. In this sense, graduation implies that donor countries may remove the more advanced developing countries from eligibility for all or some products under the Generalized System of Preferences. Within the World Bank, graduation moves a country from dependence on concessional grants to non-concessional loans from international financial institutions and private banks.

### Grameen Bank
(Literally: Bank of the Villages.) A bank founded in 1976 by Muhammad Yunus, a US-educated professor of economics, to test his methodology for providing credit and other banking services to the rural poor (especially women) of Bangladesh. Since that time the Grameen Bank and its many subsidiaries have grown and made a reputation for both themselves and the concept of microcredit. Some interesting facts about the bank: the bank is 94% owned by its borrowers and 6% by the Government of Bangladesh; total borrowers: 6.39 million; women borrowers: 96%; loan recovery rate: 98.45%.
Features of the loan methodology include: 1. Loans are made without collateral and without legally enforceable contracts. 2. Loans are made to promote self employment, housing and education, not consumption. 3. Borrowers must join a group of borrowers and attend weekly meetings. 4. Borrowers must agree to both obligatory and vol-

**G**

untary savings programs. 5. Although the loans are very small, the interest rates charged are very close to market rate. *See* microcredit.

### Granger Laws
(U.S. law) State laws passed in the late 1800s in the western and mid-western states of the U.S. that sought to regulate railroads, warehouses and grain elevators and eliminate discriminatory rates and charges. The name came from an organization of farmers established in 1867 called the National Grange of the Patrons of Husbandry (commonly called the Grange). While the group was fundamentally nonpolitical, it urged state legislation to regulate railroad rates and practices. Although most of these laws were eventually repealed or drastically changed, they served as a basis for later regulation of utilities and railroads.

### grandfather clause
(law) A contract clause in a legal document granting a formal exemption to a rule or law based on previously existing conditions or circumstances.
(WTO) A World Trade Organization (WTO) provision that allows the original contracting parties to exempt from general WTO obligations mandatory domestic legislation which is inconsistent with WTO provisions, but which existed before the WTO/GATT was signed. Newer members may also "grandfather" domestic legislation if that is agreed to in negotiating the terms of accession.

### grantee
(U.S. foreign trade zones) A public or private corporation to which the privilege of establishing, operating or maintaining a foreign trade zone has been given. *See* foreign trade zone; Foreign Trade Zone Board; Foreign Trade Zone Act; operator; zone user; subzones.

### green card
(U.S. immigration) An identity card (visa) issued by the U.S. Citizenship and Immigration Services Bureau (formerly, the U.S. Immigration and Naturalization Service) entitling a foreign national to enter and reside in the United States as a permanent resident.

### green line
*See* China green line.

### grey list
(U.S.) A list of disreputable end users in nations of concern for missile proliferation from the U.S. intelligence community. Licensing officials in the U.S. Departments of Commerce and State use this list as a cross-reference when reviewing export license applications for commodities listed in the Missile Technology Control Regime (MTCR) Equipment and Technology Annex.

### grid
(foreign exchange) Fixed margin within which exchange rates are allowed to fluctuate.

### gross
(general) 12 dozen or 144 articles.
(finance) The total amount before any deductions have been made.

### gross axle weight rating (GAWR)
(logistics) An axle manufacturer's maximum weight rating for a truck axle and the proportion of the truck's weight that may be carried by that axle. *See* gross vehicle weight rating.

### gross domestic product (GDP)
(economics) A measure of the market value of all goods and services produced within the boundaries of a nation, regardless of asset ownership. Unlike gross national product, GDP excludes receipts from that nation's business operations in foreign countries, as well as the share of reinvested earning in foreign affiliates of domestic corporations. *See* gross national product.

### gross national product (GNP)
(economics) A measure of the market value of all goods and services produced by the labor and property of a nation. Includes receipts from that nation's business operation in foreign countries, as well as the share of reinvested earnings in foreign affiliates of domestic corporations. *See* gross domestic product.

### gross ton
(measure) A unit of mass or weight measure equal to 2,240 pounds.

### gross tonnage
(shipping) The capacity of a vessel (not cargo) expressed in vessel tons. It is determined by dividing by 100 the contents, in cubic feet, of the vessels closed-in spaces. (A vessel ton is 100 cubic feet.) The register of a vessel states both gross and net tonnage.

### gross vehicle weight
(logistics) The total weight of a vehicle and its load.

### gross vehicle weight rating (GVWR)
(logistics) A truck manufacturer's stated maximum loaded weight of a vehicle including the vehicle itself, fuel, fluids and a full load of cargo. *See* gross axle weight rating.

### gross weight
(shipping) The full weight of a shipment, including goods and packaging. *See* tare weight.

### Group of Five (G-5)
Similar to the Group of Seven (G-7), with the exception of Canada and Italy.

### Group of Seven (G-7)
Group comprising the major industrialized nations in economic terms, which in view of the global economic importance of the member states have made it their objective to coordinate domestic economic policies. The coordination of economic, exchange rate and monetary policy aims is achieved both at government, central bank and also on other institutionalized levels. Member states are the USA, France, Great Britain, Germany, Japan, Canada, and Italy.

### Group of Ten (G-10)
A group of originally 10 countries (following Switzerland's accession, 11) comprising Belgium, Germany, France, Great Britain, Italy, Japan, Canada, Holland, Sweden and the United States, who within the framework of the General Arrangements to Borrow (GAB) have decided to put the equivalent of 17 billion in Special Drawing Rights (SDRs) in their various currencies at the International Monetary Fund's (IMF) disposal for granting loans. The Group of Ten plays an important role in discussions concerning international monetary policy. The Group of Ten is also called the Paris Club.

### Group of Fifteen (G-15)
The G-15, established in 1990, consists of relatively prosperous or large developing countries. The G-15 discusses the benefits of mutual cooperation in improving their international economic positions. Members include: Algeria, Argentina, Brazil, Egypt, India, Indonesia, Jamaica, Malaysia (a very active member), Mexico, Nigeria, Peru, Senegal, Venezuela, Yugoslavia, and Zimbabwe.

### Group of Twenty-Four (G-24)
A grouping of finance ministers from 24 developing country members of the International Monetary Fund. The Group, representing eight countries from each of the African, Asian, and Latin American country groupings in the Group of 77, was formed in 1971 to counterbalance the influence of the Group of Ten.

### Group of Seventy-Seven (G-77)
A grouping of developing countries which had its origins in the early 1960s. This numerical designation persists, although membership had increased to more than 120 coun-

G

tries. The G-77 functions as a caucus for the developing countries on economic matters in many forums including the United Nations.

**GSP**
*See* Generalized System of Preferences.

**GST**
(Canada) Goods and Services Tax. A Canadian tax that is payable on most goods and services (imported and domestic) at the rate of 7.0 percent.

**guanxi**
(China) Chinese for relationships or connections. More specifically, the network of business and personal relationships that support success in an endeavor. Includes connections, clout, favors given and favors owed, trust, courtesy, and gifts (not bribery).

**guarani**
The currency of Paraguay. 1G=100 centesimos.

**guarantor**
(law) An individual or legal entity that makes a guaranty, by which the guarantor agrees to be held liable for another's debt or performance. *See* guaranty.

**guaranty**
(law) A contract by which one person (the guarantor) agrees to pay another's debt or to perform another's obligation only if that other individual or legal entity fails to pay or perform. A guaranty is usually a separate contract from the principal agreement, and therefore the guarantor is secondarily liable to the third person. *See* guarantor; surety.

**Guidelines for Trade Data Interchange (GTDI)**
(computers/data interchange) A set of trade data interchange rules first published in 1981 in Europe and enhanced at later dates with the goal of achieving wider acceptance. GTDI and other standards (such as American National Standards Institute ANSI X12) seek to facilitate Electronic Data Interchange (EDI), which is the direct transfer of business data between computers. GTDI led to the UN/EDIFACT standards. Uniformity in international rules for trade data interchange, however, remains an unfulfilled goal. Competing standards and legacy systems have led to the failure of countries and companies to adopt a single standard. *See* American National Standards Institute, EDI, UN/EDIFACT.

**guilder**
The currency of:
Aruba, 1 Af = 100 cents.
Netherlands Antilles, 1 Naf = 100 cents;
Suriname, 1 Sf = 100 cents.
The former currency of the Netherlands. The new currency of the Netherlands is the European Union Euro. €1 = 100 cents.

**Gulf Cooperation Council (GCC)**
The six member countries (Saudi Arabia, Kuwait, the United Arab Emirates, Bahrain, Qatar, and Oman) of the Gulf Cooperation Council (GCC) control half the proven oil reserves outside the Soviet Union, and account for about 40 percent of all the oil moving in international trade. The GCC was created in 1981, largely in response to the outbreak of the Iran-Iraq war. In creating the GCC, the members tried to maintain the balance of power in the Gulf by strengthening multilateral cooperation in security and economic matters. As regards trade, the GCC is only a policy-coordinating forum; the Council cannot impose policies on the members. GCC headquarters are in Riyadh, Saudi Arabia. The presidency of the GCC rotates yearly among the rulers of the member countries. Contact: Gulf Cooperation Council, PO Box 7153, Riyadh 11462, Saudi Arabia; Tel: [966] (1) 482-7777; Telex: (1) 403635; Fax: [966] (1) 482-9089; Web: www.gcc-sg.org.

**hallmark**
An impression made on gold and silverware introduced in the beginning of the fourteenth century in England to identify the quality of the metal used.

**handling costs**
(logistics) Costs related to moving, transferring, and preparing inventory for shipment, but not the shipping charges themselves.

**Handymax**
(shipping) A small bulk or oil tanker vessel of 30,001 to 50,000 dwt that is a larger version of the popular Handysize vessel.

**Handysize**
(shipping) A small bulk or oil tanker vessel that is suited to tie up at a T2 type pier. These vessels are a maximum of 560 to 600ft (171-183m) in length and a maximum of 30,000 dwt. These vessels are more maneuverable and have shallower draft than larger vessels and make up the majority of the world's ocean-going cargo fleet.

**harbor fees**
(shipping) Charges assessed to users for use of a harbor, used generally for maintenance of the harbor. *See* users fees.

**harbor master**
(shipping) The person who administers and oversees the operations of a port, including harbor traffic, anchorages and berths. A harbor master typically has the experience of a certified master mariner with excellent knowledge of the port and surrounding areas.

**harbor pilot**
(shipping) A person qualified and typically licensed to guide ships through channels going into or out of a port or in specified waters.

**hard loan**
(banking) A foreign loan that must be paid in hard money.

**hard money (currency)**
(general) (a) Currency of a nation having stability in the country and abroad. Refers to currency that is accepted internationally and freely convertible. (b) Coins, in contrast with paper currency, or soft money.
(finance) Describes a situation in which interest rates are high and loans are difficult to arrange. synonymous with dear money.

**hard top container**
(shipping/logistics) A shipping container that has a roof which can be opened on hinges or lifted off. These two features facilitate loading through the top of the container, especially for shipping heavy equipment that has to be loaded from the top with a crane.

**Harmonized Standards**
Technical product specifications which have been established by various European standards organizations such as the European Committee for Standardization (CEN) and European Committee for Electrotechnical Standardization (CENELEC). *See* CE marking

**Harmonized System (HS)**
A multipurpose international goods classification system designed to be used by manufacturers, transporters, exporters, importers, customs, statisticians, and others in classifying goods moving in international trade under a single commodity code.

Developed under the auspices of the Customs Cooperation Council (CCC), an international Customs organization in Brussels, this code is a hierarchically structured product nomenclature containing approximately 5,000 headings and subheadings describing the articles moving in international trade. It is organized into 99 chapters arranged in 22 sections with the sections generally covering an industry (e.g., Section XI, Textiles and Textile Articles) and the chapters covering the various materials and products of the industry (e.g., Chapter 50—Silk; Chapter 55—Man-made Staple Fibers; Chapter 57—Carpets). The basic code contains 4-digit headings and 6-digit subheadings.

(U.S.) The United States has added digits for tariff and statistical purposes. In the United States, duty rates are in the 8-digit level; statistical suffixes at the 10-digit level. The Harmonized System (HS) supplanted the U.S. Tariff Schedule (TSUSA) in January 1989.

For the United States, the HS numbers are the numbers that are entered on the actual export and import documents. Any other commodity code classification number (SIC, SITC, end-use, etc.) are just rearrangements and transformations of the original HS numbers.

*See* Harmonized Tariff Schedule of the United States.

### Harmonized Tariff Schedule
### of the United States (HTS or HTSUS)

(U.S.) An organized listing of goods and their duty rates which is used by U.S. Customs as the basis for classifying imported products and therefore establishing the duty to be charged and providing the U.S. Census with statistical information about imports and exports. The categorization of product listings in the HTSUS is based on the international Harmonized Commodity Description and Coding System developed under the auspices of the Customs Cooperation Council (Harmonized System, HS).

Familiarity with the organization of the HTSUS facilitates the classification process. The tariff schedule is divided into various sections and chapters dealing separately with merchandise in broad product categories. These categories, for example, separately cover animal products, vegetable products, products of various basic materials such as wood, textiles, plastics, rubber, and steel and other metal products in various stages of manufacture. Other sections encompass chemicals, machinery and electrical equipment, and other specified or non-enumerated products. The last section, Section XXII, covers certain exceptions from duty and special statutory exceptions.

In Sections I through XXI, products are classifiable (1) under items or descriptions which name them, known as an eo nomine provision; (2) under provisions of general description; (3) under provisions which identify them by component material; or (4) under provisions which encompass merchandise in accordance with its actual or principal use. When two or more provisions seem to cover the same merchandise, the prevailing provision is determined in accordance with the legal notes and the General Rules of Interpretation for the tariff schedule. Also applicable are tariff classification principles contained in administrative precedents or in the case law of the U.S. Court of International Trade (formerly the U.S. Customs Court) or the U.S.Court of Appeals for the Federal Circuit Court (formerly the U.S. Court of Customs and Patent Appeals).

The Harmonized Tariff Schedules of the United States also contain two rates of duty for each commodity listed. Column 1 duty rates are low and apply to imports from countries that have achieved Most Favored Nation (MFN) trading status with the United States. Column 2 duty rates apply to imports from countries that do not have Most Favored Nation (MFN) trading status with the United States.

The Office of Tariff Affairs and Trade Agreements of the U.S. International Trade Commission is responsible for publishing the Schedule. The latest edition can be found online at http://hotdocs.usitc.gov/tariff_chapters_current/toc.html. Adobe Acrobat PDF versions, including those of prior years, are downloadable at Web: www.usitc.gov/taffairs.htm. Print and CD-ROM versions are available from the U.S. Government Printing office at http://bookstore.gpo.gov; Tel: [1] [866] 512-8000. *See* classification; Harmonized System.

### Harter Act
(shipping) Legislation protecting a ship's owner against claims for damage resulting from the behavior of the vessel's crew, provided the ship left port in a seaworthy condition, properly manned and equipped.

### hatch
(shipping) The opening in the deck of a vessel which gives access to the cargo hold.

### haulage
(shipping) The local transport of goods. Also the charge(s) made for hauling freight on carts, drays or trucks. Also called cartage or drayage.

### hawala
(banking) An informal worldwide network of businesses that offer foreign exchange and international funds transfer services to clients, but operate outside of traditional western banking channels.

Originating in India (*hawala* means "providing a code" in Hindi), the hawala system is often the only means of currency exchange and funds transfer in countries and regions where no banking services are offered to individuals and small businesses.

Hawala transactions are often simply legitimate transfers of funds from overseas workers to their families back home. However, the system is coming under scrutiny as it is also a favored conduit of funds by money launderers, drug dealers, arms dealers and terrorists.

In extremely bureaucratic countries such as India, a bank transfer might be illegal or could take as long as a month to complete. Hawala transactions, on the other hand, are often completed in as little as three days, regardless of official regulations.

Hawala dealers are often able to offer more favorable foreign exchange rates and quicker turnaround time because they typically operate outside of government control, do not use standard banking records and do not pay taxes.

As a result, hawala operations are legal and subject to government control in some countries, but entirely illegal in others. In 1994 the U.S. required hawala dealers to register with the government. The hawala system operates primarily in the Middle East, North Africa and Central, South and East Asia, but the network is worldwide.

How it works

An individual gives a local hawala dealer cash and asks that it be transferred to a named individual in a foreign country. The dealer charges the remitter a transfer fee of from 1 to 4 percent for large transactions and from 5 to 20 percent for small transactions.

The hawala dealer than calls, faxes or e-mails (in code) a counterpart in another part of the world with instructions to give the funds to the named individual who uses a password or code as identification when collecting the money. In India the codes typically involve animals, (e.g., "five pigs" or "twelve hens.")

Unlike typical western banking, the hawala dealer does not forward the funds to his counterpart. Both dealers make a record in their ledgers with the assumption that a counterbalancing transaction will occur at a later date. If one dealer has paid out a substantial sum over time to another dealer, a compensating shipment of valuable or saleable goods may be made. Such a shipment might include gold jewelry (such as 22-24 karat gold) that has an internationally known market value, or merchandise that the dealer can easily sell in his local market.

### Hawley-Smoot Act
*See* Smoot-Hawley Tariff Act of 1930.

### hazardous materials
(shipping) A substance or material which has been determined to be capable of posing a risk to health, safety, and property when transported in commerce. (U.S.) A substance or material which has been determined by the U.S. Secretary of Transportation to be capable of posing an unreasonable risk to health, safety, and property when transported in commerce and which has been so designated. Title 49, Code of Federal Regulations (U.S.) Transportation—Parts 100-199, govern the transportation of hazardous materials. Hazardous materials may be transported domestically, but they may be classified as Dangerous Goods when transported internationally by air. *See* restricted article; dangerous goods.

### hazmat
(logistics) An abbreviation for hazardous materials. *See* hazardous materials.

### heavy lift
(shipping) Articles too heavy to be lifted by a ship's tackle.

### heavy lift charge
(shipping) A charge made for lifting (onloading or offloading) articles too heavy to be lifted by a ship's tackle. Usually requiring the use of heavy lift equipment at a port.

### heavy lift vessel
(shipping) A vessel with heavy lift cranes and other equipment designed to be self-sustaining in the handling of heavy cargo.

### hedge
To offset. Also, a security that has offsetting qualities. Thus one attempts to "hedge" against inflation by the purchase of securities whose values should respond to inflationary developments. Securities having these qualities are "inflation hedges." *See* hedging; delta hedging.

### hedge ratio
(finance/foreign exchange) The amount of an underlying instrument or the number of options which are needed to hedge a covered option. The hedge ratio is determined by the size of the delta. *See* delta; delta hedging.

### hedging
(finance/foreign exchange) A type of economic insurance used by dealers in commodities, foreign exchange and securities, manufacturers, and other producers to prevent loss due to price fluctuations. Hedging consists of counterbalancing a present sale or purchase by a purchase or sale of a similar commodity or of a different commodity, usually for delivery at some future date. The desired result is that the profit or loss on a current sale or purchase be offset by the loss or profit on the future purchase or sale. *See* arbitrage; delta hedging.

### high density
(shipping) The compression of flat or standard bales of cotton to high density of approximately 32 pounds. This compression usually applies to cotton exported or shipped coast to coast.

### high security bolt seal
(security) A bolt seal consisting of a metal rod, threaded or unthreaded, flexible or rigid, with a formed head and secured with a separate locking mechanism.

### high security cable seal
(security) A cable seal consisting of a cable and a locking mechanism. On a one-piece seal, the locking or seizing mechanism is permanently attached to one end of the cable. A two-piece cable seal has a separate locking mechanism, which slips onto the cable or prefabricated cable end.

### high security padlock/handcuff seal
(security) A padlock/handcuff seal consisting of a locking body with a bail attached. Examples of this type of seal are wire shackle padlock and keyless padlock seals.

### hitchment
(shipping) The marrying of two or more portions of one shipment that originate at different geographical locations, moving under one bill of lading, from one shipper to one consignee. Authority for this service must be granted by tariff publication.

### hold
(shipping) The space below deck in a vessel used to carry cargo.

### hold for pickup
(shipping) Freight to be held at the carrier's destination location for pickup by the recipient.

### hold harmless contract
(law) An agreement by which one party accepts responsibility for all damages and other liability that arise from a transaction, relieving the other party of any such liability. A commercial tenant, for example, may agree to hold a landlord harmless for all liabilities that could arise from injuries to customers who enter the premises. A guarantor may agree to guaranty a person's debt only if that person agrees to hold the guarantor harmless from all damages that may arise if the person fails to pay the debt. A hold harmless contract provides complete indemnity. *See* guaranty; indemnity; surety.

### holder in due course
(law) An individual or legal entity (holder) who possesses a negotiable instrument, document of title, or similar document, and who took possession for value, in good faith, and without notice of any other individual's or legal entity's claim or defense against the instrument or document. A buyer, for example, who receives title to goods after remitting the contract price to the seller is a holder in due course, provided the buyer has no notice of any lien or other claim against the goods. A holder in due course is generally protected from the claims of third parties against the item transferred, and thus the only recourse of a third party is against the person that transferred the title, instrument, or other item to the holder in due course.

### hong
A Chinese transliteration from Cantonese meaning trading company. The term was primarily used in the west from the early 1800s through the 1900s to refer to Hong Kong and Macau trading firms that conducted internal trade with southern China.

### honor
(banking) To pay or to accept a draft complying with the terms of credit. *See* bill of exchange.

### hopper cars
(railroads/logistics) A rail car designed for top-loading and bottom-unloading of dry bulk commodities such as iron ore. Some hopper cars have hatched or sliding roofs for protection of cargo from the elements.

### horizontal export trading company
An export trading company which exports a range of similar or identical products supplied by a number of manufacturers or other producers. Webb-Pomerene Organizations, trade-grouped organized export trading companies, and an export trading company formed by an association of agri-

cultural cooperatives are prime examples of horizontally organized export trading companies.

### horizontal integration
(economics/management) The expansion, acquisition or merger of firms or business activities that produce or deliver similar products to similar markets. For example, a supermarket chain that purchases another supermarket chain. *See* vertical integration.

### house air waybill (HAWB)
(shipping) A bill of lading issued by a freight forwarder for consolidated air freight shipments. In documentary letter of credit transactions HAWBs are treated exactly the same as conventional air waybills, provided they indicate that the issuer itself assumes the liability as carrier or is acting as the agent of a named carrier, or if the credit expressly permits the acceptance of a HAWB. *See* air waybill; bill of lading.

### house-to-house
(shipping) A term usually used to indicate a container yard to container yard (CY/CY) shipment.

### hub and spoke routing
(shipping) Aircraft routing service pattern that feeds traffic from many cities into a central hub designed to connect with other flights to final destinations. The system maximizes operating flexibility by connecting many markets through a central hub with fewer flights than would be required to connect each pair of cities in an extensive system.

### hull
(shipping) The outer shell of a vessel usually made of steel.

### hump
(shipping) That part of a rail track which is elevated so that when a car is pushed up on "the hump" and uncoupled it runs down on the other side by gravity.

### hundredweight pricing
(shipping) Special pricing for multiple-piece shipments traveling to one destination which are rated on the total weight of the shipment (usually over 100 pounds) as opposed to rating on a per package basis.

# I

### identical merchandise
(U.S. Customs) In establishing the customs value of merchandise exported to the United States, identical merchandise is merchandise that is: (1) Identical in all respects to the merchandise being appraised, (2) Produced in the same country as the merchandise being appraised, and (3) Produced by the same person as the merchandise being appraised.
If merchandise meeting all these criteria cannot be found, then identical merchandise is merchandise satisfying the first two criteria but produced by a different person than the producer of merchandise being appraised.
Note: Merchandise can be identical to the merchandise being appraised and still show minor differences in appearance.
Exclusion: Identical merchandise does not include merchandise that incorporates or reflects engineering, development, artwork, design work, and plans and sketches provided free or at reduced cost by the buyer and undertaken in the United States.
*See* valuation; transaction value; computed value; similar merchandise.

### igloo
(air freight/logistics) An air freight cargo container (unit load device or ULD) designed to fit the interior contours (usually of an upper deck) of a specific airplane. The name comes from the fact that many of these containers are in the shape of an igloo. *See* unit load device and the appendix "Guide to Air Freight Containers."

### IMDG
*See* International Maritime Dangerous Goods Code.

### immediate delivery
(U.S. Customs) An alternate U.S. Customs entry procedure which provides for immediate release of a shipment in certain cases. Application must be made to Customs for a Special Permit for Immediate Delivery on Customs Form 3461 prior to the arrival of the merchandise. If the application is approved, the shipment is released expeditiously following arrival. An entry summary must then be filed in proper form and estimated duties deposited within 10 working days of release. *See* entry.

### immediate transportation entry
(U.S. Customs) A form of U.S. Customs entry which allows imported merchandise to be forwarded from the port of original entry to another final destination for customs clearance. Merchandise travels in bond, without appraisal, from the original port of entry to the final destination, where it is then inspected by customs. *See* entry.

### immigration
The entry of foreign nationals into a country for the purpose of establishing permanent residence. *See* green card.

### implied agency
*See* agency.

### implied conditions
(insurance) Certain implied conditions are not written into marine insurance policies, but they are so basic to understanding between underwriter and assured that the law gives them much the same effect as if written. Thus, it is implied: (1) that the assured will exercise the utmost good faith in disclosing to his underwriter all facts material to the risk when applying for insurance; (2) that the generally established usages of trade applicable to the insured subject

matter are followed; and (3) that the assured shall not contribute to loss through willful fault or negligence. *See* special marine policy.

### implied volatility
*See* volatility.

### implied warranties
(insurance) Legal decisions have established two important implied warranties in marine insurance policies, that of legality of the venture and that of seaworthiness. The latter is of little concern today since insurance policies commonly waive the warranty of seaworthiness by stating that seaworthiness is admitted as between the assured and the insurer. The insurer is not at liberty, however, to waive the implied warranty of legality. Such a waiver would be against public policy and the law of the land. *See* special marine policy.

### import
(a) To receive goods and services from abroad. (b) An imported item.

### import credit
(banking) A commercial letter of credit issued for the purpose of financing the importation of goods. *See* letter of credit.

### import duty
(customs) Any tax on items imported. *See* tariff; Harmonized Tariff Schedule of the United States.

### import license
(customs) A document required and issued by some national governments authorizing the importation of goods.

### import quota
(customs) A protective ruling establishing limits on the quantity of a particular product that can be imported. Quotas are a means of restricting imports by the issuance of licenses to importers, assigning each a quota, after determination of the total amount of any commodity which is to be imported during a period. Import licenses may also specify the country from which the importer must purchase the goods. *See* quota; tariff quotas.

### import quota auctioning
(customs) The process of auctioning the right to import specified quantities of quota-restricted goods.

### import relief
Any of several measures imposed by a government to temporarily restrict imports of a product or commodity to protect domestic producers from competition.

### import restrictions
Any one of a series of tariff and non-tariff barriers imposed by an importing nation to control the volume of goods coming into the country from other countries. May include the imposition of tariffs or import quotas, restrictions on the amount of foreign currency available to cover imports, a requirement for import deposits, the imposition of import surcharges, or the prohibition of various categories of imports. *See* tariff; non-tariff barriers.

### import sensitive producers
Domestic producers whose economic viability is threatened by competition (quality, price or service) from imported products.

### import service
*See* export service.

### import substitution
A strategy which emphasizes the replacement of imports with domestically produced goods, rather than the production of goods for export, to encourage the development of domestic industry.

### importer
The individual, firm or legal entity that brings articles of trade from a foreign source into a domestic market in the course of trade.

### importer number
(U.S. Customs) A unique 9- to 11-position alphanumeric code assigned by U.S. Customs and Border Protection to identify a person or company that imports merchandise.

### Importers Manual USA
(publication) A reference book detailing specific requirements for importing each of the 99 Chapters (categories of goods) of the Harmonized Tariff Schedule of the United States, plus extensive sections on banking, letters of credit, foreign exchange, packing, shipping, insurance, and U.S. Customs Entry. Published by World Trade Press, 1450 Grant Ave., Novato, CA 94945 USA; Tel: [1] (415) 898-1124; Fax: [1] (415) 898-1080; Web: www.worldtrade-press.com.

### imports
Commodities of foreign origin as well as goods of domestic origin returned to the producing country with no change in condition, or after having been processed and/or assembled in other countries.

(U.S.) For statistical purposes, imports to the U.S. are classified by type of transaction: (a) Merchandise entered for immediate consumption. ("duty free" merchandise and merchandise on which duty is paid on arrival); (b) Merchandise withdrawn for consumption from U.S. Customs bonded warehouses, and U.S. Foreign Trade Zones; (c) Merchandise entered into U.S. Customs bonded warehouses and U.S. Foreign Trade Zones from foreign countries.

### imports for consumption
(U.S. Customs) The total of merchandise that has physically cleared through U.S. Customs either entering domestic consumption channels immediately or entering after withdrawal for consumption from bonded warehouses under U.S. Customs custody or from U.S. Foreign Trade Zones. Many countries use the term "special imports" to designate statistics compiled on this basis. *See* consumption entry.

### imports of goods and services (U.S.)
(economics) Represent the sum of all payments for merchandise imports, military expenditures, transportation and travel costs, other private and U.S. government services, and income and service payments to foreign parent companies by their affiliates operating in the United States. By far the largest component of this category is merchandise imports, which includes all goods bought or otherwise transferred from a foreign country to the United States.

### impost
A tax, usually an import duty. *See* tariff.

### impound
(law/customs) (a) To seize or hold. (b) To place in protective custody by order of a court (e.g., impounded property, impounded records).

### in bond
(U.S. Customs) A procedure under which goods are transported or warehoused under customs supervision until they are either formally entered into the customs territory of the United States and duties paid, or until they are exported from the United States.

The procedure is so named because the cargo moves under the carrier's bond (financial liability assured by the carrier) from the gateway sea port or airport and remains "in bond" until customs releases the cargo at the inland customs point.

This procedure is used in several ways:

(1) To postpone the payment of import duties on high duty merchandise, (such as alcoholic beverages), until they are needed,

(2) To hold goods that may or may not meet a requirement of customs until a determination is made and the importer decides to enter the goods or re-export them,

(3) To effect the transport of goods originating in one foreign country through the United States for export to a third country without having to pay customs duties.

*See* temporary importation under bond.

### in bond goods
*See* in bond.

### in bond shipment
(customs) An import or export shipment which has not been cleared by U.S. Customs officials. *See* in bond.

### in-bond system
(U.S. Customs) A part of U.S. Customs' Automated Commercial System, controls merchandise from the point of unloading at the port of entry or exportation. The system works with the input of departures (from the port of unlading), arrivals, and closures (accountability of arrivals). *See* Automated Commercial System; in bond.

### in personam
(law) Against the person. In personam jurisdiction, for example, is a court's authority in a legal action to subject a person to its order or judgment.

### in rem
(law) Against the thing. In rem jurisdiction, for example, is a court's authority in a legal action to determine title to, or affect interests in, property of the parties.

### in trust (goods/documents)
(banking) In documentary collections, when a bank releases documents to the importer/buyer to allow him to inspect them prior to payment.

### inbound logistics
The entire process of planning, acquiring and controlling the flow of raw materials, components, parts, sub-assemblies and components from outside sources (vendors, suppliers and subsidiaries) into a production process. Inbound logistics can occur directly from the outside supplier to the production floor or indirectly through intermediate storage facilities. *See* logistics.

### incentive
(economics) A motivational force that stimulates people to greater activity or increased efficiency.

### incentive rate
(logistics) A special lower freight rate applied to large or heavy loads to encourage larger volume shipments.

### Inchmaree Clause
(insurance) An insurance policy extension to cover loss resulting from a latent defect of the carrying vessel's hull or machinery which is not discoverable by due diligence. (So-called for a celebrated legal decision involving a vessel of that name.) Latent defect is not, by law, recoverable from the vessel owner, and the Inchmaree Clause thus plugs a gap that would otherwise exist in complete insurance protection. Loss resulting from errors of navigation or management of the vessel by the master or the crew, and for which the vessel owner is likewise relieved of liability by law, is also covered by the Inchmaree Clause. *See* special marine policy.

### income
(economics) Money or its equivalent, earned or accrued, arising from the sale of goods or services.

### Incorporated (Inc.)
(South Africa) Designation for a private limited liability corporation with limited liability to shareholders but with joint and several liability to the directors.

(United States) Designation for a corporation with limited liability to shareholders.

### Incoterms
A codification of international rules for the uniform interpretation of common contract clauses in export/import transactions involving goods. Developed and issued by the International Chamber of Commerce (ICC) in Paris. The version which is currently valid is from 2000. The thirteen Incoterms 2000 are:

(1) Ex Works (EXW),

(2) Free Carrier (FCA),

(3) Free Alongside Ship (FAS),

(4) Free On Board FOB),

(5) Cost and Freight CFR),

(6) Cost, Insurance and Freight (CIF),

(7) Carriage Paid To (CPT),

(8) Carriage and Insurance Paid To (CIP),

(9) Delivered At Frontier (DAF),

(10) Delivered Ex Ship (DES),

(11) Delivered Ex Quay (DEQ),

(12) Delivered Duty Unpaid (DDU), and

(13) Delivered Duty Paid (DDP).

Refer to individual listings for definitions of these terms. Also refer to the Appendix Guide to Incoterms 2000. For a book fully describing responsibilities of the seller and the buyer in each term, contact: International Chamber of Commerce (ICC), 38, Cours Albert 1$^{er}$, 75008 Paris, France; Tel: [33] (1) 49-53-28-28; Fax: [33] (1) 49-53-28-59; Web: www.iccwbo.org; In U.S. contact: ICC Publishing, Inc., 156 Fifth Avenue, New York, NY 10010 USA; Tel: [1] (212) 206-1150; Fax: [1] (212) 633-6025; Web: www.iccbooksusa.com.

### indemnify
(insurance/law) To compensate for actual loss sustained. Many insurance policies and all bonds promise to "indemnify" the insureds. Under such a contract, there can be no recovery until the insured has actually suffered a loss, at which time he or she is entitled to be compensated for the damage that has occurred (i.e. to be restored to the same financial position enjoyed before the loss).

### indemnity
(insurance/law) An agreement to reimburse another individual or legal entity who incurs a loss that is covered by the agreement. An indemnity against loss may be partial or whole. A buyer may obtain indemnity insurance, for example, to insure against damage to or destruction of goods that may occur after title has passed to the buyer.

(finance) A bond protecting the insured against losses from others failing to fulfill their obligations.

(investments) An option to buy or sell a specific quantity of a stock at a state price within a given time period.

(law) An act of legislation, granting exemption from prosecution to certain people.

### independent action
(shipping) The right of a conference member to depart from the common freight rates, terms or conditions of the conference without the need for prior approval of the conference. *See* conference.

### indexed currency borrowings
(banking/finance) Borrowings in a foreign currency where the rate of interest is linked to an agreed scale.

### indexed currency option note
(banking/finance) Note denominated and paying interest in one currency but whose redemption value is linked to an exchange rate for another currency. Also called Heaven and Hell Bond.

### individual validated license
(U.S.) Written approval by the U.S. Department of Commerce granting permission, which is valid for 2 years, for the export of a specified quantity of products or technical data to a single recipient. Individual validated licenses also are required, under certain circumstances, as authorization for re export of U.S.-origin commodities to new destinations abroad. *See* United States Department of Commerce.

### indorsement
*See* endorsement.

### industrial list
The Coordinating Committee for Multilateral Export Controls (CoCom) industrial list contains dual-use items whose export are controlled for strategic reasons. *See* Coordinating Committee for Multilateral Export Controls.

### industrial policy
(economics) Encompasses traditional government policies intended to provide a favorable economic climate for the development of industry in general or specific industrial sectors. Instruments of industrial policy may include tax incentives to promote investments or exports, direct or indirect subsidies, special financing arrangements, protection against foreign competition, worker training programs, regional development programs, assistance for research and development, and measures to help small business firms. Historically, the term industrial policy has been associated with some degree of centralized economic planning or indicative planning, but this connotation is not always intended by its contemporary advocates.

### Industry Consultations Program
(U.S.) An advisory committee structure created by the Trade Act of 1974, expanded by the Trade Agreements Act of 1979, and amended by the Omnibus Trade and Competitiveness Act of 1988. Jointly sponsored by the U.S. Department of Commerce and the U.S. Trade Representative, the program includes over 500 industry executives who provide advice and information to the U.S. government on trade policy matters. The advisors focus on objectives and bargaining positions for multilateral trade negotiations, bilateral trade negotiations, and other trade-related matters. Members of the committees are appointed by the Secretary of Commerce and the U.S. Trade Representative.

The present structure consists of 17 Industry Sector Advisory Committees (ISACs), 3 Industry Functional Advisory Committees (IFACs), a Committee of Chairs, and an Industry Policy Advisory Committee (IPAC). The focus of the 3 Functional Advisory Committees are: (1) Customs Matters, (2) Standards, and (3) Intellectual Property Rights. The focus of the 17 Industry Sector Advisory Committees are: (1) Aerospace Equipment, (2) Capital Goods, (3) Chemicals and Allied Products, (4) Consumer Goods, (5) Electronics and Instrumentation, (6) Energy, (7) Ferrous Ores and Metals, (8) Footwear, Leather, and Leather Products, (9) Building Products and Other Materials, (10) Lumber and Wood Products, (11) Nonferrous Ores and Metals, (12) Paper and Paper Products, (13) Services, (14) Small and Minority Business, (15) Textiles and Apparel, (16) Transportation, Construction, and Agricultural Equipment, (17) Wholesaling and Retailing.
*See* Advisory Committee on Trade Policy and Negotiations.

### Industry Functional Advisory Committee
*See* Industry Consultations Program.

### Industry Partnership Programs (IPP)
(United States) A series of U.S. Customs and Border Protection (CBP) programs designed to engage the international trade community in a cooperative relationship with CBP in the war on drugs and terrorism. The IPP promotes the importance of employing best business practices and enhanced security measures to eliminate the trade's exposure to narcotic smugglers and vulnerability to terrorist actions. The IPP proactively works with foreign manufacturers, exporters, carriers, importers, and many other industry sectors emphasizing a seamless security conscience environment throughout the entire commercial process.

Currently, the CBP has three active Industry Partnership Programs that are designed to deter and prevent narcotics smuggling and terrorist activities via commercial cargo and conveyances, which include the Carrier Initiative Program (CIP), the Business Anti-Smuggling Coalition (BASC) and the Americas Counter Smuggling Initiative (ACSI). For more information contact the CBP Industry Partnership Programs at: Tel: [1] (202) 927-0520; E-mail: industry.partnership@dhs.gov; Web: http://www.cbp.gov/xp/cgov/import/carriers/ipp.xml.

### Industry Policy Advisory Committee
*See* Industry Consultations Program.

### Industry Sector Advisory Committee
*See* Industry Consultations Program.

### Industry Subsector Analysis
(U.S.) Overseas market research for a given industry subsector (such as cardiological equipment for the medical equipment industry) that presents basic information about a foreign market such as market size, the competitive environment, primary end users, best prospect products, and market access information. Available as individual reports from the U.S. Department of Commerce, or on the National Trade Data Bank, U.S. Dept. of Commerce, Office of Business Analysis, HCHB Room 4885, Washington, DC 20230 USA; Tel: [1] (202) 482-1986; Web: www.stat-usa.gov/tradtest.nsf.

### infant industry argument
(economics) The view that "temporary protection" for a new industry or firm in a particular country through tariff and non-tariff barriers to imports can help it to become established and eventually competitive in world markets. Historically, new industries that are soundly based and efficiently operated have experienced declining costs as output expands and production experience is acquired. However, industries that have been established and operated with heavy dependence on direct or indirect government subsidies have sometimes found it difficult to relinquish that support. The rationale underlying the Generalized System of Preferences is comparable to that of the infant industry argument. *See* Generalized System of Preferences.

### inflammable
*See* flammable.

### inflammable liquids
*See* flammable liquids.

### inflation
(economics) Loss of purchasing power of money, caused by growth of the amount of money in circulation which, if the supply of goods stays the same or only increases at a slower rate, leads to an increase in prices.

### in-flight survey (IFS)
(U.S.) A survey of U.S. and foreign travelers departing the U.S. as a means of obtaining data on visitor characteristics, travel patterns and spending habits, and for supplying data on the U.S. international travel dollar accounts as well as to meet balance of payments estimation needs. The IFS covers about 70 percent of U.S. carriers and 35 percent of foreign carriers, who voluntarily choose to participate. Sample results are expanded to universe estimates to account for non response of passengers on each sampled flight, for coverage of all flights on each major airline route, and for

all international routes. The basis for the expansion is the number of passengers departing the United States, obtained from the U.S. Citizenship and Immigration Services Bureau (formerly, the Immigration and Naturalization Service).

### informal entry
(US Customs) A simplified import entry procedure accepted at the option of Customs for any noncommercial shipment (baggage) and any commercial shipment not over $1,000 in value. *See* entry.

### informed compliance
(US Customs) A shared responsibility wherein the US Customs Service effectively communicates its requirements to the trade, and the people and businesses subject to those requirements conduct their regulated activities in conformance with US laws and regulations.

### infrastructure
(economics) The basic structure of a nation's economy, including transportation, communications, and other public services, on which the economic activity relies.

### inherent vice
(shipping/insurance) Damage to goods which one can foresee is bound to occur during any normal transit, and which arises solely because of the nature or condition of the goods shipped. Such damage is said to arise from "inherent vice" which may be defined as an internal cause rather than an external cause of damage. An example of damage from inherent vice is deterioration of imperfectly cured skins.

Exclusion of insurance coverage for inherent vice is implied in every cargo policy. This type of exclusion is reinforced by the words "from any external cause" in the "all risks" coverage. The word "risk" itself implies that only fortuitous losses are intended to be covered. Insurance protects against hazards, not certainties.

### initial margin
(finance/foreign exchange) The amount of margin which has to be deposited with the clearing house both by the buyer and the seller through the respective broker and/or bank in order to establish a position in a futures contract.

### initial negotiating right (INR)
(WTO) A right held by a World Trade Organization (WTO) country to seek compensation for an impairment of a given bound tariff rate by another WTO country. INRs stem from past negotiating concessions and allow the INR holder to seek compensation for an impairment of tariff concessions regardless of its status as a supplier of the product in question. *See* World Trade Organization (WTO).

### injury
(U.S.) A finding by the U.S. International Trade Commission that imports are causing, or are likely to cause, harm to a U.S. industry. An injury determination is the basis for a Section 201 case. It is also a requirement in all antidumping and most countervailing duty cases, in conjunction with Commerce Department determinations on dumping and subsidization. *See* dumping; countervailing duty; Section 201.

### inland bill of lading
(shipping) A bill of lading used in transporting goods overland to the exporter's international carrier. Although a through bill of lading can sometimes be used, it is usually necessary to prepare both an inland bill of lading and an ocean bill of lading for export shipments. *See* bill of lading.

### inland carrier
(shipping) A transportation line which hauls import/export traffic between ports and inland points.

### Inland Pre-Arrival Review System (InPARS)
(Canada Customs) *See* Pre-Arrival Review System (PARS).

### InPARS
(Canada Customs) *See* Pre-Arrival Review System.

### insolvency
*See* bankruptcy.

### insourcing
(logistics) The sourcing of raw materials, component parts and finished goods from within a business organization. The opposite of outsourcing. *See* outsourcing.

### inspection certificate
A document confirming that goods have been inspected for conformity to a set of industry, customer, government or carrier specifications prior to shipment. Inspection certificates are generally obtained from independent, neutral testing organizations.

### instrument
(law) Any written document that gives formal expression to a legal agreement or act. *See* financial instrument.

### instruments of international traffic (IIT)
Empty articles such as pallets, tanks, cores, containers and the like.

### insulated container
(logistics) A shipping container designed to protect sensitive cargo from extremes in temperature. These containers are not heated or refrigerated, but can, for a limited time, keep inside temperatures from exceeding certain limits. Such containers are often used to transport electronics, electronic equipment, ammunition, some foods and other sensitive goods. *See* container, and the appendix "Guide to Ocean Freight Containers."

### insurable interest
(insurance) The financial interest of an individual or business in property, even if that individual is not the owner of the property.

A typical case of insurable interest is where title to goods has passed from the seller to the buyer, but where the seller has yet to receive payment, and still has exposure for loss.

**Example 1**: When a seller sells on FOB inland point terms, he transfers the title to the buyer before the commencement of the ocean voyage. In this case the obligation to place marine and war risk insurance rests, strictly speaking, with the buyer. However, it is customary in many trades for the seller on FOB terms (or similar terms), to obtain insurance, as well as ocean freight space, for account of the buyer.

This is, in effect, an agency relationship. It can be provided for by a policy clause reading: "to cover all shipments made by or to the assured for their own account as principals, or as agents for others and in which they have an insurable interest, or for the account of others from which written instructions to insure them have been received prior to any known or reported loss, damage or accident prior to sailing of vessel."

**Example 2:** The seller on FOB or other terms, under which the title passes to the buyer at some inland point of departure, will have a financial interest in the goods until payment has been received. This situation arises when the terms of payment call for sight draft against documents, or for acceptance at 30-60-90 days sight, or for open account. Under such circumstances, the seller will be well advised to place his own insurance to protect himself in the event that the loss or damage to the shipment impairs the buyer's desire to make payment as originally contemplated. For example, the buyer may be uninsured, or the buyer's coverage may be inadequate because of under-insurance or restricted conditions. The buyer's insurance company may be less liberal in loss adjustments than would the insurer of the seller or, because of currency restrictions, a foreign company may be hampered in its ability to transmit funds. *See* contingency insurance.

**insurance**
(general) A method whereby those concerned about some form of hazard contribute to a common fund usually an insurance company, out of which losses sustained by the contributors are paid.
(law) A contractual relationship that exists when one party (the insurer), for a consideration (the premium), agrees to reimburse another party (the insured) for loss to a specified subject (the risk) caused by designated contingencies (hazards or perils), or to pay in behalf of the insured all reasonable sums for which he may be liable to a third party (the claimant).

**insurance broker**
(insurance) An individual or firm who represents buyers of insurance and deals with insurance companies or their agents in arranging for insurance coverage for the buyer.
An insurance agent represents a single insurance company whereas an insurance broker is free to obtain insurance coverage from any insurance company.

**insurance certificate**
(insurance) A document indicating the type and amount of insurance coverage in force on a particular shipment. Used to assure the consignee that insurance is provided to cover loss of or damage to the cargo while in transit.
In some cases a shipper may issue a document that certifies that a shipment has been insured under a given open policy, and that the certificate represents and takes the place of such open policy, the provisions of which are controlling.
Because of the objections that an instrument of this kind did not constitute a "policy" within the requirements of letters of credit, it has become the practice to use a special marine policy. A special marine policy makes no reference to an open policy and stands on its own feet as an obligation of the underwriting company.
*See* special marine policy; declaration; bordereau; open policy.

**insurance company**
(insurance) An organization chartered under state or provincial laws to act as an insurer. In the United States, insurance companies are usually classified as fire and marine, life, casualty, and surety companies and may write only the kinds of insurance for which they are specifically authorized by their charters.

**insurance coverage**
(insurance) The total amount of insurance that is carried.

**insurance document**
*See* insurance certificate.

**insurance policy**
(insurance) Broadly, the entire written contract of insurance. More specifically, it is the basic written or printed document, as well as the coverage forms and endorsement added to it.

**insurance premium**
(insurance) The amount paid to an insurance company for coverage under an insurance policy.

**insured**
(insurance) The person(s) protected under an insurance contract (policy).

**insured value**
(insurance) The combined value of merchandise, inland freight, ocean freight, cost of packaging, freight forwarding charges, consular fees, and insurance cost, for which insurance is obtained.

**insurer**
(insurance) The party to the insurance contract who promises to indemnify losses or provide service; the insurance company.

**integrated cargo service**
(shipping) A blend of all segments of the cargo system providing the combined services of carrier, forwarder, handlers and agents.

**integrated carriers**
(shipping) Carriers that have both air and ground fleets; or other combinations, such as sea, rail, and truck. Since they usually handle large volumes, they are often less expensive and offer more diverse services than regular carriers.

**integrated logistics**
(shipping/management) The management of logistics operations as a system rather than as individual activities. Relates to the integration of the entire supply chain management process from just-in-time manufacturing/warehousing through final distribution to the ultimate consumer. Includes the merging of warehousing, packaging, local transportation, international transportation, local market warehousing and final distribution. *See* logistics.

**integrated logistics support (ILS)**
(logistics) The process of ensuring that all requirements for a logistics system are met. This encompasses all aspects of the supply chain and includes planning, funding, facilities, personnel, hardware and software.

**intellectual property**
(law) An original work that can be copyrighted, patented, or registered as a trademark or service mark. Ownership conferring the right to possess, use, or dispose of products created by human ingenuity, including patents, trademarks and copyrights. *See* copyright; patent; service mark; trademark.

**intellectual property rights**
(law) The ownership of the right to possess or otherwise use or dispose of products created by human ingenuity. *See* copyright; patent; service mark; trademark.

**INTELSAT**
*See* International Telecommunications Satellite Organization.

**intended**
(shipping) A reference which may appear on marine/ocean bills of lading, non-negotiable sea waybills and multimodal transport documents where the carrier reserves the right to change the port of loading, the ship or the port of discharge. Examples: "intended port of shipment Hamburg," "intended ocean vessel MV Swissahoi," "intended port of discharge Hong Kong."

**inter absentee**
(law) Among absent parties. An inter absentee contract, for example, is made between parties who do not meet face-to-face.

**Interagency Group on Countertrade**
(U.S.) Established in December 1988 under Executive Order 12661, reviews policy and negotiates agreements with other countries on countertrade and offsets. The IGC operates at the Assistant Secretary level, with the Department of Commerce as chair. Membership includes 11 other agencies: the Departments of Agriculture, Defense, Energy, Justice, Labor, State, Treasury, the Agency for International Development, the Federal Emergency Management Agency, the U.S. Trade Representative, and the Office of Management and Budget. Contact: Assistant Secretary of Trade Development, U.S. Department of Commerce, 14th Street and Constitution Ave. NW, Washington, DC 20230 USA; Tel: [1] (202) 482-1461. *See* countertrade; offsets.

**Inter-American Development Bank**
A regional financial institution established in 1959 to advance the economic and social development of 27 Latin American member countries. Contact: Inter-American Development Bank, 1300 New York Avenue NW, Washing-

ton, DC 20577; Tel: [1] (202) 623-1000; Fax: [1] (202) 623-3096; E-mail: pic@iadb.org; Web: www.iadb.org.

### interbank dealings
(banking) Dealings between the banks.

### interbank offered rate (IBOR)
(banking/finance) Rate of interest offered by banks for their loans to the most creditworthy banks for a large loan, for a specific period and in a specific currency. The best known one is the London Interbank Offered Rate (LIBOR), but they also exist for Abu Dhabi (ADIBOR), Amsterdam (AIBOR), Bahrein (BIBOR), Brussels (BRIBOR), Hong Kong (HIBOR) or (HKIBOR), Kuwait (KIBOR), Luxembourg (LUXIBOR), Madrid (MIBOR), Paris (PIBOR) (occasionally known as taux interbancaire offert à Paris - TIOP), Saudi Arabia (SAIBOR), Singapore (SIBOR), 6 month SDRs (SDRIBOR), Zurich (ZIBOR) and other financial centers.

### interchange
(logistics) (a) The transfer of freight from one carrier to another. (b) The transfer of transportation equipment from one carrier to another.
(data/computers) The transfer of electronic data from one computer to another. *See* EDI, UN/EDIFACT.

### interchange agreement
(shipping) An agreement which fixes specific accountability for use and maintenance of carrier-owned equipment. It formalizes terms and conditions under which equipment will be leased, in order to protect the carrier's financial and legal interest in the operation of the leased equipment.

### interchange point
(transportation/logistics) A location where one carrier delivers freight or freight transportation equipment to another carrier. *See* interchange, interchange agreement, interchange receipt.

### interchange receipt
(logistics) A document that states the condition of equipment at the time of interchange. *See* interchange agreement, interchange point.

### intercoastal carrier
(shipping) A carrier that transports cargo between ports of one nation.
(U.S. shipping) A carrier that transports cargo between U.S. east and west coast ports. Refers specifically to water carriers that travel through the Panama Canal.

### intercorporate hauling
(logistics) The act of a carrier transporting cargo for a subsidiary and charging a fee.
(U.S. logistics) Intercorporate hauling is legal in the U.S. if the subsidiary is wholly owned by the carrier or if the carrier has common-carrier authority.

### Interessantelskab (I/S)
(Denmark, Norway) Designation for a general partnership, in which all partners have joint and several liability.

### interest arbitrage
(banking) The attempt to make a profit out of differing interest rates for various maturities and/or various instruments. *See* arbitrage.

### interline shipping
(shipping) The movement of a single shipment of freight via two or more carriers. *See* intermodal; coordinated movement; intermodal compatibility.

### interlocutory
(law) Temporary or interim. An interlocutory injunction, for example, may be granted pending trial as a temporary restraint against a party before final judgment is rendered.

### intermediate consignee
A bank, forwarding agent, or other intermediary (if any) which acts in a foreign country as an agent for the exporter,

the purchaser, or the ultimate consignee, for the purpose of effecting delivery of the export to the ultimate consignee.

### intermediate products
Goods and services consumed as inputs by a process of production, excluding fixed assets.

### intermodal compatibility
(shipping) The capability which enables a shipment to be transferred from one form of transport to another, as from airplane to highway truck, to railway freight car, to ocean vessel.

### intermodal marketing company (IMC)
(logistics) A shipping intermediary that acts as a broker by arranging, buying and selling intermodal freight services. IMCs are not carriers.

### intermodal transport
(shipping) The coordinated transport of freight, especially in connection with relatively long-haul movements using any combination of freight forwarders, piggyback, containerization, air-freight, ocean freight, assemblers, motor carriers.

### International Air Transport Association (IATA)
A trade association serving airlines, passengers, shippers, travel agents, and governments. Contact: International Air Transport Association, 800 Place Victoria, P.O. Box 113, Montreal, Quebec H4Z 1M1 Canada; Tel: [1] (514) 874-0202; Fax: [1] (514) 874-9632; Web: www.iata.org.

### International Anticounterfeiting Coalition
A non-profit organization located in Washington, DC that seeks to advance intellectual property rights protection on a worldwide basis by promoting laws, regulations, and directives designed to render theft of intellectual property rights unattractive and unprofitable. Contact: International Anticounterfeiting Coalition, 1725 K Street, NW, Suite 411, Washington, DC 20006 USA; Tel: [1] (202) 223-6667; Fax: [1] (202) 223-6668; E-mail: rwynne@iacc.org; Web: www.iacc.org.

### International Atomic Energy Agency (IAEA)
The primary international organization that enforces a system of safeguards to ensure that non-nuclear weapons states do not divert shipments of sensitive equipment from peaceful applications to the production of nuclear weapons. Before a supplier state of nuclear materials or equipment may approve an export to a non-nuclear weapons NPT (Nuclear Non-Proliferation Treaty) signatory state, it must receive assurances that the recipient will place the material under IAEA safeguards. Subsequent to shipment, the recipient state must allow IAEA officials to verify the legitimate end use of the exported materials or equipment.
IAEA, established in July 1957, gives advice and technical assistance to developing countries on nuclear power development, nuclear safety, radioactive waste management, and related efforts. Safeguards are the technical means applied by the IAEA to verify that nuclear equipment or materials are used exclusively for peaceful purposes. Contact: International Atomic Energy Agency, Vienna International Centre, Wagramer Strasse 5, A-1400, P.O. Box 100, Vienna, Austria; Tel: [43] (1) 26-000; Fax: [43] (1) 26-007; E-mail: Official.Mail@iaea.org; Web: www.iaea.org.

### International Bank for Reconstruction and Development (The World Bank)
(banking) The International Bank for Reconstruction and Finance (IBRF) was proposed at Bretton Woods on July 1944, commencing operation in June 1946. Originally established to help countries reconstruct their economies after World War II. IBRD, commonly referred to as the World Bank, now assists developing member countries by lending to government agencies, or by guaranteeing private loans for such projects as agricultural modernization or in-

frastructural development. Contact: The World Bank, 1818 H Street NW, Washington, DC 20433 USA; Tel: [1] (202) 473-1000; Fax: [1] (202) 477-6391; E-mail: pic@worldbank.org; Web: www.worldbank.org. *See* International Monetary Fund; World Bank; World Bank Group.

### international banking facility (IBF)
(U.S.) One of four categories of foreign banking in the United States. An IBF is a set of asset and liability accounts that is segregated and limited to financing international trade.

### International Buyer Program
(U.S.) (Formerly Foreign Buyer Program) A joint industry-U.S. International Trade Administration program to assist exporters in meeting qualified foreign purchasers for their product or service at trade shows held in the United States. ITA selects leading U.S. trade shows in industries with high export potential. Each show selected for the FBP receives promotion through overseas mailings, U.S. embassy and regional commercial newsletters, and other promotional techniques. ITA trade specialists counsel participating U.S. exhibitors. Contact: International Buyer Program, International Trade Administration, Department of Commerce, Washington, DC 20230 USA.

### International Center for Settlement of Investment Disputes (ICSID)
(banking) A separate organization of the World Bank which encourages greater flows of investment capital by providing facilities for the conciliation and arbitration of disputes between governments and foreign investors. The ICSID also conducts and publishes research in foreign-investment law. Contact: International Center for Settlement of Investment Disputes, 1818 H Street NW, Washington, DC 20433 USA; Tel: [1] (202) 458-1534; Fax: [1] (202) 522-2615; Web: www.worldbank.org/icsid.

### International Chamber of Commerce (ICC)
A non-governmental organization serving as a policy advocate for world business. Members in 110 countries comprise tens of thousands of companies and business organizations. The ICC aims to facilitate world trade, investment, and an international free market economy through consultation with other inter-governmental organizations.

The ICC was founded in Atlantic City in 1919. It now encompasses associations and companies from all branches of industry. As an institution of international economic self-administration, it operates through expert commissions, sub-committees and working groups to address questions which are of importance for the international business community. These include, for example, contract and delivery clauses (Incoterms); standardization of means of payment, (Uniform Rules for Collection, Uniform Customs and Practice for Documentary Credits, Uniform Rules for Demand Guarantees); arbitral jurisdiction (Rules of Conciliation and Arbitration); questions relating to such issues as competition, foreign investments, and transportation.

The ICC also offers various services to the business community such as the ATA Carnet system. The ICC publishes many books and references which are valuable to the international trade community. Contact: International Chamber of Commerce, 38 Cours Albert 1er, 75008 Paris, France; Tel: (1) 49-53-28-28; Fax: (1) 49-53-28-59; Web: www.uscib.org; For U.S. representative, contact: U.S. Council for International Business, 1212 Avenue of the Americas, New York, NY 10036; Tel: [1] (212) 354-4480, or, for ICC publications in the U.S. contact ICC Books Worldwide, Web: www.iccbooks.com. Refer to the Appendix for a list of ICC publications.

### International Cocoa Agreement
*See* international commodity agreement.

### International Coffee Agreement
*See* international commodity agreement.

### international commodity agreement
An international understanding, usually reflected in a legal instrument, relating to trade in a particular basic commodity, and based on terms negotiated and accepted by most of the countries that export and import commercially significant quantities of the commodity. Some commodity agreements (such as exists for coffee, cocoa, natural rubber, sugar, and tin) center on economic provisions intended to defend a price range for the commodity through the use of buffer stocks or export quotas or both. Other commodity agreements (such as existing agreements for jute and jute products, olive oil, and wheat) promote cooperation among producers and consumers through improved consultation, exchange of information, research and development, and export promotion.

### International Communications Satellite Organization (Intelsat)
The organization formed under a multilateral agreement which owns, maintains, and operates the global satellite system used by over 100 participating countries. COMSAT is the United States' representative to and participant in Intelsat. Contact: International Communications Satellite Organization (Intelsat), 3400 International Drive NW, Washington, DC 20008-3098 USA; Tel: [1] (202) 944-6800; Fax: [1] (202) 944-8125; Web: www.intelsat.com.

### International Company Profile (ICP)
(U.S. Dept. of Commerce) A fee-based service that provides a background report on a specific foreign firm, prepared by U.S. commercial officers overseas. ICPs provide information about the type of organization, year established, relative size, number of employees, general reputation, territory covered, language preferred, product lines handled, principal owners, financial references, and trade references. ICPs include narrative information about the reliability of the foreign firm. Cost is $100 per report. Issued by the ITA. To obtain an International Company Profile, contact the nearest Department of Commerce district office, or call [1] (800) USA-TRADE.

### International Dairy Agreement
*See* international commodity agreement.

### International Development Association (IDA)
An affiliate of the World Bank Group that was created in 1959 to lend money to developing countries at no interest and for a long repayment period. By providing development assistance through soft loans, IDA meets the needs of many developing countries that cannot afford development loans at ordinary rates of interest and in the time span of conventional loans. Contact: International Development Association, World Bank, 1818 H Street NW, Washington, DC 20433 USA; Tel: [1] (202) 473-1000; Fax:[1] (202) 477-6391; Web: www.worldbank.org/ida.

### International Electrotechnical Commission (IEC)
The IEC was established in 1906 to deal with questions related to international standardization in the electrical and electronic engineering fields. The members of the IEC are the national committees, one for each country, which are required to be as representative as possible of all electrical interests in the country concerned: manufacturers, users, governmental authorities, teaching, and professional bodies. They are composed of representatives of the various organizations which deal with questions of electrical standardization at the national level. Most of them are recognized and supported by their governments. Contact:

International Electrotechnical Commission, 3 rue de Varembé, PO Box 131, 1211 Geneva 20, Switzerland; Tel: [41] (22) 919-02-11; Fax: [41] (22) 919-03-00; E-mail: inmail@iec.ch; Web: www.iec.ch.

### International Emergency Economic Powers Act (IEEPA)

(U.S. law) The IEEPA was enacted in 1977 to extend emergency powers previously granted to the president by the Trading with the Enemy Act of 1917 (which still authorized the president to exercise extraordinary powers when the United States is at war). IEEPA enables the president, after declaring that a national emergency exists because of a threat from a source outside the United States, to investigate, regulate, compel or prohibit virtually any economic transaction involving property in which a foreign country or national has an interest.

### International Energy Agency (IEA)

The IEA was founded in 1974 as a forum for energy cooperation among 21 member nations. The IEA helps participating countries prepare to reduce the economic risks of oil supply disruptions and to reduce dependence on oil through coordinated and cooperative research efforts. Headquarters Contact: International Energy Agency, 9 rue de la Federation, 75739 Paris Cedex 15, France; Tel: [33] (1) 40 57 65 01; Fax: [33] (1) 40 57 65 59; E-mail: info@iea.org; Web: www.iea.org.

### International Federation of Freight Forwarders Associations (FIATA)

(logistics) The world's largest non-governmental trade organization in the field of transportation and logistics. FIATA's objectives are to unite the freight-forwarding industry worldwide, represent and promote the interests of the industry with other international organizations, disseminate information, offer publications about the industry to members and to the public, promote uniform forwarding documents, assist in vocational training, help develop tools for electronic commerce including electronic data interchange (EDI) and promote standard trading conditions. Contact: FIATA Secretariat, Schaffhauserstrasse 104, P.O. Box 364, CH-8152 Glattbrugg, Switzerland; Tel: [41] (43) 211 65 00; Fax: [41] (43) 211 65 65; E-mail: info@fiata.com; Web: www.fiata.com.

### International Finance Corporation (IFC)

The IFC was established in 1956 as a member of the World Bank Group. The IFC promotes capital flow into private investment in developing countries. Contact: International Finance Corporation, 2121 Pennsylvania Ave. NW, Washington, DC 20433 USA; Tel: [1] (202) 473-1000; Fax: [1] (202) 974-4384; E-mail: Webmaster@ifc.org; Web: www.ifc.org. *See* World Bank Group.

### International Frequency Registration Board (IFRB)

An organizational entity under the International Telecommunication Union (ITU). Located in Geneva, IFRB is composed of five full-time elected officials with a rotating chairmanship. IFRB maintains the International Frequency Register, monitors and analyzes all ITU records of frequency use around the world, and makes determinations as to whether or not certain systems are in compliance with the Radio Regulations. *See* International Telecommunications Union.

### international investment

*See* foreign direct investment in the U.S.

### International Jute Agreement

*See* international commodity agreement.

### International Labor Organization (ILO)

The ILO, set up in 1919, became a specialized agency of the United Nations in 1946. The ILO seeks to promote improved working and living conditions by establishing standards that reduce social injustice. Contact: International Labor Organization, 4, rue des Morillons, CH-1211, Geneva 22, Switzerland; Tel: [41] (22) 799-6111; Fax: [41] (22) 798-8685; E-mail: ilo@ilo.org; Web: www.ilo.org.

### international landing rights

*See* Freedoms of the Air.

### International Maritime Dangerous Goods Code (IMDG)

The IMDG Code, which was first published in 1965, has become the standard guide to all aspects of handling dangerous goods and marine pollutants in sea transport. Although the information in the Code is directed primarily at the mariner, its provisions affect a whole range of industries and services including manufacturers, packers, shippers, feeder services such as road and rail, and port authorities.

The IMDG Code lays down basic principles and offers detailed recommendations for individual substances, materials and articles, and a number of recommendations for good operational practice including advice on terminology, packing, labelling, stowage, segregation and handling, and emergency response action.

Available from the International Maritime Organization; 4 Albert Embankment; London SE1 7SR; United Kingdom; Tel: [44] (20) 7735-7611; Fax: [44] (20) 7587-3210; Web: www.imo.org.

### International Maritime Organization (IMO)

The International Maritime Organization, IMO, was established as a specialized agency of the United Nations in 1948. The IMO facilitates cooperation on technical matters affecting merchant shipping and traffic. It publishes "Guidelines for Packing and Securing Cargoes in Containers for Transport by Land or Sea" (Container Packing Guidelines). Contact: International Maritime Organization, 4 Albert Embankment, London SE1 7SR, UK; Tel: [44] (20) 7735-7611; Fax: [44] (20) 7587-3210; Web: www.imo.org.

### International Maritime Satellite Organization (IMSO or INMARSAT)

An international partnership of signatories from 62 nations. The partnership provides mobile satellite capacity to its signatories, who, in turn, use the capacity to provide worldwide mobile satellite services to their maritime, aeronautical and land-mobile customers—including shipping, cruise, fishing, research and offshore exploration industries, and airlines. INMARSAT began service in 1976. COMSAT is the U.S. signatory to INMARSAT. Contact: International Maritime Satellite Organization, 99 City Road, London EC1Y 1AX, UK; Tel: [44] (20) 7728-1000; Fax: [44] (20) 7728-1044; Web: www.inmarsat.org.

### International Market Insights (IMI)

(U.S.) Reports prepared by staff at American embassies and consulates covering developments in a single country that are of interest to traders and investors. Topics may include: new laws, policies and procedures, new trade regulations, and marketplace changes. Available from the National Trade Data Bank CD-ROM, online through the Department of Commerce's STAT-USA/Internet service at Web: www.stat-usa.gov, or as individual reports from the Department of Commerce. For address information, *see* National Trade Data Bank; STAT-USA; United States Department of Commerce. Tel: [1] (800) STAT-USA.

### international market research

*See* Industry Subsector Analysis.

### International Monetary Fund (IMF)

(banking/finance/foreign exchange) An international financial institution proposed at the 1944 Bretton Woods Conference and established in 1946 that seeks to stabilize the

international monetary system as a sound basis for the orderly expansion of international trade. Specifically, among other things, the Fund monitors exchange rate policies of member countries, lends them foreign exchange resources to support their adjustment policies when they experience balance of payments difficulties, and provides them financial assistance through a special "compensatory financing facility" when they experience temporary shortfalls in commodity export earnings. Membership in the fund is a prerequisite to membership in the International Bank for Reconstruction and Development. Contact: International Monetary Fund, 700 19th Street NW, Washington, DC 20431 USA; Tel: [1] (202) 623-7000; Fax: [1] (202) 623-4661; E-mail: publicaffairs@imf.org; Web: www.imf.org.
*See* Bretton-Woods Agreement; International Bank for Reconstruction and Development; World Bank Group.

### International Olive Oil Agreement
*See* international commodity agreement.

### International Organization for Standardization.
*See* International Standards Organization.

### International Partner Search (IPS)
(U.S. government) An International Trade Administration (ITA) fee-based service which locates foreign import agents and distributors for U.S. exporters. IPS provides a custom search overseas for interested and qualified foreign representatives on behalf of a U.S. exporter. Officers abroad conduct the search and prepare a report identifying up to six foreign prospects that have examined the U.S. firm's product literature and have expressed interest in representing the U.S. firm's products. Contact the nearest Department of Commerce District Office or call [1] (800) USA-TRADE. *See* United States Department of Commerce.

### International POW WOW
(U.S.) An annual trade fair, coordinated by the Travel Industry Association of America (TIA) to promote foreign tourism to the United States, which brings together over 1,200 international buyers (tour operators and wholesalers) from 55 countries. The buyers are chosen through international selection criteria and purchase packages which they sell to their respective travel retailers.

Each non-U.S. country has a chairman and the chairman has a selection committee. Each country has a quota of buyers they can send to either the U.S. or the European POW WOW. If a buyer wants to go and hasn't already been selected, they can try contacting the selection committee via the chairman. One way to find out who this is, would be to contact the Travel Industry Association of America (see address below.) U.S. sellers do not need to go through such a process. However, to have a booth at the European POW WOW they must be TIA members. They do not have to be TIA members to participate in the U.S. POW WOW. Organizer: Travel Industry Association of America, 1100 New York Ave. NW, Suite 450, Washington, DC 20005-3934 USA; Tel: [1] (202) 408-8422; Fax: [1] (202) 408-1255; E-mail: feedback@tia.org; Web: www.tia.org. The TIA coordinates the POW WOW with the U.S. Travel and Tourism Administration of the U.S. Department of Commerce.

### International Rubber Agreement (IRA)
An international agreement among natural rubber exporting and importing nations whose purpose is to stabilize the price of rubber through import quotas, thereby protecting rubber exporting countries in the developing world from the effects of extreme price fluctuations. *See* international commodity agreement.

### International Ship and Port Facility Security (ISPS) Code
The ISPS Code, developed by the International Maritime Organization (IMO), a specialized agency of the United Nations (UN), is a series of amendments to the SOLAS (Safety of Life at Sea) Convention that set new standards for security for ships engaged in international voyages as well as port facilities around the world. It aims to make shipping activities more secure against threats of terrorism, piracy and smuggling.
The ISPS Code went into effect on July 1, 2004.
The full text of the ISPS Code can be found on the Web at: www.dcmnr.gov.ie/files/marsecISPS-2003.pdf
Also, contact the IMO at: www.imo.org.

### International Standard Audiovisual Number (ISAN)
(international standard) An internationally recognized voluntary numbering system for the identification of audiovisual works. The ISAN is similar to the ISBN (International Standard Book Number) system for the identification of books.
The ISAN is a 16-digit number consisting of a 12-digit root segment and a 4-digit segment for the identification of episodes or parts when applicable. A check digit is added whenever the ISAN is presented in human-readable form.
The ISAN identifies the work rather than the content of the work or actual publications. There is no relation between the ISAN and copyright registration. The standard was developed by the International Standards Organization (ISO).
Contact: Web: www.collectionscanada.ca/iso/tc46sc9, clicking specifically on WG 1 (ISAN).

### International Standard Book Number (ISBN)
(international standard) The internationally-recognized standard numbering system for the identification of publications of all kinds.
The ISBN is a 10-digit number that identifies both the publisher and the publication. The numbering system was defined by the International Organization for Standardization (ISO) in 1970 as ISO 2108. Numbers are assigned by agencies in the U.S. and Germany.
U.S. ISBN Agency; 121 Chanlon Road; New Providence, NJ 07974 USA; Tel: [1] (877) 310-7333; Fax: [1] (908) 665-2895; Web: www.isbn.org.
International ISBN Agency, c/o EDITEUR, 39-41 North Road, London N7 9DP, UK; Tel: [44] (20) 7607-0021; Fax: [44] (20) 7607-0415; E-mail: isbn@bic.org.uk; Web: http://isbn-international.org.

### International Standard Industrial Classification
(classification system) A United Nations business enterprise classification system based upon the economic activity of the enterprise. The currently valid version is Revision 3. Contact at UNSD (United Nations Statistical Division); Web: http://unstats.un.org/unsd. Trade-related statistics can be requested at E-mail: tradestat@un.org

### International Standard Music Number (ISMN)
(international standard) An internationally recognized code used in the identification of music publications. The ISMN is similar to the ISBN (International Standard Book Number) system for the identification of books. The ISMN identifies all printed music publications, whether available for sale, hire or free of charge—whether a part, a score or an element in a multi-media kit.
The ISMN consists of four elements comprising ten digits: 1) a constant <M>, to distinguish it from other standard numbers, 2) a publisher prefix which identifies a certain music publisher, 3) a title number which identifies a certain publication and 4) a check digit which validates the number on a mathematical basis.

Items to be given an ISMN include:

Scores, miniature (study) scores, vocal scores, sets of parts, individual parts when available separately, pop folios, anthologies, multimedia when printed music is a part of the kit, song texts or lyrics when published with the music, song books (optional), microform publications, braille music publications and electronic publications.

Items not to be given ISMNs include:

Books on music, stand-alone sound or video recordings and serials.

Benefits of the ISMN system include:

Fast and unique identification, allows quick and efficient ordering and tele-ordering, speeded up distribution, creation of a music trade directory, Music in Print, support for bar coding and electronic point-of-sale systems and support for a variety of computer applications.

The International Agency is responsible for the maintenance of the ISMN system, the standard and its application. Publishers prefixes are distributed on a national or regional level by ISMN agencies. Publishers usually administer their own contingents of title numbers as received from the ISMN agency.

ISO Standard 10957 gives basic rules of the ISMN system. A more explicit ISMN Users's Manual is available free of charge from the International ISMN Agency. Contact: International ISMN Agency, Staatsbibliothek zu Berlin, Potsdamer Strasse 33, 10785 Berlin, Germany; Tel: [49] (30) 266-2338; Fax: [49] (30) 266-2378; E-mail: ismn@sbb.spk-berlin.de; Web: www.ismn-international.org.

### International Standard Musical Work Code (ISWC)

(international standard) The internationally recognized standard numbering system for the identification of musical works.

An ISWC for musical works consists of a letter followed by nine digits and a check digit, as follows:

distinguishing element (1 letter); work identifier (9 digits) and check digit (1 digit). The distinguishing element for musical works is the letter «T». In printed form the ISWC is preceded by a label and may include hyphens and dots between the elements for ease of reading. Example ISWC T-034.524.680-1

Arrangements, adaptations and translations are all given separate ISWCs. These are known collectively as versions. The system is based on the International Standards Organization ISO 15707. The International ISWC Agency is provided by CISAC (International Confederation of Societies of Authors and Composers).

Numbers may be obtained through rights societies or directly by individuals. Works in the public domain may also have a number allocated.

Contact: ISWC Administrator; International ISWC Agency; CISAC; 20-26, Boulevard du Parc; 92200 Neuilly sur Seine France; Tel: [33] 1 55 62 08 50; Fax: [33] 1 55 62 08 60; E-mail: info@iswc.org; Web: www.iswc.org.

### International Standard Recording Code (ISRC)

(international standard) The internationally recognized standard code system used to identify sound and audio-visual recordings and individual tracks on compact disks (CDs), music videos and other media, primarily to ensure royalty payments. The ISRC is contained in the subcode (Q-channel) and is unique to each track of the recording. Note that the ISRC identifies the track and not the physical product.

Each ISRC is comprised of 12 characters as follows: 2 characters to identify the country of residence of the registrant of the recording (such as FR for France); 3 characters

or digits to identify the first owner (as allocated by Phonographic Performance Ltd. for audio); 2 digits to identify the year of recording (represented as the last two digits of the year); and a 5 digit Designation Code assigned by the first owner.

The ISRC was developed by the International Standards Organization (ISO) in 1986 and is also known as ISO 3901. U.S. Contact: RIAA (Recording Industry Association of America); Web: www.riaa.com.

### International Standard Serial Number (ISSN)

(international standard) The internationally recognized standard numbering system used to identify serial publications (such as newspapers, annuals, magazines and journals).

Each ISSN is comprised of two groups of 4 digits separated by a hyphen. The eighth character is a control digit calculated using the preceding 7 digits. If the calculation equals "10" the control digit is "X" (e.g., ISSN 1234-567X).

The ISSN is simply an identifier of a specific serial. The ISSN does not identify the serial's country of origin, language, contents, frequency of publication or copyright.

The ISSN was originally established by the International Standards Organization (ISO) and is currently administered from over 60 national centers. The International Center in Paris handles central distribution of ISSNs and takes care of countries that do not have their own national center.

ISSN International Center; 20, rue Bachaumont; 75002 Paris France; Tel: [33] (1) 44 88 22 20; Fax: [33] (1) 40 26 32 43; E-mail: issnic@issn.org; Web: www.issn.org.

### International Standards Organization (ISO)

The ISO, established in 1947, is a worldwide federation of national bodies, representing approximately 90 member countries. The scope of the International Standards Organization covers standardization in all fields except electrical and electronic engineering standards, which are the responsibility of the International Electrotechnical Commission (IEC). Together, the ISO and IEC form the specialized system for worldwide standardization—the world's largest nongovernmental system for voluntary industrial and technical collaboration at the international level.

The result of ISO technical work is published in the form of International Standards. There are, for example, ISO standards for the quality grading of steel; for testing the strength of woven textiles; for storage of citrus fruits; for magnetic codes on credit cards; for automobile safety belts; and for ensuring the quality and performance of such diverse products as surgical implants, ski bindings, wire ropes, and photographic lenses.

ISO 9000 is a new series of voluntary international quality standards. Its formal name is ISO 9000 Series of Standards. Adoption of ISO standards has become a virtual prerequisite for doing business internationally. Contact: International Standards Organization, 1 rue de Varembé, PO Box 56, CH-1211 Geneva 20, Switzerland; Tel: [41] (22) 749-0111; Fax: [41] (22) 733-3430; Web: www.iso.ch. In the United States contact: International Organization for Standards, The American National Standards Institute, 1819 L Street, NW, (between 18th and 19th Streets), 6th floor, Washington, DC 20036; Tel: [1] (202) 293-8020; Fax: [1] 202 298-9287; E-mail: info@ansi.org; Web: www.ansi.org.

### International Sugar Agreement

*See* international commodity agreement.

### International Telecommunications Satellite Organization (INTELSAT)

Created in 1964 under a multilateral agreement, INTELSAT was originally a nonprofit cooperation of countries from around the world that jointly owned and operated a global communications satellite system serving the world. Currently, INTELSAT is a private corporation with a global fleet of 21 satellites (with plans to launch an additional seven), and offers wholesale Internet, broadcast, telephony and corporate network solutions to leading service providers in more than 200 countries and territories worldwide. Contact: Intelsat Global Service Corporation, 3400 International Drive, NW, Washington, D.C. 20008 USA; Tel: [1] (202) 944-6800; Fax: [1] (202) 944-8125; Web: www.intelsat.com.

### International Telecommunications Union
A specialized agency of the United Nations with responsibilities for developing operational procedures and technical standards for the use of the radio frequency spectrum, the satellite orbit, and for the international public telephone and telegraph network. There are over 160 member nations of the ITU. The Radio Regulations that result from ITU conferences have treaty status and provide the principal guidelines for world telecommunications. In the case of the U.S., they are the framework for development of the U.S. national frequency allocations and regulations. The ITU has four permanent organs: the General Secretariat, the International Frequency Registration Board (IFRB), the International Radio Consultative Committee (CCIR), and the International Telegraph and Telephone and Consultative Committee (ITTCC). Contact: International Telecommunications Union, Place des Nations, CH-1211 Geneva 20, Switzerland; Tel: [41] (22) 730-5111; Fax: [41] (22) 733-7256; E-mail: itumail@itu.int; Web: www.itu.int.

### International Tin Agreement
*See* international commodity agreement.

### International Trade Administration (ITA)
(U.S.) The trade unit of the U.S. Department of Commerce, ITA was established in 1980 to carry out the U.S. government's nonagricultural foreign trade activities and support the policy negotiations of the U.S. Trade Representative. It encourages and promotes U.S. exports of manufactured goods, administers U.S. statutes and agreements dealing with foreign trade, and advises on U.S. international trade and commercial policy. An important arm of the ITA is the United States and Foreign Commercial Service. Contact: International Trade Administration, 14th Street and Constitution Avenue NW, Washington, DC 20230 USA; Tel: [1] (202) 482-2867; Web: http//ita.doc.gov. *See* United States Department of Commerce; United States and Foreign Commercial Service; United States Trade Representative.

### International Trade Commission (ITC)
(U.S.) An independent U.S. government fact-finding agency with six commissioners who review and make recommendations concerning countervailing duty and antidumping petitions submitted by U.S. industries seeking relief from imports that benefit unfair trade practices. Known as the U.S. Tariff Commission before its mandate was broadened by the Trade Act of 1974. Contact: U.S. Department of Commerce, International Trade Commission, 500 E. Street SW, Washington, DC 20436 USA; Tel: [1] (202) 205-2000; E-mail: webmaster@usitc.gov; Web: www.usitc.gov. *See* dumping; countervailing duty.

### International Trade Data System (ITDS)
(U.S. Customs) A U.S. government multi-agency, information technology initiative that will implement an integrated, government-wide system for the electronic collection, use, and dissemination of international trade data. ITDS is being integrated with the U.S. Customs and Border Protection (CBP) modernization Automated Commercial Environment (ACE) project and will serve as the U.S. government's "single window" into international trade data collection and distribution. ITDS supports both Homeland Security (Border and Transportation Security) and the President's Management Agenda. For more information on ITDS, go to: www.itds.treas.gov.

### International Traffic in Arms Regulations
(U.S.) Regulations administered in the United States by the U.S. State Department to control the export of weapons and munitions.

### International Union for the Protection of Literary and Artistic Works
*See* Berne Convention; World Intellectual Property Organization.

### International Wheat Agreement
*See* international commodity agreement.

### interstate carrier
(shipping-U.S.) A common carrier whose business extends beyond the boundaries of one state. *See* carrier; common carrier.

### interstate commerce
(U.S.) Trade between or among several states of the United States. A seller that uses a telephone or facsimile across state lines in its transactions, or transports goods by rail or interstate roads is using interstate commerce.

### Interstate Commerce Act of 1887
(U.S. law) Federal legislation regulating the practices, rates, and rules of transportation for carriers engaged in handling interstate shipments or the movement for a fee of people across state lines.

### intervention
(banking/foreign exchange) Efforts by central banks and national governments to influence the exchange rates for its currency. Intervention is usually done in one of two ways: (1) The purchase of large amounts of a currency in order to bolster the price, or (2) The sale of large amounts of a currency to lower the price of the currency. Central banks can also raise interest rates in order to attract capital into the country or lower interest rates to discourage the flow of capital into the country.

### intervention currency
(banking/foreign exchange) The foreign currency a country uses to ensure by means of official exchange transactions that the permitted exchange rate margins are observed. Intervention usually takes the form of purchases and sales of foreign currency by the central bank or exchange equalization fund in domestic dealings with commercial banks.

### in-the-money
(foreign exchange) An option is in-the-money in the following cases: (1) Call option: market price is greater than the strike price; and (2) Put option: market price less than the strike price. For European options, replace the market price by the forward price of the underlying instrument on the expiry date of the option. *See* call option; put option; strike price; European option; out-of-the-money.

### in transit cargo
*See* transit cargo.

### intrinsic value
(commerce/economics) The value of an item independent of location or ownership.
(banking/finance/foreign exchange) The difference between the strike price of an option and the forward price of the underlying security up to maturity, as long as the option is in-the-money. The premium of an option is made up of the time value and the intrinsic value.

### inventory
(commerce/accounting/logistics) (a) A listing of raw materials, component parts, work in progress and finished goods on hand at any given moment. (b) The value of raw materials, component parts, work in progress and finished goods on hand at any given moment. *See* cycle inventory, defec-

tive goods inventory, inventory deployment, inventory in transit, inventory turns.

### inventory carrying costs
(commerce/accounting/logistics) The costs associated with maintaining goods in inventory. These include the time value of money invested in producing or purchasing the inventory, warehousing, insurance, depreciation of warehouse and equipment, obsolescence, taxes, utilities and administrative costs.

### inventory deployment
(logistics) The strategic management of inventory to minimize stock and storage levels (and thus costs) while meeting customer demand. This is achieved by dynamically monitoring supply, demand, inventory at rest and inventory in transit.

### inventory in transit
(logistics/accounting) (a) Inventory that is in the possession of carriers. (b) The value of inventory that is in the possession of carriers. Value can be defined as the either the cost or the sales value.

### inventory turns
(logistics) The number of times an inventory is replaced over a stated period of time. The annual unit calculation is: total number of units sold during a year divided by the average number of units kept in inventory during the year.

### inventory velocity
(logistics) The rate at which inventory moves through a defined cycle. For example: the speed at which inventory is sold in a retail or distribution environment; the speed at which inventory moves through the entire supply chain; the speed at which inventory moves from a receiving dock to the shipping dock. The more traditional term for inventory velocity is "turns". *See* inventory turns.

### investment climate statements
(U.S.) Reports prepared occasionally by the commercial sections of U.S. embassies for the U.S. and Foreign Commercial Service, covering 67 individual countries. The ICSs provide statistics and analysis of policies and issues effecting the climate for direct investment in the individual country. *See* United States and Foreign Commercial Service.

### investment performance requirements
(foreign investment) Special conditions imposed on direct foreign investment by recipient governments, sometimes requiring commitments to export a certain percentage of the output, to purchase given supplies locally, or to ensure the employment of a specified percentage of local labor and management.

### invisible balance
*See* invisible trade balance.

### invisible barriers to trade
Government regulations that do not directly restrict trade, but indirectly impede free trade by imposing excessive or obscure requirements on goods sold within a country, especially imported goods. These regulations are often known to business owners within the country, because they may be required to comply with them, but are often not known by foreign businesses seeking to export their products, and therefore such regulations are "invisible." Examples include labelling requirements, sanitary standards, and size or measurement standards.

### invisibles; invisible trade
(economics) Non-merchandise items such as freight, insurance, and financial services that are included in a country's balance of payments accounts (in the "current" account), even though they are not recorded as physically visible exports and imports. *See* balance of trade.

### invisible trade balance
(economics) As contrasted with the import and export of goods—the trade balance created by the import and export of services, including consulting and advisory services, transportation services, income and expenditure on travel services, insurances, licenses, earnings and interest income from international capital movements. *See* balance of trade.

### invoice
A document identifying the seller and buyer of goods or services, identifying numbers such as invoice number, date, shipping date, mode of transport, delivery and payment terms, and a complete listing and description of the goods or services being sold including prices, discounts and quantities. *See* commercial invoice.

### inward cargo manifest
A document giving the description of a ship's cargo or the contents of a rail car or truck.
(U.S. Customs) A U.S. Customs and Border Protection (CBP) document required of all carriers entering the customs territory of the United States giving a description of a ship's cargo or the contents of a rail car or truck.

### inward foreign manifest (IFM)
(U.S. Customs) A U.S. Customs mandated document requiring the complete listing by bill of lading numbers of an arriving ship's freight being imported into the United States.

### ipso jure
(law) By operation of law. Contract terms that are implied by a court from the conduct of the parties, for example, are enforceable ipso jure.

### irregular route carrier
(logistics) A motor carrier that does not follow a set route.

### irrevocable letter of credit
(banking) A letter of credit which cannot be amended or canceled without prior mutual consent of all parties to the credit. Such a letter of credit guarantees payment by the bank to the seller/exporter so long as all the terms and conditions of the credit have been met.
Documentary letters of credit issued subject to the Uniform Customs and Practice for Documentary Credits (UCPDC) Publication No. 500 are deemed to be irrevocable unless expressly marked as revocable. *See* letter of credit.

### irritating material
(shipping) Items capable of causing discomfort such as tearing, choking, vomiting and skin irritation. (UN CLASS 6.) Examples are tear gas and riot control agents. Hazards/precautions are: may cause difficulty in breathing; may burn but do not ignite readily; exposure in enclosed areas may be harmful; may cause tearing of the eyes, choking, nausea or skin irritation.

### ISIC
*See* International Standard Industrial Classification.

### ISO 1400
A family of voluntary *generic management system standards* established by the ISO (International Standards Organization) that are concerned with "environmental management." ISO 14000 is not a product or service standard. Generic means that the same standards may be applied to any organization, whether public or private, non-profit or profit-making, regardless of its size or whether it deals in a products or services. Management system means that the organization has a systematic written procedure for managing its activities. Standards means that the organization is following an internationally recognized model for setting up and operating the management system. Environmental management is what an organization does to make sure that its products and/or services will have the least harmful impact on the environment, either during produc-

tion or disposal, either by pollution or by depleting natural resources.

Adoption of ISO standards has become a virtual prerequisite for doing business internationally. *See* International Standards Organization.

### ISO 9000

A family of voluntary *generic management system standards* established by the ISO (International Standards Organization) that are concerned with "quality management." ISO 9000 is not a product or service standard. Generic means that the same standards may be applied to any organization, whether public or private, non-profit or profit-making, regardless of its size or whether it deals in a products or services. Management system means that the organization has a systematic written procedure for managing its activities. Standards means that the organization is following an internationally recognized model for setting up and operating the management system. Quality management is what an organization does to make sure that its products and/or services conform to customer requirements.

Its formal name is ISO 9000 Series of Standards. Adoption of ISO standards has become a virtual prerequisite for doing business internationally. *See* International Standards Organization.

### ISRC

*See* International Standard Recording Code.

### issuance

(banking) The establishment of a letter of credit by the issuing bank (buyer's bank) based on the buyer's application and credit relationship with the bank. *See* letter of credit; advice; amendment.

### issuance date of the documents

(shipping) Unless otherwise stipulated in a transport document, the date of issuance is deemed to be the date of shipment or loading on board of the goods.

(banking) Unless prohibited by the documentary letter of credit, documents bearing a date of issuance prior to that of the letter of credit are acceptable.

### issuing bank

(banking) The buyer's bank which establishes a letter of credit at the request of the buyer, in favor of the beneficiary (seller/exporter). Also called the buyer's bank or the opening bank. *See* advising bank; negotiating bank.

### issuing carrier

(logistics) The carrier that issues the bill of lading. Specifically, the carrier that establishes the contract for carriage.

# J

### Japan Bank for International Cooperation (JBIC)

(Japan) Japan's official provider of export credits. Contact: Japan Bank for International Cooperation, 4-1, Otemachi 1-chome, Chiyoda-ku, Tokyo 100-8144, Japan; Tel: [81] (3) 5217-3101; Fax: [81] (3) 5218-3955; Web: www.jbic.go.jp.

### Japan, Development Bank of (DBJ)

(Japan) The Development Bank of Japan was founded in 1951 to aid in developing and diversifying the Japanese economy. The DBJ is a non-profit organization owned entirely by the Japanese Government. U.S. companies may participate in DBJ funding activity under the Bank's Loan Division in the International Department. The International Department disburses loans to foreign companies under two primary loan programs: Promotion of Foreign Direct Investment in Japan and Facilities for Import Products. The other loan programs of DBJ are also available to foreign-owned companies under the principle of equal treatment of clients regardless of nationality. Contact: Development Bank of Japan; 9-1, Otemachi 1-chome; Chiyoda-ku, Tokyo 100-0004, Japan; Tel: [81] (3) 3244-1900; Web: www.dbj.go.jp

### Japan Export Information Center (JEIC)

(U.S.) Provides information on doing business in Japan, market entry alternatives, market information and research, product standards and testing requirements, tariffs and nontariff barriers. The Center maintains a commercial library and participates in private- and government-sponsored seminars on doing business in Japan. JEIC is operated by the International Trade Administration of the U.S. Department of Commerce, 14th Street and Constitution Ave. NW, Washington, DC 20230 USA; Tel: [1] (202) 482-2425 and [1] (202) 482-4524; Fax: [1] (202) 482-0469; Web: www.mac.doc.gov/japan/.

### Japan External Trade Organization (JETRO)

(Japan) Although legally under the aegis of the Ministry of International Trade and Industry (MITI), JETRO administers the export programs of the Japanese Government independently. The MITI subsidizes about 60 percent of JETRO's total annual expenditures and, technically, has final decision-making authority over JETRO management and programs. Originally established to help Japanese firms export, JETRO also assists American companies seeking to export to Japan and promotes Japanese direct investment in the United States and U.S. direct investment in Japan. JETRO offices in the U.S. have excellent trade libraries open to the public. There are seven branches throughout the U.S. Headquarters are in Tokyo: Japan External Trade Organization, Ark Mori Building, 6F 12-32, Akasaka 1-chome, Minato-ku, Tokyo 107-6006, Japan; Tel: [81] (3) 3582-5511; New York branch Tel: [1] (212) 997-0400; San Francisco branch Tel: [1] (415) 392-1333; Fax: (415) 788-6927; Web: www.jetro.go.jp.

### Japan International Cooperation Agency (JICA)

Established in August 1974 to administer the bilateral grant portion of Japan's Official Development Assistance (ODA). JICA covers both: (1) grant aid cooperation (offered without the obligation of repayment) and (2) technical cooperation (offering trainees, experts, equipment, project-type technical cooperation, and development studies). Contact: Japan International Cooperation Agency, 6-

13F, Shinjuku Maynds Tower, 1-1, Yoyogi 2-chome, Shibuya-ku, Tokyo 151-8558; Tel: [81] (3) 5352-5311; E-mail: jicagap-opinion@jica.go.jp; Web: www.jica.go.jp.

### jetsam
(shipping) Articles from a ship or ship's cargo which are thrown overboard, usually to lighten the load in times of emergency or distress and that sinks or is washed ashore. *See* flotsam.

### jettison
(shipping) To unload or throw overboard at sea a part of a ship's paraphernalia or cargo to lighten the ship in time of emergency.

### joint agent
(shipping) A person having authority to transact business for two or more transportation lines.

### joint and several guarantee
*See* aval.

### joint and several liability
(law) Liability for damages imposed on two or more individuals or legal entities who are responsible together and individually, allowing the party harmed to seek full remedy against all or any number of the wrongdoers. The availability of joint and several liability varies among countries, and some jurisdictions have placed limitations on the amount of damages for which a single person can be held liable when multiple parties could be responsible.

### joint rate
(shipping) A single through-rate on cargo moving via two or more carriers.

### joint stock company
(law) An unincorporated business association with ownership interests represented by shares of stock. These companies have characteristics of both corporations and partnerships. They are created under authority of law and are treated differently from jurisdiction to jurisdiction. *See* corporation; partnership.

### joint venture
(law) (a) A combination of two or more individuals or legal entities who undertake together a transaction for mutual gain or to engage in a commercial enterprise together with mutual sharing of profits and losses. (b) A form of business partnership involving joint management and the sharing of risks and profits as between enterprises based in different countries. If joint ownership of capital is involved, the partnership is known as an equity joint venture.

### Jones Act
(U.S. maritime law) The U.S. Merchant Marine Act of 1920 and related statutes, commonly known as the Jones Act, require that vessels used to transport passengers or cargo between U.S. ports be built in U.S. shipyards, owned by U.S. citizens, and manned by U.S. crews. The purpose and argument for the Jones Act is to maintain a national shipbuilding and repair base as well as jobs and training for U.S. mariners, and to provide maritime assets in times of national emergencies. The argument against The Jones Act is that it is discriminatory and anti-competitive. As expected, from time-to-time the Jones Act becomes a hot political issue. The Jones Act is similar to cabotage laws in place in some 50 other nations around the world that protect domestic shipping and reserve immediate coastal activity for home fleets. *See* cabotage.

### jurat
(law) A statement signed by a person authorized to take oaths certifying to the authenticity of a document or affidavit. *See* authentication; notary public.

### juridical person
*See* person, as defined by law.

### jurisdiction
(law) (a) The legal right, power or authority of a court to hear, interpret and apply the law to a case. Concurrent jurisdiction exists when two courts have simultaneous responsibility for the same case. (b) The geographic area over which a court has authority to decide cases.

### juristic act
(law) Action intended to, and capable of having, a legal effect, such as the creation, termination, or modification of a legal right. Signing a power of attorney, for example, is a juristic act because it gives legal authority to an agent.

### juristic person
*See* person, as defined by law.

### just in time
(economics/manufacturing) The principle of production and inventory control that prescribes precise controls for the movement of raw materials, component parts and work-in-progress. Goods arrive when needed (just in time) for production for use rather than becoming expensive inventory that occupies costly warehouse space.

**J**

# K

### K&R insurance
(insurance) Acronym for kidnapping and ransom insurance. Insurance coverage against the threat of kidnapping or ransom of staff working in another country.

### Kabushiki Kaisha (KK)
(Japan) Designation for a joint stock company with limited personal liability to shareholders.

### Kaizen
(Japanese management) A Japanese word meaning gradual, orderly and continuous improvement. Specifically a management theory defined in the book *Kaizen: The key to Japan's Competitive Success*, by Mr. Masaaki Imai, that promotes a personal and business culture of sustained continuous improvement. For information connect at Web: www.kaizen-institute.com.

### Kanban system
(Japanese logistics) A just-in-time inventory and production flow system developed in Japan that uses a card to signal when refurbishment is needed. It is a demand-oriented system whose purpose is to minimize raw materials and work-in-progress inventory. Kanban is a Japanese word that defines a communication signal or card.

### karbovanet
The currency of Ukraine. The abbreviation is Uak. No subcurrency is in use.

### keelage
(shipping) The charges paid by a ship entering or remaining in certain ports.

### Keidanren
(Japan) Keidanren (the Japanese Federation of Economic Organizations) was established in 1946 as a private, non-profit economic organization representing virtually all branches of economic activity in Japan. Contact: Japan Federation of Economic Organizations (Keidanren), 1-9-4, Otemachi 1-chome, Chiyoda-ku, Tokyo 100-8188, Japan; Tel: [81] (3) 5204-1500; Fax: [81] (3) 5255-6255; Web: www.keidanren.or.jp.

### keiretsu
(Japan) Keiretsu refers to the horizontally and vertically linked industrial structure of post-war Japan. (Prior to WWII they were called *zaibatsu*.) The horizontally linked groups include a broad range of industries linked via banks and general trading firms. There are eight major industrial groups, sometimes referred to as "Kigyo Shudan": Mitsubishi, Mitsui, Sumitomo, Fuyo, DKB, Sanwa, Tokai, and IBJ. The vertically linked groups (such as Toyota, Matsushita, and Sony) are centered around parent companies, with subsidiaries frequently serving as suppliers, distributors, and retail outlets. Common characteristics among the groups include crossholding of company shares, intra-group financing, joint investment, mutual appointment of officers, and other joint business activities. The keiretsu system emphasizes mutual cooperation and protects affiliates from mergers and acquisitions. Ties within groups became looser after the oil shocks of the 1970s as a result of decreasing dependence on banks for capital.

### key currency
(foreign exchange) A major currency in the global economy. Small countries, which are highly dependent on exports, orientate their exchange rate to major currencies in the global economy, the so-called key currencies. Key currencies include the U.S. dollar, the British pound sterling, the European Union Euro, the Swiss franc, the Japanese yen and the Canadian dollar.

### kidnapping and ransom insurance
*See* K&R insurance.

### kilo ton (metric ton)
(measure) A unit of mass or weight measure equal to 2,204.6 pounds.

### kilogram
(measure) A unit of mass or weight measure equal to 2.2046 lbs. Abbreviated as k, K, KS, kg, KG, kgs, or KGS.

### kina
The currency of Papua New Guinea. 1K=1 toea.

### kind or quality
*See* drawback—refund of duties.

### kip
The currency of Laos. 1K=100 at.

### kitting
(logistics) The assembly or packaging of components, parts or finished products into a new single item. This light assembly operation is sometimes performed in foreign trade zones or special economic zones. The term refers to the making of a kit (a collection of items). For example, five different types and sizes of screwdrivers might be kitted into a single set of screwdrivers for sale to consumers.

### kiwi bond
(banking/finance) Bond issued in New Zealand dollars on the New Zealand market by non New Zealand borrowers.

### knocked down (K.D.)
An article taken apart and folded or telescoped in such a manner as to reduce its bulk at least 66 2/3 percent from its normal shipping cubage when set up or assembled.

### knot
(measure) A unit of measurement of speed of a vessel in water or an airplane in air equal to one nautical mile (6082.66 feet) per hour.

### known loss
(shipping/insurance) A loss discovered before or at the time of delivery of a shipment.

### Kokusai Denshin Denwa
(Japan) The Kokusai Denshin Denwa Company, KDD, was established in 1953 but traces its history back to 1871 and the establishment of its predecessor organizations. For more than a century, the company was Japan's sole supplier of international telecommunications services and today remains Japan's leading international carrier. KDD is Japan's signatory to INTELSAT and INMARSAT.

### Kommanditgesellschaft (KG)
(Austria, Germany, Switzerland) Designation for a limited partnership in which at least one of the partners has general liability and at least one of the other partners has limited liability.

### Kommanditselskab (K/S)
(Denmark) Designation for a limited partnership in which at least one of the partners has general liability and at least one of the other partners has limited liability.

### koruna
The currency of the Czech and the Slovak Republics. 1Kcs=100 halers.

### krona
The currency of:
Iceland, 1IKr=100 aurar;
Sweden, 1SKr=100 öre.

### krone
The currency of:
Denmark, 1DKr=100 öre;
Norway, 1NKr=100 öre;
Greenland (*see* Denmark).

**kroon**
The currency of Estonia. 1Eek=100 senti.

**kwacha**
The currency of:
Malawi, 1MK=100 tambala;
Zambia, 1K=100 ngwee.

**kwanza**
The currency of Angola. 1Kz=100 lwei.

**kyat**
The currency of Myanmar (Burma). 1K=100 pyas.

**Kyoto Protocol**
An amendment to the United Nations Framework Convention on Climate Change (UNFCCC) and the result of negotiations at the third Conference of the Parties (COP-3) in Kyoto, Japan, in December of 1997. The Kyoto Protocol sets binding greenhouse gas emissions targets for carbon dioxide ($CO_2$), methane ($CH_4$), nitrous oxide ($N_2O$), hydrofluorocarbons (HFCs), perfluorocarbons (PFCs) and sulfur hexafluoride ($SF_6$).
Annex 1 (developed) countries that sign and ratify the Protocol agree to reduce emissions of the named gasses by at least five percent below 1990 levels for the 2008 to 2012 commitment period. Annex 2 (developing) countries (such as China and India) are not required to reduce emissions at all.
As of September 2006 162 countries have signed and ratified the agreement. Additionally, two countries have signed, but not ratified; two have signed, but do not intend to ratify (Australia and the United States); and 29 have not signed and not ratified the agreement.
Non ratification of the Kyoto Protocol has become a political/economic/social issue in the United States. The U.S. government's position is, in part, that exempting developing countries that have large and fast growing greenhouse gas emissions (China is the second largest emitter of greenhouse gases) would put the U.S. at an economic disadvantage. (Note that the U.S. Senate has the power to ratify the Protocol, not the president.)

# L

**lading**
(logistics) (a) The act of loading cargo or freight onto a conveyance. (b) Cargo or freight.

**lagan (also ligan)**
(shipping) Goods or wreckage attached to a buoy and cast into the sea for later salvage.

**laissez-faire**
(economics) A term used to describe minimal governmental involvement in an economy, allowing market forces and individuals to make their own decisions, with little or no regulation.

**lakh**
(South Asia term) The quantity 100,000 of any item, but especially rupees (currency).

**land**
(a) The solid part of the earth's surface. (b) To arrive at the shore, as in "to land a ship." (c) To place cargo on shore (land) from a ship. (c) To cause to come to the ground, as in "to land an airplane."

**Land Border Carrier Initiative Program (LBCIP)**
(United States) A U.S. Customs and Border Protection (CBP) program developed in 1995 to address the threat of drug smuggling along the southwest border of the U.S. The purpose of the LBCIP is to deter smugglers of illegal drugs from using land border commercial conveyances to transport their contraband. For information contact the CBP Industry Partnership Programs at [1] (202) 927-0520 or go to: www.cbp.gov.

**landbridge**
(shipping) The movement of containers from a foreign country by vessel, transiting a country by rail or truck, and then being loaded aboard another vessel for delivery to a second foreign country. An example would be a container from Shanghai which arrives in the U.S. at Tacoma, Washington and is carried by rail to New Jersey where it is shipped by ocean to London (water-rail-water operation).

**landed cost**
(shipping) The total cost of a shipment delivered to a named location. Specifically, the cost of the goods plus the cost of transportation. *See* Incoterms.

**landed price (named location)**
*See* Incoterms.

**Lanham Act of 1947**
(U.S. law) Federal legislation governing trademarks and other symbols for identifying goods sold in interstate commerce. As amended, it allows a manufacturer to protect his brand or trademark in the United States by having it recorded on a government register in the U.S. Patent Office. Also provides for the legal right to register any distinctive mark.

**lash**
*See* lighter aboard ship.

**lashing device**
(logistics) A rope, cable or other tie-down device designed to secure cargo to its transport and provide minimal shifting during its journey. Typical lashing arrangements may secure a container by running across the middle or with four individual lashing devices one attached to each corner of the top face of the container.

**LASH Vessel**
(shipping/logistics) A ship of at least 820 feet specially designed with an onboard deck crane capable of loading and

unloading lighters (barges) through a stern section of the ship that projects out over the water. Lighters are generally used in shallow water ports or where the port does not have container facilities. LASH vessels usually handle break-bulk cargo. *See* lighter aboard ship, lighter.

**lat**
The currency of Latvia. 1LvL=100 sintim.

**Latin American Free Trade Association (LAFTA)**
*See* Latin American Integration Association.

**Latin American Integration Association (LAIA)**
(regional trade alliance) LAIA was created by the 1980 Montevideo Treaty as a replacement to the Latin American Free Trade Association (LAFTA). LAFTA was rejected because members felt its rules governing integration trends were too rigid. LAIA, an association involving Argentina, Bolivia, Brazil, Chile, Colombia, Ecuador, Mexico, Paraguay, Peru, Uruguay, and Venezuela, since has declined as a major Latin American integration effort in favor of regional efforts, such as Mercosur. *See* Mercosur.

**lay order**
(customs) The period during which imported merchandise may remain at the place of unlading without some action being taken for its disposition, i.e., beyond the 5-day General Order period. *See* general order.

**lead inventory**
(logistics) The volume of inventory necessary to satisfy demand during the cycle time required to obtain a new shipment from a supplier. *See* inventory.

**League of Arab States**
*See* Arab League.

**leasehold**
(law) The temporary right to possess land. Technically a lease on land which reverts to the owner at the end of the lease term. *See* freehold.

**least developed countries (LDC's)**
(economics) Some 36 of the world's poorest countries. considered by the United Nations to be the least developed of the less developed countries. Most of them are small in terms of area and population, and some are land-locked or small island countries. They are generally characterized by low: per capita incomes, literacy levels, and medical standards; subsistence agriculture; and a lack of exploitable minerals and competitive industries. Many suffer from aridity, floods, hurricanes, and excessive animal and plant pests, and most are situated in the zone 10 to 30 degrees north latitude. These countries have little prospect of rapid economic development in the foreseeable future and are likely to remain heavily dependent upon official development assistance for many years. Most are in Africa, but a few, such as Bangladesh, Afghanistan, Laos, and Nepal, are in Asia. Haiti is the only country in the Western Hemisphere classified by the United Nations as "least developed." *See* developing countries; less developed country.

**legal entity**
(law) Any individual, proprietorship, partnership, corporation, association, or other organization that has, in the eyes of the law, the capacity to make a contract or an agreement, and the abilities to assume an obligation and to discharge an indebtedness. A legal entity is a responsible being in the eyes of the law and can be sued for damages if the performance of a contract or agreement is not met. *See* person.

**legal person**
*See* person; legal entity.

**legal tender**
(banking/currency/law) Any money that is recognized as being lawful for use by a debtor to pay a creditor, who must accept same in the discharge of a debt unless the contract between the parties specifically states that another type of money is to be used.

**lek**
The currency of Albania. 1L=100 qintars.

**lempira**
The currency of Honduras. 1L=100 centavos.

**lender of last resort**
(banking) One of the functions and a major raison d'être of a modern central bank; whereby the bank has to provide liquid assets to the banking system when the existing liquid assets of the banking system threaten to deplete.

**leone**
The currency of Sierra Leone. 1Le=100 cents.

**less developed country (LDC)**
(economics) A country showing: (1) a poverty level of income, (2) a high rate of population increase, (3) a substantial portion of its workers employed in agriculture, (4) a low proportion of adult literacy, (5) high unemployment, and (6) a significant reliance on a few items for export.
Terms such as third world, poor, developing nations, and underdeveloped have also been used to describe less developed countries.

**less than container load (LCL)**
(shipping) A shipment of cargo that does not fill a container and is merged with cargo for more than one consignee or from more than one shipper. A container may be packed with LCL cargo at a container freight station for LCL delivery.

**less than truckload (LTL)**
(shipping) A shipment weighing less than the weight required for the application of the truckload rate.

**lesser developed country (LLDC)**
(economics) The classification LLDC was developed by the United Nations to give some guidance to donor agencies and countries about an equitable allocation of foreign assistance. The criteria for designating a country an LLDC, originally adopted by the UN Committee for Development Planning in 1971, have been modified several times. Criteria have included low: per capita income, literacy, and manufacturing share of the country's total gross domestic product. There is continuing concern that the criteria should be more robust and less subject to the possibility of easy fluctuation of a country between less developed and least developed status.

**letter of assignment**
A document with which the assignor assigns rights to a third party. *See* assignment.

**letter of credit (L/C)**
(banking) Formal term: Documentary credit or documentary letter of credit.
A letter of credit is a document issued by a bank stating its commitment to pay someone (supplier/exporter/seller) a stated amount of money on behalf of a buyer (importer) so long as the seller meets very specific terms and conditions. Letters of credit are more formally called documentary letters of credit because the banks handling the transaction deal in documents as opposed to goods.
The terms and conditions listed in the credit all involve presentation of specific documents within a stated period of time, hence the formal name—documentary credits.
The documents the buyer requires in the credit may vary, but at a minimum include an invoice and a bill of lading. Other documents the buyer may specify are certificate of origin, consular invoice, insurance certificate, inspection certificate and others.
Letters of credit are the most common method of making international payments, because the risks of the transaction are shared by both the buyer and the supplier.

Documentary letters of credit are subject to the Uniform Customs and Practice for Documentary Credits (UCPDC), Brochure No. 500, of the International Chamber of Commerce (ICC) in Paris. *See* Uniform Customs and Practice.

**Basic Letters of Credit**

There are two basic forms of a letter of credit: the Revocable Credit and the Irrevocable Credit. There are also two types of irrevocable credit: the Irrevocable Credit not Confirmed, and the Irrevocable Confirmed Credit. Each type of credit has advantages and disadvantages for the buyer and for the seller. Also note that the more the banks assume risk by guaranteeing payment, the more they will charge for providing the service.

(a) **Revocable credit**—This credit can be changed or canceled by the buyer without prior notice to the supplier. Because it offers little security to the seller, revocable credits are generally unacceptable and are rarely used.

(b) **Irrevocable credit**—The irrevocable credit is one which the issuing bank commits itself irrevocably to honor, provided the beneficiary complies with all stipulated conditions. This credit cannot be changed or canceled without the consent of both the buyer and the seller. As a result, this type of credit is the most widely used in international trade. Irrevocable credits are more expensive because of the issuing bank's added liability in guaranteeing the credit. There are two types of irrevocable credits:

(1) **The Irrevocable credit not confirmed (Unconfirmed credit)**. This means that the buyer's bank which issues the credit is the only party responsible for payment to the supplier, and the supplier's bank is obliged to pay the supplier only after receiving payment from the buyer's bank. The supplier's bank merely acts on behalf of the issuing bank and therefore incurs no risk.

(2) **The Irrevocable, confirmed credit.** In a confirmed credit, the advising bank adds its guarantee to pay the supplier to that of the issuing bank. If the issuing bank fails to make payment, the advising bank will pay. If a supplier is unfamiliar with the buyer's bank which issues the letter of credit, he may insist on an irrevocable confirmed credit. These credits may be used when trade is conducted in a high risk area where there are fears of outbreak of war or social, political, or financial instability. Confirmed credits may also be used by the supplier to enlist the aid of a local bank to extend financing to enable him to fill the order. A confirmed credit costs more because the bank has added liability.

**Special Letters of Credit**

There are numerous special letters of credit designed to meet specific needs of buyers, suppliers, and intermediaries. Special letters of credit usually involve increased participation by banks, so financing and service charges are higher than those for basic letters of credit. The following is a brief description of some special letters of credit.

(a) **Standby letter of credit**—This credit is primarily a payment or performance guarantee. It is used primarily in the United States because U.S. banks are prevented by law from giving certain guarantees. Standby credits are often called non-performing letters of credit because they are only used as a backup payment method if the collection on a primary payment method is past due.

Standby letters of credit can be used, for example, to guarantee the following types of payment and performance:

- repayment of loans,
- fulfillment by subcontractors,
- securing the payment for goods delivered by third parties.

The beneficiary to a standby letter of credit can draw from it on demand, so the buyer assumes added risk.

(b) **Revolving letter of credit**—This credit is a commitment on the part of the issuing bank to restore the credit to the original amount after it has been used or drawn down. The number of times it can be utilized and the period of validity is stated in the credit. The credit can be cumulative or noncumulative. Cumulative means that unutilized sums can be added to the next installment, whereas noncumulative means that partial amounts not utilized in time expire.

(c) **Deferred payment letter of credit**—In this credit the buyer takes delivery of the shipped goods by accepting the documents and agreeing to pay the bank after a fixed period of time. This credit gives the buyer a grace period for payment.

(d) **Red clause letter of credit**—This is used to provide the supplier with some funds prior to shipment to finance production of the goods. The credit may be advanced in part or in full, and the buyer's bank finances the advance payment. The buyer, in essence, extends financing to the seller and incurs ultimate risk for all advanced credits.

(e) **Transferable Letter of Credit**—This credit allows the supplier to transfer all or part of the proceeds of the letter of credit to a second beneficiary, usually the ultimate supplier of the goods. This is a common financing tactic for middlemen and is used extensively in the Far East.

(f) **Back-to-Back Letter of Credit**—This is a new credit opened on the basis of an already existing, nontransferable credit. It is used by traders to make payment to the ultimate supplier. A trader receives a letter of credit from the buyer and then opens another letter of credit in favor of the supplier. The first letter of credit is used as collateral for the second credit. The second credit makes price adjustments from which come the trader's profit. *See* Guide to Letters of Credit Appendix.

***letter of indemnity (LOI)***

(shipping) A document which serves to protect the carrier/owner financially against possible repercussions in connection with the release of goods without presentation of an original bill of lading. A letter of indemnity (usually as an indemnity for missing bill of lading) is used in cases in which the goods arrive at the port of destination before the original bills of lading. The issuance of the letter of indemnity allows the purchaser to take immediate delivery of the goods, thus saving himself time, additional demurrage, storage expenses, insurance costs, etc.

***letter of intent***

(law) A document, such as a written memorandum, that describes the preliminary understanding between parties who intend to make a contract or join together in another action, such as a joint venture or a corporate merger.

***leu***

The currency of Romania. 1L=100 bani.

***lev***

The currency of Bulgaria. 1Lv=100 stotinki.

***leverage***

(finance/foreign exchange) In options terminology, this expresses the disproportionately large change in the premium in terms of the relative price movement of the underlying instrument.

***lex loci actus***

(law) A legal rule to apply the law of the place where a wrongful act occurred. A court may apply this law in a legal action if the parties have not expressly agreed to the law that will govern their contract and if the laws of more than one jurisdiction could apply. If a buyer and seller, for example, are located in different countries and the buyer breaches the contract, under the rule of lex loci actus the court will apply the law of the buyer's country in interpreting the contract. This rule is usually applied when the wrongful act has a greater effect in the jurisdiction where it occurred than in any other jurisdiction. *See* conflict of laws; nexus; lex loci solutionis.

### lex loci solutionis
(law) A legal rule to apply the law of the place where payment is to be made or a contract is to be performed. A country may apply this law in a legal action if the parties have not expressly agreed to the law that will govern their contract and if the laws of more than one jurisdiction could apply. If a buyer and seller, for example, are located in different countries and the buyer breaches the contract, under the law of lex loci solutionis the court will apply the law of the seller's country, which is where payment is to be made. This rule is usually applied when performance of the contract has a greater effect in the jurisdiction where it is to occur than in any other jurisdiction. *See* conflict of laws; nexus; lex loci actus.

### liberal
(economics) When referring to trade policy, "liberal" usually means relatively free of import controls or restraints and/or a preference for reducing existing barriers to trade, often contrasted with the protectionist preference for retaining or raising selected barriers to imports.

### LIBID
*See* London Interbank Bid Rate.

### LIBOR
*See* London Interbank Offered Rate.

### license
(law) A legal document conferring to the holder (licensee), the right to do something. Examples include foreign language translation rights for books, local manufacturing rights for pharmaceuticals, or use of a well-known brand name and logo in a specific market.

### licensee
(law) An individual, company or organization that acquires a license, typically for intellectual property rights such as foreign language translation rights for books, local manufacturing rights for pharmaceuticals, or use of a well-known brand name and logo in a specific market.

### licensor
(law) An individual, company or organization that grants a license. A licensor owns or has the rights to license intellectual property such as a copyright, patent or trademark. Examples of intellectual property licenses include foreign language translation rights for books, local manufacturing rights for pharmaceuticals, or use of a well-known brand name and logo in a specific market.

### licensing agreement
(law) A contract whereby the holder of a trademark, patent, or copyright transfers a limited right to use a process, sell or manufacture an article, or furnish specialized services covered by the trademark, patent or copyright to another firm.

### life-cycle processing
(economics/accounting) An accounting approach in which a company sets product prices based on recovering costs over the life cycle of the product.
(U.S.) In antidumping cases, U.S. authorities dispute the validity of this approach because projections of future yield improvements cannot be verified at the time of dumping calculations. *See* dumping.

### lift on, lift off (Lo/Lo)
(shipping) the loading and unloading of cargo from a ship using a crane.

### lift van
(shipping) A wooden or metal container used for packing household goods and personal effects. A lift van must be at least 100 cubic feet and be suitable for lifting by mechanical device.

### lighter
(shipping) An open or covered barge towed by a tugboat and used mainly in harbors and inland waterways for the transport of cargo. Lighters are used in situations where shallow water prevents the ocean going vessel from coming close to shore.

### lighter aboard ship (LASH)
(shipping) A floatable large container (lighter) used in the combined ocean and inland waterway transport of goods. Lighters are transported on specially constructed ships.

### lighterage
(shipping) (a) The loading or unloading of a ship by means of a lighter. (b) Charges assessed for lighter service.

### lilangeni
The currency of Swaziland. 1L=100 cents. The plural of lilangeni is emalangeni (E).

### LIMEAN
(banking/finance) The calculated average of the London Interbank Bid Rate (LIBID) and the London Interbank Offered Rate (LIBOR). *See* London Interbank Bid Rate; London Interbank Offered Rate.

### Limitada (Ltda.)
(Brazil, Portugal) Designation for a private limited liability corporation with limited liability to shareholders. *See* Sociedad por Quota.

### limitation period
(law) A maximum period set by statute within which a legal action can be brought or a right enforced. A statute may prohibit, for example, any individual or legal entity from bringing an action for breach of contract more than one year after the breach occurred.

### Limited (Ltd.)
(United Kingdom) Designation for a private limited liability corporation with limited liability to shareholders.
(South Africa, United States) Designation for a public corporation with limited liability to shareholders.

### limited appointment
(diplomacy) Limited appointees to the U.S. & Foreign Commercial Service (or to other foreign services) are persons from the private sector or from the federal government who are non-career officers assigned overseas for a limited time.

### limited liability
(law) Restricted liability for the obligations of a business. Liability may be limited, for example, to the amount of a partner's or shareholder's contribution to the capital of partnership or corporation.

### limited partnership
(law) A partnership in which at least one partner has general liability and at least one of the other partners has limited liability.

### Limitée (Ltée.)
(Canada) Designation for a public corporation with limited liability to shareholders.

### line haul
(shipping) The direct movement of freight between two major ports by a single ship.

### line haul vessel
(shipping) A vessel which is on a regularly defined schedule.

### Line Release System
(U.S. Customs) A part of the U.S. Customs' Automated Commercial System, is designed for the release and tracking of shipments through the use of personal computers and bar code technology. To qualify for line release, a commodity must have a history of invoice accuracy, and be selected by local Customs districts on the basis of high volume. To release the merchandise, Customs reads the bar code into a personal computer, verifies that the bar code

matches the invoice data, and enters the quantity. The cargo release is transmitted to the Automated Commercial System, which establishes an entry and the requirement for an entry summary, and provides the Automated Broker Interface system participants with release information. *See* Automated Commercial System.

(Canada Customs) A Canada Border Services Agency (CBSA) import shipment program that allows for the quick clearance of commercial shipments. The LRS processes release information before a shipment arrives at the border, thereby speeding the process of deciding to release a shipment or to refer it for examination.

The Line Release System has two release procedures called service options:
- **Prearrival Review System (PARS)** Available to importers and brokers who can send invoice and manifest information to the CBSA before a shipment arrives; and
- **Frequent Importer Release System (FIRST)** Available to importers of frequent, low-risk shipments. FIRST requires prior CBSA authorization.

For information about CBSA and the LRS, go to: www.cbsa-asfc.gc.ca or contact the CBSA's Automated Customs Information Service (ACIS) at 1-800-461-9999 for service in English or 1-800-959-2036 for service in French.

### liner
(shipping) A vessel carrying passengers and cargo that operates on a route with a fixed schedule.

### liner terms
(shipping) Conditions under which a shipping company will transport goods, including the amount payable for carriage of the goods (freight) and the cost both for loading and discharge of the vessel.

### liquidated damages
(law) A sum of money that a contracting party agrees to pay to the other party for breaching an agreement, particularly important in a contract in which damages for breach may be difficult to assess. A manufacturer, for example, that agrees to develop, produce, and sell unique products to a buyer may insist on a contract clause for liquidated damages in the event that the buyer rejects the goods without justifiable reason because the market for resale of the unique goods will be so limited that damages will be difficult to assess.

### liquidation
(U.S. Customs) The final review of a U.S. Customs entry, and determination of the rate of duty and amount of duty by Customs. Liquidation is accomplished by Customs posting a notice on a public bulletin board at the customhouse. An importer may receive an advance notice on Customs Form 4333A "Courtesy Notice" stating when and in what amount duty will be liquidated. This form is not the liquidation, and protest rights do not accrue until the notice is posted. Time limits for protesting do not start to run until the date of posting, and a protest cannot be filed before liquidation is posted.

The Customs Service may determine that an entry cannot be liquidated as entered for one reason or another. For example, the tariff classification may not be correct or may not be acceptable because it is not consistent with an established and uniform classification practice. If the change required by this determination results in a rate of duty more favorable to an importer, the entry is liquidated accordingly and a refund of the applicable amount of the deposited duties is authorized. On the other hand, a change may be necessary which imposes a higher rate of duty. For example, a claim for an exemption from duty under a duty-free provision or under a conditional exemption may be found to be insufficient for lack of the required supporting documentation. In this situation, the importer will be given an advance notice of the proposed duty rate advancement and an opportunity to validate the claim for a free rate or more favorable rate of duty.

If the importer does not respond to the notice or if the response is found to be without merit, duty is liquidated in accordance with the entry as corrected and the importer is billed for the additional duty. The port or district may find that the importer's response raises issues of such complexity that resolution by a Customs Headquarters decision through the internal advise procedure is warranted. Internal advice from Customs Headquarters may be requested by the local Customs officers on their own initiative or in response to a request by the importer.

Public Law 95-410 (Customs Procedural Reform and Simplification Act of 1978) requires that all liquidations be performed within one year from the date of consumption entry or final withdrawal on a warehouse entry. Three one-year extensions are permitted.

*See* protest; entry; classification; valuation.

### liquidation system
(U.S. Customs) A part of U.S. Customs' Automated Commercial System, closes the file on each entry and establishes a batch filing number which is essential for recovering an entry for review or enforcement purposes. An entry liquidation is a final review of the entry. Public Law 95-410 (Customs Procedural Reform and Simplification Act of 1978) requires that all liquidations be performed within one year from the date of consumption entry or final withdrawal on a warehouse entry. Three one-year extensions are permitted. *See* liquidation; Automated Commercial System.

### liquidity
(economics) (a) A company's ability to meet its obligations at all times. (b) The availability of liquid funds in an economy. (c) The possibility of being able to carry out financial transactions without influencing the market.

### lira
The currency of:
Malta, 1£M (or 1 LM)=100 cents;
The former currency of Italy, San Marino, Turkey and The Vatican. The new currency of these countries is the European Union Euro. €1 = 100 cents.

### litas
The currency of Lithuania. 1Lit=100 centai.

### Lloyd's Agency System
(insurance) The global Lloyd's Agency network consists of over 350 main Lloyd's Agents and a further 325 Lloyd's Sub-Agents. The first Lloyd's Agency appointments were made in 1811, primarily for the communication of shipping movements and casualty information. Although most Agents still carry out this function, their main role today is one of conducting or arranging surveys on ships and cargoes for insurers and commercial interests throughout the world. Almost 200 Agents have also been granted authority to adjust and settle claims arising under Lloyd's certificates of insurance. Although the Lloyd's Agency network is heavily influenced by its maritime origin, many Agents have diversified to embrace aviation, property, vehicle and liability specialties.

Many underwriters and their assureds throughout the world utilize the services of Lloyd's Agents and evidence of this is usually reflected in the wording of cargo insurance certificates, which often incorporate the clause: "In the event of loss or damage which may result in a claim under this insurance immediate notice should be given to the Lloyd's Agent at the port or place where the loss or damage is discovered, in order that he may examine the goods and issue a survey report." For information go to: www.lloydsagency.com.

**Lloyd's List**
(shipping) A leading source of worldwide maritime news and information. The print and on-line publication includes coverage of world shipping, insurance, energy and logistics markets. Lloyds List; Informa UK Ltd.; Telephone House; 69 - 77 Paul Street; London EC2A 4LQ; UK Tel: [44] (0) 20 7017 5000.
Informa Publishing Group Ltd.; PO Box 1017; Westborough, MA 01581-6017; USA; Tel: [1] (800) 493 4080. Contact at www.lloydslist.com

**Lloyd's of London**
(insurance) A market of 66 insurers (themselves syndicates) that operate under the Lloyd's of London umbrella. Each insurer specializes in a specific risk such as ocean vessels (Exxon Valdez shipwreck and oil spill in Alaska), liability (asbestos), manufacturing facilities (match and fireworks factories), buildings (World Trade Center in New York), excessive risks (1906 San Francisco Earthquake), reinsurance (the insurance of insurance companies) and retrocessions (the reinsurance of reinsurance companies). Lloyd's does not sell insurance to individuals.
Membership in a syndicate was restricted to individuals (the famous "Names") with significant net worth. Names accept *unlimited personal liability* ("down to their cufflinks") on the policies they write.
In the 1990s Lloyd's allowed "Names" to convert to "Namecos," limited liability companies, which enabled them to carry forward income tax losses or defer capital gains. Previously, Names had not been permitted by the Inland Revenue to do this because their business could not be transferred as a going concern. These tax concessions now also apply to (the otherwise obscure) Scottish limited partnership.
Lloyd's was founded in 1688 in Edward Lloyd's coffeehouse near the London docks. Insurers, merchants and ships' captains would meet to exchange gossip, trade news and shipping information. Lloyd's of London; One Lime Street; London EC3M 7HA; UK; Tel: [44] (0) 20 7327 1000; Web: www.lloyds.com.

**Lloyd's Register**
(shipping) An independent risk management organization providing risk assessment and risk mitigation solutions and management systems certification around the world. Originally founded in 1760 to survey and classify merchant ships so that insurance underwriters and other interested parties may know the quality and condition of the vessels offered by insurance or employment. Contact at Lloyd's Register; 71 Fenchurch Street; London EC3M 4BS, UK; Tel: [44] (0)20 7709 9166; www.lr.org.

**loading**
(shipping) The physical placing of cargo into carrier's container, or onto a vessel.

**load line**
(shipping) A horizontal marking (or markings) painted on the hull of an ocean-going cargo vessel that shows where the waterline is when the vessel is at full capacity. *See* Plimsoll mark for a historical perspective and illustration.

**localization**
A broad term used to describe the modification, preparation and/or translation of products, services, media or advertising for use or sale in a local market. Localization can include changes to product or service specifications, additions of content that are more appropriate for a local market, deletion of content deemed insensitive or not applicable to a local market, checking content for cultural insensitivity and the translation of books, operational manuals and advertising into a local language or dialect. Examples include converting a U.S.-made, left-hand drive automobile to right-hand drive for the Japanese market; changing the cutting patterns for clothing to reflect different body shapes (not just sizes) for another culture; making sure that translations of marketing materials are not incorrect, insensitive or contrary to the goals of the advertiser; adding coverage of local issues to Web sites; and deleting or changing references that imply that the reader or user is from a country or culture other than the "target" country or culture.

**locus**
(law) A place. The locus of arbitration, for example, is the place where arbitration proceedings are held.

**logistics**
The process of planning, implementing and controlling the flow of personnel, materials and information from the point of origin to the point of destination at the required time and in the desired condition.
(shipping) The process of planning and controlling the flow of raw materials, work in progress or finished products from the point of origin to the point of destination (either to a factory for further processing, to a warehouse for storage or to the marketplace for sale) at the required time and in the desired condition.

**logistics data interchange (LDI)**
(logistics) The electronic exchange of logistics data through a computer system. LDI is similar to electronic data interchange (EDI). *See* EDI.

**logistics resource management (LRM)**
"A new class of software for supply chain execution that provides visibility and control of integrated transportation and import export processes and delivers cost savings, trade security, and supply chain advantages to Global 2000 companies." (Definition by Arzoon, Inc., Web: www.arzoon.com.)

**Lombard rate**
(banking/finance-Germany) The interest rate applied to loans backed by collateral in the form of movable, easily-sold assets (goods or securities). Particularly used with reference to the German Bundesbank, which normally maintains its Lombard rate at about 1/2 percent above its discount rate.

**Lomé Convention**
A 1975 agreement between the European Community (EC) and 62 African, Caribbean, and Pacific (ACP) states (mostly former colonies of the EC members). The agreement covers some aid provisions as well as trade and tariff preferences for the ACP countries when shipping to the EC. The Lome Convention grew out of the 1958 Treaty of Rome's "association" with the 18 African colonies/countries that had ties with Belgium and France.

**London Interbank Bid Rate (LIBID)**
(banking/finance) The bid in a quotation representing the interest rate at which U.S. dollar deposits are retraded in London. *See* London Interbank Offered Rate; LIMEAN.

**London Interbank Offered Rate (LIBOR)**
(banking/finance) The interest rate at which banks in London are prepared to lend funds to first-class banks. It is used to determine the interest rate payable on most Eurocredits. *See* London Interbank Bid Rate; LIMEAN.

**London Metal Exchange**
(banking/finance) A commodity exchange whose members, approximately 110 in number, deal in copper, lead, zinc, and tin. Contact: London Metal Exchange, 56 Leadenhall Street, London EC3A 2 DX, UK; Tel: [44] (20)

7264-5555; Fax: [44] (20) 7680-0505; Web: www.lme.co.uk.

### London Tanker Brokers' Panel
(shipping) A body made up of representatives of six London-based shipping organizations which will make an independent assessment or award of compensation for a voyage, contract or demurrage based upon historical market information in return for a fee. The Panel also establishes the terms of reference for AFRA (Average Freight Rate Assessment) and publishes AFRA. The six member organizations are: Clarkson and Company Ltd. (www.clarksons.co.uk); John I. Jacobs PLC; Davies and Newman Wake Ltd. (E-mail: bunkers@wakemarine.ltd.uk); Howard Houlder and Partners Ltd.; E.A. Gibson Shipbrokers Ltd. (www.eagibson.co.uk); and Galbraith's Ltd. (www.galbraiths.co.uk).

### long form
A form (document) that has terms and conditions printed on the reverse (back) of the form. For example, a long form bill of lading has the terms and conditions of carriage printed on the reverse. The long form bill of lading is preferred in international transactions. *See* short form.

### long of exchange
(banking/foreign exchange) When a trader in foreign currency holds foreign bills in an amount exceeding the bills of his or her own that have been sold and remain outstanding, the trader is long of exchange.

### long ton
(measure) A unit of mass or weight measurement equal to 2,240 pounds. A short ton is 2,000 pounds.

### longshoreman
(shipping) A laborer who loads and unloads ships at a seaport. *See* stevedore; gang.

### lorry
(UK term) British for truck.

### loss of specie
(insurance) A loss when goods arrive so damaged as to cease to be a thing of the kind insured. Examples of "loss of specie" are cement arriving as rock, or textiles as rags. *See* total loss.

### loti
The currency of Lesotho. 1L=100 lisente. Plural of loti is maloti (M).

### lot labels
(shipping) Labels attached to each piece of multiple lot shipment for identification purposes.

### lower deck
(logistics) A lower, or the lowest, cargo holding area of an airplane or a ship.

### lower deck containers
(shipping) Carrier owned containers specially designed as an integral part of the aircraft to fit in the cargo compartments (lower deck) of a wide body aircraft.

### Low Value Shipment Program (LVS Program)
(Canada Customs) Also called the Courier/LVS Program. A Canada Customs program designed to streamline the processing of low-value shipments through customs while providing the courier industry with expedited release. Fundamental aspects of the Courier/LVS Program include:
- A combined cargo report and release document called the "cargo/release list" for goods valued under $1,600 CAN
- Expedited release of qualifying shipments based on the information contained on the cargo/release list
- Accounting for duties and taxes on these shipments on a consolidated monthly entry or CADEX transmission on an "F""ype entry

- Compliance verification of courier and importer records by the CBSA to validate proper and complete accounting.

For more information go to www.cbsa-asfc.gc.ca/import/courier/courier/menu-e.html.

### lump of labor fallacy
(economics) The fallacious theory that an ever-increasing population leads to an ever-increasing rate of unemployment because there are only a fixed number of jobs to go around. The resurgence of this theory is an effort by some European nations to reduce the legal workweek as a means of reducing unemployment.

### lumper
(logistics/trucking) A laborer who assists a motor carrier or truck driver in the loading or unloading of cargo. *See* lumping.

### lumping
(logistics/trucking) The assistance given to a motor carrier, specifically a truck driver, in the loading and unloading of cargo. This practice occurs most commonly in the food and produce industries. The laborers (lumpers) may be paid by the terminal operator or by the driver. *See* lumper.

### LVS (Courier LVS)
(Canada) Low Value Shipment. A Canada Border Services Agency (CBSA) program that speeds the release of low-value entries of up to C$1,600 for commercial imports by approved carriers. Information at Web: www.cbsa-asfc.gc.ca/import/courier/courier/menu-e.html.

## M

### Maastricht (Treaty)

(European Union) The popular name for the European Treaty for Economic Union. A treaty, signed in the Dutch city of Maastricht on February 7, 1992, that changed the name of the European Community (EC) to the European Union (EU) and paved the way for further European integration. In addition to the change in name, the major aims of the treaty were: 1) Monetary union. To abolish existing European currencies and replace them with the Euro. (This was achieved as of January 1, 2002.) In addition, to create a European Central Bank (ECB) to assume the various functions of the central banks of the member states in establishing monetary policy. 2) Political and military integration. To work towards a common foreign policy and a joint military force. (These goals have proved to be more controversial than monetary union as they have been seen to infringe upon the very core of national sovereignty.) And 3) Common citizenship. To establish common EU citizenship for nationals of all member states.

The ratification of the treaty was a sometimes dramatic affair during the course of 1992 and 1993. National referendums were held in France, Spain, and Ireland and twice in Denmark. The Danes initially voted to reject the treaty prompting the UK and Italy to withdraw from the European Exchange Rate Mechanism. The French voted narrowly in favor in September 1992.

Low-income countries such as Spain and Ireland, however, voted clearly for ratification as they stood to benefit the greatest from the treaty. By November 1992 all member states except Denmark and Great Britain had ratified the treaty. At a summit meeting in Edinburgh in December 1992, compromises were made which led to Danish ratification in a second referendum in May 1993 and to ratification in the UK in July 1993. The treaty was formally ratified by all member states on November 1, 1993.

*See* European Union.

### Maatschappij (Mij.)

(Netherlands) Designation for a combination of two or more persons who enter into a joint arrangement to conduct certain business activities.

### macroeconomics

(economics) (a) The study of statistics (e.g., total consumption, total employment) of the economy as a whole rather than as single economic units. (b) Synonymous with aggregate economics. *See* microeconomics.

### mail entry

(U.S. Customs) A means of shipping and entering goods into the Customs Territory of the United States. Mail entry has several advantages as well as several limitations.

(1) Duties on parcels valued at US$1,200 or less are collected by the letter carrier delivering the parcel to the addressee.

(2) No formal entry paperwork is required on duty-free merchandise not exceeding US$1,200 in value.

(3) There is no need to clear shipments personally if under US$1,200 in value.

Joint Customs and postal regulations provide that all international parcel post packages must have a Customs declaration securely attached giving an accurate description and the value of the contents. This declaration is obtained at post offices. Commercial shipments must also be accompa-

nied by a commercial invoice enclosed in the parcel bearing the declaration.

Parcels and packages not labeled or endorsed properly and found to contain merchandise subject to duty or taxes are subject to forfeiture.

If the value of a mail importation exceeds US$1,250, the addressee is notified to prepare and file a formal Customs entry (consumption entry) for it at the nearest Customs port.

A mail entry limit of US$250 has been set for a number of articles classified in sub-chapters III and IV, chapter 99, of the Harmonized Tariff Schedule of the U.S. as an exception to the above US$1,250 limit. Items on this list include billfolds, feathers, flowers, footwear, fur, gloves, handbags, headwear, leather, luggage, millinery, pillows, plastics, skins, rubber, textiles, toys, games, sports equipment and trimmings.

Unaccompanied shipments of made-to-measure suits from Hong Kong require a formal entry regardless of value.

*See* entry; consumption entry.

### mala fide

(law) In bad faith. A seller's representation that goods are usable for a particular purpose when in fact the seller knows that the goods are not is a representation made mala fide.

### manifest

(shipping) A document giving the description of a ship's cargo or the contents of a car or truck.

### Manufactured Imports and Investment Promotion Organization (MIPRO)

(Japan) A non-profit organization, established in 1978 by the joint efforts of the Japanese Government and the private sector to promote imports of foreign manufactured products by hosting exhibitions and providing market information. MIPRO's activities are broadly classified into three categories: (1) holding imported product trade exhibitions for buyers and the general public; (2) disseminating information regarding imported products and the Japanese market; and (3) promoting sales of foreign products to Japanese consumers to promote recognition of the quality of imported goods. Contact: Manufactured Imports Promotion Organization, 1-3, Higashi Ikebukuro 3-chome, Toshima-ku, Tokyo 170, Japan; Tel: [81] (3) 3988-2791; Fax: [81] (3) 3988-1629; E-mail: mipro@mipro.or.jp; Web: www.mipro.or.jp.

### manufacturing resources planning

*See* MRP.

### maquila

(Mexico) *See* maquiladora.

### maquiladora

(Mexico) A manufacturing or assembly plant located in Mexico where raw materials, component parts and support equipment (such as computers, administrative materials and transportation equipment) are imported duty- and license-free and whose production is exported, often to the United States, for low or no import duty. These plants are located primarily along the Mexico-U.S. border and enjoy other exemptions from Mexican laws governing foreign companies.

The Maquiladora program was established in 1965 after a 1942 U.S.-Mexican program to assist *Braceros* (extremely poor Mexican migrant farm workers living along the Mexican border), was abolished in 1964. In 1989 the program was liberalized further to make it an even more attractive and dynamic sector of the economy.

The maquiladora system is also called an "in-bond" or "free trade zone" program as raw materials, component parts and support equipment is imported under bond with the stipulation that it eventually be reexported.

Critics charge that these plants are notorious for environmental degradation, low wages and poor working conditions.

Proponents respond that the plants provide needed jobs to Mexican workers, provide the second largest source of foreign income to the country (after oil exports) and lessen the flow of illegal immigration to the United States.

From Spanish, the word is pronounced mah-kee-lah-DOH-rah. It is usually shortened to maquila (mah-KEE-lah).

### margin
(general) The difference between the cost of sold items and the total net sales income.

(finance) The difference between the market value of collateral pledged to secure a loan and the face value of the loan itself.

(investments—U.S.) The amount paid by the customer when he or she uses a broker credit to buy a security under Federal Reserve regulations, the initial margin required in past decades has ranged from 50 to 100 percent of the purchase price.

(finance) The spread between bid and asked rates

(foreign exchange) The good faith deposit which the writer of an option or the buyer of a forward or futures contract has to put up to cover the risk of adverse price movements.

### marginal cost
(economics) The increase in the total cost of production that results from manufacturing one more unit output.

### marine cargo insurance
(insurance) Broadly, insurance covering loss of, or damage to, goods at sea. Marine insurance typically compensates the owner of merchandise for losses in excess of those which can be legally recovered from the carrier that are sustained from fire, shipwreck, piracy, and various other causes. *See* special marine policy; all risk.

### Marine Extension Clause 1943 & 1952
(insurance) An insurance extension which broadens warehouse-to-warehouse insurance coverage by eliminating the requirement that ordinary course of transit be maintained as well as the 15- or 30-day time limit at destination. Moreover, continuation of coverage is provided when certain conditions necessitate discharge of goods from vessel at a port other than the original destination. The most recent form of Marine Extension Clause was developed in 1952. It too provides for extensions as does the 1943 version, and adds that the assured will act with reasonable dispatch. The Warehouse-to-Warehouse Clause is now found in practically all open cargo policies. *See* warehouse-to-warehouse.

### marine insurance
*See* marine cargo insurance.

### MarinePARS
(Canada Customs) *See* Pre-Arrival Review System.

### Marine Pre-Arrival Review System (MarinePARS)
(Canada Customs) *See* Pre-Arrival Review System (PARS).

### marine protection and indemnity insurance
(insurance) Insurance against legal liability of the insured for loss, damage, or expense arising out of or incident to the ownership, operation, chartering, maintenance, use, repair, or construction of any vessel, craft, or instrumentality in use in ocean or inland waterways, including liability of the insured for personal injury or death, and for loss of or damage to the property of another person.

### maritime
Business pertaining to commerce or navigation transacted upon the sea or in seaports in such matters as the court of

admiralty have jurisdiction over, concurrently with the courts of common law.

### mark
The former currency of Germany. 1DM=100 pfennig. The new currency of Germany is the European Union Euro. €1 = 100 cents.

### market access
(economics) The openness of a national market to foreign products. Market access reflects a government's willingness to permit imports to compete relatively unimpeded with similar domestically produced goods.

### Market Access Program (MAP)
(U.S.) A U.S. government program authorized by the U.S. Food, Agriculture, Conservation, and Trade Act of 1990 and administered by the U.S. Department of Agriculture's Foreign Agricultural Service. Under the MPP, surplus stocks or funds from the Commodity Credit Corporation are used to partially reimburse agricultural organizations conducting specific foreign market development projects for eligible products in specified countries. Proposals for MPP programs are developed by trade organizations and private firms. Activities financed by the programs vary from commodity to commodity, and include activities such as market research, construction of a three-story wood demonstration building, construction of a model feed mill, and consumer promotion activities. (MPP is similar to the Targeted Export Assistance (TEA) program which was repealed by the 1990 Farm Bill.) Contact: U.S. Department of Agriculture, Foreign Agriculture Service, Marketing Operations Staff, 1400 Independence Ave., Washington, DC 20250 USA; Tel: [1] (202) 720-4327; Fax: [1] (202) 720-9361; Web: www.fas.usda.gov/mos/programs/map.asp.

### market disruption
(economics) The situation created when a surge of imports in a given product area causes sales of domestically produced goods in a particular country to decline to such an extent that the domestic producers and their employees suffer major economic hardship.

### market economy
(economics) An economic system where resources are allocated and production of products determined by market forces rather than by government decree.

### Market-Oriented Cooperation Plan
(U.S./Japan) A U.S. Japan trade agreement aimed at improving long-term business relations between Japan's automotive manufacturers and U.S. auto parts suppliers.

### Market-Oriented Sector-Selective
(U.S./Japan) Bilateral trade discussions between the U.S. and Japan begun in January 1985 in an effort to remove many trade barriers at once in a given sector. MOSS talks have focused on five sectors: (1) telecommunications, (2) medical equipment and pharmaceuticals, (3) electronics, (4) forest products, and (5) auto parts. Overall, the talks focus high-level attention on reducing certain market obstacles opening communication channels to resolve follow-up disputes.

### market price
(economics) (a) The price established in the market where buyers and sellers meet to buy and sell similar products. (b) The price determined by factors of supply and demand rather than by decisions made by management.

### marking: country of origin
The physical markings on a product that indicate the country of origin where the article was produced.

(U.S. Customs) U.S. Customs laws require each imported article produced abroad to be marked in a conspicuous place as legibly, indelibly, and permanently as the nature of the article permits, with the English name of the country of origin, to indicate to the ultimate purchaser in the United States the name of the country in which the article was manufactured or produced. Articles which are otherwise specifically exempted from individual marking are an exception to this rule. *See* United States Customs Service.

**markka**
The former currency of Finland. 1Fmk=100 pennia. The new currency of Finland is the European Union Euro. €1 = 100 cents.

**marks**
(shipping) Information placed on outer surface of shipping containers or packages such as address labels, identifying numbers, box specifications, caution, or directional warnings.

**markup**
*See* premium.

**master air waybill (MAWB)**
(logistics) An air waybill of lading that covers a consolidated shipment of goods and lists the consolidator as the shipper. *See* bill of lading, air waybill.

**master's protest**
*See* captain's protest.

**matador bond**
(banking/finance) Bond issued on the Spanish market, denominated in currencies other than the peseta.

**Matchmaker Program**
(U.S.) Matchmaker trade delegations are organized and led by the U.S. International Trade Administration to help new-to-export and new-to-market firms meet prescreened prospects who are interested in their products or services in overseas markets. Matchmaker delegations usually target two major country markets in two countries and limit trips to a week or less. This approach is designed to permit U.S. firms to interview a maximum number of prospective overseas business partners with a minimum of time away from their home office. The program includes U.S. embassy support, briefings on market requirements and business practices, and interpreters' services. Matchmaker events, based on specific product themes and end-users, are scheduled for a limited number of countries each year. Contact: International Trade Administration, Department of Commerce, 14th and Constitution Ave. NW, Washington, DC 20230 USA; Tel: [1] (202) 482-2000. *See* new-to-export; new-to-market.

**material contract terms**
(law) Terms that are necessary to the agreement. Clauses that describe the goods, fix the price, and set the delivery date are examples of material contract terms.

**material safety data sheets (MSDS)**
A document prepared by a supplier or manufacturer of potentially hazardous materials and products that details safety information and procedures for handling or using a substance, material or product. Material safety data sheets typically contain: a listing of hazardous ingredients and components, proper handling procedures, first aid instructions and emergency response and reporting procedures. Such data sheets are designed to be an aid for both workers and users and are distributed with such materials and products in industrial and retail settings.

**mate's receipt**
(shipping) A declaration issued by an officer of a vessel in the name of the shipping company stating that certain goods have been received on board his vessel. A mate's receipt is not a title document. Used as an interim document until the bill of lading is issued.

**maximum payload**
(logistics) The maximum weight limit of cargo that a particular transportation vehicle can carry.

**measurement cargo**
(shipping) A cargo on which the transportation charge is assessed on the basis of measurement.

**measurement ton**
(shipping) Also known as a cargo or freight ton. A space measurement usually 40 cubic feet or one cubic meter. The cargo is assessed a certain rate for every 40 cubic feet of space it occupies.

**medium of exchange**
(economics) Any commodity (commonly money) which is widely accepted in payment for goods and services and in settlement of debts, and is accepted without reference to the standing of the person who offers it in payment.

**memorandum bill of lading**
(shipping) The duplicate copy of a bill of lading. *See* bill of lading.

**memorandum of understanding (MOU)**
(general) An informal record, document or instrument that serves as the basis of a future contact.
(U.S.) A very detailed document devised by executive branch agencies of the government in areas such as aviation and fisheries that serve as agreements between nations.

**memorandum tariff**
(shipping) Publications which contain rule and rate information extracted from official tariffs. Memorandum tariffs are published by many carriers and are available from these carriers upon request. *See* tariff.

**mercantilism**
(economics) A prominent economic philosophy in the 16th and 17th centuries that equated the accumulation and possession of gold and other international monetary assets, such as foreign currency reserves, with national wealth. Although this point of view is generally discredited among 20th and 21st century economists and trade policy experts, some contemporary politicians still favor policies designed to create trade "surpluses," such as import substitution and tariff protection for domestic industries, as essential to national economic strength.

**merchandise processing fee (MPF)**
(U.S. Customs) A user fee collected by the U.S. Customs and Border Protection (CBP) for imports as follows: 0.21 percent ad valorem on formally-entered imported merchandise (generally entries valued over US $2,000), subject to a minimum fee of $25 per entry and a maximum fee of $485 per entry. On informal entries (those valued at less than $2,000), the MPFs are: $2 for automated entries, $6 for manual entries not prepared by Customs, and $9 for manual entries that are prepared by Customs. *See* user fees.

**merchandise trade balance**
*See* balance of payments.

**merchant bank**
(banking) A term used in Great Britain for an organization that underwrites securities for corporations, advises such clients on mergers, and is involved in the ownership of commercial ventures.

**merchant's credit**
(banking) A letter of credit issued by the buyer himself. Contains no commitment whatever on the part of a bank. *See* letter of credit.

**merchant's haulage**
(shipping) The inland move from or to a port that has all arrangements made by the cargo interests (seller/exporter).

**Mercosur**
(regional trade alliance) Mercosur (Spanish; Mercosul in Portuguese) or Southern Common Market, is comprised of

Argentina, Brazil, Paraguay, and Uruguay. Mercosur is scheduled to enter into force in December 1994 for Argentina and Brazil and to enter into force in December 1995 for Paraguay and Uruguay. Mercosur, modeled similarly to the European Community's Treaty of Rome, will establish a common external tariff and eliminate barriers to trade in services. Chile has not sought entry to Mercosur, but does have an agreement with Argentina which will provide for some similar benefits.

### merry-go-round
(banking/finance/foreign exchange) The circulation of money through various sources, ending up where it started. For instance the German Central Bank recycles excess capital by selling U.S. dollars to banks under a repurchase agreement and the banks place the U.S. dollars in the Euromarket. As the financial institutions could run up a U.S. dollar debt on the Euromarket, the Central Bank must buy back the U.S. dollars and sell domestic currency to avoid an excessive increase in the mark.

### meter
(measure) A unit of linear measure equal to 39.37 inches (approximately). *See* Weights and Measures in the Appendix.

### metical
The currency of Mozambique. 1Mt=100 centavos.

### metric system
(measurement) A decimal system of weights and measures based on the meter of approximately 39.37 inches and the kilogram of approximately 2.2046 pounds. *See* Weights and Measures in the Appendix.

### metric ton
(measure) A unit of mass or weight measure equal to 2,204.6 pounds or 1,000 kilograms preferably called kiloton.

### microbridge
(shipping) A landbridge movement in which cargo originating/destined to an inland point is railed or trucked to/from the water port for a shipment to/from a foreign country. Carrier is responsible for cargo and costs from origin to destination.

### microcredit
The extension of very small loans to entrepreneurs who lack collateral, steady employment and credit history, and are therefore not considered good credit risks by traditional banks. Microcredit has existed in a number of forms for hundreds of years, but has gained notoriety in the face of defaults on massive international development loans and the rise of Muhammad Yunus' Grameen Bank (and others). Rather than filter money through bloated and corrupt bureaucracies, microcredit seeks to deliver investment money directly to those at the very bottom of the economic ladder, and has had remarkable successes, especially among women in undeveloped countries. *See also* Grameen Bank.

### microeconomics
(economics) The examination of the economic behavior of individual units in the economy, such as households or corporations. *See* macroeconomics.

### Military Critical Technologies List
(U.S.) A document listing technologies that the U.S. Defense Department considers to have current or future utility in military systems. The MCTL describes arrays of design and manufacturing know-how; keystone manufacturing, inspection, and test equipment; and goods accompanied by sophisticated operation, application, and maintenance know-how. Military justification for each entry is included in a classified version of the list. *See* United States Department of Defense.

### minibridge
(shipping) Movement of cargo from a port over water, then over land to a port on an opposite coast.

### minimum bill of lading
(shipping) Ocean bills of lading are known as minimum because they contain a clause which specifies the least charge that the carrier will make for the issuance of a lading. The charge may be a definite sum, or the current charge per ton or for any specified quantity of cargo. *See* bill of lading.

### minimum charge
(shipping) The lowest rate applicable on each type of cargo service no matter how small the shipment.

### Ministry of Economy, Trade and Industry (METI)
(Japan) METI occupies a central position in Japan's "economic bureaucracy" and is regarded as one of the three most powerful and prestigious ministries of the central government (along with the Ministry of Finance and the Ministry of Foreign Affairs). In formulating and implementing Japan's trade and industrial policies, METI is responsible for funding most of Japan's export promotion programs (although operation of these programs is left to JETRO). The Ministry also supervises the export financing programs of Japan's Export-Import Bank, operates several types of export insurance programs, supports research organizations, and facilitates various types of overseas technical and cooperation training programs. Lately, METI has assumed a role in encouraging imports of foreign products into Japan. Contact: Ministry of International Trade and Industry, 1-3-1, Kasumigaseki 1-chome, Chiyoda-ku, Tokyo 100-8901, Japan; Tel: [81] (3) 3501-1511; E-mail: webmail@meti.go.jp; Web: www.meti.go.jp.

### Ministry of Foreign Economic Relations and Trade (MOFERT)
Renamed Ministry of Foreign Economic Trade and Economic Cooperation. *See* Ministry of Foreign Economic Trade and Economic Cooperation.

### Ministry of Foreign Economic Trade and Economic Cooperation
(China) The People's Republic of China (PRC) Ministry of Foreign Economic Trade and Economic Cooperation implements national trade policies through administrative actions, drafting laws and issuing foreign trade regulations. It does not engage in foreign trade transactions but facilitates the foreign trading corporations (FTCs) which do. Contact: Ministry of Foreign Trade & Economic Cooperation (MOFTEC), 2 Dongchangan Ave., Beijing 100731, CHINA; Tel: [86] (10) 6512-1919; Fax: [86] (10) 6519-8173; Web: www.mofcom.gov.cn.

### Minitel
(France) The still used, but now outdated, French online telephone directory and information source.

### mitigation of damages
(law/insurance) A legal doctrine that charges a party who suffers contract damages with a duty to use reasonable diligence and ordinary care in attempting to minimize damages or avoid aggravating the injury. If a seller of oranges, for example, is entitled to prepayment before shipment and the buyer fails to pay, the seller should make a reasonable attempt to sell the oranges to another buyer before they spoil so as to mitigate the seller's damages. The seller may then recover from the breaching buyer the difference between the contract price and the price at which the oranges were sold to the other buyer.

The concept also applies to insurance where the insured has the responsibility to minimize damages to an insured cargo shipment.

**mixed credit**
(banking) The combining of concessional (liberal) and market-rate export credit as an export promotion mechanism.

**mixed load**
(logistics) A shipment of goods that includes regulated and exempt commodities in the same vehicle at the same time.

**modal split**
(logistics) A measure of an individual company's or organization's use of different modes of transport. Modal split can be expressed in terms of numbers of shipments, ton-miles/kilometers, expenses or revenues. For example, modal split in percentages by cost: air 34%, sea 47%, truck 19%.

**moiety claim**
(customs, law) A legal claim for compensation by an individual who provides information to a government entity that results in the recovery of unpaid duties or "ill gotten gains." Moietie is French for half, but can also mean either of two parts that may not be of equal size. Moiety claims in the US are often for 25 percent of the recovered amount.)

**monetary instrument**
*See* financial instrument.

**monetary system**
(banking) The authority of the state in matters of establishing monetary policy, including determining the monetary unit, the monetary authorities, and the ways in which money is issued and the way the money supply is controlled.

**money**
(banking) Any denomination of coin or paper currency of legal tender that passes freely as a medium of exchange; anything that is accepted in exchange for other things (e.g., precious metals). Major characteristics of money include easy recognition, uniformity in quality, easy divisibility, and a relatively high value within a small area.

**money creation**
(banking) The increase in money supply by the central or commercial banks.

**money laundering**
(law) A popular term used to describe the process by which criminals disguise the nature, location, source, ownership or control of illicitly acquired funds. Money laundering typically involves three steps: 1) Placement: Physically placing cash at a domestic or offshore location, such as in a business or bank, 2) Layering: Establishing layers of complex financial transactions to obscure the money's source, location and ownership, and 3) Integration: Establishing legitimate but false explanations as to the origin of the funds.

**money market**
(banking/finance) The market for short-term financial instruments, such as certificates of deposit, commercial paper, banker's acceptances, Treasury bills, discount notes and others. These instruments are all liquid and tend to be safe. *See* capital market, financial market.

**money market operations**
(banking) Comprises the acceptance and re-lending of deposits (*see* time deposits) on the money market.

**money supply**
(economics/banking) The amount of domestic cash and deposit money available in an economy.

**moor**
(shipping) To secure a vessel to an anchor, buoy or pier.

**moorage**
(shipping) Charges assessed for mooring a vessel to a pier or wharf.

**moral right (droit moral)**
(law) Rights of attribution and integrity granted by the laws of certain countries to the authors of literary, dramatic, musical and artistic works, as well as to film directors.
Attribution is the right of the true author, creator or film director to be identified as such on the work (such as on the cover of a book or in the credits of a film). In the same manner, non-authors are prevented from attaching their names to the legitimate artistic work of another person.
Integrity is the right of the true author, creator or film director to object to the derogatory treatment of the work or film when it amounts to a distortion or mutilation of the work or is otherwise prejudicial to the honor or reputation of the author or director.
Moral rights are different from economic rights under copyright and other laws that deal with property. In most countries where such rights are recognized, moral rights are perpetual, inalienable and descend to the heirs of the creators of the artistic works. Moral rights are not mentioned in the Berne Convention, but are common in civil law countries (especially in France), but not recognized in other countries (including the United States).
Moral rights include such rights as:
**Right of disclosure**—The right of an author to have the final decision as to when and where the work will be published (*droit de divulgation*).
Right to withdraw or retract—The right of an author, who has changed his views on a subject, to purchase, at wholesale prices, the remaining copies of a work, and to prevent the printing of more copies of the work (*droit de retrait ou de repentir*).
**Right to reply to criticism**—The right of an author to reply to a critic and to have the reply published in the same venue as that of the critic.
Moral rights are based on the concept that a creative work is an extension of the author's character and personality and is therefore not transferable as is a property right such as copyright.
Moral rights generally do not apply to computer programs, situations where the ownership of a work was originally vested in an author's employer, material used in newspapers or magazines, or reference works such as dictionaries or encyclopedias.

**Most Favored Nation (MFN)**
A non-discriminatory trade policy commitment on the part of one country to extend to another country the lowest tariff rates it applies to any other country.
(WTO) All contracting parties to the World Trade Organization (WTO) undertake to apply such treatment to one another under Article I of the treaty.
Under MFN principles, when a country agrees to cut tariffs on a particular product imported from one country, the tariff reduction automatically applies to imports of this product from any other country eligible for most-favored nation treatment. This principle of nondiscriminatory treatment of imports appeared in numerous bilateral trade agreements prior to establishment of the WTO. A country is under no obligation to extend MFN treatment to another country unless both are bilateral contracting parties of the World Trade Organization or MFN treatment is specified in a bilateral agreement.
(U.S.) The most favored nation principle was a feature of U.S. trade policy as early as 1778. Since 1923 the United States has incorporated an "unconditional" Most Favored Nation clause in its trade agreements, binding the contracting governments to confer upon each other all the most favorable trade concessions that either may grant to any other country subsequent to the signing of the agreement. The

**M**

United States now applies this provision to its trade with all of its trading partners except for those specifically excluded by law. As a result of the controversy around granting China MFN status, the U.S. has changed MFN to "Normal Trade Relations." *See* normal trade relations, Harmonized Tariff Schedule of the United States.

### mother vessel/mother ship
(shipping) A vessel (ship) that loads cargo from feeder vessels or offloads cargo to lighters without entering a port or without docking at a pier. This often occurs when the draft of the vessel is greater than the maximum depth of the channel leading to a port or of the of the port itself.

### motor carrier's terminal
(shipping) The place where loaded or empty shipping containers are received or delivered by a motor carrier and where the motor carrier maintains an equipment pool.

### motor vehicle
(shipping) Any vehicle, machine, tractor, trailer or semi-trailer propelled or drawn by mechanical power and used upon the highways in the transportation of passengers or property.

### MRP
(manufacturing/logistics) Acronym for Manufacturing Resources Planning. A materials procurement planning system that uses the production plan for finished goods to determine what raw materials and component parts will be required to make the product. MRP involves planning for the collection, stocking and distribution of raw materials and component parts in the manufacturing process. MRP focuses on materials and inventories rather than personnel and equipment. MRP software is available from a number of firms. *See* MRP II, ERP.

### MRP II
(logistics) Acronym for Manufacturing Resources Planning II. A further development of MRP which includes production planning and scheduling, shop-floor control, financial management, forecasting, order processing and performance measurement. MRP II software is available from a number of firms. *See* MRP.

### multicurrency clause
(banking) a clause in a loan agreement stating that more than one currency may be used in paying or redeeming the loan.

### Multi-Fiber Arrangement, textiles (MFA)
(WTO) An international compact under the World Trade Organization (WTO) that allows an importing signatory country to apply quantitative restrictions on textiles imports when it considers them necessary to prevent market disruption.

The MFA provides a framework for regulating international trade in textiles and apparel with the objectives of achieving "orderly marketing" of such products, and of avoiding "market disruption" in importing countries. It provides a basis on which major importers, such as the United States and the European Community, may negotiate bilateral agreements or, if necessary, impose restraints on imports from low-wage producing countries. It provides, among other things, standards for determining market disruption, minimum levels of import restraints, and annual growth of imports.

The MFA provides that such restrictions should not reduce imports to levels below those attained during the preceding year. Bilateral agreements usually allow for import growth tied to anticipated greater demand.

Since an importing country may impose such quotas unilaterally to restrict rapidly rising textiles imports, many important textiles-exporting countries consider it advantageous to enter into bilateral agreements with the principal textiles-importing countries.

The MFA went into effect on Jan. 1, 1974, was renewed in December 1977, in December 1981, and again in July 1986. It succeeded the Long-term Agreement on International Trade in Cotton Textiles ("The LTA"), which had been in effect since 1962. Whereas the LTA applied only to cotton textiles, the MFA now applies to wool, man-made (synthetic) fiber, silk blend and other vegetable fiber textiles and apparel. Note: The MFA will eventually be phased out as a result of the Uruguay Round of the General Agreement on Tariffs and Trade. *See* quotas; bilateral trade agreement; Uruguay Round; General Agreement on Tariffs and Trade.

### multilateral agreement
An international compact involving three or more parties. For example, the World Trade Organization (WTO), has been seeking to promote trade liberalization through multilateral negotiations. *See* bilateral trade agreement.

### Multilateral Investment Fund
Under the Enterprise for the Americas Initiative, the fund complements the Inter-American Development Bank. The fund provides program and project grants to advance specific, market-oriented investment policy initiatives and reforms, and encourages domestic and foreign investment in Latin America and the Caribbean. Contact: Inter-American Development Bank, 1300 New York Avenue NW, Washington, DC 20577; Tel: [1] (202) 623-1000; Fax: [1] (202) 623-3096; E-mail: pic@iadb.org; Web: www.iadb.org.

### Multilateral Investment Guarantee Agency (MIGA)
A part of the World Bank Group. MIGA encourages equity investment and other direct investment flows to developing countries through the mitigation of noncommercial investment barriers. The agency offers investors guarantees against noncommercial risks; advises developing member governments on the design and implementation of policies, programs, and procedures related to foreign investments; and sponsors a dialogue between the international business community and host governments on investment issues. Contact: Multilateral Investment Guarantee Agency, World Bank, 1818 H Street NW, Washington, DC 20433 USA; Tel: [1] (202) 473-1000; Fax: [1] (202) 522-2630; Web: www.miga.org.

### multilateral trade negotiations
(GATT/WTO) A term describing the multilateral rounds of negotiations held under the auspices of the General Agreement on Tariffs and Trade (GATT) and World Trade Organization (WTO) since 1947. Each Round represented a discrete and lengthy series of interacting bargaining sessions among the participating Contracting Parties in search of mutually beneficial agreements looking toward the reduction of barriers to world trade. The agreements ultimately reached at the conclusion of each Round became new commitments and thus amounted to an important step in the evolution of the world trading system. *See* General Agreement on Tariffs and Trade; rounds; Tokyo Round; Uruguay Round, World Trade Organization (WTO).

### multimodal transport
(shipping) Shipping which includes at least two modes of transport, such as shipping by rail and by sea.

### multinational corporation
(economics) A corporation having supplier and/or sales networks in more than one country.

### multiple-car/trailer load rate
(logistics) A special lower freight rate that applies to a bulk shipment that requires multiple trailers or rail cars.

*mutatis mutandis*
(law) Meaning changing what needs to be changed; used when cases are nearly the same except for minor details. A statute that governs one type of transaction, for example, may also be applied to another transaction with minor exceptions, in which event the statute applies mutatis mutandis. A country may apply its trademark law mutatis mutandis to service marks, in which event the same law will apply except for changes to account for such details as the use of the mark to distinguish services instead of goods.

*Naamloze Vennotschap (N.V.)*
(Belgium, Netherlands) Designation for a joint stock company with limited personal liability to shareholders.

*NAFTA*
*See* North American Free Trade Agreement.

*NAFTA Prior Disclosure*
*See* Prior Disclosure.

*naira*
The currency of Nigeria. 1N=100 kobo.

*named insured*
(insurance) Any person or firm or corporation or any of its members, specially designated by name as insured(s) in a policy, as distinguished from others who, although unnamed, are protected under some circumstances.

*National Association of Export Companies*
(U.S.) A non-profit organization established in 1965 to act as the information provider, support clearinghouse forum, and advocate for those involved in exporting and servicing exporters. Provides networking opportunities, counseling, publications, seminars, etc. Contact: Executive Director, NEXCO, PO Box 3949, Grand Central Station, New York, NY 10163 USA; Tel: [1] (877) 291-4901; Fax: [1] (646) 349-9628; Email: director@nexco.org; Web: www.nexco.org.

*National Association of State Development Agencies (NASDA)*
(U.S.) NASDA was formed in 1946 to provide a forum for directors of state economic development agencies to exchange information, compare programs, and deal with issues of mutual interest. NASDA's organization includes International Trade and Foreign Investment components. Trade activities include maintenance of a State Export Program Database. Contact: NASDA, 12884 Harbor Drive, Woodbridge, VA 22192 USA; Tel: [1] (703) 490-6777; Fax: [1] (703) 492-4404; Email: mfriedman@nasda.com; Web: www.nasda.com.

*National Customs Automation Program (NCAP)*
(U.S. Customs) A planned U.S. Customs and Border Protection (CBP) automated and electronic system for processing commercial imports into the U.S. The NCAP is the first functionality of the Automated Commercial Environment (ACE). The plan is for the NCAP to include the following existing and planned components:
1) Existing components:
(a) The electronic entry of merchandise. (b) The electronic entry summary of required information. (c) The electronic transmission of invoice information. (d) The electronic transmission of manifest information. (e) The electronic payments of duties, fees, and taxes. (f) The electronic status of liquidation and reliquidation. (g) The electronic selection of high-risk entries for examination (cargo selectivity and entry summary selectivity).
2) Planned components:
(a) The electronic filing and status of protests. (b) The electronic filing (including remote filing) of entry information with the Customs Service at any location. (c) The electronic filing of import activity summary statements and reconciliation. (d) The electronic filing of bonds. (e) The electronic penalty process. (f) The electronic filing of drawback claims, records, or entries. (g) Other related components initiated by the CBP.

Participation in the Program is voluntary.

For full information, go to: www.access.gpo.gov/uscode/title19/chapter4_subtitleiii_parti_subpartb_.html

### National Customs Brokers and Forwarders Association of America

A non-profit organization founded in 1897 which serves as the trade organization of customs brokers and international freight forwarders in the U.S. Through ongoing communications with industry trade publications and the general media, the Association projects the industry's interests and objectives. Membership includes brokers and freight forwarders in 32 affiliated associations located at major ports throughout the U.S. Contact: National Customs Brokers and Forwarders Association of America, 1200 18th Street, NW, #901 Washington, DC 20036 USA; Tel: [1] (202) 466-0222; Fax: [1] (202) 466-0226; E-mail: staff@ncbfaa.org; Web: www.ncbfaa.org.

### National Motor Freight Classification (NMFC)

(U.S. logistics) A freight classification schedule of tariffs applicable to less-than-truck-load (LTL) freight shipments. This tariff divides products into one of 18 classes and provides a standard for the pricing of domestic shipments throughout the United States. Information at Web: www.nmfta.org; Tel: [1] (703) 838-1810.

### national security controls

(U.S.) National security controls restrict exports of U.S. goods and technology which would make a significant contribution to the military potential of another country and thus be detrimental to national security.

### National Security Directive #53

(U.S.) NSD-53 deals with the export licensing process and sets specified time periods for resolving disputes on both national security and foreign policy export license applications. Under NSD-53, exports controlled on both of these grounds are subject to explicit timetables for interagency dispute resolution at the Sub-Cabinet level by the Advisory Committee on Export Policy (ACEP), and at the cabinet level by the Export Administration Review Board (EARB). The Directive requires escalation to the ACEP not later than 100 days from the filing date of the applicant's application, and if the disagreement cannot be resolved by the ACEP, for review and resolution by the EARB within 35 days of the date of the ACEP meeting. Cases not resolved by the EARB must be escalated to the president for resolution. The new procedures also permit an agency to refer a case at any stage of the dispute resolution process to the NSC for a 30 day policy review. *See* National Security Directives.

### National Security Directives (NSD)

(U.S.) NSDs provide policy or procedural guidance and are signed by the president. In 1989, the president reorganized the national security council committee process (separate from the Export Administration Review Board (EARB)). As reorganized, under the National Security Council (NSC), there are committees for Coordinating Committee for Multilateral Export Controls (CoCom), terrorism, nonproliferation, etc. NSDs were known as National Security Decision Directives, NSDDs, before President Bush's reorganization. NSD-1 reorganized the process; NSD-10 established the committees; NSD-53 deals with export licensing. The scope of coverage and the players are about the same under the NSD and NSDD processes.

### National Security Override (NSO)

(U.S.) In some cases of U.S. export law, despite a finding of foreign availability of a controlled commodity, control is maintained over exporting the commodity because it is deemed a national security sensitive item. The term national security override is used to describe this circumstance.

The term has also been used in other contexts. For example, under a November 16, 1990 directive, the president instructed the interagency control groups to move as many dual use items from the U.S. State Department's International Munitions List to the Commerce Department's Commerce Control List. In some circumstances, a national security override is applied to prevent transfer of a particular item.

*See* International Munitions List; Commerce Control List.

### National Tourism Policy Act

(U.S. law) Legislation passed in 1981 that created the U.S. Travel and Tourism Administration and required the establishment of the Tourism Policy Council and the Travel and Tourism Advisory Board.

### National Trade Data Bank (NTDB)

(CD-ROM publication/Internet service) The NTDB is an electronic database available on CD-ROM and on the World Wide Web through the U.S. Department of Commerce's fee-based STAT-USA/Internet service at Web: www.stat-usa.gov. The NTDB contains international economic and export promotion information supplied by various U.S. governmental agencies. The NTDB provides world trade data from several hundred thousand documents taken from over 20 Federal sources. Topics include: export opportunities by industry, country, and product; foreign companies or importers looking for specific products; how-to market guides; and demographic, political, and socioeconomic conditions in hundreds of countries. Source: U.S. Department of Commerce, Office of Economic Analysis, HCHB Room 4885, Washington, DC 20230 USA; Tel: [1] (202) 482-1986, [1] (800) STAT-USA; E-mail: statmail@esa.doc.gov; Web: www.stat-usa.gov.

### National Trade Estimates Report

(U.S.) An annual report by the United States Trade Representative (USTR) that identifies significant foreign barriers to and distortions of trade. Contact: Office of the United States Trade Representative, Executive Office of the President, 600 17th Street NW, Washington, DC 20508 USA; Tel: [1] (888) 473-8787; E-mail: contactustr@ustr.eop.gov; Web: www.ustr.gov.

### national treatment

(trade policy) A requirement in World Trade Organization (WTO) trade policy that member nations regulate imports in the same way they regulate domestic goods. Specifically, member nations cannot impose more stringent regulations on imports as a "non-tariff barrier" in an effort to exclude such imports. National treatment affords individuals and firms of foreign countries the same competitive opportunities, including market access, as are available to domestic parties.

### nationalization

(economics/law) The forcible acquisition, with or without compensation, of private property such as real estate, a business enterprise or an entire industry by a sovereign nation. In nationalization, social or economic equality is often stated as the motive. Nationalization is most common in socialistic and communistic countries, but also in less-developed nations where there is resentment of foreign control of major industries. Famous examples of nationalizations include: Mexico's nationalization of oil producing properties owned by U.S. firms in 1938, Great Britain's nationalization of the coal, steel and transportation industries between 1945 and 1951, Iran's nationalization of the Anglo-Iranian Oil Company in 1951, Egypt's nationalization of the Suez Canal in 1956 and Chile's nationalization of foreign-owned copper mines in 1971. *See* privatization.

**natural advantage**
(economics) Economic theory that states that a country has a competitive advantage in the production of certain products as a result of access to natural resources, transportation or climatic conditions.

**NDA**
*See* non-disclosure agreement.

**near-bank**
(banking-Canada) A financial institution, excluding standard commercial bank, such as savings bank, credit union, etc.

**negligence**
(law) Failure to do that which an ordinary, reasonable, prudent person would do, or the doing of some act that an ordinary, prudent person would not do. Reference is made of the situation, circumstances, and awareness of the parties involved.

**negotiable**
(general) Anything that can be sold or transferred to another for money or as payments of a debt. In international trade, usually refers to the transferability of a title document—such as a negotiable bill of lading.
(investments) Refers to a security, title to which is transferable by delivery.
*See* negotiable instrument.

**negotiable bill of lading**
(shipping) Bill of lading transferred by endorsement. There are three possibilities: (1) to XY & Co. or their order; (2) to the order of XY & Co.; and (3) to order, without the name of the party. In the latter case the bill remains to the order of the shipper until he endorses it.
These types of bills of lading are usually endorsed on the reverse. The opposite of a negotiable bill of lading is the straight bill of lading *See* bill of lading; endorsement.

**negotiable instrument**
(law/banking/shipping) A written document (instrument) that can be transferred merely by endorsement (signing) or delivery. Checks, bills of exchange, bills of lading and warehouse receipts (if marked negotiable), and promissory notes are examples of negotiable instruments.
(U.S.) The Uniform Negotiable Instruments Act states: "An instrument, to be negotiable, must conform to the following requirements: (1) it must be in writing and signed by the maker or drawer; (2) it must contain an unconditional promise or order to pay a certain sum in money; (3) it must be payable on demand, or at a fixed or determinable future time; (4) it must be payable to order or to bearer; and (5) where the instrument is addressed to a drawee, he must be named or otherwise indicated therein with reasonable certainty."

**negotiable warehouse receipt**
(shipping) A certificate issued by an approved warehouse that guarantees the existence and the grade of a commodity held in store. *See* negotiable instrument.

**negotiating bank**
(banking) In a letter of credit transaction, the bank that (1) receives and examines the seller's documents for adherence to the terms and conditions of the letter of credit, (2) gives value to the seller, so long as the terms of the credit have been met, and (3) forwards them to the issuing bank (the buyer's or importer's bank). Depending upon the type of credit, the negotiating bank will either credit or pay the seller/exporter immediately under the terms of the letter of credit, or credit or pay the exporter once it has received payment from the issuing bank. *See* advising bank; issuing bank.

**negotiation**
(banking) (a) The action by which a negotiable instrument is circulated (bought and sold) from one holder to another. (b) In letter of credit transactions, (1) the examination of the seller's documentation by the negotiating bank to determine if they comply with the terms and conditions of the letter of credit and (2) the giving of value for draft(s) and/or document(s) by the bank authorized to negotiate. Mere examination of the documents without giving value does not constitute a negotiation. *See* letter of credit.

**negotiation credit**
(banking) A documentary letter of credit available by negotiation. *See* letter of credit.

**NES**
*See* not elsewhere specified.

**nested**
(shipping) Packed one within another.

**net cash**
Payment for goods sold usually within a short period of time with no deduction allowed from the invoice price.

**net export of goods and services**
(economics) The excess of exports of goods and services (domestic output sold abroad, and the production abroad credit to U.S.-owned resources) over imports (U.S. purchases of foreign output, domestic production credit to foreign-owned resources, and net private cash remittances to creditors abroad).

**net foreign investment**
(economics/foreign investment) The net change in a nation's foreign assets and liabilities, including the monetary gold stocks, arising out of current trade, income on foreign investment, and cash gifts and contributions. It measures the excess of: (1) exports over imports, (2) income on U.S. public and private investment abroad over payments on foreign investment in the U.S., and (3) cash gifts and contributions of the U.S. (public and private) to foreigners over cash gifts and contributions received from abroad.
Net foreign investment may also be viewed as the acquisition of foreign assets by that country's residents, less the acquisition of that country's assets by foreign residents.

**net income**
(economics) The remains from earnings after all costs, expenses and allowances for depreciation and probable loss have been deducted.

**net loss**
(economics) The excess of expenses and losses during a specified period over revenues and gains in the same time frame.

**net national product**
(economics) Gross national product minus capital consumption (depreciation). The market value of the net output of goods and services produced by the nation's economy.

**net price**
Price after all discounts, rebates, etc., have been allowed.

**net ton (N.T.)**
(measure) A unit of mass or weight measurement equal to 2,000 pounds. Also called short ton (S.T.).

**net tonnage**
(shipping) A vessel's gross tonnage minus deductions for space occupied by accommodations for crew, machinery for navigation, the engine room, and fuel. A vessel's net tonnage represents the space available for the accommodation of passengers and the stowage of cargo.

**net weight**
(general) The weight of goods without packaging.
(shipping) The weight of merchandise without the shipper container. Also the weight of the contents of a freight car.

**neutral air waybill**
(shipping) A standard air waybill without identification of issuing carrier. *See* air waybill; bill of lading.

**neutral body**
(shipping) A regulatory entity operating within the framework of a shipping conference, established by the member carriers to act as a self-policing force to ferret out malpractices and other tariff violations. The neutral body has authority to scrutinize all documents kept by the carriers and the carriers' personnel with right of entry to all areas of the carrier's facilities including desks, briefcases, etc. Violations found are reported to the membership with significant penalties being assessed. Repeated offenses are subject to escalating penalty amounts. Revenue from penalties are used to support the cost of the neutral body activity. *See* carrier; conference.

**New Blueprint for International Trade**
(United Kingdom) Plans by the UK government to modernize customs procedures for international trade. A key objective of the Blueprint is to improve compliance, while providing greater facilitation for those traders who abide by the rules. (The New Blueprint parallels a number of U.S. initiatives, such as Informed Compliance, C-TPAT and the AMS to improve security and streamline trade procedures.) Fo information go to the UK Customs (HM Customs and Excise) Web site at: www.hmrc.gov.uk.

**newly industrializing countries (NICs)**
(economics) Relatively advanced developing countries whose industrial production and exports have grown rapidly in recent years. Examples include Brazil, Hong Kong, Korea, Mexico, Singapore, and Taiwan. The term was originated by the Organization for Economic Cooperation and Development (OECD).

**new-to-export (NTE)**
(U.S.) As defined by the United States Department of Commerce, a new-to-export action is one that results from documented assistance to a company that assists the client's first verifiable export sale. Either the company has not exported to any destination during the past 24 months or prior exports have resulted from unsolicited orders or were received through a U.S.-based intermediary. *See* United States Department of Commerce.

**new-to-market (NTM)**
(U.S.) As defined by the U.S. Department of Commerce, a reportable new-to-market export action is one that results from documented assistance to an exporter that facilitates a verifiable sale in a new foreign market. Either the company has not exported to that market during the past 24 months or previous exports to that market have resulted from unsolicited orders or were received through a U.S. based intermediary. *See* United States Department of Commerce.

**nexus**
(law) A party's connection with, or presence in, a place that is sufficient enough that it would be fair to subject the party to the jurisdiction of the court or government located there.

**NFO**
Acronym for Next Flight Out.

**NGO**
Acronym for non-government organization.
a) A private sector profit or non-profit organization. (b) A private sector non-profit organization that "pursues activities to relieve suffering, promote the interests of the poor, protect the environment, provide basic social services or undertake community development." (World Bank NGO criteria.)

**ngultrum**
The currency of Bhutan. 1Nu=100 chetrum.

**Nigerian scam**
(law) See 419 scam.

**Nippon Telegraph and Telephone Corporation (NTT)**
(Japan) NTT is Japan's largest telecommunications enterprise and was converted from a public corporation to a private enterprise in April 1985. Although competition has been allowed, the Japanese Government still owns the majority of NTT stock and postponement of a decision in NTT divestiture is an issue of considerable importance to market access by foreign companies. NTT was established in 1952. Contact: Nippon Telegraph and Telephone Corporation, 3-1, Otemachi 2-chome, Chiyoda-ku, Tokyo 100-8116, Japan; Tel: [81] (3) 3509-5111; Web: www.ntt.co.jp.

**non-disclosure agreement (NDA)**
(law) An agreement between two or more parties not to disclose trade secrets, trade practices, business or marketing plans or other proprietary or confidential information. A non-disclosure agreement is often signed by parties entering into a business negotiation or business relationship where such information is likely to be revealed.

**non-government organization**
*See* NGO.

**non-market economy**
(economics) A national economy or a country in which the government seeks to determine economic activity largely through a mechanism of central planning, as formerly in the Soviet Union, in contrast to a market economy that depends heavily upon market forces to allocate productive resources. In a "non-market" economy, production targets, prices, costs, investment allocations, raw materials, labor, international trade, and most other economic aggregates are manipulated within a national economic plan drawn up by a central planning authority, and hence the public sector makes the major decisions affecting demand and supply within the national economy.

**non-negotiable**
(law) Not transferable from one person to another. Usually refers to the transferability of a title document (e.g., non-negotiable bill of lading). Possession of a non-negotiable title document alone does not entitle the holder to receive the goods named therein (e.g., non-negotiable sea waybill, air waybill, forwarder's receipt, etc.). *See* negotiable; negotiable instrument.

**nonperforming assets**
(banking) Assets which have no financial return.

**nonperforming debt**
(banking) A debt which has no financial return (i.e. no interest is paid on it).

**nonperforming loan; nonaccruing loan**
(banking) Loan where payment of interest has been delayed for more than 90 days.

**nonstructural container**
(shipping) A unit load device composed of a bottomless rigid shell used in combination with a pallet and net assembly. Note: The expression "nonstructural container" is also used to refer to the shell part of a device.

**non-tariff barriers or measures**
(economics) Any number of import quotas or other quantitative restrictions, non-automatic import licensing, customs surcharges or other fees and charges, customs procedures, export subsidies, unreasonable standards or standards-setting procedures, government procurement restrictions, inadequate intellectual property protection and investment restrictions which deny or make market access excessively difficult for goods or services of foreign origin.
(GATT) Participants in the Tokyo Round of the General Agreement on Tariffs and Trade attempted to address these

barriers through the negotiations of a number of GATT codes, open for signature to all GATT members. Seven codes were negotiated during the Tokyo Round, covering customs valuations, import licensing, subsidies and countervailing duties, antidumping duties, standards, government procurement and trade in civil aircraft. Although the Tokyo Round codes had alleviated some of the problems caused by non-tariff measures, overall use of NTMs has increased since conclusion of the Tokyo Round.

*See* import restrictions; non-tariff barriers; Tokyo Round; General Agreement on Tariffs and Trade; World Trade Organization.

### non-vessel operating common carrier (NVOCC)

(shipping) A carrier issuing bills of lading for carriage of goods on vessels which it neither operates nor owns. NVOCCs purchase large blocks of space at discounted rates from shipping lines and resell them in smaller blocks to other shippers at a profit. NVOCCs often consolidate and transport shipments under a single bill of lading.

(U.S.) A "carrier" defined by maritime law offering an international cargo transport service through the use of underlying carriers and under their own rate structure in accordance with tariffs filed with the Federal Maritime Commission in Washington, DC. The rates filed are required only to port-to-port portion. Specific authority for the NVOCC is given in the code of Federal Regulations, Title 46, Chapter IV, Federal Maritime Commission Sub-Part B, entitled "Regulations Affecting Maritime Carriers and Related Activities." General Order 4, Amendment i, Section 510.2 (d) states:

"The term 'non-vessel operating common carrier by water' means a person who holds himself out by the establishment and maintenance of tariffs, by advertisement, solicitation, or otherwise, to provide transportation for hire by water in interstate commerce as defined in the Act, and in commerce from the United States as defined in paragraph (b) of the section; assumes responsibility or has liability imposed by law for safe transportation of shipments; and arranges in his own name with underlying water carriers for the performance of such transportation whether or not owning or controlling the means by which such transportation is affected."

### Nordic Council

(regional alliance) The Nordic Council, established in 1952, supports cooperation among Nordic countries in communications, cultural, economic, environmental, fiscal, legal and social areas. Members include: Denmark, Finland, Iceland, Norway and Sweden. Contact: Nordic Council, Store Strandstræde 18, DK-1255 Copenhagen K, Denmark; Tel: [45] (33) 96-04-00; Fax: [45] (33) 11-18-70; E-mail: info@norden.org; Web: www.norden.org.

### normal trade relations (NTR)

(trade policy) The new designation for Most Favored Nation (MFN) trading status. Although the name has changed, the privileges remain the same. (U.S. trade policy) With controversy surrounding giving Most Favored Nation status to China, it was decided that for political reasons the designation would change to Normal Trade Relations. Countries with MFN/NTR status enjoy preferred import tariff rates on goods exported to the U.S.

### North American Free Trade Agreement (NAFTA)

A free trade agreement that comprises Canada, the U.S. and Mexico. The objectives of the Agreement are to eliminate barriers to trade, promote conditions of fair competition, increase investment opportunities, provide protection for intellectual property rights and establish procedures for the resolution of disputes.

NAFTA eliminates all tariffs on goods originating in Canada, Mexico and the United States over a transition period. Rules of origin are necessary to define which goods are eligible for preferential tariff treatment.

NAFTA contains special provisions for market access, customs administration, automotive goods, textiles and apparel, energy and petrochemicals, agriculture, sanitary and phytosanitary measures, technical standards, emergency action, antidumping and countervailing duty matters, government procurement, trade in services, land transportation, telecommunications, investment, financial services, intellectual property, temporary entry for business persons, dispute settlement, administration of law and the environment.

NAFTA will produce a market exceeding 360 million consumers and a combined output of more than $6 trillion—20 percent larger than the European Community. The agreement took effect January 1, 1994.

The Commerce Department's Office of NAFTA & Inter-American affairs has its Web site at Web: www.mac.doc.gov/nafta/. This site contains the full text of the treaty, as well as resources, news items, items from the Federal Register, ways to contact this office for assistance, and links to other NAFTA-related sites on the Web. The entire text of NAFTA is also available from the U.S. Government Printing Office, Mail Stop: IDCC, 732 N. Capitol Street, NW, Washington, DC 20401; Tel: [1] (866) 512-1800, [1] (202) 512-1800; Fax: [1] (202) 512-2104; Web: www.gpoaccess.gov; or on the National Trade Data Bank on CD-ROM, Tel: [1] (202) 482-1986.

### North-South trade

(economics) Trade between developed countries (North) and developing countries (South). *See* developed countries; developing countries.

### no show

(shipping) Freight that has been booked to a ship, but has not physically arrived in time to be loaded to that ship.

### nostro account

(banking) "Our" account. An account maintained by a bank with a bank in a foreign country. Nostro accounts are kept in foreign currencies of the country which the monies are held, with the equivalent dollar value listed in another column for accounting purposes.

### notary public

(law-U.S.) A person commissioned by a state for a stipulated period (with the privilege of renewal) to administer certain oaths and to attest and certify documents, thus authorizing him or her to take affidavits and depositions. A notary is also authorized to "protect" negotiable instruments for nonpayment or nonacceptance.

The role of a notary public varies from country to country. In some countries they take on many of the responsibilities which in the U.S. an attorney would assume, while in other countries they do not exist at all.

### not elsewhere specified (N.E.S.)

(shipping) The abbreviation N.E.S. often appears in air freight tariffs. For example: "advertising matter, N.E.S.," "printed matter, N.E.S.," indicating that the rate stated in the tariff applies to all commodities within the commodity group except those appearing under their own rate. The abbreviation N.E.S., as used in air freight tariffs, is comparable to the abbreviation N.O.I.B.N. (not otherwise indexed by number) and N.O.S. (not otherwise specified) which appear in tariffs published by the surface modes.

### notify address

(shipping) Address mentioned in the transport document (bill of lading or an air waybill), to which the carrier is to give notice when goods are due to arrive.

### notify party
(shipping) Name and address of a party in the transport document (bill of lading or air waybill), usually the buyer or his agent, to be notified by the shipping company of the arrival of a shipment.

### NTR
*See* normal trade relations.

### Nuclear Energy Agency (NEA)
Promotes the safe and effective use of nuclear energy through the exchange of information among technical experts, the sharing of analytical studies, and undertaking joint research and development projects by member countries. Headquarters are in Paris, France. Contact: Nuclear Energy Agency, Le Seine-Saint Germain, 12 blvd. des Iles, 92130 Issy-les-Moulineaux, France; Tel: [33] (1) 45-24-10-10; Fax: [33] (1) 45-24-11-10; E-mail: nea@nea.fr; Web: www.nea.fr.

### Nuclear Non-Proliferation Act
(U.S. law) Among other actions, this Act made the U.S. Energy Department responsible for approving arrangements for nuclear exports and transfers. Each arrangement requires U.S. State Department concurrence, as well as consultations with the Arms Control and Disarmament Agency, the Nuclear Regulatory Commission, and the Departments of Defense and Commerce.

### Nuclear Non-Proliferation Treaty
The NPT became effective in 1970 and was intended to limit the number of states with nuclear weapons to five: the U.S., the Soviet Union, Britain, France, and China. In doing so, the NPT attempts to: (1) prevent nuclear weapons sales by not assisting other nations with nuclear weapons development; (2) halt the nuclear weapons development programs of non-nuclear weapons states; and (3) promote nuclear disarmament and the peaceful use of nuclear technologies and materials. Over 140 states have pledged not to acquire nuclear weapons and to accept the safeguards of the International Atomic Energy Agency over all their nuclear materials. The treaty, however, is not of indefinite duration. One of the provisions of the treaty was to convene a conference 25 years after entry to decide whether the treaty would continue indefinitely or be extended for a specified time.

### Nuclear Referral List
*See* Nuclear Regulatory Commission.

### Nuclear Regulatory Commission (NRC)
(U.S.) The NRC regulates the transfer of nuclear facilities, materials and parts with uniquely nuclear applications (such as items associated with nuclear reactors). The U.S. Department of Energy regulates the transfer of information relating to nuclear technology. The U.S. State Department controls defense articles and services, such as nuclear weapons design and test equipment. The U.S. Department of Commerce controls a range of dual-use items with potential nuclear application. Validated licensing controls are in effect for commodities and technical data identified to be useful in the design, development, production or use of nuclear weapons or nuclear explosive purposes. These commodities compose the "Nuclear Referral List" (NRL). Any item under national security-based licensing requirements and intended for a nuclear-related end-use/end-user is also subject to review. In addition, any commodity that will be used in a sensitive nuclear activity is also subject to validated licensing controls. License applications for U.S. export of NRL items as well as applications that may involve possible nuclear uses are reviewed by the U.S. Department of Commerce in consultation with the Department of Energy. When either Department believes that the application requires further review, the application is referred to the Subgroup on Nuclear Export Coordination (SNEC). The SNEC is comprised of representatives from State, Defense, ACDA, and the NRC. Contact: U.S. Nuclear Regulatory Commission, Office of Public Affairs (OPA), Washington, D.C. 20555 USA; Tel: [1] (800) 368-5642, or [1] (301) 415-5575; E-mail: opa@nrc.gov; Web: www.nrc.gov. *See* Nuclear Suppliers Group; Zangger Committee.

### Nuclear Suppliers Group
An organization of nuclear supplier nations which coordinates exports of nuclear materials and equipment with the International Atomic Energy Agency (IAEA) inspectorate regime. The reason for creating the NSG was to allow member states some flexibility (which they do not enjoy in the Zangger Committee) in controlling items to non-nuclear weapons states.

The NSG's independence from the Nuclear Non-Proliferation Treaty (NPT) enables NSG to enlist the cooperation of supplier states that are not signatories to the NPT and thus not involved in the nuclear export control activities of the Zangger Committee. The NSG's control list is more comprehensive than the Zangger Committee's "trigger list"; it requires the imposition of safeguards on exports of nuclear technology in addition to nuclear materials and equipment. *See* Nuclear Non-Proliferation Treaty; Zangger Committee; Nuclear Regulatory Commission.

# O

**ocean bill of lading (B/L)**
(shipping) A receipt for the cargo and a contract for transportation between a shipper and the ocean carrier. It may also be used as an instrument of ownership (negotiable bill of lading) which can be bought, sold, or traded while the goods are in transit. To be used in this manner, it must be a negotiable "Order" Bill-of-Lading.
(a) A **clean bill of lading** is issued when the shipment is received in good order. If damaged or a shortage is noted, a clean bill of lading will not be issued.
(b) An **on board bill of lading** certifies that the cargo has been placed aboard the named vessel and is signed by the master of the vessel or his representative. In letter of credit transactions, an on board bill of lading is usually necessary for the shipper to obtain payment from the bank. When all bills of lading are processed, a ship's manifest is prepared by the steamship line. This summarizes all cargo aboard the vessel by port of loading and discharge.
(c) An **inland bill of lading** (a waybill on rail or the "pro forma" bill of lading in trucking) is used to document the transportation of the goods between the port and the point of origin or destination. It should contain information such as marks, numbers, steamship line, and similar information to match with a dock receipt.
*See* bill of lading.

**ocean transport intermediary (OTI)**
(shipping) An ocean freight forwarder and NVOCC (Non Vessel Operating Common Carrier) that acts as an intermediary between shippers and shipping lines. In the U.S. OTI's are licensed according to provisions in the Ocean Shipping Reform Act of 1998 which include the responsibility to publish tariffs (charges) in an electronically accessible automated tariff system.

**OEM**
Acronym for original equipment manufacturer. (a) A manufacturer who sells equipment to a reseller for the purpose of repackaging, bundling, rebranding or co-branding. (b) (popular) The reseller of repackaged, bundled, rebranded or co-branded equipment.
In both cases, the reseller can simply repackage and resell the equipment, add value to the equipment or bundle the equipment with other products for resale. *See* VAR (value-added reseller).

**Offene Handelsgesellschaft (OHG)**
(Austria) Designation for a general partnership, in which all partners have joint and several liability.

**offer**
(law) A proposal that is made to a certain individual or legal entity to enter into a contract, that is definite in its terms, and that indicates the offeror's intent to be bound by an acceptance. For example, an order delivered to a seller to buy a product on certain terms is an offer, but an advertisement sent to many potential buyers is not. *See* acceptance; counteroffer.

**Office of Exporter Services (OEXS)**
(U.S.) Under the Commerce Department's Bureau of Industry and Security, the OEXS administerSs export licenses. The Bureau of Industry and Security (formerly the Bureau of Export Administration) provides an Internet-based export license application program free of charge called the Simplified Network Application Process (SNAP) at Web: http://snap.bis.doc.gov. Telephone support

for SNAP is also available at [1] (202) 482-4811. Contact: Office of Exporter Services, U.S. Department of Commerce, 14th and Pennsylvania NW, Washington, DC 20230 USA; Web: www.bis.doc.gov. *See* Bureau of Industry and Security.

**Office of Management and Budget (OMB)**
(U.S.) An executive office of the president which evaluates, formulates and coordinates management procedures and program objectives within and among federal departments and agencies. It also controls the administration of the federal budget. Contact: Office of Management and Budget, New Executive Office Building, 725 17th Street NW, Washington, DC 20503 USA; Tel: [1] (202) 395-3080; Fax: [1] (202 395-3888; Web: www.omb.gov.

**Office of Munitions Control**
*See* Defense Trade Controls.

**official development assistance**
(U.S.) Financial flows to developing countries and multilateral institutions provided by official agencies of national, state, or local governments. Each transaction must be:
(1) administered with the promotion of the economic development and welfare of developing countries as its main objective; and
(2) concessional in character and contain a grant element of at least 25 percent.

**offset(s)**
(general) In non-defense trade, governments sometimes impose offset requirements on foreign exporters, as a condition for approval of major sales agreements in an effort to either reduce the adverse trade impact of a major sale or to gain specified industrial benefits for the importing country. In these circumstances, offset requirements generally take one of two forms. In one formulation, an exporter may be required to purchase a specified amount of locally-produced goods or services from the importing country. For example, a commercial aircraft manufacturer seeking sales to an airline in another country might be required to purchase products as different from airplanes as canned hams. In other instances, an exporter might be required to establish manufacturing facilities in the importing country or to secure a specified percentage of the components used in manufacturing his product from established local manufacturers. *See* countertrade.
(defense related–U.S.) In trade of defense items, "offsets" are industrial compensation practices mandated by many foreign governments when purchasing U.S. defense systems. Types of offsets include mandatory coproduction, subcontractor production, technology transfer, countertrade, and foreign investment. Countries require offsets for a variety of reasons: to ease (or "offset") the burden of large defense purchases on their economies, to increase domestic employment, to obtain desired technology, or to promote targeted industrial sectors. *See* countertrade.

**offshore**
(economics/law) (a) Outside the legal or taxing jurisdiction of a country. (b) An investment, security, bank account or property located outside an individual's country of domicile. (c) A geographic region located "off the shore", but within waters under a country's control (e.g., offshore fisheries). (d) Manufacturing, production or technical support facilities located in a foreign country. (e) Contracting work carried out at sea (e.g., oil exploration and production at sea). (f) Conditions when the wind is blowing off the land. (g) Utilizing an outsourcing service provider (such as a call center) located in a foreign country. (h) Away from shore; away from land; "cruising five miles offshore," "offshore oil reserves," "an offshore island."

**offshore bank**
(banking) Bank located outside the country in question.

**offshore banking center**
(banking) Financial center where many of the financial institutions have little connection with that country's financial system. Usually established for purposes of tax avoidance. Examples are the Cayman Islands, where many of the corporations are engaged in business in the U.S. and Europe, and London, where many of the financial institutions are engaged in Eurodollar trading.

**offshore banking unit (OBU)**
(banking) Department within a bank that, in certain countries (e.g., Bahrain), is permitted to engage in specific transactions (usually Euromarket business) that ordinary domestic banks are not allowed to do.

**offshore outsourcing**
The outsourcing of a business function to a third-party vendor located in a foreign country.

**offshoring**
The relocation of an entire business process to a foreign country. The business process or function can be performed by the parent company or by a local third-party contractor. Offshoring is similar to outsourcing, but can be performed by a division or subsidiary of the offshoring company, as well as by a third-party entity. Note that offshoring can refer to either a manufacturing (production) process or a service process.

**old-to-market (OTM)**
(U.S.) A committed to export, experienced, larger-scale firm. A significant portion of manufacturing capability may be foreign sourced. Export sales volume is often in excess of 15 percent of total sales.

**on board**
(shipping) Notation on a bill of lading indicating that the goods have been loaded on board or shipped on a named ship. In the case of received for shipment bills of lading, the following four parties are authorized to add this "on board" notation: (1) the carrier, (2) the carrier's agent, (3) the master of the ship, and (4) the master's agent. *See* ocean bill of lading; bill of lading; negotiable bill of lading.

**on deck**
(shipping) Notation on a bill of lading which indicates that the goods have been loaded on the deck of the ship. In letter of credit transactions documents with an "on deck" notation will only be accepted if expressly authorized in the credit. *See* ocean bill of lading.

**on deck bill of lading**
(shipping) Bill of lading containing the notation that goods have been placed on deck.
*See* ocean bill of lading; bill of lading.

**on their face**
(banking) In letter of credit and other documentary operations banks must examine documents with reasonable care to ascertain whether or not they appear, on their face, to be in compliance with the terms or conditions of the documentary letter of credit. *See* letter of credit; documentary collection.

**online receiving**
(logistics) A freight management system where operators enter goods received information directly into computer terminals as shipments occur.

**open account**
Credit extended that is not supported by a note, mortgage, or other formal written evidence of indebtedness (e.g., merchandise for which a buyer is billed later). Because this method poses an obvious risk to the supplier, it is essential that the buyer's integrity be unquestionable.

**open bill of lading**
A legally or commercially incomplete bill of lading that requires some action to be taken for disposition according to law or practice.

**open conference**
(shipping) A shipping conference in which there are no restrictions upon membership other than ability and willingness to serve the trade. U.S. law requires all conferences serving the U.S. to be open. *See* conference; closed conference.

**open economy**
(economics) An economy free of trade restrictions.

**open-end contract**
(law) An agreement by which the buyer may purchase goods from a seller for a certain time without changes in the price or the contract terms.

**open manifest**
A manifest in which one or more bills of lading require some action that some action be taken for disposition according to law or practice.

**open policy**
(insurance) An insurance contract (policy) which remains in force until cancelled and under which individual successive shipments are reported or declared and automatically covered on or after the inception date. The open policy saves time and expense for all concerned, whether underwriter, agent or assured.
The shipper gains many advantages from the use of an open policy.
(1) He or she has automatic protection (up to the maximum limits stated in the policy) from the time shipments leave the warehouse at the place named in the policy for the commencement of transit. The policyholder warrants that shipments will be declared as soon as practicable, but unintentional failure to report will not void the insurance, since the goods are "held covered," subject to policy conditions. In effect, this is errors and omissions coverage, and it forestalls the possibility that, because of the press of business, goods may commence transit without being insured.
(2) The open policy provides a convenient way to report shipments. It also relieves the shipper from the necessity of arranging individual placings of insurance for each shipment.
(3) Under an open policy the shipper has prior knowledge of the rate of premium that will be charged and thus can be certain of the cost. This in turn facilitates his quoting a landed sales price.
(4) The use of the open policy creates a business relationship that may exist over a long period of time. This permits the insurer to learn the special requirements of its assureds and so to provide them with individualized protection, tailor-made to fit the specific situation. This may be an important factor in the case of loss adjustments at out-of-the-way ports around the world, or in overcoming problems peculiar to a given commodity.
Some letter of credit transactions require evidence of an individual "policy" covering the specified shipment. In such cases it has become the practice to use a special marine policy. *See* bordereau; declaration; special marine policy.

**open-top container**
(logistics/shipping) A shipping container that is designed to open from the top so that cargo too large to be loaded from the side can be lowered in through the roof. This type of container is especially suitable for machinery. Once loaded the container is covered with rigid panels or a tarpaulin.

**open top container**
(shipping) An ocean shipping container with an open or removable roof or top, making it possible to load large, bulky

or awkward cargo (especially machinery) from the top. After cargo has been loaded, cross braces can be attached at the roof line to stabilize the container walls and rigid panels or a tarpaulin spread to offer some protection against the elements.

### operating committees
(U.S.) There are four operating committees (OCs), which are the first step in resolving interagency disputes over the disposition of export license applications. The operating committees are: (1) the State Department's Subgroup on Nuclear Export Coordination (SNEC), (2) the State Department's working group on Missile Technology, (3) the State Department's working group on Chemical and Biological Warfare, and (4) the Department of Commerce's operating committee on all other dual-use items. Operating committees must make recommendations within 90 days of the date of the filing of an export license application. Operating committees generally meet a couple of times per month. *See* United States Department of Commerce; United States Department of State.

### Operating Differential Subsidy (ODS)
(U.S. shipping) A subsidy paid to an American flag carrier by the U.S. government to offset the higher costs of operating a U.S. flag vessel than a foreign flag vessel.

### Operation Exodus
(U.S.) A U.S. Customs and Border Protection export enforcement program that was developed in 1981 to help stem the flow of the illegal export of U.S.-sourced arms and technology to the Soviet bloc and other prohibited destinations. These enforcement activities are currently coordinated by the U.S. Customs and Border Protection's Exodus Command Center. Information on this Center can be found online at Web: www.cbp.gov/custoday/sep2000/exodus2.htm.
*See* United States Customs and Border Protection.

### operator
(U.S. foreign trade zones) A corporation, partnership or person that operates a foreign trade zone under the terms of an agreement with a foreign trade zone grantee. If there is no operator agreement and the grantee operates his own zone, the grantee is considered the operator for Customs Regulations purposes. *See* foreign trade zone; Foreign Trade Zone Board; Foreign Trade Zone Act; grantee; zone user; subzones.

### option
(general) (a) A right to take up an offer. (b) The right to choose from several different possibilities. (c) A privilege to buy or sell, receive, or deliver property, given in accordance with the terms stated, with a consideration for price. This privilege may or may not be exercised at the option holder's discretion. Failure to exercise the option leads to forfeiture of the option.
(securities) A contract giving the holder the right to buy or sell a stated number of shares of a particular security at a fixed price within a predetermined period.
(foreign exchange) The contractually agreed upon right to buy (call option) or sell (put option) a specific amount of an underlying instrument at a predetermined price on a specific date (European option) or up to a future date (American option).
*See* call option; put option; American option; European option.

### order
(law/banking/shipping) A request to deliver, sell, receive, or purchase goods or services.

### order bill
(law) A bill of lading that states that goods are consigned to the order of the person named in the bill. *See* bill of lading; ocean bill of lading.

### order cycle
(logistics) The total time and process required for the placement of an order and its final receipt by a customer. This includes order placement, order processing, production and transportation to the final destination.

### order notify
(shipping) A bill of lading term to provide for surrender of the original bill of lading before freight is surrendered; usually handled through a bank. *See* letter of credit; bill of lading; ocean bill of lading; documentary collection.

### order picking
(logistics) The process of retrieving goods from storage to fill shop or customer orders.

### order processing
(logistics) The process of fulfillment of a customer order. This includes the entire process from order receiving, invoicing and other documentation, picking, packing and shipping.

### orderly marketing agreements
International agreements negotiated between two or more governments, in which the trading partners agree to restrain the growth of trade (limit exports) in specified "sensitive" products, usually through the imposition of import quotas. Orderly Marketing Agreements are intended to ensure that future trade increases will not disrupt, threaten or impair competitive industries or their workers in importing countries.

### Ordinary Seaman
(shipping) A deck crew member in the merchant marine who is subordinate to and assists able bodied seamen and officers and keeps facilities clean. An apprentice able bodied seaman. Ordinary seaman is the first level job of six towards becoming a capitan (ordinary seaman, able-bodied seaman, third mate, second mate, chief mate, captain).

### Organization for Economic Cooperation and Development (OECD)
The OECD is the primary forum for the discussion of common economic and social issues confronting the U.S., Canada, Western Europe, Japan, Australia, and New Zealand. It was founded in 1960 as the successor to the Organization for European Economic Cooperation which oversaw European participation in the Marshall Plan. The OECD's fundamental objective is "to achieve the highest sustainable economic growth and employment and a rising standard of living in member countries while maintaining financial stability and thus contribute to the world economy." Members currently include: Australia, Austria, Belgium-Luxembourg, Canada, Denmark, Finland, France, Germany, Greece, Iceland, Ireland, Italy, Japan, the Netherlands, New Zealand, Norway, Portugal, Spain, Sweden, Switzerland, Turkey, the United Kingdom, and the United States. Contact: Organization for Economic Cooperation and Development, 2 rue Andre Pascal, F-75775 Paris Cedex 16, France; Tel: [33] (1) 45-24-82-00; Web: www.oecd.org.

### Organization of African Unity (OAU)
*See* African Union.

### Organization of American States (OAS)
The OAS is a regional organization established in April 1948 which promotes Latin American economic and social development. Members include the United States, Mexico, and most Central American, South American, and Caribbean nations. Members include: Antigua and Barbuda, Argentina, the Bahamas, Barbados, Belize, Bolivia, Brazil, Canada, Chile, Colombia, Costa Rica, Cuba (participation suspended), Dominica, Dominican Republic, Ecuador, El Salvador, Grenada, Guatemala, Guyana, Haiti, Honduras, Jamaica, Mexico, Nicaragua, Panama, Paraguay, Peru, St. Christopher-Nevis, St. Lucia, St. Vincent and the Grena-

dines, Suriname, Trinidad and Tobago, the United States, Uruguay, and Venezuela. Contact: Organization of American States, 17th Street and Constitution Avenue NW, Washington, DC 20006; Tel: [1] (202) 458-3000; Web: www.oas.org.

### Organization of Arab Petroleum Exporting Countries (OAPEC)

OAPEC was established in 1968 to safeguard the interests of its members and to provide a forum for cooperation in the petroleum industry. Approximately 25% of the annual world petroleum production is from the member states of OAPEC. OAPEC members include: Algeria, Bahrain, Egypt, Iraq, Kuwait, Libya, Qatar, Saudi Arabia, Syria, and the United Arab Emirates. Contact: Organization of Arab Petroleum Exporting Countries, P.O. Box 20501, SAFAT 13066 Kuwait; Tel: [96] (5) 484-4500; Fax: [96] (5) 481-5747; E-mail: oapec@qualitynet.net; Web: www.oapecorg.org.

### Organization of Petroleum Exporting Countries (OPEC)

An association of the world's oil-producing countries, formed in 1960. The chief purpose of OPEC is to coordinate oil production and pricing policies of its members: Algeria, Ecuador, Gabon, Indonesia, Iran, Iraq, Kuwait, Libya, Nigeria, Qatar, Saudi Arabia, the United Arab Emirates, and Venezuela. Contact: Organization of Petroleum Exporting Countries, Obere-Donaustrasse 93, A-1020 Vienna, Austria; Tel: [43] (1) 211-12-279; Fax: [43] (1) 214-98-27; Web: www.opec.org.

### Organization of the Islamic Conference (OIC)

The OIC, established in May 1971, promotes cooperation in cultural, economic, scientific and social areas among Islamic nations. Headquarters are located in Jeddah, Saudi Arabia. Members include: Afghanistan, Algeria, Bahrain, Bangladesh, Benin, Brunei, Burkina Faso, Cameroon, Chad, Comoros, Cyprus, Djibouti, Egypt, Gabon, the Gambia, Guinea, Guinea-Bissau, Indonesia, Iran, Iraq, Jordan, Kuwait, Lebanon, Libya, Malaysia, Maldives, Mali, Mauritania, Morocco, Niger, Nigeria, Oman, Pakistan, Qatar, Saudi Arabia, Senegal, Sierra Leone, Somalia, Sudan, Syria, Tunisia, Turkey, Uganda, the United Arab Emirates, and Yemen. Contact: Organization of The Islamic Conference, PO Box: 178, Jeddah-21411, Kingdom of Saudi Arabia; Tel: [966] (2) 690-0001; Fax: [966] (2) 275-1953; E-mail: info@oic-oci.org; Web: www.oic-oci.org.

### original documents

(banking/letters of credit) Unless otherwise stated in the letter of credit, the requirement for an original document may also be satisfied by the presentation of documents produced or appearing to have been produced:
(1) reprographically,
(2) by automated or computerized systems, or
(3) as carbon copies,
and marked as "originals" and where necessary appearing to be signed. *See* letter of credit.

### original equipment manufacturer (OEM)

*See* OEM.

### ORM (other regulated material)

*See* hazardous materials; restricted articles; ORM; ORM-A, B, C, D, E.

### ORM-A

(shipping) Material with an anesthetic, irritating, noxious, toxic or other properties that can cause discomfort to persons in the event of leakage. Examples are trichloroethylene, 1,1,1-trichloroethane, dry ice, chloroform, carbon tetrachloride.

### ORM-B

(shipping) Material specifically named or capable of causing significant corrosion damage from leakage. Examples are lead chloride, quicklime, metallic mercury, barium oxide.

### ORM-C

(shipping) Material specifically named and with characteristics which make it unsuitable for shipment unless properly packaged. Examples are bleaching powder, lithium batteries (for disposal), magnetized materials, sawdust, asbestos.

### ORM-D

(shipping) Material such as consumer commodities which present a limited hazard due to form, quantity and packaging. They must be materials for which exceptions are provided. Examples are chemical consumer commodities (e.g., hair spray and shaving lotion) and small arm ammunition (reclassified because of packaging).

### ORM-E

(shipping) Material that is not included in any other hazard class, but is regulated as ORM. Examples are hazardous waste and hazardous substances.

### other regulated materials

*See* ORM.

### ouguiya

The currency of Mauritania. 1UM=5 khoums.

### outbound consolidation

*See* consolidation.

### outbound logistics

(logistics) The entire process of planning and controlling the flow of products from the end of a production line to the end user. This includes both transportation and intermediate storage. *See* logistics.

### out-of-the-money

(foreign exchange) An option is out-of-the-money in the following cases:
(1) Call option: market price less than the strike price.
(2) Put option: market price greater than the strike price.
For European options, replace the market price by the forward price of the underlying instrument on the expiry date of the option. *See* call option; put option; option; in-the-money.

### output contract

(law) An agreement by which one party agrees to sell his or her entire production to the other, who agrees to purchase it.

### outright

(foreign exchange) A forward purchase or sale of foreign exchange which is not offset by a corresponding spot transaction, i.e. which has not been contracted through swaps. *See* foreign exchange.

### outsource (outsourcing)

(economics) (a) The sourcing of raw materials, component parts or finished goods from outside a business organization. The opposite of insourcing. (b) The contracting of services (such as call center services, software development or maintenance services) to an outside company. (c) The contracting of services (such as call center services) to an outside company located in a foreign country.

### outward swap

(foreign exchange) Spot purchase of foreign exchange and forward resale of the same currency against domestic currency. *See* foreign exchange.

### overland common point (OCP)

(shipping) A special rate concession made by shipping lines, rail carriers, and truckers serving the U.S. West Coast for export and import traffic intended to benefit midwest shippers and importers by equalizing rates to and from other coastal areas, and offering these Midwest companies a comparable alternative. The steamship companies lower their rates and their inland carriers pick up the terminal charges, which consist of handling charges, wharfage charges, and carloading or unloading charges. OCP rates apply to cargo shipped from or consigned to the states of North Dakota, South Dakota, Nebraska, Colorado, New Mexico and all states east thereof. OCP rates in Canada apply to the provinces of Manitoba, Ontario and Quebec.

**overnight**
(foreign exchange) Swap from settlement date until the following business day, i.e., one day or three days over the weekend. *See* foreign exchange.

**Overseas Private Investment Corporation (OPIC)**
(U.S.) A self-sustaining U.S. agency, whose purpose is to promote economic growth in developing countries by encouraging U.S. private investment in those nations. The Corporation assists American investors in three principal ways: (1) financing investment projects through direct loans and/or guaranties; (2) insuring investment projects against a broad range of political risks; and (3) providing a variety of investor services including investor counseling, country and regional information kits, computer-assisted project and investor matching, and investment missions. OPIC does not support projects that will result in the loss of domestic jobs or have a negative impact on the host country's environment or worker's rights. Contact: Overseas Private Investment Corporation, 1100 New York Ave. NW, Washington, DC 20527 USA; Tel: [1] (202) 336-8400; Fax: [1] (202) 408-9859; E-mail: info@opic.gov; Web: www.opic.gov.

**overs, short, and damaged (OSD)**
(logistics) A report that details discrepancies between a bill of lading and a shipment at hand. Extra goods are "overs," missing goods are "short," and damaged goods are listed as "damaged."

**over the counter (OTC)**
(finance) Securities trading which takes place outside the normal exchanges. In contrast to normal exchanges, it is not tied to a central set-up in any one place but is conducted mainly by telephone and telex between traders, brokers and customers.

**over the counter small package service**
*See* small package service.

**oxidizing material**
(shipping) These items are chemically reactive and will provide both heat and oxygen to support a fire. (UN CLASS 5.) Examples are calcium permanganate, calcium hypochlorite, barium perchlorate, hydrogen peroxide and ammonium nitrate. Hazards/precautions are: may ignite combustibles (wood, paper, etc.); reaction with fuels may be violent; fires may produce poisonous fumes; vapors and dusts may be irritating; contact may burn skin and eyes; and peroxides may explode from heat or contamination.

# P

**pa'anga**
The currency of Tonga. 1T$=100 seniti.

**Pacific Rim**
Refers to countries and economies bordering the Pacific ocean. Pacific Rim is an informal, flexible term which generally has been regarded as a reference to East Asia, Canada, and the United States. At a minimum, the Pacific Rim includes Canada, Japan, the People's Republic of China, Taiwan, and the United States. It may also include Australia, Brunei, Cambodia, Hong Kong/Macau, Indonesia, Laos, North Korea, South Korea, Malaysia, New Zealand, the Pacific Islands, the Philippines, Russia (or the Commonwealth of Independent States), Singapore, Thailand, and Vietnam. As an evolutionary term, usage sometimes includes Mexico, the countries of Central America, and the Pacific coast countries of South America.

**packing credit**
(banking) A monetary advance granted by a bank in connection with shipments of storable goods guaranteed by the assignment of the payment expected later on under a documentary letter of credit.

**packing list**
(shipping) A document prepared by a shipper listing the kinds and quantities of merchandise in a particular shipment. A copy of the packing list is often attached to the shipment itself (to the exterior of a package or crate) and another copy sent directly to the consignee to assist in checking the contents of the shipment when received. Also called a bill of parcels.

**pallet**
(shipping) A shallow portable platform with or without sides used to store, handle or move materials and goods in factories, warehouses, containers or vessels. Pallets are usually constructed of wood and are designed so that the prongs of a fork-lift truck can lift the pallet and its load. *See* skid, forklift truck.
(air freight) A platform with a flat metal framed undersurface on which goods are assembled and secured by nets and straps. *See* aircraft pallet.
Palletization results in more efficient use of space and better cargo handling, particularly when used as part of mechanized loading systems.

**pallet loader**
(shipping) A device employing one or more vertical lift platforms for the mechanical loading or unloading of palletized freight at planeside.

**pallet transporter**
(shipping) A vehicle for the movement of loaded pallets between the aircraft and the freight terminal or truck dock.

**palletizing**
(shipping) The loading and securing of a number of sacks, bags, boxes or drums on a pallet base.

**Panamax**
(shipping) An ocean-going cargo vessel of the maximum size possible to pass through the locks of the Panama Canal, which are 1000ft long by 110ft wide and 85ft deep. These vessels are typically of 50,000 to 80,000 dwt, 965ft (290m) in length; 106ft. (32.3m) beam; and 39.5ft (12.04m) draft.

**Paperless Master In-bond**
(United States) A U.S. Customs and Border Protection program that controls the movement and disposition of master

in-bond (MIB) shipments from the carrier's custody at the port of unlading to the same carrier's custody at the port of destination. For more information contact the CBP Industry Partnership Programs at [1] (202) 927-0520 or go to: www.cbp.gov.

**PAPS**
*See* Pre Arrival Processing System.

**par exchange rate**
(foreign exchange) The free market price of one country's money in terms of the currency of another.

**par of exchange**
(foreign exchange) The market price of money in one national currency that is exchanged at the official rate for a specific amount in another national currency, or another commodity of value (gold, silver, etc.).

**par value**
(foreign exchange) The official fixed exchange rate between two currencies or between a currency and a specific weight of gold or a basket of currencies. *See* foreign exchange.

**parallel trade (parallel imports)**
(economics) Imports of genuine copyrighted, patented or trademarked products without the authorization of the copyright, patent or trademark holder. Parallel trade is the subject of great debate, especially in the pharmaceutical industry. For example, U.S. manufacturers of pharmaceuticals sell their products for what the market will bear in local country markets around the world. In some cases licenses are granted to producers to manufacture the items locally, often at substantially lower cost, resulting in a lower local market price. This means that the same drug may sell for more in the U.S. and, for example, less in Canada. U.S. consumers, however, in an effort to save money, purchase the drug in Canada and import it into the U.S., technically in violation of U.S. import laws regarding copyrights, patents and trademarks. The pharmaceutical industry argues that this practice, while giving short-term benefit to consumers, drains profits and ultimately research and development money from the industry for new products. Also called gray market or gray market imports.

**parcel post air freight**
(shipping) An airline service through which a shipper can consolidate a number of parcel post packages (with destination postage affixed by the shipper) for shipment as air freight to the postmaster at another city for subsequent delivery within local postal zones or beyond.

**parent bank**
(banking) A bank in a major industrial country that sets up a subsidiary in a developing country.

**parent corporation**
(law) A corporation (business entity) that owns all or the majority interest of another business entity.

**Pareto Principle/Postulate**
(business theory) The concept that when a large number of individuals or organizations contribute to a result, the major part of the result comes from a minority of the contributors. The Pareto Postulate is that 20% of your effort or clients will generate 80% of your results or business. This is commonly referred to as the 80/20 rule. An actual percentage can be calculated by ranking customers or contributors by volume or any other factor. The Pareto Principle is based on the work and writings of the 19th century Italian economist Vilfredo Pareto.

**pari passu**
(law) On an equal basis without preference. Creditors who receive payment pari passu, for example, are paid in proportion to their interests without regard to whether any of the claims would have taken priority over others.

**Paris Club**
Under the International Monetary Fund's (IMF) General Agreements to Borrow (GAB), established in 1962, 10 of the wealthiest industrial members of the IMF agreed to lend funds to the IMF, up to specified amounts "when supplementary resources are needed." The finance ministers of these countries comprise the Paris Club (also called the Group of 10).

The Paris Club has become a popular designation for meetings between representatives of a developing country that wishes to renegotiate its "official" debt (normally excluding debts owed by and to the private sector without official guarantees) and representatives of the relevant creditor governments and international institutions. These meetings usually occur at the request of a debtor country that wishes to consolidate all or part of its debt service payments falling due over a specified period. Meetings are traditionally chaired by a senior official of the French Treasury Department. Comparable meetings occasionally take place in London and in New York for countries that wish to renegotiate repayment terms for their debts to private banks. These meetings are sometimes called "creditor clubs." *See* International Monetary Fund; Group of Ten.

**Paris Convention**
The Paris Convention for the Protection of Industrial Property, first adopted in 1883, is the major international agreement providing basic rights for protecting industrial property. It covers patents, industrial designs, service marks, trade names, indications of source, and unfair competition. The U.S. ratified this treaty in 1903. The treaty provides two fundamental rights:

(1) The **principle of national treatment** provides that nationals of any signatory nation shall enjoy in all other countries of the union the advantages that each nation's laws grant to its own nationals.

(2) The **right of priority** enables any resident or national of a member country to, first, file a patent application in any member country and, thereafter, to file a patent application for the same invention in any of the other member countries within 12 months of the original filing and receive benefit of the original filing date.

*See* patent; trademark; copyright; World Intellectual Property Organization; Patent Cooperation Treaty.

**Paris Union**
*See* World Intellectual Property Organization.

**parity**
(general) Equality in amount or value. For example, if the price for goods sold in two different markets is the same, the price is in parity.

(foreign exchange) Exchange relationship of a currency to a legally binding reference, i.e., to a specific amount of gold, to Special Drawing Rights (SDRs) or to other currencies. *See* special drawing right(s).

(foreign exchange/official parity) Predetermined exchange rate relationship between two currencies.

**parol**
(law) Oral expression. A parol contract, for example, is one that is verbal only and that has not be put into writing by the parties.

**PARS (Pre-Arrival Review System)**
(Canada) A Canada Revenue Agency (CRA) electronic data interchange (EDI) system that allows importers and brokers to gain shipment release information prior to the arrival of the goods in Canada. Information at: www.ccra-adrc.gc.ca.

**particular average**
(insurance) An insurance loss that affects specific interests only. There are two kinds of particular average losses: the

total loss of a part of the goods, and the arrival of goods at destination in a damaged condition.

In the first situation, it is necessary to determine how much of the total amount insured is applicable to the missing item. In homogeneous or fungible cargo—that is, cargo which is capable of mutual substitution, like oil or coal—it is frequently a matter of simple arithmetic. The value of the unit of measurement of the cargo is found by dividing the amount of insurance by the total number of units in the shipment. This value multiplied by the number of missing units gives the value of the loss.

Where a normal or trade loss is to be expected, as in cargo subject to leakage, slackage or loss of moisture during the voyage, the method of calculation is slightly different. The value of the insurance is divided by the number of units in the "expected outturn," that is, the expected arrived quantity rather than the shipped quantity. This can be determined either by the normal percentage of trade loss for similar shipments or by examinations of sound arrived cargo forming part of the shipment in question. While this method will produce a somewhat higher insured value per unit, it naturally requires the normal or trade loss to be deducted in calculating the actual shortage sustained.

*See* average; general average; with average; free of particular average; deductible average; trade loss.

### parties to the credit
(banking) At least the following three parties are involved in a documentary letter of credit transaction:
(1) Applicant (buyer/importer),
(2) Issuing bank (buyers bank), and
(3) Beneficiary (seller/exporter).

As a rule, however, the issuing bank will entrust a correspondent bank with the task of advising and authenticating the credit and, if applicable, with payment, acceptance or negotiation. The issuing bank may also request the advising bank to add its confirmation.

*See* letter of credit; confirmation; issuing bank; advising bank.

### partnership
(law) An unincorporated business owned and operated by two or more persons (partners), who may have general or limited liability in accordance with the partnership agreement. Note: The definition of status of partnership varies from country to country, and is not recognized as a business entity in some countries. *See* general partnership; limited partnership.

### Partners in Protection (PIP)
(Canada Customs) A Canada Border Services Agency (CBSA) program that is designed to enlist the co-operation of private industry in efforts to enhance border security, combat organized crime and terrorism, increase awareness of customs compliance issues and help detect and prevent contraband smuggling.

Participating organizations are asked to sign an agreement known as a Memorandum of Understanding (MOU) with the CBSA. The arrangement is based on goodwill. Participating organizations are not asked to act as a law-enforcement body, and all information exchanged is treated as confidential. Organizations and the CBSA work together to focus on security, the exchange of information and awareness.

To enhance and strengthen security processes, participating companies are asked to give a self-assessment of their security systems. This self-assessment will help CBSA identify any weaknesses in security processes and will enable the to help firms address any deficiencies. The goal is to minimize the threat of illegal activity. For information about PIP and the CBSA go to: www.cbsa-asfc.gc.ca

### passengermile/kilometer
(logistics) A passenger load factor equal to the transportation of one passenger for one mile/kilometer. A measure of a carrier's total passenger miles/kilometers in the course of a year would be the total number of passengers carried during a year multiplied by the average number of miles/kilometers each passenger traveled

### pataca
The currency of Macao. 1P=100 avos.

### patent
(law) A grant by law to an inventor of a device of the right to exclude other persons from making, using, or selling the device. The patent holder has the right to license to another person the right to make, use, or sell the device. A patent is available only for devices that embody a new idea or principle and that involve a discovery. Patent protection varies from country to country, and may not be available in some jurisdictions. A country that is a member the Paris Convention for the Protection of Industrial Property may recognize patents held in other jurisdictions. *See* copyright; service mark; trademark; Paris Convention; World Intellectual Property Organization.

### Patent Cooperation Treaty (PCT)
The PCT, is a worldwide convention, open to any Paris Convention country. The PCT entered into force in 1978. Unlike the Paris Convention, which addresses substantive intellectual property rights, the PCT addresses procedural requirements, aiming to simplify the filing, searching, and publication of international patent applications. *See* Paris Convention.

### payable in exchange
(foreign exchange) The requirement that a negotiable instrument be paid in the funds of the place from which it was originally issued.

### payee
(banking) The person or organization to whom a check or draft or note is made payable. The payee's name follows the expression "pay to the order of." *See* payer; negotiable; negotiable instrument.

### payer
(banking) The party primarily responsible for the payment of the amount owed as evidenced by a given negotiable instrument. *See* payee; negotiable; negotiable instrument.

### payload
(shipping) (a) The gross weight minus the tare of a shipping container or trailer. (b) The maximum cargo weight a container or trailer is rated to carry. (c) The gross weight minus the tare, fuel and operating personnel of a truck, vessel or aircraft. (d) The maximum cargo and passenger weight a vessel or aircraft is rated to carry. (e) The revenue producing portion of an aircraft or vessel's load including cargo and passengers.

### payments surplus
(economics) The excess of the value of a nation's exports over its imports. *See* balance of trade.

### pedimento
(Mexico) The required document for the import or export of goods from Mexico, prepared by a Mexican customs broker. For details in English, go to: www.mexicanlaws.com/new_pedimento.htm.

### penalties
(customs) The charges assessed or action taken by customs in response to a violation of a customs-enforced regulation or law.

### per diem
(general) Latin for "per day." A charge or allowance based upon a rate or cost per day.

(travel) The monetary cost or allowance given an employee to pay expenses while traveling or living at another location.

(logistics) Payment or charges based on a daily rate.

### perfect competition
(economics) A description for an industry or market unit consisting of a large number of purchasers and sellers all involved in the buying and selling of a homogeneous good, with awareness of prices and volume, no discrimination in buying and selling, and a mobility of resources.

### performance
(law) The proper fulfillment of a contract or obligation.

### performance bond
(insurance) A bond which guarantees proper fulfillment of the terms of a contract. In practice, the beneficiary of the bond (usually the buyer of services and/or goods), will claim financial restitution under the bond if the principal (supplier of the services and/or goods) fails to comply with the terms and conditions of the contract. *See* bond; surety.

### peril point
(economics) A hypothetical limit beyond which a reduction in tariff protection would cause serious injury to a domestic industry.

(U.S.) U.S. legislation in 1949 that extended the Trade Agreements Act of 1934 required the Tariff Commission to establish such "peril points" for U.S. industries, and for the president to submit specific reasons to Congress if and when any U.S. tariff was reduced below those levels. This requirement, which was an important constraint on U.S. negotiating positions in early General Agreement on Tariffs and Trade (GATT) tariff-cutting Rounds, was eliminated by the Trade Expansion Act of 1962.

### perils of the sea
(shipping) Causes of loss to cargo resulting from a shipment by sea.

(insurance) Marine insurance coverage that includes unusual action of wind and waves (often described as "stress of weather" or "heavy weather"), stranding, lightning, collision and damage by sea water when caused by insured perils such as opening of the seams of the vessel by stranding or collision. *See* special marine policy; all risk.

### perishable freight
(shipping) Freight subject to decay or deterioration.

### permanent normalized trade relations
*See* normal trade relations (NTR).

### person
(law) An individual or legal entity recognized under law as having legal rights and obligations. In the United States, for example, corporations and partnerships are examples of legal entities that are recognized as persons under the law. In countries that allow the formation of limited and unlimited liability companies, those companies are recognized as persons under the law.

### personal income
(economics) National income less various kinds of income not actually received by individuals, non-profit institutions, and so on (e.g., undistributed corporate profits, corporate taxes, employer contributions for social insurance), plus certain receipts that do not arise from production (i.e., transfer payments and government interest).

### peseta
The former currency of Spain and Andorra, 1Pts=100 centimos. The new currency of Spain and Andorra is the European Union Euro. €1 = 100 cents.

### peso
The currency of:
Argentina, 1$a=100 centavos;
Chile, 1Ch$=100 centavos;
Columbia, 1Col$=100 centavos;
Cuba, 1$=100 centavos;
Dominican Republic, 1RD$=100 centavos;
Guinea-Bissau, 1PG=100 centavos;
Mexico, 1Mex$=100 centavos;
Philippines, 1P=100 centavos;
Uruguay, 1UR$=100 centesimos.

### petrodollars
(foreign investment/banking) Huge sums of money from oil-producing nations other than the United States or Great Britain. These funds are initially converted into Eurocurrency and deposited with international banks to be used for future investment and for paying debts. These banks traditionally set limits on the sum they will accept from any one country.

### physical distribution
(logistics) The storage and movement of finished products from manufacturing facilities through the logistics chain to the ultimate consumer. *See* logistics.

### phytosanitary inspection certificate
A document indicating that a shipment of cargo has been inspected and is free from harmful pests and plant diseases. Phytosanitary inspection certificates are often required by import authorities for shipments containing plant products.

### pick/pack
(logistics) The selection of component parts or finished products from inventory and their subsequent packing for shipment.

### pickup and delivery service
(shipping) An optional service for the surface transport of shipments from shipper's door to originating carrier's terminal and from the terminal of destination to receiver's door. Pickup service, at an additional charge, is provided upon shipper's request. In air cargo shipments delivery service is provided automatically by the air carrier at an additional charge unless the shipper requests otherwise. PU&D service is provided between all airports and all local points of such airports. For service beyond the terminal area *See* truck/air service.

### pickup order
(shipping) An order from a broker (working as the agent of a consignee) to a carrier to pick up freight at a location.

### pier receipt
(shipping) *See* dock receipt.

### pier-to-pier
(shipping) Shipment of cargo by carrier from origin pier to discharge pier. Applies to container yard (CY) cargo. Drayage to/from pier is borne by customer.

### piggyback
(shipping/rail shipping) A form of intermodal transport of a truck trailer with chassis and wheels on a rail flat car. Technically called trailer on flat car (TOFC). Also called container on flatcar.

### pilferage
(shipping/insurance) The loss of goods due to steady theft in small amounts.

### pilot
(shipping) A person whose office or occupation is to steer ships, particularly along a coast, or into and out of a harbor.

### pips
(foreign exchange) In foreign exchange dealing, the last decimal places of a price quotation are called pips for purposes of simplicity (1/100th of 1 percent or 0.0001 of a unit). In futures trading the smallest possible price fluctuation upwards or downwards (1 pip) is called a tick.

### place utility
(economics/logistics) The added value given a raw material, component part or finished good as a result of a change

in its location. For example, iron ore brought to the smelter is more valuable that iron ore at the mine.

**planned order**
(logistics) In MRP (Materials Requirements Planning) and DRP (Distribution Requirements Planning) computer software systems, an order that the system automatically creates based upon projected demand, but which may be amended based upon changing demand. *See* MRP, DRP.

**platform**
(shipping) An ocean shipping or aircraft (ULD) cargo "container" consisting of a standard-sized rigid platform with fork lift pockets at the bottom and lashing devices on the sides for securing cargo to the platform. Platforms are used for oversized, bulky or awkward cargo loads that will not fit into standard containers.

**Plimsoll mark (Plimsoll line)**
(shipping) A horizontal load line (or set of horizontal load line markings) painted on the hull of an ocean-going cargo vessel that shows where the waterline is when the vessel is at full capacity. The term is named for Samuel Plimsoll, who as a member of the British Parliament, instigated the passage of the Merchant Shipping Act of 1875 which required the marking of a load line on all merchant ships. Plimsoll was a lone reformer who was vilified in the press, but persevered to end the practice of unscrupulous merchants deliberately launching overloaded "coffin ships" which were intended to sink in order that the owner could collect insurance. The technical term is the international load line. *See* draft or draught.

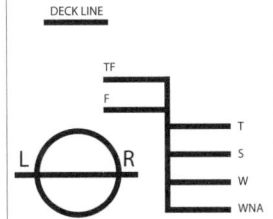

Plimsoll marks
Each horizontal mark designates a maximum vessel load as characterized by the vessel's depth in the water for various ocean zones.
TF – Tropical Fresh (zone)
F – Fresh (zone)
T – Tropical (zone)
S – Summer (zone)
W – Winter (zone)
WNA – Winter, North Atlantic
LR – Initials of the Lloyd's Register Classification Society.

**PNTR**
Acronym for permanent normal trade relations. *See* normal trade relations (NTR).

**point of origin**
(shipping) The location at which a shipment is received by a transportation line from the shipper.

**point-to-point; door-to-door**
(shipping) Designates service and rates for shipments in door-to-door service. Originating carrier spots (places) empty container at shipper's facility at carrier's expense for loading by and at expense of shipper, the delivering carrier spots the loaded container at consignee's facility at carrier's expense for unloading by and at expense of consignee. *See* demurrage; detention.

**poisonous material**
(shipping) Items that are extremely toxic to man and animals. (UN CLASS 6.) Examples are cyanogen gas, lead cyanide and parathion. Hazards/precautions are: may cause death quickly if breathed, swallowed or touched; may be flammable, explosive, corrosive or irritating; may be EXTREMELY HAZARDOUS. Look for the "Skull and Crossbones" on the label; degree of hazard key words: poison, danger, warning, highly toxic, moderately toxic, least toxic; and read the label carefully for storage and safety information.

**political risk**
(economics) Economic risk resulting from the political decisions of sovereign governments as well as political and social events in a country. Political risks includes confiscation, expropriation, nationalization, currency inconvertibility, contract frustration, war, civil unrest, revolution and annexation. Political risk can lead to the inability of a debtor to comply with a contract or to the loss, confiscation or damage to goods belonging to an exporter. An exporter may be able to cover this risk by utilizing a confirmed letter of credit or by applying for cover from export credit agencies. *See* commercial risk.

**political risk insurance**
(economics) Insurance coverage against political risk. Political risk insurance is typically provided by insurance companies, government entities and organizations such as the Inter-American Development Bank, (Web: www.iadb.org) and the Multilateral Investment Guarantee Agency (Web: www.miga.org).

**pooling**
(logistics) An agreement among a group of carriers to share freight, customers, revenues and/or profits.
(U.S. law) The U.S. Interstate Commerce Act outlaws pooling; however, the Civil Aeronautics Board allows air carriers, during strikes, to enter into profit-pooling agreements.

**port**
(shipping) (a) A harbor or haven where ships may anchor and discharge or receive cargo. (b) The left side of a ship when one is facing the bow.

**port authority**
(law) An entity of a local, state or national government that owns, manages and maintains the physical infrastructure of a seaport, airport or bus terminal. Port infrastructure can include wharfs, docks, piers, transit sheds, loading equipment and warehouses. Also known as harbor authority, port trust or port commission.

**port charge**
(shipping) A charge made for services performed at ports.

**port of call**
(shipping) A port at which a vessel loads or unloads some or all of its cargo or passengers during a voyage.

**port of discharge**
(shipping) The port at which a shipment is off-loaded by a transportation line, not to be confused with destination which may be a point further inland.

**port of embarkation**
*See* port of export.

**port of entry**
(shipping/customs) (a) The port at which passengers or cargo enter the administrative or customs territory of a country. (b) An officially designated port where a vessel may enter a country's territory and discharge passengers and cargo. (c) A port where the administrative functions of immigration and customs are handled.
(U.S. Customs) Any place designated by act of U.S. Congress, executive order of the President of the United States, or order of the U.S. Secretary of the Treasury, at which a U.S. Customs officer is assigned with authority to accept entries of merchandise, to collect duties, and to enforce the various provisions of the U.S. Customs laws.

**port of export**
(shipping) The port, airport or customs point from which an export shipment leaves a country for a voyage to a foreign country.

**port of loading**
(shipping) The port where cargo is loaded on board a vessel.

**port-of-origin air cargo clearance**
(shipping) For the convenience of exporters moving goods by air from inland U.S. cities, certain U.S. Customs formalities can now be handled at the originating airport city. This avoids delaying such procedures until the export reaches a gateway point sometimes hundreds of miles from the exporter's business.

**portfolio investment**
(foreign investment) In general, any foreign investment that is not direct investment is considered portfolio investment. Foreign portfolio investment includes the purchase of voting securities (stocks) at less than a 10 percent level, bonds, trade finance, and government lending or borrowing, excluding transactions in official reserves.

**postdated check**
(banking) A check bearing a date that has not yet arrived. Such a check cannot be paid by a bank before the date shown and must be returned to the maker or to the person attempting to use it. If presented on or after the date shown, the same check will be honored if the account contains sufficient funds.

**post importation NAFTA claim**
(NAFTA) A claim for NAFTA status for an import shipment from and to a NAFTA country (Canada, United States, Mexico) made by the importer within one year of the original customs entry.

**positive-sum**
(economics) The concept that a business transaction or negotiation can result in additional benefits or profits to both or all parties to the transaction. ALso referred to as win-win. Compare to zero-sum.

**post-shipment verifications (PSV)**
(U.S.) An inspection to determine that an exported strategic commodity is being used for the purposes for which its export was licensed. Firms or individuals representing the end user, intermediate consignees, or the purchaser may be subject to inquiries pertaining to the post-shipment verification. As part of the PSV process, the Bureau of Industry and Security (formerly the Bureau of Export Administration) forwards a cable to the U.S. embassy or consulate in the respective geographical location to conduct an on-site inspection to ensure that the commodity is physically present and used as stated in the application. Post-shipment verifications are usually conducted six-to-eight months subsequent to export of the commodity. *See* Bureau of Industry and Security.

**pound**
The currency for:
Cyprus, 1£C=100 cents;
Egypt, 1LE (or 1E£)=100 piasters=1,000 milliemes;
Falkland Islands, 1£F=100 pence;
Lebanon, 1LL (or 1L£)=100 piasters;
St. Helena (uses U.K. pound);
Syria, 1S£=100 piasters;
United Kingdom, 1£=100 pence.
The former currency of Ireland (pound or punt). The new currency of Ireland is the European Union Euro. €1 = 100 cents.

**POW WOW**
*See* International POW WOW.

**power of attorney**
(law) A written legal document by which one person (principal) authorizes another person (agent) to perform stated acts on the principal's behalf. For example: to enter into contracts, to sign documents, to sign checks, and spend money, etc.
A principal may execute a **special power of attorney** authorizing an agent to sign a specific contract or a **general**

**power of attorney** authorizing the agent to sign all contracts for the principal.
(U.S. Customs) Importers often give a limited power of attorney to their customs broker to conduct business with U.S. Customs on their behalf.
Tip: When you set up a power of attorney, make sure that it is broad enough in its language to cover the types of situations likely to arise, but not so broad that it gives more power to that individual than you intend. Power of attorney falls under "agency" law, which varies from country to country. Before giving someone power of attorney in a foreign country, be sure you understand what the local legal ramifications are. *See* agent; agency.

**pre-advice**
(banking/letters of credit) At the request of an applicant to a letter of credit, the issuing bank may give a pre-advice of issuance and/or amendment of the letter of credit. A pre-advice is usually marked with a reference such as "Full details to follow." Unless otherwise stated, the pre-advice irrevocably commits the issuing bank to issue/amend the credit in a manner consistent with said pre-advice. *See* letter of credit; advice; advising bank; issuing bank; amendment.

**Pre-Arrival Processing System (PAPS)**
(United States) A U.S. Customs Automated Commercial System (ACS) border cargo release mechanism that utilizes barcode technology to expedite the release of commercial shipments while processing each shipment through Border Cargo Selectivity (BCS) and the Automated Targeting System. (ATS). For more information go to: www.cbp.gov. *See* Automated Commercial System, Border Cargo Selectivity, Automated Targeting System.

**Pre Arrival Review System (PARS)**
(Canada Customs) A Canada Border Services Agency (CBSA) (formerly the Canada Customs Revenue Agency (CCRA) border cargo release mechanism for those importers with RMD (Release on Minimum Documentation) privileges that expedites the release of low-risk, low revenue, repetitive commercial shipments to Canada. The release information can be submitted in either paper format or by Electronic Data Interchange (EDI). PARS allows the processing of goods that require permits, licenses and certificates.
The Canadian PARS system is similar to the U.S. Pre-Arrival Processing System (PAPS) system, but where PAPS applies to shipments from Canada to the U.S., PARS applies to shipments from the U.S. to Canada.
The cargo control number is the key element of the PARS process and must be in a bar-coded format on paper release requests presented to customs for pre-arrival review. The carrier supplies the bar codes.
The PARS service option is available for goods imported into Canada by different modes of transport:
• **PARS** For goods arriving by highway and cleared at the border;
• **InPARS** For goods cleared at an inland highway "sufferance warehouse";
• **RailPARS** For goods arriving by rail;
• **MarinePARS** For goods arriving by ocean or marine freight; and
• **AirPARS** For goods arriving by air freight.
For more information, go to the Canada Border Services Agency Web site at: www.cbsa-asfc.gc.ca.

**preferences**
(law) A creditor's right to be paid before other creditors of the same debtor. A creditor who holds a secured note, for example, generally has preference over one who holds an unsecured note.

### Preferential Trade Agreement for Eastern and Southern Africa
*See* Common Market for Eastern and Southern Africa.

### pre-license checks (PLC)
(U.S.) Pre-license checks are conducted to determine that a request for a license to export a controlled commodity represents a legitimate order. Firms or individuals representing the licensee (the applicant), a consignee, the purchaser, an intermediate consignee, or the end user may be subject to inquiries pertaining to the pre-license check. As part of the process, the Bureau of Industry and Security (formerly the Bureau of Export Administration) forwards a cable to the U.S. embassy or consulate in the respective geographical location to conduct an inspection or meet with company representatives to conduct inquiries on BXA's behalf. *See* Bureau of Industry and Security.

### preliminary determination
(U.S.) The determination announcing the results of a dumping investigation conducted within 160 days (or, in extraordinarily complicated cases, 210 days) after a petition is filed or an investigation is self-initiated by the International Trade Administration (ITA). If it is determined that there is a reasonable basis to believe or suspect that the merchandise under consideration is being sold or is likely to be sold at less than fair value, liquidation of all affected entries is suspended, and the matter is referred to the International Trade Commission. "Preliminary determination" also refers to the decision by the ITC where there is a reasonable indication that an industry in the United States is materially injured, or threatened with material injury, or the establishment of an industry in the United States is materially retarded by reason of the imports of the merchandise which is the subject of the petition. The ITC must make its decision within 45 days after the date on which the petition is filed or an investigation is self-initiated by the International Trade Administration. If this determination is negative, the investigation is terminated. *See* dumping; International Trade Administration; fair value.

### premium
(general) The amount above a regular price, paid as an incentive to do something. For example, a buyer might pay a premium for quick delivery. Opposite of discount.
(insurance) The amount paid to an insurance company for coverage under an insurance policy.
(foreign exchange) (a) Premium, markup (forward premium) or contango of a forward rate against the spot rate. (b) The price at which an option sells.

### prepaid
(shipping) (a) A notation on a shipping document indicating that shipping charges have already been paid by the shipper or his agent to the carrier. (b) Also, that shipping charges are to be paid by the consignee or his agent prior to release of the shipment.

### prepaid charges
*See* prepaid freight.

### prepaid freight
(logistics) Freight for which transportation charges have been paid by the consignor (shipper) at the time of shipment. Prepaid freight charges are generally not refundable.

### prescription period
*See* limitation period.

### President's Export Council (PEC)
(U.S.) Advises the president on government policies and programs that affect U.S. trade performance; promotes export expansion; and provides a forum for discussing and resolving trade-related problems among the business, industrial, agricultural, labor, and government sectors.

The Council was established by Executive Order of the president in 1973 and was originally composed only of business executives. The Council was reconstituted in 1979 to include leaders of the labor and agricultural communities, Congress, and the Executive branch.

Twenty-eight private sector members serve "at the pleasure of the president" with no set term of office. Other members include five U.S. Senators and five Members of the House, the Secretaries of Agriculture, Commerce, Labor, State, and Treasury, the Chairman of the Export-Import Bank, and the U.S. Trade Representative. The Council reports to the president through the Secretary of Commerce. Tel: [1] (202) 482-1124; Web: www.ita.doc.gov/td/pec.

### price support
(economics) Subsidy or financial aid offered to specific growers, producers, or distributors, in accordance with governmental regulations to keep market prices from dropping below a certain minimum level.

### pricing (of a loan)
(banking/finance) Fixing the cost of a loan, i.e., the interest rate and any other charges, such as front end fees.

### prima facie
(law) A presumption of fact as true unless contradicted by other evidence. For example, unless an agreement assigning contract rights clearly states that outstanding interest payments are retained by the assignor, the right to collect such payments is deemed transferred prima facie to the assignee.

### primary-business test
(U.S. law/trucking) A test used by the U.S. Interstate Commerce Commission (ICC) to determine if a trucking operation is a bona fide private transportation firm. The test was designed as a response to certain trucking operators who had been using phony "buy and sell" arrangements to avoid interstate trucking regulations.

### prime contractor
(law) An individual or company that assumes the overall responsibility of fulfilling the terms of a contract, usually by coordinating the activities of a number of subcontractors. *See* subcontractor.

### principal
(law) An individual or legal entity who authorizes another party (agent) to act on the principal's behalf. *See* agency; agent; power of attorney.

### Prior Disclosure
(U.S. Customs) A voluntary corrected declaration made to U.S. Customs and Border Protection (CBP) in good faith by a U.S. importer or exporter who has mistakenly (but not fraudulently) violated a Customs law or made an incorrect certification. The corrected declaration or certification must be made before commencement or knowledge of a formal investigation, within 30 days of knowledge of the violation, and be accompanied by payment of any duties and merchandise processing fees (MPF) that were not properly paid. A Prior Disclosure saves the U.S. importer or exporter from paying civil or administrative penalties. Prior Disclosure is part of the CBP's "reasonable care" standard for importers.
*See* reasonable care.

### prior notice
(United States) Notification to the U.S. Food and Drug Administration (FDA) that an article of food, including animal feed or pet food, is being imported or offered for import into the United States in advance of the arrival of the article of food at the U.S. border.

Additional information on the prior notice regulation may be found on FDA's web site at www.fda.gov, select Bioterrorism Act.

For information on the U.S. Customs and Border Protection's (CBP's) procedures for prior notice, go to the CBP Web site at: www.cbp.gov.

### priority air freight
(shipping) Reserved air freight or air express service wherein shipments have a priority after mail and the small package services. Any size or weight allowed within air freight service limits is acceptable. Advanced reservations are permitted for movement on a given flight and in some cases a partial refund is paid the shipper if the shipment is not moved on the flight specified.

### priority foreign countries
*See* Special 301.

### priority logistics management
(shipping) The application of the just in time transportation theory. *See* just in time.

### priority watchlist
*See* Special 301.

### private corporation
(law) (a) A business corporation with shares that are not traded among the general public. (b) A corporation that is established by individuals to conduct business or other activities and that does not perform government functions. *See* corporation; close corporation; public corporation.

### Private Export Funding Corporation (PEFCO)
(U.S.) PEFCO works with the Export-Import Bank in using private capital to finance U.S. exports. PEFCO acts as a supplemental lender to traditional commercial banking sources by making loans to public and private borrowers located outside of the United States who require medium and/or longer-term financing of their purchases of U.S. goods and services. Contact: PEFCO, 280 Park Avenue, New York, NY 10017 USA; Tel: [1] (212) 916-0300; Fax: [1] (212) 286-0304; E-mail: info@pefco.com; Web: www.pefco.com. *See* Export-Import Bank of the United States.

### Private Limited (Pte. Ltd.)
(India, Rhodesia, Singapore) Designation for a private limited liability corporation with limited liability to shareholders.

### private limited liability corporation
*See* closely held corporation.

### private sector
(economics) That part of an economy not under direct government control and that functions within the market. Private enterprise. *See* public sector

### privatization
(economics/law) The sale of state owned and operated enterprises and assets to private individuals or groups of individuals. Privatization is the opposite of nationalization and is an effort by governments to allow market forces determine the fate of the enterprise. *See* nationalization, expropriation.

### pro forma
When coupled with the title of another document (pro forma invoice, pro forma manifest), it means an informal document presented in advance of the arrival or preparation of the required document in order to satisfy a requirement, usually a customs requirement.

### pro forma invoice
An invoice provided by a supplier prior to a sale or shipment of merchandise, informing the buyer of the kinds and quantities of goods to be sent, their value, and important specifications (weight, size, and similar characteristics). A pro forma invoice is used: (1) as a preliminary invoice together with a quotation; (2) for customs purposes in connection with shipments of samples, advertising material, etc.

(U.S. Customs) An invoice provided by the importer in lieu of a commercial invoice when a commercial invoice is not available at the time of merchandise entry. In such cases the importer must present a bond to Customs guaranteeing production of the required commercial invoice not later than 120 days from the date of entry. If the invoice is needed by Customs for statistical purposes, it must generally be produced within 50 days from the date the entry summary is required to be filed.

If the required commercial invoice is not presented to Customs before the expiration of the 120-day period, the importer incurs a liability under his bond for failure to file.
*See* invoice; commercial invoice; entry; bond.

### procurement
(a) The purchase of goods, services, supplies and equipment. (b) The process by which goods, services, supplies and equipment are purchased.

The procurement process can include: establishing the need, establishing specifications, writing a request for proposal, soliciting bids, evaluating bids, negotiating contracts, writing a purchase order, contract administration, and adding items to inventory.

### product groups
(U.S.) Commodity groupings used for export control purposes. *See* export control classification number.

### productivity
(economics) A measurement of the efficiency of production. A ratio of output to input (e.g., 10 units per man-hour).

### profit, gross
(economics/accounting) (gross profit/gross margin) Net sales less cost of goods sold (before consideration of selling and administrative expenses). Gross profit is expressed in dollar figures; gross margin is expressed as a percentage of net sales.

(U.S. Customs) For the purposes of constructed value in an antidumping duty investigation or review, the profit used is the profit normally earned by a producer, from the country of export, of the same or similar product as that under investigation. By statute, the amount of profit shall not be less than 8 percent of the sum of general expenses and cost. *See* dumping; countervailing duty.

### project license
(U.S.) A license which authorizes large-scale exports of a wide variety of commodities and technical data for specified activities. Those activities can include capital expansion, maintenance, repair or operating supplies, or the supply of materials to be used in the production of other commodities for sale. *See* Bureau of Industry and Security.

### promissory note
(banking) (a) Any written promise to pay. (b) A negotiable instrument that is evidence of a debt contracted by a borrower from a creditor, known as a lender of funds. If the instrument does not have all the qualities of a negotiable instrument, it cannot legally be transferred. *See* negotiable instrument.

### promoter of corporation
(law) Individual or entity that organizes a corporation.

### promotional rate
(shipping) A rate applying to traffic under special conditions and usually confined to movement between a limited number of cities. Early rates on fresh farm produce which helped develop increased air freight volumes from the West Coast to eastern cities are examples of promotional rates. *See* special rates.

## proof of delivery
(shipping) Information provided to payor containing name of person who signed for the package with the date and time of delivery.

## Proprietary Limited (Pty. Ltd.)
(Australia, South Africa) Designation for a private limited liability corporation with limited liability to shareholders.

## proprietor
(law) A person who has an exclusive right or interest in property or in a business.

## proprietorship
(law) A business owned by one person. The individual owner has all the rights to profits from the business as well as all the liabilities and losses. Synonymous with "individual proprietorship."

## PROSEC (Programs of Sectorial Promotion)
(Mexico) Mexican government program designed to eliminate or reduce import duties (down to 0 to 7%) in over 20 industrial sectors, especially for materials and components that are to be exported later as manufactured products.

## protectionism
(economics) The deliberate use or encouragement of restrictions on imports to enable relatively inefficient domestic producers to compete successfully with foreign producers.

## protective order
(U.S. Customs) With regard to antidumping cases, a term for the order under which most business proprietary information is made available to an attorney or other representative of a party to the proceeding. *See* dumping.

## protective service
(shipping) Many airlines offer a protective service where shippers can arrange to have their shipments under carrier surveillance at each stage of transit from origin to destination. This service can be extended to pickup and delivery. Shippers can also arrange for armed guard protection. There is usually an extra charge for various levels of protective service. *See* signature service.

## protective tariff
(customs/economics) A duty or tax imposed on imported products for the purpose of making them more expensive in comparison to domestic products, thereby giving the domestic products a price advantage. *See* tariff.

## protest
(U.S. Customs) The means by which an importer, consignee, or other designated party may challenge decisions, (usually regarding the duitable status of imported goods) made by a District Director of Customs. The importer files a protest and an application for further review on Customs Form 19 within 90 days after liquidation. If the Customs Service denies a protest, an importer has the right to litigate the matter by filing a summons with the U.S. Court of International Trade within 180 days after denial of the protest. The rules of the court and other applicable statutes and precedents determine the course of Customs litigation.
While the Customs ascertainment of duitable status is final for most purposes at the time of liquidation, a liquidation is not final until any protest which has been filed against it has been decided. Similarly, the administrative decision issued on a protest is not final until any litigation filed against it has become final.
Entries must be liquidated within one year of the date of entry unless the liquidation needs to be extended for another one-year period not to exceed a total of four years from the date of entry. The Customs Service will suspend liquidation of an entry when required by statute or court order. A suspension will remain in effect until the issue is resolved. Notifications of extensions and suspensions are given to importers, surety companies and customs brokers who are parties to the transaction. *See* entry; liquidation.
(banking) Legal procedure noting the refusal of the drawee to accept a bill of exchange (protest for non-acceptance) or to pay it (protest for non-payment). Essential in order to preserve the right of recourse on the endorser.

## protest system
(U.S. Customs) A part of U.S. Customs' Automated Commercial System, tracks protests from the date they are received through final action. *See* Automated Commercial System.

## protocol
(diplomacy) (a) A preliminary document or memorandum signed by diplomatic or commercial negotiators which is used as a basis for final negotiations, agreements conventions or treaties. (b) The etiquette and ranking of diplomatic personnel.
(U.S.) U.S. diplomatic ranking is as follows: (1) Ambassadors-at-large have a higher rank than a regular Ambassador and are higher ranked on protocol than, say, the head of the C.I.A.; (2) The Deputy Chief of Mission, almost always a career officer, has the personal rank of Minister which is one rank down from Ambassador; (3) The rank of Minister-Counselor is just a little step below Minister; (4) The Chargé d'Affaires may either be acting, or indefinite, and is regarded as the acting Ambassador when the Ambassador is out of the country or when, for political reasons, an Ambassador is not appointed to a country; (5) An Attaché may be either fairly high or fairly low; in terms of rank an Attaché can be anything; a Military Attaché is of at least medium rank, but the military hold no diplomatic rank; (6) A consulate is not a diplomatic mission, nor is it autonomous; it is established by an international organization (such as U.S. Mission to the European Communities (USEC) or NATO) or is used for reasons of diplomatic snobbery or pique.

## Protocol of Provisional Application
(GATT/WTO) A legal device that enabled the original contracting parties to accept General Agreement on Tariffs and Trade (GATT) obligations and benefits, despite the fact that some of their existing domestic legislation at that time discriminated against imports in a manner that was inconsistent with certain GATT provisions. Although meant to be "temporary," the Protocol has remained in effect; and countries that signed the PPA in 1947 continue to invoke it to defend certain practices that are otherwise inconsistent with their GATT/WTO obligations. Countries that acceded to the GATT/WTO after 1947 have also done so under the terms of the Protocol. *See* General Agreement on Tariffs and Trade, World Trade Organization (WTO).

## provenance
(law) (a) The ownership history of an item, especially a work of art. (b) The country and place of origin of a grown, mined or manufactured item.

## PTT
Acronym for Post Telephone Telegraph. The national monopoly agency or authority that provides postal, telephone and telegraph services in certain countries. Most western economies have deregulated at least their telecommunications systems and rigid monopolies rarely exist.

## public corporation
(law) (a) A business corporation with shares traded among the general public, such as through a stock exchange. (b) A corporation created by a government to administer its operations. *See* corporation; close corporation; private corporation.

P

**Public Goods**
*See* Global Public Goods.

**Public Limited Company (PLC)**
(United Kingdom) Designation for a public corporation with limited liability to shareholders.

**public sector**
(economics) That part of an economy that is not privately owned, either because it is owned by the state or because it is subject to common ownership. Includes the national government, local authorities, national industries and public corporations. *See* private sector.

**public warehouse receipt**
(logistics) A document issued by a public warehouse manager for receipt of goods into a warehouse. Public warehouse receipts can be either negotiable or non-negotiable.

**publication**
(law) (a) Offering or distributing information or materials to the public generally. (b) Communicating defamatory information to a third person.

**published rate**
(shipping) The charges for a particular class of cargo as published in a carrier's tariff.

**pula**
The currency of Botswana. 1P=100 thebe.

**pull ordering system**
(logistics) A stocking and warehousing order system where a stocking location places orders for inventory based upon its own individual needs. A pull ordering system is based upon actual demand for the product, service or component. *See* push ordering system, push strategy, pull strategy, push/pull strategy.

**pull strategy**
(logistics) A production and distribution strategy based on specific customer demand. In a pure pull strategy only goods and services actually ordered by customers are produced and shipped; there is no inventory of completed products. The term is used in many other fields to describe decision making by demand of the marketplace rather than by a central authority. *See* push ordering system, push strategy, pull ordering system, push/pull strategy.

**punt**
The former currency of Ireland. The new currency of Ireland is the European Union Euro. €1 = 100 cents.

**purchase order**
A purchaser's written offer to a supplier formally stating all terms and conditions of a proposed transaction.

**purchase price**
(U.S. Customs) A statutory term used in dumping investigations to refer to the United States sales price of merchandise which is sold or likely to be sold prior to the date of importation, by the producer or reseller of the merchandise for exportation to the United States. Certain statutory adjustments (e.g., import duties, commissions, freight) are made, if appropriate, to permit a meaningful comparison with the foreign market value of such or similar merchandise. *See* dumping.

**purchaser**
(U.S.) Within the context of export controls, the purchaser is that person abroad who has entered into the export transaction with the applicant to purchase the commodities or technical data for delivery to the ultimate consignee.

**purchasing agent**
(law) An agent who purchases goods in his/her own country on behalf of foreign buyers such as government agencies and private businesses. *See* agent; agency.

**pure market economy**
(economics) A competitive economic system of numerous buyers and sellers, where prices are determined by the free interaction of supply and demand.

**purpose built**
(U.K.) A piece of equipment, facility or vehicle designed and made to perform a specific function. Roughly translated from British to American English as "custom made." The U.S. term, however, does not necessarily refer to an item's functionality.

**push ordering system**
(logistics) A stocking and warehousing order system based on inventory deployment decisions being made by a centralized authority rather than by field locations. *See* pull ordering system, pull strategy, push strategy, push/pull strategy.

**push strategy**
(logistics) A production and distribution strategy based upon forecasts rather than on specific customer demand. The term is used in many other fields to describe centralized decision-making authority without the immediate input of data from the marketplace. *See* pull strategy, pull ordering system, push ordering system, push/pull strategy.

**push/pull strategy**
(logistics) A production and distribution strategy based upon a combination of forecasts and specific customer demand. For example, a manufacturer might purchase component parts based upon sales forecasts, but manufacture finished products only upon actual customer orders. *See* pull strategy, pull ordering system, push strategy, push ordering system.

**put**
(banking/finance) A right to redeem a debt instrument before maturity at par under specific circumstances outlined in the original agreement. *See* option; put option; call; call option.

**put option**
(banking/finance) A contract which entitles one party, at his option, to sell a specified amount of a commodity, security or foreign exchange to another party, at the price fixed in the contract, during the life of the contract. *See* option; call option; American Option; European Option.

# Q

### quadrilateral meetings
Meetings involving trade ministers from the U.S., the European Community, Canada, and Japan to discuss trade policy matters.

### quantitative restrictions (QRs)
(customs) Explicit limits, or quotas, on the physical amounts of particular commodities that can be imported or exported during a specified time period, usually measured by volume but sometimes by value. The quota may be applied on a "selective" basis, with varying limits set according to the country of origin, or on a quantitative global basis that only specifies the total limit and thus tends to benefit more efficient suppliers. Quotas are frequently ministered through a system of licensing.
(WTO) The World Trade Organization (WTO) generally prohibits the use of quantitative restrictions, except under conditions specified by other WTO articles.
*See* quotas; General Agreement on Tariffs and Trade (GATT) , World Trade Organization (WTO).

### quarantine
(shipping) (a) The term during which an arriving ship or airplane, including its passengers, crew and cargo, suspected of carrying a contagious disease, is held in isolation to prevent the possible spread of the disease. (b) The place where a ship, airplane, individual or cargo is detained during quarantine.

### quay
(shipping) A structure built for the purpose of mooring a vessel. Also called a pier.

### quetzal
The currency of Guatemala. 1Q=100 centavos.

### queue
(a) A line or group of people waiting for service, such as a line of people waiting in a teller line at a bank. (b) Paperwork in a stack waiting for processing. (c) Items on a waiting list waiting for processing or repair.

### quick response
(logistics) A logistics strategy designed to lower costs and increase response to customer demand by shortening the lead time for order fulfillment and increasing the frequency of deliveries.

### quid pro quo
(law/business) "Something for something" (Latin). A mutual consideration; securing an advantage or receiving a concession in return for a similar favor.

### quota
(customs) A limitation on the quantity of goods that may be imported into a country from all countries or from specific countries during a set period of time.
(a) **Absolute quotas** permit a limited number of units of specified merchandise to be entered or withdrawn for consumption in a country during specified periods.
(b) **Tariff-rate quotas** permit a specified quantity of merchandise to be entered or withdrawn in a country at a reduced rate during a specified period.
(U.S. Customs) In the United States, quotas are established by Presidential Proclamations, Executive Orders, or other legislation. *See* quantitative restrictions; quota system; visa.

### quota system
(U.S. Customs) A part of the U.S. Customs' Service Automated Commercial System, controls quota levels (quantities authorized) and quantities entered against those levels.

Visas control exports from the country of origin. Visa authorizations are received from other countries and quantities entered against those visas are transmitted back to them. Control of visas and quotas simplify reconciliation of other countries' exports and U.S. imports.
*See* Automated Commercial System; visa.

### quotation
(foreign exchange) The price quotation of a currency can be made either directly or indirectly. (a) The direct quotation gives the equivalent of a certain amount of foreign currency (normally in units of 100 or 1) in domestic currency. (b) In an indirect price quotation (less common) the domestic currency is valued in units of foreign currency.

Q

### radioactive materials
(shipping) Degree of hazard will vary depending on type and quantity of material. (UN CLASS 7.) Examples are thorium 232, carbon 14 and radium 226. Hazards/precautions are: avoid touching broken or damaged radioactive items; persons handling damaged items must wear rubber or plastic gloves; damaged items will be monitored and safely packaged under the surveillance of the radiological monitor; and persons having come in direct contact with damaged or broken radioactive items must move away from the spill site (but stay in the area) to be monitored and decontaminated.

### Rail Pre-Arrival Review System (RailPARS)
(Canada Customs) *See* Pre-Arrival Review System (PARS).

### rail waybill
(shipping) Freight document that indicates goods have been received for shipment by rail. A duplicate is given to the shipper as a receipt for acceptance of the goods (also called duplicate waybill). *See* bill of lading.

### RailPARS
(Canada Customs) *See* Pre-Arrival Review System.

### rand
The currency of:
Namibia, 1R=100 cents.
South Africa, 1R=100 cents;

### rate basis
(logistics) The economic factors considered when establishing a freight transportation rate. These factors at the very least include weight, bulk, packaging, equipment depreciation, freight handling by personnel, fuel, port charges, insurance and management costs.

### rate basis number
(logistics) The distance between two rate basis points. Used to determine tariff rates from a table. *See* rate basis point.

### rate basis point
(logistics) The formally named point (such as Houston, Texas) in a geographic area (such as greater Houston Texas) that serves as the identifier on a freight rate table for all departures or arrivals in that area. Carriers consider all points in the immediate geographic area to be the rate basis point.

### rate bureau
(logistics) A group of carriers that have organized for the purpose of establishing joint rates, dividing joint revenues and liabilities and publishing tariffs for participating carriers.
(U.S. law) Rate bureaus were legalized under the Reed-Bullwinkle Act for the purpose of establishing joint rates. *See* Reed-Bullwinkle Act.

### rate of exchange
(banking/foreign exchange) The amount of funds of one nation that can be bought, at a specific date, for a sum of currency of another country. Rates fluctuate often because of economic, political and other forces. *See* foreign exchange.

### reachstacker
A forklift truck-type vehicle designed to lift, move and stack ocean freigh containers in ocean, truck and rail container terminals. Reachstackers lift from the top of the container, whereas forlift trucks lift from the bottom of the container. Modern reachstackers can stack containers four high and reach back to a second row.

### real rights
(law) Rights in real estate or in items attached to real estate.

### realignment
(foreign exchange) Simultaneous and mutually coordinated re- and devaluation of the currencies of several countries. The concept was first used in 1971 for the exchange rate corrections made in a number of countries within the framework of the Smithsonian Agreement. Since then, it has mainly been used to describe the exchange rate corrections within the European Monetary System.

### reasonable care
(law) (a) The degree of care that a person of ordinary prudence and intelligence would exercise in the same or similar circumstances. In certain situations and jurisdictions, failure to exercise reasonable care is considered legal negligence. (b) A standard for determining legal duty.
(U.S. Customs) A key component of the U.S. Customs and Border Protection (CBP) Informed Compliance program that states that the importer of goods to the U.S. is expected to exercise reasonable care in his or her importing operations.

### reasonable person standard
(law) A legal test that is used to determine whether a person is liable for damages. It is based on a comparison of the person's conduct with the actions or conduct expected of a reasonable person of the same characteristics in similar circumstances.

### receipt
(law) Any written acknowledgment of value received.

### receipt point
(logistics) The place where freight or cargo enters into the care and custody of a carrier for either storage or shipment.

### received for shipment bill of lading
(shipping) A bill of lading which confirms the receipt of goods by the carrier, but not their actual loading on board. *See* bill of lading.
(banking/letters of credit) A received for shipment bill of lading can be accepted under letters of credit only if this is expressly permitted in the letter of credit, or if the credit stipulates a document covering multimodal transport. Otherwise, "received for shipment" bills of lading must show an additional "On board" notation in order to be accepted as an ocean bill of lading. *See* bill of lading; ocean bill of lading.

### receiving papers
(shipping) Paperwork that accompanies a shipment when it is brought to the dock. Usual information listed is name and address of shipper, number of pieces, commodity, weight, consignee, booking number and any special requirements, such as label cargo or temperature control.

### reciprocal defense procurement memoranda of understanding
(NATO/USA) Reciprocal memoranda of understanding (MOU) are broad bilateral umbrella MOUs that seek to reduce trade barriers on defense procurement. They usually call for the waiver of "buy national" restrictions, customs and duties to allow the contractors of the signatories to participate, on a competitive basis, in the defense procurement of the other country. These agreements were designed in the late 1970's to promote rationalization, standardization, and interoperability of defense equipment within NATO. At that time, the MOUs were also intended to reduce the large defense trade advantage the United States possessed over the European allies. The first agreements were signed in 1978. *See* memorandum of understanding.

### reciprocal trade agreement
(trade) An international agreement between two or more countries to establish mutual trade concessions that are expected to be of equal value.

### reciprocity
(general) The mutual exchange of privileges or benefits. Also called "mutuality of benefits," "quid pro quo," and "equivalence of advantages."

(international trade) The practice by which governments extend similar concessions to each other, as when one government lowers its tariffs or other barriers (non-tariff barriers) impeding its imports in exchange for equivalent concessions from a trading partner on barriers affecting its exports (a "balance of concessions"). Reciprocity has traditionally been a principal objective of negotiators in the World Trade Organization (WTO) "Rounds."

In practice, this principle applies only in negotiations between developed countries. Because of the frequently wide disparity in their economic capacities and potential, the relationship between developed and developing countries is generally not one of equivalence.

The concept of "relative reciprocity" has emerged to characterize the practice by developed countries to seek less than full reciprocity from developing countries in trade negotiations.

### Reconciliation
(U.S. Customs) An electronic process, initiated at the request of an importer, under which the elements of an entry (other than those elements related to the admissibility of the merchandise) that are undetermined at the time the importer files or transmits the documentation or information required by section 1484(a)(1)(B) of import code, or the import activity summary statement, are provided to the U.S. Customs and Border Protection (CBP) at a later time. A reconciliation is treated as an entry for purposes of liquidation, reliquidation, recordkeeping, and protest.

### reconsignment
(shipping) A change in the name of the consignor or consignee; a change in the place of delivery; a change in the destination point; or relinquishment of shipment at point of origin.

### record
(a) A document that serves as legal or commercial evidence of a transaction. (b) A collection of data elements that serve as permanent evidence of or information about past events.

### recourse
(banking) Right of claim against the joint and several guarantors (e.g., endorsers, drawers) of a bill of exchange or cheque. *See* protest; bill of exchange.

### red clause (letter of credit)
(banking) A special clause included in a documentary letter of credit which allows the seller to obtain an advance on an unsecured basis from the correspondent bank to finance the manufacture or purchase of goods to be delivered under the documentary letter of credit. Liability is assumed by the issuing bank rather than the corresponding bank. It is called red clause because red ink used to be used to draw attention to the clause. *See* letter of credit.

### redeliver
(U.S. Customs) A demand by U.S. Customs and Border Protection to return previously released merchandise to Customs custody for reexamination, reexport or destruction.

### Reed-Bullwinkle Act
(U.S. law/shipping) Legislation originally passed by the U.S. Congress in 1948 authorizing the creation of rate bureaus which would provide a sanctioned forum for domestic railroads to set agreements on rates. In the 1970 revision of the Act, Congress expressly granted railroads antitrust immunity for any collective rate-making activity accomplished in accordance with the procedures described in the Act. *See* rate bureau.

### reefer
*See* reefer container, refrigerated container.

### reefer container
(shipping) A controlled temperature refrigerated shipping container.

### reefer vessel
(shipping) A vessel with refrigerated cargo holds.

### re-engineering
(management) (a) The radical change of processes on all levels within an organization. (b) The way a company performs radical changes to processes. As opposed to gradual improvements over time, re-engineering seeks to create breakthrough changes in the way a business operates. Re-engineering is often sought by senior managers as a means of dramatically reducing labor costs, increasing productivity and increasing responsiveness to customer demand.

### re-export
(general) The export of imported goods without added value.

(U.S.) For U.S. export control purposes: the shipment of U.S. origin products from one foreign destination to another.

For U.S. statistical reporting purposes: exports of foreign-origin merchandise which have previously entered the United States for consumption or into Customs bonded warehouses for U.S. Foreign Trade Zones.

### refrigerated container (reefer)
(shipping/logistics) A temperature controlled container. Typically, an insulated container with a self-contained refrigeration unit for the shipment of perishable cargo such as food or pharmaceuticals. The term can refer to an ocean container, truck trailer, boxcar, air shipment container (unit load device or ULD) or an entire vessel. Reefer is the industry-accepted slang term.

### refund
(shipping) An amount returned to the consignor or consignee as a result of the carrier having collected charges in excess of the originally agreed upon, or legally applicable, charges.

(customs) Refund of import duties. *See* drawback.

### regional carrier
(logistics) (a) A carrier that operates regionally rather than nationally or internationally. (b) A carrier that transports passengers or cargo between small cities or between major cities and small cities or towns.

### reimbursing bank
(banking) The bank named in a documentary credit (letter of credit) from which the paying, accepting or negotiating bank may request cover after receipt of the documents in compliance with the documentary credit. The reimbursing bank is often, but not always, the issuing bank. If the reimbursing bank is not the issuing bank, it does not have a commitment to pay unless it has confirmed the reimbursement instruction. The issuing bank is not released from its commitment to pay through the nomination of a reimbursing bank. If cover from the reimbursing bank should not arrive in time, the issuing bank is obliged to pay (also any accrued interest on arrears).

### re-insurance
(insurance) The insurance of insurance companies by other insurance companies for excessive losses. For example, an insurance company might obtain insurance coverage for losses exceeding US$50 million in a single catastrophe in

order to limit its maximum liability. Furthermore, reinsurance coverage is often spread out among a group of insurance companies so as to further distribute potential liabilities for losses.

### re-invoicing
The procedure whereby an intermediary purchases goods from a vendor for sale to a third-party client, receives an invoice from the vendor and then writes a new invoice at a higher price which is presented to the third-party client.

### rejected merchandise drawback
*See* drawback.

### relative reciprocity
*See* reciprocity.

### relay
(shipping) A shipment that is transferred to its ultimate destination port after having been shipped to an intermediate point.

### Release Notification System (RNS)
(Canada Customs) RNS is a Canada Border Services Agency (CBSA) import shipment program that includes four features: automatic release notification, arrival certification, status query and automatic status.

For Canadian importers authorized to use the automatic release notification feature of RNS, data confirming release of goods is electronically transmitted in the United Nations Electronic Data Interchange for Administration, Commerce and Transportation (UNEDIFACT) message format to their EDI mailbox using a third-party EDI network, also known as a value-added network (VAN), through the Customs Internet Gateway or through CADEX telecommunication lines. The RNS message can be used to update systems to schedule deliveries or initiate the preparation of accounting data, as well as to electronically notify other parties affected by the release and ensure more timely delivery of shipments.

For importers approved to use arrival certification, two-way electronic communication can be established to notify CBSA of the arrival of commercial shipments. Importers can also verify if CBSA has processed release documents for a shipment using the status query feature or by receiving an automatic status message. For importers who choose to transmit an arrival certification message, CBSA can advise whether the goods have been released or referred for examination.

For more information, go to:
www.cbsa-asfc.gc.ca/import/servicesintro-e.html.

### Release on Minimum Documentation (RMD)
(Canada Customs) A Canada Border Services Agency (CBSA) import shipment release program where importers and brokers can post an approved amount of security (cash or bond) with the CBSA, fast-track the release of shipments and account for and pay duty and other charges after release. RMD release times for various methods of document delivery are:
• Electronic Data Interchange (EDI) 45 minutes
• EDI Machine Release 5 minutes
• Paper 2 hours
For more information about CBSA and RMD, go to:
www.cbsa-asfc.gc.ca

### released-value rate
(logistics) A reduced transportation rate given on a high-value shipment based upon the shipper's agreement to accept a set maximum carrier liability in the case of loss or damage that is less than the actual or declared value.

### relief from liability
(U.S. Customs) In cases where articles imported under temporary importation under bond (TIB), relief from liability under bond may be obtained in any case in which the articles are destroyed under Customs supervision, in lieu of exportation, within the original bond period. However, in the case of articles imported solely for testing or experimentation, destruction need not be under Customs supervision where articles are destroyed during the course of experiments or tests during the bond period or any lawful extension, but satisfactory proof of destruction shall be furnished to the district or port director with whom the customs entry was filed. *See* temporary importation under bond; drawback; in bond.

### remittance
(banking) Funds forwarded from one person to another as payment for bought items or services.

### remittance following collection
(shipping) In instances when the shipper has performed services incident to the transportation of goods a carrier will collect payment for these services from the receiver and remit such payment to the shipper. Carriers charge nominal fees for this service.

### remitter
(banking) In a documentary collection, an alternate name given to the seller who forwards documents to the buyer through banks. *See* documentary collection.

### remitting
(banking) Paying, as in remitting a payment; also canceling, as in remitting a debt.

### remitting bank
(banking) In a documentary collection, a bank which acts as an intermediary, forwarding the remitter's documents to, and payments from the collecting bank. *See* documentary collection.

### renminbi (RMB)
(People's Republic of China) Literally "people's currency." The official currency of China, issued by the Central Bank of China. As of January 1, 1994, China's dual currency system of RMB and FEC (Foreign Exchange Certificate) was united in a step toward making the RMB more freely convertible and bringing its exchange rate closer to market value.

### reorder point
(logistics) A predetermined inventory level at or below which a replenishment order is made. The reorder point inventory quantity must be sufficient to respond to customer demand for the time required to order and receive additional stock.

### reparation
(general) Repairing or keeping in repair.
(ethics/law) The making of amends or giving satisfaction to a wronged party.
(logistics) A compensation paid by a carrier to a shipper that has been overcharged.
(U.S. law) Compensation ordered by the Interstate Commerce Commission (ICC) in situations where a carrier (specifically a railroad) has charged a shipper more than is allowable by law.

Reparation claims are differentiated from overcharge claims in that they refer to an illegal amount being charged as opposed to a legal charge: the overcharge.

### replevin
(law) A legal action for recovering property brought by the owner or party entitled to repossess the property against a party who has wrongfully kept it. A seller that furnishes products to a sales representative on consignment, for example, may sue for replevin if the sales representative wrongfully retains products not sold at the end of the term of the consignment agreement.

### request for proposal (RFP)
A formal request by a company or organization (customer) presented to one or more potential vendors asking for a formal proposal to supply goods or services based upon specifications set forth in the request. An RFP typically includes specifications of the product or service required, quantities required, time and place of delivery, method of shipment, packaging, materiels to be furnished and other technical requirements. The RFP also asks for prices and payment terms for products, services and maintenance.

Proposals sent in response to an RFP assist the customer in making an educated purchasing decision. An RFP can be as simple as a one page letter of request to a multi-thousand page document outlining specifications in minute detail.

### request for quotation (RFQ)
A negotiating approach whereby the buyer asks for a price quotation from a potential seller/suppler for specific quantities of goods (or services) to specifications the buyer establishes in the request for quotation letter.

### requirement contract
(law) An agreement by which a seller promises to supply all of the specified goods or services that a buyer needs over a certain time and at a fixed price, and the buyer agrees to purchase such goods or services exclusively from the seller during that time.

### rescind
(law) To cancel a contract. A contract may, for example, give one party a right to rescind if the other party fails to perform within a reasonable time.

### rescission
*See* rescind.

### reserved freight space
(shipping) A service by some airlines enabling shippers to reserve freight space on designated flights. *See* priority air freight.

### residual restrictions
(GATT/WTO) Quantitative restrictions that have been maintained by governments before they became contracting parties to the General Agreement on Tariffs and Trade (GATT) and the World Trade Organization (WTO) and, hence, permissible under the GATT/WTO "grandfather clause." Most of the residual restrictions still in effect are maintained by developed countries against the imports of agricultural products. *See* grandfather clause; General Agreement on Tariffs and Trade, World Trade Organization (WTO).

### restitution
(law) A legal remedy for a breach of contract by which the parties are restored to their original positions before the contract was made or the breach occurred. Damages are distinguished from restitution in that damages compensate for a party who has suffered a loss. If a buyer, for example, partially pays for merchandise in advance and the seller delivers merchandise that fails to meet the buyer's specifications, the buyer may file a legal action seeking restitution, that is, a return of the advance payment to the buyer and of the goods to the seller. Alternatively, the buyer may accept the goods and may sue for damages in the amount by which the worth of the goods is less than the original contract price.

### restricted articles
(shipping) An airline term meaning a hazardous material as defined by Title 49, Code of Federal Regulations (U.S.) and Air Transport Restricted Articles Circular 6-D. Restricted articles may be transported domestically and be classified dangerous goods when transported internationally by air. *See* dangerous goods; hazardous material.

### restricted letter of credit
(banking) A letter of credit, the negotiation of which is restricted to a bank specially mentioned. *See* letter of credit.

### restrictive business practices
(economics) Actions in the private sector, such as collusion among the largest suppliers, designed to restrict competition so as to keep prices relatively high.

### restrictive endorsement
*See* endorsement.

### retaliation
Action taken by a country to restrain its imports from a country that has increased a tariff or imposed other measures that adversely affect its exports.

(WTO) The World Trade Organization, in certain circumstances, permits retaliation, although this has very rarely been practiced. The value of trade affected by such retaliatory measures should in theory, approximately equal the value affected by the initial import restriction.

### retaliatory duty
*See* retaliation.

### returned without action
(U.S.) For export control purposes, the return of an export license application without action because the application is incomplete, additional information is required, or the product is eligible for a general license. *See* Bureau of Export Administration; general license.

### revaluation
(economics) The increase of the value (restoration) of a nation's currency (that had once been devalued) in terms of the currency of another nation.

### reverse logistics
(logistics) The act of, and management systems associated with, the recovery of discarded products and packaging from the end user. Reverse logistics is based upon a heightened environmental consciousness, public policy and law. The concept is that reusable packaging, as well as outdated, damaged or defective products, can best be recycled or reused by the original manufacturer. Reverse logistics, however, is much more than recycling. It involves both product and systems designs that make recovery and reuse possible, efficient and even profitable. In reverse logistics a measure of what gets thrown away is a measure of the failure of the product design and recovery process.

### reverse preferences
Tariff advantages once offered by developing countries to imports from certain developed countries that granted them preferences. Reverse preferences characterized trading arrangements between the European Community and some developing countries prior to the advent of the Generalized System of Preferences (GSP) and the signing of the Lome Convention.

### reverse swap
(banking/trade) A swap which offsets the interest rate or currency exposure on an existing swap. It can be written with the original counterparty or with a new counterparty. In either case, it is typically executed to realize capital gains.

### Revised American Foreign Trade Definitions
A set of foreign trade terms which are considered obsolete, but still sometimes used in domestic U.S. trade. The most widely accepted international trade terms are Incoterms 2000. *See* Incoterms 2000.

### revocable letter of credit
(banking) A letter of credit which can be cancelled or altered by the drawee (buyer) after it has been issued by the drawee's bank. Due to the low level of security of this type of credit, they are extremely rare in practice. *See* letter of credit.

### revocation of antidumping duty order
### termination of suspended investigation

(U.S. Customs) An antidumping duty order may be revoked or a suspended investigation may be terminated upon application from a party to the proceeding. Ordinarily the application is considered only if there have been no sales at less than fair value for at least the two most recent years. However, the Department of Commerce may on its own initiative revoke an antidumping duty order or terminate a suspended investigation if there have not been sales at less than fair value for a period of 3 years. *See* dumping.

### revolving letter of credit

(banking) A letter of credit which is automatically restored to its full amount after the completion of each documentary exchange.

The number of utilizations and the period of time within which these must take place are specified in the documentary letter of credit. The revolving letter of credit is used when a purchaser wishes to have certain partial quantities of the ordered goods delivered at specified intervals (multiple delivery contract) and when multiple documents are presented for this purpose. Such credit may be cumulative or non-cumulative. *See* letter of credit.

### rial

The currency of:
Iran, 1Rl=100 dinars;
Oman, 1RO=1,000 baiza;
Yemen, 1YR=100 fils.

### riel

The currency of Kampuchea. 1CR=100 sen.

### ringgit

The currency of Malaysia. 1M$=100 sen.

### risk position

(banking/finance/foreign exchange) An asset or liability, which is exposed to fluctuations in value through changes in exchange rates or interest rates.

### riyal

The currency of:
Qatar, 1QR=100 dirhams;
Saudi Arabia, 1SR=100 halala.

### RNS

(Canada) Release Notification System. A Canada Revenue Agency (CRA) electronic data interchange (EDI) system that notifies importers, brokers, warehouse operators, and carriers of customs releases.

### road-rail trailer

(trucking/railroads) A semi-trailer able to function as an on-road truck trailer with pneumatic tires, or, on railroad tracks with the deployment of a steel wheel rail assembly. In some cases the road tires retract to allow the trailer chassis (container) to mount on a pair of rail bogies. Also called a bimodal trailer.

### road waybill

(shipping) Transport document that indicates goods have been received for shipment by road haulage carrier. *See* bill of lading.

### rollback

(GATT) Refers to an agreement among Uruguay Round participants to dismantle all trade-restrictive or distorting measures that are inconsistent with the provisions of the General Agreement on Tariffs and Trade (GATT). Measures subject to rollback would be phased out or brought into conformity within an agreed timeframe, no later than by the formal completion of the negotiations. The rollback agreement is accompanied by a commitment to "standstill" on existing trade-restrictive measures. Rollback is also used as a reference to the imposition of quantitative restrictions at levels less than those occurring in the present.

*See* standstill; General Agreement on Tariffs and Trade; rounds; Tokyo Round; Uruguay Round.

### roll-on, roll-off (RoRo)

(shipping) A broad category of ships designed to load and discharge cargo which rolls on wheels. Broadly interpreted, this may include train ships, trailer ships, auto, truck and trailer ferries, and ships designed to carry military vehicles.

### rollover

(finance/foreign exchange) (a) Extension of a maturing financial instrument, such as a loan or certificate of deposit. (b) Extension of a maturing foreign exchange operation through the conclusion of a swap agreement (e.g., tom/next swap). (c) Variability of an interest rate according to the appropriate, currently prevailing rates on the Euromarket (normally LIBOR) for a medium-term loan.

### rollover credit

(banking) Any line of credit that can be borrowed against up to a stated credit limit and into which repayments go for crediting. *See* letter of credit.

### rouble

The currency of Russia and throughout the Commonwealth of Independent States. 1R=100 kopecks.

### rounds (of trade negotiations)

(GATT/WTO) Cycles of multilateral trade negotiations under the General Agreement on Tariffs and Trade (GATT) and the successor World Trade Organization (WTO), culminating in simultaneous agreements among participating countries to reduce tariff and non-tariff trade barriers.

**1st Round**: 1947, Geneva (creation of the GATT);
**2nd Round**: 1949, Annecy, France (tariff reduction);
**3rd Round**: 1951, Torquay, England (accession & tariff reduction);
**4th Round**: 1956, Geneva (accession and tariff reduction);
**5th Round**: 1960-62, Geneva ("Dillon" Round; revision of GATT; addition of more countries);
**6th Round**: 1964-67, Geneva ("Kennedy" Round);
**7th Round**: 1973-79, Geneva ("Tokyo" Round);
**8th Round**: 1986-93, Geneva ("Uruguay" Round);
**9th Round**: 9th round: Launched 11/14/01 by the WTO's 142 members in a Ministerial Declaration at the Doha (Qatar) Ministerial Conference, with a target completion date of January 2005.

*See* General Agreement on Tariffs and Trade; Tokyo Round; Uruguay Round, World Trade Organization.

### route

(shipping) (a) A pathway between a point of origin and a point of destination for people, cargo or a means of transport. (b) To designate the course or direction a shipment shall move.

### routing

(shipping) (a) The chosen pathway between a point of origin and a point of destination for people, cargo or a means of transport. (b) The process of determining the most efficient pathway for a shipment from the consignor to the consignee.

### royalty

(law) Compensation for the use of a person's property based on an agreed percentage of the income arising from its use (e.g., to an author on sale of his book, to a manufacturer for use of his machinery in the factory of another person, to a composer or performer, etc.). A royalty is a payment, lease or similar right, while a residual payment is often made on properties that have not been patented or are not patentable.

### rufiyaa

The currency of Maldives. 1Rf=100 larees.

### rule of law
(law) Equal protection and equal punishment under the law for all individual in a society. Equal protection includes protection of human rights as well as property and other rights. The concept is that the rule of law reigns over government, protecting citizens against arbitrary state action, and over society generally, governing relations among private interests. It ensures that all citizens are treated equally and are subject to the law rather than the whims of the powerful. The rule of law is an essential precondition for accountability and predictability in both the public and private sector.

### rulings on imports
(U.S. Customs) An exporter, importer, or other interested party may get advance information on any matter affecting the dutiable status of merchandise by writing the District Director of Customs where the merchandise will be entered, or to the Regional Commissioner of Customs, New York Region, New York, NY 10048 USA, or to U.S. Customs and Border Protection, Office of Regulations and Rulings, Washington, DC 20229 USA. Detailed information on the procedures applicable to decisions on prospective importations is given in 19 Code of Federal Regulations part 177.
Tip: Do not depend on a small "trial" or "test" import shipments since there is no guarantee that the next shipment will receive the same tariff treatment. Small importations may slip by, particularly if they are processed under informal procedures which apply to small shipments or in circumstances warranting application of a flat rate.

### rupee
The currency of:
India, 1Re=100 paise;
Mauritius, 1MauRe=100 cents;
Nepal, 1NRe=100 paise;
Pakistan, 1PRe=100 paisas;
Seychelles, 1Re=100 cents;
Sri Lanka, 1R=100 cents.

### rupiah
The currency of Indonesia. 1Rp=100 sen.

# S

### SA8000
Social Accountability 8000. A voluntary international workplace standard and verification system covering: child labor, forced labor, health and safety, freedom of association/collective bargaining, discrimination, discipline, working hours, compensation and management systems in factories and workplaces around the world.

Successful implimentation of the standard enables international firms and organizations to present a visible social accountability management system to the marketplace and other stakeholders.

The system was developed by the Council on Economic Priorities Accreditation Agency and is maintained by Social Accountability International (SAI). SAI is an organization founded in 1996 that seeks to improve workplaces and communities around the work by developing and implementing socially responsible workplace standards.

Social Accountability International; 220 East 23rd Street, Suite 605; New York, NY 10010; USA; Tel: (212) 684-1414; Web: www.sa-intl.org.

### safeguards
(WTO) The World Trade Organization (WTO) permits two forms of multilateral safeguards: (1) a country's right to impose temporary import controls or other trade restrictions to prevent commercial injury to domestic industry, and (2) the corresponding right of exporters not to be deprived arbitrarily of access to markets.

Article XIX permits a country whose domestic industries or workers are adversely affected by increased imports to withdraw or modify concessions the country had earlier granted, to impose, for a limited period, new import restrictions if the country can establish that a product is "being imported in such increased quantities as to cause or threaten serious injury to domestic producers," and to keep such restrictions in effect for such time as may be necessary to prevent or remedy such injury. *See* General Agreement on Tariffs and Trade, World Trade Organization.

### safety stock
(logistics) (a) (technical) The average volume of inventory on hand when a new order is received. (b) (general) Raw materials, component parts or finished goods maintained in inventory specifically in anticipation of unforeseen shortages of materials or component parts or unusual demand for finished goods. The volume of safety stock held in inventory is determined by such factors as instability in supplier markets, supplier production time, order fulfillment and delivery time from the point of origin and the potential for unusual increases in demand for finished product. *See* buffer stock.

### said to contain (s.t.c.); said to weigh (s.t.w.); shipper's load and count
(shipping) Clauses in transport documents which exclude liability of the carrier for the consistency of the description of the goods or the weight of the goods actually loaded, e.g., goods in containers. This provides protection to the carrier against claims by the consignee.

### sales agreement
(law) A written document by which a seller agrees to convey property to a buyer for a stipulated price under specified conditions. *See* contract.

## sales representative
An agent who distributes, represents, services, or sells goods on behalf of sellers. *See* agent; agency.

## sales tax
A tax placed by a state or municipality on items at the time of their purchase. It may be a tax on the sale of an item every time it changes hands (value added tax, VAT), or only upon its transfer of ownership at one specific time.

In the case of a VAT, the sales of manufacturers are taxed when the items are considered to be completed goods; the sales of wholesalers are taxed when their goods are sold to retailers; and retail sales are taxed when the goods are purchased by consumers. *See* value added tax.

## salvage
(insurance) (a) Compensation paid for the rescue of a ship, its cargo or passengers from a loss at sea, (b) The act of saving a ship or its cargo from possible loss, (c) Property saved from a wreck or fire.

## salvage loss
(insurance) A method of insurance adjustment where the underwriter pays the difference between the amount of insurance and the net proceeds of the sale of damaged goods. It is sometimes incorrectly assumed that when damaged goods are sold to determine the extent of loss, the underwriter is obligated to pay the difference between the amount of insurance and the net proceeds of the sale. The salvage loss method is regularly used only if goods are justifiably sold short of destination.

## samurai bond
(banking/finance) Bond issued on the Japanese market in yen outside Japan.

## sanction
(economics) An embargo imposed against an individual country by the United Nations—or a group of nations—in an effort to influence its conduct or its policies. *See* embargo.

## sanitary certificate
A document attesting to the absence of disease or pests in a shipment of animal or plant products, especially foodstuffs. *See* phytosanitary inspection certificate.

## Saudi Arabian Standards Organization
(Saudi Arabia) SASO was established in April 1972 as the sole Saudi Arabian government organization to promulgate standards and measurements in the kingdom. Primarily, SASO promulgates standards for electrical equipment and some food products. Some of these standards have been adopted by the Gulf Cooperation Council. Contact: Saudi Arabian Standards Organization, P.O. Box 3437, Riyadh 1147 Saudi Arabia; Tel: [966] (1) 452-0000; Fax: [966] (1) 452-0086; E-mail: Enquiries@saso.org.sa; Web: www.saso.org.sa. *See* International Standards Organization.

## scanner
*See* bar code scanner.

## schilling
The former currency of Austria, 1S=100 groschen. The new currency of Austria is the European Union Euro. €1 = 100 cents.

## SDR
*See* special drawing rights.

## seal
(law) A mark or sign that is used to witness and authenticate the signing of an instrument, contract, or other document. A corporation, for example, uses a seal to authenticate its contracts and records of its corporate acts.

(shipping) A small metal strip and lead fastener used for fastening or locking the doors of a container, which is usually numbered and which provides proof that a container has not been opened since the seal was applied.

## seal number
(logistics) A number located on the plastic or metal tamper seal or tag affixed to a loaded container or truck. Seals and seal numbers are not reused. A new seal and therefore a new seal number are used each time a container or truck is sealed. *See* container.

## sea waybill
(banking) A transport document which is not a document of title/negotiable document. The sea waybill indicates the "on board" loading of the goods and can be used in cases where no ocean bill of lading, i.e. no document of title is required. For receipt of the goods, presentation of the sea waybill by the consignee named therein is not required, which can speed up processing at the port of destination. *See* bill of lading; ocean bill of lading.

## seaworthiness
(shipping) The fitness or safety of a vessel for its intended use.

## Second Mate (2nd Mate)
(shipping) The third in command officer of a ship in the merchant marine. Responsibilities include: being in charge of bridge watch, plotting the ship's course, following the plot, tracking the ship's movement, using radar, radios, maps, safety and fire-fighting equipment, and maintaining small boats. The $2^{nd}$ mate is often the navigator of a ship. Second mate is the fourth level job of six towards becoming a capitan (ordinary seaman, able-bodied seaman, third mate, second mate, chief mate, captain).

## second party logistics (2PL)
Basic domestic and international transport and warehouse management logistics handled for a company by an outside contractor.

*See also*: first-party logistics, third-party logistics, fourth-party logistics.

## Section 201
(U.S.) Section 201, the "escape clause" provision of the Trade Act of 1974, permits temporary import relief, not to exceed a maximum of eight years, to a domestic industry which is seriously injured, or threatened with serious injury, due to increased imports. Import relief, granted at the president's discretion, generally takes the form of increased tariffs or quantitative restrictions. To be eligible for section 201 relief, the International Trade Commission (ITC) must determine that: (1) the industry has been seriously injured or threatened to be injured and (2) imports have been a substantial cause (not less than any other cause) of that injury. Industries need not prove that an unfair trade practice exists, as is necessary under the antidumping and countervailing duty laws. However, under section 201, a greater degree of injury—"serious" injury— must be found to exist, and imports must be a "substantial" cause (defined as not less than any other cause) of that injury.

If the ITC finding is affirmative, the president's remedy may be a tariff increase, quantitative restrictions, or orderly marketing agreements. At the conclusion of any relief action, the Commission must report on the effectiveness of the relief action in facilitating the positive adjustment of the domestic industry to import competition. If the decision is made not to grant relief, the president must provide an explanation to the Congress. *See* escape clause; unfair trade advantage; orderly marketing agreements; adjustment assistance; International Trade Administration. *See* quantitative restrictions; International Trade Commission.

## Section 232
(U.S.) Under Section 232 of the Trade Expansion Act of 1962, as amended, the U.S. Department of Commerce determines whether articles are being imported into the U.S. in quantities or circumstances that threaten national secu-

rity. Based on the investigation report, the president can adjust imports of the article(s) in question.

The U.S. Department of Commerce must report on the effects these imports have on national security and make recommendations for action or inaction within 270 days after starting an investigation. Within 90 days of the report, the president decides whether to take action to adjust imports on the basis of national security. The president must notify Congress of his decision within 30 days.

### Section 301
(U.S.) Under Section 301 of the Trade Act of 1974, firms can complain about a foreign country's trade policies or practices that are harmful to U.S. commerce. The section empowers the United States Trade Representative (USTR) to investigate the allegations and to negotiate the removal of any trade barriers. The section requires that the World Trade Organization (WTO) dispute resolution process be invoked where applicable and, if negotiations fail, to retaliate within 180 days from the date that discovery of a trade agreement violation took place.

This provision enables the president to withdraw concessions or restrict imports from countries that discriminate against U.S. exports, subsidize their own exports to the United States, or engage in other unjustifiable or unreasonable practices that burden or discriminate against U.S. trade. *See* Super 301; Special 301.

### Section 337
(U.S.) Section 337 of the Tariff Act of 1930 requires investigations of unfair practices in import trade. Under this authority, the International Trade Commission (ITA) applies U.S. statutory and common law of unfair competition to the importation of products into the United States and their sale. Section 337 prohibits unfair competition and unfair importing practices and sales of products in the U.S., when these threaten to: (1) destroy or substantially injure a domestic industry, (2) prevent the establishment of such an industry, or (3) restrain or monopolize U.S. trade and commerce. Section 337 also prohibits infringement of U.S. patents, copyrights or registered trademarks.

### secured
(law/banking) Guaranteed as to payment by the pledge of something valuable.

### security
(general) Property pledged as collateral.
(investments) Stocks and bonds placed by a debtor with a creditor, with authority to sell for the creditor's account if the debt is not paid.
(law) (a) Any evidence of debt or right to a property. (b) An individual who agrees to make good the failure of another to pay.

### seizure
(law) The act of taking possession of property.

### self-insurance
(insurance) A system whereby a firm or individual, by setting aside an amount of monies, provides for the occurrence of losses that would ordinarily be covered under an insurance program. The monies that would normally be used for premium payments are added to this special fund for payment of losses incurred.

### seller's market
Exists when goods cannot easily be secured and when the economic forces of business tend to cause goods to be priced at the vendor's estimate of value.

### selling, general and administrative (expenses)
(U.S. Customs) In establishing valuation of an import shipment, the sum of:
(1) General and administrative expenses (such as: salaries of non-sales personnel, rent, heat, and light);

(2) Direct selling expenses (that is, expenses that can be directly tied to the sale of a specific unit, such as: credit, warranty, and advertising expenses); and
(3) Indirect selling expenses (that is, expenses which cannot be directly tied to the sale of a specific unit but which are proportionally allocated to all units sold during a certain period, such as: telephone, interest, and postal charges). *See* valuation.

### selling rate
(banking/foreign exchange) Rate at which a bank is willing to sell foreign exchange or to lend money.

### semi
*See* semitrailer.

### Semiconductor Trade Arrangement
The U.S.-Japan Semiconductor Trade Arrangement is a bilateral agreement which came into effect on August 1, 1991, replacing the prior 1986 Semiconductor Trade Arrangement. The new Arrangement contains provisions to: (1) increase foreign access to the Japanese semiconductor market; and (2) deter dumping of semiconductors by Japanese suppliers into the U.S. market, as well as in third country markets. In evaluating market access improvement, both governments agreed to pay particular attention to market share. The expectation of a 20 percent foreign market share by the end of 1992 is included in the Arrangement. The Arrangement explicitly states, however, that the 20 percent figure is not a guarantee, a ceiling, or a floor on the foreign market share.

### semitrailer
(logistics/trucking) A non-motorized cargo vehicle designed to be supported at one end by wheels and the other by a motorized vehicle such as a tractor. *See* trailer, tractor.

### senior commercial officer (SCO)
(U.S. diplomacy) The SCO is the senior U.S. and Foreign Commercial Officer at an embassy and reports in-country to the Ambassador. At major posts, this position carries the title of Commercial Counselor; in key posts, Minister Counselor. Usually reporting to the SCO are a Commercial Attaché and Commercial Officers. The latter are sometimes assigned to subordinate posts throughout the country.

### separable cost
(logistics) A cost that can be assigned to a specific portion of a business activity or operation.

### sequestration
*See* attachment.

### Serial Shipping Container Code (SSCC)
(logistics) An international and multi-industry standard numbering and bar coding system used in supply-chain management for the identification, tracking and tracing of cartons and containers. SSCC numbers contain 18 digits and identify: supplier, transporter, distributor, transporter, customer. The SSCC bar code uses UCC/EAN-128 symbology. For information, contact: GS1 (the former Uniform Code Council) at: www.gs1.org.

### service a loan
(banking) To pay interest due on a loan.

### service commitments
(shipping) Pickup and/or delivery commitments agreed to by carrier and shipper.

### service mark
(law) A mark used in sales or advertising to identify a service offered by an individual or legal entity and to distinguish that service from services offered by others. A service mark is distinguished from a trademark in that the former identifies services, while the later identifies goods. Protection for service marks varies from country to country, and may not be available in some jurisdic-

tions. Service marks are often, but not necessarily, regulated by the same laws that govern trademarks. A country that is a member the Paris Convention for the Protection of Industrial Property may recognize service marks held in other jurisdictions. *See* trademark; patent; Paris Convention; World Intellectual Property Organization.

### services
(economics) Economic activities—such as transportation, banking, insurance, tourism, space launching telecommunications, advertising, entertainment, data processing, consulting and the licensing of intellectual property—that are usually of an intangible character and often consumed as they are produced. Service industries have become increasingly important since the 1920s. Services now account for more than two-thirds of the economic activity of the United States and about 25 percent of world trade.

### servitude
(law) A charge against or burden on property that benefits a person with an interest in another property. An owner of property may grant another person, for example, a right to travel over that property to reach adjoining land, in which case the owner has created a servitude against the property. *See* easement.

### settlement date
(banking) The date on which payment for a transaction must be made.

### severability clause
(law) A contract term that provides that each portion of the agreement is independent of the others, allowing a court to invalidate a clause of the contract without voiding the entire agreement.

### shared foreign sales corporation
(U.S.) A foreign sales corporation consisting of more than one and less than 25 unrelated exporters. *See* foreign sales corporation.

### Sharia (Shari'a, Shariah)
(law) Islamic canon law. (Literally: "the right path." Pronounced shuh REE uh.) The traditional code of Islamic civil and criminal law based on the Quran (Koran), the sacred book of Islam, which Muslims consider the actual word of God (Allah). Sharia is also based on the teachings of the Prophet Muhammad and interpretations of the Prophet's teachings by certain Muslim legal scholars.

### shekel
The currency of Israel. 1IS=100 agorot.

### shelter service provider
Firms that operate in Mexico under the Maquiladora Program that provide outsourced manufacturing support for manufacturers in non-core, but critical, areas such as human resources, logistics management, procurement, accounting, payroll management and others. The providing of these services allows companies to focus on core manufacturing functions.

### shilling
The currency of:
Kenya, 1KSh=100 cents;
Somalia, 1 SoSh=100 cents;
Tanzania, 1 TSh=100 cents;
Uganda, 1USh=100 cents.
The former currency of Austria, The new currency of Austria is the European Union Euro. €1 = 100 cents.

### ship agent
(shipping) A port-based representative for a shipping line or tramp operation who handles ship arrival and departure formalities, port clearance, payment of fees, loading and unloading and local provisioning.

### ship broker
(logistics) An individual or company that acts as an intermediary between a shipper and a ship owner or operator, especially tramp ship owners and operators.

### ship chandlery
(shipping) A business that sells ships' provisions, supplies and equipment.
(general) A dealer and/or maker of wax, tallow, candles and soap.
Historic note: In the days of sailing ships, a ship's crew would collect the residual grease (called slush) from empty barrels of fried salt pork and sell it to chandlers once in port. The money so earned was called the *slush fund* and was used to purchase small necessities such as razors, soap, mirrors and tobacco. Chandlers eventually came to be suppliers of ships' provisions.

### ship's manifest
(shipping) A list, signed by the captain of a ship, of the individual shipments constituting the ship's cargo. *See* manifest.

### ship's papers
(shipping) The documents a ship must carry to meet the safety, health, immigration, commercial and customs requirements of a port of call or of international law.

### ship's stores
(shipping) The food, medical supplies, spare parts and other provisions carried for the day-to-day running of a vessel.

### shipment
(shipping) Except as otherwise provided, cargo tendered by one shipper, on one bill of lading, from one point of departure, for one consignee, to one destination, at one time, via a single port of discharge.

### shipment record
(shipping) A repository of information for each shipment that reflects all activity throughout each step of the shipment life cycle.

### shipped on deck
(shipping) Annotation in a bill of lading stating that the goods have been shipped on the deck of a ship. *See* bill of lading.

### shipper
(shipping) The company or person who ships cargo to the consignee.

### shipper's export declaration (SED)
(documentation) A form required by the export authorities of many countries to document an export of goods.
(U.S. documentation) Form required for all U.S. export shipments by mail valued at more than $500 and for non-mail shipments with declared value greater than $2,500. Also required for shipments requiring a U.S. Department of Commerce validated export license or U.S. Department of State license regardless of value of goods. Prepared by a shipper indicating the value, weight, destination, and other basic information about the shipment. The shipper's export declaration is used to control exports and compile trade statistics. The U.S. SED must be filed electronically. For information go to: www.aesdirect.gov for information about how to file an SED electronically.

### shipper's letter of instruction
(shipping) A form used by a shipper to authorize a carrier to issue a bill of lading or an air waybill on the shipper's behalf. The form contains all details of shipment and authorizes the carrier to sign the bill of lading in the name of the shipper. *See* bill of lading.

**S**

**shipper's load and count**
(shipping) A clause in, or notation on, a transport document noting that the contents of a container were loaded and counted by the shipper and not checked or verified by the carrier. Such a notation provides protection to the carrier against claims by the consignee.

**shipping point**
(logistics) The physical place where cargo begins moving aboard a vessel toward its destination.

**shipping instructions**
(shipping) Information supplied by the shipper/exporter providing detailed instructions pertaining to the shipment (e.g., shipper, consignee, bill-to party, commodity, pieces, weight, cube, etc.).

**shipping order**
(shipping) Instructions of shipper to carrier for forwarding of goods; usually the triplicate copy of the bill of lading.

**shipping weight**
(shipping) The total weight usually expressed in kilograms of shipments, including the weight of moisture content, wrappings, crates, boxes, and containers (other than cargo vans and similar substantial outer containers).

**shogun bond**
(finance) Non-resident bond issues denominated in foreign currencies on the Tokyo market. Started June 1985.

**short form bill of lading**
(shipping) A bill of lading that does not have the detailed terms and conditions of carriage printed on (usually) the reverse of the form. A deviation from a regular (long form) bill of lading since it only refers to the contract terms but does not include them. *See* bill of lading, blank back, long form.

**short of exchange**
(banking/foreign exchange) The position of a foreign exchange trader who has sold more foreign bills than the quantity of bills he or she has in possession to cover sales.

**short supply**
(U.S.) Commodities in short supply may be subject to export controls to protect the domestic economy from the excessive drain of scarce materials and to reduce the serious inflationary impact of satisfying foreign demand. Two commodities which the U.S. controls for short supply purposes are crude oil and unprocessed western red cedar.

**short ton**
(measure) A unit of mass or weight measurement equal to 2,000 pounds. A long ton is 2,240 pounds.

**short weight**
(shipping) Notation of a shipment's weight as less than that noted on the original bill of lading, indicating loss during shipment.

**shortage**
(shipping) A deficiency in quantity shipped.

**sight draft**
(banking) A financial instrument payable upon presentation or demand. A bill of exchange may be made payable, for example, at sight or after sight, which means it is payable upon presentation or demand, or within a particular period after demand is made. *See* bill of exchange.

**signature service**
(shipping) A service designed to provide continuous responsibility for the custody of shipments in transit, so named because a signature is required from each person handling the shipment at each stage of its transit from origin to destination.

**silent confirmation**
(banking/letters of credit) In addition to the commitment of the issuing bank of a letter of credit, the advising bank can, by silent confirmation, enter into its own, independent commitment to pay or accept. In contrast to the confirmed letter of credit, in this case there is no confirmation instruction given by the issuing bank. Silent confirmations are thus purely agreements between the beneficiary and the "silently confirming" bank. In order to enforce its claim, the "silently confirming" bank requires the assignment of all the rights of the beneficiary under the letter of credit. *See* letter of credit.

**similar merchandise**
(U.S. Customs) For purposes of establishing the customs value of imported merchandise, similar merchandise is merchandise that is:
(1) Produced in the same country and by the same person as the merchandise being appraised,
(2) Like merchandise being appraised in characteristics and component materials,
(3) Commercially interchangeable with the merchandise being appraised.
If merchandise meeting all these criteria cannot be found, then similar merchandise is merchandise having the same country of production, like characteristics and component materials, and commercially interchangeability, but produced by a different person.
In determining whether goods are similar, some of the factors to be considered are the quality of the goods, their reputation, and existence of a trademark.
Exclusion: Similar merchandise does not include merchandise that incorporates or reflects engineering, development, artwork, design work, and plans and sketches provided free or at reduced cost by the buyer and undertaken in the United States.
*See* valuation; transaction value; computed value; identical merchandise.

**simple average**
(insurance) Particular average. *See* particular average.

**Single European Act**
The SEA, which entered into force in July 1987, provided the legal and procedural support for achievement of the single European Market by 1992. The SEA revised the European Economic Community (EEC) Treaty and, where not already provided for in the Treaty, majority decisions were introduced for numerous votes facing the Council of Ministers, particularly those affecting establishment of the single European Market and the European financial common market. The role of the European Parliament was strengthened; decisions on fiscal matters remained subject to unanimity.

**Single Internal Market Information Service**
SIMIS, run by the the European Community Affairs Office under the United States International Trade Administration (ITA), is a clearinghouse for information on European Community activities. Contact: European Community Affairs Office, United States Department of Commerce, 14th and Constitution Ave. NW, Room 3036, Washington, DC 20230 USA; Tel: [1] (202) 482-5276; Fax: [1] (202) 482-2155.

**SITC**
*See* standard international trade classification.

**skid**
(logistics/transportation) A portable platform supported by two parallel runners that elevate the platform so that the prongs of a forklift truck can fit underneath. Skids are used to store, handle and move materials and goods in factories, warehouses, containers and vessels. A skid is different from a pallet in that it is generally higher and does not have additional cross member support beneath the runners. *See* pallet, forklift.

### sku (number)

(logistics/inventory management) Acronym for stock keeping unit. An alpha, numeric or alpha/numeric designation for the smallest unit quantity of an item (finished product, component part or raw material) that can be accepted into or sent out of inventory from a business or organization. In simple terms: an inventory or stock number, but with some caveats.

An sku (pronounced skew) is not simply a model number. For example, a retail hardware store sells light bulbs by the unit, so it is likely to have an sku number designation for a single 100-watt standard light bulb. The wholesaler, however, may sell the same item in cartons of 24 units, so is likely to have an sku designation for a carton of 24 100-watt standard light bulbs. The manufacturer, however, may only sell full pallets of 32 cartons of 24 each 100-watt standard light bulbs and is likely to have an sku designation for the same.

For ease of use, some wholesalers and retailers may incorporate a manufacturer code, manufacturer's model number, color, size and other designations into their own internal sku number system.

### sling

(shipping) A contrivance into which freight is placed to be hoisted into or out of a ship.

### slip

(shipping) A vessel's berth between two piers.

### slip seat

(logistics) The replacement of a driver who has, by regulation, reached maximum driving time, by a fresh driver.

### slip sheet

(logistics) A durable sheet of plastic or cardboard upon which goods are stacked and used as an alternative to a traditional pallet.

### slurry

(logistics/transportation) The substance that results when dry commodities (such as coal) are liquefied by the addition of a fluid for the purpose of transmission through a pipeline.

### Small Business Administration (SBA)

(U.S. government) An independent government organizations which acts as an advocate to small business, providing aid, counseling, assistance and protection. The SBA's Office of International Trade plans, develops and implements programs to encourage small business participation in international trade. The Office also coordinates the Administrations' International Trade Program with the Departments of Commerce and Agriculture, the Export-Import Bank of the United States, the Agency for International Development, and with other Federal and State agencies with private organizations concerned with international trade. Contact: Small Business Administration, 409 Third Street, SW, Washington, DC 20416 USA; Web: www.sba.gov. The SBA provides an answer desk at: SBA Answer Desk, 6302 Fairview Road, Suite 300, Charlotte, North Carolina 28210 USA; Tel: [1] (800) 827-5722; E-mail: answerdesk@sba.gov.

### small package service

(shipping) A specialized service to guarantee the delivery of small parcels within specified express time limits, e.g., same day or next day. This traffic is subject to size and weight limitations. Air carriers that also transport passengers often accept these packages at airport ticket counters with delivery at destination baggage claim area. Many carriers provide door-to-door service on a 24-hour basis.

### Smoot Hawley Tariff Act of 1930

(U.S.) The Tariff Act of 1930, also commonly known as the Smoot Hawley Tariff, was protectionist legislation that raised tariff rates on most articles imported by the United States, triggering comparable tariff increases by U.S. trading partners.

### smuggling

(customs) Conveying goods or persons, without permission, across the borders of a country or other political entities (e.g., cigarette smuggling across state lines).

### snake system

(banking/foreign exchange-obsolete) The former agreement between Belgium, The Netherlands, Luxembourg, Denmark, Sweden, Norway, and West Germany, linking the currencies of these countries together in an exchange system. The signatories agreed to limit fluctuations in exchange rates among their currencies to 2.25 percent above or below set median rates. The snake was designed to be the first stage in forming a uniform Common Market currency which was finally achieved January 1, 2002. See Euro.

### social accountability

A broad range of actions, besides voting, that citizens, consumers, stockholders and organizations can use to hold bureaucrats, governments and businesses accountable regarding social, political, economic and ethical issues. For example, on an individual level, a person can choose not to knowingly purchase goods produced in prison factories. On an organizational level, a business can choose not to purchase goods produced by child labor. The topic has gained a great deal of attention with a consumer backlash against internationally well-known firms that were employing workers in developing nations at very low wages and in sub-standard working conditions. Social accountability factors include working environment, employment compliance, safety, diversity, discrimination and equal rights, human rights, community responsibility, environmental concerns, among others. *See* Social Accountability International, SA8000.

### Social Accountability International (SAI)

Social Accountability International (SAI) is a human rights organization founded in 1996 that seeks to improve workplaces and communities around the world by developing and implementing socially responsible workplace standards. To fulfill its mission, SAI promotes "ISO-like" standards systems for social accountability. Its SA8000 (Social Accountability 8000) is a workplace standard and verification system that features certification of compliance at the facility level and support for companies seeking to implement their standards. Social Accountability International; 220 East 23rd Street, Suite 605; New York, NY 10010; USA; Tel: (212) 684-1414; Web: www.sa-intl.org.

### Sociedad Anónima (S.A.)

(Latin America, Mexico, Spain) Designation for a joint stock company with limited personal liability to shareholders.

### Sociedad a Responsabilidad Limitada (S.R.L.)

(Latin America, Mexico, Spain) Designation for a private limited liability corporation with limited liability to shareholders.

### Sociedad por Quota (S.Q.)

(Portugal) Designation for a private limited liability corporation with limited liability to shareholders. *See* Limitada.

### Società a Garanzia Limitata (S.G.L.)

(Switzerland) Designation for a private limited liability corporation with limited liability to shareholders.

### Società Cooperativa a Responsabilità (SCaRL)

(Italy, Switzerland) Designation for an incorporated association with limited liability for its members, unless its articles provide otherwise.

*Società in Accomandita Semplice (S.A.S.)*
(Italy) Designation for a limited partnership in which at least one of the partners has general liability and at least one of the other partners has limited liability.
*Società per Azioni (S.p.A.)*
(Italy) Designation for a joint stock company with limited personal liability to shareholders.
*Société (Sté.)*
(France, Luxembourg, Switzerland) General designation for a corporation, partnership, or association.
*Société Anonyme (S.A.)*
(Belgium, France, Luxembourg, Switzerland) Designation for a joint stock company with limited personal liability to shareholders.
*Société à Responsabilité Limitée (S.R.L.)*
(France, Luxembourg, Switzerland) Designation for a private limited liability corporation with limited liability to shareholders.
*Société Cooperative (Sté. Cve.)*
(Belgium, Switzerland) Designation for an incorporated association with limited liability for its members, unless its articles provide otherwise.
*Société de Personnes à Responsabilité Limitée (S.P.R.L.)*
(Belgium) Designation for a private limited liability company with limited liability to shareholders.
*Société en Commandité par Actions (S.C.)*
(France, Luxembourg) Designation for a limited partnership in which the partners have limited liability.
*Société en Commandité Simple (S.C.S.)*
(France, Luxembourg) Designation for a limited partnership in which at least one of the partners has general personal liability and at least one of the other partners has limited liability.
*Société en Nom Collectif (S.N.C.)*
(France, Luxembourg) Designation for a general partnership, in which all partners have joint and several liability.
*soft clause*
(banking) Clauses in a documentary letter of credit which make it impossible for the beneficiary (seller) to meet the conditions of the documentary letter of credit on his own and independently of the purchaser.
Example: "The goods must be accepted prior to shipment by a representative of the purchaser." The name of the representative is made known via an amendment in the documentary letter of credit at a later stage when it is either too late or very inconvenient to follow through on the requirement. It is not recommended for exporters to agree to this type of request.
*soft currency*
(banking/foreign exchange) The funds of a country that are controlled by exchange procedures, thereby having limited convertibility into gold and other currencies.
*soft loan*
(general) A loan made with easy or generous terms such as low or no interest and long payback.
(banking) This term refers to the no-interest loans granted to developing countries by the International Development Association. Such a "soft loan" carries no interest (although there is a small annual service charge), is payable in 50 years, and has an amortization rate of 1% repayable annually for the 10 years following an initial 10-year grace period, followed by 3% repayable annually for the remaining 30 years.
*sogo bank*
(banking/finance) Regional finance institutions in Japan, dealing chiefly with smaller enterprises.

*sol*
The currency of Peru. 1S=100 centavos.
*SOLAS Convention*
Acronym for Safety of Life at Sea Convention. An international convention, the result of the first International Conference on the Safety of Life at Sea, convened in London, England on November 12, 1913, as a direct result of the Titanic disaster.
The SOLAS Convention in its successive forms is regarded as the most important of all international treaties concerning the safety of merchant ships. The first version was signed on January 30, 1914 by representatives of the world's maritime powers.
The convention provided for the International Ice Patrol and included minimum standards for radio communications and lifesaving equipment on passenger ships. New versions were adopted in 1929, 1948, 1960 and 1974.
The 1960 Convention, which was adopted on June 17, 1960 and entered into force on May 26, 1965, was the first major task for the International Maritime Organization (IMO) after the Organization's creation, and it represented a considerable step forward in modernizing regulations and in keeping pace with technical developments in the shipping industry.
A completely new Convention was adopted in 1974, which included not only amendments agreed up until that date but a new amendment procedure--the tacit acceptance procedure--deigned to ensure that changes could be made within a specified (and acceptably short) period of time.
As a result, the 1974 Convention has been updated and amended on numerous occasions. The Convention in force today is sometimes referred to as SOLAS, 1974, as amended. For information contact the International Maritime Organization at www.imo.org.
*sourcing*
The location and acquisition of all the vital inputs required for an organization to operate. If an organization spends money or exchanges value for a product or service, it is sourced. An organization's vital inputs can include raw materials, component parts, intermediate parts, machinery, supplies, labor, management, production and management facilities, communications services, and utilities, as well as design, legal, accounting and other services, to name but a few.
Sourcing is a primary function of any organizational entity. Successful sourcing has three key components: 1) the acquisition of products and services of sufficient quality, 2) the securing of an uninterrupted supply of products and services, and 3) the acquisition of products and services at the most competitive prices possible. If any of these three components are deficient, the organization will suffer and possibly fail.
*Southern Africa Development Community (SADC)*
A regional economic pact comprising Angola, Botswana, Lesotho, Malawi, Mozambique, Namibia, Swaziland, Tanzania, Zambia, and Zimbabwe. Note: The Southern Africa Development Coordinating Conference (SADCC) became the Southern Africa Development Community (SADC) in August, 1992, when the 10 member countries signed a treaty to establish it and replace the SADCC. The SADC placed binding obligations on member countries with the aim of promoting economic integration towards a fully developed common market. Contact: Southern Africa Development Community, Private Bag 0095, Gaborone, Botswana; Tel: [267] 395-1863; Fax: [267] 397- 2848; E-mail: registry@sadc.int; Web: www.sadc.int.

**S**

### Southern Africa Development Coordination Conference

Note: The Southern Africa Development Coordinating Conference (SADCC) became the Southern Africa Development Community (SADC) in August, 1992, when the 10 member countries signed a treaty to establish it and replace the SADCC. *See* Southern Africa Development Community.

### Southern African Customs Union

SACU, established in 1910, includes Botswana, Lesotho, Namibia, South Africa, and Swaziland. SACU provides for the free exchange of goods within the area, a common external tariff, and a sharing of custom revenues. External tariffs, excise duties, and several rebate and refund provisions are the same for all SACU members. SACU's revenues are apportioned among its members according to a set formula. These funds constitute a significant contribution to each member's government revenues.

### Southern Common Market

*See* Mercosur.

### southern cone

The southern cone consists of Argentina, Brazil, Chile, Paraguay, and Uruguay. With the exception of Chile, these countries also comprise the Southern Common Market.

### sovereign credit

(finance) A borrowing guaranteed by the government of a sovereign state.

### sovereign risk

(finance) The risk to a lendor that the government of a sovereign state may default on its financial obligations.

### sovereignty

The rights of a nation to self determination over all that transpires within its boundaries, especially concerning the rights of its people, immigration policy, business dealings, and jurisdiction over airspace, land and maritime matters.

### space and equipment reservation

(logistics) A carrier's setting aside of cargo space and equipment for a shipper's specific future shipment.

### space arbitrage

*See* arbitrage, space.

### space request (space and equipment request)

(logistics) A shipper's asking a carrier for availability of cargo space and the equipment required to effect a shipment at a future date. This is generally the first contact a shipper makes with a carrier concerning a shipment.

### Special 301

(U.S.) The Special 301 statute requires the United States Trade Representative (USTR) to review annually the condition of intellectual property protection among U.S. trading partners. Submissions are accepted from industry after which the USTR, weighing all relevant information, makes a determination as to whether a country presents excessive barriers to trade with the United States by virtue of its inadequate protection of intellectual property. If the USTR makes a positive determination, a country may be named to the list of: (1) Priority Foreign Countries (the most egregious), (2) the Priority Watch List, or (3) the Watch List. *See* Section 301; Super 301.

### special agency

*See* agency.

### Special American Business Internship Training Program (SABIT)

(U.S. government agency) SABIT, formerly the Soviet-American Business Internship Training Program, is a program in which American companies give managers from the Confederation of Independent States (CIS) an opportunity to work in a U.S. corporate setting for up to six months. CIS business managers are referred by the U.S. Department of Commerce to sponsoring U.S. companies, which make the final selection of their interns. The SABIT program matches U.S. corporate sponsors with CIS business executives from the same industries. The CIS provides transportation; the companies provide living expenses and training in management techniques (production, distribution, marketing, accounting, wholesaling, and publishing). SABIT is funded by the U.S. Agency for International Development. Contact: U.S. Department of Commerce, SABIT Program, 1401 Constitution Avenue NW, HCHB 4318, Washington, DC 20230 USA; Tel: [1] (202) 482-0073; Fax: [1] (202) 482-2443; Web: www.mac.doc.gov/sabit/sabit.html.

### special and differential treatment

(GATT/WTO) The principle, enunciated in the Tokyo Declaration, that the Tokyo Round of the General Agreement on Tariffs and Trade (GATT) negotiations should seek to accord particular benefits to the exports of developing countries, consistent with their trade, financial, and development needs. Among proposals for special or differential treatment are reduction or elimination of tariffs applied to exports of developing countries under the Generalized System of Preferences (GSP), expansion of product and country coverage of the GSP, accelerated implementation of tariff cuts agreed to in the Tokyo Round for developing country exports, substantial reduction or elimination of tariff escalation, special provisions for developing country exports in any new codes of conduct covering nontariff measures, assurance that any new multilateral safeguard system will contain special provisions for developing country exports, and the principle that developed countries will expect less than full reciprocity for trade concessions they grant developing countries.
*See* General Agreement on Tariffs and Trade; Generalized System of Preferences, World Trade Organization.

### special commodities carrier

(logistics/trucking) A common carrier that is authorized to haul certain regulated items, such as household goods, petroleum products and hazardous materials.

### special commodity warehouse

(logistics) A warehouse designed with special facilities and authorized to store unique products such as chemicals (in tanks), grain (in elevators) and tobacco (in barns).

### special customs invoice

(customs) A country-of-import required document, similar to a commercial invoice, that contains particular information required for entry of goods into that country. Special customs invoices often itemize freight and insurance charges when a country bases import duties on the landed cost (CIF or Cost, Insurance and Freight) of a shipment.

### special drawing right(s) (SDR)

(banking) Reserve assets of the member states of the International Monetary Fund, (IMF) (Bretton-Woods system), for which they can draw an amount of SDRs proportional to their predetermined quota in the IMF. The value of an SDR is based on a currency basket (the last realignment was in January 2001: U.S.$=45%, Euro (€) =29%, Yen=15%, GB£=11%.) Some countries define the parity of their currencies in SDRs.

(banking/foreign exchange) The amount by which each member state of the IMF is permitted to have its international checking account with the International Monetary Fund go negative before the nation must ask for additional loans.

SDRs were established at the Rio de Janeiro conference of 1967. SDRs are available to governments through the Fund and may be used in transactions between the Fund and member governments.

**S**

IMF member countries have agreed to regard SDRs as complementary to gold and reserve currencies in settling their international accounts. The unit value of an SDR reflects the foreign exchange value of a "basket" of currencies of several major trading countries (the U.S. dollar, the European Union Euro, the Japanese yen, and the British pound). The SDR has become the unit of account used by the IMF and several national currencies are pegged to it. Some commercial banks accept deposits denominated in SDR's (although they are unofficial and not the same units transacted among governments and the fund). *See* International Monetary Fund.

### Special Import Measures Act (SIMA)
(Canada Customs) A Canadian law designed to protect Canadian producers and manufacturers against unfair competition from imports of low-priced dumpted or subsidized goods. For more information go to: www.cbsa-asfc.gc.ca/menu/D14-e.html.

### Specially Designated Nationals and Blocked Persons (SDN)
(U.S.) A list maintained by the U.S. Treasury's Office of Foreign Asset Control (OFAC) of individuals, organizations, countries and geographic regions with whom U.S. individuals and firms are prohibited from doing business. U.S. firms must check this list on an ongoing basis to ensure that potential customers and existing customers are not prohibited persons or entities and are not from embargoed countries or regions before transacting any business with them.

### special marine policy
(insurance) An insurance policy which is issued to cover a single shipment. The special marine policy form calls for the name of the vessel and sailing date, points of shipment and destination, nature of commodity, description of units comprising the shipment, and the amount of insurance desired. In addition, it calls for the marks and numbers of the shipment, the name of the party to whom loss shall be payable (usually the assured "or orders" thus making the instrument negotiable upon endorsement by the assured), and the applicable policy provisions. Some of these provisions are standard clauses and are incorporated by reference only, while others are specific and apply to the individual shipment in question.

A special marine policy is usually utilized on export shipments when the sale is financed through a bank by letter of credit and evidence of insurance is a part of the required documentation.

The special marine policy is generally prepared in four or more copies. The original (and duplicate if necessary) is negotiable and is forwarded with the shipping documents to the consignee. The remaining documents serve as office copies for the assured and for the insurance company.

The terms "special marine policy" and "certificate" are often used interchangeably. The practical effect of the two is the same, but a word as to their difference will be of interest.

In former years the use of "certificate" was customary. This, as the name implies, certifies that a shipment has been insured under a given open policy, and that the certificate represents and takes the place of such open policy, the provisions of which are controlling.

Because of the objections that an instrument of this kind did not constitute a "policy" within the requirements of letters of credit, it has become the practice to use a special marine policy. This makes no reference to an open policy and stands on its own feet as an obligation of the underwriting company.

In some cases, exporters insure through freight forwarders when arranging for forwarding, warehousing, documentation, ocean freight space and the other requirements of overseas trade. While this method may have the merit of simplicity, it should be emphasized that there are definite advantages in having one's own policy and that this need not entail burdensome clerical detail. *See* open policy; declaration; bordereau.

### special rates
(shipping) Rates that apply to cargo traffic under special conditions and usually at a limited number of cities. Examples of such rates are container rates, exception ratings, surface-air rates, and import rates.

### Special Trade Programs
(U.S. imports) A group of six programs that offer incentives for doing business with certain countries. The programs include: African Growth and Opportunity Act (AGOA), Andean Trade Preference Act (ATPA), Andean Trade Promotion and Drug Eradication Act (ATPDEA), Caribbean Basin Trade Partnership Act (CBTPA), Caribbean Basin Economic Recovery Act (CBERA), and Generalized Systems of Preferences (GSP). For more information, contact U.S. Customs and Border Protection at www.cbp.gov.

### specific commodity rate
(shipping) Rate applicable to certain classes of commodities, usually commodities moving in volume shipments. Hence, specific commodity rates are usually lower than the general commodity rate between the same pair of cities.

### specific rate of duty
(customs) A specified amount of duty per unit of weight or other quantity. For example 5.9 cents per pound, or 8 cents per dozen. *See* ad valorem; compound rate of duty.

### spot
*See* spot operations.

### spot cash
(banking) Immediate cash payment in a transaction, as opposed to payment at some future time.

### spot exchange
(foreign exchange) The purchase and sale of foreign exchange for delivery and payment at the time of the transaction.

### spot exchange rate
(foreign exchange) The price of one currency expressed in terms of another currency at a given moment in time.

### spot market
(foreign exchange) The market (or exchange) for a commodity or foreign exchange available for immediate delivery (usually one or two days after the transaction date).

### spot/next
(foreign exchange) Swap transaction, the spot side of which has the normal spot value date while the forward side becomes due one business day later.

### spot operations
(foreign exchange) Foreign exchange dealing in which settlement of the mutual delivery commitments is made at the latest two days (normally on the second business day) after the transaction was carried out.

### spot price
A price quotation for immediate sale and delivery of a commodity or currency.

### spot rate
The rate for purchase or sale of a commodity for immediate delivery.

### spot trading
*See* spot market; spot operations.

S

**spotting**
(shipping) The placing of a container where required to be loaded or unloaded.

**squaring (positions)**
(finance/foreign exchange) Covering an open position (securities, foreign exchange or commodities) by means of corresponding contra business.

**spur track**
(logistics/rail transport) A section of railroad track that connects a manufacturing plant or warehouse to the main railroad line. The cost of the spur and its maintenance is borne by the connected facility.

**stage**
(logistics) Positioning and preparing freight for shipment at a specific location.

**stanchion**
(shipping) (a) A vertical supporting beam that transfers force from the mast to the hull of a sailing ship. (b) A vertical supporting beam that supports decks or girders on a container vessel. (c) A vertical supporting beam that supports the roof of a shipping container.

**standard industrial classification (SIC)**
(U.S.) The classification standard underlying all establishment-based U.S. economic statistics classified by industry.

**standard industry (business) practices**
Purchase, sale, delivery and other practices that are unique to a specific industry. For example, in the printing industry, standard industry practice allows for a final delivery quantity of ten percent over or under the ordered quantity, with the final bill adjusted accordingly.

**Standard International Trade Classification, Revision 3 (SITC, Rev. 3)**
(international classification system) A United Nations-established and maintained classification and coding system developed for the compilation of international trade statistics and the promotion of international comparability of international trade statistics. The SITC code reflects: 1) the materials used in production, 2) the processing stage, 3) market practices and uses of the products, 4) the importance of the commodities in terms of world trade, and 5) technological changes. The latest revision was Revision 3 in 1986. The SITC corresponds to the following other international classifications: Classification by Broad Economic Categories (BEC), The Harmonized Commodity Description and Coding System (HS), Central Product Classification (CPC), and the International Standard Industrial Classification (ISIC). Contact at UNSD (United Nations Statistics Division); International Trade Statistics Branch; Fax: [1] (212) 963-4116; E-mail: statistics@un.org; Web: http://unstats.un.org/unsd/default.htm. *See* Harmonized System, International Standard Industrial Classification.

**standard of living**
(economics) The level of material affluence of a nation as measured by per capita output.

**standards**
As defined by the Multilateral Trade Negotiations "Agreement on Technical Barriers to Trade" (Standards Code), a standard is a technical specification contained in a document that lays down characteristics of a product such as levels of quality, performance, safety, or dimensions. Standards may include, or deal exclusively with, terminology, symbols, testing and test methods, packaging, marking, or labeling requirements as they apply to a product. *See* International Standards Organization; American National Standards Institute.

**standby commitment**
(banking) A bank commitment to loan money up to a specified amount for a specific period, to be used only in a certain contingency.

**standby letter of credit**
(banking) The standby letter of credit is very similar in nature to a guarantee. The beneficiary can claim payment in the event that the principal does not comply with its obligations to the beneficiary. Payment can usually be realized against presentation of a sight draft and written statement that the principal has failed to fulfill his obligations.
With this instrument the following payments and performances, among others, can be supported:
(1) repay funds borrowed or advanced,
(2) fulfill subcontracts, and
(3) undertake payment of invoices made on open account. *See* letter of credit.

**standing to sue**
(law) A party's interest in a controversy that is sufficient to allow the party to request a judicial resolution. A buyer who suffers damages because of the seller's breach of contract, for example, has standing to sue, but a friend of the buyer who was not a party to the contract and who has not suffered damages from the breach has no standing to sue.

**standstill**
(GATT) Standstill refers to a commitment of the General Agreement on Tariffs and Trade (GATT) contracting parties not to impose new trade-restrictive measures during the Uruguay Round negotiations. *See* rollback; General Agreement on Tariffs and Trade; Uruguay Round.

**starboard**
(shipping) The right side of a ship when one is facing the bow.

**stare decisis**
(law) A legal doctrine under which courts, in resolving current disputes, follow cases decided previously. This doctrine is followed in countries that adhere to common law principles. *See* common law.

**State Export Program Database**
(U.S.) The SEPD is a trade lead system maintained by the National Association of State Development Agencies (NASDA). The SEPD includes information on state operated trade lead systems. The SEPD can be purchased on CD-ROM for $125.00 directly from the NASDA's Web site at: www.nasda.com. *See* National Association of State Development Agencies.

**state/industry-organized, government approved (S/IOGA)**
The name of this program has recently been changed to Certified Trade Missions Program. *See* Certified Trade Missions Program.

**state trading enterprises**
Entities established by governments to import, export and/or produce certain products. Examples include: government-operated import/export monopolies and marketing boards, or private companies that receive special or exclusive privileges from their governments to engage in trading activities.

**STAT-USA**
(U.S. Dept. of Commerce) STAT-USA is a fee-funded office in the U.S. Department of Commerce that develops and operates electronic information systems to deliver government economic, business, statistical, and foreign trade information to the public, primarily through subscription online services. STAT-USA's flagship product, STAT-USA/Internet (Web: www.stat-usa.gov), is a subscription based Internet site that contains all of the information in the National Trade Data Bank (NTDB) as well as an extensive collection of do-

mestic economic data. Customers can view, print and download trade opportunity leads, market reports, economic releases and more from the State Department, the Bureau of Industry & Security, the Federal Reserve Board, the U.S. Census Bureau, and others. USA Trade Online, a joint venture with the U.S. Census Bureau and a private partner, is the latest STAT-USA product, offering trade statistics to subscribers within minutes of release. Tel: [1] (800) STAT-USA; E-mail: statmail@esa.doc.gov; Web: www.stat-usa.gov.

### state trading nations
(economics) Countries such as the former Soviet Union, the People's Republic of China, and nations of Eastern Europe that rely heavily on government entities, instead of the private sector, to conduct trade with other countries. Some of these countries, (e.g., Cuba) have long been Contracting Parties to the General Agreement on Tariffs and Trade (GATT) and now the World Trade Organization (WTO), whereas others (e.g., Poland, Hungary, and Romania), became Contracting Parties later under special Protocols of Accession. The different terms and conditions under which these countries acceded to GATT and the WTO were designed in each case to ensure steady expansion of the country's trade with other GATT/WTO countries taking into account the relative insignificance of tariffs on imports into state trading nations.

### statute of frauds
(U.S. law) A law that requires designated documents to be written in order to be enforced by a court. Contracting parties, for example, may orally agree to transfer ownership of land, but a court may not enforce that contract, and may not award damages for breach, unless the contract is written.

### steamship indemnity
(shipping) An indemnity received by an ocean carrier issued by a bank indemnifying him for any loss incurred for release of goods to the buyer without presentation of the original bill of lading.

### sterling
(a) The money of Great Britain. (b) An article made from sterling silver. Sterling silver is an alloy of silver that is 925/1000 pure. An article of sterling silver is generally marked "925".

### stern
(shipping) The rear part of a ship, boat or airplane.

### stevedore
(shipping) A person having charge of the loading and unloading of ships in port. *See* longshoreman; gang.

### stock on hand
(logistics) Inventory of raw materials, component parts or finished goods available for shipment at any given moment in time. The term generally refers to stock of finished goods.

### stop loss order
(foreign exchange) An order to buy (on a short position) or to sell (on a long position) foreign exchange if the rate rises above or falls below a specific limit. As soon as the rate reaches the prescribed limit, the order will be carried out at the next rate. Depending on the market situation, this rate can differ considerably from the limit rate.

### storage
(shipping) The keeping of goods in a warehouse.

### storage demurrage
(shipping) A charge made on property remaining on the dock past the prescribed "free-time period." *See* demurrage.

### storage in transit
(shipping) The stopping of freight traffic at a point located between the point of origin and destination to be stored and reforwarded at a later date.

### store-door delivery
(shipping) The movement of goods to the consignee's place of business, customarily applied to movement by truck.

### stores
*See* ship's stores.

### stowage
(shipping) The arranging and packing of cargo in a vessel for shipment.

### stowage instructions
(shipping) Specific instructions given by the shipper or his agent concerning the way in which cargo is to be stowed. For example, a shipper may require that his shipment be placed below deck if it may be damaged by exposure to the elements above deck, or midships if it may be damaged by the greater movement of the vessel in fore and aft sections.

### stowplan or stowage plan
(shipping) A diagram showing how cargo or containers have been or are to be placed on a vessel.

### straddle carrier
A four- or eight-wheeled vehicle designed to straddle, lift, move and stack ocean freight containers at container terminals. Straddle carriers come in different sizes, with the largest able to lift and stack 50,000kg (110,000lb) loaded containers three or four high.

### straight bill of lading
(shipping) A nonnegotiable bill of lading that designates a consignee who is to receive the goods and that obligates the carrier to deliver the goods to that consignee only. A straight bill of lading cannot be transferred by endorsement. *See* bill of lading; negotiable instrument; ocean bill of lading.

### strategic alliance
(commerce/management) An agreement made between two or more individuals, organizations or legal entities, within the same or complimentary industries, to accomplish one or more specific goals such as: increase market share, reduce costs, create new products or enter new markets. *See* joint venture.

### strategic level of controls
(U.S.) Commodity groupings used for export control purposes. *See* export control classification number.

### strike clause
(insurance) An insurance clause included in policies to cover against losses as a result of strikes.

### strike price
(finance/foreign exchange) Price at which the option buyer obtains the right to purchase (call option) or sell (put option) the underlying security or currency.

### strikes, riots and civil commotion
(insurance) An insurance policy endorsement, usually referred to as S.R.&C.C. (strikes, riots and civil commotion) coverage, which extends the insurance policy to cover damage, theft, pilferage, breakage or destruction of the insured property directly caused by strikers, locked-out workmen or persons taking part in labor disturbances, riots or civil commotions.
Destruction of and damage to property caused by vandalism, sabotage and malicious acts of person(s) regardless of (political/ideological/terroristic) intent be it accidental or otherwise is also held covered under S.R.&C.C. unless so excluded in the F.C.&S. (free of capture and seizure) warranty in the policy.

The S.R.&C.C. endorsement excludes coverage for any damage or deterioration as a result of delay or loss of market, change in temperature/humidity, loss resulting from hostilities or warlike operations, absence/shortage/ withholding power, fuel, labor during a strike (riot or civil commotion) or weapons of war that employ atomic or nuclear fusion/fission.

In order to eliminate the war cover from the marine policy it became customary to add a "free of capture and seizure" clause, stating that the policy did not cover warlike operations or its consequences, whether before or after the actual declaration of war. Currently, most open policies omit war perils from its insuring conditions and in all cases will include a F.C.&S. clause. War coverage is customarily furnished in conjunction with an open cargo policy and is written under a separate, distinct policy-the War Risk Only Policy.

*See* war risk; war risk insurance; open policy.

### striking price; exercise price
*See* strike price.

### stripping
(shipping) The unloading of cargo from a container. Also called devanning.

### Structural Impediments Initiative (SII)
(U.S./Japan) The SII was started in July 1989 to identify and solve structural problems that restrict bringing two-way trade between the U.S. and Japan into better balance.

Both the U.S. and Japanese governments chose issues of concern in the other's economy as impediments to trade and current account imbalances. The areas which the U.S. government chose included: (1) Japanese savings and investment patterns, (2) land use, (3) distribution, (4) keiretsu, (5) exclusionary business practices, and (6) pricing. Areas which the Japanese Government chose included: (1) U.S. savings and investment patterns, (2) corporate investment patterns and supply capacity, (3) corporate behavior, (4) government regulation, (5) research and development, (6) export promotion, and g) workforce education and training.

In a June 1990 report, the U.S. and Japan agreed to seven meetings in the following three years to review progress, discuss problems, and produce annual joint reports.

### stuffing
(shipping) The loading of cargo into a container.

### subcontract
(law) A contract between a party to an original contract (prime contractor) and a third party (subcontractor) to provide some or all of the goods or services required in the original contract.

### subcontractor
(law) An individual or company that contracts to provide some or all of the goods or services required by a prime contractor in satisfaction of an original contract. *See* prime contractor.

### subrogation
(insurance) The right of the insurer, upon payment of a loss, to the benefit of any rights against third parties that may be held by the assured himself. This usually involves recoveries from carriers that handled the shipment.

### subsidiary
(law) A business entity with more than 50 percent of its voting stock owned by another firm.

### subsidy
(economics) A bounty, grant or economic advantage paid by a government to producers of goods for the manufacture, production, or export of an article, often to strengthen their competitive position. Export subsidies are contingent on exports; domestic subsidies are conferred on production without reference to exports.

The subsidy may be direct (a cash grant), or indirect, low-interest export credits guaranteed by a government agency, for example), or take a less direct form (R&D support, tax breaks, loans on preferential terms, and provision of raw materials at below-market prices).

(WTO) The payment of subsidies by a national government to export producers in a major trade issue. *See* World Trade Organization.

### subzone
(U.S. foreign trade zones) A special purpose foreign trade zone established as part of a foreign trade zone project for a limited purpose that cannot be accommodated within an existing zone. Subzones are often established to serve the needs of a specific company and may be located within an existing facility of the company. *See* foreign trade zone; Foreign Trade Zone Board; Foreign Trade Zone Act; operator; grantee; zone user.

### sucre
The currency of Ecuador. 1S/=100 centavos.

### sue and labor
(insurance) The responsibility of the assured to act to keep his insured loss at a minimum. The sue and labor clause of the open cargo policy reads essentially as follows:

"In case of any loss or misfortune it shall be lawful and necessary to and for the assured, his or their factors, servants and assigns to sue, labor, and travel, for, in and about the defense, safeguard and recovery of the goods and merchandise or any part thereof ... to the charges whereof this company will contribute according to the rate and quantity of the sum herein insured."

Reasonable charges incurred for this purpose are generally collectible under the insurance policy. For example, when a shipment of canned goods arrives with some leaking cans in each of several cartons, the leaking cans must be taken out if rusting and label damage are to be minimized. The expense insured in this operation may be recovered under the insurance policy.

### Suezmax
(shipping) An ocean-going cargo vessel of the maximum size possible to pass through the locks of the Suez Canal in Egypt. This standard has evolved over time. Prior to 1967, a Suezmax was a maximum of 80,000 dwt. The canal was closed between 1967 and 1975 because of the Israel-Arab conflict. Upon reopening in 1975, after many modifications to the locks and canal itself, the maximum was increased to 150,000 dwt.

### Sufferance Warehouse
(Canada Customs) Privately owned and operated warehouse facilities licensed by the Canada Border Services Agency (CCRA) for the control, short-term storage and examination of imported goods until they are released by the CBSA or exported from Canada. This means that goods can be moved under Customs' control beyond the first point of arrival to a licensed facility for temporary storage pending Customs clearance.

There are five main types of sufferage warehouse licenses depending upon the type of goods stored and the method of transportation:

Type A—Operated by an airline, marine or railway company. Also those located at a marine wharf and operated by a harbor commission or stevedoring company.

Type B—Used for the storage of imported goods arriving by highway in commercial motor vehicles

Type C—Operated by a third-party for the storage, deconsolidation and sorting of imported shipments and for the consolidation of shipments according to their destination.

Type S—Operated by a person or persons for the storage of specific classes of imported goods arriving by any mode of transportation.

Type PS—Railway sidings owned or operated by an importer where carloads of imported goods are held pending release by the CBSA.

For details on sufferage warehouse regulations go to: www.cbsc.org/servlet/Content-Server?cid=1081944191809&page-name=CBSC_YT%2Fdisplay&lang=en&c=Regs or contact the Automated Customs Information Service (ACIS) at (800) 461-9999 (English).

### summary investigation
(U.S.) A 20-day investigation conducted immediately following filing of an antidumping petition to ascertain if the petition contains sufficient information with respect to sales at "less than fair value" and the injury or threat of material injury to a domestic industry caused by the alleged sales at "less than fair value" to warrant the initiation of an antidumping investigation. *See* dumping.

### summit conference
(diplomacy) An international meeting at which heads of government are the chief negotiators, major world powers are represented, and the meeting serves substantive rather than ceremonial purposes. The term first came into use in reference to the Geneva Big Four Conference of 1955.

### Super 301
(U.S.) This provision was enacted due to U.S. Congressional concern that the regular Section 301 procedures narrowly limit U.S. attention to the market access problems of individual sectors or companies. Super 301 sets procedures to identify and address within three years certain "priority," systemic trade restriction policies of other nations. Super 301 authority expired May 30, 1990. *See* Section 301; Special 301.

### superdeductive
*See* deductive value.

### superficies
(law) A right to build on the surface of real property. A landowner may transfer a superficies right, for example, to a developer who agrees to build on the property in exchange for an annual rent to the landowner.

### Superintendent of Documents
(U.S.) Official supplier of U.S. government documents, publications, books, etc. Government Periodicals and Subscription Services is a catalog of products and prices. Contact: Superintendent of Documents, U.S. Government Printing Office, Mail Stop: IDCC, 732 N. Capitol Street, NW, Washington, DC 20401; Tel: [1] (866) 512-1800, [1] (202) 512-1800; Fax: [1] (202) 512-2104; Web: www.gpoaccess.gov.

### supplemental carrier
(logistics) A for-hire air carrier that operates without a set schedule or designated route. Service is provided on a charter or contract basis.

### supply access
(economics/customs) Assurances that importing countries will, in the future, have fair and equitable access at reasonable prices to supplies of raw materials and other essential imports. Such assurances should include explicit constraints against the use of the export embargo as an instrument of foreign policy.

### supply chain (logistics)
The series of physical facilities, equipment, management and technology that supply goods or services from source to the ultimate consumer. For products these minimally include manufacturing plants, warehouses, distribution centers, conveyances (such as trucks, cargo aircraft, ships and trains), sales locations or methodologies (such as retail stores or Internet Web sites), computer systems and software. The processes, systems and links between these facilities are the subject of ever evolving theory, debate and great technological change. For example, computers and the Internet are part of the supply chain through inventory information systems and e-commerce ordering systems as well as Web-based delivery of information and services. *See* supply chain management.

### supply chain management
(logistics) The efficient integration of the processes, facilities and technologies involved in the movement of goods or services from source to the ultimate consumer. Modern supply chain management involves the linking of all parties in the supply chain to effectively coordinate the production of the right products or services and their delivery to the right place at the right time for the least cost. Supply chain management refers to the aggregate of the following processes: customer ordering or obtaining sales data, raw material and component parts procurement, coordination of the manufacturing process, warehousing, distribution, invoicing, shipping, receiving, inventory control and order fulfillment. *See* supply chain.

### surcharge
(shipping) A charge above the usual or customary charge.

### surety
(insurance) A bond, guaranty, or other security that protects a person, corporation, or other legal entity in cases of another's default in the payment of a given obligation, improper performance of a given contract, malfeasance of office, and others.

(law) A surety is usually a party to the contract with the principal debtor and the third person, making the surety equally liable with the debtor. In contrast, a guarantor is usually not a party to the contract between the debtor and the third person.

(U.S. Customs) Surety Bond—U.S. Customs entries must be accompanied by evidence that a bond is posted with Customs to cover any potential duties, taxes, and penalties which may accrue. Bonds may be secured through a resident U.S. surety company, but may be posted in the form of United States money or certain United States government obligations. In the event that a customs broker is employed for the purpose of making entry, the broker may permit the use of his bond to provide the required coverage. *See* bond; guaranty.

### survey
(shipping) To examine the condition of a vessel for purposes of establishing seaworthiness and/or value.

(insurance) To inspect goods as to their condition, weight and/or value in order to establish the extent of an insured loss.

### survey report
Report of an expert, issued by an independent party. *See* inspection certificate.

### sushi bond
(banking/finance) Eurodollar bonds issued by Japanese corporations on the Japanese market for Japanese investors.

### suspension of investigation
(U.S.) A decision to suspend an antidumping investigation if the exporters who account for substantially all of the imported merchandise agree to stop exports to the U.S. or agree to revise their prices promptly to eliminate any dumping margin. An investigation may be suspended at any time before a final determination is made. No agreement to suspend an investigation may be made unless effective monitoring of the agreement is practicable and is determined to be in the public interest. *See* dumping.

**S**

### suspension of liquidation

(U.S. Customs) When a preliminary determination of dumping or subsidization, or final determination after a negative preliminary determination is affirmative, there is a provision for suspension of liquidation of all entries of merchandise subject to the determination which are entered, or withdrawn from warehouse, for consumption, on or after the date of the publication of the notice in the Federal Register. Customs is directed to require a cash deposit, or the posting of a bond or other security, for each entry affected equal to the estimated amount of the subsidy or the amount by which the fair value exceeds the U.S. price. When an administrative review is completed, Customs is directed to collect the final subsidy rate or amount by which the foreign market value exceeds the U.S. price, and to require for each entry thereafter a cash deposit equal to the newly determined subsidy rate or margin of dumping. *See* liquidation; dumping.

### swap (transaction)

(banking/finance/foreign exchange) A spot purchase of foreign exchange (currency swaps), fixed or floating rate funds (interest rate swaps) or assets (asset swaps) with simultaneous forward sale or vice versa.

Pase financiero is an Argentinian system, related to the swap system, whereby persons or institutions making capital investments are given an "exchange guarantee," which guarantees that the funds can be reexchanged at a predetermined exchange rate on a specific date. The French government is recommending the term crédit croisé but it is fighting a losing battle.

(foreign exchange) Sale of one currency against another currency at a specific maturity and the simultaneous repurchase from the same counterparty at a different maturity. Normally, one of the maturity dates will be that of spot operations. *See* countertrade.

### SWIFT

(banking). Acronym for Society for Worldwide Interbank Financial Telecommunication. A co-operative organization founded in Brussels in 1973 that promotes the standardization of global communications links for data processing and a common language for international financial transactions. Specifically, the society operates secure standardized messaging services and interface software to 7,500 financial institutions in 200 countries for financial messages related to letters of credit and various other forms of international payments. As of March 2004, ten million SWIFT messages were being sent and received each business day. SWIFT has offices in 14 countries. For information go to: www.swift.com or contact at:

SWIFT (Headquarters); Avenue Adèle 1; B-1310 La Hulpe; Belgium; Tel: [32] 2 655 31 11; Fax: [32] 2 655 32 26; SWIFT BIC: SWHQ BE BB.

SWIFT (USA); 7 Times Square, 45th floor, New York, NY 10036 USA; Tel: [1] (212) 455-1800; Fax: [1] (212) 455-1817; SWIFT BIC: SWHQ US 3N

### switch

(railroads/logistics) (a) To move railway cars around a railyard or terminal. (b) To detach a railway car from one train and attach it to another.

### switch arrangements

(commerce/banking) A form of countertrade in which the seller sells on credit and then transfers the credit to a third party. *See* countertrade.

### switch engine

(railroads/logistics) A railroad engine used to move railway cars around a railyard or terminal.

### switching and terminal company

(logistics) A company that provides specialized terminal services to carriers including switching, terminal trackage, bridges or ferries. These firms sometimes operate cargo and passenger services.

### System for Tracking Export License Applications (STELA)

(U.S.) STELA is a U.S. Department of Commerce, Bureau of Industry and Security (formerly the Bureau of Export Administration) computer-generated voice unit that provides callers with the status of their license and classification applications. STELA enables a caller to check on an export license by making a telephone call to [1] (202) 482-2752. *See* Bureau of Industry and Security.

**S**

# T

### 24-Hour Rule
(U.S. Customs) An amendment to the U.S. Trade Act of 2002 requiring that sea carriers and NVOCCs (Non-Vessel Operating Common Carriers) provide U.S. Customs and Border Protection (CBP) with detailed descriptions of the contents of sea containers bound for the United States 24 hours before the container is loaded on board a vessel. The cargo information required is that which is reasonably necessary to enable high-risk shipments to be identified for purposes of ensuring cargo safety and security and preventing smuggling pursuant to the laws enforced and administered by CBP. This information must be detailed and be transmitted electronically through approved systems.

Foreign exporters to the U.S., domestic U.S. exporters and importers, and foreign importers of U.S. products are also affected by these new regulations, because the bulk of the data forwarded to CBP by the carriers and NVOCCs originates from these groups. If transmittal of information is either incomplete, misleading or not timely, it can cause a number of potentially serious problems for the trader, including: 1) CBP may issue a "No Load" order to the carrier, effectively keeping the shipment at port and subjecting the shipment to storage charges and the importer and exporter to possible lost commercial opportunities, 2) Having the shipment become the target of additional scrutiny by CBP and possibly subjecting it to intense cargo examinations, and 3) Potential denial or delays in obtaining permission to unlade the cargo at a U.S. port.

For information go to: www.cbp.gov. *See* the 24-Hour Rule section of the Security Appendix.

### table of denial orders
(U.S.) A list of individuals and firms which have been disbarred from shipping or receiving U.S. goods or technology. Firms and individuals on the list may be disbarred with respect to either controlled commodities or general destination (across-the-board) exports.

### taka
The currency of Bangladesh. 1Tk=100 paise.

### tala
The currency of Western Samoa. 1WS$=100 sene.

### tally sheet
(logistics) A record of the particulars of freight being loaded or unloaded, including quantities, descriptions and marks.

### tandem
(trucking) A vehicle, such as a tractor or semitrailer, with a close coupled pair of rear axles.

### tank car
(trucking/rail transport) A tank carried on a railway car frame for carriage by rail or by road. Tank cars are used for the shipment of bulk liquids or gases. *See* tank container.

### tank container
(logistics) A receptacle used for holding, storing or transporting liquid or gas in bulk. The typical tank container consists of a tank encased in a framework of a standard 10-, 20-, or 40-foot length container. Some tank containers are divided into separate internal sections. *See* tank car.

### tanker
(shipping/rail transport) A truck trailer, barge, container or vessel specially designed to transport bulk liquids such as crude oil, refined petroleum, liquid chemicals, cooking oil or orange juice.

### tapering rate
(logistics) A cargo shipping rate that increases with distance traveled, but not in as great a proportion as the distance traveled. For example, the rate for cargo shipped 2,000 km might only be 60 percent greater than the rate for shipping the same cargo 1,000 km.

### tare or tare weight
(shipping) The weight of a container and/or packing materials, but without the goods being shipped. The gross weight of a shipment less the net weight of the goods being shipped.

### tariff
(general) A comprehensive list or "schedule" of merchandise with applicable rates to be paid or charged for each listed article.

(shipping) A schedule of shipping rates charged, together with governing rules and regulations. A tariff sets forth a contract of carriage for the shipper, the consignee, and the carrier. Individual carriers also publish their own tariffs covering special services. International tariffs containing freight rates of the U.S. international carriers are published by the U.S. flag carriers.

(customs) A schedule of duties or taxes assessed by a government on goods as they enter (or leave) a country. Tariffs may be imposed to protect domestic industries from imported goods and/or to generate revenue. Types include ad valorem, specific, variable, or compound. In the United States, the imposition of tariffs is made on imported goods only.

Tariffs raise the prices of imported goods, thus making them less competitive within the market of the importing country. Tariffs are much less important measures of protection than they used to be.

*See* ad valorem; specific rate of duty; variable rate of duty; compound rate of duty.

### tariff anomaly
(customs) A tariff anomaly exists when the tariff on raw materials or semi-manufactured goods is higher than the tariff on the finished product.

### tariff escalation
(customs) A situation in which tariffs on manufactured goods are relatively high, tariffs on semi-processed goods are moderate, and tariffs on raw materials are nonexistent or very low.

### tariff quotas
(customs) Application of a higher tariff rate to imported goods after a specified quantity of the item has entered the country at a lower prevailing rate. *See* quota.

### tariff schedule
(customs) A comprehensive list of the goods which a country may import and the import duties applicable to each product. *See* Harmonized System; Harmonized Tariff Schedule of the United States.

### Tariff Schedule of the United States
*See* Harmonized Tariff Schedule of the United States.

### tariff trade barriers
*See* trade barriers.

### tariff war
When one nation increases the tariffs on goods imported from, or exported to another country, and that country then follows by raising tariffs itself in a retaliatory manner.

### tau
(foreign exchange) The price change of a foreign exchange option for a 1 percent change in the implied volatility.

### tax haven
(trade) A nation offering low tax rates and other incentives for individuals and businesses of other countries.

### Tax Information Exchange Agreement
An agreement concluded between the U.S. and a beneficiary country designated pursuant to the Caribbean Basin Economic Recovery Act of 1983. This agreement generally involves an expanded version of the standard exchange of information article usually included in a bilateral income tax treaty. The U.S. has similar agreements with most major trading partners. Like the standard tax treaty exchange of information article, a TIEA imposes on the agreeing countries a mutual and reciprocal obligation to exchange information relating to the enforcement of their respective tax laws.

### Technical Advisory Committee(s)
(U.S.) Voluntary groups of industry and government representatives who provide guidance and expertise to the U.S. Department of Commerce on technical and export control matters, including evaluation of technical issues; worldwide availability, use and production of technology; and licensing procedures related to specific industries. TACs have been set up for: (1) materials, (2) biotechnology, (3) computer systems, (4) electronics (formerly "semiconductors"), (5) sensors (formerly "electronic instrumentation"), (6) materials processing equipment (formerly "automated manufacturing equipment"), (7) military critical technologies, (8) telecommunications equipment, and (9) transportation and related equipment. *See* United States Department of Commerce.

### technical analysis
(economics/foreign exchange) The analysis of past price and volume trends–often with the help of chart analysis–in a market, in order to be able to make forecasts about the future price developments of the commodity being traded. Technical exchange rate analysis is often used in professional dealing for short-term foreign exchange rate forecasts.

### technical barrier to trade
A specification which sets forth stringent standards a product must meet (such as levels of quality, performance, safety, or dimensions) in order to be imported. A technical barrier to trade has the effect of adding to the cost of an imported article, thereby making it less competitive in the marketplace when compared to domestically produced articles.

### technical data
Information of any kind that can be used, or adapted for use, in the design, production, manufacture, utilization, or reconstruction of articles or materials. All software is technical data. Technical data can be either "tangible" or "intangible." Models, prototypes, blueprints or operating manuals (even if stored on recording media) are examples of tangible technical data. Intangible technical data consists of technical services, such as training, oral advice, information, guidance and consulting.

### technology transfer
The transfer of knowledge generated and developed in one place to another, where is it is used to achieve some practical end. Technology may be transferred in many ways: by giving it away (technical journals, conferences, emigration of technical experts, technical assistance programs); by industrial espionage; or by sale (patents, blueprints, industrial processes, and the activities of multinational corporations).

### TECRO/AIT Carnet
(customs) TECRO is the acronym for the Taiwan Economic and Cultural Representative Office in the United States and AIT is the acronym for the American Institute in Taiwan. TECRO/AIT Carnets are carnets issued to applicants who wish to temporarily import commercial samples and/or professional equipment to Taiwan. For further information, go to www.carnetsonline.com or in the U.S. call 1 (800) CARNETS. See also American Institute in Taiwan, ATA Carnet, carnet.

### telegraphic transfer (TT)
(banking) The electronic transfer of money from one bank to another, typically at the request of customers.

### telephony
(communications) (a) The science and technology of telecommunications. (b) The science and technology of converting voice and other audio into electrical or digital signals, which can be transmitted by wire, fiber optics or radio and reconverted to audible sound upon receipt.
Telephony ("far voice" in Greek) has entered the world of personal computers with inexpensive after market add-on boards that combine the functions of modems, sound boards, speakerphones and voice mail systems.

### telex
(communications, obsolete) Acronym for teleprinter exchange. A printed message transmitted from and to teleprinters over public telecommunications networks. Teleprinters (popularly known as telex machines) were very large and noisy character printers that operated as electric typewriters and were fed paper from a continuous roll. Telexes have been completely obsoleted by fax machines and now by e-mail and other forms of messaging such as SWIFT (for messaging between banks).

### temperature controlled ground handling
(air freight) Many of the commodities moving in air freight must be protected against sudden changes in temperatures. The temperature of a jet freighter's cabin is ideal to maintain perishables in peak condition; but the increase in the shipment of perishables by air required new strides in ground handling to protect cargoes from spoilage induced by marked differences in temperatures often encountered on the ground at points of origin and destination. To meet these needs the airlines have, at some cities, special equipment and facilities ranging from heated vans to temperature controlled holding rooms in which 100,000 pounds of perishables can be held at one time.

### temporary importation under bond (TIB)
(U.S. Customs) Temporary admission into the United States under a conditional bond for articles not imported for sale or for sale on approval.
Certain classes of goods may be admitted into the United States without the payment of duty, under bond, for their exportation within one year from the date of importation when they are not imported for sale, or for sale on approval. Generally, the amount of the bond is double the estimated duties. The one-year period for exportation may, upon application to the district or port director of Customs, be extended for one or more further periods which, when added to the initial one year, shall not exceed a total of three years. There is an exception in the case of automobiles or any parts thereof which are subject to a total period of six months which may not be extended.
Merchandise entered under TIB must be exported before expiration of the bond period, or any extension, to avoid assessment of liquidated damages in the amount of the bond. Classes of goods which may be entered under a TIB include a wide range of merchandise. Some examples are: (1) merchandise to be repaired or altered; (2) wearing apparel for use as samples; (3) articles imported by illustrators or photographers for use solely as models; (4) samples for use in taking orders; (5) articles solely for examination with a view to reproduction; (6) articles intended solely for testing; (7) automobiles and other motor vehicles, boats, balloons, racing shells etc. and the usual equipment of the

forgoing, imported by non-residents for the purposes of taking part in races; (8) locomotives and railway equipment for use in clearing obstructions; (9) containers for holding merchandise; (10) articles of special design for temporary use in connection with the manufacture of articles for export; (11) animals brought into the United States for the purposes of breeding; (12) theatrical scenery, properties and costumes; (13) works of fine art brought in by lecturers; (14) automobiles, other motor vehicles, and parts thereof brought in for show purposes.

**Relief from Liability**. Relief from liability under bond may be obtained in any case in which the articles are destroyed under Customs supervision, in lieu of exportation, within the original bond period. However, in the case of articles imported solely for testing or experimentation, destruction need not be under Customs supervision where articles are destroyed during the course of experiments or tests during the bond period or any lawful extension, but satisfactory proof of destruction shall be furnished to the district or port director with whom the customs entry was filed. *See* ATA Carnet; bond; in bond.

### tender
(shipping) (a) A small vessel which serves a larger vessel in a port for the purpose of supplying provisions and carrying passengers from ship to shore. (b) A vessel that supplies provisions to a ship at sea.

(law) (a) An offer or proposal submitted for acceptance. (b) A public offer to purchase a minimum number of shares of a publicly-traded stock for a fixed price per share. (c) An offer of money in satisfaction of a debt or obligation.

### tenor
(law/banking) The period between the formation of a debt and the date of expected payment.

### terminal
(shipping) An area at the end of a rail, ship, air or truck line which serves as a loading, unloading and transfer point for cargo or passengers, and often includes storage facilities, management offices and repair facilities.

### terminal charge
(logistics) A charge made for services performed at a terminal. Terminal charges can include those for loading, unloading, stevedores, warehousing and drayage.

### terminal delivery allowance
(logistics) A reduction in freight charges or a reduced freight rate based upon the consignor/shipper's agreement to deliver or pick up a shipment at the carrier's terminal.

### terminal handling charge (THC)
(shipping) Fees charged by ocean carriers (shipping lines) and paid by shippers (manufacturers, importers, exporters) for moving containers between container terminals and ships (onloading and offloading).

Traditionally, carriers combined ocean freight and terminal charges at ports in their freight rates. Since the introduction of THCs, freight rates have only covered port-to-port charges, while two separate THCs cover the cost of using container terminals at the port of origin and at the port of destination.

### terminal operator
(logistics) The business entity responsible for the operation of a terminal and its facilities.

### terminal pass
(logistics) A document allowing a delivering or receiving carrier to enter a terminal.

### terminal receipt
(logistics) A document that evidences proof of delivery (for the delivering carrier) and verification of receipt (for the terminal operator) of cargo or equipment at a terminal.

### terms of trade
(economics) The purchasing power of a country's exports in terms of the country's imports. Terms of trade are a measure of how much imports a country can purchase based upon its exports. Changes in the terms of trade are generally measured by comparing changes in the ratio of export prices to import prices. The terms of trade are considered to have improved when a given volume of exports can be exchanged for a larger volume of imports.

### TEU
(logistics) Acronym for twenty-foot equivalent unit. (a) A standard 20-foot international ocean shipping container. (b) A measure of a shipping container's capacity using a standard 20-foot international ocean shipping container as a measuring unit. A 40-foot container is therefore equal to two TEUs. (c) A measure of a container vessel's capacity using a standard 20-foot international ocean shipping container as the measuring unit. d) A measure of a container vessel's load using a standard 20-foot international ocean shipping container as the measuring unit.

### theta
(statistics/foreign exchange) A ratio expressing the price change of an option (i.e. the change in the premium) over a period of time (per time unit). Mathematically, this corresponds to the 1st derivative of the option premium according to the time factor.

### thing in action
(law) A right to bring a legal action to recover personal property, money, damages, or a debt. A seller, for example, who has a right to recover payment for goods and who is not in possession of the buyer's payment has a thing in action, that is, a right to procure payment by lawsuit.

### Third Country Meat Directive
A regulation by which the European Community (EC) controls meat imports based on sanitary requirements. The TCMD requires individual inspection and certification by EC veterinarians of meat plants wishing to export to the EC. *See* European Community.

### Third Mate (3rd Mate)
(shipping) The fourth in command officer on board a ship in the merchant marine. Responsibilities include: bridge watch, plotting the ship's course, following the plot, tracking the ship, using radar, radios, maps, the safety and firefighting equipment, and maintaining the small boats. Third mate is the third level job of six towards becoming a capitan (ordinary seaman, able-bodied seaman, third mate, second mate, chief mate, captain).

### third-party beneficiary
(law) An individual or legal entity that benefits from, but is not a contracting party of, a contract between two or more other individuals or legal entities. A bank, for example, that loans a business owner funds to purchase specific property is a third-party beneficiary to the sales contract between the business owner and seller.

### third party documents
(banking) In letter of credit operations, documents which indicate a party other than the beneficiary of the credit as the consignor of the goods. Banks accept third party transport documents. *See* transport documents; letter of credit.

### third-party insurance
(insurance) Liability insurance.

### third party logistics (3PL)
The integration and management of all logistics services of a complex supply chain. Also, to be the sole point of contact between a customer and its array of logistics and information service providers. This includes storage, transshipment and other value-added services as well as the

services of subcontractors. These are typically complex service chains.

*See also*: first-party logistics, second-party logistics, fourth-party logistics.

### third world countries
(economics) Developing countries, especially in Asia, Africa and Latin America, but excluding communist countries and industrial non-communist countries.

### Three Sisters
(banking) Colloquial name given to the The World Bank, the International Monetary Fund (IMF) and the World Trade Organization (WTO).

### through bill of lading
(shipping) A single bill of lading covering receipt of the cargo at the point of origin for delivery to the ultimate consignee, using two or more modes of transportation. *See* bill of lading; ocean bill of lading.

### through rate
(shipping) A shipping rate applicable from point of origin to destination. A through rate may be either a joint rate or a combination of two or more rates.

### throughput
(logistics) (a) A measure of the number of units or tonnage of shipping containers that pass through a container facility or port in a given period of time. The measure is a function of units received, units shipped and units that remain in the facility. (b) A measure of the number of units of materials or products that pass through a warehouse in a given period of time. The measure is a function of units received, units shipped and units that remain in the facility.

(computers) A measure of the processing power of a computer system based on transactions, batches or other criteria.

### tick
*See* pips.

### tied aid credit
The practice of providing grants and/or concessional loans, either alone or combined with export credits, linked to procurement from the donor country.

### tied loan
(banking) A loan made by a government agency that requires a foreign borrower to spend the proceeds in the lender's country.

### time arbitrage
*See* arbitrage, time.

### time definite services
(logistics) A freight, cargo or courier service standard specifying or guaranteeing delivery either on a specific day or time or within a set number of days or time from receipt.

### time deposits
(banking) Funds invested in a bank for a pre-determined time and at a specific interest rate. For large amounts, conditions can be freely negotiable (maturity, interest rate).

### time draft
(banking) A financial instrument that is payable at a future fixed or determinable date. *See* bill of exchange.

### time value
(finance) The value of an option if the intrinsic value is zero. It merely reflects possible price fluctuations of the underlying instrument, so that at a later point in time the option could achieve an intrinsic value.

### title
(law) A document evidencing legal ownership in goods or real estate (deed). Title can also refer to non-paper documentary rights to legal possession.

### to order
(law/banking/shipping) A term on a financial instrument or title document indicating that it is negotiable and transfer-able. For example, on a bill of lading "to order" means that it is negotiable and transferable by the person or entity whose name appears on the document.

### Tokyo Round
(GATT) The seventh round of multilateral negotiations concerning the General Agreement on Tariffs and Trade (GATT). Begun in 1973, it concluded November 1979, with agreements covering the following: (1) an improved legal framework for the conduct of world trade (which includes preferential tariff and non-tariff treatment in favor of, and among, developing countries as a permanent legal feature of the world trading system); (2) non-tariff measures (subsidies and countervailing measures; technical barriers to trade; government procurement; customs valuation; import licensing procedures; a revision of the 1967 GATT anti-dumping code); (3) bovine meat; (4) dairy products; (5) tropical products; and (6) an agreement on free trade in civil aircraft.

Participating countries (99) also agreed to reduce tariffs on thousands of industrial and agricultural products. These cuts were gradually implemented over a period of eight years ending January 1, 1987. The total value of trade affected by Tokyo Round most-favored-nation (MFN) tariff reductions, and by bindings of prevailing tariff rates, amounted to more than US$300 billion, measured on MFN imports in 1981. As a result of these cuts, the weighted average (the average tariff measured against actual trade flows) on manufactured products in the world's nine major industrial markets declined 7.0 to 4.7 percent, representing a 34 percent reduction of customs collection. This can be contrasted with the average tariff of around 40 percent at the time of GATT's establishment in the late 1940's. Since the tariff-cutting formula adopted by most industrialized countries resulted in the largest reductions generally being made in the highest duties, the customs duties of different countries were brought closer together or "harmonized."

*See* General Agreement on Tariffs and Trade; rounds; Uruguay Round; World Trade Organization.

### tolar
The currency of Slovenia. 1SiT=100 stotinev.

### tom/next
(foreign exchange) Swap transaction where the spot side becomes due on the business day following the day on which the contract was concluded and where the forward side becomes due on the day after, i.e. on the normal spot value date.

### ton
(measure) A unit of mass or weight equal to 1.1016 metric tons, 2,240 pounds, or 1,016.06 kilograms.

### ton mile
(shipping) The transport of one ton of cargo for one mile. Used most often in air cargo services.

### tonne
(measure) The French spelling of "ton" used especially in the air cargo industry to denote a metric ton of 1,000 kg or 2,204.6 lbs.

### total average inventory
(logistics) (a) (general) The average of total stock on hand over a specified period of time. (b) (technical) Average normal use inventory plus average lead inventory plus buffer stock inventory.

### total cost analysis
(logistics) A systems approach to assessing the costs and interrelationships of transportation, warehousing, inventory and customer service in relation to providing logistics services.

**total cost of distribution**
(shipping) The sum total of all the costs incurred in the distribution of goods. The total cost of distribution includes such items as: (1) Transportation charges, (2) Inventory carrying costs, (3) Warehousing expenses, (4) Packaging, (5) Insurance, (6) Product obsolescence while en route or in storage, and (7) Pilferage.

**total loss**
(insurance) An actual total loss occurs when the goods are destroyed, when the assured is irretrievably deprived of their possession or when they arrive so damaged as to cease to be a thing of the kind insured. Examples of this last, which is spoken of as a "loss of specie," are cement arriving as rock or textiles as rags. Disasters likely to give rise to total loss include fire, sinking or stranding of the vessel, collision and loss overboard in the course of loading or discharge.

**trace**
(logistics) To obtain information about the whereabouts of cargo, equipment or a container by researching its movements from its point of origin or from its last known location.

**tracer**
(shipping) (a) A request upon a transportation line to trace a shipment for the purpose of expediting its movement or establishing delivery;
(general/banking) (b) A request for an answer to a communication, or for advice concerning the status of a subject.

**track**
(logistics) (a) A pair of parallel rails providing a runway for trains. (b) To research the movement of a shipment of cargo, equipment or a container (full or empty) from its point of origin to its final delivery point. (c) To maintain current status information on a shipment of cargo, or container (full or empty) at every stage of the shipping process. The most modern tracking systems using "smart container" technology are able to identify the exact location of a shipment anywhere in the world at any time.

**tracking; tracing**
(shipping) A carrier's system of recording movement intervals of shipments from origin to destination.

**tractor**
(shipping) A vehicle with four or more wheels designed and used primarily for drawing other vehicles such as a trailer or semitrailer and not designed to carry a load itself other than part of the weight of the vehicle and load being drawn.

**Trade Act of 1974**
(U.S. law) Legislation enacted late in 1974 and signed into law in January 1975, granting the president broad authority to enter into international agreements to reduce import barriers. Major purposes were to: (1) stimulate U.S. economic growth and to maintain and enlarge foreign markets for the products of U.S. agriculture, industry, mining and commerce; (2) strengthen economic relations with other countries through open and non-discriminatory trading practices; (3) protect American industry and workers against unfair or injurious import competition; and (4) provide "adjustment assistance" to industries, workers and communities injured or threatened by increased imports. The Act allowed the president to extend tariff preferences to certain imports from developing countries and set conditions under which Most-Favored-Nation Treatment could be extended to non-market economy countries and provided negotiating authority for the Tokyo Round of multilateral trade negotiations. *See* trade adjustment assistance; most favored nation; Tokyo Round.

**Trade Act of 2002**
(U.S. law) Legislation enacted by the U.S. Congress dealing with a number of trade issues. Highlights:
• Extends and expands Trade Adjustment Assistance to U.S. workers, firms and farmers adversely affected by trade.
• Authorizes fiscal year 2003 and 2004 appropriations for the U.S. Customs and Border Protection.
• Special provisions for antiterror and narcotics interdiction.
• Provisions for the examination of mail sent out of the U.S. without a search warrent.
• Requires advance transmission of electronic cargo information to the U.S. Customs and Border Protection. (The so-called 24-Hour Rule.)
• Gives the President certain authority to negotiate trade pacts.
• Renews and enhances the benefits available to Bolivia, Ecuador, Colombia and Peru under the Andean Trade Preference Act (ATPA).
• Expands the benefits, and clarifies the provisions of, the Caribbean Basin Economic Recovery Act (CBERA) and the African Growth and Opportunity Act (AGOA).
• Renews and extends the Generalized System of Preferences (GSP) program to December 31, 2006.
• Establishes a fund for payments to the World Trade Organization (WTO) in settlement of disputes.
Full text of the Trade Act of 2002 can be found at: www.doleta.gov/tradeact/directives/107PL210.pdf.

**trade adjustment assistance (TAA)**
(U.S.) TAA for firms and workers is authorized by the 1974 Trade Act. TAA for firms is administered by the U.S. Department of Commerce; TAA for workers is administered by the U.S. Department of Labor.
Eligible firms must show that increased imports of articles like or directly competitive with those produced by the firm contributed importantly to declines in its sales and/or production and to the separation or threat of separation of a significant portion of the firm's workers. These firms receive help through Trade Adjustment Assistance Centers (TAACs), primarily in implementing adjustment strategies in production, marketing, and management.
Eligible workers must be associated with a firm whose sales or production have decreased absolutely due to increases in like or directly competitive imported products resulting in total or partial separation of the employee and the decline in the firm's sales or production. Assistance includes training, job search and relocation allowances, plus reemployment services for workers adversely affected by the increased imports. E-mail: info@taacenters.org; Web: www.taacenters.org.
*See* United States Department of Commerce; United States Department of Labor.

**Trade Agreements Act of 1979**
(U.S.) Legislation authorizing the U.S. to implement trade agreements dealing with non-tariff barriers negotiated during the Tokyo Round of the General Agreement on Tariffs and Trade (GATT), including agreements that required changes in existing U.S. laws, and certain concessions that had not been explicitly authorized by the Trade Act of 1974. The Act incorporated into U.S. law the Tokyo Round (GATT) agreements on dumping, customs valuation, import licensing procedures, government procurement practices, product standards, civil aircraft, meat and dairy products, and liquor duties. The Act also extended the president's authority to negotiate trade agreements with foreign countries to reduce or eliminate non-tariff barriers to trade.

*See* General Agreement on Tariffs and Trade; Tokyo Round.

### Trade and Development Agency (TDA)
(U.S.) Initially started as the Trade and Development Program within the Agency for International Development, the TDA was spun off as an independent agency in 1981. TDA offers tied aid and resembles Japan's tied aid funding. The program provides project planning funding only for projects that are priorities of the host country and present a good opportunity for sales of U.S. goods and services. Contact: U.S. Trade and Development Agency; 1000 Wilson Boulevard, Suite 1600, Arlington, VA 22209-3901 USA; Tel: [1] (703) 875-4357; Fax: [1] (703) 875-4009; E-mail: info@tda.gov; Web: www.tda.gov.

### trade balance
*See* current balance; balance of payments.

### trade barriers
Any one or group of tariff or non-tariff barriers to trade often classified into eight general categories: (1) import policies (tariffs and other import charges, quantitative restrictions, import licensing, and customs barriers); (2) standards, testing, labeling, and certification; (3) government procurement; (4) export subsidies; (5) lack of intellectual property protection; (6) service barriers; (7) investment barriers; and (8) other barriers (e.g., barriers encompassing more than one category or barriers affecting a single sector). *See* technical barrier to trade; tariff; quota.

### trade concordance
Trade concordance refers to the matching of Harmonized System (HS) codes to larger statistical definitions, such as the Standard Industrial Classification (SIC) code and the Standard International Trade Classification (SITC) system. The U.S. Bureau of the Census, the United Nations, as well as individual U.S. Federal and private organizations, maintain trade concordances for the purpose of relating trade and production data. *See* Harmonized System.

### trade credit
(commerce) (a) Credit extended to a customer (e.g., a businesses, a government or government agency, non-profit organization or individual) for the sale of goods or services. (b) Credit extended by one government to another for the purchase of exports. (c) The accounts receivable and/or trade acceptances of a business purchased by a bank or financial institution, at a discount for immediate payment.

### trade deficit
(economics) A nation's excess of imports over exports over a period of time.

### trade event
A promotional activity that may include a demonstration of products or services and brings together in one viewing area the principals in the purchase and sale of the products or services. As a generic term, trade events may include trade fairs, trade missions, trade shows, catalog shows, matchmaker events, foreign buyer missions, and similar functions.

### Trade Expansion Act of 1962
(U.S. law) The Act provided authority for U.S. participation in the Kennedy Round of the General Agreement on Tariffs and Trade (GATT). The legislation granted the president general authority to negotiate, on a reciprocal basis, reductions of up to 50 percent in U.S. tariffs. The Act explicitly eliminated the "Peril Point" provision that had limited U.S. negotiating positions in earlier GATT Rounds, and instead called on the Tariff Commission, the U.S. International Trade Commission, and other federal agencies to provide information regarding the probable economic effects of specific tariff concessions. This Act superseded the Trade Agreements Act of 1934, as amended. *See* General Agreement on Tariffs and Trade; peril point.

### trade fair
A stage-setting event in which firms of several nationalities present their products or services to prospective customers in a pre-formatted setting (usually a booth of a certain size which is located adjacent to other potential suppliers). A distinguishing factor between trade fairs and trade shows is size. A trade fair is generally viewed as having a larger number of participants than other trade events, or as an event bringing together related industries.

### Trade Fair Certification Program
(U.S.) The U.S. Department of Commerce Trade Fair Certification program was started in 1983 to promote selected privately organized trade shows. The program helps private sector organizations in mounting certified international fairs. The Department of Commerce assistance includes promoting the fair among foreign customers and helping exhibitors to make commercial contacts. *See* United States Department of Commerce.

### Trade Information Center
(U.S.) A U.S. government one-stop source for information on Federal programs to assist U.S. exporters; Tel: [1] (800) USA-TRADE; Fax: [1] (202) 482-4473. Contact: Trade Information Center, U.S. Department of Commerce, 14th St. and Constitution Ave. NW, Washington, DC 20230 USA; Web: www.ita.doc.gov/td/tic.

### trade lane
(logistics) A carrier route between a point of origin and a point of destination.

### trade loss
(insurance) The ordinary and unavoidable loss of weight caused by evaporation as in ore shipments. May also include shortages due to other causes which are considered normal and unavoidable. These losses are generally uninsurable.

### trade mission
Generically, a trade mission is composed of individuals who are taken as a group to meet with prospective customers overseas. Missions visit specific individuals or places with no specific stage setting other than appointments. Appointments are made with government and/or commercial customers, or with individuals who may be a stepping stone to customers.

(U.S.) International Trade Administration (ITA) trade missions are scheduled in selected countries to help participants find local agents, representatives, and distributors, to make direct sales, or to conduct market assessments. Some missions include technical seminars to support sales of sophisticated products and technology in specific markets. ITA missions include planning and publicity, appointments with qualified contacts and with government officials, market briefings and background information on contacts, as well as logistical support and interpreter service. Trade missions also are frequently organized by other Federal, State, or local agencies.

### trade name
(law) The name under which an organization conducts business, or by which the business or its goods and services are identified. It may or may not be registered as a trademark.

### Trade Negotiations Committee
(WTO/GATT) The steering group that historically has managed the GATT and WTO trade negotiation rounds. For information on the Trade Negotiations Committee for the 9th (current) round of negotiations, go to the WTO's Web site at Web: www.wto.org/english/tratop_e/dda_e/tnc_e.htm. *See* rounds (of trade negotiations), General

Agreement on Tariffs and Trade, World Trade Organization.

### Trade Opportunities Program (TOP)
(U.S.) An International Trade Administration service which provides sales leads from overseas firms seeking to buy or represent U.S. products and services. Through overseas channels, U.S. foreign commercial officers gather leads and details, including specifications, quantities, end use, and delivery deadlines. TOP leads can be obtained in an electronic format from the Commerce Department's STAT-USA hotline at [1] (800) STAT-USA or through the Department's STAT-USA/Internet service at Web: www.stat-usa.com.

### Trade Policy Committee (TPC)
(U.S.) A cabinet-level, interagency trade committee established by the Trade Expansion Act of 1962 (chaired by the U.S. Trade Representative) to provide broad guidance on trade issues. Members include the Secretaries of Commerce, State, Treasury, Agriculture, and Labor. The Committee was renewed by an Executive Order at the end of the Carter Administration. Toward the end of the first Reagan Administration, with much dissension over Japan policy between the TPC, the Senior Interagency Group (chaired by Treasury), and the other groups, the White House created the Economic Policy Council (EPC) in 1985 as a single forum to reduce tensions. *See* Economic Policy Council.

### Trade Policy Review Mechanism
The TPRM was created at the General Agreement on Tariffs and Trade (GATT) Uruguay Round mid-term ministerial meeting in Montreal. Under the TPRM, the trade policies of any GATT contracting party were subject to regularly scheduled review by the GATT Council. Reviews led to recommendations on ways to improve a contracting party's trade policies. *See* General Agreements on Tariffs and Trade; Uruguay Round.

### Trade Promotion Coordinating Committee
(U.S.) The president established the TPCC in May 1990 to unify and streamline the government's decentralized approach to export promotion. TPCC members include Departments of Commerce (as chair), State, Treasury, Agriculture, Defense, Energy, and Transportation, the Office of Management and Budget, the U.S. Trade Representative, the Council of Economic Advisers, Eximbank, the Overseas Private Investment Corporation, the U.S. Information Agency, the Agency for International Development, the Trade and Development Program, and the Small Business Administration. The TPCC chair office is at the U.S. Department of Commerce. 19 agencies are on the committee. The Trade Information Center was created as one of the main missions of the TPCC. The TPCC is not a body which would be contacted by the general public. If you have questions about what they do, or how it works, call [1] (800) USA-TRADE or visit http://tradecenter.ntis.gov/tpcc.htm.

### trade-related aspects of intellectual property rights (TRIPs)
(WTO) TRIPs refers to intellectual property rights objectives in the General Agreement on Tariffs and Trade (GATT) Uruguay Round and the successor World Trade Organization (WTO). These objectives include achieving a comprehensive agreement that would include: (1) substantive standards of protection for all areas of intellectual property (patents, trademarks, copyrights, etc.); (2) effective enforcement measures (both at the border and internally); and (3) effective dispute settlement provisions. *See* Uruguay Round, World Trade Organization.

### trade show
A trade show is a stage-setting event in which firms present their products or services to prospective customers in a pre-formatted setting (usually a booth of a certain size which is located adjacent to other potential suppliers). The firms are generally in the same industry but not necessarily of the same nationality. A distinguishing factor between trade fairs and trade shows is size. A trade show is generally viewed as a smaller assembly of participants.

### Trade Support Network (TSN)
(U.S. Customs) A group started in 1994 by the then U.S. Customs Service (now the U.S. Customs and Border Protection) to provide a forum for the discussion of significant Customs-related redesign efforts. There are over 150 members of the TSN that represent various segments of the trade community, including trade associations, importers, brokers, carriers, sureties and others.
The Network has a number of committees and sub-committees whose purpose is to identify legal, procedural or systems issues and priorities specific to the business area and to submit user requirements where appropriate.
For more information, go to: www.cbp.gov.

### trade surplus
(economics) A nation's excess of exports over imports over a period of time.

### Trade Tariff Act of 1930
(U.S. law) U.S. statutes originally enacted in 1930 and amended periodically that impose duties payable for the importation of articles into the United States and that contain schedules of the duties for specific merchandise. The Act is found at 19 United States Code, sections 1202, et seq.

### trade terms
(a) The terms of a sale. The setting of responsibilities of the buyer and seller in a sale, including: sale price, responsibility for shipping, insurance and customs duties. (b) One of the several recognized sets of definitions of trade terms. The most widely used trade terms are Incoterms 2000, which are published by the International Chamber of Commerce, which have replaced the now obsolete Revised American Foreign Trade Definitions. *See* Incoterms; International Chamber of Commerce.

### trade-weighted revaluation rate
(foreign exchange) The change in value of a currency is ascertained in terms of an index against a basket of currencies. The make-up of the currencies in the basket and their weighting are determined according to the percentage of exports of the country whose currency is to be valued with its trading partners.

### trademark
(law) A distinctive identification of a manufactured product or of a service taking the form of a name, logo, motto, and so on; a trademarked brand has legal protection and only the owner can use the mark.
A trademark is distinguished from a servicemark in that the former identifies products while the later identifies services.
Trademark protection varies from country to country, and may not be available in some jurisdictions. If trademark protection is available under the laws of a particular country, a trademark may usually be registered only if it is distinguishable from other registered trademarks and if it contains a name, brand, label, signature, word, letter, numeral, device, or any combination of these items. A country that is a member the Paris Convention for the Protection of Industrial Property may recognize trademarks held in other jurisdictions.

(U.S.) Organizations that file an application at the U.S. Patent Office and use the brand for five years may be granted a trademark. A firm may lose a trademark that has become generic. Generic names are those which consumers use to identify the product, rather than to specify a particular brand (e.g., escalator, aspirin and nylon).
*See* copyright; service mark; patent; World Intellectual Property Organization; Patent Cooperation Treaty.

**tradeoffs**
(shipping) Interaction between related activities such as the offsetting of higher costs in one area with reduced costs or other benefits in another. In air freight, for example, the classic "tradeoff" is one of time (quick delivery) versus money (greater expense).

**traffic**
(logistics) The aggregate of passengers or conveyances (e.g., automobiles, ships, trains, trucks, etc.) coming and going in a geographic area (e.g., street, port, station, truck terminal) during a set period of time (e.g., hour, day, month, year).
(commerce) The buying and selling of a commodity, especially an illicit drug or product.
(data communications) The aggregate of activity on a given communications system (e.g., telephone trunk line, Internet) during a set period of time.

**trailer**
(logistics/trucking) A non-motorized cargo vehicle supported by wheels at each of four corners and designed to be drawn by a motorized vehicle such as a tractor. *See* semi-trailer, tractor.

**trailer on flatcar (TOFC)**
(logistics/trucking/rail transport) A truck trailer or semi-trailer transported on a rail flatcar. This is a multi-modal form of transportation often used when the rail leg of the route is less costly than transportation by roadway. Also called piggyback. *See* trailer.

**tramp line**
(shipping) A transportation line operating tramp steamers.

**tramp steamer**
(shipping) A steamship which does not operate under any regular schedule from one port to another, but calls at any port where cargo may be obtained.

**transaction value**
(general) The price actually paid or payable for merchandise.
(U.S. Customs) U.S. Customs officers are required by law to determine the value of imported merchandise. Valuation is necessary for statistical purposes as well as to determine the amount of import duty which must be paid if the duty rate is stated as a percentage of value (ad valorem duty).
The transaction value of imported merchandise is the price actually paid or payable for the merchandise when sold for exportation to the United States, plus amounts for the following items if not included in the price:
(1) The packing costs incurred by the buyer.
(2) Any selling commission incurred by the buyer,
(3) The value of any assist,
(4) Any royalty or license fee that the buyer is required to pay as a condition of the sale, and
(5) The proceeds, accruing to the seller, of any subsequent resale, disposal, or use of the imported merchandise.
The amounts for the above items are added only to the extent that each is not included in the price actually paid or payable and information is available to establish the accuracy of the amount. If sufficient information is not available, then the transaction value cannot be determined and the next basis of value, in order of precedence, must be considered for appraisement.

If the transaction value cannot be used, then certain secondary bases are considered. The secondary bases of value, listed in order of precedence for use, are:
(1) Transaction value of identical merchandise,
(2) Transaction value of similar merchandise,
(3) Deductive value, and
(4) Computed value.
The order of precedence of the last two values can be reversed if the importer so requests.
*See* valuation; identical merchandise; similar merchandise; computed value; deductive value; assist.

**transferable letter of credit**
(banking) A letter of credit where the beneficiary specified in the credit has the option of instructing his bank to transfer the credit fully or in part to another beneficiary.
A letter of credit can only be transferred if it is expressly designated as "transferable" by the issuing bank. This type of letter of credit enables intermediaries (first beneficiaries) to offer security in the form of a letter of credit to their suppliers (second beneficiaries). *See* letter of credit.

**transfer of technology**
The movement of modem or scientific methods of production or distribution from one enterprise, institution or country to another, as through foreign investment, international trade licensing of patent rights, technical assistance or training.

**transfer pricing**
(law/customs) The overpricing of imports and/or underpricing of exports between affiliated companies in different countries for the purpose of transferring profits, revenues or monies out of a country in order to evade taxes.

**transfer risk**
(banking) Currency measures of foreign governments which make it impossible for the debtor to allocate and transfer foreign exchange abroad. Transfer risks can be covered through use of bank guarantees, confirmed letters of credits, export credit agencies, etc.

**transfer pricing**
(a) The setting of prices for products and services between units, subsidiaries, divisions or affiliates of the same organization. For example, a manufacturing company may establish special (lower) prices for products sold to a wholly-owned foreign subsidiary than to a non-owned foreign distributor. (b) The practice of adjusting prices for products and services within units, subsidiaries, divisions or affiliates of the same organization to take advantage of different tax rates in different countries. For example, transfers (sales) to an affiliate in a high-tax country for a high price and transfers to an affiliate in a low-tax country for a low price. The result is to transfer the organization's profits to low-tax countries for overall tax savings.

**transfers (mail, wire, cable)**
(banking) Transfers are the remittance of money by a bank to be paid to a party in another town or city. If the instruction to pay such funds is transmitted by regular mail, the term "mail transfer" is used. Wire transfer is used to designate a transfer of funds from one point to another by wire or telegraph. Cable transfer is used to designate a transfer of funds to a city or town located outside the United States by cable. Commissions or fees are charged for all typed of transfers. When transfers are made by wire or cable, the cost of transmitting the instructions to pay by wire or cable is charged to the remitter in addition to the commission.

**transit**
(logistics) (From the Latin "to go across.")
(a) A journey from one place to another. (b) To make a passage (journey) by ocean vessel. (c) A facility for the movement of passengers or cargo. (d) Local passenger service

on established routes provided to the public in urban areas by bus or light rail and with published fares.

**Transit Air Cargo Manifest**
(shipping-U.S.) Procedures under which air cargo imports move through a gateway city to the city of final U.S. Customs destination for the collection of duty and other import processing, thereby expediting shipment movements, reducing gateway congestion, and saving expense for importers, U.S. Customs and Border Protection and the airlines.

**transit cargo**
(logistics) Cargo that arrives and departs from the same transit point. The term is usually applied to air cargo that arrives and departs on the same flight. Inbound transit cargo may or may not clear customs at the transit point.

**transit zone**
(shipping) A port of entry in a coastal country that is established as a storage and distribution center for the convenience of a neighboring country lacking adequate port facilities or access to the sea. A zone is administered so that goods in transit to and from the neighboring country are not subject to the customs duties, import controls or many of the entry and exit formalities of the host country. A transit zone is a more limited facility then a free trade zone or a free port.

**transmittal letter**
(shipping) A list of the particulars of a shipment and a record of the documents being transmitted together with instructions for disposition of documents. Any special instructions are also included.

**transnational (multinational) corporation**
A business whose operations include supplier and sales networks that cross national borders.

**Trans-Pacific Stabilization Agreement (TSA)**
(logistics) An organization of twelve ocean freight carriers controlling approximately 85 percent of Pacific Ocean freight trade who seek a platform for discussing and sharing mutual concerns. The TSA is not in itself a conference and does not publish rates. The TSA enjoys antitrust immunity although the U.S. Ocean Shipping Reform Act (OSRA) of 1998 has curtailed a significant amount of the group's influence. The TSA consists of the Japan-United States Eastbound Freight Conference (JUSEFC), the Asia North America Eastbound Freight Rate Agreement (ANAERA) and four major non-conference carriers. The twelve members are: APL, Mark Island, NYK, P&O, Hapag-Lloyd, Hyundai, Hanjin, Evergreen, Yang Ming, Orient Overseas Container Lines (OOCL), Cosco and MOL (Mitsui OSK Lines).

**transparency**
The extent to which laws, regulations, agreements, and practices affecting international trade are open, clear, measurable, and verifiable.
(GATT/WTO) Some of the codes of conduct negotiated during the Tokyo Round of the General Agreement on Tariff and Trade sought to increase the transparency of nontariff barriers that impede trade. *See* General Agreement on Tariff and Trade, World Trade Organization.

**Transparency International**
A non-profit, non-governmental organization dedicated to counter corrupt international business and government practices. The organization's stated concerns include: 1) humanitarian, as corruption undermines and distorts development and leads to increasing levels of human rights abuse, 2) democratic, as corruption undermines democracies and in particular the achievements of many developing countries and countries in transition, 3) ethical, as corruption undermines a society's integrity, and 4) practical, as corruption distorts the operations of markets and deprives

ordinary people of the benefits which should flow from them. The organization is headquartered in Germany and has chapter offices around the world. Transparency International, Alt Moabit 96, 10559 Berlin, Germany; Tel: [49] (30) 343-8200; Fax: [49] (30) 3470-3912; E-mail: ti@transparency.org; Web: www.transparency.org.

**transport documents**
(shipping) All types of documents evidencing acceptance, receipt and shipment of goods. Examples: bill of lading; ocean bill of lading; air waybill; rail waybill; dock receipt; etc.

**transportation and exportation entry**
(U.S. Customs) Customs entry used when merchandise arrives in the U.S. and is destined for a foreign country. Under a transportation and exportation entry, merchandise may be transported in bond through U.S. territory. For example, a transportation and exportation entry would be used for merchandise destined for Canada, arriving in Seattle, from Japan. *See* entry; in bond.

**transship**
(logistics) The transfer of freight from one conveyance or carrier to another, or from one ship to another of different ownership.
(economics/commerce) The transfer of merchandise from the country-of-origin to an intermediary country prior to shipment to the destination country for purposes of 1) achieving a lower transport cost, 2) legally or illegally achieving new country of origin status for the merchandise or 3) circumventing the foreign trade policies of the country of origin or the country of destination.

**Travel Advisories**
(U.S.) Reports by the U.S. Department of State to inform traveling U.S. citizens of conditions abroad which may affect them adversely. Travel advisories are generally about physical dangers, unexpected arrests or detention, serious health hazards, and other conditions abroad with serious consequences for traveling U.S. citizens. Travel advisories are available at any of the U.S. passport agencies, field offices of the U.S. Department of Commerce and U.S. Embassies and consulates abroad. They are also available at the Bureau of Consular Affairs, Room 4811, N.S., U.S. Department of State, Washington, DC 20520 USA; Web: http://travel.state.gov/travel/cis_pa_tw/tw/tw_1764.html.

**Travel Industry Association of America (TIA)**
Organizer of the International POW WOW. Contact: Travel Industry Association of America, 2 Lafayette Center, 1100 New York Ave. NW, Suite 450, Washington, DC 20005-3934 USA; Tel: [1] (202) 408-8422; Fax: [1] (202) 408-1255; E-mail: feedback@tia.org; Web: www.tia.org. *See* International POW WOW.

**travel mission**
*See* trade mission.

**traveler**
(U.S.) A traveler is a person who stays for a period of less than 1 year in a country of which he or she is not a resident. Military and other government personnel and their dependents stationed outside their country of residence are not considered travelers, regardless of the length of their stay abroad; they are considered to have remained within the economy of their home country. The definition of travelers also excludes owners or employees of business enterprises who temporarily work abroad in order to further the enterprise's business, but intend to return to their country of residence within a reasonable period of time.

**traveler's checks**
(banking) A form of check especially designed for travelers, including persons on vacation and business trips. These checks are usually preprinted in denominations of US$10,

20, 50, and 100, as well as in other currencies such as the Euro and British pounds Sterling. They can be cashed and used to purchase goods and services at businesses that accept them.

### traveler's letter of credit
(banking) A letter of credit issued by a bank to a customer preparing for an extended trip. The customer pays for the letter of credit, which is issued for a specified period of time in the amount purchased. The bank furnishes a list of correspondent banks or its own foreign branches at which drafts drawn against the letter of credit will be honored. *See* letter of credit.

### Treaty of Fusion
*See* European Community.

### Treaty of Rome
The 1957 Treaty of Rome was intended to create a single market for the European Community, with free movement of goods, persons, services, and capital. Article 30 of the Treaty prohibited not only quantitative restrictions on imports but also all measures having an equivalent effect. *See* European Community.

### triangular trade
(trade) Trade between three countries, in which an attempt is made to create a favorable balance for each.

### trigger price mechanism
(U.S.) System for monitoring imported goods (particularly steel) to identify imports that are possibly being "dumped" in the United States or subsidized by the governments of exporting countries. The minimum price under this system is based on the estimated landed cost at a U.S. port of entry of the product produced by the world's most efficient producers.

Imported products entering the United States below that price may "trigger" formal anti-dumping investigations by the Department of Commerce and the U.S. International Trade Commission. The TPM was first used to protect the U.S. steel industry and was in effect between early 1978 and March 1980. It was reinstated in October 1980 and suspended for all products except for stainless steel wire in January 1982. *See* dumping.

### tri-temp
(shipping) A container that can maintain three exact temperature zones in difference compartments simultaneously.

### tropical products
Traditionally, agricultural goods of export interest to developing countries in the tropical zones of Africa, Latin America, and East Asia (coffee, tea, spices, bananas, and tropical hardwoods).

### truck/air service
(shipping) The surface movement of air freight to and from airports and origin and destination points beyond the terminal area of pickup and delivery service. A directory listing cities served is available through your local airline office.

### truck bill of lading
(logistics) A non-negotiable bill of lading used for domestic shipments by truck. This bill of lading is issued in either a short or long form but with freight rates and charges not shown. Any party may sign to verify receipt of goods unless the bill is marked as "signature service," which requires that the party named by the shipper sign to confirm delivery of goods. *See* bill of lading.

### truck load
A shipment of cargo that fills a given truck either by bulk or maximum weight.

### truckload (TL) carrier
(logistics/trucking) A trucking company that specializes in hauling a trailerload or more of freight at a time for individual shippers, typically delivering to a final destination location directly rather than to a terminal. Compare to an LTL (less than truckload) carrier that carries consolidated cargo for a number of shippers on the same truck and typically delivers the entire load to a terminal before making individual deliveries.

### trust bank (shintaku ginko)
(banking-Japan) Japanese bank involved in both lending and money management.

### trust receipt
(banking) A declaration by a client to a bank that ownership in goods released by the bank are retained by the bank, and that the client has received the goods in trust only.

Release of merchandise by a bank to a buyer in which the bank retains title to the merchandise. The buyer, who obtains the goods for manufacturing or sales purposes, is obligated to maintain the goods (or the proceeds from their sale) distinct from the remainder of his/her assets and to hold them ready for repossession by the bank.

Trust receipts are used under letters of credit or collections so that the buyer may receive the goods before paying the issuing bank or collecting bank. *See* documentary collection; letter of credit.

### tugrik
The currency of Mongolia. 1Tug=100 mongos.

### turnkey
A method of construction whereby the contractor assumes total responsibility from design through completion of the project (and then hands over the "key" to the owner).

### turnkey contract
An agreement under which a builder agrees to complete a facility so that it is ready for use when delivered to the other contracting party. A contractor may agree, for example, to build a fully equipped and operational factory under a turnkey contract. The responsibility of the contractor ends when he hands the completed installation over to the client.

### turns
(logistics) The rate at which inventory moves through a defined cycle, usually expressed as the number of inventory turns per year. Other examples: the speed at which inventory is sold in a retail or distribution environment; the speed at which inventory moves through the entire supply chain; the speed at which inventory moves from a receiving dock to the shipping dock.

### twenty-foot equivalent unit
*See* TEU.

### two-tier market
(foreign exchange) An exchange rate regime which normally insulates a country from the balance of payments effects of capital flows while it maintains a stable exchange rate for current account transactions. Capital transactions are normally required to pass through a "financial" market while current transactions go through an "official" market, though other arrangements are possible. Examples are found in Belgium and the United Kingdom, though France and Italy have experimented with such systems.

### tying arrangement
(law) A condition that a seller imposes on a buyer, requiring that if the buyer desires to purchase one product (tying product), the buyer must also agree to purchase another product (tied product), which the buyer may or may not want. The laws of some countries prohibit certain tying arrangements.

# U

**UCP**
(banking) The Uniform Customs and Practice for Documentary (Letters of) Credit. The universally accepted set of rules governing documentary (letters of) credit transactions in more than 160 countries around the world. Developed by the International Chamber of Commerce (ICC). The current version from 1993, is contained in ICC publication #500, and is referred to simply as UCP 500. *See* International Chamber of Commerce for contact information.

**ud**
(shipping) Abbreviation for upper deck.

**UL**
*See* Underwriters Laboratories, Inc.

**ULD**
*See* unit load device.

**ultimate beneficial owner (UBO)**
(U.S.) The UBO of a U.S. affiliate is that person, proceeding up the affiliate's ownership chain beginning with and including the foreign parent, that is not owned more than 50 percent by another person. The UBO consists of only the ultimate owner, other affiliated persons are excluded. If the foreign parent is not owned more than 50 percent by another person, the foreign parent and the UBO are the same. A UBO, unlike a foreign parent, may be a U.S. person.

**ultimate consignee**
(shipping) The person who is the true party in interest, receiving goods for the designated end-use.

**ultimo day**
(finance/foreign exchange) The last business day or last stock trading day of a month.

**Ultra Large Crude Carrier (ULCC)**
(shipping) An ocean-going crude oil tanker of 300,000 to 550,000 dwt. These are the largest vessels in the world and are used for carrying crude oil on long haul routes from the Arabian Gulf to Europe, America and the Far East, via the Cape of Good Hope. These vessels require custom built terminals for loading and discharge.

**ultra vires**
(law) An act performed without authority to do so. If a contract provision, for example, requires both parties to approve an assignment of the contract but one party agrees to an assignment without obtaining the other's consent, the assignment is ultra vires.

**umbrella rate**
(logistics) A shipping rate system that establishes artificially high minimum rates in order to protect less competitive carriers and carrier modes.

**unclean bill of lading**
*See* claused bill of lading; bill of lading; ocean bill of lading.

**unconfirmed**
(banking) A documentary letter of credit where the advising bank makes no commitment to pay, accept or negotiate. *See* letter of credit; silent confirmation.

**unconscionable**
(law) Unfair or oppressive. A contract with unconscionable terms, for example, favors one party over the other to such an extent that it is unjust, and if the oppressed party made the contract under duress or without meaningful negotiation as to the terms, a court may refuse to enforce it against that party.

**underdeveloped country**
(economics) A nation in which per capita real income is proportionally low when contrasted with the per capita real income of nations where industry flourishes. *See* less developed countries; least developed country; lesser developed country.

**Underwriters Laboratory Inc. (UL)**
(international standards) An independent not-for-profit product safety testing and certification organization. Founded in 1894 in the U.S., UL has developed more than 740 product safety standards and a reputation as the leader in U.S. product safety and certification. The organization is also rapidly becoming one of the most recognized conformity assessment providers in the world. Each year 16 billion UL Marks are applied to products worldwide. Contact: Underwriters Labaratory Inc, 333 Pfingsten Road, Northbrook, IL 60062-2096 USA; Tel: [1] (847) 272-8800; Customer Services: [1] (877) ULHELPS (854-3577); Fax: [1] (847) 272-8129; E-mail: CustomerService.NBK@us.ul.com; Web: www.ul.com.

**UN/EDIFACT**
(logistics) Acronym for United Nations [rules for] Electronic Data Interchange for Administration, Commerce and Transportation. A set of standards, directories and guidelines for the electronic interchange, between computer systems, of structured data and documents, especially those that relate to the international trade in goods and services. Contact: UN/EDIFACT, UN Economic Commission for Europe, Information Service, Palais des Nations, CH - 1211 Geneva 10, Switzerland; Tel: [41] (22) 917-1234; Fax: [41] (22) 917-0505; E-mail: info.ece@unece.org; Web: www.unece.org/trade/untdid. *See* EDI.

**unfair trade practice**
(general) Unusual government support to firms—such as export subsidies to certain anti-competitive practices by firms themselves—such as dumping, boycotts or discriminatory shipping arrangements— that result in competitive advantages for the benefiting firms in international trade.

(U.S.) Any act, policy, or practice of a foreign government that: (1) violates, is inconsistent with, or otherwise denies benefits to the U.S. under any trade agreement to which the United States is a party; (2) is unjustifiable, unreasonable, or discriminatory and burdens or restricts United States commerce; or (3) is otherwise inconsistent with a favorable Section 301 determination by the U.S. Trade Representative. *See* Section 301; dumping.

**Uniform Code Council (UCC)**
(international standards) (Changed name to GS1) An independent not-for-profit standards organization dedicated to the development and distribution of integrated business standards. The UCC administers the Universal Product Code (UPC) and provides other open and global standards for supply chain and business processes in its partnership with EAN (European Article Number) International. The UCC is a primary resource for businesses and provides publications and training in all aspects of identification numbers, bar coding, and electronic commerce. Contact: GS1 US, Princeton Pike Corporate Center, 1009 Lenox Drive, Suite 202, Lawrenceville, NJ 08648 USA; Tel: [1] (609) 620-0200; E-mail: [1] (609) 620-1200; Web: www.uc-council.org.

**Uniform Commercial Code (UCC)**
(U.S. law) A set of statutes purporting to provide some consistency among states' commercial laws. It includes uniform laws dealing with bills of lading, negotiable instruments, sales, stock transfers, trust receipts, and warehouse receipts.

### Uniform Customs and Practice (UCP)

(banking) Full name: Uniform Customs and Practice for Documentary Credits (UCPDC). The internationally recognized codification of rules unifying banking practice regarding documentary credits (letters of credit).

The UCPDC was developed by a working group attached to the International Chamber of Commerce (ICC) in Paris, France. It is revised and updated from time to time and the current valid version as of January 1, 1994 is ICC Publication 500 which is the 1993 edition.

It is highly recommended that all documentary credits (letters of credit) specify that they are subject to the UCPDC. *See* letter of credit; International Chamber of Commerce; and the Appendix for a listing of ICC publications that relate to the UCPDC.

### Uniform Rules for Collections (URC)

(banking) The internationally recognized codification of rules unifying banking practice regarding collection operations for drafts, their payment or non-payment, protest and for documentary collections, (documents against payment, D/P, and documents against acceptance, D/A).

The URC was developed by a working group attached to the International Chamber of Commerce (ICC) in Paris, France. It is revised and updated from time to time and the current valid version as of January 1, 1994 is ICC Publication 322.

*See* documentary collection; International Chamber of Commerce; and the Appendix for a listing of ICC publications that relate to the URC.

### Uniform Warehouse Receipts Act

(U.S. logistics) An act establishing management responsibilities and documentation requirements for public warehouses.

### unit cost

(logistics) (a) The total of all costs associated with the production of a single unit of a product or service. (b) The total of all costs associated with a production run of a product or service divided by the total number of units produced.

### United Nations Conference on Trade and Development (UNCTAD)

UNCTAD was set up in December 1964 as a permanent organ of the UN General Assembly. UNCTAD promotes international trade and seeks to increase trade between developing countries and countries with different social and economic systems. UNCTAD also examines problems of economic development within the context of principles and policies of international trade and seeks to harmonize trade, development, and regional economic policies. The Conference was first convened (UNCTAD-1) in Geneva in 1964.

### United Nations Convention on Contracts for the International Sale of Goods (CISG)

(law) A United Nations-sponsored multilateral treaty containing a commercial code that governs the rights and responsibilities of buyers and sellers in international sales contracts. The CISG was designed to foster international trade by establishing a unified legal framework for the sale of goods internationally. The CISG was finalized at a United Nations conference held in Vienna in 1980 and as a result is sometimes referred to as the Vienna Sales Convention.

There are many similarities between the U.S. UCC (Uniform Commercial Code) and the UN CISG which both serve to avoid misunderstandings when one set of rules govern the buyer and another set of rules govern the seller. The U.S. UCC is designed to avoid differences in the laws of the fifty U.S. states while the CISG is designed to avoid misunderstandings in the laws of the countries of the world.

The CISG specifically does not apply to the sale of services or labor and as a result agreements involving distribution, licensing, leasing, transportation, carriage, insurance and financing are generally not covered. The CISG does not apply to the sale of goods for consumption directly by consumers; goods sold at auction; securities or negotiable instruments; ships, vessels or aircraft; or electricity. The CISG also does not cover liabilities or injuries caused by goods.

Transactions for the sale of computer software, the sale of both goods and services, or sales of leases with purchase options are considered gray areas where the validity of the CISG is in question and subject to legal challenge. For information go to: www.uncitral.org.

### United Nations Industrial Development Organization (UNIDO)

Established in 1967, under the UN Secretariat, UNIDO serves as a specialized agency to foster industrial development in lesser developed countries through offering technical assistance in the form of expert services, supplying equipment and/or training. Contact: United Nations Industrial Development Organization, PO Box 300, 1400 Vienna, Austria; Tel: [43] (1) 26-026-0; Fax: [43] (1) 26-92-669; E-mail: unido@unido.org; Web: www.unido.org.

### United States Affiliate

(U.S. foreign investment) A U.S. business enterprise in which there is foreign direct investment–that is, in which a single foreign person owns or controls, directly or indirectly, 10 percent or more of its voting securities if the enterprise is incorporated or an equivalent interest if the enterprise is unincorporated. The affiliate is called a U.S. affiliate to denote that the affiliate is located in the U.S. (although it is owned by a foreign person). *See* foreign person; affiliate.

### United States and Foreign Commercial Service (US&FCS)

(U.S.) An agency of the U.S. Department of Commerce that helps U.S. firms compete more effectively in the global marketplace. The US&FCS (more commonly known as the U.S. Commercial Service) has a network of trade specialists in 68 U.S. cities and 66 countries worldwide. US&FCS offices provide information on foreign markets, agent/distributor location services, trade leads, and counseling on business opportunities, trade barriers and prospects abroad. Contact: Tel: [1] (800) USA-TRADE; E-mail: TIC@ita.doc.gov

### United States-Canada Free Trade Agreement FTA)

The provisions of the U.S./Canada Free Trade Agreement were adopted by the U.S. with the enactment of the FTA Implementation Act of 1988. The FTA not only reduced tariffs on imported merchandise between Canada and the U.S., but opened up new areas of trade in investment services, agriculture, and business travel. In order to be eligible for FTA treatment, goods must not enter the commerce of a third country, or, if shipped through a third country, must remain under customs control.

Several publications about the United States-Canada Free Trade Agreement are available from: the National Technical Information Service (NTIS), 5285 Port Royal Road, Springfield, VA 22161; Tel: [1] (703) 605-6040; Web: www.ntis.gov.

Other sources of information about the agreement can be obtained from the Office of North American Affairs, Office of the United States Trade Representative (USTR), 600 17th St. NW, Washington, DC 20508 USA; Tel: [1] (888) 473-8787; E-mail: contactustr@ustr.gov; Web: www.ustr.gov.

**U**

### United States Code (USC)

(U.S. law) A set of volumes containing the official compilation of U.S. law. A new edition of the USC is printed every six years with supplemental volumes issued every year. The USC is found in larger public libraries and is available for purchase from the Superintendent of Documents, U.S. Government Printing Office, Mail Stop: IDCC, 732 N. Capitol Street, NW, Washington, DC 20401; Tel: [1] (866) 512-1800, [1] (202) 512-1800; Fax: [1] (202) 512-2104; Web: www.gpoaccess.gov. There are also local offices of the U.S. Government Printing Office in major U.S. cities.

### United States Consumer Product Safety Commission (CPSC)

(United States) The CPSC is the U.S. governmental agency charged with protecting the public from unreasonable risks of serious injury or death from more than 15,000 types of consumer products under the agency's jurisdiction. Deaths, injuries and property damage from consumer product incidents cost the nation more than $700 billion annually. The CPSC is responsible for protecting consumers and families from products that pose a fire, electrical, chemical or mechanical hazard or can injure children. The CPSC's work to ensure the safety of consumer products - such as toys, cribs, power tools, cigarette lighters, and household chemicals - contributed significantly to the 30 percent decline in the rate of deaths and injuries associated with consumer products over the past 30 years. Mailing Contact: U.S. Consumer Product Safety Commission; Washington, D.C. 20207-0001. Street Contact: 4330 East-West Highway; Bethesda, Maryland 20814-4408. Tel: (800) 638-2772, Fax (301) 504-0124/ (301) 504-0025; Web: www.cpsc.gov.

### United States Custom House Guide

(publication) A comprehensive resource for importing goods to the U.S., covering three major topics: 1) Ports of Entry (U.S. and Canadian) and U.S. Import Regulations, 2) the U.S. Harmonized Tariff Schedule and 3) Trade Services Directory and Guide. Available as a print product and as an online service. Contact: Commonwealth Business Media, Inc., 400 Windsor Corporate Center, 50 Millstone Road, Suite 200, East Windsor, New Jersey 08520-1415 USA; Tel: [1] (800) 221-5488; Fax: [1] (609) 371-7718; Web: www.cbizmedia.com.

### United States Customs & Border Protection

(formerly, U.S. Customs Service) U.S. governmental agency, part of the U.S. Department of Homeland Security since 2003, whose major responsibility is to administer the Tariff Act of 1930, as amended. Primary duties include the assessment and collection of all duties, taxes and fees on imported merchandise, and the enforcement of customs and related laws and treaties. As a major enforcement organization, Customs combats smuggling and fraud on the revenue and enforces the regulations of numerous other federal agencies at ports of entry and along the land and sea borders of the U.S.

The customs territory of the United States consists of the 50 states, the District of Columbia, and Puerto Rico. The Customs Bureau has its headquarters in Washington, DC and is headed by a Commissioner of Customs. The field organization consists of seven geographical regions further divided into districts with ports of entry within each district. These organizational elements are headed respectively by regional commissioners, district directors (or area directors in the case of the New York Region), and port directors.

Contact: U.S. Customs & Border Protection, 1300 Pennsylvania Avenue NW, Washington, DC 20229 USA; Tel: [1] (202) 344-1000; Web: www.cbp.gov.

U.S. Customs regional and district offices are in Boston, Massachusetts; New York, NY; Miami, Florida; New Orleans, Louisiana; Houston, Texas; Los Angeles, California; and Chicago, Illinois.

U.S. Customs also has offices in Austria, Belgium, Canada, France, Hong Kong, Italy, Japan, Korea, Mexico, The Netherlands, Panama, Singapore, Thailand, The United Kingdom, Uruguay, and Germany. These offices are a part of the U.S. Embassy complex in each country.

### United States Customs Service

The now obsolete name of the United States Customs and Border Protection (CBP). *See* U.S. Customs and Border Protection.

### United States Department of Agriculture (DOA)

(U.S. government) An executive department which serves as the principal adviser to the president on agricultural policy. The Department works to improve and maintain farm income, implement nutrition programs and develop and expand markets abroad for U.S. agricultural products. It is also charged with inspecting and grading food products for safe consumption. Organizations within the Department of Agriculture include: Agricultural Marketing Service, Agricultural Stabilization and Conservation Service, Animal and Plant Inspection Service, the Commodity Credit Corporation, the Extension Service, the Farmers Home Administration, Federal Grain Inspection Service, the Food and Inspection Service, the Food Safety and Inspection Service, the Foreign Agricultural Service, Forest Service, Rural Electrification Administration, Soil Conservation Service. Contact: United States Department of Agriculture, 1400 Independence Ave. SW, Washington, DC 20250 USA; Tel: [1] (202) 720-2791; Web: www.usda.gov. Foreign Agricultural Service; Tel: [1] (202) 720-7115; Web: www.fas.usda.gov.

### United States Department of Commerce (DOC)

(U.S. government) An executive department which encourages and promotes the United States' economic growth, international trade, and technological advancement. The Department provides a wide variety of programs to increase American competitiveness in the world economy and to assist business. The DOC also: works to prevent unfair foreign trade competition, provides social and economic statistics and analyses, supports the increased use of scientific engineering and technological development, grants patents and registers trademarks, and provides assistance to promote domestic economic development. Organizations within the DOC include the Bureau of Industry and Security (formerly, Bureau of Export Administration), Tel: [1] (202) 482-2000; the Census Bureau, Web: www.census.gov; the Economic Development Administration, Tel: [1] (202) 482-2000; the International Trade Administration, Tel: [1] (202) 482-2000; the Minority Business Development Agency, Tel: [1] (202) 482-2000; the National Institute of Standards and Technology, Tel: [1] (301) 975-6478; the National Oceanic and Atmospheric Administration, E-mail: answers@noaa.gov; the Patent and Trademark Office, Tel: [1] (703) 308-4357 (Public Affairs) or [1] (800) 786-9199; and the Technology Administration, E-mail: Public_Affairs@ta.doc.gov. Contact: United States Department of Commerce, 1401 Constitution Ave. NW, Washington, DC 20230 USA; Tel: [1] (202) 482-2000; Web: www.commerce.gov. *See* Bureau of Industry and Security; International Trade Administration.

### United States Department of Defense

(U.S. government) A civilian executive department providing the military forces needed to deter war and protect the security of the U.S. There are three departments within the Department of Defense: the Air Force, Army, and Navy.

Contact: United States Department of Defense, The Pentagon, Washington, DC 20301 USA; Tel: [1] (703) 697-5737; Web: www.defenselink.mil.

### United States Department of Energy (DOE)
(U.S. government) An executive department created in 1977 to consolidate all major Federal energy functions into one department. The principal programmatic missions are energy programs, weapons and waste clean-up programs, and science and technology programs. Organizations under the department include the Economic Regulatory Administration, the Energy Information Administration, and the Federal Energy Regulatory Commission. Contact: United States Department of Energy, 1000 Independence Ave. SW, Washington, DC 20585 USA; Tel (toll-free within North America): [1] (800) dial-DOE (all others [1] (202) 586-5000); Fax: [1] (202) 586-4403; Web: www.energy.gov.

### United States Department of Homeland Security (DHS)
(U.S. Government) The DHS is a federal agency created under the Homeland Security Act of 2002 and mandated to protect the United States of America. The DHS coordinates and oversees the efforts of a variety of organizations working to protect U.S. infrastructure and points of entry, stop the flow of illegal drugs into the U.S., and prevent and respond to terrorist attacks on Americans.

The DHS is under the direction of the Secretary of Homeland Defense, who is nominated by the President and confirmed by the Senate. The Secretary is responsible for ensuring that the many agencies within the Department are effectively working together, and for coordinating such efforts with the President and other federal agencies.

According to the Homeland Security Act of 2002, the primary mission of the Department is to (1) prevent terrorist attacks within the United States; (2) reduce the vulnerability of the United States to terrorism; and (3) minimize the damage, and assist in the recovery, from terrorist attacks that do occur within the United States.

The agencies that make up the Department are housed in one of four major directorates: Border and Transportation Security, Emergency Preparedness and Response, Science and Technology, and Information Analysis and Infrastructure Protection.

The Border and Transportation Security directorate brings together the following:
- The U.S. Customs & Border Protection Bureau (formerly, the U.S. Customs Service of the Treasury Department)
- The U.S. Citizenship and Immigration Services Bureau (formerly, the Immigration and Naturalization Service of the Justice Department)
- The U.S. Immigration and Customs Enforcement Bureau
- The Transportation Security Administration
- Federal Law Enforcement Training Center
- Animal and Plant Health Inspection Service
- Office for Domestic Preparedness
- The Emergency Preparedness and Response directorate brings together the following:
- The Federal Emergency Management Agency (FEMA)
- Strategic National Stockpile and the National Disaster Medical System (of Health and Human Services)
- Nuclear Incident Response Team (of the Department of Energy)
- Domestic Emergency Support Teams (of the Department of Justice)
- National Domestic Preparedness Office (of the FBI)
- The Science and Technology directorate brings together the following:

- CBRN Countermeasures Programs (of the Department of Energy)
- Environmental Measurements Laboratory (of the Department of Energy)
- National BW Defense Analysis Center (of the Department of Defense)
- Plum Island Animal Disease Center (of the Department of Agriculture)

The Information Analysis and Infrastructure Protection directorate will analyze intelligence and information from other agencies (including the CIA, FBI, DIA and NSA) involving threats to homeland security and evaluate vulnerabilities in the nation's infrastructure. It will bring together:
- Critical Infrastructure Assurance Office (of the Department of Commerce)
- Federal Computer Incident Response Center
- National Communications System (of the Department of Defense)
- National Infrastructure Protection Center (of the FBI)
- Energy Security and Assurance Program (of the Department of Energy)

The Secret Service and the Coast Guard are also located in the Department of Homeland Security, remaining intact and reporting directly to the Secretary.
Contact: U.S. Department of Homeland Security, Washington, D.C. 20528; Tel: [1] (202) 282-8000; Web: www.dhs.gov.

### United States Department of Labor (DOL)
(U.S. government) An executive department which promotes and develops the welfare of U.S. wage earners, improves working conditions, and advances opportunities for profitable employment. The DOL keeps track of changes in employment, prices, and other national economic measures. Organizations under the Department include the Bureau of Labor Statistics, the Employment and Training Administration, the Employment Standards Administration, Labor-Management Standards, the Mine Safety and Health Administration, Occupational Safety and Health, and the Pension and Welfare Benefits Administration. Contact: United States Department of Labor, 200 Constitution Ave. NW, Washington, DC 20210 USA; Tel: [1] (866) 487-2365; Web: www.dol.gov.

### United States Department of State
(U.S. government) An executive department which directs U.S. foreign relations and negotiates treaties and agreements with foreign nations. Activities of the State Department are coordinated with foreign activities of other U.S. departments and agencies. Organizations within the Department include the Bureau of Consular Affairs, the Bureau of Economic and Business Affairs, the Bureau of Intelligence and Research, the Bureau of International Organization Affairs, and the Bureau of Oceans. Contact: United States Department of State, 2201 C St. NW, Washington, DC 20520 USA; Tel: [1] (202) 647-4000; Web: www.state.gov.

### United States Department of the Interior (DOI)
(U.S. government) An executive department that has responsibility for most U.S. federal government owned public lands and natural resources; the principal U.S. conservation agency. The office of Territorial and International Affairs oversees activities pertaining to U.S. territorial lands and the Freely Associated States and coordinates the international affairs of the Department. Organizations under the DOI include: the Bureau of Indian Affairs, the Bureau of Land Management, the Bureau of Mines, the Bureau of Reclamation, the Minerals Management Service, the National Park Service, the U.S. Fish and Wildlife Service, and the U.S. Geological Survey. Contact: United

States Department of the Interior, 1849 C St. NW, Washington, DC 20240 USA; Tel: [1] (202) 208-3100; E-mail: webteam@ios.doi.gov; Web: www.doi.gov.

**United States Department of the Treasury**
(U.S. government) An executive department which performs four basic functions: formulating and recommending economic, financial, tax and fiscal policies; serving as financial agent for the U.S. government; enforcing the law; and manufacturing coins and currency. The International Affairs unit is responsible for Department activities in international monetary affairs, trade and investment policy, international debt strategy, and U.S. participation in international financial institutions. The Under Secretary of the International Affairs unit acts as the U.S. Group of Seven (G-7) Deputy. Organizations within the Department include the Bureau of Alcohol, Tobacco and Firearms; the Bureau of Engraving and Printing; the Comptroller of the Currency; the Internal Revenue Service; the Office of Thrift Supervision; the U.S. Customs and Border Protection; the U.S. Mint; the U.S. Secret Service. Contact: United States Department of the Treasury, 1500 Pennsylvania Ave. NW, Washington, DC 20220 USA; Tel: [1] (202) 622-2000; Fax: [1] (202) 622-6415; Web: www.ustreas.gov. *See* Group of Seven (G-7); United States Customs Service; Bureau of Alcohol, Tobacco and Firearms.

**United States Department of Transportation (DOT)**
(U.S. government) An executive department of the U.S. government established by the Department of Transportation Act of 1966 (80 Stat 931) for the purpose of developing national transportation policies. Organizations within the Department of Transportation include the Federal Aviation Administration, the Federal Highway Administration, the Federal Railroad Administration, the Federal Transit Administration, the Maritime Administration, the National Highway Traffic Safety Administration, the Research and Special Programs Administration, the St. Lawrence Seaway Development Corporation, and the U.S. Coast Guard. Contact: United States Department of Transportation, 400 7th Street SW, Washington, DC 20590 USA; Tel: [1] (202) 366-4000; Web: www.dot.gov.

**United States Foreign Trade Definitions**
An obsolete standard of trade terms, although they are sometimes specified in U.S. domestic contracts. The international standard of trade terms is Incoterms 2000. *See* Incoterms 2000.

**United States International Trade Commission**
(U.S. government) Formerly the U.S. Tariff Commission, which was created in 1916 by an Act of Congress. Its mandate was broadened and its name changed by the Trade Act of 1974. It is an independent fact-finding agency of the U.S. government that studies the effects of tariffs and other restraints to trade on the U.S. economy. It conducts public hearings to assist in determining whether particular U.S. industries are injured or threatened with injury by dumping, export subsidies in other countries, or rapidly rising imports. It also studies the probable economic impact on specific U.S. industries of proposed reductions in U.S. tariffs and non-tariff barriers to imports. Its six members are appointed by the president with the advice and consent of the U.S. Senate for nine-year terms (six-year terms prior to 1974). Contact: International Trade Commission, 500 E Street SW, Washington, DC 20436 USA; Tel: [1] (202) 205-2000; E-mail: webposting@usitc.gov; Web: www.usitc.gov.

**United States-Japan Semiconductor Trade Arrangement**
*See* Semiconductor Trade Arrangement.

**United States Munitions List**
(U.S.) The USML identifies those items or categories of items considered to be defense articles and defense services subject to export control. The USML is similar in coverage to the International Munitions List (IML), but is more restrictive in two ways. First, the USML currently contains some dual-use items that are controlled for national security and foreign policy reasons (such as space-related or encryption-related equipment). Second, the USML contains some nuclear-related items. Under Presidential directive, most dual-use items are to be transferred from the USML to the Commerce Department's dual-use list. The Department of State, with the concurrence of Defense, designates which articles will be controlled under the USML. Items on the Munitions List face a stricter control regime and lack the safeguards to protect commercial competitiveness that apply to dual-use items. *See* International Munitions List; United States Department of State.

**United States price**
(U.S.) In the context of dumping investigations, this term refers to the price at which goods are sold in the U.S. compared to their foreign market value. The comparisons are used in the process of determining whether imported merchandise is sold at less than fair value. *See* dumping.

**United States Trade and Development Agency**
(U.S. government) An independent agency within the executive branch. Its mandate is to promote economic development in, and simultaneously export U.S. goods and services to, developing and middle-income countries. The Agency conducts feasibility studies and orientation visits, and provides trade-related training to assist U.S. firms in becoming involved in developing projects with substantial U.S. export potential. It also coordinates government-to-government technical assistance. Contact: United States Trade and Development Agency, 1000 Wilson Blvd, Suite 1600, Arlington VA 22209 USA; Tel: [1] (703) 875-4357; Fax: [1] (703) 875-4009; E-mail: info@ustda.gov; Web: www.ustda.gov.

**United States Trade Representative**
(U.S. government) A cabinet-level official with the rank of Ambassador who is the principal adviser to the president on international trade policy, and has responsibility for setting and administering overall trade policy. The U.S. Trade Representative is concerned with the expansion of U.S. exports; U.S. participation in the World Trade Organization (WTO), commodity issues; East-West and North-South trade; and direct investment related to trade. As Chairman of the U.S. Trade Policy Committee he is also the primary official responsible for U.S. participation in all international trade negotiations. Prior to the Trade Agreements Act of 1979, which created the Office of the U.S. Trade Representative, the comparable official was known as the President's Special Representative for Trade Negotiations (STR), a position first established by the Trade Expansion Act of 1962. Contact: United States Trade Representative, 600 17th St. NW, Washington, DC 20508 USA; Tel: [1] (888) 473-8787; E-mail: contactustr@ustr.gov; Web: www.ustr.gov.

**unit load**
(shipping) The strapping or banding together of a number of individual cartons, packages, sacks, drums or other cargo, often on a pallet, in order to create a single unit.

### unit load device (ULD)
(logistics/air freight)
(a) Any type of container or pallet used to load or transport cargo. (b) Any type of container or pallet used to load or transport cargo in the hold of an aircraft. ULDs vary in size and shape to fit specific vessels. *See* the appendix Guide to Air Freight Containers (ULDs).

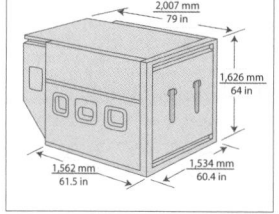

### unitization
(shipping) The practice or technique of consolidating many small pieces of freight into a single unit for easier handling.

### universal agency
*See* agency.

### Universal Copyright Convention
An international agreement that was concluded to afford copyright protection to literary and artistic works in all countries that voluntarily agree to be bound by the Convention terms. *See* copyright; trademark; service mark.

### unloading
(shipping) The physical removal of cargo from carrier's container.

### UN/LOCODE
Acronym for United Nations Code for Trade and Transport Locations. A five-character code system used to identify more than 40,000 trade and transport locations worldwide. These locations include ports, airports, railway, bus and truck terminals, and other pick-up and drop-off points for freight. The five character code consists of a two character country code (based on the ISO 3166 alpha-2 Country Code) and a three character code element for the location itself. While alpha characters are typical for the location itself, the numerals 2 to 9 may also be used. *See* www.un-ece.org/cefact/locode/service/main.htm for a complete listing of codes.

### unrestricted letter of credit
(banking) A letter of credit which may be negotiated through any bank of the beneficiary's choice. *See* letter of credit.

### upper deck
(shipping) A higher or the highest deck on a ship or airplane.

### Uruguay Round
(GATT) The eighth round of multilateral trade negotiations concerning the General Agreement on Tariffs and Trade (GATT). The Uruguay Round (so named because meetings began in Punta del Este, Uruguay in 1987) concluded in December, 1993 after seven years of talks with 117 member nations. The major goals of the Uruguay Round were to reduce barriers to trade in goods; to strengthen the role of GATT and improve the multilateral trading system; to increase the responsiveness of GATT to the evolving international economic environment; to encourage cooperation in strengthening the inter-relationship between trade and other economic policies affecting growth and development; and the establishment of a multilateral framework of principles and rules for trade in services, including the elaboration of possible disciplines for individual service sectors.

Key provisions of the Uruguay Round agreements were: a reduction of import tariffs, with an overall cut of more than 33 percent of global tariffs; a gradual reduction of 36 percent of government subsidies for farmers; a phasing-out of import protection for textile producers in industrialized countries allowing more open markets for entry of cheaper products from Third World countries; stricter anti-dumping

rules; greater global protection of intellectual property rights, including patents and copyrighted goods such as films and music. Although agriculture and other industries were brought under GATT for the first time, certain industries (such as the entertainment industry) were, in the end, excluded from the Round negotiations in order for negotiators to reach a final agreement. Particularly disappointing to many was the lack of progress in opening access to the trade of financial services, such as banking, accounting, and insurance. Most aspects of the agreement went into effect July 1, 1995.

Agreements reached at the Uruguay Round covered:

(1) **Market Access for Goods**—Tariffs to be reduced by an average of one-third, with the U.S. and other major industrial nations eliminating tariffs altogether on some products, by one-half on others, while cutting tariffs much less in the rest of the world.

(2) Agriculture—Strengthened long-term rules for agricultural trade and assures reduction of specific policies that distort agricultural trade. Addressed export subsidies, domestic subsidies, and market access. Agricultural export subsidies and some farm subsidies made subject to multilateral disciplines, and to be bound and reduced. Many non-tariff measures, including quotas to be converted to low tariffs over time.

(3) **Textiles and Clothing**—The Multi-Fiber Arrangement (MFA), a system of quotas that limits imports of textiles and apparel to the U.S. and other developed countries, to be phased out over a 10 year period. The quotas will eventually be replaced by tariffs.

(4) **Safeguards**—Provided incentives for countries to use GATT safeguard rules when import-related, serious injury problems occur.

(5) **Antidumping**—Revised the 1979 Antidumping Code, by improving provisions to define, deter, and discourage the use of dumping practices. Disputes between GATT members to be settled by binding dispute settlement.

(6) **Subsidies and Countervailing Measures**—Established clearer rules and stronger disciplines in the subsidies area while also making certain subsidies non-actionable.

(7) **Trade-related Investment Measures** (TRIMs)—Limited the ability of countries to favor domestically owned factories at the expense of foreign-owned ones. Prohibits local content and trade balancing requirements. Established a 5 to 7-year transition period for developing and least-developed countries.

(8) **Import Licensing Procedures**—More precisely defined automatic and non-automatic licensing. Signatories that adopt new procedures to notify the Import Licensing Committee within 60 days and provide information about it.

(9) **Customs Valuation**—Amendments to the Customs Valuation Code to help stem fraud, retain established minimum values, and encourage developing countries to study areas of concern in customs valuation.

(10) **Preshipment Inspection**—Regulated activities of Preshipment Inspection companies and reduced impediments to international trade resulting from the use of such companies, particularly in developing countries where they may supplement or replace national customs services.

(11) **Rules of Origin**—A program to be implemented to harmonize rules for determination of the origin of goods. Established a GATT Committee on Rules of Origin and a Customs Cooperation Council Technical Committee on Rules of Origin.

(12) **Technical Barriers to Trade**—Updated and improved rules respecting standards, technical regulations and conformity assessment procedures.

(13) **Sanitary and Phytosanitary Measures**—Established rules for the development of measures which are taken to protect human, animal or plant life or health in food safety or agriculture. Included quarantine procedures, food processing measures, meat inspection rules, procedures for approval of food additives or use of pesticides.

(14) **Services**—The General Agreement on Trade in Services (GATS) was the first multilateral, legally enforceable agreement covering trade investment in the service sectors. Principal elements included most-favored-nation treatment, national treatment, market access, transparency, and the free flow of payments and transfers.

(15) **Trade-Related Intellectual Property Rights** (TRIPs)—Established improved standards for the protection of a full range of property rights and the enforcement of those standards both internally and at the border. Covered: copyrights, patents, trademarks, industrial designs, trade secrets, integrated circuits, and geographical indications. Provided for a 20-year term of protection for most of these rights.

(16) **Dispute Settlement**—The Dispute Settlement Understanding (DSU) created new procedures for settlement of disputes arising under any of the Uruguay Round agreements.

(17) **World Trade Organization** (WTO)—Established a new organization available only to countries that were contracting parties to the GATT and that agreed and adhered to all of the Uruguay Round agreements. Encompassed and extended the then current GATT structure. The intention was for the new WTO to have a stature similar to that of the Bretton Woods financial institutions, the World Bank, and the International Monetary Fund.

(18) **GATT Articles**—Updated articles relating to balance-of-payment reform, state trading enterprises, regional trading arrangements, and waivers of obligation.

(19) **Trade Policy Review Mechanism**—Provided for regular examination of national trade policies and other economic policies bearing on international trading.

(20) **Ministerial Decisions and Declaration**—Stated the views and objectives of the Uruguay Round participants on a number of issues relating to the operation of the global trading system.

(21) **Government Procurement**—A new Agreement on Government Procurement replaced the existing agreement. Included procurement of services and construction and some coverage of subcentral governments and government-owned utilities.

*See* General Agreement on Tariffs and Trade; rounds; Tokyo Round, World Trade Organization

### U.S. ...
*See* United States ....

### U.S. person
Any person who is a citizen or national of the United States and any form of business enterprise or entity organized, chartered or incorporated under the laws of the United States or its possessions and trust territories.

### usance letter of credit
(banking) A documentary letter of credit which is not available by sight payment and which is therefore available against:
(1) acceptance of a term bill of exchange,
(2) or in certain usages by deferred payment. *See* letter of credit.

### user fees
(U.S. Customs) Assessments collected by U.S. Customs and Border Protection as part of the entry process to help defray various costs involved in the importation of goods to the United States.

(a) The **harbor maintenance fee** is an ad valorem fee assessed on cargo imports and admissions into foreign trade zones. The fee is 0.125 percent of the value of the cargo and is paid quarterly, except for imports which are paid at the time of entry. Customs deposits the harbor maintenance fee collections into the Harbor Maintenance Trust Fund. The funds are made available, subject to appropriation, to the Army Corps of Engineers for the improvement and maintenance of U.S. ports and harbors.

(b) The **merchandise processing fee** (MPF) is 0.21 percent ad valorem on formally-entered imported merchandise (generally entries valued over US $2,000), subject to a minimum fee of $25 per entry and a maximum fee of $485 per entry. On informal entries (those valued at less than $2,000), the MPFs are: $2 for automated entries, $6 for manual entries not prepared by Customs, and $9 for manual entries that are prepared by Customs.

### usuance
(banking) The time allowed for payment of an international obligation. A usuance credit is a credit available against time drafts. *See* letter of credit; usance letter of credit.

### validated export license

(U.S.) A document issued by the U.S. government authorizing the export of commodities for which written export authorization is required by law. For more information on export licensing in general, call Exporter Assistance at: [1] (202) 482-4811. Contact: Bureau of Industry and Security, U.S. Department of Commerce, 14th St. and Constitution Ave. NW, Washington, DC 20230 USA; Tel: [1] (202) 482-4811; Fax: [1] (202) 482-3617; Web: www.bis.doc.gov.

### validity

(banking) The time period for which a letter of credit is valid. After receiving notice of a letter of credit opened in his behalf, the seller/exporter/beneficiary must meet all the requirements of the letter of credit within the period of validity. *See* letter of credit.

### valuation

The fixing of value to anything.

(customs) The appraisal of the worth of imported goods by customs officials for the purpose of determining the amount of duty payable in the importing country. The WTO Customs Valuation Code obligates governments that sign it to use the "transaction value" of imported goods—or the price actually paid or payable for them—as the principal basis for valuing the goods for customs purposes.

(U.S. Customs) U.S. Customs officers are required by law to determine the value of imported merchandise. Valuation is necessary for statistical purposes as well as to determine the amount of import duty which must be paid if the duty rate is stated as a percentage of value (ad valorem duty).

Generally, the Customs value of all merchandise exported to the United States is the transaction value for the goods. The transaction value of imported merchandise is the price actually paid or payable for the merchandise when sold for exportation to the United States, plus amounts for the following items if not included in the price:

(1) The packing costs incurred by the buyer.

(2) Any selling commission incurred by the buyer,

(3) The value of any assist,

(4) Any royalty or license fee that the buyer is required to pay as a condition of the sale, and

(5) The proceeds, accruing to the seller, of any subsequent resale, disposal, or use of the imported merchandise.

The amounts for the above items are added only to the extent that each is not included in the price actually paid or payable and information is available to establish the accuracy of the amount. If sufficient information is not available, then the transaction value cannot be determined and the next basis of value, in order of precedence, must be considered for appraisement.

The secondary bases of value, listed in order of precedence for use, are:

(1) Transaction value of identical merchandise,

(2) Transaction value of similar merchandise,

(3) Deductive value, and

(4) Computed value.

The order of precedence of the last two values can be reversed if the importer so requests.

*See* transaction value; deductive value; computed value.

### valuation charges

(shipping) Transportation charges assessed shippers who declare a value of goods higher than the value of carriers' limits of liability. *See* declared value for carriage.

### valuation clause

(insurance) A clause in an insurance policy stating the value of the policy. A valuation clause commonly in use reads:

"valued premium included at amount of invoice, including all charges in the invoice and including prepaid and/or advanced and/or guaranteed freight, if any, plus _____ %." (This is usually 10% on exports.)

### value added

(economics) The amount by which the value of a product is increased at each stage of its production cycle, less the cost of materials and purchased parts and services. It is determined by subtracting from sales the costs of materials and supplies, energy costs, contract work, and so on, and it includes labor expenses, administrative and sales costs, and other operating profits. *See* value-added tax.

### value added counseling

Assessing a company's current international business operations and assisting in one or more of the following: (1) identifying and selecting the most viable markets; (2) developing an export market strategy; (3) implementing the export market strategy; and (4) increasing market presence.

### value-added tax (VAT)

(taxation) An indirect tax on consumption that is assessed on the increased value of goods at each discrete point in the chain of production and distribution, from the raw material stage to final consumption. The tax on processors or merchants is levied on the amount by which they increase the value of items they purchase and resell.

### value-added reseller

Acronym for value-added reseller. A company that combines products and/or services from several sources to produce a new product for sale. For example, a VAR might purchase computer systems from a manufacturer at a discount, add their own proprietary medical billing software and sell the resulting system to medical offices as a complete solution.

### value chain

(logistics, management) A variation of supply chain. The term is used to communicate the value each member, contributor or participant in the supply chain adds to the value of the final delivered product or service.

### value date

(banking) Fixing of a value date for accounting purposes on banking operations, i.e. the date on which the interest accrual for the respective accounting entry begins or ends.

### VAR

*See* value-added reseller.

### variable rate of duty

(customs) A tariff subject to alterations as world market prices change, the alterations are designed to assure that the import price after payment of the duty will equal a predetermined "gate" price.

### vatu

The currency of Vanuatu. 1VT=100 centimes.

### vega

(statistics/foreign exchange) The price change of a foreign exchange option for a 1 percent change in the implied volatility.

### vendor

A company or individual that supplies goods or services.

### Vennootschap onder firma

(Netherlands) Designation for a general partnership, in which all partners have joint and several liability.

**ventilated container**
(logistics) A weather-proof cargo container with protected small openings in the top and/or sides to allow for free movement of air.

**vertical export trading company**
An export trading company that integrates a range of functions taking products from suppliers to consumers.

**vertical integration**
(economics/management) The expansion, acquisition or merger of firms or business activities into different points of the same production and/or distribution path. For example, a leather shoe manufacturer who acquires a leather manufacturer and a retail shoe store chain.
*See* horizontal integration.

**Very Large Crude Carrier (VLCC)**
(shipping) An ocean-going crude oil tanker of 200,000 to 299,999 dwt. These vessels have greater flexibility than ULCCs (Ultra Large Crude Carriers) due to their smaller size, and are used extensively in the Mediterranean, West Africa and the North Sea. These vessels can sometimes be ballasted through the Suez Canal.

**vessel lift**
(shipping) A statistical term referring to a single loading or unloading of ocean freight containers from vessels at a port or terminal. The term is used to communicate the volume of container traffic (on an hourly, weekly, monthly or yearly basis) at a particular port or terminal.

**vessel ton**
(shipping/measurement) A unit of measurement in the shipping industry assuming that 100 cubic feet of cargo equals one ton.

**videoconferencing**
A conference between two or more individuals at different locations using telephone lines or computer networks to transmit and receive audio and video of the participants in real time.

**Vienna Sales Convention**
*See* United Nations Convention on Contracts for the International Sale of Goods (CISG).

**visa**
(general) A certificate or stamp placed in a passport by a foreign government's embassy, consular office or other representative. It permits the holder to either visit (tourist visa) conduct business in (business visa), work (work permit or visa) in, or immigrate (residency or immigration visa) to the issuing country for a specified time.
(customs) A license issued by the government of an exporting country for the export to a specific importing country of a certain quantity of a quota controlled commodity (such as textiles) subject to a voluntary export restriction or a voluntary restraint agreement.

**visa waiver**
A program of selected countries to eliminate their visa requirement on a test basis.

**vis major**
(law) A major force or disturbance, usually a natural cause, that a person cannot prevent despite exercise of due care. Floods and labor strikes are examples of vis major events.

**void ab initio**
(law) Invalid from the time of initiation. A contract, for example, that violates law or public policy is void ab initio, that is, it is invalid when it is made.

**void contract**
(law) An agreement that has no legal effect and that cannot be ratified or otherwise made effective. A contract that requires the performance of an illegal act, for example, is void and cannot become effective.

**voidable contract**
(law) An agreement that is valid but that one party may declare invalid because of a defect or illegality in making it. A contract that is entered into in reliance on a fraudulent misrepresentation, for example, will be enforced against the party that committed the fraud, but the party harmed by the misrepresentation may elect to void the contract.

**volatility**
(foreign exchange) The measure of the relative deviation of a price from the mean.

**volume rate**
(shipping) A rate applicable in connection with a specified volume of freight.

**voluntary export restriction**
An understanding between trading partners in which the exporting nation, in order to reduce trade friction, agrees to limit its exports of a particular good. Also called voluntary restraint agreement. *See* voluntary restraint agreements.

**voluntary restraint agreements (VRA's)**
Informal bilateral or multilateral arrangements through which exporters voluntarily restrain certain exports, usually through export quotas to avoid economic dislocation in an importing country and to avert the possible imposition of mandatory import restrictions.
These arrangements do not involve an obligation on the part of the importing country to provide "compensation" to the exporting country, as would be the case if the importing country unilaterally imposed equivalent restraints on imports. *See* voluntary export restriction; quota; visa.

# W

### war clause
(insurance) An insurance clause included in policies to cover against losses as a result of war. *See* war risk.

### war risk
(insurance) The risk to a vessel, its cargo and passengers by aggressive actions of a hostile nation or group. *See* war risk insurance.

### war risk insurance
(insurance) Insurance coverage against war risks as outlined in detail in some dozen rather specific paragraphs of an insurance policy. The policy conditions must be read for complete understanding. In general, they cover risks of capture and seizure, destruction or damage by warlike operations in prosecution of hostilities, civil wars and insurrections or in the application of sanctions under international agreements. Delay or loss of market is excluded. Loss or expense arising from detainments, nationalization of the government to or from which the goods are insured or seizure under quarantine or customs regulations is also excluded.

War risk insurance generally attaches as goods are first loaded on board a vessel at the port of shipment, and it ceases to attach as goods are landed at the intended port of discharge or on expiry of 15 days from arrival of the overseas vessel whichever first occurs. It includes transshipment and intermediate overland transit to an on-carrying overseas vessel, if any, but in no case for more than 15 days counting from midnight of the day of arrival of the overseas vessel at the intended port of discharge. If in transshipment, the 15-day period is exceeded, the insurance re-attaches as the interest is loaded on the on-carrying vessel. In case the voyage is terminated and the goods are discharged at a port or place other than the original port of discharge, such port or place shall be deemed the intended port of discharge.

The war risk policy is subject to 48 hours cancellation by either party. However, it cannot be cancelled on shipments upon which insurance has already attached. Since the cancellation provision is used at times for changing the conditions of insurance the current coverage should be studied for exact understanding of the war risk policy.

War risk insurance is routinely obtained for protection against mines and other implements of war from former wars.

### warehouse
(logistics) A secured, weatherproof building where raw materials, component parts, finished products and/or freight and cargo can be stored. There are many different types of warehouses including:

**customs bonded warehouse:** A warehouse where goods may be stored under the direct or indirect supervision of a country's import or export authorities.

**public warehouse:** A warehouse subject to government regulation where a number of different firms may store goods.

**private warehouse:** A warehouse operated by a manufacturing or trading firm, often adjacent to a manufacturing plant or port, used solely to store that firm's goods.

**special commodities warehouse:** A warehouse designed with special facilities and authorized to store unique products such as chemicals (in tanks), grain (in elevators) and tobacco (in barns).

**temperature controlled warehouse:** A warehouse that has either heating and/or refrigeration to maintain goods at a specified constant temperature.

**U.S. Customs bonded warehouse**: A federal warehouse where goods remain until duty has been collected from the importer. Goods under bond are also kept here. *See* surety; bond; in bond.

### warehouse receipt
(shipping) An instrument (document) listing the goods or commodities deposited in a warehouse. It is a receipt for the commodities listed, and for which the warehouse is the bailee. Warehouse receipts may be either non-negotiable or negotiable.

### warehouse-to-warehouse
(insurance) Insurance coverage of risks to a shipment of goods from the time the goods leave the warehouse for commencement of transit and continue during ordinary course of transit until delivered to final warehouse at destination, or until the expiration of 15 days (30 if destination is outside the limits of the port), whichever shall first occur. In the case of delay in excess of the time limit specified, if it arises from circumstances beyond his control, the assured is "held covered" if he gives prompt notice and pays additional premium. See Marine Extension Clause 1943 & 1952; currency (term) of insurance.

### warehousing
(logistics) The storing, securing and managing of raw materials, component parts or finished goods in a secure location. *See* warehouse, bonded warehouse.

### warranty
(law) A promise by a contracting party that the other party can rely on certain facts or representations as being true. A seller, for example, may warrant that certain products will meet a list of specifications furnished by the buyer.

### Warsaw Convention
(shipping) Formal name: The Convention for the Unification of Certain Rules Relating to International Carriage by Air, signed in Warsaw in 1929. An international multilateral treaty which regulates, in a uniform manner, the conditions of international transportation by air. Among other things it establishes the international liability of air carriers and establishes the monetary limits for loss, damage, and delay.

### Wassenaar Arrangement
An understanding between thirty-three nations promoting voluntary export control guidelines, as well as transparency and greater responsibility in the transfer of conventional arms and dual-use goods and technologies. Contact: Wassenaar Arrangement; Vienna Austria; Tel: [43] (1) 960-03; Fax: [43] (1) 960-031; Email: secretariat@wassenaar.org; Web: www.wassenaar.org.

### watch
a) (time measurement) A period of time during which part of a ship's crew is on duty. A ship's day is divided into five four-hour watches and two two-hour "dog" watches. The two two-hour dog watches enable the crew to avoid or "dodge" the same routine every day. Dodging the watch became known as "dogging," thence the "dog" watch. Typically, one of two or three groups of watchstanders are on duty for four hours and then off for either four or eight hours, then back to duty. *See* bells

| WATCHES AT SEA | |
|---|---|
| Middle Watch | Midnight to 4 AM (0000–0400) |
| Morning Watch | 4 AM to 8 AM (0400 – 0800) |
| Forenoon Watch | 8 AM to Noon (0800 – 1200) |
| Afternoon Watch | Noon to 4 PM (1200 – 1600) |
| First Dog Watch | 4 PM to 6 PM (1600 – 1800) |
| Second Dog Watch | 6 PM to 8 PM (1800 – 2000) |
| First Watch | 8 PM to Midnight (2000 – 0000) |

b) That part of a ship's crew that is on duty at any given time.
c) (weather) A forecast by a weather service that the conditions for a storm are present. Weather watches include those for tornados, severe thunderstorms, high winds, hurricanes, floods and flash floods.

### Watch List
*See* Special 301.

### waterway use tax
(shipping) A usage fee for vessels operating on inland waterways. The fee is generally assessed as a tax on fuel used in vessels operating on the waterway.

### waybill
(shipping) A document prepared by a transportation line at the point of a shipment, showing the point or origin, destination, route, consignor, consignee, description of shipment and amount charged for the transportation service, and forwarded with the shipment, or direct by mail, to the agent at the transfer point or waybill destination. *See* bill of lading; air waybill; ocean bill of lading.

### Webb-Pomerene Act of 1918
(U.S. law) Federal legislation exempting exporters' associations from the antitrust regulations.

### Webb-Pomerene Association
(U.S.) Associations engaged in exporting that combine the products of similar producers for overseas sales. These associations have partial exemption from U.S. anti-trust laws but may not engage in import, domestic or third country trade, or combine to export services.

### weight break
(shipping) Levels at which the freight rate per 100 pounds decreases because of substantial increases in the weight of the shipment. Examples of levels at which weight breaks occur (in pounds) are 100, 500, 1,000, 3,000, 5,000 and 10,000.

### weight ton
(measurement) (a) Short ton = 2,000 pounds, (b) Long ton = 2,240 pounds, (c) Metric ton = 2,204.68 pounds.

### weight unit qualifier
(logistics) (a) The unit of weight measure specified for use in a contract. (b) A symbol or code that represents the unit of weight measure to be used in a contract.

### weights and measures
*See* the Weights and Measures Appendix.

### West African Economic and Monetary Union
A regional alliance, WAMU (French: Union Monetaire Ouest Africaine, UEMOA) was created by treaty signed in May 1962. WAMU comprises seven French-speaking African countries: Benin, Burkina Faso, Cote d'Ivoire, Mali, Niger, Senegal, and Togo. Within WAMU, these countries share a common currency (CFA Franc) now freely convertible into the European Union Euro (€) at a fixed parity (under special arrangement with the French government), and a common Central Bank (BCEAO) responsible for the con-

duct of the Union's monetary and credit policies. There is also a common regional development bank. Commission de l'UEMOA, 380, rue Agostino Neto, 01 BP 543, Ouagadougou 01, Burkina Faso; Tél: (226) 50 31 88 73-76; Fax: (226) 50 31 88 72; E-mail: Commission@uemoa.int; Web: www.uemoa.int.

### West Africa Economic Community
*See* Economic Community of West African States.

### wharf
(shipping) A man-made structure built out from the shore into a river, bay, lake or ocean and supported by piles; providing access to vessels and used for loading and unloading cargo and passengers.

### wharfage
(shipping) (a) A charge assessed by a pier or dock owner for handling incoming or outgoing cargo, (b) The charge made for docking vessels at a wharf.

### with average (WA)
(insurance) Insurance coverage which gives the assured protection for partial damage by sea perils, if the partial damage amounts to 3% (or other percentage as specified) or more of the value of the whole shipment or of a shipping package. If the vessel has stranded, sunk, been on fire or in collision, the percentage requirement is waived and losses from sea perils are recoverable in full.

Additional named perils may be added to the WA Clause. Theft, pilferage, nondelivery, fresh water damage, sweat damage, breakage and leakage are often covered. The combination of perils needed by a particular assured will naturally depend upon the commodity being shipped and the trade involved.

In its standard form a typical with average clause may read: Subject to particular average if amounting to 3%, unless general or the vessel and/or craft is stranded, sunk, burnt, on fire and/or in collision, each package separately insured or on the whole."

The "all risk" clause is a logical extension of the broader forms of "With Average" coverage. This clause reads:

To cover against all risks of physical loss or damage from any external cause irrespective of percentage, but excluding, nevertheless, the risk of war, strikes, riots, seizure, detention and other risks excluded by the F.C.&S. (Free of Capture and Seizure) Warranty and the S.R.&C.C. (Strikes, Riots and Civil Commotion) Warranty in this policy, excepting to the extent that such risks are specifically covered by endorsement."

Some types of loss are commonly excluded and others not recoverable, even under the "all risk" clauses.

*See* average; particular average; general average; free of particular average; deductible average; all risk; special marine policy.

### with particular average
(insurance) Insurance covering also the loss of single cases or partial quantities (as opposed to free from particular average, fpa). *See* average; particular average; deductible average; all risk.

### without reserve
(shipping) A term indicating that a shipper's agent or representative is empowered to make definitive decisions and adjustments abroad without approval of the group or individual represented.

### won
The currency of:
North Korea, 1W=100 jun;
South Korea, 1W=100 jeon.

### work in progress (WIP)
(logistics) Raw materials and component parts that have entered a production cycle or process that has not been completed.

### World Administrative Radio Conference
WARC refers to the conference convened regularly by the United Nations' International Telegraphic Union (ITU) to allocate and regulate radio frequencies for the purposes of television and radio broadcasting, telephone data communications, navigation, maritime and aeronautical communication, and satellite broadcasting. *See* International Telecommunications Union.

### World Bank
(banking) The International Bank for Reconstruction and Development (IBRD), commonly referred to as the World Bank, is an intergovernmental financial institution located in Washington, DC. Its objectives are to help raise productivity and incomes and reduce poverty in developing countries. It was established in December 1945 on the basis of a plan developed at the Bretton Woods Conference of 1944. The Bank loans financial resources to credit worthy developing countries. It raises most of its funds by selling bonds in the world's major capital markets. Its bonds have, over the years, earned a quality rating enjoyed only by sound governments and leading corporations. Projects supported by the World Bank normally receive high priority within recipient governments and are usually well planned and supervised. The World Bank earns a profit, which is plowed back into its capital. Contact: World Bank, 1818 H Street NW, Washington, DC 20433 USA; Tel: [1] (202) 473-1000; Fax: [1] (202) 477-6391; E-mail: pic@worldbank.org; Web: www.worldbank.org. *See* International Bank for Reconstruction and Development; World Bank Group.

### World Bank Group
(banking) An integrated group of international institutions that provides financial and technical assistance to developing countries. The group includes the International Bank for Reconstruction and Development, the International Development Association, and the International Finance Corporation. Contact: World Bank Group, 1818 H Street NW, Washington, DC 20433; Tel: [1] (202) 473-1000; Fax: [1] (202) 477-6391; Web: www.worldbank.org.

### World Economic Forum
A Geneva, Switzerland-based non-profit organization founded in 1971 by Klaus M. Schwab, a professor of business in Switzerland. The foundation is best known for its annual meeting of business and political leaders, intellectuals and journalists, and representatives of selected NGOs, usually held in Davos, Switzerland in January of each year. World Economic Forum; 91-93 route de la Capite; CH - 1223 Cologny/Geneva Switzerland; Tel: +41 (0) 22 869 1212; Fax: +41 (0) 22 786 2744; web: www.weforum.org.

### World Intellectual Property Organization
A specialized agency of the United Nations system of organizations that seeks to promote international cooperation in the protection of intellectual property around the world through cooperation among states, and administers various "Unions," each founded on a multilateral treaty and dealing with the legal and administrative aspects of intellectual property.

WIPO administers the International Union for the Protection of Industrial Property (the "Paris Union"), which was founded in 1883 to reduce discrimination in national patent practices, the International Union for the Protection of Literary and Artistic Works (the "Bern Union"), which was founded in 1886 to provide analo-

gous functions with respect to copyrights, and other treaties, conventions and agreements concerned with intellectual property. Contact: World Intellectual Property Organization, 34, chemin des Colombettes, P.O. Box 18, CH-1211 Geneva 20, Switzerland; Tel: [41] (22) 338-9111; Fax: [41] (22) 733-5428; E-mail: wipo.mail@wipo.int; Web: www.wipo.int. *See* patent; copyright; service mark; trademark; Patent Cooperation Treaty.

### World Meteorological Organization
The WMO facilitates worldwide cooperation in establishing a network for meteorological, hydrological, and geophysical observations, for exchanging meteorological and related information, and for promoting standardization in meteorological measurements. Contact: World Meteorological Organization, 7 bis Avenue de la Paix, CP 2300, 1211 Geneva 2, Switzerland; Tel: [41] (22) 730-8111; Fax: [41] (22) 730-8181; E-mail: wmo@wmo.int; Web: www.wmo.int.

### World Tourism Organization (WTO)
An intergovernmental technical body dealing with all aspects of tourism. The WTO promotes and develops tourism as a means of contributing to economic development, international understanding, peace, and prosperity. Headquarters Contact: World Tourism Organization, Calle Capitan Haya 42, E-28020 Madrid, Spain; Tel: [34] (91) 567-8100; Fax: [34] (91) 571-3733; E-mail: omtweb@world-tourism.org; Web: www.world-tourism.org.

### world trade clubs / centers
Local or regional based organizations in the United States and around the world of importers, exporters, customs brokers, freight forwarders, attorneys, bankers, manufacturers and shippers.

Each world trade club provides different services and activities, but many provide: information services including data bases and libraries, educational services including seminars and regularly scheduled classes, meeting space, club atmosphere, dining, exhibit facilities, and trade missions. Most major cities in the world have world trade clubs. For a list of world trade clubs internationally contact: World Trade Center Association, 60 East 42nd Street, Suite 1901, New York, NY 10165 USA; Tel: [1] (212) 432-2626; Fax: [1] (212) 488-0064; Email: wtca@wtca.org; Web: http://iserve.wtca.org.

### World Trade Institute (WTI)
(Historic) Associated with Pace University (New York City) since 1997, the WTI was one of the world's foremost educational institutions and resources for the international business and financial community. Its programs included conferences and seminars, the School of International Trade & Commerce (SITC), the WTI Language Center, international training programs and academic partnership programs. Pace University ceased operations of the World Trade Institute on June 30, 2005. For archival information and links, go to http://appserv.pace.edu/execute/page.cfm?doc_id=15453.

### WorldScale
(shipping) A schedule of nominal ocean shipping freight rates for the carriage of oil in bulk intended to be used as a standard of reference to compare rates for all voyages and market levels. The oil maritime transportation industry uses the Worldscale rates to express the market level in terms of percentage of the Worldscale nominal freight rate. For example, Worldscale 100 (or Worldscale Flat) is the rate calculated and published by the Worldscale Associations. Worldscale 150, or WS 150 as it is most often used, means 150 percent of the published rate, while WS 50 means 50 percent of that rate. The Worldscale schedule was first is-

sued on September 15, 1969 as a replacement for the London-issued International Tanker Normal Freight Scale and the New York-issued American Tanker Rate Schedule. Worldscale Association (London) Ltd.; Copenhagen House; 5-10 Bury Street; London EC3A 5AT; Tel: [44] (0)20 7456 6600. WorldScale Association (New York) Inc.; 116 John Street - Suite 620; New York, NY 10038; Tel: [1] (212) 422-2786. Web: www.worldscale.co.uk.

### World Trade Organization (WTO)

The WTO is the premier international organization seeking to deal with the global rules of trade between nations. Created by the Uruguay Round of trade negotiations (1986-1994) of the GATT (General Agreement on Tariffs and Trade), the WTO was established 1 January 1995, and is comprised of 134 nations with others actively seeking membership. Contact at: World Trade Organization, rue de Lausanne 154, CH-1211 Geneva 21, Switzerland; Tel: [41] (22) 739-5111; Fax: [41] (22) 731-4206; E-mail: enquiries@wto.org; Web: www.wto.org.

WTO Objective

The WTO's stated objective is to help trade flow smoothly, freely, fairly and predictably. It does this by administering WTO trade agreements, acting as a forum for international trade negotiations, settling trade disputes, monitoring national trade policies, assisting developing countries in trade policy issues through technical assistance and training programs, and cooperation with other international organizations.

The activities of the WTO are based on the implementation of multilateral trade agreements which have been negotiated and signed by a majority of the world's trading nations, and ratified by their parliaments. These agreements are contracts guaranteeing member countries important trade rights. They also bind governments to keep their trade policies within agreed limits to the benefit of the whole.

WTO Structure

The WTO is run by its member governments. Major decisions are made by the membership as a whole, either by ministers (who meet every two years at a ministerial conference) or by officials (who meet regularly in Geneva). Decisions are normally made by consensus.

The ministerial conference can make decisions on all matters under any of the multilateral trade agreements. Day-to-day work in between the ministerial conferences is handled by three bodies: 1) The General Council, 2) The Dispute Settlement Body, and 3) The Trade Policy Review Body. All three are called The General Council, although they meet under different terms of reference.

Three more councils, each handling a different broad area of trade, report to the General Council. These are: 1) The Council for Trade in Goods (Goods Council), 2) The Council for Trade in Services (Services Council), and 3) The Council for Trade-Related Aspects of Intellectual Property (TRIPS Council).

Additional groups report to the General Council. The scope of their coverage is smaller, so they are called "committees." These committees cover such issues as trade and development, the environment, regional trading agreements, investment and competition policy, government procurement, trade facilitation, and others.

Each of the higher level councils has subsidiary bodies. For example, the Goods Council has 11 committees dealing with specific subjects such as agriculture, market access, subsidies, anti-dumping, and others.

The most difficult issues are not resolved in these upper level councils, but rather in much smaller meetings with representatives from as many as 40 countries to as few as two countries.

Successes

The WTO (and its predecessor GATT) has played a major role in the following areas: the reduction of tariffs on manufactured goods and agricultural products, the opening of banking, insurance and telecommunications markets to foreign competition, standards for the protection of intellectual property rights, food safety regulations, and bans on local preferences for government purchasing.

Challenges

With all its successes, the WTO is challenged by disputes by member nations to: 1) tariffs—lower or eliminate tariffs on agricultural, aquaculture and forest products, scientific, environmental and medical equipment, and chemicals, 2) agricultural subsidies—eliminate government subsidies to agriculture that set artificially low prices for agricultural products (thus hurting exporters), 3) intellectual property rights—either strengthen intellectual property rights (primarily proposed by advanced western nations that are home to major pharmaceutical companies) or establish exemptions from such rules (primarily proposed by developing nations that desire cheap access to drugs to treat HIV/AIDS and other health problems), 4) environment—establish more stringent rules designed to protect the environment, 5) services—continue to open up such service industries such as banking, insurance and medical technology, as well as maintain a tax-free status on Internet commerce, 6) genetically modified food products—give nations more latitude in their ability to exclude genetically altered food products based on public health or environmental concerns, 7) labor—open discussions on how international trade affects labor and possibly to establish international labor standards in the areas of child labor, health, and safety issues, and 8) transparency—make the WTO more transparent by eliminating secretive practices.

World Trade Organization; Centre William Rappard; Rue de Lausanne 154; CH-1211 Geneva 21; Switzerland; Tel: [41] (22) 739-5111; Web: www.wto.org. WTO Information and Media Relations Division; Tel: [41] (22) 739-50-07; Fax: [41] (22) 739-54-58; E-mail: enquiries@wto.org. WTO Publications; Tel: [41] (22) 739-52-08 / 739-53-08; Fax: [41] (22) 739-5792; E-mail: publications@wto.org. *See* General Agreement on Tariffs and Trade, Uruguay Round.

### World Wide Web (WWW)

(Internet) The international network of electronic links that connect personal computers with computer servers. Also referred to as 'the Web'.

### writ

(law) A judicial order to a person, often a sheriff, judge, or another officer of the law, to perform a specified act or to have the act performed. Writs of attachment, execution, and replevin are examples of writs that courts issue to require officials to carry out court judgments. *See* attachment; execution; replevin.

### writer

(foreign exchange) The party which writes an option (also known as the option seller). The writer undertakes the obligation to carry out the conditions of the options contract according to the choice of the option buyer during the whole life to maturity of the option. For this he receives a premium which is paid to him by the buyer of the option.

### WTO

*See* World Trade Organization (WTO).

### Web

*See* World Wide Web.

# X-Y-Z

### yen
The currency of Japan. 1¥=100 sen.

### yuan
The currency of China. 1¥=100 fen.

### zaibatsu
*See* keiretsu.

### zaire
The currency of Zaire. 1Z=100 makuta.

### Zangger Committee
Examines controls enacted pursuant to the Nuclear Non-proliferation Treaty by refining the list of items requiring nuclear safeguards. The Zangger Committee consists of 23 Nuclear Non-Proliferation Treaty (NPT) nuclear supplier nations and includes all nuclear weapons states except France and China. Through a series of consultations in the early 1970's, the countries of the Zangger Committee compiled a "trigger list" of nuclear materials and equipment. The shipment of any item on the list to a non-nuclear weapons state "triggers" the requirement of International Atomic Energy Agency (IAEA) safeguards. Since the Zangger Committee is associated with the NPT, its members are obligated to treat all non-nuclear weapons parties to the treaty alike. For fear of discrediting the NPT, the Zangger countries cannot target strict nuclear controls toward certain nations with questionable proliferation credentials; the NPT binds them to assist non-nuclear weapons states with peaceful atomic energy projects. *See* International Atomic Energy Agency; Nuclear Non-Proliferation Treaty.

### zero-sum
(economics) The concept that one side's gains are directly offset by the other side's losses in business or negotiations. When all the gains and losses from each side are totalled, the sum is zero. Compare to positive-sum.

### zip code
(shipping) A numerical code, established by the U.S. Postal Service, used for the purpose of routing and to identify delivery zones. Some U.S. carriers apply this code for freight in the same manner.

### zloty
The currency of Poland. 1Zl=100 groszy.

### zone
(shipping) Any one of a number of sections or districts of the United States or of the world used for the purpose of establishing proper rates for parcels, mail, and pickup and delivery.

### zone price
(logistics) The price or rate to transport mail, cargo or freight to any location within a zone. *See* zone.

### zone status
(U.S. foreign trade zones) The legal status of merchandise which has been admitted to a U.S. foreign trade zone, thereby becoming subject to the provisions of the Foreign Trade Zone Act (FTZA). *See* foreign trade zone; Foreign Trade Zone Board; Foreign Trade Zone Act; grantee; operator; zone user; subzones.

### zone user
(U.S. foreign trade zones) A corporation, partnership or party that uses a U.S. foreign trade zone for storage, handling, processing, or manufacturing merchandise in zone status, whether foreign or domestic. Usually, the zone user is the party which requests a Customs permit to admit, process or remove zone status merchandise. In subzones, the operator and zone user are usually the same party. Users pay the grantee or operator for services such as rent on facilities, storage, handling, promotion and similar services. *See* foreign trade zone; Foreign Trade Zone Board; Foreign Trade Zone Act; operator; zone user; subzones; zone status.

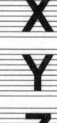

# Acronyms and Abbreviations[1]

**ACRONYMS**

## A

**AAA**
American Arbitration Association
**AAB**
Arab-African Bank
**AAEI**
American Association of Exporters and Importers
**AAPA**
American Association of Port Authorities
**AAR**
Against All Risks (insurance)
**AB**
Aktiebolag. company limited by shares. *See* Business Entities Appendix.
**ABC**
Activity-Based Costing
**ABEDA**
Arab Bank for Economic Development in Africa
**ABI**
Automated Broker Interface
American Business Initiative
**ABTA**
Association of British Travel Agents
**A/C**
Account Current
**ACC**
Arab Cooperation Council
**ACDA**
Arms Control and Disarmament Agency
**ACE**
Automated Commercial Environment
Agrupamento Complementar de Empresas. *See* Business Entities Appendix.
**ACEP**
Advisory Committee on Export Policy
**ACH**
Automated Clearinghouse
**ACI**
Advance Cargo Information
**ACP**
African, Caribbean, and Pacific Group of States
**ACS**
Automated Commercial System
**ACSI**
Americas Counter Smuggling Initiative
**ACTPN**
Advisory Committee on Trade Policy and Negotiations
**a/d**
After date
**AD**
Aktzionerno Drouzestvo. *See* Business Entities Appendix.
Anti-Dumping
**ADB**
Asian Development Bank
**ADF**
African Development Foundation
**ADS**
Agent Distributor Service
**Ad Val (or A.V.)**
Ad Valorem
**AE**
Anonymos Eteria. *See* Business Entities Appendix.
**AECA**
Arms Export Control Act
**AEIE**
Agrupamento Europeu de Interêsse Econômico. *See* Business Entities Appendix.
**AEN**
Administrative Exception Note
**AES**
Automated Export System
**AEV**
Articles of Extraordinary Value
**AfDB**
African Development Bank
**AFESD**
Arab Fund for Economic and Social Development
**AFRA**
Average Freight Rate Assessment
**AG**
Aktiengesellschaften. *See* Business Entities Appendix.
Australia Group
Andean Group
**AGVS**
Automated Guided Vehicle System
**AGX**
Agriculture Export Connections
**AID**
Agency for International Development
**AIES**
Automated Information Exchange System
**AIMS**
Agriculture Information and Marketing Services
**AIS**
Automatic Identification System
**AIT**
American Institute in Taiwan
**AL**
Arab League
**ALADI**
Asociacion Latinoamericana de Integracion
**AMB**
Ambassador

**AMF**
Arab Monetary Fund
Airport Mail Facility
**AMS**
Automated Manifest System
**AMU**
Arab Maghreb Union
**ANCOM**
Andean Common Market
**ANSI**
American National Standards Institute
**A/O**
Account Of
**AOSIS**
Alliance of Small Island States
**APAC**
Agriculture Policy Advisory Committee
Auto Parts Advisory Committee
**APEC**
Asian-Pacific Economic Cooperation
**APHIS**
Animal and Plant Health Inspection Service (U.S.)
**APO**
Administrative Protective Order
**Arabsat**
Arab Satellite Communications Organization
**a.s.**
Akciova Spolecnost. *See* Business Entities Appendix.
**A.S.**
Anonim Sirket. *See* Business Entities Appendix.
**A/S**
Aktieselskab. *See* Business Entities Appendix.
Aksjeselskap
**ASEAN**
Association of Southeast Asian Nations
**ASIC**
Application-Specific Integrated Circuit
**ASN**
Advance Shipment Notice
**ASRS**
Automated Storage and Retrieval System
**ATA Carnet**
"Admission Temporaire-Temporary Admission" Carnet
**ATF**
Alcohol, Tobacco and Firearms (and Explosives), U.S. Bureau of
**ATI**
American Traders Index
Andean Trade Initiative
**ATP**
Advanced Technology Products

---

1. Most acronyms are written in upper case letters without periods (.). However, due to different customs and practice they may be written in uppercase and/or lowercase, and with or without various punctuation. Some examples: Facsimile may be abbreviated as Fax, fax, Fax:, fax., or telefax. Foreign Exchange may be abbreviated as FX or F/X. United States of America may be abbreviated as U.S.A., U.S., USA or US.

**ACRONYMS**

**ATPI**
Andean Trade Preference Initiative
**AT&T**
American Telephone & Telegraph
**AU**
African Union
**AUTOVON**
Automatic Voice Network
**A.V. (or Ad Val)**
Ad Valorem
**avdp.**
avoirdupois (weight)

# B

**B.A.**
Buenos Aires (Argentina)
**B/A**
Bill of Adventure
**BAD**
Banque Africaine de Développement
**BADEA**
Banque Arabe de Développement Economique en Afrique
**BAF**
Bunker Adjustment Factor
**BASC**
Business Anti-Smuggling Coalition
**BATF**
Bureau of Alcohol, Tobacco, and Firearms (U.S.)
**Bbl**
Barrel
**B/C**
Bill of Credit
**BCIE**
Banco Centroamericano de Integracion Economico
**B/D**
Bank Draft
**BDEAC**
Banque de Développement des Etats de l'Afrique Centrale
**B./Dft.**
Bank Draft
**Bd. Ft. (also fbm or bf)**
Board Foot
**Bdl**
Bundle
**B/E**
Bill of Exchange
**BENELUX**
Belgium, Netherlands, Luxembourg Economic Union
**BF**
Board Foot
**BFP**
Bona Fide Purchaser
**B.H.**
Bill of Health
**BHC**
Bank Holding Company
British High Commission
**Bhd.**
Berhad. *See* Business Entities Appendix.
**BID**
Banco Interamericano de Desarrollo

**BIE**
Bureau of International Expositions
**BIMCO**
Baltic and International Maritime Council
**BIS**
Bank for International Settlements
**BIT(s)**
Bilateral Investment Treaty(ies)
**B/L**
Bill of Lading
**BLEU**
Belgium-Luxembourg Economic Union
**Bls**
Bales
**B/M**
Board measure
**B.O.**
Bad order
**BOAD**
Banque Ouest-Africaine de Développement
**BOM**
Bill of Material
**BOP**
Balance of Payments
**BOT**
Balance of Trade
**B/P**
Bill of Parcels
Bills Payable
**B/R**
Bills Receivable
**BRASS**
Border Release Advanced Screening and Selectivity
**BRITE**
Basic Research in Industrial Technologies in Europe
**B.S.**
Bill of Sale
**BSA**
Bilateral Steel Agreement
**BSEC**
Black Sea Economic Cooperation Zone
**BSP**
Business Sponsored
Between Show Promotion
**Bt**
Betéti Társaság. *See* Business Entities Appendix.
**BTN**
Brussels Tariff Nomenclature
**B/V**
Book Value
**B.V.B.A.**
Besloten Vennootschap met Beperkte Aansprakelijkheid. *See* Business Entities Appendix.
**BWS**
Bank Wire Service
Bretton-Woods System
**Bx**
Box
**BXA**
Bureau of Export Administration (U.S. Dept. of Commerce)

# C

**C**
Consulate
Commonwealth
**C.A.**
Compainía Anómima. *See* Business Entities Appendix.
**CAB**
Civil Aeronautics Board
**CACM**
Central American Common Market
**CAD/CAM**
Computer Aided Design/Computer Aided Manufacturing
Cash Against Documents
**CADEX**
Customs Automated Data Exchange
**CAEU**
Council of Arab Economic Unity
**C.A.F.**
Currency Adjustment Factor
**CAN**
(Andean) Community of Nations
**CAP**
Common Agricultural Policy
Country Action Plan
**CAR**
Commercial Activity Report
**CARICOM**
Caribbean Common Market
**CASE**
Council of American States in Europe
**CB**
Citizen's Band (mobile radio communications)
**CBD**
Commerce Business Daily
**CBERA**
Caribbean Basin Economic Recovery Act
**CBI**
Caribbean Basin Initiative
**Cbm/ (or C.B.M.)**
Cubic Meter
**CBOT**
Chicago Board of Trade
**CBP**
Customs and Border Protection, U.S. Bureau of
**CBSA**
Canada Border Services Agency
**CBSS**
Council of the Baltic Sea States
**CBW**
Chemical and Biological Weapons
**cc**
Carbon Copy (a duplicate copy)
**CCC**
Canadian Commercial Corporation
Commodity Credit Corporation
Customs Cooperation Council
China Compulsory Certification
**CCCN**
Customs Cooperation Council Nomenclature
**CCEPS**
Commercial Cash Entry Processing System

**CCL**
Commerce Control List
Commodity Control List
**C.D.**
Carried Down
Certificate of Deposit
Container Depot
**CDB**
Caribbean Development Bank
**CD-R**
Compact Disc—Rewritable
**CD-ROM**
Compact Disc—Read Only Memory
**CDT**
Center for Defense Trade
**CE**
Council of Europe
Conformité Européene
**CEA**
Council of Economic Advisors
**CEAO**
Communauté Economique de
l'Afrique Ouest (West Africa
Economic Community)
**CEEAC**
Communauté Economique des Etats de
l'Afrique Centrale (Economic
Community of Central African States)
**CEEBIC**
Central and Eastern Europe Business
Information Center
**CEI**
Central European Initiative
**Celsius**
centigrade
**CEMA**
Council for Mutual Economic
Assistance
**CEN**
Comité Européen de Normalisation
(European Committee for
Standardization)
**C. en C.**
Compainía en Comandita. *See*
Business Entities Appendix.
**C. en C. por A.**
Compainía en Comandita por Acciones.
*See* Business Entities Appendix.
**CENELEC**
Comité Européen de Normalisation
Électrotechnique (European
Committee for Electrotechnical
Standardization)
**CEO**
Chief Executive Officer
**CEPGL**
Communauté Economique des Pays
des Grands Lacs
**CEPT**
Conférence Européenne des Postes et
des Télécommunications (European
Conference of Postal and
Telecommunications
Administrations)
**CERN**
Conseil Européen pour la Recherche
Nucléaire (European Council for
Nuclear Research)

**CET (or TEC)**
Common External Tariff (Tarif
Extérieur Commun)
**C&F**
Cost and Freight
**CFIUS**
Committee on Foreign Investment in
the U.S.
**CFO**
Chief Financial Officer
**CFR**
Code of Federal Regulations
Cost and Freight
**CFS**
Country Focused Seminar
Container Freight Station
**Cft. (or CuFt.)**
Cubic Foot (Feet)
**CFTA**
Canadian Free Trade Agreement
**CG**
Consul General, Consulate General
Contadora Group
**CGM**
Compagnie Générale Maritime
**CHG**
Charge d'Affairs
**C.I.**
Cost and insurance
**Cía**
Sociedad Colectiva. *See* Business
Entities Appendix.
Cash in Advance
Central Intelligence Agency (U.S.)
**CIB**
Council for International Business
**Cie**
Compagnie
Offene Handelsgesellschaft. *See*
Business Entities Appendix.
**CIF**
Cost, Insurance and Freight
**C.I.F.& C.**
Cost, insurance, freight and
commission.
**C.I.F.C.I.**
Cost, insurance, freight, collection and
interest.
**C.I.F.I.&E.**
Cost, insurance, freight, interest, and
exchange.
**CIG**
Customs Internet Gateway
**CIM**
Convention Internationale Concernant
le Transport des Marchandises par
Chemin de Fer (The International
Convention for Transport of
Merchandise by Rail)
**CIMS**
Commercial Information Management
System
**CIO**
Congress of Industrial Organizations
**CIP**
Carriage and Insurance Paid To
Commodity Import Program
Carrier Initiative Program

**CIS**
Census Interface System
Commonwealth of Independent States
**CISG**
Convention on Contracts for the
International Sale of Goods
**CIT**
Court of International Trade
**CITA**
Committee for the Implementation of
Textile Agreements
**CITES**
Convention on International Trade in
Endangered Species in Wild Fauna
and Flora
**C.K.D.**
Completely Knocked Down
**C.L.**
Car Load
**CL**
Container Load
**CLM**
Council of Logistics Management
**CLS**
Company Limited by Shares. *See*
Business Entities Appendix.
**C. Ltda.**
Compainía de Responsabilidad
Limitada. *See* Business Entities
Appendix.
**C.M.**
Cubic Meter (capital letters);
**cm**
cm (small letters) centimeter
**CMA**
Common Monetary Agreement
Compagnie Maritime d'Affretement
**CMEA**
Council for Mutual Economic
Assistance
**CMP**
Country Marketing Plan
**C/N**
Circular Note
Credit Note
**CNUSA**
Commercial News USA
**C/O**
In Care Of
Carried Over
Cash Order
**Co.**
Company. *See* Business Entities
Appendix.
Offene Handelsgesellschaft. *See*
Business Entities Appendix.
S Corporation. *See* Business Entities
Appendix.
**COCOM**
Coordinating Committee on
Multilateral Export Controls
**C.O.D.**
Collect (cash) on delivery
**COE**
Council of Europe
**C.O.F.C.**
Container on flatcar
**COGSA**
Carriage of Goods by Sea Act

**COM**
Chief of Mission
Cost of Manufacture
**COMECON**
Council for Mutual Economic
  Assistance
**COMESA**
Common Market for Eastern and
  Southern Africa
**COMEX**
Commodity Exchange Inc. (futures
  contracts)
**COMSAT**
Communications Satellite Corporation
**Conc'd.**
Concluded
**Cont'd.**
Continued
**COO**
Chief Operating Officer
**COP**
Cost of Production
**Corp.**
Corporation, *See* Business Entities
  Appendix.
Stock Corporation. *See* Business
  Entities Appendix.
**CP**
Colombo Plan
**CPE**
Centrally Planned Economy
**C. por A.**
Companía por Acciones. *See* Sociedad
  Anónima in Business Entities
  Appendix.
**CPSC**
Consumer Product Safety Commission
  (U.S.)
**c.p.t.**
Cuideachta Phoibli Theoranta. *See*
  Business Entities Appendix.
**CPT**
Carriage Paid To
**CRP**
Continuous Replenishment Planning
**C.S.C.**
Container Service Charge
**CSCE**
Conference on Security and
  Cooperation in Europe
**CSI**
Container Security Initiative
**CSIS**
Center for Strategic and International
  Studies
**CSO**
Company Security Officer
**CSP**
Common Standard Level of Effective
  Protection
**CSR**
Continuous Synopsis Record
**CSS**
Cargo Selectivity System
Comparison Shopping Service
**CT**
Countertrade
**CTD**
Committee on Trade and Development

**CTF**
Certified Trade Fair
**CTIS**
Center for Trade and Investment
  Services
**CTM**
Certified Trade Mission
**CTP**
Composite Theoretical Performance
**C-TPAT**
Customs-Trade Partnership Against
  Terrorism
**Ctr**
Container
Currency Transaction Report
**Cu.**
Cubic (measure)
**CV**
Constructed Value
**C.V.**
Commanditaire Vennootschap. *See*
  Business Entities Appendix.
**CVD**
Countervailing Duty
**CWO**
Cash With Order
**Cwt.**
(measure) Hundredweight (100 lbs. in
  U.S., 112 lbs. in United Kingdom)
**C.Y. or CY**
Container Yard.

# D

**D/A**
Documents Against Acceptance
**DAF**
Delivered at Frontier
**D.B.A.**
Doing Business As
**DBJ**
Development Bank of Japan
**DC**
Developed Country
**DCM**
Deputy Chief of Mission
**D/D**
Delivered
**DDP**
Delivered Duty Paid
**DDU**
Delivered Duty Unpaid
**DEC**
District Export Council
**DEQ**
Delivered Ex Quay
**DES**
Delivered Ex Ship
**DFI**
Direct Foreign Investment
**DGI**
Defective Goods Inventory
**DHS**
Department of Homeland Security
  (U.S.)
**DISA**
Data Interchange Standards
  Association

**DISC**
Domestic International Sales
  Corporation (U.S.)
**DISCO**
Defense Industrial Security Clearing
  Office
**DL**
Distribution License
**DNA**
Delta Nu Alpha
**D/O**
Delivery Order
**DOA**
Department of Agriculture (U.S.)
**DOC**
Department of Commerce (U.S.)
**DOD**
Department of Defense (U.S.)
**DOE**
Department of Energy (U.S.)
**DOI**
Department of the Interior (U.S.)
**DOL**
Department of Labor (U.S.)
**DOT**
Department of Transportation (U.S.)
**D/P**
Documents Against Payment
**DPAC**
Defense Policy Advisory Committee
**DPL**
Denied Persons List (formerly, Denied
  Parties List)
**D-RAM**
Dynamic Random Access Memory
**DRP**
Distribution Requirements Planning
**DSD**
Direct Store Delivery
**DSL**
Digital Subscriber Line
**DTC**
Defense Trade Controls
**DTSA**
Defense Technology Security
  Administration
**DTWG**
Defense Trade Working Group
**DUNS**
Data Universal Numbering System
**DWT**
Deadweight Ton

# E

**Ea or ea.**
each
**EAA**
Export Administration Act
**EAAA**
Export Administration Amendments
  Act
**EAC**
Export Assistance Center
**EADB**
East African Development Bank
**EAEC**
European Atomic Energy Commission

**ACRONYMS**

**EAI**
Enterprise for the Americas Initiative
**EAN**
European Article Number Association
  International
Except As Noted
**EAPC**
Euro-Atlantic Partnership Council
**EAR**
Export Administration Regulations
**EARB**
Export Administration Review Board
**EBB**
Economic Bulletin Board
**EBRD**
European Bank for Reconstruction and
  Development
**EC**
European Community
**ECA**
Economic Commission for Africa
**ECAF**
Emergency Currency Adjustment
  Factor
**ECAFE**
Economic Commission for Asia and
  the Far East
**ECAs**
Export Credit Agencies
**ECASS**
Export Control Automated Support
  System
**ECB**
European Central Bank
**ECCN**
Export Control Classification Number;
  formerly: Export Commodity
  Classification Number
**ECE**
Economic Commission for Europe
**ECLA**
Economic Commission for Latin
  America
**ECLAC**
Economic Commission for Latin
  America and the Caribbean
**ECLS**
Export Contact List Service
**ECMT**
European Conference of Ministers of
  Transport
**ECO/COM**
Economic/Commercial Section
Economic Cooperation Organization
**ECOSOC**
Economic and Social Council
**ECOWAS**
Economic Community of West African
  States
**eCP**
e-Customs Partnership
**ECR**
Efficient Consumer Response
**ECSC**
European Coal and Steel Community
**ECU**
European Currency Unit
**ECWA**
Economic Commission for Western

Asia
**EDC**
Export Development Corporation
**EDI**
Electronic Data Interchange
**EDIFACT**
Electronic Data Interchange For
  Administration, Commerce, and
  Transportation
**EDO**
Export Development Office
**EE**
Eterorythmos Eteria. *See* Business
  Entities Appendix.
**EEA**
European Economic Area
**EEBIC**
Eastern Europe Business Information
  Center
**EEC**
European Economic Community
**EEP**
Export Enhancement Program
**EEPROM**
Electronically Erasable Programmable
  Read-Only Memory
**EEZ**
Exclusive Economic Zones
**EFT**
Electronic Funds Transfer
**EFTA**
European Free Trade Association
**EIB**
European Investment Bank
**E.I. de R.L.**
Empresa Individual de Responsibilidad
  Limitada. *See* Business Entities
  Appendix.
**EIN**
Employer Identification Number
Exporter Identification Number
**EIRL**
Eestabelecimento Individual de
  Responsabildade Limitada. *See*
  Business Entities Appendix.
**ELAIN**
Electronic License Application and
  Information Network
**ELAN**
Export Legal Assistance Network
**ELP**
Exempted Limited Partnership. *See*
  Business Entities Appendix.
**ELVIS**
Export License Voice Information
  System
**EMC**
Export Management Company
**EMS**
European Monetary System
**EMU**
European Monetary Union
**E&OE**
Errors and Omissions Excepted
**EOQ**
Economic Order Quantity
**EOTC**
European Organization for Testing and
  Certification

**EP**
European Parliament
**EPA**
Environmental Protection Agency
  (U.S.)
**EPC**
Economic Policy Council
European Patent Convention
**EPCI**
Enhanced Proliferation Control
  Initiative
**EPE**
Eteria Periorismenis Efthinis. *See*
  Business Entities Appendix.
**EPROM**
Erasable Programmable Read-Only
  Memory
**EPS**
Export Promotion Services
**EPZ**
Export Processing Zone
**ERLC**
Export Revolving Line of Credit
**ERM**
Exchange Rate Mechanism
**ESA**
European Space Agency
**ESC**
European Shippers' Council
**ESCAP**
Economic and Social Commission for
  Asia and the Pacific
**ESCWA**
Economic and Social Commission for
  Western Asia
**ESP**
Exporter's Sale Price
**ESPRIT**
European Strategic Program for
  Research and Development in
  Information Technologies
**ESSS**
Entry Summary Selectivity System
**est**
Estimate
**ETA**
Estimated Time of Arrival
**etc.**
et cetera
**ETC**
Export Trading Company
**ETD**
Estimated Time of Departure
**ETSI**
European Telecommunications
  Standards Institute
**EU**
European Union
**EUCLID**
European Cooperation for the Long-
  term in Defense
**eUCP**
Electronic Supplement to the Uniform
  Customs and Practice for
  Documentary Credits
**EURAM**
European Research in Advanced
  Materials

**A C R O N Y M S**

**EURATOM**
European Atomic Energy Community
**EURESCOM**
European Institute for Research and
  Strategic Studies In
  Telecommunications
**E.U.R.L.**
Entreprise Unipersonnelle à
  Responsabilité Limitée. *See* Business
  Entities Appendix.
**EUTELSAT**
European Telecommunications
  Satellite Organization
**EXCAPS**
Foreign Affairs/Customs Automated
  Permit System
**EXCEL**
Export Credit Enhanced Leverage
**EXIMBANK**
Export-Import Bank of the U.S.A.
**EXW**
Ex Works

# F

**1PL**
First Party Logistics
**4PL**
Fourth Party Logistics
**F**
Fahrenheit
**FAA**
Federal Aviation Administration (U.S.)
Foreign Assistance Act
**FAAS**
Foreign Affairs Administrative Support
**FAC**
Foreign Assets Control (U.S.)
**F.A.K.**
Freight All Kinds
**FAO**
(U.N.) Food and Agricultural
  Organization
**FAS**
Foreign Agricultural Service (U.S.)
Free Alongside Ship
**FAST**
Free And Secure Trade
**fax**
facsimile (fax machine or fax letter)
**FBIS**
Foreign Broadcast Information Service
**fbm (also Bd.Ft.)**
Board Foot
**FBP**
Foreign Buyer Program
**FBT**
Flatbed Trailer
**FCA**
Free Carrier
**FCIA**
Foreign Credit Insurance Association
**FCL**
Full Container Load
Full Car Load
**FCPA**
Foreign Corrupt Practices Act
**F.C.&S.**
Free of Capture and Seizure Warranty

**FDA**
Food and Drug Administration (U.S.)
**FDIC**
Federal Deposit Insurance Corporation
  (U.S.)
**FDIUS**
Foreign Direct Investment in the United
  States
**FEMA**
Federal Emergency Management
  Agency (U.S.)
**FET**
Foreign Economic Trends
**FEU**
Forty Foot Equivalent Units
**FFP**
Food For Progress
**FGI**
Finished Goods Inventory
**FI**
Free In
**FIATA**
Federation Internationale des
  Associations de Transitaires et
  Assimiles (International Federation
  of Freight Forwarders Associations)
**FIFO**
First In, First Out
**FIO**
Free In and Out
**F.I.O.S.**
Free In, Out and Stow
**FIRST**
Frequent Importers Release System
**FIT**
Foreign Independent Tour
**F.M.C. (or FMC)**
Federal Maritime Commission
**FMS**
Foreign Military Sales
**FMV**
Foreign Market Value
**FO**
Free Out
**FOB**
Free on Board
**FOR**
Free on Rail
**FOREX (also F/X)**
Foreign Exchange
**FOT**
Free on Truck
**FPA**
Free of Particular Average
**FPFS**
Fines, Penalties, and Forfeitures
  System
**FPG**
Foreign Parent Group
**FR**
Flat Rack
**FRA**
Forward/Future Rate Agreement
**FROB**
Foreign Remaining on Board
**FSC**
Foreign Sales Corporation (U.S.)
**FSI**
Flag State Implementation

Foreign Service Institute (U.S.)
**FSN**
Foreign Service National
**FSO**
Foreign Service Officer
**ft**
Foot/Feet (measure)
**FTA**
Free Trade Agreement
Free Trade Area
**FTC**
Federal Trade Commission (U.S.)
**FTI**
Foreign Traders Index
**FTL**
Full Truck Load
**FTO**
Foreign Trade Organization
**FTZ**
Foreign Trade Zone
**FTZA**
Foreign Trade Zone Act
**FTZB**
Foreign Trade Zone Board
**FTZ-SZ**
Foreign Trade Zone-Subzone
**F/X (also FOREX)**
Foreign Exchange
**FY**
Fiscal Year
**FYROM**
Former Yugoslav Republic of
  Macedonia

# G

**G-2**
Group of Two
**G-3**
Group of Three
**G-5**
Group of Five
**G-6**
Group of Six
**G-7**
Group of Seven
**G-8**
Group of Eight
**G-9**
Group of Nine
**G-10**
Group of 10
**G-11**
Group of 11
**G-15**
Group of 15
**G-19**
Group of 19
**G-24**
Group of 24
**G-30**
Group of 30
**G-33**
Group of 33
**G-77**
Group of 77
**G/A**
General Average
**GAB**
General Agreements to Borrow (Paris

Club)
**GAO**
General Accounting Office (U.S.)
**GATS**
General License - Aircraft on
  Temporary Sojourn
**GATT**
General Agreement on Tariffs and
  Trade
**GAWR**
Gross Axle Weight Rating
**G-BAGGAGE**
General License - Baggage
**GB/L**
Government Bill of Lading
**GCC**
Gulf Cooperation Council
**GCG**
General License - Shipments to
  Agencies of Cooperating
  Governments
**G-COCOM**
General License - COCOM
**G-DEST**
General License - Destination
**GDP**
Gross Domestic Product
**GEM**
Global Export Manager
**GFW**
General License - Free World
**GIT**
General License - In Transit Shipments
**GL**
General License
**GLR**
General License - Return
  (Replacement)
**GLV**
General License - Shipments of
  Limited Value
**GmbH**
Gesellschaft mit beschränkter Haftung.
  *See* Business Entities Appendix.
**G-NNR**
General License - Non-Naval Reserve
**GNP**
Gross National Product
**GO**
General Order
**GPO**
Government Printing Office (U.S.)
**G.R.I.**
General Rate Increase
**GRT**
Gross Register Ton
**GSP**
Generalized System of Preferences
**GST**
Goods and Services Tax (Canada)
**GTDA**
General License - Technical Data
**GTDI**
Guidelines for Trade Data Interchange
**GTDR**
General License - Technical Data
  Restricted
**G-TEMP**
General License - Temporary Export

**GTF-U.S.**
General License - Goods Imported for
  Display at U.S. Exhibitions or Trade
  Fairs
**GUS**
General License - Shipments to
  Personnel and Agencies of the U.S.
  Government
**GVWR**
Gross Vehicle Weight Rating
**GWP**
Gross World Product

# H

*H*
Height
**HAWB**
House Air Waybill
**HC**
High Commission (British)
**HF**
High Frequency
**H/H**
House to House
**HMHC**
Her Majesty's High Commission
**H.P.**
Horsepower
**H/P**
House to Pier
**HS**
Harmonized System
**HTS**
Harmonized Tariff Schedule
**HTSUS**
Harmonized Tariff Schedule of the U.S.
**HTWG**
High Technology Working Group

# I

**IACC**
International Anticounterfeiting
  Coalition
**IACS**
International Association of
  Classification Societies
**IADB**
Inter-American Development Bank
**IAEA**
International Atomic Energy Agency
**IAEL**
International Atomic Energy List
**IAPH**
International Association of Ports and
  Harbours
**IATA**
International Air Transport Association
**IBEC**
International Bank for Economic
  Cooperation
**IBF**
International Banking Facility
**IBM**
International Business Machines
  (Company)
**IBOR**
Interbank Offered Rate

**IBRD**
International Bank for Reconstruction
  and Development
**IC**
Import Certificate
Integrated Circuit
**ICA**
International Cocoa Agreement
International Coffee Agreement
International Commodity Agreement
**ICAO**
International Civil Aviation
  Organization
**ICC**
International Chamber of Commerce
  (Paris)
Interstate Commerce Commission
**ICEM**
Intergovernmental Committee for
  European Migration
**ICFTU**
International Confederation of Free
  Trade Unions
**ICJ**
International Court of Justice
**ICM**
Intergovernmental Committee for
  Migration
**ICO**
International Congress Office
**ICP**
Industry Consultations Program
International Company Profile
**ICRC**
International Committee of the Red
  Cross
**ICS**
International Chamber of Shipping
Investment Climate Statement
**ICSID**
International Center for Settlement of
  Investment Disputes (World Bank
  group)
**ICSU**
International Council of Scientific
  Unions
**I.D.**
Inside Diameter
**IDA**
International Development Association
**IDB**
Inter-American Development Bank
Islamic Development Bank
**IDCA**
International Development
  Cooperation Agency
**IEA**
International Energy Agency
**IEC**
International Electrotechnical
  Commission
**IEEPA**
International Emergency Economic
  Powers Act
**IEPG**
Independent European Program Group
**IESC**
International Executive Service Corps

**A C R O N Y M S**

**IFAC**
Industry Functional Advisory Committee
**IFAD**
International Fund for Agricultural Development
**IFC**
International Finance Corporation
**IFM**
Inward Foreign Manifest
**IFRB**
International Frequency Registration Board
**IFRCS**
International Federation of Red Cross and Red Crescent Societies
**IFS**
Industry Focused Seminar
In-Flight Survey
**IGAD**
Inter-Governmental Authority on Development
**IGC**
Interagency Group on Countertrade
**IGPAC**
Intergovernmental Policy Advisory Committee
**IHO**
International Hydrographic Organization
**IIB**
International Investment Bank
**IIDM**
Instituto Iberoamericano de Derecho Marítimo (Iberoamerican Institute of Maritime Law)
**IIT**
Instruments of International Traffic
**IJA**
International Jute Agreement
**IL**
Industrial List
**ILO**
International Labor Organization
**IMC**
Intermodal Marketing Company
**IMCO**
Intergovernmental Maritime Consultative Organization
**IMDG**
International Maritime Dangerous Goods Code
**IMF**
International Monetary Fund
**IMI**
International Market Insight
**IML**
International Munitions List
**IMO**
International Maritime Organization
**IMSO**
International Maritime Satellite Organization
**In.**
Inch
**Inc. (or Corp.)**
Incorporated
Corporation
C corporation, *See* Business Entities

Appendix.
Close Corporation, *See* Business Entities Appendix.
Stock Corporation. *See* Business Entities Appendix.
**info.**
Information
**INMARSAT**
International Maritime Satellite Organization
**InOC**
Indian Ocean Commission
**INPAC**
Investment Policy Advisory Committee
**INR**
Initial Negotiating Right
**INS**
Immigration and Naturalization Service
**INTELSAT**
International Telecommunications Satellite Organization
**INTERCARGO**
International Association of Dry Cargo Ship Owners
**INTERPOL**
International Criminal Police Organization
**INTERSPUTNIK**
International Organization of Space Communications
**INTERTANKO**
International Association of Independent Tanker Owners
**IOC**
International Olympic Committee
**IOGA**
Industry-Organized, Government-Approved Mission
**IOM**
International Organization for Migration
**IPAC**
Industry Policy Advisory Committee
**IPO**
Initial Public Offering (stock)
**IPP**
Industry Partnership Programs
**IPR**
Intellectual Property Rights
**IPS**
International Partner Search
**IRA**
International Rubber Agreement
**IRS**
Internal Revenue Service (U.S.)
**I/S**
Interessantelskab
**ISA**
Industry Sub-Sector Analysis
International Sugar Agreement
**ISAC**
Industry Sector Advisory Committee
**ISAN**
International Standard Audiovisual Number
**ISBN**
International Standard Book Number

**ISC**
Intermodal Service Charge
**ISDN**
Integrated Services Digital Network
**ISIC**
International Standard Industrial Classification
**ISMN**
International Standard Music Number
**ISO**
International Standards Organization
**ISPS**
International Ship and Port Facility Security
**ISRC**
International Standard Recording Code
**ISSC**
International Ship Security Certificate
**ISSN**
International Standard Serial Number
**ISWC**
International Standard Musical Work Code
**ITA**
International Tin Agreement
International Trade Administration
**ITAR**
International Traffic in Arms Regulations
**ITC**
International Trade Commission
**ITDS**
International Trade Data System
**ITT**
International Telephone & Telegraph
**ITU**
International Telecommunications Union
**IVL**
Individual Validated License
**IWC**
International Whaling Commission

# J

**JBIC**
Japan Bank for International Cooperation
**JCIT**
Joint Committee for Investment and Trade
**JDB**
Japan Development Bank
**JEIC**
Japan Export Information Center
**JETRO**
Japan External Trade Organization
**JEXIM**
The Japan Export-Import Bank
**JICA**
Japan International Cooperation Agency

# K

**K.D.**
Knocked Down
**KDD**
Kokusai Denshin Denwa
**K.D.F.**
Knocked Down Flat
**KEG**
Kommandit Erwerbsgesellschaft. *See* Business Entities Appendix.
**Kft**
Korlátolt Felelosségu Társaság. *See* Business Entities Appendix.
**KG**
Kommanditgesellschaft
**KGS (or Kilos)**
Kilogram(s)
**KK**
Kabushiki Kaisha
**Kkt**
Közkereseti Társaság. *See* Business Entities Appendix.
**k.s.**
Komanditní Spolecnost. *See* Business Entities Appendix.
**K/S**
Kommanditselskab

# L

**L**
Length
**LAES**
Latin American Economic System
**LAFTA**
Latin American Free Trade Association
**LAIA**
Latin American Integration Association
**LAS**
League of Arab States
**LASH**
Lighter Aboard Ship
**Lb(s)**
Pound(s) (weight measure)
**LBCIP**
Land Border Carrier Initiative Program
**L/C**
Letter of Credit
**LCL**
Less Than Container Load
**Lda.**
Sociedade por Quota. *See* Business Entities Appendix.
**LDC**
Less Developed Country
Limited Duration Companies. *See* Business Entities Appendix.
**LDI**
Logistics Data Interchange
**LIBID**
London Interbank Bid Rate
**LIBOR**
London Interbank Offered Rate
**LIFFE**
London International Financial Futures Exchange
**LIMEAN**
London Interbank Mean

**LLC**
Limited Liability Company. *See* Business Entities Appendix.
**LLDC**
Least Developed Country
**LLP**
Limited Liability Partnership. *See* Business Entities Appendix.
**L.O.A.**
Length Overall
**Lo/Lo**
Lift on, Lift off
**LOI**
Letter of Indemnity
**LOS**
U.N. Convention on the Law of the Sea
**LRM**
Logistics Resource Management
**L.S.**
Lump Sum
**LSM**
Lloyd's Ship Manager
**L.T.**
Long Ton (2,240 Pounds)
**Ltd.**
Limited
Corporation, *See* Business Entities Appendix.
Private Company. *See* Business Entities Appendix.
**Ltda.**
Sociedad de Responsabilidad Limitada. *See* Business Entities Appendix.
Limitada
**Ltée.**
Corporation, *See* Business Entities Appendix.
Limitée
**L.T.L.**
Less than truckload
**LVS**
Low Value Shipment

# M

**M**
Measurement
Thousand (1,000 units)
**MAP**
Market Access Program
**MARECS**
Maritime European Communications Satellite
**MAWB**
Master Air Waybill
**max.**
Maximum
**MBF or MBM**
One Thousand Board Feet
**MC**
Minister Counsellor
**MCTL**
Militarily Critical Technologies List
**M/D**
Month's Date
**MD**
Managing Director
**MDB**
Multilateral Development Bank

**MEDARABTEL**
Middle East Telecommunications Project of the International Telecommunications Union
**MERCOSUR**
Mercado Comun del Cono Sur (Southern Cone Common Market)
**METI**
Ministry of Economy, Trade and Industry (Japan)
**MFA**
Multi-Fiber Arrangement
**MFN**
Most Favored Nation
**MFT**
Per Thousand Feet
**MHW**
Ministry of Health and Welfare
**MIF**
Multilateral Investment Fund
**MIGA**
Multilateral Investment Guarantee Agency
**Mij.**
Maatschappij
**min.**
Minimum
**MIPRO**
Manufactured Imports Promotion Organization
**MITI**
Ministry of International Trade and Industry
**MKR**
Matchmaker Program
**M.O.**
Money Order
**MOCP**
Market-Oriented Cooperation Plan
**MOFERT**
Ministry of Foreign Economic Relations and Trade
**MOFTEC**
Ministry of Foreign Economic Trade and Economic Cooperation
**MOSS**
Market-Oriented, Sector-Selective
**MOU**
Memorandum of Understanding
**MPA**
Major Projects Agreement
**MPF**
Merchandise Processing Fee
**MPP**
Market Promotion Program
**MPT**
Ministry of Posts and Telecommunications
**MRA**
Mutual Recognition Agreement
**MRP**
Manufacturing Resources Planning
**MSC**
Maritime Safety Committee
**MSDS**
Material Safety Data Sheets
**MT**
Marine Terminal

**ACRONYMS**

**MTAG**
Missile Technology Advisory Group
**MTCR**
Missile Technology Control Regime
**MTEC**
Missile Technology Export Control
Group
**MTN**
Multilateral Trade Negotiations
**MTO**
Multilateral Trade Organization
**MTSA**
Maritime Transportation Security Act

# N

**N/A**
Not Applicable
Not Available
**NACC**
North Atlantic Cooperation Council
**NAEC**
National Association of Export
Companies
**NAFTA**
North American Free Trade Agreement
**NAM**
Non-Aligned Movement
**NASDA**
National Association of State
Development Agencies
**NASDAQ**
North American Securities Dealers
Automated Quotations (U.S. stock
exchange)
**NATO**
North Atlantic Treaty Organization
**N.B.**
Note Below
**NC**
Nordic Council
**NCAP**
National Customs Automation
Program (Canada)
**NCC**
National Chambers of Commerce
**NDA**
Non-Disclosure Agreement
**NEA**
Nuclear Energy Agency
**NePAD**
New Partnership for African
Development
**N.E.S.**
Not Elsewhere Specified
**NGO**
Non-Governmental Organization
**NIB**
Nordic Investment Bank
**NICs**
Newly Industrializing Countries
**NIE**
Newly Industrializing Economy
**NIPA**
National Income and Product Accounts
**NM**
Nautical Mile
**NMEs**
Nonmarket Economies

**NMFC**
National Motor Freight Classification
**NMT**
Nordic Mobile Telephone
**NNPA**
Nuclear Non-Proliferation Act
**NNPT**
Nuclear Non-Proliferation Treaty
**No**
Number
**N.O.I.B.N.**
Not Otherwise Indexed by Number
**N.O.S.**
Not Otherwise Specified
**NPT**
Nuclear Non-Proliferation Treaty
**NRC**
Nuclear Regulatory Commission (U.S.)
**NRL**
Nuclear Referral List
**NRPB**
Natural Resource Based Products
**N/S (also NSF)**
Not Sufficient Funds
**NS**
Not Subject to
**NSA**
National Security Agency (U.S.)
**NSC**
National Security Council (U.S.)
**NSD**
National Security Directive
**NSF (also N/S)**
Not Sufficient Funds
**NSG**
Nuclear Suppliers Group
**NSO**
National Security Override
**NT**
Net Ton
**NTBs**
Non-Tariff Barriers
**NTDB**
National Trade Data Bank
**NTE**
National Trade Estimates Report
New-To-Export
**NTM**
New-To-Market
**NTMs**
Non-Tariff Measures
**NTR**
Normal Trade Relations
**NTT**
Nippon Telegraph and Telephone
corporation
**N.V.**
Naamloze Vennootschap. *See* Business
Entities Appendix.
**NVOCC**
Non-Vessel Operating Common
Carrier
**NYMEX**
New York Mercantile Exchange
**NYSE**
New York Stock Exchange

# O

**OAPEC**
Organization of Arab Petroleum
Exporting Countries
**OAS**
Organization of American States
**OAU**
Organization of African Unity
**O.B.L.**
Ocean Bill of Lading
**OBR**
Overseas Business Report
**OBU**
Offshore Banking Unit
**O/C**
Overcharge
**OC**
Operating Committee
**OCP**
Overland Common Point
**O.D.**
Outside Diameter
**ODA**
Official Development Assistance
**ODS**
Operating Differential Subsidy
**OE**
Omorythmos Eteria. *See* Business
Entities Appendix.
**OECD**
Organization for Economic
Cooperation and Development
**OECS**
Organization of Eastern Caribbean
States
**OEG**
Offene Erwerbsgesellschaft. *See*
Business Entities Appendix.
**OEL**
Office of Export Licensing (U.S.)
**OEM**
Original Equipment Manufacturer
**OEXS**
Office of Exporter Services (U.S.)
**OFAC**
Office of Foreign Assets Control
**OHG**
Offene Handelsgesellschaft. *See*
Business Entities Appendix.
**OIC**
Organization of the Islamic Conference
**OIEC**
Organization for Economic
Cooperation
**OMA**
Orderly Marketing Agreement
**OMB**
Office of Management and Budget
(U.S.)
**OMC**
Office of Munitions Control
**OOD**
Drouzestvo s Ogranichena
Otgovornost. *See* Business Entities
Appendix.
**OPEC**
Organization of Petroleum Exporting
Countries

**OPIC**
Overseas Private Investment
  Corporation
**ORM**
Other Regulated Materials
**O/S**
Out of Stock
**OSD**
Overs, Short, and Damaged
**OSHA**
Occupational Safety and Health
  Administration (U.S.)
**OT**
Open Top
**O/T**
Overtime
**OTC**
Over the Counter
**OTI**
Ocean Transport Intermediary
**OTM**
Old-To-Market
**OWC**
On Wheels Charge
**Oy**
Osakeyhtiö. *See* Business Entities
  Appendix.

# P

**PAPS**
Pre-Arrival Processing System
**PARS**
Pre-Arrival Review System (Canada)
**P/A**
Power of Attorney
**PC**
Per Container
Personal Computer
**P/C**
Prices Current
Petty Cash
**PCA**
Permanent Court of Arbitration
**PCS**
Piece(s)
**PCT**
Patent Cooperation Treaty
**PEC**
President's Export Council (U.S.)
**PEFCO**
Private Export Funding Corporation
**PFSO**
Port Facility Security Officer
**PFSP**
Port Facility Security Plan
**P/H**
Pier to House
**P&I**
Principal and Interest
Protection and Indemnity
**PIP**
Post-Initiated Promotion
Partners in Protection
**Pkg(s)**
Package(s)
**P&L**
Profit and Loss

**PLC**
Pre-License Check
Public Limited Company. *See* Business
  Entities Appendix.
**P/N**
Promissory Note
**POE**
Point of Entry
**PP**
Purchase Price
**P.P.**
Prepaid (Freight Prepaid)
**P/P**
Pier to Pier
**PPA**
Protocol of Provisional Application
**P.R.C.**
People's Republic of China
**PROSEC**
Programs of Sectorial Promotion
  (Mexico)
**PSV**
Post-Shipment Verification
**p/t**
Part-time
Pte. Ltd.
Private Limited
**PT**
Per Trailer
**PT 20**
Per 20 Foot Trailer/Container
**PT 40**
Per 40 Foot Trailer/Container
**PTA**
Preferential Trade Agreement for
  Eastern and Southern Africa
**Pty. Ltd.**
Proprietary Limited. *See* Business
  Entities Appendix.
**PU&D**
Pick Up and Delivery
**Pvt. Ltd.**
Private Company. *See* Business Entities
  Appendix.

# Q

**QRs**
Quantitative Restrictions

# R

**R**
Rail Ramp
**RACE**
Research in Advanced
  Communications in Europe
**RAM**
Random Access Memory
**RBPs**
Restrictive Business Practices
**RCS**
Regular Catalog Show
**R&D**
Research and Development
**RFP**
Request for Proposal
**RFQ**
Request for Quotation

**RG**
Rio Group
**RILO**
Regional Intelligence Liaison Offices
**RMD**
Release on Minimum Documentation
  (Canada)
**RNS**
Release Notification System (Canada)
**ROM**
Read Only Memory
**RoRo**
Roll-on, Roll-off
**R.R.**
Railroad
**RSO**
Recognized Security Organizations
**Rt**
Részvénytársaság. *See* Business
  Entities Appendix.
**RWA**
Returned Without Action

# S

**2PL**
Second Party Logistics
**S.A.**
Sociedad Anónima. *See* Business
  Entities Appendix.
Sociedade Anónima. *See* Business
  Entities Appendix.
Società per Azioni. *See* Business
  Entities Appendix.
Société Anonyme. *See* Business
  Entities Appendix.
Spólka Akcyjna. *See* Business Entities
  Appendix.
**SAARC**
South Asian Association for Regional
  Cooperation
**SABIT**
Special American Business Internship
  Training Program
**SACU**
Southern African Customs Union
**SADC**
Southern African Development
  Community
**SADCC**
Southern African Development
  Coordination Conference
**S.A. de C.A.**
Sociedad Anónima de Capital Abierto.
  *See* Business Entities Appendix.
**SAI**
Social Accountability International
**S.A.R.L.**
Société à Responsabilité Limitée. *See*
  Business Entities Appendix.
**S.A.S.**
Società in Accomandita Semplice. *See*
  Business Entities Appendix.
Société par Actions Simplifée. *See*
  Business Entities Appendix.
**SASO**
Saudi Arabian Standards Organization
**SBA**
Small Business Administration

**ACRONYMS**

**S.C.**
Sociedad Colectiva. *See* Business Entities Appendix
Société en Commandite. Société Coopérative. *See* Business Entities Appendix.
**S.C.A.**
Sociedad en Comandita por Acciones. *See* Business Entities Appendix.
**SCaRL**
Società Cooperativa a Responsabilità. *See* Business Entities Appendix.
**S.C.I.**
Sociedad de Capital e Industria. *See* Business Entities Appendix.
**SCM**
Southern Common Market
**SCO**
Senior Commercial Officer
**S.C. par A.**
Société en Commandite par Actionss. *See* Business Entities Appendix.
**SCRL**
Sociedade Cooperativa. *See* Business Entities Appendix.
**S.C.S.**
Société en Commandite Simple. *See* Business Entities Appendix.
**S&D**
Special and Differential Treatment
**S. de R.L. (also Ltda.)**
Sociedad de Responsabilidad Limitada. *See* Business Entities Appendix.
**Sdn. Bhd.**
Sendirian Berhard. *See* Business Entities Appendix.
**SDR**
Special Drawing Rights (banking)
**SEA**
Single European Act
**SEACATS**
Seized Asset and Case Tracking System
**SEC**
Securities and Exchange Commission
Special Equipment Compensation
**SED**
Shipper's Export Declaration
**SEED**
Support for East European Democracy
**SELA**
Sistema Economico Latinoamericana
**SEM**
Seminar Mission
**S. en C.**
Sociedad en Comandita. *See* Business Entities Appendix.
Société en Commandite Simple. *See* Business Entities Appendix.
**S. en C.S.**
Société en Commandite Simple. *See* Business Entities Appendix.
**SEPD**
State Export Program Database
**SFO**
Solo Fair Overseas procured
**SFSC**
Shared Foreign Sales Corporation

**SFW**
Solo Fair Washington procured
**SGA**
Selling, General, and Administrative (Expenses)
**S.G.L.**
Società a Garanzia Limitata. *See* Business Entities Appendix.
**SIC**
Standard Industrial Classification
**SII**
Structural Impediments Initiative
**SIMIS**
Single Internal Market Information Service
**SIMS**
Single Internal Market Service
**SIN**
Ship Identification Number
**S/IOGA**
State/Industry-Organized, Government-Approved
**SITC**
Standard International Tariff Classification
**sku**
Stock Keeping Unit
**SLI**
Shipper's Letter of Instruction
**SM (or sm)**
Service Mark
**SMSA**
Standard Metropolitan Statistical Area
**SNC**
Société en Nom Collectif. *See* Business Entities Appendix.
**SNEC**
Subgroup on Nuclear Export Coordination
**s/o (or S.O.)**
Ship's Option, (rate yielding greater revenue; must be charged)
**SOD**
Shipped on Deck
**SOGA**
State-Organized, Government-Approved Mission
**SOLAS**
Safety of Life at Sea Convention
**S.p.A.**
Società per Azioni. *See* Business Entities Appendix.
**SPAC**
Services Policy Advisory Committee
**SPARTECA**
South Pacific Regional Trade and Economic Cooperation Agreement
**SPC**
South Pacific Commission
**SPF**
South Pacific Forum
**spol. s r.o.**
Spolecnost s Rucením Omezenym. *See* Business Entities Appendix.
**S.P.R.L.**
Société Privée a Résponsabilité Limitée. *See* Business Entities Appendix.

**Sp. z o.o.**
Spólka z Ograniczona Odpowied Zialnóscia. *See* Business Entities Appendix.
**S.Q.**
Sociedad por Quota
**S.R.&C.C.**
Strikes, Riots and Civil Commotion Warranty (all risk insurance)
**S.R.L.**
Sociedad de Responsabilidad Limitada. *See* Business Entities Appendix.
Società a Responsabilità Limitata. *See* Business Entities Appendix.
Société à Responsabilité Limitée. *See* Business Entities Appendix.
**s.r.o.**
Spolecnost s Rucením Omezenym. *See* Business Entities Appendix.
**SSA**
Sub-Saharan Africa
Ship Security Assessment
**SSAS**
Ship Security Alert System
**SSCC**
Serial Shipping Container Code
**SSO**
Ship Security Officer
**SSP**
Ship Security Plan
**STA**
Semiconductor Trade Agreement
**S.T.C.**
Said to Contain
**Sté.**
Société
**Ste. Cve.**
Société Cooperative. *See* Business Entities Appendix.
**STELA**
System for Tracking Export License Applications
**STEs**
State Trading Enterprises
**STM**
State Trade Mission
**S.T.W.**
Said to Weigh
**S.U.**
Set Up
**SWIFT**
Society for Worldwide Interbank Financial Telecommunications

# T

**3PL**
Third Party Logistics
**T.**
Ton of 2,240 lbs
**TA**
Trade Assistant
**TAA**
Trade Adjustment Assistance
**TAAC**
Trade Adjustment Assistance Center
**TAC**
Technical Advisory Committee

**TACM**
Transit Air Cargo Manifest
**TAPO**
Trade Assistance and Planning Office
**TCI**
Third Country Initiative
**TCMD**
Third Country Meat Directive
**TDA**
Trade and Development Agency (U.S.)
**TDO**
Table of Denial Orders
**TDP**
Trade and Development Program
**TEC or CET**
Tarif Extérieur Commun (common external tariff)
**Tel.**
Telephone
**Teo.**
Steoranta. *See* Business Entities Appendix.
**TEU**
Twenty foot equivalent unit. A forty foot container is equal to two (2) TEU'S.
**TFC**
Trade Fair Certification
**TFO**
Trade Fair (Overseas-Recruited)
**TFW**
Trade Fair (Washington-Recruited)
**THC**
Terminal Handling Charge
**TIA**
Travel Industry Association of America
**TIB**
Temporary Importation under Bond
**TIC**
Trade Information Center
**TIEA**
Tax Information Exchange Agreement
**TIFTs**
Trade and Investment Facilitation Talks
**TIMS**
Textiles Information Management System
**T.L.**
Total Loss (shipping)
Truckload
**T.L.S.**
Türk Limited Sirket. *See* Business Entities Appendix.
**T.M.**
Traffic Manager
**TM**
Trademark
Trade Mission
**TNC**
Trade Negotiations Committee
**T.O.F.C.**
Trailer (On Wheels) Flat Car
**TOP**
Trade Opportunities Program (U.S.)
**TPC**
Trade Policy Committee (U.S.)
**TPCC**
Trade Promotion Coordinating Committee

**TPIS**
Trade Policy Information System
**TPM**
Trigger Price Mechanism
**TPRG**
Trade Policy Review Group
**TPRM**
Trade Policy Review Mechanism
**TPSC**
Trade Policy Staff Committee
**TRA**
Trade Reference Assistant
Tax Reform Act
**TRIMs**
Trade-Related Investment Measures
**TRIPs**
Trade-Related Aspects of Intellectual Property Rights
**TRO**
Temporary Restraining Order
**TS**
Trade Specialist
**TSA**
Trans-Pacific Stabilization Agreement
**TSB**
Textile Surveillance Body
**TSN**
Trade Support Network
**TSUSA**
Tariff Schedules of the United States Annotated. Usually referred to as HTSUS or Harmonized Tariff Schedules of the United States
**TT**
Telegraphic Transfer (bank wire)
**T.T.S.**
Telegraphic transfer selling rate
**TWEA**
Trading With the Enemy Act

# U

**U.A.E.**
United Arab Emirates
**UBO**
Ultimate Beneficial Owner
**UCC**
Uniform Commercial Code
Uniform Code Council
**UCP**
Uniform Customs and Practices
**UCPDC**
Uniform Customs and Practice for Documentary Credits
**UDEAC**
Union Douaniere et Economique de l'Afrique Centrale (Customs and Economic Union of Central Africa)
**UEMOA (also WAEMU)**
Union Economique et Monetaire Ouest Africaine (West African Economic and Monetary Union)
**U.K.**
United Kingdom
**UL**
Underwriters Laboratories
**ULCC**
Ultra Large Crude Carrier

**ULD**
Unit Load Device
**UMOA**
Union Monétaire Ouest Africaine (West African Monetary Union)
**UN**
United Nations
**UNCDF**
United Nations Capital Development Fund
**UNCSTD**
United Nations Conference on Science and Technology for Development
**UNCTAD**
United Nations Conference on Trade and Development
**UNDP**
United Nations Development Program
**UNDRO**
United Nations Disaster Relief Organization
**UN/EDIFACT**
United Nations [rules for] Electronic Data Interchange for Administration, Commerce and Transportation.
**UNEP**
United Nations Environment Program
**UNESCO**
United Nations Educational, Scientific, and Cultural Organization
**UNFPA**
United Nations Fund for Population Activities
**UNGA**
United Nations General Assembly
**UNHCR**
United Nations High Commissioner for Refugees
**UNICEF**
United Nations International Children's Emergency Fund
**UNIDO**
United Nations Industrial Development Organization
**UNITAR**
United Nations Institute for Training and Research
**UN/LOCODE**
United Nations Code for Trade and Transport Locations
**UNRISD**
United Nations Research Institute for Social Development
**UNRWA**
United Nations Relief and Works Agency
**UPU**
Universal Postal Union
**URC**
Uniform Rules for Collection
**U.S. or U.S.A.**
United States of America
**USC**
United States Code
**USCS**
U.S. Customs Service (obsolete)
**USD (also US$)**
U.S. Dollar

**ACRONYMS**

**USDA**
U.S. Department of Agriculture
**USDIA**
U.S. Direct Investment Abroad
**USEC**
U.S. Mission to the European
Communities
**US&FCS**
United States and Foreign Commercial
Service
**USGPO**
U.S. Government Printing Office
**USIA**
U.S. Information Agency
**USIS**
U.S. Information Service
**USITC**
U.S. International Trade Commission
**U.S.M.C**
U.S. Maritime Commission
U.S. Marine Corps
**USML**
U.S. Munitions List
**USP**
U.S. Price
**USSR**
Union of Soviet Socialist Republics
(obsolete)
**USTDA**
U.S. Trade and Development Agency
**USTR**
United States Trade Representative
**USTTA**
United States Travel and Tourism
Administration
**USUN**
U.S. Mission to the United Nations

# V

**VAR**
Value-Added Reseller
**VAT**
Value-Added Tax
**VER**
Voluntary Export Restriction
**VHF**
Very High Frequency
**Viz**
Namely
**VL**
Variable Levy
**VLCC**
Very Large Crude Carrier
**VOA**
Voice of America
**VOIP**
Voice Over Internet Protocol
**v.o.s.**
Verejná Obchodní Spolecnost. *See*
Business Entities Appendix.
**VP**
Vice President
**VRA**
Voluntary Restraint Agreement

# W-X-Y

**W**
Width

Ton of 1000 kilos
**w/ (also W/ )**
With
**WA**
With Average
**WADB**
West African Development Bank
**WAEMU (also UEMOA)**
West African Economic and Monetary
Union
**WAMU**
West African Monetary Union
**WARC**
World Administrative Radio
Conference
**W/B**
Waybill
**WCL**
World Confederation of Labor
**WCO**
World Customs Organization
**WFG**
Wharfage
**WHO**
World Health Organization
**WIP**
Work In Progress
**WIPO**
World Intellectual Property
Organization
**WLL**
Sharika That Massouliyyah
Mahdoodah. *See* Business Entities
Appendix.
**WMD**
Weapons of Mass Destruction
**WMO**
World Meteorological Organization
**W/O**
Without
**WP**
Warsaw Pact
**W.P.A.**
With Particular Average (insurance)
**WSC**
World Shipping Council
**WTDR**
World Traders Data Report
**WTO**
World Trade Organization
World Tourism Organization
**WWW**
World Wide Web

# Z

**ZC**
Zangger Committe

# Country Codes (ISO 3166)

The following two tables list ISO (International Organization for Standardization) 2-letter, 3-letter, and numeric codes for countries of the world.

ISO codes are used in communications to identify countries where a code or abbreviation is helpful. These *are not* currency or dialing codes.

**Table 1** is sorted by country and then codes.

**Table 2** is sorted by 2-letter code, then country.

## Table 1: COUNTRY ☞ Country Code

| Country | 2-letter | 3-letter | Numeric |
|---|---|---|---|
| Afghanistan | AF | AFG | 004 |
| Åland Islands | AX | ALA | 248 |
| Albania | AL | ALB | 008 |
| Algeria | DZ | DZA | 012 |
| American Samoa | AS | ASM | 016 |
| Andorra | AD | AND | 020 |
| Angola | AO | AGO | 024 |
| Anguilla | AI | AIA | 660 |
| Antarctica | AQ | ATA | 010 |
| Antigua and Barbuda | AG | ATG | 028 |
| Argentina | AR | ARG | 032 |
| Armenia | AM | ARM | 051 |
| Aruba | AW | ABW | 533 |
| Australia | AU | AUS | 036 |
| Austria | AT | AUT | 040 |
| Azerbaijan | AZ | AZE | 031 |
| Bahamas | BS | BHS | 044 |
| Bahrain | BH | BHR | 048 |
| Bangladesh | BD | BGD | 050 |
| Barbados | BB | BRB | 052 |
| Belarus | BY | BLR | 112 |
| Belgium | BE | BEL | 056 |
| Belize | BZ | BLZ | 084 |
| Benin | BJ | BEN | 204 |
| Bermuda | BM | BMU | 060 |
| Bhutan | BT | BTN | 064 |
| Bolivia | BO | BOL | 068 |
| Bosnia and Herzegovina | BA | BIH | 070 |
| Botswana | BW | BWA | 072 |
| Bouvet Island | BV | BVT | 074 |
| Brazil | BR | BRA | 076 |
| British Indian Ocean Territory | IO | IOT | 086 |
| Brunei Darussalam | BN | BRN | 096 |
| Bulgaria | BG | BGR | 100 |
| Burkina Faso | BF | BFA | 854 |
| Burundi | BI | BDI | 108 |
| Cambodia | KH | KHM | 116 |

## Table 2: COUNTRY CODE ☞ Country

| 2-letter | Country | 3-letter | Numeric |
|---|---|---|---|
| AD | Andorra | AND | 020 |
| AE | United Arab Emirates | ARE | 784 |
| AF | Afghanistan | AFG | 004 |
| AG | Antigua and Barbuda | ATG | 028 |
| AI | Anguilla | AIA | 660 |
| AL | Albania | ALB | 008 |
| AM | Armenia | ARM | 051 |
| AN | Netherlands Antilles | ANT | 530 |
| AO | Angola | AGO | 024 |
| AQ | Antarctica | ATA | 010 |
| AR | Argentina | ARG | 032 |
| AS | American Samoa | ASM | 016 |
| AT | Austria | AUT | 040 |
| AU | Australia | AUS | 036 |
| AW | Aruba | ABW | 533 |
| AX | Åland Islands | ALA | 248 |
| AZ | Azerbaijan | AZE | 031 |
| BA | Bosnia & Herzegovina | BIH | 070 |
| BB | Barbados | BRB | 052 |
| BD | Bangladesh | BGD | 050 |
| BE | Belgium | BEL | 056 |
| BF | Burkina Faso | BFA | 854 |
| BG | Bulgaria | BGR | 100 |
| BH | Bahrain | BHR | 048 |
| BI | Burundi | BDI | 108 |
| BJ | Benin | BEN | 204 |
| BM | Bermuda | BMU | 060 |
| BN | Brunei Darussalam | BRN | 096 |
| BO | Bolivia | BOL | 068 |
| BR | Brazil | BRA | 076 |
| BS | Bahamas | BHS | 044 |
| BT | Bhutan | BTN | 064 |
| BV | Bouvet Island | BVT | 074 |
| BW | Botswana | BWA | 072 |
| BY | Belarus | BLR | 112 |
| BZ | Belize | BLZ | 084 |
| CA | Canada | CAN | 124 |
| CC | Cocos (Keeling) Isl. | CCK | 166 |

COUNTRIES

C
O
U
N
T
R
I
E
S

| Table 1: COUNTRY ☞ Country Code | | | |
|---|---|---|---|
| Country | 2-letter | 3-letter | Numeric |
| Cameroon | CM | CMR | 120 |
| Canada | CA | CAN | 124 |
| Cape Verde | CV | CPV | 132 |
| Cayman Islands | KY | CYM | 136 |
| Central African Republic | CF | CAF | 140 |
| Chad | TD | TCD | 148 |
| Chile | CL | CHL | 152 |
| China | CN | CHN | 156 |
| Christmas Island | CX | CXR | 162 |
| Cocos (Keeling) Islands | CC | CCK | 166 |
| Colombia | CO | COL | 170 |
| Comoros | KM | COM | 174 |
| Congo | CG | COG | 178 |
| Congo, Dem. Rep. of the (was Zaire) | CD | COD | 180 |
| Cook Islands | CK | COK | 184 |
| Costa Rica | CR | CRI | 188 |
| Côte d'Ivoire (Ivory Coast) | CI | CIV | 384 |
| Croatia | HR | HRV | 191 |
| Cuba | CU | CUB | 192 |
| Cyprus | CY | CYP | 196 |
| Czech Republic | CZ | CZE | 203 |
| Denmark | DK | DNK | 208 |
| Djibouti | DJ | DJI | 262 |
| Dominica | DM | DMA | 212 |
| Dominican Republic | DO | DOM | 214 |
| Ecuador | EC | ECU | 218 |
| Egypt | EG | EGY | 818 |
| El Salvador | SV | SLV | 222 |
| Equat. Guinea | GQ | GNQ | 226 |
| Eritrea | ER | ERI | 232 |
| Estonia | EE | EST | 233 |
| Ethiopia | ET | ETH | 231 |
| Falkland Islands | FK | FLK | 238 |
| Faroe Islands | FO | FRO | 234 |
| Fiji | FJ | FJI | 242 |
| Finland | FI | FIN | 246 |
| France | FR | FRA | 250 |
| French Guiana | GF | GUF | 254 |
| French Polynesia | PF | PYF | 258 |
| French Southern Territories | TF | ATF | 260 |
| Gabon | GA | GAB | 266 |

| Table 2: COUNTRY CODE ☞ Country | | | |
|---|---|---|---|
| 2-letter | Country | 3-letter | Numeric |
| CD | Congo, Dem. Rep. of the (was Zaire) | COD | 180 |
| CD | Zaire | COD | 180 |
| CF | Central African Republic | CAF | 140 |
| CG | Congo | COG | 178 |
| CH | Switzerland | CHE | 756 |
| CI | Côte d'Ivoire (Ivory Coast) | CIV | 384 |
| CI | Ivory Coast (Côte d'Ivoire) | CIV | 384 |
| CK | Cook Islands | COK | 184 |
| CL | Chile | CHL | 152 |
| CM | Cameroon | CMR | 120 |
| CN | China | CHN | 156 |
| CO | Colombia | COL | 170 |
| CR | Costa Rica | CRI | 188 |
| CS | Serbia & Montenegro | SCG | 891 |
| CU | Cuba | CUB | 192 |
| CV | Cape Verde | CPV | 132 |
| CX | Christmas Island | CXR | 162 |
| CY | Cyprus | CYP | 196 |
| CZ | Czech Republic | CZE | 203 |
| DE | Germany | DEU | 276 |
| DJ | Djibouti | DJI | 262 |
| DK | Denmark | DNK | 208 |
| DM | Dominica | DMA | 212 |
| DO | Dominican Republic | DOM | 214 |
| DZ | Algeria | DZA | 012 |
| EC | Ecuador | ECU | 218 |
| EE | Estonia | EST | 233 |
| EG | Egypt | EGY | 818 |
| EH | Western Sahara | ESH | 732 |
| ER | Eritrea | ERI | 232 |
| ES | Spain | ESP | 724 |
| ET | Ethiopia | ETH | 231 |
| FI | Finland | FIN | 246 |
| FJ | Fiji | FJI | 242 |
| FK | Falkland Islands | FLK | 238 |
| FO | Faroe Islands | FRO | 234 |
| FR | France | FRA | 250 |
| GA | Gabon | GAB | 266 |
| GB | United Kingdom | GBR | 826 |
| GD | Grenada | GRD | 308 |
| GE | Georgia | GEO | 268 |
| GF | French Guiana | GUF | 254 |

| Table 1: COUNTRY ☞ Country Code | | | |
|---|---|---|---|
| Country | 2-letter | 3-letter | Numeric |
| Gambia | GM | GMB | 270 |
| Georgia | GE | GEO | 268 |
| Germany | DE | DEU | 276 |
| Ghana | GH | GHA | 288 |
| Gibraltar | GI | GIB | 292 |
| Greece | GR | GRC | 300 |
| Greenland | GL | GRL | 304 |
| Grenada | GD | GRD | 308 |
| Guadeloupe | GP | GLP | 312 |
| Guam | GU | GUM | 316 |
| Guatemala | GT | GTM | 320 |
| Guinea | GN | GIN | 324 |
| Guinea-Bissau | GW | GNB | 624 |
| Guyana | GY | GUY | 328 |
| Haiti | HT | HTI | 332 |
| Heard & McDonald Isl. | HM | HMD | 334 |
| Holy See (Vatican) | VA | VAT | 336 |
| Honduras | HN | HND | 340 |
| Hong Kong | HK | HKG | 344 |
| Hungary | HU | HUN | 348 |
| Iceland | IS | ISL | 352 |
| India | IN | IND | 356 |
| Indonesia | ID | IDN | 360 |
| Iran | IR | IRN | 364 |
| Iraq | IQ | IRQ | 368 |
| Ireland | IE | IRL | 372 |
| Israel | IL | ISR | 376 |
| Italy | IT | ITA | 380 |
| Ivory Coast (Côte d'Ivoire) | CI | CIV | 384 |
| Jamaica | JM | JAM | 388 |
| Japan | JP | JPN | 392 |
| Jordan | JO | JOR | 400 |
| Kazakhstan | KZ | KAZ | 398 |
| Kenya | KE | KEN | 404 |
| Kiribati | KI | KIR | 296 |
| Korea, Dem. People's Rep. of (North) | KP | PRK | 408 |
| Korea, Republic of (South) | KR | KOR | 410 |
| Kuwait | KW | KWT | 414 |
| Kyrgyzstan | KG | KGZ | 417 |
| Laos (Lao People's Dem. Rep.) | LA | LAO | 418 |
| Latvia | LV | LVA | 428 |

| Table 2: COUNTRY CODE ☞ Country | | | |
|---|---|---|---|
| 2-letter | Country | 3-letter | Numeric |
| GH | Ghana | GHA | 288 |
| GI | Gibraltar | GIB | 292 |
| GL | Greenland | GRL | 304 |
| GM | Gambia | GMB | 270 |
| GN | Guinea | GIN | 324 |
| GP | Guadeloupe | GLP | 312 |
| GQ | Equat. Guinea | GNQ | 226 |
| GR | Greece | GRC | 300 |
| GS | S. Georgia and S. Sandwich Islands | SGS | 239 |
| GT | Guatemala | GTM | 320 |
| GU | Guam | GUM | 316 |
| GW | Guinea-Bissau | GNB | 624 |
| GY | Guyana | GUY | 328 |
| HK | Hong Kong | HKG | 344 |
| HM | Heard & McDonald Isl. | HMD | 334 |
| HN | Honduras | HND | 340 |
| HR | Croatia | HRV | 191 |
| HT | Haiti | HTI | 332 |
| HU | Hungary | HUN | 348 |
| ID | Indonesia | IDN | 360 |
| IE | Ireland | IRL | 372 |
| IL | Israel | ISR | 376 |
| IN | India | IND | 356 |
| IO | British Indian Ocean Territory | IOT | 086 |
| IQ | Iraq | IRQ | 368 |
| IR | Iran | IRN | 364 |
| IS | Iceland | ISL | 352 |
| IT | Italy | ITA | 380 |
| JM | Jamaica | JAM | 388 |
| JO | Jordan | JOR | 400 |
| JP | Japan | JPN | 392 |
| KE | Kenya | KEN | 404 |
| KG | Kyrgyzstan | KGZ | 417 |
| KH | Cambodia | KHM | 116 |
| KI | Kiribati | KIR | 296 |
| KM | Comoros | COM | 174 |
| KN | Saint Kitts and Nevis | KNA | 659 |
| KP | Korea, Dem. People's Rep. of (North) | PRK | 408 |
| KR | Korea, Republic of (South) | KOR | 410 |
| KW | Kuwait | KWT | 414 |
| KY | Cayman Islands | CYM | 136 |

COUNTRIES

COUNTRIES

| Table 1: COUNTRY ☞ Country Code | | | |
|---|---|---|---|
| Country | 2-letter | 3-letter | Numeric |
| Lebanon | LB | LBN | 422 |
| Lesotho | LS | LSO | 426 |
| Liberia | LR | LBR | 430 |
| Libya | LY | LBY | 434 |
| Liechtenstein | LI | LIE | 438 |
| Lithuania | LT | LTU | 440 |
| Luxembourg | LU | LUX | 442 |
| Macau | MO | MAC | 446 |
| Macedonia | MK | MKD | 807 |
| Madagascar | MG | MDG | 450 |
| Malawi | MW | MWI | 454 |
| Malaysia | MY | MYS | 458 |
| Maldives | MV | MDV | 462 |
| Mali | ML | MLI | 466 |
| Malta | MT | MLT | 470 |
| Marshall Islands | MH | MHL | 584 |
| Martinique | MQ | MTQ | 474 |
| Mauritania | MR | MRT | 478 |
| Mauritius | MU | MUS | 480 |
| Mayotte | YT | MYT | 175 |
| Mexico | MX | MEX | 484 |
| Micronesia, Federated States of | OF | FM | FSM |
| Moldova | MD | MDA | 498 |
| Monaco | MC | MCO | 492 |
| Mongolia | MN | MNG | 496 |
| Montserrat | MS | MSR | 500 |
| Morocco | MA | MAR | 504 |
| Mozambique | MZ | MOZ | 508 |
| Myanmar | MM | MMR | 104 |
| Namibia | NA | NAM | 516 |
| Nauru | NR | NRU | 520 |
| Nepal | NP | NPL | 524 |
| Netherlands | NL | NLD | 528 |
| Netherlands Antilles | AN | ANT | 530 |
| New Caledonia | NC | NCL | 540 |
| New Zealand | NZ | NZL | 554 |
| Nicaragua | NI | NIC | 558 |
| Niger | NE | NER | 562 |
| Nigeria | NG | NGA | 566 |
| Niue | NU | NIU | 570 |
| Norfolk Island | NF | NFK | 574 |
| Northern Marianas | MP | MNP | 580 |
| Norway | NO | NOR | 578 |
| Oman | OM | OMN | 512 |

| Table 2: COUNTRY CODE ☞ Country | | | |
|---|---|---|---|
| 2-letter | Country | 3-letter | Numeric |
| KZ | Kazakhstan | KAZ | 398 |
| LA | Laos (Lao People's Dem. Rep.) | LAO | 418 |
| LB | Lebanon | LBN | 422 |
| LC | Saint Lucia | LCA | 662 |
| LI | Liechtenstein | LIE | 438 |
| LK | Sri Lanka | LKA | 144 |
| LR | Liberia | LBR | 430 |
| LS | Lesotho | LSO | 426 |
| LT | Lithuania | LTU | 440 |
| LU | Luxembourg | LUX | 442 |
| LV | Latvia | LVA | 428 |
| LY | Libya | LBY | 434 |
| MA | Morocco | MAR | 504 |
| MC | Monaco | MCO | 492 |
| MD | Moldova | MDA | 498 |
| MG | Madagascar | MDG | 450 |
| MH | Marshall Islands | MHL | 584 |
| MK | Macedonia | MKD | 807 |
| ML | Mali | MLI | 466 |
| MM | Myanmar | MMR | 104 |
| MN | Mongolia | MNG | 496 |
| MO | Macau | MAC | 446 |
| MP | Northern Marianas | MNP | 580 |
| MQ | Martinique | MTQ | 474 |
| MR | Mauritania | MRT | 478 |
| MS | Montserrat | MSR | 500 |
| MT | Malta | MLT | 470 |
| MU | Mauritius | MUS | 480 |
| MV | Maldives | MDV | 462 |
| MW | Malawi | MWI | 454 |
| MX | Mexico | MEX | 484 |
| MY | Malaysia | MYS | 458 |
| MZ | Mozambique | MOZ | 508 |
| NA | Namibia | NAM | 516 |
| NC | New Caledonia | NCL | 540 |
| NE | Niger | NER | 562 |
| NF | Norfolk Island | NFK | 574 |
| NG | Nigeria | NGA | 566 |
| NI | Nicaragua | NIC | 558 |
| NL | Netherlands | NLD | 528 |
| NO | Norway | NOR | 578 |
| NP | Nepal | NPL | 524 |
| NR | Nauru | NRU | 520 |
| NU | Niue | NIU | 570 |

## Table 1: COUNTRY ☞ Country Code

| Country | 2-letter | 3-letter | Numeric |
|---|---|---|---|
| Pakistan | PK | PAK | 586 |
| Palau | PW | PLW | 585 |
| Palestinian Territory, Occupied | PS | PSE | 275 |
| Panama | PA | PAN | 591 |
| Papua New Guinea | PG | PNG | 598 |
| Paraguay | PY | PRY | 600 |
| Peru | PE | PER | 604 |
| Philippines | PH | PHL | 608 |
| Pitcairn Islands | PN | PCN | 612 |
| Poland | PL | POL | 616 |
| Portugal | PT | PRT | 620 |
| Puerto Rico | PR | PRI | 630 |
| Qatar | QA | QAT | 634 |
| Reunion | RE | REU | 638 |
| Romania | RO | ROM | 642 |
| Russian Federation | RU | RUS | 643 |
| Rwanda | RW | RWA | 646 |
| Saint Kitts and Nevis | KN | KNA | 659 |
| Saint Lucia | LC | LCA | 662 |
| Saint Pierre and Miquelon | PM | SPM | 666 |
| Saint Vincent and Grenadines | VC | VCT | 670 |
| Samoa | WS | WSM | 882 |
| San Marino | SM | SMR | 674 |
| Sao Tome and Principe | ST | STP | 678 |
| Saudi Arabia | SA | SAU | 682 |
| Senegal | SN | SEN | 686 |
| Serbia & Montenegro | CS | SCG | 891 |
| Seychelles | SC | SYC | 690 |
| Sierra Leone | SL | SLE | 694 |
| Singapore | SG | SGP | 702 |
| Slovakia | SK | SVK | 703 |
| Slovenia | SI | SVN | 705 |
| Solomon Islands | SB | SLB | 090 |
| Somalia | SO | SOM | 706 |
| South Africa | ZA | ZAF | 710 |
| S. Georgia and S. Sandwich Isl. | GS | SGS | 239 |
| Spain | ES | ESP | 724 |
| Sri Lanka | LK | LKA | 144 |
| Sudan | SD | SDN | 736 |
| Suriname | SR | SUR | 740 |

## Table 2: COUNTRY CODE ☞ Country

| 2-letter | Country | 3-letter | Numeric |
|---|---|---|---|
| NZ | New Zealand | NZL | 554 |
| OF | Micronesia, Federated States of | FM | FSM |
| OM | Oman | OMN | 512 |
| PA | Panama | PAN | 591 |
| PE | Peru | PER | 604 |
| PF | French Polynesia | PYF | 258 |
| PG | Papua New Guinea | PNG | 598 |
| PH | Philippines | PHL | 608 |
| PK | Pakistan | PAK | 586 |
| PL | Poland | POL | 616 |
| PM | Saint Pierre and Miquelon | SPM | 666 |
| PN | Pitcairn Islands | PCN | 612 |
| PR | Puerto Rico | PRI | 630 |
| PS | Palestinian Territory, Occupied | PSE | 275 |
| PT | Portugal | PRT | 620 |
| PW | Palau | PLW | 585 |
| PY | Paraguay | PRY | 600 |
| QA | Qatar | QAT | 634 |
| RE | Reunion | REU | 638 |
| RO | Romania | ROM | 642 |
| RU | Russian Federation | RUS | 643 |
| RW | Rwanda | RWA | 646 |
| SA | Saudi Arabia | SAU | 682 |
| SB | Solomon Islands | SLB | 090 |
| SC | Seychelles | SYC | 690 |
| SD | Sudan | SDN | 736 |
| SE | Sweden | SWE | 752 |
| SG | Singapore | SGP | 702 |
| SI | Slovenia | SVN | 705 |
| SJ | Svalbard and Jan Mayen Islands | SJM | 744 |
| SK | Slovakia | SVK | 703 |
| SL | Sierra Leone | SLE | 694 |
| SM | San Marino | SMR | 674 |
| SN | Senegal | SEN | 686 |
| SO | Somalia | SOM | 706 |
| SR | Suriname | SUR | 740 |
| ST | Sao Tome and Principe | STP | 678 |
| SV | El Salvador | SLV | 222 |
| SY | Syria | SYR | 760 |
| SZ | Swaziland | SWZ | 748 |
| TC | Turks and Caicos Isl. | TCA | 796 |

COUNTRIES

COUNTRIES

| Table 1: COUNTRY ☞ Country Code | | | |
|---|---|---|---|
| Country | 2-letter | 3-letter | Numeric |
| Svalbard and Jan Mayen Islands | SJ | SJM | 744 |
| Swaziland | SZ | SWZ | 748 |
| Sweden | SE | SWE | 752 |
| Switzerland | CH | CHE | 756 |
| Syria | SY | SYR | 760 |
| Taiwan | TW | TWN | 158 |
| Tajikistan | TJ | TJK | 762 |
| Tanzania | TZ | TZA | 834 |
| Thailand | TH | THA | 764 |
| Timor-Leste (East) | TL | TLS | 626 |
| Togo | TG | TGO | 768 |
| Tokelau | TK | TKL | 772 |
| Tonga | TO | TON | 776 |
| Trinidad & Tobago | TT | TTO | 780 |
| Tunisia | TN | TUN | 788 |
| Turkey | TR | TUR | 792 |
| Turkmenistan | TM | TKM | 795 |
| Turks and Caicos Islands | TC | TCA | 796 |
| Tuvalu | TV | TUV | 798 |
| Uganda | UG | UGA | 800 |
| Ukraine | UA | UKR | 804 |
| United Arab Emirates | AE | ARE | 784 |
| United Kingdom | GB | GBR | 826 |
| United States | US | USA | 840 |
| US Minor Outlying Islands | UM | UMI | 581 |
| Uruguay | UY | URY | 858 |
| Uzbekistan | UZ | UZB | 860 |
| Vanuatu | VU | VUT | 548 |
| Vatican City (Holy See) | VA | VAT | 336 |
| Venezuela | VE | VEN | 862 |
| Vietnam | VN | VNM | 704 |
| Virgin Islands (UK) | VG | VGB | 092 |
| Virgin Islands (US) | VI | VIR | 850 |
| Wallis & Futuna | WF | WLF | 876 |
| Western Sahara | EH | ESH | 732 |
| Yemen | YE | YEM | 887 |
| Yugoslavia (now Serbia & Montenegro) | YU | YUG | 891 |
| Zaire | CD | COD | 180 |
| Zambia | ZM | ZMB | 894 |
| Zimbabwe | ZW | ZWE | 716 |

| Table 2: COUNTRY CODE ☞ Country | | | |
|---|---|---|---|
| 2-letter | Country | 3-letter | Numeric |
| TD | Chad | TCD | 148 |
| TF | French Southern Territories | ATF | 260 |
| TG | Togo | TGO | 768 |
| TH | Thailand | THA | 764 |
| TJ | Tajikistan | TJK | 762 |
| TK | Tokelau | TKL | 772 |
| TL | Timor-Leste (East) | TLS | 626 |
| TM | Turkmenistan | TKM | 795 |
| TN | Tunisia | TUN | 788 |
| TO | Tonga | TON | 776 |
| TR | Turkey | TUR | 792 |
| TT | Trinidad & Tobago | TTO | 780 |
| TV | Tuvalu | TUV | 798 |
| TW | Taiwan | TWN | 158 |
| TZ | Tanzania | TZA | 834 |
| UA | Ukraine | UKR | 804 |
| UG | Uganda | UGA | 800 |
| UM | US Minor Outlying Islands | UMI | 581 |
| US | United States | USA | 840 |
| UY | Uruguay | URY | 858 |
| UZ | Uzbekistan | UZB | 860 |
| VA | Holy See (Vatican) | VAT | 336 |
| VA | Vatican City (Holy See) | VAT | 336 |
| VC | Saint Vincent and Grenadines | VCT | 670 |
| VE | Venezuela | VEN | 862 |
| VG | Virgin Islands (UK) | VGB | 092 |
| VI | Virgin Islands (US) | VIR | 850 |
| VN | Vietnam | VNM | 704 |
| VU | Vanuatu | VUT | 548 |
| WF | Wallis & Futuna | WLF | 876 |
| WS | Samoa | WSM | 882 |
| YE | Yemen | YEM | 887 |
| YT | Mayotte | MYT | 175 |
| YU | Yugoslavia (now Serbia & Montenegro) | YUG | 891 |
| ZA | South Africa | ZAF | 710 |
| ZM | Zambia | ZMB | 894 |
| ZW | Zimbabwe | ZWE | 716 |

# International Dialing Guide

This International Dialing Guide and the tables that follow have been designed to be useful to anyone, regardless of the country of origin or the country of destination of their call.

The following two pages give basic instructions for how to dial international calls, a list of points of confusion, a number of dialing examples, informa-tion regarding world time zones so you do not mis-takenly call someone at 3 am in the morning, and resources for more information.

Tables on pages that follow offer tables of inter-national access codes, a comprehensive listing of in-ternational dialing codes by country, and a table of country codes listed by code.

## HOW TO DIAL INTERNATIONAL CALLS

International direct dialing from most countries is quite easy. An international call simply consists of dial-ing a sequence of numbers as follows:

1. The International Access Code (IAC),
2. The country code,
3. The city/area code, and
4. The local subscriber (telephone) number.

Each step routes your call a step closer to the person or business you are calling.

**The International Access Code** (IAC). The IAC is a prefix used to get an international line. For example, if you are calling from the United States, the IAC is '011'. The IAC differs from country to country. For Brazil it is '00'. Some countries do not allow direct dialing for in-ternational calls and require an operator. The table on the next page lists IAC prefixes for most countries. You may need to wait for a dial tone after dialing the IAC.

**The Country Code.** Next comes the code of the country you are calling. Refer to "International Dial-ing Codes" on page 206 for a list of country codes.

**The Area Code.** This is the regional or city dial-ing code. Refer to "International Dialing Codes" on page 206 for a listing of many area codes. Note that some countries have done away with area codes, in-corporating them into individual subscriber numbers, or what are now called national numbers.

**The Local Telephone Number.** This is also called the subscriber number.

## POINTS OF CONFUSION

1. **International Access Code** When you are given an international phone number, the string of nu-merals you see may include: the IAC (International Access Code) + area code + the subscriber number. This may be confusing, especially if the IAC shown is not that of your own country, but of the country where the number originates.

For example, you may be handed a business card from a U.K. company with the following:

Tel: 00 [44] 1234-123456

In this case, the '00' is the IAC for calls originat-ing in the U.K. However, if you are calling from the U.S. you will need to use the U.S. IAC, which is '011.' See International Access Codes on the following page.

2. **Long Distance Prefix** Many telephone num-bers printed on business cards include the country's long-distance prefix (often shown in parentheses). This prefix (also known as the domestic access code or DAC) only serves domestic calling purposes.

For example, '0' serves as the long-distance pre-fix when making long-distance calls *within* Germany. You may, therefore see the following number on a business card:

[49] (0) 30 6858-8855

To make it slightly more confusing, some busi-ness cards are printed with the long-distance prefix *merged* with the area code. For example:

[49] (030) 6858-8855

In both cases, when making an *international* call to this number in Germany, you will need to omit the '0.' See International Access Codes on page 205.

3. **North American Numbering Plan (NANP)** For calls from and to NANP countries in North America and the Caribbean see below for details.

## NORTH AMERICAN NUMBERING PLAN (NANP)

A number of countries in North America and the Caribbean share what is called the North American Numbering Plan (NANP). The country code for *all* these countries is '1.' Except for the U.S. and Can-ada, each NANP country has a single area code.

International calls from outside the NANP to an NANP country use the following dialing format:

1 + 3-digit area code + 7-digit subscriber number

Calls *within* the NANP are treated simply as long-dis-tance calls requiring the long-distance prefix '1' as follows:

1 + 3-digit area code + 7-digit subscriber number.

In the case of international calls, the '1' acts as the country code, whereas for long-distance calls within the NANP, the '1' acts as the long-distance prefix.

Members of the North American Numbering plan (and their area codes) are: American Samoa (684), An-guilla (264), Antigua & Barbuda (268), Bahamas (242), Barbados (246), Bermuda (Atlantic) (441), British Virgin Islands (284), Canada (various), Cayman Islands (345), Dominica (767), Dominican Republic (809), Grenada & Carriacou (473), Guam (671), Jamaica (876), Montserrat (664), Puerto Rico (787), St. Kitts and Nevis (869), St. Lucia (758), Trinidad and Tobago (868), Turks & Caicos (649), U.S.A. (various), U.S. Virgin Islands (340).

**DIALING**

# DIALING EXAMPLES

**Example 1**

A call from London, U.K. ➡ Chicago, USA:

**00 + [1] + (312) + (local number)**

The UK's IAC is '00', the U.S.' country code is [1] and Chicago's area code is (312).

**Example 2**

A call from Denmark ➡ Sydney, Australia:

**00 + [61] + (2) + (local number)**

Denmark's IAC is '00', Australia's country code is [61] and Sydney's area code is (2).

**Example 3**

A call from the USA ➡ Vancouver, Canada:

**1 + (604) + (the local number)**

The prefix '1' is used for long-distance calls within the North American Numbering Plan (Canada, the U.S., and much of the Caribbean) and (604) is the area code for Vancouver.

**Example 4**

A call from Hong Kong ➡ Delhi, India:

**001 + [91] + (11) + (local number).**

Hong Kong's IAC is '001', India's country code is [91], and Delhi's city code is (11).

**Example 5**

A call from the USA ➡ Hong Kong:

**011 + [852] + (local number)**

The U.S.' IAC is '011', Hong Kong's country code is [852], and there are no city/area codes.

**Example 6**

A call from the USA to any city in the Dominican Republic:

**1+ (809) + (local number)**

The prefix '1' is used for long-distance calls within the North American Numbering Plan (Canada, the U.S., and the Caribbean) and (809) is the area code for the Dominican Republic.

# TIME ZONES

In the 'International Dialing Codes' table we have listed time differences between the cities listed in column three and point of reference cities listed in the fourth through ninth columns.

All cities in a given country or territory are in one time zone unless a †† symbol appears next to the country name. Find the city you wish to call in column three, and the column which corresponds to the time zone from which you are calling. Add or subtract the number shown to your own current time to find the time in that city.

**Example**: You are calling France from New York. +6 appears in the New York column for France, which means France is 6 hours *ahead* of New York. Thus, when it is 9 a.m. Monday in New York, it is 3:00 p.m. Monday in France.

**Example**: You are calling Japan from San Francisco. +17 appears in the Los Angeles column for Japan, which means Japan is 17 hours ahead of San Francisco. Thus, when it is 4:00 p.m. Monday in San Francisco, it is 9:00 a.m. Tuesday in Japan.

# DAYLIGHT SAVINGS TIME

The time differences in the table are based on Standard Time and may require adjustment if either you or the country you are calling is following Daylight Savings Time (DST) at the time you place the call.

The United States (excluding Arizona and Hawaii) is in DST from the first Sunday in April until the last Sunday in October. Many, but not all, countries north of the Tropic of Cancer also use DST during a similar period. DST is not used in most tropical areas. Countries in the southern hemisphere that follow a daylight savings period normally use it from mid-March through mid-October, their summertime.

The dates used for DST vary considerably from country to country and even from year to year. Also, in a few larger countries like the United States, Aus-

tralia, and Brazil, some regions of the country may follow daylight savings while others do not.

If you are in DST, and the country you are calling is not, *subtract* one hour from the time shown. If you are in Standard Time, and the country you are calling is currently following DST, *add* one hour to the time shown. If you and the country you are calling are both using DST, the time difference shown in the table will be correct.

**Example**: You are calling Japan from San Francisco in June. California follows DST in the summer, while Japan does not. The PST (Pacific Standard Time) column for Japan shows +17. Subtract one hour from this, to find that Japan is 16 hours ahead of San Francisco. Thus, when it is 4:00 p.m. Monday in San Francisco, it is 8:00 a.m. Tuesday in Japan.

# FOR FURTHER INFORMATION

Please note that dialing systems are changing rapidly due to the huge increase in demand for tele and data communications. This section was last updated in August 2006.

The world's most comprehensive book of international communications data is *Global Connect!*, also by World Trade Press. Its 960 pages contain telecommunications, cell communications, mobile connectivity and Internet connectivity information for 175 countries of the world, plus a series of key appendices on all aspects of communications and connectivity issues. Go to www.worldtradepress.com and select 'Books.'

*Global Connect*, in an even more expanded version, is available online at www.HowToConnect.com. This product includes the new *Global Quick Call*, an 'expert software application' for dialing international calls.

Additional resources include world time at www.globaltimeclock.com and the AmeriCom Long Distance Area Decoder at http://decoder.americom.com, which enables users to look up country codes, city codes, and area codes by country.

# INTERNATIONAL ACCESS CODES (IAC)

When making an international call *from* a country, dial its International Access Code, then the country code of the country you are calling. For details, see "How to Dial International Calls" on the preceding pages.

| Country | Code |
|---|---|
| Afghanistan | 00 |
| Albania | 00 |
| Algeria | 00 pause for tone |
| American Samoa | 011 |
| Andorra | 00 |
| Angola | 00 |
| Anguilla | 011 |
| Antigua & Barbuda | 011 |
| Argentina | 00 |
| Armenia | 00 |
| Aruba | 00 |
| Australia | 0011 |
| Australian fax calls | 0015 |
| Austria | 00 |
| Azerbaijan | 00 |
| Bahamas | 011 |
| Bahrain | 00 |
| Bangladesh | 00 |
| Barbados | 011 |
| Belarus | 8 pause 10 |
| Belgium | 00 |
| Belize | 00 |
| Benin | 00 |
| Bermuda | 011 |
| Bhutan | 00 |
| Bolivia | 00 |
| Bosnia & Herzegovina | 00 |
| Botswana | 00 |
| Brazil | 00 + carrier code (i.e., 0021) |
| Brunei | 00 |
| Bulgaria | 00 |
| Burkina Faso | 00 |
| Burma (Myanmar) | 00 |
| Burundi | 90 |
| Bulgaria | 00 |
| Cambodia | 001 |
| Cameroon | 00 |
| Canada | 011 |
| Cape Verde | 0 |
| Cayman Islands | 011 |
| Central African Republic | 00 |
| Chad | 15 |
| Chechnya | 8 pause 10 |
| Chile | 00 or carrier code + 0 |
| China (PRC) | 00 |
| Colombia | 009 |
| Comoros | 00 |
| Congo, Democratic Republic of (formerly Zaire) | 00 |
| Congo, Republic of (Brazzaville) | 00 |
| Cook Islands | 00 |
| Costa Rica | 00 |
| Côte d'Ivoire (Ivory Coast) | 00 |
| Croatia | 00 |
| Cuba | 119 |
| Cuba (Guantánamo Bay) | 00 |
| Cyprus | 00 |
| Czech Republic | 00 |
| Denmark | 00 |
| Diego Garcia | 00 |
| Djibouti | 00 |
| Dominica | 011 |
| Dominican Republic | 011 |
| East Timor | 00 |
| Ecuador | 00 |
| Egypt | 00 |
| El Salvador | 00 |
| Equatorial Guinea | 00 |
| Eritrea | 00 |
| Estonia | 00 |
| Ethiopia | 00 |
| Falkland Islands | 00 |
| Faeroe Islands | 00 |
| Fiji | 00 |
| Finland | 00 |
| France | 00 |
| French Antilles | 00 |
| French Guiana | 00 |
| French Polynesia | 00 |
| Gabon | 00 |

| Country | Code |
|---|---|
| Gambia, The | 00 |
| Georgia | 8 pause 10 |
| Germany | 00 |
| Ghana | 00 |
| Greece | 00 |
| Greenland | 00 |
| Grenada | 011 |
| Guadeloupe | 00 |
| Guam | 011 |
| Guatemala | 00 |
| Guinea | 00 |
| Guinea-Bissau | 00 |
| Guyana | 001 |
| Haiti | 00 |
| Honduras | 00 |
| Hong Kong | 001 |
| Hungary | 00 |
| Iceland | 00 |
| India | 00 |
| Indonesia | 001 |
| Iran | 00 |
| Iraq | 00 |
| Ireland | 00 |
| Israel | 00 |
| Israel public phones | 012, 013, 014 |
| Italy | 00 |
| Ivory Coast (Côte d'Ivoire) | 00 |
| Jamaica | 011 |
| Japan | 001 |
| Jordan | 00 |
| Kazakhstan | 8 pause 10 |
| Kenya | 000 |
| Kenya to Uganda | 006 |
| Kenya to Tanzania | 007 |
| Kiribati | 00 |
| Korea, South | 001 |
| Korea, North | 00 |
| Kosovo | 8 pause 10 |
| Kuwait | 00 |
| Kyrgyzstan | 00 |
| Laos | 00 |
| Latvia | 00 |
| Lebanon | 00 |
| Lesotho | 00 |
| Liberia | 00 |
| Libya | 00 |
| Liechtenstein | 00 |
| Lithuania | 00 |
| Luxembourg | 00 |
| Macau | 00 |
| Macedonia | 00 |
| Madagascar | 00 |
| Malawi | 00 |
| Malaysia | 00 |
| Maldives | 00 |
| Mali | 00 |
| Malta | 00 |
| Marshall Islands | 011 |
| Martinique | 00 |
| Mauritania | 00 |
| Mauritius | 00 |
| Mexico | 00 |
| Midway Island | 011 |
| Moldova | 00 |
| Monaco | 00 |
| Mongolia | 001 |
| Montenegro (Serbia & Montenegro) | 99 |
| Montserrat | 011 |
| Morocco | 00 |
| Mozambique | 00 |
| Myanmar (Burma) | 00 |
| Namibia | 00 |
| Nauru | 00 |
| Nepal | 00 |
| Netherlands | 00 |
| Netherlands Antilles | 00 |
| New Calidonia | 00 |
| New Zealand | 00 |
| Nicaragua | 00 |
| Niger Republic | 00 |

| Country | Code |
|---|---|
| Nigeria | 009 |
| Niue | 00 |
| Northern Mariana Islands | 011 |
| Norway | 00 |
| Oman | 00 |
| Pakistan | 00 |
| Palau | 011 |
| Palestine | 00 |
| Panama | 00 |
| Papua New Guinea | 05 |
| Paraguay | 002 |
| Peru | 00 |
| Philippines | 00 |
| Poland | 0*0 |
| Portugal | 00 |
| Puerto Rico | 011 |
| Qatar | 00 |
| Réunion | 00 |
| Romania | 00 |
| Russia | 8 pause 10 |
| Rwanda | 00 |
| St. Kitts & Nevis | 011 |
| St. Lucia | 011 |
| St. Vincent & Grenadines | 011 |
| Samoa | 0 |
| San Marino | 00 |
| São Tomé & Principe | 00 |
| Saudi Arabia | 00 |
| Senegal | 00 |
| Serbia & Montenegro | 00 |
| Seychelles | 00 |
| Sierra Leone | 00 |
| Singapore | 001 |
| Slovak Republic | 00 |
| Slovenia | 00 |
| Solomon Islands | 00 |
| Somalia | 00 |
| South Africa | 09 |
| Spain | 00 |
| Sri Lanka | 00 |
| Sudan | 00 |
| Suriname | 00 |
| Swaziland | 00 |
| Sweden | 00 |
| Switzerland | 00 |
| Syria | 00 |
| Taiwan | 002 |
| Tajikistan | 8 pause 10 |
| Tanzania | 000 |
| Tanzania to Uganda | 006 |
| Thailand | 001 |
| Thailand to Malaysia | 007 |
| Togo | 00 |
| Tonga Islands | 00 |
| Trinidad & Tobago | 011 |
| Tunisia | 00 |
| Turkey | 00 |
| Turkmenistan | 8 pause 10 |
| Turks & Caicos | 011 |
| Tuvalu | 00 |
| Uganda | 000 |
| Uganda to Kenya | 005 |
| Uganda to Tanzania | 007 |
| Ukraine | 8 pause 10 |
| United Arab Emirates | 00 |
| United Kingdom | 00 |
| United States | 011 |
| Uruguay | 00 |
| Uzbekistan | 8 pause 10 |
| Vanuatu | 00 |
| Venezuela | 00 |
| Vietnam | 00 |
| Virgin Islands (U.K.) | 011 |
| Virgin Islands (U.S.) | 011 |
| Western Sahara | 00 |
| Yugoslavia (now Serbia & Montenegro) | 00 |
| Zaire (now Dem. Rep. of Congo) | 00 |
| Zambia | 00 |
| Zimbabwe | 00 |

DIALING

# International Dialing Codes

| Country | Country Code | City Code / Area Code | Cities in Column 3 are X Hours Ahead (+) or Behind (-): | | | | | |
|---|---|---|---|---|---|---|---|---|
| | | | Los Angeles | New York | London (GMT) | Paris/ Berlin | Hong Kong | Tokyo/ Seoul |
| **Afghanistan** | [93] | ✪Kabul (20, 21, 22, 23, 24, 25) Herat (40) Jalalabad (60, 61, 62, 63, 64) Kandahar (30) Kunduz (56) Mazar-i-Sherif (50, 51, 52, 53) | +12₁/₂ | +9₁/₂ | +4₁/₂ | +3₁/₂ | -3₁/₂ | -4₁/₂ |
| **Albania** (DST) | [355] | ✪Tirana (4) | +9 | +6 | +1 | 0 | -7 | -8 |
| **Algeria** | [213] | ✪Algiers (21) Oran (41) | +9 | +6 | +1 | 0 | -7 | -8 |
| **American Samoa** | [1] | ✪Pago Pago (684)** | -3 | -6 | -11 | -12 | -19 | -20 |
| **Andorra** (DST) | [376] | ✪Andorra la Vella* | +9 | +6 | +1 | 0 | -7 | -8 |
| **Angola** | [244] | ✪Luanda * (9-digit numbers) | +9 | +6 | +1 | 0 | -7 | -8 |
| **Anguilla** | [1] | ✪ The Valley (264)** (7-digit numbers) | +4 | +1 | -4 | -5 | -12 | -13 |
| **Antigua & Barbuda** | [1] | ✪St. John's (268)** (7-digit numbers) | +4 | +1 | -4 | -5 | -12 | -13 |
| **Argentina††** | [54] | ✪Buenos Aires (11) Cordoba (351) La Plata (221) Mendoza (261) Rosario (341) | +5 | +2 | -3 | -4 | -11 | -12 |
| **Armenia** (DST) | [374] | ✪Yerevan (1) Ararat (38) | +11 | +8 | +3 | +2 | -5 | -6 |
| **Aruba** | [297] | ✪ Oranjestad (8)** | +4 | +1 | -4 | -5 | -12 | -13 |
| **Australia††** (DST) (Note: Queensland, Northern Territory, and Western Australia do not use DST.) | [61] | ✪Canberra (2) Adelaide (8) Brisbane (7) Cairns (7) Melbourne (3) Perth (8) Sydney (2) | +18 +17₁/₂ +18 +18 +18 +16 +18 | +15 +14₁/₂ +15 +15 +15 +13 +15 | +10 +9₁/₂ +10 +10 +10 +8 +10 | +9 +8₁/₂ +9 +9 +9 +7 +9 | +2 +1₁/₂ +2 +2 +2 0 +2 | +1 +1/₂ +1 +1 +1 -1 +1 |
| **Austria** (DST) | [43] | ✪Vienna (1) Graz (316) Innsbruck (512) Linz (732) Salzburg (662) | +9 | +6 | +1 | 0 | -7 | -8 |
| **Azerbaijan** (DST) | [994] | ✪Baku (12) Gandja (222) | +12 | +9 | +4 | +3 | -4 | -5 |
| **Bahamas** (DST) | [1] | ✪Nassau (242)** (7-digit numbers) | +3 | 0 | -5 | -6 | -13 | -14 |
| **Bahrain** | [973] | ✪Manama* | +11 | +8 | +3 | +2 | -5 | -6 |

DIALING

| Country | Country Code | City Code / Area Code | Cities in Column 3 are X Hours Ahead (+) or Behind (-): | | | | | |
|---------|--------------|----------------------|------------------|----------|---------------|-----------------|--------------|---------------|
| | | | Los Angeles | New York | London (GMT) | Paris/ Berlin | Hong Kong | Tokyo/ Seoul |
| Bangladesh | [880] | ✪Dhaka (2) Barisal (431) Chittagong (31) | +14 | +11 | +6 | +5 | -2 | -3 |
| Barbados | [1] | ✪Bridgetown (246)** | +4 | +1 | -4 | -5 | -12 | -13 |
| Belarus (DST) | [375] | ✪Mensk (17) Gomel (23) Gorki (22) | +10 | +7 | +2 | +1 | -6 | -7 |
| Belgium (DST) | [32] | ✪Brussels* | +9 | +6 | +1 | 0 | -7 | -8 |
| | | As of 2000, area code + local number = national number. | | | | | | |
| Belize | [501] | ✪Belmopan (8) Beliz City (2) Orange Walk (3) | +2 | -1 | -6 | -7 | -14 | -15 |
| Benin | [229] | ✪Porto-Novo* | +9 | +6 | +1 | 0 | -7 | -8 |
| Bermuda (DST) | [1] | ✪Hamilton (441)** (7-digit numbers) | +4 | +1 | -4 | -5 | -12 | -13 |
| Bhutan | [975] | ✪Thimphu (2) Paro (8) | +14 | +11 | +6 | +5 | -2 | -3 |
| Bolivia | [591] | ✪La Paz (2) ✪Sucre (4) Cochabamba (4) Santa Cruz (3) | +4 | +1 | -4 | -5 | -12 | -13 |
| Bosnia & Herzegovina(DST) | [387] | ✪Sarajevo (33) Tuzla (35) Mostar (36) | +9 | +6 | +1 | 0 | -7 | -8 |
| Botswana | [267] | ✪Gaborone* | +10 | +7 | +2 | +1 | -6 | -7 |
| Brazil†† (DST) | [55] | ✪Brasilia (61) | +5 | +2 | -3 | -4 | -11 | -12 |
| | | Belém (91) | +5 | +2 | -3 | -4 | -11 | -12 |
| | | Belo Horizonte (31) | +5 | +2 | -3 | -4 | -11 | -12 |
| | | Curitiba (41) | +5 | +2 | -3 | -4 | -11 | -12 |
| | | Manaus (92) | +4 | +1 | -4 | -5 | -12 | -13 |
| | | Porto Alegre (51) | +5 | +2 | -3 | -4 | -11 | -12 |
| | | Recife (81) | +5 | +2 | -3 | -4 | -11 | -12 |
| | | Rio de Janeiro (21) | +5 | +2 | -3 | -4 | -11 | -12 |
| | | Salvador (71) | +5 | +2 | -3 | -4 | -11 | -12 |
| | | Sao Paulo (11) | +5 | +2 | -3 | -4 | -11 | -12 |
| | | Santos (13) | +5 | +2 | -3 | -4 | -11 | -12 |
| | | Vitoria (27) | +5 | +2 | -3 | -4 | -11 | -12 |
| Brunei | [673] | ✪Bandar Seri Begawan* | +16 | +13 | +8 | +7 | 0 | -1 |
| Bulgaria (DST) | [359] | ✪Sofia (2) Varna (52) Sliven (44) Burgas (56) | +10 | +7 | +2 | +1 | -6 | -7 |
| Burkina Faso | [226] | ✪Ouagadougou* | +8 | +5 | 0 | -1 | -8 | -9 |
| Burundi | [257] | ✪Bujumbura* | +10 | +7 | +2 | +1 | -6 | -7 |
| Cambodia | [855] | ✪Phnom Penh (23) Angkor Wat (63) | +15 | +12 | +7 | +6 | -1 | -2 |

| | |
|---|---|
| ✪ Capital city | †† More than one time zone in this country. |
| (DST) = Uses Daylight Savings Time | * City/area codes not used in this country |
| Code = Country Dialing Code | ** This area code used for entire country |

**DIALING**

| Country | Country Code | City Code / Area Code | Cities in Column 3 are X Hours Ahead (+) or Behind (-): | | | | | |
|---|---|---|---|---|---|---|---|---|
| | | | Los Angeles | New York | London (GMT) | Paris/ Berlin | Hong Kong | Tokyo/ Seoul |
| **Cameroon** | [237] | ✪Yaoundé* | +9 | +6 | +1 | 0 | -7 | -8 |
| **Canada††** (DST) (The province of Saskatchewan does not observe DST.) | [1] | ✪Ottawa, ON (613) | +3 | 0 | -5 | -6 | -13 | -14 |
| | | Calgary, AB (403) | +1 | -2 | -7 | -8 | -15 | -16 |
| | | Edmonton,AB (780) | +1 | -2 | -7 | -8 | -15 | -16 |
| | | Fredericton, NB (506) | +4 | +1 | -4 | -5 | -12 | -13 |
| | | Halifax, NS (902) | +4 | +1 | -4 | -5 | -12 | -13 |
| | | London, ON (519) | +3 | 0 | -5 | -6 | -13 | -14 |
| | | Montreal, PQ (514) | +3 | 0 | -5 | -6 | -13 | -14 |
| | | Quebec City, PQ (418) | +3 | 0 | -5 | -6 | -13 | -14 |
| | | Regina, SK (306) | +1 | -2 | -7 | -8 | -15 | -16 |
| | | Saskatoon, SK (306) | +1 | -2 | -7 | -8 | -15 | -16 |
| | | St. John's, NF (709) | +4 1/2 | +1 1/2 | -3 1/2 | -4 1/2 | -11 1/2 | -12 1/2 |
| | | Toronto, ON Metro (416, 647) | +3 | 0 | -5 | -6 | -13 | -14 |
| | | Toronto Vicinity (905) | +3 | 0 | -5 | -6 | -13 | -14 |
| | | Vancouver, BC (604) | 0 | -3 | -8 | -9 | -16 | -17 |
| | | Victoria, BC (250) | 0 | -3 | -8 | -9 | -16 | -17 |
| | | Winnipeg, MB (204) | +2 | -1 | -6 | -7 | -14 | -15 |
| **Cape Verde Isl.** | [238] | ✪Praia* | +7 | +4 | -1 | -2 | -9 | -10 |
| **Cayman Islands** | [1] | ✪George Town (345)** | +3 | 0 | -5 | -6 | -13 | -14 |
| **Central African Republic** | [236] | ✪Bangui* (6-digit numbers) | +9 | +6 | +1 | 0 | -7 | -8 |
| **Chad** | [235] | ✪N'Djamena* | +9 | +6 | +1 | 0 | -7 | -8 |
| **Chagos Archipelago** | [246] | ✪Diego Garcia* | +13 | +10 | +5 | +4 | -3 | -4 |
| **Chile** (DST) | [56] | ✪Santiago (2) Concepcion (41) Punta Arenas (61) Valparaiso (32) | +4 | +1 | -4 | -5 | -12 | -13 |
| **China, People's Republic of** | [86] | ✪Beijing (10) Fuzhou (591) Guangzhou (20) Harbin (451) Nanjing (25) Zhangzhou-Fujian (596) Shanghai (21) Shenzhen-Guangdong (755) Tianjin (22) Wuhan (27) Xiamen (592) Xian (29) | +16 | +13 | +8 | +7 | 0 | -1 |
| **Colombia** | [57] | ✪Bogota (1) Barranquilla (5) Cali (2) Medellin (4) | +3 | 0 | -5 | -6 | -13 | -14 |
| **Comoros** | [269] | ✪Moroni* | +11 | +8 | +3 | +2 | -5 | -6 |
| **Congo** | [242] | ✪Brazzaville* | +9 | +6 | +1 | 0 | -7 | -8 |
| **Congo,††** **Democratic Republic of** | [243] | ✪Kinshasa (12) Lubumbashi (2) | +9 +10 | +6 +7 | +1 +2 | 0 +1 | -7 -6 | -8 -7 |
| **Cook Islands** | [682] | ✪Avarua* | -2 | -5 | -10 | -11 | -18 | -19 |

D
I
A
L
I
N
G

| Country | Country Code | City Code / Area Code | Cities in Column 3 are X Hours Ahead (+) or Behind (-): | | | | | |
|---|---|---|---|---|---|---|---|---|
| | | | Los Angeles | New York | London (GMT) | Paris/ Berlin | Hong Kong | Tokyo/ Seoul |
| Costa Rica | [506] | ✪San José* (7-digit numbers) | +2 | -1 | -6 | -7 | -14 | -15 |
| Côte d'Ivoire (Ivory Coast) | [225] | ✪Yamoussoukro* Abidjan* (national 8-digit numbers) | +8 | +5 | 0 | -1 | -8 | -9 |
| Croatia (DST) | [385] | ✪Zagreb (1) Dubrovnik (20) Split (21) | +9 | +6 | +1 | 0 | -7 | -8 |
| Cuba (DST) | [53] | ✪Havana (7) Santiago de Cuba (226) Guantanamo U.S. Naval Base (99) | +3 | 0 | -5 | -6 | -13 | -14 |
| Cyprus (DST) | [357] | ✪Nicosia * (8-digit numbers) | +10 | +7 | +2 | +1 | -6 | -7 |
| Czech Republic (DST) | [420] | ✪Prague | +9 | +6 | +1 | 0 | -7 | -8 |
| | | As of September 2002, area code + local number = 9-digit national number. | | | | | | |
| Denmark (DST) | [45] | ✪Copenhagen* (8-digit numbers) | +9 | +6 | +1 | 0 | -7 | -8 |
| Djibouti | [253] | ✪Djibouti* (6-digit numbers) | +11 | +8 | +3 | +2 | -5 | -6 |
| Dominica | [1] | ✪Roseau (767)** | +4 | +1 | -4 | -5 | -12 | -13 |
| Dominican Republic | [1] | ✪Santo Domingo (809)** | +4 | +1 | -4 | -5 | -12 | -13 |
| East Timor | [670] | ✪Dili* (7-digit numbers) | +16 | +13 | +8 | +7 | 0 | -1 |
| Ecuador | [593] | ✪Quito (2) Guayaquil (4) | +3 | 0 | -5 | -6 | -13 | -14 |
| Egypt (DST) | [20] | ✪Cairo (2) Alexandria (3) Aswan (97) Luxor (95) Port Said (66) | +10 | +7 | +2 | +1 | -6 | -7 |
| El Salvador | [503] | ✪San Salvador* | +2 | -1 | -6 | -7 | -14 | -15 |
| Equatorial Guinea | [240] | ✪Malabo (9) Bata (8) | +9 | +6 | +1 | 0 | -7 | -8 |
| Estonia (DST) | [372] | ✪Tallinn* | +10 | +7 | +2 | +1 | -6 | -7 |
| Ethiopia | [251] | ✪Addis Ababa (11) | +11 | +8 | +3 | +2 | -5 | -6 |
| Faeroe Islands (DST) | [298] | ✪Tórshavn* | +8 | +5 | 0 | -1 | -8 | -9 |
| Falkland Islands | [500] | ✪Stanley* (5-digit numbers) | +4 | +1 | -4 | -5 | -12 | -13 |
| Fiji (DST | [679] | ✪Suva* | +20 | +17 | +12 | +11 | +4 | +3 |
| Finland (DST) | [358] | ✪Helsinki (9) | +10 | +7 | +2 | +1 | -6 | -7 |

✪ Capital city
(DST) = Uses Daylight Savings Time
Code = Country Dialing Code

†† More than one time zone in this country.
* City/area codes not used in this country
** This area code used for entire country

| Country | Country Code | City Code / Area Code | Cities in Column 3 are X Hours Ahead (+) or Behind (-): | | | | | |
|---|---|---|---|---|---|---|---|---|
| | | | Los Angeles | New York | London (GMT) | Paris/ Berlin | Hong Kong | Tokyo/ Seoul |
| France (DST) | [33] | ✪Paris* | +9 | +6 | +1 | 0 | -7 | -8 |
| | | Old area codes + local number = new 9-digit national number. | | | | | | |
| French Guiana | [594] | ✪Cayenne* (9-digit numbers) | +5 | +2 | -3 | -4 | -11 | -12 |
| French Polynesia†† | [689] | ✪Papeete, Tahiti* | -2 | -5 | -10 | -11 | -18 | -19 |
| Gabon | [241] | ✪Libreville* | +9 | +6 | +1 | 0 | -7 | -8 |
| Gambia, The | [220] | ✪Banjul* | +8 | +5 | 0 | -1 | -8 | -9 |
| Georgia (DST) | [995] | ✪Tbilisi (32) | +12 | +9 | +4 | +3 | -4 | -5 |
| Germany (DST) | [49] | ✪Berlin (30) Bonn (228) Bremen (421) Cologne (221) Dresden (351) Dusseldorf (211) Essen (201) Frankfurt am Main (69) Frankfurt Oder (335) Freiburg (761) Hamburg (40) Hannover (511) Heidelberg (6221) Kiel (431) Leipzig (341) Munich (89) Potsdam (331) Stuttgart (711) Wiesbaden (611) | +9 | +6 | +1 | 0 | -7 | -8 |
| Ghana | [233] | ✪Accra (21) Kumasi (51) | +8 | +5 | 0 | -1 | -8 | -9 |
| Gibraltar (DST) | [350] | ✪Gibraltar* (5-digit numbers) | +9 | +6 | +1 | 0 | -7 | -8 |
| Greece (DST) | [30] | ✪Athens* | +10 | +7 | +2 | +1 | -6 | -7 |
| Greenland††(DST) | [299] | ✪Nuuk (Godthaab)* | +5 | +2 | -3 | -4 | -11 | -12 |
| Grenada | [1] | ✪St. George's (473)** (7-digit numbers) | +4 | +1 | -4 | -5 | -12 | -13 |
| Guadeloupe, French Antilles | [590] | ✪Basse-Terre (81) (10-digit numbers) | +4 | +1 | -4 | -5 | -12 | -13 |
| Guam | [1] | ✪Agana (671)** (7-digit numbers) | +18 | +15 | +10 | +9 | +2 | +1 |
| Guatemala(DST) | [502] | ✪Guatemala City* (7-digit numbers) | +2 | -1 | -6 | -7 | -14 | -15 |
| Guinea | [224] | ✪Conakry* | +8 | +5 | 0 | -1 | -8 | -9 |
| Guinea-Bissau | [245] | ✪Bissau* (6-digit numbers) | +8 | +5 | 0 | -1 | -8 | -9 |
| Guyana | [592] | ✪Georgetown* (7-digit numbers) | +4 | +1 | -4 | -5 | -12 | -13 |
| Haiti | [509] | ✪Port-au-Prince (6-digit numbers) | +3 | 0 | -5 | -6 | -13 | -14 |

| Country | Country Code | City Code / Area Code | Cities in Column 3 are X Hours Ahead (+) or Behind (-): | | | | | |
|---|---|---|---|---|---|---|---|---|
| | | | Los Angeles | New York | London (GMT) | Paris/ Berlin | Hong Kong | Tokyo/ Seoul |
| Honduras | [504] | ✪Tegucigalpa (7-digit numbers) | +2 | -1 | -6 | -7 | -14 | -15 |
| Hong Kong | [852] | ✪Hong Kong* (8-digit numbers) | +16 | +13 | +8 | +7 | 0 | -1 |
| Hungary (DST) | [36] | ✪Budapest (1) | +9 | +6 | +1 | 0 | -7 | -8 |
| Iceland | [354] | ✪Reykjavik (7-digit numbers) | +8 | +5 | 0 | -1 | -8 | -9 |
| India | [91] | ✪New Delhi (11) Ahmadabad (79) Bangalore (80) Chennai (Madras) (44) Hyderabad (40) Jaipur (141) Kanpur (512) Kolkata (Calcutta) (33) Lucknow (522) Mumbai (Bombay) (22) | +13½ | +10½ | +5½ | +4½ | -2½ | -3½ |
| Indonesia†† | [62] | ✪Jakarta (21) | +15 | +12 | +7 | +6 | -1 | -2 |
| | | Bandung (22) | +15 | +12 | +7 | +6 | -1 | -2 |
| | | Denpasar, Bali (36) | +16 | +13 | +8 | +7 | 0 | -1 |
| | | Padang (751) | +15 | +12 | +7 | +6 | -1 | -2 |
| | | Palu (451) | +16 | +13 | +8 | +7 | 0 | -1 |
| | | Palembang (711) | +15 | +12 | +7 | +6 | -1 | -2 |
| | | Semarang (24) | +15 | +12 | +7 | +6 | -1 | -2 |
| | | Surabaya (31) | +15 | +12 | +7 | +6 | -1 | -2 |
| | | Yogyakarta (274) | +15 | +12 | +7 | +6 | -1 | -2 |
| Iran | [98] | ✪Tehran (21) Esfahan (311) Mashhad (511) Shiraz (711) Tabriz (411) | +12½ | +9½ | +3½ | +2½ | -3½ | -4½ |
| Iraq (DST) | [964] | ✪Baghdad (1) Basra (40) Erbil (66) Sulayamaniyah (53) | +11 | +8 | +3 | +2 | -5 | -6 |
| Ireland (DST) | [353] | ✪Dublin (1) Cork (21) Galway (91) Limerick (61) Waterford (51) | +8 | +5 | 0 | -1 | -8 | -9 |
| Israel (DST) | [972] | ✪Jerusalem (2) Haifa (4) Holon (3) Ramallah (2) Tel Aviv (3) | +10 | +7 | +2 | +1 | -6 | -7 |
| Italy (DST) | [39] | ✪Rome* | +9 | +6 | +1 | 0 | -7 | -8 |
| | | '0' + area code + local number = new 10-digit national number. | | | | | | |

**DIALING**

✪ Capital city
(DST) = Uses Daylight Savings Time
Code = Country Dialing Code

†† More than one time zone in this country.
* City/area codes not used in this country
** This area code used for entire country

| Country | Country Code | City Code / Area Code | Cities in Column 3 are X Hours Ahead (+) or Behind (-): | | | | | |
|---------|--------------|-----------------------|------------------|--------------|-----------------|-----------------|---------------|---------------|
| | | | Los Angeles | New York | London (GMT) | Paris/ Berlin | Hong Kong | Tokyo/ Seoul |
| **Ivory Coast** | | See (Côte d'Ivoire) | | | | | | |
| **Jamaica** | [1] | ✪Kingston (876)** | +3 | 0 | -5 | -6 | -13 | -14 |
| **Japan** | [81] | ✪Tokyo (3) Fukuoka (92) Hiroshima (82) Kobe (78) Kyoto (75) Nagasaki (958) Nagoya (52) Osaka (66) Sapporo (11) Yamaguchi (839) Yokohama (45) | +17 | +14 | +9 | +8 | +1 | 0 |
| **Jordan** (DST) | [962] | ✪Amman (6) Irbid (2) Zerqua (9) | +10 | +7 | +2 | +1 | -6 | -7 |
| **Kazakhstan**(DST) | [7] | ✪Almaty (3272) Chimkent (325) Karaganda (3212) | +14 | +11 | +6 | +5 | -2 | -3 |
| **Kenya** | [254] | ✪Nairobi (20) Mombasa (11) | +11 | +8 | +3 | +2 | -5 | -6 |
| **Korea, North** | [850] | ✪Pyongyang (2) | +17 | +14 | +9 | +8 | +1 | 0 |
| **Korea, South** | [82] | ✪Seoul (2) Cheju (64) Inchon (32) Kwangju (62) Pusan (51) Taegu (53) | +17 | +14 | +9 | +8 | +1 | 0 |
| **Kuwait** | [965] | ✪Kuwait* | +11 | +8 | +3 | +2 | -5 | -6 |
| **Kyrgyzstan** | [996] | ✪Bishkek (312) Jalal-Abad (3722) Osh (3222) | +13 | +10 | +5 | +4 | -3 | -4 |
| **Laos** | [856] | ✪Vientiane (21) Luang Prabang (71) Svannakhet (41) | +15 | +12 | +7 | +6 | -1 | -2 |
| **Latvia** (DST) | [371] | ✪Riga (2) Daugavpils (54) Liepaja (34) | +10 | +7 | +2 | +1 | -6 | -7 |
| **Lebanon** (DST) | [961] | ✪Beirut (1) Tripoli (6) | +10 | +7 | +2 | +1 | -6 | -7 |
| **Lesotho** | [266] | ✪Maseru* | +10 | +7 | +2 | +1 | -6 | -7 |
| **Liberia** | [231] | ✪Monrovia* | +8 | +5 | 0 | -1 | -8 | -9 |
| **Libya** | [218] | ✪Tripoli (21) Benghazi (61) Misratah (51) | +10 | +7 | +2 | +1 | -6 | -7 |
| **Liechtenstein**(DST) | [423] | ✪Vaduz* | +9 | +6 | +1 | 0 | -7 | -8 |
| **Lithuania** | [370] | ✪Vilnius* | +10 | +7 | +2 | +1 | -6 | -7 |
| | | As of 2003, area code + local number = 8-digit national number | | | | | | |
| **Luxembourg**(DST) | [352] | ✪Luxembourg* | +9 | +6 | +1 | 0 | -7 | -8 |

**DIALING**

| Country | Country Code | City Code / Area Code | Cities in Column 3 are X Hours Ahead (+) or Behind (-): | | | | | |
|---|---|---|---|---|---|---|---|---|
| | | | Los Angeles | New York | London (GMT) | Paris/ Berlin | Hong Kong | Tokyo/ Seoul |
| Macau | [853] | ✪Macau* (6-digit numbers) | +16 | +13 | +8 | +7 | 0 | -1 |
| Macedonia (DST) | [389] | ✪Skopje (2) | +9 | +6 | +1 | 0 | -7 | -8 |
| Madagascar | [261] | ✪Antananarivo* (7-digit numbers) | +11 | +8 | +3 | +2 | -5 | -6 |
| Malawi | [265] | ✪Lilongwe* | +10 | +7 | +2 | +1 | -6 | -7 |
| Malaysia | [60] | ✪Kuala Lumpur (3) Johor Bahru (7) Kota Bahru (9) Melaka (6) Penang (4) | +16 | +13 | +8 | +7 | 0 | -1 |
| Maldives | [960] | ✪Malé* (6-digit numbers) | +13 | +10 | +5 | +4 | -3 | -4 |
| Mali | [223] | ✪Bamako* (6- to 7-digit numbers) | +8 | +5 | 0 | -1 | -8 | -9 |
| Malta (DST) | [356] | ✪Valletta* (8-digit numbers) | +9 | +6 | +1 | 0 | -7 | -8 |
| Marshall Islands | [692] | ✪Majuro* (7-digit numbers) | +20 | +17 | +12 | +11 | +4 | +3 |
| Martinique, French Antilles | [596] | ✪Fort-De-France* (10-digit numbers) | +4 | +1 | -4 | -5 | -12 | -13 |
| Mauritania | [222] | ✪Nouakchott* (7-digit numbers) | +8 | +5 | 0 | -1 | -8 | -9 |
| Mauritius | [230] | ✪Port Louis* (7-digit numbers) | +12 | +9 | +4 | +3 | -4 | -5 |
| Mexico†† (DST) | [52] | ✪Mexico City (55) | +2 | -1 | -6 | -7 | -14 | -15 |
| | | Acapulco (744) | +2 | -1 | -6 | -7 | -14 | -15 |
| | | Cancun (998) | +2 | -1 | -6 | -7 | -14 | -15 |
| | | Cabo San Lucas (624) | +1 | -2 | -7 | -8 | -15 | -16 |
| | | Cuidad Juarez (656) | +2 | -1 | -6 | -7 | -14 | -15 |
| | | Durango (618) | +2 | -1 | -6 | -7 | -14 | -15 |
| | | Ensenada (646) | 0 | -3 | -8 | -9 | -16 | -17 |
| | | Guadalajara (33) | +2 | -1 | -6 | -7 | -14 | -15 |
| | | Ixtapa (462) | +2 | -1 | -6 | -7 | -14 | -15 |
| | | Leon (477) | +1 | -2 | -7 | -8 | -15 | -16 |
| | | Mazatlan (669) | 0 | -3 | -8 | -9 | -16 | -17 |
| | | Mexicali (686) | +2 | -1 | -6 | -7 | -14 | -15 |
| | | Monterrey (81) | +2 | -1 | -6 | -7 | -14 | -15 |
| | | Nuevo Laredo (867) | 0 | -3 | -8 | -9 | -16 | -17 |
| | | Playa del Carmen (984) | +2 | -1 | -6 | -7 | -14 | -15 |
| | | Puebla (222) | +2 | -1 | -6 | -7 | -14 | -15 |
| | | Tijuana (664) | 0 | -3 | -8 | -9 | -16 | -17 |
| | | Veracruz (229) | +2 | -1 | -6 | -7 | -14 | -15 |
| Midway Islands | [1] | (808)** | -3 | -6 | -11 | -12 | -19 | -20 |
| Moldova (DST) | [373] | ✪Chisinau (2) Tiraspol (33) | +10 | +7 | +2 | +1 | -6 | -7 |

DIALING

✪ Capital city
(DST) = Uses Daylight Savings Time
Code = Country Dialing Code

†† More than one time zone in this country.
* City/area codes not used in this country
** This area code used for entire country

| Country | Country Code | City Code / Area Code | Cities in Column 3 are X Hours Ahead (+) or Behind (-): | | | | | |
|---|---|---|---|---|---|---|---|---|
| | | | Los Angeles | New York | London (GMT) | Paris/ Berlin | Hong Kong | Tokyo/ Seoul |
| **Monaco** (DST) | [377] | ✪Monaco* | +9 | +6 | +1 | 0 | -7 | -8 |
| **Mongolia** (DST) | [976] | ✪Ulaanbaatar (1) | +16 | +13 | +8 | +7 | 0 | -1 |
| **Montenegro** | [381] | ✪Podgorica (81) Cetinje (86) | +9 | +6 | +1 | 0 | -7 | -8 |
| **Montserrat** | [1] | ✪Plymouth (664)** (7-digit numbers) | +4 | +1 | -4 | -5 | -12 | -13 |
| **Morocco** | [212] | ✪Rabat (3) Casablanca (2) Fez (5) Marrakech (4) Tangiers (3) | +8 | +5 | 0 | -1 | -8 | -9 |
| **Mozambique** | [258] | ✪Maputo (1) Nampula (6) | +10 | +7 | +2 | +1 | -6 | -7 |
| **Myanmar (Burma)** | [95] | ✪ Yangon (1) Mandalay (2) | +14₁/₂ | +11₁/₂ | +6₁/₂ | +5₁/₂ | -1₁/₂ | -2₁/₂ |
| **Namibia** (DST) | [264] | ✪Windhoek (61) | +9 | +6 | +1 | 0 | -7 | -8 |
| **Nepal** | [977] | ✪Kathmandu (1) | +13₃/₄ | +10₃/₄ | +5₃/₄ | +4₃/₄ | -2₁/₄ | -3₁/₄ |
| **Netherlands**(DST) | [31] | ✪Amsterdam (20) ✪The Hague (Den Haag) (70) Eindhoven (40) Rotterdam (10) Utrecht (30) | +9 | +6 | +1 | 0 | -7 | -8 |
| **Netherlands Antilles** | [599] | ✪Willemstad (Curacao) (9) St. Maarten (5) | +4 | +1 | -4 | -5 | -12 | -13 |
| **New Caledonia** | [687] | ✪Nouméa* | +19 | +16 | +11 | +10 | +3 | +2 |
| **New Zealand** (DST) | [64] | ✪Wellington (4) Auckland (9) Christchurch (3) Telecom Mobile Phones (25) | +20 | +17 | +12 | +11 | +4 | +3 |
| **Nicaragua** | [505] | ✪Managua* 7-digit numbers | +2 | -1 | -6 | -7 | -14 | -15 |
| **Niger Republic** | [227] | ✪Niamey* (6-digit numbers) | +9 | +6 | +1 | 0 | -7 | -8 |
| **Nigeria** | [234] | ✪Abuja (9) ✪Lagos (1) Ibadan (22) Kano (64) | +9 | +6 | +1 | 0 | -7 | -8 |
| **Northern Mariana Isl.** | [1] | ✪Saipan (670)** | +18 | +15 | +10 | +9 | +2 | +1 |
| **Norway** (DST) | [47] | ✪Oslo* (8-digit numbers) | +9 | +6 | +1 | 0 | -7 | -8 |
| **Oman** | [968] | ✪Muscat* | +12 | +9 | +4 | +3 | -4 | -5 |
| **Pakistan** | [92] | ✪Islamabad (51) Faisalabad (41) Karachi (21) Lahore (42) | +13 | +10 | +5 | +4 | -3 | -4 |

| Country | Country Code | City Code / Area Code | Cities in Column 3 are X Hours Ahead (+) or Behind (-): | | | | | |
|---|---|---|---|---|---|---|---|---|
| | | | Los Angeles | New York | London (GMT) | Paris/ Berlin | Hong Kong | Tokyo/ Seoul |
| Palau | [680] | ✪Koror* | +17 | +14 | +9 | +8 | +1 | 0 |
| Panama | [507] | ✪Panama City* (7-digit numbers) | +3 | 0 | -5 | -6 | -13 | -14 |
| Papua New Guinea | [675] | ✪Port Moresby* (7-digit numbers) | +18 | +15 | +10 | +9 | +2 | +1 |
| Paraguay (DST) | [595] | ✪Asuncion (21) | +4 | +1 | -4 | -5 | -12 | -13 |
| Peru | [51] | ✪Lima (1) Arequipa (54) Cuzco (84) Trujillo (44) | +3 | 0 | -5 | -6 | -13 | -14 |
| Philippines | [63] | ✪Manila (2) Cebu (32) Davao (82) Quezon City (2) | +16 | +13 | +8 | +7 | 0 | -1 |
| Poland (DST) | [48] | ✪Warsaw (22) Gdansk (58) Kraków (12) Lodz (42) Wroclaw (71) | +9 | +6 | +1 | 0 | -7 | -8 |
| Portugal (DST) | [351] | ✪Lisbon* (9-digit numbers) | +8 | +5 | 0 | -1 | -8 | -9 |
| Puerto Rico | [1] | ✪San Juan (787)** | +4 | +1 | -4 | -5 | -12 | -13 |
| Qatar | [974] | ✪Doha* | +11 | +8 | +3 | +2 | -5 | -6 |
| Reunion Island | [262] | ✪St. Denis* (10-digit numbers) | +12 | +9 | +4 | +3 | -4 | -5 |
| Romania (DST) | [40] | ✪Bucharest (21) Constanta (241) Iasi (232) | +10 | +7 | +2 | +1 | -6 | -7 |
| Russia†† (DST) | [7] | ✪Moscow (095) Moscow Area (096) | +11 | +8 | +3 | +2 | -5 | -6 |
| | | Kaliningrad (011) | +11 | +8 | +3 | +2 | -5 | -6 |
| | | Novgorod (816) | +14 | +11 | +6 | +5 | -2 | -3 |
| | | Novosibirsk (383) St. Petersburg (812) | +11 | +8 | +3 | +2 | -5 | -6 |
| Rwanda | [250] | ✪Kigali* | +10 | +7 | +2 | +1 | -6 | -7 |
| St. Kitts & Nevis | [1] | ✪Basseterre (869)** | +4 | +1 | -4 | -5 | -12 | -13 |
| St. Lucia | [1] | ✪Castries (758)** | +4 | +1 | -4 | -5 | -12 | -13 |
| St. Vincent & Grenadines | [1] | ✪Kingstown (784)** | +4 | +1 | -4 | -5 | -12 | -13 |
| Samoa | [685] | ✪Apia* | -3 | -6 | -11 | -12 | -19 | -20 |
| San Marino (DST) | [378] | ✪San Marino* | +9 | +6 | +1 | 0 | -7 | -8 |
| São Tomé & Principe | [239] | ✪São Tomé* | +8 | +5 | 0 | -1 | -8 | -9 |

✪ Capital city
(DST) = Uses Daylight Savings Time
Code = Country Dialing Code

†† More than one time zone in this country.
* City/area codes not used in this country
** This area code used for entire country

D
I
A
L
I
N
G

| Country | Country Code | City Code / Area Code | Cities in Column 3 are X Hours Ahead (+) or Behind (-): | | | | | |
|---|---|---|---|---|---|---|---|---|
| | | | Los Angeles | New York | London (GMT) | Paris/ Berlin | Hong Kong | Tokyo/ Seoul |
| Saudi Arabia | [966] | ✪Riyadh (1) Jeddah (2) Makkah (Mecca) (2) | +11 | +8 | +3 | +2 | -5 | -6 |
| Senegal | [221] | ✪Dakar* (7-digit numbers) | +8 | +5 | 0 | -1 | -8 | -9 |
| Serbia & Monte-negro (former Yugoslavia) | [381] | ✪Belgrade (11) Pec (39) Novi Sad (21) | +9 | +6 | +1 | 0 | -7 | -8 |
| Seychelles | [248] | ✪Victoria (6-digit numbers) | +12 | +9 | +4 | +3 | -4 | -5 |
| Sierra Leone | [232] | ✪Freetown (22) | +8 | +5 | 0 | -1 | -8 | -9 |
| Singapore | [65] | ✪Singapore* (8-digit numbers) | +16 | +13 | +8 | +7 | 0 | -1 |
| Slovak Republic (DST) | [421] | ✪Bratislava (2) Kosice (55) | +9 | +6 | +1 | 0 | -7 | -8 |
| Slovenia (DST) | [386] | ✪Ljubljana (1) Maribor (2) | +9 | +6 | +1 | 0 | -7 | -8 |
| Solomon Islands | [677] | ✪Honiara* | +19 | +16 | +11 | +10 | +3 | +2 |
| Somalia | [252] | ✪Mogadishu (1) | +11 | +8 | +3 | +2 | -5 | -6 |
| South Africa | [27] | ✪Cape Town* ✪Pretoria | +10 | +7 | +2 | +1 | -6 | -7 |
| | | Area code + local number = new 9-digit national number. | | | | | | |
| Spain (DST) | [34] | ✪Madrid* | +9 | +6 | +1 | 0 | -7 | -8 |
| | | Area code + local number = new 9-digit national number. | | | | | | |
| Sri Lanka | [94] | ✪Colombo (11) | +13½ | +10½ | +5½ | +4½ | -2½ | -3½ |
| Sudan | [249] | ✪Khartoum (11) Port Sudan (311) | +10 | +7 | +2 | +1 | -6 | -7 |
| Suriname | [597] | ✪Paramaribo* | +5 | +2 | -3 | -4 | -11 | -12 |
| Swaziland | [268] | ✪Mbabane* ✪Lobamba* | +10 | +7 | +2 | +1 | -6 | -7 |
| Sweden (DST) | [46] | ✪Stockholm (8) Göteborg (31) Kristianstad (44) Lund (46) Malmö (40) Uppsala (18) | +9 | +6 | +1 | 0 | -7 | -8 |
| Switzerland(DST) | [41] | ✪Bern* | +9 | +6 | +1 | 0 | -7 | -8 |
| | | As of March 2002, area code + local number = new 8- to 9-digit national number. | | | | | | |
| Syria (DST) | [963] | ✪Damascus (11) Aleppo (21) | +10 | +7 | +2 | +1 | -6 | -7 |
| Taiwan | [886] | ✪Taipei (2) Kaohsiung (7) Taichung (4) Tainan (6) | +16 | +13 | +8 | +7 | 0 | -1 |
| Tajikistan | [992] | ✪Dushanbe (372) | +13 | +10 | +5 | +4 | -3 | -4 |
| Tanzania | [255] | ✪Dar es Salaam (22) | +11 | +8 | +3 | +2 | -5 | -6 |
| Thailand | [66] | ✪Bangkok* | +15 | +12 | +7 | +6 | -1 | -2 |
| | | Area code + local number = 8-digit national number. | | | | | | |

D
I
A
L
I
N
G

| Country | Country Code | City Code / Area Code | Cities in Column 3 are X Hours Ahead (+) or Behind (-): | | | | | |
|---|---|---|---|---|---|---|---|---|
| | | | Los Angeles | New York | London (GMT) | Paris/ Berlin | Hong Kong | Tokyo/ Seoul |
| Togo | [228] | ✪Lomé* (7-digit numbers) | +8 | +5 | 0 | -1 | -8 | -9 |
| Tonga | [676] | ✪Nuku'alofa** | +21 | +18 | +13 | +12 | +5 | +4 |
| Trinidad & Tobago | [1] | ✪Port-of-Spain (868)** (7-digit numbers) | +4 | +1 | -4 | -5 | -12 | -13 |
| Tunisia | [216] | ✪Tunis* | +9 | +6 | +1 | 0 | -7 | -8 |
| | | 7 + area code + local number = new 8-digit national number. | | | | | | |
| Turkey (DST) | [90] | ✪Ankara (312) Istanbul (Anatolia) 216) Istanbul (Thrace) (212) Adana (322) Antalya (242) Bursa (224) Izmir (232) | +10 | +7 | +2 | +1 | -6 | -7 |
| Turkmenistan | [993] | ✪Ashgabat (12) Mary (522) | +13 | +10 | +5 | +4 | -3 | -4 |
| Turks & Caicos Islands (DST) | [1] | ✪Grand Turk (649)** | +3 | 0 | -5 | -6 | -13 | -14 |
| Tuvalu | [688] | ✪Funafuti* (5-digit numbers) | +20 | +17 | +12 | +11 | +4 | +3 |
| Uganda | [256] | ✪Kampala (41) | +11 | +8 | +3 | +2 | -5 | -6 |
| Ukraine (DST) | [380] | ✪Kiev (44) Odessa (48) | +10 | +7 | +2 | +1 | -6 | -7 |
| | | In addition to the trunk prefix '8', long-distance calls within Ukraine add the prefix '0' to the area code (e.g., *8 (044) + subscriber number* for Kiev). | | | | | | |
| United Arab Emirates | [971] | ✪Abu Dhabi (2) Dubai (4) | +12 | +9 | +4 | +3 | -4 | -5 |
| United Kingdom (DST) | [44] | ✪London (20) Aberdeen (1224) Bath (1225) Belfast (28) Birmingham (121) Bristol (117) Cardiff (29) Edinburgh (131) Glasgow (141) Leeds (113) Liverpool (151) Manchester (161) Nottingham (115) Plymouth (1752) Sheffield (114) Swansea (1792) | +8 | +5 | 0 | -1 | -8 | -9 |

**D I A L I N G**

---

| | |
|---|---|
| ✪ Capital city | †† More than one time zone in this country. |
| (DST) = Uses Daylight Savings Time | * City/area codes not used in this country |
| Code = Country Dialing Code | ** This area code used for entire country |

**DIALING**

| Country | Country Code | City Code / Area Code | Cities in Column 3 are X Hours Ahead (+) or Behind (-): | | | | | |
|---|---|---|---|---|---|---|---|---|
| | | | Los Angeles | New York | London (GMT) | Paris/ Berlin | Hong Kong | Tokyo/ Seoul |
| United States †† (DST) (The states of Arizona and Hawaii do not observe DST.) | [1] | ✪Washington, DC (202) | +3 | 0 | -5 | -6 | -13 | -14 |
| | | Atlanta (404) | +3 | 0 | -5 | -6 | -13 | -14 |
| | | Baltimore (410) | +3 | 0 | -5 | -6 | -13 | -14 |
| | | Boston (617) | +3 | 0 | -5 | -6 | -13 | -14 |
| | | Chicago (312) (773) | +2 | -1 | -6 | -7 | -14 | -15 |
| | | Cleveland (216) | +2 | -1 | -6 | -7 | -14 | -15 |
| | | Dallas (214) (469) (972) | +2 | -1 | -6 | -7 | -14 | -15 |
| | | Denver (303) | +1 | -2 | -7 | -8 | -15 | -16 |
| | | Detroit (313) | +3 | 0 | -5 | -6 | -13 | -14 |
| | | Honolulu (808) | -2 | -5 | -10 | -11 | -18 | -19 |
| | | Houston (713) (281) | +2 | -1 | -6 | -7 | -14 | -15 |
| | | Los Angeles (213) (323) | 0 | -3 | -8 | -9 | -16 | -17 |
| | | (310) | 0 | -3 | -8 | -9 | -16 | -17 |
| | | Miami (305) (786) | +3 | 0 | -5 | -6 | -13 | -14 |
| | | Minneapolis (612) | +2 | -1 | -6 | -7 | -14 | -15 |
| | | New Orleans (504) | +2 | -1 | -6 | -7 | -14 | -15 |
| | | New York (212) (347) (646) (718) (917) | +3 | 0 | -5 | -6 | -13 | -14 |
| | | Philadelphia (215) (267) (610) | +3 | 0 | -5 | -6 | -13 | -14 |
| | | Phoenix (602) | +1 | -2 | -7 | -8 | -15 | -16 |
| | | Sacramento (916) | 0 | -3 | -8 | -9 | -16 | -17 |
| | | (530) | 0 | -3 | -8 | -9 | -16 | -17 |
| | | St. Louis (314) | +2 | -1 | -6 | -7 | -14 | -15 |
| | | Salt Lake City (801) | +1 | -2 | -7 | -8 | -15 | -16 |
| | | San Antonio (210) | +2 | -1 | -6 | -7 | -14 | -15 |
| | | San Diego (619) | 0 | -3 | -8 | -9 | -16 | -17 |
| | | San Francisco (415) | 0 | -3 | -8 | -9 | -16 | -17 |
| | | San Jose (408) | 0 | -3 | -8 | -9 | -16 | -17 |
| | | Seattle (206) | 0 | -3 | -8 | -9 | -16 | -17 |
| Uruguay | [598] | ✪Montevideo (2) | +5 | +2 | -3 | -4 | -11 | -12 |
| Uzbekistan | [998] | ✪Tashkent (71) Namangan (69) Samarkand (66) | +13 | +10 | +5 | +4 | -3 | -4 |
| Vanuatu | [678] | ✪Port Vila* (5-digit numbers) | +19 | +16 | +11 | +10 | +3 | +2 |
| Venezuela | [58] | ✪Caracas (212) Maracaibo (261) Valencia (241) | +4 | +1 | -4 | -5 | -12 | -13 |
| Vietnam | [84] | ✪Hanoi (4) Ho Chi Minh City (8) | +15 | +12 | +7 | +6 | -1 | -2 |
| Virgin Islands, British | [1] | ✪Road Town (284)** | +4 | +1 | -4 | -5 | -12 | -13 |
| Virgin Islands, U.S. | [1] | ✪Charlotte Amalie/St. Thomas (340)** | +4 | +1 | -4 | -5 | -12 | -13 |
| Yemen | [967] | ✪Sana'a (1) | +11 | +8 | +3 | +2 | -5 | -6 |
| Yugoslavia | | See Serbia, Montenegro | | | | | | |
| Zambia | [260] | ✪Lusaka (1) | +10 | +7 | +2 | +1 | -6 | -7 |
| Zimbabwe | [263] | ✪Harare (4) | +10 | +7 | +2 | +1 | -6 | -7 |

# Country Dialing Codes by Code

Do you have someone's *complete* international telephone number, but do not know the country? Perhaps you were handed a business card in an unknown language, with unknown city names and no country listing. Use this table to identify the country.

| Code | Country |
|------|---------|
| 1 | United States |
| 1 | Canada |
| 1 (242) | Bahamas |
| 1 (246) | Barbados |
| 1 (264) | Anguilla |
| 1 (268) | Antigua & Barbuda |
| 1 (284) | Virgin Islands (U.K.) |
| 1 (340) | Virgin Islands (U.S.) |
| 1 (345) | Cayman Islands |
| 1 (441) | Bermuda |
| 1 (473) | Grenada |
| 1 (649) | Turks & Caicos |
| 1 (664) | Montserrat |
| 1 (670) | N. Mariana Islands |
| 1 (671) | Guam |
| 1 (684) | American Samoa |
| 1 (758) | St. Lucia |
| 1 (767) | Dominica |
| 1 (784) | St. Vincent & Grenadines |
| 1 (787) | Puerto Rico |
| 1 (808) | Midway Islands |
| 1 (809) | Dominican Republic |
| 1 (868) | Trinidad & Tobago |
| 1 (869) | St. Kitts & Nevis |
| 1 (876) | Jamaica |
| 7 | Chechnya |
| 7 | Kazakhstan |
| 7 | Russia |
| 20 | Egypt |
| 27 | South Africa |
| 30 | Greece |
| 31 | Netherlands |
| 32 | Belgium |
| 33 | France |
| 34 | Spain |
| 36 | Hungary |
| 39 | Italy |
| 40 | Romania |
| 41 | Switzerland |
| 43 | Austria |
| 44 | United Kingdom |
| 45 | Denmark |
| 46 | Sweden |
| 47 | Norway |
| 48 | Poland |
| 49 | Germany |
| 51 | Peru |
| 52 | Mexico |
| 53 | Cuba |
| 54 | Argentina |
| 55 | Brazil |
| 56 | Chile |
| 57 | Colombia |
| 58 | Venezuela |
| 60 | Malaysia |
| 61 | Australia |
| 62 | Indonesia |
| 63 | Philippines |
| 64 | New Zealand |
| 65 | Singapore |
| 66 | Thailand |
| 81 | Japan |
| 82 | Korea, South |
| 84 | Vietnam |
| 86 | China (PRC) |
| 90 | Turkey |
| 91 | India |
| 92 | Pakistan |
| 93 | Afghanistan |
| 94 | Sri Lanka |
| 95 | Myanmar (Burma) |
| 98 | Iran |
| 99 | Greenland |
| 212 | Morocco |
| 212 | Western Sahara |
| 213 | Algeria |
| 216 | Tunisia |
| 218 | Libya |
| 220 | Gambia, The |
| 221 | Senegal |
| 222 | Mauritania |
| 223 | Mali |
| 224 | Guinea |
| 225 | Côte d'Ivoire (Ivory Coast) |
| 226 | Burkina Faso |
| 227 | Niger Republic |
| 228 | Togo |
| 229 | Benin |
| 230 | Mauritius |
| 231 | Liberia |
| 232 | Sierra Leone |
| 233 | Ghana |
| 234 | Nigeria |
| 235 | Chad |
| 236 | Central African Rep. |
| 237 | Cameroon |
| 238 | Cape Verde |
| 239 | São Tomé & Principe |
| 240 | Equatorial Guinea |
| 241 | Gabon |
| 242 | Congo (Brazzaville) |
| 243 | Congo, Democratic Republic of (Kinshasa) |
| 244 | Angola |
| 245 | Guinea-Bissau |
| 246 | Diego Garcia |
| 248 | Seychelles |
| 249 | Sudan |
| 250 | Rwanda |
| 251 | Ethiopia |
| 252 | Somalia |
| 253 | Djibouti |
| 254 | Kenya |
| 255 | Tanzania |
| 256 | Uganda |
| 257 | Burundi |
| 258 | Mozambique |
| 260 | Zambia |
| 261 | Madagascar |
| 262 | Reunion |
| 263 | Zimbabwe |
| 264 | Namibia |
| 265 | Malawi |
| 266 | Lesotho |
| 267 | Botswana |
| 268 | Swaziland |
| 269 | Comoros and Mayotte |
| 291 | Eritrea |
| 297 | Aruba |
| 298 | Faeroe Islands |
| 299 | Greenland |
| 350 | Gibraltar |
| 351 | Portugal |
| 352 | Luxembourg |
| 353 | Ireland |
| 354 | Iceland |
| 355 | Albania |
| 356 | Malta |
| 357 | Cyprus |
| 358 | Finland |
| 359 | Bulgaria |
| 370 | Lithuania |
| 371 | Latvia |
| 372 | Estonia |
| 373 | Moldova |
| 374 | Armenia |
| 375 | Belarus |
| 376 | Andorra |
| 377 | Monaco |
| 378 | San Marino |
| 379 | Vatican City |
| 380 | Ukraine |
| 381 | Kosovo |
| 381 | Serbia & Montenegro |
| 385 | Croatia |
| 386 | Slovenia |
| 387 | Bosnia & Herzegovina |
| 389 | Macedonia |
| 420 | Czech Rep. |
| 421 | Slovak Rep. |
| 423 | Liechtenstein |
| 500 | Falkland Islands |
| 501 | Belize |
| 502 | Guatemala |
| 503 | El Salvador |
| 504 | Honduras |
| 505 | Nicaragua |
| 506 | Costa Rica |
| 507 | Panama |
| 509 | Haiti |
| 590 | Guadeloupe (French Antilles) |
| 591 | Bolivia |
| 592 | Guyana |
| 593 | Ecuador |
| 594 | French Guiana |
| 595 | Paraguay |
| 596 | Martinique (French Antilles) |
| 597 | Suriname |
| 598 | Uruguay |
| 599 | Netherlands Antilles |
| 670 | East Timor |
| 673 | Brunei |
| 674 | Nauru |
| 675 | Papua New Guinea |
| 676 | Tonga |
| 677 | Solomon Islands |
| 678 | Vanuatu |
| 679 | Fiji |
| 680 | Palau |
| 681 | Wallis & Futuna |
| 682 | Cook Islands |
| 683 | Niue |
| 685 | Western Samoa |
| 687 | New Caledonia |
| 688 | Tuvalu |
| 689 | French Polynesia |
| 690 | Tokelau |
| 691 | Micronesia |
| 692 | Marshall Islands |
| 808 | Midway Islands |
| 850 | Korea, North |
| 852 | Hong Kong |
| 853 | Macau |
| 855 | Cambodia |
| 856 | Laos |
| 880 | Bangladesh |
| 886 | Taiwan |
| 960 | Maldives |
| 961 | Lebanon |
| 962 | Jordan |
| 963 | Syria |
| 964 | Iraq |
| 965 | Kuwait |
| 966 | Saudi Arabia |
| 967 | Yemen |
| 968 | Oman |
| 970 | Palestine |
| 971 | United Arab Emirates |
| 972 | Israel |
| 973 | Bahrain |
| 974 | Qatar |
| 975 | Bhutan |
| 976 | Mongolia |
| 977 | Nepal |
| 992 | Tajikistan |
| 993 | Turkmenistan |
| 994 | Azerbaijan |
| 995 | Georgia |
| 996 | Kyrgyzstan |
| 998 | Uzbekistan |

DIALING

# Currencies of the World

The table below lists the currencies and subcurrencies in use in more than 200 countries and territories around the world.

## Country Name
We have used the popular rather than the formal names of countries and territories. For example, we list Korea, South, rather than Republic of Korea.

## Currency Name
In many cases a number of countries share the same currency name, but not the same currency. To lessen confusion, we have included the country name in the currency column (e.g., Australian Dollar, U.S. Dollar, Hong Kong Dollar).

## ISO Codes
The International Organization for Standardization (ISO, not IOS) has established alpha and numeric codes for all currencies. These are the formal codes that banks and currency dealers use.

## Symbols
Most every currency in the world has a symbol or abbreviation that is more commonly used than the formal ISO codes. For example, $, £ and ¥.

## The Euro
On January 1, 2002, the Euro replaced the national currencies of 12 European Union (EU) countries including Austria, Belgium, Finland, France, Germany, Greece, Ireland, Italy, Luxembourg, the Netherlands, Portugal and Spain. At the same time, many other countries and

territories that used the former currencies of these countries converted as well. For example, French Guiana used the French franc but now also uses the Euro.

## Hard vs. Soft Currencies
Some currencies are "soft," meaning they are either legally inconvertible, or simply undesirable because they are not stable. "Hard" currencies, on the other hand, are convertible and stable and, therefore, most often used in international transactions. Hard currencies include the EU Euro, U.S. dollar, British Pound Sterling, Japanese Yen and Swiss Franc.

## Exchange Rate and Currency Information
Exchange rates can and do fluctuate, sometime wildly. The traditional method for learning about rates used to include the Monday edition of the Wall Street Journal, other major newspapers, and banks and foreign exchange firms like Thomas Cook. Now, of course, instant information is available on the Internet at services such as:

**Oanda** (www.oanda.com),
**Bloomberg** (www.bloomberg.com), and
**Universal Currency Converter** (www.xe.com).
Two other great sources of currency information include the **Pacific Exchange Rate Service** at: http://fx.sauder.ubc.ca/currency_table.html and the **UN Operational Rates of Exchange** at www.un.org/Depts/treasury.
The information below is current as of September 2006.

| Country | Currency | ISO 4217 Codes | | Symbol | Sub-Currency |
|---|---|---|---|---|---|
| | | Alpha | Numeric | | |
| Afghanistan | Afghani | AFN | 004 | Af | Af 1 = 100 puls |
| Albania | Lek | ALL | 008 | L | L1 = 100 qintars |
| Algeria | Algerian Dinar | DZD | 012 | DA | DA1= 100 centimes |
| American Samoa | U.S. Dollar | USD | 840 | US$ | US$1 = 100 cents |
| Andorra | European Union Euro | EUR | 978 | € | € 1 = 100 cents |
| Angola | Kwanza | AOA | 024 | Kz | Kz1 = 100 lwei |
| Anguilla | East Caribbean Dollar | XCD | 951 | EC$ | EC$1 = 100 cents |
| Antigua and Barbuda | East Caribbean Dollar | XCD | 951 | EC$ | EC$1 = 100 cents |
| Argentina | Argentine Peso | ARS | 032 | $ | $1 = 100 centavos |
| Armenia | Armenian Dram | AMD | 051 | n/a | 1 Dram = 100 luma |
| Aruba | Aruban Guilder | AWG | 533 | Af. | Af.1 = 100 cents |
| Australia | Australian Dollar | AUD | 036 | A$ | A$1 = 100 cent |
| Austria | European Union Euro | EUR | 978 | € | € 1 = 100 cents |
| Austria (pre-2002) | Schilling | ATS | 040 | S | S1 = 100 groschen |
| Azerbaijan | Manat | AZM | 031 | n/a | 1 Manat = 100 gopik |
| Bahamas | Bahamian Dollar | BSD | 044 | B$ | B$1 = 100 cents |
| Bahrain | Bahraini Dinar | BHD | 048 | BD | BD1 = 100 fils |

| Country | Currency | ISO 4217 Codes | | Symbol | Sub-Currency |
|---------|----------|------|--------|--------|--------------|
| | | Alpha | Numeric | | |
| **Bangladesh** | Taka | BDT | 050 | Tk | TK1 = 100 poisha |
| **Barbados** | Barbados Dollar | BBD | 052 | Bds$ | Bds$ = 100 cents |
| **Belarus** | Belarussian Ruble | BYR | 974 | BR | BR1 = 100 kopeks |
| **Belgium** | European Union Euro | EUR | 978 | € | € 1 = 100 cents |
| **Belgium (pre-2002)** | Belgium Franc | BEF | 056 | BF | BF1 = 100 centimes |
| **Belize** | Belize Dollar | BZD | 084 | BZ$ | BZ$1 = 100 cents |
| **Benin** | CFA Franc BCEAO | XOF | 952 | CFAF | CFAF 1 = 100 centimes (discontinued) |
| **Bermuda** | Bermudian Dollar | BMD | 060 | Bd$ | Bd$1 = 100 cents |
| **Bhutan** | Ngultrum | BTN | 064 | Nu | Nu1 = 100 chetrums |
| **Bolivia** | Boliviano | BOB | 068 | Bs | Bs1 = 100 centavos |
| **Bosnia-Herzegovina** | Convertible Mark | BAM | 977 | KM | KM1 = 100 pfening |
| **Botswana** | Pula | BWP | 072 | P | P1 = 100 thebe |
| **Bouvet Island** | Norwegian Krone | NOK | 578 | NKr | NKr1 = 100 øre |
| **Brazil** | Real | BRL | 986 | R$ | R$1 = 100 centavos |
| **British Indian Ocean Territory** | Pound Sterling | GBP | 826 | £ | £1 = 100 pence |
| **Brunei Darussalam** | Brunei Dollar (ringgit) | BND | 096 | B$ | B$1 = 100 cents (sen) |
| **Bulgaria** | Bulgarian Lev | BGN | 975 | Lv | Lv1 = 100 stotinki |
| **Burkina Faso** | CFA Franc BCEAO | XOF | 952 | CFAF | CFAF1 = 100 centimes (discontinued) |
| **Burundi** | Burundi Franc | BIF | 108 | FBu | FBu1 = 100 centimes |
| **Cambodia** | Riel | KHR | 116 | CR | CR1 = 100 sen |
| **Cameroon** | CFA Franc BEAC | XAF | 950 | CFAF | CFAF1 = 100 centimes (discontinued) |
| **Canada** | Canadian Dollar | CAD | 124 | Can$ | Can$1 = 100 cents |
| **Cape Verde** | Cape Verdean escudo | CVE | 132 | C.V.Esc. | C.V.Esc.1 = 100 centavos |
| **Cayman Islands** | Cayman Islands Dollar | KYD | 136 | CI$ | CI$1 = 100 cents |
| **Central African Republic** | CFA Franc BEAC | XAF | 950 | CFAF | CFAF1 = 100 centimes (discontinued) |
| **Chad** | CFA Franc BEAC | XAF | 950 | CFAF | CFAF1 = 100 centimes (discontinued) |
| **Chile** | Chilean Peso | CLP | 152 | Ch$ | Ch$1 = 100 centavos |
| **China** | Renminbi, Yuan | CNY | 156 | Y | Y1 = 10 jiao, 100 fen |
| **Christmas Island** | Australian Dollar | AUD | 036 | A$ | A$1 = 100 cents |
| **Cocos (Keeling) Islands** | Australian Dollar | AUD | 036 | A$ | A$1 = 100 cents |
| **Colombia** | Colombian Peso | COP | 170 | Col$ | Col$1 = 100 centavos |
| **Comoros** | Comorian Franc | KMF | 174 | CF | CF1 = 100 centimes (discontinued) |
| **Congo** | CFA Franc BEAC | XAF | 950 | CFAF | CFAF1 = 100 centimes (discontinued) |
| **Congo-Kinshasa (Democratic Republic of the Congo)** | Franc Congolais | CDF | 976 | n/a | 1 FC = 100 centimes |

CURRENCY

| Country | Currency | ISO 4217 Codes | | Symbol | Sub-Currency |
|---------|----------|------|---------|--------|--------------|
| | | Alpha | Numeric | | |
| **Cook Islands** | New Zealand Dollar | NZD | 554 | NZ$ | NZ$1 = 100 cents |
| **Costa Rica** | Costa Rican Colón | CRC | 188 | C | 1 Colón = 100 centimos |
| **Côte d'Ivoire** | CFA Franc BCEAO | XOF | 952 | CFAF | CFAF1 = 100 centimes (discontinued) |
| **Croatia** | Kuna | HRK | 191 | HRK | HRK1 = 100 lipas |
| **Cuba** | Cuban Peso | CUP | 192 | Cu$ | Cu$1 = 100 centavos |
| **Cyprus** | Cypriot Pound | CYP | 196 | £C | £C1 = 100 cents |
| **Cyprus, Northern** | Turkish Lira | TRL | 792 | TL | TL1 = 100 kurus |
| **Czech Republic** | Czech Koruna | CZK | 203 | Kc | K1 = 100 haleru |
| **Denmark** | Danish Krone | DKK | 208 | Dkr | Dkr1 = 100 øre |
| **Djibouti** | Djibouti franc | DJF | 262 | DF | DF1 = 100 centimes |
| **Dominica** | East Caribbean Dollar | XCD | 951 | EC$ | EC$1 = 100 cents |
| **Dominican Republic** | Dominican Republic Peso | DOP | 214 | RD$ | RD$1 = 100 centavos |
| **East Timor** | U.S. Dollar | USD | 840 | US$ | US$1 = 100 cents |
| **Ecuador** | U.S. Dollar | USD | 840 | US$ | US$1 = 100 cents |
| **Ecuador (pre-9/2002)** | Sucre | ECS | 218 | S/ | S/1 = 100 centavos |
| **Egypt** | Egyptian Pound | EGP | 818 | £E | £E1 = 100 piasters, 1,000 milliemes |
| **El Salvador** | U.S. Dollar | USD | 840 | US$ | US$1 = 100 cents |
| **Equatorial Guinea** | CFA Franc BEAC | XAF | 950 | CFAF | CFAF1 = 100 centimes (discontinued) |
| **Eritrea** | Nakfa | ERN | 232 | Nfa | Nfa1 = 100 cents |
| **Estonia** | Estonia Kroon | EEK | 233 | KR | KR1 = 100 senti |
| **Ethiopia** | Birr | ETB | 230 | Br | Br1 = 100 cents |
| **European Union** | Euro | EUR | 978 | € | € 1 = 100 cents |
| **Falkland Islands** | Falkland Pound | FKP | 238 | £F | £F1 = 100 pence |
| **Faroe Islands** | Danish Krone | DKK | 208 | Dkr | Dkr1 = 100 øre |
| **Fiji** | Fiji Dollar | FJD | 242 | F$ | F$1 = 100 cents |
| **Finland** | Euro | EUR | 978 | € | € 1 = 100 cents |
| **Finland (pre-2002)** | Markka | FIM | 246 | mk | mk1 = 100 penniä |
| **France** | Euro | EUR | 978 | € | € 1 = 100 cents |
| **France (pre-2002)** | French Franc | FRF | 250 | F or FF | F1 = 100 centimes |
| **French Guiana** | Euro | EUR | 978 | € | € 1 = 100 cents |
| **French Polynesia** | CFP Franc | XPF | 953 | CFPF | CFPF1 = 100 centimes |
| **French Southern Territories** | Euro | EUR | 978 | € | € 1 = 100 cents |
| **Gabon** | CFA Franc BEAC | XAF | 950 | CFAF | CFAF1 = 100 centimes (discontinued) |
| **Gambia** | Dalasi | GMD | 270 | D | D1 = 100 butut |
| **Gaza** | New Shekel (Israel) Jordanian Dinar | ILS JOD | 376 400 | NIS JD | NIS1 = 100 agorot JD1 = 1,000 fils |
| **Georgia** | Lari | GEL | 981 | | 1 Lari = 100 tetri |
| **Germany** | European Union Euro | EUR | 978 | € | € 1 = 100 cents |

| Country | Currency | ISO 4217 Codes | | Symbol | Sub-Currency |
| --- | --- | --- | --- | --- | --- |
| | | Alpha | Numeric | | |
| Germany (pre-2002) | Deutsche Mark | DEM | 276 | DM | DM1 = 100 pfennigs |
| Ghana | Cedi | GHC | 288 | ¢ | ¢1 = 100 psewas |
| Gibraltar | Gibraltar Pound | GIP | 292 | £G | £G1 = 100 pence |
| Greece | Euro | EUR | 978 | € | € 1 = 100 cents |
| Greece (pre-2002) | Drachma | GRD | 300 | Dr | Dr1 = 100 lepta |
| Greenland | Danish Krone | DKK | 208 | Dkr | Dkr1 = 100 øre |
| Grenada | East Caribbean Dollar | XCD | 951 | EC$ | EC$1 = 100 cents |
| Guadeloupe | Euro | EUR | 978 | € | € 1 = 100 cents |
| Guam | U.S. Dollar | USD | 840 | US$ | US$1 = 100 cents |
| Guatemala | Quetzal | GTQ | 320 | Q | Q1 = 100 centavos |
| Guinea | Guinea Franc | GNF | 324 | GF | 1 Franc = 100 centimes |
| Guinea-Bissau | CFA Franc BCEAO | XOF | 952 | CFAF | CFAF1 = 100 centimes (discontinued) |
| Guyana | Guyana Dollar | GYD | 328 | G$ | G$1 = 100 cents |
| Haiti | Gourde | HTG | 332 | G | G1 = 100 centimes |
| Heard and McDonald Islands | Australian Dollar | AUD | 036 | A$ | A$1 = 100 cents |
| Honduras | Lempira | HNL | 340 | L | L1 = 100 centavos |
| Hong Kong | Hong Kong Dollar | HKD | 344 | HK$ | HK$1 = 100 cents |
| Hungary | Forint | HUF | 348 | Ft | Ft1 = 100 fillérs (discontinued) |
| Iceland | Króna | ISK | 352 | Ikr | Ikr1 = 100 aurar |
| India | Rupee | INR | 356 | Rs | Rs1 = 100 paise |
| Indonesia | Rupiah | IDR | 360 | Rp | Rp1 = 100 sen (discontinued) |
| Iran | Rial | IRR | 364 | Rls | 1 rial = 100 dinars 10 rials = 1 toman |
| Iraq | New Iraqi Dinar | NID | 368 | ID | The sub-currency units "dirhams" and "filses" have been discontinued |
| Ireland | Euro | EUR | 978 | € | € 1 = 100 cents |
| Ireland (pre-2002) | Irish Pound | IEP | 372 | IR£ | IR£1 = 100 pence |
| Israel | New Israel Shekel | ILS | 376 | NIS | NIS1 = 100 new agorot |
| Italy | Euro | EUR | 978 | € | € 1 = 100 cents |
| Italy (pre-2002) | Italian Lira | ITL | 380 | Lit | Lit1 = 100 centesimi (not used) |
| Jamaica | Jamaican Dollar | JMD | 388 | J$ | J$1 = 100 cents |
| Japan | Yen | JPY | 392 | ¥ | ¥1 = 100 sen (not used) |
| Jordan | Jordanian Dinar | JOD | 400 | JD | JD1 = 1000 fils |
| Kazakhstan | Tenge | KZT | 398 | n/a | 1 Tenge = 100 tiyn |
| Kenya | Kenyan Shilling | KES | 404 | K Sh | K Sh1 = 100 cents |
| Kiribati | Australian Dollar | AUD | 036 | A$ | A$ 1 = 100 cents |
| Korea, North | North Korean Won | KPW | 408 | Wn | Wn1 = 100 chon |

| Country | Currency | ISO 4217 Codes Alpha | ISO 4217 Codes Numeric | Symbol | Sub-Currency |
|---|---|---|---|---|---|
| Korea, South | South Korean Won | KRW | 410 | W | W1 = 100 jeon |
| Kuwait | Kuwaiti Dinar | KWD | 414 | KD | KD1 = 1000 fils |
| Kyrgyzstan | Kyrgyzstan Som | KGS | 417 | n/a | 1 Som = 100 tyyn |
| Laos | Kip | LAK | 418 | KN | KN1 = 100 at |
| Latvia | Lat | LVL | 428 | Ls | Ls1 = 100 santims |
| Lebanon | Lebanese Pound (Livre) | LBP | 422 | L.L. | L.L.1 = 100 piastres |
| Lesotho | Loti | LSL | 426 | L (sing.) M (plu.) | 1L = 100 lisente |
| Liberia | Liberian Dollar | LRD | 430 | $ | $1 = 100 cents |
| Libya | Libyan Dinar | LYD | 434 | LD | LD1 = 1000 dirhams |
| Liechtenstein | Swiss Franc | CHF | 756 | SwF | SwF1 = 100 centimes/ rappen |
| Lithuania | Litas | LTL | 440 | n/a | 1 Litas = 100 centu |
| Luxembourg | Euro | EUR | 978 | € | € 1 = 100 cents |
| Luxembourg (pre-2002) | Luxembourg Franc | LUF | 442 | LuxF | LuxF1 = 100 centimes |
| Macau | Pataca | MOP | 446 | P | P1 = 100 avos |
| Macedonia | Denar | MKD | 807 | MKD | MKD1 = 100 deni |
| Madagascar | Malagasy Franc | MGF | 450 | FMG | 1 franc = 100 centimes |
| Malawi | Kwacha | MWK | 454 | MK | MK1 = 100 tambala |
| Malaysia | Malaysian Ringgit | MYR | 458 | RM | RM1 = 100 sen |
| Maldives | Rufiyaa | MVR | 462 | Rf or MRF | Rf1 = 100 laari or lari |
| Mali | CFA Franc BCEAO | XOF | 952 | CFAF | CFAF1 = 100 centimes (discontinued) |
| Malta | Maltese Lira | MTL | 470 | Lm | Lm1 = 100 cents |
| Marshall Islands | U.S. Dollar | USD | 840 | US$ | US$1 = 100 cents |
| Martinique | Euro | EUR | 978 | € | € 1 = 100 cents |
| Mauritania | Ouguiya | MRO | 478 | UM | UM1 = 5 khoums |
| Mauritius | Mauritius Rupee | MUR | 480 | Mau Rs | Mau Rs1 = 100 cents |
| Mayotte | Euro | EUR | 978 | € | € 1 = 100 cents |
| Mexico | Mexican Peso | MXN | 484 | Mex$ | 1 Peso = 100 centavos |
| Micronesia | U.S. Dollar | USD | 840 | US$ | US$1 = 100 cents |
| Midway Islands | U.S. Dollar | USD | 840 | US$ | US$1 = 100 cents |
| Moldova | Leu (singular) / Lei (plural) | MDL | 498 | n/a | 1 Leu = 100 bani |
| Monaco | European Union Euro | EUR | 978 | € | € 1 = 100 cents |
| Mongolia | Tugrik | MNT | 496 | Tug | Tug1 = 100 mongos |
| Montserrat | East Caribbean Dollar | XCD | 951 | EC$ | EC$1 = 100 cents |
| Morocco | Morrocan Dirham | MAD | 504 | DH | DH1 = 100 centimes |
| Mozambique | Metical | MZM | 508 | Mt | Mt1 = 100 centavos |
| Myanmar (Burma) | Kyat | MMK | 104 | K | K1 = 100 pyas |
| Namibia | Namibian Dollar South African Rand | NAD ZAR | 516 710 | N$ R | N$1 = 100 cents R1 = 100 cents |

| Country | Currency | ISO 4217 Codes | | Symbol | Sub-Currency |
|---|---|---|---|---|---|
| | | Alpha | Numeric | | |
| Nauru | Australian Dollar | AUD | 036 | A$ | A$1 = 100 cents |
| Nepal | Nepalese Rupee | NPR | 524 | NRs | NRs1 = 100 paise |
| Netherlands | Euro | EUR | 978 | € | € 1 = 100 cents |
| Netherlands (pre-2002) | Dutch Guilder (florin or gulden) | NLG | 528 | f. | f.1 = 100 cents |
| Netherlands Antilles | Antillian Guilder (florin or gulden) | ANG | 532 | Ant.f. or NAf. | Ant.f. or NAf.1 = 100 cents |
| New Caledonia | CFP Franc | XPF | 953 | CFPF | CFPF1 = 100 centimes |
| New Zealand | New Zealand Dollar | NZD | 554 | NZ$ | NZ$1 = 100 cents |
| Nicaragua | Gold Córdoba (Cordoba Oro) | NIO | 558 | C$ | C$1 = 100 centavos |
| Niger | CFA Franc BCEAO | XOF | 952 | CFAF | CFAF1 = 100 centimes (discontinued) |
| Nigeria | Naira | NGN | 566 | | 1 Naria = 100 kobo |
| Niue | New Zealand Dollar | NZD | 554 | NZ$ | NZ$1 = 100 cents |
| Norfolk Island | Australian Dollar | AUD | 036 | A$ | A$1 = 100 cents |
| Northern Marianas | U.S. Dollar | USD | 840 | US$ | US$1 = 100 cents |
| Norway | Norwegian Krone | NOK | 578 | NKr | NKr1 = 100 øre |
| Oman | Rial Omani | OMR | 512 | RO | RO1 = 1000 baizas |
| Pakistan | Pakistani Rupee | PKR | 586 | Rs | Rs1 = 100 paisa |
| Palau | U.S. Dollar | USD | 840 | US$ | US$1 = 100 cents |
| Palestinian Territory, Occupied | New Israel Shekel / Jordanian Dinar | ILS / JOD | 376 / 400 | NIS / JD | 1 Shekel = 100 agorot / JD1 = 1000 fils |
| Panama | Balboa / U.S. Dollar | PAB / USD | 590 / 840 | B / US$ | B1 = 100 centesimos / US$1 = 100 cents |
| Panama Canal Zone | U.S. Dollar | USD | 840 | US$ | US$1 = 100 cents |
| Papua New Guinea | Kina | PGK | 598 | K | K1 = 100 toeas |
| Paraguay | Guarani | PYG | 600 | | 1 Guarani = 100 centimos |
| Peru | New Sol | PEN | 604 | S/. | S/.1 = 100 centimos |
| Philippines | Philippine Peso | PHP | 608 | | 1 Peso = 100 centavos |
| Pitcairn Islands | New Zealand Dollar | NZD | 554 | NZ$ | NZ$1 = 100 cents |
| Poland | New Zloty | PLN | 985 | Z/1 | 1 Zloty = 100 groszy |
| Portugal | European Union Euro | EUR | 978 | € | € 1 = 100 cents |
| Portugal (pre-2002) | Portuguese Escudo | PTE | 620 | Esc | Esc1 = 100 centavos |
| Puerto Rico | U.S. Dollar | USD | 840 | US$ | US$1 = 100 cents |
| Qatar | Qatari Riyal (Rial) | QAR | 634 | QR | 1 = 100 dirhams |
| Reunion | Euro | EUR | 978 | € | € 1 = 100 cents |
| Romania | New Leu | RON | 946 | L | L1 = 100 bani |
| Russian Federation | Ruble | RUB | 810 | R | R1 = 100 kopecks |
| Rwanda | Rwanda Franc | RWF | 646 | RF | RF1 = 100 centimes |
| Saint Helena and Dependencies | St. Helena Pound | SHP | 654 | £S | £S1 = 100 pence |
| Saint Kitts and Nevis | East Caribbean Dollar | XCD | 951 | EC$ | EC$1 = 100 cents |

CURRENCY

| Country | Currency | ISO 4217 Codes | | Symbol | Sub-Currency |
| --- | --- | --- | --- | --- | --- |
| | | Alpha | Numeric | | |
| Saint Lucia | East Caribbean Dollar | XCD | 951 | EC$ | EC$1 = 100 cents |
| Saint Pierre and Miquelon | Euro | EUR | 978 | € | € 1 = 100 cents |
| Saint Vincent and the Grenadines | East Caribbean Dollar | XCD | 951 | EC$ | EC$1 = 100 cents |
| Samoa | Tala | WST | 882 | WS$ | WS$1 = 100 sene |
| San Marino | Euro | EUR | 978 | € | € 1 = 100 cents |
| Sao Tome and Principe | Dobra | STD | 678 | Db | Db1 = 100 centimos |
| Saudi Arabia | Saudi Riyal | SAR | 682 | SRls | SRls1 = 100 Halalat |
| Senegal | CFA Franc BCEAO | XOF | 952 | CFAF | CFAF1 = 100 centimes (discontinued) |
| Serbia & Montenegro (formerly Yugoslavia) | Dinar<br>Euro (in Montenegro) | CSD<br>EUR | 891<br>978 | Din<br>€ | Din1 = 100 paras<br>€ 1 = 100 cents |
| Seychelles | Seychelles Rupee | SCR | 690 | SR | SR1 = 100 cents |
| Sierra Leone | Leone | SLL | 694 | Le | Le1 = 100 cents |
| Singapore | Singapore Dollar | SGD | 702 | S$ | S$1 = 100 cents |
| Slovakia | Slovak Koruna | SKK | 703 | Sk | Sk1 = 100 haliers (halierov) |
| Slovenia | Tolar | SIT | 705 | SIT | SIT1 = 100 stotins (stotinov) |
| Solomon Islands | Solomon Islands Dollar | SBD | 090 | SI$ | SI$1 = 100 cents |
| Somalia | Somali Shilling | SOS | 706 | So. Sh. | So. Sh.1 = 100 cents (centesimi) |
| South Africa | Rand | ZAR | 710 | R | R1 = 100 cents |
| South Georgia and South Sandwich Islands | Pound Sterling | GBP | 826 | £ | £1 = 100 pence |
| Spain | Euro | EUR | 978 | € | €1 = 100 cents |
| Spain (pre-2002) | Peseta | ESP | 724 | Ptas | Ptas1 = 100 centimos |
| Sri Lanka | Sri Lankan Rupee | LKR | 144 | SLRs | SLRs1 = 100 cents |
| Sudan | Sudanese Dinar | SDD | 736 | n/a | 1 Dinar = 100 piastres |
| Suriname | Suriname Dollar | SRD | 740 | $Sur | $Sur1 = 100 cents |
| Svalbard and Jan Mayen Islands | Norwegian Krone | NOK | 578 | Nkr | Nkr1 = 100 øre |
| Swaziland | Lilangeni (singular) / Emalangeni (plural) | SZL | 748 | L | L1 = 100 cents |
| Sweden | Swedish Krona | SEK | 752 | Sk | Sk1 = 100 ören |
| Switzerland | Swiss Franc | CHF | 756 | SwF | SwF1 = 100 rappen/ centimes |
| Syria | Syrian Pound | SYP | 760 | £S | £S1 = 100 piasters |
| Taiwan | Taiwan Dollar | TWD | 901 | NT$ | NT$1 = 100 cents |
| Tajikistan | Somoni | TJS | 762 | n/a | 1 Somoni = 100 dirams |
| Tanzania | Tanzanian Shilling | TZS | 834 | TSh | TSh1 = 100 cents |
| Thailand | Baht | THB | 764 | Bht or Bt | Bht or Bt1 = 100 stang |
| Togo | CFA Franc BCEAO | XOF | 952 | CFAF | CFAF1 = 100 centimes (discontinued) |

CURRENCY

| Country | Currency | ISO 4217 Codes | | Symbol | Sub-Currency |
|---------|----------|---------|---------|--------|--------------|
| | | Alpha | Numeric | | |
| Tokelau | New Zealand Dollar | NZD | 554 | NZ$ | NZ$1 = 100 cents |
| Tonga | Pa'anga | TOP | 776 | PT or T$ | PT or T$1 = 100 seniti |
| Trinidad and Tobago | Trinidad and Tobago Dollar | TTD | 780 | TT$ | TT$1 = 100 cents |
| Tunisia | Tunisian Dinar | TND | 788 | TD | TD1 = 100 millimes |
| Turkey | New Turkish Lira | TRY | 949 | YTL | YTL1 = 100 new kurus |
| Turkmenistan | Manat | TMM | 795 | n/a | 1 Manat = 100 tenga or (e) |
| Turks and Caicos Islands | U.S. Dollar | USD | 840 | US$ | US$1 = 100 cents |
| Tuvalu | Australian Dollar | AUD | 036 | A$ | A$1 = 100 cents |
| Uganda | Uganda Shilling | UGX | 800 | USh | USh1 = 100 cents |
| Ukraine | Hryvnia | UAH | 980 | n/a | 1 Hryvnia = 100 kopiykas |
| United Arab Emirates | UAE Dirham | AED | 784 | Dh | Dh1 = 100 filses |
| United Kingdom | Pound Sterling | GBP | 826 | £ | £1 = 100 pence |
| United States | U.S. Dollar | USD | 840 | US$ | US$1 = 100 cents |
| United States Minor Outlying Islands | U.S. Dollar | USD | 840 | US$ | US$1 = 100 cents |
| Uruguay | Uruguayan Peso (Peso Uruguayo) | UYU | 858 | $U | $U1 = 100 centésimos |
| Uzbekistan | Uzbek Sum (s'om) | UZS | 860 | n/a | 1 Sum = 100 tiyin |
| Vanuatu | Vatu | VUV | 548 | VT | VT1 = 100 centimes |
| Vatican City | European Union Euro | EUR | 978 | € | € 1 = 100 cents |
| Venezuela | Venezuela Bolivar | VEB | 862 | Bs | Bs1 = 100 centimos |
| Vietnam | New Dong | VND | 704 | D | D1 = 100 hao, 100 xu (discontinued) |
| Virgin Islands (British) | U.S. Dollar | USD | 840 | US$ | US$1 = 100 cents |
| Virgin Islands (U.S.) | U.S. Dollar | USD | 840 | US$ | US$1 = 100 cents |
| Wallis and Futuna | CFP Franc | XPF | 953 | CFPF | CFPF1 = 100 centimes |
| Western Sahara | Morrocan Dirham | MAD | 504 | DH | DH1=100 centimes |
| | Euro (Spain) | EUR | 978 | € | € 1 = 100 cents |
| | Ouguiya (Mauritania) | MRO | 478 | UM | UM1 = 5 khoums |
| Yemen | Yemeni Rial | YER | 886 | YRls | YRlis1 = 100 fils |
| Yugoslavia (now Serbia & Montenegro) | New Dinar | YUM | 891 | Din | Din1 = 100 paras |
| | Euro (in Montenegro) | EUR | 978 | € | € 1 = 100 cents |
| Zambia | Kwacha | ZMK | 894 | ZK | ZK1 = 100 ngwee |
| Zimbabwe | Zimbabwe Dollar | ZWD | 716 | Z$ | Z$1 = 100 cents |

CURRENCY

# Business Entities Worldwide

The following is a list of the most common business entities worldwide. It is not intended to be exhaustive of all enterprises in the world. Nonprofit enterprises and informal associations have generally not been included, unless they are in common use among traders. Emphasis has been given to private enterprises, as opposed to government or civil enterprises.

The detailed legal requirements for enterprises are numerous, complex, and different from country to country. Moreover, they usually have little meaning within a general definition or comparison of enterprises. The following definitions include some of these details for purposes of giving a general idea of the relative size and complexity of the enterprises, but it is beyond the scope of this work to list and explain every single characteristic, legal nuance, and exception to the exception. For more detailed information, advice should be sought from legal counsel in the relevant country. Another source is the "Martindale-Hubbell International Law Guide." See Resources Appendix for source information.

In many countries, the words "company", "association", and "venture" have special meanings, and therefore the word "enterprise" has been used as a generic term for the concept of a group of persons who join together for purposes of conducting business for profit. Similarly, the word "incorporate" in many countries refers to the procedure for registration of a business, even a partnership; therefore usage of this word has been avoided.

**Note**: Several definitions are useful at this time:

*corporate person*
An enterprise whether incorporated or not.

*entity*
An individual or an enterprise, having an organizational presence separate from the owner, recognized by law as having rights and obligations.

*natural person*
An individual.

*joint liability*
Liability for the obligations of an enterprise imposed on two or more owners of an enterprise.

*person*
An individual or legal entity recognized under law as having legal rights and obligations.

*share or stock*
An ownership interest in an enterprise. Stock usually refers to an ownership interest evidenced by a formal document issued by the enterprise. Share has a broader meaning in that it can describe a formal interest (such as stock) as well as a less formal interest such as in a partnership. Shares can have different characteristics depending upon the type of enterprise and country of the enterprise. For example: shares can be of equal or unequal value, be voting or non-voting, or can convey limited or unlimited liability for its owner(s).

*several liability*
Liability for the full obligations of an enterprise imposed on a single owner when other owners who also share responsibility cannot or do not pay.

---

**additional liability company**
**(Russian Federation)**
An enterprise with ownership interests divided into "parts" or "shares," formed to conduct business activities, and owned by one or more natural or corporate persons (members) who are jointly and severally liable for enterprise obligations in the percentage of their respective contributions to the enterprise.

**agrupamento complementar de empresas**
(ACE) (association of business entities) **(Portugal)**
An association of natural or corporate persons in Portugal formed to facilitate and develop the economic activities of the association members for their mutual benefit. Members have unlimited liability for association obligations.

**agrupamento Europeu de interêsse econômico**
(AEIE) (European economic interest group) **(Portugal)**
An association of natural or corporate persons from different European Community countries, formed to facilitate and develop the economic activities of the association members for their mutual benefit. Members have unlimited liability for association obligations.

**Akciova Spolecnost**
(a.s.) (joint stock company) **(Czech Republic)**
An enterprise with ownership interests in the form of shares and minimal capitalization of Kc 1,000,000, formed to undertake business activities, and owned by a single entity or by two or more individuals or entities (shareholders) whose liability for enterprise obligations is limited to the price of the shares.

**Aktiebolag**
(AB) (company limited by shares)
**(Finland, Sweden)**
An enterprise with ownership interests in the form of shares and minimum capital of SEK 100,000 (private company) or SEK 500,000 (public company), owned by one or more natural or corporate persons (shareholders) who receive dividends and whose liability for enterprise obligations is limited to the price of the shares.

**Aktiengesellschaft**
(AG) (corporation limited by shares)
**(Germany, Liechtenstein)**
An enterprise with ownership interests in the form of shares, owned by one or more natural or corporate persons (shareholders) who receive dividends and whose liability for enterprise obligations is limited to the price of the shares.

**Aktiengesellschaften**
(AG) (joint stock corporation) **(Austria)**
An enterprise with ownership interests in the form of shares and having minimal capital of ATS 1,000,000, formed for commercial purposes, and owned by natural or corporate persons (stockholders) whose liability for enterprise obligations is limited to the price of the shares.

**Aktieselskab**
(A/S) (joint stock company) **(Denmark)**
An enterprise with ownership interests in the form of shares and minimum capital of DKK 500,000, formed to conduct business activities, and owned by three or more natural or corporate natural or corporate persons (shareholders) whose liability for enterprise obligations is limited to the price of the shares.

**Aktzionerno Drouzestvo**
(AD) (public limited company) **(Bulgaria)**
An enterprise with ownership interests in the form of stock, formed to conduct any business, and owned by two or more natural or corporate persons (stockholders) who receive dividends, but whose liability for enterprise obligations is limited to the price of the stock.

**anonim sirket**
(A.S.) (public company) **(Turkey)**
An enterprise with ownership interests in the form of shares that are traded publicly, formed for any lawful purpose, and

owned by five or more natural or corporate persons (share-holders) who receive dividends but whose liability for enter-prise obligations is limited to the price of the shares.

### anonymos eteria
(AE) (joint stock company) **(Greece)**
An enterprise with ownership interests in the form of shares which may be traded publicly or privately, formed for any law-ful purpose, and owned by one or more natural or corporate per-sons (shareholders) who receive dividends but who are liable only for the price of the shares.

### Anpartsselskaber
(private company) **(Denmark)**
An enterprise with ownership interests in the form of shares and minimum capital of DKK 125,000, owned by one or more natu-ral or corporate persons whose liability for enterprise obligations is limited to the price of the shares.

### Anstalt
(establishment) **(Liechtenstein)**
An enterprise in which ownership interests are placed in an undivided fund, usually formed as a holding or investment company, and owned by one or more natural or corporate members who share profits in accordance with contractual provisions in the founding documents.

### Ansvarlig Selskap
(unlimited partnership) **(Norway)**
An enterprise with ownership interests stated by contract and formed for commercial purposes by two or more natural or cor-porate natural or corporate persons who have unlimited and joint liability for enterprise obligations.

### Artel
(production cooperative) **(Russian Federation)**
An enterprise with ownership interests combined into a single fund, formed by individuals to produce goods or engage in busi-ness activities jointly for their mutual benefit. The owners con-tribute labor and property to the enterprise, profits are divided in accordance with the labor contributed, and liability for enterprise obligations is stated in the enterprise bylaws.

### Associazione in Partecipazione
(participation in association) **(Italy)**
An enterprise with ownership interests determined by contract and formed by a combination of individuals who contribute cap-ital funds and individuals who provide only services. The part-ners who provide services have unlimited and joint liability for enterprise obligations, while the liability of partners who con-tribute capital is limited to the amount of their contribution. Profit-sharing is fixed by the partnership agreement.

### Berhad
(Bhd.) (public limited liability company)
**(Malaysia)**
An enterprise with ownership interests in the form of shares that are publicly traded, owned by one or more natural or cor-porate persons who receive dividends and whose liability for enterprise obligations is limited to the price of the shares.

### Besloten Vennootschap met Beperkte Aansprakelijkheid
(B.V.B.A.) (private limited company)
**(Belgium, Netherlands)**
An enterprise with ownership interests in the form of shares that are not publicly traded, owned by one or more natural or corporate persons who receive dividends and whose liability for enterprise obligations is limited to the price of the shares.

### Betéti Társaság
(Bt) (limited partnership) **(Hungary)**
An enterprise with ownership interests determined by contract and owned by one or more general partners and one or more limited partners. General partners have unlimited and joint lia-bility for enterprise obligations, while limited partners have li-ability only to the amount of funds they have agreed to invest in the enterprise.

### C corporation
(inc. or corp.) **(United States)**
A name derived from United States tax laws to refer to a cor-poration. *See* corporation.

### Chusik-Hosea
(stock companies) **(Korea, Republic of)**
An enterprise with ownership interests in the form of shares, owned by one or more natural or corporate natural or corpo-rate persons who receive dividends and whose liability for en-terprise obligations is limited to the price of the shares.

### Close Corporation
(Inc.) **(Canada, South Africa, United States)**
An enterprise with ownership interests in the form of shares, formed for purposes of conducting business, and owned by one or more persons (shareholders) who usually restrict the power of the managing directors to operate the enterprise. The shares are usually not traded publicly and the number of shareholders is usually less than 30. In some countries, the owners must be nat-ural persons only, while in other countries corporate or natural persons may own shares in a close corporation.

### Closed Company
(private company) **(Brazil)**
A sociedade anonima having shares traded privately. *See* So-ciedade Anonima.

### closed joint stock company
**(Russian Federation)**
An enterprise with ownership interests in the form of stock that can be transferred by private sale only, owned by one to fifty natural or corporate persons (stockholders) who receive dividends and whose liability for enterprise obligations is lim-ited to the price of the stock.

### Commanditaire Vennootschap
(special partnership) **(Belgium, Netherlands)**
An enterprise with ownership interests determined by written contract, and owned by one or more general partners and one or more special partners. General partners have unlimited and joint liability for enterprise obligations, while special partners have liability only to the amount of capital they have agreed to invest in the company.

### Compañía Anóniman
(C.A.) (corporation)
**(Dominican Republic, Ecuador, Venezuela)**
*See* Sociedad Anónima.

### Compañía de Responsabilidad Limitada
(C. Ltda.) (limited liability company) **(Ecuador)**
An enterprise with ownership interests divided in shares of equal value known as participations, formed for any commer-cial purpose, and owned by at least 3 but no more than 25 members. Liability of each member for enterprise obligations is limited to the amount that the member agrees to invest in the enterprise.

### compañía en comandita
(C. en C.) (limited partnership)
**(Dominican Republic, Ecuador, Venezuela)**
An enterprise with ownership interests in the form of "parts" and formed for commercial purposes by two or more general and limited partners. General partners have unlimited and joint liability for enterprise obligations, while limited partners are li-able only to the capital that the partner has agreed to invest in the enterprise.

### compañía en comandita por acciones
(C. en C. por A.) (limited partnership with shares)
**(Dominican Republic, Ecuador, Venezuela)**
A compañía en comandita with ownership interests in the form of shares instead of "parts". *See* compañía en comandita.

### compañía por acciones
(C. por A.) (corporation) **(Dominican Republic)**
*See* Sociedad Anónima.

*Company*
(Co.) **(Australia, England, Papua New Guinea)**
An enterprise having ownership interests in the form of shares owned by natural or corporate persons whose liability is limited to the price of the shares. *See* public company; private company.

*company limited by guarantee*
**(Papua New Guinea, South Africa)**
An enterprise with ownership interests in the form of shares and owned by members who are liable for enterprise obligations in the amount stated in the formation documents.

*Company Limited by Shares*
(CLS) **(China)**
An enterprise with ownership interests in the form of shares and having minimum capital of RMB 10,000,000, formed for commercial purposes, and owned by natural or corporate persons (shareholders) whose liability for enterprise obligations is limited to the price of the shares. Shares may be sold privately or offered to the public at large.

*Compañía en Nombre Colectivo*
(compañía) (general partnership)
**(Dominican Republic, Ecuador, Venezuela)**
An enterprise with ownership interests stated by contract and formed for commercial purposes by two or more natural or corporate persons who have unlimited and joint liability for enterprise obligations.

*Corporation*
(Inc. or Corp. or Ltd. or Ltée.)
**(Bahamas, Canada, United States)**
An enterprise with ownership interests in the form of shares, formed to do business for gain, and owned by one or more natural or corporate persons (shareholders) who receive dividends but whose liability for enterprise obligations is limited to the price of the shares.

*Cuideachta Phoibli Theoranta*
(c.p.t.) **(Ireland)**
*See* Private Company.

*Drouzestvo s Ogranichena Otgovornost*
(OOD) (private limited company) **(Bulgaria)**
An enterprise with ownership interests in the form of shares and with minimum capital of 50,000 leva, formed for business purposes, and owned by one or more natural or corporate persons (shareholders) who receive dividends but whose liability for enterprise obligations is limited to the price of the shares. New members may be admitted only by approval of the existing members.

*Empresa Individual de Responsibilidad Limitada*
(E.I. de R.L.) (individual limited liability company) **(Costa Rica, El Salvador)**
An enterprise with ownership interests stated in the formation documents, formed for any lawful purpose, and owned by a single individual who may withdraw profits and whose liability for enterprise obligations is limited to the enterprise property.

*Entreprise Unipersonnelle à Responsabilité Limitée*
(E.U.R.L.) (individual limited liability company)
**(France)**
A société à responsabilité limitée formed and owned by one person (associé unique) who receives dividends and whose liability for enterprise obligations is limited to the price of the participation. *See* société à responsabilité limitée.

*Eshamli Komandit Sirket*
(special partnership with shares) **(Turkey)**
An enterprise with ownership interests in the form of shares and formed for commercial purposes by two or more general and special partners. General partners have unlimited and joint liability for enterprise obligations, while special partners are liable only to the funds that the partner has agreed to invest in the enterprise.

*estabelecimento individual de responsabilidade limitada*
(EIRL) (individual limited liability company)
**(Portugal)**
An enterprise with ownership interests stated in the formation documents, formed for any lawful purpose, having minimum capital of Euro 5,000 and owned by a single individual who may withdraw profits and whose liability for enterprise obligations is limited to the enterprise property.

*eteria periorismenis efthinis*
(EPE) (limited liability company) **(Greece)**
An enterprise with ownership interests in the form of shares that are transferred privately and owned by one or more natural or corporate persons (shareholders) whose liability for enterprise obligations is limited to the price of the shares.

*eterorythmos eteria*
(EE) (limited partnership) **(Greece)**
An enterprise with ownership interests and profit-sharing determined by written contract, formed to undertake business activities, and owned by general and limited partners. Each general partner has unlimited and joint liability for enterprise obligations, while each limited partner is liable only for the funds that the partner has agreed to invest in the enterprise.

*Exempted Limited Partnership*
(ELP) **(Bahamas)**
An enterprise that is formed and operated similarly to a limited partnership, but that is exempt from business licensee fees and government-imposed taxes for 50 years. General partners have unlimited and joint liability for enterprise obligations, while limited partners incur no liability except for the purchase of their interests.

*General Partnership*
**(Australia, Bahamas, Canada, Channel Islands, China, Cyprus, England, Hong Kong, India, Israel, Russian Federation, South Africa, Turkey, United States, Zimbabwe)**
An enterprise with ownership interests and profit-sharing fixed by contract and formed to carry on business for gain by the partners, all of whom have unlimited and joint personal liability for enterprise obligations.

*Gesellschaft mit beschränkter Haftung*
(GmbH) (limited liability company)
**(Austria, Germany, Liechtenstein)**
An enterprise with ownership interests in the form of shares that are transferred privately and owned by one or more natural or corporate persons (shareholders) whose liability for enterprise obligations is limited to the price of the shares.

*Gomei Kaisha*
(partnership corporation) **(Japan)**
An enterprise with ownership interests in the form of shares and formed for commercial purposes by two or more partners.

*Goshi Kaisha*
(limited partnership corporation) **(Japan)**
An enterprise with ownership interests in the form of shares, owned by one or more general partners and one or more special partners. General partners have unlimited and joint liability for enterprise obligations, while special partners have liability only to the amount of funds they have agreed to invest in the enterprise.

*Handelsbolag*
(general partnership) **(Sweden)**
An enterprise with ownership interests stated by contract and formed for commercial purposes by two or more natural or corporate persons who have unlimited and joint liability for enterprise obligations.

*Hapcha-Hosea*
(limited partnership) **(Korea, Republic of)**
An enterprise with ownership interests determined by contract, and owned by one or more general partners and one or

more special partners. General partners have unlimited and joint liability for enterprise obligations, while special partners have liability only to the amount of funds they have agreed to invest in the enterprise.

### Hapmyong-Hosea
(partnership) **(Korea, Republic of)**
An enterprise with ownership interests stated by contract and formed for commercial purposes by two or more natural or corporate persons who have unlimited and joint liability for enterprise obligations.

### Is Ortakligi
(business partnership) **(Turkey)**
An enterprise with ownership interests stated by contract and formed for commercial purposes by two or more natural or corporate persons who have unlimited and joint liability for enterprise obligations.

### Julkinen Osakeyhtiö-oyj
(public limited liability company) **(Finland)**
An enterprise with ownership interests in the form of shares and minimum capital of Euro 80,000, formed to conduct any business, and owned by one or more natural or corporate persons (shareholders) whose liability for enterprise obligations is limited to the price of the shares.

### Kollektif Sirket
(general partnership) **(Turkey)**
An enterprise with ownership interests stated by contract and formed for commercial or other lawful purposes by two or more natural or corporate persons who have unlimited and joint liability for enterprise obligations.

### Kollektivgesellschaft
(general partnership) **(Liechtenstein)**
An enterprise with ownership and profit-sharing interests stated by contract and formed for commercial purposes by two or more natural or corporate persons who have unlimited and joint liability for enterprise obligations.

### Komandit Sirket
(special partnership) **(Turkey)**
An enterprise with ownership interests determined by contract, and owned by one or more general partners and one or more special partners. General partners have unlimited and joint liability for enterprise obligations, while special partners have liability only to the amount of funds they have agreed to invest in the enterprise.

### Komanditní Spolecnost
(k.s.) (limited partnership) **(Czech Republic)**
An enterprise with ownership interests and profit-sharing determined by written contract, formed to undertake business activities, and owned by general and limited partners. Each general partner has unlimited and joint liability for enterprise obligations, while each limited partner is liable only to the amount of the funds that the partner has agreed to invest in the enterprise.

### Komanditno Druzestvo
(limited partnership) **(Bulgaria)**
An enterprise with ownership interests determined by written contract and formed to conclude commercial transactions by two or more individuals who decide to act in concert, but at least one of whom has unlimited liability for enterprise obligations and at least one of whom has liability limited in accordance with the partnership contract.

### Kommandit Erwerbsgesellschaft
(KEG) (limited professional association) **(Austria)**
An enterprise with ownership interests determined by contract, formed to provide professional or business services that require special regulatory licenses, and owned by partners who have limited liability for enterprise obligations.

### Kommanditbolag
(limited partnership) **(Sweden)**
An enterprise with ownership interests determined by con-

tract, and owned by one or more general partners and one or more limited partners. General partners have unlimited and joint liability for enterprise obligations, while limited partners have liability only to the amount of the funds they have agreed to invest in the enterprise.

### Kommanditgesellschaft
(limited partnership)
**(Austria, Germany, Liechtenstein)**
An enterprise with ownership interests determined by contract, formed to carry on trade or production, and owned by two or more partners. At least one partner (Komplementaer) has unlimited liability for enterprise obligations, while at least one other partner (Kommanditist) is liable only to the amount of the funds that the partner has invested in the enterprise.

### Kommanditselskap
(limited partnership) **(Norway)**
An enterprise with ownership interests determined by contract, and owned by one or more general partners and one or more limited partners. General partners have unlimited and joint liability for enterprise obligations, while limited partners have liability only to the amount of the funds they have agreed to invest in the enterprise.

### korlátolt felelosségu társaság
(Kft) (limited liability company) **(Hungary)**
An enterprise with ownership interests in the form of "parts" and minimum capital of HUF 1,000,000, formed to conduct business for profit, owned by one or more natural or corporate persons who receive dividends and whose liability for enterprise obligations is limited to the price of the parts.

### közkereseti társaság
(Kkt) (general partnership) **(Hungary)**
An enterprise with ownership interests stated by contract and formed to conduct business for profit by two or more natural or corporate persons who have unlimited and joint liability for enterprise obligations.

### közös vállalat
(joint venture) **(Hungary)**
An enterprise formed for profit from commercial activities by two or more natural or corporate persons who are liable for enterprise obligations in proportion to their respective contributions to the enterprise.

### Limited Duration Companies
(LDC) **(Bahamas)**
An enterprise with a limited duration of 30 years or less, formed to allow for automatic termination of the enterprise when the period of existence has elapsed. The formation documents determine whether ownership interests are in the form of shares or otherwise, and liability of the shareholders may be limited or unlimited.

### limited liability company
(LLC)
**(China, Russian Federation, United States)**
An enterprise with ownership interests in the form of shares, formed for commercial purposes, and owned by one or more natural or corporate persons (shareholders) but no more than the statutory maximum (usually 50 shareholders). The liability of the shareholders for enterprise obligations is limited to the price of the shares.

### limited liability partnership
(LLP) **(United States)**
An enterprise with ownership interests determined by written contract among the partners, all of whom must be professionals licensed or otherwise specially qualified to offer services regulated by law and must be permitted to offer services through a limited liability partnership. The partners remain personally liable for their own obligations, jointly and severally liable for partnership obligations, but have no liability for the actions of other partners.

***limited partnership***
**(Bahamas, Canada, Channel Islands, Cyprus, England, India, Israel, South Africa, United States, Zimbabwe)**
An enterprise with ownership interests and profit-sharing fixed by contract among the partners and formed to carry on business for gain by two or more partners. At least one partner has unlimited liability for enterprise obligations, while at least one other partner is liable only to the amount of the funds that the partner has invested in the enterprise, provided that the limited partner contributes no services and takes no part in controlling the day-to-day partnership business.

***Maatschap***
(partnership) **(Netherlands)**
An enterprise with ownership interests stated by contract and formed to conduct business or to offer services for profit by two or more natural or corporate persons who contribute labor, funds, and property to the enterprise and who have unlimited and joint liability for enterprise obligations. The formation contract may limit a partner's liability to the partner's percentage of contribution to the enterprise.

***Naamloze Vennootschap***
(N.V.) (public joint stock company)
**(Belgium, Netherlands)**
An enterprise with ownership interests in the form of shares that are publicly traded, owned by one or more natural or corporate persons who receive dividends and whose liability for enterprise obligations is limited to the price of the shares.

***Offene Erwerbsgesellschaft***
(OEG) (general professional association) **(Austria)**
An enterprise with ownership interests determined by contract, formed to provide professional or business services that require special regulatory licenses, and owned by partners who have unlimited and joint liability for enterprise obligations.

***Offene Handelsgesellschaft***
(Co. or Cie.) (general partnership)
**(Austria, Germany)**
An enterprise with ownership interests determined by contract, formed to carry on a trade or production, and owned by partners who are jointly and severally liable for enterprise obligations.

***omorythmos eteria***
(OE) (general partnership) **(Greece)**
An enterprise with ownership interests stated by contract and formed for commercial purposes by two or more natural or corporate persons (partners) who have unlimited and joint liability for enterprise actions.

***Open Company***
(public company) **(Brazil)**
A sociedade anonima having shares traded publicly through a stock exchange or otherwise in an over-the-counter market. *See* Sociedade Anonima.

***open joint stock company***
**(Russian Federation)**
An enterprise with ownership interests in the form of stock sold to the public, owned by one or more natural or corporate persons (stockholders) who receive dividends and whose liability for enterprise obligations is limited to the price of the stock.

***Ordinary Partnership***
**(England, Hong Kong, Zimbabwe)**
*See* General Partnership.

***Osakeyhtiö***
(Oy) (private limited liability company) **(Finland)**
An enterprise with ownership interests in the form of shares and minimum capital of Euro 8,000, owned by one or more natural or corporate persons whose liability for enterprise obligations is limited to the price of the shares.

***osuuskunta***
(osuus) (cooperative association) **(Finland)**
An enterprise with ownership and profit-sharing interests determined by contract, formed by five or more members who contribute their property and labor for purposes of carrying on business to their mutual benefit. The liability of the members for enterprise obligations is determined by the formation contract.

***Partnership***
**(England, United States)**
An enterprise with ownership interests determined by contract between the owners (partners) who join together for purposes of acting in concert to attain common goals. *See* general partnership, limited partnership, and limited liability partnership.

***partnership in commendam***
(limited partnership) **(Russian Federation)**
An enterprise with ownership interests and profit-sharing fixed by contract among the partners and formed to carry on business for gain by two or more partners. At least one partner has unlimited liability for enterprise obligations, while at least one other partner is liable only to the amount of the funds that the partner has agreed to invest in the enterprise.

***Private Company***
(Ltd. or Pvt. Ltd.) **(Australia, Bahamas, Channel Islands, Cyprus, England, Hong Kong, India, Israel, Nigeria, Pakistan, Zimbabwe)**
An enterprise with ownership interests in the form of shares that are not sold to the public at large, owned by natural or corporate persons (shareholders) who receive dividends but whose liability for enterprise obligations is limited to the price of the shares.

***Public Company***
(P.L.C.) **(Australia, Bahamas, Channel Islands, Cyprus, England, Hong Kong, India, Israel, Nigeria, Pakistan, Zimbabwe)**
An enterprise having ownership interests in the form of shares that are sold to the public at large and owned by natural or corporate persons (shareholders) who receive dividends but whose liability for enterprise obligations is limited to the price of the shares.

***Publikt Aktiebolag-abp***
(public limited liability company) **(Finland)**
*See* Julkinen Osakeyhtiö-oyj.

***Részvénytársaság***
(Rt) (corporation limited by shares) **(Hungary)**
An enterprise with ownership interests in the form of shares and minimum capital of HUF 10,000,000, owned by one or more natural or corporate persons (shareholders) who receive dividends and whose liability for enterprise obligations is limited to the price of the shares.

***S Corporation***
(Inc. or Co.) **(United States)**
An enterprise with special tax features, having ownership interests in the form of shares, owned by one to thirty-five natural or corporate persons (shareholders) who receive a share of annual net profits as determined by their respective share percentages, and whose liability for enterprise obligations is limited to the funds they agree to invest in the enterprise.

***Sendirian Berhard***
(Sdn. Bhd.) (private limited liability company) **(Malaysia)**
An enterprise with ownership interests in the form of shares that are privately traded only, owned by one or more natural or corporate persons who receive dividends and whose liability for enterprise obligations is limited to the price of the shares.

***sharika mossahmah***
(joint stock company) **(Bahrain, Egypt, Qatar)**
An enterprise with ownership interests in the form of stock or shares, formed for commercial purposes, and owned by natural or corporate persons (stockholders or shareholders) who receive dividends but whose liability for enterprise obligations is limited to the price of the stock or shares.

***sharika tadhamun***
(general partnership) **(Bahrain, Egypt, Qatar)**
An enterprise with ownership interests stated by contract and

formed for commercial purposes by two or more natural or corporate persons (partners) who have unlimited and joint liability for enterprise actions.

### sharika tawsiyah baseetah
(limited partnership) **(Bahrain, Egypt, Qatar)**
An enterprise with ownership interests and profit-sharing fixed by contract among the partners and formed to carry on business for gain by two or more partners. At least one partner has unlimited liability for enterprise obligations, while at least one other partner is liable only to the amount of the funds that the partner has agreed to invest in the enterprise.

### sharika tawsiyah biel-ash-nam
(partnership limited by shares)
**(Bahrain, Egypt, Qatar)**
An enterprise with ownership interests in the form of shares and formed for commercial purposes by two or more general and limited partners. General partners have unlimited and joint liability for enterprise actions, while limited partners are liable only to the price of the shares.

### sharika that massouliyyah mahdoodah
(WLL) (limited liability company)
**(Bahrain, Egypt, Qatar)**
An enterprise with ownership interests divided in shares that cannot be sold publicly, formed for any commercial purpose, having limited duration of no more than 25 years, and owned by at least two natural or corporate persons but no more than the number of members permitted by law (usually 50 or fewer). Liability of members for enterprise obligations is limited to the amount stated in the formation documents.

### Sociedad Anónima
(S.A.) (stock company)
**(Argentina, Bahamas, Bolivia, Chile, Colombia, Costa Rica, Denmark, Dominican Republic, Ecuador, El Salvador, Guatemala, Honduras, Mexico, Paraguay, Peru, Spain, Uruguay)**
An enterprise with ownership interests in the form of stock or shares, formed to sell goods or services, and owned by natural or corporate persons (stockholders or shareholders) who receive dividends based on enterprise net profits but whose liability for enterprise obligations is limited to the price of the stock or shares.

### Sociedad Anónima de Capital Abierto
(S.A. de C.A.) (public corporation) **(Costa Rica)**
A sociedad anónima registered on the Costa Rican stock exchange, having at least 50 stockholders none of whom own more than 10 percent of the shares, and with at least 10 percent of its shares transferred annually through the stock exchange. *See* Sociedad Anónima.

### Sociedad Colectiva
(S.C. or Cía) (general partnership)
**(Argentina, Bolivia, Chile, Colombia, El Salvador, Guatemala, Honduras, Peru, Uruguay)**
An enterprise with ownership interests stated by contract and formed for commercial purposes by two or more natural or corporate persons who have unlimited and joint liability for enterprise obligations.

### Sociedad Commanditaria
(limited partnership) **(Spain)**
An enterprise with ownership interests determined by contract, and owned by one or more general partners and one or more limited partners. General partners have unlimited and joint liability for enterprise obligations, while limited partners have liability only to the amount of the funds they have agreed to invest in the enterprise.

### Sociedad de Capital e Industria
(S.C.I.) (capital and industry partnership)
**(Argentina)**
An enterprise with ownership interests determined by contract and formed by a combination of individuals who contribute funds and individuals who provide only services. The partners who contribute funds have unlimited liability, while the other partners are not liable personally for enterprise obligations. Profit-sharing is fixed by the partnership agreement.

### Sociedad de Responsabilidad Limitada
(S.R.L. or S. de R.L. or Ltda.) (limited liability company)
**(Argentina, Bolivia, Brazil, Chile, Colombia, El Salvador, Honduras, Mexico, Spain)**
An enterprise with ownership interests divided in shares of equal value known as quotas, formed for any commercial purpose, and owned by no more than the number of members permitted by law (usually 50 or fewer). Liability of members for enterprise obligations is limited to the amount stated in the enterprise contract.

### Sociedad en Comandita
(S. en C.) (limited partnership) **(Argentina, Bolivia, Chile, Colombia, El Salvador, Guatemala, Honduras, Mexico, Peru, Uruguay)**
An enterprise with ownership interests stated by contract and formed for commercial purposes by two or more active and silent partners. Active partners have unlimited and joint liability for enterprise obligations, while silent partners are liable only to the funds that the partner has invested in the enterprise.

### Sociedad en Comandita por Acciones
(S.C.A.) (joint stock company) **(Argentina, Colombia, Guatemala, Honduras, Mexico)**
An enterprise having attributes of both a stock company and partnership, with ownership interests in the form of stock, and owned by active and silent partners. Active partners are liable for enterprise obligations and obligations to the same degree as in a general partnership. The liability of each silent partner is limited to the funds that the partner has agreed to invest in the enterprise.

### Sociedad en Nombre Colectivo
(general partnership) **(Mexico)**
An enterprise with ownership interests stated by contract and formed for commercial purposes by two or more natural or corporate persons who have unlimited and joint liability for enterprise obligations.

### Sociedad Regular Colectiva
(general partnership) **(Spain)**
An enterprise with ownership interests stated by contract and formed for commercial purposes by two or more natural or corporate persons who have unlimited and joint liability for enterprise obligations.

### sociedade anónima
(S.A.) (stock company) **(Brazil, Portugal)**
An enterprise with ownership interests in the form of shares, formed for any object or gain not contrary to law or public order, and owned by two or more natural or corporate persons (shareholders) who receive dividends and whose liability for enterprise obligations is limited to the price of the shares.

### sociedade cooperativa
(SCRL) (cooperative) **(Portugal)**
An enterprise with ownership interests in the form of shares and minimum capitalization of Euro 30,000, formed for commercial purposes, and owned by ten or more natural or corporate persons (shareholders) who share profits in relation to their labor contributions to the business and whose liability for enterprise obligations may be limited or unlimited as stated in the formation documents.

### sociedade em comandita por acções
(partnership with shares) **(Portugal)**
An enterprise with ownership interests in the form of shares and formed for commercial purposes by two or more general and limited partners. General partners have unlimited and joint liability for enterprise actions, while limited partners are liable only to the funds that they have agreed to invest in the enterprise.

**ENTITIES**

### sociedade em comandita simple
(limited partnership) (**Portugal**)
An enterprise with ownership interests in the form of "quotas" and formed for commercial purposes by two or more active and silent partners. Active partners have unlimited and joint liability for enterprise actions, while silent partners are liable only to the amount of funds that the partner has invested in the enterprise.

### sociedade em nome colectivo
(general partnership) (**Portugal**)
An enterprise with ownership interests stated by contract and formed for commercial purposes by two or more natural or corporate persons who have unlimited and joint liability for enterprise actions.

### sociedade por quota
(Lda.) (limited liability companyl) (**Portugal**)
An enterprise with ownership interests in the form of "quotas", formed for any commercial purpose, and owned by no more than the number of members permitted by law (usually 50 or fewer). Liability of members for enterprise obligations is limited to the amount stated in the enterprise contract.

### Società a Responsabilità Limitata
(S.R.L.) (limited liability company) (**Italy**)
An enterprise with ownership interests in the form of "quotas", having limits on the transfer of quotas, and owned by one or more natural or corporate persons (quotaholders) whose liability for enterprise obligations is limited to the price of the shares, except that a sole quotaholder that is a corporate entity has unlimited liability for enterprise obligations if the enterprise becomes insolvent.

### Società in Accomandita per Azioni
(company with liability limited per share) (**Italy**)
An enterprise with ownership interests in the form of shares, owned by one or more natural or corporate persons (partners) whose liability for enterprise obligations is limited to the price of the shares.

### Società in Accomandita Semplice
(unlimited liability share company) (**Italy**)
An enterprise with ownership interests in the form of shares, owned by one or more natural or corporate persons (partners) who have unlimited and joint liability for enterprise obligations.

### Società in Nome Collettivo
(general partnership) (**Italy**)
A enterprise with ownership interests stated by contract and formed for commercial purposes by two or more natural or corporate persons (partners) who have unlimited and joint liability for enterprise obligations.

### Società per Azioni
(S.A.) (corporation) (**Italy**)
An enterprise with ownership interests in the form of shares and minimum capital of Euro 100,000, owned by one or more natural or corporate persons who receive dividends and whose liability for enterprise obligations is limited to the price of the shares, except that a sole shareholder has unlimited liability for enterprise obligations in the event the enterprise becomes insolvent.

### Società Semplice
(simple partnership) (**Italy**)
An enterprise with ownership interests stated by written or verbal contract, formed other than for industrial or commercial purposes by two or more individuals who act severally but have unlimited and joint liability for enterprise obligations.

### Societate cu Raspundere Limitata
(limited liability company) (**Romania**)
An enterprise with ownership interests in the form of "shares" or "parts", owned by one or more natural or corporate persons whose liability for enterprise obligations is limited to the price of the shares.

### Societate in Comandita pe Actiuni
(limited joint stock company) (**Romania**)
An enterprise with ownership interests in the form of shares that are privately traded, owned by one or more natural or corporate persons who receive dividends and whose liability for enterprise obligations is limited to the price of the shares.

### Societate in Comandita Simpla
(limited partnership) (**Romania**)
An enterprise with ownership interests determined by contract, and owned by one or more general partners and one or more limited partners. General partners have unlimited and joint liability for enterprise obligations, while limited partners have liability only to the amount of the funds they have agreed to invest in the enterprise.

### Societate in Nume Colectiv
(general partnership) (**Romania**)
An enterprise with ownership interests stated by contract and formed for commercial purposes by two or more natural or corporate persons who have unlimited and joint liability for enterprise obligations.

### Societate pe Actiuni
(joint stock company) (**Romania**)
An enterprise with ownership interests in the form of shares that are publicly traded, owned by one or more natural or corporate persons who receive dividends and whose liability for enterprise obligations is limited to the price of the shares.

### Société à Responsabilité Limitée
(S.A.R.L.) (limited liability company)
(**France, Luxembourg, Morocco**)
An enterprise with ownership interests in the form of "participations", having a maximum duration of 99 years, and owned by one to fifty natural or corporate persons (associés) who receive dividends and whose liability for enterprise obligations is limited to the price of the participations.

### Société Anonyme
(S.A.) (joint stock company) (**Bahamas, Belgium, France, Lebanon, Luxembourg, Morocco**)
An enterprise with ownership interests in the form of shares, formed for any lawful purpose, and owned by natural or corporate persons (shareholders) who receive dividends but who are liable only for the price of the shares.

### Société Coopérative
(S.C.) (cooperative company) (**Belgium**)
An enterprise with ownership interests in the form of shares and minimum capitalization of BF 750,000, formed for commercial purposes, and owned by three or more natural or corporate persons (shareholders) who share profits in relation to the amount of business with the enterprise and whose liability for enterprise obligations may be limited as stated in the enterprise formation documents.

### Société en Commandite
(S. en C.) (special partnership)
(**France, Lebanon, Morocco**)
*See* Société en Commandite Simple.

### Société en Commandite par Actions
(S.C. par A.) (special partnership by shares)
(**France, Morocco**)
An enterprise with ownership interests in the form of shares and formed for commercial purposes by two or more general and limited partners. General partners have unlimited and joint liability for enterprise obligations, while limited partners are liable only to the funds that the partner has agreed to invest in the enterprise.

### Société en Commandite Simple
(S. en C.S.) (special partnership)
(**France, Lebanon, Morocco**)
An enterprise with ownership interests determined by public deed or private written contract, and owned by one or more general partners and one or more special partners. General

partners have unlimited and joint liability for enterprise obligations, while special partners have liability only to the amount of the funds they have agreed to invest in the company.

### Société en Nom Collectif
(SNC) (general partnership)
**(Belgium, France, Lebanon, Morocco)**
An enterprise with ownership interests determined by public deed or private written contract, and owned by two or more partners who have unlimited and joint liability for all enterprise obligations.

### société en participation
(joint venture) **(France)**
An enterprise formed by written or verbal contract by natural or corporate persons who agree to act in concert for a particular purpose. Partners conduct business in their own names and are personally liable for enterprise obligations.

### Société par Actions Simplifiée
(S.A.S.) (simplified shares company) **(France)**
An enterprise with ownership interests in the form of shares and minimum capital of Euro 37,000, formed by companies for the purpose of conducting business jointly, and owned by two or more corporations (shareholders) that receive dividends and that have liability for enterprise obligations limited to the price of the shares.

### Société Privée a Reponsabilité Limitée
(S.P.R.L.) (private limited company) **(Belgium)**
An enterprise with ownership interests in the form of shares and minimum capitalization of BEF 750,000, and owned by two or more members with liability limited to the amount of the funds they agreed to invest in the enterprise.

### Spolecnost s Rucením Omezenym
(s.r.o. or spol. s r.o.) (limited liability company)
**(Czech Republic)**
An enterprise with ownership interests in the form of investments agreed by the members in advance, formed to undertake business activities, and owned by one or more natural or corporate persons, to a maximum of 50. Liability of members for enterprise obligations is limited to the investment amount stated in the founding documents for the enterprise.

### spólka akcyjna
(S.A.) (joint stock company) **(Poland)**
An enterprise with ownership interests in the form of shares and minimum capital of Zl 1 billion, owned by one or more natural or corporate persons (shareholders) who receive dividends and whose liability for enterprise obligations is limited to the price of the shares.

### spólka cywilna
(civil partnership) **(Poland)**
An enterprise with ownership interests determined by private written or verbal contract, formed for business purposes but not registered nationally, and owned by two or more partners who have unlimited and joint liability for all enterprise obligations.

### spólka jawna
(registered general partnership) **(Poland)**
An enterprise with ownership interests determined by written or verbal contract, formed for commercial purposes and registered nationally, and owned by two or more partners who have unlimited and joint liability for all enterprise obligations.

### spólka komandytowa
(limited partnership) **(Poland)**
An enterprise with ownership interests determined by contract, and owned by one or more general partners and one or more special partners. General partners have unlimited and joint liability for enterprise obligations, while special partners have liability only to the amount of funds they have agreed to invest in the enterprise.

### spólka z ograniczona odpowied zialnóscia
(Sp. z o.o.) (limited liability company) **(Poland)**
An enterprise with ownership interests in the form of shares that are transferred privately, having minimum capital of Zl 40 million, and owned by one or more natural or corporate persons (shareholders) whose liability for enterprise obligations is limited to the price of the shares.

### Stock Corporation
(Inc. or Corp.) **(Philippines)**
An enterprise with ownership interests in the form of shares, owned by one or more natural or corporate persons who receive dividends and whose liability for enterprise obligations is limited to the price of the shares.

### Subiratelno Druzestvo
(sudrudzie) (general partnership) **(Bulgaria)**
An enterprise with ownership interests determined by written contract and formed to conclude commercial transactions by two or more individuals who decide to act in concert and who have unlimited and joint liability for enterprise obligations.

### Teoranta
(Teo.) **(Ireland)**
*See* Public Company.

### Trading Company
**(Brazil)**
An enterprise with ownership interests in the form of stocks, formed to manufacture goods for export only, and owned by natural or corporate persons (stockholders) whose liability is limited to the purchase of the shares.

### Treuunternehmen
(business trust) **(Liechtenstein)**
An enterprise that has both corporate and trust attributes because a natural or corporate person (trustor) places property into the trust, and the trust property is then invested or otherwise utilized to conduct the business stated in the trust documents. The trust is administered by an trustee on behalf of the trust beneficiaries.

### türk limited sirket
(T.L.S.) (limited liability company) **(Turkey)**
An enterprise with ownership interests in the form of shares that are transferred privately only, having minimum capital of TL 10,000, and owned by two to 50 natural or corporate persons (shareholders) whose liability for enterprise obligations is limited to the price of the shares.

### Vennootschap Onder Firma
(general partnership) **(Belgium, Netherlands)**
An enterprise with ownership interests stated by contract, registered to conduct business, and formed for commercial purposes by two or more natural or corporate persons who have unlimited and joint liability for enterprise obligations.

### Verejná Obchodní Spolecnost
(v.o.s.) (general commercial partnership)
**(Czech Republic)**
An enterprise with ownership interests and profit-sharing determined by written contract, formed to undertake business activities, and owned by two or more partners who have unlimited and joint liability for enterprise obligations.

### Yugen Kaisha
(joint stock corporation) **(Japan)**
An enterprise with ownership interests in the form of shares that are publicly traded, owned by one or more natural or corporate persons who receive dividends and whose liability for enterprise obligations is limited to the price of the shares.

### Yuhan-Hosea
(limited companies) **(Korea, Republic of)**
An enterprise with ownership interests in the form of "shares" that are privately transferred, owned by one or more natural or corporate persons whose liability for enterprise obligations is limited to the price of the shares.

# Weights and Measures

## LINEAR MEASURE

### U.S. CUSTOMARY LINEAR MEASURES

Many of these measures are based on those developed in medieval England, when a yard was a measure of King Edward I's waist, a rod was an actual 10-foot pole and a furlong was the width of 32 plowed rows. The mile began with the Romans measuring it as 1,000 paces. The United States is one of the few countries which still uses many of them. Our yard is now officially 3600/3937 of a meter (exactly 0.9144 meter), while a survey foot is 1200/3937 of a meter (approximately 0.3048 meter).

| | | | | |
|---|---|---|---|---|
| 1000 mil | = 1 inch (in) | | | = 2.54 centimeters |
| 12 inches (in) | = 1 foot (ft) | | | = 30.48 centimeters |
| 3 feet | = 1 yard (yd) | | | = 0.9144 meter |
| 5-1/2 yards | = 1 rod (rd), pole, or perch | = 16-1/2 ft | | = 5.029 meters |
| 40 rods | = 1 furlong (fur) | = 220 yds | = 660 ft | = 0.201 kilometers |
| 8 furlongs | = 1 statute mile (mi) | = 1,760 yds | = 5,280 ft | = 1.609 kilometers |
| 3 statute miles | = 1 league* | = 5,280 yds | = 15,840 ft | = 4.82 kilometers |

\* A league is an imprecise measure that may range from approximately 2.4 to 4.6 statute miles, but in most English-speaking countries it refers to 3 statute miles.

### GUNTER'S OR SURVEYOR'S CHAIN MEASURES

These measures are based on a 17th century British surveyor's tool that was, in fact, a 66-foot long chain composed of 100 links. They fit in with the rod and furlong already in use.

| | | | | |
|---|---|---|---|---|
| 7.92 inches | = 1 link (li) | | | = 20.12 centimeters |
| 25 links | = 1 rod (rd) | = 16-1/2 feet | | = 5.029 meters |
| 100 links | = 1 chain (ch) | = 4 rods | = 66 ft | = 20.11 meters |
| 10 chains | = 1 furlong (fur) | = 660 ft | | = 0.201 kilometers |
| 80 chains | = 1 statute mile | = 320 rods | = 5,280 ft | = 1.609 kilometers |

### NAUTICAL MEASURES

A nautical mile is based on the circumference of the earth, but the precise definition of it has varied considerably through the centuries. Most recently, a nautical mile has meant a minute (1/60) of a degree. The current International Nautical Mile, defined in 1929 and adopted by the U.S. in 1954 is slightly shorter than the U.S. Nautical Mile, which is no longer used.

| | | | |
|---|---|---|---|
| 6 feet | = 1 fathom | | = 1.82 meters |
| 120 fathoms | = 1 cable | = 720 feet | = 219.45 meters |
| 8.44 cables | = 1 International Nautical Mile | | = 1.852 kilometers |
| 1.15 statute mi | = 1 Int'l Nautical Mile | = 6,076.11549 feet | = 1.852 kilometers |

### METRIC LINEAR MEASURES

A meter is the length of the path traveled by light in a vacuum during the time interval of 1/299,794,458 second. Originally, it was one 10-millionth of a line running from the equator, through Paris to the North Pole. The metric system is also called SI (Systèm Internationale).

| | | | |
|---|---|---|---|
| 10 millimeters | = 1 centimeter (cm) | | = 0.39 inch |
| 10 centimeters | = 1 decimeter (dm) | = 100 millimeters (mm) | = 3.94 inches |
| 10 decimeters | = 1 meter (m) | = 1000 millimeters (mm) | = 39.37 inches |
| 10 meters | = 1 dekameter (dam) | | = 32.81 feet |
| 10 dekameters | = 1 hectometer (hm) | = 100 meters | = 328.1 feet |
| 10 hectometers | = 1 kilometer (km) | = 1000 meters | = 0.62 mile |

# AREA MEASURE

Squares and cubes of units are sometimes abbreviated by using "superior" figures. For example, $ft^2$ means square foot, and $m^3$ means cubic meter.

### U.S. CUSTOMARY AREA MEASURES

| | | | |
|---|---|---|---|
| 144 square inches | = 1 square feet ($ft^2$) | | = 0.093 square meter |
| 9 square feet | = 1 square yard ($yd^2$) | = 1,296 sq in | = 0.836 square meter |
| 30-1/4 square yards | = 1 square rod ($rd^2$) | = 272-1/4 sq ft | = 25.29 square meters |
| 160 square rods | = 1 acre = 4,840 $yd^2$ | = 43,560 sq ft | = 0.405 hectare |
| 640 acres | = 1 square mile ($mi^2$) | | = 2.590 square kilometers |
| 1 square mile | = 1 section (of land) | | = 2.590 square kilometers |
| 6 square miles | = 1 township* = 36 sections | = 36 sq mi | = 93.24 square kilometers |

* 6 square miles is a somewhat imprecise measure of a township, but one which is used for many practical purposes. In actuality, a township is 6 miles on each of its east and west borders which follow the meridians, making the north or south border slightly less than 6 miles long due to the curve of the earth.

### METRIC AREA MEASURES

| | | | |
|---|---|---|---|
| 100 square millimeters ($mm^2$) | = 1 square centimeter ($cm^2$) | | = 0.155 square inch |
| 10,000 square centimeters | = 1 square meter ($m^2$) | = 1,000,000 $mm^2$ | = 1.19 square yards |
| 100 square meters | = 1 are (a) | | = 119.60 square yards |
| 100 ares | = 1 hectare (ha) | = 10,000 $m^2$ | = 2.471 acres |
| 100 hectares | = 1 square kilometer ($km^2$) | = 1,000,000 $m^2$ | = 0.3861 square miles |

# VOLUME (CAPACITY) MEASURE

The American method of measuring volume is based on an Ancient Egyptian measure, a 12th century British measure and a custom of doubling each measure to find the next. Some measures dropped along the way, so this is no longer apparent. There are two official sets of volume measures in the U.S., wet and dry.

### U.S. CUSTOMARY LIQUID MEASURES

The gallon is now officially defined in terms of cubic inches, which, in turn, are defined in terms of the meter. When necessary to distinguish the liquid pint or quart from the dry pint or quart, the word "liquid" or the abbreviation "liq" should be used in combination with the name or abbreviation of the liquid unit.

| | | | |
|---|---|---|---|
| 8 fluid drams | = 1 fluid ounce | | = 29.57 milliliters |
| 4 fluid ounces (oz) | = 1 gill | | = 0.118 liter |
| 4 gills (gi) | = 1 pint (pt) | = 28.875 $in^3$ | = 0.473 liter |
| 2 pints | = 1 quart (qt) | = 57.75 $in^3$ | = 0.946 liter |
| 4 quarts | = 1 gallon (gal) | = 231 $in^3$ = 8 pts = 32 gills | = 3.785 liters |

### U.S. CUSTOMARY DRY MEASURES

The bushel is now officially defined in terms of cubic inches, which, in turn, are defined in terms of the meter. When necessary to distinguish the dry pint or quart from the liquid pint or quart; the word "dry" should be used in combination with the name or abbreviation of the dry unit.

| | | | |
|---|---|---|---|
| 2 dry pints (pt) | = 1 dry quart (qt) | = 67.2006 $in^3$ | = 1.101 liters |
| 8 dry quarts | = 1 peck (pk) | = 537.605 $in^3$ = 16 pt | = 8.81 liters |
| 4 pecks | = 1 bushel (bu)* | = 2,150.42 $in^3$ = 32 dry qt | = 35.239 liters |

* This is also called a bushel, struck measure. One bushel, heaped measure is frequently recognized as $1^1/_4$ bushels, struck measure. More precisely, one bushel, heaped is equal to 1.278 bushels, struck.

### APOTHECARIES' FLUID MEASURES

These units were once widely used in the U.S. for pharmaceutical purposes, but have largely been replaced by metric units. These measures are actually the same as those for U.S. customary wet measure (above), with some additional subdivisions.

| | | | |
|---|---|---|---|
| 60 minims (min) | = 1 fluid dram (fl dr) | = 0.2256 $in^3$ | = 3.888 grams |
| 8 fluid drams | = 1 fluid ounce (fl oz) | = 1.8047 $in^3$ | = 31.103 grams |
| 16 fluid ounces | = 1 pint (pt) | = 28.875 $in^3$ = 128 fl drs | = 0.473 liter |
| 2 pints | = 1 quart (qt) | = 57.75 $in^3$= 32 fl oz = 256 fl drs | = 0.946 liter |
| 4 quarts | = 1 gallon (gal) | = 231 $in^3$ = 128 fl oz = 1,024 fl drs | = 3.785 liters |

W&M

## *U.S. COOKING MEASURES*

| | | | |
|---|---|---|---|
| 76 drops | = 1 teaspoon | = 1-1/3 fl drams | = 4.9288 milliliters |
| 3 teaspoons | = 1 tablespoon | = 4 fl drams | = 14.786 milliliters |
| 16 tablespoons | = 1 cup | = 8 fl ounces | = 0.2366 liter |
| 2 cups | = 1 pint | = 16 fl ounces | = 0.4732 liter |
| 2 pints | = 1 quart | = 32 fl ounces | = 0.9463 liter |

## *BRITISH IMPERIAL LIQUID AND DRY MEASURES*

The British changed their definitions of capacity measures slightly in the 19th century, so that British Imperial measures having the same names as U.S. measures are slightly larger than their U.S. counterparts.

| British imperial | | cubic inches | U.S. equiv. | Metric |
|---|---|---|---|---|
| 60 minims | = 1 fluidram (fl dr) | = $0.216734$ in$^3$ | = 0.961 fl dr | = 3.552 milliliters |
| 8 fluidrams | = 1 fluidounce (fl oz) | = $1.7339$ in$^3$ | = 0.961 fl oz | = 28.412 milliliters |
| 5 fluidounces | = 1 gill | = $8.669$ in$^3$ | = 4.805 fl oz | = 142.066 milliliters |
| 4 gills | = 1 pint | = $34.678$ in$^3$ | = 1.201 fl pt | = 0.5683 liters |
| 2 pints | = 1 quart | = $69.355$ in$^3$ | = 1.201 fl qt, 1.032 dry qt | = 1.136 liters |
| 4 quarts | = 1 gallon | = $277.420$ in$^3$ | = 1.201 fl gal | = 4.546 liters |
| 2 gallons | = 1 peck | = $554.84$ in$^3$ | = 1.0314 pecks | = 9.087 liters |
| 4 pecks | = 1 bushel | = $2219.36$ in$^3$ | = 1.032 bushels | = 36.369 liters |

## *METRIC MEASURES OF CAPACITY*

The liter was derived from the kilogram, originally the volume occupied by a kilogram of water. It is now officially defined as a cubic decimeter of pure water, which is nearly the same. This one set of measures is used for all capacity measures.

| | | | | | |
|---|---|---|---|---|---|
| 10 milliliters (ml) | = 1 centiliter (cl) | = | 10 liters | = 1 dekaliter (dal) | = |
| 0.338 fluid ounce | | | 2.6417 gallons | | |
| 10 centiliters | = 1 deciliter (dl) | = | 10 dekaliters | = 1 hectoliter (hl) | = |
| 100 milliliters | = 0.21 pint | | 100 liters | = 26.417 gallons | |
| 10 deciliters | = 1 liter (l) | = | 10 hectoliters | = 1 kiloliter (kl) | = |
| 1000 milliliters | = 1.057 quarts | | 1,000 liters | = 264.17 gallons | |

# CUBIC MEASURE

## *U.S. CUSTOMARY CUBIC MEASURES*

| | | |
|---|---|---|
| 1,728 cubic inches (in$^3$) | = 1 cubic foot (ft$^3$) | = 0.028 cubic meter |
| 27 cubic feet | = 1 cubic yard (yd$^3$) | = 0.765 cubic meter |

## *METRIC*

| | | |
|---|---|---|
| 1,000 cubic millimeters (mm$^3$) | = 1 cubic centimeter | inches |
| (cm$^3$) | = 0.061 cubic inch | 1,000 cubic decimeters | = 1 cubic meter (m$^3$) |
| 1,000 cubic centimeters | = 1 cubic decimeter | = 1 stere | = 1.307 cubic yards |
| (dm$^3$) | = 61.023 cubic | | |

# WEIGHT (MASS)

When necessary to distinguish avoirdupois units from troy or apothecaries' units, the word "avoirdupois" or the abbreviation "avdp" should be used in combination with the name or abbreviation of the unit.

### AVOIRDUPOIS WEIGHT

This is the weight system in everyday use in the U.S. Historically, it is a rearrangement of the troy system. The word avoirdupois is French, meaning goods of weight. The avoirdupois pound is now officially defined as 0.45359237 kilogram.

| | | | |
|---|---|---|---|
| 27-11/32 grains | = 1 dram (dr) | | = 1.1772 grams |
| 16 drams | = 1 ounce (oz) | = 437-1/2 grains | = 28.35 grams |
| 16 ounces | = 1 pound (lb) = 256 drams | = 7,000 grains | = 0.454 kilogram |
| 100 pounds | = 1 hundredweight (cwt)* | | = 45.359 kilograms |
| 112 pounds | = 1 gross or long hundredweight* | | = 50.802 kilograms |
| 20 hundredweights | = 1 short ton (tn) | = 2,000 lbs* | = 0.907 metric ton |
| 20 gross or long hundredweights | = 1 gross or long ton | = 2,240 lbs* | = 1.016 metric tons |

*When the terms "hundredweight" and "ton" are used unmodified, they are commonly understood to mean the 100-pound hundredweight and the 2,000-pound (short) ton, respectively; these units may be designated "net" or "short" when necessary to distinguish them from the corresponding units in gross or long measure.

### TROY WEIGHT

The troy system began in Ancient Egypt and was modified over the years by Europeans. The British used the troy as the official weight system for currency, while the U.S. mint adopted it in America. These units are still used for over-the-counter sales of precious metals, although they have largely fallen into disuse, in favor of the metric system.

| | | | | | |
|---|---|---|---|---|---|
| 24 grains (gr) | = 1 pennyweight (dwt) | | | | = 1.555 grams |
| 20 pennyweights | = 1 ounce troy (oz t) | | | = 480 grains | = 31.103 grams |
| 12 ounces troy | = 1 pound troy (lb t) | = 240 dwt | = 5,760 gr | | = 0.373 kilogram |

### APOTHECARIES' WEIGHT

While one pound apothecaries' is equivalent to 1 pound troy, the apothecaries' system differs in its subdivisions. These units were once widely used in the United States for pharmaceutical purposes, but have largely been replaced by metric units, although they are still legal standards.

| | | | |
|---|---|---|---|
| 20 grains (gr) | = 1 scruple (s ap) | | = 1.296 grams |
| 3 scruples | = 1 dram apothecaries' (dr ap) | = 60 gr | = 3.888 grams |
| 8 drams apothecaries | = 1 ounce apothecaries' (oz ap) | = 24 s ap = 480 gr | = 31.103 grams |
| 12 ounces apothecaries | = 1 pound apothecaries' (lb ap) | = 96 dr ap | = 373.24 grams |
| | | | = 288 s ap |
| | | | = 5,760 grains |

### METRIC WEIGHT (MASS)

A kilogram was originally defined as the mass of one cubic decimeter of water at the temperature of maximum density, but is now a cylinder of platinum-iridium alloy of the same size.

| | | | |
|---|---|---|---|
| 10 milligrams (mg) | = 1 centigram (cg) | = 0.154 grain | |
| 10 centigrams | = 1 decigram (dg) | = 100 milligrams | = 1.543 grains |
| 10 decigrams | = 1 gram (g) | = 1,000 milligrams | = 0.035 ounce |
| 10 grams | = 1 dekagram (dag) | | = 0.353 ounce |
| 10 dekagrams | = 1 hectogram (hg) | = 100 grams | = 3.527 ounces |
| 10 hectograms | = 1 kilogram (kg) | = 1,000 grams | = 2.2046 pounds |
| 1,000 kilograms | = 1 metric ton (t) | | = 1.102 short tons |

# TEMPERATURE

| | Absolute Zero | Water Freezes/Melts | Water Boils | Average Body Temperature |
|---|---|---|---|---|
| Celsius (°C)* | -273.15°C | 0°C | 100°C | 36.8°C |
| Fahrenheit (°F)* | -459.67°F | 32°F | 212°F | 98.24°F |
| Kelvin (°K)* | 0°K | 273.15°K | 373.15°K | 309.95°K |

*All calculations at 1 atmosphere

# ConversionTable

### *Distance*

| To Convert | To | Multiply by | Conversion |
|---|---|---|---|
| millimeters (mm) | inches (in) | 0.03937 | 1mm = 0.03937in |
| centimeters (cm) | inches (in) | 0.3937 | 1cm = 10mm = 0.3937in |
| meters (m) | yards (yd) | 1.0936 | 1m = 100 cm = 1.0936yd |
| kilometers (km) | miles (mi) | 0.6214 | 1km = 1000m = 0.6214mi |
| inches (in) | millimeters (mm) | 25.4 | 1in = 25.4mm |
| inches (in) | centimeters (cm) | 2.54 | 1in = 2.54cm |
| feet (ft) | meters (m) | 0.3048 | 1ft = 12in = 0.3048m |
| yards (yd) | meters (m) | 0.9144 | 1yd = 3ft = 36in = 0.9144m |
| miles (mi) | kilometers (km) | 1.6093 | 1mi = 1760yd = 1.6093km |
| nautical miles (nm) | kilometers (km) | 1.853 | 1nm = 2025.4 yd = 1.853km |

### *Area*

| To Convert | To | Multiply by | Conversion |
|---|---|---|---|
| square centimeters ($cm^2$) | square inches ($in^2$) | 0.1550 | $1cm^2 = 0.155in^2$ |
| square meters ($m^2$) | square yards ($yd^2$) | 1.1960 | $1m^2 = 1.1960yd^2$ |
| hectare (ha) | acre | 2.4711 | 1ha = 2.4711acres |
| square kilometers ($km^2$) | square miles ($mi^2$) | 0.3861 | $1km^2 = 0.3861mi^2$ |
| square inches ($in^2$) | square centimeters ($cm^2$) | 6.4516 | $1in^2 = 6.4516cm^2$ |
| square feet ($ft^2$) | square meters ($m^2$) | 0.0929 | $1ft^2 = 0.0929m^2$ |
| square yards ($yd^2$) | square meters ($m^2$) | 0.8361 | $1yd^2 = 0.8361m^2$ |
| acre | hectare | 0.4047 | 1 acre = .4047ha |
| square mile ($mi^2$) | square kilometers ($km^2$) | 2.59 | $1mi^2 = 2.59km^2$ |

### *Volume/Capacity*

| To Convert | To | Multiply by | Conversion |
|---|---|---|---|
| cubic centimeters ($cm^3$) | cubic inches ($in^3$) | 0.0610 | $1cm^3 = 0.0610 in^3$ |
| cubic decimeters ($dm^3$) | cubic feet ($ft^3$) | 0.0353 | $1dm^3 = 1000cm^3 = = 0.0353 ft^3$ |
| cubic meters($m^3$) | cubic yards ($yd^3$) | 1.3080 | $1m^3 = 1000dm^3 = 1.3080 yd^3$ |
| liters (l) | pints (pt) | 1.76 | $1l = 1dm^3 = 1.76 pt$ |
| hectoliters (hl) | gallon (gal) | 21.997 | 1hl = 100l = 21.997 gal |
| cubic inches ($in^3$) | cubic centimeters ($cm^3$) | 16.387 | $1in^3 = 16.387 cm^3$ |
| cubic feet ($ft^3$) | cubic meters ($m^3$) | 0.0283 | $1ft^3 = 1728in^3 = 0.0283m^3$ |
| UK fluid ounces (fl oz) | millileters (ml) | 28.413 | 1 UK fl oz = 28.413ml |
| UK pints (pt) | liters (l) | 0.5683 | 1 UK pt = 20 fl oz = 0.5683 l |
| UK gallons (gal) | liters (l) | 4.54611 | 1 UK gal = 8 pt = 4.54611 l |
| USA fluid ounces (fl oz) | millileters (ml) | 29.574 | 1 USA fl oz = 1.0408 UK fl oz = 29.574 ml |
| USA pints (pt) | liters (l) | 0.47311 | 1 USA pt = 0.8327 UK pt = 0.47311 l |
| USA gallons (gal) | liters (l) | 3.78541 | 1 USA gal = 0.8327 UK gal = 3.78541 l |

### *Mass/Weight*

| To Convert | To | Multiply by | Conversion |
|---|---|---|---|
| milligrams (mg) | grains | 0.0154 | 1mg = 0.0154 grains |
| grams (g) | ounces (oz) | 0.0353 | 1g = 1000mg = 0.0353 oz |
| kilograms (kg) | pounds (lb) | 2.2046 | 1kg = 1000g = 2.2046 lbs |
| tonnes (t) | tons | 0.9842 | 1t = 1000 kg = 0.9842 tons |
| ounces (oz) | grams (g) | 28.35 | 1oz = 437.5 grain = 28.35 g |
| pounds (lb) | kilograms (kg) | 0.4536 | 1lb = 16 oz = 0.4536kg |
| stones | kilograms (kg) | 6.3503 | 1 stone = 14 lb = 6.3503kg |
| hundredweight (cwt) | kilogram (kg) | 50.802 | 1cwt = 112 lb = 50.802kg |
| long tons (UK) | tonne (t) | 1.016 | 1 long ton (UK) = 20 cwt = 1.016t |

# Glossary of Other Weights and Measures

**W & M**

### amphora
A traditional unit of volume measurement equal to the volume of an urn or jar of the same name. Amphorae were widely used as shipping containers for wine, olive oil and other liquids in the ancient Mediterranean. Amphora is the combination of two Greek words "on both sides" (referring to handles on both sides at the top) and "carry." The Greek amphora held about 39 liters (10 U.S. gallons) while the Roman amphorae held about 25 liters (about 6.7 U.S. gallons).

### apothecary weights
A variation of the traditional English troy weight system formerly used by apothecaries (pharmacists). Apothecary weights use the troy pound (of 5760 grains) which is divided into 12 ounces (of 480 grains each). Apothecary weights, however, divide the ounce into 8 drams (of 60 grains each), and each dram into 3 scruples (of 20 grains each). The apothecary weight system has been replaced by metric units.

### ASA number
Acronym for American Standards Association number. A unit of measurement of the exposure speed of photographic film emulsion. ASA 200 film is therefore exposed at twice the speed of ASA 100 film. The ASA film exposure rating system has been largely combined with the DIN (Deutsches Institut für Normung) rating system in a new ISO (International Standards Organization) composite rating (e.g., ISO 200/24°).

### avoirdupois weights
A system of weight measurement based on a pound (of 7,000 grains) divided into 16 ounces and used in most all English-speaking countries of the world. Also called the Imperial System of Weights and Measurement. Avoirdupois is French for "goods having weight" meaning that the goods were offered for sale based on weight rather than by the piece or by volume.

### baht
(a) The currency of Thailand. (b) A traditional Thai unit of weight measurement for precious metals now equal to 15 grams. (c) "Baht chain" is gold necklace chain that is almost pure (22-24 karat) gold sold in Thailand in units of 15 grams. A three-baht chain weighs 45 grams.

### bale (bl)
An imprecise measure of a large bundle of goods, especially cotton or hay. The weight varies from country to country and by commodity. In the U.S., a bale of cotton weighs between 480 and 500 pounds, while in Egypt a bale of cotton weighs 720 to 750 pounds.

### barrel (bbl/brl/bl/bo)
A unit of liquid or dry volume measurement which varies by commodity, and sometimes by country. A barrel is generally between 31 and 42 gallons. One barrel of fermented liquors is 31 gallons, one barrel of other liquids is typically 31.5 gallons, a barrel of beer is 36 gallons, one barrel of "proof spirits" is 40 gallons by U.S. federal law, and one barrel of crude oil (abbreviation is 'bo') for statistical purposes is 42 gallons (159 liters). Two common barrel measurements for dry commodities are:
1 barrel, standard for fruits, vegetables, and other dry commodities (except cranberries) = 105 dry quarts = 7,056 in$^3$ = 3.281 bushels, struck measure.
1 barrel, standard, cranberries = 86-45/64 dry quarts = 5,826 in$^3$ = 2.709 bushels, struck measure.

### Beaufort scale
(historic) A system of measurement of the force of the wind at sea designated by numbers from 0 to 12. The system was originally developed by Sir Francis Beaufort (1774-1857), a Royal Navy Commander (later admiral) in 1805-1806 while in command of the *Woolwich*, a 44-gun man-of-war. The original scale was called *Wind Force Scale and Weather Notation Coding* and was a measure of the force of wind rather than wind speed, and described the state and behavior of a "well-conditioned man-of-war" at each level (0 to 12) of force. Therefore, the Beaufort Scale measured the effect of wind on a man-of-war, rather than the wind itself. Beaufort numbers 0 through 4 described a ship's speed with all sails set and clean full, and in smooth water. Numbers 5 through 9 concerned the ship's mission, the chase, and its sail-carrying ability. Numbers 10 through 12 concerned the ship's survival. **The original Beaufort Scale:**

| WIND FORCE SCALE AND WEATHER NOTATION CODING | | |
|---|---|---|
| **Figures to Denote the Force of the Wind** | | |
| 0 | Calm | |
| 1 | Light Air | Or just sufficient to give steerage way. |
| 2 | Light Breeze | Or that in which a man-of-war with all sail set, and clean full would go in smooth water from. |
| 3 | Gentle Breeze | 3 to 4 knots |
| 4 | Moderate Breeze | 5 to 6 knots |
| 5 | Fresh Breeze | Royals, &c. |
| 6 | Strong Breeze | Or that in which a man-of-war could just carry in chase, full and by. |
| 7 | Moderate Gale | Double reefed topsails, jib, &c. |
| 8 | Fresh Gale | Treble-reefed topsails &c. |
| 9 | Strong Gale | Close-reefed topsails and courses. |
| 10 | Whole Gale | Or that with which she could scarcely bear close-reefed main-topsail and reefed fore-sail. |
| 11 | Storm | Or that which would reduce her to storm staysails. |
| 12 | Hurricane | Or that which no canvas could withstand. |

Over the course of time the original Beaufort system became associated with wind speed rather than force and effect on a sailing ship. The problem was that observers who had never been on an 1805 man-of-war, or for that matter, had never even seen the ocean, were attempting to estimate wind speed based on the system.

In 1912 the International Commission for Weather Telegraphy sought some agreement on velocity equivalents for the Beaufort scale. A uniform set of equivalents was accepted in 1926 and slightly revised in 1946. By 1955, wind velocities in knots replaced Beaufort numbers on weather maps. The Beaufort Scale is now used in both sea and land applications.

(modern) A system of measurement of wind speed, wave height, wind effects on sea and wind effects on land designated by numbers from 0 to 12.

W
&
M

| THE BEAUFORT WIND SPEED SCALE for USE AT SEA | | | | |
|---|---|---|---|---|
| Beaufort Number (Force) | Wind Speed (knots) | WMO[1] Description | Wave Height (feet) | Wind Effects Observed on Sea |
| 0 | < 1 | Calm | 0 | Calm, like a mirror |
| 1 | 1 – 3 | Light air | .25 | Ripples with appearance of scale, no foam crests |
| 2 | 4 – 6 | Light breeze | .5 – 1 | Small wavelets; crests of glassy appearance, not breaking |
| 3 | 7 – 10 | Gentle breeze | 2 – 3 | Large wavelets, crests begin to break; scattered whitecaps |
| 4 | 11 – 16 | Moderate breeze | 3.5 – 5 | Small waves, becoming longer numerous whitecaps |
| 5 | 17 – 21 | Fresh Breeze | 6 – 8 | Moderate waves, taking longer form, many whitecaps; some spray |
| 6 | 22 – 27 | Strong breeze | 9.25 – 13 | Larger waves forming; whitecaps everywhere; more spray |
| 7 | 28 – 33 | Near gale | 13.5 – 19 | Sea heaps up; white foam from breaking waves begins to be blown in streaks |
| 8 | 34 – 40 | Gale | 18 – 28 | Moderately high waves of greater length; edges of crests begin to break into spindrift; foam is blown in well-marked streaks |
| 9 | 41 – 47 | Strong gale | 23 – 32 | High waves; sea begins to roll; dense streaks of foam; spray may reduce visibility |
| 10 | 48 – 55 | Storm | 29 – 41 | Very high waves with overhanging crests; sea takes white appearance as foam is blown in very dense streaks; rolling is heavy and visibility is reduced |
| 11 | 56 – 63 | Violent storm | 39 – 46 | Exceptionally high waves; sea covered with white foam patches; visibility still more reduced |
| 12 | > 64 | Hurricane | 37 – 52 | Air filled with foam; sea completely white with driving spray; visibility greatly reduced |
| [1]World Meterogical Organization | | | | |

| THE BEAUFORT WIND SPEED SCALE for USE ON LAND U.S. National Weather Service (NWS) | | | |
|---|---|---|---|
| Beaufort Number (Force) | Terms Used in NWS Forecasts | Wind Speed (mph) | Wind Effects Observed on Land |
| 0 | Calm | < 1 | Calm, smoke rises vertically |
| 1 | Light air | 1 – 3 | Direction of wind shown by smoke, but not by wind vanes |
| 2 | Light breeze | 4 – 7 | Wind felt on face; leaves rustle; ordinary vane moved by wind |
| 3 | Gentle breeze | 8 – 12 | Leaves and small twigs in constant motion; wind extends light flag |
| 4 | Moderate breeze | 13 – 18 | Raises dust and loose paper; small branches are moved |
| 5 | Fresh Breeze | 19 – 24 | Small trees in leaf begin to sway; crested wavelets form on inland waters |
| 6 | Strong breeze | 25 – 31 | Large branches in motion; telegraph wires whistle; umbrellas used with difficulty |
| 7 | Moderate gale (or near gale) | 32 – 38 | Whole trees in motion; inconvenience in walking against wind |
| 8 | Fresh gale (or gale) | 39 – 46 | Breaks twigs off trees; generally impedes progress |
| 9 | Strong gale | 47 – 54 | Slight structural damage occurs; chimney pots and slates removed |
| 10 | Whole storm (or storm) | 55 – 63 | Trees uprooted; considerable structural damage occurs |
| 11 | Storm (or violent storm) | 64 – 72 | Very rarely experienced; accompanied by widespread damage |
| 12 | Hurricane | 73 – 136 | Devastation occurs |

### bell

A traditional unit of time measurement used on sailing ships and equal to one-half hour. A "watch" is the standard period of time a sailor is on duty and is divided into 8 bells or 4 hours. During a watch each half hour is marked by a sounding of the bell. *See* Watch.

| SHIP'S BELLS | | | |
|---|---|---|---|
| Bells | Hour (AM or PM) | | |
| 1 | 12:30 | 4:30 | 8:30 |
| 2 | 1:00 | 5:00 | 9:00 |
| 3 | 1:30 | 5:30 | 9:30 |
| 4 | 2:00 | 6:00 | 10:00 |
| 5 | 2:30 | 6:30 | 10:30 |
| 6 | 3:00 | 7:00 | 11:00 |
| 7 | 3:30 | 7:30 | 11:30 |
| 8 | 4:00 | 8:00 | 12:00 |

| SOUNDING OF SHIP'S BELLS Example: Middle Watch | |
|---|---|
| Hour | Bells |
| 00:30 | 1 bell |
| 01:00 | 2 bells |
| 01:30 | 2 bells, pause, 1 bell |
| 02:00 | 2 bells, pause, 2 bells |
| 02:30 | 2 bells, pause, 2 bells, pause, 1 bell |
| 03:00 | 2 bells, pause, 2 bells, pause, 2 bells |
| 03:30 | 2 bells, pause, 2 bells, pause, 2 bells, pause, 1 bell |
| 04:00 | 2 bells, pause, 2 bells, pause, 2 bells, pause 2 bells |

### carat (ct or c)

(a) A unit of weight or mass measurement of precious stones equal to 200 milligrams (approximately 3.086 grains). A carat is divided into 100 points. Therefore, a 10 point diamond is 1/10th of a carat. In ancient India and the Middle East, the carob sead or bean was used to weigh precious stones because of its consistent weight. The word carat is believed to be derived from carob. (b) U.K. spelling for the U.S. karat, a measure of the purity of gold in an alloy. *See also* karat.

### catty

A traditional unit of weight measurement in East and Southeast Asia equal to 4/3 pounds avoirdupois. In Malaysia the catty is still equal to 4/3 pounds. In Thailand the catty is now equal to precisely 600 grams (0.6 kilo).

### celsius (°C)

A temperature scale where water freezes at 0°C and boils at 100°C.

### cubit

An ancient unit of linear measurement based on the length of the forearm, from the elbow to the tip of the middle finger. One cubit is not a precise length, although it is usually figured between 17 and 21 inches, and most often at 18 inches.

### dan or tan

(a) A traditional Chinese unit of weight or mass measurement equal to 100 cattys or 1,600 taels. (b) A modern Chinese unit of weight or mass measurement equal to 50 kilograms or 100 jin.

### degree (symbol °)

(a) (maps and navigation) A unit of measurement for arcs and angles. A circle is divided into 360°. A degree is divided into 60 minutes (symbol '), and a minute is further divided into 60 seconds (symbol "). Degrees are used in measurement of positions of latitude and longitude on the earth (or for positions above the Earth's horizon). For example, Beijing, China is located at 39°55'North, 116°25'East.
(b) (temperature) A unit of measurement of temperature using one of numerous temperature scales.

### displacement ton

A unit used for measuring the weight of water displaced by a ship, in place of weighing the ship itself. One displacement ton is equal to a long ton, or 2,240 pounds. It is calculated by finding the number of cubic feet of water displaced and calculating the weight of the water. Loaded displacement tonnage refers to the displacement tonnage of a ship when it is carrying its usual cargo, fuel and crew load. Light displacement tonnage is the displacement tonnage of an unloaded ship, while the dead weight tonnage is the weight that the ship can carry, or the difference between the loaded displacement and the light displacement tonnage. Different types of ships are more commonly described according to one type of displacement tonnage or another.

### deadweight ton (dwt)

A term used to express the total carrying capacity of a vessel expressed in long tons of 2,240 pounds. Specifically, the deadweight tonnage of a vessel is its loaded displacement minus its light displacement. This is the vessel's capacity for cargo, fuel, supplies, passengers and crew. In modern usage the metric ton of 2,204.623 pounds is often used instead of the long ton.

### DIN number

Acronym for Deutsches Institut für Normung (a German standards agency) number. A unit of measure of the exposure speed of photographic film emulsion. DIN 24° (with a degree symbol) is equal to ASA 200. A difference of 3 in the DIN system doubles (or halves) the film speed rating. Therefore DIN 27 is equal to ASA 400. The DIN film exposure rating system has been largely combined with the ASA (American Standards Association) rating system in a new ISO (International Standards Organization) composite rating (e.g., ISO 200/24°).

### fahrenheit (°F)

A temperature scale where water freezes at 32°F and boils at 212°F.

### fathom (fth or fath)

A unit of linear measurement equal to 6 feet or two yards. The term comes from *fœthm,* Old English for outstretched arms, meaning the distance between a man's outstretched arms. The fathom is used almost exclusively in shipping as a measurement of the depth of water. Many other cultures have used this form of measurement unit (with slightly different values). They include *braza* (Spanish), *toise* (French), *klafter* (German), *favn* (Dutch), *famn* (Swedish) and *ken* (Japanese).

### FEU

Acronym for 40-foot equivalent unit. A unit of cargo capacity equal to one (1) forty-foot ocean cargo container (40' x 8' x approximately 8.5'). The term is used to quantify the carrying capacity of a container ship or the throughput volume of a port facility.

### freight ton (FT)

(a) (modern usage) A unit of weight or mass measurement equal to one metric ton (1,000 kilograms) of freight of any volume. (b) (outdated usage) A unit of volume equal to 40 cubic feet, used to measure the cargo or cargo capacity of a ship, truck, railcar or airplane. Also called a measurement ton.

W & M

### glass

A traditional unit of time measurement based on the use of an hourglass or sandglass. A "glass" was equal to the time it took sand to pass from the top to the bottom of the specially-designed glass vessel. The amount of time measured could be controlled by varying the width of the passageway from the top to the bottom, or by adding or subtracting sand. The most traditional instrument was the hourglass and was calibrated to measure one (1) hour. At sea, half-hourglasses were often used to correspond to the ship's bell time measurement in units of one-half hour.

### GMT

Acronym for Greenwich Mean Time. GMT is the designation for the standard time at longitude 0° which runs north and south and passes through the Royal Observatory at Greenwich England. Longitude 0° is also called the Prime Meridian. The usage of the term Universal Time or UT instead of GMT has come into vogue recently.

### gongli

A modern Chinese unit of linear measurement equal to two li, or 1 kilometer and often referred to as the metric li.

### grain

(a) A unit of weight or mass measurement equal to 1/60 dram or 1/7000 pound (64.799 milligrams). (b) A unit of weight or mass measurement used for weighing pearls and precious stones equal to 1/4 carat (50mg). (c) Historically, the weight of a single grain of wheat taken from the middle of the ear.

### great gross

A unit of quantity for counting commercial items typically sold at wholesale equal to a dozen gross (12 x 144) or 1,728.

### gross

A unit of quantity for counting commercial items typically sold at wholesale equal to 144.

### hank

(a) A coil of rope, wool or yarn. (b) A length of textile material whose length varies depending upon the material. A hank of wool is 560 yards, of cotton or silk 840 yards, linen 300 yards, tapestry wool 55 meters and crewel wool approximately 180 meters. (c) A number of stands of pearls, beads or other strung gem or jewelry material that have been tied together at the end to form a unit to be sold wholesale.

### horsepower (hp)

A unit of measure for the power of engines. One horsepower is equal to 746 watts or to 2,546.0756 Btu per hour. It was derived from the power needed by a horse to lift 33,000 pounds a distance of 1 foot in 1 minute or to lift 550 pounds 1 foot in 1 second.

### imperial gallon (IG)

A unit of volume measurement based on the British Imperial System equal to 1.201 U.S. liquid gallons or 4.546 liters.

### imperial units

Unit designations for the British Imperial System of weights and measures as adopted by the British Parliament in 1828. The major units of the British Imperial System are the foot of 12 inches, the pound avoirdupois of 16 ounces and the imperial pint.

### international nautical mile

A unit of distance measurement used in nautical and aeronautical navigation equal to the average distance on the earth's surface of one (1) minute of latitude. Because the Earth is not a perfect sphere this definition left the precise measurement of a nautical mile open to interpretation. As a result there were several competing definitions, including: the Admiralty Mile of 6,080 feet (1,853.18 meters), and the U.S. Nautical Mile of 6080.20 feet (1853.24 meters) (the latter was in use until 1954). However, an international conference held in Monaco in 1929 defined the nautical mile at exactly 1852 meters (6,076.11 feet or 1.1508 statute miles). This is now called the international nautical mile and is the accepted definition.

### international unit (IU) (system)

An internationally accepted system for the measurement of drugs and vitamins based upon their level of biological effect (potency) rather than their weight or volume. By agreement, for each substance to which the IU system applies, there is an established biological effect associated with a dose of 1IU of that drug or vitamin. For example, 1IU of Vitamin C is 50 micrograms (0.05mg), while 1IU of a preparation of penicillin is 0.6 microgram.

### ISO

Acronym for International Organization for Standardization. The ISO, established in 1947, is a worldwide federation of national bodies, representing approximately 90 member countries that set international standards for everything from the quality grading of steel; for testing the strength of woven textiles; for storage of citrus fruits; for magnetic codes on credit cards; for the exposure speed of photographic film; and for ensuring the quality and performance of such products as surgical implants, ski bindings, wire ropes, and photographic lenses.
International Standardization Organization, 1 rue de Varembé, PO Box 56, CH-1211 Geneva 20, Switzerland; Tel: [41] (22) 749-0111; Fax: [41] (22) 733-3430; Web: www.iso.ch. In the United States contact: International Organization for Standards, The American National Standards Institute, 25 West 43rd Street, 4th Floor, New York, NY 10036 USA; Tel: [1] (212) 642-4900; Fax: [1] (212) 398-0023; Web: www.ansi.org.

### jin (sometimes chin or gin)

(historic) A traditional Chinese unit of weight or mass measurement originally equal to 4/3 pounds. The jin was divided into 16 liang.
(contemporary) A Chinese unit of weight or mass measurement equal to 500 grams or 0.5 kilograms and divided into 10 liang.

### jo

A traditional Japanese unit of area measurement equal to a tatami mat which is 90cm x 180cm (35.46 inches x 70.92 inches). In area a jo is equal to 1.62 m3 or 1.94 square yards. The jo is used to describe the area of an apartment or house.

### karat (k)

A measure of the purity of gold in an alloy. Each karat represents a ratio of 1/24 purity, indicating how many parts out of 24 are pure. Therefore, 24 karat gold is pure, while 18 karat gold is 3/4 gold and 1/4 alloy. The system was derived from a time when a karat was used to describe 1/24 of a troy pound and 24 karat was one full troy pound. In the U.S. the abbreviation for karat is k. In the U.K. the word is spelled carat just as in carat weight of precious stones and the abbreviation for both is c.

### kelvin (°K)

A temperature scale where absolute zero is 0°K, water freezes at 273.15°K and boils at 309.95°K.

### ken

A traditional Japanese unit of length measurement equal to 1.818 meters (5.965 feet) and comparable to the English fathom. One (1) ken equals 6 shaku. The Japanese nautical equivalent of the *ken* is the *hiro*.

### knot (kn or kt)

A unit of speed (velocity) equal to one nautical mile per hour (1.852 kilometers/hour or 1.1508 miles/hour). The term is used primarily for vessels at sea and airplanes in flight. The usage "knots per hour" is incorrect. Also, a knot is not a nautical mile (distance), but rather a measure of speed. The term knots is derived from the traditional practice of measuring a ship's speed at sea using a cord with evenly-spaced knots called a log line.

### koku
A traditional Japanese unit of volume measurement equal to 180.391 liters (39.68 British imperial gallons or 6.37 cubic feet). The *koku* was originally a measure of the amount of rice required to feed an adult person for a year.

### kommerzlast
German for "commercial load." The traditional value of the term varied depending upon the commodity. In modern usage the term is defined as 3 metric tons (tonnes) or 3,000 kilograms total.

### last
(a) Traditional German term meaning "load" as in a cart or truckload of a commodity. (b) A traditional unit of weight or mass measurement equal to approximately 4,000 pounds.

### li
A traditional Chinese unit of linear measurement whose value varied from 1,760 to 2,115 feet. In modern China the *li* is 0.5 kilometers (500 meters or 1,640.5 feet). The often misquoted Confucian proverb "A journey of a thousand miles starts with a single step" is actually "A journey of a thousand *li* starts with a single step."

### liang
A traditional Chinese unit of weight or mass measurement that was equal to 1/16 catty (0.5 pound), the same as a tael. In modern China, the liang equals 50 grams (1/10 jin or 10 quin).

### livre
A traditional French and Greek unit of weight or mass measurement equal to 2 marcs or 16 onces. The traditional value of a livre varied from market to market, but was standardized in the 14th century at about 489.5 grams (1.079 pounds) and called the *livre poids de marc* or *livre de Paris*. In modern France, the *livre* is defined as 500 grams or (0.5 kilogram or 1.1023 pounds).

### long ton
A unit of weight or mass measurement equal to 2,240 pounds. Synonymous with the British ton.

### measurement ton (MTON or MT)
A unit of cargo-carrying capacity of a cargo vessel, railcar, truck or other cargo conveyance equal to 40 cubic feet (1.1326m3) of cargo capacity. In some usage this is called a freight ton. However, modern convention is to use freight ton when referring to one (1) metric ton (1,000 kilos) of freight.

### metric ton (t or MT)
A unit of weight or mass measurement equal to 1,000 kilos. Metric ton and tonne are synonymous. In the U.S. the term metric ton is used.

### nautical mile (nmi, naut mi or NM)
A unit of distance measurement used in nautical and aeronautical navigation equal to the average distance on the earth's surface of one (1) minute of latitude. Because the Earth is not a perfect sphere this definition left the precise measurement of a nautical mile open to interpretation. As a result there were several competing definitions, including: the Admiralty Mile of 6,080 feet (1,853.18 meters), and the U.S. Nautical Mile of 6080.20 feet (1853.24 meters) (the latter was in use until 1954). However, an international conference held in Monaco in 1929 defined the nautical mile at exactly 1852 meters (6,076.11 feet or 1.1508 statute miles). This is now called the international nautical mile and is the accepted definition.

### net ton (NT)
(a) Alternate term used to signify a U.S. short ton (2,000 pounds). (b) Alternate term used to signify a register ton (100 cubic feet of cargo or cargo space on board a vessel). As a result of the possible confusion it is advised that the terms short ton or register ton be used instead of net ton.

### qian
A traditional Chinese unit of weight or mass measurement equal in modern usage to 0.1 liang or 5 grams.

### ream (rm)
(modern) Five hundred (500) sheets of paper.
(historic) Four hundred and eighty (480) sheets of paper (specifically 20 quires of 24 sheets each).

### register ton (RT)
A unit of ocean shipping cargo capacity equal to 100 cubic feet. Also called the merchant marine ton. Note: the register ton abbreviation 'RT' is also used for refrigeration ton and revenue ton.

### revenue ton (tonne) (RT)
A revenue-generating cargo shipment of either one (1) metric ton (tonne) or one (1) cubic meter ($m^3$) whichever yields the greatest amount of revenue for the carrier. Revenue ton is a shipping industry billing unit and is usually used in the term revenue ton mile.

### revenue ton mile
(a) The shipment of one ton of revenue-generating cargo for one mile. (b) The shipment of one (1) revenue ton of cargo for one mile.

### Riga last
A British unit of volume equal to 80 cubic feet ($2.265m^3$) of square-sawn timber or 65 cubic feet ($1.841m^3$) of round (unsurfaced) timber. Named for Riga, the capital of Latvia which was a major port used for the export of Russian timber. A "last" can mean simply a "load" (of anything), or traditionally, a unit of mass or volume equal to 4,000 pounds, very close to the weight of 80 cubic feet ($2.265m^3$) of square-sawn timber.

### score
A unit of quantity equal to 20.

### short ton (st or tn)
A unit of weight or mass measurement equal to 2,000 pounds.

### skein
(a) A coil of yarn or cord. (b) One sixth (1/6) of a hank. The length of a skein depends upon the fiber and manufacturer.

### smoot
A unit of linear measure equal to five feet, seven inches (5' 7"). This "unit of measure" resulted from a fraternity prank at the Massachusetts Institute of Technology (MIT) in 1958 when the body length of fraternity pledge Oliver Smoot was used to measure the length of the Harvard Bridge over the Charles River in Boston. This measurement of the bridge produced a result of 364.4 smoots plus an ear (the ear is allegedly the width of the earhole in the side of the football helmet Mr. Smoot was wearing as he was dragged and measured 365 times across the bridge). Smoot markers have been repainted on the bridge ever since. Also, Boston police have been known to use these "smoot markers" to identify locations of accidents on the roadway. Adding a degree of interest (and legitimacy) to the story and this entry is that the prank possibly inspired the young man in his career choice. The very well-respected Mr. Oliver Smoot went on to become the Chairman of the Board of the American National Standards Institute (ANSI) and then president of the International Organization for Standardization (ISO), retiring in 2005.

**W & M**

W
&
M

### stone
A traditional British unit of weight or mass measurement equal to 14 pounds avoirdupois (6.3 kilograms).

### tael or tahil
A traditional unit of weight or mass measurement used in eastern Asia with different values depending upon the country or market of use. One tael equals 16 cattys. During the colonial period the tael was standardized at 4/3 (1.333) ounce avoirdupois.

### tan or dan
(a) (China traditional) A unit of weight or mass measurement equal to 100 cattys or 1,600 taels. (b) (China modern) A unit of weight or mass equal to 50 kilograms or 100 jin.

### tatami
(Japan) A unit of area equal to a traditional tatami mat which is 0.5 ken x 1 ken (90cm x 180cm) or 17.5 square feet ($1.62m^3$). This is the traditional and still used method for describing the area of rooms in apartments or homes. Also called the jo.

### TEU
Acronym for 20-foot equivalent unit. A unit of cargo capacity equal to one twenty foot ocean cargo container (20' x 8' x approximately 8.5').

### ton
(a) (U.S.) A unit of weight or mass measurement equal to 20 hundredweight of 100 pounds each or 2,000 pounds (907.185 kilograms). Also called the short ton. (b) (U.K.) A unit of weight or mass equal to 2,240 pounds (1,016.047 kilograms). Also called the long ton.

### ton, metric
A unit of weight or mass measurement equal to 1000 kilograms (2204.623 pounds avoirdupois). The metric ton is now officially called the tonne.

### ton, merchant marine
A unit of volume measurement equal to 100 cubic feet ($2.8316m^3$) used in ocean shipping. Also called a register ton.

### ton, displacement (DT or dT)
A unit of weight or mass measurement used to measure the volume of water displaced by a vessel, especially warships. The weight of sea water varies, but a displacement ton has been defined to be 35 cubic feet (0.9911m3) of water.

### ton, freight (FT)
(a) A unit of volume measurement equal to 40 cubic feet, used to measure the cargo or cargo capacity of a ship, truck, railcar or airplane. Also called a measurement ton. (b) One metric ton of freight of any volume.

### tonne (t) / metric ton
A unit of weight or mass measurement equal to 1000 kilograms. Also called a metric ton. The French spelling 'tonne' is used to distinguish it from the U.S. short ton and U.K. long ton.

### tonneau
(French) (a) A traditional French unit of weight or mass measurement equal to 2000 livres (approximately 979 kilograms or 1.079 U.S. ton). (b) A traditional French unit of volume equal to 42 cubic pieds (approximately 50.84 cubic feet, or 1440 liters). (c) A shipment of 100 cases, or 1,200 bottles of wine.

### troy
A traditional English weight system based on a troy pound of 5760 grains. The troy pound was divided into 12 ounces of 480 grains each. The troy ounce was divided into 20 pennyweight of 24 grains each.
Apothecaries used to divide the troy ounce into 8 drams (of 60 grains each) with each dram equal to 3 scruples (of 20

grains each).
Although the troy pound was abolished in 1878 to avoid confusion with the avoirdupois pound (and system) the troy ounce is still used in quoting the market price of precious metals.
The troy weight system was the numeric basis of the still current English monetary system with one (1) English (U.K.) £ (pound) equal to 20 shillings and 12 pence (pennies) to each shilling.

### USP unit
Acronym for United States Pharmacopoeia unit. A unit of weight or mass of a drug or vitamin based upon its expected biological result as established by the U.S. Food and Drug Administration. The United States Pharmacopoeia is a reference published by the U.S. Pharmacopoeia Convention describing the properties of medicinal drugs.

### wan
(a) A Chinese unit of quantity equal to 10,000. The wan is used as a unit much like the thousand (1,000) unit is used in the West. Therefore, 100 wan is 1,000,000. (b) A Chinese term used to mean an indefinitely large number.

### watch
(sailing/shipping–traditional) An assigned period of duty on a vessel equal to four hours or eight bells. The day at sea is divided into six watches of four hours each. Typically, a seaman is on duty for four hours and then off for eight hours.

### watch
a) (time measurement) A period of time during which part of a ship's crew is on duty. A ship's day starts at 12 noon and is divided into six four-hour watches: 12 noon to 4PM, 4 to 8PM, 8PM to 12 midnight, 12 midnight to 4 AM, 4 to 8AM and 8AM to 12 noon. The 4 to 8AM watch is sometimes divided into two two-hour "dog" watches, enabling the crew to avoid or "dodge" the same routine every day. Dodging the watch became known as "dogging," thence the "dog" watch. Typically, two or three groups of watchstanders are on duty for four hours and then off for either four or eight hours, then back to duty. *See also* bells.

| WATCHES AT SEA | |
|---|---|
| Middle Watch | Midnight to 4 AM (0000–0400) |
| Morning Watch | 4 AM to 8 AM (0400 – 0800) |
| Forenoon Watch | 8 AM to Noon (0800 – 1200) |
| Afternoon Watch | Noon to 4 PM (1200 – 1600) |
| First Dog Watch | 4 PM to 6 PM (1600 – 1800) |
| Second Dog Watch | 6 PM to 8 PM (1800 – 2000) |
| First Watch | 8 PM to Midnight (2000 – 0000) |

### watt
A unit of power measurement (the amount of work an appliance is capable of) equal to the power used by a current of one ampere across a potential difference of one volt.

# Guide to INCOTERMS 2000

While the terms of sale in international business often sound similar to those commonly used in domestic contracts, they often have different meanings. Confusion over these terms can result in a lost sale or a financial loss on a sale. Thus, it is essential that you understand what terms you are agreeing to before you finalize a contract.

### Incoterms 2000[1]

By the 1920s, international traders had developed a set of trade terms to describe their rights and liabilities with regard to the sale and transport of goods. These trade terms consisted of short abbreviations for lengthy contract provisions. Unfortunately, there was no uniform interpretation of them in all countries, and therefore misunderstandings often arose in cross-border transactions.

To improve this aspect of international trade, the International Chamber of Commerce (ICC) in Paris developed INCOTERMS (INternational COmmercial TERMS), a set of uniform rules for the interpretation of international commercial terms defining the costs, risks, and obligations of buyers and sellers in international transactions. First published in 1936, these rules have been periodically revised to account for changing modes of transport and document delivery. The current version is Incoterms 2000.

### Use of Incoterms

Incoterms are not implied into contracts for the sale of goods. If you desire to use Incoterms, you must specifically include them in your contract. Further, your contract should expressly refer to the rules of interpretation as defined in the latest revision of Incoterms, for example, *Incoterms 2000*, and you should ensure the proper application of the terms by additional contract provisions. Also, Incoterms are not "laws." In case of a dispute, courts and arbitrators will look at: 1) the sales contract, 2) who has possession of the goods, and 3) what payment, if any, has been made. See *International Contracts*, also by World Trade Press.

### Illustrated Guide to Incoterms

This guide was designed to give a graphic representation of the buyer's and seller's risks and costs under each Incoterm. The material on each facing page gives a summary of seller and buyer responsibilities.

parties desire the following:
1. To complete a sale of goods.
2. To indicate each contracting party's costs, risks, and obligations with regard to delivery of the goods as follows:
   a. When is the delivery completed?
   b. How does a party ensure that the other party has met that standard of performance?
   c. Which party must comply with requisite licenses and government-imposed import and export formalities?
   d. What are the mode and terms of carriage?
   e. What are the delivery terms and what is required as proof of delivery?
   f. When is the risk of loss transferred from the seller to the buyer?
   g. How will transport costs be divided between the parties?
   h. What notices are the parties required to give to each other regarding the transport and transfer of the goods?
3. To establish basic terms of transport and delivery in a short format.

### Incoterms Do Not . . .

*Incoterms 2000* are not sufficient on their own to express the full intent of the parties. They will not:
1. Apply to contracts for services.
2. Define contractual rights and obligations other than for delivery.
3. Specify details of the transfer, transport, and delivery of the goods.
4. Determine how title to the goods will be transferred.
5. Protect a party from his/her own risk of loss.
6. Cover the goods before or after delivery.
7. Define the remedies for breach of contract.

**Tip:** Incoterms can be quite useful, but their use has limitations. If you use them incorrectly, your contract may be ambiguous, if not impossible to perform. It is therefore important to understand the scope and purpose of Incoterms—when and why you might use them—before you rely on them to define such important terms as mode of delivery, customs clearance, passage of title, and transfer of risk.

### Incoterms Do . . .

*Incoterms 2000* may be included in a sales contract if the

1. INCOTERMS 2000 are Copyright © 1999 by ICC Publishing S.A. All rights reserved. The actual text of INCOTERMS 2000 is contained in ICC publication No. 560. Contact: ICC Publishing, Inc.; 156 Fifth Avenue; New York, New York 10010; Tel: +1 (212) 206-1150. ICC Publishing S.A.; 38 Cours Albert, 1er; 75008 Paris, France; Tel: +[33] (1) 49 53 29 23; e-mail: pub@iccbo.org; www.iccbooks.org.
2. This Illustrated Guide to Incoterms 2000 is © Copyright 2000-2006 by World Trade Press. All Rights Reserved. World Trade Press; 800 Lindberg Lane, Suite 190; Petaluma, CA 94952 USA; Tel: (707) 778-1124; www.worldtradepress.com, www.worldtraderef.com.

# Organization of Incoterms

Incoterms are grouped into four categories:

1. **The "E" term (EXW)**—The only term where the seller/exporter makes the goods available at his or her own premises to the buyer/importer.
2. **The "F" terms (FCA, FAS and FOB)**—Terms where the seller/exporter is responsible to deliver the goods to a carrier named by the buyer.
3. **The "C" terms (CFR, CIF, CPT and CIP)**—Terms where the seller/exporter/manufacturer is responsible for contracting and paying for carriage of the goods, but not responsible for additional costs or risk of loss or damage to the goods once they have been shipped.
   C terms evidence "shipment" (as opposed to "arrival") contracts.
4. **The "D" terms (DAF, DES, DEQ, DDU and DDP)**—Terms where the seller/exporter/manufacturer is responsible for all costs and risks associated with bringing the goods to the place of destination.
   D terms evidence "arrival" contracts.

The following table sets out these categories.

| INCOTERMS 2000 | | |
|---|---|---|
| **Group E**<br>Departure | **EXW** | Ex Works<br>(...named place) |
| **Group F**<br>Main<br>Carriage<br>Unpaid | **FCA** | Free Carrier (...named place) |
| | **FAS** | Free Alongside Ship<br>(...named port of shipment) |
| | **FOB** | Free On Board<br>(...named port of shipment) |
| **Group C**<br>Main<br>Carriage<br>Paid | **CFR** | Cost and Freight<br>(...named port of destination) |
| | **CIF** | Cost, Insurance and Freight<br>(...named port of destination) |
| | **CPT** | Carriage Paid To<br>(...named place of destination) |
| | **CIP** | Carriage and Insurance Paid To<br>(...named place of destination) |
| **Group D**<br>Arrival | **DAF** | Delivered at Frontier<br>(...named place) |
| | **DES** | Delivered Ex Ship<br>(...named port of destination) |
| | **DEQ** | Delivered Ex Quay<br>(...named port of destination) |
| | **DDU** | Delivered Duty Unpaid<br>(...named port of destination) |
| | **DDP** | Delivered Duty Paid<br>(...named port of destination) |

# Mode of transport

Not all Incoterms are appropriate for all modes of transport. Some terms were designed with sea vessels in mind while others were designed to be applicable to all modes. The following table sets out which terms are applicable for each mode of transport.

| INCOTERMS 2000 | | |
|---|---|---|
| All modes<br>of<br>transport<br>including<br>multimodal | **EXW** | Ex Works<br>(...named place) |
| | **FCA** | Free Carrier (...named place) |
| | **CPT** | Carriage Paid To<br>(...named place of destination) |
| | **CIP** | Carriage and Insurance Paid To<br>(...named place of destination) |
| | **DAF** | Delivered at Frontier<br>(...named place) |
| | **DDU** | Delivered Duty Unpaid |
| | **DDP** | Delivered Duty Paid |
| Sea and<br>inland<br>waterway<br>transport<br>only | **FAS** | Free Alongside Ship<br>(...named port of shipment) |
| | **FOB** | Free On Board<br>(...named port of shipment) |
| | **CFR** | Cost and Freight<br>(...named port of destination) |
| | **CIF** | Cost, Insurance and Freight<br>(...named port of destination) |
| | **DES** | Delivered Ex Ship<br>(...named port of destination) |
| | **DEQ** | Delivered Ex Quay<br>(...named port of destination) |

## *Helpful Definitions*

**Pre-carriage**—The initial transport of goods from the seller's premises to the main port or place of shipment. Usually by truck, rail or on inland waterway.

**Main carriage**—The primary transport of goods, generally for the longest part of the journey and generally from one country to another. Usually by sea vessel or by airplane, but can be by truck or rail or inland waterway as well.

**On-carriage**—Transport from the port or place of arrival in the country of destination to the buyer's premises. Usually by truck, rail or inland waterways.

# Notes on Incoterms

1. **Underlying Contract**—Incoterms were designed to be used within the context of a written contract for the sale of goods (not for the sale of services). Incoterms, therefore, refer to the contract of sale, rather than the contract of carriage of the goods. Buyers and sellers should specify that their contract be governed by Incoterms 2000.

2. **EXW and FCA**—If you buy Ex Works or Free Carrier you will need to arrange for the contract of carriage. Also, since the shipper will not receive a bill of lading, using a letter of credit requiring a bill of lading will not be possible.

3. **EDI: Electronic Data Interchange**—It is increasingly common for sellers to prepare and transmit documents electronically. Incoterms provides for EDI so long as buyers and sellers agree on their use in the sales contract.

4. **Insurable Interest**—Note that in many cases either the buyer or the seller is not *obligated* to provide insurance. In a number of cases neither party is obligated to provide insurance. However, both the seller and buyer should be aware that they may have insurable interest in the goods and prudence dictates purchase of insurance coverage.

5. **Customs of the Port or Trade**—Incoterms are an attempt to standardize trade terms for all nations and all trades. However, different ports and different trades have their own customs and practices. It is best if specific customs and practices are specified in the sales contract.

6. **Precise Point of Delivery**—In some cases it may not be possible for the buyer to name the precise point of delivery at contract. However, if the buyer does not do so in a timely manner, it may give the seller the option to make delivery within a range of places that is within the terms of the contract. For example, the original terms of sale may state CFR Port of Rotterdam. The Port of Rotterdam is huge and the buyer may find that a particular point within the port is best and should so state in the sales contract and in the trade term. Also, since the buyer becomes liable for the goods once they arrive, he or she may be responsible for unloading, storage and other charges once the goods have been made available at the place named.

7. **Export and Import Customs Clearance**—It is usually desirable that export customs formalities be handled by the seller and import customs formalities be handled by the buyer. However, some trade terms require that the buyer handle export formalities and others require that the seller handle import formalities. In each case the buyer and seller will have to assume risk from export and import restrictions and prohibitions. In some cases foreign exporters may not be able to obtain import licenses in the country of import. This should be researched before accepting final terms.

8. **Added Wording**—It is possible, and in many cases desirable, that the seller and buyer agree to additional wording to an Incoterm. For example, if the seller agrees to DDP terms, agreeing to pay for customs formalities and import duties, but not for VAT (Value Added Taxes) the term "DDP VAT Unpaid" may be used.

9. **Packing**—It is the responsibility of the seller to provide packaging unless the goods shipped are customarily shipped in bulk (usually commodities such as oil or grain). In most situations it is best if the buyer and seller agree in the sales contract on the type and extent of packing required. However, it may not be possible to know beforehand the type or duration of transport. As a result, it is the responsibility of the seller to provide for safe and appropriate packaging, but only to the extent that the buyer has made the circumstances of the transport known to the seller beforehand.

   If the seller is responsible for packing goods in an ocean or air freight container it is also his responsibility to pack the container properly to withstand shipment.

10. **Inspection**—These are several issues related to inspections: a) the seller is responsible for costs of inspection to make certain the quantity and quality of the shipment is in conformity with the sales contract, b) pre-shipment inspections as required by the export authority are the responsibility of the party responsible for export formalities, c) import inspections as required by the import authority are the responsibility of the party responsible for import formalities, and d) third-party inspections for independent verification of quality and quantity (if required) are generally the responsibility of the buyer. The buyer may require such an inspection and inspection document as a condition of payment.

11. **Passing of Risks and Costs**—The general rule is that risks and costs pass from the seller to the buyer once the seller has delivered the goods to the point and place named in the trade term.

**INCOTERMS**

**INCOTERMS**

# EXW
## Ex Works (... named place)

SELLER ➝
BUYER ⇢

| Seller/ Exporter Premises | Export Documents/ Formalities | Delivered (to carrier) at Named Place/Terminal/Quay | Loading Place/Port of Shipment | Onboard Ship's Rail | Onboard Ship's Rail | Discharging Place/Port of Arrival | Delivery at Named Place/ Port of Destination: Frontier/Terminal/Quay | Import Documents/ Formalities | Buyer/ Importer Premises |
|---|---|---|---|---|---|---|---|---|---|
| **SELLER'S RISKS** | | | | | | | | **BUYER'S RISKS** | |
| **SELLER'S COSTS** | | | | | | | | **BUYER'S COSTS** | |

## EXW, Ex Works (...named place)

In Ex Works, the seller/exporter/manufacturer merely makes the goods available to the buyer at the seller's "named place" of business. This trade term places the greatest responsibility on the buyer and minimum obligations on the seller.

The seller does not clear the goods for export and does not load the goods onto a truck or other transport vehicle at the named place of departure.

The parties to the transaction, however, may stipulate that the seller be responsible for the costs and risks of loading the goods onto a transport vehicle. Such a stipulation must be made within the contract of sale.

If the buyer cannot handle export formalities the Ex Works term should not be used. In such a case Free Car-

rier (FCA) is recommended.

The Ex Works term is often used when making an initial quotation for the sale of goods. It represents the cost of the goods without any other costs included.

Normal payment terms for Ex Works transactions are generally cash in advance and open account.

### Examples

EXW Ex Works ABC Factory Paris, France

EXW Ex Works XYZ Printing Plant Singapore

# EXW
# Ex Works (. . . named place)

## Incoterm Category

EXW is the only "E" Incoterm. The "E" Incoterm is where the seller/exporter makes the goods available to the buyer/importer at the seller/exporter's premises/factory/warehouse.

## Modes of Transport Covered

All modes of transport including multimodal.

## Seller's Responsibilities (summary)

1. **Goods**—Provide the goods, commercial invoice or electronic message, and other documentation as required by the sales contract.

2. **Licenses and Customs Formalities**—Provide the buyer at the buyer's request, risk and cost, every assistance in obtaining any license, authorization or documentation required for export of the goods.

3. **Carriage and Insurance**—The seller has no obligation to provide carriage of goods or insurance.

4. **Delivery**—Make the goods available to the buyer, unloaded, at the named place and on the date stipulated in the sales contract.

5. **Risk Transfer**—Assume all risks to the goods (loss or damage) until they have been made available to the buyer as above in # 4 above.

6. **Costs**—Pay all costs until the goods have been made available to the buyer in accordance with #4 above.

7. **Notice to the Buyer**—Provide sufficient notice to the buyer of the location and time of availability of the goods.

8. **Proof of Delivery, Transport Documents**—The seller has no obligation to provide the buyer with a proof of delivery or a transport document.

9. **Checking, Packing, Marking**—Pay all costs associated with checking the quality and quantity of the goods to be in conformity with the sales contract. Provide appropriate packing (unless the goods are traditionally delivered unpackaged) as required for the transport of the goods, to the extent that the buyer has made transport circumstances known to the seller prior to the execution of the sales contract. Provide marking appropriate to the packaging.

10. **Other**—Provide the buyer, at the buyer's request, risk and expense, assistance in securing documentation originating in the country of origin or of export as required for export and import. Provide the buyer at the buyer's request information necessary to obtain insurance.

## Buyer's Responsibilities (summary)

1. **Payment**—Pay for the goods as provided in the sales contract.

2. **Licenses and Customs Formalities**—Obtain at own risk and cost all export and import licenses and authorizations. Carry out all export and import formalities at own risk and cost.

3. **Carriage and Insurance**—The buyer has no obligation to the seller to provide contract of carriage or insurance.

4. **Taking Delivery**—Take delivery of the goods when they have been made available by the seller in accordance with the terms of the sales contract.

5. **Risk Transfer**—Assume all risks (loss or damage) from the time the goods have been made available by the seller in accordance with the terms of the sales contract.

6. **Costs**—Pay all costs for carriage and insurance from the time the goods have been made available by the seller in accordance with the terms of the sales contract. Pay all costs resulting from failure to take delivery at the named place and time. Pay all costs relating to export and import including duties, taxes, customs formalities and other charges including transship-ment. Reimburse the seller for costs of providing assistance in obtaining export licenses and authorizations.

7. **Notice to Seller**—If, according to the sales contract, the buyer is able to specify a time within a stipulated period, and/or specify a place of taking delivery, to give the seller sufficient notice.

8. **Proof of Delivery**—Provide the seller with evidence of having taken delivery.

9. **Inspection(s)**—Pay for the costs of pre-shipment inspection(s) including inspections required by the country of export.

10. **Other**—Pay and/or reimburse the seller for all costs associated with securing documentation originating in the country of origin or export as required for export and import.

**INCOTERMS**

**INCOTERMS**

# FCA
## Free Carrier (. . . named place)

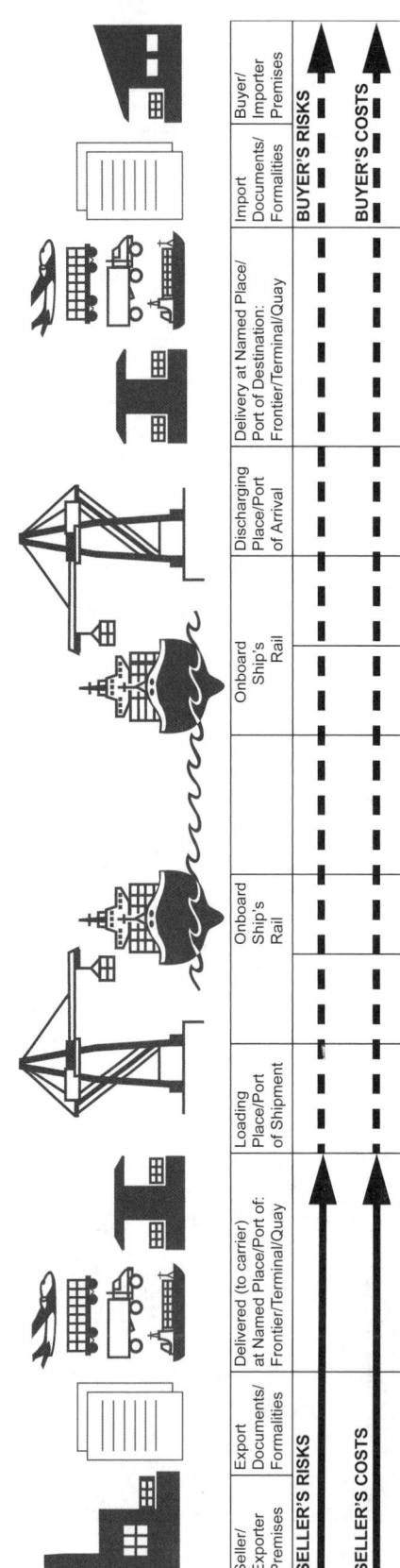

| | Seller/ Exporter Premises | Export Documents/ Formalities | Delivered (to carrier) at Named Place/Port of: Frontier/Terminal/Quay | Loading Place/Port of Shipment | Onboard Ship's Rail | Onboard Ship's Rail | Discharging Place/Port of Arrival | Delivery at Named Place/ Port of Destination: Frontier/Terminal/Quay | Import Documents/ Formalities | Buyer/ Importer Premises |
|---|---|---|---|---|---|---|---|---|---|---|
| SELLER'S RISKS | | | → | | | | | | | |
| SELLER'S COSTS | | | → | | | | | | | |
| BUYER'S RISKS | | | | | | | | | → | |
| BUYER'S COSTS | | | | | | | | | → | |

## FCA, Free Carrier (...named place)

In Free Carrier, the seller/exporter/manufacturer clears the goods for export and then delivers them to the carrier specified by the buyer at the named place.

If the named place is the seller's place of business, the seller is responsible for loading the goods onto the transport vehicle. If the named place is any other location, such as the loading dock of the carrier, the seller is not responsible for loading the goods onto the transport vehicle.

The Free Carrier term may be used for any mode of transport, including multimodal.

The "named place" in Free Carrier and all "F" terms is domestic to the seller.

"Carrier" has a specific and somewhat expanded meaning. A carrier can be a shipping line, an airline, a trucking firm, or a railway. The carrier can also be an individual or

firm who undertakes to procure carriage by any of the above methods of transport including multimodal. Therefore, a person, such as a freight forwarder, can act as a "carrier" under this term. In such a case, the buyer names the carrier or the individual who is to receive the goods.

The Free Carrier term is often used when making an initial quotation for the sale of goods.

Normal payment terms for Free Carrier transactions are generally cash in advance and open account.

### Examples
FCA Free Carrier ABC Shipping Hamburg Germany
FCA Free Carrier XYZ Air Lines SFO (San Francisco International Airport)
FCA Free Carrier AZ Freight Forwarders Tokyo Japan

# FCA
# Free Carrier (. . . named place)

## Incoterm Category

FCA is an "F" Incoterm where the seller/exporter delivers the goods export cleared to a carrier named by the buyer, but does not bear risk or costs once the goods have been handed over.

## Modes of Transport Covered

All modes of transport including multimodal.

## Seller's Responsibilities (summary)

1. **Goods**—Provide the goods, commercial invoice or electronic message, and other documentation as required by the sales contract.

2. **Licenses and Customs Formalities**—Obtain at own risk and cost all required export licenses, documentation and authorizations and carry out all export formalities and procedures.

3. **Carriage and Insurance**—The seller has no obligation to provide carriage of goods or insurance. However, if requested by buyer, the seller may contract for carriage on standard industry terms at the buyer's risk and cost. If so, the seller must notify buyer who may chose to decline the contract and notify the seller.

4. **Delivery**—Deliver the goods to the named carrier, freight forwarder or person at the named place and at the time stipulated in the sales contract. Requirements for delivery to the carrier vary depending upon the means of transport and the size of the shipment. In general, delivery is considered complete when the seller either loads the goods onto the vehicle provided, or delivers the goods to the carrier's terminal, unloaded.

5. **Risk Transfer**—Assume all risks to the goods (loss or damage) until they have been delivered to the carrier.

6. **Costs**—Pay all costs until the goods have been delivered to the carrier as well as all costs relating to export including duties, taxes and customs formalities.

7. **Notices**—Provide sufficient notice to the buyer that the goods have been delivered to the carrier.

8. **Proof of Delivery, Transport Documents**—Provide the buyer with a proof of delivery (to the carrier) or a transport document, or to assist the buyer in obtaining a transport document.

9. **Checking, Packing, Marking**—Pay all costs associated with checking the quality and quantity of the goods to be in conformity with the sales contract. Provide appropriate packing (unless the goods are traditionally delivered unpackaged) as required for the transport of the goods, to the extent that the buyer has made transport circumstances known to the seller prior to the execution of the sales contract. Provide marking appropriate to the packaging.

10. **Other**—Provide the buyer, at the buyer's request, risk and expense, assistance in securing documentation originating in the country of origin or of export as required for import or transshipment through another country. Provide the buyer at the buyer's request information necessary to obtain insurance.

## Buyer's Responsibilities (summary)

1. **Payment**—Pay for the goods as provided in the sales contract.

2. **Licenses and Customs Formalities**—Obtain all import licenses, documentation and authorizations and carry out all import formalities.

3. **Carriage and Insurance**—Provide for contract of carriage from the named place. No obligation to seller for insurance.

4. **Taking Delivery**—Take delivery of the goods as provided in the sales contract.

5. **Risk Transfer**—Assume all risk of loss or damage from the time the goods have been delivered to the carrier as provided in the sales contract.

6. **Costs**—Pay all costs for carriage and insurance from the time the goods have been delivered to the carrier as provided in the sales contract. Pay all costs resulting from failure to take delivery at the named place and time. Pay all costs relating to import formalities including duties, taxes and other charges including transshipment.

7. **Notice to Seller**—Give the seller sufficient notice of the name of the carrier, the time or period for delivery and the place of delivery.

8. **Proof of Delivery, Transport Document**—Accept the seller's proof of delivery or transport document.

9. **Inspection(s)**—Pay for the costs of pre-shipment inspection except inspections required by the country of export.

10. **Other**—Pay all costs associated with securing documentation originating in the country of origin or export as required for import. Reimburse seller for costs in providing documentation or assistance. Give the seller instructions regarding carriage.

INCOTERMS

# FAS
## Free Alongside Ship (. . . named port of shipment)

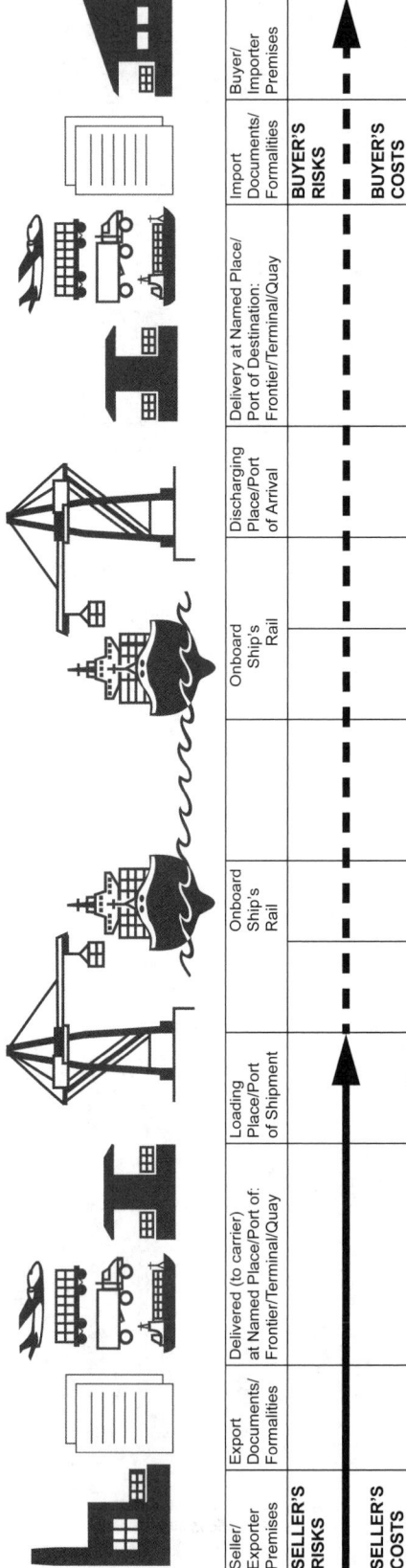

| | Seller/ Exporter Premises | Export Documents/ Formalities | Delivered (to carrier) at Named Place/Port of: Frontier/Terminal/Quay | Loading Place/Port of Shipment | Onboard Ship's Rail | | Onboard Ship's Rail | Discharging Place/Port of Arrival | Delivery at Named Place/ Port of Destination: Frontier/Terminal/Quay | Import Documents/ Formalities | Buyer/ Importer Premises |
|---|---|---|---|---|---|---|---|---|---|---|---|
| **SELLER'S RISKS** | | | | | | | | | | **BUYER'S RISKS** | |
| **SELLER'S COSTS** | | | | | | | | | | **BUYER'S COSTS** | |

## FAS, Free Alongside Ship (...named port of shipment)

In Free Alongside Ship, the seller/exporter/manufacturer clears the goods for export and then places them alongside the vessel at the "named port of shipment." [The seller's clearing the goods for export is new to Incoterms 2000.]

The parties to the transaction, however, may stipulate in their contract of sale that the buyer, instead of the seller clear the goods for export. The standard FAS term, however, requires that the seller clear the goods for export.

The Free Alongside Ship term is used only for ocean or inland waterway transport.

The "named place" in Free Alongside Ship and all "F" terms is domestic to the seller.

The Free Alongside Ship term is commonly used in the sale of bulk commodity cargo such as oil, grains, and ore. Normal payment terms for Free Carrier transactions are generally cash in advance and open account, but letters of credit are also used.

### Examples

FAS Free Alongside Ship Port Elizabeth South Africa
FAS Free Alongside Ship Le Havre France

# FAS
# Free Alongside Ship (. . . named port of shipment)

## Incoterm Category

FAS is an "F" Incoterm where the seller/exporter delivers the goods alongside a ship, and does not bear risk or costs once the goods have been handed over.

## Modes of Transport Covered

Used only for ocean or inland waterway transport.

## Seller's Responsibilities (summary)

1. **Goods**—Provide the goods, commercial invoice or electronic message, and other documentation as required by the sales contract.

2. **Licenses and Customs Formalities**—Obtain at own risk and cost any export licenses and authorizations and carry out all export formalities and procedures.

3. **Carriage and Insurance**—The seller has no obligation to the buyer to provide carriage of goods or insurance.

4. **Delivery**—Deliver the goods on the quay alongside the named vessel at the named place and at the time stipulated in the sales contract.

5. **Risk Transfer**—Assume all risks of loss or damage to the goods until they have been delivered to the port at the named place and time as provided in the sales contract.

6. **Costs**—Pay all costs until the goods have been delivered alongside the named vessel and all costs related to export formalities.

7. **Notice to the Buyer**—Provide sufficient notice to the buyer that the goods have been delivered alongside the named vessel.

8. **Proof of Delivery, Transport Documents**—Provide the buyer with a proof of delivery (to the carrier) or a transport document, or to assist the buyer in obtaining a transport document.

9. **Checking, Packing, Marking**—Pay all costs associated with checking the quality and quantity of the goods to be in conformity with the sales contract. Provide appropriate packing (unless the goods are traditionally delivered unpackaged) as required for the transport of the goods, to the extent that the buyer has made transport circumstances known to the seller prior to the execution of the sales contract. Provide marking appropriate to the packaging.

10. **Other**—Provide the buyer at the buyer's request, risk and expense any and all assistance in securing documentation originating in the country of export or of origin required for import and transshipment through another country. Provide the buyer at the buyer's request information necessary to obtain insurance.

## Buyer's Responsibilities (summary)

1. **Payment**—Pay for the goods as provided in the sales contract.

2. **Licenses and Customs Formalities**—Obtain at own risk and cost any import licenses and authorizations and carry out all import formalities.

3. **Carriage and Insurance**—Provide for contract of carriage from the named port of shipment. No obligation for insurance.

4. **Taking Delivery**—Take delivery of the goods as provided in the sales contract.

5. **Risk Transfer**—Assume all risk of loss or damage from the time the goods have been delivered alongside the ship as provided in the sales contract.

6. **Costs**—Pay all costs for carriage and insurance from the time the goods have been delivered alongside the vessel in accordance with the terms of the sales contract. Pay all costs resulting from failure of the named ship to arrive on time or to be able to take the goods. Pay all costs relating import formalities including duties, taxes and other charges including transshipment.

7. **Notice to Seller**—Give sufficient notice to the seller of the name of the vessel, the time or period for delivery and the place of delivery.

8. **Proof of Delivery, Transport Document**—Accept the seller's proof of delivery or transport document.

9. **Inspection(s)**—Pay for the costs of pre-shipment inspection except inspections required by the country of export.

10. **Other**—Pay all costs associated with securing documentation originating in the country of origin or export as required for import formalities. Reimburse seller for seller's costs in providing such documentation or assistance. Also, to give the seller instructions regarding contract for carriage.

INCOTERMS

# INCOTERMS

# FOB
## Free On Board (. . . named port of shipment)

SELLER ▶

BUYER ┇▶

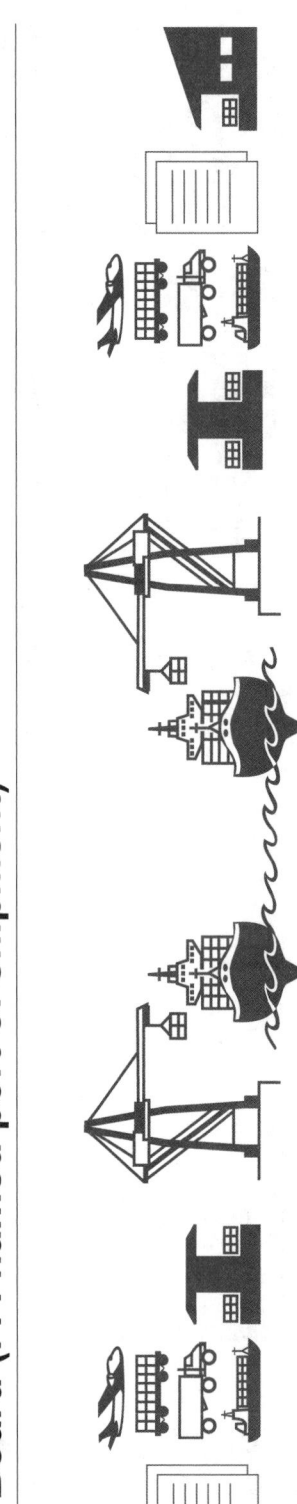

| Seller/ Exporter Premises | Export Documents/ Formalities | Delivered (to carrier) at Named Place/Port of: Frontier/Terminal/Quay | Loading Place/Port of Shipment | Onboard Ship's Rail | Onboard Ship's Rail | Discharging Place/Port of Arrival | Delivery at Named Place/ Port of Destination: Frontier/Terminal/Quay | Import Documents/ Formalities | Buyer/ Importer Premises |
|---|---|---|---|---|---|---|---|---|---|
| **SELLER'S RISKS** | | | ▲ | | | | | **BUYER'S RISKS** | |
| **SELLER'S COSTS** | | | ▲ | | | | | **BUYER'S COSTS** | |

## FOB, Free On Board (...named port of shipment)

In Free On Board, the seller/exporter/manufacturer clears the goods for export and is responsible for the costs and risks of delivering the goods past the ship's rail at the named port of shipment.

The Free On Board term is used only for ocean or inland waterway transport.

The "named place" in Free On Board and all "F" terms is domestic to the seller.

Normal payment terms for Free On Board transactions include cash in advance, open account, and letters of credit.

The Free On Board term is commonly used in the sale of bulk commodity cargo such as oil, grains, and ore where passing the ship's rail is important. However, it is also commonly used in shipping container loads of other goods.

The key document in FOB transactions is the "On Board Bill of Lading."

Sellers and buyers often confuse the Free On Board term with Free Carrier. Free On Board (FOB) does not mean loading the goods onto a truck at the seller's place of business. Free On Board is used only in reference to delivering the goods past a ship's rail in ocean or inland waterway transport. Free Carrier, on the other hand, is applicable to all modes of transport.

### Examples

FOB Free on Board "Vessel ABC" Buenos Aires Argentina

FOB Free on Board Gdansk Poland

# FOB
# Free on Board (. . . named port of shipment)

## *Incoterm Category*

FOB is an "F" Incoterm where the seller/exporter is responsible for delivering the goods, export cleared, on board a ship, and does not bear risk or costs afterwards.

## *Modes of Transport Covered*

Used only for ocean or inland waterway transport.

## *Seller's Responsibilities (summary)*

1. **Goods**—Provide the goods, commercial invoice or electronic message, and other documentation as required by the sales contract.

2. **Licenses and Customs Formalities**—Obtain at own risk and cost any export licenses and authorizations and carry out all export formalities and procedures.

3. **Carriage and Insurance**—The seller has no obligation to the buyer to provide carriage of goods or insurance.

4. **Delivery**—Deliver the goods on board the named vessel at the named port and place and at the time stipulated in the sales contract.

5. **Risk Transfer**—Assume all risks of loss or damage to the goods until they have passed the ship's rail on the named vessel as provided in the sales contract.

6. **Costs**—Pay all costs until the goods have passed the ship's rail on the named vessel as well as all costs relating to export including duties, taxes and customs formalities.

7. **Notice to the Buyer**—Provide sufficient notice to the buyer that the goods have been delivered on board the named vessel.

8. **Proof of Delivery, Transport Documents**—Provide the buyer with a proof of delivery or a transport document, or to assist the buyer in obtaining a transport document.

9. **Checking, Packing, Marking**—Pay all costs asso-

ciated with checking the quality and quantity of the goods to be in conformity with the sales contract. Provide appropriate packing (unless the goods are traditionally delivered unpackaged) as required for the transport of the goods, to the extent that the buyer has made transport circumstances known to the seller prior to the execution of the sales contract. Provide marking appropriate to the packaging.

10. **Other**—Provide the buyer at the buyer's request, risk and expense any and all assistance in securing documentation originating in the country of export or of origin required for import and transshipment through another country. Provide the buyer at the buyer's request information necessary to obtain insurance.

## *Buyer's Responsibilities (summary)*

1. **Payment**—Pay for the goods as provided in the sales contract.

2. **Licenses and Customs Formalities**—Obtain at own risk and cost any import licenses and authorizations and carry out all import formalities.

3. **Carriage and Insurance**—Provide for contract of carriage from the named port of shipment. No obligation for insurance.

4. **Taking Delivery**—Take delivery of the goods as provided in the sales contract.

5. **Risk Transfer**—Assume all risks of loss or damage from the time the goods have passed the ship's rail at the port of shipment.

6. **Costs**—Pay all costs for carriage and insurance from the time the goods have passed the ship's rail at the port of shipment in accordance with the terms of the sales contract. Pay all costs resulting from failure of the named ship to arrive on time or to be able to take the goods. Pay all costs relating to import formalities including duties, taxes and other charges including transshipment.

7. **Notice to Seller**—Give sufficient notice to the seller of the name of the vessel, the time or period for delivery and the place of delivery.

8. **Proof of Delivery, Transport Document**—Accept the seller's proof of delivery or transport document.

9. **Inspection(s)**—Pay for the costs of pre-shipment inspection except inspections required by the country of export.

10. **Other**—Pay all costs associated with securing documentation originating in the country of origin or export as required for import. Reimburse seller for seller's costs in providing such documentation or assistance.

# CFR
## Cost and Freight (. . . named port of destination)

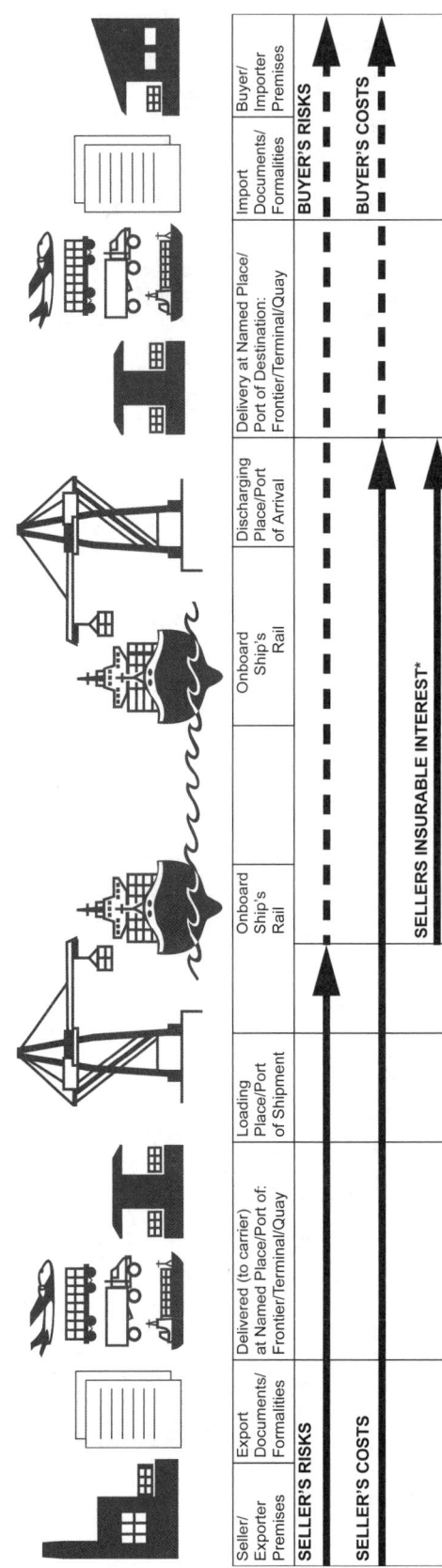

| Seller/ Exporter Premises | Export Documents/ Formalities | Delivered (to carrier) at Named Place/Port of: Frontier/Terminal/Quay | Loading Place/Port of Shipment | Onboard Ship's Rail | Onboard Ship's Rail | Discharging Place/Port of Arrival | Delivery at Named Place/ Port of Destination: Frontier/Terminal/Quay | Import Documents/ Formalities | Buyer/ Importer Premises |
|---|---|---|---|---|---|---|---|---|---|
| SELLER'S RISKS | | | | | | | | BUYER'S RISKS | |
| SELLER'S COSTS | | | | | | | | BUYER'S COSTS | |
| | | | | SELLERS INSURABLE INTEREST* | | | | | |

## CFR Cost and Freight (...named port of destination)

In Cost and Freight, the seller/exporter/manufacturer clears the goods for export and is responsible for delivering the goods past the ship's rail at the port of shipment (not destination).

The seller is also responsible for paying for the costs associated with transport of the goods to the named port of destination. However, once the goods pass the ship's rail at the port of shipment, the buyer assumes responsibility for risk of loss or damage as well as any additional transport costs.

The Cost and Freight term is used only for ocean or inland waterway transport.

The "named port of destination" in Cost and Freight and all "C" terms is domestic to the buyer.

Normal payment terms for Cost and Freight transactions include cash in advance, open account, and letters of credit.

The Cost and Freight term is commonly used in the sale of oversize and overweight cargo that will not fit into an ocean freight container or exceeds weight limitations of such containers. The term is also used for LCL (less than container load) cargo and for the shipment of goods by rail in boxcars to the ocean carrier.

### *Insurance Note

While the seller may not be legally responsible for the goods once they pass the ship's rail in the port of shipment, he may have "insurable interest" during the voy-

age. Prudence may dictate purchase of additional insurance coverage.

### Examples

CFR Cost and Freight Port-au-Prince Haiti

CFR Cost and Freight Bombay India

# CFR
# Cost and Freight (. . . named port of destination)

## Incoterm Category
**CFR is a "C" Incoterm** where the seller is responsible for contracting and paying for carriage of the goods, but not responsible for additional costs or risk of loss or damage to the goods once they have been shipped. C terms evidence "shipment" (as opposed to "arrival") contracts.

## Modes of Transport Covered
Used only for ocean or inland waterway transport.

## Seller's Responsibilities (summary)
1. **Goods**—Provide the goods, commercial invoice or electronic message, and other documentation as required by the sales contract.
2. **Licenses and Customs Formalities**—Obtain at own risk and cost any export licenses and authorizations and carry out all export formalities and procedures.
3. **Carriage and Insurance**—Contract for and pay all costs of carriage by sea vessel to the named port of destination. No obligation to provide insurance.
4. **Delivery**—Deliver the goods on board the named vessel at the named port and on the date or within the time period stipulated in the sales contract.
5. **Risk Transfer**—Assume all risks of loss or damage to the goods until they have passed over the ship's rail at the port of shipment.
6. **Costs**—Pay all costs until the goods have been delivered to the named port of shipment and passed over the ship's rail plus costs of loading, carriage to the port of destination and normal unloading. Also to pay all costs relating to export including duties, taxes and customs formalities.
7. **Notice to the Buyer**—Provide sufficient notice to the buyer that the goods have been delivered on board the named vessel.
8. **Proof of Delivery, Transport Documents**—Pro-

vide the buyer with a transport document that will allow the buyer to claim the goods at the destination and (unless otherwise agreed) allow the buyer to sell the goods while in transit through the transfer of the transport document or by notification to the sea carrier.
9. **Checking, Packing, Marking**—Pay all costs associated with checking the quality and quantity of the goods to be in conformity with the sales contract. Provide appropriate packing (unless the goods are traditionally delivered unpackaged) as required for the transport of the goods, to the extent that the buyer has made transport circumstances known to the seller prior to the execution of the sales contract. Provide marking appropriate to the packaging.
10. **Other**—Provide the buyer at the buyer's request, risk and expense any and all assistance in securing documentation originating in the country of export or of origin required for import and transshipment (as necessary). Provide the buyer at the buyer's request information necessary to obtain insurance.

## Buyer's Responsibilities (summary)
1. **Payment**—Pay for the goods as provided in the sales contract.
2. **Licenses and Customs Formalities**—Obtain and pay costs of all import licenses and authorizations and carry out all import formalities.
3. **Carriage and Insurance**—No obligation to the seller.
4. **Taking Delivery**—Take delivery of the goods at the port of destination as provided in the sales contract.
5. **Risk Transfer**—Assume all risk of loss or damage from the time the goods have passed over the ship's rail at the port of shipment.
6. **Costs**—Pay all additional costs for the goods once they have passed over the ship's rail at the port of shipment, including unloading, lighterage and wharfage at the port of destination. Pay all costs relating to import formalities including duties, taxes and other charges including transshipment.
7. **Notice to Seller**—If, according to the sales contract, the buyer is able to specify a time for shipping and/or specify a port of destination, to give the seller sufficient notice.
8. **Proof of Delivery, Transport Document**—Accept the seller's transport document so long as it is in conformity with the sales contract.
9. **Inspection(s)**—Pay for the costs of pre-shipment inspection except inspections required by the country of export.
10. **Other**—Pay all costs of securing documentation from the country of origin or export as required for import. Reimburse seller for costs in providing such documentation or assistance.

# CIF
## Cost, Insurance and Freight (... named port of destination)

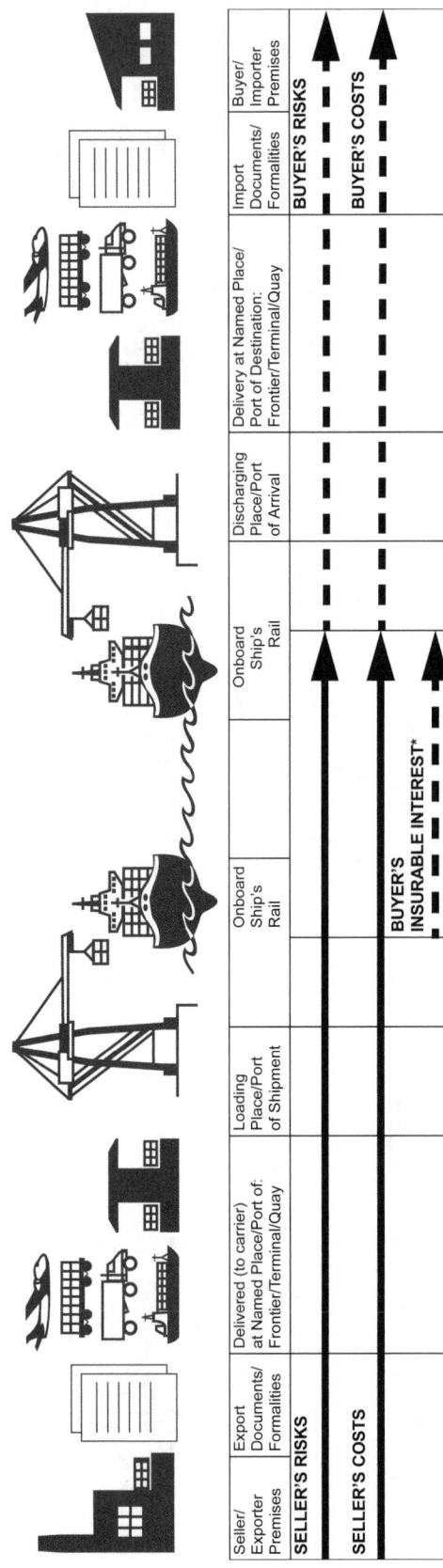

| Seller/ Exporter Premises | Export Documents/ Formalities | Delivered (to carrier) at Named Place/Port of: Frontier/Terminal/Quay | Loading Place/Port of Shipment | Onboard Ship's Rail | Onboard Ship's Rail | Discharging Place/Port of Arrival | Delivery at Named Place/ Port of Destination: Frontier/Terminal/Quay | Import Documents/ Formalities | Buyer/ Importer Premises |
|---|---|---|---|---|---|---|---|---|---|
| SELLER'S RISKS | | | | | | | | BUYER'S RISKS | |
| SELLER'S COSTS | | | | | | | | BUYER'S COSTS | |
| | | | | | BUYER'S INSURABLE INTEREST* | | | | |

## CIF Cost, Insurance and Freight (...named port of destination)

In Cost, Insurance and Freight, the seller/exporter/manufacturer clears the goods for export and is responsible for delivering the goods past the ship's rail at the port of shipment (not destination).

The seller is responsible for paying for the costs associated with transport of the goods to the named port of destination. However, once the goods pass the ship's rail at the port of shipment, the buyer assumes responsibility for risk of loss or damage as well as any additional transport costs.

The seller is also responsible for procuring and paying for marine insurance in the buyer's name for the shipment.

The Cost, Insurance and Freight term is used only for ocean or inland waterway transport.

The "named port of destination" in Cost, Insurance and Freight and all "C" terms is domestic to the buyer. Normal payment terms for Cost, Insurance and Freight transactions include cash in advance, open account, and letters of credit.

### *Insurance Note

While the seller is responsible for procuring and paying for insurance co ver during the voyage to the named port of destination, the buyer may exercise prudence and purchase additional insurance coverage.

### Examples

CIF Cost, Insurance and Freight Hong Kong

CIF Cost, Insurance and Freight Port of New York

# CIF
# Cost, Insurance and Freight (. . . named port of destination)

## Incoterm Category

CIF is a "C" Incoterm where the seller is responsible for contracting and paying for carriage and insurance of the goods, but not responsible for additional costs or risk of loss or damage to the goods once they have been shipped. C terms evidence "shipment" (as opposed to "arrival") contracts.

## Modes of Transport Covered

Used only for ocean or inland waterway transport.

## Seller's Responsibilities (summary)

1. **Goods**—Provide the goods, commercial invoice or electronic message, and other documentation as required by the sales contract.

2. **Licenses and Customs Formalities**—Obtain at own risk and cost any export licenses and authorizations and carry out all export formalities and procedures.

3. **Carriage and Insurance**—Contract for and pay costs of carriage by sea or inland waterway and insurance for 110 percent of the value of the contract to the named port of destination. The insurance policy must allow the buyer to make claim directly from the insurer. Deliver the insurance document to the buyer.

4. **Delivery**—Deliver the goods on board the named vessel at the named port and at the date or within the time period stipulated in the sales contract.

5. **Risk Transfer**—Assume all risks of loss or damage to the goods until they have passed over the ship's rail at the port of shipment.

6. **Costs**—Pay all costs of carriage and insurance until the goods have been delivered to the named port of shipment and passed over the ship's rail, plus costs of loading, carriage to the port of destination and normal unloading. Also to pay all costs relating to export in-

cluding duties, taxes and customs formalities.

7. **Notice to the Buyer**—Provide sufficient notice to the buyer that the goods have been delivered on board the named vessel.

8. **Proof of Delivery, Transport Documents**—Provide the buyer with a transport document that will allow the buyer to claim the goods at the destination and (unless otherwise agreed) allow the buyer to sell the goods while in transit through the transfer of the transport document or by notification to the sea carrier.

9. **Checking, Packing, Marking**—Pay all costs associated with checking the quality and quantity of the goods to be in conformity with the sales contract. Provide appropriate packing (unless the goods are traditionally delivered unpackaged) as required for the transport of the goods, to the extent that the buyer has made transport circumstances known to the seller prior to the execution of the sales contract. Provide marking appropriate to the packaging.

10. **Other**—Provide the buyer at the buyer's request, risk and cost any and all assistance in securing documentation originating in the country of export or of origin required for import and for transshipment.

## Buyer's Responsibilities (summary)

1. **Payment**—Pay for the goods as provided in the sales contract.

2. **Licenses and Customs Formalities**—Obtain and pay costs of all import licenses and authorizations and carry out all import formalities.

3. **Carriage and Insurance**—No obligation to the seller to pay for carriage or insurance.

4. **Taking Delivery**—Take delivery of the goods at the port of destination as provided in the sales contract.

5. **Risk Transfer**—Assume all risk of loss or damage from the time the goods have passed over the ship's rail at the port of shipment.

6. **Costs**—Pay all supplemental costs for the goods once they have passed over the ship's rail at the port of shipment, including unloading, lighterage and wharfage at the port of destination. Pay all costs relating to import formalities including duties, taxes and other charges including transshipment.

7. **Notice to Seller**—If, according to the sales contract, the buyer is able to specify a time for shipping and/or specify a port of destination, to give the seller sufficient notice.

8. **Proof of Delivery, Transport Document**—Accept the seller's transport document so long as it is in conformity with the sales contract.

9. **Inspection(s)**—Pay for the costs of pre-shipment inspection except inspections required by the country of export.

10. **Other**—Pay costs of securing documentation from the country of origin or export as required for import. Reimburse seller such costs. Provide information necessary to obtain insurance.

INCOTERMS

# INCOTERMS

## CPT
## Carriage Paid To (. . . named place of destination)

SELLER ⟶
BUYER ⇢

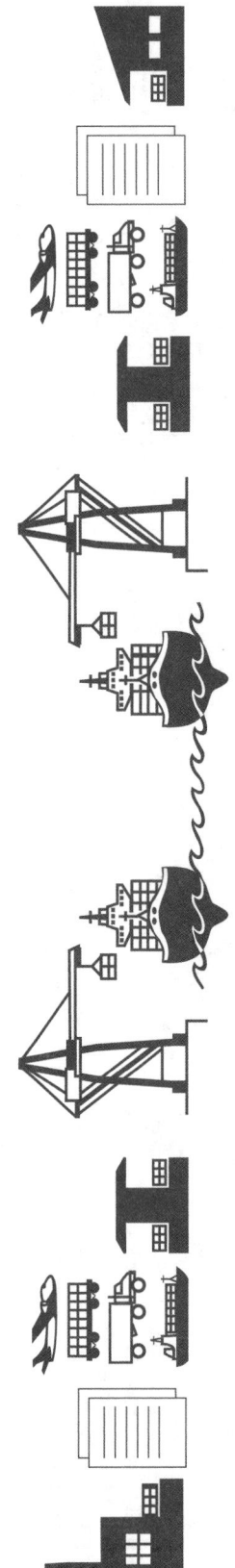

| Seller/ Exporter Premises | Export Documents/ Formalities | Delivered (to carrier) at Named Place/Port of: Frontier/Terminal/Quay | Loading Place/Port of Shipment | Onboard Ship's Rail | Onboard Ship's Rail | Discharging Place/Port of Arrival | Delivery at Named Place/ Port of Destination: Frontier/Terminal/Quay | Import Documents/ Formalities | Buyer/ Importer Premises |
|---|---|---|---|---|---|---|---|---|---|
| SELLER'S RISKS | | | | | | | | BUYER'S RISKS | |
| SELLER'S COSTS | | | | | | | | BUYER'S COSTS | |

BUYER'S and SELLER'S INSURABLE INTEREST*

## CPT Carriage Paid To (...named place of destination)

In Carriage Paid To, the seller/exporter/manufacturer clears the goods for export, delivers them to the carrier, and is responsible for paying for carriage to the named place of destination. However, once the seller delivers the goods to the carrier, the buyer becomes responsible for all additional costs.

In Incoterms 2000 the seller is also responsible for the costs of unloading, customs clearance, duties, and other costs if such costs are included in the cost of carriage such as in small package courier delivery.

The seller is not responsible for procuring and paying for insurance cover.

The CPT term is valid for any form of transport including multimodal.

The "named place of destination" in CPT and all "C" terms is domestic to the buyer, but is not necessarily the final delivery point.

The Carriage Paid To term is often used in sales where the shipment is by air freight, containerized ocean freight, courier shipments of small parcels, and in "ro-ro" (roll-on, roll-off) shipments of motor vehicles.

A "carrier" can be a shipping line, airline, trucking firm, railway or also an individual or firm who undertakes to procure carriage by any of the above methods of transport including multimodal. Therefore, a person, such as a freight forwarder, can act as a "carrier" under this term. If subsequent carriers are used for the carriage to the agreed destination, the risk passes when the goods have been delivered to the first carrier.

### *Insurance Note
While neither the buyer nor seller have obligation for providing insurance during the main voyage, both may have "insurable interest" and prudence may dictate purchase of insurance coverage.

# CPT
## Carriage Paid To ( . . . named place of destination)

### Incoterm Category

**CPT is a "C" Incoterm** where the seller is responsible for contracting and paying for carriage of the goods, but not responsible for additional costs or risk of loss or damage to the goods once they have been shipped. C terms evidence "shipment" (as opposed to "arrival") contracts.

### Modes of Transport Covered

All modes of transport including multimodal.

### Seller's Responsibilities (summary)

1. **Goods**—Provide the goods, commercial invoice or electronic message, and other documentation as required by the sales contract.

2. **Licenses and Customs Formalities**—Obtain at own risk and cost any export licenses and authorizations and carry out all export formalities and procedures.

3. **Carriage and Insurance**—Contract for and pay all costs of carriage to the agreed point at the named place of destination. No obligation to provide insurance.

4. **Delivery**—Deliver the goods to the carrier (or first of multiple carriers) for carriage to the named place of destination within the time period stipulated in the sales contract.

5. **Risk Transfer**—Assume all risks of loss or damage to the goods until they have been delivered to the carrier or first of multiple carriers.

6. **Costs**—Pay all costs until the goods have been delivered to the carrier plus costs of loading, carriage to the place of destination and normal unloading. Also to pay all costs related to export including duties, taxes and customs formalities. Pay the costs of unloading, customs clearance, duties, and other costs if such costs are included in the cost of carriage.

7. **Notice to the Buyer**—Provide sufficient notice to the buyer that the goods have been delivered to the carrier.

8. **Proof of Delivery, Transport Documents**—Provide the buyer with a transport document.

9. **Checking, Packing, Marking**—Pay all costs associated with checking the quality and quantity of the goods to be in conformity with the sales contract. Provide appropriate packing (unless the goods are traditionally delivered unpackaged) as required for the transport of the goods, to the extent that the buyer has made transport circumstances known to the seller prior to the execution of the sales contract. Provide marking appropriate to the packaging.

10. **Other**—Provide the buyer at the buyer's request, risk and expense any and all assistance in securing documentation originating in the country of export or of origin required for import and for transshipment (as necessary). Provide the buyer at the buyer's request information necessary to obtain insurance.

### Buyer's Responsibilities (summary)

1. **Payment**—Pay for the goods as provided in the sales contract.

2. **Licenses and Customs Formalities**—Obtain and pay costs of all import licenses and authorizations and carry out all import formalities.

3. **Carriage and Insurance**—No obligation to the seller for either carriage or insurance.

4. **Taking Delivery**—Take delivery of the goods from the carrier at the place of destination as provided in the sales contract.

5. **Risk Transfer**—Assume all risk of loss or damage from the time the goods have been delivered to the carrier by the seller.

6. **Costs**—Pay all additional costs (not covered in the seller's contract of carriage in Seller's #6) for the goods once they have been delivered to the carrier, including unloading, lighterage and wharfage at the place of destination. Pay all costs relating to import formalities including duties, taxes and other charges including transshipment.

7. **Notice to Seller**—If, according to the sales contract, the buyer is able to specify a time for shipping and/or specify a place of destination, to give the seller sufficient notice.

8. **Proof of Delivery, Transport Document**—Accept the seller's transport document so long as it is in conformity with the sales contract.

9. **Inspection(s)**—Pay for the costs of pre-shipment inspection(s) except inspections required by the country of export.

10. **Other**—Pay all costs associated with securing documentation from the country of origin or export as required for import. Reimburse seller for costs in providing such documentation or assistance.

INCOTERMS

# CIP
## Carriage and Insurance Paid To (... named place of destination)

**SELLER** → **BUYER** ⇢

INCOTERMS

| Seller/ Exporter Premises | Export Documents/ Formalities | Delivered (to carrier) at Named Place/Port of: Frontier/Terminal/Quay | Loading Place/Port of Shipment | Onboard Ship's Rail | Onboard Ship's Rail | Discharging Place/Port of Arrival | Delivery at Named Place/ Port of Destination: Frontier/Terminal/Quay | Import Documents/ Formalities | Buyer/ Importer Premises |
|---|---|---|---|---|---|---|---|---|---|
| **SELLER'S RISKS** | | | | | | | | **BUYER'S RISKS** | |
| **SELLER'S COSTS** | | | | | | | | **BUYER'S COSTS** | |
| | | | | **BUYER'S INSURABLE INTEREST\*** | | | | | |

## CIP Carriage and Insurance Paid To (...named place of destination)

In Carriage and Insurance Paid To, the seller/exporter clears the goods for export, delivers them to the carrier, and is responsible for paying for carriage and insurance to the named place of destination. However, once the goods are delivered to the carrier, the buyer is responsible for all additional costs.

In Incoterms 2000 the seller is also responsible for the costs of unloading, customs clearance, duties, and other costs if such costs are included in the cost of carriage such as in small package courier delivery.

The seller is responsible for procuring and paying for insurance cover.

The CIP term is valid for any form of transport including multimodal.

The "named place of destination" in CIP and all "C" terms is domestic to the buyer, but is not necessarily the final delivery point.

The Carriage and Insurance Paid To term is often used in sales where the shipment is by air freight, containerized ocean freight, courier shipments of small parcels, and in "ro-ro" (roll-on, roll-off) shipments of motor vehicles. A "carrier" can be a shipping line, airline, trucking firm, railway or also an individual or firm who undertakes to procure carriage by any of the above methods of transport including multimodal. Therefore, a person, such as a freight forwarder, can act as a "carrier" under this term. If subsequent carriers are used for the carriage to the agreed destination, the risk passes when the goods have been delivered to the first carrier.

### *Insurance Note
While the seller is responsible for insurance coverage during the main voyage, the buyer may have additional "insurable interest" and prudence may dictate purchase of additional coverage.

# CIP
# Carriage and Insurance Paid To (... named place of destination)

## Incoterm Category

**CIP is a "C" Incoterm** where the seller is responsible for contracting and paying for carriage and insurance of the goods, but not responsible for additional costs or risk of loss or damage to the goods once they have been shipped. C terms evidence "shipment" (as opposed to "arrival") contracts.

## Modes of Transport Covered

All modes of transport including multimodal.

## Seller's Responsibilities (summary)

1. **Goods**—Provide the goods, commercial invoice or electronic message, and other documentation as required by the sales contract.

2. **Licenses and Customs Formalities**—Obtain at own risk and cost any export licenses and authorizations and carry out all export formalities and procedures.

3. **Carriage and Insurance**—Contract for and pay all costs of carriage and insurance to the named place of destination. The insurance policy or document must allow the buyer to make a claim directly from the insurer. Deliver the insurance document to the buyer.

4. **Delivery**—Deliver the goods to the carrier (or first of multiple carriers) for carriage to the named place of destination within the time period stipulated in the sales contract.

5. **Risk Transfer**—Assume all risks of loss or damage to the goods until they have been delivered to the carrier or first of multiple carriers.

6. **Costs**—Pay all costs until the goods have been delivered to the carrier, plus costs of loading, carriage, insurance to the named place of destination plus normal unloading. Also to pay all costs relating to export including duties, taxes and customs

formalities. Pay the costs of unloading, customs clearance, duties, and other costs if such costs are included in the cost of carriage.

7. **Notice to the Buyer**—Provide sufficient notice to the buyer that the goods have been delivered to the carrier.

8. **Proof of Delivery, Transport Documents**—Provide the buyer with a transport document.

9. **Checking, Packing, Marking**—Pay all costs associated with checking the quality and quantity of the goods to be in conformity with the sales contract. Provide appropriate packing (unless the goods are traditionally delivered unpackaged) as required for the transport of the goods, to the extent that the buyer has made transport circumstances known to the seller prior to the execution of the sales contract. Provide marking appropriate to the packaging.

10. **Other**—Provide the buyer at the buyer's request, risk and expense any and all assistance in securing documentation originating in the country of export or of origin required for import and for transshipment (as necessary). Provide the buyer with information necessary to procure additional insurance.

## Buyer's Responsibilities (summary)

1. **Payment**—Pay for the goods as provided in the sales contract.

2. **Licenses and Customs Formalities**—Obtain and pay costs of all import licenses and authorizations and carry out all import formalities.

3. **Carriage and Insurance**—No obligation to the seller for either carriage or insurance.

4. **Taking Delivery**—Take delivery of the goods from the carrier at the place of destination as provided in the sales contract.

5. **Risk Transfer**—Assume all risk of loss or damage from the time the goods have been delivered to the carrier by the seller.

6. **Costs**—Pay all additional costs (not covered in the seller's contract of carriage in Seller's #6) for the goods once they have been delivered to the carrier, including unloading, lighterage and wharfage at the place of destination. Pay all costs relating to import formalities including duties, taxes and other charges including transshipment.

7. **Notice to Seller**—If, according to the sales contract, the buyer is able to specify a time for shipping and/or specify a place of destination, to give the seller sufficient notice.

8. **Proof of Delivery, Transport Document**—Accept the seller's transport document so long as it is in conformity with the sales contract.

9. **Inspection(s)**—Pay for the costs of pre-shipment inspection(s) except inspections required by the country of export.

10. **Other**—Pay all costs associated with securing documentation from the country of origin or export required for import. Reimburse seller for costs in providing such documentation or assistance.

INCOTERMS

**INCOTERMS**

# DAF
## Delivered At Frontier (. . . named place)

SELLER →     BUYER ▪ ▪ ▪ ▶

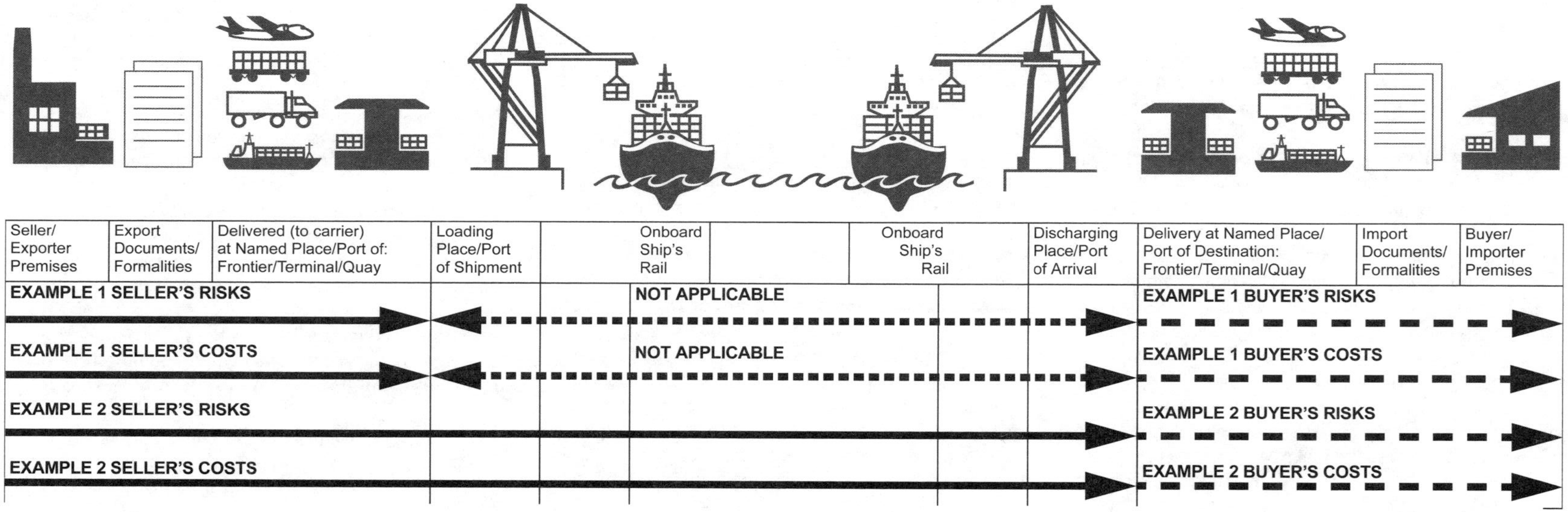

| Seller/ Exporter Premises | Export Documents/ Formalities | Delivered (to carrier) at Named Place/Terminal/Quay | Loading Place/Port of Shipment | Onboard Ship's Rail | Onboard Ship's Rail | Discharging Place/Port of Arrival | Delivery at Named Place/ Port of Destination: Frontier/Terminal/Quay | Import Documents/ Formalities | Buyer/ Importer Premises |
|---|---|---|---|---|---|---|---|---|---|
| | EXAMPLE 1 SELLER'S RISKS | | | NOT APPLICABLE | | | EXAMPLE 1 BUYER'S RISKS | | |
| | EXAMPLE 1 SELLER'S COSTS | | | NOT APPLICABLE | | | EXAMPLE 1 BUYER'S COSTS | | |
| | EXAMPLE 2 SELLER'S RISKS | | | | | | EXAMPLE 2 BUYER'S RISKS | | |
| | EXAMPLE 2 SELLER'S COSTS | | | | | | EXAMPLE 2 BUYER'S COSTS | | |

## DAF Delivered At Frontier (...named place)

In Delivered At Frontier, the seller/exporter/manufacturer clears the goods for export and is responsible for making them available to the buyer at the named point and place at the frontier, not unloaded, and not cleared for import.

In the DAF term, naming the precise point, place, and time of availability at the frontier is very important as the buyer must make arrangements to unload and secure the goods in a timely manner.

Frontier can mean any frontier including the frontier of export.

The DAF term is valid for any mode of shipment, so long as the final shipment to the named place at the frontier is by land.

The seller is not responsible for procuring and paying for insurance cover.

### Example 1

DAF Laredo, Texas. Seller is in Dallas, Texas, buyer is in Mexico City, Mexico. The shipment travels by truck from Dallas to the frontier at Laredo, Texas USA where the buyer takes possession and trucks the goods to Mexico City.

### Example 2

DAF Basel Switzerland. Seller is in Dallas, Texas, buyer is in Bern Switzerland. The shipment travels by truck from Dallas to Port Arthur, by ship to Le Havre, France and then by rail to the frontier in Basel where the buyer takes possession and transports the goods to the city of Bern.

# DAF
# Delivered at Frontier (. . . named place)

## Incoterm Category

DAF is a "D" Incoterm where the seller is responsible for all costs associated with delivering the goods to the named point and place of destination. "D" terms evidence "arrival" (as opposed to "shipment") contracts.

## Modes of Transport Covered

Used for all modes of transport so long as the final shipment to the named place at the frontier is by land.

## Seller's Responsibilities (summary)

1. **Goods**—Provide the goods, commercial invoice or electronic message, and other documentation as required by the sales contract.
2. **Licenses and Customs Formalities**—a) Obtain at own risk and cost any export licenses and authorizations required to enable the buyer to deal with export formalities at the named frontier. And, if transshipped, b) Carry out all export formalities and procedures required to bring the goods to the named frontier.
3. **Carriage and Insurance**—Contract for and pay all costs of carriage and transshipment (if necessary) to the named place. No obligation to provide insurance.
4. **Delivery**—Make the goods available to the buyer unloaded at the frontier at the named point and place and on the date or period specified in the sales contract.
5. **Risk Transfer**—Assume all risks of loss or damage to the goods until they have been made available to the buyer at the named point place and time at the frontier.
6. **Costs**—Pay all costs until the goods have been delivered at the frontier, including carriage, and all prior to delivery export formalities.
7. **Notice to the Buyer**—Provide sufficient notice of dispatch and projected arrival that the buyer can take appropriate action to arrange pick-up of the goods.
8. **Proof of Delivery, Transport Documents**—Provide the buyer with documentary evidence of delivery at the frontier. At the buyer's request, risk and cost, provide a through document of transport to the named place of destination.
9. **Checking, Packing, Marking**—Pay all costs associated with checking the quality and quantity of the goods to be in conformity with the sales contract. Provide appropriate packing (unless the goods are traditionally delivered unpackaged) as required for the transport of the goods, to the extent that the buyer has made transport circumstances known to the seller prior to the execution of the sales contract. Provide marking appropriate to the packaging.
10. **Other**—Provide the buyer at the buyer's request, risk and expense any and all assistance in securing documentation originating in the country of export or of origin required for import. Provide the buyer with information necessary to obtain insurance.

## Buyer's Responsibilities (summary)

1. **Payment**—Pay for the goods as provided in the sales contract.
2. **Licenses and Customs Formalities**—Obtain and pay costs of all import licenses and authorizations and carry out all import formalities.
3. **Carriage and Insurance**—No obligation to the seller for either carriage or insurance.
4. **Taking Delivery**—Take delivery of the goods once they are made available at the frontier.
5. **Risk Transfer**—Assume all risk of loss or damage from the time the goods have been delivered at the named point, place and time at the frontier.
6. **Costs**—Pay all costs for the goods once they have been delivered to the frontier including unloading. Pay all costs relating to import formalities including duties, taxes and formalities. Pay for transport from the frontier to the final destination.
7. **Notice to Seller**—If, according to the sales contract, the buyer is able to specify a time for and/or a place of delivery, to give the seller sufficient notice.
8. **Proof of Delivery, Transport Document**—Accept the seller's transport document so long as it is in conformity with the sales contract.
9. **Inspection(s)**—Pay for the costs of pre-shipment inspection(s) except inspections required by the country of export.
10. **Other**—Pay all costs associated with securing documentation from the country of origin or export required for import. Reimburse seller for costs in providing such documentation or assistance. Provide the seller with any authorizations, permits, documents or other information required for obtaining a through transport document.

INCOTERMS

**INCOTERMS**

# DES
## Delivered Ex Ship (. . . named port of destination)

SELLER →   BUYER →

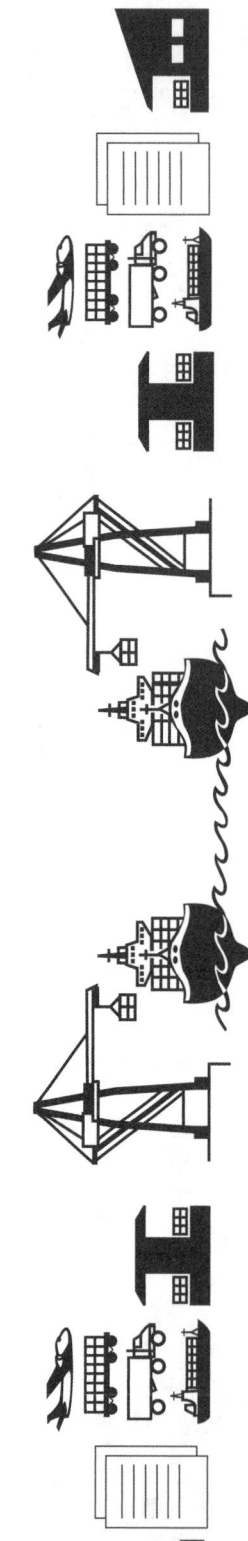

| Seller/ Exporter Premises | Export Documents/ Formalities | Delivered (to carrier) at Named Place/Port of: Frontier/Terminal/Quay | Loading Place/Port of Shipment | Onboard Ship's Rail | | Onboard Ship's Rail | Discharging Place/Port of Arrival | Delivery at Named Place/ Port of Destination: Frontier/Terminal/Quay | Import Documents/ Formalities | Buyer/ Importer Premises |
|---|---|---|---|---|---|---|---|---|---|---|
| **SELLER'S RISKS** | | | | | | | | **BUYER'S RISKS** | | |
| **SELLER'S COSTS** | | | | | | | | **BUYER'S COSTS** | | |

## DES Delivered Ex Ship (...named port of destination)

In Delivered Ex Ship, the seller/exporter/manufacturer clears the goods for export and is responsible for making them available to the buyer on board the ship at the named port of destination, not cleared for import.

The seller is thus responsible for all costs of getting the goods to the named port of destination prior to unloading.

The DES term is used only for shipments of goods by ocean or inland waterway or by multimodal transport where the final delivery is made on a vessel at the named port of destination.

All forms of payment are used in DES transactions.

*Examples*
DES Delivered Ex Ship Port of Calcutta
DES Delivered Ex Ship Port of New York

# DES
## Delivered Ex Ship (... named port of destination)

### Incoterm Category

DES is a "D" Incoterm where the seller is responsible for all costs associated with delivering the goods to the named port of destination. "D" terms evidence "arrival" (as opposed to "shipment") contracts.

### Modes of Transport Covered

Used only for ocean or inland waterway transport.

### Seller's Responsibilities (summary)

1. **Goods**—Provide the goods, commercial invoice or electronic message, and other documentation as required by the sales contract.

2. **Licenses and Customs Formalities**—Obtain at own risk and cost any export licenses and authorizations and carry out all export formalities and procedures, including those associated with transshipment to the named port of destination.

3. **Carriage and Insurance**—Contract for and pay all costs of carriage and transshipment (if necessary) to the named place and port of destination. No obligation to provide insurance.

4. **Delivery**—Make the goods available to the buyer uncleared for import on board the vessel at the named place and port on the date or within the time period specified in the sales contract.

5. **Risk Transfer**—Assume all risks of loss or damage to the goods until they have been made available to the buyer at the named place and port.

6. **Costs**—Pay all costs until the goods have been delivered, including all export formalities, carriage and transshipment (if necessary) to the named place and port.

7. **Notice to the Buyer**—Provide sufficient notice of dispatch and projected arrival that the buyer can take appropriate action to arrange pick-up of the goods.

8. **Proof of Delivery, Transport Documents**—Pro-vide the buyer with the delivery order and/or a trans-port document enabling the buyer to take delivery of the goods at the port of destination.

9. **Checking, Packing, Marking**—Pay all costs asso-ciated with checking the quality and quantity of the goods to be in conformity with the sales contract. Provide appropriate packing (unless the goods are traditionally delivered unpackaged) as required for the transport of the goods, to the extent that the buyer has made transport circumstances known to the seller prior to the execution of the sales contract. Provide marking appropriate to the packaging.

10. **Other**—Provide the buyer at the buyer's request, risk and expense any and all assistance in securing docu-mentation originating in the country of export or of origin required for import. Provide the buyer with in-formation necessary to obtain insurance.

### Buyer's Responsibilities (summary)

1. **Payment**—Pay for the goods as provided in the sales contract.

2. **Licenses and Customs Formalities**—Obtain and pay costs of all import licenses and authorizations and carry out all import formalities.

3. **Carriage and Insurance**—No obligation to the seller for either carriage or insurance.

4. **Taking Delivery**—Take delivery of the goods once they are made available at the port.

5. **Risk Transfer**—Assume all risk of loss or damage from the time the goods have been made available at the port.

6. **Costs**—Pay all costs for the goods once they have been made available at the port including unloading. Pay all costs relating to import formalities including duties, taxes and other charges.

7. **Notice to Seller**—If, according to the sales contract, the buyer is able to specify a time for and/or a place of delivery, to give the seller sufficient notice.

8. **Proof of Delivery, Transport Document**—Accept the seller's transport document so long as it is in con-formity with the sales contract.

9. **Inspection(s)**—Pay for the costs of pre-shipment in-spection(s) except inspections required by the country of export.

10. **Other**—Pay all costs associated with securing docu-mentation from the country of origin or export re-quired for import. Reimburse seller for costs in providing such documentation or assistance.

# DEQ
## Delivered Ex Quay (. . . named port of destination)

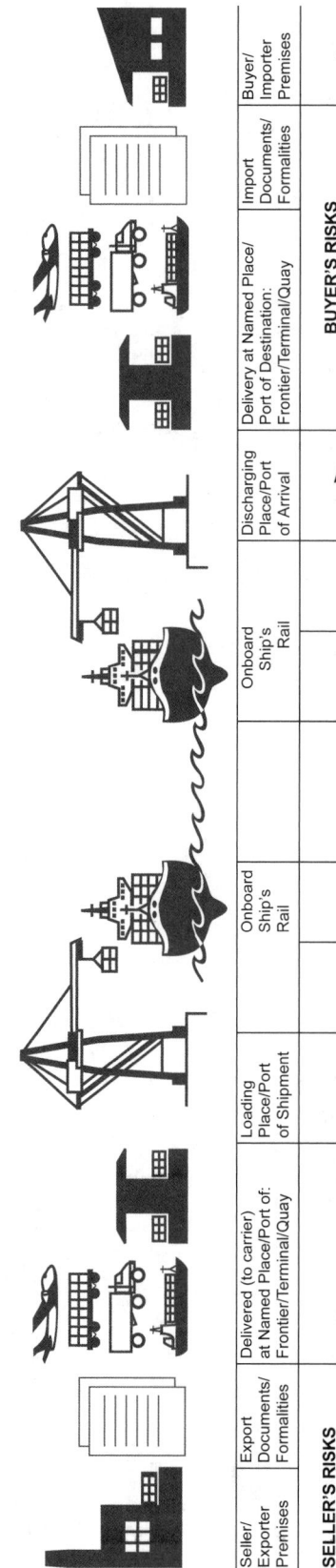

| Seller/ Exporter Premises | Export Documents/ Formalities | Delivered (to carrier) at Named Place/Port of: Frontier/Terminal/Quay | Loading Place/Port of Shipment | Onboard Ship's Rail | | Onboard Ship's Rail | Discharging Place/Port of Arrival | Delivery at Named Place/ Port of Destination: Frontier/Terminal/Quay | Import Documents/ Formalities | Buyer/ Importer Premises |
|---|---|---|---|---|---|---|---|---|---|---|
| SELLER'S RISKS | | | | | | | | BUYER'S RISKS | | |
| SELLER'S COSTS | | | | | | | | BUYER'S COSTS | | |

## DEQ Delivered Ex Quay (...named port of destination)

In Delivered Ex Quay, the seller/exporter/manufacturer clears the goods for export and is responsible for making them available to the buyer on the quay (wharf) at the named port of destination, not cleared for import.

The buyer, therefore, assumes all responsibilities for import clearance, duties, and other costs upon import as well as transport to the final destination. This is new for Incoterms 2000.

The DEQ term is used only for shipments of goods arriving at the port of destination by ocean or by inland waterway.

All forms of payment are used in DEQ transactions.

### Examples

DEQ Delivered Ex Quay Alexandria Egypt
DEQ Delivered Ex Quay Stockholm Sweden

# DEQ
# Delivered Ex Quay (. . . named port of destination)

## Incoterm Category

DEQ is a "D" Incoterm where the seller is responsible for all costs associated with delivering the goods to the quay (wharf) at the named port of destination. "D" terms evidence "arrival" (as opposed to "shipment") contracts.

## Modes of Transport Covered

Used only for ocean or inland waterway transport.

## Seller's Responsibilities (summary)

1. **Goods**—Provide the goods, commercial invoice or electronic message, and other documentation as required by the sales contract.

2. **Licenses and Customs Formalities**—Obtain at own risk and cost any export licenses and authorizations and carry out all export formalities and procedures, including those associated with transshipment to the named port of destination.

3. **Carriage and Insurance**—Contract for and pay all costs of carriage and transshipment (if necessary) to the named place, port and quay (wharf) of destination. No obligation to provide insurance.

4. **Delivery**—Make the goods available to the buyer at the named port and quay on the date or within the period specified in the sales contract.

5. **Risk Transfer**—Assume all risks of loss or damage to the goods until they have been made available to the buyer at the named port and quay (wharf).

6. **Costs**—Pay all costs until the goods have been delivered, including carriage, unloading, all export and import formalities, duties and taxes and transshipment (if necessary) to the named port and quay (wharf).

7. **Notice to the Buyer**—Provide sufficient notice of dispatch and projected arrival that the buyer can take appropriate action to arrange pick-up of the goods.

8. **Transport Documents**—Provide the buyer with the delivery order and/or a transport document enabling the buyer to take possession at the port of destination.

9. **Checking, Packing, Marking**—Pay all costs associated with checking the quality and quantity of the goods to be in conformity with the sales contract. Provide appropriate packing (unless the goods are traditionally delivered unpackaged) as required for the transport of the goods, to the extent that the buyer has made transport circumstances known to the seller prior to the execution of the sales contract. Provide marking appropriate to the packaging.

10. **Other**—Pay all costs associated with securing documentation originating in the country of importation required to for import clearance of the goods. Provide the buyer with information necessary to obtain insurance.

## Buyer's Responsibilities (summary)

1. **Payment**—Pay for the goods as provided in the sales contract.

2. **Licenses and Customs Formalities**—Obtain and pay costs of all import licenses and authorizations and carry out all import formalities.

3. **Carriage and Insurance**—No obligation to the seller for either carriage or insurance.

4. **Taking Delivery**—Take delivery of the goods once they are made available at the quay.

5. **Risk Transfer**—Assume all risk of loss or damage from the time the goods have been made available at the quay wharf).

6. **Costs**—Pay all costs for the goods once they have been made available at the quay (wharf).

7. **Notice to Seller**—If, according to the sales contract, the buyer is able to specify a time for and/or a place of delivery, to give the seller sufficient notice.

8. **Proof of Delivery, Transport Document**—Accept the seller's delivery order or transport document so long as it is in conformity with the sales contract.

9. **Inspection(s)**—Pay for the costs of pre-shipment inspection(s) except inspections required by the country of export.

10. **Other**—Pay all costs associated with securing documentation from the country of origin or export required for import. Reimburse seller for costs in providing such documentation or assistance.

INCOTERMS

# DDU
## Delivered Duty Unpaid (. . . named place of destination)

| | SELLER | BUYER |
|--|--|--|

| Seller/ Exporter Premises | Export Documents/ Formalities | Delivered (to carrier) at Named Place/Port of: Frontier/Terminal/Quay | Loading Place/Port of Shipment | Onboard Ship's Rail | Onboard Ship's Rail | Discharging Place/Port of Arrival | Delivery at Named Place/Port of Destination: Frontier/Terminal/Quay | Import Documents/ Formalities | Buyer/ Importer Premises |
|--|--|--|--|--|--|--|--|--|--|
| SELLER'S RISKS | | | | | | | | BUYER'S RISKS | |
| SELLER'S COSTS | | | | | | | | BUYER'S COSTS | |

## DDU Delivered Duty Unpaid (...named place of destination)

In Delivered Duty Unpaid, the seller/exporter/manufacturer clears the goods for export and is responsible for making them available to the buyer at the named place of destination, not cleared for import.

The seller, therefore, assumes all responsibilities for delivering the goods to the named place of destination, but the buyer assumes all responsibility for import clearance, duties, administrative costs, and any other costs upon import as well as transport to the final destination.

The DDU term can be used for any mode of transport. However, if the seller and buyer desire that delivery should take place on board a sea vessel or on a quay (wharf), the DES or DEQ terms are recommended.

All forms of payment are used in DDU transactions.

The DDU term is used when the named place of destination (point of delivery) is other than the seaport or airport.

### Examples
DDU Delivered Duty Unpaid New York New York USA
DDU Delivered Duty Unpaid Hamburg Germany

# DDU
## Delivered Duty Unpaid (. . . named place of destination)

### Incoterm Category
**DES is a "D" Incoterm** where the seller is responsible for all costs associated with delivering the goods to the named point and place of destination. "D" terms evidence "arrival" (as opposed to "shipment") contracts.

### Modes of Transport Covered
All modes of transport including multimodal.

### Seller's Responsibilities (summary)
1. **Goods**—Provide the goods, commercial invoice or electronic message, and other documentation as required by the sales contract.
2. **Licenses and Customs Formalities**—Obtain at own risk and cost any export licenses and authorizations and carry out all export formalities and procedures, including those associated with transshipment to the named port of destination.
3. **Carriage and Insurance**—Contract for and pay all costs of carriage and transshipment (if necessary) to the named destination. No obligation to provide insurance.
4. **Delivery**—Make the goods available to the buyer at the named destination on the date or within the period specified in the sales contract.
5. **Risk Transfer**—Assume all risks of loss or damage to the goods until they have been made available to the buyer at the named destination.
6. **Costs**—Pay all costs until the goods have been delivered to the named destination, including carriage, all export formalities, export duties and taxes, and transshipment (if necessary) to the named destination.
7. **Notice to the Buyer**—Provide sufficient notice of dispatch and projected arrival that the buyer can take appropriate action to arrange pick-up of the goods.
8. **Proof of Delivery, Transport Documents**—Provide the buyer with the delivery order and/or a trans-

port document enabling the buyer to take delivery at the named place of destination.
9. **Checking, Packing, Marking**—Pay all costs associated with checking the quality and quantity of the goods to be in conformity with the sales contract. Provide appropriate packing (unless the goods are traditionally delivered unpackaged) as required for the transport of the goods, to the extent that the buyer has made transport circumstances known to the seller prior to the execution of the sales contract. Provide marking appropriate to the packaging.
10. **Other**—Provide the buyer at the buyer's request, risk and expense any and all assistance in securing documentation originating in the country of export or of origin required for import. Provide the buyer with information necessary to obtain insurance.

### Buyer's Responsibilities (summary)
1. **Payment**—Pay for the goods as provided in the sales contract.
2. **Licenses and Customs Formalities**—Obtain and pay costs of all import licenses, documentation and authorizations and carry out all import formalities.
3. **Carriage and Insurance**—No obligation to the seller for either carriage or insurance.
4. **Taking Delivery**—Take delivery of the goods once they are made available at the named destination.
5. **Risk Transfer**—Assume all risk of loss or damage from the time the goods have been made available at the named place of destination.
6. **Costs**—Pay all costs for the goods once they have been made available at the named place of destination. Pay all costs relating to import formalities including duties, taxes and other charges.
7. **Notice to Seller**—If, according to the sales contract, the buyer is able to specify a time for and/or a place of delivery, to give the seller sufficient notice.
8. **Proof of Delivery, Transport Document**—Accept the seller's transport document so long as it is in conformity with the sales contract.
9. **Inspection(s)**—Pay for the costs of pre-shipment inspection(s) except inspections required by the country of export.
10. **Other**—Pay all costs associated with securing documentation from the country of origin or export required for import. Reimburse seller for costs in providing such documentation or assistance.

**INCOTERMS**

# DDP
## Delivered Duty Paid (. . . named place of destination)

SELLER → BUYER

| Seller/ Exporter Premises | Export Documents Formalities | Delivered at named place of: Frontier/Terminal/Quay | Loading Port of Shipment | Onboard Ship's Rail | Onboard Ship's Rail | Discharging Port of Arrival | Delivery at named place of destination: Frontier/Terminal/Quay | Import Documents Formalities | Buyer/ Importer Premises |
|---|---|---|---|---|---|---|---|---|---|
| **SELLER'S RISKS** | | | | | | | | | **BUYER'S RISKS** |
| **SELLER'S COSTS** | | | | | | | | | **BUYER'S COSTS** |

## DDP Delivered Duty Paid (...named place of destination)

In Delivered Duty Paid, the seller/exporter/manufacturer clears the goods for export and is responsible for making them available to the buyer at the named place of destination, cleared for import, but not unloaded from the transport vehicle.

The seller, therefore, assumes all responsibilities for delivering the goods to the named place of destination, including all responsibility for import clearance, duties, and other costs payable upon import.

The DDP term can be used for any mode of transport.

All forms of payment are used in DDP transactions.

The DDP term is used when the named place of destination (point of delivery) is other than the seaport or airport.

### Examples
DDP Delivered Duty Paid Chicago USA
DDP Delivered Duty Paid VAT Unpaid Paris France

# DDP
# Delivered Duty Paid (. . . named place of destination)

## Incoterm Category

DDP is a "D" Incoterm where the seller is responsible for all costs associated with delivering the goods to the named point and place of destination. "D" terms evidence "arrival" (as opposed to "shipment") contracts.

## Modes of Transport Covered

All modes of transport including multimodal.

## Seller's Responsibilities (summary)

1. **Goods**—Provide the goods, commercial invoice or electronic message, and other documentation as required by the sales contract.
2. **Licenses and Customs Formalities**—Obtain at own risk and cost any export and import licenses and authorizations and carry out all export and import formalities and procedures, including those associated with transshipment to the named port of destination.
3. **Carriage and Insurance**—Contract for and pay all costs of carriage and transshipment (if necessary) to the named destination. No obligation to provide insurance.
4. **Delivery**—Make the goods available to the buyer not unloaded at the named destination on the date or within the period specified in the sales contract.
5. **Risk Transfer**—Assume all risks of loss or damage to the goods until they have been made available to the buyer at the named destination.
6. **Costs**—Pay all costs until the goods have been delivered to the named destination, including carriage, all export and import formalities and transshipment (if necessary) to the named destination.
7. **Notice to the Buyer**—Provide sufficient notice of dispatch and projected arrival that the buyer can take appropriate action to arrange unloading of the goods.
8. **Proof of Delivery, Transport Documents**—Pro-
vide the buyer with the delivery order and/or a transport document enabling the buyer to take delivery at the named place of destination.
9. **Checking, Packing, Marking**—Pay all costs associated with checking the quality and quantity of the goods to be in conformity with the sales contract. Provide appropriate packing (unless the goods are traditionally delivered unpackaged) as required for the transport of the goods, to the extent that the buyer has made transport circumstances known to the seller prior to the execution of the sales contract. Provide marking appropriate to the packaging.
10. **Other**—Pay all costs associated with securing documentation necessary for to make the goods available to the buyer at the named place of destination. Provide the buyer with information necessary to obtain insurance.

## Buyer's Responsibilities (summary)

1. **Payment**—Pay for the goods as provided in the sales contract.
2. **Licenses and Customs Formalities**—Provide the seller at the seller's request, risk and cost any and all assistance in securing licenses, documentation and authorizations necessary to import the goods.
3. **Carriage and Insurance**—No obligation to the seller for either carriage or insurance.
4. **Taking Delivery**—Take delivery of the goods once they are made available at the named destination.
5. **Risk Transfer**—Assume all risk of loss or damage from the time the goods have been made available at the named place of destination.
6. **Costs**—Pay all costs for the goods once they have been made available at the named place of destination.
7. **Notice to Seller**—If, according to the sales contract, the buyer is able to specify a time for and/or a place of delivery, to give the seller sufficient notice.
8. **Proof of Delivery, Transport Document**—Accept the seller's transport document so long as it is in conformity with the sales contract.
9. **Inspection(s)**—Pay for the costs of pre-shipment inspection(s) except inspections required by the country of export.
10. **Other**—Provide the seller, at the seller's request, risk and cost any and all assistance in securing import and other documentation necessary for the seller to make the goods available to buyer at the named destination.

**INCOTERMS**

# Guide to Letters of Credit[1]

## Letters of Credit Defined

A documentary credit is the written promise of a bank, undertaken on behalf of a buyer, to pay a seller the amount specified in the credit provided the seller complies with the terms and conditions set forth in the credit. The terms and conditions of a documentary credit revolve around two issues: (1) the presentation of documents that evidence title to goods shipped by the seller, and (2) payment.

In simple terms, banks act as intermediaries to collect payment from the buyer in exchange for the transfer of documents that enable the holder to take possession of the goods.

Documentary credits provide a high level of protection and security to both buyers and sellers engaged in international trade. The seller is assured that payment will be made by a party independent of the buyer so long as the terms and conditions of the credit are met. The buyer is assured that payment will be released to the seller only after the bank has received the title documents called for in the credit.

Documentary credits are so named because of the importance of documents in the transaction. Letter of credit (L/C) is the historic and popular term used for a documentary credit because such credits were and are transmitted in the form of a letter from the buyer's bank. Both "documentary credit" and "letter of credit" will be used for our discussions.

## Types of Credits

There are a number of different types of standard and special documentary credits. Each type contains a variety of features designed to meet the different needs of buyers, sellers, or the banks involved.

For example, standard documentary credits can be either revocable (may be cancelled by the buyer), or irrevocable (may not be cancelled by the buyer), or confirmed (a second bank, in addition to the buyer's bank, guarantees payment) or unconfirmed (payment guaranteed only by the issuing bank). The most popular variation for sellers is the irrevocable confirmed credit because it cannot be cancelled by the buyer, and a second bank (usually the seller's bank) adds its guarantee of payment to that of the buyer's bank. Standard credits are discussed later in this section.

Specialized credits include revolving credits, red clause credits, standby credits, transferable credits, and back-to-back credits. These are also discussed later in this section.

This section is designed as an introduction to letters of credit. It is not comprehensive. To learn more about letters of credit and other types of international payments see *A Short Course in International Payments*, also available from World Trade Press.

## Limitations of Letters of Credit

Although documentary credits provide good protection and are the preferred means of payment in many international transactions, they do have limitations. They do not, for example, ensure that the goods actually shipped are as ordered nor do they insulate buyers and sellers from other disagreements or complaints arising from their relationship. It is up to the parties to settle questions of this nature between themselves.

Advantages, disadvantages, and issues for both buyer and seller will be discussed later in this section. Please note that these issues can have a significant impact on a given transaction. An incomplete understanding of the subject can be more dangerous than no knowledge at all.

## Role of Banks

It is important to note, and not for the last time, that a fundamental principle of documentary credits is that banks deal in documents and not goods. Banks are responsible for issues relating to documents and the specific wording of the documentary credit as opposed to issues relating to the goods themselves.

Therefore, banks are not concerned if a shipment is in conformity with the documents, only that the documents are in conformity with the wording of the credit.

## The Uniform Customs and Practice

Although documentary credits, in one form or another, have been in use for a long time, questions arose about how to effect transactions in a practical, fair, and uniform manner.

The Uniform Customs and Practice for Documentary Credits (UCP) is the internationally recognized codification of rules unifying banking practice regarding documentary credits. The UCP was developed by a working committee attached to the International Chamber of Commerce (ICC) in Paris. It is revised and updated from time to time; the current valid version is ICC publication No. 500. See the Resources Appendix for contact information for the ICC.

---

1. This section has been excerpted from the book *A Short Course in International Payments*, ISBN 1-885073-50-X, also by Edward G. Hinkelman and available from World Trade Press.

## Parties to the Transaction

There are four main parties to a basic documentary letter of credit transaction. Note that each party has multiple names. The name used for each party to the transaction depends upon who is speaking. Businesspeople like to use the names buyer, seller, buyer's bank and seller's bank. The banks prefer to use the names applicant, beneficiary, issuing bank, and advising bank. The four parties are:

### The Buyer (Applicant/Importer)

The buyer initiates the documentary credit process by applying to his bank to open a documentary credit naming the seller as the beneficiary. The buyer, therefore, may be called the buyer in commercial terms, the importer in economic terms, and the applicant in banking terms. They are all one and the same.

### The Issuing (Buyer's) Bank

Upon instructions from the buyer, th e issuing bank (typically the buyer's regular business bank) issues a documentary credit naming the seller as the beneficiary and sends it to the advising bank (typically the seller's bank).

### The Advising (Seller's) Bank

Upon instructions from the issuing bank and the buyer, the advising bank (typically the seller's bank) advises the seller of the credit. The advising bank is typically the seller's regular business bank and is in the seller's country.

### The Seller (Beneficiary/Exporter)

The seller receives notification (advice) of the credit from the advising bank, complies with the terms and conditions of the credit, and gets paid. The seller is the beneficiary of the documentary credit. The seller, therefore, may be called the seller in commercial terms, the exporter in economic terms, and the beneficiary in banking terms. They are all one and the same.

## Basic Documentary Credit Procedure

Documentary credit procedure involves the step-by-step exchange of documents giving title to the goods for either cash or a contracted promise to pay at a later time. There are four basic steps in the procedure.

### Issuance

Issuance describes the process of the buyer's applying for and opening a documentary credit at the issuing bank and the issuing bank's formal notification of the seller through the advising bank.

### Amendment

Amendment describes the process whereby the terms and conditions of a documentary credit may be modified after the credit has been issued.

### Utilization

This describes the procedure for the seller's shipping of goods, transfer of documents from the seller to the buyer through the banks, and transfer of payment from the buyer to the seller through the banks (settlement).

### Settlement

Settlement (a subpart of utilization) describes the different ways in which payment may be effected to the seller from the buyer through the banks.

**Note:** Specific issues relating to applying for a credit, confirmed vs. unconfirmed credits, special types of credits, settlement, correspondent and confirming banks will be discussed later.

## Issuance

### Procedure

Refer to the diagram on the facing page for each numbered step.

### Buyer and Seller

1. The buyer and seller agree on the terms of sale: (a) specifying a documentary credit as the means of payment, (b) naming an advising bank (usually the seller's bank), and (c) listing required documents.

### Buyer (Applicant/Importer)

2. The buyer applies to his bank (issuing bank) and opens a documentary credit naming the seller as beneficiary based on specific terms and conditions that are listed in the credit.

### Issuing (Buyer's) Bank

3. The issuing bank sends the documentary credit to the advising bank named in the credit.

### Advising (Seller's) Bank

4. The advising bank informs (advises) the seller of the documentary credit.

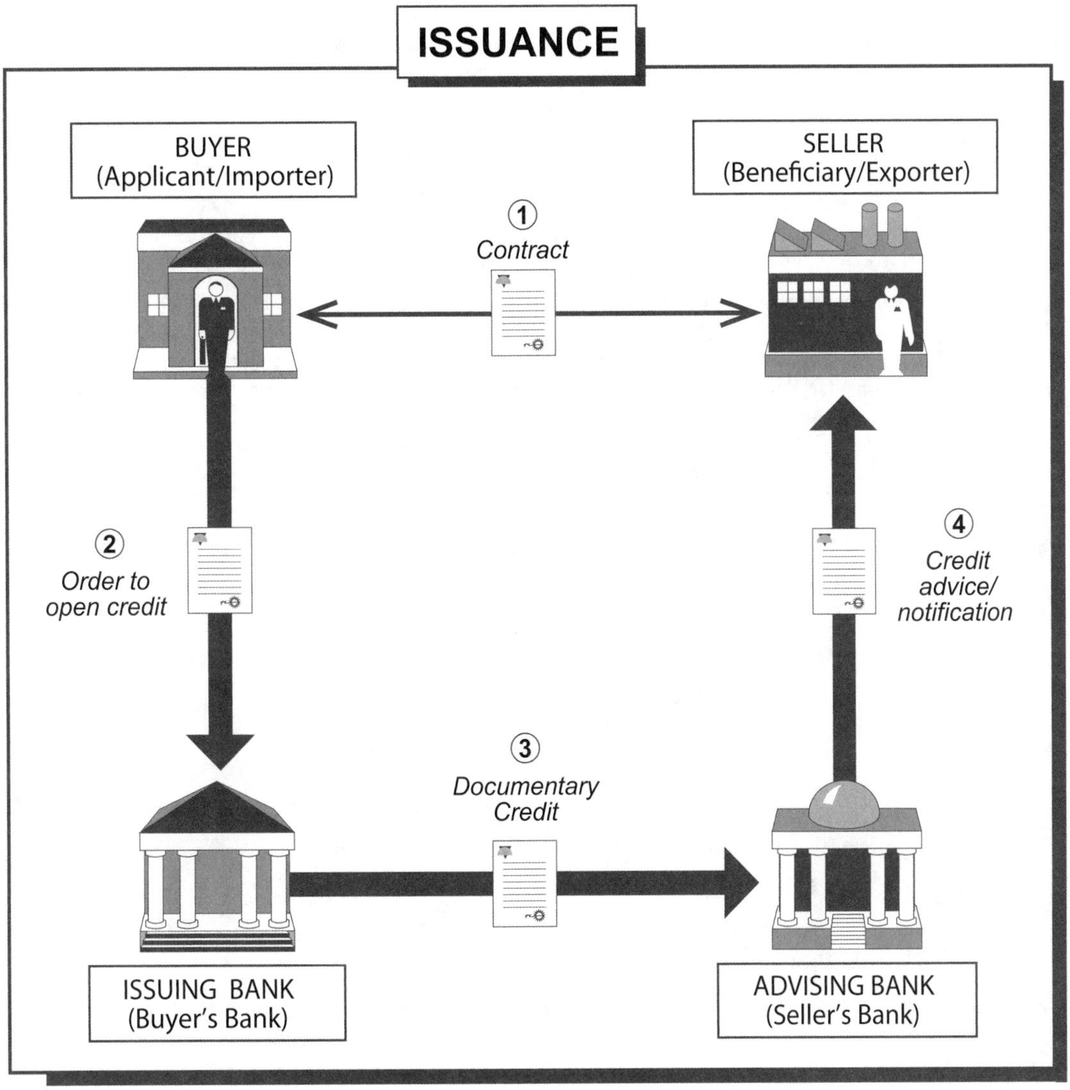

# ISSUANCE

BUYER
(Applicant/Importer)

SELLER
(Beneficiary/Exporter)

① Contract

② Order to
open credit

③ Documentary
Credit

④ Credit
advice/
notification

ISSUING BANK
(Buyer's Bank)

ADVISING BANK
(Seller's Bank)

## Amendment

When the seller receives the documentary credit it must be examined closely to determine if the terms and conditions (1) reflect the agreement of the buyer and seller, and (2) can be met within the time stipulated.

Upon examination, the seller may find problems. Some examples:

1. The seller might disagree with the terms and conditions. For example, the transaction price listed in the credit may be lower than the originally agreed upon price, or perhaps the buyer has specified that the total price is to include shipping, whereas the seller originally quoted a price without shipping.

2. The seller might find himself unable to meet specific requirements of the credit. For example, the time may be too short to effect shipment, or certain documents may not be available.

If the buyer still wants to proceed with the transaction, but with modification to the terms of the credit, he or she should contact the buyer immediately and request an amendment.

Amendments must be authorized by the buyer and issued by the issuing bank to the seller through the same channel as the original documentary letter of credit. This can be an involved undertaking so any amendments should be initiated only when necessary and as soon as a problem is identified.

### Procedure

Refer to the diagram on the facing page for each numbered step.

### Seller

1. The seller requests that the buyer make an amendment to the credit. This can be effected by a telephone call, a fax letter, or by face-to-face negotiation.

### Buyer

2. If the buyer agrees, the buyer orders the issuing bank to issue the amendment.

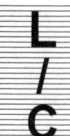

### Issuing Bank

3. The issuing bank amends the credit and notifies the advising bank of the amendment.

### Advising Bank

4. The advising bank notifies the seller of the amendment.

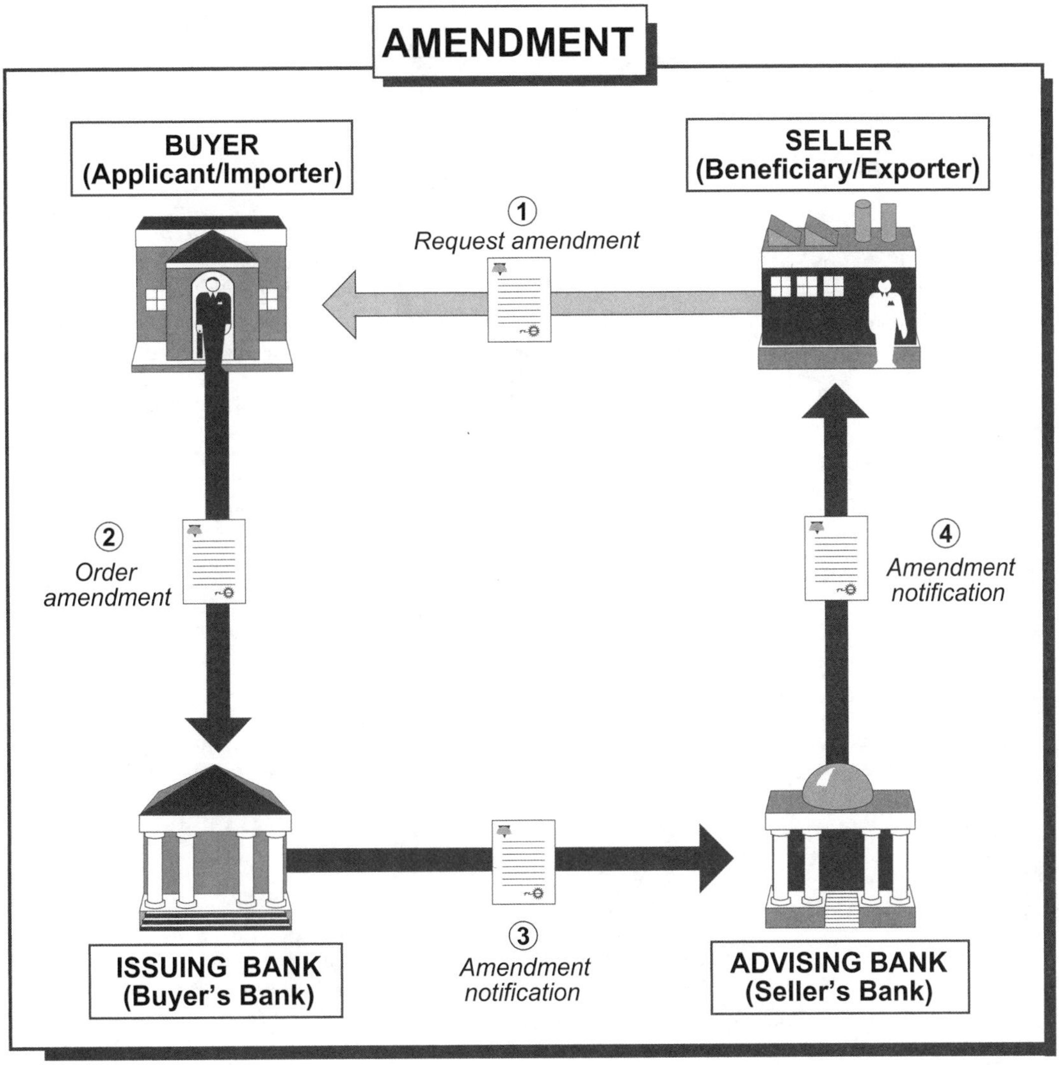

# AMENDMENT

**BUYER**
**(Applicant/Importer)**

**SELLER**
**(Beneficiary/Exporter)**

① Request amendment

② Order amendment

④ Amendment notification

**ISSUING BANK**
**(Buyer's Bank)**

③ Amendment notification

**ADVISING BANK**
**(Seller's Bank)**

L/C

# Utilization

### Procedure

Refer to the diagram on the facing page for each numbered step.

## Seller

1.  The seller (beneficiary) ships the goods to the buyer and obtains a negotiable transport document (negotiable bill of lading) from the shipping firm/agent.

2.  The seller prepares and presents a document package to his bank (the advising bank) consisting of (a) the negotiable transport document, and (b) other documents (e.g., commercial invoice, insurance document, certificate of origin, inspection certificate, etc.) as required by the buyer in the documentary credit.

## Advising Bank

3.  The advising bank (a) reviews the document package making certain the documents are in conformity with the terms of the credit and (b) pays the seller (based upon the terms of the credit).

4.  The advising bank sends the documentation package by mail or by courier to the issuing bank.

## Issuing Bank

5.  The issuing bank (a) reviews the document package making certain the documents are in conformity with the terms of the credit, (b) pays the advising bank (based upon the terms of the credit), and (c) advises the buyer that the documents have arrived.

## Buyer

6.  The buyer (a) reviews the document package making certain the documents are in conformity with the terms of the credit, and (b) makes a cash payment (signs a sight draft) to the issuing bank, or if the collection order allows, signs an acceptance (promise to pay at a future date).

## Issuing Bank

7.  The issuing bank sends the document package by mail or courier to the buyer who then takes possession of the shipment.

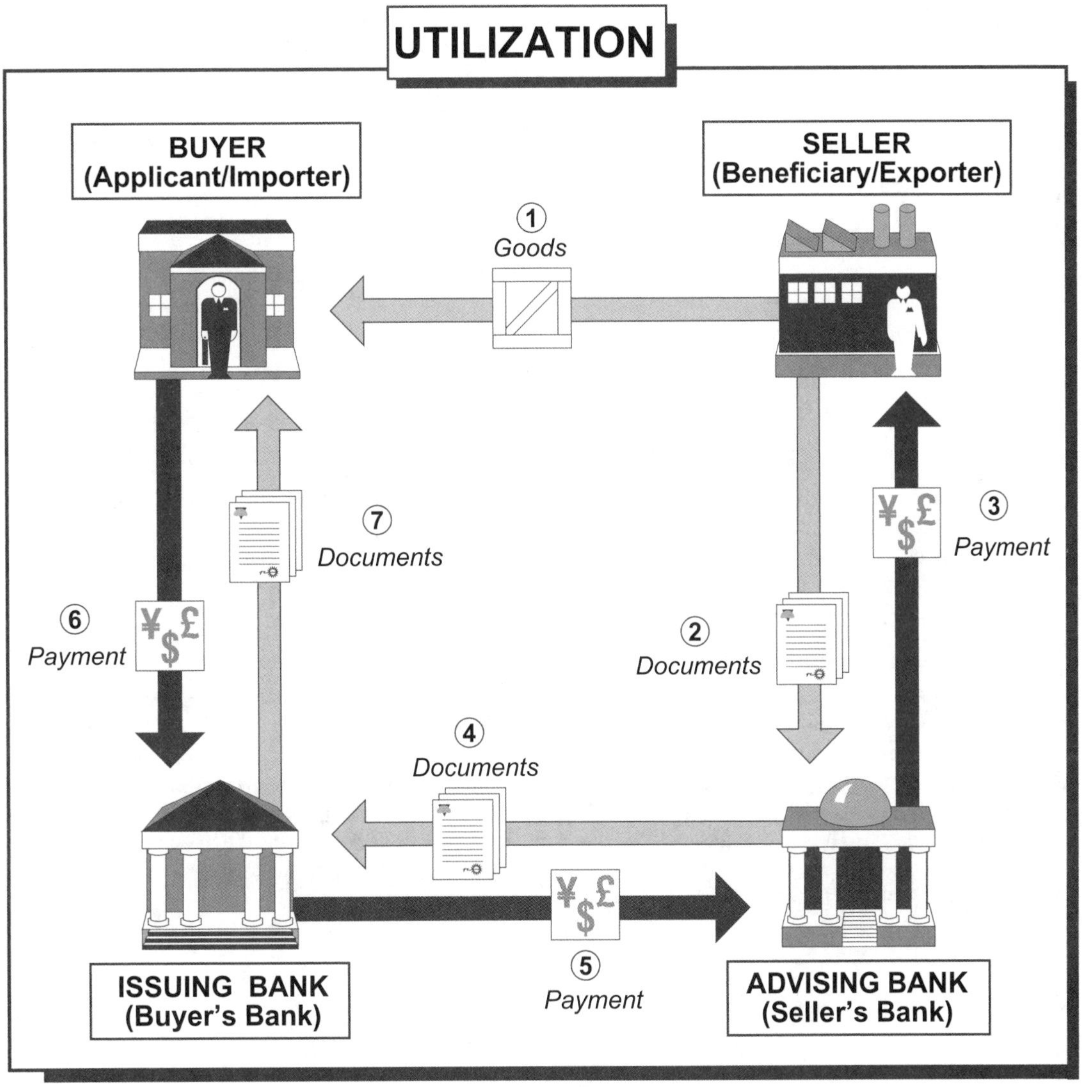

# UTILIZATION

**BUYER
(Applicant/Importer)**

**SELLER
(Beneficiary/Exporter)**

(1) *Goods*

(7) *Documents*

(3) *Payment*

(6) *Payment*

(2) *Documents*

(4) *Documents*

(5) *Payment*

**ISSUING  BANK
(Buyer's Bank)**

**ADVISING BANK
(Seller's Bank)**

## Settlement (Availability)

Settlement and availability refer to the availability of proceeds (funds) to the beneficiary (seller) after presentation of documents under the credit. Each of the following forms of payment availability must be specified in the original credit, and be accepted by the seller. For example, if the original agreement between the buyer and seller calls for a sight credit (immediate availability of funds to the seller) and a usance credit (funds available in 30, 60 or 90 days) is prescribed in the credit presented to the seller, the seller may reject the credit and the transaction.

### The Sight Credit (Settlement by Payment)

In a sight credit (confirmed sight credit) the value of the credit is available to the beneficiary as soon as the terms and conditions of the credit have been met (as soon as the prescribed document package has been presented to and checked by the confirming bank). When foreign exchange is at issue, several days may pass between the time of beneficiary's presentation of documents and the actual transfer of funds to the beneficiary's account.

In a sight credit (unconfirmed), the value of the credit is made available to the beneficiary once the advising bank has received the funds from the issuing bank.

### The Usance Credit (Settlement by Acceptance)

In a usance credit the beneficiary presents the required document package to the bank along with a time draft drawn on the issuing, advising, or a third bank for the value of the credit. Once the documents have made their way to the buyer and found to be in order, the draft is accepted by the bank upon which it is drawn (the draft is now called an acceptance) and it is returned to the seller who holds it until maturity.

The seller has the option of selling the acceptance by discounting its value. The discount charged will be in some proportion to the time to maturity of the draft and the perceived risk associated with its collection. The buyer pays the draft at maturity to its holder.

### The Deferred Payment Credit (Settlement by Negotiation)

In a deferred payment credit the buyer accepts the documents and agrees to pay the bank after a set period of time. Essentially, this gives the buyer time (a grace period) between delivery of the goods and payment. The issuing bank makes the payment at the specified time, when the terms and conditions of the credit have been met.

Deferred payment credits are often used in transactions involving food or drugs that require inspection prior to import and approval by a government agency. In this case the bank will release the documents to the importer/buyer against a trust receipt. The bank holds the title documents to the goods and still owns the merchandise. Once the goods have been approved by the government agency, the bank transfers the titles documents to the buyer, charges the buyer's account, and pays the seller.

L
/
C

# Opening a Documentary Credit

## The Importance of Wording

The success or failure of a documentary credit transaction can turn upon the wording of the documentary credit itself. As such, the buyer (whose responsibility it is to open the credit) should adhere to the greatest extent possible to the terms and conditions of the original contractual agreement, keeping the specifications clear and concise and as simple as possible.

## Refer to Documents

The buyer's instructions to the issuing bank should be given in clear, professional wording, and should pertain only to documentation, not to the goods themselves. It is very important to demand documents in the credit that clearly reflect the agreements reached.

**Example 1:** Require confirmation that goods are shipped by Conference vessel no more than twenty years old, rather than that the goods be shipped by Conference vessel no more than twenty years old.

**Example 2:** Require confirmation that the goods were packaged in double-strength, waterproof containers, rather than requiring that the goods be packaged in double-strength, waterproof containers.

**Example 3:** Require proof of notification to the buyer (such as a copy of the communication) that goods were shipped, rather than requiring that the buyer be notified that the goods were shipped.

Remember, the banks are concerned only with the documents presented, not with whether a party has complied with the contract clauses when they check compliance with the documentary credit terms.

## Be Clear and Concise

The wording in a documentary credit should be simple but specific. The more detailed the documentary credit is, the more likely the seller will reject it as too difficult to fulfill. It is also more likely that the banks will find a discrepancy in the details, thus voiding the credit, even though simpler terms might have been found to be in compliance with the credit.

The buyer should, however, completely and precisely set forth the details of the agreement as it relates to credit terms and conditions and the presentation of documents.

## Do Not Specify Impossible Documentation

The documentary credit should not require documents that the seller cannot obtain; nor should it call for details in a document that are beyond the knowledge of the issuer of the document. The documents specified should be limited to those required to smoothly and completely conclude an international sale of goods.

L
/
C

## Documentary Credit Application

### Procedure

Refer to the application form on the facing page for each numbered step.

 Buyer

1. **Beneficiary** Always write the seller's company name and address completely and correctly. A simple mistake here may result in the seller preparing inconsistent or improper documentation on the other end.

2. **Amount** State the actual amount of the credit. You may state a maximum amount in a situation where actual count or quantity is in question. You also may use the words APPROXIMATE, CIRCA, or ABOUT to indicate an acceptable 10 percent plus or minus amount from the stated amount. If you use such wording, you will need to be consistent and use it also in connection with the quantity as well.

3. **Validity Period** The validity and period for presentation of the documents following shipment of the goods should be sufficiently long to allow the exporter time to prepare the necessary documents and send them to the bank.

4. **Beneficiary's Bank** Either leave blank to indicate that the issuing bank may freely select the correspondent bank or name the seller's bank.

5. **Type of Payment Availability** Sight drafts, time drafts, or deferred payment may be used, as previously agreed to by the seller and buyer.

6. **Desired Documents** The buyer specifies which documents are needed. Buyer can list, for example, a bill of lading, a commercial invoice, a certificate of origin, certificates of analysis, and so on.

7. **Notify Address** An address is given for notification of the imminent arrival of goods at the port or airport of destination. This address can also be used for notification of damage to the shipment while en route. The buyer's business or shipping agent is most often used.

8. **Merchandise Description** A short, precise description of the goods is given, along with quantity. Note the comments in number two above concerning approximate amounts.

9. **Confirmation Order** If the foreign beneficiary (exporter) insists on having the credit confirmed by a bank in his or her country it will be so noted in this space.

| | |
|---|---|
| Sender<br>Argentine Trading Company<br>Lavalle 1716, Piso 2<br>1048 Buenos Aires<br>Argentina<br><br>Our reference   AB/02 | **Instructions**<br>to open a Documentary Credit<br><br><br>Buenos Aires, 30th September 2006<br>Place / Date |

| | |
|---|---|
| Please open the following<br><br>[X] irrevocable    [ ] revocable documentary credit | **Argentine Bank Corporation**<br>Documentary Credits<br>P.O. Box 1040<br>Buenos Aires, Argentina |

**(1)** Beneficiary
American Import-Export Co., Inc.
123 Main Street
San Francisco, California
USA

**(4)** Beneficiary's bank (if known)
US Domestic Bank
525 Main Street
San Francisco, CA 94105
USA

**(2)** Amount
US$180,000.--

**(3)** Date and place of expiry
25th November 2006 in San Francisco

Please advise this bank
[ ] by letter
[X] by letter, cabling main details in advance
[ ] by telex / telegram with full text of credit

| Partial shipments | Transhipment | Terms of shipment (FOB, CR&CIF) |
|---|---|---|
| [X] allowed   [ ] not allowed | [ ] allowed   [X] not allowed | CIF Buenos Aires |

| Despatch from / Taking in charge at | For transportation to | Latest date of shipment | Documents must be presented not later than |
|---|---|---|---|
| Oakland | Buenos Aires | 10th Nov 2006 | **(3)** 15 days after date of despatch |

**Beneficiary may dispose of the credit amount as follows**

[X] at sight upon presentation of documents **(5)**
[ ] after ............days, calculated from date of ...........................

[ ] by a draft due ...........................
drawn on   [ ] you   [ ] your correspondents
which you / your correspondents will please accept

**against surrender of the following documents (6)**

[X] invoice      (....3......copies)

Shipping document
[X] sea:   bill of lading, to order, endorsed in blank
[ ] rail:   dublicate waybill
[ ] air:   air consignment note
[ ]

[X] insurance policy, certificte    (................ copies)
covering the following risks:
   "all risks including war up to
[ ] Additional documents    final destination in
   Argentina
[X] Confirmation of the carrier that the
   ship is not more than 15 years old
[X] packing

| | |
|---|---|
| Notify address in bill of lading / goods addressed to<br>Argentine Trading Company **(7)**<br>Lavalle 1716, Piso 2<br>1048 Buenos Aires   Argentina | Goods insured by    [ ] us      [X] seller |

Goods

400 "Computers model Pentium 4 as per specifications on pro forma
     invoice no. 74/1853 dd 10th September 2006"

**(8)**    at US$450.00 per unit

Your correspondents to advise beneficiary   [ ] adding their confirmation   [X] without adding their confirmation   **(9)**
Payments to be debited to our...U.S. Dollars...........account no....10-32679150

NB.The applicable text is marked by [X]

Signature .......... Argentine Trading Company

For mailing please see overleaf

L/C

## Details on Parties and Procedures

 The Buyer (Importer/Applicant)

Since a documentary credit is a pledge by the bank to make payment to the seller, the bank will want to evaluate the creditworthiness of the buyer. If the buyer's credit and relationship with the bank is excellent, the bank will issue a credit for the full value. If the buyer's relationship is good, but perhaps not excellent, the bank will require that the buyer pledge a percentage of the value of the documentary credit in cash funds. If the buyer's relationship with the bank is less established, the bank will require that the buyer pledge 100 percent of the value of the documentary credit in cash funds in advance.

It is essential that the application for the documentary credit be in conformity with the underlying sales contract between the buyer and the seller. The buyer's instructions to the issuing bank must be clear with respect to the type of credit, the amount, duration, required documents, shipping date, expiration date, and beneficiary.

 The Issuing (Buyer's) Bank

Upon receiving the buyer's application, the opening bank checks the credit of the applicant, determines whether cash security is necessary, and scrutinizes the contents of the application to see whether they generally are consistent with national and international banking and legal requirements. If the application is satisfactory to the bank, the buyer and the opening bank will sign an agreement to open a documentary credit. The credit must be written and signed by an authorized person of the issuing bank.

The issuing bank usually sends the original documentary credit to the seller (called the beneficiary) through an advising bank, which may be a branch or correspondent bank of the issuing (opening) bank. The seller may request that a particular bank be the advising bank, or the buyer's bank may select one of its correspondent banks in the seller's country.

 The Advising (Seller's) Bank

Upon receipt of the credit from the issuing bank, the advising bank informs the seller that the credit has been issued.

The advising bank will examine the credit upon receipt. The advising bank, however, examines the terms of the credit itself; it does not determine whether the terms of the credit are consistent with those of the contract between the buyer and seller, or whether the description of goods is correctly stated in accordance with the contract. The advising bank then forwards the credit to the seller.

If the advising bank is simply "advising the credit," it is under no obligation or commitment to make payment, and it will so advise the seller. In some cases the advising bank confirms (adds its guarantee to pay) the seller. In this case it becomes the confirming bank.

If the advising bank confirms the credit it must pay without recourse to the seller when the documents are presented, provided they are in order and the credit requirements are met.

 The Seller/Exporter/Beneficiary

In addition to assessing the reputation of the buyer prior to signing a sales contract, the seller should also assess the reputation of the buyer's (issuing) bank before agreeing to rely upon that bank for payment in a documentary credit. It is not unknown for sellers to receive fictitious documentary credits from non-existent banks and to realize their mistake after shipment.

The seller must carefully review all conditions the buyer has stipulated in the documentary credit. If the seller cannot comply with one or more of the provisions, or if the terms of the credit are not in accordance with those of the contract, the buyer should be notified immediately and asked to make an amendment to the credit.

The seller should also scrutinize the credit to make certain that it does not contain provisions that specify documents such as acceptance reports, progress reports, etc. that have to be signed or approved by the buyer. By refusing to sign such documents, the buyer can block payment.

After reaching agreement, the seller is well-advised to provide the buyer with a sample of the final product specified in the credit for confirmation of quality, suitability, etc.

# Complying With the Documentary Credit

 Seller/Exporter/Beneficiary

Upon receipt of the documentary credit, the seller should immediately and carefully examine it to ensure it conforms to the original sales contract with the buyer and that all the conditions stated in the credit can be met. If any of its conditions have to be amended, which can be time-consuming, the seller should immediately contact the buyer.

## Examining the Documentary Credit

The following is a checklist for the seller's examination of the credit:

1. The buyer's and seller's names and addresses are correct. ❏

2. The amount of the credit is in accordance with the contract, including unit prices, shipping charges, handling costs, and total invoice amounts. ❏

3. The merchandise description is consistent with the sales contract. ❏

4. The credit's payment availability agrees with the contract conditions. ❏

5. The shipping, expiration, and presentation dates allow sufficient time for processing the order, shipping the merchandise, and preparing the documents for presentation to the bank. ❏

6. Partial shipments or transshipments are specified correctly. ❏

7. The point of dispatch, taking charge of the goods, loading on board, or of discharge at final destination are as agreed. ❏

8. Insurance coverage and party to pay charges are as agreed.

9. Instructions on whom the drafts are to be drawn, and in what tenor (maturity dates), are correct. ❏

10. The credit is confirmed or unconfirmed as agreed. ❏

11. There are no unacceptable conditions. ❏

12. The specified documents can be obtained in the form required. ❏

13. The issuing (or confirming) bank is known to the seller. ❏

## Revocable vs. Irrevocable Documentary Credits

Documentary credits may be issued by the buyer and issuing bank as revocable or irrevocable. (The buyer must indicate either revocable or irrevocable on the application form to the issuing bank.) Each has a distinct advantage for buyers and sellers.

### Revocable Credit

A revocable documentary credit gives the buyer and/or issuing bank the ability to amend or cancel the credit at any time right up to the moment of intended payment without approval by, or notice to, the seller. Revocable credits are, therefore, of great advantage to the buyer.

Revocable credits are, conversely, of great disadvantage to the seller as the credit may be canceled at any time, even while the goods are in transit, giving the seller no security whatsoever. Although revocable credits are sometimes used between affiliated firms, sellers are advised never to accept a revocable credit as a payment method.

### Irrevocable Credit

An irrevocable documentary credit constitutes a firm contractual obligation on the part of the issuing bank to honor the terms of payment of the credit as issued. The buyer and issuing bank cannot amend or cancel the credit without the express approval of the seller.

Irrevocable credits are of advantage to the seller. As long as the seller complies with the terms of the credit, payment will be made by the issuing bank. Virtually all documentary credits issued today are irrevocable and so state on their face (on the face of the documentary credit itself). Sellers are advised to insist upon an irrevocable credit from the buyer.

## Confirmed vs. Unconfirmed Documentary Credits

Payment under an irrevocable documentary credit is guaranteed by the issuing bank. However, from the seller's perspective, this guarantee may have limited value as the issuing bank may be (1) in a foreign country, (2) beholden to the buyer, (3) small and unknown to the seller, or (4) subject to unknown foreign exchange control restrictions. The seller, therefore, might wish that another, more local bank add its guarantee (confirmation) of payment to that of the issuing bank.

Within the category of irrevocable credits there are two further options for the buyer and seller. These are the irrevocable unconfirmed credit and the irrevocable confirmed credit. Once again, each has a distinct advantage for buyers and sellers.

### Unconfirmed (or Advised) Documentary Credit

Under an unconfirmed documentary credit only the issuing bank assumes the undertaking to pay, thus payment is the sole responsibility of the issuing bank. An unconfirmed documentary credit will be communicated (advised) to the seller through a bank most likely located in the seller's country, and the related shipping and other documents will usually be presented to that bank for eventual payment. However, the final responsibility for payment rests with the issuing bank alone. The advising bank may or may not negotiate the seller's draft depending on the degree of political and financial risk anticipated in the issuing bank's country, as well as the credit standing of the issuing bank.

In dealing with a readily identifiable issuing bank in a developed country, an unconfirmed documentary credit is very probably an acceptable, safe instrument for most sellers. If you have any doubt about the issuing bank and its standing, you can check the name through a local bank with an international department.

**Note**: Some countries (most notably China) do not permit confirmation of letters of credit issued by their banks, deeming that the credit of their national financial institutions should not be questioned by others.

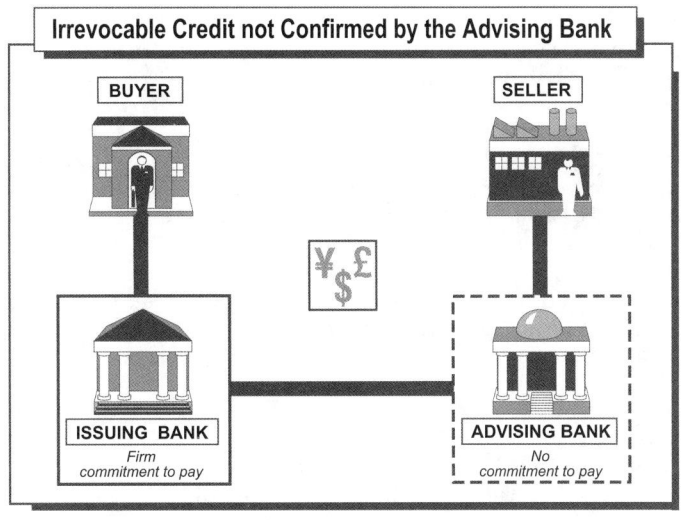

Irrevocable Credit not Confirmed by the Advising Bank

## Confirmed Documentary Credit

Confirmed letters of credit carry the commitment to pay of both the issuing and the advising banks. The advising bank adds its undertaking to pay to that of the issuing bank, and its commitment is independent of that of the issuing bank. Therefore, when documents conforming to the requirements of the confirmed documentary credit are presented in a timely manner, the payment from the advising bank to the seller is final in all respects as far as the seller is concerned.

Confirmed, irrevocable letters of credit give the seller the greatest protection, since sellers can rely on the commitment of two banks to make payment. The confirming bank will pay even if the issuing bank cannot or will not honor the draft for any reason whatever. In accordance with the additional risk assumed by the banks, however, confirmed, irrevocable letters of credit are more expensive than unconfirmed letters of credit. Confirmed, irrevocable letters of credit are used most frequently in transactions involving buyers in developing countries.

L/I/C

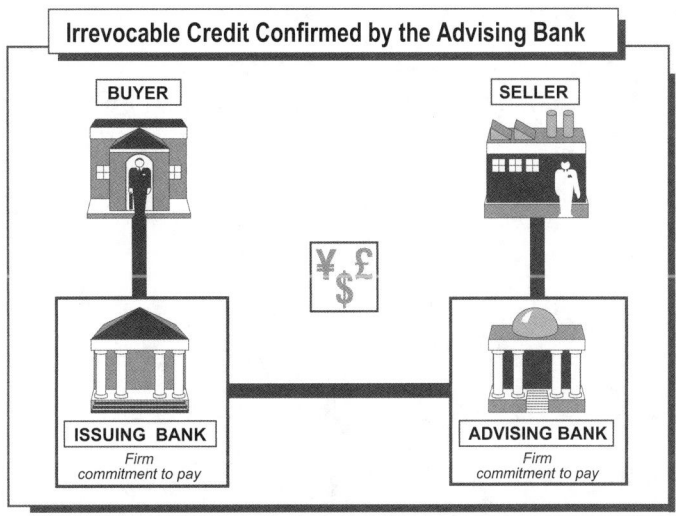

Irrevocable Credit Confirmed by the Advising Bank

## Special Letters of Credits

There are several special credits designed to meet the specific needs of buyers, suppliers, and intermediaries. Special credits involve increased participation by banks, so financing and service charges are higher. Each of the credits listed below is explained in greater detail in the pages that follow.

### Standby Credit

Standby credits are often called nonperforming letters of credit because they are only used if the collection on a primary payment method is past due. Standby credits can be used to guarantee repayment of loans, fulfillment by subcontractors, and securing the payment for goods delivered by third parties.

### Revolving Credit

This is a commitment on the part of the issuing bank to restore the credit to the original amount after it has been used or drawn down. This credit is used in cases where a buyer wishes to have certain quantities of the ordered goods delivered at specified intervals, such as in a multiple delivery contract.

### Red Clause Credit

A red clause credit has a special clause (red clause) that authorizes the confirming bank to make advances to the beneficiary (seller) prior to the presentation of the shipping documents. In this credit the buyer, in essence, extends financing to the seller and incurs ultimate risk for all sums advanced under the credit.

### Transferable Credit

A transferable credit is one where the original beneficiary transfers all or part of the proceeds of an existing credit to another party (typically the ultimate supplier of the goods). It is normally used by middlemen as a financing tool.

### Back-to-Back Credit

This is a new credit opened on the basis of an already existing, nontransferable credit. It is used by traders to make payment to the ultimate supplier. A trader receives a documentary credit from the buyer and then opens another documentary credit in favor of the ultimate supplier. The first documentary credit is used as collateral for the second credit. The second credit makes price adjustments from which comes the trader's profit.

L
/
C

# Computer Terms

Over the course of the past decade computers and computer technology have had a significant impact upon international trade. Some points: 1) Virtually every firm conducting trade uses computers, 2) Many firms now use specialized import/export document software, 3) Many countries require compliance documents to be filed electronically, and 4) The Internet has created a whole new field of cross-border trade.

This glossary of computer terms is not meant to be exhaustive. Rather, it is designed to offer the user a solid base in understanding the basic terms of comput-ing with an emphasis upon Internet technology and e-commerce.

Note that many terms are listed by their acronym when common usage dictates. In some instances the full term is spelled out with a cross reference to the main entry.

For a comprehensive glossary/encyclopedia we recommend the Osborne/McGraw-Hill *Computer Desktop Encyclopedia*, by Alan Freedman, or the *Microsoft Computer Dictionary* by Microsoft Press.

---

**access provider**
(Internet) *See* ISP (Internet Service Provider).

**Acrobat**
(computers) Computer software from Adobe Systems, Inc. that allows documents to be sent from one computer to another and printed regardless of platform and without losing formatting, fonts or graphics, all of which are embedded in the transmitted document. The transmitted document is called a PDF (Portable Document Format). Acrobat Distiller is the software used to create a PDF, while Acrobat Reader is the software used to display and print *.pdf documents. Acrobat Reader can be downloaded for free from the Adobe Web site (www.adobe.com). *See* PDF, platform.

**AltaVista**
(computers/Internet) An Internet search engine. Connect at www.altavista.com. *See* keyword search, search engine.

**American Standard Code for Information Interchange**
*See* ASCII.

**analog**
The representation of data in continuous quantities, as opposed to digital, which is the representation of data in discrete units. The most common explanation of analog vs. digital uses clocks. An analog clock has hour, minute, and second hands that display time in a continuous manner. The information displayed is in a constant state of change. A digital clock, on the other hand, displays time in discrete units such as hour, minute, and second. It shows one second, then the next, and then the next.
(wireless) A voice transmission characterized by continuous change and flow achieved by modulating its frequency and amplitude. Analog wireless service is being replaced by digital, because digital signals are more secure, transmit and receive signals with less noise and interference, and importantly, are faster and more reliable for data communications, which is the future of wireless.

**AOL**
(Internet) Acronym for America Online. An online information service that combines access to the Internet, e-mail, databases, and other features to more than 20 million subscribers worldwide. Connect at www.aol.com.

**applet**
(computers/Internet) a) A small or simple computer application (program). b) Specifically, a small application program written in Java programming language. Applets are embedded into the HTML of a Web page and are downloaded to, and then executed by, the local computer's browser. Applets generally run faster than other Web applications because they do not need to send user requests back to the server. *See* Java.

**application (software)**
(computers) Short for "application program." Computer software designed to perform a specific function directly for the user. An application typically manipulates data and then supplies results to the user. Examples of common applications include: word processors, spreadsheets, accounting and database programs. Web browsers and graphics software are also considered to be applications. Compare to "systems software," which includes programming languages and operating systems that are required to run applications software.

**ASCII**
(computers) Acronym for American Standard Code for Information Interchange. A binary data coding system developed by the American National Standards Institute (ANSI) to represent the letters of the Western alphabet, Arabic numbers and commonly used symbols (such as punctuation marks) with a value that can be manipulated by a computer for data communications and data processing. Not included are accents and letters not used in English. Pronounced "ask-ee," this coding system assigns a 7-digit binary number to represent each of these 128 alphanumeric characters.

**attachment (e-mail)**
(Internet) A text, graphic, audio, video, or other data file that is sent along with an e-mail on the Internet. In most e-mail systems one selects "Attach" from a menu and then selects a specific file or document to attach. Attachments are often compressed when the file size is large.

**B2B**
(commerce/e-commerce) Acronym for business-to-business. Commerce in goods, services, or information that takes place between business enterprises. Contrast to the exchange of goods, services, or information between businesses and private individuals (B2C or business-to-consumer). Business-to-business is a term associated with the pre-Internet "old" economy whereas B2B is a term associated with the "new" Internet economy. B2B sales on the Internet are expected to grow at a faster rate than the B2C sector.

**B2C**
(commerce/e-commerce) Acronym for business-to-consumer. Commerce in goods, services, or information that takes place between a business enterprise and a private individual. Contrast to the exchange of goods between companies (B2B or business-to-business).

**COMPUTERS**

### backup
(computers) A duplicate copy of a computer file such as a company database or application program. A backup is made for security purposes in case of loss of data because of an equipment failure, fire, theft, or other causes. Many businesses keep backup copies of important files off-site in a secure location such as a bank safety deposit box. Also used as a verb: to backup a file.

### band
(wireless) A range of radio frequencies between two defined limits that are used for a specific purpose.

### bandwidth
(computers/Internet) The data transmission capacity of an electric communications channel or connection. The more bandwidth, the more data can be transferred in a given period of time. Bandwidth is measured in bits per second (bps).
The technical definition of bandwidth refers to the difference between the highest and lowest frequency that a connection can transmit and is measured in hertz (Hz) or cycles per second. The greater the difference between these two values the more data can be sent in a given period of time. Bandwidth differs greatly depending upon a number of factors. LANs (local area networks) used in many office environments are much faster than WANs (wide area networks) such as dial-up modems, DSL, and T1-3 lines as used in most Internet connections. The following chart gives a sampling of bandwidth for the most common network configurations.

**WAN Connections—Bandwidth**
**Switched Services**
Dial-up modems: 9.6, 14.4, 28.8, 33.6
   and 56 Kbps.
ISDN: BRI 64-128 Kbps
       PRI 1.544 Mbps
**Unswitched Private Lines**
T1: 1.5 Mbps
T3: 44.7 Mbps
DSL: 144 Kbps to 52 Mbps.
**LAN Connections—Bandwidth**
Ethernet (10 BaseT): 10 Mbps
Fast Ethernet (100 BaseT): 100 Mbps
Gigabit Ethernet: 1,000 Mbps
Token Ring: 4, 16 Mbps
ATM: 25, 45, 155, 622, 2,488 Mbps+

### banner ad
(Internet) A graphic image of generally 460 pixels wide by 60 pixels high (also 460 x 55 or 392 x 72 pixels) used on a Web page to advertise a product or service. Many banner ads are now animated and/or hot linked to an advertiser's Web site.

### baud
(computers/Internet) a) (common usage) A measure of data transfer speed of a computer modem expressed as the number of bits the modem can send or receive per second. b) (technical) A unit of signaling speed related to the number of times per second that the carrier signal can shift value, expressed as the number of state-transitions or symbols that can be transmitted per second on a connection. This value can be different from the number of bits that can be moved per second. For example, a modem running at 300 baud can move 4 bits per baud or 1,200 bps. The true technical baud rate depends on the type of connection. *See* bandwidth.

### beta version
(computer software) The final (or near final), pre-release version of computer hardware or software used for qual-

ity assurance testing. Beta testing is often conducted by individuals in real-world settings to help identify problems or "bugs" that still exist in the product. Final revisions are then made before the product is released to the general public.

### binary
(computers) a) Two parts or things. b) A base-two system of representing data. In modern computing, all data (text, images, audio, and video) is stored, read, and processed by the computer in the form of ON and OFF electrical impulses. This binary system (ON or OFF) can also be represented as 1 (ON) or 0 (OFF), or as TRUE (1) or FALSE (0). Each byte of data is represented by a series of these ON, OFF electrical impulses. For example, the letter "A" is "01000001." The representation of data in binary form is the basis of modern digital computers, digital audio recordings, and digital wireless communications. *See* bit, byte.

### bit
(computers) Contraction of binary digit. The smallest element of data storage on a computer. In a binary system (0 or 1, OFF or ON) a bit represents either 0 or 1, OFF or ON.

### bookmark
(Internet) A hyperlink marker that serves as a shortcut to a particular Web site or a specific page of content within a Web site. Web browsers enable users to automatically bookmark favorite Web sites or pages for quick retrieval at a later date.

### boot
(computers) To start a computer and its operating system software. To start application software, the term "launch" is used; as in "launch Microsoft Word."

### bps
(computers) Acronym for bits per second. *See* bandwidth, bit.

### bricks and clicks
(Internet) A business that combines a physical location open to the public (bricks and mortar) with an Internet e-commerce presence (click of a mouse).

### bricks and mortar
(Internet) A business with a physical location (building) open to the public, especially retail locations, as opposed to a business that operates only on the Internet.

### broadband
(computers/Internet) High-speed data transmission over a network. Broadband is generally considered to be a speed of 1.544 Mbps (T1 line) or faster. *See* bandwidth, DSL, ISDN, T1-3.

### broadcast
(Internet) To transmit data to anyone with access to a receiver (radio, television or computer with Internet access). Radio and television are early examples of broadcast; their signals can be accessed by anyone with a radio or television receiver. A Web site can be considered a form of broadcast message as it is available to anyone with access to the Internet. Some consider e-mail sent in bulk to everyone on a network as broadcast, but others consider it to be a bulk point-to-point communication.

### browser
*See* Web browser.

### bug
(computers) An error or problem in computer software or hardware that cannot be fixed by the user.

### business-to-business
*See* B2B.

### business-to-consumer
*See* B2C.

### byte
(computers) Contraction of binary table. A unit of computer storage that consists of 8 bits and that generally represents a single character (a, b, c, 1, 2, 3, $, %, etc.). Computer storage (either in RAM, disk space, or file sizes) is generally stated in either kilobytes (KB or thousands of bytes), megabytes (MB or millions of bytes), or gigabytes (GB or billions of bytes). *See* bit.

### carrier
(wireless) A company that provides telephone, wireless, and/or other communications services.

### CD-R
(computers) Acronym for Compact Disk-Recordable. A recordable compact disk (CD) used for recording data or music that can be written (recorded) only once. Once recorded, a CD-R can be used (played) in a standard CD-ROM computer drive. CD-Rs are used for backup storage of data and as a pre-master for the replication of CD-ROMs in bulk. *See* CD-ROM, CD-RW, DVD.

### CD-ROM
(computers) Compact Disk-Read Only Memory. A storage medium using the compact disk format and used to record data, text, graphics, and/or audio files. The most common data capacities for CD-ROM disks are 650 and 700 MB. Note that computer CD-ROM drives can play both CD-ROM and audio CDs but that audio CD players can play only audio CDs. CD-ROMs provide more stable data storage than floppy disks and other magnetic storage mediums and are used extensively for the distribution of computer software, games, and other data.

### CD-RW
(computers) Acronym for Compact Disk-ReWriteable. A recordable compact disk (CD) used for recording data or music that can be written (recorded) multiple times. Once recorded, a CD-RW can be used (played) in a standard CD-ROM computer drive. *See* CD-R, CD-ROM, DVD.

### cellular
(wireless) A wireless communications system and technology that divides a service area into a multitude of cells, each with a cell site (base station). Cellular calls are transferred from cell site to cell site as the user travels from cell to cell.

### cellular phone
(wireless) A wireless radiotelephone that operates within the service area of a cellular network.

### central processing unit
*See* CPU.

### chip
(computers) A set of miniaturized electronic circuits used to process or store data. There are many types of chips designed for specific functions. Chip, microchip, and integrated circuit are used interchangeably.

### COMDEX
(computers) Contraction of Computer Dealers Exposition. (Historic note: last show was 2004.) Up until 2004, the U.S.'s largest and most important trade shows for computers and computer-related products and services. COMDEX/Fall was the original show and was about twice the size of COMDEX/Spring. Both took place in Las Vegas, Nevada, USA. The shows were produced by the Japanese-owned Softbank Corporation (www.comdex.com). Softbank Corporation is trying to regroup and produce shows in the future.

### comma delimited
(computers) A database record format that separates data fields in a record with a comma. In some cases the data content of each field is surrounded with quotes. For example: "World Trade Press", "800 Lindberg Lane", "Suite 190", "Petaluma", "CA", "94952", "USA", "Publisher". *See* tab delimited.

### compression
(computers) The encoding of data to reduce storage space. There are different compression methods and programs but they all work on the same basis of finding repeatable patterns of binary data (0s and 1s) and replacing them with a code and marker system. Compression is especially popular in sending large files (attachments) by e-mail. WinZip (www.winzip.com) is one example of a popular compression utility.

### CompuServe
(Internet) An online information service that combines access to the Internet, e-mail, databases, and other features. CompuServe is one of the oldest online services and is geared to business users, especially in the airline, insurance, and legal industries. CompuServe was acquired by AOL (www.aol.com) in 1998. Connect at http://webcenters.netscape.compuserve.com.

### CPU
(computers) Acronym for central processing unit. a) The processor or computing unit of a computer. In modern PCs the CPU is contained on a single small computer chip. b) (popular) The computer as opposed to the monitor, keyboard and mouse. *See* chip, hardware, Pentium, software.

### crash
(computers) An event that renders a computer temporarily inoperable. Most computer crashes are the result of 1) an overload of instructions or data, 2) a conflict in software, or 3) a hardware failure. Most computer crashes can be resolved by re-booting (restarting) the computer. Also called an abend (contraction of abnormal end).

### cross platform
(computers) A computer application (software) that is able to operate on all or a variety of different computer hardware or software platforms. The ability of an application to run across various platforms has become a hot topic in the age of Internet and wireless technology.

### cyberspace
(Internet) A popular term used to describe the aggregate of information available on the Internet and other computer networks. The term was originally coined by William Gibson in his 1984 novel *Neuromancer* and (interestingly) referred to a futuristic computer network comprised of the minds (not computers!) of all the people who were "plugged" in.

### database
(general) An organization of related files in a structured format that enables easy access and manipulation. Examples range from a paper card file to a computer database. (computer software) A computer application designed to organize, store and retrieve data from a database.
Modern computer databases can store any form of binary data including text, images, audio and video. Many data driven Web sites are built around powerful relational database software (such as Oracle, IBM's DB2, Microsoft's SQL Server or freeware's MySQL) and allow for dynamically updated information to be displayed on the Web site.

**COMPUTERS**

**debug**
(computers) To fix an error or problem in computer software or hardware. *See* bug.

**default**
(computers) The preestablished setting of a piece of computer hardware or software. For example, the default opening screen for a word-processing application might be a "New" document. Many default settings can be changed through user customization, often from a "Preferences," "User Preferences," or "Settings" menu.

**digital**
(computers) a) The representation of data in numerical form, usually in a binary system. b) Anything relating to numerical systems.

**digital subscriber line**
*See* DSL.

**discussion group**
*See* newsgroup.

**domain name**
*See* Internet domain name.

**dot-com**
(Internet) a) The period "." followed by the commercial (com) domain of an Internet domain name or e-mail address. b) Anything related to the Internet industry or economy. c) A company that does business on the Internet.

**down**
(computers/Internet) a) A computer that has not been turned on or that is not in operational condition. b) A Web site that is not operational. *See* up.

**download**
(Internet/computers) The transfer of computer documents or data files from a remote (host) computer to a local (client) computer over a network. To download means to receive and to upload means to transmit. *See* upload.

**DSL**
(Internet) Digital Subscriber Line. A technology that dramatically increases the data transmission capacity of telephone lines into homes and offices. DSL is one of the most popular forms of Internet access because it provides "always on" operation and uses existing telephone lines. DSL speeds, however, are a function of the distance between the subscriber and the telecom central office. The greater the distance, the slower the speed. There are many versions of DSL, but the two main groupings of service are Asymmetric DSL (including ADSL, RADSL, G.Lite, and VDSL) and Symmetric DSL (including HDSL, HDSL-2, SDSL, and IDSL). Asymmetric DSL features fast download and slow upload of data and is used primarily for Internet connections. Symmetric DSL features fast speeds in both directions but is used only where the distance from the telecom office is short. *See* bandwidth, E1, E3, ISDN, modem, T1-3.

**dual band**
(telecommunications) A mobile phone (handset) that is capable of sending and receiving signals in both 800 MHz cellular and 1900 MHz PCS frequencies. *See* dual mode, PCS.

**dual mode**
(wireless) A mobile phone (handset) that is capable of operating on analog and digital wireless networks. *See* dual band.

**DVD**
(computers) Acronym for Digital Video Disk. A portable storage medium used to store large volumes of data. DVDs are the same physical size as CDs, but are double-sided and hold from 2.6 GB to 17 GB of data (in contrast to the typical 650 MB capacity of CDs). Originally designed for video distribution, DVDs have become important in the computer industry for backup storage of large databases, computer graphics audio and video. DVDs come in a variety of formats and storage capacities. Many feel that DVDs will eventually replace CD-ROMs. *See* CD-ROM.

**E1, E2, E3**
(Internet, European standard) A dedicated digital circuit connection leased from a telecommunications provider that provides 2.048 Mbps (E1), 8.448 Mbps (E2) or 44.736 Mbps (E3) data transmission capacity. E1-E3 lines are used for high speed private networks and connections to the Internet. E3 lines can handle full-screen, full-motion video. *See also* T1, T2, T3.

**e-business**
(Internet) Short for electronic business. An umbrella term for doing business online. In addition to simply processing transactions online (e-commerce), e-business includes all aspects of conducting business online including: buying, selling, marketing, advertising, order tracking, shipment tracking, and customer service. *See* e-commerce.

**e-commerce**
(Internet) Short for electronic commerce. Business transactions conducted on the Internet. The sale of goods or services online. E-commerce is a subset of e-business and generally refers specifically to the ability to process a transaction online. E-commerce also includes electronic data interchange (EDI) which is the structured exchange of business documents (e.g., inquiries, purchase orders, invoices, compliance documents, etc.) between computers.

**EDI**
(computers/Internet) Acronym for Electronic Data Interchange. The electronic communication of business-transaction information and documentation between businesses and between businesses and governmental entities. EDI includes transmission of purchase orders, order confirmations, invoices and compliance documents. Modern EDI involves direct links into supplier ordering systems and government regulatory authorities.

**Electronic Data Interchange (EDI)**
*See* EDI.

**e-mail**
(Internet) Short for electronic-mail. The transmission of electronic messages over a network from one computer to another, especially over the Internet. *See* attachment, spam.

**e-mail attachment**
*See* attachment.

**e-mail blast**
(Internet) A large number of e-mail advertising messages sent at the same time. *See* attachment, spam.

**encryption**
(computers) The encoding of data for security while in transmission.

**e-tailing**
(Internet) Short for electronic retailing. Business-to-consumer (B2C) sales over the Internet. *See* B2C, e-business, e-commerce.

**Ethernet**
(computers) The most popular LAN (local area network) technology currently in use. Many PCs, most peripherals (such as laser printers), and all Macintosh computers come standard with an Ethernet port (RJ-45 connector) for connecting to a LAN or to a DSL or cable modem for Internet access.

Ethernet is available in three bandwidths:
Ethernet: 10BaseT (10 Mbps)
Fast Ethernet: 100BaseT (100 Mbps)
Gigabit Ethernet: 1,000BaseT (1,000 Mbps)
*See* bandwidth.

### Excite
(computers/Internet) An Internet portal and search engine. Connect at www.excite.com. *See* search engine, keyword search.

### Explorer
*See* Internet Explorer.

### eXtensible Markup Language
*See* XML.

### extensions
*See* Internet domain name, top-level domain, URL.

### extranet
(Internet) A Web site with limited access, designed and maintained specifically for communicating with clients and customers rather than with the general public. An extranet uses the Internet as its delivery system, but restricts access via passwords. An extranet can be used to deliver vendor inventory information, specialized content such as research, or any other private data. Access to an extranet site may be free or on a paid subscription basis.

### FAQ
(Internet) Acronym for Frequently Asked Questions. A list of commonly asked questions, with answers, maintained on a Web site to assist users with fundamental content, navigation, and usage information. It is considered a breach of netiquette (etiquette of the Internet) to call or e-mail asking a question that is answered in the FAQ section.

### fiber optics
(telecommunications) Wire or cable made from glass fiber and designed to transmit digital signals (audio, video, or other data) as pulses of light. Fiber optics is becoming the preferred technology in telecommunications for systems requiring higher bandwidths and/or lengthy transmission distances. For example, thousands of electrical links (using copper wires) can be replaced by a single optical fiber.

### firewall
(Internet) Computer software, or more commonly, a combination of computer hardware, software, and security measures designed to keep a computer or computer network secure from intruders. *See* hacker, virus.

### flame
(Internet) A critical, often abusive message that is delivered by e-mail. For example, a flame may be received by someone who has abused the netiquette (etiquette of the Internet) by using public forums for advertising.

### floppy disk
(computers) A flexible magnetic storage medium housed in a paper envelope or plastic shell. Also called a "diskette," floppy disks have come in a number of different physical sizes that each have varying storage capacity. The standard sizes are:
8" in a flexible envelope: 100-500KB storage
5.25" in a flexible envelope: 100KB-1.2MB storage
3.5" in a rigid case: 400KB-2.8MB storage
Today, only the 3.5" disk is still widely used and many predict that it too will disappear within a few years because of its limited storage capacity. *See* CD-ROM, DVD, hard disk.

### frequently asked questions
*See* FAQ.

### FTP
(Internet) File Transfer Protocol. A standard protocol for transferring computer files over the Internet. FTP is often used by Web developers to upload their files to a host server. An FTP transfer is generally performed with a utility program or from within a Web browser. *See* upload.

### GB
*See* gigabyte.

### gigabyte (GB)
(computers) One billion bytes. *See* byte.

### Global Positioning System
*See* GPS.

### Global System for Mobile Communications
*See* GSM.

### Google
(computers/Internet) An Internet portal and the world's most widely-used search engine. Connect at www.google.com. *See* keyword search, search engine.

### Gopher
(Internet) An application program that searches the Internet for file names and other information and presents its findings in a hierarchical format. Developed at the University of Minnesota (USA), home to the "Golden Gophers," Gopher was a big step forward in the development of the Internet and paved the way for the Hypertext Transfer Protocol (HTTP). It remains available at many universities and most recent Web browsers still incorporate support for the protocol. Note: Gopher is both the name of a burrowing animal and a slang term for "Go fer (for)" as in "go get it."

### GPS
Acronym for Global Positioning System. A worldwide satellite-based radio navigation system consisting of 24 Earth orbit satellites operated by the U.S. Department of Defense and used to provide three- and four-dimensional position, time, and velocity information to military and civilian users who have GPS receivers. The system has two levels of service.
**Standard Positioning Service** is available to anyone in possession of a GPS receiver (available for as little as US$100) and allows the user to establish their Earth location in latitude and longitude within a proximity of 10 meters.
**Precise Positioning Service** is a highly accurate military positioning, velocity and timing service available only to the U.S. military and other authorized users.
How GPS works: Each of the 24 satellites contains a computer, atomic clock, and radio. The strategic positioning of these satellites enables a GPS receiver on Earth to establish location by communicating with at least three of the orbiting satellites within its "field of view." If contact can be made from a fourth satellite, altitude data can also be obtained. GPS is used in various industries including navigation (ocean and land), energy exploration, and environment monitoring. GPS is the essential component in automobiles equipped with navigation systems.

### graphic user interface
*See* GUI.

### GSM
(wireless) Global System for Mobile Communications. The predominant worldwide standard for digital wireless service. GSM operates at either 900 or 1800 MHz and is used extensively in Europe and in more than 120 countries. GSM is a TDMA (Time Division Multiple Access) technology and allows a number of calls to take place on

**C O M P U T E R S**

a single channel or frequency at the same time. For more information, contact GSM World at www.gsmworld.com.

### GUI
(computers) Acronym for Graphical User Interface. Pronounced "goo-ey." A graphics-based as opposed to a text-based interface used to communicate with a computer. A text-based interface uses words and alphanumeric commands, whereas a GUI uses icons, pull-down menus and a computer mouse for navigation, giving commands and operating the machine. The three major operating system GUIs are Windows (for the PC), Mac OS (for the Macintosh) and Motif (for UNIX).

### hacker
(computers) a) A highly-skilled and clever computer programmer who writes programs in assembly or systems-level languages. The term refers to the programmer's "hacking away" at tedious computer code when writing complex programs. b) (popular usage) A mischievous person who seeks unauthorized entry into computer systems. Such entry can be benign (simply for the satisfaction of succeeding) or malicious (for the purpose of doing harm). *See* virus.

### Handheld Devices Markup Language
*See* HDML.

### hard disk
(computers) A rigid magnetic storage medium that is fixed within a computer in a sealed compartment. A hard disk can also be contained in an external device or in a removable cartridge. In the mid-1980s hard disks for PCs had storage capacities of 5 to 20 MB. By the year 2000 most PCs came standard with 5 to 20 GB hard disks. *See* gigabyte, megabyte.

### hardware
(computers/logistics) Machines and equipment. In the field of computers, hardware refers to physical equipment such as CPUs, keyboards, monitors, disk drives, modems, and cables. *See also* software.

### HDML
(computers) Handheld Devices Markup Language. A computer language and coding system used to enable wireless devices such as cell phones, wireless pagers, and other handheld devices with small display screens to view information from the Internet. HDML is a version of HTML (HyperText Markup Language) and a subset of WAP (Wireless Application Protocol). *See* HTML, WAP.

### home page
(Internet) The first page viewed (main access page) on an Internet Web site. All other pages are accessed from the home page. The home page of a well-designed Web site enables the user to intuitively understand and navigate through the content of the site.

### Hotmail
(Internet) A Web-based e-mail provider that enables users to send and receive messages from any computer connected to the Internet. Users get a special Hotmail e-mail address (_____@hotmail.com) that they can use from home, an office, or from an Internet café anywhere in the world. This is a favorite of travelers as the e-mail address is permanent and is free of charge. Connect at www.hotmail.com.

### HTML
(Internet) HyperText Markup Language. The computer language used for creating hyperlinked or hypertext documents on the World Wide Web. This computer language (also called a document format) enables users to view content in a Web browser and navigate within a Web site

and to other Web sites by clicking hyperlinked text or graphics.

### HTTP
(Internet) Acronym for HyperText Transfer Protocol. The communications protocol used by computers and Web browsers to connect to Web servers and move HTML files across the Internet. For example, to establish a connection with the World Trade Press Web server, one types http as a prefix to the Web domain name (http://www.worldtradepress.com) in the address field of a Web browser.

### hyperlink
(Internet) A link between two text or graphic objects. Pointing with the computer's cursor and clicking a hyperlink will transfer you to a specified page, file (text, graphic, audio, or video), or Web site. Hyperlinks are generally identified in computer documents by underlined colored text (often blue) or by graphic buttons. Hyperlinks form the foundation for navigation on the World Wide Web. Hyperlink and hypertext are used interchangeably. *See* hypertext.

### hypertext
(Internet) A single word or text passage on a Web page that has been hyperlinked to a related text occurrence, page, file (text, graphic, audio, or video), or Web site. Hypertext passages are often referred to as a "link" or "hyperlink." Hypertext links are generally identified in computer documents by underlined colored text (usually blue). Hypertext and hyperlink are used interchangeably. *See* hyperlink.

### HyperText Markup Language
*See* HTML.

### hypertext transfer protocol
*See* HTTP.

### IE
(Internet) Acronym for Internet Explorer. *See* Internet Explorer.

### Infoseek
(computers/Internet) An Internet portal and search engine. Connect at www.infoseek.com. *See* search engine, keyword search.

### Integrated Services Digital Network
*See* ISDN.

### Interface
(computers) a) The connection of two or more computer devices such as a computer and a printer, or a keyboard and a computer. b) The connection between an individual computer, its operating system software, application software, and the user. c) (popular usage) To work with another individual or organization.

### Internet
(computers/Internet) The world's largest, fastest-growing, and most important computer network. Specifically, a worldwide network made up of smaller networks that provides access to all those connected to any part of the network.

The original Internet was started in 1969 as the ARPAnet and was designed as a series of high-speed links between educational and research institutions. By the 1990s commercial and other traffic increased exponentially and the Internet became an economic and cultural phenomenon.

While the Internet's exact future is unclear, the following is generally understood to be true: 1) Internet use will continue to grow, 2) the Internet is by far the world's greatest source of information, and 3) the Internet holds untold opportunities for commerce and education. *See* World Wide Web.

### Internet address
(Internet) a) An individual's e-mail address on the Internet. b) An individual Web site address (URL) on the Internet. *See* e-mail, Internet domain name, URL.

### Internet discussion group
*See* newsgroup.

### Internet domain name
(Internet) The address of an Internet Web site. Technically, an organization's domain name combined with a top-level domain (TLD). TLDs are extensions to the domain name such as ".com", ".org", ".net", etc. For example: www.worldtradepress.com. Note that no two organizations can hold the same Internet domain name and that trademarked names can only be used by the trademark holder. One can register an Internet domain name at any number of Web sites, but the most important register is Network Solutions (www.networksolutions.com). An Internet domain name is one of the components of a URL.

### Internet Explorer
(Internet) The Web browser developed by Microsoft Corporation (www.microsoft.com), and referred to simply as Explorer or IE. In the late 1990s to early 2000s, IE gained a marked ascendancy in usage over the previously standard Netscape browser, to the point that Netscape's usage became trivial. Recently, the free Mozilla Firefox browser has begun to take market share from IE, although IE is still the dominant browser worldwide.

### Internet Service Provider
*See* ISP.

### intranet
(Internet) A private computer network designed for use by one company or organization. For example, a company might design and maintain an intranet to share databases and provide intra-company e-mail services for its employees. An intranet operates on the same principles as the Internet. *See* Internet, extranet.

### ISDN
(Internet) Integrated Services Digital Network. A technology that dramatically increases the data transmission capacity of telephone lines into homes and offices. With ISDN one can send analog and digital data over the same network at transmission rates of up to 128 Kbps. *See* bandwidth, DSL, E1, E3, modem, T1-3.

### ISP
(Internet) Internet Service Provider. A firm that provides clients with direct access to the Internet. ISPs may provide other services such as Web hosting and Web site design and building. Online services such as AOL and CompuServe also provide Internet access as part of their service offering. For a directory of ISPs see "List of ISPs" at www.thelist.com.

### Java
(Internet) A programming language developed by Sun Microsystems (www.sun.com) designed to run on all computer operating systems, especially in Web applications. A Java "applet" is a Java program that is first downloaded from the host Web server to a user's local computer, where it runs after being called from a Web page. A Java "servlet" is a Java program that resides on and operates from a Web server. *See* applet.

### KB
*See* kilobyte.

### Kbps
(computers/Internet) Acronym for kilo (1,000) bits per second. *See* bandwidth, bit.

### keyword search
(Internet) A search for information or documents on the World Wide Web based on use of a single word, phrase, or combination of words in a search engine. By modifying the keywords and their sequence one can often obtain different search results.

### kilobyte (KB)
(computers) One thousand bytes. *See* byte.

### LAN
(computers) Acronym for Local Area Network. A computer network that is shared by computers and devices within a relatively small area. A LAN may serve two or three users or it may be used by hundreds, but the geographic area served ranges typically from a single office to part or all of a single floor of a building.

### laptop
(computers) A small, portable, battery-operated computer with integrated screen and keyboard.

### link
*See* hyperlink.

### Linux
(computers) An open-source, free-of-charge computer operating system, with Unix-like features and interface, that has been slowly but surely gaining in popularity and usage, especially for web servers. In addition, Linux desktop and mobile-phone applications have been appearing with more frequency. The Linux operating system has a reputation for being reliable and secure, with the added benefits of no-to-low cost and no vendor lock-in. Linux has become a preferred alternative to Microsoft Windows.

### local area network
*See* LAN.

### Lycos
(computers/Internet) An Internet portal and search engine. Connect at www.lycos.com. *See* keyword search, search engine.

### Mac OS
(computers) Short for Macintosh Operating System. The operating system used on Macintosh computers. The Mac OS is especially popular in desktop publishing, design, and graphics-related industries.

### MB
*See* megabyte.

### Mbps
(computers) Acronym for mega (1,000,000) bits per second. *See* bandwidth, bit.

### megabyte (MB)
(computers) One million bytes. *See* byte.

### menu
(computers) An on-screen list of computer functions or operations that may be selected by the user.

### mobile e-commerce
(Internet) Electronic commerce that uses a wireless device as the access point (as opposed to a PC that is connected by landlines to the Internet). Examples of wireless devices used in mobile e-commerce include cellular telephones, beepers, and PDAs (Personal Digital Assistants) with Internet access.

### mobile Web
(wireless) Access to the World Wide Web from a mobile wireless device such as a cellular phone, beeper, or PDA (Personal Digital Assistant). Mobile Web promises to be a

**COMPUTERS**

huge area for growth because of users' ability to gain instant access to information and mobile e-mail.

### modem
(computers/Internet) Contraction of Modulator-Demodulator. An electronic hardware device that connects a computer communications port to a telephone line or TV cable and thence to other computers or computer networks including the Internet. Technically, a modem is a digital-to-analog and analog-to-digital device that converts a computer's digital pulses to audio frequencies that can be transmitted over a telephone line and vice-versa. A modem is only one way in which a user can connect to the Internet. Modern modems connect to the Internet at speeds of up to 56,000 bps, slower than ISDN, DSL and T1, T2, and T3 lines.

### Mozilla Firefox
An open-source, free web browser developed, maintained and enhanced by the Mozilla Foundation. As of late 2006, Firefox has become the second most-used web browser worldwide (behind Microsoft's Internet Explorer), with an estimated worldwide usage of 12 percent. *See* Internet Explorer.

### Navigator
*See* Netscape Navigator.

### Netscape Navigator
(Internet) The Web browser developed by Netscape Communications Corporation (www.netscape.com), now part of AOL Time Warner (www.aol.com). It has steadily been losing worldwide market share to Internet Explorer, which since 1999 is the most widely used Web browser.

### network
(computers) A group of linked computers. A network can link as few as two computers in a small office (a Local Area Network), several hundred or thousand computers in a company wide network (a Wide Area Network), or tens of millions of computers on the Internet. *See* extranet, Internet, intranet, LAN (Local Area Network), WAN (Wide Area Network).

### New Economy
(Internet) The economy associated with the Internet. *See* B2B, B2C, e-commerce, Old Economy.

### newsgroup
(Internet) A message board on an Internet Web site or portal. Also known as an Internet discussion group. A newsgroup is generally topic-specific and starts with a single user posting a query or comment that is followed by comments and queries by other users. Newsgroups have become an extremely popular addition to Web sites that wish to foster communications among and with members or users.

### offline
(Internet) Not connected to the Internet.
(computers) a) Describes a device (such as a laser printer) that is not connected to a computer. b) Describes a device that is not in ready mode.
(general) Not available for use.

### Old Economy
(Internet) a) The pre-Internet economy. b) The economy associated with "bricks and mortar" businesses. *See* New Economy.

### online
(Internet) Connected to the Internet.
(computers) a) Describes a device (such as a laser printer) that is connected to a computer. b) Describes a device that is in ready mode.
(general) Available for use.

### online service
(Internet) A business entity that provides access to the Internet, proprietary databases and e-mail services to its users. Several of the largest online services include:
America Online (AOL) (www.aol.com)
CompuServe (www.compuserve.com)
DIALOG (online databases) (www.dialog.com)
Dow Jones Interactive (business, finance and news) (www.dowjones.com)
LEXIS-NEXIS (legal and news information) (www.lexis-nexis.com)
WESTLAW (legal databases) (http://web2.westlaw.com)

### operating system (OS)
(computers) The primary software program that manages a computer's basic functions and controls the execution of application programs. All application software must conform to certain standards of a computer's operating system to function. Also called system software. The most common operating systems are Windows (for Intel/IBM PC-compatible computers), Mac OS (for Macintosh), and UNIX and Linux (for PC and UNIX computers).

### OS
*See* operating system.

### PC
(computers) a) Personal Computer. Specifically a personal computer (laptop or desktop) running Windows or DOS. b) Any laptop or desktop personal computer. c) Acronym for printed circuit.

### PCS
(wireless) Personal Communication Services. A second-generation digital wireless two-way voice, messaging, and data communications service operating at 1900 MHz. PCS is usually packaged with call waiting, voice mail, and caller ID service features.

### PDA
(computers) Personal Digital Assistant. A handheld, battery-powered computing device used to store addresses, personal calendars, and notes. PDA and wireless technologies are merging to create combination PDA, wireless phone, and Internet-accessible devices.

### PDF
Acronym for Portable Document Format. *See* Acrobat.

### Pentium
(computers) The world's dominant series of 32-bit CPU microprocessor chips manufactured by the Intel Corporation (www.intel.com) and used in PCs (personal computers). Pentium can refer to either the chip or a computer that uses the chip.

### personal digital assistant
*See* PDA.

### PIN
(wireless) Personal Identity Number. A code number used as a security password by the authorized owner or user for accessing a wireless phone, bank accounts, and other services and accounts.

### pixel
(computers) Contraction of Picture (slang "pix") Element. The smallest element of visual information that can be used to make an image on a computer monitor or TV screen. The more pixels, the higher the resolution of a monitor. A pixel on a color monitor is made up of red, blue, and green dots of varying intensity that converge at the same point.

### platform
(computers) a) A specific computer hardware architecture. For example, the PC, Macintosh, or UNIX plat-

forms. b) A specific computer software architecture. For example, the Windows platform, or the Mac OS platform. The terms "platform," "operating system," and "environment" are often used interchangeably. *See* cross platform, operating system.

### plug and play
(computers) Specialized computer software that recognizes when a new hardware component has been plugged into the computer system and that initializes and installs the component for immediate use with the system.

### portal
(Internet) A Web site that provides a wide variety of services to the user including Web search functionality, directories, news, e-mail, databases, discussion groups, online shopping, and links to other sites. The term was originally used to refer to all-purpose sites such as AOL and CompuServe, but is now more commonly used to refer to vertical market sites that cover specific industries or topics.

### pull-down menu
(computers) An on-screen list of computer functions or operations accessed by selecting (clicking) a single main menu title.

### RAM
(computers) Random Access Memory. Memory chips that plug into a computer's motherboard and that serve as the computer's primary but temporary workspace. Generally, the larger the files that are in use at one time, the more RAM a computer needs to operate. For example, a computer needs more RAM to process graphics files than textual word-processing files. Most new computers (as of 2002) are made with a standard minimum of 128 MB (megabytes) of RAM and allow for additional upgrades. Note that storage of data in RAM is temporary and is lost when the computer is turned off. *See* ROM (Read Only Memory).

### Random Access Memory
*See* RAM.

### Read Only Memory
*See* ROM.

### real time
(computers) a) A measure of computational time that relates to achieving a result in an external process. b) A computer system that interacts with and gives an immediate result to external input. Explanation: A computer will continue to perform a task until the task has been completed. However, some tasks must be performed very quickly to have any value. For example, a GPS (Global Positioning System) device held by a hiker in the remote wilderness could take as long as several seconds to compute location coordinates to the user and still be useful. However, a jet airplane traveling at 1,000 miles per hour (more than a mile every four seconds!) must make this calculation in much less time to be useful. In another example, a video-conferencing camera is considered to operate in real time, even though it takes a very small amount of time for the video image to move over the phone lines. In popular usage, a computational operation that takes "essentially" no time is considered to happen in real time.

### re-boot
(computers) To restart (turn off, then turn on) a computer. This resets the computer, often resolving conflicts in the processing. *See* boot.

### ROM
(computers) Read Only Memory. Memory chips built into the motherboard of a computer that permanently store data, instructions, and routines for the operation of the computer. ROM cannot be altered by the user and is not lost when the computer is turned off. *See* RAM.

### search engine
(Internet) Computer software designed by a company and offered online to search the Internet for information based upon keywords entered by the user. Search engines do not reside on the user's computer, but rather at the online location of the respective company. Major search engines on the Web include:
AltaVista (www.altavista.com)
Excite (www.excite.com)
Google (www.google.com)
Infoseek (www.infoseek.com)
Lycos (www.lycos.com)
WebCrawler (www.webcrawler.com)
Yahoo! (www.yahoo.com)

### server
(Internet) A computer connected to a network so its data and programs can be shared by multiple users of the other connected computers. Server can refer to either or both the hardware or the software that runs the computer itself. Some of the many types of servers include: Application Server (runs application software for multiple computers); Database Server (maintains a database accessed by multiple users); Remote Access Server (provides access to information to multiple remote users); and Web Server (provides World Wide Web access to the Internet).

### software
(computers) A series of instructions that run on a computer. Software can be either "system software" that runs the computer itself, or "application software" that interacts with and performs specific tasks for the user. *See* application (software), system software, operating system.

### spam
(Internet) Unsolicited e-mail, usually mass e-mail messages promoting a political or social message or advertising a product. Named after the canned meat by-product SPAM (which is a registered trademark of Hormel Corporation). The use of mass e-mailings is the subject of great controversy. Some feel that unsolicited e-mail is a violation of the basic values of the Internet, while others have built legitimate businesses on such "mailings." *See* e-mail.

### streaming audio
(computers/Internet) Digital audio transmission over a data network such as the Internet. Streaming audio is a one-way data transmission.

### streaming video
(computers/Internet) Digital video transmission over a data network such as the Internet. Streaming video is a one-way data transmission.

### system
(computers) A group of computer components and peripherals that work together to perform a task.

### system software
(computers) The primary software program that manages a computer's basic functions and controls the execution of application programs. All application software must conform to certain standards of a computer's operating system software to function. Also called operating system. The most common operating systems are Windows (for Intel/IBM PC-compatible computers), Mac OS (for

**COMPUTERS**

C
O
M
P
U
T
E
R
S

Macintosh), and UNIX and Linux (for PC and UNIX computers).

**T1**

(Internet) A dedicated digital circuit connection leased from a telecommunications provider that provides 1.544 Mbps data transmission capacity. T1 lines are used for high speed private networks and connections to the Internet. *See* bandwidth, DSL, E1, E2, E3, ISDN, modem, T2, T3.

**T2**

(Internet) A dedicated digital circuit connection leased from a telecommunications provider that provides 3.152 Mbps data transmission capacity. T2 lines are used for high speed private networks and connections to the Internet. *See* bandwidth, DSL, E1, E2, E3, ISDN, modem, T1, T3.

**T3**

(Internet) A dedicated digital circuit connection leased from a telecommunications provider that provides 44.736 Mbps data transmission capacity. T3 lines are used for ultra high speed private networks and connections to the Internet. T3 lines can handle full-screen, full-motion video. The European equivalent is E3. *See* bandwidth, DSL, E1, E3, ISDN, modem, T1, T2.

**tab delimited**

(computers) A database record format that separates data fields in a record with a tab. Tab delimited formatting, unlike comma delimited formatting, does not use quotation marks around each field of data content. *See* comma delimited.

**top-level domain**

(Internet) The primary organizational category of a domain name. All domain names are organized into categories that are assigned and administered by ICANN (Internet Corporation for Assigned Names and Numbers). The top-level domain is indicated by the extension at the end of a domain name and is intended to describe the nature of the domain name owner. Top-level domains include:

.com —commercial (business entities)
.net —network
.org —organization (non-government organization)
.edu —U.S. educational institution
.gov —U.S. government (federal, state, or local)
.mil —U.S. military

The exponential surge in domain name registrations has led to the introduction of new top-level domains, some of which include:

.biz —business entity
.pro —professional
.museum —museum
.info —information service
.name —individual person

Many countries are permitted to have top-level domains, indicated by two-letter extensions. A few examples include:

.ca —Canada
.fr —France
.uk —United Kingdom

**tri-band (mode) phone**

(wireless) A mobile phone (handset) that is capable of operating on digital 800 MHz and 1900 MHz frequencies as well as analog 800 MHz frequency.

**UNIX**

(computers) A computer operating system used extensively in workstations and servers in scientific and academic environments and especially on the Internet. UNIX is especially popular because of its stability and ability to

multitask; although it has been losing usage to the more recent Linux operating system. *See* Linux, Mac OS, operating system, Windows.

**up**

(computers/Internet) a) A computer that has been turned on or that is in operational condition. b) A Web site that is operational. *See* down.

**upload**

(Internet/computers) The transfer of computer documents or files from a local (client) computer to a remote computer over a network. To download means to receive and to upload means to transmit. *See* download.

**URL**

(Internet) Acronym for Uniform Resource Locator. The address and/or route to a file, document, or Web site on the Internet. A URL is typed into the "address" window of a Web browser to access a particular Web domain or Web page on the Internet. For example:

http://www.worldtradepress.com

is the URL for World Trade Press.

Specifically, a URL is a series of letters, characters, and numbers that contain 1) a protocol prefix, 2) port number, 3) domain name, 4) subdirectory name, and 5) file name. The port number is almost always a default and does not need to be included. As a result, a user need only type in the protocol prefix and domain name to gain access to a Web site or page. There are more than 10 protocol prefixes, but the most common are:

http: —World Wide Web server
ftp: —file transfer protocol server
news: —Usenet newsgroups
mailto: —e-mail
gopher: —Gopher service
file: —file on local system

In many cases a specific page is stored in a subdirectory on the domain. For example:

http://www.worldtradepress.com/catalog/dictionary.html

is the specific Web page for the World Trade Press Dictionary of International Trade. This URL can be broken up as follows:

http: —protocol prefix
// —separators
www.worldtradepress.com/ —domain name
catalog/ —subdirectory name
dictionary.html —document name

*See* Internet domain name, top-level domain.

**Usenet**

(Internet) Contraction of User Network. An Internet-based bulletin board network that provides access to newsgroups and group e-mail.

**user interface**

(computers) The means of communication between a user and a computer. This includes the computer keyboard, mouse, text commands (such as "Ctrl S" to save) and pull-down menus and other hyperlinked commands that enter data or tell the computer what to do. *See* GUI.

**virus**

(computers) A software program designed maliciously to infect and harm computer files. A computer virus is distinguished by its ability to attach itself to other programs and self-replicate. Typically, a virus arrives hidden within or attached to a file, program, e-mail, or e-mail attachment. Some viruses simply display a harmless message when activated, while others are designed to do severe damage to computer files and system software. A virus can be activated automatically or by a trigger event such as a date, time, or sequence of keyboard strokes. A number of anti-virus programs are available and can be especially helpful because many viruses operate on similar principles that can be detected by the anti-virus software. However, it is wise to regularly update this software (often with direct downloads from Web sites) as new viruses are invented and discovered daily. *See* hacker.

### VOIP (Voice Over Internet Protocol)
(telecommunications) The technology of transmitting telephone calls over a data network such as the Internet. VOIP technology offers the promise of eliminating long distance telephone charges. Also called IP telephony.

### WAN
(computers) Wide Area Network. A data communications network that serves a very large geographic area such as a state, province, or country. *See* extranet, Internet, intranet, LAN (Local Area Network), network.

### WAP
(computers/Internet) Wireless Application Protocol. A set of communications protocols designed to provide e-mail, Internet Relay Chat (IRC), and Web content to wireless devices such as cellular phones, beepers, and wireless PDAs (Personal Digital Assistants). The development of WAP was initially spurred by four major manufacturers of wireless products: Motorola, Nokia, Ericsson, and Unwired Planet. WAP technology is based on WML (Wireless Markup Language), which is a derivative of HDML and HTML designed for small screen displays. *See* HDML, HTML.

### Web
*See* World Wide Web.

### Web browser
(Internet) An application program that enables the user to access the World Wide Web on the Internet. To view a particular Web site or page, the user types its Internet address (URL) into the "Address" window of the Web browser. Today's popular browsers enable the user to view graphics and text as well as listen to audio files and see video files that reside on the World Wide Web. Technically a browser is a client application that uses the HyperText Transfer Protocol (HTTP) to enable the user to make requests of Web servers. Popular browsers include Microsoft Internet Explorer and Mozilla Firefox, both of which support e-mail. *See* Internet Explorer.

### Webcrawler
(computers/Internet) An Internet portal and search engine. Connect at www.webcrawler.com. *See* keyword search, search engine.

### Web page
(Internet) A document on the World Wide Web. A Web page is maintained on a Web site. *See* Web site, home page.

### Web server
(computers/Internet) A computer with an operating system and server software designed to provide World Wide Web (WWW) services on the Internet. After an organization's Web site data is loaded onto its Web server, it is accessible to anyone accessing the WWW. A Web server can be located in an organization's offices or at a third-party hosting service.

### Web site
(Internet) A collection of files on a server that are accessible on the World Wide Web. The term is used both to denote the server that contains files and the collection of files that relate to a specific URL. A Web site is composed of a "home page" and other data files that can be accessed from the home page.

### wide area network
*See* WAN.

### Windows
(computers) The dominant IBM PC-compatible computer operating system developed by Microsoft Corporation (www.microsoft.com). Windows comes in a number of variations including Windows 95, Windows 98, Windows 2000 and Windows XP. *See* Linux, Mac OS, operating system, PC, UNIX.

### Wintel
(computers) Contraction of Windows Intel. A general reference to the dominant computing environment of PCs using Intel CPUs and Windows operating systems. *See* PC, Windows.

### Wireless Application Protocol
*See* WAP.

### World Wide Web (WWW) (Web)
(Internet) a) The aggregation of documents that can be accessed via the Internet. b) The aggregation of hypertext servers (HTTP servers) that can be accessed via the Internet. c) The system of accessing files and documents on the Internet using hypertext links.
The Web operates using the HTTP protocol and provides graphic capability. The Internet, on the other hand, is the network of computer networks and servers on which the Web resides and operates. The Web was developed at the European Center for Nuclear Research (CERN) between 1989 and 1991 as a means of sharing data on nuclear research.

### WWW
*See* World Wide Web.

### XML
(Internet) Acronym for eXtensible Markup Language. An open standard computer language used for defining data elements on a Web page. XML is considered the successor language to HTML (HyperText Markup Language) because of its ability to define content and function as if it were a database. In HTML the Web developer defines how text and graphic elements are displayed, whereas in XML the developer defines what these text and graphic elements contain. In HTML the developer can use only predefined tags, whereas in XML the developer can create and define the tags.

### Yahoo
(computers/Internet) An Internet portal and search engine. Connect at www.yahoo.com.

### zip
(computers/Internet) A popular method of compressing a computer file or group of files. Compression of large documents makes them easier to store or send via e-mail as an attachment. After being "zipped" a file has the suffix ".zip" appended to its name. When extracted, the file returns to its normal size and can be opened using the original application program. Most computers and browsers come equipped with a zip utility and *.zip files can be extracted (uncompressed) simply by double-clicking the document icon or name.

# Resources for International Trade

## BOOKS & DIRECTORIES

### Air Freight Directory
Directory of Air Freight, Air Cargo and Freight Forwarders and Carriers. Bimonthly. $109 annually for either print or web versions, and $160 annually for a print/web combination subscription. Available from: Aircargo Communities Inc. (ACI), 437 Rozzi Place, South San Francisco, CA 94080 USA; Tel: [1] (866) 952-9050; Fax: [1] (650) 952-9051; E-mail: sales@aircargocommunities.com; Web: www.aircargocommunities.com.

### American Association of Port Authorities' (AAPA) Port Industry Services Directory
AAPA's official, comprehensive and authoritative port industry directory and virtual registry of the most important port services & equipment companies throughout the western hemisphere and throughout the world. Includes listings by categories, an alphabetical directory and ports from around the world. Published online and in print, and updated weekly at www.aapadirectory.com.

### Basic Guide to Exporting
Designed to help U.S. firms learn the costs and risks associated with exporting and to develop a strategy for exporting. Sources of assistance throughout the federal and state governments as well as the private sector. $19.95 softcover. 3rd Edition. ISBN 1-885073-83-6. Available from: World Trade Press, 1450 Grant Ave., Suite 204, Novato, CA 94945 USA; Tel: [1] (415) 898-1124 or [1] (800) 833-8586; Fax: [1] (415) 898-1080; Web: www.worldtradepress.com.

### Black's Law Dictionary
Considered a standard in the field. Lists over 10,000 entries updated to reflect recent developments in the law. Includes pronunciation guides. By Henry Campbell Black. $50. Softcover. Abridged 8th Edition. Available from: West Group, PO Box 64833, St. Paul, MN 55164-0833 USA; Tel: [1] (800) 344-5008; Web: www.west.thomson.com.

### Breaking into the Trade Game: A Small Business Guide to Exporting
Designed to assist America businesses develop international markets. Both a comprehensive how-to manual and reference book providing the reader with the contacts and resources to ease entry into markets around the world. Also highlights export success stories of small businesses. The full text of the Guide is available on the SBA's Web Site at www.sba.gov/oit/info/Guide-To-Exporting. Print versions free of charge can be requested from the SBA Answer Desk, 200 North College Street, Suite A-2015, Charlotte, NC 28202 USA; Tel: [1] (800) UASK-SBA; E-mail: answerdesk@sba.gov.

### 19 Code of Federal Regulations (CFR)
Two volumes. Vol. 1 contains regulations of the U.S. Customs & Border Protection Agency, Dept. of Homeland Security. Vol. 2 contains regulations of the International Trade Commission, International Trade Administration, Department of Commerce. Topics covered include packing and stamping, marking; customs financial and accounting procedure; customs bond; air commerce regulations; trademarks, trade names, and copyrights, etc. Available from the U.S. Government Printing Office at: Tel: [1] (866) 512-1800; Web: http://bookstore.gpo.gov.

### Directory of United States Exporters
Directory of U.S. export firms, export executives, and products exported. Available from Commonwealth Business Media. Contact at: Tel: [1] Tel: [1] (877) 203-5277; E-mail: customerservice@cbizmedia.com; Web: www.cbizmedia.com/prodserv/products/?pub=DEI. A free electronic index on CD-ROM is included. A CD-ROM version, as well as a downloadable PDF version, of the Directory can be ordered from this Web site.

### Directory of United States Importers
Directory of U.S. import firms, import executives, and products imported. Available from Commonwealth Business Media. Contact at: Tel: [1] Tel: [1] (877) 203-5277; E-mail: customerservice@cbizmedia.com; Web: www.cbizmedia.com/prodserv/products/?pub=DEI. A free electronic index on CD-ROM is included. A CD-ROM version, as well as a downloadable PDF version, of the Directory can be ordered from this Web site.

### Europa World Year Book
Provides analytical, statistical, and directory information on each country's economic, social and political structure. ISBN: 1857433068. Annual. $1025 (2005 edition). Available from: Taylor & Francis Group Ltd, 2 Park Square, Milton Park, Abingdon, Oxford OX14 4RN, UK; Tel: +44 (0) 20 7017 6000; Fax: +44 (0) 20 7017 6699; Web: http://search.tandf.co.uk/bookscatalogue.asp.

### Export Reference Guide
A reference guide used by exporters and freight forwarders as a source of country specific shipping document and import information. CD-ROM version is updated monthly, and the Web version is updated weekly. Available from: BNA, 1231 25th Street NW; Washington, DC 20037 USA; Tel: [1] (800) 372-1033; www.bna.com.

### Export Sales and Marketing Manual
Step-by-step procedural manual for marketing U.S. products world-wide. The manual contains illustrations, flow charts, worksheets, and samples of export contracts, shipping documents, and effective international correspondence. By John Jagoe. $295.00 within U.S., $345 outside U.S. 2006 edition available in print (ISBN 0-943677-63-7) and CD-ROM (ISBN 0-943677-64-5). Available directly from Export Institute USA's Web site at www.exportinstitute.com. Address: Export Institute USA, 6901 West 84th St., Suite 359, Minneapolis, MN 55438 USA; Tel: (from within the U.S.) [1] (800) 943-3171, (from outside the U.S.) (952) 943-1505; E-mail: jrj@exportinstitute.com; Web: www.exportinstitute.com.

### Exporters' Encyclopedia - Reference Book
A comprehensive reference manual detailing trade regulations, documentation requirements, transportation, key contacts, etc. for 220 world markets. Sections cover export order, markets and know-how, communication data, information sources and services, and transportation data. ISBN 1-56203-006-X. Available from: The D&B Corporation, 103 JFK Parkway, Short Hills, NJ 07078 USA; Tel: (from within the U.S.) [1] (800) 624-5669, (from outside the U.S.) [1] (973) 921-5500; E-mail: custserv@dnb.com; Web: http:www.dnb.com. Subscriptions include twice-monthly country-specific trade updates and access to free consultations with export specialists.

### Foreign Trade Zone Manual
A U.S. government reference manual for grantees, operators, and users of U.S. Foreign Trade Zones and customs brokers. Available from the U.S. Government Printing Of-

fice at: Tel: [1] (866) 512-1800; Web: http://book-store.gpo.gov.

### Gestures: The Do's and Taboo's of Body Language Around the World

A humorous and informative book on gestures and body language around the world. The first half of the book illustrates gestures and describes what each gestures means in different countries. The second half presents a country by country listing of gestures and body language. $16.95. By Roger Axtell. ISBN: 0-471-18342-3. Other books by Roger Axtell: Do's and Taboos Around the World, 2nd Edition; Do's and Taboos of International Trade: A Small Business Primer; Do's and Taboos of Hosting International Visitors. Available in many bookstores, and also from the publisher at: John Wiley and Sons, Inc., Customer Care Center, 1 Wiley Drive, Somerset, NJ 08875-1272 USA; Tel: [1] (800) 225-5945; Fax: [1] (732) 302-2300; E-mail: custserv@wiley.com; Web: www.wiley.com.

### Global Road Warrior (book and CD-ROM)

175-country handbook for the international business traveler. Thousands of facts and tips for surviving and succeeding while "on the road internationally." Includes detailed "techno travel" information on Internet access, using mobile phones, electrical requirements, and local support numbers for hardware and software vendors. Softcover, 3 volumes, 3840 pages, $245.00 (ISBN 1-885073-96-8). Also available on CD-ROM (ISBN 1-885073-97-6) for both PC and Mac users for $195.00. Available from: World Trade Press, 1450 Grant Ave., Suite 204, Novato, CA 94945 USA; Tel: [1] (415) 898-1124 or (800) 833-8586; Fax: [1] (415) 898-1080; Web: www.globalroadwarrior.com, www.worldtradepress.com.

### Harmonized Tariff Schedule of the United States (HTS or HTSUS)

(USA) An organized listing of goods and their duty rates which is used by U.S. Customs & Border Protection Agency as the basis for classifying imported products and therefore establishing the duty to be charged and providing the U.S. Census with statistical information about imports and exports. The categorization of product listings in the HTSUS is based on the international Harmonized Commodity Description and Coding System developed under the auspices of the Customs Cooperation Council (Harmonized System, HS). Available from the U.S. Government Printing Office at: Tel: [1] (866) 512-1800; Web: http://bookstore.gpo.gov.

### Importer's Manual USA (4th Edition)

A comprehensive reference for importing to the United States. Topics include U.S. Customs Entry and Clearance; International Banking, Letters of Credit; Foreign Exchange; International Law; Packing, Shipping and Insurance; and Commodity Index. Import how-to for 99 commodity groups. ISBN 1-885073-93-3. Hardbound, 960 pages, includes illustrations, photographs. $145.00. Also available on CD-ROM (ISBN 1-885073-98-4) for both PC and Mac users for $145.00. By Edward G. Hinkelman. World Trade Press, 1450 Grant Ave., Suite 204, Novato, CA 94945 USA; Tel: [1] (415) 898-1124 or [1] (800) 833-8586; Fax: [1] (415) 898-1080; Web: www.worldtradepress.com.

### International Business Transactions

From the "In a Nutshell" series, a succinct exposition of the law for those who are not specialists in international trade. Traces legal aspects of an international business transaction from first idea to negotiated conclusion. By Ralph H. Folsom, Michael Wallace, John Spanogle, Jr. ISBN: 031415101X. 7th edition available for $26.50 from major online bookstores, such as Amazon (www.amazon.com)

and Barnes & Noble (www.barnesandnoble.com).

### Law Digest, The

Contains information on the legal systems of countries around the world. Included are digests of the laws of the 50 states, the District of Columbia, Puerto Rico and the US Virgin Islands, summaries of the laws of 82 countries, the complete texts of over 50 Uniform and Model Acts and International Conventions. Annual. Available from: Martindale-Hubbell, Customer Relations Dept., 121 Chanlon Road, New Providence, NJ 07974 USA; E-mail: info@martindale.com; Tel: [1] (800) 526-4902; Fax: [1] (908) 771-8704; Web: www.martindale.com/xp/Martindale/Products/Law_Digest/law_digest.xml. A CD-ROM version is scheduled for Spring of 2007.

The Law Digest is also available through LEXIS®-NEXIS®. The Digest is found in the MARHUB library on the LEXIS®-NEXIS® service. Web: www.lexis.com.

### National Trade Data Bank (NTDB)

(CD-ROM/Internet) Contains international economic and export promotion information supplied by 15 U.S. agencies. Data are updated monthly. The NTDB contains data from the Departments of Agriculture (Foreign Agricultural Service), Commerce (Bureau of the Census, Bureau of Economic Analysis, Office of Administration, and National Institute for Standards and Technology), Energy, Labor (Bureau of Labor Statistics), the Central Intelligence Agency, Eximbank, Federal Reserve System, U.S. International Trade Commission, Overseas Private Investment Corporation, Small Business Administration, the U.S. Trade Representative, and the University of Massachusetts. Source: U.S. Department of Commerce, Office of Economic Analysis, HCHB Room 4885, Washington, DC 20230 USA; Tel: [1] (202) 482-1986; Web: www.stat-usa.gov.

### Official Export Guide

Gives comprehensive export information from source to market for shippers, freight forwarders, and transportation companies. Features marketing, shipping, and documentation information. Includes country profiles with trade data to find new markets, surveys of major world ports, and Export Administration regulations. The Guide is available from Commonwealth Business Media, Inc. in a subscription service either online (at www.officialexportguide.com) or in print; changes are published in biweekly updates available to both online and print subscribers. E-mail: customerservice@cbizmedia.com.

### Paperboard Packaging Resource Directory

(Formerly, the Official Container Directory) The Paperboard Packaging Resource Directory is an annually-updated resource supporting the paperboard converting industry. Can be purchased directly at www.packaging-online.com/paperboardpackaging; Advantar Marketing Services, Customer Service Dept., 131 W. 1st St., Duluth, MN 55802 USA; Fax: [1] (218) 723-9146.

### Reference Book for Exporters

Providing both general and specific guidance, this manual has been helping exporters get the export process right for over 50 years. Available in online, print, and CD-ROM versions. Available from: Croner, 145 London Road, Kingston upon Thames, Surrey KT2 6SR, Tel: +44 (0)20 8547-3333; Fax: +44 (0)20 8547-2637; E-mail: info@croner.co.uk; Web: www.croner.co.uk.

### Bank Directory, Intl. Edition

Lists banks located around the world with addresses of branches and other information. Included are Central Bank and trade association information for each country and each US state. 5 Volumes (includes Worldwide Correspondence Guide). Biannual. $684.00. Can be ordered directly at www.accuitysolutions.com. Available from: Accuity Solutions; Tel: [1] (800) 321-3373 or [1] (847) 676-9600; E-mail: custserv@AccuitySolutions.com; Web: www.accuitysolutions.com.

### Trade Shows Worldwide
Details of conventions, conferences, trade shows and expositions. Five-year date and location information provided. U.S., Canada, and 60 other countries. 23rd edition. ISBN: 0-7876-8968-8. $459.00. Available from: Thomson Gale, Inbound Sales, 27500 Drake Road, Farmington Hills, MI 4833; Tel: [1] (800) 877-GALE (4253); Fax: [1] (800) 414-5043; E-mail: gale.salesassistance@thomson.com; Web: www.gale.com.

### Transportation Telephone Tickler
Since 1949, this is the industry's fundamental guide to services and suppliers. Provides contact information for 24,000 suppliers of 160 types of transportation services in the U.S., Canada, the Caribbean, and parts of Latin America. Four volumes (2006 edition), $149.95 for the 2006 print version plus online subscription to TicklerOnline.com (updated weekly). Available from: Commonwealth Business Media, 400 Windsor Corporate Park, 50 Millstone Road, Suite 200, East Windsor, NJ 08520-1415 USA; Tel (toll-free in U.S.): [1] 888-215-6084; Fax: [1] (609) 371-7883; E-mail: customerservice@cbizmedia.com; Web: www.tickleronline.com.

### U.S. Customs House Guide
Comprehensive reference, first published in 1862, that provides information necessary to document, ship and distribute goods to market. Profiles of U.S. and Canadian ports. Updated harmonized tariff schedules, customs regulations and directories of services. Available in both online (www.customhouseguide.com) and print subscriptions. Subscriptions include free updates. Available from: Commonwealth Business Media; Tel: [1] (888) 215-6084; Fax: [1] (609) 371-7883; Web: www.customhouseguide.com.

### World Business Directory
Contains information on about 136,000 trade-oriented businesses in 180 countries. 11th edition. ISBN: 0-7876-6488-X. $750.00. Available from: Thomson Gale, 27500 Drake Road, Farmington Hills, MI 48331 USA; Tel: [1] (800) 877-GALE (4253); Fax: [1] (248) 699-8049; E-mail: gale.salesassistance@thomson.com; Web: www.gale.com.

### World Directory of Trade and Business Journals
Provides contact information and extensive details on the activities, publications and membership of more than 1,700 trade and business journals worldwide. 3rd Edition. ISBN: 1-84264-416-5. $650.00. Available from: Thomson Gale, 27500 Drake Road, Farmington Hills, MI 48331 USA; Tel: [1] (800) 877-GALE (4253); Fax: [1] (248) 699-8049; E-mail: gale.salesassistance@thomson.com; Web: www.gale.com.

### Worldwide Corporate Tax Guide
Summarizes the corporate tax systems in over 140 countries. Revised annually. Available from: Ernst & Young Product Sales. Web: www.ey.com/global/Content.nsf/International/Tax_-_Library. Also available as a downloadable Adobe Acrobat PDF file free of charge at this Web site.

## International Chamber of Commerce Publications

**ICC Publishing (France)**
International Chamber of Commerce (ICC)
38 Cours Albert 1$^{er}$
75008 Paris, France
Tel: [33] (1) 49-53-28-28
Fax: [33] (1) 49-53-29-42
www.iccwbo.org

**ICC Books**
1212 Avenue of the Americas, 18th Floor
New York, NY 10036 USA
Tel: [1] (212) 703-5066
Fax: [1] (212) 944-0012
www.iccbooksusa.com

### Trade Reference

#### Guide to Export-Import Basics
Describes the process of international trade, from how to prepare the sales contract, how to arrange for international transport, questions of agency, distributorship and franchising. ICC No. 641, ISBN: 92-842-1309-6, softcover, 352 pages, $65.00.

#### A to Z of International Trade
ICC No. 623, ISBN: 92-842-1277-4, softcover, 335 pages, $65.00

#### Free Trade Agreements for Americans
Extracts the important generally applicable provisions found in the nine U.S. free trade agreements in effect or pending congressional ratification as of November 2004. These are compared with each other and to the two basic models against which they are written. This huge quantity of data becomes manageable through this process of focusing on similarities and highlighting differences. ICC No. 972, paperback, 2004 Edition, 88 pages, $50.00.

### International Commercial Transactions
Presents a legal framework within which rules of law, general principles, standard contracts and commercial practice are shown to interact to the benefit of the parties involved in international trade transactions. ICC No. 624, hardcover, ISBN: 92-842-1351-7, 40 pages, $165.00

#### Key Words in International Trade
Contains more than 3000 business words and expressions, translated into English, German, Spanish, French, and Italian. Separate alphabetical indexes are also included for all languages. ICC No. 417/4, softcover, 424 pages, $75.00

### Banking— Letters of Credit

#### Uniform Customs and Practice for Documentary Credits, UCP 500
World standard rules and procedures for using documentary letters of credit. A key document for bankers, lawyers, importers, exporters and the logistics industry. ICC No. 500, softcover, ISBN: 92-842-1155-7, 60 pages, $14.95. Available in e-book version for $25.00.

#### ICC Guide to Documentary Credit Operations
ICC's popular Guide to Documentary Credit Operations offers a total explanation of the documentary credit process. Each stage of the process is illustrated by colorful, easy-to-read diagrams and supported by concrete examples of how it applies in practice. 117 pages. ICC No. 515, softcover, ISBN: 92-842-1159-X, 117 pages, $49.95

#### International Standard Banking Practice for the Examination of Documents Under Documentary Credits
Explains how the practices articulated in ICC's UCP for Documentary Credits are applied in everyday practice by documentary credit practitioners around the world. ICC No. 645, softcover, ISBN: 92-842-1314-2, 108 pages, $25.95. Available in e-book version for $25.00.

### *Documentary Credit Law Throughout the World*
Annotated compilation of national laws on documentary credits (letters of credit) in more than 35 countries. ICC No. 633, softcover, $65.00. Available in e-book version for $65.00.

### *Collected Opinions of the ICC Banking Commission, 1995-2001*
ICC No. 632, hardcover, ISBN: 92-842-1297-9, 576 pages, $150.00

### *Standard Documentary Credit Forms for UCP 500*
Authoritative sourcebook for forms to use with the UCP 500. ICC No. 516, softcover, ISBN: 92-842-1160-3, 76 pages, $34.95

### *International Standby Practices ISP98*
ICC No. 590, softcover, ISBN: 92-842-1247-2, 76 pages, $14.95

### *UCP 500 & 400 Compared*
This publication was developed as a vehicle from which to train managers, supervisors and practitioners of international trade in critical areas of the new UCP 500 Rules. It pays particular attention to those Articles that have been the source of litigation. ICC No. 511, softcover, ISBN: 92-842-1157-3, 134 pages, $39.95

## Banking—eUCP

### *ICC Guide to the eUCP*
A guide to the workings of documentary credits when presented in electronic form. ICC No. 639, ISBN: 92-842-1308-8, softcover, 250 pages, $75.00

### *UCP 500 + eUCP Comprehensive Book Version*
Full texts of the UCP 500 and the twelve supplemental articles to the UCP 500 that cover the electronic presentation of documents in documentary credits. Also included are selected "Opinions of the ICC Banking Commission" and "ICC Banking Commission Decisions and Policy Statements". ICC No. 500/2, softcover, ISBN: 92-842-1306-1, 100 pages, $24.95

### *eUCP Supplement Leaflet Version*
The twelve supplimental articles to the UCP 500 that cover the electronic presentation of documents in documentary credits. ICC No. 500/4, leaflet, 4 pages, $5.00

### *UCP 500 + eUCP Comprehensive Leaflet Version*
The UCP 500 and the twelve supplimental articles to the UCP 500 that cover the electronic presentation of documents in documentary credits.
ICC No. 500/5, leaflet, 8 pages, $3.95

### *eUCP Supplement, Booklet Version*
ICC No. 500/3, leaflet, ISBN: 92-842-1307-X, 16 pages, sold in packs of 10 booklets, $72.50. Available in e-book version for $20.00

## Banking—Uniform Rules for Collections

### *ICC Uniform Rules for Collections*
This publication describes the conditions governing collections, including those for the presentation, payment and the acceptance terms. The Articles also specify the responsibility of the bank regarding protest, case of need and actions to protect the merchandise. An aid to everyday banking operations. ICC No. 522, booklet, ISBN: 92-842-1184-0, 32 pages, $12.95

### *ICC Guide to Collection Operations*
ICC No. 561, softcover, ISBN: 92-842-1214-6, 112 pages, $49.95

### *A Commentary, URC 522*
ICC No. 550, softcover, ISBN: 92-842-1201-5, 48 pages, $25.95

## Uniform Rules for Demand Guarantees

### *Uniform Rules for Demand Guarantees*
In 28 articles sets out the liabilities and responsibilities of principals, beneficiaries and guarantors of demand guarantees. ICC No. 458, softcover booklet, ISBN: 92-842-1094-1, 20 pages, $12.95. Also available as an e-book for $20.00

### *A User's Handbook to the URDG*
Sets out the procedures involved in the issue, presentation and demand for payment of demand guarantees and counter guarantees under the URDG. ICC No. 631, softcover, 190 pages, $65.00

## Banking—Uniform Rules for Bank-toBank Reinbursements

### *ICC Guide to Bank-to-Bank Reinbursements under Documentary Credits*
ICC No. 575, softcover, ISBN: 92-842-1232-4, 79 pages, $49.95

### *ICC Uniform Rules for Bank-to-Bank Reinbursements Under Documentary Credits*
ICC No. 525, booklet, ISBN: 92-842-1185-9, 31 pages, $12.95. Also available as an e-book for $20.00

### *A Commentary, URR 525*
ICC No. 551, softcover, ISBN: 92-842-1203-0, 40 pages, $25.95

## Incoterms

### *Incoterms 2000*
Defines the thirteen Incoterms (International Commercial Terms) and specifies respective rights and obligations of buyer and seller in international transactions.
ICC No. 560, softcover, ISBN: 92-842-1199-9, 127 pages, $44.95. Also available as an e-book for $50.00

### *Incoterms 2000 Wall Chart*
ICC No. 614, 12"x24" poster, $100.00

### *ICC Guide to Incoterms 2000*
Describes how Incoterms work in daily practice. ICC No. 620, softcover, ISBN: 92-842-1269-3, 192 pages, $75.00

### *Incoterms for Americans*
Answers questions about Incoterms transactions based on American customary practice. ICC No. 967, softcover, 140 pages, $65.00

### *Incoterms 2000 Multimedia Expert*
ICC No. 616. Incoterms 2000 Multimedia Expert is available from the ICC main office in Paris. Please contact them by E-mail: pub@iccwbo.org for details about this product. CD-ROM, $150.00

### *A Forum of Experts*
ICC No. 617, softcover 132 pages, $49.95

## International Law and Arbitration

### *International Chamber of Commerce Arbitration*
The definitive text on the workings of the world's foremost arbitration institution, the ICC International Court of Arbitration. By Craig, Park, and Paulsson. ICC No. 594, hardcover, ISBN: 92-842-1251-0, 952 pages, $200.00

### *Arbitration*
Money Laundering, Corruption and Fraud
ICC No. 651, softcover, ISBN: 92-842-1320-7, 192 pages, $75.00

### *Collection of ICC Arbitral Awards, 1996-2000*
ICC No. 647, hardcover, ISBN: 92 842 0316 3, 600 pages, $225.00

RESOURCES

### *ICC Force Majeure Clause 2003 and ICC Hardship Clause 2003*
ICC No. 650, softcover, ISBN: 92-842-1319-3, 24 pages, $25.00. Also available as an e-book for $25.00

### *UNIDROIT Principles of International Commercial Contracts*
ICC No. 642, softcover, ISBN: 92-842-1310-X, 156 pages, $75.00

### *Collection of ICC Arbitral Awards, 1986-1990*
ICC No. 514, hardcover, ISBN: 92-842-0161-6, 578 pages, $225.00

### *Resolving International Intellectual Property Disputes*
ICC No. 592, softcover, ISBN: 92-842-1249-9, 207 pages, $75.00

### *Arbitration, Finance and Insurance*
ICC No. 627, softcover, ISBN: 92-842-1292-8, 82 pages, $75.00

### *Transfer of Ownership in International Trade*
ICC No. 546, hardcover, ISBN: 92-842-1197-2, 437 pages, $125.00

## Model International Commercial Contracts

### *ICC Model Turnkey Contract for the Supply of an Industrial Plant*
CD-ROM included. ICC No. 653, softcover, ISBN: 92-842-1323-1, 120 pages, $75.00

### *ICC Short Form Model Contracts*
CD-ROM included. ICC No. 634, softcover, ISBN: 92-842-1299-5, 40 pages, $75.00

### *ICC Model Commercial Agency Contract*
CD-ROM included. ICC No. 644, softcover, ISBN: 92-8421313-4, 64 pages, $75.00

### *ICC Model Distributorship Contract*
ICC No. 646, softcover, ISBN: 92-842-1315-0, 68 pages, $75.00

### *The ICC Model International Franchasing Contract*
ICC No. 557, softcover, ISBN: 92-842-1211-1, 76 pages, $75.00

### *ICC Model Occasional Intermediary Contract*
ICC No. 619, softcover, ISBN: 92-842-1272-3, 36 pages, $75.00

## Commercial Fraud and Counterfeiting

### *Private Commercial Bribery*
ICC No. 953, ISBN: 92-842-1322-3, 656 pages, $125.00

### *Fighting Corruption*
ICC No. 652, ISBN: 92 842 1261 3, 241 pages, $75.00

### *Preventing Financial Instrument Fraud*
ICC No. 648, softcover, ISBN: 92-842-1317-7, 119 pages, $100.00

### *Anti-Counterfeiting Technology*
ICC No. 630, softcover, ISBN: 92-842-1293-6, 80 pages, $75.00

# World Trade Press Publications

**World Trade Press**
800 Lindberg Lane, Suite 190
Petaluma, California (CA) 94952 USA
Tel: [1] (707) 778-1124 x 3 (sales)
Toll-free in USA: (800) 833-8586
Fax: [1] (707) 778-1329
E-mail: sales@worldtradepress.com
Web: www.worldtradepress.com
World Trade Press is one of the world's foremost publishers of professional books, e-content, software and maps for the international trade community. The company was founded in 1993 and currently offers more than 65 print products, plus maps and e-content for web delivery.

## General Reference Books

### *Dictionary of International Trade, 7th Edition*
"Handbook of the Global Trade Community" This is the most respected and largest-selling dictionary of trade in the world. It is in use in more than 100 countries by importers, exporters, bankers, shippers, logistics professionals, attorneys, economists, government officials and students. ISBN: 1-885073-72-0
Softcover, 688 pages, 7"x10", $60.00

### *Importer's Manual USA (4th Edition)*
A comprehensive reference for importing to the United States. Topics include U.S. Customs Entry and Clearance; International Banking, Letters of Credit; Foreign Exchange; International Law; Packing, Shipping and Insurance; and Commodity Index. Import how-to for 99 commodity groups. ISBN 1-885073-93-3. Hardbound, 960 pages, includes illustrations, photographs. $145.00. By Edward G. Hinkelman.

### *Global Road Warrior (book and CD-ROM)*
175-country handbook for the international business traveler. Thousands of facts and tips for surviving and succeeding while "on the road internationally." Includes detailed "techno travel" information on Internet access, electrical requirements, and local support numbers for hardware and software vendors. ISBN 1-885073-96-8. Softcover, three volumes, 3840 pages, $245.00. Also available as a 175-country CD-ROM for both PC and Mac.

### *A Basic Guide to Exporting, 3rd Edition*
This is the most respected and best-selling introduction to exporting from the USA. It is designed to help new to export firms understand the elements of the export process, learn about the costs and risks and develop a strategy for success. ISBN: 1-885073-83-6
Softcover, 188 pages, 8.5"x11", $19.95

### *Pocket Guide to Mobile Connectivity*
Worldwide solutions for telecommunications, cell communications, Internet connectivity, Mobile connectivity and wi-fi. Softcover, 160 pages, 4.25"x7.5", $22.00, ISBN: 1-885073-70-4

### *Global Connect! 4th Edition*
The world's first truly comprehensive guide to international telecommunications, cell communications, Internet connectivity and mobile connectivity. Contains more than 20 general reference features plus thirteen categories of coverage for 175 countries. ISBN: 1-885073-94-1. Hardcover, 960 pages, 6.5"x9", $88.00.

### *Services, The Export of the 21st Century*
This book is designed to help domestic USA service providers "go international."
Softcover, 173 pages, $19.95, ISBN: 1-885073-41-0

## Short Course Series

Short Course books are stand-alone training modules that teach the key skills of international trade. Each covers a single topic and is designed as a practical guide with immediate real world application. Each is written from an international perspective for an international audience. Content focuses on the universal needs of all business people, regardless of whether they are a buyer or seller, or dealing in products or services. These books are as useful to someone from Asia as to someone from Europe or the Americas.

*International Business Culture*
Building Your International Business Through Cultural Awareness. Softcover, 184 pages, 7"x10", $19.95
By Charles Mitchell, ISBN: 1-885073-54-2

*International Business Ethics*
Combining Ethics and Profits in Global Business
Softcover, 184 pages, 7"x10", $24.95
By Charles Mitchell, ISBN: 1-885073-63-1

*International Business Plans*
Charting a Strategy for Success in Global Commerce
Softcover, 184 pages, 7"x10", $24.95
By Robert L. Brown, MBA, J.D., Ph.D. and Alan S. Gutterman, MBA, J.D., Ph.D., ISBN: 1-885073-62-3

*International Contracts, 2nd Edition*
Drafting the International Sales Contract
Softcover, 184 pages, 7"x10", $24.95
By Karla C. Shippey, J.D., ISBN: 1-885073-55-0

*International Economics*
Understanding the Dynamics of the International Marketplace. Softcover, 184 pages, 7"x10", $19.95
By Jeffrey Curry, MBA, Ph.D, ISBN: 1-885073-53-4

*International Intellectual Property Rights*
Protecting Your Brands, Marks, Copyrights, Patents, Designs and Related Rights Worldwide
Softcover, 184 pages, 7"x10", $24.95
By Karla C. Shippey, J.D., ISBN: 1-885073-56-9

*International Joint Ventures*
How to Negotiate, Establish and Manage an International Joint Venture. Softcover, 184 pages, 7"x10", $24.95
By Alan S. Gutterman, MBA, Ph.D.,
ISBN: 1-885073-61-5

*International Marketing*
Approaching and Penetrating the International Marketplace. Softcover, 184 pages, 7"x10", $19.95
By Jeffrey Curry, MBA, Ph.D, ISBN: 1-885073-52-6

*International Marketing Blunders*
Marketing Mistakes Made by Companies that Should Have Known Better
Softcover, 184 pages, 7"x10", $24.95
By Michael D. White, ISBN: 1-885073-60-7

*International Negotiating*
Planning and Conducting International Business Negotiations. Softcover, 184 pages, 7"x10", $19.95
By Jeffrey Curry, MBA, Ph.D, ISBN: 1-885073-51-8

*International Payments, 2nd Edition*
Letters of Credit, Documentary Collections and Cyber Payments in International Transactions
Softcover, 184 pages, 7"x10", $24.95
By Edward G. Hinkelman, ISBN: 1-885073-50-X

*International Trade Documentation*
The Documents of Exporting, Importing, Shipping and Banking. Softcover, 184 pages, 7"x10", $24.95
By Edward G. Hinkelman, ISBN: 1-885073-59-3

## Country Business Guides (CBG)

Each CBG offers a comprehensive view of a country's business life and covers 25 key topics. Included are chapters on the economy, natural resources, business formation and entities, foreign investment, labor, business practices and etiquette, trade fairs, law, business travel, personal and business taxation, important addresses, maps and more. Each Country Business Guide is $24.95.

*Argentina Business*
Softcover, 7"x10", 372 pages, ISBN 1-885073-75-5

*Australia Business*
Softcover, 7"x10", 328 pages, ISBN 1-885073-03-8

*Canada Business*
Softcover, 7"x10", 304 pages, ISBN 1-885073-13-5

*China Business*
Softcover, 7"x10", 418pages, ISBN 0-9631864-3-4

*Hong Kong Business*
Softcover, 7"x10", 305pages, ISBN 0-9631864-7-7

*Japan Business*
Softcover, 7"x10", 374 pages, ISBN 0-9631864-2-6

*Korea Business*
Softcover, 7"x10", 331 pages, ISBN 0-9631864-4-2

*Mexico Business*
Softcover, 7"x10",488 pages, ISBN 1-885073-47-X

*Philippines Business*
Softcover, 7"x10", 342 pages, ISBN 1-885073-08-9

*Singapore Business*
Softcover, 7"x10", 309 pages, ISBN 0-9631864-6-9

*Taiwan Business*
Softcover, 7"x10", 310 pages, ISBN 0-9631864-5-0

*USA Business*
Softcover, 7"x10", 507 pages, ISBN 1-885073-01-1

## Passport to the World Series

These are pocket-sized guides to the business, culture, etiquette and communication styles of a country. They are designed to help businesspeople avoid cultural faux-pas, learn about a country's values and beliefs and develop an effective negotiating style. Twenty-five countries.
All Passport Series books softcover, 96 pages, 4.25"x7" and cost only $6.95.

*Passport Argentina*
By Andrea Campbell, ISBN 1-885073-21-6

*Passport Brazil*
By Elizabeth Ann Herrington, ISBN 1-885073-18-6

*Passport China*
By Jenni Lee, ISBN 1-885073-89-5

*Passport France*
By Nadine Joseph, ISBN 1-885073-29-1

*Passport Germany*
By Roland Flamini, 4.25"x7", ISBN 1-885073-20-8

*Passport Hong Kong*
By Andrew Grzeskowiak, ISBN 1-885073-31-3

*Passport India*
By Manoj Joshi, ISBN 1-885073-23-2

*Passport Indonesia*
By Gregory Cole, ISBN 1-885073-37-2

*Passport Israel*
By Donna Rosenthal, ISBN 1-885073-22-4

*Passport Italy*
By Claudia Gioseffi, ISBN 1-885073-34-8

*Passport Japan*
By Dean Engel and Ken Murakami, ISBN 1-885073-95-X

*Passport Korea*
By Kevin Keating, ISBN 1-885073-39-9

*Passport Mexico*
By Randy Malat, ISBN 1-885073-91-7

*Passport Philippines*
By Luis H. Francia, ISBN 1-885073-40-2

*Passport Poland*
By Natalia Kissel, ISBN 1-885073-33-X

*Passport Russia*
By Charles Mitchell, ISBN 1-885073-32-1

*Passport Singapore*
By Alexandra Kett, ISBN 1-885073-38-0

RESOURCES

**Passport South Africa**
By Charles Mitchell, ISBN 1-885073-19-4

**Passport Spain**
By Himilce Novas, ISBN 1-885073-35-6

**Passport Switzerland**
By François Micheloud, ISBN 1-885073-88-7

**Passport Taiwan**
By Jeffrey E. Curry, ISBN 1-885073-27-5

**Passport Thailand**
By Naomi Wise, ISBN 1-885073-26-7

**Passport United Kingdom**
By Timothy Harper, ISBN 1-885073-28-3

**Passport USA**
Softcover, 96 pages, 4.25"x7", ISBN 1-885073-15-1

**Passport Vietnam**
By Jeffrey E. Curry and Jim Chinh Nguyen,
ISBN 1-885073-25-9

# PERIODICALS & REPORTS

### AAPA Seaports Magazine
The American Association of Port Authorities' (AAPA) semi-annual magazine for the entire port industry. Published in January & September in print and online. Provides editorial review of industry issues, news and events, feature articles of interest to the port industry at large, and the latest updates of port data, statistics and personnel changes throughout the industry. Available from: SEA-PORTS PUBLICATIONS GROUP, Commonwealth Business Media, Inc., Ray Venturino, Publisher, 33 Washington Street, 13th Floor, Newark, NJ 07102-3107; Tel: [1] (973) 848-7207; Email: rventurino@joc.com; Web: www.aapaseaports.com.

### Background Notes
A series of publications by the U.S. State Department providing an overview of a country's history, people, political conditions, economy and foreign relations. Each publication also includes map of country and travel notes. Available from the U.S. Government Printing Office at: Tel: [1] (866) 512-1800; Fax: [1] (202) 512-2104; E-Mail: ContactCenter@gpo.gov; Web: http://bookstore.gpo.gov./subjects/sb-093.jsp.

### Business Beijing (China)
Business Beijing magazine provides the most comprehensive and up-to-date information on trade, investment and business policies in the People's Republic of China. Published once a month by the Beijing Municipal Foreign Economic & Trade Commission. Business Beijing publishes a full range of analysis, news, features and graphic data about the business climate in China, with special emphasis on the capital Beijing. Also includes an archive of back issues. Subscription information is available at: http://www.btmbeijing.com/contents/en/business; Tel: +86 010 6515-5020; Fax: +86 010 6515-5019

### Economist, The
Current affairs and business magazine (the publishers call it a newspaper). Includes reports, analysis, and comments on key events in business, finance, science and technology. Special surveys focus on specific countries, industries or markets. Available in a weekly print edition and online. Contact at Economist Intelligence Unit at www.eiu.com.

### Economist Intelligence Unit
Research reports, country profiles, newsletters, and on-line information to help companies operate and expand abroad. Also, individual country studies, quarterly country reports, and forecasts. Contact the Economist Intelligence Unit, Ltd. online at www.eiu.com for subscription and advertising information; Economist Intelligence Unit, 26 Red Lion Square London WC1R 4HQ United Kingdom; Tel: + 44 (0) 20 7576 8181; Fax: + 44 (0) 20 7576 8476; E-mail: london@eiu.com; Web: http://www.eiu.com.

### Exporter, The
Monthly reports on the business of exporting. Available from: The Exporter, 26 Broadway, Suite 776, New York, NY 10004 USA; Tel: [1] (212) 269-2016; Fax: [1] (212) 269-2740; E-mail: exporter@exporter.com; Web: www.exporter.com.

### Financial Times (of London)
Daily newspaper specifically for those in the economic and financial sector. Covers current news and information of financial and political issues. Also includes stock tables, graphs, and commentary. Contact the Financial Times online at www.ft.com for subscription information specific to the country or continent of delivery.

### Foreign Labor Trends
A series of reports on specific countries of the world, providing an overview of the labor sector of a country's economy. Includes information on labor standards, conditions of employment, human resource development and labor relations. Available from the U.S. Government Printing Office at: Tel: [1] (866) 512-1800; Web: http://bookstore.gpo.gov.

### Foreign Traders Index (FTI)
The foreign traders index, which is part of the National Trade Data Bank (NTDB), identifies foreign firms that are interested in importing U.S. products. The FTI includes background information on foreign companies, address, contact person, sales figures, size of company, and products by SIC code. Contact: U.S. Department of Commerce, HCHB Room 4885, Washington, DC 20230 USA; Tel: [1] (202) 482-1986; Fax: [1] (202) 482-2164; Web: www.statusa.gov.

### Multimodal Business
Bi-weekly (24 issues annually, by e-mail and hard copy). From ports to rail and trucking, Multimodal Business keeps you up to date on the logistical and financial impact of new security regulations and burdensome requirements for shippers, carriers and equipment providers. Multimodal Business also provides unrivaled coverage of bottlenecks in the US transportation system, case studies on how other companies are succeeding and crucial intelligence on the availability of containers, chassis and other equipment at major intermodal hubs. Tel: [1] (202) 775-0240; Fax: [1] (202) 872-8045; E-mail: sales@argusmediagroup.com; Web: www.fieldston.com.

### International Company Profiles (ICPs)
U.S. government fee-based service which provides a background report on a specific foreign firm, prepared by U.S. commercial officers overseas. ICPs provide information about the type of organization, year established, size, number of employees, reputation, language preferred, product lines, principal owners, financial and trade references. ICPs include narrative information about the reliability of the foreign firm. Issued by the International Trade Administration (U.S. Dept. of Commerce). To obtain an International Company Profile, contact your nearest Dept. of Commerce district office, or call [1] (800) USA-TRADE; Web: http://trade.gov/cs.

### Journal of Commerce
The Journal of Commerce is published in both print and online versions. Subscription to the print version includes full access to the online version, which contains an exten-

sive archive of articles. The JoC has information on domestic and foreign economic developments plus export opportunities, shipyards, agricultural trade leads, and trade fair information. Feature articles on tariff and non-tariff barriers, licensing controls, joint ventures, and trade legislation in foreign countries. Contact: The Journal of Commerce, 33 Washington Street, Newark, N.J. 07102 USA; Tel: [1] (888) 215-6084 or (from outside the U.S.) (973) 848-7259; E-mail: customerservice@cbizmedia.com; Web: www.joc.com.

### OAG Cargo Guide Worldwide
A basic reference publication for shipping freight by air. It contains current domestic and international cargo flight schedules, including pure cargo, wide body, and combination passenger-cargo flights. Each monthly issue also contains information on air carriers' special services, labeling, airline and aircraft decodings, air carrier and freight forwarders directory, cargo charter information, Worldwide City Directory, small package services, interline air freight agreements, aircraft loading charts and more. Includes the OAG Cargo Guide Rules Supplement with regulations by country, documentary requirements and aircraft-loading restrictions. $299.00 for annual subscription. Can be purchased from OAG Worldwide, Ltd. online at http://www.oag.com/oag/website/com/en/Home/Product+Catalog/Products; Tel: (from within the U.S.) [1] (800) DIA-LOAG, (from outside the U.S.) [1] (630) 515-5307; E-mail: custsvc@oag.com.

### Pacific Shipper
Weekly news magazine for the trans-Pacific shipping industry. $199 annual subscription. Available from Commonwealth Business Media, Inc. Contact at: Tel: [1] (888) 215-6084; Fax: [1] (609) 371-7883; E-mail: customerservice@cbizmedia.com; Web: www.pacificshipper.com

### Gulf Shipper
Weekly news magazine for the Gulf shipping industry. $69 annual subscription. Available from Commonwealth News Media, Inc. Contact at: Tel: [1] (888) 215-6084; Fax: [1] (609) 371-7883; E-mail: customerservice@cbizmedia.com; Web: www.gulfshipper.com

### Florida Shipper
Weekly news magazine for the Florida shipping industry. $69 annual subscription. Available from Commonwealth News Media, Inc. Contact at: Tel: [1] (888) 215-6084; Fax: [1] (609) 371-7883; E-mail: customerservice@cbizmedia.com; Web: www.floridashipper.com

### Wall Street Journal
National and international finance and business. A more conservative tone. Also publishes a European and Asian edition as well as the Asian Wall Street Journal Weekly. Available in print and/or online subscriptions. Print subscription (subscribe directly at http://subscribe.wsj.com/wsjie): $99/year, published weekdays. Online subscription (go to http://interactive.wsj.com): $99/year. Available from: The Wall Street Journal, 200 Burnett Road, Chicopee, MA 01020 USA; Tel: 1-800-JOURNAL (1-800-568-7625) OR 1-800-369-2834; Fax: 1-800-975-8618; E-mail: wsj.service@dowjones.com OR onlinejournal@wsj.com; Web: www.wsj.com.

### World Trade Magazine
Provides information to help exporters increase global sales. Targeted to U.S. executives who ship and source worldwide. Subscribe through www.worldtrademag.com. World Trade Magazine, BNP Media, 2401 W. Big Beaver Rd., Suite 700, Troy, MI 48084 USA; Tel: [1] (248) 362-3700; Fax: [1] (248) 244-6439

### World Wide Shipping Guide
Complete up-to-date information on an international scale. Provides name, address, services offered, telephone, fax numbers, key personnel, E-mail & Website addresses for over 60,000 companies in the domestic and international freight transportation industry. Includes complete glossary of maritime terms and foreign trade definitions. Updated annually. One Year Subscription $95.00, Two Year Subscription $175.00, One Year USA CD-ROM including (3) Quarterly Updates $165.00, and One Year Foreign CD-ROM including (3) Quarterly Updates $195.00 Tel: [1] (845) 358-3813; Fax: [1] (845) 358-3854; E-mail: bob@wwship.com; Web: www.wwship.

## COUNTRY SERIES BOOKS

### Country Business Guides
Each book presents a comprehensive view of a country's business life, covering 25 topics important to international business. Included are chapters on the economy and natural resources, business formation, business entities, demographics, foreign investment, labor, business practices and etiquette, trade fairs, business law, industry reviews, business travel, personal and business taxation, opportunities, important addresses, maps and more. Available from: World Trade Press, 1450 Grant Ave., Suite 204, Novato, CA 94945 USA; Tel: [1] (415) 898-1124 or [1] (800) 833-8586; Fax: [1] (415) 898-1080; Web: www.worldtradepress.com.

### Country Reports
Detailed and continually updated analysis of the financial, political, and economic climate in 189 countries around the world. Single issue: $245.00. Annual subscription: $525.00. Available from the Economist Intelligence Unit, Ltd. directly from their online bookstore at http://store.eiu.com (home page www.eiu.com).

### Culture Shock Series
A series of roughly 50 country-specific books devoted to helping the business person visiting or working in a particular country to wisely handle various cultural situations. Provides survival guide for expatriates and suggestions on dealing with culture shock. Available from: Graphic Arts

Center Publishing Company; 3019 NW Yeon, Portland, OR 97210 USA; Tel: [1] (503) 226-2402; Fax: [1] (503) 223-1410; E-mail: sales@gacpc.com; Web: www.gacpc.com. Also available from major online bookstores such as Amazon (www.amazon.com) and Barnes and Noble (www.barnesandnoble.com).

### Doing Business in ... Guides
Comprehensive guides by PricewaterhouseCoopers on approximately 80 countries worldwide from Antigua to Zimbabwe. Chapters discuss investment climate, doing business, audits, accounting, and taxation, and include helpful appendix items. Each publication is $39.95. Entire set is available for $695.00. Can be ordered directly from the Web site at www.pwcglobal.com. Tel: [1] (800) 579-1646 OR [1] (646) 394-3508.

### Passport to the World
Pocket-sized guides to the business, culture, etiquette and communication styles of a country. Designed to help businesspeople avoid cultural faux-pas, learn about a country's values and beliefs and develop an effective negotiating style. Twenty-four countries. Softcover, $6.95 each. World Trade Press, 1450 Grant Ave., Suite 204, Novato, CA 94945 USA; Tel: [1] (415) 898-1124 or [1] (800) 833-8586; Fax: [1] (415) 898-1080; Web: www.worldtradepress.com.

**RESOURCES**

# ASSOCIATIONS

### Air Transport Association of America (ATA)
The trade and service organization for the U.S. scheduled airlines. ATA acts on behalf of the airlines in activities ranging from improvement in air safety to planning for the airlines' role in national defense. ATA works with the airlines, the Government, and shippers in developing standards and techniques in all phases of air cargo. ATA is a source of information on cargo matters ranging from air freight packaging practices, automation, and freight lift capacity, data on air freight growth, and statistical data on air cargo services. Contact: Air Transport Association of America, 1301 Pennsylvania Ave. NW, Suite 1100, Washington, DC 20004-1707 USA; Tel: [1] (202) 626-4000; E-mail: ata@airlines.org; Web: www.airlines.org.

### American Association of Exporters and Importers (AAEI)
A trade association which advises members of legislation regarding importing and exporting. Provides information to the international trade community and fights against protectionism. Hosts seminars and conferences for importers and exporters. Contact: American Association of Exporters and Importers, 1050 17th Street, NW, Washington, DC 20036 USA; Tel: [1] (202) 857-8009; Fax: [1] (202) 857-7843; Web: www.aaei.org.

### Canadian Institute of Traffic and Transportation (C.I.T.T.)
Since 1958, the C.I.T.T. has been helping individuals working in logistics. With the maturation of logistics as a crucial element of business, the C.I.T.T. has evolved from an academic institution into a well-developed professional association that certifies logistics professionals. Contact at: C.I.T.T., 10 King Street East, Suite 400, Toronto, ON M5C 1C3 Canada; Tel: [1] (416) 363-5696; Fax: [1] (416) 363-5698; Email: info@citt.ca; Web: www.citt.ca.

### Council of Supply Chain Management Professionals
A non-profit organization of individuals throughout the world who have interests and/or responsibilities in logistics and the related functions that make up the logistics profession. Its purpose is to enhance the development of the logistics profession through logistics professionals by providing them with educational opportunities and relevant information through a variety of programs, services, and activities. Contact: Council of Logistics Management, 2805 Butterfield Road, Suite 200, Oak Brook, Illinois 60523 USA; Tel: [1] (630) 574-0985; Fax: [1] (630) 574-0989; E-mail: cscmpadmin@cscmp.org; Web: http://www.cscmp.org.

### Federation of International Trade Associations (FITA)
Can assist you in locating an international trade association in your geographic area. Contact: Federation of International Trade Associations, 11800 Sunrise Valley Drive, Suite 210, Reston, VA 20191 USA; [1] (800) 969-FITA (3482) or [1] (703) 620-1588; E-mail: info@fita.org; Fax: [1] (703) 620-4922; Web: www.fita.org.

### Intermodal Association of North America (IANA)
The IANA is North America's leading industry trade association representing the combined interests of the intermodal freight industry. The IANA promotes the benefits of intermodal transportation, provides a forum to discuss common issues and innovations; fosters professional development; participates in governmental proceedings impacting the industry; and informs and educates lawmakers and other public sector representatives about intermodal-ism. Contact at: IANA, Suite 1100, 11785 Beltsville Drive Calverton, MD 20705 USA; Tel: [1] (301) 982-3400; Fax: [1] (301) 982-4815; E-mail: iana@intermodal.org; Web: www.intermodal.org.

### International Air Transport Association
The trade and service organization for airlines of more than 100 countries serving international routes. IATA activities on behalf of shippers in international air freight include development of containerization programs, freight handling techniques and, for some airlines, uniform rates and rules. Contact: IATA, Route de l'Aeroport 33, PO Box 416, 15 Airport, CH-1215 Geneva Switzerland; Tel: [41] (22) 799-2525; Fax: [41] (22) 798-3553; Web: www.iata.org.

### International Chamber of Commerce (ICC)
The ICC is the world's only truly global business organization and acts as the voice of world business championing the global economy as a force for economic growth, job creation and prosperity.
The ICC covers a broad spectrum, from arbitration and dispute resolution to making the case for open trade and the market economy system, business self-regulation, fighting corruption and combating commercial crime.
Importantly, the ICC is the creator and publisher of extremely important documents promoting the standardization of international business terms (Incoterms 2000), documentary credits (UCP 500), documentary collections (URC), and many others. Refer to the major listing of ICC publications in this section.

### ICC Publishing (France)
International Chamber of Commerce (ICC)
38 Cours Albert 1$^{er}$
75008 Paris, France
Tel: [33] (1) 49-53-28-28; Fax: [33] (1) 49-53-29-42
www.iccwbo.org

### ICC Publishing, Inc. (USA)
1212 Avenue of the Americas, 18th Floor
New York, NY 10036 USA
Tel: [1] (212) 703-5066
Fax: [1] (212) 944-0012
www.iccbooksusa.com

### International Civil Aviation Organization
The ICAO is an agency of the United Nations. It was organized to insure orderly worldwide technical development of civil aviation. Contact: ICAO, Public Information Office, 999 University Street, Montreal, Quebec H3C 5H7 Canada; Tel: [1] (514) 954-8219; Fax: [1] (514) 954-6077; E-mail: icaohq@icao.int; Web: www.icao.int.

### International Society of Logistics (SOLE)
Non-profit international professional society composed of individuals organized to enhance the art and science of logistics technology, education and management. There are over 90 SOLE chapters in more than 50 countries. Chapters conduct technical meetings, symposia and workshops, all designed to provide members with opportunities for professional advancement. Contact at: SOLE - The International Society of Logistics, 8100 Professional Place, Suite 111, Hyattsville, Maryland 20785 USA; Tel: [1] (301) 459-8446; Fax: [1] (301) 459-1522; E-mail: solehq@erols.com; Web: www.sole.org.

### National Association of Export Companies (NEXCO)
An information provider, support clearinghouse, forum, and advocate for those involved in exporting and servicing exporters. Provides networking opportunities, counseling, publications, seminars, etc. Contact: NEXCO, PO Box

3949, Grand Central Station, New York, NY 10163 USA; Tel: [1] (877) 291-4901; Fax: [1] (646) 349-9628; Email: director@nexco.org.; Web: www.nexco.org.

**National Association of Foreign Trade Zones**
A U.S. based trade association of operators and users of U.S. Foreign Trade Zones. Contact: National Association of Foreign Trade Zones, 1001 Connecticut Ave. NW, Suite 350, Washington, DC 20036 USA; Tel: [1] (202) 331-1950; Fax: [1] (202) 331-1994; E-mail: info@naftz.org; Web: www.naftz.org.

**National Customs Brokers & Forwarders Association of America**
A non-profit organization which serves as the trade organization of customs brokers and international freight forwarders in the U.S. Through ongoing communications with industry trade publications and the general media, the Association projects the industry's interests and objectives. Membership includes brokers and freight forwarders in 32 affiliated associations located at major ports throughout the U.S. Contact: National Customs Brokers & Forwarders Association of America, Inc., 1200 18th Street NW, #901, Washington, DC 20036 USA: Tel: [1] (202) 466-0222; Fax: [1] (202) 466-0226; E-mail: staff@ncbfaa.org; Web: www.ncbfaa.org.

**National Foreign Trade Council**
Trade association that deals exclusively with U.S. public policy affecting international trade and investment. The Council consists of about 500 U.S. manufacturing and service corporations that have international operations of interest. Contact: National Foreign Trade Council, 1625 K St. NW, Suite 1090, Washington, DC 20006 USA; Tel: [1] (202) 887-0278; Fax: [1] (202) 452-8160; E-mail: nftcinformation@nftc.org; Web: www.nftc.org.

**Association of Women in International Trade (WIIT)**
The Association of Women in International Trade (WIIT) is the premier non-partisan professional organization in Washington, D.C. for individuals -- particularly women -- who share a strong interest and expertise in the field of international trade. In addition to its first-rate substantive programs, WIIT is recognized for its range of professional development supports. It is the only trade organization in the Washington, DC area that keeps you ahead on trade news while also expanding your professional skills and opportunities. Web: www.wiit.org

**Small Business Exporters Association**
A trade association representing small- and medium-size exporters. Contact: Small Business Exporters Association, 1156 15th Street NW, Suite 1100, Washington, DC 20005 USA; Tel: [1] (202) 659-9320 OR [1] (800) 345-6728, x211; Web: www.sbea.org.

**Supply-Chain Council**
Global, non-profit trade association open to all types of organizations. Sponsors and supports educational programs includ-

ing conferences, retreats, benchmarking studies, and development of the Supply-Chain Operations Reference-model (SCOR), the process reference model designed to improve users' efficiency and productivity. The Council is dedicated to improving the supply chain efficiency of its practitioner members. Contact at: Supply-Chain Council, Inc., 1400 Eye Street NW, Suite 1050, Washington, DC USA 20005; Tel: [1] (202) 962-0440; Fax: [1] (202) 962-3939; E-mail: info@supply-chain.org; Web: www.supply-chain.org.

**U.S. Chamber of Commerce, International Division**
Represents American business. It lobbies the U.S. Government for specific trade policies and sponsors a number of conferences. Contact: U.S. Chamber of Commerce, International Division, 1615 H Street NW, Washington, DC 20062-2000 USA; Tel: [1] (202) 659-6000; Web: www.us-chamber.com/International.

**U.S. Council for International Business**
A membership organization which is the official U.S. affiliate of the International Chamber of Commerce. The council also oversees the Interstate Commerce Commission's Temporary Admission Carnet System. Provides a number of programs available for members: Court of Arbitration; Counterfeiting Intelligence Bureau; Institute of International Business and Law Practice; International Environmental Bureau. Address: Contact: United States Council for International Business, 1212 Avenue of the Americas, New York, NY 10036 USA; Tel: [1] (212) 354-4480; E-mail: info@uscib.org; Web: www.uscib.org.

**Washington International Trade Association (WITA)**
A non-profit, voluntary organization dedicated to providing a neutral forum in the nation's capital for the open discussion of international trade issues. WITA has over 800 members consisting of business executives, consultants, lawyers, federal officials, diplomats and academics. Through an extensive series of programs, WITA keeps its members informed of the latest positions taken by the Administration and Congress on trade policy, rules and regulations governing international trade, and views of U.S. trade policy from abroad. Contact: Washington International Trade Association, 1300 Pennsylvania Ave., NW, Suite 350 Washington, DC 20004 USA; Tel: [1] (202) 312-1600; Fax: [1] (202) 312-1601; E-mail: wita@wita.org; Web: www.wita.org.

**World Trade Centers Association**
Located around the world. World Trade Center members receive office support services, consultant services, conferences and reciprocal membership services at WTCs globally. Administers NETWORK, a trade lead data bank system. Contact: World Trade Centers Association, 60 East 42nd Street, Suite 1901, New York, NY 10165 USA; Tel: [1] (212) 432-2626; Fax: [1] (212) 488-0064; E-mail: wtca@wtca.org; Web: http://iserve.wtca.org.

# Academic Institutions

## United States

**Center for Logistics Management (University of Nevada, Reno)**
Offers an undergraduate degree in logistics management as well as graduate degrees with emphasis in this area. The program is integrated with key business courses yielding well-rounded graduates in logistics management. Contact at: Center for Logistics Management, College of Business Administration, University of Nevada at Reno, Reno, NV 89557 USA; Tel: [1] (775) 784-8050; E-mail: palmerjm@unr.edu; Web: www.unr.edu/coba/logis/program.html

**Centers for International Business Education and Research (CIBERs)**
CIBERs were created under the U.S. Omnibus Trade and Competitiveness Act of 1988. Administered by the U.S. Department of Education, the CIBER program links the manpower and information needs of U.S. business with the international education, language training, and research capacities of universities across the U.S. The 30 universities listed below were designated as centers that serve as regional and national resources to business, students, and academics.

**Brigham Young University (Utah)**
www.byu.edu
**Columbia University (New York)**
www.columbia.edu
**Duke University (North Carolina)**
www.duke.edu
**Florida International University**
www.fiu.edu
**Georgia Institute of Technology**
www.gatech.edu
**Indiana University**
www.indiana.edu
**Michigan State University**
www.msu.edu
Ohio State University
www.osu.edu
**Purdue University (Indiana)**
www.purdue.edu
**San Diego State University**
www.sdsu.edu
**Temple University (Philadelphia, Pennsylvania)**
www.temple.edu
**Texas A&M University**
www.tamu.edu
**Thunderbird (Glendale, Arizona)**
www.t-bird.edu
**University of California at Los Angeles (UCLA)**
www.ucla.edu
**University of Colorado at Denver**
www.cudenver.edu
**University of Connecticut**
www.uconn.edu
**University of Florida**
www.ufl.edu
**University of Hawaii at Manoa**
www.uhm.hawaii.edu
**University of Illinois at Urbana-Champaign**
www.uiuc.edu
**University of Kansas**
www.ku.edu
**University of Memphis (Tennessee)**
www.memphis.edu
**University of Michigan**
www.umich.edu
**University of North Carolina**
www.unc.edu
**University of Pennsylvania**
www.upenn.edu
**University of Pittsburgh (Pennsylvania)**
www.pitt.edu
**University of South Carolina**
www.sc.edu
**University of Southern California**
www.usc.edu
University of Texas at Austin
www.utexas.edu
**University of Washington**
www.washington.edu
**University of Wisconsin**
www.wisc.edu

### Certificates in International Trade (The International Import-Export Institute)

The International Import-Export Institute (IIEI) is the only organization authorized by the Certification Board of Governors to administer its certification standards program to the international trade community worldwide. IIEI offers various online certification programs depending on the specific industry need being addressed. Here are some of the certifi-

cations available: Certified Exporter® (CE®); Certified International Trade Documentation Specialist® (CITDS®); Certified International Trade Finance Specialist® (CITFS®); Certified International Trade Logistics Specialist® (CITLS®); Certified International Trade Marketing Specialist® (CITMS®); Certified International Trade Professional® (CITP®); Certified International Trade Manager® (CITM®). Contact at: The International Import-Export Institute, 11225 N. 28th Dr., Suite B201, Phoenix, AZ 85029 USA; Tel: [1] (800) 474-8013 OR [1] (602) 648-5750; Fax: [1] (602) 648-5755; E-mail: info@expandglobal.com; Web: www.intlimport-export.com.

### Department of Marketing and Supply Chain Management (Michigan State University)

This department is a leader in creating, integrating, and disseminating marketing, procurement, manufacturing, and logistics knowledge. Offers strong research-based knowledge products; excellence in education to executives, Ph.D., MBA, and undergraduate students; and an integrated, dynamic, and forward-oriented vision of competition in the next millennium. Contact at: Michigan State University, The Eli Broad College of Business, Department of Marketing & Supply Chain Management, 370 North Business Complex, Michigan State University, East Lansing, MI 48824 USA; Tel: [1] (517) 353-6381; Fax: [1] (517) 432-1112; E-mail: msc@msu.edu; Web: www.bus.msu.edu/msc/

### Department of Supply Chain & Information Systems (SC&IS) (Penn State University)

SC&IS is a boundary-spanning field of study of supply chain networks. The program integrates source (strategic procurement and supply management), make (manufacturing and service operations), delivery (demand fulfillment), and return (reverse logistics, recycle, and remanufacture) processes, along with information systems as the critical enabler of supply chain efficiencies and responsiveness. These core processes encompass activities such as information management; purchasing; inventory flow scheduling and control; logistics-production coordination; transportation systems operation and infrastructure; and customer service, order fulfillment, and distribution facilities management. The following degrees are offered: B.A., MBA, Executive MBA, M.S., and Ph.D. Contact at: Department of Supply Chain & Information Systems, The Smeal College of Business, The Pennsylvania State University, 454 Business Building, University Park, PA 16802 USA; Tel: [1] (814) 865-1866; Fax: [1] (814) 863-7067; E-mail: scis@smeal.psu.edu; Web: www.smeal.psu.edu/scis/index.html

### Executive Masters in International Logistics (EMIL) (Georgia Tech University)

The EMIL program focuses on the total optimization of the logistics value chain, and helps global companies design creative new solutions for critical issues in global logistics by educating their supply chain executives. This unique 18-month Masters program keeps key employees on-the-job while teaching them practical techniques for decreasing logistics costs and improving supply chain efficiencies. Contact at: EMIL Program, School of Industrial and Systems Engineering, Georgia Institute of Technology, 765 Ferst Drive, Atlanta, Georgia 30332 USA; Fax: (404) 894-2301; Email: emil@isye.gatech.edu; Web: www.emil.gatech.edu/

### Global Logistics Programs (California State University, Long Beach)

The Certified Global Logistics Specialist (GLS™) program, the Certified Global Logistics Employee (GLE™) program, and the Master of Arts in Global Logistics program prepare individuals for positions in the international trade and logistics industry. Course work covers industry segments such as: Freight Forwarders, Custom Brokers, Trucking and Distribution companies, NVOCC's (Non-Vessel Operating Carrier), Import and Export companies, Air Cargo companies, and more. The programs were developed by the university's Center for International Trade and Transportation, which is a congressionally designated multidisciplinary center for multimodal transportation studies and integrated logistics research, education, training, policy analysis, and technology transfer. Contact at: Center for International Trade and Transportation, California State University, Long Beach, 1000 Studebaker Road, Suite 3, Long Beach, Ca 90815 USA; Tel: [1] (562) 296-1170; Fax: [1] (562) 296-1171; E-mail: mvenieris@uces.csulb.edu; Web: www.uces.csulb.edu/CITT/Home/Home.aspx

### Global Supply Chain Management Programs (Loeb-Sullivan School of International Business & Logistics)
The Loeb-Sullivan School provides specialized programs in global supply chain management and related fields. Offers the following: M.S. in Global Supply Chain Management; Post-Graduate Diploma Program; Certificate Program; Management Development Program. Contact at: Loeb-Sullivan School of International Business & Logistics, Castine, ME 04420 USA; Tel: [1] (800) 227-8465; E-mail: info.ls@mma.edu; Web: http://ibl.mainemaritime.edu.

### Global Trade, Transportation, and Logistics Studies (University of Washington)
The graduate certificate program in Global Trade, Transportation, and Logistics (GTTL) provides for the study of activities involved in the flow of goods from point of origin to point of consumption on a global scale. Included are the management of the intermodal connections among maritime, aviation, and overland modes of transport; environmental and energy concerns; advancements in telecommunications; and the legal, regulatory, and technological infrastructures that facilitate global commerce and transportation. Contact at: Global Trade, Transportation, and Logistics Studies, University of Washington, Loew Hall, Room 313, Box 352193, Seattle, WA 98195-2193 USA; Tel: [1] (206) 616-5778; E-mail: gttl@u.washington.edu; Web: http://depts.washington.edu/~gttl

### International Intermodal Transportation Center (New Jersey Institute of Technology)
The Center was established by the Intermodal Surface Transportation Efficiency Act of 1991 (ISTEA). It is one of three national university centers under the U.S. Department of Transportation University Transportation Centers Program. The Center works closely with public and private sector transportation stakeholders to facilitate economic development and quality of life improvements efforts linked to intermodal transportation. Contact at: 287 Tiernan Hall, New Jersey Institute of Technology, University Heights, Newark, NJ 07102 USA; Tel: [1] (973) 596-5274; Fax: [1] (973) 596-6454; Web: http://transportation.njit.edu/iitc/Home/

### Graduate Certificate in International Trade Policy (George Washington University)
Contact at: Elliott School of International Affairs, Office of Graduate Admissions, The George Washington University, 1957 E Street, NW. Suite 301, Washington, D.C. 20052 USA; Tel: [1] (202) 994-6240; Fax: [1] (202) 994-0335; Web: Web: www.gwu.edu/~elliott/academicprograms/gc/itp.html

### Master of Arts in International Trade Policy (Monterey Institute of International Studies)
Candidates gain a strong academic foundation in the field of international trade laws and institutions combined with professional skills training similar to that offered by law

schools or medical schools. Contact at: Belinda Yeomans, Enrollment Manager; Tel: [1] (831) 647-6543; E-mail: gsips@miis.edu; Web: http://policy.miis.edu/programs/maitp.html

### World Trade Institute (of Pace University)
(Historic) The oldest accredited academic institution in the United States teaching subjects of international trade and commerce. The Institute was closed on June 30, 2005. For more information, see http://appserv.pace.edu/execute/page.cfm?doc_id=15453

## Belgium

### M.S. in Transportation and Logistics (European University - Antwerp)
Combines core MBA studies with a specialized curriculum in Transportation and Logistics. Contact at: European University, International Management Institute Center for Management Studies, Transportation and Logistics, Jacob Jordaensstraat 77, 2018 Antwerpen, Belgium; E-mail:itmma@ua.ac.be; Tel: [32] (3) 218-5431; Fax: [32] (3) 218-5868

## Canada

### Transportation and Logistics (University of British Columbia)
Degree offered: M.Sc. Two-year program, in which candidate chooses one area of specialization, including Transportation and Logistics. Ph.D also offered. Contact at: Centre for Transportation Studies, Sauder School of Business, University of British Columbia, 2053 Main Mall, Vancouver, B.C. Canada V6T 1Z2; Tel: [1] (604) 822-4510; Fax: [1] (604) 822-4977; Web: www.sauder.ubc.ca/cts

## China

### Master of Economics in International Trade (Tsinghua University, Beijing)
Contact at: Tsinghua University, Department of Economics, Foreign Students Office, Beijing, 100084 People's Republic of China; Tel: [86] (10) 6278-4857; Fax: [86] (10) 6277-1134; E-mail: info@tsinghua.edu.cn; Web: http://econ.em.tsinghua.edu.cn/english.asp

### Master's in International Trade (Nankai University, China)
Degrees Offered: M.A. in International Trade; M.A. in International Trade Law; M.A. in International Trade Policy. Contact at: Nankai University, Institute of International Insurance, Office for Int'l Academic Exchanges, Tianjin, 300071 China; Tel: [86] (22) 2350-8632; Fax: [86] (22) 2350-2990; E-mail: manager@nankai.edu.cn; Web: www.nankai.edu.cn

## France

### International Supply Management Program (ESSEC Business School)
1-year program in French and English. Courses cover the stakes, product cost and performance analysis, technology and supplies, marketing, negotiations, quality and certification, sourcing, international logistics, information systems, contract law, agrifood supplies and forward markets. Degrees Offered: M.S. in International Supply Management. Contact at: ESSEC Business School, Avenue Bernard Hirsch, B.P. 50105, Cergy-Pontoise, 95021 France; Tel: 33 (0)1 34 43 30 00; Fax: 33 (0)1 34 43 30 01; E-mail: essecinfo@essec.fr; Web: www.eseec.fr

### Masters in Logistics and International Transportation (Lille Catholic University)
Contact at: Lille Catholic University, 60 Boulevard

Vauban, Lille Cedex, BP 109 France; Tel: [33] (3) 2013-4000; Fax: [33] (3) 2013-4001; E-mail: saio@fupl.asso.fr; Web: www.univ-catholille.fr/

### MBA and Executive Master's (IEMI - European Institute of International Management)

In French and English. Degrees Offered: MBA; Executive Master - International Business; Executive Master - European Affairs; Executive Master - South American Trade; Executive Master - East West Trade; Executive Master - Chinese Business; Executive Master - International Sports Management. Internships and job placement, accredited programs. Contact at: IEMI - European Institute of International Management, MBA and Executive Master, 52, Rue St Lazare, 75009 Paris, FRANCE; Tel: [33] 145-265-928; Fax: [33] 145-265-929; E-mail: info@iemi.com; Web: www.iemi.com

### M.Sc. in Procurement and Supply-Chain Management (Ecole de Management, Grenoble)

One-year postgraduate program. In French. Contact at: Grenoble Ecole de Management, 12 rue Pierre Semard, Grenoble 38003, France; E-mail: info@grenoble-em.com; Tel: [33] 476-706-060; Fax: [33] 476-706-099; Web: www.grenoble-em.com

## India

### Master's and Ph.D in International Trade and Development (Jawaharlal Nehru University, India)

Contact at: Jawaharlal Nehru University, School Of International Studies, New Mehrauli Road, New Delhi 110067 India; E-mail: query@mail.jnu.ac.in; Web: www.nju.ac.in/

## Korea

### Department of International Trade (of Korea University's Seochang Campus)

The Department of International Trade was established in 1980 and offers over 30 courses. The curriculum includes internships and case studies as well as traditional classroom work. Proficiency in English is an important goal of the curriculum. Subjects of study include business English, international marketing and finance, international trade law, trade blocs and international business strategies. Contact at: Korea University, 1, 5-Ka, Anam-dong Sungbuk-ku, Seoul, 136-701 Republic of Korea; Tel: [82] (2) 3290-1152; Fax: [82] (2) 922-5820; Web: www.korea.ac.kr

### Master's and PhD. in International Trade (Chonbuk National University)

Contact at: Chonbuk National University, International Trade, 664-14, 1 Ga, Duck-jin dong, Chon-ju, Chonbuk, 56-756 Republic of Korea; Tel: [82] (65) 22 70 20 98; Fax: [82] (65) 22 70 20 99; E-mail: master@cbnu.edu; Web: www.cbnu.edu

## Mexico

### M.S. in International Business Administration (Alliant International University - Mexico)

Research Areas: International trade; international business; NAFTA; organizational development; cross-cultural management. Program combines theoretical approaches with hands-on, practical experience, providing students with personalized attention. Contact at: Alliant Mexico (Universidad Internacional de Mexico, A.C.), Alvaro Obregon #110, Colonia Roma, CP 06700, Mexico City, Mexico; Tel: (52-55) 5264-2187; Fax: (52-55) 5264-2188; E-mail: mexicoregistrar@alliant.edu; Web: www.alliantmexico.edu

## Netherlands

### European Logistics, Transport and Distribution (Arnhem Business School)

Degrees Offered: M.Sc. Contact at: Arnhem Business School, European Transport and Logistics, P.O. Box 5171, ED Arnhem, 6802 The Netherlands; Tel: [31] (26) 369-1333; Fax: [31] (26) 369-1367; E-mail: international.arnhem@han.nl; Web: www.abs.han.nl

### Maritime Economics and Logistics Program (Erasmus University - Rotterdam)

10-month, fully accredited international MSc Programme. Research Areas: International Shipping; Port Management; Transport Economics and Policy; Logistics Management and Transport EDI/MIS; Quantitative Methods; International Economics; E-shipping; Maritime Law and Marine Insurance; Port Privatisation Port Project Appraisal; Ship Investment and Finance; Quality Assurance in Shipping; Shipbroking and Chartering; Container Terminal Management ; Supply Chain Management; Public/Private Partnerships in Transport. Contact at: Erasmus University, P.O. Box 1738, Rotterdam, 3000 DR, The Netherlands; Tel: [31] (10) 408-1137; Fax: [31] (10) 408-9156; E-mail: sic@oos.eur.nl; Web: www.eur.nl

### Master's in Logistics Management (Rotterdam Business School)

Program designed in co-operation with business community. Strong focus on personal competency development. Research Areas: Managing Logistic Enterprises; Human Factors of Internal and External Clients; Enterprise Resource Planning (ERP); Inventory Strategy and Management; Planning and Forecasting; The Consequences of IT and E-Business in the Logistics Sector; Supply Chain Management; Successful Performance. Contact at: PO Box 25035, 3001 HA Rotterdam, The Netherlands; Tel: +31 (0)10 452-6663; Fax: +31 (0)10 453 6001; E-mail: administration.rbs@hro.nl; Web: www.RotterdamBusinessSchool.nl

## Portugal

### Master's in International Trade (Universidade do Minho)

Contact at: Universidade do Minho, School of Economics and Management, Campus de Gualtar, 4710 - 057 Braga Portugal; Fax: 00 351 253-676-375; Tel: 00 351 253-604-510; E-mail: sec@eeg.uminho.pt; Web: www.eeg.uminho.pt

## Taiwan

### Department of International Trade (Tamkang University)

Undergraduate and Masters programs. Contact at: Tamkang University, 151 Ying Chuan Road, Tamsui, Taipei, Taiwan 251, Republic of China; Tel: [886] (2) 2621-5656 ext. 2018; Fax: [886] (2) 2625-3021; E-mail: academic@mail.tku.edu.tw; Web: www.acad.tku.edu.tw

## Turkey

### Department of International Trade (Bogazici University)

This program is designed to meet the needs of students moving into positions of international responsibility. The interdisciplinary nature of the program prepares students as future business professionals who can function effectively in the dynamic and complex environment of the global marketplace. Most courses are conducted in English. Contact at: Bogazici University, 34342 Bebek, Istanbul, Turkey; Tel: [90] (212) 359-5400; Web: www.boun.edu.tr/undergraduate/applied_disciplines/international_trade.html

### United Kingdom

*Diploma in Port and Shipping Administration (Cardiff Business School)*

This diploma is aimed at professionals who are already working in the port and shipping fields, and at qualified people who wish to do so. It is recognised worldwide as a professional qualification for those employed in the port and shipping industries. The program is designed to equip students with a knowledge of the techniques employed in the management and operation of modern ports and ships. Contact at: Cardiff University, Cardiff Business School, Cardiff Business School, Cardiff University, Aberconway Building, Colum Drive, Cardiff, CF10 3EU, UK; Fax: +44(0) 29 2087 4419; Tel: +44(0) 29 2087 4000; Web: www.cardiff.ac.uk/carbs/

*European and International Trade Law (Glasgow Caledonian University)*

Degrees Offered: LL.M. - European and International Trade Law; Pg.Dip. - European and International Trade Law. Contact at: Glasgow Caledonian University, Faculty of Business, European and International Trade Law, Glasgow Caledonian University, Cowcaddens Road, Glasgow, G4 0BA, Scotland, UK; Tel: +44 141 331- 8675; Fax: +44 141 331-8676; E-mail: international@gcal.ac.uk; Web: www.gcal.ac.uk

*Master's in International Economics and Trade (London Metropolitan University)*

This program provides students with a thorough understanding of the evolution and practice of the global economy. It is based on a foundation of international economics theory and focuses on flows in trade, including financial services between nations, corporations, and markets and their impact on growth, trade and development. Contact at: London Metropolitan University, International Office, London Metropolitan University, 166-220 Holloway Road, London N7 8DB UK; Tel: +44 (0) 20 7133 3317; Fax: +44 (0) 20 7133 2240 E-mail: international@londonmet.ac.uk Web: www.londonmet.ac.uk/

*Transport, Trade and Finance (City University of London)*

Course work contentrates on the following areas: finance, international trade, logistics, economics, and international logistics. Contact at: City University of London, Cass Business School, 106 Bunhill Row, London EC1Y 8TZ UK; Tel: +44 (0) 20 7040 8600; Web: www.cass.city.ac.uk

## OTHER INFORMATION SOURCES

*Air Cargo, Inc. (ACI)*

A ground service corporation established and jointly owned by 17 U.S. scheduled airlines. In addition to its airline owners, ACI also serves over 53 air freight forwarders and international air carriers. One of ACI's major functions is to facilitate the surface movement of air freight by negotiating and supervising the performance of a nationwide series of contracts under which trucking companies provide both local pickup and delivery service at airport cities and over-the-road truck service to move air freight to and from points not directly served by the airlines. ACI also makes available, in many cities, low cost, disposable containers for shippers' use. Contact: Aircargo Communities Inc. (ACI), 437 Rozzi Place, South San Francisco, CA 94080 USA; Tel: [1] (866) 952-9050; Fax: [1] (650) 952-9051; E-mail: sales@aircargocommunities.com; Web: www.air-cargo-inc.com.

*Boskage Commerce Publications*

More than 100 policy and procedure guidelines written by the leading U.S. Customs compliance expert. Fine and penalty proof techniques for handling U.S. Customs business. Functional guide for training new and existing employees. Free customizable software included. Boskage Commerce Publications, Ltd., P.O. Box 337, Allegan, MI 49010 USA; Tel: [1] (269) 673-7242 or [1] (888) 880-4088; E-mail: inquiries@boskage.com; Fax: [1] (269) 673-5901; Web: www.boskage.com.

*PIERS (Port Import Export Reporting Service) www.piers.com*

PIERS maintains the most comprehensive database of import/export information on cargoes moving through ports in the U.S., Mexico, Latin America, and Asia. Collects data from over 25,000 bills of lading every day. PIERS helps in finding new suppliers, new markets and new business opportunities; benchmarking performance against the competition; defending intellectual property against infringement and counterfeiting; understanding international trade trends and forecasts; supporting strategic decision-making; and arbitrating trade disputes. Part of the Commonwealth Business Media, Inc.

*STAT-USA*

STAT-USA is a fee-funded office in the U.S. Department of Commerce that develops and operates electronic information systems to deliver government economic, business, statistical, and foreign trade information to the public, primarily through subscription on-line services. STAT-USA's flagship product, STAT-USA/Internet, is a subscription based Internet site that contains the international trade information of the National Trade Data Bank (NTDB) as well as an extensive collection of domestic economic data. Customers can view, print, and download trade opportunity leads, market reports, economic releases, and more from the State Department, the Bureau of Export Administration, the Federal Reserve Board, the US Census Bureau, and others. USA Trade On-line, a joint venture with the US Census Bureau and a private partner, is the latest STAT-USA product, offering trade statistics to subscribers within minutes of release. Contact STAT-USA online at www.stat-usa.gov.

*World Trade Center Clubs*

Local and regional based organizations around the world of importers, exporters, customs brokers, freight forwarders, attorneys, bankers, manufacturers and shippers. Each world trade club provides different services and activities, but many provide information services including data bases and libraries, educational services including seminars and regularly scheduled classes, meeting space, club atmosphere, dining, exhibit facilities, and trade missions. Most major cities in the world have World Trade Clubs. For a list of world trade clubs internationally, go online at http://iserve.wtca.org. World Trade Centers Association, 60 East 42nd Street, Suite 1901, New York, NY 10165 USA; Tel: [1] (212) 432-2626; Fax: [1] (212) 488-0064; Web: http://iserve.wtca.org.

# Web Resources

## General Travel Sites

**Alta Vista Babelfish Translation Services**                 **http://babelfish.altavista.com**
Free on-line translation service. Translates from Spanish, German, Dutch, French, Italian, Russian, Korean, Chinese, and Portuguese to English, and from English to these other languages.

**Best Country Reports**                        **www.BestCountryReports.com**
A massive 225-country database available in country- and topic-specific report form covering culture, business culture, business practices, marketing, travel, communications, trade, trade documentation, business, media, demographics, and more. Modest download fees from $5 to $25 per report.

**Business Traveller**                          **www.btonline.com**
The online version of the monthly magazine for business travelers featuring country profiles, plus hotel, airline, and special perks information.

**Center for Disease Control and Prevention**              **www.cdc.gov**
The U.S. Government's site for disease control and global immunization information.

**CIA World Factbook**                          **www.odci.gov/cia/publications/factbook**
Published by the U.S. Central Intelligence Agency (CIA). An excellent reference for general country-by-country information. Covers the people, government, economy, transportation, defense and communications of other countries. Contains maps and helpful appendices.

**Consular Information Sheets and Travel Warnings**         **http://travel.state.gov/travel/cis_pa_tw/ tw/tw_1764.html**
U.S. Department of State country information sheets apprising travelers of current events and dangers affecting international travel safety. Also contact information for US consulates abroad.

**Embassies and Consulates**                    **http://usembassy.state.gov**
Links to United States embassies and consulates worldwide.

**Expedia Travel**                              **www.expedia.com**
Microsoft's online travel service featuring a fare finder, discounts, destination information, vacation packages, maps, global guidebook search, accommodations, transportation and travel merchandise.

**Foreign Language for Travelers**              **www.travlang.com/languages**
Foreign languages for travelers, including electronic speaking dictionaries and translation software. Also, information provided on worldwide hotels and currency exchange rates.

**Global Road Warrior**                         **www.globalroadwarrior.com**
A 175-country travel and business information resource for the international business communicator and traveler. Contains pragmatic information on communications, mobile connectivity, business services, technical support, business culture, travel facts, color maps and city centers for each country. Subscription-based.

**iGo.com**                                     **www.igo.com**
A major supplier of mobile connectivity and technology products for business travelers.

**Konexx**                                      **www.konexx.com**
Comprehensive supplier of computer and telephone interface products and accessories. Also has online tech support for products.

**Maps.com**                                    **www.maps.com**
Specializing in maps, Maps.com provides digital maps, travel guides and gear, an online map store, driving directions and an address locator.

**Magellan's**                                  **www.magellans.com**
A major mail order supplier of tech and non-tech travel products. Many mobile connectivity products. They also have an excellent print catalog you can order through their Web site.

**Lonely Planet Online**                        **www.lonelyplanet.com**
A travel guide to many destinations around the world, mostly aimed at the budget and adventure traveler, but with many helpful tips and insights useful to the businessperson.

**Project Visa**                                **http://projectvisa.com**
Comprehensive site with up-to-date information on embassies, consulates, and visa requirements worldwide.

**Targus International**                         **www.targus.com**
Major supplier of mobile computing cases and accessories.

**TeleAdapt**                                   **www.teleadapt.com**
TeleAdapt is a major worldwide supplier of mobile connectivity products for the business traveler, such as electrical and telephone plug adapters and much more.

**Travel Document Systems**                     **www.traveldocs.com**
TDS is a leading visa and passport processing agency. Clients include travel professionals, tour operators, and cruise lines, as well as corporate and individual international travelers. TDS specializes in travel that involves visas for more than one country.

**Travelocity**                                 **www.travelocity.com**
Online travel service with air, hotel, and car reservations, maps, weather, currency converter, electronic ticketing, destination guide, consolidator fares, travel agency locator and travel headlines.

**W E B S I T E S**

**Walkabout Travel Gear**                                    www.walkabouttravelgear.com
Supplier of useful items of travel gear as well as mobile connectivity products. See photos of how the products work and order them online.

**World Maps**                                              www.mapquest.com
Create driving directions and maps, or purchase maps on this Web site.

**World Time Information**                                  www.worldtime.com
Features an interactive world atlas and information on local time worldwide for countries around the world.

**World Travel Guide**                                     www.wtgonline.com
A extensive travel site with key information for most countries, including some business protocol and contact information. Contains separate guides relating to cities, weather, airports, events; also, has an online bookstore.

# International Trade Related Sites

**A to Z Freight Gateway**                                 www.azfreight.com
An air freight industry Web site containing listings of airlines, cargo handling agents, sales agents, airports, cargo agents, freight forwarders, couriers, services and supplies.

**Alibaba Trade Leads**                                    www.alibaba.com
Big marketplace for global trade and a leading provider of online marketing services for importers and exporters. Headquartered in Hong Kong, the service covers more than 200 countries worldwide. Trade leads can be bought and sold; the leads are organized and searchable by business types and categories.

**AllBusiness Directory**                                  www.allbusiness.com/biz-directory
AllBusiness.com is an online media and e-commerce company, helping entrepreneurs, small and growing businesses, consultants and business professionals save time and money by addressing real-world business questions and presenting practical solutions. The site offers resources including how-to articles, business forms, contracts and agreements, expert advice, blogs, business news, business directory listings, product comparisons, business guides, a small business association and more.

**Asian Business Watch**                                   www.asianbusinesswatch.com
Japan-based web site containing comprehensive news, as well as many categories of links relating to importing/exporting, travelling, or investing in Asia.

**ATA and TECRO/AIT Carnets**                              www.carnetsonline.com
Apply online for duty-free and tax-free temporary entry of merchandise, including commercial samples, professional equipment and items for trade shows into participating foreign countries. 24-hour turnaround is often possible.

**BizEurope**                                              www.bizeurope.com
A business portal providing trade leads, company information and contacts, import and export information, individual country guides, a directory of World Trade Centers, and more.

**Business Wire**                                          www.businesswire.com
A newswire service listing the day's business headlines in industry-specific categories. Also provides news on current and upcoming trade shows.

**Cal Trade Report**                                       www.caltradereport.com
Long time international trade journalist Michael White's excellent international trade and business news e-letter and Web site. Reports news from broad sources throughout California (USA), the USA and the world on developments, trends, and activities that impact California and international trade activities.

**Cargo Insurance and US Customs Bonds**                   www.roanoketrade.com
Control risk by controlling the insurance on shipments; obtain Customs bonds; find out what is available for freight forwarders, customs brokers and shippers. Note: goods imported into the US must clear US Customs under a US Customs Bond. A great website for staying current on e-bond developments in ACE (Automated Commercial Environment).

**Cargo Ports of the World**                               www.hal-pc.org/~nugent/port.html
Provides links to web sites of ports and terminals around the world and contains information on vessel traffic and cargo types that individual ports allow.

**Centre for International Trade**                          www.centretrade.com
Includes rules, regulations, tariffs, trade opportunities, finance, management, transportation, resource and travel information. The 3,500 members come from every corner of the world and include embassies, government agencies, trade associations, companies, firms and individuals.

**Directory of Freight Forwarding Services**               http://forwarders.com
Directories cover air freight, shipping, rail freight, trucking, specialized transportation, logistics management, customs brokers, international trade, export documentation and licensing, letters of credit, etc.

**Dow Jones & Company**                                    www.dowjones.com
Website includes indexes, business publications, financial information services, investor relations, Wall Street Journal services, press releases and a directory.

**Expo DataBase**                                          www.expodatabase.com
Online database containing about 20,000 tradeshow and exhibition dates worldwide with detailed exhibition particulars, around 6,000 organisers and over 2,000 exhibition centres.

**Federation of Intl. Trade Associations**                 www.fita.org
Provides over 1,000 links to websites related to international trade. The site has a useful page called "The Trading Hub: Import and Export Trade Leads from Around the World."

**Foreign Trade Online**                                   www.foreign-trade.com
A global B2B trade portal that helps companies around the world expand their business beyond their own borders. The

**WEBSITES**

service helps manufacturers, exporters, and companies planning to export to market themselves cost-effectively on a global scale by providing qualified foreign buyers with information about their products and services. Also helps importers to locate their product sourcing from around the world. Trade leads can be posted on the site.

### Global Business Centre                              www.glreach.com/gbc
A guide to Web sites around the world, arranged by language in topic-specific directories. Provides links to interesting Web sites, especially those not written in English. The site is organized according to subject matter within each language: business, culture, online publications and e-zines (electronic magazines), index (lists of sites in this online language community), leisure, jobs, shopping and travel.

### Global Connector                        www.kelley.in.edu/connector/gc_home.cfm
Part of the University of Indiana's Kelley School of Business. Menu-driven utility that lets you target by country or industry. Returns online links.

### Global Business Network (GBN)                       www.gbn.org
Membership-based organization made up of individuals and organizations worldwide. Through its WorldView service, GBN brings this network together through: meetings and events; learning journeys; the GBN Book Club; and publications, commentary, and conversations. Services also include consulting and customized offerings as well as scenario training.

### Global Edge                              http://globaledge.msu.edu/ibrd/ibrd.asp
Links to trade information. Includes regional and country information. Maintained by the Center for International Business Education and Research of Michigan State University (USA).

### Global Industrial Buying Guide                       www.tgrnet.com
Site of the Thomas Global Register, an extensive and regularly update directory of worldwide industrial product information. Visitors can search for over 700,000 industrial suppliers, organized by 11,000 industrial product classifications, in 10 languages, and from 28 countries. Companies are listed free of charge.

### Global Trade, Transportation & Logistics Directory -- http://depts.washington.edu/gttl/links.htm
Directory of links to organizations related to global trade, transportation, and logistics. Site is published and maintained by the University of Washington. Links are organized under the following categories: Global Trade, Transportation, Air, Shipping, Ports, Railways, Trucking and GPS, Logistics, Software & Technology, Communications, News/ Periodicals/ Journals, Organizations, Legislation, Universities & Colleges, Public Sector, Private Sector.

### IMEX Exchange                              www.imex.com
Dedicated to promoting international trade on the Internet. The site offers publications, informational links, marketing/ business consulting services, and joint venture information.

### InfoAmericas                              www.infoamericas.com
InfoAmericas provides market research, competitive intelligence and strategic consulting services throughout Latin America. Delivers on-the-ground research and intelligence capabilities. In English, Spanish, and Portuguese.

### International Chamber of Commerce (ICC)           www.iccwbo.org
The ICC represents businesses and chambers of commerce worldwide and facilitates contacts with intergovernmental organizations and other international bodies. The ICC also is the source of important publications on international banking, letters of credit and mediation.

### International Monetary Fund (IMF)                       www.imf.org
Official Web site of the IMF includes news releases, publications, fund rates, data standards and index.

### International Trade Centre (United Nations)           www.intracen.org
The International Trade Centre (ITC) is the technical cooperation agency of the United Nations Conference on Trade and Development (UNCTAD) and the World Trade Organization (WTO) for operational, enterprise-oriented aspects of trade development. The ITC supports the business sectors of developing and transition economies. The site provides global programs, advisory and training services, information sources, and tools and products.

### Internet Service Providers                       www.thelist.com
A listing of internet service providers (ISPs) and their service parameters within a specified country; listings include Web links to the individual ISP sites.

### Journal of Commerce                              www.joc.com
The daily Journal of Commerce online. Includes a plenitude of information about trade.

### Kompass                              www.kompass.com
Originating in Switzerland, this worldwide business group publishes a database of more than 1.9 million companies in 70 countries, referenced by 54,000 product and service keywords, 750,000 trade names, and 3.5 million executive names. Provides contact information, financial profiles, and lists of company products. General leads are free; specific information is fee-based. Also publishes 50 CD-ROMs.

### LogisticsWorld Directory                       www.logisticsworld.com
The LogisticsWorld Directory™ offers service and contact information from various companies and organizations in the transportation, logistics, and supply chain industry. Directory listings are free. The site includes the following categories: Transportation, Logistics, Freight, Trucking, Software, Consulting, Warehousing, Supply Chain, Import/Export, technology, Manufacturing, Services, Trade/Finance, International, and others.

### Massachusetts Inst. for Social and Economic Research   http://www.umass.edu/miser
Internationally known for research on foreign trade data. MISER has developed the only non-Federal contributions to the National Trade Data Bank (NTDB). MISER has also developed an MIS system for foreign trade data to help potential exporters locate the best foreign markets for their products.

### Nafta Home Page                              www.mac.doc.gov/nafta
Web site about the North American Free Trade Agreement provided by the U.S. International Trade Administration.

### National Ass'n of Foreign Trade Zones                  www.naftz.org
Official site of the National Association of FTZs, including descriptions of FTZs and how to establish one. Provides case studies, an event calendar, a member directory and a listing of zones and subzones in the U.S.

**WEBSITES**

**National Technical Information Service**                    **www.ntis.gov**
The National Technical Information Service is the Federal Government's central source for the sale of scientific, technical, engineering, and related business information produced by or for the U.S. Government and complementary material from international sources.

**Pangea.Net**                                               **www.pangea.net**
Comprehensive source and reference for international business activities -- from information collection and strategy development through tactical implementation. PANGAEA.NET is the online service of PANGAEA®, International Consultants, a global consultancy with expertise in strategic positioning, branding, competitive intelligence, multicultural advertising and consumer psychographics for the largest consumer products/services companies in the world.

**PIERS (Port Import Export Reporting Service)**             **www.piers.com**
PIERS maintains the most comprehensive database of import/export information on cargoes moving through ports in the U.S., Mexico, Latin America, and Asia. Collects data from over 25,000 bills of lading every day. PIERS helps in finding new suppliers, new markets and new business opportunities; benchmarking performance against the competition; defending intellectual property against infringement and counterfeiting; understanding international trade trends and forecasts; supporting strategic decision-making; and arbitrating trade disputes. Part of the Commonwealth Business Media, Inc.

**Planet Business**                                          **www.planetbiz.com**
Contains a directory organized by continent, trade zone, and name of business, with links to "gateway" business search/portal sites all over the world. Intended for Importers, Exporters, Traders and Distributors.

**Seaports of the World**                                    **www.seaportsinfo.com**
A directory with links for seaports, port authorities and port industry information for the Western Hemisphere.

**TradeMatch**                                               **www.expo.co.uk**
Helps companies worldwide to make business contacts and gain new markets, partners, and customers overseas. Divided into three sections: Exporters, Importers, and Services. Free registration.

**Tradeport**                                                **www.tradeport.org**
An international trade Web site funded by the California Export Assistance Center and the U.S. Department of Commerce provides information on trade leads, market and industry research, events and trade shows, trade tutorial and other information.

**Trade Show News Network**                                  **www.tsnn.com**
Leading online resource for the trade show and exhibition industry worldwide, with the most widely consulted internet database containing data on more than 15,000 trade shows and conferences and more than 30,000 seminars.

**The Trade Lead Zone**                                      **www.tradezone.com**
Tradezone.com provides international trade services for manufacturers, importers/exporters, trade service businesses and opportunity seekers. Includes import-export trade leads, the International Traders Bulletin Board, traders Web sites and Web site advertising services. Contains a Global Trade Lead database that can be searched for leads or in which company information can be placed free of charge.

**United Nations Online**                                    **www.un.org**
Official site of the United Nations.

**Women's Global Business Alliance -- Peer Counsel**         **www.wgba-business.com**
Member-based organization for senior-level executive women worldwide. Provides executive women with direct and personal connections to an elite group of peers, thought leaders, and some of the world's most renowned business executives and change agents. Members exchange views on critical business issues and share tools that impact the bottom line.

**World Bank**                                               **www.worldbank.org**
The World Bank, headquartered in Washington D.C., provides loans, policy advice, technical assistance and knowledge sharing services to low and middle income countries to reduce poverty.

**World Chambers Network**                                   **www.worldchambers.com**
A listing of chambers of commerce worldwide. Contains additional resources relating to international trade. Includes over 12,000 registered Chambers of Commerce and Industry & Boards of Trade (CCIs).

**World Trade Centers Association**                          **http://world.wtca.org**
A complete listing of world trade centers worldwide, their services and membership information.

**World Trade Organization (WTO)**                           **www.wto.org**
Official Web site of the WTO contains trade topics, resources, and membership information.

**World Trade Magazine**                                     **www.worldtrademag.com**
Source of news and information for US companies doing business in the global marketplace. Targeted to U.S. executives shipping and sourcing worldwide. Core coverage areas include: banking, finance and insurance; cargo transportation and logistics; economic development; technology; international marketing and protocol; foreign exchange; tips on travel; cultural considerations; political risk analysis; and demographics.

**World Trade Press**                                        **www.worldtradepress.com**
Worldwide publisher of professional books, CD-ROMs, Internet-based applications, and databases for international trade.

**World Trade Ref**                                          **www.worldtraderef.com**
A major subscriber-based (also available by license) online resource for international trade consisting of 50 data sets. Includes the entire contents of the Dictionary of International Trade, complete USA import an export requirements, USA denied parties list, BIS requirements, more than 3000 trade terms translated into eight languages, ports and airports of the world, ocean and air shipping containers, import and export documentation requirements for countries of the world, measurement converters and a great deal more. Subscription-based.

**WEBSITES**

# European Union Resources

**Euro Pages**                                              **www.europages.com**
Contains the European Business Directory, which can be searched to find and contact suppliers, and the EuroPages Marketplace, which can be used to sell or buy used and new equipment, discontinued stock, or promotional affairs. Covers 600,000 companies in 35 European countries. In 25 languages.

**Europa - European Union**                                **www.europa.eu.int**
Site of the European Union. Many links and menus relating to doing business in the EU. In all EU languages.

**European Customs Authorities**                           **http://www.zollkriminalamt.de/gb/**
German site containing a useful menu of links to customs authorities in Europe and North America, as well as to international anti-fraud organizations.

**European Union in the U.S.**                             **www.eurunion.org**
Site of the Delegation of the European Commission to the U.S. Includes links relating to doing business and business news, as well as comprehensive links to EU-related web sites.

**EUROSTAT**                                               **http://epp.eurostat.ec.europa.eu**
Eurostat's mission is to provide the European Union with a high-quality statistical information service to enable comparisons between countries and regions. The site also includes a comprehensive news service.

# NAFTA-Related Resources

**Office of NAFTA and Inter-American Affairs**             **www.mac.doc.gov/NAFTA**
The U.S. government's NAFTA site. In addition to law and regulations, contains news, export assistance, and additional resources.

**NAFTA Resources - Mexico**                              **http://lanic.utexas.edu/la/mexico/nafta**
Published by the Latin American Network Information Center of the University of Texas. Has academic resources, documents and publications, news, and other NAFTA-related resources. In English, Spanish, and Portuguese.

**NAFTA Secretariat**                                     **www.nafta-sec-alena.org**
Official site of the NAFTA Secretariat. Provides English, Spanish, and French versions.

# Broker Services

**Go Global**                                             **http://goglobalinc.com**
Global Import/Export Brokers™, an Texas-based import/export brokerage, specializes in linking international buyers and sellers. Offers custom product searches, international market research and export management services.

# Country-Specific Sources

## ARGENTINA

**Fundacíon Invertir Argentina**                          **www.invertir.com**
Comprehensive Web site covering topics related to doing business in Argentina.

**Grippo Argentina Directory**                            **www.grippo.com**
A search engine for Argentina with links to other search engines. Links are usually in Spanish.

**Latinworld - Argentina**                                **www.latinworld.com/sur/argentina**
Latinworld provides links to business information in Argentina, as well as North, Central and South American countries, the Caribbean, and Spain.

**Trade Leads Online**                                    **www.tradeline.com.ar**
A Web site for companies interested in exporting to or importing from Argentina and the Mercosur countries.

## AUSTRALIA

**Austrade**                                              **www.austrade.gov.au**
The Australian Trade Commission online; includes export and investment information, international business guide, general information, supplier database, Austrade offices, trade shows, importing from Australia and a link to the Australian stock exchange.

**Australia Department of Foreign Affairs and Trade**     **www.dfat.gov.au**
Searchable collection of detailed information on services, travel, trade policy, and foreign policy.

**TradeData International**                               **www.tradedata.net**
Marketing information service based on details of internationally traded goods. Up-to-date information on thousands of products, covering imports and exports for a wide range of countries. Offers reports providing a vast range of international trade statistics. TradeData reports assist you in identifying market opportunities, monitoring competitors, identifying new sources of cheaper material inputs, monitoring growth, volatility and seasonal behavior, assessing possible dumping of imported products, and monitoring price/quantity relationships.

**Web Wombat**                                           **www.webwombat.com.au**
An Australian search engine, with the largest online database of searchable information on Australia.

WEBSITES

## AUSTRIA

**Austrian Worldport**                                    www.worldport.at/index.html
An index of company names and Austrian business information, including: marketing, legal, investment, business travel, addresses and on-line services.

**AustroNaut**                                    www.austronaut.at
An Austrian Web search engine in German for various categories including business.

## BELGIUM

**Belgian and Luxembourg Exports**                                    www.belgiumexports.com
Overview of exporting and importing companies, links to importers and detailed company profiles.

**Scoot, the Belgium Business Directory**                                    www.scoot.be
A quick find guide (in French and Flemish) to companies, searchable by product, service, or company name, with identical local sites for the Netherlands and the United Kingdom.

**Webwatch**                                    www.webwatch.be
A comprehensive Belgian search engine and directory, available in French, Flemish, and English versions.

## BOLIVIA

**Bolivian Law**                                    http://natlaw.com/interam/bo/
The National Law Center for Inter-American free trade provides links to Bolivia's Central Bank, Bolivian statistics, business information, country information, industrial and commercial information and law.

**Bolivia Web**                                    www.boliviaweb.com/
This Web site for Bolivia includes business, communications, government, and travel links, as well as a chat room and classifieds.

**Latinworld - Bolivia**                                    www.latinworld.com/sur/bolivia
Latinworld provides links to business information in Bolivia, as well as North, Central and South American countries, the Caribbean, and Spain.

## BRAZIL

**BrazilBiz**                                    www.brazilbiz.com.br
A Brazilian business to business directory for products and services; includes a business center for companies interested in buying, business opportunities as well as an international business directory.

**Brazil Exporters**                                    www.brazilexporters.com
This Web site has assisted hundreds of thousands of business people worldwide do business with Brazil. Contains an on-line directory of Brazilian exporters, plus other business resources.

**BrazilTradeNet**                                    www.braziltradenet.gov.br
BrazilTradeNet is maintained by the Ministry of External Relations of Brazil to offer foreign enterprises easy contact with Brazilian companies wishing to export or to establish business ventures. Offers information on trade fairs and other events in Brazil.

**Brazilian Web Resources**                                    www.brazilcham.com/
                                    other_brazilian_web_resources.htm

A member directory searchable by name or product/service description; includes government sites, financial institutions and media. Published by the Brazilian American Chamber of Commerce.

**InfoBrazil**                                    www.infobrazil.com/
Quality, independent and diverse English-language analysis and opinion articles about Brazilian issues and current affairs. Attracts a wide array of guest columnists, including political, entrepreneurial and community leaders, business and investment executives, advisors, consultants, sports and entertainment personalities, and well-informed "players" in Brazilian affairs

## BULGARIA

**Bulgaria.Com**                                    www.bulgaria.com
Business, services, travel, government, history, art, news, chat rooms and links are all included in this business and general information site.

**Bulgarian Industrial Association**                                    http://b2b.bia-bg.com
Directory for regional associations, branch chambers, economic focus, legal framework, investments, calendar, regulations, customs, tariffs and a Bulgarian company directory. In Bulgarian and English.

## CANADA

**Canada Business Directory**                                    www.cdnbusinessdirectory.com
Directory of businesses organized by province.

**Department of Foreign Affairs**                                    www.dfait-maeci.gc.ca
**and International Trade**
Official Web site of the Department of Foreign Affairs with links to trade, investment, market information, exporting programs and services, plus a directory.

**W E B S I T E S**

**Small Business Canada**       http://sbinfocanada.about.com
Comprehensive site covering all aspects of starting a business in Canada..

**Statistics Canada**       www.statcan.ca
Comprehensive government site producing statistics on Canadian population, resources, economy, society, and culture. International Trade is one of the numerous categories economic statistics.

**Strategis**       http://strategis.ic.gc.ca/engdoc/main.html
Canadian government site that includes company directories; industry and professional associations; sector analysis and statistics; information on international trade, legislation, regulation, financial management, provinces and territories.

**Team Canada Inc. / ExportSource.CA**       www.exportsource.ca
Canada's most comprehensive source of information and practical tools for new or experienced exporters.

## CHILE

**ChileNet**       www.chilenet.cl
Includes a Chilean Yellow Pages directory, as well as various links relating to business opportunities in Chile. Very comprehensive. In English, Spanish, and Portuguese.

**ProChile**       www.prochile.cl
Comprehensive database of companies and products from Chile and up-to-date information for international businesses seeking opportunities in trade and investment. In Spanish, sponsored by the Chilean Trade Commission.

**Latinworld - Chile**       www.latinworld.com/sur/chile
Latinworld provides links to business information in Chile, as well as North, Central and South American countries, the Caribbean, and Spain.

## CHINA

**BLI Internet Center for Chinese Products**       www.buildlink.com
Build Link International provides listings of Chinese products, companies, investment opportunities, joint ventures, product bidding and general information. In English.

**China Council for the Promotion of International Trade**       www.ccpit.org
The CCPIT comprises enterprises and organizations representing the economic and trade sectors in China. It is the most important and the largest institution for the promotion of foreign trade in China. Includes categories such as Trade Leads, Foreign Trade, and Foreign Investment. In English and Chinese.

**China Daily Biz News**       www.chinadaily.com.cn/bizchina/
bizchina.html
The business section of the online China Daily news service. Numerous categories of links cover all major business and industrial sectors and services. In English and Chinese.

**China Investment and Trade Links**       www.china-inc.com/link/tradelink.html
Investment and trade links, links on competitive zones for foreign investment, as well as an extensive business directory organized by business types and categories.

**China Today**       www.chinatoday.com
Provides links to banking and finance, culture, diplomatic missions, government agencies and services, health, international trade, investment and business opportunities, products, legal services and law, mass media and publications, real estate and more.

**US-China Chamber of Commerce**       www.usccc.org
Nonprofit, bi-national membership organization. Conducts seminars, conferences, workshops, executive briefings, trade missions and networking events - to identify the various trends critical for successful economic development between the U.S. and China.þ Aids both American and Chinese companies in locating business partners.

## COLOMBIA

**Colombian Trade News**       www.coltrade.org
The Colombian Government Trade Bureau in Washington, DC USA supplies information on trade and economy, industrial sectors, commercial laws, trade agreements, trading with Colombia, news and events, trade shows. Also offers weblinks.

**Latinworld - Colombia**       www.latinworld.com/sur/colombia
Latinworld provides links to business information in Paraguay, as well as North, Central and South American countries, the Caribbean, and Spain.

## CUBA

**CubaFirst**       www.cubafirst.com
Comprehensive investment guide for Cuba. Categories include: How to do business in cuba; foreign investment in cuba; investment application; banking regulations; free zones and industrial parks; commercial relations with foreign firms; administrative tariffs; real estate & building; and a business consulting gallery.

**LatinWorld - Cuba**       www.latinworld.com/caribe/cuba
Links to Cuba including companies, exporters, organizations, products, services, economy, culture, government and politics, internet resources, news and travel.

**WEBSITES**

## CZECH REPUBLIC

**Czech Republic Business Guide**  http://czech.kiwano.net
Provides information relating to real estate, human resources, banking, taxes and auditing, corporate legal issues, communications, transportation, health care, travel and tourism.

## DENMARK

**Danish Exporters**  www.danishexporters.dk
Denmark's official Export Directory. A Danish government site; includes information about investing in Denmark, legal framework, organizations and media.

**Invest in Denmark**  www.investindk.com
The Royal Danish Ministry of Foreign Affairs provides news and information, facts and figures, Denmark investment information, company profiles and business networks and links.

## ECUADOR

**EcuadorExports.COM**  www.ecuadorexports.com
A recent site, Ecuador Exports.com aims to be the world's top resource for Ecuador business, economy, trade, and product and services information.

**go4EcuadorBusiness.COM**  http://go4ecuadorbusiness.COM
This site provides a searchable directory of businesses, products, and trade leads. In English.

**Latinworld - Ecuador**  www.latinworld.com/sur/ecuador
Latinworld provides links to business information in Ecuador, as well as North, Central and South American countries, the Caribbean, and Spain.

## EGYPT

**American Chamber of Commerce in Egypt**  www.amcham.org.eg/Publications/BusinessMonthly/Business_Monthly.asp

Online business monthly publication; covers chamber's activities, committees, events, meetings, trade missions and more. Highest circulation English language business magazine in Egypt.

**Egyptian Exporters Association**  www.expolink.org
Nonprofit organization providing services to exporters and assisting companies who want to import.

**Egyptian Trading Directory**  www.egtrade.com
Free service that can be used to locate factories, import and export companies, agents, banks, hotels, insurance companies, and maritime companies in Egypt. Visitors can sign up for regular e-mail with company listing updates for a specific field of interest.

## FINLAND

**Contact Finland**  www.contactfinland.fi
A guide to Finnish business services, organizations and authorities. Published by the Central Chamber of Commerce of Finland.

**The Nordic Pages**  www.markovits.com/nordic
The Nordic Pages provide resource links for Scandinavian countries, including Finland.

## FRANCE

**Business-in-Europe**  www.business-in-europe.com
An extensive Web directory of sites to assist in doing business in France. Includes: Web site addresses, industry-by-industry guide, contacts in France as well as news.

**Invest in France**  www.afii.fr
Works with a vast global network to provide international firms with a wide range of services to make their operations in France a success and promote France to business leaders worldwide.

**Ministry of Foreign Affairs**  www.france.diplomatie.fr
Site of the ministry responsible for diplomacy and foreign affairs. In French, English, Spanish, and German.

**Ministry of Foreign Trade**  www.exporter.gouv.fr/exporter
Site of the French Foreign Trade Ministry. Has excellent menus of links relating to business sectors and a comprehensive news service. In French, English, German, Spanish, and Chinese.

## GERMANY

**Abacho**  www.abacho.de
A German search engine and portal in the German language.

**DeTeMedien**  www.teleauskunft.de
German Telekom posts a yellow-page directory comprising all of Germany. In German.

**German Business Center**  www.guj-wpo.de
Business news, stock market, politics, economy, and private business news from Germany (in German).

WEBSITES

**German Resources** **www.uni-karlsruhe.de/Outerspace/VirtualLibrary**
Excellent menu of links covering all aspects of German society and culture, including business and technology. Maintained by the Universitat Karlsruhe.

**Germany Info** **www.germany.info**
Published by the Germany Embassy in the U.S. The Business section contains information on business operations in Germany and the German economy. Includes answers to tax questions.

**Deutsche Messe AG** **www.messe.de**
A search engine and portal in German and English that offers a supplier database searchable by company, brand name, or product; also contains a business center with economic and business information, and trade fairs taking place at the Hannover Convention Center.

**BusinessLink** **www.businesslink.ch**
A product and services search engine, convention guide and buyer contact list for Switzerland and Germany (in German).

## GREECE

**Hellenic Foreign Trade Board** **www.hepo.gr**
Trade Board services, publications, economic and commercial offices, Greek investment information and Greek exports. In Greek and English.

**Go Greece** **www.gogreece.com**
Internet directory of links to Greek travel, business, finance, education, news, government, and more. In English

## GUATEMALA

**Guatemala Online** **www.quetzalnet.com**
Includes the following categories: Business Guide, Traditional Investment Areas, Non-Traditional Investment Areas, Business Assistance and Support Institutions, and Tourism. Provides links to Guatemalan business and trade-related web sites.

**Guatemalan Yellow Pages** **www.paginasamarillas.com**
Directory of businesses, with contact information. In Spanish and English. Click on the Guatemala link to access that country's yellow pages.

**Latinworld - Guatemala** **www.latinworld.com/centro/guatemala/**
Latinworld provides links to business information in Guatemala, as well as North, Central and South American countries, the Caribbean, and Spain.



## HONDURAS

**Honduras Internet Directory** **www.hondirectorio.com**
Links to all manner of Honduras related information, including business, industry, and technology.

**Hondu-Web** **www.marrder.com/hw**
Includes the online version of the Honduras This Week magazine, as well as content on travel and industry. In English

**In-Honduras** **www.in-honduras.com**
Comprehensive search engine and portal for Honduras. In English.

**Latinworld - Honduras** **www.latinworld.com/centro/honduras/**
Latinworld provides links to business information in Honduras, as well as North, Central and South American countries, the Caribbean, and Spain.

## HONG KONG

**Hong Kong Trade Development Council** **www.tdc.org.hk**
The Hong Kong Trade Development Council (HKTDC) promotes Hong Kong's trade in goods and services. The Web site offers a products and services catalog, HKTDC business information, media information and more. Visitors can subscribe to a free newsletter.

**Hong Kong and Chinese Stocks Live** **www.int.quamnet.com**
This stock site includes daily quotes from the Hang Seng index with daily market reports. The mainland Chinese stock market is also covered.

**SMENet** **www.sme-cma.org.hk**
A comprehensive, menu-driven series of links to Hong Kong-based businesses (including small to medium-sized). Maintained by the Chinese Manufacturers' Association of Hong Kong.

## HUNGARY

**Hungary Around the Clock** **www.hatc.hu**
An online guide to news and business information in Hungary. In English.

**Hungarian Yellowpages** **www.yellowpages.hu**
Hungarian yellow page search directory in Hungarian, English, and German.

## INDIA

**Link India**                                                    www.linkindia.net
Comprehensive search engine and portal for India.

**India Business Directory**                          www.india-invest.com/directory.htm
Presents a directory of indian companies having a presence on the Web.

**IndiaMart**                                                    www.indiamart.com
A massive Web directory with links to 60,000 Indian businesses (manufacture and exporters, importers and buyers and service providers), including foreign business, apparel and textiles, travel and tourism.

**India Trade Zone**                                        www.indiatradezone.com
Extensive site that lets you search products, companies and trade leads. Connects Indian exporters and importers to their counterparts across the world.

**Trade India**                                                 www.trade-india.com
A major reference site containing an Exporters Yellow Pages, Indian Importers Directory, Top 1,000 Companies of India, Trade Leads, Newsletters, Forums, Links, Forex Watch and more.

**WebIndia**                                                    www.webindia.com
WebIndia is a leading Indian business and technology consultancy. The site helps Indian businesses successfully sell products, explore import and export opportunities, and exploit the possibilities of technical collaboration with the Internet as the medium. Contains a Biz Portal directory of Indian businesses, with contact information.

## INDONESIA

**Indonesia Yellow Pages**                             www.yellowpages.co.id
Yellow-page listings of Indonesian companies and businesses. In English.

**National Agency for Export Development**       www.nafed.go.id
The Ministry of Trade of Indonesia provides information on resources, trade fairs, offers, and links to other sources as well as maintaining a bulletin board dedicated to these topics.

## IRAN

**Doing Business in Iran**                         www.iraniantrade.org/doinbiz/index.asp
Helpful online guide. Produced by the Iranian Trade Association (ITA), a California-based advocacy group. ITA provides Iranian advocacy, trade, and conference services to its global membership. ITA's prime directive is to empower the Iranian American community to join its advocacy campaign against U.S. unilateral and extra-territorial trade sanctions on Iran. In support of its advocacy program, ITA provides trade information on Iran and promotes Iranian conferences worldwide.

**Iran Trade Point Network**                           www.irtp.com
Excellent web portal with news, reports, reference materials, and numerous categories of links.

## IRELAND

**Finfacts Irish Finance and Business Portal**        www.finfacts.ie
This Web site is a major portal to Irish business and financial sites, including those providing stock market analysis.

**Investment and Development Agency**             www.idaireland.com
Information on investment in Ireland, with profiles on a range of service and manufacturing based industries, a directory of overseas companies currently doing business in Ireland, and statistics and demographics on the Irish labor force and local business environment.

**Irish Financial Sector**                         http://ireland.iol.ie/~rclapham/finance.html
An index for associations, banking, budgets and tax, government, investment, legal, life assurance, media and news, PLC's (corporations), securities, stock brokers, and travel.

**Swift Guide to Ireland**                              http://swift.kerna.ie
A database of more than 3,000 sites sectioned by business category.

## ISRAEL

**Export & International Cooperation Institute**        www.export.gov.il
Important internet portal designed to help with business and trading opportunities in Israel. Numerous categories and links, as well as news and forums. In Hebrew, English, and French.

**Globes -- Israel's Business Arena**              www.globes.co.il
Israel's business in daily headlines, economic analysis and Tel Aviv stock exchange reports. Includes a Start-up Guide and Venture Capital category, as well as a comprehensive directory of sources of information and assistance for those interested in Israel's high-tech industry.

## ITALY

**ANIBO Italian Buyers**                                http://anibo.com
The National Association of Italian Buying Offices provides a listing of member Italian purchasing agents with contact information, e-mail links and some Web links.

**WEBSITES**

**Invest in Italy**                                    www.investinitaly.com/
Site maintained by the Italian Trade Commission. Content includes incentives, location opportunities, and specific information for investors.

**Italy - Industry / Trade Worlds**                    www.italyindustry.com
An index of Italian companies searchable by product or industry, with product specific sub sites and free URL submission.

**Made In italy Official Portal**                    www.italtrade.com
Produced by the Italian Institute for Foreign Trade, a puublic agency entrusted with promoting trade, business opportunities and industrial co-operation between Italian and foreign companies, mostly by organizing the participation of Italian firms in fairs, exhibitions, workshops and bilateral meetings in more than 100 countries. Comprehensive Web site.

## JAPAN

**Investing in Japan**                                    www.investjapan.org
This site was launched by the Japan External Trade Organization (JETRO) in 2001. Includes features such as a cost simulation model to help estimate start-up costs in establishing a new operation in Japan, an overview of Japan's regional transportation infrastructure, information regarding regulations on establishing new enterprises, and more. In English.

**Japan Export and Trade Consultants**                    www.jetc.com
Resources for developing your business in Japan; includes trade leads, directories of Japanese companies, business protocols, trade fairs, classifieds and business tips. In English.

**Japan Information Network**                    http://jin.jcic.or.jp
The business and economy section of this comprehensive site contains menu-driven information on various aspects of doing business in Japan, including labor laws and taxation. Up-to-date statistics are also provided. In English and Japanese.

**JETRO**                                    www.jetro.go.jp
The Japan External Trade Organization is a non-profit, government-supported organization which promotes building trade and economic relationships; their Web site includes business information, useful links, publications, and latest developments.

**Statistics Bureau**                    www.stat.go.jp/english/index.htm
Very comprehensive site published by the Japanese Ministry of Internal Affairs and Communications. Has Japanese and English versions.

## KOREA

**Business Korea Plaza**                                    www.bizkorea.com
The Korean Exporters' Catalog; search for products offered by manufacturers and exporters from Korea. Visitors can ask for assistance over the Internet.

**EC21**                                    www.ec21.com
This site, run by the Korean International Trade Association, assists international business people in meeting at any time to exchange information on their companies and products, and to buy or sell desired products and services. Includes a Trade Leads section as well as a Company Directory and Product Catalogs. In Korean, English, and Chinese.

**Korea International Trade Association**                    www.kita.org
KITA's Web site includes trade opportunities, a company directory, a digital catalog, trade information and Korean business information; offered in Korean and English.

**KOTRA**                                    http://english.kotra.or.kr
The Korea Trade and Investment Promotion Agency Web site; links to Korean products, export, trade fairs, investment guide and opportunities and a directory.

**Buy Korea**                                    www.buykorea.org
Korea's global e-trade channel. Provides trade leads and online directory for Korean products. In Korean and English.

## LEBANON

**Business@Lebanon.com**                    www.lebanon.com/business
A Web site which includes links to Lebanese weekly business reports, the Beirut stock exchange, real estate, financial information, import-export, tour and hotel guide and a business directory.

**Lebanon Index**                                    www.lebindex.com
A search engine and portal for Lebanon; categories include business, government, banking and finance, tourism, and industry and trade.

## LIBYA

**ArabNet**                                    www.arab.net/libya
Overview, history, geography, business, culture, government and transport information about Libya. In English

**Libya Online**                                    www.libyaonline.com/economic
The business and economics section of Libya Online. Categories include: news, services, Libyan Business Directory, Laws and Regulations, GPC Decisions, Tenders, and Events and Announcements.

**Libyan Yellow Pages**                    http://www.yellowpages.ly
Directory of businesses with contact information. Official partner of the Federation of the Libyan Chambers of Commerce. In English.

**MBendi**  www.mbendi.co.za
Electronic encyclopedia of business and communication data for Africa. Links to countries, companies, events, industries, organizations, personalities, stock exchanges, publications, projects, products and country-specific data.

## MALAYSIA

**Malaysia Yellow Pages**  www.yellowpages.com.my
Comprehensive business directory with contact information. In English.

## MEXICO

**MaqGuide**  www.maqguide.com
MaqGuide.com is a registered business directory in over 800 search engines, advertises in trade publications, sponsors and exhibits at numerous tradeshows, conferences and international trade development meetings and participates in a link exchange with international trade Web sites throughout the global manufacturing community.

**BancoMext**  www.bancomext.com
Export directory, business opportunities, export and investment offices in Mexico, trade leads, Mexican government agencies, resource centers, universities and research institutes, trade shows, news sources, NAFTA information, and regional information. Sponsored by the Mexican Export Bank.

**Mexico Connect**  www.mexconnected.com
Mexican Trade and Business Forum, listing Mexican products and services and providing a forum for business practices and problems of Mexican trade; refer to home page at www.mexconnected.com for general information on working and living in Mexico. Also contains the Mexico Connect online magazine.

## MOROCCO

**ArabNet**  www.arab.net/morocco
General country information, with culture, business and government links.

**MBendi**  www.mbendi.co.za
A large electronic encyclopedia of business and communication information in Africa. Links to countries, companies, events, industries, organizations, personalities, stock exchanges, publications, projects, products and country-specific information.

**Morocco - Menara**  www.menara.ma
Index of Moroccan websites, e-mail addresses, classified ads, personal ads, events, business opportunities, Moroccan yellow pages and job offers (mostly in French).

## NETHERLANDS

**Dutch Yellow Pages**  www.dmo.com
Organized for quick location of businesses in the Netherlands. In Dutch and English.

**FENEDEX - The Dutch Export Site**  www.export.nl
A yellow-page directory of nearly 7,000 Dutch exporting companies and their international business partners, including corporate identity, products, and services, searchable by country, business category or alphabetical name. Export information is also available. In Dutch and English.

## NEW ZEALAND

**National Business Review Online**  www.nbr.co.nz
A large business internet site. Includes instant news, markets, global update, politics and polls.

**New Zealand Trade and Enterprise**  www.nzte.govt.nz
Information on importing, exporting and investing. Published by New Zealand's Economic and Trade Development Agency.

**UBD**  www.ubd.co.nz
Contains an online directory of New Zealand businesses, as well as import and export categories.

## NICARAGUA

**Centramerica Nicaragua**  http://directory.centramerica.com/nicaragua_asp/main.asp

Includes a business directory and links to economy, government, laws, demographics, news services, maps, related sites and events in Nicaragua.

**Nicaragua Yellow Pages**  www.paginasamarillas.com
Directory of Latin American businesses with contact information. Click on the Nicaragua link . In Spanish.

**Latinworld - Nicaragua**  www.latinworld.com/centro/nicaragua/
Latinworld provides links to business information in Nicaragua, as well as North, Central and South American countries, the Caribbean, and Spain.

**WEBSITES**

## NIGERIA

**MBendi** www.mbendi.co.za
A large electronic encyclopedia of business and communication information in Africa, searchable by country; includes information on companies, events, industries, organizations, personalities, stock exchanges, publications, projects, products and country information.

**E-Nigeria.NET** www.e-nigeria.net
General information site that contains a complete trade nework facility featuring buyers and sellers of different products and services.

## NORWAY

**Norway Online Information Service** www.norway.org
Business information on this Web site includes links to the Norwegian Trade Council in North America, industry attaches, products made in Norway, oil production, the fishing industry, Norwegian shipping, the stock exchange, exchange rates, statistics and yellow pages.

**ODIN** http://odin.dep.no
Official Documentation and Information from Norway (ODIN) is the central Web server for the Norwegian government, the office of the Prime Minister and the ministries. In Norwegian and English.

## PAKISTAN

**PakistanBiz** www.PakistanBiz.com
Very comprehensive web site includes the following categories: Exporters Directory, Trade Index, Investment Guide, Export Guide, Trade Directory, Buyer's Guide, and B2B Marketing Tools.

## PANAMA

**Centramerica Panama** http://directory.centramerica.com/panama_asp/main.asp
Includes a business directory and links to economy, government, laws, demographics, news services, maps, related sites and events in Panama.

**Latinworld - Panama** www.latinworld.com/centro/panama/
Latinworld provides links to business information in Panama, as well as North, Central and South American countries, the Caribbean, and Spain.

## PARAGUAY

**Latinworld - Paraguay** www.latinworld.com/sur/paraguay
Latinworld provides links to business information in Paraguay, as well as North, Central and South American countries, the Caribbean, and Spain.

## PERU

**Latinworld - Peru** www.latinworld.com/sur/peru
Latinworld provides links to business information in Peru, as well as North, Central and South American countries, the Caribbean, and Spain.

**U.S. Embassy in Lima** http://peru.usembassy.gov
Links to USAID, agricultural service, consular section, commercial service and weekly topics.

## PHILIPPINES

**Filipino Directory Online** www.filipino-directory.com
A large site providing links for everything related to the Philippines including business and investment opportunities.

**Philexport** www.philexport.ph
An export oriented site for importers of products made in the Philippines. The database includes information for most products made in the Philippines.

## POLAND

**Poland Business Network** www.polandbusinessnetwork.pl
This site includes extensive Polish business news coverage as well as a directory of Polish businesses and other business-related categories. In English.

**Poland - Export & Import Offers** www.export-import.pl
Comprehensive directory of Polish companies. This site enables businesses to link up with Polish companies for purposes of exporting to and importing from Poland. In Polish, English, German, Russian, French, and Spanish.

## PORTUGAL

**go4PortugalBusiness** http://go4portugalbusiness.com
Huge and comprehensive site consisting of extensive directories of Portuguese businesses, trade leads, and import and export sections.

**PortugalExporters** www.portugalinbusiness.com
Portuguese-government site providing information and links relating to Portuguese business opportunities, goods and services, companies, and foreign markets. Very comprehensive database.

**Portugal Offer** www.portugaloffer.com
Helps you business directly with Portuguese companies; contacts, products and services offered by the nation's top businesses so that you can find a supplier, customer, agent or partner in Portugal.

## ROMANIA

**Embassy of Romania in U.S.** www.roembus.org
Information on consular services, embassy news, travel tips, trade and business, news and media, and links to other official Romanian sites.

**Romanian Yellow Pages** www.romanianyellowpages.com
Directory of businesses with contact information. In English and Romanian.

**Trade Romania** www.trade-romania.biz
Contains a comprehensive directory of Romanian businesses. In addition, visitors to this site can buy and sell trade leads, place offers, and access real estates investment opportunities. The Romanian stock market is also covered.

## RUSSIA

**RusMarket Business Portal** www.rusmarket.com
Extensive site with the following categories: Business Directory, Marketplae, Business News, Exhibitions, Partners, B2B, among others.

**Russia on the Net** www.ru
A Russian Web directory and search engine. The Business category includes companies, banks and finance, products and services, electronic commerce, news and references.

**American Chamber of Commerce in Russia** www.amcham.ru
In addition to news, events, and marketing information, has detailed advice on various aspects of doing business Russia, with links to other Russian business-related sites.

**Russia Today** www.einnews.com/russia
Daily news and business updates concerning Russia and the CIS. In English.

## SAUDI ARABIA

**ArabNet** www.arab.net
A large source of information for the Middle East, including Saudi Arabia.

**U.S.-Saudi Arabian Business Council** www.us-saudi-business.org
Basic facts about Saudi Arabia, economy, doing business in Saudi Arabia, business regulations and procedures, joint venture opportunities, key contacts and certification procedures.

## SINGAPORE

**Singapore Yellow Pages** www.yellowpages.com.sg
A yellow-page directory of businesses in Singapore, organized by business category. Also contains various "resource" links.

**The Green Book** www.thegreenbook.com
The Singapore Industrial, Commercial, and Consumer Guide directs users to chambers of commerce, news, the Singapore government, products and services, brand names, and company information for most businesses in Singapore.

**International Enterprise Singapore** www.iesingapore.com
The government trade promotion site of Singapore featuring business matching, trade promotion, import and export information, foreign market information, information services, trade statistics, trade news and trade policy watch.

## SLOVAKIA

**Guide to the Slovak Republic** www.slovakia.org
An internet-based information site dedicated to presenting objective and non-partisan information about Slovak politics, society, history, culture, economy and links to government sites.

**Slovensko.com** www.slovensko.com/business/
Internet guide to Slovakia. Contains up-to-date news and business information. Numerous links to sites related to doing business in the Slovakia, including directories of businesses and consultants.

**U.S. Embassy in Slovakia** www.usis.sk
The U.S. Embassy provides news, a daily Washington file, U.S. information service, commercial services, a contact list, USAID information, consular section and information about Slovakia.

## SLOVENIA

**Slovenia Yellow Pages** http://yellow2.eunet.si/yellowpage/a/index.html

An internet directory of Slovenian businesses.

**WEBSITES**

## SOUTH AFRICA

**ExiNet**  www.exinet.co.za/business.htm
Links to trade, travel, Web search, environment, events, professional services and yellow pages. Trade link includes manufacturers, exporters, importers and distributors, freight clearing and forwarding agents, investments and trade opportunities.

**South African Business Directory**  http://iafrica.com/directories/business
A business directory searchable by sector or business name.

## SPAIN

**Camerdata Online**  www.camerdata.es
Spanish chambers of commerce, Euro chambers, a Spanish company directory, a business information area, commercial offers and a business guide. In Spanish.

**Invest in Spain**  www.interes.org
Web site of INTERES Invest in Spain, the new Spanish Investment Promotion Agency, serving as the reference point for foreign investors.

**Spanish Yellow Pages**  www.paginas-amarillas.es
Directory of businesses, with contact information. In Spanish.

## SWEDEN

**Swedish American Chambers of Commerce**  www.sacc-usa.org
This site represents the 18 regional chambers in the U.S.

**Swedish Web Sites**  http://katalogen.sunet.se/index-en.html
A search engine of Swedish Web pages searchable by category or by key words. Has an extensive business section. In English.

**The Swedish Page**  www.inetmedia.nu/sweden
Directory of Swedish sites including business, economy, politics, and education. Also, an address book. In English.

**Swedish Trade Council**  www.swedishtrade.com/other
An informative Web site for the foreign company wishing to do business in Sweden; offers company search, an export directory, sector information, business news, investment advice, legal information, and a listing of relevant publications. In English.

## SWITZERLAND

**SwissInfo**  www.swissinfo.org
Huge internet portal, including an alphabetical listing of Swiss companies under the Business category. In English, German, French, Italian, Spanish, Portuguese, Japanese, Arabic, and Chinese.

**Swisstrade**  www.swisstrade.com
Links to Swiss export services and companies, manufacturing pool and the Federal Office for Economic Development and Labor. In English, German, and French.

**Swiss Search Engine**  www.search.ch
A search engine offered in German, English, French and Italian languages; search all of Switzerland or by specific region.

## TAIWAN

**China Productivity Center (CPC)**  www.cpc.org.tw
Homepage for the CPC, a statutory body in Taiwan. The CPC assists Taiwan enterprises to upgrade quality and productivity, gives Taiwan's enterprises competitiveness information and promotes economic growth. The CPC also publishes directories in English and guides to international trade in Chinese.

**Taiwan Trade Media**  www.cens.com/
The largest suppliers' online information database for Taiwan.

**Taiwan Commerce Online**  http://Taiwan-Commerce.com
The Taiwan Commerce search engine includes global trade, a trade bulletin board, business service, technology, world news, financial services and trade exhibition information. In Chinese and English.

**TransWorld Trade Net**  www.ttnet.net
An extensive databank of matching trade opportunities and trade information; enter keywords of products or companies.

## THAILAND

**Exporters Directory**  http://exporter.thaitrade.com
Thailand's Exporters Directory is a handy and helpful platform where buyers can meet more than five thousand Thai exporters. Products are divided into 17 categories. In English.

**Thailand Board of Investment**  www.boi.go.th
Big web site offering information about investing in Thailand. In Thai and English.

**Thailand Exports**  www.thailand.com/exports/index.php
A site developed by the Thailand Department of Export Promotion. Includes an extensive set of links as well as trade tools and a news service.

**WEBSITES**

## TURKEY

**Turkey Business Links**                               www.eurasianet.org/resource/turkey/
                                                         links/business.shtml
This part of the EurasiaNet web site contains various categories of links relating to Turkish business.

**Trade Turkey**                                         www.tradeturkey.com
Huge internet portal including a business directory and trade leads.

## UKRAINE

**UkraineBiz**                                           www.ukrainebiz.com
A free informational site describing services and products available for export to and from the Ukraine operated by the Center for Economic Initiatives. Companies are listed free of charge.

**Ukrainian Yellow Pages**                              http://www.ukraine.org/
                                                         www.ukrainet.lviv.ua/yellow/pages.htm
Directory of businesses, with contact information. In English and Ukrainian.

## UNITED ARAB EMIRATES (U.A.E.)

**Go Dubai**                                             www.godubai.com
A guide to Dubai and the United Arab Emirates, with information on travel facilities, a searchable database of companies, local business news, and more.

## UNITED KINGDOM

**British Exporters**                                    www.export.co.uk
A database of British companies with listings by company name or business classification; users must register company data in order to use the directory.

**British Promotional Merchandise Ass'n**               www.promotionalmerchandise.org.uk
A source directory of British promotional merchandise manufacturers and suppliers with listings by product category.

**Scoot Business Finder**                                www.scoot.co.uk
A quick find guide to companies, searchable by product, service, or company name, with identical local sites for Belgium and Holland.

**The Business Information Zone**                        www.thebiz.co.uk
Business information, products and services on the Internet as well as database listings for companies and organizations not yet on the internet. The extensive business directory is organized into business types.

**UK Electronic Yellow Pages**                          http://search.yell.com
A yellow-page directory of businesses in the United Kingdom.

## UNITED STATES

**Bureau of Industry and Security**                      www.bis.doc.gov
Formerly, The Bureau of Export Administration. Regulates the export of sensitive goods and technologies; enforces export control, antiboycott, and public safety laws; cooperates with other countries on export control and strategic trade issues; and monitors the viability of the U.S. defense industrial base.

**BuyUSA.gov**                                           www.buyusa.gov
Published by the U.S. Commercial Service. Contains specific sites for the majority of countries. Each country-specific site is in English and the language of the selected country. Information is provided by more than 1,800 trade professionals in 105 U.S. cities and 151 U.S. Embassies, Consulates and Trade Centers around the world.

**Export Import Bank of the U.S.**                       www.exim.gov
Provides information regarding loans for U.S. exporters and purchasers of U.S. goods and services, and insurance against foreign buyer defaults.

**Foreign Trade Statistics**                             www.census.gov/foreign-trade/www
The U.S. Census Bureau provides foreign trade statistics for the U.S.; includes country trade data, export classification assistance, profile of U.S. export companies, export seminars and more.

**Hoovers Online**                                       www.hoovers.com
Searchable database of 12 million companies, with in-depth coverage of 40,000 of the world's top business enterprises. Staff of 80 editors delivers comprehensive company, industry, and market intelligence. Updated daily.

**International Trade Administration**                   www.ita.doc.gov
A Web site by the U.S. Department of Commerce providing leads to exporters, trade development information, market access and compliance as well as import regulations.

**Library of International Trade Resources**            www.litr.com
Online service providing both interactive information access and customized consultation services. The providers have expertise in the areas of antidumping, the textile and apparel quota regime, import and export market research, and economic and statistical analysis.

**MSU-CIBER (Michigan State University**                http://ciber.msu.edu
Designated as a national resource center in international business education by the U.S. Department of Education. Target audience includes students, faculty, practicing mangers and public policy makers. Offers hundreds of links to international trade-related sites.

**WEBSITES**

**The Export Yellow Pages**      **www.exportyellowpages.com**
The Export Yellow Pages is a public-private partnership of the U.S. Department of Commerce and Global Publishers LLC. This site gives US exporters and service providers a simple, fast, and convenient way to establish contacts and conduct business. The Export Yellow Pages is administered by the Export Trading Company Affairs, International Trade Administration. Includes the U.S. Trade Assistance Directory.

**STAT-USA**      **www.stat-usa.gov**
Important research tool provided by the U.S. Federal Government. Contains the National Trade Database (NTDB), which groups both business and economic information in electronic libraries, including trade statistics, overseas contacts, market research reports, daily economic releases, and procurement information. Annual fee.

**Tariff Affairs and Related Matters (USITC)**      **www.usitc.gov/tata/index.htm**
The U.S. International Trade Commission publishes the Harmonized Tariff Schedule Annotated (HTSA). The HTSA provides tariff rates and statistical categories for all merchandise imported into the United States.

**ThomasNet**      **www.thomasregister.com**
Covers 173,000 North American manufacturers. Users can place orders online, view and download Computer Aided Design (CAD) drawings, and view thousands of online company catalogs and websites. Currently free.

**Trade Information Center**      **www.trade.gov/td/tic**
Provides information about federal export assistance programs and country market information. Part of the International Trade Administration of the U.S. Department of Commerce.

**TradePort**      **www.tradeport.org**
TradePort is a repository of free information and resources for businesses that seek to conduct international trade to and from California. Contains an online newsletter. In English, Japanese, Chinese, and Italian.

**U.S. Council for International Business**      **www.uscib.org**
U.S. affiliate of the International Chamber of Commerce (ICC). Among the premier pro-trade, pro-market liberalization organizations. Membership includes over 300 multinational companies, law firms and business associations. Provides access to international policy makers and regulatory authorities.

**U.S. Customs and Border Protection**      **www.cbp.gov**
Comprehensive information of U.S. import/export procedures, documentation and programs, C-TPAT, 24-Hour Rule and other security-related programs.

**U.S. Department of Commerce**      **www.commerce.gov**
The gateway for links to all the main agencies and bureaus within the Department of Commerce.

**U.S. Government Export Portal**      **www.export.gov**
The U.S. government's portal to all export-related assistance and market information offered by the federal government. Extremely comprehensive. Contains a free monthly newsletter.

## VENEZUELA

**Latin World -- Venezuela**      **www.latinworld.com/sur/venezuela**
Comprehensive all-purpose directory, with categories for business and export/import.

**Venezuela Export**      **www.venexport.com/**
A directory of exporters, searchable by name or sector.

## VIETNAM

**Vietnam Business Center**      **www.usvietnam.com**
A resource for Vietnam market intelligence information. Provides news, market research, facts and figures. Visitors can find business partners and explore trade opportunities at the site's Trade Exchange Center, which is a destination for buyers and sellers, importers and exporters to find trade opportunities and promote business online. A search feature can locate hundreds of businesses in the Business Directory. Visitors can request custom market intelligence information.

**VVG Vietnam**      **www.vvg-vietnam.com**
The Vietnam Venture Group site provides Web links related to business formation and investment advice, and provides access to business consultants, investment counselors, purchasing and export agents, and market entry service providers. Also contains articles on business and Investment.

**WEBSITES**

# Guide to Trade Documents[1]

Documents play a key role in international transactions. Both buyers and sellers need documents for bookkeeping, accounting, taxation, export and import formalities, as well as making payment using letters of credit and other documentary payment methods.

This section gives examples of the most common documents used in international trade. It is not an exhaustive listing. Specialized trades, special circumstances and different countries of origin and destination may require additional documentation. For more information contact your local logistics company representative or refer to *A Short Course in International Trade Documentation*, also by World Trade Press.

Following a general discussion of a) document categories, b) transport documents and c) documents and international payments; sample documents will be presented and defined, key elements listed, and cautions offered concerning important issues and common problems. Emphasis will be given to issues regarding letters of credit.

## Document Categories

Documents for international trade fall into several overlapping categories:

### Transaction Document(s)

The key transaction document is the invoice or commercial invoice. This document is used by all parties to the transaction for accounting and bookkeeping purposes. It is also required for export and import formalities as well as most banking and payment procedures.

### Export Documents

These are documents required by the customs or national export authority of the country of export and vary greatly from country to country. Included are licenses, permits, export declarations, inspection certificates, commercial invoices and sometimes transport documents.

### Transport Documents

These are documents issued by a shipping line, air cargo carrier, trucking company or freight forwarder that detail the terms of transport for cargo. The key transport document is the bill of lading.

### Inspection Documents

These documents are generally issued by third party inspection firms at the request of the buyer to certify the quality and quantities of a shipment. Inspection documents are also issued to satisfy country export and import requirements.

### Insurance Documents

These documents evidence insurance coverage of a shipment and can be in the form of a policy or a certificate.

### Banking / Payment Documents

Banking and payment documents include letters of credit, amendments to letters of credit, various advices, plus virtually all the other documents used in trade (bills of lading, commercial invoice, insurance document, inspection certificates, etc.).

### Import Documents

These are documents required by the customs authority of the country of import and vary greatly from country to country. The minimum documentation requirement is an entry form and a commercial invoice. However, many other forms may be required, especially if the imported merchandise is sensitive (e.g., animals, weapons, drugs, food), if the importer is requesting special tariff treatment under an import program (e.g., GSP, NAFTA) or if the import comes from certain countries.

---

1. This section has been excerpted from the book Short Course in International Trade Documentation, ISBN 1-885073-59-3, also by Edward G. Hinkelman and available from World Trade Press.

# Transport Documents

## Bills of lading

A bill of lading is a document issued by a carrier to a shipper, signed by the captain, agent, or owner of a vessel, furnishing written evidence regarding receipt of the goods (cargo), the conditions on which transportation is made (contract of carriage), and the engagement to deliver goods at the prescribed port of destination to the lawful holder of the bill of lading.

A bill of lading is, therefore, both a receipt for merchandise and a contract to deliver it as freight. There are a number of different types of bills of lading and a number of issues that relate to them as a group of documents.

## Straight bill of lading (non-negotiable)

A straight bill of lading indicates that the shipper will deliver the goods to the consignee. The document itself does not give title to the goods (making it "non-negotiable"). The consignee need only identify himself to claim the goods. A straight bill of lading is often used when payment for the goods has already been made in advance or in cases where the goods are shipped on open account. A straight bill of lading, therefore, cannot be transferred by endorsement.

## Shipper's order bill of lading (negotiable)

A shipper's order bill of lading is a title document to the goods, issued "to the order of" a party, usually the shipper, whose endorsement is required to effect its negotiation. Because it is negotiable, it can be bought, sold, or traded while goods are in transit. These are highly favored for documentary credit transactions. The buyer usually needs the original or a copy as proof of ownership to take possession of the goods.

## Blank endorsed negotiable bill of lading

A blank endorsed negotiable bill of lading is one that has been endorsed without naming an endorsee. In simple terms, the person in possession of the document may claim possession of the goods.

## Air waybill

An air waybill is a form of bill of lading used for the air transport of goods and is not negotiable.

## Clean bill of lading

A clean bill of lading is one where the carrier has noted that the merchandise has been received in apparent good condition (no apparent damage, loss, etc.) and that does not bear such notations as "Shipper's Load and Count," etc.

Most forms of documentary payment require a "clean" bill of lading in order for the seller to obtain payment. There are, however, some circumstances in some trades, in which transport documents with special clauses are acceptable.

## Claused bill of lading

A claused bill of lading is one which contains notations that specify a shortfall in quantity or deficient condition of the goods and/or packaging. Opposite of clean bill of lading.

## Originals

Some bills of lading are issued in "sets of originals." In documentary credit transactions the "full set" of original transport documents (one or more) must usually be presented for payment (especially if they are negotiable documents).

## On board

An "on board" notation on a bill of lading means that the goods have in fact been loaded on board or shipped on a named vessel. This notation may be made by the carrier, his agent, the master of the ship, or his agent. Unless expressly authorized, the transport document issued by the carrier must reflect that it is "on board" in order for the seller to obtain payment under a documentary credit.

## On deck

An "on deck" notation means that the goods have been secured on the deck of the vessel rather than in its hold, and therefore subject to wind and weather. Such a notation is generally not acceptable in documentary credit transactions unless specifically authorized. If the transport document shows that the goods are loaded on deck, any accompanying insurance document must show cover against "on deck" risks. Bear in mind, however, that certain dangerous cargo (including certain chemicals and live animals) are often carried on deck.

# Documents and International Payments

Documents are an integral part of all international payment methods, including documentary letters of credit, documents against payment, and documents against acceptance.

The documents called for by a payment type will differ somewhat according to the nature of the goods and the countries of export and import. Some documents, however, such as the commercial invoice and a bill of lading, are specified in all transactions.

## Consistency Among Documents

One of the major issues in the preparation, presentation, and verification of documentation by sellers, buyers, and banks in payment situations is consistency among the documents.

**Example**: In examining the documentation for a letter of credit transaction involving the sale of five pieces of machinery, the buyer noticed that the commercial invoice listed the net weight as 12,140 kilograms and the gross weight as 12,860 kilograms. The bill of lading, however, listed the gross weight as 9,612 kilograms. What happened to the other 3,248 kilograms? Did the seller make a mistake in preparing the commercial invoice? Did the shipping company make a mistake in preparing the bill of lading? Did the seller forget to ship one or more pieces of machinery? Did the shipping company misplace some machinery? Did someone steal the machinery?

In the above example, the seller should have noticed the inconsistency before forwarding the documents to the advising bank. The advising bank should have noticed the inconsistency before forwarding the documents to the issuing bank. The issuing bank should have noticed the inconsistency before forwarding the documents to the buyer. The buyer will most certainly reject this documentation.

## Documentation Consistency Checklist

The following is a list of points of consistency buyers, sellers, and banks should all be aware of when preparing, presenting, and checking documents for documentary payment transactions:

1. Name and address of shipper
2. Name and address of buyer/consignee
3. Issuer name and address
4. Description of the goods, quantities, units
5. Country of origin of the goods
6. Country of destination of the goods
7. Invoice numbers, documentary credit numbers
8. Certifications
9. Legalizations
10. Shipping marks and numbers
11. Net weight, gross weight, volume
12. Number of crates, cartons, or containers

## Ambiguity as to issuers of documents

If terms such as "first class," "well-known," "qualified," "independent," "official," "competent," or "local" are used in a documentary credit to refer to the issuer of a required document (e.g., inspection certificate or certificate of origin), banks are authorized to accept whatever documents are presented, provided that on their face they appear to be in compliance with the credit and were not issued and signed by the seller (beneficiary).

## Originals

The originals of specified documents should be provided unless copies are called for or allowed. If more than one set of originals is required, the buyer should specify in the credit how many are necessary.

Unless otherwise noted in the documentary credit, banks are authorized to accept documents as originals, even if they were produced or appear to have been produced on a copy machine, by a computerized system, or are carbon copies, provided they have the notation "Original" and are, when necessary, signed.

## Named carrier

A transport document must appear on its face to have been issued by a named carrier, or his agent. This does not mean that the applicant must name the carrier in the documentary credit application. It merely means that the transport document must indicate the name of the carrier.

## Authentication

Unless otherwise noted in the documentary credit, banks are authorized to accept documents that are authenticated, validated, legalized, visaed, or certified so long as the document appears on its face to satisfy the requirement. This means that the banks are not responsible for the verification of the certification or authorized signature. Certificates must usually bear the signature of the issuer.

## Signature

Banks are authorized to accept documents that have been signed by facsimile, perforated signature, stamp, symbol, or any other mechanical or electronic method.

## Unspecified issuers or contents of documents

If the credit does not name a specific issuer or specific contents of a document (other than transport documents, insurance documents, and the commercial invoice), banks are authorized to accept documents as presented so long as the data contained in the documents are consistent with the credit and other stipulated documents.

## Issuance date vs. documentary credit date

Unless otherwise noted in the documentary credit, banks are authorized to accept documents dated prior to the issuance date of the credit, so long as all other terms of the credit have been satisfied.

DOCUMENTS

# Commercial Invoice

## Definition

The commercial invoice is the key accounting document describing the commercial transaction between the buyer and the seller.

## ✔ Key Elements

The commercial invoice includes the following elements:

1. Name and address of seller
2. Name and address of buyer
3. Date of issuance
4. Invoice number
5. Order or contract number
6. Quantity and description of the goods
7. Unit price, total price, other agreed upon charges, and total invoice amount stated in the currency of the contract or letter of credit (e.g., US$, €, ¥, etc.)
8. Shipping details including: weight of the goods, number of packages, and shipping marks and numbers
9. Terms of delivery and payment
10. Signature of company representative filling out the form
11. Any other information as required in the sales contract or letter of credit (e.g., country of origin)

## Cautions & Notes for Documentary Letters of Credit

In transactions involving a documentary letter of credit it is vitally important that the description of the goods in the commercial invoice correspond precisely to the description of goods in the credit.

The invoice amount should match exactly (or at least should not exceed) the amount specified in the credit. Banks have the right to refuse invoices issued for amounts in excess of the amount stated in the credit. For this, as well as other reasons, the invoice should be made out in the same currency as the credit.

The exception: when a documentary credit specifies "about" in relation to the currency amount and quantity of merchandise, in which case the invoice may specify an amount equal to plus or minus 10 percent of the stipulated amount of the credit.

Unless otherwise stipulated in the documentary credit, the commercial invoice must be made out in the name of the applicant (buyer). The exception: In a transferable documentary credit the invoice may be made out to a third party.

The buyer, seller, and bank(s) should all carefully check for discrepancies in the invoice. The details specified therein should not be inconsistent with those of any other documents, and should exactly conform to the specifications of the credit.

DOCUMENTS

# Commercial Invoice

| 1. Exporter Name and Address | | 2. Shipper Name and Address | |
|---|---|---|---|
| World Trade Press<br>800 Lindberg Lane, Suite 190<br>Petaluma, California 94952 USA | | World Trade Press<br>800 Lindberg Lane, Suite 190<br>Petaluma, California 94952 USA | |

| 3. Seller E.I.N. (Tax ID)<br>94-1234567 | 4. Date<br>September 18, 2006 | 5. Invoice #<br>2006-12516 | 6. Ship Date<br>September 20, 2006 |
|---|---|---|---|

| 7. Forwarder Name and Address | 8. Ship to Name and Address<br>Map Import Company<br>26th Floor, Office Tower, Convention Plaza<br>1 Harbour Road<br>Wanchai, Hong Kong, China SAR |
|---|---|
| 9. International Consignee Name and Address | 10. Buyer Name and Address<br>Map Import Company<br>26th Floor, Office Tower, Convention Plaza<br>1 Harbour Road<br>Wanchai, Hong Kong, China SAR |
| 11. Affiliate Name and Address | 12. Carrier Name and Address<br>XYZ Air Freight Company<br>1234 Cargo Street<br>Oakland, California 94### USA |

| 13. Port of Export<br>Oakland, California USA | 14. Country of Export<br>USA | 15. Country of Manufacture<br>USA | 16. Final Country of Destination<br>Hong Kong China SAR |
|---|---|---|---|
| 17. Customer Account Number<br>12,345 | 18. AWB#<br>AWB123456789 | 19. Shipment # | 20. Terms of Payment<br>Prepaid |
| 21. Terms of Sale<br>Prepaid | 22. Terms of Delivery<br>CIF | 23. Currency of Sale<br>USD | 24. Letter of Credit # |
| 25. Method of Transportation<br>Air Freight | 26. # of Pkgs/items/load<br>Hong Kong | 27. Gross Weight<br>126 lbs. | 28. Other Reference # |

| Item | Commodity Description | SKU | COO | QTY | Unit Price | Net Weight | Total Price |
|---|---|---|---|---|---|---|---|
| #1 | World Map 140" x 90" Vinyl | | | 4 | US$1,750.00 | | US$7,000.00 |
| #2 | World Map 120" x 70" Vinyl | | | 10 | US$1,250.00 | | US$12,500.00 |
| #3 | World Map 90" x 60" Vinyl | | | 20 | US$600.00 | | US$12,000.00 |
| #4 | USA Map 90" x 60" Vinyl | | | 5 | US$600.00 | | US$3,000.00 |

| | |
|---|---|
| Sub Total | US$34,500.00 |
| Shipping and Handling Costs | US$1,800.00 |
| Insurance Costs | US$300.00 |
| Total Invoice Value | US$36,600.00 |

Kathleen B. Shipper, Shipping Manager

Name and Title of Authorizing Person

*K.B. Shipper*         September 20, 2006

Signature of Authorizing Person       Date

DOCUMENTS

# Marine/Ocean/Port-to-Port Bill of Lading

## Definition

A marine bill of lading is a transport document covering port-to-port shipments of goods (for carriage of goods solely by sea).

## ✔ Key Elements

A completed marine bill of lading contains the following elements:

1. Name of carrier with a signature identified as that of carrier, or ship's master, or agent for or on behalf of either the carrier or ship's master
2. An indication or notation that the goods have been loaded "on board" or shipped on a named vessel. Also, the date of issuance or date of loading
3. An indication of the port of loading and the port of discharge
4. A sole original, or if issued in multiple originals, the full set of originals
5. The terms and conditions of carriage or a reference to the terms and conditions of carriage in another source or document
6. In a documentary letter of credit, no indication that the document is subject to a charter party and/or an indication that the named vessel is propelled by sail only
7. Meets any other stipulations of the sales contract or documentary letter of credit

## Cautions & Notes for Documentary Letters of Credits

If the document includes the notation "intended vessel" it must also contain an "on board" notation of a named vessel along with the date of loading, even if the named vessel is the same as the intended vessel.

If the document indicates a place where the goods were received by the carrier different from the port of loading, the document must also contain an "on-board" notation indicating the port of loading as named in the credit and the named vessel, along with the date.

If a documentary credit calls for a port-to-port shipment but does not call specifically for a marine bill of lading, the banks will accept a transport document, however named, that contains the above information. Banks will normally accept the following documents under this title: ocean bill of lading, combined transport bill of lading, short form bill of lading, or received for shipment bill of lading, provided it carries the notation "on board."

If the documents are drawn up "to the order of" the exporter or "to order" they must be endorsed.

If the documentary credit prohibits transshipment this document will be rejected if it specifically states that the goods will be transshipped.

Since this is a negotiable instrument, it may be endorsed and transferred to a third party while the goods are in transit.

DOCUMENTS

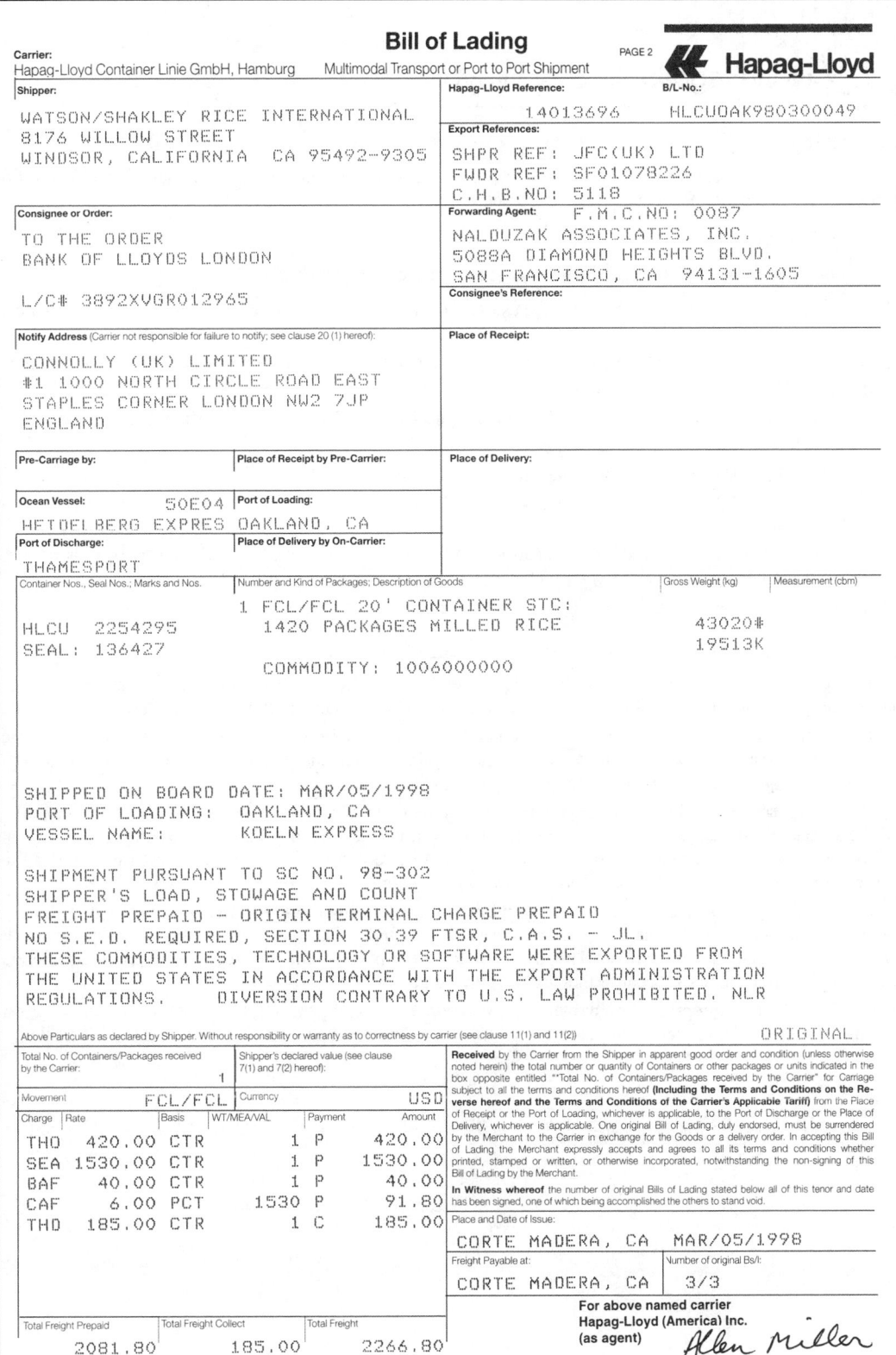

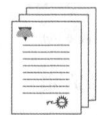

# Non-Negotiable Sea Waybill

## Definition

A non-negotiable sea waybill is a transport document covering port-to-port shipments. It is not a title document, is not negotiable and cannot be endorsed.

## ✔ Key Elements

A completed non-negotiable sea waybill contains the following elements:

1. Name of carrier with a signature identified as that of carrier, or ship's master, or agent for or on behalf of either the carrier or ship's master
2. An indication or notation that the goods have been loaded "on board" or shipped on a named vessel. Also, the date of issuance or date of loading
3. An indication of the port of loading and the port of discharge as specified in the original sales contract or documentary credit
4. A sole original, or if issued in multiple originals, the full set of originals
5. The terms and conditions of carriage or a reference to the terms and conditions of carriage in another source or document
6. In a documentary letter of credit, no indication that the document is subject to a charter party and/or an indication that the named vessel is propelled by sail only
7. Meets any other stipulations of the sales contract or documentary credit

## Cautions & Notes for Documentary Letters of Credit

If the document includes the notation "intended vessel" it must also contain an "on board" notation of a named vessel along with the date of loading, even if the named vessel is the same as the intended vessel.

If the document indicates a place where the goods were received by the carrier different from the port of loading, the document must also contain an "on-board" notation indicating the port of loading as named in the documentary letter of credit and the named vessel, along with the date.

If the documentary credit calls for a port-to-port shipment but does not call specifically for a marine bill of lading, the banks will accept a transport document, however named, that contains the above information. Banks will normally accept the following documents under this title: ocean bill of lading, combined transport bill of lading, short form bill of lading, or received for shipment bill of lading, provided it carries the notation "on board."

Because they are not title documents, sea waybills eliminate many of the inconveniences of a bill of lading and offer advantages in situations where the rigid security of a bill of lading is not required. Waybills reduce the opportunity for fraud—although they do not by any means eliminate it—and they remove the problems of goods arriving ahead of documents (because they travel with the goods).

Sea waybills are appropriate for shipments between associated companies, for shipments to an agent for sale at destination on an open account basis, and for shipments between companies that have established mutual trust.

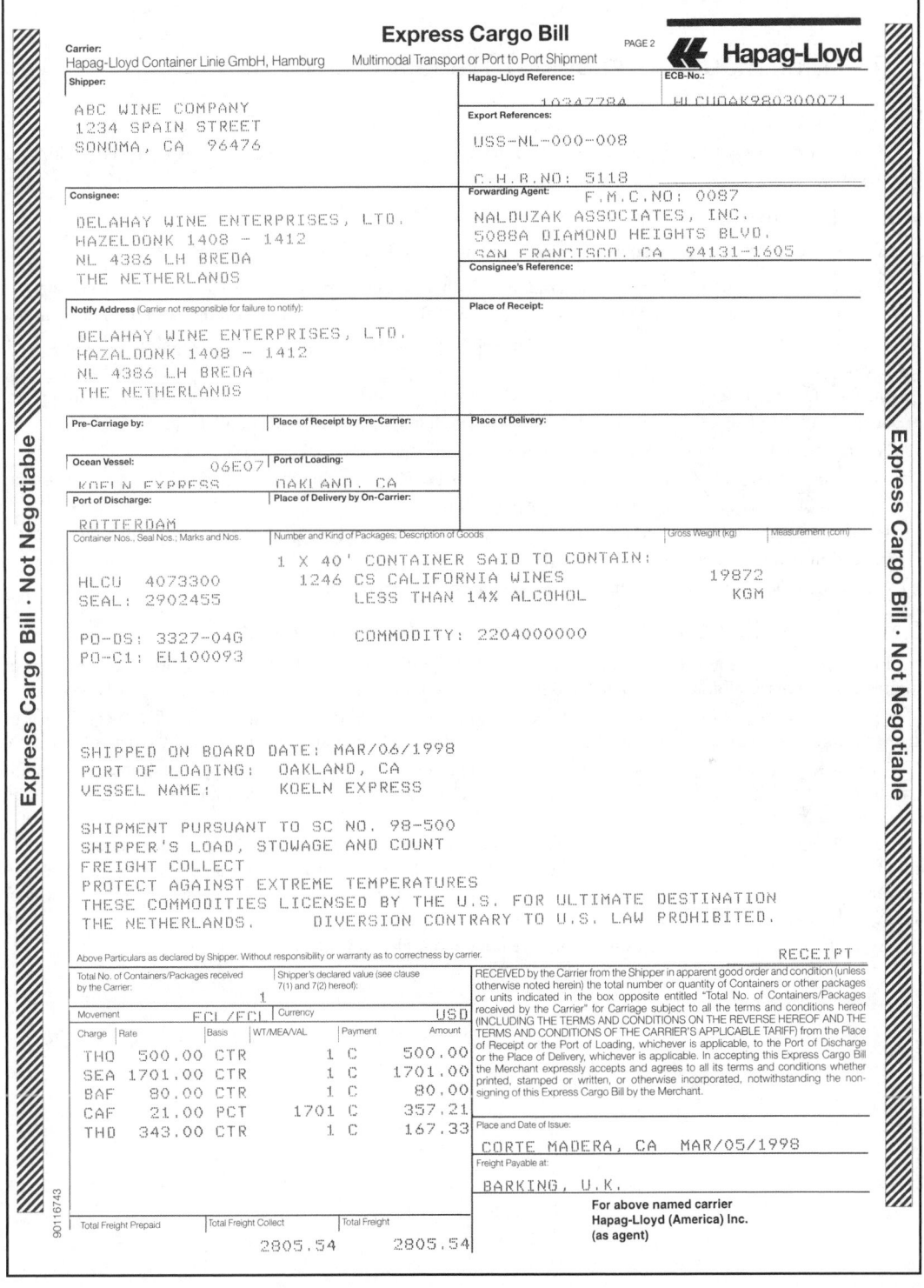

## Express Cargo Bill

Carrier:
Hapag-Lloyd Container Linie GmbH, Hamburg

Multimodal Transport or Port to Port Shipment   PAGE 2

**Hapag-Lloyd**

| | |
|---|---|
| **Shipper:**<br>ABC WINE COMPANY<br>1234 SPAIN STREET<br>SONOMA, CA  96476 | **Hapag-Lloyd Reference:** 10347784  **ECB-No.:** HLCU0AK980300071<br>**Export References:**<br>USS-NL-000-008<br>C.H.R.NO: 5118  F.M.C.NO: 0087 |
| **Consignee:**<br>DELAHAY WINE ENTERPRISES, LTD.<br>HAZELDONK 1408 - 1412<br>NL 4386 LH BREDA<br>THE NETHERLANDS | **Forwarding Agent:**<br>NALDUZAK ASSOCIATES, INC.<br>5088A DIAMOND HEIGHTS BLVD.<br>SAN FRANCISCO, CA  94131-1605<br>**Consignee's Reference:** |
| **Notify Address** (Carrier not responsible for failure to notify):<br>DELAHAY WINE ENTERPRISES, LTD.<br>HAZELDONK 1408 - 1412<br>NL 4386 LH BREDA<br>THE NETHERLANDS | **Place of Receipt:** |
| **Pre-Carriage by:**  **Place of Receipt by Pre-Carrier:** | **Place of Delivery:** |
| **Ocean Vessel:** 06E07  **Port of Loading:**<br>KOELN EXPRESS  OAKLAND, CA | |
| **Port of Discharge:**  **Place of Delivery by On-Carrier:**<br>ROTTERDAM | |

| Container Nos., Seal Nos.; Marks and Nos. | Number and Kind of Packages; Description of Goods | Gross Weight (kg) | Measurement (cbm) |
|---|---|---|---|
| HLCU   4073300<br>SEAL: 2902455<br><br>PO-DS: 3327-04G<br>PO-C1: EL100093 | 1 X 40' CONTAINER SAID TO CONTAIN:<br>1246 CS CALIFORNIA WINES<br>LESS THAN 14% ALCOHOL<br><br>COMMODITY: 2204000000 | 19872<br>KGM | |

SHIPPED ON BOARD DATE: MAR/06/1998
PORT OF LOADING:  OAKLAND, CA
VESSEL NAME:       KOELN EXPRESS

SHIPMENT PURSUANT TO SC NO. 98-500
SHIPPER'S LOAD, STOWAGE AND COUNT
FREIGHT COLLECT
PROTECT AGAINST EXTREME TEMPERATURES
THESE COMMODITIES LICENSED BY THE U.S. FOR ULTIMATE DESTINATION
THE NETHERLANDS.       DIVERSION CONTRARY TO U.S. LAW PROHIBITED.

Above Particulars as declared by Shipper. Without responsibility or warranty as to correctness by carrier.

**RECEIPT**

Total No. of Containers/Packages received by the Carrier:  1

Shipper's declared value (see clause 7(1) and 7(2) hereof):

| Movement | | | FCI/FCI | Currency | | USD |
|---|---|---|---|---|---|---|
| Charge | Rate | Basis | WT/MEA/VAL | Payment | | Amount |
| THO | 500.00 | CTR | 1 | C | | 500.00 |
| SEA | 1701.00 | CTR | 1 | C | | 1701.00 |
| BAF | 80.00 | CTR | 1 | C | | 80.00 |
| CAF | 21.00 | PCT | 1701 | C | | 357.21 |
| THD | 343.00 | CTR | 1 | C | | 167.33 |

RECEIVED by the Carrier from the Shipper in apparent good order and condition (unless otherwise noted herein) the total number or quantity of Containers or other packages or units indicated in the box opposite entitled "Total No. of Containers/Packages received by the Carrier" for Carriage subject to all the terms and conditions hereof (INCLUDING THE TERMS AND CONDITIONS ON THE REVERSE HEREOF AND THE TERMS AND CONDITIONS OF THE CARRIER'S APPLICABLE TARIFF) from the Place of Receipt or the Port of Loading, whichever is applicable, to the Port of Discharge or the Place of Delivery, whichever is applicable. In accepting this Express Cargo Bill the Merchant expressly accepts and agrees to all its terms and conditions whether printed, stamped or written, or otherwise incorporated, notwithstanding the non-signing of this Express Cargo Bill by the Merchant.

**Place and Date of Issue:**
CORTE MADERA, CA   MAR/05/1998

**Freight Payable at:**
BARKING, U.K.

**For above named carrier**
**Hapag-Lloyd (America) Inc.**
**(as agent)**

| Total Freight Prepaid | Total Freight Collect | Total Freight |
|---|---|---|
| | 2805.54 | 2805.54 |

90116743

# Multimodal (Combined) Transport Document

## Definition

A multimodal transport document is a bill of lading covering two or more modes of transport, such as shipping by rail and by sea.

## ✔ Key Elements

A completed multimodal transport document contains the following elements:

1. Name of carrier or multimodal transport operator with a signature identified as that of carrier, transport operator, or ship's master, or agent for or on behalf of either the carrier, transport operator, or ship's master
2. An indication that the shipment has been "dispatched," "taken in charge," or "loaded on board," along with a date
3. Indication of the place of receipt of the shipment that may be different from the place of actual loading "on board" and the place of delivery of the shipment, which may be different from the place of discharge
4. A sole original, or if issued in multiple originals, the full set of originals
5. The terms and conditions of carriage or a reference to the terms and conditions of carriage in another source or document other than the multimodal transport document
6. In a documentary letter of credit, no indication that the document is subject to a charter party and/or an indication that the named vessel is propelled by sail only
7. Meets any other stipulations of the sales contract or documentary letter of credit

## Cautions & Notes for Documentary Letters of Credit

In multimodal situations the contract of carriage and liability is for a combined transport from the place of shipment to the place of delivery. Thus, the document evidences receipt of goods and not shipment on board.

The date of issuance of the document is deemed to be the date of dispatch unless there is a specific date of dispatch, taking in charge, or loading on board, in which case the latter date is deemed to be the date of dispatch.

Even if a documentary letter of credit prohibits transshipment, banks will accept a multimodal transport document that indicates that transshipment will or may take place, provided that the entire carriage is covered by one transport document.

A combined transport document issued by a freight forwarder is acceptable unless the documentary letter of credit stipulates otherwise or unless the credit specifically calls for a "marine bill of lading." The issuing freight forwarder accepts carrier responsibility for performance of the entire contract of carriage and liability for loss or damage wherever and however it occurs.

As a rule, multimodal transport documents are not negotiable instruments.

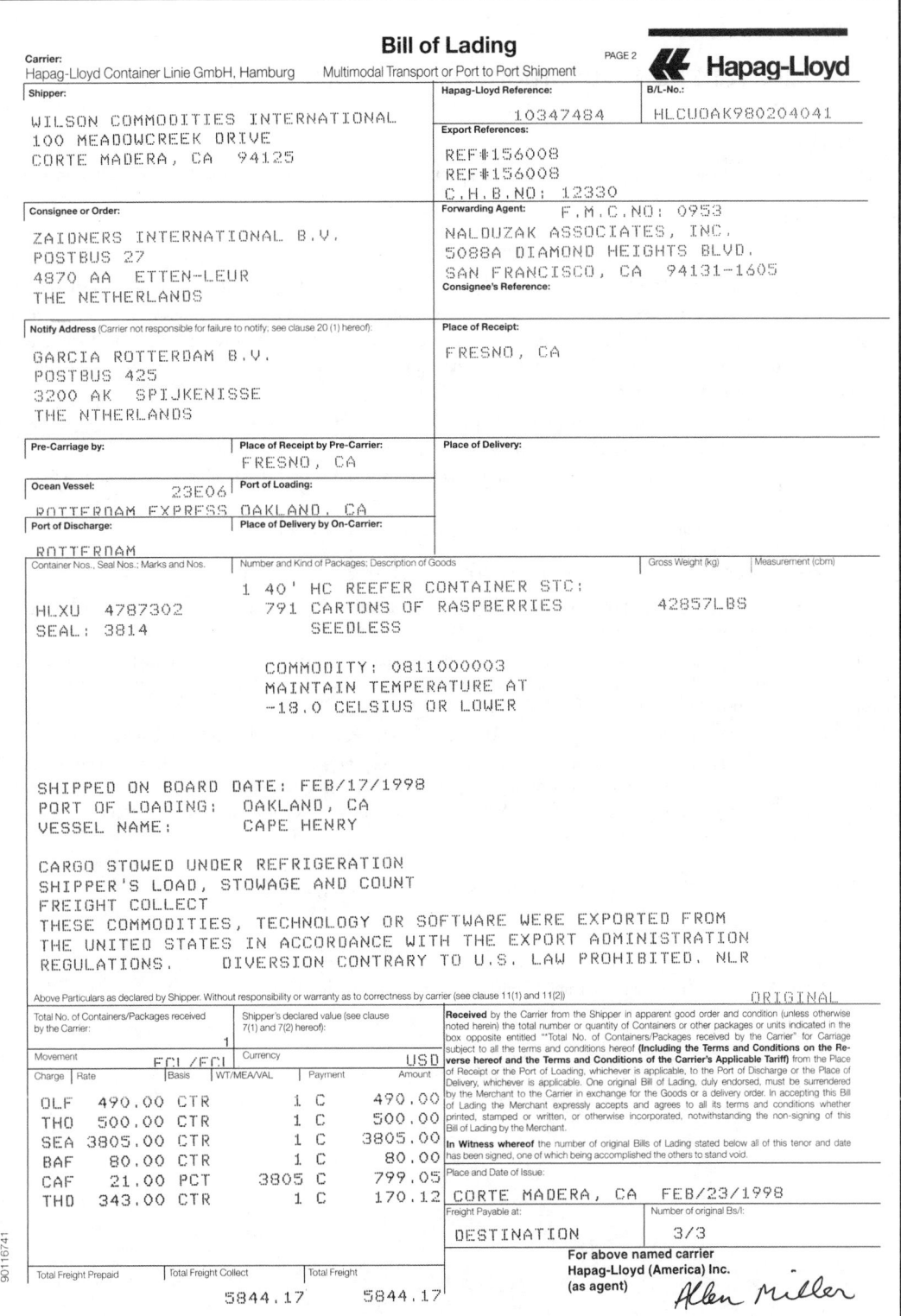

## Bill of Lading

PAGE 2     **Hapag-Lloyd**

Carrier:
Hapag-Lloyd Container Linie GmbH, Hamburg    Multimodal Transport or Port to Port Shipment

| Shipper: | Hapag-Lloyd Reference: | B/L-No.: |
|---|---|---|
| WILSON COMMODITIES INTERNATIONAL<br>100 MEADOWCREEK DRIVE<br>CORTE MADERA, CA 94125 | 10347484 | HLCUOAK980204041 |

Export References:
REF#156008
REF#156008
C.H.B.NO: 12330

| Consignee or Order: | Forwarding Agent:   F.M.C.NO: 0953 |
|---|---|
| ZAIDNERS INTERNATIONAL B.V.<br>POSTBUS 27<br>4870 AA ETTEN-LEUR<br>THE NETHERLANDS | NALDUZAK ASSOCIATES, INC.<br>5088A DIAMOND HEIGHTS BLVD.<br>SAN FRANCISCO, CA 94131-1605<br>Consignee's Reference: |

| Notify Address (Carrier not responsible for failure to notify; see clause 20 (1) hereof): | Place of Receipt: |
|---|---|
| GARCIA ROTTERDAM B.V.<br>POSTBUS 425<br>3200 AK SPIJKENISSE<br>THE NTHERLANDS | FRESNO, CA |

| Pre-Carriage by: | Place of Receipt by Pre-Carrier:<br>FRESNO, CA | Place of Delivery: |
|---|---|---|
| Ocean Vessel: 23E06<br>ROTTERDAM EXPRESS | Port of Loading:<br>OAKLAND, CA | |
| Port of Discharge:<br>ROTTERDAM | Place of Delivery by On-Carrier: | |

| Container Nos., Seal Nos.; Marks and Nos. | Number and Kind of Packages; Description of Goods | Gross Weight (kg) | Measurement (cbm) |
|---|---|---|---|
| HLXU 4787302<br>SEAL: 3814 | 1 40' HC REEFER CONTAINER STC:<br>791 CARTONS OF RASPBERRIES<br>SEEDLESS<br><br>COMMODITY: 0811000003<br>MAINTAIN TEMPERATURE AT<br>-18.0 CELSIUS OR LOWER | 42857LBS | |

SHIPPED ON BOARD DATE: FEB/17/1998
PORT OF LOADING: OAKLAND, CA
VESSEL NAME: CAPE HENRY

CARGO STOWED UNDER REFRIGERATION
SHIPPER'S LOAD, STOWAGE AND COUNT
FREIGHT COLLECT
THESE COMMODITIES, TECHNOLOGY OR SOFTWARE WERE EXPORTED FROM
THE UNITED STATES IN ACCORDANCE WITH THE EXPORT ADMINISTRATION
REGULATIONS. DIVERSION CONTRARY TO U.S. LAW PROHIBITED. NLR

                                                          ORIGINAL

Above Particulars as declared by Shipper. Without responsibility or warranty as to correctness by carrier (see clause 11(1) and 11(2))

Received by the Carrier from the Shipper in apparent good order and condition (unless otherwise noted herein) the total number or quantity of Containers or other packages or units indicated in the box opposite entitled "Total No. of Containers/Packages received by the Carrier" for Carriage subject to all the terms and conditions hereof **(including the Terms and Conditions on the Reverse hereof and the Terms and Conditions of the Carrier's Applicable Tariff)** from the Place of Receipt or the Port of Loading, whichever is applicable, to the Port of Discharge or the Place of Delivery, whichever is applicable. One original Bill of Lading, duly endorsed, must be surrendered by the Merchant to the Carrier in exchange for the Goods or a delivery order. In accepting this Bill of Lading the Merchant expressly accepts and agrees to all its terms and conditions whether printed, stamped or written, or otherwise incorporated, notwithstanding the non-signing of this Bill of Lading by the Merchant.

**In Witness whereof** the number of original Bills of Lading stated below all of this tenor and date has been signed, one of which being accomplished the others to stand void.

| Total No. of Containers/Packages received by the Carrier | Shipper's declared value (see clause 7(1) and 7(2) hereof): |
|---|---|
| 1 | |

| Movement | FCL/FCL | Currency | USD |

| Charge | Rate | Basis | WT/MEA/VAL | Payment | Amount |
|---|---|---|---|---|---|
| OLF | 490.00 | CTR | 1 | C | 490.00 |
| THO | 500.00 | CTR | 1 | C | 500.00 |
| SEA | 3805.00 | CTR | 1 | C | 3805.00 |
| BAF | 80.00 | CTR | 1 | C | 80.00 |
| CAF | 21.00 | PCT | 3805 | C | 799.05 |
| THD | 343.00 | CTR | 1 | C | 170.12 |

Place and Date of Issue:
CORTE MADERA, CA    FEB/23/1998

| Freight Payable at:<br>DESTINATION | Number of original Bs/l:<br>3/3 |
|---|---|

For above named carrier
Hapag-Lloyd (America) Inc.
(as agent)    *Allen Miller*

| Total Freight Prepaid | Total Freight Collect | Total Freight |
|---|---|---|
| | 5844.17 | 5844.17 |

90116741

**DOCUMENTS**

# Air Transport Document (Air Waybill)

## Definition

An air waybill is a non-negotiable transport document covering transport of cargo from airport to airport.

## ✔ Key Elements

A completed air waybill contains the following elements:

1. Name of carrier with a signature identified as that of carrier or named agent for or on behalf of the carrier
2. An indication that the goods have been accepted for carriage. Also, the date of issuance or date of loading
3. In a documentary letter of credit, an indication of the actual date of dispatch if required by the documentary letter of credit, or, if the actual date of dispatch is not required by the credit, the issuance date of the document is deemed to be the date of shipment
4. An indication of the airport of departure and airport of destination
5. Appears on its face to be the original for consignor/shipper
6. The terms and conditions of carriage or a reference to the terms and conditions of carriage in another source or document
7. Meets any other stipulations of the sales contract or documentary letter of credit

## Cautions & Notes for Documentary Letters of Credit

Information contained in the "for carrier use only" box concerning flight number and date are not considered to be the actual flight number and date.

Since air waybills are issued in three originals—one for the issuing carrier, one for the consignee (buyer), and one for the shipper (seller)—a documentary credit should not require presentation in more than one original, nor should it call for a "full set of original air waybills."

The air waybill is not a negotiable document. It indicates only acceptance of goods for carriage.

The air waybill must name a consignee (who can be the buyer), and it should not be required to be issued "to order" and/or "to be endorsed." Since it is not negotiable, and it does not evidence title to the goods, in order to maintain some control of goods not paid for by cash in advance, sellers often consign air shipments to their sales agents, or freight forwarders' agents in the buyer's country.

The air waybill should not be required to indicate an "actual flight date" since IATA regulations specify that reservations requested by the shipper shall not be inserted under "Flight/Date."

## Definitions

**Master Air Waybill** A shipper's contract of carriage with an airline.

**House Air Waybill** A shipper's contract of carriage with the logistics firm.

**085** | BSL | **7260 2751**                                          085-7260-2751

| Shipper's Name and Address | Shipper's account Number |
|---|---|

SWISS EXPORT LTD
AIRFREIGHT DIVISION
ZUERICH

NOT NEGOTIABLE
**AIRWAYBILL**
AIR CONSIGNMENT NOTE

**swissair** ✚

Issued by: Swiss Air Transport Co., Ltd., Zurich, Switzerland
Member of IATA (International Air Transport Association)

Copies 1, 2 and 3 of this Air Waybill are originals and have the same validity

| Consignee's Name and Address | Consignee's account Number |
|---|---|

IMPORT KONTOR
VIENNA

Phone: 633 7876

It is agreed that the goods described herein are accepted in apparent good order and conditio (except as noted) for carriage SUBJECT O THE CONDITIONS OF CONTRACT ON THE REVERSE HEREOF. THE SHIPPER'S ATTENTION IS DRAWN TO THE NOTICE CONCERNING CARRIERS' LIMITATION OF LIABILITY. Shipper may increase such limitation of liability by declaring a higher value for carriage and paying a supplemental charge if required.

| Issuing Carrier's Agent Name and City | Accounting information |
|---|---|

FORWARDING LTD
BASLE

| Agent's IATA Code | Account No. |
|---|---|
| 81-4 0000 | |

Airport of Departure (Addr. of the Carrier) and requested Routing
BSL-VIE

| to | By first Carrier | Routing and Destination | to | by | to | by | Currency | CHGS Code | WT/VAL PPD COLL | Other PPD COLL | Declared Value for Carriage | Declared Value for Customs |
|---|---|---|---|---|---|---|---|---|---|---|---|---|
| VIE | SWISSAIR | | | | | | SFR | | CO | PP | NVD | |

| Airport of Destination | Flight/Date | For Carrier Use only | Flight/Date | Amount of Insurance | INSURANCE - If carrier offers insurance and such insurance is requested in accordance with conditions on reverse hereof, indicate amount to be insured in figures in box marked amount of insurance. |
|---|---|---|---|---|---|
| VIENNA | SR436/8.7. | | | | |

Handling Informatio

| No of Pieces RCP | Gross Weight | kg lb | Rate Class | Commodity Item No | Chargeabl Weight | Rate | Charge | Total | Nature and Quantity of Goods (incl. Dimensions or Volume) |
|---|---|---|---|---|---|---|---|---|---|
| 8 | 200,6 | K | C | 6750 | 201 | 1.90 | | 381.90 | CHEMICALS NOT RESTRICTED CONTRACT No 100-15-2 |
| 8 | 200,6 | | | | | | | | |

| Prepaid | Weight Charge | Collect | Other Charges |
|---|---|---|---|
| | | 381.90 | AWA 15.00 |

Valuation Charge

Tax

| Total Other Charges Due Agent |
|---|
| 15.00 |

Total other Charges Due Carrie

Shipper certifies that the particulars on the face hereof are correct and that insofar as any part of the consignment contains dangerous goods, such part is properly described by name and is in proper condition for carriage by air according to the applicable Dangerous Goods Regulations.

SWISS EXPORT LTD / p p Forwarding LTD
-------------------------------------------
Signature of Shipper or his Agent

| Total Prepaid | Total Collect |
|---|---|
| 15.00 | 381.90 |

| Currency Conversion Rates | cc charges in Dest. Currency |
|---|---|

07.07.          BASLE          Forwarding LTD
--------------------------------------------------
Executed on        (Date)    at    (Place)    Signature of Issuing Carrier or its Agent

Charges at Destination

| For Carrier's Use only at Destination | Total collect Charges |
|---|---|

085-7260 2751

## No. 3 - ORIGINAL for SHIPPER

Form 30.301
Printed in the Fed. Rep. Germany - Bartsch Verlag, Munich-Ottobrunn 600j (III)

# Insurance Document (or Certificate)

## Definition

A document indicating the type and amount of insurance coverage in force on a particular shipment. In documentary credit transactions the insurance document is used to assure the consignee that insurance is provided to cover loss of or damage to cargo while in transit subject to policy terms and conditions.

## ✔ Key Elements

A completed insurance document includes the following elements:

1. The name of the insurance company
2. Policy number
3. Description of the merchandise insured
4. Points of origin and destination of the shipment. Coverage is indicated by the terms of sale. For example, for goods sold "FOB," coverage commences once the cargo is on board the vessel and continues until the consignee takes possession at either the seaport or in-land port of destination.
5. Conditions of coverage, exclusions, and deductible, if applicable.
6. A signature by the insurance carrier, underwriter or agent for same
7. Indication that the cover is effective at the latest from the date of loading of the goods on board a transport vessel or the taking in charge of the goods by the carrier, as indicated by the transport document (bill of lading, etc.)
8. Statement of the sum insured
9. In a documentary letter of credit, specifies coverage for at least 110 percent of either: (a) the CIF or CIP value of the shipment, if such can be determined from the various documents on their face, otherwise, (b) the amount of the payment, acceptance or negotiation specified in the documentary credit, or (c) the gross amount of the commercial invoice
10. Is presented as the sole original, or if issued in more than one original, the full set of originals

## Cautions & Notes

In documentary credit transactions the insurance currency should be consistent with the currency of the documentary credit.

Documentary credit transactions indicating CIF (Cost Insurance Freight) or CIP (Carriage and Insurance Paid) pricing should list an insurance document in the required documentation.

"Cover notes" issued by insurance brokers (as opposed to insurance companies, underwriters, or their agents) are not accepted in letter of credit transactions unless authorized specifically by the credit terms.

## In Case of Loss or Shortfall

The consignee should always note on the delivery document any damage or shortfall prior to signing for receipt of the goods. The consignee has the responsibility to make reasonable efforts to minimize loss. This includes steps to prevent further damage to the shipment. Expenses incurred in such efforts are almost universally collectible under the insurance policy. Prompt notice of loss is essential.

The original copy of the insurance certificate is a negotiable document and is required in the filing of a claim.

Copies of documents necessary to support an insurance claim include the insurance policy or certificate, bill of lading, invoice, packing list, and a survey report (usually prepared by a claims agent).

# Special Marine Policy

**ACE USA**

No. _____

Open Policy No. _____ of

$ _____

| SERVICE OFFICE: | | ORIGINAL | (ORIGINAL AND DUPLICATE ISSUED ONE OF WHICH BEING ACCOMPLISHED, THE OTHER TO BE NULL AND VOID) |
|---|---|---|---|

(PLACE & DATE) _____

This Company, in consideration of a premium as agreed, and subject to the Terms and Conditions printed or stamped hereon and/or attached hereto, does insure, lost or not lost _____ .

For account of whom it may concern; to be shipped by the vessel _____ , and connecting conveyances.

MARKS AND NUMBERS

From _____

To _____ .

Lawful Goods Consisting Of _____ ,

_____ , Number of _____

Valued at **Sum hereby insured**

Inv. #

Loss, if any, payable to **Assured**      or order.    B/L #

## TERMS AND CONDITIONS - SEE ALSO BACK HEREOF

**WAREHOUSE TO WAREHOUSE:** This insurance attaches from the time the goods leave the Warehouse and/or Store at the place named in the Policy for the commencement of the transit and continues during the ordinary course of transit, including customary transshipment if any, until the goods are discharged overside from the overseas vessel at the final port. Thereafter the insurance continues whilst the goods are in transit and/or awaiting transit until delivered to final warehouse at the destination named in the Policy or until the expiry of 15 days (or 30 days if the destination to which the goods are insured is outside the port) whichever shall first occur. The time limits referred to above to be reckoned from midnight of the day on which the discharge overside of the goods hereby insured from the overseas vessel is completed. Held covered at a premium to be arranged in the event of transshipment, if any, other than as above and/or in the event of delay in excess of the above time limits arising from circumstances beyond the control of the Assured. NOTE -- IT IS NECESSARY FOR THE ASSURED TO GIVE PROMPT NOTICE TO THESE ASSURERS WHEN THEY BECOME AWARE OF AN EVENT FOR WHICH THEY ARE "HELD COVERED" UNDER THIS POLICY AND THE RIGHT TO SUCH COVER IS DEPENDENT ON COMPLIANCE WITH THIS OBLIGATION.

**SHORE CLAUSE:** Where this insurance by its terms covers while on docks, wharves or elsewhere on shore, and/or during land transportation, it shall include the risks of collision, derailment, overturning or other accident to the conveyance, fire, lightning, sprinkler leakage, cyclones, hurricanes, earthquakes, floods (meaning the rising of navigable waters), and/or collapse or subsidence of docks or wharves, even though the insurance be otherwise F.P.A.

**BOTH TO BLAME CLAUSE:** Where goods are shipped under a Bill of Lading containing the so-called "Both to Blame Collision" Clause, these Assurers agree as to all losses covered by this insurance, to indemnify the Assured for this Policy's proportion of any amount (not exceeding the amount insured) which the Assured may be legally bound to pay to the shipowners under such clause. In the event that such liability is asserted the Assured agrees to notify these Assurers who shall have the right at their own cost and expense to defend the Assured against such claim.

**MACHINERY CLAUSE:** When the property insured under this Policy includes a machine consisting when complete for sale or use of several parts, then in case of loss or damage covered by this insurance to any part of such machine, these Assurers shall be liable only for the proportion of the insured value of the part lost or damaged, or at the Assured's option, for the cost and expense, including labor and forwarding charges, of replacing and repairing the lost or damaged part; but in no event shall these Assurers be liable for more than the insured value of the complete machine.

**LABELS CLAUSE:** In case of damage affecting labels, capsules or wrappers, these Assurers, if liable therefor under the terms of this policy, shall not be liable for more than an amount sufficient to pay the cost of new labels, capsules or wrappers, and the cost of reconditioning the goods, but in no event shall these Assurers be liable for more than the insured value of the damaged merchandise.

**DELAY CLAUSE:** Warranted free of claim for loss of market or for loss, damage or deterioration arising from delay, whether caused by a peril insured against or otherwise, unless expressly assumed in writing hereon.

**AMERICAN INSTITUTE CLAUSES:** This insurance, in addition to the foregoing, is also subject to the following American Institute Cargo Clauses, current forms:

1. CRAFT, ETC. 3. WAREHOUSE & FORWARDING CHARGES,   4.GENERAL AVERAGE 6. BILL OF LADING, ETC. 8. CONSTRUCTIVE TOTAL LOSS   10. EXTENDED R.A.C.E.
2. DEVIATION    PACKAGES TOTALLY LOST LOADING, ETC. 5.EXPLOSION     7. INCHMAREE      9. CARRIER      11. CHEMICAL, BIOLOGICAL, ELECTROMAGNETIC EXCLUSION

**PERILS CLAUSE:** Touching the adventures and perils which this Company is contented to bear, and takes upon itself, they are of the seas, assailing thieves, jettisons, barratry of the master and mariners, and all other like perils, losses and misfortunes (illicit or contraband trade excepted in all cases), that have or shall come to the hurt, detriment or damage of the said goods and merchandise, or any part thereof.

**AVERAGE TERMS:** ON DECK AND SUBJECT TO AN "ON DECK" BILL OF LADING -- (which must be so declared by the Assured): Free of Particular Average unless caused by the vessel being stranded, sunk, burnt, on fire or in collision, but including jettison and/or washing overboard irrespective of percentage. EXCEPT WHILE SUBJECT TO AN "ON DECK" BILL OF LADING:

**ALL RISK STANDARD WORDING:** To cover against all risks of physical loss or damage from any external cause irrespective of percentage, but excluding, nevertheless, the risks of war, strikes, riots, seizure, detention and other risks excluded by the F.C.& S. (Free of Capture & Seizure) Warranty and the S.R. & C.C. (Strikes, Riots, and Civil Commotions) Warranty policy, excepting to the extent that such risks are specifically covered by endorsement.

This Policy is extended to include the provisions of the following clauses as if the current form of each were endorsed hereon:

American Institute Clauses -

F.C. & S. Warranty
Marine Extension Clauses
S.R.&C.C. Endorsement
War Risk Insurance
Nuclear Exclusion

Where appropriate -

South America 60-Day Clause

**PARAMOUNT WARRANTIES: THE FOLLOWING WARRANTIES SHALL BE PARAMOUNT AND SHALL NOT BE MODIFIED OR SUPERSEDED BY ANY OTHER** PROVISION INCLUDED HEREIN OR STAMPED OR ENDORSED HEREON UNLESS SUCH OTHER PROVISION REFERS SPECIFICALLY TO THE RISKS EXCLUDED BY THESE WARRANTIES AND EXPRESSLY ASSUMES THE SAID RISKS C.& S.(a) NOTWITHSTANDING ANYTHING HEREIN CONTAINED TO THE CONTRARY THIS INSURANCE IS WARRANTED FREE FROM: (a) capture, seizure, arrest, restraint, detainment, confiscation, preemption, requisition or nationalization, and the consequences thereof or any attempt thereat, whether in time of peace or war and whether lawful or otherwise; (b) all loss, damage or expense, whether in time of peace or war, caused by (i) any weapon or war employing atomic or nuclear fission and/or fusion or other reaction or radioactive force or matter or (ii) any mine or torpedo; (c) all consequences of hostilities or warlike operations (whether there be a declaration of war or not), but this warranty shall not exclude collision or contact with aircraft, or with rockets or similar missiles (other than weapons of war) or with any fixed or floating object (other than a mine or torpedo), stranding, heavy weather, fire or explosion unless caused directly (and independently of the nature of the voyage or service which the vessel concerned or, in the case of a collision, any other vessel involved therein, is performing) by a hostile act by or against a belligerent power; and for the purposes of this warranty "power" includes any authority maintaining naval, military or air forces in association with a power; (d) the consequences of civil war, revolution, rebellion, insurrection, or civil strife arising therefrom; or from the consequences of the imposition of martial law, military or usurped power; or piracy. S.R.&C.C. (b) Notwithstanding anything herein contained to the contrary, this insurance is warranted free from loss, damage or expense caused by or resulting from: (1) strikes, lockouts, labor disturbances, riots, civil commotions, or the acts of any person or persons taking part in any such occurrences or disorders, (2) vandalism, sabotage or malicious act, which shall be deemed also to encompass the act or acts of one or more persons, whether or not agents of a sovereign power, carried out for political, terroristic or ideological purposes and whether any loss, damage or expense resulting therefrom is accidental or intentional.

**ECONOMIC SANCTIONS AND EMBARGO PROGRAMS OF THE UNITED STATES:** This policy excludes loss otherwise payable to an individual, organization, or authority that is the subject of any trade embargo or other trade sanction imposed by the United States Government; or that arises out of any trade in, or shipment of, any goods or merchandise prohibited by such embargo or sanction, whether or not deemed lawful under the laws of another nation.

DRAFT

DOCUMENTS

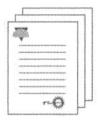

# Certificate of Origin

## Definition

A document issued by a certifying authority stating the country of origin of goods.

## ✔ Key Elements

A certificate of origin should include the following elements:

1. Key details (typically consignor, consignee, and description of goods) regarding the shipment. Also, such details to be in conformity with other documents (e.g., documentary credit, commercial invoice)
2. A statement of origin of the goods
3. The name, signature and/or stamp or seal of the certifying authority

A NAFTA Certificate of Origin includes the following elements:

1. Name and address of exporter
2. Blanket period of shipment (for multiple shipments of identical goods for a specified period of up to one year)
3. Name and address of importer
4. Name and address of producer
5. Description of goods
6. Harmonized Tariff Schedule classification number up to six digits
7. Preference criteria (one of six criteria of rules of origin of the goods)
8. Indication of whether the exporter is the producer of the goods
9. Regional Value Content indication
10. Country of origin of goods
11. Exporter company name, date and authorized signature

## Cautions & Notes

If you are the buyer (importer) the import authority of your country may require a certificate of origin. If so, make certain that you require it of the seller in the form and content as specified by your country's customs authority.

A certificate of origin can be the key document required for obtaining special (reduced) tariff rates for imports from countries listed as beneficiaries to programs such as the GSP (Generalized Systems of Preferences) or NAFTA (North American Free Trade Area).

In a documentary letter of credit buyers should avoid the use of such terms as "first class," "well-known," "qualified," "independent," "official," "competent," or "local" when referring to the certifying authority. It is preferable to name the required certifying authority. Use of vague terminology will result in the bank's acceptance of any relevant document that appears "on its face" to be in compliance with the documentary credit, so long as it was not issued and signed by the beneficiary (seller).

In certain countries the certificate of origin is prepared by the seller (beneficiary to the documentary credit) on a standard form and then certified (with a signature, stamp or seal) by the certifying authority.

Certifying authorities most often used are city and regional chambers of commerce and chambers of commerce and industry.

DOCUMENTS

| Exporteur<br>Exportateur<br>Esportatore<br>Exporter | Nr.<br>No.  201884 |
|---|---|
| MUELLER AG<br>Birsstrasse 26<br>4132 Muttenz / Switzerland | **URSPRUNGSZEUGNIS<br>CERTIFICAT D'ORIGINE<br>CERTIFICATO D'ORIGINE<br>CERTIFICATE OF ORIGIN** |

**Empfänger**
Destinataire
Destinatario
Consignee

ADILMA TRADING CORPORATION
27, Nihonbashi, Chiyoda-Ku

TOKYO 125 / Japan

**SCHWEIZERISCHE EIDGENOSSENSCHAFT<br>CONFÉDÉRATION SUISSE<br>CONFEDERAZIONE SVIZZERA<br>SWISS CONFEDERATION**

**Ursprungsstaat**
Pays d'origine
Paese d'origine        SWITZERLAND
Country of origin

---

**Angaben über die Beförderung (Ausfüllung freigestellt)**
Informations relatives au transport (mention facultative)
Informazioni riguardanti il trasporto (indicazione facoltativa)
Particulars of transport (optional declaration)

**Bemerkungen**
Observations
Osservazioni
Observations

LETTER OF CREDIT NR. 064204

---

**Zeichen, Nummern, Anzahl und Art der Packstücke; Warenbezeichnung**
Marques, numéros, nombre et nature des colis; désignation des marchandises
Marche, numeri, numero e natura dei colli; designazione delle merci
Marks, numbers, number and kind of packages; description of the goods

**Nettogewicht**
Poids net
Peso netto
Net weight
kg, l, m³
etc./ecc.

| | | | |
|---|---|---|---|
| ADILMA TRADING | 6 cases | CYLINDER- | |
| VIA TOKYO | | PRESS | 12'140,0 kg |
| NR. 1-6 | | COMPLETELY | |
| ORDER 0-535/1 | | ASSEMBLED | |

**Bruttogewicht**
Poids brut
Peso lordo
Gross weight

12'860,0 kg

---

**Die unterzeichnete Handelskammer bescheinigt den Ursprung oben bezeichneter Ware**
La Chambre de commerce soussignée certifie l'origine des marchandises désignées ci-dessus
La sottoscritta Camera di commercio certifica l'origine delle merci summenzionate
The undersigned Chamber of commerce certifies the origin of the above mentioned goods

Basel, 2 6. 04.

**Basler Handelskammer<br>Chambre de Commerce de Bâle<br>Camera di Commercio di Basilea<br>Basle Chamber of Commerce**

## Inspection Certificate

## Definition

A document issued by an authority indicating that goods have been inspected (typically according to a set of industry, customer, government, or carrier specifications) prior to shipment and the results of the inspection.

Inspection certificates are generally obtained from neutral testing organizations (e.g., a government entity or independent service company). In some cases the inspection certificate can come from the manufacturer or shipper, but not from the forwarder or logistics firm.

## ✔ Key Elements

An inspection certificate should include the following elements:

1. Key details (typically consignor, consignee, and description of goods) regarding the shipment. Also, such details to be in conformity with other documents (e.g., documentary credit, commercial invoice, etc.)
2. Date of the inspection
3. Statement of sampling methodology
4. Statement of the results of the inspection
5. The name, signature and/or stamp or seal of the inspecting entity

## Cautions & Notes

In the case of certain countries and certain commodities the inspection certificate must be issued by an appropriate government entity.

In a documentary letter of credit buyers should avoid the use of such terms as "first class," "well-known," "qualified," "independent," "official," "competent," or "local" when referring to an acceptable inspection authority. It is preferable to agree beforehand as to a specific inspection organization or entity and for the buyer to name the required certifying organization or entity in the documentary credit.

Use of vague terminology (as above) will result in the bank's acceptance of any relevant document that appears "on its face" to be in compliance with the documentary credit, so long as it was not issued by the beneficiary (seller).

DOCUMENTS

 **SGS Supervise (Suisse) S.A.**

May 10, 19..

Hardstrasse 1
Postfach 4149
**CH-4002 Basel**
Tel. (+41-61) 271 36 11
Fax (+41-61) 271 40 48
Telex : 962 457 SGS

## Certificate No 1407/ 012488

| | | |
|---|---|---|
| BUYER | : | TA PING CO. LTD. YACHT BUILDING |
| | | 18-5, HARBOUR STREET, TAIPEI, TAIWAN |
| SELLER | : | SWISS EXPORT LTD. AIRFREIGHT DIVISION |
| | | 8008 ZUERICH,SWITZERLAND |
| LETTER OF CREDIT NBR. | : | FB-03-45786-9 |
| GOODS | : | MACHINERY PARTS, as designated below |
| CONTRACT NBR. | : | FA12345WO79PE |
| IMPORT PERMIT NUMBER | : | TW-2395-497-0006, as declared |
| SERVICES REQUIRED | : | FINAL PRE-SHIPMENT INSPECTION |

This is to certify that, at buyers' request and based on the specifications submitted to us, we have inspected the following goods:

1. <u>MATERIAL DESIGNATION</u>
   1 LOT ACCESSORIES AND SPARE PARTS FOR FOOD PROCESSING MACHINERY, as detailed in seller's commercial invoice and corresponding packing list both dated April 29, 19

2. <u>INSPECTIONS PERFORMED AND FINDINGS</u>
   2.1. Material identification for conformity with the specifications submitted to us.
   2.2. Visual inspection on workmanship, finish and condition.
   2.3. Quantitative and completeness checks.
   2.4. Dimensional checks at random, where applicable.
   2.5. Packing inspection: The packing, consisting of 5 plywood cases, is considered adequate to ship the goods by air to Taipei under normal conditions of transport and handling.
   2.6. Marking inspection: The shipping marks include: **SWISS EXPORT 0405/1-5**
   2.7. Loading details as per Air Waybill No. BSL 122077 issued by PANALPINA LTD BASLE-AIRPORT on 4 MAY ..

3. <u>INSPECTION RESULTS AND CONCLUSION</u>
   Based on the inspections performed, we certify the goods to be new, of good workmanship and finish, free from apparent damage or defect, and that the shipment is fully in compliance with the contract requirements in specification, quantity, quality, proper packing and marking.

5. <u>DATE AND PLACE OF INSPECTION</u>
   April 30, 19.. on seller's premises in Zurich, Switzerland with subsequent review of loading details.
   ----------------------------------------------------------

This certificate is evidence of and reports on our findings at the time and place of inspection. It does not release buyers or sellers from their contractual obligations.

SGS SUPERVISE (SUISSE) SA
BASLE OFFICE, SWITZERLAND

As Member of SOCIETE GENERALE
DE SURVEILLANCE S.A. (SGS)
Geneva, Switzerland

**DOCUMENTS**

# Regional Trade Pact Import/Export Declaration

## Definition

A standardized export/import document used in common by members of a regional trade group containing compliance, administrative and statistical information.

## Issued By

This document is typically issued by the exporter/seller.

## ✔ Key Elements

The typical trade pact import/export declaration contains the following elements:

1. Name and address of exporter/seller/consignor
2. Name and address of importer/buyer/consignee
3. Description and value of the goods
4. A statement of origin of the goods
5. Country of destination of the goods
6. Carrier and means of transport
7. Other compliance, administrative and statistical information

## Cautions & Notes

This document is used as an export declaration when exporting from any trade pact member country to a non-member country and as both an import and export declaration when transporting goods across country borders within the trade group.

Because of its standardized format, this document is often linked to a computer system for the electronic transfer of information to export and import authorities within the trade group.

## The EU (European Union) SAD (Single Administrative Document)

This document is a prime example of a regional trade pact import/export declaration. It was established by the European Community Council in 1988 with the goals of standardizing customs documentation and simplifying international transactions.

This particular document is used as an import/export declaration and also for the declaration of goods in transit within EU and EFTA (European Free Trade Area) countries. It may be submitted by computer directly to the customs authorities in all the 15 EU member nations.

Countries outside of the EU have shown interest in using the SAD and some have already adopted the format for their import documentation (e.g., Bulgaria).

DOCUMENTS

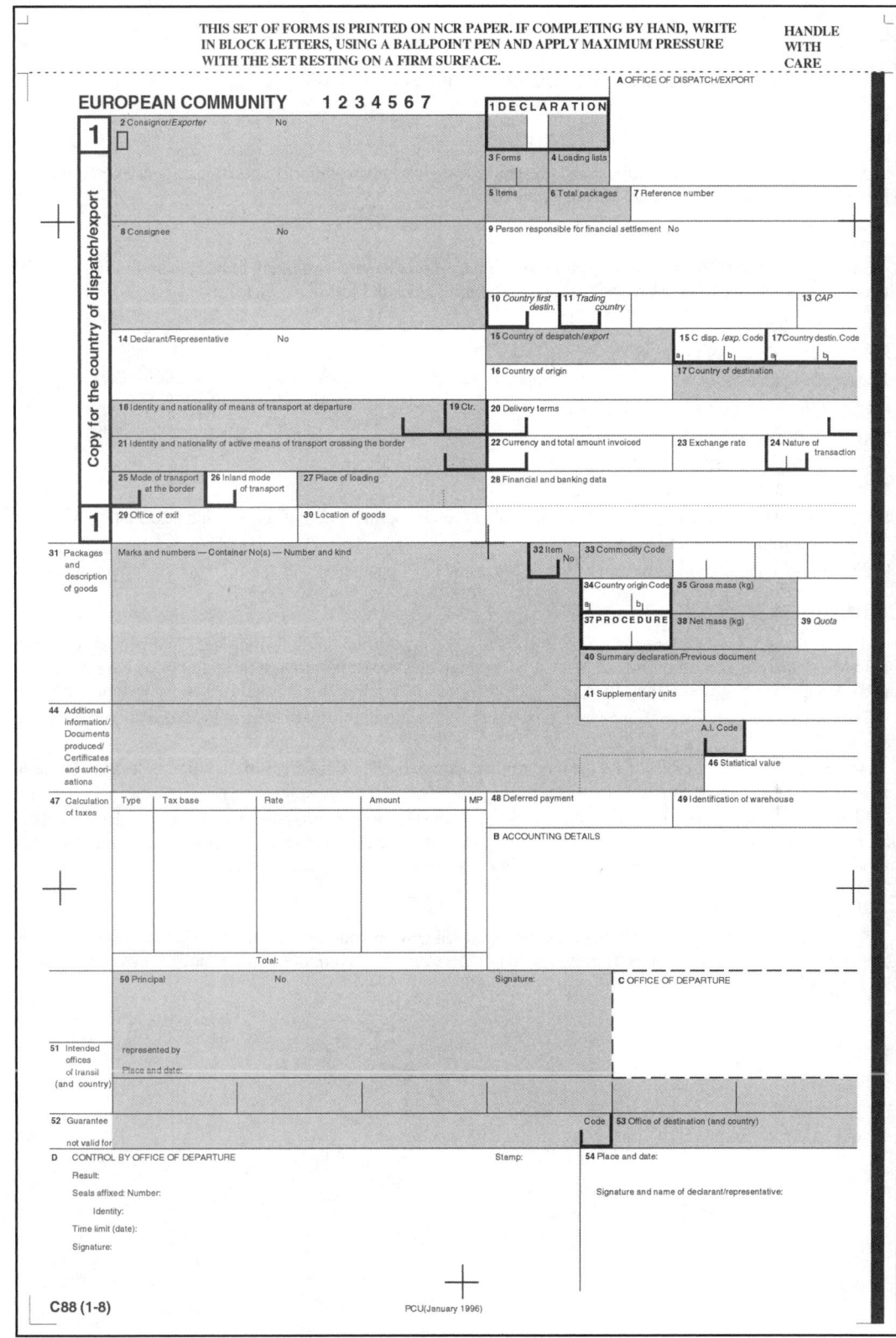

 # Shipper's Export Declaration (SED)

## Definition

A document prepared by the shipper and presented to a government authority specifying goods exported along with their quantities, weight, value, and destination.

## ✔ Key Elements

Each country has its own export declaration form. Certain elements are likely to be required in the SED for all countries. The shipper's export declaration typically includes the following elements:

1. Name and address of seller
2. Name and address of buyer
3. Date of issuance
4. Export license number (if required, based upon country of export requirements and goods exported)
5. Country of origin of the goods shipped
6. Country of final destination of the goods
7. Quantity and description of the goods
8. Country of export statistical classification number (some countries do not require this information for shipments under a certain level)
9. Shipping details including: weight of the goods, number of packages, and shipping marks and numbers

## Cautions & Notes

(United States) As of October 18, 2003 exports of goods classified on the Commerce Control List (CCL) or the USML (United States Munitions List) must be reported electronically through the Automated Export System (AES). Mandatory electronic filing for all U.S. exports became a requirement in mid 2004. (www.cbp.gov)

The shipper's export declaration is used by a nation's customs authority to control exports and compile trade statistics.

An SED is usually not required by the buyer in a documentary letter of credit transaction unless the buyer is responsible for export formalities.

Many nations impose strict controls on exports (e.g., high technology, armaments and drugs) and use the SED as a means of export control. Because many exports can be diverted to "unfriendly" nations and individuals, it is considered the responsibility of the exporter to know his cargo, destination, customer, end-use, and end-user.

## Electronic Filing

Some nations (such as the United States) have instituted new procedures that require exporters to submit their Shipper's Export Declarations electronically. This involves using a computer with a modem or other form of Internet connection.

DOCUMENTS

U.S. DEPARTMENT OF COMMERCE – Economics and Statistics Administration – U.S. CENSUS BUREAU – BUREAU OF EXPORT ADMINISTRATION

FORM **7525-V** (7-18-2003)      **SHIPPER'S EXPORT DECLARATION**      OMB No. 0607-0152

**1a.** U.S. PRINCIPAL PARTY IN INTEREST (USPPI)(Complete name and address)

ZIP CODE

**2.** DATE OF EXPORTATION

**3.** TRANSPORTATION REFERENCE NO.

**b.** USPPI'S EIN (IRS) OR ID NO.

**c.** PARTIES TO TRANSACTION
☐ Related    ☐ Non-related

**4a.** ULTIMATE CONSIGNEE *(Complete name and address)*

**b.** INTERMEDIATE CONSIGNEE *(Complete name and address)*

**5a.** FORWARDING AGENT *(Complete name and address)*

**5b.** FORWARDING AGENT'S EIN (IRS) NO.

**6.** POINT (STATE) OF ORIGIN OR FTZ NO.

**7.** COUNTRY OF ULTIMATE DESTINATION

**8.** LOADING PIER *(Vessel only)*

**9.** METHOD OF TRANSPORTATION *(Specify)*

**14.** CARRIER IDENTIFICATION CODE

**15.** SHIPMENT REFERENCE NO.

**10.** EXPORTING CARRIER

**11.** PORT OF EXPORT

**16.** ENTRY NUMBER

**17.** HAZARDOUS MATERIALS
☐ Yes    ☐ No

**12.** PORT OF UNLOADING *(Vessel and air only)*

**13.** CONTAINERIZED *(Vessel only)*
☐ Yes    ☐ No

**18.** IN BOND CODE

**19.** ROUTED EXPORT TRANSACTION
☐ Yes    ☐ No

**20.** SCHEDULE B DESCRIPTION OF COMMODITIES *(Use columns 22–24)*

| D/F or M (21) | SCHEDULE B NUMBER (22) | QUANTITY – SCHEDULE B UNIT(S) (23) | SHIPPING WEIGHT (Kilograms) (24) | VIN/PRODUCT NUMBER/ VEHICLE TITLE NUMBER (25) | VALUE (U.S. dollars, omit cents) (Selling price or cost if not sold) (26) |
|---|---|---|---|---|---|
| | | | | | |

**27.** LICENSE NO./LICENSE EXCEPTION SYMBOL/AUTHORIZATION

**28.** ECCN *(When required)*

**29.** Duly authorized officer or employee

The USPPI authorizes the forwarder named above to act as forwarding agent for export control and customs purposes.

**30.** I certify that all statements made and all information contained herein are true and correct and that I have read and understand the instructions for preparation of this document, set forth in the **"Correct Way to Fill Out the Shipper's Export Declaration."** I understand that civil and criminal penalties, including forfeiture and sale, may be imposed for making false or fraudulent statements herein, failing to provide the requested information or for violation of U.S. laws on exportation (13 U.S.C. Sec. 305; 22 U.S.C. Sec. 401; 18 U.S.C. Sec. 1001; 50 U.S.C. App. 2410).

Signature

**Confidential** – Shipper's Export Declarations (or any successor document) wherever located, shall be exempt from public disclosure unless the Secretary determines that such exemption would be contrary to the national interest (Title 13, Chapter 9, Section 301 (g)).

Title

Export shipments are subject to inspection by U.S. Customs Service and/or Office of Export Enforcement.

Date

**31.** AUTHENTICATION *(When required)*

Telephone No. (Include Area Code)

E-mail address

This form may be printed by private parties provided it conforms to the official form. For sale by the Superintendent of Documents, Government Printing Office, Washington, DC 20402, and local Customs District Directors. The **"Correct Way to Fill Out the Shipper's Export Declaration"** is available from the U.S. Census Bureau, Washington, DC 20233.

DOCUMENTS

 Carnet

## Definition

A document that allows the temporary importation of merchandise into member countries while eliminating the value-added taxes (VAT), duties, and the posting of security normally required at the time of importation.

## ✔ Key Elements

1. Document can be used for goods traveling as "Commercial Samples," "Professional Equipment," or "Exhibitions and Fairs"
2. Valid for a period of up to one year
3. Can be used for as many trips to member countries as required during the validity period
4. Can be used in over 90 member countries and territories
5. Carnets are issued in the name of the company or individual with title to the goods, also known as the "Holder"
6. All fees are paid in the Holder's country prior to the first departure
7. Security in the amount of 40% of the value of the goods is required and can be placed using cash (certified check) or a surety bond
8. Cash deposits are returned and bonds are terminated upon cancellation of a Carnet
9. Document is made up of several colored sheets of paper including a green cover which serves as the registration of goods, yellow exportation and re-importation counterfoils for use in the Holder's country, and white importation and re-exportation counterfoils and corresponding vouchers for use in foreign countries
10. Carnet is presented to the customs authorities of the Holder's country upon exportation of the goods, upon importation into a foreign country, upon re-exportation from the foreign country, and upon re-importation into the Holder's country
11. Carnets have become widely used in the past decade. Obtaining a carnet has become simple, especially through new automated systems such as www.carnetsonline.com

## Cautions and Notes

Prior to the first exportation from the Holder's country, the Carnet Holder (company or individual whose name appears on the Carnet) or an Authorized Representative must ensure that the green cover of the document is validated by the customs authority of the Holder's country.

Goods not re-exported from the foreign country by midnight of the expiration date or the date noted by the foreign customs authority as the "final date for re-exportation" (whichever is earlier) are subject to a claim from foreign customs.

Vehicles shipped on an ATA Carnet require additional security.

Taiwan accepts the TECRO/AIT Carnet through a bi-lateral agreement with the United States.

**A.T.A. CARNET FOR TEMPORARY ADMISSION OF GOODS**
*CARNET A.T.A. POUR L'ADMISSION TEMPORAIRE DE MARCHANDISES*
**CUSTOMS CONVENTION ON THE A.T.A. CARNET FOR THE TEMPORARY ADMISSION OF GOODS**
*CONVENTION DOUANIERE SUR LE CARNET A.T.A. POUR L'ADMISSION TEMPORAIRE DE MARCHANDISES*
**CONVENTION ON TEMPORARY ADMISSION** / *CONVENTION RELATIVE À L'ADMISSION TEMPORAIRE*
(Before completing the Carnet, please read Notes on cover page 3 / *Avant de remplir le carnet, lire la notice en page 3 de la couverture*)

Issuing Association / *Association émettrice*

INTERNATIONAL GUARANTEE CHAIN / *CHAÎNE DE GARANTIE INTERNATIONALE*
ICC W.C.F.

**A. HOLDER AND ADDRESS** / *Titulaire et adresse*
International Export Company
4376 Commerce Center Drive
Dallas, TX 75201

**G. FOR ISSUING ASSOCIATION USE** / *Réservé à l'association émettrice*
**FRONT COVER** / *Couverture*
a) **A.T.A. CARNET No.** *Carnet A.T.A. N°* **US3/0619998**
Number of continuation sheets: / *Nombre de feuilles supplémentaires:*

**B. REPRESENTED BY*** / *Représenté par*
Jack Meacham or any other authorized representative

b) **ISSUED BY** / *Délivré par*
**United States Council for International Business**

**C. INTENDED USE OF GOODS** / *Utilisation prévue des marchandises*
Commercial Samples
Exhibitions & Fairs

c) **VALID UNTIL** / *Valable jusqu'au*
2007 | 12 | 14
year / *année* | month / *mois* | day (inclusive) / *jour (Inclus)*

P. This Carnet may be used in the following countries/customs territories under the guarantee of the associations listed on page 4 of the cover:/ *Ce carnet est valable dans les pays/ territoires douaniers ci-après, sous la garantie des associations reprises en page quatre de la couverture:*

**EUROPEAN UNION**
AUSTRIA (AT), BELGIUM (BE), CYPRUS (CY), CZECH REPUBLIC (CZ), DENMARK (DK), ESTONIA (EE), FINLAND (FI), FRANCE (FR), GERMANY (DE), GREECE (GR), HUNGARY (HU), IRELAND (IE), ITALY (IT), LATVIA (LV), LITHUANIA (LT), LUXEMBOURG (LU), MALTA (MT), NETHERLANDS (NL), POLAND (PL), PORTUGAL (PT), SLOVAKIA (SK), SLOVENIA (SI), SPAIN (ES), SWEDEN (SE), UNITED KINGDOM (GB)

**OTHER COUNTRIES**
ALGERIA (DZ), ANDORRA (AD), AUSTRALIA (AU), BELARUS (BY), BULGARIA (BG), CANADA (CA), CHINA (CN), CROATIA (HR), GIBRALTAR (GI), HONG KONG, CHINA (HK), ICELAND (IS), INDIA (IN), ISRAEL (IL), IVORY COAST (CI), JAPAN (JP), KOREA (KR), LEBANON (LB), MACEDONIA (MK), MALAYSIA (MY), MAURITIUS (MU), MONGOLIA (MN), MOROCCO (MA), NEW ZEALAND (NZ), NORWAY (NO), ROMANIA (RO), RUSSIA (RU), SENEGAL (SN), SERBIA (CS), SINGAPORE (SG), SOUTH AFRICA (ZA), SRI LANKA (LK), SWITZERLAND (CH), THAILAND (TH), TUNISIA (TN), TURKEY (TR), UNITED STATES (US)

The Holder of this Carnet and his representative will be held responsible for compliance with the laws and regulations of the country/customs territory of departure and the countries/customs territories of importation./ *A charge pour le titulaire et son représentant de se conformer aux lois et règlements du pays/territoire douanier de départ et des pays/territoires douaniers d'importation.*

**H. CERTIFICATE BY CUSTOMS AT DEPARTURE**
*Attestation de la douane, au départ*
a) Identification marks have been affixed as indicated in column 7 against the following items No(s). of the General List
*Apposé les marques d'identification mentionnées dans la colonne 7 en regard du (des) numéro(s) d'ordre suivant(s) de la liste générale*
b) **GOODS EXAMINED*** / *Vérifié les marchandises* Yes / Oui ☐ No / Non ☐
c) Registered under Reference No.* / *Enregistré sous le numéro*
d) Customs Office / *Bureau de douane* — Place / *Lieu* — Date (year/month/day) / *Date (année/mois/jour)* — Signature and Stamp / *Signature et timbre*

**I.** Signature of authorized official and Issuing Association stamp / *Signature du délégué et timbre de l'association émettrice*
Issuer: Lisa Higgins
Schaumburg, IL   2006/12/15
*Lisa Higgins*
Place and Date of Issue (year/month/day) / *Lieu et date d'émission (année/mois/jour)*
**J.**
X_____X
Signature of Holder / *Signature du titulaire*

*If applicable / *S'il y a lieu*    N1 (11/12/04)

**AFTER FINAL USE, RETURN THIS CARNET TO USCIB**
1212 AVENUE OF THE AMERICAS, NEW YORK, NY 10036
*(A RETOURNER A LA CHAMBRE EMETTRICE IMMEDIATEMENT APRES UTILISATION)*

DOCUMENTS

 # Packing List

## Definition

A packing list is a document prepared by the shipper listing the kinds and quantities of merchandise in a particular shipment.

A copy of the packing list is often attached to the shipment itself and another copy is sent directly to the consignee to assist in checking the shipment when received. Also called a bill of parcels.

## ✔ Key Elements

The packing list includes the following elements:

1. Name and address of seller
2. Name and address of buyer
3. Date of issuance
4. Invoice number
5. Order or contract number
6. Quantity and description of the goods
7. Shipping details including: weight of the goods, number of packages, and shipping marks and numbers
8. Quantity and description of contents of each package, carton, crate or container
9. Any other information as required in the sales contract or documentary credit (e.g., country of origin)

## Cautions & Notes

The packing list is a more detailed version of the commercial invoice but without price information. The type of each container is identified, as well as its individual weight and measurements. The packing list is attached to the outside of its respective container in a waterproof envelope marked "Packing List" or "Packing List Enclosed," and is immediately available to authorities in both the countries of export and import.

Although not required in all transactions, it is required by some countries and some buyers.

# Cargo Vessels

## Vessel Classification

In order to be registered, an ocean-going ship must be certified to be of a particular type and size and be maintained to certain minimum standards. While most states (national governments) do not insist that ships be "classed," without a "class" category there would be considerable difficulties in operating a ship, as "class" is a requirement of most insurance companies and shippers using the vessel.

### Classification Societies

(shipping) Classification societies are organizations that survey and classify ships, both during their construction and operation. They are the principal means by which standards of construction and maintenance are enforced, and ship certificates can be issued by Flag States. Classification societies are licensed by "Flag States" to undertake this work on their behalf. The principal classification societies are:

- **American Bureau of Shipping (U.S.) (ABS)**
  www.eagle.org
- **Bureau Veritas (France) (BV)**
  www.bureauveritas.com
- **China Classification Society (CCS)**
  www.ccs.org.cn
- **Det Norske Veritas (Norway) (DNV)**
  www.dnv.com
- **Germanischer Lloyd (Germany) (GL)**
  www.glc.de
- **Hellenic Register of Shipping (Greece) (HRS)**
  www.hrs.gr
- **Indian Register of Shipping (India) (IRS)**
  www.irclass.org
- **Korean Register of Shipping (Korea) (KRS)**
  www.krs.co.kr
- **Lloyd's Register of Shipping (UK) (LR)**
  www.lr.org
- **Nippon Kaiji Kyokai (Japan) Class NK**
  www.classnk.or.jp
- **Polski Rejestr Statkow (Poland) (PRS)**
  www.prs.gda.pl
- **Registro Italiano Navale (Italy) (RINA)**
  www.rina.org

### Vessel Classification by Type of Cargo

Vessels are typed in general categories as follows:

- **Oil Tankers**
  Designed for transporting crude oil
- **Bulk Carriers**
  Designed to carry bulk solids such as grains, fertilizer and ores or bulk liquids such as refined petroleum products, chemicals and orange juice
- **General Cargo Ships**
  Designed to carry break bulk cargo
- **Containerships**
  Designed to transport standard-sized ocean freight containers
- **Other Types of Ships**
  Liquified gas carriers
  Chemical tankers
  Miscellaneous tankers
  Ferries and passenger ships
  Other miscellaneous ships

### Vessel Glossary

**Aframax**
(shipping) An ocean-going crude oil tanker vessel of standard size between 80,001 and 120,000 dwt that is the largest crude oil tanker size in the AFRA (Average Freight Rate Assessment) tanker rate system.

**Capesize**
(shipping) An ocean-going cargo vessel that is physically too large to fit through the locks of either the Panama or Suez Canals and therefore must voyage via Cape Horn at the southernmost tip of South America to get to or from the Atlantic and Pacific Oceans, or the Cape of Good Hope at the southernmost tip of South Africa to get to and from the Indian and Atlantic Oceans. Capesize vessels generally serve deepwater terminals handling raw materials, such as iron ore and coal.

**Handysize**
(shipping) A small bulk or oil tanker vessel that is suited to tie up at a T2 type pier. These vessels are a maximum of 10,000 to 30,000 dwt. These vessels are more maneuverable and have shallower draft than larger vessels and therefore make up the majority of the world's ocean-going cargo fleet.

**Handymax**
(shipping) A small bulk or oil tanker vessel of 30,001 to 50,000 dwt that is a larger version of the popular Handysize vessel.

**Panamax**
(shipping) An ocean-going cargo vessel of the maximum size possible to pass through the locks of the Panama Canal, which are 1000ft long by 110ft wide and 85ft deep. These vessels are typically of 50,001 to 80,000 dwt; 965ft (290m) in length; 106ft. (32.2m) beam; and 39.5ft (12.04m) draft.

**Suezmax**
(shipping) An ocean-going cargo vessel of the maximum size possible to pass through the locks of the Suez Canal in Egypt. This standard has evolved over time. Prior to 1967, a Suezmax was a maximum of 80,000 dwt. The canal was closed between 1967 and 1975 because of the Israel-Arab conflict. Upon reopening in 1975, after many modifications to the locks and canal itself, the maximum was increased to 200,000 dwt.

**Very Large Crude Carrier (VLCC)**
(shipping) An ocean-going crude oil tanker of 200,001 to 350,000dwt. These vessels have greater flexibility than ULCCs due to their smaller size and are used extensively in the Mediterranean, West Africa and the North Sea. These vessels can sometimes be ballasted through the Suez Canal.

**Ultra Large Crude Carrier (ULCC)**
(shipping) An ocean-going crude oil tanker of 350,000+dwt. These are the largest vessels in the world and are used for carrying crude oil on long haul routes from the Arabian Gulf to Europe, America and the Far East, via the Cape of Good Hope. These vessels require custom built terminals for loading and discharge.

# Vessel Types

Ocean-going vessels are classified by the type of cargo they carry and their size expressed as dwt or deadweight tonnage. In some cases, a vessel is classified by its length and width. Since each classification society has slightly different standards, the size range for each vessel type may vary.

## Bulk Carriers

These vessels carry dry (grains, fertilizers, phophates and ores) or wet (chemicals, orange juice, refined petroleum products) bulk cargo.

### Bulk Carrier
A ship with a single deck designed to carry homogenous loose cargo.

### Handysize
Size: 10,000 – 30,000 dwt
These are small bulk carriers that make up the majority of the world's short haul fleet. Handysize can refer either to a bulk carrier or tanker.

### Handymax
Size: 30,001 – 50,000 dwt
These are a larger version of the Handysize vessels and popular for both bulk and crude carriers. These vessels have a large variation in size and characteristics.

### Panamax
Size: 50,001 – 80,000 dwt
This is the maximum size ship that can pass through the locks of the Panama Canal. Locks are 1000ft long by 110ft wide and 85ft deep. Panamax dimensions are: overall length (LOA) of 965ft (290m); beam of 106ft (32.2m); draft of 39.5ft (12.04m).

### Capesize
Size: 80,001 dwt and larger
These are vessels that are too large to pass through the locks of either the Panama or Suez Canals. As a result, these vessels must travel around the Cape of Good Hope in South Africa or Cape Horn in South America to their destinations. These vessels also require deep-water ports.

### Very Large Ore Carriers (VL Ore Carriers)
Size: 200,000 dwt and larger
These vessels are the largest bulk carriers and cannot pass through either the Panama or Suez canals.

## Tankers

These vessels carry refined petroleum products in numerous bulk tanks for safety and in order to carry a number of different products in a single voyage.
Tankers of less than 100,000 dwt are referred to as either "clean" or "dirty". Clean tankers carry refined petroleum products such as gasoline, kerosene, jet fuels, or chemicals. The so-called dirty vessels transport products such as heavy fuel oils or crude oil. Larger tankers usually only carry crude oil.

### Coastal
Size: 3,001 dwt – 10,000 dwt
These are the smallest tankers and are generally used in coastal waters requiring a shallow draft. Coastal tankers typically carry kerosene, heating oils, fuels and chemicals.

### Small
Size: 10,001 dwt – 19,000 dwt
This is the next size up tanker and is still often used in coastal waters. These also typically carry kerosene, heating oils, fuels and chemicals.

### Handy or Handysize
Size: 19,001 dwt – 25,000 dwt
Alternate: 10,000 – 34,999 dwt
This is a popular-sized tanker, but typically not used in very long voyages

### Medium or Handymax
Size: 25,001 – 45,000 dwt
Alternate: 35,000 – 49,999 dwt
This is a larger "Handy" sized vessel.

### Long Range One (LRI)
Size: 45,001 – 70,000 dwt
Alternate: 45,000 to 79,999 dwt

### Long Range Two (LRII)
Size: 70,001 – 100,000+ dwt
Alternate: 80,000 – 159,999 dwt

## Crude Oil Carriers

These vessels carry bulk crude oil in tanks.
Tankers of less than 100,000 dwt are referred to as either "clean" or "dirty". Clean tankers carry refined petroleum products such as gasoline, kerosene or jet fuels, or chemicals. The so-called dirty vessels transport products such as heavy fuel oils or crude oil. Larger tankers usually only carry crude oil.

### Panamax
Size: 50,001 – 80,000 dwt
Approximate 32.2m beam limitation
This is the maximum size ship that can pass through the locks of the Panama Canal. Locks are 1000ft long by 110ft wide and 85ft deep. Panamax dimensions are: overall length (LOA) of 965ft (290m); beam of 106ft (32.2m); draft of 39.5ft (12.04m).

### Aframax
Size: 80,001 – 120,000 dwt
This is the largest crude oil tanker size in the AFRA (Average Freight Rate Assessment) tanker rate system.

### Suezmax
Size: 120,001 – 200,000 dwt
This is the maximum size crude oil ship that can pass through the Suez Canal in Egypt.

### Very Large Crude Carrier (VLCC)
Size: 200,001 – 350,000 dwt
These are very large crude oil carriers that transport crude oil from the Gulf, West Africa, the North Sea and Prudhoe Bay to destinations in the United States, Mediterranean Europe and Asia. Although VLCCs are otherwise too large, it is possible to ballast these vessels through the Suez Canal.

### Ultra Large Crude Carrier (ULCC)
Size: 321,000+ dwt
These are the largest man-made vessels that move. Currently, the largest ULCC is 564,939 dwt. These ships sail the longest routes, typically from the Gulf to Europe, the United States and Asia. They are so large that they require custom-built terminals for loading and unloading.

# Traditional Freighter

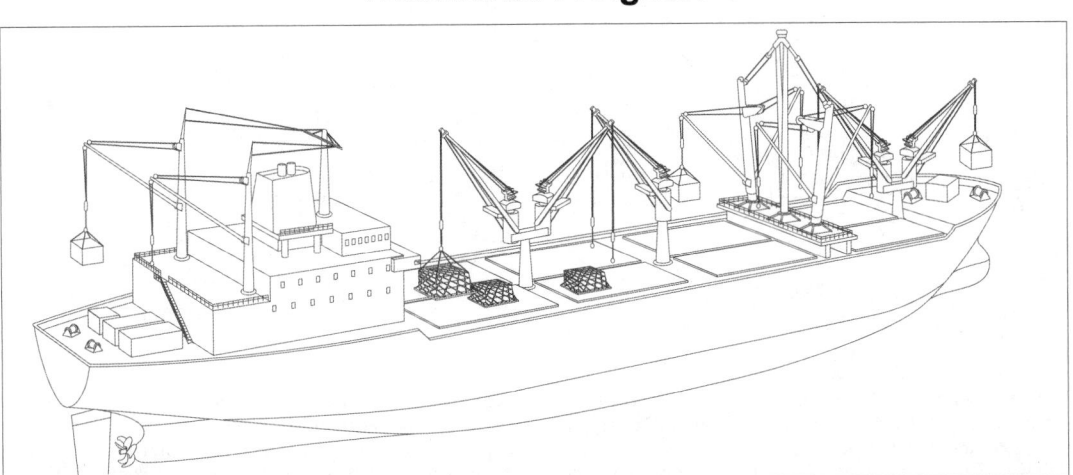

The term freighter is broadly used to describe any vessel that carries freight. However, a traditional freighter carries break bulk cargo as opposed to containerized cargo.

**Distinguishing Features:** Traditional freighters have deck-mounted cranes used to transfer cargo from a wharf to the vessel.

**Size or Length:** Traditional freighters range in length from 250ft (76.2m) to 600ft (182.88m). The "Liberty Ships" of WWII were 441ft (134.4m) in length and 56ft (17m) wide.

**Types of Cargo:** All types of break bulk (as opposed to wet or dry bulk or containerized) cargo.

**How Cargo is Loaded:** Freighters utilize numerous deck-mounted cranes to transfer uncontainerized cargo such as cartons, bales, drums, palletized cargo, machinery and vehicles from a wharf or lighter onto the vessel, where longshoremen or stevedores, in a very time-consuming process, stow the cargo into the holds.

**Note:** Traditional freighters are for the most part obsolete, but are still used in remote parts of the world. Some have been converted to carry containers and dry bulk cargo such as grain, coal, phosphates, fertilizers, and animal feeds. For the most part, they have been sold as scrap metal.

# Container Vessel

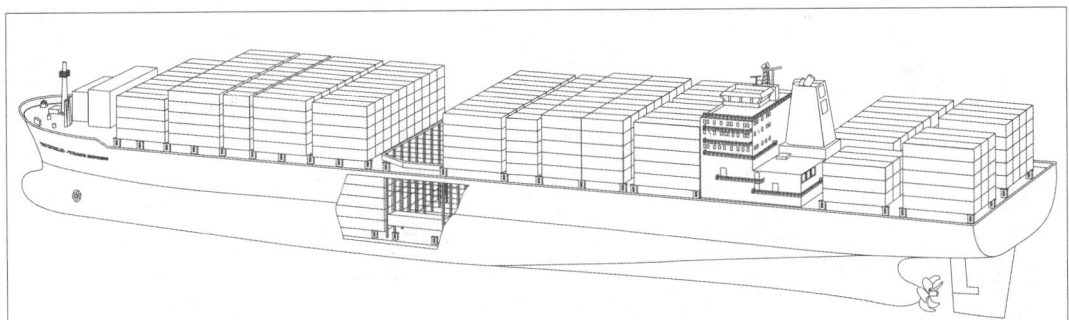

A Container Vessel is designed to carry uniform-sized ocean freight containers of 20ft (6m) or 40ft (12m) length, 8ft width, and 8.5ft to 9.5ft height.

**Distinguishing Features:** Containers are loaded into tall slots that extend from three to six containers below deck to three to six containers above deck. The containers are then connected at the corners with locking devices.

**Size or Length:** Container ships vary dramatically in size and capacity. While most vessel specifications are given in length and width, container vessel specifications are in TEUs or twenty-foot equivalent units (how many standard 20 foot containers the vessel can carry). Very small container vessels might carry as few as 20 TEUs, but modern vessels typically carry 1,000 TEUs or more. Currently, the largest container vessel in the world is 1,060ft (323m) long, 138ft (42m) wide, has a draught of 47.5ft (14.5m) when fully laden and has a capacity of 8,063 TEUs.

**Types of Cargo:** Container vessels carry any cargo that can be stowed into any of the following container types: general purpose, high cube, hardtop, open top, flat, platform, insulated, ventilated, bulk, refrigerated (reefer) and tank-type containers. Containerized cargo can include merchandise in cartons, bales, drums, as well as cars, furniture, electronics, food, livestock, chemicals and machinery. Oversize cargo such as heavy machinery, trucks, earth moving equipment and pleasure boats can be placed in or on open-top, open-side or flat rack containers or secured to the tops of several containers in a row.

**How Cargo is Loaded:** Individual containers are loaded by port-based cranes.

# Container Vessel with Deck Cranes

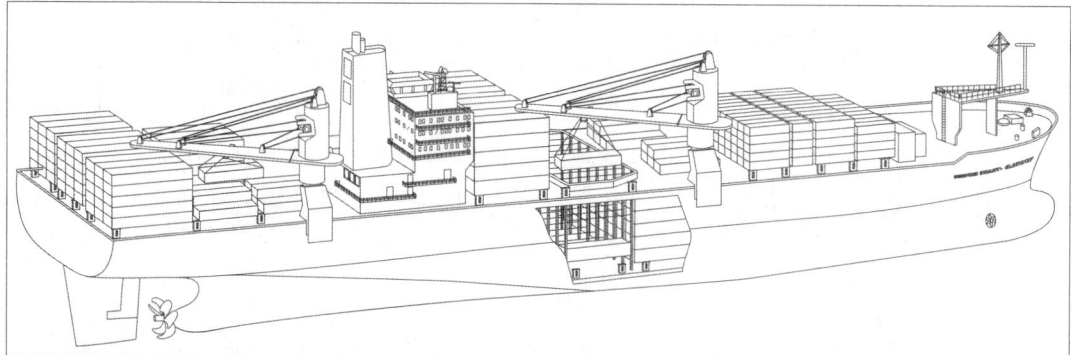

A Container Vessel is designed to carry uniform-sized ocean freight containers of 20ft (6m) or 40ft (12m) length, 8ft width, and 8.5ft to 9.5ft height.

**Distinguishing Features:** Containers are loaded into tall slots that extend from three to five containers below deck to three to five containers above deck. This specific type of vessel also has a number of deck-mounted cranes for on and off loading of containers.

**Size or Length:** Container ships vary dramatically in size and capacity. While most vessel specifications are given in length and width, container vessel specifications are in TEUs or twenty-foot equivalent units (how many standard 20-foot containers the vessel can carry). Very small container vessels might carry as few as 20 TEUs, but modern vessels typically carry 1,000 TEUs or more. Currently, the largest container vessel in the world has a capacity of 8,063 TEUs, but does not have deck cranes.

**Types of Cargo:** Container vessels carry any cargo that can be stowed into any of the following container types: general purpose, high cube, hardtop, open top, flat, platform, insulated, ventilated, bulk, refrigerated (reefer) and tank. Cargo can include merchandise of all kinds, cars, furniture, electronics, food, livestock, chemicals, machinery, and products packed in cartons, bales and drums. Oversize cargo such as heavy machinery, trucks, earth moving equipment and pleasure boats can be placed in or on opentop, open-side or flat rack containers or secured above deck on top of other containers.

**How Cargo is Loaded:** Individual containers are loaded by ship- or port-based cranes.

# Ro-Ro (Roll-on Roll-off) Vessel

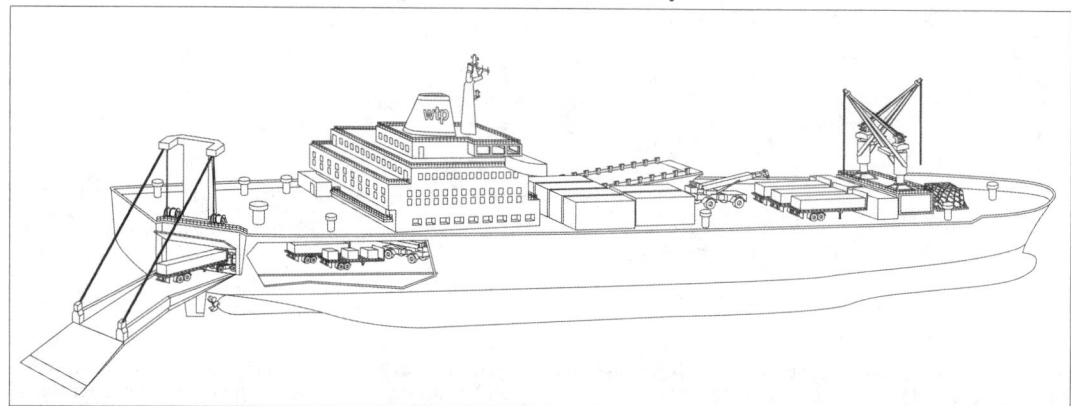

A Ro-Ro (Roll-on Roll-off) vessel is designed to transport motor vehicles or any other rolling stock

**Distinguishing Features**: Ro-Ro vessels have a hinged ramp, typically offset at the stern, that allows motor vehicles (automobiles, trucks, trailers, farm tractors, etc.) to drive on and off the vessel.

A Ro-Ro differs from a ferry in that a ferry is designed to carry vehicles and their individual drivers short to medium distances, whereas a Ro-Ro is designed to carry vehicles for wholesale transport without drivers for long distances. For example, a Ro-Ro would be used by an automobile manufacturer such as Honda or Volkswagen to transport hundreds of vehicles at a time across oceans to sell in another country.

Ro-Ro vessels may have as many as eight interior decks, all of which are accessible by interior rampways.

Ro-Ro vessels may also have deck cranes and/or the ability to carry standard ocean containers on deck.

**Size or Length**: Ro-Ro vessels are typically very large. The largest Ro-Ro vessel is 789.34ft (240.6m) in length, with a tonnage of 67,140 gross tons and 34,376 dwt.

**Types of Cargo**: Motor vehicles, trucks, buses, tractors, bulldozers, yachts, heavy plant equipment, rail cars, and general cargo. Oversize cargo can be loaded on flatbed or lowboy trailers or placed on deck.

**How Cargo is Loaded**: Motor vehicles and rolling stock are driven on or rolled onto the vessel via a hinged ramp at the stern.

# Heavy Lift Vessel

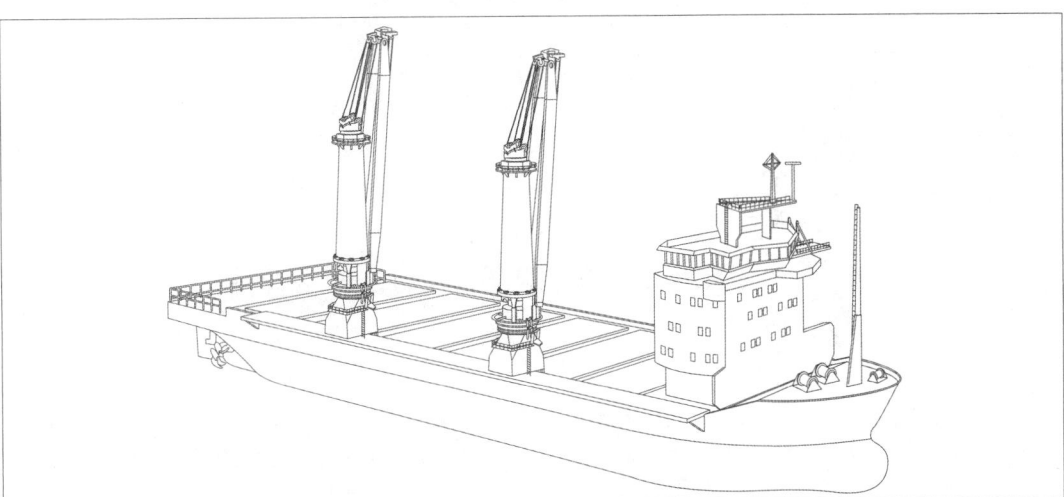

A Heavy Lift Vessel is designed to carry extremely large and/or heavy items that cannot be transported in or on other vessels. Semi-submersible types are designed to transport, lift and unload very large floating objects, including damaged ships. Ro-Ro/heavy lift vessels also exist.

**Distinguishing Features:** Heavy lift vessels have extremely large cargo decks, unusual deck and pilothouse configurations to accommodate unusual types of cargo and very high-capacity on-deck cranes.

**Size or Length:** Varies by vessel and type of cargo. A large heavy lift vessel can measure 584.6ft (178.20m) in length and 137.8ft (42m) in width.

**Types of Cargo:** High-value, complex cargoes such as: transformers, locomotives, rockets, crushers, semi-submersible rigs, jack-ups, oil platforms, bridge spans, TLPs (tension leg platforms) and SPAR buoys, etc.

**How Items are Loaded:** Cargo is loaded by onboard cranes or shore-based cranes. Conventional loading is the by over-the-top Lo-Lo (Load-on/Load-off). Some heavy lift vessels also have Ro-Ro capabilities.

# LNG (Liquified Natural Gas) Carrier

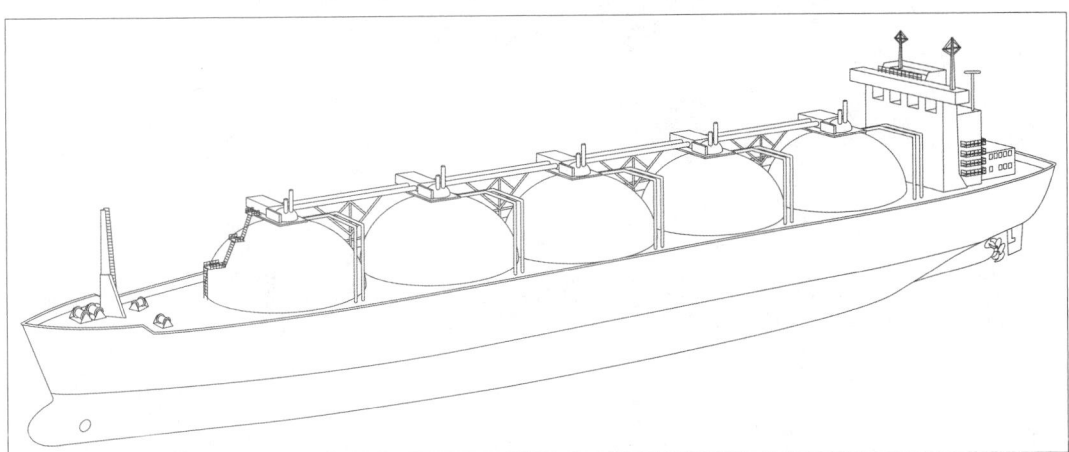

An LNG (Liquified Natural Gas) Carrier is designed to transport natural gas that has been cooled at high pressure and extremely low temperature (-260°F/-162°C) until it contracts into a liquid. LNG compresses to 1/600th of its original volume.

**Distinguishing Features:** LNG spherical storage tanks are positioned half below and half above the deck.

**Size or Length:** A conventional LNG carrier has a carrying capacity of 135,000 cubic meters (4,767,480 cuft). The largest LNG tanker has a capacity of 145,000 cubic meters (5,120,627 cuft).

**Types of Cargo:** Liquified Natural Gas

**How LNG is Loaded:** The LNG is loaded and unloaded through pumps at specialized terminals. The liquid is then turned back into gas and fed into pipelines for distribution.

**Safety Note:** Although LNG is a dangerous cargo, LNG tankers have an exceptional safety record, primarily because they are staffed with the best officers and crews available.

**U.S. LNG Vessel Note:** Due to the dangerous nature of the cargo, U.S. Coast Guard coordinates protection for each trip to a U.S. LNG port, including helicopter patrol, police divers, marine patrol, environmental police, firefighting tugs, city police boats and Coast Guard vessels. Bridges are closed as tankers pass underneath. An established zone of security extends 500 yards on each side, two miles ahead and a mile behind the tanker.

# Crude Oil Tanker

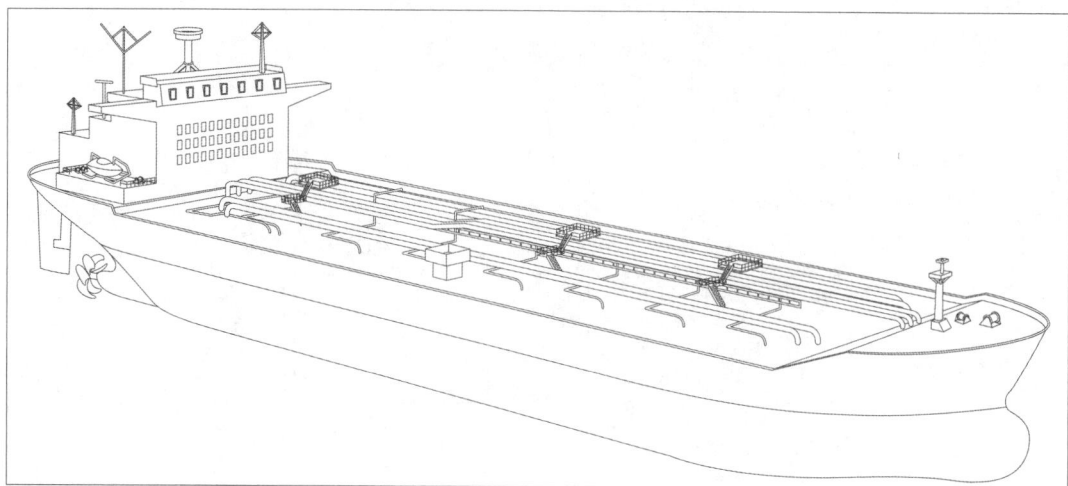

A Crude Oil Tanker is a liquid bulk vessel designed specifically to carry crude oil.

**Distinguishing Features:** Oil tankers come in all sizes, but the larger "supertankers" are truly giant vessels. The deck of a tanker is covered with pipes and pumps used to transport the crude oil from ship to shore or from hold to hold. All modern oil tankers are double-hulled to protect against oil spills in case of a collision.

**Size or Length:** Crude oil tankers fall into different categories of size (dwt = deadweight tons):
Panamax Crude Carrier: 50,001–80,000dwt with a 32.2m beam limitation;

Aframax Crude Carrier: 80,001–120,000 dwt;
Suezmax Crude Carrier: 120,001–200,000 dwt;
Very Large Crude Carrier (VLCC): 200,001–350,000 dwt;
Ultra Large Crude Carrier (ULCC): 350,001+ dwt.
The largest ULCC is 564,939 dwt.

**Types of Cargo:** Crude Oil

**How Cargo is Loaded:** Oil tankers load their cargo by gravity from the shore or by shore pumps, and discharge using onboard pumps.

# Dry Bulk Carrier

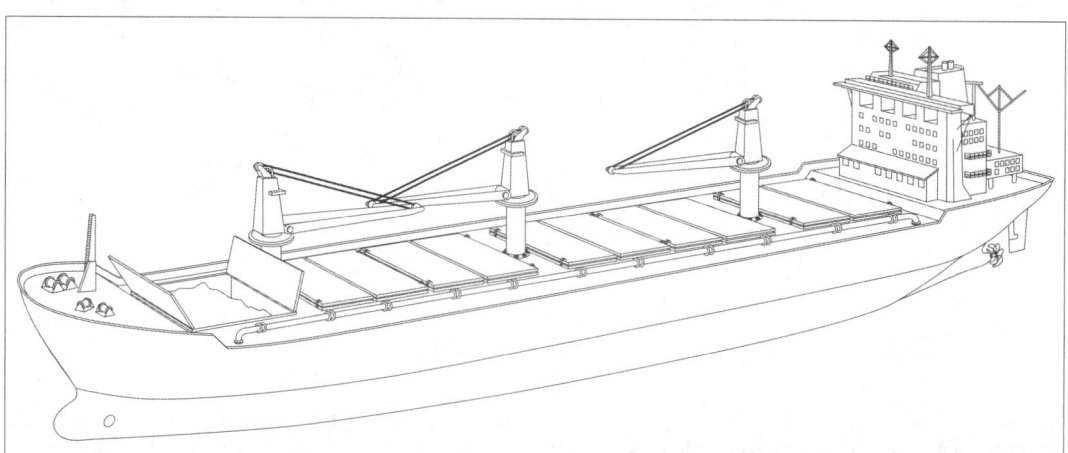

A Bulk Carrier is designed to carry dry bulk cargo.

**Distinguishing Features:** A bulk carrier typically has a flush deck with numerous waterproof hatches covering holds into which bulk cargo is stored. Some bulk carriers have deck cranes.

**Size or Length:** Bulk carrier vessels vary greatly in size depending upon the intended cargo and regions served. They range from 10,000 dwt (deadweight tons) to 364,000 dwt in capacity. The longest bulk carrier is 1125ft (343m) in length.

**Types of Cargo:** Coal, phosphates, iron and other ores, cocoa, grains, fertilizers, animal feeds, scrap metal or other dry, loose cargo.

**How Cargo is Loaded:** Cargo can be loaded by terminal-based gravity chutes or by shore- or ship-based overhead vacuum pumps, which suck the cargo in and out of the holds of the ship.

**Note:** Special types of bulk carriers are designed for use on the Great Lakes area of the U.S. and Canada. These vessels transport potash, cement, salt, grain, coal, stone and iron ore.

# Canal Barge with Propulsion

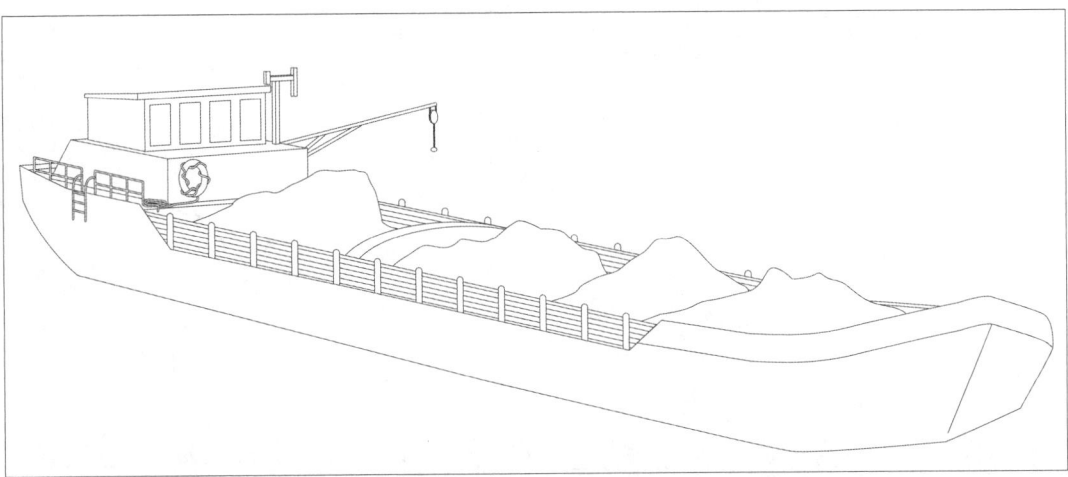

A Canal Barge is designed to carry cargo on the specific canals or waterways it navigates (i.e. Mississippi River, Rhine River, etc.). At issue are the width and length of the waterway's locks (if any) and the depth of the waterway. As a result, barges designed for one waterway may not work on another.

Almost all barges are designed for superior cargo carrying capacity. Freight barges can carry cargo inside the hull or on the deck. Barges are categorized by their physical size, the type of cargo they carry, and the waterways they can travel (i.e., oceans, coasts, lakes, bays, sounds, rivers).

Barges are manufactured with propulsion (see illustration above) or without propulsion (see illustration below).

An oil barge is categorized by its barrel or tonnage cargo capacity, its cubic area for cargo, or its deadweight tonnage (dwt).

**Distinguishing Features**: U.S. river barges are usually flat-bottomed, rectangular in shape, without propulsion and pushed or pulled by powerful tugboat-type vessels.

U.S./Canada Great Lakes barges are often full-sized ships that are long and narrow and have their own propulsion.

European barges are long and narrow to fit through canals and inland waterways. They are also designed to ride low in the water. These barges have special low-draught propulsion systems.

**Size or Length:** Varies to suit the canal or waterway. Except for the busiest canals, most canals in Europe allow a maximum beam size of about 14ft (4.27m) for barges.

**Types of Cargo:** Almost anything: crude oil, asphalt, clean oils, gasoline, chemicals, soy bean oil, corn oil, molasses, tallow, dry and dry bulk cargo (containers, lumber, steel, coal, construction equipment, grain, rice, sugar, sand, gravel, railcars, etc.).

**How Items are Loaded:** Varies by cargo. Typically by a land-based or floating crane for heavy-lift items; by spouting systems fed by conveyors (for grains); by pumps (for liquids); and loading ramps (for vehicles or rolling stock).

# Barge without Propulsion

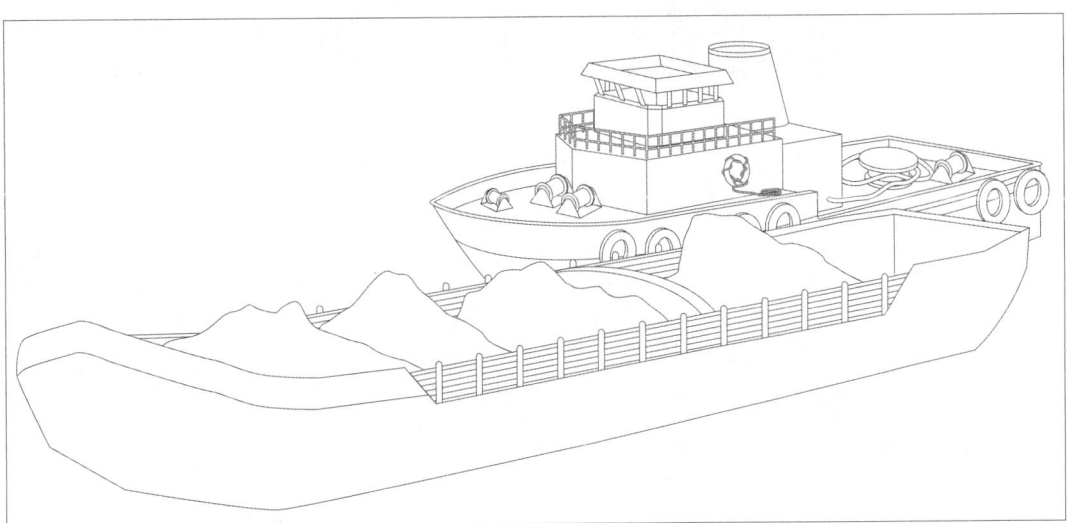

# Ship to Shore Container Crane

CRANES

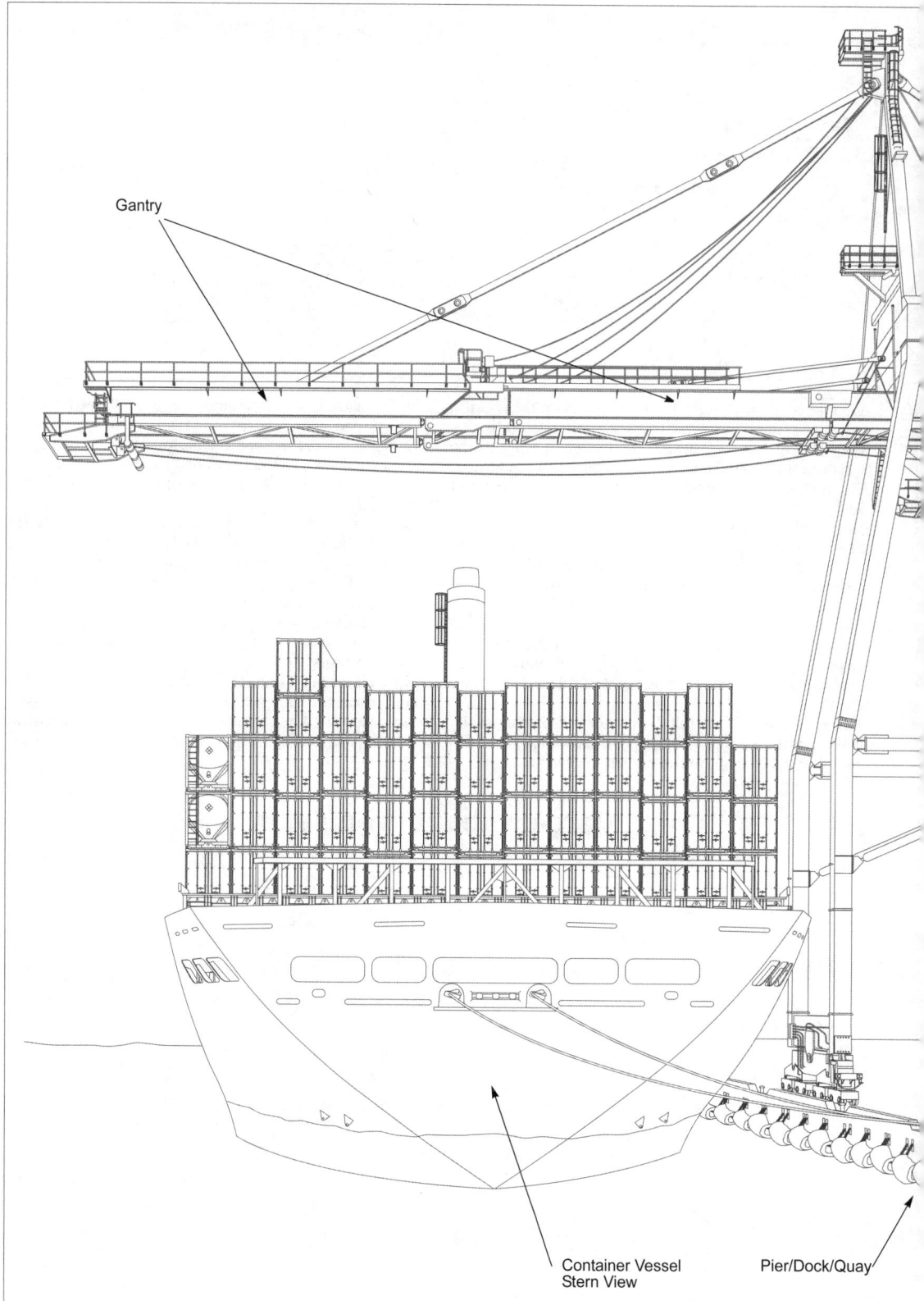

Gantry

Container Vessel
Stern View

Pier/Dock/Quay

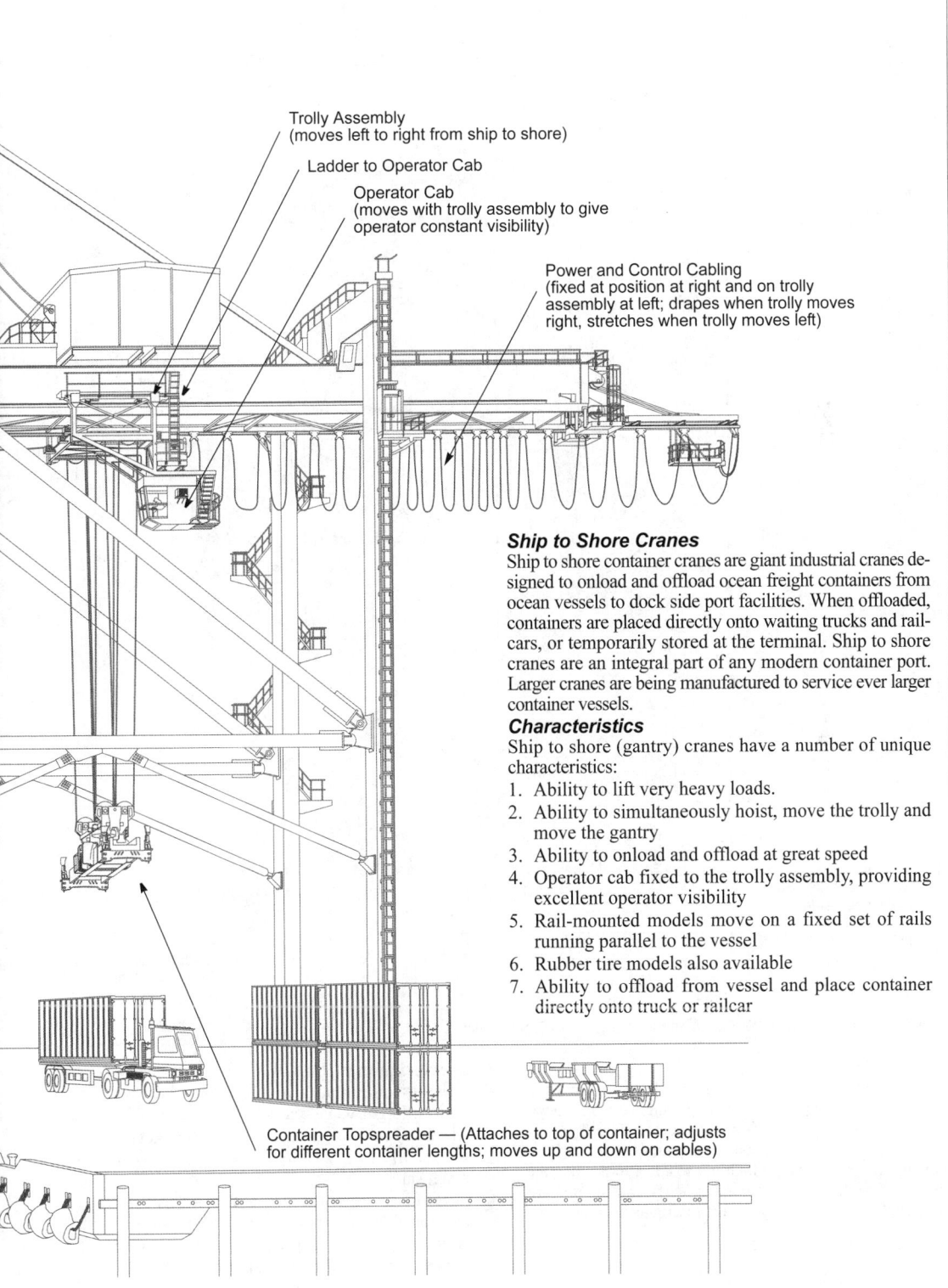

Trolly Assembly
(moves left to right from ship to shore)

Ladder to Operator Cab

Operator Cab
(moves with trolly assembly to give
operator constant visibility)

Power and Control Cabling
(fixed at position at right and on trolly
assembly at left; drapes when trolly moves
right, stretches when trolly moves left)

Container Topspreader — (Attaches to top of container; adjusts
for different container lengths; moves up and down on cables)

## Ship to Shore Cranes

Ship to shore container cranes are giant industrial cranes designed to onload and offload ocean freight containers from
ocean vessels to dock side port facilities. When offloaded,
containers are placed directly onto waiting trucks and railcars, or temporarily stored at the terminal. Ship to shore
cranes are an integral part of any modern container port.
Larger cranes are being manufactured to service ever larger
container vessels.

## Characteristics

Ship to shore (gantry) cranes have a number of unique
characteristics:

1. Ability to lift very heavy loads.
2. Ability to simultaneously hoist, move the trolly and
   move the gantry
3. Ability to onload and offload at great speed
4. Operator cab fixed to the trolly assembly, providing
   excellent operator visibility
5. Rail-mounted models move on a fixed set of rails
   running parallel to the vessel
6. Rubber tire models also available
7. Ability to offload from vessel and place container
   directly onto truck or railcar

# Straddle Carrier
# for Ocean Cargo Containers

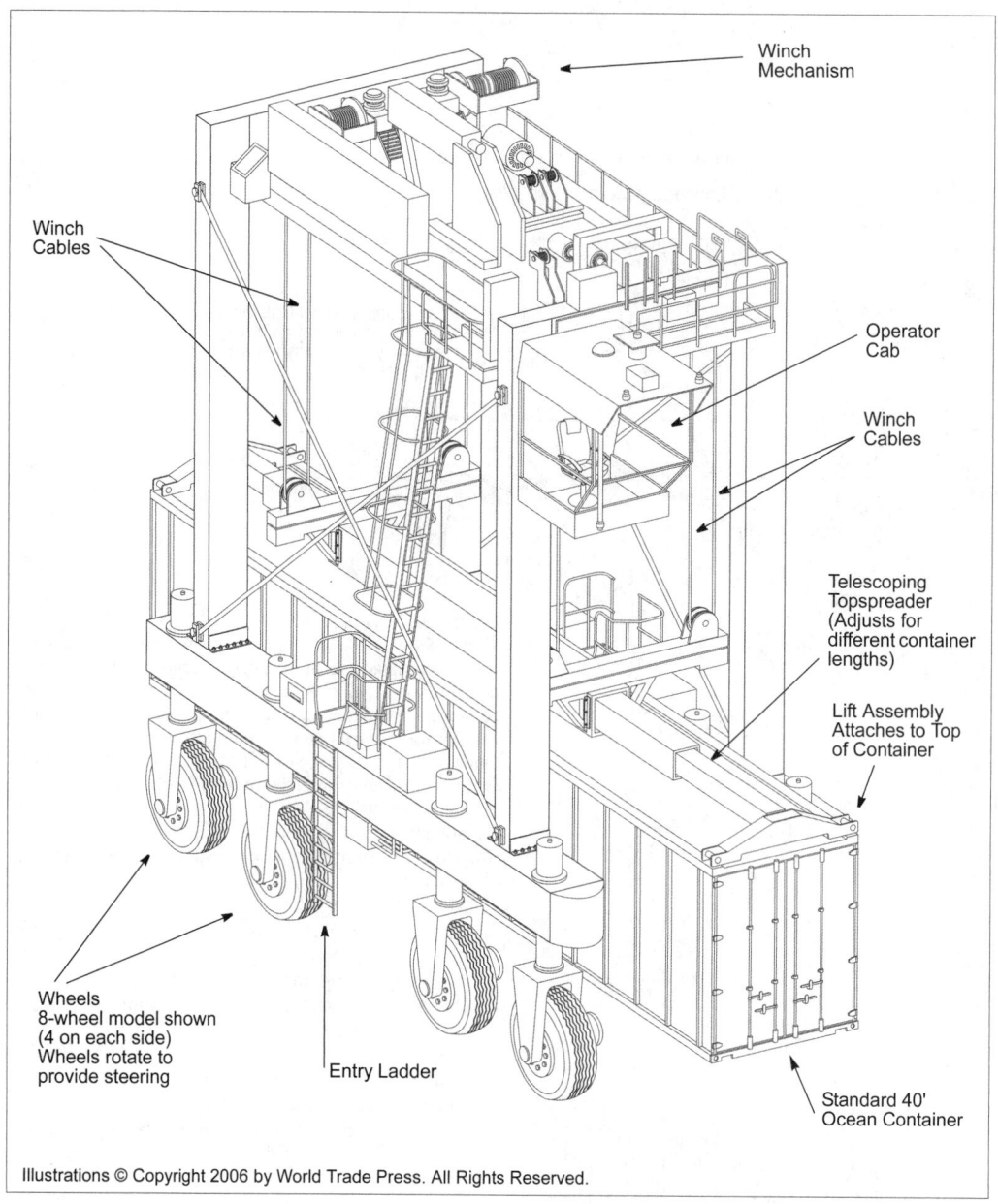

Winch Mechanism

Winch Cables

Operator Cab

Winch Cables

Telescoping Topspreader (Adjusts for different container lengths)

Lift Assembly Attaches to Top of Container

Wheels
8-wheel model shown
(4 on each side)
Wheels rotate to
provide steering

Entry Ladder

Standard 40'
Ocean Container

### Straddle Carrier
Straddle (container) carriers are designed to lift, move and stack loaded and empty ocean freight containers. Although they are also used in railyards and truck terminals, their primary use is at ocean port container terminals.

Straddle carriers became popular in the late 1960s when the volume of container traffic grew quickly and the need to move containers efficiently in port terminals became a priority.

### Characteristics
Straddle carriers have a number of unique characteristics:
1. Four- or eight-wheel models
2. Ability of multiple wheels to rotate for steering
3. Ability to move a container at greater speed than a reach stacker
4. Operator cab located as high as 40 feet (10 meters) above the ground providing excellent operator visibility
5. Ability to operate deep within rows of containers (so long as there is sufficient gap between rows)
6. The ability to lift very heavy loads (often heavier loads than most reach stackers)

# Reach Stacker
# for Ocean Cargo Containers

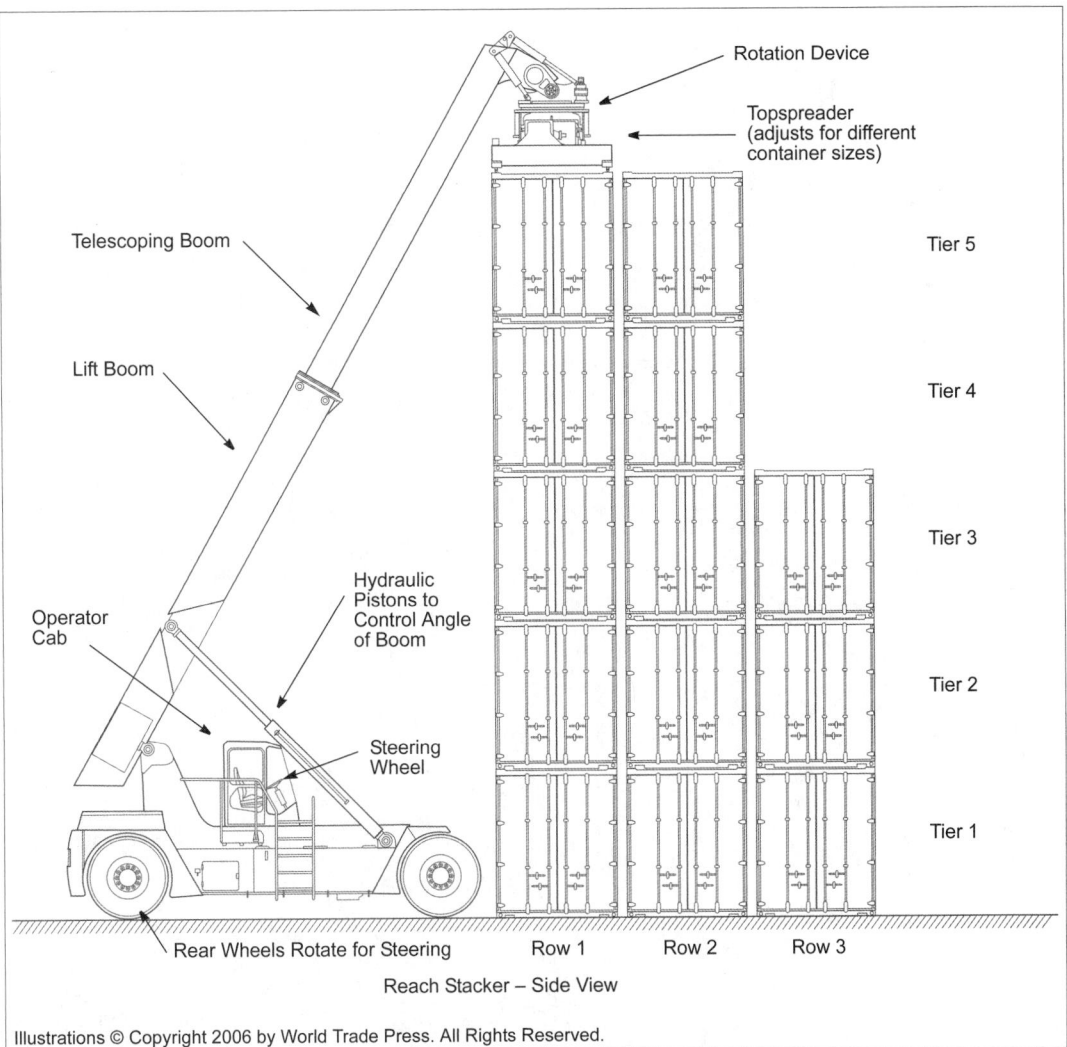

Rotation Device

Topspreader
(adjusts for different
container sizes)

Telescoping Boom

Lift Boom

Hydraulic
Pistons to
Control Angle
of Boom

Operator
Cab

Steering
Wheel

Tier 5

Tier 4

Tier 3

Tier 2

Tier 1

Rear Wheels Rotate for Steering    Row 1    Row 2    Row 3

Reach Stacker – Side View

**CRANES**

## Reach Stacker

Reach stackers are forkliff-like industrial trucks used to move and stack loaded and empty ocean freight containers. Reach stackers are available from a number of manufacturers and in a number of different configurations and have become common pieces of equipment in ocean and inland waterway terminals, railyards and truck terminals. They are versatile and, while more expensive than forklift trucks, are less expensive than straddle cranes.

Reach stackers are somewhat similar to fortlift trucks, but are different in a number of ways:

1. Reach stackers lift from the top of a container rather than the bottom.
2. Reach stackers have greater lift capacity than most forklift trucks. 100,000 lbs (45,360kg), vs. about 5,000 pounds (2,268kg) for a typical warehouse fork lift.
3. Reach stackers will typically stack containers to 4-, 5-, or 6-high; higher than most forklift trucks.

## Characteristics

Reach stackers have a number of unique characteristics:

1. Extremely heavy ballasted base
2. Telescoping boom
3. Adjustable topspreader to accommodate different sized containers
4. Ability to rotate the container
5. Ability to sideshift the container
6. All weather cab with operator comforts

## Capabilities

Reach stacker capability categories are:

1. Lift capability for 1st to 3rd tiers in 1st row.
2. Lift capacity for higher tiers in 1st row.
3. Lift capacity for various tiers in 2nd and 3rd rows.
4. Turning radius.
5. Length of telescoping boom.
6. Adjustable topspreader.
7. Rotation and sideshift capabilities.

Note: New curved boom models allow higher stacking in back rows.

**CRANES**

# Guide to Ocean Freight Containers

## Introduction

Container specifications listed are virtually standardized world-wide. However, the possibility exists that individual container manufacturers and shipping lines will have container specifications which vary somewhat from those listed in this section. Be certain to inquire about precise specifications from your shipping line or forwarder when you arrange for a shipment.

## Values / Details

All values listed in the tables are given in metric. Ft and lbs values are for easy reference only.

All details listed are nominal figures. Apart from the tolerances given on internal dimensions below the tare weight can vary +/- 2%.

## General Information

### External and Minimum Internal Dimensions

The following table gives the overall external dimensions as standardized in ISO 668 and the minimum internal dimensions and door openings for General Purpose Containers as standardized in ISO 1496-1.

|  | Length | | Width | Height | | |
|---|---|---|---|---|---|---|
| **Dimensions** | 20'<br>6,058 mm | 40'<br>12,192 mm | 8'<br>2,438 mm | 8'6"<br>2,438 mm | 8'6"<br>2,438 mm | 9'6"<br>2,896 mm |
| **Minimum Internal Dimensions** | 5,867 mm<br>19'3" | 11,998 mm<br>39' 4 3/8" | 2,330 mm<br>7'7 3/4" | 2,197 mm<br>7'2 1/2" | 2,350 mm<br>7'8 1/2" | 2,655 mm<br>8'8 1/2" |
| **Minimun Door Opening Dimensions** | - | - | 2,286 mm<br>7'6" | 2,134 mm<br>7' | 2,261 mm<br>7'5" | 2,566 mm<br>8'5" |

### Internal Dimensions

The internal dimensions and door openings of most containers exceed the above given dimensions. However, the dimensions mentioned on the following pages are nominal figures. Because of production tolerances a difference in measurements is possible:

| Tolerances | Length | Width | Height |
|---|---|---|---|
| **Maximum Difference** | 10 mm<br>3/8" | 10 mm<br>3/8" | 10 mm<br>3/8" |

### Maximum Gross Weights

**20' containers:**
24,000 kg (52,910 lbs) according to the latest issue of ISO 668;
30, 480 kg (67,200 lbs) valid for most Hapag-Lloyd 20' containers; exceeds ISO minimum standards.
**40' containers:**
30,480 kg (67,200 lbs).

### Floor Loads

A container floor is capable of carrying a fork-lift truck with a maximum axle load of 5,460 kg (12,040 lbs), if the contact area per wheel is at least 142 cm2 (22 sq.in) (ISO 1496/I).

### Concentrated Loads

When stowing heavy cargo in containers other than flats or platforms due care has to be taken that concentrated loads will not exceed the strength of the bottom construction of the container.
The maximum spreaded load should not exceed
—for 20' containers 4 ts per running meter in length (3' 3.5")
—for 40' containers 3 ts per running meter in length.

### Gooseneck Tunnel on 40' Containers

All Hapag-Lloyd 40' containers are fitted with a Gooseneck tunnel to enable the transport on Gooseneck chassis.

### Timber Treatment

Exposed timber is treated according to Australian requirements (exceptions: 40' flats and platforms).

CONTAINERS

# General Purpose Container

## 20'

- Suitable for any general cargo.
- Containers may be equipped with liner bags suitable for bulk cargo, e.g. malt.
- Fork-lift pockets on a number of containers.
- Various lashing devices on the top and bottom longitudinal rails and the corner posts.

Lashing devices have a permissible load of 1,000 kg (2,205 lbs) each.
- Note permissable weight limits for road and rail transport.

## General Purpose Container

## 20'

| Construction | Inside Dimensions | | | Door Opening | | Weights | | | Capacity |
|---|---|---|---|---|---|---|---|---|---|
| | Length | Width | Height | Width | Height | Max. Gross | Tare | Max. Payload | |
| | mm<br>ft | mm<br>ft | mm<br>ft | mm<br>ft | mm<br>ft | kg<br>lbs | kg<br>lbs | kg<br>lbs | m³<br>cu.ft. |
| **8'6" high** | | | | | | | | | |
| Steel container with corrugated walls and wooden floor | 5,895<br>19'4¹/₈" | 2,350<br>7'8¹/₂" | 2,392<br>7'10¹/₈" | 2,340<br>7'8¹/₈" | 2,292<br>7'6¹/₄" | 30,480<br>67,200 | 2,250<br>4,960 | 28,230<br>62,240 | 33.2<br>1,172 |
| | 5,895<br>19'4" | 2,350<br>7'8¹/₂" | 2,385<br>7'9⁷/₈" | 2,338<br>7'8" | 2,292<br>7'6¹/₄" | 24,000<br>52,910 | 2,250<br>4,960 | 21,750<br>47,950 | 33.2<br>1,172 |
| | 5,879<br>19'3³/₈" | 2,330<br>7'7³/₄" | 2,370<br>7'9¹/₄" | 2,330<br>7'7³/₄" | 2,290<br>7'6¹/₈" | 24,000<br>52,910 | 2,250<br>4,960 | 21,750<br>47,950 | 33.0<br>1,165 |
| | 5,889<br>19'3⁷/₈" | 2,346<br>7'8³/₈" | 2,372<br>7'9³/₈" | 2,330<br>7'7³/₄" | 2,272<br>7'5¹/₂" | 24,000<br>52,910 | 2,360<br>5,200 | 21,640<br>47,710 | 32.8<br>1,158 |
| | 5,885<br>19'4" | 2,350<br>7'8¹/₂" | 2,403<br>7'10⁵/₈" | 2,338<br>7'8" | 2,292<br>7'6¹/₄" | 24,000<br>52,910 | 2,150<br>4,740 | 21,850<br>48,170 | 33.15<br>1,170 |
| | 5,884<br>19'3⁵/₈" | 2,335<br>7'8" | 2,390<br>7'10" | 2,335<br>7'8" | 2,292<br>7'6¹/₄" | 24,000<br>52,910 | 2,200<br>4,850 | 21,800<br>48,060 | 33.1<br>1,169 |
| | 5,899<br>19'4¹/₄" | 2,350<br>7'8¹/₂" | 2,394<br>7'10¹/₄" | 2,338<br>7'8" | 2,280<br>7'5³/₄" | 24,000<br>52,910 | 2,180<br>4,810 | 21,820<br>48,100 | 33.2<br>1,172 |
| | 5,891<br>19'3⁷/₈" | 2,330<br>7'7³/₄" | 2,376<br>7'9¹/₂" | 2,330<br>7'7³/₄" | 2,272<br>7'5¹/₂" | 24,000<br>52,910 | 2,300<br>5,070 | 21,700<br>47,840 | 33.0<br>1,165 |
| | 5,880<br>19'3¹/₂" | 2,330<br>7'7³/₄" | 2,380<br>7'9⁵/₈" | 2,330<br>7'7³/₄" | 2,275<br>7'5¹/₂" | 24,000<br>52,910 | 2,300<br>5,070 | 21,700<br>47,840 | 33.0<br>1,165 |

CONTAINERS

## General Purpose Container       **20'**

| Construction | Inside Dimensions | | | Door Opening | | Weights | | | Capacity |
|---|---|---|---|---|---|---|---|---|---|
| | Length | Width | Height | Width | Height | Max. Gross | Tare | Max. Payload | |
| | mm ft | mm ft | mm ft | mm ft | mm ft | kg lbs | kg lbs | kg lbs | m³ cu.ft. |
| **8'6" high** | | | | | | | | | |
| Steel container with corrugated walls and wooden floor | 5,895 19'4¹/₈" | 2,350 7'8¹/₂" | 2,392 7'10¹/₈" | 2,340 7'8¹/₈" | 2,292 7'6¹/₄" | 30,480 67,200 | 2,250 4,960 | 28,230 62,240 | 33.2 1,172 |
| | 5,895 19'4" | 2,350 7'8¹/₂" | 2,385 7'9⁷/₈" | 2,338 7'8" | 2,292 7'6¹/₄" | 24,000 52,910 | 2,250 4,960 | 21,750 47,950 | 33.2 1,172 |
| | 5,879 19'3³/₈" | 2,330 7'7³/₄" | 2,370 7'9¹/₄" | 2,330 7'7³/₄" | 2,290 7'6¹/₈" | 24,000 52,910 | 2,250 4,960 | 21,750 47,950 | 33.0 1,165 |
| | 5,889 19'3⁷/₈" | 2,346 7'8³/₈" | 2,372 7'9³/₈" | 2,330 7'7³/₄" | 2,272 7'5¹/₂" | 24,000 52,910 | 2,360 5,200 | 21,640 47,710 | 32.8 1,158 |
| | 5,885 19'4" | 2,350 7'8¹/₂" | 2,403 7'10⁵/₈" | 2,338 7'8" | 2,292 7'6¹/₄" | 24,000 52,910 | 2,150 4,740 | 21,850 48,170 | 33.15 1,170 |
| | 5,884 19'3⁵/₈" | 2,335 7'8" | 2,390 7'10" | 2,335 7'8" | 2,292 7'6¹/₄" | 24,000 52,910 | 2,200 4,850 | 21,800 48,060 | 33.1 1,169 |
| | 5,899 19'4¹/₄" | 2,350 7'8¹/₂" | 2,394 7'10¹/₄" | 2,338 7'8" | 2,280 7'5³/₄" | 24,000 52,910 | 2,180 4,810 | 21,820 48,100 | 33.2 1,172 |
| | 5,891 19'3⁷/₈" | 2,330 7'7³/₄" | 2,376 7'9¹/₂" | 2,330 7'7³/₄" | 2,272 7'5¹/₂" | 24,000 52,910 | 2,300 5,070 | 21,700 47,840 | 33.0 1,165 |
| | 5,880 19'3¹/₂" | 2,330 7'7³/₄" | 2,380 7'9⁵/₈" | 2,330 7'7³/₄" | 2,275 7'5¹/₂" | 24,000 52,910 | 2,300 5,070 | 21,700 47,840 | 33.0 1,165 |

CONTAINERS

# General Purpose Container                                    40'

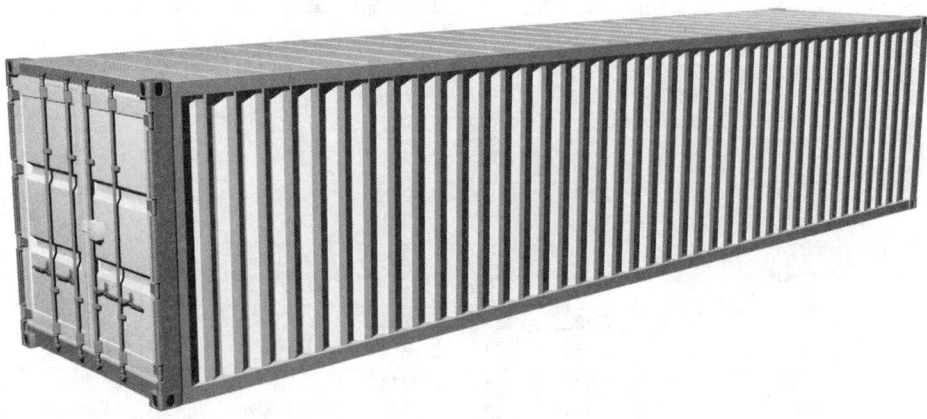

- Suitable for any general cargo.
- Various lashing devices on the top and bottom longitudinal rails and the corner posts.
  Lashing devices have a permissible load of 1,000 kg (2,205 lbs) each.
- Note permissable weight limits for road and rail transport.

## General Purpose Container                                    40'

| Construction | Inside Dimensions | | | Door Opening | | Weights | | | Capacity |
|---|---|---|---|---|---|---|---|---|---|
| | Length | Width | Height | Width | Height | Max. Gross | Tare | Max. Payload | |
| | mm<br>ft | mm<br>ft | mm<br>ft | mm<br>ft | mm<br>ft | kg<br>lbs | kg<br>lbs | kg<br>lbs | m³<br>cu.ft. |
| **8'6" high** | | | | | | | | | |
| Steel container with corrugated walls and wooden floor | 12,029<br>39'5¹/₂" | 2,350<br>7'8¹/₂" | 2,392<br>7'10¹/₈" | 2,340<br>7'8¹/₂" | 2,292<br>7'6¹/₄" | 30,480<br>67,200 | 3,780<br>8,330 | 26,700<br>58,870 | 67.7<br>2,390 |
| | 12,024<br>39'5³/₈" | 2,350<br>7'8¹/₂" | 2,387<br>7'10" | 2,340<br>7'8¹/₈" | 2,292<br>7'6¹/₄" | 30,480<br>67,200 | 3,810<br>8,400 | 26,670<br>58,800 | 67.7<br>2,390 |
| | 12,033<br>39'5³/₄" | 2,350<br>7'8¹/₂" | 2,394<br>7'10¹/₄" | 2,338<br>7'8" | 2,280<br>7'5³/₄" | 30,480<br>67,200 | 3,800<br>8,377 | 26,680<br>58,823 | 67.7<br>2,390 |

CONTAINERS

# High Cube General Purpose Container      **40'**

**9'6"**
**2.9m**

- Especially for light, voluminous cargo and overheight cargo up to maximum 2.70 m (8'10$^1/_4$") (see table).
- Numerous lashing devices on the top and bottom longitudinal rails and the corner posts.

- Lashing devices have a permissible load of 1,000 kg (2,205 lbs) each.
- Consider overheight for inland transportation.
- Note permissable weight limits for road and rail transport.

## High Cube General Purpose Container      **40'**

| Construction | Inside Dimensions | | | Door Opening | | Weights | | | Capacity |
|---|---|---|---|---|---|---|---|---|---|
| | Length | Width | Height | Width | Height | Max. Gross | Tare | Max. Payload | |
| | mm<br>ft | mm<br>ft | mm<br>ft | mm<br>ft | mm<br>ft | kg<br>lbs | kg<br>lbs | kg<br>lbs | m³<br>cu.ft. |
| **9'6" high** | | | | | | | | | |
| Steel container with corrugated walls and wooden floor | 12,024<br>39'5³/₈" | 2,350<br>7'8¹/₂" | 2,697<br>8'10¹/₈" | 2,340<br>7'8¹/₈" | 2,597<br>8'6¹/₄" | 30,480<br>67,200 | 4,020<br>8,860 | 26,460<br>58,340 | 76.3<br>2,694 |
| | 12,024<br>39'5³/₈" | 2,350<br>7'8¹/₂" | 2,697<br>8'10¹/₈" | 2,338<br>7'8" | 2,585<br>8'5³/₄" | 30,480<br>67,200 | 4,020<br>8,860 | 26,460<br>58,340 | 76.3<br>2,694 |

# Hardtop Container

## 20'

CONTAINERS

- This container type has been especially designed and developed for
  —heavy loads
  —high and excessively high loads
  —loading, e.g. by crane, through roof opening and door side.
- The steel roof of some series is lifted with fork-lift rings so that it can be removed by using a fork-lift. The weight of the steel roof is approx. 450 kg (990 lbs).
- With the roof removed and the door header swung out, it is much easier to load cargo using a crane via the door side.
- In case your cargo is overheight, the roof sections can be lashed to a sidewall inside the container using only some 13 cm (5 $^1/_8$") of space.
- If required, disposable tarpaulins can be provided for the transport which can be fastened to the walls on the outside using lashing devices.
- The capacity of the container floor exceeds the ISO 1496/1 standard by 33%, so that a fork-lift whose front axle weight does not exceed 7,280 kg (16,000 lbs) can be used inside.
- The hardtop container provides many lashing devices to fasten goods. The lashing devices on the corner posts and on the longitudinal rails of the roof and floor are capable of bearing loads of up to 2,000 kg (4,410 lbs) each, and those in the middle of the side walls up to 500 kg (1,100 lbs) each. Lashing to the side walls can only be done after the roof has been closed.

- This container type has been designed for heavy loads. While considering the technical data (including the permissible spreaded load limitations) please bear in mind the prevalent weight restrictions for land transport.
- Note permissable weight limits for road and rail transport.

## Hardtop Container       20'

| Construction | Inside Dimensions | | | | Weights | | | Capacity |
|---|---|---|---|---|---|---|---|---|
| | Length | Width | Height | | Max. | Tare | Max. | |
| | | | Middle | Side | Gross | | Payload | |
| | mm<br>ft | mm<br>ft | mm<br>ft | mm<br>ft | kg<br>lbs | kg<br>lbs | kg<br>lbs | m³<br>cu.ft. |

### 8'6" high

| Steel<br>container<br>with<br>corrugated<br>walls and wooden<br>floor | 5,886<br>19'3¾" | 2,342<br>7'8⅛" | 2,388<br>7'10" | 2,313<br>7'7" | 30,480<br>67,200 | 2,700<br>5,950 | 27,780<br>61,250 | 32.8<br>1,160 |
|---|---|---|---|---|---|---|---|---|
| | 5,886<br>19'3¾" | 2,342<br>7'8⅛" | 2,388<br>7'10" | 2,313<br>7'7" | 30,480<br>67,200 | 2,700<br>5,950 | 27,780<br>61,250 | 32.8<br>1,160 |
| | 5,886<br>19'3¾" | 2,342<br>7'8⅛" | 2,375<br>7'9½" | 2,330<br>7'7¾" | 30,480<br>67,200 | 2,590<br>5,710 | 27,890<br>61,490 | 32.8<br>1,160 |
| | 5,871<br>19'3⅛" | 2,338<br>7'8" | 2,390<br>7'10" | 2,335<br>7'8" | 24,000<br>52,910 | 2,580<br>5,690 | 21,420<br>47,220 | 32.8<br>1,158 |

### Roof Opening

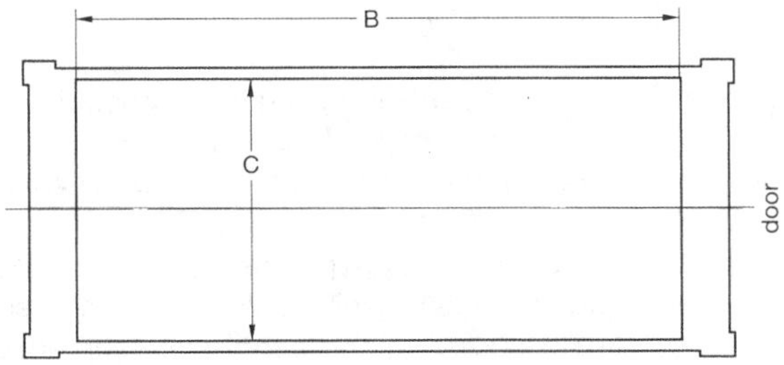

### Door Opening

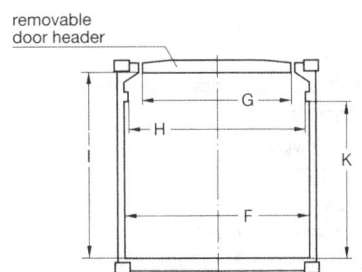

removable
door header

## Hardtop Container  Roof Openings      20'

| Roof Openings | | Door Openings | | | | | Roof Inside Container | | |
|---|---|---|---|---|---|---|---|---|---|
| Length | Width | Width | | | Height | | Reduced Width | | |
| B<br>Between<br>Gusset<br>Plates<br>mm<br>ft | C<br>Max.<br>Width<br>mm<br>ft | F<br>Max.<br>Width<br>mm<br>ft | G<br>At<br>Door<br>Header<br>mm<br>ft | H<br>Between<br>Top Longi-<br>tudinal<br>Rails<br>mm<br>ft | I<br>Up to<br>Door<br>Header<br>mm<br>ft | K<br>Up to Top<br>Longitudi-<br>nal Rail<br>mm<br>ft | Inside<br>Width<br>mm<br>ft | Width of<br>Roof<br>Opening<br>mm<br>ft | Width of<br>Door<br>Opening<br>mm<br>ft |
| 5,590<br>18'4" | 2,208<br>7'2⅞" | 2,336<br>7'8" | 1,896<br>6'2⅝" | 2,208<br>7'2⅞" | 2,276<br>7'5⅝" | 2,220<br>7'⅜" | 2,209<br>7'3" | 2,142<br>7'¼" | 2,206<br>7'2⅞" |
| 5,590<br>18'4" | 2,208<br>7'2⅞" | 2,336<br>7'8" | 1,896<br>6'2⅝" | 2,208<br>7'2⅞" | 2,292<br>7'6¼" | 2,220<br>7'⅜" | 2,209<br>7'3" | 2,142<br>7'¼" | 2,206<br>7'2⅞" |
| 5,590<br>18'4" | 2,208<br>7'2⅞" | 2,336<br>7'8" | 1,896<br>6'2⅝" | 2,208<br>7'2⅞" | 2,280<br>7'5¾" | 2,231<br>7'3¾" | 2,215<br>7'3⅛" | 2,148<br>7'½" | 2,212<br>7'3" |
| 5,616<br>18'5⅛" | 2,206<br>7'2⅞" | 2,335<br>7'8" | 1,890<br>6'2⅜" | 2,206<br>7'2⅞" | 2,292<br>7'6¼" | 2,225<br>7'3½" | 2,250<br>7'4½" | 2,180<br>7'1¾" | 2,250<br>7'4½" |

CONTAINERS

# Hardtop Container         **40'**

**C O N T A I N E R S**

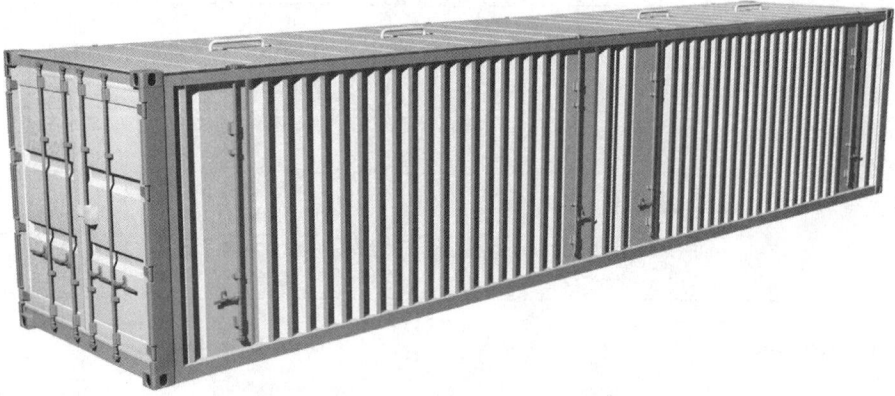

- The 40' hardtop container has particularly been constructed for:
  —long loads which cannot be transported in the 20' hardtop container
  —heavy loads
  —high and excessively high loads
  —loading, e.g. by crane, through roof opening and door side.
- The roof can be removed by using a fork-lift. The weight of the steel roof is approx. 450 kg (990 lbs) each section.
- With the roof removed and the door-header swung out, it is much easier to load cargo using a crane via the door side.
- In case your cargo is overheight, the roof sections can be lashed to a sidewall inside the container using only some 13 cm (5 $1/_8$") of space.
- If required, disposable tarpaulins can be provided for the transport which can be fastened to the walls on the outside using lashing devices.
- The capacity of the container floor exceeds the ISO 1496/1 standard by 33%, so that a fork-lift whose front axle weight does not exceed 7,280 kg (16,000 lbs) can be used inside.
- The hardtop container provides many lashing devices to fasten goods. The lashing devices on the corner posts and on the longitudinal rails of the roof and floor are capable of bearing loads of up to 2,000 kg (4,410 lbs) each, and those in the middle of the side walls up to 500 kg (1,100 lbs) each. Lashing to the side walls can only be done after the roof has been closed.

- The roof can easily be raised by about 70 mm (2 $3/_4$"), using the roof locking devices so that the door-header can be swung out without removing the roof.
- This container type has been designed for heavy loads. While considering the technical data (including the permissible spreaded load limitations) please bear in mind the prevalent weight restrictions for land transport.
- Note permissable weight limits for road and rail transport.

## Hardtop Container 40'

| Construction | Inside Dimensions | | | | Weights | | | Capacity |
|---|---|---|---|---|---|---|---|---|
| | Length | Width | Height | | Max. | Tare | Max. | |
| | | | Middle | Side | Gross | | Payload | |
| | mm<br>ft | mm<br>ft | mm<br>ft | mm<br>ft | kg<br>lbs | kg<br>lbs | kg<br>lbs | $m^3$<br>cu.ft. |
| **8'6" high** | | | | | | | | |
| Steel container with corrugated walls and wooden floor | 12,020<br>39'5 1/4" | 2,342<br>7'8 1/8" | 2,388<br>7'10" | 2,313<br>7'7" | 30,480<br>67,200 | 4,700<br>10,360 | 25,780<br>56,840 | 67.2<br>2,374 |
| | 12,020<br>39'5 1/4" | 2,342<br>7'8 1/8" | 2,388<br>7'10" | 2,313<br>7'7" | 30,480<br>67,200 | 4,700<br>10,360 | 25,780<br>56,840 | 67.2<br>2,374 |

**Roof Opening**

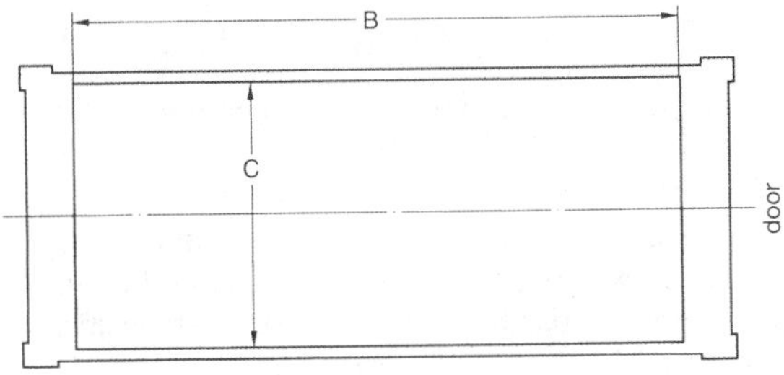


**Door Opening**

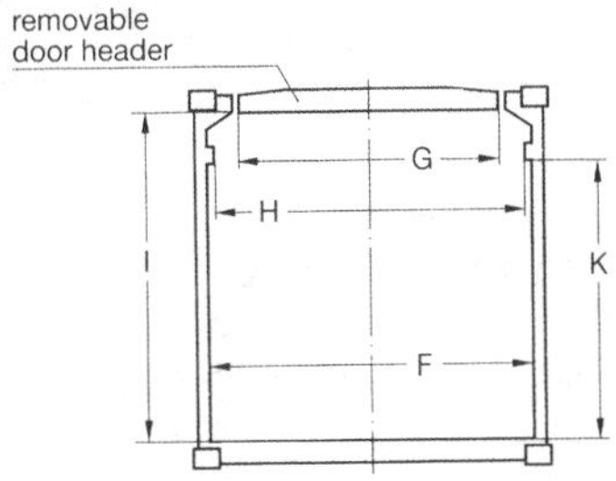


## Hardtop Container 40'

| Roof Openings | | Door Openings | | | | | Roof Inside Container | | |
|---|---|---|---|---|---|---|---|---|---|
| Length | Width | Width | | | Height | | Reduced Width | | |
| B<br>Between Gusset Plates<br>mm<br>ft | C<br>Max. Width<br>mm<br>ft | F<br>Max. Width<br>mm<br>ft | G<br>At Door Header<br>mm<br>ft | H<br>Between Top Longitudinal Rails<br>mm<br>ft | I<br>Up to Door Header<br>mm<br>ft | K<br>Up to Top Longitudinal Rail<br>mm<br>ft | Inside Width<br>mm<br>ft | Width of Roof Opening<br>mm<br>ft | Width of Door Opening<br>mm<br>ft |
| 11,724<br>38'5" | 2,208<br>7'2 7/8" | 2,336<br>7'8" | 1,896<br>6'2 5/8" | 2,208<br>7'2 7/8" | 2,292<br>7'6 1/4" | 2,220<br>7'3 3/8" | 2,209<br>7'3" | 2,142<br>7' 3/8" | 2,206<br>7'2 7/8" |
| 11,724<br>38'5" | 2,208<br>7'2 7/8" | 2,336<br>7'8" | 1,896<br>6'2 5/8" | 2,208<br>7'2 7/8" | 2,276<br>7'5 5/8" | 2,220<br>7'3 3/8" | 2,209<br>7'3" | 2,142<br>7' 3/8" | 2,206<br>7'2 7/8" |

# Open Top Container       20'

- Especially for:
  —overheight cargo
  —loading from top side, e.g. by crane
  —loading from door side, e.g. with cargo hanging from overhead tackle.
- Door header can be swung out on all open top containers.
- If required, disposable tarpaulins can be provided. For fastening tarpaulins, lashing bars are available on the outside of the walls. Using one way tarpaulins requires the corner castings to be accessible.
- Fork-lift pockets on a number of containers (please see footnote 1).

- The capacity of the floor for use of fort-lift trucks exceeds the ISO standards by 33% on all 20' open top containers.
- Numerous lashing devices are located on the top and bottom longitudinal rails and the corner posts. Lashing devices have a permissible load of 1,000 kg (2,205 lbs) each.
- Dimensions of roof and door openings are on the next page.
- Note permissable weight limits for road and rail transport.
- 
- 
- 
- 

## Open Top Container Dimensions       20'

| Construction | Inside Dimensions | | | | Weights | | | Capacity |
|---|---|---|---|---|---|---|---|---|
| | Length | Width | Height | | Max. | Tare | Max. | |
| | | | Middle | Side | Gross | | Payload | |
| | mm<br>ft | mm<br>ft | mm<br>ft | mm<br>ft | kg<br>lbs | kg<br>lbs | kg<br>lbs | m³<br>cu.ft. |
| **8'6" high** | | | | | | | | |
| Steel container with corrugated walls, removable tarpaulin and wooden floor | 5,895<br>19'4" | 2,350<br>7'8½" | 2,394<br>7'10¼" | 2,364<br>7'9" | 24,000<br>52,910 | 2,100<br>4,630 | 21,900<br>48,280 | 32.45<br>1,146 |
| | 5,877<br>19'3⅜" | 2,335<br>7'8" | 2,369<br>7'9¼" | 2,309<br>7'6⅞" | 24,000<br>52,910 | 2,200<br>4,850 | 21,800<br>48,060 | 32.4<br>1,140 |
| | 5,895<br>19'4" | 2,330<br>7'7¾" | 2,329<br>7'7¾" | — | 24,000<br>52,910 | 2,200<br>4,850 | 21,800<br>48,060 | 32.0<br>1,130 |
| | 5,888<br>19'3¾" | 2,345<br>7'8⅛" | 2,365<br>7'9" | 2,315<br>7'7⅛" | 30,480<br>67,200 | 2,250<br>4,960 | 28,230<br>62,240 | 32.0<br>1,130 |

## Roof and Door Openings of Open Top Containers 20'

### Types:

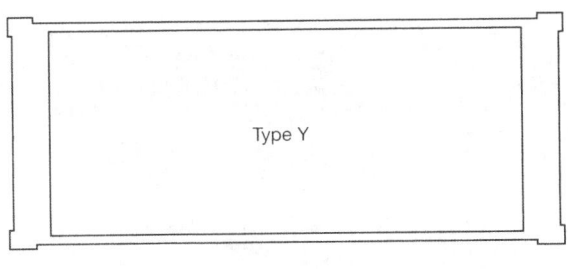

Type Y

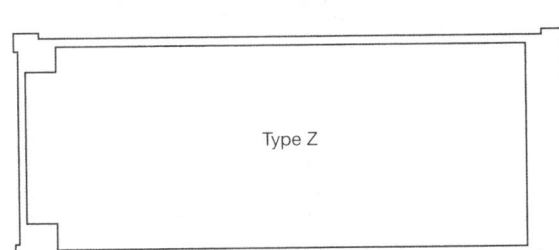

Type Z

### Door Openings:

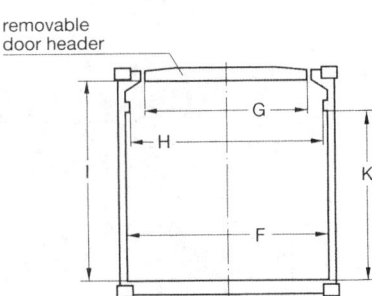

removable door header

### Roof Openings:

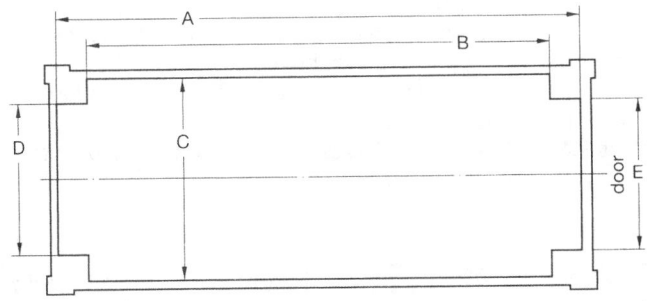

## Roof and Door Openings of Open Top Containers 20'

| Type | Roof Openings | | | | | Door Openings | | | | |
|---|---|---|---|---|---|---|---|---|---|---|
| | Length | | Width | | | Width | | | Height | |
| | A Max. Length | B Between Gusset Plates | C Max. Width | D Front End between Gusset Plates | E Door End, between Gusset Plates | F Max. Width | G At Door Header | H Between Top Longitudinal Rails | I Up to Door Header | K Up to Top Longitudinal Rail |
| | mm ft | mm ft | mm ft | mm ft | mm ft | mm ft | mm ft | mm ft | mm ft | mm ft |
| Z | 5,583 18'3³/₄" | 5,488 18" | 2,230 7'3³/₄" | 1,928 6'3⁷/₈" | — | 2,335 7'8" | 1,928 6'3⁷/₈" | 2,230 7'3³/₄" | 2,291 7'6¹/₄" | 2,194 7'2³/₈" |
| Z | 5,660 18'6⁷/₈" | 5,440 17'10¹/₈" | 2,208 7'2⁷/₈" | 1,860 6'1¹/₄" | — | 2,335 7'8" | 1,848 6'¹³/₄" | 2,208 7'2⁷/₈" | 2,290 7'6¹/₈" | 1,889 6'2³/₈" |
| Z | 5,770 18'11¹/₈" | 5,452 17'10⁵/₈" | 2,232 7'3⁷/₈" | — | 1,904 6'3" | 2,305 7'6³/₄" | 1,834 6'¹/₈" | 2,208 7'3⁷/₈" | 2,218 7'3¹/₄" | 2,033 6'8" |
| Z | 5,415 17'9¹/₈" | 5,360 17'7" | 2,205 7'2³/₄" | — | 1,880 6'2" | 2,335 7'8" | 1,880 6'2" | 2,205 7'2³/₄" | 2,280 7'5³/₄" | 2,125 6'11⁵/₈" |

## Open Top Container                                                    40'

- Especially for:
  —overheight cargo
  —loading from top side, e.g. by crane
  —loading from door side, e.g. with cargo
  hanging from overhead tackle.
- Door header can be swung out on all open top containers.
- If required, disposable tarpaulins can be provided. For fastening tarpaulins, lashing bars are available on the outside of the walls. Using one way tarpaulins requires the corner castings to be accessible.

- The capacity of the floor for use of fort-lift trucks exceeds the ISO standards by 33% on all 40' open top containers.
- Numerous lashing devices are located on the top and bottom longitudinal rails and the corner posts.
  Lashing devices have a permissible load of 1,000 kg (2,205 lbs) each.
- Dimensions of roof and door openings follow in two pages.
- Note permissable weight limits for road and rail transport.
-

## Open Top Container Dimensions                                        40'

| Construction | Inside Dimensions | | | | Weights | | | Capacity |
|---|---|---|---|---|---|---|---|---|
| | Length | Width | Height | | Max. | Tare | Max. | |
| | | | Middle | Side | Gross | | Payload | |
| | mm | mm | mm | mm | kg | kg | kg | m³ |
| | ft | ft | ft | ft | lbs | lbs | lbs | cu.ft. |
| **8'6" high** | | | | | | | | |
| Steel container with corrugated walls, removable tarpaulin and wooden floor | 12,023 | 2,335 | 2,378 | 2,318 | 30,480 | 3,800 | 26,680 | 66.7 |
| | 39'5³/₈" | 7'8" | 7'9⁵/₈" | 7'7¹/₄" | 67,200 | 8,380 | 58,820 | 2,354 |
| | 12,038 | 2,338 | 2,363 | 2,313 | 30,480 | 3,650 | 26,830 | 66.7 |
| | 39'5⁷/₈" | 7'8" | 7'9" | 7'7¹/₈" | 67,200 | 8,050 | 59,150 | 2,354 |
| | 12,025 | 2,330 | 2,360 | 2,325 | 30,480 | 3,890 | 26,590 | 66.0 |
| | 39'5¹/₂" | 7'7³/₄" | 7'8⁷/₈" | 7'7¹/₂" | 67,200 | 8,580 | 58,620 | 2,330 |
| | 12,038 | 2,336 | 2,370 | 2,320 | 30,480 | 3,700 | 26,780 | 65.3 |
| | 39'5⁷/₈" | 7'8" | 7'9¹/₄" | 7'7¹/₄" | 67,197 | 8,157 | 59,040 | 2,306 |
| | 12,029 | 2,342 | 2,376 | 2,326 | 30,480 | 3,810 | 26,670 | 65.5 |
| | 39'5¹/₂" | 7'8¹/₈" | 7'9¹/₂" | 7'7¹/₂" | 67,200 | 8,400 | 58,800 | 2,310 |
| | 12,022 | 2,346 | 2,365 | 2,315 | 30,480 | 3,740 | 26,740 | 65.3 |
| | 39'5¹/₄" | 7'8³/₈" | 7'9¹/₈" | 7'7¹/₈" | 67,200 | 8,250 | 58,950 | 2,306 |
| | 12,007 | 2,315 | 2,362 | 2,317 | 30,480 | 3,950 | 26,530 | 65.0 |
| | 39'4³/₄" | 7'7¹/₈" | 7'9" | 7'7¹/₄" | 67,200 | 8,710 | 58,490 | 2,295 |
| | 12,005 | 2,330 | 2,380 | 2,340 | 30,480 | 4,350 | 26,130 | 65.5 |
| | 39'4⁵/₈" | 7'7³/₄" | 7'9⁵/₈" | 7'8¹/₈" | 67,200 | 9,590 | 57,610 | 2,315 |

## Open Top Container Dimensions 40'

| Construction | Inside Dimensions | | | | Weights | | | Capacity |
|---|---|---|---|---|---|---|---|---|
| | Length | Width | Height | | Max. | Tare | Max. | |
| | | | Middle | Side | Gross | | Payload | |
| | mm ft | mm ft | mm ft | mm ft | kg lbs | kg lbs | kg lbs | m³ cu.ft. |

### 8'6" high

| Steel container with corrugated walls, removable tarpaulin and wooden floor | 12,023 39'5³/₈" | 2,335 7'8" | 2,378 7'9⁵/₈" | 2,318 7'7¹/₄" | 30,480 67,200 | 3,800 8,380 | 26,680 58,820 | 66.7 2,354 |
|---|---|---|---|---|---|---|---|---|
| | 12,038 39'5⁷/₈" | 2,338 7'8" | 2,363 7'9" | 2,313 7'7¹/₈" | 30,480 67,200 | 3,650 8,050 | 26,830 59,150 | 66.7 2,354 |
| | 12,025 39'5¹/₂" | 2,330 7'3³/₄" | 2,360 7'8⁷/₈" | 2,325 7'7¹/₂" | 30,480 67,200 | 3,890 8,580 | 26,590 58,620 | 66.0 2,330 |
| | 12,038 39'5⁷/₈" | 2,336 7'8" | 2,370 7'9¹/₄" | 2,320 7'7¹/₄" | 30,480 67,197 | 3,700 8,157 | 26,780 59,040 | 65.3 2,306 |
| | 12,029 39'5¹/₂" | 2,342 7'8¹/₈" | 2,376 7'9¹/₂" | 2,326 7'7¹/₂" | 30,480 67,200 | 3,810 8,400 | 26,670 58,800 | 65.5 2,310 |
| | 12,022 39'5¹/₄" | 2,346 7'8³/₈" | 2,365 7'9¹/₈" | 2,315 7'7¹/₈" | 30,480 67,200 | 3,740 8,250 | 26,740 58,950 | 65.3 2,306 |
| | 12,007 39'4³/₄" | 2,315 7'7¹/₈" | 2,362 7'9" | 2,317 7'7¹/₄" | 30,480 67,200 | 3,950 8,710 | 26,530 58,490 | 65.0 2,295 |
| | 12,005 39'4⁵/₈" | 2,330 7'3³/₄" | 2,380 7'9⁵/₈" | 2,340 7'8¹/₈" | 30,480 67,200 | 4,350 9,590 | 26,130 57,610 | 65.5 2,315 |

CONTAINERS

## Roof and Door Openings of Open Top Containers    40'

### Types:

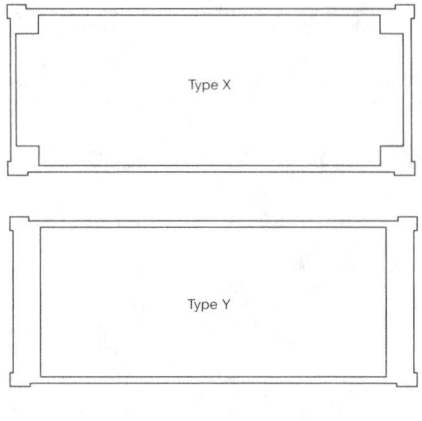

### Door Openings:

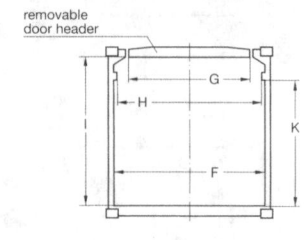

### Roof Opening:

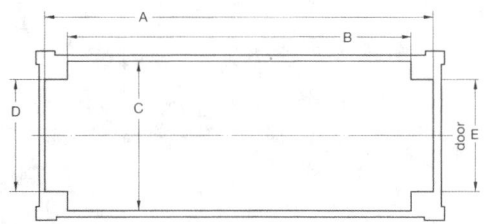

C O N T A I N E R S

## Roof and Door Openings of Open Top Containers    40'

| Type | Roof Openings | | | | | Door Openings | | | | |
|---|---|---|---|---|---|---|---|---|---|---|
| | Length | | Width | | | Width | | | Height | |
| | A Max. Length | B Between Gusset Plates | C Max. Width | D Front End between Gusset Plates mm ft | E Door End, between Gusset Plates mm ft | F Max. Width | G At Door Header | H Between Top Longitudinal Rails | I Up to Door Header mm ft | K Up to Top Longitudinal Rail |
| | mm ft | mm ft | mm ft | | | mm ft | mm ft | mm ft | | mm ft |
| Z | 11,800 38'8⅝" | 11,317 37'1½" | 2,205 7'2¾" | 1,728 5'8" | — | 2,335 7'8" | 1,840 6'½" | 2,205 7'2¾" | 2,287 7'6" | 1,889 6'2⅜" |
| Z | 11,787 38'8" | 11,563 37'11¼" | 2,208 7'2⅞" | 1,850 6'7⅞" | — | 2,335 7'8" | 1,844 6'5⅝" | 2,208 7'2⅞" | 2,287 7'6" | 1,896 6'2⅝" |
| X | 11,917 39'1⅛" | 10,837 35'6⅝" | 2,128 6'11¾" | 1,600 5'3" | 1,816 5'11½" | 2,330 7'7¾" | 1,816 5'11½" | 2,128 6'11⅞" | 2,201 7'2⅝" | 1,957 6'5" |
| Y | — | 11,550 37'10⅝" | 2,220 7'3⅜" | — | — | 2,336 7'8" | 1,845 6'5⅝" | 2,220 7'3⅜" | 2,292 7'6¼" | 2,125 6'11⅝" |
| Z | 11,544 37'10½" | 11,444 37'6½" | 2,230 7'3¾" | — | 1,885 6'2⅛" | 2,336 7'8" | 1,885 6'2⅛" | 2,230 7'3¾" | 2,280 7'5¾" | 2,146 7'½" |
| Z | 11,550 37'10¾" | 11,515 37'9⅜" | 2,205 7'2¾" | — | 1,880 6'2" | 2,335 7'8" | 1,880 6'2" | 2,205 7'2¾" | 2,280 7'5¾" | 2,125 6'11⅝" |
| Y | — | 11,379 37'4" | 2,205 7'2¾" | — | — | 2,315 7'7⅛" | 1,855 6'1" | 2,205 7'2¾" | 2,266 7'5¼" | 1,957 6'5" |
| X | 11,825 38'9½" | 11,496 37'8⅝" | 2,100 6'10⅝" | 1,774 5'9⅞" | 1,774 5'9⅞" | 2,335 7'8" | 1,750 5'8⅞" | 2,100 6'10⅝" | 2,180 7'1¾" | 2180 7'1¾" |

# Flat                                              40'

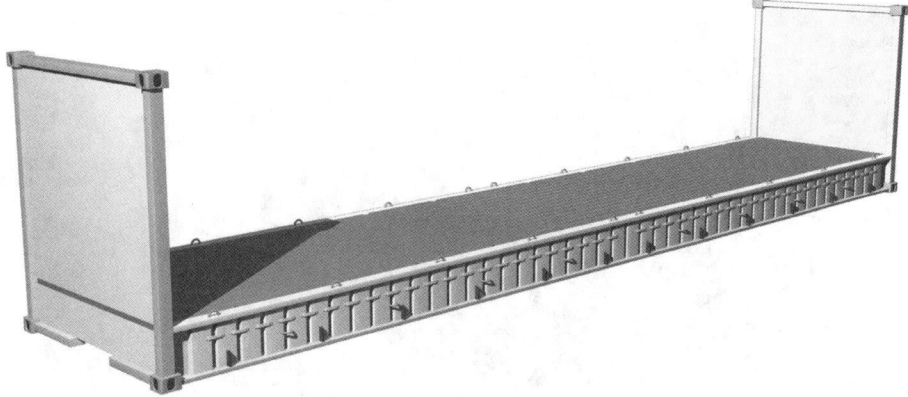

- Especially for heavy loads and overwidth cargo.
- Higher loadings possible.
- Strong bottom construction with fixed endwalls (which allow bracing and lashing of cargo as well as stacking).
- Gooseneck tunnel on both ends of 40' flats.
- Numerous very strong lashing devices on the corner posts, longitudinal rails and the floor. Lashing devices on the longitudinal rails and on the floor of 40' containers have a permissible load of 4,000 kg respectively (8,820 lbs) each.

- Maximum payload can only be used if distributed over the total floor area of the flat. If concentration of heavy load on a small part floor area is required please contact representative for stowage advice.
- Flats are delivered without stanchions. If stancions are required, please contact representative upon booking.
- Note permissable weight limits for road and rail transport.

**Flat**                                              **40'**

| Construction | Inside Dimensions | | | | | | Weights | | |
|---|---|---|---|---|---|---|---|---|---|
| | Length of floor mm ft | Width between Corner Posts mm ft | Width of Floor mm ft | Width between Stanchions mm ft | Height mm ft | Height of Bottom mm ft | Max. Gross kg lbs | Tare kg lbs | Max. Payload kg lbs |
| **8'6" high** | | | | | | | | | |
| Steelframe with fixed endwalls and softwood floor | 12,008 39'4³/₄" | 11,712 38'5¹/₈" | 2,318 7'7¹/₄" | 2,232 7'3⁷/₈" | 1,981 6'6" | 610 2' | 30,480 67,200 | 4,750 10,470 | 25,730 56,730 |
| | 11,990 39'4" | 11,722 38'5¹/₂" | 2,400 7'10¹/₂" | 2,202 7'2³/₄" | 1,981 6'6" | 610 2' | 30,480 67,200 | 5,100 11,240 | 25,380 55,960 |
| | 11,990 39'4" | 11,758 38'6⁷/₈" | 2,338 7'8" | 2,228 7'3³/₄" | 1,981 6'6" | 610 2' | 30,480 67,200 | 4,200 9,265 | 26,280 57,935 |
| | 12,010 39'4⁷/₈" | 11,832 38'9⁷/₈" | 2,228 7'3³/₄" | 2,228 7'3³/₄" | 1,981 6'6" | 610 2' | 30,480 67,200 | 4,200 9,265 | 26,280 57,935 |
| | 12,086 39'7⁷/₈" | 11,826 38'9⁵/₈" | 2,224 7'3¹/₂" | 2,224 7'3¹/₂" | 1,981 6'6" | 610 2' | 30,480 67,200 | 4,200 9,265 | 26,280 57,935 |
| | 12,010 39'4⁷/₈" | 11,826 38'9⁵/₈" | 2,244 7'4³/₈" | 2,204 7'2³/₄" | 1,981 6'6" | 610 2' | 30,480 67,200 | 4,200 9,265 | 26,280 57,935 |
| **9'6" high** | | | | | | | | | |
| Steel container with collapsible endwalls and softwood floor | 12,060 39'6³/₄" | 11,660 38'3¹/₈" | 2,365 7'9¹/₈" | 2,200 7'2⁵/₈" | 2,245 7'4³/₈" | 648 2'1¹/₂" | 45,000 99,210 | 5,700 12,570 | 39,300 86,640 |

CONTAINERS

# Flat                                                20'

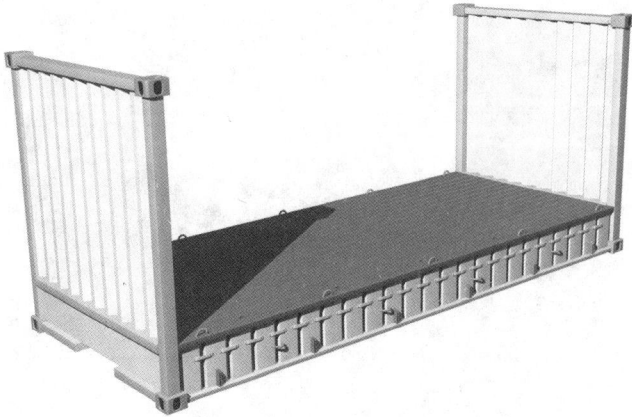

- Especially for heavy and overwidth cargo.
- Strong bottom construction with fixed endwalls (which allow bracing and lashing of cargo as well as stacking).
- Fork-lift pockets on a number of 20' flats
- Numerous very strong lashing devices on the corner posts, longitudinal rails and on the floor. Lashing devices on the longitudinal rails of 20' containers have a permissible load of 2,000 kg or 4,000 kg respectively (4,410 lbs or 8,820 lbs respectively) each.

- Maximum payload can only be used if distributed over the total floor area.
  If concentration of heavy load on a small part floor area is required please contact representative for stowage advice.
- Flats are delivered without stanchions. If stancions are required, please contact representative upon booking.
- Note permissable weight limits for road and rail transport.

## Flat                                              20'

| Construction | Inside Dimensions | | | | | | Weights | | |
|---|---|---|---|---|---|---|---|---|---|
| | Length of floor mm ft | Width between Corner Posts mm ft | Width of floor mm ft | Width between Stanchions mm ft | Height mm ft | Height of Bottom mm ft | Max. Gross kg lbs | Tare kg lbs | Max. Payload kg lbs |
| **8' high** | | | | | | | | | |
| Steelframe with fixed endwalls and softwood floor | 5,918 19'5" | 5,625 18'5³/₈" | 2,398 7'10³/₈" | 2,208 7'2⁷/₈" | 2,172 7'1¹/₂" | 265 10¹/₂" | 24,000 52,910 | 2,800 6,170 | 21,200 46,740 |
| **8'6" high** | | | | | | | | | |
| Steelframe with fixed endwalls and softwood floor | 5,902 19'4³/₈" | 5,700 18'8³/₈" | 2,358 7'8⁷/₈" | 2,235 7'4" | 2,276 7'5⁵/₈" | 315 1³/₈" | 24,000 52,910 | 2,720 6,000 | 21,280 46,910 |
| | 5,980 19'7³/₈" | 5,698 18'8³/₈" | 2,230 7'3³/₄" | 2,245 7'4³/₈" | 2,255 7'4³/₄" | 336 1¹/₄" | 24,000 52,910 | 2,500 5,510 | 21,500 47,400 |
| | 5,962 19'6³/₄" | 5,672 18'7¹/₄" | 2,242 7'4¹/₄" | 2,242 7'4¹/₄" | 2,261 7'5" | 330 1'1" | 30,000 66,140 | 2,200 4,850 | 27,800 61,290 |
| Steel container with collapsible endwalls and softwood floors. | 5,956 19'6¹/₂" | 5,658 18'6³/₄" | 2,418 7'11¹/₈" | 2,181 7'1⁷/₈" | 2,320 7'7³/₈" | 271 10⁵/₈" | 33,050 72,860 | 3,045 6,710 | 30,005 66,150 |

# Platform       20' / 40'

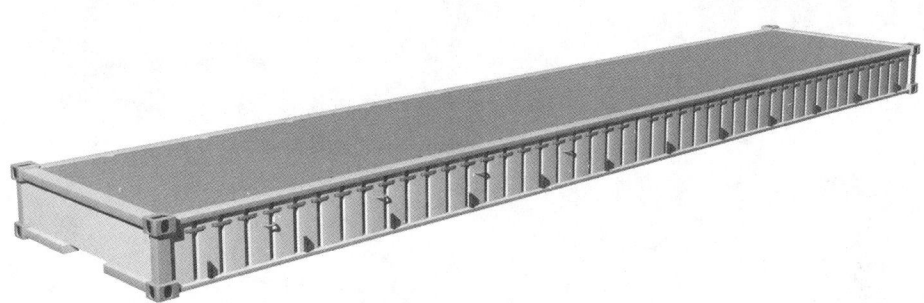

- Especially for heavy loads and oversized cargo.
- Strong bottom construction.
- Gooseneck tunnel on both ends of all 40' platforms.
- Numerous very strong lashing devices on the longitudinal rails. Lashing devices have a permissible load of 3,000 kg (6,615 lbs) each.

- Transport of heavy loads concentrated on a small load transfer area is possible. Contact your representative for details.

## Platform Dimensions       20'

| Construction | Dimensions | | | Weights | | |
|---|---|---|---|---|---|---|
| | Length<br><br>mm<br>ft | Width<br><br>mm<br>ft | Height<br>of bottom<br>mm<br>ft | Max.<br>Gross<br>kg<br>lbs | Tare<br><br>kg<br>lbs | Max.<br>Payload<br>kg<br>lbs |
| **1'1¼" high** | | | | | | |
| Steelframe with softwood floor | 6,058<br>20' | 2,438<br>8' | 335<br>1'1¼" | 24,000<br>52,910 | 2,100<br>4,630 | 21,900<br>48,280 |

## Platform Dimensions       40'

| Construction | Dimensions | | | Weights | | |
|---|---|---|---|---|---|---|
| | Length<br><br>mm<br>ft | Width<br><br>mm<br>ft | Height<br>of bottom<br>mm<br>ft | Max.<br>Gross<br>kg<br>lbs | Tare<br><br>kg<br>lbs | Max.<br>Payload<br>kg<br>lbs |
| **2' high** | | | | | | |
| Steelframe with softwood floor | 12,192<br>40' | 2,438<br>8' | 610<br>2' | 45,000<br>99,210" | 4,200<br>9,260 | 40,800<br>89,950 |

CONTAINERS

# Insulated Container                                     20' / 40'

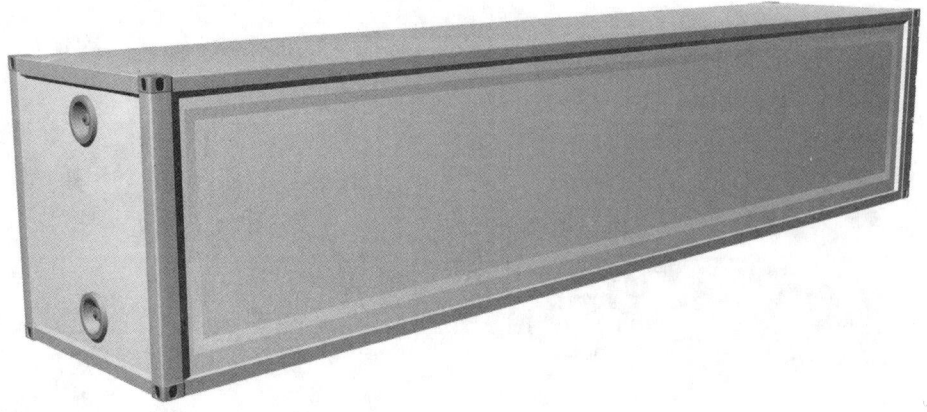

**Porthole Type**
- Especially for cargo which needs constant temperatures above or below freezing point.
- Walls in "sandwich-construction", with Polyurethane foam to provide maximum insulation.
- Temperature is controlled by ship's/terminal's cooling plant or "clip-on" unit.
- The air, delivered at the correct temperature, is circulated in the container through two aperatures in the front wall (supply air via the lower aperature, return air via the upper aperature).
- Possible temperatures inside the 20' containers, depending on specification of respective cooling device, from about +12°C to -25°C (+54°F to -14°F).
- Please note maximum stowage height in below table and as indicated by red line inside container in order to ensure proper ventilation.
- Possible temperatures inside the 40' containers, depending on specification of respective cooling device, from about +13°C to -22°C (+57°F to -8°F).
- Note permissable weight limits for road and rail transport.

## Insulated Container 20'

| Construction | Inside Dimensions | | | Door Opening | | Weights | | | Capacity |
|---|---|---|---|---|---|---|---|---|---|
| | Length | Width | Max. Stowable Height | Width | Height | Max. Gross | Tare | Max. Payload | |
| | mm ft | mm ft | mm ft | mm ft | mm ft | kg lbs | kg lbs | kg lbs | m³ cu.ft. |

### 8' high

| Construction | Length | Width | Max. Stowable Height | Width | Height | Max. Gross | Tare | Max. Payload | Capacity |
|---|---|---|---|---|---|---|---|---|---|
| Steelframe. Walls: outside plywood, coated with GRP, inside GRP shell | 5,652 18'6½" | 2,235 7'4" | 2,000 6'6¾" | 2,235 7'4" | 2,083 6'10" | 20,320 44,800 | 2,500 5,510 | 17,820 39,290 | 26.35 930 |
| | 5,652 18'6½" | 2,235 7'4" | 2,000 6'6¾" | 2,235 7'4" | 2,083 6'10" | 24,000 52,910 | 2,450 5,400 | 21,550 47,510 | 26.3 930 |
| Steelframe. Walls outside and inside GRP. | 5,652 18'6½" | 2,235 7'8" | 2,000 6'6¾" | 2,218 7'3¼" | 2,083 6'10" | 20,320 44,800 | 2,633 5,800 | 17,687 39,000 | 26.3 930 |
| Steelframe. Walls outside and inside stainless steel. | 5,724 18'9⅜" | 2,286 7'6" | 2,014 6'7¼" | 2,286 7'6" | 2,067 6'9⅜" | 24,000 52,910 | 2,550 5,620 | 21,450 47,290 | 26.4 933 |

## Insulated Container 40'

| Construction | Inside Dimensions | | | Door Opening | | Weights | | | Capacity |
|---|---|---|---|---|---|---|---|---|---|
| | Length | Width | Max. Stowage Height | Width | Height | Max. Gross | Tare | Max. Payload | |
| | mm ft | mm ft | mm ft | mm ft | mm ft | kg lbs | kg lbs | kg lbs | m³ cu.ft. |

### 8' high

| Construction | Length | Width | Max. Stowage Height | Width | Height | Max. Gross | Tare | Max. Payload | Capacity |
|---|---|---|---|---|---|---|---|---|---|
| Steelframe. Walls: outside/inside: GRP coated plywood/stainless steel and aluminum/ aluminum | 11,750 38'6⅝" | 2,250 7'4½" | 2,080 6'9⅞" | 2,250 7'4½" | 2,180 7'1⅞" | 30,480 67,200 | 4,650 10,250 | 25,830 56,950 | 58.4 2,060 |
| | 11,840 38'10⅛" | 2,286 7'6" | 2,120 6'11½" | 2,286 7'6" | 2,195 7'2⅜" | 30,480 67,200 | 3,850 8,490 | 26,630 58,710 | 60.6 2,140 |

CONTAINERS

## Ventilated Container       40'

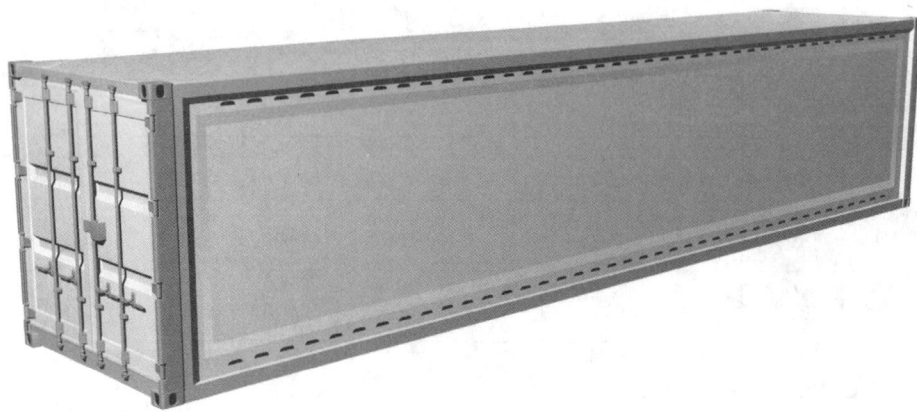

- Especially for cargo that needs ventilation.
- Natural ventilation is provided by openings in top and bottom longitudinal rails. The labyrinth construction of these ventilation openings ensures weather-proofness.

- Numerous lashing devices on the top and bottom longitudinal rails and the corner posts. Lashing devices have a permissible load of 1,000 kg (2,205 lbs) each.
- Note permissable weight limits for road and rail transport.

## Ventilated Container       20'

| Construction | Inside Dimensions | | | Door Opening | | Weights | | | Capacity |
|---|---|---|---|---|---|---|---|---|---|
| | Length | Width | Height | Width | Height | Max. Gross | Tare | Max. Payload | |
| | mm ft | mm ft | mm ft | mm ft | mm ft | kg lbs | kg lbs | kg lbs | m³ cu.ft. |
| **8'6" high** | | | | | | | | | |
| Steelframe. Walls: plywood, coated with GRP, wooden floor. | 5,930 19'5¹/₂" | 2,358 7'8⁷/₈" | 2,375 7'9¹/₂" | 2,335 7'8" | 2,292 7'6¹/₄" | 24,000 52,910 | 2,400 5,290 | 21,600 47,620 | 33.7 1,190 |
| Steel container with corrugated walls and wooden floor. | 5,888 19'3³/₄" | 2,346 7'8³/₈" | 2,392 7'10¹/₈" | 2,334 7'7⁷/₈" | 2,290 7'6¹/₈" | 30,480 67,200 | 2,400 5,290 | 28,080 61,910 | 33.0 1,167 |

CONTAINERS

# Bulk Container                                      20'

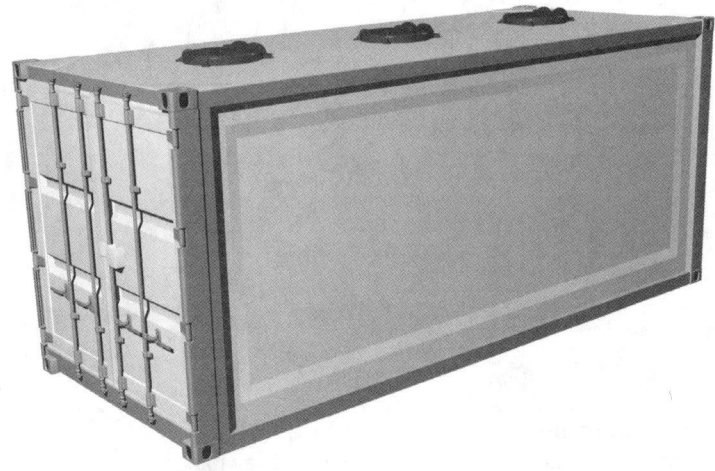

- Especially for dry bulk cargos, e.g. malt.
- Three manholes for top loading of each container. Distance centerline to centerline manhole 1.83 m (6').
- One discharge opening in each door wing. On demand, short discharge tubes can be installed to move the cargo in desired directions.
- Fastening of linerbag possible.

- Fork-lift pockets on a number of the containers.
- Lashing devices on the top longitudinal rails.
- Roof openings 455 mm (18") discharge door openings 340 x 380 mm ( 13.5" x 15").
- Note permissable weight limits for road and rail transport.

## Bulk Container                                      20'

| Construction | Inside Dimensions | | | Door Opening | | Weights | | | Capacity |
|---|---|---|---|---|---|---|---|---|---|
| | Length | Width | Height | Width | Height | Max. Gross | Tare | Max. Payload | |
| | mm<br>ft | mm<br>ft | mm<br>ft | mm<br>ft | mm<br>ft | kg<br>lbs | kg<br>lbs | kg<br>lbs | m³<br>cu.ft. |
| **8'6" high** | | | | | | | | | |
| Steelframe.<br>Walls: plywood,<br>coated with GRP. | 5,934<br>19'5½" | 2,358<br>7'8¾" | 2,340<br>7'8⅛" | 2,335<br>7'8" | 2,292<br>7'6¼" | 24,000<br>52,910 | 2,450<br>5,400 | 21,550<br>47,510 | 32.9<br>1,162 |
| | 5,931<br>19'5½" | 2,358<br>7'8¾" | 2,326<br>7'7⅝" | 2,335<br>7'8" | 2,292<br>7'6¼" | 24,000<br>52,910 | 2,370<br>5,220 | 21,630<br>47,690 | 32.9<br>1,162 |

CONTAINERS

## Refrigerated Container 20'

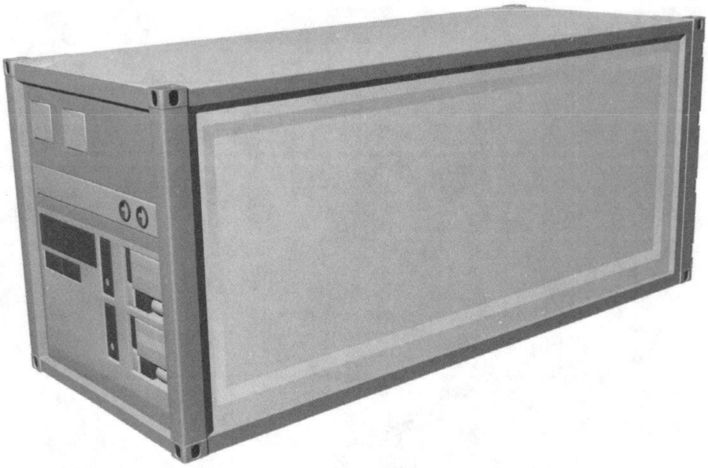



**Temperature Controlled Container**

- Especially for cargo that needs constant temperatures above or below freezing point.
- Controlled fresh-air supply is possible. Containers are ATO-approved (formerly SPRENGER).
- Walls in "sandwich-construction", with Polyurethane foam to provide maximum insulation.
- The reefer unit is a compact-design compressor unit with aircooled condenser. It switches automatically from cooling to heating operation (and vice versa), if a change of the outside temperatures makes it necessary.
- Please note maximum stowage height in below table and as indicated by red line inside container in order to ensure proper ventilation.
- Possible voltages:
  380V/50 Hz to 460 V/60Hz
  200 V/50 Hz to 220 V/60 Hz
- Refer to technical specifications and illustrations of electric plugs on refrigerated containers at the end of this chapter.
- Note permissable weight limits for road and rail transport.
- Permissable temperature setting:
  +25°C to -25°C (+77°F to -13°F).
- The set temperatures can be kept as long as the difference between outside and cargo temperatures does not exceed the following limits: for heating 42°C (76°F)
  for cooling 65°C (117°F).

### Refrigerated Container 20'

| Construction | Inside Dimensions | | | | Door Opening | | Weights | | | Capacity |
|---|---|---|---|---|---|---|---|---|---|---|
| | Length mm ft | Width mm ft | Height mm ft | Max. Stowable Height mm ft | Width mm ft | Height mm ft | Max. Gross kg lbs | Tare kg lbs | Max. Payload kg lbs | m³ cu.ft. |
| **8'6" high** | | | | | | | | | | |
| Steelframe. Walls: outside plywood, coated with GRP, inside GRP, inside stainless steel | 5,340<br>17'6 1/4" | 2,200<br>7'2 5/8" | 2,254<br>7'4 3/4" | 2,154<br>7' 3/4" | 2,200<br>7'2 5/8" | 2,220<br>7'3 3/8" | 24,000<br>52,910 | 3,380<br>7,450 | 20,620<br>45,460 | 26.4<br>932 |
| Steelframe. Walls outside and inside stainless steel | 5,479<br>17'11 5/8" | 2,286<br>7'6" | 2,257<br>7'4 7/8" | 2,157<br>7' 7/8" | 2,286<br>7'6" | 2,220<br>7'3 3/8" | 30,480<br>67,200 | 3,160<br>6,970 | 27,320<br>60,230 | 28.3<br>1,000 |
| | 5,459<br>17'10 7/8" | 2,295<br>7'6 1/8" | 2,268<br>7'6" | 2,168<br>7'1 3/8" | 2,291<br>7'6 1/8" | 2,259<br>7'4 7/8" | 30,480<br>67,200 | 3,050<br>6,720 | 27,430<br>60,480 | 28.4<br>1,003 |
| | 5,448<br>17'10 1/2" | 2,290<br>7'6 1/8" | 2,264<br>7'5 1/8" | 2,164<br>7'1 1/8" | 2,286<br>7'6" | 2,260<br>7'5" | 30,480<br>67,200 | 3,060<br>6,750 | 27,420<br>60,450 | 28.3<br>1,000 |

# Refrigerated Container      40'

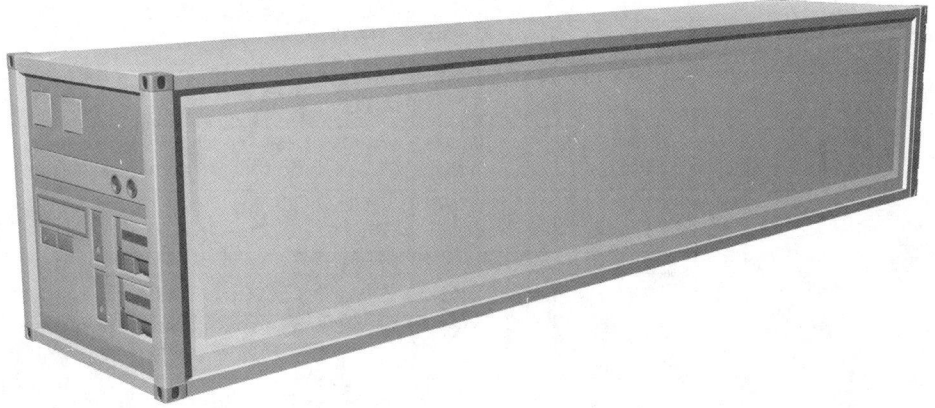

- Especially for cargo which needs constant temperatures above or below freezing point.
- Controlled fresh-air supply is possible. Containers are ATO-approved (formerly SPRENGER).
- Walls in "sandwich-construction", with Polyurethane foam to provide maximum insulation.
- The reefer unit is a compact-design compressor unit with aircooled condenser. It switches automatically from cooling to heating operation (and vice versa), if a change of the outside temperatures makes it necessary.
- Please note maximum stowage height in below table and as indicated by red line inside container in order to ensure proper ventilation.
- Possible voltages:
  380V/50 Hz to 460 V/60Hz
  200 V/50 Hz to 220 V/60 Hz
- Technical specifications and illustrations of electric plugs for refrigerated containers at the end of this chapter.
- Note permissable weight limits for road and rail transport.
- Possible temperature setting:
  +25°C to -25°C (+77°F to -13°F).
- Diesel generators are installed on some 40' containers to provide a power supply.
- The set temperatures can be kept as long as the difference between outside and cargo temperatures does not exceed the following limits:
  for heating 42°C (76°F)
  for cooling 60°C (108°F)

CONTAINERS

## Refrigerated Container 40'

| Construction | Inside Dimensions | | | | Door Opening | | Weights | | | Capacity |
|---|---|---|---|---|---|---|---|---|---|---|
| | Length<br>mm<br>ft | Width<br>mm<br>ft | Height<br>mm<br>ft | Max. Stowable Height<br>mm<br>ft | Width<br>mm<br>ft | Height<br>mm<br>ft | Max. Gross<br>kg<br>lbs | Tare<br>kg<br>lbs | Max. Payload<br>kg<br>lbs | m³<br>cu.ft. |

### 8' high

| Construction | Length mm / ft | Width mm / ft | Height mm / ft | Max. Stowable Height mm / ft | Door Width mm / ft | Door Height mm / ft | Max. Gross kg / lbs | Tare kg / lbs | Max. Payload kg / lbs | Capacity m³ / cu.ft. |
|---|---|---|---|---|---|---|---|---|---|---|
| Steelframe. Walls: outside plywood, coated with GRP, inside GRP shell | 11,141<br>36'4 5/8" | 2,197<br>7'2 1/2" | 2,216<br>7'3 1/4" | 2,096<br>6'10 1/2" | 2,197<br>7'2 1/2" | 2,173<br>7'1 1/2" | 30,480<br>67,200 | 6,010<br>13,250 | 24,470<br>53,950 | 54.2<br>1,920 |
| | 11,141<br>36'4 5/8" | 2,197<br>7'2 1/2" | 2,216<br>7'3 1/4" | 2,096<br>6'10 1/2" | 2,197<br>7'2 1/2" | 2,173<br>7'1 1/2" | 30,480<br>67,200 | 6,010<br>13,250 | 24,470<br>53,950 | 54.2<br>1,920 |
| Steelframe. Walls: outside plywood coated with GRP, inside stainless steel | 11,141<br>36'4 5/8" | 2,197<br>7'2 1/2" | 2,216<br>7'3 1/4" | 2,096<br>6'10 1/2" | 2,197<br>7'2 1/2" | 2,173<br>7'1 1/2" | 30,480<br>67,200 | 6,010<br>13,250 | 24,470<br>53,950 | 54.2<br>1,920 |
| | 11,140<br>36'4 5/8" | 2,226<br>7'3 5/8" | 2,221<br>7'3 3/8" | 2,101<br>6'10 5/8" | 2,226<br>7'3 5/8" | 2,173<br>7'1 1/2" | 30,480<br>67,200 | 6,010<br>13,250 | 24,470<br>53,950 | 55.0<br>1,945 |
| Steelframe. Walls: outside aluminum, inside stainless steel | 11,170<br>36'7 3/4" | 2,286<br>7'6" | 2,235<br>7'4" | 2,115<br>6'11 1/4" | 2,286<br>7'6" | 2,200<br>7'2 5/8" | 30,480<br>67,200 | 5,200<br>11,460 | 25,280<br>55,740 | 57.3<br>2,023 |
| | 11,192<br>36'8 5/8" | 2,286<br>7'6" | 2,240<br>7'5 1/4" | 2,120<br>6'11 1/2" | 2,286<br>7'6" | 2,195<br>7'2 3/8" | 30,480<br>67,200 | 5,200<br>11,460 | 25,280<br>55,740 | 57.3<br>2,023 |
| | 11,572<br>37'11 5/8" | 2,286<br>7'6" | 2,254<br>7'4 3/4" | 2,134<br>7' | 2,286<br>7'6" | 2,207<br>7'2 7/8" | 30,480<br>67,200 | 4,400<br>9,700 | 26,080<br>57,500 | 59.64<br>2,106 |
| Steelframe. Rails aluminum. Walls: outside aluminum, inside stainless steel | 11,558<br>37'11" | 2,286<br>7'6" | 2,188<br>7'1 7/8" | 2,068<br>6'9 3/8" | 2,286<br>7'6" | 2,161<br>7'1" | 30,480<br>67,200 | 4,140<br>9,130 | 26,340<br>58,070 | 57.8<br>2,023 |

# High Cube Refrigerated Container                    40'

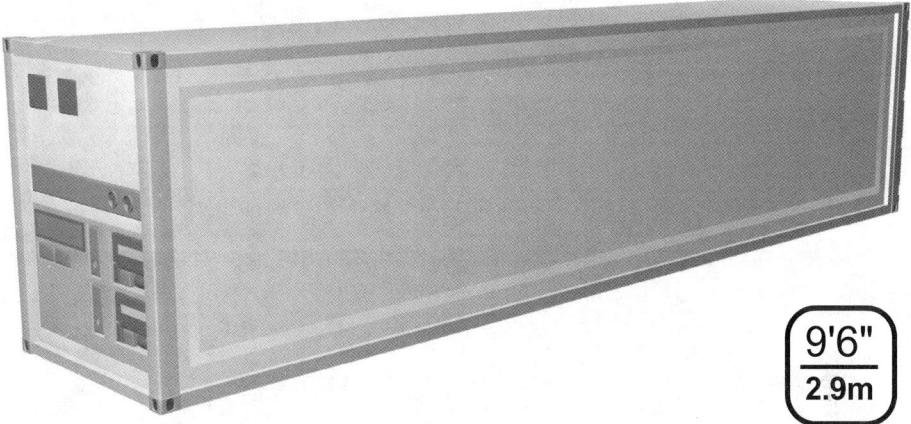

9'6"
2.9m

**CONTAINERS**

- Particularly suitable for voluminous light-weight cargoes (e.g., fruit, flowers, ferns).
- Especially for cargo that needs constant temperatures above or below freezing point.
- Controlled fresh-air supply is possible. Containers are ATO-approved (formerly SPRENGER).
- Walls in "sandwich-construction", with Polyurethane foam to provide maximum insulation.
- The reefer unit is a compact-design compressor unit with aircooled condenser. It switches automatically from cooling to heating operation (and vice versa), if a change of the outside temperatures makes it necessary.
- Possible voltages:
  380V/50 Hz to 460 V/60Hz
- Technical specifications and illustrations of electric plugs for refrigerated containers at the end of this chapter.
- Note permissable weight limits for road and rail transport.
- Permissable temperature setting:
  +25°C to -25°C (+77°F to -13°F).
- The set temperatures can be kept as long as the difference between outside and cargo temperatures does not exceed the following limits:
  for heating 42°C (76°F)
  for cooling 60°C (108°F)

## High Cube Refrigerated Container 40'

| Construction | Inside Dimensions | | | | Door Opening | | Weights | | | Capacity |
|---|---|---|---|---|---|---|---|---|---|---|
| | Length | Width | Height | Max. Stowage Height | Width | Height | Max. Gross | Tare | Max. Payload | |
| | mm ft | mm ft | mm ft | mm ft | mm ft | mm ft | kg lbs | kg lbs | kg lbs | m³ cu.ft. |

### 9'6" high — without Diesel Generator Set

| Construction | Length | Width | Height | Max. Stow. Ht. | Width | Height | Max. Gross | Tare | Max. Payload | Capacity |
|---|---|---|---|---|---|---|---|---|---|---|
| Steelframes. Rails: Aluminum. Walls: outside aluminum, inside stainless steel. | 11,634 / 38'2" | 2,288 / 7'6¹/₈" | 2,498 / 8'2³/₈" | 2,378 / 7'9⁵/₈" | 2,288 / 7'6¹/₈" | 2,517 / 8'3¹/₈" | 30,480 / 67,200 | 4,180 / 9,220 | 26,300 / 57,980 | 66.5 / 2348 |
| | 11,568 / 37'11³/₈" | 2,290 / 7'6¹/₈" | 2,509 / 8'2³/₄" | 2,389 / 7'10" | 2,290 / 7'6¹/₈" | 2,473 / 8'1³/₈" | 32,480 / 71,600 | 4,240 / 9,350 | 28,240 / 62,250 | 66.4 / 2,345 |
| | 11,580 / 37'11¹/₈" | 2,288 / 7'6¹/₈" | 2,498 / 8'2³/₈" | 2,378 / 7'9⁵/₈" | 2,288 / 7'6¹/₈" | 2,517 / 8'3¹/₈" | 30,480 / 67,200 | 4,180 / 9,220 | 26,300 / 57,980 | 66.2 / 2370 |
| | 11,580 / 37'11⁷/₈" | 2,290 / 7'6¹/₈" | 2,513 / 8'3" | 2,393 / 7'10¹/₄" | 2,290 / 7'6¹/₈" | 2,522 / 8'3¹/₄" | 30,480 / 67,200 | 4,180 / 9,220 | 26,300 / 57,980 | 67.0 / 2,370 |
| | 11,580 / 37'11⁷/₈" | 2,286 / 7'6" | 2,528 / 8'11¹/₂" | 2,408 / 7'10³/₄" | 2,286 / 7'6" | 2,545 / 8'4¹/₈" | 30,480 / 67,200 | 4,000 / 8,820 | 26,480 / 58,380 | 67.0 / 2,366 |
| | 11,580 / 37'11⁷/₈" | 2,286 / 7'6" | 2,515 / 8'3" | 2,395 / 7'10¹/₄" | 2,286 / 7'6" | 2,535 / 8'3³/₄" | 30,480 / 67,200 | 4,150 / 9,150 | 26,330 / 58,050 | 67.0 / 2,366 |
| | 11,580 / 37'11⁷/₈" | 2,286 / 7'6" | 2,515 / 8'3" | 2,395 / 7'10¹/₄" | 2,286 / 7'6" | 2,535 / 8'3³/₄" | 30,480 / 67,200 | 6,000 / 13,230 | 24,480 / 53,970 | 67.0 / 2,366 |
| Steelframe. Walls outside and inside GRP. | 11,575 / 37'11⁵/₈" | 2,294 / 7'6¹/₄" | 2,560 / 8'4³/₄" | 2,440 / 8' | 2,286 / 7'6" | 2,570 / 8'5¹/₈" | 32,500 / 71,650 | 4,300 / 9,480 | 28,200 / 62,170 | 68.0 / 2,400 |
| | 11,575 / 37'11⁵/₈" | 2,294 / 7'6¹/₄" | 2,560 / 8'4³/₄" | 2,440 / 8' | 2,286 / 7'6" | 2,570 / 8'5¹/₈" | 32,500 / 71,650 | 4,240 / 9,350 | 28,260 / 62,300 | 68.0 / 2,400 |
| | 11,578 / 37'11³/₄" | 2,295 / 7'6³/₈" | 2,550 / 8'4³/₈" | 2,425 / 7'11¹/₂" | 2,290 / 7'6¹/₈" | 2,560 / 8'4³/₄" | 30,480 / 67,200 | 4,640 / 10,230 | 25,840 / 56,970 | 67.8 / 2,394 |
| | 11,578 / 37'11³/₄" | 2,295 / 7'6³/₈" | 2,550 / 8'4³/₈" | 2,425 / 7'11¹/₂" | 2,290 / 7'6¹/₈" | 2,560 / 8'4³/₄" | 30,480 / 67,200 | 4,580 / 10,100 | 25,900 / 57,100 | 67.8 / 2,394 |

CONTAINERS

# Tank Container 20'

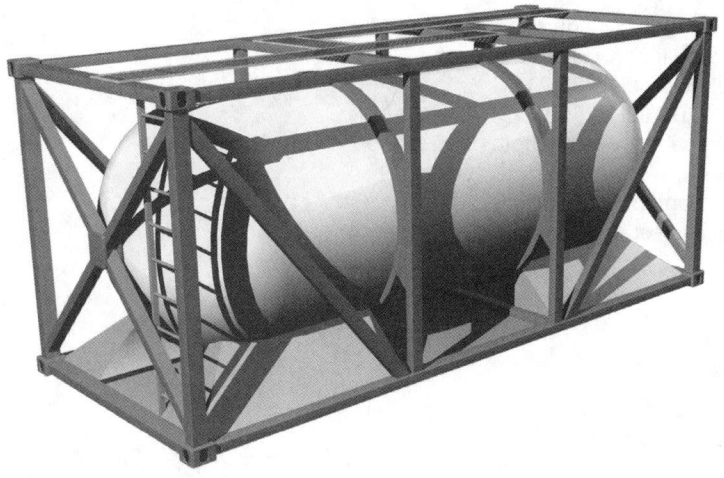

- Separate tank fleets are available for:
  CHEMICAL PRODUCTS, e.g.:
  —Flammables
  —Oxidising agents
  —Toxic substances
  —Corrosives
    FOODSTUFFS, e.g.:
  —Alcohols
  —Fruit juices
  —Edible oils
  —Food additives
- Tanks must be filled to not less than 80% of their capacity to avoid dangerous surg/swells during transport.
  Tanks must not be filled to 100% of their capacity. Sufficient ullage space shall be left—which must be determined depending on the thermal expansion of the product to be carried.
- Certain dangerous products must be carried in tanks having no openings below the surface level of the liquid. Such tanks must be discharged through a syphon pipe by either pressure or pumping.
- National road/rail weight limitations have to be maintained when arranging land transport.
- For the cleaning of tanks and disposal of residues tariff rules apply. Tanks moving in a dedicated service are exempted from such rules until the dedication is terminated.
- For more details contact your representative.

CONTAINERS

# Electric Plugs

The following are electric plug configurations for refrigerated containers.

- Depending on power sources refrigerated containers are equipped with 1 or 2 plugs 380V/50Hz to 460V/60Hz (32 A), 200V/50Hz to 220V/60Hz (60A).
- There are fixed cables with a length of 15 m (49 ft).
- Couplings for adapters are available.
- Adapters are subject to corresponding safety regulations.

Earth Contact

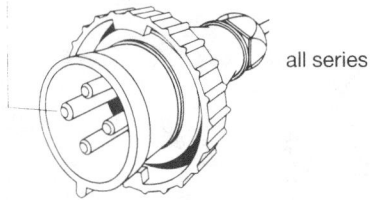

all series

### 380/460 V plugs
- 4 poles according to CEE.
- According to ISO 1496-2 annex M.
- Earth contact in 3rd position according to socket.

Earth Contact

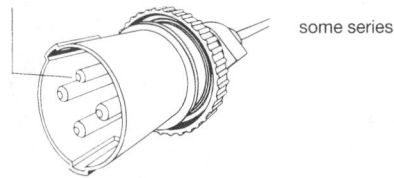

some series

### 200/220 V plugs
- 4 poles
- According to ISO 1496-2 annex O.
- Position of earth contact according to illustration.

# Seaports of the World

The following is a listing of 815 of the most active seaports and inland ports in the world. Several thousand additional ports exist yet more than 99 percent of the world's trade moves through these ports. We have omitted fishing ports and small ports that primarily handle private pleasure craft.

### Arrangement of Listings

Listings are in alpha sequence by country and then by port. We also include: UN/LOCODE, Latitude and Longitude, GMT Offset, Telephone and Web URL (as available).

### UN/LOCODE

UN/LOCODE is the acronym for United Nations Code for Trade and Transport Locations. It is a geographic coding system developed by the UNECE (United Nations Economic Commission for Europe) for more than 40,000 locations worldwide.

The UN/LOCODE is a combination of a 2-character country code and a three character location code. The first two digits refer to the country location based on the ISO 3166 alpha-2 Country Code. Refer to the Country Codes section for a complete listing of country codes.

The next three characters are normally three letters and refer to a specific location in the country. In some cases, where the letter options have been exhausted, the numerals 2-9 may be used. All 40,000 UN/LOCODEs can be found at www.un-ece.org/cefact/locode/service/main.htm.

### Latitude / Longitude

Latitude and Longitude are expressed as coordinates in the following format: Latitude 00° 00' N or S / Longitude 00° 00' E or W.

Latitude refers to degrees (°) and minutes (') N (North) or S (South) of the Equator (0°), with the North Pole at 90° North Latitude and the South Pole at 90° South Latitude.

Longitude refers to degrees (°) and minutes (') E (East) or W (West) of the Prime Meridian (0°), which runs North and South through the original site of the Royal Observatory at Greenwich, England. Note that 180° East and West Longitude refer to the same meridian: the international date line which runs North and South through the middle of the Pacific ocean.

### GMT Offset

This refers to the local time zone of the port as + (hours ahead) or - (hours behind) GMT (Greenwich Mean Time).

### Contact Information

Telephone numbers are listed in the format: [country code] (city code) subscriber number. Refer to the Dialing Guide for information about making international calls.

Web URLs are available for many, but all not ports. If you have information regarding these ports please contact us at info@worldtradepress.com.

### Additional Information

Additional information can be found at:
www.portfocus.com;

www.hal-pc.org/~nugent/port.html;

www.ports.com and www.seacompanion.com.

## Albania

**Port of Durres (Durazzo)**
UN/LOCODE: AL DRZ
Latitude/Longitude: 41° 19' N / 19° 28' E
GMT Offset: +1
Web: www.nrlmry.navy.mil/~cannon/medports/Durres/index.html

**Port of Sarande**
UN/LOCODE: AL SAR
Latitude/Longitude: 39° 53' N / 20° 0' E
GMT Offset: +1

**Port of Shengjin**
UN/LOCODE: AL SHG
Latitude/Longitude: 41° 49' N / 19° 36' E
GMT Offset: +1

**Port of Vlore (Valona, Vlone)**
UN/LOCODE: AL VOA
Latitude/Longitude: 40° 29' N / 19° 29' E
GMT Offset: +1

## Algeria

**Port of Annaba (Ex Bone)**
UN/LOCODE: DZ AAE
Latitude/Longitude: 36° 58' N / 7° 47' E
GMT Offset: +1
Web: http://portfocus.com/algeria/annaba/index.html

**Port of Arzew**
UN/LOCODE: DZ AZW
Latitude/Longitude: 35° 50' N / 0° 8' W
GMT Offset: +1
Telephone: [213] (34) 211-807
Web: www.portdebejaia.com.dz

**Port of Bejaia (Ex Bougie)**
UN/LOCODE: DZ BJA
Latitude/Longitude: 36° 45' N / 5° 5' E
GMT Offset: +1
Telephone: [213] (34) 211-807
Web: www.portdebejaia.com.dz

**Port of Dellys**
UN/LOCODE: DZ DEL
Latitude/Longitude: 36° 55' N / 3° 55' E
GMT Offset: +1

**Port of Ghazaouet**
UN/LOCODE: DZ GHA
Latitude/Longitude: 35° 6' N / 1° 52' W
GMT Offset: +1
Telephone: [213] (43) 321220

**Port of Mostaganem**
UN/LOCODE: DZ MOS
Latitude/Longitude: 35° 56' N / 0° 5' E
GMT Offset: +1

**Port of Oran**
UN/LOCODE: DZ ORN
Latitude/Longitude: 35° 43' N / 0° 39' W
GMT Offset: +1

**Port of Skikda (Ex Philippeville)**
UN/LOCODE: DZ SKI
Latitude/Longitude: 36° 53' N / 6° 54' E
GMT Offset: +1
Telephone: [213] (38) 756-827
Web: www.skikda-port.com

**Port of Tenes**
UN/LOCODE: DZ TEN
Latitude/Longitude: 36° 35' N / 1° 18' E
GMT Offset: +1
Telephone: [213] (27) 757276

SEAPORTS

## American Samoa

**Port of Pago Pago**
*UN/LOCODE:* . . . . . . . . . . . . . . . . . . . AS PPG
*Latitude/Longitude:* . . . . . . . . 14° 17' S / 170° 41' E
*GMT Offset:* . . . . . . . . . . . . . . . . . . . . . . . . . . -11

## Angola

**Port of Cabinda**
*UN/LOCODE:* . . . . . . . . . . . . . . . . . . . AO CAB
*Latitude/Longitude:* . . . . . . . . . 5° 32' S / 12° 11' E
*GMT Offset:* . . . . . . . . . . . . . . . . . . . . . . . . . . +1
*Telephone:* . . . . . . . . . . . . . . [244] (31) 52216
*Web:* . . www.marineafric.com/english/gen-info/ports/
port_angola.htm#cabinda
**Port of Lobito**
*UN/LOCODE:* . . . . . . . . . . . . . . . . . . . AO LOB
*Latitude/Longitude:* . . . . . . . . 12° 20' S / 13° 34' E
*GMT Offset:* . . . . . . . . . . . . . . . . . . . . . . . . . . +1
*Telephone:* . . . . . . . . . . . . . . [244] (72) 22710
*Web:* . . http://portfocus.com/angola/lobito/index.html
**Port of Luanda**
*UN/LOCODE:* . . . . . . . . . . . . . . . . . . . AO LAD
*Latitude/Longitude:* . . . . . . . . . 8° 48' S / 13° 15' E
*GMT Offset:* . . . . . . . . . . . . . . . . . . . . . . . . . . +1
*Telephone:* . . . . . . . . . . . . . . [244] (2) 311-178
*Web:* . http://portfocus.com/angola/luanda/index.html
**Port of Namibe**
*UN/LOCODE:* . . . . . . . . . . . . . . . . . . . AO MSZ
*Latitude/Longitude:* . . . . . . . . 15° 11' S / 12° 7' E
*GMT Offset:* . . . . . . . . . . . . . . . . . . . . . . . . . . +1
**Port of Porto Amboim**
*UN/LOCODE:* . . . . . . . . . . . . . . . . . . . AO PBN
*Latitude/Longitude:* . . . . . . . . 10° 44' S / 13° 45' E
*GMT Offset:* . . . . . . . . . . . . . . . . . . . . . . . . . . +1
**Port of Soyo-Quinfuquena Termina**
*UN/LOCODE:* . . . . . . . . . . . . . . . . . . . AO SOQ
*Latitude/Longitude:* . . . . . . . . . 6° 20' S / 12° 14' E
*GMT Offset:* . . . . . . . . . . . . . . . . . . . . . . . . . . +1
*Telephone:* . . . . . . . . . . . . . . [244] (32) 239-1031

## Argentina

**Port of Bahia Blanca**
*UN/LOCODE:* . . . . . . . . . . . . . . . . . . . AR BHI
*Latitude/Longitude:* . . . . . . . . 38° 47' S / 62° 16' W
*GMT Offset:* . . . . . . . . . . . . . . . . . . . . . . . . . . -3
*Web:* . . . . . www.bblanca.com.ar/puerto/i_index.html
**Port of Buenos Aires**
*UN/LOCODE:* . . . . . . . . . . . . . . . . . . . AR BUE
*Latitude/Longitude:* . . . . . . . . 34° 36' S / 58° 22' W
*GMT Offset:* . . . . . . . . . . . . . . . . . . . . . . . . . . -3
*Telephone:* . . . . . . . . . . . . . . [54] (11) 4331-4407
*Web:* . . . . . . . . . . . . . . . www.consejoportuario.com.ar
**Port of Comodoro Rivadavia**
*UN/LOCODE:* . . . . . . . . . . . . . . . . . . . AR CRD
*Latitude/Longitude:* . . . . . . . . 45° 51' S / 67° 26' W
*GMT Offset:* . . . . . . . . . . . . . . . . . . . . . . . . . . -3
*Telephone:* . . . . . . . . . . . . . . [54] (297) 447-3096
*Web:* . . . . . . . . . www.puertocomodororivadavia.com
**Port of Concepcion del Uruguay**
*UN/LOCODE:* . . . . . . . . . . . . . . . . . . . AR COU
*Latitude/Longitude:* . . . . . . . . 32° 25' S / 58° 13' W
*GMT Offset:* . . . . . . . . . . . . . . . . . . . . . . . . . . -3
**Port of Mar del Plata**
*UN/LOCODE:* . . . . . . . . . . . . . . . . . . . AR MDQ
*Latitude/Longitude:* . . . . . . . . 38° 0' S / 57° 32' W
*GMT Offset:* . . . . . . . . . . . . . . . . . . . . . . . . . . -3
**Port of Necochea**
*UN/LOCODE:* . . . . . . . . . . . . . . . . . . . AR NEC
*Latitude/Longitude:* . . . . . . . . 38° 31' S / 58° 46' W
*GMT Offset:* . . . . . . . . . . . . . . . . . . . . . . . . . . -3
*Web:* . . . www.heinlein.com.ar/ports/necocheagrain.htm

**Port of Rio Gallegos**
*UN/LOCODE:* . . . . . . . . . . . . . . . . . . . AR RGL
*Latitude/Longitude:* . . . . . . . . 51° 37' S / 68° 58' W
*GMT Offset:* . . . . . . . . . . . . . . . . . . . . . . . . . . -3
**Port of Rosario**
*UN/LOCODE:* . . . . . . . . . . . . . . . . . . . AR ROS
*Latitude/Longitude:* . . . . . . . . 32° 57' S / 60° 33' W
*GMT Offset:* . . . . . . . . . . . . . . . . . . . . . . . . . . -3
*Web:* . . . www.heinlein.com.ar/ports/rosariograin.htm
**Port of Santa Fe**
*UN/LOCODE:* . . . . . . . . . . . . . . . . . . . AR SFN
*Latitude/Longitude:* . . . . . . . . 31° 39' S / 60° 42' W
*GMT Offset:* . . . . . . . . . . . . . . . . . . . . . . . . . . -3
*Telephone:* . . . . . . . . . . . . . . [54] (342) 455-4393
*Web:* . . . . . . . . . . . . . . . . . . . . . www.puertosfe.com
**Port of Ushuaia**
*UN/LOCODE:* . . . . . . . . . . . . . . . . . . . AR USH
*Latitude/Longitude:* . . . . . . . . 54° 49' S / 68° 18' W
*GMT Offset:* . . . . . . . . . . . . . . . . . . . . . . . . . . -3
*Telephone:* . . . . . . . . . . . . . . [54] (2901) 42-4022
*Web:* . .http://portfocus.com/argentina/ushuaia/index.html

## Aruba

**Port of Oranjestad**
*UN/LOCODE:* . . . . . . . . . . . . . . . . . . . AW ORJ
*Latitude/Longitude:* . . . . . . . . . 12° 31' N / 70° 2' W
*GMT Offset:* . . . . . . . . . . . . . . . . . . . . . . . . . . -4
*Telephone:* . . . . . . . . . . . . . . . . . . . [297] (8) 26633
*Web:* . http://home.houston.rr.com/nugent/aruba.html

## Australia

**Port of Adelaide**
*UN/LOCODE:* . . . . . . . . . . . . . . . . . . . AU PAE
*Latitude/Longitude:* . . . . . . . . 34° 51' S / 138° 30' E
*GMT Offset:* . . . . . . . . . . . . . . . . . . . . . . . . . . +0
*Telephone:* . . . . . . . . . . . . . . [61] (8) 8248-9300
*Web:* . . www.flindersports.com.au/portfacilities2.html
**Port of Brisbane**
*UN/LOCODE:* . . . . . . . . . . . . . . . . . . . AU BNE
*Latitude/Longitude:* . . . . . . . . 27° 27' S / 153° 4' E
*GMT Offset:* . . . . . . . . . . . . . . . . . . . . . . . . . . +10
*Telephone:* . . . . . . . . . . . . . . [61] (7) 3258-4888
*Web:* . . . . . . . . . . . . . . . . . . . . www.portbris.com.au
**Port of Cairns**
*UN/LOCODE:* . . . . . . . . . . . . . . . . . . . AU CNS
*Latitude/Longitude:* . . . . . . . . 16° 56' S / 145° 47' E
*GMT Offset:* . . . . . . . . . . . . . . . . . . . . . . . . . . +10
*Telephone:* . . . . . . . . . . . . . . [61] (7) 4052-3888
*Web:* . . . . . . . . . . . . . . . . . . www.cairnsport.com.au
**Port of Darwin**
*UN/LOCODE:* . . . . . . . . . . . . . . . . . . . AU DRW
*Latitude/Longitude:* . . . . . . . . 12° 28' S / 130° 50' E
*GMT Offset:* . . . . . . . . . . . . . . . . . . . . . . . . . . +10
*Telephone:* . . . . . . . . . . . . . . [61] (8) 8922-0660
*Web:* . . . . . . . . . . . . . . . www.darwinport.nt.gov.au
**Port of Devonport**
*UN/LOCODE:* . . . . . . . . . . . . . . . . . . . AU DPO
*Latitude/Longitude:* . . . . . . . . 41° 11' S / 146° 22' E
*GMT Offset:* . . . . . . . . . . . . . . . . . . . . . . . . . . +10
*Telephone:* . . . . . . . . . . . . . . [61] (3) 6421-4911
*Web:* . . . . . . . . . . . . . . . . . . . . . . . . . . . . . . . . . . .
**Port of Fremantle**
*UN/LOCODE:* . . . . . . . . . . . . . . . . . . . AU FRE
*Latitude/Longitude:* . . . . . . . . 32° 3' S / 115° 44' E
*GMT Offset:* . . . . . . . . . . . . . . . . . . . . . . . . . . +8
*Telephone:* . . . . . . . . . . . . . . [61] (8) 9430-3555
*Web:* . . . . . . . . . . . . . . . . . www.freport.wa.gov.au
**Port of Geelong**
*UN/LOCODE:* . . . . . . . . . . . . . . . . . . . AU GEX
*Latitude/Longitude:* . . . . . . . . 38° 9' S / 144° 22' E
*GMT Offset:* . . . . . . . . . . . . . . . . . . . . . . . . . . +10
*Telephone:* . . . . . . . . . . . . . . [61] (3) 5226-6300
*Web:* . . . . . . . . . . . . . . . . . . www.tollports.com.au

**Port of Hobart**
UN/LOCODE: . . . . . . . . . . . . . . . . . . . . AU HBA
Latitude/Longitude: . . . . . . . 42° 53' S / 147° 20' E
GMT Offset: . . . . . . . . . . . . . . . . . . . . . . . . +10
Telephone: . . . . . . . . . . . . . . [61] (3) 6235-1000
Web: . . . . . . . . . . . . . . . . . . www.hpc.com.au

**Port of Mackay**
UN/LOCODE: . . . . . . . . . . . . . . . . . . . . AU MKY
Latitude/Longitude: . . . . . . . 21° 6' S / 149° 14' E
GMT Offset: . . . . . . . . . . . . . . . . . . . . . . . . +10
Telephone: . . . . . . . . . . . . . . [61] (7) 4955-8155
Web: . . . . . . . . . . . . . . . . www.mackayports.com

**Port of Melbourne**
UN/LOCODE: . . . . . . . . . . . . . . . . . . . . AU MEL
Latitude/Longitude: . . . . . . . 37° 50' S / 144° 58' E
GMT Offset: . . . . . . . . . . . . . . . . . . . . . . . . +10
Telephone: . . . . . . . . . . . . . . [61] (3) 9628-7555
Web: . . . . . . . . . . . . . www.portofmelbourne.com

**Port of Sydney**
UN/LOCODE: . . . . . . . . . . . . . . . . . . . . AU SYD
Latitude/Longitude: . . . . . . . 33° 55' S / 151° 12' E
GMT Offset: . . . . . . . . . . . . . . . . . . . . . . . . +10
Telephone: . . . . . . . . . . . . . . [61] (2) 9296-4999
Web: . . . . . . . . . . . . . . . . www.sydports.com.au/

**Port of Townsville**
UN/LOCODE: . . . . . . . . . . . . . . . . . . . . AU TSV
Latitude/Longitude: . . . . . . . 19° 15' S / 146° 50' E
GMT Offset: . . . . . . . . . . . . . . . . . . . . . . . . +10
Telephone: . . . . . . . . . . . . . . [61] (7) 4781-1500
Web: . . . . . . . . . . . . . www.townsville-port.com.au

## Azerbaijan

**Port of Baku**
UN/LOCODE: . . . . . . . . . . . . . . . . . . . . AZ BAK
Latitude/Longitude: . . . . . . . . 40° 20' N / 49° 51' E
GMT Offset: . . . . . . . . . . . . . . . . . . . . . . . . +4
Telephone: . . . . . . . . . . . . . [996] (12) 934-668

## Bahamas

**Port of Nassau**
UN/LOCODE: . . . . . . . . . . . . . . . . . . . . BS NAS
Latitude/Longitude: . . . . . . . . 25° 5' N / 77° 20' W
GMT Offset: . . . . . . . . . . . . . . . . . . . . . . . . -5
Telephone: . . . . . . . . . . . . . . [1] (809) 322-2049

## Bahrain

**Port of Mina Salman**
UN/LOCODE: . . . . . . . . . . . . . . . . . . . . BH MIN
Latitude/Longitude: . . . . . . . . 26° 12' N / 50° 37' E
GMT Offset: . . . . . . . . . . . . . . . . . . . . . . . . +3
Telephone: . . . . . . . . . . . . . . . . [973] 725-555
Web: . . . . . . . . . . . . . . www.bahrainports.gov.bh

**Port of Sitra**
UN/LOCODE: . . . . . . . . . . . . . . . . . . . . BH SIT
Latitude/Longitude: . . . . . . . . . 26° 9' N / 50° 40' E
GMT Offset: . . . . . . . . . . . . . . . . . . . . . . . . +3

## Bangladesh

**Port of Chittagong**
UN/LOCODE: . . . . . . . . . . . . . . . . . . . . BD CGP
Latitude/Longitude: . . . . . . . . 22° 19' N / 91° 48' E
GMT Offset: . . . . . . . . . . . . . . . . . . . . . . . . +6
Telephone: . . . . . . . . . . . . . . [880] (31) 723-721
Web: . . . . . . . . . . . . . . . . . . www.cpa.gov.bd

**Port of Mongla**
UN/LOCODE: . . . . . . . . . . . . . . . . . . . . BD MGL
Latitude/Longitude: . . . . . . . . 22° 29' N / 89° 35' E
GMT Offset: . . . . . . . . . . . . . . . . . . . . . . . . +6
Web: . . . . . . www.citechco.net/starpath/mongla.html

## Barbados

**Port of Bridgetown**
UN/LOCODE: . . . . . . . . . . . . . . . . . . . . BB BGI
Latitude/Longitude: . . . . . . . . . 13° 6' N / 59° 38' W
GMT Offset: . . . . . . . . . . . . . . . . . . . . . . . . -4
Telephone: . . . . . . . . . . . . . . [1] (246) 430-4700
Web: . . . . . . . . . . . . . . . . www.barbadosport.com

## Belgium

**Port of Antwerp**
UN/LOCODE: . . . . . . . . . . . . . . . . . . . . BE ANR
Latitude/Longitude: . . . . . . . . 51° 14' N / 4° 23' E
GMT Offset: . . . . . . . . . . . . . . . . . . . . . . . . +1
Telephone: . . . . . . . . . . . . . . [32] (3) 205-2011
Web: . . . . . . . . . . . . . . www.portofantwerp.be/

**Port of Bruges**
UN/LOCODE: . . . . . . . . . . . . . . . . . . . . BE BGS
Latitude/Longitude: . . . . . . . . 51° 13' N / 3° 13' E
GMT Offset: . . . . . . . . . . . . . . . . . . . . . . . . +1
Telephone: . . . . . . . . . . . . . . [32] (50) 444-211

**Port of Brussels (Bruxelles)**
UN/LOCODE: . . . . . . . . . . . . . . . . . . . . BE BRU
Latitude/Longitude: . . . . . . . . 50° 52' N / 4° 21' E
GMT Offset: . . . . . . . . . . . . . . . . . . . . . . . . +1
Telephone: . . . . . . . . . . . . . . [32] (2) 420-6700
Web: . . . . . . www.portdebruxelles.irisnet.be

**Port of Ghent**
UN/LOCODE: . . . . . . . . . . . . . . . . . . . . BE GNE
Latitude/Longitude: . . . . . . . . 51° 2' N / 3° 44' E
GMT Offset: . . . . . . . . . . . . . . . . . . . . . . . . +1
Telephone: . . . . . . . . . . . . . . [32] (9) 251-0550
Web: . . . . . . . . . . . . . . . . . . www.portghent.com

**Port of Liege**
UN/LOCODE: . . . . . . . . . . . . . . . . . . . . BE LGG
Latitude/Longitude: . . . . . . . . 50° 40' N / 5° 34' E
GMT Offset: . . . . . . . . . . . . . . . . . . . . . . . . +1
Telephone: . . . . . . . . . . . . . . [32] (4) 232-9797
Web: . . . . . . . . . . www.liege.port-autonome.be

**Port of Zeebrugge**
UN/LOCODE: . . . . . . . . . . . . . . . . . . . . BE ZEE
Latitude/Longitude: . . . . . . . . 51° 20' N / 3° 13' E
GMT Offset: . . . . . . . . . . . . . . . . . . . . . . . . +1
Telephone: . . . . . . . . . . . . . . [32] (50) 543-211
Web: . . . . . . . . . . . . . . www.portofzeebrugge.be/

## Belize

**Port of Belize City**
UN/LOCODE: . . . . . . . . . . . . . . . . . . . . BZ BZE
Latitude/Longitude: . . . . . . . . 17° 29' N / 88° 11' W
GMT Offset: . . . . . . . . . . . . . . . . . . . . . . . . -6
Telephone: . . . . . . . . . . . . . . . . [501] (2) 73-571

## Benin

**Port of Cotonou**
UN/LOCODE: . . . . . . . . . . . . . . . . . . . . BJ COO
Latitude/Longitude: . . . . . . . . . 6° 20' N / 2° 32' E
GMT Offset: . . . . . . . . . . . . . . . . . . . . . . . . +1
Telephone: . . . . . . . . . . . . . . . . [229] 312-119
Web: . . . . . . . . . . . . www.otal.com/benin/benin.htm

## Bermuda

**Port of Hamilton**
UN/LOCODE: . . . . . . . . . . . . . . . . . . . . BM BDA
Latitude/Longitude: . . . . . . . . 32° 17' N / 64° 47' W
GMT Offset: . . . . . . . . . . . . . . . . . . . . . . . . -4

**Port of St Georges**
UN/LOCODE: . . . . . . . . . . . . . . . . . . . . BM SGE
Latitude/Longitude: . . . . . . . . 32° 22' N / 64° 42' W
GMT Offset: . . . . . . . . . . . . . . . . . . . . . . . . -4

SEAPORTS

## Brazil

**Port of Belem**
UN/LOCODE: .................... BR BEL
Latitude/Longitude: ......... 1° 28' S / 48° 29' W
GMT Offset: ................................-3
Telephone: ............. [55] (91) 216-2073
Web: ........ www.cdp.com.br/porto_belem.aspx

**Port of Fortaleza**
UN/LOCODE: .................... BR FOR
Latitude/Longitude: ......... 3° 41' S / 38° 33' W
GMT Offset: ................................-3
Telephone: ............. [55] (85) 263-2433
Web: ............... www.docasdoceara.com.br

**Port of Imbituba**
UN/LOCODE: .................... BR IBB
Latitude/Longitude: ......... 28° 13' S / 48° 38' W
GMT Offset: ................................-3
Telephone: ............. [55] (91) 322-186
Web: ........ www.cdp.com.br/porto_itaituba.aspx

**Port of Manaus**
UN/LOCODE: .................... BR MAO
Latitude/Longitude: ......... 3° 8' S / 60° 0' W
GMT Offset: ................................-4
Telephone: ............. [55] (92) 232-4250

**Port of Paranagua**
UN/LOCODE: .................... BR PNG
Latitude/Longitude: ......... 25° 30' S / 48° 30' W
GMT Offset: ................................-3
Telephone: ............. [55] (41) 420-1100
Web: ................. www.pr.gov.br/portos

**Port of Porto Alegre**
UN/LOCODE: .................... BR POA
Latitude/Longitude: ......... 30° 5' S / 51° 15' W
GMT Offset: ................................-3
Telephone: ............. [55] (512) 245-733

**Port of Recife**
UN/LOCODE: .................... BR REC
Latitude/Longitude: ......... 8° 4' S / 34° 52' W
GMT Offset: ................................-3
Telephone: ............. [55] (81) 3419-1900
Web: ............. www.portodorecife.pe.gov.br

**Port of Rio De Janeiro**
UN/LOCODE: .................... BR RIO
Latitude/Longitude: ......... 22° 54' S / 43° 12' W
GMT Offset: ................................-3
Telephone: ............. [55] (21) 2219-8600
Web: ................. www.portosrio.gov.br

**Port of Rio Grande**
UN/LOCODE: .................... BR RIG
Latitude/Longitude: ......... 32° 3' S / 52° 5' W
GMT Offset: ................................-3
Telephone: ............. [55] (53) 231-1366
Web: ............. www.portoriogrande.com.br

**Port of Salvador**
UN/LOCODE: .................... BR SSA
Latitude/Longitude: ......... 13° 1' S / 38° 35' W
GMT Offset: ................................-3
Telephone: ............. [55] (71) 320-1299
Web: ........ www.codeba.com.br/porto_ssa.php

**Port of Santos**
UN/LOCODE: .................... BR SSZ
Latitude/Longitude: ......... 23° 56' S / 46° 19' W
GMT Offset: ................................-3
Telephone: ............. [55] (13) 3233-6565
Web: ............. www.portodesantos.com.br

**Port of Vitoria**
UN/LOCODE: .................... BR VIX
Latitude/Longitude: ......... 20° 19' S / 40° 17' W
GMT Offset: ................................-3
Telephone: ............. [55] (27) 3132-7360
Web: ............. www.portodevitoria.com.br

## Brunei Darussalam

**Port of Kuala Belait**
UN/LOCODE: .................... BN KUB
Latitude/Longitude: ......... 4° 38' N / 114° 12' E
GMT Offset: ................................+8
Telephone: ............. [673] (3) 335-298

**Port of Muara**
UN/LOCODE: .................... BN MUA
Latitude/Longitude: ......... 5° 1' N / 115° 4' E
GMT Offset: ................................+8
Telephone: ............. [673] (2) 770-222
Web: ........ www.brunet.bn/gov/ports/lkpage.htm

## Bulgaria

**Port of Varna**
UN/LOCODE: .................... BG VAR
Latitude/Longitude: ......... 43° 12' N / 27° 57' E
GMT Offset: ................................+2
Telephone: ............. [359] (52) 602-191
Web: ................. www.port-varna.bg

## Cambodia

**Port of Kompongsom**
UN/LOCODE: .................... KH KOS
Latitude/Longitude: ......... 10° 38' N / 103° 30' E
GMT Offset: ................................+7

**Port of Phnom Penh**
UN/LOCODE: .................... KH PNH
Latitude/Longitude: ......... 11° 35' N / 104° 55' E
GMT Offset: ................................+7

**Port of Sihanoukville**
UN/LOCODE: .................... KH SIH
Latitude/Longitude: ......... 10° 38' N / 103° 29' E
GMT Offset: ................................+7
Telephone: ............. [855] (34) 933-416
Web: ................. www.pas.gov.kh

## Cameroon

**Port of Douala**
UN/LOCODE: .................... CM DLA
Latitude/Longitude: ......... 4° 3' N / 9° 42' E
GMT Offset: ................................+1
Telephone: ............. [237] 422-888
Web: ... www.otal.com/cameroon/cameroon.htm#psi

**Port of Kribi**
UN/LOCODE: .................... CM KBI
Latitude/Longitude: ......... 2° 56' N / 9° 56' E
GMT Offset: ................................+1

**Port of Tiko**
UN/LOCODE: .................... CM TKC
Latitude/Longitude: ......... 4° 4' N / 9° 24' E
GMT Offset: ................................+1

## Canada

**Fraser River Port (Port of New Westminster)**
UN/LOCODE: .................... CA NWE
Latitude/Longitude: ......... 49° 21' N / 122° 54' E
GMT Offset: ................................-8
Telephone: ............. [1] (604) 524-6655
Web: ....... www.fraserportauthority.com/index.html

**Port of Becancour**
UN/LOCODE: .................... CA BEC
Latitude/Longitude: ......... 46° 24' N / 72° 23' W
GMT Offset: ................................-5
Telephone: ............. [1] (819) 294-6656
Web: ................. www.spipb.com/accueil.php

**Port of Churchill**
UN/LOCODE: .................... CA CHV
Latitude/Longitude: ......... 58° 47' N / 94° 12' W
GMT Offset: ................................-6
Telephone: ............. [1] (204) 675-8823
Web: ........ www.omnitrax.com/portservice.shtml

SEAPORTS

**Port of Halifax**
UN/LOCODE: .................... CA HAL
Latitude/Longitude: ....... 44° 39' N / 63° 34' W
GMT Offset: .................................-4
Telephone: .............. [1] (902) 426-8222
Web: .............. www.portofhalifax.ca

**Port of Hamilton**
UN/LOCODE: .................... CA HAM
Latitude/Longitude: ....... 43° 17' N / 79° 50' W
GMT Offset: .................................-5
Telephone: .............. [1] (905) 525-4330
Web: .............. www.hamiltonport.ca

**Port of Prince Rupert**
UN/LOCODE: .................... CA PRR
Latitude/Longitude: ....... 54° 19' N / 130° 20' W
GMT Offset: .................................-8
Telephone: .............. [1] (604) 627-7545
Web: .............. www.rupertport.com

**Port of Sept Iles (Seven Is.)**
UN/LOCODE: .................... CA SEI
Latitude/Longitude: ....... 50° 11' N / 66° 23' W
GMT Offset: .................................-5
Telephone: .............. [1] (418) 968-1231
Web: .............. www.portsi.com

**Port of St Johns**
UN/LOCODE: .................... CA SJF
Latitude/Longitude: ....... 47° 34' N / 52° 42' W
GMT Offset: .................................-4
Telephone: .............. [1] (709) 772-4664
Web: .............. www.sjpa.com

**Port of Sydney**
UN/LOCODE: .................... CA SYD
Latitude/Longitude: ....... 46° 9' N / 60° 12' W
GMT Offset: .................................-4
Telephone: .............. [1] (902) 794-3073

**Port of Thunder Bay**
UN/LOCODE: .................... CA THU
Latitude/Longitude: ....... 48° 25' N / 89° 13' W
GMT Offset: .................................-6
Telephone: .............. [1] (807) 345-6400
Web: ...... www.portauthority.thunder-bay.on.ca

**Port of Toronto**
UN/LOCODE: .................... CA TOR
Latitude/Longitude: ....... 43° 38' N / 79° 23' W
GMT Offset: .................................-5
Telephone: .............. [1] (416) 863-2000
Web: .............. www.torontoport.com/

**Port of Trois-Rivieres**
UN/LOCODE: .................... CA TRR
Latitude/Longitude: ....... 46° 22' N / 72° 34' W
GMT Offset: .................................-5
Telephone: .............. [1] (819) 378-2887
Web: .............. www.porttr.com

**Port of Vancouver**
UN/LOCODE: .................... CA VAN
Latitude/Longitude: ....... 49° 17' N / 123° 7' W
GMT Offset: .................................-8
Telephone: .............. [1] (604) 666-3226
Web: .............. www.portvancouver.com/

**Port of Windsor**
UN/LOCODE: .................... CA WND
Latitude/Longitude: ....... 42° 19' N / 83° 4' W
GMT Offset: .................................-5
Telephone: .............. [1] (519) 258-5741
Web: .............. www.portwindsor.com

## Cape Verde

**Port of Mindelo**
UN/LOCODE: .................... CV MIN
Latitude/Longitude: ....... 16° 53' N / 25° 0' W
GMT Offset: .................................-1
Web: .............. www.enapor.cv

## Cayman Islands

**Port of Georgetown, Grand Cayman**
UN/LOCODE: .................... KY GEC
Latitude/Longitude: ....... 19° 18' N / 81° 23' W
GMT Offset: .................................-5

## Chile

**Port of Antofagasta**
UN/LOCODE: .................... CL ANF
Latitude/Longitude: ....... 23° 39' S / 70° 25' W
GMT Offset: .................................-4
Telephone: .............. [56] (55) 223-171
Web: .............. www.puertoantofagasta.cl

**Port of Arica**
UN/LOCODE: .................... CL ARI
Latitude/Longitude: ....... 18° 28' S / 70° 20' W
GMT Offset: .................................-4
Telephone: .............. [56] (58) 255-078
Web: .............. www.puertoarica.cl

**Port of Chanaral**
UN/LOCODE: .................... CL CNR
Latitude/Longitude: ....... 26° 21' S / 70° 38' W
GMT Offset: .................................-4
Web: .............. www.directemar.cl

**Port of Iquique**
UN/LOCODE: .................... CL IQQ
Latitude/Longitude: ....... 20° 12' S / 70° 9' W
GMT Offset: .................................-4
Telephone: .............. [56] (57) 422-582
Web: .............. www.directemar.cl

**Port of Puerto Montt**
UN/LOCODE: .................... CL PMC
Latitude/Longitude: ....... 41° 28' S / 72° 57' W
GMT Offset: .................................-4
Telephone: .............. [56] (65) 252-247
Web: .............. www.empormontt.cl/

**Port of Punta Arenas**
UN/LOCODE: .................... CL PUQ
Latitude/Longitude: ....... 53° 10' S / 70° 54' W
GMT Offset: .................................-4
Telephone: .............. [56] (61) 221-050
Web: .............. www.directemar.cl

**Port of San Antonio**
UN/LOCODE: .................... CL SAI
Latitude/Longitude: ....... 33° 35' S / 71° 37' W
GMT Offset: .................................-4
Web: .............. www.saiport.cl/

**Port of San Vicente**
UN/LOCODE: .................... CL SVE
Latitude/Longitude: ....... 36° 44' S / 73° 9' W
GMT Offset: .................................-4
Telephone: .............. [56] (41) 797-600
Web: .............. www.ptotalsve.cl

**Port of Talcahuano**
UN/LOCODE: .................... CL TAL
Latitude/Longitude: ....... 36° 41' S / 73° 6' W
GMT Offset: .................................-4
Telephone: .............. [56] (41) 797-600
Web: .............. www.ptotalsve.cl

**Port of Valparaiso**
UN/LOCODE: .................... CL VAP
Latitude/Longitude: ....... 33° 2' S / 71° 38' W
GMT Offset: .................................-4
Telephone: .............. [56] (32) 448-800
Web: .............. www.vap.cl

SEAPORTS

## China

**Port of Dalian**
*UN/LOCODE:* . . . . . . . . . . . . . . . . . . . . CN DLC
*Latitude/Longitude:* . . . . . . . 38° 55' N / 121° 40' E
*GMT Offset:* . . . . . . . . . . . . . . . . . . . . . . . . +8
*Web:* . . . . . . . . . . . . . www.portdalian.com.cn

**Port of Fuzhou**
*UN/LOCODE:* . . . . . . . . . . . . . . . . . . . . CN FOC
*Latitude/Longitude:* . . . . . . . . 26° 3' N / 119° 18' E
*GMT Offset:* . . . . . . . . . . . . . . . . . . . . . . . . +8
*Telephone:* . . . . . . . . . . . . . . [86] (591) 682-312
*Web:* . . . . . . . . . . . www.infomarine.gr/china/fuzhou

**Port of Guangzhou**
*UN/LOCODE:* . . . . . . . . . . . . . . . . . . . . CN CAN
*Latitude/Longitude:* . . . . . . . 23° 6' N / 113° 14' E
*GMT Offset:* . . . . . . . . . . . . . . . . . . . . . . . . +8
*Telephone:* . . . . . . . . . . . . [86] (20)-8221-2732
*Web:* . . . . . . http://portfocus.com/china/guangzhou/
index.html

**Port of Haikou**
*UN/LOCODE:* . . . . . . . . . . . . . . . . . . . . CN HAK
*Latitude/Longitude:* . . . . . . . 20° 1' N / 110° 16' E
*GMT Offset:* . . . . . . . . . . . . . . . . . . . . . . . . +8
*Telephone:* . . . . . . . . . . . . . . [86] (750) 662-345
*Web:* . . . . . . . . . www.infomarine.gr/china/haikou

**Port of Huangpu**
*UN/LOCODE:* . . . . . . . . . . . . . . . . . . . . CN HUA
*Latitude/Longitude:* . . . . . . . . 23° 5' N / 113° 25' E
*GMT Offset:* . . . . . . . . . . . . . . . . . . . . . . . . +8
*Telephone:* . . . . . . . . . . . . . . [86] (20) 227-8553

**Port of Lianyungang**
*UN/LOCODE:* . . . . . . . . . . . . . . . . . . . . CN LYG
*Latitude/Longitude:* . . . . . . . 34° 44' N / 119° 27' E
*GMT Offset:* . . . . . . . . . . . . . . . . . . . . . . . . +8
*Telephone:* . . . . . . . . . . . . [86] (518) 238-3193
www.lygport.com.cn

**Port of Nantong**
*UN/LOCODE:* . . . . . . . . . . . . . . . . . . . . CN NTG
*Latitude/Longitude:* . . . . . . . . 32° 0' N / 120° 48' E
*GMT Offset:* . . . . . . . . . . . . . . . . . . . . . . . . +8
*Web:* . . . . . . . . . . . . . . . . www.ntport.com.cn

**Port of Ningbo**
*UN/LOCODE:* . . . . . . . . . . . . . . . . . . . . CN NGB
*Latitude/Longitude:* . . . . . . . 29° 52' N / 121° 31' E
*GMT Offset:* . . . . . . . . . . . . . . . . . . . . . . . . +8
*Web:* . . . . . . . . . . . . . . . . www.nbport.com.cn

**Port of Qingdao**
*UN/LOCODE:* . . . . . . . . . . . . . . . . . . . . CN TAO
*Latitude/Longitude:* . . . . . . . . 36° 3' N / 120° 20' E
*GMT Offset:* . . . . . . . . . . . . . . . . . . . . . . . . +8
*Telephone:* . . . . . . . . . . . . . [86] (532) 222-878
*Web:* . http://portfocus.com/china/qingdao/index.html

**Port of Qinhuangdao**
*UN/LOCODE:* . . . . . . . . . . . . . . . . . . . . CN SHP
*Latitude/Longitude:* . . . . . . 40° 0' N / 119° 30' E
*GMT Offset:* . . . . . . . . . . . . . . . . . . . . . . . . +8

**Port of Shanghai**
*UN/LOCODE:* . . . . . . . . . . . . . . . . . . . . CN SHA
*Latitude/Longitude:* . . . . . . . 31° 14' N / 121° 28' E
*GMT Offset:* . . . . . . . . . . . . . . . . . . . . . . . . +8
*Telephone:* . . . . . . . . . . . . . [86] (21) 6323-0184
*Web:* . . . . . . . . . . . . . www.portshanghai.com.cn

**Port of Shantou**
*UN/LOCODE:* . . . . . . . . . . . . . . . . . . . . CN SWA
*Latitude/Longitude:* . . . . . . . 23° 20' N / 116° 45' E
*GMT Offset:* . . . . . . . . . . . . . . . . . . . . . . . . +8
*Telephone:* . . . . . . . . . . . . . . [86] (754) 827-5421
*Web:* . . . . . . . . . . www.infomarine.gr/china/shantou

**Port of Tianjin**
*UN/LOCODE:* . . . . . . . . . . . . . . . . . . . . CN TSN
*Latitude/Longitude:* . . . . . . . . 39° 6' N / 117° 10' E
*GMT Offset:* . . . . . . . . . . . . . . . . . . . . . . . . +8
*Telephone:* . . . . . . . . . . . . [86] (22)-2570-5733
*Web:* . . . http://portfocus.com/china/tianjin/index.html

**Port of Xiamen**
*UN/LOCODE:* . . . . . . . . . . . . . . . . . . . . CN XMN
*Latitude/Longitude:* . . . . . . . . 24° 27' N / 118° 2' E
*GMT Offset:* . . . . . . . . . . . . . . . . . . . . . . . . +8
*Telephone:* . . . . . . . . . . . . . . . [86] (592) 43116
*Web:* . . . . . . . . . . www.infomarine.gr/china/xiamen

**Port of Zhanjiang**
*UN/LOCODE:* . . . . . . . . . . . . . . . . . . . . CN ZHA
*Latitude/Longitude:* . . . . . . . 21° 11' N / 110° 24' E
*GMT Offset:* . . . . . . . . . . . . . . . . . . . . . . . . +8
*Telephone:* . . . . . . . . . . . . . . [86] (759) 250-103
*Web:* . . . . . . . . . . . . . . . . . . www.zjgport.com.cn

## Colombia

**Port of Barranquilla**
*UN/LOCODE:* . . . . . . . . . . . . . . . . . . . . CO BAQ
*Latitude/Longitude:* . . . . . . . 10° 58' N / 74° 47' W
*GMT Offset:* . . . . . . . . . . . . . . . . . . . . . . . . -5
*Telephone:* . . . . . . . . . . . . . . [57] (5) 379-9555
*Web:* . . . . . . . . . . . . . . . . . . www.sprb.com.co

**Port of Buenaventura**
*UN/LOCODE:* . . . . . . . . . . . . . . . . . . . . CO BUN
*Latitude/Longitude:* . . . . . . . . 3° 53' N / 77° 5' W
*GMT Offset:* . . . . . . . . . . . . . . . . . . . . . . . . -5
*Web:.* www.navescolombia.com/ports/buenaventura.htm

**Port of Cartagena**
*UN/LOCODE:* . . . . . . . . . . . . . . . . . . . . CO CTG
*Latitude/Longitude:* . . . . . . . 10° 26' N / 75° 33' W
*GMT Offset:* . . . . . . . . . . . . . . . . . . . . . . . . -5
*Telephone:* . . . . . . . . . . . . . . [57] (5) 660-7534
*Web:* . . . . . . . . . . www.puertocartagena.com/

**Port of Puerto Bolivar**
*UN/LOCODE:* . . . . . . . . . . . . . . . . . . . . CO PBO
*Latitude/Longitude:* . . . . . . . . 12° 16' N / 71° 58' W
*GMT Offset:* . . . . . . . . . . . . . . . . . . . . . . . . -5
*Telephone:* . . . . . . . . . . . . . . [57] (5) 856-2131
*Web:* . . . www.navescolombia.com/ports/pbolivar.htm

**Port of Tumaco**
*UN/LOCODE:* . . . . . . . . . . . . . . . . . . . . CO TCO
*Latitude/Longitude:* . . . . . . . . 1° 49' N / 78° 45' W
*GMT Offset:* . . . . . . . . . . . . . . . . . . . . . . . . -5
*Telephone:* . . . . . . . . . . . . . . [57] (30) 272-457
*Web:* . . . www.navescolombia.com/ports/tumaco.htm

**Port of Turbo**
*UN/LOCODE:* . . . . . . . . . . . . . . . . . . . . CO TRB
*Latitude/Longitude:* . . . . . . . . . . 8° 0' N / 76° 50' W
*GMT Offset:* . . . . . . . . . . . . . . . . . . . . . . . . -5
*Telephone:* . . . . . . . . . . . . . . [57] (94) 868-2025
*Web:* . . . . . www.navescolombia.com/ports/turbo.htm

## Comoros

**Port of Moroni**
*UN/LOCODE:* . . . . . . . . . . . . . . . . . . . . KM YVA
*Latitude/Longitude:* . . . . . . . 11° 42' S / 43° 44' E
*GMT Offset:* . . . . . . . . . . . . . . . . . . . . . . . . +3

**Port of Mutsamudu**
*UN/LOCODE:* . . . . . . . . . . . . . . . . . . . . KM MUT
*Latitude/Longitude:* . . . . . . . 12° 10' S / 44° 24' E
*GMT Offset:* . . . . . . . . . . . . . . . . . . . . . . . . +3

# Congo

**Port of Pointe Noire**
*UN/LOCODE:* . . . . . . . . . . . . . . . . . . . . . . . CG PNR
*Latitude/Longitude:* . . . . . . . . . 4° 47' S / 11° 49' E
*GMT Offset:* . . . . . . . . . . . . . . . . . . . . . . . . . . +1
*Telephone:* . . . . . . . . . . . . . . . . . . . [242] 940-953
*Web:* . . . . . . . . . www.otal.com/congo/congo.htm#psi

# Congo, Democratic Republic of

**Port of Banana**
*UN/LOCODE:* . . . . . . . . . . . . . . . . . . . . . . . ZR BNW
*Latitude/Longitude:* . . . . . . . . . . . 6° 1' S / 12° 25' E
*GMT Offset:* . . . . . . . . . . . . . . . . . . . . . . . . . . +1

**Port of Boma**
*UN/LOCODE:* . . . . . . . . . . . . . . . . . . . . . . . ZR BOA
*Latitude/Longitude:* . . . . . . . . . . . 5° 51' S / 13° 3' E
*GMT Offset:* . . . . . . . . . . . . . . . . . . . . . . . . . . +1

# Costa Rica

**Port of Caldera**
*UN/LOCODE:* . . . . . . . . . . . . . . . . . . . . . . . CR CAL
*Latitude/Longitude:* . . . . . . . . . 9° 54' N / 84° 43' W
*GMT Offset:* . . . . . . . . . . . . . . . . . . . . . . . . . . -6
*Web:* . . . . . . . . . . . www.cocatram.org.ni/puertosca/
pto_caldera_cr.html

**Port of Golfito**
*UN/LOCODE:* . . . . . . . . . . . . . . . . . . . . . . . CR GLF
*Latitude/Longitude:* . . . . . . . . . 8° 37' N / 83° 10' W
*GMT Offset:* . . . . . . . . . . . . . . . . . . . . . . . . . . -6
*Web:* . . . . . . . . . . . www.cocatram.org.ni/puertosca/
pto_golfito_cr.html

**Port of Puntarenas**
*UN/LOCODE:* . . . . . . . . . . . . . . . . . . . . . . . CR PAS
*Latitude/Longitude:* . . . . . . . . . 9° 58' N / 84° 50' W
*GMT Offset:* . . . . . . . . . . . . . . . . . . . . . . . . . . -6
*Web:* . . . . . . . . . . . www.cocatram.org.ni/puertosca/
pto_puntarenas_cr.html

**Port of Quepos**
*UN/LOCODE:* . . . . . . . . . . . . . . . . . . . . . . . CR XQP
*Latitude/Longitude:* . . . . . . . . . 9° 25' N / 84° 10' W
*GMT Offset:* . . . . . . . . . . . . . . . . . . . . . . . . . . -6

**Port of San Jose**
*UN/LOCODE:* . . . . . . . . . . . . . . . . . . . . . . . CR SJO
*Latitude/Longitude:* . . . . . . . . . 13° 55' N / 90° 50' W
*GMT Offset:* . . . . . . . . . . . . . . . . . . . . . . . . . . -6

# Cote D'Ivoire (Ivory Coast)

**Port of Abidjan**
*UN/LOCODE:* . . . . . . . . . . . . . . . . . . . . . . . CI ABJ
*Latitude/Longitude:* . . . . . . . . . 5° 18' N / 4° 0' W
*GMT Offset:* . . . . . . . . . . . . . . . . . . . . . . . . . . +0
*Telephone:* . . . . . . . . . . . . . . . . . [225] 2123-8000
*Web:* . . . . . . . . . . . . . . . . . . . . . . . www.paa-ci.org

# Croatia (Hrvatska)

**Port of Dubrovnik**
*UN/LOCODE:* . . . . . . . . . . . . . . . . . . . . . . . HR DBV
*Latitude/Longitude:* . . . . . . . . . . 42° 39' N / 18° 5' E
*GMT Offset:* . . . . . . . . . . . . . . . . . . . . . . . . . . +1
*Telephone:* . . . . . . . . . . . . . . . [385] (20) 418-511
*Web:* . . . . . . . . . www.portauthority.hr/dubrovni.html

**Port of Omisalj**
*UN/LOCODE:* . . . . . . . . . . . . . . . . . . . . . . . HR OMI
*Latitude/Longitude:* . . . . . . . . . 45° 12' N / 14° 33' E
*GMT Offset:* . . . . . . . . . . . . . . . . . . . . . . . . . . +1
*Web:* . . . . . . . . . . . . . www.jadroagent.hr/omisalj.htm

**Port of Ploce**
*UN/LOCODE:* . . . . . . . . . . . . . . . . . . . . . . . HR PLE
*Latitude/Longitude:* . . . . . . . . . 43° 3' N / 17° 26' E
*GMT Offset:* . . . . . . . . . . . . . . . . . . . . . . . . . . +1
*Telephone:* . . . . . . . . . . . . . . [385] (20) 603-180
*Web:* . . . . . . . . . www.port-authority-ploce.hr

**Port of Pula**
*UN/LOCODE:* . . . . . . . . . . . . . . . . . . . . . . . HR PUY
*Latitude/Longitude:* . . . . . . . . . 44° 51' N / 13° 51' E
*GMT Offset:* . . . . . . . . . . . . . . . . . . . . . . . . . . +1
*Web:* . . . . . . . . . . . www.jadroagent.hr/pula.htm

**Port of Rijeka Bakar**
*UN/LOCODE:* . . . . . . . . . . . . . . . . . . . . . . . HR RJK
*Latitude/Longitude:* . . . . . . . . . 45° 19' N / 14° 26' E
*GMT Offset:* . . . . . . . . . . . . . . . . . . . . . . . . . . +1
*Telephone:* . . . . . . . . . . . . . . [385] (51) 351-111
*Web:* . . . . . . . . . www.portauthority.hr/english/rijeka/
port_rijeka_authority.shtml

**Port of Sibenik**
*UN/LOCODE:* . . . . . . . . . . . . . . . . . . . . . . . HR SIB
*Latitude/Longitude:* . . . . . . . . . 43° 44' N / 15° 53' E
*GMT Offset:* . . . . . . . . . . . . . . . . . . . . . . . . . . +1
*Web:* . . . . . . . . . . . www.jadroagent.hr/sibenik.htm

**Port of Split**
*UN/LOCODE:* . . . . . . . . . . . . . . . . . . . . . . . HR SPU
*Latitude/Longitude:* . . . . . . . . . 43° 31' N / 16° 26' E
*GMT Offset:* . . . . . . . . . . . . . . . . . . . . . . . . . . +1
*Telephone:* . . . . . . . . . . . . . . [385] (21) 362-501
*Web:* . . . . . . . . . www.portauthority.hr/split.html

**Port of Zadar**
*UN/LOCODE:* . . . . . . . . . . . . . . . . . . . . . . . HR ZAD
*Latitude/Longitude:* . . . . . . . . . 44° 7' N / 15° 14' E
*GMT Offset:* . . . . . . . . . . . . . . . . . . . . . . . . . . +1
*Telephone:* . . . . . . . . . . . . . . [385] (23) 314-520
*Web:* . . . . . . . . . www.portauthority.hr/zadar.html

# Cuba

**Port of Cienfuegos**
*UN/LOCODE:* . . . . . . . . . . . . . . . . . . . . . . . CU CFG
*Latitude/Longitude:* . . . . . . . . . 22° 9' N / 80° 27' W
*GMT Offset:* . . . . . . . . . . . . . . . . . . . . . . . . . . -5

**Port of Manzanillo**
*UN/LOCODE:* . . . . . . . . . . . . . . . . . . . . . . . CU MZO
*Latitude/Longitude:* . . . . . . . . . 20° 20' N / 77° 12' W
*GMT Offset:* . . . . . . . . . . . . . . . . . . . . . . . . . . -5

**Port of Mariel**
*UN/LOCODE:* . . . . . . . . . . . . . . . . . . . . . . . CU MAR
*Latitude/Longitude:* . . . . . . . . . 23° 1' N / 82° 46' W
*GMT Offset:* . . . . . . . . . . . . . . . . . . . . . . . . . . -5

**Port of Matanzas**
*UN/LOCODE:* . . . . . . . . . . . . . . . . . . . . . . . CU QMA
*Latitude/Longitude:* . . . . . . . . . 23° 3' N / 81° 34' W
*GMT Offset:* . . . . . . . . . . . . . . . . . . . . . . . . . . -5

**Port of Nuevitas**
*UN/LOCODE:* . . . . . . . . . . . . . . . . . . . . . . . CU NVT
*Latitude/Longitude:* . . . . . . . . . 21° 33' N / 77° 16' W
*GMT Offset:* . . . . . . . . . . . . . . . . . . . . . . . . . . -5

**Port of Santiago de Cuba**
*UN/LOCODE:* . . . . . . . . . . . . . . . . . . . . . . . CU SCU
*Latitude/Longitude:* . . . . . . . . . 19° 50' N / 75° 52' W
*GMT Offset:* . . . . . . . . . . . . . . . . . . . . . . . . . . -5

# Cyprus

**Port of Akrotiri**
*UN/LOCODE:* . . . . . . . . . . . . . . . . . . . . . . . CY AKT
*Latitude/Longitude:* . . . . . . . . . 34° 34' N / 33° 2' E
*GMT Offset:* . . . . . . . . . . . . . . . . . . . . . . . . . . +2
*Telephone:* . . . . . . . . . . . . . . [357] (22) 817-200
*Web:* . . . . . . . . . . . . . . . . . . . . . . . www.cpa.gov.cy

SEAPORTS

**Port of Famagusta**
*UN/LOCODE:* . . . . . . . . . . . . . . . . . . . . . CY FMG
*Latitude/Longitude:* . . . . . . . . . 35° 7' N / 33° 57' E
*GMT Offset:* . . . . . . . . . . . . . . . . . . . . . . . . +2
*Telephone:* . . . . . . . . . . . . . . [357] (22) 817-200
*Web:* . . . . . . . . . . . . . . . . . . . . www.cpa.gov.cy

**Port of Kyrenia**
*UN/LOCODE:* . . . . . . . . . . . . . . . . . . . . . CY KYR
*Latitude/Longitude:* . . . . . . . . . 35° 20' N / 33° 19' E
*GMT Offset:* . . . . . . . . . . . . . . . . . . . . . . . . +2
*Telephone:* . . . . . . . . . . . . . . [357] (22) 817-200
*Web:* . . . . . . . . . . . . . . . . . . . . www.cpa.gov.cy

**Port of Larnaca**
*UN/LOCODE:* . . . . . . . . . . . . . . . . . . . . . CY LAT
*Latitude/Longitude:* . . . . . . . . . 35° 3' N / 32° 24' E
*GMT Offset:* . . . . . . . . . . . . . . . . . . . . . . . . +2
*Telephone:* . . . . . . . . . . . . . . [357] (22) 756-100
*Web:* . . . . . . . . . . . . . . . . . . . . www.cpa.gov.cy

**Port of Limassol**
*UN/LOCODE:* . . . . . . . . . . . . . . . . . . . . . CY LMS
*Latitude/Longitude:* . . . . . . . . . 34° 39' N / 33° 1' E
*GMT Offset:* . . . . . . . . . . . . . . . . . . . . . . . . +2
*Telephone:* . . . . . . . . . . . . . . [357] (22) 817-200
*Web:* . . . . . . . . . . . . . . . . . . . . www.cpa.gov.cy

**Port of Paphos**
*UN/LOCODE:* . . . . . . . . . . . . . . . . . . . . . CY PFO
*Latitude/Longitude:* . . . . . . . . . 34° 45' N / 32° 24' E
*GMT Offset:* . . . . . . . . . . . . . . . . . . . . . . . . +2
*Telephone:* . . . . . . . . . . . . . . [357] (22) 817-200
*Web:* . . . . . . . . . . . . . . . . . . . . www.cpa.gov.cy

**Port of Vassiliko**
*UN/LOCODE:* . . . . . . . . . . . . . . . . . . . . . CY VAS
*Latitude/Longitude:* . . . . . . . . . 34° 43' N / 33° 19' E
*GMT Offset:* . . . . . . . . . . . . . . . . . . . . . . . . +2
*Telephone:* . . . . . . . . . . . . . . [357] (22) 817-200
*Web:* . . . . . . . . . . . . . . . . . . . . www.cpa.gov.cy

## Denmark
**Port of Aarhus**
*UN/LOCODE:* . . . . . . . . . . . . . . . . . . . . . DK AAR
*Latitude/Longitude:* . . . . . . . . . 56° 10' N / 10° 13' E
*GMT Offset:* . . . . . . . . . . . . . . . . . . . . . . . . +2
*Telephone:* . . . . . . . . . . . . . . [45] (86) 133-266
*Web:* . . . . . . . . . . . . . . . . . . . . www.aarhushavn.dk

**Port of Esbjerg**
*UN/LOCODE:* . . . . . . . . . . . . . . . . . . . . . DK EBJ
*Latitude/Longitude:* . . . . . . . . . 55° 28' N / 8° 26' E
*GMT Offset:* . . . . . . . . . . . . . . . . . . . . . . . . +1
*Telephone:* . . . . . . . . . . . . . . [45] (75) 124-144
*Web:* . . . . . . . . . . . . . . . . . www.port-of-esbjerg.dk/

**Port of Fredericia**
*UN/LOCODE:* . . . . . . . . . . . . . . . . . . . . . DK FRC
*Latitude/Longitude:* . . . . . . . . . 55° 33' N / 9° 45' E
*GMT Offset:* . . . . . . . . . . . . . . . . . . . . . . . . +1
*Telephone:* . . . . . . . . . . . . . . [45] (79) 215-000
*Web:* . . . . . . . . . . . . . . . . . . . . www.adp-as.dk

**Port of Frederikshavn**
*UN/LOCODE:* . . . . . . . . . . . . . . . . . . . . . DK FDH
*Latitude/Longitude:* . . . . . . . . . 57° 28' N / 10° 33' E
*GMT Offset:* . . . . . . . . . . . . . . . . . . . . . . . . +1
*Telephone:* . . . . . . . . . . . . . . [45] (96) 204-700
*Web:* . . . . . . . . www.frederikshavnhavn.dk/en

**Port of Grenaa**
*UN/LOCODE:* . . . . . . . . . . . . . . . . . . . . . DK GRE
*Latitude/Longitude:* . . . . . . . . . 56° 25' N / 10° 56' E
*GMT Offset:* . . . . . . . . . . . . . . . . . . . . . . . . +1
*Telephone:* . . . . . . . . . . . . . . [45] (87) 587-600
*Web:* . . . . . . . . . . . . . . . . www.port-of-grenaa.com

**Port of Odense**
*UN/LOCODE:* . . . . . . . . . . . . . . . . . . . . . DK ODE
*Latitude/Longitude:* . . . . . . . . . 55° 25' N / 10° 23' E
*GMT Offset:* . . . . . . . . . . . . . . . . . . . . . . . . +1
*Telephone:* . . . . . . . . . . . . . . [45] (66) 120-792
*Web:* . . . . . . . . . . . . . . . . . . . . www.odensehavn.dk

## Djibouti
**Port of Djibouti**
*UN/LOCODE:* . . . . . . . . . . . . . . . . . . . . . DJ JIB
*Latitude/Longitude:* . . . . . . . . . 11° 36' N / 43° 8' E
*GMT Offset:* . . . . . . . . . . . . . . . . . . . . . . . . +3
*Web:* . . . . . . . . . . . . . . . . www.pmaesa.org/djibouti

## Dominica
**Port of Portsmouth**
*UN/LOCODE:* . . . . . . . . . . . . . . . . . . . . . DM POR
*Latitude/Longitude:* . . . . . . . . . 15° 34' N / 61° 28' W
*GMT Offset:* . . . . . . . . . . . . . . . . . . . . . . . . -4

**Port of Roseau**
*UN/LOCODE:* . . . . . . . . . . . . . . . . . . . . . DM RSU
*Latitude/Longitude:* . . . . . . . . . 15° 17' N / 61° 24' W
*GMT Offset:* . . . . . . . . . . . . . . . . . . . . . . . . -4

## Dominican Republic
**Port of Barahona**
*UN/LOCODE:* . . . . . . . . . . . . . . . . . . . . . DO BRX
*Latitude/Longitude:* . . . . . . . . . 18° 12' N / 71° 4' W
*GMT Offset:* . . . . . . . . . . . . . . . . . . . . . . . . -4
*Telephone:* . . . . . . . . . . . . . . [1] (809) 524-2384
*Web:* . . . www.fschad.com/dominicanports/barahona/
index.html

**Port of La Romana**
*UN/LOCODE:* . . . . . . . . . . . . . . . . . . . . . DO LRM
*Latitude/Longitude:* . . . . . . . . . 18° 27' N / 69° 1' W
*GMT Offset:* . . . . . . . . . . . . . . . . . . . . . . . . -4
*Telephone:* . . . . . . . . . . . . . . [1] (809) 556-3285
*Web:* . . www.fschad.com/dominicanports/la_romana/
index.html

**Port of Puerto Plata**
*UN/LOCODE:* . . . . . . . . . . . . . . . . . . . . . DO POP
*Latitude/Longitude:* . . . . . . . . . 19° 49' N / 70° 42' W
*GMT Offset:* . . . . . . . . . . . . . . . . . . . . . . . . -4
*Telephone:* . . . . . . . . . . . . . . [1] (809) 539-6339
*Web:* . . . . . . . www.amarit.com.do/pi_puertoplata.asp

**Port of San Pedro de Macoris**
*UN/LOCODE:* . . . . . . . . . . . . . . . . . . . . . DO SPM
*Latitude/Longitude:* . . . . . . . . . 18° 26' N / 69° 18' W
*GMT Offset:* . . . . . . . . . . . . . . . . . . . . . . . . -4
*Telephone:* . . . . . . . . . . . . . . [1] (809) 529-2069
*Web:* . . www.fschad.com/dominicanports/san_pedro/
index.html

**Port of Santo Domingo**
*UN/LOCODE:* . . . . . . . . . . . . . . . . . . . . . DO SDQ
*Latitude/Longitude:* . . . . . . . . . 18° 28' N / 18° 28' N
*GMT Offset:* . . . . . . . . . . . . . . . . . . . . . . . . -4
*Telephone:* . . . . . . . . . . . . . . [1] (809) 682-8792
*Web:* www.fschad.com/dominicanports/santo_domingo/
index.html

## Ecuador
**Port of Esmeraldas**
*UN/LOCODE:* . . . . . . . . . . . . . . . . . . . . . EC ESM
*Latitude/Longitude:* . . . . . . . . . 1° 0' N / 79° 38' W
*GMT Offset:* . . . . . . . . . . . . . . . . . . . . . . . . -5
*Telephone:* . . . . . . . . . . . . . . [593] (6) 711-996

**Port of Guayaquil**
*UN/LOCODE:* . . . . . . . . . . . . . . . . . . . . . EC GYE
*Latitude/Longitude:* . . . . . . . . . 2° 16' S / 79° 54' W
*GMT Offset:* . . . . . . . . . . . . . . . . . . . . . . . . -5
*Telephone:* . . . . . . . . . . . . . . [593] (4) 480-459
*Web:* . . . . . . . . . . . . . www1.puertodeguayaquil.com

**Port of La Libertad**
UN/LOCODE: . . . . . . . . . . . . . . . . . . . . EC LLD
Latitude/Longitude: . . . . . . . . 2° 12' S / 80° 55' W
GMT Offset: . . . . . . . . . . . . . . . . . . . . . . . . . -5
Telephone: . . . . . . . . . . . . . . . [593] (4) 785-781

**Port of Manta**
UN/LOCODE: . . . . . . . . . . . . . . . . . . . . EC MEC
Latitude/Longitude: . . . . . . . . 0° 55' S / 80° 43' W
GMT Offset: . . . . . . . . . . . . . . . . . . . . . . . . . -5
Web: . . . . . . . . . . . . . . . . . . www.apmanta.gov.ec

**Port of Puerto Bolivar**
UN/LOCODE: . . . . . . . . . . . . . . . . . . . . EC PBO
Latitude/Longitude: . . . . . . . . . 3° 15' S / 80° 1' W
GMT Offset: . . . . . . . . . . . . . . . . . . . . . . . . . -5
Telephone: . . . . . . . . . . . . . . . [593] (7) 920-483

**Port of San Lorenzo**
UN/LOCODE: . . . . . . . . . . . . . . . . . . . . EC SLR
Latitude/Longitude: . . . . . . . . 1° 10' S / 78° 50' W
GMT Offset: . . . . . . . . . . . . . . . . . . . . . . . . . -5

## Egypt

**Port of Alexandria**
UN/LOCODE: . . . . . . . . . . . . . . . . . . . . EG EDK
Latitude/Longitude: . . . . . . . . 31° 8' N / 29° 49' E
GMT Offset: . . . . . . . . . . . . . . . . . . . . . . . . . +2
Web: . . . . . . . . . . . . . . . . . . www.astrans.com.eg

**Port of Damietta**
UN/LOCODE: . . . . . . . . . . . . . . . . . . . . EG DAM
Latitude/Longitude: . . . . . . . . 31° 28' N / 31° 45' E
GMT Offset: . . . . . . . . . . . . . . . . . . . . . . . . . +2
Telephone: . . . . . . . . . . . . . . . [20] (57) 325-940
Web: . . . . . . . . . . . . . . . . . . www.astrans.com.eg

**Port of Suez (Al Suweis)**
UN/LOCODE: . . . . . . . . . . . . . . . . . . . . . . EG
Latitude/Longitude: . . . . . . . . 29° 58' N / 32° 33' E
GMT Offset: . . . . . . . . . . . . . . . . . . . . . . . . . +2
Telephone: . . . . . . . . . . . . . . . [20] (62) 220-740
Web: . . . . . . . . . . . . . . . . . . www.astrans.com.eg

**Port Said**
UN/LOCODE: . . . . . . . . . . . . . . . . . . . . EG PSD
Latitude/Longitude: . . . . . . . . 31° 16' N / 32° 19' E
GMT Offset: . . . . . . . . . . . . . . . . . . . . . . . . . +2
Telephone: . . . . . . . . . . . . . . . [20] (66) 223-892
Web: . . . . . . . . . . . . . . . . . . www.astrans.com.eg

## El Salvador

**Port of Acajutla**
UN/LOCODE: . . . . . . . . . . . . . . . . . . . . SV AQJ
Latitude/Longitude: . . . . . . . . 13° 35' N / 89° 50' W
GMT Offset: . . . . . . . . . . . . . . . . . . . . . . . . . -6
Telephone: . . . . . . . . . . . . . . . . . [503] 887-3681
Web: . . . . . . . . . . . . www.cocatram.org.ni/puertosca/
pto_acajutla_elsalvador.html

**Port of La Libertad**
UN/LOCODE: . . . . . . . . . . . . . . . . . . . . SV LLD
Latitude/Longitude: . . . . . . . . 13° 28' N / 89° 20' W
GMT Offset: . . . . . . . . . . . . . . . . . . . . . . . . . -6

**Port of La Union**
UN/LOCODE: . . . . . . . . . . . . . . . . . . . . SV LUN
Latitude/Longitude: . . . . . . . . 13° 20' N / 87° 50' W
GMT Offset: . . . . . . . . . . . . . . . . . . . . . . . . . -6

## Equatorial Guinea

**Port of Bata**
UN/LOCODE: . . . . . . . . . . . . . . . . . . . . GQ BSG
Latitude/Longitude: . . . . . . . . . . 1° 52' N / 9° 46' E
GMT Offset: . . . . . . . . . . . . . . . . . . . . . . . . . +1

**Port of Luba**
UN/LOCODE: . . . . . . . . . . . . . . . . . . . . GQ LUB
Latitude/Longitude: . . . . . . . . . . 3° 28' N / 8° 33' E
GMT Offset: . . . . . . . . . . . . . . . . . . . . . . . . . +1

## Eritrea

**Port of Assab**
UN/LOCODE: . . . . . . . . . . . . . . . . . . . . ER ASA
Latitude/Longitude: . . . . . . . . . 13° 1' N / 42° 44' E
GMT Offset: . . . . . . . . . . . . . . . . . . . . . . . . . +3
Web: . . . http://home.planet.nl/~hans.mebrat/eritrea-
assab.htm

**Port of Massawa**
UN/LOCODE: . . . . . . . . . . . . . . . . . . . . ER MSW
Latitude/Longitude: . . . . . . . . 15° 37' N / 39° 28' E
GMT Offset: . . . . . . . . . . . . . . . . . . . . . . . . . +3
Telephone: . . . . . . . . . . . . . . . [291] (1) 552-931

## Estonia

**Port of P‰ornu**
UN/LOCODE: . . . . . . . . . . . . . . . . . . . . EE PYA
Latitude/Longitude: . . . . . . . . 58° 23' N / 24° 29' E
GMT Offset: . . . . . . . . . . . . . . . . . . . . . . . . . +2

**Port of Tallinn**
UN/LOCODE: . . . . . . . . . . . . . . . . . . . . EE TLL
Latitude/Longitude: . . . . . . . . 59° 27' N / 24° 46' E
GMT Offset: . . . . . . . . . . . . . . . . . . . . . . . . . +2
Telephone: . . . . . . . . . . . . . . . [372] (6) 318-555
Web: . . . . . . . . . . . . . . . . . . www.portoftallinn.com

## Faroe Islands

**Port of Klaksvik**
UN/LOCODE: . . . . . . . . . . . . . . . . . . . . FO KVI
Latitude/Longitude: . . . . . . . . . 62° 14' N / 6° 35' W
GMT Offset: . . . . . . . . . . . . . . . . . . . . . . . . . . 0
Telephone: . . . . . . . . . . . . . . . . . [298] 455-101
Web: . . . . . . . . . . . . . . . . . . . . . www.klhavn.fo

**Port of Tvoroyri**
UN/LOCODE: . . . . . . . . . . . . . . . . . . . . FO TVO
Latitude/Longitude: . . . . . . . . . 61° 34' N / 6° 48' W
GMT Offset: . . . . . . . . . . . . . . . . . . . . . . . . . . 0

## Fiji

**Port of Labasa**
UN/LOCODE: . . . . . . . . . . . . . . . . . . . . FJ LBS
Latitude/Longitude: . . . . . . . . 16° 26' S / 179° 14' E
GMT Offset: . . . . . . . . . . . . . . . . . . . . . . . . . +12

**Port of Lautoka**
UN/LOCODE: . . . . . . . . . . . . . . . . . . . . FJ LTK
Latitude/Longitude: . . . . . . . . 17° 36' S / 177° 26' E
GMT Offset: . . . . . . . . . . . . . . . . . . . . . . . . . +12
Telephone: . . . . . . . . . . . . . . . . . [679] 330-4725
Web: . . . . . . . . . . . . . . . . . . www.portofsuva.com

**Port of Levuka**
UN/LOCODE: . . . . . . . . . . . . . . . . . . . . FJ LEV
Latitude/Longitude: . . . . . . . . 17° 41' S / 178° 51' E
GMT Offset: . . . . . . . . . . . . . . . . . . . . . . . . . +12

**Port of Savusavu**
UN/LOCODE: . . . . . . . . . . . . . . . . . . . . FJ SVU
Latitude/Longitude: . . . . . . . . 16° 49' S / 179° 18' E
GMT Offset: . . . . . . . . . . . . . . . . . . . . . . . . . +12

**Port of Suva**
UN/LOCODE: . . . . . . . . . . . . . . . . . . . . FJ SUV
Latitude/Longitude: . . . . . . . . . 18° 8' S / 178° 26' E
GMT Offset: . . . . . . . . . . . . . . . . . . . . . . . . . +12
Telephone: . . . . . . . . . . . . . . . . . [679] 330-4725
Web: . . . . . . . . . . . . . . . . . . www.portofsuva.com

**SEAPORTS**

## Finland

**Port of Hamina**
UN/LOCODE: . . . . . . . . . . . . . . . . . . . . . . . FI HMN
Latitude/Longitude: . . . . . . . . 60° 34' N / 27° 11' E
GMT Offset: . . . . . . . . . . . . . . . . . . . . . . . . . . . +2
Telephone: . . . . . . . . . . . . . . . [358] (5)-225-5400
Web: . . . . . . . . . . . . . . . . . . www.portofhamina.fi

**Port of Helsinki**
UN/LOCODE: . . . . . . . . . . . . . . . . . . . . . . . FI HEL
Latitude/Longitude: . . . . . . . . 60° 10' N / 24° 57' E
GMT Offset: . . . . . . . . . . . . . . . . . . . . . . . . . . . +2
Telephone: . . . . . . . . . . . . . . . . [358] (9) 173-331
Web: . . . . . . . . . . . . . . . . . . www.portofhelsinki.fi

**Port of Kokkola**
UN/LOCODE: . . . . . . . . . . . . . . . . . . . . . . . FI KOK
Latitude/Longitude: . . . . . . . . . 63° 50' N / 23° 8' E
GMT Offset: . . . . . . . . . . . . . . . . . . . . . . . . . . . +2
Telephone: . . . . . . . . . . . . . . . [358] (6) 824-2400
Web: . . . . . . . . . . . . . . . . . www.port.of.kokkola.fi

**Port of Kotka**
UN/LOCODE: . . . . . . . . . . . . . . . . . . . . . . . FI KTK
Latitude/Longitude: . . . . . . . . 60° 28' N / 26° 57' E
GMT Offset: . . . . . . . . . . . . . . . . . . . . . . . . . . . +2
Telephone: . . . . . . . . . . . . . . . [358] (5) 234-4280

**Port of Loviisa**
UN/LOCODE: . . . . . . . . . . . . . . . . . . . . . . . FI LOV
Latitude/Longitude: . . . . . . . . 60° 24' N / 26° 16' E
GMT Offset: . . . . . . . . . . . . . . . . . . . . . . . . . . . +2

**Port of Oulu**
UN/LOCODE: . . . . . . . . . . . . . . . . . . . . . . . FI OUL
Latitude/Longitude: . . . . . . . . . 65° 0' N / 25° 25' E
GMT Offset: . . . . . . . . . . . . . . . . . . . . . . . . . . . +2
Telephone: . . . . . . . . . . . . . . . [358] (8) 5584-2750
Web: . . . . . . . . . . . . . . . . . . . www.ouluport.com/

**Port of Pori**
UN/LOCODE: . . . . . . . . . . . . . . . . . . . . . . . FI POR
Latitude/Longitude: . . . . . . . . 61° 36' N / 21° 29' E
GMT Offset: . . . . . . . . . . . . . . . . . . . . . . . . . . . +0
Telephone: . . . . . . . . . . . . . . . . [358] (2) 621-2600
Web: . . . . . . . . . . . . . . . . . . . . www.pori.fi/port/

**Port of Rauma**
UN/LOCODE: . . . . . . . . . . . . . . . . . . . . . . . FI RAU
Latitude/Longitude: . . . . . . . . . 61° 8' N / 21° 30' E
GMT Offset: . . . . . . . . . . . . . . . . . . . . . . . . . . . +2
Telephone: . . . . . . . . . . . . . . . . [358] (2) 834-4712
Web: . . . . . . . . . . . . . . . . . www.portofrauma.com/

**Port of Turku**
UN/LOCODE: . . . . . . . . . . . . . . . . . . . . . . . FI TKU
Latitude/Longitude: . . . . . . . . 60° 27' N / 22° 15' E
GMT Offset: . . . . . . . . . . . . . . . . . . . . . . . . . . . +2
Telephone: . . . . . . . . . . . . . . . . [358] (2) 126-7411
Web: . . . . . . . . . . . . . . . . . . . www.port.turku.fi/

**Port of Uusikaupunki**
UN/LOCODE: . . . . . . . . . . . . . . . . . . . . . . . FI UKI
Latitude/Longitude: . . . . . . . . 60° 48' N / 21° 24' E
GMT Offset: . . . . . . . . . . . . . . . . . . . . . . . . . . . +2

**Port of Varkaus**
UN/LOCODE: . . . . . . . . . . . . . . . . . . . . . . . FI VRK
Latitude/Longitude: . . . . . . . . 62° 17' N / 27° 44' E
GMT Offset: . . . . . . . . . . . . . . . . . . . . . . . . . . . +2
Telephone: . . . . . . . . . . . . . . . . [358] (7) 257-9411

## France

**Port of Bordeaux**
UN/LOCODE: . . . . . . . . . . . . . . . . . . . . . . . FR BOD
Latitude/Longitude: . . . . . . . . . 44° 50' N / 0° 34' W
GMT Offset: . . . . . . . . . . . . . . . . . . . . . . . . . . . +1
Telephone: . . . . . . . . . . . . . . . . [33] 556-905-800
Web: . . . . . . . . . . . . . . . . . . www.bordeaux-port.fr

**Port of Boulogne Sur Mer**
UN/LOCODE: . . . . . . . . . . . . . . . . . . . . . . . FR BOL
Latitude/Longitude: . . . . . . . . . 50° 45' N / 1° 34' E
GMT Offset: . . . . . . . . . . . . . . . . . . . . . . . . . . . +1
Telephone: . . . . . . . . . . . . . . . . [33] 321-305-323
Web: . . . . . . . . . . . . . . . . . . www.portboulogne.com

**Port of Cherbourg**
UN/LOCODE: . . . . . . . . . . . . . . . . . . . . . . . FR CER
Latitude/Longitude: . . . . . . . . . 49° 38' N / 1° 38' W
GMT Offset: . . . . . . . . . . . . . . . . . . . . . . . . . . . +1
Telephone: . . . . . . . . . . . . . . . . [33] 333-233-225
Web: . . . . . . . . . . . . . . . . . www.port-cherbourg.com

**Port of Dunkerque**
UN/LOCODE: . . . . . . . . . . . . . . . . . . . . . . . FR DKK
Latitude/Longitude: . . . . . . . . . 51° 3' N / 2° 22' E
GMT Offset: . . . . . . . . . . . . . . . . . . . . . . . . . . . +1
Telephone: . . . . . . . . . . . . . . . . [33] 328-287-401
Web: . . . . . . . . . . . . . . . . . www.portdedunkerque.fr

**Port of La Rochelle-Pallice**
UN/LOCODE: . . . . . . . . . . . . . . . . . . . . . . . FR LPE
Latitude/Longitude: . . . . . . . . . 46° 9' N / 1° 10' W
GMT Offset: . . . . . . . . . . . . . . . . . . . . . . . . . . . +1
Telephone: . . . . . . . . . . . . . . . . [33] 546-005-360
Web: . . . . . . . . . . . . . . . . . . www.larochelle.port.fr

**Port of Le Havre**
UN/LOCODE: . . . . . . . . . . . . . . . . . . . . . . . FR LEH
Latitude/Longitude: . . . . . . . . . 49° 30' N / 0° 7' W
GMT Offset: . . . . . . . . . . . . . . . . . . . . . . . . . . . +1
Web: . . . . . . . . . . . . . . . . . . . . www.havre-port.fr

**Port of Marseille**
UN/LOCODE: . . . . . . . . . . . . . . . . . . . . . . . FR MRS
Latitude/Longitude: . . . . . . . . . 43° 19' N / 5° 22' E
GMT Offset: . . . . . . . . . . . . . . . . . . . . . . . . . . . +1
Telephone: . . . . . . . . . . . . . . . . [33] 491-394-000
Web: . . . . . . . . . . . . . . . . . . www.marseille-port.fr

**Port of Nantes**
UN/LOCODE: . . . . . . . . . . . . . . . . . . . . . . . FR NTE
Latitude/Longitude: . . . . . . . . . 47° 14' N / 1° 34' W
GMT Offset: . . . . . . . . . . . . . . . . . . . . . . . . . . . +1
Web: . . . . . . . . . . . . . . . . . . . . www.nantes.port.fr

**Port of Paris**
UN/LOCODE: . . . . . . . . . . . . . . . . . . . . . . . FR PAR
Latitude/Longitude: . . . . . . . . . 48° 57' N / 2° 16' E
GMT Offset: . . . . . . . . . . . . . . . . . . . . . . . . . . . +1
Telephone: . . . . . . . . . . . . . . . . [33] 140-582-999
Web: . . . . . . . . . . . . . . . . . . . . www.paris-ports.fr

**Port of Rouen**
UN/LOCODE: . . . . . . . . . . . . . . . . . . . . . . . FR URO
Latitude/Longitude: . . . . . . . . . 49° 28' N / 1° 4' E
GMT Offset: . . . . . . . . . . . . . . . . . . . . . . . . . . . +1
Telephone: . . . . . . . . . . . . . . . . [33] 235-525-456
Web: . . . . . . . . . . . . . . . . . . . . www.rouen.port.fr

**Port of St Malo**
UN/LOCODE: . . . . . . . . . . . . . . . . . . . . . . . FR SML
Latitude/Longitude: . . . . . . . . . 48° 39' N / 2° 1' W
GMT Offset: . . . . . . . . . . . . . . . . . . . . . . . . . . . +1

**Port of St Nazaire**
UN/LOCODE: . . . . . . . . . . . . . . . . . . . . . . . FR SNR
Latitude/Longitude: . . . . . . . . . 47° 14' N / 1° 34' W
GMT Offset: . . . . . . . . . . . . . . . . . . . . . . . . . . . +0
Web: . . . . . . . . . . . . . . . . . . . . www.nantes.port.fr

**Port of Strasbourg**
UN/LOCODE: . . . . . . . . . . . . . . . . . . . . . FR SXB
Latitude/Longitude: . . . . . . . . . 48° 34' N / 7° 42' E
GMT Offset: . . . . . . . . . . . . . . . . . . . . . . . . . . +1
Telephone: . . . . . . . . . . . . . . . [33] 388-217-474
Web: . . . . . . . . . . . . . . . . www.strasbourg.port.fr

**Port of Toulon**
UN/LOCODE: . . . . . . . . . . . . . . . . . . . . . FR TLN
Latitude/Longitude: . . . . . . . . . . 43° 7' N / 5° 55' E
GMT Offset: . . . . . . . . . . . . . . . . . . . . . . . . . . +1
Web: www.nrlmry.navy.mil/~cannon/medports/Toulon/
index.html

## French Guiana

**Port of Cayenne**
UN/LOCODE: . . . . . . . . . . . . . . . . . . . . . GF CAY
Latitude/Longitude: . . . . . . . . 4° 56' N / 52° 20' W
GMT Offset: . . . . . . . . . . . . . . . . . . . . . . . . . . -3

## French Polynesia

**Port of Papeete**
UN/LOCODE: . . . . . . . . . . . . . . . . . . . . . PF PPT
Latitude/Longitude: . . . . . . . 17° 33' S / 149° 34' W
GMT Offset: . . . . . . . . . . . . . . . . . . . . . . . . . . +10
Telephone: . . . . . . . . . . . . . . . . . (689) 505-454
Web: . . . . . . . . . . . . . . . . www.portdepapeete.pf

## Gabon

**Port Gentil**
UN/LOCODE: . . . . . . . . . . . . . . . . . . . . GA POG
Latitude/Longitude: . . . . . . . . . . 0° 43' S / 8° 48' E
GMT Offset: . . . . . . . . . . . . . . . . . . . . . . . . . . +1
Telephone: . . . . . . . . . . . . . . . . . [241] 752-711
Web: . . . . . www.otal.com/gabon/gabon.htm#luanda

**Port of Cap Lopez**
UN/LOCODE: . . . . . . . . . . . . . . . . . . . . GA CLZ
Latitude/Longitude: . . . . . . . . . . 0° 38' S / 8° 42' E
GMT Offset: . . . . . . . . . . . . . . . . . . . . . . . . . . +1

**Port of Libreville**
UN/LOCODE: . . . . . . . . . . . . . . . . . . . . GA LBV
Latitude/Longitude: . . . . . . . . . . 0° 17' N / 9° 30' E
GMT Offset: . . . . . . . . . . . . . . . . . . . . . . . . . . +1

**Port of Owendo**
UN/LOCODE: . . . . . . . . . . . . . . . . . . . . GA OWE
Latitude/Longitude: . . . . . . . . . . 0° 17' N / 9° 30' E
GMT Offset: . . . . . . . . . . . . . . . . . . . . . . . . . . +1

## Gambia

**Port of Banjul**
UN/LOCODE: . . . . . . . . . . . . . . . . . . . . GM BJL
Latitude/Longitude: . . . . . . . . 13° 27' N / 16° 34' W
GMT Offset: . . . . . . . . . . . . . . . . . . . . . . . . . . +0
Telephone: . . . . . . . . . . . . . . . . [220] 229-940
Web: . . . . . . . . . . . . . . . . . . www.gamport.gm

## Georgia

**Port of Batumi**
UN/LOCODE: . . . . . . . . . . . . . . . . . . . . GE BUS
Latitude/Longitude: . . . . . . . . 41° 39' N / 41° 38' E
GMT Offset: . . . . . . . . . . . . . . . . . . . . . . . . . . +3
Telephone: . . . . . . . . . . . . . . [995] (222) 76269
Web: . . . . . . . . . . . . . . . . . www.batumiport.com

## Germany

**Port of Brake**
UN/LOCODE: . . . . . . . . . . . . . . . . . . . . DE BKE
Latitude/Longitude: . . . . . . . . 53° 20' N / 8° 29' E
GMT Offset: . . . . . . . . . . . . . . . . . . . . . . . . . . +1
Telephone: . . . . . . . . . . . . . . [49] (4401) 9140
Web: . . . . . . . . . . . . . . . . . www.brake-port.de/

**Port of Bremen**
UN/LOCODE: . . . . . . . . . . . . . . . . . . . . DE BRE
Latitude/Longitude: . . . . . . . . . . 53° 7' N / 8° 45' E
GMT Offset: . . . . . . . . . . . . . . . . . . . . . . . . . . +1
Telephone: . . . . . . . . . . . . . . [49] (421) 397-8504
Web: . . . . . . . . . . . . . . . . . www.bremen-ports.de

**Port of Bremerhaven**
UN/LOCODE: . . . . . . . . . . . . . . . . . . . . DE BRV
Latitude/Longitude: . . . . . . . . 53° 33' N / 8° 35' E
GMT Offset: . . . . . . . . . . . . . . . . . . . . . . . . . . +1
Telephone: . . . . . . . . . . . . . . [49] (471) 947-4600
Web: . . . . . . . . . . . . . . . . . www.bremen-ports.de

**Port of Duisburg**
UN/LOCODE: . . . . . . . . . . . . . . . . . . . . DE DUI
Latitude/Longitude: . . . . . . . . 51° 27' N / 6° 43' E
GMT Offset: . . . . . . . . . . . . . . . . . . . . . . . . . . +1
Telephone: . . . . . . . . . . . . . . [49] (203) 803-232
Web: . . . . . . . . . . . . . . . . . . . www.duisport.de

**Port of Dusseldorf**
UN/LOCODE: . . . . . . . . . . . . . . . . . . . . DE DUS
Latitude/Longitude: . . . . . . . . 51° 13' N / 6° 47' E
GMT Offset: . . . . . . . . . . . . . . . . . . . . . . . . . . +1

**Port of Emden**
UN/LOCODE: . . . . . . . . . . . . . . . . . . . . DE EME
Latitude/Longitude: . . . . . . . . 53° 21' N / 7° 12' E
GMT Offset: . . . . . . . . . . . . . . . . . . . . . . . . . . +1
Telephone: . . . . . . . . . . . . . . [49] (4921) 51770
Web: . . . . . . . . . . . . . . . . . . www.emden-port.de

**Port of Hamburg**
UN/LOCODE: . . . . . . . . . . . . . . . . . . . . DE HAM
Latitude/Longitude: . . . . . . . . 53° 33' N / 9° 59' E
GMT Offset: . . . . . . . . . . . . . . . . . . . . . . . . . . +1
Web: . . . . . . . . . . . . www.hafen-hamburg.de

**Port of Karlsruhe**
UN/LOCODE: . . . . . . . . . . . . . . . . . . . . DE KAE
Latitude/Longitude: . . . . . . . . . . 49° 3' N / 8° 20' E
GMT Offset: . . . . . . . . . . . . . . . . . . . . . . . . . . +1
Telephone: . . . . . . . . . . . . . . [49] (721) 599-5760

**Port of Kiel**
UN/LOCODE: . . . . . . . . . . . . . . . . . . . . DE KEL
Latitude/Longitude: . . . . . . . . 54° 19' N / 10° 10' E
GMT Offset: . . . . . . . . . . . . . . . . . . . . . . . . . . +1
Telephone: . . . . . . . . . . . . . . [49] (431) 982-2141
Web: . . . . . . . . . . . . . . . . . www.port-of-kiel.de

**Port of Lubeck**
UN/LOCODE: . . . . . . . . . . . . . . . . . . . . DE LBC
Latitude/Longitude: . . . . . . . . 53° 52' N / 10° 41' E
GMT Offset: . . . . . . . . . . . . . . . . . . . . . . . . . . +1
Telephone: . . . . . . . . . . . . . . . [49] (451) 7900
Web: . . . . . . . . . . . . . . . . . . . . www.hafen.de

**Port of Mannheim**
UN/LOCODE: . . . . . . . . . . . . . . . . . . . . DE MHG
Latitude/Longitude: . . . . . . . . 49° 32' N / 8° 30' E
GMT Offset: . . . . . . . . . . . . . . . . . . . . . . . . . . +1

**Port of Rostock**
UN/LOCODE: . . . . . . . . . . . . . . . . . . . . DE RSK
Latitude/Longitude: . . . . . . . . . . 54° 9' N / 12° 8' E
GMT Offset: . . . . . . . . . . . . . . . . . . . . . . . . . . +1
Telephone: . . . . . . . . . . . . . . [49] (381) 350-4000
Web: . . . . . . . . . . . . . . . . . www.rostock-port.de

## Ghana

**Port of Takoradi**
UN/LOCODE: . . . . . . . . . . . . . . . . . . . . GH TKD
Latitude/Longitude: . . . . . . . . . . 4° 53' N / 1° 45' W
GMT Offset: . . . . . . . . . . . . . . . . . . . . . . . . . . +0
Telephone: . . . . . . . . . . [49] (233) 2220-2563
Web: . http://portfocus.com/ghana/takoradi/index.html

**Port of Tema**
UN/LOCODE: . . . . . . . . . . . . . . . . . . . . GH TEM
Latitude/Longitude: . . . . . . . . . . 5° 38' N / 0° 1' E
GMT Offset: . . . . . . . . . . . . . . . . . . . . . . . . . . +0
Telephone: . . . . . . . . . . . . . [49] (233) 2220-2563

**S E A P O R T S**

## Gibraltar

**Port of Gibraltar**
*UN/LOCODE:* . . . . . . . . . . . . . . . . . . . GI GIB
*Latitude/Longitude:* . . . . . . . . . 36° 8' N / 5° 21' W
*GMT Offset:* . . . . . . . . . . . . . . . . . . . . . . +1
*Telephone:* . . . . . . . . . . . . . . . [350] 77254
*Web:* . . . . . . . . . . . . . . . www.gibraltarport.com

## Greece

**Port of Eleusis**
*UN/LOCODE:* . . . . . . . . . . . . . . . . . . GR EEU
*Latitude/Longitude:* . . . . . . . . . 38° 2' N / 23° 33' E
*GMT Offset:* . . . . . . . . . . . . . . . . . . . . . . +2
*Telephone:* . . . . . . . . . . . . . . [30] 210-554-6671

**Port of Iraklion (Heraklion)**
*UN/LOCODE:* . . . . . . . . . . . . . . . . . . GR HER
*Latitude/Longitude:* . . . . . . . . . 35° 16' N / 25° 9' E
*GMT Offset:* . . . . . . . . . . . . . . . . . . . . . . +2
*Telephone:* . . . . . . . . . . . . . . [30] 281-022-6176
*Web:* . . . . . . . . . . . . . . . www.portheraklion.gr

**Port of Kavala**
*UN/LOCODE:* . . . . . . . . . . . . . . . . . . GR KVA
*Latitude/Longitude:* . . . . . . . . . 40° 55' N / 24° 25' E
*GMT Offset:* . . . . . . . . . . . . . . . . . . . . . . +2
*Telephone:* . . . . . . . . . . . . . . [30] 251-022-3716

**Port of Patras**
*UN/LOCODE:* . . . . . . . . . . . . . . . . . . GR GPA
*Latitude/Longitude:* . . . . . . . . . 38° 15' N / 21° 45' E
*GMT Offset:* . . . . . . . . . . . . . . . . . . . . . . +2
*Telephone:* . . . . . . . . . . . . . . [30] 261-034-1002

**Port of Piraeus**
*UN/LOCODE:* . . . . . . . . . . . . . . . . . . GR PIR
*Latitude/Longitude:* . . . . . . . . . 37° 57' N / 23° 38' E
*GMT Offset:* . . . . . . . . . . . . . . . . . . . . . . +2
*Telephone:* . . . . . . . . . . . . . . [30] 210-428-6842
*Web:* . . . . . . . . . . . . . . . www.olp.gr

**Port of Thessaloniki**
*UN/LOCODE:* . . . . . . . . . . . . . . . . . . GR SKG
*Latitude/Longitude:* . . . . . . . . . 40° 38' N / 22° 56' E
*GMT Offset:* . . . . . . . . . . . . . . . . . . . . . . +2
*Telephone:* . . . . . . . . . . . . . . [30] 231-059-3129
*Web:* . . . . . . . . . . . . . . . www.thpa.gr

**Port of Volos**
*UN/LOCODE:* . . . . . . . . . . . . . . . . . . GR VOL
*Latitude/Longitude:* . . . . . . . . . 39° 22' N / 22° 57' E
*GMT Offset:* . . . . . . . . . . . . . . . . . . . . . . +2
*Telephone:* . . . . . . . . . . . . . . [30] 242-103-1115
*Web:* . . . . . . . . . . . . . . . www.port-volos.gr

## Greenland

**Port of Holsteinsborg  Sisimiut**
*UN/LOCODE:* . . . . . . . . . . . . . . . . . . GL
*Latitude/Longitude:* . . . . . . . . . 66° 56' N / 53° 40' W
*GMT Offset:* . . . . . . . . . . . . . . . . . . . . . . -3

**Port of Kangerdluarssoruseg**
*UN/LOCODE:* . . . . . . . . . . . . . . . . . . GL FHN
*Latitude/Longitude:* . . . . . . . . . 66° 58' N / 50° 57' W
*GMT Offset:* . . . . . . . . . . . . . . . . . . . . . . -3

**Port of Nanortalik**
*UN/LOCODE:* . . . . . . . . . . . . . . . . . . GL JNN
*Latitude/Longitude:* . . . . . . . . . 60° 8' N / 45° 14' W
*GMT Offset:* . . . . . . . . . . . . . . . . . . . . . . -3

**Port of Narsarsuaq**
*UN/LOCODE:* . . . . . . . . . . . . . . . . . . GL UAK
*Latitude/Longitude:* . . . . . . . . . 61° 9' N / 45° 25' W
*GMT Offset:* . . . . . . . . . . . . . . . . . . . . . . -3

**Port of Nuuk (Godthaab)**
*UN/LOCODE:* . . . . . . . . . . . . . . . . . . GL GOH
*Latitude/Longitude:* . . . . . . . . . 64° 10' N / 51° 44' W
*GMT Offset:* . . . . . . . . . . . . . . . . . . . . . . -3

## Guadeloupe

**Port of Gustavia**
*UN/LOCODE:* . . . . . . . . . . . . . . . . . . GP GUS
*Latitude/Longitude:* . . . . . . . . . 17° 54' N / 62° 51' W
*GMT Offset:* . . . . . . . . . . . . . . . . . . . . . . -4
*Telephone:* . . . . . . . . . . . . . . [590] 276-697

## Guam

**Port of Apra (Agana)**
*UN/LOCODE:* . . . . . . . . . . . . . . . . . . GU APR
*Latitude/Longitude:* . . . . . . . . . 13° 27' N / 144° 37' E
*GMT Offset:* . . . . . . . . . . . . . . . . . . . . . . +10
*Telephone:* . . . . . . . . . . . . . . [1] (671) 477-5931

## Guatemala

**Port of Champerico**
*UN/LOCODE:* . . . . . . . . . . . . . . . . . . GT CHR
*Latitude/Longitude:* . . . . . . . . . 14° 18' N / 91° 55' W
*GMT Offset:* . . . . . . . . . . . . . . . . . . . . . . -6

**Port of Puerto Barrios**
*UN/LOCODE:* . . . . . . . . . . . . . . . . . . GT PBR
*Latitude/Longitude:* . . . . . . . . . 15° 43' N / 88° 37' W
*GMT Offset:* . . . . . . . . . . . . . . . . . . . . . . -6
*Telephone:* . . . . . . . . . . . . . . [502] 360-5632
*Web:* . . . . . . . . . . . . . . . www.cpn.gob.gt

**Port of Santo Tomas De Castilla**
*UN/LOCODE:* . . . . . . . . . . . . . . . . . . GT STC
*Latitude/Longitude:* . . . . . . . . . 15° 42' N / 88° 37' W
*GMT Offset:* . . . . . . . . . . . . . . . . . . . . . . -6
*Telephone:* . . . . . . . . . . . . . . [502] 360-5632
*Web:* . . . . . . . . . . . . . . . www.cpn.gob.gt

## Guinea

**Port Kamsar**
*UN/LOCODE:* . . . . . . . . . . . . . . . . . . GN KMR
*Latitude/Longitude:* . . . . . . . . . 10° 39' N / 14° 37' W
*GMT Offset:* . . . . . . . . . . . . . . . . . . . . . . +0

**Port of Conakry**
*UN/LOCODE:* . . . . . . . . . . . . . . . . . . GN CKY
*Latitude/Longitude:* . . . . . . . . . 9° 31' N / 13° 43' W
*GMT Offset:* . . . . . . . . . . . . . . . . . . . . . . +0
*Telephone:* . . . . . . . . . . . . . . [224] 442-737
*Web:* . . . . . www.otal.com/guinea/guinea.htm#abidjan

## Guinea-Bissau

**Port of Bissau**
*UN/LOCODE:* . . . . . . . . . . . . . . . . . . GW BXO
*Latitude/Longitude:* . . . . . . . . . 11° 51' N / 15° 35' W
*GMT Offset:* . . . . . . . . . . . . . . . . . . . . . . -1

## Guyana

**Port of Georgetown**
*UN/LOCODE:* . . . . . . . . . . . . . . . . . . GY GEO
*Latitude/Longitude:* . . . . . . . . . 6° 49' N / 58° 10' W
*GMT Offset:* . . . . . . . . . . . . . . . . . . . . . . -4
*Telephone:* . . . . . . . . . . . . . . [592] 227-8545

**Port of New Amsterdam**
*UN/LOCODE:* . . . . . . . . . . . . . . . . . . GY QSK
*Latitude/Longitude:* . . . . . . . . . 6° 14' N / 57° 31' W
*GMT Offset:* . . . . . . . . . . . . . . . . . . . . . . -4
*Telephone:* . . . . . . . . . . . . . . [592] 226-0329

## Haiti

**Port Au Prince**
*UN/LOCODE:* . . . . . . . . . . . . . . . . . . HT PAP
*Latitude/Longitude:* . . . . . . . . . 18° 33' N / 72° 21' W
*GMT Offset:* . . . . . . . . . . . . . . . . . . . . . . -5

**Port of Cap Haitien**
*UN/LOCODE:* . . . . . . . . . . . . . . . . . . HT CAP
*Latitude/Longitude:* . . . . . . . . . 19° 46' N / 72° 11' W
*GMT Offset:* . . . . . . . . . . . . . . . . . . . . . . -5

**Port of Miragoane**
UN/LOCODE: . . . . . . . . . . . . . . . . . . . . . HT MIR
Latitude/Longitude: . . . . . . . . 18° 28' N / 73° 6' W
GMT Offset: . . . . . . . . . . . . . . . . . . . . . . . . . -5

## Honduras

**Port of La Ceiba**
UN/LOCODE: . . . . . . . . . . . . . . . . . . . . HN LCE
Latitude/Longitude: . . . . . . . . 15° 46' N / 86° 50' W
GMT Offset: . . . . . . . . . . . . . . . . . . . . . . . . . -6
Web: . . . . . . . . . www.enp.hn/Puertos/Puertos.htm

**Port of Puerto Castilla**
UN/LOCODE: . . . . . . . . . . . . . . . . . . . . HN PCA
Latitude/Longitude: . . . . . . . . 16° 1' N / 86° 3' W
GMT Offset: . . . . . . . . . . . . . . . . . . . . . . . . . -6
Web: . . . . . . . . . www.enp.hn/Puertos/Puertos.htm

**Port of Puerto Cortes**
UN/LOCODE: . . . . . . . . . . . . . . . . . . . . HN PCR
Latitude/Longitude: . . . . . . . . 15° 51' N / 87° 56' W
GMT Offset: . . . . . . . . . . . . . . . . . . . . . . . . . -6
Web: . . . . . . . . . www.enp.hn/Puertos/Puertos.htm

**Port of San Lorenzo**
UN/LOCODE: . . . . . . . . . . . . . . . . . . . . HN SLO
Latitude/Longitude: . . . . . . . . 13° 24' N / 87° 25' W
GMT Offset: . . . . . . . . . . . . . . . . . . . . . . . . . -6
Web: . . . . . . . . . www.enp.hn/Puertos/Puertos.htm

**Port of Tela**
UN/LOCODE: . . . . . . . . . . . . . . . . . . . . HN TEA
Latitude/Longitude: . . . . . . . . 15° 47' N / 87° 27' W
GMT Offset: . . . . . . . . . . . . . . . . . . . . . . . . . -6

## Hong Kong

**Port of Hong Kong**
UN/LOCODE: . . . . . . . . . . . . . . . . . . . . HK HKG
Latitude/Longitude: . . . . . . . . 22° 18' N / 114° 10' E
GMT Offset: . . . . . . . . . . . . . . . . . . . . . . . . . +8
Telephone: . . . . . . . . . . . . . . . . [852] 2852-4346
Web: . . . . . . . . . . . . . www.info.gov.hk/mardep/

## Iceland

**Port of Akureyri**
UN/LOCODE: . . . . . . . . . . . . . . . . . . . . IS AKU
Latitude/Longitude: . . . . . . . . 65° 41' N / 18° 3' W
GMT Offset: . . . . . . . . . . . . . . . . . . . . . . . . . +0
Telephone: . . . . . . . . . . . . . . . . . [354] 626-699
Web: . . . . . . . . . . . . . . . . . . . . . . . www.port.is

**Port of Isafjordur - hofn**
UN/LOCODE: . . . . . . . . . . . . . . . . . . . . IS ISA
Latitude/Longitude: . . . . . . . . 66° 5' N / 23° 6' W
GMT Offset: . . . . . . . . . . . . . . . . . . . . . . . . . +0

**Port of Keflavik**
UN/LOCODE: . . . . . . . . . . . . . . . . . . . . IS KEV
Latitude/Longitude: . . . . . . . . 64° 0' N / 22° 33' W
GMT Offset: . . . . . . . . . . . . . . . . . . . . . . . . . +0
Telephone: . . . . . . . . . . . . . . . . . [354] 421-4575
Web: . . . . . . . . . www.randburg.com/is/portkefl

**Port of Raufarhofn**
UN/LOCODE: . . . . . . . . . . . . . . . . . . . . IS RAU
Latitude/Longitude: . . . . . . . . 66° 27' N / 15° 54' W
GMT Offset: . . . . . . . . . . . . . . . . . . . . . . . . . +0

**Port of Reykjavik**
UN/LOCODE: . . . . . . . . . . . . . . . . . . . . IS REY
Latitude/Longitude: . . . . . . . . 64° 8' N / 21° 56' W
GMT Offset: . . . . . . . . . . . . . . . . . . . . . . . . . +0
Telephone: . . . . . . . . . . . . . . . . [354] 525-8900
Web: . . . . . . . http://portfocus.com/iceland/reykjavik/

**Port of Straumsvik**
UN/LOCODE: . . . . . . . . . . . . . . . . . . . . IS STR
Latitude/Longitude: . . . . . . . . 64° 3' N / 22° 3' W
GMT Offset: . . . . . . . . . . . . . . . . . . . . . . . . . +0

**Port of Vestmannaeyjar - hofn**
UN/LOCODE: . . . . . . . . . . . . . . . . . . . . IS VES
Latitude/Longitude: . . . . . . . . 63° 26' N / 20° 16' W
GMT Offset: . . . . . . . . . . . . . . . . . . . . . . . . . +0

## India

**Port of Bombay (Mumbai)**
UN/LOCODE: . . . . . . . . . . . . . . . . . . . . IN BOM
Latitude/Longitude:
GMT Offset: . . . . . . . . . . . . . . . . . . . . . . . . +5.5
Web: . . . . . . . . . . www.mumbaiporttrust.com

**Port of Calcutta**
UN/LOCODE: . . . . . . . . . . . . . . . . . . . . IN CCU
Latitude/Longitude: . . . . . . . . 22° 32' N / 88° 22' E
GMT Offset: . . . . . . . . . . . . . . . . . . . . . . . . +5.5
Telephone: . . . . . . . . . . . . . . [91] (33) 220-3451
www.portofcalcutta.com

**Port of Cochin**
UN/LOCODE: . . . . . . . . . . . . . . . . . . . . IN COK
Latitude/Longitude: . . . . . . . . . 9° 58' N / 76° 15' E
GMT Offset: . . . . . . . . . . . . . . . . . . . . . . . . . +6
Telephone: . . . . . . . . . . . . . . [91] (484) 666-871
Web: . . . . . . . . . . . . . . . . www.cochinport.com

**Port of Kandla**
UN/LOCODE: . . . . . . . . . . . . . . . . . . . . IN IXY
Latitude/Longitude: . . . . . . . . 23° 0' N / 70° 12' E
GMT Offset: . . . . . . . . . . . . . . . . . . . . . . . . +5.5
Telephone: . . . . . . . . . . . . . [91] (2836) 221-347
Web: . . . . . . . . . . . . . www.kandlaport.gov.in

**Port of Nhava Sheva (Jawaharlal Nehru)**
UN/LOCODE: . . . . . . . . . . . . . . . . . . . . IN NSA
Latitude/Longitude: . . . . . . . . 18° 57' N / 72° 58' E
GMT Offset: . . . . . . . . . . . . . . . . . . . . . . . . . +6
Telephone: . . . . . . . . . . . . . . [91] (22) 724-2623
Web: . . . . . . . . . . . . . . . . . . www.jnport.com

**Port of Vishakhapatnam**
UN/LOCODE: . . . . . . . . . . . . . . . . . . . . IN VTZ
Latitude/Longitude: . . . . . . . . 17° 41' N / 83° 18' E
GMT Offset: . . . . . . . . . . . . . . . . . . . . . . . . . +6
Telephone: . . . . . . . . . . . . . . [91] (891) 256-4841
Web: . . . . . . . . . . . . . . . . . . http://vizagport.com

## Indonesia

**Port of Cilacap, Java**
UN/LOCODE: . . . . . . . . . . . . . . . . . . . . ID CXP
Latitude/Longitude: . . . . . . . . . 8° 44' S / 109° 0' E
GMT Offset: . . . . . . . . . . . . . . . . . . . . . . . . . +7
Telephone: . . . . . . . . . . . . . . [62] (282) 21334

**Port of Cirebon, Java**
UN/LOCODE: . . . . . . . . . . . . . . . . . . . . ID CBN
Latitude/Longitude: . . . . . . . . . 6° 41' S / 108° 33' E
GMT Offset: . . . . . . . . . . . . . . . . . . . . . . . . . +7
Telephone: . . . . . . . . . . . . . . [62] (231) 209-723
Web: . . . . . . . . . . . . . . www.cirebonport.co.id

**Port of Jakarta, Java**
UN/LOCODE: . . . . . . . . . . . . . . . . . . . . ID JKT
Latitude/Longitude: . . . . . . . . . 6° 10' S / 106° 50' E
GMT Offset: . . . . . . . . . . . . . . . . . . . . . . . . . +7
Telephone: . . . . . . . . . . . . . . [62] (21) 430-1080

**Port of Kupang, Timor**
UN/LOCODE: . . . . . . . . . . . . . . . . . . . . ID KOE
Latitude/Longitude: . . . . . . . . 10° 10' S / 123° 34' E
GMT Offset: . . . . . . . . . . . . . . . . . . . . . . . . . +8
Telephone: . . . . . . . . . . . . . . [62] (391) 21790

**Port of Palembang, Sumatra**
UN/LOCODE: . . . . . . . . . . . . . . . . . . . . ID PLM
Latitude/Longitude: . . . . . . . . . 2° 59' S / 104° 45' E
GMT Offset: . . . . . . . . . . . . . . . . . . . . . . . . . +7
Telephone: . . . . . . . . . . . . . . [62] (711) 710-472

**Port of Semarang, Java**
UN/LOCODE: . . . . . . . . . . . . . . . . . . . . . ID SRG
Latitude/Longitude: . . . . . . . . 6° 53' S / 110° 24' E
GMT Offset: . . . . . . . . . . . . . . . . . . . . . . . . . +7
Telephone: . . . . . . . . . . . . . . [62] (24) 544-491

**Port of Surabaya, Java**
UN/LOCODE: . . . . . . . . . . . . . . . . . . . . . ID SUB
Latitude/Longitude: . . . . . . . . 7° 13' S / 112° 44' E
GMT Offset: . . . . . . . . . . . . . . . . . . . . . . . . . +7
Telephone: . . . . . . . . . . . . [62] (31) 328-32265
Web: . . . . . . . . . . . . . . . . . . . . . www.tps.co.id

**Port of Ujung Pandang, Sulawesi**
UN/LOCODE: . . . . . . . . . . . . . . . . . . . . . ID UPG
Latitude/Longitude: . . . . . . . . 5° 8' S / 119° 24' E
GMT Offset: . . . . . . . . . . . . . . . . . . . . . . . . . +8
Telephone: . . . . . . . . . . . . . . [62] (411) 316-447

## Iran

**Port of Abadan**
UN/LOCODE: . . . . . . . . . . . . . . . . . . . . . IR ABD
Latitude/Longitude: . . . . . . . . 30° 20' N / 48° 20' E
GMT Offset: . . . . . . . . . . . . . . . . . . . . . . . . . +4
Telephone: . . . . . . . . . . . . . . [98] (631) 216-151

**Port of Bandar Abbas**
UN/LOCODE: . . . . . . . . . . . . . . . . . . . . . IR BND
Latitude/Longitude: . . . . . . . . 27° 11' N / 56° 17' E
GMT Offset: . . . . . . . . . . . . . . . . . . . . . . . . . +4

**Port of Bandar Anzali**
UN/LOCODE: . . . . . . . . . . . . . . . . . . . . . IR BAZ
Latitude/Longitude: . . . . . . . . 37° 28' N / 49° 28' E
GMT Offset: . . . . . . . . . . . . . . . . . . . . . . . . . +4
Telephone: . . . . . . . . . . . . . . [98] (21) 880-9281

**Port of Bandar Mahshahr**
UN/LOCODE: . . . . . . . . . . . . . . . . . . . . . IR MRX
Latitude/Longitude: . . . . . . . . 30° 27' N / 49° 20' E
GMT Offset: . . . . . . . . . . . . . . . . . . . . . . . . . +4

**Port of Bushehr**
UN/LOCODE: . . . . . . . . . . . . . . . . . . . . . IR BUZ
Latitude/Longitude: . . . . . . . . 28° 59' N / 50° 50' E
GMT Offset: . . . . . . . . . . . . . . . . . . . . . . . . . +4
Telephone: . . . . . . . . . . . . [98] (771) 253-0079
Web: . . . . . . . . . http://portfocus.com/iran/bushehr/

**Port of Imam Khomeini**
UN/LOCODE: . . . . . . . . . . . . . . . . . . . . . IR BKM
Latitude/Longitude: . . . . . . . . 30° 25' N / 40° 4' E
GMT Offset: . . . . . . . . . . . . . . . . . . . . . . . . . +4
Telephone: . . . . . . . . . . . . . . [98] (21) 312-8342
Web: . . . . . . . . . . . . . . . . . www.khomeiniport.com

**Port of Khorramshahr**
UN/LOCODE: . . . . . . . . . . . . . . . . . . . . . IR KHO
Latitude/Longitude: . . . . . . . . 30° 26' N / 48° 11' E
GMT Offset: . . . . . . . . . . . . . . . . . . . . . . . . . +4
Telephone: . . . . . . . . . . . . . . [98] (21) 880-9281

**Port of Lavan**
UN/LOCODE: . . . . . . . . . . . . . . . . . . . . . IR LVP
Latitude/Longitude: . . . . . . . . 26° 47' N / 53° 20' E
GMT Offset: . . . . . . . . . . . . . . . . . . . . . . . . . +4
Telephone: . . . . . . . . . . . . . . [98] (21) 615-3083

**Port of Sirri Island**
UN/LOCODE: . . . . . . . . . . . . . . . . . . . . . IR SXI
Latitude/Longitude: . . . . . . . . 25° 54' N / 54° 33' E
GMT Offset: . . . . . . . . . . . . . . . . . . . . . . . . . +4

## Iraq

**Port of Basra**
UN/LOCODE: . . . . . . . . . . . . . . . . . . . . . IQ BSR
Latitude/Longitude: . . . . . . . . 30° 33' N / 47° 47' E
GMT Offset: . . . . . . . . . . . . . . . . . . . . . . . . . +3

**Port of Khor al Zubair**
UN/LOCODE: . . . . . . . . . . . . . . . . . . . . . IQ KAZ
Latitude/Longitude: . . . . . . . . 30° 11' N / 47° 54' E
GMT Offset: . . . . . . . . . . . . . . . . . . . . . . . . . +3

**Port of Umm Qasr**
UN/LOCODE: . . . . . . . . . . . . . . . . . . . . . IQ UQR
Latitude/Longitude: . . . . . . . . 24° 54' N / 51° 35' E
GMT Offset: . . . . . . . . . . . . . . . . . . . . . . . . . +4

## Ireland

**Port of Arklow**
UN/LOCODE: . . . . . . . . . . . . . . . . . . . . . IE ARK
Latitude/Longitude: . . . . . . . . 52° 48' N / 6° 9' W
GMT Offset: . . . . . . . . . . . . . . . . . . . . . . . . . +0
Telephone: . . . . . . . . . . . . . . [353] (402) 32466

**Port of Cork**
UN/LOCODE: . . . . . . . . . . . . . . . . . . . . . IE ORK
Latitude/Longitude: . . . . . . . . 51° 50' N / 8° 17' W
GMT Offset: . . . . . . . . . . . . . . . . . . . . . . . . . +0
Telephone: . . . . . . . . . . . . . . [353] (21) 427-3125
Web: . . . . . . . . . . . . . . . . . www.portofcork.ie

**Port of Drogheda**
UN/LOCODE: . . . . . . . . . . . . . . . . . . . . . IE DRO
Latitude/Longitude: . . . . . . . . 53° 43' N / 6° 18' W
GMT Offset: . . . . . . . . . . . . . . . . . . . . . . . . . +0
Telephone: . . . . . . . . . . . . . . [353] (41) 983-8378
Web: . . . . . . . . . . . . . . . . . www.droghedaport.ie

**Port of Dublin**
UN/LOCODE: . . . . . . . . . . . . . . . . . . . . . IE DUB
Latitude/Longitude: . . . . . . . . 53° 21' N / 6° 16' W
GMT Offset: . . . . . . . . . . . . . . . . . . . . . . . . . +0
Telephone: . . . . . . . . . . . . . . [353] (1) 874-8771

**Port of Foynes**
UN/LOCODE: . . . . . . . . . . . . . . . . . . . . . IE FOV
Latitude/Longitude: . . . . . . . . 52° 36' N / 9° 6' W
GMT Offset: . . . . . . . . . . . . . . . . . . . . . . . . . +0
Web: . . . . . . . . . . . . . . . . . www.sfpc.ie

**Port of Galway**
UN/LOCODE: . . . . . . . . . . . . . . . . . . . . . IE GWY
Latitude/Longitude: . . . . . . . . 53° 16' N / 9° 3' W
GMT Offset: . . . . . . . . . . . . . . . . . . . . . . . . . +0
Telephone: . . . . . . . . . . . . . . [353] (91) 562-329

**Port of Limerick**
UN/LOCODE: . . . . . . . . . . . . . . . . . . . . . IE LMK
Latitude/Longitude: . . . . . . . . 52° 40' N / 8° 38' W
GMT Offset: . . . . . . . . . . . . . . . . . . . . . . . . . +0
Telephone: . . . . . . . . . . . . . . [353] (61) 315-377
Web: . . . . . . . . . . . . . . . . . www.sfpc.ie

**Port of New Ross**
UN/LOCODE: . . . . . . . . . . . . . . . . . . . . . IE NRS
Latitude/Longitude: . . . . . . . . 52° 23' N / 6° 56' W
GMT Offset: . . . . . . . . . . . . . . . . . . . . . . . . . +0
Telephone: . . . . . . . . . . . . . . [353] (51) 21303

**Port of Waterford**
UN/LOCODE: . . . . . . . . . . . . . . . . . . . . . IE WAT
Latitude/Longitude: . . . . . . . . 52° 15' N / 7° 7' W
GMT Offset: . . . . . . . . . . . . . . . . . . . . . . . . . +0
Telephone: . . . . . . . . . . . . . . [353] (51) 74907

## Israel

**Port of Ashdod**
UN/LOCODE: . . . . . . . . . . . . . . . . . . . . . IL ASH
Latitude/Longitude: . . . . . . . . 31° 50' N / 34° 38' E
GMT Offset: . . . . . . . . . . . . . . . . . . . . . . . . . +2
Telephone: . . . . . . . . . . . . . . [972] (8) 856-1255
Web: . . . . . . . . . . . . . . . . . www.ashdodport.org.il

**Port of Ashkelon**
UN/LOCODE: . . . . . . . . . . . . . . . . . . . . . IL AKL
Latitude/Longitude: . . . . . . . . 31° 38' N / 34° 32' E
GMT Offset: . . . . . . . . . . . . . . . . . . . . . . . . . +2
Telephone: . . . . . . . . . . . . . . [972] (3) 561-0292
Web: . . . . . . . . www.unishipping.co.il/ashkelon.html

**Port of Eilat**
UN/LOCODE: . . . . . . . . . . . . . . . . . . . . . . . IL ETH
Latitude/Longitude: . . . . . . . . 29° 32' N / 34° 57' E
GMT Offset: . . . . . . . . . . . . . . . . . . . . . . . . . . . +2
Telephone: . . . . . . . . . . . . . . . [972] (8) 638-5332
Web: . . . . . . . . . www.israports.org.il/ports/Eilat.asp

**Port of Hadera**
UN/LOCODE: . . . . . . . . . . . . . . . . . . . . . IL HAD
Latitude/Longitude: . . . . . . . . . 32° 28' N / 34° 53' E
GMT Offset: . . . . . . . . . . . . . . . . . . . . . . . . . . . +2
Telephone: . . . . . . . . . . . . . . . . [972] (6) 332-976

**Port of Haifa**
UN/LOCODE: . . . . . . . . . . . . . . . . . . . . . . IL HFA
Latitude/Longitude: . . . . . . . . . 32° 49' N / 35° 0' E
GMT Offset: . . . . . . . . . . . . . . . . . . . . . . . . . . . +2
Telephone: . . . . . . . . . . . . . . . [972] (4) 855-8558
Web: . . . . . . . . . . . . . . . . . www.haifaport.org.il

## Italy

**Port of Augusta**
UN/LOCODE: . . . . . . . . . . . . . . . . . . . . . IT AUG
Latitude/Longitude: . . . . . . . . 37° 13' N / 15° 14' E
GMT Offset: . . . . . . . . . . . . . . . . . . . . . . . . . . . +1
Telephone: . . . . . . . . . . . . . . . [39] (0931) 978-922
Web: . . . . . . . . . . . www.harbours.net/augusta/

**Port of Bagnoli**
UN/LOCODE: . . . . . . . . . . . . . . . . . . . . . . IT BLN
Latitude/Longitude: . . . . . . . . . 40° 48' N / 14° 10' E
GMT Offset: . . . . . . . . . . . . . . . . . . . . . . . . . . . +1
Telephone: . . . . . . . . . . . . . . [39] (081) 723-2272

**Port of Bari**
UN/LOCODE: . . . . . . . . . . . . . . . . . . . . . . IT BRI
Latitude/Longitude: . . . . . . . . . . 41° 8' N / 16° 52' E
GMT Offset: . . . . . . . . . . . . . . . . . . . . . . . . . . . +1
Telephone: . . . . . . . . . . . . . . [39] (080) 216-860
Web: . . . . . . . . . . . . . . . . . . www.porto.bari.it

**Port of Brindisi**
UN/LOCODE: . . . . . . . . . . . . . . . . . . . . . . IT BDS
Latitude/Longitude: . . . . . . . . 40° 39' N / 17° 56' E
GMT Offset: . . . . . . . . . . . . . . . . . . . . . . . . . . . +1
Telephone: . . . . . . . . . . . . . . [39] (083) 121-022
Web: . . . . . www.informare.it/harbs/brindisi/idxuk.asp

**Port of Gela**
UN/LOCODE: . . . . . . . . . . . . . . . . . . . . . IT GEA
Latitude/Longitude: . . . . . . . . . . 37° 4' N / 14° 15' E
GMT Offset: . . . . . . . . . . . . . . . . . . . . . . . . . . . +1
Telephone: . . . . . . . . . . . . . . [39] (0933) 917-755
Web: . . . . . . . . . . . . www.harbours.net/gela

**Port of Genoa**
UN/LOCODE: . . . . . . . . . . . . . . . . . . . . . IT GOA
Latitude/Longitude: . . . . . . . . . 44° 24' N / 8° 54' E
GMT Offset: . . . . . . . . . . . . . . . . . . . . . . . . . . . +1
Telephone: . . . . . . . . . . . . . . [39] (010) 241-2891
Web: . . . . . . . . . . . . . . . www.porto.genova.it

**Port of La Spezia**
UN/LOCODE: . . . . . . . . . . . . . . . . . . . . . IT SPE
Latitude/Longitude: . . . . . . . . . . 44° 1' N / 9° 51' E
GMT Offset: . . . . . . . . . . . . . . . . . . . . . . . . . . . +1
Telephone: . . . . . . . . . . . . . . [39] (0187) 546-320
Web: . . . . . . . . . . . . . www.porto.la-spezia.it

**Port of Livorno**
UN/LOCODE: . . . . . . . . . . . . . . . . . . . . . . IT LIV
Latitude/Longitude: . . . . . . . . . 43° 33' N / 10° 20' E
GMT Offset: . . . . . . . . . . . . . . . . . . . . . . . . . . . +1
Telephone: . . . . . . . . . . . . . . [39] (0586) 249-411
Web: . . . . . . . . . . . . . . . www.portauthority.li.it

**Port of Messina**
UN/LOCODE: . . . . . . . . . . . . . . . . . . . . . IT MSN
Latitude/Longitude: . . . . . . . . . 38° 11' N / 15° 34' E
GMT Offset: . . . . . . . . . . . . . . . . . . . . . . . . . . . +1
Web: . . . . . . . . . . . . www.harbours.net/messina

**Port of Milazzo**
UN/LOCODE: . . . . . . . . . . . . . . . . . . . . . IT MLZ
Latitude/Longitude: . . . . . . . . 38° 13' N / 15° 16' E
GMT Offset: . . . . . . . . . . . . . . . . . . . . . . . . . . . +1
Telephone: . . . . . . . . . . . . . . [39] (090) 928-1110
Web: . . . . . . . . . . . www.harbours.net/milazzo

**Port of Napoli (Naples)**
UN/LOCODE: . . . . . . . . . . . . . . . . . . . . . IT NAP
Latitude/Longitude: . . . . . . . . 40° 50' N / 14° 15' E
GMT Offset: . . . . . . . . . . . . . . . . . . . . . . . . . . . +1
Telephone: . . . . . . . . . . . . . . [39] (081) 206-929
Web: . . . . . . www.informare.it/harbs/napoli/idxuk.asp

**Port of Palermo**
UN/LOCODE: . . . . . . . . . . . . . . . . . . . . . IT PMO
Latitude/Longitude: . . . . . . . . . 38° 7' N / 13° 20' E
GMT Offset: . . . . . . . . . . . . . . . . . . . . . . . . . . . +1
Telephone: . . . . . . . . . . . . . . [39] (091) 627-7111
Web: . . . . . . . . . . . . . . www.harbours.net/palermo

**Port of Sarroch (Porto Foxi)**
UN/LOCODE: . . . . . . . . . . . . . . . . . . . . . IT PFX
Latitude/Longitude: . . . . . . . . . . 39° 5' N / 9° 2' E
GMT Offset: . . . . . . . . . . . . . . . . . . . . . . . . . . . +1
Telephone: . . . . . . . . . . . . . . [39] (070) 900-057

**Port of Savona**
UN/LOCODE: . . . . . . . . . . . . . . . . . . . . . IT SVN
Latitude/Longitude: . . . . . . . . . 44° 18' N / 8° 29' E
GMT Offset: . . . . . . . . . . . . . . . . . . . . . . . . . . . +1
Telephone: . . . . . . . . . . . . . . [39] (019) 85541
Web: . . . . . . . . . . . . . . . . . . . www.porto.sv.it

**Port of Taranto**
UN/LOCODE: . . . . . . . . . . . . . . . . . . . . . IT TAR
Latitude/Longitude: . . . . . . . . 40° 29' N / 17° 13' E
GMT Offset: . . . . . . . . . . . . . . . . . . . . . . . . . . . +1
Telephone: . . . . . . . . . . . . . . [39] (099) 470-7527
Web: . . . . . . . . . . . . . . . . . www.port.taranto.it

**Port of Trieste**
UN/LOCODE: . . . . . . . . . . . . . . . . . . . . . . IT TRS
Latitude/Longitude: . . . . . . . . 45° 39' N / 13° 45' E
GMT Offset: . . . . . . . . . . . . . . . . . . . . . . . . . . . +1
Telephone: . . . . . . . . . . . . . . [39] (0586) 788-121
Web: . . . . . . . . . . . . . . . . . www.porto.trieste.it

**Port of Venice**
UN/LOCODE: . . . . . . . . . . . . . . . . . . . . . IT VCE
Latitude/Longitude: . . . . . . . . 45° 26' N / 12° 20' E
GMT Offset: . . . . . . . . . . . . . . . . . . . . . . . . . . . +1
Telephone: . . . . . . . . . . . . . . [39] (041) 533-4111
Web: . . . . . . . . . . . . . . . . . www.port.venice.it

**Porto Torres**
UN/LOCODE: . . . . . . . . . . . . . . . . . . . . . IT PTO
Latitude/Longitude: . . . . . . . . . 40° 51' N / 8° 24' E
GMT Offset: . . . . . . . . . . . . . . . . . . . . . . . . . . . +1
Telephone: . . . . . . . . . . . . . . [39] (079) 502-258

## Jamaica

**Port Antonio**
UN/LOCODE: . . . . . . . . . . . . . . . . . . . . . JM POT
Latitude/Longitude: . . . . . . . . 18° 12' N / 76° 27' W
GMT Offset: . . . . . . . . . . . . . . . . . . . . . . . . . . . -5
Telephone: . . . . . . . . . . . . . . [1] (876) 922-0290
Web: . . . . . . . . . . . . www.portantoniojamaica.com

**Port Esquivel**
UN/LOCODE: . . . . . . . . . . . . . . . . . . . . . JM PEV
Latitude/Longitude: . . . . . . . . . 17° 53' N / 77° 8' W
GMT Offset: . . . . . . . . . . . . . . . . . . . . . . . . . . . -5
Telephone: . . . . . . . . . . . . . . [1] (876) 922-0290
Web: . . . http://portfocus.com/jamaica/port_esquivel/

**Port of Kingston**
UN/LOCODE: . . . . . . . . . . . . . . . . . . . . . JM KIN
Latitude/Longitude: . . . . . . . . 17° 59' N / 76° 50' W
GMT Offset: . . . . . . . . . . . . . . . . . . . . . . . . . . . -5
Telephone: . . . . . . . . . . . . . . [1] (809) 922-6766
Web: . . . . . . . . . . . . . . . . . www.portofkingston.org/

S
E
A
P
O
R
T
S

**Port of Montego Bay**
*UN/LOCODE:* . . . . . . . . . . . . . . . . . . . . . . . JM MBJ
*Latitude/Longitude:* . . . . . . . . 18° 30' N / 77° 56' W
*GMT Offset:* . . . . . . . . . . . . . . . . . . . . . . . . . . . -5
*Web:* . . . http://portfocus.com/jamaica/montego_bay/
index.html

**Port of Ocho Rios**
*UN/LOCODE:* . . . . . . . . . . . . . . . . . . . . . . JM OCJ
*Latitude/Longitude:* . . . . . . . . 18° 25' N / 18° 25' N
*GMT Offset:* . . . . . . . . . . . . . . . . . . . . . . . . . . . -5
*Web:* . http://portfocus.com/jamaica/ocho_rios/index.html/

**Port of Rocky Point**
*UN/LOCODE:* . . . . . . . . . . . . . . . . . . . . . . JM ROP
*Latitude/Longitude:* . . . . . . . . 17° 38' N / 77° 14' W
*GMT Offset:* . . . . . . . . . . . . . . . . . . . . . . . . . . . -5
*Web:* http://portfocus.com/jamaica/rocky_point/index.html

# Japan

**Port of Akita, Akita**
*UN/LOCODE:* . . . . . . . . . . . . . . . . . . . . . . . JP AXT
*Latitude/Longitude:* . . . . . . . . 39° 45' N / 140° 3' E
*GMT Offset:* . . . . . . . . . . . . . . . . . . . . . . . . . . . +9
*Telephone:* . . . . . . . . . . . . . . . . [81] (18)866-2164
*Web:* . . . . . . . . www.city.akita.akita.jp/city/in/hb/port

**Port of Amagasaki, Hyogo**
*UN/LOCODE:* . . . . . . . . . . . . . . . . . . . . . . JP AMA
*Latitude/Longitude:* . . . . . . . . 34° 42' N / 135° 24' E
*GMT Offset:* . . . . . . . . . . . . . . . . . . . . . . . . . . . +9
*Telephone:* . . . . . . . . . . . . . . . . [81] (6) 412-1361

**Port of Chiba, Chiba**
*UN/LOCODE:* . . . . . . . . . . . . . . . . . . . . . . JP CHB
*Latitude/Longitude:* . . . . . . . . 35° 36' N / 140° 7' E
*GMT Offset:* . . . . . . . . . . . . . . . . . . . . . . . . . . . +9
*Telephone:* . . . . . . . . . . . . . . . . [81] (43) 223-3000
*Web:* . www.pref.chiba.jp/business/kowan/chibaport-
e.html

**Port of Hachinohe, Aomori**
*UN/LOCODE:* . . . . . . . . . . . . . . . . . . . . . . JP HHE
*Latitude/Longitude:* . . . . . . . . 40° 33' N / 141° 33' E
*GMT Offset:* . . . . . . . . . . . . . . . . . . . . . . . . . . . +9
*Web:* www.pref.aomori.jp/kowankuko/english/minato/
hachinohe/hachinohe.htm

**Port of Hakodate, Hokkaido**
*UN/LOCODE:* . . . . . . . . . . . . . . . . . . . . . . JP HKD
*Latitude/Longitude:* . . . . . . . . 41° 47' N / 140° 42' E
*GMT Offset:* . . . . . . . . . . . . . . . . . . . . . . . . . . . +9
*Telephone:* . . . . . . . . . . . . . . . . [81] (138) 223-101
*Web:* . . www.hk.hkd.mlit.go.jp/port/m_hakodate.html

**Port of Higashiharima, Hyogo**
*UN/LOCODE:* . . . . . . . . . . . . . . . . . . . . . . JP HHR
*Latitude/Longitude:* . . . . . . . . 34° 43' N / 134° 45' E
*GMT Offset:* . . . . . . . . . . . . . . . . . . . . . . . . . . . +9
*Telephone:* . . . . . . . . . . . . . . . . [81] (78) 341-7711

**Port of Himeji, Hyogo**
*UN/LOCODE:* . . . . . . . . . . . . . . . . . . . . . . JP HIM
*Latitude/Longitude:* . . . . . . . . 34° 47' N / 134° 41' E
*GMT Offset:* . . . . . . . . . . . . . . . . . . . . . . . . . . . +9
*Telephone:* . . . . . . . . . . . . . . . . [81] (792) 350-176

**Port of Hiroshima, Hiroshima**
*UN/LOCODE:* . . . . . . . . . . . . . . . . . . . . . . JP HIJ
*Latitude/Longitude:* . . . . . . . . 34° 20' N / 132° 25' E
*GMT Offset:* . . . . . . . . . . . . . . . . . . . . . . . . . . . +9
*Telephone:* . . . . . . . . . . . . . . . . [81] (82) 228-2111
*Web:* . . www.pref.hiroshima.jp/kukou/kouwan/minato

**Port of Kawasaki, Kanagawa**
*UN/LOCODE:* . . . . . . . . . . . . . . . . . . . . . . JP KWS
*Latitude/Longitude:* . . . . . . . . 35° 32' N / 139° 46' E
*GMT Offset:* . . . . . . . . . . . . . . . . . . . . . . . . . . . +9
*Telephone:* . . . . . . . . . . . . . . . . [81] (44) 200-2111
*Web:* . . . www.city.kawasaki.jp/english/minato_e.htm

**Port of Kinuura, Aichi**
*UN/LOCODE:* . . . . . . . . . . . . . . . . . . . . . . JP KNU
*Latitude/Longitude:* . . . . . . . . 34° 52' N / 136° 57' E
*GMT Offset:* . . . . . . . . . . . . . . . . . . . . . . . . . . . +9
*Telephone:* . . . . . . . . . . . . . . . . [81] (52) 961-2111
*Web:* www.pref.aichi.jp/kensetsu-somu/kinuura-komu

**Port of Kobe, Hyogo**
*UN/LOCODE:* . . . . . . . . . . . . . . . . . . . . . . JP UKB
*Latitude/Longitude:* . . . . . . . . 34° 40' N / 135° 12' E
*GMT Offset:* . . . . . . . . . . . . . . . . . . . . . . . . . . . +9
*Telephone:* . . . . . . . . . . . . . . . . [81] (78) 231-4672
*Web:* . www.city.kobe.jp/cityoffice/39/port/index_e.htm

**Port of Kushiro, Hokkaido**
*UN/LOCODE:* . . . . . . . . . . . . . . . . . . . . . . JP KUH
*Latitude/Longitude:* . . . . . . . . 42° 58' N / 144° 21' E
*GMT Offset:* . . . . . . . . . . . . . . . . . . . . . . . . . . . +9
*Telephone:* . . . . . . . . . . . . . . . . [81] (154) 235-151
*Web:* . . . . . . . . . . www.worldportsource.com/ports/
JPN_Port_of_Kushiro_1446.php

**Port of Mizushima, Okayama**
*UN/LOCODE:* . . . . . . . . . . . . . . . . . . . . . . JP MIZ
*Latitude/Longitude:* . . . . . . . . 34° 31' N / 133° 45' E
*GMT Offset:* . . . . . . . . . . . . . . . . . . . . . . . . . . . +9
*Telephone:* . . . . . . . . . . . . . . . . [81] (864) 447-141
*Web:* . . www.pref.okayama.jp/kurashiki/mizu/port.htm

**Port of Moji, Fukuoka**
*UN/LOCODE:* . . . . . . . . . . . . . . . . . . . . . . JP MOJ
*Latitude/Longitude:* . . . . . . . . 33° 57' N / 130° 58' E
*GMT Offset:* . . . . . . . . . . . . . . . . . . . . . . . . . . . +9
*Telephone:* . . . . . . . . . . . . . . . . [81] (93) 321-5941

**Port of Nagoya, Aichi**
*UN/LOCODE:* . . . . . . . . . . . . . . . . . . . . . . JP NGO
*Latitude/Longitude:* . . . . . . . . 35° 5' N / 136° 53' E
*GMT Offset:* . . . . . . . . . . . . . . . . . . . . . . . . . . . +9
*Telephone:* . . . . . . . . . . . . . . . . [81] (52) 654-7840
*Web:* . . . . . . . . . . . . . . . . . . . . www.port-of-nagoya.jp

**Port of Osaka, Osaka**
*UN/LOCODE:* . . . . . . . . . . . . . . . . . . . . . . JP OSA
*Latitude/Longitude:* . . . . . . . . 34° 39' N / 135° 26' E
*GMT Offset:* . . . . . . . . . . . . . . . . . . . . . . . . . . . +9
*Telephone:* . . . . . . . . . . . . . . . . [81] (6) 6615-7211
*Web:* . . . . . . . . . . . . . . . . . . . . . . . . . www.optc.or.jp

**Port of Sakai, Osaka**
*UN/LOCODE:* . . . . . . . . . . . . . . . . . . . . . . JP SAK
*Latitude/Longitude:* . . . . . . . . 34° 34' N / 135° 27' E
*GMT Offset:* . . . . . . . . . . . . . . . . . . . . . . . . . . . +9
*Telephone:* . . . . . . . . . . . . . . . . [81] (722) 385-241

**Port of Sakata**
*UN/LOCODE:* . . . . . . . . . . . . . . . . . . . . . . JP SKT
*Latitude/Longitude:* . . . . . . . . 38°56' N / 139°48' E
*GMT Offset:* . . . . . . . . . . . . . . . . . . . . . . . . . . . +9
*Telephone:* . . . . . . . . . . . . . . . . [81] (23) 630-2629
*Web:* . www.city.sakata.yamagata.jp/sakata_tmp/port/
index-e.htm

**Port of Shimizu, Shizuoka**
*UN/LOCODE:* . . . . . . . . . . . . . . . . . . . . . . JP SMZ
*Latitude/Longitude:* . . . . . . . . 35° 0' N / 138° 30' E
*GMT Offset:* . . . . . . . . . . . . . . . . . . . . . . . . . . . +9
*Telephone:* . . . . . . . . . . . . . . . . [81] (543) 532-203
*Web:* . . . . . . . . . . . . . . . . . . . . www.portofshimizu.com

**Port of Tokyo**
*UN/LOCODE:* . . . . . . . . . . . . . . . . . . . . . . JP TYO
*Latitude/Longitude:* . . . . . . . . 35° 43' N / 139° 46' E
*GMT Offset:* . . . . . . . . . . . . . . . . . . . . . . . . . . . +9
*Telephone:* . . . . . . . . . . . . . . . . [81] (3) 5320-5524
*Web:* . . . . . . . . . . . . . . . . . . . . www.kouwan.metro.tokyo.jp

**Port of Tomakomai, Hokkaido**
*UN/LOCODE:* . . . . . . . . . . . . . . . . . . . . . . JP TMK
*Latitude/Longitude:* . . . . . . . . 42° 35' N / 141° 35' E
*GMT Offset:* . . . . . . . . . . . . . . . . . . . . . . . . . . . +9
*Telephone:* . . . . . . . . . . . . . . . . [81] (144) 345-551
*Web:* . . . . . . . http://portfocus.com/japan/tomakomai/

SEAPORTS

# Jordan

**Port of Aqaba (El Akaba)**
*UN/LOCODE:* . . . . . . . . . . . . . . . . . . . . . . JO AQJ
*Latitude/Longitude:* . . . . . . . . . 29° 31' N / 35° 1' E
*GMT Offset:* . . . . . . . . . . . . . . . . . . . . . . . . . +2
*Telephone:* . . . . . . . . . . . . . . . [962] (3) 201-403
*Web:* . . . . . . . . . . . . . . . . www.aqabaports.com.jo

# Kenya

**Port of Lamu**
*UN/LOCODE:* . . . . . . . . . . . . . . . . . . . . KE LAU
*Latitude/Longitude:* . . . . . . . . . 2° 17' S / 40° 54' E
*GMT Offset:* . . . . . . . . . . . . . . . . . . . . . . . . . +3
*Telephone:* . . . . . . . . . . . . . . . [254] (41) 312-211
*Web:* . . . . . . . . . . . . . . . . . . . . . www.kpa.co.ke

**Port of Mombasa**
*UN/LOCODE:* . . . . . . . . . . . . . . . . . . . . KE MBA
*Latitude/Longitude:* . . . . . . . . . 4° 4' S / 39° 40' E
*GMT Offset:* . . . . . . . . . . . . . . . . . . . . . . . . . +3
*Telephone:* . . . . . . . . . . . . . . . [254] (41) 312-211
*Web:* . . . . . . . . . . . . . . . . . . . . . www.kpa.co.ke

# Kiribati

**Port of Tarawa**
*UN/LOCODE:* . . . . . . . . . . . . . . . . . . . . KI TRW
*Latitude/Longitude:* . . . . . . . . . 1° 25' N / 172° 54' E
*GMT Offset:* . . . . . . . . . . . . . . . . . . . . . . . . . +12

# Korea (North)

**Port of Chongjin**
*UN/LOCODE:* . . . . . . . . . . . . . . . . . . . . KP CHO
*Latitude/Longitude:* . . . . . . . . 41° 46' N / 129° 49' E
*GMT Offset:* . . . . . . . . . . . . . . . . . . . . . . . . . +9

**Port of Haeju**
*UN/LOCODE:* . . . . . . . . . . . . . . . . . . . . KP HAE
*Latitude/Longitude:* . . . . . . . . . 38° 0' N / 125° 42' E
*GMT Offset:* . . . . . . . . . . . . . . . . . . . . . . . . . +9

**Port of Nampo**
*UN/LOCODE:* . . . . . . . . . . . . . . . . . . . . KP NAM
*Latitude/Longitude:* . . . . . . . . 38° 44' N / 125° 25' E
*GMT Offset:* . . . . . . . . . . . . . . . . . . . . . . . . . +9

**Port of Wonsan**
*UN/LOCODE:* . . . . . . . . . . . . . . . . . . . . KP WON
*Latitude/Longitude:* . . . . . . . . 39° 10' N / 127° 26' E
*GMT Offset:* . . . . . . . . . . . . . . . . . . . . . . . . . +9

# Korea (South)

**Port of Busan (Pusan)**
*UN/LOCODE:* . . . . . . . . . . . . . . . . . . . . KR PUS
*Latitude/Longitude:* . . . . . . . . . 35° 5' N / 129° E
*GMT Offset:* . . . . . . . . . . . . . . . . . . . . . . . . . +9
*Telephone:* . . . . . . . . . . . . . . . [82] (51) 999-3000
*Web:* . . . . . . . . . . . . . . . . . . . . . www.busanpa.com

**Port of Chinhae**
*UN/LOCODE:* . . . . . . . . . . . . . . . . . . . . KR CHF
*Latitude/Longitude:* . . . . . . . . . 35° 7' N / 128° 42' E
*GMT Offset:* . . . . . . . . . . . . . . . . . . . . . . . . . +9
*Telephone:* . . . . . . . . . . . . . . . [82] (551) 456177
*Web:* http://portfocus.com/korea_south/chinhae/index.html

**Port of Inchon**
*UN/LOCODE:* . . . . . . . . . . . . . . . . . . . . KR INC
*Latitude/Longitude:* . . . . . . . . 37° 28' N / 126° 37' E
*GMT Offset:* . . . . . . . . . . . . . . . . . . . . . . . . . +9
*Telephone:* . . . . . . . . . . . . . . . [82] (32) 883-4061
*Web:* www.samsunglobal.com/PortInfo/inchon/inchon.asp

**Port of Masan**
*UN/LOCODE:* . . . . . . . . . . . . . . . . . . . . KR MAS
*Latitude/Longitude:* . . . . . . . . 35° 11' N / 128° 36' E
*GMT Offset:* . . . . . . . . . . . . . . . . . . . . . . . . . +9
*Telephone:* . . . . . . . . . . . . . . . [82] (551) 456-177
*Web:* . . http://masan.momaf.go.kr/eng/welcome/welcome.html

**Port of Mokpo**
*UN/LOCODE:* . . . . . . . . . . . . . . . . . . . . KR MOK
*Latitude/Longitude:* . . . . . . . . 34° 46' N / 126° 23' E
*GMT Offset:* . . . . . . . . . . . . . . . . . . . . . . . . . +9
*Telephone:* . . . . . . . . . . . . . . . [82] (631) 421-301
*Web:* www.samsunglobal.com/PortInfo/mokpo/mokpo.asp

**Port of Pohang**
*UN/LOCODE:* . . . . . . . . . . . . . . . . . . . . KR KPO
*Latitude/Longitude:* . . . . . . . . . 36° 2' N / 129° 26' E
*GMT Offset:* . . . . . . . . . . . . . . . . . . . . . . . . . +9
*Telephone:* . . . . . . . . . . . . . . . [82] (54) 242-1812
*Web:* . . . . . . . . . . . . . http://pohang.momaf.go.kr/eng/

**Port of Tonghae**
*UN/LOCODE:* . . . . . . . . . . . . . . . . . . . . KR TGH
*Latitude/Longitude:* . . . . . . . . 37° 30' N / 129° 9' E
*GMT Offset:* . . . . . . . . . . . . . . . . . . . . . . . . . +9
*Telephone:* . . . . . . . . . . . . . . . [82] (394) 521-0313
*Web:* www.samsunglobal.com/PortInfo/donghae/donghae.asp

**Port of Ulsan**
*UN/LOCODE:* . . . . . . . . . . . . . . . . . . . . KR USN
*Latitude/Longitude:* . . . . . . . . 35° 27' N / 129° 23' E
*GMT Offset:* . . . . . . . . . . . . . . . . . . . . . . . . . +9
*Telephone:* . . . . . . . . . . . . . . . [82] (52) 228-5572
*Web:* . . . . . . . . . . . . . http://ulsan.momaf.go.kr

**Port of Yosu**
*UN/LOCODE:* . . . . . . . . . . . . . . . . . . . . KR YOS
*Latitude/Longitude:* . . . . . . . . 34° 44' N / 127° 45' E
*GMT Offset:* . . . . . . . . . . . . . . . . . . . . . . . . . +9
*Web:* www.samsunglobal.com/portinfo/yosu/yosu.asp

# Kuwait

**Port of Mina al Ahmadi**
*UN/LOCODE:* . . . . . . . . . . . . . . . . . . . . KW MEA
*Latitude/Longitude:* . . . . . . . . . 29° 4' N / 48° 10' E
*GMT Offset:* . . . . . . . . . . . . . . . . . . . . . . . . . +3

**Port of Mina Saud**
*UN/LOCODE:* . . . . . . . . . . . . . . . . . . . . KW MIS
*Latitude/Longitude:* . . . . . . . . 28° 45' N / 48° 24' E
*GMT Offset:* . . . . . . . . . . . . . . . . . . . . . . . . . +3

**Port of Shuwaikh**
*UN/LOCODE:* . . . . . . . . . . . . . . . . . . . . KW SWK
*Latitude/Longitude:* . . . . . . . . 29° 21' N / 47° 56' E
*GMT Offset:* . . . . . . . . . . . . . . . . . . . . . . . . . +3
*Web:* . . . . . . . . . . . . . . . . . . . . . www.kpa.com.kw

# Latvia

**Port of Liepaya**
*UN/LOCODE:* . . . . . . . . . . . . . . . . . . . . LV LPX
*Latitude/Longitude:* . . . . . . . . 56° 30' N / 21° 0' E
*GMT Offset:* . . . . . . . . . . . . . . . . . . . . . . . . . +2
*Web:* . . . . . . . . . . . . . . . . . . . . . www.lsez.lv

**Port of Riga**
*UN/LOCODE:* . . . . . . . . . . . . . . . . . . . . SU RIX
*Latitude/Longitude:* . . . . . . . . 56° 58' N / 24° 6' E
*GMT Offset:* . . . . . . . . . . . . . . . . . . . . . . . . . +2
*Telephone:* . . . . . . . . . . . . . . . [371] 732-9224
*Web:* www.rto.lv/RigaCommercialFreePort.htm

**Port of Ventspils**
*UN/LOCODE:* . . . . . . . . . . . . . . . . . . . . LV VNT
*Latitude/Longitude:* . . . . . . . . 57° 24' N / 21° 33' E
*GMT Offset:* . . . . . . . . . . . . . . . . . . . . . . . . . +2
*Telephone:* . . . . . . . . . . . . . . . [371] 362-3324
*Web:* . . . . . . . . . . . . . . . . . . . . . www.vbp.lv

# Lebanon

**Port of Beirut**
*UN/LOCODE:* . . . . . . . . . . . . . . . . . . . . LB BEY
*Latitude/Longitude:* . . . . . . . . 33° 54' N / 35° 30' E
*GMT Offset:* . . . . . . . . . . . . . . . . . . . . . . . . . +2
*Telephone:* . . . . . . . . . . . . . . . [961] (1) 580-211

SEAPORTS

**Port of Chekka**
UN/LOCODE: ...................... LB CHK
Latitude/Longitude: ......... 34° 18' N / 35° 36' E
GMT Offset: .............................. +2
Telephone: ............... [961] (1) 430-502

**Port of Selaata**
UN/LOCODE: ...................... LB SEL
Latitude/Longitude: ......... 34° 17' N / 35° 40' E
GMT Offset: .............................. +2
Telephone: ............... [961] (6) 642-787

**Port of Sidon**
UN/LOCODE: ...................... LB SDN
Latitude/Longitude: ......... 33° 30' N / 35° 21' E
GMT Offset: .............................. +2
Telephone: ............... [961] (7) 720-019

**Port of Tripoli**
UN/LOCODE: ...................... LB KYE
Latitude/Longitude: ......... 34° 28' N / 35° 49' E
GMT Offset: .............................. +2

## Liberia

**Port of Buchanan**
UN/LOCODE: ...................... LR UCN
Latitude/Longitude: ......... 5° 54' N / 10° 4' W
GMT Offset: .............................. +0

**Port of Greenville**
UN/LOCODE: ...................... LR GRE
Latitude/Longitude: ......... 4° 59' N / 9° 3' W
GMT Offset: .............................. +0

**Port of Monrovia**
UN/LOCODE: ...................... LR MLW
Latitude/Longitude: ......... 6° 20' N / 10° 50' W
GMT Offset: .............................. +0
Telephone: ................... [231] 221-577
Web: ........... www.otal.com/liberia/liberia.htm

## Libya

**Port of Bingazi (Benghazi)**
UN/LOCODE: ...................... LY BEN
Latitude/Longitude: ......... 32° 6' N / 20° 3' E
GMT Offset: .............................. +2
Telephone: ............... [218] (61) 92017

**Port of Derna**
UN/LOCODE: ...................... LY DNF
Latitude/Longitude: ......... 32° 46' N / 22° 39' E
GMT Offset: .............................. +2

**Port of Marsa El Brega**
UN/LOCODE: ...................... LY LMQ
Latitude/Longitude: ......... 30° 25' N / 19° 34' E
GMT Offset: .............................. +2
Web: ................... www.libyanet.de/

**Port of Misurata**
UN/LOCODE: ...................... LY MRA
Latitude/Longitude: ......... 32° 22' N / 15° 13' E
GMT Offset: .............................. +2
Telephone: ............... [231] (51) 24457

**Port of Ras Lanuf**
UN/LOCODE: ...................... LY RLA
Latitude/Longitude: ......... 30° 31' N / 18° 35' E
GMT Offset: .............................. +2

**Port of Tobruk**
UN/LOCODE: ...................... LY TOB
Latitude/Longitude: ......... 32° 4' N / 24° 0' E
GMT Offset: .............................. +2

**Port of Tripoli**
UN/LOCODE: ...................... LY TIP
Latitude/Longitude: ......... 32° 54' N / 13° 13' E
GMT Offset: .............................. +2
Telephone: ............... [231] (21) 47011

**Port of Zuara**
UN/LOCODE: ...................... LY ZUA
Latitude/Longitude: ......... 32° 55' N / 12° 7' E
GMT Offset: .............................. +2

## Lithuania

**Port of Klaipeda**
UN/LOCODE: ...................... LT KLJ
Latitude/Longitude: ......... 55° 43' N / 21° 7' E
GMT Offset: .............................. +0
Telephone: ............... [370] (46) 499-799
Web: ........... www.portofklaipeda.lt/en.php

## Madagascar

**Port of Antsiranana**
UN/LOCODE: ...................... MG DIE
Latitude/Longitude: ......... 12° 13' S / 49° 19' E
GMT Offset: .............................. +3

**Port of Majunga (Mahajanga)**
UN/LOCODE: ...................... MG MJN
Latitude/Longitude: ......... 15° 43' S / 46° 20' E
GMT Offset: .............................. +3
Telephone: ............... [216] (20) 422-328

**Port of Toamasina**
UN/LOCODE: ...................... MG TOA
Latitude/Longitude: ......... 18° 8' S / 49° 22' E
GMT Offset: .............................. +0

**Port of Tulear (Toliara)**
UN/LOCODE: ...................... MG TLE
Latitude/Longitude: ......... 23° 21' S / 43° 40' E
GMT Offset: .............................. +3

## Malaysia

**Port Dickson**
UN/LOCODE: ...................... MY PDI
Latitude/Longitude: ......... 2° 31' N / 101° 47' E
GMT Offset: .............................. +8
Telephone: ............... [60] (6) 471-405
Web: ... www.portsworld.com/Ports/portdickson.htm

**Port Kelang**
UN/LOCODE: ...................... MY PKL
Latitude/Longitude: ......... 3° 0' N / 101° 24' E
GMT Offset: .............................. +8
Telephone: ............... [60] (3) 3169-8888
Web: ................... www.pka.gov.my

**Port of Bintulu, Sarawak**
UN/LOCODE: ...................... MY BTU
Latitude/Longitude: ......... 3° 16' N / 112° 59' E
GMT Offset: .............................. +8
Telephone: ............... [60] (86) 253-888
Web: ................... www.bpa.gov.my

**Port of Kota Kinabalu, Sabah**
UN/LOCODE: ...................... MY BKI
Latitude/Longitude: ......... 5° 59' N / 116° 0' E
GMT Offset: .............................. +8
Telephone: ............... [60] (88) 256-155
Web: ... www.portsworld.com/Ports/kotakinabalu.htm

**Port of Kuantan (Tanjong Gelang)**
UN/LOCODE: ...................... MY KUA
Latitude/Longitude: ......... 3° 58' N / 103° 26' E
GMT Offset: .............................. +8
Telephone: ............... [60] (9) 583-3201
Web: ................... www.lpktn.gov.my/

**Port of Kuching, Sarawak**
UN/LOCODE: ...................... MY KCH
Latitude/Longitude: ......... 1° 34' N / 110° 21' E
GMT Offset: .............................. +8
Telephone: ............... [60] (82) 482-144
Web: ... www.portsworld.com/Ports/kuchingport.htm

**Port of Kudat, Sabah**
*UN/LOCODE:* . . . . . . . . . . . . . . . . . . . . . MY KUD
*Latitude/Longitude:* . . . . . . . 6° 53' N / 116° 51' E
*GMT Offset:* . . . . . . . . . . . . . . . . . . . . . . . . . . +8
*Telephone:* . . . . . . . . . . . . . . [60] (88) 256-155
*Web:* . . . http://portfocus.com/malaysia/kudat/index.html

**Port of Labuan, Sabah**
*UN/LOCODE:* . . . . . . . . . . . . . . . . . . . . . MY LBU
*Latitude/Longitude:* . . . . . . . . . 5° 17' N / 115° 15' E
*GMT Offset:* . . . . . . . . . . . . . . . . . . . . . . . . . . +8
*Telephone:* . . . . . . . . . . . . . . [60] (87) 421-699
*Web:* . . . . www.portsworld.com/Ports/labuanport.htm

**Port of Lahad Datu, Sabah**
*UN/LOCODE:* . . . . . . . . . . . . . . . . . . . . . MY LDU
*Latitude/Longitude:* . . . . . . . . . . 5° 2' N / 118° 20' E
*GMT Offset:* . . . . . . . . . . . . . . . . . . . . . . . . . . +8
*Telephone:* . . . . . . . . . . . . . . . [60] (89) 81244
*Web:* .http://portfocus.com/malaysia/lahad_datu/index.html

**Port of Lumut**
*UN/LOCODE:* . . . . . . . . . . . . . . . . . . . . . MY LUM
*Latitude/Longitude:* . . . . . . . . . 4° 16' N / 100° 39' E
*GMT Offset:* . . . . . . . . . . . . . . . . . . . . . . . . . . +8
*Telephone:* . . . . . . . . . . . . . . [60] (5) 683-5477
*Web:* . . . . . . . . . . . . . . . . . . www.lumutport.com

**Port of Miri, Sarawak**
*UN/LOCODE:* . . . . . . . . . . . . . . . . . . . . . MY MYY
*Latitude/Longitude:* . . . . . . . . . 4° 26' N / 113° 55' E
*GMT Offset:* . . . . . . . . . . . . . . . . . . . . . . . . . . +8
*Telephone:* . . . . . . . . . . . . . . . [60] (85) 33301

**Port of Pasir Gudang, Johor**
*UN/LOCODE:* . . . . . . . . . . . . . . . . . . . . . MY PGU
*Latitude/Longitude:* . . . . . . . . . 1° 26' N / 103° 54' E
*GMT Offset:* . . . . . . . . . . . . . . . . . . . . . . . . . . +8
*Telephone:* . . . . . . . . . . . . . . [60] (7) 251-7721
*Web:* . . . . . . . . . . . . . . . . . . . . www.lpj.gov.my

**Port of Penang (Georgetown)**
*UN/LOCODE:* . . . . . . . . . . . . . . . . . . . . . MY PEN
*Latitude/Longitude:* . . . . . . . . . 5° 25' N / 100° 21' E
*GMT Offset:* . . . . . . . . . . . . . . . . . . . . . . . . . . +8
*Telephone:* . . . . . . . . . . . . . . [60] (4) 210-2211
*Web:* . . . . . . . . . . . . . . . www.penangport.com.my

**Port of Sandakan, Sabah**
*UN/LOCODE:* . . . . . . . . . . . . . . . . . . . . . MY SDK
*Latitude/Longitude:* . . . . . . . . . . 5° 50' N / 118° 7' E
*GMT Offset:* . . . . . . . . . . . . . . . . . . . . . . . . . . +8
*Telephone:* . . . . . . . . . . . . . . [60] (89) 612-411

**Port of Sibu, Sarawak**
*UN/LOCODE:* . . . . . . . . . . . . . . . . . . . . . MY SBW
*Latitude/Longitude:* . . . . . . . . . 2° 18' N / 111° 49' E
*GMT Offset:* . . . . . . . . . . . . . . . . . . . . . . . . . . +8
*Telephone:* . . . . . . . . . . . . . . [60] (84) 319-009

**Port of Tawau, Sabah**
*UN/LOCODE:* . . . . . . . . . . . . . . . . . . . . . MY TWU
*Latitude/Longitude:* . . . . . . . . . 4° 14' N / 117° 52' E
*GMT Offset:* . . . . . . . . . . . . . . . . . . . . . . . . . . +8
*Telephone:* . . . . . . . . . . . . . . [60] (89) 773-700
*Web:* . . . http://portfocus.com/malaysia/tawau/index.html

## Malta

**Port of Valetta**
*UN/LOCODE:* . . . . . . . . . . . . . . . . . . . . . MT MLA
*Latitude/Longitude:* . . . . . . . . . . . 35° 54' N / 014° 31'
*GMT Offset:* . . . . . . . . . . . . . . . . . . . . . . . . . . +1
*Telephone:* . . . . . . . . . . . . . . . [356] 2122-2203
*Web:* . . . . . . . . www.mma.gov.mt/ports_valletta.htm

## Martinique

**Port of Fort de France**
*UN/LOCODE:* . . . . . . . . . . . . . . . . . . . . . MQ FDF
*Latitude/Longitude:* . . . . . . . . . 14° 36' N / 61° 4' W
*GMT Offset:* . . . . . . . . . . . . . . . . . . . . . . . . . . -4

## Mauritania

**Port of Nouadhibou**
*UN/LOCODE:* . . . . . . . . . . . . . . . . . . . . . MR NDB
*Latitude/Longitude:* . . . . . . . . . 20° 49' N / 17° 3' W
*GMT Offset:* . . . . . . . . . . . . . . . . . . . . . . . . . . +0

**Port of Nouakchott**
*UN/LOCODE:* . . . . . . . . . . . . . . . . . . . . . MR NKC
*Latitude/Longitude:* . . . . . . . . . 18° 2' N / 16° 2' W
*GMT Offset:* . . . . . . . . . . . . . . . . . . . . . . . . . . +0
*Telephone:* . . . . . . . . . . . . . . . . [222] 251-453
*Web:* . . . . . www.otal.com/mauritania/mauritania.htm

## Mauritius

**Port Louis**
*UN/LOCODE:* . . . . . . . . . . . . . . . . . . . . . MU PLU
*Latitude/Longitude:* . . . . . . . . . 20° 9' S / 57° 30' E
*GMT Offset:* . . . . . . . . . . . . . . . . . . . . . . . . . . +4
*Telephone:* . . . . . . . . . . . . . . . . [230] 206-5400
*Web:* . . . . . . . . . . . . . . . . . . . . www.mauport.com

## Mexico

**Port of Acapulco**
*UN/LOCODE:* . . . . . . . . . . . . . . . . . . . . . MX ACA
*Latitude/Longitude:* . . . . . . . . . 16° 51' N / 99° 56' W
*GMT Offset:* . . . . . . . . . . . . . . . . . . . . . . . . . . -6
*Web:* . . http://portfocus.com/mexico/acapulco/index.html

**Port of Coatzacoalcos**
*UN/LOCODE:* . . . . . . . . . . . . . . . . . . . . . MX COA
*Latitude/Longitude:* . . . . . . . . . 18° 8' N / 94° 25' W
*GMT Offset:* . . . . . . . . . . . . . . . . . . . . . . . . . . -6
*Web:* . . . . . . . . . . . . . . . . . . www.apicoatza.com

**Port of Guaymas**
*UN/LOCODE:* . . . . . . . . . . . . . . . . . . . . . MX GYM
*Latitude/Longitude:* . . . . . . . 27° 55' N / 110° 53' W
*GMT Offset:* . . . . . . . . . . . . . . . . . . . . . . . . . . -7
*Telephone:* . . . . . . . . . . . . . . . [52] (622) 22250
*Web:* . http://portfocus.com/mexico/guaymas/index.html

**Port of La Paz**
*UN/LOCODE:* . . . . . . . . . . . . . . . . . . . . . MX LAP
*Latitude/Longitude:* . . . . . . . 24° 10' N / 110° 19' W
*GMT Offset:* . . . . . . . . . . . . . . . . . . . . . . . . . . -7
*Telephone:* . . . . . . . . . . . . . . . [52] (682) 20243
*Web:* . . . . . . . www.bajaport.com/ptopich.html#lapaz

**Port of Lazaro Cardenas**
*UN/LOCODE:* . . . . . . . . . . . . . . . . . . . . . MX LZC
*Latitude/Longitude:* . . . . . . . 17° 53' N / 102° 10' W
*GMT Offset:* . . . . . . . . . . . . . . . . . . . . . . . . . . -6
*Telephone:* . . . . . . . . . . . . . . [52] (753) 532-2064
*Web:* . . . . . . . www.puerto-lazarocardenas.com.mx

**Port of Manzanillo**
*UN/LOCODE:* . . . . . . . . . . . . . . . . . . . . . MX ZLO
*Latitude/Longitude:* . . . . . . . . . 19° 3' N / 104° 20' W
*GMT Offset:* . . . . . . . . . . . . . . . . . . . . . . . . . . -7
*Telephone:* . . . . . . . . . . . . . . [52] (333) 23061
*Web:* . . . . . . . . . . . www.apimanzanillo.com.mx

**Port of Mazatlan**
*UN/LOCODE:* . . . . . . . . . . . . . . . . . . . . . MX MZT
*Latitude/Longitude:* . . . . . . . 23° 11' N / 106° 26' W
*GMT Offset:* . . . . . . . . . . . . . . . . . . . . . . . . . . -7
*Telephone:* . . . . . . . . . . . . . . [52] (669) 982-3019
*Web:* . . . . . . . . . . . . www.apimazatlan.com.mx

**Port of Progreso**
*UN/LOCODE:* . . . . . . . . . . . . . . . . . . . . . MX PGO
*Latitude/Longitude:* . . . . . . . . . 21° 17' N / 89° 39' W
*GMT Offset:* . . . . . . . . . . . . . . . . . . . . . . . . . . -6
*Telephone:* . . . . . . . . . . . . . . [52] (969) 935-0095
*Web:* . . . . . . . . . . . . www.puerto-progreso.com.mx

**SEAPORTS**

**Port of Salina Cruz**
UN/LOCODE: . . . . . . . . . . . . . . . . . . . . . . MX SCX
Latitude/Longitude: . . . . . . . . 16° 10' N / 95° 12' W
GMT Offset: . . . . . . . . . . . . . . . . . . . . . . . . . . . -6
Telephone: . . . . . . . . . . . . . [52] (971) 413-2501
Web: . . . . . . . . . . . . . . . . www.apisal.com.mx

**Port of Tampico**
UN/LOCODE: . . . . . . . . . . . . . . . . . . . . . MX TAM
Latitude/Longitude: . . . . . . . 22° 16' N / 97° 47' W
GMT Offset: . . . . . . . . . . . . . . . . . . . . . . . . . . . -6
Web: . . . . . . . . . . . . www.puertodetampico.com.mx

**Port of Topolobampo**
UN/LOCODE: . . . . . . . . . . . . . . . . . . . . . MX TPB
Latitude/Longitude: . . . . . . . 25° 36' N / 109° 3' W
GMT Offset: . . . . . . . . . . . . . . . . . . . . . . . . . . . -7
Telephone: . . . . . . . . . . . . . [52] (668) 862-0494
Web: http://portfocus.com/mexico/topolobampo/index.html

**Port of Tuxpan**
UN/LOCODE: . . . . . . . . . . . . . . . . . . . . . MX TUX
Latitude/Longitude: . . . . . . . 20° 57' N / 97° 24' W
GMT Offset: . . . . . . . . . . . . . . . . . . . . . . . . . . . -6
Telephone: . . . . . . . . . . . . . . . . [52] (688) 2266
Web: . . . . . . . . . . . . . . . www.tuxpanport.com.mx

**Port of Veracruz**
UN/LOCODE: . . . . . . . . . . . . . . . . . . . . . MX VER
Latitude/Longitude: . . . . . . . . 19° 12' N / 96° 8' W
GMT Offset: . . . . . . . . . . . . . . . . . . . . . . . . . . . -6
Telephone: . . . . . . . . . . . . . . . [52] (29) 321-319
Web: . . . . . . . . . . . . . . . . . . . . www.apiver.com

## Micronesia
**Port of Pohnpei (Ex Ponape)**
UN/LOCODE: . . . . . . . . . . . . . . . . . . . . . . FM PNI
Latitude/Longitude: . . . . . . . . 6° 55' N / 158° 10' E
GMT Offset: . . . . . . . . . . . . . . . . . . . . . . . . . . +11
Telephone: . . . . . . . . . . . . . . . . [691] 320-2793

## Monaco
**Port of Monaco**
UN/LOCODE: . . . . . . . . . . . . . . . . . . . . . MC MON
Latitude/Longitude: . . . . . . . . 43° 44' N / 7° 27' E
GMT Offset: . . . . . . . . . . . . . . . . . . . . . . . . . . . +1
Web: . . . . . . . . http://portfocus.com/monaco/index.html

## Montenegro
**Port of Bar**
UN/LOCODE: . . . . . . . . . . . . . . . . . . . . . . YU BAR
Latitude/Longitude: . . . . . . . . . . 42° 5' N / 19° 3' E
GMT Offset: . . . . . . . . . . . . . . . . . . . . . . . . . . . +1
Telephone: . . . . . . . . . . . . . . . . [381] (85) 11382
Web: . . . . . . . . . . . . . . . http://www.lukabar.cg.yu/

## Montserrat
**Port of Plymouth**
UN/LOCODE: . . . . . . . . . . . . . . . . . . . . . MS PLY
Latitude/Longitude: . . . . . . . . 16° 42' N / 62° 13' W
GMT Offset: . . . . . . . . . . . . . . . . . . . . . . . . . . . -4

## Morocco
**Port of Agadir**
UN/LOCODE: . . . . . . . . . . . . . . . . . . . . . MA AGA
Latitude/Longitude: . . . . . . . . 30° 26' N / 9° 38' W
GMT Offset: . . . . . . . . . . . . . . . . . . . . . . . . . . . +0
Telephone: . . . . . . . . . . . . . . . [212] (4) 884-2934
Web: . www.mtpnet.gov.ma/infrastructure/patrimoine/
port/p_AGADIR.htm

**Port of Casablanca**
UN/LOCODE: . . . . . . . . . . . . . . . . . . . . . MA CAS
Latitude/Longitude: . . . . . . . . 33° 36' N / 7° 37' W
GMT Offset: . . . . . . . . . . . . . . . . . . . . . . . . . . . +0
Web: . www.mtpnet.gov.ma/infrastructure/patrimoine/
port/p_CASABLANCA.htm

**Port of El Jadida**
UN/LOCODE: . . . . . . . . . . . . . . . . . . . . . . MA ELJ
Latitude/Longitude: . . . . . . . . 33° 16' N / 33° 16' N
GMT Offset: . . . . . . . . . . . . . . . . . . . . . . . . . . . +0
Web: . www.mtpnet.gov.ma/infrastructure/patrimoine/
port/p_ELJADIDA.htm

**Port of Kenitra**
UN/LOCODE: . . . . . . . . . . . . . . . . . . . . . MA NNA
Latitude/Longitude: . . . . . . . . . 34° 16' N / 6° 35' W
GMT Offset: . . . . . . . . . . . . . . . . . . . . . . . . . . . +0
Telephone: . . . . . . . . . . . . . . . . [212] (3) 71345
Web: . www.mtpnet.gov.ma/infrastructure/patrimoine/
port/p_KENITRA.htm

**Port of Mohammedia**
UN/LOCODE: . . . . . . . . . . . . . . . . . . . . . MA MOH
Latitude/Longitude: . . . . . . . . 33° 45' N / 7° 22' W
GMT Offset: . . . . . . . . . . . . . . . . . . . . . . . . . . . +0
Web: . www.mtpnet.gov.ma/infrastructure/patrimoine/
port/p_MOHAMMEDIA.htm

**Port of Safi**
UN/LOCODE: . . . . . . . . . . . . . . . . . . . . . . MA SFI
Latitude/Longitude: . . . . . . . . . 32° 19' N / 9° 12' W
GMT Offset: . . . . . . . . . . . . . . . . . . . . . . . . . . . +0
Telephone: . . . . . . . . . . . . . . [212] (4) 446-2136
Web: . www.mtpnet.gov.ma/infrastructure/patrimoine/
port/p_SAFI.htm

**Port of Tangier**
UN/LOCODE: . . . . . . . . . . . . . . . . . . . . . MA TNG
Latitude/Longitude: . . . . . . . . . 35° 47' N / 5° 48' W
GMT Offset: . . . . . . . . . . . . . . . . . . . . . . . . . . . +0
Telephone: . . . . . . . . . . . . . . [212] (3) 993-7495
Web: . www.mtpnet.gov.ma/infrastructure/patrimoine/
port/p_TANGER.htm

## Mozambique
**Port of Beira**
UN/LOCODE: . . . . . . . . . . . . . . . . . . . . . MZ BEW
Latitude/Longitude: . . . . . . . . 19° 46' S / 34° 50' E
GMT Offset: . . . . . . . . . . . . . . . . . . . . . . . . . . . +2
Web: . . . . . . . . . http://www.tallships.co.za/beira.htm

**Port of Inhambane**
UN/LOCODE: . . . . . . . . . . . . . . . . . . . . . . MZ INH
Latitude/Longitude: . . . . . . . . 23° 52' S / 35° 23' E
GMT Offset: . . . . . . . . . . . . . . . . . . . . . . . . . . . +2

**Port of Maputo**
UN/LOCODE: . . . . . . . . . . . . . . . . . . . . MZ MPM
Latitude/Longitude: . . . . . . . . 25° 59' S / 32° 36' E
GMT Offset: . . . . . . . . . . . . . . . . . . . . . . . . . . . +2
Telephone: . . . . . . . . . . . . . . . [258] (1) 427-173
Web: . . . . . . . . . . . . . . . . . www.portmaputo.com

**Port of Matola**
UN/LOCODE: . . . . . . . . . . . . . . . . . . . . . MZ MAT
Latitude/Longitude: . . . . . . . . 25° 58' S / 32° 30' E
GMT Offset: . . . . . . . . . . . . . . . . . . . . . . . . . . . +2

**Port of Nacala**
UN/LOCODE: . . . . . . . . . . . . . . . . . . . . . MZ MNC
Latitude/Longitude: . . . . . . . . 14° 32' S / 40° 40' E
GMT Offset: . . . . . . . . . . . . . . . . . . . . . . . . . . . +2
Telephone: . . . . . . . . . . . . . . . [258] (6) 212-927
Web: . . . . . . . . . . . . . . www.ports.co.za/nacala.php

**Port of Pemba**
UN/LOCODE: . . . . . . . . . . . . . . . . . . . . . MZ POL
Latitude/Longitude: . . . . . . . . 12° 57' S / 40° 30' E
GMT Offset: . . . . . . . . . . . . . . . . . . . . . . . . . . . +2

**Port of Quelimane**
UN/LOCODE: . . . . . . . . . . . . . . . . . . . . . MZ UEL
Latitude/Longitude: . . . . . . . . 17° 53' S / 36° 53' E
GMT Offset: . . . . . . . . . . . . . . . . . . . . . . . . . . . +2
Telephone: . . . . . . . . . . . . . . . [258] (4) 212-994

## Myanmar

**Port of Bassein**
UN/LOCODE: . . . . . . . . . . . . . . . . . . . . . MM BSX
Latitude/Longitude: . . . . . . . . 16° 45' N / 94° 43' E
GMT Offset: . . . . . . . . . . . . . . . . . . . . . . . . . +6

**Port of Mawlamyine (Moulmein)**
UN/LOCODE: . . . . . . . . . . . . . . . . . . . . MM MNU
Latitude/Longitude: . . . . . . . . 16° 29' N / 97° 37' E
GMT Offset: . . . . . . . . . . . . . . . . . . . . . . . . . +6

**Port of Yangon**
UN/LOCODE: . . . . . . . . . . . . . . . . . . . . MM RGN
Latitude/Longitude: . . . . . . . . 16° 47' N / 96° 15' E
GMT Offset: . . . . . . . . . . . . . . . . . . . . . . . . . +6

## Namibia

**Port of Luderitz**
UN/LOCODE: . . . . . . . . . . . . . . . . . . . . . NA LUD
Latitude/Longitude: . . . . . . . . . 26° 39' S / 15° 9' E
GMT Offset: . . . . . . . . . . . . . . . . . . . . . . . . . +2
Telephone: . . . . . . . . . . . . . . . [264] (63) 312-337
Web: . . . . . . . . . . . . www.ports.co.za/luderitz.php

**Port of Walvis Bay**
UN/LOCODE: . . . . . . . . . . . . . . . . . . . . NA WVB
Latitude/Longitude: . . . . . . . . 22° 57' S / 14° 30' E
GMT Offset: . . . . . . . . . . . . . . . . . . . . . . . . . +2
Telephone: . . . . . . . . . . . . . . . . [264] (64) 28390
Web: . . . . . . . . . . . . www.ports.co.za/walvis-bay.php

## Nauru

**Port of Nauru Island**
UN/LOCODE: . . . . . . . . . . . . . . . . . . . . . NR INU
Latitude/Longitude: . . . . . . . . . 0° 32' S / 166° 55' E
GMT Offset: . . . . . . . . . . . . . . . . . . . . . . . . . +12

## Netherlands

**Port of Amsterdam**
UN/LOCODE: . . . . . . . . . . . . . . . . . . . . . NL AMS
Latitude/Longitude: . . . . . . . . . 52° 22' N / 4° 54' E
GMT Offset: . . . . . . . . . . . . . . . . . . . . . . . . . +1
Telephone: . . . . . . . . . . . . . . . [31] (20) 523-4500
Web: . . . . . . . . . . . . . . . www.amsterdamports.nl

**Port of Delfzijl**
UN/LOCODE: . . . . . . . . . . . . . . . . . . . . . NL DZL
Latitude/Longitude: . . . . . . . . . 53° 20' N / 6° 56' E
GMT Offset: . . . . . . . . . . . . . . . . . . . . . . . . . +1
Telephone: . . . . . . . . . . . . . . . [31] (59) 664-0400
Web: . . . . . . . www.groningen-seaports.com/engels/

**Port of Dordrecht**
UN/LOCODE: . . . . . . . . . . . . . . . . . . . . . NL DOR
Latitude/Longitude: . . . . . . . . . 51° 49' N / 4° 40' E
GMT Offset: . . . . . . . . . . . . . . . . . . . . . . . . . +1
Telephone: . . . . . . . . . . . . . . . . [31] (78) 134-211

**Port of Eemshaven**
UN/LOCODE: . . . . . . . . . . . . . . . . . . . . . NL EEM
Latitude/Longitude: . . . . . . . . . 53° 27' N / 6° 50' E
GMT Offset: . . . . . . . . . . . . . . . . . . . . . . . . . +1
Web: . . . . . . . . . . www.groningen-seaports.com

**Port of Groningen**
UN/LOCODE: . . . . . . . . . . . . . . . . . . . . . NL GRQ
Latitude/Longitude: . . . . . . . . . 53° 13' N / 6° 34' E
GMT Offset: . . . . . . . . . . . . . . . . . . . . . . . . . +1
Telephone: . . . . . . . . . . . . . . . [31] (59) 664-0400
Web: . . . . . . . . . . www.groningen-seaports.com

**Port of Ijmuiden**
UN/LOCODE: . . . . . . . . . . . . . . . . . . . . . NL IJM
Latitude/Longitude: . . . . . . . . . 52° 27' N / 4° 35' E
GMT Offset: . . . . . . . . . . . . . . . . . . . . . . . . . +1

**Port of Rotterdam**
UN/LOCODE: . . . . . . . . . . . . . . . . . . . . NL RTM
Latitude/Longitude: . . . . . . . . . 51° 55' N / 4° 24' E
GMT Offset: . . . . . . . . . . . . . . . . . . . . . . . . . +1
Telephone: . . . . . . . . . . . . . . . [31] (10) 252-1111
Web: . . . . . . . . . . . . . . www.portofrotterdam.com/

**Port of Terneuzen**
UN/LOCODE: . . . . . . . . . . . . . . . . . . . . . NL TNZ
Latitude/Longitude: . . . . . . . . . 51° 20' N / 3° 50' E
GMT Offset: . . . . . . . . . . . . . . . . . . . . . . . . . +1
Telephone: . . . . . . . . . . . . . . . [31] (11) 562-0997
Web: . . . . . . . . . . . . . . www.zeeland-seaports.com

## Netherlands Antilles

**Port of Kralendijk, Bonaire**
UN/LOCODE: . . . . . . . . . . . . . . . . . . . . . AN KRA
Latitude/Longitude: . . . . . . . . . 12° 9' N / 68° 17' W
GMT Offset: . . . . . . . . . . . . . . . . . . . . . . . . . -4
Telephone: . . . . . . . . . . . . . . . . . [599] (7) 8151

**Port of Philipsburg**
UN/LOCODE: . . . . . . . . . . . . . . . . . . . . . AN PHI
Latitude/Longitude: . . . . . . . . . 18° 5' N / 63° 10' W
GMT Offset: . . . . . . . . . . . . . . . . . . . . . . . . . -4

**Port of Willemstad**
UN/LOCODE: . . . . . . . . . . . . . . . . . . . . . AN WIL
Latitude/Longitude: . . . . . . . . . 12° 6' N / 68° 56' W
GMT Offset: . . . . . . . . . . . . . . . . . . . . . . . . . -4
Telephone: . . . . . . . . . . . . . . . . . [599] 434-5999
Web: . . . . . . . . . . . . . . . . . . . . . www.curports.com

## New Caledonia

**Port of Noumea**
UN/LOCODE: . . . . . . . . . . . . . . . . . . . . NC NOU
Latitude/Longitude: . . . . . . . . 22° 16' S / 166° 27' E
GMT Offset: . . . . . . . . . . . . . . . . . . . . . . . . . +11
Telephone: . . . . . . . . . . . . . . . . . . [687] 275-966

**Port of Thio**
UN/LOCODE: . . . . . . . . . . . . . . . . . . . . . NC THI
Latitude/Longitude: . . . . . . . . 21° 37' S / 166° 15' E
GMT Offset: . . . . . . . . . . . . . . . . . . . . . . . . . +11

## New Zealand

**Port of Auckland**
UN/LOCODE: . . . . . . . . . . . . . . . . . . . . NZ AKL
Latitude/Longitude: . . . . . . . . 36° 51' S / 174° 45' E
GMT Offset: . . . . . . . . . . . . . . . . . . . . . . . . . +12
Telephone: . . . . . . . . . . . . . . . . . [64] (9) 366-0055
Web: . . . . . . . . . . . . . . . . . . . . . www.poal.co.nz

**Port of Dunedin**
UN/LOCODE: . . . . . . . . . . . . . . . . . . . . NZ DUD
Latitude/Longitude: . . . . . . . . 45° 55' S / 170° 30' E
GMT Offset: . . . . . . . . . . . . . . . . . . . . . . . . . +12

**Port of Tauranga**
UN/LOCODE: . . . . . . . . . . . . . . . . . . . . NZ TRG
Latitude/Longitude: . . . . . . . . 37° 39' S / 176° 11' E
GMT Offset: . . . . . . . . . . . . . . . . . . . . . . . . . +12
Telephone: . . . . . . . . . . . . . . . [64] (7) 575-1899
Web: . . . . . . . . . . www.port-tauranga.co.nz/

**Port of Wellington**
UN/LOCODE: . . . . . . . . . . . . . . . . . . . . NZ WLG
Latitude/Longitude: . . . . . . . . 41° 17' S / 174° 47' E
GMT Offset: . . . . . . . . . . . . . . . . . . . . . . . . . +12
Telephone: . . . . . . . . . . . . . . . [64] (4) 495-3800
Web: . . . . . . . . . . . . . . . www.centreport.co.nz

## Nicaragua

**Port of Bluefields**
UN/LOCODE: . . . . . . . . . . . . . . . . . . . . . NI BEF
Latitude/Longitude: . . . . . . . . . 12° 1' N / 83° 45' W
GMT Offset: . . . . . . . . . . . . . . . . . . . . . . . . . -6
Telephone: . . . . . . . . . . . . . . . [505] (822) 2632

**Port of Corinto**
UN/LOCODE: ................... NI CIO
Latitude/Longitude: ........ 12° 30' N / 87° 11' W
GMT Offset: .................................... -6
Telephone: ............... [505] (342) 2768
Web: .............. www.epn.com.ni/corinto.php

**Port of El Bluff**
UN/LOCODE: ................... NI ELB
Latitude/Longitude: ........ 12° 0' N / 83° 41' W
GMT Offset: .................................... +0
Telephone: ............... [505] (822) 2632
Web: .............. www.epn.com.ni/bluff.php

**Port of Puerto Cabezas**
UN/LOCODE: ................... NI PUZ
Latitude/Longitude: ........ 14° 1' N / 83° 23' W
GMT Offset: .................................... -6
Telephone: ............... [505] (282) 2331
Web: ....... www.epn.com.ni/puerto_cabezas.php

**Port of Puerto Sandino**
UN/LOCODE: ................... NI PSN
Latitude/Longitude: ........ 12° 12' N / 86° 46' W
GMT Offset: .................................... -6
Telephone: ............... [505] (312) 2212
Web: .......... www.epn.com.ni/sandino.php

**Port of San Juan Del Sur**
UN/LOCODE: ................... NI SJS
Latitude/Longitude: ........ 11° 14' N / 85° 52' W
GMT Offset: .................................... -6
Telephone: ............... [505] (458) 2336
Web: ......... www.epn.com.ni/san_juan_sur.php

## Nigeria

**Port Harcourt**
UN/LOCODE: ................. NG PHC
Latitude/Longitude: .......... 4° 46' N / 7° 0' E
GMT Offset: .................................... +1
Telephone: ............... [234] (84) 300-370
Web: ........... www.aboutnpa.co.uk/Ports.htm

**Port of Calabar**
UN/LOCODE: ................. NG CBQ
Latitude/Longitude: ......... 4° 58' N / 8° 19' E
GMT Offset: .................................... +1
Telephone: ............... [234] (87) 225-111
Web: ........... www.aboutnpa.co.uk/Ports.htm

**Port of Lagos**
UN/LOCODE: ................. NG LOS
Latitude/Longitude: .......... 6° 27' N / 3° 24' E
GMT Offset: .................................... +1
Telephone: ............... [234] (1) 545-2820
Web: ........... www.aboutnpa.co.uk/Ports.htm

**Port of Onne**
UN/LOCODE: ................. NG ONN
Latitude/Longitude: .......... 4° 39' N / 7° 9' E
GMT Offset: .................................... +1
Telephone: ............... [234] (84) 820-461

**Port of Sapele**
UN/LOCODE: ................. NG SPL
Latitude/Longitude: ......... 5° 55' N / 5° 45' E
GMT Offset: .................................... +1

**Port of Tin Can**
UN/LOCODE: ................. NG TIN
Latitude/Longitude: .......... 6° 25' N / 3° 18' E
GMT Offset: .................................... +1
Telephone: ............... [234] (1) 804-100
Web: ........... www.aboutnpa.co.uk/Ports.htm

**Port of Warri**
UN/LOCODE: ................. NG WAR
Latitude/Longitude: .......... 5° 30' N / 5° 44' E
GMT Offset: .................................... +1
Telephone: ............... [234] (53) 254-173
Web: ........... www.aboutnpa.co.uk/Ports.htm

## Northern Mariana Islands

**Port of Saipan**
UN/LOCODE: ................... MP SPN
Latitude/Longitude: ........ 15° 13' N / 145° 44' E
GMT Offset: .................................... +10
Telephone: ............... [1] (670) 234-8315

## Norway

**Port of Bergen**
UN/LOCODE: ................... NO BGO
Latitude/Longitude: .......... 60° 24' N / 5° 19' E
GMT Offset: .................................... +1
Telephone: ............... [47] (55) 568-950
Web: .............. http://www.bergenhavn.no

**Port of Drammen**
UN/LOCODE: ................... NO DRM
Latitude/Longitude: ........ 59° 45' N / 10° 13' E
GMT Offset: .................................... +1
Telephone: ............... [47] (32) 208-650
Web: .............. http://www.drammenhavn.no

**Port of Hammerfest**
UN/LOCODE: ................... NO HFT
Latitude/Longitude: ........ 70° 40' N / 23° 40' E
GMT Offset: .................................... +1

**Port of Harstad**
UN/LOCODE: ................... NO HRD
Latitude/Longitude: ........ 68° 48' N / 16° 39' E
GMT Offset: .................................... +1

**Port of Haugesund**
UN/LOCODE: ................... NO HAU
Latitude/Longitude: .......... 59° 25' N / 5° 16' E
GMT Offset: .................................... +1

**Port of Kristiansand**
UN/LOCODE: ................... NO KRS
Latitude/Longitude: .......... 58° 9' N / 8° 0' E
GMT Offset: .................................... +1
Telephone: ............... [47] (38) 006-000
Web: .............. http://kristiansand-havn.no

**Port of Larvik**
UN/LOCODE: ................... NO LAR
Latitude/Longitude: .......... 59° 3' N / 10° 2' E
GMT Offset: .................................... +1
Telephone: ............... [47] (33) 165-750
Web: .............. www.larvik.havn.no

**Port of Oslo**
UN/LOCODE: ................... NO OSL
Latitude/Longitude: ........ 59° 54' N / 10° 43' E
GMT Offset: .................................... +1
Telephone: ............... [47] (22) 910-000
Web: .............. www.ohv.oslo.no

**Port of Porsgrunn**
UN/LOCODE: ................... NO POR
Latitude/Longitude: .......... 59° 8' N / 9° 39' E
GMT Offset: .................................... +1

**Port of Stavanger**
UN/LOCODE: ................... NO SVG
Latitude/Longitude: .......... 58° 58' N / 5° 44' E
GMT Offset: .................................... +1
Telephone: ............... [47] (51) 501-200
Web: .............. www.stavanger-havn.no

**Port of Trondheim**
UN/LOCODE: ................... NO TRD
Latitude/Longitude: ........ 63° 25' N / 10° 24' E
GMT Offset: .................................... +1
Telephone: ............... [47] (73) 528-015

# Pakistan

**Port of Karachi**
UN/LOCODE: ..................... PK KHI
Latitude/Longitude: ......... 24° 49' N / 66° 59' E
GMT Offset: ............................ +5
Telephone: ................ [92] (21) 205-887
Web: ..................... www.kpt.gov.pk

**Port of Muhammad Bin Qasim**
UN/LOCODE: ..................... PK BQM
Latitude/Longitude: ......... 24° 46' N / 67° 21' E
GMT Offset: ............................ +5
Telephone: ................ [92] (21) 473-9100
Web: ..................... http://www.qict.net

# Panama

**Port of Colon**
UN/LOCODE: ................. PA ONX
Latitude/Longitude: ......... 9° 22' N / 79° 55' W
GMT Offset: ............................ -5
Web: ......... http://portfocus.com/panama/colon/

**Port of Cristobal**
UN/LOCODE: ..................... PA CTB
Latitude/Longitude: ......... 9° 21' N / 79° 55' W
GMT Offset: ............................ -5
Telephone: ................ [507] 232-6025

**Port of Vacamonte**
UN/LOCODE: ..................... PA VAC
Latitude/Longitude: ......... 8° 51' N / 79° 40' W
GMT Offset: ............................ -5

# Papua New Guinea

**Port Moresby**
UN/LOCODE: ..................... PG POM
Latitude/Longitude: ......... 9° 29' S / 147° 9' E
GMT Offset: ............................ +10
Telephone: ................ [675] 211-400

**Port of Kieta**
UN/LOCODE: ..................... PG KIE
Latitude/Longitude: ......... 6° 13' S / 155° 38' E
GMT Offset: ............................ +10

**Port of Lae**
UN/LOCODE: ..................... PG LAE
Latitude/Longitude: ......... 6° 44' S / 146° 59' E
GMT Offset: ............................ +10

**Port of Madang**
UN/LOCODE: ..................... PG MAG
Latitude/Longitude: ......... 5° 13' S / 145° 49' E
GMT Offset: ............................ +10

**Port of Rabaul**
UN/LOCODE: ..................... PG RAB
Latitude/Longitude: ......... 4° 12' S / 152° 10' E
GMT Offset: ............................ +10

# Peru

**Port of Callao**
UN/LOCODE: ................. PE CLL
Latitude/Longitude: ......... 12° 3' S / 77° 10' W
GMT Offset: ............................ -5
Telephone: ................ [51] (1) 429-9210
Web: www.enapu.com.pe/spn/terminal_portcallao.htm

**Port of Chimbote**
UN/LOCODE: ..................... PE CHM
Latitude/Longitude: ......... 9° 5' S / 78° 37' W
GMT Offset: ............................ -5
Telephone: ................ [51] (1) 429-9210
Web: ............ http://www.enapu.com.pe/spn/
terminal_portchimbote.htm

**Port of Ilo**
UN/LOCODE: ..................... PE ILO
Latitude/Longitude: ......... 17° 39' S / 71° 21' W
GMT Offset: ............................ +0
Telephone: ................ [51] (1) 429-9210
Web: ............ http://www.enapu.com.pe/spn/
terminal_portilo.htm

**Port of Matarani**
UN/LOCODE: ..................... PE MRI
Latitude/Longitude: ......... 17° 0' S / 72° 7' W
GMT Offset: ............................ -5

**Port of Paita**
UN/LOCODE: ..................... PE PAI
Latitude/Longitude: ......... 5° 5' S / 81° 7' W
GMT Offset: ............................ -5
Telephone: ................ [51] (1) 429-9210
Web: ............ http://www.enapu.com.pe/spn/
terminal_portpaita.htm

**Port of Salaverry**
UN/LOCODE: ..................... PE SVY
Latitude/Longitude: ......... 8° 13' S / 78° 59' W
GMT Offset: ............................ -5
Telephone: ................ [51] (1) 429-9210
Web: ............ http://www.enapu.com.pe/spn/
terminal_portsalaverry.htm

**Port of Talara**
UN/LOCODE: ..................... PE TYL
Latitude/Longitude: ......... 4° 35' S / 81° 17' W
GMT Offset: ............................ -5

# Philippines

**Port of Batangas**
UN/LOCODE: ..................... PH BTG
Latitude/Longitude: ......... 13° 45' N / 121° 3' E
GMT Offset: ............................ +8
Web: ............ http://www.ppa.com.ph

**Port of Cagayan de Oro, Mindanao**
UN/LOCODE: ..................... PH CGY
Latitude/Longitude: ......... 8° 30' N / 124° 39' E
GMT Offset: ............................ +8
Telephone: ................ [63] (32) 232-3401
Web: ............ http://www.ppa.com.ph

**Port of Cebu**
UN/LOCODE: ..................... PH CEB
Latitude/Longitude: ......... 10° 18' N / 123° 53' E
GMT Offset: ............................ +8
Telephone: ................ [63] (32) 232-1461
Web: ..................... www.cpa.gov.ph

**Port of Davao, Mindanao**
UN/LOCODE: ..................... PH DVO
Latitude/Longitude: ......... 7° 4' N / 125° 38' E
GMT Offset: ............................ +8
Web: ..................... www.ppa.com.ph

**Port of Iligan, Mindanao**
UN/LOCODE: ..................... PH IGN
Latitude/Longitude: ......... 8° 15' N / 124° 12' E
GMT Offset: ............................ +8
Web: ..................... www.ppa.com.ph

**Port of Iloilo**
UN/LOCODE: ..................... PH ILO
Latitude/Longitude: ......... 10° 41' N / 122° 35' E
GMT Offset: ............................ +8
Web: ..................... www.ppa.com.ph

**Port of Jolo**
UN/LOCODE: ..................... PH JOL
Latitude/Longitude: ......... 6° 3' N / 121° 0' E
GMT Offset: ............................ +8

**Port of Legaspi, Davao**
UN/LOCODE: ..................... PH LGP
Latitude/Longitude: ......... 13° 9' N / 123° 45' E
GMT Offset: ............................ +8
Web: ..................... www.ppa.com.ph

**Port of Manila**
UN/LOCODE: . . . . . . . . . . . . . . . . . . . . PH MNL
Latitude/Longitude: . . . . . . . 14° 35' N / 120° 58' E
GMT Offset: . . . . . . . . . . . . . . . . . . . . . . . . +8
Telephone: . . . . . . . . . . . . [63] (2) 528-6000
Web: . . . . . . . . . . . . www.asianterminals.com.ph

**Port of Puerto Princesa, Palawan**
UN/LOCODE: . . . . . . . . . . . . . . . . . . . PH PPS
Latitude/Longitude: . . . . . . . . 9° 44' N / 118° 43' E
GMT Offset: . . . . . . . . . . . . . . . . . . . . . . . . +8

**Port of San Fernando, Luzon**
UN/LOCODE: . . . . . . . . . . . . . . . . . . . PH SFE
Latitude/Longitude: . . . . . . . 16° 37' N / 120° 18' E
GMT Offset: . . . . . . . . . . . . . . . . . . . . . . . . +8
Web: . . . . . . . . . . . . . . . . . . www.ppa.com.ph/

**Port of Subic Bay**
UN/LOCODE: . . . . . . . . . . . . . . . . . . . PH SFS
Latitude/Longitude: . . . . . . . 14° 49' N / 120° 18' E
GMT Offset: . . . . . . . . . . . . . . . . . . . . . . . . +8
Telephone: . . . . . . . . . . . . [63] (47) 222-5456

**Port of Zamboanga, Mindanao**
UN/LOCODE: . . . . . . . . . . . . . . . . . . . PH ZAM
Latitude/Longitude: . . . . . . . . 6° 54' N / 122° 4' E
GMT Offset: . . . . . . . . . . . . . . . . . . . . . . . . +8
Web: . . . . . . . . . . . . . . . . . . . www.ppa.com.ph

## Poland

**Port of Gdansk**
UN/LOCODE: . . . . . . . . . . . . . . . . . . . PL GDN
Latitude/Longitude: . . . . . . . . 54° 21' N / 18° 39' E
GMT Offset: . . . . . . . . . . . . . . . . . . . . . . . . +1
Telephone: . . . . . . . . . . . . . [48] (58) 343-9300
Web: . . . . . . . . . . . . . . . . . www.portgdansk.pl

**Port of Gdynia**
UN/LOCODE: . . . . . . . . . . . . . . . . . . . PL GDY
Latitude/Longitude: . . . . . . . . 54° 32' N / 18° 34' E
GMT Offset: . . . . . . . . . . . . . . . . . . . . . . . . +1
Telephone: . . . . . . . . . . . . . [48] (58) 627-4002
Web: . . . . . . . . . . . . . . . . . www.port.gdynia.pl

**Port of Kolobrzeg**
UN/LOCODE: . . . . . . . . . . . . . . . . . . . PL KOL
Latitude/Longitude: . . . . . . . . 54° 11' N / 15° 34' E
GMT Offset: . . . . . . . . . . . . . . . . . . . . . . . . +1
Telephone: . . . . . . . . . . . . . . [48] (965) 23350
Web: www.polfracht.pl/polfracht/psal/localinf/kolo/port-kolo.htm

**Port of Swinoujscie**
UN/LOCODE: . . . . . . . . . . . . . . . . . . . PL SWI
Latitude/Longitude: . . . . . . . . 53° 55' N / 14° 15' E
GMT Offset: . . . . . . . . . . . . . . . . . . . . . . . . +1
Telephone: . . . . . . . . . . . . . [48] (91) 327-7200
Web: . . . . . . . . . . . . . . . . . . . www.phs.com.pl

**Port of Szczecin**
UN/LOCODE: . . . . . . . . . . . . . . . . . . . PL SZZ
Latitude/Longitude: . . . . . . . . 53° 25' N / 14° 32' E
GMT Offset: . . . . . . . . . . . . . . . . . . . . . . . . +1
Telephone: . . . . . . . . . . . . . [48] (22) 826-9229
Web: . . . . . . . . . . . . . . . . www.port.szczecin.pl

**Port of Ustka**
UN/LOCODE: . . . . . . . . . . . . . . . . . . . PL UST
Latitude/Longitude: . . . . . . . . 54° 35' N / 16° 52' E
GMT Offset: . . . . . . . . . . . . . . . . . . . . . . . . +1
Telephone: . . . . . . . . . . . . . . [48] (59) 144-430
Web: www.polfracht.pl/polfracht/psal/localinf/ust/por-tust.htm

## Portugal

**Port of Aveiro**
UN/LOCODE: . . . . . . . . . . . . . . . . . . . PT AVE
Latitude/Longitude: . . . . . . . . 40° 39' N / 8° 45' W
GMT Offset: . . . . . . . . . . . . . . . . . . . . . . . . +1
Telephone: . . . . . . . . . . . . . [351] (234) 393-300
Web: . . . . . . . . . . . . . . . . www.portodeaveiro.pt

**Port of Funchal, Madeira**
UN/LOCODE: . . . . . . . . . . . . . . . . . . . PT FNC
Latitude/Longitude: . . . . . . . . 32° 38' N / 16° 55' W
GMT Offset: . . . . . . . . . . . . . . . . . . . . . . . . 0

**Port of Horta**
UN/LOCODE: . . . . . . . . . . . . . . . . . . . PT HOR
Latitude/Longitude: . . . . . . . . 38° 32' N / 28° 39' W
GMT Offset: . . . . . . . . . . . . . . . . . . . . . . . . -1

**Port of Leixoes**
UN/LOCODE: . . . . . . . . . . . . . . . . . . . PT LEI
Latitude/Longitude: . . . . . . . . 41° 11' N / 8° 43' W
GMT Offset: . . . . . . . . . . . . . . . . . . . . . . . . +1
Telephone: . . . . . . . . . . . . . [351] (22) 999-0700
Web: . . . . . . . . . . . . . . . . . . . . . www.apdl.pt

**Port of Lisbon**
UN/LOCODE: . . . . . . . . . . . . . . . . . . . PT LIS
Latitude/Longitude: . . . . . . . . . 38° 42' N / 9° 6' W
GMT Offset: . . . . . . . . . . . . . . . . . . . . . . . . +1
Telephone: . . . . . . . . . . . . . [351] (21) 361-1000
Web: . . . . . . . . . . . . . . . . www.portodelisboa.com

**Port of Ponta Delgada**
UN/LOCODE: . . . . . . . . . . . . . . . . . . . PT PDL
Latitude/Longitude: . . . . . . . . 37° 44' N / 25° 40' W
GMT Offset: . . . . . . . . . . . . . . . . . . . . . . . . -1
Telephone: . . . . . . . . . . . . . [351] (296) 282-638
Web: . . . http://sapp.telepac.pt/albano.agency/PORT-INFO.htm

**Port of Portimao**
UN/LOCODE: . . . . . . . . . . . . . . . . . . . PT PRM
Latitude/Longitude: . . . . . . . . . 37° 6' N / 8° 32' W
GMT Offset: . . . . . . . . . . . . . . . . . . . . . . . . +1
Web: . . . . . . . . . . . . . www.algarvenet.pt/porto

**Port of Praia da Vitoria**
UN/LOCODE: . . . . . . . . . . . . . . . . . . . PT PRV
Latitude/Longitude: . . . . . . . . 38° 44' N / 27° 3' W
GMT Offset: . . . . . . . . . . . . . . . . . . . . . . . . +1

**Port of Setubal**
UN/LOCODE: . . . . . . . . . . . . . . . . . . . PT SET
Latitude/Longitude: . . . . . . . . 38° 30' N / 8° 55' W
GMT Offset: . . . . . . . . . . . . . . . . . . . . . . . . +1
Telephone: . . . . . . . . . . . . . [351] (265) 542-000
Web: . . . . . . . . . . . . . . . . www.portodesetubal.pt

**Port of Viana Do Castelo**
UN/LOCODE: . . . . . . . . . . . . . . . . . . . PT VDC
Latitude/Longitude: . . . . . . . . 41° 41' N / 8° 48' W
GMT Offset: . . . . . . . . . . . . . . . . . . . . . . . . +1

## Puerto Rico

**Port of Guanica Harbour**
UN/LOCODE: . . . . . . . . . . . . . . . . . . . PR GUX
Latitude/Longitude: . . . . . . . . 17° 57' N / 66° 54' W
GMT Offset: . . . . . . . . . . . . . . . . . . . . . . . . -4

**Port of Guayanilla**
UN/LOCODE: . . . . . . . . . . . . . . . . . . . PR GUY
Latitude/Longitude: . . . . . . . . 18° 0' N / 66° 46' W
GMT Offset: . . . . . . . . . . . . . . . . . . . . . . . . -4

**Port of Las Mareas (Guayama)**
UN/LOCODE: . . . . . . . . . . . . . . . . . . . PR LAM
Latitude/Longitude: . . . . . . . . 17° 55' N / 66° 10' W
GMT Offset: . . . . . . . . . . . . . . . . . . . . . . . . -4

**Port of Ponce**
UN/LOCODE: . . . . . . . . . . . . . . . . . . . PR PSE
Latitude/Longitude: . . . . . . . . 17° 58' N / 66° 37' W
GMT Offset: . . . . . . . . . . . . . . . . . . . . . . . . -4

## Qatar

**Port of Doha**
UN/LOCODE: . . . . . . . . . . . . . . . . . . . QA DOH
Latitude/Longitude: . . . . . . . . 29° 23' N / 47° 48' E
GMT Offset: . . . . . . . . . . . . . . . . . . . . . . . . +3

SEAPORTS

**Port of Halul**
UN/LOCODE: . . . . . . . . . . . . . . . . . . . . . . QA HAL
Latitude/Longitude: . . . . . . . . 25° 40' N / 52° 25' E
GMT Offset: . . . . . . . . . . . . . . . . . . . . . . . . +3

**Port of Ras Laffan**
UN/LOCODE: . . . . . . . . . . . . . . . . . . . . . QA RLF
Latitude/Longitude: . . . . . . . . . 25° 56'N / 51° 37' E
GMT Offset: . . . . . . . . . . . . . . . . . . . . . . . . +3
Telephone: . . . . . . . . . . . . . . . [974] 473-3443
Web: . . . . . . . http://portfocus.com/qatar/ras_laffan/

**Port of Umm Said**
UN/LOCODE: . . . . . . . . . . . . . . . . . . . . QA UMS
Latitude/Longitude: . . . . . . . . 24° 54' N / 51° 34' E
GMT Offset: . . . . . . . . . . . . . . . . . . . . . . . . +3

# Reunion
**Port of Pointe des Galets**
UN/LOCODE: . . . . . . . . . . . . . . . . . . . . . RE PDG
Latitude/Longitude: . . . . . . . . 20° 55' S / 55° 17' E
GMT Offset: . . . . . . . . . . . . . . . . . . . . . . . . +4

# Romania
**Port of Braila**
UN/LOCODE: . . . . . . . . . . . . . . . . . . . . . RO BRA
Latitude/Longitude: . . . . . . . . . 45° 15' N / 27° 59' E
GMT Offset: . . . . . . . . . . . . . . . . . . . . . . . . +2
Telephone: . . . . . . . . . . . . . . [40] (239) 613-712

**Port of Constanta**
UN/LOCODE: . . . . . . . . . . . . . . . . . . . . . RO CND
Latitude/Longitude: . . . . . . . . . 44° 10' N / 28° 39' E
GMT Offset: . . . . . . . . . . . . . . . . . . . . . . . . +2
Telephone: . . . . . . . . . . . . . . [40] (241) 611-540
Web: . . . . . . . . . . . . . . www.constantza-port.ro

**Port of Mangalia**
UN/LOCODE: . . . . . . . . . . . . . . . . . . . . RO MAG
Latitude/Longitude: . . . . . . . . 43° 49' N / 28° 35' E
GMT Offset: . . . . . . . . . . . . . . . . . . . . . . . . +2
Telephone: . . . . . . . . . . . . . . . [40] (241) 12678

**Port of Sulina**
UN/LOCODE: . . . . . . . . . . . . . . . . . . . . . RO SUL
Latitude/Longitude: . . . . . . . . . 45° 10' N / 29° 40' E
GMT Offset: . . . . . . . . . . . . . . . . . . . . . . . . +2
Telephone: . . . . . . . . . . . . . . [40] (240) 543-243

# Russian Federation
**Port of Kaliningrad**
UN/LOCODE: . . . . . . . . . . . . . . . . . . . . SU KGD
Latitude/Longitude: . . . . . . . . 54° 53' N / 20° 31' E
GMT Offset: . . . . . . . . . . . . . . . . . . . . . . . . +2
Telephone: . . . . . . . . . . . . [7] (0112) 444-856
Web: . . . . . . . . . . www.transmarine.ru/portinfor.htm

**Port of Kholmsk**
UN/LOCODE: . . . . . . . . . . . . . . . . . . . . RU KHO
Latitude/Longitude: . . . . . . . . . 47° 3' N / 142° 5' E
GMT Offset: . . . . . . . . . . . . . . . . . . . . . . . +11
Telephone: . . . . . . . . . . . . . . . [7] (42434) 22361

**Port of Murmansk**
UN/LOCODE: . . . . . . . . . . . . . . . . . . . RU MMK
Latitude/Longitude: . . . . . . . . 51° 29' N / 140° 47' E
GMT Offset: . . . . . . . . . . . . . . . . . . . . . . . . +3

**Port of Nakhodka**
UN/LOCODE: . . . . . . . . . . . . . . . . . . . . RU NJK
Latitude/Longitude: . . . . . . . . 42° 48' N / 132° 53' E
GMT Offset: . . . . . . . . . . . . . . . . . . . . . . . . +9
Telephone: . . . . . . . . . . . . . . . [7] (42366) 57702

**Port of Nevelsk**
UN/LOCODE: . . . . . . . . . . . . . . . . . . . . RU NEV
Latitude/Longitude: . . . . . . . . 46° 40' N / 141° 51' E
GMT Offset: . . . . . . . . . . . . . . . . . . . . . . . +11

**Port of Novorossiysk**
UN/LOCODE: . . . . . . . . . . . . . . . . . . . . RU NVS
Latitude/Longitude: . . . . . . . . 44° 43' N / 37° 47' E
GMT Offset: . . . . . . . . . . . . . . . . . . . . . . . . +3
Telephone: . . . . . . . . . . . . . [7] (86134) 11495

**Port of St Petersburg**
UN/LOCODE: . . . . . . . . . . . . . . . . . . . . RU LED
Latitude/Longitude: . . . . . . . . 59° 53' N / 30° 13' E
GMT Offset: . . . . . . . . . . . . . . . . . . . . . . . . +3
Telephone: . . . . . . . . . . . . . [7] (812) 251-5954
Web: . . . . . . . . . . . . . . www.seaport.spb.ru

**Port of Tuapse**
UN/LOCODE: . . . . . . . . . . . . . . . . . . . . RU TUA
Latitude/Longitude: . . . . . . . . 44° 6' N / 39° 4' E
GMT Offset: . . . . . . . . . . . . . . . . . . . . . . . . +3
Telephone: . . . . . . . . . . . . . [7] (86167) 76400
Web: . . . . . . . . . www.tuapseport.ru/Eng/index.asp

**Port of Vladivostok**
UN/LOCODE: . . . . . . . . . . . . . . . . . . . . RU VVO
Latitude/Longitude: . . . . . . . . 43° 10' N / 132° 0' E
GMT Offset: . . . . . . . . . . . . . . . . . . . . . . . +10
Telephone: . . . . . . . . . . . . . [7] (81278) 24750
Web: . . www.apec.adwin.ru/engl/vlad_mor_torg_port.htm

**Port of Vyborg**
UN/LOCODE: . . . . . . . . . . . . . . . . . . . . RU VYG
Latitude/Longitude: . . . . . . . . 60° 42' N / 28° 44' E
GMT Offset: . . . . . . . . . . . . . . . . . . . . . . . . +3
Telephone: . . . . . . . . . . . . . [7] (81278) 24750
Web: . . . . . . . . . . . www.vyborg.ru/org/baff/55.htm

# Saint Kitts and Nevis
**Port of Basseterre**
UN/LOCODE: . . . . . . . . . . . . . . . . . . . . KN BAS
Latitude/Longitude: . . . . . 17° 18' N / 62° 43' W
GMT Offset: . . . . . . . . . . . . . . . . . . . . . . . . -4

# Saint Lucia
**Port of Castries (St Lucia)**
UN/LOCODE: . . . . . . . . . . . . . . . . . . . . LC SLU
Latitude/Longitude: . . . . . . . . 14° 1' N / 61° 0' W
GMT Offset: . . . . . . . . . . . . . . . . . . . . . . . . -4

**Port of Vieux Fort**
UN/LOCODE: . . . . . . . . . . . . . . . . . . . . LC VIF
Latitude/Longitude: . . . . . . . . 13° 43' N / 60° 58' W
GMT Offset: . . . . . . . . . . . . . . . . . . . . . . . . -4

# Saint Vincent and the Grenadines
**Port of Kingstown**
UN/LOCODE: . . . . . . . . . . . . . . . . . . . . VC KTN
Latitude/Longitude: . . . . . . . . 13° 9' N / 61° 14' W
GMT Offset: . . . . . . . . . . . . . . . . . . . . . . . . -4
Telephone: . . . . . . . . . . . . . [1] (784)-456-1830
Web: . . . . . . . . . . . . . . . . www.svgpa.com

# Samoa
**Port of Apia**
UN/LOCODE: . . . . . . . . . . . . . . . . . . . WS APW
Latitude/Longitude: . . . . . . . 13° 50' S / 171° 45' W
GMT Offset: . . . . . . . . . . . . . . . . . . . . . . . -11
Telephone: . . . . . . . . . . . . . . . . [685] 23552
Web: . . . . . www.samoalive.com/Samoaseaports.htm

# Sao Tome and Principe
**Port of Santo Antonio**
UN/LOCODE: . . . . . . . . . . . . . . . . . . . . ST SAA
Latitude/Longitude: . . . . . . . . . 1° 39' N / 7° 27' E
GMT Offset: . . . . . . . . . . . . . . . . . . . . . . . . +0

**Port of Sao Tome**
UN/LOCODE: . . . . . . . . . . . . . . . . . . . . ST TMS
Latitude/Longitude: . . . . . . . . . 0° 21' N / 6° 45' E
GMT Offset: . . . . . . . . . . . . . . . . . . . . . . . . +0

SEAPORTS

## Saudi Arabia

**Port of Damman**
*UN/LOCODE:* .................... SA DMN
*Latitude/Longitude:* ......... 26° 30' N / 50° 12' E
*GMT Offset:* ............................... +3
*Telephone:* ................. [966] (3) 858-3199
*Web:* .................... www.ports.gov.sa/

**Port of Dhuba**
*UN/LOCODE:* ..................... SA DHU
*Latitude/Longitude:* ......... 27° 21' N / 35° 42' E
*GMT Offset:* ............................... +3
*Telephone:* ................. [966] (4) 432-1060
*Web:* .................... www.ports.gov.sa/

**Port of Gizan**
*UN/LOCODE:* ..................... SA GIZ
*Latitude/Longitude:* ......... 16° 54' N / 42° 29' E
*GMT Offset:* ............................... +3
*Telephone:* ................. [966] (7) 317-1000
*Web:* .................... www.ports.gov.sa/

**Port of Jeddah**
*UN/LOCODE:* ..................... SA JED
*Latitude/Longitude:* ......... 21° 28' N / 39° 10' E
*GMT Offset:* ............................... +3
*Telephone:* ................. [966] (2) 647-1200
*Web:* .................... www.ports.gov.sa/

**Port of Jubail**
*UN/LOCODE:* ..................... SA JUB
*Latitude/Longitude:* ......... 27° 4' N / 49° 40' E
*GMT Offset:* ............................... +3
*Telephone:* ................. [966] (3) 357-8000
*Web:* ......... www.ports.gov.sa/Kfipj/Index.htm

**Port of Rabigh**
*UN/LOCODE:* ..................... SA RAB
*Latitude/Longitude:* ......... 22° 44' N / 38° 59' E
*GMT Offset:* ............................... +3
*Telephone:* ................. [966] (2) 422-3200

**Port of Ras al Mishab**
*UN/LOCODE:* ..................... SA RAM
*Latitude/Longitude:* ......... 28° 6' N / 48° 37' E
*GMT Offset:* ............................... +3

**Port of Ras Tanura**
*UN/LOCODE:* ..................... SA RTA
*Latitude/Longitude:* ......... 26° 39' N / 50° 10' E
*GMT Offset:* ............................... +3
*Telephone:* ................. [966] (3) 673-4252

**Port of Yanbu**
*UN/LOCODE:* ..................... SA YNB
*Latitude/Longitude:* ......... 24° 5' N / 38° 3' E
*GMT Offset:* ............................... +3
*Telephone:* ................. [966] (4) 322-2100
*Web:* .................... www.ports.gov.sa/

## Senegal

**Port of Dakar**
*UN/LOCODE:* ..................... SN DKR
*Latitude/Longitude:* ......... 14° 40' N / 17° 26' W
*GMT Offset:* ............................... +0
*Telephone:* ................. [221] 849-4545
*Web:* .................... www.portdakar.sn

## Serbia

**Port of Kotor**
*UN/LOCODE:* ..................... YU KOT
*Latitude/Longitude:* ......... 42° 27' N / 18° 36' E
*GMT Offset:* ............................... +1
*Telephone:* ................. [381] (82) 14950

## Seychelles

**Port Victoria**
*UN/LOCODE:* ..................... SC POV
*Latitude/Longitude:* ......... 4° 37' S / 55° 28' E
*GMT Offset:* ............................... +4

## Sierra Leone

**Port of Freetown**
*UN/LOCODE:* ..................... SL FNA
*Latitude/Longitude:* ......... 8° 30' N / 13° 14' W
*GMT Offset:* ............................... +0
*Telephone:* ................. [232] (22) 229-308
*Web:* .......... www.otal.com/sierra/sierra.htm

**Port of Pepel**
*UN/LOCODE:* ..................... SL PEP
*Latitude/Longitude:* ......... 8° 34' N / 13° 3' W
*GMT Offset:* ............................... +0

## Singapore

**Port of Singapore**
*UN/LOCODE:* ..................... SG SIN
*Latitude/Longitude:* ......... 1° 16' N / 103° 50' E
*GMT Offset:* ............................... +8
*Telephone:* ................. [65] 6375-1600
*Web:* .................... www.mpa.gov.sg/

## Slovenia

**Port of Izola**
*UN/LOCODE:* ..................... SI IZO
*Latitude/Longitude:* ......... 45° 31' N / 13° 41' E
*GMT Offset:* ............................... +1

**Port of Koper**
*UN/LOCODE:* ..................... SI KOP
*Latitude/Longitude:* ......... 45° 31' N / 13° 44' E
*GMT Offset:* ............................... +1
*Telephone:* ................. [386] (5) 665-6100
*Web:* .................... www.luka-kp.si

**Port of Piran**
*UN/LOCODE:* ..................... SI PIR
*Latitude/Longitude:* ......... 45° 31' N / 13° 36' E
*GMT Offset:* ............................... +1

## Solomon Islands

**Port of Honiara**
*UN/LOCODE:* ..................... SB HIR
*Latitude/Longitude:* ......... 9° 25' S / 159° 57' E
*GMT Offset:* ............................... +11

**Port of Noro, New Georgia**
*UN/LOCODE:* ..................... SB NOR
*Latitude/Longitude:* ......... 8° 13' S / 157° 12' E
*GMT Offset:* ............................... +11

**Port of Viru Harbour**
*UN/LOCODE:* ..................... SB VIU
*Latitude/Longitude:* ......... 8° 30' S / 157° 43' E
*GMT Offset:* ............................... +11

**Port of Yandina, Pavuvu Island**
*UN/LOCODE:* ..................... SB XYA
*Latitude/Longitude:* ......... 9° 4' S / 159° 14' E
*GMT Offset:* ............................... +11

## Somalia

**Port of Berbera**
*UN/LOCODE:* ..................... SO BBO
*Latitude/Longitude:* ......... 10° 26' N / 45° 1' E
*GMT Offset:* ............................... +3

**Port of Kismayu**
*UN/LOCODE:* ..................... SO KMU
*Latitude/Longitude:* ......... 0° 23' S / 42° 33' E
*GMT Offset:* ............................... +3

**Port of Merca**
*UN/LOCODE:* ..................... SO MER
*Latitude/Longitude:* ......... 1° 43' N / 44° 46' E
*GMT Offset:* ............................... +3

**Port of Mogadishu**
*UN/LOCODE:* . . . . . . . . . . . . . . . . . . . . SO MGQ
*Latitude/Longitude:* . . . . . . . . . . 2° 1' N / 45° 21' E
*GMT Offset:* . . . . . . . . . . . . . . . . . . . . . . . . . . +3
*Telephone:* . . . . . . . . . . . . . . . . [252] (1) 30081

## South Africa

**Port Elizabeth**
*UN/LOCODE:* . . . . . . . . . . . . . . . . . . . . ZA PLZ
*Latitude/Longitude:* . . . . . . . . 33° 57' S / 25° 39' E
*GMT Offset:* . . . . . . . . . . . . . . . . . . . . . . . . . . +2
*Telephone:* . . . . . . . . . . . . . . [27] (41) 507-1710
*Web:* . . . . . www.npa.co.za/Ports/Port%20Elizabeth/
Index.htm

**Port of Cape Town**
*UN/LOCODE:* . . . . . . . . . . . . . . . . . . . . ZA CPT
*Latitude/Longitude:* . . . . . . . . 33° 54' S / 18° 26' E
*GMT Offset:* . . . . . . . . . . . . . . . . . . . . . . . . . . +2
*Telephone:* . . . . . . . . . . . . . . [27] (21) 449-2612
*Web:* www.npa.co.za/Ports/Cape%20Town/index.htm

**Port of Durban**
*UN/LOCODE:* . . . . . . . . . . . . . . . . . . . . ZA DUR
*Latitude/Longitude:* . . . . . . . . . . 29° 53' S / 31° 2' E
*GMT Offset:* . . . . . . . . . . . . . . . . . . . . . . . . . . +2
*Telephone:* . . . . . . . . . . . . . . [27] (31) 361-8822
*Web:* . . . . . . www.npa.co.za/Ports/Durban/Index.htm

**Port of Mossel Bay**
*UN/LOCODE:* . . . . . . . . . . . . . . . . . . . . ZA MZY
*Latitude/Longitude:* . . . . . . . . . . 34° 10' S / 22° 9' E
*GMT Offset:* . . . . . . . . . . . . . . . . . . . . . . . . . . +2
*Telephone:* . . . . . . . . . . . . . . [27] (44) 604-6271
*Web:* www.npa.co.za/Ports/Mossel%20Bay/index.htm

**Port of Richards Bay**
*UN/LOCODE:* . . . . . . . . . . . . . . . . . . . . ZA RCB
*Latitude/Longitude:* . . . . . . . . 28° 48' S / 32° 2' E
*GMT Offset:* . . . . . . . . . . . . . . . . . . . . . . . . . . +2
*Telephone:* . . . . . . . . . . . . . . [27] (35) 905-3203
*Web:* . . . . . . www.npa.co.za/Ports/Richards%20Bay/
index.htm

**Port of Saldanha Bay**
*UN/LOCODE:* . . . . . . . . . . . . . . . . . . . . ZA SDB
*Latitude/Longitude:* . . . . . . . . 33° 2' S / 17° 58' E
*GMT Offset:* . . . . . . . . . . . . . . . . . . . . . . . . . . +2
*Telephone:* . . . . . . . . . . . . . . [27] (22) 701-4303
*Web:* . . . . www.npa.co.za/Ports/Saldanha/Index.htm

## Spain

**Port of Aviles**
*UN/LOCODE:* . . . . . . . . . . . . . . . . . . . . ES AVS
*Latitude/Longitude:* . . . . . . . . 43° 35' N / 5° 56' W
*GMT Offset:* . . . . . . . . . . . . . . . . . . . . . . . . . . +1
*Telephone:* . . . . . . . . . . . . . . [34] (985) 541-111

**Port of Barcelona**
*UN/LOCODE:* . . . . . . . . . . . . . . . . . . . . ES BCN
*Latitude/Longitude:* . . . . . . . . 41° 20' N / 2° 10' E
*GMT Offset:* . . . . . . . . . . . . . . . . . . . . . . . . . . +1
*Telephone:* . . . . . . . . . . . . . . [34] (93) 298-6119
*Web:* . . . . . . . . . . . . . . . . . . . . . . www.apb.es

**Port of Bilbao**
*UN/LOCODE:* . . . . . . . . . . . . . . . . . . . . ES BIO
*Latitude/Longitude:* . . . . . . . . 43° 17' N / 2° 55' W
*GMT Offset:* . . . . . . . . . . . . . . . . . . . . . . . . . . +1
*Telephone:* . . . . . . . . . . . . . . [34] (94) 487-1200
*Web:* . . . . . . . . . . . . . . . . . . www.bilbaoport.es

**Port of Cadiz**
*UN/LOCODE:* . . . . . . . . . . . . . . . . . . . . ES CAD
*Latitude/Longitude:* . . . . . . . . 36° 31' N / 6° 18' W
*GMT Offset:* . . . . . . . . . . . . . . . . . . . . . . . . . . +1
*Telephone:* . . . . . . . . . . . . . . [34] (956) 240-400
*Web:* . . . . . . . . . . . . . . . . . . www.puertocadiz.com

**Port of Cartagena**
*UN/LOCODE:* . . . . . . . . . . . . . . . . . . . . ES CAR
*Latitude/Longitude:* . . . . . . . . 37° 37' N / 0° 59' W
*GMT Offset:* . . . . . . . . . . . . . . . . . . . . . . . . . . +1
*Telephone:* . . . . . . . . . . . . . . [34] (968) 325-800
*Web:* . . . . . . . . . . . . . . . . . . . . . . www.apc.es

**Port of Castellon**
*UN/LOCODE:* . . . . . . . . . . . . . . . . . . . . ES CAS
*Latitude/Longitude:* . . . . . . . . 39° 58' N / 0° 1' W
*GMT Offset:* . . . . . . . . . . . . . . . . . . . . . . . . . . +1
*Telephone:* . . . . . . . . . . . . . . [34] (964) 281-140
*Web:* . . . . . . . . . . . . . . . . . . www.portcastello.com

**Port of Ceuta**
*UN/LOCODE:* . . . . . . . . . . . . . . . . . . . . ES CEU
*Latitude/Longitude:* . . . . . . . . 35° 53' N / 5° 17' W
*GMT Offset:* . . . . . . . . . . . . . . . . . . . . . . . . . . +1
*Telephone:* . . . . . . . . . . . . . . [34] (956) 527-000
*Web:* . . . . . . . . . . . . . . . . . . www.puertodeceuta.com

**Port of Huelva**
*UN/LOCODE:* . . . . . . . . . . . . . . . . . . . . ES HUV
*Latitude/Longitude:* . . . . . . . . 37° 16' N / 6° 55' W
*GMT Offset:* . . . . . . . . . . . . . . . . . . . . . . . . . . +1
*Telephone:* . . . . . . . . . . . . . . [34] (900) 213-100
*Web:* . . . . . . . . . . . . . . . . . . www.puertohuelva.com

**Port of Las Palmas**
*UN/LOCODE:* . . . . . . . . . . . . . . . . . . . . ES LPA
*Latitude/Longitude:* . . . . . . . . 28° 5' N / 15° 27' W
*GMT Offset:* . . . . . . . . . . . . . . . . . . . . . . . . . . +0
*Telephone:* . . . . . . . . . . . . . . [34] (928) 300-400
*Web:* . . . . . . . . . . . . . . . . . . www.palmasport.es

**Port of Malaga**
*UN/LOCODE:* . . . . . . . . . . . . . . . . . . . . ES AGP
*Latitude/Longitude:* . . . . . . . . 36° 43' N / 4° 25' W
*GMT Offset:* . . . . . . . . . . . . . . . . . . . . . . . . . . +1
*Telephone:* . . . . . . . . . . . . . . [34] (95) 221-0595
*Web:* . . . . . . . . . . . . . . . . . . www.puertomalaga.com

**Port of Pasajes**
*UN/LOCODE:* . . . . . . . . . . . . . . . . . . . . ES PAS
*Latitude/Longitude:* . . . . . . . . 43° 20' N / 1° 56' W
*GMT Offset:* . . . . . . . . . . . . . . . . . . . . . . . . . . +1
*Web:* . . . . . . . . . . . . . . . . . . www.puertopasajes.net

**Port of Santa Cruz de Tenerife**
*UN/LOCODE:* . . . . . . . . . . . . . . . . . . . . ES SCT
*Latitude/Longitude:* . . . . . . . . 28° 28' N / 16° 14' W
*GMT Offset:* . . . . . . . . . . . . . . . . . . . . . . . . . . +0
*Telephone:* . . . . . . . . . . . . . . [34] (922) 277-850
*Web:* . . . . . . . . . www.puertosdetenerife.org/

**Port of Santander**
*UN/LOCODE:* . . . . . . . . . . . . . . . . . . . . ES SDR
*Latitude/Longitude:* . . . . . . . . 43° 28' N / 3° 49' W
*GMT Offset:* . . . . . . . . . . . . . . . . . . . . . . . . . . +1
*Telephone:* . . . . . . . . . . . . . . [34] (942) 215-109
*Web:* . . . . . . . . . . . . . . . . . . www.puertosantander.es

**Port of Tarragona**
*UN/LOCODE:* . . . . . . . . . . . . . . . . . . . . ES TAR
*Latitude/Longitude:* . . . . . . . . 41° 5' N / 1° 14' E
*GMT Offset:* . . . . . . . . . . . . . . . . . . . . . . . . . . +1
*Telephone:* . . . . . . . . . . . . . . [34] (901) 116-658
*Web:* . . . . . . . . . . . . . . . . . . www.porttarragona.es

**Port of Valencia**
*UN/LOCODE:* . . . . . . . . . . . . . . . . . . . . ES VLC
*Latitude/Longitude:* . . . . . . . . 39° 27' N / 0° 18' W
*GMT Offset:* . . . . . . . . . . . . . . . . . . . . . . . . . . +1
*Web:* . . . . . . . . . . . . . . . . . . www.valenciaport.com

**Port of Vigo**
*UN/LOCODE:* . . . . . . . . . . . . . . . . . . . . ES VGO
*Latitude/Longitude:* . . . . . . . . 42° 14' N / 8° 42' W
*GMT Offset:* . . . . . . . . . . . . . . . . . . . . . . . . . . +1
*Telephone:* . . . . . . . . . . . . . . [34] (986) 268-000
*Web:* . . . . . . . . . . . . . . . . . . www.apvigo.com

SEAPORTS

## Sri Lanka

**Port of Colombo**
*UN/LOCODE:* . . . . . . . . . . . . . . . . . . LK CMB
*Latitude/Longitude:* . . . . . . . . . 6° 56' N / 79° 50' E
*GMT Offset:* . . . . . . . . . . . . . . . . . . . . . . . +6
*Telephone:* . . . . . . . . . . . . . . [94] (11) 242-1201
*Web:* . . . . . . . . . . . . . . . . . . . . . www.slpa.lk

**Port of Jaffna**
*UN/LOCODE:* . . . . . . . . . . . . . . . . . . LK JAF
*Latitude/Longitude:* . . . . . . . . . 9° 40' N / 80° 1' E
*GMT Offset:* . . . . . . . . . . . . . . . . . . . . . . . +6

**Port of Trincomalee**
*UN/LOCODE:* . . . . . . . . . . . . . . . . . . LK TRR
*Latitude/Longitude:* . . . . . . . . . 8° 36' N / 81° 15' E
*GMT Offset:* . . . . . . . . . . . . . . . . . . . . . . . +6

## St. Helena

**Port of Georgetown**
*UN/LOCODE:* . . . . . . . . . . . . . . . . . . SH ASI
*Latitude/Longitude:* . . . . . . . . . 7° 56' S / 14° 25' W
*GMT Offset:* . . . . . . . . . . . . . . . . . . . . . . . +0

**Port of Jamestown**
*UN/LOCODE:* . . . . . . . . . . . . . . . . . . SH SHN
*Latitude/Longitude:* . . . . . . . 15° 56' S / 5° 43' W
*GMT Offset:* . . . . . . . . . . . . . . . . . . . . . . . +0

## St. Pierre and Miquelon

**Port of St Pierre**
*UN/LOCODE:* . . . . . . . . . . . . . . . . . . PM FSP
*Latitude/Longitude:* . . . . . . 46° 47' N / 56° 10' W
*GMT Offset:* . . . . . . . . . . . . . . . . . . . . . . . -4

## Sudan

**Port Sudan**
*UN/LOCODE:* . . . . . . . . . . . . . . . . . . SD PZU
*Latitude/Longitude:* . . . . . . . . . 19° 37' N / 37° 14' E
*GMT Offset:* . . . . . . . . . . . . . . . . . . . . . . . +2
*Telephone:* . . . . . . . . . . . . . . [249] (311) 824-232
*Web:* . . . . . . http://portfocus.com/sudan/port_sudan/

## Suriname

**Port of Moengo**
*UN/LOCODE:* . . . . . . . . . . . . . . . . . . SR MOJ
*Latitude/Longitude:* . . . . . . . . . 5° 39' N / 54° 25' W
*GMT Offset:* . . . . . . . . . . . . . . . . . . . . . . . -3

**Port of New Nickerie**
*UN/LOCODE:* . . . . . . . . . . . . . . . . . . SR ICK
*Latitude/Longitude:* . . . . . . . . . 5° 57' N / 56° 59' W
*GMT Offset:* . . . . . . . . . . . . . . . . . . . . . . . -3

**Port of Paramaribo**
*UN/LOCODE:* . . . . . . . . . . . . . . . . . . SR PBM
*Latitude/Longitude:* . . . . . . . . . 5° 59' N / 55° 9' W
*GMT Offset:* . . . . . . . . . . . . . . . . . . . . . . . -3

**Port of Paranam**
*UN/LOCODE:* . . . . . . . . . . . . . . . . . . SR PRM
*Latitude/Longitude:* . . . . . . . . . 5° 38' N / 55° 5' W
*GMT Offset:* . . . . . . . . . . . . . . . . . . . . . . . -3

**Port of Wageningen**
*UN/LOCODE:* . . . . . . . . . . . . . . . . . . SR AGI
*Latitude/Longitude:* . . . . . . . . . 5° 46' N / 56° 41' W
*GMT Offset:* . . . . . . . . . . . . . . . . . . . . . . . -3

## Sweden

**Port of Gavle**
*UN/LOCODE:* . . . . . . . . . . . . . . . . . . SE GVX
*Latitude/Longitude:* . . . . . . . . . 60° 41' N / 17° 11' E
*GMT Offset:* . . . . . . . . . . . . . . . . . . . . . . . +1
*Telephone:* . . . . . . . . . . . . . . [46] (26) 178-843
*Web:* . . . . . . . . . . . . . . . . www.gavle.se/hamn

**Port of Goteborg**
*UN/LOCODE:* . . . . . . . . . . . . . . . . . . SE GOT
*Latitude/Longitude:* . . . . . . 57° 42' N / 11° 57' E
*GMT Offset:* . . . . . . . . . . . . . . . . . . . . . . . +1
*Telephone:* . . . . . . . . . . . . . . [46] (31) 731-2000
*Web:* . . . . . . . . . . . . . . . . . www.portgot.se/

**Port of Halmstad**
*UN/LOCODE:* . . . . . . . . . . . . . . . . . . SE HAD
*Latitude/Longitude:* . . . . . . . . . 56° 40' N / 12° 52' E
*GMT Offset:* . . . . . . . . . . . . . . . . . . . . . . . +1
*Telephone:* . . . . . . . . . . . . . . [46] (35) 155-300
*Web:* . . . . . . . . . . . www.halmstadharbour.se

**Port of Kalmar**
*UN/LOCODE:* . . . . . . . . . . . . . . . . . . SE KLR
*Latitude/Longitude:* . . . . . . . . . 56° 40' N / 16° 20' E
*GMT Offset:* . . . . . . . . . . . . . . . . . . . . . . . +1
*Telephone:* . . . . . . . . . . . . . . [46] (480) 56200

**Port of Karlshamn**
*UN/LOCODE:* . . . . . . . . . . . . . . . . . . SE KAN
*Latitude/Longitude:* . . . . . . . . . 56° 10' N / 14° 52' E
*GMT Offset:* . . . . . . . . . . . . . . . . . . . . . . . +1
*Telephone:* . . . . . . . . . . . . . . [46] (455) 83000

**Port of Malmo**
*UN/LOCODE:* . . . . . . . . . . . . . . . . . . SE MMA
*Latitude/Longitude:* . . . . . . . . . 55° 37' N / 13° 0' E
*GMT Offset:* . . . . . . . . . . . . . . . . . . . . . . . +1
*Telephone:* . . . . . . . . . . . . . . [46] (40) 680-4100
*Web:* . . . . . . . . www.cmport.se/CMP/se/se_docs.nsf

**Port of Solvesborg**
*UN/LOCODE:* . . . . . . . . . . . . . . . . . . SE SOL
*Latitude/Longitude:* . . . . . . . . . 56° 3' N / 14° 35' E
*GMT Offset:* . . . . . . . . . . . . . . . . . . . . . . . +1
*Telephone:* . . . . . . . . . . . . . . [46] (456) 42240
*Web:* . . . . . . . . . . . . . . . . www.stuverihamn.se

**Port of Stockholm**
*UN/LOCODE:* . . . . . . . . . . . . . . . . . . SE STO
*Latitude/Longitude:* . . . . . . . . . 59° 19' N / 18° 3' E
*GMT Offset:* . . . . . . . . . . . . . . . . . . . . . . . +1
*Telephone:* . . . . . . . . . . . . . . [46] (8) 670-2600
*Web:* . . . . . . . . . . . www.portsofstockholm.com

**Port of Sundsvall**
*UN/LOCODE:* . . . . . . . . . . . . . . . . . . SE SDL
*Latitude/Longitude:* . . . . . . 62° 25' N / 17° 20' E
*GMT Offset:* . . . . . . . . . . . . . . . . . . . . . . . +1
*Telephone:* . . . . . . . . . . . . . . [46] (60) 123-180
*Web:* . . . . . . . . . . . . . . www.sundsvallshamn.se/

## Switzerland

**Port of Basel**
*UN/LOCODE:* . . . . . . . . . . . . . . . . . . CH BSL
*Latitude/Longitude:* . . . . . . . . . 47° 33' N / 7° 34' E
*GMT Offset:* . . . . . . . . . . . . . . . . . . . . . . . +1
*Telephone:* . . . . . . . . . . . . . . [41] (61) 631-4545

## Syria

**Port of Baniyas**
*UN/LOCODE:* . . . . . . . . . . . . . . . . . . SY BAN
*Latitude/Longitude:* . . . . . . . . . 35° 15' N / 35° 56' E
*GMT Offset:* . . . . . . . . . . . . . . . . . . . . . . . +3
*Telephone:* . . . . . . . . . . . . . . [963] (43) 711-300

**Port of Latakia**
*UN/LOCODE:* . . . . . . . . . . . . . . . . . . SY LTK
*Latitude/Longitude:* . . . . . . . . . 35° 31' N / 35° 47' E
*GMT Offset:* . . . . . . . . . . . . . . . . . . . . . . . +3
*Telephone:* . . . . . . . . . . . . . . [963] (41) 223-900
*Web:* . . . . . . . . . . . . www.mot.gov.sy/en/m_latk.htm

**Port of Tartous**
*UN/LOCODE:* . . . . . . . . . . . . . . . . . . SY TTS
*Latitude/Longitude:* . . . . . . . . . 34° 53' N / 35° 45' E
*GMT Offset:* . . . . . . . . . . . . . . . . . . . . . . . +3
*Telephone:* . . . . . . . . . . . . . . [963] (43) 329-852
*Web:* . . . . . . . . . . . . . www.mot.gov.sy/en/m_tar.htm

## Taiwan

**Port of Hualien**
*UN/LOCODE:* ................... TW HUN
*Latitude/Longitude:* ........ 23° 59' N / 121° 38' E
*GMT Offset:* ............................ +8
*Telephone:* ............ [886] (3) 833-3513
*Web:* ..................... www.hlhb.gov.tw

**Port of Kaohsiung**
*UN/LOCODE:* ................... TW KHH
*Latitude/Longitude:* ........ 22° 37' N / 120° 16' E
*GMT Offset:* ............................ +8
*Telephone:* ............ [886] (07) 562-2127
*Web:* ..................... www.khb.gov.tw

**Port of Keelung (Chilung)**
*UN/LOCODE:* ................... TW KEL
*Latitude/Longitude:* ........ 25° 9' N / 121° 44' E
*GMT Offset:* ............................ +8
*Telephone:* ............ [886] (2) 2420-6100
*Web:* ..................... www.klhb.gov.tw

**Port of Suao**
*UN/LOCODE:* ................... TW SUO
*Latitude/Longitude:* ....... 24° 35' N / 121° 51' E
*GMT Offset:* ............................ +8
*Telephone:* ............ [886] (39) 965-121

**Port of Taichung**
*UN/LOCODE:* ................... TW TXG
*Latitude/Longitude:* ........ 24° 17' N / 120° 30' E
*GMT Offset:* ............................ +8
*Telephone:* ............ [886] (4) 2656-2611
*Web:* ..................... www.tchb.gov.tw/

## Tanzania

**Port of Dar Es Salaam Port Authority**
*UN/LOCODE:* ................... TZ DAR
*Latitude/Longitude:* ........ 6° 50' S / 39° 17' E
*GMT Offset:* ............................ +3
*Telephone:* ............ [255] (22) 211-0401
*Web:* ..... www.tanzaniaports.com/Daresalaam.htm

**Port of Kilwa Masoko**
*UN/LOCODE:* ................... TZ KIM
*Latitude/Longitude:* ........ 8° 56' S / 39° 31' E
*GMT Offset:* ............................ +3
*Web:* ........ www.robmarine.com/PortsTZ10.html

**Port of Lindi**
*UN/LOCODE:* ................... TZ LDI
*Latitude/Longitude:* ........ 10° 0' S / 39° 44' E
*GMT Offset:* ............................ +3
*Web:* ........ www.robmarine.com/PortsTZ11.html

**Port of Mtwara**
*UN/LOCODE:* ................... TZ MYW
*Latitude/Longitude:* ........ 10° 16' S / 40° 12' E
*GMT Offset:* ............................ +3
*Telephone:* ............ [255] (59) 333-125
*Web:* ........ www.tanzaniaports.com/Mtwara.htm

**Port of Pangani**
*UN/LOCODE:* ................... TZ PAN
*Latitude/Longitude:* ........ 5° 27' S / 39° 0' E
*GMT Offset:* ............................ +3
*Web:* ........ www.robmarine.com/PortsTZ12.html

**Port of Tanga**
*UN/LOCODE:* ................... TZ TGT
*Latitude/Longitude:* ........ 5° 4' S / 39° 8' E
*GMT Offset:* ............................ +3
*Telephone:* ............ [255] (53) 43078
*Web:* ........ www.tanzaniaports.com/Tanga.htm

**Port of Zanzibar**
*UN/LOCODE:* ................... TZ ZNZ
*Latitude/Longitude:* ........ 6° 10' S / 39° 11' E
*GMT Offset:* ............................ +3
*Web:* ........ www.robmarine.com/PortsTZ14.html

## Thailand

**Port of Bangkok**
*UN/LOCODE:* ................... TH BKK
*Latitude/Longitude:* ........ 13° 26' N / 100° 35' E
*GMT Offset:* ............................ +7
*Telephone:* ............ [66] (2) 249-0399

**Port of Laem Chabang**
*UN/LOCODE:* ................... TH LCH
*Latitude/Longitude:* ........ 13° 5' N / 100° 53' E
*GMT Offset:* ............................ +7
*Telephone:* ............ [66] (38) 490-000

**Port of Pattani**
*UN/LOCODE:* ................... TH PAN
*Latitude/Longitude:* ........ 6° 57' N / 101° 18' E
*GMT Offset:* ............................ +7

**Port of Phuket**
*UN/LOCODE:* ................... TH HKT
*Latitude/Longitude:* ........ 7° 49' N / 98° 24' E
*GMT Offset:* ............................ +7
*Web:* ...... www.tpni.co.th/content/phuket_port.htm

**Port of Sattahip**
*UN/LOCODE:* ................... TH SAT
*Latitude/Longitude:* ........ 12° 35' N / 100° 55' E
*GMT Offset:* ............................ +7

**Port of Songkhla**
*UN/LOCODE:* ................... TH SGZ
*Latitude/Longitude:* ........ 7° 14' N / 100° 35' E
*GMT Offset:* ............................ +7
*Telephone:* ............ [66] (74) 331-158
*Web:* ........ www.tpni.co.th/content/songkla.htm

**Port of Sriracha**
*UN/LOCODE:* ................... TH SRI
*Latitude/Longitude:* ........ 13° 7' N / 100° 52' E
*GMT Offset:* ............................ +7
*Telephone:* ............ [66] (2) 719-9631
*Web:* ..................... www.srirachaport.com/

## Togo

**Port of Kpeme**
*UN/LOCODE:* ................... TG KPE
*Latitude/Longitude:* ........ 6° 12' N / 1° 30' E
*GMT Offset:* ............................ 0

**Port of Lome**
*UN/LOCODE:* ................... TG LFW
*Latitude/Longitude:* ........ 6° 8' N / 1° 17' E
*GMT Offset:* ............................ 0
*Telephone:* ............ [228] 274-742
*Web:* ............ www.otal.com/togo/togo.htm

## Tonga

**Port of Neiafu**
*UN/LOCODE:* ................... TO NEI
*Latitude/Longitude:* ........ 18° 39' S / 173° 59' W
*GMT Offset:* ............................ +13

**Port of Nuku*alofa-Tongatapu**
*UN/LOCODE:* ................... TO TBU
*Latitude/Longitude:* ........ 21° 8' S / 175° 11' W
*GMT Offset:* ............................ +13

**Port of Pangai**
*UN/LOCODE:* ................... TO PAN
*Latitude/Longitude:* ........ 19° 50' S / 174° 23' W
*GMT Offset:* ............................ +13

## Trinidad and Tobago

**Port of Point Fortin**
*UN/LOCODE:* ................... TT PTF
*Latitude/Longitude:* ........ 10° 12' N / 61° 42' W
*GMT Offset:* ............................ -4

SEAPORTS

**Port of Point Lisas**
UN/LOCODE: .......................... TT PTS
Latitude/Longitude: ........ 10° 22' N / 61° 29' W
GMT Offset: ................................. -4
Telephone: ............. [1] (868) 636-2201
Web: ..................... www.plipdeco.com/

**Port of Pointe a Pierre**
UN/LOCODE: .......................... TT PTP
Latitude/Longitude: ........ 10° 19' N / 61° 29' W
GMT Offset: ................................. -4

**Port of Scarborough/Tobago**
UN/LOCODE: .......................... TT SCA
Latitude/Longitude: ........ 11° 11' N / 60° 44' W
GMT Offset: ................................. -4

**Port of Spain**
UN/LOCODE: .......................... TT POS
Latitude/Longitude: ........ 10° 39' N / 61° 32' W
GMT Offset: ................................. -4
Telephone: ............. [1] (868) 625-2644
Web: ..................... www.patnt.com

**Port of Tembladora**
UN/LOCODE: .......................... TT TEM
Latitude/Longitude: ........ 10° 14' N / 61° 36' W
GMT Offset: ................................. -4

## Tunisia

**Port of Bizerte**
UN/LOCODE: .......................... TN BIZ
Latitude/Longitude: ........ 37° 17' N / 9° 54' E
GMT Offset: ................................. +1
Web: www.nrlmry.navy.mil/~cannon/medports/Bizerte/index.html

**Port of Gabes**
UN/LOCODE: .......................... TN GAE
Latitude/Longitude: ........ 33° 57' N / 10° 4' E
GMT Offset: ................................. +1

**Port of La Goulette Nord**
UN/LOCODE: .......................... TN LGN
Latitude/Longitude: ........ 36° 49' N / 10° 18' E
GMT Offset: ................................. +1

**Port of Sfax**
UN/LOCODE: .......................... TN SFA
Latitude/Longitude: ........ 34° 44' N / 10° 46' E
GMT Offset: ................................. +1
Web: . www.nrlmry.navy.mil/~cannon/medports/Sfax/index.html

**Port of Sousse**
UN/LOCODE: .......................... TN SUS
Latitude/Longitude: ........ 35° 50' N / 10° 38' E
GMT Offset: ................................. +1
Web: www.nrlmry.navy.mil/~cannon/medports/Sousse/index.html

**Port of Tunis**
UN/LOCODE: .......................... TN TUN
Latitude/Longitude: ........ 36° 49' N / 10° 15' E
GMT Offset: ................................. +1
Telephone: ............. [216] (71) 243-737
Web: www.nrlmry.navy.mil/~cannon/medports/Tunis/index.html

## Turkey

**Port of Derince, Kocaeli**
UN/LOCODE: .......................... TR DRC
Latitude/Longitude: ........ 40° 44' N / 29° 50' E
GMT Offset: ................................. +2
Telephone: ............. [90] (262) 223-1574

**Port of Dikili, Izmir**
UN/LOCODE: .......................... TR DIK
Latitude/Longitude: ........ 39° 0' N / 26° 50' E
GMT Offset: ................................. +2
Telephone: ............. [90] (232) 671-4400
Web: ..... www.armamarine.com/port_of_dikili.html

**Port of Gemlik**
UN/LOCODE: .......................... TR GEM
Latitude/Longitude: ........ 40° 25' N / 29° 7' E
GMT Offset: ................................. +2
Telephone: ............. (224) 513 45 21
Web: ..................... www.gemport.com.tr

**Port of Hopa, Artvin**
UN/LOCODE: .......................... TR HOP
Latitude/Longitude: ........ 42° 24' N / 41° 25' E
GMT Offset: ................................. +2
Telephone: ............. [90] (466) 351-2259
Web: ... http://portfocus.com/turkey/hopa/index.html

**Port of Iskenderun, Hatay**
UN/LOCODE: .......................... TR ISK
Latitude/Longitude: ........ 36° 38' N / 36° 10' E
GMT Offset: ................................. +2
Telephone: ............. [90] (326) 614-0047
Web: ...... http://portfocus.comturkey/iskenderun/index.html

**Port of Istanbul**
UN/LOCODE: .......................... TR IST
Latitude/Longitude: ........ 41° 1' N / 28° 59' E
GMT Offset: ................................. +2
Web: . www.nrlmry.navy.mil/~cannon/medports/Istanbul/index.html

**Port of Trabzon**
UN/LOCODE: .......................... TR TZX
Latitude/Longitude: ........ 41° 1' N / 39° 46' E
GMT Offset: ................................. +2
Telephone: ............... [90] (462) 321-1156
Web: . http://portfocus.com/turkey/trabzon/index.html

## Turks and Caicos Islands

**Port of Grand Turk Island**
UN/LOCODE: .......................... TC GDT
Latitude/Longitude: ........ 21° 26' N / 71° 8' W
GMT Offset: ................................. -5

**Port of Providenciales**
UN/LOCODE: .......................... TC PLS
Latitude/Longitude: ........ 21° 30' N / 72° 30' W
GMT Offset: ................................. -5

## Tuvalu

**Port of Funafuti**
UN/LOCODE: .......................... TV FUN
Latitude/Longitude: ........ 8° 31' S / 179° 13' W
GMT Offset: ................................. +12

## Ukraine

**Port of Berdyansk**
UN/LOCODE: .......................... UA ERD
Latitude/Longitude: ........ 46° 45' N / 36° 48' E
GMT Offset: ................................. +2

**Port of Kherson**
UN/LOCODE: .......................... UA KHE
Latitude/Longitude: ........ 46° 37' N / 32° 37' E
GMT Offset: ................................. +2
Telephone: ............... [380] (552) 265-085
Web: ........ www.ceebd.co.uk/ceebd/kherson.htm

**Port of Odessa**
UN/LOCODE: .......................... UA ODS
Latitude/Longitude: ........ 46° 30' N / 30° 46' E
GMT Offset: ................................. +2
Web: ..................... www.port.odessa.ua

**Port of Reni**
UN/LOCODE: .......................... UA RNI
Latitude/Longitude: ........ 45° 26' N / 28° 18' E
GMT Offset: ................................. +2
Telephone: ............... [380] (4840) 30726

**Port of Sevastopol**
*UN/LOCODE:* . . . . . . . . . . . . . . . . . . . . . . UA SVP
*Latitude/Longitude:* . . . . . . . . 44° 37' N / 33° 32' E
*GMT Offset:* . . . . . . . . . . . . . . . . . . . . . . . . . . +0
*Web:* . . . . . . . . . . . . . . www.dias-co.com/ports/?6

# United Arab Emirates

**Port of Ajman**
*UN/LOCODE:* . . . . . . . . . . . . . . . . . . . . . . AE AJM
*Latitude/Longitude:* . . . . . . . . . . . . . . . . . . . . . . .
*GMT Offset:* . . . . . . . . . . . . . . . . . . . . . . . . . . +4
*Telephone:* . . . . . . . . . . . . . . . [971] (6) 747-0111
*Web:* . . . . . . . . . . . . . . . . . www.ajmanport.gov.ae

**Port of Das Island**
*UN/LOCODE:* . . . . . . . . . . . . . . . . . . . . . . AE DAS
*Latitude/Longitude:* . . . . . . . . 25° 9' N / 52° 52' E
*GMT Offset:* . . . . . . . . . . . . . . . . . . . . . . . . . . +4

**Port of Dubai**
*UN/LOCODE:* . . . . . . . . . . . . . . . . . . . . . . AE DXB
*Latitude/Longitude:* . . . . . . . . 25° 15' N / 55° 16' E
*GMT Offset:* . . . . . . . . . . . . . . . . . . . . . . . . . . +4
*Telephone:* . . . . . . . . . . . . . . . [971] (4) 881-5000
*Web:* . . . . . . . . . . . . . . . . . . . . www.dpa.co.ae/

**Port of Fujairah**
*UN/LOCODE:* . . . . . . . . . . . . . . . . . . . . . . AE FJR
*Latitude/Longitude:* . . . . . . . . 25° 10' N / 56° 21' E
*GMT Offset:* . . . . . . . . . . . . . . . . . . . . . . . . . . +4
*Telephone:* . . . . . . . . . . . . . . . [971] (9) 222-8833
*Web:* . . . . . . . . . . . . . . . . . . www.fujairahport.ae

**Port of Jebel Ali**
*UN/LOCODE:* . . . . . . . . . . . . . . . . . . . . . . AE JEA
*Latitude/Longitude:* . . . . . . . . . . 25° 0' N / 55° 3' E
*GMT Offset:* . . . . . . . . . . . . . . . . . . . . . . . . . . +4
*Telephone:* . . . . . . . . . . . . . . . [971] [4] 881-5000
*Web:* . . . . . . . . . . . . . . . . . . . . www.dpa.co.ae

**Port of Khor Al Fakkan**
*UN/LOCODE:* . . . . . . . . . . . . . . . . . . . . . . AE KLF
*Latitude/Longitude:* . . . . . . . . 25° 21' N / 56° 22' E
*GMT Offset:* . . . . . . . . . . . . . . . . . . . . . . . . . . +4
*Telephone:* . . . . . . . . . . . . . . . [971] (6) 528-1666
*Web:* . . . . . www.sharjahports.gov.ae/khorfakan.htm

**Port of Mina Saqr**
*UN/LOCODE:* . . . . . . . . . . . . . . . . . . . . . . AE MSA
*Latitude/Longitude:* . . . . . . . . 25° 58' N / 56° 3' E
*GMT Offset:* . . . . . . . . . . . . . . . . . . . . . . . . . . +4

**Port of Mina Zayed**
*UN/LOCODE:* . . . . . . . . . . . . . . . . . . . . . . AE MZD
*Latitude/Longitude:* . . . . . . . . 24° 32' N / 54° 23' E
*GMT Offset:* . . . . . . . . . . . . . . . . . . . . . . . . . . +4
*Telephone:* . . . . . . . . . . . . . . . . [971] (2) 6730600

**Port Rashid**
*UN/LOCODE:* . . . . . . . . . . . . . . . . . . . . . . AE PRA
*Latitude/Longitude:* . . . . . . . . 25° 16' N / 55° 16' E
*GMT Offset:* . . . . . . . . . . . . . . . . . . . . . . . . . . +4

# United Kingdom

**Port of Aberdeen**
*UN/LOCODE:* . . . . . . . . . . . . . . . . . . . . . . GB ABD
*Latitude/Longitude:* . . . . . . . . . . 57° 8' N / 2° 4' W
*GMT Offset:* . . . . . . . . . . . . . . . . . . . . . . . . . . +0
*Telephone:* . . . . . . . . . . . . . . . [44] (1224) 597-000
*Web:* . . . . . . . . . http://www.aberdeen-harbour.co.uk

**Port of Belfast**
*UN/LOCODE:* . . . . . . . . . . . . . . . . . . . . . . GB BEL
*Latitude/Longitude:* . . . . . . . . 54° 36' N / 5° 56' W
*GMT Offset:* . . . . . . . . . . . . . . . . . . . . . . . . . . +0
*Telephone:* . . . . . . . . . . . . . . . [44] (28) 9055-4422
*Web:* . . . . . . . . . . . . . . www.belfast-harbour.co.uk

**Port of Bristol**
*UN/LOCODE:* . . . . . . . . . . . . . . . . . . . . . . GB BRS
*Latitude/Longitude:* . . . . . . . . 51° 30' N / 2° 43' W
*GMT Offset:* . . . . . . . . . . . . . . . . . . . . . . . . . . +0
*Telephone:* . . . . . . . . . . . . . . . [44] (117) 982-0000
*Web:* . . . . . . . . . . . . . . . . . . www.bristolport.co.uk

**Port of Dover**
*UN/LOCODE:* . . . . . . . . . . . . . . . . . . . . . . GB DVR
*Latitude/Longitude:* . . . . . . . . . 51° 7' N / 1° 18' E
*GMT Offset:* . . . . . . . . . . . . . . . . . . . . . . . . . . +0
*Telephone:* . . . . . . . . . . . . . . . [44] (1304) 240-400
*Web:* . . . . . . . . . . . . . . . . . . www.doverport.co.uk

**Port of Falmouth**
*UN/LOCODE:* . . . . . . . . . . . . . . . . . . . . . . GB FAL
*Latitude/Longitude:* . . . . . . . . . 50° 9' N / 5° 4' W
*GMT Offset:* . . . . . . . . . . . . . . . . . . . . . . . . . . +0
*Telephone:* . . . . . . . . . . . . . . . [44] (1326) 313-816
*Web:* . . . . . . . . www.tamlyn-shipping.co.uk/info.htm

**Port of Felixstowe**
*UN/LOCODE:* . . . . . . . . . . . . . . . . . . . . . . GB FXT
*Latitude/Longitude:* . . . . . . . . 51° 57' N / 1° 21' E
*GMT Offset:* . . . . . . . . . . . . . . . . . . . . . . . . . . +0
*Telephone:* . . . . . . . . . . . . . . . [44] (1394) 604-500
*Web:* . . . . . . . . . . www.portoffelixstowe.co.uk

**Port of Glasgow**
*UN/LOCODE:* . . . . . . . . . . . . . . . . . . . . . . GB GLW
*Latitude/Longitude:* . . . . . . . . 55° 52' N / 4° 21' W
*GMT Offset:* . . . . . . . . . . . . . . . . . . . . . . . . . . +0
*Telephone:* . . . . . . . . . . . . . . . [44] (141) 221-8733
*Web:* . . . . . . . . . . . . . . . . . . www.clydeport.co.uk

**Port of Grangemouth**
*UN/LOCODE:* . . . . . . . . . . . . . . . . . . . . . . GB GRG
*Latitude/Longitude:* . . . . . . . . . 56° 1' N / 3° 43' W
*GMT Offset:* . . . . . . . . . . . . . . . . . . . . . . . . . . +0
*Telephone:* . . . . . . . . . . . . . . . [44] (1324) 482-591
*Web:* . . . . . www.forthports.co.uk/ports/grangemouth

**Port of Hull**
*UN/LOCODE:* . . . . . . . . . . . . . . . . . . . . . . GB HUL
*Latitude/Longitude:* . . . . . . . . 53° 44' N / 0° 14' W
*GMT Offset:* . . . . . . . . . . . . . . . . . . . . . . . . . . +0
*Telephone:* . . . . . . . . . . . . . . . [44] (1482) 327-171
*Web:* . . . . www.abports.co.uk/custinfo/ports/hull.htm

**Port of Leith**
*UN/LOCODE:* . . . . . . . . . . . . . . . . . . . . . . GB LEI
*Latitude/Longitude:* . . . . . . . . 55° 59' N / 3° 10' W
*GMT Offset:* . . . . . . . . . . . . . . . . . . . . . . . . . . +0
*Telephone:* . . . . . . . . . . . . . . . [44] (131) 555 8750
*Web:* . . . . . . . . . . . www.forthports.co.uk/ports/leith/

**Port of Liverpool**
*UN/LOCODE:* . . . . . . . . . . . . . . . . . . . . . . GB LIV
*Latitude/Longitude:* . . . . . . . . . 53° 28' N / 3° 2' W
*GMT Offset:* . . . . . . . . . . . . . . . . . . . . . . . . . . +0
*Telephone:* . . . . . . . . . . . . . . . [44] (151) 949-6000
*Web:* . . . . . . . . . . . . . . . www.portofliverpool.co.uk

**Port of London**
*UN/LOCODE:* . . . . . . . . . . . . . . . . . . . . . . GB LON
*Latitude/Longitude:* . . . . . . . . . 51° 30' N / 0° 5' W
*GMT Offset:* . . . . . . . . . . . . . . . . . . . . . . . . . . +0
*Telephone:* . . . . . . . . . . . . . . . [44] (20) 7743 7900
*Web:* . . . . . . . . . . . . . . www.portoflondon.co.uk/

**Port of Manchester**
*UN/LOCODE:* . . . . . . . . . . . . . . . . . . . . . . GB MNC
*Latitude/Longitude:* . . . . . . . . 53° 29' N / 2° 14' W
*GMT Offset:* . . . . . . . . . . . . . . . . . . . . . . . . . . +0

**Port of Peterhead BayS**
*UN/LOCODE:* . . . . . . . . . . . . . . . . . . . . . . GB PHD
*Latitude/Longitude:* . . . . . . . . 57° 30' N / 1° 47' W
*GMT Offset:* . . . . . . . . . . . . . . . . . . . . . . . . . . +0
*Telephone:* . . . . . . . . . . . . . . . [44] (1779) 474-020
*Web:* . . . . . . . . . . . . . . www.peterhead-bay.co.uk

SEAPORTS

### Port of Plymouth
*UN/LOCODE:* . . . . . . . . . . . . . . . . . . . . . . GB PLY
*Latitude/Longitude:* . . . . . . . . . . 50° 22' N / 4° 9' W
*GMT Offset:* . . . . . . . . . . . . . . . . . . . . . . . . . . +0
*Telephone:* . . . . . . . . . . . . . . [44] (1752) 662191
*Web:* . . . .www.abports.co.uk/custinfo/ports/plym.htm

### Port of Portsmouth
*UN/LOCODE:* . . . . . . . . . . . . . . . . . . . . . GB PME
*Latitude/Longitude:* . . . . . . . . . . 50° 48' N / 1° 7' W
*GMT Offset:* . . . . . . . . . . . . . . . . . . . . . . . . . . +0
*Telephone:* . . . . . . . . . . . . . [44] (23) 9229 7391
*Web:* . . . . . . . . . . . . . www.portsmouth-port.co.uk/

### Port of Scapa Flow
*UN/LOCODE:* . . . . . . . . . . . . . . . . . . . . . GB SFW
*Latitude/Longitude:* . . . . . . . . . . 58° 53' N / 3° 5' W
*GMT Offset:* . . . . . . . . . . . . . . . . . . . . . . . . . . +0

### Port of Southampton
*UN/LOCODE:* . . . . . . . . . . . . . . . . . . . . . GB SOU
*Latitude/Longitude:* . . . . . . . . . 50° 54' N / 1° 24' W
*GMT Offset:* . . . . . . . . . . . . . . . . . . . . . . . . . . +0
*Telephone:* . . . . . . . . . . . . . . [44] (23) 8070-1701
*Web:* . . . . . . . . . . . . . . . . . . . . www.sct.uk.com

### Port of Sullom Voe
*UN/LOCODE:* . . . . . . . . . . . . . . . . . . . . . GB SUL
*Latitude/Longitude:* . . . . . . . . . 60° 27' N / 1° 17' W
*GMT Offset:* . . . . . . . . . . . . . . . . . . . . . . . . . . +0
*Telephone:* . . . . . . . . . . . . . . [44] (1806) 244-200
*Web:* . . . . . . . . http://content.shetland.gov.uk/ports

### Port of Tees
*UN/LOCODE:* . . . . . . . . . . . . . . . . . . . . . GB TEE
*Latitude/Longitude:* . . . . . . . . . . 54° 39' N / 1° 8' W
*GMT Offset:* . . . . . . . . . . . . . . . . . . . . . . . . . . +0
*Telephone:* . . . . . . . . . . . . . . [44] (1642) 877-000
*Web:* . . . . . . . . . . . . . . . . . . . . www.thpal.co.uk

### Port of Tyne
*UN/LOCODE:* . . . . . . . . . . . . . . . . . . . . . GB TYN
*Latitude/Longitude:* . . . . . . . . . . 55° 1' N / 1° 24' W
*GMT Offset:* . . . . . . . . . . . . . . . . . . . . . . . . . . +0
*Telephone:* . . . . . . . . . . . . . . [44] (191) 455-2671
*Web:* . . . . . . . . . . . . . . . . . www.portoftyne.com

## United States

### Port Everglades
*UN/LOCODE:* . . . . . . . . . . . . . . . . . . . . . US PEF
*Latitude/Longitude:* . . . . . . . . . . 26° 5' N / 80° 5' W
*GMT Offset:* . . . . . . . . . . . . . . . . . . . . . . . . . . -5
*Telephone:* . . . . . . . . . . . . . . [1] (954) 523-4304
*Web:* . . . . . . . . . . . . . . . www.porteverglades.org

### Port of Anacortes
*UN/LOCODE:* . . . . . . . . . . . . . . . . . . . . . US AOT
*Latitude/Longitude:* . . . . . . . . 48° 31' N / 122° 36' W
*GMT Offset:* . . . . . . . . . . . . . . . . . . . . . . . . . . -8
*Telephone:* . . . . . . . . . . . . . . [1] (360) 293-3134
*Web:* . . . . . . . . . . . . . . . www.portofanacortes.net

### Port of Ashtabula
*UN/LOCODE:* . . . . . . . . . . . . . . . . . . . . . US ASF
*Latitude/Longitude:* . . . . . . . . 41° 54' N / 80° 48' W
*GMT Offset:* . . . . . . . . . . . . . . . . . . . . . . . . . . -6
*Web:* . . http://www.greatlakes-seaway.com/en/ports/
portofashtabula.html

### Port of Baltimore
*UN/LOCODE:* . . . . . . . . . . . . . . . . . . . . . US BAL
*Latitude/Longitude:* . . . . . . . . 39° 17' N / 76° 35' W
*GMT Offset:* . . . . . . . . . . . . . . . . . . . . . . . . . . -5
*Telephone:* . . . . . . . . . . . . . . [1] (410) 385-4480
*Web:* . . . . . . . . . . . . . . . www.mpa.state.md.us

### Port of Baton Rouge
*UN/LOCODE:* . . . . . . . . . . . . . . . . . . . . . US BTR
*Latitude/Longitude:* . . . . . . . . 30° 28' N / 91° 12' W
*GMT Offset:* . . . . . . . . . . . . . . . . . . . . . . . . . . -6
*Telephone:* . . . . . . . . . . . . . . [1] (225) 342-1660
*Web:* . . . . . . . . . . . . . . . . . . . www.portgbr.com

### Port of Beaumont
*UN/LOCODE:* . . . . . . . . . . . . . . . . . . . . . US BPT
*Latitude/Longitude:* . . . . . . . . . . 30° 5' N / 94° 5' W
*GMT Offset:* . . . . . . . . . . . . . . . . . . . . . . . . . . -6
*Telephone:* . . . . . . . . . . . . . . [1] (409) 835-5367
*Web:* . . . . . . . . . . . . . . www.portofbeaumont.com

### Port of Boston
*UN/LOCODE:* . . . . . . . . . . . . . . . . . . . . . US BOS
*Latitude/Longitude:* . . . . . . . . . 42° 21' N / 71° 5' W
*GMT Offset:* . . . . . . . . . . . . . . . . . . . . . . . . . . -5
*Telephone:* . . . . . . . . . . . . . . [1] (617) 973-5354
*Web:* . . . . . . . . . . . . . . www.massport.com/ports/

### Port of Charleston
*UN/LOCODE:* . . . . . . . . . . . . . . . . . . . . . US CHS
*Latitude/Longitude:* . . . . . . . . 32° 47' N / 79° 56' W
*GMT Offset:* . . . . . . . . . . . . . . . . . . . . . . . . . . -5
*Telephone:* . . . . . . . . . . . . . . [1] (803) 723-8651
*Web:* . . . . . . . . . . . . . www.port-of-charleston.com/

### Port of Chicago
*UN/LOCODE:* . . . . . . . . . . . . . . . . . . . . . US CHI
*Latitude/Longitude:* . . . . . . . . 41° 50' N / 87° 38' W
*GMT Offset:* . . . . . . . . . . . . . . . . . . . . . . . . . . -6
*Telephone:* . . . . . . . . . . . . . . [1] (773) 646-4400
*Web:* . . . . . . www.theportofchicago.com/index1a.html

### Port of Cleveland
*UN/LOCODE:* . . . . . . . . . . . . . . . . . . . . . US CLE
*Latitude/Longitude:* . . . . . . . . 41° 31' N / 81° 43' W
*GMT Offset:* . . . . . . . . . . . . . . . . . . . . . . . . . . -5
*Telephone:* . . . . . . . . . . . . . . [1] (216) 241-8004
*Web:* . . . . . . . . . . . . . . www.portofcleveland.com

### Port of Corpus Christi
*UN/LOCODE:* . . . . . . . . . . . . . . . . . . . . . US CRP
*Latitude/Longitude:* . . . . . . . . 27° 48' N / 97° 23' W
*GMT Offset:* . . . . . . . . . . . . . . . . . . . . . . . . . . -6
*Telephone:* . . . . . . . . . . . . . . [1] (361) 882-5633
*Web:* . . . . . . . . . . . www.portofcorpuschristi.com

### Port of Detroit
*UN/LOCODE:* . . . . . . . . . . . . . . . . . . . . . US DET
*Latitude/Longitude:* . . . . . . . . . 42° 20' N / 83° 2' W
*GMT Offset:* . . . . . . . . . . . . . . . . . . . . . . . . . . -5
*Telephone:* . . . . . . . . . . . . . . [1] (313) 331-3842
*Web:* . . . . . . . . . . . . . . . . . www.portdetroit.com/

### Port of Duluth
*UN/LOCODE:* . . . . . . . . . . . . . . . . . . . . . US DLH
*Latitude/Longitude:* . . . . . . . . . . 46° 44' N / 92° 6' W
*GMT Offset:* . . . . . . . . . . . . . . . . . . . . . . . . . . -6
*Telephone:* . . . . . . . . . . . . . . [1] (218) 727-8525
*Web:* . . . . . . . . . . . . . . . . . . www.duluthport.com

### Port of Freeport
*UN/LOCODE:* . . . . . . . . . . . . . . . . . . . . . US FRP
*Latitude/Longitude:* . . . . . . . . 28° 57' N / 95° 21' W
*GMT Offset:* . . . . . . . . . . . . . . . . . . . . . . . . . . -6
*Telephone:* . . . . . . . . . . . . . . [1] (409) 233-2667
*Web:* . . . . . . . . . . . . . . . . . www.portfreeport.com

### Port of Honolulu
*UN/LOCODE:* . . . . . . . . . . . . . . . . . . . . . US HNL
*Latitude/Longitude:* . . . . . . . . 21° 19' N / 157° 52' W
*GMT Offset:* . . . . . . . . . . . . . . . . . . . . . . . . . . -10
*Telephone:* . . . . . . . . . . . . . . [1] (808) 527-2764
*Web:* . . . www.hawaii.gov/dot/harbors/oahu/oahu.htm

### Port of Houston
*UN/LOCODE:* . . . . . . . . . . . . . . . . . . . . . US HOU
*Latitude/Longitude:* . . . . . . . . 29° 45' N / 95° 20' W
*GMT Offset:* . . . . . . . . . . . . . . . . . . . . . . . . . . -6
*Telephone:* . . . . . . . . . . . . . . [1] (713) 670-2400
*Web:* . . . . . . . . . . . . . . . . . www.portofhouston.com

### Port of Huntington - Tri-State (WV)
*UN/LOCODE:* . . . . . . . . . . . . . . . . . . . . . US HTS
*GMT Offset:* . . . . . . . . . . . . . . . . . . . . . . . . . . -5

**Port of Jacksonville**
UN/LOCODE: . . . . . . . . . . . . . . . . US JAX
Latitude/Longitude: . . . . . . . 30° 20' N / 81° 40' W
GMT Offset: . . . . . . . . . . . . . . . . . . . . . . . . . . . -5
Telephone: . . . . . . . . . . . . . [1] (904) 630-3080
Web: . . . . . . . . . . . . . . . . . . www.jaxport.com/

**Port of Lake Charles**
UN/LOCODE: . . . . . . . . . . . . . . . . US LCH
Latitude/Longitude: . . . . . . . 30° 13' N / 93° 15' W
GMT Offset: . . . . . . . . . . . . . . . . . . . . . . . . . . . -6
Telephone: . . . . . . . . . . . . . [1] (337) 439-3661
Web: . . . . . . . . . . . . . . . . . . . www.portlc.com

**Port of Long Beach**
UN/LOCODE: . . . . . . . . . . . . . . . . US LGB
Latitude/Longitude: . . . Latitude: 33° 76 N / 118° 21'
GMT Offset: . . . . . . . . . . . . . . . . . . . . . . . . . . . -8
Telephone: . . . . . . . . . . . . . [1] (562) 437-0041
Web: . . . . . . . . . . . . . . . . . . www.polb.com

**Port of Los Angeles**
UN/LOCODE: . . . . . . . . . . . . . . . . US LAX
Latitude/Longitude: . . . . . . . 33° 43' N / 118° 16' W
GMT Offset: . . . . . . . . . . . . . . . . . . . . . . . . . . . -8
Telephone: . . . . . . . . . . . . . [1] (310) 732-3840
Web: . . . . . . . . . . . . . www.portoflosangeles.org

**Port of Memphis**
UN/LOCODE: . . . . . . . . . . . . . . . . US MEM
Latitude/Longitude: . . . . . . . 35° 04' N / 90° 10' W
GMT Offset: . . . . . . . . . . . . . . . . . . . . . . . . . . . -6
Telephone: . . . . . . . . . . . . . [1] (901) 948-4422
Web: . . http://portfocus.com/united_states_america/
memphis_tn/

**Port of Miami**
UN/LOCODE: . . . . . . . . . . . . . . . . US MIA
Latitude/Longitude: . . . . . . . 25° 46' N / 80° 10' W
GMT Offset: . . . . . . . . . . . . . . . . . . . . . . . . . . . -5
Telephone: . . . . . . . . . . . . . [1] (305) 371-7678
Web: . . . . . www.co.miami-dade.fl.us/portofmiami/

**Port of Mobile**
UN/LOCODE: . . . . . . . . . . . . . . . . US MOB
Latitude/Longitude: . . . . . . . . 30° 40' N / 88° 2' W
GMT Offset: . . . . . . . . . . . . . . . . . . . . . . . . . . . -6
Telephone: . . . . . . . . . . . . . [1] (334) 441-7001
Web: . . . . . . . . . . . . . . . . . . . www.asdd.com/

**Port of New Orleans**
UN/LOCODE: . . . . . . . . . . . . . . . . . . . US
Latitude/Longitude: . . . . . . . . 29° 57' N / 90° 4' W
GMT Offset: . . . . . . . . . . . . . . . . . . . . . . . . . . . -6
Telephone: . . . . . . . . . . . . . [1] (504) 522-2551
Web: . . . . . . . . . . . . . . . . . . www.portno.com/

**Port of New York**
UN/LOCODE: . . . . . . . . . . . . . . . . US NYC
Latitude/Longitude: . . . . . . . . 40° 43' N / 74° 0' W
GMT Offset: . . . . . . . . . . . . . . . . . . . . . . . . . . . -5
Telephone: . . . . . . . . . . . . . [1] (908) 629-5566
Web: . . . . . . . . . . . . . . . . . . www.panynj.gov/

**Port of Newport News**
UN/LOCODE: . . . . . . . . . . . . . . . . US NNS
Latitude/Longitude: . . . . . . . . . 36° 59' N / 76° 26' W
GMT Offset: . . . . . . . . . . . . . . . . . . . . . . . . . . . -5
Telephone: . . . . . . . . . . . . . [1] (757) 683-8000
Web: www.vaports.com/Facilities/FAC-term-nnmt.htm

**Port of Norfolk**
UN/LOCODE: . . . . . . . . . . . . . . . . US ORF
Latitude/Longitude: . . . . . . . 36° 51' N / 76° 19' W
GMT Offset: . . . . . . . . . . . . . . . . . . . . . . . . . . . -5
Telephone: . . . . . . . . . . . . . [1] (757) 683-8000
Web: . . www.vaports.com/Facilities/FAC-term-nit.htm

**Port of Oakland**
UN/LOCODE: . . . . . . . . . . . . . . . . US OAK
Latitude/Longitude: . . . . . . . 37° 50' N / 122° 18' W
GMT Offset: . . . . . . . . . . . . . . . . . . . . . . . . . . . -8
Telephone: . . . . . . . . . . . . . [1] (510) 627-1100
Web: . . . . . . . . . . . . www.portofoakland.com/

**Port of Pascagoula**
UN/LOCODE: . . . . . . . . . . . . . . . . US PGL
Latitude/Longitude: . . . . . . . . . 30° 21' N / 88° 34' W
GMT Offset: . . . . . . . . . . . . . . . . . . . . . . . . . . . -6
Telephone: . . . . . . . . . . . . . [1] (412) 201-7330
Web: . . . . . . . . . . . www.portofpascagoula.com

**Port of Philadelphia**
UN/LOCODE: . . . . . . . . . . . . . . . . US PHL
Latitude/Longitude: . . . . . . . 39° 57' N / 75° 10' W
GMT Offset: . . . . . . . . . . . . . . . . . . . . . . . . . . . -5
Telephone: . . . . . . . . . . . . . [1] (215) 426-2441
Web: . . . . . . . . . . . . . . . www.philaport.com

**Port of Pittsburgh**
UN/LOCODE: . . . . . . . . . . . . . . . . US PIT
Latitude/Longitude: . . . . . . . 44° 45' N / 80° W
GMT Offset: . . . . . . . . . . . . . . . . . . . . . . . . . . . -5
Telephone: . . . . . . . . . . . . . [1] (412) 201-7330
Web: . . . . . . . . . . www.port.pittsburgh.pa.us

**Port of Plaquemine (Louisiana)**
UN/LOCODE: . . . . . . . . . . . . . . . . US PLQ
Latitude/Longitude: . . . . . . . . 30½ 13' N / 91½ 18' W
GMT Offset: . . . . . . . . . . . . . . . . . . . . . . . . . . . -6
Telephone: . . . . . . . . . . . . . [1] (504) 682-0081
Web: . . . . . . . . . . . . www.lded.state.la.us/

**Port of Port Arthur**
UN/LOCODE: . . . . . . . . . . . . . . . . US POA
Latitude/Longitude: . . . . . . . . 28° 52' N / 93° 56' W
GMT Offset: . . . . . . . . . . . . . . . . . . . . . . . . . . . -6
Telephone: . . . . . . . . . . . . . [1] (409) 983-2029
Web: . . . . . . . . . . . . . www.portofportarthur.com

**Port of Portland (Maine)**
UN/LOCODE: . . . . . . . . . . . . . . . . US PWM
Latitude/Longitude: . . . . . . . 43° 39' N / 70° 14' W
GMT Offset: . . . . . . . . . . . . . . . . . . . . . . . . . . . -5
Telephone: . . . . . . . . . . . . . [1] (207) 541-6900
Web: . . . . . . . . . . . . www.portofportlandmaine.org

**Port of Portland (Oregon)**
UN/LOCODE: . . . . . . . . . . . . . . . . US PDX
Latitude/Longitude: . . . . . . . 45° 30' N / 122° 40' W
GMT Offset: . . . . . . . . . . . . . . . . . . . . . . . . . . . -8
Telephone: . . . . . . . . . . . . . [1] (503) 944-7000
Web: . . . . . . . . . . . . . www.portofportland.com/

**Port of Richmond (CA)**
UN/LOCODE: . . . . . . . . . . . . . . . . US RCH
Latitude/Longitude: . . . . . . . 37° 56' N / 122° 25' W
GMT Offset: . . . . . . . . . . . . . . . . . . . . . . . . . . . -8
Telephone: . . . . . . . . . . . . . [1] (510) 215-4600
Web: . . . . . . . . . . www.ci.richmond.ca.us/port

**Port of Richmond (VA)**
UN/LOCODE: . . . . . . . . . . . . . . . . US RIC
Latitude/Longitude: . . . . . . . 37° 27' N / 77° 25' W
GMT Offset: . . . . . . . . . . . . . . . . . . . . . . . . . . . -5
Telephone: . . . . . . . . . . . . . [1] (804) 646-2020
Web: . . . . . . . . . . . . . www.portofrichmond.com

**Port of Savannah**
UN/LOCODE: . . . . . . . . . . . . . . . . US SAV
Latitude/Longitude: . . . . . . . 32° 2' N / 81° 7' W
GMT Offset: . . . . . . . . . . . . . . . . . . . . . . . . . . . -5
Telephone: . . . . . . . . . . . . . [1] (912) 964-3811
Web: . . . . . . . . . . . . . . . www.gaports.com

**Port of Seattle**
UN/LOCODE: . . . . . . . . . . . . . . . . US SEA
Latitude/Longitude: . . . . . . . 47° 36' N / 122° 20' W
GMT Offset: . . . . . . . . . . . . . . . . . . . . . . . . . . . -8
Telephone: . . . . . . . . . . . . . [1] (206) 728-3000
Web: . . . . . . . . . . . . . . . www.portseattle.org/

**Port of South Louisiana**
UN/LOCODE: . . . . . . . . . . . . . . . . US LUA
GMT Offset: . . . . . . . . . . . . . . . . . . . . . . . . . . . -6
Telephone: . . . . . . . . . . . . . [1] (888) SLA-PORT
Web: . . . . . . . . . . . . . . . . . . www.portsl.com

**Port of Tacoma**
*UN/LOCODE:* . . . . . . . . . . . . . . . . . . . . US ACI
*Latitude/Longitude:* . . . . . . 47° 14' N / 122° 28' W
*GMT Offset:* . . . . . . . . . . . . . . . . . . . . . . . . . . -8
*Telephone:* . . . . . . . . . . . . . [1] (206) 383-5841
*Web:* . . . . . . . . . . . . . . http://portoftacoma.com/

**Port of Tampa**
*UN/LOCODE:* . . . . . . . . . . . . . . . . . . US TPA
*Latitude/Longitude:* . . . . . . . 27° 57' N / 82° 28' W
*GMT Offset:* . . . . . . . . . . . . . . . . . . . . . . . . . . -5
*Telephone:* . . . . . . . . . . . . . [1] (813) 248-1924
*Web:* . . . . . . . . . . . . . . . . . . . www.tampaport.com

**Port of Valdez**
*UN/LOCODE:* . . . . . . . . . . . . . . . . . . . . US VDZ
*Latitude/Longitude:* . . . . . . . 61° 7' N / 146° 21' W
*GMT Offset:* . . . . . . . . . . . . . . . . . . . . . . . . . . -9
*Telephone:* . . . . . . . . . . . . . [1] (907) 835-4564
*Web:* . . . . . . . . . . . . . . www.ci.valdez.ak.us/port/

**Port of Wilmington (DE)**
*UN/LOCODE:* . . . . . . . . . . . . . . . . . . . . US ILM
*Latitude/Longitude:* . . . . . . . 39° 45' N / 75° 30' W
*GMT Offset:* . . . . . . . . . . . . . . . . . . . . . . . . . . -5
*Telephone:* . . . . . . . . . . . . . [1] (302) 571-4600
*Web:* . . . . . . . . . . . www.portofwilmingtonde.com/

**Port of Wilmington (NC)**
*UN/LOCODE:* . . . . . . . . . . . . . . . . . . . . US ILG
*Latitude/Longitude:* . . . . . . . 34° 14' N / 77° 57' W
*GMT Offset:* . . . . . . . . . . . . . . . . . . . . . . . . . . -5
*Telephone:* . . . . . . . . . . . . . [1] (910) 763-1621
*Web:* . . . . . . . . . . . . . . . . . . . www.ncports.com

**Port of Yakutat**
*UN/LOCODE:* . . . . . . . . . . . . . . . . . . . . US YAK
*Latitude/Longitude:* . . . . . . 59° 29' N / 139° 49' W
*GMT Offset:* . . . . . . . . . . . . . . . . . . . . . . . . . . -10

**Port of Texas City**
*UN/LOCODE:* . . . . . . . . . . . . . . . . . . . . US TXT
*Latitude/Longitude:* . . . . . . . 29° 22' N / 94° 53' W
*GMT Offset:* . . . . . . . . . . . . . . . . . . . . . . . . . . -6
*Telephone:* . . . . . . . . . . . . . [1] (409) 945-4461
*Web:* . . . . . . . . . . . . . . . . . . . www.railporttc.com

## Uruguay

**Port of Fray Bentos**
*UN/LOCODE:* . . . . . . . . . . . . . . . . . . . . UY FZB
*Latitude/Longitude:* . . . . . . . . 33° 6' S / 58° 19' W
*GMT Offset:* . . . . . . . . . . . . . . . . . . . . . . . . . . -3
*Web:* www.cennave.com.uy/home/content/view/259/151/

**Port of Montevideo**
*UN/LOCODE:* . . . . . . . . . . . . . . . . . . . . UY MVD
*Latitude/Longitude:* . . . . . . . 34° 55' S / 56° 13' W
*GMT Offset:* . . . . . . . . . . . . . . . . . . . . . . . . . . -3
*Telephone:* . . . . . . . . . . . . . [598] (2) 916-1901
*Web:* www.cennave.com.uy/home/content/view/267/160/

**Port of Nueva Palmira**
*UN/LOCODE:* . . . . . . . . . . . . . . . . . . . . UY NVP
*Latitude/Longitude:* . . . . . . . 33° 52' S / 58° 20' W
*GMT Offset:* . . . . . . . . . . . . . . . . . . . . . . . . . . -3
*Web:* www.cennave.com.uy/home/content/view/260/153/

**Port of Paysandu**
*UN/LOCODE:* . . . . . . . . . . . . . . . . . . . . UY PDU
*Latitude/Longitude:* . . . . . . . . 32° 18' S / 58° 6' W
*GMT Offset:* . . . . . . . . . . . . . . . . . . . . . . . . . . -3
*Web:* www.cennave.com.uy/home/content/view/258/154/

## Vanuatu

**Port of Santo**
*UN/LOCODE:* . . . . . . . . . . . . . . . . . . . . VU SAN
*Latitude/Longitude:* . . . . . . . 15° 31' S / 167° 11' E
*GMT Offset:* . . . . . . . . . . . . . . . . . . . . . . . . . +11

**Port Vila**
*UN/LOCODE:* . . . . . . . . . . . . . . . . . . . . VU VLI
*Latitude/Longitude:* . . . . . . . 17° 45' S / 168° 18' E
*GMT Offset:* . . . . . . . . . . . . . . . . . . . . . . . . . +11

## Venezuela

**Port of Bajo Grande/Maracaibo L**
*UN/LOCODE:* . . . . . . . . . . . . . . . . . . . . VE BJV
*Latitude/Longitude:* . . . . . . . . 10° 31' N / 71° 36' W
*GMT Offset:* . . . . . . . . . . . . . . . . . . . . . . . . . . -4
*Telephone:* . . . . . . . . . . . . . [58] (61) 201-111

**Port of La Guaira**
*UN/LOCODE:* . . . . . . . . . . . . . . . . . . . . VE LAG
*Latitude/Longitude:* . . . . . . . . 10° 38' N / 67° 7' W
*GMT Offset:* . . . . . . . . . . . . . . . . . . . . . . . . . . -4
*Telephone:* . . . . . . . . . . . . . [58] (31) 25364
*Web:* . . . . . http://portfocus.com/venezuela/la_guaira/

**Port of La Salina**
*UN/LOCODE:* . . . . . . . . . . . . . . . . . . . . VE LSV
*Latitude/Longitude:* . . . . . . . . 10° 22' N / 71° 27' W
*GMT Offset:* . . . . . . . . . . . . . . . . . . . . . . . . . . -4
*Telephone:* . . . . . . . . . . . . . [58] (61) 201-111

**Port of Maracaibo**
*UN/LOCODE:* . . . . . . . . . . . . . . . . . . . VE MAR
*Latitude/Longitude:* . . . . . . . . 10° 42' N / 71° 39' W
*GMT Offset:* . . . . . . . . . . . . . . . . . . . . . . . . . . -4
*Telephone:* . . . . . . . . . . . [58] (261) 723-1721
*Web:* . . . . . . . . . . . www.puertodemaracaibo.com

**Port of Matanzas**
*UN/LOCODE:* . . . . . . . . . . . . . . . . . . . . VE MTV
*Latitude/Longitude:* . . . . . . . . 8° 18' N / 62° 50' W
*GMT Offset:* . . . . . . . . . . . . . . . . . . . . . . . . . . -4

**Port of Palua**
*UN/LOCODE:* . . . . . . . . . . . . . . . . . . . . VE PLA
*Latitude/Longitude:* . . . . . . . . . 8° 22' N / 62° 42' W
*GMT Offset:* . . . . . . . . . . . . . . . . . . . . . . . . . . -4

**Port of Puerto Cabello**
*UN/LOCODE:* . . . . . . . . . . . . . . . . . . . . VE PBL
*Latitude/Longitude:* . . . . . . . . 10° 29' N / 68° 1' W
*GMT Offset:* . . . . . . . . . . . . . . . . . . . . . . . . . . -4
*Telephone:* . . . . . . . . (58)(42) 617616, 619103
*Web:* . http://portfocus.com/venezuela/puerto_cabello/

**Port of Puerto La Cruz**
*UN/LOCODE:* . . . . . . . . . . . . . . . . . . . . VE PCZ
*Latitude/Longitude:* . . . . . . . . 10° 13' N / 64° 38' W
*GMT Offset:* . . . . . . . . . . . . . . . . . . . . . . . . . . -4
*Telephone:* . . . . . . . . . . . . . [58] (81) 660-534

**Port of Puerto Sucre**
*UN/LOCODE:* . . . . . . . . . . . . . . . . . . . . VE PSU
*Latitude/Longitude:* . . . . . . . . 10° 27' N / 64° 11' W
*GMT Offset:* . . . . . . . . . . . . . . . . . . . . . . . . . . -4
*Web:* . . . . . . . . . . . . www.seaport.com.ve/ports.asp

**Port of Punta Cardon**
*UN/LOCODE:* . . . . . . . . . . . . . . . . . . . . VE PCN
*Latitude/Longitude:* . . . . . . . . 11° 38' N / 70° 14' W
*GMT Offset:* . . . . . . . . . . . . . . . . . . . . . . . . . . -4
*Telephone:* . . . . . . . . . . . . . [58] (69) 451-921
*Web:* . . . . . . . . . . . . www.seaport.com.ve/ports.asp

## Viet Nam

**Port of Da Nang**
*UN/LOCODE:* . . . . . . . . . . . . . . . . . . . VN DAD
*Latitude/Longitude:* . . . . . . . . 16° 6' N / 108° 18' E
*GMT Offset:* . . . . . . . . . . . . . . . . . . . . . . . . . +7

**Port of Haiphong**
*UN/LOCODE:* . . . . . . . . . . . . . . . . . . . VN HPH
*Latitude/Longitude:* . . . . . . . 20° 52' N / 106° 41' E
*GMT Offset:* . . . . . . . . . . . . . . . . . . . . . . . . . +7
*Telephone:* . . . . . . . . . . . . . [84] (31) 42637

**Port of Ho Chi Minh City**
*UN/LOCODE:* . . . . . . . . . . . . . . . . . . . VN SGN
*Latitude/Longitude:* . . . . . . . 10° 50' N / 106° 45' E
*GMT Offset:* . . . . . . . . . . . . . . . . . . . . . . . . . +7
*Telephone:* . . . . . . . . . . . . . [84] (8) 872-9999
*Web:* . . . . . . . . . . . . . . . . . . . www.vict-vn.com

**SEAPORTS**

**Port of Hongai**
*UN/LOCODE:* ..................... VN HON
*Latitude/Longitude:* ........ 20° 57' N / 107° 6' E
*GMT Offset:* ............................. +7
*Telephone:* ................ [84] (133) 25394

**Port of Nha Trang**
*UN/LOCODE:* ..................... VN NHA
*Latitude/Longitude:* ........ 12° 12' N / 109° 13' E
*GMT Offset:* ............................. +7

## Virgin Islands (U.S.)

**Port of Christiansted, St. Croix**
*UN/LOCODE:* ..................... VI CTD
*Latitude/Longitude:* ........ 17° 45' N / 64° 41' W
*GMT Offset:* ............................. -4

**Port of Limetree Bay**
*UN/LOCODE:* ..................... VI LIB
*Latitude/Longitude:* ........ 17° 41' N / 64° 44' W
*GMT Offset:* ............................. -4

**Port of St Thomas Island**
*UN/LOCODE:* ..................... VI STT
*Latitude/Longitude:* ........ 18° 20' N / 64° 56' W
*GMT Offset:* ............................. -4

## Yemen

**Port of Aden**
*UN/LOCODE:* ..................... YE ADE
*Latitude/Longitude:* ........ 12° 48' N / 44° 54' E
*GMT Offset:* ............................. +3
*Telephone:* ................ [967] (2) 202-666
*Web:* ................... www.portofaden.com

**Port of Hodeidah**
*UN/LOCODE:* ..................... YE HOD
*Latitude/Longitude:* ........ 14° 48' N / 42° 55' E
*GMT Offset:* ............................. +3
*Telephone:* ................ [967] (3) 211-603

**Port of Mokha**
*UN/LOCODE:* ..................... YE MOK
*Latitude/Longitude:* ........ 13° 21' N / 43° 12' E
*GMT Offset:* ............................. +3
*Telephone:* ................ [967] (3) 211-603

**Port of Mukalla**
*UN/LOCODE:* ..................... YE MKX
*Latitude/Longitude:* ......... 14° 31' N / 49° 7' E
*GMT Offset:* ............................. +3
*Telephone:* ................ [967] (5) 302856

SEAPORTS

# Cargo Aircraft Specifications

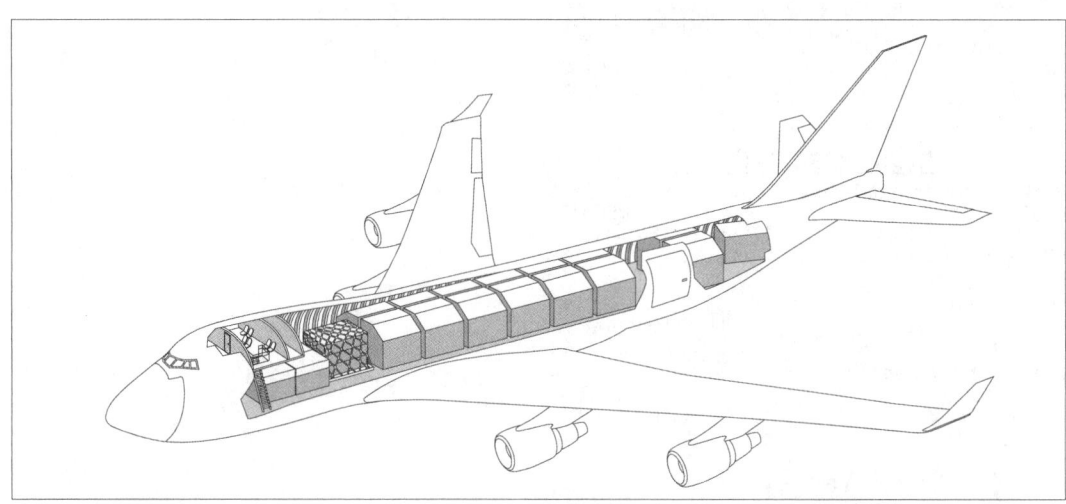

## Resources

### Airbus SAS (www.airbus.com)
Web site for the major European aerospace company. Contains information, photos, multi-media items and technical specifications for all current and out-of-production Airbus aircraft.

Airbus SAS is a global company with design and manufacturing facilities in France, Germany, the UK and Spain as well as subsidiaries in the U.S., China and Japan. Headquartered in Toulouse, France, Airbus is a joint EADS Company with BAE Systems of the UK.

### Air Cargo News (www.aircargonews.net)
An award-winning newsletter published every two weeks with over 100,000 readers in more than 170 countries. Annual subscription varies from US $50 to US $209 (depending on destination). The Web site has additional resources for users in the air cargo industry.

### AirFax (www.airtrading.com)
An aviation marketletter that provides up-to-date, accurate and comprehensive information on the worldwide availability of commercial transport aircraft. Two editions of the marketletter are produced: a Jet Transport Aircraft edition that provides information on the availability of DC-9 and larger jet aircraft, and a Regional & Commuter Aircraft edition that provides similar information for turboprop and regional jet aircraft.

### Airliners.NET
This Web site has a comprehensive database of photos, illustrations and general specifications for all current and out-of-production commercial aircraft, including freighters. Technical information is found at www.airliners.net/info.

### A-Z Worldwide Airfreight Directory (www.azfreight.com)
Online resource for air cargo professionals. Includes a directory (by country) of airports, airlines, airline sales agents, cargo agents, freight forwarders, cargo handling agents, charter brokers, express operators/couriers, services and suppliers to air cargo agents/operators and services and suppliers to the freighter/airports industries.

### Boeing Corporation (www.boeing.com)
Web site for the American aerospace company. Contains information, photos, multi-media items and technical specifications for all current and out-of-production Boeing aircraft, including those acquired through the 1997 merger with McDonnell Douglas.

### Civil Jet Aircraft Design (www.bh.com/companions/034074152X)
This Web site has a database of downloadable files (in HTML and Microsoft Excel formats) containing specifications for the 70 most important commercial aircraft currently flying. Information is separated into three categories: 1) Aircraft specification and mass data; 2) Aircraft geometric data; and 3) Aircraft performance data. Data are intended for undergraduate students of aeronautical design and for professionals in the industry.

### Freighter Reference Guide
An electronic Adobe PDF format guide produced by the Boeing Corporation that provides general information on freighter aircraft (including non-Boeing aircraft) that are currently in service throughout the world. The "Freighter Aircraft Specifications and Capabilities" section separates freighter aircraft into five categories based on each type's maximum payload capability. Within each category, aircraft are arranged alphabetically by manufacturer, and in turn, by ascending model variants. The payload-range information shown is based on typical international freighter mission rules, nominal performance (i.e., no degradation for age or OEW growth), zero winds, sea-level takeoff and ISA conditions. The Guide can be downloaded from many sites, including the International Air Cargo Association's site at www.tiaca.org/cm/G2/I138/S8.

### Freighters Online (www.freightersonline.com)
Comprehensive, free Web site that provides access to specifications for all freighter aircraft and utility freighters, with cross-referencing and search capabilities. Includes complete listings of aircraft and freighters, ULDs and pallets characteristics, wingspans, loading specifications, structural payloads and fuel capacities.

# MD 11

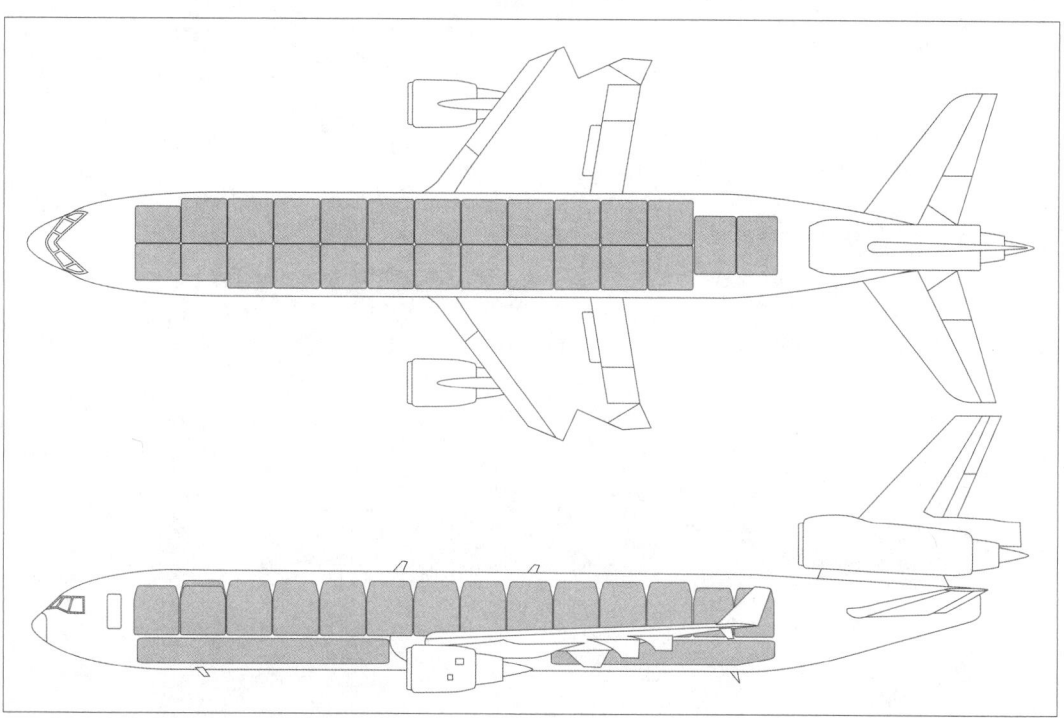

## MD-11 General Specifications

*Manufacturer*
McDonnell Douglas
(merged with Boeing Corporation in 1997)

*First flight*
January 10, 1990

*Wingspan*
169ft 6in/51.66m

*Length*
200ft 10 in/61.21m

*Height*
57ft 9in/17.6m

*Ceiling*
41,000ft

*Range*
6,500nm/12,038km

*Weight*
Passenger: 295,600lbs/134,082kg

*Power Plant*
Three Pratt & Whitney PW4460/62
-or- General Electric CF6-80C2

*Speed*
550 knots/1,017km/h/ 0.83mach

*Crew*
2

*Accommodation*
285-323-410 in three, two or one class configuration

## MD-11F (Freighter)

*Maximum Takeoff Weight*
272,070kg (502,000lb)

*Maximum Landing Weight*
213,870kg (471,500lb)

*Structural Payload*
93,170kg (205,400lb)

*Usable Volume*
433m³ (15,653ft³)

*Maximum Stack Height*
98.25in (249.5cm)

*Forward Cargo Door*
140in wide by 103.5in high (356cm x 263cm)

*Lower Deck Capacity*
5,566ft³ (158m³) of containerized or bulk cargo

*ULD Accomodation*
All standard industry containers.

# Airbus A300-600F

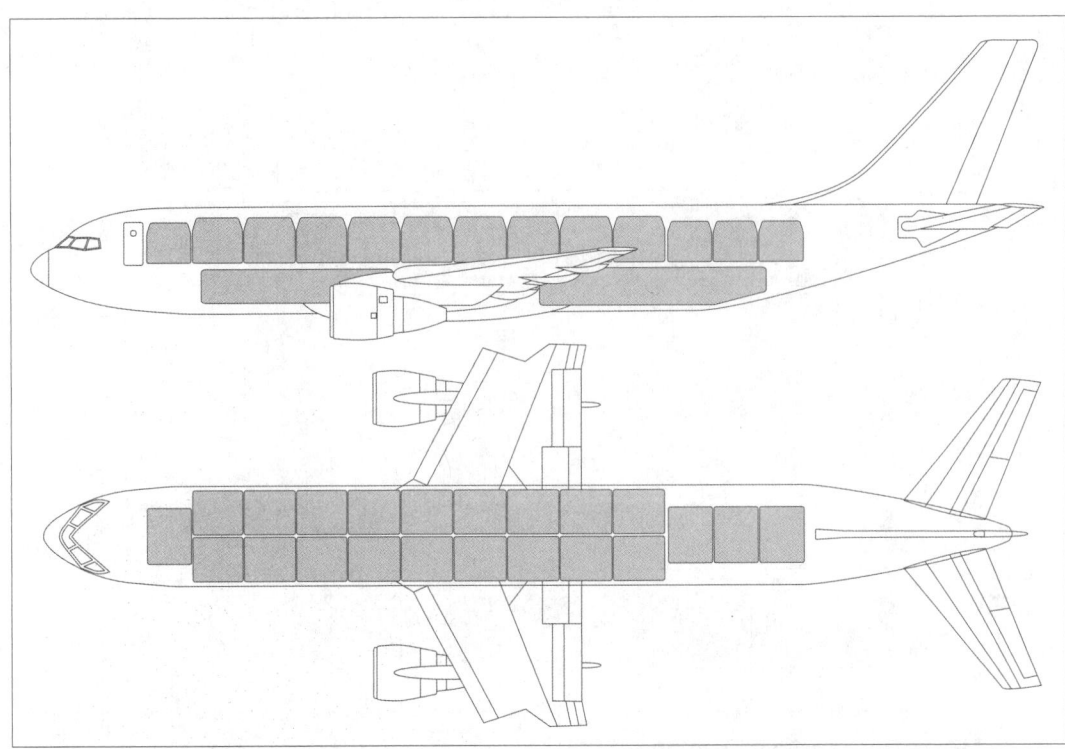

## Airbus A300-600F General Specifications

**Manufacturer**
Airbus Industries

**First flight**
2001

**Wingspan**
147ft 1in/44.84m

**Length**
177ft 5in/54.10m

**Height**
54ft. 3in/16.54m

**Ceiling**
41,000ft

**Range**
1,950-2,650nm/3,650-4,850km

**Weight**
300,900lbs /136,363kg

**Power Plant**
Four Rolls Royce Trent 556

**Speed**
549knots /1,017km/h/0.82mach

**Crew**
2

**Payload**
120,200lbs/54,636kg

## Airbus A300-600 Freighter + Payload Mode

**Maximum Takeoff Weight**
168,000kg (370,400lb)

**Maximum Landing Weight**
143,300kg (315,500lb)

**Bulk Hold Volume**
11.27m³ (398ft³)

### A300 and A310 Freighter Conversions

Typical conversion includes: installation of a 141in x 101in (3.58m x 2.57m) main deck cargo door, floor reinforcement, a main deck cargo loading system, safety barrier net, smoke curtain, and additional fire-suppression equipment.

**Cargo Loads for Converted Aircraft**

Typical cargo loads for converted aircraft are:
A300 — 48 tonnes on up to 25 88in x 125in pallets, 21 carried on the main deck and four in the forward underfloor hold, or alternatively, up to 21 pallets on the main deck plus up to 23 LD3 containers in the underfloor holds.
A310 — 40 tonnes on up to 19 pallets, 16 on the main deck and three in the forward underfloor hold, or alternatively, up to 16 pallets on the main deck plus up to 15 LD3 containers in the underfloor holds.

# Boeing 727-100

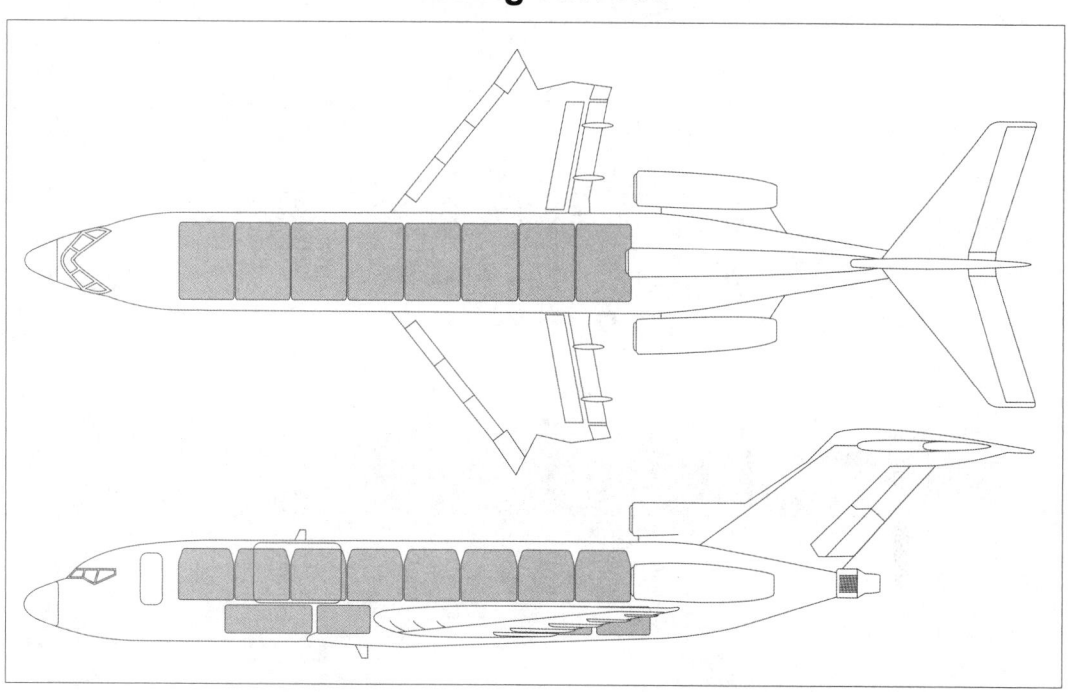

## Boeing 727 General Specifications

*Manufacturer*
Boeing Corporation

*First flight*
February 9, 1963

*Wingspan*
108ft/ 32.91m

*Length*
133ft 2in/40.59m

*Height*
34ft/10.36m

*Ceiling*
40,000ft

*Range*
3,000nm /5,556 km

*Weight*
80,600lbs /36,560kg

*Power Plant*
Three Pratt & Whitney JT8D7

*Speed*
529 knots /980 km/h /mach 0.80

*Crew*
3

*Accommodation*
94-131 in two or one class configuration

## Boeing 727-100 Freighter

*Maximum Takeoff Weight*
72,580kg (160,000lb)

*Maximum Landing Weight*
62,510kg (137,800lb)

*Structural Payload*
15,650kg (34,500lb)

*Usable Volume*
99m³ (3,496ft³)

## Boeing 727-200 Freighter

*Maximum Takeoff Weight*
78,020kg (172,000lb)

*Maximum Landing Weight*
66,0400kg (150,000lb)

*Structural Payload*
na

*Usable Volume*
137m³ (4,838ft³)

AIRPLANES

# Boeing 747 Freighter

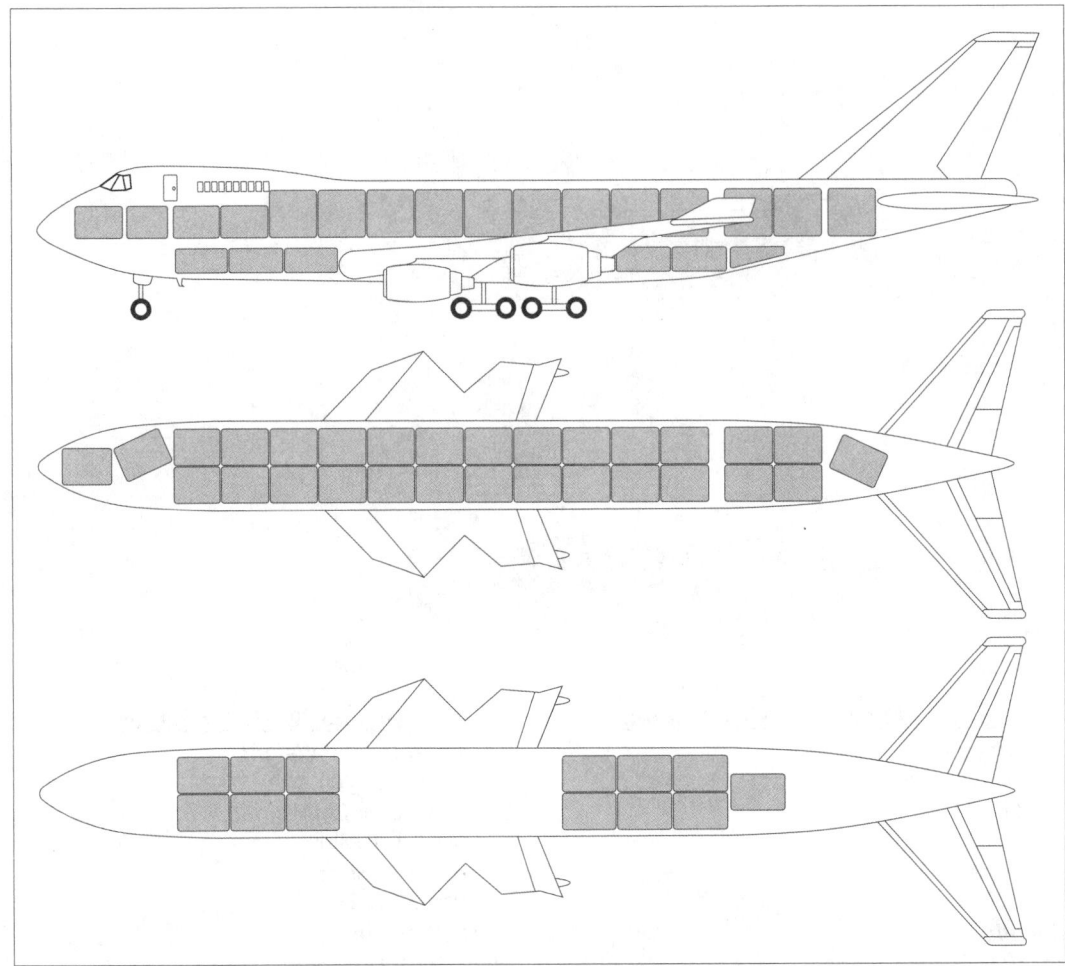

## Boeing 747 General Specifications

**Manufacturer**
Boeing Corporation

**Cargo Volume, Main Deck**
21,347ft³ (605m³)
30 pallets, 96x125in (244 x 318cm)

**Cargo Volume, Lower Deck**
5,600ft³ (159m³)
32 LD-1 containers

**Cargo Volume, Bulk Cargo**
520ft³ (15m³)

**Maximum Payload**
248,300lbs (112,630kg)
Optional 273,300lbs (123,970kg) available with maximum take-off-weight limitation

**Engines Maximum Thrust**
Pratt & Whitney PW4062 –63,300lb (281.57 kN)
Rolls-Royce RB211-524H2-T – 59,500 lb (264.67 kN)
General Electric CF6-80C2B5F – 62,100lb (276.23 kN)

**Maximum Fuel Capacity**
53,765 U.S. gal (203,515 L)

**Maximum Takeoff Weight**
875,000lb (396,900kg)

**Maximum Range**
4,445 nautical miles (8,232km)
Typical city range:
Paris-New York
New York-Frankfurt
London-Beijing
Toyky-Sydney

**Typical Cruise Speed at 35,000 feet**
0.845mach, 560mph (901km/h)

**Wing Span**
211ft 5in (64.4m)

**Overall Length**
231ft 10in (70.7m)

**Tail Height**
63ft 8in (19.4m)

**Interior Cabin Width**
20 ft (6.1m)

**AIRPLANES**

# Boeing 757-200

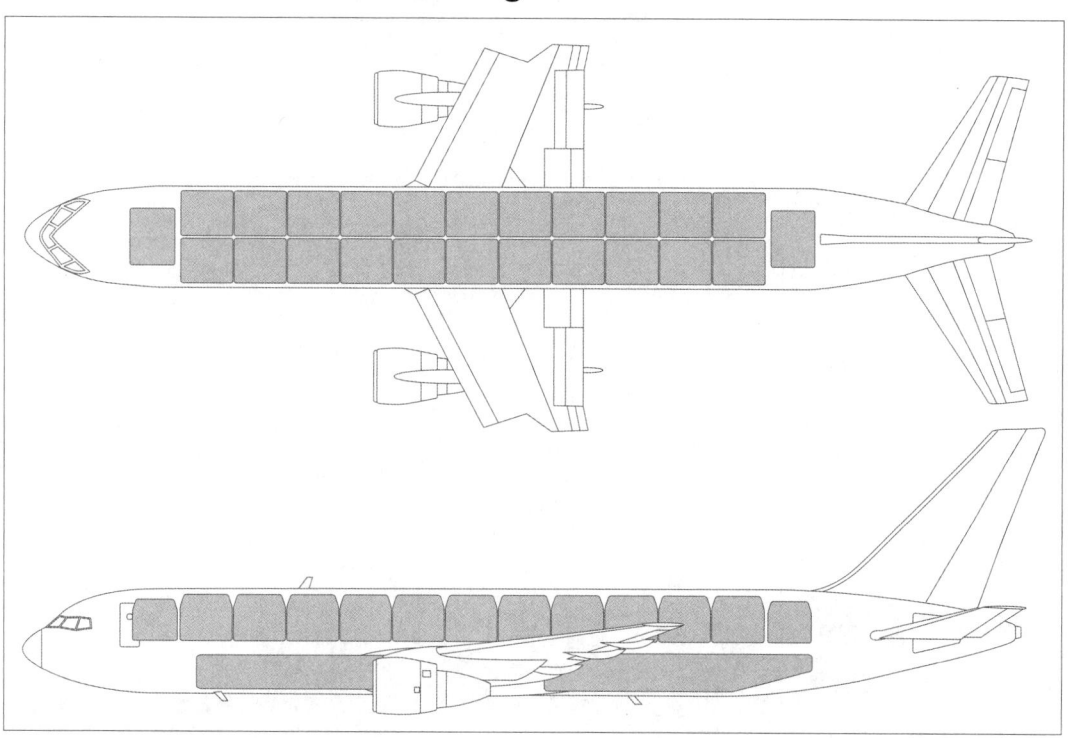

## Boeing 757 General Specifications

**Manufacturer**
Boeing Corporation

**First flight**
February 19, 1982

**Wingspan**
124ft 10in/38.05m

**Length**
155ft 3in/47.32m

**Height**
44 ft. 6in/13.56m

**Ceiling**
41,000ft

**Range**
3,928nm /7,275 km

**Weight**
128,730lbs /58,391 kg

**Power plant**
Two RollsRoyce RB211535C / RB211535E4 -or-
Pratt & Whitney PW2037 / PW2040

**Speed**
530knots /982km/h/0.80mach

**Crew**
2

**Accommodation**
192-239 in two or one class configuration

## Boeing 757-200 Freighter

**Maximum Takeoff Weight**
115,670kg (255,000lb)

**Maximum Landing Weight**
95,260kg (210,000lb)

**Structural Payload**
31,750kg (70,000lb)

**Usable Volume**
187m$^3$ (6,603ft$^3$)

**A I R P L A N E S**

# Boeing 767-300

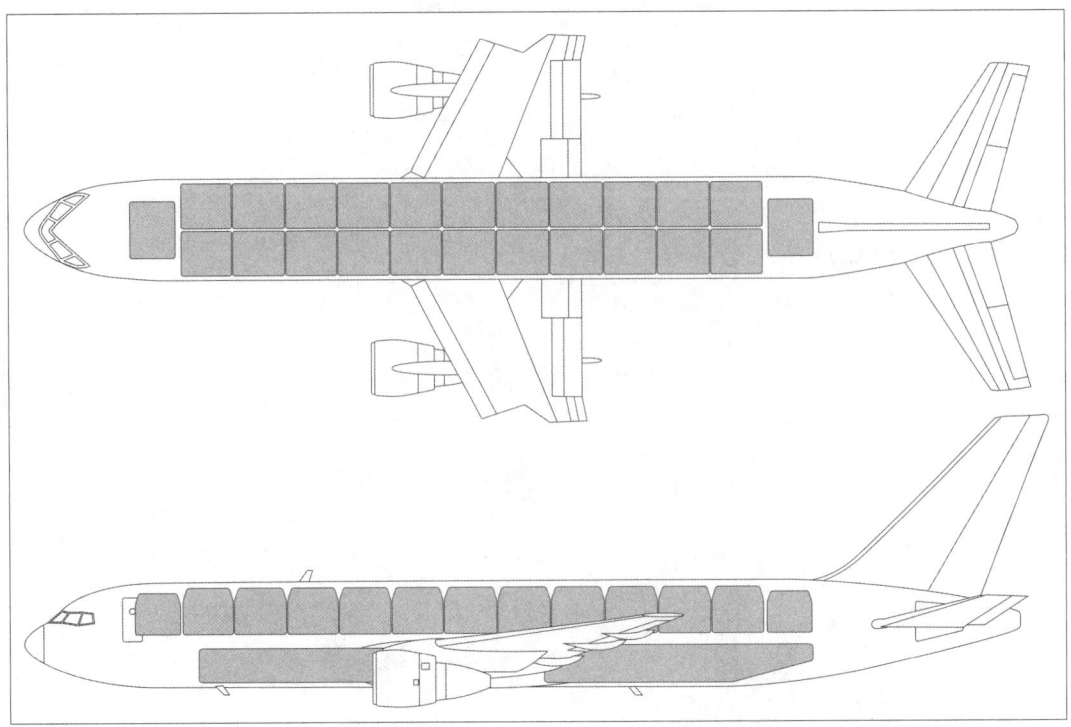

## Boeing 767 General Specifications

*Manufacturer*
Boeing Corporation

*First flight:*
January 30, 1986

*Wingspan:*
156 ft 1in/47.6m

*Length:*
180 ft 3in/54.9m

*Height:*
52 ft/15.8m

*Ceiling:*
41,000ft

*Range:*
6,115nm /11,325km

*Weight:*
196,000lbs /88,904kg
(199,600lbs /90,537kg -extended range)

*Power plant:*
Two Pratt & Whitney PW4062 -or- General Electric
CF6-80C2B7F -or- Rolls Royce RB211-514H

*Speed:*
530knots/982km/h /0.80mach

*Crew:*
2

*Accommodation:*
218-269-351 in three, two or one class passenger
configuration / 60.5 tons as freighter

## Boeing 300 Freighter

*Maximum Takeoff Weight*
188,880kg (412,000lb)

*Maximum Landing Weight*
147,870kg (326,000lb)

*Structural Payload*
54,840kg (120,900lb)

*Usable Volume*
336m³ (11,865ft³)

# Douglas DC-8

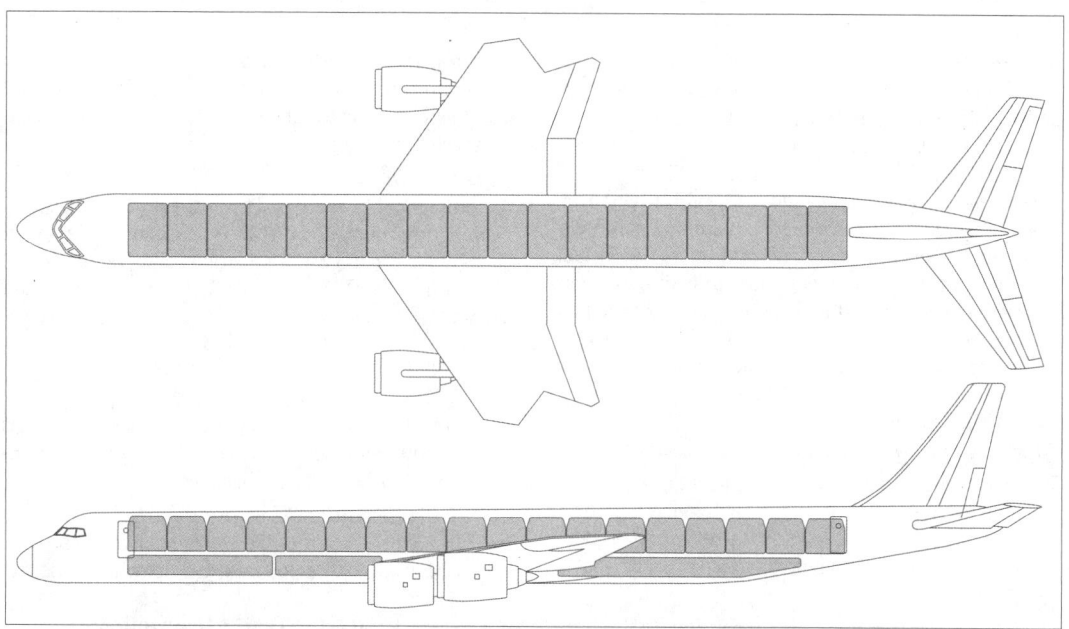

## DC-8 General Specifications

**Manufacturer**
McDonnell-Douglas Corporation, now Boeing Corporation

**First flight:**
May 30, 1958

**Wingspan:**
142ft 5in/43.41m

**Length:**
150ft 6in/45.87m

**Height:**
42ft 4in/12.91m

**Ceiling:**
35,000ft

**Range:**
4,800nm /8,890km

**Weight:**
126,525lbs /57,391kg (-30) -to-
153,749 lbs / 69,739 kg (-63)

**Power plant:**
Four Pratt & Whitney JT3D

**Speed:**
500 knots / 926 km/h / 0.76mach

**Crew:**
3

**Accommodation:**
132-144-179 in three, two or one class configuration (Freighter: 17 tons)

## DC-8 Model 62AF

**Maximum Takeoff Weight**
147,420kg (335,000lb)

**Maximum Landing Weight**
113,400kg (250,000lb)

**Structural Payload**
42,640kg (94,000lb)

**Usable Volume**
198m³ (6,992ft³)

## DC-8 Model 62AFa

**Maximum Takeoff Weight**
158,760kg (350,000lb)

**Maximum Landing Weight**
113,400kg (250,000lb)

**Structural Payload**
42,640kg (94,000lb)

**Usable Volume**
198m³ (6,992ft³)

## DC-8 Model 63AF

**Maximum Takeoff Weight**
161,030kg (355,000lb)

**Maximum Landing Weight**
124,740kg (275,000lb)

**Structural Payload**
52,620kg (116,000lb)

**Usable Volume**
252m³ (8,900ft³)

# Guide to Air Freight Containers (ULDs)

## Introduction

The following guide to air freight containers has been developed from materials supplied by the International Air Transport Association (IATA), air cargo carriers and container manufacturers. It should be noted that producing a truly comprehensive guide is a problematic task. While it would appear that there is a limited number of cargo aircraft operating in the world, there are in fact, many aircraft types and many more aircraft cargo configurations. Each aircraft and configuration may require customized containers. The guide that follows contains illustrations and specifications of the most common containers in use today. Many of these containers can be used in multiple aircraft.

## ULD (Unit Load Devices)

While in the ocean freight cargo business the word "container" is widely accepted, in the air freight cargo business the proper term is "unit load device", or more commonly ULD. However, both terms are used.

## IATA

The International Air Transport Association (IATA) is the primary source of industry wide technical information for ULDs. Their "ULD Technical Manual" contains the specifications manufacturers usually follow in making containers for airlines. The book can be obtained from:

**IATA**
800 Place Victoria, PO Box 113
Montreal H4Z 1M1, Quebec Canada
Tel: [1] (514) 874-0202; Fax: [1] (514) 874-9632
or
**IATA**
77 Robinson Road, #05-00SIA Building
Singapore 068896
Tel: [65] 6438-4555; Fax: [65] 6438-4666

## Your Air Freight Forwarder

The practical source of information concerning ULDs for your shipment will most likely come from your air carrier or air freight forwarder. They will be best equipped to assist you in selecting the appropriate ULD for your needs.

## Values / Details

All values listed in illustrations and tables are given in metric. Ft and lbs values are for easy reference only.

## Openings / Doors

While airlines may be quite rigid about external dimensions and maximum gross weights, there are many styles of door openings that are permissible. ULD manufacturers produce products with hinged doors, folding aluminum panels as well as reinforced nylon curtains.

## Pallets / Nettings

Pallets are in common use in most aircraft cargo configurations. All require the use of restraining devices. The most common type is a flexible netting of which there are numerous designs. Ask your air carrier or freight forwarder for details.

## Maximum Gross Weights

Maximum gross weights vary from ULD type, ULD manufacturer, aircraft and air carrier. Be certain to confirm weight maximums.

## ULD Markings

According to IATA all ULDs must carry the following marking information: 1) ULD Type Code, 2) Maximum Gross Weight (MGW) in kilograms and pounds and 3) The actual Tare Weight (TARE) in kilograms and pounds. Example:

| | | |
|---|---|---|
| UAK | 1 2 3 4 | XB |
| MGW | 6,033 kg | 13,300 lb |
| TARE | 216 kg | 476 lb |

For marking non-structural aircraft containers MGW is optional. The actual TARE shall be the sum of the components aircraft pallet, net and container.

## IATA ULD Identification Codes

Prior to October 1, 1993 the IATA Identification Code consisted of nine (9) alpha numeric elements in the following sequence:

| Position | Character Type | Description |
|---|---|---|
| 1 | alphabetic | ULD Category |
| 2 | alphabetic | Base Dimensions |
| 3 | alphabetic | Contour or Compatibility |
| 4,5,6,7 | numeric | Serial Number |
| 8,9 | alpha-numeric | Owner/Registrant |

Effective October 1, 1993 the IATA Identification Code consists of nine (9) or ten (10) alpha-numeric elements in the following sequence:

| Position | Character Type | Description |
|---|---|---|
| 1 | alphabetic | ULD Category |
| 2 | alphabetic | Base Dimensions |
| 3 | alphabetic | Contour or Compatibility |
| 4,5,6,7,8 | (see Note below) | Serial Number |
| 9, 10 | alpha-numeric | Owner/Registrant |

Note: The serial number consists of four or five numerics.

## ULD Type Code

IATA uses three letter codes (in upper case letters) to describe key characteristics of ULDs. Examples are AKE, DPN and RKE. Each of the three letter code positions describes particular characteristics of the ULD.

## Position 1

The Position 1 letter describes the container as:
1. certified as to airworthiness or non-certified
2. structural unit or non-structural
3. fitted with equipment for refrigeration, insulation or thermal control (Thermal) or not fitted with refrigeration, insulation or thermal control
4. containers, pallets, nets, pallet/net/non-structural igloo assembly

The Code List for Position 1 is as follows:

A   Certified Aircraft Container
D   Non-Certified Aircraft Container
F   Non-Certified Aircraft Pallet
G   Non-Certified Aircraft Pallet Net
J   Thermal Non-Structural Igloo
H   Horse Stalls
K   Cattle Stalls
M   Thermal Non-Certified Aircraft Container
N   Certified Aircraft Pallet Net
P   Certified Aircraft Pallet
R   Thermal Certified Aircraft Container
U   Non-Structural Container
V   Automobile Transport Equipment

The following are obsolete codes that are still found on some older ULDs.

(B) Certified Main Deck Aircraft Container
(C) Non-Aircraft Container
(E) Non-Certified Main Deck Aircraft Container
(S) Structural Igloo— Solid Doors
(T) Structural Igloo—Other Closures
     (other than solid doors)

## Position 2

The Position 2 letter describes the base dimensions of the container. For containers manufactured after October 1, 1990 the following code letters are used:

A   2,235 x 3,175 mm (88 x 125 in)
B   2,235 x 2,743 mm (88 x 108 in)
E   1,346 x 2,235 mm (53 x 88 in)
F   2,438 x 2,991 mm (96 x 117.75 in)
G   2,438 x 6,058 mm (96 x 238.5 in)
H   2,438 x 9,125 mm (96 x 359.25 in)
J   2,438 x 12,192 mm (96 x 480 in)
K   1,534 x 1,562 mm (60.4 x 61.5 in)
L   1,534 x 3,175 mm (60.4 x 125 in)
M   2,438 x 3,175 mm (96 x 125 in)
N   1,562 x 2,438 mm (61.5 x 96 in)
P   1,198 x 1,534 mm (47 x 60.4 in)
Q   1,534 x 2,438 mm (60.4 x 96 in)
R   2,438 x 4,938 mm (96 x 196 in)
X   Miscellaneous sizes largest dimension between 2,438 mm and 3,175 mm (between 96 in and 125 in)
Y   Miscellaneous sizes largest dimension 2,438 mm (96 in)
Z   Miscellaneous sizes largest dimension >3,175mm (>125 in)

## Position 3

The Position 3 letter describes the container's contour, fork lift capability, and in the case of pallets and nets, the restraint system into which the unit is classified. The Position 3 codes are extremely complex and are not within the scope of this publication. Refer to the IATA "ULD Technical Manual" for complete information.

### Notes on ULD Guide

1. IATA (International Air Transport Association) and ATA (Air Transport Association of America) have different designations for air containers. For example: A US Type LD-3 is equivalent to the IATA Type 8 container. We list the IATA designation first and then the ATA designation second.

2. This guide lists and illustrates the primary air containers in use today. There are other types not listed that can be found in the IATA ULD Technical Manual.

3. Specifications listed in metric measures of kilos and millimeters (kg, mm) are official IATA specifications. Pounds and inches are listed only as a point of reference.

4. L x W x H = Length x Width x Height.

5. Specifications listed are taken from IATA's "ULD Technical Manual." In practice, these specifications (dimensions and weight) may vary according to special aircraft configurations and ULD manufacturers.

6. ULDs are generally classified as lower deck containers or upper deck containers. Lower deck containers generally have smaller base dimensions than upper deck containers as a result of the curvature of the airplane body.

7. Since a great deal of cargo is carried on commercial passenger flights, there are generally more lower deck than upper deck containers.

## Main Deck Pallet with Net—IATA Type 1/1S—IATA Prefix: PG

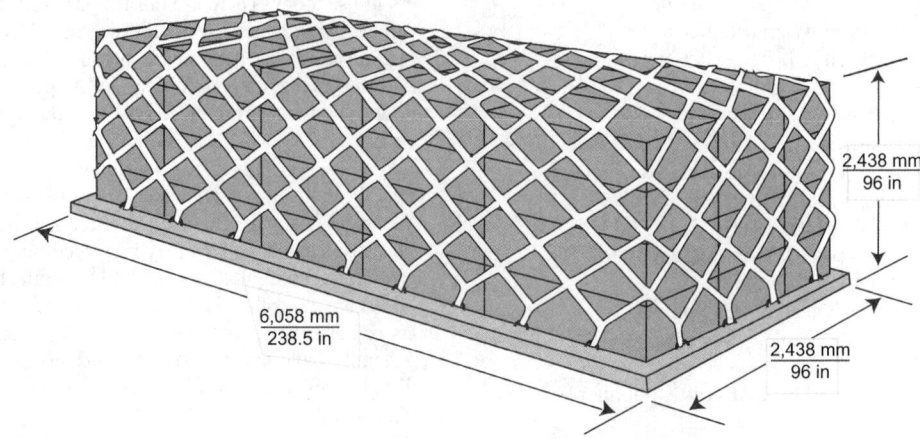

**Maximum Gross Weight**
13,608 kg / 30,000 lb

**Volume**
33.25 m³ / 1,174 ft³

**Tare**
400 kg / 882 lb

**External Dimensions**
(L x W x H)
6,058 mm x 2,438 mm x 2,438 mm
(238.5 in x 96 in x 96 in)

**Aircraft Accepted For**
DC10-30 Freighter, 747F

## Main Deck Pallet with Net—IATA Type 2/2Q—IATA Prefix: PM

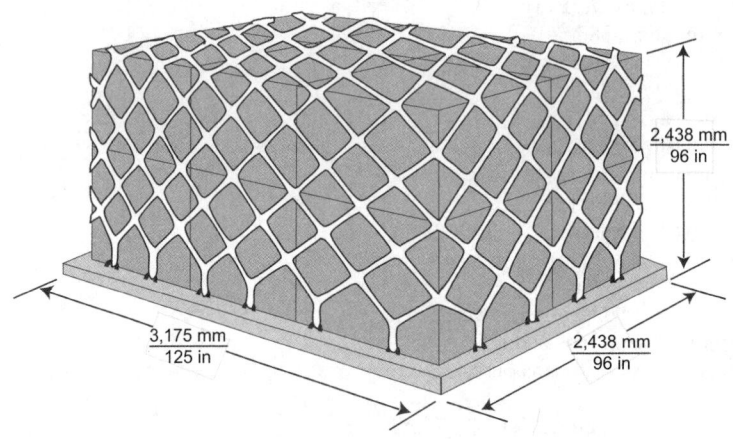

**Maximum Gross Weight**
6,804 kg / 15,000 lb

**Volume**
17.16 m³ / 606 ft³

**Tare**
130 kg / 287 lb

**External Dimensions**
(L x W x H)
3,175 mm x 2,438 mm x 2,438 mm
(125 in x 96 in x 96 in)

**Aircraft Accepted For**
DC10-30 Freighter, 747F

# Main Deck Pallet with Net—IATA Type 2H—IATA Prefix: PM

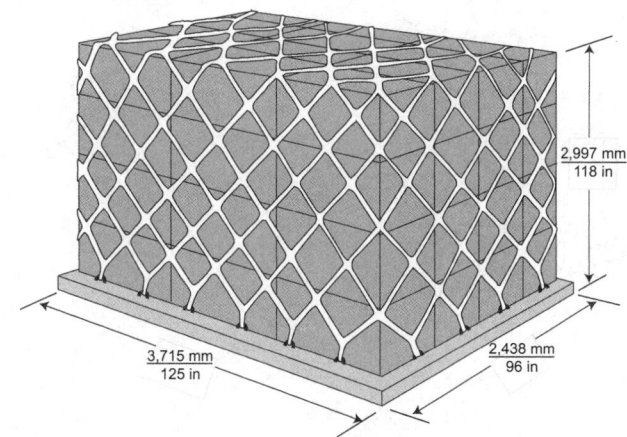

**Maximum Gross Weight**
6,804 kg / 15,000 lb

**Volume**
21.16 m³ / 747 ft³

**Tare**
130 kg / 287 lb

**External Dimensions**
(L x W x H)
3,715 mm x 2,438 mm x 2,997 mm
(125 in x 96 in x 118in)

**Aircraft Accepted For:**
DC10-30 Freighter, 747F

# Pallet with Net—IATA Type 2WA—IATA Prefix: PM

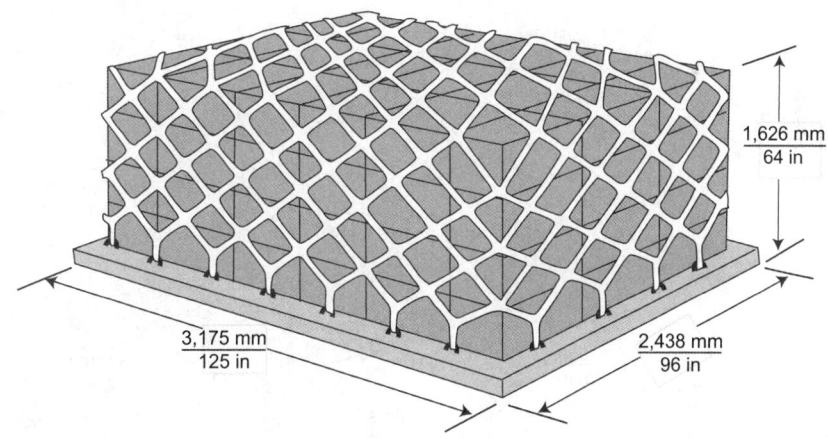

**Maximum Gross Weight**
5,035 kg / 11,100 lb

**Volume**
15.8 m³ / 557 ft³

**Tare**
130 kg / 287 lb

**External Dimensions**
(L x W x H)
3,715 mm x 2,438 mm x 1,626 mm
(125 in x 96 in x 64 in)

**Aircraft Accepted For:**
DC10-30, Freighter, DC10-30, 747, 747F

## Pallet with Net—IATA Type 5—IATA Prefix: PA

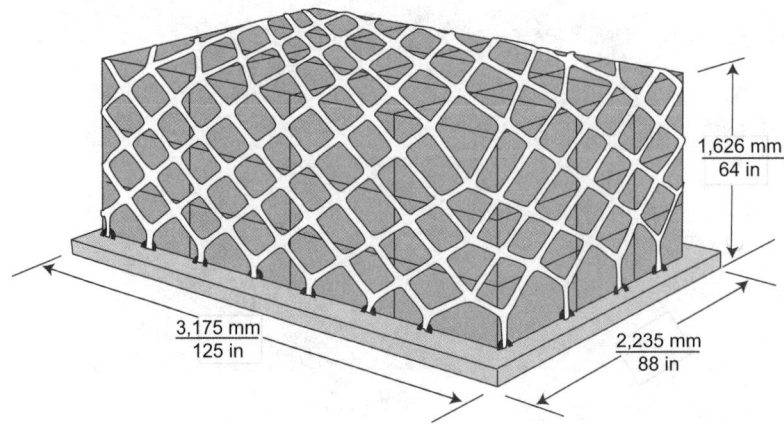

**ULD**

**Maximum Gross Weight**
4,626 kg / 10,200 lb

**Volume**
9.91 m³ / 350 ft³

**Tare**
120 kg / 264 lb

**External Dimensions**
(L x W x H)
3,715 mm x 2,235 mm x 1,626 mm
(125 in x 88 in x 64 in)

**Aircraft Accepted For:**
DC10-30 Freighter, DC10-30
747, 747F, 777, 767-300

## Lower Deck Pallet with Net—IATA Type 6—IATA Prefix: PL

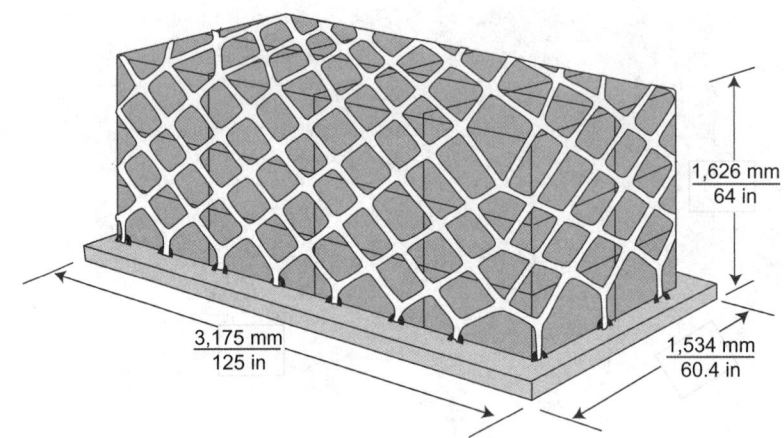

**Maximum Gross Weight**
3,175 kg / 7,000 lb

**Volume**
6.94 m³ / 245 ft³

**Tare**
90 kg / 198 lb

**External Dimensions**
(L x W x H)
3,175 mm x 1,534 mm x 1,626 mm
(125 in x 60.4 in x 64 in)

**Aircraft Accepted For:**
DC10, DC10-30 Freighter, 747, 777

# Lower Deck Container—IATA Type 2BG—IATA Prefix: AMU

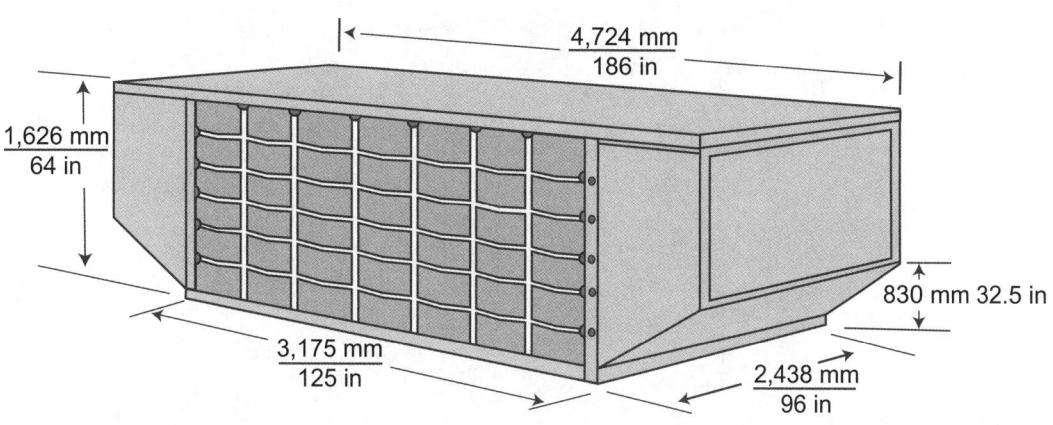

**Maximum Gross Weight**
6,033 kg / 13,300 lb

**Volume**
13.7 m³ / 480 ft³

**Tare**
200 kg / 440 lb

**External Dimensions**
(L x W x H)
3,175 mm x 2,438 mm x 1,626 mm
(125 in x 96 in x 64 in)

**Aircraft Accepted For:**
747, 747F

# Main Deck Container—IATA Type 2/2Q—IATA Prefix: AMA

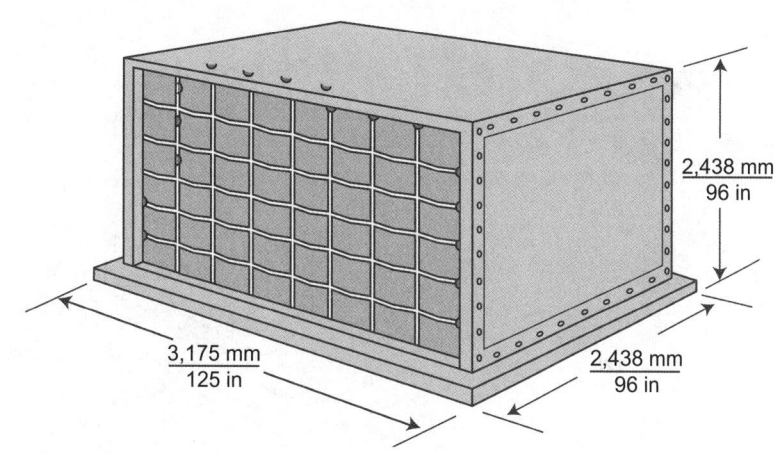

**Maximum Gross Weight**
6,804 kg / 15,000 lb

**Volume**
17.16 m³ / 606 ft³

**Tare**
260 kg / 572 lb

**External Dimensions**
(L x W x H)
3,175 mm x 2,438 mm x 2,438 mm
(125 in x 96 in x 96 in)

**Aircraft Accepted For:**
747F

ULD

## Upper Deck Container—IATA Type 5—IATA Prefix AAK—ATA: LD-7

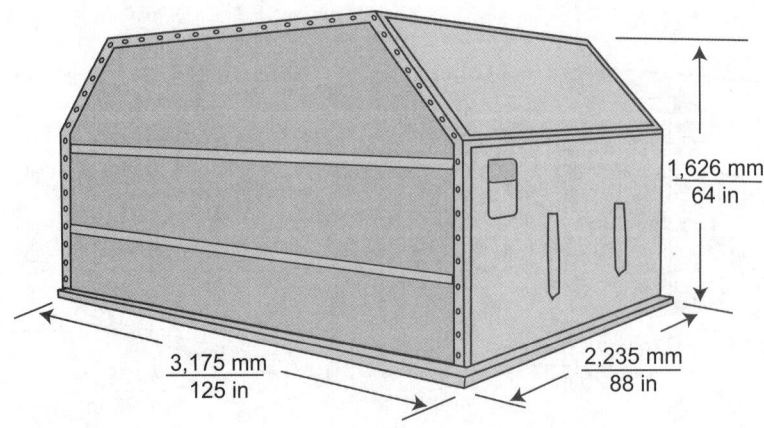

**Maximum Gross Weight**
6,033 kg / 13,300 lb

**Volume**
9.91 m³ / 350 ft³

**Tare**
200 kg / 440 lb

**External Dimensions**
(L x W x H)
3,175 mm x 2,235 mm x 1,626 mm
(125 in x 88 in x 64 in)

**Aircraft Accepted For**

## Container—IATA Type 5—IATA Prefix AAP—ATA: LD-9

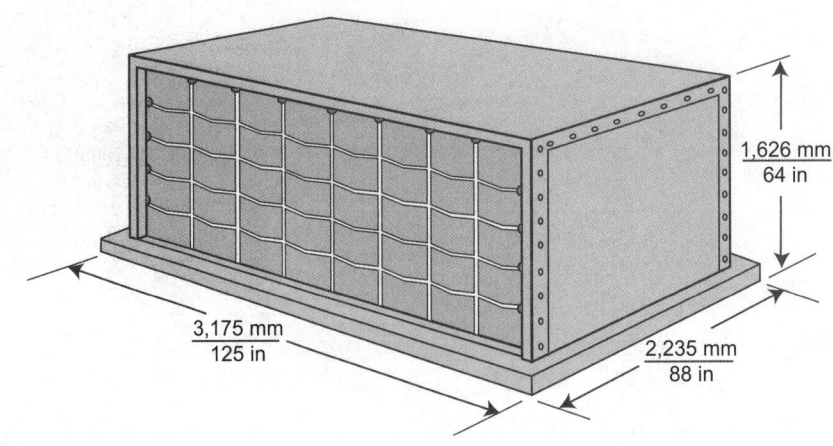

**Maximum Gross Weight**
6,033 kg / 13,300 lb

**Volume**
9.91 m³ / 350 ft³

**Tare**
200 kg / 440 lb

**External Dimensions**
(L x W x H)
3,175 mm x 2,235 mm x 1,626 mm
(125 in x 88 in x 64 in)

**Aircraft Accepted For:**
747, 747F, L1011

## Lower Deck Container—IATA Type 6B—IATA Prefix: AQ—ATA: LD-8

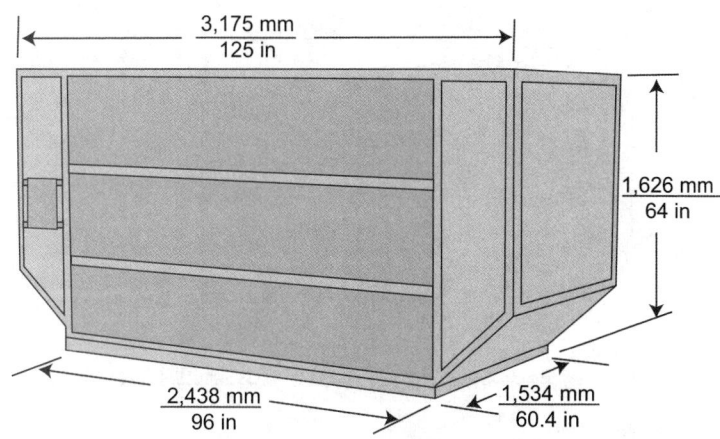

**Maximum Gross Weight**
2,449 kg / 5,400 lb

**Volume**
6.94 m³ / 245 ft³

**Tare**
120 kg / 264 lb

**External Dimensions**
(L x W x H)
2,438 mm x 1,534 mm x 1,626 mm
(96 in x 60.4 in x 64 in)

**Aircraft Accepted For:**
777, 767

## Lower Deck Container—IATA Type 6—IATA Prefix: ALF—ATA: LD-6

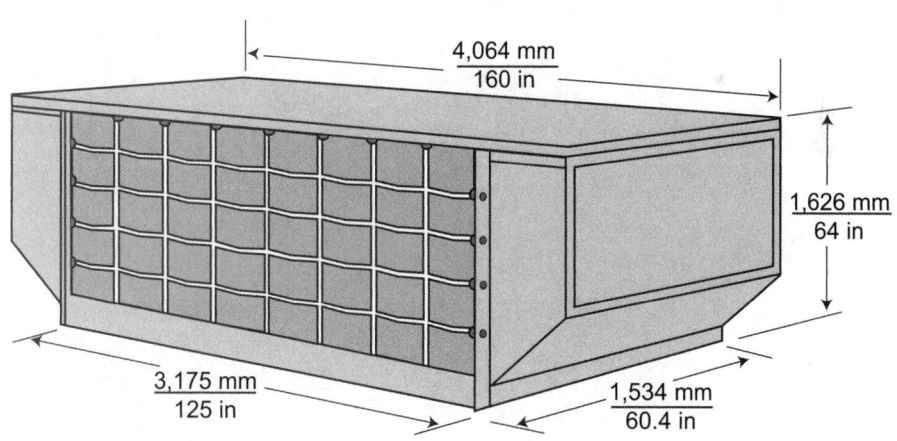

**Maximum Gross Weight**
3,175 kg / 7,000 lb

**Volume**
6.94 m³ / 245 ft³

**Tare**
180 kg / 397 lb

**External Dimensions**
(L x W x H)
3,175 mm x 1,534 mm x 1,626 mm
(125 in x 60.4 in x 64 in)

**Aircraft Accepted For:**
747, 747F, L1011

U
L
D

## Lower Deck Container—IATA Type 8—IATA Prefix AK—ATA: LD-3

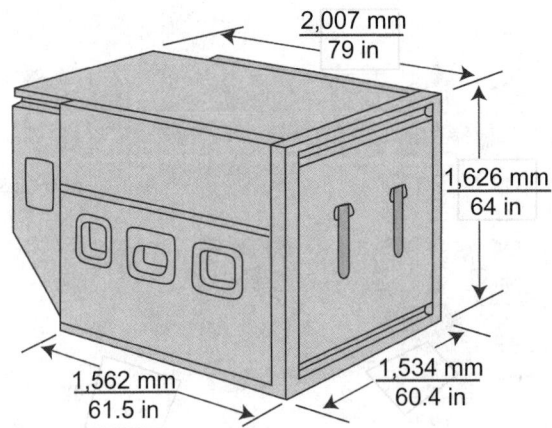

**Maximum Gross Weight**
1,588 kg / 3,500 lb

**Volume**
4.53 m³ / 160 ft³

**Tare**
70 kg / 154 lb

**External Dimensions**
(L x W x H)
1,562 mm x 1,534 mm x 1,626 mm
(61.5 in x 60.4 in x 64 in)

**Aircraft Accepted For:**
DC10-30 Freighter, DC10, 747, 777, 767

## Lower Deck Container—IATA Type 8D—Prefix: APA—APA: LD-2

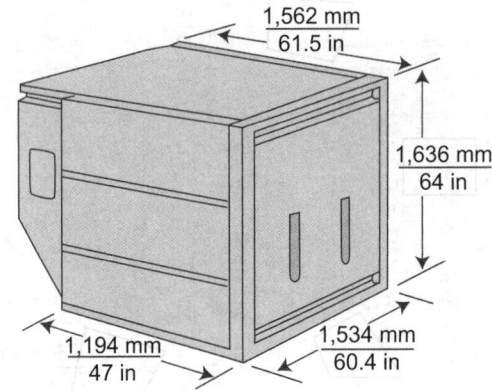

**Maximum Gross Weight**
1,225 kg / 2,700 lb

**Volume**
3.4 m³ / 120 ft³

**Tare**
60 kg / 132 lb

**External Dimensions**
(L x W x H)
1,194 mm x 1,534 mm x 1,626 mm
(47 in x 60.4 in x 64 in)

**Aircraft Accepted For:**
777, 767

# World Airports by IATA Code

## List 1 of 2:
## IATA Code...Airport/location...Country

### Notes

1. The following is a list of more than 10,000 three-letter IATA (International Air Transport Association) codes and their respective locations.
2. IATA codes are primarily used to identify airports, but are also used to identify transshipment, pick-up and delivery locations; cities; bus and train stations; as well as harbors and ports.
3. Approximately ten percent of these locations are major international airports. The balance are municipal and remote airfields and other locations.
4. Locations in the U.S., Canada, and Australia generally have a two-letter state or province notation (e.g., CA for California).
5. Global location codes are added, re-assigned, or deleted at the rate of approximately ten to twelve per month. This list is current as of April 2004.
6. For the most up-to-date information, refer to www.iata.org.

### Abbreviations

AAF ............................ Army Air Field
AFB ............................. Air Force Base
AFS ........................... Air Force Station
AHP ........................... Army Heliport
Arpt ................................... Airport
CGS .................... Coast Guard Station
Cnty.................................... County
Fld .................................... Field
HP ................................. Heliport
HVC ................... Hovercraft Terminal
Int'l ................................ International
Is ...................................... Island
Mt ..................................... Mount
NAS ...................... Naval Air Station
PT ...................................... Point
RR Stn.............Railway Station/Service
RAF .......................... Royal Air Force
SPB ............................ Sea Plane Base
Stn ................................... Station
Svc .................................... Service
USAF ............. United States Air Force

## A

| Code | Airport/location | Country |
|------|------------------|---------|
| AAA | Anaa | F. Polynesia |
| AAB | Arrabury | Australia |
| AAC | Al Arish | Egypt |
| AAD | Ad-Dabbah | Sudan |
| AAE | Annaba | Algeria |
| AAF | Apalachicola Municipal, FL | USA |
| AAG | Arapoti | Brazil |
| AAH | Aachen/Merzbruck | Germany |
| AAI | Arraias | Brazil |
| AAJ | Awaradam/Cayana Arpt | Suriname |
| AAK | Aranulka | Kiribati |
| AAL | Aalborg/Civil/Military | Denmark |
| AAM | Mala Mala | S. Africa |
| AAN | Al Ain Int'l | UAE |
| AAO | Anaco | Venezuela |
| AAP | Houston/Andrau Airpark, TX | USA |
| AAQ | Anaapa | Russia |
| AAR | Aarhus/Tirstrup | Denmark |
| AAS | Apalapsili | Indonesia |
| AAT | Altay | China |
| AAU | Asau | Samoa |
| AAV | Alah | Philippines |
| AAW | Abbottabad | Pakistan |
| AAX | Araxa | Brazil |
| AAY | Al Ghayclah | Yemen |
| AAZ | Quetzaltenanac | Guatemala |
| ABA | Abakan | Russia |
| ABB | Abingdon/RAF | UK |
| ABD | Abadan | Iran |
| ABE | Allentown/Lehigh Int'l, PA | USA |
| ABF | Abaiang | Kiribati |
| ABG | Abingdon | Australia |
| ABH | Alpha | Australia |
| ABI | Abilene Municipal, TX | USA |
| ABJ | Abidjan | Côte D'Ivoire |
| ABK | Kabri Dar | Ethiopia |
| ABL | Ambler, AK | USA |
| ABM | Barnaga | Australia |
| ABN | Alnina | Suriname |
| ABO | Aboisso | Côte D'Ivoire |
| ABP | Atkamba | Papua New Guinea |
| ABQ | Albuquerque Int'l, NM | USA |
| ABR | Aberdeen Municipal, SD | USA |
| ABS | Abu Simbel | Egypt |
| ABT | Al-Baha/Al-Aqiq | Saudi Arabia |
| ABU | Atambua | Indonesia |
| ABV | Abuja Int'l | Nigeria |
| ABW | Abau | Papua New Guinea |
| ABX | Albury | Australia |
| ABY | Albany, GA | USA |
| ABZ | Aberdeen/Dyce | UK |
| ACA | Acapulco/G. Alvarez Int'l | Mexico |
| ACB | Bellaire/Antrim County, MI | USA |
| ACC | Accra/Kotoka | Ghana |
| ACD | Acandi | Colombia |
| ACE | Lanzarote | Spain |
| ACH | Altenirhein | Switzerland |
| ACI | Alderney | UK |
| ACK | Nantucket, MA | USA |
| ACL | Aguaclara | Colombia |
| ACM | Arica | Colombia |
| ACN | Ciudad Acuna Int'l | Mexico |
| ACO | Ascona | Switzerland |
| ACR | Araracuara | Colombia |
| ACS | Achinsk | Russia |
| ACT | Waco, TX | USA |
| ACU | Achutupo | Panama |
| ACV | Arcata, CA | USA |
| ACY | Atlantic City, NJ | USA |
| ADA | Adana/Sakirpasa | Turkey |
| ADB | Izmir/Adnan Menderes | Turkey |
| ADC | Altenburg | Germany |
| ADD | Addis Ababa/Bole | Ethiopia |
| ADE | Aden Int'l | Yemen |
| ADF | Adiyaman/Incirlik | Turkey |
| ADG | Adrian/Lenawee County, MI | USA |
| ADH | Aidan | Russia |
| ADI | Aranclis | Namibia |
| ADJ | Amman/Marka (Civil) | Jordan |
| ADK | Adak Is/NAS, AK | USA |
| ADL | Adelaide | Australia |
| ADM | Ardmore, OK | USA |
| ADN | Andes | Colombia |
| ADO | Andamooka | Australia |
| ADP | Anuradhapura | Sri Lanka |
| ADQ | Kodiak Arpt, AK | USA |
| ADR | Andrews, SC | USA |
| ADS | Dallas, TX | USA |
| ADT | Ada, OK | USA |
| ADU | Arclabil | Iran |
| ADV | Andover | UK |
| ADW | Camp Springs, MD | USA |
| ADX | St Andrews/Leuchars | UK |
| ADY | Alidays | S. Africa |
| ADZ | San Andres Is | Colombia |
| AEA | Abernama Atoll | Kiribati |
| AED | Aleneva, AK | USA |
| AEG | Aek Godang | Indonesia |
| AEH | Abecher | Chad |
| AEK | Aseki | Papua New Guinea |
| AEL | Albert Lea, MN | USA |
| AEO | Aioun El Atrouss | Mauritania |
| AEP | Buenos Aires/Newbery | Argentina |
| AER | Adler/Sochi | Russia |
| AES | Aalesund/Vigra | Norway |
| AET | Allakaket, AK | USA |
| AEX | Alexandria, LA | USA |
| AEY | Akureyri | Iceland |
| AFA | San Rafael | Argentina |
| AFD | Port Alfred | S. Africa |
| AFF | Colorado Springs, USAF Academy, CO | USA |
| AFI | Amalfi | Colombia |
| AFL | Alta Floresta | Brazil |
| AFN | Jaffrey/Municipal, NH | USA |
| AFO | Afton/Municipal, WY | USA |
| AFR | Afore | Papua New Guinea |
| AFT | Afutara/Atutara | Solomon Is |
| AFW | Dallas/Fort Worth, TX | USA |
| AFY | Afyon | Turkey |
| AGA | Agadir/Agadir Almassira | Morocco |
| AGB | Augsburg, Muehlhausen | Germany |
| AGC | Pittsburgh/Allegheny, PA | USA |
| AGD | Anggi | Indonesia |
| AGE | Wangerooge/Fluglplatz | Germany |
| AGF | Agen/La Garenne | France |
| AGG | Angoram | Papua New Guinea |
| AGH | Helsingborg | Sweden |
| AGI | Wageningen | Suriname |
| AGJ | Aguni | Japan |
| AGK | Kagua | Papua New Guinea |
| AGL | Wanigela | Papua New Guinea |
| AGM | Tasiilaq | Greenland |
| AGN | Angoon, AK | USA |
| AGO | Magnolia/Municipal, AK | USA |
| AGP | Malaga | Spain |
| AGQ | Agrinion | Greece |
| AGR | Agra/Kheria | India |
| AGS | Augusta, GA | USA |
| AGT | Ciudad del Este | Paraguay |
| AGU | Aguascalientes | Mexico |
| AGV | Acarigua | Venezuela |
| AGW | Agnew | Australia |
| AGX | Agatti Is | India |
| AGY | Argyle Downs | Australia |
| AGZ | Aggeneys | S. Africa |
| AHA | Okinawa/Naha AFB | Japan |
| AHB | Ablitia | Saudi Arabia |
| AHC | Amedee/AAF, CA | USA |
| AHD | Ardmore/Downtown, OK | USA |
| AHE | Ahe | F. Polynesia |
| AHF | Arapahoe/Municipal, NE | USA |

| Code | Airport | Country |
|------|---------|---------|
| AHH | Amery/Municipal, WI | USA |
| AHI | Amahai | Indonesia |
| AHL | Aishaiton | Guyana |
| AHN | Athens, GA | USA |
| AHO | Alghero | Italy |
| AHS | Ahuas | Honduras |
| AHT | Amchitka, AK | USA |
| AHU | Al Hoceima | Morocco |
| AHY | Ambatolahy | Madagascar |
| AHZ | Alpe D Huez | France |
| AIA | Alliance, NE | USA |
| AIB | Anita Bay, AK | USA |
| AIC | Airok | Marshall Is |
| AID | Anderson/Municipal, IN | USA |
| AIE | Aiome | Papua New Guinea |
| AIF | Assis | Brazil |
| AIG | Yalinga | Central African Rep |
| AII | Alisabieh | Djibouti |
| AIK | Aiken/Municipal, SC | USA |
| AIL | Ailigandi | Panama |
| AIM | Ailuk Is | Marshall Is |
| AIN | Wainwright, AK | USA |
| AIO | Atlantic, IA | USA |
| AIP | Ailinglapalap Is. | Marshall Is |
| AIR | Aripuana | Brazil |
| AIS | Arorae Is | Kiribati |
| AIT | Aitutaki | Cook Is |
| AIU | Atiu Is | Cook Is |
| AIV | Aliceville, AL | USA |
| AIW | Ai-Ais | Namibia |
| AIY | Atlantic City/Bader Field, NJ | USA |
| AIZ | Kaiser/Lake Ozark, MO | USA |
| AJA | Ajaccio/Campo Dell Oro | France |
| AJF | Jouf | Saudi Arabia |
| AJI | Agri/Agri | Turkey |
| AJJ | Akioujt | Mauritania |
| AJL | Aizawl | India |
| AJN | Anjouan/Ouant | Comoros |
| AJO | Aljouf | Yemen |
| AJR | Arvidsiaur | Sweden |
| AJS | Abreojos | Mexico |
| AJU | Aracap | Brazil |
| AJY | Agades/Manu Dayak | Niger |
| AKA | Ankang | China |
| AKB | Atka, AK | USA |
| AKC | Akron/Fulton Int'l, OH | USA |
| AKD | Akola | India |
| AKE | Akieni | Gabon |
| AKF | Kufrah | Libya |
| AKG | Anguganak | Papua New Guinea |
| AKH | Gastonia, NC | USA |
| AKI | Akiak, AK | USA |
| AKJ | Asahikawa/Akhiolk SPB | Japan |
| AKK | Akhiok, AK | USA |
| AKL | Auckland | New Zealand |
| AKM | Zakouma | Chad |
| AKN | King Salmon, AK | USA |
| AKO | Akron, CO | USA |
| AKP | Anaktuvuk, AK | USA |
| AKQ | Astraksetra | Indonesia |
| AKR | Akure | Nigeria |
| AKS | Auki/Gwaunaru'u | Solomon Is |
| AKT | Akrotiri | Cyprus |
| AKU | Aksu | China |
| AKV | Akulivik, QC | Canada |
| AKW | Klawock, AK | USA |
| AKX | Aktyubinsk | Kazakhstan |
| AKY | Sittwe/Civil | Myanmar |
| ALA | Almaty | Kazakhstan |
| ALB | Albany, NY | USA |
| ALC | Alicante | Spain |
| ALD | Alerta | Peru |
| ALE | Alpine, TX | USA |
| ALF | Alta/Lufthavn | Norway |
| ALG | Algiers-Houari Boumediene | Algeria |
| ALH | Albany | Australia |
| ALI | Alice, TX | USA |
| ALJ | Alexander Bay/Koftdoorn | S. Africa |
| ALK | Asela | Ethiopia |
| ALL | Albenga | Italy |
| ALM | Alamogordo, NM | USA |
| ALN | Alton, IL | USA |
| ALO | Waterloo, IA | USA |
| ALP | Aleppo/Nejrab | Syria |
| ALQ | Alegrete/Federal | Brazil |
| ALR | Alexandra | New Zealand |
| ALS | Alamosa, CO | USA |
| ALT | Alenquer | Brazil |
| ALU | Alula | Somalia |
| ALV | Andorra La Vella | Andorra |
| ALW | Walla Walla, WA | USA |
| ALX | Alexander City, AL | USA |
| ALY | Alexandria/Nouzha | Egypt |
| ALZ | Alitak/SPB, AK | USA |
| AMA | Amarillo, TX | USA |
| AMB | Ambilobe | Madagascar |
| AMC | Am Timan | Chad |
| AMD | Ahmadabad | India |
| AME | Alto Molocue | Mozambique |
| AMF | Ama | Papua New Guinea |
| AMG | Amboin | Papua New Guinea |
| AMH | Arba Mintch | Ethiopia |
| AMI | Mataram/Selaparang | Indonesia |
| AMJ | Almenara | Brazil |
| AMK | Durango/Animas Airpark, CO | USA |
| AML | Puerto Armuellas | Panama |
| AMM | Amman/Queen Alia Int'l | Jordan |
| AMN | Alma/Gratiot Com Municipality, MI | USA |
| AMO | Mao | Chad |
| AMP | Ampanihy | Madagascar |
| AMQ | Ambon/Pattimura | Indonesia |
| AMR | Arno | Marshall Is |
| AMS | Amsterdam/Schiphol | Netherlands |
| AMT | Amata | Australia |
| AMU | Amanab | Papua New Guinea |
| AMV | Amderma | Russia |
| AMW | Ames, IA | USA |
| AMX | Ammaroo | Australia |
| AMY | Ambatomainty | Madagascar |
| AMZ | Ardmore | New Zealand |
| ANA | Anaheim, CA | USA |
| ANB | Anniston, AL | USA |
| ANC | Anchorage Int'l, AK | USA |
| AND | Anderson, SC | USA |
| ANE | Angers/Marce | France |
| ANF | Antotagasta/Cerro Moreno | Chile |
| ANG | Angouleme | France |
| ANH | Anuha Is | Solomon Is |
| ANI | Aniak, AK | USA |
| ANJ | Zanaga | Congo, DR |
| ANK | Ankara/Etimesgut | Turkey |
| ANL | Andulo | Angola |
| ANM | Antalaha/Antsirabato | Madagascar |
| ANN | Annette Is, AK | USA |
| ANO | Angoche | Mozambique |
| ANP | Annapolis/Lee, MD | USA |
| ANQ | Angola, IN | USA |
| ANR | Antwerp/Deurne | Belgium |
| ANS | Andahuaylas | Peru |
| ANT | St Anton | Austria |
| ANU | V.C. Bird Int'l | Antigua & Barbuda |
| ANV | Anvik, AK | USA |
| ANW | Ainsworth, NE | USA |
| ANX | Andenes | Norway |
| ANY | Anthony, KS | USA |
| ANZ | Angus Downs | Australia |
| AOA | Aroa | Papua New Guinea |
| AOB | Annanberg | Papua New Guinea |
| AOD | Abou Deia | Chad |
| AOE | Eskisehir/Anadolu Univ. | Turkey |
| AOG | Anshan | China |
| AOH | Lima, OH | USA |
| AOI | Ancona/Falconara | Italy |
| AOJ | Aomori | Japan |
| AOK | Karpathos | Greece |
| AOL | Paso De Los Libres | Argentina |
| AON | Arona | Papua New Guinea |
| AOO | Altoona, PA | USA |
| AOR | Mor Setar | Malaysia |
| AOS | Amook, AK | USA |
| AOT | Aosta/Corrado Gex | Italy |
| AOU | Attopeu | Laos |
| APA | Denver, CO | USA |
| APB | Apolo | Bolivia |
| APC | Napa, CA | USA |
| APE | San Juan Aposento | Peru |
| APF | Naples, FL | USA |
| APG | Aberdeen, MD | USA |
| APH | Bowling Green, VA | USA |
| API | Apiay | Colombia |
| APK | Apataki | F. Polynesia |
| APL | Nampula | Mozambique |
| APN | Alpena, MI | USA |
| APO | Apartacto | Colombia |
| APP | Asapa | Papua New Guinea |
| APQ | Arapiraca | Brazil |
| APR | April River | Papua New Guinea |
| APS | Anapolis | Brazil |
| APT | Jasper/Marion County, TN | USA |
| APU | Apucarana | Brazil |
| APV | Apple Valley, CA | USA |
| APW | Apia/Faleolo | Samoa |
| APX | Arapongas | Brazil |
| APY | Alto Parnatiba | Brazil |
| APZ | Zapala | Argentina |
| AQA | Araraquara | Brazil |
| AQB | Quiche/Quiche Arpt | Guatemala |
| AQG | Anqing | China |
| AQI | Qaisumah | Saudi Arabia |
| AQJ | Aqaba | Jordan |
| AQM | Ariquemes | Brazil |
| AQP | Arequipa/Rodriguez Ballon | Peru |
| AQQ | Apalachicola, FL | USA |
| AQS | Saqani | Fiji |
| AQY | Alyeska, AK | USA |
| ARA | New Iberia, LA | USA |
| ARB | Ann Arbor, MI | USA |
| ARC | Arctic Village, AK | USA |
| ARD | Alor Is | Indonesia |
| ARE | Arecibo | Puerto Rico |
| ARF | Acaricuara | Colombia |
| ARG | Walnut Ridge, AR | USA |
| ARH | Arkhan,elsk | Russia |
| ARI | Anica/Chacalluta | Chile |
| ARJ | Arso | Indonesia |
| ARK | Arusha | Tanzania |
| ARL | Arty | Burkina Faso |
| ARM | Armidale | Australia |
| ARN | Stockholm/Arlanda | Sweden |
| ARO | Arboletas | Colombia |
| ARP | Aragip | Papua New Guinea |
| ARQ | Arauquita | Colombia |
| ARR | Alto Rio Senguerr | Argentina |
| ARS | Aragarcas | Brazil |
| ART | Watertown, NY | USA |
| ARU | Aracatuba | Brazil |
| ARV | Minocqua, WI | USA |
| ARW | Arad | Romania |
| ARX | Asbury Park, NJ | USA |
| ARY | Ararat | Australia |
| ARZ | N'Zeto | Angola |
| ASA | Assab | Eritrea |
| ASB | Ashgabat | Turkmenistan |
| ASC | Ascension | Bolivia |
| ASD | Andros Town | Bahamas |
| ASE | Aspen, CO | USA |
| ASF | Astrakhan | Russia |
| ASG | Ashburton | New Zealand |
| ASH | Nashua, NH | USA |
| ASI | Georgetown | St. Helena |
| ASJ | Amami O Shima | Japan |
| ASK | Yamoussoukro | Côte D'ivoire |
| ASL | Marshall, TX | USA |
| ASM | Asmara Int'l | Eritrea |
| ASN | Talladega, AL | USA |
| ASO | Asosa | Ethiopia |
| ASP | Alice Springs | Australia |
| ASQ | Austin, NV | USA |
| ASR | Kayseri | Turkey |
| AST | Astoria, OR | USA |
| ASU | Asuncion/Silvio Pettirossi | Paraguay |
| ASV | Amboseli | Kenya |
| ASW | Aswan | Egypt |
| ASX | Ashland, WI | USA |
| ASY | Ashley, ND | USA |
| ASZ | Asirim | Papua New Guinea |
| ATA | Anta | Peru |
| ATB | Atbara | Seychelles |
| ATC | Arthur's Town | Bahamas |
| ATD | Atoifi | Solomon Is |
| ATE | Antlers, OK | USA |
| ATF | Ambato/Chachoan | Ecuador |
| ATG | Attock | Pakistan |
| ATH | Athens-Eleftherios Venizelos | Greece |
| ATI | Artigas | Uruguay |
| ATJ | Antsirabe | Madagascar |
| ATK | Atqasuk, AK | USA |
| ATL | Atlanta/Hartsfield, GA | USA |
| ATM | Altamira | Brazil |
| ATN | Namatanai | Papua New Guinea |
| ATO | Athens/Ohio University, OH | USA |
| ATP | Aitape/Airstrip | Papua New Guinea |
| ATQ | Amritsar/Raja Sansi | India |
| ATR | Atar/Mouakchott | Mauritania |
| ATS | Artesia, NM | USA |
| ATT | Atmautluak, AK | USA |
| ATU | Attu Is/Casco Cove, AK | USA |
| ATV | Ati | Chad |
| ATW | Appleton, WI | USA |
| ATX | Atbasar | Kazakhstan |
| ATY | Watertown, SD | USA |
| ATZ | Assiut | Egypt |

| | | |
|---|---|---|
| **AUA** | Aruba/Reina Beatrix | Aruba |
| **AUB** | Itauba | Brazil |
| **AUC** | Arauca | Colombia |
| **AUD** | Augustus Downs | Australia |
| **AUE** | Abu Rudeis | Egypt |
| **AUF** | Auxerre/Auxerre Branches | France |
| **AUG** | Augusta, ME | USA |
| **AUH** | Abu Dhabi Int'l | UAE |
| **AUI** | Aua Is | Papua New Guinea |
| **AUJ** | Ambunti | Papua New Guinea |
| **AUK** | Alakanuk, AK | USA |
| **AUL** | Aur Is | Marshall Is |
| **AUM** | Austin, MN | USA |
| **AUN** | Auburn, CA | USA |
| **AUO** | Auburn, AL | USA |
| **AUP** | Agaun | Papua New Guinea |
| **AUQ** | Atuona | F. Polynesia |
| **AUR** | Aurillac | France |
| **AUS** | Austin, TX | USA |
| **AUT** | Atauro | Indonesia |
| **AUU** | Aurukun Mission | Australia |
| **AUV** | Aumo | Papua New Guinea |
| **AUW** | Wausau, WI | USA |
| **AUX** | Araguaina | Brazil |
| **AUY** | Aneityum | Vanuatu |
| **AUZ** | Aurora/Municipal, IL | USA |
| **AVB** | Aviano | Italy |
| **AVF** | Avoriaz | France |
| **AVG** | Auvergne | Australia |
| **AVI** | Ciego De Avila | Cuba |
| **AVK** | Arvaikheer | Mongolia |
| **AVL** | Asheville/Municipal, NC | USA |
| **AVN** | Avignon/Avignon-Caum | France |
| **AVO** | Avon Park/Municipal, FL | USA |
| **AVP** | Scranton, OH | USA |
| **AVU** | Avu Avu | Solomon Is |
| **AVV** | Avalon | Australia |
| **AVW** | Tucson/Avra Valley, AZ | USA |
| **AVX** | Avalon, CA | USA |
| **AWA** | Awassa | Ethiopia |
| **AWB** | Awaba | Papua New Guinea |
| **AWD** | Aniwa | Vanuatu |
| **AWE** | Alowe | Gabon |
| **AWG** | Washington, IA | USA |
| **AWH** | Awareh | Ethiopia |
| **AWI** | Wainwright, AK | USA |
| **AWK** | Wake Is | Wake/Midway Is |
| **AWM** | W Memphis/Municipal, AR | USA |
| **AWN** | Afton Downs | Australia |
| **AWO** | Arlington, WA | USA |
| **AWP** | Austral Downs | Australia |
| **AWR** | Awar | Papua New Guinea |
| **AWZ** | Ahwaz | Iran |
| **AXA** | Anguilla/Wallblake | Anguilla |
| **AXB** | Alexandria Bay, NY | USA |
| **AXC** | Aramac | Australia |
| **AXD** | Alexandroupolis-Demokritos | Greece |
| **AXE** | Xanxere | Brazil |
| **AXG** | Algona, IA | USA |
| **AXK** | Ataq | Yemen |
| **AXL** | Alexandria | Australia |
| **AXM** | Armenia/El Eden | Colombia |
| **AXN** | Alexandria, MN | USA |
| **AXP** | Spring Point | Bahamas |
| **AXR** | Arutua | F. Polynesia |
| **AXS** | Altus/Municipal, OK | USA |
| **AXT** | Akita | Japan |
| **AXU** | Axum | Ethiopia |
| **AXV** | Wapakoneta/Armstrong, OH | USA |
| **AXX** | Angel Fire, NM | USA |
| **AYA** | Ayapel | Colombia |
| **AYC** | Ayacucho | Colombia |
| **AYD** | Alroy Downs | Australia |
| **AYE** | Fort Devens, MA | USA |
| **AYG** | Yaguara | Colombia |
| **AYH** | Alconbury/RAF | UK |
| **AYI** | Yan | Colombia |
| **AYK** | Arkalyk | Kazakstan |
| **AYL** | Anthony Lagoon | Australia |
| **AYN** | Anyang | China |
| **AYO** | Ayoias | Paraguay |
| **AYP** | Ayacucho/Yanamilla | Peru |
| **AYQ** | Ayers Rock/COnnellan | Australia |
| **AYR** | Ayr | Australia |
| **AYS** | Waycross/Ware County, GA | USA |
| **AYT** | Antalya | Turkey |
| **AYU** | Aiyura | Papua New Guinea |
| **AYW** | Ayawasi | Indonesia |
| **AYZ** | Amityville/Zahns, NY | USA |
| **AZB** | Amazon Bay | Papua New Guinea |
| **AZD** | Yazd | Iran |
| **AZG** | Apatzingan | Mexico |
| **AZI** | Abu Dhalbi/Bateen | UAE |
| **AZN** | Andizhan | Uzbekistan |
| **AZO** | Kalamazoo, MI | USA |
| **AZP** | Mexico City/Atizapan | Mexico |
| **AZR** | Adrar | Algeria |
| **AZT** | Zapatoca | Colombia |
| **AZZ** | Ambriz | Andorra |

# B

| | | |
|---|---|---|
| **BAA** | Bialla | Papua New Guinea |
| **BAB** | Beale/AFB, CA | USA |
| **BAC** | Barranca De Upia | Colombia |
| **BAD** | Barksdale/AFB, LA | USA |
| **BAE** | Barcelonnette | France |
| **BAF** | Westfield/Barnes, MA | USA |
| **BAG** | Baguic,/Loakan | Philippines |
| **BAH** | Bahrain/Int'l | Bahrain |
| **BAI** | Buenos Aires | Costa Rica |
| **BAJ** | Bali | Papua New Guinea |
| **BAK** | Baku | Azerbaijan |
| **BAL** | Batman | Turkey |
| **BAM** | Battle Mountain, NV | USA |
| **BAN** | Basongo | Congo, DR |
| **BAO** | Ban Mak Khaen/Udorn | Thailand |
| **BAP** | Baibara | Papua New Guinea |
| **BAQ** | Barranquilla/E Cortissoz | Colombia |
| **BAR** | Baker/AAF, AK | USA |
| **BAS** | Balalae | Solomon Is |
| **BAT** | Barretos | Brazil |
| **BAU** | Bauru | Brazil |
| **BAV** | Baotou | China |
| **BAW** | Biawonque | Gabon |
| **BAX** | Barnaul | Russia |
| **BAY** | Baia Mare | Romania |
| **BAZ** | Barbelos | Brazil |
| **BBA** | Balmaceda/Teniente Vicial | Chile |
| **BBB** | Benson/Municipal, MN | USA |
| **BBC** | Bay City, TX | USA |
| **BBD** | Brady/Curtis Fld, TX | USA |
| **BBE** | Big Bell | Australia |
| **BBF** | Burlington, MA | USA |
| **BBG** | Butaritari | kiribati |
| **BBH** | Barth | Germany |
| **BBI** | Bhubaneswar | India |
| **BBJ** | Bitiburg Air Base | Germany |
| **BBK** | Kasane | Botswana |
| **BBL** | Babolsar | Iran |
| **BBM** | Battambang | Cambodia |
| **BBN** | Bario | Malaysia |
| **BBO** | Berbera | Somalia |
| **BBP** | Bembridge | UK |
| **BBQ** | Barbuda | Antigua & Barbuda |
| **BBR** | Basse Terre/Baillif | Gaudeloupe |
| **BBS** | Blackbushe | UK |
| **BBT** | Berberati | Central African Rep |
| **BBU** | Bucharest/Baneasa | Romania |
| **BBV** | Bereby | Côte D'Ivoire |
| **BBW** | Broken Bow Municipal, NE | USA |
| **BBX** | Blue Bell/Wings Fld, PA | USA |
| **BBY** | Bambari | Central African Rep |
| **BBZ** | Zambezi | Zambia |
| **BCA** | Baracoa | Cuba |
| **BCB** | Virginia Tech Arpt, VA | USA |
| **BCC** | Bear Creek, AK | USA |
| **BCD** | Bacolod | Philippines |
| **BCE** | Bryce Canyon, UT | USA |
| **BCF** | Bouca | Central African Rep |
| **BCG** | Bemichi | Guyana |
| **BCH** | Baucau/English Madeira | Indonesia |
| **BCI** | Barcaidine | Australia |
| **BCJ** | Baca Grande, CO | USA |
| **BCK** | Bolwarra | Australia |
| **BCL** | Barra Colorado | Costa Rica |
| **BCM** | Bacau | Romania |
| **BCN** | Barcelona | Spain |
| **BCO** | Jinka | Ethiopia |
| **BCP** | Bambu | Papua New Guinea |
| **BCQ** | Brack | Libya |
| **BCR** | Boca Do Acre | Brazil |
| **BCS** | Belle Chasse/Southern Seaplane, LA | USA |
| **BCT** | Boca Raton/Public, FL | USA |
| **BCU** | Bauchi | Nigeria |
| **BCV** | Belmopan | Belize |
| **BCW** | Benguera Is | Mozambique |
| **BCX** | Beloreck | Russia |
| **BCY** | Buichi | Ethiopia |
| **BCZ** | Bickerton Is | Australia |
| **BDA** | Hamilton/Int'l | Bermuda |
| **BDB** | Bundaberg | Australia |
| **BDC** | Barra Do COrda | Brazil |
| **BDD** | Badu Is | Australia |
| **BDE** | Baudette/Int'l, MN | USA |
| **BDF** | Bradford/Rinkenberg, IL | USA |
| **BDG** | Blanding, UT | USA |
| **BDH** | Bandar Lengeh | Iran |
| **BDI** | Bird Is | Seychelles |
| **BDJ** | Banjarmasin/Sjamsudin Noor | Indonesia |
| **BDK** | Bondaukou/Soko | Côte D'Ivoire |
| **BDL** | Hartford/Bradley Int'l, CT | USA |
| **BDM** | Bandirma | Turkey |
| **BDN** | Badin/Talhar | Pakistan |
| **BDO** | Bandung/Husein Sastranegara | Indonesia |
| **BDP** | Elhadrapur | Nepal |
| **BDQ** | Vadodara | India |
| **BDR** | Bridgeport/Sikorsky Memorial, CT | USA |
| **BDS** | Brindisi/Papola Casale | Italy |
| **BDT** | Gbadolite | Congo, DR |
| **BDU** | Bardufoss | Norway |
| **BDV** | Moba | Congo, DR |
| **BDW** | Bedford Downs | Australia |
| **BDX** | Broadus, MT | USA |
| **BDY** | Bandon/State, OR | USA |
| **BDZ** | Baindoung | Papua New Guinea |
| **BEA** | Bereina | Papua New Guinea |
| **BEB** | Benbecula | UK |
| **BEC** | Wichita, KS | USA |
| **BED** | Bedford/Hanscom Fld, MA | USA |
| **BEE** | Beagle Bay | Australia |
| **BEF** | Bluefields | Netherlands |
| **BEG** | Belgrade/Becigrad | Yugoslavia |
| **BEH** | Benton Harbor/Ross Fld, MI | USA |
| **BEI** | Beica | Ethiopia |
| **BEJ** | Berau | Indonesia |
| **BEK** | careh | India |
| **BEL** | Belem/Val De Cans | Brazil |
| **BEN** | Benghazi/Benina Intl | Libya |
| **BEO** | Newcastle/Belmont | Australia |
| **BEP** | Beliary | India |
| **BEQ** | Bury St Edmunds/Honington | UK |
| **BES** | Brest/Guipavas | France |
| **BET** | Bethel, AK | USA |
| **BEU** | Bedourie | Australia |
| **BEV** | Beer Sheba | Israel |
| **BEW** | Beira | Mozambique |
| **BEX** | Benson/RAF | UK |
| **BEY** | Beirut/Int'l | Lebanon |
| **BEZ** | Beru | Kiribati |
| **BFB** | Blue Fox Bay, AK | USA |
| **BFC** | Bloomfield | Australia |
| **BFD** | Bradford, PA | USA |
| **BFE** | Bielefeid | Germany |
| **BFF** | Scottsbluff, Heilig Fld, NE | USA |
| **BFG** | Bullfrog Basin, UT | USA |
| **BFH** | Curitiba./Bacacher; | Brazil |
| **BFI** | Seattle, Boeing Fld, WA | USA |
| **BFJ** | Ba | Fiji |
| **BFK** | Denver/Buckley ANGB, CO | USA |
| **BFL** | Bakersfield/Meadows Fld, CA | USA |
| **BFM** | Mobile/Dwntwn Arpt, AL | USA |
| **BFN** | Bloemfontein Int'l | South Africa |
| **BFO** | Buffalo Range | Zimbabwe |
| **BFP** | Beaver Falls Arpt, PA | USA |
| **BFQ** | Bahia Pinas | Panama |
| **BFR** | Bedford, IN | USA |
| **BFS** | Belfast/Belfast Int'l Arpt | UK |
| **BFT** | Beaufort/County, SC | USA |
| **BFU** | Bengbu | China |
| **BFV** | Buri Ram | Thailand |
| **BFW** | Silver Bay, MN | USA |
| **BFX** | Bafoussam | Cameroon |
| **BFZ** | Bedford/Thurleigh (Military) | UK |
| **BGA** | Bucaramanga/Palo Negro | Colombia |
| **BGB** | Booue | Gabon |
| **BGC** | Braganca | Portugal |
| **BGD** | Hutchinson County Arpt, TX | USA |
| **BGE** | Bainbridge/Decatur County, GA | USA |
| **BGF** | Bangui | Central African Rep |
| **BGG** | Bongouanou | Chile |
| **BGH** | Boghe/Abbaye | Mauritania |
| **BGI** | Bridgetown/Grantley Adams Int'l | Barbados |
| **BGJ** | Borgarfiordur Eystri | Iceland |

| Code | Airport | Country |
|---|---|---|
| **BGK** | Big Creek | Belize |
| **BGL** | Baglung | Nepal |
| **BGM** | Binghamton, NY | USA |
| **BGN** | Brueggen/R.A.F. | Germany |
| **BGO** | Bergen/Flesland | Norway |
| **BGP** | Bongo | Gabon |
| **BGQ** | Big Lake, AK | USA |
| **BGR** | Bangor Int'l Arpt, ME | USA |
| **BGS** | Big Spring, Webb/AFB, TX | USA |
| **BGT** | Bagdad, AZ | USA |
| **BGU** | Bangassou | Central African Rep |
| **BGV** | Bento Goncalves | Brazil |
| **BGW** | Baghdad/Al Muthana | Iraq |
| **BGX** | Bage | Brazil |
| **BGY** | Milan/Milano/Ono Al Serio | Italy |
| **BGZ** | Braga | Portugal |
| **BHA** | Bahia De Caraquez | Ecuador |
| **BHB** | Bar Harbour, ME | USA |
| **BHC** | Bhurban/Bhurban HP | Pakistan |
| **BHD** | Belfast/Belfast City Arpt | UK |
| **BHE** | Blenheim | New Zealand |
| **BHF** | Bahia Cupica | Cocos (Keeling) Is |
| **BHG** | Brus Laguna | Honduras |
| **BHH** | Bisha | Saudi Arabia |
| **BHI** | Bahia Blanca/Comandante | Argentina |
| **BHJ** | Bhuj/Rudra Mata | India |
| **BHK** | Bukhara | Uzbekistan |
| **BHL** | Bahla Angeles | Mexico |
| **BHM** | Birmingham/Int'l, AL | USA |
| **BHN** | Beinan | Yemen |
| **BHO** | Bhopal | India |
| **BHP** | Bhojpur | Nepal |
| **BHQ** | Broken Hill | Australia |
| **BHR** | Bharatpur | Nepal |
| **BHS** | Bathurst/Raglan | Australia |
| **BHT** | Brighton Downs | Australia |
| **BHU** | Bhavnagar | India |
| **BHV** | Bahawaipur | Pakistan |
| **BHW** | Sargodha/Bhagatanwala | Pakistan |
| **BHX** | Birmingham/Int'l | UK |
| **BHY** | Beil-tai | China |
| **BIA** | Bastia/Poretta | France |
| **BIB** | Baidoa | Somalia |
| **BIC** | Big Creek, AK | USA |
| **BID** | Block Is, RI | USA |
| **BIE** | Beatrice, NE | USA |
| **BIF** | Biggs/AAF, TX | USA |
| **BIG** | Big Delta/Intermediate Fld, AK | USA |
| **BIH** | Bishop, CA | USA |
| **BII** | Bikini Atoll/Enyu Airfield | Marshall Is |
| **BIJ** | Biliau | Papua New Guinea |
| **BIK** | Biak/Mokmer | Indonesia |
| **BIL** | Billings/Int'l, MT | USA |
| **BIM** | Bimini/Int'l | Bahamas |
| **BIN** | Bamiyan | Afghanistan |
| **BIO** | Bilbao | Spain |
| **BIP** | Bulimba | Australia |
| **BIQ** | Biarritz/Biarritz Parme | France |
| **BIR** | Biratnagar | Nepal |
| **BIS** | Bismarck, ND | USA |
| **BIT** | Baitadi | Nepal |
| **BIU** | Bildudalur | Iceland |
| **BIV** | Bria | Costa Rica |
| **BIW** | Billiluna | Australia |
| **BIX** | Keesler/AFB, MS | USA |
| **BIY** | Bisho | South Africa |
| **BIZ** | Bimin | Papua New Guinea |
| **BJA** | Bejaia | Algeria |
| **BJB** | Bopord | Iran |
| **BJC** | Broomfield/Jeffco, CO | USA |
| **BJD** | Bakkafjordur | Iceland |
| **BJF** | Batsfjord | Norway |
| **BJG** | Bolaang | Indonesia |
| **BJH** | Bajhang | Nepal |
| **BJI** | Bemidji, MN | USA |
| **BJJ** | Wooster/Wayne Cnty. Arpt, OH | USA |
| **BJK** | Berijina | Indonesia |
| **BJL** | Banjul/Yundum Int'l | The Gambia |
| **BJM** | Bujumbura/Int'l | Burundi |
| **BJN** | Bajone | Mozambique |
| **BJO** | Bermejo | Bolivia |
| **BJP** | Braganca Paulista | Brazil |
| **BJR** | Bahar Dar | Ethiopia |
| **BJU** | Bajura Arpt | Nepal |
| **BJV** | Bodrum./Milas Arpt | Turkey |
| **BJW** | Bajawa | Indonesia |
| **BJX** | Lecin/Guanajuato/Del Bajic | Mexico |
| **BJY** | Belgrade/Batapica | Yugoslavia |
| **BJZ** | Baclajoz/Talaveral La Real | Spain |
| **BKA** | Moscow/Bykovo | Russia |
| **BKB** | Bikaner | India |
| **BKC** | Buckland, AK | USA |
| **BKD** | Breckenridge/Stephens Cnty., TX | USA |
| **BKE** | Baker/Baker Mncpl Arpt, OR, | USA |
| **BKF** | Brooks Lake, AK | USA |
| **BKH** | Kekaha/Barking Sands, HI | USA |
| **BKI** | Kota Kinabalu | Malaysia |
| **BKJ** | Boke | Guinea |
| **BKK** | Bangkok/Int'l | Thailand |
| **BKL** | Cleveland, Burke Arpt, OH | USA |
| **BKM** | Bakalalan | Malaysia |
| **BKN** | Birni Nkoni | Niger |
| **BKO** | Bamako | Mali |
| **BKP** | Barkly Downs | Australia |
| **BKQ** | Blackall | Australia |
| **BKR** | Bokoro | Chad |
| **BKS** | Bengkulu/Padangkemiling | Indonesia |
| **BKT** | Blackstone/AAF, VA | USA |
| **BKU** | Betioky | Madagascar |
| **BKV** | Brooksville, FL | USA |
| **BKW** | Beckley, WV | USA |
| **BKX** | Brookings, SD | USA |
| **BKY** | Bukavu/Kamenbe | Congo, DR |
| **BKZ** | Bukoba | Tanzania |
| **BLA** | Barcelona | Venezuela |
| **BLB** | Balboa | Panama |
| **BLC** | Bali | Cameroon |
| **BLD** | Boulder City, CO | USA |
| **BLE** | Boriange/Dala | Sweden |
| **BLF** | Bluefield, Mercer County Arpt, WV | USA |
| **BLG** | Belaga | Malaysia |
| **BLH** | Blythe Arpt, CA | USA |
| **BLI** | Bellingham/Int'l Arpt, WA | USA |
| **BLJ** | Batna | Algeria |
| **BLK** | Blackpool | UK |
| **BLL** | Billund/Lufthavn | Denmark |
| **BLM** | Belmar-Farmdale, NJ | USA |
| **BLN** | Benalla | Australia |
| **BLO** | Blonduos | Iceland |
| **BLP** | Bellavista | Peru |
| **BLQ** | Bologna/Guglielmo Marconi | Italy |
| **BLR** | Bangalore,/Hindustan | India |
| **BLS** | Bollon | Australia |
| **BLT** | Blackwater | Australia |
| **BLU** | Blue Canyon, CA | USA |
| **BLV** | Scott/AFB, IL | USA |
| **BLW** | Waimanalo/Bellows Fld, HI | USA |
| **BLX** | Belluno | Italy |
| **BLY** | Belmullet | Ireland |
| **BLZ** | Blantyre/Chileka | Malawi |
| **BMA** | Stockholm/Bromma | Sweden |
| **BMB** | Bumba | Congo, DR |
| **BMC** | Brigham City, UT | USA |
| **BMD** | Belo | Madagascar |
| **BME** | Broome | Australia |
| **BMF** | Bakourna | Central African Rep |
| **BMG** | Bloomington, IN | USA |
| **BMH** | Bomai | Papua New Guinea |
| **BMI** | Bloomington/Normal, IL | USA |
| **BMJ** | Baramita | Guyana |
| **BMK** | Borkum | Germany |
| **BML** | Berlin Municipal Arpt, NH | USA |
| **BMM** | Bitam | Gabon |
| **BMN** | Bamerny | Iraq |
| **BMO** | Bhamo | Myanmar |
| **BMP** | Brampton Is | Australia |
| **BMQ** | Bamburi | Kenya |
| **BMR** | Baitrum | Germany |
| **BMS** | Brumado | Brazil |
| **BMT** | Beaumont/Municipal, TX | USA |
| **BMU** | Bima | Indonesia |
| **BMV** | Banmethuot/Phung-Duc | Vietnam |
| **BMW** | Bordj Badji Mokintar | Algeria |
| **BMX** | Big Mountain, AK | USA |
| **BMY** | Belep Is | New Caledonia |
| **BMZ** | Bamu | Papua New Guinea |
| **BNA** | Nashville/Int'l, TN | USA |
| **BNB** | Boende | Congo, DR |
| **BNC** | Beni | Congo, DR |
| **BND** | Bandar Abbas | Iran |
| **BNE** | Brisbane/Int'l | Australia |
| **BNF** | Warm Spring Bay/SPB, AK | USA |
| **BNG** | Banning, CA | USA |
| **BNH** | Hartford/Barnes, CT | USA |
| **BNI** | Benin City | Nigeria |
| **BNJ** | Cologne/Bann/Off-line Pt. | Germany |
| **BNK** | Ballina | Australia |
| **BNL** | Barnwell, SC | USA |
| **BNM** | Bodinumu | Papua New Guinea |
| **BNN** | Bronnoysund/Bronnoy | Norway |
| **BNO** | Burns Municipal Arpt, OR | USA |
| **BNP** | Bannu | Pakistan |
| **BNQ** | Baganga | Philippines |
| **BNR** | Banfora | Burkina Faso |
| **BNS** | Barinas | Venezuela |
| **BNT** | Bundi | Papua New Guinea |
| **BNU** | Biumenau | Brazil |
| **BNV** | Boana | Papua New Guinea |
| **BNW** | Boone Municipal, IA | USA |
| **BNX** | Banja Luka | Bosnia Hercegovina |
| **BNY** | Bellona | Solomon Is |
| **BNZ** | Banz | Papua New Guinea |
| **BOA** | Boma | Congo, DR |
| **BOB** | Bora Bora/Motu-mute | F. Polynesia |
| **BOC** | Bocas Del Tore, | Panama |
| **BOD** | Bordeaux/Merignac | France |
| **BOE** | Boundji | Congo, DR |
| **BOF** | Bolling/AFB, DC | USA |
| **BOG** | Bogota/Eldorado | Colombia |
| **BOH** | Bournemouth/Int'l | UK |
| **BOI** | Boise, Boise Air Terminal, ID | USA |
| **BOJ** | Bourgas | Bulgaria |
| **BOK** | Brookings, OR | USA |
| **BOL** | Bally Kelly | UK |
| **BOM** | Mumbai | India |
| **BON** | Bonaire/Int'l | Netherlands Antilles |
| **BOO** | Bodo | Norway |
| **BOP** | Bouar | Central African Rep |
| **BOQ** | Boku | Papua New Guinea |
| **BOR** | Belfort/Fontaine | France |
| **BOS** | Boston/Logan Int'l, MA | USA |
| **BOT** | Boset | Papua New Guinea |
| **BOU** | Bourges | France |
| **BOV** | Boang | Papua New Guinea |
| **BOW** | Bartow Municipal, FL | USA |
| **BOX** | Borroloola | Australia |
| **BOY** | Bobo Dioulasso/Borgo | Burkina Faso |
| **BOZ** | Bozoum | Central African Rep |
| **BPA** | Bethpage/Grumman, NY | USA |
| **BPB** | Boridi | Papua New Guinea |
| **BPC** | Bamenda | Cameroon |
| **BPD** | Bapi | Papua New Guinea |
| **BPE** | Bagan | Myanmar |
| **BPF** | Batuna Aerodrome | Solomon Is |
| **BPG** | Barra Do Garcas | Brazil |
| **BPH** | Bislig | Philippines |
| **BPI** | Big Piney, WY | USA |
| **BPK** | Mountain Home, AR | USA |
| **BPN** | Balikipapan/Sepingan | Indonesia |
| **BPS** | Porto Seguro | Brazil |
| **BPT** | Beaumont, TX | USA |
| **BPU** | Beppu | Japan |
| **BPX** | Bangda | China |
| **BPY** | Besalampy | Madagascar |
| **BQA** | Baler | Philippines |
| **BQB** | Bussellton/Bussellton Arpt | Australia |
| **BQE** | Bubaque | Guinea Bissau |
| **BQH** | London/Biggin Hill | UK |
| **BQI** | Bagani | Namibia |
| **BQK** | Brunswick/Glynco, GA | USA |
| **BQL** | Boulia | Australia |
| **BQN** | Aguadilla/Borinquen | Puerto Rico |
| **BQO** | Bouna/Tehini | Côte D'Ivoire |
| **BQQ** | Barra | Brazil |
| **BQS** | Blagoveschensk | Russia |
| **BQT** | Brest | Belarus |
| **BQU** | Bequia | St. Vincent & Grenadines |
| **BQV** | Gustavus/Bartlett SPB, AK | USA |
| **BQW** | Balgo Hills | Australia |
| **BRA** | Barreiras | Brazil |
| **BRB** | Barreirinhas | Brazil |
| **BRC** | San Carlos DeBariloche | Argentina |
| **BRD** | Brainerd, MN | USA |
| **BRE** | Bremen | Germany |
| **BRF** | Bradford | UK |
| **BRG** | Whitesburg/Municipal, KY | USA |
| **BRH** | Brahman | Papua New Guinea |
| **BRI** | Bari/Palese Macchie | Italy |
| **BRJ** | Bright | Australia |
| **BRK** | Bourke | Australia |
| **BRL** | Burlington, IA | USA |
| **BRM** | Barquisimeto | Venezuela |
| **BRN** | Berne/Belp | Switzerland |
| **BRO** | Brownsville/Int'l, TX | USA |
| **BRP** | Biaru | Papua New Guinea |
| **BRQ** | Brno/Turany | Czech Rep |
| **BRR** | Barra/North Bay | UK |
| **BRS** | Bristol/Lulsgate | UK |
| **BRT** | Bathurst Is | Australia |
| **BRU** | Brussels/National | Belgium |

| | | |
|---|---|---|
| BRV | Bremerhaven | Germany |
| BRW | Barrow/Metro., AK | USA |
| BRX | Barahona | Dominican Rep |
| BRY | Bardstown/Samuels Fld, KY | USA |
| BRZ | Borotou | Côte D'Ivoire |
| BSA | Bossaso | Somalia |
| BSB | Brasilia/Int'l | Brazil |
| BSC | Bahia Solano | Colombia |
| BSD | Baoshan | China |
| BSE | Sematan | Malaysia |
| BSF | Bradshaw/AAF, HI | USA |
| BSG | Bata | Equatorial Guinea |
| BSH | Brighton | UK |
| BSI | Blairsville, PA | USA |
| BSJ | Bairnsdale | Australia |
| BSK | Biskra | Algeria |
| BSL | Basel/Mulhouse | Switzerland |
| BSN | Bossangoa | Central African Rep |
| BSO | Basco | Philippines |
| BSP | Bensbach | Papua New Guinea |
| BSQ | Bisbee/Municipal, AZ | USA |
| BSR | Basra/Int'l | Iraq |
| BSS | Balsas | Brazil |
| BST | Bost | Afghanistan |
| BSU | Basankusu | Congo, DR |
| BSV | Besakoa | Madagascar |
| BSW | Boswell Bay, AK | USA |
| BSX | Bassein | Myanmar |
| BSY | Bardera | Somalia |
| BSZ | Bartletts, AK | USA |
| BTA | Bertoua | Cameroon |
| BTB | Betou | Congo, DR |
| BTC | Batticaloa | Sri Lanka |
| BTD | Brunette Downs | Australia |
| BTE | Bonthe | Sierra Leone |
| BTF | Bountiful, UT | USA |
| BTG | Batangafo | Central African Rep |
| BTH | Batam/HaNadirr, | Indonesia |
| BTI | Barter Is, AK | USA |
| BTJ | Banda Aceh/Blang Bintang | Indonesia |
| BTK | Bratsk | Russia |
| BTL | Battle Creek/Kellogg, MI | USA |
| BTM | Butte, Mooney Arpt, MT | USA |
| BTN | Bennettsville, SC | USA |
| BTO | Botopasie | Suriname |
| BTP | Butler/Graham Fld, PA | USA |
| BTQ | Butare | Rwanda |
| BTR | Baton Rouge/Ryan Fld, LA | USA |
| BTS | Bratislava/Ivanka | Slovakia |
| BTT | Bettles Arpt, AK | USA |
| BTU | Bintulu | Malaysia |
| BTV | Burlington/Int'l, VT | USA |
| BTW | BaLicin | Indonesia |
| BTX | Betoota | Australia |
| BTY | Beatty, NV | USA |
| BTZ | Bursa | Turkey |
| BUA | Buka | Papua New Guinea |
| BUB | Burwell/Municipal, NE | USA |
| BUC | Burketown | Australia |
| BUD | Budapest/Ferihegy | Hungary |
| BUF | Buffalo Int'l Arpt, NY | USA |
| BUG | Benguela/GV Deslandes | Angola |
| BUI | Bokondini | Indonesia |
| BUJ | Boussaada | Algeria |
| BUK | Albuq | Yemen |
| BUL | Bulolo | Papua New Guinea |
| BUM | Butler, MO | USA |
| BUN | Buenaventura | Colombia |
| BUO | Burao | Somalia |
| BUP | Bhatinda | India |
| BUQ | Bulawayo | Zimbabwe |
| BUR | Burbank, CA | USA |
| BUS | Batumi | Georgia |
| BUT | Burtonwood | UK |
| BUU | Buyo | Côte D'Ivoire |
| BUV | Bella Union | Uruguay |
| BUW | Baubau/Beto Ambiri | Indonesia |
| BUY | Bunbury | Australia |
| BUZ | Bushehr | Iran |
| BVA | Beauvais | France |
| BVB | Boa Vista | Brazil |
| BVC | Boa Vista/Rabil | Cape Verde Is |
| BVD | Beaver Inlet/Sea Port, AK | USA |
| BVE | Brive-La-Gaillarde/Laroche | France |
| BVF | Bua/Dama | Fiji |
| BVG | Berlevag | Norway |
| BVH | Vilhena | Brazil |
| BVI | Birdsville | Australia |
| BVK | Huacaraje | Bolivia |
| BVL | Baures | Bolivia |

| | | |
|---|---|---|
| BVM | Belmonte | Brazil |
| BVO | Bartlesville, OK | USA |
| BVP | Bolovip | Papua New Guinea |
| BVR | Brava | Cape Verde Is |
| BVS | Breves | Brazil |
| BVU | Beluga, AK | USA |
| BVW | Batavia Downs | Australia |
| BVX | Batesvilie/Municipal | Australia |
| BVY | Beverly, MA | USA |
| BVZ | Beverley Springs | Australia |
| BWA | Bhairawa | Nepal |
| BWB | Barrow Is | Australia |
| BWC | Brawley, CA | USA |
| BWD | Brownwood, TX | USA |
| BWE | Braunschweig | Germany |
| BWF | Barrow-In-Furness/Walney Isl | UK |
| BWG | Bowling Green, KY | USA |
| BWH | Butterworth | Malaysia |
| BWI | Baltimore, MD | USA |
| BWJ | Bawan | Papua New Guinea |
| BWK | Bol | Croatia |
| BWL | Backwell, OK | USA |
| BWM | Bowman, ND | USA |
| BWN | Bandar Seri Begawan | Brunei |
| BWO | Balakovo | Russia |
| BWP | Bewani | Papua New Guinea |
| BWQ | Brewarrina | Australia |
| BWS | Blaine, WA | USA |
| BWT | Burnie/Burnie Wynyard | Australia |
| BWU | Bankstown | Australia |
| BWY | Woodbridge | UK |
| BXA | Bogalusa/George R Carr, LA | USA |
| BXB | Babo | Indonesia |
| BXC | Boxborough, MA | USA |
| BXD | Bade | Indonesia |
| BXE | Bakel | Senegal |
| BXH | Balhash | Kazakstan |
| BXI | Boundiali | Côte D'Ivoire |
| BXJ | Burundai | Kazakstan |
| BXK | Buckeye, AZ | USA |
| BXL | Blue Lagoon | Fiji |
| BXM | Batom | Indonesia |
| BXN | Bodrum/Imisk Arpt | Turkey |
| BXR | Barn | Iran |
| BXS | Borrego Springs, CA | USA |
| BXT | Bontang | Indonesia |
| BXU | Butuan | Philippines |
| BXV | Breiddalsvilk | Iceland |
| BXX | Borama | Somalia |
| BXZ | Bunsil | Papua New Guinea |
| BYA | Boundary, AK | USA |
| BYB | Dibaa | Oman |
| BYC | Yacuiba | Bolivia |
| BYD | Beidah | Yemen |
| BYG | Buffalo, WY | USA |
| BYH | Blytheville/AFB, AR | USA |
| BYI | Burley, ID | USA |
| BYK | Bouake | Côte D'Ivoire |
| BYL | Bella Yeila | Liberia |
| BYM | Bayamo/C.M. de Cespedes | Cuba |
| BYN | Bayankhongor | Mongolia |
| BYQ | Bunyu | Indonesia |
| BYR | Laeso Is Arpt | Denmark |
| BYS | Fort Irwin/AAF, CA | USA |
| BYT | Bantry | Ireland |
| BYU | Bayreuth | Germany |
| BYW | Blakely Is, WA | USA |
| BYX | Baniyala | Australia |
| BZA | Bonanza/San Pedro | Netherlands |
| BZB | Bazaruto Is | Mozambique |
| BZC | Buzios | Brazil |
| BZD | Balranald | Australia |
| BZE | Belize City/Goldson Int'l | Belize |
| BZG | Bydgoszcz | Poland |
| BZH | Bumi Hills | Zimbabwe |
| BZI | Balikesir | Turkey |
| BZK | Briansk | Russia |
| BZL | Barisal | Bangladesh |
| BZM | Bergen Op Zoom | Netherlands |
| BZN | Bozeman, MT | USA |
| BZO | Boizano | Italy |
| BZP | Bizant | Australia |
| BZR | Beziers/Vias | France |
| BZS | Washington/Buzzards Pt S., DC | USA |
| BZT | Brazoria/Hinkles Ferry, TX | USA |
| BZU | Buta | Congo, DR |
| BZV | Brazzaville/Maya-Maya | Congo, DR |
| BZY | Beitsy | Macau |
| BZZ | RAF Brize Norton | UK |

# C

| | | |
|---|---|---|
| CAA | Catacamas | Honduras |
| CAB | Cabinda | Angola |
| CAC | Cascavel | Brazil |
| CAD | Cadillac, MI | USA |
| CAE | Columbia, SC | USA |
| CAF | Carauari | Brazil |
| CAG | Cagliari/Elmas | Italy |
| CAH | Ca Mau | Vietnam |
| CAI | Cairo/Int'l | Egypt |
| CAJ | Canaima | Venezuela |
| CAK | Akron, OH | USA |
| CAL | Campbeltown/Machrihanish | UK |
| CAM | Camiri | Bolivia |
| CAN | Guangzhou | China |
| CAO | Clayton, NM | USA |
| CAP | Cap Haitien | Haiti |
| CAQ | Caucasia | Colombia |
| CAR | Caribou, ME | USA |
| CAS | Casablanca/Anfa | Morocco |
| CAT | Cat Is | Bahamas |
| CAU | Caruaru | Brazil |
| CAV | Cazombo | Andorra |
| CAW | Campos/B. Lisandro | Brazil |
| CAX | Carlisle | UK |
| CAY | Cayenne/Rochambeau | F. Guiana |
| CAZ | Cobar | Australia |
| CBA | Corner Bay, AK | USA |
| CBB | Cochabamba/J Wilsterman | Bolivia |
| CBC | Cherrabun | Australia |
| CBD | Car Niconar | India |
| CBE | Cumberland/Wiley Ford, MD | USA |
| CBF | Council Bluffs, IA | USA |
| CBG | Cambridge, MN | UK |
| CBH | Bechar | Algeria |
| CBI | Cape Barren Is | Australia |
| CBJ | Cabo Rojo | Dominican Rep |
| CBK | Colby/Municipal, KS | USA |
| CBL | Ciudad Boliva | Venezuela |
| CBM | Columbus/AFB, MS | USA |
| CBN | Cirebon/Penggung | Indonesia |
| CBO | Cotabato/Awang | Philippines |
| CBP | Coirribra | Portugal |
| CBQ | Calabar | Nigeria |
| CBR | Canberra | Australia |
| CBS | Cabimas/Oro Negro | Venezuela |
| CBT | Catumbela | Andorra |
| CBU | Cottbus/Flugplatz | Germany |
| CBV | Coban | Guatemala |
| CBW | Campo Mourac | Brazil |
| CBX | Condobolin | Australia |
| CBY | Canobie | Australia |
| CBZ | Cabin Creek, AK | USA |
| CCA | Chaffee/AFB, AR | USA |
| CCB | Upland/Cable, CA | USA |
| CCC | Cayo Coco | Cuba |
| CCD | Los Angeles/Century City, CA | USA |
| CCE | St Martin/Grand Case | Gaudeloupe |
| CCF | Carcassonne/Salvaza | France |
| CCG | Crane County Arpt, TX | USA |
| CCH | Chile Chico | Chile |
| CCI | Concordia | Brazil |
| CCJ | Calicut | India |
| CCK | Cocos Iss | Cocos (Keeling) Is |
| CCL | Chinchilla | Australia |
| CCM | Criciuma | Brazil |
| CCN | Chakcharan | Afghanistan |
| CCO | Carimagua | Colombia |
| CCP | Concepcion/Carriel Sur | Chile |
| CCQ | Cachoeira | Brazil |
| CCR | Concord, CA | USA |
| CCS | Caracas/Simon Bolivar | Venezuela |
| CCT | Colonia Catriel | Argentina |
| CCU | Calcutta/N. S. Chandra | India |
| CCV | Craig Cove | Vanuatu |
| CCW | Cowell | Australia |
| CCX | Caceres | Brazil |
| CCY | Charles City, IA | USA |
| CCZ | Chub Cay | Bahamas |
| CDA | Cooinda | Australia |
| CDB | Cold Bay, AK | USA |
| CDC | Cedar City, UT | USA |
| CDD | Cauquira | Honduras |
| CDE | Caledonia | Panama |
| CDF | Cortina d'Ampezzo/Fiames | Italy |
| CDG | Paris/Charles De Gaulle | France |
| CDH | Camden, AR | USA |

| Code | Location | Country |
|------|----------|---------|
| CDI | Cachoeiro Itapernirim | Brazil |
| CDJ | Conceicao Do Araguaia | Brazil |
| CDK | CedarKey/Lewis, FL | USA |
| CDL | Candle, AK | USA |
| CDN | Camden/Woodward Fld, SC | USA |
| CDO | Cradock | S. Africa |
| CDP | Cuddapain | India |
| CDQ | Croydon | Australia |
| CDR | Chadron, NE | USA |
| CDS | Childress, TX | USA |
| CDU | Camden | Australia |
| CDV | Cordova, AK | USA |
| CDW | Caldwell, NJ | USA |
| CDY | Cagayan De Sulu | Philippines |
| CEA | Wichita/Cessna Aircraft Fld, KS | USA |
| CEB | Cebu | Philippines |
| CEC | Crescent City, CA | USA |
| CED | Ceduna | Australia |
| CEE | Cherepovets | Russia |
| CEF | Chicopee/Westover Arpt, MA | USA |
| CEG | Chester | UK |
| CEH | Chelinda | Malawi |
| CEI | Chiang Rai | Thailand |
| CEJ | Chernigov | Ukraine |
| CEK | Chelyabinsk | Russia |
| CEL | Cape Eleuthera | Bahamas |
| CEM | Central, AK | USA |
| CEN | Ciudad Obregon | Mexico |
| CEO | Waco Kungo | Angola |
| CEP | Concepcion | Bolivia |
| CEQ | Cannes/Mandelieu | France |
| CER | Cherbourg/Maupertus | France |
| CES | Cessnock | Australia |
| CET | Cholet/Le Pontreau | France |
| CEU | Clemson, SC | USA |
| CEV | Connersville/Mettle Fld, IN | USA |
| CEW | Crestview, FL | USA |
| CEX | Chena Hot Springs, AK | USA |
| CEY | Murray/Calloway County, KY | USA |
| CEZ | Cortez, CO | USA |
| CFA | Coffee Point, AK | USA |
| CFC | Cacador | Brazil |
| CFD | Bryan/Coulter Fld, TX | USA |
| CFE | Clermont-Ferrand/Aulriat | France |
| CFF | Cafunfo | Angola |
| CFG | Cienfuegos | Cuba |
| CFH | Clifton Hills | Australia |
| CFI | Camfield | Australia |
| CFN | Donegal | Ireland |
| CFO | Confreza | Brazil |
| CFP | Carpentaria Downs | Australia |
| CFQ | Creston, BC | Canada |
| CFR | Caen/Carpiquet | France |
| CFS | Coffs Harbour | Australia |
| CFT | Clitton/Morenci, AZ | USA |
| CFU | Kerkyra/Corfu/Ioannis | Greece |
| CFV | Coffeyvifle, KS | USA |
| CGA | Craig/SPB, AK | USA |
| CGB | Cuiaba/M. Rondon | Brazil |
| CGC | Cape Gloucester | Papua New Guinea |
| CGD | Changde | China |
| CGE | Cambridge, MD | USA |
| CGF | Cleveland, OH | USA |
| CGG | Casiguran | Philippines |
| CGH | Sao Paulo/Congonhas | Brazil |
| CGI | Cape Girardeau, MO | USA |
| CGJ | Chingola | Zambia |
| CGK | Jakarta/Soekarno Int'l | Indonesia |
| CGM | Camiguin/Mamoajao | Philippines |
| CGN | Cologne/Cologne/Bonn | Germany |
| CGO | Zhengzhou | China |
| CGP | Chittagong/Patenga | Bangladesh |
| CGQ | Changchun | China |
| CGR | Campo Grande/Int'l | Brazil |
| CGS | College Park, MD | USA |
| CGT | Chinguitti | Mauritania |
| CGU | Ciudad Guayana | Venezuela |
| CGV | Caiguna | Australia |
| CGX | Chicago, IL | USA |
| CGY | Cagayan De Oro/Lumbia | Philippines |
| CGZ | Casa Grande/Municipal, AZ | USA |
| CHA | Chattanooga, TN | USA |
| CHB | Chilas | Pakistan |
| CHC | Christchurch | New Zealand |
| CHD | Williams/AFB, AZ | USA |
| CHE | Caherciveen/Reenroe | Ireland |
| CHF | Chinhae | S. Korea |
| CHG | Chaoyang/Chaoyang Arpt | China |
| CHH | Chachapoyas | Peru |
| CHI | Chicago, IL | USA |
| CHJ | Chipinge | Zimbabwe |
| CHK | Chickasha/Municipal, OK | USA |
| CHL | Challis, ID | USA |
| CHM | Chimbote | Peru |
| CHN | Chongju/Air Base | S. Korea |
| CHO | Charlottesville, VA | USA |
| CHP | Circle Hot Springs, AK | USA |
| CHQ | Souda/Khania | Greece |
| CHR | Chateauroux | France |
| CHS | Charleston/AFB, SC | USA |
| CHT | Chatham Is/Karewa | New Zealand |
| CHU | Chuathbaluk, AK | USA |
| CHV | Chaves | Portugal |
| CHW | Jiuquan | China |
| CHX | Changuinola | Panama |
| CHY | Choiseul Bay | Solomon Is |
| CHZ | Chiloquin/State, OR | USA |
| CIA | Rome/Roma/Ciampino | Italy |
| CIB | Catalina Is, CA | USA |
| CIC | Chico, CA | USA |
| CID | Cedar Rapids, IA | USA |
| CIE | Collie | Australia |
| CIF | Chifeng | China |
| CIG | Craig/Craig-Molfat, CO | USA |
| CIH | Changzhi | China |
| CIJ | Cobija/E. Beltram | Bolivia |
| CIK | Chalkyitsik, AK | USA |
| CIL | Council/Melsing Creek, AK | USA |
| CIM | Cimitarra | Colombia |
| CIN | Carroll, IA | USA |
| CIO | Concepcion/MCAL Lopez | Paraguay |
| CIP | Chipata | Zambia |
| CIQ | Chiquimula | Guatemala |
| CIR | Cairo, IL | USA |
| CIS | Canton Is | Kiribati |
| CIT | Shirrikent | Kazakstan |
| CIU | Sault Ste Marie, MI | USA |
| CIV | Chomley, AK | USA |
| CIW | Canouan Is. St. Vincent & Grenadines | |
| CIX | Chiclayo/Connel Ruiz | Peru |
| CIY | Comiso | Italy |
| CIZ | Coan | Brazil |
| CJA | Cajamarca | Peru |
| CJB | Coimbatore/Peelamedu | India |
| CJC | Calama/El Loa | Chile |
| CJD | Candilejas | Colombia |
| CJH | Chilko Lake, BC | Canada |
| CJJ | Cheong Ju City Arpt | S. Korea |
| CJL | Chitral | Pakistan |
| CJM | Chumphon Arpt | Thailand |
| CJN | El Cajon, CA | USA |
| CJS | Ciudad Juarez/A. Gonzaiez | Mexico |
| CJU | Cheju/Cheju Int'l Arpt | S. Korea. |
| CKA | Cherokee/Kegelman AF, OK | USA |
| CKB | Clarksburg, WV | USA |
| CKC | Cherkassy | Ukraine |
| CKD | Crooked Creek, AK | USA |
| CKE | Clear Lake, CA | USA |
| CKG | Chongqing | China |
| CKH | Chokurdah | Russia |
| CKI | Croker Is | Australia |
| CKK | Cherokee, AR | USA |
| CKL | Chkalovsky | Russia |
| CKM | Clarksdale/Fletcher Fld, MS | USA |
| CKN | Crookston, MN | USA |
| CKO | Comelio Procopio | Brazil |
| CKR | Crane Is, WA | USA |
| CKS | Carajas | Brazil |
| CKT | Sarakhs | Iran |
| CKU | Cordova/City, AK | USA |
| CKV | Clarksville, TN | USA |
| CKX | Chicken, AK | USA |
| CKY | Conakry | Guinea |
| CKZ | Canakkaie | Turkey |
| CLA | Comilla | Bangladesh |
| CLB | Castlebar | Ireland |
| CLC | Clearlake/Metroport, TX | USA |
| CLD | Carlsbad, CA | USA |
| CLE | Cleveland, OH | USA |
| CLF | Coltishall | UK |
| CLG | Coalinga, CA | USA |
| CLH | Coolah | Australia |
| CLI | Clintonville, WI | USA |
| CLJ | Cluj/Napoca | Romania |
| CLK | Clinton/Municipal, OK | USA |
| CLL | College Stn, TX | USA |
| CLM | Port Angeles, WA | USA |
| CLN | Carolina | Brazil |
| CLO | Cali/Alfonso B. Aragon | Colombia |
| CLP | Clarks Point, AK | USA |
| CLQ | Colima | Myanmar |
| CLR | Calipatria, CA | USA |
| CLS | Chehalis/Centralia, WA | USA |
| CLT | Charlotte, NC | USA |
| CLU | Columbus Municipal, IN | USA |
| CLV | Caldas Novas | Brazil |
| CLW | Clearwater/Executive, FL | USA |
| CLX | Clorinda | Argentina |
| CLY | Calvi/Ste Catherine | France |
| CLZ | Calabozo | Venezuela |
| CMA | Cunnamuila | Australia |
| CMB | Colombo/Bandaranayake | Sri Lanka |
| CMC | Camocim | Brazil |
| CMD | Cootamundra | Australia |
| CME | Ciudad Del Carmen | Mexico |
| CMF | Chambery/Aix-Les-Bains | France |
| CMG | Corumba/Int'l | Brazil |
| CMH | Columbus, OH | USA |
| CMI | Champaign, IL | USA |
| CMJ | Chi Mei | Taiwan |
| CMK | Club Makokola | Malawi |
| CML | Camooweal | Australia |
| CMM | Carmelita | Guatemala |
| CMN | Casablanca/Mohamed V | Morocco |
| CMO | Obbia | Somalia |
| CMP | Santana Do Araguaia | Brazil |
| CMQ | Clermont | Australia |
| CMR | Coirnar/Colmar-Houssen | France |
| CMS | Scusciuban | Somalia |
| CMT | Cameta | Brazil |
| CMU | Kundiawa | Papua New Guinea |
| CMV | Coromandel | New Zealand |
| CMW | Camaguey/Ign Agramonte | Cuba |
| CMX | Hancock, MI | USA |
| CMY | Sparta/AAF, WI | USA |
| CMZ | Caia | Mozambique |
| CNA | Cananea | Mexico |
| CNB | Coonamble | Australia |
| CNC | Coconut Is | Australia |
| CND | Constanta/Kogainiceanu | Romania |
| CNE | Canon City, CO | USA |
| CNF | Belo Horizonte/T. Neves | Brazil |
| CNG | Cognac/Chateau Bernard | France |
| CNH | Claremont/Municipal, NH | USA |
| CNI | Changhai | China |
| CNJ | Cloncurry | Australia |
| CNK | Concordia, KS | USA |
| CNL | Sindal/Flyveplads | Denmark |
| CNM | Carlsbad, NM | USA |
| CNN | Chulman | Russia |
| CNO | Chino, CA | USA |
| CNP | Neerlerit Inaat | Greenland |
| CNQ | Corrientes/Camba Punta | Argentina |
| CNR | Chanaral | Chile |
| CNS | Cairns, CA | Australia |
| CNT | Charata | Argentina |
| CNU | Chanute, KS | USA |
| CNV | Canavieiras | Brazil |
| CNW | Waco/James Connall, TX | USA |
| CNX | Chiang Mai/Int'l | Thailand |
| CNY | Moab, UT. | USA |
| CNZ | Cangamba | Angola |
| COA | Columbia, CA | USA |
| COB | Coolibah | Australia |
| COC | Concordia | Argentina |
| COD | Cody, WY | USA |
| COE | Coeur D'Alene, ID. | USA |
| COF | Cocoa/AFB, FL | USA |
| COG | Condoto/Mandinga | Colombia |
| COH | Cooch Behar | India |
| COI | Cocoa/Merritt Is, FL | USA |
| COJ | Coonabarabran | Australia |
| COK | Cochin | India |
| COL | Colt Is | UK |
| COM | Coleman, TX | USA |
| CON | Concord, NH | USA |
| COO | Cotonou/Cadjehoun | Benin |
| COP | Cooperstown, NY | USA |
| COQ | Choibalsan | Mongolia |
| COR | Cordoba/Pajas Blancas | Argentina |
| COS | Colorado Springs, CO | USA |
| COT | Cotulla, TX | USA |
| COU | Columbia, MO | USA |
| COV | Covilha | Portugal |
| COW | Coquimbo | Chile |
| COX | Congo Town | Bahamas |
| COY | Coolawanyah | Australia |
| COZ | Constanza | Dominican Rep |
| CPA | Cape Palmas/A. Tubman | Liberia |
| CPB | Capurgana | Colombia |
| CPC | San Martin Del-os Andes | Argentina |
| CPD | Coober Pedy | Australia |
| CPE | Campeche/Campeche Int'l | Mexico |

| Code | Location | Country |
|------|----------|---------|
| CPF | Cepu | Indonesia |
| CPG | Carmen De Patagones | Argentina |
| CPH | Copenhagen/Kastrup | Denmark |
| CPI | Cape Orford | Papua New Guinea |
| CPL | Chaparral | Colombia |
| CPM | Compton, CA | USA |
| CPN | Cape Rodney | Papua New Guinea |
| CPO | Copiapo/Chamonate | Chile |
| CPQ | Campinas/Int'l | Brazil |
| CPR | Casper, WY | USA |
| CPS | St Louis, IL | USA |
| CPT | Cape Town Int'l | S. Africa |
| CPU | Cururupu | Brazil |
| CPV | Campina Grande/J. Suassuna | Brazil |
| CPX | Culebra | Puerto Rico |
| CQA | Canarana/Canarana Arpt | Brazil |
| CQF | Calais | France |
| CQN | Chattanooga/Daisy, TN | USA |
| CQP | Cape Flattery | Australia |
| CQS | Costa Marques | Brazil |
| CQT | Caquetania | Colombia |
| CQV | Colville Municipal, WA | USA |
| CQX | Chatham Municipal, MA | USA |
| CRA | Craiciva | Romania |
| CRB | Collarenebri | Australia |
| CRC | Cartago | Colombia |
| CRD | Comodoro Rivadavia | Argentina |
| CRE | Myrtle Beach, SC | USA |
| CRF | Carnot | Central African Rep |
| CRG | Jacksonville, FL | USA |
| CRH | Cherribah | Australia |
| CRI | Crooked Is | Bahamas |
| CRJ | Coorabie | Australia |
| CRK | Luzon Is/Clark Field | Philippines |
| CRL | Brussels | Belgium |
| CRM | Catarman/National | Philippines |
| CRN | Cromarty | UK |
| CRO | Corcoran, CA | USA |
| CRP | Corpus Christi, TX | USA |
| CRQ | Caravelas | Brazil |
| CRR | Ceres | Argentina |
| CRS | Corsicana, TX | USA |
| CRT | Crossett/Municipal, AR | USA |
| CRU | Carriacou Is | Grenada |
| CRV | Crotone | Italy |
| CRW | Charleston, WV | USA |
| CRX | Corinth/Roscoe Turner, MS | USA |
| CRY | Cariton Hill | Australia |
| CRZ | Chardzhou | Turkmenistan |
| CSA | Colonsay Is | UK |
| CSB | Caransebes | Romania |
| CSC | Canas | Costa Rica |
| CSD | Cresswell Downs | Australia |
| CSE | Crested Butte, CO | USA |
| CSF | Creil/AFB | France |
| CSG | Columbus Metropolitan, GA | USA |
| CSI | Casino | Australia |
| CSJ | Cape St Jacques | Vietnam |
| CSK | Cap Skirring | Senegal |
| CSL | San Luis Obispo/AAF, CA | USA |
| CSM | Clinton, OK | USA |
| CSN | Carson City, NV | USA |
| CSO | Cochstedt | Germany |
| CSP | Cape Spencer/Coast Guard HP, AK | USA |
| CSQ | Creston, IA | USA |
| CSR | Casuarito | Colombia |
| CSS | Cassilandia | Brazil |
| CST | Castaway | Fiji |
| CSU | Santa Cruz Do Sul | Brazil |
| CSV | Crossville, TN | USA |
| CSW | Colorado do Oeste | Brazil |
| CSX | Changsha | China |
| CSY | Cheboksary | Russia |
| CTA | Catania/Fontanarossa | Italy |
| CTB | Cut Bank, MT | USA |
| CTC | Catamarca | Argentina |
| CTD | Chitre | Panama |
| CTE | Carti | Panama |
| CTF | Coatepeque | Guatemala |
| CTG | Cartagena/Rafael Nunez | Colombia |
| CTH | Coatesville, PA | USA |
| CTI | Cuito Cuanavale | Angola |
| CTK | Canton, SD | USA |
| CTL | Charleville | Australia |
| CTM | Cheturnal | Mexico |
| CTN | Cookitown | Australia |
| CTO | Calverton, NY | USA |
| CTP | Carutapera | Brazil |
| CTQ | Santa Vitoria/Do Palmar | Brazil |
| CTR | Cattle Creek | Australia |
| CTS | Sapporo/Chitose | Japan |
| CTT | Le Castellet | France |
| CTU | Chengdu | China |
| CTW | Cottonwood, AZ | USA |
| CTX | Cortland, NY | USA |
| CTY | Cross City, FL | USA |
| CTZ | Clinton/Sampson County, NC | USA |
| CUA | Ciudad Constitucion | Mexico |
| CUB | Columbia, SC | USA |
| CUC | Cucuta/Camilo Dazo | Colombia |
| CUD | Caloundra | Australia |
| CUE | Cuenca | Ecuador |
| CUF | Cuneo/Levaldigi | Italy |
| CUG | Cudal | Australia |
| CUH | Cushing/Municipal, OK | USA |
| CUI | Currillo | Colombia |
| CUJ | Culion | Philippines |
| CUK | Caye Caulker | Belize |
| CUL | Cuhacan/F.D. Bachigualato | Mexico |
| CUM | Cumana | Venezuela |
| CUN | Cancun | Mexico |
| CUO | Caruru | Colombia |
| CUP | Carupano | Venezuela |
| CUQ | Coen | Australia |
| CUR | Curacao/Halo | Netherlands Antilles |
| CUS | Columbus/Municipal, NM | USA |
| CUT | Cutral | Argentina |
| CUU | Chihuahua/G.F. Villalobos | Mexico |
| CUV | Casigua | Venezuela |
| CUW | Cube CoveAK | USA |
| CUX | Corpus Christi/Cuddihy Fld, TX | USA |
| CUY | Cue | Australia |
| CUZ | Cuzio/Velazco Astete | Peru |
| CVA | Pittsburgh/Civic HP, PA | USA |
| CVB | Chungribu | Papua New Guinea |
| CVC | Cleve | Australia |
| CVE | Covenas | Colombia |
| CVF | Courchevel | France |
| CVG | Cincinnati, KY | USA |
| CVH | Caviahue | Argentina |
| CVI | Caleta Olivia | Argentina |
| CVJ | Cuernavaca | Mexico |
| CVL | Cape Vogel | Papua New Guinea |
| CVM | Ciudad Victoria | Mexico |
| CVN | Clovis/Municipal, NM | USA |
| CVO | Albany, OR | USA |
| CVQ | Carnarvon | Australia |
| CVR | Culver City/Hughes, CA | USA |
| CVS | Clovis/AFB, NM | USA |
| CVT | Coventry/Baginton | UK |
| CVU | Corvo Is | Portugal |
| CWA | Mosinee, WI | USA |
| CWB | Curitiba/Afonso Pena | Brazil |
| CWC | Chernovtsy | Ukraine |
| CWF | Chenault Airpark, LA | USA |
| CWG | Callaway Gardens, GA | USA |
| CWI | Clinton, IA | USA |
| CWL | Cardiff | UK |
| CWO | Ft Wolter/AAF, TX | USA |
| CWP | Campbellpore | Pakistan |
| CWR | Cowarie | Australia |
| CWS | Center Is, WA | USA |
| CWT | Cowra | Australia |
| CWW | Corowa | Australia |
| CXA | Caicara De Oro | Venezuela |
| CXB | Cox's Bazar | Bangladesh |
| CXC | Chitina Arpt, AK | USA |
| CXF | Coldfoot, AK | USA |
| CXH | Vancouver/Coal Harbour, BC | Canada |
| CXI | Christmas Is | Kiribati |
| CXJ | Camas Do Sul/C.D. Bugres | Brazil |
| CXL | Calexico/Int'l, CA | USA |
| CXN | Candala | Somalia |
| CXO | Conroe, TX | USA |
| CXP | Cilacap/Tunggul Wuiung | Indonesia |
| CXQ | Christmas Creek | Australia |
| CXT | Charters Towers | Australia |
| CXY | Cat Cays | Bahamas |
| CYA | Les Cayes | Haiti |
| CYB | Cayman Brac | Cayman Is |
| CYC | Caye Chapel | Belize |
| CYE | Crystal Lake, PA | USA |
| CYF | Chefornak/SPB, AK | USA |
| CYG | Corryong | Australia |
| CYI | Chiayi | Taiwan |
| CYL | Coyoles | Honduras |
| CYM | Chatham/SPB, AK | USA |
| CYO | Cayo Largo Del Sur | Cuba |
| CYP | Calbayog | Philippines |
| CYR | Colonia | Uruguay |
| CYS | Cheyenne, WY | USA |
| CYT | Yakatapa/Intermediate, AK | USA |
| CYU | Cuyo | Philippines |
| CYX | Cherskiy | Russia |
| CYZ | Cauayan | Philippines |
| CZA | Chichen Itza | Mexico |
| CZB | Cruz Alta/Carios Ruhl | Brazil |
| CZC | Copper Centre, AK | USA |
| CZD | Cozad Municipal, NE | USA |
| CZE | Coro | Venezuela |
| CZF | Cape Romanzof, AK | USA |
| CZH | Corozal | Belize |
| CZJ | Corazon De Jesus | Panama |
| CZK | Cascade Locks, OR | USA |
| CZL | Constantine | Algeria |
| CZM | Cozumel | Mexico |
| CZN | Chisana/Chisana Fld, AK | USA |
| CZO | Chistochina, AK | USA |
| CZP | Cape Pole, AK | USA |
| CZS | Cruzeiro Do Sul/Campo Int'l | Brazil |
| CZT | Carrizo Springs, TX | USA |
| CZU | Corozal | Colombia |
| CZW | Czestochowa | Poland |
| CZX | Changzhou | China |
| CZY | Cluny | Australia |
| CZZ | Campo, CA | USA |

# D

| Code | Location | Country |
|------|----------|---------|
| DAA | Fort Belvoir/Davison/AAF, VA | USA |
| DAB | Daytona Beach/Regional, FL | USA |
| DAC | Dhaka/Zia Int'l | Bangladesh |
| DAD | Da Nang | Vietnam |
| DAE | Daparizo | India |
| DAF | Daup | Papua New Guinea |
| DAG | Barstow-Daggett, CA | USA |
| DAH | Dathina | Yemen |
| DAI | Darjeelino | India |
| DAJ | Dauan Is | Australia |
| DAK | Dakhla Oasis/Dakhla | Egypt |
| DAL | Dallas, TX | USA |
| DAM | Damascus/Int'l | Syria |
| DAN | Danville, VA | USA |
| DAP | Darchula | Nepal |
| DAR | Dar Es Salaam/Int'l | Tanzania |
| DAS | Great Bear Lake, NT | Canada |
| DAT | Datong | China |
| DAU | Daru | Papua New Guinea |
| DAV | David/Enrique Maiek | Panama |
| DAX | Daxian | China |
| DAY | Dayton, OH | USA |
| DAZ | Darwaz | Afghanistan |
| DBA | Dalbandin | Pakistan |
| DBD | Dhanbad | India |
| DBM | Debra Marcos | Ethiopia |
| DBN | Dublin/Municipal, GA | USA |
| DBO | Dubbo | Australia |
| DBP | Debepare | Papua New Guinea |
| DBQ | Dubuque, IA | USA |
| DBS | Dubois, ID | USA |
| DBT | Debra Tabor | Ethiopia |
| DBV | Dubrovnik | Croatia |
| DBY | Dallby | Australia |
| DCA | Washington D.C. | USA |
| DCF | Dominica/Cane Field | Dominica |
| DCI | Decimomannu/Ratsu | Italy |
| DCK | Dahl Creek/Dahl Creek Arpt, AK | USA |
| DCM | Castres/Mazamet | France |
| DCR | Decatur/Decatur Hi-Way, IN | USA |
| DCS | Doncaster/Finningley | UK |
| DCT | Duncan Town | Bahamas |
| DCU | Decatur, AL | USA |
| DDC | Dodge City, KS | USA |
| DDG | Dandong | China |
| DDI | Daydream Is | Australia |
| DDL | ACARS | n/a |
| DDM | Dodoirna | Papua New Guinea |
| DDN | Delta Downs | Australia |
| DDP | Dorado/Dorado Beach | Puerto Rico |
| DDU | Dadu | Pakistan |
| DEA | Dera Ghazi Khan | Pakistan |
| DEB | Debrecen | Hungary |
| DEC | Decatur, IL | USA |
| DED | Dehra Dun | India |
| DEE | Deering, Deering Arpt, AK | USA |
| DEH | Decorah, IA | USA |
| DEI | Denis Is | Seychelles |
| DEL | Delhi/Indira Gandhi Inti | India |
| DEM | Dembidollo | Ethiopia |

**AIRPORTS-1-**

| Code | Location | Country |
|------|----------|---------|
| DEN | Denver, CO | USA |
| DEO | Dearborn/Hyatt Regency HP, MI | USA |
| DEP | Deparizo | India |
| DER | Derim | Papua New Guinea |
| DES | Desroches | Seychelles |
| DET | Detroit, MI | USA |
| DEZ | Deirezzor/Al Jafrah | Syria |
| DFI | Defiance, OH | USA |
| DFP | Drumduff | Australia |
| DFW | Dallas/Fort Worth, TX | USA |
| DGA | Dangriga | Belize |
| DGB | Danger Bay, AK | USA |
| DGC | Degalthbur | Ethiopia |
| DGD | Dalgaranga | Australia |
| DGE | Mudgee | Australia |
| DGF | Douglas Lake, BC | Canada |
| DGG | Daugo | Papua New Guinea |
| DGL | Douglas Municipal, AZ | USA |
| DGM | Dongguan | China |
| DGN | Dahigren/NAF, VA | USA |
| DGO | Durango/Guadalupe Victoria | Mexico |
| DGP | Daugavpils | Latvia |
| DGR | Dargaville | New Zealand |
| DGT | Dumaguete | Philippines |
| DGU | Dedougou | Burkina Faso |
| DGW | Douglas, WY | USA |
| DHA | Dhahran | Saudi Arabia |
| DHD | Durham Downs | Australia |
| DHF | Abu Dhabi/Al Dhafra Military Arpt | UAE |
| DHI | Dhangarhi | Nepal |
| DHL | Dhala | Yemen |
| DHM | Dharamsala/Gaggal Arpt | India |
| DHN | Dothan, AL | USA |
| DHR | Den Helder/De Kooy | Netherlands |
| DHT | Dalhart, TX | USA |
| DIB | Dibrugarh/Chabua | India |
| DIC | Dili | Congo, DR |
| DIE | Antsiranana/Arrachart | Madagascar |
| DIG | Dicling | China |
| DIJ | Dijon | France |
| DIK | Dickinson, ND | USA |
| DIL | Dili/Comoro | Indonesia |
| DIM | Dimboko/Ville | Côte D'Ivoire |
| DIN | Dien Sien Phu/Gialam | Vietnam |
| DIO | Diomede Is, AK | USA |
| DIP | Diapaga | Burkina Faso |
| DIQ | Divinopolis | Brazil |
| DIR | Dire Dawa/Aba Tenna D Yilma | Ethiopia |
| DIS | Loubomo | Congo, DR |
| DIU | Diu | India |
| DIV | Divo | Côte D'Ivoire |
| DIX | Phila. Nexrad, PA | USA |
| DIY | Diyarbakir | Turkey |
| DJA | Djougou | Benin |
| DJB | Jambi/Sultan Taha Syarifudn | Indonesia |
| DJE | Djerba/Zarzis | Tunisia |
| DJG | Djanet | Algeria |
| DJJ | Jayapura/Sentani | Indonesia |
| DJM | Djambala | Congo, DR |
| DJN | Delta Junction, AK | USA |
| DJO | Daloa | Côte D'Ivoire |
| DJU | Djupivogur | Iceland |
| DKI | Dunk Is | Australia |
| DKK | Dunkirk, NY | USA |
| DKR | Dakar/Yoff | Senegal |
| DKS | Dikson | Russia |
| DKV | Docker River | Australia |
| DKX | Knoxville Downtown, TN | USA |
| DLA | Douala | Cameroon |
| DLB | Dalbertis | Papua New Guinea |
| DLC | Dalian | China |
| DLD | Geilo/Dagali | Norway |
| DLE | Dote/Tavaux | France |
| DLF | Del Rio/AFB, TX | USA |
| DLG | Dillingham/Municipal, AK | USA |
| DLH | Duluth, MN | USA |
| DLI | Dalat/Lienkinang | Vietnam |
| DLJ | Batna | Algeria |
| DLK | Dulkaninna | Australia |
| DLL | Dillon, SC | USA |
| DLM | Dataman | Turkey |
| DLN | Dillon, MT | USA |
| DLO | Dolorni, AK | USA |
| DLS | The Dalles, OR | USA |
| DLU | Dali City/Dali | China |
| DLV | Delissaville | Australia |
| DLY | Dillons Bay | Vanuatu |
| DLZ | Dalanzadgad | Mongolia |
| DMA | Tucson/AFB, AZ | USA |
| DMB | Zhambyl | Kazakstan |
| DMD | Doomadgee | Australia |
| DME | Moscow/Domodedovo | Russia |
| DMM | Dammam/King Fahad | Saudi Arabia |
| DMN | Deming, NM | USA |
| DMO | Sedalia, MO | USA |
| DMR | Dharnar | Yemen |
| DMT | Diamantino | Brazil |
| DMU | Dimapur | India |
| DMX | Des Moines Nexrad, IA | USA |
| DNA | Okinawa/Kadena AFB | Japan |
| DNB | Dunbar | Australia |
| DNC | Danane | Côte D'Ivoire |
| DND | Dundee/Riverside | UK |
| DNE | Dallas North Arpt, TX | USA |
| DNF | Derna/Martuba | Libya |
| DNG | Doongan | Australia |
| DNH | Dunhuang | China |
| DNI | Wad Medani | Somalia |
| DNK | Dnepropetrovsk | Ukraine |
| DNL | Augusta, GA | USA |
| DNM | Denham | Australia |
| DNN | Dalton/Municipal, GA | USA |
| DNO | Dianopolis | Brazil |
| DNP | Dang | Nepal |
| DNQ | Deniliquin | Australia |
| DNR | Dinard | France |
| DNS | Denison, IA | USA |
| DNT | Santa Ana / HP, CA | USA |
| DNU | Dinangat | Papua New Guinea |
| DNV | Danville/Vermilion County, IL | USA |
| DNX | Dinder/Galegu | Sudan |
| DNZ | Denizli/Cardak | Turkey |
| DOA | Doany | Madagascar |
| DOB | Dobo/Dobo Arpt | Indonesia |
| DOC | Dornoch | UK |
| DOD | Dodoma | Tanzania |
| DOE | Djoemoe | Suriname |
| DOF | Dora Bay, AK | USA |
| DOG | Dongola | Sudan |
| DOH | Doha Int'l Arpt | Qatar |
| DOI | Doini | Papua New Guinea |
| DOK | Donetsk | Ukraine |
| DOL | Deauville/St Gatien | France |
| DOM | Dominica/Melville Hail | Oman |
| DON | Dos Lagunas | Guatemala |
| DOO | Dorobisoro | Papua New Guinea |
| DOP | Dolpa | Nepal |
| DOR | Dori | Burkina Faso |
| DOS | Dios | Papua New Guinea |
| DOU | Dourados | Brazil |
| DOV | Dover/AFB, DE | USA |
| DOX | Dongara | Australia |
| DPA | West Chicago, IL | USA |
| DPC | Data Processing Ctr. | n/a |
| DPE | Dieppe/Saint Aubin | France |
| DPG | Dugway/AAF, UT | USA |
| DPI | Dipolog | Philippines |
| DPO | Devonpori | Australia |
| DPS | Denpasar, Bali/N. Rai | Indonesia |
| DPU | Dumpu | Papua New Guinea |
| DRA | Mercury, NV | USA |
| DRB | Derby | Australia |
| DRC | Dinco | Angola |
| DRD | Dorunda Stn | Australia |
| DRE | Drummond Is, MI | USA |
| DRF | Drift River, AK | USA |
| DRG | Deering, AK | USA |
| DRH | Dabra | Indonesia |
| DRI | De Ridder/Beauregard Parish, LA | USA |
| DRJ | Drietabbetje | Suriname |
| DRM | Drama | Greece |
| DRN | Dirranbandi | Australia |
| DRO | Durango, CO | USA |
| DRR | Durrie | Australia |
| DRS | Dresden/Klotzsche | Germany |
| DRT | Del Rio, TX | USA |
| DRU | Drummond, MT | USA |
| DRW | Darwin Arpt | Australia |
| DRY | Drysdale River | Australia |
| DSC | Dschang | Cameroon |
| DSD | La Desirade | Gaudeloupe |
| DSE | Dessie/Combolcha | Ethiopia |
| DSG | Dilasag | Philippines |
| DSI | Destin, FL | USA |
| DSK | Dera Ismail Khan | Pakistan |
| DSL | Daru | Sierra Leone |
| DSM | Des Moines, IA | USA |
| DSN | Dongsheng | China |
| DSV | Dansville, NY | USA |
| DTA | Delta, UT | USA |
| DTD | Datadawai | Indonesia |
| DTE | Dael/Camarines Norte | Philippines |
| DTH | Death Valley, CA | USA |
| DTL | Detroit Lakes/Municipal, MN | USA |
| DTM | Dortmund/Wickede | Germany |
| DTN | Shreveport, LA | USA |
| DTO | Denton Municipal Arpt, TX | USA |
| DTR | Decatur Is, WA | USA |
| DTS | Destin, Ft Walton Beach, FL | USA |
| DTW | Detroit, MI | USA |
| DTX | Detroit Nexrad, MI | USA |
| DUA | Durant/Eaker, OK | USA |
| DUB | Dublin | Ireland |
| DUC | Duncan/Halliburton, OK | USA |
| DUD | Dunedin | New Zealand |
| DUE | Dunce | Angola |
| DUF | Duck/Pine Is Arpt, OK | USA |
| DUG | Douglas, AZ | USA |
| DUI | Duisburg | Germany |
| DUJ | Dubois/Jefferson County, PA | USA |
| DUK | Dukuduk | S. Africa |
| DUM | Dumai | Indonesia |
| DUN | Dundas | Greenland |
| DUR | Durban/Durban Int'l | S. Africa |
| DUS | Duesseldorf | Germany |
| DUT | Dutch Harbor/Emergency Fld, AK | USA |
| DVA | Deva | Romania |
| DVL | Devils Lake, ND | USA |
| DVN | Davenport, IA | USA |
| DVO | Davao | Philippines |
| DVP | Davenport Downs | Australia |
| DVR | Daly River | Australia |
| DVT | Phoenix, AZ | USA |
| DWA | Dwangwa | Malawi |
| DWB | Soalaia | Madagascar |
| DWF | Daylon/Wright/AFB | USA |
| DWH | Houston, TX | USA |
| DWN | Oklahoma City/Dntwn, OK | USA |
| DWS | Orlando/Walt Disney World, FL | USA |
| DXA | Deux Alpes | France |
| DXB | Dubai | UAE |
| DXD | Dixie | Australia |
| DXR | Danbury, CT | USA |
| DYA | Dysart | Australia |
| DYG | Dayong | China |
| DYL | Doylestown | Australia |
| DYM | Diamantina Lakes | Australia |
| DYR | Anadyr | Russia |
| DYS | Abilene/Dyess/AFB, TX | USA |
| DYU | Dushanbe | Tajikistan |
| DYW | Daly Waters | Australia |
| DZA | Dzaoudzi | Mayotte |
| DZN | Zhezkazgan/Zhezhazgan | Kazakstan |
| DZO | Durazno | Uruguay |
| DZU | Dazu | China |

# E

| Code | Location | Country |
|------|----------|---------|
| EAA | Eagle, Eagle Arpt, AK | USA |
| EAB | Abbse | Yemen |
| EAE | Ernae | Vanuatu |
| EAM | Nelran | Saudi Arabia |
| EAN | Wheatland/Phifer Fld, WY | USA |
| EAR | Kearney, NE | USA |
| EAS | San Sebastian | Spain |
| EAT | Wenatchee, WA | USA |
| EAU | Eau Claire, WI | USA |
| EAX | Pleasant Nexrad, MO | USA |
| EBA | Elba Is/Marina Di Campe. | Italy |
| EBB | Entebbe | Uganda |
| EBD | El Obeid | Sudan |
| EBG | El Bagre | Colombia |
| EBJ | Esbjerg | Denmark |
| EBM | El Borma | Tunisia |
| EBN | Ebadon | Marshall Is |
| EBO | Ebon/Ebon Arpt | Marshall Is |
| EBR | Baton Rouge/Downtown, LA | USA |
| EBS | Webster City, IA | USA |
| EBU | St Etienne/Boutheon | France |
| EBW | Ebolowa | Cameroon |
| ECA | East Tawas, MI | USA |
| ECG | Elizabeth City, NC | USA |
| ECH | Echuca | Australia |
| ECN | Ercan | Cyprus |
| ECO | El Encanto | Colombia |

| Code | Location | Country |
|---|---|---|
| ECR | El Charco | Colombia |
| ECS | Newcastle/Mondell, WY | USA |
| EDA | Edna Bay, AK | USA |
| EDB | Eldebba | Sudan |
| EDD | Erldunda | Australia |
| EDE | Edenton/Municipal, NC | USA |
| EDF | Anchorage/Elmendorl/AFB, AK | USA |
| EDG | Edgewood/Weide/AAF, MD | USA |
| EDI | Edinburgh/Turnhouse | UK |
| EDK | El Dorado, KS | USA |
| EDL | Eldoret | Kenya |
| EDM | La Roche/Les Ajoncs | France |
| EDO | Edremit/Korfez | Turkey |
| EDQ | Erandique | Honduras |
| EDR | Edward River | Australia |
| EDW | Edwards/AFB, CA | USA |
| EED | Needles, CA | USA |
| EEK | Eek, AK | USA |
| EEN | Brattleboro, VT | USA |
| EEO | Meeker, Meeker Arpt, CO | USA |
| EET | Alabaster, Shelby County, AL | USA |
| EEW | Neenah, WI | USA |
| EFB | Eight Fathom Bight, AK | USA |
| EFC | Belle Fourche, SD | USA |
| EFD | Ellington, TX | USA |
| EFG | Efogi | Papua New Guinea |
| EFK | Newport, UT | USA |
| EFL | Kefalhnia/Argostolion | Greece |
| EFO | East Fork, AK | USA |
| EFW | Jefferson/Municipal, IA | USA |
| EGA | Engati | Papua New Guinea |
| EGC | Bergerac/Roumanieres | France |
| EGE | Vail, CO | USA |
| EGI | Valparaiso, FL | USA |
| EGL | Negrielli | Ethiopia |
| EGM | Sege | Sweden |
| EGN | Geneina | Sudan |
| EGO | Belgorod | Russia |
| EGP | Eagle Pass/Maverick, TX | USA |
| EGS | Egilsstadir | Iceland |
| EGV | Eagle River, WI | USA |
| EGX | Egegik, AK | USA |
| EHL | El Bolson | Argentina |
| EHM | Cape Newenham, AK | USA |
| EHR | Henderson City, KY | USA |
| EHT | East Hartford/Rentschler, CT | USA |
| EIA | Eia/Popondetta | Papua New Guinea |
| EIB | Eisenach | Germany |
| EIE | Eniseysk | Russia |
| EIH | Einasieigh | Australia |
| EIL | Fairbanks/Eielson/AFB, AK | USA |
| EIN | Eindhoven | Netherlands |
| EIS | Beef Is | Virgin Is (British) |
| EIY | Ein Yahav | Israel |
| EJA | Barrancabermeia/Vrgs | Colombia |
| EJH | Wedjh | Saudi Arabia |
| EKA | Eureka/Murray Fld, CA | USA |
| EKB | Ekibastuz | Kazakstan |
| EKD | Elkedra | Australia |
| EKE | Ekereku | Guyana |
| EKI | Elkhart/Municipal, IN | USA |
| EKN | Elkins, WV | USA |
| EKO | Elko, NV | USA |
| EKT | Eskilstuna | Sweden |
| EKX | Elizabethtown, KY | USA |
| ELA | Eagle Lake, TX | USA |
| ELB | El Banco/San Bernado | Colombia |
| ELC | Elcho Is | Australia |
| ELD | El Dorado, AR | USA |
| ELE | El Real | Panama |
| ELF | El Fasher | Somalia |
| ELG | El Golea | Algeria |
| ELH | North Eleuthera/Int'l | Bahamas |
| ELI | Elim, AK | USA |
| ELJ | El Recreo | Colombia |
| ELK | Elk City/Municipal, OK | USA |
| ELL | Ellisras | S. Africa |
| ELM | Elmira, NY | USA |
| ELN | Ellensburg, WA | USA |
| ELO | Eldorado | Argentina |
| ELP | El Paso, TX | USA |
| ELQ | Gassim | Saudi Arabia |
| ELR | Elelim | Indonesia |
| ELS | East London | S. Africa |
| ELT | Tour Sinai City | Egypt |
| ELU | El Oued | Algeria |
| ELV | Elfin Cove/SPB, AK | USA |
| ELW | Ellamar, AK | USA |
| ELX | El Tigre | Venezuela |
| ELY | Ely, NV | USA |
| ELZ | Wellsville, NY | USA |
| EMA | Nottingham | UK |
| EMB | San Francisco/Embarcadero, CA | USA |
| EMD | Emerald | Australia |
| EME | Ernden | Germany |
| EMG | Empangeni | S. Africa |
| EMI | Emirau | Papua New Guinea |
| EMK | Emmonak, AK | USA |
| EMM | Kemerer, WY | USA |
| EMN | Nema | Mauritania |
| EMO | Emo | Papua New Guinea |
| EMP | Emporia, KS | USA |
| EMS | Embessa | Papua New Guinea |
| EMT | El Monte, CA | USA |
| EMX | El Maiten | Argentina |
| EMY | El Minya | Egypt |
| ENA | Kenai, AK | USA |
| ENB | Eneabba West | Australia |
| ENC | Nancy/Essey | France |
| END | Enid/AFB, OK | USA |
| ENE | Ende | Indonesia |
| ENF | Enontekiö | Finland |
| ENH | Enshi | China |
| ENI | El Nido | Philippines |
| ENJ | El Naranjo | Guatemala |
| ENK | Enniskillen/St Angelo | UK |
| ENL | Centralia/Municipal, IL | USA |
| ENN | Nenana, AK | USA |
| ENO | Encarnacion | Paraguay |
| ENQ | Coronel E Solo Cano AB | Honduras |
| ENS | Enschede/Twente | Netherlands |
| ENT | Enewetak Is | Marshall Is |
| ENU | Enugu | Nigeria |
| ENV | Wendover, UT | USA |
| ENW | Kenosha, WI | USA |
| ENX | Albany Nexrad, NY | USA |
| ENY | Yan'an | China |
| EOH | Medellin/E. O. Herrera | Colombia |
| EOI | Eday | UK |
| EOK | Keokuk, IA | USA |
| EOR | El Dorado | Venezuela |
| EOS | Neosho, MO | USA |
| EOZ | Elorza | Venezuela |
| EPG | Weeping Water/Browns, NE | USA |
| EPH | Ephrata, WA | USA |
| EPI | Epi | Vanuatu |
| EPK | Episkopi | Cyprus |
| EPL | Epinal/Mirecourt | France |
| EPN | Epena | Congo, DR |
| EPO | Eastport, ME | USA |
| EPR | Esperance | Australia |
| EPS | El Portillo | Dominican Rep |
| EPT | Eliptarnin | Papua New Guinea |
| EPZ | Santa Teresa, NM | USA |
| EQS | Esquel | Argentina |
| EQY | Monroe, Monroe Arpt, NC | USA |
| ERA | Erigavo | Somalia |
| ERB | Ernabella | Australia |
| ERC | Erzincan | Turkey |
| ERD | Berdyansk | Ukraine |
| ERE | Erave | Papua New Guinea |
| ERF | Erfurt/Bindersleben | Germany |
| ERH | Errachidla | Morocco |
| ERI | Erie, PA | USA |
| ERM | Erechim/C. Kraemer | Brazil |
| ERN | Eirunepe | Brazil |
| ERO | Eldred Rock/Coast Guard, AK | USA |
| ERR | Errol, NH | USA |
| ERS | Windhoek/Eros | Namibia |
| ERT | Erdenet | Mongolia |
| ERU | Erume | Papua New Guinea |
| ERV | Kerrville, TX | USA |
| ERZ | Erzurum | Turkey |
| ESA | Esa'Ala | Papua New Guinea |
| ESB | Ankara/Esenboga | Turkey |
| ESC | Escanaba, MI | USA |
| ESD | Eastsound/Orcas Is, WA | USA |
| ESE | Ensenada | Mexico |
| ESF | Alexandria, LA | USA |
| ESG | Mariscal Estigarribia | Paraguay |
| ESH | Shoreham By Sea/Shoreham | UK |
| ESI | Espinosa | Brazil |
| ESK | Eskisehir | Turkey |
| ESL | Elista | Russia |
| ESM | Esmeraidas | Ecuador |
| ESN | Easton, MD | USA |
| ESO | Espanola, MI | USA |
| ESP | East Stroudsburg/B. Pocono, PA | USA |
| ESR | El Salvador | Chile |
| ESS | Essen | Germany |
| EST | Estherville, IA | USA |
| ESU | Essaouira | Morocco |
| ESW | Easton/State, WA | USA |
| ESX | Las Vegas Nexrad, NV | USA |
| ETB | West Send, WI | USA |
| ETD | Etadunna | Australia |
| ETE | Genda Wuha | Ethiopia |
| ETH | Elat/J. Hozman | Israel |
| ETN | Eastland/Municipal, TX | USA |
| ETR | Esltree | UK |
| ETS | Enterprise/Municipal, AL | USA |
| ETZ | Metz/Nancy/Lorraine | France |
| EUA | Eua/Kaufana | Tonga |
| EUC | Eucla | Australia |
| EUE | Eureka | USA |
| EUF | Eufaula | USA |
| EUG | Eugene, OR | USA |
| EUM | Neumuenster | Germany |
| EUN | Laayoune/Hassan I | Morocco |
| EUO | Paratebueno | Colombia |
| EUX | St Eustatius | Netherlands Antilles |
| EVA | Evadale/Landing Strip, TX | USA |
| EVE | Harstad-Narvik/Evenes | Norway |
| EVG | Sveg | Sweden |
| EVH | Evans Head | Australia |
| EVM | Eveleth, MN | USA |
| EVN | Yerevan | Armenia |
| EVO | Eva Downs | Australia |
| EVV | Evansville, IN | USA |
| EVW | Evanston, WY | USA |
| EVX | Evreux | France |
| EWB | Fail River, MA | USA |
| EWE | Ewer | Indonesia |
| EWI | Enarotali | Indonesia |
| EWK | Newton, KS | USA |
| EWN | New Bern, NC | USA |
| EWO | Ewo | Congo, DR |
| EWR | Newark, NJ | USA |
| EWX | San Antonio Nexrad, TX | USA |
| EWY | Newbury/Greenham/RAF | UK |
| EXI | Excursion Inlet/SPB, AK | USA |
| EXM | Exmouth Gulf | Australia |
| EXT | Exeter Arpt | UK |
| EYE | Indianapolis, Eagle Creek, IN | USA |
| EYL | Yelimane | Mali |
| EYP | El Yopal | Colombia |
| EYR | Yerington, NV | USA |
| EYS | Eflye Springs | Kenya |
| EYW | Key West, FL | USA |
| EZE | Buenos Aires/Ministro Pistarini | Argentina |
| EZF | Shannon Arpt, VA | USA |
| EZS | Elazig | Turkey |

# F

| Code | Location | Country |
|---|---|---|
| FAA | Faranah | Guinea |
| FAB | Farnborough | UK |
| FAC | Faaite | F. Polynesia |
| FAE | Faroe Iss/Vagar | Faroe Islands |
| FAF | Feiker/AAF, VA | USA |
| FAG | Fagurholsmyri | Iceland |
| FAH | Farah | Afghanistan |
| FAI | Fairbanks Int'l, AK | USA |
| FAJ | Fajardo | Puerto Rico |
| FAK | False Is, AK | USA |
| FAL | Roma/Falcon State, TX | USA |
| FAM | Farmington, MO | USA |
| FAN | Farsund/Lista | Norway |
| FAO | Faro | Portugal |
| FAQ | Freida River | Papua New Guinea |
| FAR | Fargo, ND | USA |
| FAS | Faskrudsfjordur | Iceland |
| FAT | Fresno, CA | USA |
| FAV | Fakarava | F. Polynesia |
| FAY | Fayetteville, NC | USA |
| FBD | Faizabad | Afghanistan |
| FBE | Francisco Beltrao | Brazil |
| FBG | Fort Bragg/AAF, NC | USA |
| FBK | Fairbanks/Ft Wainwright, AK | USA |
| FBL | Faribault/Municipal, MN | USA |
| FBM | Lubumbashi/Luano | Congo, DR |
| FBR | Fort Bridger, WY | USA |
| FBU | Oslo/Fornebu | Norway |
| FBY | Fairbury/Municipal, NE | USA |
| FCA | Kalispell, MT | USA |
| FCB | Ficksburg | S. Africa |
| FCH | Fresno-Chandler, CA | USA |
| FCM | Minneapolis, Flying Cloud Arpt, MN | USA |

AIRPORTS -1-

**AIRPORTS -1-**

| Code | Location | Country |
|---|---|---|
| FCO | Rome/Roma/Fiumicino | Italy |
| FCS | Colorado Springs/AAF, CO | USA |
| FCT | Yakima/Firing Center/AAF, WA | USA |
| FCX | Roanoke Nexrad, VA | USA |
| FCY | Forrest City/Municipal, AR | USA |
| FDE | Forde/Bringeland | Norway |
| FDF | Fort De France/Lamentin | Martinique |
| FDH | Friedrichshafen | Germany |
| FDK | Frederick, MD | USA |
| FDR | Frederick, OK | USA |
| FDU | Bandundu | Congo, DR |
| FDY | Findlay, OH | USA |
| FEA | Fetlar | UK |
| FEB | Sanfebagar | Nepal |
| FEC | Feira De Santana | Brazil |
| FEG | Fercana | Uzbekistan |
| FEJ | Feijo | Brazil |
| FEK | Ferkessedougou | Côte D'Ivoire |
| FEL | Fuerstenfeldbruck | Germany |
| FEN | Fernando De Noronha | Brazil |
| FEP | Freeport/Albertus, IL | USA |
| FER | Fercusons Gulf | Kenya |
| FET | Fremont, NE | USA |
| FEW | Cheyenne/AFB, WY | USA |
| FEZ | Fez/Sars | Morocco |
| FFA | Kill Devil Hills/First Flight, NC | USA |
| FFC | Atlanta, Falcon Fld, GA | USA |
| FFD | Fairford/RAF | UK |
| FFL | Fairfield, IA | USA |
| FFM | Fergus Falls, MN | USA |
| FFO | Dayton/AFB, OH | USA |
| FFT | Frankfort, KY | USA |
| FFU | Furtaeulu | Chile |
| FFZ | Mesa/Falcon Fld, AZ | USA |
| FGD | Fderik | Mauritania |
| FGI | Apia/Fagali I | Samoa |
| FGL | Fox Glacier | New Zealand |
| FGU | Fangatau | F. Polynesia |
| FHR | Friday Harbor Arpt, WA | USA |
| FHU | Libby/AAF, AZ | USA |
| FHZ | Fakahina | F. Polynesia |
| FIC | Fire Cove, AK | USA |
| FID | Fishers Is, NY | USA |
| FIE | Fair Isle | UK |
| FIG | Fria | Guinea |
| FIH | Kinshasa/N'Djili | Congo, DR |
| FIK | Finke | Australia |
| FIL | Fillmore/Municipal, UT | USA |
| FIN | Finschhafen | Papua New Guinea |
| FIT | Fitchburg Municipal, MA | USA |
| FIV | Five Finger, AK | USA |
| FIZ | Fitzroy Crossing | Australia |
| FJR | Fujairah Int'l Arpt | UAE |
| FKB | Karlsruhe/Baden Baden | Germany |
| FKH | Fakenham/Sculthorp/RAF | Georgia |
| FKI | Kisangani | Congo, DR |
| FKJ | Fukui | Japan |
| FKL | Franklin, PA | USA |
| FKN | Franklin Municipal, VA | USA |
| FKQ | Fak Fak/Torea | Indonesia |
| FKS | Fukushima Arpt | Japan |
| FLA | Florencia, CO | USA |
| FLB | Floriano | Brazil |
| FLC | Falls Creek | Australia |
| FLD | Fond Du Lac Arpt, WI | USA |
| FLE | Fort Lee/AAF, VA | USA |
| FLF | Flensburg/Schaferhaus | Germany |
| FLG | Flagstaff/Pulliam Arpt, AZ | USA |
| FLH | Flotta | UK |
| FLI | Flateyri | Iceland |
| FLJ | Falls Bay, AK | USA |
| FLL | Fort Lauderdale Int'l, FL | USA |
| FLM | Filadelfia | Paraguay |
| FLN | Florianopolis | Brazil |
| FLO | Florence Regional Arpt, SC | USA |
| FLP | Flippin | Australia |
| FLR | Florence/Peretola | Italy |
| FLS | Flinders Is | Australia |
| FLT | Flat, AK | USA |
| FLU | Flushing, NY | USA |
| FLV | Sherman/AAF, KS | USA |
| FLW | Flores Is/Santa Cruz | Portugal |
| FLX | Fallon/Municipal, NV | USA |
| FLY | Finley | Australia |
| FMA | Formosa | Argentina |
| FMC | Five Mile, AK | USA |
| FME | Tipton/AAF, MD | USA |
| FMG | Flaminoo | Costa Rica |
| FMH | Otis/AFB, MA | USA |
| FMI | Kalemie | Congo, DR |
| FMN | Farmington Municipal, NM | USA |
| FMO | Muenster | Germany |
| FMS | Fort Madison, IA | USA |
| FMY | Fort Myers, FL | USA |
| FNA | Freetown | Sierra Leone |
| FNB | Neulbrandenburg | Germany |
| FNC | Funchal/Madeira | Portugal |
| FNE | Fane | Papua New Guinea |
| FNG | Fada N'Gourma | Burkina Faso |
| FNH | Fincha | Ethiopia |
| FNI | Nimes/Garons | France |
| FNJ | Pyongyang/Sunan | N. Korea |
| FNK | Fin Creek, AK | USA |
| FNL | Fort Collins, CO | USA |
| FNR | Funter Bay/SPB, AK | USA |
| FNT | Flint Int'l Arpt, MI | USA |
| FOA | Foula | UK |
| FOB | Fort Bragg, CA | USA |
| FOC | Fuzhou | China |
| FOD | Fort Dodge, IA | USA |
| FOE | Forbes/AFB, KS | USA |
| FOG | Foggia | Italy |
| FOK | Westhampton, NY | USA |
| FOM | Foumban | Cameroon |
| FON | Fortuna | Costa Rica |
| FOO | Numfoor | Indonesia |
| FOP | Forest Park/Morris/AAF, GA | USA |
| FOR | Fortaieza/Pinto Martins | Brazil |
| FOS | Forrest | Australia |
| FOT | Forster | Australia |
| FOU | Fougamou | Gabon |
| FOX | Fox, AK | USA |
| FOY | Foya | Liberia |
| FPO | Freeport | Bahamas |
| FPR | Fort Pierce Int'l, FL | USA |
| FPY | Perry-Foley, FL | USA |
| FRA | Frankfurt/Int'l | Germany |
| FRB | Forbes | Australia |
| FRC | Franca | Brazil |
| FRE | Fera Is | Solomon Is |
| FRF | Frankfurt AFB | Germany |
| FRG | Farmingdale, NY | USA |
| FRH | French Lick, IN | USA |
| FRI | Marshall/AAF, KS | USA |
| FRJ | Frejus | France |
| FRK | Fregate Is | Seychelles |
| FRL | Forli/Luigi Ridolfi | Italy |
| FRM | Fairmont, MN | USA |
| FRN | Bryant/AAF, AK | USA |
| FRO | Floro | Norway |
| FRP | Fresh Water Bay, AK | USA |
| FRQ | Feramin | Papua New Guinea |
| FRR | Front Royal/Warren County, VA | USA |
| FRS | Flores/Santa Elena | Guatemala |
| FRT | Frutillar | Chile |
| FRU | Bishkek | Kyrgyzstan |
| FRW | Francistown | Botswana |
| FRY | Fryeburg, ME | USA |
| FRZ | Fritziar | Germany |
| FSC | Figari | France |
| FSD | Sioux Falls, SD | USA |
| FSI | Henry Post/AAF, OK | USA |
| FSK | Forl Scott, KS | USA |
| FSL | Fossil Downs | Australia |
| FSM | Fort Smith Municipal, AR | USA |
| FSN | Fort Sheridan/AAF, IL | USA |
| FSP | St Pierre | St. Pierre and Miquelon |
| FSS | Kinloss/RAF | UK |
| FST | Fort Stockton, TX | USA |
| FSU | Fort Sumner, NM | USA |
| FSW | Fort Madison, IA | USA |
| FTA | Futuna Is Arpt | Vanuatu |
| FTG | Denver Nexrad, CO | USA |
| FTI | Fitiuta | American Samoa |
| FTK | Godman/AAF, KY | USA |
| FTL | Fortuna Ledge, AK | USA |
| FTU | Fort Dauphin | Madagascar |
| FTW | Fort Worth, TX | USA |
| FTX | Owando | Congo, DR |
| FTY | Fulton County, GA | USA |
| FUB | Fulleborn | Papua New Guinea |
| FUE | Fuerteventura | Spain |
| FUG | Fuyang | China |
| FUJ | Fukue | Japan |
| FUK | Fukuoka | Japan |
| FUL | Fullerton Municipal, CA | USA |
| FUM | Fuma | Papua New Guinea |
| FUN | Funafuti Atol Int'l | Tuvalu |
| FUO | Fucishan | China |
| FUT | Futuna Is | Wallis and Futuna Is |
| FVE | Frenchville, N Aroostook, ME | USA |
| FVL | Flora Valley/Flora Valey | Australia |
| FVR | Forrest River Arpt | Australia |
| FVX | Farmville, VA | USA |
| FWA | Fort Wayne Int'l, IN | USA |
| FWD | Ft Worth, TX | USA |
| FWH | Carswell/AFB, TX | USA |
| FWL | Farewell, AK | USA |
| FWM | Fort William/ HPHP | UK |
| FWN | Sussex, Sussex Arpt, NJ | USA |
| FWS | Dfw Nexrad, TX | USA |
| FXE | Fort Lauderdale Executive, FL | USA |
| FXM | Flaxman Is, AK | USA |
| FXO | Cuamba | Mozambique |
| FXY | Forest City/Municipal, IA | USA |
| FYM | Fayetteville/Municipal, TN | USA |
| FYN | Fuyun | China |
| FYT | Faya | Chad |
| FYU | Fort Yukon, AK | USA |
| FYV | Fayetteville Municipal, AR | USA |
| FZO | Bristol/Filton | UK |

# G

| Code | Location | Country |
|---|---|---|
| GAA | Guarrial | Colombia |
| GAB | Gabbs, NV | USA |
| GAC | Gracias | Honduras |
| GAD | Gadsden/Municipal, AL | USA |
| GAE | Gabes | Tunisia |
| GAF | Gafsa/Ksar | Tunisia |
| GAG | Gage, OK | USA |
| GAH | Gayndah | Australia |
| GAI | Gaithersburg, MD | USA |
| GAJ | Yamagata/Junmachi | Japan |
| GAK | Gakona, AK | USA |
| GAL | Galena, AK | USA |
| GAM | Gambell, AK | USA |
| GAN | Gan Is/Gan/Seenu | Maldives |
| GAO | Guantanamo/Los Canos | Cuba |
| GAP | Gusap | Papua New Guinea |
| GAQ | Gao | Mali |
| GAR | Garaina | Papua New Guinea |
| GAS | Garissa | Kenya |
| GAT | Gap/Tallard | France |
| GAU | Gauhati/Borlhar | India |
| GAV | Gag Is | Indonesia |
| GAW | Gangaw | Myanmar |
| GAX | Gamba | Gabon |
| GAY | Gaya | India |
| GAZ | Guasopa | Papua New Guinea |
| GBA | Big Bay | Vanuatu |
| GBB | Gara Djebilet | Algeria |
| GBC | Gasuke | Papua New Guinea |
| GBD | Great Bend, KS | USA |
| GBE | Gaborone/Sir Seretse Khama Int'l | Botswana |
| GBF | Negarbo | Papua New Guinea |
| GBG | Galesburg, GBG | USA |
| GBH | Galbraith Lake, AK | USA |
| GBI | Grand Bahama/Aux Ab | Bahamas |
| GBJ | Marie Galante/Les Bases | Gaudeloupe |
| GBK | Gbangbatok | Sierra Leone |
| GBL | Goulburn Is | Australia |
| GBM | Garbaharey | Somalia |
| GBN | Gila Bend/AAF, AZ | USA |
| GBO | Baltimore-Greenbelt, MD | USA |
| GBP | Gamboola | Australia |
| GBR | Great Barrington, MA | USA |
| GBS | Port Fitzroy | New Zealand |
| GBU | Khashm El Girba | Somalia |
| GBV | Gibb River | Australia |
| GBZ | Great Barrier Is | New Zealand |
| GCA | Guacamaya | Colombia |
| GCC | Campbell County Arpt, WY | USA |
| GCI | Guernsey | UK |
| GCJ | Johannesburg/Grand Central | S. Africa |
| GCK | Garden City, KS | USA |
| GCM | Grand Cayman Is Int'l | Cayman Is |
| GCN | Grand Canyon Natl. Park, AZ | USA |
| GCY | Greenville/Municipal, TN | USA |
| GDA | Gounda | Central African Rep |
| GDC | Greenville/Donaldson Cntr, SC | USA |
| GDD | Gordon Downs | Australia |
| GDE | Gode/Iddidole | Ethiopia |
| GDG | Magelagachi | Russia |
| GDH | Golden Horn/SPB, AK | USA |
| GDI | Gordil | Central African Rep |

| Code | Name | Country |
|------|------|---------|
| GDJ | Gandajika | Congo, DR |
| GDL | Guadalajara/Miguel Hidal | Mexico |
| GDM | Gardner/Municipal, MA | USA |
| GDN | Gdansk-Rebiechowo | Poland |
| GDO | Guasdualito/Vare Maria | Venezuela |
| GDP | Guadalupe | Brazil |
| GDQ | Gondar | Ethiopia |
| GDT | Grand Turk Is | Turks & Caicos Is |
| GDV | Glendive, MT | USA |
| GDW | Gladwin, MI | USA |
| GDX | Magadan | Russia |
| GDZ | Gelenclzilk | Russia |
| GEA | Noumea/Magenta | New Caledonia |
| GEB | Gebe | Indonesia |
| GEC | Geatkale | Cyprus |
| GED | Georgetown, DE | USA |
| GEE | George Town | Australia |
| GEF | Geva Airstrip | Solomon Is |
| GEG | Spokane Int'l Arpt, WA | USA |
| GEI | Green Iss | Papua New Guinea |
| GEK | Ganes Creek, AK | USA |
| GEL | Santo Angelo/Sepe Tiaraju | Brazil |
| GEO | Georgetown/Cheddi Jagan Int'l Guyana | |
| GER | Nueva Gerona/Rafael Cabrera | Cuba |
| GES | General Safflos/Buayan | Philippines |
| GET | Geraldton | Australia |
| GEV | Gallivare | Sweden |
| GEW | Gewoia | Papua New Guinea |
| GEX | Geelong | Australia |
| GEY | Greybull, WY | USA |
| GFA | Malmstrom/AFB, MT | USA |
| GFB | Togiak Fish, AK | USA |
| GFD | Greenfeid/Pope Fld, IN | USA |
| GFE | Grenfell | Australia |
| GFF | Griffith | Australia |
| GFK | Grand Forks Int'l, ND | USA |
| GFL | Glens Falls, NY | USA |
| GFN | Grafton | Australia |
| GFO | Bartica | Guyana |
| GFR | Granville | France |
| GFY | Grootfontein | Namibia |
| GGB | Golden Gate Bridge, CA | USA |
| GGC | Lumbala | Angola |
| GGD | Gregory Downs | Australia |
| GGE | Georgetown, SC | USA |
| GGG | Gladewater, TX | USA |
| GGL | Gilgal | Colombia |
| GGN | Gagnoa | Côte D'Ivoire |
| GGO | Guiglo | Côte D'Ivoire |
| GGR | Garoe | Somalia |
| GGS | Gobernador Gregores | Argentina |
| GGT | George Town/Exurna Int'l | Bahamas |
| GGW | Glasgow Int'l Arpt, MT | USA |
| GHA | Ghardaia Nournerate | Algeria |
| GHB | Governors Harbour | Bahamas |
| GHC | Great Harbour | Bahamas |
| GHD | Ghimbi | Ethiopia |
| GHE | Garachine | Panama |
| GHF | Gebelstacit | Germany |
| GHK | Gush Katif | Israel |
| GHM | Centerville MunicipalTN | USA |
| GHN | Guanghan | China |
| GHT | Ghat | Libya |
| GHU | Gualeguaychu | Argentina |
| GHW | Glenwood Asos, MN | USA |
| GIB | Gibraltar North Front | Gibraltar |
| GIC | Boigu Is | Australia |
| GID | Gitega | Benin |
| GIF | Winter Haven/Gilbert Fld, FL | USA |
| GIG | Rio De Janeiro Int'l | Brazil |
| GII | Siguin | Guinea |
| GIL | Gilgit | Pakistan |
| GIM | Miele Mimbale | Gabon |
| GIR | Girardot | Colombia |
| GIS | Gisborne | New Zealand |
| GIT | Geita | Tanzania |
| GIY | Giyani | S. Africa |
| GIZ | Gizan | Saudi Arabia |
| GJA | Guanaja | Honduras |
| GJL | Jijel Achouat | Algeria |
| GJM | Gualara-Mirim | Brazil |
| GJR | Gjogur | Iceland |
| GJT | Grand Junction/Walker Fld, CO | USA |
| GKA | Goroka | Papua New Guinea |
| GKE | Geilenkirchen | Germany |
| GKH | Gorkha | Nepal |
| GKL | Great Keppel Is | Australia |
| GKN | Gulkana Arpt, AK | USA |
| GKO | Kongoboumba | Gabon |
| GKT | Gatlinburg, TN | USA |
| GLA | Glasgow/Int'l | UK |
| GLC | Geladi | Ethiopia |
| GLD | Goodland, Renner Fld, KS | USA |
| GLE | Gainesville/Municipal, TX | USA |
| GLF | Golfito | Costa Rica |
| GLG | Glengyie | Australia |
| GLH | Greenville, MS | USA |
| GLI | Glen Innes | Australia |
| GLK | Galcaio | Somalia |
| GLL | Gol/Klanten | Norway |
| GLM | Gienormiston | Australia |
| GLN | Goulimime | Morocco |
| GLO | Gloucester/Staverton Private | UK |
| GLP | Guigubip | Papua New Guinea |
| GLQ | Glennallen, AK | USA |
| GLR | Gaylord, Otsego County, MI | USA |
| GLS | Galveston, Scholes Fld, TX | USA |
| GLT | Gladstone | Australia |
| GLV | Golovin, AK | USA |
| GLW | Glasgow/Municipal, KY | USA |
| GLX | Galela/Gamarmalamu | Indonesia |
| GLY | Goldsworthy | Australia |
| GLZ | Breda/Gilze-Rijen | Netherlands |
| GMA | Gemena | Congo, DR |
| GMB | Gambela | Ethiopia |
| GMC | Guerima | Colombia |
| GME | Gomel | Belarus |
| GMI | Gasmata Is | Papua New Guinea |
| GMM | Gamboma | Congo, DR |
| GMN | Greymouth | New Zealand |
| GMR | Gambier Is | F. Polynesia |
| GMS | Guimaraes | Brazil |
| GMT | Granite Mountain, AK | USA |
| GMU | Greenville, SC | USA |
| GMV | Monument Valley, UT | USA |
| GMY | Rheindahlen | Germany |
| GNA | Grodna | Belarus |
| GNB | Grenoble/Saint Geoirs | France |
| GND | Grenada/Point Saline Int'l | Grenada |
| GNE | Ghent/Industrie-Zone | Belgium |
| GNG | Gooding, ID | USA |
| GNI | Green Is | Taiwan |
| GNM | Guanambi | Brazil |
| GNN | Ghinnir | Ethiopia |
| GNR | General Roca | Argentina |
| GNS | Gunungsitoli/Binaka | Indonesia |
| GNT | Grants-Milan, NM | USA |
| GNU | Goodnews Bay, AK | USA |
| GNV | Gainesville, FL | USA |
| GNZ | Ghanzi | Botswana |
| GOA | Genoa/Cristoforo Colombo | Italy |
| GOB | Goba | Ethiopia |
| GOC | Gora | Papua New Guinea |
| GOE | Gonalia | Papua New Guinea |
| GOF | Goodfellow/AFB, TX | USA |
| GOG | Golbabis | Namibia |
| GOH | Nuuk | Greenland |
| GOI | Goa/Dabolim | India |
| GOJ | Nizhniy Novgorod | Russia |
| GOK | Guthrie, OK | USA |
| GOL | Gold Beach/State, OR | USA |
| GOM | Goma | Congo, DR |
| GON | New London, CT | USA |
| GOO | Goondiwindi | Australia |
| GOP | Gorakhpur | India |
| GOQ | Golmud | China |
| GOR | Gore | Ethiopia |
| GOS | Gosford | Australia |
| GOT | Goteborg/Landvetter | Sweden |
| GOU | Garoua | Cameroon |
| GOV | Gove/Nhulunbuy | Australia |
| GOY | Gal Oya/Amparai | Sri Lanka |
| GOZ | Gorna Orechovitsa | Bulgaria |
| GPA | Araxos/Patrai | Greece |
| GPB | Guarapuava/Tancredo Thornaz Faria Brazil | |
| GPI | Guapi | Colombia |
| GPL | Guapiles | Costa Rica |
| GPN | Garden Point | Australia |
| GPO | General Pico | Argentina |
| GPS | Galapagos Is/Baltra | Ecuador |
| GPT | Biloxi Regional Arpt, MS | USA |
| GPZ | Grand Rapids, MN | USA |
| GQJ | Machrihanish/RAF | UK |
| GQQ | Galion, OH | USA |
| GRA | Gamarra | Colombia |
| GRB | Green Bay, Austin Straubel Int'l Arpt, WI | USA |
| GRC | Grand Cess | Liberia |
| GRD | Greenwood County Arpt, SC | USA |
| GRE | Greenville/Municipal, IL | USA |
| GRF | Ft. Lewis Gray/AAF, WA | USA |
| GRG | Gardez | Afghanistan |
| GRH | Garuahi | Papua New Guinea |
| GRI | Grand Is, NE | USA |
| GRJ | George | S. Africa |
| GRK | Ft. Hood Gray/AAF, TX | USA |
| GRL | Garasa | Papua New Guinea |
| GRM | Grand Marais Municipal, MN | USA |
| GRN | Gordon Municipal, NE | USA |
| GRO | Gerona/Costa Brava | Spain |
| GRP | Gurupi | Brazil |
| GRQ | Groningen/Eelde | Netherlands |
| GRR | Kent County Int'l Arpt, MI | USA |
| GRS | Grosseto/Baccarini | Italy |
| GRT | Guirat | Pakistan |
| GRU | Sao Paulo/Guarulhos Int'l | Brazil |
| GRV | Groznyj | Russia |
| GRW | Graciosa Is | Portugal |
| GRX | Granada | Spain |
| GRY | Grimsey | Iceland |
| GRZ | Graz/Thalerhof | Austria |
| GSA | Long Pasia | Malaysia |
| GSB | Seymour Johnson/AFB, NC | USA |
| GSC | Gascoyne Junction | Australia |
| GSE | Gothenburg/Saeve | Sweden |
| GSH | Goshen Municipal Arpt, IN | USA |
| GSI | Guadalcanal | Solomon Is |
| GSL | Taltheilei Narrows, NT | Canada |
| GSM | Gheshm | Iran |
| GSN | Mount Gunson | Australia |
| GSO | Piedmont Triad/Int'l, NC | USA |
| GSP | Greenville, SC | USA |
| GSQ | Shark El Oweinat | Egypt |
| GSR | Gardo | Somalia |
| GSS | Sabi Sabi | S. Africa |
| GST | Gustavus, AK | USA |
| GSU | Gedaref | Somalia |
| GSY | Grimsby/Binbrook | UK |
| GTA | Gatokae Aerodrom | Solomon Is |
| GTB | Genting | Malaysia |
| GTC | Green Turtle | Bahamas |
| GTE | Groote Eylandt/Alyangula | Australia |
| GTF | Great Falls Int'l Arpt, MT | USA |
| GTG | Grantsburg/Municipal, WI | USA |
| GTI | Guettin | Germany |
| GTK | SungeiTekai | Malaysia |
| GTN | Mount Cook/Glentanner | New Zealand |
| GTO | Gorontalo/Tolotio | Indonesia |
| GTR | Columbus, MS | USA |
| GTS | Granites | Australia |
| GTT | Georgetown | Australia |
| GTW | Zlin/Holesov | Czech Rep |
| GTY | Gettysburg, PA | USA |
| GUA | Guatemala City/La Aurora | Guatemala |
| GUB | Guerrero Negro | Mexico |
| GUC | Gunnison, CO | USA |
| GUD | Goundam | Mali |
| GUE | Guriaso | Papua New Guinea |
| GUF | Gulf Shores/Edwards, AL | USA |
| GUG | Guari | Papua New Guinea |
| GUH | Gunnedah | Australia |
| GUI | Guiria | Venezuela |
| GUJ | Guaratingueta | Brazil |
| GUL | Goulburn | Australia |
| GUM | Guam/A.B. Won Pat Infl. | Guam |
| GUN | Montgomery/Gunter/AFB, AL | USA |
| GUO | Gualaco | Honduras |
| GUP | Gallup Municipal Arpt, NM | USA |
| GUQ | Guanare | Venezuela |
| GUR | Alotau/Gurney | Papua New Guinea |
| GUS | Grissom/AFB, IN | USA |
| GUT | Guetersloh | Germany |
| GUU | Grundarfjordur | Iceland |
| GUV | Mougulu | Papua New Guinea |
| GUW | Atyrau | Kazakstan |
| GUX | Guna | India |
| GUY | Guymon, OK | USA |
| GUZ | Guarapari | Brazil |
| GVA | Geneva Cointrin | Switzerland |
| GVE | Gordonsville/Municipal, VA | USA |
| GVI | Green River | Papua New Guinea |
| GVL | Gainesville/Gilmer Memorial, GA | USA |
| GVP | Greenvale | Australia |
| GVR | Governador Valadares | Brazil |
| GVT | Greenville Majors, TX | USA |
| GVW | Kansas City, Richards-Gebaur Arpt, MO | USA |
| GVX | Gavie/Sandviken AFB | Sweden |
| GWA | Gwa | Myanmar |
| GWD | Gwadar | Pakistan |
| GWE | Gweru | Zimbabwe |

**AIRPORTS -1-**

| Code | Location | Country |
|------|----------|---------|
| GWL | Gwalior | India |
| GWN | Gnarowein | Papua New Guinea |
| GWO | Greenwood/Leflore, MS | USA |
| GWS | Glenwood Springs, CO | USA |
| GWT | Westerland/Sylt | Germany |
| GWV | Glendale,WV | USA |
| GWW | Berlin/RAF Gatow | Germany |
| GWY | Galway Cammore | Ireland |
| GXF | Seiyun | Yemen |
| GXG | Negage | Andorra |
| GXH | Mildenhall/NAF | UK |
| GXQ | Coyhaique/Ten. Vidal | Chile |
| GXX | Yagoua | Cameroon |
| GXY | Greeley/Weld County, CO | USA |
| GYA | Guayaramerin | Bolivia |
| GYE | Guayaquil/Simon Bolivar | Ecuador |
| GYI | Gisenyi | Rwanda |
| GYL | Argyle | Australia |
| GYM | Guaymas | Mexico |
| GYN | Goiania/Santa Genoveva | Brazil |
| GYP | Gympie | Australia |
| GYR | Goodyear Municipal, AZ | USA |
| GYY | Gary Regional, IN | USA |
| GZA | Gaza Strip/Gaza Int'l Occupied Palestinian Territory | |
| GZH | Evergreen, Middleton Fld, AL | USA |
| GZI | Ghazni | Afghanistan |
| GZM | Gozo | Malta |
| GZO | Gizo/Nusatope | Solomon Is |

## H

| Code | Location | Country |
|------|----------|---------|
| HAA | Hasvik | Norway |
| HAB | Hamilton/Marion County, AL | USA |
| HAC | Hachijo Jima | Japan |
| HAD | Halmstad/AFB | Sweden |
| HAE | Havasupai, AZ | USA |
| HAF | Half Moon, CA | USA |
| HAH | Moroni/Prince Said Ibrahim Int'l | Comoros |
| HAI | Three Rivers/Dr Haines, MI | USA |
| HAJ | Hanover | Germany |
| HAK | Haikou | China |
| HAL | Halah | Namibia |
| HAM | Hamburg/Fuhlsbuettel | Germany |
| HAN | Hanoi/Noibai | Vietnam |
| HAO | Hamilton, OH | USA |
| HAP | Long Is | Australia |
| HAQ | Hanimaadhoo | Maldives |
| HAR | Harrisburg Skyport, PA | USA |
| HAS | Hail | Saudi Arabia |
| HAT | Heathlands | Australia |
| HAU | Haugesund/Karmoy | Norway |
| HAV | Havana/Jose Marti Int'l | Cuba |
| HAW | Haverfordwest | UK |
| HAX | Muskogee/Hatbox Fld, OK | USA |
| HAY | Haycock, AK | USA |
| HAZ | Hatzfeldthaven | Papua New Guinea |
| HBA | Hobart Arpt | Australia |
| HBB | Hobbs/Industrial Airpark, NM | USA |
| HBC | Hanus Bay, AK | USA |
| HBE | Alexandria/Borg El Arab | Egypt |
| HBG | Hattiesburg, MS | USA |
| HBH | Hobart Bay, AK | USA |
| HBI | Harbour Is | Bahamas |
| HBL | Babelegi/ HP | S. Africa |
| HBN | Phu-bon | Vietnam |
| HBO | Humboldt Municipal, NE | USA |
| HBR | Hobart Municipal Arpt, OK | USA |
| HBT | Hafr Albatin | Saudi Arabia |
| HBX | Hubli | India |
| HCA | Big Spring/Howard Cnty, TX | USA |
| HCB | Shoal Cove, AK | USA |
| HCC | Hudson/Columbia Cnty, NY | USA |
| HCM | Eil | Somalia |
| HCN | Hengchun | Taiwan |
| HCQ | Halls Creek | Australia |
| HCR | Holy Cross, AK | USA |
| HCS | Johannesburg/HP | S. Africa |
| HCW | Cheraw, SC | USA |
| HDA | Hidden Falls, AK | USA |
| HDB | Heidelberg | Germany |
| HDD | Hyderabad | Pakistan |
| HDE | Brewster Fld Arpt, NE | USA |
| HDF | Heringsdorf | Germany |
| HDH | Oahu/Dillingham Airfield, HI | USA |
| HDM | Hamadan | Iran |
| HDN | Hayden/Yampa Valley, CO | USA |

| Code | Location | Country |
|------|----------|---------|
| HDO | Hondo, TX | USA |
| HDQ | Atlanta/Headquarters | n/a |
| HDS | Hoedspruit | S. Africa |
| HDY | Hat Yai | Thailand |
| HEA | Herat | Afghanistan |
| HEB | Henzada | Myanmar |
| HED | Herendeen, AK | USA |
| HEE | Helena/Thompson-Robbins, AR | USA |
| HEH | Heho | Myanmar |
| HEI | Heide/Buesum | Germany |
| HEK | Heihe | China |
| HEL | Helsinki/Vantaa | Finland |
| HEM | Helsinki/Malmi | Finland |
| HEN | Hendon | UK |
| HEO | Haeloao | Papua New Guinea |
| HER | Heraklion/Iraklio | Greece |
| HES | Hermiston/State, OR | USA |
| HET | Hohhot | China |
| HEW | Athens/Athinai/Hellinikon | Greece |
| HEX | Santo Domingo/Herrera | Dominican Republic |
| HEY | Hanchey/AHP, AL | USA |
| HEZ | Natchez/Hardy-Anders, MS | USA |
| HFA | Haifa/U Michaeli | Israel |
| HFD | Hartford-Brainard Arpt, CT | USA |
| HFE | Hefei | China |
| HFF | Mackall/AAF, NC | USA |
| HFN | Hornafjordur | Iceland |
| HFS | Hagfors | Sweden |
| HFT | Hammerfest | Norway |
| HGA | Hargeisa | Somalia |
| HGD | Hughenden | Australia |
| HGH | Hangzhou | China |
| HGL | Helgoland | Germany |
| HGN | Mae Hong Son | Thailand |
| HGO | Korhogo | Côte D'Ivoire |
| HGR | Hagerstown, MD | USA |
| HGS | Freetown/Hastings | Sierra Leone |
| HGT | Jolon/Hunter/AAF, CA | USA |
| HGU | Mount Hagen/Kagamuga | Papua New Guinea |
| HGX | HuStn/GlvStn Nexrad, TX | USA |
| HGZ | Hogatza, AK | USA |
| HHE | Hachinohe AB | Japan |
| HHF | Canadian/Hemphill, TX | USA |
| HHH | Hilton Head, SC | USA |
| HHI | Wheeler/AFB, HI | USA |
| HHN | Hahn | Germany |
| HHP | Hong Kong / HP | Hong Kong |
| HHQ | Hua Hin | Thailand |
| HHR | Hawthorne, CA | USA |
| HHZ | Hikueru | F. Polynesia |
| HIB | Chisholm-Hibbing Arpt, MN | USA |
| HIC | Pretoria/iscor HP | S. Africa |
| HID | Horn Is | Australia |
| HIE | Whitefield, NH | USA |
| HIF | Hill/AFB, UT | USA |
| HIG | Highbury | Australia |
| HIH | Hook Is | Australia |
| HII | Lake Havasu City, AZ | USA |
| HIJ | Hiroshima/Int'l | Japan |
| HIK | Hickam/AFB, HI | USA |
| HIL | Shillavo | Ethiopia |
| HIN | Chinju/Sacheon | S. Korea |
| HIO | Hillsboro, OR | USA |
| HIP | Headingly | Australia |
| HIR | Honiara/Henderson | Solomon Is |
| HIS | Hayman Is | Australia |
| HIT | Hivaro | Papua New Guinea |
| HIW | Hiroshima/Hiroshima West | Japan |
| HIX | Hiva Oa | F. Polynesia |
| HJR | Khajuraho | India |
| HJT | Khujirt | Mongolia |
| HKA | Blytheville Municipal, AR | USA |
| HKB | Healy Lake, AK | USA |
| HKD | Hakodate | Japan |
| HKG | Hong Kong Int'l | Hong Kong |
| HKK | Hokitika | New Zealand |
| HKN | Hoskins | Papua New Guinea |
| HKS | Jackson, Hawkins Fld, MS | USA |
| HKT | Phuket/Int'l | Thailand |
| HKV | Haskovo | Bulgaria |
| HKY | Hickory, NC | USA |
| HLA | Lanseria | S. Africa |
| HLB | Batesville/Hillenbrand, IN | USA |
| HLC | Hill City, KS | USA |
| HLD | Hailar | China |
| HLF | Hultsfred/AFB | Sweden |
| HLG | Wheeling, WV | USA |
| HLH | Ulanhot | China |
| HLI | Hollister, CA | USA |

| Code | Location | Country |
|------|----------|---------|
| HLJ | Shauliaj | Lithuania |
| HLL | Hillside | Australia |
| HLM | Holland/Park Township, MI | USA |
| HLN | Heiena, MT | USA |
| HLP | Jakarta/Halim Penclana Kusuma | Indonesia |
| HLR | Ft. Hood/AAF, TX | USA |
| HLS | St Helens | Australia |
| HLT | Hamilton | Australia |
| HLU | Houailou | New Caledonia |
| HLV | Helenvaie | Australia |
| HLW | Hluhluwe | S. Africa |
| HLX | Hillsville, VA | USA |
| HLY | Holyhead | UK |
| HLZ | Hamilton | New Zealand |
| HMA | Malmo/Malmo City HVC | Sweden |
| HME | Hassi-Messaoud | Algeria |
| HMG | Hermannsburg | Australia |
| HMI | Hami | China |
| HMJ | Khmeinitskiy | Ukraine |
| HMM | Hamilton/Ravalli County, MT | USA |
| HMN | Holloman/AFB, NM | USA |
| HMO | Hermosillo/Gen Pesqueira Garcia | Mexico |
| HMR | Hamar/Hamar Arpt | Norway |
| HMS | Hanford., WA | USA |
| HMT | Hemet/Ryan Fld, CA | USA |
| HMV | Hemavan | Sweden |
| HNA | Moriolka/Hanamaki | Japan |
| HNB | Huntingburg, IN | USA |
| HNC | Hatteras, NC | USA |
| HND | Tokyo/Haneda | Japan |
| HNE | Tahneta Pass Lodge, AK | USA |
| HNG | Hienghene | New Caledonia |
| HNH | Hoonah, AK | USA |
| HNI | Heiweni | Papua New Guinea |
| HNK | Hinchinbrook Is | Australia |
| HNL | Honolulu/Int'l, HI | USA |
| HNM | Hana, HI | USA |
| HNN | Honinabi | Papua New Guinea |
| HNO | Hercegnovi | Yugoslavia |
| HNS | Haines Arpt, AK | USA |
| HNX | Hanna, WY | USA |
| HNY | Hengyang | China |
| HOA | Hola | Kenya |
| HOB | Hobbs, NM | USA |
| HOC | Komako | Papua New Guinea |
| HOD | Hodeidah/Hodeidah Arpt | Yemen |
| HOE | Houeisay | Laos |
| HOF | Hofuf/Al Hasa | Saudi Arabia |
| HOG | Holguir/Frank Pais | Cuba |
| HOH | Hohenems | Austria |
| HOI | Hao Is | F. Polynesia |
| HOK | Hooker Creek | Australia |
| HOL | Holikachu, AK | USA |
| HOM | Homer Arpt, AK | USA |
| HON | Huron, SD | USA |
| HOO | Quanduc/Nhon Co | Vietnam |
| HOP | Campbell/AAF, KY | USA |
| HOQ | Hof | Germany |
| HOR | Horta | Portugal |
| HOS | Chos Malal/Oscar Reguera | Argentina |
| HOT | Hot Springs, AR | USA |
| HOU | Houston, Hobby Arpt, TX | USA |
| HOV | Orsta-Volda/Hovden | Norway |
| HOW | Ft. Kobbe/Howard AFB | Panama |
| HOX | Homalin | Myanmar |
| HOY | Hoy Is | UK |
| HPA | Ha'Apai/Salote Pilolevu | Tonga |
| HPB | Hooper Bay, AK | USA |
| HPE | Hope Vale | Australia |
| HPH | Haiphong/Catbi | Vietnam |
| HPN | Westchester County, NY | USA |
| HPR | Pretoria/Central Hpr | S. Africa |
| HPT | Hampton/Municipal, IA | USA |
| HPV | Kauai Is/Princeville, HI | USA |
| HPY | Baytown, TX | USA |
| HQM | Hoquiam, WA | USA |
| HRA | Mansehra | Pakistan |
| HRB | Harbin | China |
| HRC | Zhairem | Kazakstan |
| HRD | Harstad | Norway |
| HRE | Harare Kutsaga | Zimbabwe |
| HRG | Hurghada | Egypt |
| HRJ | Chaurjlnari | Nepal |
| HRK | Kharkov | Ukraine |
| HRL | Harlingen/Valley Int'l, TX | USA |
| HRM | Hassi R Mel/Tilrempt | Algeria |
| HRN | Heron Is / HP | Australia |
| HRO | Harrison, AR | USA |
| HRR | Herrera | Colombia |

| Code | Airport | Country |
|---|---|---|
| HRS | Harrismith | S. Africa |
| HRT | Harrogate/Linton-On-Ouse | UK |
| HRY | Henbury | Australia |
| HRZ | Horizontina | Brazil |
| HSB | Harrisburg/Raleigh, NC | USA |
| HSC | Shaoguan | China |
| HSE | Hatteras, Mitchell Fld, NC | USA |
| HSG | Saga | Japan |
| HSH | Las Vegas/Henderson Sky Harbor, NV | USA |
| HSI | Hastings Municipal, NE | USA |
| HSL | Huslia, AK | USA |
| HSM | Horsham | Australia |
| HSN | Zhoushan | China |
| HSP | Hot Springs/Ingalls, VA | USA |
| HSS | Hissar | India |
| HST | Homestead/AFB, FL | USA |
| HSV | Huntsville, AL | USA |
| HSZ | Hsinchu | Taiwan |
| HTA | Chita | Russia |
| HTB | Terre-de-Bas | Gaudeloupe |
| HTF | Hatfeild | UK |
| HTG | Hatanga | Russia |
| HTH | Hawthorne, NV | USA |
| HTI | Hamilton Is | Australia |
| HTL | Houghton Lake, MI | USA |
| HTN | Hotan | China |
| HTO | East Hampton, NY | USA |
| HTR | Hateruma | Japan |
| HTS | Huntington, WV | USA |
| HTU | Hopetoun | Australia |
| HTV | Huntsville, TX | USA |
| HTW | Chesapeake/Huntington County, OH | USA |
| HTZ | Hato Corozal | Colombia |
| HUA | Huntsville/Redstone/AAF | USA |
| HUB | Humbert River | Australia |
| HUC | Humacao/Humacao Arpt | Puerto Rico |
| HUD | Humboldt, IA | USA |
| HUE | Humera | Ethiopia |
| HUF | Terre Haute, IN | USA |
| HUG | Huelnuetenango | Guatemala |
| HUH | Huahine/Flying Boat | French Polynesia |
| HUI | Hue/Phu Bai | Vietnam |
| HUJ | Hugo, OK | USA |
| HUK | Hukuntsi | Botswana |
| HUL | Houlton Int'l, ME | USA |
| HUM | Houma-Terrebonne, LA | USA |
| HUN | Hualien | Taiwan |
| HUQ | Houn | Libya |
| HUS | Hughes/Municipal, AK | USA |
| HUT | Hutchinsen, KS | USA |
| HUU | Huanuco | Peru |
| HUV | Hudiksvall | Sweden |
| HUX | Huatulco | Mexico |
| HUY | Humberside | UK |
| HUZ | Huizinou | China |
| HVA | Analalava | Madagascar |
| HVB | Hervey Bay | Australia |
| HVD | Khovd | Mongolia |
| HVE | Hanksville/Intermediate, UT | USA |
| HVG | Honningsvag/Valan | Norway |
| HVK | Holmavik | Iceland |
| HVM | Hvammstangi | Iceland |
| HVN | Tweed-New Haven, CT | USA |
| HVR | Havre City-County, MT | USA |
| HVS | Hartsville, SC | USA |
| HWA | Hawabango | Papua New Guinea |
| HWD | Hayward Air Terminal, CA | USA |
| HWI | Hawk Inlet/SPB, AK | USA |
| HWK | Hawker/Wilpena Pound | Australia |
| HWN | Hwange Nat Park | Zimbabwe |
| HWO | Hollywood-North Perry, FL | USA |
| HWV | Shirley, Brookhaven Arpt, NY | USA |
| HXX | Hay | Australia |
| HYA | Hyannis-Barnstable, MA | USA |
| HYC | High Wycombe (MOD) | UK |
| HYD | Hyderabad/Begumpet | India |
| HYF | Hayfields | Papua New Guinea |
| HYG | Hydaburg/SPB, AK | USA |
| HYL | Hollis/SPB, AK | USA |
| HYN | Huangyan | China |
| HYR | Hayward Municipal, WI | USA |
| HYS | Hays/Municipal, KS | USA |
| HYV | Hyvinkää | Finland |
| HZB | Hazebrouck, Merville/Calonne | France |
| HZG | Hartzhong | China |
| HZK | Husavik | Iceland |
| HZL | HazletonPA | USA |
| HZV | Hazyview | S. Africa |

# I

| Code | Airport | Country |
|---|---|---|
| IAA | Igarka | Russia |
| IAB | Mcconnell/AFB, KS | USA |
| IAD | Dulles Int'l, DC | USA |
| IAG | Niagara Falls Int'l, NY | USA |
| IAH | Houston George Bush Int'l, TX | USA |
| IAM | In Amenas | Algeria |
| IAN | Kiana/Bob Barker Memorial, AK | USA |
| IAQ | Bahregan | Iran |
| IAR | Yaroslavl | Russia |
| IAS | Iasi | Romania |
| IAT | IATA Traffic Svcs | n/a |
| IAU | Iaura | Papua New Guinea |
| IBA | Ibadan/(NAW) | Nigeria |
| IBE | Ibague | Colombia |
| IBI | Iboki | Papua New Guinea |
| IBO | Illbo | Mozambique |
| IBP | Iberia | Peru |
| IBZ | Ibiza | Spain |
| ICA | Icabaru | Venezuela |
| ICI | Cicia | Fiji |
| ICK | Nieuw Nickerie | Suriname |
| ICL | Clarinda, IA | USA |
| ICN | Incheon | S. Korea |
| ICO | Sicogon Is | Philippines |
| ICR | Nicaro | Cuba |
| ICT | Wichita Mid-Continent, KS | USA |
| ICY | Icy Bay, AK | USA |
| IDA | Idaho Falls, Fanning Fld, ID | USA |
| IDB | Idre | Sweden |
| IDF | Idiofa | Congo, DR |
| IDG | Ida Grove/Municipal, IA | USA |
| IDI | Indiana, PA | USA |
| IDK | Indulkana | Australia |
| IDN | Indagen | Papua New Guinea |
| IDO | Santa Isabel do Morro | Brazil |
| IDP | Independence, KS | USA |
| IDR | Indore | India |
| IDY | Ile d'Yeu | France |
| IEG | Zielona Gora/Babimost | Poland |
| IEJ | Lejima | Japan |
| IEN | Pine Ridge, SD | USA |
| IEV | Kiev/Zhulhany | Ukraine |
| IFA | Iowa Falls, IA | USA |
| IFF | Iffley | Australia |
| IFJ | Isafjordur | Iceland |
| IFL | Innisfail | Australia |
| IFN | Isfahan | Iran |
| IFO | Ivanci-Frankovsk | Ukraine |
| IFP | Bullhead City/Int'l, AZ | USA |
| IGA | Inagua | Bahamas |
| IGB | Ingeniero Jacobacci | Argentina |
| IGC | Charleston/AFB, SC | USA |
| IGE | Iguela | Gabon |
| IGG | Igiugig, AK | USA |
| IGH | Ingham | Australia |
| IGM | Kingman, AZ | USA |
| IGN | Iligan/Maria Cristina | Philippines |
| IGO | Chigorodo | Colombia |
| IGR | Iguazu/Cataratas | Argentina |
| IGU | Iguassu Falls/Cataratas | Brazil |
| IGX | Chapel Hill/Williams, NC | USA |
| IHA | Niihama | Japan |
| IHN | Oishn | Yemen |
| IHO | Ithosy | Madagascar |
| IHU | Ihu | Papua New Guinea |
| IIA | Inishmaian | Ireland |
| IIN | Nishinoomote | Japan |
| IIS | Nissan Is | Papua New Guinea |
| IJD | Willimantic/Windham, CT | USA |
| IJK | Izhevsk | Russia |
| IJU | Ijui/J.Batista Bos Filho | Brazil |
| IJX | Jacksonville, IL | USA |
| IKB | Wilkesboro/Wilkes County, NC | USA |
| IKI | Iki | Japan |
| IKK | Kankakee, IL | USA |
| IKL | Ikela | Congo, DR |
| IKO | Nikolski/AFS, AK | USA |
| IKP | Inkerman | Australia |
| IKR | Kirtland/AFB, NM | USA |
| IKS | Tiksi | Russia |
| IKT | Irkutsk | Russia |
| ILA | Illaga | Indonesia |
| ILB | Ilha Solteira | Brazil |
| ILE | Killeen/Municipal, TX | USA |
| ILF | Ilford, MB | Canada |
| ILG | Wilmington, DE | USA |

| Code | Airport | Country |
|---|---|---|
| ILH | Illishern/Illis Airbase | Germany |
| ILI | Iliamna Arpt, AK | USA |
| ILK | Ilaka | Madagascar |
| ILL | Willmar, MN | USA |
| ILM | Wilmington, New Hanover Int'l, NC | USA |
| ILN | Wilmington, Airborne Airpark, OH | USA |
| ILO | Ioilo/Mandurriao | Philippines |
| ILP | Ile Des Pins | New Caledonia |
| ILQ | Ilo | Peru |
| ILR | Ilorin | Nigeria |
| ILU | Kilaguni | Kenya |
| ILX | Ileg | Papua New Guinea |
| ILY | Islay/Glenegedaie | UK |
| ILZ | Zilina | Slovakia |
| IMA | Iamalele | Papua New Guinea |
| IMB | Imbaimadai | Guyana |
| IMD | Imonda | Papua New Guinea |
| IMF | Imphal/Mun | India |
| IMG | Inhaminga | Mozambique |
| IMI | Ine Is | Marshall Is |
| IMK | Simikot | Nepal |
| IML | Imperial Municipal, NE | USA |
| IMM | Immokalee, FL | USA |
| IMN | Imane | Papua New Guinea |
| IMO | Zemio | Central African Rep |
| IMP | Imperatriz | Brazil |
| IMT | Iron Mountain, MI | USA |
| IMZ | Nimroz | Afghanistan |
| INA | Inta | Russia |
| INB | Independence | Belize |
| INC | Yinchuan | China |
| IND | Indianapolis Int'l, IN | USA |
| INE | Chinde | Mozambique |
| INF | In Guezzam | Algeria |
| ING | Lago Argentina | Argentina |
| INH | Inhambane | Mozambique |
| INI | Nis | Yugoslavia |
| INJ | Injune | Australia |
| INK | Wink, TX | USA |
| INL | Int'l Falls, MN | USA |
| INM | Innamiricka | Australia |
| INN | Innsbruck/Kranebitten | Austria |
| INO | Inongo | Congo, DR |
| INQ | Inisheer | Ireland |
| INR | Sault Ste Marie/Kincheloe/AFB, MI | USA |
| INS | Indian Springs, NV | USA |
| INT | Winston Salem, NC | USA |
| INU | Nauru Arpt | Nauru |
| INV | Inverness/Dalcross | UK |
| INW | Winslow Municipal, AZ | USA |
| INX | Inanwatan | Indonesia |
| INY | Inyati | S. Africa |
| INZ | In Salah North | Algeria |
| IOA | Ioannina | Greece |
| IOK | Iokea | Papua New Guinea |
| IOM | Isle Of Man/Ronaldsway | UK |
| ION | Imptondo | Congo, DR |
| IOP | Ioma | Papua New Guinea |
| IOR | Inishmore/Kilronan | Ireland |
| IOU | Ile Ouen | New Caledonia |
| IOW | Iowa City Municipal, IA | USA |
| IPA | Ipota | Vanuatu |
| IPC | Easter Is/Mataveri inE | Chile |
| IPE | Ipil | Philippines |
| IPG | Ipiranga | Brazil |
| IPH | Ipoh | Malaysia |
| IPI | Ipiales/San Luis | Colombia |
| IPL | Imperial County, CA | USA |
| IPN | Ipatinga/Usiminas | Brazil |
| IPT | Williamsport, PA | USA |
| IPU | Ipiau | Brazil |
| IPW | Ipswich | UK |
| IQM | Cierno | China |
| IQN | Qingyang | China |
| IQQ | Iquique/Cavancha | Chile |
| IQT | Iquitos/CF, Secada | Peru |
| IRA | KiraKira | Solomon Is |
| IRB | Iraan/Municipal, TX | USA |
| IRC | Circle/Circle City, AK | USA |
| IRD | Ishurdi | Bangladesh |
| IRE | Irece | Brazil |
| IRG | Lockhart River | Australia |
| IRI | Iringa/Nduli | Tanzania |
| IRJ | La Riola | Argentina |
| IRK | Kirksvite Municipal, MO | USA |
| IRN | Iriona | Honduras |
| IRO | Birao | Central African Rep |
| IRP | Isro/Matari | Congo, DR |
| IRS | Sturgis/Kirsch Municipal, MI | USA |

AIRPORTS -1-

| | | |
|---|---|---|
| ISA | Mount Isa | Australia |
| ISB | Islamabad Int'l | Pakistan |
| ISC | Isles Of Scilly-St Marys | UK |
| ISD | Iscuande | Colombia |
| ISE | Isparta | Turkey |
| ISG | Ishigaki | Japan |
| ISH | Ischia | Italy |
| ISI | Isisford | Australia |
| ISJ | Isla Mujeres | Mexico |
| ISK | Nasik/Gandhinagar | India |
| ISL | Isabel Pass, AK | USA |
| ISM | Kissimmee/Municipal, FL | USA |
| ISN | Williston/Sloulin Fld Int'l, ND | USA |
| ISO | Kinston-Stallings, NC | USA |
| ISP | Long Is MacArthur, NY | USA |
| ISQ | Manistique, MI | USA |
| ISS | Wiscasset, ME | USA |
| IST | Istanbul/Ataturk | Turkey |
| ISW | Wisconsin Rapids, WI | USA |
| ITA | Itacoatiara | Brazil |
| ITB | Itaituba | Brazil |
| ITE | Itubera | Brazil |
| ITH | Ithaca, NY | USA |
| ITI | Itambacuri | Brazil |
| ITJ | Itaiai | Brazil |
| ITK | Tokarna | Papua New Guinea |
| ITM | Osaka/Itami | Japan |
| ITN | Itaburia | Brazil |
| ITO | Hilo Int'l, HI | USA |
| ITP | Itaperuna | Brazil |
| ITQ | Itaqui | Brazil |
| ITR | Itumbiara | Brazil |
| IUE | Niue Is/Hanan | Niue Is |
| IUL | Ilu | Indonesia |
| IUM | Summit Lake, BC | Canada |
| IUS | Inus | Papua New Guinea |
| IVA | Ambanja | Madagascar |
| IVC | Invercargill | New Zealand |
| IVG | Ivangrad | Yugoslavia |
| IVH | Ivishak, AK | USA |
| IVL | Ivalo | Finland |
| IVO | Chivoo | Colombia |
| IVR | Inverell | Australia |
| IVW | Inverway | Australia |
| IWA | Ivanova | Russia |
| IWD | Ironwood/Gogebic County, MI | USA |
| IWH | Lawn Hill | Australia |
| IWI | Wiscasset, ME | USA |
| IWJ | Iwami | Japan |
| IWO | Iwo Jima Vol/Airbase | Japan |
| IWS | Lakeside, TX | USA |
| IXA | Agartala/Singerbhil | India |
| IXB | Bagdogra | India |
| IXC | Chandigarh | India |
| IXD | Allahabad/Bamrauli | India |
| IXE | Mangalore/Balpe | India |
| IXG | Belgaum/Sambre | India |
| IXH | Kailashahar | India |
| IXI | Lilabari | India |
| IXJ | Jammu/Satwari | India |
| IXK | Keshod | India |
| IXL | Leh | India |
| IXM | Madurai | India |
| IXN | Khowai | India |
| IXP | Pathankot | India |
| IXQ | Kamalpur | India |
| IXR | Ranchi | India |
| IXS | Silchar/Kumbhirgram | India |
| IXT | Pasighat | India |
| IXU | Aurangabad/Chikkalthana | India |
| IXV | Along | India |
| IXW | Jamshedpur/Sonari | India |
| IXY | Kandla | India |
| IXZ | Port Blair | India |
| IYK | Inyokern, CA | USA |
| IZG | Fryeburg, Eastern Slopes Regional Arpt, ME | USA |
| IZO | Izumo | Japan |
| IZT | Ixtepec | Mexico |

## J

| | | |
|---|---|---|
| JAA | Jalalabad | Afghanistan |
| JAB | Jabiru | Australia |
| JAC | Jackson Hole, WY | USA |
| JAD | Jandakot | Australia |
| JAE | Atlanta/Technology Park, GA | USA |
| JAF | JaUna/Kankesanturai | Sri Lanka |

| | | |
|---|---|---|
| JAG | Jacobabad | Pakistan |
| JAH | Aubagne/Agora Helipad | France |
| JAI | Jaipur/Sanganeer | India |
| JAJ | Atlanta/Perimeter Mall, GA | USA |
| JAK | Jacmel | Haiti |
| JAL | Jalapa | Mexico |
| JAM | Jambol | Bulgaria |
| JAN | Jackson Int'l, MS | USA |
| JAO | Atlanta/Beaver Ruin, GA | USA |
| JAP | Punta Renes | Costa Rica |
| JAQ | Jacquinot Bay | Papua New Guinea |
| JAS | Jasper/County, TX | USA |
| JAT | Jabot | Marshall Is |
| JAU | Jaula | Peru |
| JAV | Ilulissat | Greenland |
| JAX | Jacksonville Int'l, FL | USA |
| JBC | Boston / HP, MA | USA |
| JBK | Berkeley, CA | USA |
| JBP | Los Angeles/Commerce Bus. Plaza, CA | USA |
| JBR | Jonesboro, AR | USA |
| JBS | Pleasanton/Hacienda Bus-Park HP, CA | USA |
| JBT | Bethel/City Landing, AK | USA |
| JCA | Cannes/Croisette HP | France |
| JCB | Joacaba | Brazil |
| JCC | San Francisco/China Basin HP, CA | USA |
| JCD | St Croix Is/Downtown HP | Virgin Is (US) |
| JCH | Qasigiannguit | Greenland |
| JCI | Kansas City/Johnson Industrial, MO | USA |
| JCJ | Cheju/Chu Ja HP | S. Korea |
| JCK | Julia Creek | Australia |
| JCM | Jacobina | Brazil |
| JCO | Cominc / HP | Malta |
| JCR | Jacareacanga | Brazil |
| JCT | Junction, TX | USA |
| JCU | Ceuta/Ceuta HP | Spain |
| JCX | Los Angeles/Citicorp Plaza HP, CA | USA |
| JCY | Johnson, TX | USA |
| JDF | Juiz De Fora/Francisco De Assis | Brazil |
| JDH | Jodhpur | India |
| JDM | Miami/Downtown HP, FL | USA |
| JDN | Jordan, MT | USA |
| JDO | Juazeiro Do Norte/Regional Do Carin. Brazil | |
| JDP | Paris / HP | France |
| JDT | Minneapolis/Downtown HP | USA |
| JDX | Houston/Cntrl Bus. District, TX | USA |
| JDY | Downey / HP, CA | USA |
| JDZ | Jingdezhen | China |
| JED | Jeddah/King Abdul Aziz Int'l Arpt | Saudi Arabia |
| JEE | Jeremie | Haiti |
| JEF | Jefferson City, MO | USA |
| JEG | Aasiaat | Greenland |
| JEJ | Jeh | Marshall Is |
| JEM | Emeryville / HP, CA | USA |
| JEQ | Jequie | Brazil |
| JER | Jersey | UK |
| JEV | Eviry HP | France |
| JFK | Kennedy Int'l, NY | USA |
| JFM | Fremantle/ HP | Australia |
| JFN | Jefferson/Ashtabula, OH | USA |
| JFR | Paamiut | Greenland |
| JGA | Jamnagar/Govardhanpur | India |
| JGB | Jagdaipur | India |
| JGC | Grand Canyon / HP, AZ | USA |
| JGE | Geoie HP | S. Korea |
| JGL | Atlanta/Galleria, GA | USA |
| JGN | Jiayuguan | China |
| JGO | Oeqertarsuaq | Greenland |
| JGP | Houston/Greenway Plaza HP, TX | USA |
| JGQ | Houston/Transco Twr Galleria, TX | USA |
| JGR | Groennedal/ HP | Greenland |
| JGX | Glendale / HP, CA | USA |
| JHB | Johor Bahru/Sultan Ismail Int'l | Malaysia |
| JHC | Garden City/Is HP, NY | USA |
| JHE | Helsingborg/ HP | Sweden |
| JHG | Jinghong/Gasa | China |
| JHM | Kapalua, HI | USA |
| JHN | Nanchang | China |
| JHQ | Shute Harbour HP | Australia |
| JHS | Sisimiut | Greenland |

| | | |
|---|---|---|
| JHW | Jamestown, NY | USA |
| JHY | Cambridge/Hyatt Regency HP, MA | USA |
| JI0 | Ontario/Int'l HP, CA | USA |
| JIA | Juina | Brazil |
| JIB | Djibouti/Ambouli | Côte D'Ivoire |
| JID | Los Angeles/City Of Industry HP, CA | USA |
| JIJ | Jijig/Jigiga | Ethiopia |
| JIK | Ikaria Is/Ikaria | Greece |
| JIL | Jilin | China |
| JIM | Jimma | Ethiopia |
| JIN | Jinja | Uganda |
| JIP | Jpjapa | Ecuador |
| JIR | Jin | Nepal |
| JIU | Jiujiang | China |
| JIW | Jiwani | Pakistan |
| JJI | Juanjui | Peru |
| JJN | Jinjiang | China |
| JJU | Qaqortoq / HP | Greenland |
| JKG | Jonkoping/Axamo | Sweden |
| JKH | Chios/Khios | Greece |
| JKL | Jackson/Carroll, KY | USA |
| JKR | Janakpur | Nepal |
| JKV | Jacksonville, TX | USA |
| JLA | Cooper Lodge/Quartz Creek, AK | USA |
| JLB | Long Beach / HP, CA | USA |
| JLD | Landskrona/ HP | Sweden |
| JLH | Arlington Heights/US AHP, IL | USA |
| JLN | Joplin, MO | USA |
| JLO | Jesolo | Italy |
| JLP | Juan Les Pins | France |
| JLR | Jalbalpur | India |
| JLS | Jales | Brazil |
| JLX | Los Angeles/Union Stn HP, CA | USA |
| JMA | Houston/Marriot Astrodome, TX | USA |
| JMB | Jamba | Angola |
| JMC | Sausalito/Marin County, CA | USA |
| JMD | Dallas/Market Centre HP, TX | USA |
| JMH | Schaumburg/Marriott HP, IL | USA |
| JMK | Mikonos | Greece |
| JMM | Malmo/Malmo Harbour HP | Sweden |
| JMN | Mankato/Municipal HP, MN | USA |
| JMO | Jornsom | Nepal |
| JMS | Jamestown, ND | USA |
| JMU | Jiarnusi | China |
| JMY | Freetown/Mammy Yoko HP | Sierra Leone |
| JNA | Januaria | Brazil |
| JNB | Johannesburg Int'l | S. Africa |
| JNG | Jining | China |
| JNH | Dallas/North Park Inn HP, TX | USA |
| JNI | Junin | Argentina |
| JNN | Nanortalik | Greenland |
| JNP | Newport Beach / HP, CA | USA |
| JNS | Narsaq/ HP | Greenland |
| JNU | Juneau Int'l, AK | USA |
| JNW | Newport, OR | USA |
| JNX | Naxos | Greece |
| JNZ | Jinzhou | China |
| JOC | Santa Ana/Centerport HP, CA | USA |
| JOE | Joensuu | Finland |
| JOG | Yogyakarta/Adisutjipto | Indonesia |
| JOH | Port Saint Johns | S. Africa |
| JOI | Joinville/Cubatao | Brazil |
| JOK | Josrikar-Cia | Russia |
| JOL | Jolo | Philippines |
| JOM | Njombe | Tanzania |
| JON | Johnston Is | Wake/Midway Is |
| JOP | Josephstaal | Papua New Guinea |
| JOR | Orange/The City HP, CA | USA |
| JOS | Jos | Nigeria |
| JOT | Joliet Municipal, IL | USA |
| JPA | Joato Pessoa/Castro Pinto | Brazil |
| JPD | Pasadena / HP, CA | USA |
| JPN | Washington/Pentagon Army, DC | USA |
| JPR | Ji-Parana | Brazil |
| JPT | Houston/Park Ten HP, TX | USA |
| JPU | Paris/La Defense HP | France |
| JQE | Jaque | Panama |
| JRA | New York/West 30th St HP, NY | USA |
| JRB | New York/Downtown Manhattan HP, NY | USA |
| JRC | Rochester/Municipal HP, MN | USA |
| JRD | Riverside/ HP, CA | USA |
| JRE | New York/East 60th Street HP, NY | USA |
| JRH | Jorhat/Rowriah | India |

| | | |
|---|---|---|
| JRK | Arsuk | Greenland |
| JRN | Juruena | Brazil |
| JRO | Kilimanjaro | Tanzania |
| JRS | Jerusalem, Occupied Palestinian Territory | |
| JSA | Jaisalmer | India |
| JSD | Stratford/Sikorsky HP, CT | USA |
| JSG | San Rafael HP, CA | USA |
| JSH | Sitia | Greece |
| JSI | Skiathos Is | Greece |
| JSK | Saint Cloud HP, MN | USA |
| JSL | Atlantic City/Steel Pier HP, NJ | USA |
| JSM | Jose De San Martin | Argentina |
| JSN | Los Angeles/Sherman Oaks HP, CA | USA |
| JSO | Sodertalje/Sodertalje HP | Sweden |
| JSP | Cheju/Sogwipo HP | S. Korea |
| JSR | Jessore | Bangladesh |
| JSS | Spetsai Is | Gaudeloupe |
| JST | Johnstown-Cambria, PA | USA |
| JSU | Manihsoq / HP | Greenland |
| JSY | Syros Is | Greece |
| JSZ | Saint Tropez / HP | France |
| JTI | Jalai | Brazil |
| JTO | Thousand Oaks / HP, CA | USA |
| JTR | Thira | Greece |
| JTY | Astypalaia Is | Greece |
| JUA | Juara | Brazil |
| JUB | Juba | Sudan |
| JUC | Los Angeles/Universal City HP, CA | USA |
| JUI | Juist | Germany |
| JUJ | Jujuy/El Cadilial | Argentina |
| JUL | Juliaca | Peru |
| JUM | Jumla | Nepal |
| JUN | Jundah | Australia |
| JUO | Jurado | Colombia |
| JUP | Upland/Cable HP, CA | USA |
| JUR | Jurien Bay | Australia |
| JUT | Juticalpa | Honduras |
| JUV | Upernavik/ HP | Greenland |
| JUZ | Juzhou | China |
| JVA | Ankavandra | Madagascar |
| JVI | Manville/Kupper, NJ | USA |
| JVL | Janesville, WI | USA |
| JWA | Jwaneng | Botswana |
| JWC | Los Angeles/Warner Cntr Bus. Plaza, CA | USA |
| JWH | Houston/Westchase Hilton HP, TX | USA |
| JWL | Houston/Woodlawns, TX | USA |
| JXN | Jackson-Reynolds Municipal, MI | USA |
| JYO | Leesburg/Godfrey, VA | USA |
| JYV | Jyvaskyla | Finland |

# K

| | | |
|---|---|---|
| KAA | Kasama | Zambia |
| KAB | Kariba | Zimbabwe |
| KAC | Kameshli | Syria |
| KAD | Kaduna | Nigeria |
| KAE | Kake/SPB, AK | USA |
| KAF | Karato | Papua New Guinea |
| KAG | Kangnung/Air Base | S. Korea |
| KAH | Melbourne HP | Australia |
| KAI | Kaieteur | Guyana |
| KAJ | Kajaani | Finland |
| KAK | Kar | Papua New Guinea |
| KAL | Kallag, AK | USA |
| KAM | Kamaran Is | Yemen |
| KAN | Kano/Aminu Kano Int'l | Nigeria |
| KAO | Kuusamo | Finland |
| KAP | Kapanga | Congo, DR |
| KAQ | Kamulai | Papua New Guinea |
| KAR | Kamarang | Guyana |
| KAS | Karasburg | Namibia |
| KAT | Kaitaia | New Zealand |
| KAU | Kauhava | Finland |
| KAV | Kavanayen | Venezuela |
| KAW | Kawthaung | Myanmar |
| KAX | Kalbarri | Australia |
| KAY | Wakaya Is | Fiji |
| KAZ | Kau | Indonesia |
| KBA | Kabala | Sierra Leone |
| KBB | Kirkimbie | Australia |
| KBC | Birch Creek, AK | USA |
| KBD | Kimberley Downs | Australia |
| KBE | Bell Is/Hot Springs SPB, AK | USA |

| | | |
|---|---|---|
| KBF | Karubaga | Indonesia |
| KBG | Kabaiega Falls | Uganda |
| KBH | Kalat | Pakistan |
| KBI | Kribi | Cameroon |
| KBJ | Kings Canyon | Australia |
| KBK | Klag Bay, AK | USA |
| KBL | Kabul/Khwaja Rawash | Afghanistan |
| KBM | Kabwurn | Papua New Guinea |
| KBN | Kabinda | Congo, DR |
| KBO | Kabalo | Congo, DR |
| KBP | Kiev/Borispol | Ukraine |
| KBQ | Kasungu | Malawi |
| KBR | Kota Bharu/Pengkalan Chepa | Malaysia |
| KBS | Bo | Sierra Leone |
| KBT | Kaben | Marshall Is |
| KBU | Kotabaru | Indonesia |
| KBV | Krabi | Thailand |
| KBW | Chignik, Chignik Bay, AK | USA |
| KBX | Kambuaya | Indonesia |
| KBY | Streaky Bay | Australia |
| KBZ | Kaikoura | New Zealand |
| KCA | Kucla | China |
| KCB | Kasikasirna/Tepoe Airstrip | Suriname |
| KCC | Coffman Cove, AK | USA |
| KCD | Kamur | Indonesia |
| KCE | Collinsville | Australia |
| KCF | Kadanwari | Pakistan |
| KCG | Chignik, Fisheries, AK | USA |
| KCH | Kuching | Malaysia |
| KCI | Kon | Indonesia |
| KCJ | Komaio | Papua New Guinea |
| KCK | Kansas City/Fairfax, KS | USA |
| KCL | Chignik/Lagoon, AK | USA |
| KCM | Kahramanmaras | Turkey |
| KCN | Chernofski/SPB, AK | USA |
| KCO | Kocaeli/Cengiz Topel | Turkey |
| KCP | Kamenets-Podolskiy | Ukraine |
| KCQ | Chignik, AK | USA |
| KCR | Colorado Creek, AK | USA |
| KCS | Kings Creek Stn | Australia |
| KCU | Masindi | Uganda |
| KCZ | Kochi | Japan |
| KDA | Kolda | Senegal |
| KDB | Kambaida | Australia |
| KDC | Kandi | Benin |
| KDD | Khuzdar | Pakistan |
| KDE | Koroba | Papua New Guinea |
| KDF | Kouba | Algeria |
| KDG | Kardjali | Bulgaria |
| KDH | Kandahar | Afghanistan |
| KDI | Kendan/Wolter Monginsidi | Indonesia |
| KDJ | N'Djole | Gabon |
| KDK | Kodiak/Municipal, AK | USA |
| KDL | Kardla | Estonia |
| KDM | Kaadedhclhoo | Maldives |
| KDN | Ndende | Gabon |
| KDO | Kadhdhoo | Maldives |
| KDP | Kandep | Papua New Guinea |
| KDQ | Kamberatoro | Papua New Guinea |
| KDR | Kandrian | Papua New Guinea |
| KDS | Kamaran Downs | Australia |
| KDU | Skardu | Pakistan |
| KDV | Kandavu | Fiji |
| KEA | Keisah | Indonesia |
| KEB | Nanwalek, AK | USA |
| KEC | Kasenga | Congo, DR |
| KED | Kaedi | Mauritania |
| KEE | Kelle | Congo, DR |
| KEF | Reykjavik Int'l | Iceland |
| KEG | Keglsugi | Papua New Guinea |
| KEH | Kenmore Air Harbor, WA | USA |
| KEi | Kepi | Indonesia |
| KEJ | Kemerovo | Russia |
| KEK | Ekwok, AK | USA |
| KEL | Kiel/Holtenau Civilian | Germany |
| KEM | Kemi/Tornio | Finland |
| KEN | Kenema | Sierra Leone |
| KEO | Odienne | Côte D'Ivoire |
| KEP | Nepalganj | Nepal |
| KEQ | Kebar | Indonesia |
| KER | Kerman | Iran |
| KES | Kelsey, MB | Canada |
| KET | Keng Tung | Myanmar |
| KEU | Kelly Bar, AK | USA |
| KEV | Kuorevesi/Halli | Finland |
| KEW | Keewaywin, ON | Canada |
| KEX | Kanabea | Papua New Guinea |
| KEY | Kericho | Kenya |
| KFA | Kiffa | Mauritania |
| KFG | Kalkurung | Australia |

| | | |
|---|---|---|
| KFP | False Pass, AK | USA |
| KFS | Kastamonu | Turkey |
| KGA | Kananga | Congo, DR |
| KGB | Konge | Papua New Guinea |
| KGC | Kingscote | Australia |
| KGD | Kaliningrad | Russia |
| KGE | Kagau | Solomon Is |
| KGF | Karaganda | Kazakstan |
| KGG | Kedougou | Senegal |
| KGH | Yongai | Papua New Guinea |
| KGI | Kalgoorlie | Australia |
| KGJ | Karonga | Malawi |
| KGK | New Koliganek, AK | USA |
| KGL | Kigali/Gregoire Kayibanda | Rwanda |
| KGM | Kungum | Papua New Guinea |
| KGN | Kasongo Lunda | Congo, DR |
| KGO | Kirovograd | Ukraine |
| KGP | Kogalym Int'l | Russia |
| KGR | Kulgera | Australia |
| KGS | Kos | Greece |
| KGU | Keningau | Malaysia |
| KGW | Kagi | Papua New Guinea |
| KGX | Grayling, AK | USA |
| KGY | Kingaroy | Australia |
| KGZ | Glacier Creek, AK | USA |
| KHA | Khaneh | Iran |
| KHC | Kerch | Ukraine |
| KHD | Khorramabad | Iran |
| KHE | Kherson | Ukraine |
| KHG | Kashi | China |
| KHH | Kaohsiung/Int'l | Taiwan |
| KHI | Karachi/Quaid-E-Azam Int'l | Pakistan |
| KHJ | Kauhajoki | Finland |
| KHK | Khark Is | Iran |
| KHL | Khulna | Bangladesh |
| KHM | Khamti | Myanmar |
| KHN | Nanchang | China |
| KHO | Khoka Moya | S. Africa |
| KHR | Kharkhorin | Mongolia |
| KHS | Khasab | Oman |
| KHT | Khost | Afghanistan |
| KHU | Kremenchug | Ukraine |
| KHV | Khaloarovsk/Novyy | Russia |
| KHW | Khwai River Lodge | Botswana |
| KIA | Kaiapit | Papua New Guinea |
| KIB | Ivanof Bay/SPB, AK | USA |
| KIC | King City, Mesa Del Rey, CA | USA |
| KID | Kristianstad/Everod | Sweden |
| KIE | Kieta/Aropa | Papua New Guinea |
| KIF | Kingfisher Lake, ON | Canada |
| KIG | Koinghaas | S. Africa |
| KIH | Kish Is | Iran |
| KIJ | Niigata | Japan |
| KIK | Kirkuk | Iraq |
| KIL | Kilwa | Congo, DR |
| KIM | Kimberley | S. Africa |
| KIN | Kingston/Norman Manley | Jamaica |
| KIO | Kili Is | Marshall Is |
| KIP | Wichita Falls/Kickapoo, KS | USA |
| KIQ | Kira | Papua New Guinea |
| KIR | Kerry | Ireland |
| KIS | Kisumu | Kenya |
| KIT | Kithira | Greece |
| KIV | Chisinau | Moldova, Republic of |
| KIW | Kitwe/Southdowns | Zambia |
| KIX | Osaka/Kansai Int'l | Japan |
| KIY | Kilwa | Tanzania |
| KIZ | Kikinonda | Papua New Guinea |
| KJA | Krasnoiarsk | Russia |
| KJK | Kortrijk/Wevelgem | Belgium |
| KJP | Kerama | Japan |
| KJU | Kamiraba | Papua New Guinea |
| KKA | Koyuk, AK | USA |
| KKB | Kitoi Bay/SPB, AK | USA |
| KKC | Khon Kaen | Thailand |
| KKD | Kokoda | Papua New Guinea |
| KKE | Kerikeri | New Zealand |
| KKF | Kagvik Creek, AK | USA |
| KKG | Konawaruk | Guyana |
| KKH | Kongiganak, AK | USA |
| KKI | Akiachak/SPB, AK | USA |
| KKJ | Kita Kyushu/Kokura | S. Korea |
| KKK | Kalalkalket/AFS, AK | USA |
| KKL | Karluk Lake SPB, AK | USA |
| KKM | Lop Bun | Thailand |
| KKN | Kirkenes/Hoeybuktmoen | Norway |
| KKO | Kaikohe | New Zealand |
| KKP | Koolburra | Australia |
| KKR | Kaukura Atoll | F. Polynesia |
| KKT | Kentland, IN | USA |
| KKU | Ekuk, AK | USA |

| Code | Name | Country |
|------|------|---------|
| KKW | Kikwit | Congo, DR |
| KKX | Kikaiga Shima | Japan |
| KKY | Kilkenny | Ireland |
| KKZ | Koh Kong | Cambodia |
| KLA | Kampala | Uganda |
| KLB | Kalabo | Zambia |
| KLC | Kaolack | Senegal |
| KLD | Kalinin/Migalovo | Russia |
| KLE | Kaele | Cameroon |
| KLF | Kaluga | Russia |
| KLG | Kalskag/Municipal, AK | USA |
| KLH | Kolhapur | India |
| KLI | Kota Koli | Congo, DR |
| KLJ | Klaipeda | Lithuania |
| KLK | Kalokol | Kenya |
| KLL | Levelock, AK | USA |
| KLN | Larsen/SPB, AK | USA |
| KLO | Kalibo | Philippines |
| KLP | Kelp Bay, AK | USA |
| KLQ | Keluang | Indonesia |
| KLR | Kalmar | Sweden |
| KLS | Kelso, Longview, WA | USA |
| KLT | Kaiserslautern | Germany |
| KLU | Klagenfurt | Austria |
| KIU | Kiunga | Kenya |
| KLV | Karlovy Vary | Czech Rep |
| KLW | Klawock, AK | USA |
| KLX | Kalamata | Greece |
| KLY | Kalima | Congo, DR |
| KLZ | Kleinzee | S. Africa |
| KMA | Kerema | Papua New Guinea |
| KMB | Koinambe | Papua New Guinea |
| KMC | King Khalid Military | Saudi Arabia |
| KMD | Mandji | Gabon |
| KME | Kamembe | Rwanda |
| KMF | Kamina | Papua New Guinea |
| KMG | Kunming | China |
| KMH | Kuruman | S. Africa |
| KMI | Miyazaki | Japan |
| KMJ | Kumamoto | Japan |
| KMK | Makabana | Congo, DR |
| KML | Kamileroi | Australia |
| KMM | Kimam | Indonesia |
| KMN | Kamina | Congo, DR |
| KMO | Manolkotak/SPB, AK | USA |
| KMP | Keetmanshoop/J.G.H. Van Der Wath | Namibia |
| KMQ | Konnatsu | Japan |
| KMR | Karinnui | Papua New Guinea |
| KMS | Kumasi | Ghana |
| KMT | Kampot | Cambodia |
| KMU | Kismayu | Somalia |
| KMV | Kalemyo | Myanmar |
| KMW | Kostroma | Russia |
| KMX | Khamis Mushat | Saudi Arabia |
| KMY | Moser Bay, AK | USA |
| KMZ | Kaoma | Zambia |
| KNA | Vina del Mar | Chile |
| KNB | Kanab, UT | USA |
| KNC | Ji'An | China |
| KND | Kindu | Congo, DR |
| KNE | Kanainj | Papua New Guinea |
| KNF | Kings Lynn/Marham/RAF | UK |
| KNG | Kaimana/Utarom | Indonesia |
| KNH | Kinmen/Shang-Yi | Taiwan |
| KNI | Katanning | Australia |
| KNJ | Kindamba | Congo, DR |
| KNK | Kakhonak, AK | USA |
| KNL | Kelanoa | Papua New Guinea |
| KNM | Kaniama | Congo, DR |
| KNN | Kankan | Guinea |
| KNO | Knokke/Het Zoute | Belgium |
| KNP | Capanda | Angola |
| KNQ | Kone | New Caledonia |
| KNR | Kangan/Jam | Iran |
| KNS | King Is | Australia |
| KNT | Kennett Municipal, MO | USA |
| KNU | Kanpur | India |
| KNV | Knights Inlet, BC | Canada |
| KNW | New Stuyahok, AK | USA |
| KNX | Kununurra | Australia |
| KNY | Kinoosao, SK | Canada |
| KNZ | Kenieba | Mali |
| KOA | Kona/Keahole, HI | USA |
| KOB | Koutaba | Cameroon |
| KOC | Koumac | New Caledonia |
| KOD | Kotabangun | Indonesia |
| KOE | Kupang/El Tari | Indonesia |
| KOF | Komatipoort | S. Africa |
| KOG | Khong | Laos |
| KOH | Koolatah | Australia |
| KOI | Kirkwall | UK |
| KOJ | Kagoshima | Japan |
| KOK | Kokkola/Pietarsaari/Kruunupyy | Finland |
| KOL | Kounnala | Central African Rep |
| KOM | Korno-Manda | Papua New Guinea |
| KON | Kontum | Vietnam |
| KOO | Kongolo | Congo, DR |
| KOP | Nakhon Phanom | Thailand |
| KOQ | Koethen | Germany |
| KOR | Kokoro | Papua New Guinea |
| KOS | Sihanoukville | Cambodia |
| KOT | Kotlik, AK | USA |
| KOU | Koulamoutou | Gabon |
| KOV | Kokshetau | Kazakstan |
| KOW | Ganzhou | China |
| KOX | Kokonao/Timuka | Indonesia |
| KOY | Olga Bay/SPB, AK | USA |
| KOZ | Ouzinkie/SPB, AK | USA |
| KPA | Koplago | Papua New Guinea |
| KPB | Point Baker/SPB, AK | USA |
| KPC | Port Clarence, AK | USA |
| KPD | King Of Prussia, PA | USA |
| KPE | Yapsiei | Papua New Guinea |
| KPG | Kurupung | Guyana |
| KPH | Pauloff Harbor/SPB, AK | USA |
| KPI | Kapit | Malaysia |
| KPK | Parks/SPB, AK | USA |
| KPM | Kompiam | Papua New Guinea |
| KPN | Kipnulk, AK | USA |
| KPO | Pohang/Air Base | S. Korea |
| KPP | Kalpowar | Australia |
| KPR | Port Williams/SPB, AK | USA |
| KPS | Kempsey | Australia |
| KPT | Jackpot, NV | USA |
| KPV | Perryville/SPB, AK | USA |
| KPY | Port Bailey/SPB, AK | USA |
| KQA | Akutan, AK | USA |
| KQB | Koonibba | Australia |
| KQL | Kol | Papua New Guinea |
| KRA | Kerang | Australia |
| KRB | Karumba | Australia |
| KRC | Kerinci/Depati Parbo | Indonesia |
| KRD | Kurundi | Australia |
| KRE | Kirundo | Benin |
| KRF | Kramfors/Flygplats | Sweden |
| KRG | Karasabai | Guyana |
| KRH | Redhill | UK |
| KRI | Kikori | Papua New Guinea |
| KRJ | Karawari | Papua New Guinea |
| KRK | Krakow | Poland |
| KRL | Korla | China |
| KRM | Karanambo | Guyana |
| KRN | Kiruna | Sweden |
| KRO | Kurgan | Russia |
| KRP | Karup/Military | Denmark |
| KRQ | Kramatorsk | Ukraine |
| KRR | Krasnodar | Russia |
| KRS | Kristiansand/Kjevik | Norway |
| KRT | Khartoum/Civil | Sudan |
| KRU | Kerau | Papua New Guinea |
| KRV | Kerio Valley | Kenya |
| KRW | Turkmanbashi | Turkmenistan |
| KRX | Kar Kar | Papua New Guinea |
| KRY | Karamay | China |
| KRZ | Kiri | Congo, DR |
| KSA | Kosrae | Micronesia |
| KSB | Kasanombe | Papua New Guinea |
| KSC | Kosice/Barca | Slovakia |
| KSD | Karlstad/Flygplats | Sweden |
| KSE | Kasese | Uganda |
| KSF | Kassel/Calden | Germany |
| KSG | Kisengan | Papua New Guinea |
| KSH | Kermanshah | Iran |
| KSI | Kissidougou | Guinea |
| KSJ | Kasos Is | Greece |
| KSK | Karlskoga | Sweden |
| KSL | Kassala | Sudan |
| KSM | Saint Marys, AK | USA |
| KSN | Kostanay | Kazakstan |
| KSO | Kastoria/Aristotelis | Greece |
| KSP | Kosipe | Papua New Guinea |
| KSQ | Karshi | Uzbekistan |
| KSR | Sanoy River, AK | USA |
| KSS | Skasso | Mali |
| KST | Kosti | Sudan |
| KSU | Kristiansund/Kvernberget | Norway |
| KSV | Springvale | Australia |
| KSW | Kiryat Shmona | Israel |
| KSX | Yasuru | Papua New Guinea |
| KSY | Kars | Turkey |
| KSZ | Kotlas | Russia |
| KTA | Karratha | Australia |
| KTB | Thorne Bay, AK | USA |
| KTC | Katiola | Côte D'Ivoire |
| KTD | Kitadaito Is | Japan |
| KTE | Kerteh | Malaysia |
| KTF | Takalka | New Zealand |
| KTG | Ketapang/Rahadi Usmaman | Indonesia |
| KTH | Tikchik/SPB, AK | USA |
| KTI | Kratie | Cambodia |
| KTK | Kanua | Papua New Guinea |
| KTL | Kitale | Kenya |
| KTM | Kathmandu/Tribhuvan | Nepal |
| KTN | Ketchikan/Int'l, AK | USA |
| KTO | Kato | Guyana |
| KTP | Kingston/Tinson | Jamaica |
| KTQ | Kitee | Finland |
| KTR | Katherine/Tindal | Australia |
| KTS | Teller Mission, Brevig Mission, AK | USA |
| KTT | Kittilä | Finland |
| KTU | Kota | India |
| KTV | Kamarata | Venezuela |
| KTW | Katowice/Pyrzowice | Poland |
| KTX | Koutiala | Mali |
| KTZ | Kwun Tong | Hong Kong |
| KUA | Kuantan | Malaysia |
| KUB | Koala Belait | Brunei |
| KUC | Kuria | Kiribati |
| KUD | Kudat | Malaysia |
| KUE | Kukundu | Solomon Is |
| KUF | Samara | Russia |
| KUG | Kubin Is | Australia |
| KUH | Kushiro | Japan |
| KUI | Kawau Is | New Zealand |
| KUJ | Kushimoto | Japan |
| KUK | Kasigluk, AK | USA |
| KUL | Kuala Lumpur/Kuala Lumpur Infl | Malaysia |
| KUM | Yakushima | Japan |
| KUN | Kaunas/Int'l | Lithuania |
| KUO | Kuopio | Finland |
| KUP | Kupiano | Papua New Guinea |
| KUQ | Kuri | Papua New Guinea |
| KUR | Kuran-O-Munjan | Afghanistan |
| KUS | Kulusuk | Greenland |
| KUT | Kutaisi | Georgia |
| KUU | Kulu/Shuntar | India |
| KUV | Kunsan/Air Base | S. Korea |
| KUW | Kugururok River, AK | USA |
| KUY | Kamusi/Kamusi Arpt | Papua New Guinea |
| KUZ | Kusan/Air Base | S. Korea |
| KVA | Kavala/Megas Alexandros | Greece |
| KVB | Skovde | Sweden |
| KVC | King Cove, AK | USA |
| KVD | Gyancizha | Azerbaijan |
| KVE | Kitava | Papua New Guinea |
| KVG | Kavieng | Papua New Guinea |
| KVK | Kirovsk | Russia |
| KVL | Kivalina, AK | USA |
| KVU | Korolevu | Fiji |
| KVX | Kirov | Russia |
| KWA | Kwajalein | Marshall Is |
| KWB | Karimunjawa | Indonesia |
| KWD | Kawadjia | Central African Rep |
| KWE | Guiyang | China |
| KWF | Waterfall/SPS, AK | USA |
| KWG | Krivoy Rog | Ukraine |
| KWH | Khwahan | Afghanistan |
| KWI | Kuwait Int'l | Kuwait |
| KWJ | Kwangju/Air Base | S. Korea |
| KWK | Kwigillingok, AK | USA |
| KWL | Guilin | China |
| KWM | Kowanyama | Australia |
| KWN | Quinhagak/Kwinhagak, AK | USA |
| KWO | Kawito | Papua New Guinea |
| KWP | Village/SPB, AK | USA |
| KWR | Kwai Harbour | Solomon Is |
| KWS | Kwailabesi Aerodrom | Solomon Is |
| KWT | Kwethluk, AK | USA |
| KWU | Mansion House | New Zealand |
| KWV | Kurwina | Papua New Guinea |
| KWX | Kiwai Is | Papua New Guinea |
| KWY | Kiwayu | Kenya |
| KWZ | Kolwezi | Congo, DR |
| KXA | Kasaan SPB, AK | USA |
| KXD | Klerksdorp | S. Africa |
| KXF | Koro Is | Fiji |
| KXK | Komsomolsk Na Amure | Russia |
| KXR | Karoola | Papua New Guinea |

| Code | Airport | Country |
|------|---------|---------|
| KYA | Konya | Turkey |
| KYB | Yangoonabie | Australia |
| KYD | Orchid Is | Taiwan |
| KYE | Tripoli/Kleyate | Lebanon |
| KYF | Yeelirrie | Australia |
| KYI | Yalata Mission | Australia |
| KYK | Karuk, AK | USA |
| KYL | Key Largo/Port Largo, FL | USA |
| KYN | Milton Keynes | UK |
| KYO | Tampa/Topp Of Tampa, FL | USA |
| KYP | Kyaulkpyu | Myanmar |
| KYS | Kayes | Mali |
| KYT | Kyauktaw | Myanmar |
| KYU | Koyukuk, AK | USA |
| KYX | Yalumet | Papua New Guinea |
| KYZ | Kyzyl | Russia |
| KZB | Zachar Bay/SPB, AK | USA |
| KZC | Kompong-Chhna | Cambodia |
| KZD | Krakor | Cambodia |
| KZF | Kaintiba | Papua New Guinea |
| KZG | Kitzingen | Germany |
| KZH | Kizhuyak, AK | USA |
| KZI | Kozani/Philippos | Greece |
| KZK | Kompong Thorn | Cambodia |
| KZN | Kazan | Russia |
| KZO | Kzyl-Orda | Kazakstan |
| KZS | Kastelorizo | Greece |

# L

| Code | Airport | Country |
|------|---------|---------|
| LAA | Lamar Municipal, CO | USA |
| LAB | Lablab | Papua New Guinea |
| LAC | Pulau Layang-Layang Is | Malaysia |
| LAD | Luanda/4 de Fevereiro | Angola |
| LAE | Lae/Nadzab | Papua New Guinea |
| LAF | Lafayette-Purdue, IN | USA |
| LAG | La Guaira | Venezuela |
| LAH | Labuha/Taliabu | Indonesia |
| LAI | Lannion/Servel | France |
| LAJ | Lages | Brazil |
| LAK | Aklavik, NT | Canada |
| LAL | Lakeland, FL | USA |
| LAM | Los Alamos, NM | USA |
| LAN | Lansing, MI | USA |
| LAO | Laoag | Philippines |
| LAP | La Paz/Leon | Mexico |
| LAQ | Beida/La Braq | Libya |
| LAR | Laramie, WY | USA |
| LAS | Las Vegas, NV | USA |
| LAT | La Unbe | Colombia |
| LAU | Lamu | Kenya |
| LAV | Lalomalava | Samoa |
| LAW | Lawton, OK | USA |
| LAX | Los Angeles Int'l, CA | USA |
| LAY | Ladysmith | S. Africa |
| LAZ | Bom Jesus Da Lapa | Brazil |
| LBA | Leeds Bradford/Yeadon | UK |
| LBB | Lubbock Int'l, TX | USA |
| LBC | Luebeck/Blankensee | Germany |
| LBD | Khudzhand | Tajikistan |
| LBE | Latrobe, PA | USA |
| LBF | North Platte, NE | USA |
| LBG | Paris/Le Bourget | France |
| LBH | Sydney/Palm Beach SPB | Australia |
| LBI | Albi/Le Sequestre | France |
| LBJ | Labuan Bajo/Mutiara | Indonesia |
| LBK | Lilboi | Kenya |
| LBL | Liberal/Municipal, KS | USA |
| LBM | Lualbo | Mozambique |
| LBN | Lake Baringo | Kenya |
| LBO | Lusambo | Congo, DR |
| LBP | Long Banga | Malaysia |
| LBQ | Lambarene | Gabon |
| LBR | Labrea | Brazil |
| LBS | Labasa | Fiji |
| LBT | Lumberton, NC | USA |
| LBU | Labuan | Malaysia |
| LBV | Libreville | Gabon |
| LBW | Long Bawan/Juvai Semaring | Indonesia |
| LBX | Lubang | Philippines |
| LBY | La Baule/Montoir | France |
| LBZ | Lukapa | Angola |
| LCA | Larnaca | Cyprus |
| LCB | Pontes e Lacerda | Brazil |
| LCC | Lecce/Galatina | Italy |
| LCD | Louis Trichardt | S. Africa |
| LCE | La Ceiba/Goloson Int'l | Honduras |

| Code | Airport | Country |
|------|---------|---------|
| LCF | Rio Dulce/Las Vegas | Guatemala |
| LCG | La Coruna | Spain |
| LCH | Lake Charles, LA | USA |
| LCI | Laconia, NH | USA |
| LCJ | Lodz/Lodz Lublinek | Poland |
| LCK | Rickenbacker, OH | USA |
| LCL | La Colorna | Cuba |
| LCM | La Cumbre | Argentina |
| LCN | Balcanoona | Australia |
| LCO | Lague | Congo |
| LCP | Loncope | Argentina |
| LCR | La Chorrera | Colombia |
| LCS | Las Canas | Costa Rica |
| LCV | Lucca | Italy |
| LCY | London/London City Arpt | UK |
| LDA | Maida | India |
| LDB | Londrina | Brazil |
| LDC | Linderan Is | Australia |
| LDE | Lourdes/Tarbes | France |
| LDH | Lord Howe Is | Australia |
| LDI | Lindi/Kikwetu | Tanzania |
| LDJ | Linden, NJ | USA |
| LDK | Lidkoping/Hovby | Sweden |
| LDM | Ludington/Mason Cnty, MI | USA |
| LDN | Lamidanda | Nepal |
| LDO | Ladouanie | Suriname |
| LDR | Lodar | Yemen |
| LDS | Leeds, MT | USA |
| LDU | Lahad Datu | Malaysia |
| LDV | Landivisiau | France |
| LDW | Lansdowne | Australia |
| LDX | St Laurent du Maroni | F. Guiana |
| LDY | Londonderry/Eglinton | UK |
| LDZ | Londolozi | S. Africa |
| LEA | Learmonth | Australia |
| LEB | Hanover, NH | USA |
| LEC | Lencois/Chapada Diamantina | Brazil |
| LED | St Petersburg/Pulkovo | Russia |
| LEE | Leesburg, FL | USA |
| LEF | Lebakeng | Lesotho |
| LEG | Aleg | Mauritania |
| LEH | Le Havre/Octeville | France |
| LEI | Almeria | Spain |
| LEJ | Leipzig/Halle | Germany |
| LEK | Labe | Guinea |
| LEL | Lake Evella | Australia |
| LEM | Lemmon, SD | USA |
| LEN | Leon | Spain |
| LEO | Leconi | Gabon |
| LEP | Leopoldina | Brazil |
| LEQ | Lands End | UK |
| LER | Leinster | Australia |
| LES | Lesobeng | Lesotho |
| LET | Leticia/Gen. A.V. Cobo | Colombia |
| LEU | Seo De Urgel/Aeroport De La Seu | Spain |
| LEV | Bureta/Levuka Airfield | Fiji |
| LEW | Auburn, ME | USA |
| LEX | Lexington-Blue Grass, KY | USA |
| LEY | Lelystad | Netherlands |
| LEZ | La Esperanza | Honduras |
| LFI | Langley/AFB, VA | USA |
| LFK | Nacogdoches, TX | USA |
| LFN | Louisburg, NC | USA |
| LFO | Kelafo/Callaf/Kelafo | Ethiopia |
| LFP | Lakefield | Australia |
| LFR | La Fria | Venezuela |
| LFT | Lafayette, LA | USA |
| LFW | Lome/Tokoin | Togo |
| LGA | New York-La Guardia, NY | USA |
| LGB | Long Beach, CA | USA |
| LGC | La Grange/Calloway, GA | USA |
| LGD | La Grande, OR | USA |
| LGE | Lake Gregory | Australia |
| LGF | Laguna/AAF, AZ | USA |
| LGG | Liege/Bierset | Belgium |
| LGH | Leigh Creek | Australia |
| LGI | Deadmans Cay | Bahamas |
| LGK | Langkawi | Malaysia |
| LGL | Long Lellang | Malaysia |
| LGM | Laiagam | Papua New Guinea |
| LGN | Linga Linga | Papua New Guinea |
| LGO | Langeoog | Germany |
| LGP | Legaspi | Philippines |
| LGQ | Lago Agrio | Ecuador |
| LGR | Cochrane | Chile |
| LGS | Malargue | Argentina |
| LGT | Las Gaviotas | Colombia |
| LGU | Logan, UT | USA |
| LGW | London/Gatwick | UK |
| LGX | Lugh Ganane | Somalia |

| Code | Airport | Country |
|------|---------|---------|
| LGY | Lagunillas | Venezuela |
| LGZ | Leguizamo | Colombia |
| LHA | Lahr | Germany |
| LHB | Lost Harbor, AK | USA |
| LHD | Lake Hood/SPB, AK | USA |
| LHE | Lahore | Pakistan |
| LHG | Lightning Ridge | Australia |
| LHI | Lereh | Indonesia |
| LHK | Guanghua | China |
| LHN | Lishan | Taiwan |
| LHP | Lehu | Papua New Guinea |
| LHQ | Lancaster, Fairfield County Arpt, OH | USA |
| LHR | London/Heathrow | UK |
| LHS | Las Heras | Argentina |
| LHV | Lock Haven, PA | USA |
| LHW | Lanzhou | China |
| LHX | La Junta, CO | USA |
| LIA | Liangping | China |
| LIB | Limbunya | Australia |
| LIC | Limon Municipal, CO | USA |
| LID | Leiden/Valkenburg | Netherlands |
| LIE | Libenge | Congo, DR |
| LIF | Lifou | New Caledonia |
| LIG | Limoges/Bellegarde | France |
| LIH | Kauai Is/Lihue, HI | USA |
| LII | Mulia | Indonesia |
| LIJ | Long Is, AK | USA |
| LIK | Likiep Is | Marshall Is |
| LIL | Lille/Lesquin | France |
| LIM | Lima/J Chavez Int'l | Peru |
| LIN | Milan/Linate | Italy |
| LIO | Limon | Costa Rica |
| LIP | Lins | Brazil |
| LIQ | Lisala | Congo, DR |
| LIR | Liberia | Costa Rica |
| LIS | Lisboa Portela | Portugal |
| LIT | Little Rock, AR | USA |
| LIU | Linosa HP | Italy |
| LIV | Livengood, AK | USA |
| LIW | Loikaw | Myanmar |
| LIX | Likoma Is | Malawi |
| LIY | Wright/AAF, GA | USA |
| LIZ | Loring/AFB, ME | USA |
| LJA | Lodja | Congo, DR |
| LJC | Louisville/Intercontinental, KY | USA |
| LJG | Lijiang City/Lijiang | China |
| LJN | Lake Jackson, TX | USA |
| LJU | Ljubljana/Brnik | Slovenia |
| LKA | Larantuka | Indonesia |
| LKB | Lakeba | Fiji |
| LKC | Lekana | Congo, DR |
| LKD | Lakeland Downs | Australia |
| LKE | Lake Union SPB, WA | USA |
| LKG | Lokichoggio | Kenya |
| LKI | Duluth/Lakeside USAF, MN | USA |
| LKK | Kulik Lake, AK | USA |
| LKL | Lakselv/Banak | Norway |
| LKN | Leknes | Norway |
| LKO | Lucknow/Amausi | India |
| LKP | Lake Placid, NY | USA |
| LKR | Las Khoreh | Somalia |
| LKS | LakesideTX | USA |
| LKT | Lakota | Côte D'Ivoire |
| LKU | Lake Rudolf | Kenya |
| LKV | Lakeview, OR | USA |
| LKY | Lake Manyara | Tanzania |
| LKZ | Brandon/Lakenheath/RAF | UK |
| LLA | Lulea/Kallax | Sweden |
| LLE | Malelane | S. Africa |
| LLG | Chillagoe | Australia |
| LLH | Las Limas | Honduras |
| LLI | Lalibela | Ethiopia |
| LLL | Lissadell | Australia |
| LLM | Long Lama | Malaysia |
| LLN | Kelila | Indonesia |
| LLP | Linda Downs | Australia |
| LLQ | Monticello, AR | USA |
| LLS | Las Lomitas | Argentina |
| LLU | Alluitsup Paa | Greenland |
| LLW | Lilongwe Int'l | Malawi |
| LLX | Lyndonville, VT | USA |
| LLY | Mount Holly, NJ | USA |
| LMA | Lake Minchumina, AK | USA |
| LMB | Salima | Malawi |
| LMC | Lamacarena | Colombia |
| LMD | Los Menucos | Argentina |
| LME | Le Mans/Arnage | France |
| LMG | Lamassa | Papua New Guinea |
| LMH | Limon | Honduras |
| LMI | Lumi | Papua New Guinea |

**AIRPORTS-1-**

| Code | Location | Country |
|---|---|---|
| LMK | Limerick | Ireland |
| LML | Lae Is | Marshall Is |
| LMM | Los Mochis/Federal | Mexico |
| LMN | Limbang | Malaysia |
| LMO | Lossiernouth/RAF | UK |
| LMP | Lampedusa | Italy |
| LMQ | Marsa Brega | Libya |
| LMR | Lime Acres | S. Africa |
| LMS | Louisville, MS | USA |
| LMT | Klamath Falls Int'l, OR | USA |
| LMX | Lopez De Micay | Colombia |
| LMY | Lake Murray | Papua New Guinea |
| LMZ | Palma | Mozambique |
| LNA | West Palm Beach, FL | USA |
| LNB | Lamen Bay | Vanuatu |
| LNC | Lengbati | Papua New Guinea |
| LND | Lander, WY | USA |
| LNE | Lonorore | Vanuatu |
| LNF | Munbil | Papua New Guinea |
| LNG | Lese | Papua New Guinea |
| LNH | Lake/NASh | Australia |
| LNI | Lonely/Dew Stn, AK | USA |
| LNK | Lincoln, NE | USA |
| LNM | Langimar | Papua New Guinea |
| LNN | Willoughby, OH | USA |
| LNO | Leonora | Australia |
| LNP | Wise, VA | USA |
| LNQ | Loani | Papua New Guinea |
| LNR | Lone Rock, WI | USA |
| LNS | Lancaster, PA | USA |
| LNV | Lihir Is | Papua New Guinea |
| LNX | Smolensk | Russia |
| LNY | Lanai City, HI | USA |
| LNZ | Linz/Hoersching | Austria |
| LOA | Lorraine | Australia |
| LOB | Los Andes | Chile |
| LOC | Lock | Australia |
| LOD | Longana | Vanuatu |
| LOE | Loei | Thailand |
| LOF | Loen | Marshall Is |
| LOG | Longview, WA | USA |
| LOH | Loja | Ecuador |
| LOI | Lontras/Helmuth Baungartem | Brazil |
| LOK | Lodwar | Kenya |
| LOL | Lovelock, NV | USA |
| LOM | Lagos de Moreno | Mexico |
| LOO | Laghouat-L'Mekrareg | Algeria |
| LOQ | Lobatse | Botswana |
| LOR | Ft. Rucker-Army HP, AL | USA |
| LOS | Lagos/Murtala Muhammed | Nigeria |
| LOT | Chicago Nexrad, IL | USA |
| LOU | Louisville, KY | USA |
| LOV | Monclova | Mexico |
| LOW | Louisa, VA | USA |
| LOX | Los Tablones | Guatemala |
| LOY | Loyangalani | Kenya |
| LOZ | London, KY | USA |
| LPA | Las Palmas | Spain |
| LPB | La Paz/El Alto | Bolivia |
| LPC | Lompoc, CA | USA |
| LPD | La Pedrera | Colombia |
| LPE | La Primavera | Colombia |
| LPG | La Plata | Argentina |
| LPH | Lochgliphead / HP | UK |
| LPI | Linkoping | Sweden |
| LPJ | Pijiguaos | Venezuela |
| LPK | Lipetsk | Russia |
| LPL | Liverpool/Speke | UK |
| LPM | Lamap | Vanuatu |
| LPN | Leron Plains | Papua New Guinea |
| LPO | Laporte/Municipal, IN | USA |
| LPP | Lappeenranta | Finland |
| LPQ | Luang Prabang | Laos |
| LPS | Lopez Is, WA | USA |
| LPT | Lampang | Thailand |
| LPU | Long Apung | Indonesia |
| LPW | Little Port Walter, AK | USA |
| LPX | Liepaya/Int'l | Latvia |
| LPY | Le Puy/Loudes | France |
| LQK | Pickens, SC | USA |
| LQM | Puerto Leguizamo | Colombia |
| LQN | Qala Nau | Afghanistan |
| LRA | Larisa | Greece |
| LRB | Leribe | Lesotho |
| LRC | Laarbruch/RAF | Germany |
| LRD | Laredo Int'l, TX | USA |
| LRE | Longreach | Australia |
| LRF | Little Rock/AFB, AR | USA |
| LRG | Lora Lai | Pakistan |
| LRH | La Rochelle/Laleu | France |
| LRI | Lorica | Colombia |

| Code | Location | Country |
|---|---|---|
| LRJ | Lemars/Municipal, IA | USA |
| LRK | Lincoln Rock/Cst Guard, AK | USA |
| LRL | Niamtougou/Lama-Kara | Togo |
| LRM | La Romana | Dominican Rep |
| LRN | Larson/AFB, WA | USA |
| LRO | Lathrop/Sharpe/AAF, CA | USA |
| LRQ | Laurie River, MB | Canada |
| LRR | Lar | Iran |
| LRS | Leros | Greece |
| LRT | Lorient/Lann Bilhoue | France |
| LRU | Las Cruces Int'l, NM | USA |
| LRV | Los Roques | Venezuela |
| LRX | Elko Nexrad, NV | USA |
| LSA | Losuia | Papua New Guinea |
| LSB | Lordsburg, NM | USA |
| LSC | La Serena/La Florida | Chile |
| LSD | Creech/AAF, KY | USA |
| LSE | La Crosse, WI | USA |
| LSF | Lawson/AAF, GA | USA |
| LSH | Lashio | Myanmar |
| LSI | Shetland Iss | UK |
| LSJ | Long Is | Papua New Guinea |
| LSK | Lusk, WY | USA |
| LSL | Los Chiles | Costa Rica |
| LSM | Long Semado/Lawas | Malaysia |
| LSN | Los Banos, CA | USA |
| LSO | Les Sables/Talmont | France |
| LSP | Las Piedras/Josefa Camejo | Venezuela |
| LSQ | Los Angeles | Chile |
| LSR | Lost River, AK | USA |
| LSS | Terre-de-Haut | Gaudeloupe |
| LST | Launceston | Australia |
| LSU | Long Sukang | Malaysia |
| LSV | Nellis/AFB, NV | USA |
| LSW | Lhoksumawe/Malikussaleh | Indonesia |
| LSX | Lhok Sukon | Indonesia |
| LSY | Lismore | Australia |
| LSZ | Mali Losinj | Croatia |
| LTA | Tzaneen/Letaba | S. Africa |
| LTB | Latrobe | Australia |
| LTC | Lai | Chad |
| LTD | Ghadames | Libya |
| LTF | Leitre | Papua New Guinea |
| LTG | Langtang | Nepal |
| LTH | Lathrop Wells, NV | USA |
| LTI | Altai | Mongolia |
| LTK | Latakia | Syria |
| LTL | Lastourville | Gabon |
| LTM | Lethem | Guyana |
| LTN | London/Luton Int'l Arpt | UK |
| LTO | Loreto | Mexico |
| LTP | Lyndhurst | Australia |
| LTQ | Paris/Le Touquet | France |
| LTR | Letterkenny | Ireland |
| LTS | Altus/AFB, OK | USA |
| LTT | Saint Tropez/La Mole | France |
| LTV | Lotusvaie | Australia |
| LTW | Leonardtown/St Marys County, MD | USA |
| LTX | Wilmington Nexrad, NC | USA |
| LUA | Lukla | Nepal |
| LUB | Lumid Pau | Guyana |
| LUC | Laucata Is | Fiji |
| LUD | Luderitz | Namibia |
| LUE | Lucenec | Slovakia |
| LUF | Luke/AFB, AZ | USA |
| LUG | Lugano | Switzerland |
| LUH | Ludhiana | India |
| LUI | La Union | Honduras |
| LUJ | Lusikisiki | S. Africa |
| LUK | Cincinnati, OH | USA |
| LUL | Laurel/Hester/Noble Fld, MS | USA |
| LUM | Luxi/Mangshi | China |
| LUN | Lusaka | Zambia |
| LUO | Luena | Angola |
| LUP | Kalaupapa, HI | USA |
| LUQ | San Luis | Argentina |
| LUR | Cape Lisburne, AK | USA |
| LUS | Lusanga | Congo, DR |
| LUT | Laura Stn | Australia |
| LUU | Laura | Australia |
| LUV | Langgur | Indonesia |
| LUW | Luwuk/Bubung | Indonesia |
| LUX | Luxembourg | Luxembourg |
| LUY | Lushoto | Tanzania |
| LUZ | Lushan | China |
| LVA | Laval/Entrammes | France |
| LVB | Uvramento/Dos Galpoes | Brazil |
| LVD | Lime Village, AK | USA |
| LVI | Livingstone | Zambia |

| Code | Location | Country |
|---|---|---|
| LVK | Livermore, CA | USA |
| LVL | Lawrenceville, VA | USA |
| LVM | Livingston, MT | USA |
| LVO | Laverlon | Australia |
| LVP | Lavan | Iran |
| LVS | Las Vegas, NM | USA |
| LVX | Louisville Nexrad, KY | USA |
| LWA | Lwbak | Philippines |
| LWB | Lewisburg, WV | USA |
| LWC | Lawrence, KS | USA |
| LWE | Lewoleba | Indonesia |
| LWI | Lowai | Papua New Guinea |
| LWK | Shetland Iss, Lerwick/Tingwall | UK |
| LWL | Wells/Harriet Fld, NV | USA |
| LWM | Lawrence, MA | USA |
| LWN | Gyoumri | Armenia |
| LWO | Lvov/Snilow | Ukraine |
| LWR | Leeuwarden | Netherlands |
| LWS | Lewiston, ID | USA |
| LWT | Lewistown, MT | USA |
| LWV | Lawreneeville, IL | USA |
| LWY | Lawas | Malaysia |
| LXA | Lhasa | China |
| LXG | Luang Namtha | Laos |
| LXI | Linxi | China |
| LXN | Lexington, NE | USA |
| LXR | Luxor | Egypt |
| LXS | Lemnos | Greece |
| LXU | Lukulu | Zambia |
| LXV | Leadville, CO | USA |
| LYA | Luoyang | China |
| LYB | Little Cayman | Cayman Is |
| LYC | Lycksele | Sweden |
| LYE | Lyneham/RAF | UK |
| LYG | Lianyungang | China |
| LYH | Lynchburg, VA | USA |
| LYI | Linyi | China |
| LYK | Lunyuk | Indonesia |
| LYN | Lyon/Bron | France |
| LYO | Lyons, KS | USA |
| LYP | Faisalabad | Pakistan |
| LYR | Longyearbyen/Svalbard | Svalbard and Jan Mayen Is |
| LYS | Lyon-Satolas | France |
| LYT | Lady Elliot Is | Australia |
| LYU | Ely, MN | USA |
| LYX | Lydd/Lydd Int'l | UK |
| LZA | Luiza | Congo, DR |
| LZC | Lazaro Cardenas | Mexico |
| LZD | Lanzhou/Lanzhoudong | China |
| LZH | Liuzhou | China |
| LZI | Luozi | Congo, DR |
| LZK | North Little Rock, AR | USA |
| LZM | Luzamba | Angola |
| LZO | Luzhou | China |
| LZR | Lizard Is | Australia |

# M

| Code | Location | Country |
|---|---|---|
| MAA | Chennai | India |
| MAB | Maraba | Brazil |
| MAC | Macon/Smart, GA | USA |
| MAD | Madrid/Barajas | Spain |
| MAE | Madera, CA | USA |
| MAF | Midland Int'l, TX | USA |
| MAG | Madang | Papua New Guinea |
| MAH | Menorea | Spain |
| MAI | Mangochi | Malawi |
| MAJ | Majuro/Amata Kabua Int'l | Marshall Is |
| MAK | Malakal | Sudan |
| MAL | Mangole | Indonesia |
| MAM | Matamoros | Mexico |
| MAN | Manchester/Ringway | UK |
| MAO | Manaus-Eduardo Gomes Int'l | Brazil |
| MAP | Mamai | Papua New Guinea |
| MAQ | Mae Sot | Thailand |
| MAR | Maracailbo/La Chwila | Venezuela |
| MAS | Manus Is | Papua New Guinea |
| MAT | Matadi | Congo, DR |
| MAU | Maupiti | F. Polynesia |
| MAV | Maloelap Is | Marshall Is |
| MAW | Malden, MO | USA |
| MAX | Matam | Senegal |
| MAY | Mangrove Cay | Bahamas |
| MAZ | Mayaguez/Eugenic M De Hostos | Puerto Rico |
| MBA | Mombasa/Moi Int'l | Kenya |
| MBB | Marble Bar | Australia |

| Code | Airport | Location |
|------|---------|----------|
| MBC | Mbigou | Gabon |
| MBD | Mmabatho/Int'l | S. Africa |
| MBE | Monbetsu | Japan |
| MBF | Mount Buffalo | Australia |
| MBG | Mobridge Municipal, SD | USA |
| MBH | Maryborough | Australia |
| MBI | Mbeya | Tanzania |
| MBJ | Montego Bay/Sangster Int'l | Jamaica |
| MBK | Matupa | Brazil |
| MBL | Manistee/Blacker, MI | USA |
| MBM | Mikambati | S. Africa |
| MBN | Mt Barnett | Australia |
| MBO | Mamburao | Philippines |
| MBP | Moyobamba | Peru |
| MBQ | Mbarara | Uganda |
| MBR | Mbout | Mauritania |
| MBS | Bay City, MI | USA |
| MBT | Masbate | Philippines |
| MBU | Mbambanakira | Solomon Is |
| MBV | Masa | Papua New Guinea |
| MBW | Moorabbin | Australia |
| MBX | Maribor/Slivnica | Slovenia |
| MBY | Moberly, MO | USA |
| MBZ | Maues | Brazil |
| MCA | Macenta | Guinea |
| MCB | Mccomb, MS | USA |
| MCC | Mcclellan/AFB, CA | USA |
| MCD | Mackinac Is, MI | USA |
| MCE | Merced, CA | USA |
| MCF | MacDill/AFB, FL | USA |
| MCG | Mcgrath, AK | USA |
| MCH | Machala | Ecuador |
| MCI | Kansas City Int'l, MO | USA |
| MCJ | Maicao | Colombia |
| MCK | Mccook, NE | USA |
| MCL | Mt Mckinley, AK | USA |
| MCM | Monte Carlo/ HP | Monaco |
| MCN | Macon, GA | USA |
| MCO | Orlando Int'l, FL | USA |
| MCP | Macapa/Int'l | Brazil |
| MCQ | Miskolc | Hungary |
| MCR | Melchor De Menco | Guatemala |
| MCS | Monte Caseros/Seelb | Argentina |
| MCT | Muscat | Oman |
| MCU | Montlucon/Gueret (Lepaud) | France |
| MCV | Mcarthur River | Australia |
| MCW | Mason City, IA | USA |
| MCX | Makhachkala | Russia |
| MCY | Sunshine Coast/Maroochydore | Australia |
| MCZ | Maceio/Palmares | Brazil |
| MDA | Martindale/AAF, TX | USA |
| MDB | Melinda | Belize |
| MDC | Manado/Samratulangi | Indonesia |
| MDD | Midland Airpark, TX | USA |
| MDE | Medellin/Jose Marie Cordova | Colombia |
| MDF | Medford, WI | USA |
| MDG | Muclarijiang | China |
| MDH | Carbondale, IL | USA |
| MDI | Makurdi | Nigeria |
| MDJ | Madras, OR | USA |
| MDK | Mbandaka | Congo, DR |
| MDL | Mandalay/Annisaton | Myanmar |
| MDM | Munduku | Papua New Guinea |
| MDN | Jefferson Proving Grnd., IN | USA |
| MDO | Middleton Is, AK | USA |
| MDP | Mindiptana | Indonesia |
| MDQ | Mar Del Plata | Argentina |
| MDR | Medfra, AK | USA |
| MDS | Middle Caicos | Turks & Caicos Is |
| MDT | Harrisburg Int'l, PA | USA |
| MDU | Mendi | Papua New Guinea |
| MDV | Medoueneu | Gabon |
| MDW | Chicago/Midway, IL | USA |
| MDX | Mereedes | Argentina |
| MDY | Midway Is/Sand Is Field | U.S. Minor Outlying Islands |
| MDZ | Mendoza/El Plumerillo | Argentina |
| MEA | Macae | Brazil |
| MEB | Melbourne/Essendon | Australia |
| MEC | Manta | Ecuador |
| MED | Madinah/Mohammad Bin Abdulaziz | Saudi Arabia |
| MEE | Mare | New Caledonia |
| MEG | Malange | Angola |
| MEH | Mehamn | Norway |
| MEI | Meridian, MS | USA |
| MEJ | Meadville, PA | USA |
| MEK | Meknes | Morocco |
| MEL | Melbourne | Australia |
| MEM | Memphis Int'l, TN | USA |
| MEN | Mende/Brenoux | France |
| MEO | Manteo/Dare County Regional, NC | USA |
| MEP | Mersing | Malaysia |
| MEQ | Meulaboh/Seunagan | Indonesia |
| MER | Merced-Castle/AFB, CA | USA |
| MES | Medan/Polonia | Indonesia |
| MET | Moreton | Australia |
| MEU | Monte Dourado | Brazil |
| MEV | Minden/Douglas County, NV | USA |
| MEW | Mwelka | Congo, DR |
| MEX | Mexico City/Juarez Int'l | Mexico |
| MEY | Meghauli | Nepal |
| MEZ | Messina | S. Africa |
| MFA | Mafia | Tanzania |
| MFB | MonFt | Colombia |
| MFC | Mafeteng | Lesotho |
| MFD | Mansfield, OH | USA |
| MFE | Mcallen, TX | USA |
| MFF | Moanda | Gabon |
| MFG | Muzaffarabad | Pakistan |
| MFH | Mesquite, NV | USA |
| MFI | Marshfield, WI | USA |
| MFJ | Moala | Fiji |
| MFK | Matsu | Taiwan |
| MFL | Mount Full Stop | Australia |
| MFM | Macau | Macau |
| MFN | Milford Sound | New Zealand |
| MFO | Manguna | Papua New Guinea |
| MFP | Manners Creek | Australia |
| MFQ | Maradi | Niger |
| MFR | Medford, OR | USA |
| MFS | Miraflores | Colombia |
| MFT | Machu Picchu | Peru |
| MFU | Mfuwe | Zambia |
| MFV | Melfa, VA | USA |
| MFW | Magaruque | Mozambique |
| MFX | Meribel | France |
| MFY | Mayfa'ah | Yemen |
| MFZ | Mesalia/Sandino | Papua New Guinea |
| MGA | Managua | Nicaragua |
| MGB | Mount Gambier | Australia |
| MGC | Michigan City, IN | USA |
| MGE | Marietta/AFB, GA | USA |
| MGF | Maringa | Brazil |
| MGG | Margarima | Papua New Guinea |
| MGH | Margate | Australia |
| MGI | Matagorda/AFB, TX | USA |
| MGJ | Montgomery, NY | USA |
| MGK | Mong Ton | Myanmar |
| MGL | Dusseldorf/Monchen-Gladbach | Germany |
| MGM | Montgomery, AL | USA |
| MGN | Magangue/Baracoa | Colombia |
| MGO | Manega | Gabon |
| MGP | Manga | Papua New Guinea |
| MGQ | Mogadishu/Int'l | Somalia |
| MGR | Moultrie/Thornasville, GA | USA |
| MGS | Mangaia Is | Cook Is |
| MGT | Milingimbi | Australia |
| MGU | Manaung | Myanmar |
| MGV | Margaret River | Australia |
| MGW | Morgantown, WV | USA |
| MGX | Moabi | Australia |
| MGY | Dayton, OH | USA |
| MGZ | Myeik | Myanmar |
| MHA | Mahdia | Guyana |
| MHB | Auckland | New Zealand |
| MHC | Macmahon Camp 4 | Australia |
| MHD | Mashad | Iran |
| MHE | Mitchell, SD | USA |
| MHF | Morichal | Colombia |
| MHG | Marinheim | Germany |
| MHH | Marsh Harbour/Int'l | Bahamas |
| MHI | Musha | Djibouti |
| MHJ | Misrak Gashamo | Ethiopia |
| MHK | Manhattan, KS | USA |
| MHL | Marshall/Memorial, MO | USA |
| MHM | Minchumina/Intermediate, AK | USA |
| MHN | Mullen, NE | USA |
| MHO | Mount House | Australia |
| MHP | Minsk/Minsk Int'l | Belarus |
| MHQ | Mariehamn/Aland Is | Finland |
| MHR | Mather/AFB, CA | USA |
| MHS | Mount Shasta, CA | USA |
| MHT | Manchester, NH | USA |
| MHU | Mount Hotham | Australia |
| MHV | Mojave, CA | USA |
| MHW | Monteagudo | Bolivia |
| MHX | Manihiki Is | Cook Is |
| MHY | Morehead | Papua New Guinea |
| MHZ | Mildenhall/RAF | UK |
| MIA | Miami Int'l, FL | USA |
| MIB | Minot/AFB, ND | USA |
| MIC | Minneapolis-Crystal, MN | USA |
| MID | Merida/Rejon | Mexico |
| MIE | Muncie, IN | USA |
| MIF | Monahans/Roy Hurd, TX | USA |
| MIG | Munich/Neubiberg Ab | Germany |
| MIH | Mitchell Plateau | Australia |
| MII | Marilia/Dr Gastao Vidigal | Brazil |
| MIJ | Mili Is | Marshall Is |
| MIK | Mikkeli | Finland |
| MIM | Merimbula | Australia |
| MIN | Minnipa | Saudi Arabia |
| MIO | Miami, FL | USA |
| MIP | Mitspeh Ramon | Israel |
| MIQ | Omaha/Millard, NE | USA |
| MIR | Monastir/Int'l | Tunisia |
| MIS | Misima Is | Papua New Guinea |
| MIT | Shatter, CA | USA |
| MIU | Maiduguri | Nigeria |
| MIV | Miliville, NJ | USA |
| MIW | Marshalltown, IA | USA |
| MIX | Miriti | Colombia |
| MIY | Mittiebah | Australia |
| MIZ | Mainoru | Australia |
| MJA | Manja | Madagascar |
| MJB | Mejit Is | Marshall Is |
| MJC | Man | Côte D'Ivoire |
| MJD | Mohenjodaro | Pakistan |
| MJE | Majkin | Marshall Is |
| MJF | Mosjoen/Kjaerstad | Norway |
| MJG | Mayajigua | Cuba |
| MJH | Malma | Saudi Arabia |
| MJI | Mitiga | Libya |
| MJJ | Moki | Papua New Guinea |
| MJK | Monkey Mia/Shark Bay | Australia |
| MJL | Mouila | Gabon |
| MJM | Mbuji Mayi | Congo, DR |
| MJN | Majunga/Amborovy | Madagascar |
| MJO | Mount Etjo Lodge | Namibia |
| MJP | Manjinnup | Australia |
| MJQ | Jackson, MN | USA |
| MJR | Miramar | Argentina |
| MJS | Maganja Da Costa | Mozambique |
| MJT | Mytilene | Greece |
| MJU | Mamuju | Indonesia |
| MJV | Murcia/San Javier | Spain |
| MJW | Mahenye | Zimbabwe |
| MJX | Toms River/Robert J Miller, NJ | USA |
| MJY | Mangunjaya | Indonesia |
| MJZ | Mirnyj | Russia |
| MKA | Marianske Lazne | Czech Rep |
| MKB | Mekambo | Gabon |
| MKC | Kansas City/Downtown, MO | USA |
| MKD | Chagni | Ethiopia |
| MKE | Milwaukee, WI | USA |
| MKF | Mckenna/AAF, OH | USA |
| MKG | Muskegon, MI | USA |
| MKH | Mokhotlong | Lesotho |
| MKI | M'Boki | Central African Rep |
| MKJ | Makoua | Congo, DR |
| MKK | Hoolehua-Molokai, HI | USA |
| MKL | Jackson, TN | USA |
| MKM | Mukah | Malaysia |
| MKN | Malekolon | Papua New Guinea |
| MKO | Muskogee, OK | USA |
| MKP | Makemo | F. Polynesia |
| MKQ | Merauke/Mopah | Indonesia |
| MKR | Meekatharra | Australia |
| MKS | Mekane Selam | Ethiopia |
| MKT | Mankato, MN | USA |
| MKU | Makokou | Gabon |
| MKV | Mt Cavenagh | Australia |
| MKW | Manokwari/Rendani | Indonesia |
| MKX | Mukalla | Yemen |
| MKY | Mackay | Australia |
| MKZ | Malacca | Malaysia |
| MLA | Malta Int'l | Malta |
| MLB | Melbourne Int'l, FL | USA |
| MLC | McAlester, OK | USA |
| MLD | Malad City, ID | USA |
| MLE | Male/Int'l | Maldives |
| MLF | Milford, UT | USA |
| MLG | Malang | Indonesia |
| MLH | Basel/Mulhouse | Switzerland |
| MLI | Quad-City, IL | USA |
| MLJ | Milledgeville, GA | USA |
| MLK | Malta, MT | USA |
| MLL | Marshall, AK | USA |

| | | |
|---|---|---|
| MLM | Morelia | Mexico |
| MLN | Melilla | Spain |
| MLO | Milos | Greece |
| MLP | Malabang | Philippines |
| MLQ | Malalaua | Papua New Guinea |
| MLR | Millicent | Australia |
| MLS | Milles City, MT | USA |
| MLT | Millinocket, ME | USA |
| MLU | Monroe, LA | USA |
| MLV | Merluna | Australia |
| MLW | Monrovia/Sprigg Payne | Liberia |
| MLX | Malatya | Turkey |
| MLY | Manley Hot Springs, AK | USA |
| MLZ | Melo | Uruguay |
| MMB | Memanbetsu | Japan |
| MMC | Ciudad Mante | Mexico |
| MMD | Minami Daito | Japan |
| MME | Teesside | UK |
| MMF | Marnte | Cameroon |
| MMG | Mount Magnet | Australia |
| MMH | Mammoth Lakes, CA | USA |
| MMI | Athens, TN | USA |
| MMJ | Matsumoto | Japan |
| MMK | Murmansk | Russia |
| MML | Marshall, MN | USA |
| MMM | Middlemount | Australia |
| MMN | Stow, MA | USA |
| MMO | Maio | Cape Verde Is |
| MMP | Mompos | Colombia |
| MMQ | Mbala | Zambia |
| MMR | Camp Maybry AHP, TX | USA |
| MMS | Marks/Selts, MS | USA |
| MMT | Columbia, SC | USA |
| MMU | Morristown, NJ | USA |
| MMV | Mal | Papua New Guinea |
| MMW | Moma | New Zealand |
| MMX | Malmo/Sturup | Sweden |
| MMY | Miyake Jima/Hirara | Japan |
| MMZ | Maimana | Afghanistan |
| MNA | Melangguane | Indonesia |
| MNB | Moanda | Congo, DR |
| MNC | Nacala | Mozambique |
| MND | Medina | Colombia |
| MNE | Mungeranie | Australia |
| MNF | Mana Is. | Fiji |
| MNG | Maningrida | Australia |
| MNH | Minnenya | Sri Lanka |
| MNI | Montserrat/Bramble | Montserrat |
| MNJ | Mananjary | Madagascar |
| MNK | Maiana | Kiribati |
| MNL | Manila/Int'l | Philippines |
| MNM | Menominee, MI | USA |
| MNN | Marion, OH | USA |
| MNO | Manono | Congo, DR |
| MNP | Maron | Papua New Guinea |
| MNQ | Monto | Australia |
| MNR | Mongu | Zambia |
| MNS | Mansa | Zambia |
| MNT | Minto, AK | USA |
| MNU | Maulmyine | Myanmar |
| MNV | Mountain Valley | Australia |
| MNW | Macdonald Downs | Australia |
| MNX | Manicore | Brazil |
| MNY | Mono | Solomon Is |
| MNZ | Manassas, VA | USA |
| MOA | Moa/Orestes Acosta | Chile |
| MOB | Mabile, AL | USA |
| MOC | Montes Claros | Brazil |
| MOD | Modesto, CA | USA |
| MOE | Momeik | Myanmar |
| MOF | Maumere/Waioti | Indonesia |
| MOG | Mong Hsat | Myanmar |
| MOH | Mohanban | India |
| MOI | Mitiaro Is | Cook Is |
| MOJ | Moengo | Suriname |
| MOK | Mankono | Côte D'Ivoire |
| MOL | Molde | Norway |
| MOM | Moudieria | Mauritania |
| MON | Mount Cook | New Zealand |
| MOO | Moomba | Australia |
| MOP | Mount Pleasant, MI | USA |
| MOQ | Morondava | Madagascar |
| MOR | Morristown, TN | USA |
| MOS | Moses Point, AK | USA |
| MOT | Minot Int'l, ND | USA |
| MOU | Mountain Village, AK | USA |
| MOV | Moranbah | Australia |
| MOX | Morris, MN | USA |
| MOY | Monterrey | Colombia |
| MOZ | Moorea/Ternae | F. Polynesia |
| MPA | Mpacha | Namibia |

| | | |
|---|---|---|
| MPB | Miami/SPB, FL | USA |
| MPC | Muko-Muko | Indonesia |
| MPD | Mirpur Khas | Pakistan |
| MPE | Madison/Griswold, CT | USA |
| MPF | Mapoda | Papua New Guinea |
| MPG | Makini | Papua New Guinea |
| MPH | Caticlan/Malay | Philippines |
| MPI | Mannitupo | Panama |
| MPJ | Morrilton, AR | USA |
| MPK | Mokpo | S. Korea |
| MPL | Montpellier/Frejorgues | France |
| MPM | Maputo Int'l | Mozambique |
| MPN | Mount Pleasant | Falkland Is |
| MPO | Mt Pocono, PA | USA |
| MPP | Mulatupo | Panama |
| MPQ | Maan | Jordan |
| MPR | Mcpherson, KS | USA |
| MPS | Mount Pleasant, TX | USA |
| MPT | Maliana | Indonesia |
| MPU | Mapua | Papua New Guinea |
| MPV | Barre, VT | USA |
| MPW | Mariupol | Ukraine |
| MPX | Miyanmin | Papua New Guinea |
| MPY | Maripasoula | F. Guiana |
| MPZ | Mt Pleasant, IA | USA |
| MQA | Mandora | Australia |
| MQC | Miquelon | St. Pierre and Miquelon |
| MQD | Maquinchao | Argentina |
| MQE | Marqua | Australia |
| MQF | Magnitogorsk | Russia |
| MQG | Midgard | Namibia |
| MQH | Minacu | Brazil |
| MQI | Quincy, MA | USA |
| MQJ | Balikesir/Merkez | Turkey |
| MQK | San Matias | Bolivia |
| MQM | Monida, MT | USA |
| MQN | Mo I Rana/Rossvoll | Norway |
| MQO | Moundou | Chad |
| MQR | Mosquera | Colombia |
| MQS | Mustique Is | St. Vincent & Grenadines |
| MQT | Marquette, MI | USA |
| MQU | Mariquita | Colombia |
| MQW | Mc Rae, GA | USA |
| MQX | Makale | Ethiopia |
| MQY | Smyrna, TN | USA |
| MRA | Misurata | Libya |
| MRB | Martinsburg, WV | USA |
| MRC | Columbia, TN | USA |
| MRD | Merida/A Carnevalli | Venezuela |
| MRE | Mara Lodges | Kenya |
| MRF | Marfa, TX | USA |
| MRG | Mareeba | Australia |
| MRH | May River | Papua New Guinea |
| MRI | Anchorage, AK | USA |
| MRJ | Mareala | Honduras |
| MRK | Marco Is, FL | USA |
| MRL | Miners Lake | Australia |
| MRM | Manare | Papua New Guinea |
| MRN | Morganton/Lenoir, NC | USA |
| MRO | Masterton | New Zealand |
| MRP | Marla | Australia |
| MRQ | Marinduque | Philippines |
| MRR | Macara | Ecuador |
| MRS | Marseille/Marignane | France |
| MRT | Moroak | Australia |
| MRU | Mauritius/Int'l | Mauritius |
| MRV | Minerainye Vody | Russia |
| MRW | Maribo/Lufthavn | Denmark |
| MRX | Bandar Mahshahr | Iran |
| MRY | Monterey, CA | USA |
| MRZ | Moree | Australia |
| MSA | Muskrat Dam, ON | Canada |
| MSB | Marigot/SPB | Gaudeloupe |
| MSC | Mesa/Falcon Fld, AZ | USA |
| MSD | Mt Pleasant, UT | USA |
| MSE | Manston/Kent Int'l | UK |
| MSF | Mount Swan | Australia |
| MSG | Matsaile | Lesotho |
| MSH | Masirah | Oman |
| MSI | Masalembo | Indonesia |
| MSJ | Misawa | Japan |
| MSK | Mastic Point | Bahamas |
| MSL | Florence, AL | USA |
| MSM | Masi Manimba | Congo, DR |
| MSN | Madison, WI | USA |
| MSO | Missoula Int'l, MT | USA |
| MSP | Minneapolis-St Paul Int'l, MN | USA |
| MSQ | Minsk Int'l | Belarus |
| MSR | Mus | Turkey |
| MSS | Massena, NY | USA |
| MST | Maastricht/Aachen | Netherlands |

| | | |
|---|---|---|
| MSU | Maseru/Moshoeshoe Int'l | Lesotho |
| MSV | Monticello/Int'l, NY | USA |
| MSW | Massawa | Eritrea |
| MSX | Mossendjo | Congo, DR |
| MSY | New Orleans Int'l, LA | USA |
| MSZ | Namibe | Angola |
| MTA | Matamata | New Zealand |
| MTB | Monte Libano, CO | Colombia |
| MTC | Mt Clemens, MI | USA |
| MTD | Mt Sandford | Australia |
| MTE | Monte Alegre | Brazil |
| MTF | Mizan Teferi | Ethiopia |
| MTG | Mato Grosso | Brazil |
| MTH | Marathon, FL | USA |
| MTI | Mosteiros | Cape Verde Is |
| MTJ | Montrose, CO | USA |
| MTK | Makin Is | Kiribati |
| MTL | Maitland | Australia |
| MTM | Metlakatia/SPB, AK | USA |
| MTN | Baltimore, MD | USA |
| MTO | Mattoon, IL | USA |
| MTP | Montauk, NY | USA |
| MTQ | Mitchell | Australia |
| MTR | Monteria/S. Jeronimo | Colombia |
| MTS | Manzini/Int'l | Swaziland |
| MTT | Minatitlan | Mexico |
| MTU | Montepuez | Mozambique |
| MTV | Mota Lava | Vanuatu |
| MTW | Manitowoc, WI | USA |
| MTX | Fairbanks, AK | USA |
| MTY | Monterrey | Mexico |
| MTZ | Masada | Israel |
| MUA | Munda | Solomon Is |
| MUB | Maun | Botswana |
| MUC | Munich | Germany |
| MUD | Mueda | Mozambique |
| MUE | Kamuela, HI | USA |
| MUF | Muting | Indonesia |
| MUG | Mulege | Mexico |
| MUH | Mersa Matruh | Egypt |
| MUI | Muir/AAF, PA | USA |
| MUJ | Mui | Ethiopia |
| MUK | Mauke Is | Cook Is |
| MUL | Moultrie, GA | USA |
| MUM | Mumias | Kenya |
| MUN | Maturin/Quiriquire | Venezuela |
| MUO | Mountain Home/AFB, ID | USA |
| MUP | Mulga Park | Australia |
| MUQ | Muccan | Australia |
| MUR | Marudi | Malaysia |
| MUS | Marcus Is | Japan |
| MUT | Muscatine, IA | USA |
| MUU | Mount Union, PA | USA |
| MUV | Philadelphia/Mustin Alf, PA | USA |
| MUW | Mascara | Algeria |
| MUX | Multan | Pakistan |
| MUY | Mouyiondzi | Congo |
| MUZ | Musoma | Tanzania |
| MVA | Myvatn/Reykiahlid | Iceland |
| MVB | Franceville/Mvengue | Gabon |
| MVC | Monroeville, AL | USA |
| MVD | Montevideo/Carrasco | Uruguay |
| MVE | Montevideo, MN | USA |
| MVF | Mossoro/Dixsept Rosado | Brazil |
| MVG | Mevang | Gabon |
| MVH | Macksville | Australia |
| MVI | Manetai | Papua New Guinea |
| MVJ | Mandeville/Mariboro | Jamaica |
| MVK | Mulka | Australia |
| MVL | Morrisville, VT | USA |
| MVM | Kayenta, AZ | USA |
| MVN | Mt Vernon, IL | USA |
| MVO | Mongo | Chad |
| MVP | Mitu | Colombia |
| MVQ | Mogilev | Belarus |
| MVR | Maroua/Salarn | Cameroon |
| MVS | Mucuri | Brazil |
| MVT | Mataiva | F. Polynesia |
| MVU | Musigrave | Australia |
| MVV | Megeve | France |
| MVW | Mount Vernon, WA | USA |
| MVX | Minvoul | Gabon |
| MVY | Martha's Vineyard, MA | USA |
| MVZ | Masvingo | Zimbabwe |
| MWA | Marion, IL | USA |
| MWB | Morawa | Australia |
| MWC | Milwaukee, WI | USA |
| MWD | Mianwali | Pakistan |
| MWE | Merowe | Sudan |
| MWF | Malewo | Vanuatu |
| MWG | Marawaka | Papua New Guinea |

| Code | Location | Country |
|---|---|---|
| MWH | Moses Lake, WA | USA |
| MWI | Maramuni | Papua New Guinea |
| MWJ | Matthews Ridge | Guyana |
| MWK | Matak | Indonesia |
| MWL | Mineral Wells, TX | USA |
| MWM | Windom, MN | USA |
| MWN | Mwadui | Tanzania |
| MWO | Middletown, OH | USA |
| MWP | Mountain | Nepal |
| MWQ | Magwe | Myanmar |
| MWR | Motswari Airfield | S. Africa |
| MWS | Mount Wilson, CA | USA |
| MWT | Moolawatana | Australia |
| MWU | Mussau | Papua New Guinea |
| MWV | Mundulkiri | Cambodia |
| MWY | Miranda Downs | Australia |
| MWZ | Mwanza | Tanzania |
| MXA | Manila/Municipal, AR | USA |
| MXB | Masamba | Indonesia |
| MXC | Monticello, UT | USA |
| MXD | Marion Downs | Australia |
| MXE | Maxton, NC | USA |
| MXF | Maxwell/AFB, AL | USA |
| MXG | Marlborough, MA | USA |
| MXH | Moro | Papua New Guinea |
| MXI | Mati | Philippines |
| MXJ | Minna | Nigeria |
| MXK | Mindik | Papua New Guinea |
| MXL | Mexicali | Mexico |
| MXM | Morombe | Madagascar |
| MXN | Morlaix/Ploujean | France |
| MXO | Monticello, IA | USA |
| MXP | Milan//Malpensa | Italy |
| MXQ | Mitichell River | Australia |
| MXR | Mirgorod | Ukraine |
| MXS | Maota Savaii Is | Samoa |
| MXT | Maintirano | Madagascar |
| MXU | Mullewa | Australia |
| MXV | Moron | Mongolia |
| MXW | Mandalgobi | Mongolia |
| MXX | Mora | Sweden |
| MXY | McCarthy, AK | USA |
| MXZ | Meixian | China |
| MYA | Moruya | Australia |
| MYB | Mayoumba | Gabon |
| MYC | Maracay | Venezuela |
| MYD | Malindi | Kenya |
| MYE | Miyakojima | Japan |
| MYF | San Diego, CA | USA |
| MYG | Mayaguana | Bahamas |
| MYH | Marble Canyon, AZ | USA |
| MYI | Murray Is | Australia |
| MYJ | Matsuyama | Japan |
| MYK | May Creek, AK | USA |
| MYL | Mccall, ID | USA |
| MYM | Monkey Mountain | Guyana |
| MYN | Marelb | Yemen |
| MYO | Myroodah | Australia |
| MYP | Mary | Turkmenistan |
| MYQ | Mysore | India |
| MYR | Myrtle Beach/AFB, SC | USA |
| MYS | Moyale | Ethiopia |
| MYT | Myitkyina | Myanmar |
| MYU | Mekoryuk/Ellis Fld, AK | USA |
| MYV | Marysville, CA | USA |
| MYW | Mtwara | Tanzania |
| MYX | Menyamya | Papua New Guinea |
| MYY | Miri | Malaysia |
| MYZ | Monkey Bay | Malawi |
| MZA | Muzattarnagar | India |
| MZB | Mocimboa Praia | Mozambique |
| MZC | Mitzic | Gabon |
| MZD | Mendez | Ecuador |
| MZE | Manatee | Belize |
| MZF | Mzamba (Wild Coast Sun) | S. Africa |
| MZG | Makung | Taiwan |
| MZH | Merzifon | Turkey |
| MZI | Mopti | Mali |
| MZJ | Marana, AZ | USA |
| MZK | Marakei | Kiribati |
| MZL | Manizales/Santaguida | Colombia |
| MZM | Metz/Frescaty | France |
| MZN | Minj | Papua New Guinea |
| MZO | Manzanillo/Sierra Maestra | Cuba |
| MZP | Motueka | New Zealand |
| MZQ | Mkuze | S. Africa |
| MZR | Mazar-I-Sharif | Afghanistan |
| MZS | Mostyn | Malaysia |
| MZT | Mazatian/Gen Ralael Bueina | Mexico |
| MZU | Muzaffarpur | India |
| MZV | Mulu | Malaysia |
| MZX | Mena | Ethiopia |
| MZY | Mossel Bay | S. Africa |
| MZZ | Marion, IN | USA |

# N

| Code | Location | Country |
|---|---|---|
| NAA | Narrabri | Australia |
| NAB | Albany/NAS, GA | USA |
| NAC | Naracoorte | Australia |
| NAD | Macanal | Colombia |
| NAE | Natitingou | Benin |
| NAF | Banaina | Indonesia |
| NAG | Nagpur/Sonegaon | India |
| NAH | Naha | Indonesia |
| NAI | Annat | Guyana |
| NAJ | Nalkinichevan | Azerbaijan |
| NAK | Nakhon Ratchasima | Thailand |
| NAL | Nalchik | Russia |
| NAM | Namlea | Indonesia |
| NAN | Nandi/Int'l | Fiji |
| NAO | Nanchong | China |
| NAP | Naples/Capodichino | Italy |
| NAQ | Qaanaaq | Greenland |
| NAR | Nare | Colombia |
| NAS | Nassau/Int'l | Bahamas |
| NAT | Natal/Augusto Severo | Brazil |
| NAU | Napuka Is | F. Polynesia |
| NAV | Nevsehir | Turkey |
| NAW | Narathiwat | Thailand |
| NAX | Barbers Point, HI | USA |
| NAY | Beijing/Nanyuan | China |
| NBA | Nambaiyufa | Papua New Guinea |
| NBB | Barrancominas | Colombia |
| NBC | Naberevnye Chelny | Russia |
| NBE | Dallas/NAS, TX | USA |
| NBG | New Orleans/NAS, LA | USA |
| NBH | Nambucca Heads | Australia |
| NBJ | Barin/NAS, AL | USA |
| NBL | San Bias | Panama |
| NBO | Nairobi/Jorno Kenyatta Int'l | Kenya |
| NBP | New York/Battery Pk, NY | USA |
| NBQ | Kings Bay/NAS, GA | USA |
| NBR | Nambour | Australia |
| NBU | Glenview/NAS, IL | USA |
| NBV | Cana Brava | Brazil |
| NBW | Guantanamo/NAS | Cuba |
| NBX | Nabire | Indonesia |
| NCA | North Caicos | Turks & Caicos Is |
| NCE | Nice | France |
| NCG | Nueva Casas Grandes | Mexico |
| NCH | Nachingwea | Tanzania |
| NCI | Necocli | Colombia |
| NCL | Newcastle | UK |
| NCN | New Chenega, AK | USA |
| NCO | Quonset Point/NAS, RI | USA |
| NCP | Luzonis/NAS | Philippines |
| NCR | San Carlos | Netherlands |
| NCS | Newcastle | S. Africa |
| NCT | Nicoya/Guanacaste | Costa Rica |
| NCU | Nukus | Uzbekistan |
| NCY | Annecy | France |
| NDA | Bandanatra | Indonesia |
| NDB | Nouadhilbou | Mauritania |
| NDC | Nanded | India |
| NDD | Sumbe | Angola |
| NDE | Mandera | Kenya |
| NDF | Ndalatandos | Angola |
| NDG | Qiqihar | China |
| NDI | Namudi | Papua New Guinea |
| NDJ | Ndjamena | Tonga |
| NDK | Namdrik Is | Marshall Is |
| NDL | Ndele | Central African Rep |
| NDM | Mendi | Ethiopia |
| NDN | Nadunumu | Papua New Guinea |
| NDP | Pensacola/NAS, FL | USA |
| NDR | Nador | Morocco |
| NDS | Sandstone | Australia |
| NDU | Rundu | Namibia |
| NDV | Anacostia/USN HP, DC | USA |
| NDY | Sanday | UK |
| NDZ | Nordholz-Spieka | Germany |
| NEA | Glynco/NAS, GA | USA |
| NEC | Necochea | Argentina |
| NED | Winner, SD | USA |
| NEF | Neftekamsk | Russia |
| NEG | Negril | Jamaica |
| NEJ | Nejjo | Ethiopia |
| NEK | Nelkernt | Ethiopia |
| NEL | Lakehurst, NJ | USA |
| NEN | Whitehouse, FL | USA |
| NER | Neryungri | Russia |
| NES | New York/E. 34 St Landing, NY | USA |
| NET | New Bight | Bahamas |
| NEU | Sam Neua | Laos |
| NEV | Nevis/Newcastle | St. Kitts and Nevis |
| NEW | New Orleans, LA | USA |
| NEX | Charleston Nise, SC | USA |
| NFB | Detroit NAF, MI | USA |
| NFG | Nefteyugansk | Russia |
| NFL | Fallon/NAS, NV | USA |
| NFO | Niuafo'ou/Mata'aho | Tonga |
| NFR | Nafoora | Libya |
| NFW | Ft. Worth/NAS, TX | USA |
| NGA | Young | Australia |
| NGB | Ningbo | China |
| NGC | Grand Canyon/North Rim, AZ | USA |
| NGD | Anegada | Virgin Is (British) |
| NGE | Ngaoundere | Cameroon |
| NGI | Ngau Is | Fiji |
| NGL | Ngala | S. Africa |
| NGM | Guam/Agana/NAS | Guam |
| NGN | Nargana | Panama |
| NGO | Nagoya/Koniaki AFS | Japan |
| NGP | Corpus Christi/NAS, TX | USA |
| NGR | Ningerum | Papua New Guinea |
| NGS | Nagasaki | Japan |
| NGU | Norfolk/NAS, VA | USA |
| NGV | Ngiva | Angola |
| NGW | Corpus Christi/NAS, TX | USA |
| NGX | Manang | Nepal |
| NGZ | Alameda/NAS, CA | USA |
| NHA | Nha Trang | Vietnam |
| NHD | Minhad Ab/Military | UAE |
| NHF | New Halfa | Somalia |
| NHK | Patuxent River/NAS, MD | USA |
| NHS | Nushki | Pakistan |
| NHT | Northolt/RAF | UK |
| NHV | Nuku Hiva | F. Polynesia |
| NHX | Foley, AL | USA |
| NHZ | Brunswick/NAS, ME | USA |
| NIA | Nimba | Liberia |
| NIB | Nikolai, AK | USA |
| NIC | Nicosia | Cyprus |
| NID | China Lake/NAS, CA | USA |
| NIE | Niblack, AK | USA |
| NIF | Nifty | Australia |
| NIG | Nikunau | Kiribati |
| NIK | Mokolo Koba | Senegal |
| NIM | Niamey/Diori Hamani | Niger |
| NIN | Ninilchik, AK | USA |
| NIO | Niolki | Congo, DR |
| NIP | Jacksonvill/NAS, FL | USA |
| NIR | Beeville/NAS, TX | USA |
| NIS | Simberi Is | Papua New Guinea |
| NIT | Niort/Souche | France |
| NIX | Nioro | Mali |
| NJA | Atsugi/NAS | Japan |
| NJC | Nizhnevartovsk | Russia |
| NJK | El Centro/NAF, CA | USA |
| NKA | Nkan | Gabon |
| NKB | Noonkanbah | Australia |
| NKC | Nouakchott | Mauritania |
| NKD | Sinalk | Indonesia |
| NKG | Nanking | China |
| NKI | Naukiti, AK | USA |
| NKL | Nkolo | Congo, DR |
| NKN | Nankina | Papua New Guinea |
| NKS | Nkongsamba | Cameroon |
| NKT | Cherry Point/MCAS, NC | USA |
| NKU | Nkaus | Lesotho |
| NKV | Nichen Cove, AK | USA |
| NKX | Miramar/NAS, CA | USA |
| NKY | Nkayi/Yokangassi | Congo, DR |
| NLA | Ndola | Zambia |
| NLC | Lemoore/NAS, CA | USA |
| NLD | Nuevo Laredo/Int'l | Mexico |
| NLE | Niles, MI | USA |
| NLF | Darnley Is | Australia |
| NLG | Nelson Lagoon, AK | USA |
| NLK | Norfolk Is | Norfolk Is |
| NLL | Nullagine | Australia |
| NLO | Kinshasa/N'Dolo | Congo, DR |
| NLP | Neispruit | S. Africa |
| NLS | Nicholson | Australia |
| NLU | Mexico City/Santa Lucia | Mexico |
| NLV | Nikolaev | Ukraine |
| NMA | Namangan | Uzbekistan |
| NMB | Daman | India |
| NMC | Norman's Cay | Bahamas |

AIRPORTS-1-

| | | |
|---|---|---|
| NME | Nightmute, AK | USA |
| NMG | San Miguel | Panama |
| NMM | Meridian/NAS, MS | USA |
| NMN | Nomane | Papua New Guinea |
| NMP | New Moon | Australia |
| NMR | Nappa Merry | Australia |
| NMS | Namsang | Myanmar |
| NMT | Namtu | Myanmar |
| NMU | Namu | Marshall Is |
| NNA | Kenitra/NAF | Morocco |
| NNB | Santa Ana | Solomon Is |
| NND | Nangade | Mozambique |
| NNG | Nanning | China |
| NNI | Narnutoni | Namibia |
| NNK | Naknek, AK | USA |
| NNL | Nondalton, AK | USA |
| NNM | Naryan-Mar | Russia |
| NNR | Spiddal/Connemara | Ireland |
| NNT | Nan | Thailand |
| NNU | Nanuque | Brazil |
| NNX | Nunukan | Indonesia |
| NNY | Nanyang | China |
| NNZ | Point Sur, CA | USA |
| NOA | Nowra | Australia |
| NOB | Nosara Beach | Costa Rica |
| NOC | Knock Int'l | Ireland |
| NOD | Norden | Germany |
| NOE | Norddeich | Germany |
| NOG | Nogales | Mexico |
| NOH | Chicago/NAS, IL | USA |
| NOI | Novoirossijsk | Russia |
| NOJ | Nojabrxsk | Russia |
| NOK | Nova Xavantina | Brazil |
| NOL | Nakolik River, AK | USA |
| NOM | Nomad River | Papua New Guinea |
| NON | Nonouti | Kiribati |
| NOO | Naoro | Papua New Guinea |
| NOP | Mactan Is | Philippines |
| NOR | Nordfjordur | Iceland |
| NOS | Nossi-be/Fascene | Madagascar |
| NOT | Novato, CA | USA |
| NOU | Nourrea/Tontouta | New Caledonia |
| NOV | Huambo | Andorra |
| NOW | Port Angeles., WA | USA |
| NOZ | Novokuzinetsk | Russia |
| NPA | Pensacola/NAS, FL | USA |
| NPE | Napier-Hastings | New Zealand |
| NPG | Nipa | Papua New Guinea |
| NPH | Nephi, UT | USA |
| NPL | New Plymouth | New Zealand |
| NPO | Nangapinoh | Indonesia |
| NPP | Napperby | Australia |
| NPT | Newport/State, TI | USA |
| NPU | San Pedro Uraba | Colombia |
| NQA | Memphis/NAS, TN | USA |
| NQI | Kingsville/NAS, TX | USA |
| NQL | Niquelandia | Brazil |
| NQT | Nottingham | UK |
| NQU | Nuqui | Colombia |
| NQX | Key West/NAS, FL | USA |
| NQY | Newquay-St Mawgan | UK |
| NRA | Narrandera | Australia |
| NRB | Mayport/NAF, FL | USA |
| NRC | Crows Landing/NAS, CA | USA |
| NRD | Norderney | Germany |
| NRE | Namrole | Indonesia |
| NRG | Narrogin | Australia |
| NRI | Shangri-la, OK | USA |
| NRK | Norrkoping/Kungsangen | Sweden |
| NRL | North Ronaldsay | UK |
| NRM | Nara | Mali |
| NRQ | N'Fliquinha | Angola |
| NRR | Roosevelt/NAS | Puerto Rico |
| NRS | Imperial Beach/NAF, CA | USA |
| NRT | Tokyo/Narita | Japan |
| NRV | Guam/USCG Shore St | Guam |
| NRY | Newry | Australia |
| NSA | Noosa | Australia |
| NSB | Bimini/North SPB | Bahamas |
| NSE | Milton, FL | USA |
| NSF | Andrews/NAF, MD | USA |
| NSH | Now Shahr | Iran |
| NSI | Yaaunde/Nsimalen | Cameroon |
| NSK | Noril'sk | Russia |
| NSM | Norseman | Australia |
| NSN | Nelson | New Zealand |
| NSO | Scone | Australia |
| NSP | Sangley Point/NAF | Philippines |
| NST | Nakhon Si Thammarat | Thailand |
| NSV | Noosaville | Australia |
| NSX | N. Sound/Virgin Gorda/Hovercraft/ | |

| | | |
|---|---|---|
| | Launch Pt | Virgin Is (British) |
| NSY | Sigonella/NAF | Italy |
| NTA | Natadola | Fiji |
| NTB | Notodden | Norway |
| NTC | Santa Carolina | Mozambique |
| NTD | Point Mugu/NAS, CA | USA |
| NTE | Nantes | France |
| NTG | Nantong | China |
| NTI | Bintuni | Indonesia |
| NTJ | Manti, UT | USA |
| NTL | Newcastle/Williamtown | Australia |
| NTM | Miracema Do Norte | Brazil |
| NTN | Normanton | Australia |
| NTO | Santo Antao | Cape Verde Is |
| NTR | Monterrey/Aeropuerto Del None | |
| | | Mexico |
| NTT | Niuatoputapu/Kuini Lavenia | Tonga |
| NTU | Oceana/NAS, VA | USA |
| NTX | Natuna Ranai | Indonesia |
| NTY | Sun City/Pilansberg | S. Africa |
| NUB | Numbulwar | Australia |
| NUC | San Clemente/NAF, CA | USA |
| NUD | En Nahud | Somalia |
| NUE | Nuernberg | Germany |
| NUG | Nuguria | Papua New Guinea |
| NUH | Nunchia | Colombia |
| NUI | Nuiqsut, AK | USA |
| NUK | Nukutavake | F. Polynesia |
| NUL | Nulato, AK | USA |
| NUN | Saufley/NAS, FL | USA |
| NUP | Nunapitchuk, AK | USA |
| NUQ | Mountain View, CA | USA |
| NUR | Nullarbor | Australia |
| NUS | Norsup | Vanuatu |
| NUT | Nutuve | Papua New Guinea |
| NUU | Nakuru | Kenya |
| NUW | Whidbey Is/NAS, WA | USA |
| NUX | Novy Urengoy | Russia |
| NVA | Neiva/La Marguita | Colombia |
| NVD | Nevada, MO | USA |
| NVG | Nueva Guinea | Netherlands |
| NVK | Narvik/Framnes | Norway |
| NVP | Novo Aripuana | Brazil |
| NVR | Novgorod | Russia |
| NVS | Nevers | France |
| NVT | Navegantes | Brazil |
| NVY | Neyveli | India |
| NWA | Moheli | Comoros |
| NWH | Newport, NH | USA |
| NWI | Norwich | UK |
| NWP | Argentia, NS | Canada |
| NWS | New York/Pier 11/SPB, NY | USA |
| NWT | Nowata | Papua New Guinea |
| NWU | Bermuda/NAS | Bermuda |
| NXP | Twenty-Nine Palms, Marine Corps Air-Ground Combat Cntr, CA | USA |
| NXX | Willow Grove/NAS, PA | USA |
| NYC | New York, NY | USA |
| NYE | Nyeri | Kenya |
| NYG | Quantico-MCAF, VA | USA |
| NYI | Sunyani | Ghana |
| NYK | Nanyuki | Kenya |
| NYL | Yuma/MCAS, AZ | USA |
| NYM | Nadym | Russia |
| NYN | Nyingan | Australia |
| NYO | Stockholm/Skavsta | Sweden |
| NYU | Nyaung-u | Myanmar |
| NZA | Nzagi | Angola |
| NZC | Cecil/NAS, FL | USA |
| NZE | Nzerekore | Guinea |
| NZO | Nzola | Kenya |
| NZW | South Weymouth, MA | USA |
| NZY | North Is/NAS, CA | USA |

# O

| | | |
|---|---|---|
| OAG | Orange/Springhill | Australia |
| OAJ | Jacksonville, NC | USA |
| OAK | Oakland Int'l, CA | USA |
| OAL | Cacoal | Brazil |
| OAM | Oamaru | New Zealand |
| OAN | Olanchito | Honduras |
| OAR | Fritzsche/AAF, CA | USA |
| OAX | Oaxaca | Mexico |
| OBA | Oban | Australia |
| OBC | Obock | Djibouti |
| OBD | Obano | Indonesia |
| OBE | Okeechobee, FL | USA |

| | | |
|---|---|---|
| OBF | Oberpfaffenhofen | Germany |
| OBI | Odibos | Brazil |
| OBK | Northbrook, IL | USA |
| OBL | Zoersel | Belgium |
| OBM | Morobe | Papua New Guinea |
| OBN | Oban/Connei | UK |
| OBO | Obihiro | Japan |
| OBS | Aubenas/Vals-Lanas | France |
| OBT | Oakland, MD | USA |
| OBU | Kobuk, AK | USA |
| OBX | Obo | Papua New Guinea |
| OBY | Ittoqqortoormiit | Greenland |
| OCA | Ocean Reef, FL | USA |
| OCC | Coca | Ecuador |
| OCE | Ocean City, MD | USA |
| OCF | Ocala, FL | USA |
| OCH | Lufkin, TX | USA |
| OCI | Oceanic, AK | USA |
| OCJ | Ocho Rios/Boscobel | Jamaica |
| OCN | Oceanside, CA | USA |
| OCV | Ocana/Aguasclaras | Colombia |
| OCW | Washington, NC | USA |
| ODA | Ouadda | Central African Rep |
| ODB | Cordoba | Spain |
| ODD | Oodnadatta | Australia |
| ODE | Odense/Beldringe | Denmark |
| ODH | Odiham/RAF | UK |
| ODJ | Ouanda Dialle | Central African Rep |
| ODL | Cordillo Downs | Australia |
| ODN | Long Seridan | Malaysia |
| ODR | Ord River | Australia |
| ODS | Odessa/Central | Ukraine |
| ODW | Oak Harbor, WA | USA |
| ODX | Ord/Sharp Fld, NE | USA |
| ODY | Oudoni | Laos |
| OEA | Vincennes/Oneal, IN | USA |
| OEC | Ocussi | Indonesia |
| OEL | Orel | Russia |
| OEM | Paloemeu/Vincent Fayks | Suriname |
| OEO | Osceola, WI | USA |
| OER | Ornskoldsvik | Sweden |
| OES | San Antonio Oeste | Argentina |
| OFF | Offutt/AFB, NE | USA |
| OFI | Ouango Fitini | Côte D'Ivoire |
| OFJ | Olafsfjordur | Iceland |
| OFK | Norfolk, NE | USA |
| OFP | Ashland, VA | USA |
| OFU | Ofu | American Samoa |
| OGA | Ogallala/Searle Fld, NE | USA |
| OGB | Orangeburg, SC | USA |
| OGD | Ogden, UT | USA |
| OGE | Ogeranang | Papua New Guinea |
| OGG | Kahului, HI | USA |
| OGL | Ogle | Guyana |
| OGN | Yonaguni Jima | Japan |
| OGO | Abengourou | Côte D'Ivoire |
| OGR | Bonger | Chad |
| OGS | Ogdensburg Int'l, NY | USA |
| OGV | Ongava Game Reserve | Namibia |
| OGX | Ouargla | Algeria |
| OGZ | Vladikavkaz | Russia |
| OHA | Ohakea/RAF | New Zealand |
| OHC | Northeast Cape/AFS, AK | USA |
| OHD | Ohrid | Macedonia |
| OHI | Oshakati | Namibia |
| OHO | Okhotsk | Russia |
| OHP | Oban/ HP | UK |
| OHR | Wylk Auf Foehr | Germany |
| OHT | Kohat | Pakistan |
| OHX | Nashville Nexrad, TN | USA |
| OIA | Ourilandia | Brazil |
| OIC | Norwich/Eaten | Australia |
| OIL | Oil City, PA | USA |
| OIM | Oshima | Japan |
| OIR | Okushiri | Japan |
| OIT | Oita | Japan |
| OJC | Kansas City Exec, KS | USA |
| OKA | Okinawa/Naha | Japan |
| OKB | Orchid Beach/Fraser Is | Australia |
| OKC | Oklahoma City, OK | USA |
| OKD | Sapporo/Okadarna | Japan |
| OKE | Okino Erabu | Japan |
| OKF | Okaukuejo | Namibia |
| OKG | Okoyo | Congo, DR |
| OKH | Oakham/Cottesmor/RAF | UK |
| OKI | Oki Is | Japan |
| OKJ | Okayama | Japan |
| OKK | Kokorno, IN | USA |
| OKL | Oksibil | Indonesia |
| OKM | Okmulgee, OK | USA |
| OKN | Okondja | Gabon |

| Code | City | Country |
|------|------|---------|
| OKO | Tokyo/Yokota AFB | Japan |
| OKP | Oksapimin | Papua New Guinea |
| OKQ | Okaba | Indonesia |
| OKR | Yorke Is. | Australia |
| OKS | Oshkosh, NE | USA |
| OKT | Oktiabrskij | Russia |
| OKU | Mokuti Lodge | Namibia |
| OKV | Winchester, VA | USA |
| OKX | NY City Nexrad, NY | USA |
| OKY | Oakey | Australia |
| OLA | Orland | Norway |
| OLB | Olbia/Costa Smeraida | Italy |
| OLD | Old Town, ME | USA |
| OLE | Olean, NY | USA |
| OLF | Wolf Point Int'l, MT | USA |
| OLH | Old Harbor/SPB, AK | USA |
| OLI | Olafsvik/Rif | Iceland |
| OLJ | Olpoi | Vanuatu |
| OLM | Olympia, WA | USA |
| OLN | Colonia Sarmiento | Argentina |
| OLO | Olomouc | Czech Rep |
| OLP | Olympic Dam | Australia |
| OLQ | Olsobip | Papua New Guinea |
| OLS | Nogales Int'l, AZ | USA |
| OLU | Columbus, NE | USA |
| OLV | Olive Branch, MS | USA |
| OLY | Olney, IL | USA |
| OLZ | Oelwen, IA | USA |
| OMA | Omaha, NE | USA |
| OMB | Omboue | Gabon |
| OMC | Ormoc | Philippines |
| OMD | Oranjemund | Namibia |
| OME | Nome, AK | USA |
| OMF | Mafraq/King Hussein (RJAF) | Jordan |
| OMG | Omega | Namibia |
| OMH | Urmieh | Iran |
| OMJ | Omura | Japan |
| OMK | Omak, WA | USA |
| OML | Omkalai | Papua New Guinea |
| OMM | Marmul | Oman |
| OMN | Osmanabad | India |
| OMO | Mostar | Bosnia Hercegovina |
| OMR | Oradea | Romania |
| OMS | Omsk | Russia |
| OMY | Oddor Meanche | Cambodia |
| ONA | Winona, MN | USA |
| ONB | Ononge | Papua New Guinea |
| OND | Ondangwa | Namibia |
| ONE | Onepusu | Solomon Is |
| ONG | Mornington | Australia |
| ONH | Oneonta/Municipal, NY | USA |
| ONI | Moanamani | Indonesia |
| ONJ | Odate Noshiro | Japan |
| ONL | O'Neill, NE | USA |
| ONM | Socorro, NM | USA |
| ONN | Onion Bay, AK | USA |
| ONO | Ontario, OR | USA |
| ONP | Newport, OR | USA |
| ONQ | Zonguldak | Turkey |
| ONR | Monkira | Australia |
| ONS | Onsiow | Australia |
| ONT | Ontario Int'l, CA | USA |
| ONU | Ono I Lau | Fiji |
| ONX | Colon | Panama |
| ONY | Olney, TX | USA |
| OOA | Oskaloosa, IA | USA |
| OOL | Gold Coast | Australia |
| OOM | Cooma | Australia |
| OOR | Mooraberree | Australia |
| OOT | Onotoa | Kiribati |
| OPA | Kopasker | Iceland |
| OPB | Open Bay | Papua New Guinea |
| OPF | Miami-Opa Locka, FL | USA |
| OPI | Oenpeili | Australia |
| OPL | Opelousas, LA | USA |
| OPO | Porto | Portugal |
| OPS | Sinop | Brazil |
| OPU | Balimo | Papua New Guinea |
| OPW | Opuwa | Namibia |
| ORA | Oran | Argentina |
| ORB | Orebro | Sweden |
| ORC | Orocue | Colombia |
| ORD | Chicago/O'Hare Int'l, IL | USA |
| ORE | Orange, MA | USA |
| ORF | Norfolk Int'l, VA | USA |
| ORG | Paramaribo/Zorg En Hoop | Suriname |
| ORH | Worcester, MA | USA |
| ORI | Port Lions/SPB, AK | USA |
| ORJ | Orinduik | Guyana |
| ORK | Cork | Ireland |
| ORL | Orlando Exec, FL | USA |
| ORM | Northampton | Georgia |
| ORN | Oran/Es Senia | Algeria |
| ORO | Yoro | Honduras |
| ORP | Orapa | Botswana |
| ORQ | Norwalk / HP, CT | USA |
| ORR | Yorketown | Australia |
| ORS | Orpheus Is Resort/Waterport | Australia |
| ORT | Northway, AK | USA |
| ORU | Oruro | Bolivia |
| ORV | Noorvik/Curtis Memorial, AK | USA |
| ORW | Ormara | Pakistan |
| ORX | Oriximina | Brazil |
| ORY | Paris/Orly | France |
| ORZ | Orange Walk | Belize |
| OSB | Osage Beach, MD | USA |
| OSC | Wurtsmith/AFB, MI | USA |
| OSD | Ostersund/Froesoe | Sweden |
| OSE | Omora | Papua New Guinea |
| OSG | Ossima | Papua New Guinea |
| OSH | Oshkosh, WI | USA |
| OSI | Osijek | Croatia |
| OSK | Oskarshamn | Sweden |
| OSL | Oslo/Gardermoen | Norway |
| OSM | Mosul | Iraq |
| OSN | Osan/Air Base | S. Korea |
| OSP | Slupsk/Recizikowo | Poland |
| OSR | Ostrava/Mosnov | Czech Rep |
| OSS | Osh | Kyrgyzstan |
| OST | Ostend | Belgium |
| OSU | Colurribus, OH | USA |
| OSW | Orsk | Russia |
| OSX | Kosciusko/Attala County, MS | USA |
| OSY | Namsos/Lufthavn | Norway |
| OSZ | Koszalin | Poland |
| OTA | Mota | Ethiopia |
| OTC | Bol | Chad |
| OTD | Contadora | Panama |
| OTG | Worthington, MN | USA |
| OTH | North Bend, OR | USA |
| OTI | Morotai Is | Indonesia |
| OTJ | Otjiwarongo | Namibia |
| OTL | Boutilimit | Mauritania |
| OTM | Ottumwa, IA | USA |
| OTN | Oaktown, IN | USA |
| OTO | Otto/Vor, NM | USA |
| OTP | Bucharest/Otopeni Int'l | Romania |
| OTR | Coto 47 | Costa Rica |
| OTS | Anacortes, WA | USA |
| OTU | Otu | Colombia |
| OTY | Oria | Papua New Guinea |
| OTZ | Kotzebue, AK | USA |
| OUA | Ouagadougou/Aeroport | Burkina Faso |
| OUD | Oujda/Les Angades | Morocco |
| OUE | Ouesso | Cocos (Keeling) Is |
| OUG | Ouahigouya | Burkina Faso |
| OUH | Ouctshoorn | S. Africa |
| OUI | Ban Houei | Laos |
| OUK | Outer Skerries | UK |
| OUL | Oulu | Finland |
| OUM | Oum Hadjer | Chad |
| OUN | Norman, OK | USA |
| OUR | Batouri | Cameroon |
| OUS | Ourinhos | Brazil |
| OUT | Bousso | Chad |
| OUU | Ouanga | Gabon |
| OUZ | Zouerate | Mauritania |
| OVA | Bekily | Madagascar |
| OVB | Novosibirsk | Russia |
| OVD | Asturias | Spain |
| OVE | Oroville, CA | USA |
| OVL | Ovalle | Chile |
| OVS | Boscobel, WI | USA |
| OWA | Owatonna, MN | USA |
| OWB | Owensboro, KY | USA |
| OWD | Norwood, MA | USA |
| OWE | Owendo | Gabon |
| OWK | Norridgewock, ME | USA |
| OWY | Owyhee, NV | USA |
| OXB | Bissau/Osvaldo Vieira | Guinea Bissau |
| OXC | Oxford, CT | USA |
| OXD | Oxford, OH | USA |
| OXF | Oxford/Kidlington | UK |
| OXO | Orientos | Australia |
| OXR | Oxnard, CA | USA |
| OXV | Knoxville, IA | USA |
| OXY | Morney | Australia |
| OYA | Goya | Argentina |
| OYE | Oyem | Gabon |
| OYG | Moyo | Uganda |
| OYK | Ciapoclue | Brazil |
| OYL | Moyale | Kenya |
| OYN | Ouyen | Australia |
| OYO | Tres Arroyos | Argentina |
| OYP | St Georges de Ioyapock | French Guiana |
| OYS | Yosemite Ntl Park, CA | USA |
| OZA | Ozona, TX | USA |
| OZC | Ozamis City/Labo | Philippines |
| OZH | Zaporozhye | Ukraine |
| OZI | Codazzi | Colombia |
| OZP | Moron | Spain |
| OZR | Cairns/AAF, AL | USA |
| OZZ | Ouarzazate | Morocco |

# P

| Code | City | Country |
|------|------|---------|
| PAA | Pa-an | Myanmar |
| PAB | Bilaspur | India |
| PAC | Panama City/Paitilia | Panama |
| PAD | Paderborn/Lippstadt | Germany |
| PAE | Everett, WA | USA |
| PAF | Pakulha | Uganda |
| PAG | Pagadian | Philippines |
| PAH | Paducah, KY | USA |
| PAI | Pailin | Cambodia |
| PAJ | Para Chinar | Pakistan |
| PAK | Hanapepe/Port Allen, HI | USA |
| PAL | Palanquero | Colombia |
| PAM | Tyndall/AFB, FL | USA |
| PAN | Pattani | Thailand |
| PAO | Palo Alto, CA | USA |
| PAP | Port Au Prince | Haiti |
| PAQ | Palmer, AK | USA |
| PAS | Paros | Greece |
| PAT | Patna | India |
| PAU | Pauk | Myanmar |
| PAV | Paulo Afonso | Brazil |
| PAW | Pambwa | Papua New Guinea |
| PAX | Port De Paix | Haiti |
| PAY | Pamol | Malaysia |
| PAZ | Poza Rica/Tajin | Mexico |
| PBA | Barrow/Point Barrow, AK | USA |
| PBB | Paranaiba | Brazil |
| PBC | Puebla/Huejotsingo | Mexico |
| PBD | Porbandar | India |
| PBE | Puerto Berrio | Colombia |
| PBF | Pine Bluff, AR | USA |
| PBG | Plattsburgh/AFB, NY | USA |
| PBH | Paro | Bhutan |
| PBI | West Palm Beach, FL | USA |
| PBJ | Paama | Vanuatu |
| PBK | Pack Creek, AK | USA |
| PBL | Puerto Cabello | Venezuela |
| PBM | Paramaribo/Zandenj Int'l | Suriname |
| PBN | Porto Amboim | Angola |
| PBO | Paraburdoo | Australia |
| PBP | Punta Istilta | Costa Rica |
| PBQ | Pimenta Bueno | Brazil |
| PBR | Puerto Barrios | Guatemala |
| PBS | Patong Beach | Thailand |
| PBU | Putao | Myanmar |
| PBV | Porto Dos Gauchos | Brazil |
| PBW | Palibelo | Indonesia |
| PBX | Porto Alegre Do Norte | Brazil |
| PBZ | Plettenberg Bay | S. Africa |
| PCA | Portage Creek, AK | USA |
| PCB | Pondok Cabe | Indonesia |
| PCC | Puerto Rico | Colombia |
| PCD | Prairie Du Chien, WI | USA |
| PCE | Painter Creek, AK | USA |
| PCG | Paso Calballos | Guatemala |
| PCH | Palacios | Honduras |
| PCK | Porcupine Creek, AK | USA |
| PCL | Pucallpa/Capitan Rolden | Peru |
| PCM | Playa del Carmen | Mexico |
| PCN | Picton/Koromiko | New Zealand |
| PCO | Punta Colorada | Mexico |
| PCP | Principe | Sao Tome and Principe |
| PCR | Puerto Carreno | Colombia |
| PCS | Picos | Brazil |
| PCT | Princeton, NJ | USA |
| PCU | Picayune, MS | USA |
| PCV | Dunta Chivato | Mexico |
| PDA | Puerto Ininda | Colombia |
| PDB | Pedro Bay, AK | USA |
| PDC | Mueo | New Caledonia |
| PDE | Panclie Pandie | Australia |
| PDF | Prado | Brazil |
| PDG | Padang/Tabing | Indonesia |

**A I R P O R T S -1-**

| Code | Location | Country |
|------|----------|---------|
| PDI | Pindiu | Papua New Guinea |
| PDK | Atlanta, GA | USA |
| PDL | Ponta Delgada/Nordela | Portugal |
| PDN | Parndana | Australia |
| PDO | Pendopo | Indonesia |
| PDP | Punta Del Este | Uruguay |
| PDR | Presidente Dutra/Mun | Brazil |
| PDS | Piedras Negras | Mexico |
| PDT | Pendleton, OR | USA |
| PDU | Paysandu | Uruguay |
| PDV | Plovcliv | Bulgaria |
| PDX | Portland Int'l, OR | USA |
| PDZ | Pedernales | Venezuela |
| PEA | Penneshaw | Australia |
| PEB | Pebane | Mozambique |
| PEC | Pelican/SPB, AK | USA |
| PEE | Perm | Russia |
| PEF | Peenemuende | Germany |
| PEG | Perugia/Sant Egidio | Italy |
| PEH | Pehuajo | Argentina |
| PEI | Pereira/Matecana | Colombia |
| PEK | Beijing | China |
| PEL | Pelaneng | Lesotho |
| PEM | Puerto Madonado | Peru |
| PEN | Penang Int'l | Malaysia |
| PEO | Penn Yan, NY | USA |
| PEP | Peppimenarti | Australia |
| PEQ | Pecos City, TX | USA |
| PER | Perth | Australia |
| PES | Petrozavodsk | Russia |
| PET | Pelotas/Federal | Brazil |
| PEU | Puerto Lempira | Honduras |
| PEW | Peshawar | Pakistan |
| PEX | Pechora | Russia |
| PEY | Pencing | Australia |
| PEZ | Penza | Russia |
| PFA | Pat Warren, AK | USA |
| PFB | Passo Fundo | Brazil |
| PFC | Pacific City, OR | USA |
| PFD | Port Frederick, AK | USA |
| PFJ | Patreksfjordur | Iceland |
| PFN | Panama City, FL | USA |
| PFO | Paphos Int'l | Cyprus |
| PFR | Ilebo | Congo, DR |
| PGA | Page, AZ | USA |
| PGB | Pangoa | Papua New Guinea |
| PGC | Petersburg, WV | USA |
| PGD | Punta Gorda, FL | USA |
| PGE | Yegepa | Papua New Guinea |
| PGF | Perpignan/Llabanere | France |
| PGG | Progresso | Brazil |
| PGH | Pantnagar | India |
| PGI | Chitato | Angola |
| PGK | Pangkalpinang | Indonesia |
| PGL | Pascagoula, MS | USA |
| PGM | Port Graham, AK | USA |
| PGN | Pangia | Papua New Guinea |
| PGO | Pagosa Springs, CO | USA |
| PGP | Porto Alegre | Sao Tome and Principe |
| PGR | Paragould/Mun | Australia |
| PGS | Peach Springs, AZ | USA |
| PGV | Greenville, NC | USA |
| PGX | Perigueux/Bassillac | France |
| PGZ | Ponta Grossa/Sant'Ana | Brazil |
| PHA | Phan Rang | Vietnam |
| PHB | Parnailba/Santos Dumont | Brazil |
| PHC | Port Harcourt | Nigeria |
| PHD | New Philadelphia, OH | USA |
| PHE | Port Hedland | Australia |
| PHF | Hampton, VA | USA |
| PHH | Phan Thiet | Vietnam |
| PHI | Pinheiro | Brazil |
| PHJ | Porl Hunter | Australia |
| PHK | Pahokee, FL | USA |
| PHL | Philadelphia Int'l, PA | USA |
| PHM | Boeblingen | Germany |
| PHN | Port Huron Int'l, MI | USA |
| PHO | Point Hope, AK | USA |
| PHP | Philip, SD | USA |
| PHR | Pacific Harbor | Fiji |
| PHS | Phitsanulok | Thailand |
| PHT | Paris, TN | USA |
| PHU | Phu Vinh | Vietnam |
| PHW | Phalaborwa | S. Africa |
| PHX | Phoenix Int'l, AZ | USA |
| PHZ | Phi Phi Is | Thailand |
| PIA | Peoria, IL | USA |
| PIB | Laurel, MS | USA |
| PIC | Pine Cay | Turks & Caicos Is |
| PID | Nassau/Paradise Is | Bahamas |
| PIE | St Petersburg- Clearwater Int'l, FL | USA |

| Code | Location | Country |
|------|----------|---------|
| PIF | Pingtung | Taiwan |
| PIG | Pitinga | Brazil |
| PIH | Pocatello, ID | USA |
| PII | Fairbanks/Phillips Fld, AK | USA |
| PIK | Glasgow | UK |
| PIL | Pilar | Paraguay |
| PIM | Pine Mountain, GA | USA |
| PIN | Parintins | Brazil |
| PIO | Pisco | Peru |
| PIP | Pilot Point, AK | USA |
| PIQ | Pipillipai | Guyana |
| PIR | Pierre, SD | USA |
| PIS | Poitiers/Biard | France |
| PIT | Pittsburgh Int'l, PA | USA |
| PIU | Ptura | Peru |
| PIV | Pirapora | Brazil |
| PIW | Pilkwitonei, MB | Canada |
| PIX | Pico Is | Portugal |
| PIZ | Point Lay, AK | USA |
| PJB | Payson, AZ | USA |
| PJC | Pedro Juan Caballero | Paraguay |
| PJG | Panjgur | Pakistan |
| PJM | Puerto Jimenez | Costa Rica |
| PJS | Port San Juan, AK | USA |
| PJZ | Puerto Juarez | Mexico |
| PKA | Napaskiak/SPB, AK | USA |
| PKB | Parkersburg, WV | USA |
| PKC | Petropavlovsk-Kamchats | Russia |
| PKD | Park Rapids, MN | USA |
| PKE | Parkes | Australia |
| PKF | Park Falls, WI | USA |
| PKG | Pangkor | Malaysia |
| PKH | Porto Cheli Kheli/Alexion | Greece |
| PKJ | Playa Grande | Guatemala |
| PKK | Palkokku | Myanmar |
| PKL | Pakatoa Is | New Zealand |
| PKM | Port Kaituma | Guyana |
| PKN | Pangkalanbuun | Indonesia |
| PKO | Parakou | Benin |
| PKP | Puka Puka | F. Polynesia |
| PKR | Pokhara | Nepal |
| PKS | Paksane | Laos |
| PKT | Port Keats | Australia |
| PKU | Pekanbaru/Simpang Tiga | Indonesia |
| PKV | Pskov | Russia |
| PKW | Selebi-Phikwe | Botswana |
| PKY | Palangkaraya | Indonesia |
| PKZ | Pakse | Laos |
| PLA | Planaclas | Colombia |
| PLB | Plattsburgh, NY | USA |
| PLC | Pianeta Rica | Colombia |
| PLD | Playa Samara | Costa Rica |
| PLE | Paiela | Papua New Guinea |
| PLF | Pala | Chad |
| PLG | La Plagne | France |
| PLH | Plymouth | UK |
| PLI | Palm Is | St. Vincent & Grenadines |
| PLJ | Placencia | Belize |
| PLL | Ponta Pelada | Brazil |
| PLM | Palembang/Mahmud Badaruddin II | Indonesia |
| PLN | Pellston, MI | USA |
| PLO | Port Lincoln | Australia |
| PLP | La Palma | Panama |
| PLQ | Palanga | Italy |
| PLR | Pell City, AK | USA |
| PLS | Providenciales/Int'l | Turks & Caicos Is |
| PLT | Plato | Colombia |
| PLU | Belo Horizonte/Pampulha | Brazil |
| PLV | Poll | Ukraine |
| PLW | Palu/Mutiara | Indonesia |
| PLX | Semipalatinsk | Kazakstan |
| PLY | Plymouth, IN | USA |
| PLZ | Port Elizabeth | S. Africa |
| PMA | Pemba/Wawi | Tanzania |
| PMB | Pembina/Intermediate, ND | USA |
| PMC | Puerto Moritt/Tepual | Chile |
| PMD | Palmdale, CA | USA |
| PME | Portsmouth | UK |
| PMF | Milan/Milano/Parma | Italy |
| PMG | Ponta Pora/Int'l | Brazil |
| PMH | Portsmouth, OH | USA |
| PMI | Palma Mallorca | Spain |
| PMK | Palm Is | Australia |
| PML | Port Moller/AFS, AK | USA |
| PMM | Phanom Sarakham | Thailand |
| PMN | Pumani | Papua New Guinea |
| PMO | Palermo/Punta Raisi | Italy |
| PMP | Pimaga | Papua New Guinea |
| PMQ | Perito Moreno | Argentina |
| PMR | Palmerston North | New Zealand |

| Code | Location | Country |
|------|----------|---------|
| PMS | Palmyra | Syria |
| PMT | Paramakotoi | Guyana |
| PMU | Paimiut/SPB, AK | USA |
| PMV | Porlarnar | Venezuela |
| PMW | Palmas | Brazil |
| PMX | Palmer, MA | USA |
| PMY | Puerto Madryn/El Tehuelche | Argentina |
| PMZ | Palmar/Palmar Sur | Costa Rica |
| PNA | Pamplona | Spain |
| PNB | Porto Nacional | Brazil |
| PNC | Ponca City, OK | USA |
| PND | Punta Gorda | Belize |
| PNE | Philadelphia, PA | USA |
| PNF | Peterson's Point, AK | USA |
| PNG | Paranagua | Brazil |
| PNH | Phnom Penh/Pochentong | Cambodia |
| PNI | Pohnpei | Micronesia |
| PNK | Pontianak/Supadio | Indonesia |
| PNL | Pantelleria | Italy |
| PNM | Princeton, MN | USA |
| PNN | Princeton, ME | USA |
| PNO | Pinotepa Nacional | Mexico |
| PNP | Popondetta/Girua | Papua New Guinea |
| PNQ | Poona/Lohegaon | India |
| PNR | Pointe-Noire | Congo, DR |
| PNS | Pensacola, FL | USA |
| PNT | Puerto Natales/Teniente J. Gallardo | Chile |
| PNU | Panguitch, UT | USA |
| PNV | Panevezys | Lithuania |
| PNX | Sherman-Denison, TX | USA |
| PNY | Pondicherry | India |
| PNZ | Petrolina/Int'l | Brazil |
| POA | Porto Alegre/Salgado Filhe | Brazil |
| POB | Pope/AFB, NC | USA |
| POC | La Verne, CA | USA |
| POD | Podor | Senegal |
| POE | Polk/AAF, LA | USA |
| POF | Poplar Bluff, MO | USA |
| POG | Port Gentil | Gabon |
| POH | Pocahontas, IA | USA |
| POI | Potosi | Bolivia |
| POJ | Patos De Minas | Brazil |
| POL | Pemba | Mozambique |
| POM | Port Moresby/Int'l | Papua New Guinea |
| PON | Poptun | Guatemala |
| POO | Pocos De Calclas | Brazil |
| POP | Puerto Plata/La Union | Dominican Republic |
| POQ | Polk Inlet, AK | USA |
| POR | Pori | Finland |
| POS | Port Of Spain | Trinidad and Tobago |
| POT | Port Antonio/Ken Jones | Jamaica |
| POU | Poughkeepsie, NY | USA |
| POV | Presov | Slovakia |
| POW | Portoroz/Secovlje | Slovenia |
| POX | Paris/Paris Cergy Pontoise | France |
| POY | Lovell, WY | USA |
| POZ | Pozan/Lawica | Poland |
| PPA | Pampa/Perry Lefors Fld, TX | USA |
| PPB | Presidente Prudente/A. De Barros | Brazil |
| PPC | Prospect Creek, AK | USA |
| PPD | Humacao/Palmas Del Mar | Puerto Rico |
| PPE | Puerto Penasco | Mexico |
| PPF | Parsons, KS | USA |
| PPG | Pago Pago/Int'l | American Samoa |
| PPH | Peraitepuy | Venezuela |
| PPI | Port Pirie | Australia |
| PPJ | Pulau Panlang | Indonesia |
| PPK | Petropavlovsk | Kazakstan |
| PPL | Phaplu | Nepal |
| PPM | Pompano Beach, FL | USA |
| PPN | Popayan/Machangara | Colombia |
| PPO | Powell Point | Bahamas |
| PPP | Proserpine | Australia |
| PPQ | Paraparaumu | New Zealand |
| PPR | Pasir Pangarayan | Indonesia |
| PPS | Puerto Princesa | Philippines |
| PPT | Papeete/Faaa | F. Polynesia |
| PPU | Papun | Myanmar |
| PPV | Port Protection, AK | USA |
| PPW | Papa Westray | UK |
| PPX | Param | Papua New Guinea |
| PPY | Pouso Alegre | Brazil |
| PPZ | Puerto Paez | Venezuela |
| PQC | Phu Quoc/Duong Dang | Vietnam |
| PQI | Presque Isle, ME | USA |
| PQL | Pascagoula, Lott Int'l Arpt, MS | USA |
| PQM | Palenque | Mexico |

| Code | Location | Country |
|---|---|---|
| PQQ | Port Macquarie | Australia |
| PQS | Pilot Stn, AK | USA |
| PRA | Parana | Argentina |
| PRB | Paso Robles, CA | USA |
| PRC | Prescott, AZ | USA |
| PRD | Pardoo | Australia |
| PRE | Pore | Colombia |
| PRF | Port Johnson | Australia |
| PRG | Prague/Ruzyne | Czech Rep |
| PRH | Phrae | Thailand |
| PRI | Praslin Is | Seychelles |
| PRJ | Capri | Italy |
| PRK | Prieska | S. Africa |
| PRL | Port Oceanic, AK | USA |
| PRM | Portimao | Portugal |
| PRN | Pristina | Yugoslavia |
| PRO | Perry, IA | USA |
| PRP | Propriano | France |
| PRQ | Pres. Roque Saenz Pena | Argentina |
| PRR | Paruima | Guyana |
| PRS | Parasi | Solomon Is |
| PRT | Point Retreat/Coast Guard HP, AK | USA |
| PRU | Prome | Myanmar |
| PRV | Prerov | Czech Rep |
| PRW | Prentice, WI | USA |
| PRX | Paris, TX | USA |
| PRY | Pretoria | S. Africa |
| PRZ | Prineville, OR | USA |
| PSA | Florence/Pisa/Gal Galilei | Italy |
| PSB | Bellefonte, PA | USA |
| PSC | Pasco, WA | USA |
| PSD | Port Said | Egypt |
| PSE | Ponce/Mercedita | Puerto Rico |
| PSF | Pittsfield, MA | USA |
| PSG | Petersburg, AK | USA |
| PSH | St Peter | Germany |
| PSI | Pasni | Pakistan |
| PSJ | Poso/Kasiguncu | Indonesia |
| PSK | Dublin, VA | USA |
| PSL | Perth/Scone | UK |
| PSM | Pease/AFB, NH | USA |
| PSN | Palestine, TX | USA |
| PSO | Pasto/Cano | Colombia |
| PSP | Palm Springs, CA | USA |
| PSQ | Philadelphia/SPB, PA | USA |
| PSR | Pescara/Liberi | Italy |
| PSS | Posadas | Argentina |
| PST | Preston | Cuba |
| PSU | Putussibau | Indonesia |
| PSV | Papa Stour | UK |
| PSW | Passos | Brazil |
| PSX | Palacios, TX | USA |
| PSY | Port Stanley | Falkland Is |
| PSZ | Puerto Suarez | Somalia |
| PTA | Port Alsworth, AK | USA |
| PTB | Petersburg, VA | USA |
| PTC | Port Alice, AK | USA |
| PTD | Port Alexander, AK | USA |
| PTE | Port Stephens | Australia |
| PTF | Malololailal | Fiji |
| PTG | Pietersburg | S. Africa |
| PTH | Port Heiden, AK | USA |
| PTI | Port Douglas | Australia |
| PTJ | Portland | Australia |
| PTK | Pontiac, MI | USA |
| PTL | Port Armstrong, AK | USA |
| PTM | Palmanto | Venezuela |
| PTN | Morgan City/Municipal HP, LA | USA |
| PTO | Pato Branco | Brazil |
| PTP | Pointe A Pitre/Le Raizet | Gaudeloupe |
| PTR | Pleasant Harbour, AK | USA |
| PTS | Pittsburg, KS | USA |
| PTT | Pratt Municipal, KS | USA |
| PTU | Platinum, AK | USA |
| PTV | Porterville, CA | USA |
| PTW | Pottstown, PA | USA |
| PTX | Pitalito | Colombia |
| PTY | Panama City/Tocumen Int'l | Panama |
| PTZ | Pastaza | Ecuador |
| PUA | Puas | Papua New Guinea |
| PUB | Pueblo, CO | USA |
| PUC | Price, UT | USA |
| PUD | Puerto Deseado | Argentina |
| PUE | Puerto Obaldia | Panama |
| PUF | Pau/Uzein | France |
| PUG | Port Augusta | Australia |
| PUH | Pochutla | Mexico |
| PUI | Pureni | Papua New Guinea |
| PUJ | Punta Cana | Dominican Rep |
| PUK | Pukarua | F. Polynesia |
| PUL | Poulsbo, WA | USA |
| PUM | Pomala | Indonesia |
| PUN | Punia | Congo, DR |
| PUO | Prudhoe Bay, AK | USA |
| PUP | Po | Burkina Faso |
| PUQ | Punta Arenas/Pres Ibanez | Chile |
| PUR | Puerto Rico | Somalia |
| PUS | Pusan/Kimhae Int'l Arpt | S. Korea |
| PUT | Puttaparthi/Puttaprathe | India |
| PUU | Puerto Asis | Colombia |
| PUV | Pourn | New Caledonia |
| PUW | Pullman, WA | USA |
| PUX | Puerto Varas | Chile |
| PUY | Pula | Croatia |
| PUZ | Puerto Cabezas | Netherlands |
| PVA | Providencia | Colombia |
| PVC | Provincetown, MA | USA |
| PVD | Providence, RI | USA |
| PVE | El Porvenir | Panama |
| PVF | Placerville, CA | USA |
| PVG | Shanghai/Pu Dong | China |
| PVH | Porto Velho/Belmonte | Brazil |
| PVI | Paranavai | Brazil |
| PVK | Preveza/Lefkas/Aktion | Greece |
| PVN | Pleven | Bulgaria |
| PVO | Portoviejo | Ecuador |
| PVR | Puerto Vallarta/Ordaz | Mexico |
| PVS | Providemya | Russia |
| PVU | Provo, UT | USA |
| PVW | Plainview, TX | USA |
| PVX | Provedenia | Russia |
| PVY | Pope Vanoy, AK | USA |
| PVZ | Painesville, OH | USA |
| PWA | Oklahoma City, OK | USA |
| PWD | Plentywood, MT | USA |
| PWE | Pevek | Russia |
| PWI | Pawi/Beles | Ethiopia |
| PWK | Chicago/Pal-Waukee, IL | USA |
| PWL | Purwokerto | Indonesia |
| PWM | Portland Int'l, ME | USA |
| PWN | Pitts Town | Bahamas |
| PWO | Pweto | Congo, DR |
| PWQ | Pavloclar | Kazakstan |
| PWR | Port Walter, AK | USA |
| PWT | Bremerton, WA | USA |
| PXL | Polacca, AZ | USA |
| PXM | Puerto Escondido | Myanmar |
| PXO | Porto Santo | Portugal |
| PXU | Pleiku | Vietnam |
| PYA | Puerto Boyaca | Colombia |
| PYB | Jeypore | India |
| PYC | Playon Chico | Panama |
| PYE | Penrhyn Island | Cook Is |
| PYH | Puerto Ayacucho | Venezuela |
| PYJ | Polyarnyl | Russia |
| PYL | Perry/SPB, AK | USA |
| PYM | Plymouth, MA | USA |
| PYN | Payan | Colombia |
| PYO | Putumayo | Ecuador |
| PYR | Pyrgos/Andravida | Greece |
| PYV | Yaviza | Panama |
| PYX | Pattaya | Thailand |
| PZA | Paz De Ariporo/Casanare | Colombia |
| PZB | Pietermaritzburg | S. Africa |
| PZE | Penzance/ HP | UK |
| PZH | Zhob | Pakistan |
| PZK | Puka Puka Is/Attol | Cook Is |
| PZL | Phinda/Zulu Inyaia | S. Africa |
| PZO | Puerto Ordaz | Venezuela |
| PZQ | Presque Isle/Rogers, M! | USA |
| PZU | Port Sudan | Sudan |
| PZY | Piestany | Slovakia |

# Q

| Code | Location | Country |
|---|---|---|
| QAC | Castro | Brazil |
| QAD | Pordenone | Italy |
| QAE | Arzew | Algeria |
| QAG | El Ghazaciuet | Algeria |
| QAH | Alcantara | Brazil |
| QAI | Aime | France |
| QAJ | Ajman City | UAE |
| QAK | Barbacena | Brazil |
| QAL | Alessandria | Italy |
| QAM | Amiens/Glisy | France |
| QAN | Nedroma | Algeria |
| QAO | Agrigento | Italy |
| QAP | Apapa | Nigeria |
| QAQ | L'Aquila | Italy |
| QAR | Arnhem/Bus Svc | Netherlands |
| QAS | Ech Cheliff | Algeria |
| QAT | Abeokuta | Nigeria |
| QAU | Bebedouro | Brazil |
| QAV | Benjamin Constant | Brazil |
| QAW | Anniston/Ft Mcclellan Bus Trml, AL | USA |
| QAX | Alaa | Nigeria |
| QAY | Alba Iufla | Romania |
| QAZ | Zakopane | Poland |
| QBA | Budva | Yugoslavia |
| QBB | BelAbbes | Algeria |
| QBC | Bella Coola, BC | Canada |
| QBD | Barra Do Pirai | Brazil |
| QBE | Bega/Off-line Pt | Australia |
| QBF | Vail Van Svc, CO | USA |
| QBG | Pancevo | Yugoslavia |
| QBH | Levaliois | France |
| QBI | Bitola | Macedonia |
| QBJ | Bordj-Bou-Arreri | Algeria |
| QBK | Betim | Brazil |
| QBL | Bani-walid | Libya |
| QBM | Bourg-St Maurice | France |
| QBN | Barra Mansa | Brazil |
| QBO | Bochum | Germany |
| QBP | Ain Beida | Algeria |
| QBQ | Besancon | France |
| QBR | Bandar Khomeini | Iran |
| QBS | Brescia | Italy |
| QBT | Bettioua | Algeria |
| QBU | Bauchi | Nigeria |
| QBV | Benevento | Italy |
| QBW | Batemans Bay | Australia |
| QBX | Sobral | Brazil |
| QBY | Bistrita/Nasaud | Romania |
| QBZ | Bouira | Algeria |
| QCA | Makkah | Saudi Arabia |
| QCB | Chiba City | Japan |
| QCC | Camacari | Brazil |
| QCD | Campo Born | Brazil |
| QCE | Copper Mountain/Van Svc, CO | USA |
| QCF | Birigui | Brazil |
| QCG | Cataguases | Brazil |
| QCH | Colatina | Brazil |
| QCI | Playa deLos Cristianos | Spain |
| QCJ | Botucatu | Brazil |
| QCK | Cabo Frio | Brazil |
| QCL | Caltanissetta | Italy |
| QCM | Como | Italy |
| QCN | Canela | Brazil |
| QCO | Colon | Chile |
| QCP | Currais Novos | Brazil |
| QCQ | Caraguatatuba | Brazil |
| QCR | Curitibanos | Brazil |
| QCS | Cosenza | Italy |
| QCT | Bacita | Nigeria |
| QCU | Akunnaaq | Greenland |
| QCV | Guarulhos | Brazil |
| QCW | Wilton, CT/Off-line Pt | USA |
| QCX | Sao Caetano Do Sul | Brazil |
| QCY | Coningsby/RAF | UK |
| QCZ | Catanzaro | Italy |
| QDA | Charqueada | Brazil |
| QDB | Cachoeira Do Sul | Brazil |
| QDC | Dracena | Brazil |
| QDD | Botosani | Romania |
| QDE | Catanduva | Brazil |
| QDF | Conselheiro Lafaiete | Brazil |
| QDG | Ostro Weikopolski | Poland |
| QDH | Ashford/Int'l RR Stn | UK |
| QDI | Dornbirn | Austria |
| QDJ | Djelfa | Algeria |
| QDK | Chattanooga/Greyhound Bus Svc, TN | USA |
| QDN | Eden | Australia |
| QDO | Icoaraci | Brazil |
| QDP | Dom Pedrito | Brazil |
| QDQ | Duque De Caxias | Brazil |
| QDR | Dera'a | Syria |
| QDS | Itajuba | Brazil |
| QDT | Sedrata | Algeria |
| QDU | Dusseldorf/Stn | Germany |
| QDV | Jundiai | Brazil |
| QDW | Diadema | Brazil |
| QDX | Damietta | Egypt |
| QDY | Andong | S. Korea |
| QDZ | Saida | Algeria |
| QEA | Teramo | Italy |
| QEB | Maebashi | Japan |
| QEC | Elmarj City | Libya |

AIRPORTS -1-

**AIRPORTS-1-**

| Code | Name | Country |
|------|------|---------|
| QED | Medea | Algeria |
| QEE | Ebeye | Marshall Is |
| QEF | Egeisbach | Germany |
| QEG | Ribera Grande | Portugal |
| QEH | El Hadjar | Algeria |
| QEI | Crailsheim | Germany |
| QEJ | Elgarhbolli | Libya |
| QEK | El Mahalla El Kobra | Egypt |
| QEL | Wellington | Australia |
| QEM | Elmanzala | Egypt |
| QEN | SITA | - |
| QEO | Bielsko-Baila | Poland |
| QEP | Tarnobrzeg | Poland |
| QEQ | Embrach | Switzerland |
| QER | Shehr | Yemen |
| QES | SITA | - |
| QET | Taedok | S. Korea |
| QEU | Parnamirim | Brazil |
| QEV | Courbevoie | France |
| QEW | Nottingham | UK |
| QEX | Emmerich | Germany |
| QEY | Qeqertarsuatsiaat | Greenland |
| QEZ | Pomezia | Italy |
| QFA | Aalsmeer | Netherlands |
| QFB | Freburg | Germany |
| QFC | Creteil | France |
| QFD | Boufarik | Algeria |
| QFE | Ft. Benning, GA | USA |
| QFF | Brooklyn, NJ | USA |
| QFG | Eqalugaiarsuit | Greenland |
| QFH | Frederkshavn/Bus Svc | Denmark |
| QFI | Iginniarfik | Greenland |
| QFJ | Alluitsup Paa | Greenland |
| QFK | Selje/Harbour | Norway |
| QFL | Freilassing | Germany |
| QFM | Meet Ghamr | Egypt |
| QFN | Narsaq Kujalleq | Greenland |
| QFO | Duxford | UK |
| QFQ | Maloy/Harbour | Norway |
| QFR | Frosinone | Italy |
| QFS | Sao Francisco | Brazil |
| QFT | Qassiarsulk | Greenland |
| QFU | Corralejo | Spain |
| QFV | Bergen/Harbour Pier | Norway |
| QFW | Ft. Washington, PA/Off-line Pt | USA |
| QFX | Igaliku | Chile |
| QFY | Fukuyama | Japan |
| QFZ | Saarbruecken/HBF RR | Germany |
| QGA | Guaira | Brazil |
| QGB | Limeira | Brazil |
| QGC | Lencois Paulista | Brazil |
| QGD | Monte Alegre | Brazil |
| QGE | Guelma | Algeria |
| QGF | Monte Negro | Brazil |
| QGG | Agedabia | Libya |
| QGH | Gherian | Libya |
| QGI | Ilha Do Governador | Brazil |
| QGJ | Nova Friburgo | Brazil |
| QGK | Palmares | Brazil |
| QGL | St Gallen | Switzerland |
| QGM | Cheighourn Laid | Algeria |
| QGN | Tarragona | Spain |
| QGO | Gorizia | Italy |
| QGP | Garanhuns | Brazil |
| QGQ | Attu | Greenland |
| QGR | Kangerluk | Greenland |
| QGS | Alagoinhas | Brazil |
| QGT | Moriguchi | Japan |
| QGU | Gifu AB | Japan |
| QGV | Frankfurt/Neu Isenburg | Germany |
| QGW | Neustadt/Glawe | Germany |
| QGX | Gerga | Egypt |
| QGY | Gyor | Hungary |
| QGZ | Yokkaichi | Japan |
| QHA | Hasselt | Belgium |
| QHB | Piracicaba | Brazil |
| QHC | Rolandia | Brazil |
| QHD | Hahnweide/RR | Germany |
| QHE | Sato Bento Do Sul | Brazil |
| QHF | Saa Sebastiao Do Cai | Brazil |
| QHG | Sete Lagoas | Brazil |
| QHH | El Harrouche | Algeria |
| QHI | Chonburi | Thailand |
| QHJ | Hjoerring/Bus Svc | Denmark |
| QHK | Shahrkord | Iran |
| QHL | Castanhal | Brazil |
| QHM | Hama | Syria |
| QHN | Taguatinga | Brazil |
| QHO | Oak Brook, IL/Off-line Pt | USA |
| QHP | Taubate | Brazil |
| QHQ | Cham | Germany |

| Code | Name | Country |
|------|------|---------|
| QHR | Harar | Ethiopia |
| QHS | Horns | Syria |
| QHT | Terezopolis | Brazil |
| QHU | Husum | Germany |
| QHV | Novo Hamburgo | Brazil |
| QHW | Brooklyn, NJ | USA |
| QHX | Sohag | Egypt |
| QHY | Hachioji City | Japan |
| QHZ | Hoofddorp | Netherlands |
| QIA | Itauna | Brazil |
| QIB | Ibiruba/Off-line Pt | Brazil |
| QIC | Siracusa | Italy |
| QID | Tres Coracoes | Brazil |
| QIE | Istres | France |
| QIF | Isleworth | UK |
| QIG | Iguatu | Brazil |
| QIH | Tres Rios | Brazil |
| QII | Lindau | Germany |
| QIJ | Gijon | Spain |
| QIK | Ikoyi | Norway |
| QIL | Sig | Algeria |
| QIM | Ain Mlila | Algeria |
| QIN | Mersin | Turkey |
| QIO | Ain Temouchent | Algeria |
| QIP | Simbach | Germany |
| QIQ | Rio Claro | Brazil |
| QIR | Irbid/Off-line Pt | Jordan |
| QIS | Mito | Japan |
| QIT | Itapetinga | Brazil |
| QIU | Ciucladela | Spain |
| QIV | Ismailia | Egypt |
| QIW | Umm Alquwain | UAE |
| QIX | Quixada | Brazil |
| QIY | Beclarra Is. | Australia |
| QIZ | Bizerte | India |
| QJA | Jaragua Do Sul | Brazil |
| QJB | Jubail | Saudi Arabia |
| QJC | Thimbu | Bhutan |
| QJD | Jindaloyne | Australia |
| QJE | Kitsissuarsuit | Greenland |
| QJF | Atammik | Greenland |
| QJG | Itilleq | Greenland |
| QJH | Gassimiut | Greenland |
| QJI | ikarniut | Greenland |
| QJJ | Dalton/FlightLink Bus Svc, GA | USA |
| QJK | Ajaokuta | Nigeria |
| QJL | Kjoellefjord | Norway |
| QJM | Brusque | Brazil |
| QJN | Jounieh | Lebanon |
| QJO | Campos Do Jorclao | Brazil |
| QJP | Puchon City | S. Korea |
| QJQ | Jal Edib | Lebanon |
| QJR | La Junquera | Spain |
| QJS | Saelby | Denmark |
| QJT | Napasoq/Off-line Pt | Greenland |
| QJU | Jullundur | India |
| QJV | Skagen/Limousine Svc | Denmark |
| QJW | Kjellerup/Bus Svc | Denmark |
| QJX | Nong Khai | Thailand |
| QJY | Kolobrzeg/Bus Svc | Poland |
| QJZ | Nantes/RR | France |
| QKA | Cachoeirinha | Brazil |
| QKB | Breckenridge/Van Svc, CO | USA |
| QKC | Karaj | Iran |
| QKD | Elk | Poland |
| QKE | Kabwe | Zambia |
| QKF | Kirefeld | Germany |
| QKG | Chalkis | Greece |
| QKH | Kharian | Pakistan |
| QKI | Kielce | Poland |
| QKJ | Khenchela | Algeria |
| QKK | Karasjok | Norway |
| QKL | Cologne/Stn | Germany |
| QKM | Gurni City | S. Korea |
| QKN | Kairouan | Tunisia |
| QKO | Khoms | Libya |
| QKP | Kruger National Park | S. Africa |
| QKQ | Anklam | Germany |
| QKR | Kourou | F. Guiana |
| QKS | Keystone/Van Svc, CO | USA |
| QKT | Kangaamiut | Greenland |
| QKU | Cologne/RR | Germany |
| QKV | Osaka/Off-line Pt | Japan |
| QKW | Kanazawa | Japan |
| QKX | Kautokeino | Norway |
| QKY | Wakayama | Japan |
| QKZ | Konstanz | Germany |
| QLA | Lasham | UK |
| QLB | Lajeado | Brazil |
| QLC | Gilwice | Poland |
| QLD | Blida | Algeria |

| Code | Name | Country |
|------|------|---------|
| QLE | Leeton/Bus Svc | Australia |
| QLF | Lahti | Finland |
| QLG | Landshut | Germany |
| QLH | Kelsterbach | Germany |
| QLI | Limassol | Cyprus |
| QLJ | Lucerne | Switzerland |
| QLK | El Kala | Algeria |
| QLL | Sao Leopoldo | Brazil |
| QLM | La Munoza | Spain |
| QLN | Sulmona | Italy |
| QLO | Loerrach | Germany |
| QLP | La Spezia | Italy |
| QLQ | Lerida | Spain |
| QLR | Leiria | Portugal |
| QLS | Lausanne | Switzerland |
| QLT | Latina | Italy |
| QLU | Lublin | Poland |
| QLV | Olivos | Argentina |
| QLW | Lavras | Brazil |
| QLX | Lauterach | Austria |
| QLY | Playa Blanca | Spain |
| QLZ | Ikast/Bus Svc | Denmark |
| QMA | Matanzas | Cuba |
| QMB | Panambi | Brazil |
| QMC | Mairipora | Brazil |
| QMD | Madaba | Jordan |
| QME | Messina | Italy |
| QMF | Mafra | Brazil |
| QMG | Maghnia | Algeria |
| QMH | Cum El Bouaghi | Algeria |
| QMI | Mogi Das Cruzes | Brazil |
| QMJ | Masjed Soleyman | Iran |
| QMK | Niacornaarsuk | Greenland |
| QML | Mirpur | Pakistan |
| QMM | Marina Di Massa | Italy |
| QMN | Mbabane/Off-line Pt/(DCA HQ) | Swaziland |
| QMO | Mons | Belgium |
| QMP | Macon/FlightLink Bus Svc, GA | USA |
| QMQ | Murzuq | Libya |
| QMR | Marsala | Italy |
| QMS | Masan | S. Korea |
| QMT | Mostaganem | Algeria |
| QMU | Moutiers | France |
| QMV | Montvale, NJ | USA |
| QMW | Mohammadia | Algeria |
| QMZ | Mainz | Germany |
| QNA | Ballina | Australia |
| QNB | Anand | India |
| QNC | Neuchatel | Switzerland |
| QND | NoviSad | Yugoslavia |
| QNE | Rio Negrinho | Brazil |
| QNF | Faridabad | India |
| QNG | Nagano | Japan |
| QNH | Canoinhas | Brazil |
| QNI | Onitsha | Norway |
| QNJ | Annemasse | France |
| QNK | Nsukka | Norway |
| QNL | Neuilly-Sur-Seine | France |
| QNM | Namur | Belgium |
| QNN | Marina | Nigeria |
| QNO | Ascoli Piceno | Italy |
| QNP | Ayja Napa | Cyprus |
| QNQ | Malmo Town | Sweden |
| QNR | Santa Cruz Rio Pardo | Brazil |
| QNS | Canoas | Brazil |
| QNT | Niteroi | Brazil |
| QNU | Nuoro | Italy |
| QNV | Novalguacu | Brazil |
| QNW | Nawanshahar | India |
| QNX | Macon | France |
| QNY | New York/Marine Air Terminal, NY | USA |
| QNZ | Nara City | Japan |
| QOA | Mococa | Brazil |
| QOB | Ansbach/Katterbach | Germany |
| QOC | Osasco | Brazil |
| QOD | Osvaldo Cruz/Off-line Pt | Brazil |
| QOE | Noervenich | Germany |
| QOF | Kiev/Darnitsa Bus Stn | Ukraine |
| QOG | Homburg | Germany |
| QOH | Kiev/Hotel Rus Bus Stn | Ukraine |
| QOI | Cotia | Brazil |
| QOJ | Sac Borja | Brazil |
| QOK | Oeksfjord | Norway |
| QOL | Collo | Algeria |
| QOM | Ornlya | Japan |
| QON | Arlon | Belgium |
| QOO | Otsu City | Japan |
| QOP | Codroipo | Italy |
| QOQ | Saarloq | Greenland |

| Code | Location | Country |
|------|----------|---------|
| QOR | Ordu | Turkey |
| QOS | Oristano | Italy |
| QOT | Otaru | Japan |
| QOU | Oued Rhiou | Algeria |
| QOV | Comuna Providencia | Chile |
| QOW | Owerri | Nigeria |
| QOX | Memmingen | Germany |
| QOY | Lorriza | Poland |
| QOZ | Oued Zenati | Algeria |
| QPA | Padova | Italy |
| QPB | Campobasso | Italy |
| QPC | Plock | Poland |
| QPD | Pinar Del Rio | Colombia |
| QPE | Petropolis | Brazil |
| QPF | Pompeia | Brazil |
| QPG | Singapore/Paya Lebar | Seychelles |
| QPH | Palapye | Botswana |
| QPI | Palmira | Colombia |
| QPJ | Pecs | Hungary |
| QPK | Strausberg | Germany |
| QPL | Ploiesti | Romania |
| QPM | Opoie | Poland |
| QPN | Piatra Neamt | Romania |
| QPO | Potenza | Italy |
| QPP | Berlin | Germany |
| QPQ | Pinamar | Argentina |
| QPR | Prato | Italy |
| QPS | Pirassununga/Off-line Pt. | Brazil |
| QPU | Porto Uniao | Brazil |
| QPV | PerisheR Valley/Bus Svc | Australia |
| QPW | Kangaiatsiaq | Greenland |
| QPZ | Piacenza | Italy |
| QQA | Britrail Rail Zone A | UK |
| QQB | Britrail Rail Zone B | UK |
| QQC | Britrail Rail Zone C | UK |
| QQD | Dover/RR | UK |
| QQE | Britrail Rail Zone E | UK |
| QQF | Britrail Rail Zone F | UK |
| QQG | Britrail Rail Zone G | UK |
| QQH | Harwich/RR | UK |
| QQI | Britrail Rail Zone I | UK |
| QQJ | Britrail Rail Zone J | UK |
| QQK | London Kings Cross/RR | UK |
| QQL | Britrail Rail Zone L | UK |
| QQM | Manchester Piccadilly/RR | UK |
| QQN | Birminaham-New Street/RR | UK |
| QQO | Britrail Rail Zone O | UK |
| QQP | London-Paddington/RR | UK |
| QQR | Ramsgate/RR | UK |
| QQS | Britrail Rail Zone S | UK |
| QQT | Britrail Rail Zone T | UK |
| QQU | London Euston/RR | UK |
| QQV | Britrail Rail Zone V | UK |
| QQW | London/London-Waterloo | UK |
| QQX | Bath/RR | UK |
| QQY | York/RR | UK |
| QQZ | Britrail Rail Zone Z | Georgia |
| QRA | Johannesburg/Randgermiston | S. Africa |
| QRB | Ravensburg | Germany |
| QRC | Rancagua | Chile |
| QRD | Andradas | Brazil |
| QRE | Carazinho | Brazil |
| QRF | Bragado | Argentina |
| QRG | Ragusa | Italy |
| QRH | Rotterdam/Central Stn | Netherlands |
| QRI | Rize | East Timor |
| QRJ | Cariacica | Brazil |
| QRK | Aricos | Brazil |
| QRL | Marbella | Spain |
| QRM | Narromine | Australia |
| QRN | Muroran | Japan |
| QRO | Queretaro | Myanmar |
| QRP | Gramado | Brazil |
| QRQ | Marmaris | Turkey |
| QRR | Warren | Australia |
| QRS | Resita | Romania |
| QRT | Rieti | Italy |
| QRU | Rio Do Sul | Brazil |
| QRV | Arras | France |
| QRW | Warri | Nigeria |
| QRX | Narooma | Australia |
| QRY | Ikeraasarsuk | Greenland |
| QRZ | Resende | Brazil |
| QSA | Sabadell | Spain |
| QSB | Sac Bernardo Do Campo | Brazil |
| QSC | Sac Carlos | Brazil |
| QSD | Sac Goncad | Brazil |
| QSE | Santo Andre | Brazil |
| QSF | Setif | Algeria |
| QSG | Sonderborg | Denmark |
| QSH | Seeheim | Germany |
| QSI | Moshi | Tanzania |
| QSJ | Sao Joao Del Rei | Brazil |
| QSK | Souk Ahras | Algeria |
| QSL | Suru-Lere | Nigeria |
| QSM | Uetersen/Off-line Pt | Germany |
| QSN | San Nicolas Ban | Cuba |
| QSO | Sousse | Tunisia |
| QSP | Reserved/Network Service Code | |
| QSQ | Sidon | Lebanon |
| QSR | Salerno | Italy |
| QSS | Sassan | Italy |
| QST | Izmil | Turkey |
| QSU | Mansoura | Egypt |
| QSV | Sovata | Romania |
| QSW | Sweida | Syria |
| QSX | New Amsterdam | Guyana |
| QSY | Ruedesheim/Off-line Pt | Germany |
| QSZ | Shizijoka City | Japan |
| QTC | Caserta | Italy |
| QTD | Timbauba | Brazil |
| QTE | Sac Goncalo Amarante | Brazil |
| QTF | Qatif | Saudi Arabia |
| QTG | Tupi Paulista | Brazil |
| QTH | Thredbo/Bus Svc | Australia |
| QTI | Termini Imere | Italy |
| QTJ | Chartres | France |
| QTK | Rothenburg/Off-line Pt. | Germany |
| QTL | Caratinga | Brazil |
| QTM | Tomakomaj | Japan |
| QTN | San Antonjo | Chile |
| QTO | Skitube/Bus Svc. | Australia |
| QTP | Tana | Norway |
| QTR | Tartous | Syria |
| QTS | Englewood, CO/Off-line Pt | USA |
| QTT | Tanta | Egypt |
| QTU | Itu | Brazil |
| QTW | Taejon | S. Korea |
| QTX | Arbatax | Italy |
| QTY | Tsu | Japan |
| QTZ | Coatzacoalcos | Mexico |
| QUA | Puttgarden | Germany |
| QUB | Ubari | Libya |
| QUC | Puerto la Cruz | Venezuela |
| QUD | Damanhour | Egypt |
| QUE | Qullissat | Greenland |
| QUF | Tallinn/Pirita Harbour | Estonia |
| QUG | Chichester Goodwood | UK |
| QUH | Shebeen El Korn | Egypt |
| QUI | Chuquicamata | Chile |
| QUJ | Uijongbu | S. Korea |
| QUL | Ulm | Germany |
| QUM | Qum | Iran |
| QUN | Chun Chon City/Air Base | S. Korea |
| QUO | Uyo | Nigeria |
| QUP | Saqqaq | Greenland |
| QUQ | Caceres | Spain |
| QUR | Muriae | Brazil |
| QUS | Gusau | Nigeria |
| QUT | Utsunomiya AB | Japan |
| QUU | Chung-Mu City | S. Korea |
| QUV | Aappilattoq | Greenland |
| QUW | Ammassivik | Greenland |
| QUX | Caudebec en Caux | France |
| QUY | Wyton/RAF | UK |
| QUZ | Puerto de la Luz | Spain |
| QVA | Varese | Italy |
| QVB | Uniao Da Vitoria | Brazil |
| QVC | Vicosa | Brazil |
| QVD | Salo | Finland |
| QVE | Forssa | Finland |
| QVF | Karkkila | Finland |
| QVG | Vilgenis | France |
| QVH | Vila Velha | Brazil |
| QVI | Valbonne | France |
| QVJ | Vraidebria | Bulgaria |
| QVK | Valkeakoski | Finland |
| QVL | Victoria Is | Nigeria |
| QVM | Hämeenlinna | Finland |
| QVN | Avellino | Italy |
| QVO | Havoeysund | Norway |
| QVP | Avare | Brazil |
| QVQ | Verden | Germany |
| QVR | Volta Redonda | Brazil |
| QVS | Tervakoski | Finland |
| QVT | Riihimäki | Finland |
| QVU | Vaduz | Liechtenstein |
| QVV | Heinola | Finland |
| QVW | Kotka | Finland |
| QVX | Ghazaouet | Algeria |
| QVY | Kouvola/Bus Stn. | Finland |
| QVZ | Hamina | Finland |
| QWA | Oshawa, ON | Canada |
| QWB | Berlin/HBF Railway Svc | Germany |
| QWC | Berlin/Berlin Zoo | Germany |
| QWD | Mittenwaid | Germany |
| QWE | Berlin/Fredrichstr. Railway Svc | Germany |
| QWF | Ft. Collins Bus Svc, CO | USA |
| QWG | Charlotte/Wilgrove Air Park, NC | USA |
| QWH | Loveland Bus Svc, CO | USA |
| QWI | Schleswig | Germany |
| QWJ | Americana | Brazil |
| QWK | Wloclawek | Poland |
| QWL | Crankenback Villeage/Bus Svc | Australia |
| QWM | Longmont Bus Svc, CO | USA |
| QWN | Astorga | Brazil |
| QWO | Holstelbro/Bus Svc. | Denmark |
| QWP | Winter Park/Van Svc, CO | USA |
| QWQ | Struer/Bus Svc | Denmark |
| QWR | Donauwoerth | Germany |
| QWS | Nowy Targ | Poland |
| QWT | Talavera de la Reina | Spain |
| QWU | Wuerzburg | Germany |
| QWV | Valevo | Yugoslavia |
| QWW | Navalmoral de a Mata | Spain |
| QWX | Merida | Spain |
| QWY | Albany/Bus Svc, NY | USA |
| QWZ | Best/Bus Svc. | Netherlands |
| QXB | Aix-en-Provence | France |
| QXC | Caxias | Brazil |
| QXD | Cachoeiro Itapemirim | Brazil |
| QXE | Sora | Italy |
| QXF | Vestbjerg/Bus Svc | Denmark |
| QXG | Angers/RR | France |
| QXH | Schoenhagen | Germany |
| QXI | Loviisa | Finland |
| QXJ | Porvoo | Finland |
| QXK | St. Genis/Bus Svc. | France |
| QXN | SITA Network | - |
| QXO | Tokyo | Japan |
| QXP | Struga | Macedonia |
| QXQ | Stalowa Wola | Poland |
| QXR | Radom | Poland |
| QXS | SITA Aircom | - |
| QXT | SITA Network | - |
| QXV | Svendborg/RR | Denmark |
| QXW | Alfenas | Brazil |
| QXZ | Woergi/Bus Svc | Austria |
| QYA | Anyang | S. Korea |
| QYB | Yaba | Nigeria |
| QYC | Drachten/Bus Svc. | Netherlands |
| QYD | Gdynia | Poland |
| QYE | Enschede/RR | Netherlands |
| QYF | German Railways Zone F/RR | Germany |
| QYG | Germany/RR | Germany |
| QYH | Hengelo/RR | Netherlands |
| QYI | Hilversum/RR | Netherlands |
| QYJ | German Railways Zone J/RR | Germany |
| QYK | Koyang | Kuwait |
| QYL | Almelo/RR | Netherlands |
| QYM | Amersfoort/RR | Netherlands |
| QYN | Byron Bay | Australia |
| QYO | Olsztyin | Poland |
| QYP | Apeldoorn/RR | Netherlands |
| QYQ | Sulsted/Bus Svc | Denmark |
| QYR | Troyes | France |
| QYS | Yasoudj | Netherlands |
| QYT | Paterswolde/Bus Svc. | Netherlands |
| QYV | Deventer/RR | Netherlands |
| QYW | Cannes/Vieux Port | France |
| QYY | Bialystok | Poland |
| QYZ | Heerenveen/Bus Svc. | Netherlands |
| QZA | Zarqa | Jordan |
| QZB | Zermatt | Switzerland |
| QZC | Smiggin Holes/Bus Svc | Australia |
| QZD | Szeged | Hungary |
| QZE | Mont Louis | France |
| QZF | Font Romeu | France |
| QZG | La Llagone | France |
| QZH | Les Angles | France |
| QZI | Tizi Ouzou | Algeria |
| QZJ | Loimaa | Finland |
| QZK | Mantsala | Finland |
| QZL | Zliten | Libya |
| QZM | Bullocks Flat/Bus Svc. | Australia |
| QZN | Relizane | Algeria |
| QZO | Arezzo | Italy |

AIRPORTS-1-

| Code | Location | Country |
|---|---|---|
| QZP | GC Apollo, ON/Off-line Pt. | Canada |
| QZQ | Zahleh | Lebanon |
| QZR | Aprilia | Italy |
| QZS | Soeroeya | Norway |
| QZT | Zawia Town | Libya |
| QZU | Rauma | Finland |
| QZV | Roissy-en-France | France |
| QZZ | Zagazeeg | Egypt |

# R

| Code | Location | Country |
|---|---|---|
| RAA | Rakanda | Papua New Guinea |
| RAB | Rabaui/Tokua | Papua New Guinea |
| RAC | Racine, WI | USA |
| RAD | Tortola/Road Town | Virgin Is (British) |
| RAE | Arar | Saudi Arabia |
| RAG | Raglan | New Zealand |
| RAH | Rafha | Saudi Arabia |
| RAI | Praia/Francisco Mendes | Cape Verde Island |
| RAJ | Raikot/Civil | India |
| RAK | Marrakeeh/Menara | Morocco |
| RAL | Riverside, CA | USA |
| RAM | Ramingining | Australia |
| RAN | Ravenna/La Spreta | Italy |
| RAO | Ribeirao Preto/Leite Lopes | Brazil |
| RAP | Rapid City, SD | USA |
| RAQ | Raha/Sugimanuru | Indonesia |
| RAR | Rarotonga | Cook Is |
| RAS | Rasht | Iran |
| RAT | Raduzhnyi | Russia |
| RAU | Rangpur | Bangladesh |
| RAV | Cravo None | Colombia |
| RAW | Arawa | Papua New Guinea |
| RAX | Oram | Papua New Guinea |
| RAY | Rothesay / HP | UK |
| RAZ | Rawala Kot | Pakistan |
| RBA | Rabat/Sale | Morocco |
| RBB | Borba | Brazil |
| RBC | Robinvale | Australia |
| RBD | Dallas-Redbird, TX | USA |
| RBE | Ratanakiri | Cambodia |
| RBF | Big Bear, CA | USA |
| RBG | Roseburg, OR | USA |
| RBH | Brooks Lodge, AK | USA |
| RBI | Rabi | Fiji |
| RBJ | Rebun | Japan |
| RBK | Rancho, CA | USA |
| RBL | Red Bluff, CA | USA |
| RBM | Straubing/Wallmuhle | Germany |
| RBN | Ft. Jelferson, FL | USA |
| RBO | Robore | Bolivia |
| RBP | Rabaraba | Papua New Guinea |
| RBQ | Rurrenabaque | Bolivia |
| RBR | Rio Branco/Pres. Medici | Brazil |
| RBS | Orbost | Australia |
| RBT | Marsabit | Kenya |
| RBU | Roebourne | Australia |
| RBV | Ramata | Solomon Is |
| RBY | Ruby, AK | USA |
| RCA | Ellsworth/AFB, SD | USA |
| RCB | Richards Bay | S. Africa |
| RCE | Roche Harbor, WA | USA |
| RCH | Riohacha | Colombia |
| RCK | Rockdale/Coffield, TX | USA |
| RCL | Redcliffe | Vanuatu |
| RCM | Richmond | Australia |
| RCN | American River | Australia |
| RCO | RocheFt./Saint Agnant | France |
| RCQ | Reconquista | Argentina |
| RCR | Rochester, IN | USA |
| RCS | Rochester | UK |
| RCT | Reed City, MI | USA |
| RCU | Rio Cuarto | Argentina |
| RCY | Rum Cay | Bahamas |
| RDA | Rockhampton Downs | Australia |
| RDB | Red Dog, AK | USA |
| RDC | Redencao | Brazil |
| RDD | Redding, CA | USA |
| RDE | Mercley | Indonesia |
| RDG | Reading, PA | USA |
| RDK | Red Oak, IA | USA |
| RDM | Redmond, OR | USA |
| RDR | Grand Forks/AFB, ND | USA |
| RDS | Rincon de los Sauces | Argentina |
| RDT | Richard Toll | Senegal |
| RDU | Raleigh-Durham Int'l, NC | USA |
| RDV | Red Devil, AK | USA |

| Code | Location | Country |
|---|---|---|
| RDZ | Rodez/Marcillac | France |
| REA | Reaci | F. Polynesia |
| REB | Rechlin | Germany |
| REC | Recife/Guararapes Int'l | Brazil |
| RED | Red Lodge, MT | USA |
| REE | Reese/AFB, TX | USA |
| REG | Reggio Calabria/Tito Menniti | Italy |
| REH | Rehoboth Beach, DE. | USA |
| REI | Regina | F. Guiana |
| REL | Trelew | Argentina |
| REN | Orenburg | Russia |
| REO | Rome, OR | USA |
| REP | Siern Reap | Cambodia |
| RER | Retallnuleu/Base Aerea Del Sur | Guatemala |
| RES | Resistencia | Argentina |
| RET | Rost/Stollport | Norway |
| REU | Reus | Spain |
| REW | Rewa | India |
| REX | Reynosa/Gen Lucio Blanco | Mexico |
| REY | Reyes | Bolivia |
| REZ | Resende | Brazil |
| RFA | Rafai | Central African Rep |
| RFD | Rockford, IL | USA |
| RFG | Refugio/Rooke Fld, TX | USA |
| RFK | Anguilla/Rollang Fld, MS | USA |
| RFN | Raufarhofn | Iceland |
| RFP | Raiatea | F. Polynesia |
| RFR | Rio Frio | Costa Rica |
| RFS | Rosita | Netherlands |
| RGA | Rio Grande | Argentina |
| RGE | Porgera | Papua New Guinea |
| RGH | Balurghat | India |
| RGI | Rangiroa | F. Polynesia |
| RGL | Rio Gallegos Int'l | Argentina |
| RGN | Yangon/Mingaladon | Myanmar |
| RGR | Ranger, TX | USA |
| RGT | Rengat/Japura | Jamaica |
| RGX | Reno Nexrad, NV | USA |
| RHA | Reykholar | Iceland |
| RHD | Rio Hondo | Argentina |
| RHE | Reims | France |
| RHG | Ruhengeri | Rwanda |
| RHI | Rhinelander, WI | USA |
| RHL | Roy Hill | Australia |
| RHO | Rhodes/Diagoras/Paradisi | Greece |
| RHP | Ramechhap | Nepal |
| RHV | San Jose, CA | USA |
| RIA | Santa Maria/Base Aerea | Brazil |
| RIB | Riberalta/Gen Buech | Bolivia |
| RIC | Richmond Int'l, VA | USA |
| RID | Richmond, IN | USA |
| RIE | Rice Lake, WI | USA |
| RIF | Richfield/Reynolds, UT | USA |
| RIG | Rio Grande | Brazil |
| RIJ | Rioja | Peru |
| RIK | Carrillo | Costa Rica |
| RIL | Rifle, CO | USA |
| RIM | Rodriguez De Men. | Peru |
| RIN | Ringi Cove | Solomon Is |
| RIR | Riverside, CA | USA |
| RIS | Rishin | Japan |
| RIT | Rio Tigre | Panama |
| RIV | March/AFB, CA | USA |
| RIW | Riverton, WY | USA |
| RIX | Riga/Int'l | Latvia |
| RIY | Riyan Mulkalla | Yemen |
| RIZ | Rio Aizucar | Panama |
| RJA | Rajahmundry | India |
| RJB | Rajbiraj | Nepal |
| RJH | Raishahi | Bangladesh |
| RJI | Rajouri | India |
| RJK | Rijelka | Croatia |
| RJN | Rafsanian | Iran |
| RKC | Yreka, CA | USA |
| RKD | Rockland, ME | USA |
| RKE | Copenhagen/Roskilde | Denmark |
| RKH | Rock Hill, SC | USA |
| RKI | Rokot | Indonesia |
| RKO | Spora | Indonesia |
| RKP | Rockport, TX | USA |
| RKR | Poteau/Robert S Kerr, OK | USA |
| RKS | Rock Springs, WY | USA |
| RKT | Ras Al Khaimah Int'l | UAE |
| RKU | Yule Is/Kairuku | Papua New Guinea |
| RKV | Reykjavik Domestic | Iceland |
| RKW | Rockwood/Municipal, TN | USA |
| RKY | Rokeby | Australia |
| RLA | Rolla/National, MO | USA |
| RLD | Richland, WA | USA |
| RLG | Rostock-Laage/Laane | Germany |

| Code | Location | Country |
|---|---|---|
| RLI | Anniston/Reilly AHP, AL | USA |
| RLP | Rosella Plains | Australia |
| RLT | Arlit | Niger |
| RLU | Bornite, AK | USA |
| RLX | Charleston, WV. | USA |
| RMA | Roma | Australia |
| RMB | Buraimi | Oman |
| RMC | Rockford/Machesney, IL | USA |
| RMD | Ramagundam | India |
| RME | Griffiss/AFB, NY | USA |
| RMG | Rome, GA | USA |
| RMI | Rimini/Miramare | Italy |
| RMK | Renmark | Australia |
| RML | Colombo/Ratmalana | Sri Lanka |
| RMN | Rurriginae | Papua New Guinea |
| RMP | Rampart, AK | USA |
| RMS | Ramstein | Germany |
| RNB | Ronneby/Kallinge | Sweden |
| RNC | Mcminnville, TN | USA |
| RND | Randolph/AFB, TX | USA |
| RNE | Roanne/Renaison | France |
| RNG | Rangely, CO | USA |
| RNH | New Richmond, WI | USA |
| RNI | Corn Is | Netherlands |
| RNJ | Yororijima | Japan |
| RNL | Rennell | Solomon Is |
| RNN | Bornholm/Ronne | Denmark |
| RNO | Reno Int'l, NV | USA |
| RNP | Rongelap Is | Marshall Is |
| RNR | Robinson River | Papua New Guinea |
| RNS | Rennes/St Jacques | France |
| RNT | Renton, WA | USA |
| RNU | Ranau | Malaysia |
| RNZ | Rensselaer, IN | USA |
| ROA | Roanoke, VA | USA |
| ROB | Monrovia/Roberts Int'l | Liberia |
| ROC | Rochester Int'l, NY | USA |
| ROD | Roberlson | S. Africa |
| ROG | Rogers, AR | USA |
| ROH | Robinhood | Australia |
| ROI | Roi Et Arpt | Thailand |
| ROK | Rockhampton | Australia |
| ROL | Roosevelt, UT | USA |
| RON | Rondon | Colombia |
| ROO | Rondonopolis | Brazil |
| ROP | Rota | Northern Mariana Is |
| ROR | Koror/Airai | Palau |
| ROS | Rosario/Fisherton | Argentina |
| ROT | Rotorua | New Zealand |
| ROU | Rousse | Bulgaria |
| ROV | Rostov | Russia |
| ROW | Roswell, NM | USA |
| ROX | Roseau/Municipal, MN | USA |
| ROY | Rio Mayo | Argentina |
| RPA | Rolpa | Nepal |
| RPB | Roper Bar | Australia |
| RPE | Sabine Pass, TX | USA |
| RPM | Ngukurr | Australia |
| RPN | Rosh Pina | Israel |
| RPR | Raipur | India |
| RPV | Roper Valley | Australia |
| RPX | Roundup, MT | USA |
| RRE | Marree | Australia |
| RRF | Tampa Bay Exec., FL | USA |
| RRG | Rodriguesis | Mauritius |
| RRI | Barora | Solomon Is |
| RRK | Rourkela | India |
| RRL | Merrill/Municipal, WI | USA |
| RRM | Marromeu | Mozambique |
| RRN | Serra Norte | Brazil |
| RRO | Sorrento | Italy |
| RRS | Poros | Norway |
| RRT | Warroad, MN. | USA |
| RRV | Robinson River | Australia |
| RSA | Santa Rosa | Argentina |
| RSB | Poseberth | Australia |
| RSD | Rock Sound/S Eleuthera | Bahamas |
| RSE | Sydney/Au-Rose Bay. | Australia |
| RSG | Serra Pelada | Brazil |
| RSH | Russian/SPB, AK | USA |
| RSI | Rio Sidra | Panama |
| RSJ | Rosario/SPB, AK | USA |
| RSK | Ransiki | Indonesia |
| RSL | Russell, KS | USA |
| RSN | Ruston, LA. | USA |
| RSP | Raspberry Strait, AK. | USA |
| RSS | Roseires, SD | USA |
| RST | Rochester, MN | USA |
| RSU | Yosu | S. Korea |
| RSW | Ft. Myers Int'l, FL. | USA |
| RSX | Rouses Point, NY | USA |

| | | |
|---|---|---|
| RTA | Rotuma Is. | Fiji |
| RTB | Roatan | Honduras |
| RTC | Ratinagiri | India |
| RTD | Rotunda, FL. | USA |
| RTE | Marguerite Bay, AK. | USA |
| RTG | Ruteng | Indonesia |
| RTI | Roti | Indonesia |
| RTL | Spirit Lake, IA. | USA |
| RTM | Rotterdam/Zestienhoven | Netherlands |
| RTN | Raton, NM | USA |
| RTP | Rutland Plains | Australia |
| RTS | Rottnest Is | Australia |
| RTW | Saratov. | Russia |
| RTX | Portland Nexrad, OR. | USA |
| RTY | Merty. | Australia |
| RUA | Anua | Uganda |
| RUE | Russellville/Municipal, AR. | USA |
| RUF | Yurut | Indonesia |
| RUG | Rugao. | China |
| RUH | Riyadh/King Khaled Int'l | Saudi Arabia |
| RUI | Ruidoso/Municipal, NM. | USA |
| RUK | Rukumkot. | Nepal |
| RUM | Rumjatar. | Nepal |
| RUN | St Denis de la Reunion | Reunion Is |
| RUP | Rupsi | India |
| RUR | Rurutu. | F. Polynesia |
| RUS | Marau Sound. | Solomon Is |
| RUT | Rutland, VT | USA |
| RUU | Ruti | Papua New Guinea |
| RUV | Rubelsanto. | Guatemala |
| RUY | Copan. | Honduras |
| RVA | Farafangana | Madagascar |
| RVC | Rivercess. | Liberia |
| RVD | Rio Verde | Brazil |
| RVE | Saravena. | Colombia |
| RVH | St Petersburg/Rzhevka. | Russia |
| RVN | Rovaniemi | Finland |
| RVO | Reivilo. | S. Africa |
| RVR | Green River, UT | USA |
| RVS | Tulsa, OK. | USA |
| RVY | Rivera. | Uruguay |
| RWB | Rowan Bay, AK. | USA |
| RWF | Redwood Falls, MN. | USA |
| RWI | Rocky Mount, NC | USA |
| RWL | Rawlins, WY | USA |
| RWN | Rovirio | Ukraine |
| RWP | Rawalpindi | Pakistan |
| RXA | Raudha. | Yemen |
| RXS | Roxas City | Philippines |
| RYB | Rybirisk. | Russia |
| RYK | Rahim Yar Khan | Pakistan |
| RYN | Royan/Medis | France |
| RYO | Rio Turbio. | Argentina |
| RYV | Watertown, WI | USA |
| RZA | Santa Cruz. | Argentina |
| RZE | Rzeszow/Jasionka | Poland |
| RZH | Lancaster/Quartz Hill, CA | USA |
| RZN | Ryazan. | Russia |
| RZR | Ramsar. | Iran |
| RZZ | Roanoke Rapids, NC | USA |

# S

| | | |
|---|---|---|
| SAA | Saratoga/Shively, WY | USA |
| SAB | Saba Is | Netherlands Antilles |
| SAC | Sacramento Exec, CA | USA |
| SAD | Safford, AZ. | USA |
| SAE | Sangir. | Indonesia |
| SAF | Santa Fe, NM | USA |
| SAG | Sagwon, AK. | USA |
| SAH | Sana'a/Sana'a Int'l. | Yemen |
| SAI | San Marino. | San Marino |
| SAJ | Sirajganj | Bangladesh |
| SAK | Saudarkrokur/Comalapa Int'l | Iceland |
| SAL | San Salvador. | El Salvador |
| SAM | Salamo. | Papua New Guinea |
| SAN | San Diego Int'l, CA | USA |
| SAP | San Pedro Sula/RMorales | Honduras |
| SAQ | San Andros | Bahamas |
| SAR | Sparta/ComMunicipality, IL | USA |
| SAS | Salton City, CA. | USA |
| SAT | San Antonio Int'l, TX | USA |
| SAU | Sawu | Indonesia |
| SAV | Savannah Int'l, GA | USA |
| SAW | Sabiha Gokcen | Turkey |
| SAX | Sambu | Panama |
| SAY | Siena | Italy |
| SAZ | Sasstown | Liberia |

| | | |
|---|---|---|
| SBA | Santa Barbara, CA. | USA |
| SBB | Santa Barbara Ba | Venezuela |
| SBC | Selbang. | Papua New Guinea |
| SBD | Norton/AFB, CA. | USA |
| SBE | Suabi. | Papua New Guinea |
| SBF | Sardeh Band | Afghanistan |
| SBG | Sabang/Cut Bau. | Indonesia |
| SBH | St Barthelemy. | Gaudeloupe |
| SBI | Koundara/Sambailo. | Guinea |
| SBJ | Sao Mateus | Brazil |
| SBK | St Brieuc/Tremuson | Eritrea |
| SBL | Santa Aria/Yacuma | Bolivia |
| SBM | Sheboygan, WI | USA |
| SBN | South Bend, IN. | USA |
| SBO | Salina, UT. | USA |
| SBP | San Luis Obispo, CA. | USA |
| SBQ | Sibi. | Pakistan |
| SBR | Saibai Is | Australia |
| SBS | Steamboat Springs, CO. | USA |
| SBT | San Bernardino/Tri-City, CA | USA |
| SBU | Springbok | S. Africa |
| SBV | Sabah | Papua New Guinea |
| SBW | Sibu. | Malaysia |
| SBX | Shelby, MT | USA |
| SBY | Salisbury, MD | USA |
| SBZ | Sibiu | Romania |
| SCA | Santa Catalina | Colombia |
| SCB | Scribner/State, NE | USA |
| SCC | Deadhorse, AK. | USA |
| SCD | Suiaco. | Honduras |
| SCE | State College, PA. | USA |
| SCG | Spring Creek. | Australia |
| SCH | Schenectady, NY | USA |
| SCI | San Cristobal | Venezuela |
| SCJ | Smith Cove, AK. | USA |
| SCK | Stockton, CA. | USA |
| SCL | Santiago/Arturo M. Benitez. | Chile |
| SCM | Scammon Bay/SPB, AK. | USA |
| SCN | Saarbruecken/Ensheim. | Germany |
| SCO | Aktau. | Kazakstan |
| SCP | St Crepin | Eritrea |
| SCQ | Santiago De Compostela | Spain |
| SCR | Scranton/Municipal, PA | USA |
| SCS | Shetland Iss/Scatsta | UK |
| SCT | Socotra | Yemen |
| SCU | Santiago/Antonio Maceo. | Cuba |
| SCV | Suceava/Salcea. | Romania |
| SCW | SyklyvKar | Russia |
| SCX | Salina Cruz. | Mexico |
| SCY | San Cristobal/Arpt | Ecuador |
| SCZ | Santa Cruz | Solomon Is |
| SDA | Baghdad/Saddam Int'l. | Iraq |
| SDB | Saldanha Bay. | S. Africa |
| SDC | Sandcreek | Guyana |
| SDD | Lubango | Angola |
| SDE | Santiago Del Estero. | Argentina |
| SDF | Louisville, KY | USA |
| SDG | Sanandaj. | Iran |
| SDH | Santa Rosa Copan | Honduras |
| SDI | Saidor | Papua New Guinea |
| SDJ | Sendai. | Japan |
| SDK | Sandakan | Malaysia |
| SDL | Sundsvall | Sweden |
| SDM | San Diego/Brown Fld, CA. | USA |
| SDN | Sandane/Anda. | Norway |
| SDO | Ryotsu Sado Is. | Japan |
| SDP | Sand Point/Municipal, AK. | USA |
| SDQ | Santo Domingo | Dominican Rep |
| SDR | Santander. | Spain |
| SDS | Sado Shima | Japan |
| SDT | Saidu Sharif | Pakistan |
| SDU | Rio De Janeiro/S. Dumont | Brazil |
| SDV | Tel Aviv Yafo/Sde Dov | Israel |
| SDW | Sandwip | Bangladesh |
| SDX | Sedona, AZ | USA |
| SDY | Sidney-Richland, MT. | USA |
| SEA | Seattle, WA. | USA |
| SEB | Sebha | Libya |
| SEC | Serre Chevalier | Eritrea |
| SED | Sedom/Min'hat Hashnayim. | Israel |
| SEE | San Diego-Gillespie, CA | USA |
| SEG | Selinsgrove, PA | USA |
| SEH | Senggeh | Indonesia |
| SEI | Senhor Do Bonfirn. | Brazil |
| SEJ | Seyclisfjordur | Iceland |
| SEK | Ksar Es Souk | Morocco |
| SEL | Seoul/Kimp'O Int'l Arpt. | S. Korea |
| SEM | Craig/AFB, AL | USA |
| SEN | Southend | UK |
| SEO | Seguela. | Côte D'Ivoire |
| SEP | Stephenville, TX | USA |

| | | |
|---|---|---|
| SEQ | Sungai Pakning. | Indonesia |
| SER | Seymour/Freeman Municipal, IN | USA |
| SES | Selma/Selfield, AL | USA |
| SET | San Esteban | Honduras |
| SEU | Seronera | Tanzania |
| SEV | Severodoneck. | Ukraine |
| SEW | Siwa | Egypt |
| SEX | Sembach. | Germany |
| SEY | Selibaby. | Mauritania |
| SEZ | Mahe Is | Seychelles |
| SFA | Sfax/Sfax El Maou | Tunisia |
| SFB | Sanford, FL | USA |
| SFC | St Francois | Gaudeloupe |
| SFD | San Fernando De Apure | Venezuela |
| SFE | San Fernando. | Philippines |
| SFF | Spokane, WA | USA |
| SFG | St Martin/Esperance. | Gaudeloupe |
| SFH | San Felipe. | Mexico |
| SFI | Safi. | Morocco |
| SFJ | Kangerlussuaq | Greenland |
| SFK | Soure. | Brazil |
| SFL | Sao Filipe. | Cape Verde Is |
| SFM | Sanford, ME | USA |
| SFN | Santa Fe | Argentina |
| SFO | San Francisco Int'l, CA. | USA |
| SFP | Surfers Paradise. | Australia |
| SFQ | Sanliurfa. | Turkey |
| SFR | San Fernando, CA. | USA |
| SFS | Subic Bay/Int'l Airpt. | Philippines |
| SFT | Skelleftea. | Sweden |
| SFU | Safia. | Papua New Guinea |
| SFV | Santa Fe Do Sul | Brazil |
| SFW | Santa Fe | Panama |
| SFX | San Felix | Venezuela |
| SFZ | Smithfield/North Central, RI | USA |
| SGA | Sheghnan | Afghanistan |
| SGB | Singaua | Papua New Guinea |
| SGC | Surgut | Russia |
| SGD | Sonderborg/Lufthavn | Denmark |
| SGE | Siegen/Segerland Arpt. | Germany |
| SGF | Springfield, MO | USA |
| SGG | Simanggang | Malaysia |
| SGH | Springfield, OH | USA |
| SGI | Sargodha/Sargodha Arpt. | Pakistan |
| SGJ | Sagarai | Papua New Guinea |
| SGK | Sangapi | Papua New Guinea |
| SGL | Manila/Sangley Pt/NAS | Philippines |
| SGM | San Ignacio. | Mexico |
| SGN | Ho Chi Minh | Vietnam |
| SGO | St George | Australia |
| SGP | Shay Gap | Australia |
| SGQ | Sanggata | Indonesia |
| SGR | Houston-SugarLand, TX | USA |
| SGS | Santa Sanga | Philippines |
| SGT | Stuttgart, AR | USA |
| SGU | Saint George/Municipal, UT | USA |
| SGV | Sierra Grande | Argentina |
| SGW | Saginaw Bay, AK. | USA |
| SGX | Songea | Tanzania |
| SGY | Skagway/Municipal, AK. | USA |
| SGZ | Songkhla | Thailand |
| SHA | Shanghai/Hongqiao | China |
| SHB | Nakashibetsu | Japan |
| SHC | Indaselassie | Ethiopia |
| SHD | Staunton, VA | USA |
| SHE | Shenyang | China |
| SHF | Shanhaiguan. | China |
| SHG | Shungnak, AK. | USA |
| SHH | Shishmaref, AK. | USA |
| SHI | Shimojishima. | Japan |
| SHJ | Sharjah Int'l | UAE |
| SHK | Sehonghong. | Lesotho |
| SHL | Shillong | India |
| SHM | Shirahama. | Japan |
| SHN | Shelton, WA | USA |
| SHO | Sokcho/Solak | S. Korea |
| SHP | Qinhuangdao | China |
| SHQ | Southport. | Australia |
| SHR | Sheridan, WY | USA |
| SHS | Shashi | China |
| SHT | Shepparton | Australia |
| SHU | Smith Point | Australia |
| SHV | Shreveport, LA | USA |
| SHW | Sharurah | Saudi Arabia |
| SHX | Shageluk, AK. | USA |
| SHY | Shinyanga | Tanzania |
| SHZ | Seshutes | Lesotho |
| SIA | Xi An | China |
| SIB | Sibiti | Colombia |
| SIC | Sinop/Sinop Arpt. | Turkey |
| SID | Sal/Amilcar Cabrai Int'l | Cape Verde Is |

A
I
R
P
O
R
T
S
-1-

| Code | Location | Country |
|---|---|---|
| SIE | Sines | Portugal |
| SIF | Simara | Nepal |
| SIG | San Juan/Isla Grande | Puerto Rico |
| SIH | Silgadi Doti | Nepal |
| SII | Sidi Ifni | Morocco |
| SIJ | Siglufjordur | Iceland |
| SIK | Sikeston/Memorial, MO | USA |
| SIL | Sila | Papua New Guinea |
| SIM | Simbas | Papua New Guinea |
| SIN | Singapore | Singapore |
| SIO | Smithton | Australia |
| SIP | Simferopol | Ukraine |
| SIQ | Singkep/Dabo | Indonesia |
| SIR | Sion | Switzerland |
| SIS | Sishen | S. Africa |
| SIT | Sitka, AK | USA |
| SIU | Siuna | Netherlands |
| SIV | Sullivan/County, IN | USA |
| SIW | Sibisa | Indonesia |
| SIX | Singleton | Australia |
| SIY | Montague, CA | USA |
| SIZ | Sissano | Papua New Guinea |
| SJA | San Juan | Peru |
| SJB | San Joacluin | Bolivia |
| SJC | San Jose Int'l, CA | USA |
| SJD | San Jose Cabo/Los Cabos | Mexico |
| SJE | San Jose Del Gua | Colombia |
| SJF | Kangerlussuaq | Greenland |
| SJF | St John Is | Virgin Is (US) |
| SJG | San Pedro Jagua | Colombia |
| SJI | San Jose/Meguire Fld | Philippines |
| SJJ | Saraievo/Butmir..Bosnia Hercegovina | |
| SJK | Sao Jose Dos Campos | Brazil |
| SJL | Sao Gabriel/Da Cachoeira | Brazil |
| SJM | San Juan | Dominican Rep |
| SJN | St Johns, AZ | USA |
| SJO | San Jose/Juan Santamaria Int'l | Costa Rica |
| SJP | Sap Jose Do Rio Preto | Brazil |
| SJQ | Seskeke | Zambia |
| SJR | San Juan D Ur | Colombia |
| SJS | San Jose | Bolivia |
| SJT | San Angelo, TX | USA |
| SJU | San Juan Int'l, PR | USA |
| SJV | San Javier | Bolivia |
| SJW | Shijiazhuang/Daguocun | China |
| SJX | Sartaneja | Belize |
| SJY | Seinäjoki/Ilmajoki | Finland |
| SJZ | Sao Jorge Is | Portugal |
| SKA | Fairchild/AFB, WA | USA |
| SKB | St Kitts/Gldn Rck | St. Kitts and Nevis |
| SKC | Suki | Papua New Guinea |
| SKD | Samarkand | Uzbekistan |
| SKE | Skien | Norway |
| SKF | Kelly/AFB, TX | USA |
| SKG | Thessaloniki/Makedonia | Greece |
| SKH | Surkhet | Nepal |
| SKI | Skikda | Algeria |
| SKJ | Sitkinak Is/CGS, AK | USA |
| SKK | Shaktoolik, AK | USA |
| SKL | Isle Of Skye/Broadford | UK |
| SKM | Skeldon | Guyana |
| SKN | Stokmarknes/Skagen | Norway |
| SKO | Sokoto | Nigeria |
| SKP | Skople | Macedonia |
| SKQ | Sekakes | Lesotho |
| SKR | Shakiso | Ethiopia |
| SKS | Vojens/Skrydstrup/Military | Denmark |
| SKT | Sialkot | Pakistan |
| SKU | Skiros | Greece |
| SKV | Santa Katarina/Mount Sinai | Egypt |
| SKW | Skwentna/Intermediate, AK | USA |
| SKX | Saransk | Russia |
| SKY | Sandusky/G. Sandusky, OH | USA |
| SKZ | Sukkur | Pakistan |
| SLA | Salta/Gen Belgrano | Argentina |
| SLB | Storm Lake, IA | USA |
| SLC | Salt Lake City Int'l, UT | USA |
| SLD | Sliac | Slovakia |
| SLE | Salem, OR | USA |
| SLF | Sulayel | Saudi Arabia |
| SLG | Siloam Springs/Smith Fld, AR | USA |
| SLH | Sola | Vanuatu |
| SLI | Solwezi | Zambia |
| SLJ | Chandler/Stellar Air Park, AZ | USA |
| SLK | Saranac Lake, NY | USA |
| SLL | Salatah | Oman |
| SLM | Salamanca/Matacan | Spain |
| SLN | Salina, KS | USA |
| SLO | Salem-Leckrone, IL | USA |
| SLP | San Lus Potosi | Mexico |
| SLQ | Sleetmute, AK | USA |
| SLR | Sulphur Springs, TX | USA |
| SLS | Silistra | Bulgaria |
| SLT | Salida, CO | USA |
| SLU | St Lucia/Vigie | St. Lucia |
| SLV | Simia | India |
| SLW | Saltillo | Mexico |
| SLX | Salt Cay | Tonga |
| SLY | Salehard | Russia |
| SLZ | Sao Luiz/Mal. C. Machado | Brazil |
| SMA | Santa Maria/Vila Do Porto | Portugal |
| SMB | Cerro Sombrero | Chile |
| SMC | Santa Maria | Colombia |
| SMD | Ft. Wayne/Smith Fld, IN | USA |
| SME | Somerset/Pulaski County, KY | USA |
| SMF | Sacramento, CA | USA |
| SMG | Santa Maria | Peru |
| SMH | Sapmanga | Papua New Guinea |
| SMI | Samos | Greece |
| SMJ | Sim | Papua New Guinea |
| SMK | St Michael, AK | USA |
| SML | Stella Maris/Estate Airstrip | Bahamas |
| SMM | Serrporna | Malaysia |
| SMN | Salmon, AK | USA |
| SMO | Santa Monica, CA | USA |
| SMP | Stockholm | Papua New Guinea |
| SMQ | Sampit | Indonesia |
| SMR | Santa Marta/S. Bolivar | Colombia |
| SMS | Sainte Marie | Madagascar |
| SMT | Sun Moon Lake | Taiwan |
| SMU | Sheep Mountain, ID | USA |
| SMV | St Moritz/Samedan | Switzerland |
| SMW | Smara | Morocco |
| SMX | Santa Maria, CA | USA |
| SMY | Simenti | Senegal |
| SMZ | Stoelmans Eiland | Suriname |
| SNA | Santa Ana, CA | USA |
| SNB | Snake Bay | Australia |
| SNC | Salinas | Ecuador |
| SND | Seno | Laos |
| SNE | Sao Nicolau/Prgca | Cape Verde Is |
| SNF | San Felipe | Venezuela |
| SNG | San Ignacio De Velasco | Bolivia |
| SNH | Stanthorpe | Australia |
| SNI | Sinoe/R.E. Murray | Liberia |
| SNJ | San Julian | Cuba |
| SNK | Snyder/Winston Fld, TX | USA |
| SNL | Shawnee/Municipal, OK | USA |
| SNM | San Ignacio De M | Bolivia |
| SNN | Shannon | Ireland |
| SNO | Sakon Nakhon | Thailand |
| SNP | St Paul Is, AK | USA |
| SNQ | San Quintin | Mexico |
| SNR | St Nazaire/Montoir | France |
| SNS | Salinas, CA | USA |
| SNT | Sabana De Torres | Colombia |
| SNU | Santa Clara | Cuba |
| SNV | Santa Eiena | Venezuela |
| SNW | Thandwe | Myanmar |
| SNX | Sabana De Mar | Dominican Rep |
| SNY | Sidney, NE | USA |
| SNZ | Santa Cruz | Brazil |
| SOA | Soc Trang | Vietnam |
| SOB | Saarmelleek/Srmhk/Btn | Hungary |
| SOC | Solo City/Adi Surnarmo | Indonesia |
| SOD | Sorocaba | Brazil |
| SOE | Souanke | Congo |
| SOF | Sofia | Bulgaria |
| SOG | Sogndal | Norway |
| SOH | Solita | Colombia |
| SOI | South Molle Is | Australia |
| SOJ | Sorkjosen | Norway |
| SOK | Semongkong | Lesotho |
| SOL | Solomon, AK | USA |
| SOM | San Tome/El Tigre | Venezuela |
| SON | Espiritu Santo/Pekoa | Vanuatu |
| SOO | Soderhamn | Sweden |
| SOP | Southern Pines/Pinehurst, NC | USA |
| SOQ | Sorong/Jefman | Indonesia |
| SOR | X Thaurah | Syria |
| SOT | Sodankyla | Finland |
| SOU | Southampton | UK |
| SOV | Seldovia, AK | USA |
| SOW | Show Low, AZ | USA |
| SOX | Sogamoso | Colombia |
| SOY | Stronsay | UK |
| SOZ | Soienzara | France |
| SPA | Spartanburg Memorial, SC | USA |
| SPB | St Thomas/SPB | Virgin Is (US) |
| SPC | Santa Cruiz De La Palma | Spain |
| SPD | Saidpur | Bangladesh |
| SPE | Sepulot | Malaysia |
| SPF | Spearfish, SD | USA |
| SPG | St Petersburg, FL | USA |
| SPH | Sopu | Papua New Guinea |
| SPI | Springfield, IL | USA |
| SPJ | Sparta | Greece |
| SPL | Schiphol | Netherlands |
| SPM | Spangdahlem | Germany |
| SPN | Saipan/Int'l | Northern Mariana Is |
| SPO | San Pabio | Spain |
| SPP | Menongue | Angola |
| SPQ | San Pedro/Catalina SPB, CA | USA |
| SPR | San Pedro | Belize |
| SPS | Sheppard/AFB, TX | USA |
| SPT | Sipitang | Malaysia |
| SPU | Split | Croatia |
| SPV | Sepik Plains | Papua New Guinea |
| SPW | Spencer, IA | USA |
| SPX | Houston/Spaceland, TX | USA |
| SPY | San Pedro | Côte D'Ivoire |
| SPZ | Springdale/Springdale Municipal, AR | USA |
| SQA | Santa Ynez, CA | USA |
| SQB | Santa Ana | Colombia |
| SQC | Southern Cross | Australia |
| SQD | Sinop | Turkey |
| SQE | San Luis De Pale | Colombia |
| SQF | Solano | Colombia |
| SQG | Sintang | Indonesia |
| SQH | Son-La/Na-San | Vietnam |
| SQI | Sterling Rockfalls, IL | USA |
| SQJ | Shehdi | Ethiopia |
| SQK | Sidi Barani | Egypt |
| SQL | San Carlos, CA | USA |
| SQM | Sao Miguel Araguaia | Brazil |
| SQN | Sanana | Indonesia |
| SQO | Storurnan/Gunnarn | Sweden |
| SQP | Starcke | Australia |
| SQQ | Siauliai/Int'l | Lithuania |
| SQR | Soroako | Indonesia |
| SQS | San Ignacio/Matthew Spain | Belize |
| SQT | Samarai Is/China Straits Airstrip | Papua New Guinea |
| SQU | Saposcia | Peru |
| SQV | Sequim/Valley Arpt, WA | USA |
| SQW | Skive/Skive Arpt | Denmark |
| SQX | Sao Miguel Do Oeste | Brazil |
| SQY | Sao Lourenco Do Sul | Brazil |
| SQZ | Scampton/RAF Stn | UK |
| SRA | Santa Rosa | Brazil |
| SRB | Santa Rosa | Bolivia |
| SRC | Searcy, AR | USA |
| SRD | San Ramon | Bolivia |
| SRE | Sucre | Bolivia |
| SRF | Hamilton/AAF, CA | USA |
| SRG | Semarang/Achmad Uani | Indonesia |
| SRH | Sarh | Chad |
| SRI | Samarinda/Temindung | Indonesia |
| SRJ | San Borja/Capitan G Q Guardia | Bolivia |
| SRK | Sierra Leone | Sierra Leone |
| SRL | Santa Rosalia | Mexico |
| SRM | Sandringham | Australia |
| SRN | Strahan | Australia |
| SRO | Santana Ramos | Colombia |
| SRP | Stord/Stord Airporl | Norway |
| SRQ | Sarasota, FL | USA |
| SRR | Stradbroke Is | Australia |
| SRS | San Marcos | Colombia |
| SRT | Soroti | Uganda |
| SRU | Santa Cruz/Skypark, CA | USA |
| SRV | Stony River, AK | USA |
| SRW | Salisbury/Rowan County, NC | USA |
| SRX | Sert | Libya |
| SRY | Sary/Dashte Naz | Iran |
| SRZ | Santa Cruz/El Trompillo | Bolivia |
| SSA | Salvador/Arpt Luis R. Magalhaes | Brazil |
| SSB | St Croix Is/SPB | Virgin Is (US) |
| SSC | Shaw/AFB, SC | USA |
| SSD | San Felipe | Colombia |
| SSE | Sholapur | India |
| SSF | San Antonio, TX | USA |
| SSG | Malabo/Santa Isabel | Equatorial Guinea |
| SSH | Sharm El Sheikh/Ophira | Egypt |
| SSI | Brunswick, GA | USA |
| SSJ | Sandnessjoen/Stokka | Norway |
| SSK | Sturt Creek | Australia |
| SSL | Santa Rosalia | Colombia |
| SSN | Seoul/Seoul Air Base | S. Korea |

| Code | Location | Country |
|---|---|---|
| SSO | Sac, Lourenco | Brazil |
| SSP | Silver Plains | Australia |
| SSQ | La Sarre, QC | Canada |
| SSR | Sara | Vanuatu |
| SSS | Siassi | Papua New Guinea |
| SST | Santa Teresita | Argentina |
| SSU | White Sulphur Sprng, WV | USA |
| SSV | Siasi | Philippines |
| SSW | Stuart Is, WA | USA |
| SSX | Samsun | Turkey |
| SSY | M'Banza Congo | Angola |
| SSZ | Santos | Brazil |
| STA | Stauning/Lufthavn | Denmark |
| STB | Santa Barbara Ed/L Dlcias | Venezuela |
| STC | St Cloud, MN | USA |
| STD | Santo Domingo | Venezuela |
| STE | Stevens Point, WI | USA |
| STF | Stephen Is | Australia |
| STG | St George Is, AK | USA |
| STH | Strathmore | Australia |
| STI | Santiago/Mun | Dominican Rep |
| STJ | St Joseph, MO | USA |
| STK | Sterling/Crosson Fld, CO | USA |
| STL | St Louis Int'l, MO | USA |
| STM | Santarem/Eduardo Gomes | Brazil |
| STN | London/Stansted | UK |
| STP | St Paul-Dwntnw, MN | USA |
| STQ | St Marys, PA | USA |
| STR | Stuttgart/Echterdingen | Germany |
| STS | Santa Rosa, CA | USA |
| STT | St Thomas Is | Virgin Is (US) |
| STU | Santa Cruz | Belize |
| STV | Surat | India |
| STW | Stavropol | Russia |
| STX | St Croix Is | Virgin Is (US) |
| STY | Saito | Uruguay |
| STZ | Santa Terezinha/Confresa | Brazil |
| SUA | Stuart/Witham Fld, FL | USA |
| SUB | Surabaya/Juanda | Indonesia |
| SUC | Sundance/Schloredt, WY | USA |
| SUD | Stroud, OK | USA |
| SUE | Sturgeon Bay, WI | USA |
| SUF | Lamezia-Terme/S Eufernia | Italy |
| SUG | Surigao | Philippines |
| SUH | Sur | Oman |
| SUI | Sukhumi/Babusheri | Georgia |
| SUJ | Satu Mare | Romania |
| SUK | Samchok | S. Korea |
| SUL | Sui | Pakistan |
| SUM | Sumter/Municipal, SC | USA |
| SUN | Hailey, ID | USA |
| SUO | Sun River, OR | USA |
| SUP | Sumeneo/Trunojoyo | Indonesia |
| SUQ | Sucua | Ecuador |
| SUR | Summer Beaver, ON | Canada |
| SUS | St Louis-Spirit Of St Louis, MO | USA |
| SUT | Sumbawanga | Tanzania |
| SUU | Travis/AFB, CA | USA |
| SUV | Suva/Nausori | Fiji |
| SUW | Superior/Richard 1 Bong, WI | USA |
| SUX | Sioux City, IA | USA |
| SUY | Sudureyri | Iceland |
| SUZ | Suria | Papua New Guinea |
| SVA | Savoonga, AK | USA |
| SVB | Sambava | Madagascar |
| SVC | Silver City, NM | USA |
| SVD | St Vincent/E-T. Joshua | St. Vincent & Grenadines |
| SVE | Susanville, CA | USA |
| SVF | Save | Benin |
| SVG | Stavanger/Sola | Norway |
| SVH | Statesville/Municipal, NC | USA |
| SVI | San Vicente | Colombia |
| SVJ | Svolvaer/Helle | Norway |
| SVK | Silver Creek | Belize |
| SVL | Savonlinna | Finland |
| SVM | St Paul's Mission | Australia |
| SVN | Hunter/AAF, GA | USA |
| SVO | Moscow | Russia |
| SVP | Kuito | Angola |
| SVQ | Sevilla | Spain |
| SVR | Svay Rieng | Cambodia |
| SVS | Stevens Village, AK | USA |
| SVT | Savuti | Botswana |
| SVU | Savusavu | Fiji |
| SVV | San Salvador De | Venezuela |
| SVW | Sparrevohn/AFS, AK | USA |
| SVX | Ekaterinburg | Russia |
| SVY | Savo | Solomon Is |
| SVZ | San Antonio | Venezuela |
| SWA | Shantou | China |
| SWB | Shaw River | Australia |
| SWC | Stawell | Australia |
| SWD | Seward, AK | USA |
| SWE | Siwea | Papua New Guinea |
| SWF | Newburgh, NY | USA |
| SWG | Satwag | Papua New Guinea |
| SWH | Swan Hill | Australia |
| SWI | Swindon | UK |
| SWJ | South West Bay | Vanuatu |
| SWK | Milan/Milano/Segrate | Italy |
| SWL | Spanish Wells | Bahamas |
| SWM | Suia-Missu | Brazil |
| SWN | Sahiwal | Pakistan |
| SWO | Stillwater, OK | USA |
| SWP | Swakopmund | Namibia |
| SWQ | Sumbawa/Brang Bidji | Indonesia |
| SWR | Silur | Papua New Guinea |
| SWS | Swansea | UK |
| SWT | Strzhewoi | Russia |
| SWU | Su Won City/Su Won Arpt | S. Korea |
| SWV | Shikarpur | Pakistan |
| SWW | Sweetwater, TX | USA |
| SWX | Shakawe | Botswana |
| SWY | Sitiawan | Malaysia |
| SWZ | Sydney/Sydney West | Australia |
| SXA | Sialum | Papua New Guinea |
| SXB | Strasbourg/Entzineim | France |
| SXC | Catalina Is, CA | USA |
| SXD | Sophia Antipolis | France |
| SXE | Sale | Australia |
| SXF | Berlin/Schoenefeld | Germany |
| SXG | Senanga | Zambia |
| SXH | Sehuiea | Papua New Guinea |
| SXI | Sirri Is | Iran |
| SXJ | Shanshan | China |
| SXK | Saumlaki | Indonesia |
| SXL | Sligo | Ireland |
| SXM | St Maarten/Princ. Juliana | Netherlands Antilles |
| SXN | Sua pan | Botswana |
| SXO | Sao Felix Do Araguaia | Brazil |
| SXP | Sheldon Point/Sheldon SPB, AK | USA |
| SXQ | Soldotna, AK | USA |
| SXR | Srinagar | India |
| SXS | Sahabat 16 | Malaysia |
| SXT | Taman Negara | Malaysia |
| SXU | Soddu | Ethiopia |
| SXV | Salem | India |
| SXW | Sauren | Papua New Guinea |
| SXX | Sao Fefix DO Xingu | Brazil |
| SXY | Sidney, NY | USA |
| SXZ | Slirt | Turkey |
| SYA | Shemya/Shemya/AFB, AK | USA |
| SYB | Seal Bay, AK | USA |
| SYC | Shiringayoc | Peru |
| SYD | Sydney | Australia |
| SYE | Sadah | Yemen |
| SYF | Silva Bay, BC | Canada |
| SYG | Svalbard/Spitsberg | Norway |
| SYH | Syangboche | Nepal |
| SYI | Shelbyville/Bomar Fld, AK | USA |
| SYJ | Sirjan | Iran |
| SYK | Stykkisholmur | Iceland |
| SYL | San Miguei/Roberts/AAF, CA | USA |
| SYM | Simao | China |
| SYN | Stanton/Carleton, MN | USA |
| SYO | Shonai | Japan |
| SYP | Santiago | Panama |
| SYQ | San Jose/Tobias Bolanos Intl | Costa Rica |
| SYR | Syracuse Int'l, NY | USA |
| SYS | Sunchon/Yosu | S. Korea |
| SYT | Saint Yan/Charolais Bourgogne | France |
| SYU | Sue Is/Warraber Is | Australia |
| SYV | Sylvester, GA | USA |
| SYW | Sehwen Sharif | Pakistan |
| SYX | Sanya | China |
| SYY | Stornoway | UK |
| SYZ | Shiraz | Iran |
| SZA | Soyo | Angola |
| SZB | Kuala Lumpur/Sultan Alodul Aziz Shah | Malaysia |
| SZC | Santa Cruz/Guanacaste | Costa Rica |
| SZD | Sheffield | UK |
| SZE | Semera/Semera Arpt | Ethiopia |
| SZF | Samsun/Carsamba | Turkey |
| SZG | Salzburg | Austria |
| SZH | Senipah | Indonesia |
| SZI | Zaisan | Kazakstan |
| SZJ | Siguanea | Cuba |
| SZK | Skukuza | S. Africa |
| SZL | Whiteman/AFB, MO | USA |
| SZM | Sesnem | Namibia |
| SZN | Santa Barbara, CA | USA |
| SZO | Shanzinou | China |
| SZP | Santa Paula, CA | USA |
| SZQ | Saenz Pena | Argentina |
| SZR | Stara Zagora | Bulgaria |
| SZS | Stewart Is | New Zealand |
| SZT | S.Cristobal del- Casas/San Cristobal Arpt | Mexico |
| SZU | Segou | Mali |
| SZV | Suzhou | China |
| SZW | Schwerin/Parchim Arpt | Germany |
| SZX | Shenzhen | China |
| SZY | Szymany/Mazury | Poland |
| SZZ | Szczecin/Goleniow | Poland |

# T

| Code | Location | Country |
|---|---|---|
| TAA | Tarapaina | Solomon Is |
| TAB | Tobago | Trinidad and Tobago |
| TAC | Tacloban/D1. Rornualdez | Philippines |
| TAD | Trinidad, CO | USA |
| TAE | Taegu/Air Base | S. Korea |
| TAG | Tagbilaran | Philippines |
| TAH | Tanna | Vanuatu |
| TAI | Taiz/AlJanad | Yemen |
| TAJ | Aitape/Tadji | Papua New Guinea |
| TAK | Takamatsu | Japan |
| TAL | Tanana, AK | USA |
| TAM | Tampico/Gen F Javier Mina | Mexico |
| TAN | Tangalooma | Australia |
| TAO | Oingdao | China |
| TAP | Tapachula Int'l | Mexico |
| TAQ | Tarcoola | Australia |
| TAR | Taranto/M. A. Grottag | Italy |
| TAS | Tashkent | Uzbekistan |
| TAT | Tatry/Poprad | Slovakia |
| TAU | Tauramena | Colombia |
| TAV | Tau | American Samoa |
| TAW | Tacuarembo | Uruguay |
| TAX | Taliabu | Indonesia |
| TAY | Tartu/Raadi | Estonia |
| TAZ | Tashauz | Turkmenistan |
| TBA | Tabibuga | Papua New Guinea |
| TBB | Tuy Hoa | Vietnam |
| TBC | Tuba City, AZ | USA |
| TBD | Timbiqui | Colombia |
| TBE | Timbunke | Papua New Guinea |
| TBF | Tabiteuea North | Kiribati |
| TBG | Tabubil | Papua New Guinea |
| TBH | Tablas | Philippines |
| TBI | The Bight | Bahamas |
| TBJ | Tabarka/7 Novembre | Tunisia |
| TBK | Timber Creek | Australia |
| TBL | Tableland | Australia |
| TBM | Tumbang Samba | Indonesia |
| TBN | Forney/AAF, MO | USA |
| TBO | Talbora | Tanzania |
| TBP | Tumbes | Peru |
| TBQ | Tarabo | Papua New Guinea |
| TBR | Statesboro/Municipal, GA | USA |
| TBS | Tbilisi/Novo Alexeyevka | Georgia |
| TBT | Tabatinga/Int'l | Brazil |
| TBU | Nuku'Alofa/Fija'Arnotu Intl | Tonga |
| TBV | Tabal | Marshall Is |
| TBW | Tambov | Russia |
| TBX | Taabo | Côte D'Ivoire |
| TBY | Tsabong | Botswana |
| TBZ | Tabriz | Iran |
| TCA | Tennant Creek | Australia |
| TCB | Treasure Cay | Bahamas |
| TCC | Tucumcari, NM | USA |
| TCD | Tarapaca | Colombia |
| TCE | Tuicea | Romania |
| TCF | Tocoa | Honduras |
| TCG | Tacheng | China |
| TCH | Tehibanga | Gabon |
| TCJ | Torembi Arpt | Papua New Guinea |
| TCK | Tinboli Arpt | Papua New Guinea |
| TCL | Tuscaloosa, AL | USA |
| TCM | McChord/AFB, WA | USA |
| TCN | Tehuacan | Mexico |
| TCO | Turnaco/La Florida | Colombia |
| TCP | Taba/Talba Int'l | Egypt |
| TCQ | Tacna | Peru |

AIRPORTS -1-

| Code | Name | Country |
|---|---|---|
| TCR | Tuticorin | India |
| TCS | Truth Or Consequences, NM | USA |
| TCT | Takotna, AK | USA |
| TCU | Thaba Nchu | S. Africa |
| TCV | Tete | Mozambique |
| TCW | Tocumwal | Australia |
| TCX | Tabas | Iran |
| TCY | Terrace Bay | Namibia |
| TDA | Trinidad | Colombia |
| TDB | Tetabedi | Papua New Guinea |
| TDD | Trinidad | Bolivia |
| TDG | Tandag | Philippines |
| TDJ | Tadjoura | Djibouti |
| TDK | Taldy-Kurgan | Kazakstan |
| TDL | Tandil | Argentina |
| TDN | Thecia/Thecia Stn | Australia |
| TDO | Toledo, WA | USA |
| TDR | Theodore | Australia |
| TDT | Tanda Tula | S. Africa |
| TDV | Tanandava | Madagascar |
| TDW | Annarillo/Tradewind, TX | USA |
| TDZ | Toledo, OH | USA |
| TEA | Tela | Honduras |
| TEB | Teterboro, NJ | USA |
| TEC | Telemaco Borba | Brazil |
| TED | Thisted/Lufthavn | Denmark |
| TEE | Tbessa | Algeria |
| TEF | Teller | Australia |
| TEG | Tenkodogo | Burkina Faso |
| TEH | Tetlin, AK | USA |
| TEI | Tezu | India |
| TEK | Tatitlek, AK | USA |
| TEL | Telupid | Malaysia |
| TEM | Temora | Australia |
| TEN | Tongren | China |
| TEO | Terapo | Papua New Guinea |
| TEP | Teptelp | Papua New Guinea |
| TEQ | TeKirdag/Corlu | Turkey |
| TER | Terceira Is/Laies | Portugal |
| TES | Tessenei | Eritrea |
| TET | Tete/Matunda | Mozambique |
| TEU | Te Anau/Manapouri | New Zealand |
| TEX | Telluride, CO | USA |
| TEY | Thingeyn | Iceland |
| TEZ | Tezpur/Salonibari | India |
| TFA | Tilfalmin | Papua New Guinea |
| TFF | Tete | Brazil |
| TFI | Tufl | Papua New Guinea |
| TFL | Teofilo Otoni | Brazil |
| TFM | Telefornin | Papua New Guinea |
| TFN | Tenerife | Spain |
| TFR | Ramadan | Ecuador |
| TFS | Tenerife Sur | Spain |
| TFT | Taftan | Pakistan |
| TFX | Great Falls Nexrad, MT | USA |
| TFY | Tarlaya | Morocco |
| TGA | Tengah | Singapore |
| TGB | Tagloita | Philippines |
| TGD | Poelgorica,/Golubovci | Yugoslavia |
| TGE | Tuskegee/Sharpe Fld, AL | USA |
| TGF | Tignes | France |
| TGG | Kuala Terengganu/Sultan Mahmood | Malaysia |
| TGH | Tongoa | Vanuatu |
| TGI | Tinge Maria | Peru |
| TGJ | Tiga | New Caledonia |
| TGL | Tagula | Papua New Guinea |
| TGM | Tirgu Mures | Romania |
| TGN | Traralgon/La Trobe Regional | Australia |
| TGO | Tongliao | China |
| TGQ | Tangara da Serra | Brazil |
| TGR | Touggourt | Algeria |
| TGS | Chokwe | Mozambique |
| TGT | Tanga | Tanzania |
| TGU | Tegucigalpa/Toncontin | Honduras |
| TGV | Targovishte | Bulgaria |
| TGX | Tingrela | Côte D'Ivoire |
| TGZ | Tuxtia Gutierrez/Llano San Juan | Mexico |
| THA | Tullahoma/Northern, TN | USA |
| THB | Thalba-Tselka | Lesotho |
| THC | Tchien | Liberia |
| THE | Teresina | Brazil |
| THF | Berlin/Tempelhof | Germany |
| THG | Thangool | Australia |
| THH | Taharoa | New Zealand |
| THI | Tichitt | Mauritania |
| THK | Thakhek | Laos |
| THL | Tachilek | Myanmar |
| THM | Thompsonfield, MO | USA |
| THN | Trollhattan/Private | Sweden |
| THO | Thorshofn | Iceland |
| THP | Thermopolis/Hot Springs, WY | USA |
| THR | Tehran-Mehrabad | Iran |
| THS | Sukinothai | Thailand |
| THT | Tamchakett | Mauritania |
| THU | Pituffik | Greenland |
| THV | York, PA | USA |
| THY | Thohoyandou | S. Africa |
| THZ | Tahoua | Niger |
| TIA | Tirana/Rinas | Albania |
| TIB | Tibu | Colombia |
| TIC | Tinak Is | Marshall Is |
| TID | Tiaret | Algeria |
| TIE | Tippi | Ethiopia |
| TIF | Taif | Saudi Arabia |
| TIG | Tingwon | Papua New Guinea |
| TIH | Tikehau Atoll | F. Polynesia |
| TII | Tirinkot | Afghanistan |
| TIJ | Tijuana/Rodriguez | Mexico |
| TIK | Tinker/AFB, OK | USA |
| TIL | Inverlake, AB | Canada |
| TIM | Tembagapura/Timika | Indonesia |
| TIN | Tindouf | Algeria |
| TIO | Tilin | Myanmar |
| TIP | Tripoli/Int'l | Libya |
| TIQ | Tinian | Northern Mariana Is |
| TIR | Tirupati | India |
| TIS | Thursday Is | Australia |
| TIU | Timaru | New Zealand |
| TIV | Tivat | Yugoslavia |
| TIW | Tacoma-Narrows, WA | USA |
| TIX | Titusville, FL | USA |
| TIY | Tidjikia | Mauritania |
| TIZ | Tari | Papua New Guinea |
| TJA | Tarija | Bolivia |
| TJB | Tanjung Balai | Indonesia |
| TJC | Ticantiki | Panama |
| TJG | Tanjung Warukin | Indonesia |
| TJH | Toyooka/Tapma | Japan |
| TJI | Trujillo/Capiro | Honduras |
| TJK | Tokat | Turkey |
| TJM | Tyumen | Russia |
| TJN | Takume | F. Polynesia |
| TJQ | Tanjung Pandan/Bulutumbang | Indonesia |
| TJS | Tanjung Selor | Indonesia |
| TJV | Thanjavur | India |
| TKA | Talkeetna, AK | USA |
| TKB | Tekadu | Papua New Guinea |
| TKC | Tiko | Cameroon |
| TKD | Takoradi | Ghana |
| TKE | Tenakee Springs/Tenakee SPB, AK | USA |
| TKF | Truckee, CA | USA |
| TKG | Bandar Lampung/Branti | Indonesia |
| TKH | Takhli | Thailand |
| TKI | Tokeen, AK | USA |
| TKK | Truk | Micronesia |
| TKL | Taku Lodge/Taku SPB, AK | USA |
| TKM | Tikal/El Peten | Guatemala |
| TKN | Tokunoshima | Japan |
| TKO | Tlokoeng | Lesotho |
| TKP | Takapoto | F. Polynesia |
| TKQ | Kigoma | Tanzania |
| TKR | Thakurgaon | Bangladesh |
| TKS | Tokushima AB | Japan |
| TKT | Tak | Thailand |
| TKU | Turku | Finland |
| TKV | Tatakoto | F. Polynesia |
| TKW | Tekin | Papua New Guinea |
| TKX | Takaroa | F. Polynesia |
| TKY | Turkey Creek | Australia |
| TKZ | Tokoroa | New Zealand |
| TLA | Teller, AK | USA |
| TLB | Tarbela | Pakistan |
| TLC | Toluca | Mexico |
| TLD | Tuli Lodge | Botswana |
| TLE | Tulear | Madagascar |
| TLF | Telida, AK | USA |
| TLG | Tulagi Is | Solomon Is |
| TLH | Tallahassee, FL | USA |
| TLI | Tolitoli/Lalos | Indonesia |
| TLJ | Tatalina/Tatalina AFS, AK | USA |
| TLK | Taiknafjordur | Iceland |
| TLL | Tallinn/Ulemiste | Estonia |
| TLM | Tlemcen/Zenata | Algeria |
| TLN | Toulon/Hyeres | France |
| TLO | Tol | Papua New Guinea |
| TLP | Tumolbil | Papua New Guinea |
| TLR | Tulare, CA | USA |
| TLS | Toulouse/Blagnac | France |
| TLT | Tuluksak, AK | USA |
| TLU | Tolu | Colombia |
| TLV | Tel Aviv-Ben Gurion Int'l | Israel |
| TLW | Talasea | Papua New Guinea |
| TLX | Talca | Chile |
| TLZ | Catalao | Brazil |
| TMA | Tifton/Henry Tift Myers, GA | USA |
| TMB | Miami Exec, FL | USA |
| TMC | Tambolaka | Indonesia |
| TMD | Timbedra | Mauritania |
| TME | Tame | Colombia |
| TMG | Tomanggong | Malaysia |
| TMH | Tanah Merah/Tanah Merah | Indonesia |
| TMI | Tumling Tar | Nepal |
| TMJ | Termez | Uzbekistan |
| TMK | Tarnky | Vietnam |
| TML | Tamale | Ghana |
| TMM | Tamatave | Madagascar |
| TMN | Tamana Is | Kiribati |
| TMO | Tumeremo | Venezuela |
| TMP | Tampere/Pirkkala | Finland |
| TMQ | Tambao | Burkina Faso |
| TMR | Tamanrasset/Aguemar | Algeria |
| TMS | Sao Tome Is | Sao Tome and Principe |
| TMT | Trombetas | Brazil |
| TMU | Tambor | Costa Rica |
| TMW | Tamworth | Australia |
| TMX | Timimoun | Algeria |
| TMY | Tiom | Indonesia |
| TMZ | Thames | New Zealand |
| TNA | Jinan | China |
| TNB | Tanah Grogot | Indonesia |
| TNC | Tin City/AFS, AK | USA |
| TND | Trinidad | Cuba |
| TNE | Tanegashima | Japan |
| TNF | Toussus Le Noble | France |
| TNG | Tangier/Boukhalef | Morocco |
| TNH | Tonghua/Tonghua Liuhe | China |
| TNI | Satna | India |
| TNJ | Tanjung Pinang/Kidjang | Indonesia |
| TNK | Tununak, AK | USA |
| TNL | Ternopol | Laos |
| TNM | Teniente R. Marsh | Antarctica |
| TNN | Tainan | Taiwan |
| TNO | Tamarindo | Costa Rica |
| TNP | Twentynine Palms, CA | USA |
| TNQ | Teraina | Kiribati |
| TNR | Antananarivo | Madagascar |
| TNS | Tungsten, NT | Canada |
| TNT | Miami/Dade Collier, FL | USA |
| TNU | Newton, IA | USA |
| TNV | Tabuaeran | Kiribati |
| TNX | Stung Treng | Cambodia |
| TOA | Torrance, CA | USA |
| TOB | Tobruk | Libya |
| TOC | Toccoa, GA | USA |
| TOD | Tioman | Malaysia |
| TOE | Tozeur/Nefta | Tunisia |
| TOG | Togiak Village, AK | USA |
| TOH | Torres/Torres Airstrip | Vanuatu |
| TOI | Troy, AL | USA |
| TOJ | Madrid/Torrejon AFB | Spain |
| TOK | Torokina | Papua New Guinea |
| TOL | Toledo, OH | USA |
| TOM | Tombouctou | Mali |
| TON | Tonu | Papua New Guinea |
| TOO | San Vito | Costa Rica |
| TOP | Topeka, KS | USA |
| TOQ | Tocopilla/Barriles | Chile |
| TOR | Torrington, WY | USA |
| TOS | Tromso/Langnes | Norway |
| TOT | Totness/Coronie | Suriname |
| TOU | Touho | New Caledonia |
| TOV | Tortola/West End SPB | Virgin Islands (British) |
| TOW | Toledo | Brazil |
| TOX | Tobolsk | Russia |
| TOY | Toyama | Japan |
| TOZ | Touba/Mahana | Côte D'Ivoire |
| TPA | Tampa Int'l, FL | USA |
| TPC | Tarapoa | Ecuador |
| TPE | Taipei/Chiang Kai Shek | Taiwan |
| TPF | Tampa/Peter O'Knight, FL | USA |
| TPG | Taiping | Malaysia |
| TPH | Tonopah, NV | USA |
| TPI | Tapini | Papua New Guinea |
| TPJ | Tapiejung | Nepal |
| TPK | Tapaktuan | Indonesia |
| TPL | Temple/Draughon-Miller, TX | USA |
| TPN | Tiputini | Ecuador |
| TPO | Tanalian Point, AK | USA |

| | | |
|---|---|---|
| TPP | Tarapoto | Peru |
| TPQ | Tepic | Mexico |
| TPR | Tom Price | Australia |
| TPS | Trapani/Birgi | Italy |
| TPT | Tapeta | Iran |
| TPU | Tikapur | Nepal |
| TQE | Tekamah, Tekamah Municipal Arpt, NE | USA |
| TQN | Taluqan | Afghanistan |
| TQR | San Domino Is | Italy |
| TQS | Tres Esquinas | Colombia |
| TRA | Taramaprina/Tarama | Japan |
| TRB | Turbo/Gonzalo | Colombia |
| TRC | Torreon | Mexico |
| TRD | Trondheim/Vaernes | Norway |
| TRE | Tiree | UK |
| TRF | Oslo/Sandefjord | Norway |
| TRG | Tauranga | New Zealand |
| TRH | Trona, CA | USA |
| TRI | Bristol, TN | USA |
| TRJ | Tarakbits | Papua New Guinea |
| TRK | Tarakan | Indonesia |
| TRL | Terrell, TX | USA |
| TRM | Palm Springs-Thermal, CA | USA |
| TRN | Turin/Citta Di Torino | Italy |
| TRO | Taree | Australia |
| TRP | Tree Point/Cst Guard Heliport, AK | USA |
| TRQ | Tarauaca | Brazil |
| TRR | Trincomalee/China Bay | Sri Lanka |
| TRS | Trieste/Dei Legionari | Italy |
| TRT | Tremonton, UT | USA |
| TRU | Trujillo | Peru |
| TRV | Trivandrum/Int'l | India |
| TRW | Tarawa/Bonriki | Kiribati |
| TRX | Trenton/Memorial, MO | USA |
| TRY | Tororo | Uganda |
| TRZ | Tiruchirapally/Civil | India |
| TSA | Taipei/Sung Shan | Taiwan |
| TSB | Tsumeb | Namibia |
| TSC | Taisha | Ecuador |
| TSD | Tshipise | S. Africa |
| TSE | Astana | Kazakstan |
| TSF | Venice/Treviso | Italy |
| TSG | Tanacross/Intermediate, AK | USA |
| TSH | Tshikapa | Congo, DR |
| TSI | Tsili Tsili | Papua New Guinea |
| TSJ | Tsushima | Japan |
| TSK | Taskul | Papua New Guinea |
| TSL | Tamuin | Myanmar |
| TSM | Taos, NM | USA |
| TSN | Tiarijin | China |
| TSO | Isles Of Scilly/Tresco | UK |
| TSP | Tehachapi/Kern County, CA | USA |
| TSQ | Torres | Brazil |
| TSR | Timisoara | Romania |
| TSS | New York/E. 34th St Heiliport, NY | USA |
| TST | Trang | Thailand |
| TSU | Tabiteuea South | Kiribati |
| TSV | Townsville | Australia |
| TSW | Tsewi | Papua New Guinea |
| TSX | Tanjung Santan | Indonesia |
| TSY | Tasikmalaya/Cibeureum | Indonesia |
| TSZ | Tsetserleg | Mongolia |
| TTA | Tan Tan | Morocco |
| TTB | Tortoli/Arbatax | Italy |
| TTC | Taltal | Chile |
| TTD | Portland-Troutdale, OR | USA |
| TTE | Ternate/Babullah | Indonesia |
| TTG | Tartagal | Argentina |
| TTH | Thumrait | Oman |
| TTI | Tetiaroa Is | F. Polynesia |
| TTJ | Tottori | Japan |
| TTK | Tottenham Hale Stn | UK |
| TTL | Turtle Is | Fiji |
| TTM | Tablon De Tamara | Colombia |
| TTN | Trenton, NJ | USA |
| TTO | Britton/Municipal, SD | USA |
| TTQ | Tortuquero | Costa Rica |
| TTR | Tana Toraja | Indonesia |
| TTS | Tsaratanana | Madagascar |
| TTT | Taitung | Taiwan |
| TTU | Tetuan/Sania Ramel | Morocco |
| TUA | Tulcan | Ecuador |
| TUB | Tubuai | F. Polynesia |
| TUC | Tueuman/Benj Matienzo | Argentina |
| TUD | Tambacounda | Senegal |
| TUE | Tupile | Panama |
| TUF | Tours/St Symphorien | France |
| TUG | Tuguegarao | Philippines |
| TUH | Tullahoma/Arnold AFS, TN | USA |
| TUI | Turaif | Saudi Arabia |

| | | |
|---|---|---|
| TUJ | Turn | Ethiopia |
| TUK | Turbat | Pakistan |
| TUL | Tulsa Int'l, OK | USA |
| TUM | Tumut | Australia |
| TUN | Tunis/Carthage | Tunisia |
| TUO | Taupo | New Zealand |
| TUP | Tupelo, MS | USA |
| TUQ | Tougan | Burkina Faso |
| TUR | Tucurui | Brazil |
| TUS | Tucson Int'l, AZ | USA |
| TUT | Tauta | Papua New Guinea |
| TUU | Tabuk | Saudi Arabia |
| TUV | Tucupita | Venezuela |
| TUW | Tubala | Panama |
| TUX | Tumbler Ridge, BC | Canada |
| TUY | Tulum | Mexico |
| TUZ | Tucuma | Brazil |
| TVA | Morafenobe | Madagascar |
| TVC | Traverse City, MI | USA |
| TVF | Thief River Falls/Regional, MN | USA |
| TVI | Thomasville/Municipal, GA | USA |
| TVL | South Lake Tahoe, CA | USA |
| TVR | Vicksburg, Tallulah Rgnl. Arpt, LA | USA |
| TVU | Taveuni/Matei | Fiji |
| TVY | Dawe | Myanmar |
| TWA | Twin Hills, AK | USA |
| TWB | Toowoomba | Australia |
| TWD | Port Townsend, WA | USA |
| TWE | Taylor, AK | USA |
| TWF | Twin Falls, ID | USA |
| TWH | Catalina Is/Two Harbors, CA | USA |
| TWM | Two Harbors, MN | USA |
| TWN | Tewantin | Australia |
| TWP | Torwood | Australia |
| TWT | Tawitawi | Philippines |
| TWU | Tawau | Malaysia |
| TWX | Topeka Nexrad, KS | USA |
| TWY | Tawa | Papua New Guinea |
| TWZ | Mount Cook/Pulkalki/Twizel | New Zealand |
| TXF | Te ixeira de Freitas | Brazil |
| TXG | Taichung | Taiwan |
| TXK | Texarkana, AR | USA |
| TXL | Berlin/Tegel | Germany |
| TXM | Terminabuan | Indonesia |
| TXN | Tunxl | China |
| TXR | Tanbar | Australia |
| TXU | Tabou | Côte D'Ivoire |
| TYA | Tula | Russia |
| TYB | Tibooburra | Australia |
| TYD | Tyncia | Russia |
| TYE | Tyonek, AK | USA |
| TYF | Torsby/Torsby Arpt | Sweden |
| TYG | Thylungra | Australia |
| TYL | Talara | Peru |
| TYM | Staniel Cay | Bahamas |
| TYN | Taiyuan | China |
| TYP | Tobermorey | Australia |
| TYR | Tyler, TX | USA |
| TYS | Knoxville, TN | USA |
| TYT | Treinta-y-Tres | Uruguay |
| TYZ | Taylor, AZ | USA |
| TZA | Belize City/Mun | Belize |
| TZL | Tuzia/Tuzla Int'l | Bosnia Hercegovina |
| TZM | Tizimin | Mexico |
| TZN | South Andros | Bahamas |
| TZX | Trabzon | Turkey |

# U

| | | |
|---|---|---|
| UAC | San Luis Rio Colorado | Mexico |
| UAE | Mount Aue | Papua New Guinea |
| UAH | Lia Hulka | F. Polynesia |
| UAI | Suai | Indonesia |
| UAK | Narsarsuaq | Greenland |
| UAL | Luau | Andorra |
| UAM | Guam/Anderson AFB | Guam |
| UAO | Aurora State Arpt, OR | USA |
| UAP | Lia Pou | F. Polynesia |
| UAQ | San Juan | Argentina |
| UAS | Samburu | Kenya |
| UAX | Uaxactun | Guatemala |
| UBA | Uberaba | Brazil |
| UBB | Mabuiag Is | Australia |
| UBI | Buin | Papua New Guinea |
| UBJ | Ube | Japan |
| UBP | Ubon Ratchathani | Thailand |
| UBR | Ubrub | Indonesia |

| | | |
|---|---|---|
| UBS | Columbus/Lowrides County, MS. | USA |
| UBT | Ubatuba | Brazil |
| UBU | Kalumburu | Australia |
| UCA | Utica, NY | USA |
| UCC | Yucca Flat, NV | USA |
| UCE | Eunice, LA | USA |
| UCK | Lutsk | Ukraine |
| UCN | Buchanan | Liberia |
| UCT | Ukhta | Russia |
| UCY | Union City/Everett-Stewart, TN | USA |
| UDA | Unclarra | Australia |
| UDD | Palm Springs/Bermuda Dunes, CA | USA |
| UDE | Uden/Volkel | Netherlands |
| UDI | Uberlandia/Eduardo Gomes | Brazil |
| UDJ | Uzhgorod | Ukraine |
| UDN | Udine/Airfield | Italy |
| UDO | Udomxay | Laos |
| UDR | Udaipur/Dabok | India |
| UEE | Queenstown | Australia |
| UEL | Quelimane | Mozambique |
| UEO | Kumejima | Japan |
| UES | Waukesha, WI | USA |
| UET | Quetta | Pakistan |
| UEX | Grand Is Nexrad, NE | USA |
| UFA | Ufa | Russia |
| UGA | Bulgan | Mongolia |
| UGB | Pilot Point/Ugashik Bay, AK | USA |
| UGC | Urgench | Uzbekistan |
| UGI | Uganik, AK | USA |
| UGN | Chicago-Waukegan, IL | USA |
| UGO | Uige | Andorra |
| UGS | Ugashik, AK | USA |
| UGU | Zugapa | Indonesia |
| UHE | Uherske Hradiste | Czech Rep |
| UHF | Upper Heyford/RAF | UK |
| UIB | Quibdo | Colombia |
| UIH | Qui Nhon | Vietnam |
| UII | Utila | Honduras |
| UIK | Ust-Llimsk | Russia |
| UIL | Quillayute, WA | USA |
| UIN | Quincy, IL | USA |
| UIO | Quito/Mariscal Sucr | Ecuador |
| UIP | Quimper/Pluguffan | France |
| UIQ | Quine Hill | Vanuatu |
| UIR | Quirincli | Australia |
| UIT | Jaluit Is | Marshall Is |
| UIZ | Utica/Berz-Macomb, MI | USA |
| UJE | Ujae Is | Marshall Is |
| UKA | Ukunda | Kenya |
| UKB | Kobe | Japan |
| UKI | Ukiah, CA | USA |
| UKK | Ust-Kamenogorsk | Kazakstan |
| UKN | Waukon/Municipal, IA | USA |
| UKR | Mukeiras | Yemen |
| UKT | Quakertown/Upper Bucks, PA | USA |
| UKU | Nuku | Papua New Guinea |
| UKX | Ust-Kut | Russia |
| UKY | Kyoto | Japan |
| ULA | San Julian | Argentina |
| ULB | Ulei/Los Cerrillos | Vanuatu |
| ULC | Santiago | Chile |
| ULD | Ulundi | S. Africa |
| ULE | Sule | Papua New Guinea |
| ULG | Ulgit | Mongolia |
| ULI | Ulithi | Micronesia |
| ULL | Mull | UK |
| ULM | New Ulm, MN | USA |
| ULN | Ulaaribaatar/Buyant Uhaa | Mongolia |
| ULO | Ulaangom | Mongolia |
| ULP | Quilpie | Australia |
| ULQ | Tulua/Farfan | Colombia |
| ULS | Mulatos | Colombia |
| ULU | Gulu | Uganda |
| ULX | Ulusaba | S. Africa |
| ULY | Ulyanovsk | Russia |
| ULZ | Liliastai | Mongolia |
| UMA | Punta De Maisi | Colombia |
| UMB | Umnak Is/North Shore, AK | USA |
| UMC | Umba | Papua New Guinea |
| UMD | Uummannaq | Greenland |
| UME | Umea/Flygplats | Sweden |
| UMI | Quincemil | Peru |
| UMM | Summit, AK | USA |
| UMR | Woomera | Australia |
| UMT | Umiat, AK | USA |
| UMU | Umuarama/Ernesto Geisel | Brazil |
| UMY | Sumy | Ukraine |
| UNC | Unguia | Colombia |
| UND | Kunduz | Afghanistan |
| UNE | Gachas Nek | Lesotho |

# V

| | | |
|---|---|---|
| UNG | Kiunga | Papua New Guinea |
| UNI | Union Isl | St. Vincent & Grenadines |
| UNK | Unalakleet, AK | USA |
| UNN | Ranong | Thailand |
| UNO | West Plains Municipal Arpt, MO | USA |
| UNR | Underkhaan | Mongolia |
| UNS | Umnak Is/Umnak, AK | USA |
| UNT | Unst Shetland Iss | UK |
| UNU | Juneau/Dodge County, AK | USA |
| UNV | State College, PA | USA |
| UOL | Buol | Indonesia |
| UON | Muong Sai | Laos |
| UOS | Sewanee/Franklin County, TN | USA |
| UOX | Oxford/University-Oxford, MS | USA |
| UPA | Punta Alegre | Colombia |
| UPC | Puerto La Cruz | Spain |
| UPF | Pforheim | Germany |
| UPG | Ujung Pandang/Hasanudin | Indonesia |
| UPL | Upala | Costa Rica |
| UPN | Uruapan | Mexico |
| UPP | Upolu Point, HI | USA |
| UPR | Uplara | Papua New Guinea |
| UPV | Upavon | UK |
| UQE | Queen, AK | USA |
| URA | Uralsk | Kazakstan |
| URB | Urubupunga/Ernesto Pochier | Brazil |
| URC | Urumqi | China |
| URD | Burg Feuerstein | Germany |
| URE | Kuressaare | Estonia |
| URG | Uruguaiana/Ruben Berta | Brazil |
| URI | Uribe | Colombia |
| URJ | Uraj | Russia |
| URM | Uriman | Venezuela |
| URN | Urgoon | Afghanistan |
| URO | Rouen/Boos | France |
| URR | Urrao | Colombia |
| URS | Kursk | Russia |
| URT | Surat Thani | Thailand |
| URU | Uroubi | Papua New Guinea |
| URY | Gurayat | Saudi Arabia |
| URZ | Unuzgan | Afghanistan |
| USC | Union South Carolina, SC | USA |
| USH | Ushuaia/Islas Malvinas | Argentina |
| USI | Mabaruma | Guyana |
| USK | Usinsk | Russia |
| USL | Useless Loop | Australia |
| USM | Koh Sannui | Thailand |
| USN | Uisan | S. Korea |
| USO | Usino | Papua New Guinea |
| USQ | Usak | Turkey |
| USS | Sancti Spiritus | Cuba |
| UST | St Augustine, FL | USA |
| USU | Busuanga | Philippines |
| UTA | Mutare | Zimbabwe |
| UTB | Muttaburra | Australia |
| UTC | Utrecht/Soesterberg | Netherlands |
| UTD | Nutwood Downs | Australia |
| UTE | Butterworth | S. Africa |
| UTG | Outhing | Iceland |
| UTH | Udon Thani | Thailand |
| UTI | Kouvola/Utti | Finland |
| UTK | Utirik Is | Marshall Is |
| UTL | Torremolinos | Spain |
| UTN | Upington | S. Africa |
| UTO | Indian Mountain AFS, AK | USA |
| UTP | Utapato | Thailand |
| UTR | Uttaradit | Thailand |
| UTS | Huntsville, TX | USA |
| UTT | Umtata | S. Africa |
| UTU | Ustupo | Panama |
| UTW | Queenstown | S. Africa |
| UUA | Buguima | Russia |
| UUD | Ulan-Ude | Russia |
| UUK | Kuparuk, AK | USA |
| UUN | Baruun-Urt | Mongolia |
| UUS | Yuzhno-Sakhalinsk | Russia |
| UUU | Manumu | Papua New Guinea |
| UVA | Uvaide/Garner Fld, TX | USA |
| UVE | Ouvea | New Caledonia |
| UVF | St Lucia/Hewanorra | St. Lucia |
| UVL | Kharga | Egypt |
| UVO | Llvol | Papua New Guinea |
| UWA | Ware, MA | USA |
| UWE | Wiesbaden | Germany |
| UWP | Wuppertal | Germany |
| UYL | Nyala | Somalia |
| UYN | Yulin | China |
| UZC | Uzice/Ponikve | Yugoslavia |
| UZH | Unayzah | Saudi Arabia |
| UZU | Cunuzu Cuatia | Argentina |

| | | |
|---|---|---|
| VAA | Vaasa | Finland |
| VAB | Yavarate | Colombia |
| VAC | Varrelbusch | Germany |
| VAD | Moody/AFB, GA | USA |
| VAF | Valence/Chalpeuil | France |
| VAG | Varginha/M. B. Trompowsky | Brazil |
| VAH | Vallegrande | Bolivia |
| VAI | Vanimo | Papua New Guinea |
| VAK | Chevak, AK | USA |
| VAL | Vaienca | Brazil |
| VAN | Van | Turkey |
| VAO | Suavanao Airstrip | Solomon Is |
| VAP | Valparaiso | Chile |
| VAR | Varna | Bulgaria |
| VAS | Sivas | Turkey |
| VAT | Vatomandry | Madagascar |
| VAU | Vatulkoula | Fiji |
| VAV | Vava'u/Lupepau'u | Tonga |
| VAW | Vandoe | Norway |
| VAY | Mount Holly, South Jersey, NJ | USA |
| VAZ | Val D'Isere | France |
| VBG | Vandenberg/AFB, CA | USA |
| VBS | Brescia/Montichiari | Italy |
| VBV | Vanuabalavu | Fiji |
| VBY | Visby/Flygplats | Sweden |
| VCA | Can Tho | Vietnam |
| VCB | View Cove, AK | USA |
| VCC | Limbe | Cameroon |
| VCD | Victoria River Downs | Australia |
| VCE | Venice/Marco Polo | Italy |
| VCF | Valcheta | Argentina |
| VCH | Vichadero | Uruguay |
| VCP | Sao Paud/Viracopos | Brazil |
| VCR | Carora | Venezuela |
| VCT | Victoria, TX | USA |
| VCV | George/AFB, CA | USA |
| VDA | Ovda | Israel |
| VDB | Fagernes/Valdres | Norway |
| VDC | Vitoria Da Conquista | Brazil |
| VDD | Vienna/Danubelpier Hov | Austria |
| VDE | Valverde/Hierro | Spain |
| VDI | Vidalia/Municipal, GA | USA |
| VDM | Viedma | Argentina |
| VDP | Valle De Pascua | Venezuela |
| VDR | Villa Dolores | Argentina |
| VDS | Vadso | Norway |
| VDU | Refugio/O'Connor Oilfield, TX | USA |
| VDZ | Valdez/Municipal, AK | USA |
| VEE | Venetie, AK | USA |
| VEG | Mailkwalk | Guyana |
| VEJ | Vejle | Denmark |
| VEL | Vernal, UT | USA |
| VER | Veracruz/Las Bajadas | Mexico |
| VEV | Barakoma | Solomon Is |
| VEX | Tioga/Municipal, ND | USA |
| VEY | Vestmannaeyjar | Iceland |
| VFA | Victoria Falls | Zimbabwe |
| VGA | Vijayawada | India |
| VGD | Vologida | Russia |
| VGG | Vangrieng | Laos |
| VGO | Vigo | Spain |
| VGS | General Villegas | Argentina |
| VGT | Las Vegas/North Air Terminal, NV | USA |
| VGZ | Villagarzon | Colombia |
| VHC | Saurimo | Angola |
| VHM | Vilhelmina | Sweden |
| VHN | Van Horn/Cullberson County, TX | USA |
| VHY | Vichy/Charmeil | France |
| VHZ | Vahitahi | F. Polynesia |
| VIA | Videira | Brazil |
| VIB | Villa Constitucion | Mexico |
| VIC | Vicenza | Italy |
| VID | Vidin | Bulgaria |
| VIE | Vienna Int'l | Austria |
| VIG | El Vigia | Venezuela |
| VIH | Vichy, MO | USA |
| VII | Vinh City | Vietnam |
| VIJ | Virgin Gorda | Virgin Is (British) |
| VIK | Kavik/Airstrip, AK | USA |
| VIL | Dakhla | Morocco |
| VIN | Vinnica | Ukraine |
| VIQ | Viqueque | Indonesia |
| VIR | Durban/Virginia | S. Africa |
| VIS | Visalia, CA | USA |
| VIT | Vitoria | Spain |

| | | |
|---|---|---|
| VIU | Viru/Viru Harbour | Solomon Is |
| VIV | Vivigani | Papua New Guinea |
| VIX | Vitoria/Euroo Sales | Brazil |
| VJB | Xai Xai | Mozambique |
| VJI | Abingdon/Virginia Highlands, VA | USA |
| VJQ | Gurue | Mozambique |
| VKG | Rach Gia | Vietnam |
| VKO | Moscow/Vnukovo | Russia |
| VKS | Vicksburg, MS | USA |
| VKT | Vorkuta | Russia |
| VKW | West Kavik, AK | USA |
| VLA | Vandalia, IL | USA |
| VLC | Valencia | Spain |
| VLD | Valdosta, GA | USA |
| VLE | Valle, AZ | Australia |
| VLG | Villa Gesell | Argentina |
| VLI | Port Vila/Bauerfield | Vanuatu |
| VLK | Volgodonsk | Russia |
| VLL | Valladolid | Spain |
| VLM | Villamontes | Bolivia |
| VLN | Valencia | Venezuela |
| VLO | Vallejo/Stolport, CA | USA |
| VLP | Vila Rica/Mun | Brazil |
| VLR | Vallenar | Chile |
| VLS | Valesdir | Vanuatu |
| VLU | Velikiye Luki | Russia |
| VLV | Valera/Carvajal | Venezuela |
| VME | Villa Mercedes | Argentina |
| VMI | Vallemi/INC | Paraguay |
| VMU | Baimuru | Papua New Guinea |
| VNA | Saravane | Laos |
| VNC | Venice, FL | USA |
| VND | Vangaindrano | Madagascar |
| VNE | Vannes/Meucon | Eritrea |
| VNG | Viengxay | Laos |
| VNO | Vilnius/Int'l | Lithuania |
| VNR | Vanrook | Australia |
| VNS | Varanasi | India |
| VNX | Vilanculos | Mozambique |
| VNY | Los Angeles-Van Nuys, CA | USA |
| VOG | Volgograd | Russia |
| VOH | Vohemar | Madagascar |
| VOI | Voinjama | Liberia |
| VOK | Camp Douglas, WI | USA |
| VOL | Volos/Nea Anchialos | Greece |
| VOT | Votuporanga | Brazil |
| VOZ | Voronezh | Russia |
| VPC | Cartersville, GA | USA |
| VPE | Ongiva | Angola |
| VPN | Vopnafjordur | Iceland |
| VPS | Elglin/AFB, FL | USA |
| VPY | Chimoio | Mozambique |
| VPZ | Valparaiso, IN | USA |
| VQN | Volens, VA | USA |
| VQS | Vieques | Puerto Rico |
| VRA | Varadero/Juan Gualberto Gomez | Cuba |
| VRB | Vero Beach, FL | USA |
| VRC | Virac | Philippines |
| VRE | Vredendal | S. Africa |
| VRK | Varkaus | Finland |
| VRL | Vila Real | Portugal |
| VRN | Verona/Villafranca | Italy |
| VRS | Versailles, MO | USA |
| VRU | Vryburg | S. Africa |
| VRX | Vermillion Area, LA | USA |
| VRY | Vaeroy/Stolport | Norway |
| VSA | Villahermosa/Capitan Carlos Perez | Mexico |
| VSE | Viseu | Portugal |
| VSF | Springfield, VT | USA |
| VSG | Lugansk | Ukraine |
| VSO | Phuoclong | Vietnam |
| VST | Vasteras/Hasslo | Sweden |
| VTA | Victoria | Honduras |
| VTB | Vitebsk | Belarus |
| VTE | Vientiane/Wattav | Laos |
| VTF | Vatulele | Fiji |
| VTG | Vung Tau | Vietnam |
| VTL | Vittel | Eritrea |
| VTN | Valentine, NE | USA |
| VTU | Las Tunas | Cuba |
| VTX | Los Angeles Nexrad, CA | USA |
| VTZ | Vishakhapatnam | India |
| VUO | Vancouver, Pearson Airpark, WA | USA |
| VUP | Valledupar | Colombia |
| VUS | Velikij Ustyug | Russia |
| VUW | Eugene Is, LA | USA |
| VVB | Mahanoro | Madagascar |
| VVC | Villavicencio/La Vanguardia | Colombia |
| VVI | Santa Cruz/Viru Viru Int'l | Bolivia |

| | | |
|---|---|---|
| **VVK** | Vastervik | Sweden |
| **VVO** | Vladivostok | Russia |
| **VVZ** | Illizi | Algeria |
| **VXC** | Lichinga | Mozambique |
| **VXE** | Sao Vicente/San Pedro | Cape Verde Is |
| **VXO** | Vaxjo | Sweden |
| **VYD** | Vryheid | S. Africa |
| **VYS** | Peru/Illinois Valley Regional, IL | USA |

# W

| | | |
|---|---|---|
| **WAA** | Wales, AK | USA |
| **WAB** | Wabag | Papua New Guinea |
| **WAC** | Waca | Ethiopia |
| **WAD** | Andriamena | Madagascar |
| **WAE** | Wadi Ad Dawasir | Saudi Arabia |
| **WAF** | Wana | Pakistan |
| **WAG** | Wanganui | New Zealand |
| **WAH** | Wahpeton, ND | USA |
| **WAI** | Antsohihy | Madagascar |
| **WAJ** | Wawoi Falls | Papua New Guinea |
| **WAK** | Ankazoabo | Madagascar |
| **WAL** | Wallops Is, VA | USA |
| **WAM** | Ambatondrazalka | Madagascar |
| **WAN** | Waverney | Australia |
| **WAO** | Wabo | Papua New Guinea |
| **WAP** | Alto Palena | Chile |
| **WAQ** | Antsalova | Madagascar |
| **WAR** | Waris | Indonesia |
| **WAT** | Waterford | Ireland |
| **WAU** | Wauchope | Australia |
| **WAV** | Wave Hill/Kalkgurung | Australia |
| **WAW** | Warszawa-Okecie | Poland |
| **WAX** | Zwara | Libya |
| **WAY** | Waynesburg/Green County, PA | USA |
| **WAZ** | Warwick | Australia |
| **WBA** | Wahai | Indonesia |
| **WBB** | Stebbins, AK | USA |
| **WBC** | Wapolu | Papua New Guinea |
| **WBD** | Befandriana | Madagascar |
| **WBE** | Bealanana | Madagascar |
| **WBG** | Schieswig-Jagel | Germany |
| **WBI** | Boulder/Broker Inn, CO | USA |
| **WBM** | Wapenamanda | Papua New Guinea |
| **WBN** | Woburn/Cummings Park, MA | USA |
| **WBO** | Beroroha | Madagascar |
| **WBQ** | Beaver, AK | USA |
| **WBR** | Big Rapids, MI | USA |
| **WBU** | Boulder/Metro, CO | USA |
| **WBW** | Wilkes-Barre/Wyoming Valle, PA | USA |
| **WCA** | Castro/Gamboa | Chile |
| **WCH** | Chaiten | Chile |
| **WCR** | Chandalar, AK | USA |
| **WDA** | Wadi Ain | Yemen |
| **WDB** | Deep Bay, AK | USA |
| **WDG** | Enid, OK | USA |
| **WDH** | Windhoek/H. Kutako Int'l | Namibia |
| **WDI** | Wondai | Australia |
| **WDN** | Waldron Is, WA | USA |
| **WDR** | Winder, GA | USA |
| **WDT** | Woensdrecht | Netherlands |
| **WDY** | Kodiak, AK | USA |
| **WEA** | Weatherford/Parker County, TX | USA |
| **WED** | Wedau | Papua New Guinea |
| **WEE** | Weifang | China |
| **WEH** | Weihai | China |
| **WEI** | Weipa | Australia |
| **WEL** | Welkom | S. Africa |
| **WEM** | West Malling | UK |
| **WEP** | Wearn | Papua New Guinea |
| **WES** | Weasua | Iran |
| **WET** | Wagethe | Indonesia |
| **WEW** | Wee Waa | Australia |
| **WEX** | Wexford/Castlebridge | Ireland |
| **WEY** | West Yellowstone, MT | USA |
| **WFB** | Ketchikan/Waterfront SPB, AK | USA |
| **WFI** | Fianarantsoa | Madagascar |
| **WFK** | Frenchville, ME | USA |
| **WGA** | Wagga Wagga/Forrest Hill | Australia |
| **WGB** | Bahawainagar | Pakistan |
| **WGC** | Warrangal | India |
| **WGE** | Walgett | Australia |
| **WGL** | Isle Baltra | Ecuador |
| **WGN** | Waitangi | New Zealand |
| **WGO** | Winchester/Municipal, VA | USA |
| **WGP** | Waingapu/Mau Hau | Indonesia |
| **WGT** | Wangaratta | Australia |
| **WGU** | Wagau | Papua New Guinea |
| **WGY** | Wagny | Gabon |
| **WHD** | Hyder/SPB, AK | USA |
| **WHF** | Wadi Halfa | Somalia |
| **WHH** | Boulder/Hiltons Har H, CO | USA |
| **WHK** | Whakatane | New Zealand |
| **WHL** | Welshpool | Australia |
| **WHO** | Franz Josef | New Zealand |
| **WHP** | Los Angeles/Whiteman, CA | USA |
| **WHS** | Whalsay | UK |
| **WHT** | Wharton, TX | USA |
| **WHU** | Wuhu | China |
| **WIC** | Wick | UK |
| **WID** | Wildenrath | Germany |
| **WIE** | Wiesbaden/Air Base | Germany |
| **WIH** | Walaba | Vanuatu |
| **WIK** | Surfdale | New Zealand |
| **WIL** | Nairobi/Wilson | Kenya |
| **WIN** | Winton | Australia |
| **WIO** | Wilcannia | Australia |
| **WIR** | Wairoa | New Zealand |
| **WIT** | Wittenoom | Australia |
| **WIU** | Witu | Papua New Guinea |
| **WJA** | Woja | Marshall Is |
| **WJF** | Lancaster, CA | USA |
| **WJR** | Wajir | Kenya |
| **WJU** | Wonju | S. Korea |
| **WKA** | Wanaka | New Zealand |
| **WKB** | Warracknabeal | Australia |
| **WKI** | Hwange | Zimbabwe |
| **WKJ** | Wakkanai/Hokkaido | Japan |
| **WKK** | Aleknagik, AK | USA |
| **WKL** | Waikoloa/Waikoloa Arpt, HI | USA |
| **WKN** | Wakunai | Papua New Guinea |
| **WKR** | Walker's Cay | Bahamas |
| **WLA** | Walial | Australia |
| **WLB** | Labouchere Bay, AK | USA |
| **WLC** | Walcha | Australia |
| **WLD** | Winfield, KS | USA |
| **WLG** | Wellington/Int'l | New Zealand |
| **WLI** | Wollogorang | Australia |
| **WLK** | Selawilk, AK | USA |
| **WLM** | Waltham, MA | USA |
| **WLN** | Little Naukati, AK | USA |
| **WLO** | Waterloo | Australia |
| **WLR** | Loring, AK | USA |
| **WLS** | Wallis Is | Wallis and Futuna Is |
| **WLW** | Willows/Glenn County, CA | USA |
| **WMA** | Mandritsara | Madagascar |
| **WMB** | Warmarnboof | Australia |
| **WMC** | Winnemucca, NV | USA |
| **WMD** | Mandabe | Madagascar |
| **WME** | Mount Keith | Australia |
| **WMH** | Mountain Home, AR | USA |
| **WMK** | Meyers Chuck/SPB, AK | USA |
| **WML** | Malaimbandy | Madagascar |
| **WMN** | Maroantsetra | Madagascar |
| **WMO** | White Mountain, AK | USA |
| **WMP** | Mampikony | Madagascar |
| **WMR** | Mananara | Madagascar |
| **WMV** | Madirovalo | Madagascar |
| **WMX** | Wamena | Indonesia |
| **WNA** | Napakiak/SPB, AK | USA |
| **WNC** | Nichen Cove/SPB, AK | USA |
| **WND** | Windarra | Australia |
| **WNE** | Wora Na Ye | Gabon |
| **WNN** | Wunnummin Lake, ON | Canada |
| **WNP** | Naga | Philippines |
| **WNR** | Windorah | Australia |
| **WNS** | Nawabshah | Pakistan |
| **WNU** | Wanuma | Papua New Guinea |
| **WNZ** | Werizinou | China |
| **WOA** | Wonenara | Papua New Guinea |
| **WOB** | Suttonheath/Woodbridge/RAF | UK |
| **WOD** | Wood River, AK | USA |
| **WOE** | Woensdrecht/AB | Netherlands |
| **WOG** | Woodgreen | Australia |
| **WOI** | Wologissi | Liberia |
| **WOK** | Wonken | Venezuela |
| **WOL** | Wollongong | Australia |
| **WON** | Wondoola | Australia |
| **WOO** | Woodchopper, AK | USA |
| **WOT** | Wonan | Taiwan |
| **WOW** | Willow, AK | USA |
| **WPA** | Puerto Aisen | Chile |
| **WPB** | Port Berge | Madagascar |
| **WPC** | Pincher Creek, AB | Canada |
| **WPK** | Wrotham Park | Australia |
| **WPL** | Powell Lake, BC | Canada |
| **WPM** | Wipim | Papua New Guinea |
| **WPO** | Paonia/North Fork Valley, CO | USA |
| **WPR** | Porvenir | Chile |
| **WPS** | Persepolis | Iran |
| **WPU** | Puerto Williams | Chile |
| **WRA** | Warder | Ethiopia |
| **WRB** | Robins/AFB, GA | USA |
| **WRE** | Whangarei | New Zealand |
| **WRG** | Wrangell/SPB, AK | USA |
| **WRH** | Wrench Creek, AK | USA |
| **WRI** | Mcguire/AFB, NJ | USA |
| **WRL** | Worland, WY | USA |
| **WRO** | Wroclaw/Strachowice | Poland |
| **WRW** | Warrawagine | Australia |
| **WRY** | Westray | UK |
| **WSA** | Wasua | Papua New Guinea |
| **WSB** | Steamboat Bay/SPB, AK | USA |
| **WSD** | White Sands/Condron/AAF, NM | USA |
| **WSE** | Santa Cecilia | Ecuador |
| **WSF** | Sarichef, AK | USA |
| **WSG** | Washington/County, PA | USA |
| **WSH** | Shirley/Brookhaven, NY | USA |
| **WSJ** | San Juan/SPB, AK | USA |
| **WSM** | Wiseman, AK | USA |
| **WSN** | South Naknek, AK | USA |
| **WSO** | Washabo | Suriname |
| **WSP** | Waspam | Netherlands |
| **WSR** | Wasior | Indonesia |
| **WST** | Westerly, RI | USA |
| **WSU** | Wasu | Papua New Guinea |
| **WSX** | Westsound, WA | USA |
| **WSY** | Airlie Beach/Whitsunday Airstrip | Australia |
| **WSZ** | Westport | New Zealand |
| **WTA** | Tambohorano | Madagascar |
| **WTC** | New York/World Trade Center, NY | USA |
| **WTD** | West End | Bahamas |
| **WTE** | Wotje Is | Marshall Is |
| **WTK** | Noatak, AK | USA |
| **WTL** | Tuntutuliak, AK | USA |
| **WTN** | Waddington/RAF Stn | UK |
| **WTO** | Wotho Is | Marshall Is |
| **WTP** | Woitape | Papua New Guinea |
| **WTR** | White River, AZ | USA |
| **WTS** | Tsiroanomandidy | Madagascar |
| **WTT** | Wantoat | Papua New Guinea |
| **WTZ** | Whitianga | New Zealand |
| **WUD** | Wudinna | Australia |
| **WUG** | Wau | Papua New Guinea |
| **WUH** | Wuhan | China |
| **WUM** | Wasum | Papua New Guinea |
| **WUN** | Wiluna | Australia |
| **WUS** | Wuyishan | China |
| **WUU** | Wau | Sudan |
| **WUV** | Wuvulu Is | Papua New Guinea |
| **WUX** | Wuxi | China |
| **WUZ** | Wuzhou/Changzhoudao | China |
| **WVB** | Walvis Bay/Rooikop | Namibia |
| **WVI** | Watsonville, CA | USA |
| **WVK** | Manakara | Madagascar |
| **WVL** | Waterville/Robert Lafleur, ME | USA |
| **WVN** | Wilhelmshaven | Germany |
| **WWA** | Wasilia, AK | USA |
| **WWD** | Wildwood/Cape May County, NJ | USA |
| **WWI** | Woodie Woodie | Australia |
| **WWK** | Wewak/Boram | Papua New Guinea |
| **WWP** | Whale Pass, AK | USA |
| **WWR** | West Woodward, OK | USA |
| **WWS** | Wildwood/USAF HP, AK | USA |
| **WWT** | Newtok, AK | USA |
| **WWY** | West Wyalong | Australia |
| **WXF** | Braintree/Wether Fld/RAF | UK |
| **WXN** | Wanxian | China |
| **WYA** | Whyalla | Australia |
| **WYB** | Yes Bay/SPB, AK | USA |
| **WYE** | Yengema | Sierra Leone |
| **WYN** | Wyndham | Australia |
| **WYS** | West Yellowstone, MT | USA |
| **WZY** | Nassau/Seaplane Base | Bahamas |
| **XAB** | Abbeville | France |

# X

| | | |
|---|---|---|
| **XAC** | Arcachon/Teste de Buch | France |
| **XAD** | Churchill/RR, MB | Canada |
| **XAG** | Agde/Off-line Pt | France |
| **XAH** | Silkeborg/RR Stn | Denmark |
| **XAI** | Aix Les Bains | France |
| **XAJ** | Hirlshals/Bus Svc | Denmark |
| **XAK** | Herning/RR | Denmark |

| Code | Location | Country |
|------|----------|---------|
| XAL | Alamos | Mexico |
| XAM | Amboise | France |
| XAN | Alencon | France |
| XAP | Chapeco | Brazil |
| XAQ | Broenclersev/Bus Svc | Denmark |
| XAR | Aribinda | Burkina Faso |
| XAS | Ales | France |
| XAT | Antibes | France |
| XAU | Saul | F. Guiana |
| XAV | Alberwille | France |
| XAW | Capreol/RR, ON | Canada |
| XAX | Montreal/Dorval RR, QC | Canada |
| XAY | Xayabury | Laos |
| XAZ | Campbellton/RR, NB | Canada |
| XBA | Bareges | France |
| XBB | Blubber Bay, BC | Canada |
| XBC | Briancon | France |
| XBE | Bearskin Lake, ON | Canada |
| XBF | Bellegarde | France |
| XBG | Bogande | Burkina Faso |
| XBH | Bethune | France |
| XBI | Bourg D'Oisans | France |
| XBJ | Birjand | Iran |
| XBK | Bourg En Bresse | France |
| XBL | Buno Bedelle | Ethiopia |
| XBM | Beaulieu Sur Mer | France |
| XBN | Biniguni | Papua New Guinea |
| XBO | Boulsa | Burkina Faso |
| XBP | La Baule Les Pins | France |
| XBQ | Blois | France |
| XBR | Brockville, ON | Canada |
| XBS | Boulogne Sur Mer | France |
| XBT | Boulogne Billancourt | France |
| XBU | Banyuls Sur Mer | France |
| XBV | Beaune | France |
| XBW | Killineq, QC | Canada |
| XBX | Bernay | France |
| XBY | Bayonne | France |
| XBZ | Bandol | France |
| XCB | Cambrai | France |
| XCC | Creusot Montceau MON | France |
| XCD | Chalon Sur Saone | France |
| XCE | Cerbere | France |
| XCF | Chamonix Mont Blanc | France |
| XCG | Cagnes Sur Mer | France |
| XCH | Christmas Is | Christmas Is |
| XCI | Chambord/RR, QC | Canada |
| XCJ | Marigot | Gaudeloupe |
| XCK | St Die | France |
| XCL | Cluff Lake, SK | Canada |
| XCM | Chatham, ON | Canada |
| XCN | Coron | Philippines |
| XCO | Colac | Australia |
| XCP | Compiegne/Margny | France |
| XCQ | Chamrousse | France |
| XCR | Chalons Sur Marne | France |
| XCS | Caussade | France |
| XCT | La Ciotat | France |
| XCU | Collioure/Off-line Pt | France |
| XCV | Chantilly | France |
| XCW | Chaumont | France |
| XCX | Chatellerault/Targe | France |
| XCY | Chateau Thierry | France |
| XCZ | Charleville Mezieres | France |
| XDA | Dax/Seyresse | France |
| XDB | Lille/Lille Europe Rail Svc | France |
| XDC | Dives Cabourg | France |
| XDD | Gaspe/RR, QC | Canada |
| XDE | Diebougou | Burkina Faso |
| XDG | Halifax/RR. NS | Canada |
| XDH | Jasper/RR, AB | Canada |
| XDI | Digne | France |
| XDJ | Djibo | Burkina Faso |
| XDK | Dunkerque/Ghyvelde | France |
| XDL | Chandler/RR, QC | Canada |
| XDM | Drummondville/RR, QC | Canada |
| XDN | Douai | France |
| XDO | Grande-Riviere/RR, QC | Canada |
| XDP | Moncton/RR, NB | Canada |
| XDQ | London/RR, ON | Canada |
| XDR | Dreux | France |
| XDS | Ottawa/RR, ON | Canada |
| XDT | Paris/C.de G. ITGV Rail Sve | France |
| XDU | Hervey/RR, QC | Canada |
| XDV | Prince George/RR, BC | Canada |
| XDW | Prince Rupert/RR, BC | Canada |
| XDX | Sarnia/RR, ON | Canada |
| XDY | Sudbury/Jet RR, ON | Canada |
| XDZ | The Pas/RR, MB | Canada |
| XEA | Vancouver/RR, BC | Canada |
| XEB | Evian Les Bains | France |
| XEC | Windsor/RR, ON | Canada |
| XED | Disneyland Paris-RR | France |
| XEE | Lac Edouard/RR, QC | Canada |
| XEF | Winnipeg/RR, MB | Canada |
| XEG | Kingston/RR, ON | Canada |
| XEH | Ladysmith/RR, BC | Canada |
| XEI | Tsukuba | Japan |
| XEJ | Langford/RR, BC | Canada |
| XEK | Melville/RR, SK | Canada |
| XEL | New Carlisle/RR, QC | Canada |
| XEM | New Richmond/RR, QC | Canada |
| XEN | Xingcheng | China |
| XEO | Ocatsut/Harbour | Greenland |
| XEP | Epernay | France |
| XEQ | Tasiuasaq/Harbour | Greenland |
| XER | Strasbourg/Bus Svc | France |
| XES | Lake Geneva/Municipal, WI | USA |
| XET | Karisruhe/Baden Baden/Bus Svc | Germany |
| XEX | Paris/Aerogare des Invalides | France |
| XEY | Miramichi/RR, NB | Canada |
| XFA | Lille/Lille Flanders Rail Svc | France |
| XFB | Fontainebieau | France |
| XFC | Fredericton Junction/RR, NB | Canada |
| XFD | Stratford/RR, ON | Canada |
| XFE | Parent/RR, QC | Canada |
| XFF | Calais/Frethun RR | France |
| XFG | Perce/RR, QC | Canada |
| XFI | Port-Daniel/RR, QC | Canada |
| XFK | Senneterre/RR, QC | Canada |
| XFL | Shawinigan/RR, QC | Canada |
| XFM | Shawnigan/RR, BC | Canada |
| XFN | Xiangan | China |
| XFO | Taschereau/RR, QC | Canada |
| XFQ | Weymont/RR, QC | Canada |
| XFS | Alexandria/RR, ON | Canada |
| XFV | Brantford/RR, ON | Canada |
| XFW | Hamburg/Finkenwerder | Germany |
| XFX | Foix | France |
| XFY | Quebec/Sainte-Foy Rail Svc, QC | Canada |
| XFZ | Quebec/Charny, QC | Canada |
| XGA | Gaoua | Burkina Faso |
| XGB | Paris/Gare Montparnasse | France |
| XGF | St Gervais Le Fayet | France |
| XGG | Gorom-Gorom | Burkina Faso |
| XGJ | Cobourg/RR, ON | Canada |
| XGK | Coteau/RR, QC | Canada |
| XGL | Granville Lake, MB | Canada |
| XGM | Grantham/RR | UK |
| XGN | Xangongo | Angola |
| XGO | Santiago | Brazil |
| XGR | Kangiqsualuijuaq, QC | Canada |
| XGT | Gueret/Saint Laurent | France |
| XGV | St Gilles Croix De Vie | France |
| XGW | Gananoque/RR, ON | Canada |
| XGY | Grimsby/RR, ON | Canada |
| XHE | Hyeres | France |
| XHM | Georgetown/RR, ON | Canada |
| XHR | Timbo/Ott-Line Point | Brazil |
| XHS | Chemainus/RR, BC | Canada |
| XHU | Huntingdon/RR | UK |
| XHY | Hendaye | France |
| XI0 | St Marys/RR, ON | Canada |
| XIA | Guelph/RR, ON | Canada |
| XIB | Ingersoll/RR, ON | Canada |
| XIC | Xichang | China |
| XID | Maxvifle/RR, ON | Canada |
| XIE | Xienglorn | Laos |
| XIF | Napanee/RR, ON | Canada |
| XIG | Xinguara/Mun | Brazil |
| XII | Prescott/RR, ON | Canada |
| XIL | Xilinhot | China |
| XIM | Saint Hyacinthe/RR, QC | Canada |
| XIN | Xingning | China |
| XIP | Woodstock/RR, ON | Canada |
| XIQ | Ilimanaq/Harbour | Greenland |
| XIS | Dionisio Cerqueira | Brazil |
| XIY | Xi An/Xianyang | China |
| XJE | Vojens/RR | Denmark |
| XJL | Joliette/RR, QC | Canada |
| XJQ | Jonquiere/RR, QC | Canada |
| XJT | Tours/RR | France |
| XJZ | St Jean De Luz | France |
| XKA | Kantchari | Burkina Faso |
| XKH | Xieng Khouang | Laos |
| XKL | Kuala Lumpur/KUL Sentral Rail | Malaysia |
| XKO | Kemano, BC | Canada |
| XKS | Kasabonika, ON | Canada |
| XKT | Kennedy Town | Hong Kong |
| XKU | Kusadasi | Turkey |
| XKV | Sackville/RR, NB | Canada |
| XKY | Kaya | Burkina Faso |
| XLA | La Bastide Puylaurent | France |
| XLB | Lac Brochet, MB | Canada |
| XLC | Fictious Point/Off-line Pt | USA |
| XLD | Landerneau | France |
| XLE | Lens | France |
| XLF | Leaf Bay, QB | Canada |
| XLG | Lognes | France |
| XLH | Luchon | France |
| XLI | St Louis | France |
| XLJ | Quebec/Quebec Stn Rail Svc, QC | Canada |
| XLK | Quebec/Levis Rail Svc, QC | Canada |
| XLM | Montreal/St. Lambert Rail Svc, QC | Canada |
| XLN | Laon/Chambry | France |
| XLO | Long Xuyen | Vietnam |
| XLP | Matapedia/RR, QC | Canada |
| XLQ | Toronto/Guildwood Rail Svc, ON | Canada |
| XLR | Libourne/Artiques de Lussac | France |
| XLS | St Louis | Senegal |
| XLT | Ax Les Thermes | France |
| XLU | Leo | Burkina Faso |
| XLV | Niagara Falls/RR, ON | Canada |
| XLW | Lernwerder | Germany |
| XLX | Lisieux | France |
| XLY | Aldershot/RR, ON | Canada |
| XLZ | Truro/RR, NS | Canada |
| XMA | Maramag | Philippines |
| XMB | M'Bahiakro | Côte D'Ivoire |
| XMC | Mallacoota | Australia |
| XMD | Madison, SD | USA |
| XME | Maubeuge | France |
| XMF | Montbelliard | France |
| XMG | Mahendranagar | Nepal |
| XMH | Manihi | F. Polynesia |
| XMI | Masasi | Tanzania |
| XMJ | Mont De Marsan | France |
| XMK | Montelimar | France |
| XML | Minlaton | Australia |
| XMM | Monaco Monte Carlo | France |
| XMN | Xiamen | China |
| XMO | Modane | France |
| XMP | Maemillan Pass, YT | Canada |
| XMQ | Morzine | France |
| XMR | Marmande/Off-line Pt | France |
| XMS | Macas | Ecuador |
| XMT | Menton | France |
| XMU | Moulin Sur Allier | France |
| XMV | Pichanal | Argentina |
| XMW | Montauban | France |
| XMX | Ledesma | Argentina |
| XMY | Yam Is | Australia |
| XMZ | Macclesfield/RR | UK |
| XNA | Fayetteville/Northwest Arkansas, AR | USA |
| XNE | Newport (Gwent)/RR | UK |
| XNG | Quang Ngai | Vietnam |
| XNK | Newark Northgate/RR | UK |
| XNM | Nottingham/RR | UK |
| XNN | Xining | China |
| XNO | Northallerton/RR | UK |
| XNR | Aalbenraa/Bus Svc | Denmark |
| XNS | Ansan | Kuwait |
| XNT | Xingtai | China |
| XNU | Nouna | Burkina Faso |
| XNV | Nuneaton/RR | UK |
| XOE | Sao Jose | Brazil |
| XOG | Orange | France |
| XOK | Oakville/Rail Svc, ON | Canada |
| XON | Carleton/RR, QC | Canada |
| XOP | Poitiers/RR | France |
| XOS | Mosconi | Argentina |
| XOX | Cheonan | Kuwait |
| XOY | Aulnoye | France |
| XPA | Pama | Burkina Faso |
| XPB | Parksville/RR, BC | Canada |
| XPD | San Pedro | Argentina |
| XPF | Penrith/RR | UK |
| XPG | Paris/Gare du Nord RR | France |
| XPH | Port Hope/RR, ON | Canada |
| XPK | Pukatawagan, MB | Canada |
| XPL | Comayagua/Palmerola Air Base | Honduras |
| XPM | Pontorson Mt St Michel | France |
| XPN | Brampton/RR, ON | Canada |
| XPP | Poplar River, MB | Canada |
| XPR | Pine Ridge, SD | USA |

| | | |
|---|---|---|
| XPS | Provins | France |
| XPT | Preston/RR | UK |
| XPU | West Kuparuk, AK | USA |
| XPV | Port Vendres | France |
| XPW | Didcot Parkway/RR | UK |
| XPX | Pointe-aux-Trembles/RR, QC | Canada |
| XPZ | Saint-Tropez/Harbour | France |
| XQB | Basingstoke/RR | UK |
| XQD | Bedford/RR | UK |
| XQG | Berwick/RR | UK |
| XQH | Nottingham/RR | UK |
| XQI | Nottingham/RR Stn. | UK |
| XQL | Lancaster/RR Stn. | UK |
| XQM | Market Harborough/RR Stn. | UK |
| XQP | Quepos | Costa Rica |
| XQT | Lichfield T.V./RR Stn. | UK |
| XQU | Qualicurn, BC | Canada |
| XQW | Motherwell/RR Stn. | UK |
| XQY | St Quentin en Yvelines | France |
| XRA | Graasten/Bus Svc. | Denmark |
| XRB | Ararangua | Brazil |
| XRC | Runcom/RR Stn. | UK |
| XRE | Reading | UK |
| XRG | Rugeley T.V./RR Stn. | UK |
| XRI | Riom | France |
| XRM | Armentieres | France |
| XRN | Redon. | France |
| XRO | La Roche Sur Yon | France |
| XRP | Riviere-a-Pierre/RR Stn., QC | Canada |
| XRR | Ross River, YT. | Canada |
| XRS | Les Ares | France |
| XRT | Rambouillet | France |
| XRU | Rugby/RR Stn. | UK |
| XRX | Roubaix | France |
| XRY | Jerez De La Frontera/La Parra | |
| | | Spain |
| XSA | Sinoe/AFC | Liberia |
| XSB | St Malo | France |
| XSC | South Caicos/Int'l. | Turks & Caicos Is |
| XSD | Tonopah/Test Range, NV | USA |
| XSE | Sebba | Burkina Faso |
| XSF | Sens | France |
| XSG | St Omer | France |
| XSH | Tours/RR Stn. | France |
| XSI | South Indian Lake, MB | Canada |
| XSJ | St Quentin | France |
| XSK | St Raphael | France |
| XSL | Sarlat/Domme | France |
| XSM | St Marys, MD. | USA |
| XSN | Sallanches | France |
| XSO | Siocon | Philippines |
| XSP | Singapore/Seletar | Singapore |
| XSQ | Selestat | France |
| XSR | Salisbury/RR Stn. | UK |
| XSS | Soissons | France |
| XST | Saintes | France |
| XSU | Saumur | France |
| XSV | Senlis | France |
| XSW | Sedan | France |
| XSX | Seclin | France |
| XSY | Sete | France |
| XSZ | Setubal | Portugal |
| XTB | Tarbes/Laloubere. | France |
| XTC | St Claude | France |
| XTE | La Tour De Carol | France |
| XTG | Thargomindah | Australia |
| XTH | Thionvifle | France |
| XTK | Thirsk/RR Stn. | UK |
| XTL | Tadoule Lake, MB | Canada |
| XTN | Tourcoing | France |
| XTO | Taroom | Australia |
| XTR | Tara | Australia |
| XTS | Thonon Les Bains | France |
| XTT | Paris/Etoile | France |
| XTU | Tulle | France |
| XTY | Strathroy/RR Stn., ON. | Canada |
| XUY | Auray | France |
| XUZ | Xuzhou | China |
| XVA | Stockport/RR Stn. | UK |
| XVB | Stafford/RR Stn. | UK |
| XVC | Crewe/RR Stn. | UK |
| XVD | Vendome | France |
| XVE | Versailles | France |
| XVF | Villefranche Sur Saone | France |
| XVG | Darlington/RR Stn. | UK |
| XVH | Peterborough/RR Stn. | UK |
| XVI | Vienne | France |
| XVJ | Stevenage/RR Stn. | UK |
| XVL | Vinh Long | Vietnam |
| XVN | Verdun | France |
| XVO | Vesoul | France |

| | | |
|---|---|---|
| XVP | Villepinte | France |
| XVR | Valloire. | France |
| XVS | Valenciennes/RR Stn. | France |
| XVT | Vitre | France |
| XVU | Durham/RR Stn. | UK |
| XVV | Belleville/RR Stn., ON | Canada |
| XVW | Wolverhampton-RR | UK |
| XVX | Vejle/RR Stn. | Denmark |
| XVZ | Vierzon | France |
| XWA | Watford/RR Stn., ON | Canada |
| XWB | Stirling/RR Stn. | UK |
| XWD | Wakefield Westgate/RR Stn. | UK |
| XWE | Wellingborough/RR Stn. | UK |
| XWH | Stoke on Trent/RR Stn. | UK |
| XWI | Wigan N.W./RR Stn. | UK |
| XWN | Warrington B.Q./RR Stn. | UK |
| XWO | Woking/RR Stn. | UK |
| XWS | Swindon/RR Stn. | UK |
| XWY | Wyoming/RR Stn., ON | Canada |
| XXB | Bhadohi. | India |
| XXF | Scenic Flight | New Zealand |
| XXH | Helicopter Scenic | New Zealand |
| XXP | Potsdam | Germany |
| XXS | Skiplane Scenic | New Zealand |
| XYA | Yandina | Solomon Is |
| XYD | Lyon/Lyon Part-Dieu Rail Svc. | France |
| XYE | Ye. | Myanmar |
| XYL | Lyon/Lyon Perrache Rail Svc | |
| | | France |
| XYR | Yellow River | Papua New Guinea |
| XYT | Toulouse/Montaudran | France |
| XYV | Lyon/Lyon Satolas Rail Svc. | France |
| XZA | Zabre. | Burkina Faso |
| XZB | Casselman/RR Stn., ON | Canada |
| XZC | Glencoe/RR Stn., ON | Canada |
| XZK | Amherst/RR Stn., NS. | Canada |
| XZL | Edmonton/RR Stn., AB | Canada |
| XZP | Pass (Generic), QC | Canada |
| XZR | Rail (Generic), QC | Canada |
| XZY | Alzey | Germany |

# Y

| | | |
|---|---|---|
| YAA | Anahim Lake, BC | Canada |
| YAB | Arctic Bay, NU | Canada |
| YAC | Cat Lake, ON | Canada |
| YAD | Moose Lake, MB | Canada |
| YAE | Alta Lake, BC | Canada |
| YAF | Asbestos Hill, QC | Canada |
| YAG | Ft. Frances/Mun, ON. | Canada |
| YAH | La Grande, QC. | Canada |
| YAI | Chillan | Chile |
| YAJ | Lyall Harbour, BC | Canada |
| YAK | Yakutat, AK. | USA |
| YAL | Alert Bay, BC | Canada |
| YAM | Sault Ste Marie, ON. | Canada |
| YAN | Yangambi | Congo, DR |
| YAO | Yaounde/Yaciunde Arpt. | Cameroon |
| YAP | Yap | Micronesia |
| YAQ | Maple Bay, BC | Canada |
| YAR | Lagrange 3, QC | Canada |
| YAS | Yasawa Is | Fiji |
| YAT | Attawapiskat, ON | Canada |
| YAU | Kattiniq/Donaldson Lak, QC | Canada |
| YAV | Miners Bay, BC | Canada |
| YAW | Shearwater, NS | Canada |
| YAX | Angling Lake, ON. | Canada |
| YAY | St Anthony, NF | Canada |
| YAZ | Tofino, BC | Canada |
| YBA | Banff, AB. | Canada |
| YBB | Pelly Bay, NU | Canada |
| YBC | Baie Comeau, QC | Canada |
| YBD | New Westminster, BC | Canada |
| YBE | Uranium City, SK | Canada |
| YBF | Bamfield, BC | Canada |
| YBG | Bagotville, QC | Canada |
| YBH | Bull Harbour, BC | Canada |
| YBI | Black Tickle, NF | Canada |
| YBJ | Bale Johan Beetz, QC. | Canada |
| YBK | Baker Lake, NT | Canada |
| YBL | Campbell River, BC | Canada |
| YBM | Bronson Creek, BC | Canada |
| YBN | Borden, ON | Canada |
| YBO | Bobquinn Lake, BC | Canada |
| YBP | Yibin. | China |
| YBQ | Telegraph Harbour, BC | Canada |
| YBR | Brandon, MB | Canada |
| YBS | Opapamiska Lake/Musselwhite, | |

| | | |
|---|---|---|
| | ON | Canada |
| YBT | Brochet, MB | Canada |
| YBU | Nipawin, SK. | Canada |
| YBV | Berens River, MB | Canada |
| YBW | Springbank, AB. | Canada |
| YBX | Blanc Sablon, QC | Canada |
| YBY | Bonnyville, AB. | Canada |
| YBZ | Toronto/Downtown RR Stn., ON | |
| | | Canada |
| YCA | Courtenay, BC. | Canada |
| YCB | Cambridge Bay, NT | Canada |
| YCC | Cornwall/Regional, ON | Canada |
| YCD | Nanaimo, BC. | Canada |
| YCE | Centralia, ON | Canada |
| YCF | Cortes Bay, BC | Canada |
| YCG | Castlegar, BC | Canada |
| YCH | Miramichi, NB | Canada |
| YCI | Caribou Is, ON | Canada |
| YCJ | Cape St James, BC | Canada |
| YCK | Colville Lake, NT. | Canada |
| YCL | Charlo, NB. | Canada |
| YCM | St Catharines, ON. | Canada |
| YCN | Cochrane, ON. | Canada |
| YCO | Coppermine, NU. | Canada |
| YCP | Blue River, BC. | Canada |
| YCQ | Chetwynd, BC. | Canada |
| YCR | Cross Lake, MB | Canada |
| YCS | Chesterfield Inlet, NU | Canada |
| YCT | Coronation, AB | Canada |
| YCV | Cartierville, QC | Canada |
| YCW | Chilliwack, BC. | Canada |
| YCX | Gagetown, NB | Canada |
| YCY | Clyde River, NU | Canada |
| YCZ | Fairmount Springs, BC. | Canada |
| YDA | Dawson, YT | Canada |
| YDB | Burwash Landings, YT. | Canada |
| YDC | Drayton Valley, AB | Canada |
| YDE | Paradise River, NF | Canada |
| YDF | Deer Lake, NF. | Canada |
| YDG | Djgby, NS. | Canada |
| YDH | Daniels Harbour, NF. | Canada |
| YDI | Davis Inlet, NF. | Canada |
| YDJ | Hatchet Lake, SK | Canada |
| YDK | Main Duck Is, ON | Canada |
| YDL | Dease Lake, BC | Canada |
| YDN | Dauphin, MB. | Canada |
| YDO | Dolbeau/St Methode, QC. | Canada |
| YDP | Nain, NF | Canada |
| YDQ | Dawson Creek, BC. | Canada |
| YDR | Broadview, SK. | Canada |
| YDS | Desolation Sound, BC | Canada |
| YDT | Vancouver/Boundary Bay, BC | |
| | | Canada |
| YDU | Kasba Lake, NT | Canada |
| YDV | Bloodvein, MB. | Canada |
| YDW | Obre Lake, NT | Canada |
| YDX | Doc Creek, BC | Canada |
| YEC | Yechon/Air Base | S. Korea |
| YED | Edmonton Namao, AB. | Canada |
| YEG | Edmonton Int'l, AB | Canada |
| YEI | Bursa | Turkey |
| YEK | Arviat, NU | Canada |
| YEL | Elliot Lake, ON | Canada |
| YEM | Manitowaning/East Manitoulin, | |
| | ON | Canada |
| YEN | Estevan, SK | Canada |
| YEO | Yeovilton-RNAS | UK |
| YEP | Estevan Point, BC | Canada |
| YEQ | Yenkis | Papua New Guinea |
| YER | Ft. Severn, ON | Canada |
| YET | Edson, AB | Canada |
| YEU | Eureka, MB | Canada |
| YEV | Inuvik, NT | Canada |
| YEY | Amos, QC | Canada |
| YFA | Ft. Albany, ON. | Canada |
| YFB | Iqaluit, NT | Canada |
| YFC | Fredericton, NB. | Canada |
| YFE | Forestville, QC | Canada |
| YFG | Fontanges, QC | Canada |
| YFH | Ft. Hope, ON. | Canada |
| YFJ | Snare Lake, NT. | Canada |
| YFL | Ft. Reliance, NT | Canada |
| YFO | Flin Flon, MB | Canada |
| YFR | Ft. Resolution, NT. | Canada |
| YFS | Ft. Simpson, NT | Canada |
| YFT | Makkovik Arpt | Canada |
| YFX | Fox Harbour (St Lewis), NG | |
| | | Canada |
| YGA | Gagnon, QC | Canada |
| YGB | Gillies Bay, BC | Canada |
| YGC | Grande Cache, AB. | Canada |

| Code | Location | Country |
|------|----------|---------|
| YGE | Gorge Harbor, BC | Canada |
| YGG | Ganges Harbor, BC | Canada |
| YGH | Ft. Good Hope, NT | Canada |
| YGJ | Yonago/Miho | Japan |
| YGK | Kingston, ON | Canada |
| YGL | La Grande, QC | Canada |
| YGM | Gimli, MB | Canada |
| YGN | Greenway Sound, BC | Canada |
| YGO | Gods Narrows, MB | Canada |
| YGP | Gaspe, QC | Canada |
| YGQ | Geraldton, ON | Canada |
| YGR | Iles De La MadeleineQC | Canada |
| YGS | Germansen, BC | Canada |
| YGT | Igloolik, BC | Canada |
| YGV | Havre St Pierre, QC | Canada |
| YGW | Kuujjuarapik, QC | Canada |
| YGX | Gillam, MB | Canada |
| YGY | Deception, QC | Canada |
| YGZ | Grise Fiord, NU | Canada |
| YHA | Port Hope Simpson, NF | Canada |
| YHB | Hudson Bay, SK | Canada |
| YHC | Hakai Pass, BC | Canada |
| YHD | Dryden, ON | Canada |
| YHE | Hope, BC | Canada |
| YHF | Hearst, OH | Canada |
| YHG | Charlottetown, NF | Canada |
| YHH | Campbell River/Harbor SPB, BC | Canada |
| YHI | Holman, NT | Canada |
| YHK | Gjoa Haven, NU | Canada |
| YHM | Hamilton, ON | Canada |
| YHN | Hornepayne, ON | Canada |
| YHO | Hopedale, NF | Canada |
| YHP | Poplar Hill, ON | Canada |
| YHR | Chevery, QC | Canada |
| YHS | Secheit, BC | Canada |
| YHT | Haines Junction, YT | Canada |
| YHU | Montreal-St. Hubert, QC | Canada |
| YHY | Hay River, NT | Canada |
| YHZ | Halifax Int'l, NS | Canada |
| YIB | Atikokan, ON | Canada |
| YIF | Pakuashipi, QC | Canada |
| YIG | Big Bay Marina, BC | Canada |
| YIH | Yichang, QC | China |
| YIK | Ivujivik, QC | Canada |
| YIN | Yining | China |
| YIO | Pond Inlet, NU | Canada |
| YIP | Detroit-Willow Run, MI | USA |
| YIV | Is Lake, MB | Canada |
| YIW | Yiwu | China |
| YJF | Ft. Liard, NT | Canada |
| YJN | St Jean, QC | Canada |
| YJO | Johnny Mountain, BC | Canada |
| YJP | Jasper-Hinton, AB | Canada |
| YJT | Stephenville, NF | Canada |
| YKA | Kamloops. BC | Canada |
| YKC | Collins Bay, SK | Canada |
| YKD | Kincardine, ON | Canada |
| YKE | Knee Lake, MB | Canada |
| YKF | Kitchener, ON | Canada |
| YKG | Kangirsuk, QC | Canada |
| YKI | Kennosao Lake, MB | Canada |
| YKJ | Key Lake, SK | Canada |
| YKK | Kitkatla, BC | Canada |
| YKL | Schefferville, QC | Canada |
| YKM | Yakima, WA | USA |
| YKN | Yankton/Chan Gurney, SD | USA |
| YKQ | Waskaganish, QC | Canada |
| YKS | Yakutsk | Russia |
| YKT | Kierritu, BC | Canada |
| YKU | Chisasibi, QC | Canada |
| YKX | Kirkland Lake, ON | Canada |
| YKY | Kindersley, SK | Canada |
| YKZ | Toronto Buttonville, ON | Canada |
| YLA | Langara, BC | Canada |
| YLB | Lac Biche, AB | Canada |
| YLC | Kimmirut, NT | Canada |
| YLD | Chapleau, ON | Canada |
| YLE | Wha Ti/Lac La Martre, NT | Canada |
| YLF | LaForges, QC | Canada |
| YLG | Yalgoo | Australia |
| YLH | Lansdowne House, ON | Canada |
| YLI | Ylivieska | Finland |
| YLJ | Meadow Lake, SK | Canada |
| YLL | Lloydminister, AB | Canada |
| YLM | Clinton Creek, YT | Canada |
| YLN | Yilan | China |
| YLO | Shilo-YLP Mingan, MB | Canada |
| YLP | Mingan, QC | Canada |
| YLQ | La Tuclue, QC | Canada |
| YLR | Leaf Rapids, MB | Canada |
| YLS | Lebel-Sur-Quevillon, QC | Canada |
| YLT | Alert, NU | Canada |
| YLW | Kelowna, BC | Canada |
| YLX | Long Point, ON | Canada |
| YMA | Mayo, YT | Canada |
| YMB | Merritt, BC | Canada |
| YMC | Maricourt Airstrip, QC | Canada |
| YMD | Mould Bay, NT | Canada |
| YME | Matane, QC | Canada |
| YMF | Montagne Harbor, BC | Canada |
| YMG | Manitouwadge, ON | Canada |
| YMH | Mary's Harbour, NF | Canada |
| YMI | Minaki, ON | Canada |
| YMJ | Moose Jaw, SK | Canada |
| YML | Murray Bay, QC | Canada |
| YMM | Ft. Mcmurray, AB | Canada |
| YMN | Makkovik, NF | Canada |
| YMO | Moosonee, ON | Canada |
| YMP | Port McNeil, BC | Canada |
| YMR | Merry Is, BC | Canada |
| YMS | Yurimaguas | Peru |
| YMT | Chibougamau, QC | Canada |
| YMW | Maniwaki, QC | Canada |
| YMX | Montreal/Mirabel, QC | Canada |
| YMY | Montreal/Downtown RR Stn., QC | Canada |
| YNA | Natashquan, QC | Canada |
| YNB | Yanbu | Saudi Arabia |
| YNC | Wemindpi, QC | Canada |
| YND | Gatineati, ON | Canada |
| YNE | Norway House, MB | Canada |
| YNF | Corner Brook/Deer Lake, NF | Canada |
| YNG | Youngstown, OH | USA |
| YNH | Hudson's Hope, BC | Canada |
| YNI | Nitchequon, QC | Canada |
| YNJ | Yanji | China |
| YNK | Nootka Sound, BC | Canada |
| YNL | Points North Landing, SK | Canada |
| YNM | Matagami, QC | Canada |
| YNO | North Spirit Lake, ON | Canada |
| YNR | Arnes, MB | Canada |
| YNS | Nemiscau, QC | Canada |
| YNT | Yantai/Laishan | China |
| YNZ | Yancheng | China |
| YOA | Ekati, NT | Canada |
| YOC | Old Crow, YT | Canada |
| YOD | Cold Lake, AB | Canada |
| YOE | Falher, AB | Canada |
| YOG | Ogoki, ON | Canada |
| YOH | Oxford House, MB | Canada |
| YOJ | High Level, AB | Canada |
| YOK | Yokohama | Japan |
| YOL | Yola | Nigeria |
| YOO | Oshawa, ON | Canada |
| YOP | Rainbow Lake, AB | Canada |
| YOS | Owen Sound/Billy Bishop Regional, ON | Canada |
| YOT | Yotvata | Israel |
| YOW | Ottawa Int'l, ON | Canada |
| YOY | Valcartier, QC | Canada |
| YPA | Prince Albert,SK | Canada |
| YPB | Port Allberni, BC | Canada |
| YPC | Paulatuk, NT | Canada |
| YPD | Parry Sound, ON | Canada |
| YPE | Peace River, AB | Canada |
| YPF | Esquimalt, BC | Canada |
| YPG | Portage La Prairie, MB | Canada |
| YPH | Inulkjualk, QC | Canada |
| YPI | Port Simpson, BC | Canada |
| YPJ | Aupaluk, QC | Canada |
| YPL | Pickle Lake, ON | Canada |
| YPM | Pikangikum, ON | Canada |
| YPN | Port Menier, MB | Canada |
| YPO | Peawanuck, ON | Canada |
| YPP | Pine Point, NT | Canada |
| YPQ | Peterborough, ON | Canada |
| YPR | Prince Rupert, BC | Canada |
| YPS | Port Hawkesbury, NS | Canada |
| YPT | Pender Harbor, BC | Canada |
| YPW | Powell River, BC | Canada |
| YPX | Povungnituk, QC | Canada |
| YPY | Ft. Chipewyan, AB | Canada |
| YPZ | Burns Lake, BC | Canada |
| YQA | Muskoka, ON | Canada |
| YQB | Quebec, QC | Canada |
| YQC | Quaqtaq, QC | Canada |
| YQD | The Pas, MB | Canada |
| YQE | Kimberley, QC | Canada |
| YQF | Red Deer, AB | Canada |
| YQG | Windsor, ON | Canada |
| YQH | Watson Lake, YT | Canada |
| YQI | Yarmouth, NS | Canada |
| YQK | Kenora, ON | Canada |
| YQL | Lethbridge, AB | Canada |
| YQM | Moncton, NB | Canada |
| YQN | Nakina, ON | Canada |
| YQQ | Comox, BC | Canada |
| YQR | Regina, SK | Canada |
| YQS | St Thomas/Pembroke Area, ON | Canada |
| YQT | Thunder Bay, ON | Canada |
| YQU | Grande Prairie, AB | Canada |
| YQV | Yorkton, SK | Canada |
| YQW | North Battleford, SK | Canada |
| YQX | Gander Int'l, NF | Canada |
| YQY | Sydney, NS | Canada |
| YQZ | Ouesnel, BC | Canada |
| YRA | Rae Lakes, NT | Canada |
| YRB | Resolute, NT | Canada |
| YRD | Dean River, BC | Canada |
| YRE | Resolution Is, NU | Canada |
| YRF | Cartwright, NF | Canada |
| YRG | Rigolet, NF | Canada |
| YRI | Riviere Du Loup, QC | Canada |
| YRJ | Roberval, QC | Canada |
| YRL | Red Lake, ON | Canada |
| YRM | Rocky Mountain House, AB | Canada |
| YRN | Rivers Inlet, BC | Canada |
| YRO | Ottawa/Rockcliffe St, ON | Canada |
| YRQ | Trois-Rivieres, QC | Canada |
| YRR | Stuart Is, BC | Canada |
| YRS | Red Sucker Lake, MB | Canada |
| YRT | Rankin Inlet, NT | Canada |
| YRV | Revelstoke, BC | Canada |
| YSA | Sable Is, NS | Canada |
| YSB | Sudbury, ON | Canada |
| YSC | Sherbrooke, QC | Canada |
| YSD | Suffield, AB | Canada |
| YSE | Squamish, BC | Canada |
| YSF | Stony Rapids, SK | Canada |
| YSG | Lutselke/Snowdrift, NT | Canada |
| YSH | Smith Falls, ON | Canada |
| YSI | Sans Souci, ON | Canada |
| YSJ | Saint John, NB | Canada |
| YSK | Sanikiluaq, NU | Canada |
| YSL | St Leonard, NB | Canada |
| YSM | Ft. Smith, NT | Canada |
| YSN | Salmon Arm, BC | Canada |
| YSO | Postville, NF | Canada |
| YSP | Marathon, ON | Canada |
| YSQ | Spring Is, BC | Canada |
| YSR | Nanisivik, NU | Canada |
| YSS | Slate Is, ON | Canada |
| YST | Ste Therese Point, MB | Canada |
| YSU | Summerside, PE | Canada |
| YSY | Saglek, NF | Canada |
| YSX | Shearwater, BC | Canada |
| YSY | Sachs Harbour, NT | Canada |
| YSZ | Squirrel Cove, BC | Canada |
| YTA | Pembroke, ON | Canada |
| YTB | Hartley Bay, BC | Canada |
| YTC | Sturdee, BC | Canada |
| YTD | Thicket Portage, MB | Canada |
| YTE | Cape Dorset, NT | Canada |
| YTF | Alma, QC | Canada |
| YTG | Sullivan Say, BC | Canada |
| YTH | Thompson, MB | Canada |
| YTI | Triple Is, BC | Canada |
| YTJ | Terrace Bay, ON | Canada |
| YTK | Tuiugak, QC | Canada |
| YTL | Big Trout, ON | Canada |
| YTN | Riviere Au Tonnerre, QC | Canada |
| YTO | Guildwood/Toronto, ON | Canada |
| YTP | Tofino/Seaplane Base, BC | Canada |
| YTQ | Tasiujuaq, QC | Canada |
| YTR | Trenton, ON | Canada |
| YTS | Timmins, ON | Canada |
| YTT | Tisdale, SK | Canada |
| YTU | Tasu, BC | Canada |
| YTX | Telegraph Creek, BC | Canada |
| YTZ | Toronto/Toronto Is, ON | Canada |
| YUA | Yuanmou | China |
| YUB | Tukloyaktuk, NT | Canada |
| YUD | Umiujaq, QC | Canada |
| YUE | Yuendurnu | Australia |
| YUL | Montreal Int'l, QC | Canada |
| YUM | Yuma Int'l, AZ | USA |
| YUT | Repulse Bay, NU | Canada |
| YUX | Hall Beach, NU | Canada |
| YUY | Rouyn, QC | Canada |
| YVA | Moroni/Iconi | Comoros |
| YVB | Bonaventure, QC | Canada |

| Code | Location | Country |
|------|----------|---------|
| YVC | La Ronge, SK | Canada |
| YVD | Yeva | Papua New Guinea |
| YVE | Vernon, BC. | Canada |
| YVG | Vermilion, AB | Canada |
| YVM | Qikiqtarjuaq, NU | Canada |
| YVO | Val D'Or, QC. | Canada |
| YVP | Kuujjuaq, QC | Canada |
| YVQ | Norman Wells, NT. | Canada |
| YVR | Vancouver Int'l, BC | Canada |
| YVT | Buffalo Narrows, SK | Canada |
| YVV | Wiarton, ON. | Canada |
| YVZ | Deer Lake, ON | Canada |
| YWA | Petawawa, ON | Canada |
| YWB | Kangiqsujuaq, QC. | Canada |
| YWF | Halifax/Dwtown Waterfront HP, NS. | Canada |
| YWG | Winnipeg Int'l, MB | Canada |
| YWH | Victoria Harbour, BC | Canada |
| YWJ | Deline, NT | Canada |
| YWK | Wabush, NF. | Canada |
| YWL | Williams Lake, BC. | Canada |
| YWM | Williams Harbour, NF | Canada |
| YWN | Winisk, ON. | Canada |
| YWO | Lupin, NT | Canada |
| YWP | Welbequie, ON | Canada |
| YWQ | Chute-Des-Passes, QC | Canada |
| YWR | White River, ON. | Canada |
| YWS | Whistler, BC | Canada |
| YWV | Wainwright Arpt, AB | Canada |
| YWY | Wrigley, NT. | Canada |
| YXC | Cranbrook, BC. | Canada |
| YXD | Edmonton, AB | Canada |
| YXE | Saskatoon, SK. | Canada |
| YXF | Snake River, YT | Canada |
| YXH | Medicine Hat, AB. | Canada |
| YXI | Kilialoe, ON | Canada |
| YXJ | Fort St John, BC | Canada |
| YXK | Rimouski, QC | Canada |
| YXL | Sioux Lookout, ON | Canada |
| YXN | Whale Cove, NU | Canada |
| YXP | Pangnirtung, NU | Canada |
| YXQ | Beaver Creek, YT | Canada |
| YXR | Earlton, ON | Canada |
| YXS | Prince George, BC | Canada |
| YXT | Terrace, BC | Canada |
| YXU | London, ON | Canada |
| YXX | Abbotsford, BC | Canada |
| YXY | Withehorse, YT | Canada |
| YXZ | Wawa, ON | Canada |
| YY | Clyde, NT | Canada |
| YYA | Big Bay Yacht Club, BC | Canada |
| YYB | North Bay, ON | Canada |
| YYC | Calgary Int'l, AB | Canada |
| YYD | Smithers, BC | Canada |
| YYE | Ft. Nelson, BC | Canada |
| YYF | Penticton, BC. | Canada |
| YYG | Charlottetown, PE | Canada |
| YYH | Spence Bay Arpt, NU | Canada |
| YYI | Rivers, MB | Canada |
| YYJ | Victoria Int'l, BC | Canada |
| YYL | Lynn Lake, MB. | Canada |
| YYM | Cowley, AB. | Canada |
| YYN | Swift Current, SK. | Canada |
| YYQ | Churchill, MB | Canada |
| YYR | Goose, NF | Canada |
| YYT | St. John's, NF. | Canada |
| YYU | Kapuskasing, ON | Canada |
| YYW | Armstrong, ON | Canada |
| YYY | Mont Joli, QC. | Canada |
| YYZ | Toronto-Pearson Int'l., ON | Canada |
| YZA | Ashcrott, BC. | Canada |
| YZC | Beatton River, BC | Canada |
| YZE | Gore Bay, ON | Canada |
| YZF | Yellowknife, NT | Canada |
| YZG | Salluit, QC | Canada |
| YZH | Slave Lake, AB | Canada |
| YZM | Buchans, NF | Canada |
| YZP | Sandspit, BC | Canada |
| YZR | Sarnia, ON. | Canada |
| YZS | Coral Harbour, NT. | Canada |
| YZT | Port Hardy, BC. | Canada |
| YZU | Whitecourt, AB. | Canada |
| YZV | Sept-Iles, QC. | Canada |
| YZW | Teslin, YT. | Canada |
| YZX | Greenwood, NS. | Canada |
| YZY | Mackenzie, BC. | Canada |

# Z

| Code | Location | Country |
|------|----------|---------|
| ZAA | Alice Arm, BC. | Canada |
| ZAB | Boukadir | Algeria |
| ZAC | York Landing. | Mongolia |
| ZAD | Zadar. | Croatia |
| ZAE | El Eulma | Algeria |
| ZAF | Arles/RR Stn. | France |
| ZAG | Zagreb/Pleso | Croatia |
| ZAH | Zahedan | Iran |
| ZAI | Embarcacion | Argentina |
| ZAJ | Zaranj | Afghanistan |
| ZAK | Chiusa/Klausen/Bus Stn | Italy |
| ZAL | Valdivia/Pichoy | Chile |
| ZAM | Zamboanga | Philippines |
| ZAN | Aghios Nicolaos | Greece |
| ZAO | Cahors/Laberande. | France |
| ZAP | Appenzell | Switzerland |
| ZAQ | Nuremberg/HBF Railway Svc | Germany |
| ZAR | Zaria | Nigeria |
| ZAS | Arenshausen/RR Stn. | Germany |
| ZAT | Zhaotong. | China |
| ZAU | Aue/RR Stn. | Germany |
| ZAV | Aveiro | Portugal |
| ZAW | Nyikobing Mors/Bus Svc. | Denmark |
| ZAX | Angermuende/RR Stn. | Germany |
| ZAY | Antwerp/De Keyserlei Bus Stn | Belgium |
| ZAZ | Zaragoza. | Spain |
| ZBA | Basel/Mulhouse/German Railway Svc. | Switzerland |
| ZBB | Esbjerg/RR Stn. | Denmark |
| ZBC | Birmingham/Colmore Row Bus Stn | UK |
| ZBD | Bad Brambach/RR Stn. | Germany |
| ZBE | Zabreh/Dolni Benesov. | Czech Rep |
| ZBF | Bathurst, NB. | Canada |
| ZBG | Elblag | Poland |
| ZBH | Severac Le Chateau/RR Stn. | France |
| ZBI | Berriane | Algeria |
| ZBJ | Fredericia/RR Stn. | Denmark |
| ZBK | Zabljak. | Yugoslavia |
| ZBL | Biloela | Australia |
| ZBM | Bromont, QC | Canada |
| ZBN | Bozen/Bus Stn | Italy |
| ZBO | Bowen. | Australia |
| ZBP | Baltimore/Baltimore Rail, MD | USA |
| ZBQ | Odense/RR Stn. | Denmark |
| ZBR | Chah-Bahar | Iran |
| ZBS | Mesa/Bus Svc, AZ. | USA |
| ZBT | Kolding/RR Stn. | Denmark |
| ZBU | Aarhus/Limousine Svc. | Denmark |
| ZBV | Vail/Eagle/Beaver Creek Van Svc, CO. | USA |
| ZBW | Atibaia. | Brazil |
| ZBX | Szombathely. | Hungary |
| ZBY | Sayaboury | Laos |
| ZBZ | Bad Saizurigen/RR Stn. | Germany |
| ZCA | Amsberg | Germany |
| ZCB | Aschaffenburg | Germany |
| ZCC | Baden-Baden | Germany |
| ZCD | Bamberg/Off-line Pt. | Germany |
| ZCE | Berchtesgaden. | Germany |
| ZCF | Bergheim (Cologne) | Germany |
| ZCG | Bergisch Gladbach | Germany |
| ZCH | Bergkamen/Off-line Pt. | Germany |
| ZCI | Bocholt | Germany |
| ZCJ | Bottrop. | Germany |
| ZCK | Bruehl | Germany |
| ZCL | Zacatecas/La Calera | Mexico |
| ZCM | Castrop-Rauxel | Germany |
| ZCN | Celle | Germany |
| ZCO | Temuco | Chile |
| ZCP | Coburg | Germany |
| ZCQ | Curico | Chile |
| ZCR | Dachau | Germany |
| ZCS | Darmstact | Germany |
| ZCT | Delmenhorst. | Germany |
| ZCU | Detmold. | Germany |
| ZCV | Dinslaken | Germany |
| ZCW | Dormagen. | Germany |
| ZCX | Dorsten | Germany |
| ZCY | Dueren | Germany |
| ZCZ | Erlangen | Germany |
| ZDA | Aarau. | Switzerland |
| ZDB | Adelboden | Switzerland |
| ZDC | Aiale | Switzerland |
| ZDD | Arbon. | Switzerland |

| Code | Location | Country |
|------|----------|---------|
| ZDE | Arosa | Switzerland |
| ZDF | Nablus | West Bank |
| ZDG | Baden | Switzerland |
| ZDH | Basel/Mulhouse/SBB Railway Svc | Switzerland |
| ZDI | Bellinzona | Switzerland |
| ZDJ | Berne | Switzerland |
| ZDK | Biel/Bienne | Switzerland |
| ZDL | Brig. | Switzerland |
| ZDM | Ramallah | West Bank |
| ZDN | Brno/Bus Svc | Czech Rep |
| ZDO | Buchs SG | Switzerland |
| ZDP | Burgdorf. | Switzerland |
| ZDQ | Champery | Switzerland |
| ZDR | Chateau-d-Oex. | Switzerland |
| ZDS | Chasso | Switzerland |
| ZDT | Chur. | Switzerland |
| ZDU | Dundee/ScotRail. | UK |
| ZDV | Davos. | Switzerland |
| ZDW | Delemont. | Switzerland |
| ZDX | Dietikon | Switzerland |
| ZDY | Gaza Strip | Occupied Palestinian Ter |
| ZDZ | Einsiedeln | Switzerland |
| ZEA | Eschweiler. | Germany |
| ZEB | Esslingen. | Germany |
| ZEC | Secunda | S. Africa |
| ZED | Euskirchen. | Germany |
| ZEE | Fulda | Germany |
| ZEF | Fuerth. | Germany |
| ZEG | Senggo | Indonesia |
| ZEH | Garbsen. | Germany |
| ZEI | Garmisch-Partenkirchen | Germany |
| ZEJ | Gelsenkirchen. | Germany |
| ZEK | Gladbeck | Germany |
| ZEL | Bella Bella, BC | Canada |
| ZEM | East Main, QC. | Canada |
| ZEN | Zenag. | Papua New Guinea |
| ZEO | Savi Ragha | Pakistan |
| ZEP | London/Victoria Railway Stn | UK |
| ZEQ | Dewsbury/Bus Stn | UK |
| ZER | Zero | India |
| ZES | Goeppingen | Germany |
| ZET | Goslar | Germany |
| ZEU | Goettingen. | Germany |
| ZEV | Grevenbroich | Germany |
| ZEW | Gummersbach | Germany |
| ZEX | Guetersloh. | Germany |
| ZEY | Hagen | Germany |
| ZEZ | Hameln | Germany |
| ZFA | Faro, YT. | Canada |
| ZFB | Old Ft. Bay, QC. | Canada |
| ZFC | Bradford/Bus Stn. | UK |
| ZFD | Fond Du Lac, SK | Canada |
| ZFE | Beltsville, MO/Off-line Pt. | USA |
| ZFF | Tulsa/Off-Line Pt (Fedex), OK. | USA |
| ZFG | Sheffield/Bus Svc | UK |
| ZFH | Milton Keynes/Bus Svc | UK |
| ZFI | Chesterfield/Bus Svc | UK |
| ZFJ | Rennes/Gare de Rennes. | France |
| ZFL | South Trout Lake, ON | Canada |
| ZFM | Ft. Mcpherson, NT | Canada |
| ZFN | Tulita/Ft. Norman, NT. | Canada |
| ZFO | Franconia, VA. | USA |
| ZFP | Veszprem | Hungary |
| ZFQ | Bordeaux/Gare de Bordeaux | France |
| ZFR | Frankfurt/Oder/RR Stn. | Germany |
| ZFS | Sabre-Tech, FL. | USA |
| ZFT | Ft. Lauderdale/RR Stn., FL | USA |
| ZFV | Philadelphia/Philadelphia Rail, P. | USA |
| ZFW | Fairview, AB | Canada |
| ZFZ | Buffalo/Buffalo Depew RR, NY | USA |
| ZGA | Gera/RR Stn. | Germany |
| ZGB | Nottingham/Bus Svc. | UK |
| ZGC | Lanzhou/Zhongchuan | China |
| ZGD | Groton/New London Rail, CT | USA |
| ZGE | Goerlitz/RR Stn. | Germany |
| ZGF | Grand Forks, BC. | Canada |
| ZGG | Glasgow/ScotRail | UK |
| ZGH | Copenhagen/RR Stn. | Denmark |
| ZGI | Gods River, MB. | Canada |
| ZGJ | Brugge. | Belgium |
| ZGK | Leuven. | Belgium |
| ZGL | South Galway | Australia |
| ZGM | Ngoma. | Zambia |
| ZGN | Gutenfuerst/RR Stn. | Germany |
| ZGO | Gotha/RR Stn. | Germany |
| ZGP | Mechelen. | Belgium |
| ZGQ | Tournai. | Belgium |
| ZGR | Little Grand Rapids, MB. | Canada |
| ZGS | Gethsemani, QC. | Canada |
| ZGT | Gerstungen/RR Stn. | Germany |

| Code | Name | Country |
|------|------|---------|
| ZGU | Gaua | Vanuatu |
| ZGV | Wavre | Belgium |
| ZGW | Greifswald/RR Stn. | Germany |
| ZGX | Viborg/RR Stn. | Denmark |
| ZHA | Zhanjiang | China |
| ZHB | Engelberg | Switzerland |
| ZHC | Philadelphia/N Philadelphia Rail Station, PA | USA |
| ZHD | Fluelen | Switzerland |
| ZHE | Frauenfeld | Switzerland |
| ZHF | Fribourg | Switzerland |
| ZHG | Glarus | Switzerland |
| ZHH | Gossau SG | Switzerland |
| ZHI | Grenchen | Switzerland |
| ZHJ | Grindelwald | Switzerland |
| ZHK | Gstaad | Switzerland |
| ZHL | Heerbrugg | Switzerland |
| ZHM | Shamshernagar | Bangladesh |
| ZHN | Herzogenbuchsee | Switzerland |
| ZHO | Houston/Bus Stn, BC | Canada |
| ZHP | High Prairie, AB | Canada |
| ZHQ | Halberstadt/RR Stn. | Germany |
| ZHR | Kandersteg | Switzerland |
| ZHS | Klosters | Switzerland |
| ZHT | Geneva-Cornavin/RR Stn. | Switzerland |
| ZHU | Kreuzlingen | Switzerland |
| ZHV | La Chaux-de-Fonds | Switzerland |
| ZHW | Langenthal | Switzerland |
| ZHX | Tubarao | Brazil |
| ZHY | Geneva Aeroport/RR Stn. | Switzerland |
| ZHZ | Halle/RR Stn. | Germany |
| ZIA | Trento | Italy |
| ZIB | Nyborg/RR Stn. | Denmark |
| ZIC | Victoria | Chile |
| ZID | Aarhus/Bus Svc. | Denmark |
| ZIG | Ziguinchor | Senegal |
| ZIH | Ixtapa/Zihuatanejo/Int'l | Mexico |
| ZIJ | Sjaelland/RR Stn. | Denmark |
| ZIM | Odense/Bus Svc | Denmark |
| ZIN | Interlaken | Switzerland |
| ZIO | Solingen-Ohligs/RR Stn. | Germany |
| ZIR | Randers/RR Stn. | Denmark |
| ZIS | Zhongshan | China |
| ZIT | Zittau/RR Stn. | Germany |
| ZIV | Inverness/ScotRail | UK |
| ZJA | Le Locle | Switzerland |
| ZJC | Lenzburg | Switzerland |
| ZJD | Lenzerheide/Lai | Switzerland |
| ZJG | Jenpeg, MB | Canada |
| ZJH | Aarhus/RR Stn. | Denmark |
| ZJI | Locarno | Switzerland |
| ZJL | Lyss | Switzerland |
| ZJM | Martigny | Switzerland |
| ZJN | Swan River, MB | Canada |
| ZJO | San Jose/Bus Svc, CA | USA |
| ZJP | Montreux | Switzerland |
| ZJQ | Morges | Switzerland |
| ZJS | Jena/RR Stn. | Germany |
| ZJU | Olten | Switzerland |
| ZJV | Pontresina | Switzerland |
| ZJW | Rapperswil | Switzerland |
| ZJZ | Rorschach | Switzerland |
| ZKA | Sargans | Switzerland |
| ZKB | Kasaba Bay | Zambia |
| ZKC | Sarnen | Switzerland |
| ZKD | Moscow/Leningradsky RR Stn. | Russia |
| ZKE | Kaschechewan, ON | Canada |
| ZKF | St Margrethen | Switzerland |
| ZKG | Kegaska, QC | Canada |
| ZKH | St Moritz | Switzerland |
| ZKI | Saas Fee | Switzerland |
| ZKJ | Schaffhausen | Switzerland |
| ZKK | Schwyz | Switzerland |
| ZKL | Steenkool | Indonesia |
| ZKM | Sette Cama | Gabon |
| ZKN | Skive/RR Stn. | Denmark |
| ZKO | Sierre/Siders | Switzerland |
| ZKP | Kasompe | Zambia |
| ZKQ | Kotor | Yugoslavia |
| ZKR | Karlovasi | Greece |
| ZKS | Solothurn | Switzerland |
| ZKT | Komotini | Greece |
| ZKU | Sursee | Switzerland |
| ZKV | Thalwil | Switzerland |
| ZKW | Wetzikon | Switzerland |
| ZKX | Uzwil | Switzerland |
| ZKY | Verbier | Switzerland |
| ZKZ | Vevey | Switzerland |
| ZLA | Villars | Switzerland |
| ZLB | Visp | Switzerland |
| ZLC | Waedenswil/Off-line Pt | Switzerland |
| ZLD | Weinfelden | Switzerland |
| ZLE | Wengen | Switzerland |
| ZLF | Wettingen | Switzerland |
| ZLG | El Gouera | Mauritania |
| ZLH | Wil | Switzerland |
| ZLI | Winterthur | Switzerland |
| ZLJ | Yverdon | Switzerland |
| ZLK | St Petersburg/Moscovskiy Railway Stn | Russia |
| ZLL | Zofingen | Switzerland |
| ZLM | Zug | Switzerland |
| ZLN | Le Mans/RR Stn. | France |
| ZLO | Manzanillo | Mexico |
| ZLP | Zurich/HBF Railway Svc | Switzerland |
| ZLQ | Zurich | Switzerland |
| ZLR | Linares | Chile |
| ZLS | Liverpool Street Stn/RR Stn. | UK |
| ZLT | La Tabatiere, QC | Canada |
| ZLU | Ludwigslust/RR Stn. | Germany |
| ZLX | London/British Rail Terminal | UK |
| ZLY | Albany/Allbany NY Rail, NY | USA |
| ZLZ | Leeds/Bus Svc | UK |
| ZMA | Mansfield/Bus Svc | UK |
| ZMB | Hamburg/RR Stn. | Germany |
| ZMD | Sena Madureira | Brazil |
| ZME | Newark/Metropark Rail, NJ | USA |
| ZMG | Magdeburg/RR Stn. | Germany |
| ZMH | 108 Mile Ranch, BC | Canada |
| ZMI | Naples/Mergellina Railway Svc | Italy |
| ZML | Milwaukee/Rail Svc., WI | USA |
| ZMM | Zamora | Mexico |
| ZMO | Modena/Bus Stn | Italy |
| ZMP | Manchester/Manchester Bus Stn. | UK |
| ZMR | Meran/Bus Stn | Italy |
| ZMS | Florence/S.M. Novella Rail.Svc | Italy |
| ZMT | Masset, BC | Canada |
| ZMU | Munich/HBF Railway Svc | Germany |
| ZMV | Melville, NY/Off-line Pt | USA |
| ZNA | Nanaimo/Harbour, BC | Canada |
| ZNB | Hamm | Germany |
| ZNC | Nyac, AK | USA |
| ZND | Zinder | Niger |
| ZNE | Newman | Australia |
| ZNF | Hanau | Germany |
| ZNG | Negginan, MB | Canada |
| ZNH | Hettlingen | Germany |
| ZNI | Heidenheim | Germany |
| ZNJ | Heilbronn | Germany |
| ZNK | Herford | Germany |
| ZNL | Herne | Germany |
| ZNM | Herten | Germany |
| ZNN | Hilden | Germany |
| ZNO | Hildesheim | Germany |
| ZNP | Huerth | Germany |
| ZNQ | Ingolstadt | Germany |
| ZNR | Iserlohn | Germany |
| ZNS | Kempten | Germany |
| ZNT | Kerpen | Germany |
| ZNU | Namu, BC | Canada |
| ZNV | Koblenz | Germany |
| ZNW | Limburg | Germany |
| ZNX | Lagenfeld | Germany |
| ZNY | Langenhagen | Germany |
| ZNZ | Zanzibar/Kisauni | Tanzania |
| ZOA | Level | Germany |
| ZOB | Lippstadt | Germany |
| ZOC | Luedenscheid | Germany |
| ZOD | Ludwigsburg | Germany |
| ZOE | Ludwigshafen | Germany |
| ZOF | Ocean Falls, BC | Canada |
| ZOG | Lueneburg/RR Stn. | Germany |
| ZOH | Luenen | Germany |
| ZOI | Marburg An Der Lahn | Germany |
| ZOJ | Marl | Germany |
| ZOK | Meerbusch | Germany |
| ZOL | Menden | Germany |
| ZOM | Minden | Germany |
| ZON | Moers | Germany |
| ZOO | Muelhefm An Der Ruhr | Germany |
| ZOP | Neunkirchen/Ott^line Pt | Germany |
| ZOQ | Neuss | Germany |
| ZOR | Neustadt-Weinstrasse | Germany |
| ZOS | Osorno/Canal Balo | Chile |
| ZOT | Neu-Ulm | Germany |
| ZOU | Neuwied | Germany |
| ZOV | Norderstedt | Germany |
| ZOW | Nordhorn | Germany |
| ZOX | Oberammergau | Germany |
| ZOY | Oberhausen | Germany |
| ZOZ | Offerbach | Germany |
| ZPA | Offenburg | Germany |
| ZPB | Sachigo Lake, ON | Canada |
| ZPC | Pucon | Chile |
| ZPD | Oldenburg | Germany |
| ZPE | Osnabrueck/RR Stn. | Germany |
| ZPF | Passau | Germany |
| ZPG | Peine | Germany |
| ZPH | Zephyrhills, FL. | USA |
| ZPI | Pirmasens | Germany |
| ZPJ | Ratingen | Germany |
| ZPK | Ravensburg | Germany |
| ZPL | Recklinghausen | Germany |
| ZPM | Regensburg/RR Stn. | Germany |
| ZPN | Remscheid/Offline Pt | Germany |
| ZPO | Pine House, SK | Canada |
| ZPP | Reutlingen | Germany |
| ZPQ | Rheine/Bentlage | Germany |
| ZPR | Rosenheim | Germany |
| ZPS | Ruesselsheim | Germany |
| ZPT | Saarlouis | Germany |
| ZPU | Salzgitter | Germany |
| ZPV | Schwaebisch Gmuend/ Off-line Pt | Germany |
| ZPW | Schweinfurt | Germany |
| ZPX | Schwerte | Germany |
| ZPY | Siegburg | Germany |
| ZPZ | Sindelfingen/Off-line Pt. | Germany |
| ZQA | Singen | Germany |
| ZQB | Solingen | Germany |
| ZQC | Speyer | Germany |
| ZQD | Stade | Germany |
| ZQE | Stolberg | Germany |
| ZQF | Trier | Germany |
| ZQG | Troisdorf | Germany |
| ZQH | Tuebingen | Germany |
| ZQI | Unna | Germany |
| ZQJ | Velbert | Germany |
| ZQK | Viersen | Germany |
| ZQL | Villingen-Schwenningen | Germany |
| ZQM | Voelklingen | Germany |
| ZQN | Queenstown/Frankton | New Zealand |
| ZQO | Waiblingen | Germany |
| ZQP | Wesel | Germany |
| ZQQ | Wetzlar | Germany |
| ZQR | Witten | Germany |
| ZQS | Queen Charlotte Is, BC | Canada |
| ZQT | Wolfenbuettel | Germany |
| ZQU | Wolfsburg/Off-line Pt. | Germany |
| ZQV | Worms | Germany |
| ZQW | Zweibruecken | Germany |
| ZQX | Nias | Indonesia |
| ZRA | Atlantic City/Rail Svc., NJ. | USA |
| ZRB | Frankfurt/HBF Railway Svc | Germany |
| ZRC | San Pedro de Alcantara/Bus Stn | Spain |
| ZRD | Richmond/Richmond VA Rail, VA | USA |
| ZRE | Rethymno | Greece |
| ZRF | Rockford/Park & Ride Bus Svc., IL | USA |
| ZRG | Bratislava/Bus Svc | Slovakia |
| ZRH | Zurich | Switzerland |
| ZRI | Serui/Yendosa | Indonesia |
| ZRJ | Round Lake, ON. | Canada |
| ZRK | Rockford/Van Galder Bus Terminal, IL | USA |
| ZRL | Lancaster/Lancaster PA RR Stn. | USA |
| ZRM | Sarmi | Indonesia |
| ZRN | Nyon | Switzerland |
| ZRO | Reggio Nell Emilia/Bus Svc. | Italy |
| ZRP | Newark/Newark NJ Rail. | USA |
| ZRS | Zurs/Lech/Flexenpass HP | Austria |
| ZRT | Hartford/Hartford CT Rail | USA |
| ZRU | Boston/Boston RT128 Rail, MA | USA |
| ZRV | Providence/Providence Rail, RI. | USA |
| ZRW | Rastatt/Bus Svc | Germany |
| ZRX | Riesa/RR Stn. | Germany |
| ZRZ | Washington/New Carrolton RR, DC. | USA |
| ZSA | San Salvador | Bahamas |
| ZSB | Salzburg/German Railway Svc | Austria |
| ZSC | Schoena/RR Stn. | Germany |
| ZSD | Schwanheide/RR Stn. | Germany |
| ZSE | St Pierre dela Reunion | Reunion Is |
| ZSF | Springfield, MA RR. | USA |
| ZSG | Sonneberg/RR Stn. | Germany |
| ZSH | Santa Fe/Bus Stn, NM | USA |
| ZSI | Sassnitz/RR Stn. | Germany |
| ZSJ | Sandy Lake, ON | Canada |
| ZSK | Pasewalk/RR Stn. | Germany |
| ZSL | Sligo/Bus Stn. | Ireland |
| ZSM | Santa Clara/Bus Svc, CA. | USA |

| Code | Description | Country |
|------|-------------|---------|
| ZSN | Stendal/RR Stn. | Germany |
| ZSO | Suhl/RR Stn. | Germany |
| ZSP | St Paul, QC | Canada |
| ZSQ | Salzwedel/RR Stn. | Germany |
| ZSR | Schwerin/RR Stn. | Germany |
| ZSS | Sassandra | Côte D'Ivoire |
| ZST | Stewart, BC | Canada |
| ZSU | Dessau/RR Stn. | Germany |
| ZSV | St Louis/Rail Svc., MO | USA |
| ZSW | Prince Rupert/SealCove, BC | Canada |
| ZSX | Straisund/RR Stn. | Germany |
| ZSY | Scottsdale/Bus Svc, AZ | USA |
| ZSZ | Swakopmund/RR Stn. | Namibia |
| ZTA | Tureira | F. Polynesia |
| ZTB | Tete-a-La Baleine, QC | Canada |
| ZTC | Turin/Bus Svc. | Italy |
| ZTD | Schenectady/Schenectady Rail, NY | USA |
| ZTE | Rochester/Rochester NY Rail | USA |
| ZTF | Westchester County/ Stamford RR Stn., NY | USA |
| ZTG | Aalborg/RR Stn. | Denmark |
| ZTH | Zakinthos Is | Greece |
| ZTJ | Princeton/Princeton JT Rail, NJ | USA |
| ZTK | Thun | Switzerland |
| ZTL | Telluride/Bus Stn, CO | USA |
| ZTM | Shamattawa, MB. | Canada |
| ZTN | Philadelphia/Trenton RR Stn., PA | USA |
| ZTO | Boston/Boston South Rail, MA. | USA |
| ZTP | Itapetininga. | Brazil |
| ZTR | Zhitomir. | Ukraine |
| ZTS | Tahsis, BC | Canada |
| ZTT | Cottbus/RR Stn. | Germany |
| ZTW | Tsuen Wan/RR Stn. | Hong Kong |
| ZTY | Boston/BKBAY Rail, MA. | USA |
| ZTZ | Chemnitz/RR Stn. | Germany |
| ZUA | Utica/Utica NY Rail | USA |
| ZUC | Ignace, ON. | Canada |
| ZUD | Ancud. | Chile |
| ZUE | Zuenoula | Côte D'Ivoire |
| ZUG | Harrisburg/Rail, PA | USA |
| ZUH | Zhuhai/Zhuhai Arpt | China |
| ZUL | Zilfi. | Saudi Arabia |
| ZUM | Churchill Falls, NF | Canada |
| ZUN | Chicago/Union Railway Svc, IL | USA |
| ZUO | Dutch Rail Zone 16/Rail Svc | Netherlands |
| ZUP | Dutch Rail Zone 17/Rail Svc | Netherlands |
| ZUQ | Dutch Rail Zone 18/Rail Svc | Netherlands |
| ZUR | Dutch Rail Zone 19/Rail Svc | Netherlands |
| ZUS | Dutch Rail Zone 20/Rail Svc | Netherlands |
| ZUT | Dutch Rail Zone 21/Rail Svc | Netherlands |
| ZUU | Dutch Rail Zone 22/Rail Svc | Netherlands |
| ZUV | Dutch Rail Zone 23/Rail Svc | Netherlands |
| ZUW | Dutch Rail Zone 24/Rail Svc | Netherlands |
| ZUX | Dutch Rail Zone 25/Rail Svc | Netherlands |
| ZUY | Dutch Rail Zone 26/Rail Svc | Netherlands |
| ZUZ | Dutch Rail Zone 27/Rail Svc | Netherlands |
| ZVA | Miandrivazo | Madagascar |
| ZVE | New Haven/New Haven Rail, CT. | USA |
| ZVG | Springvale. | Australia |
| ZVH | Veldhoven/RR Stn. | Netherlands |
| ZVK | Savannakhet | Laos |
| ZVL | Dutch Rail Zone 01/Rail Svc | Netherlands |
| ZVM | Hanover/Messe-BF Railway Svc | Germany |
| ZVN | Dutch Rail Zone 03/Rail Svc | Netherlands |
| ZVO | Dutch Rail Zone 04/Rail Svc | Netherlands |
| ZVP | Dutch Rail Zone 05/Rail Svc | Netherlands |
| ZVQ | Dutch Rail Zone 06/Rail Svc | Netherlands |
| ZVR | Hanover/HBF Railway Svc. | Germany |
| ZVS | Dutch Rail Zone 08/Rail Svc | Netherlands |
| ZVT | Dutch Rail Zone 09/Rail Svc | Netherlands |
| ZVU | Dutch Rail Zone 10/Rail Svc | Netherlands |
| ZVV | Dutch Rail Zone 11/Rail Svc | Netherlands |
| ZVW | Dutch Rail Zone 12/Rail Svc | Netherlands |
| ZVX | Dutch Rail Zone 13/Rail Svc | Netherlands |
| ZVY | Dutch Rail Zone 14/Rail Svc | Netherlands |
| ZVZ | Dutch Rail Zone 15/Rail Svc | Netherlands |
| ZWA | Andapa | Madagascar |
| ZWB | Hampton/Williamsburg Rail, VA | USA |
| ZWD | Warnemuende/RR Stn. | Germany |
| ZWG | Weingarten | Germany |
| ZWH | Windhoek/RR Stn. | Namibia |
| ZWI | Wilmington/Wilmington Rail, DE | USA |
| ZWK | Suwalki | Poland |
| ZWL | Wollaston Lake, SK | Canada |
| ZWM | Wismar/RR Stn. | Germany |
| ZWN | Wittenberg/RR Stn. | Germany |
| ZWO | Dutch Rail Zone 02/Rail Svc | Netherlands |
| ZWP | West Palm Beach/RR Stn., FL | USA |
| ZWQ | Dutch Rail Zone 07/Rail Svc | Netherlands |
| ZWS | Stuttgart/RR Stn. | Germany |
| ZWT | Wittenberg/RR Stn. | Germany |
| ZWU | Washington/Washington DC RR Stn. | USA |
| ZWW | Hampton/Newport News Rail, VA | USA |
| ZWX | Dutch Rail Zone 28/Rail Svc | Netherlands |
| ZWY | Dutch Rail Zone 29/Rail Svc | Netherlands |
| ZWZ | Dutch Rail Zone 30/Rail Svc | Netherlands |
| ZXA | Aberdeen/ScotRail | UK |
| ZXB | Jan Mayen | Svalbard and Jan Mayen Is |
| ZXC | Bangsiund | Norway |
| ZXD | Vikna | Norway |
| ZXE | Edinburgh/ScotRail. | UK |
| ZXF | Roervik. | Norway |
| ZXG | Gravik. | Norway |
| ZXH | Soerfjord | Norway |
| ZXI | Roeddey | Norway |
| ZXJ | Fore | Norway |
| ZXK | Baasmo. | Norway |
| ZXL | Skjerstad | Norway |
| ZXM | Rognan | Norway |
| ZXN | Leka | Norway |
| ZXO | Fauske. | Norway |
| ZXP | Perth/ScotRail. | UK |
| ZXQ | Solstad. | Norway |
| ZXR | Hemnes. | Norway |
| ZXS | Buffalo/Exchange St Railway Svc., NY | USA |
| ZYA | Amsterdam/RR Stn. | Netherlands |
| ZYC | Gizycio. | Poland |
| ZYE | Eindhoven/RR Stn. | Netherlands |
| ZYH | The Hague/Holland Spoor RR Stn. | Netherlands |
| ZYI | Zunyi | China |
| ZYL | Syllnet/Civil | Bangladesh |
| ZYM | Arnhem/RR Stn. | Netherlands |
| ZYO | Roosendaal/RR Stn. | Netherlands |
| ZYP | New York/Penn Rail, NY | USA |
| ZYQ | Syracuse/NY Rail, NY | USA |
| ZYR | Brussels/Midi Railway Stn | Belgium |
| ZYT | Maastricht/RR Stn. | Netherlands |
| ZYU | Utrecht/RR Stn. | Netherlands |
| ZYZ | Antwerp | Belgium |
| ZZA | Azzazga. | Algeria |
| ZZB | Barka | Algeria |
| ZZC | Cherchell | Algeria |
| ZZD | Dra El Mizan | Algeria |
| ZZE | Uzice | Yugoslavia |
| ZZF | Mystery Flight | Australia |
| ZZH | Cranzahl/RR Stn. | Germany |
| ZZI | Elite Mystery Night | Australia |
| ZZJ | Mystery Night | Australia |
| ZZK | Khemis Miliana | Algeria |
| ZZL | Larba Nath Iraten | Algeria |
| ZZM | Borcj Menatiel | Algeria |
| ZZP | Pozarevac. | Yugoslavia |
| ZZQ | Cheung Sha Wan. | Hong Kong |
| ZZR | Kherrata. | Algeria |
| ZZS | M'Sila | Algeria |
| ZZT | Taher | Algeria |
| ZZU | Mzuzu | Malawi |
| ZZV | Zanesville, OH | USA |

# World Airports by Airport

## List 2 of 2:
## Airport/Location...Country...IATA Code

### Notes

1. The following is a list of more than 10,000 airports and locations worldwide and their three-letter IATA (International Air Transport Association) codes.
2. IATA codes are primarily used to identify airports, but are also used to identify transshipment, pick-up and delivery locations; cities; bus and train stations; as well as harbors and ports.
3. Approximately ten percent of these locations are major international airports. The balance are municipal and remote airfields and other locations.
4. Locations in the U.S., Canada, and Australia generally have a two-letter state or province notation (e.g., CA for California).
5. Global location codes are added, reassigned, or deleted at the rate of approximately ten to twelve per month. This list is current as of January 2002.
6. For the most up-to-date information, refer to www.iata.org.

### Abbreviations

| | |
|---|---|
| AAF | Army Air Field |
| AFB | Air Force Base |
| AFS | Air Force Station |
| AHP | Army Heliport |
| Arpt | Airport |
| CGS | Coast Guard Station |
| Cnty | County |
| Fld | Field |
| HP | Heliport |
| HVC | Hovercraft Terminal |
| Int'l | International |
| Is | Island |
| Mt | Mount |
| NAS | Naval Air Station |
| PT | Point |
| RR Stn | Railway Station/Service |
| RAF | Royal Air Force |
| SPB | Sea Plane Base |
| Stn | Station |
| Svc | Service |
| USAF | United States Air Force |

## A

Albina . . . . . . . . . . . . . . . . . Suriname . . ABN
108 Mile Ranch, BC . . . . . . Canada . . ZMH
Aachen/Merzbruck . . . . . . . Germany . . AAH
Aalbenraa/Bus Svc. . . . . . . Denmark . . XNR
Aalborg/Civil/Military . . . . . Denmark . . AAL
Aalborg/RR Stn. . . . . . . . . . Denmark . . ZTG
Aalesund/Vigra . . . . . . . . . . . Norway . . AES
Aalsmeer . . . . . . . . . . . . . Netherlands . . QFA
Aappilattoq . . . . . . . . . . . Greenland . .QUV
Aarau . . . . . . . . . . . . . . . . Switzerland . . ZDA
Aarhus/Bus Svc. . . . . . . . . . Denmark . . ZID
Aarhus/Limousine Svc . . . . . Denmark . . ZBU
Aarhus/RR Stn. . . . . . . . . . Denmark . . ZJH
Aarhus/Tirstrup . . . . . . . . . Denmark . . AAR
Aasiaat . . . . . . . . . . . . . . . Greenland . . JEG
Abadan . . . . . . . . . . . . . . . . . . . . Iran . . ABD
Abaiang . . . . . . . . . . . . . . . . .Kiribati . . ABF
Abakan . . . . . . . . . . . . . . . . . . Russia . . ABA
Abau . . . . . . . . . Papua New Guinea . . ABW
Abbeville . . . . . . . . . . . . . . . . France . . XAB
Abbotsford, BC . . . . . . . . . . Canada . . YXX
Abbottabad . . . . . . . . . . . . . Pakistan . . AAW
Abbse . . . . . . . . . . . . . . . . . . Yemen . . EAB
Abecher . . . . . . . . . . . . . . . . . . Chad . . AEH
Abengourou . . . . . . . . . . Côte D'Ivoire . OGO
Abeokuta . . . . . . . . . . . . . . . Nigeria . . QAT
Aberdeen Municipal, SD. . . . . USA . . ABR
Aberdeen, MD. . . . . . . . . . . . . USA . . APG
Aberdeen/Dyce. . . . . . . . . . . . . .UK . . ABZ
Aberdeen/ScotRail . . . . . . . . . . . .UK . . ZXA
Abernama Atoll . . . . . . . . . . . .Kiribati . . AEA
Abidjan . . . . . . . . . . . . . . Côte D'Ivoire . . ABJ
Abilene Municipal, TX . . . . . . USA . . ABI
Abilene/Dyess/AFB, TX . . . . . . USA . .DYS
Abingdon. . . . . . . . . . . . . . Australia . .ABG
Abingdon/RAF . . . . . . . . . . . . . .UK . . ABB
Abingdon/Virginia Highlands, VAUSA . . VJI
Ablitia . . . . . . . . . . . . . . Saudi Arabia . AHB
Aboisso . . . . . . . . . . . . . Côte D'Ivoire . ABO
Abou Deia . . . . . . . . . . . . . . . . .Chad . . AOD
Abreojos . . . . . . . . . . . . . . . Mexico . . AJS
Abu Dhabi Int'l. . . . . . . . . . . . UAE . .AUH
Abu Dhabi/Al Dhafra Military Arpt . . .
. . . . . . . . . . . . . . . . . . . . . . . . UAE . .DHF
Abu Dhalbi/Bateen. . . . . . . . . . . UAE . . AZI
Abu Rudeis . . . . . . . . . . . . . . . Egypt . . AUE
Abu Simbel . . . . . . . . . . . . . . . Egypt . . ABS
Abuja Int'l . . . . . . . . . . . . . . . Nigeria . . ABV
Acandi . . . . . . . . . . . . . . . . . Colombia . . ACD
Acapulco/G. Alvarez Int'l . . . . Mexico . . ACA
Acaricuara . . . . . . . . . . . . . Colombia . . ARF
Acarigua . . . . . . . . . . . . . Venezuela . . AGV
ACARS . . . . . . . . . . . . . . . . . . . . . . n/a . . DDL
Accra/Kotoka . . . . . . . . . . . . . Ghana . . ACC
Achinsk . . . . . . . . . . . . . . . . . . Russia . . ACS
Achutupo. . . . . . . . . . . . . . . . Panama . .ACU
Ad-Dabbah . . . . . . . . . . . . . . . Sudan . . AAD
Ada, OK. . . . . . . . . . . . . . . . . . . USA . . ADT
Adak Is/NAS, AK. . . . . . . . . . . USA . . ADK
Adana/Sakirpasa . . . . . . . . . Turkey . . ADA
Addis Ababa/Bole . . . . . . . Ethiopia . . ADD
Adelaide. . . . . . . . . . . . . . . Australia . . ADL
Adelboden . . . . . . . . . . . Switzerland . . ZDB
Aden Int'l . . . . . . . . . . . . . . . . Yemen . . ADE
Adiyaman/Incirlik. . . . . . . . . . Turkey . . ADF
Adler/Sochi. . . . . . . . . . . . . . . Russia . . AER
Adrar . . . . . . . . . . . . . . . . . . . Algeria . . AZR
Adrian/Lenawee County, MI. . . . USA . . ADG
Aek Godang . . . . . . . . . . . Indonesia . . AEG
Afore . . . . . . . . . Papua New Guinea . . AFR
Afton Downs . . . . . . . . . . . Australia . . AWN
Afton/Municipal, WY . . . . . . . . USA . . AFO
Afutara/Atutara . . . . . . . . Solomon Is . . AFT

Afyon . . . . . . . . . . . . . . . . . . . Turkey. . .AFY
Agades/Manu Dayak. . . . . . . . . Niger. . .AJY
Agadir/Agadir Almassira . . . .Morocco. . AGA
Agartala/Singerbhil . . . . . . . . . .India. . . IXA
Agatti Is . . . . . . . . . . . . . . . . . . India. . . AGX
Agaun . . . . . . . . Papua New Guinea . . AUP
Agde/Off-line Pt. . . . . . . . . . . . France. . XAG
Agedabia . . . . . . . . . . . . . . . . . Libya. . QGG
Agen/La Garenne. . . . . . . . . . France. . AGF
Aggeneys . . . . . . . . . . . . . . . S. Africa . AGZ
Aghios Nicolaos . . . . . . . . . . Greece. .ZAN
Agnew . . . . . . . . . . . . . . . . .Australia. .AGW
Agra/Kheria . . . . . . . . . . . . . . . India. . AGR
Agri/Agri. . . . . . . . . . . . . . . . . Turkey. . . .AJI
Agrigento . . . . . . . . . . . . . . . . . Italy. . QAO
Agrinion . . . . . . . . . . . . . . . . .Greece. . AGQ
Aguaclara. . . . . . . . . . . . . . . Colombia. . ACL
Aguadilla/Borinquen . . . . . Puerto Rico . BQN
Aguascalientes . . . . . . . . . . . Mexico. . AGU
Aguni . . . . . . . . . . . . . . . . . . . Japan. . .AGJ
Ahe. . . . . . . . . . . . . . . . . . .F. Polynesia . . AHE
Ahmadabad. . . . . . . . . . . . . . . India. . AMD
Ahuas . . . . . . . . . . . . . . . .Honduras. . AHS
Ahwaz . . . . . . . . . . . . . . . . . . . .Iran. . AWZ
Ai-Ais . . . . . . . . . . . . . . . . . Namibia. . AIW
Aiale. . . . . . . . . . . . . . . . . Switzerland. . ZDC
Aiamosa, CO . . . . . . . . . . . . . . . USA. . ALS
Aidan . . . . . . . . . . . . . . . . . . . Russia. . ADH
Aljouf . . . . . . . . . . . . . . . . . . .Yemen. . . AJO
Aiken/Municipal, SC. . . . . . . . . USA. . AIK
Ailigandi . . . . . . . . . . . . . . . .Panama. . . AIL
Ailinglapalap Is . . . . . . . . Marshall Is . . AIP
Ailuk Is . . . . . . . . . . . . . . .Marshall Is . . AIM
Aime. . . . . . . . . . . . . . . . . . . France. . . QAI
Ain Beida . . . . . . . . . . . . . . . . Algeria. . QBP
Ain Mlila . . . . . . . . . . . . . . . . .Algeria. . QIM
Ain Temouchent . . . . . . . . . . Algeria. . QIO
Ainsworth, NE. . . . . . . . . . . . . . USA. . ANW
Aiome . . . . . . . . Papua New Guinea . . AIE
Aioun El Atrouss . . . . . . . Mauritania. . AEO
Airlie Beach/Whitsunday Airstrip
. . . . . . . . . . . . . . . . . . . . .Australia. . WSY
Airok . . . . . . . . . . . . . . . . .Marshall Is . . AIC
Aishaiton . . . . . . . . . . . . . . . Guyana. . .AHL
Aitape/Airstrip . . Papua New Guinea . . ATP
Aitape/Tadji . . . . . Papua New Guinea . . TAJ
Aitutaki . . . . . . . . . . . . . . . . . Cook Is . . AIT
Aix Les Bains . . . . . . . . . . . . . France. . XAI
Aix-en-Provence . . . . . . . . . . France. . QXB
Aiyura . . . . . . . . Papua New Guinea . . AYU
Aizawi . . . . . . . . . . . . . . . . . . . India. . AJL
Ajaccio/Campo Dell Oro . . . . . France. . AJA
Ajaokuta . . . . . . . . . . . . . . . . Nigeria. .QJK
Ajman City . . . . . . . . . . . . . . . UAE. .QAJ
Akhiok, AK . . . . . . . . . . . . . . . USA. .AKK
Akiachak/SPB, AK . . . . . . . . . USA. . KKI
Akiak, AK. . . . . . . . . . . . . . . . USA. . AKI
Akieni . . . . . . . . . . . . . . . . . Gabon. . AKE
Akioujt. . . . . . . . . . . . . . . Mauritania. . AJJ
Akita. . . . . . . . . . . . . . . . . . . Japan. . AXT
Aklavik, NT. . . . . . . . . . . . . Canada. . LAK
Akola . . . . . . . . . . . . . . . . . . . India. . AKD
Akron, CO. . . . . . . . . . . . . . . . USA. . AKO
Akron, OH. . . . . . . . . . . . . . . . USA. . CAK
Akron/Fulton Int'l, OH. . . . . . . USA. . AKC
Akrotiri . . . . . . . . . . . . . . . . . Cyprus. . .AKT
Aksu. . . . . . . . . . . . . . . . . . . . China. . AKU
Aktau . . . . . . . . . . . . . . . . Kazakstan. . SCO
Aktyubinsk . . . . . . . . . . . . Kazakstan. . AKX
Akulivik, QC. . . . . . . . . . . . . Canada. . AKV
Akunnaaq. . . . . . . . . . . . . . Greenland. . QCU
Akure . . . . . . . . . . . . . . . . . Nigeria. . AKR
Akureyri . . . . . . . . . . . . . . . . Iceland. . AEY
Akutan, AK. . . . . . . . . . . . . . . USA. . KQA
Al Ain Int'l . . . . . . . . . . . . . . . UAE. . AAN
Al Arish. . . . . . . . . . . . . . . . . Egypt. . AAC
Al Ghayclah. . . . . . . . . . . . . .Yemen. . .AAY
Al Hoceima . . . . . . . . . . . . .Morocco. . AHU
Al-Baha/Al-Aqiq . . . . . . Saudi Arabia . .ABT

| Airport | Location | Code |
|---|---|---|
| Alaa | Nigeria | QAX |
| Alabaster, Shelby County, AL | USA | EET |
| Alagoinhas | Brazil | QGS |
| Alah | Philippines | AAV |
| Alakanuk, AK | USA | AUK |
| Alameda/NAS, CA | USA | NGZ |
| Alamogordo, NM | USA | ALM |
| Alamos | Mexico | XAL |
| Alba Iufla | Romania | QAY |
| Albany | Australia | ALH |
| Albany Nexrad, NY | USA | ENX |
| Albany, GA | USA | ABY |
| Albany, NY | USA | ALB |
| Albany, OR | USA | CVO |
| Albany/Allbany NY Rail, NY | USA | ZLY |
| Albany/Bus Svc, NY | USA | QWY |
| Albany/NAS, GA | USA | NAB |
| Albenga | Italy | ALL |
| Albert Lea, MN | USA | AEL |
| Alberville | France | XAV |
| Albi/Le Sequestre | France | LBI |
| Albuq | Yemen | BUK |
| Albuquerque Int'l, NM | USA | ABQ |
| Albury | Australia | ABX |
| Alcantara | Brazil | QAH |
| Alconbury/RAF | UK | AYH |
| Alderney | UK | ACI |
| Aldershot/RR Stn., ON | Canada | XLY |
| Aleg | Mauritania | LEG |
| Alegrete/Federal | Brazil | ALQ |
| Aleknagik, AK | USA | WKK |
| Alencon | France | XAN |
| Aleneva, AK | USA | AED |
| Alenquer | Brazil | ALT |
| Aleppo/Nejrab | Syria | ALP |
| Alert Bay, BC | Canada | YAL |
| Alert, NU | Canada | YLT |
| Alerta | Peru | ALD |
| Ales | France | XAS |
| Alessandria | Italy | QAL |
| Alexander Bay/Koftdoorn | S. Africa | ALJ |
| Alexander City, AL | USA | ALX |
| Alexandra | New Zealand | ALR |
| Alexandria | Australia | AXL |
| Alexandria Bay, NY | USA | AXB |
| Alexandria, LA | USA | AEX |
| Alexandria, LA | USA | ESF |
| Alexandria, MN | USA | AXN |
| Alexandria/Borg El Arab | Egypt | HBE |
| Alexandria/Nouzha | Egypt | ALY |
| Alexandria/RR Stn., ON | Canada | XFS |
| Alexandroupolis-Demokritos | Greece | AXD |
| Alfenas | Brazil | QXW |
| Alghero | Italy | AHO |
| Algiers-Houari Boumediene | Algeria | ALG |
| Algona, IA | USA | AXG |
| Alicante | Spain | ALC |
| Alice Arm, BC | Canada | ZAA |
| Alice Springs | Australia | ASP |
| Alice, TX | USA | ALI |
| Aliceville, AL | USA | AIV |
| Alidays | S. Africa | ADY |
| Alisabieh | Djibouti | AII |
| Alitak/SPB, AK | USA | ALZ |
| Allahabad/Bamrauli | India | IXD |
| Allakaket, AK | USA | AET |
| Allentown/Lehigh Int'l, PA | USA | ABE |
| Alliance, NE | USA | AIA |
| Ailuitsup Paa | Greenland | LLU |
| Ailuitsup Paa | Greenland | QFJ |
| Alma, QC | Canada | YTF |
| Alma/Gratiot ComMunicipality, MI | USA | AMN |
| Almaty | Kazakstan | ALA |
| Almelo/RR | Netherlands | QYL |
| Almenara | Brazil | AMJ |
| Almeria | Spain | LEI |
| Along | India | IXV |
| Alor Is | Indonesia | ARD |
| Alotau/Gurney | Papua New Guinea | GUR |
| Alowe | Gabon | AWE |
| Alpe D Huez | France | AHZ |
| Alpena, MI | USA | APN |
| Alpha | Australia | ABH |
| Alpine, TX | USA | ALE |
| Alroy Downs | Australia | AYD |
| Alta Floresta | Brazil | AFL |
| Alta Lake, BC | Canada | YAE |
| Alta/Lufthavn | Norway | ALF |
| Altai | Mongolia | LTI |
| Altamira | Brazil | ATM |
| Altay | China | AAT |
| Altenburg | Germany | ADC |
| Altenirhein | Switzerland | ACH |
| Alto Molocue | Mozambique | AME |
| Alto Palena | Chile | WAP |
| Alto Parnatiba | Brazil | APY |
| Alto Rio Senguerr | Argentina | ARR |
| Alton, IL | USA | ALN |
| Altoona, PA | USA | AOO |
| Altus/AFB, OK | USA | LTS |
| Altus/Municipal, OK | USA | AXS |
| Alula | Somalia | ALU |
| Alyeska, AK | USA | AQY |
| Alzey | Germany | XZY |
| Am Timan | Chad | AMC |
| Ama | Papua New Guinea | AMF |
| Amahai | Indonesia | AHI |
| Amalfi | Colombia | AFI |
| Amami O Shima | Japan | ASJ |
| Amanab | Papua New Guinea | AMU |
| Amarillo, TX | USA | AMA |
| Amata | Australia | AMT |
| Amazon Bay | Papua New Guinea | AZB |
| Ambanja | Madagascar | IVA |
| Ambato/Chachoan | Ecuador | ATF |
| Ambatolahy | Madagascar | AHY |
| Ambatomainty | Madagascar | AMY |
| Ambatondrazaka | Madagascar | WAM |
| Ambilobe | Madagascar | AMB |
| Ambler, AK | USA | ABL |
| Amboin | Papua New Guinea | AMG |
| Amboise | France | XAM |
| Ambon/Pattimura | Indonesia | AMQ |
| Amboseli | Kenya | ASV |
| Ambriz | Andorra | AZZ |
| Ambunti | Papua New Guinea | AUJ |
| Amchitka, AK | USA | AHT |
| Amderma | Russia | AMV |
| Amedee/AAF, CA | USA | AHC |
| American River | Australia | RCN |
| Americana | Brazil | QWJ |
| Amersfoort/RR | Netherlands | QYM |
| Amery/Municipal, WI | USA | AHH |
| Ames, IA | USA | AMW |
| Amherst/RR Stn., NS | Canada | XZK |
| Amiens/Glisy | France | QAM |
| Amityville/Zahns, NY | USA | AYZ |
| Amman/Marka (Civil) | Jordan | ADJ |
| Amman/Queen Alia Int'l | Jordan | AMM |
| Ammaroo | Australia | AMX |
| Ammassivik | Greenland | QUW |
| Amook, AK | USA | AOS |
| Amos, QC | Canada | YEY |
| Ampanihy | Madagascar | AMP |
| Amritsar/Raja Sansi | India | ATQ |
| Amsberg | Germany | ZCA |
| Amsterdam/RR Stn | Netherlands | ZYA |
| Amsterdam/Schiphol | Netherlands | AMS |
| Anaa | F. Polynesia | AAA |
| Anaapa | Russia | AAQ |
| Anaco | Venezuela | AAO |
| Anacortes, WA | USA | OTS |
| Anacostia/USN HP, DC | USA | NDV |
| Anadyr | Russia | DYR |
| Anaheim, CA | USA | ANA |
| Anahim Lake, BC | Canada | YAA |
| Anaktuvuk, AK | USA | AKP |
| Analalava | Madagascar | HVA |
| Anand | India | QNB |
| Anapolis | Brazil | APS |
| Anchorage Int'l, AK | USA | ANC |
| Anchorage, AK | USA | MRI |
| Anchorage/Elmendorl/AFB, AK | USA | EDF |
| Ancona/Falconara | Italy | AOI |
| Ancud | Chile | ZUD |
| Andahuaylas | Peru | ANS |
| Andamooka | Australia | ADO |
| Andapa | Madagascar | ZWA |
| Andenes | Norway | ANX |
| Anderson, SC | USA | AND |
| Anderson/Municipal, IN | USA | AID |
| Andes | Colombia | ADN |
| Andizhan | Uzbekistan | AZN |
| Andong | S. Korea | QDY |
| Andorra La Vella | Andorra | ALV |
| Andover | UK | ADV |
| Andradas | Brazil | QRD |
| Andrews, SC | USA | ADR |
| Andrews/NAF, MD | USA | NSF |
| Andriamena | Madagascar | WAD |
| Andros Town | Bahamas | ASD |
| Andulo | Angola | ANL |
| Anegada | Virgin Is (British) | NGD |
| Aneityum | Vanuatu | AUY |
| Angel Fire, NM | USA | AXX |
| Angermuende/RR Stn. | Germany | ZAX |
| Angers/Marce | France | ANE |
| Angers/RR | France | QXG |
| Anggi | Indonesia | AGD |
| Angling Lake, ON | Canada | YAX |
| Angoche | Mozambique | ANO |
| Angola, IN | USA | ANQ |
| Angoon, AK | USA | AGN |
| Angorarn | Papua New Guinea | AGG |
| Angouleme | France | ANG |
| Anguganak | Papua New Guinea | AKG |
| Anguilla/Rollang Fld, MS | USA | RFK |
| Anguilla/Wallblake | Anguilla | AXA |
| Angus Downs | Australia | ANZ |
| Aniak, AK | USA | ANI |
| Anica/Chacalluta | Chile | ARI |
| Anita Bay, AK | USA | AIB |
| Aniwa | Vanuatu | AWD |
| Anjouan/Ouant | Comoros | AJN |
| Ankang | China | AKA |
| Ankara/Esenboga | Turkey | ESB |
| Ankara/Etimesgut | Turkey | ANK |
| Ankavandra | Madagascar | JVA |
| Ankazoabo | Madagascar | WAK |
| Anklam | Germany | QKQ |
| Ann Arbor, MI | USA | ARB |
| Annaba | Algeria | AAE |
| Annanberg | Papua New Guinea | AOB |
| Annapolis/Lee, MD | USA | ANP |
| Annarillo/Tradewind, TX | USA | TDW |
| Annat | Guyana | NAI |
| Annecy | France | NCY |
| Annemasse | France | QNJ |
| Annette Is, AK | USA | ANN |
| Anniston, AL | USA | ANB |
| Anniston/Ft Mcclellan Bus Trml, AL | USA | QAW |
| Anniston/Reilly AHP, AL | USA | RLI |
| Anqing | China | AQG |
| Ansan | Kuwait | XNS |
| Ansbach/Katterbach | Germany | QOB |
| Anshan | China | AOG |
| Anta | Peru | ATA |
| Antalaha/Antsirabato | Madagascar | ANM |
| Antalya | Turkey | AYT |
| Antananarivo | Madagascar | TNR |
| Anthony Lagoon | Australia | AYL |
| Anthony, KS | USA | ANY |
| Antibes | France | XAT |
| Antlers, OK | USA | ATE |
| Antotagasta/Cerro Moreno | Chile | ANF |
| Antsalova | Madagascar | WAQ |
| Antsirabe | Madagascar | ATJ |
| Antsiranana/Arrachart | Madagascar | DIE |
| Antsohihy | Madagascar | WAI |
| Antwerp | Belgium | ZYZ |
| Antwerp/De Keyserlei Bus Stn | Belgium | ZAY |
| Antwerp/Deurne | Belgium | ANR |
| Anua | Uganda | RUA |
| Anuha Is | Solomon Is | ANH |
| Anuradhapura | Sri Lanka | ADP |
| Anvik, AK | USA | ANV |
| Anyang | China | AYN |
| Anyang | S. Korea | QYA |
| Aomori | Japan | AOJ |
| Aosta/Corrado Gex | Italy | AOT |
| Apalachicola Municipal, FL | USA | AAF |
| Apalachicola, FL | USA | AQQ |
| Apalapsili | Indonesia | AAS |
| Apapa | Nigeria | QAP |
| Apartacto | Colombia | APO |
| Apataki | F. Polynesia | APK |
| Apatzingan | Mexico | AZG |
| Apeldoorn/RR | Netherlands | QYP |
| Apia/Fagali I | Samoa | FGI |
| Apia/Faleolo | Samoa | APW |
| Apiay | Colombia | API |
| Apolo | Bolivia | APB |
| Appenzell | Switzerland | ZAP |
| Apple Valley, CA | USA | APV |
| Appleton, WI | USA | ATW |
| April River | Papua New Guinea | APR |
| Aprilia | Italy | QZR |
| Apucarana | Brazil | APU |

AIRPORTS -2-

| | | |
|---|---|---|
| Aqaba | Jordan | AQJ |
| Aracap | Brazil | AJU |
| Aracatuba | Brazil | ARU |
| Arad | Romania | ARW |
| Aragarcas | Brazil | ARS |
| Aragip | Papua New Guinea | ARP |
| Araguaina | Brazil | AUX |
| Aramac | Australia | AXC |
| Aranclis | Namibia | ADI |
| Aranulka | Kiribati | AAK |
| Arapahoe/Municipal, NE | USA | AHF |
| Arapiraca | Brazil | APQ |
| Arapongas | Brazil | APX |
| Arapoti | Brazil | AAG |
| Arar | Saudi Arabia | RAE |
| Araracuara | Colombia | ACR |
| Ararangua | Brazil | XRB |
| Araraquara | Brazil | AQA |
| Ararat | Australia | ARY |
| Arauca | Colombia | AUC |
| Arauquita | Colombia | ARQ |
| Arawa | Papua New Guinea | RAW |
| Araxa | Brazil | AAX |
| Araxos/Patrai | Greece | GPA |
| Arba Mintch | Ethiopia | AMH |
| Arbatax | Italy | QTX |
| Arboletas | Colombia | ARO |
| Arbon | Switzerland | ZDD |
| Arcachon/Teste de Buch | France | XAC |
| Arcata, CA | USA | ACV |
| Arclabil | Iran | ADU |
| Arctic Bay, NU | Canada | YAB |
| Arctic Village, AK | USA | ARC |
| Ardmore | New Zealand | AMZ |
| Ardmore, OK | USA | ADM |
| Ardmore/Downtown, OK | USA | AHD |
| Arecilbo | Puerto Rico | ARE |
| Arenshausen/RR Stn. | Germany | ZAS |
| Arequipa/Rodriguez Ballon | Peru | AQP |
| Arezzo | Italy | QZO |
| Argentia, NS | Canada | NWP |
| Argyle | Australia | GYL |
| Argyle Downs | Australia | AGY |
| Aribinda | Burkina Faso | XAR |
| Arica | Colombia | ACM |
| Aricos | Brazil | QRK |
| Aripuana | Brazil | AIR |
| Ariquernes | Brazil | AQM |
| Arkalyk | Kazakstan | AYK |
| Arkhanelsk | Russia | ARH |
| Arles/RR Stn. | France | ZAF |
| Arlington Heights/US AHP, IL | USA | JLH |
| Arlington, WA | USA | AWO |
| Arlit | Niger | RLT |
| Arlon | Belgium | QON |
| Armenia/El Eden | Colombia | AXM |
| Armentieres | France | XRM |
| Armidale | Australia | ARM |
| Armstrong, ON | Canada | YYW |
| Arnes, MB | Canada | YNR |
| Arnhem/Bus Svc. | Netherlands | QAR |
| Arnhem/RR Stn. | Netherlands | ZYM |
| Arno | Marshall Is. | AMR |
| Aroa | Papua New Guinea | AOA |
| Arona | Papua New Guinea | AON |
| Arorae Is | Kiribati | AIS |
| Arosa | Switzerland | ZDE |
| Arrabury | Australia | AAB |
| Arraias | Brazil | AAI |
| Arras | France | QRV |
| Arso | Indonesia | ARJ |
| Arsuk | Greenland | JRK |
| Artesia, NM | USA | ATS |
| Arthur's Town | Bahamas | ATC |
| Artigas | Uruguay | ATI |
| Arty | Burkina Faso | ARL |
| Aruba/Reina Beatrix | Aruba | AUA |
| Arusha | Tanzania | ARK |
| Arutua | F. Polynesia | AXR |
| Arvaikheer | Mongolia | AVK |
| Arviat, NU | Canada | YEK |
| Arvidsiaur | Sweden | AJR |
| Arzew | Algeria | QAE |
| Asahikawa/Akhiolk SPB | Japan | AKJ |
| Asapa | Papua New Guinea | APP |
| Asau | Samoa | AAU |
| Asbestos Hill, QC | Canada | YAF |
| Asbury Park, NJ | USA | ARX |
| Ascension | Bolivia | ASC |
| Aschaffenburg | Germany | ZCB |
| Ascoli Piceno | Italy | QNO |

| | | |
|---|---|---|
| Ascona | Switzerland | ACO |
| Aseki | Papua New Guinea | AEK |
| Asela | Ethiopia | ALK |
| Ashburton | New Zealand | ASG |
| Ashcrott, BC | Canada | YZA |
| Asheville/Municipal, NC | USA | AVL |
| Ashford/Int'l RR | UK | QDH |
| Ashgabat | Turkmenistan | ASB |
| Ashland, VA | USA | OFP |
| Ashland, WI | USA | ASX |
| Ashley, ND | USA | ASY |
| Asirim | Papua New Guinea | ASZ |
| Asmara/Int'l Arpt | Eritrea | ASM |
| Asosa | Ethiopia | ASO |
| Aspen, CO | USA | ASE |
| Assab | Eritrea | ASA |
| Assis | Brazil | AIF |
| Assiut | Egypt | ATZ |
| Astana | Kazakstan | TSE |
| Astorga | Brazil | QWN |
| Astoria, OR | USA | AST |
| Astrakhan | Russia | ASF |
| Astraksetra | Indonesia | AKQ |
| Asturias | Spain | OVD |
| Astypalaia Is | Greece | JTY |
| Asuncion/Silvio Pettirossi. | Paraguay | ASU |
| Aswan | Egypt | ASW |
| Atambua | Indonesia | ABU |
| Atammik | Greenland | QJF |
| Ataq | Yemen | AXK |
| Atar/Mouakchott | Mauritania | ATR |
| Atauro | Indonesia | AUT |
| Atbara | Seychelles | ATB |
| Atbasar | Kazakstan | ATX |
| Athens, GA | USA | AHN |
| Athens, TN | USA | MMI |
| **Athens-Eleftherios Venizelos** | | |
| Int'l | Greece | ATH |
| Athens/Athinai/Hellinikon | Greece | HEW |
| Athens/Ohio University, OH | USA | ATO |
| Ati | Chad | ATV |
| Atibaia | Brazil | ZBW |
| Atikokan, ON | Canada | YIB |
| Atiu Is | Cook Is | AIU |
| Atka, AK | USA | AKB |
| Atkamba | Papua New Guinea | ABP |
| Atlanta, Falcon Fld, GA | USA | FFC |
| Atlanta, GA | USA | PDK |
| Atlanta/Beaver Ruin, GA | USA | JAO |
| Atlanta/Galleria, GA | USA | JGL |
| Atlanta/Hartsfield, GA | USA | ATL |
| Atlanta/Headquarters | USA | HDQ |
| Atlanta/Perimeter Mall, GA | USA | JAJ |
| Atlanta/Technology Park, GA | USA | JAE |
| Atlantic City, NJ | USA | ACY |
| Atlantic City/Bader Fld, NJ | USA | AIY |
| Atlantic City/Rail Svc., NJ | USA | ZRA |
| Atlantic City/Steel Pier HP, NJ | USA | JSL |
| Atlantic, IA | USA | AIO |
| Atmautluak, AK | USA | ATT |
| Atoifi | Solomon Is | ATD |
| Atqasuk, AK | USA | ATK |
| Atsugi/NAS | Japan | NJA |
| Attawapiskat, ON | Canada | YAT |
| Attock | Pakistan | ATG |
| Attopeu | Laos | AOU |
| Attu | Greenland | QGQ |
| Attu Is/Casco Cove, AK | USA | ATU |
| Atuona | F. Polynesia | AUQ |
| Atyrau | Kazakstan | GUW |
| Aua Is | Papua New Guinea | AUI |
| Aubagne/Agora Helipad | France | JAH |
| Aubenas/Vals-Lanas | France | OBS |
| Auburn, AL | USA | AUO |
| Auburn, CA | USA | AUN |
| Auburn, ME | USA | LEW |
| Auckland | New Zealand | AKL |
| Auckland | New Zealand | MHB |
| Aue/RR Stn. | Germany | ZAU |
| Augsburg, Muehlhausen | Germany | AGB |
| Augusta, GA | USA | AGS |
| Augusta, GA | USA | DNL |
| Augusta, ME | USA | AUG |
| Augustus Downs | Australia | AUD |
| Auki/Gwanaru'u | Solomon Is | AKS |
| Aulnoye | France | XOY |
| Aupaluk, QC | Canada | YPJ |
| Aur Is | Marshall Is | AUL |
| Aurangabad/Chikkalthana | India | IXU |
| Auray | France | XUY |
| Aurillac | France | AUR |

| | | |
|---|---|---|
| Aurno | Papua New Guinea | AUV |
| Aurora State Arpt, OR | USA | UAO |
| Aurora/Municipal, IL | USA | AUZ |
| Aurukun Mission | Australia | AUU |
| Austin, MN | USA | AUM |
| Austin, NV | USA | ASQ |
| Austin, TX | USA | AUS |
| Austral Downs | Australia | AWP |
| Auvergne | Australia | AVG |
| Auxerre/Auxerre Branches | France | AUF |
| Avalon | Australia | AVV |
| Avalon, CA | USA | AVX |
| Avare | Brazil | QVP |
| Aveiro | Portugal | ZAV |
| Avellino | Italy | QVN |
| Aviano | Italy | AVB |
| Avignon/Avignon-Caum | France | AVN |
| Avon Park/Municipal, FL | USA | AVO |
| Avoriaz | France | AVF |
| Avu Avu | Solomon Is | AVU |
| Awaba | Papua New Guinea | AWB |
| Awar | Papua New Guinea | AWR |
| Awaradam/Cayana Arpt | Suriname | AAJ |
| Awareh | Ethiopia | AWH |
| Awassa | Ethiopia | AWA |
| Ax Les Thermes | France | XLT |
| Axurn | Ethiopia | AXU |
| Ayacucho | Colombia | AYC |
| Ayacucho/Yanamilla | Peru | AYP |
| Ayapel | Colombia | AYA |
| Ayawasi | Indonesia | AYW |
| Ayers Rock/Connellan | Australia | AYQ |
| Ayja Napa | Cyprus | QNP |
| Ayoias | Paraguay | AYO |
| Ayr | Australia | AYR |
| Azzazga | Algeria | ZZA |

# B

| | | |
|---|---|---|
| Ba | Fiji | BFJ |
| Baasmo | Norway | ZXK |
| Babelegi/ HP | S. Africa | HBL |
| Babo | Indonesia | BXB |
| Babolsar | Iran | BBL |
| Baca Grande, CO | USA | BCJ |
| Bacau | Romania | BCM |
| Bacita | Nigeria | QCT |
| Backwell, OK | USA | BWL |
| Baclajoz/Talaveral La Real | Spain | BJZ |
| Bacolod | Philippines | BCD |
| Bad Brambach/RR Stn. | Germany | ZBD |
| Bad Saizurigen/RR Stn. | Germany | ZBZ |
| Bade | Indonesia | BXD |
| Baden | Switzerland | ZDG |
| Baden-Baden | Germany | ZCC |
| Badin/Talhar | Pakistan | BDN |
| Badu Is | Australia | BDD |
| Bafoussarn | Cameroon | BFX |
| Bagan | Myanmar | BPE |
| Baganga | Philippines | BNQ |
| Bagani | Namibia | BQI |
| Bagdad, AZ | USA | BGT |
| Bagdogra | India | IXB |
| Bage | Brazil | BGX |
| Baghdad/Al Muthana | Iraq | BGW |
| Baghdad/Saddam Int'l | Iraq | SDA |
| Baglung | Nepal | BGL |
| Bagotville, QC | Canada | YBG |
| Baguic,/Loakan | Philippines | BAG |
| Bahar Dar | Ethiopia | BJR |
| Bahawainagar | Pakistan | WGB |
| Bahawaipur | Pakistan | BHV |
| Bahia Blanca/Comandante | Argentina | BHI |
| Bahia Cupica | Cocos (Keeling) Is | BHF |
| Bahia De Caraquez | Ecuador | BHA |
| Bahia Pinas | Panama | BFQ |
| Bahia Solano | Colombia | BSC |
| Bahla Angeles | Mexico | BHL |
| Bahrain/Int'l | Bahrain | BAH |
| Bahregan | Iran | IAQ |
| Baia Mare | Romania | BAY |
| Baibara | Papua New Guinea | BAP |
| Baidoa | Somalia | BIB |
| Baie Comeau, QC | Canada | YBC |
| Baimuru | Papua New Guinea | VMU |
| Bainbridge/Decatur County, GA | USA | BGE |

| | | |
|---|---|---|
| Baindoung | Papua New Guinea | BDZ |
| Bairnsdale | Australia | BSJ |
| Baitadi | Nepal | BIT |
| Baitrum | Germany | BMR |
| Bajawa | Indonesia | BJW |
| Bajhang | Nepal | BJH |
| Bajone | Mozambique | BJN |
| Bajura Arpt | Nepal | BJU |
| Bakalalan | Malaysia | BKM |
| Bakel | Senegal | BXE |
| Baker Lake, NT | Canada | YBK |
| Baker, Baker Municipal Arpt, OR USA | | BKE |
| Baker/AAF, AK | USA | BAR |
| Bakersfield/Meadows Fld, CA | USA | BFL |
| Bakkafjordur | Iceland | BJD |
| Bakourna | Central African Rep | BMF |
| Baku | Azerbaijan | BAK |
| Balakovo | Russia | BWO |
| Balalae | Solomon Is | BAS |
| Balboa | Panama | BLB |
| Balcanoona | Australia | LCN |
| Bale Johan Beetz, QC | Canada | YBJ |
| Baler | Philippines | BQA |
| Balgo Hills | Australia | BQW |
| Balhash | Kazakstan | BXH |
| Bali | Papua New Guinea | BAJ |
| Bali | Cameroon | BLC |
| BaLicin | Indonesia | BTW |
| Balikesir | Turkey | BZI |
| Balikesir/Merkez | Turkey | MQJ |
| Balikipapan/Sepingan | Indonesia | BPN |
| Balimo | Papua New Guinea | OPU |
| Ballina | Australia | BNK |
| Ballina | Australia | QNA |
| Bally Kelly | UK | BOL |
| Balmaceda/Teniente Vicial | Chile | BBA |
| Balranald | Australia | BZD |
| Balsas | Brazil | BSS |
| Baltimore, MD | USA | BWI |
| Baltimore, MD | USA | MTN |
| Baltimore-Greenbelt, MD | USA | GBO |
| Baltimore/Baltimore Rail, MD | USA | ZBP |
| Balurghat | India | RGH |
| Bamako | Mali | BKO |
| Bambari | Central African Rep | BBY |
| Bamberg/Off-line Pt | Germany | ZCD |
| Bambu | Papua New Guinea | BCP |
| Bamburi | Kenya | BMQ |
| Bamenda | Cameroon | BPC |
| Bamerny | Iraq | BMN |
| Bamfield, BC | Canada | YBF |
| Bamiyan | Afghanistan | BIN |
| Bamu | Papua New Guinea | BMZ |
| Ban Houei | Laos | OUI |
| Ban Mak Khaen/Udorn | Thailand | BAO |
| Banaina | Indonesia | NAF |
| Banda Aceh/Blang Bintang | | |
| | Indonesia | BTJ |
| Bandanatra | Indonesia | NDA |
| Bandar Abbas | Iran | BND |
| Bandar Khomeini | Iran | QBR |
| Bandar Lampung/Branti | Indonesia | TKG |
| Bandar Lengeh | Iran | BDH |
| Bandar Mahshahr | Iran | MRX |
| Bandar Seri Begawan | Brunei | BWN |
| Bandirma | Turkey | BDM |
| Bandol | France | XBZ |
| Bandon/State, OR | USA | BDY |
| Bandundu | Congo, DR | FDU |
| Bandung/Husein Sastranegara | | |
| | Indonesia | BDO |
| Banff, AB | Canada | YBA |
| Banfora | Burkina Faso | BNR |
| Bangalore/Hindustan | India | BLR |
| Bangassou | Central African Rep | BGU |
| Bangda | China | BPX |
| Bangkok Int'l | Thailand | BKK |
| Bangor Int'l Arpt, ME | USA | BGR |
| Bangsiund | Norway | ZXC |
| Bangui | Central African Rep | BGF |
| Bani-walid | Libya | QBL |
| Baniyala | Australia | BYX |
| Banja Luka | Bosnia Hercegovina | BNX |
| Banjarmasin/Sjamsudin Noor | | |
| | Indonesia | BDJ |
| Banjul/Yundum Int'l | The Gambia | BJL |
| Bankstown | Australia | BWU |
| Banmethuot/Phung-Duc | Vietnam | BMV |
| Banning, CA | USA | BNG |
| Bannu | Pakistan | BNP |
| Bantry | Ireland | BYT |
| Banyuls Sur Mer | France | XBU |
| Banz | Papua New Guinea | BNZ |
| Baoshan | China | BSD |
| Baotou | China | BAV |
| Bapi | Papua New Guinea | BPD |
| Bar Harbour, ME | USA | BHB |
| Baracoa | Cuba | BCA |
| Barahona | Dominican Rep | BRX |
| Barakorna | Solomon Is | VEV |
| Baramita | Guyana | BMJ |
| Barbacena | Brazil | QAK |
| Barbelos | Brazil | BAZ |
| Barbers Point, HI | USA | NAX |
| Barbuda | Antigua & Barbuda | BBQ |
| Barcaidine | Australia | BCI |
| Barcelona | Spain | BCN |
| Barcelona | Venezuela | BLA |
| Barcelonnette | France | BAE |
| Bardera | Somalia | BSY |
| Bardstown/Samuels Fld, KY | USA | BRY |
| Bardufoss | Norway | BDU |
| Bareges | France | XBA |
| Bari/Palese Macchie | Italy | BRI |
| Barin/NAS, AL | USA | NBJ |
| Barinas | Venezuela | BNS |
| Bario | Malaysia | BBN |
| Barisal | Bangladesh | BZL |
| Barka | Algeria | ZZB |
| Barkly Downs | Australia | BKP |
| Barksdale/AFB, LA | USA | BAD |
| Barn | Iran | BXR |
| Barnaga | Australia | ABM |
| Barnaul | Russia | BAX |
| Barnwell, SC | USA | BNL |
| Barora | Solomon Is | RRI |
| Barquisimeto | Venezuela | BRM |
| Barra | Brazil | BQQ |
| Barra Colorado | Costa Rica | BCL |
| Barra Do Corda | Brazil | BDC |
| Barra Do Garcas | Brazil | BPG |
| Barra Do Pirai | Brazil | QBD |
| Barra Mansa | Brazil | QBN |
| Barra/North Bay | UK | BRR |
| Barranca De Upia | Colombia | BAC |
| Barrancabermeia/Vrgs | Colombia | EJA |
| Barrancominas | Colombia | NBB |
| Barranquilla/E Cortissoz | Colombia | BAQ |
| Barre, VT | USA | MPV |
| Barreiras | Brazil | BRA |
| Barreirinhas | Brazil | BRB |
| Barretos | Brazil | BAT |
| Barrow Is | Australia | BWB |
| Barrow-In-Furness/Walney Isl | UK | BWF |
| Barrow/Metro., AK | USA | BRW |
| Barrow/Point Barrow, AK | USA | PBA |
| Barstow-Daggett, CA | USA | DAG |
| Barter Is, AK | USA | BTI |
| Barth | Germany | BBH |
| Bartica | Guyana | GFO |
| Bartlesville, OK | USA | BVO |
| Bartletts, AK | USA | BSZ |
| Bartow Municipal, FL | USA | BOW |
| Baruun-Urt | Mongolia | UUN |
| Basankusu | Congo, DR | BSU |
| Basco | Philippines | BSO |
| Basel/Mulhouse | Switzerland | BSL |
| Basel/Mulhouse | Switzerland | MLH |
| Basel/Mulhouse/German Railway | | |
| Svc | Switzerland | ZBA |
| Basel/Mulhouse/SBB Railway | | |
| Svc | Switzerland | ZDH |
| Basingstoke/RR Stn | UK | XQB |
| Basongo | Congo, DR | BAN |
| Basra/Int'l | Iraq | BSR |
| Basse Terre/Baillif | Gaudeloupe | BBR |
| Bassein | Myanmar | BSX |
| Bastia/Poretta | France | BIA |
| Bata | Equatorial Guinea | BSG |
| Batam/HaNadirr, | Indonesia | BTH |
| Batangafo | Central African Rep | BTG |
| Batavia Downs | Australia | BVW |
| Batemans Bay | Australia | QBW |
| Batesvilie,/Municipal | Australia | BVX |
| Batesville/Hillenbrand, IN | USA | HLB |
| Bath/RR | UK | QQX |
| Bathurst Is | Australia | BRT |
| Bathurst, NB | Canada | ZBF |
| Bathurst/Raglan | Australia | BHS |
| Batman | Turkey | BAL |
| Batna | Algeria | BLJ |
| Batna | Algeria | DLJ |
| Batom | Indonesia | BXM |
| Baton Rouge/Downtown, LA | USA | EBR |
| Baton Rouge/Ryan Fld, LA | USA | BTR |
| Batouri | Cameroon | OUR |
| Batsfjord | Norway | BJF |
| Battambang | Cambodia | BBM |
| Batticaloa | Sri Lanka | BTC |
| Battle Creek/Kellogg, MI | USA | BTL |
| Battle Mountain, NV | USA | BAM |
| Batumi | Georgia | BUS |
| Batuna Aerodrome | Solomon Is | BPF |
| Baubau/Beto Ambiri | Indonesia | BUW |
| Baucau/English Madeira | Indonesia | BCH |
| Bauchi | Nigeria | BCU |
| Bauchi | Nigeria | QBU |
| Baudette/Int'l, MN | USA | BDE |
| Baures | Bolivia | BVL |
| Bauru | Brazil | BAU |
| Bawan | Papua New Guinea | BWJ |
| Bay City, MI | USA | MBS |
| Bay City, TX | USA | BBC |
| Bayamo/C.M. de Cespedes | Cuba | BYM |
| Bayankhongor | Mongolia | BYN |
| Bayonne | France | XBY |
| Bayreuth | Germany | BYU |
| Baytown, TX | USA | HPY |
| Bazaruto Is | Mozambique | BZB |
| Beagle Bay | Australia | BEE |
| Bealanana | Madagascar | WBE |
| Beale/AFB, CA | USA | BAB |
| Bear Creek, AK | USA | BCC |
| Bearskin Lake, ON | Canada | XBE |
| Beatrice, NE | USA | BIE |
| Beatton River, BC | Canada | YZC |
| Beatty, NV | USA | BTY |
| Beaufort/County, SC | USA | BFT |
| Beaulieu Sur Mer | France | XBM |
| Beaumont, TX | USA | BPT |
| Beaumont/Municipal, TX | USA | BMT |
| Beaune | France | XBV |
| Beauvais | France | BVA |
| Beaver Creek, YT | Canada | YXQ |
| Beaver Falls Arpt, PA | USA | BFP |
| Beaver Inlet/Sea Port, AK | USA | BVD |
| Beaver, AK | USA | WBQ |
| Bebedouro | Brazil | QAU |
| Bechar | Algeria | CBH |
| Beckley, WV | USA | BKW |
| Beclarra Is | Australia | QIY |
| Bedford Downs | Australia | BDW |
| Bedford, IN | USA | BFR |
| Bedford/Hanscom Fld, MA | USA | BED |
| Bedford/RR Stn | UK | XQD |
| Bedford/Thurleigh (Military) | UK | BFZ |
| Bedourie | Australia | BEU |
| Beef Is | Virgin Is (British) | EIS |
| Beer Sheba | Israel | BEV |
| Beeville/NAS, TX | USA | NIR |
| Befandriana | Madagascar | WBD |
| Bega/Off-line Pt | Australia | QBE |
| Beica | Ethiopia | BEI |
| Beida/La Braq | Libya | LAQ |
| Beidah | Yemen | BYD |
| Beijing | China | PEK |
| Beijing/Nanyuan | China | NAY |
| Beil-tai | China | BHY |
| Beinan | Yemen | BHN |
| Beira | Mozambique | BEW |
| Beirut/Int'l | Lebanon | BEY |
| Beitsy | Macau | BZY |
| Bejaia | Algeria | BJA |
| Bekily | Madagascar | OVA |
| BelAbbes | Algeria | QBB |
| Belaga | Malaysia | BLG |
| Belem/Val De Cans | Brazil | BEL |
| Belep Is | New Caledonia | BMY |
| Belfast/Belfast City Arpt | UK | BHD |
| Belfast/Belfast Int'l Arpt | UK | BFS |
| Belfort/Fontaine | France | BOR |
| Belgaum/Sambre | India | IXG |
| Belgorod | Russia | EGO |
| Belgrade/Batapica | Yugoslavia | BJY |
| Belgrade/Becigrad | Yugoslavia | BEG |
| Beliary | India | BEP |
| Belize City/Goldson Int'l | Belize | BZE |
| Belize City/Mun | Belize | TZA |
| Bell Is/Hot Springs SPB, AK | USA | KBE |
| Bella Bella, BC | Canada | ZEL |
| Bella Coola, BC | Canada | QBR |
| Bella Union | Uruguay | BUV |
| Bella Yeila | Liberia | BYL |

**Bellaire**/Antrim County, MI ... USA .. ACB
**Bellavista** ... Peru .. BLP
**Belle Chasse**/Southern Seaplane, LA ... USA .. BCS
**Belle Fourche**, SD ... USA .. EFC
**Bellefonte**, PA ... USA .. PSB
**Bellegarde** ... France .. XBF
**Belleville**/RR Stn., ON ... Canada .. XVV
**Bellingham**/Int'l Arpt, WA ... USA ... BLI
**Bellinzona** ... Switzerland ... ZDI
**Bellona** ... Solomon Is .. BNY
**Belluno** ... Italy .. BLX
**Belmar-Farmdale**, NJ ... USA .. BLM
**Belmonte** ... Brazil .. BVM
**Belmopan** ... Belize .. BCV
**Belmullet** ... Ireland ... BLY
**Belo** ... Madagascar .. BMD
**Belo Horizonte**/Pampulha ... Brazil .. PLU
**Belo Horizonte**/T. Neves ... Brazil .. CNF
**Beloreck** ... Russia .. BCX
**Beltsville**, MO/Off-line Pt ... USA .. ZFE
**Beluga**, AK ... USA .. BVU
**Bembridge** ... UK .. BBP
**Bemichi** ... Guyana .. BCG
**Bemidji**, MN ... USA ... BJI
**Benalla** ... Australia .. BLN
**Benbecula** ... UK .. BEB
**Benevento** ... Italy .. QBV
**Bengbu** ... China .. BFU
**Benghazi**/Benina Intl ... Libya .. BEN
**Bengkulu**/Padangkemiling ... Indonesia .. BKS
**Benguela**/GV Deslandes ... Angola .. BUG
**Benguera Is** ... Mozambique .. BCW
**Beni** ... Congo, DR .. BNC
**Benin City** ... Nigeria ... BNI
**Benjamin Constant** ... Brazil .. QAV
**Bennettsville**, SC ... USA .. BTN
**Bensbach** ... Papua New Guinea .. BSP
**Benson**/Municipal, MN ... USA .. BBB
**Benson**/RAF ... UK .. BEX
**Bento Goncalves** ... Brazil .. BGV
**Benton Harbor**/Ross Fld, MI ... USA .. BEH
**Beppu** ... Japan .. BPU
**Bequia Arpt**St. Vincent & Grenadines .. BQU
**Berau** ... Indonesia ... BEJ
**Berbera** ... Somalia .. BBO
**Berberati** ... Central African Rep .. BBT
**Berchtesgaden** ... Germany .. ZCE
**Berdyansk** ... Ukraine .. ERD
**Bereby** ... Côte D'Ivoire .. BBV
**Bereina** ... Papua New Guinea .. BEA
**Berens River**, MB ... Canada .. YBV
**Bergen Op Zoom** ... Netherlands .. BZM
**Bergen**/Flesland ... Norway .. BGO
**Bergen**/Harbour Pier ... Norway .. QFV
**Bergerac**/Roumanieres ... France .. EGC
**Bergheim** (Cologne) ... Germany .. ZCF
**Bergisch Gladbach** ... Germany .. ZCG
**Bergkamen**/Off-line Pt ... Germany .. ZCH
**Berijina** ... Indonesia ... BJK
**Berkeley**, CA ... USA ... JBK
**Berlevag** ... Norway .. BVG
**Berlin** ... Germany .. QPP
**Berlin Municipal Arpt**, NH ... USA .. BML
**Berlin**/Berlin Zoo Railway Sta ... Germany . QWC
**Berlin**/Fredrichstr. Railway Sta ... Germany . QWE
**Berlin**/HBF Railway Sta ... Germany . QWB
**Berlin**/RAF Gatow ... Germany . GWW
**Berlin**/Schoenefeld ... Germany .. SXF
**Berlin**/Tegel ... Germany ... TXL
**Berlin**/Tempelhof ... Germany .. THF
**Bermejo** ... Bolivia .. BJO
**Bermuda**/NAS ... Bermuda . NWU
**Bernay** ... France .. XBX
**Berne** ... Switzerland ... ZDJ
**Berne**/Belp ... Switzerland .. BRN
**Beroroha** ... Madagascar . WBO
**Berriane** ... Algeria ... ZBI
**Bertoua** ... Cameroon .. BTA
**Beru** ... Kiribati .. BEZ
**Berwick**/RR Stn ... UK .. XQG
**Besakoa** ... Madagascar .. BSV
**Besalampy** ... Madagascar .. BPY
**Besancon** ... France .. QBQ
**Best**/Bus Svc ... Netherlands . QWZ
**Bethel**, AK ... USA .. BET
**Bethel**/City Landing, AK ... USA ... JBT
**Bethpage**/Grumman, NY ... USA .. BPA
**Bethune** ... France .. XBH
**Betim** ... Brazil .. QBK
**Betioky** ... Madagascar .. BKU
**Betoota** ... Australia .. BTX
**Betou** ... Congo, DR .. BTB
**Bettioua** ... Algeria .. QBT
**Bettles Arpt**, AK ... USA .. BTT
**Beverley Springs** ... Australia .. BVZ
**Beverly**, MA ... USA .. BVY
**Bewani** ... Papua New Guinea . BWP
**Beziers**/Vias ... France .. BZR
**Bhadohi** ... India .. XXB
**Bhairawa** ... Nepal . BWA
**Bhamo** ... Myanmar . BMO
**Bharatpur** ... Nepal .. BHR
**Bhatinda** ... India .. BUP
**Bhavnagar** ... India .. BHU
**Bhojpur** ... Nepal .. BHP
**Bhopal** ... India .. BHO
**Bhubaneswar** ... India ... BBI
**Bhuj**/Rudra Mata ... India .. BHJ
**Bhurban**/Bhurban HP ... Pakistan .. BHC
**Biak**/Mokmer ... Indonesia ... BIK
**Bialla** ... Papua New Guinea .. BAA
**Bialystok** ... Poland .. QYY
**Biarritz**/Biarritz Parme ... France .. BIQ
**Biaru** ... Papua New Guinea .. BRP
**Biawonque** ... Gabon . BAW
**Bickerton Is** ... Australia .. BCZ
**Biel**/Bienne ... Switzerland .. ZDK
**Bielefeld** ... Germany .. BFE
**Bielsko-Baila** ... Poland . QEO
**Big Bay** ... Vanuatu .. GBA
**Big Bay Marina**, BC ... Canada .. YIG
**Big Bay Yacht Club**, BC .. Canada .. YYA
**Big Bear**, CA ... USA .. RBF
**Big Bell** ... Australia .. BBE
**Big Creek** ... Belize .. BGK
**Big Creek**, AK ... USA ... BIC
**Big Delta**/Intermediate Fld, AK . USA .. BIG
**Big Lake**, AK ... USA . BGQ
**Big Mountain**, AK ... USA .. BMX
**Big Piney**, WY ... USA ... BPI
**Big Rapids**, MI ... USA . WBR
**Big Spring**, Webb/AFB, TX ... USA .. BGS
**Big Spring**/Howard County, TX USA .. HCA
**Big Trout**, ON ... Canada .. YTL
**Biggs**/AAF, TX ... USA ... BIF
**Bikaner** ... India .. BKB
**Bikini Atoll**/Enyu Airfield . Marshall Is ... BII
**Bilaspur** ... India .. PAB
**Bilbao** ... Spain .. BIO
**Bildudalur** ... Iceland .. BIU
**Biliau** ... Papua New Guinea ... BIJ
**Billiluna** ... Australia .. BIW
**Billings**/Int'l, MT ... USA ... BIL
**Billund**/Lufthavn ... Denmark .. BLL
**Biloela** ... Australia .. ZBL
**Biloxi Regional Arpt**, MS ... USA .. GPT
**Bima** ... Indonesia . BMU
**Bimin** ... Papua New Guinea ... BIZ
**Bimini**/Int'l ... Bahamas .. BIM
**Bimini**/North SPB ... Bahamas .. NSB
**Binghamton**, NY ... USA . BGM
**Biniguni** ... Papua New Guinea .. XBN
**Bintulu** ... Malaysia .. BTU
**Bintuni** ... Indonesia ... NTI
**Birao** ... Central African Rep ... IRO
**Biratnagar** ... Nepal ... BIR
**Birch Creek**, AK ... USA ... KBC
**Bird Is** ... Seychelles ... BDI
**Birdsville** ... Australia ... BVI
**Birigui** ... Brazil .. QCF
**Birjand** ... Iran .. XBJ
**Birminaham**-New Street/RR ... UK . QQN
**Birmingham**/Colmore Row Bus Stn. ... UK .. ZBC
**Birmingham**/Int'l ... UK .. BHX
**Birmingham**/Int'l, AL ... USA . BHM
**Birni Nkoni** ... Niger .. BKN
**Bisbee**/Municipal, AZ ... USA .. BSQ
**Bisha** ... Saudi Arabia .. BHH
**Bishkek** ... Kyrgyzstan .. FRU
**Bisho** ... South Africa ... BIY
**Bishop**, CA ... USA ... BIH
**Biskra** ... Algeria .. BSK
**Bislig** ... Philippines .. BPH
**Bismarck**, ND ... USA ... BIS
**Bissau**/Osvaldo Vieira Guinea Bissau .. OXB
**Bistrita**/Nasaud ... Romania .. QBY
**Bitam** ... Gabon . BMM
**Bitiburg Air Base** ... Germany ... BBJ
**Bitola** ... Macedonia ... QBI
**Biumenau** ... Brazil .. BNU
**Bizant** ... Australia .. BZP
**Bizerte** ... India ... QIZ
**Black Tickle**, NF ... Canada ... YBI
**Blackall** ... Australia .. BKQ
**Blackbushe** ... UK .. BBS
**Blackpool** ... UK .. BLK
**Blackstone**/AAF, VA ... USA .. BKT
**Blackwater** ... Australia .. BLT
**Blagoveschensk** ... Russia .. BQS
**Blaine**, WA ... USA .. BWS
**Blairsville**, PA ... USA ... BSI
**Blakely Is**, WA ... USA .. BYW
**Blanc Sablon**, QC ... Canada ... YBX
**Blanding**, UT ... USA .. BDG
**Blantyre**/Chileka ... Malawi ... BLZ
**Blenheim** ... New Zealand . BHE
**Blida** ... Algeria .. QLD
**Block Is**, RI ... USA ... BID
**Bloemfontein Int'l** ... South Africa .. BFN
**Blois** ... France .. XBQ
**Blonduos** ... Iceland .. BLO
**Bloodvein**, MB ... Canada .. YDV
**Bloomfield** ... Australia .. BFC
**Bloomington**, IN ... USA .. BMG
**Bloomington**/Normal, IL ... USA ... BMI
**Blubber Bay**, BC ... Canada .. XBB
**Blue Bell**/Wings Fld, PA ... USA .. BBX
**Blue Canyon**, CA ... USA .. BLU
**Blue Fox Bay**, AK ... USA .. BFB
**Blue Lagoon** ... Fiji .. BXL
**Blue River**, BC ... Canada .. YCP
**Bluefield**/Mercer County Arpt, WV ... USA ... BLF
**Bluefields** ... Netherlands ... BEF
**Blythe Arpt**, CA ... USA .. BLH
**Blytheville Municipal**, AR ... USA .. HKA
**Blytheville**/AFB, AR ... USA .. BYH
**Bo** ... Sierra Leone .. KBS
**Boa Vista** ... Brazil .. BVB
**Boa Vista**/Rabil ... Cape Verde Is . BVC
**Boana** ... Papua New Guinea . BNV
**Boang** ... Papua New Guinea . BOV
**Bobo Dioulasso**/Borgo ... Burkina Faso . BOY
**Bobquinn Lake**, BC ... Canada .. YBO
**Boca Do Acre** ... Brazil .. BCR
**Boca Raton**/Public, FL ... USA .. BCT
**Bocas Del Tore**, ... Panama .. BOC
**Bocholt** ... Germany ... ZCI
**Bochum** ... Germany .. QBO
**Bodinumu** ... Papua New Guinea . BNM
**Bodo** ... Norway .. BOO
**Bodrum**./Milas Arpt ... Turkey ... BJV
**Bodrum**/Imisk Arpt ... Turkey .. BXN
**Boeblingen** ... Germany .. PHM
**Boende** ... Congo, DR . BNB
**Bogalusa**/George R Carr, LA ... USA .. BXA
**Bogande** ... Burkina Faso . XBG
**Boghe**/Abbaye ... Mauritania .. BGH
**Bogota**/Eldorado ... Colombia .. BOG
**Boigu Is** ... Australia ... GIC
**Boise**/Boise Air Terminal, ID ... USA ... BOI
**Boizano** ... Italy .. BZO
**Boke** ... Guinea ... BKJ
**Bokondini** ... Indonesia ... BUI
**Bokoro** ... Chad .. BKR
**Boku** ... Papua New Guinea . BOQ
**Bol** ... Croatia .. BWK
**Bol** ... Chad .. OTC
**Bolaang** ... Indonesia .. BJG
**Bolling**/AFB, DC ... USA .. BOF
**Bollon** ... Australia .. BLS
**Bologna**/Guglielmo Marconi ... Italy .. BLQ
**Bolovip** ... Papua New Guinea .. BVP
**Bolwarra** ... Australia .. BCK
**Bom Jesus Da Lapa** ... Brazil ... LAZ
**Boma** ... Congo, DR . BOA
**Bomai** ... Papua New Guinea . BMH
**Bonaire**/Int'l ... Netherlands Antilles . BON
**Bonanza**/San Pedro ... Netherlands ... BZA
**Bonaventure**, QC ... Canada .. YVB
**Bondaukou**/Soko ... Côte D'Ivoire . BDK
**Bonger** ... Chad .. OGR
**Bongo** ... Gabon .. BGP
**Bongouanou** ... Chile .. BGG
**Bonnyville**, AB ... Canada .. YBY
**Bontang** ... Indonesia .. BXT
**Bonthe** ... Sierra Leone .. BTE

AIRPORTS -2-

| | | |
|---|---|---|
| Boone Municipal, IA.........USA. BNW | Brantford/RR Stn., ON..... Canada .. XFV | Brus Laguna............Honduras.. BHG |
| Booue .....................Gabon.. BGB | Brasilia/Int'l....................Brazil .. BSB | Brusque .................. Brazil.. QJM |
| Bopord........................Iran..BJB | Bratislava/Bus Svc........ Slovakia ..ZRG | Brussels ................ Belgium.. CRL |
| Bora Bora/Motu-mute .. F. Polynesia .. BOB | Bratislava/Ivanka ......... Slovakia .. BTS | Brussels/Midi Railway Stn . Belgium.. ZYR |
| Borama..................Somalia.. BXX | Bratsk .....................Russia .. BTK | Brussels/National ......... Belgium.. BRU |
| Borba ......................Brazil.. RBB | Brattleboro, VT.............. USA .. EEN | Bryan/Coulter Fld, TX .........USA.. CFD |
| Borcj Menatiel..............Algeria . ZZM | Braunschweig ......... Germany . BWE | Bryant/AAF, AK ...............USA.. FRN |
| Bordeaux/Gare de Bordeaux .France.. ZFQ | Brava............. Cape Verde Is .. BVR | Bryce Canyon, UT.............USA.. BCE |
| Bordeaux/Merignac........France.. BOD | Brawley, CA.................. USA .. BWC | Bua/Dama ....................Fiji.. BVF |
| Borden, ON................Canada.. YBN | Brazoria/Hinkles Ferry, TX..... USA .. BZT | Bubaque........... Guinea Bissau .. BQE |
| Bordj Badji Mokintar...... Algeria . BMW | Brazzaville/Maya-Maya.. Congo, DR .. BZV | Bucaramanga/Palo Negro  Colombia.. BGA |
| Bordj-Bou-Arreri ......... Algeria .. QBJ | Breckenridge/Stephens County, | Buchanan...............Liberia.. UCN |
| Borgarfiordur Eystri ...... Iceland.. BGJ | TX.....................USA .. BKD | Buchans, NF ............ Canada.. YZM |
| Boriange/Dala.............Sweden.. BLE | Breckenridge/Van Svc, CO ... USA .. QKB | Bucharest/Baneasa ...... Romania.. BBU |
| Boridi .........Papua New Guinea.. BPB | Breda/Gilze-Rijen........ Netherlands .. GLZ | Bucharest/Otopeni Int'l... Romania.. OTP |
| Borkum .................Germany.. BMK | Breiddalsvilk ............. Iceland.. BXV | Buchs SG ............. Switzerland.. ZDO |
| Bornholm/Ronne .........Denmark.. RNN | Bremen ................. Germany . BRE | Buckeye, AZ...............USA.. BXK |
| Bornite, AK ...................USA.. RLU | Bremerhaven ........... Germany . BRV | Buckland, AK................USA.. BKC |
| Borotou ..............Côte D'Ivoire .. BRZ | Bremerton, WA.............. USA . PWT | Budapest/Ferihegy .........Hungary.. BUD |
| Borrego Springs, CA........USA.. BXS | Brescia .....................Italy . QBS | Budva .................Yugoslavia.. QBA |
| Borroloola ............ Australia.. BOX | Brescia/Montichiari ..........Italy .. VBS | Buenaventura ........... Colombia.. BUN |
| Boscobel, WI ...............USA.. OVS | Brest .................... Belarus . BQT | Buenos Aires ..........Costa Rica .. BAI |
| Boset .........Papua New Guinea.. BOT | Brest/Guipavas ........... France .. BES | Buenos Aires/Ministro Pistarini |
| Bossangoa..... Central African Rep.. BSN | Breves .....................Brazil .. BVS | .....................Argentina..EZE |
| Bossaso ..................Somalia.. BSA | Brewarrina ............. Australia . BWQ | Buenos Aires/Newbery .. Argentina..AEP |
| Bost ...................Afghanistan.. BST | Brewster Fld Arpt, NE ....... USA .. HDE | Buffalo Int'l Arpt, NY..........USA.. BUF |
| Boston/HP, MA...............USA.. JBC | Bria .....................Costa Rica .. BIV | Buffalo Narrows, SK ...... Canada.. YVT |
| Boston/BKBAY Rail, MA.......USA.. ZTY | Briancon ...................France . XBC | Buffalo Range .......... Zimbabwe.. BFO |
| Boston/Boston RT128 Rail, MA .USA.. ZRU | Briansk ....................Russia . BZK | Buffalo, WY ..................USA.. BYG |
| Boston/Boston South Rail, MA ..USA.. ZTO | Bridgeport/Sikorsky Memorial, | Buffalo/Buffalo Depew RR, NY .USA.. ZFZ |
| Boston/Logan Int'l, MA.......USA.. BOS | CT.................... USA .. BDR | Buffalo/Exchange St Railway |
| Boswell Bay, AK .............USA..BSW | Bridgetown/Grantley Adams Int'l | Svc., NY ...............USA..ZXS |
| Botopasie ...............Suriname.. BTO | .................... Barbados .. BGI | Buguima.................Russia.. UUA |
| Botosani .................Romania.. QDD | Brig ................. Switzerland .. ZDL | Buichi ..................Ethiopia.. BCY |
| Bottrop ..................Germany.. ZCJ | Brigham City, UT ......... USA . BMC | Buin ...........Papua New Guinea .. UBI |
| Botucatu ...................Brazil.. QCJ | Bright .................. Australia .. BRJ | Bujumbura/Int'l ..........Burundi.. BJM |
| Bouake ..............Côte D'Ivoire.. BYK | Brighton....................UK .. BSH | Buka ...........Papua New Guinea .. BUA |
| Bouar ......... Central African Rep.. BOP | Brighton Downs ........ Australia .. BHT | Bukavu/Kamenbe ..... Congo, DR ..BKY |
| Bouca ......... Central African Rep.. BCF | Brindisi/Papola Casale.........Italy .. BDS | Bukhara ...............Uzbekistan.. BHK |
| Boufarik ...................Algeria.. QFD | Brisbane/Int'l ........... Australia .. BNE | Bukoba ..................Tanzania.. BKZ |
| Bouira .....................Algeria.. QBZ | Bristol, TN ................. USA .. TRI | Bulawayo ...............Zimbabwe.. BUQ |
| Boukadir ...................Algeria.. ZAB | Bristol/Filton...............UK .. FZO | Bulgan ..................Mongolia.. UGA |
| Boulder City, CO.............USA.. BLD | Bristol/Lulsgate.............UK .. BRS | Bulimba ..................Australia.. BIP |
| Boulder/Broker Inn, CO.......USA.. WBI | Britrail Rail Zone A..........UK . QQA | Bull Harbour, BC ........ Canada.. YBH |
| Boulder/Hiltons Har H, CO .....USA.. WHH | Britrail Rail Zone B..........UK . QQB | Bullfrog Basin, UT...........USA.. BFG |
| Boulder/Metro, CO...........USA.. WBU | Britrail Rail Zone C..........UK . QQC | Bullhead City/Int'l, AZ. .......USA.. IFP |
| Boulia ...................Australia.. BQL | Britrail Rail Zone E..........UK . QQE | Bullocks Flat/Bus Svc .....Australia.. QZM |
| Boulogne Billancourt......France.. XBT | Britrail Rail Zone F..........UK . QQF | Bulolo ..........Papua New Guinea .. BUL |
| Boulogne Sur Mer .......France.. XBS | Britrail Rail Zone G..........UK . QQG | Bumba ...............Congo, DR . BMB |
| Boulsa ..............Burkina Faso.. XBO | Britrail Rail Zone I ..........UK .. QQI | Bumi Hills ..............Zimbabwe.. BZH |
| Bouna/Tehini ..........Côte D'Ivoire.. BQO | Britrail Rail Zone J..........UK .. QQJ | Bunbury ..................Australia.. BUY |
| Boundary, AK................USA.. BYA | Britrail Rail Zone L..........UK .. QQL | Bundaberg ...............Australia.. BDB |
| Boundiali ............Côte D'Ivoire.. BXI | Britrail Rail Zone O ..........UK .. QQO | Bundi ...........Papua New Guinea .. BNT |
| Boundji ..............Congo, DR.. BOE | Britrail Rail Zone S..........UK .. QQS | Buno Bedelle ............ Ethiopia.. XBL |
| Bountiful, UT ................USA.. BTF | Britrail Rail Zone T..........UK .. QQT | Bunsil ..........Papua New Guinea .. BXZ |
| Bourg D'Oisans ...........France.. XBI | Britrail Rail Zone V..........UK .. QQV | Bunyu ..................Indonesia.. BYQ |
| Bourg En Bresse .........France.. XBK | Britrail Rail Zone Z ...... Georgia .. QQZ | Buol ...................Indonesia.. UOL |
| Bourg-St Maurice .........France..QBM | Britton/Municipal, SD ........ USA .. TTO | Buraimi .....................Oman.. RMB |
| Bourgas ..................Bulgaria.. BOJ | Brive-La-Gaillarde/Laroche  France .. BVE | Burao ...................Somalia.. BUO |
| Bourges ...................France.. BOU | Brize Norton/RAF ............UK .. BZZ | Burbank, CA ................USA.. BUR |
| Bourke ..................Australia.. BRK | Brno/Bus Svc ..........Czech Rep .. ZDN | Bureta/Levuka Airfield .........Fiji.. LEV |
| Bournemouth/Int'l ...........UK.. BOH | Brno/Turany ..........Czech Rep .. BRQ | Burg Feuerstein.......... Germany.. URD |
| Boussaada..................Algeria.. BUJ | Broadus, MT ................ USA .. BDX | Burgdorf................Switzerland.. ZDP |
| Bousso .......................Chad.. OUT | Broadview, SK ............ Canada .. YDR | Buri Ram .................Thailand.. BFV |
| Boutilimit ..............Mauritania.. OTL | Brochet, MB................ Canada .. YBT | Burketown ...............Australia.. BUC |
| Bowen ...................Australia.. ZBO | Brockville, ON ............ Canada .. XBR | Burley, ID ....................USA.. BYI |
| Bowling Green, KY...........USA.. BWG | Broenclersev/Bus Svc ... Denmark ..XAQ | Burlington, IA ...............USA.. BRL |
| Bowling Green, VA...........USA.. APH | Broken Bow Municipal, NE .. USA .. BBW | Burlington, MA ..............USA.. BBF |
| Bowman, ND ................USA.. BWM | Broken Hill ............... Australia ..BHQ | Burlington/Int'l, VT ...........USA.. BTV |
| Boxborough, MA.............USA.. BXC | Bromont, QC.............. Canada ..ZBM | Burnie/Burnie Wynyard.....Australia.. BWT |
| Bozeman, MT...............USA.. BZN | Bronnoysund/Bronnoy .... Norway .. BNN | Burns Lake, BC............ Canada..YPZ |
| Bozen/Bus Stn...............Italy.. ZBN | Bronson Creek, BC....... Canada ..YBM | Burns Municipal Arpt, OR.... USA.. BNO |
| Bozoum ........ Central African Rep.. BOZ | Brookings, OR ............ USA .. BOK | Bursa ....................Turkey.. BTZ |
| Brack .....................Libya.. BCQ | Brookings, SD ............ USA .. BKX | Bursa ....................Turkey... YEI |
| Bradford ....................UK.. BRF | Brooklyn, NJ .............. USA .. QFF | Burtonwood .................UK..BUT |
| Bradford, PA.................USA.. BFD | Brooklyn, NJ .............. USA ..QHW | Burundai ...............Kazakstan.. BXJ |
| Bradford/Bus Stn .............UK.. ZFC | Brooks, AK ................. USA .. BKF | Burwash Landings, YT ... Canada.. YDB |
| Bradford/Rinkenberg, IL ........USA.. BDF | Brooks Lodge, AK............ USA .. RBH | Burwell/Municipal, NE ........USA.. BUB |
| Bradshaw/AAF, HI ............USA.. BSF | Brooksville, FL.............. USA .. BKV | Bury St Edmunds/Honington... UK.. BEQ |
| Brady/Curtis Fld, TX ..........USA.. BBD | Broome .................. Australia ..BME | Bushehr ......................Iran.. BUZ |
| Braga .....................Portugal.. BGZ | Broomfield/Jeffco, CO ....... USA .. BJC | Busselton/Bussellton Arpt...Australia.. BQB |
| Bragado ..................Argentina.. QRF | Brownsville/Int'l, TX ........ USA .. BRO | Busuanga ...............Philippines.. USU |
| Braganca .................Portugal.. BGC | Brownwood, TX............ USA .. BWD | Buta ...................Congo, DR.. BZU |
| Braganca Paulista ........ Brazil .. BJP | Brueggen/R.A.F. ........ Germany ..BGN | Butare ...................Rwanda.. BTQ |
| Brahman .......Papua New Guinea.. BRH | Bruehl .................. Germany ..ZCK | Butaritari ..................Kiribati.. BBG |
| Brainerd, MN ...............USA.. BRD | Brugge .................. Belgium ..ZGJ | Butler, MO....................USA.. BUM |
| Braintree/Wether Fld/RAF .....UK.. WXF | Brumado ...................Brazil ..BMS | Butler/Graham Fld, PA .........USA.. BTP |
| Brampton Is ..............Australia.. BMP | Brunette Downs ......... Australia ..BTD | Butte/Mooney Arpt, MT .......USA.. BTM |
| Brampton/RR Stn., ON ..... Canada.. XPN | Brunswick, GA ............. USA ..SSI | Butterworth .............. Malaysia.. BWH |
| Brandon, MB .............Canada.. YBR | Brunswick/Glynco, GA ....... USA ..BQK | Butterworth ..............S. Africa.. UTE |
| Brandon/Lakenheath/RAF .....UK...LKZ | Brunswick/NAS, ME ........ USA ..NHZ | Butuan ................Philippines.. BXU |

AIRPORTS-2-

| | | |
|---|---|---|
| Buyo | Côte D'Ivoire | BUU |
| Buzios | Brazil | BZC |
| Bydgoszcz | Poland | BZG |
| Byron Bay | Australia | QYN |

# C

| | | |
|---|---|---|
| Ca Mau | Vietnam | CAH |
| Cabimas/Oro Negro | Venezuela | CBS |
| Cabin Creek, AK | USA | CBZ |
| Cabinda | Angola | CAB |
| Cabo Frio | Brazil | QCK |
| Cabo Rojo | Dominican Rep. | CBJ |
| Cacador | Brazil | CFC |
| Caceres | Brazil | CCX |
| Caceres | Spain | QUU |
| Cachoeira | Brazil | CCQ |
| Cachoeira Do Sul | Brazil | QDB |
| Cachoeirinha | Brazil | QKA |
| Cachoeira Itapemirim | Brazil | QXD |
| Cachoeiro Itapernirim | Brazil | CDI |
| Cacoal | Brazil | OAL |
| Cadillac, MI | USA | CAD |
| Caen/Carpiquet | France | CFR |
| Cafunfo | Angola | CFF |
| Cagayan De Oro/Lumbia | Philippines | CGY |
| Cagayan De Sulu | Philippines | CDY |
| Cagliari/Elmas | Italy | CAG |
| Cagnes Sur Mer | France | XCG |
| Caherciveen/Reenroe | Ireland | CHE |
| Cahors/Laberande | France | ZAO |
| Caia | Mozambique | CMZ |
| Caicara De Oro | Venezuela | CXA |
| Caiguna | Australia | CGV |
| Cairns, CA | Australia | CNS |
| Cairns/AAF, AL | USA | OZR |
| Cairo, IL | USA | CIR |
| Cairo/Int'l | Egypt | CAI |
| Cajamarca | Peru | CJA |
| Calabar | Nigeria | CBQ |
| Calabozo | Venezuela | CLZ |
| Calais | France | CQF |
| Calais/Frethun RR Stn. | France | XFF |
| Calama/El Loa | Chile | CJC |
| Calbayog | Philippines | CYP |
| Calcutta/N. S. Chandra | India | CCU |
| Caldas Novas | Brazil | CLV |
| Caldwell, NJ | USA | CDW |
| Caledonia | Panama | CDE |
| Caleta Olivia | Argentina | CVI |
| Calexico/Int'l, CA | USA | CXL |
| Calgary Int'l, AB | Canada | YYC |
| Cali/Alfonso B. Aragon | Colombia | CLO |
| Calicut | India | CCJ |
| Calipatria, CA | USA | CLR |
| Callaway Gardens, GA | USA | CWG |
| Caloundra | Australia | CUD |
| Caltanissetta | Italy | QCL |
| Calverton, NY | USA | CTO |
| Calvi/Ste Catherine | France | CLY |
| Camacari | Brazil | QCC |
| Camaguey/Ign Agramonte | Cuba | CMW |
| Camas Do Sul/C.D. Bugres | Brazil | CXJ |
| Cambrai | France | XCB |
| Cambridge Bay, NT | Canada | YCB |
| Cambridge, MD | USA | CGE |
| Cambridge, MN | UK | CBG |
| Cambridge/Hyatt Regency HP, MA | USA | JHY |
| Camden | Australia | CDU |
| Camden, AR | USA | CDH |
| Camden/Woodward Fld, SC | USA | CDN |
| Cameta | Brazil | CMT |
| Camfield | Australia | CFI |
| Camiguin/Mamoajao | Philippines | CGM |
| Camiri | Bolivia | CAM |
| Camocim | Brazil | CMC |
| Camooweal | Australia | CML |
| Camp Douglas, WI | USA | VOK |
| Camp Maybry AHP, TX | USA | MMR |
| Camp Springs, MD | USA | ADW |
| Campbell County Arpt, WY | USA | GCC |
| Campbell River, BC | Canada | YBL |
| Campbell River/Harbor SPB, BC | Canada | YHH |
| Campbell/AAF, KY | USA | HOP |
| Campbellpore | Pakistan | CWP |
| Campbellton/RR Stn., NB | Canada | XAZ |

| | | |
|---|---|---|
| Campbeltown/Machrihanish | UK | CAL |
| Campeche/Campeche Int'l | Mexico | CPE |
| Campina Grande/J. Suassuna | Brazil | CPV |
| Campinas/Int'l | Brazil | CPQ |
| Campo Born | Brazil | QCD |
| Campo Grande/Int'l | Brazil | CGR |
| Campo Mourac | Brazil | CBW |
| Campo, CA | USA | CZZ |
| Campobasso | Italy | QPB |
| Campos Do Jorclao | Brazil | QJO |
| Campos/B. Lisandro | Brazil | CAW |
| Can Tho | Vietnam | VCA |
| Cana Brava | Brazil | NBV |
| Canadian/Hemphill, TX | USA | HHF |
| Canaima | Venezuela | CAJ |
| Canakkaie | Turkey | CKZ |
| Cananea | Mexico | CNA |
| Canarana/Canarana Arpt | Brazil | CQA |
| Canas | Costa Rica | CSC |
| Canavieiras | Brazil | CNV |
| Canberra | Australia | CBR |
| Cancun | Mexico | CUN |
| Candala | Somalia | CXN |
| Candilejas | Colombia | CJD |
| Candle, AK | USA | CDL |
| Canela | Brazil | QCN |
| Cangamba | Angola | CNZ |
| Cannes/Croisette HP | France | JCA |
| Cannes/Mandelieu | France | CEQ |
| Cannes/Vieux Port | France | QYW |
| Canoas | Brazil | QNS |
| Canobie | Australia | CBY |
| Canoinhas | Brazil | QNH |
| Canon City, CO | USA | CNE |
| Canouan Is | St. Vincent & Grenadines | CIW |
| Canton Is | Kiribati | CIS |
| Canton, SD | USA | CTK |
| Cap Haitien | Haiti | CAP |
| Cap Skirring | Senegal | CSK |
| Capanda | Angola | KNP |
| Cape Barren Is | Australia | CBI |
| Cape Dorset, NT | Canada | YTE |
| Cape Eleuthera | Bahamas | CEL |
| Cape Flattery | Australia | CQP |
| Cape Girardeau, MO | USA | CGI |
| Cape Gloucester | Papua New Guinea | CGC |
| Cape Lisburne, AK | USA | LUR |
| Cape Newenham, AK | USA | EHM |
| Cape Orford | Papua New Guinea | CPI |
| Cape Palmas/A. Tubman | Liberia | CPA |
| Cape Pole, AK | USA | CZP |
| Cape Rodney | Papua New Guinea | CPN |
| Cape Romanzof, AK | USA | CZF |
| Cape Spencer/Coast Guard HP, AK | USA | CSP |
| Cape St Jacques | Vietnam | CSJ |
| Cape St James, BC | Canada | YCJ |
| Cape Town Int'l | S. Africa | CPT |
| Cape Vogel | Papua New Guinea | CVL |
| Capreol/RR Stn., ON | Canada | XAW |
| Capri | Italy | PRJ |
| Capurgana | Colombia | CPB |
| Caquetania | Colombia | CQT |
| Car Niconar | India | CBD |
| Caracas/Simon Bolivar | Venezuela | CCS |
| Caraguatatuba | Brazil | QCQ |
| Carajas | Brazil | CKS |
| Caransebes | Romania | CSB |
| Caratinga | Brazil | QTL |
| Carauari | Brazil | CAF |
| Caravelas | Brazil | CRQ |
| Carazinho | Brazil | QRE |
| Carbondale, IL | USA | MDH |
| Carcassonne/Salvaza | France | CCF |
| Cardiff | UK | CWL |
| careh | India | BEK |
| Cariacica | Brazil | QRJ |
| Caribou Is, ON | Canada | YCI |
| Caribou, ME | USA | CAR |
| Carimagua | Colombia | CCO |
| Carlsbad, NM | USA | CNM |
| Cariton Hill | Australia | CRY |
| Carleton/RR Stn., QC | Canada | XON |
| Carlisle | UK | CAX |
| Carlsbad, CA | USA | CLD |
| Carmelita | Guatemala | CMM |
| Carmen De Patagones | Argentina | CPG |
| Carnarvon | Australia | CVQ |
| Carnot | Central African Rep. | CRF |

| | | |
|---|---|---|
| Carolina | Brazil | CLN |
| Carora | Vanuatu | VCR |
| Carpentaria Downs | Australia | CFP |
| Carriacou Is | Grenada | CRU |
| Carrillo | Costa Rica | RIK |
| Carrizo Springs, TX | USA | CZT |
| Carroll, IA | USA | CIN |
| Carson City, NV | USA | CSN |
| Carswell/AFB, TX | USA | FWH |
| Cartagena/Rafael Nunez | Colombia | CTG |
| Cartago | Colombia | CRC |
| Cartersville, GA | USA | VPC |
| Carti | Panama | CTE |
| Cartierville, QC | Canada | YCV |
| Cartwright, NF | Canada | YRF |
| Caruaru | Brazil | CAU |
| Carupano | Venezuela | CUP |
| Caruru | Colombia | CUO |
| Carutapera | Brazil | CTP |
| Casa Grande/Mncpl, AZ | USA | CGZ |
| Casablanca/Anfa | Morocco | CAS |
| Casablanca/Mohamed V | Morocco | CMN |
| Cascade Locks, OR | USA | CZK |
| Cascavel | Brazil | CAC |
| Caserta | Italy | QTC |
| Casigua | Venezuela | CUV |
| Casiguran | Philippines | CGG |
| Casino | Australia | CSI |
| Casper, WY | USA | CPR |
| Casselman/RR Stn., ON | Canada | XZB |
| Cassilandia | Brazil | CSS |
| Castanhal | Brazil | QHL |
| Castaway | Fiji | CST |
| Castlebar | Ireland | CLB |
| Castlegar, BC | Canada | YCG |
| Castres/Mazamet | France | DCM |
| Castro | Brazil | QAC |
| Castro/Gamboa | Chile | WCA |
| Castrop-Rauxel | Germany | ZCM |
| Casuarito | Colombia | CSR |
| Cat Cays | Bahamas | CXY |
| Cat Is | Bahamas | CAT |
| Cat Lake, ON | Canada | YAC |
| Catacamas | Honduras | CAA |
| Cataguases | Brazil | QCG |
| Catalao | Brazil | TLZ |
| Catalina Is, CA | USA | CIB |
| Catalina Is, CA | USA | SXC |
| Catalina Is/Two Harbors, CA | USA | TWH |
| Catamarca | Argentina | CTC |
| Catanduva | Brazil | QDE |
| Catania/Fontanarossa | Italy | CTA |
| Catanzaro | Italy | QCZ |
| Catarman/National | Philippines | CRM |
| Caticlan/Malay | Philippines | MPH |
| Cattle Creek | Australia | CTR |
| Catumbela | Andorra | CBT |
| Cauayan | Philippines | CYZ |
| Caucasia | Colombia | CAQ |
| Caudebec en Caux | France | QUX |
| Cauquira | Honduras | CDD |
| Caussade | France | XCS |
| Caviahue | Argentina | CVH |
| Caxias | Brazil | QXC |
| Caye Caulker | Belize | CUK |
| Caye Chapel | Belize | CYC |
| Cayenne/Rochambeau | French Guiana | CAY |
| Cayman Brac | Cayman Is | CYB |
| Cayo Coco | Cuba | CCC |
| Cayo Largo Del Sur | Cuba | CYO |
| Cazombo | Andorra | CAV |
| Cebu | Philippines | CEB |
| Cecil/NAS, FL | USA | NZC |
| Cedar City, UT | USA | CDC |
| Cedar Rapids, IA | USA | CID |
| CedarKey/Lewis, FL | USA | CDK |
| Ceduna | Australia | CED |
| Celle | Germany | ZCN |
| Center Is, WA | USA | CWS |
| Centerville/Mncpl Arpt, TN | USA | GHM |
| New York, NY | USA | NYC |
| Central, AK | USA | CEM |
| Centralia, ON | Canada | YCE |
| Centralia/Municipal, IL | USA | ENL |
| Cepu | Indonesia | CPF |
| Cerbere | France | XCE |
| Ceres | Argentina | CRR |
| Cerro Sombrero | Chile | SMB |
| Cessnock | Australia | CES |
| Ceuta/Ceuta HP | Spain | JCU |

| | | |
|---|---|---|
| Chachapoyas | Peru | CHH |
| Chadron, NE | USA | CDR |
| Chaffee/AFB, AR | USA | CCA |
| Chagni | Ethiopia | MKD |
| Chah-Bahar | Iran | ZBR |
| Chaiten | Chile | WCH |
| Chakcharan | Afghanistan | CCN |
| Chalkis | Greece | QKG |
| Chalkyitsik, AK | USA | CIK |
| Challis, ID | USA | CHL |
| Chalon Sur Saone | France | XCD |
| Chalons Sur Marne | France | XCR |
| Cham | Germany | QHQ |
| Chambery/Aix-Les-Bains | France | CMF |
| Chambord/RR Stn., QC | Canada | XCI |
| Chamonix Mont Blanc | France | XCF |
| Champaign, IL | USA | CMI |
| Champery | Switzerland | ZDQ |
| Chamrousse | France | XCQ |
| Chanaral | Chile | CNR |
| Chandalar, AK | USA | WCR |
| Chandigarh | India | IXC |
| Chandler/RR Stn., QC | Canada | XDL |
| Chandler/Stellar Air Park, AZ | USA | SLJ |
| Changchun | China | CGQ |
| Changde | China | CGD |
| Changhai | China | CNI |
| Changsha | China | CSX |
| Changuinola | Panama | CHX |
| Changzhi | China | CIH |
| Changzhou | China | CZX |
| Chantilly | France | XCV |
| Chanute, KS | USA | CNU |
| Chaoyang/Chaoyang Arpt. | China | CHG |
| Chaparral | Colombia | CPL |
| Chapeco | Brazil | XAP |
| Chapel Hill/Williams, NC | USA | IGX |
| Chapleau, ON | Canada | YLD |
| Charata | Argentina | CNT |
| Chardzhou | Turkmenistan | CRZ |
| Charles City, IA | USA | CCY |
| Charleston Nise, SC | USA | NEX |
| Charleston, WV | USA | CRW |
| Charleston, WV | USA | RLX |
| Charleston/AFB, SC | USA | CHS |
| Charleston/AFB, SC | USA | IGC |
| Charleville | Australia | CTL |
| Charleville Mezieres | France | XCZ |
| Charlo, NB | Canada | YCL |
| Charlotte, NC | USA | CLT |
| Charlotte/Wilgrove Air Park, NC | USA | QWG |
| Charlottesville, VA | USA | CHO |
| Charlottetown, NF | Canada | YHG |
| Charlottetown, PE | Canada | YYG |
| Charqueada | Brazil | QDA |
| Charters Towers | Australia | CXT |
| Chartres | France | QTJ |
| Chasso | Switzerland | ZDS |
| Chateau Thierry | France | XCY |
| Chateau-d-Oex | Switzerland | ZDR |
| Chateauroux | France | CHR |
| Chatellerault/Targe | France | XCX |
| Chatham Is/Karewa | New Zealand | CHT |
| Chatham Municipal, MA | USA | CQX |
| Chatham, ON | Canada | XCM |
| Chatham/SPB, AK | USA | CYM |
| Chattanooga, TN | USA | CHA |
| Chattanooga/Daisy, TN | USA | CQN |
| Chattanooga/Greyhound Bus Svc, TN | USA | QDK |
| Chaumont | France | XCW |
| Chaurjlnari | Nepal | HRJ |
| Chaves | Portugal | CHV |
| Cheboksary | Russia | CSY |
| Chefornak/SPB, AK | USA | CYF |
| Chehalis/Centralia, WA | USA | CLS |
| Cheighourn Laid | Algeria | QGM |
| Cheju/Cheju Int'l Arpt | S. Korea | CJU |
| Cheju/Chu Ja HP | S. Korea | JCJ |
| Cheju/Sogwipo HP | S. Korea | JSP |
| Chelinda | Malawi | CEH |
| Chelyabinsk | Russia | CEK |
| Chemainus/RR Stn., BC | Canada | XHS |
| Chemnitz/RR Stn. | Germany | ZTZ |
| Chena Hot Springs, AK | USA | CEX |
| Chenault Airpark, LA | USA | CWF |
| Chengdu | China | CTU |
| Chennai | India | MAA |
| Cheonan | Kuwait | XOX |
| Cheong Ju City/Arpt | S. Korea | CJJ |
| Cheraw, SC | USA | HCW |
| Cherbourg/Maupertus | France | CER |
| Cherchell | Algeria | ZZC |
| Cherepovets | Russia | CEE |
| Cherkassy | Ukraine | CKC |
| Chernigov | Ukraine | CEJ |
| Chernofski/SPB, AK | USA | KCN |
| Chernovtsy | Ukraine | CWC |
| Cherokee, AR | USA | CKK |
| Cherokee/Kegelman AF, OK | USA | CKA |
| Cherrabun | Australia | CBC |
| Cherribah | Australia | CRH |
| Cherry Point/MCAS, NC | USA | NKT |
| Cherskiy | Russia | CYX |
| Chesapeake/Huntington Cnty, OH | USA | HTW |
| Chester | UK | CEG |
| Chesterfield Inlet, NU | Canada | YCS |
| Chesterfield/Bus Svc | UK | ZFI |
| Cheturnal | Mexico | CTM |
| Chetwynd, BC | Canada | YCQ |
| Cheung Sha Wan | Hong Kong | ZZQ |
| Chevak, AK | USA | VAK |
| Chevery, QC | Canada | YHR |
| Cheyenne, WY | USA | CYS |
| Cheyenne/AFB, WY | USA | FEW |
| Chi Mei | Taiwan | CMJ |
| Chiang Mai/Int'l | Thailand | CNX |
| Chiang Rai | Thailand | CEI |
| Chiayi | Taiwan | CYI |
| Chiba City | Japan | QCB |
| Chibougamau, QC | Canada | YMT |
| Chicago Nexrad, IL | USA | LOT |
| Chicago, IL | USA | CGX |
| Chicago, IL | USA | CHI |
| Chicago-Waukegan, IL | USA | UGN |
| Chicago/Midway, IL | USA | MDW |
| Chicago/NAS, IL | USA | NOH |
| Chicago/O'Hare Int'l, IL | USA | ORD |
| Chicago/Pal-Waukee, IL | USA | PWK |
| Chicago/Union Railway Svc, IL | USA | ZUN |
| Chichen Itza | Mexico | CZA |
| Chichester Goodwood | UK | QUG |
| Chickasha/Municipal, OK | USA | CHK |
| Chicken, AK | USA | CKX |
| Chiclayo/Connel Ruiz | Peru | CIX |
| Chico, CA | USA | CIC |
| Chicopee/Westover Arpt, MA | USA | CEF |
| Chifeng | China | CIF |
| Chignik, AK | USA | KCQ |
| Chignik, Chignik Bay, AK | USA | KBW |
| Chignik, Fisheries, AK | USA | KCG |
| Chignik/Lagoon, AK | USA | KCL |
| Chigorodo | Colombia | IGO |
| Chihuahua/G.F. Villalobos | Mexico | CUU |
| Chilas | Pakistan | CHB |
| Childress, TX | USA | CDS |
| Chile Chico | Chile | CCH |
| Chilko Lake, BC | Canada | CJH |
| Chillagoe | Australia | LLG |
| Chillan | Chile | YAI |
| Chilliwack, BC | Canada | YCW |
| Chiloquin/State, OR | USA | CHZ |
| Chimbote | Peru | CHM |
| Chimoio | Mozambique | VPY |
| China Lake/NAS, CA | USA | NID |
| Chinchilla | Australia | CCL |
| Chinde | Mozambique | INE |
| Chingola | Zambia | CGJ |
| Chinguitti | Mauritania | CGT |
| Chinhae | S. Korea | CHF |
| Chinju/Sacheon | S. Korea | HIN |
| Chino, CA | USA | CNO |
| Chios/Khios | Greece | JKH |
| Chipata | Zambia | CIP |
| Chipinge | Zimbabwe | CHJ |
| Chiquimula | Guatemala | CIQ |
| Chisana/Chisana Fld, AK | USA | CZN |
| Chisasibi, QC | Canada | YKU |
| Chisholm-Hibbing Arpt, MN | USA | HIB |
| Chisinau | Moldova | KIV |
| Chistochina, AK | USA | CZO |
| Chita | Russia | HTA |
| Chitato | Angola | PGI |
| Chitina Arpt, AK | USA | CXC |
| Chitral | Pakistan | CJL |
| Chitre | Panama | CTD |
| Chittagong/Patenga | Bangladesh | CGP |
| Chiusa/Klausen/Bus Stn. | Italy | ZAK |
| Chivoo | Colombia | IVO |
| Chkalovsky | Russia | CKL |
| Choibalsan | Mongolia | COQ |
| Choiseul Bay | Solomon Is | CHY |
| Chokurdah | Russia | CKH |
| Chokwe | Mozambique | TGS |
| Cholet/Le Pontreau | France | CET |
| Chomley, AK | USA | CIV |
| Chonburi | Thailand | QHI |
| Chongju/Air Base | S. Korea | CHN |
| Chongqing | China | CKG |
| Chos Malal/Oscar Reguera | Argentina | HOS |
| Christchurch | New Zealand | CHC |
| Christmas Creek | Australia | CXQ |
| Christmas Is | Kiribati | CXI |
| Christmas Is | Christmas Is | XCH |
| Chuathbaluk, AK | USA | CHU |
| Chub Cay | Bahamas | CCZ |
| Chulman | Russia | CNN |
| Chumphon Arpt | Thailand | CJM |
| Chun Chon City/Air Base | S. Korea | QUN |
| Chung-Mu City | S. Korea | QUU |
| Chungribu | Papua New Guinea | CVB |
| Chuquicamata | Chile | QUI |
| Chur | Switzerland | ZDT |
| Churchill Falls, NF | Canada | ZUM |
| Churchill, MB | Canada | YYQ |
| Churchill/RR Stn., MB | Canada | XAD |
| Chute-Des-Passes, QC | Canada | YWQ |
| Ciapoclue | Brazil | OYK |
| Cicia | Fiji | ICI |
| Ciego De Avila | Cuba | AVI |
| Cienfuegos | Cuba | CFG |
| Cierno | China | IQM |
| Cilacap/Tunggul Wuiung | Indonesia | CXP |
| Cimitarra | Colombia | CIM |
| Cincinnati, KY | USA | CVG |
| Cincinnati, OH | USA | LUK |
| Circle Hot Springs, AK | USA | CHP |
| Circle/Circle City, AK | USA | IRC |
| Cirebon/Penggung | Indonesia | CBN |
| Ciucladela | Spain | QIU |
| Ciudad Acuna Int'l | Mexico | ACN |
| Ciudad Boliva | Venezuela | CBL |
| Ciudad Constitucion | Mexico | CUA |
| Ciudad Del Carmen | Mexico | CME |
| Ciudad del Este | Paraguay | AGT |
| Ciudad Guayana | Venezuela | CGU |
| Ciudad Juarez/A. Gonzaiez | Mexico | CJS |
| Ciudad Mante | Mexico | MMC |
| Ciudad Obregon | Mexico | CEN |
| Ciudad Victoria | Mexico | CVM |
| Claremont/Municipal, NH | USA | CNH |
| Clarinda, IA | USA | ICL |
| Clarks Point, AK | USA | CLP |
| Clarksburg, WV | USA | CKB |
| Clarksdale/Fletcher Fld, MS | USA | CKM |
| Clarksville, TN | USA | CKV |
| Clayton, NM | USA | CAO |
| Clear Lake, CA | USA | CKE |
| Clearlake/Metroport, TX | USA | CLC |
| Clearwater/Executive, FL | USA | CLW |
| Clemson, SC | USA | CEU |
| Clermont | Australia | CMQ |
| Clermont-Ferrand/Aulriat | France | CFE |
| Cleve | Australia | CVC |
| Cleveland, Burke Arpt, OH | USA | BKL |
| Cleveland, OH | USA | CGF |
| Cleveland, OH | USA | CLE |
| Clifton Hills | Australia | CFH |
| Clinton Creek, YT | Canada | YLM |
| Clinton, IA | USA | CWI |
| Clinton, OK | USA | CSM |
| Clinton/Municipal, OK | USA | CLK |
| Clinton/Sampson County, NC | USA | CTZ |
| Clintonville, WI | USA | CLI |
| Clitton/Morenci, AZ | USA | CFT |
| Cloncurry | Australia | CNJ |
| Clorinda | Argentina | CLX |
| Clovis/AFB, NM | USA | CVS |
| Clovis/Municipal, NM | USA | CVN |
| Club Makokola | Malawi | CMK |
| Cluff Lake, SK | Canada | XCL |
| Cluj/Napoca | Romania | CLJ |
| Cluny | Australia | CZY |
| Clyde River, NU | Canada | YCY |
| Clyde, NT | Canada | YY |
| Coalinga, CA | USA | CLG |
| Coan | Brazil | CIZ |
| Coatepeque | Guatemala | CTF |
| Coatesville, PA | USA | CTH |
| Coatzacoalcos | Mexico | QTZ |
| Coban | Guatemala | CBV |

**Cobar** ... Australia .. CAZ
**Cobija**/E. Beltram ... Bolivia ... CIJ
**Cobourg**/RR Stn., ON ... Canada .. XGJ
**Coburg** ... Germany .. ZCP
**Coca** ... Ecuador .. OCC
**Cochabamba**/J Wilsterman .. Bolivia .. CBB
**Cochin** ... India .. COK
**Cochrane** ... Chile .. LGR
**Cochrane**, ON ... Canada .. YCN
**Cochstedt** ... Germany .. CSO
**Cocoa**/AFB, FL ... USA .. COF
**Cocoa**/Merritt Is, FL ... USA .. COI
**Coconut Is** ... Australia .. CNC
**Cocos Iss** ... Cocos (Keeling) Is .. CCK
**Codazzi** ... Colombia ... OZI
**Codroipo** ... Italy .. QOP
**Cody**, WY ... USA .. COD
**Coen** ... Australia .. CUQ
**Coeur D'Alene**, ID ... USA .. COE
**Coffee Point**, AK ... USA .. CFA
**Coffeyvifle**, KS ... USA .. CFV
**Coffman Cove**, AK ... USA .. KCC
**Coffs Harbour** ... Australia .. CFS
**Cognac**/Chateau Bernard ... France .. CNG
**Coimbatore**/Peelamedu ... India .. CJB
**Coirnar**/Colmar-Houssen ... France .. CMR
**Coirribra** ... Portugal .. CBP
**Colac** ... Australia .. XCO
**Colatina** ... Brazil .. QCH
**Colby**/Municipal, KS ... USA .. CBK
**Cold Bay**, AK ... USA .. CDB
**Cold Lake**, AB ... Canada .. YOD
**Coldfoot**, AK ... USA .. CXF
**Coleman**, TX ... USA. COM
**Colima** ... Myanmar .. CLQ
**Collarenebri** ... Australia .. CRB
**College Park**, MD ... USA .. CGS
**College Stn**, TX ... USA ... CLL
**Collie** ... Australia ... CIE
**Collins Bay**, SK ... Canada .. YKC
**Collinsville** ... Australia .. KCE
**Collioure**/Off-line Pt ... France .. XCU
**Collo** ... Algeria .. QOL
**Cologne**/Bonn/Off-line Pt ... Germany .. BNJ
**Cologne**/Cologne/Bonn Mtrpltn. ... Germany .. CGN
**Cologne**/RR ... Germany .. QKU
**Cologne**/Stn ... Germany .. QKL
**Colombo**/Bandaranayake .. Sri Lanka .. CMB
**Colombo**/Ratmalana ... Sri Lanka .. RML
**Colon** ... Panama .. ONX
**Colon** ... Chile .. QCO
**Colonia** ... Uruguay .. CYR
**Colonia Catriel** ... Argentina .. CCT
**Colonia Sarmiento** ... Argentina .. OLN
**Colonsay Is** ... UK .. CSA
**Colorado Creek**, AK ... USA .. KCR
**Colorado do Oeste** ... Brazil. CSW
**Colorado Springs**, CO ... USA .. COS
**Colorado Springs**/USAF Academy, CO ... USA .. AFF
**Colorado Springs**/AAF, CO ... USA .. FCS
**Colt Is** ... UK .. COL
**Coltishall** ... UK .. CLF
**Columbia**, CA ... USA .. COA
**Columbia**, MO ... USA .. COU
**Columbia**, SC ... USA .. CAE
**Columbia**, SC ... USA .. CUB
**Columbia**, SC ... USA .. MMT
**Columbia**, TN ... USA .. MRC
**Columbus Metropolitan**, GA .. USA .. CSG
**Columbus Municipal**, IN ... USA .. CLU
**Columbus**, MS ... USA .. GTR
**Columbus**, NE ... USA .. OLU
**Columbus**, OH ... USA .. CMH
**Columbus**/AFB, MS ... USA .. CBM
**Columbus**/Lowrides County, MS ... USA .. UBS
**Columbus**/Municipal, NM ... USA .. CUS
**Colurribus**, OH ... USA .. OSU
**Colville Lake**, NT ... Canada .. YCK
**Colville Municipal**, WA ... USA .. CQV
**Comayagua**/Palmerola Air Base ... Honduras .. XPL
**Comelio Procopio** ... Brazil .. CKO
**Comilla** ... Bangladesh .. CLA
**Cominc** / HP ... Malta .. JCO
**Comiso** ... Italy ... CIY
**Como** ... Italy. QCM
**Comodoro Rivadavia** ... Argentina .. CRD
**Comox**, BC ... Canada .. YQQ

**Compiegne**/Margny ... France .. XCP
**Compton**, CA ... USA .. CPM
**Comuna Providencia** ... Chile . QOV
**Conakry** ... Guinea .. CKY
**Conceicao Do Araguaia** ... Brazil .. CDJ
**Concepcion** ... Bolivia .. CEP
**Concepcion**/Carriel Sur ... Chile .. CCP
**Concepcion**/MCAL Lopez ... Paraguay .. CIO
**Concord**, CA ... USA .. CCR
**Concord**, NH ... USA .. CON
**Concordia** ... Brazil .. CCI
**Concordia** ... Argentina . COC
**Concordia**, KS ... USA .. CNK
**Condobolin** ... Australia .. CBX
**Condoto**/Mandinga ... Colombia . COG
**Confreza** ... Brazil .. CFO
**Congo Town** ... Bahamas .. COX
**Coningsby**/RAF ... UK .. QCY
**Connersville**/Mettle Fld, IN ... USA .. CEV
**Conroe**, TX ... USA .. CXO
**Conselheiro Lafaiete** ... Brazil .. QDF
**Constanta**/Kogainiceanu ... Romania .. CND
**Constantine** ... Algeria .. CZL
**Constanza** ... Dominican Rep .. COZ
**Contadora** ... Panama .. OTD
**Coober Pedy** ... Australia .. CPD
**Cooch Behar** ... India . COH
**Cooinda** ... Australia .. CDA
**Cookitown** ... Australia .. CTN
**Coolah** ... Australia .. CLH
**Coolawanyah** ... Australia .. COY
**Coolibah** ... Australia .. COB
**Cooma** ... Australia . OOM
**Coonabarabran** ... Australia .. COJ
**Coonamble** ... Australia .. CNB
**Cooper Lodge**/Quartz Creek, AK ... USA .. JLA
**Cooperstown**, NY ... USA .. COP
**Coorabie** ... Australia .. CRJ
**Cootamundra** ... Australia . CMD
**Copan** ... Honduras .. RUY
**Copenhagen**/Kastrup ... Denmark .. CPH
**Copenhagen**/RR Stn. ... Denmark .. ZGH
**Copenhagen**/Roskilde ... Denmark .. RKE
**Copiapo**/Chamonate ... Chile .. CPO
**Copper Centre**, AK ... USA .. CZC
**Copper Mountain**/Van Svc, CO USA .. QCE
**Coppermine**, NU ... Canada .. YCO
**Coquimbo** ... Chile . COW
**Coral Harbour**, NT ... Canada .. YZS
**Corazon De Jesus** ... Panama .. CZJ
**Corcoran**, CA ... USA . CRO
**Cordillo Downs** ... Australia .. ODL
**Cordoba** ... Spain .. ODB
**Cordoba**/Pajas Blancas ... Argentina . COR
**Cordova**, AK ... USA .. CDV
**Cordova**/City, AK ... USA .. CKU
**Corinth**/Roscoe Turner, MS ... USA .. CRX
**Cork** ... Ireland .. ORK
**Corn Is** ... Netherlands .. RNI
**Corner Bay**, AK ... USA .. CBA
**Corner Brook**/Deer Lake, NF Canada .. YNF
**Cornwall**/Regional, ON ... Canada .. YCC
**Coro** ... Venezuela .. CZE
**Coromandel** ... New Zealand . CMV
**Coron** ... Philippines .. XCN
**Coronation**, AB ... Canada .. YCT
**Coronel E Solo Cano AB** Honduras .. ENQ
**Corowa** ... Australia .CWW
**Corozal** ... Belize .. CZH
**Corozal** ... Colombia .. CZU
**Corpus Christi**, TX ... USA .. CRP
**Corpus Christi**/Cuddihy Fld, TX ... USA .. CUX
**Corpus Christi**/NAS, TX ... USA .. NGP
**Corpus Christi**/NAS, TX ... USA . NGW
**Corralejo** ... Spain .. QFU
**Corrientes**/Camba Punta .. Argentina . CNQ
**Corryong** ... Australia .. CYG
**Corsicana**, TX ... USA .. CRS
**Cortes Bay**, BC ... Canada .. YCF
**Cortez**, CO ... USA .. CEZ
**Cortina d'Ampezzo**/Fiames ... Italy .. CDF
**Cortland**, NY ... USA .. CTX
**Corumba**/Int'l ... Brazil . CMG
**Corvo Is** ... Portugal .. CVU
**Cosenza** ... Italy .. QCS
**Costa Marques** ... Brazil .. CQS
**Cotabato**/Awang ... Philippines .. CBO

**Coteau**/RR Stn., QC ... Canada .. XGK
**Cotia** ... Brazil ... QOI
**Coto 47** ... Costa Rica . OTR
**Cotonou**/Cadjehoun ... Benin .. COO
**Cottbus**/Flugplatz ... Germany .. CBU
**Cottbus**/RR Stn. ... Germany ... ZTT
**Cottonwood**, AZ ... USA .. CTW
**Cotulla**, TX ... USA .. COT
**Council Bluffs**, IA ... USA .. CBF
**Council**/Melsing Creek, AK ... USA ... CIL
**Courbevoie** ... France .. QEV
**Courchevel** ... France .. CVF
**Courtenay**, BC ... Canada .. YCA
**Covenas** ... Colombia .. CVE
**Coventry**/Baginton ... UK .. CVT
**Covilha** ... Portugal .. COV
**Cowarie** ... Australia .. CWR
**Cowell** ... Australia .. CCW
**Cowley**, AB ... Canada .. YYM
**Cowra** ... Australia .. CWT
**Cox's Bazar** ... Bangladesh .. CXB
**Coyhaique**/Ten. Vidal ... Chile .. GXQ
**Coyoles** ... Honduras ... CYL
**Cozad Municipal**, NE ... USA .. CZD
**Cozumel** ... Mexico .. CZM
**Cradock** ... S. Africa . CDO
**Craiciva** ... Romania .. CRA
**Craig Cove** ... Vanuatu .. CCV
**Craig**/AFB, AL ... USA .. SEM
**Craig**/Craig-Molfat, CO ... USA ... CIG
**Craig**/SPB, AK ... USA .. CGA
**Crailsheim** ... Germany ... QEI
**Cranbrook**, BC ... Canada .. YXC
**Crane County** Arpt, TX ... USA .. CCG
**Crane Is**, WA ... USA .. CKR
**Crankenback Villeage**/Bus Svc ... Australia .. QWL
**Cranzahl**/RR Stn. ... Germany ... ZZH
**Cravo None** ... Colombia .. RAV
**Creech**/AAF, KY ... USA .. LSD
**Creil**/AFB ... France .. CSF
**Crescent City**, CA ... USA .. CEC
**Cresswell Downs** ... Australia .. CSD
**Crested Butte**, CO ... USA .. CSE
**Creston**, BC ... Canada .. CFQ
**Creston**, IA ... USA .. CSQ
**Crestview**, FL ... USA .. CEW
**Creteil** ... France .. QFC
**Creusot Montceau Mont** ... France .. XCC
**Crewe**/RR Stn. ... UK .. XVC
**Cricluma** ... Brazil .. CCM
**Croker Is** ... Australia .. CKI
**Cromarty** ... UK .. CRN
**Crooked Creek**, AK ... USA .. CKD
**Crooked Is** ... Bahamas ... CRI
**Crookston**, MN ... USA .. CKN
**Cross City**, FL ... USA ... CTY
**Cross Lake**, MB ... Canada .. YCR
**Crossett**/Municipal, AR ... USA .. CRT
**Crossville**, TN ... USA .. CSV
**Crotone** ... Italy .. CRV
**Crows Landing**/NAS, CA ... USA .. NRC
**Croydon** ... Australia .. CDQ
**Cruz Alta**/Carios Ruhl ... Brazil .. CZB
**Cruzeiro Do** Sul/Campo Int'l .. Brazil .. CZS
**Crystal Lake**, PA ... USA .. CYE
**Cuamba** ... Mozambique .. FXO
**Cube CoveAK** ... USA .. CUW
**Cucuta**/Camilo Dazo ... Colombia .. CUC
**Cudal** ... Australia .. CUG
**Cuddapain** ... India .. CDP
**Cue** ... Australia .. CUY
**Cuenca** ... Ecuador .. CUE
**Cuernavaca** ... Mexico ... CVJ
**Cuhacan**/F.D. Bachigualato .. Mexico ... CUL
**Cuiaba**/M. Rondon ... Brazil .. CGB
**Cuito Cuanavale** ... Angola ... CTI
**Culebra** ... Puerto Rico . CPX
**Culion** ... Philippines ... CUJ
**Culver City**/Hughes, CA ... USA .. CVR
**Cum El** Bouaghi ... Algeria .. QMH
**Cumana** ... Venezuela .. CUM
**Cumberland**/Wiley Ford, MD ... USA .. CBE
**Cuneo**/Levaldigi ... Italy .. CUF
**Cunnamuila** ... Australia .. CMA
**Cunuzu Cuatia** ... Argentina .. UZU
**Curacao**/Halo ... Netherlands Antilles . CUR
**Curico** ... Chile .. ZCQ
**Curitiba**./Bacacher; ... Brazil ... BFH
**Curitiba**/Afonso Pena ... Brazil .. CWB
**Curitibanos** ... Brazil .. QCR

A I R P O R T S -2-

| Location | Country | Code |
|---|---|---|
| Currais Novos | Brazil | QCP |
| Currillo | Colombia | CUI |
| Cururupu | Brazil | CPU |
| Cushing/Municipal, OK | USA | CUH |
| Cut Bank, MT | USA | CTB |
| Cutral | Argentina | CUT |
| Cuyo | Philippines | CYU |
| Cuzio/Velazco Astete | Peru | CUZ |
| Czestochowa | Poland | CZW |

# D

| Location | Country | Code |
|---|---|---|
| Da Nang | Vietnam | DAD |
| Dabra | Indonesia | DRH |
| Dachau | Germany | ZCR |
| Dadu | Pakistan | DDU |
| Dael/Camarines Norte | Philippines | DTE |
| Dahigren/NAF, VA | USA | DGN |
| Dahl Creek/Dahl Creek Arpt, AK | USA | DCK |
| Dakar/Yoff | Senegal | DKR |
| Dakhla | Morocco | VIL |
| Dakhla Oasis/Dakhla | Egypt | DAK |
| Dalanzadgad | Mongolia | DLZ |
| Dalat/Lienkinang | Vietnam | DLI |
| Dalbandin | Pakistan | DBA |
| Dalbertis | Papua New Guinea | DLB |
| Dalgaranga | Australia | DGD |
| Dalhart, TX | USA | DHT |
| Dali City/Dali | China | DLU |
| Dalian | China | DLC |
| Dallas North Arpt, TX | USA | DNE |
| Dallas, TX | USA | ADS |
| Dallas, TX | USA | DAL |
| Dallas/DFW Redbird, TX | USA | RBD |
| Dallas/Fort Worth, TX | USA | AFW |
| Dallas-Fort Worth, TX | USA | DFW |
| Dallas/Market Centre HP, TX | USA | JMD |
| Dallas/NAS, TX | USA | NBE |
| Dallas/North Park Inn HP, TX | USA | JNH |
| Dallby | Australia | DBY |
| Daloa | Côte D'Ivoire | DJO |
| Dalton/FlightLink Bus Svc, GA | USA | QJJ |
| Dalton/Municipal, GA | USA | DNN |
| Daly River | Australia | DVR |
| Daly Waters | Australia | DYW |
| Daman | India | NMB |
| Damanhour | Egypt | QUD |
| Damascus/Int'l | Syria | DAM |
| Damierta | Egypt | QDX |
| Dammarn/King Fahad | Saudi Arabia | DMM |
| Danane | Côte D'Ivoire | DNC |
| Danbury, CT | USA | DXR |
| Dandong | China | DDG |
| Dang | Nepal | DNP |
| Danger Bay, AK | USA | DGB |
| Dangriga | Belize | DGA |
| Daniels Harbour, NF | Canada | YDH |
| Dansville, NY | USA | DSV |
| Danville, VA | USA | DAN |
| Danville/Vermilion County, IL | USA | DNV |
| Daparizo | India | DAE |
| Dar Es Salaam/Int'l | Tanzania | DAR |
| Darchula | Nepal | DAP |
| Dargaville | New Zealand | DGR |
| Darjeelino | India | DAI |
| Darlington/RR Stn | UK | XVG |
| Darmstact | Germany | ZCS |
| Darnley Is | Australia | NLF |
| Daru | Papua New Guinea | DAU |
| Daru | Sierra Leone | DSL |
| Darwaz | Afghanistan | DAZ |
| Darwin Arpt | Australia | DRW |
| Data Processing Ctr | n/a | DPC |
| Datadawai | Indonesia | DTD |
| Dataman | Turkey | DLM |
| Dathina | Yemen | DAH |
| Datong | China | DAT |
| Dauan Is | Australia | DAJ |
| Daugavpils | Latvia | DGP |
| Daugo | Papua New Guinea | DGG |
| Daup | Papua New Guinea | DAF |
| Dauphin, MB | Canada | YDN |
| Davao | Philippines | DVO |
| Davenport Downs | Australia | DVP |
| Davenport, IA | USA | DVN |
| David/Enrique Maiek | Panama | DAV |
| Davis Inlet, NF | Canada | YDI |
| Davos | Switzerland | ZDV |
| Dawe | Myanmar | TVY |
| Dawson Creek, BC | Canada | YDQ |
| Dawson, YT | Canada | YDA |
| Dax/Seyresse | France | XDA |
| Daxian | China | DAX |
| Daydream Is | Australia | DDI |
| Daylon/Wright/AFB | USA | DWF |
| Dayong | China | DYG |
| Dayton, OH | USA | DAY |
| Dayton, OH | USA | MGY |
| Dayton/AFB, OH | USA | FFO |
| Daytona Beach/Regional, FL | USA | DAB |
| Dazu | China | DZU |
| De Ridder/Beauregard Parish, LA | USA | DRI |
| Deadhorse, AK | USA | SCC |
| Deadmans Cay | Bahamas | LGI |
| Dean River, BC | Canada | YRD |
| Dearborn/Hyatt Regency HP, MI | USA | DEO |
| Dease Lake, BC | Canada | YDL |
| Death Valley, CA | USA | DTH |
| Deauville/St Gatien | France | DOL |
| Debepare | Papua New Guinea | DBP |
| Debra Marcos | Ethiopia | DBM |
| Debra Tabor | Ethiopia | DBT |
| Debrecen | Hungary | DEB |
| Decatur Is, WA | USA | DTR |
| Decatur, AL | USA | DCU |
| Decatur, IL | USA | DEC |
| Decatur/Decatur Hi-Way, IN | USA | DCR |
| Deception, QC | Canada | YGY |
| Decimomannu/Ratsu | Italy | DCI |
| Decorah, IA | USA | DEH |
| Dedougou | Burkina Faso | DGU |
| Deep Bay, AK | USA | WDB |
| Deer Lake, NF | Canada | YDF |
| Deer Lake, ON | Canada | YVZ |
| Deering, AK | USA | DRG |
| Deering, Deering Arpt, AK | USA | DEE |
| Defiance, OH | USA | DFI |
| Degalthbur | Ethiopia | DGC |
| Dehra Dun | India | DED |
| Deirezzor/Al Jafrah | Syria | DEZ |
| Del Rio, TX | USA | DRT |
| Del Rio/AFB, TX | USA | DLF |
| Delemont | Switzerland | ZDW |
| Delhi/Indira Gandhi Int'l | India | DEL |
| Deline, NT | Canada | YWJ |
| Delissaville | Australia | DLV |
| Delmenhorst | Germany | ZCT |
| Delta Downs | Australia | DDN |
| Delta Junction, AK | USA | DJN |
| Delta, UT | USA | DTA |
| Dembidollo | Ethiopia | DEM |
| Deming, NM | USA | DMN |
| Den Helder/De Kooy | Netherlands | DHR |
| Denham | Australia | DNM |
| Deniliquin | Australia | DNQ |
| Denis Is | Seychelles | DEI |
| Denison, IA | USA | DNS |
| Denizli/Cardak | Turkey | DNZ |
| Denpasar, Bali/N. Rai | Indonesia | DPS |
| Denton/Municipal Arpt, TX | USA | DTO |
| Denver Nexrad, CO | USA | FTG |
| Denver, CO | USA | APA |
| Denver, CO | USA | DEN |
| Denver/Buckley ANGB, CO | USA | BFK |
| Deparizo | India | DEP |
| Dera Ghazi Khan | Pakistan | DEA |
| Dera Ismaii Khan | Pakistan | DSK |
| Dera'a | Syria | QDR |
| Derby | Australia | DRB |
| Derim | Papua New Guinea | DER |
| Derna/Martuba | Libya | DNF |
| Des Moines Nexrad, IA | USA | DMX |
| Des Moines, IA | USA | DSM |
| Desolation Sound, BC | Canada | YDS |
| Desroches | Seychelles | DES |
| Dessau/RR Stn | Germany | ZSU |
| Dessie/Combolcha | Ethiopia | DSE |
| Destin, FL | USA | DSI |
| Destin, Ft Walton Beach, FL | USA | DTS |
| Detmold | Germany | ZCU |
| Detroit Lakes/Municipal, MN | USA | DTL |
| Detroit NAF, MI | USA | NFB |
| Detroit Nexrad, MI | USA | DTX |
| Detroit, MI | USA | DET |
| Detroit, MI | USA | DTW |
| Detroit-Willow Run, MI | USA | YIP |
| Deux Alpes | France | DXA |
| Deva | Romania | DVA |
| Deventer/RR | Netherlands | QYV |
| Devils Lake, ND | USA | DVL |
| Devonpori | Australia | DPO |
| Dewsbury/Bus Stn | UK | ZEQ |
| Dfw Nexrad, TX | USA | FWS |
| Dhahran | Saudi Arabia | DHA |
| Dhaka/Zia Int'l | Bangladesh | DAC |
| Dhala | Yemen | DHL |
| Dhanbad | India | DBD |
| Dhangarhi | Nepal | DHI |
| Dharamsala/Gaggal Arpt | India | DHM |
| Dharnar | Yemen | DMR |
| Diadema | Brazil | QDW |
| Diamantina Lakes | Australia | DYM |
| Dianopolis | Brazil | DNO |
| Diapaga | Burkina Faso | DIP |
| Diarnantino | Brazil | DMT |
| Dibaa | Oman | BYB |
| Dibrugarn/Chabua | India | DIB |
| Dickinson, ND | USA | DIK |
| Dicling | China | DIG |
| Didcot Parkway/RR Stn | UK | XPW |
| Diebougou | Burkina Faso | XDE |
| Dien Sien Phu/Gialam | Vietnam | DIN |
| Dieppe/Saint Aubin | France | DPE |
| Dietikon | Switzerland | ZDX |
| Digne | France | XDI |
| Dijon | France | DIJ |
| Dikson | Russia | DKS |
| Dilasag | Philippines | DSG |
| Dili | Congo, DR | DIC |
| Dili/Comoro | Indonesia | DIL |
| Dillingharn/Municipal, AK | USA | DLG |
| Dillon, MT | USA | DLN |
| Dillon, SC | USA | DLL |
| Dillons Bay | Vanuatu | DLY |
| Dimapur | India | DMU |
| Dimbokro/Ville | Côte D'Ivoire | DIM |
| Dinangat | Papua New Guinea | DNU |
| Dinard | France | DNR |
| Dinco | Angola | DRC |
| Dinder/Galegu | Sudan | DNX |
| Dinslaken | Germany | ZCV |
| Diomede Is, AK | USA | DIO |
| Dionisio Cerqueira | Brazil | XIS |
| Dios | Papua New Guinea | DOS |
| Dipolog | Philippines | DPI |
| Dire Dawa/Aba Tenna D Yilma | Ethiopia | DIR |
| Dirranbandi | Australia | DRN |
| Disneyland Paris-RR | France | XED |
| Diu | India | DIU |
| Dives Cabourg | France | XDC |
| Divinopolis | Brazil | DIQ |
| Divo | Côte D'Ivoire | DIV |
| Dixie | Australia | DXD |
| Diyarbakir | Turkey | DIY |
| Djambala | Congo, DR | DJM |
| Djanet | Algeria | DJG |
| Djelfa | Algeria | QDJ |
| Djerba/Zarzis | Tunisia | DJE |
| Djgby, NS | Canada | YDG |
| Djibo | Burkina Faso | XDJ |
| Djibouti/Ambouli | Côte D'Ivoire | JIB |
| Djoemoe | Suriname | DOE |
| Djougou | Benin | DJA |
| Djupivogur | Iceland | DJU |
| Dnepropetrovsk | Ukraine | DNK |
| Doany | Madagascar | DOA |
| Dobo/Dobo Arpt | Indonesia | DOB |
| Doc Creek, BC | Canada | YDX |
| Docker River | Australia | DKV |
| Dodge City, KS | USA | DDC |
| Dodoirna | Papua New Guinea | DDM |
| Dodoma | Tanzania | DOD |
| Doha/Int'l Arpt | Qatar | DOH |
| Doini | Papua New Guinea | DOI |
| Dolbeau/St Methode, QC | Canada | YDO |
| Dolorni, AK | USA | DLO |
| Dolpa | Nepal | DOP |
| Dom Pedrito | Brazil | QDP |
| Dominica/Cane Field | Dominica | DCF |
| Dominica/Melville Hail | Oman | DOM |
| Donauwoerth | Germany | QWR |
| Doncaster/Finningley | UK | DCS |
| Donegal | Ireland | CFN |
| Donetsk | Ukraine | DOK |
| Dongara | Australia | DOX |
| Dongguan | China | DGM |
| Dongola | Sudan | DOG |

AIRPORTS -2-

| | | |
|---|---|---|
| Dongsheng | China | DSN |
| Doomadgee | Australia | DMD |
| Doongan | Australia | DNG |
| Dora Bay, AK | USA | DOF |
| Dorado/Dorado Beach | Puerto Rico | DDP |
| Dori | Burkina Faso | DOR |
| Dormagen | Germany | ZCW |
| Dornbirn | Austria | QDI |
| Dornoch | UK | DOC |
| Dorobisoro | Papua New Guinea | DOO |
| Dorsten | Germany | ZCX |
| Dortmund/Wickede | Germany | DTM |
| Dorunda Stn | Australia | DRD |
| Dos Lagunas | Guatemala | DON |
| Dote/Tavaux | France | DLE |
| Dothan, AL | USA | DHN |
| Douai | France | XDN |
| Douala | Cameroon | DLA |
| Douglas Lake, BC | Canada | DGF |
| Douglas Municipal, AZ | USA | DGL |
| Douglas, AZ | USA | DUG |
| Douglas, WY | USA | DGW |
| Dourados | Brazil | DOU |
| Dover/AFB, DE | USA | DOV |
| Dover/RR | UK | QQD |
| Downey/HP, CA | USA | JDY |
| Doylestown | Australia | DYL |
| Dra El Mizan | Algeria | ZZD |
| Dracena | Brazil | QDC |
| Drachten/Bus Svc | Netherlands | QYC |
| Drama | Greece | DRM |
| Drayton Valley, AB | Canada | YDC |
| Dresden/Klotzsche | Germany | DRS |
| Dreux | France | XDR |
| Drietabbetje | Suriname | DRJ |
| Drift River, AK | USA | DRF |
| Drumduff | Australia | DFP |
| Drummond Is, MI | USA | DRE |
| Drummond, MT | USA | DRU |
| Drummondville/RR Stn., QC | | |
| | Canada | XDM |
| Dryden, ON | Canada | YHD |
| Drysdale River | Australia | DRY |
| Dschang | Cameroon | DSC |
| Dubai | UAE | DXB |
| Dubbo | Australia | DBO |
| Dublin | Ireland | DUB |
| Dublin, VA | USA | PSK |
| Dublin/Municipal, GA | USA | DBN |
| Dubois, ID | USA | DBS |
| Dubois/Jefferson County, PA | USA | DUJ |
| Dubrovnik | Croatia | DBV |
| Dubuque, IA | USA | DBQ |
| Duck/Pine Is Arpt, OK | USA | DUF |
| Dueren | Germany | ZCY |
| Duesseldorf | Germany | DUS |
| Dugway/AAF, UT | USA | DPG |
| Duisburg | Germany | DUI |
| Dukuduk | S. Africa | DUK |
| Dulkaninna | Australia | DLK |
| Dulles Int'l, DC | USA | IAD |
| Duluth, MN | USA | DLH |
| Duluth/Lakeside USAF, MN | USA | LKI |
| Dumaguete | Philippines | DGT |
| Dumai | Indonesia | DUM |
| Dumpu | Papua New Guinea | DPU |
| Dunbar | Australia | DNB |
| Duncan Town | Bahamas | DCT |
| Duncan/Halliburton, OK | USA | DUC |
| Dunce | Angola | DUE |
| Dundas | Greenland | DUN |
| Dundee/Riverside | UK | DND |
| Dundee/ScotRail | UK | ZDU |
| Dunedin | New Zealand | DUD |
| Dunhuang | China | DNH |
| Dunk Is | Australia | DKI |
| Dunkerque/Ghyvelde | France | XDK |
| Dunkirk, NY | USA | DKK |
| Dunta Chivato | Mexico | PCV |
| Duque De Caxias | Brazil | QDQ |
| Durango, CO | USA | DRO |
| Durango/Animas Airpark, CO | USA | AMK |
| Durango/Guadalupe Victoria | Mexico | DGO |
| Durant/Eaker, OK | USA | DUA |
| Durazno | Uruguay | DZO |
| Durban/Durban Int'l | S. Africa | DUR |
| Durban/Virginia | S. Africa | VIR |
| Durham Downs | Australia | DHD |
| Durham/RR Stn | UK | XVU |
| Durrie | Australia | DRR |
| Dushanbe | Tajikistan | DYU |
| Dusseldorf/Monchen-Gladbach | | |

| | | |
|---|---|---|
| | Germany | MGL |
| Dusseldorf/Stn | Germany | QDU |
| Dutch Harbor/Emergency Fld, AK | | |
| | USA | DUT |
| Dutch Rail Zone 01 | Netherlands | ZVL |
| Dutch Rail Zone 02 | Netherlands | ZWO |
| Dutch Rail Zone 03 | Netherlands | ZVN |
| Dutch Rail Zone 04 | Netherlands | ZVO |
| Dutch Rail Zone 05 | Netherlands | ZVP |
| Dutch Rail Zone 06 | Netherlands | ZVQ |
| Dutch Rail Zone 07 | Netherlands | ZWQ |
| Dutch Rail Zone 08 | Netherlands | ZVS |
| Dutch Rail Zone 09 | Netherlands | ZVT |
| Dutch Rail Zone 10 | Netherlands | ZVU |
| Dutch Rail Zone 11 | Netherlands | ZVV |
| Dutch Rail Zone 12 | Netherlands | ZVW |
| Dutch Rail Zone 13 | Netherlands | ZVX |
| Dutch Rail Zone 14 | Netherlands | ZVY |
| Dutch Rail Zone 15 | Netherlands | ZVZ |
| Dutch Rail Zone 16 | Netherlands | ZUO |
| Dutch Rail Zone 17 | Netherlands | ZUP |
| Dutch Rail Zone 18 | Netherlands | ZUQ |
| Dutch Rail Zone 19 | Netherlands | ZUR |
| Dutch Rail Zone 20 | Netherlands | ZUS |
| Dutch Rail Zone 21 | Netherlands | ZUT |
| Dutch Rail Zone 22 | Netherlands | ZUU |
| Dutch Rail Zone 23 | Netherlands | ZUV |
| Dutch Rail Zone 24 | Netherlands | ZUW |
| Dutch Rail Zone 25 | Netherlands | ZUX |
| Dutch Rail Zone 26 | Netherlands | ZUY |
| Dutch Rail Zone 27 | Netherlands | ZUZ |
| Dutch Rail Zone 28 | Netherlands | ZWX |
| Dutch Rail Zone 29 | Netherlands | ZWY |
| Dutch Rail Zone 30 | Netherlands | ZWZ |
| Duxford | UK | QFO |
| Dwangwa | Malawi | DWA |
| Dysart | Australia | DYA |
| Dzaoudzi | Mayotte | DZA |

# E

| | | |
|---|---|---|
| Eagle Lake, TX | USA | ELA |
| Eagle Pass/Maverick, TX | USA | EGP |
| Eagle River, WI | USA | EGV |
| Eagle, Eagle Arpt, AK | USA | EAA |
| Earlton, ON | Canada | YXR |
| East Fork, AK | USA | EFO |
| East Hampton, NY | USA | HTO |
| East Hartford/Rentschler, CT | USA | EHT |
| East London | S. Africa | ELS |
| East Main, QC | Canada | ZEM |
| East Stroudsburg/B. Pocono, PA | USA | ESP |
| East Tawas, MI | USA | ECA |
| Easter Is/Mataveri inE | Chile | IPC |
| Eastland/Municipal, TX | USA | ETN |
| Easton, MD | USA | ESN |
| Easton/State, WA | USA | ESW |
| Eastport, ME | USA | EPO |
| Eastsound/Orcas Is, WA | USA | ESD |
| Eau Claire, WI | USA | EAU |
| Ebadon | Marshall Is | EBN |
| Ebeye | Marshall Is | QEE |
| Ebolowa | Cameroon | EBW |
| Ebon/Ebon Arpt | Marshall Is | EBO |
| Ech Cheliff | Algeria | QAS |
| Echuca | Australia | ECH |
| Eday | UK | EOI |
| Eden | Australia | QDN |
| Edenton/Municipal, NC | USA | EDE |
| Edgewood/Weide/AAF, MD | USA | EDG |
| Edinburgh/ScotRail | UK | ZXE |
| Edinburgh/Turnhouse | UK | EDI |
| Edmonton Int'l, AB | Canada | YEG |
| Edmonton Namao, AB | Canada | YED |
| Edmonton, AB | Canada | YXD |
| Edmonton/RR Stn., AB | Canada | XZL |
| Edna Bay, AK | USA | EDA |
| Edremit/Korfez | Turkey | EDO |
| Edson | Canada | YET |
| Edward River | Australia | EDR |
| Edwards/AFB, CA | USA | EDW |
| Eek, AK | USA | EEK |
| Eflye Springs | Kenya | EYS |
| Efogi | Papua New Guinea | EFG |
| Egegik, AK | USA | EGX |
| Egeisbach | Germany | QEF |
| Egilsstadir | Iceland | EGS |

| | | |
|---|---|---|
| El Ghazaciuet | Algeria | QAG |
| El Harrouche | Algeria | QHH |
| El Yopal | Colombia | EYP |
| Eia/Popondetta | Papua New Guinea | EIA |
| Elba Is/Marina Di Campe | Italy | EBA |
| Eight Fathom Bight, AK | USA | EFB |
| Eil | Somalia | HCM |
| Ein Yahav | Israel | EIY |
| Einasieigh | Australia | EIH |
| Eindhoven | Netherlands | EIN |
| Eindhoven/RR Stn | Netherlands | ZYE |
| Einsiedeln | Switzerland | ZDZ |
| Eirunepe | Brazil | ERN |
| Eisenach | Germany | EIB |
| Ekaterinburg | Russia | SVX |
| Ekati, NT | Canada | YOA |
| Ekereku | Guyana | EKE |
| Ekibastuz | Kazakstan | EKB |
| Ekuk, AK | USA | KKU |
| Ekwok, AK | USA | KEK |
| El Bagre | Colombia | EBG |
| El Banco/San Bernado | Colombia | ELB |
| El Bolson | Argentina | EHL |
| El Borma | Tunisia | EBM |
| El Cajon, CA | USA | CJN |
| El Centro/NAF, CA | USA | NJK |
| El Charco | Colombia | ECR |
| El Dorado | Venezuela | EOR |
| El Dorado, AR | USA | ELD |
| El Dorado, KS | USA | EDK |
| El Encanto | Colombia | ECO |
| El Eulma | Algeria | ZAE |
| El Fasher | Somalia | ELF |
| El Golea | Algeria | ELG |
| El Gouera | Mauritania | ZLG |
| El Hadjar | Algeria | QEH |
| El Kala | Algeria | QLK |
| El Mahalla El Kobra | Egypt | QEK |
| El Maiten | Argentina | EMX |
| El Minya | Egypt | EMY |
| El Monte, CA | USA | EMT |
| El Naranjo | Guatemala | ENJ |
| El Nido | Philippines | ENI |
| El Obeid | Sudan | EBD |
| El Oued | Algeria | ELU |
| El Paso, TX | USA | ELP |
| El Portillo | Dominican Rep | EPS |
| El Porvenir | Panama | PVE |
| El Real | Panama | ELE |
| El Recreo | Colombia | ELJ |
| El Salvador | Chile | ESR |
| El Tigre | Venezuela | ELX |
| El Vigia | Venezuela | VIG |
| Elat/J. Hozman | Israel | ETH |
| Elazig | Turkey | EZS |
| Elblag | Poland | ZBG |
| Elcho Is | Australia | ELC |
| Eldebba | Sudan | EDB |
| Eldorado | Argentina | ELO |
| Eldoret | Kenya | EDL |
| Eldred Rock/Coast Guard, AK | USA | ERO |
| Elelim | Indonesia | ELR |
| Elfin Cove/SPB, AK | USA | ELV |
| Elgarhbolli | Libya | QEJ |
| Eglin/AFB, FL | USA | VPS |
| Elhadrapur | Nepal | BDP |
| Elim, AK | USA | ELI |
| Eliptarnin | Papua New Guinea | EPT |
| Elista | Russia | ESL |
| Elite Mystery Night | Australia | ZZI |
| Elizabeth City, NC | USA | ECG |
| Elizabethtown, KY | USA | EKX |
| Elk | Poland | QKD |
| Elk City/Municipal, OK | USA | ELK |
| Elkedra | Australia | EKD |
| Elkhart/Municipal, IN | USA | EKI |
| Elkins, WV | USA | EKN |
| Elko Nexrad, NV | USA | LRX |
| Elko, NV | USA | EKO |
| Ellamar, AK | USA | ELW |
| Ellensburg, WA | USA | ELN |
| Ellington, TX | USA | EFD |
| Elliot Lake, ON | Canada | YEL |
| Ellisras | S. Africa | ELL |
| Ellsworth/AFB, SD | USA | RCA |
| Elmanzala | Egypt | QEM |
| Elmarj City | Libya | QEC |
| Elmira, NY | USA | ELM |
| Elorza | Venezuela | EOZ |
| Ely, MN | USA | LYU |
| Ely, NV | USA | ELY |

| | | |
|---|---|---|
| Embarcacion | Argentina | ZAI |
| Embessa | Papua New Guinea | EMS |
| Embrach | Switzerland | QEQ |
| Emerald | Australia | EMD |
| Emeryville/HP, CA | USA | JEM |
| Emirau | Papua New Guinea | EMI |
| Emmerich | Germany | QEX |
| Emmonak, AK | USA | EMK |
| Emo | Papua New Guinea | EMO |
| Empangeni | S. Africa | EMG |
| Emporia, KS | USA | EMP |
| En Nahud | Somalia | NUD |
| Enarotali | Indonesia | EWI |
| Encarnacion | Paraguay | ENO |
| Ende | Indonesia | ENE |
| Eneabba West | Australia | ENB |
| Enewetak Is | Marshall Is | ENT |
| Engati | Papua New Guinea | EGA |
| Engelberg | Switzerland | ZHB |
| Englewood, CO/Off-line Pt | USA | QTS |
| Enid, OK | USA | WDG |
| Enid/AFB, OK | USA | END |
| Eniseysk | Russia | EIE |
| Enniskillen/St Angelo | UK | ENK |
| Enontekiö | Finland | ENF |
| Enschede/RR | Netherlands | QYE |
| Enschede/Twente | Netherlands | ENS |
| Ensenada | Mexico | ESE |
| Enshi | China | ENH |
| Entebbe | Uganda | EBB |
| Enterprise/Municipal, AL | USA | ETS |
| Enugu | Nigeria | ENU |
| Epena | Congo, DR | EPN |
| Epernay | France | XEP |
| Ephrata, WA | USA | EPH |
| Epi | Vanuatu | EPI |
| Epinal/Mirecourt | France | EPL |
| Episkopi | Cyprus | EPK |
| Eqalugaiarsuit | Greenland | QFG |
| Erandique | Honduras | EDQ |
| Erave | Papua New Guinea | ERE |
| Ercan | Cyprus | ECN |
| Erdenet | Mongolia | ERT |
| Erechim/C. Kraemer | Brazil | ERM |
| Erfurt/Bindersleben | Germany | ERF |
| Erie, PA | USA | ERI |
| Erigavo | Somalia | ERA |
| Erlangen | Germany | ZCZ |
| Erldunda | Australia | EDD |
| Ernabella | Australia | ERB |
| Ernae | Vanuatu | EAE |
| Ernden | Germany | EME |
| Errachidla | Morocco | ERH |
| Errol, NH | USA | ERR |
| Erume | Papua New Guinea | ERU |
| Erzincan | Turkey | ERC |
| Erzurum | Turkey | ERZ |
| Esa'Ala | Papua New Guinea | ESA |
| Esbjerg | Denmark | EBJ |
| Esbjerg/RR Stn | Denmark | ZBB |
| Escanaba, MI | USA | ESC |
| Eschweiler | Germany | ZEA |
| Eskilstuna | Sweden | EKT |
| Eskisehir | Turkey | ESK |
| Eskisehir/Anadolu Univ. | Turkey | AOE |
| Esltree | UK | ETR |
| Esmeraidas | Ecuador | ESM |
| Espanola, NM | USA | ESO |
| Esperance | Australia | EPR |
| Espinosa | Brazil | ESI |
| Espiritu Santo/Pekoa | Vanuatu | SON |
| Esquel | Argentina | EQS |
| Esquimalt, BC | Canada | YPF |
| Essaouira | Morocco | ESU |
| Essen | Germany | ESS |
| Esslingen | Germany | ZEB |
| Estevan Point, BC | Canada | YEP |
| Estevan, SK | Canada | YEN |
| Estherville, IA | USA | EST |
| Etadunna | Australia | ETD |
| Eua/Kaufana | Tonga | EUA |
| Eucla | Australia | EUC |
| Eufaula | USA | EUF |
| Eugene Is, LA | USA | VUW |
| Eugene, OR | USA | EUG |
| Eunice, LA | USA | UCE |
| Eureka | USA | EUE |
| Eureka, MB | Canada | YEU |
| Eureka/Murray Fld, CA | USA | EKA |
| Euskirchen | Germany | ZED |
| Eva Downs | Australia | EVO |

| | | |
|---|---|---|
| Evadale/Landing Strip, TX | USA | EVA |
| Evans Head | Australia | EVH |
| Evanston, WY | USA | EVW |
| Evansville, IN | USA | EVV |
| Eveleth, MN | USA | EVM |
| Everett, WA | USA | PAE |
| Evergreen, Middleton Fld, AL | USA | GZH |
| Evian Les Bains | France | XEB |
| Eviry/HP | France | JEV |
| Evreux | France | EVX |
| Ewer | Indonesia | EWE |
| Ewo | Congo, DR | EWO |
| Excursion Inlet/SPB, AK | USA | EXI |
| Exeter Arpt | UK | EXT |
| Exmouth Gulf | Australia | EXM |

# F

| | | |
|---|---|---|
| Faaite | F. Polynesia | FAC |
| Fada N'Gourma | Burkina Faso | FNG |
| Fagernes/Valdres | Norway | VDB |
| Fagurholsmyri | Iceland | FAG |
| Fail River, MA | USA | EWB |
| Fair Isle | UK | FIE |
| Fairbanks/Int'l Arpt, AK | USA | FAI |
| Fairbanks, AK | USA | MTX |
| Fairbanks/Eielson/AFB, AK | USA | EIL |
| Fairbanks/Ft Wainwright, AK | USA | FBK |
| Fairbanks/Phillips Fld, AK | USA | PII |
| Fairbury/Municipal, NE | USA | FBY |
| Fairchild/AFB, WA | USA | SKA |
| Fairfield, IA | USA | FFL |
| Fairford/RAF | UK | FFD |
| Fairmont, MN | USA | FRM |
| Fairmount Springs, BC | Canada | YCZ |
| Fairview, AB | Canada | ZFW |
| Faisalabad | Pakistan | LYP |
| Faizabad | Afghanistan | FBD |
| Fajardo | Puerto Rico | FAJ |
| Fak Fak/Torea | Indonesia | FKQ |
| Fakahina | F. Polynesia | FHZ |
| Fakarava | F. Polynesia | FAV |
| Fakenham/Sculthorp/RAF | Georgia | FKH |
| Falher, AB | Canada | YOE |
| Fallon/Municipal, NV | USA | FLX |
| Fallon/NAS, NV | USA | NFL |
| Falls Bay, AK | USA | FLJ |
| Falls Creek | Australia | FLC |
| False Is, AK | USA | FAK |
| False Pass, AK | USA | KFP |
| Fane | Papua New Guinea | FNE |
| Fangatau | F. Polynesia | FGU |
| Farafangana | Madagascar | RVA |
| Farah | Afghanistan | FAH |
| Faranah | Guinea | FAA |
| Farewell, AK | USA | FWL |
| Fargo, ND | USA | FAR |
| Faribault/Municipal, MN | USA | FBL |
| Faridabad | India | QNF |
| Farmingdale, NY | USA | FRG |
| Farmington Municipal, NM | USA | FMN |
| Farmington, MO | USA | FAM |
| Farmville, VA | USA | FVX |
| Farnborough | UK | FAB |
| Faro | Portugal | FAO |
| Faro, YT | Canada | ZFA |
| Faroe Iss/Vagar | Faroe Islands | FAE |
| Farsund/Lista | Norway | FAN |
| Faskrudsfjordur | Iceland | FAS |
| Fauske | Norway | ZXO |
| Faya | Chad | FYT |
| Fayetteville Municipal, AR | USA | FYV |
| Fayetteville, NC | USA | FAY |
| Fayetteville/Municipal, TN | USA | FYM |
| Fayetteville/Northwest Arkansas, AR | USA | XNA |
| Fderik | Mauritania | FGD |
| Feijo | Brazil | FEJ |
| Feiker/AAF, VA | USA | FAF |
| Feira De Santana | Brazil | FEC |
| Fera Is | Solomon Is | FRE |
| Feramin | Papua New Guinea | FRQ |
| Fercana | Uzbekistan | FEG |
| Fercusons Gulf | Kenya | FER |
| Fergus Falls, MN | USA | FFM |
| Ferkessedougou | Côte D'Ivoire | FEK |
| Fernando De Noronha | Brazil | FEN |
| Fetlar | UK | FEA |

| | | |
|---|---|---|
| Fez/Sais | Morocco | FEZ |
| Fianarantsoa | Madagascar | WFI |
| Ficksburg | S. Africa | FCB |
| Figari | France | FSC |
| Filadelfia | Paraguay | FLM |
| Fillmore/Municipal, UT | USA | FIL |
| Fin Creek, AK | USA | FNK |
| Fincha | Ethiopia | FNH |
| Findlay, OH | USA | FDY |
| Finke | Australia | FIK |
| Finley | Australia | FLY |
| Finschhafen | Papua New Guinea | FIN |
| Fire Cove, AK | USA | FIC |
| Fishers Is, NY | USA | FID |
| Fitchburg Municipal, MA | USA | FIT |
| Fitiuta | American Samoa | FTI |
| Fitzroy Crossing | Australia | FIZ |
| Five Finger, AK | USA | FIV |
| Five Mile, AK | USA | FMC |
| Flagstaff/Pulliam Fld, AZ | USA | FLG |
| Flaminoo | Costa Rica | FMG |
| Flat, AK | USA | FLT |
| Flateyri | Iceland | FLI |
| Flaxman Is, AK | USA | FXM |
| Flensburg/Schaferhaus | Germany | FLF |
| Flin Flon, MB | Canada | YFO |
| Flinders Is | Australia | FLS |
| Flint Int'l Arpt, MI | USA | FNT |
| Flippin | Australia | FLP |
| Flora Valley/Flora Vale | Australia | FVL |
| Florence Regional Arpt, SC | USA | FLO |
| Florence, AL | USA | MSL |
| Florence/Peretola | Italy | FLR |
| Florence/Pisa/Gal Galilei | Italy | PSA |
| Florence/S.M. Novella Rail.Svc | Italy | ZMS |
| Florencia, CO | USA | FLA |
| Flores Is/Santa Cruz | Portugal | FLW |
| Flores/Santa Elena | Guatemala | FRS |
| Floriano | Brazil | FLB |
| Florianopolis | Brazil | FLN |
| Floro | Norway | FRO |
| Flotta | UK | FLH |
| Fluelen | Switzerland | ZHD |
| Flushing, NY | USA | FLU |
| Foggia | Italy | FOG |
| Foix | France | XFX |
| Foley, AL | USA | NHX |
| Fond Du Lac Arpt, WI | USA | FLD |
| Fond Du Lac, SK | Canada | ZFD |
| Font Romeu | France | QZF |
| Fontainebieau | France | XFB |
| Fontanges, QC | Canada | YFG |
| Forbes | Australia | FRB |
| Forbes/AFB, KS | USA | FOE |
| Forde/Bringeland | Norway | FDE |
| Fore | Norway | ZXJ |
| Forest City/Municipal, IA | USA | FXY |
| Forest Park/Morris/AAF, GA | USA | FOP |
| Forestville, QC | Canada | YFE |
| Forl Scott, KS | USA | FSK |
| Forli/Luigi Ridolfi | Italy | FRL |
| Formosa | Argentina | FMA |
| Forney/AAF, MO | USA | TBN |
| Forrest | Australia | FOS |
| Forrest City/Municipal, AR | USA | FCY |
| Forrest River Arpt | Australia | FVR |
| Forssa | Finland | QVE |
| Forster | Australia | FOT |
| Fort Belvoir/Davison/AAF, VA | USA | DAA |
| Fort Bragg, CA | USA | FOB |
| Fort Bragg/AAF, NC | USA | FBG |
| Fort Bridger, WY | USA | FBR |
| Fort Collins, CO | USA | FNL |
| Fort Dauphin | Madagascar | FTU |
| Fort De France/Lamentin, Martinique | | FDF |
| Fort Devens, MA | USA | AYE |
| Fort Dodge, IA | USA | FOD |
| Fort Irwin/AAF, CA | USA | BYS |
| Fort Lauderdale/Executive, FL | USA | FXE |
| Fort Lauderdale Int'l, FL | USA | FLL |
| Fort Lee/AAF, VA | USA | FLE |
| Fort Madison, IA | USA | FMS |
| Fort Madison, IA | USA | FSW |
| Fort Myers, FL | USA | FMY |
| Fort Pierce Int'l, FL | USA | FPR |
| Fort Sheridan/AAF, IL | USA | FSN |
| Fort Smith Municipal, AR | USA | FSM |
| Fort St John, BC | Canada | YXJ |
| Fort Stockton, TX | USA | FST |
| Fort Sumner, NM | USA | FSU |
| Fort Wayne/Mncpl/Baer Fld, IN | | |

........................... USA .. FWA
**Fort William**/ HPHP ........... UK. FWM
**Fort Worth**, TX ............... USA .. FTW
**Fort Yukon**, AK ............... USA .. FYU
**Fortaieza**/Pinto Martins ....... Brazil .. FOR
**Fortuna** ............... Costa Rica .. FON
**Fortuna Ledge**, AK ........... USA ... FTL
**Fossil Downs** ........... Australia ... FSL
**Fougamou** ............... Gabon .. FOU
**Foula** ........................ UK .. FOA
**Foumban** ............... Cameroon .. FOM
**Fox Glacier** .......... New Zealand .. FGL
**Fox Harbour** (St Lewis), NG
........................ Canada .. YFX
**Fox**, AK ...................... USA .. FOX
**Foya** ...................... Liberia .. FOY
**Franca** .................... Brazil .. FRC
**Franceville**/Mvengue ........ Gabon .. MVB
**Francisco Beltrao** .......... Brazil .. FBE
**Francistown** ............ Botswana .. FRW
**Franconia**, VA ............... USA .. ZFO
**Frankfort**, KY ................ USA ... FFT
**Frankfurt AFB** ........... Germany .. FRF
**Frankfurt**/HBF Railway Svc Germany .. ZRB
**Frankfurt**/Int'l ............. Germany .. FRA
**Frankfurt**/Neu Isenburg .... Germany .. QGV
**Frankfurt**/Oder/RR Stn ..... Germany .. ZFR
**Franklin Municipal**, VA ....... USA .. FKN
**Franklin**, PA ................. USA ... FKL
**Franz Josef** ......... New Zealand. WHO
**Frauenfeld** ............ Switzerland .. ZHE
**Freburg** ................. Germany .. QFB
**Fredericia**/RR Stn ......... Denmark ... ZBJ
**Frederick**, MD ............... USA .. FDK
**Frederick**, OK ................ USA .. FDR
**Fredericton Junction**/RR Stn.,
NB ..................... Canada .. XFC
**Fredericton**, NB ............ Canada .. YFC
**Frederkshavn**/Bus Svc .... Denmark .. QFH
**Freeport** ............... Bahamas .. FPO
**Freeport**/Albertus, IL .......... USA .. FEP
**Freetown** ............. Sierra Leone .. FNA
**Freetown**/Hastings ..... Sierra Leone .. HGS
**Freetown**/Mammy Yoko HP
.................... Sierra Leone .. JMY
**Fregate Is** ............. Seychelles .. FRK
**Freida River** .... Papua New Guinea .. FAQ
**Freilassing** .............. Germany .. QFL
**Frejus** ..................... France ... FRJ
**Fremantle**/ HP ........... Australia .. JFM
**Fremont**, NE ................. USA .. FET
**French Lick**, IN .............. USA .. FRH
**Frenchville**, ME .............. USA .. WFK
**Frenchville**, N Aroostook, ME .. USA .. FVE
**Fresh Water Bay**, AK ......... USA .. FRP
**Fresno**, CA ................... USA .. FAT
**Fresno-Chandler**, CA ......... USA .. FCH
**Fria** ...................... Guinea ... FIG
**Fribourg** .............. Switzerland .. ZHF
**Friday Harbor** Arpt, WA ....... USA .. FHR
**Friedrichshafen** ......... Germany .. FDH
**Fritziar** .................. Germany .. FRZ
**Fritzsche**/AAF, CA ............ USA .. OAR
**Front Royal**/Warren County, VA. USA .. FRR
**Frosinone** ...................... Italy .. QFR
**Frutillar** ....................... Chile .. FRT
**Fryeburg**, Eastern Slopes
Regional Arpt, ME ........... USA ... IZG
**Fryeburg**, ME ................ USA .. FRY
**Ft Wolter**/AAF, TX ............ USA . CWO
**Ft Worth**, TX ................. USA .. FWD
**Ft. Albany**, ON ............ Canada .. YFA
**Ft. Benning**, GA ............. USA .. FBG
**Ft. Chipewyan**, AB ........ Canada .. YPY
**Ft. Collins** Bus Svc, CO ....... USA . QWF
**Ft. Frances**/Mun, ON ....... Canada .. YAG
**Ft. Good Hope**, NT ........ Canada .. YGH
**Ft. Hood Gray**/AAF, TX ........ USA .. GRK
**Ft. Hood**/AAF, TX ............. USA .. HLR
**Ft. Hope**, ON .............. Canada .. YFH
**Ft. Jelferson**, FL ............. USA .. RBN
**Ft. Kobbe**/Howard AFB .... Panama . HOW
**Ft. Lauderdale**/RR Stn., FL .... USA ... ZFT
**Ft. Lewis Gray**/AAF, WA ...... USA .. GRF
**Ft. Liard**, NT ............. Canada .. YJF
**Ft. Mcmurray**, AB .......... Canada . YMM
**Ft. Mcpherson**, NT ........ Canada .. ZFM
**Ft. Myers**/SW Florida Reg, FL .. USA . RSW
**Ft. Nelson**, BC ............ Canada .. YYE
**Ft. Reliance**, NT ........... Canada ... YFL
**Ft. Resolution**, NT ........ Canada .. YFR
**Ft. Rucker**/Ozark/Army HP, AL. USA .. LOR
**Ft. Severn**, ON ........... Canada .. YER
**Ft. Simpson**, NT ........... Canada .. YFS
**Ft. Smith**, NT ............. Canada .. YSM
**Ft. Washington**, PA/Off-line Pt . USA . QFW
**Ft. Wayne**/Smith Fld, IN ....... USA . SMD
**Ft. Worth**/NAS, TX ........... USA . NFW
**Fucishan** ................... China .. FUO
**Fuerstenfeldbruck** ...... Germany .. FEL
**Fuerteventura** ............. Spain .. FUE
**Fuerth** ................. Germany .. ZEF
**Fujairah**/Int'l Arpt ............ UAE .. FJR
**Fukue** ..................... Japan .. FUJ
**Fukui** ...................... Japan .. FKJ
**Fukuoka** ................... Japan .. FUK
**Fukushima Arpt** ........... Japan .. FKS
**Fukuyama** ................. Japan .. QFY
**Fulda** ................... Germany .. ZEE
**Fulleborn** ...... Papua New Guinea .. FUB
**Fullerton Municipal**, CA ..... USA .. FUL
**Fulton County**, GA .......... USA .. FTY
**Fuma** .......... Papua New Guinea .. FUM
**Funafuti Atol Int'l** .......... Tuvalu .. FUN
**Funchal**/Madeira .......... Portugal .. FNC
**Funter Bay**/SPB, AK ......... USA .. FNR
**Furtaeulu** ................... Chile .. FFU
**Futuna Is** ...... Wallis and Futuna Is .. FUT
**Futuna Is** Arpt ............ Vanuatu .. FTA
**Fuyang** .................... China .. FUG
**Fuyun** ..................... China .. FYN
**Fuzhou** .................... China .. FOC

# G

**Gabbs**, NV ................... USA .. GAB
**Gabes** .................... Tunisia .. GAE
**Gaborone**/Sir Seretse
Khama Int'l ........... Botswana .. GBE
**Gachas Nek** ............. Lesotho .. UNE
**Gadsden**/Municipal, AL ....... USA .. GAD
**Gafsa**/Ksar ............... Tunisia .. GAF
**Gag Is** .................. Indonesia .. GAV
**Gage**, OK ................... USA . GAG
**Gagetown**, NB ............ Canada .. YCX
**Gagnoa** ............. Côte D'Ivoire . GGN
**Gagnon**, QC ............. Canada .. YGA
**Gainesville**, FL ............. USA .. GNV
**Gainesville**/Gilmer Memorial,
GA ......................... USA .. GVL
**Gainesville**/Municipal, TX ..... USA .. GLE
**Gaithersburg**, MD ............ USA .. GAI
**Gakona**, AK .................. USA .. GAK
**Gal Oya**/Amparai ......... Sri Lanka . GOY
**Galapagos Is**/Baltra ....... Ecuador .. GPS
**Galbraith Lake**, AK .......... USA .. GBH
**Galcaio** ................. Somalia .. GLK
**Galela**/Gamarmalamu ..... Indonesia .. GLX
**Galena**, AK .................. USA .. GAL
**Galesburg**, GBG ............ USA . GBG
**Galion**, OH .................. USA . GQQ
**Gallivare** ............... Sweden .. GEV
**Gallup Municipal** Arpt, NM .... USA .. GUP
**Galveston**, Scholes Fld, TX .... USA .. GLS
**Galway Cammore** .......... Ireland . GWY
**Gamarra** .............. Colombia .. GRA
**Gamba** .................. Gabon .. GAX
**Gambela** ............... Ethiopia . GMB
**Gambell**, AK .................. USA . GAM
**Gambier Is** ........... F. Polynesia . GMR
**Gamboma** ............ Congo, DR . GMM
**Gamboola** ............. Australia .. GBP
**Gan Is**/Gan/Seenu ......... Maldives .. GAN
**Gananoque**/RR Stn., ON ... Canada . XGW
**Gandajika** ............ Congo, DR .. GDJ
**Gander Int'l**, NF ........... Canada .. YQX
**Ganes Creek**, AK ............ USA .. GEK
**Gangaw** ............... Myanmar . GAW
**Ganges Harbor**, BC ....... Canada . YGG
**Ganzhou** ................. China . KOW
**Gao** ........................ Mali . GAQ
**Gaoua** ............. Burkina Faso .. XGA
**Gap**/Tallard ................ France . GAT
**Gara Djebilet** .............. Algeria .. GBB
**Garachine** ............... Panama .. GHE
**Garaina** ........ Papua New Guinea .. GAR
**Garanhuns** ................. Brazil . QGP
**Garasa** ........ Papua New Guinea .. GRL
**Garbaharey** .............. Somalia .. GBM
**Garbsen** ................ Germany .. ZEH
**Garden City**, KS ............ USA .. GCK
**Garden City**/Is HP, NY ........ USA ... JHC
**Garden Point** ........... Australia .. GPN
**Gardez** ............... Afghanistan .. GRG
**Gardner**/Municipal, MA ........ USA .. GDM
**Gardo** .................. Somalia .. GSR
**Garissa** .................. Kenya .. GAS
**Garmisch-Partenkirchen** Germany ... ZEI
**Garoe** ................... Somalia .. GGR
**Garoua** ............... Cameroon .. GOU
**Garuahi** ........ Papua New Guinea . GRH
**Gary Regional**, IN ........... USA .. GYY
**Gascoyne Junction** ...... Australia .. GSC
**Gasmata Is** ..... Papua New Guinea .. GMI
**Gaspe**, QC ................ Canada .. YGP
**Gaspe**/RR Stn., QC ........ Canada .. XDD
**Gassim** .............. Saudi Arabia .. ELQ
**Gassimiut** .............. Greenland ... QJH
**Gastonia**, NC ................ USA .. AKH
**Gasuke** ........ Papua New Guinea . GBC
**Gatineati**, ON ............ Canada .. YND
**Gatlinburg**, TN ............... USA .. GKT
**Gatokae Aerodrom** .... Solomon Is .. GTA
**Gaua** .................... Vanuatu .. ZGU
**Gauhati**/Borlhar ............. India .. GAU
**Gavie**/Sandviken AFB ...... Sweden .. GVX
**Gaya** ...................... India .. GAY
**Gaylord**, Otsego County, MI .... USA .. GLR
**Gayndah** ............... Australia .. GAH
**Gaza Strip** . Occupied Palestinian Ter .. ZDY
**Gaza Strip**/Gaza Int'l
.......... Occupied Palestinian Ter . GZA
**Gbadolite** ............ Congo, DR .. BDT
**Gbangbatok** ......... Sierra Leone . GBK
**GC Apollo**, ON/Off-line Pt ... Canada .. QZP
**Gdansk**/Rebiechowo ........ Poland .. GDN
**Gdynia** .................. Poland .. QYD
**Geatkale** ................. Cyprus .. GEC
**Gebe** ................. Indonesia .. GEB
**Gebelstacit** ............. Germany .. GHF
**Gedaref** ................. Somalia .. GSU
**Geelong** ............... Australia .. GEX
**Geilenkirchen** ........... Germany .. GKE
**Geilo**/Dagali .............. Norway ... DLD
**Geita** ................... Tanzania ... GIT
**Geladi** .................. Ethiopia .. GLC
**Gelenclzilk** ............... Russia .. GDZ
**Gelsenkirchen** .......... Germany ... ZEJ
**Gemena** ............. Congo, DR . GMA
**Genda Wuha** ............ Ethiopia ... ETE
**Geneina** ................. Sudan .. EGN
**General Pico** ........... Argentina .. GPO
**General Roca** .......... Argentina .. GNR
**General Safflos**/Buayan . Philippines .. GES
**General Villegas** ....... Argentina .. VGS
**Geneva Aeroport**/RR Stn.
..................... Switzerland ... ZHY
**Geneva Cointrin** ...... Switzerland .. GVA
**Geneva-Cornavin**/RR Stn.
..................... Switzerland ... ZHT
**Genoa**/Cristoforo Colombo ...... Italy .. GOA
**Genting** ................ Malaysia ... GTB
**Geoie HP** ............... S. Korea .. JGE
**George** ................. S. Africa .. GRJ
**George Town** ........... Australia .. GEE
**George Town**/Exuma Int'l
........................ Bahamas .. GGT
**George**/AFB, CA ............. USA .. VCV
**Georgetown** ........... St. Helena .. ASI
**Georgetown** ............ Australia ... GTT
**Georgetown**, DE .............. USA .. GED
**Georgetown**, SC .............. USA .. GGE
**Georgetown**/Cheddi Jagan Int'l
......................... Guyana .. GEO
**Georgetown**/RR Stn., ON .. Canada .. XHM
**Gera**/RR Stn ............. Germany .. ZGA
**Geraldton** .............. Australia .. GET
**Geraldton**, ON ............ Canada .. YGQ
**Gerga** .................... Egypt .. QGX
**German Railways Zone F**/RR
....................... Germany .. QYF
**German Railways Zone J**/RR
....................... Germany ... QYJ
**Germansen**, BC .......... Canada .. YGS
**Germany**/RR ............. Germany .. QYG
**Gerona**/Costa Brava ......... Spain .. GRO
**Gerstungen**/RR Stn ....... Germany ... ZGT
**Gethsemani**, QC .......... Canada .. ZGS
**Gettysburg**, PA .............. USA .. GTY

| | | |
|---|---|---|
| Geva Airstrip | Solomon Is. | GEF |
| Gewoia | Papua New Guinea | GEW |
| Ghadames | Libya | LTD |
| Ghanzi | Botswana | GNZ |
| Ghardaia Nournerate | Algeria | GHA |
| Ghat | Libya | GHT |
| Ghazaouet | Algeria | QVX |
| Ghazni | Afghanistan | GZI |
| Ghent/Industrie-Zone | Belgium | GNE |
| Gherian | Libya | QGH |
| Gheshm | Iran | GSM |
| Ghimbi | Ethiopia | GHD |
| Ghinnir | Ethiopia | GNN |
| Gibb River | Australia | GBV |
| Gibraltar/North Front | Gibraltar | GIB |
| Gienormiston | Australia | GLM |
| Gifu AB | Japan | QGU |
| Gijon | Spain | QIJ |
| Gila Bend/AAF, AZ | USA | GBN |
| Gilgal | Colombia | GGL |
| Gilgit | Pakistan | GIL |
| Gillam, MB | Canada | YGX |
| Gillies Bay, BC | Canada | YGB |
| Gilwice | Poland | QLC |
| Gimli, MB | Canada | YGM |
| Girardot | Colombia | GIR |
| Gisborne | New Zealand | GIS |
| Gisenyi | Rwanda | GYI |
| Gitega | Benin | GID |
| Giyani | S. Africa | GIY |
| Gizan | Saudi Arabia | GIZ |
| Gizo/Nusatope | Solomon Is | GZO |
| Gizycio | Poland | ZYC |
| Gjoa Haven, NU | Canada | YHK |
| Gjogur | Iceland | GJR |
| Glacier Creek, AK | USA | KGZ |
| Gladbeck | Germany | ZEK |
| Gladewater, TX | USA | GGG |
| Gladstone | Australia | GLT |
| Gladwin, MI | USA | GDW |
| Glarus | Switzerland | ZHG |
| Glasgow | UK | PIK |
| Glasgow Int'l Arpt, MT | USA | GGW |
| Glasgow/Int'l | UK | GLA |
| Glasgow/Municipal, KY | USA | GLW |
| Glasgow/ScotRail | UK | ZGG |
| Glen Innes | Australia | GLI |
| Glencoe/RR Stn., ON | Canada | XZC |
| Glendale / HP, CA | USA | JGX |
| Glendale,WV | USA | GWV |
| Glendive, MT | USA | GDV |
| Glengyie | Australia | GLG |
| Glennallen, AK | USA | GLQ |
| Glens Falls, NY | USA | GFL |
| Glenview/NAS, IL | USA | NBU |
| Glenwood Asos, MN | USA | GHW |
| Glenwood Springs, CO | USA | GWS |
| Gloucester/Staverton Private | UK | GLO |
| Glynco/NAS, GA | USA | NEA |
| Gnarowein | Papua New Guinea | GWN |
| Goa/Dabolim | India | GOI |
| Goba | Ethiopia | GOB |
| Gobernador Gregores | Argentina | GGS |
| Gode/Iddidole | Ethiopia | GDE |
| Godman/AAF, KY | USA | FTK |
| Gods Narrows, MB | Canada | YGO |
| Gods River, MB | Canada | ZGI |
| Goeppingen | Germany | ZES |
| Goerlitz/RR Stn | Germany | ZGE |
| Goettingen | Germany | ZEU |
| Goiania/Santa Genoveva | Brazil | GYN |
| Gol/Klanten | Norway | GLL |
| Golbabis | Namibia | GOG |
| Gold Beach/State, OR | USA | GOL |
| Gold Coast | Australia | OOL |
| Golden Gate Bridge, CA | USA | GGB |
| Golden Horn/SPB, AK | USA | GDH |
| Goldsworthy | Australia | GLY |
| Golfito | Costa Rica | GLF |
| Golmud | China | GOQ |
| Golovin, AK | USA | GLV |
| Goma | Congo, DR | GOM |
| Gomel | Belarus | GME |
| Gonalia | Papua New Guinea | GOE |
| Gondar | Ethiopia | GDQ |
| Goodfellow/AFB, TX | USA | GOF |
| Gooding, ID | USA | GNG |
| Goodland, Renner Fld, KS | USA | GLD |
| Goodnews Bay, AK | USA | GNU |
| Goodyear Municipal, AZ | USA | GYR |
| Goondiwindi | Australia | GOO |

| | | |
|---|---|---|
| Goose, NF | Canada | YYR |
| Gora | Papua New Guinea | GOC |
| Gorakhpur | India | GOP |
| Gordil | Central African Rep | GDI |
| Gordon Downs | Australia | GDD |
| Gordon Municipal, NE | USA | GRN |
| Gordonsville/Municipal, VA | USA | GVE |
| Gore | Ethiopia | GOR |
| Gore Bay, ON | Canada | YZE |
| Gorge Harbor, BC | Canada | YGE |
| Gorizia | Italy | QGO |
| Gorkha | Nepal | GKH |
| Gorna Orechovitsa | Bulgaria | GOZ |
| Goroka | Papua New Guinea | GKA |
| Gorom-Gorom | Burkina Faso | XGG |
| Gorontalo/Tolotio | Indonesia | GTO |
| Gosford | Australia | GOS |
| Goshen Municipal Arpt, IN | USA | GSH |
| Goslar | Germany | ZET |
| Gossau SG | Switzerland | ZHH |
| Goteborg/Landvetter | Sweden | GOT |
| Gotha/RR Stn | Germany | ZGO |
| Gothenburg/Saeve | Sweden | GSE |
| Goulburn | Australia | GUL |
| Goulburn Is | Australia | GBL |
| Goulimime | Morocco | GLN |
| Gounda | Central African Rep | GDA |
| Goundam | Mali | GUD |
| Gove/Nhulunbuy | Australia | GOV |
| Governador Valadares | Brazil | GVR |
| Governors Harbour | Bahamas | GHB |
| Goya | Argentina | OYA |
| Gozo | Malta | GZM |
| Graasten/Bus Svc | Denmark | XRA |
| Gracias | Honduras | GAC |
| Graciosa Is | Portugal | GRW |
| Grafton | Australia | GFN |
| Gramado | Brazil | QRP |
| Granada | Spain | GRX |
| Grand Bahama/Aux Ab | Bahamas | GBI |
| Grand Canyon/HP, AZ | USA | JGC |
| Grand Canyon National Park, AZ | USA | GCN |
| Grand Canyon/North Rim, AZ | USA | NGC |
| Grand Cayman Is Int'l | Cayman Is | GCM |
| Grand Cess | Liberia | GRC |
| Grand Forks Int'l, ND | USA | GFK |
| Grand Forks, BC | Canada | ZGF |
| Grand Forks/AFB, ND | USA | RDR |
| Grand Is Nexrad, NE | USA | UEX |
| Grand Is, NE | USA | GRI |
| Grand Junction/Walker Fld, CO | USA | GJT |
| Grand Marais/Municipal, MN | USA | GRM |
| Grand Rapids, MN | USA | GPZ |
| Grand Rapids/Kent County Int'l Arpt, MI | USA | GRR |
| Grand Turk Is | Turks & Caicos Is | GDT |
| Grande Cache, AB | Canada | YGC |
| Grande Prairie, AB | Canada | YQU |
| Grande-Riviere/RR Stn., QC | Canada | XDO |
| Granite Mountain, AK | USA | GMT |
| Granites | Australia | GTS |
| Grantham/RR Stn | UK | XGM |
| Grants-Milan, NM | USA | GNT |
| Grantsburg/Municipal, WI | USA | GTG |
| Granville | France | GFR |
| Granville Lake, MB | Canada | XGL |
| Gravik | Norway | ZXG |
| Grayling, AK | USA | KGX |
| Graz/Thalerhof | Austria | GRZ |
| Great Barrier Is | New Zealand | GBZ |
| Great Barrington, MA | USA | GBR |
| Great Bear Lake, NT | Canada | DAS |
| Great Bend, KS | USA | GBD |
| Great Falls Int'l Arpt, MT | USA | GTF |
| Great Falls Nexrad, MT | USA | TFX |
| Great Harbour | Bahamas | GHC |
| Great Keppel Is | Australia | GKL |
| Greeley/Weld County, CO | USA | GXY |
| Green Bay, Austin Straubel Int'l, WI | USA | GRB |
| Green Is | Taiwan | GNI |
| Green Iss | Papua New Guinea | GEI |
| Green River | Papua New Guinea | GVI |
| Green River, UT | USA | RVR |
| Green Turtle | Bahamas | GTC |
| Greenfeid/Pope Fld, IN | USA | GFD |
| Greenvale | Australia | GVL |
| Greenville Majors, TX | USA | GVT |
| Greenville, MS | USA | GLH |

| | | |
|---|---|---|
| Greenville, NC | USA | PGV |
| Greenville, SC | USA | GMU |
| Greenville, SC | USA | GSP |
| Greenville/Donaldson Center, SC | USA | GDC |
| Greenville/Municipal, IL | USA | GRE |
| Greenville/Municipal, TN | USA | GCY |
| Greenway Sound, BC | Canada | YGN |
| Greenwood County Arpt, SC | USA | GRD |
| Greenwood, NS | Canada | YZX |
| Greenwood/Leflore, MS | USA | GWO |
| Gregory Downs | Australia | GGD |
| Greifswald/RR Stn | Germany | ZGW |
| Grenada/Point Saline Int'l | Grenada | GND |
| Grenchen | Switzerland | ZHI |
| Grenfell | Australia | GFE |
| Grenoble/Saint Geoirs | France | GNB |
| Grevenbroich | Germany | ZEV |
| Greybull, WY | USA | GEY |
| Greymouth | New Zealand | GMN |
| Griffiss/AFB, NY | USA | RME |
| Griffith | Australia | GFF |
| Grimsby/Binbrook | UK | GSY |
| Grimsby/RR Stn., ON | Canada | XGY |
| Grimsey | Iceland | GRY |
| Grindelwald | Switzerland | ZHJ |
| Grise Fiord, NU | Canada | YGZ |
| Grissom/AFB, IN | USA | GUS |
| Grodna | Belarus | GNA |
| Groennedal/ HP | Greenland | JGR |
| Groningen/Eelde | Netherlands | GRQ |
| Groote Eylandt/Alyangula | Australia | GTE |
| Grootfontein | Namibia | GFY |
| Grosseto/Baccarini | Italy | GRS |
| Groton/New London Rail, CT | USA | GZD |
| Groznyj | Russia | GRV |
| Grundarfjordur | Iceland | GUU |
| Gstaad | Switzerland | ZHK |
| Guacamaya | Colombia | GCA |
| Guadalajara/Miguel Hidal | Mexico | GDL |
| Guadalcanal | Solomon Is | GSI |
| Guadalupe | Brazil | GDP |
| Guaira | Brazil | QGA |
| Gualaco | Honduras | GUO |
| Gualara-Mirim | Brazil | GJM |
| Gualeguaychu | Argentina | GHU |
| Guam/A.B. Won Pat Infl | Guam | GUM |
| Guam/Agana/NAS | Guam | NGM |
| Guam/Anderson AFB | Guam | UAM |
| Guam/USCG Shore St | Guam | NRV |
| Guanaja | Honduras | GJA |
| Guanambi | Brazil | GNM |
| Guanare | Venezuela | GUQ |
| Guanghan | China | GHN |
| Guanghua | China | LHK |
| Guangzhou | China | CAN |
| Guantanamo/Los Canos | Cuba | GAO |
| Guantanamo/NAS | Cuba | NBW |
| Guapi | Colombia | GPI |
| Guapiles | Costa Rica | GPL |
| Guarapari | Brazil | GUZ |
| Guarapuava/Tancredo Thornaz Faria | Brazil | GPB |
| Guaratingueta | Brazil | GUJ |
| Guari | Papua New Guinea | GUG |
| Guarrial | Colombia | GAA |
| Guarulhos | Brazil | QCV |
| Guasdualito/Vare Maria | Venezuela | GDO |
| Guasopa | Papua New Guinea | GAZ |
| Guatemala City/La Aurora | Guatemala | GUA |
| Guayaquil/Simon Bolivar | Ecuador | GYE |
| Guayaramerin | Bolivia | GYA |
| Guaymas | Mexico | GYM |
| Guelma | Algeria | QGE |
| Guelph/RR Stn., ON | Canada | XIA |
| Gueret/Saint Laurent | France | XGT |
| Guerima | Colombia | GMC |
| Guernsey | UK | GCI |
| Guerrero Negro | Mexico | GUB |
| Guetersloh | Germany | GUT |
| Guetersloh | Germany | ZEX |
| Guettin | Germany | GTI |
| Guiglo | Côte D'Ivoire | GGO |
| Guigubip | Papua New Guinea | GLP |
| Guildwood/Toronto, ON | Canada | YTO |
| Guilin | China | KWL |
| Guimaraes | Brazil | GMS |
| Guirat | Pakistan | GRT |

| Airport | Country | Code |
|---|---|---|
| Guiria | Venezuela | GUI |
| Guiyang | China | KWE |
| Gulf Shores/Edwards, AL | USA | GUF |
| Gulkana Arpt, AK | USA | GKN |
| Gulu | Uganda | ULU |
| Gummersbach | Germany | ZEW |
| Guna | India | GUX |
| Gunnedah | Australia | GUH |
| Gunnison, CO | USA | GUC |
| Gunungsitoli/Binaka | Indonesia | GNS |
| Gurayat | Saudi Arabia | URY |
| Guriaso | Papua New Guinea | GUE |
| Gurni City | S. Korea | QKM |
| Gurue | Mozambique | VJQ |
| Gurupi | Brazil | GRP |
| Gusap | Papua New Guinea | GAP |
| Gusau | Nigeria | QUS |
| Gush Katif | Israel | GHK |
| Gustavus, AK | USA | GST |
| Gustavus/Bartlett SPB, AK | USA | BQV |
| Gutenfuerst/RR Stn. | Germany | ZGN |
| Guthrie, OK. | USA | GOK |
| Guymon, OK. | USA | GUY |
| Gwa | Myanmar | GWA |
| Gwadar | Pakistan | GWD |
| Gwalior | India | GWL |
| Gweru | Zimbabwe | GWE |
| Gyancizha | Azerbaijan | KVD |
| Gympie | Australia | GYP |
| Gyor | Hungary | QGY |
| Gyoumri | Armenia | LWN |

# H

| Airport | Country | Code |
|---|---|---|
| Ha'Apai/Salote Pilolevu | Tonga | HPA |
| Hachijo Jima | Japan | HAC |
| Hachinohe AB | Japan | HHE |
| Hachioji City | Japan | QHY |
| Haeloao | Papua New Guinea | HEO |
| Hafr Albatin | Saudi Arabia | HBT |
| Hagen | Germany | ZEY |
| Hagerstown, MD | USA | HGR |
| Hagfors | Sweden | HFS |
| Hahn | Germany | HHN |
| Hahnweide/RR. | Germany | QHD |
| Haifa/U Michaeli | Israel | HFA |
| Haikou | China | HAK |
| Hail | Saudi Arabia | HAS |
| Hailar | China | HLD |
| Hailey, ID | USA | SUN |
| Haines Arpt, AK | USA | HNS |
| Haines Junction, YT | Canada | YHT |
| Haiphong/Catbi | Vietnam | HPH |
| Hakai Pass, BC | Canada | YHC |
| Hakodate | Japan | HKD |
| Halah | Namibia | HAL |
| Halberstadt/RR Stn. | Germany | ZHQ |
| Half Moon, CA | USA | HAF |
| Halifax/Int'l Arpt, NS | Canada | YHZ |
| Halifax/Dwtown Waterfront HP, NS | Canada | YWF |
| Halifax/RR Stn.. NS | Canada | XDG |
| Hall Beach, NU | Canada | YUX |
| Halle/RR Stn. | Germany | ZHZ |
| Halls Creek | Australia | HCQ |
| Halmstad/AFB | Sweden | HAD |
| Hama | Syria | QHM |
| Hamadan | Iran | HDM |
| Hamar/Hamar Arpt | Norway | HMR |
| Hamburg/Finkenwerder | Germany | XFW |
| Hamburg/Fuhlsbuettel | Germany | HAM |
| Hamburg/RR Stn. | Germany | ZMB |
| Hämeenlinna | Finland | QVM |
| Hameln | Germany | ZEZ |
| Hami | China | HMI |
| Hamilton | Australia | HLT |
| Hamilton | New Zealand | HLZ |
| Hamilton Is | Australia | HTI |
| Hamilton, OH | USA | HAO |
| Hamilton, ON | Canada | YHM |
| Hamilton/AAF, CA | USA | SRF |
| Hamilton/Int'l | Bermuda | BDA |
| Hamilton/Marion County, AL | USA | HAB |
| Hamilton/Ravalli County, MT | USA | HMM |
| Hamina | Finland | QVZ |
| Hamm | Germany | ZNB |
| Hammerfest | Norway | HFT |
| Hampton, VA | USA | PHF |
| Hampton/Municipal, IA | USA | HPT |
| Hampton/Newport News Rail, VA | USA | ZWW |
| Hampton/Williamsburg Rail, VA | USA | ZWB |
| Hana, HI | USA | HNM |
| Hanapepe/Port Allen, HI | USA | PAK |
| Hanau | Germany | ZNF |
| Hanchey/AHP, AL | USA | HEY |
| Hancock, MI. | USA | CMX |
| Hanford., WA. | USA | HMS |
| Hangzhou | China | HGH |
| Hanimaadhoo | Maldives | HAQ |
| Hanksville/Intermediate, UT | USA | HVE |
| Hanna, WY | USA | HNX |
| Hanoi/Noibai. | Vietnam | HAN |
| Hanover | Germany | HAJ |
| Hanover, NH | USA | LEB |
| Hanover/HBF Railway Svc | Germany | ZVR |
| Hanover/Messe-BF Railway Sev | Germany | ZVM |
| Hanus Bay, AK | USA | HBC |
| Hao Is | F. Polynesia | HOI |
| Harar | Ethiopia | QHR |
| Harare Kutsaga | Zimbabwe | HRE |
| Harbin | China | HRB |
| Harbour Is | Bahamas | HBI |
| Hargeisa | Somalia | HGA |
| Harlingen/Valley Int'l, TX | USA | HRL |
| Harlzhong | China | HZG |
| Harrisburg/Int'l Arpt, PA | USA | MDT |
| Harrisburg Skyport, PA | USA | HAR |
| Harrisburg/Rail, PA | USA | ZUG |
| Harrisburg/Raleigh, NC | USA | HSB |
| Harrismith | S. Africa | HRS |
| Harrison, AR | USA | HRO |
| Harrogate/Linton-On-Ouse | UK | HRT |
| Harstad | Norway | HRD |
| Harstad-Narvik/Evenes | Norway | EVE |
| Hartford-Brainard Arpt, CT | USA | HFD |
| Hartford/Barnes, CT | USA | BNH |
| Hartford/Bradley Int'l, CT | USA | BDL |
| Hartford/Hartford CT Rail | USA | ZRT |
| Hartley Bay, BC | Canada | YTB |
| Hartsville, SC | USA | HVS |
| Harwich/RR | UK | QQH |
| Haskovo | Bulgaria | HKV |
| Hasselt | Belgium | QHA |
| Hassi R'Mel/Tilrempt | Algeria | HRM |
| Hassi-Messaoud | Algeria | HME |
| Hastings Municipal, NE | USA | HSI |
| Hasvik | Norway | HAA |
| Hat Yai | Thailand | HDY |
| Hatanga | Russia | HTG |
| Hatchet Lake, SK. | Canada | YDJ |
| Hateruma | Japan | HTR |
| Hatfeild | UK | HTF |
| Hato Corozal | Colombia | HTZ |
| Hatteras/Mitchell Fld, NC | USA | HSE |
| Hatteras, NC | USA | HNC |
| Hattiesburg, MS | USA | HBG |
| Hatzfeldthaven | Papua New Guinea | HAZ |
| Haugesund/Karmoy | Norway | HAU |
| Havana/Jose Marti Int'l | Cuba | HAV |
| Havasupai, AZ | USA | HAE |
| Haverfordwest | UK | HAW |
| Havoeysund | Norway | QVO |
| Havre City-County, MT | USA | HVR |
| Havre St Pierre, QC. | Canada | YGV |
| Hawabango | Papua New Guinea | HWA |
| Hawk Inlet/SPB, AK. | USA | HWI |
| Hawker/Wilpena Pound | Australia | HWK |
| Hawthorne, CA. | USA | HHR |
| Hawthorne, NV. | USA | HTH |
| Hay | Australia | HXX |
| Hay River, NT | Canada | YHY |
| Haycock, AK. | USA | HAY |
| Hayden/Yampa Valley, CO | USA | HDN |
| Hayfields | Papua New Guinea | HYF |
| Hayman Is | Australia | HIS |
| Hays/Municipal, KS | USA | HYS |
| Hayward Air Terminal, CA. | USA | HWD |
| Hayward Municipal, WI | USA | HYR |
| Hazebrouck/Merville/Calonne | France | HZB |
| HazletonPA | USA | HZL |
| Hazyview | S. Africa | HZV |
| Headingly | Australia | HIP |
| Healy Lake, AK | USA | HKB |
| Hearst, OH | Canada | YHF |
| Heathlands | Australia | HAT |
| Heerbrugg | Switzerland | ZHL |
| Heerenveen/Bus Svc | Netherlands | QYZ |
| Hefei | China | HFE |
| Heho | Myanmar | HEH |
| Heide/Buesum | Germany | HEI |
| Heidelberg | Germany | HDB |
| Heidenheim | Germany | ZNI |
| Heiena, MT | USA | HLN |
| Heihe | China | HEK |
| Heilbronn | Germany | ZNJ |
| Heinola | Finland | QVV |
| Heiweni | Papua New Guinea | HNI |
| Helena/Thompson-Robbins, AR. | USA | HEE |
| Helenvaie | Australia | HLV |
| Helgoland | Germany | HGL |
| Helicopter Scenic | New Zealand | XXH |
| Helsingborg | Sweden | AGH |
| Helsingborg/ HP. | Sweden | JHE |
| Helsinki/Malmi | Finland | HEM |
| Helsinki/Vantaa | Finland | HEL |
| Hemavan | Sweden | HMV |
| Hemet/Ryan Fld, CA | USA | HMT |
| Hemnes | Norway | ZXR |
| Henbury | Australia | HRY |
| Hendaye | France | XHY |
| Henderson City, KY. | USA | EHR |
| Hendon | UK | HEN |
| Hengchun | Taiwan | HCN |
| Hengelo/RR | Netherlands | QYH |
| Hengyang | China | HNY |
| Henry Post/AAF, OK. | USA | FSI |
| Henzada | Myanmar | HEB |
| Heraklion/Iraklio. | Greece | HER |
| Herat | Afghanistan | HEA |
| Hercegnovi | Yugoslavia | HNO |
| Herendeen, AK. | USA | HED |
| Herford | Germany | ZNK |
| Heringsdorf | Germany | HDF |
| Hermannsburg | Australia | HMG |
| Hermiston/State, OR. | USA | HES |
| Hermosillo/Gen Pesqueira Garcia | Mexico | HMO |
| Herne | Germany | ZNL |
| Herning/RR Stn. | Denmark | XAK |
| Heron Is / HP | Australia | HRN |
| Herrera | Colombia | HRR |
| Herten | Germany | ZNM |
| Hervey Bay | Australia | HVB |
| Hervey/RR Stn., QC. | Canada | XDU |
| Herzogenbuchsee | Switzerland | ZHN |
| Hettlingen | Germany | ZNH |
| Hickam/AFB, HI | USA | HIK |
| Hickory, NC | USA | HKY |
| Hidden Falls, AK. | USA | HDA |
| Hienghene | New Caledonia | HNG |
| High Level, AB | Canada | YOJ |
| High Prairie, AB | Canada | ZHP |
| High Wycombe (MOD) | UK | HYC |
| Highbury | Australia | HIG |
| Hikueru | F. Polynesia | HHZ |
| Hilden | Germany | ZNN |
| Hildesheim | Germany | ZNO |
| Hill City, KS | USA | HLC |
| Hill/AFB, UT. | USA | HIF |
| Hillsboro, OR. | USA | HIO |
| Hillside | Australia | HLL |
| Hillsville, VA. | USA | HLX |
| Hilo Int'l, HI | USA | ITO |
| Hilton Head, SC | USA | HHH |
| Hilversum/RR | Netherlands | QYI |
| Hinchinbrook Is | Australia | HNK |
| Hirlshals/Bus Svc. | Denmark | XAJ |
| Hiroshima/Hiroshima West | Japan | HIW |
| Hiroshima/Int'l | Japan | HIJ |
| Hissar | India | HSS |
| Hiva Oa | F. Polynesia | HIX |
| Hivaro | Papua New Guinea | HIT |
| Hjoerring/Bus Svc. | Denmark | QHJ |
| Hluhluwe | S. Africa | HLW |
| Ho Chi Minh | Vietnam | SGN |
| Hobart Arpt | Australia | HBA |
| Hobart Bay, AK. | USA | HBH |
| Hobart Municipal Arpt, OK. | USA | HBR |
| Hobbs, NM | USA | HOB |
| Hobbs/Industrial Airpark, NM | USA | HBB |
| Hodeidah/Hodeidah Arpt | Yemen | HOD |
| Hoedspruit | S. Africa | HDS |
| Hof | Germany | HOQ |
| Hofuf/Al Hasa | Saudi Arabia | HOF |
| Hogatza, AK. | USA | HGZ |
| Hohenems | Austria | HOH |
| Hohhot | China | HET |

| | | |
|---|---|---|
| Hokitilka | New Zealand | HKK |
| Hola | Kenya | HOA |
| Holguir./Frank Pais | Cuba | HOG |
| Holikachu, AK | USA | HOL |
| Holland/Park Township, MI | USA | HLM |
| Hollis/SPB, AK | USA | HYL |
| Hollister, CA | USA | HLI |
| Holloman/AFB, NM | USA | HMN |
| Hollywood-North Perry, FL | USA | HWO |
| Holman, NT | Canada | YHI |
| Holmavik | Iceland | HVK |
| Holstelbro/Bus Svc | Denmark | QWO |
| Holy Cross, AK | USA | HCR |
| Holyhead | UK | HLY |
| Homalin | Myanmar | HOX |
| Homburg | Germany | QOG |
| Homer Arpt, AK | USA | HOM |
| Homestead/AFB, FL | USA | HST |
| Hondo, TX | USA | HDO |
| Hong Kong / HP | Hong Kong | HHP |
| Hong Kong Int'l | Hong Kong | HKG |
| Honiara/Henderson | Solomon Is | HIR |
| Honinabi | Papua New Guinea | HNN |
| Honningsvag/Valan | Norway | HVG |
| Honolulu/Int'l, HI | USA | HNL |
| Hoofddorp | Netherlands | QHZ |
| Hook Is | Australia | HIH |
| Hooker Creek | Australia | HOK |
| Hoolehua/Molokai, HI | USA | MKK |
| Hoonah, AK | USA | HNH |
| Hooper Bay, AK | USA | HPB |
| Hope Vale | Australia | HPE |
| Hope, BC | Canada | YHE |
| Hopedale, NF | Canada | YHO |
| Hopetoun | Australia | HTU |
| Hoquiam, WA | USA | HQM |
| Horizontina | Brazil | HRZ |
| Horn Is | Australia | HID |
| Hornafjordur | Iceland | HFN |
| Hornepayne, ON | Canada | YHN |
| Horns | Syria | QHS |
| Horsham | Australia | HSM |
| Horta | Portugal | HOR |
| Hoskins | Papua New Guinea | HKN |
| Hot Springs, AR | USA | HOT |
| Hot Springs/Ingalls, VA | USA | HSP |
| Hotan | China | HTN |
| Houailou | New Caledonia | HLU |
| Houeisay | Laos | HOE |
| Houghton Lake, MI | USA | HTL |
| Houlton Int'l, ME | USA | HUL |
| Houma-Terrebonne, LA | USA | HUM |
| Houn | Libya | HUQ |
| Houston George Bush, TX | USA | IAH |
| Houston/Hobby Arpt, TX | USA | HOU |
| Houston, TX | USA | DWH |
| Houston-SugarLand, TX | USA | SGR |
| Houston/Andrau Airpark, TX | USA | AAP |
| Houston/Bus Stn, BC | Canada | ZHO |
| Houston/Central Bus. District, TX | USA | JDX |
| Houston/Greenway Plaza HP, TX | USA | JGP |
| Houston/Marriot Astrodome, TX | USA | JMA |
| Houston/Park Ten HP, TX | USA | JPT |
| Houston/Spaceland, TX | USA | SPX |
| Houston/Transco Twr Galleria, TX | USA | JGQ |
| Houston/Westchase Hilton HP, TX | USA | JWH |
| Houston/Woodlawns, TX | USA | JWL |
| Hoy Is | UK | HOY |
| Hsinchu | Taiwan | HSZ |
| Hua Hin | Thailand | HHQ |
| Huacaraje | Bolivia | BVK |
| Huahine/Flying Boat, French Polynesia | | HUH |
| Hualien | Taiwan | HUN |
| Huambo | Andorra | NOV |
| Huangyan | China | HYN |
| Huanuco | Peru | HUU |
| Huatulco | Mexico | HUX |
| Hubli | India | HBX |
| Hudiksvall | Sweden | HUV |
| Hudson Bay, SK | Canada | YHB |
| Hudson's Hope, BC | Canada | YNH |
| Hudson/Columbia County, NY | USA | HCC |
| Hue/Phu Bai | Vietnam | HUI |
| Huelnuetenango | Guatemala | HUG |

| | | |
|---|---|---|
| Huerth | Germany | ZNP |
| Hughenden | Australia | HGD |
| Hughes/Municipal, AK | USA | HUS |
| Hugo, OK | USA | HUJ |
| Huizinou | China | HUZ |
| Hukuntsi | Botswana | HUK |
| Hultsfred/AFB | Sweden | HLF |
| Humacao/Humacao Arpt Puerto Rico | | HUC |
| Humacao/Palmas Del Mar | Puerto Rico | PPD |
| Humberside | UK | HUY |
| Humbert River | Australia | HUB |
| Humboldt Municipal, NE | USA | HBO |
| Humboldt, IA | USA | HUD |
| Humera | Ethiopia | HUE |
| Hunter/AAF, GA | USA | SVN |
| Huntingburg, IN | USA | HNB |
| Huntingdon/RR Stn | UK | XHU |
| Huntington, WV | USA | HTS |
| Huntsville, AL | USA | HSV |
| Huntsville, TX | USA | HTV |
| Huntsville, TX | USA | UTS |
| Huntsville/Redstone/AAF | USA | HUA |
| Hurghada | Egypt | HRG |
| Huron, SD | USA | HON |
| Husavik | Iceland | HZK |
| Huslia, AK | USA | HSL |
| HuStn/GlvStn Nexrad, TX | USA | HGX |
| Husum | Germany | QHU |
| Hutchinsen, KS | USA | HUT |
| Hutchinson County Arpt, TX | USA | BGD |
| Hvammstangi | Iceland | HVM |
| Hwange | Zimbabwe | WKI |
| Hwange Nat Park | Zimbabwe | HWN |
| Hyannis-Barnstable, MA | USA | HYA |
| Hydaburg/SPB, AK | USA | HYG |
| Hyder/SPB, AK | USA | WHD |
| Hyderabad | Pakistan | HDD |
| Hyderabad/Begumpet | India | HYD |
| Hyeres | France | XHE |
| Hyvinkää | Finland | HYV |

# I

| | | |
|---|---|---|
| Iamalele | Papua New Guinea | IMA |
| Iasi | Romania | IAS |
| IATA Traffic Svcs | n/a | IAT |
| Iaura | Papua New Guinea | IAU |
| Ibadan/(NAW) | Nigeria | IBA |
| Ibague | Colombia | IBE |
| Iberia | Peru | IBP |
| Ibiruba/Off-line Pt | Brazil | QIB |
| Ibiza | Spain | IBZ |
| Iboki | Papua New Guinea | IBI |
| Icabaru | Venezuela | ICA |
| Icy Bay, AK | USA | ICY |
| Ida Grove/Municipal, IA | USA | IDG |
| Idaho Falls, Fanning Fld, ID | USA | IDA |
| Iffley | Australia | IFF |
| Igloolik, BC | Canada | YGT |
| Ignace, ON | Canada | ZUC |
| Iguela | Gabon | IGE |
| Iiorin | Nigeria | ILR |
| Ijui/J.Batista Bos Filho | Brazil | IJU |
| Ikaria Is/Ikaria | Greece | JIK |
| ikarniut | Greenland | QJI |
| Ikast/Bus Svc | Denmark | QLZ |
| Ikela | Congo, DR | IKL |
| Iki | Japan | IKI |
| Ilaka | Madagascar | ILK |
| Ile Des Pins | New Caledonia | ILP |
| Ile Ouen | New Caledonia | IOU |
| Ilebo | Congo, DR | PFR |
| Ileg | Papua New Guinea | ILX |
| Iles De La Madeleine, QC | Canada | YGR |
| Ilford, MB | Canada | ILF |
| Ilha Solteira | Brazil | ILB |
| Iliamna Arpt, AK | USA | ILI |
| Iligan/Maria Cristina | Philippines | IGN |
| Illaga | Indonesia | ILA |
| Illbo | Mozambique | IBO |
| Illishern/Illis Airbase | Germany | ILH |
| Illizi | Algeria | VVZ |
| Ilo | Peru | ILQ |
| Ilu | Indonesia | IUL |
| Imane | Papua New Guinea | IMN |
| Imbaimadai | Guyana | IMB |
| Immokalee, FL | USA | IMM |

| | | |
|---|---|---|
| Imonda | Papua New Guinea | IMD |
| Imperatriz | Brazil | IMP |
| Imperial Beach/NAF, CA | USA | NRS |
| Imperial County, CA | USA | IPL |
| Imperial Municipal, NE | USA | IML |
| Imphal/Mun | India | IMF |
| Imptondo | Congo, DR | ION |
| In Amenas | Algeria | IAM |
| In Guezzam | Algeria | INF |
| In Salah North | Algeria | INZ |
| Inagua | Bahamas | IGA |
| Inanwatan | Indonesia | INX |
| Incheon | S. Korea | ICN |
| Indagen | Papua New Guinea | IDN |
| Indaselassie | Ethiopia | SHC |
| Independence | Belize | INB |
| Independence, KS | USA | IDP |
| Indian Mountain AFS, AK | USA | UTO |
| Indian Springs, NV | USA | INS |
| Indiana, PA | USA | IDI |
| Indianapolis/Int'l Arpt, IN | USA | IND |
| Indianapolis, Eagle Creek, IN | USA | EYE |
| Indore | India | IDR |
| Indulkana | Australia | IDK |
| Ine Is | Marshall Is | IMI |
| Ingeniero Jacobacci | Argentina | IGB |
| Ingersoll/RR Stn., ON | Canada | XIB |
| Ingham | Australia | IGH |
| Ingolstadt | Germany | ZNQ |
| Inhambane | Mozambique | INH |
| Inhaminga | Mozambique | IMG |
| Inisheer | Ireland | INQ |
| Inishmaian | Ireland | IIA |
| Inishmore/Kilronan | Ireland | IOR |
| Injune | Australia | INJ |
| Inkerman | Australia | IKP |
| Innamiricka | Australia | INM |
| Innisfail | Australia | IFL |
| Innsbruck/Kranebitten | Austria | INN |
| Int'l Falls, MN | USA | INL |
| Inta | Russia | INA |
| Interlaken | Switzerland | ZIN |
| Inulkjualk, QC | Canada | YPH |
| Inus | Papua New Guinea | IUS |
| Inuvik, NT | Canada | YEV |
| Invercargill | New Zealand | IVC |
| Inverell | Australia | IVR |
| Inverlake, AB | Canada | TIL |
| Inverness/Dalcross | UK | INV |
| Inverness/ScotRail | UK | ZIV |
| Inverway | Australia | IVW |
| Inyati | S. Africa | INY |
| Inyokern, CA | USA | IYK |
| Ioannina | Greece | IOA |
| Ioilo/Mandurriao | Philippines | ILO |
| Iokea | Papua New Guinea | IOK |
| Iowa City Municipal, IA | USA | IOW |
| Iowa Falls, IA | USA | IFA |
| Ipatinga/Usiminas | Brazil | IPN |
| Ipiales/San Luis | Colombia | IPI |
| Ipiau | Brazil | IPU |
| Ipil | Philippines | IPE |
| Ipiranga | Brazil | IPG |
| Ipoh | Malaysia | IPH |
| Ipota | Vanuatu | IPA |
| Ipswich | UK | IPW |
| Iqaluit, NT | Canada | YFB |
| Iquique/Cavancha | Chile | IQQ |
| Iquitos/CF, Secada | Peru | IQT |
| Iraan/Municipal, TX | USA | IRB |
| Irbid/Off-line Pt | Jordan | QIR |
| Irece | Brazil | IRE |
| Iringa/Nduli | Tanzania | IRI |
| Iriona | Honduras | IRN |
| Irkutsk | Russia | IKT |
| Iron Mountain, MI | USA | IMT |
| Ironwood/Gogebic County, MI | USA | IWD |
| Is Lake, MB | Canada | YIV |
| Isabel Pass, AK | USA | ISL |
| Isafjordur | Iceland | IFJ |
| Ischia | Italy | ISH |
| Iscuande | Colombia | ISD |
| Iserlohn | Germany | ZNR |
| Isfahan | Iran | IFN |
| Ishigalki | Japan | ISG |
| Ishurdi | Bangladesh | IRD |
| Isisford | Australia | ISI |
| Isla Mujeres | Mexico | ISJ |
| Islamabad Int'l | Pakistan | ISB |
| Islay/Glenegedaie | UK | ILY |
| Isle Baltra | Ecuador | WGL |

AIRPORTS-2-

| Airport | Country | Code |
|---|---|---|
| Isle Of Man/Ronaldsway | UK | IOM |
| Isle Of Skye/Broadford | UK | SKL |
| Isles Of Scilly/St Marys | UK | ISC |
| Isles Of Scilly/Tresco | UK | TSO |
| Isleworth | UK | QIF |
| Ismailia | Egypt | QIV |
| Isparta | Turkey | ISE |
| Isro/Matari | Congo, DR | IRP |
| Istanbul/Ataturk | Turkey | IST |
| Istres | France | QIE |
| Itaburia | Brazil | ITN |
| Itacoatiara | Brazil | ITA |
| Itaiai | Brazil | ITJ |
| Itaituba | Brazil | ITB |
| Itajuba | Brazil | QDS |
| Itambacuri | Brazil | ITI |
| Itaperuna | Brazil | ITP |
| Itapetinga | Brazil | QIT |
| Itaqui | Brazil | ITQ |
| Itauba | Brazil | AUB |
| Itauna | Brazil | QIA |
| Ithaca, NY | USA | ITH |
| Ithosy | Madagascar | IHO |
| Itilleq | Greenland | QJG |
| Ittoqqortoormiit | Greenland | OBY |
| Itu | Brazil | QTU |
| Itubera | Brazil | ITE |
| Itumbiara | Brazil | ITR |
| Ivalo | Finland | IVL |
| Ivanci-Frankovsk | Ukraine | IFO |
| Ivangrad | Yugoslavia | IVG |
| Ivanova | Russia | IWA |
| Ivishak, AK | USA | IVH |
| Iwami | Japan | IWJ |
| Iwo Jima Vol/Iwo Jima Airbase | Japan | IWO |
| Ixtapa/Zihuatanejo/Int'l | Mexico | ZIH |
| Ixtepec | Mexico | IZT |
| Izhevsk | Russia | IJK |
| Izmil | Turkey | QST |
| Izmir/Adnan Menderes | Turkey | ADB |
| Izumo | Japan | IZO |

# J

| Airport | Country | Code |
|---|---|---|
| Jabiru | Australia | JAB |
| Jabot | Marshall Is | JAT |
| Jacareacanga | Brazil | JCR |
| Jackpot, NV | USA | KPT |
| Jackson Hole, WY | USA | JAC |
| Jackson/Int'l Arpt, MS | USA | JAN |
| Jackson/Hawkins Fld, MS | USA | HKS |
| Jackson, MN | USA | MJQ |
| Jackson, TN | USA | MKL |
| Jackson/Reynolds Municipal, MI | USA | JXN |
| Jackson/Carroll, KY | USA | JKL |
| Jacksonvill/NAS, FL | USA | NIP |
| Jacksonville/Mtrpltn, FL | USA | JAX |
| Jacksonville/Craig Mncpl FL | USA | CRG |
| Jacksonville, IL | USA | IJX |
| Jacksonville, NC | USA | OAJ |
| Jacksonville, TX | USA | JKV |
| Jacmel | Haiti | JAK |
| Jacobabad | Pakistan | JAG |
| Jacobina | Brazil | JCM |
| Jacquinot Bay | Papua New Guinea | JAQ |
| Jaffrey/Municipal, NH | USA | AFN |
| Jagdaipur | India | JGB |
| Jaipur/Sanganeer | India | JAI |
| Jaisalmer | India | JSA |
| Jakarta/Halim Penclana Kusuma | Indonesia | HLP |
| Jakarta/Soekarno Int'l | Indonesia | CGK |
| Jal Edib | Lebanon | QJQ |
| Jalai | Brazil | JTI |
| Jalalabad | Afghanistan | JAA |
| Jalapa | Mexico | JAL |
| Jalbalpur | India | JLR |
| Jales | Brazil | JLS |
| Jaluit Is | Marshall Is | UIT |
| Jamba | Angola | JMB |
| Jambi/Sultan Taha Syarifudn | Indonesia | DJB |
| Jambol | Bulgaria | JAM |
| Jamestown, ND | USA | JMS |
| Jamestown, NY | USA | JHW |
| Jammu/Satwari | India | IXJ |
| Jamnagar/Govardhanpur | India | JGA |

| Airport | Country | Code |
|---|---|---|
| Jamshedpur/Sonari | India | IXW |
| Jan Mayen ...... | Svalbard and Jan Mayen Is | ZXB |
| Janakpur | Nepal | JKR |
| Jandakot | Australia | JAD |
| Janesville, WI | USA | JVL |
| Januaria | Brazil | JNA |
| Jaque | Panama | JQE |
| Jaragua Do Sul | Brazil | QJA |
| Jasper-Hinton, AB | Canada | YJP |
| Jasper/County, TX | USA | JAS |
| Jasper/Marion County, TN | USA | APT |
| Jasper/RR Stn., AB | Canada | XDH |
| Jaula | Peru | JAU |
| JaUna/Kankesanturai | Sri Lanka | JAF |
| Jayapura/Sentani | Indonesia | DJJ |
| Jeddah/King Abdul Aziz Int'l Arpt | Saudi Arabia | JED |
| Jefferson City, MO | USA | JEF |
| Jefferson Proving Grnd., IN | USA | MDN |
| Jefferson/Ashtabula, OH | USA | JFN |
| Jefferson/Municipal, IA | USA | EFW |
| Jeh | Marshall Is | JEJ |
| Jena/RR Stn. | Germany | ZJS |
| Jenpeg, MB | Canada | ZJG |
| Jequie | Brazil | JEQ |
| Jeremie | Haiti | JEE |
| Jerez De La Frontera/La Parra | Spain | XRY |
| Jersey | UK | JER |
| Jerusalem | Occupied Palestinian Ter | JRS |
| Jesolo | Italy | JLO |
| Jessore | Bangladesh | JSR |
| Jeypore | India | PYB |
| Ji'An | China | KNC |
| Ji-Parana | Brazil | JPR |
| Jiarnusi | China | JMU |
| Jiayuguan | China | JGN |
| Jijel Achouat | Algeria | GJL |
| Jijig/Jigiga | Ethiopia | JIJ |
| Jilin | China | JIL |
| Jimma | Ethiopia | JIM |
| Jin | Nepal | JIR |
| Jinan | China | TNA |
| Jindaloyne | Australia | QJD |
| Jingdezhen | China | JDZ |
| Jinghong/Gasa | China | JHG |
| Jining | China | JNG |
| Jinja | Uganda | JIN |
| Jinjiang | China | JJN |
| Jinka | Ethiopia | BCO |
| Jinzhou | China | JNZ |
| Jiujiang | China | JIU |
| Jiuquan | China | CHW |
| Jiwani | Pakistan | JIW |
| Joacaba | Brazil | JCB |
| Joato Pessoa/Castro Pinto | Brazil | JPA |
| Jodhpur | India | JDH |
| Joensuu | Finland | JOE |
| Johannesburg Int'l | S. Africa | JNB |
| Johannesburg/Grand Central | S. Africa | GCJ |
| Johannesburg/HP | S. Africa | QRA |
| Johnny Mountain, BC | Canada | YJO |
| Johnson, TX | USA | JCY |
| Johnston Is | Wake/Midway Is | JON |
| Johnstown-Cambria, PA | USA | JST |
| Johor Bahru/Sultan Ismail Int'l | Malaysia | JHB |
| Joinville/Cubatao | Brazil | JOI |
| Joliet Municipal, IL | USA | JOT |
| Joliette/RR Stn., QC | Canada | XJL |
| Jolo | Philippines | JOL |
| Jolon/Hunter/AAF, CA | USA | HGT |
| Jonesboro, AR | USA | JBR |
| Jonkoping/Axamo | Sweden | JKG |
| Jonquiere/RR Stn., QC | Canada | XJQ |
| Joplin, MO | USA | JLN |
| Jordan, MT | USA | JDN |
| Jorhat/Rowriah | India | JRH |
| Jornsom | Nepal | JMO |
| Jos | Nigeria | JOS |
| Jose De San Martin | Argentina | JSM |
| Josephstaal | Papua New Guinea | JOP |
| Josrikar-Ola | Russia | JOK |
| Jouf | Saudi Arabia | AJF |
| Jounieh | Lebanon | QJN |
| Jpjapa | Ecuador | JIP |
| Juan Les Pins | France | JLP |
| Juanjui | Peru | JJI |
| Juara | Brazil | JUA |

| Airport | Country | Code |
|---|---|---|
| Juazeiro Do Norte/Regional Do Cariri | Brazil | JDO |
| Juba | Sudan | JUB |
| Jubail | Saudi Arabia | QJB |
| Juina | Brazil | JIA |
| Juist | Germany | JUI |
| Juiz De Fora/Francisco De Assis | Brazil | JDF |
| Jujuy/El Cadilial | Argentina | JUJ |
| Julia Creek | Australia | JCK |
| Juliaca | Peru | JUL |
| Jullundur | India | QJU |
| Jumia | Nepal | JUM |
| Junction, TX | USA | JCT |
| Jundah | Australia | JUN |
| Jundiai | Brazil | QDV |
| Juneau/Int'l, AK | USA | JNU |
| Juneau/Dodge County, AK | USA | UNU |
| Junin | Argentina | JNI |
| Jurado | Colombia | JUO |
| Jurien Bay | Australia | JUR |
| Juruena | Brazil | JRN |
| Juticalpa | Honduras | JUT |
| Juzhou | China | JUZ |
| Jwaneng | Botswana | JWA |
| Jyvaskyla | Finland | JYV |

# K

| Airport | Country | Code |
|---|---|---|
| Kaadedhclhoo | Maldives | KDM |
| Kabaiega Falls | Uganda | KBG |
| Kabala | Sierra Leone | KBA |
| Kabalo | Congo, DR | KBO |
| Kaben | Marshall Is | KBT |
| Kabinda | Congo, DR | KBN |
| Kabri Dar | Ethiopia | ABK |
| Kabul/Khwaja Rawash | Afghanistan | KBL |
| Kabwe | Zambia | QKE |
| Kabwurn | Papua New Guinea | KBM |
| Kadanwari | Pakistan | KCF |
| Kadhdhoo | Maldives | KDO |
| Kaduna | Nigeria | KAD |
| Kaedi | Mauritania | KED |
| Kaele | Cameroon | KLE |
| Kagau | Solomon Is | KGE |
| Kagi | Papua New Guinea | KGW |
| Kagoshima | Japan | KOJ |
| Kagua | Papua New Guinea | AGK |
| Kagvik Creek, AK | USA | KKF |
| Kahramanmaras | Turkey | KCM |
| Kahului, HI | USA | OGG |
| Kaiapit | Papua New Guinea | KIA |
| Kaieteur | Guyana | KAI |
| Kaikohe | New Zealand | KKO |
| Kaikoura | New Zealand | KBZ |
| Kailashahar | India | IXH |
| Kaimana/Utarom | Indonesia | KNG |
| Kaintiba | Papua New Guinea | KZF |
| Kairouan | Tunisia | QKN |
| Kaiser/Lake Ozark, MO | USA | AIZ |
| Kaiserslautern | Germany | KLT |
| Kaitaia | New Zealand | KAT |
| Kajaani | Finland | KAJ |
| Kake/SPB, AK | USA | KAE |
| Kakhonak, AK | USA | KNK |
| Kalabo | Zambia | KLB |
| Kalakalket/AFS, AK | USA | KKK |
| Kalamata | Greece | KLX |
| Kalamazoo, MI | USA | AZO |
| Kalat | Pakistan | KBH |
| Kalaupapa, HI | USA | LUP |
| Kalbarri | Australia | KAX |
| Kalemie | Congo, DR | FMI |
| Kalemyo | Myanmar | KMV |
| Kalgoorlie | Australia | KGI |
| Kalibo | Philippines | KLO |
| Kalima | Congo, DR | KLY |
| Kalinin/Migalovo | Russia | KLD |
| Kaliningrad | Russia | KGD |
| Kalispell, MT | USA | FCA |
| Kalkurung | Australia | KFG |
| Kallag, AK | USA | KAL |
| Kalmar | Sweden | KLR |
| Kalokol | Kenya | KLK |
| Kalpowar | Australia | KPP |
| Kalskag/Municipal, AK | USA | KLG |
| Kaluga | Russia | KLF |

| Location | Country | Code |
|---|---|---|
| Kalumburu | Australia | UBU |
| Kamalpur | India | IXQ |
| Kamaran Downs | Australia | KDS |
| Kamaran Is | Yemen | KAM |
| Kamarang | Guyana | KAR |
| Kamarata | Venezuela | KTV |
| Kambaida | Australia | KDB |
| Kamberatoro | Papua New Guinea | KDQ |
| Kambuaya | Indonesia | KBX |
| Kamembe | Rwanda | KME |
| Kamenets-Podolskiy | Ukraine | KCP |
| Kameshli | Syria | KAC |
| Kamileroi | Australia | KML |
| Kamina | Papua New Guinea | KMF |
| Kamina | Congo, DR | KMN |
| Kamiraba | Papua New Guinea | KJU |
| Kamloops, BC | Canada | YKA |
| Kampala | Uganda | KLA |
| Kampot | Cambodia | KMT |
| Kamuela, HI | USA | MUE |
| Kamulai | Papua New Guinea | KAQ |
| Kamur | Indonesia | KCD |
| Kamusi/Kamusi Arpt | Papua New Guinea | KUY |
| Kanab, UT | USA | KNB |
| Kanabea | Papua New Guinea | KEX |
| Kanainj | Papua New Guinea | KNE |
| Kananga | Congo, DR | KGA |
| Kanazawa | Japan | QKW |
| Kandahar | Afghanistan | KDH |
| Kandavu | Fiji | KDV |
| Kandep | Papua New Guinea | KDP |
| Kandersteg | Switzerland | ZHR |
| Kandi | Benin | KDC |
| Kandla | India | IXY |
| Kandrian | Papua New Guinea | KDR |
| Kangaamiut | Greenland | QKT |
| Kangaatsiaq | Greenland | QPW |
| Kangan/Jam | Iran | KNR |
| Kangerluk | Greenland | QGR |
| Kangerlussuaq | Greenland | SFJ |
| Kangerlussuaq | Greenland | SJF |
| Kangiqsualujjuaq, QC | Canada | XGR |
| Kangiqsujuaq, QC | Canada | YWB |
| Kangirsuk, QC | Canada | YKG |
| Kangnung/Air Base | S. Korea | KAG |
| Kaniama | Congo, DR | KNM |
| Kankakee, IL | USA | IKK |
| Kankan | Guinea | KNN |
| Kano/Aminu Kano Int'l | Nigeria | KAN |
| Kanpur | India | KNU |
| Kansas City/Johnson Exec, KS | USA | OJC |
| Kansas City/Int'l, MO | USA | MCI |
| Kansas City, Richards-Gebaur Arpt, MO | USA | GVW |
| Kansas City/Downtown, MO | USA | MKC |
| Kansas City/Fairfax, KS | USA | KCK |
| Kansas City/Johnson Industrial, MO | USA | JCI |
| Kantchari | Burkina Faso | XKA |
| Kanua | Papua New Guinea | KTK |
| Kaohsiung/Int'l | Taiwan | KHH |
| Kaolack | Senegal | KLC |
| Kaorna | Zambia | KMZ |
| Kapalua, HI | USA | JHM |
| Kapanga | Congo, DR | KAP |
| Kapit | Malaysia | KPI |
| Kapuskasing, ON | Canada | YYU |
| Kar | Papua New Guinea | KAK |
| Kar Kar | Papua New Guinea | KRX |
| Karachi/Quaid-E-Azam Int'l. | Pakistan | KHI |
| Karaganda | Kazakstan | KGF |
| Karaj | Iran | QKC |
| Karamay | China | KRY |
| Karanambo | Guyana | KRM |
| Karasabai | Guyana | KRG |
| Karasburg | Namibia | KAS |
| Karasjok | Norway | QKK |
| Karato | Papua New Guinea | KAF |
| Karawari | Papua New Guinea | KRJ |
| Kardjali | Bulgaria | KDG |
| Kardla | Estonia | KDL |
| Kariba | Zimbabwe | KAB |
| Karimunjawa | Indonesia | KWB |
| Karinnui | Papua New Guinea | KMR |
| Karisruhe/Baden Baden/ Bus Svc | Germany | XET |
| Karkkila | Finland | QVF |
| Karlovasi | Greece | ZKR |
| Karlovy Vary | Czech Rep | KLV |
| Karlskoga | Sweden | KSK |
| Karlsruhe/Baden Baden | Germany | FKB |
| Karlstad/Flygplats | Sweden | KSD |
| Karluk Lake SPB, AK | USA | KKL |
| Karonga | Malawi | KGJ |
| Karoola | Papua New Guinea | KXR |
| Karpathos | Greece | AOK |
| Karratha | Australia | KTA |
| Kars | Turkey | KSY |
| Karshi | Uzbekistan | KSQ |
| Karubaga | Indonesia | KBF |
| Karuk, AK | USA | KYK |
| Karumba | Australia | KRB |
| Karup/Military | Denmark | KRP |
| Kasaan SPB, AK | USA | KXA |
| Kasaba Bay | Zambia | ZKB |
| Kasabonika, ON | Canada | XKS |
| Kasama | Zambia | KAA |
| Kasane | Botswana | BBK |
| Kasanombe | Papua New Guinea | KSB |
| Kasba Lake, NT | Canada | YDU |
| Kaschechewan, ON | Canada | ZKE |
| Kasenga | Congo, DR | KEC |
| Kasese | Uganda | KSE |
| Kashi | China | KHG |
| Kasigluk, AK | USA | KUK |
| Kasikasirna/Tepoe Airstrip | Suriname | KCB |
| Kasompe | Zambia | ZKP |
| Kasongo Lunda | Congo, DR | KGN |
| Kasos Is | Greece | KSJ |
| Kassala | Sudan | KSL |
| Kassel/Calden | Germany | KSF |
| Kastamonu | Turkey | KFS |
| Kastelorizo | Greece | KZS |
| Kastoria/Aristotelis | Greece | KSO |
| Kasungu | Malawi | KBQ |
| Katanning | Australia | KNI |
| Katherine/Tindal | Australia | KTR |
| Kathmandu/Tribhuvan | Nepal | KTM |
| Katiola | Côte D'Ivoire | KTC |
| Kato | Guyana | KTO |
| Katowice/Pyrzowice | Poland | KTW |
| Kattiniq/Donaldson Lak, QC | Canada | YAU |
| Kau | Indonesia | KAZ |
| Kauai Is/Lihue, HI | USA | LIH |
| Kauai Is/Princeville, HI | USA | HPV |
| Kauhajoki | Finland | KHJ |
| Kauhava | Finland | KAU |
| Kaukura Atoll | F. Polynesia | KKR |
| Kaunas/Int'l | Lithuania | KUN |
| Kautokeino | Norway | QKX |
| Kavala/Megas Alexandros | Greece | KVA |
| Kavanayen | Venezuela | KAV |
| Kavieng | Papua New Guinea | KVG |
| Kavik/Airstrip, AK | USA | VIK |
| Kawadjia | Central African Rep | KWD |
| Kawau Is | New Zealand | KUI |
| Kawito | Papua New Guinea | KWO |
| Kawthaung | Myanmar | KAW |
| Kaya | Burkina Faso | XKY |
| Kayenta, AZ | USA | MVM |
| Kayes | Mali | KYS |
| Kayseri | Turkey | ASR |
| Kazan | Russia | KZN |
| Kearney, NE | USA | EAR |
| Kebar | Indonesia | KEQ |
| Kedougou | Senegal | KGG |
| Keesler/AFB, MS | USA | BIX |
| Keetmanshoop/ J.G.H. Van Der Wath | Namibia | KMP |
| Keewaywin, ON | Canada | KEW |
| Kefalhnia/Argostolion | Greece | EFL |
| Kegaska, QC | Canada | ZKG |
| Keglsugi | Papua New Guinea | KEG |
| Keisah | Indonesia | KEA |
| Kekaha/Barking Sands, HI | USA | BKH |
| Kelafo/Callaf/Kelafo | Ethiopia | LFO |
| Kelanoa | Papua New Guinea | KNL |
| Kelila | Indonesia | LLN |
| Kelle | Congo, DR | KEE |
| Kelly Bar, AK | USA | KEU |
| Kelly/AFB, TX | USA | SKF |
| Kelowna, BC | Canada | YLW |
| Kelp Bay, AK | USA | KLP |
| Kelsey, MB | Canada | KES |
| Kelso, Longview, WA | USA | KLS |
| Kelsterbach | Germany | QLH |
| Keluang | Indonesia | KLQ |
| Kemano, BC | Canada | XKO |
| Kemerer, WY | USA | EMM |
| Kemerovo | Russia | KEJ |
| Kemi/Tornio | Finland | KEM |
| Kempsey | Australia | KPS |
| Kempten | Germany | ZNS |
| Kenai, AK | USA | ENA |
| Kendan/Wolter Monginsidi | Indonesia | KDI |
| Kenema | Sierra Leone | KEN |
| Keng Tung | Myanmar | KET |
| Kenieba | Mali | KNZ |
| Keningau | Malaysia | KGU |
| Kenitra/NAF | Morocco | NNA |
| Kenmore Air Harbor, WA | USA | KEH |
| Kennedy/Int'l, NY | USA | JFK |
| Kennedy Town | Hong Kong | XKT |
| Kennett Municipal, MO | USA | KNT |
| Kennosao Lake, MB | Canada | YKI |
| Kenora, ON | Canada | YQK |
| Kenosha, WI | USA | ENW |
| Kentland, IN | USA | KKT |
| Keokuk, IA | USA | EOK |
| Kepi | Indonesia | KEi |
| Kerama | Japan | KJP |
| Kerang | Australia | KRA |
| Kerau | Papua New Guinea | KRU |
| Kerch | Ukraine | KHC |
| Kerema | Papua New Guinea | KMA |
| Kericho | Kenya | KEY |
| Kerikeri | New Zealand | KKE |
| Kerinci/Depati Parbo | Indonesia | KRC |
| Kerio Valley | Kenya | KRV |
| Kerkyra/I. Kapodistrias | Greece | CFU |
| Kerman | Iran | KER |
| Kermanshah | Iran | KSH |
| Kerpen | Germany | ZNT |
| Kerrville, TX | USA | ERV |
| Kerry | Ireland | KIR |
| Kerteh | Malaysia | KTE |
| Keshod | India | IXK |
| Ketapang/Rahadi Usmaman | Indonesia | KTG |
| Ketchikan/Int'l, AK | USA | KTN |
| Ketchikan/Waterfront SPB, AK | USA | WFB |
| Key Lake, SK | Canada | YKJ |
| Key Largo/Port Largo, FL | USA | KYL |
| Key West, FL | USA | EYW |
| Key West/NAS, FL | USA | NQX |
| Keystone/Van Svc, CO | USA | QKS |
| Khajuraho | India | HJR |
| Khaloarovsk/Novyy | Russia | KHV |
| Khamis Mushat | Saudi Arabia | KMX |
| Khamti | Myanmar | KHM |
| Khaneh | Iran | KHA |
| Kharga | Egypt | UVL |
| Kharian | Pakistan | QKH |
| Khark Is | Iran | KHK |
| Kharkhorin | Mongolia | KHR |
| Kharkov | Ukraine | HRK |
| Khartoum/Civil | Sudan | KRT |
| Khasab | Oman | KHS |
| Khashm El Girba | Somalia | GBU |
| Khemis Miliana | Algeria | ZZK |
| Khenchela | Algeria | QKJ |
| Kherrata | Algeria | ZZR |
| Kherson | Ukraine | KHE |
| Khmeinitskiy | Ukraine | HMJ |
| Khoka Moya | S. Africa | KHO |
| Khoms | Libya | QKO |
| Khon Kaen | Thailand | KKC |
| Khong | Laos | KOG |
| Khorramabad | Iran | KHD |
| Khost | Afghanistan | KHT |
| Khovd | Mongolia | HVD |
| Khowai | India | IXN |
| Khudzhand | Tajikistan | LBD |
| Khujirt | Mongolia | HJT |
| Khulna | Bangladesh | KHL |
| Khuzdar | Pakistan | KDD |
| Khwahan | Afghanistan | KWH |
| Khwai River Lodge | Botswana | KHW |
| Kiana/Bob Barker Memorial, AK | USA | IAN |
| Kiel/Holtenau Civilian | Germany | KEL |
| Kielce | Poland | QKI |
| Kierritu, BC | Canada | YKT |
| Kieta/Aropa | Papua New Guinea | KIE |
| Kiev/Borispol | Ukraine | KBP |
| Kiev/Darnitsa Bus Stn | Ukraine | QOF |
| Kiev/Hotel Rus Bus Stn | Ukraine | QOH |
| Kiev/Zhulhany | Ukraine | IEV |
| Kiffa | Mauritania | KFA |
| Kigali/Gregoire Kayibanda | Rwanda | KGL |
| Kigoma | Tanzania | TKQ |
| Kikaiga Shima | Japan | KKX |

| | | |
|---|---|---|
| Kikinonda | Papua New Guinea | KIZ |
| Kikori | Papua New Guinea | KRI |
| Kikwit | Congo, DR | KKW |
| Kilaguni | Kenya | ILU |
| Kili Is | Marshall Is | KIO |
| Kilialoe, ON. | Canada | YXI |
| Kilimanjaro | Tanzania | JRO |
| Kilkenny | Ireland | KKY |
| Kill Devil Hills/First Flight, NC | USA | FFA |
| Killeen/Municipal, TX | USA | ILE |
| Killineq, QC. | Canada | XBW |
| Kilwa | Congo, DR | KIL |
| Kilwa | Tanzania | KIY |
| Kimam | Indonesia | KMM |
| Kimberley | S. Africa | KIM |
| Kimberley Downs | Australia | KBD |
| Kimberley, BC | Canada | YQE |
| Kimmirut, NT | Canada | YLC |
| Kincardine, ON | Canada | YKD |
| Kindamba | Congo, DR | KNJ |
| Kindersley, SK | Canada | YKY |
| Kindu | Congo, DR | KND |
| King City, Mesa Del Rey, CA. | USA | KIC |
| King Cove, AK | USA | KVC |
| King Is | Australia | KNS |
| King Khalid Military City | Saudi Arabia | KMC |
| King Of Prussia, PA | USA | KPD |
| King Salmon, AK. | USA | AKN |
| Kingaroy | Australia | KGY |
| Kingfisher Lake, ON | Canada | KIF |
| Kingman, AZ. | USA | IGM |
| Kings Bay/NAS, GA | USA | NBQ |
| Kings Canyon | Australia | KBJ |
| Kings Creek Stn. | Australia | KCS |
| Kings Lynn/Marham/RAF | UK | KNF |
| Kingscote | Australia | KGC |
| Kingston, ON | Canada | YGK |
| Kingston/Norman Manley | Jamaica | KIN |
| Kingston/RR Stn., ON. | Canada | XEG |
| Kingston/Tinson | Jamaica | KTP |
| Kingsville/NAS, TX | USA | NQI |
| Kinloss/RAF | UK | FSS |
| Kinmen/Shang-Yi | Taiwan | KNH |
| Kinoosao, SK | Canada | KNY |
| Kinshasa/N'Djili. | Congo, DR | FIH |
| Kinshasa/N'Dolo. | Congo, DR | NLO |
| Kinston/Stallings Fld, NC. | USA | ISO |
| Kipnulk, AK. | USA | KPN |
| Kira | Papua New Guinea | KIQ |
| KiraKira | Solomon Is | IRA |
| Kirefeld | Germany | QKF |
| Kiri | Congo, DR | KRZ |
| Kirkenes/Hoeybuktmoen | Norway | KKN |
| Kirkimbie | Australia | KBB |
| Kirkland Lake, ON | Canada | YKX |
| Kirksvite Municipal, MO | USA | IRK |
| Kirkuk | Iraq | KIK |
| Kirkwall | UK | KOI |
| Kirov | Russia | KVX |
| Kirovograd | Ukraine | KGO |
| Kirovsk | Russia | KVK |
| Kirtland/AFB, NM. | USA | IKR |
| Kiruna | Sweden | KRN |
| Kirundo | Benin | KRE |
| Kiryat Shmona | Israel | KSW |
| Kisangani | Congo, DR | FKI |
| Kisengan | Papua New Guinea | KSG |
| Kish Is | Iran | KIH |
| Kismayu | Somalia | KMU |
| Kissidougou | Guinea | KSI |
| Kissimmee/Municipal, FL | USA | ISM |
| Kisumu | Kenya | KIS |
| Kita Kyushu/Kokura | S. Korea | KKJ |
| Kitadaito Is | Japan | KTD |
| Kitale | Kenya | KTL |
| Kitava | Papua New Guinea | KVE |
| Kitchener, ON. | Canada | YKF |
| Kitee | Finland | KTQ |
| Kithira | Greece | KIT |
| Kitkatla, BC. | Canada | YKK |
| Kitoi Bay/SPB, AK. | USA | KKB |
| Kitsissuarsuit | Greenland | QJE |
| Kittilä | Finland | KTT |
| Kitwe/Southdowns | Zambia | KIW |
| Kitzingen | Germany | KZG |
| Kiunga | Kenya | KIU |
| Kiunga | Papua New Guinea | UNG |
| Kivalina, AK | USA | KVL |
| Kiwai Is | Papua New Guinea | KWX |
| Kiwayu | Kenya | KWY |

| | | |
|---|---|---|
| Kizhuyak, AK. | USA | KZH |
| Kjellerup/Bus Svc. | Denmark | QJW |
| Kjoellefjord | Norway | QJL |
| Klag Bay, AK | USA | KBK |
| Klagenfurt | Austria | KLU |
| Klaipeda | Lithuania | KLJ |
| Klamath Falls Int'l, OR. | USA | LMT |
| Klawock, AK | USA | AKW |
| Klawock, AK | USA | KLW |
| Kleinzee | S. Africa | KLZ |
| Klerksdorp | S. Africa | KXE |
| Klosters | Switzerland | ZHS |
| Knee Lake, MB | Canada | YKE |
| Knights Inlet, BC | Canada | KNV |
| Knock Int'l | Ireland | NOC |
| Knokke/Het Zoute | Belgium | KNO |
| Knoxville Downtown, TN | USA | DKX |
| Knoxville, IA | USA | OXV |
| Knoxville, TN | USA | TYS |
| Koala Belait | Brunei | KUB |
| Kobe | Japan | UKB |
| Koblenz | Germany | ZNV |
| Kobuk, AK | USA | OBU |
| Kocaeli/Cengiz Topel | Turkey | KCO |
| Kochi | Japan | KCZ |
| Kodiak Arpt, AK. | USA | ADQ |
| Kodiak, AK. | USA | WDY |
| Kodiak/Municipal, AK | USA | KDK |
| Koethen | Germany | KOQ |
| Kogalym Int'l. | Russia | KGP |
| Koh Kong | Cambodia | KKZ |
| Koh Sannui | Thailand | USM |
| Kohat | Pakistan | OHT |
| Koinambe | Papua New Guinea | KMB |
| Koinghaas | S. Africa | KIG |
| Kokkola/Pietarsaari/Kruunupyy | Finland | KOK |
| Kokoda | Papua New Guinea | KKD |
| Kokonao/Timuka. | Indonesia | KOX |
| Kokorno, IN | USA | OKK |
| Kokoro | Papua New Guinea | KOR |
| Kokshetau | Kazakstan | KOV |
| Kol | Papua New Guinea | KQL |
| Kolda | Senegal | KDA |
| Kolding/RR Stn. | Denmark | ZBT |
| Kolhapur | India | KLH |
| Kolobrzeg/Bus Svc. | Poland | QJY |
| Kolwezi | Congo, DR | KWZ |
| Komaio | Papua New Guinea | KCJ |
| Komako | Papua New Guinea | HOC |
| Komatipoort | S. Africa | KOF |
| Komotini | Greece | ZKT |
| Kompiam | Papua New Guinea | KPM |
| Kompong Thorn | Cambodia | KZK |
| Kompong-Chhna | Cambodia | KZC |
| Kon | Indonesia | KCI |
| Kona/Keahole, HI. | USA | KOA |
| Konawaruk | Guyana | KKG |
| Kone | New Caledonia | KNQ |
| Konge | Papua New Guinea | KGB |
| Kongiganak, AK. | USA | KKH |
| Kongoboumba | Gabon | GKO |
| Kongolo | Congo, DR | KOO |
| Konnatsu | Japan | KMQ |
| Konstanz | Germany | QKZ |
| Kontum | Vietnam | KON |
| Konya | Turkey | KYA |
| Koolatah | Australia | KOH |
| Koolburra | Australia | KKP |
| Koonibba | Australia | KQB |
| Kopasker | Iceland | OPA |
| Koplago | Papua New Guinea | KPA |
| Korhogo | Côte D'Ivoire | HGO |
| Korla | China | KRL |
| Korno-Manda | Papua New Guinea | KOM |
| Kornsornolsk Na Amure | Russia | KXK |
| Koro Is | Fiji | KXF |
| Koroba | Papua New Guinea | KDE |
| Korolevu | Fiji | KVU |
| Koror/Airai | Palau | ROR |
| Kortrijk/Wevelgem | Belgium | KJK |
| Kos | Greece | KGS |
| Kosciusko/Attala County, MS | USA | OSX |
| Kosice/Barca | Slovakia | KSC |
| Kosipe | Papua New Guinea | KSP |
| Kosrae | Micronesia | KSA |
| Kostanay | Kazakstan | KSN |
| Kosti | Sudan | KST |
| Kostroma | Russia | KMW |
| Koszalin | Poland | OSZ |
| Kota | India | KTU |

| | | |
|---|---|---|
| Kota Bharu/Pengkalan Chepa | Malaysia | KBR |
| Kota Kinabalu | Malaysia | BKI |
| Kota Koli | Congo, DR | KLI |
| Kotabangun | Indonesia | KOD |
| Kotabaru | Indonesia | KBU |
| Kotka | Finland | QVW |
| Kotlas | Russia | KSZ |
| Kotlik, AK | USA | KOT |
| Kotor | Yugoslavia | ZKQ |
| Kotzebue, AK. | USA | OTZ |
| Kouba | Algeria | KDF |
| Koulamoutou | Gabon | KOU |
| Koumac | New Caledonia | KOC |
| Koundara/Sambailo | Guinea | SBI |
| Kounnala | Central African Rep | KOL |
| Kourou | F. Guiana | QKR |
| Koutaba | Cameroon | KOB |
| Koutiala | Mali | KTX |
| Kouvola/Bus Stn | Finland | QVY |
| Kouvola/Utti | Finland | UTI |
| Kowanyama | Australia | KWM |
| Koyang | Kuwait | QYK |
| Koyuk, AK. | USA | KKA |
| Koyukuk, AK | USA | KYU |
| Kozani/Philippos. | Greece | KZI |
| Krabi | Thailand | KBV |
| Krakor | Cambodia | KZD |
| Krakow | Poland | KRK |
| Kramatorsk | Ukraine | KRQ |
| Kramfors/Flygplats | Sweden | KRF |
| Krasnodar | Russia | KRR |
| Krasnoiarsk. | Russia | KJA |
| Kratie | Cambodia | KTI |
| Kremenchug | Ukraine | KHU |
| Kreuzlingen | Switzerland | ZHU |
| Kribi | Cameroon | KBI |
| Kristiansand/Kjevik | Norway | KRS |
| Kristianstad/Everod | Sweden | KID |
| Kristiansund/Kvernberget | Norway | KSU |
| Krivoy Rog | Ukraine | KWG |
| Kruger National Park | S. Africa | QKP |
| Ksar Es Souk | Morocco | SEK |
| Kuala Lumpur/Kuala Lumpur Infl | Malaysia | KUL |
| Kuala Lumpur/KUL Sentral Rail | Malaysia | XKL |
| Kuala Lumpur/Sultan Alodul Aziz Shah | Malaysia | SZB |
| Kuala Terengganu/ Sultan Mahmood | Malaysia | TGG |
| Kuantan | Malaysia | KUA |
| Kubin Is | Australia | KUG |
| Kuching | Malaysia | KCH |
| Kucla | China | KCA |
| Kudat | Malaysia | KUD |
| Kufrah | Libya | AKF |
| Kugururok River, AK. | USA | KUW |
| Kuito | Angola | SVP |
| Kukundu | Solomon Is | KUE |
| Kulgera | Australia | KGR |
| Kulik Lake, AK. | USA | LKK |
| Kulu/Shuntar | India | KUU |
| Kulusuk | Greenland | KUS |
| Kumamoto | Japan | KMJ |
| Kumasi | Ghana | KMS |
| Kumejima | Japan | UEO |
| Kundiawa | Papua New Guinea | CMU |
| Kunduz | Afghanistan | UND |
| Kungum | Papua New Guinea | KGM |
| Kunming | China | KMG |
| Kunsan/Air Base | S. Korea | KUV |
| Kununurra | Australia | KNX |
| Kuopio | Finland | KUO |
| Kuorevesi/Halli | Finland | KEV |
| Kupang/El Tari | Indonesia | KOE |
| Kuparuk, AK. | USA | UUK |
| Kupiano | Papua New Guinea | KUP |
| Kuran-O-Munjan | Afghanistan | KUR |
| Kuressaare | Estonia | URE |
| Kurgan | Russia | KRO |
| Kuri | Papua New Guinea | KUQ |
| Kuria | Kiribati | KUC |
| Kursk | Russia | URS |
| Kuruman | S. Africa | KMH |
| Kurundi | Australia | KRD |
| Kurupung | Guyana | KPG |
| Kurwina | Papua New Guinea | KWV |
| Kusadasi | Turkey | XKU |
| Kusan/Air Base. | S. Korea | KUZ |
| Kushimoto | Japan | KUJ |

| | | |
|---|---|---|
| Kushiro | Japan | KUH |
| Kutaisi | Georgia | KUT |
| Kuujjuaq, QC | Canada | YVP |
| Kuujjuarapik, QC | Canada | YGW |
| Kuusamo | Finland | KAO |
| Kuwait Int'l | Kuwait | KWI |
| Kwai Harbour | Solomon Is. | KWR |
| Kwailabesi Aerodrom. | Solomon Is. | KWS |
| Kwajalein | Marshall Is. | KWA |
| Kwangju/Air Base | S. Korea | KWJ |
| Kwethluk, AK | USA | KWT |
| Kwigillingok, AK | USA | KWK |
| Kwun Tong | Hong Kong | KTZ |
| Kyauktaw | Myanmar | KYT |
| Kyaulkpyu | Myanmar | KYP |
| Kyoto | Japan | UKY |
| Kyzyl | Russia | KYZ |
| Kzyl-Orda | Kazakstan | KZO |

# L

| | | |
|---|---|---|
| L'Aquila | Italy | QAQ |
| La Bastide Puylaurent | France | XLA |
| La Baule Les Pins | France | XBP |
| La Baule/Montoir | France | LBY |
| La Ceiba/Goloson Int'l | Honduras | LCE |
| La Chaux-de-Fonds | Switzerland | ZHV |
| La Chorrera | Colombia | LCR |
| La Ciotat | France | XCT |
| La Colorna | Cuba | LCL |
| La Coruna | Spain | LCG |
| La Crosse, WI. | USA | LSE |
| La Cumbre | Argentina | LCM |
| La Desirade | Gaudeloupe | DSD |
| La Esperanza | Honduras | LEZ |
| La Fria | Venezuela | LFR |
| La Grande, OR. | USA | LGD |
| La Grande, QC | Canada | YAH |
| La Grande, QC | Canada | YGL |
| La Grange/Calloway, GA. | USA | LGC |
| La Guaira | Venezuela | LAG |
| La Junquera | Spain | QJR |
| La Junta, CO. | USA | LHX |
| La Llagone | France | QZG |
| La Munoza | Spain | QLM |
| La Palma | Panama | PLP |
| La Paz/El Alto | Bolivia | LPB |
| La Paz/Leon. | Mexico | LAP |
| La Pedrera | Colombia | LPD |
| La Plagne | France | PLG |
| La Plata | Argentina | LPG |
| La Primavera | Colombia | LPE |
| La Riola | Argentina | IRJ |
| La Roche Sur Yon | France | XRO |
| La Roche/Les Ajoncs | France | EDM |
| La Rochelle/Laleu | France | LRH |
| La Romana | Dominican Rep. | LRM |
| La Ronge, SK | Canada | YVC |
| La Sarre, QC | Canada | SSQ |
| La Serena/La Florida | Chile | LSC |
| La Spezia | Italy | QLP |
| La Tabatiere, QC | Canada | ZLT |
| La Tour De Carol | France | XTE |
| La Tuclue, QC | Canada | YLQ |
| La Unbe | Colombia | LAT |
| La Union | Honduras | LUI |
| La Verne, CA. | USA | POC |
| Laarbruch/RAF | Germany | LRC |
| Laayoune/Hassan I | Morocco | EUN |
| Labasa | Fiji | LBS |
| Labe | Guinea | LEK |
| Lablab | Papua New Guinea | LAB |
| Labouchere Bay, AK | USA | WLB |
| Labrea | Brazil | LBR |
| Labuan | Malaysia | LBU |
| Labuan Bajo/Mutiara. | Indonesia | LBJ |
| Labuha/Taliabu | Indonesia | LAH |
| Lac Biche, AB. | Canada | YLB |
| Lac Brochet, MB | Canada | XLB |
| Lac Edouard/RR Stn., QC | Canada | XEE |
| Laconia, NH | USA | LCI |
| Ladouanie. | Suriname | LDO |
| Lady Elliot Is. | Australia | LYT |
| Ladysmith | S. Africa | LAY |
| Ladysmith/RR Stn., BC. | Canada | XEH |
| Lae Is | Marshall Is. | LML |
| Lae/Nadzab | Papua New Guinea | LAE |
| Laeso Is Arpt. | Denmark | BYR |

| | | |
|---|---|---|
| Lafayette, LA. | USA | LFT |
| Lafayette-Purdue, IN | USA | LAF |
| LaForges, QC | Canada | YLF |
| Lagenfeld | Germany | ZNX |
| Lages | Brazil | LAJ |
| Laghouat/L'Mekrareg | Algeria | LOO |
| Lago Agrio | Ecuador | LGQ |
| Lago Argentina | Argentina | ING |
| Lagos de Moreno | Mexico | LOM |
| Lagos/Murtala Muhammed | Nigeria | LOS |
| Lagrande 3, QC | Canada | YAR |
| Lague | Congo | LCO |
| Laguna/AAF, AZ | USA | LGF |
| Lagunillas | Venezuela | LGY |
| Lahad Datu | Malaysia | LDU |
| Lahore | Pakistan | LHE |
| Lahr | Germany | LHA |
| Lahti | Finland | QLF |
| Lai | Chad | LTC |
| Laiagam | Papua New Guinea | LGM |
| Lajeado | Brazil | QLB |
| Lake Baringo | Kenya | LBN |
| Lake Charles, LA | USA | LCH |
| Lake Evella | Australia | LEL |
| Lake Geneva/Municipal, WI | USA | XES |
| Lake Gregory | Australia | LGE |
| Lake Havasu City, AZ. | USA | HII |
| Lake Hood/SPB, AK. | USA | LHD |
| Lake Jackson, TX | USA | LJN |
| Lake Manyara | Tanzania | LKY |
| Lake Minchumina, AK | USA | LMA |
| Lake Murray | Papua New Guinea | LMY |
| Lake Placid, NY | USA | LKP |
| Lake Rudolf | Kenya | LKU |
| Lake Union SPB, WA. | USA | LKE |
| Lake Nash | Australia | LNH |
| Lakeba | Fiji | LKB |
| Lakefield | Australia | LFP |
| Lakeland Downs | Australia | LKD |
| Lakeland, FL | USA | LAL |
| Lakeside, TX | USA | IWS |
| LakesideTX | USA | LKS |
| Lakeview, OR | USA | LKV |
| Lakota | Côte D'Ivoire | LKT |
| Lakselv/Banak. | Norway | LKL |
| Lalibela | Ethiopia | LLI |
| Lalomalava | Samoa | LAV |
| Lamacarena | Colombia | LMC |
| Lamap. | Vanuatu | LPM |
| Lamar Municipal, CO | USA | LAA |
| Lamassa | Papua New Guinea | LMG |
| Lambarene | Gabon | LBQ |
| Lamen Bay | Vanuatu | LNB |
| Lamezia-Terme/S Eufernia | Italy | SUF |
| Lamidanda | Nepal | LDN |
| Lampang | Thailand | LPT |
| Lampedusa | Italy | LMP |
| Lamu | Kenya | LAU |
| Lanai City, HI. | USA | LNY |
| Lancaster, CA | USA | WJF |
| Lancaster, Fairfield County Arpt, OH | USA | LHQ |
| Lancaster, PA | USA | LNS |
| Lancaster/Lancaster PA Rail. | USA | ZRL |
| Lancaster/Quartz Hill, CA | USA | RZH |
| Lancaster/RR Stn. | UK | XQL |
| Lander, WY | USA | LND |
| Landerneau | France | XLD |
| Landivisiau | France | LDV |
| Lands End | UK | LEQ |
| Landshut | Germany | QLG |
| Landskrona/ HP | Sweden | JLD |
| Langara, BC. | Canada | YLA |
| Langenhagen | Germany | ZNY |
| Langenthal | Switzerland | ZHW |
| Langeoog | Germany | LGO |
| Langford/RR Stn., BC | Canada | XEJ |
| Langgur | Indonesia | LUV |
| Langimar | Papua New Guinea | LNM |
| Langkawi | Malaysia | LGK |
| Langtang | Nepal | LTG |
| Lannion/Servel | France | LAI |
| Lansdowne | Australia | LDW |
| Lansdowne House, ON | Canada | YLH |
| Lanseria | S. Africa | HLA |
| Lansing, MI | USA | LAN |
| Lanzarote | Spain | ACE |
| Lanzhou | China | LHW |
| Lanzhou/Lanzhoudong | China | LZD |

| | | |
|---|---|---|
| Lanzhou/Zhongchuan | China | ZGC |
| Laoag | Philippines | LAO |
| Laon/Chambry | France | XLN |
| Laporte/Municipal, IN. | USA | LPO |
| Lappeenranta | Finland | LPP |
| Lar | Iran | LRR |
| Laramie, WY | USA | LAR |
| Larantuka | Indonesia | LKA |
| Larba Nath Iraten | Algeria | ZZL |
| Laredo/Int'l, TX | USA | LRD |
| Larisa | Greece | LRA |
| Larnaca | Cyprus | LCA |
| Larsen/SPB, AK. | USA | KLN |
| Larson/AFB, WA | USA | LRN |
| Las Canas | Costa Rica | LCS |
| Las Cruces/Int'l, NM | USA | LRU |
| Las Gaviotas | Colombia | LGT |
| Las Heras | Argentina | LHS |
| Las Khoreh | Somalia | LKR |
| Las Limas | Honduras | LLH |
| Las Lomitas | Argentina | LLS |
| Las Palmas | Spain | LPA |
| Las Piedras/Josefa Camejo | Venezuela | LSP |
| Las Tunas | Cuba | VTU |
| Las Vegas Nexrad, NV | USA | ESX |
| Las Vegas, NM | USA | LVS |
| Las Vegas, NV. | USA | LAS |
| Las Vegas/Henderson Sky Harbor, NV | USA | HSH |
| Las Vegas/North Air Terminal, NV | USA | VGT |
| Lasham | UK | QLA |
| Lashio | Myanmar | LSH |
| Lastourville | Gabon | LTL |
| Latakia | Syria | LTK |
| Lathrop Wells, NV | USA | LTH |
| Lathrop/Sharpe/AAF, CA | USA | LRO |
| Latina | Italy | QLT |
| Latrobe | Australia | LTB |
| Latrobe, PA. | USA | LBE |
| Laucata Is | Fiji | LUC |
| Launceston | Australia | LST |
| Laura | Australia | LUU |
| Laura Stn | Australia | LUT |
| Laurel, MS | USA | PIB |
| Laurel/Hester/Noble Fld, MS. | USA | LUL |
| Laurie River, MB. | Canada | LRQ |
| Lausanne | Switzerland | QLS |
| Lauterach | Austria | QLX |
| Laval/Entrammes | France | LVA |
| Lavan. | Iran | LVP |
| Laverlon | Australia | LVO |
| Lavras | Brazil | QLW |
| Lawas | Malaysia | LWY |
| Lawn Hill | Australia | IWH |
| Lawrence, KS | USA | LWC |
| Lawrence, MA | USA | LWM |
| Lawrenceville, VA | USA | LVL |
| Lawreneeville, IL | USA | LWV |
| Lawson/AAF, GA | USA | LSF |
| Lawton, OK. | USA | LAW |
| Lazaro Cardenas | Mexico | LZC |
| Icoaraci. | Brazil | QDO |
| Idiofa | Congo, DR | IDF |
| Idre | Sweden | IDB |
| Le Castellet | France | CTT |
| Le Havre/Octeville | France | LEH |
| Le Locle | Switzerland | ZJA |
| Le Mans/Arnage. | France | LME |
| Le Mans/RR Stn. | France | ZLN |
| Le Puy/Loudes | France | LPY |
| Leadville, CO. | USA | LXV |
| Leaf Bay, QB | Canada | XLF |
| Leaf Rapids, MB. | Canada | YLR |
| Learmonth | Australia | LEA |
| Lebakeng | Lesotho | LEF |
| Lebel-Sur-Quevillon, QC. | Canada | YLS |
| Lecce/Galatina | Italy | LCC |
| Lecin/Guanajuato/Del Bajic. | Mexico | BJX |
| Leconi | Gabon | LEO |
| Ledesma | Argentina | XMX |
| Leeds Bradford/Yeadon | UK | LBA |
| Leeds, MT | USA | LDS |
| Leeds/Bus Svc | UK | ZLZ |
| Leesburg, FL | USA | LEE |
| Leesburg/Godfrey, VA. | USA | JYO |
| Leeton/Bus Svc | Australia | QLE |
| Leeuwarden | Netherlands | LWR |
| Legaspi | Philippines | LGP |
| Leguizamo | Colombia | LGZ |
| Leh | India | IXL |

| | | |
|---|---|---|
| Lehu | Papua New Guinea | LHP |
| Leiden/Valkenburg | Netherlands | LID |
| Leigh Creek | Australia | LGH |
| Leinster | Australia | LER |
| Leipzig/Halle | Germany | LEJ |
| Leiria | Portugal | QLR |
| Leitre | Papua New Guinea | LTF |
| Iejima | Japan | IEJ |
| Leka | Norway | ZXN |
| Lekana | Congo, DR | LKC |
| Leknes | Norway | LKN |
| Lelystad | Netherlands | LEY |
| Lemars/Municipal, IA | USA | LRJ |
| Lemmon, SD | USA | LEM |
| Lemnos | Greece | LXS |
| Lemoore/NAS, CA | USA | NLC |
| Lencois Paulista | Brazil | QGC |
| Lencois/Chapada Diamantina | Brazil | LEC |
| Lengbati | Papua New Guinea | LNC |
| Lens | France | XLE |
| Lenzburg | Switzerland | ZJC |
| Lenzerheide/Lai | Switzerland | ZJD |
| Leo | Burkina Faso | XLU |
| Leon | Spain | LEN |
| Leonardtown/St Marys County, MD | SA | LTW |
| Leonora | Australia | LNO |
| Leopoldina | Brazil | LEP |
| Lereh | Indonesia | LHI |
| Leribe | Lesotho | LRB |
| Lerida | Spain | QLQ |
| Lernwerder | Germany | XLW |
| Leron Plains | Papua New Guinea | LPN |
| Leros | Greece | LRS |
| Les Angles | France | QZH |
| Les Ares | France | XRS |
| Les Cayes | Haiti | CYA |
| Les Sables/Talmont | France | LSO |
| Lese | Papua New Guinea | LNG |
| Lesobeng | Lesotho | LES |
| Lethbridge, AB | Canada | YQL |
| Lethem | Guyana | LTM |
| Leticia/Gen. A.V. Cobo | Colombia | LET |
| Letterkenny | Ireland | LTR |
| Leuven | Belgium | ZGK |
| Levaliois | France | QBH |
| Level | Germany | ZOA |
| Levelock, AK | USA | KLL |
| Lewisburg, WV | USA | LWB |
| Lewiston, ID | USA | LWS |
| Lewistown, MT | USA | LWT |
| Lewoleba | Indonesia | LWE |
| Lexington, NE | USA | LXN |
| Lexington-Blue Grass, KY | USA | LEX |
| Igaliku | Chile | QFX |
| Igarka | Russia | IAA |
| Iginniarfik | Greenland | QFI |
| Igiugig, AK | USA | IGG |
| Iguassu Falls/Cataratas | Brazil | IGU |
| Iguatu | Brazil | QIG |
| Iguazu/Cataratas | Argentina | IGR |
| Lhasa | China | LXA |
| Lhok Sukon | Indonesia | LSX |
| Lhoksumawe/Malikussaleh Indonesia | | LSW |
| Ihu | Papua New Guinea | IHU |
| Lia Hulka | F. Polynesia | UAH |
| Lia Pou | F. Polynesia | UAP |
| Liangping | China | LIA |
| Lianyungang | China | LYG |
| Libby/AAF, AZ | USA | FHU |
| Libenge | Congo, DR | LIE |
| Liberal/Municipal, KS | USA | LBL |
| Liberia | Costa Rica | LIR |
| Libourne/Artiques de Lussac | France | XLR |
| Libreville | Gabon | LBV |
| Lichfield T.V./RR Stn | UK | XQT |
| Lichinga | Mozambique | VXC |
| Lidkoping/Hovby | Sweden | LDK |
| Liege/Bierset | Belgium | LGG |
| Liepaya/Int'l | Latvia | LPX |
| Lifou | New Caledonia | LIF |
| Lightning Ridge | Australia | LHG |
| Lihir Is | Papua New Guinea | LNV |
| Lijiang City/Lijiang | China | LJG |
| Likiep Is | Marshall Is | LIK |
| Likoma Is | Malawi | LIX |
| Lilabari | India | IXI |
| Lilboi | Kenya | LBK |
| Liliastai | Mongolia | ULZ |
| Lille/Lesquin | France | LIL |
| Lille/Lille Europe Rail Svc | France | XDB |

| | | |
|---|---|---|
| Lille/Lille Flanders Rail Svc | France | XFA |
| Lilongwe/Int'l | Malawi | LLW |
| Lima, OH | USA | AOH |
| Lima/J Chavez Int'l | Peru | LIM |
| Limassol | Cyprus | QLI |
| Limbang | Malaysia | LMN |
| Limbe | Cameroon | VCC |
| Limbunya | Australia | LIB |
| Limburg | Germany | ZNW |
| Lime Acres | S. Africa | LMR |
| Lime Village, AK | USA | LVD |
| Limeira | Brazil | QGB |
| Limerick | Ireland | LMK |
| Limoges/Bellegarde | France | LIG |
| Limon | Costa Rica | LIO |
| Limon | Honduras | LMH |
| Limon Municipal, CO | USA | LIC |
| Linares | Chile | ZLR |
| Lincoln Rock/Coast Guard, AK | | |
| | USA | LRK |
| Lincoln, NE | USA | LNK |
| Linda Downs | Australia | LLP |
| Lindau | Germany | QII |
| Linden, NJ | USA | LDJ |
| Lindernan Is | Australia | LDC |
| Lindi/Kikwetu | Tanzania | LDI |
| Linga Linga | Papua New Guinea | LGN |
| Linkoping | Sweden | LPI |
| Linosa HP | Italy | LIU |
| Lins | Brazil | LIP |
| Linxi | China | LXI |
| Linyi | China | LYI |
| Linz/Hoersching | Austria | LNZ |
| Lipetsk | Russia | LPK |
| Lippstadt | Germany | ZOB |
| Lisala | Congo, DR | LIQ |
| Lisboa Portela | Portugal | LIS |
| Lishan | Taiwan | LHN |
| Lisieux | France | XLX |
| Lismore | Australia | LSY |
| Lissadell | Australia | LLL |
| Little Cayman | Cayman Is | LYB |
| Little Grand Rapids, MB | Canada | ZGR |
| Little Naukati, AK | USA | WLN |
| Little Port Walter, AK | USA | LPW |
| Little Rock, AR | USA | LIT |
| Little Rock/AFB, AR | USA | LRF |
| Liuzhou | China | LZH |
| Livengood, AK | USA | LIV |
| Livermore, CA | USA | LVK |
| Liverpool Street Stn/RR Stn | UK | ZLS |
| Liverpool/Speke | UK | LPL |
| Livingston, MT | USA | LVM |
| Livingstone | Zambia | LVI |
| Livol | Papua New Guinea | UVO |
| Lizard Is | Australia | LZR |
| Ljubljana/Brnik | Slovenia | LJU |
| Ikerasaarsuk | Greenland | QRY |
| Ikoyi | Norway | QIK |
| Ile d'Yeu | France | IDY |
| Ilha Do Governador | Brazil | QGI |
| Ilimanaq/Harbour | Greenland | XIQ |
| Lloydminster, AB | Canada | YLL |
| Ilulissat | Greenland | JAV |
| Inongo | Congo, DR | INO |
| Loani | Papua New Guinea | LNQ |
| Lobatse | Botswana | LOQ |
| Locarno | Switzerland | ZJI |
| Lochgliphead / HP | UK | LPH |
| Lock | Australia | LOC |
| Lock Haven, PA | USA | LHV |
| Lockhart River | Australia | IRG |
| Lodar | Yemen | LDR |
| Lodja | Congo, DR | LJA |
| Lodwar | Kenya | LOK |
| Lodz/Lodz Lublinek | Poland | LCJ |
| Loei | Thailand | LOE |
| Loen | Marshall Is | LOF |
| Loerrach | Germany | QLO |
| Logan, UT | USA | LGU |
| Lognes | France | XLG |
| Loikaw | Myanmar | LIW |
| Loimaa | Finland | QZJ |
| Loja | Ecuador | LOH |
| Lokichoggio | Kenya | LKG |
| Ioma | Papua New Guinea | IOP |
| Lome/Tokoin | Togo | LFW |
| Lompoc, CA | USA | LPC |
| Loncopue | Argentina | LCP |
| Londolozi | S. Africa | LDZ |
| London Euston/RR | UK | QQU |

| | | |
|---|---|---|
| London Kings Cross/RR | UK | QQK |
| London, KY | USA | LOZ |
| London, ON | Canada | YXU |
| London/Paddington/RR | UK | QQP |
| London/Biggin Hill | UK | BQH |
| London/British Rail Terminal | UK | ZLX |
| London/Gatwick Arpt | UK | LGW |
| London/Heathrow Arpt | UK | LHR |
| London/London City Arpt | UK | LCY |
| London/London-Waterloo | UK | QQW |
| London/Luton Int'l Arpt | UK | LTN |
| London/RR Stn., ON | Canada | XDQ |
| London/Stansted | UK | STN |
| London/Victoria RR Stn | UK | ZEP |
| Londonderry/Eglinton | UK | LDY |
| Londrina | Brazil | LDB |
| Lone Rock, WI | USA | LNR |
| Lonely/Dew Stn, AK | USA | LNI |
| Long Apung | Indonesia | LPU |
| Long Banga | Malaysia | LBP |
| Long Bawan/Juvai Semaring | | |
| | Indonesia | LBW |
| Long Beach/HP, CA | USA | JLB |
| Long Beach, CA | USA | LGB |
| Long Is | Australia | HAP |
| Long Is | Papua New Guinea | LSJ |
| Long Is MacArthur, NY | USA | ISP |
| Long Is, AK | USA | LIJ |
| Long Lama | Malaysia | LLM |
| Long Lellang | Malaysia | LGL |
| Long Pasia | Malaysia | GSA |
| Long Point, ON | Canada | YLX |
| Long Semado/Lawas | Malaysia | LSM |
| Long Seridan | Malaysia | ODN |
| Long Sukang | Malaysia | LSU |
| Long Xuyen | Vietnam | XLO |
| Longana | Vanuatu | LOD |
| Longmont Bus Svc, CO | USA | QWM |
| Longreach | Australia | LRE |
| Longview, WA | USA | LOG |
| Longyearbyen/Svalbard | | |
| | Svalbard and Jan Mayen Is | LYR |
| Lonorore | Vanuatu | LNE |
| Lontras/Helmuth Baungartem | Brazil | LOI |
| Lop Bun | Thailand | KKM |
| Lopez De Micay | Colombia | LMX |
| Lopez Is, WA | USA | LPS |
| Lora Lai | Pakistan | LRG |
| Lord Howe Is | Australia | LDH |
| Lordsburg, NM | USA | LSB |
| Loreto | Mexico | LTO |
| Lorica | Colombia | LRI |
| Lorient/Lann Bilhoue | France | LRT |
| Loring, AK | USA | WLR |
| Loring/AFB, ME | USA | LIZ |
| Lorraine | Australia | LOA |
| Lorriza | Poland | QOY |
| Los Alamos, NM | USA | LAM |
| Los Andes | Chile | LOB |
| Los Angeles | Chile | LSQ |
| Los Angeles/Int'l, CA | USA | LAX |
| Los Angeles/Nexrad, CA | USA | VTX |
| Los Angeles/Van Nuys, CA | USA | VNY |
| Los Angeles/Century City, CA | | |
| | USA | CCD |
| Los Angeles/Citicorp Plaza HP, CA | | |
| | USA | JCX |
| Los Angeles/City Of Industry HP, CA | | |
| | USA | JID |
| Los Angeles/Commerce Bus. Plaza, CA | | |
| | USA | JBP |
| Los Angeles/Sherman Oaks HP, CA | | |
| | USA | JSN |
| Los Angeles/Union Stn HP, CA | USA | JLX |
| Los Angeles/Universal City HP, CA | | |
| | USA | JUC |
| Los Angeles/Warner Cntr Bus. Plaza, CA | | |
| | USA | JWC |
| Los Angeles/Whiteman, CA | USA | WHP |
| Los Banos, CA | USA | LSN |
| Los Chiles | Costa Rica | LSL |
| Los Menucos | Argentina | LMD |
| Los Mochis/Federal | Mexico | LMM |
| Los Roques | Venezuela | LRV |
| Los Tablones | Guatemala | LOX |
| Lossiernouth/RAF | UK | LMO |
| Lost Harbor, AK | USA | LHB |
| Lost River, AK | USA | LSR |
| Losuia | Papua New Guinea | LSA |
| Lotusvaie | Australia | LTV |
| Loubomo | Congo, DR | DIS |

| Location | Country | Code |
|---|---|---|
| Louis Trichardt | S. Africa | LCD |
| Louisa, VA | USA | LOW |
| Louisburg, NC | USA | LFN |
| Louisville Nexrad, KY | USA | LVX |
| Louisville, KY | USA | LOU |
| Louisville, KY | USA | SDF |
| Louisville, MS | USA | LMS |
| Louisville/Intercontinental, KY | USA | LJC |
| Lourdes/Tarbes | France | LDE |
| Loveland Bus Svc, CO | USA | QWH |
| Lovell, WY | USA | POY |
| Lovelock, NV | USA | LOL |
| Loviisa | Finland | QXI |
| Lowai | Papua New Guinea | LWI |
| Loyangalani | Kenya | LOY |
| Itapetininga | Brazil | ZTP |
| Lualbo | Mozambique | LBM |
| Luanda/4 de Fevereiro | Angola | LAD |
| Luang Namtha | Laos | LXG |
| Luang Prabang | Laos | LPQ |
| Luau | Andorra | UAL |
| Lubang | Philippines | LBX |
| Lubango | Angola | SDD |
| Lubbock/Int'l, TX | USA | LBB |
| Lublin | Poland | QLU |
| Lubumbashi/Luano | Congo, DR | FBM |
| Lucca | Italy | LCV |
| Lucenec | Slovakia | LUE |
| Lucerne | Switzerland | QLJ |
| Luchon | France | XLH |
| Lucknow/Amausi | India | LKO |
| Luderitz | Namibia | LUD |
| Ludhiana | India | LUH |
| Ludington/Mason County, MI | USA | LDM |
| Ludwigsburg | Germany | ZOD |
| Ludwigshafen | Germany | ZOE |
| Ludwigslust/RR Stn | Germany | ZLU |
| Luebeck/Blankensee | Germany | LBC |
| Luedenscheid | Germany | ZOC |
| Luena | Angola | LUO |
| Lueneburg/RR Stn | Germany | ZOG |
| Luenen | Germany | ZOH |
| Lufkin, TX | USA | OCH |
| Lugano | Switzerland | LUG |
| Lugansk | Ukraine | VSG |
| Lugh Ganane | Somalia | LGX |
| Luiza | Congo, DR | LZA |
| Lukapa | Angola | LBZ |
| Luke/AFB, AZ | USA | LUF |
| Lukla | Nepal | LUA |
| Lukulu | Zambia | LXU |
| Lulea/Kallax | Sweden | LLA |
| Lumbala | Angola | GGC |
| Lumberton, NC | USA | LBT |
| Lumi | Papua New Guinea | LMI |
| Lumid Pau | Guyana | LUB |
| Lunyuk | Indonesia | LYK |
| Luoyang | China | LYA |
| Luozi | Congo, DR | LZI |
| Lupin, NT | Canada | YWO |
| Lusaka | Zambia | LUN |
| Lusambo | Congo, DR | LBO |
| Lusanga | Congo, DR | LUS |
| Lushan | China | LUZ |
| Lushoto | Tanzania | LUY |
| Lusikisiki | S. Africa | LUJ |
| Lusk, WY | USA | LSK |
| Lutselke/Snowdrift, NT | Canada | YSG |
| Lutsk | Ukraine | UCK |
| Luwuk/Bubung | Indonesia | LUW |
| Luxembourg | Luxembourg | LUX |
| Luxi/Mangshi | China | LUM |
| Luxor | Egypt | LXR |
| Luzamba | Angola | LZM |
| Luzhou | China | LZO |
| Luzon Is/Clark Field | Philippines | CRK |
| Luzonis/NAS | Philippines | NCP |
| Ivanof Bay/SPB, AK | USA | KIB |
| Lvov/Snilow | Ukraine | LWO |
| Ivujivik, QC | Canada | YIK |
| Lwbak | Philippines | LWA |
| Lyall Harbour, BC | Canada | YAJ |
| Lycksele | Sweden | LYC |
| Lydd/Lydd Int'l | UK | LYX |
| Lynchburg, VA | USA | LYH |
| Lyndhurst | Australia | LTP |
| Lyndonville, VT | USA | LLX |
| Lyneham/RAF | UK | LYE |
| Lynn Lake, MB | Canada | YYL |
| Lyon-Satolas | France | LYS |
| Lyon/Bron | France | LYN |
| Lyon/Lyon Part-Dieu Rail Svc. | France | XYD |
| Lyon/Lyon Perrache Rail Svc | France | XYL |
| Lyon/Lyon Satolas Rail Svc | France | XYV |
| Lyons, KS | USA | LYO |
| Lyss | Switzerland | ZJL |

# M

| Location | Country | Code |
|---|---|---|
| M'Bahiakro | Côte D'Ivoire | XMB |
| M'Banza Congo | Angola | SSY |
| M'Boki | Central African Rep | MKI |
| M'Sila | Algeria | ZZS |
| Maan | Jordan | MPQ |
| Maastricht/Aachen | Netherlands | MST |
| Maastricht/RR Stn | Netherlands | ZYT |
| Mabaruma | Guyana | USI |
| Mabile, AL | USA | MOB |
| Mabuiag Is | Australia | UBB |
| Macae | Brazil | MEA |
| Macanal | Colombia | MCP |
| Macapa/Int'l | Brazil | MCP |
| Macara | Ecuador | MRR |
| Macas | Ecuador | XMS |
| Macau | Macau | MFM |
| Macclesfield/RR Stn | UK | XMZ |
| MacDill/AFB, FL | USA | MCF |
| Macdonald Downs | Australia | MNW |
| Maceio/Palmares | Brazil | MCZ |
| Macenta | Guinea | MCA |
| Machala | Ecuador | MCH |
| Machrihanish/RAF | UK | GQJ |
| Machu Picchu | Peru | MFT |
| Mackall/AAF, NC | USA | HFF |
| Mackay | Australia | MKY |
| Mackenzie, BC | Canada | YZY |
| Mackinac Is, MI | USA | MCD |
| Macksville | Australia | MVH |
| Macmahon Camp 4 | Australia | MHC |
| Macon | France | QNX |
| Macon, GA | USA | MCN |
| Macon/FlightLink Bus Svc, GA | USA | QMP |
| Macon/Smart, GA | USA | MAC |
| Mactan Is | Philippines | NOP |
| Madaba | Jordan | QMD |
| Madang | Papua New Guinea | MAG |
| Madera, CA | USA | MAE |
| Madinah/Mohammad Bin Abdulaziz | Saudi Arabia | MED |
| Madirovalo | Madagascar | WMV |
| Madison, SD | USA | XMD |
| Madison, WI | USA | MSN |
| Madison/Griswold, CT | USA | MPE |
| Madras, OR | USA | MDJ |
| Madrid/Barajas | Spain | MAD |
| Madrid/Torrejon AFB | Spain | TOJ |
| Madurai | India | IXM |
| Mae Hong Son | Thailand | HGN |
| Mae Sot | Thailand | MAQ |
| Maebashi | Japan | QEB |
| Maemillan Pass, YT | Canada | XMP |
| Mafeteng | Lesotho | MFC |
| Mafia | Tanzania | MFA |
| Mafra | Brazil | QMF |
| Mafraq/King Hussein (RJAF) | Jordan | OMF |
| Magadan | Russia | GDX |
| Magangue/Baracoa | Colombia | MGN |
| Maganja Da Costa | Mozambique | MJS |
| Magaruque | Mozambique | MFW |
| Magdeburg/RR Stn | Germany | ZMG |
| Magelagachi | Russia | GDG |
| Maghnia | Algeria | QMG |
| Magnitogorsk | Russia | MQF |
| Magnolia/Municipal, AK | USA | AGO |
| Magwe | Myanmar | MWQ |
| Mahanoro | Madagascar | VVB |
| Mahdia | Guyana | MHA |
| Mahe Is | Seychelles | SEZ |
| Mahendranagar | Nepal | XMG |
| Mahenye | Zimbabwe | MJW |
| Maiana | Kiribati | MNK |
| Maicao | Colombia | MCJ |
| Maida | India | LDA |
| Maiduguri | Nigeria | MIU |
| Mailkwalk | Guyana | VEG |
| Maimana | Afghanistan | MMZ |
| Main Duck Is, ON. | Canada | YDK |
| Mainoru | Australia | MIZ |
| Maintirano | Madagascar | MXT |
| Mainz | Germany | QMZ |
| Maio | Cape Verde Is | MMO |
| Mairipora | Brazil | QMC |
| Maitland | Australia | MTL |
| Majkin | Marshall Is | MJE |
| Majunga/Amborovy | Madagascar | MJN |
| Majuro/Amata Kabua Int'l | Marshall Is | MAJ |
| Makabana | Congo, DR | KMK |
| Makale | Ethiopia | MQX |
| Makemo | F. Polynesia | MKP |
| Makhachkala | Russia | MCX |
| Makin Is | Kiribati | MTK |
| Makini | Papua New Guinea | MPG |
| Makkah | Saudi Arabia | QCA |
| Makkovik Arpt | Canada | YFT |
| Makkovik, NF | Canada | YMN |
| Makokou | Gabon | MKU |
| Makoua | Congo, DR | MKJ |
| Makung | Taiwan | MZG |
| Makurdi | Nigeria | MDI |
| Mal | Papua New Guinea | MMV |
| Mala Mala | S. Africa | AAM |
| Malabang | Philippines | MLP |
| Malabo/Santa Isabel | Equatorial Guinea | SSG |
| Malacca | Malaysia | MKZ |
| Malad City, ID | USA | MLD |
| Malaga | Spain | AGP |
| Malaimbandy | Madagascar | WML |
| Malakal | Sudan | MAK |
| Malalaua | Papua New Guinea | MLQ |
| Malang | Indonesia | MLG |
| Malange | Angola | MEG |
| Malargue | Argentina | LGS |
| Malatya | Turkey | MLX |
| Malden, MO | USA | MAW |
| Male/Int'l | Maldives | MLE |
| Malekolon | Papua New Guinea | MKN |
| Malelane | S. Africa | LLE |
| Malewo | Vanuatu | MWF |
| Mali Losinj | Croatia | LSZ |
| Maliana | Indonesia | MPT |
| Malindi | Kenya | MYD |
| Mallacoota | Australia | XMC |
| Malma | Saudi Arabia | MJH |
| Malmo Town | Sweden | QNQ |
| Malmo/Malmo City HVC | Sweden | HMA |
| Malmo/Malmo Harbour HP | Sweden | JMM |
| Malmo/Sturup | Sweden | MMX |
| Malmstrom/AFB, MT | USA | GFA |
| Maloelap Is | Marshall Is | MAV |
| Malololailal | Fiji | PTF |
| Maloy/Harbour | Norway | QFQ |
| Malta/Int'l | Malta | MLA |
| Malta, MT | USA | MLK |
| Mamai | Papua New Guinea | MAP |
| Mamburao | Philippines | MBO |
| Mammoth Lakes, CA | USA | MMH |
| Mampikony | Madagascar | WMP |
| Mamuju | Indonesia | MJU |
| Man | Côte D'Ivoire | MJC |
| Mana Is | Fiji | MNF |
| Manado/Samratulangi | Indonesia | MDC |
| Managua | Nicaragua | MGA |
| Manakara | Madagascar | WVK |
| Mananara | Madagascar | WMR |
| Manang | Nepal | NGX |
| Mananjary | Madagascar | MNJ |
| Manare | Papua New Guinea | MRM |
| Manassas, VA | USA | MNZ |
| Manatee | Belize | MZE |
| Manaung | Myanmar | MGU |
| Manaus/Eduardo Gomes Int'l | Brazil | MAO |
| Manchester Piccadilly/RR | UK | QQM |
| Manchester, NH | USA | MHT |
| Manchester/Manchester Bus Stn | UK | ZMP |
| Manchester/Ringway | UK | MAN |
| Mandabe | Madagascar | WMD |
| Mandalay/Annisaton | Myanmar | MDL |
| Mandalgobi | Mongolia | MXW |
| Mandera | Kenya | NDE |
| Mandeville/Mariboro | Jamaica | MVJ |
| Mandji | Gabon | KMD |
| Mandora | Australia | MQA |
| Mandritsara | Madagascar | WMA |
| Manega | Gabon | MGO |
| Manetai | Papua New Guinea | MVI |
| Manga | Papua New Guinea | MGP |
| Mangaia Is | Cook Is | MGS |
| Mangalore/Balpe | India | IXE |

AIRPORTS -2-

| | | |
|---|---|---|
| Mangochi | Malawi | MAI |
| Mangole | Indonesia | MAL |
| Mangrove Cay | Bahamas | MAY |
| Manguna | Papua New Guinea | MFO |
| Mangunjaya | Indonesia | MJY |
| Manhattan, KS | USA | MHK |
| Manicore | Brazil | MNX |
| Manihi | F. Polynesia | XMH |
| Manihiki Is | Cook Is | MHX |
| Manila/Int'l | Philippines | MNL |
| Manila/Municipal, AR | USA | MXA |
| Manila/Sangley Pt/NAS | Philippines | SGL |
| Maningrida | Australia | MNG |
| Manistee/Blacker, MI | USA | MBL |
| Manistique, MI | USA | ISQ |
| Manitouwadge, ON | Canada | YMG |
| Manitowaning/East Manitoulin, ON | Canada | YEM |
| Manitowoc, WI | USA | MTW |
| Maniwaki, QC | Canada | YMW |
| Manizales/Santaguida | Colombia | MZL |
| Manja | Madagascar | MJA |
| Manjinnup | Australia | MJP |
| Mankato, MN | USA | MKT |
| Mankato/Municipal HP, MN | USA | JMN |
| Mankono | Côte D'Ivoire | MOK |
| Manley Hot Springs, AK | USA | MLY |
| Manners Creek | Australia | MFP |
| Mannitupo | Panama | MPI |
| Manokwari/Rendani | Indonesia | MKW |
| Manolkotak/SPB, AK | USA | KMO |
| Manono | Congo, DR | MNO |
| Mansa | Zambia | MNS |
| Mansehra | Pakistan | HRA |
| Mansfield, OH | USA | MFD |
| Mansfield/Bus Svc | UK | ZMA |
| Mansion House | New Zealand | KWU |
| Mansoura | Egypt | QSU |
| Manston/Kent Int'l | UK | MSE |
| Manta | Ecuador | MEC |
| Manteo/Dare County Regional, NC | USA | MEO |
| Manti, UT | USA | NTJ |
| Mantsala | Finland | QZK |
| Manumu | Papua New Guinea | UUU |
| Manus Is | Papua New Guinea | MAS |
| Manville/Kupper, NJ | USA | JVI |
| Manzanillo | Mexico | ZLO |
| Manzanillo/Sierra Maestra | Cuba | MZO |
| Manzini/Int'l | Swaziland | MTS |
| Mao | Chad | AMO |
| Maota Savaii Is | Samoa | MXS |
| Maple Bay, BC | Canada | YAQ |
| Mapoda | Papua New Guinea | MPF |
| Mapua | Papua New Guinea | MPU |
| Maputo Int'l | Mozambique | MPM |
| Maquinchao | Argentina | MQD |
| Mar Del Plata | Argentina | MDQ |
| Mara Lodges | Kenya | MRE |
| Maraba | Brazil | MAB |
| Maracailbo/La Chwila | Venezuela | MAR |
| Maracay | Venezuela | MYC |
| Maradi | Niger | MFQ |
| Marakei | Kiribati | MZK |
| Maramag | Philippines | XMA |
| Maramuni | Papua New Guinea | MWI |
| Marana, AZ | USA | MZJ |
| Marathon, FL | USA | MTH |
| Marathon, ON | Canada | YSP |
| Marau Sound | Solomon Is | RUS |
| Marawaka | Papua New Guinea | MWG |
| Marbella | Spain | QRL |
| Marble Bar | Australia | MBB |
| Marble Canyon, AZ | USA | MYH |
| Marburg An Der Lahn | Germany | ZOI |
| March/AFB, CA | USA | RIV |
| Marco Is, FL | USA | MRK |
| Marcus Is | Japan | MUS |
| Mare | New Caledonia | MEE |
| Mareala | Honduras | MRJ |
| Mareeba | Australia | MRG |
| Marelb | Yemen | MYN |
| Marfa, TX | USA | MRF |
| Margaret River | Australia | MGV |
| Margarima | Papua New Guinea | MGG |
| Margate | Australia | MGH |
| Marguerite Bay, AK | USA | RTE |
| Marianske Lazne | Czech Rep | MKA |
| Maribo/Lufthavn | Denmark | MRW |
| Maribor/Slivnica | Slovenia | MBX |

| | | |
|---|---|---|
| Maricourt Airstrip, QC | Canada | YMC |
| Marie Galante/Les Bases | | |
| | Gaudeloupe | GBJ |
| Mariehamn/Aland Is | Finland | MHQ |
| Marietta/AFB, GA | USA | MGE |
| Marigot | Gaudeloupe | XCJ |
| Marigot/SPB | Gaudeloupe | MSB |
| Marilia/Dr Gastao Vidigal | Brazil | MII |
| Marina | Nigeria | QNN |
| Marina Di Massa | Italy | QMM |
| Marinduque | Philippines | MRQ |
| Maringa | Brazil | MGF |
| Marinheim | Germany | MHG |
| Marion Downs | Australia | MXD |
| Marion, IL | USA | MWA |
| Marion, IN | USA | MZZ |
| Marion, OH | USA | MNN |
| Maripasoula | F. Guiana | MPY |
| Mariquita | Colombia | MQU |
| Mariscal Estigarribia | Paraguay | ESG |
| Mariupol | Ukraine | MPW |
| Market Harborough/RR Stn | UK | XQM |
| Marks/Selts, MS | USA | MMS |
| Marl | Germany | ZOJ |
| Marla | Australia | MRP |
| Marlborough, MA | USA | MXG |
| Marmande/Off-line Pt | France | XMR |
| Marmaris | Turkey | QRQ |
| Marmul | Oman | OMM |
| Marnte | Cameroon | MMF |
| Maroantsetra | Madagascar | WMN |
| Maron | Papua New Guinea | MNP |
| Maroua/Salam | Cameroon | MVR |
| Marqua | Australia | MQE |
| Marquette, MI | USA | MQT |
| Marrakeeh/Menara | Morocco | RAK |
| Marree | Australia | RRE |
| Marromeu | Mozambique | RRM |
| Marsa Brega | Libya | LMQ |
| Marsabit | Kenya | RBT |
| Marsala | Italy | QMR |
| Marseille/Marignane | France | MRS |
| Marsh Harbour/Int'l | Bahamas | MHH |
| Marshall, AK | USA | MLL |
| Marshall, MN | USA | MML |
| Marshall, TX | USA | ASL |
| Marshall/AAF, KS | USA | FRI |
| Marshall/Memorial, MO | USA | MHL |
| Marshalltown, IA | USA | MIW |
| Marshfield, WI | USA | MFI |
| Martha's Vineyard, MA | USA | MVY |
| Martigny | Switzerland | ZJM |
| Martindale/AAF, TX | USA | MDA |
| Martinsburg, WV | USA | MRB |
| Marudi | Malaysia | MUR |
| Mary | Turkmenistan | MYP |
| Mary's Harbour, NF | Canada | YMH |
| Maryborough | Australia | MBH |
| Marysville, CA | USA | MYV |
| Masa | Papua New Guinea | MBV |
| Masada | Israel | MTZ |
| Masalembo | Indonesia | MSI |
| Masamba | Indonesia | MXB |
| Masan | S. Korea | QMS |
| Masasi | Tanzania | XMI |
| Masbate | Philippines | MBT |
| Mascara | Algeria | MUW |
| Maseru/Moshoeshoe Int'l | Lesotho | MSU |
| Mashad | Iran | MHD |
| Masi Manimba | Congo, DR | MSM |
| Masindi | Uganda | KCU |
| Masirah | Oman | MSH |
| Masjed Soleyman | Iran | QMJ |
| Mason City, IA | USA | MCW |
| Massawa | Eritrea | MSW |
| Massena, NY | USA | MSS |
| Masset, BC | Canada | ZMT |
| Masterton | New Zealand | MRO |
| Mastic Point | Bahamas | MSK |
| Masvingo | Zimbabwe | MVZ |
| Matadi | Congo, DR | MAT |
| Matagami, QC | Canada | YNM |
| Matagorda/AFB, TX | USA | MGI |
| Mataiva | F. Polynesia | MVT |
| Matak | Indonesia | MWK |
| Matam | Senegal | MAX |
| Matamata | New Zealand | MTA |
| Matamoros | Mexico | MAM |
| Matane, QC | Canada | YME |
| Matanzas | Cuba | QMA |
| Matapedia/RR Stn., QC | Canada | XLP |

| | | |
|---|---|---|
| Mataram/Selaparang | Indonesia | AMI |
| Mather/AFB, CA | USA | MHR |
| Mati | Philippines | MXI |
| Mato Grosso | Brazil | MTG |
| Matsaile | Lesotho | MSG |
| Matsu | Taiwan | MFK |
| Matsumoto | Japan | MMJ |
| Matsuyama | Japan | MYJ |
| Matthews Ridge | Guyana | MWJ |
| Mattoon, IL | USA | MTO |
| Matupa | Brazil | MBK |
| Maturin/Quiriquire | Venezuela | MUN |
| Maubeuge | France | XME |
| Maues | Brazil | MBZ |
| Mauke Is | Cook Is | MUK |
| Maulmyine | Myanmar | MNU |
| Maumere/Waioti | Indonesia | MOF |
| Maun | Botswana | MUB |
| Maupiti | F. Polynesia | MAU |
| Mauritius/Int'l | Mauritius | MRU |
| Maxton, NC | USA | MXE |
| Maxvifle/RR Stn., ON | Canada | XID |
| Maxwell/AFB, AL | USA | MXF |
| May Creek, AK | USA | MYK |
| May River | Papua New Guinea | MRH |
| Mayaguana | Bahamas | MYG |
| Mayaguez/Eugenic M De Hostos | | |
| | Puerto Rico | MAZ |
| Mayajigua | Cuba | MJG |
| Mayfa'ah | Yemen | MFY |
| Mayo, YT | Canada | YMA |
| Mayoumba | Gabon | MYB |
| Mayport/NAF, FL | USA | NRB |
| Mazar-I-Sharif | Afghanistan | MZR |
| Mazatian/Gen Ralael Bueina | Mexico | MZT |
| Mbabane/Off-line Pt/(DCA HQ) | | |
| | Swaziland | QMN |
| Mbala | Zambia | MMQ |
| Mbambanakira | Solomon Is | MBU |
| Mbandaka | Congo, DR | MDK |
| Mbarara | Uganda | MBQ |
| Mbeya | Tanzania | MBI |
| Mbigou | Gabon | MBC |
| Mbout | Mauritania | MBR |
| Mbuji Mayi | Congo, DR | MJM |
| Mc Rae, GA | USA | MQW |
| McAlester, OK | USA | MLC |
| Mcallen, TX | USA | MFE |
| Mcarthur River | Australia | MCV |
| Mccall, ID | USA | MYL |
| McCarthy, AK | USA | MXY |
| McChord/AFB, WA | USA | TCM |
| Mcclellan/AFB, CA | USA | MCC |
| Mccomb, MS | USA | MCB |
| Mcconnell/AFB, KS | USA | IAB |
| Mccook, NE | USA | MCK |
| Mcgrath, AK | USA | MCG |
| Mcguire/AFB, NJ | USA | WRI |
| Mckenna/AAF, OH | USA | MKF |
| Mcminnville, TN | USA | RNC |
| Mcpherson, KS | USA | MPR |
| Meadow Lake, SK | Canada | YLJ |
| Meadville, PA | USA | MEJ |
| Mechelen | Belgium | ZGP |
| Medan/Polonia | Indonesia | MES |
| Medea | Algeria | QED |
| Medellin/E. O. Herrera | Colombia | EOH |
| Medellin/Jose Marie Cordova | | |
| | Colombia | MDE |
| Medford, OR | USA | MFR |
| Medford, WI | USA | MDF |
| Medfra, AK | USA | MDR |
| Medicine Hat, AB | Canada | YXH |
| Medina | Colombia | MND |
| Medouneu | Gabon | MDV |
| Meekatharra | Australia | MKR |
| Meeker, Meeker Arpt, CO | USA | EEO |
| Meerbusch | Germany | ZOK |
| Meet Ghamr | Egypt | QFM |
| Megeve | France | MVV |
| Meghauli | Nepal | MEY |
| Mehamn | Norway | MEH |
| Meixian | China | MXZ |
| Mejit Is | Marshall Is | MJB |
| Mekambo | Gabon | MKB |
| Mekane Selam | Ethiopia | MKS |
| Meknes | Morocco | MEK |
| Mekoryuk/Ellis Fld, AK | USA | MYU |
| Melangguane | Indonesia | MNA |
| Melbourne | Australia | MEL |
| Melbourne HP | Australia | KAH |

| Airport | Country | Code |
|---|---|---|
| Melbourne Int'l, FL | USA | MLB |
| Melbourne/Essendon | Australia | MEB |
| Melchor De Menco | Guatemala | MCR |
| Melfa, VA | USA | MFV |
| Melilla | Spain | MLN |
| Melinda | Belize | MDB |
| Melo | Uruguay | MLZ |
| Melville, NY/Off-line Pt. | USA | ZMV |
| Melville/RR Stn., SK | Canada | XEK |
| Memanbetsu | Japan | MMB |
| Memmingen | Germany | QOX |
| Memphis/Int'l, TN | USA | MEM |
| Memphis/NAS, TN | USA | NQA |
| Mena | Ethiopia | MZX |
| Mende/Brenoux | France | MEN |
| Menden | Germany | ZOL |
| Mendez | Ecuador | MZD |
| Mendi | Papua New Guinea | MDU |
| Mendi | Ethiopia | NDM |
| Mendoza/El Plumerillo | Argentina | MDZ |
| Menominee, MI | USA | MNM |
| Menongue | Angola | SPP |
| Menorea | Spain | MAH |
| Menton | France | XMT |
| Menyamya | Papua New Guinea | MYX |
| Meran/Bus Stn. | Italy | ZMR |
| Merauke/Mopah | Indonesia | MKQ |
| Merced, CA | USA | MCE |
| Merced-Castle/AFB, CA | USA | MER |
| Mercley | Indonesia | RDE |
| Mercury, NV | USA | DRA |
| Mereedes | Argentina | MDX |
| Meribel | France | MFX |
| Merida | Spain | QWX |
| Merida/A Carnevalli | Venezuela | MRD |
| Merida/Rejon | Mexico | MID |
| Meridian, MS | USA | MEI |
| Meridian/NAS, MS | USA | NMM |
| Merimbula | Australia | MIM |
| Merluna | Australia | MLV |
| Merowe | Sudan | MWE |
| Merrill/Municipal, WI | USA | RRL |
| Merritt, BC | Canada | YMB |
| Merry Is, BC | Canada | YMR |
| Mersa Matruh | Egypt | MUH |
| Mersin | Turkey | QIN |
| Mersing | Malaysia | MEP |
| Merty | Australia | RTY |
| Merzifon | Turkey | MZH |
| Mesa/Bus Svc, AZ | USA | ZBS |
| Mesa/Falcon Fld, AZ | USA | FFZ |
| Mesa/Falcon Fld, AZ | USA | MSC |
| Mesalia/Sandino | | |
| | Papua New Guinea | MFZ |
| Mesquite, NV | USA | MFH |
| Messina | S. Africa | MEZ |
| Messina | Italy | QME |
| Metlakatia/SPB, AK | USA | MTM |
| Metz/Frescaty | France | MZM |
| Metz/Nancy/Lorraine | France | ETZ |
| Meulaboh/Seunagan | Indonesia | MEQ |
| Mevang | Gabon | MVG |
| Mexicali | Mexico | MXL |
| Mexico City/Atizapan | Mexico | AZP |
| Mexico City/Juarez Int'l | Mexico | MEX |
| Mexico City/Santa Lucia | Mexico | NLU |
| Meyers Chuck/SPB, AK | USA | WMK |
| Mfuwe | Zambia | MFU |
| Miami/Exec, FL | USA | TMB |
| Miami/Int'l, FL | USA | MIA |
| Miami, FL | USA | MiO |
| Miami-Opa Locka, FL | USA | OPF |
| Miami/Dade Collier, FL | USA | TNT |
| Miami/Downtown HP, FL | USA | JDM |
| Miami/SPB, FL | USA | MPB |
| Miandrivazo | Madagascar | ZVA |
| Mianwali | Pakistan | MWD |
| Michigan City, IN | USA | MGC |
| Middle Caicos | Turks & Caicos Is | MDS |
| Middlemount | Australia | MMM |
| Middleton Is, AK | USA | MDO |
| Middletown, OH | USA | MWO |
| Midgard | Namibia | MQG |
| Midland Airpark, TX | USA | MDD |
| Midland/Int'l, TX | USA | MAF |
| Midway Is/Sand Is Field | | |
| | U.S. (Minor Outlying Islands) | MDY |
| Miele Mimbale | Gabon | GIM |
| Mikambati | S. Africa | MBM |
| Mikkeli | Finland | MIK |
| Mikonos | Greece | JMK |
| Milan//Malpensa | Italy | MXP |
| Milan//Linate | Italy | LIN |
| Milan/Milano/Ono Al Serio | Italy | BGY |
| Milan/Milano/Parma | Italy | PMF |
| Milan/Milano/Segrate | Italy | SWK |
| Mildenhall/NAF | UK | GXH |
| Mildenhall/RAF | UK | MHZ |
| Milford Sound | New Zealand | MFN |
| Milford, UT | USA | MLF |
| Mili Is | Marshall Is | MIJ |
| Milingimbi | Australia | MGT |
| Miliville, NJ | USA | MIV |
| Milledgeville, GA | USA | MLJ |
| Milles City, MT | USA | MLS |
| Millicent | Australia | MLR |
| Millinocket, ME | USA | MLT |
| Milos | Greece | MLO |
| Milton Keynes | UK | KYN |
| Milton Keynes/Bus Svc | UK | ZFH |
| Milton, FL | USA | NSE |
| Milwaukee, WI | USA | MKE |
| Milwaukee, WI | USA | MWC |
| Milwaukee/Rail Svc., WI | USA | ZML |
| Minacu | Brazil | MQH |
| Minaki, ON | Canada | YMI |
| Minami Daito | Japan | MMD |
| Minatitlan | Mexico | MTT |
| Minchumina/Intermediate, AK | USA | MHM |
| Minden | Germany | ZOM |
| Minden/Douglas County, NV | USA | MEV |
| Mindik | Papua New Guinea | MXK |
| Mindiptana | Indonesia | MDP |
| Minerainye Vody | Russia | MRV |
| Mineral Wells, TX | USA | MWL |
| Miners Bay, BC | Canada | YAV |
| Miners Lake | Australia | MRL |
| Mingan, QC | Canada | YLP |
| Minhad Ab/Military | UAE | NHD |
| Minj | Papua New Guinea | MZN |
| Minlaton | Australia | XML |
| Minna | Nigeria | MXJ |
| Minneapolis/Flying Cloud Arpt, MN | USA | FCM |
| Minneapolis/Crystal, MN | USA | MIC |
| Minneapolis/St Paul Int'l, MN | USA | MSP |
| Minneapolis/Downtown HP | USA | JDT |
| Minnenya | Sri Lanka | MNH |
| Minnipa | Saudi Arabia | MIN |
| Minocqua, WI | USA | ARV |
| Minot Int'l, ND | USA | MOT |
| Minot/AFB, ND | USA | MIB |
| Minsk Int'l | Belarus | MSQ |
| Minsk/Minsk Int'l | Belarus | MHP |
| Minto, AK | USA | MNT |
| Minvoul | Gabon | MVX |
| Miquelon | St. Pierre and Miquelon | MQC |
| Miracema Do Norte | Brazil | NTM |
| Miraflores | Colombia | MFS |
| Miramar | Argentina | MJR |
| Miramar/NAS, CA | USA | NKX |
| Miramichi, NB | Canada | YCH |
| Miramichi/RR Stn., NB | Canada | XEY |
| Miranda Downs | Australia | MWY |
| Mirgorod | Ukraine | MXR |
| Miri | Malaysia | MYY |
| Miriti | Colombia | MIX |
| Mirnyj | Russia | MJZ |
| Mirpur | Pakistan | QML |
| Mirpur Khas | Pakistan | MPD |
| Misawa | Japan | MSJ |
| Misima Is | Papua New Guinea | MIS |
| Miskolc | Hungary | MCQ |
| Misrak Gashamo | Ethiopia | MHJ |
| Missoula/Int'l, MT | USA | MSO |
| Misurata | Libya | MRA |
| Mitchell | Australia | MTQ |
| Mitchell Plateau | Australia | MIH |
| Mitchell, SD | USA | MHE |
| Mitiaro Is | Cook Is | MOI |
| Mitchell River | Australia | MQX |
| Mitiga | Libya | MJI |
| Mito | Japan | QIS |
| Mitspeh Ramon | Israel | MIP |
| Mittenwaid | Germany | QWD |
| Mittiebah | Australia | MIY |
| Mitu | Colombia | MVP |
| Mitzic | Gabon | MZC |
| Miyake Jima/Hirara | Japan | MMY |
| Miyakojima | Japan | MYE |
| Miyanmin | Papua New Guinea | MPX |
| Miyazaki | Japan | KMI |
| Mizan Teferi | Ethiopia | MTF |
| Mkuze | S. Africa | MZQ |
| Mmabatho/Int'l | S. Africa | MBD |
| Mo I Rana/Rossvoll | Norway | MQN |
| Moa/Orestes Acosta | Chile | MOA |
| Moab, UT. | USA | CNY |
| Moabi | Australia | MGX |
| Moala | Fiji | MFJ |
| Moanamani | Indonesia | ONI |
| Moanda | Gabon | MFF |
| Moanda | Congo, DR | MNB |
| Moba | Congo, DR | BDV |
| Moberly, MO. | USA | MBY |
| Mobile/Dwntwn Arpt, AL | USA | BFM |
| Mobridge Municipal, SD | USA | MBG |
| Mocimboa Praia | Mozambique | MZB |
| Mococa | Brazil | QOA |
| Modane | France | XMO |
| Modena/Bus Stn. | Italy | ZMO |
| Modesto, CA | USA | MOD |
| Moengo | Suriname | MOJ |
| Moers | Germany | ZON |
| Mogadishu/Int'l | Somalia | MGQ |
| Mogi Das Cruzes | Brazil | QMI |
| Mogilev | Belarus | MVQ |
| Mohammadia | Algeria | QMW |
| Mohanban | India | MOH |
| Moheli | Comoros | NWA |
| Mohenjodaro | Pakistan | MJD |
| Mojave, CA | USA | MHV |
| Mokhotlong | Lesotho | MKH |
| Moki | Papua New Guinea | MJJ |
| Mokolo Koba | Senegal | NIK |
| Mokpo | S. Korea | MPK |
| Mokuti Lodge | Namibia | OKU |
| Molde | Norway | MOL |
| Moma | New Zealand | MMW |
| Mombasa/Moi Int'l | Kenya | MBA |
| Momeik | Myanmar | MOE |
| Mompos | Colombia | MMP |
| Monaco-Monte Carlo | France | XMM |
| Monahans/Roy Hurd, TX | USA | MIF |
| Monastir/Int'l | Tunisia | MIR |
| Monbetsu | Japan | MBE |
| Monclova | Mexico | LOV |
| Moncton, NB | Canada | YQM |
| Moncton/RR Stn., NB | Canada | XDP |
| MonFt. | Colombia | MFB |
| Mong Hsat | Myanmar | MOG |
| Mong Ton | Myanmar | MGK |
| Mongo | Chad | MVO |
| Mongu | Zambia | MNR |
| Monida, MT. | USA | MQM |
| Monkey Bay | Malawi | MYZ |
| Monkey Mia/Shark Bay | Australia | MJK |
| Monkey Mountain | Guyana | MYM |
| Monkira | Australia | ONR |
| Mono | Solomon Is | MNY |
| Monroe, LA | USA | MLU |
| Monroe, Monroe Arpt, NC | USA | EQY |
| Monroeville, AL. | USA | MVC |
| Monrovia/Roberts Int'l | Liberia | ROB |
| Monrovia/Sprigg Payne | Liberia | MLW |
| Mons | Belgium | QMO |
| Mont De Marsan | France | XMJ |
| Mont Joli, QC. | Canada | YYY |
| Mont Louis | France | QZE |
| Montague Harbor, BC | Canada | YMF |
| Montague, CA | USA | SIY |
| Montauban | France | XMW |
| Montauk, NY | USA | MTP |
| Montbelliard | France | XMF |
| Monte Alegre | Brazil | MTE |
| Monte Alegre | Brazil | QGD |
| Monte Carlo/ HP | Monaco | MCM |
| Monte Caseros/Seelb | Argentina | MCS |
| Monte Dourado | Brazil | MEU |
| Monte Libano, CO | Colombia | MTB |
| Monte Negro | Brazil | QGF |
| Monteagudo | Bolivia | MHW |
| Montego Bay/Sangster Int'l | Jamaica | MBJ |
| Montelimar | France | XMK |
| Montepuez | Mozambique | MTU |
| Monterey, CA | USA | MRY |
| Monteria/S. Jeronimo | Colombia | MTR |
| Monterrey | Colombia | MOY |
| Monterrey | Mexico | MTY |
| Monterrey/Aeropuerto Del None | | |
| | Mexico | NTR |
| Montes Claros | Brazil | MOC |
| Montevideo, MN | USA | MVE |

| | | |
|---|---|---|
| Montevideo/Carrasco | Uruguay | MVD |
| Montgomery, AL | USA | MGM |
| Montgomery, NY | USA | MGJ |
| Montgomery/Gunter/AFB, AL | USA | GUN |
| Monticello, AR | USA | LLQ |
| Monticello, IA | USA | MXO |
| Monticello, UT | USA | MXC |
| Monticello/Int'l, NY | USA | MSV |
| Montlucon/Gueret (Lepaud) | France | MCU |
| Monto | Australia | MNQ |
| Montpellier/Frejorgues | France | MPL |
| Montreal/Int'l, QC | Canada | YUL |
| Montreal-St. Hubert, QC | Canada | YHU |
| Montreal/Dorval RR Stn., QC | Canada | XAX |
| Montreal/Downtown RR Stn., QC | Canada | YMY |
| Montreal/Mirabel, QC | Canada | YMX |
| Montreal/St. Lambert Rail Svc, QC | Canada | XLM |
| Montreux | Switzerland | ZJP |
| Montrose, CO | USA | MTJ |
| Montserrat/Bramble | Montserrat | MNI |
| Montvale, NJ | USA | QMV |
| Monument Valley, UT | USA | GMV |
| Moody/AFB, GA | USA | VAD |
| Moolawatana | Australia | MWT |
| Moomba | Australia | MOO |
| Moorabbin | Australia | MBW |
| Mooraberree | Australia | OOR |
| Moorea/Ternae | F. Polynesia | MOZ |
| Moose Jaw, SK | Canada | YMJ |
| Moose Lake, MB | Canada | YAD |
| Moosonee, ON. | Canada | YMO |
| Mopti | Mali | MZI |
| Mor Setar | Malaysia | AOR |
| Mora | Sweden | MXX |
| Morafenobe | Madagascar | TVA |
| Moranbah | Australia | MOV |
| Morawa | Australia | MWB |
| Moree | Australia | MRZ |
| Morehead | Papua New Guinea | MHY |
| Morelia | Mexico | MLM |
| Moreton | Australia | MET |
| Morgan City/Municipal HP, LA | USA | PTN |
| Morganton/Lenoir, NC | USA | MRN |
| Morgantown, WV | USA | MGW |
| Morges | Switzerland | ZJQ |
| Morichal | Colombia | MHF |
| Moriguchi | Japan | QGT |
| Moriolka/Hanamaki | Japan | HNA |
| Morlaix/Ploujean | France | MXN |
| Morney | Australia | OXY |
| Mornington | Australia | ONG |
| Moro | Papua New Guinea | MXH |
| Moroak | Australia | MRT |
| Morobe | Papua New Guinea | OBM |
| Morombe | Madagascar | MXM |
| Moron | Mongolia | MXV |
| Moron | Spain | OZP |
| Morondava | Madagascar | MOQ |
| Moroni/Iconi | Comoros | YVA |
| Moroni/Prince Said Ibrahim In | Comoros | HAH |
| Morotai Is | Indonesia | OTI |
| Morrilton, AR | USA | MPJ |
| Morris, MN. | USA | MOX |
| Morristown, NJ | USA | MMU |
| Morristown, TN | USA | MOR |
| Morrisville, VT | USA | MVL |
| Moruya | Australia | MYA |
| Morzine | France | XMQ |
| Mosconi | Argentina | XOS |
| Moscow | Russia | SVO |
| Moscow/Bykovo | Russia | BKA |
| Moscow/Domodedovo | Russia | DME |
| Moscow/Leningradsky RR Stn. | Russia | ZKD |
| Moscow/Vnukovo | Russia | VKO |
| Moser Bay, AK | USA | KMY |
| Moses Lake, WA | USA | MWH |
| Moses Point, AK | USA | MOS |
| Moshi | Tanzania | QSI |
| Mosinee, WI | USA | CWA |
| Mosjoen/Kjaerstad | Norway | MJF |
| Mosquera | Colombia | MQR |
| Mossel Bay | S. Africa | MZY |
| Mossendjo | Congo, DR | MSX |
| Mossoro/Dixsept Rosado | Brazil | MVF |
| Mostaganem | Algeria | QMT |
| Mostar | Bosnia Hercegovina | OMO |

| | | |
|---|---|---|
| Mosteiros | Cape Verde Is | MTI |
| Mostyn | Malaysia | MZS |
| Mosul | Iraq | OSM |
| Mota | Ethiopia | OTA |
| Mota Lava | Vanuatu | MTV |
| Motherwell/RR Stn. | UK | XQW |
| Motswari Airfield | S. Africa | MWR |
| Motueka | New Zealand | MZP |
| Moudieria | Mauritania | MOM |
| Mougulu | Papua New Guinea | GUV |
| Mouila | Gabon | MJL |
| Mould Bay, NT | Canada | YMD |
| Moulin Sur Allier | France | XMU |
| Moultrie, GA | USA | MUL |
| Moultrie/Thornasville, GA. | USA | MGR |
| Moundou | Chad | MQO |
| Mount Aue | Papua New Guinea | UAE |
| Mount Buffalo | Australia | MBF |
| Mount Cook | New Zealand | MON |
| Mount Cook/Glentanner | New Zealand | GTN |
| Mount Cook/Pulkalki/Twizel | New Zealand | TWZ |
| Mount Etjo Lodge | Namibia | MJO |
| Mount Full Stop | Australia | MFL |
| Mount Gambier | Australia | MGB |
| Mount Gunson | Australia | GSN |
| Mount Hagen/Kagamuga | Papua New Guinea | HGU |
| Mount Holly, NJ | USA | LLY |
| Mount Holly, South Jersey, NJ | USA | VAY |
| Mount Hotham | Australia | MHU |
| Mount House | Australia | MHO |
| Mount Isa | Australia | ISA |
| Mount Keith | Australia | WME |
| Mount Magnet | Australia | MMG |
| Mount Pleasant | Falkand Is | MPN |
| Mount Pleasant, MI | USA | MOP |
| Mount Pleasant, TX | USA | MPS |
| Mount Shasta, CA | USA | MHS |
| Mount Swan | Australia | MSF |
| Mount Union, PA | USA | MUU |
| Mount Vernon, WA | USA | MVW |
| Mount Wilson, CA | USA | MWS |
| Mountain | Nepal | MWP |
| Mountain Home, AR | USA | BPK |
| Mountain Home, AR | USA | WMH |
| Mountain Home/AFB, ID | USA | MUO |
| Mountain Valley | Australia | MNV |
| Mountain View, CA | USA | NUQ |
| Mountain Village, AK | USA | MOU |
| Moutiers | France | QMU |
| Mouyiondzi | Congo | MUY |
| Moyale | Ethiopia | MYS |
| Moyale | Kenya | OYL |
| Moyo | Uganda | OYG |
| Moyobamba | Peru | MBP |
| Mpacha | Namibia | MPA |
| Mt Barnett | Australia | MBN |
| Mt Cavenagh | Australia | MKV |
| Mt Clemens, MI | USA | MTC |
| Mt Mckinley, AK | USA | MCL |
| Mt Pleasant, IA | USA | MPZ |
| Mt Pleasant, UT | USA | MSD |
| Mt Pocono, PA | USA | MPO |
| Mt Sandford | Australia | MTD |
| Mt Vernon, IL | USA | MVN |
| Mtwara | Tanzania | MYW |
| Muccan | Australia | MUQ |
| Muclarijiang | China | MDG |
| Mucuri | Brazil | MVS |
| Mudgee | Australia | DGE |
| Mueda | Mozambique | MUD |
| Muelhefm An Der Ruhr | Germany | ZOO |
| Muenster | Germany | FMO |
| Mueo | New Caledonia | PDC |
| Mui | Ethiopia | MUJ |
| Muir/AAF, PA | USA | MUI |
| Mukah | Malaysia | MKM |
| Mukalla | Yemen | MKX |
| Mukeiras | Yemen | UKR |
| Muko-Muko | Indonesia | MPC |
| Mulatos | Colombia | ULS |
| Mulatupo | Panama | MPP |
| Mulege | Mexico | MUG |
| Mulga Park | Australia | MUP |
| Mulia | Indonesia | LII |
| Mulka | Australia | MVK |
| Mull | UK | ULL |
| Mullen, NE | USA | MHN |
| Mullewa | Australia | MXU |

| | | |
|---|---|---|
| Multan | Pakistan | MUX |
| Mulu | Malaysia | MZV |
| Mumbai | India | BOM |
| Mumias | Kenya | MUM |
| Munbil | Papua New Guinea | LNF |
| Muncie, IN. | USA | MIE |
| Munda | Solomon Is | MUA |
| Munduku | Papua New Guinea | MDM |
| Mundulkiri | Cambodia | MWV |
| Mungeranie | Australia | MNE |
| Munich | Germany | MUC |
| Munich/HBF Railway Svc | Germany | ZMU |
| Munich/Neubierg Ab | Germany | MIG |
| Muong Sai | Laos | UON |
| Murcia/San Javier | Spain | MJV |
| Muriae | Brazil | QUR |
| Murmansk | Russia | MMK |
| Muroran | Japan | QRN |
| Murray Bay, QC | Canada | YML |
| Murray Is | Australia | MYI |
| Murray/Calloway County, KY | USA | CEY |
| Murzuq | Libya | QMQ |
| Mus | Turkey | MSR |
| Muscat | Oman | MCT |
| Muscatine, IA. | USA | MUT |
| Musha | Djibouti | MHI |
| Musigrave | Australia | MVU |
| Muskegon, MI | USA | MKG |
| Muskogee, OK. | USA | MKO |
| Muskogee/Hatbox Fld, OK | USA | HAX |
| Muskoka, ON. | Canada | YQA |
| Muskrat Dam, ON. | Canada | MSA |
| Musoma | Tanzania | MUZ |
| Mussau | Papua New Guinea | MWU |
| Mustique Is St. Vincent & Grenadines | | MQS |
| Mutare | Zimbabwe | UTA |
| Muting | Indonesia | MUF |
| Muttaburra | Australia | UTB |
| Muzaffarabad | Pakistan | MFG |
| Muzaffarpur | India | MZU |
| Muzattarnagar | India | MZA |
| Mwadui | Tanzania | MWN |
| Mwanza | Tanzania | MWZ |
| Mwelka | Congo, DR | MEW |
| Myeik | Myanmar | MGZ |
| Myitkyina | Myanmar | MYT |
| Myroodah | Australia | MYO |
| Myrtle Beach, SC | USA | CRE |
| Myrtle Beach/AFB, SC. | USA | MYR |
| Mysore | India | MYQ |
| Mystery Flight | Australia | ZZF |
| Mystery Night | Australia | ZZJ |
| Mytilene | Greece | MJT |
| Myvatn/Reykiahlid | Iceland | MVA |
| Mzamba (Wild Coast Sun) | S. Africa | MZF |
| Mzuzu | Malawi | ZZU |

# N

| | | |
|---|---|---|
| N'Djole | Gabon | KDJ |
| N'Fliquinha | Angola | NRQ |
| N'Zeto | Angola | ARZ |
| N. Sound/Virgin Gorda/Hovercraft/Launch Pt. | Virgin Is (British) | NSX |
| Naberevnye Chelny | Russia | NBC |
| Nabire | Indonesia | NBX |
| Nablus | West Bank | ZDF |
| Nacala | Mozambique | MNC |
| Nachingwea | Tanzania | NCH |
| Nacogdoches, TX | USA | LFK |
| Nador | Morocco | NDR |
| Nadunumu | Papua New Guinea | NDN |
| Nadym | Russia | NYM |
| Nafoora | Libya | NFR |
| Naga | Philippines | WNP |
| Nagano | Japan | QNG |
| Nagasaki | Japan | NGS |
| Nagoya/Koniaki AFS | Japan | NGO |
| Nagpur/Sonegaon | India | NAG |
| Naha | Indonesia | NAH |
| Nain, NF. | Canada | YDP |
| Nairobi/Jorno Kenyatta Int'l. | Kenya | NBO |
| Nairobi/Wilson | Kenya | WIL |
| Nakashibetsu | Japan | SHB |
| Nakhon Phanom | Thailand | KOP |
| Nakhon Ratchasima | Thailand | NAK |
| Nakhon Si Thammarat | Thailand | NST |
| Nakina, ON | Canada | YQN |

| | | |
|---|---|---|
| Naknek, AK | USA | NNK |
| Nakolik River, AK | USA | NOL |
| Nakuru | Kenya | NUU |
| Nalchik | Russia | NAL |
| Nalkinichevan | Azerbaijan | NAJ |
| Namangan | Uzbekistan | NMA |
| Namatanai | Papua New Guinea | ATN |
| Nambaiyufa | Papua New Guinea | NBA |
| Nambour | Australia | NBR |
| Namdrik Is | Marshall Is | NDK |
| Namlea | Indonesia | NAM |
| Nampula | Mozambique | APL |
| Namrole | Indonesia | NRE |
| Namsang | Myanmar | NMS |
| Namsos/Lufthavn | Norway | OSY |
| Namtu | Myanmar | NMT |
| Namu | Marshall Is | NMU |
| Namu, BC | Canada | ZNU |
| Namudi | Papua New Guinea | NDI |
| Namur | Belgium | QNM |
| Nan | Thailand | NNT |
| Nanaimo, BC | Canada | YCD |
| Nanaimo/Harbour, BC | Canada | ZNA |
| Nanchang | China | JHN |
| Nanchang | China | KHN |
| Nanchong | China | NAO |
| Nancy/Essey | France | ENC |
| Nanded | India | NDC |
| Nandi/Int'l | Fiji | NAN |
| Nangade | Mozambique | NND |
| Nangapinoh | Indonesia | NPO |
| Nanisivik, NU | Canada | YSR |
| Nankina | Papua New Guinea | NKN |
| Nanking | China | NKG |
| Nanning | China | NNG |
| Nanortalik | Greenland | JNN |
| Nantes | France | NTE |
| Nantes/RR | France | QJZ |
| Nantong | China | NTG |
| Nantucket, MA | USA | ACK |
| Nanuque | Brazil | NNU |
| Nanwalek, AK | USA | KEB |
| Nanyang | China | NNY |
| Nanyuki | Kenya | NYK |
| Naoro | Papua New Guinea | NOO |
| Napa, CA | USA | APC |
| Napakiak/SPB, AK | USA | WNA |
| Napanee/RR Stn., ON | Canada | XIF |
| Napaskiak/SPB, AK | USA | PKA |
| Napasoq/Off-line Pt | Greenland | QJT |
| Napier-Hastings | New Zealand | NPE |
| Naples, FL | USA | APF |
| Naples/Capodichino | Italy | NAP |
| Naples/Mergellina Railway Svc. | Italy | ZMI |
| Nappa Merry | Australia | NMR |
| Napperby | Australia | NPP |
| Napuka Is | F. Polynesia | NAU |
| Nara | Mali | NRM |
| Nara City | Japan | QNZ |
| Naracoorte | Australia | NAC |
| Narathiwat | Thailand | NAW |
| Nare | Colombia | NAR |
| Nargana | Panama | NGN |
| Narnbucca Heads | Australia | NBH |
| Narnibe | Angola | MSZ |
| Narnutoni | Namibia | NNI |
| Narooma | Australia | QRX |
| Narrabri | Australia | NAA |
| Narrandera | Australia | NRA |
| Narrogin | Australia | NRG |
| Narromine | Australia | QRM |
| Narsaq Kujalleq | Greenland | QFN |
| Narsaq/ HP | Greenland | JNS |
| Narsarsuaq | Greenland | UAK |
| Narvik/Framnes | Norway | NVK |
| Naryan-Mar | Russia | NNM |
| Nashua, NH | USA | ASH |
| Nashville Nexrad, TN | USA | OHX |
| Nashville/Int'l, TN | USA | BNA |
| Nasik/Gandhinagar | India | ISK |
| Nassau/Int'l | Bahamas | NAS |
| Nassau/Paradise Is | Bahamas | PID |
| Nassau/Seaplane Base | Bahamas | WZY |
| Natadola | Fiji | NTA |
| Natal/Augusto Severo | Brazil | NAT |
| Natashquan, QC | Canada | YNA |
| Natchez/Hardy-Anders, MS | USA | HEZ |
| Natitingou | Benin | NAE |
| Natuna Ranai | Indonesia | NTX |
| Naukiti, AK | USA | NKI |
| Nauru Arpt | Nauru | INU |

| | | |
|---|---|---|
| Navalmoral de a Mata | Spain | QWW |
| Navegantes | Brazil | NVT |
| Nawabshah | Pakistan | WNS |
| Nawanshahar | India | QNW |
| Naxos | Greece | JNX |
| Ndalatandos | Angola | NDF |
| Ndele | Central African Rep | NDL |
| Ndende | Gabon | KDN |
| Ndjamena | Tonga | NDJ |
| Ndola | Zambia | NLA |
| Necochea | Argentina | NEC |
| Necocli | Colombia | NCI |
| Nedroma | Algeria | QAN |
| Needles, CA | USA | EED |
| Neenah, WI | USA | EEW |
| Neerlerit Inaat | Greenland | CNP |
| Neftekamsk | Russia | NEF |
| Nefteyugansk | Russia | NFG |
| Negage | Andorra | GXG |
| Negarbo | Papua New Guinea | GBF |
| Negginan, MB | Canada | ZNG |
| Negrielli | Ethiopia | EGL |
| Negril | Jamaica | NEG |
| Neispruit | S. Africa | NLP |
| Neiva/La Marguita | Colombia | NVA |
| Nejjo | Ethiopia | NEJ |
| Nelkernt | Ethiopia | NEK |
| Nellis/AFB, NV | USA | LSV |
| Nelran | Saudi Arabia | EAM |
| Nelson | New Zealand | NSN |
| Nelson Lagoon, AK | USA | NLG |
| Nema | Mauritania | EMN |
| Nemiscau, QC | Canada | YNS |
| Nenana, AK | USA | ENN |
| Neosho, MO | USA | EOS |
| Nepalganj | Nepal | KEP |
| Nephi, UT | USA | NPH |
| Neryungri | Russia | NER |
| Neu-Ulm | Germany | ZOT |
| Neuchatel | Switzerland | QNC |
| Neuilly-Sur-Seine | France | QNL |
| Neulbrandenburg | Germany | FNB |
| Neumuenster | Germany | EUM |
| Neunkirchen/Off-line Pt. | Germany | ZOP |
| Neuss | Germany | ZOQ |
| Neustadt-Weinstrasse | Germany | ZOR |
| Neustadt/Glawe | Germany | QGW |
| Neuwied | Germany | ZOU |
| Nevada, MO | USA | NVD |
| Nevers | France | NVS |
| Nevis/Newcastle | St. Kitts and Nevis | NEV |
| Nevsehir | Turkey | NAV |
| New Amsterdam | Guyana | QSX |
| New Bern, NC | USA | EWN |
| New Bight | Bahamas | NET |
| New Carlisle/RR Stn., QC | Canada | XEL |
| New Chenega, AK | USA | NCN |
| New Halfa | Somalia | NHF |
| New Haven/New Haven Rail, CT | | |
| | USA | ZVE |
| New Iberia, LA | USA | ARA |
| New Koliganek, AK | USA | KGK |
| New London, CT | USA | GON |
| New Moon | Australia | NMP |
| New Orleans Int'l, LA | USA | MSY |
| New Orleans, LA | USA | NEW |
| New Orleans/NAS, LA | USA | NBG |
| New Philadelphia, OH | USA | PHD |
| New Plymouth | New Zealand | NPL |
| New Richmond, WI | USA | RNH |
| New Richmond/RR Stn., QC | | |
| | Canada | XEM |
| New Stuyahok, AK | USA | KNW |
| New Ulm, MN | USA | ULM |
| New Westminster, BC | Canada | YBD |
| New York/La Guardia, NY | USA | LGA |
| New York/Battery Pk, NY | USA | NBP |
| New York/Downtown Manhattan | | |
| HP, NY | USA | JRB |
| New York/E. 34 St Landing, NY. | USA | NES |
| New York/E. 34th St Heliport, NY | | |
| | USA | TSS |
| New York/East 60th Street HP, NY | | |
| | USA | JRE |
| New York/Marine Air Terminal, NY | | |
| | USA | QNY |
| New York/Penn Rail, NY | USA | ZYP |
| New York/Pier 11/SPB, NY | USA | NWS |
| New York/West 30th St HP, NY | | |
| | USA | JRA |
| New York/World Trade Center, NY | | |

| | | |
|---|---|---|
| | USA | WTC |
| Newark Northgate/RR Stn. | UK | XNK |
| Newark, NJ | USA | EWR |
| Newark/Metropark Rail, NJ | USA | ZME |
| Newark/Newark NJ Rail | USA | ZRP |
| Newburgh, NY | USA | SWF |
| Newbury/Greenham/RAF | UK | EWY |
| Newcastle | UK | NCL |
| Newcastle | S. Africa | NCS |
| Newcastle/Belmont | Australia | BEO |
| Newcastle/Mondell, WY | USA | ECS |
| Newcastle/Williamtown | Australia | NTL |
| Newman | Australia | ZNE |
| Newport (Gwent)/RR Stn. | UK | XNE |
| Newport Beach / HP, CA | USA | JNP |
| Newport, NH | USA | NWH |
| Newport, OR | USA | JNW |
| Newport, OR | USA | ONP |
| Newport, UT | USA | EFK |
| Newport/State, RI | USA | NPT |
| Newquay-St Mawgan | UK | NQY |
| Newry | Australia | NRY |
| Newtok, AK | USA | WWT |
| Newton, IA | USA | TNU |
| Newton, KS | USA | EWK |
| Neyveli | India | NVY |
| Ngala | S. Africa | NGL |
| Ngaoundere | Cameroon | NGE |
| Ngau Is | Fiji | NGI |
| Ngiva | Angola | NGV |
| Ngoma | Zambia | ZGM |
| Ngukurr | Australia | RPM |
| Nha Trang | Vietnam | NHA |
| Niacornaarsuk | Greenland | QMK |
| Niagara Falls/Int'l, NY | USA | IAG |
| Niagara Falls/RR Stn., ON | Canada | XLV |
| Niamey/Diori Hamani | Niger | NIM |
| Niamtougou/Lama-Kara | Togo | LRL |
| Nias | Indonesia | ZQX |
| Niblack, AK | USA | NIE |
| Nicaro | Cuba | ICR |
| Nice | France | NCE |
| Nichen Cove, AK | USA | NKV |
| Nichen Cove/SPB, AK | USA | WNC |
| Nicholson | Australia | NLS |
| Nicosia | Cyprus | NIC |
| Nicoya/Guanacaste | Costa Rica | NCT |
| Nieuw Nickerie | Suriname | ICK |
| Nifty | Australia | NIF |
| Nightmute, AK | USA | NME |
| Niigata | Japan | KIJ |
| Niihama | Japan | IHA |
| Nikolaev | Ukraine | NLV |
| Nikolai, AK | USA | NIB |
| Nikolski/AFS, AK | USA | IKO |
| Nikunau | Kiribati | NIG |
| Niles, MI | USA | NLE |
| Nimba | Liberia | NIA |
| Nimes/Garons | France | FNI |
| Nimroz | Afghanistan | IMZ |
| Ningbo | China | NGB |
| Ningerum | Papua New Guinea | NGR |
| Ninilchik, AK | USA | NIN |
| Niolki | Congo, DR | NIO |
| Nioro | Mali | NIX |
| Niort/Souche | France | NIT |
| Nipa | Papua New Guinea | NPG |
| Nipawin, SK | Canada | YBU |
| Niquelandia | Brazil | NQL |
| Nis | Yugoslavia | INI |
| Nishinoomote | Japan | IIN |
| Nissan Is | Papua New Guinea | IIS |
| Nitchequon, QC | Canada | YNI |
| Niteroi | Brazil | QNT |
| Niuafo'ou/Mata'aho | Tonga | NFO |
| Niuatoputapu/Kuini Lavenia | Tonga | NTT |
| Niue Is/Hanan | Niue Is | IUE |
| Nizhnevartovsk | Russia | NJC |
| Nizhniy Novgorod | Russia | GOJ |
| Njornbe | Tanzania | JOM |
| Nkan | Gabon | NKA |
| Nkaus | Lesotho | NKU |
| Nkayi/Yokangassi | Congo, DR | NKY |
| Nkolo | Congo, DR | NKL |
| Nkongsamba | Cameroon | NKS |
| Noatak, AK | USA | WTK |
| Noervenich | Germany | QOE |
| Nogales | Mexico | NOG |
| Nogales/Int'l, AZ | USA | OLS |
| Nojabrxsk | Russia | NOJ |
| Nomad River | Papua New Guinea | NOM |

| | | |
|---|---|---|
| Nomane | Papua New Guinea | NMN |
| Nome, AK | USA | OME |
| Nondalton, AK | USA | NNL |
| Nong Khai | Thailand | QJX |
| Nonouti | Kiribati | NON |
| Noonkanbah | Australia | NKB |
| Noorvik/Curtis Memorial, AK | USA | ORV |
| Noosa | Australia | NSA |
| Noosaville | Australia | NSV |
| Nootka Sound, BC | Canada | YNK |
| Norddeich | Germany | NOE |
| Norden | Germany | NOD |
| Norderney | Germany | NRD |
| Norderstedt | Germany | ZOV |
| Nordfjordur | Iceland | NOR |
| Nordholz-Spieka | Germany | NDZ |
| Nordhorn | Germany | ZOW |
| Norfolk/Int'l, VA | USA | ORF |
| Norfolk Is | Norfolk Is | NLK |
| Norfolk, NE | USA | OFK |
| Norfolk/NAS, VA | USA | NGU |
| Noril'sk | Russia | NSK |
| Norman Wells, NT | Canada | YVQ |
| Norman's Cay | Bahamas | NMC |
| Norman, OK | USA | OUN |
| Normanton | Australia | NTN |
| Norridgewock, ME | USA | OWK |
| Norrkoping/Kungsangen | Sweden | NRK |
| Norseman | Australia | NSM |
| Norsup | Vanuatu | NUS |
| North Battleford, SK | Canada | YQW |
| North Bay, ON | Canada | YYB |
| North Bend, OR | USA | OTH |
| North Caicos | Turks & Caicos Is | NCA |
| North Eleuthera/Int'l | Bahamas | ELH |
| North Is/NAS, CA | USA | NZY |
| North Little Rock, AR | USA | LZK |
| North Platte, NE | USA | LBF |
| North Ronaldsay | UK | NRL |
| North Spirit Lake, ON | Canada | YNO |
| Northallerton/RR Stn | UK | XNO |
| Northampton | Georgia | ORM |
| Northbrook, IL | USA | OBK |
| Northeast Cape/AFS, AK | USA | OHC |
| Northolt/RAF | UK | NHT |
| Northway, AK | USA | ORT |
| Norton/AFB, CA | USA | SBD |
| Norwalk/HP, CT | USA | ORQ |
| Norway House, MB | Canada | YNE |
| Norwich | UK | NWI |
| Norwich/Eaten | Australia | OIC |
| Norwood, MA | USA | OWD |
| Nosara Beach | Costa Rica | NOB |
| Nossi-be/Fascene | Madagascar | NOS |
| Notodden | Norway | NTB |
| Nottingham | UK | EMA |
| Nottingham | UK | NQT |
| Nottingham | UK | QEW |
| Nottingham/Bus Svc | UK | ZGB |
| Nottingham/RR Stn | UK | XNM |
| Nottingham/RR Stn | UK | XQH |
| Nottingham/RR Stn | UK | XQI |
| Nouadhilbou | Mauritania | NDB |
| Nouakchott | Mauritania | NKC |
| Noumea/Magenta | New Caledonia | GEA |
| Nouna | Burkina Faso | XNU |
| Nourrea/Tontouta | New Caledonia | NOU |
| Nova Friburgo | Brazil | QGJ |
| Nova Xavantina | Brazil | NOK |
| Novalguacu | Brazil | QNV |
| Novato, CA | USA | NOT |
| Novgorod | Russia | NVR |
| NoviSad | Yugoslavia | QND |
| Novo Aripuana | Brazil | NVP |
| Novo Hamburgo | Brazil | QHV |
| Novoirossijsk | Russia | NOI |
| Novokuzinetsk | Russia | NOZ |
| Novosibirsk | Russia | OVB |
| Novy Urengoy | Russia | NUX |
| Now Shahr | Iran | NSH |
| Nowata | Papua New Guinea | NWT |
| Nowra | Australia | NOA |
| Nowy Targ | Poland | QWS |
| Nsukka | Norway | QNK |
| Nuernberg | Germany | NUE |
| Nueva Casas Grandes | Mexico | NCG |
| Nueva Gerona/Rafael Cabrera | Cuba | GER |
| Nueva Guinea | Netherlands | NVG |
| Nuevo Laredo/Int'l | Mexico | NLD |
| Nuguria | Papua New Guinea | NUG |

| | | |
|---|---|---|
| Nuiqsut, AK | USA | NUI |
| Nuku | Papua New Guinea | UKU |
| Nuku Hiva | F. Polynesia | NHV |
| Nuku'Alofa/Fija'Amotu Int'l | Tonga | TBU |
| Nukus | Uzbekistan | NCU |
| Nukutavake | F. Polynesia | NUK |
| Nulato, AK | USA | NUL |
| Nullagine | Australia | NLL |
| Nullarbor | Australia | NUR |
| Numbulwar | Australia | NUB |
| Numfoor | Indonesia | FOO |
| Nunapitchuk, AK | USA | NUP |
| Nunchia | Colombia | NUH |
| Nuneaton/RR Stn | UK | XNV |
| Nunukan | Indonesia | NNX |
| Nuoro | Italy | QNU |
| Nuqui | Colombia | NQU |
| Nuremberg/HBF Railway Svc | Germany | ZAQ |
| Nushki | Pakistan | NHS |
| Nutuve | Papua New Guinea | NUT |
| Nutwood Downs | Australia | UTD |
| Nuuk | Greenland | GOH |
| NY City Nexrad, NY | USA | OKX |
| Nyac, AK | USA | ZNC |
| Nyala | Somalia | UYL |
| Nyaung-u | Myanmar | NYU |
| Nyborg/RR Stn | Denmark | ZIB |
| Nyeri | Kenya | NYE |
| Nyikobing Mors/Bus Svc | Denmark | ZAW |
| Nyingan | Australia | NYN |
| Nyon | Switzerland | ZRN |
| Nzagi | Angola | NZA |
| Nzerekore | Guinea | NZE |
| Nzola | Kenya | NZO |

# O

| | | |
|---|---|---|
| O'Neill, NE | USA | ONL |
| Oahu/Dillingham Airfield, HI | USA | HDH |
| Oak Brook, IL/Off-line Pt | USA | QHO |
| Oak Harbor, WA | USA | ODW |
| Oakey | Australia | OKY |
| Oakham/Cottesmor/RAF | UK | OKH |
| Oakland Int'l, CA | USA | OAK |
| Oakland, MD | USA | OBT |
| Oaktown, IN | USA | OTN |
| Oakville/Rail Svc, ON | Canada | XOK |
| Oamaru | New Zealand | OAM |
| Oaxaca | Mexico | OAX |
| Oban | Australia | OBA |
| Oban/ HP | UK | OHP |
| Oban/Connei | UK | OBN |
| Obano | Indonesia | OBD |
| Obbia | Somalia | CMO |
| Oberammergau | Germany | ZOX |
| Oberhausen | Germany | ZOY |
| Oberpfaffenhofen | Germany | OBF |
| Obihiro | Japan | OBO |
| Obo | Papua New Guinea | OBX |
| Obock | Djibouti | OBC |
| Obre Lake, NT | Canada | YDW |
| Ocala, FL | USA | OCF |
| Ocana/Aguasclaras | Colombia | OCV |
| Ocatsut/Harbour | Greenland | XEO |
| Ocean City, MD | USA | OCE |
| Ocean Falls, BC | Canada | ZOF |
| Ocean Reef, FL | USA | OCA |
| Oceana/NAS, VA | USA | NTU |
| Oceanic, AK | USA | OCI |
| Oceanside, CA | USA | OCN |
| Ocho Rios/Boscobel | Jamaica | OCJ |
| Ocussi | Indonesia | OEC |
| Odate Noshiro | Japan | ONJ |
| Oddor Meanche | Cambodia | OMY |
| Odense/Beldringe | Denmark | ODE |
| Odense/Bus Svc | Denmark | ZIM |
| Odense/RR Stn | Denmark | ZBQ |
| Odessa/Central | Ukraine | ODS |
| Odibos | Brazil | OBI |
| Odienne | Côte D'Ivoire | KEO |
| Odiham/RAF | UK | ODH |
| Oeksfjord | Norway | QOK |
| Oelwen, IA | USA | OLZ |
| Oenpeili | Australia | OPI |
| Oeqertarsuaq | Greenland | JGO |
| Offenburg | Germany | ZPA |

| | | |
|---|---|---|
| Offerfbach | Germany | ZOZ |
| Offutt/AFB, NE | USA | OFF |
| Ofu | American Samoa | OFU |
| Ogallala/Searle Fld, NE | USA | OGA |
| Ogden, UT | USA | OGD |
| Ogdensburg Int'l, NY | USA | OGS |
| Ogeranang | Papua New Guinea | OGE |
| Ogle | Guyana | OGL |
| Ogoki, ON | Canada | YOG |
| Ohakea/RAF | New Zealand | OHA |
| Ohrid | Macedonia | OHD |
| Oil City, PA | USA | OIL |
| Oingdao | China | TAO |
| Oishn | Yemen | IHN |
| Oita | Japan | OIT |
| Okaba | Indonesia | OKQ |
| Okaukuejo | Namibia | OKF |
| Okayama | Japan | OKJ |
| Okeechobee, FL | USA | OBE |
| Okhotsk | Russia | OHO |
| Oki Is | Japan | OKI |
| Okinawa/Kadena AFB | Japan | DNA |
| Okinawa/Naha | Japan | OKA |
| Okinawa/Naha AFB | Japan | AHA |
| Okino Erabu | Japan | OKE |
| Oklahoma City, OK | USA | OKC |
| Oklahoma City, OK | USA | PWA |
| Oklahoma City/Downtown, OK | USA | DWN |
| Okmulgee, OK | USA | OKM |
| Okondja | Gabon | OKN |
| Okoyo | Congo, DR | OKG |
| Oksapimin | Papua New Guinea | OKP |
| Oksibil | Indonesia | OKL |
| Oktiabrskij | Russia | OKT |
| Okushiri | Japan | OIR |
| Olafsfjordur | Iceland | OFJ |
| Olafsvik/Rif | Iceland | OLI |
| Olanchito | Honduras | OAN |
| Olbia/Costa Smeraida | Italy | OLB |
| Old Crow, YT | Canada | YOC |
| Old Ft. Bay, QC | Canada | ZFB |
| Old Harbor/SPB, AK | USA | OLH |
| Old Town, ME | USA | OLD |
| Oldenburg | Germany | ZPD |
| Olean, NY | USA | OLE |
| Olga Bay/SPB, AK | USA | KOY |
| Olive Branch, MS | USA | OLV |
| Olivos | Argentina | QLV |
| Olney, IL | USA | OLY |
| Olney, TX | USA | ONY |
| Olomouc | Czech Rep | OLO |
| Olpoi | Vanuatu | OLJ |
| Olsobip | Papua New Guinea | OLQ |
| Olsztyin | Poland | QYO |
| Olten | Switzerland | ZJU |
| Olympia, WA | USA | OLM |
| Olympic Dam | Australia | OLP |
| Omaha, NE | USA | OMA |
| Omaha/Millard, NE | USA | MIQ |
| Omak, WA | USA | OMK |
| Omboue | Gabon | OMB |
| Omega | Namibia | OMG |
| Omora | Papua New Guinea | OSE |
| Omsk | Russia | OMS |
| Omura | Japan | OMJ |
| Ondangwa | Namibia | OND |
| Oneonta/Municipal, NY | USA | ONH |
| Onepusu | Solomon Is | ONE |
| Ongava Game Reserve | Namibia | OGV |
| Ongiva | Angola | VPE |
| Onion Bay, AK | USA | ONN |
| Onitsha | Norway | QNI |
| Ono I Lau | Fiji | ONU |
| Ononge | Papua New Guinea | ONO |
| Onotoa | Kiribati | OOT |
| Onsiow | Australia | ONS |
| Ontario Int'l, CA | USA | ONT |
| Ontario, OR | USA | ONO |
| Ontario/Int'l HP, CA | USA | JIO |
| Oodnadatta | Australia | ODD |
| Opapamiska Lake/Musselwhite, ON | Canada | YBS |
| Opelousas, LA | USA | OPL |
| Open Bay | Papua New Guinea | OPB |
| Opoie | Poland | QPM |
| Opuwa | Namibia | OPW |
| Oradea | Romania | OMR |
| Oram | Papua New Guinea | RAX |
| Oran | Argentina | ORA |
| Oran/Es Senia | Algeria | ORN |
| Orange | France | XOG |

| | | |
|---|---|---|
| Orange Walk | Belize | ORZ |
| Orange, MA | USA | ORE |
| Orange/Springhill | Australia | OAG |
| Orange/The City HP, CA | USA | JOR |
| Orangeburg, SC | USA | OGB |
| Oranjemund | Namibia | OMD |
| Orapa | Botswana | ORP |
| Orbost | Australia | RBS |
| Orchid Beach/Fraser Is | Australia | OKB |
| Orchid Is | Taiwan | KYD |
| Ord River | Australia | ODR |
| Ord/Sharp Fld, NE | USA | ODX |
| Ordu | Turkey | QOR |
| Orebro | Sweden | ORB |
| Orel | Russia | OEL |
| Orenburg | Russia | REN |
| Oria | Papua New Guinea | OTY |
| Orientos | Australia | OXO |
| Orinduik | Guyana | ORJ |
| Oristano | Italy | QOS |
| Oriximina | Brazil | ORX |
| Orland | Norway | OLA |
| Orlando Exec, FL | USA | ORL |
| Orlando Int'l, FL | USA | MCO |
| Orlando/Walt Disney World, FL | USA | DWS |
| Ormara | Pakistan | ORW |
| Ormoc | Philippines | OMC |
| Ornkalai | Papua New Guinea | OML |
| Ornlya | Japan | QOM |
| Ornskoldsvik | Sweden | OER |
| Orocue | Colombia | ORC |
| Oroville, CA | USA | OVE |
| Orpheus Is Resort/Waterport | | |
| | Australia | ORS |
| Orsk | Russia | OSW |
| Orsta-Volda/Hovden | Norway | HOV |
| Oruro | Bolivia | ORU |
| Osage Beach, MD | USA | OSB |
| Osaka/Itami | Japan | ITM |
| Osaka/Kansai Int'l | Japan | KIX |
| Osaka/Off-line Pt | Japan | QKV |
| Osan/Air Base | S. Korea | OSN |
| Osasco | Brazil | QOC |
| Osceola, WI | USA | OEO |
| Osh | Kyrgyzstan | OSS |
| Oshakati | Namibia | OHI |
| Oshawa, ON | Canada | QWA |
| Oshawa, ON | Canada | YOO |
| Oshima | Japan | OIM |
| Oshkosh, NE | USA | OKS |
| Oshkosh, WI | USA | OSH |
| Osijek | Croatia | OSI |
| Oskaloosa, IA | USA | OOA |
| Oskarshamn | Sweden | OSK |
| Oslo/Fornebu | Norway | FBU |
| Oslo/Gardermoen | Norway | OSL |
| Oslo/Sandefjord | Norway | TRF |
| Osmanabad | India | OMN |
| Osnabrueck/RR Stn. | Germany | ZPE |
| Osorno/Canal Balo | Chile | ZOS |
| Ossima | Papua New Guinea | OSG |
| Ostend | Belgium | OST |
| Ostersund/Froesoe | Sweden | OSD |
| Ostrava/Mosnov | Czech Rep. | OSR |
| Ostro Weikopolski | Poland | QDG |
| Osvaldo Cruz/Off-line Pt | Brazil | QOD |
| Otaru | Japan | QOT |
| Otis/AFB, MA | USA | FMH |
| Otjiwarongo | Namibia | OTJ |
| Otsu City | Japan | QOO |
| Ottawa Int'l, ON | Canada | YOW |
| Ottawa/RR Stn., ON | Canada | XDS |
| Ottawa/Rockcliffe St, ON | Canada | YRO |
| Otto/Vor, NM | USA | OTO |
| Ottumwa, IA | USA | OTM |
| Otu | Colombia | OTU |
| Ouadda | Central African Rep. | ODA |
| Ouagadougou/Aeroport | | |
| | Burkina Faso | OUA |
| Ouahigouya | Burkina Faso | OUG |
| Ouanda Dialle | Central African Rep. | ODJ |
| Ouanga | Gabon | OUU |
| Ouango Fitini | Côte D'Ivoire | OFI |
| Ouargla | Algeria | OGX |
| Ouarzazate | Morocco | OZZ |
| Ouctshoorn | S. Africa | OUH |
| Oudoni | Laos | ODY |
| Oued Rhiou | Algeria | QOU |
| Oued Zenati | Algeria | QOZ |
| Ouesnel, BC | Canada | YQZ |
| Ouesso | Cocos (Keeling) Is | OUE |

| | | |
|---|---|---|
| Oujda/Les Angades | Morocco | OUD |
| Oulu | Finland | OUL |
| Oum Hadjer | Chad | OUM |
| Ourilandia | Brazil | OIA |
| Ourinhos | Brazil | OUS |
| Outer Skerries | UK | OUK |
| Outhing | Iceland | UTG |
| Ouvea | New Caledonia | UVE |
| Ouyen | Australia | OYN |
| Ouzinkie/SPB, AK | USA | KOZ |
| Ovalle | Chile | OVL |
| Ovda | Israel | VDA |
| Owando | Congo, DR | FTX |
| Owatonna, MN | USA | OWA |
| Owen Sound/Billy Bishop, | | |
| ON | Canada | YOS |
| Owendo | Gabon | OWE |
| Owensboro, KY | USA | OWB |
| Owerri | Nigeria | QOW |
| Owyhee, NV | USA | OWY |
| Oxford House, MB | Canada | YOH |
| Oxford, CT | USA | OXC |
| Oxford, OH | USA | OXD |
| Oxford/Kidlington | UK | OXF |
| Oxford/University-Oxford, MS | USA | UOX |
| Oxnard, CA | USA | OXR |
| Oyem | Gabon | OYE |
| Ozamis City/Labo | Philippines | OZC |
| Ozona, TX | USA | OZA |

# P

| | | |
|---|---|---|
| Pa-an | Myanmar | PAA |
| Paama | Vanuatu | PBJ |
| Paamiut | Greenland | JFR |
| Pacific City, OR | USA | PFC |
| Pacific Harbor | Fiji | PHR |
| Pack Creek, AK | USA | PBK |
| Padang/Tabing | Indonesia | PDG |
| Paderborn/Lippstadt | Germany | PAD |
| Padova | Italy | QPA |
| Paducah, KY | USA | PAH |
| Pagadian | Philippines | PAG |
| Page, AZ | USA | PGA |
| Pago Pago/Int'l | American Samoa | PPG |
| Pagosa Springs, CO | USA | PGO |
| Pahokee, FL | USA | PHK |
| Paiela | Papua New Guinea | PLE |
| Pailin | Cambodia | PAI |
| Paimiut/SPB, AK | USA | PMU |
| Painesville, OH | USA | PVZ |
| Painter Creek, AK | USA | PCE |
| Pakatoa Is | New Zealand | PKL |
| Paksane | Laos | PKS |
| Pakse | Laos | PKZ |
| Pakuashipi, QC | Canada | YIF |
| Pakulha | Uganda | PAF |
| Pala | Chad | PLF |
| Palacios | Honduras | PCH |
| Palaclos, TX | USA | PSX |
| Palanga | Italy | PLQ |
| Palangkaraya | Indonesia | PKY |
| Palanquero | Colombia | PAL |
| Palapye | Botswana | QPH |
| Palembang/Mahmud | | |
| Badaruddin II | Indonesia | PLM |
| Palenque | Mexico | PQM |
| Palermo/Punta Raisi | Italy | PMO |
| Palestine, TX | USA | PSN |
| Palibelo | Indonesia | PBW |
| Palkokku | Myanmar | PKK |
| Palm Is | St. Vincent & Grenadines | PLI |
| Palm Is | Australia | PMK |
| Palm Springs, CA | USA | PSP |
| Palm Springs-Thermal, CA | USA | TRM |
| Palm Springs/Bermuda Dunes, | | |
| CA | USA | UDD |
| Palma | Mozambique | LMZ |
| Palma Mallorca | Spain | PMI |
| Palmanto | Venezuela | PTM |
| Palmar/Palmar Sur | Costa Rica | PMZ |
| Palmares | Brazil | QGK |
| Palmas | Brazil | PMW |
| Palmdale, CA | USA | PMD |
| Palmer, AK | USA | PAQ |
| Palmer, MA | USA | PMX |
| Palmerston North | New Zealand | PMR |
| Palmira | Colombia | QPI |

| | | |
|---|---|---|
| Palmyra | Syria | PMS |
| Palo Alto, CA | USA | PAO |
| Paloemeu/Vincent Fayks | Suriname | OEM |
| Palu/Mutiara | Indonesia | PLW |
| Pama | Burkina Faso | XPA |
| Pambwa | Papua New Guinea | PAW |
| Pamol | Malaysia | PAY |
| Pampa/Perry Lefors Fld, TX | USA | PPA |
| Pamplona | Spain | PNA |
| Panama City, FL | USA | PFN |
| Panama City/Paitilia | Panama | PAC |
| Panama City/Tocumen Int'l | Panama | PTY |
| Panambi | Brazil | QMB |
| Pancevo | Yugoslavia | QBG |
| Panclie Pandie | Australia | PDE |
| Panevezys | Lithuania | PNV |
| Pangia | Papua New Guinea | PGN |
| Pangkalanbuun | Indonesia | PKN |
| Pangkalpinang/Pangkalpinang | | |
| | Indonesia | PGK |
| Pangkor | Malaysia | PKG |
| Pangnirtung, NU | Canada | YXP |
| Pangoa | Papua New Guinea | PGB |
| Panguitch, UT | USA | PNU |
| Panjgur | Pakistan | PJG |
| Pantelleria | Italy | PNL |
| Pantnagar | India | PGH |
| Paonia/North Fork Valley, CO | USA | WPO |
| Papa Stour | UK | PSV |
| Papa Westray | UK | PPW |
| Papeete/Faaa | F. Polynesia | PPT |
| Paphos Int'l | Cyprus | PFO |
| Papun | Myanmar | PPU |
| Para Chinar | Pakistan | PAJ |
| Paraburdoo | Australia | PBO |
| Paradise River, NF | Canada | YDE |
| Paragould/Mun | Australia | PGR |
| Parakou | Benin | PKO |
| Param | Papua New Guinea | PPX |
| Paramakotoi | Guyana | PMT |
| Paramaribo/Zandenj Int'l | Suriname | PBM |
| Paramaribo/Zorg En Hoop | | |
| | Suriname | ORG |
| Parana | Argentina | PRA |
| Paranagua | Brazil | PNG |
| Paranaiba | Brazil | PBB |
| Paranavai | Brazil | PVI |
| Paraparaumu | New Zealand | PPQ |
| Parasi | Solomon Is | PRS |
| Paratebueno | Colombia | EUO |
| Pardoo | Australia | PRD |
| Parent/RR Stn., QC | Canada | XFE |
| Parintins | Brazil | PIN |
| Paris / HP | France | JDP |
| Paris, TN | USA | PHT |
| Paris, TX | USA | PRX |
| Paris/Aerogare des Invalides | France | XEX |
| Paris/C.de G. ITGV Rail Sve | France | XDT |
| Paris/Charles De Gaulle | France | CDG |
| Paris/Etoile | France | XTT |
| Paris/Gare du Nord RR Stn. | France | XPG |
| Paris/Gare Montparnasse | France | XGB |
| Paris/La Defense HP | France | JPU |
| Paris/Le Bourget | France | LBG |
| Paris/Le Touquet | France | LTQ |
| Paris/Orly | France | ORY |
| Paris/Paris Cergy Pontoise | France | POX |
| Park Falls, WI | USA | PKF |
| Park Rapids, MN | USA | PKD |
| Parkersburg, WV | USA | PKB |
| Parkes | Australia | PKE |
| Parksville/RR Stn., BC | Canada | KPK |
| Parksville/RR Stn., BC | Canada | XPB |
| Parnailba/Santos Dumont | Brazil | PHB |
| Parnamirim | Brazil | QEU |
| Parndana | Australia | PDN |
| Paro | Bhutan | PBH |
| Paros | Greece | PAS |
| Parry Sound, ON | Canada | YPD |
| Parsons, KS | USA | PPF |
| Paruima | Guyana | PRR |
| Pasadena / HP, CA | USA | JPD |
| Pascagoula, Lott Int'l Arpt, MS | USA | PQL |
| Pascagoula, MS | USA | PGL |
| Pasco, WA | USA | PSC |
| Pasewalk/RR Stn. | Germany | ZSK |
| Pasighat | India | IXT |
| Pasir Pangarayan | Indonesia | PPR |
| Pasni | Pakistan | PSI |
| Paso Calballos | Guatemala | PCG |
| Paso De Los Libres | Argentina | AOL |

| | | |
|---|---|---|
| Paso Robles, CA | USA | PRB |
| Pass (Generic), QC | Canada | XZP |
| Passau | Germany | ZPF |
| Passo Fundo | Brazil | PFB |
| Passos | Brazil | PSW |
| Pastaza | Ecuador | PTZ |
| Pasto/Cano | Colombia | PSO |
| Pat Warren, AK | USA | PFA |
| Paterswolde/Bus Svc | Netherlands | QYT |
| Pathankot | India | IXP |
| Patna | India | PAT |
| Pato Branco | Brazil | PTO |
| Patong Beach | Thailand | PBS |
| Patos De Minas | Brazil | POJ |
| Patreksfjordur | Iceland | PFJ |
| Pattani | Thailand | PAN |
| Pattaya | Thailand | PYX |
| Patuxent River/NAS, MD | USA | NHK |
| Pau/Uzein | France | PUF |
| Pauk | Myanmar | PAU |
| Paulatuk, NT | Canada | YPC |
| Paulo Afonso | Brazil | PAV |
| Pauloff Harbor/SPB, AK | USA | KPH |
| Pavloclar | Kazakstan | PWQ |
| Pawi/Beles | Ethiopia | PWI |
| Payan | Colombia | PYN |
| Paysandu | Uruguay | PDU |
| Payson, AZ | USA | PJB |
| Paz De Ariporo/Casanare | Colombia | PZA |
| Peace River, AB | Canada | YPE |
| Peach Springs, AZ | USA | PGS |
| Pease/AFB, NH | USA | PSM |
| Peawanuck, ON | Canada | YPO |
| Pebane | Mozambique | PEB |
| Pechora | Russia | PEX |
| Pecos City, TX | USA | PEQ |
| Pecs | Hungary | QPJ |
| Pedernales | Venezuela | PDZ |
| Pedro Bay, AK | USA | PDB |
| Pedro Juan Caballero | Paraguay | PJC |
| Peenemuende | Germany | PEF |
| Pehuajo | Argentina | PEH |
| Peine | Germany | ZPG |
| Pekanbaru/Simpang Tiga | Indonesia | PKU |
| Pelaneng | Lesotho | PEL |
| Pelican/SPB, AK | USA | PEC |
| Pell City, AK | USA | PLR |
| Pellston, MI | USA | PLN |
| Pelly Bay, NU | Canada | YBB |
| Pelotas/Federal | Brazil | PET |
| Pemba | Mozambique | POL |
| Pemba/Wawi | Tanzania | PMA |
| Pembina/Intermediate, ND | USA | PMB |
| Pembroke, ON | Canada | YTA |
| Penang/Int'l | Malaysia | PEN |
| Pencing | Australia | PEY |
| Pender Harbor, BC | Canada | YPT |
| Pendleton, OR | USA | PDT |
| Pendopo | Indonesia | PDO |
| Penn Yan, NY | USA | PEO |
| Penneshaw | Australia | PEA |
| Penrhyn Island | Cook Is. | PYE |
| Penrith/RR Stn. | UK | XPF |
| Pensacola, FL | USA | PNS |
| Pensacola/NAS, FL | USA | NDP |
| Pensacola/NAS, FL | USA | NPA |
| Penticton, BC | Canada | YYF |
| Penza | Russia | PEZ |
| Penzance/ HP | UK | PZE |
| Peoria, IL | USA | PIA |
| Peppimenarti | Australia | PEP |
| Peraitepuy | Venezuela | PPH |
| Perce/RR Stn., QC | Canada | XFG |
| Pereira/Matecana | Colombia | PEI |
| Perigueux/Bassillac | France | PGX |
| PerisheR Valley/Bus Svc | Australia | QPV |
| Perito Moreno | Argentina | PMQ |
| Perm | Russia | PEE |
| Perpignan/Llabanere | France | PGF |
| Perry, IA | USA | PRO |
| Perry-Foley, FL | USA | FPY |
| Perry/SPB, AK | USA | PYL |
| Perryville/SPB, AK | USA | KPV |
| Persepolis | Iran | WPS |
| Perth | Australia | PER |
| Perth/Scone | UK | PSL |
| Perth/ScotRail | UK | ZXP |
| Peru/Illinois Valley Regional, IL | USA | VYS |
| Perugia/Sant Egidio | Italy | PEG |
| Pescara/Liberi | Italy | PSR |
| Peshawar | Pakistan | PEW |

| | | |
|---|---|---|
| Petawawa, ON | Canada | YWA |
| Peterborough, ON | Canada | YPQ |
| Peterborough/RR Stn. | UK | XVH |
| Petersburg, AK | USA | PSG |
| Petersburg, VA | USA | PTB |
| Petersburg, WV | USA | PGC |
| Peterson's Point, AK | USA | PNF |
| Petrolina/Int'l | Brazil | PNZ |
| Petropavlovsk | Kazakstan | PPK |
| Petropavlovsk-Kamchats | Russia | PKC |
| Petropolis | Brazil | QPE |
| Petrozavodsk | Russia | PES |
| Pevek | Russia | PWE |
| Pforheim | Germany | UPF |
| Phalaborwa | S. Africa | PHW |
| Phan Rang | Vietnam | PHA |
| Phan Thiet | Vietnam | PHH |
| Phanom Sarakham | Thailand | PMM |
| Phaplu | Nepal | PPL |
| Phi Phi Is | Thailand | PHZ |
| Philadelphia Int'l, PA | USA | PHL |
| Philadelphia, PA | USA | PNE |
| Philadelphia/Mustin Alf, PA | USA | MUV |
| Philadelphia/N Philadelphia RR Stn., PA | USA | ZHC |
| Philadelphia/Philadelphia Rail, PA | USA | ZFV |
| Philadelphia/SPB, PA | USA | PSQ |
| Philadelphia/Trenton RR Stn., PA | USA | ZTN |
| Philip, SD | USA | PHP |
| Phinda/Zulu Inyaia | S. Africa | PZL |
| Phitsanulok | Thailand | PHS |
| Phnom Penh/Pochentong | Cambodia | PNH |
| Phoenix/Int'l, AZ | USA | PHX |
| Phoenix, AZ | USA | DVT |
| Phrae | Thailand | PRH |
| Phu Quoc/Duong Dang | Vietnam | PQC |
| Phu Vinh | Vietnam | PHU |
| Phu-bon | Vietnam | HBN |
| Phuket/Int'l | Thailand | HKT |
| Phuoclong | Vietnam | VSO |
| Piacenza | Italy | QPZ |
| Pianeta Rica | Colombia | PLC |
| Piatra Neamt | Romania | QPN |
| Picayune, MS | USA | PCU |
| Pichanal | Argentina | XMV |
| Pickens, SC | USA | LQK |
| Pickle Lake, MB | Canada | YPL |
| Pico Is | Portugal | PIX |
| Picos | Brazil | PCS |
| Picton/Koromiko | New Zealand | PCN |
| Piedmont Triad/Int'l, NC | USA | GSO |
| Piedras Negras | Mexico | PDS |
| Pierre, SD | USA | PIR |
| Piestany | Slovakia | PZY |
| Pietermaritzburg | S. Africa | PZB |
| Pietersburg | S. Africa | PTG |
| Pijiguaos | Venezuela | LPJ |
| Pikangikum, ON | Canada | YPM |
| Pilar | Paraguay | PIL |
| Pilkwitonei, MB | Canada | PIW |
| Pilot Point, AK | USA | PIP |
| Pilot Point/Ugashik Bay, AK | USA | UGB |
| Pilot Stn, AK | USA | PQS |
| Pimaga | Papua New Guinea | PMP |
| Pimenta Bueno | Brazil | PBQ |
| Pinamar | Argentina | QPQ |
| Pinar Del Rio | Colombia | QPD |
| Pincher Creek, AB | Canada | WPC |
| Pindiu | Papua New Guinea | PDI |
| Pine Bluff, AR | USA | PBF |
| Pine Cay | Turks & Caicos Is | PIC |
| Pine House, SK | Canada | ZPO |
| Pine Mountain, GA | USA | PIM |
| Pine Point, NT | Canada | YPP |
| Pine Ridge, SD | USA | IEN |
| Pine Ridge, SD | USA | XPR |
| Pingtung | Taiwan | PIF |
| Pinheiro | Brazil | PHI |
| Pinotepa Nacional | Mexico | PNO |
| Pipillipai | Guyana | PIQ |
| Piracicaba | Brazil | QHB |
| Pirapora | Brazil | PIV |
| Pirassununga/Off-line Pt. | Brazil | QPS |
| Pirmasens | Germany | ZPI |
| Pisco | Peru | PIO |
| Pitalito | Colombia | PTX |
| Pitinga | Brazil | PIG |
| Pitts Town | Bahamas | PWN |

| | | |
|---|---|---|
| Pittsburg, KS | USA | PTS |
| Pittsburgh/Int'l, PA | USA | PIT |
| Pittsburgh/Allegheny, PA | USA | AGC |
| Pittsburgh/Civic HP, PA | USA | CVA |
| Pittsfield, MA | USA | PSF |
| Pituffik | Greenland | THU |
| Placencia | Belize | PLJ |
| Placerville, CA | USA | PVF |
| Plainview, TX | USA | PVW |
| Planaclas | Colombia | PLA |
| Platinum, AK | USA | PTU |
| Plato | Colombia | PLT |
| Plattsburgh, NY | USA | PLB |
| Plattsburgh/AFB, NY | USA | PBG |
| Playa Blanca | Spain | QLY |
| Playa del Carmen | Mexico | PCM |
| Playa de Los Cristianos | Spain | QCI |
| Playa Grande | Guatemala | PKJ |
| Playa Samara | Costa Rica | PLD |
| Playon Chico | Panama | PYC |
| Pleasant Harbour, AK | USA | PTR |
| Pleasant Nexrad, MO | USA | EAX |
| Pleasanton/Hacienda Bus-Park HP, CA | USA | JBS |
| Pleiku | Vietnam | PXU |
| Plentywood, MT | USA | PWD |
| Plettenberg Bay | S. Africa | PBZ |
| Pleven | Bulgaria | PVN |
| Plock | Poland | QPC |
| Ploiesti | Romania | QPL |
| Plovcliv | Bulgaria | PDV |
| Plymouth | UK | PLH |
| Plymouth, IN | USA | PLY |
| Plymouth, MA | USA | PYM |
| Po | Burkina Faso | PUP |
| Pocahontas, IA | USA | POH |
| Pocatello, ID | USA | PIH |
| Pochutla | Mexico | PUH |
| Pocos De Calclas | Brazil | POO |
| Podor | Senegal | POD |
| Poelgorica,/Golubovci | Yugoslavia | TGD |
| Pohang/Air Base | S. Korea | KPO |
| Pohnpei | Micronesia | PNI |
| Point Baker/SPB, AK | USA | KPB |
| Point Hope, AK | USA | PHO |
| Point Lay, AK | USA | PIZ |
| Point Mugu/NAS, CA | USA | NTD |
| Point Retreat/Coast Guard HP, AK | USA | PRT |
| Point Sur, CA | USA | NNZ |
| Pointe A Pitre/Le Raizet | Gaudeloupe | PTP |
| Pointe-aux-Trembles/RR Stn., QC | Canada | XPX |
| Pointe-Noire | Congo, DR | PNR |
| Points North Landing, SK | Canada | YNL |
| Poitiers/Biard | France | PIS |
| Poitiers/RR Stn. | France | XOP |
| Pokhara | Nepal | PKR |
| Polacca, AZ | USA | PXL |
| Polk Inlet, AK | USA | POQ |
| Polk/AAF, LA | USA | POE |
| Poll | Ukraine | PLV |
| Polyarnyl | Russia | PYJ |
| Pomala | Indonesia | PUM |
| Pomezia | Italy | QEZ |
| Pompano Beach, FL | USA | PPM |
| Pompeia | Brazil | QPF |
| Ponca City, OK | USA | PNC |
| Ponce/Mercedita | Puerto Rico | PSE |
| Pond Inlet, NU | Canada | YIO |
| Pondicherry | India | PNY |
| Pondok Cabe | Indonesia | PCB |
| Ponta Delgada/Nordela | Portugal | PDL |
| Ponta Grossa/Sant'Ana | Brazil | PGZ |
| Ponta Pelada | Brazil | PLL |
| Ponta Pora/Int'l | Brazil | PMG |
| Pontes e Lacerda | Brazil | LCB |
| Pontiac, MI | USA | PTK |
| Pontianak/Supadio | Indonesia | PNK |
| Pontorson Mt St Michel | France | XPM |
| Pontresina | Switzerland | ZJV |
| Poona/Lohegaon | India | PNQ |
| Popayan/Machangara | Colombia | PPN |
| Pope Vanoy, AK | USA | PVY |
| Pope/AFB, NC | USA | POB |
| Poplar Bluff, MO | USA | POF |
| Poplar Hill, ON | Canada | YHP |
| Poplar River, MB | Canada | XPP |
| Popondetta/Girua | Papua New Guinea | PNP |

| | | |
|---|---|---|
| Poptun | Guatemala | PON |
| Porbandar | India | PBD |
| Porcupine Creek, AK | USA | PCK |
| Pordenone | Italy | QAD |
| Pore | Colombia | PRE |
| Porgera | Papua New Guinea | RGE |
| Pori | Finland | POR |
| Porl Hunter | Australia | PHJ |
| Porlarnar | Venezuela | PMV |
| Poros | Norway | RRS |
| Port Alexander, AK | USA | PTD |
| Port Alfred | S. Africa | AFD |
| Port Alice, AK | USA | PTC |
| Port Allberni, BC | Canada | YPB |
| Port Alsworth, AK | USA | PTA |
| Port Angeles, WA | USA | CLM |
| Port Angeles, WA | USA | NOW |
| Port Antonio/Ken Jones | Jamaica | POT |
| Port Armstrong, AK | USA | PTL |
| Port Au Prince | Haiti | PAP |
| Port Augusta | Australia | PUG |
| Port Bailey/SPB, AK | USA | KPY |
| Port Berge | Madagascar | WPB |
| Port Blair | India | IXZ |
| Port Clarence, AK | USA | KPC |
| Port De Paix | Haiti | PAX |
| Port Douglas | Australia | PTI |
| Port Elizabeth | S. Africa | PLZ |
| Port Fitzroy | New Zealand | GBS |
| Port Frederick, AK | USA | PFD |
| Port Gentil | Gabon | POG |
| Port Graham, AK | USA | PGM |
| Port Harcourt | Nigeria | PHC |
| Port Hardy, BC | Canada | YZT |
| Port Hawkesbury, NS | Canada | YPS |
| Port Hedland | Australia | PHE |
| Port Heiden, AK | USA | PTH |
| Port Hope Simpson, NF | Canada | YHA |
| Port Hope/RR Stn., ON | Canada | XPH |
| Port Huron/Int'l, MI | USA | PHN |
| Port Johnson | Australia | PRF |
| Port Kaiturna | Guyana | PKM |
| Port Keats | Australia | PKT |
| Port Lincoln | Australia | PLO |
| Port Lions/SPB, AK | USA | ORI |
| Port Macquarie | Australia | PQQ |
| Port McNeil, BC | Canada | YMP |
| Port Menier, MB | Canada | YPN |
| Port Moller/AFS, AK | USA | PML |
| Port Moresby/Int'l | | |
| | Papua New Guinea | POM |
| Port Oceanic, AK | USA | PRL |
| Port Of Spain | Trinidad and Tobago | POS |
| Port Pirie | Australia | PPI |
| Port Protection, AK | USA | PPV |
| Port Said | Egypt | PSD |
| Port Saint Johns | S. Africa | JOH |
| Port San Juan, AK | USA | PJS |
| Port Simpson, BC | Canada | YPI |
| Port Stanley | Falkland Is | PSY |
| Port Stephens | Australia | PTE |
| Port Sudan | Sudan | PZU |
| Port Townsend, WA | USA | TWD |
| Port Vendres | France | XPV |
| Port Vila/Bauerfield | Vanuatu | VLI |
| Port Walter, AK | USA | PWR |
| Port Williams/SPB, AK | USA | KPR |
| Port-Daniel/RR Stn., QC | Canada | XFI |
| Portage Creek, AK | USA | PCA |
| Portage La Prairie, MB | Canada | YPG |
| Porterville, CA | USA | PTV |
| Portimao | Portugal | PRM |
| Portland | Australia | PTJ |
| Portland Int'l, ME | USA | PWM |
| Portland Int'l, OR | USA | PDX |
| Portland Nexrad, OR | USA | RTX |
| Portland-Troutdale, OR | USA | TTD |
| Porto | Portugal | OPO |
| Porto Alegre | | |
| | Sao Tome and Principe | PGP |
| Porto Alegre Do Norte | Brazil | PBX |
| Porto Alegre/Salgado Filhe | Brazil | POA |
| Porto Amboim | Angola | PBN |
| Porto Cheli Kheli/Alexion | | |
| | Greece | PKH |
| Porto Dos Gauchos | Brazil | PBV |
| Porto Nacional | Brazil | PNB |
| Porto Santo | Portugal | PXO |
| Porto Seguro | Brazil | BPS |
| Porto Uniao | Brazil | QPU |
| Porto Velho/Belmonte | Brazil | PVH |

| | | |
|---|---|---|
| Portoroz/Secovlje | Slovenia | POW |
| Portoviejo | Ecuador | PVO |
| Portsmouth | UK | PME |
| Portsmouth, OH | USA | PMH |
| Porvenir | Chile | WPR |
| Porvoo | Finland | QXJ |
| Posadas | Argentina | PSS |
| Poseberth | Australia | RSB |
| Poso/Kasiguncu | Indonesia | PSJ |
| Postville, NF | Canada | YSO |
| Poteau/Robert S Kerr, OK | USA | RKR |
| Potenza | Italy | QPO |
| Potosi | Bolivia | POI |
| Potsdam | Germany | XXP |
| Pottstown, PA | USA | PTW |
| Poughkeepsie, NY | USA | POU |
| Poulsbo, WA | USA | PUL |
| Pourn | New Caledonia | PUV |
| Pouso Alegre | Brazil | PPY |
| Povungnituk, QC | Canada | YPX |
| Powell Lake, BC | Canada | WPL |
| Powell Point | Bahamas | PPO |
| Powell River, BC | Canada | YPW |
| Poza Rica/Tajin | Mexico | PAZ |
| Pozan/Lawica | Poland | POZ |
| Pozarevac | Yugoslavia | ZZP |
| Prado | Brazil | PDF |
| Prague/Ruzyne | Czech Rep | PRG |
| Praia/Francisco Mendes | | |
| | Cape Verde Is | RAI |
| Prairie Du Chien, WI | USA | PCD |
| Praslin Is | Seychelles | PRI |
| Prato | Italy | QPR |
| Pratt Municipal, KS | USA | PTT |
| Prentice, WI | USA | PRW |
| Prerov | Czech Rep | PRV |
| Pres. Roque Saenz Pena | Argentina | PRQ |
| Prescott, AZ | USA | PRC |
| Prescott/RR Stn., ON | Canada | XII |
| Presidente Dutra/Mun | Brazil | PDR |
| Presidente Prudente/ | | |
| A. De Barros | Brazil | PPB |
| Presov | Slovakia | POV |
| Presque Isle, ME | USA | PQI |
| Presque Isle/Rogers, MI | USA | PZQ |
| Preston | Cuba | PST |
| Preston/RR Stn. | UK | XPT |
| Pretoria | S. Africa | PRY |
| Pretoria/Central Hpr | S. Africa | HPR |
| Pretoria/iscor HP | S. Africa | HIC |
| Preveza/Lefkas/Aktion | Greece | PVK |
| Price, UT | USA | PUC |
| Prieska | S. Africa | PRK |
| Prince Albert,SK | Canada | YPA |
| Prince George, BC | Canada | YXS |
| Prince George/RR Stn., BC | | |
| | Canada | XDV |
| Prince Rupert, BC | Canada | YPR |
| Prince Rupert/RR Stn., BC | Canada | XDW |
| Prince Rupert/SealCove, BC | | |
| | Canada | ZSW |
| Princeton, ME | USA | PNN |
| Princeton, MN | USA | PNM |
| Princeton, NJ | USA | PCT |
| Princeton/Princeton JT Rail, NJ | USA | ZTJ |
| Principe | Sao Tome and Principe | PCP |
| Prineville, OR | USA | PRZ |
| Pristina | Yugoslavia | PRN |
| Progresso | Brazil | PGG |
| Prome | Myanmar | PRU |
| Propriano | France | PRP |
| Proserpine | Australia | PPP |
| Prospect Creek, AK | USA | PPC |
| Provedenia | Russia | PVX |
| Providemya | Russia | PVS |
| Providence, RI | USA | PVD |
| Providence/Providence Rail, RI | USA | ZRV |
| Providencia | Colombia | PVA |
| Providenciales | Turks & Caicos Is | PLS |
| Provincetown, MA | USA | PVC |
| Provins | France | XPS |
| Provo, UT | USA | PVU |
| Prudhoe Bay, AK | USA | PUO |
| Pskov | Russia | PKV |
| Ptura | Peru | PIU |
| Puas | Papua New Guinea | PUA |
| Pucallpa/Capitan Rolden | Peru | PCL |
| Puchon City | S. Korea | QJP |
| Pucon | Chile | ZPC |
| Puebla/Huejotsingo | Mexico | PBC |
| Pueblo, CO | USA | PUB |

| | | |
|---|---|---|
| Puerto Aisen | Chile | WPA |
| Puerto Armuellas | Panama | AML |
| Puerto Asis | Colombia | PUU |
| Puerto Ayacucho | Venezuela | PYH |
| Puerto Barrios | Guatemala | PBR |
| Puerto Berrio | Colombia | PBE |
| Puerto Boyaca | Colombia | PYA |
| Puerto Cabello | Venezuela | PBL |
| Puerto Cabezas | Netherlands | PUZ |
| Puerto Carreno | Colombia | PCR |
| Puerto de la Luz | Spain | QUZ |
| Puerto Deseado | Argentina | PUD |
| Puerto Escondido | Myanmar | PXM |
| Puerto Ininda | Colombia | PDA |
| Puerto Jimenez | Costa Rica | PJM |
| Puerto Juarez | Mexico | PJZ |
| Puerto la Cruz | Venezuela | QUC |
| Puerto La Cruz | Spain | UPC |
| Puerto Leguizamo | Colombia | LQM |
| Puerto Lempira | Honduras | PEU |
| Puerto Madonado | Peru | PEM |
| Puerto Madryn/El Tehuelche | | |
| | Argentina | PMY |
| Puerto Moritt/Tepual | Chile | PMC |
| Puerto Natales/Teniente J. | | |
| Gallardo | Chile | PNT |
| Puerto Obaldia | Panama | PUE |
| Puerto Ordaz | Venezuela | PZO |
| Puerto Paez | Venezuela | PPZ |
| Puerto Penasco | Mexico | PPE |
| Puerto Plata/La Union | | |
| | Dominican Rep | POP |
| Puerto Princesa | Philippines | PPS |
| Puerto Rico | Colombia | PCC |
| Puerto Rico | Somalia | PUR |
| Puerto Suarez | Somalia | PSZ |
| Puerto Vallarta/Ordaz | Mexico | PVR |
| Puerto Varas | Chile | PUX |
| Puerto Williams | Chile | WPU |
| Puka Puka | F. Polynesia | PKP |
| Puka Puka Is/Attol | Cook Is | PZK |
| Pukarua | F. Polynesia | PUK |
| Pukatawagan, MB | Canada | XPK |
| Pula | Croatia | PUY |
| Pulau Layang-Layang Is | Malaysia | LAC |
| Pulau Panlang | Indonesia | PPJ |
| Pullman, WA | USA | PUW |
| Pumani | Papua New Guinea | PMN |
| Punia | Congo, DR | PUN |
| Punta Alegre | Colombia | UPA |
| Punta Arenas/Pres Ibanez | Chile | PUQ |
| Punta Cana | Dominican Rep | PUJ |
| Punta Colorada | Mexico | PCO |
| Punta De Maisi | Colombia | UMA |
| Punta Del Este | Uruguay | PDP |
| Punta Gorda | Belize | PND |
| Punta Gorda, FL | USA | PGD |
| Punta Istilta | Costa Rica | PBP |
| Punta Renes | Costa Rica | JAP |
| Pureni | Papua New Guinea | PUI |
| Purwokerto | Indonesia | PWL |
| Pusan/Kimhae Int'l Arpt | S. Korea | PUS |
| Putao | Myanmar | PBU |
| Puttaparthi/Puttaprathe | India | PUT |
| Puttgarden | Germany | QUA |
| Putumayo | Ecuador | PYO |
| Putussibau | Indonesia | PSU |
| Pweto | Congo, DR | PWO |
| Pyongyang/Sunan | N. Korea | FNJ |
| Pyrgos/Andravida | Greece | PYR |

# Q

| | | |
|---|---|---|
| Qaanaaq | Greenland | NAQ |
| Qaisumah | Saudi Arabia | AQI |
| Qala Nau | Afghanistan | LQN |
| Qaqortoq/HP | Greenland | JJU |
| Qasigiannguit | Greenland | JCH |
| Qassiarsulk | Greenland | QFT |
| Qatif | Saudi Arabia | QTF |
| Qeqertarsuatsiaat | Greenland | QEY |
| Qikiqtarjuaq, NU | Canada | YVM |
| Qingyang | China | IQN |
| Qinhuangdao | China | SHP |
| Qiqihar | China | NDG |
| Quad-City, IL | USA | MLI |
| Quakertown/Upper Bucks, PA | USA | UKT |
| Qualicurn, BC | Canada | XQU |

**AIRPORTS**

**-2-**

| | | |
|---|---|---|
| Quanduc/Nhon Co | Vietnam | HOO |
| Quang Ngai | Vietnam | XNG |
| Quantico/NAS, VA | USA | NYG |
| Quaqtaq, QC | Canada | YQC |
| Quebec, QC | Canada | YQB |
| Quebec/Charny, QC | Canada | XFZ |
| Quebec/Levis Rail Svc, QC | Canada | XLK |
| Quebec/Quebec Stn Rail Svc, QC | Canada | XFY |
| Queen Charlotte Is, BC | Canada | ZQS |
| Queen, AK | USA | UQE |
| Queenstown | Australia | UEE |
| Queenstown | S. Africa | UTW |
| Queenstown/Frankton New Zealand | ZQN |
| Quelimane | Mozambique | UEL |
| Quepos | Costa Rica | XQP |
| Queretaro | Myanmar | QRO |
| Quetta | Pakistan | UET |
| Quetzaltenanac | Guatemala | AAZ |
| Qui Nhon | Vietnam | UIH |
| Quibdo | Colombia | UIB |
| Quiche/Quiche Arpt | Guatemala | AQB |
| Quillayute, WA | USA | UIL |
| Quilpie | Australia | ULP |
| Quimper/Pluguffan | France | UIP |
| Quincemil | Peru | UMI |
| Quincy, IL | USA | UIN |
| Quincy, MA | USA | MQI |
| Quine Hill | Vanuatu | UIQ |
| Quinhagak/Kwinhagak, AK | USA | KWN |
| Quirincli | Australia | UIR |
| Quito/Mariscal Sucr | Ecuador | UIO |
| Quixada | Brazil | QIX |
| Qullissat | Greenland | QUE |
| Qum | Iran | QUM |
| Quonset Point/NAS, RI | USA | NCO |

# R

| | | |
|---|---|---|
| Rabaraba | Papua New Guinea | RBP |
| Rabat/Sale | Morocco | RBA |
| Rabaui/Tokua | Papua New Guinea | RAB |
| Rabi | Fiji | RBI |
| Rach Gia | Vietnam | VKG |
| Racine, WI | USA | RAC |
| Radom | Poland | QXR |
| Raduzhnyi | Russia | RAT |
| Rae Lakes, NT | Canada | YRA |
| Rafai | Central African Rep. | RFA |
| Rafha | Saudi Arabia | RAH |
| Rafsanian | Iran | RJN |
| Raglan | New Zealand | RAG |
| Ragusa | Italy | QRG |
| Raha/Sugimanuru | Indonesia | RAQ |
| Rahim Yar Khan | Pakistan | RYK |
| Raiatea | F. Polynesia | RFP |
| Raikot/Civil | India | RAJ |
| Rail (Generic), QC | Canada | XZR |
| Rainbow Lake, AB | Canada | YOP |
| Raipur | India | RPR |
| Raishahi | Bangladesh | RJH |
| Rajahmundry | India | RJA |
| Rajbiraj | Nepal | RJB |
| Rajouri | India | RJI |
| Rakanda | Papua New Guinea | RAA |
| Raleigh-Durham Int'l, NC | USA | RDU |
| Ramadan | Ecuador | TFR |
| Ramagundarn | India | RMD |
| Ramallah | West Bank | ZDM |
| Ramata | Solomon Is | RBV |
| Rambouillet | France | XRT |
| Ramechhap | Nepal | RHP |
| Ramingining | Australia | RAM |
| Rampart, AK | USA | RMP |
| Ramsar | Iran | RZR |
| Ramsgate/RR | UK | QQR |
| Ramstein | Germany | RMS |
| Ranau | Malaysia | RNU |
| Rancagua | Chile | QRC |
| Ranchi | India | IXR |
| Rancho, CA | USA | RBK |
| Randers/RR Stn | Denmark | ZIR |
| Randolph/AFB, TX | USA | RND |
| Rangely, CO | USA | RNG |
| Ranger, TX | USA | RGR |
| Rangiroa | F. Polynesia | RGI |
| Rangpur | Bangladesh | RAU |
| Rankin Inlet, NT | Canada | YRT |

| | | |
|---|---|---|
| Ranong | Thailand | UNN |
| Ransiki | Indonesia | RSK |
| Rapid City, SD | USA | RAP |
| Rapperswil | Switzerland | ZJW |
| Rarotonga | Cook Is | RAR |
| Ras Al Khaimah Int'l | UAE | RKT |
| Rasht | Iran | RAS |
| Raspberry Strait, AK | USA | RSP |
| Rastatt/Bus Svc | Germany | ZRW |
| Ratanakiri | Cambodia | RBE |
| Ratinagiri | India | RTC |
| Ratingen | Germany | ZPJ |
| Raton, NM | USA | RTN |
| Raudha | Yemen | RXA |
| Raufarhofn | Iceland | RFN |
| Rauma | Finland | QZU |
| Ravenna/La Spreta | Italy | RAN |
| Ravensburg | Germany | QRB |
| Ravensburg | Germany | ZPK |
| Rawala Kot | Pakistan | RAZ |
| Rawalpindi | Pakistan | RWP |
| Rawlins, WY | USA | RWL |
| Reaci | F. Polynesia | REA |
| Reading | UK | XRE |
| Reading, PA | USA | RDG |
| Rebun | Japan | RBJ |
| Rechlin | Germany | REB |
| Recife/Guararapes Int'l | Brazil | REC |
| Recklinghausen | Germany | ZPL |
| Reconquista | Argentina | RCQ |
| Red Bluff, CA | USA | RBL |
| Red Deer, AB | Canada | YQF |
| Red Devil, AK | USA | RDV |
| Red Dog, AK | USA | RDB |
| Red Lake, ON | Canada | YRL |
| Red Lodge, MT | USA | RED |
| Red Oak, IA | USA | RDK |
| Red Sucker Lake, MB | Canada | YRS |
| Redcliffe | Vanuatu | RCL |
| Redding, CA | USA | RDD |
| Redencao | Brazil | RDC |
| Redhill | UK | KRH |
| Redmond, OR | USA | RDM |
| Redon | France | XRN |
| Redwood Falls, MN | USA | RWF |
| Reed City, MI | USA | RCT |
| Reese/AFB, TX | USA | REE |
| Refugio/O'Connor Oilfield, TX | USA | VDU |
| Refugio/Rooke Fld, TX | USA | RFG |
| Regensburg/RR Stn | Germany | ZPM |
| Reggio Calabria/Tito Menniti | Italy | REG |
| Reggio Nell Emilia/Bus Svc | Italy | ZRO |
| Regina | F. Guiana | REI |
| Regina, SK | Canada | YQR |
| Rehoboth Beach, DE | USA | REH |
| Reims | France | RHE |
| Reivilo | S. Africa | RVO |
| Relizane | Algeria | QZN |
| Remscheid/Offline Pt | Germany | ZPN |
| Rengat/Japura | Jamaica | RGT |
| Renmark | Australia | RMK |
| Rennell | Solomon Is | RNL |
| Rennes/Gare de Rennes | France | ZFJ |
| Rennes/St Jacques | France | RNS |
| Reno Int'l, NV | USA | RNO |
| Reno Nexrad, NV | USA | RGX |
| Rensselaer, IN | USA | RNZ |
| Renton, WA | USA | RNT |
| Repulse Bay, NU | Canada | YUT |
| Resende | Brazil | QRZ |
| Resende | Brazil | REZ |
| Reserved/Network Service Code | - | QSP |
| Resistencia | Argentina | RES |
| Resita | Romania | QRS |
| Resolute, NT | Canada | YRB |
| Resolution Is, NU | Canada | YRE |
| Retallnuleu/Base Aerea Del Sur | Guatemala | RER |
| Rethymno | Greece | ZRE |
| Reus | Spain | REU |
| Reutlingen | Germany | ZPP |
| Revelstoke, BC | Canada | YRV |
| Rewa | India | REW |
| Reyes | Bolivia | REY |
| Reykholar | Iceland | RHA |
| Reykjavik Domestic | Iceland | RKV |
| Reykjavik Int'l | Iceland | KEF |
| Reynosa/Gen Lucio Blanco | Mexico | REX |
| Rheindahlen | Germany | GMY |
| Rheine/Bentlage | Germany | ZPQ |
| Rhinelander, WI | USA | RHI |

| | | |
|---|---|---|
| Rhodes/Diagoras/Paradisi | Greece | RHO |
| Ribeirao Preto/Leite Lopes | Brazil | RAO |
| Ribera Grande | Portugal | QEG |
| Riberalta/Gen Buech | Bolivia | RIB |
| Rice Lake, WI | USA | RIE |
| Richard Toll | Senegal | RDT |
| Richards Bay | S. Africa | RCB |
| Richfield/Reynolds, UT | USA | RIF |
| Richland, WA | USA | RLD |
| Richmond | Australia | RCM |
| Richmond Int'l, VA | USA | RIC |
| Richmond, IN | USA | RID |
| Richmond/Richmond VA Rail, VA | USA | ZRD |
| Rickenbacker, OH | USA | LCK |
| Riesa/RR Stn | Germany | ZRX |
| Rieti | Italy | QRT |
| Rifle, CO | USA | RIL |
| Riga/Int'l | Latvia | RIX |
| Rigolet, NF | Canada | YRG |
| Riihimäki | Finland | QVT |
| Rijelka | Croatia | RJK |
| Rimini/Miramare | Italy | RMI |
| Rimouski, QC | Canada | YXK |
| Rincon de los Sauces | Argentina | RDS |
| Ringi Cove | Solomon Is | RIN |
| Rio Aizucar | Panama | RIZ |
| Rio Branco/Pres. Medici | Brazil | RBR |
| Rio Claro | Brazil | QIQ |
| Rio Cuarto | Argentina | RCU |
| Rio De Janeiro Int'l | Brazil | GIG |
| Rio De Janeiro/S. Dumont | Brazil | SDU |
| Rio Do Sul | Brazil | QRU |
| Rio Dulce/Las Vegas | Guatemala | LCF |
| Rio Frio | Costa Rica | RFR |
| Rio Gallegos Int'l | Argentina | RGL |
| Rio Grande | Argentina | RGA |
| Rio Grande | Brazil | RIG |
| Rio Hondo | Argentina | RHD |
| Rio Mayo | Argentina | ROY |
| Rio Negrinho | Brazil | QNE |
| Rio Sidra | Panama | RSI |
| Rio Tigre | Panama | RIT |
| Rio Turbio | Argentina | RYO |
| Rio Verde | Brazil | RVD |
| Riohacha | Colombia | RCH |
| Rioja | Peru | RIJ |
| Riom | France | XRI |
| Rishin | Japan | RIS |
| Rivera | Uruguay | RVY |
| Rivercess | Liberia | RVC |
| Rivers Inlet, BC | Canada | YRN |
| Rivers, MB | Canada | YYI |
| Riverside / HP, CA | USA | JRD |
| Riverside, CA | USA | RAL |
| Riverside, CA | USA | RIR |
| Riverton, WY | USA | RIW |
| Riviere Au Tonnerre, QC | Canada | YTN |
| Riviere Du Loup, QC | Canada | YRI |
| Riviere-a-Pierre/RR Stn., QC | Canada | XRP |
| Riyadh/King Khaled Int'l | Saudi Arabia | RUH |
| Riyan Mulkalla | Yemen | RIY |
| Rize | East Timor | QRI |
| Roanne/Renaison | France | RNE |
| Roanoke Nexrad, VA | USA | FCX |
| Roanoke Rapids, NC | USA | RZZ |
| Roanoke, VA | USA | ROA |
| Roatan | Honduras | RTB |
| Roberlson | S. Africa | ROD |
| Roberval, QC | Canada | YRJ |
| Robinhood | Australia | ROH |
| Robins/AFB, GA | USA | WRB |
| Robinson River | Papua New Guinea | RNR |
| Robinson River | Australia | RRV |
| Robinvale | Australia | RBC |
| Robore | Bolivia | RBO |
| Roche Harbor, WA | USA | RCE |
| Rochefort/Saint Agnant | France | RCO |
| Rochester | UK | RCS |
| Rochester/Int'l, NY | USA | ROC |
| Rochester, IN | USA | RCR |
| Rochester, MN | USA | RST |
| Rochester/Municipal HP, MN | USA | JRC |
| Rochester/Rochester NY Rail | USA | ZTE |
| Rock Hill, SC | USA | RKH |
| Rock Sound/S Eleuthera | Bahamas | RSD |
| Rock Springs, WY | USA | RKS |

**Rockdale**/Coffield, TX ... USA .. RCK
**Rockford**, IL ... USA .. RFD
**Rockford**/Machesney, IL ... USA .. RMC
**Rockford**/Park & Ride Bus Svc., IL ... USA .. ZRF
**Rockford**/Van Galder Bus Terminal, IL ... USA .. ZRK
**Rockhampton** ... Australia .. ROK
**Rockhampton Downs** ... Australia .. RDA
**Rockland**, ME ... USA .. RKD
**Rockport**, TX ... USA .. RKP
**Rockwood**/Municipal, TN ... USA .. RKW
**Rocky Mount**, NC ... USA .. RWI
**Rocky Mountain** House, AB ... Canada .. YRM
**Rodez**/Marcillac ... France .. RDZ
**Rodriguesis** ... Mauritius .. RRG
**Rodriguez De** Men ... Peru .. RIM
**Roebourne** ... Australia .. RBU
**Roeddey** ... Norway ... ZXI
**Roervik** ... Norway .. ZXF
**Rogers**, AR ... USA .. ROG
**Rognan** ... Norway .. ZXM
**Roi Et** Arpt ... Thailand .. ROI
**Roissy-en-France** ... France .. QZV
**Rokeby** ... Australia .. RKY
**Rokot** ... Indonesia ... RKI
**Rolandia** ... Brazil .. QHC
**Rolla**/National, MO ... USA .. RLA
**Rolpa** ... Nepal .. RPA
**Roma** ... Australia .. RMA
**Roma**/Falcon State, TX ... USA ... FAL
**Rome**, GA ... USA . RMG
**Rome**, OR ... USA .. REO
**Rome**/Roma/Ciampino ... Italy ... CIA
**Rome**/Roma/Fiumicino ... Italy .. FCO
**Rondon** ... Colombia .. RON
**Rondonopolis** ... Brazil .. ROO
**Rongelap Is** ... Marshall Is .. RNP
**Ronneby**/Kallinge ... Sweden .. RNB
**Roosendaal**/RR Stn. ... Netherlands .. ZYO
**Roosevelt**, UT ... USA .. ROL
**Roosevelt**/NAS ... Puerto Rico .. NRR
**Roper Bar** ... Australia .. RPB
**Roper Valley** ... Australia .. RPV
**Rorschach** ... Switzerland ... ZJZ
**Rosario**/Fisherton ... Argentina .. ROS
**Rosario**/SPB, AK ... USA .. RSJ
**Roseau**/Municipal, MN ... USA .. ROX
**Roseburg**, OR ... USA .. RBG
**Roseires**, SD ... USA .. RSS
**Rosella Plains** ... Australia .. RLP
**Rosenheim** ... Germany .. ZPR
**Rosh Pina** ... Israel .. RPN
**Rosita** ... Netherlands .. RFS
**Ross River**, YT ... Canada .. XRR
**Rost**/Stollport ... Norway .. RET
**Rostock**-Laage/Laane ... Germany .. RLG
**Rostov** ... Russia .. ROV
**Roswell**, NM ... USA . ROW
**Rota** ... Northern Mariana Is .. ROP
**Rothenburg**/Off-line Pt ... Germany .. QTK
**Rothesay**/HP ... UK .. RAY
**Roti** ... Indonesia ... RTI
**Rotorua** ... New Zealand .. ROT
**Rotterdam**/Central Stn. .. Netherlands .. QRH
**Rotterdam**/Zestienhoven ... Netherlands .. RTM
**Rottnest Is** ... Australia .. RTS
**Rotuma Is** ... Fiji .. RTA
**Rotunda**, FL ... USA .. RTD
**Roubaix** ... France .. XRX
**Rouen**/Boos ... France .. URO
**Round Lake**, ON ... Canada ... ZRJ
**Roundup**, MT ... USA .. RPX
**Rourkela** ... India .. RRK
**Rouses Point**, NY ... USA .. RSX
**Rousse** ... Bulgaria .. ROU
**Rouyn**, QC ... Canada .. YUY
**Rovaniemi** ... Finland .. RVN
**Rovirio** ... Ukraine . RWN
**Rowan Bay**, AK ... USA .. RWB
**Roxas City** ... Philippines .. RXS
**Roy Hill** ... Australia .. RHL
**Royan**/Medis ... France .. RYN
**Rubelsanto** ... Guatemala .. RUV
**Ruby**, AK ... USA .. RBY
**Ruedesheim**/Off-line Pt. ... Germany .. QSY
**Ruesselsheim** ... Germany .. ZPS
**Rugao** ... China .. RUG
**Rugby**/RR Stn. ... UK .. XRU
**Rugeley** T.V./RR Stn. ... UK .. XRG
**Ruhengeri** ... Rwanda . RHG
**Ruidoso**/Municipal, NM ... USA .. RUI
**Rukumkot** ... Nepal .. RUK
**Rum Cay** ... Bahamas .. RCY
**Rumjatar** ... Nepal . RUM
**Runcom**/RR Stn. ... UK .. XRC
**Rundu** ... Namibia .. NDU
**Rupsi** ... India .. RUP
**Rurrenabaque** ... Bolivia .. RBQ
**Rurriginae** ... Papua New Guinea . RMN
**Rurutu** ... F. Polynesia .. RUR
**Russell**, KS ... USA .. RSL
**Russellville**/Municipal, AR ... USA .. RUE
**Russian**/SPB, AK ... USA .. RSH
**Ruston**, LA ... USA .. RSN
**Ruteng** ... Indonesia .. RTG
**Ruti** ... Papua New Guinea .. RUU
**Rutland Plains** ... Australia .. RTP
**Rutland**, VT ... USA .. RUT
**Ryazan** ... Russia .. RZN
**Rybirisk** ... Russia .. RYB
**Ryotsu Sado** Is. ... Japan .. SDO
**Rzeszow**/Jasionka ... Poland .. RZE

# S

**S.Cristobal del- Casas**/San Cristobal Arpt. ... Mexico .. SZT
**Saa Sebastiao Do Cai** ... Brazil .. QHF
**Saarbruecken**/Ensheim .. Germany .. SCN
**Saarbruecken**/HBF RR. .. Germany .. QFZ
**Saarloq** ... Greenland . QOQ
**Saarlouis** ... Germany .. ZPT
**Saarmelleek**/Srmhk/Btn. ... Hungary .. SOB
**Saas Fee** ... Switzerland ... ZKI
**Saba Is** ... Netherlands Antilles .. SAB
**Sabadell** ... Spain .. QSA
**Sabah** ... Papua New Guinea .. SBV
**Sabana De Mar** ... Dominican Rep .. SNX
**Sabana De Torres** ... Colombia .. SNT
**Sabang**/Cut Bau ... Indonesia .. SBG
**Sabi Sabi** ... S. Africa .. GSS
**Sabiha Gokcen** ... Turkey . SAW
**Sabine Pass**, TX ... USA .. RPE
**Sable Is**, NS ... Canada .. YSA
**Sabre-Tech**, FL ... USA .. ZFS
**Sac Bernardo Do Campo** ... Brazil .. QSB
**Sac Borja** ... Brazil .. QOJ
**Sac Carlos** ... Brazil .. QSC
**Sac Goncad** ... Brazil .. QSD
**Sac Goncalo Amarante** ... Brazil .. QTE
**Sac Lourenco** ... Brazil .. SSO
**Sachigo Lake**, ON ... Canada .. ZPB
**Sachs Harbour**, NT ... Canada .. YSY
**Sackville**/RR Stn., NB ... Canada .. XKV
**Sacramento Exec**, CA ... USA .. SAC
**Sacramento**, CA ... USA .. SMF
**Sadah** ... Yemen .. SYE
**Sado Shima** ... Japan .. SDS
**Saelby** ... Denmark .. QJS
**Saenz Pena** ... Argentina .. SZQ
**Safford**, AZ ... USA .. SAD
**Safi** ... Morocco ... SFI
**Safia** ... Papua New Guinea .. SFU
**Saga** ... Japan .. HSG
**Sagarai** ... Papua New Guinea .. SGJ
**Saginaw Bay**, AK ... USA . SGW
**Saglek**, NF ... Canada .. YSV
**Sagwon**, AK ... USA .. SAG
**Sahabat 16** ... Malaysia .. SXS
**Sahiwal** ... Pakistan . SWN
**Saibai Is** ... Australia .. SBR
**Saida** ... Algeria .. QDZ
**Saidor** ... Papua New Guinea ... SDI
**Saidpur** ... Bangladesh .. SPD
**Saidu Sharif** ... Pakistan .. SDT
**Saint Cloud**/HP, MN ... USA .. JSK
**Saint George**/Municipal, UT ... USA .. SGU
**Saint Hyacinthe**/RR Stn., QC ... Canada .. XIM
**Saint John**, NB ... Canada .. YSJ
**Saint Marys**, AK ... USA .. KSM
**Saint Tropez** / HP ... France .. JSZ
**Saint Tropez**/La Mole ... France .. LTT
**Saint Yan**/Charolais Bourgogne S ... France .. SYT
**Saint-Tropez**/Harbour ... France ... XPZ
**Sainte Marie** ... Madagascar .. SMS
**Saintes** ... France ... XST
**Saipan**/Int'l. ... Northern Mariana Is . SPN
**Saito** ... Uruguay ... STY
**Sakon Nakhon** ... Thailand .. SNO
**Sal**/Amilcar Cabrai Int'l ... Cape Verde Is .. SID
**Salamanca**/Matacan ... Spain .. SLM
**Salamo** ... Papua New Guinea . SAM
**Salatah** ... Oman ... SLL
**Saldanha Bay** ... S. Africa . SDB
**Sale** ... Australia ... SXE
**Salehard** ... Russia ... SLY
**Salem** ... India ... SXV
**Salem**, OR ... USA ... SLE
**Salem-Leckrone**, IL ... USA ... SLO
**Salerno** ... Italy .. QSR
**Salida**, CO ... USA .. SLT
**Salima** ... Malawi .. LMB
**Salina Cruz** ... Mexico .. SCX
**Salina**, KS ... USA ... SLN
**Salina**, UT ... USA .. SBO
**Salinas** ... Ecuador .. SNC
**Salinas**, CA ... USA .. SNS
**Salisbury**, MD ... USA ... SBY
**Salisbury**/RR Stn. ... UK .. XSR
**Salisbury**/Rowan County, NC .. USA .. SRW
**Sallanches** ... France .. XSN
**Salluit**, QC ... Canada .. YZG
**Salmon Arm**, BC ... Canada .. YSN
**Salmon**, AK ... USA .. SMN
**Salo** ... Finland .. QVD
**Salt Cay** ... Tonga ... SLX
**Salt Lake City**/Int'l, UT ... USA ... SLC
**Salta**/Gen Belgrano ... Argentina ... SLA
**Saltillo** ... Mexico .. SLW
**Salton City**, CA ... USA ... SAS
**Salvador**/Arpt Luis R. Magalhaes ... Brazil ... SSA
**Salzburg** ... Austria .. SZG
**Salzburg**/German Railway Svc ... Austria ... ZSB
**Salzgitter** ... Germany ... ZPU
**Salzwedel**/RR Stn. ... Germany .. ZSQ
**Sam Neua** ... Laos .. NEU
**Samara** ... Russia ... KUF
**Samarai Is**/China Straits Airstrip ... Papua New Guinea . SQT
**Samarinda**/Temindung ... Indonesia ... SRI
**Samarkand** ... Uzbekistan .. SKD
**Sambava** ... Madagascar .. SVB
**Sambu** ... Panama ... SAX
**Samchok** ... S. Korea .. SUK
**Samos** ... Greece ... SMI
**Sampit** ... Indonesia .. SMQ
**Samsun** ... Turkey ... SSX
**Samsun**/Carsamba ... Turkey ... SZF
**San Andres Is** ... Colombia ... ADZ
**San Andros** ... Bahamas ... SAQ
**San Angelo**, TX ... USA ... SJT
**San Antonio** ... Venezuela ... SVZ
**San Antonio**/Int'l, TX ... USA ... SAT
**San Antonio Nexrad**, TX ... USA .. EWX
**San Antonio Oeste** ... Argentina .. OES
**San Antonio**, TX ... USA ... SSF
**San Antonjo** ... Chile .. QTN
**San Bernardino**/Tri-City, CA ... USA ... SBT
**San Bias** ... Panama ... NBL
**San Borja**/Capitan G Q Guardia ... Bolivia ... SRJ
**San Carlos** ... Netherlands .. NCR
**San Carlos** DeBariloche/Int'l ... Argentina .. BRC
**San Carlos**, CA ... USA ... SQL
**San Clemente**/NAF, CA ... USA .. NUC
**San Cristobal** ... Venezuela ... SCI
**San Cristobal**/Arpt ... Ecuador .. SCY
**San Diego**/Int'l, CA ... USA .. SAN
**San Diego**, CA ... USA .. MYF
**San Diego-Gillespie**, CA ... USA ... SEE
**San Diego**/Brown Fld, CA ... USA .. SDM
**San Domino** Is. ... Italy .. TQR
**San Esteban** ... Honduras ... SET
**San Felipe** ... Mexico ... SFH
**San Felipe** ... Venezuela ... SNF
**San Felipe** ... Colombia .. SSD
**San Felix** ... Venezuela ... SFX
**San Fernando** ... Philippines ... SFE
**San Fernando De Apure** ... Venezuela ... SFD

AIRPORTS -2-

| Name | Location | Code |
|---|---|---|
| San Fernando, CA | USA | SFR |
| San Francisco/Int'l, CA | USA | SFO |
| San Francisco/China Basin HP, CA | USA | JCC |
| San Francisco/Embarcadero, CA | USA | EMB |
| San Ignacio | Mexico | SGM |
| San Ignacio De M. | Bolivia | SNM |
| San Ignacio De Velasco | Bolivia | SNG |
| San Ignacio/Matthew Spain | Belize | SQS |
| San Javier | Bolivia | SJV |
| San Joacluin | Bolivia | SJB |
| San Jose | Bolivia | SJS |
| San Jose Cabo/Los Cabos | Mexico | SJD |
| San Jose Del Gua | Colombia | SJE |
| San Jose/Int'l, CA | USA | SJC |
| San Jose, CA | USA | RHV |
| San Jose/Bus Svc, CA | USA | ZJO |
| San Jose/Juan Santamaria Int'l | Costa Rica | SJO |
| San Jose/Meguire Fld | Philippines | SJI |
| San Jose/Tobias Bolanos Intl | Costa Rica | SYQ |
| San Juan | Peru | SJA |
| San Juan | Dominican Rep. | SJM |
| San Juan | Argentina | UAQ |
| San Juan Aposento | Peru | APE |
| San Juan D Ur | Colombia | SJR |
| San Juan/Int'l, PR | USA | SJU |
| San Juan/Isla Grande | Puerto Rico | SIG |
| San Juan/SPB, AK | USA | WSJ |
| San Julian | Cuba | SNJ |
| San Julian | Argentina | ULA |
| San Luis | Argentina | LUQ |
| San Luis De Pale | Colombia | SQE |
| San Luis Obispo, CA | USA | SBP |
| San Luis Obispo/AAF, CA | USA | CSL |
| San Luis Rio Colorado | Mexico | UAC |
| San Lus Potosi | Mexico | SLP |
| San Marcos | Colombia | SRS |
| San Marino | San Marino | SAI |
| San Martin Del-os Andes | Argentina | CPC |
| San Matias | Bolivia | MQK |
| San Miguei/Roberts/AAF, CA | USA | SYL |
| San Miguel | Panama | NMG |
| San Nicolas Ban | Cuba | QSN |
| San Pabio | Spain | SPO |
| San Pedro | Belize | SPR |
| San Pedro | Côte D'Ivoire | SPY |
| San Pedro | Argentina | XPD |
| San Pedro de Alcantara /Bus Stn | Spain | ZRC |
| San Pedro Jagua | Colombia | SJG |
| San Pedro Sula/RMorales. | Honduras | SAP |
| San Pedro Uraba | Colombia | NPU |
| San Pedro/Catalina SPB, CA | USA | SPQ |
| San Quintin | Mexico | SNQ |
| San Rafael | Argentina | AFA |
| San Rafael HP, CA | USA | JSG |
| San Ramon | Bolivia | SRD |
| San Salvador | El Salvador | SAL |
| San Salvador | Bahamas | ZSA |
| San Salvador De | Venezuela | SVV |
| San Sebastian | Spain | EAS |
| San Tome/El Tigre | Venezuela | SOM |
| San Vicente | Colombia | SVI |
| San Vito | Costa Rica | TOO |
| Sana'a/Sana'a Int'l | Yemen | SAH |
| Sanana | Indonesia | SQN |
| Sanandaj | Iran | SDG |
| Sancti Spiritus | Cuba | USS |
| Sand Point/Municipal, AK | USA | SDP |
| Sandakan | Malaysia | SDK |
| Sandane/Anda | Norway | SDN |
| Sanday | UK | NDY |
| Sandcreek | Guyana | SDC |
| Sandnessjoen/Stokka | Norway | SSJ |
| Sandringham | Australia | SRM |
| Sandspit, BC | Canada | YZP |
| Sandstone | Australia | NDS |
| Sandusky/G. Sandusky, OH | USA | SKY |
| Sandwip | Bangladesh | SDW |
| Sandy Lake, ON | Canada | ZSJ |
| Sanfebagar | Nepal | FEB |
| Sanford, FL | USA | SFB |
| Sanford, ME | USA | SFM |
| Sangapi | Papua New Guinea | SGK |
| Sanggata | Indonesia | SGQ |
| Sangir | Indonesia | SAE |
| Sangley Point/NAF | Philippines | NSP |
| Sanikiluaq, NU | Canada | YSK |
| Sanliurfa | Turkey | SFQ |
| Sanoy River, AK | USA | KSR |
| Sans Souci, ON | Canada | YSI |
| Santa Ana | Solomon Is | NNB |
| Santa Ana | Colombia | SQB |
| Santa Ana / HP, CA | USA | DNT |
| Santa Ana, CA | USA | SNA |
| Santa Ana/Centerport HP, CA | USA | JOC |
| Santa Aria/Yacuma | Bolivia | SBL |
| Santa Barbara Ba | Venezuela | SBB |
| Santa Barbara Ed/L Dlcias | Venezuela | STB |
| Santa Barbara, CA | USA | SBA |
| Santa Barbara, CA | USA | SZN |
| Santa Carolina | Mozambique | NTC |
| Santa Catalina | Colombia | SCA |
| Santa Cecilia | Ecuador | WSE |
| Santa Clara | Cuba | SNU |
| Santa Clara/Bus Svc, CA | USA | ZSM |
| Santa Cruiz De La Palma | Spain | SPC |
| Santa Cruz | Argentina | RZA |
| Santa Cruz | Solomon Is | SCZ |
| Santa Cruz | Brazil | SNZ |
| Santa Cruz | Belize | STU |
| Santa Cruz Do Sul | Brazil | CSU |
| Santa Cruz Rio Pardo | Brazil | QNR |
| Santa Cruz/El Trompillo | Bolivia | SRZ |
| Santa Cruz/Guanacaste. | Costa Rica | SZC |
| Santa Cruz/Skypark, CA | USA | SRU |
| Santa Cruz/Viru Viru Int'l | Bolivia | VVI |
| Santa Eiena | Venezuela | SNV |
| Santa Fe | Argentina | SFN |
| Santa Fe | Panama | SFW |
| Santa Fe Do Sul | Brazil | SFV |
| Santa Fe, NM | USA | SAF |
| Santa Fe/Bus Stn, NM | USA | ZSH |
| Santa Isabel do Morro | Brazil | IDO |
| Santa Katarina/Mount Sinai | Egypt | SKV |
| Santa Maria | Colombia | SMC |
| Santa Maria | Peru | SMG |
| Santa Maria, CA | USA | SMX |
| Santa Maria/Base Aerea | Brazil | RIA |
| Santa Maria/Vila Do Porto | Portugal | SMA |
| Santa Marta/S. Bolivar | Colombia | SMR |
| Santa Monica, CA | USA | SMO |
| Santa Paula, CA | USA | SZP |
| Santa Rosa | Argentina | RSA |
| Santa Rosa | Brazil | SRA |
| Santa Rosa | Bolivia | SRB |
| Santa Rosa Copan | Honduras | SDH |
| Santa Rosa, CA | USA | STS |
| Santa Rosalia | Mexico | SRL |
| Santa Rosalia | Colombia | SSL |
| Santa Sanga | Philippines | SGS |
| Santa Teresa, NM | USA | EPZ |
| Santa Teresita | Argentina | SST |
| Santa Terezinha/Confresa | Brazil | STZ |
| Santa Vitoria/Do Palmar | Brazil | CTQ |
| Santa Ynez, CA | USA | SQA |
| Santana Do Araguaia | Brazil | CMP |
| Santana Ramos | Colombia | SRO |
| Santander | Spain | SDR |
| Santarem/Eduardo Gomes | Brazil | STM |
| Santiago | Panama | SYP |
| Santiago | Chile | ULC |
| Santiago | Brazil | XGO |
| Santiago De Compostela | Spain | SCQ |
| Santiago Del Estero | Argentina | SDE |
| Santiago/Antonio Maceo | Cuba | SCU |
| Santiago/Arturo M. Benitez | Chile | SCL |
| Santiago/Mun | Dominican Rep | STI |
| Santo Andre | Brazil | QSE |
| Santo Angelo/Sepe Tiaraju. | Brazil | GEL |
| Santo Antao | Cape Verde Is | NTO |
| Santo Domingo | Dominican Rep | SDQ |
| Santo Domingo | Venezuela | STD |
| Santo Domingo/Herrera | Dominican Rep | HEX |
| Santos | Brazil | SSZ |
| Sanya | China | SYX |
| Sao Caetano Do Sul | Brazil | QCX |
| Sao Fefix Do Xingu | Brazil | SXX |
| Sao Felix Do Araguaia | Brazil | SXO |
| Sao Filipe | Cape Verde Is | SFL |
| Sao Francisco | Brazil | QFS |
| Sao Gabriel/Da Cachoeira | Brazil | SJL |
| Sao Joao Del Rei | Brazil | QSJ |
| Sao Jorge Is | Portugal | SJZ |
| Sao Jose | Brazil | XOE |
| Sao Jose Dos Campos | Brazil | SJK |
| Sao Leopoldo | Brazil | QLL |
| Sao Lourenco Do Sul | Brazil | SQY |
| Sao Luiz/Mal. C. Machado | Brazil | SLZ |
| Sao Mateus | Brazil | SBJ |
| Sao Miguel Araguaia | Brazil | SQM |
| Sao Miguel Do Oeste | Brazil | SQX |
| Sao Nicolau/Prgca | Cape Verde Is | SNE |
| Sao Paud/Viracopos | Brazil | VCP |
| Sao Paulo/Congonhas | Brazil | CGH |
| Sao Paulo/Guarulhos Int'l | Brazil | GRU |
| Sao Tome Is. Sao Tome and Principe | | TMS |
| Sao Vicente/San Pedro | Cape Verde Is | VXE |
| Sap Jose Do Rio Preto | Brazil | SJP |
| Sapmanga | Papua New Guinea | SMH |
| Saposcia | Peru | SQU |
| Sapporo/Chitose | Japan | CTS |
| Sapporo/Okadarna | Japan | OKD |
| Saqani | Fiji | AQS |
| Saqqaq | Greenland | QUP |
| Sara | Vanuatu | SSR |
| Saraievo/Butmir | Bosnia Hercegovina | SJJ |
| Sarakhs | Iran | CKT |
| Saranac Lake, NY | USA | SLK |
| Saransk | Russia | SKX |
| Sarasota, FL | USA | SRQ |
| Saratoga/Shively, WY | USA | SAA |
| Saratov | Russia | RTW |
| Saravane | Laos | VNA |
| Saravena | Colombia | RVE |
| Sardeh Band | Afghanistan | SBF |
| Sargans | Switzerland | ZKA |
| Sargodha/Bhagatanwala | Pakistan | BHW |
| Sargodha/Sargodha Arpt | Pakistan | SGI |
| Sarh | Chad | SRH |
| Sarichef, AK | USA | WSF |
| Sarlat/Domme | France | XSL |
| Sarmi | Indonesia | ZRM |
| Sarnburu | Kenya | UAS |
| Sarnen | Switzerland | ZKC |
| Sarnia, ON | Canada | YZR |
| Sarnia/RR Stn., ON | Canada | XDX |
| Sartaneja | Belize | SJX |
| Sary/Dashte Naz | Iran | SRY |
| Saskatoon, SK | Canada | YXE |
| Sassan | Italy | QSS |
| Sassandra | Côte D'Ivoire | ZSS |
| Sassnitz/RR Stn. | Germany | ZSI |
| Sasstown | Liberia | SAZ |
| Satna | India | TNI |
| Sato Bento Do Sul | Brazil | QHE |
| Satu Mare | Romania | SUJ |
| Satwag | Papua New Guinea | SWG |
| Saudarkrokur/Comalapa Int'l | Iceland | SAK |
| Saufley/NAS, FL | USA | NUN |
| Saul | F. Guiana | XAU |
| Sault Ste Marie, MI | USA | CIU |
| Sault Ste Marie, ON | Canada | YAM |
| Sault Ste Marie/Kincheloe/AFB, MI | USA | INR |
| Saumlaki | Indonesia | SXK |
| Saumur | France | XSU |
| Sauren | Papua New Guinea | SXW |
| Saurimo | Angola | VHC |
| Sausalito/HP, CA | USA | JMC |
| Savannah Int'l, GA | USA | SAV |
| Savannakhet | Laos | ZVK |
| Save | Benin | SVF |
| Savi Ragha | Pakistan | ZEO |
| Savo | Solomon Is | SVY |
| Savonlinna | Finland | SVL |
| Savoonga, AK | USA | SVA |
| Savusavu | Fiji | SVU |
| Savuti | Botswana | SVT |
| Sawu | Indonesia | SAU |
| Sayaboury | Laos | ZBY |
| Scammon Bay/SPB, AK | USA | SCM |
| Scampton/RAF Stn. | UK | SQZ |
| Scenic Flight | New Zealand | XXF |
| Schaffhausen | Switzerland | ZKJ |
| Schaumburg/Marriott HP, IL | USA | JMH |
| Schefferville, QC | Canada | YKL |
| Schenectady, NY | USA | SCH |
| Schenectady/Schenectady Rail, NY | USA | ZTD |
| Schieswig-Jagel | Germany | WBG |
| Schiphol | Netherlands | SPL |
| Schleswig | Germany | QWI |

| Location | Country | Code |
|---|---|---|
| Schoena/RR Stn. | Germany | ZSC |
| Schoenhagen | Germany | QXH |
| Schwaebisch Gmuend/Off-line Pt | Germany | ZPV |
| Schwanheide/RR Stn. | Germany | ZSD |
| Schweinfurt | Germany | ZPW |
| Schwerin/Parchim Arpt | Germany | SZW |
| Schwerin/RR Stn. | Germany | ZSR |
| Schwerte | Germany | ZPX |
| Schwyz | Switzerland | ZKK |
| Scone | Australia | NSO |
| Scott/AFB, IL | USA | BLV |
| Scottsbluff, Heilig Fld, NE | USA | BFF |
| Scottsdale/Bus Svc, AZ | USA | ZSY |
| Scranton, OH | USA | AVP |
| Scranton/Municipal, PA | USA | SCR |
| Scribner/State, NE | USA | SCB |
| Scusciuban | Somalia | CMS |
| Seal Bay, AK | USA | SYB |
| Searcy, AR. | USA | SRC |
| Seattle/Boeing Fld, WA | USA | BFI |
| Seattle, WA | USA | SEA |
| Sebba | Burkina Faso | XSE |
| Sebha | Libya | SEB |
| Secheit, BC | Canada | YHS |
| Seclin | France | XSX |
| Secunda | S. Africa | ZEC |
| Sedalia, MO. | USA | DMO |
| Sedan | France | XSW |
| Sedom/Min'hat Hashnayim | Israel | SED |
| Sedona, AZ | USA | SDX |
| Sedrata | Algeria | QDT |
| Seeheim | Germany | QSH |
| Sege | Sweden | EGM |
| Segou | Mali | SZU |
| Seguela | Côte D'Ivoire | SEO |
| Sehonghong | Lesotho | SHK |
| Sehuiea | Papua New Guinea | SXH |
| Sehwen Sharif. | Pakistan | SYW |
| Seinäjoki/Ilmajoki | Finland | SJY |
| Seiyun | Yemen | GXF |
| Sekakes | Lesotho | SKQ |
| Selawilk, AK | USA | WLK |
| Selbang | Papua New Guinea | SBC |
| Seldovia, AK | USA | SOV |
| Selebi-Phikwe | Botswana | PKW |
| Selestat | France | XSQ |
| Selibaby | Mauritania | SEY |
| Selinsgrove, PA. | USA | SEG |
| Selje/Harbour. | Norway | QFK |
| Selma/Selfield, AL | USA | SES |
| Semarang/Achmad Uani. | Indonesia | SRG |
| Sematan | Malaysia | BSE |
| Sembach | Germany | SEX |
| Semera/Semera Arpt | Ethiopia | SZE |
| Semipalatinsk | Kazakstan | PLX |
| Semongkong | Lesotho | SOK |
| Sena Madureira | Brazil | ZMD |
| Senanga | Zambia | SXG |
| Sendai | Japan | SDJ |
| Senggeh | Indonesia | SEH |
| Senggo | Indonesia | ZEG |
| Senhor Do Bonfirn | Brazil | SEI |
| Senipah | Indonesia | SZH |
| Senlis | France | XSV |
| Senneterre/RR Stn., QC | Canada | XFK |
| Seno | Laos | SND |
| Sens | France | XSF |
| Seo De Urgel/Aeroport De La Seu | Spain | LEU |
| Seoul/Kimp'O Int'l Arpt | S. Korea | SEL |
| Seoul/Seoul Air Base | S. Korea | SSN |
| Sepik Plains | Papua New Guinea | SPV |
| Sept-Iles, QC | Canada | YZV |
| Sepulot | Malaysia | SPE |
| Sequim/Valley Arpt, WA. | USA | SQV |
| Seronera | Tanzania | SEU |
| Serra Norte. | Brazil | RRN |
| Serra Pelada | Brazil | RSG |
| Serre Chevalier. | Eritrea | SEC |
| Serrporna | Malaysia | SMM |
| Sert | Libya | SRX |
| Serui/Yendosa | Indonesia | ZRI |
| Sesheke | Zambia | SJQ |
| Seshutes | Lesotho | SHZ |
| Sesnem | Namibia | SZM |
| Sete | France | XSY |
| Sete Lagoas. | Brazil | QHG |
| Setif | Algeria | QSF |
| Sette Cama | Gabon | ZKM |
| Setubal | Portugal | XSZ |
| Severac Le Chateau/RR Stn. | France | ZBH |
| Severodoneck | Ukraine | SEV |
| Sevilla. | Spain | SVQ |
| Sewanee/Franklin County, TN | USA | UOS |
| Seward, AK | USA | SWD |
| Seyclisfjordur | Iceland | SEJ |
| Seymour Johnson/AFB, NC. | USA | GSB |
| Seymour/Freeman Municipal, IN | USA | SER |
| Sfax/Sfax El Maou | Tunisia | SFA |
| Shageluk, AK | USA | SHX |
| Shahrkord | Iran | QHK |
| Shakawe | Botswana | SWX |
| Shakiso | Ethiopia | SKR |
| Shaktoolik, AK | USA | SKK |
| Shamattawa, MB | Canada | ZTM |
| Shamshernagar | Bangladesh | ZHM |
| Shanghai/Hongqiao | China | SHA |
| Shanghai/Pu Dong | China | PVG |
| Shangri-la, OK | USA | NRI |
| Shanhaiguan | China | SHF |
| Shannon | Ireland | SNN |
| Shannon Arpt, VA | USA | EZF |
| Shanshan | China | SXJ |
| Shantou | China | SWA |
| Shanzinou | China | SZO |
| Shaoguan | China | HSC |
| Sharjah Int'l. | UAE | SHJ |
| Shark El Oweinat | Egypt | GSQ |
| Sharm El Sheikh/Ophira. | Egypt | SSH |
| Sharurah | Saudi Arabia | SHW |
| Shashi | China | SHS |
| Shatter, CA. | USA | MIT |
| Shauliaj | Lithuania | HLJ |
| Shaw River | Australia | SWB |
| Shaw/AFB, SC | USA | SSC |
| Shawinigan/RR Stn., QC. | Canada | XFL |
| Shawnee/Municipal, OK. | USA | SNL |
| Shawnigan/RR Stn., BC | Canada | XFM |
| Shay Gap | Australia | SGP |
| Shearwater, BC | Canada | YSX |
| Shearwater, NS | Canada | YAW |
| Shebeen El Korn | Egypt | QUH |
| Sheboygan, WI. | USA | SBM |
| Sheep Mountain, ID | USA | SMU |
| Sheffield | UK | SZD |
| Sheffield/Bus Svc. | UK | ZFG |
| Sheghnan | Afghanistan | SGA |
| Shehdi | Ethiopia | SQJ |
| Shehr | Yemen | QER |
| Shelby, MT. | USA | SBX |
| Shelbyville/Bomar Fld, AK | USA | SYI |
| Sheldon Point/Sheldon SPB, AK | USA | SXP |
| Shelton, WA. | USA | SHN |
| Shemya/Shemya/AFB, AK. | USA | SYA |
| Shenyang | China | SHE |
| Shenzhen | China | SZX |
| Sheppard/AFB, TX | USA | SPS |
| Shepparton | Australia | SHT |
| Sherbrooke, QC. | Canada | YSC |
| Sheridan, WY | USA | SHR |
| Sherman-Denison, TX | USA | PNX |
| Sherman/AAF, KS. | USA | FLV |
| Shetland Is | UK | LSI |
| Shetland Is, Lerwick/Tingwall | UK | LWK |
| Shetland Iss/Scatsta | UK | SCS |
| Shijiazhuang/Daguocun | China | SJW |
| Shikarpur. | Pakistan | SWV |
| Shillavo | Ethiopia | HIL |
| Shillong | India | SHL |
| Shilo-YLP Mingan, MB. | Canada | YLO |
| Shimojishima | Japan | SHI |
| Shinyanga | Tanzania | SHY |
| Shirahama | Japan | SHM |
| Shiraz | Iran | SYZ |
| Shiringayoc | Peru | SYC |
| Shirley, Brookhaven Arpt, NY | USA | HWV |
| Shirley/Brookhaven, NY | USA | WSH |
| Shirrikent | Kazakstan | CIT |
| Shishmaref, AK | USA | SHH |
| Shizijoka City | Japan | QSZ |
| Shoal Cove, AK | USA | HCB |
| Sholapur | India | SSE |
| Shonai | Japan | SYO |
| Shoreham By Sea/Shoreham | UK | ESH |
| Show Low, AZ | USA | SOW |
| Shreveport, LA | USA | DTN |
| Shreveport, LA | USA | SHV |
| Shungnak, AK. | USA | SHG |
| Shute Harbour/HP. | Australia | JHQ |
| Sialkot | Pakistan | SKT |
| Sialum | Papua New Guinea | SXA |
| Siasi. | Philippines | SSV |
| Siassi | Papua New Guinea | SSS |
| Siauliai/Int'l | Lithuania | SQQ |
| Sibi | Pakistan | SBQ |
| Sibisa | Indonesia | SIW |
| Sibiti. | Colombia | SIB |
| Sibiu. | Romania | SBZ |
| Sibu. | Malaysia | SBW |
| Sicogon Is | Philippines | ICO |
| Sidi Barani | Egypt | SQK |
| Sidi Ifni | Morocco | SII |
| Sidney, NE | USA | SNY |
| Sidney, NY | USA | SXY |
| Sidney-Richland, MT | USA | SDY |
| Sidon | Lebanon | QSQ |
| Siegburg. | Germany | ZPY |
| Siegen/Segerland Arpt. | Germany | SGE |
| Siena | Italy | SAY |
| Siern Reap. | Cambodia | REP |
| Sierra Grande | Argentina | SGV |
| Sierra Leone | Sierra Leone | SRK |
| Sierre/Siders. | Switzerland | ZKO |
| Sig | Algeria | QIL |
| Siglufjordur | Iceland | SIJ |
| Sigonella/NAF | Italy | NSY |
| Siguanea | Cuba | SZJ |
| Siguin | Guinea | GII |
| Sihanoukville | Cambodia | KOS |
| Sikeston/Memorial, MO | USA | SIK |
| Sila | Papua New Guinea | SIL |
| Silchar/Kumbhirgram. | India | IXS |
| Silgadi Doti | Nepal | SIH |
| Silistra | Bulgaria | SLS |
| Silkeborg/RR Stn. | Denmark | XAH |
| Siloam Springs/Smith Fld, AR | USA | SLG |
| Silur | Papua New Guinea | SWR |
| Silva Bay, BC | Canada | SYF |
| Silver Bay, MN. | USA | BFW |
| Silver City, NM. | USA | SVC |
| Silver Creek. | Belize | SVK |
| Silver Plains | Australia | SSP |
| Sim | Papua New Guinea | SMJ |
| Simanggang | Malaysia | SGG |
| Simao | China | SYM |
| Simara | Nepal | SIF |
| Simbach | Germany | QIP |
| Simbas | Papua New Guinea | SIM |
| Simberi Is. | Papua New Guinea | NIS |
| Simenti | Senegal | SMY |
| Simferopol. | Ukraine | SIP |
| Simia | India | SLV |
| Simikot | Nepal | IMK |
| Sinalk | Indonesia | NKD |
| Sindal/Flyveplads. | Denmark | CNL |
| Sindelfingen/Off-line Pt | Germany | ZPZ |
| Sines | Portugal | SIE |
| Singapore | Singapore | SIN |
| Singapore/Paya Lebar | Seychelles | QPG |
| Singapore/Seletar | Singapore | XSP |
| Singaua. | Papua New Guinea | SGB |
| Singen | Germany | ZQA |
| Singkep/Dabo | Indonesia | SIQ |
| Singleton | Australia | SIX |
| Sinoe/AFC. | Liberia | XSA |
| Sinoe/R.E. Murray | Liberia | SNI |
| Sinop | Brazil | OPS |
| Sinop | Turkey | SQD |
| Sinop/Sinop Arpt | Turkey | SIC |
| Sintang | Indonesia | SQG |
| Siocon | Philippines | XSO |
| Sion | Switzerland | SIR |
| Sioux City, IA | USA | SUX |
| Sioux Falls, SD | USA | FSD |
| Sioux Lookout, ON | Canada | YXL |
| Sipitang | Malaysia | SPT |
| Siracusa | Italy | QIC |
| Sirajganj | Bangladesh | SAJ |
| Sirjan | Iran | SYJ |
| Sirri Is | Iran | SXI |
| Sishen | S. Africa | SIS |
| Sisimiut. | Greenland | JHS |
| Sissano | Papua New Guinea | SIZ |
| SITA | - | QEN |
| SITA | - | QES |
| SITA Aircom | - | QXS |
| SITA Network | - | QXN |
| SITA Network | - | QXT |
| Sitia | Greece | JSH |
| Sitiawan | Malaysia | SWY |

AIRPORTS -2-

| Airport | Country | Code |
|---|---|---|
| Sitka, AK | USA | SIT |
| Sitkinak Is/CGS, AK | USA | SKJ |
| Sittwe/Civil | Myanmar | AKY |
| Siuna | Netherlands | SIU |
| Sivas | Turkey | VAS |
| Siwa | Egypt | SEW |
| Siwea | Papua New Guinea | SWE |
| Sjaelland/RR Stn. | Denmark | ZIJ |
| Skagen/Limousine Svc. | Denmark | QJV |
| Skagway/Municipal, AK | USA | SGY |
| Skardu | Pakistan | KDU |
| Skasso | Mali | KSS |
| Skeldon | Guyana | SKM |
| Skelleftea | Sweden | SFT |
| Skiathos Is | Greece | JSI |
| Skien | Norway | SKE |
| Skikda | Algeria | SKI |
| Skiplane Scenic | New Zealand | XXS |
| Skiros | Greece | SKU |
| Skitube/Bus Svc | Australia | QTO |
| Skive/RR Stn. | Denmark | ZKN |
| Skive/Skive Arpt | Denmark | SQW |
| Skjerstad | Norway | ZXL |
| Skople | Macedonia | SKP |
| Skovde | Sweden | KVB |
| Skukuza | S. Africa | SZK |
| Skwentna/Intermediate, AK | USA | SKW |
| Slate Is, ON | Canada | YSS |
| Slave Lake, AB | Canada | YZH |
| Sleetmute, AK | USA | SLQ |
| Sliac | Slovakia | SLD |
| Sligo | Ireland | SXL |
| Sligo/Bus Stn. | Ireland | ZSL |
| Slirt | Turkey | SXZ |
| Slupsk/Recizikowo | Poland | OSP |
| Smara | Morocco | SMW |
| Smiggin Holes/Bus Svc | Australia | QZC |
| Smith Cove, AK | USA | SCJ |
| Smith Falls, ON | Canada | YSH |
| Smith Point | Australia | SHU |
| Smithers, BC | Canada | YYD |
| Smithfield/North Central, RI | USA | SFZ |
| Smithton | Australia | SIO |
| Smolensk | Russia | LNX |
| Smyrna, TN | USA | MQY |
| Snake Bay | Australia | SNB |
| Snake River, YT | Canada | YXF |
| Snare Lake, NT | Canada | YFJ |
| Snyder/Winston Fld, TX | USA | SNK |
| Soalaia | Madagascar | DWB |
| Sobral | Brazil | QBX |
| Soc Trang | Vietnam | SOA |
| Socorro, NM | USA | ONM |
| Socotra | Yemen | SCT |
| Sodankyla | Finland | SOT |
| Soddu | Ethiopia | SXU |
| Soderhamn | Sweden | SOO |
| Sodertalje/Sodertalje HP | Sweden | JSO |
| Soerfjord | Norway | ZXH |
| Soeroeya | Norway | QZS |
| Sofia | Bulgaria | SOF |
| Sogamoso | Colombia | SOX |
| Sogndal | Norway | SOG |
| Sohag | Egypt | QHX |
| Soienzara | France | SOZ |
| Soissons | France | XSS |
| Sokcho/Solak | S. Korea | SHO |
| Sokoto | Nigeria | SKO |
| Sola | Vanuatu | SLH |
| Solano | Colombia | SQF |
| Soldotna, AK | USA | SXQ |
| Solingen | Germany | ZQB |
| Solingen-Ohligs/RR Stn. | Germany | ZIO |
| Solita | Colombia | SOH |
| Solo City/Adi Surnarmo. | Indonesia | SOC |
| Solomon, AK | USA | SOL |
| Solothurn | Switzerland | ZKS |
| Solstad | Norway | ZXQ |
| Solwezi | Zambia | SLI |
| Somerset/Pulaski County, KY | USA | SME |
| Son-La/Na-San | Vietnam | SQH |
| Sonderborg | Denmark | QSG |
| Sonderborg/Lufthavn | Denmark | SGD |
| Songea | Tanzania | SGX |
| Songkhla | Thailand | SGZ |
| Sonneberg/RR Stn. | Germany | ZSG |
| Sophia Antipolis | France | SXD |
| Sopu | Papua New Guinea | SPH |
| Sora | Italy | QXE |
| Sorkjosen | Norway | SOJ |
| Soroako | Indonesia | SQR |
| Sorocaba | Brazil | SOD |
| Sorong/Jefman | Indonesia | SOQ |
| Soroti | Uganda | SRT |
| Sorrento | Italy | RRO |
| Souanke | Congo | SOE |
| Souda/Khania | Greece | CHQ |
| Souk Ahras | Algeria | QSK |
| Soure | Brazil | SFK |
| Sousse | Tunisia | QSO |
| South Andros | Bahamas | TZN |
| South Bend, IN | USA | SBN |
| South Caicos/Int'l. Turks & Caicos Is | | XSC |
| South Galway | Australia | ZGL |
| South Indian Lake, MB | Canada | XSI |
| South Lake Tahoe, CA | USA | TVL |
| South Molle Is | Australia | SOI |
| South Naknek, AK | USA | WSN |
| South Trout Lake, ON | Canada | ZFL |
| South West Bay | Vanuatu | SWJ |
| South Weymouth, MA | USA | NZW |
| Southampton | UK | SOU |
| Southend | UK | SEN |
| Southern Cross | Australia | SQC |
| Southern Pines/Pinehurst, NC. USA | | SOP |
| Southport | Australia | SHQ |
| Sovata | Romania | QSV |
| Soyo | Angola | SZA |
| Spangdahlem | Germany | SPM |
| Spanish Wells | Bahamas | SWL |
| Sparrevohn/AFS, AK | USA | SVW |
| Sparta | Greece | SPJ |
| Sparta/AAF, WI. | USA | CMY |
| Sparta/ComMunicipality, IL | USA | SAR |
| Spartanburg Memorial, SC. | USA | SPA |
| Spearfish, SD | USA | SPF |
| Spence Bay Arpt, NU. | Canada | YYH |
| Spencer, IA | USA | SPW |
| Spetsai Is | Gaudeloupe | JSS |
| Speyer | Germany | ZQC |
| Spiddal/Connemara | Ireland | NNR |
| Spirit Lake, IA | USA | RTL |
| Split | Croatia | SPU |
| Spokane/Int'l Arpt, WA | USA | GEG |
| Spokane, WA. | USA | SFF |
| Spora | Indonesia | RKO |
| Spring Creek | Australia | SCG |
| Spring Is, BC. | Canada | YSQ |
| Spring Point | Bahamas | AXP |
| Springbank, AB | Canada | YBW |
| Springbok | S. Africa | SBU |
| Springdale/Springdale Municipal, AR | USA | SPZ |
| Springfield, IL | USA | SPI |
| Springfield, MA RR | USA | ZSF |
| Springfield, MO | USA | SGF |
| Springfield, OH. | USA | SGH |
| Springfield, VT | USA | VSF |
| Springvale | Australia | KSV |
| Springvale | Australia | ZVG |
| Squamish, BC. | Canada | YSE |
| Squirrel Cove, BC | Canada | YSZ |
| Srinagar | India | SXR |
| St Andrews/Leuchars | UK | ADX |
| St Anthony, NF | Canada | YAY |
| St Anton | Austria | ANT |
| St Augustine, FL | USA | UST |
| St Barthelemy | Gaudeloupe | SBH |
| St Brieuc/Tremuson | Eritrea | SBK |
| St Catharines, ON | Canada | YCM |
| St Claude | France | XTC |
| St Cloud, MN | USA | STC |
| St Crepin | Eritrea | SCP |
| St Croix Is | Virgin Is (US) | STX |
| St Croix Is/Downtown HP | Virgin Is (US) | JCD |
| St Croix Is/SPB | Virgin Is (US) | SSB |
| St Denis de la Reunion. Reunion Is | | RUN |
| St Die | France | XCK |
| St Etienne/Boutheon | France | EBU |
| St Eustatius | Netherlands Antilles | EUX |
| St Francois | Gaudeloupe | SFC |
| St Gallen | Switzerland | QGL |
| St George | Australia | SGO |
| St George Is, AK. | USA | STG |
| St Georges de Loyapock F. Guiana | | OYP |
| St Gervais Le Fayet | France | XGF |
| St Gilles Croix De Vie | France | XGV |
| St Helens | Australia | HLS |
| St Jean De Luz | France | XJZ |
| St Jean, QC | Canada | YJN |
| St John Is | Virgin Is (US) | SJF |
| St Johns, AZ | USA | SJN |
| St Joseph, MO. | USA | STJ |
| St Kitts/Gldn Rck ..St. Kitts and Nevis | | SKB |
| St Laurent du Maroni | F. Guiana | LDX |
| St Leonard, NB | Canada | YSL |
| St Louis | France | XLI |
| St Louis | Senegal | XLS |
| St Louis Int'l, MO | USA | STL |
| St Louis, IL | USA | CPS |
| St Louis-Spirit Of St Louis, MO. | USA | SUS |
| St Louis/Rail Svc., MO | USA | ZSV |
| St Lucia/Hewanorra | St. Lucia | UVF |
| St Lucia/Vigie | St. Lucia | SLU |
| St Maarten/Princ. Juliana | Netherlands Antilles | SXM |
| St Malo | France | XSB |
| St Margrethen | Switzerland | ZKF |
| St Martin/Esperance | Gaudeloupe | SFG |
| St Martin/Grand Case | Gaudeloupe | CCE |
| St Marys, MD | USA | XSM |
| St Marys, PA. | USA | STQ |
| St Marys/RR Stn., ON | Canada | XI0 |
| St Michael, AK. | USA | SMK |
| St Moritz | Switzerland | ZKH |
| St Moritz/Samedan | Switzerland | SMV |
| St Nazaire/Montoir | France | SNR |
| St Omer | France | XSG |
| St Paul Is, AK. | USA | SNP |
| St Paul's Mission | Australia | SVM |
| St Paul, QC. | Canada | ZSP |
| St Paul-Downtown, MN | USA | STP |
| St Peter | Germany | PSH |
| St Petersburg, FL. | USA | SPG |
| St Petersburg/Clearwater Int'l, FL | USA | PIE |
| St Petersburg/Moscovskiy Railway Stn | Russia | ZLK |
| St Petersburg/Pulkovo. | Russia | LED |
| St Petersburg/Rzhevka | Russia | RVH |
| St Pierre .... St. Pierre and Miquelon | | FSP |
| St Pierre dela Reunion. Reunion Is | | ZSE |
| St Quentin | France | XSJ |
| St Quentin en Yvelines | France | XQY |
| St Raphael | France | XSK |
| St Thomas Is | Virgin Is (US) | STT |
| St Thomas/Pembroke Area, ON | Canada | YQS |
| St Thomas/SPB. | Virgin Is (US) | SPB |
| St Vincent/E-T. Joshua .St. Vincent & Grenadines | | SVD |
| St. Genis/Bus Svc | France | QXK |
| St. John's, NF | Canada | YYT |
| Stade | Germany | ZQD |
| Stafford/RR Stn. | UK | XVB |
| Stalowa Wola | Poland | QXQ |
| Staniel Cay | Bahamas | TYM |
| Stanthorpe | Australia | SNH |
| Stanton/Carleton, MN | USA | SYN |
| Stara Zagora | Bulgaria | SZR |
| Starcke | Australia | SQP |
| State College, PA | USA | SCE |
| State College, PA | USA | UNV |
| Statesboro/Municipal, GA | USA | TBR |
| Statesville/Municipal, NC | USA | SVH |
| Stauning/Lufthavn | Denmark | STA |
| Staunton, VA | USA | SHD |
| Stavanger/Sola | Norway | SVG |
| Stavropol | Russia | STW |
| Stawell | Australia | SWC |
| Ste Therese Point, MB | Canada | YST |
| Steamboat Bay/SPB, AK. | USA | WSB |
| Steamboat Springs, CO. | USA | SBS |
| Stebbins, AK. | USA | WBB |
| Steenkool | Indonesia | ZKL |
| Stella Maris/Estate Airstrip Bahamas. | | SML |
| Stendal/RR Stn. | Germany | ZSN |
| Stephen Is | Australia | STF |
| Stephenville, NF. | Canada | YJT |
| Stephenville, TX | USA | SEP |
| Sterling Rockfalls, IL | USA | SQI |
| Sterling/Crosson Fld, CO | USA | STK |
| Stevenage/RR Stn. | UK | XVJ |
| Stevens Point, WI | USA | STE |
| Stevens Village, AK. | USA | SVS |
| Stewart Is | New Zealand | SZS |
| Stewart, BC | Canada | ZST |
| Stillwater, OK. | USA | SWO |
| Stirling/RR Stn. | UK | XWB |
| Stockholm | Papua New Guinea | SMP |
| Stockholm/Arlanda | Sweden | ARN |
| Stockholm/Bromma | Sweden | BMA |

| | | |
|---|---|---|
| Stockholm/Skavsta | Sweden | NYO |
| Stockport/RR Stn. | UK | XVA |
| Stockton, CA | USA | SCK |
| Stoelmans Eiland | Suriname | SMZ |
| Stoke on Trent/RR Stn. | UK | XWH |
| Stokmarknes/Skagen | Norway | SKN |
| Stolberg | Germany | ZQE |
| Stony Rapids, SK | Canada | YSF |
| Stony River, AK | USA | SRV |
| Stord/Stord Arpt. | Norway | SRP |
| Storm Lake, IA | USA | SLB |
| Stornoway | UK | SYY |
| Storurnan/Gunnarn | Sweden | SQO |
| Stow, MA | USA | MMN |
| Stradbroke Is | Australia | SRR |
| Strahan | Australia | SRN |
| Straisund/RR Stn. | Germany | ZSX |
| Strasbourg/Bus Svc | France | XER |
| Strasbourg/Entzineim | France | SXB |
| Stratford/RR Stn., ON | Canada | XFD |
| Stratford/Sikorsky HP, CT | USA | JSD |
| Strathmore | Australia | STH |
| Strathroy/RR Stn., ON. | Canada | XTY |
| Straubing/Wallmuhle | Germany | RBM |
| Strausberg | Germany | QPK |
| Streaky Bay | Australia | KBY |
| Stronsay | UK | SOY |
| Stroud, OK | USA | SUD |
| Struer/Bus Svc | Denmark | QWQ |
| Struga | Macedonia | QXP |
| Strzhewoi | Russia | SWT |
| Stuart Is, BC | Canada | YRR |
| Stuart Is, WA. | USA | SSW |
| Stuart/Witham Fld, FL | USA | SUA |
| Stung Treng | Cambodia | TNX |
| Sturdee, BC. | Canada | YTC |
| Sturgeon Bay, WI | USA | SUE |
| Sturgis/Kirsch Municipal, MI | USA | IRS |
| Sturt Creek | Australia | SSK |
| Stuttgart, AR. | USA | SGT |
| Stuttgart/Echterdingen | | |
| | Germany | STR |
| Stuttgart/RR Stn. | Germany | ZWS |
| Stykkisholmur. | Iceland | SYK |
| Su Won City/Su Won Arpt | S. Korea | SWU |
| Sua pan | Botswana | SXN |
| Suabi | Papua New Guinea | SBE |
| Suai. | Indonesia | UAI |
| Suavanao Airstrip | Solomon Is. | VAO |
| Subic Bay/Int'l Airpt | Philippines | SFS |
| Suceava/Salcea | Romania | SCV |
| Sucre | Bolivia | SRE |
| Sucua | Ecuador | SUQ |
| Sudbury, ON. | Canada | YSB |
| Sudbury/Jet RR Stn., ON | Canada | XDY |
| Sudureyri | Iceland | SUY |
| Sue Is/Warraber Is | Australia | SYU |
| Suffield, AB. | Canada | YSD |
| Suhl/RR Stn. | Germany | ZSO |
| Sui | Pakistan | SUL |
| Suia-Missu | Brazil | SWM |
| Suiaco | Honduras | SCD |
| Sukhumi/Babusheri | Georgia | SUI |
| Suki | Papua New Guinea | SKC |
| Sukinothai | Thailand | THS |
| Sukkur | Pakistan | SKZ |
| Sulayel | Saudi Arabia | SLF |
| Sule. | Papua New Guinea | ULE |
| Sullivan Say, BC | Canada | YTG |
| Sullivan/County, IN. | USA | SIV |
| Sulmona | Italy | QLN |
| Sulphur Springs, TX | USA | SLR |
| Sulsted/Bus Svc | Denmark | QYQ |
| Sumbawa/Brang Bidji. | Indonesia | SWQ |
| Sumbawanga | Tanzania | SUT |
| Sumbe | Angola | NDD |
| Sumeneo/Trunojoyo. | Indonesia | SUP |
| Summer Beaver, ON | Canada | SUR |
| Summerside, PE. | Canada | YSU |
| Summit Lake, BC | Canada | IUM |
| Summit, AK. | USA | UMM |
| Sumy | Ukraine | UMY |
| Sun City/Pilansberg | S. Africa | NTY |
| Sun Moon Lake. | Taiwan | SMT |
| Sun River, OR | USA | SUO |
| Sunchon/Yosu | S. Korea | SYS |
| Sundance/Schloredt, WY | USA | SUC |
| Sundsvall | Sweden | SDL |
| Sungai Pakning | Indonesia | SEQ |
| SungeiTekai | Malaysia | GTK |
| Sunshine Coast/Maroochydore | | |

| | | |
|---|---|---|
| | Australia | MCY |
| Sunyani | Ghana | NYI |
| Superior/Richard 1 Bong, WI. | USA | SUW |
| Sur | Oman | SUH |
| Surabaya/Juanda | Indonesia | SUB |
| Surat | India | STV |
| Surat Thani | Thailand | URT |
| Surfdale | New Zealand | WIK |
| Surfers Paradise | Australia | SFP |
| Surgut. | Russia | SGC |
| Suria | Papua New Guinea | SUZ |
| Surigao. | Philippines | SUG |
| Surkhet. | Nepal | SKH |
| Surnter/Municipal, SC. | USA | SUM |
| Sursee | Switzerland | ZKU |
| Suru-Lere. | Nigeria | QSL |
| Susanville, CA | USA | SVE |
| Sussex, Sussex Arpt, NJ | USA | FWN |
| Suttonheath/Woodbridge/RAF. | UK | WOB |
| Suva/Nausori | Fiji | SUV |
| Suwalki | Poland | ZWK |
| Suzhou | China | SZV |
| Svalbard/Spitsberg | Norway | SYG |
| Svay Rieng | Cambodia | SVR |
| Sveg | Sweden | EVG |
| Svendborg/RR | Denmark | QXV |
| Svolvaer/Helle. | Norway | SVJ |
| Swakopmund | Namibia | SWP |
| Swakopmund/RR Stn. | Namibia | ZSZ |
| Swan Hill | Australia | SWH |
| Swan River, MB | Canada | ZJN |
| Swansea | UK | SWS |
| Sweetwater, TX | USA | SWW |
| Sweida | Syria | QSW |
| Swift Current, SK. | Canada | YYN |
| Swindon. | UK | SWI |
| Swindon/RR Stn. | UK | XWS |
| Syangboche | Nepal | SYH |
| Sydney | Australia | SYD |
| Sydney, NS | Canada | YQY |
| Sydney/Au-Rose Bay | Australia | RSE |
| Sydney/Palm Beach SPB. | Australia | LBH |
| Sydney/Sydney West | Australia | SWZ |
| SyklyvKar | Russia | SCW |
| Syllnet/Civil | Bangladesh | ZYL |
| Sylvester, GA | USA | SYV |
| Syracuse Int'l, NY. | USA | SYR |
| Syracuse/NY Rail, NY | USA | ZYQ |
| Syros Is | Greece | JSY |
| Szczecin/Goleniow | Poland | SZZ |
| Szeged | Hungary | QZD |
| Szombathely | Hungary | ZBX |
| Szymany/Mazury | Poland | SZY |

# T

| | | |
|---|---|---|
| Taabo | Côte D'Ivoire | TBX |
| Taba/Talba Int'l | Egypt | TCP |
| Tabal | Marshall Is | TBV |
| Tabarka/7 Novembre | Tunisia | TBJ |
| Tabas | Iran | TCX |
| Tabatinga/Int'l | Brazil | TBT |
| Tabibuga | Papua New Guinea | TBA |
| Tabiteuea North. | Kiribati | TBF |
| Tabiteuea South | Kiribati | TSU |
| Tablas | Philippines | TBH |
| Tableland | Australia | TBL |
| Tablon De Tamara | Colombia | TTM |
| Tabou | Côte D'Ivoire | TXU |
| Tabriz | Iran | TBZ |
| Tabuaeran | Kiribati | TNV |
| Tabubil | Papua New Guinea | TBG |
| Tabuk | Saudi Arabia | TUU |
| Tacheng | China | TCG |
| Tachilek | Myanmar | THL |
| Tacloban/D1. Romualdez | | |
| | Philippines | TAC |
| Tacna | Peru | TCQ |
| Tacoma-Narrows, WA | USA | TIW |
| Tacuarembo | Uruguay | TAW |
| Tadjoura. | Djibouti | TDJ |
| Tadoule Lake, MB | Canada | XTL |
| Taedok | S. Korea | QET |
| Taegu/Air Base. | S. Korea | TAE |
| Taejon | S. Korea | QTW |
| Taftan | Pakistan | TFT |
| Tagbilaran | Philippines | TAG |
| Tagloita. | Philippines | TGB |

| | | |
|---|---|---|
| Taguatinga | Brazil | QHN |
| Tagula | Papua New Guinea | TGL |
| Taharoa. | New Zealand | THH |
| Taher | Algeria | ZZT |
| Tahneta Pass Lodge, AK | USA | HNE |
| Tahoua | Niger | THZ |
| Tahsis, BC. | Canada | ZTS |
| Taichung | Taiwan | TXG |
| Taif | Saudi Arabia | TIF |
| Taiknafjordur | Iceland | TLK |
| Tainan | Taiwan | TNN |
| Taipei/Chiang Kai Shek | Taiwan | TPE |
| Taipei/Sung Shan. | Taiwan | TSA |
| Taiping | Malaysia | TPG |
| Taisha | Ecuador | TSC |
| Taitung | Taiwan | TTT |
| Taiyuan | China | TYN |
| Taiz/AlJanad | Yemen | TAI |
| Tak | Thailand | TKT |
| Takalka | New Zealand | KTF |
| Takamatsu | Japan | TAK |
| Takapoto | F. Polynesia | TKP |
| Takaroa | F. Polynesia | TKX |
| Takhli | Thailand | TKH |
| Takoradi | Ghana | TKD |
| Takotna, AK | USA | TCT |
| Taku Lodge/Taku SPB, AK | USA | TKL |
| Takume | F. Polynesia | TJN |
| Talara | Peru | TYL |
| Talasea | Papua New Guinea | TLW |
| Talavera de la Reina | Spain | QWT |
| Talbora | Tanzania | TBO |
| Talca | Chile | TLX |
| Taldy-Kurgan | Kazakstan. | TDK |
| Taliabu | Indonesia | TAX |
| Talkeetna, AK. | USA | TKA |
| Talladega, AL. | USA | ASN |
| Tallahassee, FL | USA | TLH |
| Tallinn/Pirita Harbour | Estonia. | QUF |
| Tallinn/Ulemiste | Estonia. | TLL |
| Taltal | Chile. | TTC |
| Taltheilei Narrows, NT | Canada. | GSL |
| Taluqan | Afghanistan. | TQN |
| Tamale. | Ghana. | TML |
| Taman Negara | Malaysia. | SXT |
| Tamana Is. | Kiribati. | TMN |
| Tamanrasset/Aguemar. | Algeria. | TMR |
| Tamarindo | Costa Rica | TNO |
| Tamatave | Madagascar. | TMM |
| Tambacounda | Senegal. | TUD |
| Tambao | Burkina Faso | TMQ |
| Tambolaka | Indonesia. | TMC |
| Tambor | Costa Rica | TMU |
| Tambov | Russia. | TBW |
| Tamchakett | Mauritania. | THT |
| Tame | Colombia. | TME |
| Tampa Bay/Exec., FL | USA. | RRF |
| Tampa/Int'l, FL. | USA. | TPA |
| Tampa/Peter O'Knight, FL | USA. | TPF |
| Tampa/Topp Of Tampa, FL | USA. | KYO |
| Tampere/Pirkkala | Finland. | TMP |
| Tampico/Gen F Javier Mina. | Mexico. | TAM |
| Tamworth | Australia. | TMW |
| Tan Tan | Morocco. | TTA |
| Tana | Norway. | QTP |
| Tana Toraja | Indonesia. | TTR |
| Tanacross/Intermediate, AK. | USA. | TSG |
| Tanah Grogot | Indonesia. | TNB |
| Tanah Merah/Tanah Merah | | |
| | Indonesia. | TMH |
| Tanalian Point, AK | USA. | TPO |
| Tanana, AK | USA. | TAL |
| Tanandava | Madagascar. | TDV |
| Tanbar | Australia. | TXR |
| Tanda Tula | S. Africa | TDT |
| Tandag | Philippines. | TDG |
| Tandil | Argentina. | TDL |
| Tanegashima | Japan. | TNE |
| Tanga | Tanzania. | TGT |
| Tangalooma | Australia. | TAN |
| Tangara da Serra | Brazil. | TGQ |
| Tangier/Boukhalef | Morocco. | TNG |
| Tanjung Balai | Indonesia. | TJB |
| Tanjung Pandan/Bulutumbang | | |
| | Indonesia. | TJQ |
| Tanjung Pinang/Kidjang | Indonesia. | TNJ |
| Tanjung Santan | Indonesia. | TSX |
| Tanjung Selor | Indonesia. | TJS |
| Tanjung Warukin | Indonesia. | TJG |
| Tanna | Vanuatu. | TAH |
| Tanta | Egypt. | QTT |

**AIRPORTS-2-**

| Airport | Country | Code |
|---|---|---|
| Taos, NM | USA | TSM |
| Tapachula Int'l | Mexico | TAP |
| Tapaktuan | Indonesia | TPK |
| Tapeta | Iran | TPT |
| Tapiejung | Nepal | TPJ |
| Tapini | Papua New Guinea | TPI |
| Tara | Australia | XTR |
| Tarabo | Papua New Guinea | TBQ |
| Tarakan | Indonesia | TRK |
| Tarakbits | Papua New Guinea | TRJ |
| Taramaprina/Tarama | Japan | TRA |
| Taranto/M. A. Grottag | Italy | TAR |
| Tarapaca | Colombia | TCD |
| Tarapaina | Solomon Is | TAA |
| Tarapoa | Ecuador | TPC |
| Tarapoto | Peru | TPP |
| Tarauaca | Brazil | TRQ |
| Tarawa/Bonriki | Kiribati | TRW |
| Tarbela | Pakistan | TLB |
| Tarbes/Laloubere | France | XTB |
| Tarcoola | Australia | TAQ |
| Taree | Australia | TRO |
| Targovishte | Bulgaria | TGV |
| Tari | Papua New Guinea | TIZ |
| Tarija | Bolivia | TJA |
| Tarlaya | Morocco | TFY |
| Tarnbohorano | Madagascar | WTA |
| Tarnky | Vietnam | TMK |
| Tarnobrzeg | Poland | QEP |
| Tarnuin | Myanmar | TSL |
| Taroom | Australia | XTO |
| Tarragona | Spain | QGN |
| Tartagal | Argentina | TTG |
| Tartous | Syria | QTR |
| Tartu/Raadi | Estonia | TAY |
| Taschereau/RR Stn., QC | Canada | XFO |
| Tashauz | Turkmenistan | TAZ |
| Tashkent | Uzbekistan | TAS |
| Tasiilaq | Greenland | AGM |
| Tasikmalaya/Cibeureum | Indonesia | TSY |
| Tasiuasaq/Harbour | Greenland | XEQ |
| Tasiujuaq, QC | Canada | YTQ |
| Taskul | Papua New Guinea | TSK |
| Tasu, BC | Canada | YTU |
| Tatakoto | F. Polynesia | TKV |
| Tatalina/Tatalina AFS, AK | USA | TLJ |
| Tatitlek, AK | USA | TEK |
| Tatry/Poprad | Slovakia | TAT |
| Tau | American Samoa | TAV |
| Taubate | Brazil | QHP |
| Taupo | New Zealand | TUO |
| Tauramena | Colombia | TAU |
| Tauranga | New Zealand | TRG |
| Tauta | Papua New Guinea | TUT |
| Taveuni/Matei | Fiji | TVU |
| Tawa | Papua New Guinea | TWY |
| Tawau | Malaysia | TWU |
| Tawitawi | Philippines | TWT |
| Taylor, AK | USA | TWE |
| Taylor, AZ | USA | TYZ |
| Tbessa | Algeria | TEE |
| Tbilisi/Novo Alexeyevka | Georgia | TBS |
| Tchien | Liberia | THC |
| Te Anau/Manapouri | New Zealand | TEU |
| Te ixeira de Freitas | Brazil | TXF |
| Teesside | UK | MME |
| Tegucigalpa/Toncontin | Honduras | TGU |
| Tehachapi/Kern County, CA | USA | TSP |
| Tehibanga | Gabon | TCH |
| Tehran-Mehrabad | Iran | THR |
| Tehuacan | Mexico | TCN |
| Tekadu | Papua New Guinea | TKB |
| Tekamah, Tekamah Municipal Arpt, NE | USA | TQE |
| Tekin | Papua New Guinea | TKW |
| TeKirdag/Corlu | Turkey | TEQ |
| Tel Aviv Yafo/Sde Dov | Israel | SDV |
| Tel Aviv-Ben Gurion Int'l | Israel | TLV |
| Tela | Honduras | TEA |
| Telefornin | Papua New Guinea | TFM |
| Telegraph Creek, BC | Canada | YTX |
| Telegraph Harbour, BC | Canada | YBQ |
| Telemaco Borba | Brazil | TEC |
| Telida, AK | USA | TLF |
| Teller | Australia | TEF |
| Teller Mission, Brevig Mission, AK | USA | KTS |
| Teller, AK | USA | TLA |
| Telluride, CO | USA | TEX |
| Telluride/Bus Stn, CO | USA | ZTL |
| Telupid | Malaysia | TEL |
| Tembagapura/Timika | Indonesia | TIM |
| Temora | Australia | TEM |
| Temple/Draughon-Miller, TX | USA | TPL |
| Temuco | Chile | ZCO |
| Tenakee Springs/Tenakee SPB, AK | USA | TKE |
| Tenerife | Spain | TFN |
| Tenerife Sur | Spain | TFS |
| Tengah | Singapore | TGA |
| Teniente R. Marsh | Antarctica | TNM |
| Tenkodogo | Burkina Faso | TEG |
| Tennant Creek | Australia | TCA |
| Teofilo Otoni | Brazil | TFL |
| Tepic | Mexico | TPQ |
| Teptelp | Papua New Guinea | TEP |
| Teraina | Kiribati | TNQ |
| Teramo | Italy | QEA |
| Terapo | Papua New Guinea | TEO |
| Terceira Is/Laies | Portugal | TER |
| Teresina | Brazil | THE |
| Terezopolis | Brazil | QHT |
| Termez | Uzbekistan | TMJ |
| Termini Imere | Italy | QTI |
| Ternate/Babullah | Indonesia | TTE |
| Terninabuan | Indonesia | TXM |
| Ternopol | Laos | TNL |
| Terrace Bay | Namibia | TCY |
| Terrace Bay, ON | Canada | YTJ |
| Terrace, BC | Canada | YXT |
| Terre Haute, IN | USA | HUF |
| Terre-de-Bas | Gaudeloupe | HTB |
| Terre-de-Haut | Gaudeloupe | LSS |
| Terrell, TX | USA | TRL |
| Tervakoski | Finland | QVS |
| Teslin, YT | Canada | YZW |
| Tessenei | Eritrea | TES |
| Tetabedi | Papua New Guinea | TDB |
| Tete | Mozambique | TCV |
| Tete | Brazil | TFF |
| Tete-a-La Baleine, QC | Canada | ZTB |
| Tete/Matunda | Mozambique | TET |
| Teterboro, NJ | USA | TEB |
| Tetiaroa Is | F. Polynesia | TTI |
| Tetlin, AK | USA | TEH |
| Tetuan/Sania Ramel | Morocco | TTU |
| Tewantin | Australia | TWN |
| Texarkana, AR | USA | TXK |
| Tezpur/Salonibari | India | TEZ |
| Tezu | India | TEI |
| Thaba Nchu | S. Africa | TCU |
| Thakhek | Laos | THK |
| Thakurgaon | Bangladesh | TKR |
| Thalba-Tselka | Lesotho | THB |
| Thalwil | Switzerland | ZKV |
| Thames | New Zealand | TMZ |
| Thandwe | Myanmar | SNW |
| Thangool | Australia | THG |
| Thanjavur | India | TJV |
| Thargomindah | Australia | XTG |
| The Bight | Bahamas | TBI |
| The Dalles, OR | USA | DLS |
| The Hague/Holland Spoor RR Stn. | Netherlands | ZYH |
| The Pas, MB | Canada | YQD |
| The Pas/RR Stn., MB | Canada | XDZ |
| Thecia/Thecia Stn | Australia | TDN |
| Theodore | Australia | TDR |
| Thermopolis/Hot Springs, WY | USA | THP |
| Thessaloniki/Makedonia | Greece | SKG |
| Thicket Portage, MB | Canada | YTD |
| Thief River Falls/Regional, MN | USA | TVF |
| Thimbu | Bhutan | QJC |
| Thingeyn | Iceland | TEY |
| Thionvifle | France | XTH |
| Thira | Greece | JTR |
| Thirsk/RR Stn. | UK | XTK |
| Thisted/Lufthavn | Denmark | TED |
| Thohoyandou | S. Africa | THY |
| Thompson, MB | Canada | YTH |
| Thompsonfield, MO | USA | THM |
| Thonon Les Bains | France | XTS |
| Thornasville/Municipal, GA | USA | TVI |
| Thorne Bay, AK | USA | KTB |
| Thorshofn | Iceland | THO |
| Thousand Oaks / HP, CA | USA | JTO |
| Thredbo/Bus Svc | Australia | QTH |
| Three Rivers/Dr Haines, MI | USA | HAI |
| Thun | Switzerland | ZTK |
| Thunder Bay, ON | Canada | YQT |
| Thurnrait | Oman | TTH |
| Thursday Is | Australia | TIS |
| Thylungra | Australia | TYG |
| Tiaret | Algeria | TID |
| Tiarijin | China | TSN |
| Tibooburra | Australia | TYB |
| Tibu | Colombia | TIB |
| Ticantiki | Panama | TJC |
| Tichitt | Mauritania | THI |
| Tidjikia | Mauritania | TIY |
| Tifton/Henry Tift Myers, GA | USA | TMA |
| Tiga | New Caledonia | TGJ |
| Tignes | France | TGF |
| Tijuana/Rodriguez | Mexico | TIJ |
| Tikal/El Peten | Guatemala | TKM |
| Tikapur | Nepal | TPU |
| Tikchik/SPB, AK | USA | KTH |
| Tikehau Atoll | F. Polynesia | TIH |
| Tiko | Cameroon | TKC |
| Tiksi | Russia | IKS |
| Tilfalmin | Papua New Guinea | TFA |
| Tilin | Myanmar | TIO |
| Timaru | New Zealand | TIU |
| Timbauba | Brazil | QTD |
| Timbedra | Mauritania | TMD |
| Timber Creek | Australia | TBK |
| Timbiqui | Colombia | TBD |
| Timbo/Off-Line Point | Brazil | XHR |
| Timbunke | Papua New Guinea | TBE |
| Timimoun | Algeria | TMX |
| Timisoara | Romania | TSR |
| Timmins, ON | Canada | YTS |
| Tin City/AFS, AK | USA | TNC |
| Tinak Is | Marshall Is | TIC |
| Tinboli Arpt | Papua New Guinea | TCK |
| Tindouf | Algeria | TIN |
| Tinge Maria | Peru | TGI |
| Tingrela | Côte D'Ivoire | TGX |
| Tingwon | Papua New Guinea | TIG |
| Tinian | Northern Mariana Is | TIQ |
| Tinker/AFB, OK | USA | TIK |
| Tioga/Municipal, ND | USA | VEX |
| Tiom | Indonesia | TMY |
| Tioman | Malaysia | TOD |
| Tippi | Ethiopia | TIE |
| Tipton/AAF, MD | USA | FME |
| Tiputini | Ecuador | TPN |
| Tirana/Rinas | Albania | TIA |
| Tiree | UK | TRE |
| Tirgu Mures | Romania | TGM |
| Tirinkot | Afghanistan | TII |
| Tiruchirapally/Civil | India | TRZ |
| Tirupati | India | TIR |
| Tisdale, SK | Canada | YTT |
| Titusville, FL | USA | TIX |
| Tivat | Yugoslavia | TIV |
| Tizi Ouzou | Algeria | QZI |
| Tizimin | Mexico | TZM |
| Tlemcen/Zenata | Algeria | TLM |
| Tlokoeng | Lesotho | TKO |
| Tobago | Trinidad and Tobago | TAB |
| Tobermorey | Australia | TYP |
| Tobolsk | Russia | TOX |
| Tobruk | Libya | TOB |
| Toccoa, GA | USA | TOC |
| Tocoa | Honduras | TCF |
| Tocopilla/Barriles | Chile | TOQ |
| Tocurnwal | Australia | TCW |
| Tofino, BC | Canada | YAZ |
| Tofino/Seaplane Base, BC | Canada | YTP |
| Togiak Fish, AK | USA | GFB |
| Togiak Village, AK | USA | TOG |
| Tokarna | Papua New Guinea | ITK |
| Tokat | Turkey | TJK |
| Tokeen, AK | USA | TKI |
| Tokoroa | New Zealand | TKZ |
| Tokunoshima | Japan | TKN |
| Tokushima AB | Japan | TKS |
| Tokyo | Japan | QXO |
| Tokyo/Haneda | Japan | HND |
| Tokyo/Narita | Japan | NRT |
| Tokyo/Yokota AFB | Japan | OKO |
| Tol | Papua New Guinea | TLO |
| Toledo | Brazil | TOW |
| Toledo, OH | USA | TDZ |
| Toledo, OH | USA | TOL |
| Toledo, WA | USA | TDO |
| Tolitoli/Lalos | Indonesia | TLI |
| Tolu | Colombia | TLU |
| Toluca | Mexico | TLC |
| Tom Price | Australia | TPR |
| Tomakomaj | Japan | QTM |
| Tomanggong | Malaysia | TMG |

| | | |
|---|---|---|
| Tombouctou ................ Mali . . TOM | Trombetas ................. Brazil . . TMT | Tuy Hoa .................. Vietnam. . . TBB |
| Toms River/Robert J Miller, NJ. .USA . . MJX | Tromso/Langnes ........... Norway . . TOS | Tuzia/Tuzla Int'l . . Bosnia Herzegovina . . TZL |
| Tonghua/Tonghua Liuhe ..... China . . TNH | Trona, CA ................... USA . . TRH | Tweed-New Haven, CT ........ USA . . HVN |
| Tongliao .................. China . . TGO | Trondheim/Vaernes ......... Norway . . TRD | Twenty-Nine Palms, Marine Corps |
| Tongoa .................. Vanuatu . . TGH | Troy, AL .................... USA . . TOI | Air-Ground Combat Ctr., CA. . . USA. . NXP |
| Tongren .................. China . . TEN | Troyes .................... France . QYR | Twentynine Palms, CA ....... USA. . . TNP |
| Tonopah, NV ............... USA . . TPH | Truckee, CA ................. USA . . TKF | Twin Falls, ID ............. USA . . TWF |
| Tonopah/Test Range, NV ...... USA . . XSD | Trujillo .................... Peru . . TRU | Twin Hills, AK ............. USA . . TWA |
| Tonu .......... Papua New Guinea . . TON | Trujillo/Capiro .......... Honduras . . TJI | Two Harbors, MN .......... USA. . . TWM |
| Toowoomba .............. Australia . . TWB | Truk ................. Micronesia . . TKK | Tyler, TX ................ USA. . . TYR |
| Topeka Nexrad, KS. .......... USA . . TWX | Truro/RR Stn., NS ......... Canada . XLZ | Tyncia ................. Russia. . TYD |
| Topeka, KS ................ USA . . TOP | Truth Or Consequences, NM  USA . . TCS | Tyndall/AFB, FL ............ USA. . . PAM |
| Torembi Arpt . . . Papua New Guinea . . TCJ | Tsabong ................. Botswana . . TBY | Tyonek, AK ................ USA. . . TYE |
| Torokina ...... Papua New Guinea . . TOK | Tsaratanana .......... Madagascar . TTS | Tyumen .................. Russia. . TJM |
| Toronto Buttonville, ON . . Canada . . YKZ | Tsetserleg ............. Mongolia . . TSZ | Tzaneen/Letaba ........... S. Africa . . LTA |
| Toronto/Pearson Int'l., ON. . Canada . . YYZ | Tsewi ......... Papua New Guinea . . TSW | |
| Toronto/Downtown RR Stn., ON. . . . | Tshikapa ............. Congo, DR . TSH | |
| ........................ Canada . . YBZ | Tshipise .............. S. Africa . TSD | |
| Toronto/Guildwood Rail Svc, ON | Tsili Tsili ...... Papua New Guinea . . TSI | **U** |
| ........................ Canada . . XLQ | Tsiroanomandidy ..... Madagascar . WTS | |
| Toronto/Toronto Is, ON ..... Canada . . YTZ | Tsu .................... Japan . QTY | |
| Tororo .................. Uganda . . TRY | Tsuen Wan/RR Stn. ...... Hong Kong . ZTW | Uaxactun ............. Guatemala. . UAX |
| Torrance, CA. .............. USA . . TOA | Tsukuba ................. Japan . . XEI | Ubari .................. Libya. . QUB |
| Torremolinos .............. Spain . . UTL | Tsumeb ............... Namibia . . TSB | Ubatuba ............... Brazil.. . UBT |
| Torreon .................. Mexico . . TRC | Tsushima ................ Japan . . TSJ | Ube ................... Japan. . . UBJ |
| Torres .................... Brazil . . TSQ | Tuba City, AZ ............. USA . TBC | Uberaba ............... Brazil. . UBA |
| Torres/Torres Airstrip. ........ Vanuatu . . TOH | Tubala ................. Panama . TUW | Uberlandia/Eduardo Gomes . . Brazil. . UDI |
| Torrington, WY ............. USA . . TOR | Tubarao .................. Brazil . ZHX | Ubon Ratchathani .......... Thailand. . UBP |
| Torsby/Torsby Arpt ........ Sweden . . TYF | Tubuai ............. F. Polynesia . TUB | Ubrub ................ Indonesia. . UBR |
| Tortola/Road Town . . Virgin Is (British) . . RAD | Tucson Int'l, AZ ........... USA . . TUS | Udaipur/Dabok. ............. India. . UDR |
| Tortola/West End SPB | Tucson/AFB, AZ ........... USA . DMA | Uden/Volkel ......... Netherlands. . UDE |
| ................ Virgin Is (British) . . TOV | Tucson/Avra Valley, AZ ...... USA . AVW | Udine/Airfield. .............. Italy. . UDN |
| Tortoli/Arbatax. .............. Italy . . TTB | Tucuma ................. Brazil . TUZ | Udomxay ................ Laos. . UDO |
| Tortuquero ........... Costa Rica . . TTQ | Tucumcari, NM ........... USA . . TCC | Udon Thani .............. Thailand. . UTH |
| Torwood ................ Australia . . TWP | Tucupita .............. Venezuela . TUV | Uetersen/Off-line Pt ....... Germany. . QSM |
| Totness/Coronie .......... Suriname . . TOT | Tucurui .................. Brazil . TUR | Ufa ................... Russia. . UFA |
| Tottenham Hale Stn .......... UK . . TTK | Tuebingen ............. Germany . ZQH | Uganik, AK ............... USA. . UGI |
| Tottori ..................... Japan . . TTJ | Tueuman/Benj Matienzo. . . Argentina . TUC | Ugashik, AK .............. USA. . UGS |
| Touba/Mahana ........ Côte D'Ivoire. . TOZ | Tufi ............. Papua New Guinea . TFI | Uherske Hradiste ...... Czech Rep . UHE |
| Tougan ............... Burkina Faso . . TUQ | Tuguegarao .......... Philippines . TUG | Uige .................. Andorra. . UGO |
| Touggourt. ................. Algeria . . TGR | Tuicea ................. Romania . TCE | Uijongbu ................ S. Korea . QUJ |
| Touho ............. New Caledonia . . TOU | Tuiugak, QC. ............. Canada . . YTK | Uisan .................. S. Korea . USN |
| Toulon/Hyeres. ............. France . . TLN | Tukloyaktuk, NT. ......... Canada . . YUB | Ujae Is .............. Marshall Is . . UJE |
| Toulouse/Blagnac .......... France . . TLS | Tula .................... Russia . TYA | Ujung Pandang/Hasanudin |
| Toulouse/Montaudran ....... France . . XYT | Tulagi Is .............. Solomon Is . TLG | .................... Indonesia. . UPG |
| Tour Sinai City. .............. Egypt . . ELT | Tulare, CA. ................ USA . TLR | Ukhta .................. Russia. . UCT |
| Tourcoing ................. France . . XTN | Tulcan ................. Ecuador . TUA | Ukiah, CA ................ USA. . UKI |
| Tournai ................. Belgium . . ZGQ | Tulear ............... Madagascar . TLE | Ukunda ................. Kenya. . UKA |
| Tours/RR Stn. ............. France . . XJT | Tuli Lodge ............. Botswana . TLD | Ulaangom .............. Mongolia. . ULO |
| Tours/RR Stn. ............. France . . XSH | Tulita/Ft. Norman, NT ...... Canada . ZFN | Ulaaribaatar/Buyant Uhaa . Mongolia. . ULN |
| Tours/St Symphorien ....... France . . TUF | Tullahoma/Arnold AFS, TN .... USA . TUH | Ulan-Ude. ............... Russia. . UUD |
| Toussus Le Noble .......... France . . TNF | Tullahoma/Northern, TN ..... USA . THA | Ulanhot ................. China. . HLH |
| Townsville ............... Australia . . TSV | Tulle. .................... France . XTU | Ulei/Los Cerrillos. ......... Vanuatu. . ULB |
| Toyama ................... Japan . . TOY | Tulsa/Int'l, OK ............ USA . TUL | Ulgit .................. Mongolia. . ULG |
| Toyooka/Tapma ............ Japan . . TJH | Tulsa, OK ................ USA . RVS | Ulithi ................. Micronesia. . ULI |
| Tozeur/Nefta ............. Tunisia . . TOE | Tulsa/Off-Line Pt (Fedex), OK . . USA . ZFF | Ulm ................... Germany. . QUL |
| Trabzon .................. Turkey . . TZX | Tulua/Farfan ............ Colombia . ULQ | Ulundi ................. S. Africa . ULD |
| Trang ................... Thailand . . TST | Tuluksak, AK. ............ USA . TLT | Ulusaba. ................ S. Africa . ULX |
| Trapani/Birgi .............. Italy . . TPS | Tulum ................. Mexico . TUY | Ulyanovsk .............. Russia. . ULY |
| Traralgon/La Trobe Regional | Tumbang Samba. ......... Indonesia . TBM | Umba .......... Papua New Guinea . UMC |
| ................... Australia . . TGN | Tumbes ................. Peru . TBP | Umea/Flygplats .......... Sweden. . UME |
| Traverse City, MI ........... USA . . TVC | Tumbler Ridge, BC ....... Canada . TUX | Umiat, AK ............... USA. . UMT |
| Travis/AFB, CA ............. USA . . SUU | Tumeremo ............. Venezuela . TMO | Umm Alquwain ........... UAE. . QIW |
| Treasure Cay ........... Bahamas . . TCB | Tumling Tar ............. Nepal . TMI | Umnak Is/North Shore, AK . . . . USA. . UMB |
| Tree Point/Cst Guard Heliport, AK | Tumolbil ....... Papua New Guinea . TLP | Umnak Is/Umnak, AK. ....... USA. . UNS |
| ..................... USA . . TRP | Tumut ................. Australia . TUM | Umuarama/Ernesto Geisel. .. Brazil. . UMU |
| Treinta-y-Tres ........... Uruguay . . TYT | Tungsten, NT ........... Canada . TNS | Unalakleet, AK. ........... USA. . UNK |
| Trelew .................. Argentina . . REL | Tunis/Carthage. ........... Tunisia . TUN | Unayzah ............ Saudi Arabia . UZH |
| Tremonton, UT. ............. USA . . TRT | Tuntutuliak, AK. .......... USA . WTL | Unclarra ................ Australia. . UDA |
| Trento .................... Italy . . ZIA | Tununak, AK ............. USA . TNK | Underkhaan ............ Mongolia. . UNR |
| Trenton, NJ ............... USA . . TTN | Tunxi ................... China . TXN | Unguia. ................ Colombia. . UNC |
| Trenton, ON ............. Canada . . YTR | Tupelo, MS. .............. USA . TUP | Uniao Da Vitoria. .......... Brazil. . QVB |
| Trenton/Memorial, MO. ....... USA . . TRX | Tupi Paulista .............. Brazil . QTG | Union City/Everett-Stewart, TN . USA. . UCY |
| Tres Arroyos ............. Argentina . . OYO | Tupile .................. Panama . TUE | Union Isl . . . St. Vincent & Grenadines . . UNI |
| Tres Coracoes ............. Brazil . . QID | Turaif ............. Saudi Arabia . TUI | Union South Carolina, SC. . . . . USA. . USC |
| Tres Esquinas ........... Colombia . . TQS | Turbat ............... Pakistan . TUK | Unna .................. Germany. . ZQI |
| Tres Rios. ................. Brazil . . QIH | Turbo/Gonzalo .......... Colombia . TRB | Unst Shetland Is ............ UK. . UNT |
| Trier ................... Germany . . ZQF | Tureira ............. F. Polynesia . ZTA | Unuzgan ............. Afghanistan. . URZ |
| Trieste/Dei Legionari. .......... Italy . . TRS | Turin/Bus Svc. .............. Italy . ZTC | Upala ................ Costa Rica . UPL |
| Trincomalee/China Bay . . . Sri Lanka . . TRR | Turin/Citta Di Torino ......... Italy . TRN | Upavon ................. UK. . UPV |
| Trinidad ................ Colombia . . TDA | Turkey Creek ............ Australia . TKY | Upernavik/ HP ........... Greenland. . JUV |
| Trinidad .................. Bolivia . . TDD | Turkmanbashi ....... Turkmenistan . KRW | Upington ............... S. Africa . UTN |
| Trinidad .................... Cuba . . TND | Turku ................. Finland . TKU | Upland/Cable HP, CA ......... USA. . JUP |
| Trinidad, CO .............. USA . . TAD | Turn ................. Ethiopia . TUJ | Upland/Cable, CA .......... USA. . CCB |
| Triple Is, BC ............. Canada . . YTI | Turnaco/La Florida ....... Colombia . TCO | Uplara ......... Papua New Guinea . UPR |
| Tripoli/Int'l. ............... Libya . . TIP | Turtle Is ................. Fiji . TTL | Upolu Point, HI ........... USA. . UPP |
| Tripoli/Kleyate ........... Lebanon . . KYE | Tuscaloosa, AL ............ USA . TCL | Upper Heyford/RAF. ......... UK. . UHF |
| Trivandrum/Int'l ............. India . . TRV | Tuskegee/Sharpe Fld, AL. .... USA . TGE | Uraj .................. Russia. . URJ |
| Trois-Rivieres, QC ........ Canada . . YRQ | Tuticorin ................ India . TCR | Uralsk ................ Kazakhstan. . URA |
| Troisdorf ................ Germany . . ZQG | Tuxtia Gutierrez/Llano San Juan | Uranium City, SK ......... Canada. . YBE |
| Trollhattan/Private ......... Sweden . . THN | .................... Mexico . . TGZ | Urgench .............. Uzbekistan. . UGC |

**Urgoon** ... Afghanistan .. URN
**Uribe** ... Colombia ... URI
**Uriman** ... Venezuela .. URM
**Urmieh** ... Iran . OMH
**Urniujaq**, QC ... Canada .. YUD
**Urntata** ... S. Africa .. UTT
**Uroubi** ... Papua New Guinea .. URU
**Urrao** ... Colombia .. URR
**Uruapan** ... Mexico .. UPN
**Urubupunga**/Ernesto Pochier . Brazil .. URB
**Uruguaiana**/Ruben Berta ... Brazil .. URG
**Urumqi** ... China .. URC
**Usak** ... Turkey .. USQ
**Useless Loop** ... Australia .. USL
**Ushuaia**/Islas Malvinas ... Argentina .. USH
**Usino** ... Papua New Guinea .. USO
**Usinsk** ... Russia .. USK
**Ust-Kamenogorsk** ... Kazakstan .. UKK
**Ust-Kut** ... Russia .. UKX
**Ust-Llimsk** ... Russia ... UIK
**Ustupo** ... Panama .. UTU
**Utapato** ... Thailand .. UTP
**Utica**, NY ... USA .. UCA
**Utica**/Berz-Macomb, MI ... USA ... UIZ
**Utica**/Utica NY Rail ... USA .. ZUA
**Utila** ... Honduras ... UII
**Utirik Is** ... Marshall Is .. UTK
**Utrecht**/RR Stn. ... Netherlands .. ZYU
**Utrecht**/Soesterberg ... Netherlands .. UTC
**Utsunomiya AB** ... Japan .. QUT
**Uttaradit** ... Thailand .. UTR
**Uummannaq** ... Greenland .. UMD
**Uvaide**/Garner Fld, TX ... USA .. UVA
**Uvramento**/Dos Galpoes ... Brazil ... LVB
**Uyo** ... Nigeria .. QUO
**Uzhgorod** ... Ukraine .. UDJ
**Uzice** ... Yugoslavia .. ZZE
**Uzice**/Ponikve ... Yugoslavia .. UZC
**Uzwil** ... Switzerland .. ZKX

# V

**V.C. Bird Int'l** ... Antigua & Barbuda .. ANU
**Vaasa** ... Finland .. VAA
**Vadodara** ... India .. BDQ
**Vadso** ... Norway .. VDS
**Vaduz** ... Liechtenstein .. QVU
**Vaeroy**/Stolport ... Norway .. VRY
**Vahitahi** ... F. Polynesia .. VHZ
**Vaienca** ... Brazil .. VAL
**Valevo** ... Yugoslavia . QWV
**Vail Van** Svc, CO ... USA .. QBF
**Vail**, CO ... USA .. EGE
**Vail**/Eagle/Beaver Creek Van Svc, CO ... USA .. ZBV
**Val D'Isere** ... France .. VAZ
**Val D'Or**, QC ... Canada .. YVO
**Valbonne** ... France ... QVI
**Valcartier**, QC ... Canada .. YOY
**Valcheta** ... Argentina .. VCF
**Valdez**/Municipal, AK ... USA .. VDZ
**Valdivia**/Pichoy ... Chile .. ZAL
**Valdosta**, GA ... USA .. VLD
**Valence**/Chalpeuil ... France .. VAF
**Valencia** ... Spain .. VLC
**Valencia** ... Venezuela .. VLN
**Valenciennes**/RR Stn. ... France .. XVS
**Valentine**, NE ... USA .. VTN
**Valera**/Carvajal ... Venezuela .. VLV
**Valesdir** ... Vanuatu .. VLS
**Valkeakoski** ... Finland .. QVK
**Valladolid** ... Spain ... VLL
**Valle De** Pascua ... Venezuela .. VDP
**Valle**, AZ ... Australia .. VLE
**Valledupar** ... Colombia .. VUP
**Vallegrande** ... Bolivia .. VAH
**Vallejo**/Stolport, CA ... USA .. VLO
**Vallemi**/INC ... Paraguay ... VMI
**Vallenar** ... Chile .. VLR
**Valloire** ... France .. XVR
**Valparaiso** ... Chile .. VAP
**Valparaiso**, FL ... USA ... EGI
**Valparaiso**, IN ... USA .. VPZ
**Valverde**/Hierro ... Spain .. VDE
**Van** ... Turkey .. VAN
**Van Horn**/Cullberson County, TX ... USA .. VHN
**Vancouver**/Int'l, BC ... Canada .. YVR
**Vancouver**, Pearson Airpark, WA ... USA .. VUO
**Vancouver**/Boundary Bay, BC ... Canada .. YDT
**Vancouver**/Coal Harbour, BC ... Canada .. CXH
**Vancouver**/RR Stn., BC ... Canada .. XEA
**Vandalia**, IL ... USA .. VLA
**Vandenberg**/AFB, CA ... USA .. VBG
**Vandoe** ... Norway .. VAW
**Vangaindrano** ... Madagascar .. VND
**Vangrieng** ... Laos . VGG
**Vanimo** ... Papua New Guinea ... VAI
**Vannes**/Meucon ... Eritrea .. VNE
**Vanrook** ... Australia .. VNR
**Vanuabalavu** ... Fiji .. VBV
**Varadero**/Juan Gualberto Gomez ... Cuba .. VRA
**Varanasi** ... India .. VNS
**Varese** ... Italy .. QVA
**Varginha**/M. B. Trompowsky ... Brazil .. VAG
**Varkaus** ... Finland .. VRK
**Varna** ... Bulgaria .. VAR
**Varrelbusch** ... Germany .. VAC
**Vasteras**/Hasslo ... Sweden .. VST
**Vastervik** ... Sweden .. VVK
**Vatomandry** ... Madagascar .. VAT
**Vatulele** ... Fiji .. VTF
**Vatulkoula** ... Fiji .. VAU
**Vava**'u/Lupepau'u ... Tonga .. VAV
**Vaxjo** ... Sweden .. VXO
**Vejle** ... Denmark .. VEJ
**Vejle**/RR Stn. ... Denmark .. XVX
**Velbert** ... Germany .. ZQJ
**Veldhoven**/RR Stn. ... Netherlands .. ZVH
**Velikij Ustyug** ... Russia .. VUS
**Velikiye Luki** ... Russia .. VLU
**Vendome** ... France .. XVD
**Venetie**, AK ... USA .. VEE
**Venice**, FL ... USA .. VNC
**Venice**/Marco Polo ... Italy .. VCE
**Venice**/Treviso ... Italy .. TSF
**Veracruz**/Las Bajadas ... Mexico .. VER
**Verbier** ... Switzerland .. ZKY
**Verden** ... Germany . QVQ
**Verdun** ... France .. XVN
**Vermilion**, AB ... Canada .. YVG
**Vermillion Area**, LA ... USA .. VRX
**Vernal**, UT ... USA .. VEL
**Vernon**, BC ... Canada .. YVE
**Vero Beach**, FL ... USA .. VRB
**Verona**/Villafranca ... Italy .. VRN
**Versailles** ... France .. XVE
**Versailles**, MO ... USA .. VRS
**Vesoul** ... France .. XVO
**Vestbjerg**/Bus Svc ... Denmark .. QXF
**Vestmannaeyjar** ... Iceland .. VEY
**Veszprern** ... Hungary .. ZFP
**Vevey** ... Switzerland .. ZKZ
**Viborg**/RR Stn. ... Denmark .. ZGX
**Vicenza** ... Italy .. VIC
**Vichadero** ... Uruguay .. VCH
**Vichy**, MO ... USA ... VIH
**Vichy**/Charmeil ... France .. VHY
**Vicksburg**, MS ... USA .. VKS
**Vicksburg**/Tallulah Rgnl. Arpt, LA ... USA .. TVR
**Vicosa** ... Brazil .. QVC
**Victoria** ... Honduras .. VTA
**Victoria** ... Chile ... ZIC
**Victoria Falls** ... Zimbabwe .. VFA
**Victoria Harbour**, BC ... Canada . YWH
**Victoria**/Int'l, BC ... Canada .. YYJ
**Victoria Is** ... Nigeria .. QVL
**Victoria River Downs** ... Australia .. VCD
**Victoria**, TX ... USA .. VCT
**Vidalia**/Municipal, GA ... USA ... VDI
**Videira** ... Brazil .. VIA
**Vidin** ... Bulgaria ... VID
**Viedma** ... Argentina . VDM
**Viengxay** ... Laos .. VNG
**Vienna Int'l** ... Austria .. VIE
**Vienna**/Danubelpier Hov. ... Austria .. VDD
**Vienne** ... France .. XVI
**Vientiane**/Wattav ... Laos .. VTE
**Vieques** ... Puerto Rico .. VQS
**Viersen** ... Germany .. ZQK
**Vierzon** ... France .. XVZ
**View Cove**, AK ... USA .. VCB
**Vigo** ... Spain . VGO
**Vijayawada** ... India .. VGA
**Vikna** ... Norway ... ZXD
**Vila Real** ... Portugal ... VRL
**Vila Rica**/Mun ... Brazil ... VLP
**Vila Velha** ... Brazil .. QVH
**Vilanculos** ... Mozambique .. VNX
**Vilgenis** ... France .. QVG
**Vilhelmina** ... Sweden .. VHM
**Vilhena** ... Brazil .. BVH
**Villa Constitucion** ... Mexico ... VIB
**Villa Dolores** ... Argentina .. VDR
**Villa Gesell** ... Argentina ... VLG
**Villa Mercedes** ... Argentina .. VME
**Villagarzon** ... Colombia .. VGZ
**Village**/SPB, AK ... USA .. KWP
**Villahermosa**/Capitan Carlos Perez ... Mexico ... VSA
**Villamontes** ... Bolivia .. VLM
**Villars** ... Switzerland ... ZLA
**Villavicencio**/La Vanguardia ... Colombia .. VVC
**Villefranche Sur Saone** ... France ... XVF
**Villepinte** ... France ... XVP
**Villingen-Schwenningen** ... Germany ... ZQL
**Vilnius**/Int'l ... Lithuania .. VNO
**Vina del** Mar ... Chile .. KNA
**Vincennes**/Oneal, IN ... USA .. OEA
**Vinh City** ... Vietnam ... VII
**Vinh Long** ... Vietnam ... XVL
**Vinnica** ... Ukraine ... VIN
**Viqueque** ... Indonesia .. VIQ
**Virac** ... Philippines .. VRC
**Virgin Gorda** ... Virgin Is (British) ... VIJ
**Virginia Tech** Arpt, VA ... USA .. BCB
**Viru**/Viru Harbour ... Solomon Is .. VIU
**Visalia**, CA ... USA ... VIS
**Visby**/Flygplats ... Sweden ... VBY
**Viseu** ... Portugal ... VSE
**Vishakhapatnam** ... India ... VTZ
**Visp** ... Switzerland ... ZLB
**Vitebsk** ... Belarus ... VTB
**Vitoria Da Conquista** ... Brazil .. VDC
**Vitoria** ... Spain ... VIT
**Vitoria**/Euroo Sales ... Brazil ... VIX
**Vitre** ... France ... XVT
**Vittel** ... Eritrea ... VTL
**Vivigani** ... Papua New Guinea .. VIV
**Vladikavkaz** ... Russia .. OGZ
**Vladivostok** ... Russia .. VVO
**Voelklingen** ... Germany .. ZQM
**Vohemar** ... Madagascar .. VOH
**Voinjama** ... Liberia ... VOI
**Vojens**/RR Stn. ... Denmark ... XJE
**Vojens**/Skrydstrup/Military .. Denmark ... SKS
**Volens**, VA ... USA .. VQN
**Volgodonsk** ... Russia ... VLK
**Volgograd** ... Russia .. VOG
**Vologida** ... Russia .. VGD
**Volos**/Nea Anchialos ... Greece ... VOL
**Volta Redonda** ... Brazil .. QVR
**Vopnafjordur** ... Iceland .. VPN
**Vorkuta** ... Russia ... VKT
**Voronezh** ... Russia .. VOZ
**Votuporanga** ... Brazil .. VOT
**Vraidebria** ... Bulgaria ... QVJ
**Vredendal** ... S. Africa . VRE
**Vryburg** ... S. Africa . VRU
**Vryheid** ... S. Africa . VYD
**Vung Tau** ... Vietnam .. VTG

# W

**W Memphis**/Municipal, AR ... USA .. AWM
**Wabag** ... Papua New Guinea . WAB
**Wabo** ... Papua New Guinea . WAO
**Wabush**, NF ... Canada .. YWK
**Waca** ... Ethiopia .. WAC
**Waco Kungo** ... Angola .. CEO
**Waco**, TX ... USA ... ACT
**Waco**/James Connall, TX ... USA .. CNW
**Wad Medani** ... Somalia ... DNI
**Waddington**/RAF Stn ... UK .. WTN
**Wadi Ad** Dawasir ... Saudi Arabia . WAE
**Wadi Ain** ... Yemen .. WDA
**Wadi Halfa** ... Somalia .. WHF
**Waedenswil**/Off-line Pt .. Switzerland ... ZLC
**Wagau** ... Papua New Guinea . WGU
**Wageningen** ... Suriname ... AGI

AIRPORTS -2-

| | | |
|---|---|---|
| Wagethe | Indonesia | WET |
| Wagga Wagga/Forrest Hill | Australia | WGA |
| Wagny | Gabon | WGY |
| Wahai | Indonesia | WBA |
| Wahpeton, ND | USA | WAH |
| Waiblingen | Germany | ZQO |
| Waikoloa/Waikoloa Arpt, HI | USA | WKL |
| Waimanalo/Bellows Fld, HI | USA | BLW |
| Waingapu/Mau Hau | Indonesia | WGP |
| Wainwright Arpt, AB | Canada | YWV |
| Wainwright, AK | USA | AIN |
| Wainwright, AK | USA | AWI |
| Wairoa | New Zealand | WIR |
| Waitangi | New Zealand | WGN |
| Wajir | Kenya | WJR |
| Wakaya Is | Fiji | KAY |
| Wakayama | Japan | QKY |
| Wake Is | Wake/Midway Is | AWK |
| Wakefield Westgate/RR Stn | UK | XWD |
| Wakkanai/Hokkaido | Japan | WKJ |
| Wakunai | Papua New Guinea | WKN |
| Walaba | Vanuatu | WIH |
| Walcha | Australia | WLC |
| Waldron Is, WA | USA | WDN |
| Wales, AK | USA | WAA |
| Walgett | Australia | WGE |
| Walial | Australia | WLA |
| Walker's Cay | Bahamas | WKR |
| Walla Walla, WA | USA | ALW |
| Wallis Is | Wallis and Futuna Is | WLS |
| Wallops Is, VA | USA | WAL |
| Walnut Ridge, AR | USA | ARG |
| Waltham, MA | USA | WLM |
| Walvis Bay/Rooikop | Namibia | WVB |
| Wamena | Indonesia | WMX |
| Wana | Pakistan | WAF |
| Wanaka | New Zealand | WKA |
| Wanganui | New Zealand | WAG |
| Wangaratta | Australia | WGT |
| Wangerooge/Flugplatz | Germany | AGE |
| Wanigela | Papua New Guinea | AGL |
| Wantoat | Papua New Guinea | WTT |
| Wanurna | Papua New Guinea | WNU |
| Wanxian | China | WXN |
| Wapakoneta/Armstrong, OH | USA | AXV |
| Wapenamanda | Papua New Guinea | WBM |
| Wapolu | Papua New Guinea | WBC |
| Warder | Ethiopia | WRA |
| Ware, MA | USA | UWA |
| Waris | Indonesia | WAR |
| Warm Spring Bay/SPB, AK | USA | BNF |
| Warmarnboof | Australia | WMB |
| Warn | Nigeria | QRW |
| Warnemuende/RR Stn | Germany | ZWD |
| Warracknabeal | Australia | WKB |
| Warrangal | India | WGC |
| Warrawagine | Australia | WRW |
| Warren | Australia | QRR |
| Warrington B.Q./RR Stn | UK | XWN |
| Warroad, MN | USA | RRT |
| Warszawa/Okecie | Poland | WAW |
| Warwick | Australia | WAZ |
| Washabo | Suriname | WSO |
| Washington D.C. | USA | DCA |
| Washington, IA | USA | AWG |
| Washington, NC | USA | OCW |
| Washington/Buzzards Pt S., DC | USA | BZS |
| Washington/County, PA | USA | WSG |
| Washington/New Carrolton RR, DC | USA | ZRZ |
| Washington/Pentagon Army, DC | USA | JPN |
| Washington/Washington DC Rail | USA | ZWU |
| Wasilia, AK | USA | WWA |
| Wasior | Indonesia | WSR |
| Waskaganish, QC | Canada | YKQ |
| Waspam | Netherlands | WSP |
| Wasu | Papua New Guinea | WSU |
| Wasua | Papua New Guinea | WSA |
| Wasum | Papua New Guinea | WUM |
| Waterfall/SPS, AK | USA | KWF |
| Waterford | Ireland | WAT |
| Waterloo | Australia | WLO |
| Waterloo, IA | USA | ALO |
| Watertown, NY | USA | ART |
| Watertown, SD | USA | ATY |
| Watertown, WI | USA | RYV |
| Waterville/Robert Lafleur, ME | USA | WVL |
| Watford/RR Stn., ON | Canada | XWA |
| Watson Lake, YT | Canada | YQH |

| | | |
|---|---|---|
| Watsonville, CA | USA | WVI |
| Wau | Papua New Guinea | WUG |
| Wau | Sudan | WUU |
| Wauchope | Australia | WAU |
| Waukesha, WI | USA | UES |
| Waukon/Municipal, IA | USA | UKN |
| Wausau, WI | USA | AUW |
| Wave Hill/Kalkgurung | Australia | WAV |
| Waverney | Australia | WAN |
| Wavre | Belgium | ZGV |
| Wawa, ON | Canada | YXZ |
| Wawoi Falls | Papua New Guinea | WAJ |
| Waycross/Ware County, GA | USA | AYS |
| Waynesburg/Green County, PA | USA | WAY |
| Wearn | Papua New Guinea | WEP |
| Weasua | Iran | WES |
| Weatherford/Parker County, TX | USA | WEA |
| Webster City, IA | USA | EBS |
| Wedau | Papua New Guinea | WED |
| Wedjh | Saudi Arabia | EJH |
| Wee Waa | Australia | WEW |
| Weeping Water/Browns, NE | USA | EPG |
| Weifang | China | WEE |
| Weihai | China | WEH |
| Weinfelden | Switzerland | ZLD |
| Weingarten | Germany | ZWG |
| Weipa | Australia | WEI |
| Welbequie, ON | Canada | YWP |
| Welkorn | S. Africa | WEL |
| Wellingborough/RR Stn | UK | XWE |
| Wellington | Australia | QEL |
| Wellington/Int'l | New Zealand | WLG |
| Wells/Harriet Fld, NV | USA | LWL |
| Wellsville, NY | USA | ELZ |
| Welshpool | Australia | WHL |
| Wemindpi, QC | Canada | YNC |
| Wenatchee, WA | USA | EAT |
| Wendover, UT | USA | ENV |
| Wengen | Switzerland | ZLE |
| Werizinou | China | WNZ |
| Wesel | Germany | ZQP |
| West Chicago, IL | USA | DPA |
| West End | Bahamas | WTD |
| West Kavik, AK | USA | VKW |
| West Kuparuk, AK | USA | XPU |
| West Malling | UK | WEM |
| West Palm Beach, FL | USA | LNA |
| West Palm Beach, FL | USA | PBI |
| West Palm Beach/RR Stn., FL | USA | ZWP |
| West Plains Municipal Arpt, MO | USA | UNO |
| West Send, WI | USA | ETB |
| West Woodward, OK | USA | WWR |
| West Wyalong | Australia | WWY |
| West Yellowstone, MT | USA | WEY |
| West Yellowstone, MT | USA | WYS |
| Westchester County, NY | USA | HPN |
| Westchester County/Stamford RR Stn., NY | USA | ZTF |
| Westerland/Sylt | Germany | GWT |
| Westerly, RI | USA | WST |
| Westfield/Barnes, MA | USA | BAF |
| Westhampton, NY | USA | FOK |
| Westport | New Zealand | WSZ |
| Westray | UK | WRY |
| Westsound, WA | USA | WSX |
| Wettingen | Switzerland | ZLF |
| Wetzikon | Switzerland | ZKW |
| Wetzlar | Germany | ZQQ |
| Wewak/Boram | Papua New Guinea | WWK |
| Wexford/Castlebridge | Ireland | WEX |
| Weymont/RR Stn., QC | Canada | XFQ |
| Wha Ti/Lac La Martre, NT | Canada | YLE |
| Whakatane | New Zealand | WHK |
| Whale Cove, NU | Canada | YXN |
| Whale Pass, AK | USA | WWP |
| Whalsay | UK | WHS |
| Whangarei | New Zealand | WRE |
| Wharton, TX | USA | WHT |
| Wheatland/Phifer Fld, WY | USA | EAN |
| Wheeler/AFB, HI | USA | HHI |
| Wheeling, WV | USA | HLG |
| Whidbey Is/NAS, WA | USA | NUW |
| Whistler, BC | Canada | YWS |
| White Mountain, AK | USA | WMO |
| White River, AZ | USA | WTR |
| White River, ON | Canada | YWR |
| White Sands/Condron/AAF, NM | USA | WSD |
| White Sulphur Sprng, WV | USA | SSU |
| Whitecourt, AB | Canada | YZU |
| Whitefield, NH | USA | HIE |

| | | |
|---|---|---|
| Whitehouse, FL | USA | NEN |
| Whiteman/AFB, MO | USA | SZL |
| Whitesburg/Municipal, KY | USA | BRG |
| Whitianga | New Zealand | WTZ |
| Whyalla | Australia | WYA |
| Wiarton, ON | Canada | YVV |
| Wichita Falls/Kickapoo, KS | USA | KIP |
| Wichita Mid-Continent, KS | USA | ICT |
| Wichita, KS | USA | BEC |
| Wichita/Cessna Aircraft Fld, KS | USA | CEA |
| Wick | UK | WIC |
| Wiesbaden | Germany | UWE |
| Wiesbaden/Air Base | Germany | WIE |
| Wigan N.W./RR Stn | UK | XWI |
| Wil | Switzerland | ZLH |
| Wilcannia | Australia | WIO |
| Wildenrath | Germany | WID |
| Wildwood/Cape May County, NJ | USA | WWD |
| Wildwood/USAF HP, AK | USA | WWS |
| Wilhelmshaven | Germany | WVN |
| Wilkes-Barre/Wyoming Valle, PA | USA | WBW |
| Wilkesboro/Wilkes County, NC | USA | IKB |
| Williams Harbour, NF | Canada | YWM |
| Williams Lake, BC | Canada | YWL |
| Williams/AFB, AZ | USA | CHD |
| Williamsport, PA | USA | IPT |
| Willimantic/Windham, CT | USA | IJD |
| Williston/Sloulin Fld Int'l, ND | USA | ISN |
| Willmar, MN | USA | ILL |
| Willoughby, OH | USA | LNN |
| Willow Grove/NAS, PA | USA | NXX |
| Willow, AK | USA | WOW |
| Willows/Glenn County, CA | USA | WLW |
| Wilmington Nexrad, NC | USA | LTX |
| Wilmington, Airborne Airpark, OH | USA | ILN |
| Wilmington, DE | USA | ILG |
| Wilmington, New Hanover Int'l, NC | USA | ILM |
| Wilmington/Wilmington Rail, DE | USA | ZWI |
| Wilton, CT/Off-line Pt | USA | QCW |
| Wiluna | Australia | WUN |
| Winchester, VA | USA | OKV |
| Winchester/Municipal, VA | USA | WGO |
| Windarra | Australia | WND |
| Winder, GA | USA | WDR |
| Windhoek/Eros | Namibia | ERS |
| Windhoek/H. Kutako Int'l | Namibia | WDH |
| Windhoek/RR Stn | Namibia | ZWH |
| Windom, MN | USA | MWM |
| Windorah | Australia | WNR |
| Windsor, ON | Canada | YQG |
| Windsor/RR Stn., ON | Canada | XEC |
| Winfield, KS | USA | WLD |
| Winisk, ON | Canada | YWN |
| Wink, TX | USA | INK |
| Winnemucca, NV | USA | WMC |
| Winner, SD | USA | NED |
| Winnipeg/Int'l, MB | Canada | YWG |
| Winnipeg/RR Stn., MB | Canada | XEF |
| Winona, MN | USA | ONA |
| Winslow Municipal, AZ | USA | INW |
| Winston Salem, NC | USA | INT |
| Winter Haven/Gilbert Fld, FL | USA | GIF |
| Winter Park/Van Svc, CO | USA | QWP |
| Winterthur | Switzerland | ZLI |
| Winton | Australia | WIN |
| Wipim | Papua New Guinea | WPM |
| Wiscasset, ME | USA | ISS |
| Wiscasset, ME | USA | IWI |
| Wisconsin Rapids, WI | USA | ISW |
| Wise, VA | USA | LNP |
| Wiseman, AK | USA | WSM |
| Wismar/RR Stn | Germany | ZWM |
| Withehorse, YT | Canada | YXY |
| Witten | Germany | ZQR |
| Wittenberg/RR Stn | Germany | ZWT |
| Wittenberge/RR Stn | Germany | ZWN |
| Wittenoom | Australia | WIT |
| Witu | Papua New Guinea | WIU |
| Wloclawek | Poland | QWK |
| Woburn/Cummings Park, MA | USA | WBN |
| Woensdrecht | Netherlands | WDT |
| Woensdrecht/AB | Netherlands | WOE |
| Woergi/Bus Svc | Austria | QXZ |
| Woitape | Papua New Guinea | WTP |

| | | |
|---|---|---|
| Woja | Marshall Is. | WJA |
| Woking/RR Stn. | UK | XWO |
| Wolf Point Int'l, MT. | USA. | OLF |
| Wolfenbuettel | Germany | ZQT |
| Wolfsburg/Off-line Pt | Germany | ZQU |
| Wollaston Lake, SK | Canada | ZWL |
| Wollogorang | Australia | WLI |
| Wollongong | Australia | WOL |
| Wologissi | Liberia | WOI |
| Wolverhampton/RR | UK | XVW |
| Wonan | Taiwan | WOT |
| Wondai | Australia | WDI |
| Wondoola | Australia | WON |
| Wonenara | Papua New Guinea | WOA |
| Wonju | S. Korea | WJU |
| Wonken | Venezuela | WOK |
| Wood River, AK | USA | WOD |
| Woodbridge | UK | BWY |
| Woodchopper, AK | USA | WOO |
| Woodgreen | Australia | WOG |
| Woodie Woodie | Australia | WWI |
| Woodstock/RR Stn., ON. | Canada | XIP |
| Woomera | Australia | UMR |
| Wooster, Wayne County Arpt, OH | | |
| | USA | BJJ |
| Wora Na Ye | Gabon | WNE |
| Worcester, MA | USA | ORH |
| Worland, WY. | USA | WRL |
| Worms | Germany | ZQV |
| Worthington, MN. | USA | OTG |
| Wotho Is | Marshall Is. | WTO |
| Wotje Is | Marshall Is. | WTE |
| Wrangell/SPB, AK | USA | WRG |
| Wrench Creek, AK | USA | WRH |
| Wright/AAF, GA. | USA | LIY |
| Wrigley, NT | Canada | YWY |
| Wroclaw/Strachowice. | Poland | WRO |
| Wrotham Park | Australia | WPK |
| Wudinna | Australia | WUD |
| Wuerzburg | Germany | QWU |
| Wuhan | China | WUH |
| Wuhu | China | WHU |
| Wunnummin Lake, ON | Canada | WNN |
| Wuppertal | Germany | UWP |
| Wurtsmith/AFB, MI | USA | OSC |
| Wuvulu Is | Papua New Guinea | WUV |
| Wuxi | China | WUX |
| Wuyishan | China | WUS |
| Wuzhou/Changzhoudao | China | WUZ |
| Wylk Auf Foehr. | Germany | OHR |
| Wyndharn | Australia | WYN |
| Wyoming/RR Stn., ON. | Canada | XWY |
| Wyton/RAF | UK | QUY |

# X

| | | |
|---|---|---|
| X Thaurah | Syria | SOR |
| Xai Xai | Mozambique | VJB |
| Xangongo | Angola | XGN |
| Xanxere | Brazil | AXE |
| Xayabury | Laos | XAY |
| Xi An | China | SIA |
| Xi An/Xianyang | China | XIY |
| Xiamen | China | XMN |
| Xiangan | China | XFN |
| Xichang | China | XIC |
| Xieng Khouang | Laos | XKH |
| Xienglorn | Laos | XIE |
| Xilinhot | China | XIL |
| Xingcheng | China | XEN |
| Xingning | China | XIN |
| Xingtai | China | XNT |
| Xinguara/Mun. | Brazil | XIG |
| Xining | China | XNN |
| Xuzhou | China | XUZ |

# Y

| | | |
|---|---|---|
| Yaaunde/Nsimalen | Cameroon | NSI |
| Yaba | Nigeria | QYB |
| Yacuiba | Bolivia | BYC |
| Yagoua | Cameroon | GXX |
| Yaguara | Colombia | AYG |
| Yakatapa/Intermediate, AK. | USA | CYT |
| Yakima, WA | USA | YKM |
| Yakima/Firing Center/AAF, WA | USA | FCT |
| Yakushima | Japan | KUM |
| Yakutat, AK | USA | YAK |
| Yakutsk | Russia | YKS |
| Yalata Mission | Australia | KYI |
| Yalgoo | Australia | YLG |
| Yalinga | Central African Rep | AIG |
| Yalumet | Papua New Guinea | KYX |
| Yam Is | Australia | XMY |
| Yamagata/Junmachi | Japan | GAJ |
| Yamoussoukro | Côte D'ivoire | ASK |
| Yan | Colombia | AYI |
| Yan'an | China | ENY |
| Yanbu | Saudi Arabia | YNB |
| Yancheng | China | YNZ |
| Yandina | Solomon Is | XYA |
| Yangambi | Congo, DR | YAN |
| Yangon/Mingaladon | Myanmar | RGN |
| Yangoonabie | Australia | KYB |
| Yanji | China | YNJ |
| Yankton/Chan Gurney, SD. | USA | YKN |
| Yantai/Laishan | China | YNT |
| Yaounde/Yaciunde Arpt | Cameroon | YAO |
| Yap | Micronesia | YAP |
| Yapsiei | Papua New Guinea | KPE |
| Yarmouth, NS | Canada | YQI |
| Yaroslavl | Russia | IAR |
| Yasawa Is | Fiji | YAS |
| Yasoudj | Netherlands | QYS |
| Yasuru | Papua New Guinea | KSX |
| Yavarate | Colombia | VAB |
| Yaviza | Panama | PYV |
| Yazd | Iran | AZD |
| Ye | Myanmar | XYE |
| Yechon/Air Base | S. Korea | YEC |
| Yeelirrie | Australia | KYF |
| Yegepa | Papua New Guinea | PGE |
| Yelimane | Mali | EYL |
| Yellow River | Papua New Guinea | XYR |
| Yellowknife, NT | Canada | YZF |
| Yengema | Sierra Leone | WYE |
| Yenkis | Papua New Guinea | YEQ |
| Yeovilton | UK | YEO |
| Yerevan | Armenia | EVN |
| Yerington, NV | USA | EYR |
| Yes Bay/SPB, AK | USA | WYB |
| Yeva | Papua New Guinea | YVD |
| Yibin | China | YBP |
| Yichang, QC | China | YIH |
| Yilan | China | YLN |
| Yinchuan | China | INC |
| Yining | China | YIN |
| Yiwu | China | YIW |
| Ylivieska | Finland | YLI |
| Yogyakarta/Adisutjipto | Indonesia | JOG |
| Yokkaichi | Japan | QGZ |
| Yokohama | Japan | YOK |
| Yola | Nigeria | YOL |
| Yonago/Miho | Japan | YGJ |
| Yonaguni Jima | Japan | OGN |
| Yongai | Papua New Guinea | KGH |
| York Landing | Mongolia | ZAC |
| York, PA | USA | THV |
| York/RR | UK | QQY |
| Yorke Is | Australia | OKR |
| Yorketown | Australia | ORR |
| Yorkton, SK | Canada | YQV |
| Yoro | Honduras | ORO |
| Yororijima | Japan | RNJ |
| Yosemite Ntl Park, CA | USA | OYS |
| Yosu | S. Korea | RSU |
| Yotvata | Israel | YOT |
| Young | Australia | NGA |

# Z

| | | |
|---|---|---|
| Youngstown, OH | USA | YNG |
| Yreka, CA | USA | RKC |
| Yuanmou | China | YUA |
| Yucca Flat, NV. | USA | UCC |
| Yuendurnu | Australia | YUE |
| Yule Is/Kairuku | Papua New Guinea | RKU |
| Yulin | China | UYN |
| Yuma/Int'l, AZ | USA | YUM |
| Yuma/MCAS, AZ | USA | NYL |
| Yurimaguas | Peru | YMS |
| Yurut | Indonesia | RUF |
| Yuzhno-Sakhalinsk | Russia | UUS |
| Yverdon | Switzerland | ZLJ |
| | | |
| Zabljak | Yugoslavia | ZBK |
| Zabre | Burkina Faso | XZA |
| Zabreh/Dolni Benesov | Czech Rep | ZBE |
| Zacatecas/La Calera | Mexico | ZCL |
| Zachar Bay/SPB, AK | USA | KZB |
| Zadar | Croatia | ZAD |
| Zagazeeg | Egypt | QZZ |
| Zagreb/Pleso | Croatia | ZAG |
| Zahedan | Iran | ZAH |
| Zahleh | Lebanon | QZQ |
| Zaisan | Kazakstan | SZI |
| Zakinthos Is | Greece | ZTH |
| Zakopane | Poland | QAZ |
| Zakouma | Chad | AKM |
| Zambezi | Zambia | BBZ |
| Zamboanga | Philippines | ZAM |
| Zamora | Mexico | ZMM |
| Zanaga | Congo, DR | ANJ |
| Zanesville, OH. | USA | ZZV |
| Zanzibar/Kisauni | Tanzania | ZNZ |
| Zapala | Argentina | APZ |
| Zapatoca | Colombia | AZT |
| Zaporozhye | Ukraine | OZH |
| Zaragoza | Spain | ZAZ |
| Zaranj | Afghanistan | ZAJ |
| Zaria | Nigeria | ZAR |
| Zarqa | Jordan | QZA |
| Zawia Town | Libya | QZT |
| Zemio | Central African Rep | IMO |
| Zenag | Papua New Guinea | ZEN |
| Zephyrhills, FL | USA | ZPH |
| Zermatt | Switzerland | QZB |
| Zero | India | ZER |
| Zhairem | Kazakstan | HRC |
| Zhambyl | Kazakstan | DMB |
| Zhanjiang | China | ZHA |
| Zhaotong | China | ZAT |
| Zhengzhou | China | CGO |
| Zhezkazgan/Zhezhazgan | Kazakstan | DZN |
| Zhitomir | Ukraine | ZTR |
| Zhob | Pakistan | PZH |
| Zhongshan | China | ZIS |
| Zhoushan | China | HSN |
| Zhuhai/Zhuhai Arpt | China | ZUH |
| Zielona Gora/Babimost | Poland | IEG |
| Ziguinchor | Senegal | ZIG |
| Zilfi | Saudi Arabia | ZUL |
| Zilina | Slovakia | ILZ |
| Zinder | Niger | ZND |
| Zittau/RR Stn. | Germany | ZIT |
| Zlin/Holesov | Czech Rep | GTW |
| Zliten | Libya | QZL |
| Zoersel | Belgium | OBL |
| Zofingen | Switzerland | ZLL |
| Zonguldak | Turkey | ONQ |
| Zouerate | Mauritania | OUZ |
| Zuenoula | Côte D'Ivoire | ZUE |
| Zug | Switzerland | ZLM |
| Zugapa | Indonesia | UGU |
| Zunyi | China | ZYI |
| Zurich | Switzerland | ZLQ |
| Zurich | Switzerland | ZRH |
| Zurich/HBF Railway Svc. | Switzerland | ZLP |
| Zurs/Lech/Flexenpass HP. | Austria | ZRS |
| Zwara | Libya | WAX |
| Zweibruecken | Germany | ZQW |

# Guide to Truck Trailers

## Introduction

This guide to truck trailers has been developed from materials supplied by a number of trucking firms and international trailer manufacturers. It is designed to show the main types of truck trailers used in international trade and to give readers an insight into common trailer configurations and dimensions.

This guide is not designed to illustrate every type of truck trailer manufactured worldwide. It is also not designed to list the dimensions of every type of trailer, nor to list size and weight limits for trailers in every country, state and province worldwide.

## Trailer Types

In the 110 or so years since motor vehicles were modified to carry merchandise rather than just people, specialty trucks and truck trailers have been developed to transport every type of commodity imaginable. There are, however, ten basic types of trailers used in international trade. Almost all trailers in existence are a variation of these trailer types. They are:

- Freight Van
- Refrigerated Van (Reefer)
- Container Carrier
- Platform Trailer
- Tanker
- Livestock Trailer
- Dry Bulk Trailer
- Furniture Van
- Auto Transporter
- Timber Trailer

## Trailer Manufacturers

While there are but ten types of trailers, there are many variations of each type of trailer. Trailer manufacturers offer a wide variety of custom-built (purpose-built) trailers for every need imaginable. In addition, it is not unusual for a manufacturer to make one type of trailer, but with different dimensions, features and options for special applications.

Note that while there is a limited number of truck and tractor manufacturers worldwide, there are many more manufacturers of truck trailers. While only large industrialized countries have truck and engine manufacturers, most medium-sized countries have at least one or several trailer manufacturers. As a result, a truly comprehensive worldwide guide to truck trailers would require a volume of its own.

## National, State and Provincial Roadway Requirements

One factor affecting truck trailers is the body of national, state and provincial requirements regulating motor vehicles, commercial trucking and highway safety. Each country has its own requirements based on its roadways, bridges, topography, weather conditions, etc.

In addition, state and provincial governments also regulate trucking. It is not at all uncommon for a country to have different requirements for each state and province (i.e., Canada and the USA).

## Notes

Every effort has been made to accurately describe the different trailer types listed. However:

- Different trailer manufacturers worldwide produce a variety of models designed for specific applications.
- Weight and capacity data are a function of trailer manufacturer, model and roadway requirements.
- While many of the dimensions listed in this guide relate to the North American market, the trailer types themselves are universal. Every trailer type listed has its equivalent in every country.
- Be certain to inquire about precise specifications for a trailer type from your logistics provider prior to making final decisions regarding a shipment.

## Guide to Truck Trailer Dimensions

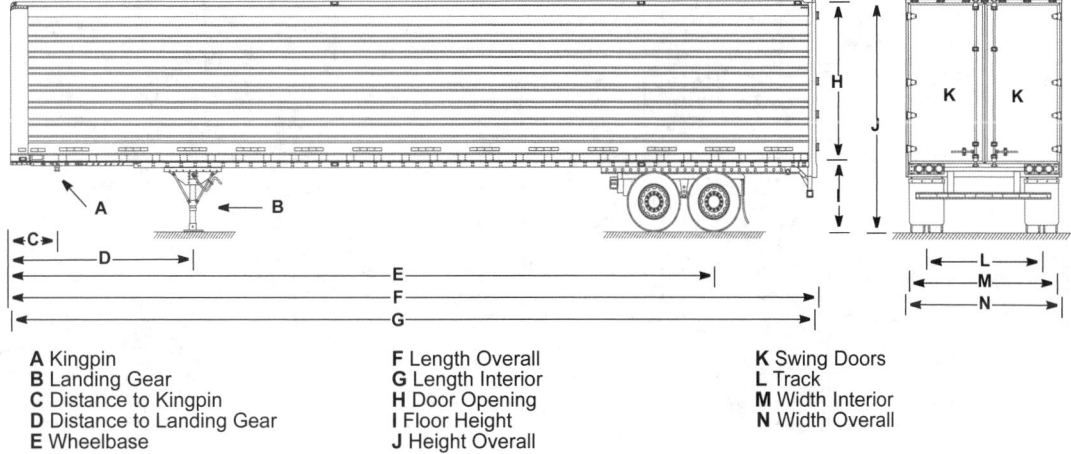

| | | |
|---|---|---|
| **A** Kingpin | **F** Length Overall | **K** Swing Doors |
| **B** Landing Gear | **G** Length Interior | **L** Track |
| **C** Distance to Kingpin | **H** Door Opening | **M** Width Interior |
| **D** Distance to Landing Gear | **I** Floor Height | **N** Width Overall |
| **E** Wheelbase | **J** Height Overall | |

# Freight (Van, Box) Trailer

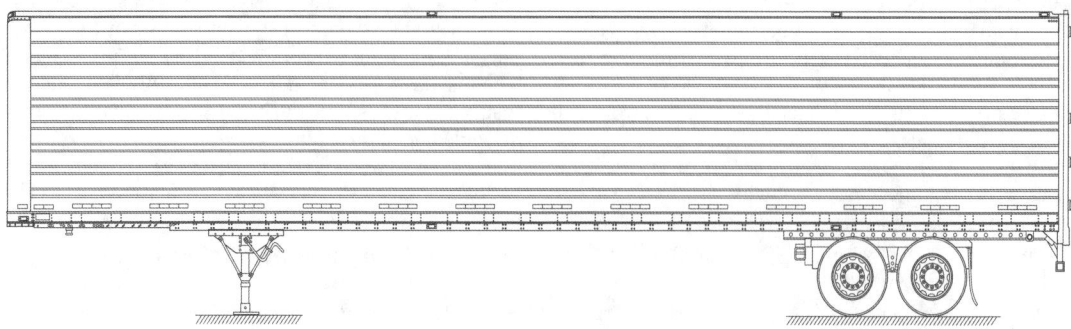

## Use
- Freight trailers (also called dry vans or simply "boxes") are designed to carry virtually any kind of boxed, crated, or palletized freight.

## Configurations
- Standard lengths: 28', 32', 36', 40', 42', 43', 45', 48' and 53'.
- Standard widths: 96"–102"
- Standard heights: 12.5'–13.5' overall.
- Shorter trailers are typically used for local deliveries or in tandem "truck trains."
- Standard axle/wheel configuration: 2-axle/8-wheel. For heavier loads: 3-axle/12-wheel or 4-axle/16-wheel configurations are also available.

## Features and Options
- Rear swing doors or roll up doors.
- One or two side doors, rollerbeds.

## Notes
- Freight trailers are manufactured worldwide by a multitude of local and international firms.

- Dimensional, weight and capacity data are a function of cargo requirements, trailer manufacturer, trailer model and national, state and provincial roadway requirements.

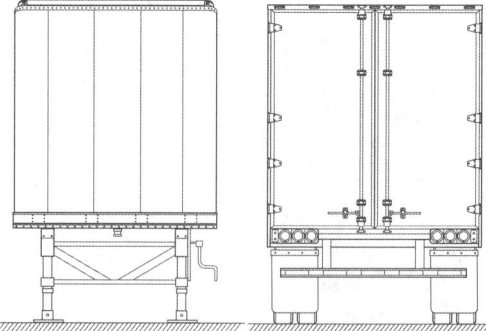

Front View - Trailer above "Landing Gear" below

Rear View (Note swing doors)

## Standard Dimensions

| OVERALL | | | INTERIOR | | | REAR SWING DOOR | | CAPACITY (volume) | TARE |
|---|---|---|---|---|---|---|---|---|---|
| Length | Width | Height | Length | Width | Height | Width | Height | | |
| 40' | 96" | 12'6" | 39'6" | 92.5" | 94.5" | 92" | 92" | 2,398 cu ft | 11,300 lbs |
| | 96" | 13'0" | 39'6" | 92.5" | 100.5" | 92" | 98" | 2,550 cu ft | 11,400 lbs |
| | 96" | 13'6" | 39'6" | 92.5" | 106.5" | 92" | 104" | 2,702 cu ft | 11,500 lbs |
| 42' / 43' | 96" | 12'6" | 41'6"/42'6" | 92.5" | 94.5" | 92" | 92" | 2,549 cu ft | 11,800/12,000 lbs |
| | 96" | 13'0" | 41'6"/42'6" | 92.5" | 100.5" | 92" | 98" | 2,711 cu ft | 11,900/12,100 lbs |
| | 96" | 13'6" | 41'6"/42'6" | 92.5" | 106.5" | 92" | 104" | 2,873 cu ft | 12,000/12,200 lbs |
| 45' | 96" | 12'6" | 44'6" | 92.5" | 94.5" | 92" | 92" | 2,701 cu ft | 12,400 lbs |
| | 96" | 13'0" | 44'6" | 92.5" | 100.5" | 92" | 98" | 2,873 cu ft | 12,500 lbs |
| | 96" | 13'6" | 44'6" | 92.5" | 106.5" | 92" | 106" | 3,044 cu ft | 12,600 lbs |
| | 102" | 13'6" | 44'6" | 92.5" | 106.5" | 98" | 106" | 3,242 cu ft | 12,950 lbs |
| 48' | 96" | 13'6" | 47'6" | 92.5" | 106.5" | 92" | 106.5" | 3,250 cu ft | 13,200 lbs |
| | 102" | 13'6" | 47'6" | 98.5" | 100.625" | 98" | 100.625" | 3,464 cu ft | 13,500 lbs |
| | | 13'6" | 47'6" | 98.5" | 108" | 98" | 108" | 3,509 cu ft | 13,500 lbs |
| 53' | 102" | 13'6" | 47'6" | 98.5" | 107.375" | 94" | 102" | 3,489 cu ft | 14,400 lbs |
| 48' Wedge | 102" | 13'6" | 47'6" | 98.5" 98.5" | Front 108" Rear 110" | 98" | 110" | 3,542 cu ft | 13,500 lbs |
| 53' Wedge | 102" | 13'6" | 52'6" | 98.5" | Front 108" Rear 110" | 98" | 110" | 3,914 cu ft | 14,400 lbs |

# Reefer (Refrigerated) Van

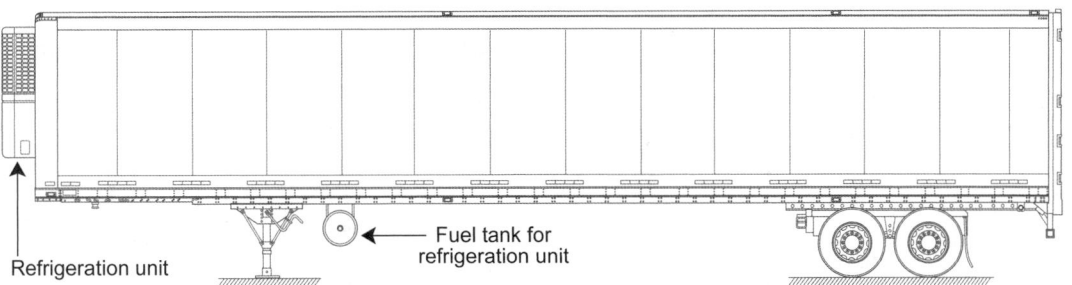

Refrigeration unit

Fuel tank for refrigeration unit

## Use

- Reefers are insulated and refrigerated trailers designed to transport perishable items.
- Commodities transported include vegetables, fruits, milk, juices, meats and poultry

## Configurations

- Standard lengths: 28', 32', 36', 40', 48' and 53'.
- Standard widths: 96"–102".
- Standard heights: 12.5'–13.5' overall.
- Shorter trailers are typically used for local deliveries or in tandem "truck trains."
- Standard axle/wheel configuration: 2-axle/8-wheel. For heavier loads: 3-axle/12-wheel or 4-axle/16-wheel configurations are also available.

## Features and Options

- Rear swing doors or roll up doors.
- One or two side doors.
- Moveable bulkheads, liftgates, and temperature recording and monitoring systems.
- Single or multi-temperature models.
- A wide variety of refrigeration units are available.

## Notes

- Freight trailers are manufactured worldwide by a multitude of local and international firms.

- Dimensional, weight and capacity data are a function of cargo requirements, trailer manufacturer, trailer model and national, state and provincial roadway requirements.

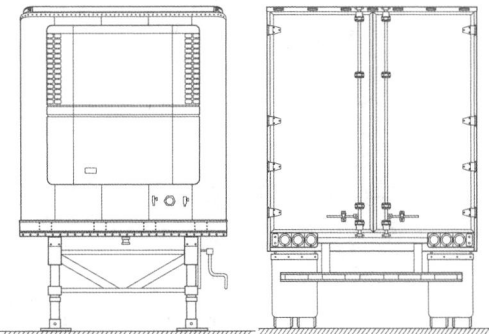

Front View
(Note refrigeration unit at top)

Rear View
(Note swing doors

## Standard Dimensions

| TYPE | OVERALL | | | INTERIOR | | | VOLUME (approximate) | AIRFLOW (approximate) | REFRIGERATION CAPACITY |
|---|---|---|---|---|---|---|---|---|---|
| | Length | Width | Height | Length | Width | Height | | | |
| Single or Multi Temp | 28' | 96" | 13'6" | 27'3" | 90" | 104.5" | 1,780 cu ft | 2,500 - 3,500 cfm | 20,000 - 60,000 BTU |
| Single or Multi Temp | 32' | 96" | 13'6" | 31'3" | 90" | 104.5" | 2,040 cu ft | 2,500 - 3,500 cfm | 20,000 - 60,000 BTU |
| Single or Multi Temp | 36' | 96" | 13'6" | 35'3" | 90" | 104.5" | 2,300 cu ft | 2,500 - 3,500 cfm | 20,000 - 60,000 BTU |
| Single or Multi Temp | 40' | 96" | 13'6" | 39'3" | 90" | 104.5" | 2,560 cu ft | 2,500 - 3,500 cfm | 20,000 - 60,000 BTU |
| Single or Multi Temp | 48' | 96" | 13'6" | 47'3" | 90" | 104.5" | 3,080 cu ft | 2,500 - 3,500 cfm | 20,000 - 60,000 BTU |
| Single or Multi Temp | 53' | 102" | 13'6" | 52'3" | 97.4" | 104.5" | 3,693 cu ft | 2,500 - 3,500 cfm | 20,000 - 60,000 BTU |

TRUCK TRAILERS

# Container Skeletal Carrier

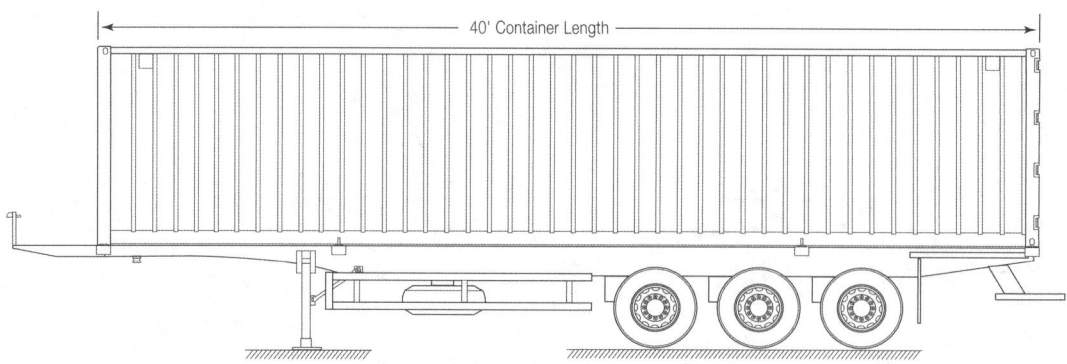

Side View - With 40' container mounted on top

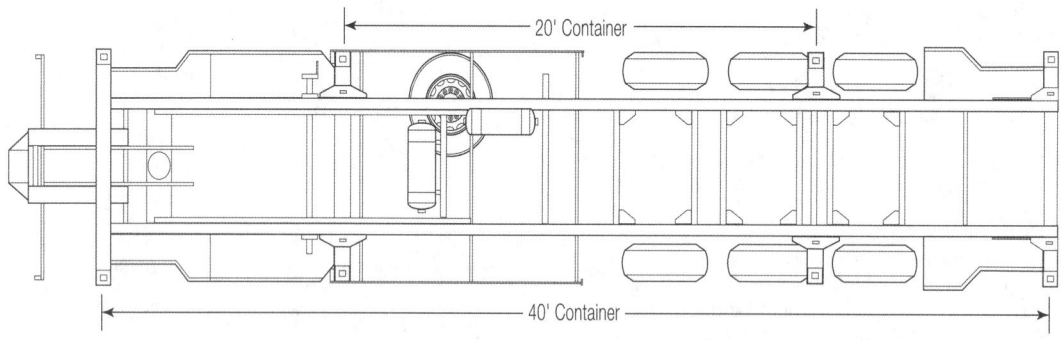

Top View (Note positioning for 20' and 40' containers)

## Use

- Container carriers are designed to transport standard international cargo containers of 20'—45'.
- Some models are able to transport non-standard and oversize containers.

## Configurations

- Models designed to transport a single specific size container (20', 40', 45', etc.)
- Models designed in adjustable ("zoom") configurations to work with a range of different sized standard and non-standard containers.
- Standard axle/wheel configuration: 2-axle/8-wheel. For heavier loads: 3-axle/12-wheel configurations are also available.
- Specially designed brackets hold the container to the carrier.

## Notes

- Container carriers are manufactured worldwide by a multitude of local and international firms.
- Dimensional, weight and capacity data are a function of cargo requirements, trailer manufacturer, trailer model and national, state and provincial roadway requirements.

## Standard Dimensions

| OVERALL | | | CONTAINER SIZES | TARE | NET CAPACITY | GROSS CAPACITY |
|---|---|---|---|---|---|---|
| Length | Width | Height | | | | |
| 41.5' | 98" | 51.5" | 20' – 40' | 12,100 lbs / 5,500 kg | 71,390 lbs / 32,450 kg | 83,600 lbs / 38,000 kg |

# Platform (Flat Bed) Trailer

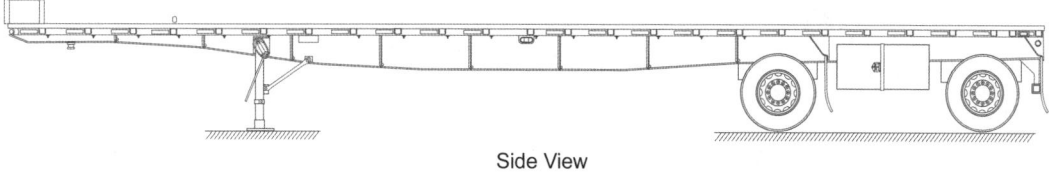

Side View

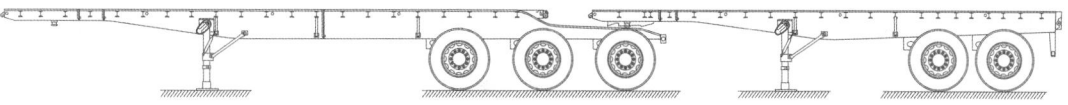

Tandem Side View

## Use

- Platform (flat bed) trailers are designed to transport oversize cargo that normally would not fit into standard freight trailers.
- Platform trailers are used especially for the transport of goods that must be loaded from the side or top of the trailer.
- Standard cargo for platform trailers includes: ocean freight containers, machinery, construction equipment, lumber, plywood, steel, pipe and rebar.

## Variations

- Standard lengths: 26', 40', 42', 45', and 48'.
- Extendible lengths: see below.

## Notes

- Different trailer manufacturers worldwide produce a variety of models designed for different freight configurations.

- Dimensional, weight and capacity data are a function of cargo requirements, trailer manufacturer, trailer model and national, state and provincial roadway requirements.

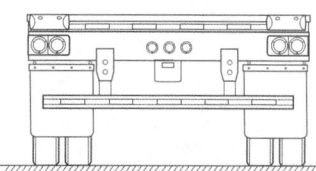

Platform Trailer
Rear View

## Standard Dimensions

| TYPE | OVERALL | | TARE | WEIGHT CAPACITY |
| --- | --- | --- | --- | --- |
| | Length | Width | | |
| Platform | 26' | 96" | 6,100 lbs. | 50,000 - 55,000 lbs. |
| Platform | 40' | 96" | 10,800 lbs. | 50,000 - 55,000 lbs. |
| Platform | 42' | 96" | 11,050 lbs. | 50,000 - 55,000 lbs. |
| Platform | 45' | 96" | 12,420 lbs. | 50,000 - 55,000 lbs. |
| Platform | 45' | 102" | 12,870 lbs. | 50,000 - 55,000 lbs. |
| Platform | 48' | 102" | 13,430 lbs. | 50,000 - 55,000 lbs. |
| Platform | 48' triaxle | 102" | 15,460 lbs. | 50,000 - 55,000 lbs. |
| Extendible | 40'–65' | 96" | 15,900 lbs | NOTE:<br>Extendible Length/Weight Capacity<br>(decreases in extended position)<br>40'/80,000 lbs<br>50'/48,000 lbs<br>55'/35,000 lbs<br>60'/30,000 lbs<br>65'/27,000 lbs<br>70'/25,000 lbs |
| Extendible | 40'–65' | 102" | 16,500 lbs | |
| Extendible | 45'–70' | 96" | 16,800 lbs | |
| Extendible | 45'–73' | 96"/102" | 16,990/17,250 lbs | |
| Extendible | 48'–76' | 96"/102" | 17,400/17,650 lbs | |
| Extendible– Single Drop | 45'–65' | 96" | 17,500 lbs | |
| Extendible– Triaxle | 45'–75' | 102" | 22,570 lbs | |

TRUCK TRAILERS

# Platform Dropdeck/Gooseneck Trailers

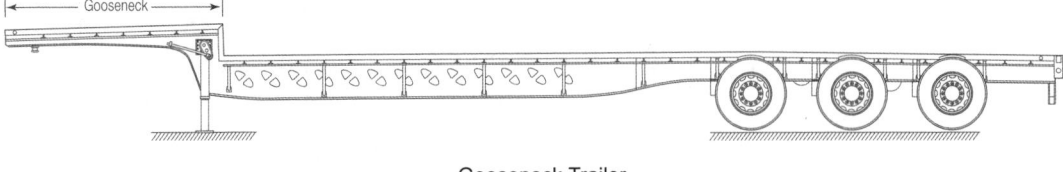

Gooseneck Trailer
Single

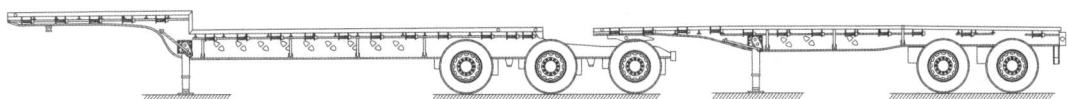

Gooseneck Trailer
Tandem

## Use

- Platform (gooseneck, low deck, dropdeck) trailers are designed to transport oversize cargo that normally would not fit into standard freight trailers.
- Platform trailers are especially used for the transport of goods that must be loaded from the side or top of the trailer.
- Standard cargo for platform trailers includes: ocean freight containers, machinery, heavy construction equipment, lumber, plywood, steel, pipe and rebar.

## Variations

- Standard lengths: 40', 42', 45', and 48'.

## Features and Options

- Also available as tandems

## Notes

- Different trailer manufacturers worldwide produce a variety of models designed for different freight configurations.
- Dimensional, weight and capacity data are a function of cargo requirements, trailer manufacturer, trailer model and national, state and provincial roadway requirements.

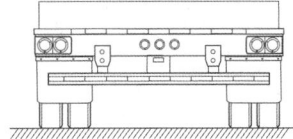

Gooseneck Trailer
Rear View

## Standard Dimensions

| TYPE | OVERALL | | TARE | WEIGHT CAPACITY |
|------|---------|---------|------|-----------------|
|  | Length | Width |  |  |
| Dropdeck | 40' | 96" | 12,800 lbs. | 70,000 lbs. |
| Dropdeck | 42' | 96" | 13,200 lbs. | 70,000 lbs. |
| Dropdeck | 45' | 96" | 13,600 lbs. | 66,000 lbs. |
| Dropdeck | 48' | 196" | 13,060 lbs. | 66,000 lbs. |
| Dropdeck | 48' | 102" | 13,350 lbs. | 66,000 lbs. |
| Dropdeck | 48' | 102" | 14,100 lbs. | 66,000 lbs. |
| Lowbed | 40' | 96" | 15,900 lbs | 70,000 lbs. |
| Lowbed | 40' | 96" | 16,500 lbs | 70,000 lbs. |
| Lowbed | 40' | 102" | 16,800 lbs | 70,000 lbs. |
| Lowbed | 41.5' | 102" | 16,990/17,250 lbs | 70,000 lbs. |

# Tanker Trailer

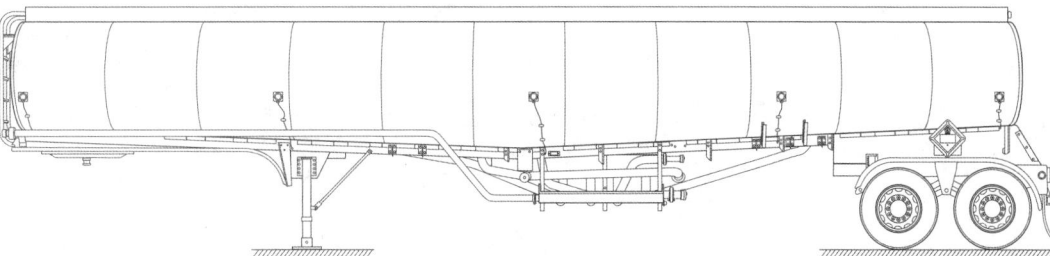

## Use
- Tanker trailers are designed to carry a wide variety of fluid cargo.
- Standard cargo for tankers includes: refined gasoline, heating oil, natural gas, acids, industrial chemicals, caustic soda, clay slurry, cooking oils, corn syrup, orange juice, milk, and other foodstuffs.
- Some fluid cargo requires specially designed tanker trailers. For example, tankers designed to transport caustic soda and certain acids require sidewalls, exterior paint and fittings that will withstand the corrosive effects of the cargo.

## Variations
- Standard lengths: 40', 42', 43', 45', 48' and 53'.
- Standard axle/wheel configuration: 2-axle/8-wheel. For heavier loads: 3-axle/12-wheel or 4-axle/16-wheel configurations are also available.

## Features and Options
- Multiple compartments (1-7)
- Discharge pumps
- Metering equipment
- Insulated tanks
- Pressure tanks
- Ladders
- Walkways
- Hose carriers
- Belly cabinets.

## Notes
- Different trailer manufacturers worldwide produce a variety of models designed for different freight configurations.
- Dimensional, weight and capacity data are a function of cargo requirements, trailer manufacturer, trailer model and national, state and provincial roadway requirements.

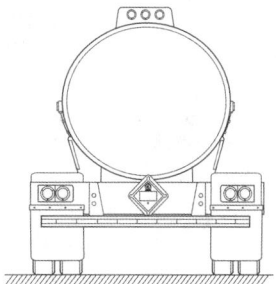

Tanker Trailer
Rear View

## Standard Dimensions

| OVERALL | | | TARE | BULKHEADS | CAPACITY |
|---|---|---|---|---|---|
| Length | Width | Height | | | |
| 28'–53' | 96"102" | 12'–13'6" | Varies | 1–7 | 3,000–9500 gallons |

**TRUCK TRAILERS**

# TRUCK TRAILERS

# Livestock Trailer

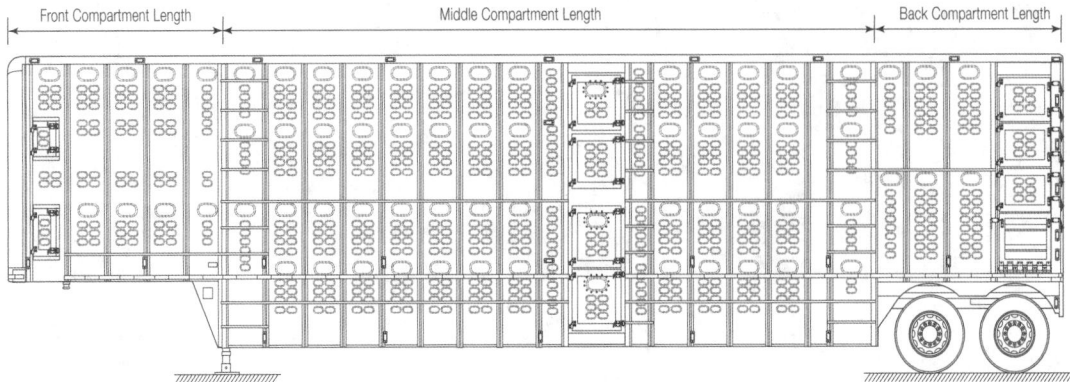

Front Compartment Length | Middle Compartment Length | Back Compartment Length

## Use
- Livestock trailers are designed to carry cattle, calves, sheep, hogs, goats and other livestock.
- This type of trailer is not used for horses or poultry

## Variations
- Standard lengths: 40', 46', 48', and 53'.
- Standard widths: 96"–102".
- Multi-deck options (2- and 3-deck) are available for the transport of small, medium and large animals.
- Standard axle/wheel configuration: 2-axle/8-wheel. For heavier loads: 3-axle/12-wheel or 4-axle/16-wheel configurations are also available.

## Features and Options
- Ventilation holes on sides
- Rear and side doors designed based on type of livestock to be transported
- Interior ramps to lower-, mid- and upper-decks

## Notes
- Different trailer manufacturers worldwide produce a variety of models designed for the transport of specific types of livestock.
- Dimensional, weight and capacity data are a function of cargo requirements, trailer manufacturer, trailer model and national, state and provincial roadway requirements.

## Standard Trailer Dimensions

| OVERALL DIMENSIONS | | |
|---|---|---|
| Length | Width | Height |
| 46' | 102" | 13'6" |
| 48' | 102" | 13'6" |
| 53' | 102" | 13'6" |

## Typical Livestock Deck Heights

| LIVESTOCK | DECK HEIGHT |
|---|---|
| Cattle | 69" - 71" |
| Calves | 66" - 67" |
| Sheep | 34" - 35" |
| Hogs | 35" - 36" |

## Livestock Decking Configurations

### Cattle/Calf Model
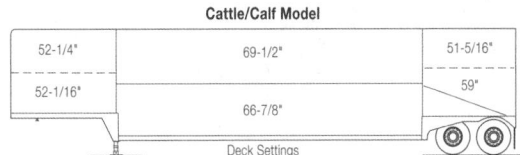

### Cattle/Hog Model
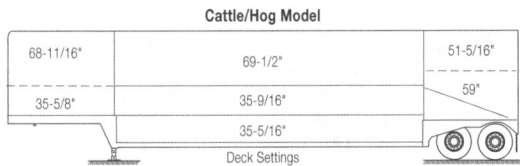

### Fat Cattle Model
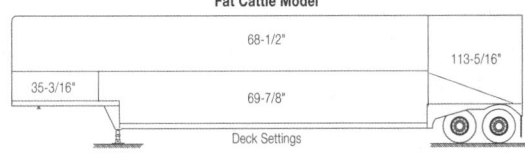

### Sheep Model
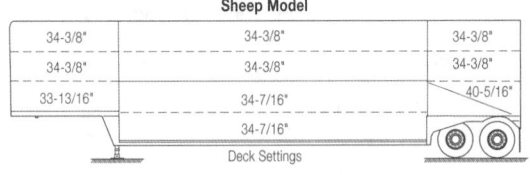

### Tri-Axle Cattle Model
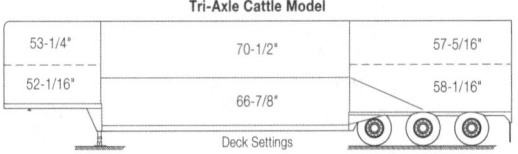

Source: Wilson Trailer Co. www.wilsontrailer.com

# Dry Bulk Trailer (Hopper)

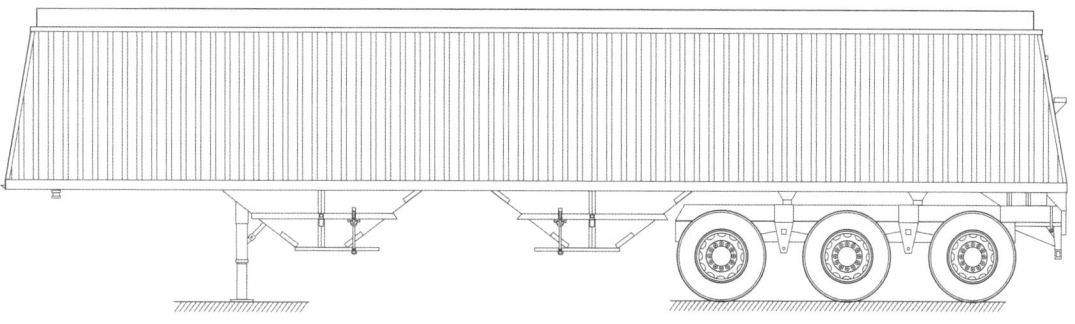

Dry Bulk (Grain) Trailer - Single

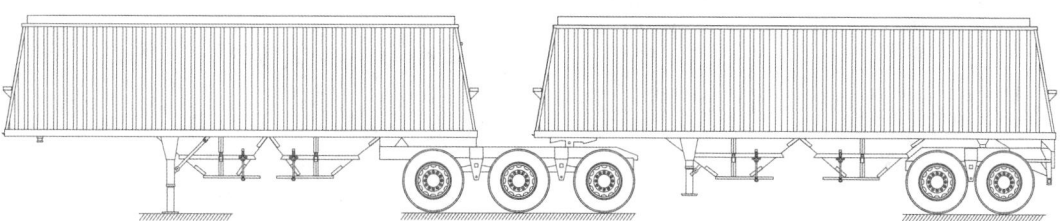

Dry Bulk (Grain) Trailer - Tandem

## Use

- Dry bulk trailers are designed to carry dry free-flowing commodities including grain, shelled corn, cornmeal, feeds, hulled rice, beans, gravel, limestone (loose and pulverized), and sand.

## Variations

- Standard lengths: 26' to 42'.
- Standard widths: 96"–102".
- Hopper configurations: single, double and triple.
- Open and closed end configurations.
- Steel and aluminum models.
- Available as singles, tandems, and three trailer truck "trains".

## Notes

- Dry bulk trailers use rolled tarpaulin tops rather than rigid tops.
- Typical dry bulk trailers use hoppers to unload, however, others emply conveyor systems.
- Different trailer manufacturers worldwide produce a variety of models designed for different freight configurations.
- Dimensional, weight and capacity data are a function of cargo requirements, trailer manufacturer, trailer model and national, state and provincial roadway requirements.

## Standard Dimensions

| TYPE | OVERALL (lead unit) | | | OVERALL (rear unit) | | | TARE WEIGHT | CAPACITY | | HOPPERS | |
|---|---|---|---|---|---|---|---|---|---|---|---|
| | Length | Width | Height | Length | Width | Height | | Lead Unit | Rear Unit | Lead | Rear |
| Single (closed end) | 42' | 102" | 132" (75" wall) | – | – | – | 13,800 lbs | 2,150 cu ft | – | 2 | – |
| Single (open end) | 45' | 102" | 136" (79" wall) | – | – | – | 12,900 lbs | 2,138 cu ft | – | 3 | – |
| Single (open end) | 36' | 102" | 132" (75" wall) | – | – | – | 10,100 lbs | 1,700 cu ft | – | 2 | – |
| Single (open end) | 40' | 102" | 132" (75" wall) | – | – | – | 10,500 lbs | 1,900 cu ft | – | 2 | – |
| Single (open end) | 42' | 102" | 132" (75" wall) | – | – | – | 10,900 lbs | 2,000 cu ft | – | 2 | – |
| Tandem (open end) | 27'10" | 102" | 140" (83" wall) | 30' | 102" | 140" (83" wall) | 20,500 lbs | 1,485 cu ft | 1,605 cu ft | 2 | 2 |
| Tandem (open end) | 36' | 102" | 124" (67" wall) | 40' | 102" | 124" (67" wall) | 20,000 lbs | 1,500 cu ft | 1,700 cu ft | 2 | 2 |
| Tandem (closed end) | 28' | 102" | 136" (79" wall) | 30' | 102" | 136" (79" wall) | 22,800 lbs | 1,365 cu ft | 1,450 cu ft | 2 | 2 |
| Tandem (closed end) | 36' | 102" | 124" (67" wall) | 40' | 102" | 124" (67" wall) | 21,000 lbs | 1,500 cu ft | 1,700 cu ft | 2 | 2 |

**TRUCK TRAILERS**

# Deep Drop Furniture/Electronics Van

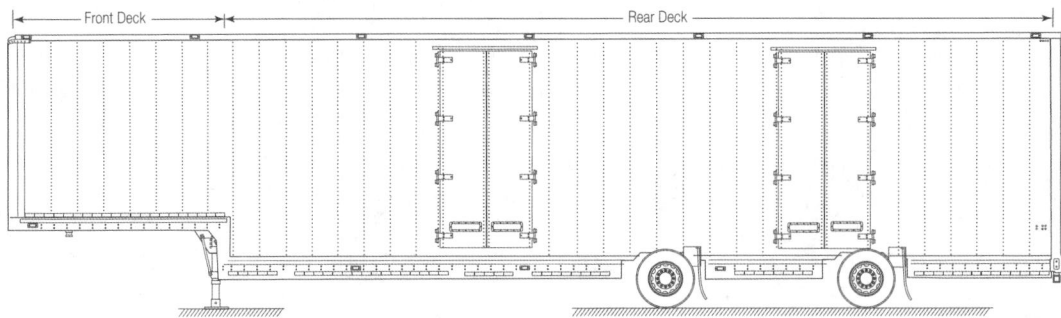

## Use
- Deep drop vans are specially designed to transport large, bulky and relatively light cargo (weight to volume).
- Deep drop vans are used especially in the transport of furniture, household goods and electronics.

## Variations
- Standard lengths: 45', 48' and 53' overall.
- Standard heights: 13'6" overall.
- Standard widths: 96"–102" overall.
- Rear door(s): Swing doors are standard.
- Side doors: 1 or 2 side swing doors are standard depending upon the length of the trailer.

## Features and Options
- Lower rear deck to facilitate loading and create greater cargo capacity
- Air ride suspensions to protect fragile cargo.
- Lockable belly compartments.
- Ramps.

## Notes
- Different trailer manufacturers worldwide produce a variety of models designed for different freight configurations.
- Dimensional, weight and capacity data are a function of cargo requirements, trailer manufacturer, trailer model and national, state and provincial roadway requirements.

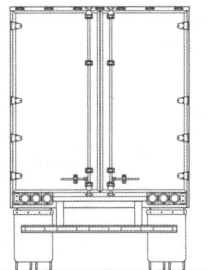

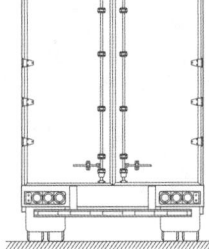

Standard Freight Van
Rear View
(Note higher deck
and lower overall height)

Deepdrop Furniture Van
Rear View
(Note lower deck
and greater overall height)

## Standard Dimensions

| OVERALL | | | INTERIOR | | | REAR SWING DOOR | | VOLUME | TARE |
|---|---|---|---|---|---|---|---|---|---|
| Length | Width | Height | Length | Width | Height | Width | Height | | |
| 45' | 96" | 13'6" | 44'7" | 92.5" | 106"/123" | 92" | 119" | 3,420 cu ft | 13,500 lbs |
| 48' | 102" | 13'6" | 47'7" | 98.5" | 106"/122" | 98" | 118" | 3,789 cu ft | 14,250 lbs |
| 53' | 102" | 13'6" | 52'7" | 98.5" | 106"/119" | 98" | 119" | 4,395 cu ft | 15,000 lbs |

T
R
U
C
K

T
R
A
I
L
E
R
S

# Auto Transport Tractor – Trailer

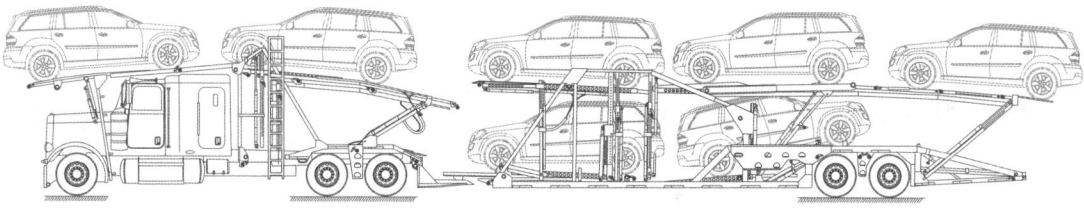

## Use
- Auto transport tractor trailers are designed to transport automobiles, sport utility vehicles, and small vans, from manufacturing plants to distributors, from manufacturing plants to ports, but most commonly from seaports (Ro-Ro vessels) to inland distributors.

## Variations
- Auto transporters come in two general configurations:
  1) Truck tractor trailer combinations where the truck tractor transports up to three vehicles and the trailer transports up to six vehicles, and
  2) Trailers designed to transport up to nine vehicles pulled by a standard truck tractor.
- Specially designed covered auto transport trailers are available for the transport of high value automobiles.

## Notes
- A substantial market has energed for the transport of private party automobiles in household relocation and the transport of specialty and high value vehicles domestically and internationally.
- Different trailer manufacturers worldwide produce a variety of models designed for different freight configurations.
- Dimensional, weight and capacity data are a function of cargo requirements, trailer manufacturer, trailer model and national, state and provincial roadway requirements.

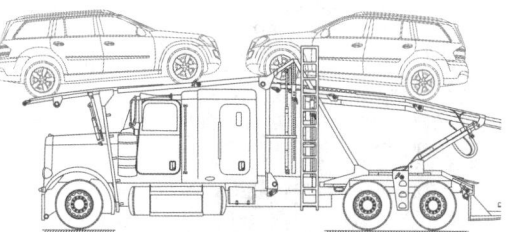

Auto Tractor
Side View Detail
(Note automobiles
on top of tractor)

## Standard Dimensions

| TYPE | OVERALL | | | TARE | VEHICLES TRANSPORTED |
|---|---|---|---|---|---|
| | Length | Width | Height | | |
| Tractor (only) | 29' | 102" | varies | n/a | 3 |
| Trailer (only) | 46'6" | 102" | varies | n/a | 6 |
| Tractor-Trailer Combined | 75'6" | 102" | varies | n/a | 9 |

**TRUCK TRAILERS**

# Timber (Logger) Trailer

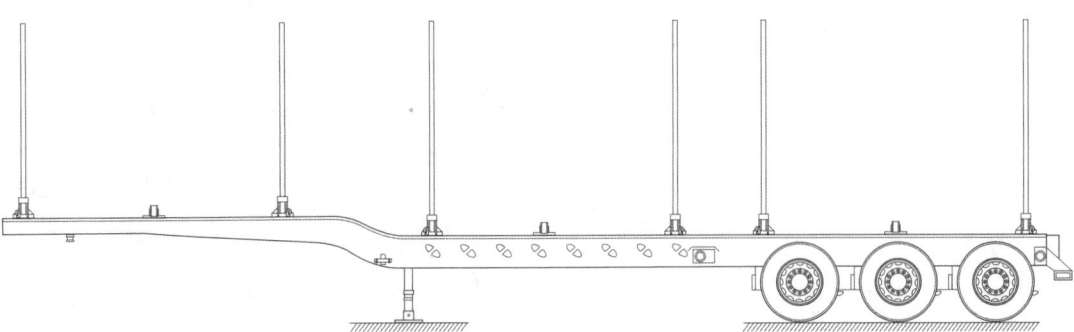

## Use
- Timber (logger) trailers are designed to carry raw timber from logging operations to sawmills (domestic or international), or to barge or ocean-going vessels for export.

## Variations
- Logging trailers are essentially a flat bed trailer, or trailer chassis with extremely rigid vertical stakes along its perimeter to hold logs in place.
- Trailer dimensions are dependent upon road access to the logging operation, species being harvested, sawmill requirements, distance to the sawmill or export loading center and other factors.
- Standard lengths: Singles: 40'–53'. Tandems: 28'–32'.
- Standard axle configuration: 2-axle/8-wheel. For heavier loads: 3-axle/12-wheel, or 4-axle/16-wheel configurations are also available.
- Logging trailers are available in both single trailer and tandem trailer configurations.

## Features and Options
- Some logging trailers are equipped with loading cranes.

## Notes
- Logs are held in place with chains and chain tighteners.
- Different trailer manufacturers worldwide produce a variety of models designed for different freight configurations.

- Dimensional, weight and capacity data are a function of cargo requirements, trailer manufacturer, trailer model and national, state and provincial roadway requirements.

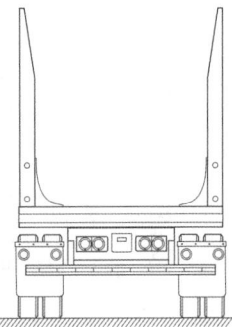

Timber (Logger) Trailer
Rear View
(Note stakes for holding logs in place)

## Standard Dimensions

| OVERALL | | | WHEEL BASE | AXLES | DROP | STAKE HEIGHT | CAPACITY |
|---|---|---|---|---|---|---|---|
| Length | Width | Height | | | | | |
| 48' | 102" | 12'9" | 37'6.5" | 5 | 50" | 8'7" | 25,000 lbs (actual load dependent upon diameter and shape of logs) |
| 48'8" | 102" | 13'10" | 38'1.5" | 3 | 59.5" | 8'10.5" | 25,000 lbs (actual load dependent upon diameter and shape of logs) |
| 48'8" | 102" | 13'10" | 38'1.5" | 3 | 55.75" | 9'3" | 22,500 lbs (actual load dependent upon diameter and shape of logs) |
| 50' | 114"* | 15'* | 38'1.5" | 3 | 58" | 10'2" | 22,500 lbs (actual load dependent upon diameter and shape of logs) |

* Non-US interstate highway configuration.

# Guide to Railcars

## Introduction
This guide to railcars has been developed from materials obtained from a number of railcar manufacturers worldwide. It is designed to illustrat e the main types of railcars used in international trade and to give readers an insight into common configurations, dimensions and options.

## Railcar Types
In the almost 200 years since the railroad was invented specialty railcars have been developed to transport every type of commodity imaginable. There are, however, nine basic types of railcars used in international trade. They are: Boxcar, Refrigerated Boxcar (Reefer), Flatcar, Tanker, Container Carrier, Gondola, Hopper, Center Partition Railcar, Auto Transporter.

## Railcar Manufacturers
While there are but nine types of railcars, there are many variations of each. Railcar manufacturers offer a wide variety of custom-built (purpose-built) models for every need imaginable. In addition, manufacturers design base models with variations in length, width, height and with special features and options.

Manufacturers also offer similar base models with different wheel and truck configurations for use on different domestic and international railway systems.

## Railway Requirements
Factors affecting railcar design specifications include railway beds, curves, track, railway gauge, bridges and tunnels, and condition of the system as a whole.
*   The quality, composition and condition of railway beds affect the weight and speed of a railway car.
*   Railway curves affect turning radius requirements.
*   Railway track type determines wheel requirements.
*   Railway gauge determines the width between wheels.
*   Bridges and tunnels determine maximum height.
*   The condition of the railway system determines gross weights and load limits for railcar configurations.

## Railway Gauge
Rail gauge is the measure of the distance between the two rails of a railroad.
*   **Standard gauge** (or international gauge) is 4' 8½" and is used in 60 percent of the world's rail systems.
*   **Broad gauge** are railways that are greater than 4' 8½" in width.
*   **Narrow gauge** are any railways that are less than 4' 8½" in width.
*   **Dual gauge** are railways that have three or four rails positioned such that trains of two different gauges can use it.
*   A **break of gauge** is where railways of two different gauges meet.

## Notes
Every effort has been made to accurately describe the different types of railcars listed. However:
*   Different railcar manufacturers worldwide produce a variety of models designed for specific applications.
*   Weight and capacity data are a function of railcar manufacturer, railcar model, and rail system requirements.
*   The Dimensions, Weight/Capacity, and Curve Negotiability Radius data are valid only for the specific railcar make and model listed.
*   While different national and regional rail systems will have specialized requirements for railcar specifications, every type of railcar in this guide has an equivalent in every rail system worldwide.
*   Be certain to inquire about precise specifications for a railcar type from your logistics provider prior to making final decisions regarding a shipment.

## Acknowledgement
We wish to thank the Greenbrier Companies, Inc. for their contribution of general information about railcars, railcar specifications, and especially for their exceptional railcar illustrations for the samples provided. (www.gbrx.com)

**RAILCARS**

## Guide to Railcar Terminology and Dimensions

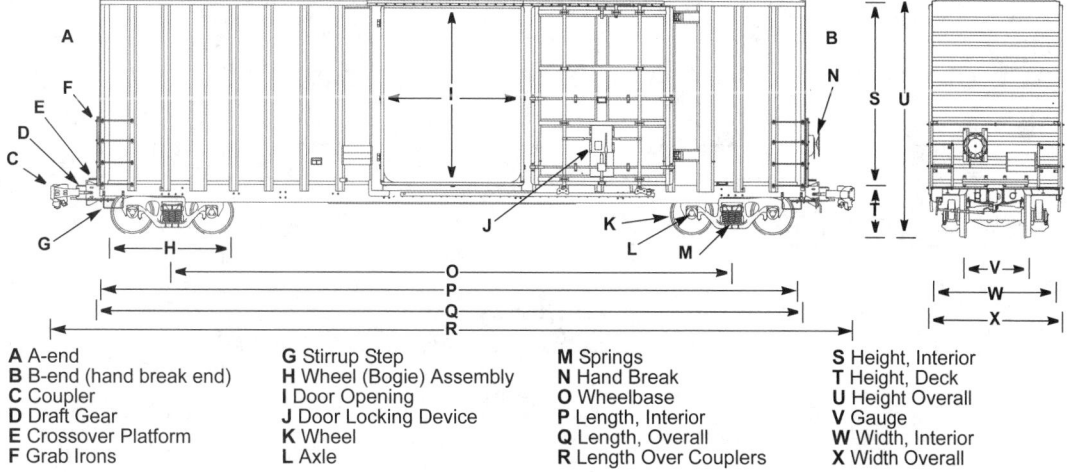

| | |
|---|---|
| **A** A-end | **G** Stirrup Step |
| **B** B-end (hand break end) | **H** Wheel (Bogie) Assembly |
| **C** Coupler | **I** Door Opening |
| **D** Draft Gear | **J** Door Locking Device |
| **E** Crossover Platform | **K** Wheel |
| **F** Grab Irons | **L** Axle |

| | |
|---|---|
| **M** Springs | **S** Height, Interior |
| **N** Hand Break | **T** Height, Deck |
| **O** Wheelbase | **U** Height Overall |
| **P** Length, Interior | **V** Gauge |
| **Q** Length, Overall | **W** Width, Interior |
| **R** Length Over Couplers | **X** Width Overall |

# Boxcar

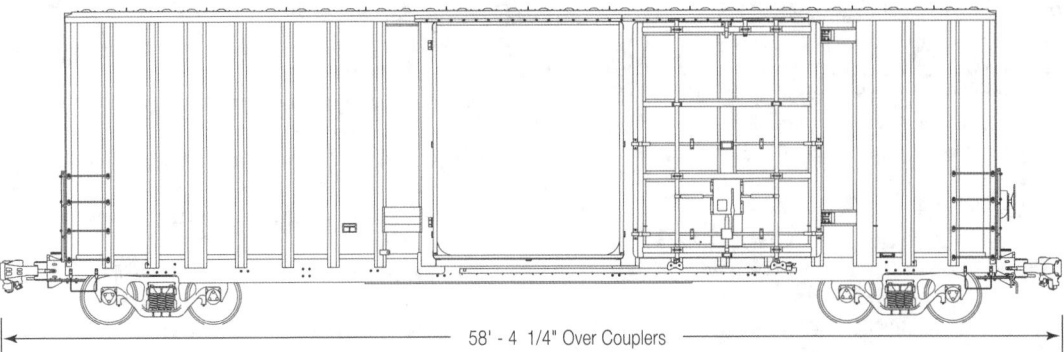

58' - 4 1/4" Over Couplers

## Use
- Boxcars are the most common type of cargo railcar in use worldwide and are designed to carry boxed, crated or palletized freight of all kinds.
- Common commodities transported include: paper products, canned goods, bulky freight.

## Key Features and Options
- Boxcars come in 50, 60, and 86-foot lengths with load capacities ranging from 70 to 105 tons.
- Single or double doors with plug or sliding configuration, cushioned or non-cushioned under-frames, insulated or non-insulated interiors. Box cars may also be equipped with various interior loading devices such as belt-rails or moveable bulkheads to secure loads.

## Notes
- Different railcar manufacturers worldwide produce a variety of models designed for specific applications.
- Weight and capacity data are a function of railcar manufacturer, railcar model, and rail system requirements.

- The following Dimensions, Weight/Capacity, and Curve Negotiability Radius data are valid for the Greenbrier Plate F Boxcar for Paper Products.

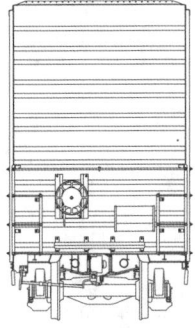

Boxcar
Rear View

## Dimensions

| Length, inside | 50' 6" | 15.4m |
|---|---|---|
| Length, over couplers | 58' 4$^{1}/_{4}$" | 17.79m |
| Total wheel base | 46' 8" | 14.22m |
| Height, inside | 13' $^{13}/_{16}$" | 3.98m |
| Height (extreme) | 16' 11$^{9}/_{16}$" | 5.18m |
| Door opening height | 12' 4" | 3.76m |
| Door opening width | 10' | 3.05m |
| Width, inside | 9' 6" | 2.90m |
| Width (extreme) | 10' 7$^{5}/_{8}$" | 3.24m |

## Weight/Capacity (estimated)

| Cubic capacity | 6,269 cu ft | 177.5m³ |
|---|---|---|
| Light weight | 74,200 lbs | 33,657kg |
| Gross rail load | 286,000 lbs | 129,727kg |
| Load limit | 211,800 lbs | 96,071kg |

## Curve Negotiability Radius

| Uncoupled | 150' | 45.72m |
|---|---|---|
| Coupled to like car | 203' | 61.87m |
| Coupled to base car | 230' | 70.10m |

Illustration and specifications courtesy The Greenbrier Companies, Inc.

# High Cube Boxcar

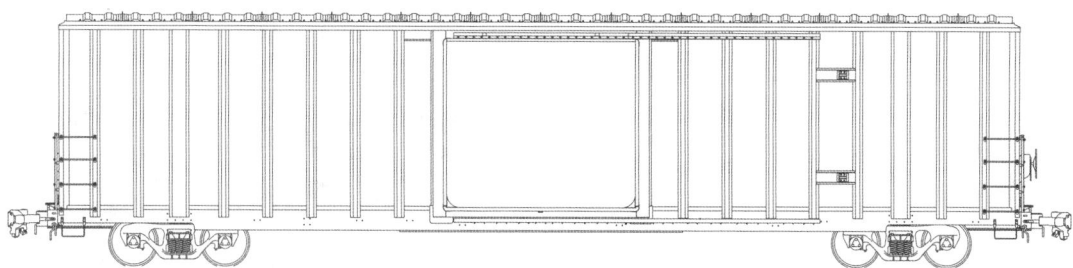

## Use
- Boxcars are the most common type of cargo railcar in use worldwide and are designed to carry boxed, crated or palletized freight of all kinds.
- Common commodities transported include: paper products, forest products, canned goods, food products.
- High cube boxcars are designed for transporting extremely bulky loads.

### Key Features and Options
- Box cars come in 50, 60, and 86-foot lengths with load capacities ranging from 70 to 105 tons.
- Single or double doors with plug or sliding configuration, cushioned or non-cushioned under-frames, insulated or non-insulated interiors. Box cars may also be equipped with various interior loading devices such as belt-rails or moveable bulkheads to secure loads.

### Notes
- Different railcar manufacturers worldwide produce a variety of models designed for specific applications.

- Weight and capacity data are a function of railcar manufacturer, railcar model, and rail system requirements.
- The following Dimensions, Weight/Capacity, and Curve Negotiability Radius data are valid for the Greenbrier 60' High-Cube Boxcar.

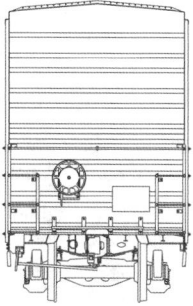

High Cube Boxcar
Rear View

**RAILCARS**

### Dimensions

| Length, inside | 60' 9" | 18.52m |
|---|---|---|
| Length, over couplers | 67' 10½" | 20.69m |
| Height, inside | 11' 5⅜" | 3.49m |
| Height (extreme) | 15' 9" | 4.80m |
| Door opening height | 10' 4" | 3.15m |
| Door opening width | 12' 0" | 3.66m |
| Width, inside | 9' 6" | 2.90m |
| Width (extreme) | 10' 7½" | 3.24m |

### Weight/Capacity (estimated)

| Cubic capacity | 6,607 cu ft | 187m³ |
|---|---|---|
| Light weight | 79,300 lbs | 35,970kg |
| Gross rail load | 286,000 lbs | 129,727kg |
| Load limit | 206,700 lbs | 93,758kg |

### Curve Negotiability Radius

| Uncoupled | 180' | 54.86m |
|---|---|---|
| Coupled to like car | 180' | 54.86m |
| Coupled to base car | 229' | 69.80m |

Illustration and specifications courtesy The Greenbrier Companies, Inc.

# Refrigerated Boxcar (Reefer)

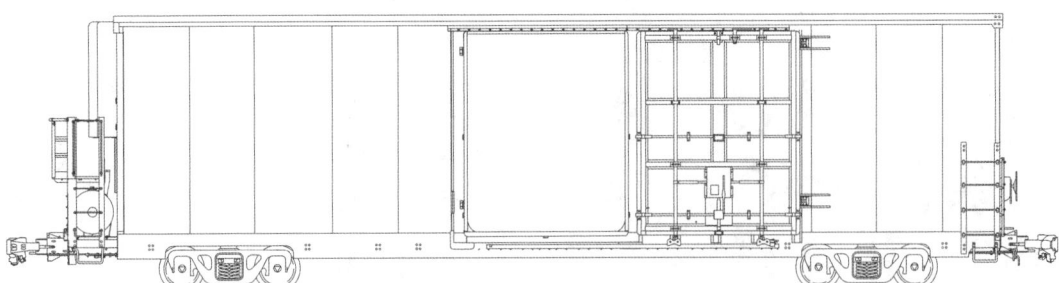

## Use
- Reefers (refrigerated) boxcars are designed to carry perishable freight at specific temperatures.
- Common commodities transported in reefer boxcars include vegetables, fruit, orange and other juices, milk, meat and poultry.

## Features and Options
- Reefers can be cooled with ice, a mechanical refrigeration system, or carbon dioxide (as dry ice or in liquid form).
- Some shipments of fruits and vegetables require only insulated and ventilated boxcars to remove the heat created in the ripening process.
- Available in a multitude of lengths.
- Meat reefers are equipped with specialized beef rails.
- Dairy and poultry products require specialized interior racks to ensure cooled air circulates.

## Notes
- Different railcar manufacturers worldwide produce a variety of models designed for specific applications.

- Weight and capacity data are a function of railcar manufacturer, railcar model, and rail system requirements.
- The following Dimensions, Weight/Capacity, and Curve Negotiability Radius data are valid only for listed railcar.

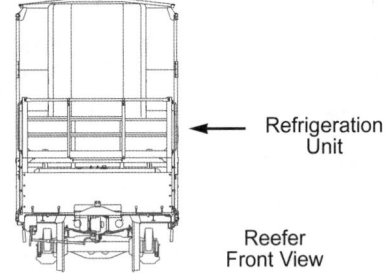

← Refrigeration Unit

Reefer
Front View

## Dimensions

| | | |
|---|---|---|
| Length, inside | 50' 6" | 15.4m |
| Length, over couplers | 58' 4$^1/_4$" | 17.79m |
| Total wheel base | 46' 8" | 14.22m |
| Height (inside | n/a | n/a |
| Height (extreme) | 16' 11$^9/_{16}$" | 5.18m |
| Door opening height | 12' 4" | 3.76m |
| Door opening width | 10' | 3.05m |
| Width inside | n/a | n/a |
| Width (extreme) | 10' 7$^5/_8$" | 3.24m |

## Weight/Capacity (estimated)

| | | |
|---|---|---|
| Cubic capacity | n/a | n/a |
| Light weight | n/a | n/a |
| Gross rail load | n/a | n/a |
| Load limit | n/a | n/a |

## Curve Negotiability Radius

| | | |
|---|---|---|
| Uncoupled | 150' | 45.72m |
| Coupled to like car | 203' | 61.87m |
| Coupled to base car | 230' | 70.10m |

RAILCARS

# Container Stack Railcar

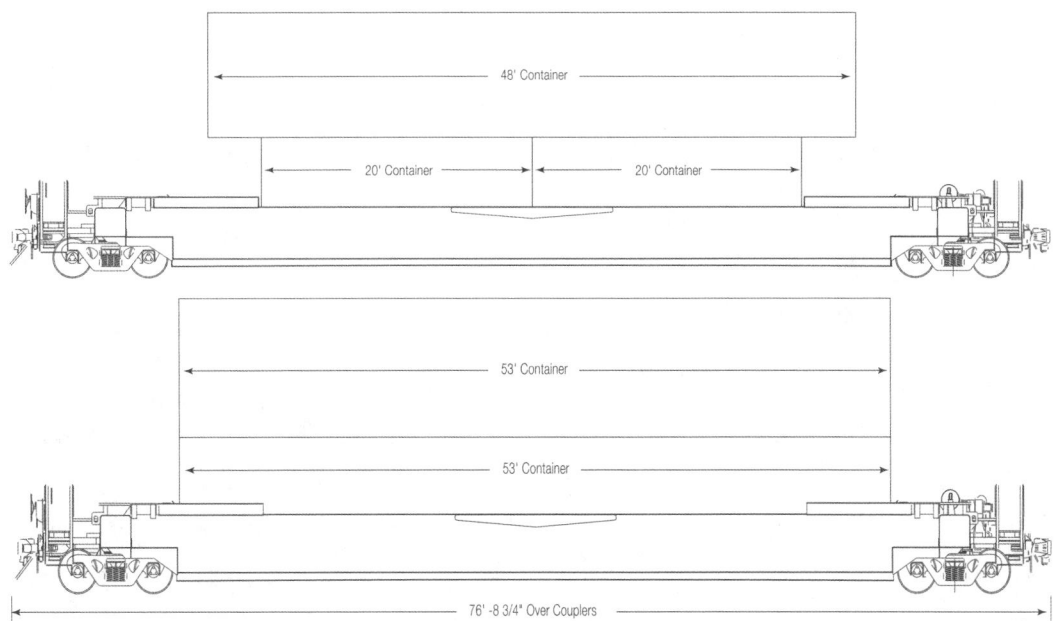

## Use

- Designed to carry international standard 20', 40', 45', 48', and 53' ocean freight containers in various stacking combinations.

## Notes

- Different railcar manufacturers worldwide produce a variety of models designed for different container and stacking configurations.
- Weight and capacity data are a function of railcar manufacturer, railcar model, and rail system requirements.
- The following Dimensions, Weight/Capacity, and Curve Negotiability Radius data are valid for the Greenbrier Husky-Stack 53' Container Car.

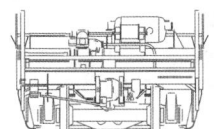

Container Stack
Railcar
Front View

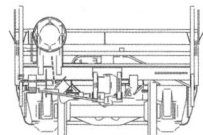

Container Stack
Railcar
Rear View

## Dimensions

| Length over couplers | 76' 8³/₄" | 23.387m |
|---|---|---|
| Length between truck centers | 62' 7" | 19.08m |
| Well size | 53' x 102' ³/₈" | 16.15m x 31.2m |
| Width extreme, over platforms | 10' 8" | 3.25m |
| Height, rail to container surface (empty car) | 12 ¹/₁₆" | 0.306m |
| Height, rail to centerline coupler | 2' 10¹/₂" | 0.876m |
| Height, extreme | 20' 2" | 6.147m |
| Top of side sill to top of rail (empty car) | 60" | 1.52m |

## Weight/Capacity

| Light weight | 50,500 lbs. | 22,906kg |
|---|---|---|
| Gross rail load | 220,000 lbs. | 99,790kg |
| Load limit (for 220,000 lb GRL) | 169,500 lbs. | 76,884kg |

## Curve Negotiability Radius

| Coupled to 40' base car | 300' | 91.5m |
|---|---|---|
| Coupled to like car | 304' | 92.7m |
| Uncoupled | 180' | 54.9m |

Illustration and specifications courtesy The Greenbrier Companies, Inc.

RAILCARS

# Flat Car

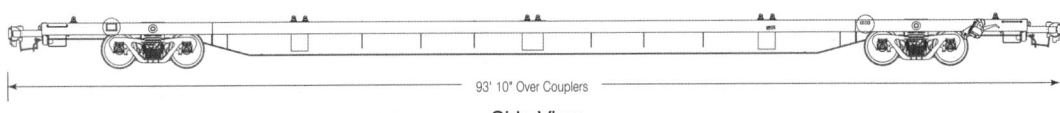

93' 10" Over Couplers

Side View

Top View

## Use

- Flatcars are designed to transport oversize goods and cargo that must be loaded from the side or top.
- Standard cargo for platform trailers includes: ocean freight containers, intermodal truck trailers, machinery, farm equipment, heavy construction equipment, lumber, plywood, steel, steel products, spooled wire, pipe and rebar.

## Features and Options

- Available in numerous lengths.
- Features large flat cargo surface that will accommodate virtually any commodity that is not subject to damage from the elements.
- Multiple tie downs.

## Notes

- Different railcar manufacturers worldwide produce a variety of models designed for different container and stacking configurations.
- Weight and capacity data are a function of railcar manufacturer, railcar model, and rail system requirements.

- The following Dimensions, Weight/Capacity, and Curve Negotiability Radius data are valid for the Greenbrier Heavy Duty Flatcar.

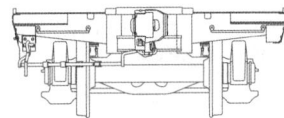

Flat Car
Rear View

## Dimensions

| Length, over end sill | 85' 2$\frac{1}{2}$" | 25.97m |
|---|---|---|
| Length, over couplers | 90' 6$\frac{1}{4}$" | 27.59m |
| Length, between truck centers | 66' 0" | 20.12m |
| Height, rail to pedestal support | 3'11" | 1.2m |
| Width, extreme | 9' 10$\frac{1}{4}$" | 3m |
| Width, over side sills | 9' 1" | 2.77m |

## Weight/Capacity

| Light weight | 60,000 lbs | 27,216kg |
|---|---|---|
| Gross rail load | 286,000 lbs | 129,727kg |
| Load limit | 226,000 lbs | 102,512kg |

## Curve Negotiability Radius

| Uncoupled | 180' | 54.86m |
|---|---|---|
| Coupled to like car | 214' | 65.23m |
| Coupled to 40' base car | 350' | 106.68m |

Illustration and specifications courtesy The Greenbrier Companies, Inc.

# Tanker

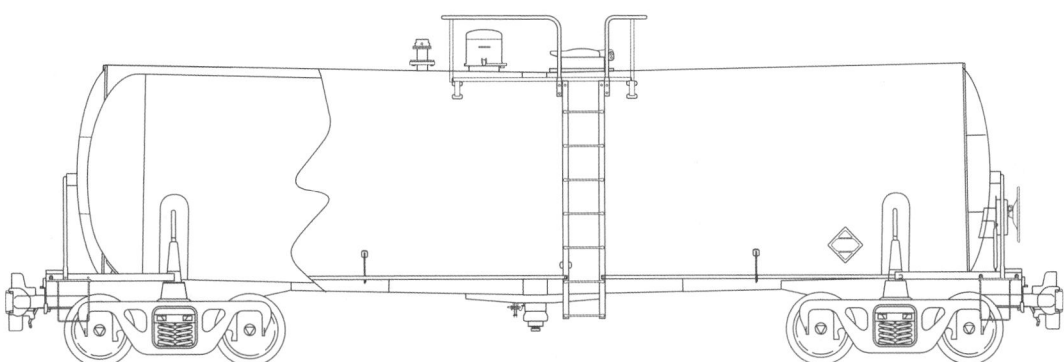

## Use
- Tankers are designed to carry bulk liquids.
- Common commodities transported in tankers include refined gasoline, heating oil, alcohol, industrial chemicals, acids (sulfuric acid, oleum, phosphoric acid, hydrochloric acid, ferric chloride, hydrofluosilic acid), clay slurry, corn syrup and other foodstuffs.

## Key Features and Options
- Product-specific linings and coatings are specially selected to protect tank shell integrity and product purity. Many cars are fitted with loading and unloading devices on a single nozzle, protecting workers and the environment.
- Acid cars are specially designed and constructed tankers that feature high-bake epoxy linings, acid resistant coatings and special acid resistant fittings and unloading systems.

## Notes
- Different railcar manufacturers worldwide produce a variety of models designed for different container and stacking configurations.

- Weight and capacity data are a function of railcar manufacturer, railcar model, and rail system requirements.
- The following Dimensions, Weight/Capacity, and Curve Negotiability Radius data are valid for a particular model gasoline/methane tanker

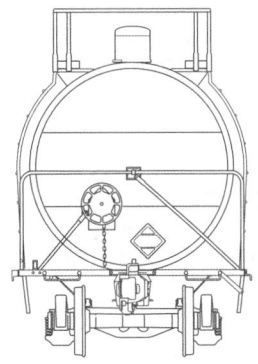

Tanker Car
Rear View

**RAILCARS**

## Dimensions

| | | |
|---|---|---|
| Length over couplers | 59' 9" | 18.21m |
| Length over strikers | 57' 1$\frac{1}{2}$" | 17.41m |
| Truck centers | 46' 3$\frac{1}{4}$" | 14.10m |
| Height, extreme | 15' 5" | 4.70m |
| Width, extreme | 10' 7$\frac{1}{2}$" | 3.24m |

## Weight/Capacity

| | | |
|---|---|---|
| Light weight | 65,700 lbs | 29,801kg |
| Gross rail load | 263,000 lbs | 119,295kg |
| Shell full capacity | 30,000 gallons | 113,562liters |

## Tank

| | | |
|---|---|---|
| Inside diameter | 9'11$\frac{1}{8}$" | 3.03m |
| Length over tank heads | 53' 10$\frac{13}{16}$" | 16.43m |
| Tank slope | $\frac{1}{4}$" per foot | - |
| Plate thickness | $\frac{7}{16}$" | 1.11cm |
| Manway nozzle | 20" | 50.8cm |

# Hopper Car

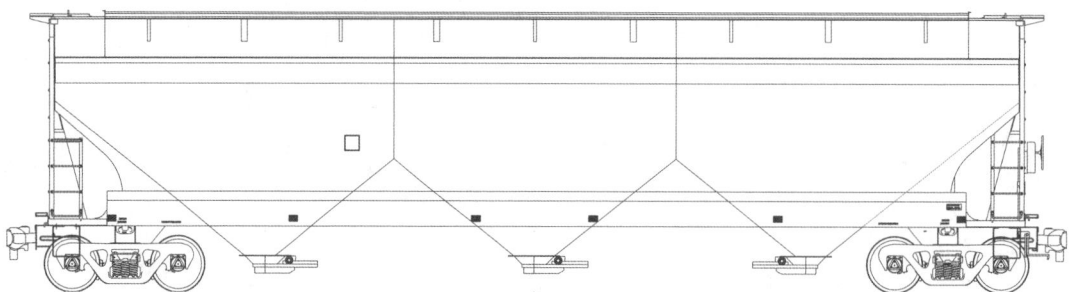

## Use

- Hopper cars are designed to transport free flowing dry bulk commodities.
- Common commodities transported include grains, industrial minerals, plastic pellets, crushed rock, gravel and sand.

## Features and Options

- Hopper cars are available in both covered and uncovered configurations.
- Hopper cars have the advantage of bulk loading from the top and bulk unloading through hoppers on the bottom.
- Special interior linings are available to protect specialty commodities.

## Notes

- Different railcar manufacturers worldwide produce a variety of models designed for different container and stacking configurations.
- Weight and capacity data are a function of railcar manufacturer, railcar model, and rail system requirements.

- The following Dimensions, Weight/Capacity, and Curve Negotiability Radius data are valid for the Greenbrier Covered Hopper for Grain Service.

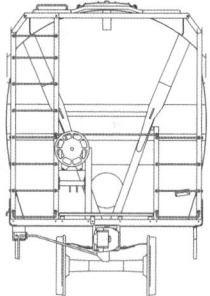

Hopper Car
Rear View

## Dimensions

| Length over couplers | 58' 0" | 17.68m |
|---|---|---|
| Length between truck centers | 52' 10$^{1}/_{8}$" | 16.11m |
| Length, inside | 45' 5$^{1}/_{2}$" | 13.18m |
| Height, extreme | 15' 6" | 4.72m |
| Height, rail to center line coupler | 34$^{1}/_{2}$" | 0.876m |
| Width, extreme | 10' 8" | 3.25m |

## Weight/Capacity

| Light weight | 61,500 lbs | 27,896kg |
|---|---|---|
| Gross rail load | 286,000 lbs | 129,727kg |
| Load limit | 224,500 lbs | 101,831kg |
| Capacity | 5,250 cu ft | 149m$^3$ |

## Curve Negotiability Radius

| Uncoupled | 150' | 45.72m |
|---|---|---|
| Coupled to like car | 199' | 60.66m |
| Coupled to base car | 197' | 60m |

Illustration and specifications courtesy The Greenbrier Companies, Inc.

# Gondola (Mill Gondola) Railcar

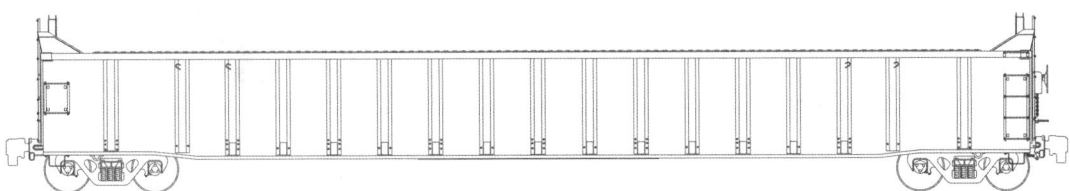

## Use

- Mill gondolas are extremely sturdy railcars designed to transport iron and steel scrap, steel ingots, coiled steel, sheet steel, pipes and other steel products.
- Aggregate gondolas are designed to transport industrial minerals, crushed rock and gravel.

### Key Features and Options

- Standard lengths range from 48' to 66'.
- Standard wall heights range from 5' to 6' for mill gondolas and higher for aggregate gondolas.
- Mill gondolas are designed primarily for the steel industry.
- Options include cross bars, load restraining devices, and wooden troughs for handling specialty cargo.
- Aggregate gondolas typically do not have internal bracing in order to facilitate top unloading.

## Notes

- Different railcar manufacturers worldwide produce a variety of models designed for different container and stacking configurations.
- Weight and capacity data are a function of railcar manufacturer, railcar model, and rail system requirements.
- The following Dimensions, Weight/Capacity, and Curve Negotiability Radius data are valid for the Greenbrier Mill Type Gondola.

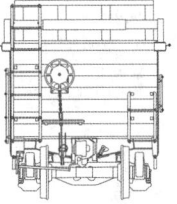

Gondola
Rear View

**R A I L C A R S**

## Dimensions

| Length, inside | 66' 0" | 20.12m |
|---|---|---|
| Length over couplers | 71' 3¹/₂" | 21.73m |
| Length between truck centers | 57' 2" | 17.42m |
| Width, inside between side sheets | 8' 10¹/₂" | 24.65m |
| Height, inside | 5' 9" | 1.75m |
| Height, top of rail to top of chord | 9' 3³/₈" | 2.83m |
| Height, top of rail to top end extension | 12' 6³/₈" | 3.82m |
| Width, inside between stake pockets extended | 8' 0" | 2.44m |

## Weight/Capacity (estimated)

| Cubic capacity | 3,366 cu ft | 95.31m³ |
|---|---|---|
| Light weight | 75,000 lbs | 34,019kg |
| Gross rail weight | 286,000 lbs | 129,727kg |
| Load limit | 211,000 lbs | 95,708kg |

## Curve Negotiability Radius

| Uncoupled | 180' | 54.86m |
|---|---|---|
| Coupled to like car (275' minimum) | 279' | 85m |
| Coupled to 40' base car (275' minimum) | 276' | 84.12m |

Illustration and specifications courtesy The Greenbrier Companies, Inc.

# Center Partition Railcar

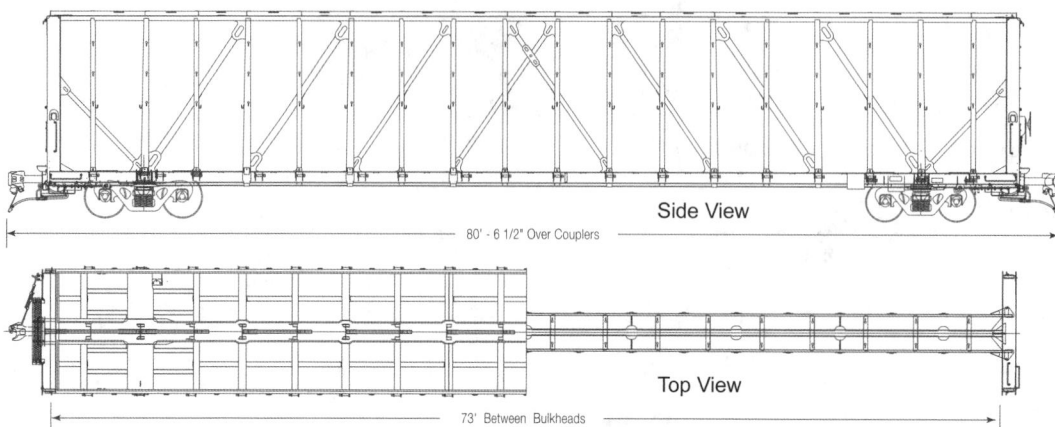

Side View

80' - 6 1/2" Over Couplers

Top View

73' Between Bulkheads

## Use
- Center partition railcars (also called centerbeam flatcars) are designed to transport lumber, plywood, building materials and other packaged products.

## Key Features and Options
- Decks are canted towards the center of the railcar and have floor risers suitable for packages without preattached dunnage.
- A center partition runs the length of the railcar. Packaged products can be secured to this partition.
- Products can be loaded from either side of the car.

## Notes
- Different railcar manufacturers worldwide produce a variety of models designed for different container and stacking configurations.

- Weight and capacity data are a function of railcar manufacturer, railcar model, and rail system requirements.
- The following Dimensions, Weight/Capacity, and Curve Negotiability Radius data are valid for the Greenbrier Center Partition Car.

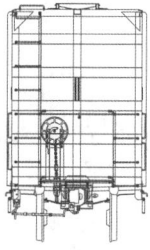

Center Partition Railcar
Rear View

## Dimensions

| Length, between bulkheads | 73' 0" | 22.25m |
|---|---|---|
| Length, over couplers | 80' 6½" | 24.55m |
| Length, over strikers | 75' 9" | 23.09m |
| Width, over floor side sills | 9' 0" | 2.74m |
| Width, over floor risers | 9' 3³/₈" | 2.83m |
| Width, extreme (over winch ratchet gears) | 9' 8⅝" | 2.96m |
| Clear bundle height (nominal) | 11' 5" | 3.48m |
| Height, top of rail to top of riser | 3' 9¼" | 1.15m |
| Height, maximum | 15' 5¾" | 4.72m |
| Truck centers | 60' 0" | 18.29m |
| Length of risers | 4' 1" | 1.24m |

## Weight/Capacity

| Light weight | 61,000 lbs | 27,669kg |
|---|---|---|
| Load capacity | 225,000 lbs | 102,058kg |
| Gross rail load | 286,000 lbs | 129,727kg |

## Curve Negotiability Radius

| Uncoupled | 180' | 54.86m |
|---|---|---|
| Coupled to like car | 218' | 66.45m |
| Coupled to 40' base car | 276' | 84.12m |

Illustration and specifications courtesy The Greenbrier Companies, Inc.

**RAILCARS**

# Auto Carrier

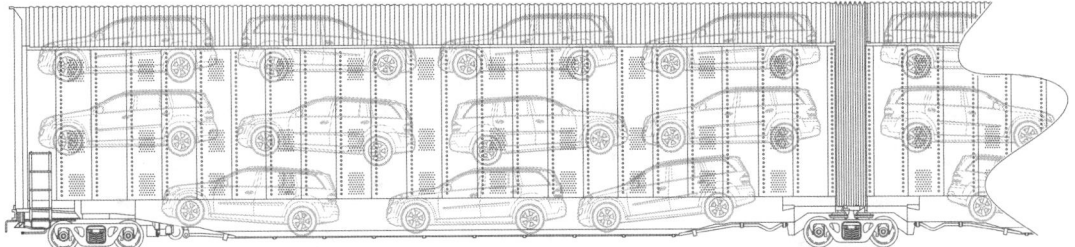

## Use

- Autocarriers are designed to transport automobiles from and to automobile manufacturing plants, ocean import/export facilities, and distribution centers. Rail auto carriers are the most efficient way to transport large numbers of automobiles long distances by land.
- Motor vehicles transported include passenger automobiles, SUVs, pickups and minivans.

## Features and Options

- Autocarriers feature adjustable decks that can be moved to bi-level or tri-level to accommodate automotive industry model changes.
- Interior ladders to prevent roof access.

## Notes

- Different railcar manufacturers worldwide produce a variety of models designed for different container and stacking configurations.

- Weight and capacity data are a function of railcar manufacturer, railcar model, and rail system requirements.
- The following Dimensions, Weight/Capacity, and Curve Negotiability Radius data are valid for the Greenbrier Auto-Max II®.

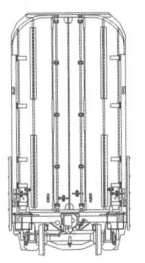 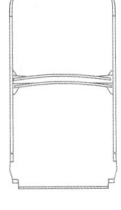 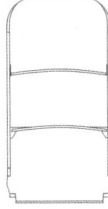

| Auto Carrier Rear View | Bi-Level Configuration | Tri-Level Configuration |

## Dimensions (approximate)

| | | |
|---|---|---|
| Overall length of 2-unit car, over couplers | 145' 4" | 44.30m |
| Overall length, inside | 141' 3¼" | 43.06m |
| Width, outside at center of units | 10' 0" | 3.05m |
| Width, outside, extreme at end of cars | 10' 8" | 3.25m |
| Width, inside, between side posts | 9' 3½" | 2.83m |
| Width, clearance at doorways | 8' 5" | 2.57m |
| Height, extreme (maximum) | 20' 2" | 6.15m |
| Truck centers | 64' 0" | 19.5m |

## Weight/Capacity (estimated)

| | | |
|---|---|---|
| Based on 44,346 lb end trucks and 58,451 lb intermediate truck lightweight | | |
| Light weight | 148,000 lbs | 67,132kg |
| Net capacity (starred) | 112,000 lbs | 50,802kg |
| Gross rail load | 260,000 lbs | 117,934kg |

## Curve Negotiability Radius

| | | |
|---|---|---|
| Uncoupled (horizontal) | 180' | 54.86m |
| Coupled to like car | 245' | 74.68m |
| Coupled to 40' base car | 299' | 91.14m |
| Uncoupled (vertical) | 1250' | 381m |

Illustration and specifications courtesy The Greenbrier Companies, Inc.

**RAILCARS**

**RAILCARS**

# Sourcing

## Key Components

### Sourcing Defined

Sourcing is the location, acquisition and management of all the vital inputs required for an organization to operate. This includes raw materials, component parts, products, labor in all its forms, location and services.

Sourcing, therefore, is a key function of any business enterprise or organization. And, while successful sourcing does not necessarily translate to a successful business, unsuccessful sourcing almost always translates to a failed enterprise.

A key to understanding sourcing is that whether it is: a) a product or service; b) purchased in small lots or large quantities; c) picked up by a staff member from a local store during a lunch break, or sent along a 10,000-mile supply chain; or d) acquired domestically or from a foreign supplier, it is sourcing.

### What is Sourced?

If an organization spends money on it, it is sourced. A small list of what is sourced includes:

* raw materials
* component parts
* intermediate products
* supplies
* tools
* machinery
* motor vehicles
* energy
* production facilities rented or owned
* regional office locations rented or owned
* office equipment
* office furniture
* information technology equipment
* computer software
* production labor
* management labor
* sales labor
* temporary labor
* communications services
* information technology services
* design and engineering services
* legal and accounting services
* marketing services
* graphics services
* call centers and help desks

### Key Components of Sourcing

Successful sourcing has three key components:

1) **Sufficient Quality**

The acquisition of products and services of sufficient quality. This means that the products and services need to be of a quality sufficient for the requirements of the job. If the quality of any component is too low, the final product or service will suffer. If the quality is too high, the sale price of the final product or service may be uncompetitive in an open market.

2) **Uninterrupted Supply**

The uninterrupted supply of products and services. This means that the products and services need to consistently get to where they are required when needed. For products, the importance of this component has led in the past decade to the spectacular rise of the logistics industry, especially since the advent of "just in time"

manufacturing and service delivery. For services, the importance of this component has, in part, led to the rise of the outsourcing "industry."

3) **Competitive Prices**

The acquisition of products and services at the most competitive prices possible. If an organization pays less for its inputs than its competition (but based on #1 and #2 above), then it has a competitive advantage. If it pays more, it is put at a competitive disadvantage.

If any of these three components are deficient, the organization will suffer and possibly fail.

### Vertical Integration vs. Outsourcing

For many years most businesses operated on the assumption that "vertical integration"—the ownership of all aspects of making, selling and delivering a product or service—was best. For a number of industries and businesses, this remains true. A new management dictum, however, is that the key to success in the new global marketplace is the control and development of a firm's core competencies, while it outsources the rest.

### Local vs. Distance Sourcing

At one end of the spectrum, an organization can be located in a small town, hire local people, purchase local supplies and sell all of its products and services locally.

At the other extreme, an organization might have multiple sales, development, and manufacturing locations around the world; purchase raw materials, component parts and services from many countries; and also sell its products and services in many countries. The key factor is that an organization needs to be competitive in the markets it chooses to service. However, many "local" businesses now find that they are facing global competition, whether they like it or not, and whether they are ready for it or not.

### Where From? Where To?

Raw materials, products and services are sourced from everywhere on earth. They can come from a local, regional or domestic supplier; from a supplier in a neighboring country; or from across the globe. The key factor is that an organization needs to be efficient in its sourcing.

Also, the products or services resulting from the merger of sourced products and services can be sold locally, regionally, domestically, or anywhere across the globe. The key factor in the latter case is that the products or services be competitive (quality and price) in the global marketplace.

### Dynamic Tension Between Quality and Price

The dynamic tension in most organizations is how to source all the needed inputs without paying too much, or by paying the least amount possible. An organization that is able to source more efficiently than its competitors will have a market advantage. It is this drive to develop a competitive advantage that drives businesses to source products and services from every corner of the globe.

### Outsourcing vs. Offshore Outsourcing

Outsourcing has become a popular term in the media, as well as in public and political discourse. Unfortunately, as a result of the emotional and political nature of some arguments, the term has been misused and confused with other related terms. Following sections will define and describe all major forms of sourcing, especially as they relate to international trade.

# The Future of Offshoring and Offshore Outsourcing

### Offshore Outsourcing is the Future

Outsourcing and offshore outsourcing have been an integral part of business enterprises and organizations for thousands of years. They're here to stay. While some businesses will find that it is to their advantage to maintain full in-house control of all aspects of their business operations, most businesses will find that it will become an absolute necessity to outsource certain operations in order to be globally competitive. The real question is: how will businesses, individuals, governments and societies use, adapt and thrive in the face of the globalization of labor?

### The Globalization of Offshore Outsourcing

Offshore outsourcing is not just a U.S. opportunity but a global opportunity. Just as U.S. firms outsource to India, Indian companies outsource to China. Just as German firms outsource to Romania, Romanian companies outsource to Vietnam. What is often lost in the heated U.S. public debate about offshoring, however, is that India, China, Germany and Romania all outsource to the U.S.

### Integral to Future Success

Offshore outsourcing will quickly become an integral part of virtually every successful business organization operating anywhere in the world. Businesses will define what they do best, organize the whole, work their core competencies and outsource the rest. Those who do not will lag behind their forward-thinking competitors. They will have higher relative costs, lower productivity, and less innovation and therefore find it impossible to compete in the global marketplace. Initially, offshore outsourcing will be complex and fraught with uncertainties. The success rate for projects will be low (currently reported at 30% to 70%). Over time, methodologies will evolve so that individuals and businesses alike located anywhere in the world will be able to purchase whatever goods and services they need in a true "world market" of products, services and labor.

### "Transformational Outsourcing"

Enlightened organizations, those with strategic vision, understand that offshore outsourcing is not just about cheap wages abroad. "Transformational outsourcing" describes the benefits that accrue to a business or organization that uses offshore outsourcing in a transformational process to save money; make better use of its highly skilled domestic staff and other resources; increase efficiency, productivity and quality; grow its domestic and global markets; employ more staff domestically; and emerge as an innovative and profitable global leader in its field.

### Transformational Phases

Success in Transformational Outsourcing does not happen all at once. An organization must be willing to commit to three process phases:
- **Initial Phase** Conduct initial research. Start the process. Make mistakes. Learn from mistakes. Stick with it. Learn how it works.
- **Benefits Phase** Make it work. Decrease costs. Gain productivity. Normalize processes.
- **Transformational Phase** Attend to the firm's core competencies. Repurpose staff and resources at home. Develop new and innovative products. Extend global reach. Become a global leader.

### Embrace Offshore Outsourcing!

Businesses that have embraced outsourcing are like those that have embraced successful technologies. The early adopters have lost a lot of time and money in developing a knowledge and process base. Firms that stick with it and learn how to do it are on the cusp of a dramatic change in what many believe will be a huge growth in productivity, with offshore outsourcing as a catalyst.

### Not Just for Businesses

Offshore outsourcing can also benefit non-profit NGOs (non-governmental organizations) such as international relief agencies. Effective NGOs ask questions similar to those asked by for-profit businesses: What is the goal of the organization? What are the organization's core competencies? What would it look like if the organization were efficient in the delivery of its "product or service"? Whether an organization's goals are to build housing for the poor, offer medical services to the needy, stop or restrict child labor, offer educational services, or promote human rights for women, there is every reason to do so efficiently. "Profit" for an NGO is doing more good for more people. Outsourcing and offshoring can help.

### Giants Beware

The future will see more small, highly efficient businesses that know how to exploit the benefits of outsourcing and offshoring and, in the process, challenge larger more entrenched firms. These small firms, with a core cadre of highly skilled staff, will use their knowledge of offshoring as a competitive advantage, enabling them to more easily scale their operations up or down as market conditions, clients and contracts dictate.

### Struggling Mid-Sized Manufacturers

The future will see the acquisition of more and more struggling mid-sized manufacturers by firms that are knowledgeable and efficient in transformational outsourcing. New owners will make the changes their predecessors refused or didn't know how to make, and in the process become competitive in the global marketplace.

### The "Global Laborplace"

The rise of information technology, development of the Internet and a dramatic increase in fiber-optic communications has led to a lowering of barriers to individuals entering the "Global Laborplace." The rise of this Global Laborplace will, in time, have a more dramatic effect on worldwide prosperity than has free trade in goods.

### "Global Labor Arbitrage"

As offshore outsourcing increases and a true global market for labor emerges, businesses will see salaries in India, China, Romania, Vietnam and other countries rise. This will lead to the development of new offshore operations in even less-developed economies and, in turn, to salaries increasing in these countries as well. This ongoing "global labor arbitrage" will lead towards a global leveling of salaries.

### Economic and Social Impact

The rise of offshore outsourcing promises to have one of the most dramatic impacts on world economic and social structures since the Industrial Revolution and the lowering of trade barriers after World War II.
As individuals enter the marketplace, unhindered by social structures and oppressive governments, we will see an increase in global living standards. This will lead to increased educational opportunities, the growth of literacy, the development of stronger social structures and, hopefully, a beneficial change in the nature of international relations.

# Sourcing Glossary

"Outsourcing" has become a popular term in the media, as well as in public and political discourse. Unfortunately, as a result of the emotional nature of some arguments, the term has been misused and confused with other terms.

This primer on sourcing terminology is in two parts:

1) Core Definitions, and 2) Other Sourcing Terminology. The five Core Definitions must be learned in order to have an understanding of the topic as a whole. Other Sourcing Terminology covers the many different types and variations of "sourcing," plus related terms.

## 5 Core Definitions

### sourcing

The location and acquisition of all the vital inputs required for an organization to operate. If an organization spends money or exchanges value for a product or service, it is sourced. An organization's vital inputs can include raw materials, component parts, intermediate parts, machinery, supplies, labor, management, production and management facilities, communications services, and utilities, as well as design, legal, accounting and other services, to name but a few.

Sourcing is a primary function of any organizational entity. Successful sourcing has three key components: 1) the acquisition of products and services of sufficient quality, 2) the securing of an uninterrupted supply of products and services, and 3) the acquisition of products and services at the most competitive prices possible. If any of these three components are deficient, the organization will suffer and possibly fail.

Examples of sourcing include:
- Purchasing a single ball-point pen from a corner stationary store
- Importing a 40-foot container load of ball-point pens directly from a manufacturer in a foreign country
- Hiring a retail sales clerk by placing a "Help Wanted" sign in a store window
- Contracting with a local firm to provide 100 inbound telemarketers for a short-term advertising campaign
- Contracting with a foreign firm to provide 100 inbound telemarketers for an ongoing advertising campaign
- Contracting out the manufacturing of component parts or a complete product to a local company
- Contracting out the manufacturing of component parts or a complete product to a company in a foreign country
- Hiring call-center personnel to work in-house
- Contracting call center operations to a local company
- Contracting call center operations to a company in a foreign country

### outsourcing

The contracting of the management and/or execution of a business function to an outside third-party contractor or subcontractor. Outsourcing can refer to either a product or service, but most commonly refers to services. Outsourcing has been a feature of the business world for hundreds of years and is simply a more modern term for "contracting out."

Note that the business function can be outsourced to either a domestic or foreign third-party contractor. The key factor here is that the service be performed by an "outside" third-party contractor, not simply by a department or division of the same company. See domestic outsourcing and offshore outsourcing below.

Benefits of outsourcing:
- The acquisition of specialized services required on a limited or temporary basis
- Quick solution to a temporary overload of work
- Ability to concentrate the organization's focus on its core competencies
- Potential to save money

Almost any business function can be outsourced, including:
- Accounting and tax preparation services
- Legal services
- Medical and legal transcription
- X-ray analysis
- Blood and urine analysis
- Data entry
- Graphic arts
- Advertising and marketing
- Telemarketing
- Call center 'help desks'
- Research and development
- Manufacturing of component parts
- Manufacturing of complete products

### domestic outsourcing

The outsourcing of a business function to a domestic third-party contractor.

Examples of domestic outsourcing include:
- Contracting year-end accounting and tax preparation work to a local accountant or accounting firm
- Contracting document shredding to an outside service that shreds the documents on location in a purpose-built truck and then disposes of the shredded paper
- Contracting telemarketing operations to a third-party company located in a less costly part of the country
- Contracting the machining of complex component parts to a local machine shop with specialized equipment and know-how
- Contracting the manufacture of a completed product to a domestic manufacturing firm

### offshore outsourcing

The outsourcing of a business function to a third-party vendor located in a foreign country.

Examples of offshore outsourcing include:
- A domestic accounting firm contracts accounting and tax preparation work to a firm located in a foreign country
- Contracting call-center operations to a foreign company
- Contracting software development to a foreign company

### offshoring

The relocation of an entire business process to a foreign country. The business process or function can be performed by the parent company or by a local third-party contractor. Offshoring is similar to outsourcing, but can be performed by a division or subsidiary of the offshoring company, as well as by a third-party entity.

Note that offshoring can refer to either a manufacturing (production) process or a service process. See production offshoring and services offshoring.

Examples of offshoring include:
- Moving a manufacturing operation to another country
- Moving a call-center operation to another country

**SOURCING**

# Other Sourcing Terminology

**Editor's Note:**
1. For terms related to pricing, refer to the "Pricing Models for Service Outsourcing" section that follows.
2. The outsourcing industry is experiencing significant growth in the volume of services outsourced, the types of services outsourced, and the development of new terminology to describe these services. In some cases, new terminology describes a unique service offering; in other cases, a term helps individuals understand a component of the process to make better decisions; in still other cases, a term was coined by service providers to add value to the services they offer.
3. This glossary lists the most commonly used terms in the industry, as those terms were in usage at the time of publication. Given the dynamic nature of the industry, new terms and meanings are being invented all the time.

### back-office outsourcing

The outsourcing of a company's administrative functions such as payroll, billing or purchasing. 'Back office' refers to the administrative functions of a business that do not involve face-to-face contact with customers. A subset of BPO (business-process outsourcing).

### backsourcing

Bringing an outsourced process back in-house after it has been performed by another firm. Backsourcing can occur for a multitude of reasons: expiration of a contract, poor performance, higher than expected costs, adverse client reactions, political and/or economic instability in the vendor's country and concerns about data security, among others.

### barriers to outsourcing

A company's internal resistance to outsourcing. These include a firm's concerns regarding a project or process that is too important to outsource, the potential loss of control over a project or process, data security issues, the compromise of intellectual property rights, the loss of customer loyalty and the welfare of current staff.

### benchmark

A standard used for comparison; a standard by which something can be measured or judged; a measurement or standard that serves as a point of reference by which process performance is measured. Benchmarking is a structured method designed to identify the best practices, products or services from industry and government, and to compare and adapt them to an organization's operations. Such an approach is aimed at identifying more efficient and effective processes for achieving intended results and suggesting goals for program output, product/service quality and process improvement.

### best practices

The processes, practices and systems acknowledged as producing the best results in an industry, organization, process or sub-process. Operating according to best practices is recognized as a means of improving and maximizing an organization's overall performance, efficiency and results.

### bestshoring / rightshoring

The offshoring of a business process to a foreign country based upon criteria that give one specific location or country key advantages over another.

### bodyshopping

(a) The use of outsourced or offshore outsourced resources or personnel to perform specific tasks within a business function without the intent of offshoring the entire business function. (b) The hiring of outside consultants on a free-lance basis. (c) The hiring of talent (employees) from another organization.

### business process outsourcing (BPO)

The outsourcing of a company's entire business process to another company located domestically or in a foreign country. BPO is generally divided into two categories:

1) back-office outsourcing, and 2) front-office outsourcing. Back-office outsourcing includes internal business functions such as payroll, billing and purchasing. Front-office outsourcing includes customer-related functions such as technical support, marketing and sales.
Examples of business process outsourcing include:
• A computer printer manufacturer outsourcing the maintenance and repair, and stocking of replacement parts, to a third-party logistics company
• A software maker outsourcing its entire customer support process to another company
• A company outsourcing its payroll and human resources functions to an outside firm
Benefits of business process outsourcing include:
• Possible lower costs
• The ability to concentrate on core competencies
• The ability to acquire specialized skills that would be difficult to replicate within an organization

### captive center

A company-owned or controlled operation either domestic or foreign. In the case of offshore outsourcing, a project or process may be performed overseas, but by a department, division or subsidiary of the company itself.

### captive design house

A product or process design firm (design or development organization) working exclusively for one client. A captive design house can be wholly owned by a parent company or be an independent company under exclusive contract to another firm. If the captive design house is located in a foreign country the facility is typically called an offshore development center (ODC).

### commoditization of services

The process by which the delivery of a service from one vendor becomes indistinguishable from that of another vendor, with the only real difference being price.

### core competencies

(a) The most essential set of skills an organization possesses enabling it to be successful. (b) The skills an organization possesses that differentiate it from other organizations in its industry or field.
Core competencies are what an organization does best, and (hopefully) better than anyone else. Core competencies might be R&D, design, production, management, customer relations, distribution, sales or after-the-sale services.

### cosourcing (co-sourcing)

The performance of a business function utilizing both internal staff and outside resources working together. The outside resources can be either independent consultants or direct employees of a vendor firm. Co-sourcing is useful in situations where very specialized knowledge is required to find solutions to very specialized problems.

### cottage industry

A business in which goods are produced primarily in the

homes of the individuals performing the work.
(a) Manufacturing or assembly work performed by individuals in their homes rather than in a firm's factory or workshop. Cottage industry workers are provided with the materials and are paid on a piecework basis. Also called the "Domestic System."
(b) An individually owned, home-based small business enterprise that typically requires the labor of only one or several individuals.
"Cottage industry" generally refers to individuals working in their homes for a larger organization and paid on a piecework basis. "Home-based" business refers to a small business enterprise operated out of the owner's home.
Examples of cottage industry (a) include:
• Hand knitting to set patterns, colors and sizes
• Rug weaving to set patterns, colors and sizes
• Clothing assembly of pre-cut components
• Assembly of component parts for a sub-manufacturer
Examples of cottage industry (b) include:
• Baking pies for sale to retailers
• Custom dressmaking and clothing alterations
• Home-based upholstery work
Benefits of cottage industry include:
• Lower facilities costs for the contracting company
• Greater staff retention
• Elimination of commute time and expenses
• Predetermined manufacturing/assembly costs
• Work time flexibility

### critical competencies
Operations a business performs that are required for the successful day-to-day functioning of the business. The most common examples are invoicing, payroll and fulfillment. While all businesses must perform these functions, it is a firm's "core" (rather than critical) competencies that distinguish it from other firms in the same industry.

### deliverable
A tangible outcome that is produced by a vendor for a client. "Deliverables" can be documents, plans, computer systems, buildings or other physical products, or achievement of service standards.

### due diligence
The systematic investigation, verification and evaluation of information in order to facilitate a decision regarding a proposed transaction. Performing a due diligence investigation is a standard operating procedure prior to: purchasing a business, investing in a business, awarding an important contract, investing venture capital, loaning money or offering securities. Due diligence can include checking financial references, background checks on key individuals, interviewing current and past clients, checking the legal status of a company and on-site evaluations.

### front office outsourcing
The outsourcing of a customer-related function such as technical support, marketing or sales. A subset of business process outsourcing (BPO).

### functional process outsourcing
The outsourcing of internal functions that support a company's staff (as opposed to functions that support the company's customers) such as human resources, accounting, staff travel and facilities services. Also, the outsourcing of the related supporting technologies and the supply chain that feeds into them.

### gainsharing (gain-sharing)
A relationship between a client and vendor whereby both parties share financially in the value created as a result of the association. An example of gainsharing is where an outside firm audits a company's shipping records for the purpose of identifying overcharges, applying for refunds and sharing the resulting revenue.

### governance
The oversight and management of an outsourcing relationship. Governance procedures are designed to ensure efficient execution, guidance and oversight of a project and relationship.

### homesourcing / homeshoring
The contracting of service work to employees or contractors who work remotely from their home, rather than from a company facility. While "cottage industry" refers to products, "homesourcing" typically refers to services.
Homesourcing is a combination of telecommuting and outsourcing. The individual can be an independent contractor or a full-time staff member of the contracting company. Homesourcing requires that the home location have adequate telephone and Internet connectivity. In one of the more publicized examples, all of the airline JetBlue's agents work from their homes (mostly in Utah).
Examples of homesourcing include:
• Remote call center agents
• Remote sales agents
Benefits of homesourcing include:
• Lower facility costs for the contracting company
• Greater staff retention
• Elimination of commute time and expenses
• Work time flexibility

### insourcing
The opposite of outsourcing, the term is used in two ways:
(a) The location and acquisition of services, specialized skills, raw materials or manufacturing capabilities from an internal department, division or subsidiary of a company. Insourcing generally refers to the insourcing of services, but can also include materials, component parts, or manufacturing capabilities. This meaning includes bringing back 'in-house' a previously outsourced process. Insourcing has the advantages of:
• Maintaining control over a process, patents, intellectual property and specialized knowledge
• Using existing internal resources and capabilities
• Reducing costs or keeping profits within a company
Examples of insourcing (a) include:
• The purchase of raw materials from a wholly owned subsidiary
• The purchase of intermediate products or component parts from another division of a company
• One department's use of the creative services of another department of the same company.
(b) The movement of jobs into a country from a foreign company. Also more conventionally known as foreign direct investment. In this context, what is outsourced from one country is insourced to another. From the standpoint of the company creating the jobs, this form of insourcing is simply production offshoring. However, from the standpoint of the country gaining the jobs, it is insourcing.
Examples of insourcing (b) include:
• Establishing a manufacturing facility in a country where production is expected to be sold
Benefits of insourcing (b) include:
• To the company creating the jobs: all the advantages of production offshoring
• To the country gaining the jobs: jobs, technological know-how, economic activity, and foreign investment

### internal outsourcing

A form of insourcing. See shared services.

### knowledge process outsourcing (KPO)

Another term for research process outsourcing (RPO).

### mission critical

Any operation, data or system that is fundamental to the success of a project or endeavor. Such functions cannot tolerate intervention, compromise or shutdown without causing the endeavor to fail. For example, R&D and product design might be a firm's core competencies, but an e-commerce firm's computer system is mission-critical.

### milestone

(project management) A scheduled event that marks the completion of a defined phase of work or the transfer of a deliverable. A milestone event is a project checkpoint designed to help evaluate progress and make decisions related to payments and the future of a project.

### nearshoring

The offshoring of a business process or manufacturing plant to a lower cost foreign location that is in close geographic proximity to the contracting company.

Examples of nearshoring include:

- A German company outsourcing production or services to a company in Poland or the Czech Republic
- A U.S. company outsourcing production or services to a company in Mexico
- A Japanese company outsourcing production or services to a company in China

Benefits of nearshoring include:

- Lower travel and communications costs
- Closer control over the process
- Lower transportation costs to a product's eventual market
- Tax and tariff advantages, especially if the nearshore country is within a trade agreement region where the eventual product will be sold. For example, a Canadian company nearshoring production to Mexico for products that will be sold in the U.S.

### near sourcing

The contracting of a business function to an outside third-party contractor or subcontractor that is located in close domestic proximity to the contracting company.

### non-disclosure agreement (NDA)

A formal written agreement between two or more parties not to disclose trade secrets, trade practices, business or marketing plans, or other proprietary or confidential information, during a set period of time. A non-disclosure agreement is often signed by parties about to enter into business negotiations or a relationship where proprietary information will, or is likely, to be revealed.

### offshore

(economics/law) (a) Outside the legal or taxing jurisdiction of a country. (b) An investment, security, bank account or property located outside an individual's country of domicile. (c) A geographic region located "off the shore," but within waters under a country's control (e.g. offshore fisheries). (d) Manufacturing, production or technical support facilities located in a foreign country. (e) Contracting work carried out at sea (e.g. oil exploration and production at sea). (f) Conditions when the wind is blowing off the land. (g) Utilizing an outsourcing service provider (such as a call center) located in a foreign country. (h) Away from shore; away from land; "cruising five miles offshore," "offshore oil reserves," "an offshore island."

### offshore development center (ODC)

A product or process development center located in a foreign country. The ODC can be wholly owned by a company in another country, a wholly independent design group contracting to a number of foreign entities, or be independently owned but work exclusively for one foreign entity.

### offshore service provider (OSP)

A service provider located in a foreign country.

### open outsourcing

The contracting of computer programming work to third-party programmers (often individuals rather than companies) who create derivative programs and applications based upon open source computer code. Companies that turn to open outsourcing typically do not have the technical know-how to perform the work internally.

In the past few years, a web-based marketplace has developed with the purpose of linking software buyers and open-source software coders. One web-based business, RentA-Coder (www.rentacoder.com) bills itself as "...an international marketplace where people who need custom software developed can find coders in a safe and business-friendly environment. Buyers can cherry pick from a pool of 138,306 coders...enabling them to hire a coder across the country or across the globe...from the comfort of their computers."

Examples of open outsourcing include:

- Development of websites, handheld/PDA applications, server-based applications and database applications

Benefits of open outsourcing include:

- Low cost work often performed by the actual programmer without need to pay organizational overhead
- Low or no cost for a license to the original code
- Retention of copyright to the resulting product
- No royalty or run-time fees for the resulting product
- No long-term obligations to a software vendor
- Ability to pay for work on a freelance or piecework basis

Challenges of open outsourcing include:

- Inconsistent or poor quality programming work by unknown or unqualified individuals
- Possible inclusion of code from unlicensed copyrighted sources
- Lack of programmer accountability

Other on-line marketplaces for this form of outsourcing include:

- www.wzgoal.com
- www.rentacoder.com
- www.odesk.com
- www.getacoder.com
- www.vividminds.net
- www.ifreelance.com
- www.offshorexperts.com

Disclaimer: The sources listed above are for informational purposes only. Neither the author nor World Trade Press assume any responsibility for any services provided by these marketplaces.

### open source (open sourcing)

A computer program whose source code is freely available to any individual or organization for their use or modification. While open source is "free software," the term has an additional meaning: that the software is available for modification. One of the issues behind the open source "movement" (refer to the Open Source Initiative at www.opensource.org) is whether the "product" resulting from modifications made by an individual or organization should also be "free." The Open Source Initiative has a 10 point "Open Source Definition" available at its web site.

Regardless of questions concerning the commercialization of derivative products, individuals and organizations can use open source code for internal benefit.

Note: While the concept of "open source" has been evolving to include applications in agriculture, health, pharmaceuticals, government and media, its primary meaning lies in "open source computer software."

Examples of open sourcing include:

- Netscape's Mozilla browser (open-source since 1998)
- Linux, Eclipse, Apache servers
- Sun Microsystems OpenSPARC T1

Benefits of open sourcing include:

- Low or no cost for a license to the original code
- No royalty or run-time fees for the resulting product
- No contractual obligations to a software vendor
- Payment for work on a freelance or piecework basis

### out-tasking

(a) Another term for outsourcing or contracting out. (b) The outsourcing of selective tasks that require urgent or professional attention on short- to medium-term contracts. Out-tasking often involves direct management and decision-making of the process by the company that lets the contracts.

Examples of out-tasking include:

- Application installation
- System administration
- Security
- System back-up

Benefits of out-tasking include:

- Immediate attention to specialized tasks
- Potential cost reduction compared to in-house execution
- Amelioration of a worsening situation
- Greater ability to focus on a firm's main activities

### onshore

(a) Inside the legal or taxing jurisdiction of a country. (b) An investment, security, bank account or property located in an individual's country of domicile. (c) A geographic region located within waters under a country's control. (d) Manufacturing, production or technical support facilities located domestically. (e) Utilizing an outsourcing service provider (such as a call center) located domestically.

### preferred provider

An arrangement whereby a client agrees that a particular vendor shall have the right to bid on subsequent contracts without having to resubmit its qualifications and, where other factors are substantially equal, be offered a contract for the new services required.

### production offshoring

The relocation of manufacturing production to a foreign country. In production offshoring the production can be performed by either a division or subsidiary of the offshoring company, or by an unrelated third-party entity.

Benefits of production offshoring can include:

- Decreased labor costs
- Lower general costs of doing business
- Local government tax breaks and incentives
- Lower manufacturing costs for production destined for sale in the company's home market
- Lower transportation costs for production destined for sale in the country of manufacture
- Avoidance of import duties for products to be sold in the country of manufacture
- Avoidance of home-country environmental regulations
- Avoidance of home-country labor regulations
- Lower transportation costs for raw materials required in the production process

### project creep

The addition of features or tasks to a project after the project specifications and budget have been approved by both parties. Project creep is an inevitable feature of outsourcing relationships and should be anticipated in the original contract. Project creep is usually charged on a cost plus basis.

### research process outsourcing (RPO)

The outsourcing of an entire research project, often in medicine, genetics, pharmaceuticals or nanotechnology. RPO is a specialized type of outsourcing requiring a high degree of specialized knowledge and the facilities to carry out the research. RPO is distinguished from other outsourcing in that it requires analytical and decision-making skills. This is a new trend for offshore outsourcing. Research process outsourcing is also known as knowledge process outsourcing (KPO).

Examples of RPO include:

- Medical R&D
- Pharmaceutical R&D
- Nanotechnology R&D
- Genetics R&D

### scope of services

A systematic listing of services to be provided in an outsourcing agreement. This list is developed by the client and includes a description of each service to be performed in enough detail to enable a service provider to fully understand client requirements. The structure of the scope of services statement is dependent upon the types of services to be performed. Similar to 'job specifications' or 'product specifications,' when a product is involved. The scope of services statement will include the type of service to be performed, the manner in which it is to be performed and required standards of performance.

### service level agreement (SLA)

A contract or contract addendum between a client and a service provider that specifies, in measurable terms, the type, quantity and quality of the services the vendor will provide. An SLA can include provisions about the quantity or volume of services to be provided, but more often references the quality of services such as response time, availability and customer satisfaction.

For example, an SLA might require a vendor to answer incoming "Help Desk" calls within 30 seconds, or require that a quality survey of clients result in a minimum 94 percent "satisfactory" rating. Many SLAs have penalty clauses if base standards are not met. However, it is considered counterproductive for a client to assess these charges for two reasons: 1) it creates a strain on the relationship with the vendor, and 2) the client should place greater emphasis on supporting remedial actions than collecting penalties.

SLAs are typically composed of three elements:

1. A description of the services to be performed,
2. A description, in measurable terms, of the quality standards of delivery for each service to be performed, and
3. A pricing formula for each service or each service unit to be performed.

### services offshoring

The relocation of a company's service function to a foreign country. In services offshoring, the services can be performed by either a division or subsidiary of the offshoring company, or by an unrelated third-party entity.

Examples of service offshoring include:

- An appliance manufacturer transferring its help desk call center to a foreign company

- A publisher transferring its desktop publishing department functions to a foreign company

Benefits of services offshoring include:
- Potential reduction in labor costs

### service provider (vendor)

An individual or business organization that provides outsourcing services; a vendor of services (usually a business). The terms contractor, provider, vendor and partner are used interchangeably, but each may carry special significance depending upon the user.

### shared services

The standardization and centralization of an internal service function for a number of business units within a larger organization. Shared services typically refer to the centralization of "back office" administrative functions. Shared services are used in organizations as small as a two-location retail chain, and in the largest multinational firms. In some instances a company is acquired knowing that the savings from shared services alone will result in a significant benefit to the acquiring organization. Some refer to shared services as a form of 'internal outsourcing.'

Examples of shared services include:
- Payroll administration
- Human resources administration
- Computer network maintenance
- Graphic arts design and production
- Purchasing administration
- Marketing management
- Logistics management

Benefits of shared services include:
- Lower costs associated with not having to replicate the same services across divisions of an organization
- Greater control over the services performed
- Greater ease in applying standards across an organizational structure

### sole provider

An arrangement whereby one particular vendor (provider) has been chosen to be the only supplier of specific products or services to a client.

### specification

A clear and accurate written description of the technical requirements for a material, product or service being purchased or performed. Specifications also include requirements related to the performance of the materials or products, or standards related to the delivery of services. A specification often includes a means for determining whether a requirement has been satisfied or a standard met. Specifications can be in the form of written descriptions, drawings, prints, commercial designations, published industry standards and other descriptive references.

### statement of work

A clear and accurate written statement of what a contractor is to accomplish to satisfy the terms of a contract. Includes a scope of services statement, other deliverables, and terms and conditions. The statement of work serves to establish an agreement between the client and contractor about the specific nature of the work to be performed.

### strategic outsourcing

The outsourcing of service functions as part of a firm's overall strategic plan of redirecting its resources to concentrate on core competencies or highest-value activities.

### supply chain

The series of physical facilities, equipment, management and technology that supply goods or services from source to the ultimate consumer. For products, these minimally include manufacturing plants, warehouses, distribution centers, conveyances (such as trucks, cargo aircraft, ships and trains), sales locations or methodologies (such as retail stores or Internet Web sites), computer systems and software. The processes, systems and links between these facilities are the subject of ever evolving theory, debate and great technological change. For example, computers and the Internet are part of the supply chain through inventory information systems and e-commerce ordering systems. Also refers to the web-based delivery of information and services.

### tactical outsourcing

The outsourcing of service functions to achieve operational efficiencies. Compare to strategic outsourcing.

### transaction

(a) The smallest unit of a business activity. An individual business event. (b) The interaction between a buyer and a seller for the sale of a product or service.

In service outsourcing, a transaction is a defined interaction, usually between a service provider and a client's customers. For example, an interaction between a call center operator and a client's customer. Transactions are a common pricing unit in a services outsourcing agreement.

### transformational outsourcing

An innovative business model whereby a firm uses outsourcing as a means of repositioning itself in the marketplace in order to concentrate on core competencies and become a global leader in its field.

### trigger

An event that precipitates an action on the part of a party to a contract. For example, in an offshore outsourcing service agreement, a customer survey "satisfactory" rating of 92 percent might be established as the minimum acceptable rating. If the rating goes below 92 percent, it would trigger a review; if it goes below 89 percent it might require specific remedial steps to be taken; and if it goes below 85 percent for 90 days it might be cause for termination of the contract.

In the case of offshore outsourcing contracts, triggers can relate to service standards, quality standards, volume of services performed by the vendor, and promptness of payments from the client company, to name but a few. A trigger can initiate a project, start a new phase of a project, initiate remedial actions or end a project.

### value proposition

a) A statement describing the unique added value an organization offers its customers and potential customers in differentiating itself from its competitors. Value propositions usually distinguish a firm based upon its operational excellence, product leadership, customer intimacy or pricing.

b) A statement of the value an organization seeks to gain from committing itself to a course of action. For example, the value proposition for outsourcing a firm's call center might be "saving US$1 million per year, which will be reinvested in research and development."

### vendor

A supplier of property, goods or services. The seller.

### your mess for less

A sales and marketing promotional statement that offers potential clients the opportunity to outsource a messy internal problem and pay less for a successful outcome in the process. The term was coined as a means of selling financial decision-makers (CFOs and controllers) on the virtues of outsourcing without having to go into technical detail about how it is to be accomplished (especially with IT services contracts).

# Challenges and Issues

Offshore outsourcing can be difficult–for both the client and the vendor. The parties to the arrangement are likely to be separated by 15,000 kilometers and ten time zones, come from different cultures, speak different languages, operate in different legal and economic systems and have different agendas. The failure rate is estimated at 30 to 70 percent. Even the most sophisticated firms fall victim to the host of problems that confront outsourcing relationships. Offshoring and offshore outsourcing are strategic decisions organizations make that can produce significant benefits, or monumental problems—problems that can cripple even the most established and otherwise strongest firms. This section outlines major issues that confront any organization that seeks to offshore or offshore outsource.

## Getting it Right

### Why Outsource?

The first question an organization has to ask itself is "Why should we outsource? If business, profits, client relations and labor relations are all good, why outsource at all?"

The fact is that not all companies will benefit from outsourcing or offshore outsourcing. The nature of a business may be such that there is no advantage to be gained. Also, a firm may be too small or not be in a position to handle the complexities of the process itself.

For example, there may be no economies of scale. If one full-time office person in a small firm can handle invoicing, general ledger, payroll, accounts receivable and accounts payable, little is likely to be gained from outsourcing these functions. Indeed, potential disadvantages may overwhelm any potential benefits. For these firms, maintaining full in-house control of a function may be best.

On the other hand, upon careful examination, a company may see vast potential benefits to offshore outsourcing; benefits that are compelling enough to invest the time, money and resources required to establish a viable outsourcing operation or relationship. As with other business decisions, an analysis of what an organization might gain compared to what it might cost, in both financial and other terms, will help it to make an informed decision.

### Good and Bad Reasons to Outsource

While offshore outsourcing can be a good path for an organization to follow, doing it for the wrong reasons can be just as bad as or worse than not doing it at all. For example:

- The fact that other organizations in the same industry are outsourcing may not in itself be a good enough reason. Outsourcing decisions are best made on a case-by-case basis.
- Outsourcing simply for the sake of saving money may not be a good enough reason either. Experienced firms report that it is best to have several compelling reasons to outsource.
- Some firms feel that dumping an unsuccessful project on an outside firm will resolve the issue. If the problem is well defined, and the vendor is well chosen, this might actually work. Often, however, firms are in such dire situations because they have not defined the problem well enough for their own people to succeed. Firms that are not able to define the problem or project well are often the same firms that are not able to choose or direct outside vendors well.

### Unrealistic Expectations

Most firms start an offshore outsourcing relationship with unreasonable expectations. Or, they are unaware of the dynamic tension that is part of any relationship between a service buyer and seller. Some examples include:

1. A firm's expectation that it will successfully achieve two potentially conflicting outcomes: a) obtain better quality and service, and b) pay less than they would if the services were performed in-house.
2. A vendor's expectation that it will be able to perform a service to a client's often unrealistic expectations and still make a profit.
3. A client's expectation that signing an outsourcing contract will cure all its problems. Outsourcing relationships have to be managed and nurtured to succeed.
4. A firm's expectation that a relationship will work without taking the time to investigate whether the relationship has a reasonable expectation of working.
5. A firm's expectation that it can go into offshore outsourcing with a quick-fix idea to resolve a problem rather than with a long-term strategy to develop capabilities and expand globally.
6. A firm's expectation that it can enter into a relationship with a vendor from a foreign culture 9,000 miles away, who speaks a different language, with the same success it experiences with a domestic vendor.

### Establishing Realistic Goals

Every company will have its own reasons to outsource services. It's best, however, to articulate these reasons and turn them into specific written goals. While saving money is a reasonable goal, it is recommended that saving money alone be one-third or less the reason a firm commits to offshore outsourcing. If necessary, refer to the "The Future of Offshoring and Offshore Outsourcing" on the second page of this chapter for ideas.

A key benefit of establishing realistic short-, medium- and long-term goals is that they can be turned into milestones and triggers for assessment of the vendor's and client's progress in developing both the process and the relationship.

### What to Outsource, What to Keep?

Some firms are prone to think that if some outsourcing is good, then more is always better. This is not the case.

The first step in determining what to outsource is to identify the organization's "core competencies." Core competencies are what an organization does best and, hopefully, better than anyone else. Core competencies might be research and development, design, production, management, customer relations, distribution, sales, service, etc. The first rule is to keep control of your core competencies.

Another factor relates to "mission critical" functions of an organization. Mission critical functions are those without which an organization will fail. For example, R&D and product design might be a firm's core competencies, but customer contact might be a mission-critical function. The second rule is not to outsource mission-critical functions.

### Where Do We Start?

The most realistic place to start is to outsource discrete non-mission critical projects. This will give the organization an opportunity to learn firsthand the challenges and issues of the process.

**SOURCING**

# Country Issues

While offshore outsourcing of services has become common, and most problem stories appear to relate more to vendors than countries, there are a number of country issues that should be taken into account prior to making a decision to work with a vendor from a particular country.

## Political Environment and Policies

The political structure of a nation consists of its political institutions and the ideological base upon which they are formed. At the ends of the spectrum are representative democracies based on the rule of law vs. totalitarian dictatorships based upon the whims of a pathological personality, and free-market economies vs. heavily socialist or communist countries.

In between, however, are countries where the political structure is neither black nor white, but one of many shades of gray that transcend simple designations of pro-business or anti-business. As experienced international businesspeople know, a country's political environment will have a significant impact upon the ability of a foreign firm to do business with vendors located in that country.

In some countries, for example, if a foreign-owned firm hires an "agent," regardless of any contract stating otherwise, that person is considered an "employee" and is accorded all the rights of an employee under that nation's employment laws. This might include extraordinary severance pay upon termination.

Conducting business in communist nations twenty years ago was a practical impossibility; now, countries like China and Vietnam, once so intolerant of market economies and private enterprise, welcome investment from, and business relations with, foreign-based companies.

In some less developed nations, political interference in business by the head of state as well as other unreliable political structures can make it difficult or impossible to form sustained relationships with local businesses.

One of the greatest uncertainties in doing business with a company in a foreign country is that there may be a change in executive or legislative power that threatens a major shift in a country's attitude towards business or international business. This is a factor covered in "Country Risk" below.

## Economic Environment and Policies

The economic structure of a nation consists of its policies and regulation of business; the ease of business formation and maintenance; the regulation and taxation of foreign investment, imports and exports; personal and business taxation; and its labor and environmental regulations.

For example, from independence until 1992, India was primarily a socialist nation that created a negative political and economic environment for business. However, since that time, the country has dramatically changed political and economic policies to be more favorable to business formation and international trade. The result has been a dramatic increase in business formation, foreign investment and employment. (A provocative question years ago was: "Why is it that Indians are successful wherever they go in the world, but not in India?")

## Legal System and Transparency

A country's legal system coupled with "the rule of law" is the base upon which its people can live, work and thrive; knowing with certainty the rights and responsibilities of all citizens and legal entities, including government itself. Laws and regulations that define business transactions that are fair and balanced, known to the people, and enforced with equality, are a necessary component of a healthy business environment. Simply put, individuals and businesses need to know what the rules are.

"Transparency" is the clarity with which a law, regulation or policy is both understood and can be depended upon by people in a society. Transparency implies openness in a system such that the policy-making and decision-making processes are open to view and subject to public scrutiny. Transparency diminishes the capacity of a government, organization or private business to practice or harbor deception or deceit.

## Infrastructure

In the case of the offshore outsourcing of services, the most important infrastructure issue is communications. This includes telecommunications, but more importantly, Internet connectivity and bandwidth. In fact, one of the main reasons India has become a powerhouse of service outsourcing is that a huge communications infrastructure was developed during the dot-com boom which was sold off very inexpensively during the dot-com bust. This communications infrastructure provides low cost and exceptional quality bandwidth for Indian companies and the foreign firms that do business with them.

In the case of offshoring involving product manufacturing, the list of issues becomes longer and more complex. They include: office and industrial real estate availability and costs; proximity to and quality of ports, airports, rail lines and highways; availability and reliability of electricity and other power sources; proximity to sources of raw materials; expatriate housing; and public transportation to name but a few.

## Culture

Many businesspeople experience "culture shock" when visiting and trying to do business in other countries. The differences in culture can be significant and difficult to comprehend for those new to the process. This is why "nearshoring" has become very popular. German firms nearshore to Eastern Europe because they have cultural, linguistic and historical ties to Eastern Europe. U.S. firms nearshore to Canada for the same reasons.

It has become common knowledge that misunderstanding the culture of a foreign *supplier* can make it impossible to do business. Offshore outsourcing has turned the tables somewhat: foreign suppliers have to understand the culture of their foreign client country in order to perform the offshored services. When there are significant cultural differences, both the client company and the vendor company will have to work hard to make the relationship work. In the offshoring of services, however, it remains the responsibility of the foreign vendor/supplier to adapt to the needs of its international clients.

## Language

There are at least three language-related issues:

The first is that if the client and the offshore vendor speak different languages, it will be difficult to communicate needs, problems and solutions. This may result in delays, especially problematic in the case of an emergency. The client will likely have to engage translators and interpreters, or hire someone at its home office that speaks the language. Conversely, the client may encourage its vendor to hire at least one individual who speaks the client's language to be the contact person.

The second is that the work performed may need to be done in the client's language. For example: call centers, help desks, outbound and inbound telemarketing, editorial research, etc. In this case it is best to outsource to a country that has a large pool of workers who speak the required language. This is why India and the Philippines have become offshore outsourcing hubs for the U.S., UK, Australia, Canada and New Zealand. Both countries have large pools of English speakers. In the case of performing editorial work, the Philippines may have an advantage over India with U.S. firms because of its close cultural ties over the past 100 plus years.

The third is that while vendor employees may speak the language, they may not speak it well, or they may speak with a strong accent. This is especially an issue where vendor staff will have regular contact with client company customers, such as in the case of call centers and help desks. In some cases the accents and intonation may be so difficult to understand that it is off-putting to client customers. Some firms have brought call center operations back in house as a result of customer complaints. In turn, this has led to the development of "accent and intonation" training programs, especially for Indian call-center workers.

### Country Risk

Country risk is a group of risk factors associated with trading with, operating in, lending to, or holding the assets of an individual, business or governmental entity of a particular country. A number of organizations that specialize in country risk analysis create composite indexes of country risk based upon the type of transaction contemplated with a legal person or entity of another country.

Country risk can be based on a multitude of factors including a country's economic and political policies, government intervention in the business community, legal system and enforcement, transparency, copyright and patent law and enforcement, inflation, exchange rates, bribery, regional issues such as political and civil unrest, war, and crime among others.

### Time Zone Issues

Differences in time zones between client and vendor locations can have a positive, negative or neutral effect on an offshore outsourcing relationship. For example, if your organization is outsourcing medical or legal transcription, it would be convenient to transmit raw data at the end of your work day, have the offshore organization transcribe the material during its normal work day, and transmit the "product" back to you prior to the start of your next day. Obviously, if the work is important, and labor rates are reasonable, the vendor will perform services at any time of night or day. Call centers in India and the Philippines operate 24 hours a day, 365 days a year.

### Geographic Proximity

Geographic proximity, like time zone issues, can have a positive, negative or neutral effect on an offshore outsourcing relationship.

- If a project requires individuals to travel back and forth on a regular basis between client and vendor, it will be convenient and less costly to have close proximity.
- If a project requires physical goods or paper documents to be sent regularly between client and vendor, it will also be convenient to have close proximity (the world's top courier services are working overtime to make this a non issue!).
- If the entire project can be managed by teleconference and the transmission of documents over the Internet, proximity is neutral.

In the case of the offshoring of product manufacturing, the proximity of raw materials, component parts, and markets and the relative tax advantages will have a much greater effect on the value of locating at an offshore site.

## Vendor Selection

### Vendor Selection

Vendor selection can be likened to choosing a spouse. There should be a certain amount of "chemistry" between the two, trust has to be built and maintained, honest communication is foundational, there should be a mutual desire for a long-term relationship, both parties want to prosper and thrive, and either party can ask for a divorce if the marriage really isn't working.

At the same time, breaking the marriage can create a great deal of stress for both parties, hardship on children and relatives (employees and customers), financial hardship for everyone, potential psychological problems, and there is no guarantee that the next relationship or marriage will work out any better!

To develop the analogy further, as in marriage, client-vendor relationships work best when both parties enter the relationship as mature individuals, independent in their own right, conscious and communicative of their needs, with eyes open, the ability to negotiate and compromise and a strong desire to work out issues as they come up.

Furthermore, while marriages are covenantal and business relationships are contractual, neither will work unless both parties commit to both the letter and intent of their agreement.

Finally, as we shall see, like selecting a spouse, selecting a vendor is not an exact science.

### Establishing Needs, Understanding Costs

The first step in selecting a vendor is establishing your needs as the client company. What do we want to offshore

outsource? Why do we want to outsource? What are our short-, medium- and long-term goals?

Answers to these questions will change over the vendor selection process; however, it is best to have a "base line" understanding of the 'what and why' at the very beginning.

A next step is to calculate your total internal costs of the services as they are currently being performed in house. For large organizations with clearly defined departments, this may be a straightforward procedure. For smaller organizations, it may be a challenge to identify all the costs of performing the service or procedure. Is is best to identify all these costs accurately so that you enter the process (and later negotiations) with firm knowledge.

Once again, your understanding of these costs is likely to change over time, but it is best to have a base point understanding from the beginning.

### Service Specifications and Expectations

A key part of the vendor selection, evaluation and retention process is establishing a service specifications and expectations list. This is the detailed "what" you propose to offshore outsource. The most easily understood parallel is a 'job description' for an employee. A prudent and fair employer-employee relationship will have a written description of what is expected from the employee.

The service specifications and expectations document will be a complete list of everything the vendor is expected to do, perhaps even how they will do it, and certainly how well they will do it. A high degree of specificity will be required.

For example, "Handle incoming technical calls" may be what you want to have happen, but your service specifications document will need to answer these questions:

- Who will be answering the phone?
- What will be the level of training of the people answering the phone?
- What will be the language skills of the people answering the phone?
- What will be the average time that the phone rings before it is answered?
- What will be the maximum time that the phone rings before it is answered?
- What will be the average time it takes to handle the incoming call?
- What will be the minimum acceptable customer service rating received from clients who call with questions?

### Non-Disclosure Agreement

At the very beginning of negotiations with potential vendors it is imperative to enter into a non-disclosure agreement (NDA). An NDA is an agreement between two or more parties not to disclose trade secrets, trade practices, business or marketing plans or other proprietary or confidential information, either before, during or even a number of years after entering into the NDA and/or an eventual contractual agreement for the delivery of services. A non-disclosure agreement is often signed by parties entering into a business negotiation or business relationship where such information is likely to be revealed. Sample non-disclosure agreements can be found on the web.

### Request for Proposal (RFP)

Once you have established that a potential vendor meets your basic standards for performing the required services, and a non-disclosure agreement is in place, send a request for proposal (RFP). An RFP will ask the firm for a formal proposal to perform work based upon the service standards outlined in the "Service Standards and Expectations" document. If asking for pricing, be specific enough about what you want so that the vendor can accurately establish pricing. While it is best to be very clear about asking for everything, it is also good to manage expectations about what is possible.

### Vendor Evaluation

Choosing a vendor for an offshore outsourcing relationship requires great care, especially if the vendor services will be replacing established services that play a key role in the success of the organization.

Regardless of the size of the transaction, outsourcing relationships are generally medium to long term. It is therefore advisable that your organization establish a formal vendor evaluation process. At the very least, these questions should be asked:

1. Do we have an immediate positive, negative or neutral feeling about the potential vendor's people and organization?
2. Will this vendor sign a non-disclosure agreement?
3. Is the political environment of the vendor's country conducive to conducting business?
4. Is the economic and business environment of the vendor's country conducive to conducting business?
5. Is the legal system of the vendor's country conducive to conducting business?
6. Is the geographic proximity of the vendor a positive, negative or neutral issue?
7. Is the time zone differential of the vendor's country a positive, negative or neutral issue?
8. Are cultural considerations a positive, negative or neutral issue?
9. Do we have personal safety issues regarding staff visiting the potential vendor's country and place of business?
10. Are there any issues regarding infrastructure (especially telecommunications and Internet bandwidth) in the potential vendor's country, locale or place of business?
11. Does this vendor have experience delivering the same or similar services?
12. What is this vendor's market share of this service area?
13. Are the vendor's employees qualified to do the work required?
14. Will the vendor's employees have to be trained to perform the required services?
15. Does this vendor have people who speak our language?
16. How do we feel about the person who has been chosen by the vendor to be our point of contact?
17. Is this vendor financially stable?
18. Are we too small or too large a client for this vendor to properly service?
19. Is this vendor large enough to handle our workload?
20. Will this vendor have to hire additional personnel to handle our workload?
21. Does this vendor have a high employee turnover rate?
22. Does this vendor take care of its employees well enough that we can expect a low turnover rate over time?
23. Will this vendor require additional physical space to handle our work? Is that space readily available?
24. Are we confident that the vendor can properly handle data security issues?
25. Does this vendor already have data security measures in place?
26. Are we confident that the vendor will properly handle intellectual property rights issues?
27. Can we get the level of support we need from this vendor?
28. Do we trust the management and staff of the vendor?
29. Does this vendor really understand what we need?
30. Does this vendor have environmental polices that are consistent with our needs (for moral and public-relations reasons)?
31. Does this vendor have employment, personnel and human resource policies that are consistent with our needs (for moral and public-relations reasons)?
32. Does this vendor have references that can be checked and relied upon?
33. What are the strengths and weaknesses of this vendor?
34. What warranties or guarantees can be obtained from this vendor that the work will be performed according to specifications?
35. Do our expectations match their likely performance?
36. Do their expectations match their likely outcome?

### Due Diligence

At the point where a potential vendor is seriously being considered as a supplier, the client company should perform a due diligence investigation. Due diligence in offshore outsourcing is the investigation and evaluation of a potential vendor prior to establishing a contractual relationship.

Due diligence can include checking financial references, performing background checks on key management of the firm, interviewing current and past clients of the firm, checking the legal status of the company and conducting on-location site evaluations, to name but a few.

# Client–Vendor Relationship

Most offshore outsourcing arrangements for services are treated as simple vendor–purchaser arrangements and are handled by the drafting of a straightforward contract for services between unrelated parties.

In other cases, however, the client-vendor relationship may be more complex. Here are a number of possible relationships that may occur:

1. Client and vendor are unrelated parties and the vendor has similar relationships with other firms.
2. Client and vendor are unrelated parties and there is an exclusivity clause whereby the vendor will not provide products or services to:
   a) any other firm,
   b) any other firm in the same industry, or
   c) any firm on a specified list.
3. Client and vendor are related parties and the vendor is a wholly owned subsidiary of the client company, but is structured as its own legal entity in the foreign country and is subject to local laws.
4. Client and vendor are related parties and the vendor is a partially-owned subsidiary of the client company, but is structured as its own legal entity with partial local ownership and is subject to local laws.
5. Client and vendor are related parties and the vendor is wholly or partially owned by the vendor's national, provincial or regional government, or by its military.

# Data Security

Data security has become one of the public's greatest concerns about outsourcing, especially when it involves personal and financial data such as social security numbers, bank account numbers, passwords, credit card information and sensitive medical data.

As a result, client firms are taking a number of steps to ensure the security of their client data. These include:

1. Writing client-vendor contracts with very specific clauses about how the vendor is to handle data security.
2. On-site inspections to make sure the vendor's data security procedures are being followed.
3. Ongoing monitoring of the vendor's policies and procedures regarding data security.

From the client's perspective, the vendor must do whatever it takes to adequately protect whatever critical data is passed in the course of the working relationship. The vendor must also ensure that such data is protected after project completion.

All outsourcing contracts now have strict provisions regarding data security. In cases where data security is a major issue (such as with financial, legal and medical data), vendors are required to develop and present a written security procedure, including provisions for the physical location of data, hardware and software, vetting of key personnel, vetting of regular staff, as well as the specific means for protecting that data using guards, access keys and encryption.

In one interesting example, an Indian firm (headed by an American) that prepares tax returns for U.S. accounting firms has designed an ingenious hardware and software system whereby the Indian tax preparers never get access to the customer's name, Social Security number, or address. Also, the tax preparers' computers themselves have been configured so that there is no removable media and no data ports that would enable the tax preparer to download data.

# Intellectual Property Rights Issues

Intellectual property issues are related to but different from data security issues. Intellectual property rights (IPR) include copyrights, patents, trademarks and business processes, but often include business plans as well.

A client firm considering outsourcing needs to understand completely its exposure to risk of losing control of its IPR. It will need to: a) understand local laws related to IPR registration and protection, b) establish a contractual framework for protection, c) have trust in its vendor, and d) monitor the relationship for possible violations.

If your firm has significant intellectual property rights that might in any way be compromised in an offshore outsourcing relationship, you will need to consult with an IPR attorney in your home country and possibly one in the vendor's country.

At the very least, a client company will want to have a non-disclosure agreement signed by the vendor, prior to the commencement of the project.

### Copyright

A copyright is an intangible right granted by law to the creator or owner of a literary, musical or artistic production to prevent any other person from copying, publishing and selling those works. However, the works that can be copyrighted, the requirements for claiming a copyright, the extent of enforcement, and the time during which a copyright is effective vary from country to country.

### Patent

A patent is a grant by law to an inventor or owner of a device of the right to exclude other persons from making, using, or selling the device. The patent holder has the right to license to another person the right to make, use, or sell the device. A patent is available only for devices that embody a new idea or principle and that involve a discovery. However, patent protection varies from country to country, and may not be available in some jurisdictions.

### Trademarks

A trademark is a distinctive identification of a manufactured product or of a service taking the form of a name, logo or motto. A trademarked brand has legal protection and only the owner or licensee can use the mark. A trademark is distinguished from a servicemark in that the former identifies products while the latter identifies services. Trademark protection, however, varies from country to country, and may not be available in some jurisdictions.

### Business Process

A business process is a collection of related, structured activities—a chain of events—that produce a specific service or product for a particular customer or customers. A firm's business processes are often part of the firm's competitive advantage over other firms in the same business. Business processes are closely held secrets of a firm, because they are often very difficult to protect legally. This is one of the key reasons why some firms refuse to outsource—they are simply unwilling to share such business processes with any other firm.

### Non-Disclosure Agreement

A non-disclosure agreement is an agreement between two or more parties not to disclose trade secrets, trade practices, business or marketing plans or other proprietary or

**S O U R C I N G**

confidential information. A non-disclosure agreement is often signed by parties entering into a business negotiation or business relationship where such information is likely to be revealed.

### Ownership of Information and Deliverables

Outsourcing contracts often produce a "product." For example, statistical results of making tens of thousands of call center calls and marketing information gained from

such call center calls are just two examples. In addition, there may well be a specific product resulting from market research, editorial writing, editing or graphic arts that results from the outsourcing contract.

Ownership of such data and product should be established in the original outsourcing contract. The client company also must be aware of copyright and related laws in the vendor's country.

# Ongoing Project Management

Project management is the coordinated application of diverse management skills to achieve a project's predetermined objectives of scope, quality, time and cost; essentially, how a project is managed to achieve a satisfactory result. Modern project management is broken down into five process groups:

1. Initiating the project
2. Planning the project
3. Executing the project
4. Controlling the project
5. Closing down the project

Since offshore outsourcing contracts are typically for medium- to long-term periods, planning, executing and controlling the project are major ongoing issues.

### The Main Contact Person

It is imperative that the client and vendor each have a main contact person who is responsible for managing the project and the relationship. The main contact people must be able to speak the same language well, be available to each other at relatively short notice, be in regular communication, preferably know each other personally, have established trust for each other, and be able to communicate honestly about problems and solutions. Each should have the responsibility of monitoring and tracking the project and making sure that the contract terms are being fulfilled. For best results, each contact person should have the authority and power to make day-to-day project and business decisions.

### Client and Vendor Teams

The client and vendor should each establish a project team. Team members are chosen based upon their technical skills, their ability to work with other people, their ability to move the project along, their problem-solving abilities, and their sensitivity to each other's issues. Names, titles, contact information, duties and roles of each team member should be clearly communicated to the other side at the very beginning of the project.

### Milestones

Milestones are checkpoints at stated periods in the performance of a project that allow both parties to evaluate progress towards achieving the stated goals of the project. Establish milestones in the original service contract before the project is started. Also, an individual in the client company, usually the main contact person, should have responsibility for monitoring the project to assess if the milestones are being met.

### Reporting

Both parties to the relationship must establish minimum and mutually agreeable communication and reporting standards to keep everyone informed of progress and problems. Reporting standards vary from organization to organization, from project to project and from industry to industry. Reporting is different from assessing the completion of milestones in that reporting is an ongoing process that communicates all matters of import to the other party.

A statement of the reporting points and procedure should be part of the original contract for services. The procedure itself should be in place from the moment the contract begins. Being on top of reporting is an integral part of the ongoing management of a project.

### Triggers

A trigger is an event that precipitates an action on the part of either party to a contract. For example, in an offshore outsourcing service agreement, a customer satisfaction survey rating of 92 percent might be established as the minimum acceptable rating. If the rating goes below 92 percent, it would trigger a review; if it goes below 89 percent, it might require specific remedial steps to be taken; and if it goes below 85 percent for 90 days, it might be cause for cancellation of the contract.

Triggers can relate to service standards, quality standards, volume of services performed and promptness of payments, to name but a few. A trigger can initiate a project, start a new phase of a project, initiate remedial actions or end a project.

### Remedial Steps

Every organization that has developed a service function internally has done so in an iterative process of taking steps, making adjustments, taking new steps, and making new adjustments, until the process has been refined. This refers to both process and people. A vendor that is new to the work will likely need to go through some of the same steps to achieve the quality level required. It is unrealistic to expect vendors to perform service functions faultlessly from the start. Therefore, expect that some remedial actions will need to be taken, especially at the beginning of a project.

### Contingency Plan

A contingency plan is an organized and coordinated course of action that will be followed in case the outsourcing agreement is not performed or not performed to the satisfaction of the client.

An integral part of outsourcing is establishing such a contingency plan at the same time that the relationship with the vendor is established. The idea of developing a plan for what to do if the great new relationship, for which all have high hopes, doesn't work, is counterintuitive to some, but must be done. Your contingency plan will include specific steps that you will take in case of the occurrence of any number of performance problems with the vendor. Make a list of everything that could possibly go wrong and develop a contingency plan for each.

### Quarterly Reviews

A review is an assessment of performance related to the progress of a project. A review is an analysis undertaken at a fixed point in time to determine if stated objectives are being met. A review can be formal or informal, verbal or written. Such reviews are used as a basis for decision-making. Just like annual employee performance reviews, they are vital to both parties' understanding of the status of a project.

# Pricing Models for Service Outsourcing

There are many pricing models for the outsourcing of services. Pricing options are dependent upon the nature of the services to be performed, the expected term of the contract, the relationship of the parties, payment considerations, client and vendor needs, and other factors. Here is a sampling:

## Unit Pricing

In this pricing model the client and vendor agree upon a unit price for work to be performed to a stated standard. The client simply pays based upon its usage of the service. Examples include:
- Cost per page for typesetting
- Cost per incoming help desk call
- Cost per unit for each tax return prepared
- Cost per unit for each x-ray evaluated

## Fixed Price

In this pricing model the client pays a fixed price for the completion of a project, regardless of how long it takes to complete. The advantage to the client is that the costs are predictable. The advantage to the vendor is the possibility of completing the project in less time than originally estimated. The disadvantage to the client is that the market price for such work might decrease over time and the client will be saddled with the relatively higher costs for the term of the contract. The disadvantage to the vendor is that true costs may escalate over time to the point that there is not enough revenue to cover costs.

This model is best when the specifications and scope of the project are clear to both parties. This model provides maximum incentive to the vendor to control costs and perform the services as effectively as possible. Examples include:
- Development of computer code to perform a particular function that is well understood by both parties
- Development of a fully functioning e-commerce web site with specific features for a specified group of products
- Ongoing maintenance of a web site that was created by the same vendor
- Handling incoming help desk inquiries when the nature of the inquiries is well known to both parties

## Variable Price

In this pricing model the client pays a fixed unit price for a specified standard service, but pays additional fees depending upon successively higher levels of service performed. Example:
- Client pays a modest unit fee for each outbound telemarketing call made, an additional charge for each telemarketing contact made, an additional charge for each sales appointment made, an additional charge for each product or service order placed and an additional charge for each firm sale made.

## Cost Plus Price (Time and Materials Plus)

In this pricing model the client agrees to pay the vendor actual costs for labor, materials and overhead, plus a fixed percentage of total costs as profit. This model is often used for performing services that require an unknown amount of work such as research and development projects. In this model a vendor will typically supply a full-time project team, a project manager, equipment and infrastructure based upon project specifications.

Cost plus contracts are usually monitored through weekly or monthly time sheets and detailed progress reports.

The disadvantage to the client is that this model does not provide incentives for the vendor to perform the service with the greatest efficiency. Therefore, cost plus pricing without some element of cost control is not recommended. If cost plus pricing is needed due to special requirements of the work, then a "Not to Exceed" clause is recommended. Cost plus pricing is a good model when there are many unknowns to the project, the client and vendor have experience working together, AND the client trusts the vendor to perform efficiently.
Examples include:
- Product development
- Software development
- Biotechnology research

## Not to Exceed (NTE)

A clause inserted into a services contract that states that vendor billing of the client shall be no greater than a stated amount on a project- or service-unit basis. NTE clauses are typical in cost plus pricing contracts.

## Performance-Based Pricing

In this pricing model the client agrees to pay the vendor on a "sliding-scale" basis with greater pay for greater performance based upon either quality or volume. Performance-based pricing establishes financial incentives that encourage the vendor to perform efficiently or effectively. The vendor may also be financially penalized for under performance. Example:
- A vendor is paid a standard rate for operating a client's customer help desk to a stated standard, an additional sum if the operation achieves customer satisfaction ratings above a certain level, and a penalty if the customer satisfaction drops below a certain level.

## Risk-Reward Share Pricing

In this pricing model the client agrees to share profits or 'rewards' with the vendor based on the business outcome of the project itself. As a result, both client and vendor have a financial interest in the success of the relationship. Example:
- A company with proprietary content or data (such as a publishing company) enters into an agreement with a web developer to create and maintain an e-commerce web site where the publisher retains copyright to the content and the vendor retains rights to the programming, but both parties share the revenue or profits from e-commerce at the site.

## Fixed Price + Cost Plus (Time and Materials)

In this pricing model it is anticipated that there will be two aspects of service delivery, and two costs. The first aspect, generally the bulk of the service to be performed, is known and understood by both parties. This is performed on a fixed-price basis. It is also understood, however, that there is another aspect to the project that is less understood by both parties. This part is performed on a cost plus price basis. Example:
- A client contracts with a vendor to develop an e-commerce web site with standard and known functionality. However, the client also wishes to have other, but as yet unspecified, functionality added as the e-commerce site is being developed.

## Project Creep

Project creep is the addition of features or tasks to an original project after the project specifications and budget have been approved by both parties. Project creep is a virtually inevitable feature of outsourcing relationships and should be anticipated in the original contract. Project creep is usually charged on a cost plus basis.

S O U R C I N G

**SOURCING**

# Billing Models for Service Outsourcing

### Milestone Based Billing

A milestone is a scheduled event that signals the completion of a contract deliverable. In this billing model the vendor invoices the client at the completion of each contract milestone event. From the client's perspective, paying for milestones achieved is often preferable to simply paying for vendor time spent working.
Example:

- A client contracts with a vendor for the development of ten e-commerce web sites and is invoiced one-tenth of the contract amount upon completion of each site.

### Monthly Billing

In this billing model the vendor sends the client a bill at the end of each month for services provided. This option works well for ongoing contracts whether they be based on unit, variable or other pricing models with the exception of fixed price upon completion contracts. Monthly billing is the preferred model for both clients and vendors as it enables both to exercise a degree of control over the process.

### Payment Upon Completion

In this billing and payment model it is assumed that the client-vendor relationship consists of a single, well-defined, small- to medium-sized project, or that the relationship is ongoing but proceeds on a project-by-project basis. The client incorporates product specifications into its contract with the vendor along with a clause that specifies payment upon completion. This billing model usually includes some sort of up front "good faith" or deposit payment.

### Half at Contract - Half Upon Completion

In this billing and payment model it is assumed that the client-vendor relationship consists of a single, well-defined project, or that the relationship is ongoing but proceeds on a project-by-project basis. However, rather than full payment upon completion, the client firm transfers a "good faith" or deposit payment to the vendor at the beginning. While the percentages or fractions paid up front vary, this is a very common billing model for individual projects.

# Payment Options for Service Outsourcing

### Prepayment

Prepayment is when a client pays the full contract price in advance of the fulfillment of the contract by the vendor. Obviously, this is very much in favor of the vendor and to the disadvantage of the client. This option is almost unheard of in offshore outsourcing as the client effectively loses all control over the vendor, the process and the outcome once the payment has been made.

### Payment by Check

Payment by check for international service contracts is uncommon. There are a number of clear disadvantages to both parties with payments by check:

- Mailing or sending a physical check by courier adds time and adds risk of loss
- Mailing or sending a physical check by courier adds expense as international courier costs are often greater than bank wire transfer fees
- From the vendor's perspective, once the check has been received, it may be drawn on insufficient funds
- Vendors receiving a check drawn on a bank in a foreign country must wait until their own bank collects the funds. This can take from one to several weeks.

An alternative is for the vendor to have an account with a bank that is domestic to the client. This benefits the client by saving courier costs, lowering the risk of loss and decreasing the amount of time it takes for funds to be fully credited to the vendor's account.

### Payment by Bank Wire Transfer

Payment by bank wire transfer is perhaps the most common and effective payment method for offshore outsourcing contracts. It has a number of advantages:

- Payments rarely take more than a few days or a week to be received.
- Bank fees for international bank wires generally cost the sender about US$25-50 and the recipient about US$10-20. These are modest amounts when the payments are for tens of thousands of dollars.
- The bank provides immediate documentation so the client can offer proof of transfer to the vendor.

An alternative is a bank wire transfer, but to a vendor account at a bank that is domestic to the client. This has the benefit of saving the client bank wire transfer fees as domestic transfers usually cost only US$10, and of decreasing the amount of time it takes for funds to be credited to the vendor's account.

### Retainer

A retainer is a fee paid in advance by a client to a service provider. A retainer has three specific functions:

1. To commit the client financially to the service provider,
2. With acceptance of the payment, to commit the service provider to perform certain services over a specified period of time, and
3. To act as a deposit against which the service provider's fees are charged as they are earned.

In this billing and payment model the client often has unspecified, but regularly occurring periodic needs for the provider's services. Payment of the (usually) monthly retainer ensures that the client will get the attention it needs when vital services need to be performed. In some cases the retainer is sufficient to have one or several dedicated staff members at the vendor's place of business working on client projects on an ongoing basis.
Examples include:

- A client pays an attorney a monthly fee with the expectation that it will require legal services on a regular basis
- A client pays a call center vendor a monthly retainer based upon the expectation that it will require at least that amount of vendor services each month

### Letters of Credit

Letters of credit are not used in payment for service contracts as they require presentation of documents (usually a Bill of Lading) that evidence title to goods shipped by the seller. The issue, of course, is that with service contracts, there are no goods being shipped and therefore no documents that evidence title to goods. While a document can be created that evidences title to a copyright, patent or business process, banks require a document that evidences title to goods specifically.

### Documentary Collections

Similarly, documentary collections are not used in payment for service contracts as they also require presentation of a document (usually a Bill of Lading) that evidences title to goods shipped by the seller. Once again, there are no goods being shipped.

# Negotiating & Maintaining Relationships

## Tips For Negotiating and Maintaining Long-Term Supplier Relationships

The purpose of these tips is to support the development and maintenance of long-term client-vendor relationships. As such, it is understood that both parties to the transaction have something to gain from the transaction and have a reason to continue the relationship.

### Before You Start Negotiating

1. Are you negotiating a short-term or long-term relationship? The amount of time you invest in developing and maintaining a relationship will be proportional to its projected term and importance to your firm.
2. Understand what it is that you are negotiating for before you start. Don't go into a negotiating session without a specific list of points of negotiation. Get the input or feedback of a second individual regarding your points of negotiation.
3. Create or develop a vision of what you want to accomplish from a successful outsourcing relationship.
4. Create or develop a vision of what you want to accomplish as a result of negotiations.
5. Identify all the key components of what has to happen for the vision(s) to become reality.
6. Identify all the objections, barriers and problems the other side might have to your proposal or ideas and create responses for each prior to negotiating.
7. Research and understand the country-of-origin price structure, as well as your own country's price structure, for similar services before you start negotiating.
8. Learn your supplier's costs. Research local labor rates, employment taxes, required and expected employee benefits, office rental rates, Internet connectivity rates and the local costs of equipment and supervision. It is unlikely that you will be able to ascertain all costs, but the more knowledgeable you are about a potential business partner's costs, the better you will be at negotiating the best deal.

### While You Are Negotiating

9. Negotiate from the standpoint that a partnership is being created, not just a client-vendor relationship.
10. Don't get tied into thinking that business can only be done with one potential supplier. Your attachment to a single deal or relationship is likely to drive the price up, or keep it from coming down. Create options for alternative relationships even if you are not likely to use them.
11. Be prepared to walk away from a negotiation if you are truly uncomfortable with the potential supplier or its people, or if there is no opportunity to get what you need. This may be difficult, especially if a great deal of time has been invested in developing the relationship, but do it if necessary.
12. Understand that negotiations are not just with a company, but with real people. You don't have to give up what you need in order to treat the other party with care and respect.
13. Do not get in a position where you have a greater need to purchase the service than the vendor has to sell it.
14. Look at the long-term consequences of any action you take. Don't take "ethical short cuts." The consequences are likely to out weight any immediate advantage. Take the initiative to set a standard for "right dealing."

15. Make sure that your supplier gets enough compensation both to provide the services you require and make a reasonable profit. If they don't stay in business, how can they do the work for you?
16. Consider that if you make too tough a deal with your supplier today (perhaps by your taking advantage of a supplier's temporary weakness) it may come back to haunt you, when your supplier (who will know exactly what happened) may be tempted to get even.
17. Ask your supplier what he or she needs—besides money—to make the project run smoothly. Listen carefully and take note of the issues that come up. You may be surprised at how easy it is to help a supplier with something that costs you little or nothing.
18. Give your supplier what it needs to make the project work. Be aware that a supplier can find creative ways to increase costs to compensate for tensions due to problematic clients.
19. Establish what it is that you (as the client) need in order to make the project successful. Differentiate between window-dressing items and real needs. Let your supplier know what is important to you.
20. Understand the supplier's issues and problems without necessarily taking them on as your own.
21. Handle difficult issues at the beginning of negotiations when everyone wants the relationship to work, rather than after work has started. Handling tough issues early on will give an indication of how the supplier handles problems. If the parties can't handle such issues early on, it is unlikely that they will be able to handle them later.
22. Isolate problems when appropriate; group problems when appropriate.
23. Don't back the supplier into a corner unless you are confident about what you're doing and understand the potential consequences.
24. Consider negotiating for an exclusive or industry exclusive with your supplier. What advantage or disadvantage might such an arrangement give your firm?
25. Remember that it is always easier to get someone to say "Yes" than it is to get them to do what they said "Yes" to.
26. Regardless of the culture and a country's laws, a contract is only as good as those who sign it.

### Ongoing 'Negotiating' and Maintenance

27. Ongoing supplier relationships are more like partnerships than simple client-vendor relationships. If you want this to be the case, be sure to treat your supplier with the respect and care of a partner.
28. Actively look for ways to support each other. Are there business opportunities that can be shared? Do you have information that will help your supplier? Are you familiar with new equipment, technology or processes that will help your supplier? Do you have information about competitors that is appropriate to share?
29. Don't approach the relationship as a "zero-sum game" where someone has to lose for someone else to win. Look for "win-win" solutions.
30. Is it feasible or worthwhile to have an ownership position in the vendor company? Will having an ownership position bring value to either company?

**SOURCING**

# Contractual Framework

The following provisions are suggested for a "standard" international contract for the offshore outsourcing of services. Not every provision is applicable to every contractual arrangement and some contracts will require additional provisions. The goal of this checklist is to ensure that you have considered and defined your relationship with the other party as clearly as possible, and that you have provided for as many contingencies as may be anticipated.

Regardless of who drafts the contract, be aware of the key provisions because it is up to you to insist on the protection of your own interests. Although the laws of many countries will imply certain terms to encourage fair dealing, the law is generally applied through costly and time-consuming legal processes, whether court, arbitration or mediation proceedings. The best course of action is to define all the provisions of your relationship in writing in the original contract.

### Contract Validity

The client company must ensure the validity of any contract established with an offshore vendor. Understanding the local validity of contract terms is part of the due diligence process.

### Disclaimer

This section is not a substitute for the services of a competent attorney. In some cases you will need to consult with an attorney in your home country as well as with an attorney in the vendor's country.

## The Business Process Outsourcing Contract Checklist

1. **Contract Date**
2. **Identification of Parties**
3. **Scope of Agreement**
   - **Single Agreement vs. Master Agreement**
   - **Independent Contractor Agreement**
4. **Scope of Services**
   - **Services Description**
   - **Methodology**
   - **Service Volumes**
   - **Start and End Dates of Services**
5. **Service Standards**
   - **Standards Statement**
   - **Benchmarking**
   - **Remedies**
6. **Fees and Payments**
   - **Pricing of Services**
   - **Price Controls**
   - **Invoice Preparation and Delivery**
   - **Payment Due Dates**
   - **Method of Payment**
   - **Medium of Exchange**
   - **Exchange Rates**
   - **Late Payments**
   - **Records and Audits**
7. **Other Costs and Charges**
   - **Transportation and Courier Charges**
   - **Insurance**
   - **Taxes**
8. **Errors and Mistakes**
9. **Human Resources**
   - **Vetting of Employee Qualifications**
   - **Status of Vendor Employees**
   - **Transference of Employees**
   - **Transferred Employees**
   - **Seconded Employees**
   - **Terminated Employees**
10. **Technological Requirements**
11. **Trigger Events**
    - **Milestones**
12. **Intellectual Property Rights (IPR)**
    - **Protection of Existing Client IPR**
    - **Ownership of Service Deliverables**
13. **Data Security**
    - **Vetting of Employees for Security**
    - **Security Standards**
    - **Security Procedures**
    - **Data Privacy**
14. **Disaster Recovery**
15. **Business Continuity**
16. **Inspection Rights**
17. **Audit Rights**
18. **Non Disclosure**
19. **Client Support Given to Vendor**
20. **Reporting**
21. **Transfer of Deliverables**
22. **Exclusivity**
23. **Change Provisions**
24. **Warranties**
25. **Limitation of Liability**
26. **Consequential Damages**
27. **Indemnification**
28. **Disclaimers**
29. **Dispute Resolution**
30. **Termination and Cancellation**
    - **Triggers**
    - **Effects of Termination or Expiration**
    - **Housekeeping**
    - **Transition Services**
31. **Limitation of Relationship Between the Parties**
32. **Enforcement and Remedies**
33. **Arbitration Provisions**
34. **Essence of Time**
35. **Cancellation**
36. **Liquidated Damages**
37. **Attorneys' Fees**
38. **Force Majeure**
39. **Inurement and Assignment**
40. **Conditions Precedent**
41. **Governing Law**
42. **Choice of Forum**
43. **Severability of Provisions**
44. **Integration of Provisions**
45. **Notices**
46. **Vendor's Contact Person**
47. **Client's Contact Person**
48. **Authority to Bind**
49. **Acceptance and Execution**

# Outsourcing Powerhouses

S
O
U
R
C
I
N
G

## United States

India and China may be in the news, but the United States is the world's top outsourcing powerhouse. More services are exported from the U.S. than from any country in the world. Also, lost in the trade 'deficit in products' debate is the fact that the U.S. has the world's greatest trade surplus in services.

Service exports from the U.S., however, are different from those exported from India and China. While India is becoming a powerhouse in the export of low- and medium-skilled services such as call centers and mid-level programming, the U.S. is the leader in more innovative services such as product design, research and development, pharmaceuticals, information systems, financial services and franchising, to name but a few.

While India and China both have increased their offerings of higher level services, the U.S. is expected to maintain its lead in service exports that require specialized knowledge, specialized facilities and advanced analytical and decision-making skills.

### Pros of Outsourcing to The United States
1. Highly educated workforce
2. Very high worker productivity in relation to most other countries
3. Exceptional system of higher education
4. World technology leader
5. World leader in innovation and entrepreneurship
6. Highly developed infrastructure
7. Highly developed intellectual property rights laws
8. Stable and transparent financial and banking system
9. Low value of the U.S. dollar relative to other world currencies
10. Political stability

### Cons of Outsourcing to The United States
1. Relatively high cost of labor compared to certain other nations
2. Lack of foreign-language skills (mitigated by the growth of English as the world's lingua franca)

### Services Outsourced to the U.S. (U.S. Service Exports)
U.S. service exports tend to be higher value-added services including:
- Advertising
- Architectural design
- Banking services
- Biomedical R&D
- Biotech R&D
- Higher Education
- Engineering services
- Environmental technologies
- Insurance services
- Knowledge services
- Large-scale construction services
- Legal services
- Medical services (including "cutting edge" surgical procedures)
- Financial services (financial "product" development)
- Pharmaceutical R&D
- Product design
- Security services
- Software design
- Technology R&D
- Telecommunications services
- Travel and tourism services

### Locations of Major Universities
Centers of service outsourcing are often located in and adjacent to university cities and towns. These centers of higher learning provide the setting for creative thinking, research centers and an educated workforce.

The United States has the best university system in the world. While other countries have universities rated in the top 100 worldwide, no other country has so many universities in that ranking. Beyond the exalted top 100 schools, there are literally hundreds of other top colleges and universities throughout the nation. Here is just a sampling:
- New England Area (Harvard University, Massachusetts Institute of Technology, Brown University, Dartmouth College, Yale University, Tufts University, Northeastern University, Brandeis University, Trinity, Bowdin College, Boston College, Boston University)
- New York Area (Columbia University, Princeton University, New York University, Cornell, Rensselaer Polytechnic Institute, Colgate)
- Other Eastern Seaboard (University of Pennsylvania, Johns Hopkins University, Carnegie Mellon University, Georgetown, University of Virginia)
- Mid-West (University of Chicago, Northwestern, University of Wisconsin, University of Michigan)
- California (California Institute of Technology, University of California at Berkeley, Stanford University, University of California at Los Angeles, Scripps)
- The South (Rice, Duke, Tulane, University of Texas-Austin)

### International Firms that Outsource Services to The United States
Virtually every "Global 500" firm has interests in or outsources to the U.S.
- Alcatel, BP Global, Barclays Bank, British Airways
- Cable & Wireless PLC
- EMI Music Publishing, Exel Global Logistics
- Dresdner Bank, GeoLogistics Corporation
- Hannover Re Group, Hapag-Lloyd
- Hellman Worldwide Logistics, HSBC Bank
- Lenovo (Chinese maker of the Think Pad laptop)
- Nortel Networks Corporation
- Ogilvy & Mather (design, PR, marketing)
- Samsung, SAP, Schenker Logistics
- Senator International, Sony, Siemens AG
- Toyota, Virgin Atlantic Airways

### Major Centers of Outsourcing
- California (information technology, biotechnology, environmental technologies, financial services, product design, large-scale construction services, filmmaking, music, creative services related to the film industry)
- New England (information technology, medical services, architectural design services, education)
- Texas (medical services, large-scale construction services)
- Research Triangle including Raleigh, Durham, and Chapel Hill areas of North Carolina (information technology)
- New York (banking, financial services, insurance)

**SOURCING**

# India

Since dramatic changes to India's laws related to trade and foreign investment were made in the early 1990s, and the dramatic increase in fibre-optic communications capabilities during the 'dot-com boom' (and their sale at bargain basement prices after the 'bust'), the entrepreneurial energies of an entire nation have been unleashed to dramatic effect.

## Pros of Outsourcing to India
1. Very highly educated workforce coupled with low salaries and related costs
2. Growing expertise in global methodologies
3. Increased ability to handle large, turnkey projects
4. Strong non-partisan government support of key globally outsourced industries
5. Stable, democratic government (the world's largest democracy)
6. Huge pool of English-speakers
7. Time-zone differential with Europe/America is a positive for certain tasks and projects (example: transcription of legal proceedings recorded during the day in the U.S. and transcribed during the U.S. night (the Indian day) in India)

## Cons of Outsourcing to India
1. Rapidly rising salaries
2. High attrition rates of workers assigned to outsourced projects
3. Inconsistent quality
4. Concern over capacity of Indian infrastructure and resources to cope with the outsourcing boom
5. Time-zone differential with Europe/America is a negative for tasks and projects that would otherwise benefit from concurrent communications
6. Concern over security of critical data
7. Anxiety over potential confrontation with nuclear rival Pakistan

## Services Outsourced to India
- Computer software (design, production, maintenance)
- Call center services (help desks, inbound telemarketing, outbound telemarketing)
- Pharmaceutical research
- Financial services ('back room services' including: payroll-processing, general-ledger services, financial-statement preparation, tax-preparation)
- Health care (primarily medical billing and coding)
- E-governance (delivery of government services via electronic technologies)

## Locations of Major Universities
- University of Calcutta (capital of the State of West Bengal, in eastern India)
- University of Madras (modern name "Chennai"; capital of the State of Tamil Nadu, on the Bay of Bengal)
- University of Mumbai (capital of western Indian State of Maharashtra)
- University of Delhi
- University of Hyderabad (capital of the State of Andhra Pradesh in south-central India)
- Jawaharlal Nehru University of New Delhi
- Indira Gandhi Open University of New Delhi
- Bangalore University (capital of the State of Karnataka in southern India)
- Shahu Ji Maharaj University of Kanpur (Kanpur is the largest industrial metropolis of the State of Uttar Pradesh)
- University of Kerala in Thiruvananthapuram (Trivan-

drum is the capital of the State of Kerala on extreme southwest coast)
- University of Pune (cultural capital of the western Indian State of Maharashtra)
- University of Rajasthan in Jaipur (Jaipur is the capital of Rajasthan State, northwestern India)

## International/U.S. Firms that Outsource Services to India
Some jokingly argue that it might be easier to list firms that have yet to outsource to India. There are literally thousands of the world's premier firms outsourcing services to India. The following is a very small sampling:
- 3M, Aftek, Agilent
- Alcatel, Amazon.com
- Amdocs, American Express, Avaya, Aviva
- BMC Software, Boeing, British Airways
- Citicorp (and thousands of other banks and financial institutions)
- Cigna, Coca-Cola, Cognizant, Convergys
- EDS, eFunds
- General Electric, Ericsson
- Fidelity Investments
- Flextronics Software Systems
- General Electric, General Motors, Gillette
- HCL technologies, Hewlett-Packard
- Hitachi Metals, HSBC Global Technology
- IBM
- I-Flex, Infosys, Lucent
- Microsoft
- Nestle, New York Life, Niksun, Nokia, Nortel
- Pepsi
- SAP, Sasken, SIEMENS, Sybase, Syntel
- TIBCO
- Veritas, Vertex, Xerox
- Zensar

## Major Centers of Outsourcing
- Bangalore (capital of the State of Karnataka in southern India); main center of IT service providers
- Chennai (formerly Madras; capital of the State of Tamil Nadu, on the Bay of Bengal); main center of IT outsourcing after Bangalore; IT services and financial services dominate outsourced services
- Gurgaon (in northern Indian State of Haryana; one of Delhi's four major satellite cities); major call center region as well as a focus of financial services and software development; fastest-growing destination of outsourced services in India
- Hyderabad (capital of the State of Andhra Pradesh in south-central India); emerging IT and biotech hub; destination for IT services and pharmaceutical research; call-center industry also important
- Mumbai (formerly Bombay; capital of western Indian State of Maharashtra, and most populous city of India); main financial center of India; financial services dominate, with growing IT and healthcare industries
- Pune (cultural capital of the western Indian State of Maharashtra); fast-growing software industry; most prominent region for Business Process Outsourcing (BPO) companies
- Kolkata (formerly Calcutta; capital of the State of West Bengal, in eastern India); IT services and industrial manufacturing; lower IT and related salary levels are making it more attractive for outsourcing relative to other destinations in India

# China

China is rapidly establishing itself as the manufacturing capital of the world. Manufactured goods from China are distributed to every nation. Furthermore, these are not just cheap, low-quality products, but increasingly high-quality, world-class products.

The country is less known as an offshore outsourcing powerhouse for a number of compelling reasons, topped by its lack of English speakers. However, two trends are appearing: Indian firms are starting to subcontract lower level software development to China, and U.S., Indian and other international firms are setting up offshore outsourcing operations in China with a view to the long term.

### Pros of Outsourcing to China

1. Strong internal IT networks and infrastructure
2. Completion of massive telecommunications expansion
3. More networking capacity than competing countries
4. Large pool of software programmers with 100,000 new programmers added each year
5. Labor costs 60% to 90% lower than those of most developed nations
6. IT salaries less than those in India or other competing countries
7. Salaries increasing less rapidly than in India and other competing countries

### Cons of Outsourcing to China

1. Lack of English-speaking environment (English is, however, becoming China's second language)
2. A 'cultural gap' between the West and Chinese firms
3. Concern over protection of intellectual property rights, despite China's entry into the WTO in 2001
4. Inability to handle large, turnkey projects
5. Lack of expertise in software project management
6. Perception that industrial espionage and corruption are endemic
7. Lack of transparency in government, administration, management, banking, finance and trade
8. Concerns related to human rights issues
9. Perception that Chinese tradition of 'saving face' means problems may not be timely identified
10. Chinese IT firms currently lack the ability to scale up to levels already achieved by Indian IT firms
11. Authoritarian government with erratic application of international laws and regulations relating to international trade
12. Time-zone differential with Europe/America is a negative for tasks and projects that would otherwise benefit from concurrent communications

### Services Outsourced to China

Most outsourcing to China consists of product and component manufacturing, with services such as computer software development, including the following, a distant second:

- Computer software services (primarily low-level programming such as maintenance and porting)
- Web development
- Software migration
- Re-engineering
- Localization
- Product and software testing

### Locations of Major Universities

Centers of service outsourcing are often located in and adjacent to university cities and towns. These centers of higher learning provide the setting for research centers and an educated workforce.

- Beijing Institute of Technology
- Beijing Medical University
- Beijing Normal University
- Beijing Science & Technology University
- Beijing University of Aeronautics & Astronautics
- China Agricultural University
- Dalian University of Technology
- Fudan University
- Harbin Institute of Technology
- Huazhong University of Science & Technology
- Jilin University
- Nanjing University
- Nan'kai University
- Northwest Polytechnic University
- Peking University
- Renmin University of China
- Shanghai Jiaotong University
- Southeast University
- Tianjin University
- Tongji University
- Tsinghua University
- University of Science & Technology of China
- Wuhan University
- Xi'an Jiaotong University
- Zhejiang University
- Zhongshan University

### International Firms that Outsource to China

Because of their geographic proximity, Japan, Korea and India are the prime customers of Chinese services. The following is an abbreviated list of companies that outsource to China (as such information is not readily available):

- Accenture
- Advanced Micro Devices
- Airbus
- BearingPoint
- Canon
- Hewlett-Packard
- Honda
- IBM
- Intel Corporation
- Microsoft
- NEC
- Nikon, Nissan
- Nypro Plastics
- Owings Mills
- Pioneer
- Texas Instruments
- Qualcomm

### Major Centers of Outsourcing

- Beijing (capital of China, northern China)
- Chengdu (capital of Sichuan Province, southwest China)
- Guangdong (aka 'Canton' Province in southeastern China; main cities Guangzhou and Shenzhen)
- Shandong Province (eastern China; main city Tai'an)
- Shanghai (eastern China; largest and wealthiest city in China)
- Shenyang (capital of Liaoning Province, northeastern China)
- Tianjin (municipality with provincial-level status, northern China)
- Xi'an (capital of Shaanxi Province, north-central China)

# The Philippines

The Philippines has a long history of political, military, social and business connections with the United States dating from the Spanish-American War of 1898 after which the country was ceded to the U.S. by Spain. During World War II the Philippines was promised independence in exchange for support of the U.S. war effort against Japan.

During the entire Twentieth Century, U.S. culture and the English language became popular and pervasive. As a result, there are both cultural connections and significant English language skills that foster development of the offshore outsourcing industry by U.S. firms.

Still, in relative terms, the country is small, with much of the country consisting of remote regions separated by bodies of water. In addition, there are internal cultural divisions and a continuing insurgency in the South.

## Pros of Outsourcing to The Philippines

1. Traditionally strong English-speaking skills, including American-style diction and pronunciation (but see "Cons" below)
2. Some Spanish-speaking language skills (a bonus for American-sourced call centers)
3. Home to the largest population of certified accountants in Asia (with many trained to work with multiple accounting standards)
4. Ongoing improvements in the last decade in education and training of IT workers
5. Competitively low labor and other costs
6. Good telecommunications infrastructure
7. Reasonable physical infrastructure
8. Committed and generous non-partisan federal and local government support for export-oriented service industries

## Cons of Outsourcing to The Philippines

1. Decline in English-speaking skills in past two decades due to legally mandated use of Filipino and Tagalog as main mediums of instruction in schools
2. Potentially insufficient number of post-secondary graduates relative to the growth in outsourcing fields, especially in relation to China and India

## Services Outsourced to The Philippines

The Philippines has become a major center for the offshore outsourcing of financial services. Also, the country has become very popular for the outsourcing of services that require high English-language proficiency, such as:

- Animation and graphics
- Business intelligence
- Call centers (most important of outsourced services, primarily for U.S. firms)
- Technology help desks
- Data entry and word processing
- Transcription
- Typesetting and book formatting
- Editorial services, including press release writing
- Medical and legal transcription
- Internet research and surveillance
- Financial services (accounting, accounts receivable collection, accounts payable administration, payroll processing, asset management, financial analysis and auditing, inventory control and purchasing, expense and revenue reporting, financial reporting, tax reporting, and other finance-related services such as financial leasing, credit card administration, factoring and stock brokerage)
- Computer software (research, analysis, design, programming, QA, software customization, re-engineering, conversion, installation, maintenance, training)
- IT-related services (database management, supply-chain management, back-office processing, data transcription)
- Long-distance warehouse and inventory management

## Locations of Major Universities

- Ateneo de Manila University (Manila)
- Ateneo de Naga University (in Naga City, most prominent city in Province of Camarines Sur, east-central Philippines)
- University of Cebu (in Cebu City, in Cebu Province on Cebu Island, eastern central Philippines)
- University of Southeastern Philippines (in Davao, most prominent city on the island of Mindanao, southeastern Philippines)
- University of the Philippines (Manila)
- Polytechnic University of the Philippines (Manila)
- Silliman University (in Dumaguete, the capital city of Negros Oriental in Central Visayas Province)
- Technological University of the Philippines (Manila)

## International Firms that Outsource Services to The Philippines

- Accenture, Autodesk, AIG
- American Express, AOL
- Bank of America
- Barnes & Noble
- Caltex, Chevron, Citigroup
- Dell Computer Company
- Hewlett Packard
- FedEx
- General Electric
- IBM, Intel
- JP Morgan Chase
- Lexis Nexis, Lloyds Register
- Motorola
- Northwest Airlines
- Procter & Gamble
- Royal Philips Electronics
- Sykes
- Trend Micro
- Walt Disney Company
- Xlibris

## Major Centers of Outsourcing

- Baguio City, Bacolod City
- Cagayan de Oro
- Cebu (on Cebu Island, east-central Philippines)
- Clark (the former U.S. military base in Pampanga province)
- Davao (on the island of Mindanao, south-east Philippines)
- Dumaguete (capital city of Negros Oriental in Central Visayas Province)
- Iloilo / Bacolod (Bacolod is in the Province of Negros Occidental, central Philippines; Iloilo City is across a narrow strait from Bacolod in the Western Visayas region, on southeastern Panay Island)
- Lipa (in province of Batangas, on Mindanao Island)
- Manila (capital city)
- Naga (in the Province of Camarines Sur, east-central Philippines)
- Subic Bay Freeport Zone (former site of major U.S. Naval base; on west coast of Luzon Island)
- Tacloban (largest city in Eastern Visayas Province, and capital city of Leyte)

# Eastern Europe and Russia

Eastern Europe and Russia have become the top choices for Western European companies wishing to nearshore service operations. Many Western European countries share historical, cultural and linguistic ties with Eastern Europe. Furthermore, distances are short, especially compared to doing business with firms in India and China. Germany is clearly the leader in offshoring operations to Eastern European firms. Companies from the Americas are also finding Eastern Europe to be a great supplier of services, especially when used in conjunction with their Western European operations.

## Pros of Outsourcing to Eastern Europe

1. Highly educated and skilled workforces (some of the world's best universities are in Eastern Europe and Russia)
2. Lower salaries and costs relative to Western Europe and The Americas
3. Mature infrastructure
4. Ability to do big, turnkey projects
5. Smaller time-zone differences compared with Asia (a positive for projects that would benefit from concurrent communications)
6. European language skills and western culture
7. Attractive regulatory environment
8. Growing transparency in management, administration, banking, finance, trade and government
9. Political stability, especially compared to the 1980s and 1990s
10. Non-partisan government support for export-oriented service industries
11. On a per-capita basis, Romania has more IT graduates than the U.S., 2 times more than Russia, 7 times more than India and 12 times more than China.
12. Reputation of Russian computer programmers as the best or among the best in the world

## Cons of Outsourcing to Eastern Europe

1. Higher salaries and costs relative to IT work performed in India, China and the Philippines
2. English-language skills not as developed as in India
3. Lack of protection of intellectual property rights
4. Continued concerns related to data security and industrial espionage
5. Vestiges of communist-era thinking
6. Unstable economies (some)
7. Top-quality talent migrating to other countries

## Services Outsourced to Eastern Europe

**Note:** Most outsourcing to Eastern Europe consists of product and component manufacturing, primarily by German firms, with services such as computer software development and call centers a distant second; including the following industries:

* Application maintenance
* Computer software development
* Cartography development
* Database development and maintenance
* Multi-lingual call centers and help desks (primarily for Western European clients)
* Financial services (payroll processing, write-up and general-ledger services, financial-statement preparation, tax-preparation services)
* Telecommunications software development
* Web and e-commerce design and development
* Legacy application development and maintenance
* QA testing

## Locations of Major Universities

* Charles University of Prague (Prague University) (Czech Republic)
* Czech Technical University in Prague (Bohemian Polytechnica; Eské Vysoké Uení Technické)
* Masaryk University in Brno (Czech Republic)
* Budapest University of Technology and Economics (Hungary)
* Central European University (Budapest, Hungary)
* University of Bucharest (Romania)
* Polytechnic University of Bucharest (Romania)
* American University (Sofia, Bulgaria)
* Sofia University (Bulgaria)
* Technical University of Sofia (Bulgaria)
* Kraków University of Technology (Politechnika Krakowska, PK) (Poland)
* Lublin University of Technology (Politechnika Lubelska, PL) (Poland)
* Warsaw University of Technology (Politechnika Warszawska, PW) (Poland)
* Riga Technical University (Latvia)
* University of Latvia (Riga, Latvia)
* Moscow Institute of Physics and Technology (Russia)
* Moscow State Technical University (Russia)
* Far Eastern National University (Russia)
* Saint Petersburg State Institute of Technology (Russia)

## International Firms that Outsource to Eastern Europe

* Accenture, AirFrance, Alcatel
* Boeing, BT Cellnet
* Caterpillar, Check Point
* Citibank, Cisco
* Daewoo Electronics
* Dell Computer Company, Deutsche Bank
* Deutsche Telekom
* Fiserv, France Telecom Mobiles
* Freescale
* General Electric, Genpact
* IBM, Internet Security Systems
* LG Electronics
* Lotus
* Microsoft
* Ness, Novell
* Oracle
* Samsung, SAP
* Siemens
* Tivoli
* U.S. Department of Energy
* Wipro

## Major Centers of Outsourcing

* Baltic States of Estonia, Latvia and Lithuania
* Bratislava (Slovak Republic)
* Bucharest (Romania)
* Budapest (Hungary)
* Kazan (Russia)
* Kiev (Ukraine)
* Lublin (Poland)
* Minsk (Belarus)
* Moscow (Russia)
* Prague (Czech Republic)
* Riga (Latvia)
* Saint Petersburg (Russia)
* Sofia (Bulgaria)
* Warsaw (Poland)

# Information Sources for Outsourcing

## Books

**The Offshore Nation: Strategies for Success in Global Outsourcing and Offshoring**
Atul Vashistha, Avinash Vashistha; 2006; McGraw-Hill; ISBN: 0071468129

**The Black Book of Outsourcing: How to Manage the Changes, Challenges, and Opportunities**
Douglas Brown, Scott Wilson; 2005; Wiley; ISBN: 0471718890

**IT, Software and Services: Outsourcing and Offshoring**
Robin Sood; 2005; AiAiYo Books, LLC; ISBN: 0976067439

**Multisourcing: Moving Beyond Outsourcing to Achieve Growth And Agility**
Linda Cohen, Allie Young; 2005; Harvard Business School Press; ISBN: 1591397979

**Outsourcing for Radical Change**
Jane C. C. Linder; 2003; AMACOM; ISBN: 0814472184

**Smartsourcing: Driving Innovation and Growth Through Outsourcing**
Thomas M. Koulopoulos, Tom Roloff; 2006; Platinum Press; ISBN: 159337514X

**The Outsourcing Revolution: Why It Makes Sense and How to Do It Right**
Michael F. Corbett; 2004; Dearborn Trade; ISBN: 0793192145

**The World is Flat**
**A Brief History of the Twenty-First Century**
Thomas L. Friedman, 2005; Farrar, Straus and Giroux; ISBN: 0374292884

**The Outsourcing Handbook: How to Implement a Successful Outsourcing Process**
Mark J. Power, Kevin Descouza, Carlo Bonifazi; 2006; Kogan Page; ISBN: 0749444304

## Organizations

**The Outsourcing Institute**
www.outsourcing.com
A neutral professional association dedicated solely to outsourcing. A global source for outsourcing information, consulting and networking opportunities. Free membership.

**European Outsourcing Association (The "€OA")**
www.e-oa.net
A pan-European federation of country-specific bodies operating as independent nonprofit organizations whose shared objective is to leverage effective business and process outsourcing. The €OA is the voice, forum and champion for Europe's business outsourcing community.

**Global Outsourcing Institute**
www.goinstitute.org
A peer-to-peer exchange for IT and Business Process Outsourcing Professionals.

**International Association of Outsourcing Professionals**
www.outsourcingprofessional.org
A global membership-based organization that seeks to shape the future of outsourcing as a management practice, as a profession, and as an industry. IAOP was formed in early 2005 by a consortium of leading companies involved in outsourcing as customers, providers, and advisors. Today, its global membership includes over 250 organizations from around the world representing a cross-section of industries and functional activities.

**National Outsourcing Association (NOA)**
www.noa.co.uk
The NOA is a UK-based organization that operates as a trade association, an independent 'not-for-profit' body whose objective is to leverage effective outsourcing by: promoting best practices, service, and innovation in the application and development of outsourcing.

## Articles

**Foreign Outsourcing: Economic Implications and Policy Responses**
CRS Report for Congress; Order Code RL32484
Updated June 21, 2005; Available free at:
Congressional Research Service, The Library of Congress
http://fpc.state.gov/documents/organization/50272.pdf

**Outsourcing Innovation**
March 21, 2005
www.businessweek.com/magazine/content/05_12/b3925601.htm

**Growth in Services Outsourcing to India: Propellant or Drain on the U.S. Economy?**
By William Greene, U.S. International Trade Commission, January 2006
http://hotdocs.usitc.gov/docs/pubs/research_working_papers/EC200601A.pdf

**The Outsourcing Bogeyman**
By Daniel W. Drezner, Foreign Affairs, May/June 2004
www.foreignaffairs.org/20040501faessay83304/daniel-w-drezner/the-outsourcing-bogeyman.html

## Web Resources

**Your Own Keyword Search**
There are now so many web resources related to outsourcing and offshoring that we can recommend only that you use an advanced web search for the keywords that are important to your search. Examples of keywords are:
• outsourcing, offshoring, nearshoring, BPO
• programming, typesetting (or other function)
• India, Philippines, Canada (or other country name)

**www.outsource2india.com.**
Pioneers in using the Internet exclusively to market and sell Indian software development services.

**www.networkworld.com/topics/outsourcing.html**
Network World's web research and information site, with numerous articles and links, as well as an e-forum.

**www.cio.com/sourcing/outsourcing/index.html**
CIO Magazine's web resource for outsourcing. Contains feature articles, columns, research reports, and case studies, as well as related links and upcoming events.

**www.softwareprojects.org**
Free courses on software project management, software selection and software development, plus lots of other resources and information.

**www.outsourceit2philippines.com**
A site run by IT experts in all fields, serving a portfolio of corporations throughout the Philippines.

**Offshore Outsourcing World**
www.enterblog.com
A daily news magazine focused on offshore outsourcing.

# Global Supply Chain Security

## Historical Perspective

International traders have had to deal with issues related to individual, cargo and information security since the beginning of time:

- Traveling to unknown lands put traders at risk of injury or death by accident, disease, drowning, thirst, starvation, bandits, or at the hands of warring tribes.
- Traders could lose their trade goods to shipwrecks, bandits, warring armies, dishonest ship captains, or even to corrupt 4th century customs officials.
- The popular term "information is power" may be new, but the concept itself is centuries old. Traders protected information as they protected their lives.

No single event: the death of an individual trader, the loss of an individual trader's goods, or even the loss of an entire ship and its cargo, however, would have a severe impact on the economy of an individual country or city state.

## September 11, 2001

The international trading system, however, has become much more complex over time. Economies are linked and intertwined in ways impossible to imagine hundreds of years ago. The advantages workers, businesses and national economies have enjoyed as a result of free trade, the division of labor, the industrial revolution, the technological revolution, open financial markets, cheap travel, and better communications have improved our living standards, but also made us ever more dependent upon the smooth running of the international trading system.

The terrorist attacks on New York and Washington, DC on September 11, 2001 have put security in an entirely new perspective. The very fabric of international trade and the economies of developed and developing countries alike depend upon stability not just in financial and commodity markets, but in security as well.

In addition to the horrible loss of life, the events of 9/11 have cost the world economy hundreds of billions of dollars and been the direct and indirect cause of tens of thousands of business bankruptcies, tens of millions of lost jobs, regional and national recessions and added costs to the cost of doing business worldwide.

## The New World Order

The new security initiatives enacted since 9/11 are here to stay; they are permanent. Companies are well advised to embrace security; the voluntary programs of today will be the mandatory programs of tomorrow.

Since 9/11, the United States has taken the worldwide lead in addressing cargo security issues. C-TPAT, FAST, CSI, the "24-Hour Rule" and other initiatives are likely to become worldwide standards, not just specific to the United States.

Today, security encompasses loss prevention, personal travel safety, terrorism, data security and commercial espionage.

## The Security Appendix

In preparing six editions of the *Dictionary of International Trade* over a period of 12 years, no single issue has proved to be as complex as security. While the field of security itself has been in existence for centuries, cargo loss, terrorism, data security and commercial espionage have grown both in importance and complexity. The field is changing at a rapid rate—new issues, new government regulations and new fields of practice make reporting on security a continuing work in progress.

My apologies to our international readers who do not trade with the U.S. The bulk of this Appendix concentrates on security initiatives by the U.S. Government, especially the U.S. Bureau of Customs and Border Protection.

## Security Table of Contents

Security and the Supply Chain ................. 582

### C-TPAT
### Customs-Trade Partnership Against Terrorism
C-TPAT .................................... 584
C-TPAT for Importers ....................... 589
C-TPAT for Sea Carriers .................... 592
C-TPAT for Rail Carriers ................... 595
C-TPAT for Highway Carriers ................ 598
C-TPAT for Foreign Manufacturers ........... 602
C-TPAT for Air Carriers .................... 605
C-TPAT for Air Freight Consolidators ....... 608
C-TPAT for Licensed Customs Brokers ........ 611
C-TPAT for U.S. Marine or Port Terminal .... 613
FAST (Free and Secure Trade) ............... 616
FAST U.S./Canada ........................... 618
FAST U.S./Mexico ........................... 620

C-TPAT Seal Requirements ................... 623

### CSI
### Container Security Initiative
Container Security Initiative (CSI) ......... 626

### U.S. BIOTERRORISM ACT
U.S. FDA Food Facility Registration ......... 628

### IMO
### (International Maritime Organization)
International Ship and Port Facility (ISPS) Code ... 630

### SECURITY CHECKLISTS
Data Security .............................. 632
Industrial Espionage ....................... 634

### GLOSSARY
Glossary of Security Terms ................. 637

### ACE e-Manifest
Automated Commercial Environment e-Manifest .. 583

### PAPS and PARS
Pre-Arrival Processing System (PAPS) ........ 650
Pre-Arrival Review System (PARS) ........... 650

### Automated Manifest System
Automated Manifest System (AMS) ............ 625

### Advance Manifest Regulations
"2-Hour Rule" "24-Hour Rule" ............... 652

# Security and the Supply Chain

Securing the supply chain means providing appropriate security at all times, at every facility and for every means of conveyance.

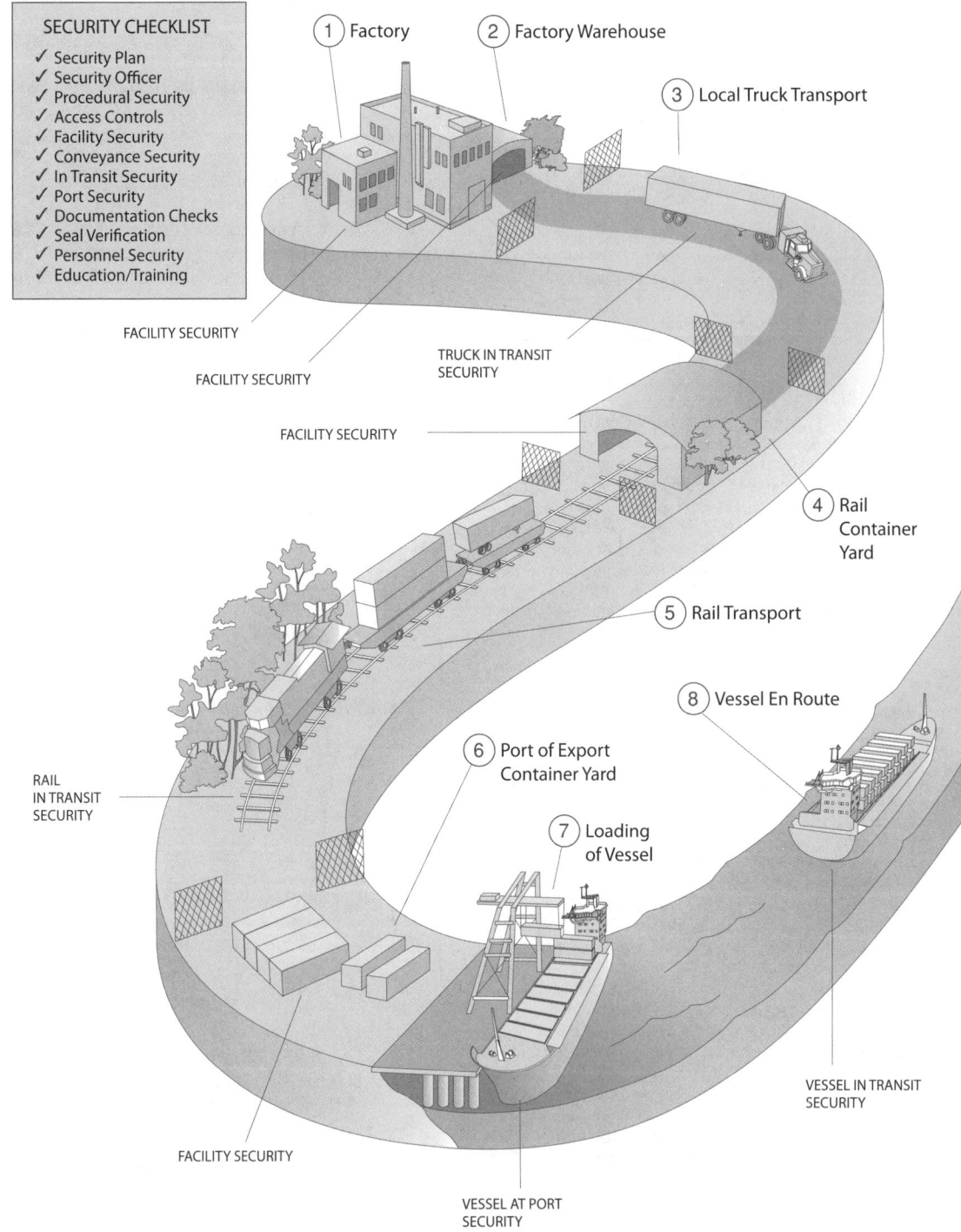

**SECURITY CHECKLIST**

✓ Security Plan
✓ Security Officer
✓ Procedural Security
✓ Access Controls
✓ Facility Security
✓ Conveyance Security
✓ In Transit Security
✓ Port Security
✓ Documentation Checks
✓ Seal Verification
✓ Personnel Security
✓ Education/Training

1 Factory
2 Factory Warehouse
3 Local Truck Transport
4 Rail Container Yard
5 Rail Transport
6 Port of Export Container Yard
7 Loading of Vessel
8 Vessel En Route

FACILITY SECURITY

FACILITY SECURITY

TRUCK IN TRANSIT SECURITY

FACILITY SECURITY

RAIL IN TRANSIT SECURITY

VESSEL IN TRANSIT SECURITY

FACILITY SECURITY

VESSEL AT PORT SECURITY

SECURITY

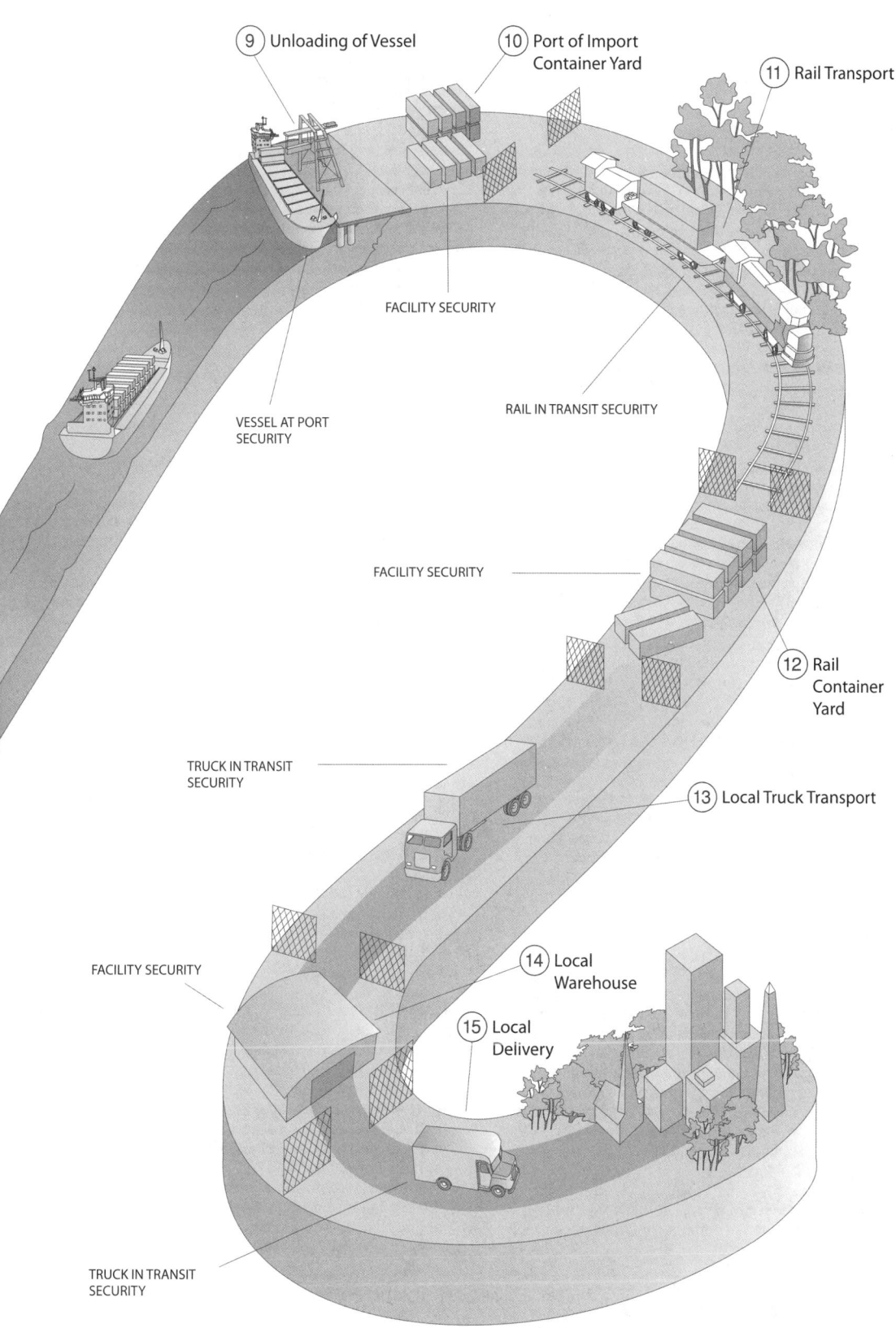

⑨ Unloading of Vessel

⑩ Port of Import Container Yard

⑪ Rail Transport

FACILITY SECURITY

VESSEL AT PORT SECURITY

RAIL IN TRANSIT SECURITY

FACILITY SECURITY

⑫ Rail Container Yard

TRUCK IN TRANSIT SECURITY

⑬ Local Truck Transport

FACILITY SECURITY

⑭ Local Warehouse

⑮ Local Delivery

TRUCK IN TRANSIT SECURITY

SECURITY

# C-TPAT[1]

## Customs-Trade Partnership Against Terrorism

(Affecting United States importers, carriers and international exporters to the U.S.)

### What is C-TPAT?

The C-TPAT (Customs-Trade Partnership Against Terrorism) is a voluntary United States Customs and Border Protection (CBP) business initiative designed to build cooperative relationships that strengthen overall supply chain and border security.

The C-TPAT initiative recognizes that CBP can provide the highest level of security to the public and to other stakeholders only through close cooperation with the ultimate owners of the supply chain: importers, carriers, brokers, warehouse operators and manufacturers.

Through this initiative, Customs is asking businesses to ensure the integrity of their security practices and communicate their security guidelines to their business partners within the supply chain.

### CBP's Vision for C-TPAT

CBP recognizes that a safe and secure supply chain is the most critical part of its work in keeping the U.S. safe. For this reason, CBP is seeking a strong anti-terrorism partnership with the trade community through C-TPAT. Trade partners will have a commitment to both trade security and trade compliance, which are rooted in the same business practices. CBP wants to work closely with companies whose good business practices ensure supply chain security and compliance with trade laws.

### Who is Eligible for C-TPAT?

Currently, open enrollment for C-TPAT is available for the following business types related to the U.S. import supply chain cargo handling and movement:

- U.S. Importers of record
- U.S./Canada Highway Carriers
- U.S./Mexico Highway Carriers
- Rail Carriers
- Sea Carriers
- Air Carriers
- U.S. Marine Port Authority/Terminal Operators
- U.S. Air Freight Consolidators, Ocean Transportation Intermediaries and Non-Vessel Operating Common Carriers (NVOCC)
- Mexican manufacturers
- Certain Invited Foreign Manufacturers
- Licensed U.S. Customs Brokers

Utilizing risk management principles, C-TPAT seeks to enroll compliant low-risk companies who are directly responsible for importing, transporting, and coordinating commercial import cargo into the United States. The goal is to identify compliant trusted import traders who have good supply chain security procedures and controls to reduce screening of their imported cargo. In turn, this enables CBP to focus screening efforts on import cargo transactions involving unknown or high-risk import traders. CBP will be consulting with the trade community to develop the most effective approach for each sector to participate in C-TPAT.

### The Application Process

Businesses must apply to participate in C-TPAT. Participants complete an online electronic application on www.cbp.gov that includes submission of corporate information, a supply chain security profile, and an acknowledgement of an agreement to voluntarily participate.

In completing the supply chain security profile, companies must conduct a comprehensive self-assessment of their supply chain security procedures using the C-TPAT security criteria or guidelines jointly developed by CBP and the trade community for their specific enrollment category. The criteria or guidelines, available for review in this section and on the CBP website, encompass the following areas:

- Business Partner Requirements,
- Procedural Security,
- Physical Security,
- Personnel Security,
- Education and Training,
- Access Controls,
- Manifest Procedures,
- Information Security, and
- Conveyance Security.

See C-TPAT Online Application Instructions on the pages that follow.

Upon satisfactory completion of the C-TPAT Online application and supply chain security profile, participants will be assigned a CBP C-TPAT Supply Chain Security Specialist (SCSS). A SCSS will contact the participant to begin the C-TPAT validation process.

### The Benefits of Participation in C-TPAT

C-TPAT offers trade-related businesses an opportunity to play an active role in the war against terrorism. By participating in this first worldwide supply chain security initiative, companies will ensure a more secure and expeditious supply chain for their employees, suppliers and customers. Beyond these essential security benefits, CBP will offer benefits to certain certified C-TPAT member categories, including:

- A reduced number of CBP inspections (reduced border delay times).
- Priority processing for CBP inspections. (Front of the Line processing for inspections when possible.)
- Assignment of a C-TPAT Supply Chain Security Specialist (SCSS) who will work with the company to validate and enhance security throughout the company's international supply chain.
- Potential eligibility for CBP Importer Self-Assessment program (ISA) with an emphasis on self-policing, not CBP audits.
- Eligibility to attend C-TPAT supply chain security training seminars.

It is clear that security issues will play an ever more important role in international trade logistics. Today's voluntary programs may become mandatory programs in the future. Many companies recognize that participation in C-TPAT is part of a "best practices" approach to achieving leadership in their industry.

### How the Partnership Works

- CBP C-TPAT account managers will contact participants to begin joint work on establishing or updating account action plans to reflect C-TPAT commitments.
- Action plans will track participants' progress in making security improvements, communicating C-TPAT criteria or guidelines to business partners, and establishing improved security relationships with other companies.

---

1. C-TPAT requirements are evolving. The information contained in this section was current as of September 2006. For the latest information refer to the U.S. Customs and Border Protection (CBP) Web site at: www.cbp.gov. (The editorial content for this article is based on CBP material.)

- Failure to meet C-TPAT commitments will result in suspension of C-TPAT benefits. Benefits will be reinstated upon correcting deficiencies in compliance and/or security.

### CBP Expectations of Participants

CBP expects C-TPAT participants to make a real commitment toward the common goal of creating a more secure and efficient supply chain through partnership. CBP understands that it has entered a new era and requires the assistance of private industry to ensure increased vigilance throughout the supply chain. CBP recognizes that just as it protects the trade and U.S. borders, businesses must ensure that their brands, employees and customers are protected to the best of their abilities.

### Confidentiality of Data

CBP has stated that all information on supply chain security submitted by companies applying for the C-TPAT program will be confidential. CBP will not disclose a company's participation in C-TPAT.

### C-TPAT Costs of Participation

Firstly, C-TPAT participation is voluntary. Secondly, CBP recognizes that not all companies are in a position to meet C-TPAT minimum security criteria or guidelines.

All eligible companies that import into the U.S. or provide import cargo movement or handling services should assess their supply chain security procedures to determine if they can qualify. CBP intent is to not impose security requirements that will be cost prohibitive. For this reason, CBP has worked in concert with the trade community in developing security criteria and guidelines that reflect a realistic business perspective. Potential C-TPAT participants may find that they already have many of these guidelines in place.

That said, enhanced security and C-TPAT participation will cost money. Also, those firms that have historically had few or no security guidelines in place will find that there will be added costs of getting "up to speed" organizationally.

C-TPAT is also not intended to create any new 'liabilities' for companies beyond existing trade laws and regulations. However, joining C-TPAT will commit companies to follow through on actions specified in the signed agreement. These actions include self-assessing security systems, submitting security questionnaires, developing security enhancement plans, and communicating C-TPAT guidelines to companies in the supply chain. If a company fails to uphold its C-TPAT commitments, CBP would take action to suspend benefits or cancel participation.

### Viability for Small- and Medium-Sized Companies

Initially, it was mostly large companies that rely heavily on international supply chains that applied and became active participants in the program.

CBP, however, encourages all companies to take an active role in promoting supply chain and border security. In that regard, C-TPAT is not just a big-company program. Medium and small companies should evaluate the requirements and benefits of C-TPAT carefully in deciding whether to apply for the program. Moreover, even without official participation in C-TPAT, companies should still consider employing C-TPAT guidelines in their security practices.

### Must vs. Should

Note that C-TPAT Security Criteria and Security Guidelines use the words "must" and "should" a great deal. These words have specific, yet logical and intuitive meanings. "Must" means that it is a requirement. A business will not achieve program participation status unless the requirement is met. "Should" means that while the procedure is likely considered to be an industry "best practice" it is not necessarily a requirement for program participation. Businesses can anticipate, however, that over time, more "shoulds" will become "musts."

### Recommendations vs. Guidelines vs. Criteria

The C-TPAT program has continued to evolve. When the program was first established, CBP issued what were called "Security Recommendations." These "Recommendations" evolved into "Security Guidelines."

In late October 2004, CBP, in discussion with the trade community, began drafting more clearly-defined, minimum-security criteria for businesses wishing to participate in the C-TPAT program. After months of dialogue, CBP developed minimum-security criteria designed to accomplish two important goals: first, to offer flexibility for accommodating the diverse business models represented within the international supply chain; and second, to achieve CBP's twin goals of security and facilitation.

"Security Criteria" are now the established minimum security requirements for participation in the C-TPAT program. Security Criteria have been established for: Importers, Rail Carriers, Foreign Manufacturers, Highway Carriers and Sea Carriers. For other groups, the "Security Guidelines" remain in effect.

### Supply Chain Security Best Practices Catalog

On March 9, 2006, the U.S. Customs and Border Protection issued its long-awaited "Supply Chain Security Best Practices Catalog." This is a 56-page booklet that is organized based on C-TPAT Security Criteria. The best practices included in the catalog are those that have been identified through more than 1,400 validations and site visits by CBP C-TPAT Supply Chain Security Specialists (SCSS).

"Best Practices" are defined as:

1. Security measures that exceed the C-TPAT Security Criteria,
2. Incorporate management support,
3. Have written policies and practices that govern their use,
4. Employ a system of checks and balances, and
5. Have measures in place to ensure continuity.

The catalog is essentially a statement of what CBP considers to be practices that will meet or exceed its Security Criteria, and has therefore become very popular in the industry.

Available online at: www.cbp.gov/linkhandler/cgov/import/ commercial_enforcement/ctpat/ctpat_best_practices.ctt/ ctpat_best_practices.pdf.

### C-TPAT Security Link Portal

The C-TPAT Security Link Portal is a secure, full-service, Internet web portal that will allow qualifying C-TPAT participants to:

- Enter new applications.
- Instantly submit information updates and add new information.
- Maintain a "living" Supply Chain Security Profile that can be updated as needed and must be updated and re-certified on a yearly basis.
- Communicate directly with CBP C-TPAT and/or their designated C-TPAT Supply Chain Security Specialists using a secure system.
- Receive information directly from CBP to include cargo security alerts and sanitized intelligence information.
- Maintain a list of authorized users.

All C-TPAT participants will be required to use the C-TPAT Security Link Portal to ensure that all company information and Supply Security Profile information is accurate and complete.

C-TPAT participants and certified members will be required to enter, update, and maintain several key fields of information to assist in the verification of program eligibility. This includes the posting of current C-TPAT Supply Chain Security Profile and business profile information.

CBP is using 128 bit Secure Sockets Layer (SSL) encryption. SSL uses a system that uses two keys to encrypt data. Both Netscape Navigator and Internet Explorer support SSL, and

SECURITY

many Web sites use the protocol to obtain confidential user information, such as credit card numbers.

To access the C-TPAT Security Link Portal:

1. Go to: https://ctpat.cbp.dhs.gov/. For information on the C-TPAT Security Link Portal, visit the www.cbp.gov C-TPAT web page at: www.cbp.gov/xp/cgov/import/commercial_enforcement/ctpat/
2. Go to the Status Verification section to Generate an SVI.
3. Read and accept the Consent to Use Company Name terms and conditions that appear on the introductory screen for the SVI. Active acceptance of the Agreement (i.e., selecting the "I Accept" box) will be required to access the SVI.

For more information on the C-TPAT Security Link Portal, go to: www.cbp.gov/xp/cgov/import/commercial_enforcement/ctpat/implement_portal.

### C-TPAT Status Verification Interface (SVI)

As stated in the C-TPAT Security Criteria, Certified C-TPAT partners need to verify the participation status of other eligible C-TPAT business partners. To address this need, CBP has created the Status Verification Interface (SVI). The SVI allows consenting certified C-TPAT partners to verify the participation status of other consenting certified C-TPAT partners. Each party must have consented to the release of their company name among the C-TPAT membership. The SVI is the point of electronic access to verify the C-TPAT status of another Status Verification Interface Participant (SVIP).

Access to the C-TPAT SVI is now found in the C-TPAT Security Link Portal. SVI Access is granted to certified C-TPAT partners who meet the specific SVIP criteria.

To qualify as a SVIP, participants must have:

- Access to the Internet C-TPAT Security Link Portal;
- Achieved certification status as a C-TPAT participant;
- Generated an SVI alpha-numeric status identification number (ID) in the C-TPAT Security Link Portal;
- Accepted the terms of the electronic C-TPAT CONSENT TO USE COMPANY NAME form found in the C-TPAT Security Link Portal.

For SVI instructions, frequently asked questions, SVI fact sheet and/or access to the SVI interface go to: www.cbp.gov/xp/cgov/import/commercial_enforcement/ctpat/svi.

### For More Information on C-TPAT

For ongoing information and updates on the C-TPAT program, go to the U.S. Customs and Border Protection Web site at www.cbp.gov.

# C-TPAT Online Application Instructions

For important instructions for submitting an online C-TPAT application go to: www.cbp.gov/xp/cgov/import/commercial_enforcement/ctpat/online_app/ and select "Instructions for Completing the C-TPAT Online Application.

The Online Application itself can be found at: https://ctpat.cbp.dhs.gov/CompanyProfile.aspx

### Part 1 Summary
- Complete the Company Profile information
- Read and Agree to the terms of the C-TPAT Agreement to Voluntarily Participate.
- Save your submission.
- Wait for an e-mail confirming your submission and granting C-TPAT Security Link Portal access using a temporary password.

Note: Companies will have 60 days to complete their Online C-TPAT Application using the C-TPAT Security Link Portal.

### Part 2 Summary
- Login to the C-TPAT Security Link Portal using your e-mail address and temporary password.
- Change your Temporary Password.
- Complete the structured Online Supply Chain Security Profile
- Save your Security Profile submission.

Note: Companies will have 60 days to complete their Online Application using the C-TPAT Security Link Portal.

## Part 1

1. Select/verify your C-TPAT Business Type and click Next. The Application Exception Token field is reserved for future use and does not apply to most applicants.
2. Enter/verify your C-TPAT Business Code and click Next. You may select Cancel Profile at any point in the process to stop your application submission.
3. Enter/verify your Company Name, and click Next.
4. Enter/verify your complete Company Physical Address and Mailing Address if applicable, and click Next.
5. Select the term that best describes Company's Ownership Type, Years in Business range, and Number of Employees range, and click Next.
6. Select Add Contact to enter Company Points of Contact (POC).
7. Enter Company Points of Contact (POC).

You must enter at least one (1) company officer as a contact. They do not have to be the primary POC. Consultants/Contractors may be entered as an alternate POC with additional information required.

The Primary POC must be a Company Employee and is designated by checking the POC field.

Select the contact type.

8. Use Add Contact to enter additional company Points of Contact (POC).

You may add an unlimited number of POC.

Select the contact type.

Warning: Each POC you add will have access to your C-TPAT Security Link web portal information and can change information.

Be sure to limit your C-TPAT Security Link Portal POC access to those personnel that are part of your company's C-TPAT program management team.

9. Enter Company Identification (ID) numbers.

The ID fields vary according to your Business Type.

10. Review/verify the summary of company information.
11. Read/review the Online C-TPAT Agreement for your Business Type.
12. If you accept the Online C-TPAT Agreement and wish to continue with your application, Click "I Agree".
13. You will receive an e-mail with instructions on how to Login and continue with your application.

## Part 2

### Initial Portal Login, Change Password

1. The "User Name" is the user's e-mail address that was provided to the C-TPAT program.

The Password will be the Temporary Password that is sent to you via e-mail after successful completion of Part 1 of the C-TPAT Online Application.

2. First time Users will be required to Change their Temporary password.

Users with Expired Passwords will be required to Change their old password.

Passwords will expire every 90 days.

3. If the User is designated as a Company Contact for more than one company, a list of companies will appear.

The User must select the company name and click continue to proceed.

4. Review Home Screen Fields.

### Security Profile Completion

1. Place the Cursor on the Partner Menu and Select Security Profile.
2. The C-TPAT Supply Chain Security Profile is now required to be maintained in the structured template found in their C-TPAT Security Link Web Portal Security Profile section.

   Participants must provide a narrative description of the procedures they use to ensure adherence to C-TPAT Security Criteria or Guidelines as applicable for their C-TPAT enrollment category.

   For information on C-TPAT Security Criteria or Guidelines, refer to the C-TPAT web page located at http://www.cbp.gov/xp/cgov/import/commercial_enforcement/ctpat/.
3. In the Text Box for each section, C-TPAT participants must provide a narrative description of the security procedures in place. Give examples.

   Any back-up documentation may be uploaded in the Documents section via the C-TPAT Partner Document Exchange function.

Answers such as Non-Applicable or Does Not Apply are NOT acceptable. If you feel that a section does not apply to your situation, give a succinct explanation of why you feel this does not apply to your company.

4. Participants navigate through the Supply Chain Security Profile Sections selecting the "Next" button or by clicking on the blue hyperlink for the section.

   Clicking "Save" will ensure all work is updated.
5. After all Security Profile Sections have been completed, you will be able to Submit your Security Profile for review.
6. If any of the Supply Chain Security Profile sections are BLANK, an error message will be generated.
7. Your completed Security Profile will be assigned to and reviewed by a C-TPAT Supply Chain Security Specialist.

   For each section of the Security Profile, any comments made by the C-TPAT Supply Chain Security Specialist reviewer will appear in the Comment section.

   The block also indicates whether the section is Critical and whether the section is Approved or Rejected.

   Section Approval/Rejection is also designated by a Green "Check" (Approval) or a Red "X" (Rejected).
8. Rejected sections must be corrected and sufficient information provided.

# C-TPAT Validation Process

## Validation Basics

### C-TPAT Validation

C-TPAT validation is a process through which U.S. Customs and Border Protection (CBP) meets with program participant representatives, and visits selected domestic and foreign sites, to verify that the supply chain security measures contained in the C-TPAT participant's security profile are accurate and being followed.

### Goals of C-TPAT Validation

Since the decision to provide expedited release of cargo, and/or a reduced number of examinations, may be directly linked to a company's C-TPAT documentation, the principal goal of a validation is to ensure that the company's C-TPAT security profile is reliable, accurate and effective.

CBP expects, however, that validations will also provide a forum through which CBP and a C-TPAT participant can build a stronger partnership by discussing supply chain security issues, sharing "best practices," and cooperatively developing solutions to address potential vulnerabilities. The face-to-face nature of a validation encourages both CBP and the C-TPAT participant to better understand the role each plays in securing U.S. borders against international terrorism.

### Validation vs. Audit

A C-TPAT validation is not a CBP audit. Whereas CBP routinely performs audits in a variety of operational areas (e.g. trade compliance, NAFTA), C-TPAT validations do not measure a company's adherence to existing government rules and regulations. Instead, the validation is focused on the verification of supply chain security processes and procedures that a company voluntarily agrees to verify or perform under the auspices of the C-TPAT program.

Validations are meant to be focused and concise. Although they may extend beyond two weeks on some occasions due to CBP planning and travel, CBP maintains that they will not involve more than ten working days of a company's time.

### Which Participants Will Get a Validation?

CBP plans on validating the security profiles of all C-TPAT participants. Normally a company's initial validation will occur within three years of becoming a certified member of C-TPAT.

### Validation Scheduling

The order in which a C-TPAT participant's profile will be selected for validation will be based on risk management principles. Validations may be initiated based on import volume, security related anomalies, strategic threat posed by geographic regions, or other risk related information. Alternatively, a validation may be performed as a matter of routine program oversight. CBP Headquarters will provide C-TPAT participants with approximately (30) thirty days advance notice prior to the beginning of any validation. The C-TPAT SCSS will work with the company's C-TPAT point of contact to schedule all validation visits.

### Reporting of Validation Findings

At the conclusion of a validation, company management will be briefed on the findings of the validation. Additionally, a written Validation Report will be prepared and presented to the company shortly thereafter.

### Impact of Validation Findings

If the validation findings are satisfactory, the results will increase the level of benefits provided to importer participants. If the validation findings reveal significant weaknesses in the company's application of C-TPAT guidelines or criteria, some or all of the participant's C-TPAT benefits may be suspended or removed until corrective action is implemented and verified.

### Role of Security Criteria or Guidelines

C-TPAT security criteria or guidelines were developed jointly by CBP and the trade community. Participating companies must use these criteria or guidelines to assess their own supply chain security programs. The criteria or guidelines are used to measure the company's overall commitment to C-TPAT and viability in the program. The validation process ensures the company's C-TPAT commitment includes physical and procedural security requirements that enhance and verify supply chain security.

## Process Guidelines

### I. Introduction

The Customs-Trade Partnership Against Terrorism (C-TPAT) program is U.S. Customs and Border Protection's (CBP) premier trade security program. The purpose of C-TPAT is to partner with the trade community for the purpose of securing the U.S. and international supply chains from possible intrusion by terrorist organizations. C-TPAT requires the trade company participant to document and validate their supply chain security procedures in relation to existing CBP C-TPAT criteria or guidelines as applicable. CBP requires that C-TPAT company participants develop an internal validation process to ensure the existence of security measures documented in their Supply Chain Security Profile and in any supplemental information provided to CBP. As a part of the C-TPAT process, CBP C-TPAT Supply Chain Security Specialists (SCSS) and the C-TPAT participant will jointly conduct a validation of the company's supply chain security procedures. The validation process is essential to verifying the company's commitment to C-TPAT.

## II. Objective
The purpose of the validation is to ensure that the C-TPAT participant's international supply chain security measures contained in the C-TPAT participant's security profile have been implemented and are being followed in accordance with established C-TPAT criteria or guidelines. The validation team evaluates the status and effectiveness of key security measures in the participant's profile to make recommendations and recognize best practices where appropriate.

## III. Validation Principles
The guiding principle of the C-TPAT program is enhancing and ensuring supply chain security though a government-industry partnership. The C-TPAT program is voluntary and designed to share information that will protect the supply chain from being compromised by terrorists and terrorist organizations. The validation process will enable CBP and the C-TPAT participant to jointly review the participant's C-TPAT security profile to ensure that security actions in the profile are being effectively executed. Throughout the process there will also be the opportunity to discuss security issues and to share "best practices" with the ultimate goal of securing the international supply chain.

C-TPAT validations are not audits. In addition, they will be focused, concise, and will last not longer than ten working days.

Based on the participant's C-TPAT security profile and the recommendations of the validation team, CBP Headquarters will also oversee the specific security elements to be validated.

## IV. Conducting a Validation
### A. Validation Selection Process
To ensure accuracy, the security profiles of C-TPAT participants will be validated. The C-TPAT participant's security profile will be selected for validation based on the company's import supply chain risk. Validations may be initiated based on many factors including: security related anomalies, strategic threat posed by geographic regions, other risk related information, or strategic import volume. Unannounced validations will not be conducted. C-TPAT participants will be given approximately thirty days advance written notice along with a request for any supporting documentation that is needed.

### B. Validation Teams
A validation team consisting of C-TPAT SCSS and a representative(s) of the C-TPAT participant will conduct C-TPAT validation visits.

SCSS on a validation team are composed of trained CBP specialists knowledgeable in international supply chain security matters. SCSS receive supply chain security training to assist them in working with industry representatives to promote effective supply chain security programs.

Generally, the lead SCSS performing the validation will be the company's assigned C-TPAT representative responsible for reviewing and assessing the company's security profile and other accessible information to determine the scope of the validation. This will help ensure that the validation is effective, focused, and limited in duration.

### C. Validation Procedures
The SCSS validation team leader will provide the company with a written notification of the scheduled validation. The notice will be issued at least thirty days prior to the start of the validation and will include a request for supporting documentation or materials, if any. The validation team leader will also contact the C-TPAT participant to establish a single point of contact at the corporate level.

Prior to the commencement of the validation, the C-TPAT SCSS team will review the participant's C-TPAT security profile, any supplemental information received from the company, and any CBP headquarters instructions, to determine the intended scope of the validation.

In preparation for the validation, the validation team may also consider specific C-TPAT security criteria and guidelines. The security criteria and guidelines are used to determine the sufficiency of specific aspects of a participant's C-TPAT security profile. It is understood that the criteria and guidelines are not inclusive with respect to effective security practices.

C-TPAT Security Criteria and Guidelines are available for each C-TPAT enrollment category at www.cbp.gov.

### D. Validation Venue
Under normal circumstances, the validation will begin with a briefing of C-TPAT participant company officials via phone or at the company's primary U.S. office location. The validation team will discuss the participant's role in the C-TPAT program. The validation team will also focus on the scope of the validation including validation visit locations throughout the company's international supply chain. If additional information is required to validate a portion of a C-TPAT participant's supply chain, the validation team will coordinate the required request with the company officials.

### E. Validation Visit
A validation visit is a detailed review of the participant's import supply chain security procedures to determine if sufficient security procedures are in place to meet current C-TPAT guidelines or criteria. The specific sites of the validation visits will be determined based on the C-TPAT SCSS validation risk analysis and coordinated with the C-TPAT participant representative. A validation may require multiple visits at foreign locations. Individual validation visits are usually performed in no more than one day.

### F. Validation Report
Validation visit findings are documented in a Validation Report and forwarded to the C-TPAT participant. The report findings will identify supply chain security recommendations or best practices. If significant supply chain security weaknesses or recommendations are found, a participant's C-TPAT benefits may be suspended or removed depending on the circumstances. If a company has their C-TPAT benefits suspended, C-TPAT will recommend that the company implement an action plan containing corrective actions to address specific supply chain security weaknesses.

# C-TPAT Security Criteria and Guidelines
The following sections include CBP C-TPAT Security Criteria and Security Guidelines that may be used by the C-TPAT Validation Team in the planning phase of an on-site validation. These Criteria and Guidelines, therefore, will be helpful in the pre-validation review of key aspects of a participant's C-TPAT security profile. Therefore, prior to conducting an on-site validation, the validation team may review and discuss appropriate security recommendations contained in these criteria and guidelines in the context of the participant's C-TPAT security profile. This will assist the team in limiting the scope of the validation and in customizing the validation to the C-TPAT participant involved.

# C-TPAT for Importers[1]

## C-TPAT Security Criteria for Importers[2]

### C-TPAT Security Criteria Importers

Importers must conduct a comprehensive assessment of their international supply chains based upon the following C-TPAT security criteria. Where an importer outsources or contracts elements of their supply chain, such as a foreign facility, conveyance, domestic warehouse, or other elements, the importer must work with these business partners to ensure that pertinent security measures are in place and adhered to throughout their supply chain. The supply chain for C-TPAT purposes is defined from point of origin (manufacturer/supplier/vendor) through to point of distribution – and recognizes the diverse business models C-TPAT members employ. C-TPAT recognizes the complexity of international supply chains and endorses the application and implementation of security measures based upon risk analysis. Therefore, the program allows for flexibility and the customization of security plans based on the member's business model.

Appropriate security measures, as listed throughout this document, must be implemented and maintained throughout the importer's supply chains - based on risk.

### Business Partner Requirement

Importers must have written and verifiable processes for the selection of business partners including manufacturers, product suppliers and vendors.

#### Security procedures

For those business partners eligible for C-TPAT certification (carriers, ports, terminals, brokers, consolidators, etc.) the importer must have documentation (e.g., C-TPAT certificate, SVI number, etc.) indicating whether these business partners are or are not C-TPAT certified.

For those business partners not eligible for C-TPAT certification, importers must require their business partners to demonstrate that they are meeting C-TPAT security criteria via written/electronic confirmation (e.g., contractual obligations; via a letter from a senior business partner officer attesting to compliance; a written statement from the business partner demonstrating their compliance with C-TPAT security criteria or an equivalent WCO accredited security program administered by a foreign customs authority; or, by providing a completed importer security questionnaire).Based upon a documented risk assessment process, non-C-TPAT eligible business partners must be subject to verification of compliance with C-TPAT security criteria by the importer.

#### Point of Origin

Importers must ensure business partners develop security processes and procedures consistent with the C-TPAT security criteria to enhance the integrity of the shipment at point of origin. Periodic reviews of business partners' processes and facilities should be conducted based on risk, and should maintain the security standards required by the importer.

#### Participation / Certification in Foreign Customs Administrations Supply Chain Security Programs

Current or prospective business partners who have obtained a certification in a supply chain security program being administered by foreign Customs Administration should be required to indicate their status of participation to the importer.

### Other Internal criteria for selection

Internal requirements, such as financial soundness, capability of meeting contractual security requirements, and the ability to identify and correct security deficiencies as needed, should be addressed by the importer. Internal requirements should be assessed against a risk-based process as determined by an internal management team.

### Container Security

Container integrity must be maintained to protect against the introduction of unauthorized material and/or persons. At point of stuffing, procedures must be in place to properly seal and maintain the integrity of the shipping containers. A high security seal must be affixed to all loaded containers bound for the U.S. All seals must meet or exceed the current PAS ISO 17712 standards for high security seals.

### Container Inspection

Procedures must be in place to verify the physical integrity of the container structure prior to stuffing, to include the reliability of the locking mechanisms of the doors. A seven-point inspection process is recommended for all containers:
- Front wall
- Left side
- Right side
- Floor
- Ceiling/Roof
- Inside/outside doors
- Outside/Undercarriage

#### Container Seals

Written procedures must stipulate how seals are to be controlled and affixed to loaded containers - to include procedures for recognizing and reporting compromised seals and/or containers to US Customs and Border Protection or the appropriate foreign authority. Only designated employees should distribute container seals for integrity purposes.

#### Container Storage

Containers must be stored in a secure area to prevent unauthorized access and/or manipulation. Procedures must be in place for reporting and neutralizing unauthorized entry into containers or container storage areas.

### Physical Access Controls

Access controls prevent unauthorized entry to facilities, maintain control of employees and visitors, and protect company assets. Access controls must include the positive identification of all employees, visitors, and vendors at all points of entry.

#### Employees

An employee identification system must be in place for positive identification and access control purposes. Employees should only be given access to those secure areas needed for the performance of their duties. Company management or security personnel must adequately control the issuance and removal of employee, visitor and vendor identification badges. Procedures for the issuance, removal and changing of access devices (e.g., keys, key cards, etc.) must be documented.

SECURITY

---

1. C-TPAT requirements are evolving. For the latest information refer to the CBP Web site at: www.cbp.gov.
2. These security criteria became effective March 25, 2005 and were current as of September 2006.

**SECURITY**

### Visitors
Visitors must present photo identification for documentation purposes upon arrival. All visitors should be escorted and visibly display temporary identification.

### Deliveries (including mail)
Proper vendor ID and/or photo identification must be presented for documentation purposes upon arrival by all vendors. Arriving packages and mail should be periodically screened before being disseminated.

### Challenging and Removing Unauthorized Persons
Procedures must be in place to identify, challenge and address unauthorized/unidentified persons.

## Personnel Security
Processes must be in place to screen prospective employees and to periodically check current employees.

### Pre-Employment Verification
Application information, such as employment history and references must be verified prior to employment.

### Background checks / investigations
Consistent with foreign, federal, state, and local regulations, background checks and investigations should be conducted for prospective employees. Once employed, periodic checks and reinvestigations should be performed based on cause, and/or the sensitivity of the employee's position.

### Personnel Termination Procedures
Companies must have procedures in place to remove identification, facility, and system access for terminated employees.

## Procedural Security
Security measures must be in place to ensure the integrity and security of processes relevant to the transportation, handling, and storage of cargo in the supply chain.

### Documentation Processing
Procedures must be in place to ensure that all information used in the clearing of merchandise/cargo, is legible, complete, accurate, and protected against the exchange, loss or introduction of erroneous information. Documentation control must include safeguarding computer access and information.

### Manifesting Procedures
To help ensure the integrity of cargo received from abroad, procedures must be in place to ensure that information received from business partners is reported accurately and timely.

### Shipping & Receiving
Arriving cargo should be reconciled against information on the cargo manifest. The cargo should be accurately described, and the weights, labels, marks and piece count indicated and verified. Departing cargo should be verified against purchase or delivery orders. Drivers delivering or receiving cargo must be positively identified before cargo is received or released.

### Cargo Discrepancies
All shortages, overages, and other significant discrepancies or anomalies must be resolved and/or investigated appropriately. Customs and/or other appropriate law enforcement agencies must be notified if illegal or suspicious activities are detected - as appropriate.

## Security Training and Threat Awareness
A threat awareness program should be established and maintained by security personnel to recognize and foster awareness of the threat posed by terrorists at each point in the supply chain. Employees must be made aware of the procedures the company has in place to address a situation and how to report it. Additional training should be provided to employees in the shipping and receiving areas, as well as those receiving and opening mail.

Additionally, specific training should be offered to assist employees in maintaining cargo integrity, recognizing internal conspiracies, and protecting access controls. These programs should offer incentives for active employee participation.

## Physical Security
Cargo handling and storage facilities in domestic and foreign locations must have physical barriers and deterrents that guard against unauthorized access. Importers should incorporate the following C-TPAT physical security criteria throughout their supply chains as applicable.

### Fencing
Perimeter fencing should enclose the areas around cargo handling and storage facilities. Interior fencing within a cargo handling structure should be used to segregate domestic, international, high value, and hazardous cargo. All fencing must be regularly inspected for integrity and damage.

### Gates and Gate Houses
Gates through which vehicles and/or personnel enter or exit must be manned and/or monitored. The number of gates should be kept to the minimum necessary for proper access and safety.

### Parking
Private passenger vehicles should be prohibited from parking in or adjacent to cargo handling and storage areas.

### Building Structure
Buildings must be constructed of materials that resist unlawful entry. The integrity of structures must be maintained by periodic inspection and repair.

### Locking Devices and Key Controls
All external and internal windows, gates and fences must be secured with locking devices. Management or security personnel must control the issuance of all locks and keys.

### Lighting
Adequate lighting must be provided inside and outside the facility including the following areas: entrances and exits, cargo handling and storage areas, fence lines and parking areas.

### Alarms Systems & Video Surveillance Cameras
Alarm systems and video surveillance cameras should be utilized to monitor premises and prevent unauthorized access to cargo handling and storage areas.

## Information Technology Security

### Password Protection
Automated systems must use individually assigned accounts that require a periodic change of password. IT security policies, procedures and standards must be in place and provided to employees in the form of training.

### Accountability
A system must be in place to identify the abuse of IT including improper access, tampering or the altering of business data. All system violators must be subject to appropriate disciplinary actions for abuse.

# Importer - C-TPAT Agreement to Voluntarily Participate

This Agreement is made between _____ (hereinafter referred to as "the Importer") and U.S. Customs and Border Protection (hereinafter referred to as "CBP") to participate in the Customs-Trade Partnership Against Terrorism (C-TPAT), a voluntary and cooperative partnership established to achieve the goals of building more secure and more efficient borders.

This Agreement between the Importer and CBP is intended to enhance the joint efforts of the Importer and CBP to protect the supply chain, identify security gaps, and implement specific security measures and best practices.

### Specifically, the Importer agrees to:

1. Conduct a comprehensive assessment of the Importer's global supply chain(s) based upon established C-TPAT security criteria to include: Business Partner Requirements, Cargo Security, Container Security, Physical Access Controls, Personnel Security, Procedural Security, Security Training/Threat Awareness, Physical Security, and Information Technology Security. The supply chain is defined from point of origin (manufacturer/supplier/vendor) to point of distribution.
2. Develop a written and verifiable process for determining risk throughout the Importer's global supply chain(s) based upon the Importer's business model (e.g., volume, country of origin, routing, potential terrorist threat, etc.)
3. Implement and maintain appropriate security measures throughout the Importer's global supply chain(s) in a written and verifiable format that is consistent with C-TPAT security criteria and based upon risk analysis as determined by the Importer's business model.
4. Complete and upload the Importer's Supply Chain Security Profile document.
5. Develop and implement a written and verifiable process for the selection of all business partners in the Importer's global supply chain(s) including manufacturers, product suppliers, and vendors based upon C-TPAT security criteria regarding Business Partner Requirements. Where the Importer outsources or contracts elements of their supply chain(s), the Importer must ensure that appropriate security measures are in place, effective, and complied with.
6. Develop and implement a periodic Self-Assessment Program in a written and verifiable format to ensure that appropriate security measures consistent with C-TPAT security criteria are maintained and are sufficient throughout the Importer's global supply chain(s), and implement changes as necessary or needs arise.
7. Notify CBP at industry.partnership@dhs.gov of all changes and/or modifications to the Importer's information on file including Official Company Name, Street Address, Company Point of Contact, Telephone Number, Fax Number, and E-Mail.

### Upon acceptance, review, and/or certification in the C-TPAT, CBP will:

1. Provide feedback and guidance to the Importer on the information provided in the Supply Chain Security Profile within 60 days of receipt.
2. Provide technical assistance and recommendations to the Importer to improve the Importer's supply chain(s) pursuant to C-TPAT security criteria.
3. Provide incentives and benefits to include expedited processing of C-TPAT shipments.
4. Assign a C-TPAT supply chain specialist to serve as the CBP liaison for validations, security issues, procedural updates, communication, and training.
5. Ensure all information provided by the Importer to CBP will remain confidential. CBP will not disclose the Importer's identity as a C-TPAT partner without the Importer's consent.

This Agreement will be administered pursuant to a plan jointly developed by CBP and the Importer.

This Agreement is subject to review and acceptance by CBP and the Importer and may be terminated upon written notice by either party.

This Agreement cannot, by law, exempt the Importer from any statutory or regulatory sanctions in the event that discrepancies are discovered during a physical examination of cargo or the review of documents associated with the Importer's transactions with CBP.

This Agreement does not relieve the Importer of any responsibilities with respect to United States law, including CBP regulations.

# General Items

## FAQs

For a list of 43 "Frequently Asked Questions and Answers Regarding Minimum Security Criteria for Importers" refer to: http://www.cbp.gov/xp/cgov/import/commercial_enforcement/ctpat/security_criteria/criteria_importers/questions.xml.

## C-TPAT Application

Instructions for submitting an online C-TPAT application are at: www.cbp.gov/xp/cgov/import/commercial_enforcement/ctpat/online_app/. Select "Instructions for Completing the C-TPAT Online Application.

The C-TPAT Online Application itself can be found at: https://ctpat.cbp.dhs.gov/CompanyProfile.aspx

## For More Information

For more information about C-TPAT for importers go to: www.cbp.gov. Search for "C-TPAT for Importers."

# C-TPAT for Sea Carriers[1]

## C-TPAT Security Criteria for Sea Carriers[2]

Sea carriers must conduct a comprehensive assessment of their security practices based upon the following C-TPAT minimum-security criteria. Where a sea carrier does not control a specific element of the cargo transportation service it has contracted to provide, such as a marine terminal operator or a time chartered vessel with whom it has contracted, the sea carrier must work with these business partners to seek to ensure that pertinent security measures are in place and adhered to. The sea carrier is responsible for exercising prudent oversight for all cargo loaded on board its vessel, pursuant to applicable law and regulations and the terms of this program. C-TPAT recognizes the complexity of international supply chains and security practices, and endorses the application and implementation of security measures based upon risk.[3] Therefore, the program allows for flexibility and the customization of security plans based on the member's business model. Security measures, as listed throughout this document, must be implemented and maintained as appropriate to the carrier's business model and risk understanding. CBP's C-TPAT validation process shall include a review of the carrier's assessment and program.

C-TPAT recognizes that sea carriers are already subject to defined security mandates created under the International Ship and Port Security Code (ISPS) and the Maritime Transportation Security Act (MTSA). It is not the intention of C-TPAT to duplicate these vessel and facility security requirements, rather, C-TPAT seeks to build upon the ISPS and MTSA foundation and require additional security measures and practices which enhance the overall security throughout the international supply chain.

ISPS and MTSA compliance are a prerequisite for C-TPAT sea carrier membership, and only vessels in compliance with the applicable ISPS code requirements may be utilized by C-TPAT members. Marine terminals operated by C-TPAT members must also comply with ISPS code requirements. The Physical Access Controls and Physical Security provisions of these criteria are satisfied for ISPS regulated vessels and port facilities by those vessels' or facilities' compliance with the ISPS Code and Coast Guard regulations.

### Business Partner Requirements

Sea carriers must have written and verifiable procedures for the screening of carrier's agents and service providers contracted to provide transportation services for the carrier. Sea carriers must also have screening procedures for new customers, beyond financial soundness issues to include indicators of whether the customer appears to be a legitimate business and/or posses a security risk. Sea carriers shall also have procedures to review their customer's requests that could affect the safety of the vessel or the cargo or otherwise raise significant security questions, including unusual customer demands, such as specific stowage placement aboard the vessel (beyond a request for below deck or on deck stowage).

### Security procedures

Sea carriers must have written or web-based procedures for screening new customers to whom they issue bills of lading, which identify specific factors or practices, the presence of which would trigger additional scrutiny by the sea carrier, up to and including a detailed physical inspection of the exterior of the suspect customer's container prior to loading onto the vessel. These procedures may also include a referral to CBP or other competent authorities for further review. CBP will work in partnership with the sea carriers to identify specific information regarding what factors, practices or risks are relevant.

Sea carriers should ensure that contract vessel services providers commit to C-TPAT security recommendations. Periodic reviews of the security commitments of the service providers should be conducted.[4]

## Container Security

For all containers in the sea carrier's custody, container integrity must be maintained to protect against the introduction of unauthorized material and/or persons. Sea carriers must have procedures in place to maintain the integrity of the shipping containers while in their custody. A high security seal must be affixed to all loaded containers bound for the U.S. All seals used or distributed by the sea carrier must meet or exceed the current PAS ISO 17712 standards for high security seals.[5]

Sea carriers and/or their marine terminal operators must have processes in place to comply with seal verification rules and seal anomaly reporting requirements once promulgated and mandated by the U.S. government.

### Container Inspection

The requirement to inspect all containers prior to stuffing (to include the reliability of the locking mechanisms of the doors) is placed upon the importers through the C-TPAT Minimum Security Criteria for Importers dated March 25, 2005. Sea carriers must visually inspect all U.S.-bound empty containers, to include the interior of the container, at the foreign port of lading.

### Container Seals

Written procedures must stipulate how seals in the sea carrier's possession are to be controlled. Procedures should also exist for recognizing and reporting compromised seals and/or containers to US Customs and Border Protection or the appropriate foreign authority consistent with the seal anomaly reporting requirements once promulgated and mandated by the U.S. government.

---

1. C-TPAT requirements are evolving. For the latest information refer to the CBP Web site at: www.cbp.gov.
2. These security criteria for Sea Carriers became effective March 1, 2006 and were current as of September 2006.
3. Sea carriers shall have a documented and verifiable process for assessing security vulnerabilities within their operations based on their business model (i.e., volume, country of origin, routing, security alerts via open source information, ports identified by U.S. Coast Guard as having inadequate security, past security incidents, etc.).
4. An ISPS regulated vessel operator or port facility is not expected under these criteria to show a carrier or other third party its ship or port security plan. It is recognized that under the ISPS Code relevant portions of an ISPS security plan are not subject to inspection without the contracting government's agreement.
5. When a container has been affixed with a high security seal that meets or exceeds the current PAS ISO 17712 standards and the shipper or carrier wishes to apply a supplementary, additional seal to the container to provide enhanced level of security, such supplementary seals do not have to meet the PAS ISO 17712 standards.

### Container Storage

The sea carrier must store containers in their custody in a secure area to prevent unauthorized access and/or manipulation. Procedures must be in place for reporting detected, unauthorized entry into containers or container storage areas to appropriate local law enforcement officials.

## Physical Access Controls

The sea carrier shall establish access controls to prevent unauthorized entry to its vessels and cargo facilities, maintain control of employees and visitors, and protect company assets. Access controls must include the positive identification of all employees, visitors, service providers, government officials and vendors at all restricted access points of entry. Shore employees and service providers should only have access to those areas of the vessel where they have legitimate business. Vessel and facility access controls are governed by the International Ship and Port Security Code and MTSA. The Physical Access Control provisions of these criteria are satisfied for ISPS regulated vessels and port facilities by those vessels' or facilities' compliance with the ISPS Code and MTSA regulations.

### Boarding and Disembarking of Vessels

Consistent with the vessel's ISPS security plan, all crew, employees, vendors and visitors may be subject to a search when boarding or disembarking vessels. A vessel visitor log must be maintained and a temporary visitor pass must be issued as required by the vessel's security plan. All crewmembers, employees, vendors and visitors, including government officials, must display proper identification, as required by the applicable ISPS/MTSA security plan.

### Employees

An employee identification system must be in place for positive identification and access control purposes. Employees should only be given access to those secure areas needed for the performance of their duties. Company management or security personnel must adequately control the issuance and removal of employee, visitor and vendor identification badges. Procedures for the issuance, removal and changing of access devices (e.g. keys, key cards, etc.) must be documented.

### Visitors / Vendors / Service Providers

Visitors, vendors, government officials, and service providers must present photo identification for documentation purposes upon arrival at carrier's vessels or cargo facilities, and a visitor log must be maintained. Measures described by the approved ISPS/MTSA security plan addressing the escort of visitors and service providers, including, when appropriate, the use of temporary identification will be followed.

### Challenging and Removing Unauthorized Persons

Procedures must be in place to identify, challenge and address unauthorized/unidentified persons.

## Personnel Security

In compliance with applicable laws and regulations for that location, written and verifiable processes must be in place to screen prospective employees and to periodically check current employees.

### Pre-Employment Verification

Application information, such as employment history and references must be verified prior to employment.

### Background Checks / Investigations

Depending on the sensitivity of the position, background checks and investigations shall be conducted for prospective employees as appropriate and as required by foreign, federal, state and local regulations. Once employed, periodic checks and reinvestigations should be performed based on cause, and/or the sensitivity of the employee's position.

### Personnel Termination Procedures

Companies must have procedures in place to remove identification, facility, and system access for terminated employees.

### Crewmen Control – Deserter/Absconder Risk

CBP will work with the U.S. Coast Guard and sea carriers to identify specific factors which may indicate when a crewman poses a potential risk of desertion/absconding. When such factors are identified and provided to the carriers, the carrier shall provide this information to its vessel masters and to the vessels under charter to the carrier, and such vessels shall establish procedures to address the potential risk of desertion/absconding. Added security measures appropriate to the risk present should be employed upon arrival into the U.S. port/territories.

### Deserter/Absconder Notifications

Vessel masters must account for all crewmen prior to the vessel's departure from a U.S. port. If the vessel master discovers that a crewman has deserted or absconded, the vessel master must report this finding by the most practical means to CBP immediately upon discovery and prior to the vessel's departure.

## Procedural Security

Security measures must be in place to ensure the integrity and security of processes relevant to the transportation, handling, and storage of cargo. Consistent with the carrier's ISPS Code security plan, procedures must be in place to prevent unauthorized personnel from gaining access to the vessel. In those geographic areas where risk assessments warrant checking containers for human concealment in containers, such procedures should be designed to address the particular, identified risk at the load port or the particular port facility. CBP will inform the sea carriers when it is aware of a high risk of human concealment or stowaways at particular ports or geographic regions. Documented procedures must also include pre-departure vessel security sweeps for stowaways at the foreign load port, and during normal watch activity while en route to the United States as warranted by risk conditions at the foreign load port.

### Passenger and Crew

Sea carriers must ensure compliance with the U.S. Coast Guard Notice of Arrival and Departure requirements so that accurate, timely and advanced transmission of data associated with international passengers and crew is provided to the U.S. government and CBP.

### Bill of Lading / Manifesting Procedures

Procedures must be in place to ensure that the information in the carrier's cargo manifest accurately reflects the information provided to the carrier by the shipper or its agent, and is filed with CBP in a timely manner. Documentation control must include safeguarding computer access and information. Bill of lading information filed with CBP should show the first foreign port (place) where the sea carrier takes possession of the cargo destined for the United States.

### BAPLIEs

At the request of CBP, sea carriers will provide a requested BAPLIE and/or stowage plan, in a format readily available. Such requests will be made on a voyage specific basis when CBP requires additional voyage information and will be honored by the sea carrier in a timely manner. CBP recognizes that these are not regulated documents and that the data included may not always match the manifest filing.

### Cargo

Customs and/or other appropriate law enforcement agencies must be notified if illegal or highly suspicious activities are detected - as appropriate.

SECURITY

### Security Training and Awareness

A security awareness program should be established and maintained by the carrier to recognize and foster awareness of security vulnerabilities to vessels and maritime cargo. Employees must be made aware of the procedures the sea carrier has in place to report a security concern or incident. Additionally, specific training should be offered to assist employees in maintaining vessel and cargo integrity, recognizing internal conspiracies, and protecting access controls.

### Physical Security

Carriers shall establish written and verifiable procedures to prevent unauthorized personnel from gaining access to its vessels, including concealment in containers, and to prevent tampering with cargo conveyances while they are in the carrier's custody. Such measures are covered by a vessel's and a port facility's ISPS security plan. Physical Security provisions of these criteria are satisfied for ISPS regulated vessels and port facilities by those vessels' or facilities' compliance with the ISPS Code and MTSA regulations. Non-ISPS Code regulated cargo handling and storage facilities and container yards operated by the carrier, in domestic and foreign locations, must have physical barriers and deterrents that guard against unauthorized access. Sea carriers should incorporate the following C-TPAT physical security criteria as applicable.

#### Fencing

Perimeter fencing should enclose the areas around cargo handling and storage facilities, container yards, and terminals. All fencing must be regularly inspected for integrity and damage.

#### Gates and Gate Houses

Gates through which vehicles and/or personnel enter or exit must be manned and/or monitored and secured when not in use.

#### Parking

Private passenger vehicles should be prohibited from parking in or adjacent to cargo handling and storage areas, and vessels.

#### Building Structure

Buildings must be constructed of materials that resist unlawful entry. The integrity of structures must be maintained by periodic inspection and repair.

#### Locking Devices and Key Controls

All external and internal windows, gates and fences must be secured with locking devices. Management or security personnel must control the issuance of all locks and keys.

#### Lighting

Adequate lighting must be provided inside and outside the facility including the following areas: entrances and exits, cargo handling and storage areas, fence lines and parking areas. While at port, the pier and waterside of the vessel must be adequately illuminated.

#### Alarms Systems & Video Surveillance Cameras

At those locations determined appropriate by the carrier's risk assessment, alarm systems and video surveillance cameras should be utilized to monitor premises and prevent unauthorized access to vessels, cargo handling and storage areas.

### Information Technology Security

#### Password Protection

Automated systems must use individually assigned accounts that require a periodic change of password. IT security policies, procedures and standards must be in place and provided to employees in the form of training.

#### Accountability

A system must be in place to identify the abuse of IT including improper access, tampering or the altering of business data. All system violators must be subject to appropriate disciplinary actions for abuse.

### Security Assessment, Response and Improvement

Carriers and CBP have a mutual interest in security assessments and improvements, and recognize that specific, implemented security procedures may be found in the future to have weaknesses or be subject to circumvention. When a security shortcoming or security incident is identified, the Carrier and CBP officials will meet in an effort to ascertain what led to the breakdown and to formulate mutually agreed remedial measures. If CBP determines that the security incident raises substantial concerns or a security weakness requires substantial remediation, CBP headquarters officials will meet with the carrier's senior management to discuss such concerns and to identify appropriate remedial measures to be taken.

While CBP has the authority to suspend or remove a sea carrier from the C-TPAT program for substantial non-compliance with the security criteria of the program, such authority is exercised only in the most serious circumstances.

# Sea Carrier General Items

### FAQs

For a list of seven Frequently Asked Questions and Answers Regarding Minimum Security Criteria for Sea Carriers" go to: http://www.cbp.gov/xp/cgov/import/commercial_enforcement/ctpat/security_criteria/sea_carrier_criteria/sea_carrier_security_faq.xml.

### C-TPAT Application

Instructions for submitting an online C-TPAT application are at: www.cbp.gov/xp/cgov/import/commercial_enforcement/ctpat/online_app/. Select "Instructions for Completing the C-TPAT Online Application."

The C-TPAT Online Application itself can be found at: https://ctpat.cbp.dhs.gov/CompanyProfile.aspx

### Agreement to Voluntarily Participate

The Sea Carrier Agreement to Voluntarily Participate is similar to the "Importer - C-TPAT Agreement to Voluntarily Participate" on page 593. The Sea Carrier Agreement can be found as part of the C-TPAT Online Application at: https://ctpat.cbp.dhs.gov/CompanyProfile.aspx

### For More Information

For more information about C-TPAT go to: www.cbp.gov. Search for "C-TPAT for Sea Carriers."

# C-TPAT for Rail Carriers[1]

## C-TPAT Security Criteria for Rail Carriers[2]

Rail carriers must conduct a comprehensive assessment of their security practices based upon the following C-TPAT minimum-security criteria. Recognizing that rail carriers do not control their shippers and have a common carrier obligation to transport goods tendered to them, rail carriers shall work with their shippers on their security practices as set forth in these criteria.

These minimum security criteria are fundamentally designed to be the building blocks for rail carriers to institute effective security practices designed to optimize supply chain performance to mitigate the risk of loss, theft, and contraband smuggling that could potentially introduce terrorists and implements of terrorism into the global supply chain.

Rail carriers should periodically assess their degree of vulnerability to risk and should prescribe security measures to strengthen or adjust their security posture to prevent security breaches and internal conspiracies. The determination and scope of criminal elements targeting world commerce through internal conspiracies requires companies to elevate their security practices.

C-TPAT recognizes the complexity of international supply chains and security practices, and endorses the application and implementation of security measures based upon risk. Therefore, the program allows for flexibility and the customization of security plans based on the member's business model. Security measures, as listed throughout this document, must be implemented and maintained as appropriate to the carrier's business model and risk understanding.

### Business Partner Requirements

Rail carriers must have written and verifiable processes for the screening of new business partners, including carrier's agents, sub-contracted rail carriers, and service providers, as well as screening procedures for new customers, beyond financial soundness issues to include security indicators. These processes apply to business partners and service providers not eligible for C-TPAT membership.

#### Security Procedures[3]

- Written procedures must exist to address specific factors or practices, the presence of which would trigger additional scrutiny by the rail carrier. U.S. Customs and Border Protection (CBP) will work in partnership with the rail carriers to identify specific information regarding what factors, practices or risks are relevant.
- For those business partners eligible for C-TPAT certification (importers, ports, terminals, brokers, consolidators, etc.) the Rail carrier must have documentation (e.g., C-TPAT certificate, SVI number, etc.) indicating whether these business partners are or are not C-TPAT certified. Non-C-TPAT business partners may be subject to additional scrutiny by the Rail carrier. Rail carriers should institute appropriate security procedures for their contract service providers.

- Rail carriers have a common carrier responsibility for all cargo loaded aboard their rail cars; they must communicate the importance of security to their employees as a fundamental aspect of their security policies.
- Rail carriers should strongly encourage that contract service providers and shippers commit to C-TPAT security recommendations.

### Rolling Stock Security

Rail carriers shall have procedures to protect against the introduction of unauthorized personnel and material.[4]

- It is recognized that even though a carrier may not "exercise control" over the loading of rail cars and the contents of the cargo, rail carriers must be vigilant to guard against stowaways, and the smuggling of implements of terrorism and contraband. The rail carrier shall have procedures in place to guard against the loading of contraband while trains are in transit to the border, even in regards to unforeseen train stops.
- Rail carriers must have procedures in place for reporting unauthorized entry into rail cars, and locomotives.
- Rail carriers must maintain inventory information and movement records on each rail car and use the physical rail car tracking technology that is inherent to the North American rail network system.

### Inspection Procedures

- Rail personnel should be trained to inspect their rail cars and locomotives for anomalies. Training in conveyance searches should be adopted as part of the company's on-the-job training program. Training that is held should be recorded or documented in a personnel file of the employee that attended the training.
- A systematic inspection must be made prior to reaching the U.S. border.
- During required on-ground safety inspections of rolling stock entering the U.S., conduct security inspections for any apparent signs of tampering, sabotage, attached explosives, contraband, stowaways, and other unusual or prohibited items. It is understood that railroads must comply with the Federal Railroad Safety Act and the Hazardous Materials Transportation Act.
- CBP will work in partnership with the rail carriers to identify specific information regarding what factors, practices or risks are relevant including the use of non-intrusive gamma ray technology or other inspections.

### Conveyance Tracking and Monitoring Procedures

- Rail carriers must maintain, to the extent feasible and practicable, locomotive and rail car integrity while the train is en route to the U.S. border by maintaining inventory information and movement records for each rail

S E C U R I T Y

---

1. C-TPAT requirements are evolving. For the latest information refer to the CBP Web site at: www.cbp.gov.
2. These Rail Carrier Security Criteria became effective August 28, 2006, and were current as of September 2006.
3. C-TPAT recognizes that rail carriers are common carriers and are already subject to defined security mandates created under the Department of Transportation, such as the Federal Railroad Safety Act and the Hazardous Materials Transportation Act, as well as the Customs and Border Patrol (CBP) Trade Act of 2002, Maritime Transportation Security Act, FDA 2002 Bio-Terrorism Act, and other applicable federal requirements of the TSA. It is not the intention of C-TPAT to duplicate these security requirements rather C-TPAT seeks to build upon the government security measures and industry practices already in place.
4. For purposes of this document, the term rolling stock is used to denote locomotives and rail-cars.

car. Rail carriers must record unannounced or unforeseen train stops.
- Rail carriers must utilize existing tracking and monitoring processes to track conveyances while they are en route to the U.S. border. Unannounced or unforeseen train stops shall be documented.
- Railroad supervision must ensure that tracking and monitoring processes are being adhered to.

### Seals
The sealing of rail cars, and intermodal maritime containers, along with continuous seal integrity are crucial elements of a secure supply chain, and remain a critical aspect of a rail carrier's commitment to C-TPAT. To the extent practical, a high security seal should be affixed to all loaded rail cars bound for the U.S. All seals must meet or exceed the current PAS ISO 17712 standards for high security seals. Rail carriers crossing the U.S. border must also fully comply with seal verification rules and seal anomaly reporting requirements once promulgated and mandated by the U.S. government.
- Clearly defined written procedures must stipulate how seals in the rail carrier's possession are to be controlled during transit. These written procedures should be briefed to all rail crewmembers and there should be a mechanism to ensure that these procedures are understood and are being followed. These procedures must include:

## Physical Access Controls
To the extent practical, rail carriers should institute access controls to prevent unauthorized entry to rail property and rail cars and should maintain control of employees and visitors. Access controls should include the positive identification of employees, visitors, service providers, and vendors. Rail companies should also conduct spot inspections of motor vehicles on railroad property where international shipments are handled.

### Employees
An employee identification system must be in place for positive identification and access control purposes. Employees should only be given access to high security areas such as dispatch centers if necessary for the performance of their duties. Railroad supervision or railroad police must adequately control the issuance and removal of employee, visitor and vendor identification badges. Procedures for the issuance, removal and changing of access devices (e.g. keys, key cards, etc.) must be documented. Establish employee identification measures for all employees. Conduct spot checks of identification as threat conditions warrant.

### Visitors, Vendors and Service Providers
To the extent feasible and practicable, and as threat conditions warrant, restrict the access of contractors and visitors to non-public areas of company-designated critical infrastructure and monitor the activities of visitors in or around such infrastructure.

### Challenging and Removing Unauthorized Persons
Procedures must be in place to identify, challenge and address unauthorized/unidentified persons.

### Unauthorized Persons
- Implement measures to deter unauthorized entry and increase the probability of detection at company-designated critical infrastructure. Provide safety and security training for employees at facilities where international shipments are handled.
- Establish procedures to detect or deter unmanifested material and unauthorized personnel from gaining access to trains crossing into the United States.

- Reinforce the need for employees to immediately report to the proper authorities all suspicious persons, activities, or objects encountered.
- Focus proactive community safety and security outreach and trespasser abatement programs in areas adjacent to company-designated critical infrastructure to reduce the likelihood of unauthorized individuals on company property and to enhance public awareness of the importance for reporting suspicious activity.

## Personnel Security
Written and verifiable processes must be in place to screen prospective rail employees and to periodically check current employees.

### Pre-Employment Verification / Background Checks / Investigations
Application information, such as employment history and references must be verified prior to employment.

### Background Checks / Investigations
Depending on the sensitivity of the position, background checks and investigations shall be conducted for current and prospective employees as appropriate and as required by foreign, federal, state and local regulations. Conduct background checks on all new railroad employees. Once employed, periodic checks and reinvestigations should be performed based on cause, and/or the sensitivity of the employee's position.

### Personnel Termination Procedures
Companies must have procedures in place to remove identification, facility, and system access for terminated employees.

## Procedural Security
Security measures must be in place to ensure the integrity and security of processes relevant to the transportation, handling, and storage of cargo in the supply chain. Procedures must be in place to prevent, detect, or deter unmanifested material and unauthorized personnel from gaining access to rail cars and locomotives.

Security procedures should be implemented that restrict access to the rail car and locomotive and prevent the lading of contraband while en-route from facilities in international locations to the United States.

Procedures must be in place to record and immediately report all anomalies regarding train crew personnel to U.S. Customs and Border Protection. Likewise, rail companies should investigate all suspicious activity and report it to the proper authority.

### Bill of Lading/Manifesting Procedures
Procedures must be in place to ensure that the information in the carrier's cargo manifest accurately reflect the information provided to the carrier by the shipper or its agent, and is filed with CBP in a timely manner. Documentation control must include safeguarding computer access and information.

### Reporting Train Crew Personnel
Identify all personnel on the train as required by CBP.

### Reporting Suspicious Cargo
All instances of suspicious cargo shipments should be reported immediately to the nearest CBP port-of-entry or other nearest appropriate authority.

## Physical Security
Procedures must be in place to prevent, detect, or deter unmanifested material and unauthorized personnel from gaining access to conveyance, including concealment in rail cars. Rail carriers should incorporate the following C-TPAT physical security criteria throughout their supply chains as applicable.

### *Fencing*
Perimeter fencing should enclose areas deemed by the rail carrier to be a critical infrastructure.

### *Parking*
Privately owned vehicles should be monitored when parked in close proximity to rolling stock that crosses the international border.

### *Building Structure*
Buildings must be constructed of materials that resist unlawful entry. The integrity of structures must be maintained by periodic inspection and repair.

### *Lighting*
Adequate lighting must be provided where appropriate, for entrances and exits.

### *Alarms Systems & Video Surveillance Cameras*
Where appropriate, alarm systems and video surveillance cameras should be utilized to monitor premises and prevent unauthorized access to rail property.

## Security Training and Threat Awareness
A threat awareness program should be established and maintained by security personnel to recognize and foster awareness of the threat posed by drug smugglers and terrorists. Employees must be made aware of the procedures the rail carrier has in place to address a situation and how to report it. Additionally, specific training should be offered to assist employees in maintaining rolling stock integrity, recognizing internal conspiracies, and protecting access controls.

- Establish an employee security awareness-training program to include procedures to recognize suspicious activity and report security concerns.
- During required on-ground safety inspections of international shipments inspect for any apparent signs of tampering, sabotage, attached explosives, and other suspicious items. Train employees to recognize suspicious activity and report security concerns found during inspections and in transit.
- Implement a policy to preclude unnecessary disclosure of sensitive information.

## Information & Technology Security

### *Password Protection*
Measures should be taken to protect electronic assets, including advising employees of the need to protect passwords and computer access. Automated systems must use individually assigned accounts that require a periodic change of password. IT security policies, procedures and standards must be in place.

### *Accountability*
IT security policies, procedures, and standards must be in place to address the abuse of IT including improper access, sharing, tampering or the altering of business data. All system violators must be subject to appropriate disciplinary actions for abuse.

# Rail Carrier General Items

## C-TPAT Application
Instructions for submitting an online C-TPAT application are at: www.cbp.gov/xp/cgov/import/commercial_enforcement/ctpat/online_app/. Select "Instructions for Completing the C-TPAT Online Application."
The C-TPAT Online Application itself can be found at: https://ctpat.cbp.dhs.gov/CompanyProfile.aspx

## Agreement to Voluntarily Participate
The Rail Carrier Agreement to Voluntarily Participate is similar to the "Importer - C-TPAT Agreement to Voluntarily Participate" on page 593. The Sea Carrier Agreement can be found as part of the C-TPAT Online Application at: https://ctpat.cbp.dhs.gov/CompanyProfile.aspx

## For More Information
For more information about C-TPAT go to: www.cbp.gov. Search for "C-TPAT for Rail Carriers."

SECURITY

# C-TPAT for Highway Carriers[1]

## C-TPAT Security Criteria for Highway Carriers[2]

The supply chain for highway carriers for C-TPAT purposes is defined from point of origin from the yard or where the tractors and trailers are stored, through pickup at the manufacturer/supplier/vendor, through to the point of distribution – and recognizes the diverse business models C-TPAT members employ.

These minimum security criteria are fundamentally designed to be the building blocks for highway carriers to institute effective security practices designed to optimize supply chain performance to mitigate the risk of loss, theft, and contraband smuggling that could potentially introduce dangerous elements into the global supply chain.

On a quarterly basis, or as circumstances dictate such as during periods of heightened alert, security breach or incident, Highway carriers should routinely assess their degree of vulnerability to risk and should prescribe security measures to strengthen or adjust their security posture to prevent security breaches and internal conspiracies. The determination and scope of criminal elements targeting world commerce through internal conspiracies requires companies, and in particular, highway carriers to elevate their security practices, especially if the highway carrier has the exclusive benefit of enrollment in the Free and Secure Trade (FAST) program.

C-TPAT recognizes the complexity of international supply chains and security practices, and endorses the application and implementation of security measures based upon risk.[3] Therefore, the program allows for flexibility and the customization of security plans based on the member's business model.

Appropriate security measures, as listed throughout this document, must be implemented and maintained.

### Business Partner Requirements

Highway carriers must have written and verifiable processes for the screening of business partners, including carrier's agents, sub-contracted highway carriers, and service providers, as well as screening procedures for new customers, beyond financial soundness issues to include security indicators, such as business references and professional associations.

#### Security Procedures

- Written procedures must exist for screening business partners, which identify specific factors or practices, the presence of which would trigger additional scrutiny by the highway carrier.
- For those business partners eligible for C-TPAT certification (importers, ports, terminals, brokers, consolidators, etc.) the highway carrier must have documentation (e.g., C-TPAT certificate, SVI number, etc.) indicating whether these business partners are or are not C-TPAT certified. Non-C-TPAT business partners may be subject to additional scrutiny by the highway carrier.
- Highway carriers should ensure that contract service providers commit to C-TPAT security recommendations through contractual agreements. For U.S. bound shipments, C-TPAT highway carriers that subcontract transportation services to other highway carriers, must use other C-TPAT approved highway carriers or carriers under direct control of the certified C-TPAT carrier through a written contract.
- Likewise, current or prospective business partners who have obtained a certification in a supply chain security program being administered by a foreign Customs Administration should be required to indicate their status of participation to the highway carrier.
- As highway carriers have the ultimate responsibility for all cargo loaded aboard their trailer or conveyance, they must communicate the importance of supply chain security and maintaining chain of custody as fundamental aspects of any company security policy.

### Conveyance Security

Conveyance (tractor and trailer) integrity procedures must be maintained to protect against the introduction of unauthorized personnel and material.

#### Conveyance Inspection Procedures

- Using a checklist, drivers should be trained to inspect their conveyances for natural or hidden compartments. Training in conveyance searches should be adopted as part of the company's on-the-job training program.
- Conveyance inspections must be systematic and should be completed upon entering and departing from the truck yard and at the last point of loading prior to reaching the U.S. border.
- To counter internal conspiracies, supervisory personnel or a security manager, held accountable to senior management for security, should search the conveyance after the driver has conducted a search. These searches should be random, documented, based on risk, and should be conducted at the truck yard and after the truck has been loaded and en route to the U.S. border.
- Written procedures must exist which identify specific factors or practices, which may deem a shipment from a certain shipper of greater risk.
- The following systematic practices should be considered when conducting training on conveyances. Highway carriers must visually inspect all empty trailers, to include the interior of the trailer, at the truck yard and at the point of loading, if possible. The following inspection process is recommended for all trailers and tractors:

  **Tractors:**
  - Bumper/tires/rims
  - Doors/tool compartments
  - Battery box
  - Air breather
  - Fuel tanks
  - Interior cab compartments/sleeper
  - Faring/roof

  **Trailers:**
  - Fifth wheel area - check natural compartment/skid plate
  - Exterior - front/sides
  - Rear - bumper/doors

---

1. C-TPAT requirements are evolving. For the latest information refer to the CBP Web site at: www.cbp.gov.
2. These security criteria for highway carriers became effective March 13, 2006 and were current as of September 2006.
3. Truck Carriers shall have a documented and verifiable process for determining risk throughout their supply chains based on their business model (i.e., volume, country of origin, routing, C-TPAT membership, potential terrorist threat via open source information, having inadequate security, past security incidents, etc.).

- Front wall
- Left side
- Right side
- Floor
- Ceiling/Roof
- Inside/outside doors
- Outside/Undercarriage

### Trailer Security

- For all trailers in the highway carrier's custody, trailer integrity must be maintained, to protect against the introduction of unauthorized material and/or persons. Highway carriers must have procedures in place to maintain the integrity of their trailers at all times.
- It is recognized that even though a carrier may not "exercise control" over the loading of trailers and the contents of the cargo, highway carriers must be vigilant to help ensure that the merchandise is legitimate and that there is no loading of contraband at the loading dock/ manufacturing facility. The highway carrier must ensure that while in transit to the border, no loading of contraband has occurred, even in regards to unforeseen vehicle stops.[1]
- Trailers must be stored in a secure area to prevent unauthorized access and/or manipulation. Procedures must be in place for reporting and neutralizing unauthorized entry into trailers, tractors or storage areas.
- The carrier must notify U.S. Customs and Border Protection of any structural changes, such as a hidden compartment, discovered in trailers, tractors or other rolling-stock equipment that crosses the border. Notification should be made immediately to CBP, and in advance of the conveyance crossing the border. Notifications can be telephonically made to CBP's Anti-Terrorism Contraband Enforcement Team (A-TCET) at the port.

### Container Security

- When transporting a container or trailer for a C-TPAT importer, a high security seal that meets or exceed the current PAS ISO 17712 standards for high security seals must be utilized.

### Conveyance Tracking and Monitoring Procedures

- Highway Carriers must ensure that conveyance and trailer integrity is maintained while the conveyance is en route transporting cargo to the U.S. border by utilizing a tracking and monitoring activity log or equivalent technology. If driver logs are utilized, they must reflect that trailer integrity was verified.
- Predetermined routes should be identified, and procedures should consist of random route checks along with documenting and verifying the length of time between the loading point/trailer pickup, the U.S. border, and the delivery destinations, during peak and non-peak times. Drivers should notify the dispatcher of any route delays due to weather, traffic and/or rerouting.
- Highway Carrier management must perform a documented, periodic, and unannounced verification process to ensure the logs are maintained and conveyance tracking and monitoring procedures are being followed and enforced.
- During Department of Transportation Inspections (DOT) or other physical inspections on the conveyance as required by state, local or federal law, drivers must report and document any anomalies or unusual structural modifications found on the conveyance. In addition,

Highway Carrier management should perform a documented, periodic, and unannounced verification process to ensure the logs are maintained and conveyance tracking and monitoring procedures are being followed and enforced.

### Trailer Seals

- The sealing of trailers, to include continuous seal integrity, are a crucial element of a secure supply chain, and remains a critical part of a carrier's commitment to C-TPAT. A high security seal must be affixed to all loaded trailers bound for the U.S. All seals must meet or exceed the current PAS ISO 17712 standards for high security seals.
- Based on risk, a high security barrier bolt seal may be applied to the door handle and/or a cable seal must be applied to the two vertical bars on the trailer doors.
- Clearly defined written procedures must stipulate how seals in the highway carrier's possession are to be controlled during transit. These written procedures should be briefed to all drivers and there should be a mechanism to ensure that these procedures are understood and are being followed. These procedures must include:
  - Verifying that the seal is intact, and if it exhibits evidence of tampering along the route.
  - Properly documenting the original and second seal numbers.
  - Verifying that the seal number and location of the seal is the same as stated by the shipper on the shipping documents.
  - If the seal is removed in-transit to the border, even by government officials, a second seal must be placed on the trailer, and the seal change must be documented.
  - The driver must immediately notify the dispatcher that the seal was broken, by whom; and the number of the second seal that is placed on the trailer.
  - The carrier must make immediate notification to the shipper, the customs broker and/or the importer of the placement of the second seal.

## Less-than Truck Load (LTL)

- LTL carriers must use a high security padlock or similarly appropriate locking device when picking up local freight in an international LTL environment. LTL carriers must ensure strict controls to limit the access to keys or combinations that can open these padlocks.
- After the freight from the pickup and delivery run is sorted, consolidated and loaded onto a line haul carrier destined to the cross the border into the U.S., the trailer must be sealed with a high security seal which meets or exceeds the current PAS ISO 17712 standard for high security seals.
- In LTL or Pickup and Delivery (P&D) operations that do not use consolidation hubs to sort or consolidate freight prior to crossing the U.S. border, the importer and/or highway carrier must use ISO 17712 high security seals for the trailer at each stop, and to cross the border.
- Written procedures must be established to record the change in seals, as well as stipulate how the seals are controlled and distributed, and how discrepancies are noted and reported. These written procedures should be maintained at the terminal/local level.
- In the LTL and non-LTL environment, procedures should also exist for recognizing and reporting compromised

---

1. C-TPAT recognizes the unique situation of the cross-border cartage industry in the Laredo, Texas corridor and encourages and endorses carriers to work within the supply chain to make a reasonable effort to ensure the integrity of trailers, especially during the cross-border segment.

seals and/or trailers to U.S. Customs and Border Protection or the appropriate foreign authority.

## Physical Access Controls

Access controls prevent unauthorized entry to trucks, trailers and facilities, maintain control of employees and visitors, and protect company assets. Access controls must include the positive identification of all employees, visitors, service providers, and vendors at all points of entry. Employees and service providers should only have access to those areas of a facility where they have legitimate business.

### Employees

An employee identification system must be in place for positive identification and access control purposes. Employees should only be given access to those secure areas needed for the performance of their duties. Company management or security personnel must adequately control the issuance and removal of employee, visitor and vendor identification badges. Procedures for the issuance, removal and changing of access devices (e.g. keys, key cards, etc.) must be documented.

### Visitors/Vendors/Service Providers

Visitors, vendors, and service providers must present photo identification for documentation purposes upon arrival, and a log must be maintained. All visitors and service providers should visibly display temporary identification.

### Challenging and Removing Unauthorized Persons

Procedures must be in place to identify, challenge and address unauthorized/unidentified persons.

## Personnel Security

Written and verifiable processes must be in place to screen prospective employees and to periodically check current employees.

### Pre-Employment Verification

Application information, such as employment history and references must be verified prior to employment.

### Background Checks/Investigations

Consistent with foreign, federal, state, and local regulations, background checks and investigations should be conducted for prospective employees. Once employed, periodic checks and reinvestigations should be performed based on cause, and/or the sensitivity of the employee's position.

### Personnel Termination Procedures

Companies must have procedures in place to remove identification, facility, and system access for terminated employees.

## Procedural Security

Security measures must be in place to ensure the integrity and security of processes relevant to the transportation, handling, and storage of cargo in the supply chain. Procedures must be in place to prevent, detect, or deter unmanifested material and unauthorized personnel from gaining access to the conveyance including concealment in trailers.

Security procedures should be implemented that restrict access to the conveyance and prevent the lading of contraband while en-route from facilities in international locations to the United States.

Procedures must be in place to record and immediately report all anomalies regarding truck drivers to U.S. Customs and Border Protection. If local, federal, or state laws and union rules permit, conducting random screening of truck driver luggage and personal effects should occur.

### Documentation Processing

Procedures must be in place to ensure that all information used in the clearance of merchandise/cargo, is legible, complete, accurate, and protected against the exchange, loss or introduction of erroneous information. Measures, such as using a locked filing cabinet, should also be taken to secure the storage of unused forms, including manifests, to prevent unauthorized use of such documentation

### Document Review

Personnel should be trained to review manifests and other documents in order to identify or recognize suspicious cargo shipments that:

- Originate from or are destined to unusual locations
- Paid by cash or a certified check
- Have unusual routing methods
- Exhibit unusual shipping/receiving practices
- Provide vague, generalized or poor information

All instances of a suspicious cargo shipment should be reported immediately to the nearest U.S. Customs and Border Protection port-of-entry.

### Bill of Lading/Manifesting Procedures

Bill of lading information filed with CBP should show the first foreign location/facility where the highway carrier takes possession of the cargo destined for the United States. Additionally, to help ensure the integrity of cargo received from abroad, procedures must be in place to ensure that information received from business partners is reported accurately and timely.

### Cargo

Cargo must be properly marked and manifested to include accurate weight and piece count. Customs and/or other appropriate law enforcement agencies must be notified if illegal or suspicious activities are detected - as appropriate.

## Physical Security

Procedures must be in place to prevent, detect, or deter unmanifested material and unauthorized personnel from gaining access to conveyance, including concealment in trailers. Cargo handling and storage facilities, trailer yards, etc., must have physical barriers and deterrents that guard against unauthorized access. Highway carriers should incorporate the following C-TPAT physical security criteria throughout their supply chains as applicable.

### Fencing

Perimeter fencing should enclose the entire truck yard or terminal, especially areas where tractors, trailers and other rolling stock are parked or stored. All fencing must be regularly inspected for integrity and damage.

### Gates and Gate Houses

Gates through which all vehicles and/or personnel enter or exit must be manned and/or monitored. The number of gates should be kept to the minimum necessary for proper access and safety.

### Parking

Private passenger vehicles must be prohibited from parking in close proximity to parking and storage areas for tractors, trailers and other rolling stock that cross the international border.

### Building Structure

Buildings must be constructed of materials that resist unlawful entry. The integrity of structures must be maintained by periodic inspection and repair.

### Locking Devices and Key Controls

All external and internal windows, gates and fences must be secured with locking devices. Management or security personnel must control the issuance of all locks and keys, to include the locks and keys for tractors. When parked in the yard, doors to tractors should be locked and the windows should be closed to prevent unauthorized access.

### *Lighting*

Adequate lighting must be provided inside and outside the facility including the following areas: entrances and exits, parking or storage areas for tractors, trailers, rolling stock, and fences.

### *Alarm Systems & Video Surveillance Cameras*

Alarm systems and video surveillance cameras should be utilized to monitor premises and prevent unauthorized access to vessels, cargo handling and storage areas, based on risk.

## Security Training and Threat Awareness

A threat awareness program should be established and maintained by security personnel to recognize and foster awareness of the threat posed by drug smugglers and terrorists at each point in the supply chain. Employees must be made aware of the procedures the highway carrier has in place to address a situation and how to report it.

Additionally, specific training should be offered to assist employees in maintaining trailer and tractor integrity, recognizing internal conspiracies, and protecting access controls. These programs should offer incentives for active employee participation.

## Information & Technology Security

### *Password Protection*

Measures should be taken to protect electronic assets, including advising employees of the need to protect passwords and computer access. Automated systems must use individually assigned accounts that require a periodic change of password. IT security policies, procedures and standards must be in place and provided to employees in the form of training.

### *Accountability*

A system must be in place to identify the abuse of IT including improper access, tampering or the altering of business data. All system violators must be subject to appropriate disciplinary actions for abuse.

### *FAST Transponder Controls*

Transponders or any technology provided to the highway carrier by U.S. Customs and Border Protection to utilize the Free and Secure Trade (FAST) program must be protected against misuse, compromise, theft, tampering, altering or duplication.[1]

C-TPAT highway carriers must have documented procedures in place to manage the ordering, issuance, activation, and deactivation of FAST transponders. C-TPAT highway carriers are prohibited from requesting FAST transponders for any highway carrier company that is not owned and controlled by the C-TPAT approved highway carrier.

C-TPAT highway carriers are also prohibited from requesting FAST transponders for any owner-operator not under written contract to provide exclusive transportation services for the C-TPAT highway carrier.

# Highway Carrier General Items

## FAQs

For a list of seven Frequently Asked Questions and Answers Regarding Minimum Security Criteria for Highway Carriers" refer to: http://www.cbp.gov/xp/cgov/import/ commercial_enforcement/ctpat/security_criteria/ hwy_carrier_criteria/hwy_security_faq.xml.

## C-TPAT Application

Instructions for submitting an online C-TPAT application are at: www.cbp.gov/xp/cgov/import/commercial_enforcement/ctpat/ online_app/. Select "Instructions for Completing the C-TPAT Online Application."

The C-TPAT Online Application itself can be found at: https://ctpat.cbp.dhs.gov/CompanyProfile.aspx

## Agreement to Voluntarily Participate

The Highway Carrier Agreement to Voluntarily Participate is similar to the "Importer - C-TPAT Agreement to Voluntarily Participate" on page 593. The Highway Carrier Agreement can be found as part of the C-TPAT Online Application at: https://ctpat.cbp.dhs.gov/CompanyProfile.aspx

## For More Information

For more information about C-TPAT go to: www.cbp.gov. Search for "C-TPAT for Highway Carriers."

---

1.  Any misuse of FAST technology, to include loaning FAST transponders to external carriers will result in suspension or removal from the FAST Program. FAST is a benefit based on trust and confidence.

# C-TPAT for Foreign Manufacturers[1]

## C-TPAT Security Criteria for Foreign Manufacturers[2]

These minimum security criteria are fundamentally designed to be the building blocks for foreign manufacturers to institute effective security practices designed to optimize supply chain performance to mitigate the risk of loss, theft, and contraband smuggling that could potentially introduce terrorists and implements of terrorism into the global supply chain. The determination and scope of criminal elements targeting world commerce through internal conspiracies requires companies, and in particular, foreign manufacturers to elevate their security practices.

At a minimum, on a yearly basis, or as circumstances dictate such as during periods of heightened alert, security breach or incident, foreign manufacturers must conduct a comprehensive assessment of their international supply chains based upon the following C-TPAT security criteria. Where a foreign manufacturer out-sources or contracts elements of their supply chain, such as another foreign facility, warehouse, or other elements, the foreign manufacturer must work with these business partners to ensure that pertinent security measures are in place and are adhered to throughout their supply chain. The supply chain for C-TPAT purposes is defined from point of origin (manufacturer/supplier/vendor) through to point of distribution – and recognizes the diverse business models C-TPAT members employ.

C-TPAT recognizes the complexity of international supply chains and security practices, and endorses the application and implementation of security measures based upon risk.[3] Therefore, the program allows for flexibility and the customization of security plans based on the member's business model.

Appropriate security measures, as listed throughout this document, must be implemented and maintained throughout the Foreign manufacturer's supply chains - based on risk.[4]

### Business Partner Requirements

Foreign manufacturers must have written and verifiable processes for the selection of business partners including carriers, other manufacturers, product suppliers and vendors (parts and raw material suppliers, etc.).

#### Security procedures

For those business partners eligible for C-TPAT certification (carriers, importers, ports, terminals, brokers, consolidators, etc.) the foreign manufacturer must have documentation (e.g., C-TPAT certificate, SVI number, etc.) indicating whether these business partners are or are not C-TPAT certified.

For those business partners not eligible for C-TPAT certification, the foreign manufacturer must require that their business partners demonstrate that they are meeting C-TPAT security criteria via written/electronic confirmation (e.g., contractual obligations; via a letter from a senior business partner officer attesting to compliance; a written statement from the business partner demonstrating their compliance with C-TPAT security criteria or an equivalent World Customs Organization (WCO) accredited security program administered by a foreign customs authority; or, by providing a completed foreign manufacturer security questionnaire). Based upon a documented risk assessment process, non-C-TPAT eligible business partners must be subject to verification of compliance with C-TPAT security criteria by the foreign manufacturer.

#### Point of Origin

Foreign manufacturers must ensure that business partners develop security processes and procedures consistent with the C-TPAT security criteria to enhance the integrity of the shipment at point of origin, assembly or manufacturing. Periodic reviews of business partners' processes and facilities should be conducted based on risk, and should maintain the security standards required by the foreign manufacturer.

#### Participation/Certification in a Foreign Customs Administration Supply Chain Security Program

Current or prospective business partners who have obtained a certification in a supply chain security program being administered by foreign Customs Administration should be required to indicate their status of participation to the foreign manufacturer.

#### Security Procedures

On U.S. bound shipments, foreign manufacturers should monitor that C-TPAT carriers that subcontract transportation services to other carriers use other C-TPAT approved carriers, or non-C-TPAT carriers that are meeting the C-TPAT security criteria as outlined in the business partner requirements.

As the foreign manufacturer is responsible for loading trailers and containers, they should work with the carrier to provide reassurance that there are effective security procedures and controls implemented at the point-of-stuffing.

### Container and Trailer Security

Container and trailer integrity must be maintained to protect against the introduction of unauthorized material and/or persons. At the point-of-stuffing, procedures must be in place to properly seal and maintain the integrity of the shipping containers and trailers. A high security seal must be affixed to all loaded containers and trailers bound for the U.S. All seals must meet or exceed the current PAS ISO 17712 standard for high security seals.

In those geographic areas where risk assessments warrant checking containers or trailers for human concealment or smuggling, such procedures should be designed to address this risk at the manufacturing facility or point-of-stuffing.

#### Container Inspection

Procedures must be in place to verify the physical integrity of the container structure prior to stuffing, to include the reliability of the locking mechanisms of the doors. A seven-point inspection process is recommended for all containers:
- Front wall
- Left side

---

1. C-TPAT requirements are evolving. For the latest information refer to the CBP Web site at: www.cbp.gov.
2. These security criteria for foreign manufacturers become effective August 29, 2006 and were current as of September 2006.
3. Foreign manufacturers shall have a documented and verifiable process for determining risk throughout their supply chains based on their business model (i.e., volume, country of origin, routing, C-TPAT membership, potential terrorist threat via open source information, having inadequate security, past security incidents, etc.).
4. Foreign manufacturer shall have a documented and verifiable process for determining risk throughout their supply chains based on their business model (i.e., volume, country of origin, routing, potential terrorist threat via open source information, etc.).

- Right side
- Floor
- Ceiling/Roof
- Inside/outside doors
- Outside/Undercarriage

### Trailer Inspection

Procedures must be in place to verify the physical integrity of the trailer structure prior to stuffing, to include the reliability of the locking mechanisms of the doors. The following five-point inspection process is recommended for all trailers:

- Fifth wheel area - check natural compartment/skid plate
- Exterior - front/sides
- Rear - bumper/doors
- Front wall
- Left side

### Container and Trailer Seals

The sealing of trailers and containers, to include continuous seal integrity, are crucial elements of a secure supply chain, and remains a critical part of a foreign manufacturers' commitment to C-TPAT. The foreign manufacturer must affix a high security seal to all loaded trailers and containers bound for the U.S. All seals must meet or exceed the current PAS ISO 17712 standards for high security seals.

Written procedures must stipulate how seals are to be controlled and affixed to loaded containers and trailers, to include procedures for recognizing and reporting compromised seals and/or containers/trailers to US Customs and Border Protection or the appropriate foreign authority. Only designated employees should distribute seals for integrity purposes.

### Container and Trailer Storage

Containers and trailers under foreign manufacturer control or located in a facility of the foreign manufacturer must be stored in a secure area to prevent unauthorized access and/or manipulation. Procedures must be in place for reporting and neutralizing unauthorized entry into containers/trailers or container/trailer storage areas.

## Physical Access Controls

Access controls prevent unauthorized entry to facilities, maintain control of employees and visitors, and protect company assets. Access controls must include the positive identification of all employees, visitors, and vendors at all points of entry.

### Employees

An employee identification system must be in place for positive identification and access control purposes. Employees should only be given access to those secure areas needed for the performance of their duties. Company management or security personnel must adequately control the issuance and removal of employee, visitor and vendor identification badges. Procedures for the issuance, removal and changing of access devices (e.g. keys, key cards, etc.) must be documented.

### Visitors

Visitors must present photo identification for documentation purposes upon arrival. All visitors should be escorted and should visibly display temporary identification.

### Deliveries (including mail)

Proper vendor ID and/or photo identification must be presented for documentation purposes upon arrival by all vendors. Arriving packages and mail should be periodically screened before being disseminated.

### Challenging and Removing Unauthorized Persons

Procedures must be in place to identify, challenge and address unauthorized/unidentified persons.

## Personnel Security

Processes must be in place to screen prospective employees and to periodically check current employees.

### Pre-Employment Verification

Application information, such as employment history and references must be verified prior to employment.

### Background Checks / Investigations

Consistent with foreign regulations, background checks and investigations should be conducted for prospective employees. Once employed, periodic checks and reinvestigations should be performed based on cause, and/or the sensitivity of the employee's position.

### Personnel Termination Procedures

Companies must have procedures in place to remove identification, facility, and system access for terminated employees.

## Procedural Security

Security measures must be in place to ensure the integrity and security of processes relevant to the transportation, handling, and storage of cargo in the supply chain.

### Documentation Processing

Procedures must be in place to ensure that all information used in the clearing of merchandise/cargo, is legible, complete, accurate, and protected against the exchange, loss or introduction of erroneous information. Documentation control must include safeguarding computer access and information.

### Manifesting Procedures

To help ensure the integrity of cargo, procedures must be in place to ensure that information received from business partners is reported accurately and timely.

### Shipping and Receiving

Departing cargo being shipped should be reconciled against information on the cargo manifest. The cargo should be accurately described, and the weights, labels, marks and piece count indicated and verified. Departing cargo should be verified against purchase or delivery orders. Drivers delivering or receiving cargo must be positively identified before cargo is received or released. Procedures should also be established to track the timely movement of incoming and outgoing goods.

### Cargo Discrepancies

All shortages, overages, and other significant discrepancies or anomalies must be resolved and/or investigated appropriately. Customs and/or other appropriate law enforcement agencies must be notified if anomalies, illegal or suspicious activities are detected - as appropriate.

## Physical Security

Cargo handling and storage facilities in international locations must have physical barriers and deterrents that guard against unauthorized access. Foreign manufacturer should incorporate the following C-TPAT physical security criteria throughout their supply chains as applicable.

### Fencing

Perimeter fencing should enclose the areas around cargo handling and storage facilities. Interior fencing within a cargo handling structure should be used to segregate domestic, international, high value, and hazardous cargo. All fencing must be regularly inspected for integrity and damage.

### Gates and Gate Houses

Gates through which vehicles and/or personnel enter or exit must be manned and/or monitored. The number of gates should be kept to the minimum necessary for proper access and safety.

### Parking

Private passenger vehicles should be prohibited from parking in or adjacent to cargo handling and storage areas.

**SECURITY**

**SECURITY**

### Building Structure
Buildings must be constructed of materials that resist unlawful entry. The integrity of structures must be maintained by periodic inspection and repair.

### Locking Devices and Key Controls
All external and internal windows, gates and fences must be secured with locking devices. Management or security personnel must control the issuance of all locks and keys.

### Lighting
Adequate lighting must be provided inside and outside the facility including the following areas: entrances and exits, cargo handling and storage areas, fence lines and parking areas.

### Alarms Systems and Video Surveillance Cameras
Alarm systems and video surveillance cameras should be utilized to monitor premises and prevent unauthorized access to cargo handling and storage areas.

## Information Technology Security

### Password Protection
Automated systems must use individually assigned accounts that require a periodic change of password. IT security policies, procedures and standards must be in place and provided to employees in the form of training.

### Accountability
A system must be in place to identify the abuse of IT including improper access, tampering or the altering of business data. All system violators must be subject to appropriate disciplinary actions for abuse.

## Security Training and Threat Awareness
A threat awareness program should be established and maintained by security personnel to recognize and foster awareness of the threat posed by terrorists and contraband smugglers at each point in the supply chain. Employees must be made aware of the procedures the company has in place to address a situation and how to report it. Additional training should be provided to employees in the shipping and receiving areas, as well as those receiving and opening mail. Additionally, specific training should be offered to assist employees in maintaining cargo integrity, recognizing internal conspiracies, and protecting access controls. These programs should offer incentives for active employee participation.

# Foreign Manufacturers General Items

## C-TPAT Application
Instructions for submitting an online C-TPAT application are at: www.cbp.gov/xp/cgov/import/commercial_enforcement/ctpat/online_app/. Select "Instructions for Completing the C-TPAT Online Application."
The C-TPAT Online Application itself can be found at: https://ctpat.cbp.dhs.gov/CompanyProfile.aspx

## Agreement to Voluntarily Participate
The Foreign Manufacturer Agreement to Voluntarily Participate is similar to the "Importer - C-TPAT Agreement to Voluntarily Participate" on page 593. The Sea Carrier Agreement can be found as part of the C-TPAT Online Application at:
https://ctpat.cbp.dhs.gov/CompanyProfile.aspx

## For More Information
For more information about C-TPAT go to: www.cbp.gov. Search for "C-TPAT for Foreign Manufacturers."

# C-TPAT for Air Carriers[1]

## C-TPAT Security Guidelines for Air Carriers[2]

### C-TPAT Qualifications for Air Carriers

1. Active Air Carrier transporting cargo shipments to the U.S.
2. Have an active Airline Code registered with CBP.
3. Possess a valid continuous international carrier bond registered with CBP.
4. Have a designated company officer that will be the primary cargo security officer responsible for C-TPAT.
5. Commit to maintaining C-TPAT Security Guidelines for Air Carriers.
6. Create and provide CBP with a C-TPAT supply chain security profile, which identifies how the Air Carrier will meet, maintain and enhance internal policy to meet the C-TPAT Security Guidelines for Air Carriers.

### C-TPAT Security Guidelines for Air Carriers

Air Carriers must conduct a comprehensive assessment of their international supply chains based upon the following C-TPAT security guidelines. Where an Air Carrier outsources or contracts elements of their supply chain, such as a conveyance, foreign facility, domestic warehouse, or other elements, the Air Carrier must work with these business partners to ensure that pertinent security measures are in place and adhered to throughout their supply chain. The supply chain for C-TPAT purposes is defined from point of origin (manufacturer/supplier/vendor) through to point of distribution and recognizes the diverse business models C-TPAT members employ.

C-TPAT recognizes the complexity of international supply chains and endorses the application and implementation of security measures based upon risk analysis. Therefore, the program allows for flexibility and the customization of security plans based on the member's business model.

As listed throughout this document appropriate security measures, based on risk, must be implemented and maintained throughout the Air Carrier's supply chains.

### Conveyance Security

Aircraft integrity must be maintained to protect against the introduction of unauthorized personnel and material. Conveyance security procedures must include the physical search of all readily accessible areas, securing all internal/external compartments and panels and reporting cases in which unmanifested materials or signs of tampering are discovered.

### Business Partner Requirements

Air Carriers must have written and verifiable processes for the screening and selection of business partners including customers, contractors, and vendors. Ensure that contracted service provider companies who provide security, transportation, and cargo handling services commit to C-TPAT Security Guidelines. Periodically review the performance of the service providers to detect weakness or potential weaknesses in security.

### C-TPAT Business Partners

For those business partners eligible for C-TPAT certification (cross border carriers, U.S. ports, terminals, importers, brokers, consolidators, etc.) the C-TPAT Air Carrier must have documentation (e.g., C-TPAT certificate, SVI number, etc.) indicating the business partners are C-TPAT certified.

### Business Partners Not Eligible for C-TPAT

For those business partners not eligible for C-TPAT certification, C-TPAT Air Carriers must require their business partners to demonstrate that they are meeting C-TPAT security guidelines via written/electronic confirmation (e.g., contractual obligations; via a letter from a senior business partner officer attesting to compliance; or a written statement demonstrating their compliance with C-TPAT security guidelines or an equivalent World Customs Organization (WCO) accredited security program administered by a foreign customs authority; or, by providing a completed security questionnaire). Based upon a documented risk assessment process, non-C-TPAT eligible business partners must be subject to verification of compliance with C-TPAT security guidelines by the C-TPAT Air Carrier.

## Security Procedures

### Point of Origin

C-TPAT Air Carriers must ensure business partners develop security processes and procedures consistent with the C-TPAT security guidelines to enhance the integrity of the shipment at point of origin. Periodic reviews of business partners' processes and facilities should be conducted based on risk and should maintain the security standards required by the U.S./Mexico Air Carrier.

### Participation/Certification in Foreign Customs Administrations Supply Chain Security Programs

Current or prospective business partners who have obtained a certification in a supply chain security program being administered by foreign Customs Administration should be required to indicate their status of participation to the C-TPAT Air Carrier.

### Service Provider Screening and Selection Procedures

The C-TPAT Air carrier should have documented service provider screening and selection procedures to screen the contracted service provider for validity, financial soundness, ability to meet contractual security requirements, and the ability to identify and correct security deficiencies as needed. Service Provider procedures should utilize a risk-based process as determined by an internal management team.

### Customer Screening Procedures

The C-TPAT Air Carrier should have documented procedures to screen prospective customers for validity, financial soundness, the ability to meet contractual security requirements, and the ability to identify and correct security deficiencies as needed. Customer screening procedures should utilize a risk-based process as determined by an internal management team.

## Container Security

Cargo container integrity must be maintained to protect against the introduction of unauthorized material and/or persons. At point of stuffing, procedures must be in place to verify cargo containers are properly secured.

### Container Inspection

Procedures must be in place to verify the physical integrity of the cargo containers prior to stuffing. An inspection process is recommended for all containers:

---

1. C-TPAT requirements are evolving. For the latest information refer to the CBP Web site at: www.cbp.gov.
2. These security guidelines for Air Carriers became effective April 24, 2006 and were current as of September 2006.

- Top
- Bottom
- Inside
- Outside

## Physical Access Controls

Access controls prevent unauthorized entry to facilities, maintain control of employees and visitors, and protect company assets. Access controls must include the positive identification of all employees, visitors and vendors at all points of entry.

### Employees

An employee identification system must be in place for positive identification and access control to its aircraft, both abroad and in the United States. Employees should only be given access to those secure areas needed for the performance of their duties. Company management or security personnel must adequately control the issuance and removal of employee, visitor and vendor identification badges. Procedures for the issuance, removal and changing of access devices (e.g. keys, key cards, etc.) must be documented.

### Visitors Controls

Visitors must present photo identification for documentation purposes upon arrival. All visitors should be escorted and visibly display temporary identification.

### Deliveries (including mail)

Proper vendor ID and/or photo identification must be presented for documentation purposes upon arrival by all vendors. Arriving packages and mail should be periodically screened before being disseminated.

### Challenging and Removing Unauthorized Persons

Procedures must be in place to identify, challenge and address unauthorized/unidentified persons.

## Personnel Security

Processes must be in place to screen prospective employees and to periodically check current employees. Maintain a current permanent employee list (foreign and domestic), which includes the name, date of birth, national identification number or social security number, position held and submit such information to CBP upon written request, to the extent permitted by law.

### Pre-Employment Verification

Application information, such as employment history and references must be verified prior to employment.

### Background Checks / Investigations

Consistent with foreign, federal, state and local regulations, background checks and investigations should be conducted for prospective employees. Periodic checks and reinvestigations should be performed based on cause and/or the sensitivity of the employee's position.

### Personnel Termination Procedures

Companies must have procedures in place to remove identification; facility and system access for terminated employees.

## Procedural Security

Security measures must be in place to ensure the integrity and security of processes relevant to the transportation, handling and storage of cargo in the supply chain. Implement a Positive Baggage Identification Match (PBIM) program. The Carrier's SOP will describe in detail a plan to ensure that all checked baggage has an accompanying passenger checked in and boarded onto the aircraft. Maintain constant control of all baggage from the check-in point to the aircraft and from the aircraft to the CBP baggage examination area.

### Documentation Processing

Procedures must be in place to ensure that all documentation used in the clearing of merchandise/cargo is legible, complete, accurate and protected against the exchange, loss or introduction of erroneous information. Documentation control must include safeguarding computer access and information.

### Manifesting Procedures

To help ensure the integrity of cargo received from abroad, procedures must be in place to ensure that information received from business partners is reported accurately and timely. Ensure that all air waybills and other documentation submitted for cargo is complete and a system in place to verify the accuracy of the weight, marks and quantity of the cargo received for shipment. Participate in the Advanced Passenger Information System (APIS) and the air Automated Manifest System (AMS).

### Shipping & Receiving

Arriving cargo should be reconciled against information on the cargo manifest. The cargo should be accurately described, weighed, labeled, marked, counted and verified. Departing cargo should be checked against purchase or delivery orders. Drivers delivering or receiving cargo must be positively identified before cargo is received or released.

### Cargo Discrepancies

All shortages, overages and other significant discrepancies or anomalies must be resolved and/or investigated appropriately. CBP and/or other appropriate law enforcement agencies must be notified if illegal or suspicious activities are detected.

## Security Training and Threat Awareness

A threat awareness program should be established and maintained by security personnel to recognize and foster awareness of the threat posed by terrorists at each point in the supply chain. Employees must be made aware of the procedures the company has in place to address a situation and how to report it. Additional training should be provided to employees in the shipping and receiving areas, as well as those receiving and opening mail.

Additionally, specific training should be offered to assist employees in maintaining cargo integrity, recognizing internal conspiracies and protecting access controls. These programs should offer incentives for active employee participation. Conduct periodic unannounced security checks to ensure that all procedures are being performed in accordance with defined guidelines.

## Physical Security

Cargo handling and storage facilities in domestic and foreign locations must have physical barriers and deterrents that guard against unauthorized access. Air Carriers should incorporate the following C-TPAT physical security guidelines throughout their supply chains as applicable.

### Fencing

Perimeter fencing should enclose the areas around cargo handling and storage facilities. Interior fencing within a cargo handling structure should be used to segregate domestic, international, high value and hazardous cargo. All fencing must be regularly inspected for integrity and damage.

### Gates and Gate Houses

Gates through which vehicles and/or personnel enter or exit must be manned and/or monitored. The number of gates should be kept to the minimum necessary for proper access and safety.

### Parking

Private passenger vehicles should be prohibited from parking in or adjacent to cargo handling and storage areas.

### Building Structure
Buildings must be constructed of materials that resist unlawful entry. The integrity of structures must be maintained by periodic inspection and repair.

### Locking Devices and Key Controls
All external and internal windows, gates and fences must be secured with locking devices. Management or security personnel must control the issuance of all locks and keys.

### Lighting
Adequate lighting must be provided inside and outside the facility including the following areas: entrances and exits, cargo handling and storage areas, fence lines and parking areas.

### Alarms Systems & Video Surveillance Cameras
Alarm systems and video surveillance cameras should be utilized to monitor premises and prevent unauthorized access to cargo handling and storage areas.

## Information Technology Security
Information Technology (IT) integrity must be maintained to protect data from unauthorized access or manipulation.

### Password Protection
Automated systems must use individually assigned accounts that require a periodic change of password. IT security policies, procedures and standards must be in place and provided to employees in the form of training.

### Accountability
A system must be in place to identify the abuse of IT including improper access, tampering or the altering of business data. All system violators must be subject to appropriate disciplinary actions for abuse.

# Air Carrier General Items

## C-TPAT Application
Instructions for submitting an online C-TPAT application are at: www.cbp.gov/xp/cgov/import/commercial_enforcement/ctpat/online_app/. Select "Instructions for Completing the C-TPAT Online Application."
The C-TPAT Online Application itself can be found at: https://ctpat.cbp.dhs.gov/CompanyProfile.aspx

## Agreement to Voluntarily Participate
The Air Carrier Agreement to Voluntarily Participate is similar to the "Importer - C-TPAT Agreement to Voluntarily Participate" on page 593. The Highway Carrier Agreement can be found as part of the C-TPAT Online Application at: https://ctpat.cbp.dhs.gov/CompanyProfile.aspx

## For More Information
For more information about C-TPAT go to: www.cbp.gov. Search for "C-TPAT for Air Carriers."

SECURITY

# C-TPAT for Air Freight Consolidators[1]

## Ocean Transportation Intermediaries and NVOCCs

## C-TPAT Security Guidelines for Air Freigh Consolidators, Ocean Transport Intermediaries and Non_vessel Operating Common Carriers (NVOCC)[2]

**SECURITY**

### C-TPAT Qualifications for Air Freight Consolidators, Ocean Transportation Intermediaries and Non-Vessel Operating Common Carriers (NVOCC)

1. Be an active Air Freight Consolidator, Ocean Transportation Intermediary or Non-Vessel Operating Common Carrier (NVOCC).
2. Have a business office staffed in the U.S.
3. If applicable, have an active Federal Maritime Commission (FMC) issued Organization Number or an International Air Transport Association (IATA) issued Organization Number in the following format.
   • ###### FMC Organization Number
   • ###### IATA Organization Number
4. Possess a valid continuous international carrier bond and/or in bond/export consolidator bond (IBEC) registered with CBP.
5. Have a designated company officer that will be the primary cargo security officer responsible for C-TPAT.
6. Commit to maintaining C-TPAT supply chain security guidelines as outlined in the C-TPAT consolidator agreement.
7. Create and provide CBP with a C-TPAT supply chain security profile, which identifies how the consolidator will meet, maintain and enhance internal policy to meet the C-TPAT consolidator security guidelines.

### C-TPAT Security Guidelines for Consolidators

Consolidators must conduct a comprehensive assessment of their international supply chains based upon the following C-TPAT security guidelines. Where a consolidator out sources or contracts elements of their supply chain, such as a foreign facility, conveyance, domestic warehouse, or other elements, the consolidator must work with these business partners to ensure that pertinent security measures are in place and adhered to throughout their supply chain. The supply chain for C-TPAT purposes is defined from point of origin (manufacturer/supplier/vendor) through to point of distribution and recognizes the diverse business models C-TPAT members employ.

C-TPAT recognizes the complexity of international supply chains and endorses the application and implementation of security measures based upon risk analysis. Therefore, the program allows for flexibility and the customization of security plans based on the member's business model.

Appropriate security measures, as listed throughout this document, must be implemented and maintained throughout the consolidator's supply chains.

### Business Partner Requirements

Consolidators must have written and verifiable processes for the screening and selection of business partners including foreign consolidators, customers, contractors, carriers, and vendors. Ensure that contracted service provider companies who provide transportation, cargo handling, and security services commit to C-TPAT Security Guidelines. Periodically review the performance of the service providers to detect weakness or potential weaknesses in security.

## Security Procedures

### Point of Origin

C-TPAT Consolidators must ensure business partners develop security processes and procedures consistent with the C-TPAT security guidelines to enhance the integrity of the shipment at point of origin. Periodic reviews of business partners' processes and facilities should be conducted based on risk and should maintain the security standards required by the Consolidator.

### Participation/Certification in Foreign Customs Administrations Supply Chain Security Programs

Current or prospective business partners who have obtained a certification in a supply chain security program being administered by foreign Customs Administration should be required to indicate their status of participation to the C-TPAT Consolidator.

### Service Provider Screening and Selection Procedures

The C-TPAT Consolidator should have documented service provider screening and selection procedures to screen the contracted service provider for validity, financial soundness, ability to meet contractual security requirements, and the ability to identify and correct security deficiencies as needed. Service Provider procedures should utilize a risk-based process as determined by an internal management team.

### Customer Screening Procedures

The C-TPAT Consolidator should have documented procedures to screen prospective customers for validity, financial soundness, the ability of meeting contractual security requirements, and the ability to identify and correct security deficiencies as needed. Customer screening procedures should utilize a risk-based process as determined by an internal management team.

## Container Security

Consolidators should ensure that all contracted service providers have procedures in place to maintain container integrity. Container integrity must be maintained to protect against the introduction of unauthorized material and/or persons. At point of stuffing, procedures must be in place to properly seal and maintain the integrity of the shipping containers. A high security seal must be affixed to all loaded C-TPAT importer containers bound for the U.S. All seals must meet or exceed the current PAS ISO 17712 standards for high security seals.

---

1. C-TPAT requirements are evolving. For the latest information refer to the CBP Web site at: www.cbp.gov.
2. These security guidelines for Air Freight Consolidators, Ocean Transport Intermediaries and Non-Vessel Operating Common Carriers (NVOCCs) became effective April 24, 2006 and were current as of September 2006.

### Container Inspection

Procedures must be in place to verify the physical integrity of the container structure prior to stuffing, to include the reliability of the locking mechanisms of the doors. A seven-point inspection process is recommended for all containers:

- Front wall
- Left side
- Right side
- Ceiling/Roof
- Inside/Outside doors
- Outside/Undercarriage

### Container Seals

Written procedures must stipulate how seals are to be controlled and affixed to loaded containers. Procedures must be in place for recognizing and reporting compromised seals and/or containers to U.S. Customs and Border Protection or the appropriate foreign authority. Only designated employees should distribute container seals for integrity purposes.

### Container Storage

Containers must be stored in a secure area to prevent unauthorized access and/or manipulation. Procedures must be in place for reporting and neutralizing unauthorized entry into containers or container storage areas.

## Physical Access Controls

Access controls prevent unauthorized entry to facilities, maintain control of employees and visitors and protect company assets. Access controls must include the positive identification of all employees, visitors and vendors at all points of entry.

### Employees

An employee identification system must be in place for positive identification and access control purposes. Employees should only be given access to those secure areas needed for the performance of their duties. Company management or security personnel must adequately control the issuance and removal of employee, visitor and vendor identification badges. Procedures for the issuance, removal and changing of access devices (e.g. keys, key cards, etc.) must be documented.

### Visitors Controls

Visitors must present photo identification for documentation purposes upon arrival. All visitors should be escorted and visibly display temporary identification.

### Deliveries (including mail)

Proper vendor ID and/or photo identification must be presented for documentation purposes upon arrival by all vendors. Arriving packages and mail should be periodically screened before being disseminated.

### Challenging and Removing Unauthorized Persons

Procedures must be in place to identify, challenge and address unauthorized/unidentified persons.

## Personnel Security

Processes must be in place to screen prospective employees and to periodically check current employees. Maintain a current permanent employee list (foreign and domestic), which includes the name, date of birth, national identification number or social security number, position held and submit such information to CBP upon written request, to the extent permitted by law.

### Pre-Employment Verification

Application information, such as employment history and references must be verified prior to employment.

### Background Checks / Investigations

Consistent with foreign, federal, state and local regulations, background checks and investigations should be conducted for prospective employees. Periodic checks and reinvestiga-

tions should be performed based on cause and/or the sensitivity of the employee's position.

### Personnel Termination Procedures

Companies must have procedures in place to remove identification; facility and system access for terminated employees.

## Procedural Security

Security measures must be in place to ensure the integrity and security of processes relevant to the transportation, handling and storage of cargo in the supply chain.

### Documentation Processing

Procedures must be in place to ensure that all documentation used in the movement of merchandise/cargo is legible, complete, accurate and protected against the exchange, loss or introduction of erroneous information. Documentation control must include safeguarding computer access and information.

### Manifesting Procedures

To help ensure the integrity of cargo received from abroad, procedures must be in place to ensure that information received from business partners is reported accurately and timely.

### Shipping & Receiving

Arriving cargo should be reconciled against information on the cargo manifest. The cargo should be accurately described, weighed, labeled, marked, counted and verified. Departing cargo should be checked against purchase or delivery orders. Drivers delivering or receiving cargo must be positively identified before cargo is received or released.

### Cargo Discrepancies

All shortages, overages and other significant discrepancies or anomalies must be resolved and/or investigated appropriately. CBP and/or other appropriate law enforcement agencies must be notified if illegal or suspicious activities are detected.

## Security Training and Threat Awareness

A threat awareness program should be established and maintained by security personnel to recognize and foster awareness of the threat posed by terrorists at each point in the supply chain. Employees must be made aware of the procedures the company has in place to address a situation and how to report it. Additional training should be provided to employees in the shipping and receiving areas, as well as those receiving and opening mail.

Additionally, specific training should be offered to assist employees in maintaining cargo integrity, recognizing internal conspiracies and protecting access controls. These programs should offer incentives for active employee participation.

## Physical Security

Cargo handling and storage facilities in domestic and foreign locations must have physical barriers and deterrents that guard against unauthorized access. Consolidators should incorporate the following C-TPAT physical security guidelines throughout their supply chains as applicable.

### Fencing

Perimeter fencing should enclose the areas around cargo handling and storage facilities. Interior fencing within a cargo handling structure should be used to segregate domestic, international, high value and hazardous cargo. All fencing must be regularly inspected for integrity and damage.

### Gates Gate Houses

Gates through which vehicles and/or personnel enter or exit must be manned and/or monitored. The number of gates should be kept to the minimum necessary for proper access and safety.

SECURITY

**SECURITY**

### Parking
Private passenger vehicles should be prohibited from parking in or adjacent to cargo handling and storage areas.

### Building Structure
Buildings must be constructed of materials that resist unlawful entry. The integrity of structures must be maintained by periodic inspection and repair.

### Locking Devices and Key Controls
All external and internal windows, gates and fences must be secured with locking devices. Management or security personnel must control the issuance of all locks and keys.

### Lighting
Adequate lighting must be provided inside and outside the facility including the following areas: entrances and exits, cargo handling, storage areas, fence lines and parking areas.

### Alarms Systems & Video Surveillance Cameras
Alarm systems and video surveillance cameras should be utilized to monitor premises and prevent unauthorized access to cargo handling and storage areas.

## Information Technology Security
Information Technology (IT) integrity must be maintained to protect data from unauthorized access or manipulation.

### Password Protection
Automated systems must use individually assigned accounts that require a periodic change of password. IT security policies, procedures and standards must be in place and provided to employees in the form of training.

### Accountability
A system must be in place to identify the abuse of IT including improper access, tampering or the altering of business data. All system violators must be subject to appropriate disciplinary actions for abuse.

# Air Freight Consolidators General Items

## C-TPAT Application
Instructions for submitting an online C-TPAT application are at: www.cbp.gov/xp/cgov/import/commercial_enforcement/ctpat/online_app/. Select "Instructions for Completing the C-TPAT Online Application."
The C-TPAT Online Application itself can be found at: https://ctpat.cbp.dhs.gov/CompanyProfile.aspx

## Agreement to Voluntarily Participate
The Air Freight Consolidator Agreement to Voluntarily Participate is similar to the "Importer - C-TPAT Agreement to Voluntarily Participate" on page 593. The Highway Carrier Agreement can be found as part of the C-TPAT Online Application at:
https://ctpat.cbp.dhs.gov/CompanyProfile.aspx

## For More Information
For more information about C-TPAT go to: www.cbp.gov. Search for "C-TPAT for Air Freight Consolidators."

# C-TPAT for Licensed Customs Brokers[1]

## C-TPAT Security Guidelines for Licensed U.S. Customs Brokers[2]

### C-TPAT Application Qualifications for Brokers

1. Be an active U.S. Licensed Customs Broker.
2. Have a business office staffed in the US.
3. Have an active U.S. Customs Broker's License and Filer Code of record ID(s) in either of the following formats:
##### Customs Broker's License Serial Number
### Filer Code
4. Have a designated company officer that will be the primary cargo security officer responsible for C-TPAT.
5. Commit to maintaining CBP's C-TPAT Security Guidelines for Brokers.
6. Create and provide CBP with a C-TPAT supply chain security profile, which identifies how the broker will meet, maintain and enhance internal policy to meet the C-TPAT Security Guidelines for Brokers.

### Penalties For The Providing of False Information

The failure to provide true, accurate and complete information in an application may result in denial of this application. Severe penalties are provided by law for knowingly and willfully falsifying or concealing a material fact or using any false document in submitting this application. If you are found in violation of the terms and conditions of this program, we may cancel your privileges and you may be subject to fines, penalties and criminal charges.

### C-TPAT Security Guidelines for Brokers

Brokers must conduct a comprehensive assessment of their international supply chains based upon the following C-TPAT security guidelines. Where a broker outsources or contracts elements of their supply chain, such as a foreign facility, conveyance, domestic warehouse, or other elements, the broker must work with these business partners to ensure that pertinent security measures are in place and adhered to throughout their supply chain. The supply chain for C-TPAT purposes is defined from point of origin (manufacturer/supplier/vendor) through to point of distribution and recognizes the diverse business models C-TPAT members employ.

C-TPAT recognizes the complexity of international supply chains and endorses the application and implementation of security measures based upon risk analysis. Therefore, the program allows for flexibility and the customization of security plans based on the member's business model.

As listed throughout this document appropriate security measures, based on risk, must be implemented and maintained throughout the broker's supply chains.

### Business Partner Requirements

Brokers must have written and verifiable processes for the screening selection of business partners including customers, contractors, carriers, and vendors. Ensure that contract companies who provide transportation, security, and cargo handling related services commit to C-TPAT Security Guidelines. Periodically review the performance of the service providers to detect weakness or potential weaknesses in security.

## Security Procedures

### Service Provider Screening and Selection Procedures

The C-TPAT Broker should have documented service provider screening and selection procedures to screen the contracted service provider for validity, financial soundness, ability to meet contractual security requirements, and the ability to identify and correct security deficiencies as needed. Service Provider procedures should utilize a risk-based process as determined by an internal management team.

### Customer Screening Procedures

The C-TPAT Broker should have documented procedures to screen prospective customers for validity, financial soundness, the ability to meet contractual security requirements, and the ability to identify and correct security deficiencies as needed. Customer screening procedures should utilize a risk-based process as determined by an internal management team.

## Physical Access Controls

Access controls prevent unauthorized entry to facilities, maintain control of employees and visitors and protect company assets. Access controls must include the positive identification of all employees, visitors and vendors at all points of entry.

### Employees

An employee identification system must be in place for positive identification and access control purposes. Employees should only be given access to those secure areas needed for the performance of their duties. Company management or security personnel must adequately control the issuance and removal of employee, visitor and vendor identification badges. Procedures for the issuance, removal and changing of access devices (e.g. keys, key cards, etc.) must be documented.

### Visitors Controls

Visitors must present photo identification for documentation purposes upon arrival. All visitors should be escorted and visibly display temporary identification.

### Deliveries (including mail)

Proper vendor ID and/or photo identification must be presented for documentation purposes upon arrival by all vendors. Arriving packages and mail should be periodically screened before being disseminated.

### Challenging and Removing Unauthorized Persons

Procedures must be in place to identify, challenge and address unauthorized/unidentified persons.

## Personnel Security

Processes must be in place to screen prospective employees and to periodically check current employees. Maintain a current permanent employee list (foreign and domestic), which includes the name, date of birth, national identification number or social security number, position held and submit such information to CBP upon written request, to the extent permitted by law.

---

1. C-TPAT requirements are evolving. For the latest information refer to the CBP Web site at: www.cbp.gov.
2. These security guidelines for Licensed Customs Brokers become effective April 24, 2006 and were current as of September 2006.

**SECURITY**

### Pre-Employment Verification
Application information, such as employment history and references must be verified prior to employment.

### Background Checks / Investigations
Consistent with foreign, federal, state and local regulations, background checks and investigations should be conducted for prospective employees. Periodic checks and reinvestigations should be performed based on cause and/or the sensitivity of the employee's position.

### Personnel Termination Procedures
Companies must have procedures in place to remove identification; facility and system access for terminated employees.

## Procedural Security
Security measures must be in place to ensure the integrity and security of processes relevant to the transportation, handling and storage of cargo in the supply chain.

### Documentation Processing
Procedures must be in place to ensure that all documentation used in the clearing of merchandise/cargo is legible, complete, accurate and protected against the exchange, loss or introduction of erroneous information. Documentation control must include safeguarding computer access and information.

### Manifesting Procedures
To help ensure the integrity of cargo received from abroad, procedures must be in place to ensure that information received from business partners is reported accurately and timely.

### Cargo Discrepancies
All shortages, overages and other significant discrepancies or anomalies must be resolved and/or investigated appropriately. CBP and/or other appropriate law enforcement agencies must be notified if illegal or suspicious activities are detected.

## Security Training and Threat Awareness
A threat awareness program should be established and maintained by security personnel to recognize and foster awareness of the threat posed by terrorists at each point in the supply chain. Employees must be made aware of the procedures the company has in place to address a situation and how to report it. Additional training should be provided to employees in sensitive areas.

Additionally, specific training should be offered to assist employees in recognizing internal conspiracies and protecting access controls. These programs should offer incentives for active employee participation.

## Physical Security
Brokers should incorporate the following C-TPAT physical security guidelines throughout their facilities as applicable.

### Building Structure
Buildings must be constructed of materials that resist unlawful entry. The integrity of structures must be maintained by periodic inspection and repair.

### Locking Devices and Key Controls
All external and internal windows, gates and fences must be secured with locking devices. Management or security personnel must control the issuance of all locks and keys.

### Lighting
Adequate lighting must be provided inside and outside the facility including the following areas: entrances and exits, fence lines and parking areas.

### Alarms Systems & Video Surveillance Cameras
Alarm systems and video surveillance cameras should be utilized to monitor premises and prevent unauthorized access to cargo handling and storage areas.

## Information Technology Security
Information Technology (IT) integrity must be maintained to protect data from unauthorized access or manipulation.

### Password Protection
Automated systems must use individually assigned accounts that require a periodic change of password. IT security policies, procedures and standards must be in place and provided to employees in the form of training.

### Accountability
A system must be in place to identify the abuse of IT including improper access, tampering or the altering of business data. All system violators must be subject to appropriate disciplinary actions for abuse.

# Licensed Customs Broker General Items

## C-TPAT Application
Instructions for submitting an online C-TPAT application are at: www.cbp.gov/xp/cgov/import/commercial_enforcement/ctpat/online_app/. Select "Instructions for Completing the C-TPAT Online Application."
The C-TPAT Online Application itself can be found at: https://ctpat.cbp.dhs.gov/CompanyProfile.aspx

## Agreement to Voluntarily Participate
The Licensed Customs Broker Agreement to Voluntarily Participate is similar to the "Importer - C-TPAT Agreement to Voluntarily Participate" on page 593. The Highway Carrier Agreement can be found as part of the C-TPAT Online Application at:
https://ctpat.cbp.dhs.gov/CompanyProfile.aspx

## For More Information
For more information about C-TPAT go to: www.cbp.gov. Search for "C-TPAT for Licensed Customs Brokers."

# C-TPAT for U.S. Marine or Port Terminal[1]

## C-TPAT Security Guidelines for
## U.S. Marine or Port Terminal Operators[2]

### C-TPAT Qualifications for U.S. Marine or Port Terminal Operators

1. Be an active U.S. Marine or Port Terminal Operator.
2. Have a business office staffed in the U.S.
3. Have an active Federal Maritime Commission (FMC) Marine Terminal Operator (MTO) Number:
   • ###### FMC MTO Number (6 digits)
4. Have a designated company officer that will be the primary cargo security officer responsible for C-TPAT.
5. Commit to maintaining CBP's C-TPAT supply chain security guidelines as outlined in the C-TPAT U.S. Marine or Port Terminal Operator agreement.
6. Create and provide CBP with a C-TPAT supply chain security profile, which identifies how the U.S. Marine or Port Terminal Operator will meet, maintain and enhance internal policy to meet the C-TPAT U.S. Marine or Port Terminal Operator security guidelines.

### C-TPAT Security Guidelines for U.S. Marine or Port Terminal Operators

U.S. Marine or Port Terminal Operators must conduct a comprehensive assessment of their international supply chains based upon the following C-TPAT security guidelines. Where a U.S. Marine or Port Terminal Operator outsources or contracts elements of their supply chain, such as a conveyance, foreign facility, domestic warehouse or other elements, the U.S. Marine or Port Terminal Operator must work with these business partners to ensure that pertinent security measures are in place and adhered to throughout their supply chain. The supply chain for C-TPAT purposes is defined from point of origin (manufacturer/supplier/vendor) through to point of distribution and recognizes the diverse business models C-TPAT members employ.

C-TPAT recognizes the complexity of international supply chains and endorses the application and implementation of security measures based upon risk analysis. Therefore, the program allows for flexibility and the customization of security plans based on the member's business model.

As listed throughout this document appropriate security measures, based on risk, must be implemented and maintained throughout the U.S. Marine or Port Terminal Operator's supply chains.

### Conveyance Security

Conveyance/vessel integrity must be maintained to protect against the introduction of unauthorized personnel and material. Conveyance/vessel security procedures must include the physical search of all readily accessible areas, securing all internal/external compartments, panels and reporting cases in which unmanifested materials, or signs of tampering are discovered. Prior to arrival at first U.S. port, search the vessel, prepare a vessel search checklist and secure all areas as appropriate. While at port, the pier and waterside of vessel must be adequately illuminated. Limit shore employees and service providers to those areas of the vessel where they have legitimate business.

### Business Partner Requirements

U.S. Marine or Port Terminal Operators must have written and verifiable processes for the screening and selection of business partners including customers, contractors, and vendors. Ensure that contracted service provider companies who provide security, transportation, and cargo handling services commit to C-TPAT Security Guidelines. Periodically review the performance of the service providers to detect weakness or potential weaknesses in security.

## Security Procedures

### Service Provider Screening and Selection Procedures

The C-TPAT U.S. Marine or Port Terminal Operators should have documented service provider screening and selection procedures to screen the contracted service provider for validity, financial soundness, ability to meet contractual security requirements, and the ability to identify and correct security deficiencies as needed. Service Provider procedures should utilize a risk-based process as determined by an internal management team.

### Customer Screening Procedures

The C-TPAT U.S. Marine or Port Terminal Operators should have documented procedures to screen prospective customers for validity, financial soundness, ability of meeting contractual security requirements, and the ability to identify and correct security deficiencies as needed. Customer screening procedures should utilize a risk-based process as determined by an internal management team.

## Container Security

Container integrity should be verified to check for the introduction of unauthorized material and/or persons.

### Container Inspection

Procedures must be in place to verify the physical integrity of the cargo container structure prior to loading, to include the reliability of the locking mechanisms of the doors. An inspection process is recommended for all full and empty containers:

• Full:
  • Left side
  • Right side
  • Roof
  • Outside doors, hinges, hasps
  • Undercarriage
• Empty:
  • Front wall
  • Left side
  • Right side
  • Floor
  • Ceiling/Roof
  • Inside/Outside doors, hinges, hasps
  • Outside/Undercarriage

---

1. C-TPAT requirements are evolving. For the latest information refer to the CBP Web site at: www.cbp.gov.
2. These security guidelines for U.S. Marine or Port Terminal Operators became effective April 24, 2006 and were current as of September 2006.

**SECURITY**

### Container Seals
Written procedures must stipulate how seals are to be controlled and affixed to loaded containers. Procedures must be in place for recognizing and reporting compromised seals and/or containers to US Customs and Border Protection or the appropriate foreign authority. Only designated employees should distribute container seals for integrity purposes.

### Container Storage
Containers must be stored in a secure area to prevent unauthorized access and/or manipulation. Procedures must be in place for reporting and neutralizing unauthorized entry into containers or container storage areas.

## Physical Access Controls
Access controls prevent unauthorized entry to conveyances and facilities, maintain control of employees, visitors and protect company assets. Access controls must include the positive identification of all employees, visitors and vendors at all points of entry.

### Employees
An employee identification system must be in place for positive identification and access. Employees should only be given access to those secure areas needed for the performance of their duties. Company management or security personnel must adequately control the issuance and removal of employee, visitor and vendor identification badges. Procedures for the issuance, removal and changing of access devices (e.g. keys, key cards, etc.) must be documented.

### Visitors Controls
Visitors must present photo identification for documentation purposes upon arrival. All visitors should be escorted and visibly display temporary identification.

### Deliveries (including mail)
Proper vendor ID and/or photo identification must be presented for documentation purposes upon arrival by all vendors. Arriving packages and mail should be periodically screened before being disseminated.

### Challenging and Removing Unauthorized Persons
Procedures must be in place to identify, challenge and address unauthorized/unidentified persons.

## Personnel Security
Processes must be in place to screen prospective employees and to periodically check current employees. Maintain a current permanent employee list, which includes the name, date of birth, national identification number or social security number, position held, and submit such information to CBP upon written request, to the extent permitted by law.

### Pre-Employment Verification
Application information, such as employment history and references must be verified prior to employment.

### Background Checks / Investigations
Consistent with foreign, federal, state and local regulations, background checks and investigations should be conducted for prospective employees. Periodic checks and reinvestigations should be performed based on cause and/or the sensitivity of the employee's position.

### Personnel Termination Procedures
Companies must have procedures in place to remove identification, facility, and system access for terminated employees.

## Procedural Security
Security measures must be in place to ensure the integrity and security of processes relevant to the transportation, handling and storage of cargo in the supply chain.

### Documentation Processing
Procedures must be in place to ensure that all documentation used in the clearing of merchandise/cargo, is legible, complete, accurate and protected against the exchange, loss or introduction of erroneous information. Documentation control must include safeguarding computer access and information.

### Manifesting Procedures
To help ensure the integrity of cargo received from abroad, procedures must be in place to ensure that information received from business partners is reported accurately and timely. Ensure that all bills of lading and other documentation submitted for cargo is complete and a system in place to verify the accuracy of the weight, marks and quantity of the shipment.

### Shipping & Receiving
Arriving cargo should be reconciled against information on the cargo manifest. The cargo should be accurately described, weighed, labeled, marked, counted and verified. Departing cargo should be checked against purchase or delivery orders. Drivers delivering or receiving cargo must be positively identified before cargo is received or released.

### Cargo Discrepancies
All shortages, overages and other significant discrepancies or anomalies must be resolved and/or investigated appropriately. CBP and/or other appropriate law enforcement agencies must be notified if illegal or suspicious activities are detected.

## Security Training and Threat Awareness
A threat awareness program should be established and maintained by security personnel to recognize and foster awareness of the threat posed by terrorists at each point in the supply chain. Employees must be made aware of the procedures the company has in place to address a situation and how to report it. Additional training should be provided to employees in the shipping and receiving areas, as well as those receiving and opening mail.

Additionally, specific training should be offered to assist employees in maintaining cargo integrity, recognizing internal conspiracies and protecting access controls. These programs should offer incentives for active employee participation. Conduct periodic unannounced security checks to ensure that all procedures are being performed in accordance with defined guidelines.

## Physical Security
Cargo handling and storage facilities in domestic and foreign locations must have physical barriers and deterrents that guard against unauthorized access. U.S./Canada Highway Carriers should incorporate the following C-TPAT physical security guidelines throughout their supply chains as applicable.

### Fencing
Perimeter fencing should enclose the areas around cargo handling and storage facilities. Interior fencing within a cargo handling structure should be used to segregate domestic, international, high value, and hazardous cargo. All fencing must be regularly inspected for integrity and damage.

### Gates and Gate Houses
Gates through which vehicles and/or personnel enter or exit must be manned and/or monitored. The number of gates should be kept to the minimum necessary for proper access and safety.

### Parking
Private passenger vehicles should be prohibited from parking in or adjacent to cargo handling and storage areas.

### Building Structure

Buildings must be constructed of materials that resist unlawful entry. The integrity of structures must be maintained by periodic inspection and repair.

### Locking Devices and Key Controls

All external and internal windows, gates and fences must be secured with locking devices. Management or security personnel must control the issuance of all locks and keys.

### Lighting

Adequate lighting must be provided inside and outside the facility including the following areas: entrances and exits, cargo handling and storage areas, fence lines and parking areas.

### Alarms Systems & Video Surveillance Cameras

Alarm systems and video surveillance cameras should be utilized to monitor premises and prevent unauthorized access to cargo handling and storage areas.

## Information Technology Security

Information Technology (IT) integrity must be maintained to protect data from unauthorized access or manipulation.

### Password Protection

Automated systems must use individually assigned accounts that require a periodic change of password. IT security policies, procedures and standards must be in place and provided to employees in the form of training.

### Accountability

A system must be in place to identify the abuse of IT including improper access, tampering or the altering of business data. All system violators must be subject to appropriate disciplinary actions for abuse.

# U.S. Marine or Port Terminal Operator General Items

## C-TPAT Application

Instructions for submitting an online C-TPAT application are at: www.cbp.gov/xp/cgov/import/commercial_enforcement/ctpat/online_app/. Select "Instructions for Completing the C-TPAT Online Application."

The C-TPAT Online Application itself can be found at: https://ctpat.cbp.dhs.gov/CompanyProfile.aspx

## Agreement to Voluntarily Participate

The U.S. Marine or Port Terminal Operator Agreement to Voluntarily Participate is similar to the "Importer - C-TPAT Agreement to Voluntarily Participate" on page 593. The Highway Carrier Agreement can be found as part of the C-TPAT Online Application at: https://ctpat.cbp.dhs.gov/CompanyProfile.aspx

## For More Information

For more information about C-TPAT go to: www.cbp.gov. Search for "C-TPAT for Port Terminal Operators."

**SECURITY**

# Free and Secure Trade (FAST)[1]

## Free And Secure Trade (FAST)

### FAST Overview

The Free and Secure Trade (FAST) program is a Border Accord Initiative between the United States, Mexico, and Canada designed to ensure security and safety while enhancing the economic prosperity of each country. In developing this program, Mexico, Canada and the United States have agreed to coordinate, to the maximum extent possible, their commercial processes for clearance of commercial shipments at the border. This will promote free and secure trade by using common risk-management principles, supply chain security, industry partnership, and advanced technology to improve the efficiency of screening and clearing commercial traffic at our shared borders.

Eligibility for the FAST program requires participants (carrier, drivers, importers, and southern border manufacturers) to submit an application, agreement, and security profile depending on their role in the Customs and Trade Partnership Against Terrorism (C-TPAT) and FAST programs. The FAST program allows known low risk participants to receive expedited border processing. This enables U.S. Customs and Border Protection (CBP) to re-direct security efforts and inspections where they are needed most - on commerce that is high risk, or unknown risk - while ensuring the movement of legitimate, low-risk commerce.

When decisions are made to elevate the national threat level, all CBP personnel must be cognizant of the heightened threat of terrorism as well a mandated increase in examinations of cargo and conveyances. Elevated alert levels should have no adverse impact on FAST processing. While other conveyances and cargo will be subject to a greater degree of inspection, FAST shipments are considered known low risk. As such, their processing should continue under normal guidelines during heightened alert levels.

### FAST Benefits

The FAST program is voluntary. The benefits for those that apply and are accepted into the FAST program include:

1. Dedicated lanes (where available) for greater speed and efficiency in the clearance of FAST Trans-border shipments;
2. Reduced number of examinations for continued compliance with Customs FAST requirements as well as secondary priority processing;
3. A strong and ongoing partnership with the Canadian Partners in Protection (PIP) and CBP C-TPAT administrations;
4. Enhanced supply chain security and safety while protecting the economic prosperity of the United States, Mexico, and Canada; and,
5. For carrier participants, the knowledge that they are transporting shipments for a C-TPAT approved importer, and on the southern border, a C-TPAT manufacturer.

### Basic Participation Requirements

FAST is a clearance process for known low-risk shipments, thus, any truck using FAST lane processing must be a C-TPAT approved carrier, carrying qualifying goods from a C-TPAT approved importer, and the driver in the possession of a valid FAST Commercial Driver Registration ID Card. Although FAST participation requirements along the northern and southern border are very similar, on the southern border

there are two additional requirements. The manufacturer must be an approved C-TPAT participant, and they must also adhere to CBP high security seal requirements.

C-TPAT is a joint government business initiative to build cooperative relationships that strengthen overall supply chain and border security. C-TPAT recognizes that CBP can provide the highest level of security only through close cooperation with the ultimate owners of the supply chain, importers, carriers, brokers, warehouse operators and manufacturers. Through this initiative, CBP asks businesses to ensure the integrity of their security practices and communicate their security guidelines to their business partners within the supply chain.

### 1. Importer Registration

Importers must complete an application for C-TPAT participation with CBP. Importers authorized to use the FAST program for clearance into the United States will have a demonstrated history of complying with all relevant legislative and regulatory requirements, and will have made a commitment to security enhancing business practices as required by C-TPAT.

### 2. Carrier Registration

Carriers must complete the FAST Highway Carrier Application Process requirements that include corporate information, a security profile, and a written Highway Carrier Agreement.

**Northern Border**: In order to qualify for FAST Highway Carrier membership into the U.S. and Canada, two separate applications must be submitted to each country's respective FAST Processing Centers. Each country will perform an independent risk assessment and each country will issue independent approvals for participation. For the United States, a FAST approved carrier will have met all aspects of C-TPAT through the FAST registration process.

**Southern Border**: To qualify for the U.S./Mexico border highway carriers agreement, the carrier must have demonstrated a history of complying with all relevant legislative and regulatory requirements set forth by CBP. The applying carrier must have made a commitment to security-enhancing business practices as required by C-TPAT and use drivers that are in possession of a valid FAST commercial driver card when using FAST clearance.

### 3. Commercial Driver Application

Two separate driver application processes exist for FAST, 1) Northern Border and 2) Southern Border. For northern border applicants, drivers must complete a FAST Commercial Driver Application for the United States and Canada. The application will first be risk assessed by a Canadian consortium of the Canada Border Service Agency (CBSA), Citizenship and Immigration Service for Canada (CIC), and Canada's Agence de Revenu (ARC). Upon approval from Canada, CBP will conduct a full U.S. based risk assessment. Applicants identified as low risk will report to an enrollment center where they will be interviewed, have their original identification and citizenship documents reviewed, fingerprinted and have a digital photo taken. Low-risk applicants will then be issued a FAST Commercial Driver Card.

The procedure for the southern border is similar however the FAST driver application is submitted to the Mellon Financial

---

1. C-TPAT and FAST requirements are evolving. The information in this section was current as of September 2006. For the latest information refer to the U.S. Customs and Border Protection (CBP) Web site at: www.cbp.gov. The editorial content for this article is based on U.S. Customs and Border Protection material.

Corporation in Pittsburgh, Pennsylvania prior to being forwarded to the CBP risk assessment center in St Albans, Vermont. Applicants identified as low risk will report to an enrollment center where they will be interviewed, have their original identification and citizenship documents reviewed, fingerprinted and have a digital photo taken. Low-risk applicants will then be issued a FAST – Commercial Driver Card.

### FAST Processing Availability
The initial phase of FAST processing for U.S. bound commercial shipments began in December 2002 at the port of Detroit, Michigan. Today, CBP has implemented FAST processing at the following northern and southern border crossings:

**Northern Border**
Alexandria Bay, New York
Blaine, Washington
Buffalo, New York
Champlain, New York
Derby Line, Vermont
Detroit, Michigan
Highgate Springs, Vermont
Houlton, Maine
Massena, New York
Ogdensburg, New York
Oroville, Washington
Pembina, North Dakota
Port Huron, Michigan
Portal, North Dakota
Sweetgrass, Montana

**Southern Border**
Brownsville, Texas
Calexico, California
Del Rio, Texas
Douglas, Arizona
Eagle Pass, Texas
El Paso, Texas
Laredo, Texas
Nogales, Arizona
Otay Mesa, California
Pharr, Texas
Rio Grande City, Texas
San Luis, Arizona
Santa Teresa, New Mexico
Tecate, California
Future FAST expansion sites include:

**Northern Border**
Calais, Maine
Sault Ste Marie, Michigan
International Falls, Minnesota

### Cargo Release Method(s)
The two cargo release methods for FAST eligible shipments are the Free and Secure Trade system formerly known as the National Customs Automated Prototype (NCAP), additionally the Pre-Arrival Processing System (PAPS) is also recognized as eligible method of cargo release processing for FAST.

1. **FAST** - FAST is the first fully electronic and completely paperless cargo release mechanism put into place by CBP. Paperless processing is achieved through advanced electronic data transmissions and transponder technology. FAST is highly automated and allows for the expedited release of highly compliant cargo from major importers, reducing congestion at our land borders.

2. **Pre Arrival Processing System (PAPS)** -The Pre-Arrival Processing System (PAPS) is an ACS (Automated Commercial System) border cargo release system that utilizes barcode technology to expedite the release of commercial shipments while still processing each shipment through Border Cargo Selectivity (BCS) and the Automated Targeting System (ATS).

Each PAPS shipment requires a unique barcode label, which the carrier attaches to the invoice and the truck manifest while the merchandise is still in Canada or Mexico. The barcode consists of the Standard Carrier Alpha Code (SCAC) and Pro-Bill number or entry number. The licensed U.S. Customs broker in the United States must indicate this sequencing of SCAC code and unique number (Pro Bill, Entry number or unique set of numbers) in the BCS entry in ACS. Upon the truck's arrival at the border, the CBP officer scans the barcode, which automatically retrieves the entry information from ACS. If no examination is required, the CBP officer then releases the truck, reducing the carrier's wait time and easing congestion at the U.S. border.

### Additional Information
In addition to the FAST information found on the CBP web site, see FAST information on the Canada Border Security Agency web site at www.cbsa-asfc.gc.ca or contact a representative at any of the designated FAST sites.

# FAST U.S./Canada[1]

## Free and Secure Trade (FAST)

### Overview
The FAST program is a bilateral initiative between the United States and Canada designed to ensure security and safety while enhancing the economic prosperity of both countries. In developing this program, Canada and the United States have agreed to harmonize, to the maximum extent possible, their commercial processes for clearance of commercial shipments at the border. This will promote free and secure trade by using common risk-management principles, supply chain security, industry partnership, and advanced technology to improve the efficiency of screening and clearing commercial traffic at our shared border.

### Objectives
FAST is an ambitious program both in terms of its scope and its implementation date. For the United States and Canada, the initiative's objectives promise to revolutionize the processing of transborder trade:

1. The program aims to increase the integrity of supply chain security by offering expedited clearance to carriers and importers enrolled in Customs Trade Partnership Against Terrorism (C-TPAT) or Canada's Partners in Protection (PIP).

2. It's designed to streamline and to integrate registration processes for drivers, carriers, and importers; minimizing paperwork and ensuring only low risk participants are enrolled as members.

---

1. C-TPAT and FAST requirements are evolving. The information in this section was current as of September 2006. For the latest information refer to the U.S. Customs and Border Protection (CBP) Web site at: www.cbp.gov. The editorial content for this article is based on U.S. Customs and Border Protection material.

SECURITY

3. The initiative seeks to expedite the clearance of transborder shipments of compliant partners by reducing Customs information requirements, dedicating lanes at major crossings to FAST participants, using common technology, and physically examining cargo transported by these low-risk clients with minimal frequency.

4. The program is a catalyst for both Customs administrations to participate in the enhanced technologies by using transponders, which would make it easier to clear low risk shipments, and would mitigate the cost of program participation for FAST partners.

### Benefits

FAST approved U.S./Canada highway carriers will benefit from:

1. Dedicated lanes (where available) for greater speed and efficiency in the clearance of FAST transborder shipments.

2. Reduced number of examinations for continued compliance with Customs FAST requirements.

3. A strong and ongoing partnership with the Canadian (PIP) and Customs (C-TPAT) administrations.

4. Enhanced supply chain security and safety while protecting the economic prosperity of both countries.

5. The knowledge that they are carrying shipments for a C-TPAT approved importer.

6. A head start for the upcoming modifications to FAST that will expand eligible electronic cargo release methods. The FAST processing of Pre Arrival Processing System (PAPS) is currently in use and will commence at expanded locations along the northern border during the year.

### Inauguration

The initial phase of FAST for U.S. and Canada bound commercial shipments began in December 2002. FAST processing is currently available for qualifying commercial shipments at the following U.S./Canadian ports:

| U.S. Border | Canada Border |
|---|---|
| Alexandria Bay, New York | Landsdowne, Quebec |
| Buffalo, New York | Fort Erie, Ontario |
| Blaine, Washington | Douglas, British Columbia |
| Calais, Maine | St. Stephen, New Brunswick |
| Champlain, New York | Lacolle, Quebec |
| Derby Line, Vermont | Stanstead Place, Quebec |
| Detroit, Michigan | Windsor, Ontario |
| Highgate Springs, Vermont | Phillipsburg, Quebec |
| Houlton, Maine | Woodstock, New Brunswick |
| International Falls, Washington | Fort Frances, Manitoba |
| Lewiston, New York | Queenston, Ontario |
| Massena, New York | Cornwall, Ontario |
| Ogdensburg, New York | Prescott, Ontario |
| Oroville, Washington | Osoyoos, British Columbia |
| Pembina, North Dakota | Emerson Junction, Manitoba |
| Portal, North Dakota | Bienfait, Saskatchewan |
| Sault Ste Marie, Michigan | Sault Ste Marie, Ontario |
| Sweetgrass, Montana | Coutts, Alberta |

### Qualifications

FAST is a harmonized clearance process for shipments of known compliant importer. Thus, any truck using FAST lane processing must be a C-TPAT approved carrier, carrying qualifying goods from a C-TPAT approved importer, and the driver must possess a valid FAST-Commercial Driver Card. FAST processing is based upon advanced electronic transmission of information. The following are the key components:

- **Importer Registration**
  Importers will complete separate applications to the Customs administrations. Importers authorized to use the FAST program for clearance into the United States will have a demonstrated history of complying with all relevant legislative and regulatory requirements, and will have made a commitment to security enhancing business practices as required by C-TPAT.

- **Carrier Registration**
  Carriers will complete the FAST U.S./Canada Border Highway Carrier Application Process requirements that include corporate information, a security profile, and a written U.S./Canada Border Highway Carrier Agreement. In order to qualify for FAST Highway Carrier membership into the U.S. and Canada, two separate applications must be submitted to each country's respective FAST Processing Centers. Each country will perform an independent risk assessment and each country will issue independent approvals for participation. For the United States, a FAST approved carrier will have met all aspects of C-TPAT through the FAST registration process.

- **Commercial Driver Application**
  Drivers will complete a U.S./Canada FAST Commercial Driver Application for the U.S. and Canada. The application will be risk assessed by the customs and immigration services of both countries. Applicants identified as low risk will report to an enrollment center where they will be interviewed, have their original identification and citizenship documents reviewed, fingerprinted and have a digital photo taken. Low-risk applicants will then be issued a FAST – Commercial Driver Identification Card.

### Cargo Release Methods

The two present cargo release methods for FAST shipments are the National Customs Automated Prototype (NCAP) and the PAPS. NCAP/FAST processing for FAST began in December 2002. The FAST processing of PAPS shipments is currently taking place.

1. **FAST** - FAST is the first completely paperless cargo release mechanism put into place by U.S. Customs and Border Protection. This paperless processing is achieved through electronic data transmissions and transponder technology. FAST is highly automated and allows for the expedited release of highly compliant cargo from major importers, reducing congestion at our land borders.

2. **The Pre-Arrival Processing System (PAPS)** - PAPS is a Customs Automated Commercial System (ACS) border cargo release mechanism that utilizes barcode technology to expedite the release of commercial shipments while processing each shipment through Border Cargo Selectivity (BCS) and the Automated Targeting System (ATS).

# FAST U.S./Mexico[1]

## Free and Secure Trade (FAST)

### Overview

The FAST program is a bilateral initiative between the United States and Mexico designed to ensure security and safety while enhancing the economic prosperity of both countries. In developing this program, Mexico and the United States have agreed to coordinate to the maximum extent possible, their commercial processes for clearance of commercial shipments at the border. This will promote free and secure trade by using common risk-management principles, supply chain security, industry partnership, and advanced technology to improve the efficiency of screening and clearing commercial traffic at our shared border.

### Objectives

FAST is an ambitious program both in terms of its scope and its implementation dates. For the United States and Mexico, the initiative's objectives promise to revolutionize the processing of transborder trade:

1. The program aims to increase the integrity of supply chain security by offering expedited clearance to carriers and importers enrolled in Customs Trade Partnership Against Terrorism (C-TPAT).
2. It's designed to streamline and to integrate registration processes for drivers, carriers, and importers, minimizing paperwork and ensuring only low risk participants are enrolled as members.
3. The initiative seeks to expedite the clearance of transborder shipments of compliant partners by reducing Customs information requirements, dedicating lanes at major crossings to FAST participants, using common technology, and physically examining cargo transported by these low-risk clients with minimal frequency.
4. The program is a catalyst for both Customs administrations to participate in the enhanced technologies by using transponders, which would make it easier to clear low risk shipments, and would mitigate the cost of program participation for FAST partners.

### Benefits

FAST approved U.S./Mexico highway carriers will benefit from:

1. Dedicated lanes (where available) for greater speed and efficiency in the clearance of FAST transborder shipments.
2. Reduced number of examinations for continued compliance with Customs FAST requirements.
3. A strong and ongoing partnership with the Mexican and Customs (C-TPAT) administrations.
4. Enhanced supply chain security and safety while protecting the economic prosperity of both countries.
5. The knowledge that they are carrying shipments for a C-TPAT approved importer.
6. A head start for the upcoming modifications to FAST that will expand eligible electronic cargo release methods. The FAST processing of Pre-Arrival Processing System (PAPS) is currently in use and will commence at locations along the U.S./Mexico border this year.

### Inauguration

The initial phase of FAST for the United States and Mexico bound commercial shipments began on September 27, 2003 at the Port of El Paso, Texas. Additional dedicated FAST lane processing is available at the following locations:

### FAST Southern Border Operations

| U.S. Border | Mexico Border |
| --- | --- |
| Brownsville, Texas | Matamoros, Tamaulipas |
| Calexico, California | Mexicali, Baja California |
| Del Rio, Texas | Villa Acuna, Coahila |
| Douglas, Arizona | Agua Prieta, Sonora |
| Eagle Pass, Texas | Piedras Negras, Coahuila |
| El Paso, Texas | Ciudad Juarez, Chihuahua |
| Hidalgo, Texas | Reynosa, Tamaulipas |
| Laredo, Texas | Nuevo Laredo, Tamaulipas |
| Nogales, Arizona | Nogales, Sonora |
| Otay Mesa, California | Tijuana, Baja California |
| Rio Grande City, Texas | Cd. Camargo, Tamaulipas |
| San Luis, Arizona | San Luis, Sonora |
| Santa Teresa, New Mexico | San Jeronimo, Chihuahua |
| Tecate, California | Tecate, Baja California |

### Qualifications

FAST is a harmonized clearance process for shipments of known compliant importer. Thus, any truck using FAST lane processing must be a C-TPAT approved carrier, carrying qualifying goods from a C-TPAT approved manufacturer, importer, and the driver must possess a valid FAST-Commercial Driver Card. FAST processing is based upon advanced electronic transmission of information. The following are the key components:

- **Manufacturer Registration**
  Mexican manufacturers who are C-TPAT certified will be allowed to participate in the FAST program along the U.S./Mexico Border. Mexican related party manufacturers that are whole or majority owned subsidiaries of current C-TPAT importers that are controlled by the C-TPAT importer and are included in the importer's C-TPAT security profile will be eligible for FAST processing upon completion of the C-TPAT Importer Related Party Manufacturer Information by the C-TPAT importer. Mexican related party manufacturers who are NOT included in the C-TPAT importer's security profile must go through the entire application process for C-TPAT certification. Once certified, these parties will be eligible for FAST processing. Please note that per FAST requirements, Mexican manufacturers must ensure that high security mechanical seals are used on all loaded containers or trailers destined for the United States, and where appropriate, must follow ISO/PSA standard 17712. Refer to U.S./Mexico Border C-TPAT/FAST Seal Requirements for more information.

SECURITY

---

1. C-TPAT and FAST requirements are evolving. The information in this section was current as of September 2006. For the latest information refer to the U.S. Customs and Border Protection (CBP) Web site at: www.cbp.gov.
   Note: The editorial content for this article is based on U.S. Customs and Border Protection material.

- **Importer Registration**
  Importers will complete a FAST Application to Customs and Border Protection in the United States. Importers authorized to use the FAST program for clearance into the United States will have a demonstrated history of complying with all relevant legislative and regulatory requirements, and will have made a commitment to security enhancing business practices as required by C-TPAT. Please note that per FAST requirements, importers participating in FAST have responsibilities to ensure that high security mechanical seals are used on all loaded containers or trailers destined for the United States, and where appropriate, must follow ISO/PSA standard 17712. Refer to U.S./Mexico Border C-TPAT/FAST Seal Requirements for more information.

- **Carrier Registration**
  Carriers will complete the FAST U.S./Mexico Border Highway Carrier Application Process requirements that include corporate information, a security profile, and a written U.S./Mexico Border Highway Carrier Agreement. In order to qualify for FAST Highway Carrier membership into the United States and Mexico, a carrier application must be submitted to the FAST Processing Center. An independent risk assessment will be performed and once the assessment is complete, an approval for FAST participation will be authorized. For the United States, a FAST approved carrier will have met all aspects of C-TPAT through the FAST registration process. Carriers must ensure that all of their employed drivers are in possession of a valid FAST Commercial Driver Identification Card or other identification issued only by CBP. Please note that per FAST requirements, carriers participating in FAST have responsibilities to ensure that high security mechanical seals are used on all loaded containers or trailers destined for the U.S., and where appropriate, must follow ISO/PSA standard 17712. Refer to U.S./Mexico Border C-TPAT/FAST Seal Requirements for more information.

- **Commercial Driver Application**
  Drivers must complete a single FAST U.S./Mexico Border Commercial Driver Application for the United States and Mexico. CBP will assess the application for risk. Applicants identified as low risk will report to an enrollment center where they will be interviewed, have their original identification and citizenship documents reviewed, fingerprinted and have a digital photo taken. Low-risk applicants will then be issued a FAST – Commercial Driver Identification Card.

- **FAST Driver Enrollment Centers**
  FAST commercial driver enrollment centers are operational at the ports of:
  - Otay Mesa, California
  - Calexico, California
  - Nogales, Arizona
  - El Paso, Texas
  - Laredo, Texas
  - Pharr, Texas
  - Brownsville, Texas

### Cargo Release Methods

Two present cargo release methods exist for FAST processing. The first method is FAST, which is the modified version of the National Customs Automated Prototype (NCAP) and the Pre-Arrival Processing System (PAPS). More detailed information on these two release methods may be obtained from Federal Register Notice Volume 68, Number 186, published on September 25, 2003, titled the Modification to the Free and Secure Trade Prototype. The initial implementation of the FAST prototype began in December 16, 2002 in Detroit, Michigan. Both cargo release methods are the only accepted electronic transactions available for FAST processing.

1. **FAST** - Modified NCAP/Prototype is the first complete paperless cargo release mechanism put into place by U.S. Customs and Border Protection. This paperless processing is achieved through electronic data transmissions and transponder technology. FAST is highly automated and allows for the expedited release of highly compliant cargo from major importers, reducing congestion at our land borders.

2. **The Pre-Arrival Processing System (PAPS)** - PAPS is a Customs Automated Commercial System (ACS) border cargo release mechanism that utilizes barcode technology to expedite the release of commercial shipments while processing each shipment through Border Cargo Selectivity (BCS) and the Automated Targeting System (ATS).

### Additional Information

For additional information, reference the www.CBP.gov web address or contact a local CBP FAST representative at any of the FAST sites indicated. Designated FAST team members are available to answer questions at designated FAST ports.

# C-TPAT Seal Requirements[1]

C-TPAT (Customs-Trade Partnership Against Terrorism) importers, carriers and manufacturers who wish to qualify for expedited processing and other related benefits under the U.S./Mexico FAST initiative will be required to adhere to the following procedures, protocols and standards with regards to the use of high-security seals.

## MANUFACTURER

- The manufacturer shall be responsible for the sealed container/trailer until such a time as the carrier assumes control.
- Seals are to be affixed at manufacturer point of origin (loading). Seals will be of the high security type as per ISO guidelines (ISO/PSA 17712, Freight Containers-Mechanical Seals), adopted May 2003.
- Establish verifiable security systems for cargo storage and handling facilities and container yards in order to prevent the improper manipulation and transportation or handling of cargo and/or containers/trailers.
- Ensure a system is in place to verify seal numbers, weights and quantity of cargo received, when practical.
- Safeguard the use of seals and maintain a log of seal numbers issued and used.
- Ensure that all manifests and/or bills of lading or other documentation (including electronic data transmissions) submitted for cargo to be shipped are complete and includes all pertinent seal information.

### Seal Integrity Responsibilities

- Seals are to be affixed by a responsible, designated representative of the manufacturing entity.
  NOTE: A responsible, designated representative is defined as an employee who maintains a position of trust (i.e. security personnel) within the business and has received appropriate instruction and training in the proper use and application of high-security seals).
- Access to seals will be strictly controlled by the responsible party and shall be issued at random in order to avoid seals being affixed in sequential order.
- Seals shall be stored in a secure location (locked cabinet, safe, etc.) until such a time as their use is warranted.
- Access to such secure locations must be restricted to those parties responsible for the inventory and affixing of seals.
- A log must be maintained in order to account for all seals under the control of the manufacturer/importer.
  NOTE: A standardized log is currently under development. In the interim, any entity responsible for the sealing of cargo should use and maintain an accounting system of its own design.

## CARRIER/DRAYAGE

- Upon receipt of container/trailer, ensure that all seal information is true and correct as reflected on manifests, bills of lading or other documentation related to the movement of cargo.
- Establish verifiable security systems for cargo storage and handling facilities, container yards and conveyances operated by the carrier to prevent the improper manipulation and transportation of cargo and/or containers/trailers.
- Establish procedures for reporting any discrepancies or anomalies related to seal integrity.

### Seal Integrity Responsibilities

- Seals will be of the high-security type as per ISO guidelines (ISO/PSA 17712, Freight Containers-Mechanical Seals), adopted May 2003.
- All seals that are removed from a cargo container/trailer for legitimate intermediate examinations (customs inspection, conveyance damage surveys, law enforcement activity, etc.) must be placed in the container just inside the doors, in plain view, before a new seal is affixed to the container.
- Establish a system for annotating and reporting any changes due to legitimate intermediate examination purposes as described above.
- Seals are to be affixed by a responsible, designated representative of the carrier.
  NOTE: A responsible, designated representative is defined as an employee who maintains a position of trust (i.e. security personnel) within the business and has received appropriate instruction and training in the proper use and application of high-security seals.
- Access to seals will be strictly controlled by the responsible party and shall be issued at random in order to avoid seals being affixed in sequential order.
- Seals shall be stored in a secure location (locked cabinet, safe, etc.) until such a time as their use is warranted.
- Access to such secure locations must be restricted to those parties responsible for the inventory and affixing of seals.
- A log must be maintained in order to account for all seals under the control of the carrier.
  NOTE: A standardized log is currently under development. In the interim, any entity responsible for the sealing of cargo should use and maintain an accounting system of their own design.
- Establish a system to ensure verification of seal numbers and types and that all pertinent seal information is reflected on all manifests, bills of lading or other documentation (including electronic data transmissions) related to the movement of cargo.

## IMPORTER

- Ensure that all related parties are aware of security guidelines and procedures as they relate to the use of seals and seal integrity.
- Establish a system to ensure all related parties/business partners adhere to established security guidelines and procedures relating to the use of seals and seal integrity.
- Establish procedures for reporting any seal discrepancies or anomalies to CBP.

SECURITY

---

1. The editorial content for this article is based on U.S. Customs and Border Protection (CBP) material and was current as of September 2006.
For the latest information refer to the U.S. Customs and Border Protection (CBP) Web site at: www.cbp.gov.

# C-TPAT
# Enrollment-Maintenance-Validation (EMV) Process[1]

## C-TPAT Enrollment

1. Establish a C-TPAT portal account;
2. Gather and input company profile information to the Company's C-TPAT portal account;
3. Perform thorough onsite review of each physical facility in the United States and abroad, verify existing security policies and procedures, and identify areas for security improvement in the Core Areas of Supply Chain Security (SCS):
   -Facility, personnel, shipping, receiving, data and documentation, information systems, cargo and container tracking, seals, vendors and service providers, self-policing, and training.
4. Gather and input company security profile information to the Company's C-TPAT portal account. (Must provide sufficient detail and responses to all questions.)
5. Transmit all data to U.S. Customs and Border Protection (CBP) via the company's C-TPAT portal account.
6. Prepare an Implementation Task List to cover and manage all areas of improvement.
7. Document a comprehensive SCS Manual covering all Core Areas of SCS, including all implementation and maintenance tools.
8. Establish a Supply Chain Task Force including representatives from various Company departments to oversee implementation, maintenance and monitoring of all Core Areas of SCS.

## C-TPAT Maintenance and Implementation

1. Educate all Company employees on the maintenance and the implementation of SCS;
2. Notify all vendors and service providers on their requirements for SCS;
3. Notify all Customers on the Company's commitment to SCS;
4. Complete the scheduled tasks on the Company's Implementation Task List;
5. Regularly update and maintain the SCS Manual and Implementation Task List;
6. Monitor the Maintenance of existing procedures;
7. On a monthly basis, self-audit at least one chapter from the SCS Manual;
8. On an annual basis self-audit or professionally review the Company's entire SCS Program;
9. On an annual basis, update the company's C-TPAT portal account;
10. Be aware of and know about the latest changes in CBP Supply Chain Security standards and requirements.

## C-TPAT Validation

1. Conduct an on-site re-assessment of each physical facility in the United States and abroad;
2. Update the SCS Manual and Implementation Task List;
3. Assemble all evidence of continuous implementation and maintenance of SCS, including all audit checklists, logs (training, visitor, warehouse, truck, etc...) and reports;
4. Prepare formal presentation for official validation by CBP;
5. Retain professional representation to support the Company's preparation and presentation process.

Courtesy of:
**Zisser Customs Law Group**
C-TPAT Specialists
International Trade Law Consulting and Management
2297 Niels Bohr Court, Suite 114
San Diego, California 92154
Tel: [1] (619) 671-0376
E-mail: solutions@zissergroup.com
Web: www.zissergroup.com

---

1. Note: The EMV Process as described in this sidebar is not a U.S. Customs and Border Protection (CBP) program. The EMV Process was developed by the Zisser Customs Law Group (a private law firm) as an aid to organizations seeking to be part of the CBP C-TPAT Program.

# Container Security Initiative (CSI)[1]

### Why Was the CSI Developed?
The Container Security Initiative (CSI) was developed by U.S. Customs, now the U.S. Bureau of Customs and Border Protection (CBP), in the aftermath of the terrorist attacks of September 11, 2001. CSI addresses the threat to border security and global trade posed by the potential for terrorist use of a maritime container to deliver a weapon.

### How Does CSI Work?
CSI is a security regime designed to ensure that all containers that pose a potential risk for terrorism are identified and inspected at foreign ports before they are placed on vessels destined for the United Sates.

CBP has stationed multidisciplinary teams of U.S. officers from both CBP and Immigration and Customs Enforcement (ICE) to work together with host foreign government counterparts at CSI ports. Their mission is to target and prescreen containers and to develop additional investigative leads related to the terrorist threat to cargo destined to the United States.

The concept is to prevent terrorist threats from being carried out and to make U.S. borders the last line of defense, not the first.

Announced in January 2002, CSI was first implemented in the ports shipping the greatest volume of containers to the United States. CBP has entered into bilateral discussions with all the foreign governments where high volume ports are located and is now expanding to additional ports in strategic locations.

### CSI Core Elements
1. Identify high-risk containers. CBP uses automated targeting tools to identify containers that pose a potential risk for terrorism, based on advance information and strategic intelligence.
2. Prescreen and evaluate containers before they are shipped. Containers are screened as early in the supply chain as possible, generally at the port of departure.
3. Use technology to prescreen high-risk containers to ensure that screening can be done rapidly without slowing down the movement of trade. This technology includes large-scale X-ray and gamma ray machines and radiation detection devices.
4. Use smarter, more secure containers, which will allow CBP officers at United States ports of arrival to identify containers that have been tampered with during transit.

### Program Reciprocity
Through CSI, CBP officers work with host customs administrations to establish security criteria for identifying high-risk containers. Those administrations use non-intrusive inspection (NII) and radiation detection technology to screen high-risk containers before they are shipped to U.S. ports.

CSI is a reciprocal program, and offers CSI participant countries the opportunity to send their customs officers to major U.S. ports to target ocean-going, containerized cargo to be exported to their countries. Likewise, CBP shares information on a bilateral basis with its CSI partners. Japan and Canada currently station their customs personnel in some U.S. ports as part of the CSI program.

### CSI Goals
CBP's goal is to have 50 operational CSI ports by the end of fiscal year 2006. At that time, approximately 90 percent of all transatlantic and transpacific cargo imported into the United States will be subjected to prescreening.

CSI continues to expand to strategic locations around the world. The World Customs Organization (WCO), the European Union (EU), and the G8 support CSI expansion and have adopted resolutions implementing CSI security measures introduced at ports throughout the world.

### Countries Committed to CSI
At this writing, forty four ports in twenty five countries are participating in the CSI initiative.

## Operational CSI Ports by Operational Date
Currently operational ports and the month and year they became operational are:
- Halifax, Montreal, and Vancouver, Canada (03/02)
- Rotterdam, The Netherlands (09/02/02)
- Le Havre, France (12/02/02)
- Marseille, France (01/07/05)
- Bremerhaven, Germany (02/02/03)
- Hamburg, Germany (02/09/03)
- Antwerp, Belgium (02/23/03)
- Zeebrugge, Belgium (10/29/04)
- Singapore (03/10/03)
- Yokohama, Japan (03/24/03)
- Tokyo, Japan (05/21/04)
- Hong Kong (05/05/03)
- Gothenburg, Sweden (05/23/03)
- Felixstowe, United Kingdom (U.K.) (05/24/03)
- Liverpool, Thamesport, Tilbury, and Southampton, U.K. (11/01/04)
- Genoa, Italy (06/16/03)
- La Spezia, Italy (06/23/03)
- Livorno, Italy (12/30/04)
- Naples, Italy (09/30/04)
- Gioia Tauro, Italy (10/31/04)
- Pusan, Korea (08/04/03)
- Durban, South Africa (12/01/03)
- Port Klang, Malaysia (03/08/04)
- Tanjung Pelepas, Malaysia (8/16/04)
- Piraeus, Greece (07/27/04)
- Algeciras, Spain (07/30/04)
- Nagoya and Kobe, Japan (08/06/04)
- Laem Chabang, Thailand (8/13/04)
- Dubai; United Arab Emirates (UAE) (03/26/05)
- Shanghai (04/28/05)
- Shenzhen (06/24/05)
- Kaohsiung (07/25/05)
- Santos, Brazil (09/22/05)
- Colombo, Sri Lanka (09/29/05)
- Buenos Aires, Argentina (11/17/05)
- Lisbon, Portugal (12/14/05)
- Port Salalah, Oman (03/08/06)
- Puerto Cortes, Honduras (03/25/06)

## Operational CSI Ports by Region
### In the Americas
- Montreal, Vancouver and Halifax, Canada
- Santos, Brazil
- Buenos Aires, Argentina
- Puerto Cortes, Honduras

### In Europe
- Rotterdam, The Netherlands

---

1. The editorial content for this article is based on U.S. Customs and Border Protection material. (CBP) information was current as of September 2006.
   For the latest information refer to the U.S. Customs and Border Protection (CBP) Web site at: www.cbp.gov.

SECURITY

- Bremerhaven and Hamburg, Germany
- Antwerp and Zeebrugge, Belgium
- Le Havre and Marseille, France
- Gothenburg, Sweden
- La Spezia, Genoa, Naples, Gioia Tauro, and Livorno, Italy
- Felixstowe, Liverpool, Thamesport, Tilbury, and Southampton, United Kingdom (U.K.)
- Piraeus, Greece
- Algeciras, Spain
- Lisbon, Portugal

### In Asia and the East
- Singapore
- Yokohama, Tokyo, Nagoya and Kobe, Japan
- Hong Kong, SAR China
- Pusan, South Korea
- Port Klang and Tanjung Pelepas, Malaysia
- Laem Chabang, Thailand
- Dubai, United Arab Emirates (UAE)
- Shenzhen and Shanghai, China
- Kaohsiung, Taiwan
- Colombo, Sri Lanka
- Port Salalah, Oman

### In Africa
- Durban, South Africa

### Minimum Standards for CSI Expansion
The following standards must be present in a potential CSI port to be considered for inclusion in the CSI program:

1. The seaport must have regular, direct and substantial container traffic to ports in the United States.
2. The CBP Administration must be able to inspect cargo originating, transiting, exiting or being transshipped through a country.
3. The port must have or make non-intrusive inspection (NII) equipment (gamma or X-ray) and radiation detection equipment available for use at or near the potential CSI port. This equipment is necessary to meet the objective of quickly screening containers without disrupting the flow of legitimate trade.
4. The port must commit to establish a risk management system to identify potential high-risk containers and to the automation of that system. This system should include a mechanism to validate threat assessments and identify best practices.
5. The port must commit to share critical data, intelligence and risk management information with the United States Customs and Border Protection (CBP) in order to do collaborative targeting, and develop an automated mechanism for these exchanges.
6. The port must conduct a thorough port assessment to ascertain vulnerable links in its infrastructure and commit to resolving port infrastructure vulnerabilities.
7. The port must commit to maintain integrity programs, and identify and combat breaches in integrity.

### U.S. CBP Officers Abroad
Along with the host country, CBP officers deployed in foreign countries will be targeting only cargo containers destined for or transiting through the United States. Only those U.S.-bound containers identified as potential threats will be examined either by NII or physical exams. Host-country officials will conduct the examination and CBP officers will observe the security screening.

U.S. CBP Officers at CSI ports abroad will not be armed nor will they have arrest powers. The officers will be working jointly with the host country authorities to screen U.S.-bound containers. They will operate in accordance with the guidelines of the host country and the terms of the declaration of principles to implement CSI.

The staffing levels of CBP offices at each port will be determined by the size of the port, the number of containers (TEUs) shipped monthly and annually, the availability of specialized equipment and by other security factors. Staffing levels will be assessed as the program develops, and adjustments will be made as necessary.

### Will CSI Delay the Flow of Goods?
CBP maintains that the CSI will not delay the transport of containers. Containers typically sit on the pier for several days waiting to be exported. CSI will target containers and screen them during this period before they depart. The CBP expects to use this waiting time at the port of export to do their work. Obviously, there will be a burden on exporters to get containers to the port in sufficient time for CBP and local officials to do their work.

CBP maintains that high-risk containers will be searched, either prior to export to the U.S. or in the U.S. It's a question of where and when, not if.

On the other hand, the movement of low-risk cargo and containers may become even more efficient as a result of the Initiative as these too will be prescreened.

### Is CSI a Trade Barrier?
While some exporters to the U.S. feel that CSI might become a trade barrier, the ultimate trade barrier would be a terrorist attack using shipping containers that would halt all trade.

Consensus opinion is that the CSI is similar to security measures at airports that protect individual passengers, aircraft and crew. It is simply one of the costs of doing business.

CBP maintains that high risk containers will be inspected regardless. CSI is merely a program that screens containers before they depart for U.S. ports of entry rather than after they arrive on U.S. shores.

### Benefits to Being a CSI Port
The CSI is a deterrent to terrorist organizations that may seek to target a foreign port. It provides a significant measure of security for the participating port as well as the United States. CSI will also provide better security for the global trading system as a whole. If terrorists were to carry out an attack on a seaport using a cargo container, the maritime trading system would likely grind to a halt until seaport security is improved. Those seaports participating in the CSI will be able to begin handling containerized cargo far sooner than other ports that haven't taken steps to enhance security. In short, CSI is an insurance policy against the threat of a terrorist attack, not just to the U.S., but to the CSI port and to the trading system as a whole.

### Economic Advantages to CSI Ports
Economic advantages to CSI ports fall into several categories:

1. **Non-intrusive inspection of containers and expedited clearance in U.S. ports**
   The advantages of inspecting containers at the earliest possible point in the supply chain will be a benefit to a CSI port and those foreign exporters using that port. The integrity of the shipment will be better ensured by using pre-arrival information and non-intrusive inspection equipment at foreign port locations, thus expediting their clearance upon arrival in the United States.
2. **A terrorist attack resulting from a non-CSI port**
   In the event of a terrorist attack using a cargo container, CSI ports would experience the least disruption because they have CSI in place. In the event of a terrorist attack, the CSI ports would have a competitive advantage.
3. **Eventual CSI requirement for all ports**
   A reasonable expectation is that all goods or containers shipped to the U.S. will have to pass through a CSI port

prior to their shipment. If this become the case, shippers from non-CSI ports will first have to ship to a CSI port for inspection. This will add additional costs to their shipments.

### Expedited CBP Processing of CSI Cargo

Pre-screened U.S.-bound sea cargo will get expedited processing through CBP upon arrival to the United States. CBP has determined that if a shipment has already been jointly examined by the U.S. and the host country's customs officials, it means one less shipment that CBP officers will have to worry about at a U.S. port. It will allow CBP to focus more attention on high-risk shipments that have not been pre-screened.

New technology, such as tamper-evident seals, are expected to be placed on containers that have been pre-screened overseas to assist in this process. CBP reserves the right to inspect any cargo container that arrives in the United States, whether it has been prescreened or not. However, this will occur only if additional information has become available or the integrity of a seal is compromised.

### Equipment and Costs

CSI implementation requires the host country to have NII (non-intrusive inspection) equipment (including gamma or X-ray imaging equipment) to help scan containers. Many of the ports and major exporting countries already have large container screening machines. In fact, some ports already have extremely sophisticated detection technology in operation.

The host country will determine who pays for the direct cost of screening and unloading containers. In the U.S., however, the importer pays the costs associated with moving, inspecting, and unloading containers.

The CBP does not believe that CSI will entail substantial new costs to the host nations. CBP will pay to deploy officers and computers in foreign seaports, and many host nations already have screening and detection technology in place. To the extent that additional detector or IT equipment is needed to implement CSI, CBP believes that the investment is well worth it. CBP considers it insurance; CSI protects both the port and the national economy of a CSI host country.

### Model Laws and Regulations for Host Countries

When discussing the implementation of CSI, a nation depends upon its native laws and customs. The CBP response has been to draft separate and unique declarations with each participating port to accommodate differences. In addition, as CSI is a cooperative effort, CBP is willing to assist foreign governments in reviewing existing laws and crafting new legislation to support implementation if they so desire.

### CSI's Effect on Trade/Time/Paperwork

CSI is expected to have a significant long-term global impact on trade and trade security. Through collaborative targeting and analysis, international trade will become more secure in each CSI port.

Exports destined for or transiting the U.S., must be compliant with the U.S. 24-hour rule, which requires 14 data elements to be reported 24 hours prior to loading aboard a vessel destined for the U.S.

### Delays as a Result of the CSI

The CBP maintains that the targeting and examination of shipments will be accomplished during the lag time between arrival at the foreign port and ship loading for departure to a U.S. port. Therefore, in theory, it will not take more time to export products. Obviously, shipments not in compliance will face delays.

**SECURITY**

# Registration of Food Facilities[1]

## U.S. Food and Drug Administration (FDA)

### Introduction

On June 12, 2002, the U.S. Public Health Security and Bioterrorism Preparedness and Response Act of 2002 (the Bioterrorism Act) was signed into law. Among its many provisions is a requirement that domestic U.S. and foreign food facilities register with the U.S. Food and Drug Administration (FDA).

In the event of a potential or actual bioterrorism incident or an outbreak of food-borne illness, facility registration information will help the FDA to determine the location and source of the event and permit the agency to quickly notify those facilities that may be affected.

The registration deadline for existing facilities was December 12, 2003. New facilities and foreign facilities that plan to export food or food products to the U.S. should register as soon as possible.

### Who Must Register?

Owners, operators or agents in charge of domestic or foreign facilities that manufacture, process, pack or hold food for human or animal consumption in the United States are required to register the facility with the FDA.

Domestic U.S. facilities are required to register whether or not food from the facility enters U.S. interstate commerce. Certain food facilities are exempt. (See below.)

### Examples of FDA-Regulated Foods

Examples of "food" as defined by the regulation include:

- Food and food additives for humans or animals
- Dietary supplements and dietary ingredients
- Infant formula
- Beverages (including alcoholic beverages and bottled water)
- Fruits and vegetables
- Fish and seafood
- Dairy products and shell eggs
- Raw agricultural commodities for use as food or components of food
- Canned foods
- Live food animals
- Bakery goods, snack food, and candy (including chewing gum)

Food contact substances and pesticides are not "food" for purposes of the rule. Thus, a facility that manufactures, processes, packs or holds a food contact substance or a pesticide is not required to register with the FDA.

### Registration Fees

There are no registration fees required for either the initial registration or for updates of any registration.

### Firms Offering Registration Services

Various third-party firms offer their services to assist domestic and/or foreign facilities to register with the FDA. These firms are not affiliated with the FDA, nor has the FDA contracted with any firms to register facilities. While the registration process is simple, foreign registrants must have a U.S. agent.

### Exempted Facilities

A foreign facility is exempt from registering if food from the facility undergoes further processing (including packaging) by another facility before the food is exported to the United States. The first facility is not exempted from registration if the processing or packaging activities of the subsequent facility are limited to affixing a label to a package or other *de minimis* activity. The facility that conducts the *de minimis* activity must also register. The following domestic and foreign facilities also do not need to register:

- **Private residences** of individuals, even though food may be manufactured/processed, packed or held there.
- **Non-bottled drinking water collection and distribution establishments and structures**, such as municipal water systems.
- **Transport vehicles** that hold food only in the usual course of their business as carriers.
- **Farms**, i.e., facilities devoted to the growing and harvesting of crops, the raising of animals (including seafood), or both.
- **Restaurants**, i.e., facilities that prepare and sell food directly to consumers for immediate consumption, including pet shelters, kennels and veterinary facilities that provide food directly to animals.
- **Retail food establishments** that sell food directly to consumers as their primary function.
- **Nonprofit food establishments**, which are charitable entities and that prepare or serve food directly to the consumer or otherwise provide food or meals for consumption by humans or animals in the U.S.
- **Fishing vessels** that harvest and transport fish.
- **Facilities regulated exclusively and throughout the entire facility by the U.S. Department of Agriculture**, that is, facilities handling only meat, poultry or egg products.

### How Long Does it Take to Register?

The FDA estimates that it takes one or two hours of a manager's time to read and understand the regulations. In addition, filling out a registration form should take less than two hours of a staff worker's time and an additional 15 minutes of an owner, operator or agent-in-charge's time to certify the registration before submission. This assumes access to the Internet and the ability to read and write in English.

### Required Information

Each registration must include:

- Name, physical address, phone number of the facility;
- Parent company's name, physical address, phone number (if applicable);
- Name, address and phone number of the owner, operator or agent in charge;
- All trade names the facility uses;
- Food product categories as identified in the FDA's regulation, 21 CFR 170.3;
- A statement certifying that the information submitted is true and accurate;
- Name and contact information of the person submitting the certification statement;
- A statement certifying that the person submitting the registration, if not the owner, operator or agent in charge, is authorized to register the facility;
- Name of foreign facility's U.S. agent and the agent's address, phone number and emergency phone number (unless the facility designates another person to serve as the emergency contact); and
- Emergency contact information including emergency phone number.

---

1. The editorial content for this article is based on U.S. Food and Drug Administration (FDA) and U.S. Customs and Border Protection (CBP) material and was current as of September 2006.

### U.S. Agent for Foreign Facilities
A foreign facility must designate a U.S. agent (for example a facility's importer or broker), who must live or maintain a place of business in the U.S. and be physically present in the U.S., for purposes of registration.

### Registration Process
Registrants must register or update a registration on FDA Form 3537. Registrations can be submitted electronically via the Internet, through surface mail on a paper form or a CD-ROM, or by fax.

**Internet Registration** Facilities are encouraged to register online via the Internet at www.fda.gov, which can accept electronic registrations from anywhere in the world 24 hours a day, 7 days a week. This Web site is available for registrations from wherever the Internet is accessible.

Electronic registration is faster and more convenient than other forms of registration. A registering facility will receive confirmation of electronic registration and its registration number instantaneously once all the required fields on the registration screen are filled in.

**Mail and Fax Registration** Registration by mail may take several weeks to several months, depending on the speed of the mail system and the number of paper registrations that FDA has to enter manually.

Form 3537 is available for download for registration by mail, FAX, or CD-ROM.

If a facility does not have access to the Internet, a paper copy of the form may be obtained from the FDA by calling: (in the U.S.) (800) 216-7331 or (301) 575-0156 (7:30 a.m.-11 p.m. Eastern Time) or by mailing a request to:

U.S. Food and Drug Administration
HFS-681
5600 Fishers Lane
Rockville, MD 20857 USA

When the form has been filled out completely and legibly, it can be mailed to the above address or faxed to (301) 210-0247.

**Assistance** Registration assistance is available:
- Online at: www.fda.gov/furls
- In the U.S call: (800) 216-7331 or (301) 575-0156
- From elsewhere call: (301) 575-0156
- Fax questions to: (301) 210-0247
- E-mail questions to: esgprep@fda.gov.

The online registration help desk is staffed from 7:30 a.m. until 11p.m. U.S. Eastern Time.

Registration is required only once for each food facility.

**Registration Number** Possession of a registration number means that the owner of the facility has registered with the FDA. Assignment of a registration number does not convey FDA approval or endorsement of the facility or its products.

**Optional Information** The FDA also asks for certain optional information on the registration form. This information will help the FDA communicate more effectively with facilities that may be the target of an actual or potential terrorist threat or other food-related emergency. Although recommended, this information is not required.

### Registration of Multiple Food Facilities
The FDA will accept multiple registrations submitted on CD-ROM (CD-R or CD-RW). Form 3537 must be submitted as a PDF (Portable Document Format) and be accompanied by one signed hard copy of the certification statement.

Each submission on the CD-ROM must use the same preferred mailing address in the appropriate block on Form 3537. There is no maximum number of registrations that may be submitted in this manner. However, each registration on a CD-ROM must have a unique file name up to 32 characters long, the first part of which may be used to identify the parent company. If the information does not conform to these specifications, FDA will not process the registration(s) and will return the CD-ROM for correction.

### Privacy of Registration Information
The list of registered facilities, registration documents, and information derived from the list or the documents that would reveal the identity or location of a specific registered person are not subject to disclosure under the U.S. Freedom of Information Act (FOIA).

### Changes to Registration Information
If a required element of a facility's registration information changes (e.g., change of operator, agent in charge or U.S. agent), the owner, operator or agent in charge, or an authorized individual, must submit an update to the facility's registration within 60 days of the change through the Internet at: www.fda.gov/furls or through the paper update process.

If a facility goes out of business, its registration must be canceled using Form 3537a, either through the Internet, at: www.fda.gov, or through the paper process.

### New Ownership of a Registered Facility
If a registered facility is sold or otherwise changes ownership, the former owner must cancel the facility's registration within 60 days of the change (using Form 3537a), and the new owner must re-register the facility using Form 3537. Both cancellation and re-registration may be completed through the Internet or through the paper process.

### Failure to Register
Failure of a domestic U.S. or foreign facility to register, update required elements, or cancel its registration is a prohibited act under the Federal Food, Drug, and Cosmetic Act. The U.S. Federal government can bring a civil action to ask a court to enjoin persons who commit a prohibited act, or it can bring a criminal action in Federal court to prosecute persons who are responsible for the commission of a prohibited act.

If a foreign facility is required to register but fails to do so, food from that foreign facility that is offered for import into the U.S. is subject to being held at the port of entry for the article unless otherwise directed by the FDA or the U.S. Customs and Border Protection (CBP).

### For More Information
For general information on the FDA Registration Rule, refer to: www.cfsan.fda.gov/~furls/ffrmqa.html#requirement
For greater detail and text of the rule itself, refer to: www.cfsan.fda.gov/~furls/ffregfr.html.

**SECURITY**

# International Ship and Port Facility Security[1]

## (ISPS) Code

### Introduction
The International Ship and Port Facility Security (ISPS) Code sets new standards for security for ships at sea as well as port facilities around the world. It aims to make shipping activities more secure against threats of terrorism, piracy and smuggling.

Security at sea has been a concern to governments, shipping lines, port authorities and importers and exporters for years. The terrorist attacks of September 11, 2001, however, provided the catalyst for formalizing tough new security measures.

In December of 2002, the International Maritime Organization (IMO), a specialized agency of the United Nations (UN), organized a conference to discuss issues related to security at sea. At this conference, representatives from 150 nations (the Contracting Governments) participated in drafting amendments to the Safety of Life at Sea (SOLAS) Convention, and the ISPS Code was adopted.

Changes to the SOLAS Convention include amendments to Chapters V and XI, and Chapter XI was divided into Chapters XI-1 and XI-2. The new Chapter XI-2 provides the umbrella ISPS regulations. The Code itself is divided into two parts. Part A presents mandatory requirements, Part B contains guidance regarding the provisions of Chapter XI-2 of the Convention and part A of the Code.

### ISPS Code Overview
The Code aims, among other things, to establish an international framework for co-operation between Contracting Governments, government agencies, local administrations and the shipping and port industries to detect security threats and take preventive measures against security incidents affecting ships or port facilities used in international trade and to establish relevant roles and responsibilities at the national and international level. ISPS provisions relating to port facilities relate solely to the ship/port interface. Also, ISPS provisions do not extend to the actual response to attacks or to any necessary activities after such an attack.

In addition, for each ship and port authority affected, the ISPS Code requires:
- Implementation of a Ship Security Plan (SSP),
- Implementation of a Port Facility Security Plan (PFSP),
- Appointment of a Ship Security Officer (SSO),
- Appointment of a Company Security Officer (CSO),
- Appointment of a Port Facility Security Officer (PFSO),
- Installation of ship alarms, and
- Installation of shipboard Automatic Identification Systems (AIS).

### Enforcement Date
The ISPS Code went into effect on July 1, 2004.

### ISPS Code Full Text
The full text of the ISPS Code can be found on the Web at: www.dcmnr.gov.ie/files/marsecISPS-2003.pdf

### Application of the ISPS Code
The ISPS Code applies to ships and ports of signatory nations to the SOLAS Convention as well as ships that call upon ports of contracting nations: Specifically:
- Ships engaged on international voyages including:
  -Passenger ships, including high-speed passenger craft
  -Cargo ships, including high-speed craft, of 500 gross tonnage and upwards

  -Mobile offshore drilling units
- Port facilities serving such ships engaged on international voyages

This represents about 55,000 ships and 10,000 to 20,000 port facilities worldwide that need to be certified. The ISPS Code does not apply to warships, naval auxiliaries or other ships owned or operated by a SOLAS Convention Contracting Government and used only on Government non-commercial service. The ISPS Code does not directly impact importers, exporters, NVOCCs or air, rail and truck carriers.

### Ship Owning Companies
Individual ship-owning companies are required to appoint a Company Security Officer (CSO), develop a Ship Security Plan (SSP) for each vessel and appoint a Ship Security Officer (SSO) for each vessel. A company's SSP must contain a clear statement emphasizing the ship master's overriding authority and responsibility to make decisions with respect to the safety and security of the ship and to request the assistance of the ship company or of any Contracting Government as may be necessary.

### The Ship Security Plan (SSP) and International Ship Security Certificate (ISSC)
Flag states (countries of registry of ships) are responsible for approving Ship Security Plans, compliance with SOLAS and the ISPS Code through verification audit, issuing an International Ship Security Certificate (ISSC) and continuous monitoring of ownership, classification and operator information. A flag state may appoint a recognized security organization to act on its behalf.

### Port Authorities
Port authorities are responsible for establishing a Port Facility Security Plan (PFSP) and to act upon the security levels set by the Contracting Government within whose territory it is located. The Port Authority must also provide an interface with the Ship Security Office of vessels calling on the port.

### Contracting Governments and Security Levels
Contracting Governments are responsible for setting security levels (see definitions of security levels which follow) and provide guidance for protection from security incidents.

### "White List" Ports
The IMO has stated that it will publish a "White List" of ports with accepted Port Facility Security Plans (PFSP). If a ship comes from a port which is not on the IMO "White List" the government responsible for a "White List" port may take this as "clear grounds" that the ship may not be in compliance with the ISPS Code. Such vessels may be subject to control and compliance measures. In extreme cases this may even lead to the ship being denied entry into port.

### "White List" Ships
The International Association of Classification Societies (IACS) also publishes a "White List" of ships issued with an International Ship Security Certificate (ISSC) by member societies. A ship not having a valid ISSC will, by definition, be outside ISPS Code requirements.

### "Black List"
The IMO does not issue a "black list" of any kind. There is no IMO list of ports or flag states that are not in compliance.

### U.S. Pre-Arrival Requirements
The United States has imposed pre-arrival requirements in addition to those of the International Maritime Organization

---

1.  The editorial content for this article is based on International Maritime Organization (IMO) material ans was current as of September 2006.

(IMO). Be aware of various U.S. Navigation & Vessel Inspection Circulars (NAVIC), specifically NAVIC 10-02 (www.uscg.mil/hq/g-m/nvic). Information on U.S. cargo security requirements can be found at (www.cbp.gov). Continuous Synopsis Record (CSR)

A new regulation, XI-1/5 requires ships to be issued a CSR which is intended to provide an on-board record of the history of the ship.

### Non-Compliance With the ISPS Code

**International**: As of July 2, 2004 any vessel unable to produce the necessary ISPS certification risks being detained by a port authority until she can show she is implementing the code on board.

**United States:** In the U.S., ship owners were required to have their Ship Security Plans (SSPs) by December 29, 2003. As of July 2, 2004, ships cannot enter U.S. waters without a valid ISPS International Ship Security Certificate. Also, their arrival must be announced 48 hours before entry into U.S. waters.

### IMO Security Model Courses

The IMO has developed the following model courses:
ISPS - Company Security Officer
ISPS - Port Facility Security Officer
ISPS - Ship Security Officer

## ISPS Definitions

### Ship Security Plan (SSP)

A plan developed to ensure the application of measures on board a ship designed to protect persons on board, cargo, cargo transport units, ship's stores or the ship from the risks of a security incident.

The SSP must address issues such as:

*   Measures to prevent weapons, dangerous substances and devices from being taken aboard ship
*   Identification of restricted areas
*   Measures for prevention of unauthorized access to the ship
*   Procedures for responding to security threats
*   Procedures for evacuation in case of security threats
*   Duties of shipboard personnel assigned security responsibilities
*   Procedures for auditing security activities
*   Procedures for security training, drills and exercises
*   Procedures for interfacing with port facility security activities
*   Procedures for the periodic review of the SSP
*   Procedures for reporting security incidents
*   Identification of the Ship Security Officer (SSO)
*   Issues related to ship security equipment

### Port Facility Security Plan (PFSP)

A plan developed to ensure the application of measures designed to protect the port facility and ships, persons, cargo, cargo transport units and ship's stores within the port facility from the risks of a security incident. The ISPS (Section 16) offers guidelines for developing the PFSP.

### Ship Security Officer (SSO)

The person on board a ship, accountable to the master, designated by the Company as responsible for the security of the ship, including implementation and maintenance of the Ship Security Plan (SSP) and for liaison with the Company Security Officer (CSO) and Port Facility Security Officer(s) (PFSO). Note that the ISPS Code does not specify who the SSO shall be. Appointment of the SSO will take into account such factors as existing workloads, aptitude and suitability for the job. Appropriate training must also be given. The SSO may be the ship's master. The ISPS (Section 12) offers guidelines for developing the SSO job description.

### Company Security Officer (CSO)

The person designated by the Company for ensuring that a ship security assessment is carried out; that a Ship Security Plan (SSP) is developed, submitted for approval, and thereafter implemented and maintained and for liaison with Port Facility Security Officer(s) (PFSO) and the Ship Security Officer (SSO). Note that the ISPS Code does not specify who the CSO shall be. Appointment of the CSO will take into account such factors as existing workloads, aptitude and suitability for the job. Appropriate training must also be given. The ISPS (Section 11) offers guidelines for developing the CSO job description.

### Port Facility Security Officer (PFSO)

The person designated as responsible for the development, implementation, revision and maintenance of the Port Facility Security Plan (PFSP) and for liaison with the Ship Security Officer(s) (SSO) and Company Security Officer(s) (CSO). The ISPS (Section 17) offers guidelines for developing the PFSO job description.

### Security Level 1

Normal. The level for which minimum appropriate protective security measures shall be maintained at all times.

### Security Level 2

Heightened. The level for which appropriate additional protective security measures shall be maintained for a period of time as a result of heightened risk of a security incident.

### Security Level 3

Exceptional. The level for which further specific protective security measures shall be maintained for a limited period of time when a security incident is probable or imminent, although it may not be possible to identify the specific target.

### The International Maritime Organization (IMO)

The IMO is a specialized agency of the United Nations that is responsible for measures to improve the safety of shipping and to prevent marine pollution from ships. It was established by means of a Convention adopted under the auspices of t he United Nations in Geneva on March 17, 1948 and met for the first time in January 1959. It currently has 163 Member States. IMO's governing body is the Assembly which is made up of all 163 Member States and meets normally once every two years. It adopts the budget for the next biennium together with technical resolutions and recommendations prepared by subsidiary bodies during the previous two years. The Council acts as governing body in between Assembly sessions. It prepares the budget and work program for the Assembly. The main technical work is carried out by the Maritime Safety, Marine Environment Protection, Legal, Technical Co-operation and Facilitation Committees and a number of sub-committees. For complete information go to: www.imo.org.

SECURITY

# Data Security

Information security is one of the hottest topics in the world of connected computers. The primary targets for information theft are government and business documents of interest to intelligence services, business documents of interest to competitors, credit card data, and other identification documents of interest to thieves.

The following sections offer suggestions for individuals, businesses and government agencies that wish to protect their sensitive data. Note that password protection and encryption (especially for mobile data) are just the beginning of a comprehensive data security regime.

## Computer Data Security

1. Install a personal firewall application and passwords on your computer to prevent hackers and/or tampering that might jeopardize your computer's general security.
2. Install anti-virus software, such as Norton or McAfee, on your computer. Schedule your anti-virus application to update its virus definitions daily. Set your anti-virus program to scan your computer at least once weekly.
3. At regular intervals, back up all data onto a removable storage device such as a CD/DVD or memory stick. These should be password protected.
4. Install encryption software for computers with sensitive data.

## Mobile Data Security

### Mobile Use Policy Considerations

Policy makers should consider devices owned by the firm or user devices that can access corporate networks when setting up the firm's security policies. Considerations should include:

1. Wireless local area networking
2. Public hotspots
3. Home networks
4. Corporate networks
5. Mobile phones
6. Reporting theft or loss of devices
7. Approved connections
8. Authentication credentials and their use
9. Notifying Human Resource and IT departments when staff are laid off or leave the company

### Standard Configuration for Laptop Security

1. Personal firewall
2. Anti-virus software
3. Disk encryption
4. Spyware detector
5. VPN (virtual private network) clients

### Threats to Laptops and PDAs

1. Loss or theft
2. Password theft
3. Viruses
4. Data theft through "line sniffing"
5. Mobile code vulnerabilities for users using the Web
6. Vulnerabilities for devices using wireless services or those that have enabled a wireless port

### Countermeasures for Wireless Laptops/PDAs

1. Label devices with phone number, address or email to assist in recovery.
2. Set up password enforcement.
3. Install anti-virus software.
4. Encrypt content to secure data when in stand-alone mode.
5. Establish company policy that restricts wireless users

from sending and receiving e-mails with proprietary or sensitive information.
6. Disable the device's WIFI/Bluetooth port to reduce risk of unauthorized people intercepting sensitive data.
7. Encrypt data link or employ other measures (e.g., electronic shielding bag) to secure data as it moves between devices for Web and wireless.
8. Create VPN (virtual private network) for extremely sensitive data.
9. Avoid use at multi-firm meetings where security cannot be assured.

## Securing Laptop/PDA for Travel

### Before you Go

1. Back up your entire hard drive/memory card and any sensitive data in case you lose your device.
2. Take only the data you will need for business purposes, and leave the rest at home or at the office.
3. Leave backup copies of your data at home or at your office.
4. Install firewall software on your home or business computer to prevent unauthorized individuals or information from entering your computer system.
5. Make sure you have updated virus protection software installed on your computer.
6. Password protect your computer login as well as your files and make sure that your password contains a mix of random alpha-numeric characters.
7. Insure your laptop before you travel.
8. Remember that computer bags are like beacons to thieves. Extra security awareness is required.
9. Bring your operating system's restore CD in case your operating system becomes corrupt.
10. If your laptop has a CD or DVD burner, bring some extra blank CD-RWs or DVD-Rs so that you can back up important data safely while on the road.
11. Make sure you bring the proper phone lines and power cord adapters for mobile connectivity.
12. Purchase an Anti-theft Device such as a motion sensor alarm or a key cable security lock from any number of suppliers. When in doubt, keep the device with you at all times while you travel.
13. Anti-theft tracking software provides a last line of defense against loss of your device and data. Unlike encryption that prevents access to sensitive files, theft tracking software and hardware come into play after your laptop/PDA is stolen.

### On the Road.

1. Carry backup disks in your suitcase, not your laptop carrying case.
2. Carry memory sticks on your person as you travel, not in your laptop case.
3. If leaving your laptop/PDA at the hotel, be sure to lock it in a safe. If data on the device is not sensitive, use a cable lock and attach it to an immovable object.
4. Always be aware of your surroundings and keep the laptop/PDA out of sight when possible. It may have cost you a few thousand, but a thief will be happy to take a hundred for it.

### Airport Security

1. At airport security, expect to be asked to demonstrate that your laptop/PDA operates.
2. Computers are often stolen from busy x-ray machines while distracted travelers try to get through security. Keep an eye on it and pick it up quickly once it has

passed through the x-ray machine.

3. If you fear for your highly sensitive documents, back them up on a CD-RW or DVD-R.

4. If you must go through the metal detector again, ask one of the guards to hold on to your computer while you go do this. Do not leave your laptop on the x-ray machine rack.

5. Some countries do not permit foreign nationals to enter the country with encryption software on their computer.

6. When standing in an airport or even a hotel lobby, make it as difficult as possible for a thief to snatch your computer equipment.

### Security on Transport

1. Always keep your laptop/PDA close at hand.

2. Pack your laptop in an inconspicuous bag, perhaps even in your suitcase. PDAs are designed to fit in pockets so make use of this feature.

3. If you plan on taking a nap or for overnight trips on trains or buses, be sure your laptop is secured in advance.

4. Keep data back ups and special connection cords packed separately.

### International Rights of Inspection

Data may not only be confiscated by authorities, but also monitored and intercepted at will by government officials. Business travelers who travel into countries where the environment is hostile, or where rights to privacy might be questioned, should take appropriate measures to ensure that data is secure. Contact the embassy of the country you will be traveling to and ask what procedures to expect—then act accordingly.

Note: When visiting developing countries, do not be surprised if the seizure of your computer becomes an opportunity for the solicitation of bribes.

# E-commerce Security

E-commerce is an increasingly utilized means of conducting business. Precautions to make sure that e-commerce transactions remain secure include the following:

### E-Commerce Computer Security

1. Install a personal firewall application on your computer to prevent unauthorized access to your accounts, passwords, and credit card numbers.

2. Never give out your password or personal data online unless you are absolutely sure of the destination site.

3. Beware of "look alike" sites that appear to be brand-name sites. Verify the site name in the address line of your browser. For example, the address for IBM is www.ibm.com, not www.wearedatathieves/ibm.com.

4. When making a financial transaction online, make sure it occurs over a secure connection. The most common secure-connection method is SSL (secure-socket layer). You'll know if your connection is over SSL if the website address starts with "https://" and you see a locked padlock icon in the lower right corner of your browser. In addition, look for a seal of security from a brand-name authorizing entity.

5. On auction sites, use the host software to verify the reliability of sellers.

### Website Hosting Security

If your company hosts any website from its own server:

1. Install firewall to divide the internal network from any external networks.

2. Install anti-virus program on all machines within the network in addition to servers.

3. Make sure all updates and patches are installed on the operating system that is hosting your website and database application.

4. At regular intervals, back up all data onto a removable storage device such as DLT tape, CD/DVD or memory sticks/chips.

5. Ensure that all transactions are done over a minimum of a 128-bit encrypted SSL (secure socket layer) connection.

6. Purchase security certificate authority to assure customers that your website is authentic and that SSL encryption secures all transactions.

### E-mail Security

In most cases, generic e-mail that you send or receive through a regular e-mail account is not secured or encrypted to protect the content. Therefore, any personal information you include in an e-mail is at risk of being intercepted by unauthorized individuals.

1. Do not send sensitive, personal, or financial information unless it is encrypted on a secure Web site and is assured encryption from a trusted source. A Web site is said to be encrypted if the web address contains https://, and if a locked padlock symbol appears in the lower right corner of your browser.

2. Caution: Even encrypted Web sites do not offer full protection and are said by some to offer a false sense of security.

3. For top security needs, proprietary "scrambling" software should be applied so that even if data is intercepted it is undecipherable.

### Internet Cafés

1. Do not send credit card or other personal information from internet café computers (or at least make sure the connection is secure).

2. When using an Internet café computer, never check the "save password" box on your email or sign-in screen.

3. When you are finished, make sure you log off from any account into which you have logged.

4. Before you leave, delete any files you saved on that computer's hard drive.

5. Empty the "trash" and clear the computer's cache as well as the search bar before leaving.

**SECURITY**

# Industrial Espionage

Where commercial analysts gather information about competitors through public sources and media, more aggressive competitors use subversive tactics to garner confidential or proprietary information. Known as commercial or industrial espionage, these tactics can undercut profit potential, market share, undermine negotiations, or even cause bankruptcy for the targeted company. Espionage by competitors (or in some cases, national governments) seeks to acquire anything from manufacturing processes, new product ideas, research and development findings, future plans, proposals, bid information, marketing prospects and strategies, and other corporate data.

### When is Industrial Espionage Noticed?
1. When a rival introduces a very similar product.
2. When others in the company red flag suspicious or illegal behavior.
3. When items, blueprints, schematics, proposals, documents are noticed altered or missing.
4. When extortion occurs for the return of stolen information.

## The Perpetrators

**Employees**: Basic espionage can be sitting right in front of you in the form of employees stealing documents, files, company or trade secrets on their own accord. These freelancers work on their own and decide which information may be of value to someone else. They then turn around and sell the information to the highest bidder or where it will do your firm the most damage.

Competitors may also pay employees of a target company to collect information or steal data. Further yet, the competitor may hire away an upper-level employee to fill a leadership role, and may even hire a whole team to start up a new team within its own ranks.

**Contractors**: In this case, the perpetrating company or government hires outside help in the form of an investigative firm, an information broker, hackers, or thieves to come up with pertinent information about the competitor. Computer hackers can do serious damage without leaving an obvious trace. Competitors often target information they know to be in development.

**Foreign Intelligence**: Foreign governments often engage their own "intelligence" services to acquire trade or research secrets for their own national purposes or industries.

## Espionage Tactics

Trade secrets can get into the hands of competitors through any number of means. Typically, proprietary information gets funneled to the wrong channels through employees—deliberate or not—telecommunications interceptions, and reverse engineering (the act of duplicating an existing product, component, or subassembly). The following list provides the most common methods in use:

### Traditional Espionage
1. **Theft**
   Stealing information or goods to use for the competition.
2. **Blackmail**
   Extortion through the use of threat or intimidation, i.e., by exposing critical information. This can also take the form of "denial of service" threats to an e-commerce firm.
3. **Mole Planting**

An agent who establishes a trusted cover within a company long before beginning any espionage.
4. **Eavesdropping**
   Listening in on private conversations, intercepting WIFI transmissions, or tapping email. Even small gifts given to you for your office or that you can carry in your pocket (anything from pens to picture frames) can conceal hidden cameras, surveillance, or recording devices. Large firms regularly "sweep" their offices for listening devices.
5. **Seduction**
   An age-old technique using sexual offers or advances to lure information out of an individual.
6. **Bribery**
   To influence someone by offering money or a favor to glean information or to prompt illegal or corrupt action.
7. **Foreign Intelligence Recruits**
   A foreign intelligence service recruits volunteers, agents or co-optees to gather information. With the demise of the "cold war" many intelligence officers re-engineered themselves into commercial agents.
8. **Hiring Competitor's Employees**
   Hiring away key employees from a competitor to collect new data, skill sets, or information.
9. **Bogus Job Interviews**
   Interviews of "job candidates" solely for the purpose of collecting information on their current employers.
10. **Bogus Purchase Negotiations**
    Companies or teams that pose as buyers in order to glean critical information about a company.
11. **Research Under False Pretenses**
    Collecting open-source or public materials or databases with false user names to hide the fact that the information collector is in fact a competitor.
12. **Corporate Communications Intercepts**
    Intercepting phone and fax transmissions, particularly international fax transmissions, which make up about 50 percent of all overseas communications, via foreign government-controlled telephone companies.
13. **Using Familial Connections**
    Conversations with unsuspecting relatives working for competing companies.
14. **Trade Fair Conversations**
    Establishing contact at trade fairs, especially with experts who have a high level of technical understanding. Agents may perform fact finding by sitting near potential targets and starting casual conversation, thus establishing a relationship for later use, or through threats of all kinds.
15. **Using Commonalities**
    Targeting individuals with common language, cultural heritage or religion for fact-finding missions.
16. **Naturalized Citizens**
    Foreign governments pressuring or appealing to naturalized citizens to provide information for patriotic or loyalty reasons, or by threatening family members in the home country.
17. **Repatriating Naturalized Citizens**
    Repatriation of naturalized citizens to employ processes and methods used by foreign companies.
18. **Government Debriefing**
    Government debriefing of its citizens to acquire information upon their return from a foreign country
19. **"Dumpster Diving"**
    Going through discarded materials to find pertinent

information. This common form of espionage has sent the sales of paper shredders skyrocketing.

**Solicitation and Marketing**

Marketing and requests by foreign entities to gain access to proprietary information or R & D through service offers, i.e. software support, purchasing or sales, or via employment applications, internships, or other means.

20. **Outsourcing / Delocalization**

Foreign outsourcing can exploit methods, processes, or information. Delocalizing under license often leads to a loss of security in countries unbound by copyright or trademark laws.

21. **Front Companies**

Foreign governments may own private companies (such as import-export firms), joint ventures, or may establish exchange or friendship organizations in other countries in order to gather intelligence from foreigners who have frequent contact with targeted firms or organizations.

22. **Joint Ventures & Bidding Process**

Foreign purchasers may prompt companies to provide copious amounts of data in the bidding process, compromising valuable proprietary information.

23. **Close Proximity**

Joint ventures and strategic alliances may put unscrupulous personnel in close proximity with a firm's key personnel or technology and may allow them to gain access to areas or information outside of their work agreement.

24. **Mergers and Acquisitions**

Mergers and acquisitions often allow new company owners/partners to acquire certain technologies not in their prior possession.

25. **Negotiating**

Sellers need to be aware that buyers may make excessive technology information demands during negotiations. Non-disclosure agreements are helpful here, but not a cure-all, especially in countries with minimal legal protection for foreign firms.

26. **Third-Party Acquisition**

Third-party acquisition of companies and technology often indicates a diversion or a transfer of technology. Sometimes, final recipients turn out to be embargoed individuals, businesses or countries that cannot otherwise get the technology themselves. Freight forwarders in the country of export may serve as decoys by providing the eventual foreign recipient with a local address to bypass local laws for export.

27. **Import-Export Front**

Import-export companies may be involved with illegal exporting of sensitive or illegal documents, data, or other items in the country of export.

28. **Altered Products or False Certification**

Domestic companies serve as fronts for getting export-controlled products to an undisclosed end user by falsifying end-user certificates and purchasing modified products altered in the manufacturing process to satisfy export-controlled specifications. This is quite common in high-tech exports and encryption devices.

29. **University Research**

Information collectors are often placed at university research facilities by foreign government intelligence services or even by commercial competitors.

### Computer Espionage

30. **Copying Files**

To copy computer files and pass them on to other individuals, businesses or governments.

31. **Computer Hacking**

Attempts to illegally gain access to a computer file or network or to do so without proper authorization.

32. **Information Requests**

Requests for sensitive information, particularly via the Internet, to unsuspecting low- or mid-level personnel.

### Visitor Espionage

33. **"Wired" Visitors**

Company visitors fitted with recording devices, video cameras, or cameras. Beware of visitors who ask unusually expert questions or seek otherwise unnecessary access to restricted areas.

34. **Conversation Detours**

Conversation "detours" during interviews or informational conferences to subjects not agreed upon in advance and covering sensitive topics.

35. **Visitor Status**

Downplaying or disguising a visitor's status or technical skill to gain access for a tour or visit.

### Travel Espionage

36. **Luggage or Laptop Search/Theft**

Foreign business people are targets for numerous ploys. Briefcases and luggage in hotel rooms can be searched for sensitive data and copied; the same applies to security checkpoints or border crossings

37. **Tapped Room Phones**

Phone, WIFI, and fax intercepts are often employed through the traveler's hotel phone or point of contact.

## Countermeasures

The following countermeasures are a starting point for security consideration and by no means represent all available measures. Depending upon the size and scope of your activities, you may need to consider only a few or all. Companies with much at stake should engage a professional security firm or security consultants to protect their assets and proprietary information. Note: Some security problems must be tolerated due to the expense of prevention or impact upon a firm's marketing image.

### Building Entry Points

1. **Alarm**

Install alarms with motion detectors in high-risk areas and with dial-up alerts to security firm or police when alarm goes off.

2. **Control Points**

Employ security personnel to control entry ways, check visitors in and out, or man doorways to sensitive areas; install surveillance cameras to monitor comings and goings.

3. **Keys and Locks**

Any sensitive area, especially research and development facilities, should have special keys. Doors in those areas and to stairwells should be locked at all times and connected to burglar and fire alarms. When an employee is terminated or leaves, ensure that all keys are returned and accounted for; erase magnetic key cards; check ceiling and ventilation entry points.

4. **High-Tech Access Control**

Employ biometric scanners that measure parts of the anatomy; e.g., fingerprints, handprints, voice, or retinas work well for high-risk, high-tech companies.

### Data Storage

5. **Safe**

Store sensitive documents, backup disks, laptops or PDAs with sensitive information in an immovable safe.

6. **Off-site Storage**

SECURITY

Store sensitive archives off site in a secure location.

## Information Disposal

7. **Cross-Cut Shredders**
   These shredders hinder even the most patient thief from resurrecting paper records; consider placing next to copiers and fax machines for immediate disposal, especially in areas that churn out sensitive documents; other types of costly shredders that handle larger items are also available.
8. **Trash Protection**
   Secure dumpster areas with proper lighting, fencing, locks, and surveillance.
9. **Overwrite Software**
   Replace previously stored data on a hard drive or disk with random data.
10. **Degaussers**
    Used for removal of all data from disks, tapes, or hard disks by electro-magnetic realignment.
11. **Computer Disposal**
    Computers that hold sensitive data should have the hard drive removed and destroyed. Do not reformat and sell.

## Surveillance Equipment

12. **Electronic surveillance**
    Utilize Internet/email security and CCTV video monitoring (where legal).
13. **Listening and Interception Devices**
    Regularly sweep offices with bug detectors.

## Telecommunications

14. **Telephones**
    The simplest models offer the fewest possibilities for others to listen in; use landlines and avoid cell phones and cordless phones for sensitive conversations.
15. **Photocopy/Fax Machines**
    Be aware that agents can insert an internal computer chip that surreptitiously records information.
16. **Encryption**
    Voice encryption programs will encrypt calls between individuals when both have the encryption device installed.

## Policies

17. **Agreements**
    Employ trade secret non-disclosure and non-compete agreements for all employees with access to sensitive information.
18. **Secure Computing**
    Develop a "Secure Computing Policy" that restricts information abuse.
19. **Awareness**
    Establish awareness training to detect espionage.
20. **Due Diligence**
    Establish due diligence background checks for hiring, outsourcing, or prospective visitors or business teams. Note: Different jurisdictions can restrain the amount and use of information collected.
21. **"At Risk" Employees**
    Management needs to be aware of employees suffering from substance abuse, financial problems, or extreme personal stress, which may prompt illegal activity within the company.
22. **Crisis Management**
    Develop a "Crisis Management Policy" for fire, systems malfunctions, industrial sabotage, natural disaster and terrorist threats.
23. **Continuity**
    Establish "Business Continuity Guidelines" in the event of death or employment separation of key personnel.
24. **Review**
    Review policies frequently and always immediately

after an incident has occurred.

## Computers

25. **Install Firewall**
    To protect your data and system, install firewall software on your computers. Maintain integrity of firewall and patches on a regular basis.
26. **Passwords**
    Regularly change passwords. Disable "save password" function on log-in scripts.
27. **Scan Network Frequently**
    Scan company networks regularly and directly in advance of new product releases.
28. **Install Integrity Checker**
    Allows system administrator to check if programs have been altered in any way and show sign of any suspicious activity.
29. **Use Encryption**
    Code software so that unauthorized users cannot read or change data, especially for e-mail and archiving.
30. **Back Up Files**
    Randomly restore files each week to ensure your back-up method is working properly.
31. **Steganography & Digital Watermarking**
    These techniques allow firms to control digital content by secreting identifying information within graphics. These are key to copyright/trade mark protection online.

## Meetings

32. **Secure Room**
    Assume any room you use is insecure unless otherwise proven to be secure.
33. **Security Sweep**
    Screen for surveillance devices before sensitive meetings. Scan for bugs, laser lights, concealed transmitters, video surveillance, or miniaturized camera lenses.

## Business Travelers

34. **Secure Sensitive Materials**
    Secure laptop computers and any sensitive materials or documents.
35. **Exercise Vigilance**
    Maintain awareness that your phone line, office equipment, or room may be tapped or subject to eavesdropping at any time by the least suspected person.

# Glossary of Security Terms

Security is a very broad field. Up until the mid 1970s, security was primarily concerned with loss prevention (from a logistics and retail perspective), labor unrest and military issues. Since that time, data security, cyber security, industrial espionage and terrorism have become the hot new issues facing companies and governments alike.

In researching these related topics, we have found a multitude of "security" glossaries, each attempting to cover a particular field, with few succeeding, and none that deal with all the topics in a comprehensive manner. The best glossaries available relate to the relatively new field of data security and the ever changing field of military security.

A comprehensive listing of security terms would fill an entire reference book. This glossary does not attempt to be as comprehensive for security as the *Dictionary of International Trade* is for trade and logistics. The emphasis of this glossary is to introduce the international trade and logistics reader to a sampling of key terms used primarily in supply chain management and data security.

Some terms are so elemental to trade and security that they appear in both the A-Z section and this glossary. For example: dual use, Customs-Trade Partnership Against Terrorism, Free And Secure Trade and others.

Clearly, supply chain security is a developing field. Subsequent editions of this Dictionary will have a number of terms removed and a number of terms added. I welcome your suggestions. (e-mail at: ed@worldtradepress.com. Please place "DIT" or "Security" in the subject field of your e-mail.)

Useful glossaries online include:
Data: www.isse.gmu.edu/~csis/glossary/merged_glossary.html
Logistics: www.eyefortransport.com/glossary/ab.shtml

# A

### access
(general) (a) The right, ability or privilege to approach or enter a building, property or secure area (e.g., access to a container facility). (b) The right, ability or privilege of communicating with an individual (especially an important or powerful individual).
(computers) (a) The ability or privilege to enter and use a computer system (e.g., access to the Internet). (b) The ability or privilege to obtain, see, read, write or edit a computer file.

### access control
(general) (a) Procedures and controls that limit the right, ability or privilege to approach or enter a building, property or secure area (e.g., access to a container facility). (b) Procedures and controls that limit the right, ability or privilege of communicating with an individual (especially an important or powerful individual).
(computers) (a) Procedures and controls established to grant, deny, identify and monitor user access to computer information systems through the use of hardware, software, physical access and password systems.
(b) Procedures and controls that limit the right, ability or privilege to obtain, see, read, write or edit a computer file.

### alpha radiation
The most energetic but least penetrating form of radiation. Alpha radiation can be stopped by a sheet of paper and cannot penetrate human skin. However, if an alpha-emitting isotope is inhaled or ingested, it will cause highly concentrated local damage.

### antivirus software
(computers) A software application that detects and prevents known computer viruses and known computer virus types from infecting a computer or network. Some antivirus programs are able to repair computer systems after being infected. Because a steady stream of new viruses are being detected all the time, a user's antivirus software must be updated on a regular basis. The most effective way of doing this is to subscribe to an online service that automatically updates your computer through an Internet connection.

### attack
The act of trying to bypass security controls on a system. The fact that an attack is made does not necessarily mean that it will succeed. The degree of success depends on the vulnerability of the system or activity and the effectiveness of countermeasures.

### audit trail
A chronological record of system activities that is sufficient to enable the reconstruction, reviewing, and examination of the sequence of environments and activities surrounding or leading to an operation, a procedure, or an event in a transaction from its inception to final results.

### authenticate
(a) To verify the identity of a user, device, or other entity in a computer system, often as a prerequisite to allowing access to resources in a system. (b) To verify the integrity of data that has been stored, transmitted, or otherwise exposed to possible unauthorized modification.

### authorization
(a) The process of granting an individual the right to have access to restricted areas. (b) The process of granting a user the right to have access to a computer system.

# B

### back door
A hidden or disguised entry point to a software, hardware or network system created by the software's author, publisher or hardware manufacturer. A back door can be benign for legitimate purposes such as maintenance or be malicious to damage the system. In a typical situation, a sequence of programming characters permits full access to a system manager account, enabling the user total access to the system. Also called trap door.

### background investigation
An formal inquiry concerning an individual, typically prior to employment. A background investigation can include collecting and analyzing (where permitted by law) information regarding: education, employment, military service, criminal and financial records as well as personal interviews of the subject and of people with knowledge of the subject.

### backup
(computers) A duplicate copy of a computer file such as a company database or application program. A backup is made for security purposes in case of loss of data because of an equipment failure, fire, theft, corruption of files or other causes. Backup copies of computer files are stored on an external medium, such as a CD-R, DVD or magnetic tape. Many businesses keep multiple backup copies of important files in various off-site locations such as bank safety deposit boxes. Also used as a verb: to backup a file.

### bacteria
Any of numerous single-celled organisms, that multiply by cell division, free-living or parasitic, that break down the wastes and bodies of dead organisms, making their components avail-

able for reuse by other organisms. Bacteria are necessary for both digestion and fermentation. Bacteria can also be helpful to humans by breaking down organic matter in sewage and in other forms of pollution. Bacteria, however, can also cause disease in humans, plants or animals and be used in bioterrorism attacks. Examples include anthrax, cholera, plaque, tularemia and Q fever.

### beta radiation
High-energy electrons (beta particles) emitted from certain radioactive material. Can pass through 1 to 2 centimeters of water or human flesh, but can be shielded by a thin sheet of aluminum. Beta particles are more deeply penetrating than alpha particles and can damage skin tissue and internal organs.

### biological agent
Living organisms, or the material derived from them, that cause disease in, or harm to, humans, animals or plants, or cause deterioration of material. Biological agents may be found as liquid droplets, aerosols, or dry powders. A biological agent can be adapted and used as a terrorist weapon, such as anthrax, tularemia, cholera, plaque and botulism. Three different types of biological agents exist: bacteria, viruses and toxins.

### biological weapons
Infectious agents or toxins which are pathogenic to human beings. These may include numerous naturally occurring viruses, bacteria or fungi previously known to science as well as genetically engineered organisms previously unknown to humans. These substances possess the common ability to kill or incapacitate large numbers of people. Biological weapons are defined as any micro-organism, virus, infectious substance or toxin capable of causing death, disease or other biological malfunction in a human, animal, plant or other living organism. Toxins are poisonous substances produced by a living organism, but in some cases can also be man-made. The danger of biological weapons is amplified by the fact that exposure to the agents would probably not be diagnosed until symptoms appeared. Comprehensive or quick field detection and identification methods do not currently exist for these agents. Not only may an accurate diagnosis be difficult to accomplish quickly, but the value of medical treatment for some agents may be diminished once symptoms have developed. Personal protection generally consists of immunization or the application of some other post-incident medical treatment, such as the use of antibiotics. A chemical protective mask may also protect personnel from biological agents.

### biometric access control
Any of numerous systems that control access to physical facilities or computer systems using biometric parameters (unique physical identification characteristics) such as fingerprints, hand geometry or retinal scans. Where a PIN or password may be lost, forgotten, stolen, changed or reissued, most biometric parameters cannot.

### biometric identification
The positive identification of a unique individual using biometric parameters (unique physical identification characteristics) such as fingerprints, hand geometry or retinal scans.

### biometric reader
An electronic device capable of identifying one or more of an individual's biometric parameters (unique physical identification characteristics) such as fingerprints, hand geometry or retinal scans.

### blister agent
A chemical agent, also called a vesicant, which causes severe blistering and burns to the eyes, skin and tissues of the respiratory tract. Exposure occurs through liquid or vapor contact. Also referred to as mustard agents; examples include mustard and lewisite.

### blood agent
A chemical agent that interferes with the ability of blood to transport oxygen and causes asphyxiation. These substances injure a person by interfering with cellular respiration (the exchange of oxygen and carbon dioxide between blood and tissues). Common examples are hydrogen cyanide and cyanogen chloride.

### breach
(law) A failure to perform a promised or legal act or obligation.
(security) The successful defeat of security controls resulting in the penetration of a physical facility or computer system.

# C

### card reader
An electronic device used to read information encoded on various types of media represented by badge technologies (magnetic stripe, capacitance, proximity, Wiegand-effect, etc.).

### CBRNE
Chemical, Biological, Radiological, Nuclear and Explosive.

### central station
A monitoring facility that is typically located outside the facility it is monitoring. A facility or area usually manned by security personnel and designed to accept all signals from the organization's intrusion detection systems, access control, closed circuit TV and security forces to determine threat and issue an appropriate response.

### challenge/response
A security procedure used in both human-to-human contact as well as in a system-to-server computer authentication where one communicator demands/requests authentication from another communicator and the latter replies with either a pre-established response, or a computed response using an authentication token.

### chemical agent
A chemical substance intended for use in military operations to kill, seriously injure or incapacitate personnel through its physiological effects.
There are five classes of chemical agents, all of which produce incapacitation, serious injury, or death: (1) nerve agents, (2) blister agents, (3) blood agents, (4) choking agents, and (5) irritating agents.

### choking agent
A chemical substance that causes damage to the tissues of the respiratory system and the eyes. In extreme cases, membranes swell and lungs become filled with liquid, which can result in asphyxiation resembling drowning. Death results from lack of oxygen; hence, the victim is "choked". Common examples are chlorine and phosgene. A protective mask is sufficient to provide protection, provided that the atmosphere contains sufficient oxygen to support life.

### cipher
(a) A message written in code. (b) A system of encryption. (c) An algorithm for encryption or decryption of a message.

### closed area
A physical space such as a room, floor of a building, whole facility or fenced area access to which is restricted to certain employees or personnel who have been given special clearance.

### Company Security Officer (CSO)
The person designated by a company to ensure that a Ship Security Assessment (SSA) is carried out; that a Ship Security Plan (SSP) is developed, submitted for approval, and thereafter implemented and maintained; and to act as liaison with Port Facility Security Officer(s) (PFSO) and the Ship Security Officer (SSO). Note that the International Ship and Port Facility Security (ISPS) Code does not specify who the CSO shall

be. Appointment of the CSO will take into account such factors as existing workloads, aptitude and suitability for the job. Appropriate training must also be given. (International Ship and Port Facility Security (ISPS) Code definition from the International Maritime Organization.)

### compromise
(security) (a) A violation of a security policy, in which an unauthorized disclosure of, or loss of control over, sensitive information may have occurred. (b) The breaching of secrecy and/or security.

### computer security
Measures and controls that ensure confidentiality, integrity, and availability of information systems assets, including hardware, software, firmware and information being processed, stored, and communicated.

### Container Security Initiative (CSI)
(U.S. Customs) A U.S. Customs and Border Protection (CBP) initiative that serves to protect the global trading system and the trade lanes between CSI ports and the U.S.

Under the CSI program, a team of CBP officers is deployed to work with host nation counterparts to identify and examine all U.S.-bound containers that pose a potential threat for terrorism before they are shipped to the United States. The concept is to prevent terrorist threats from being carried out and to make U.S. borders the last line of defense, not the first.

The CSI is founded on four core elements:
1. Using intelligence and automated information to identify and target containers that pose a risk for terrorism;
2. Pre-screening those containers that pose a risk at the port of departure before they arrive at U.S. ports;
3. Using detection technology to quickly pre-screen containers that pose a risk; and
4. Using smarter, tamper-evident containers.

*See also* the CSI section in the Security appendix.

### contamination
(a) The deposit and/or absorption of radioactive material or biological or chemical agents on and by structures, areas, personnel or objects. (b) Food and/or water made unfit for human or animal consumption by the presence of environmental chemicals, radioactive elements, bacteria or organisms in decomposing material (including the food substance itself), or waste, in food or water.

### contingency plan
A plan for emergency response, backup operations and post-disaster recovery, maintained as a part of a security program that will ensure the availability of critical resources and facilitate the continuity of operations in an emergency situation. Synonymous with disaster plan or emergency plan.

### cookie
Information stored by a Web site server on a user's computer as a small text file that indicates what Web pages the user has visited and shows other user/client data such as preferences and passwords. Cookies enable a Web site to monitor and exploit the patterns and preferences of visitors to the site.

### corporate security officer (CSO)
A company employee charged with the responsibility of administering security policy. A CSO may also: develop company security policy, enter into security-related contracts, make assessments of security issues and hire/fire other security personnel.

### corrosive material
A liquid or solid chemical agent that can cause chemical harm at an incident scene, causing visible destruction or irreversible alterations in human skin tissue at the site of contact.

### counterintelligence
Information gathered and activities conducted to protect against espionage, other intelligence activities, sabotage or assassinations conducted for or on behalf of foreign powers, organizations or persons, or international terrorist activities.

### countermeasure
An action or procedure that reduces a risk, threat, vulnerability or attack through elimination, prevention or mitigation of damage.

### counterterrorism
Offensive measures taken by civilian and military agencies of the government to prevent, deter, and respond to terrorism.

### covert collection
The acquisition of information and intelligence through concealment, disguise or deception.

### covert operation
The collection of intelligence or any other activity conducted through concealment, disguise or deception.

### covert threat
An intention or determination to cause harm to an individual, facility, system, organization or government through concealment, disguise, or deception.

### crack (Crack)
(a) To break into a safe, computer system or other locked compartment, room or system. (b) To successfully defeat a cryptographer's code. (c) A popular hacking tool used to decode encrypted passwords.

### crash
(computers) An event that renders a computer temporarily inoperable. The majority of computer crashes are the result of: 1) an overload of instructions or data, 2) a conflict in software, or 3) a hardware failure. Most computer crashes can be resolved by re-booting (restarting) the computer. Also called an abend (contraction of: abnormal end).

### crisis management
Measures to identify, acquire, and plan the use of resources to anticipate, prevent, and/or resolve a threat.

### critical assets
Any facility, equipment, service, network, data, application program, resource or infrastructure considered essential to the operations or mission of a company, organization or government that warrant measures and precautions to ensure its continued efficient operation, protection from disruption, degradation or destruction, and timely restoration.

### cryptography
(a) The encoding (enciphering) and decoding (deciphering) of messages in secret code (cipher). (b) The art, science and discipline of transforming data in order to hide its information content, prevent its undetected modification and/or prevent its unauthorized use by anyone other than the holder of the decryption code.

### Customs-Trade Partnership Against Terrorism (C-TPAT)
(U.S. Customs) A voluntary United States Customs and Border Protection (CBP) business initiative designed to encourage importers, carriers, brokers, warehouse operators and manufacturers to ensure the integrity of the supply chain by strengthening their security practices and communicating their security guidelines to their business partners within the supply chain.

Individual businesses must apply to CBP to participate. Accepted participants must sign an agreement that commits them to the following actions: 1) Conduct a comprehensive self-assessment of their supply chain security using C-TPAT security guidelines. 2) Submit a supply chain security profile questionnaire to CBP. 3) Develop and implement a program to enhance security throughout their supply chain in accordance with C-TPAT guidelines. 4) Communicate C-TPAT guidelines to other companies in their supply chain and work toward building the guidelines into relationships with these companies.

SECURITY

C-TPAT offers businesses an opportunity to play an active role in the war against terrorism. By participating in this first worldwide supply chain security initiative, companies will ensure a more secure supply chain for their employees, suppliers and customers. Beyond these essential security benefits, CBP will offer other potential benefits to C-TPAT members, including:

- Expedited release of cargo
- A reduced number of inspections (reduced border times)
- Eligibility for account-based processes (e.g., bimonthly/monthly payments)
- An emphasis on self-policing, not CBP verifications

For ongoing information and updates on the C-TPAT program, go to the U.S. Customs and Border Protection Web site at www.cbp.gov.
*See also* the C-TPAT section in the Security Appendix.

### cyberbreach
(computers) An unauthorized or illegal breach of a computer system or network resulting in damage or having the potential for damage.

### cyber crime
A criminal act through use of a computer and a computer network. Cyber crime can include the destruction, disclosure or modification of data; theft of physical property, computer services, passwords and credit card numbers; fraud; or mounting a denial of service attack.

### cyber security
(a) Measures taken by an individual, organization or government to safeguard against attack, theft, crime, sabotage or espionage over a computer network.
(b) A department or organization whose responsibility is providing cyber security.

### cyber terrorism
The unlawful use of computers and computer networks by individuals or groups against persons or property to intimidate or coerce an individual, organization or government, or any segment thereof, in the furtherance of political, religious, ideological or social objectives.

# D

### data driven attack
(computers) An attack upon a computer system where damaging code is buried in innocuous-seeming data that passes through a firewall and is then activated behind the firewall.

### decipher
*See* decrypt.

### decontaminate
To break down, neutralize or remove a chemical, biological or radioactive material posing a threat to equipment, personnel or the environment.

### decrypt
(a) To decipher or decode. (b) To transform encrypted text or data (ciphertext) into its original text or data (plaintext).

### degausser
(a) An electrical device used to demagnetize objects.
(b) An electrical device that generates a strong magnetic field used to erase data from various magnetic storage media.

### demon dialer
(computers/telephony) A computer program that repeatedly calls the same telephone number. Demon dialers are benign and legitimate for access to a bulletin board system (BBS) or malicious when used a in a denial of service attack.

### denial of service attack (DOS)
A computerized assault on a network designed to flood it with so many requests that legitimate traffic is slowed or completely stopped.

### dirty bomb
A bomb which combines conventional explosives with nuclear radioactive material which is dispersed upon detonation. The radioactive material is generally obtained from low-grade nuclear isotopes such as those used in medicine or research. The explosion of such a bomb leaves some radioactive contamination, but little physical destruction.

### dual use item
(a) Any raw material, compound, part, component, finished good, computer hardware, software or technology that has both military and commercial utility.
(b) A product or technology developed for civilian use that also has potential for military application or to produce weapons of mass destruction. Dual use items are not weapons and are often traded for perfectly legitimate civilian purposes.

### due diligence
(commerce) The process of discovery of all aspects related to the risks and value of a business that is to be purchased. This includes research into all matters related to financial, product, management, facility, personnel and legal issues of the company.
(export control) The process of discovery of all aspects related to the risks associated with the export of a controlled material, component, product or technology. This includes ascertaining whether the item is on a control list, whether the purchaser is on a Denied Persons List, and whether there is likelihood that a controlled shipment is being diverted for unlawful purposes.

# E

### economic intelligence
The product resulting from the collection, processing, integration, analysis, evaluation and interpretation of available economic, business and commercial information concerning a market, company or national economy. Also, information and knowledge obtained through observation, investigation, analysis or understanding.

### effectively owned or controlled
A business, organization or other entity controlled by another individual, business, organization, government or other entity. One entity is effectively owned or controlled by another when it is either wholly owned, or controlled, either directly or indirectly, whether exercised or exercisable, through the election, appointment or tenure of the officers, or a majority of the officers of the board of directors of that entity by any means (e.g., ownership, contract, or operation of law, or equivalent power for unincorporated organizations).

### e-mail bombs
(computers) Malicious computer code designed to bombard a targeted e-mail address with an overwhelming number of e-mails in an effort to use up the recipient's disk space or overload an e-mail or Web server.

### emergency response (HAZMAT)
A response effort by employees outside the immediate release area or by other designated responders (e.g., mutual aid groups, local fire departments, etc.) to an occurrence which results, or is likely to result, in an uncontrolled release of a hazardous substance.
Responses to incidental releases of hazardous substances where the substance can be absorbed, neutralized or otherwise controlled at the time of release by employees in the immediate release area or by maintenance personnel are not considered to be emergency responses.

Responses to releases of hazardous substances where there is no potential safety or health hazard (i.e., fire, explosion or chemical exposure) are not considered to be emergency responses.

### encipher
*See* encrypt.

### encrypt
(a) To encipher or encode. (b) To transform original text or data (plaintext) into a code (ciphertext) that is unreadable to those without a decryption table or decryption algorithm.

### enhanced due diligence (EDD)
(export control) The process of discovery of all aspects related to the risks associated with the export of a controlled material, component, product or technology. This includes ascertaining whether the item is on a control list, whether the purchaser is on a Denied Persons List, and whether there is likelihood that a controlled shipment is being diverted for unlawful purposes.

### environmental emergencies
Incidents involving the release (or potential release) of hazardous materials into the environment which require immediate action.

### environmental hazard
A condition capable of posing an unreasonable risk to air, water, or soil quality, and to plants or wildlife.

### escort
A cleared employee or staff person, designated by a company, organization or military unit, who accompanies a non-cleared individual into a restricted facility, accompanies a shipment of classified material to its destination, or accompanies a prominent person to a destination.

### espionage
The overt, covert or clandestine practice of spying or using spies to obtain intelligence about the plans and activities of a foreign government, military unit or commercial enterprise. *See* industrial espionage.

### ethernet sniffing
The use of specialized software to monitor and capture data from an Ethernet interface. The software scans packets for data that fits certain criteria, i.e. words like "login," "user name" or "password." Ethernet sniffing can also be used for other industrial espionage purposes such as scanning for and collecting data on products, processes and marketing plans.

### EU Data Protection Directive
A European Union (EU) law stating that personal data from EU countries can only be transferred to non-EU countries that provide an acceptable level of privacy protection. Details at: http://ec.europa.eu/index_en.htm. *See also* Safe Harbor Agreement.

### explosive detection device
An electronic device designed to detect the presence of explosive materials either through detection of the physical property of explosives themselves or their constituent chemicals. Such devices can detect: dynamite, Semtex, RDX, HMX, NC, PETN, EGDN, TNT, ANFO (ammonium nitrate fuel oil), smokeless powder, black powder and other explosives, on skin, cloth, cartons, plastic, metal, rubber, soil, paper, paint and other surfaces.

# F

### facility
A building, plant, laboratory, office, warehouse, storage facility, or other structure that, combined with services, utilities and a unifying function, form an operating entity. The term is also used to describe military sites, ports, airports, communications structures and power generating plants.

### FAST
(United States/Canada/Mexico) Acronym for Free And Secure Trade. The first completely paperless cargo release mechanism put into place by U.S. Customs and Border Protection. This paperless processing is achieved through electronic data transmissions and transponder technology. FAST is highly automated and allows for the expedited release of highly compliant cargo from major importers, reducing congestion at U.S. land borders with Canada and Mexico. For more information, refer to FAST in the Security section of this dictionary or contact U.S. Customs and Border Protection at: www.cbp.gov.

### firewall
(computers) Computer software, or more commonly, a combination of computer hardware, software and security measures designed to keep a computer or computer network secure from intruders.

### flooding program
(computers) Malicious computer code designed to bombard a targeted system, network or Web site with an overwhelming number of requests in an effort to slow down or shut down the system.

### forensics
The science and practice of examining physical evidence and applying the properties of that evidence to the resolution of legal issues, particularly identifying the commission, natures and perpetrators of crimes.

### front company
A company used to mask the identity, true character or activity of the actual controlling agent. Front companies are used to launder money for drug traffickers, crime syndicates and other criminals; illegally purchase and export military hardware; and purchase and illegally export dual use raw materials, components, parts and technology. A front company can be a total sham without any other business activities or a full-fledged operation with legitimate business activities.

# G

### gamma radiation
High-energy, ionizing radiation that travels at the speed of light with great penetrating power. It can cause skin burns, severe injury to internal organs and have long-term, physiological effects. (FEMA-SS)

# H

### hacker
(computers) (a) A highly-skilled computer programmer who writes programs in assembly or systems-level languages. The term refers to the programmer's "hacking away" at tedious computer code when writing complex programs. (b) A mischievous person who seeks unauthorized benign entry into computer systems for the satisfaction of succeeding. (c) A person who seeks unauthorized entry into computer systems for criminal purposes such as disrupting a system, stealing telephone account or credit card numbers or stealing passwords to gain unpaid access to Web-based services.

### Hazard Classes 1-9
A series of nine descriptive terms that have been established by the UN Committee of Experts to categorize the hazardous nature of chemical, physical, and biological materials. These categories are:
1. Explosives,
2. Non-flammable and flammable gases,
3. Flammable liquids,
4. Flammable solids,

5. Oxidizing materials,
6. Poisons, irritants, and disease causing materials,
7. Radioactive materials,
8. Corrosive materials, and
9. Miscellaneous hazardous materials

### hazardous materials (substances)
Any substance exposure to which results or may result in adverse effects on the health or safety of humans or animals.

Any chemical or biological material or agent or disease-causing agent which after release into the environment and upon exposure, ingestion, inhalation or assimilation into any person, either directly from the environment or indirectly by ingestion through food chains, will or may reasonably be anticipated to cause death, disease, behavioral abnormalities, cancer, genetic mutation, physiological malfunctions (including malfunctions in reproduction) or physical deformations in such persons or their offspring.

### HAZMAT
Acronym for hazardous materials.

### HAZMAT Team
An organized group of employees, designated by the employer, who are expected to perform work to handle and control actual or potential leaks or spills of hazardous substances requiring possible close approach to the substance. The team members perform responses to releases or potential releases of hazardous substances for the purpose of control or stabilization of the incident. A HAZMAT team is not a fire brigade nor is a typical fire brigade a HAZMAT team. A HAZMAT team, however, may be a separate component of a fire brigade or fire department.

### hijacking
(transportation) The seizing control of a vehicle in transit, such as a truck or airplane, either to rob it or divert it.

(computers) The seizing control of an active, authenticated computer session to masquerade as a user, intercept responses or otherwise use system resources.

### hoax tactic
A false threat (such as a bomb threat) designed to disrupt operations at a facility, adversely affect morale and force staff and customers to evacuate a facility leaving them open to attack.

### hostage tactic
The kidnapping of an individual or group in order to make demands against the safety of those taken.

### hot standby
Backup redundant equipment kept in a power-on mode and running in order to replace the function of other primary equipment if such equipment should fail.

# I

### identification
Evidence of identity.

### improvised nuclear device (IND)
A device incorporating radioactive materials designed to result in the formation of an explosive nuclear yield. Such devices may be fabricated from lower grade nuclear isotopes such as those used in medicine or research or may result from the seizure or theft of weapons-grade nuclear material.

### industrial espionage
The overt, covert or clandestine practice of gathering proprietary information about the plans and activities of a commercial enterprise by government or non-government personnel of the same or different nation for the purpose of improving the competitive position of another commercial enterprise.

### industrial security
Measures or controls taken by a commercial enterprise to protect its physical, financial and intellectual assets from attack, theft, crime, sabotage or espionage.

### information
Any communication or representation of knowledge, such as facts, data or opinions in any medium or form, including textual, numerical, graphic, cartographic, narrative or audiovisual.

### information security
Measures or controls taken by an individual, organization, commercial enterprise or government entity to protect proprietary or sensitive information stored or communicated in any manner, medium or form against unauthorized access, modification or theft, including measures necessary to detect, document, and counter such threats.

### information security officer (ISO)
The individual charged with the responsibility of implementing an organization's information security policy.

### infrastructure
(national) (a) The foundation upon which economic development is based. (b) A nation's public system of highways, ports, airports, telephone networks, computer networks, public buildings, dams, reservoirs, power generating plants, sewage treatment facilities, bridges, emergency services (including medical, police, fire, and rescue), and other utilities required for economic activity. (c) The above, plus a nation's private system of financial institutions, educational institutions, health care facilities, computer networks, media, professional associations, social institutions (such as churches, synagogues, girl scouts and parent-teacher associations) and continuity of government and the rule of law.

(business) (a) The foundation upon which a business organization operates and thrives. (b) A company's physical facilities, patents, trademarks, copyrights, human resources, computer systems, networks and strength and continuity of leadership required to operate and thrive.

### insider
A person whose position within an organization gives him or her access to material information about company finances, marketing plans, specialized technical data or a computer system's operations or safeguards that is not available to the public or to others within the organization.

### insider attack
(computers) (a) An assault upon the integrity of a computer system or network instigated or carried out by an insider. (b) An assault upon the integrity of a computer system or network carried out from inside a protected network.

### intelligence
The product resulting from the collection, evaluation, analysis, integration and interpretation of all available information and knowledge about a subject obtained through observation, investigation, analysis or understanding.

### International Ship and Port Facility Security (ISPS) Code
The ISPS Code, developed by the International Maritime Organization (IMO), a specialized agency of the United Nations (UN), is a series of amendments to the SOLAS (Safety of Life at Sea) Convention that set new standards for security for ships engaged in international voyages as well as port facilities around the world. It aims to make shipping activities more secure against threats of terrorism, piracy and smuggling.

The ISPS Code went into effect on July 1, 2004.

The full text of the ISPS Code can be found on the Web at: www.dcmnr.gov.ie/files/marsecISPS-2003.pdf

Also, contact the IMO at: www.imo.org.

### intruder
A person who successfully gains unauthorized access to a physical space or a computer system or network.

### intrusion detection
The detection of break-ins or attempted break-ins of a secured physical space or secured computer system or network either through security personnel or by an electronic security system.

### IP number/address
(computers) Acronym for Internet Protocol number. A numeric address consisting of four numbers separated by periods that uniquely identifies a certain computer on the Internet.

### IP sniffing
The use of a sniffer program to steal network addresses from network packets. Harmful data can then be transmitted using the trusted network addresses.

### IP splicing / hijacking
(computers) The interception of an active, established IP session that is co-opted by the unauthorized user. IP splicing attacks occur after an authentication has been made, permitting the attacker to assume the role of an already authorized user.

# J

No entries.

# K

### kidnapping
The unlawful act of capturing a person against their will, removal of the victim to another place, and holding them in false imprisonment.

### key
Any device or code whose possession entitles the holder to a means of access. A value used in combination with an algorithm to code or decode data.
In encryption, a key is a string of bits used to encode (encrypt) and/or decode (decrypt) a file. You can enter a key in either alphanumeric or condensed (hexadecimal) format.
In network access, a key is the token, or authentication tool, that a device utilizes to send and receive challenges and responses during the user authentication process.
A key may also be a small, hardware device that can be inserted into a computing device.

### Known Shipper Program
(United States) A U.S. Transportation Security Administration (TSA) rule that allows well-established shippers to send freight in the cargo holds of passenger airliners. Other shippers must ship cargo on all-cargo planes or use ground transportation. For information go to: www.tsa.gov.

# L

### least privilege
The principle that each subject in a system be granted the most restrictive set of privileges (or lowest clearance) needed for the performance of authorized tasks. The application of this principle limits the damage that can result from accident, error or unauthorized use.

### level of protection
The degree to which an asset (person, equipment, object, etc.) is protected against injury or damage from an attack.

### logging
The process of noting and recording all activities and events that occur on a computer system or network.

### logic bomb
A resident computer program that triggers the perpetration of an unauthorized act when particular states of the system are realized.

### loophole
An error of omission or oversight in software or hardware design that permits the circumvention of system security. Different from a bug.

# M

### mail bomb (e-mail bomb)
(a) A bomb or incendiary device delivered in a posted letter or package. (b) An overwhelmingly large amount of e-mail sent to a user's e-mail address in an attempt to crash the user's e-mail program.

### malicious user
(computers) A computer user who wishes to cause harm or injury to a computer system or network, or commit an unlawful act against the owners of a computer system or network. A malicious user can cause damage to the operational abilities of the system or network or steal passwords, codes or credit card numbers, or gain access to unauthorized data.

### MIS security
Measures or controls taken by an organization to safeguard and protect a Management Information System (MIS) against unauthorized use, modification or destruction; disclosure of data; or a denial of service.

# N

### national security
Measures adopted by the government of a nation to protect the safety of its citizens, guard against military or terrorist attack and prevent the unauthorized disclosure of sensitive or classified information that might threaten or embarrass the nation.

### National Security Institute
The National Security Institute (NSI), established in 1985, provides a variety of professional information and security awareness services to defense contractor, government and industrial security executives throughout the United States. NSI's central business is helping clients interpret and implement government security directives and establish sound security strategies that effectively safeguard classified and proprietary information. This is accomplished through the publication of newsletters, special reports, seminars and electronically via their Web site at: http://nsi.org.

### NBC
Acronym for Nuclear, Biological and/or Chemical.

### need-to-know
The necessity for access to, knowledge of, or possession of classified or proprietary information required to carry out official duties.

### nerve agent
A substance that interferes with the central nervous system. Exposure is primarily through contact with a nerve agent in liquid form through skin and eyes, and secondarily through inhalation of the nerve agent in vapor form. Three distinct symptoms are associated with nerve agents: pinpoint pupils, an extreme headache and severe tightness in the chest. Examples of nerve agents are sarin, soman, tabun, and VX agent.

### network security
Measures or controls taken by an organization to protect a computer network from: unauthorized access, modification and information disclosure, and physical impairment or destruction.

**network security officer**
An employee of an organization charged with the responsibility of ensuring that its computer network is protected from: unauthorized access, modification and information disclosure; physical impairment or destruction; and the provision of assurance that the network continues to perform its critical functions correctly.

**network worm**
*See* worm.

**nuclear radiation**
Particulate and electromagnetic radiation emitted from atomic nuclei in various nuclear processes. The important types of nuclear radiation, from a weapon standpoint, are alpha and beta particles, gamma rays and neutrons. All nuclear radiation is ionizing radiation, but the reverse is not true; X-rays for example, are included among ionizing radiation, but they are not nuclear radiation since they do not originate from atomic nuclei.

# O

**one-time password**
In network security, a password that is issued and used only one time for a challenge-response authentication process. One-time passwords cannot be reused.

**operations security**
The systematic process by which an organization, government or other entity identifies, controls access to, and protects information about its operations and activities to deny or mitigate an adversary's or competitor's ability to compromise the operation or activity.

**opt in**
To explicitly consent to participate in an activity, program or offering such as an online newsletter or online advertising e-mail program.

**opt out**
To explicitly decline to participate in an activity, program or offering such as an online newsletter or online advertising e-mail program.

**Orange Book**
(a) The Phillips/Sony specification document (it has an orange cover) for Compact Disc Magneto-Optical (CD-MO) and Write-Once (CD-WO) systems. Specifically, the standards by which recordable CDs (Compact Disks) are recorded.
(b) Popular name for the U.S. Department of Defense Trusted Computer System Evaluation Criteria book published by the U.S. National Computer Security Center, a division of the NSA (U.S. National Security Agency). The Orange Book contains a uniform set of basic requirements and evaluation classes for assessing degrees of assurance in the effectiveness of hardware and software security controls built into systems. These criteria are intended for use in the design and evaluation of systems that will process and/or store sensitive or classified data. This document is Government Standard DoD 5200.28-STD. For detailed information as well as the full text of the Orange Book, go to: www.dynamoo.com/orange/index.htm.
(c) The United Nations (UN) book: Classification and Testing of Dangerous Goods.

**overt collection**
The legal acquisition of information via public sources.

**overt operation**
The collection of intelligence or any other activity conducted openly, without concealment.

**overt threat**
An intention or determination to cause harm to an individual, facility, system, organization or government that is conducted openly, without concealment or disguise.

# P

**PAPS**
*See* Pre Arrival Processing System.

**PARS**
*See* Pre Arrival Review System.

**passive attack**
An attack upon a physical facility or computer system that does not result in destruction or theft of property or data. For example, an attack that monitors data. Synonymous with surveillance or eavesdropping.

**password**
A private alpha and/or numeric character string used by an individual to verify identity and gain access to a computer, network, server or physical facility.

**penetration**
The successful unauthorized access to a computer, network or physical facility.

**phishing**
(computers) The malicious use of e-mail messages, online advertisements and fraudulent Web sites to deceive people into revealing personal information such as account passwords, social security numbers and credit card numbers. For example, a phisher sends out e-mail messages purporting to be from a well-known and trusted company such as eBay, AOL or Citibank. (This is also called spoofing.) A link in the e-mail takes the unsuspecting user to a phony Web site with the look and feel of the trusted company. There the user is conned into entering sensitive data such as account passwords or credit card numbers, which the phisher then uses to commit acts of fraud. Phishers may also prompt users to supply sensitive information directly in an e-mail. To prevent such fraud, users should note the url of the linked Web site. Ebay's url, for example, is www.ebay.com, not some long string of letters. Also, users should be aware that legitimate companies never ask users for sensitive information in e-mails. For more information, go to the Anti-Phishing Working Group Web site at: www.antiphishing.org/index.html. *See also* social engineering, spoofing.

**phisher**
(computers) A criminal who commits acts of fraud by phishing.

**phracker**
An individual who combines phone phreaking with computer hacking.

**phreaker**
(a) An individual fascinated by the telephone system. (b) A criminal who hacks telephone company computer systems in order to make free phone calls, impersonate directory assistance, divert calls to numbers of the perpetrator's choice or otherwise disrupt telephone service to legitimate subscribers.

**phreaking**
The criminal act of hacking telephone company computer systems in order to make free phone calls, impersonate directory assistance, divert calls to numbers of the perpetrator's choice or otherwise disrupt telephone service to legitimate subscribers.

**physical security**
Physical barriers and control procedures designed to protect assets and personnel from harm, damage, theft, espionage or sabotage, through unauthorized access to facilities, equipment, material or documents.

**piggy back**
(logistics) The transportation of truck trailers and containers on specially equipped railroad flatcars. Also called trailer on flatcar.

(security) The gaining of unauthorized access to a physical facility or computer system by or through another individual's legitimate access. For example, the driver of an unauthorized vehicle might closely follow an authorized vehicle through an automated gate into a restricted area.

### PIN
Acronym for Personal Identification Number. An individual user's private code used in conjunction with an access control system during the authentication process. PINs are used in a wide variety of security situations including bank check and credit cards, telephone cards, library cards and company identification cards.

### piracy
Piracy consists of any of the following acts:
(a) Any illegal acts of violence or detention, or any act of depredation, committed for private ends by the crew or the passengers of a private ship or a private aircraft, and directed:
   (i) On the high seas, against another ship or aircraft, or against persons or property on board such ship or aircraft;
   (ii) Against a ship, aircraft, persons or property in a place outside the jurisdiction of any State;
(b) Any act of voluntary participation in the operation of a ship or of an aircraft with knowledge of facts making it a pirate ship or aircraft;
(c) Any act inciting or of intentionally facilitating an act described in paragraphs (a) or (b) above.
Source: Article 101 of the 1982 United Nations Convention on the Law of the Sea (UNCLOS).

### pollutant
A substance or mixture which after release into the environment and upon exposure to any organism will or may reasonably be anticipated to cause adverse effects in such organisms or their offspring.

### Port Facility Security Officer (PFSO)
The person designated as responsible for the development, implementation, revision and maintenance of the Port Facility Security Plan (PFSP) and for liaison with the Ship Security Officer(s) (SSO) and Company Security Officer(s) (CSO). (International Ship and Port Facility Security (ISPS) Code definition from the International Maritime Organization.)

### Port Facility Security Plan (PFSP)
A plan developed to ensure the application of measures designed to protect the port facility and ships, persons, cargo, cargo transport units and ship's stores within the port facility from the risks of a security incident. (International Ship and Port Facility Security (ISPS) Code definition from the International Maritime Organization.)

### Pre-Arrival Processing System (PAPS)
(United States) A U.S. Customs and Border Protection Automated Commercial System (ACS) border cargo release mechanism that utilizes barcode technology to expedite the release of commercial shipments while processing each shipment through Border Cargo Selectivity (BCS) and the Automated Targeting System. (ATS). For more information, go to: www.cbp.gov. *See* Automated Commercial System, Border Cargo Selectivity, Automated Targeting System.

### Pre-Arrival Review System (PARS)
The Pre-Arrival Review System (PARS) is a Canada Border Services Agency (CBSA) (formerly the Canada Customs Revenue Agency (CCRA)) border cargo release mechanism for those importers with RMD (Release on Minimum Documentation) privileges that expedites the release of commercial shipments to Canada. The Canadian PARS system is similar to the U.S. Pre-Arrival Processing System (PAPS) system, but where PAPS applies to shipments from Canada to the U.S., PARS applies to shipments from the U.S. to Canada. For more information, go to

the Canada Border Services Agency Web site at: www.cbsa-asfc.gc.ca.

### pretexting
The practice of getting an individual's personal information under false pretenses. Pretexting tactics include calls to individuals, banks, credit card firms, telephone companies, or places of employment to gain personal information. Pretexters seek to obtain Social Security Numbers (SSNs), telephone records, bank records, drivers' licenses and other information to falsely obtain credit, steal assets, or investigate individuals. Pretexting is against the law in the U.S.

### private key
(a) In secret key cryptology, a code (password or key) the sender and recipient both agree upon in advance and use for both encryption and decryption of future messages. *See* secret key cryptology.
(b) In public key cryptology, one of two codes (passwords or keys) the sender or recipient uses to encrypt or decrypt a message. The other is the public key. *See* public key cryptology.

### probe
Any effort to gather information about a physical facility or computer system for the purpose of gaining unauthorized access at a later time.

### proprietary information
Privately held information developed by a company that is related to its business, products or activities and that is not available to the public, without restriction, from another source. Proprietary information includes a range of categories of information including: client lists, computer programs, trade secrets, financial statements, marketing plans, research and development data, performance specifications, marketing plans and manufacturing processes.
Unlike proprietary information, patents, trademarks and copyrights are publicly known, but also publicly protected.

### proxy
(a) A person authorized to act for another.
(b) An intermediary software application that acts as both a server and a client for the purposes of making requests on behalf of other clients. For example, a firewall proxy provides Internet services that are outside of the firewall to internal users, essentially controlling access to services in both directions.

### public key
In public key cryptology one of two codes (passwords or keys) used to encrypt or decrypt a message. The user releases the public key so that anyone can use it to encrypt a message to be sent back to the user. However, only the user's private key is able to decrypt the sender's message. Compare private key.

### public key cryptology
A two-key cryptology system (also known as dual-key cryptology) in which encryption and decryption are performed with public and private keys (codes or passwords), allowing users who do not know each other to securely send and receive messages.
For example: George has a mathematically connected key pair (code). One half of the key pair is made public (the public key) while the other half is kept private (the private key). Anyone in possession of George's public key can send him a message encrypted using George's public key. Upon receipt, George, the only one in possession of the private key, decrypts the message.
Also known as asymmetrical key encryption.
Public key cryptology contrasts with secret key cryptology where the sender and recipient must agree upon and use the same private key for encryption and decryption.

### purge
(computers) The complete removal of session data from a computer, computer system, disk drive or peripheral device with storage capacity at the end of a session. A purge is per-

formed in such a way that there is assurance proportional to the sensitivity of the data that the data may not be reconstructed.

# Q

No entries.

# R

### radiation
Energy that is radiated or transmitted in the form of rays or waves or particles. There are three types of nuclear radiation: (1) alpha, (2) beta, and (3) gamma. Radiation is the cause of one of the six types of harm (*See* TRACEM). (Refers to nuclear radiation, not radiation as a type of heat transfer.)

### radio frequency identification (RFID) tag
(logistics) A small integrated circuit (microprocessor) connected to an antenna which can respond to an interrogating radio frequency (RF) signal with simple identifying information, or with more complex information depending on the size and complexity of the integrated circuit. Unlike bar codes which assign a number (product number, sku number, etc.) to a product or package, RFID tags attach a unique electronic code to each product, carton of products, pallet or shipping container. RFID technology is at the core of sophisticated inventory management systems and is used in smart pallets and smart containers.
*See* smart containers, smart pallets.

### radiological threat
The threat to human, animal and plant life, and economic and social systems by radiological (nuclear) dispersion devices such as dirty bombs.

### recovery
(general) The long-term activities beyond the initial crisis period and emergency response phase of a disaster that focus on returning individuals, organizations, governments or nations to a normal status or to reconstitute these systems to a new condition that is less vulnerable.
(computers) The restoration of a computer system's lost data or the reconciliation of conflicting or erroneous data after a system failure.

### remote attack
(computers) A malicious attack targeting a computer, system or network other than the computer the attacker is logged on to.

### restricted area
A controlled access area established for the purpose of safeguarding valuable assets or sensitive material. A restricted area can be a room, the floor of a building, an entire building or an entire facility.

### ricin
(Ricinus communis) A highly toxic plant protein derived from the coat of castor oil plant seeds (castor beans). If eaten, ricin acts as a violent irritant and is deadly. Considered a bioweapon, the Russian KGB developed a particularly potent form said to have been used by the Bulgarian Secret Service to assassinate defectors during the Cold War. As little as one milligram of ricin can kill an adult.

### risk
The exposure to danger, loss or damage to life, health, property or the environment. The probability or likelihood of sustaining loss or damage to life, health, property or the environment.

### risk analysis
The process of identifying security risks, vulnerabilities and threats, determining their likelihood and magnitude, and identifying areas needing safeguards. Risk analysis is a part of risk management. Risk analysis lists risks in rank order of severity as well as costs to the organization of implementing countermeasures. Synonymous with risk assessment.

### risk assessment
Synonymous with risk analysis.

### risk avoidance
A risk management philosophy and planning process that seeks to avoid activities that carry risk. *See* risk mitigation.

### risk management
The total process of identifying, measuring, controlling, and eliminating or minimizing negative events that may affect a system, facility or organization. Risk management includes risk analysis, cost benefit analysis, system selection, implementation, testing, evaluation and review.

### risk mitigation
A risk management planning process where actions are taken to reduce the impact of a possible risk

# S

### Safe Harbor Agreement
(personal data security) An agreement between the United States and the European Union (EU) that sets standards for U.S. companies regarding the transfer and handling of personal data originating from EU companies. Background: The 1998 European Commission Directive on Data Protection prohibits the transfer of personal data to non-European Union nations that do not meet the European "adequacy" standard for privacy protection. While the U.S. and the EU share the goal of enhancing privacy protection for their citizens, each takes a different approach to privacy. The U.S. uses a sectorial approach that relies on a mix of legislation, regulation and self regulation. The European Union, however, relies on comprehensive legislation that, for example, requires creation of government data protection agencies, registration of data bases with those agencies, and in some instances prior approval before personal data processing may begin.
U.S. firms that register and receive a Safe Harbor certification from the U.S. Department of Commerce and abide by the agreement are deemed by the EU to provide adequate privacy protection as defined by the Directive. For a list of the seven principles, answers to FAQs and other details go to: www.export.gov/safeharbor.

### seal, cargo
(security) A closure incorporating a metal strip or wire and a fastener that must be broken to be opened, thus indicating tampering. Cargo seals are used for securing shipping containers, rail freight cars, truck doors and doors leading to restricted areas.

### secret key cryptology
A single key cryptology system where the sender and recipient must agree upon and use the same private key (code or password) for encryption and decryption. Also called symmetric cryptology. *See* public key cryptology.

### security
(a) The state of being free from danger, fear or anxiety. (b) Measures or controls taken by an individual, organization or government to be free from attack, theft, crime, sabotage or espionage. (c) A department or organization whose responsibility is providing security. (d) A guarantee that an obligation will be met. (e) Something pledged that an obligation will be met.

### security evaluation
An evaluation done to assess the degree of trust that can be placed in systems for the secure handling of access, informa-

tion or goods. Security evaluations include assessments of human, hardware, software and physical systems.

### security in depth
A security program consisting of layered and complementary security controls sufficient to deter and detect unauthorized entry and movement within a computer system or physical facility.

### Security Level 1
The level for which minimum appropriate protective security measures shall be maintained at all times. (International Ship and Port Facility Security (ISPS) Code definition from the International Maritime Organization.)

### Security Level 2
The level for which appropriate additional protective security measures shall be maintained for a period of time as a result of heightened risk of a security incident. (International Ship and Port Facility Security (ISPS) Code definition from the International Maritime Organization.)

### Security Level 3
The level for which further specific protective security measures shall be maintained for a limited period of time when a security incident is probable or imminent, although it may not be possible to identify the specific target. (International Ship and Port Facility Security (ISPS) Code definition from the International Maritime Organization.)

### security policy
The set of laws, rules and practices that regulate how an organization manages and protects people, information, facilities and goods.

### security requirements
The types and levels of protection necessary for people, information, facilities and goods to meet security policy.

### security safeguards
The protective measures and controls that are prescribed to meet the security requirements of a system or organization. These safeguards may include but are not limited to: hardware and software security features, operating procedures, accountability procedures, access and distribution controls, management constraints, personnel security, and physical structures, areas, and devices.

### security violation
An instance where security has been circumvented, defeated or attacked unlawfully or without authorization.

### Ship Security Officer (SSO)
The person on board a ship, accountable to the master, designated by the Company as responsible for the security of the ship, including implementation and maintenance of the Ship Security Plan (SSP) and for liaison with the Company Security Officer (CSO) and Port Facility Security Officer(s) (PFSO). Note that the ISPS Code does not specify who the SSO shall be. Appointment of the SSO will take into account such factors as existing workloads, aptitude and suitability for the job. Appropriate training must also be given. The SSO may be the ship's master. (International Ship and Port Facility Security (ISPS) Code definition from the International Maritime Organization.)

### Ship Security Plan (SSP)
A plan developed to ensure the application of measures on board a ship to protect persons on board, cargo, cargo transport units, ship's stores or the ship from the risks of a security incident. (International Ship and Port Facility Security (ISPS) Code definition from the International Maritime Organization.)

### Smart and Secure Tradelanes (SST)
Launched by the Strategic Council on Security Technology (SCST), Smart and Secure Trade Lanes (SST) is an industry-driven, supply chain security initiative. The SST initiative focuses on deploying an end-to-end supply chain security solution—from point of origin to point of delivery—across multiple global trade lanes.

SST incorporates new, more secure business practices and advanced technologies with over 65 partners such as terminal operators, carriers, service providers and shippers in a global information network for intermodal container security.

### smart card
A credit-card-sized plastic device with an embedded microprocessor that stores and transfers data. The data stored can serve as identification, hold personal information such as medical history, or store digital cash. Access to the card requires a code. The card can be programmed to self destruct if an incorrect password is entered too many times.

Contrast to a "dumb card" that has a magnetic strip or barcode that relies upon access to a computer network to get information.

### smart container
(logistics) An ocean or air (ULD) shipping container equipped with devices capable of monitoring and transmitting the following to a central location: worldwide location; interior and exterior temperatures; exposure to light, radiation and chemicals; and inventory data (through Radio Frequency Identification (RFID) Tags and transponders on cartons).

U.S. Customs and Border Protection is considering the use of smart containers as a requirement for participation in the "Customs-Trade Partnership Against Terrorism" (C-TPAT) initiative.

### smart pallet
(logistics) A shipping pallet equipped with an electronic device (Radio Frequency Identification (RFID) Tag) that allows it to be tracked within a facility or while in transit.

### smart seal
(logistics) A combination cargo container seal and electronic device that continuously relays the container's physical location and alerts monitoring personnel if the cargo seal has been broken (implying tampering with the container).

### sniffing
(computers) The use of a sniffer program to passively collect (steal) network addresses from network packets. Harmful data can then be transmitted using the trusted network addresses.

### social engineering
(computers) Any of various techniques used to trick individuals into giving out passwords, user names, addresses or other important information in order to fraudulently gain access to computer systems, bank or credit card accounts, and physical facilities for the purpose of defrauding individuals, companies and organizations.

Social engineering is typically carried out by telephone or in Internet chat rooms. Methodologies include posing as a telephone company employee, a forgetful employee of the same company, a journalist, or an administrator of a bank, credit card company, or Internet service provider (ISP). *See also* phishing, spoofing.

### spoofing
(computers) (a) To gain access to a system by posing as an authorized user. (b) To make an e-mail communication appear that it is coming from a sender other than the actual sender.

# T

### 24-Hour Rule
(U.S. Customs) An amendment to the U.S. Trade Act of 2002 requiring that sea carriers and NVOCCs (Non-Vessel Operating Common Carriers) provide U.S. Customs and Border Protection (CBP) with detailed descriptions of the contents of sea containers bound for the United States 24 hours before the container is loaded on board a vessel. The

SECURITY

cargo information required is that which is reasonably necessary to enable high-risk shipments to be identified for purposes of ensuring cargo safety and security and preventing smuggling pursuant to the laws enforced and administered by CBP. This information must be detailed and be transmitted electronically through approved systems.

Foreign exporters to the U.S., domestic U.S. exporters and importers, and foreign importers of U.S. products are also affected by these new regulations, because the bulk of the data forwarded to CBP by the carriers and NVOCCs originates from these groups. If transmittal of information is either incomplete, misleading or not timely, a number of potentially serious problems for the trader can arise, including: 1) CBP may issue a "No Load" order to the carrier, effectively keeping the shipment at port and subjecting the shipment to storage charges and the importer and exporter to possible lost commercial opportunities, 2) Having the shipment become the target of additional scrutiny by CBP and possibly subjecting it to intense cargo examinations, and 3) Potential denial or delays in obtaining permission to unlade the cargo at a U.S. port.

For more information, go to: www.cbp.gov. *See also* the 24-Hour Rule section of the Security Appendix.

### terrorism
The unlawful use of force or violence by individuals, groups or governments against persons or property to intimidate or coerce a government or governments, a civilian population or any segment thereof, in the furtherance of political, religious, ideological or social objectives. Acts of terrorism can include murder, assassination, kidnapping, hijacking, bombing, theft, fraud, and various acts of cyber-terrorism.

### toxins
A class of biological poison resulting from the by-product of living organisms. A toxin may be obtained naturally, that is, from secretions of various organisms, or synthetically.

### threat
A capability, intention, methodology or warning of an adversary to cause harm. A circumstance, event or vulnerability with the potential to cause harm.

Threats can be to persons, groups, organizations, companies, governments, facilities, critical infrastructure, computer or information systems, food sources, water sources or the environment.

Threats can be both foreign and domestic and can come from individuals, groups, governments, biological factors, chemical factors and the environment.

### toxicity
The ability of a substance to produce injury once it reaches a susceptible site in or on the body.

### TRACEM
Acronym used to identify six types of harm one may encounter at a terrorist incident: Thermal, Radioactive, Asphyxiation, Chemical, Etiological and Mechanical.

### Trojan Horse
(computers) A seemingly harmless or benign software program that contains and conceals malicious code designed to collect, falsify or destroy information in a user's computer. Trojan Horses are non-replicating codes that might, for example, steal personal information and send it to a thief, launch a distributed denial of service attack, or erase a hard drive. A Trojan Horse can also conceal a self-replicating virus or worm. Named after the large wooden horse filled with Greek soldiers left by the Greeks outside Troy during the Trojan War. *See* virus, worm.

# U

### user
(computers) (a) A person that interacts directly with a computer system. (b) A person that has a login account on a computer system, application program or Web site. (c) A person who submits a request to a computer system. A user is considered to be a distinct entity from operators, programmers, administrators and security personnel.

### user ID
(computers) Short for user identification. A unique character string that identifies an individual to a computer system, application program or Web site as a valid user. Authentication, on the other hand, is the process by which a user establishes that they are who they say they are and that they have the right to use a computer system. *See* authentication, password.

# V

### virus
(biology) The simplest type of microorganism, lacking a system for their own metabolism, that replicates itself only within the cells of living hosts. Many viruses are pathogenic (producing or capable of producing diseases). Types of viruses include smallpox, Ebola, Marburg and Lassa fever.

(computers) A self-propagating Trojan Horse. A software program designed maliciously to infect and harm computer files. A computer virus is distinguished by its ability to attach itself to other programs and self-replicate. Typically, a virus arrives hidden within or attached to a file, program, e-mail or e-mail attachment. Some viruses simply display a harmless message when activated, while others are designed to do severe damage to computer files and system software. A virus can be activated automatically or by a trigger event such as a date, time or sequence of keyboard strokes. Viruses are typically passed through boot sectors of disks and through files and cause problems on individual computers, whereas worms cause problems on networks. A number of anti-virus programs are available and can be especially helpful because many viruses operate on similar principles that can be detected by the anti-virus software. However, it is wise to regularly update this software (often with direct downloads from Web sites), as new viruses are invented and discovered daily. *See* Trojan Horse, worm.

### vulnerability analysis
The systematic examination of systems in order to determine the adequacy of security measures, identify security deficiencies and provide data from which to predict the effectiveness of proposed security measures.

# W-X-Y-Z

### weapons of mass destruction (WMD)
(security) A broad family of weapons characterized by their broad-sweeping intended effects of inflicting mass casualties and/or physical destruction. Includes nuclear, chemical, biological and radiological weapons, but excludes the means of transporting or propelling the weapon where such means is a separable and divisible part of the weapon.

### worm
(computers) A software program designed maliciously to harm computer systems. Specifically, a software program that is designed to self-replicate and self-propagate in computer network environments causing them to consume memory and slow or crash the network in the process. *See also*: Trojan Horse, Virus.

# Manifest and Cargo Release Methods[1]

## Automated Commercial Environment (ACE)

### Introduction

The Automated Commercial Environment (ACE) is the next generation of U.S. Customs and Border Protection (CBP) border processing technology designed to facilitate legitimate trade while strengthening border security.

### Integrated On-Line Access

The ACE Secure Data Portal, essentially a customized Web page, connects CBP, the trade community, and participating government agencies by providing a single, centralized, on-line access point for communications and information related to cargo shipments.

### Periodic Payments

With the ACE account-based system, monthly payment and statement capabilities are available. Duties and fees no longer have to be paid on a transaction-per-transaction basis, and companies can more easily track their activities through customized account views and reports that better meet their business needs. ACE periodic payment users have the ability to wait until the 15th working day of the next month to pay for shipments released during the previous calendar month. This provides a potentially significant cash flow benefit. To date, more than US$6 billion in duties and fees have been paid through the ACE monthly statement process since the first payment was made in July 2004. A total of $709.7 million in payments were collected via August 21, 2006 monthly statements, representing approximately 26 percent of adjusted total statement collections.

### ACE Account Facts

There are currently more than 3,200 ACE portal accounts, including more than 600 importer accounts, more than 400 broker accounts, and more than 2,200 carrier accounts. Nonportal ACE accounts are also available, which enable importers to use authorized brokers with ACE portal accounts to make payments without the importer creating a separate ACE portal account.

### Electronic Manifests (e-Manifests)

All carriers are required to submit manifests detailing shipment, carrier, and other information to enter the United States. e-Manifests are simply electronically filed manifests. The e-Manifest feature is available at all ACE land border ports. To date, nearly 25,000 truck e-Manifests have been filed through a certified Electronic Data Interchange (EDI) or the ACE Secure Data Portal. More than 330 companies are currently certified to file e-Manifests through EDI.

EDI certification is not needed to file e-Manifests through the portal. Parties may submit e-Manifests with CBP directly at no charge, or authorized brokers, service providers, or other third parties designated by the carrier may also be used to help with filings, usually for a fee. **In 2007, CBP will begin to make the filing of e-Manifests mandatory, on a port-by-port basis.** In the coming months, check the CBP Web site at www.cbp.gov and the Federal Register for notices that will detail which ports will b ecome mandatory, on what dates. Notice will be provided a minimum of 90 days before a mandatory policy is implemented.

### ACE Locations

Total number of ACE ports: 47

States where ACE is deployed: Arizona, California, Michigan, Minnesota, New Mexico, New York, North Dakota, Texas, and Washington. CBP is working to finish deployment at all 98 land-border ports. Eventually ACE will reach all ports when, in the coming years, capabilities are deployed for air, rail, and sea cargo processing.

## ACE e-Manifest

The Trade Act of 2002 mandated that U.S. import cargo information must be sent electronically to US Customs and Border Protection (CBP) prior to its arrival into the United States. To satisfy this requirement, CBP used Pre-Arrival Processing System (PAPS), Border Release Advanced Selectivity System (BRASS), electronic in-bond QP/WP, Customs Automated Forms Entry System (CAFES), and Free and Secure Trade Program (FAST).

Soon it will be mandatory for all carriers to file their manifest electronically to comply with the Trade Act. Once this requirement has been mandated, the use of PAPS, CAFES, QP/WP, BRASS, and FAST can continue, however, CBP will no longer accept those processes as satisfying the Trade Act (one exception, FAST-NCAP (National Customs Automation Program) will still satisfy the Trade Act requirements). Thus, carriers, importers, and brokers should continue using these processes to ensure that arriving trucks are cleared from the port of entry as expeditiously as possible.

The ACE e-Manifest is now operational in the truck environment on a voluntary basis along both the Northern and Southern Border, but, as stated above, will be mandatory on a port-by-port basis by 2007.

The electronic transmission of information with the ACE e-Manifest Truck only replaces the requirement to present a paper manifest. The transmission of the e-Manifest still requires either an Entry or an In-bond movement authorization for the goods to proceed.

## How to Apply for ACE

If your company has Internet access, your company is eligible.

### Step 1: Fill out the ACE Application

- Applications can be found at:
  www.cbp.gov/modernization
  or by sending an e-mail to ACENow@dhs.gov
- Fill out all required application fields on your computer
- Print out the completed application

### Step 2: Return the ACE Application to CBP

- Mail the completed application to:
  ACE Secure Data Portal -- ACE Applications
  U.S. Customs and Border Protection
  Beauregard Building, Room A-314-3
  7681 Boston Boulevard
  Springfield, VA 22153
  CBP ACE Portal Support Center: (703) 921-6000

---

1. The editorial content for this article is based on U.S. Customs and Border Protection material (www.cbp.gov) and was current as of September 2006.

**SECURITY**

# Pre-Arrival Processing System (PAPS)

The Pre-Arrival Processing System (PAPS) is a U.S. Bureau of Customs and Border Protection border cargo release mechanism that utilizes barcode technology to expedite the release of commercial shipments to the U.S. while still processing each shipment through Border Cargo Selectivity (BCS) and the Automated Targeting System (ATS). PAPS has become mandatory for truck carriers at land border ports of entry to the U.S.

Each PAPS shipment requires a unique barcode label, which the carrier attaches to CBP 7533 (Inward Cargo Manifest) and the invoice while the merchandise is still in Canada. The barcode consists of the U.S. Standard Carrier Alpha Code (SCAC) and Pro-Bill number. This information is then transmitted by fax or Electronic Data Interchange (EDI) to a Customs broker in the U.S., who prepares a BCS entry in ACS (Automated Commercial System). Upon the truck's arrival at the border, the Customs Inspector scans the barcode, which automatically retrieves the entry information from ACS. If no examination is required, the Inspector then releases the truck from the primary booth, reducing the carrier's wait time and easing congestion at the U.S. border.

### How to use PAPS

1. To obtain your U.S. Standard Carrier Alpha Code (SCAC), contact the National Motor Freight Traffic Association (NMFTA) at (703) 838-1868 or at www.NMFTA.org
2. Email a copy of your NMFTA letter of notification (in pdf or tif format) with your assigned SCAC to: AMS.SCAC@DHS.gov, or
   Fax a copy of your NMFTA letter of notification with your assigned SCAC to: CBP SCAC Processing; Bureau of Customs and Border Protection; Fax: (703) 650-3650
3. Create a PAPS barcode: Some carriers develop their own and others use commercial printers. Remember, the SCAC, Number, and Check Digit should be continuous without spaces or dashes.
4. Place an original barcode label on a blank manifest (CF7533) and deliver it to a CBP office at your border crossing. Place the label in column 1. The purpose of this is to ensure CBP can scan your company's PAPS bar codes.
5. Contact your customs broker. Notify them that your company will be participating in PAPS and you will need their 3-digit filer code. You and your broker should then develop a method to fax the commercial invoices, with PAPS bar codes, to them while the goods are still in Canada.
6. Develop a fax cover sheet with your broker to alert them that your SCAC and pro-bill number must be entered in advance of arrival. Include the ETA for conveyance.

**Note**: PAPS is for U.S.-bound commercial vehicles and is not interchangeable with the Canadian PARS System, which is for Canadian-bound commercial traffic. For information go to the CBP Web site at: www.cbp.gov.

### Updated PAPS Procedures, Invoices and Release Dates

As of January 18, 2005 an invoice with or without an affixed barcode will no longer be required for primary clearance. Transmission of the invoice and PAPS information via FAX or EDI to the customhouse broker is still required. The broker continues to be responsible for maintaining the invoice copies and shall make them available upon demand of a CBP Officer. PAPS entries are not considered to be paperless and require documentation at the time of entry. For release purposes at primary processing locations a properly completed and signed CBP 7533 with a barcode containing the required PAPS information is sufficient. Due to this change in processing, CBP release stamps are not required to be placed on CBP 7533 or invoices for PAPS entries. The electronic release date retained in the Automated Commercial System (ACS) and transmitted to the filer via ABI will be the date of record for release date purposes. Entry date calculations will be made using the electronic release date in ACS.

# Pre-Arrival Review System (PARS)

The Pre-Arrival Review System (PARS) is a Canada Border Services Agency (CBSA) (formerly the Canada Customs Revenue Agency (CCRA)) border cargo release mechanism for those importers with RMD (Release on Minimum Documentation) privileges. PARS expedites the release of commercial shipments to Canada.

The Canadian PARS system is similar to the U.S. Pre-Arrival Processing System (PAPS) system, but where PAPS applies to shipments from Canada to the U.S., PARS applies to shipments from the U.S. to Canada.

The key element of PARS is a bar-coded cargo control number, which the carrier or U.S. exporter applies to the top right-hand corner of the original CBSA invoice for each shipment. Other required documents must also be provided: certificate(s) of origin, invoices, declarations, etc. The PARS can process goods that require permits or certificates.

A copy of the complete set of documentation, including the bar-coded invoice, is sent to the Canadian importer or broker by facsimile before arrival of the shipment in Canada.

The importer or broker then submits their import request to CBSA. "PARS" must be clearly marked by the importer or customs broker on the PARS release package.

When the documentation is received by the CBSA, a Customs officer enters data into the automated CBSA computer system.

A recommendation to release or refer is made in the Customs Commercial System (CCS). This recommendation will remain in effect for a limited period of time.

When the shipment arrives at the point of importation, the carrier/driver presents the bar-coded original release documentation to a CBSA inspector who scans the bar code into CBSA's automated system.

The system displays the status of the shipment as "to release" or "to refer".

If the status of the shipment is "to release", the CCRA inspector releases the goods to the driver. The customs inspector date-stamps the invoice copies and returns the stamped invoice photocopy to the carrier as proof of clearance.

If the status is "to refer", the shipment will be referred to an inspector who will follow normal examination procedures.

For more information, go to the Canada Border Services Agency Web site at: www.cbsa-asfc.gc.ca, call (613) 946-4278, or fax to (613) 957-9717.

# Automated Manifest System (AMS)

## Introduction

The Automated Manifest System (AMS) is a U.S. Customs and Border Protection (CBP) multi-modular cargo inventory control and release notification system. AMS interfaces directly with Customs Cargo Selectivity and In-Bond systems, and indirectly with Automated Broker Interface (ABI), allowing faster identification and release of low risk shipments. AMS speeds the flow of cargo and entry processing and provides participants with electronic authorization to move cargo release prior to arrival. AMS facilitates the intermodal movement and delivery of cargo by rail and trucks through the In-bond system. Carriers, port authorities, service bureaus, freight forwarders and container freight stations can participate in AMS. AMS reduces reliance on paper documents and speeds the processing of manifest and waybill data. As a result, cargo remains on the dock for less time, participants realize faster tracking, and Customs provides better service to the importing community.

For details on Sea, Air and Rail AMS, go to: www.cbp.gov and enter Automated Manifest System (AMS) in the "Search" field. You can also call the Automated Commercial System (ACS) Client Representative Branch at (703) 650-3500.

## Sea AMS

Sea AMS allows participants to transmit manifest data electronically prior to vessel arrival. CBP can then determine in advance whether the shipment merits examination or immediate release. Upon notification from CBP, the carrier can make decisions on staging cargo and the importer can arrange for examination, release and distribution of the merchandise. All this can be accomplished before the vessel arrives. Sea AMS allows you to communicate with other AMS participants, other government agencies, container freight stations, and non-vessel commercial carriers.

### With Sea AMS you can:
- File inward manifest data electronically.
- Get electronic cargo release days before vessel arrival.
- Benefit from electronic arrival of a vessel at each port of call.
- Amend, delete, or re-add bill of lading data electronically.
- Participate in the Paperless Master In-bond program.
- Receive electronic in-bond authorizations.
- Designate secondary parties to receive carrier status notifications: designate AMS service center, FIRMS location, rail carrier, truck carrier, terminal operator, or another ocean carrier.
- Transfer custodial bond liability electronically.
- Request and receive electronic authorizations for Permits to Transfer (PTT).
- Receive notification of APHIS, other government agency, and Customs holds.
- Receive batch numbers with transmissions from AMS to enhance tracking ability.

## Air AMS

Air AMS allows carriers to "arrive" an in-bond shipment and to file in-bond, permit to proceed, and local transfers electronically. The carrier obtains notifications of releases, in-bond authorizations, general order, permit to proceed, and local transfer authorization upon flight departure or arrival from the last foreign port. Air waybill data can be transmitted in any sequence. Carriers have the option to transmit bills at random or group them by flight. Amendments to any air waybill information can also be transmitted electronically through AMS. Air AMS increases data reliability and electronic enforcement capability by standardizing the way the trade community and CBP communicate.

### With Air AMS you can:
- File and amend air waybills electronically.
- Communicate flight departures electronically.
- File permit to proceed, in-bond, and local transfers electronically, often in the original bill.
- "Arrive" an in-bond shipment at the port of destination.
- Use the air waybill number as the in-bond control number.
- Designate a freight forwarder or deconsolidator to act as an agent for the carrier.
- Receive cargo status notifications as soon as Customs is notified that the flight has departed from the last foreign port.
- Designate cargo as General Order through AMS.
- Receive electronic authorization from the initial arrival port to the final destination.

### Freight Forwarders and Deconsolidators can:
- File air waybill information electronically for non-automated air carriers.
- Update existing air manifest data once designated as an agent by the carrier.
- Receive all cargo status notifications for the non-automated carriers serviced.

## Rail AMS

Rail AMS is a cargo release notification system for rail carriers. Using a unique bill of lading number, the rail carrier electronically transmits bill information to CBP. When all bills on a train are assigned, the rail carrier transmits a "consist" of the bills and containers in standing car order. This allows Customs an opportunity to review the submitted documentation and determine, in advance, whether the merchandise merits examination or release. The carrier, upon receiving a release from Customs, is able to make decisions on staging cargo, and the importer can arrange for examination, release, and further distribution of the merchandise. The U.S. Department of Agriculture has access to Rail AMS to review manifest data electronically and perform other functions. Similar capability is planned for other agencies.

### With Rail AMS you can:
- Send Customs a "train enroute, one hour out" message within one-hour of reaching the border. This prompts Customs to release the carrier's status messages.
- Participate in Automated Line Release.
- Receive electronic authorization for multi-transit border or in-transit border moves.
- Specify a broker in the bill of lading—the broker will then receive the bill of lading in Customs CATAIR format, as well as status notifications pertaining to the bill.
- File inward manifest data electronically.
- Amend, delete, or re-add bill of lading data electronically.
- Participate in Paperless Master In-bond program.
- Receive electronic in-bond authorizations.
- Designate secondary parties to receive carrier status notifications.
- Receive notification of APHIS, other government agency, and Customs holds and removals.

SECURITY

# Advance Manifest Rules[1]

## for Cargo Information
## "2-Hour Rule" "24-Hour Rule" Etc.

(Affecting United States importers and exporters and their trading partners.)

Introductory Note: The following is an overview of the basic provisions of the U.S. Customs and Border Protection (CBP) advance cargo information requirements (known as the "24-Hour Rule"). For actual text of the "Final Rule," a series of FAQs (Frequently Asked Questions) with answers, plus additional information go to the CBP Web site at: www.cbp.gov. Please note that the rules and their enforcement are evolving and therefore subject to change.

### Background

In response to the terrorist attacks in New York and Washington, DC on September 11, 2001, the U.S. government made substantive changes to the structure of numerous governmental agencies and enacted laws designed to better secure the country against possible future terrorist attacks.

The 200-plus year old U.S. Customs Service was renamed the Bureau of Customs and Border Protection, (CBP) and was consolidated, along with a number of other existing government agencies into the new Department of Homeland Security (DMS). Importantly, the Trade Act of 2002 (section 343(a)) required that the CBP establish rules for the mandatory collection of electronic cargo information prior to the arrival of cargo in the United States (inbound cargo or imports) or its departure from the United States (outbound cargo or exports) by any mode of commercial transportation (sea, air, rail or truck).

On December 5, 2003, U.S. Customs and Border Protection (CBP) published a notice (Final Rule) in the Federal Register (68 FR 68140) announcing changes in the Customs Regulations to require the advance electronic presentation of information for cargo in all modes of transportation, both inbound and outbound.

### The New Regulations ("Final Rule")

68 FR 68140 amends the Customs Regulations to provide that the Bureau of Customs and Border Protection (CBP) must receive, by way of a CBP-approved electronic data interchange system (EDI), information pertaining to cargo (manifest data) before the cargo is either brought into or sent from the United States by any mode of commercial transportation (sea, air, rail or truck).

The cargo information required is that which is reasonably necessary to enable high-risk shipments to be identified for purposes of ensuring cargo safety and security and preventing smuggling pursuant to the laws enforced and administered by CBP. These regulations are specifically intended to effectuate the provisions of section 343(a) of the Trade Act of 2002, as amended by the Maritime Transportation Security Act of 2002.

### Who is Affected?

Carriers and NVOCCs (non-vessel operating common carriers) are directly affected by the new regulations. Both groups must comply by sending manifest data to CBP according to the regulations (details follow).

Foreign exporters to the U.S., domestic exporters and importers, and foreign importers of U.S. products are also affected by these new regulations, because the bulk of the data forwarded to CBP by the carriers and NVOCCs originates from these groups. If transmittal of information is either incomplete, misleading or not timely, it can cause a number of potentially serious problems including:

1. CBP may issue a "No Load" order to the carrier, effectively keeping the shipment at port and subjecting the shipment to storage charges and the importer and exporter to possible lost commercial opportunities.
2. Having the shipment become the target of additional scrutiny by CBP and possibly subjecting it to intense cargo examinations.
3. Potential denial or delays in obtaining permission to unlade the cargo at a U.S. port.

Obviously, importers and exporters will need to work closely with their foreign counterparts, carriers, NVOCCs and logistics firms to ensure compliance.

It should be noted that these new regulations are for the purpose of national security and that CBP is taking a very firm stance regarding compliance.

### Inbound Transmission Times

The regulations require that carriers send the required data to the CBP using the AMS (Automated Manifest System) and that the data be received by CBP according to the following timetable:

| | Inbound - Transmission Received by CBP in AMS |
|---|---|
| Vessel | 24 hours (before lading at foreign port) for non-bulk shipments<br>24 hours before arrival for bulk shipments |
| Air | 4 hours before "Wheels up" from NAFTA (Canada and Mexico) and Central and South America above the equator |
| Rail | 2 hours before arrival in U.S. |
| Truck | 1 hour before arrival for non-Free and Secure Trade (FAST) participants<br>30 minutes before arrival for FAST participants |

The time requirements for bulk and break-bulk carriers to submit their cargo declaration information to CBP in SEA AMS is as follows:

| Cargo Declaration Data (CBP Form 1302) Including FROB* | | |
|---|---|---|
| Type of Cargo | Qualifier | Time of Receipt by CBP in AMS |
| Containerized | NONE | 24 hours prior to loading |
| Break Bulk (non-exempt) | NONE | 24 hours prior to loading |
| Bulk Cargo | Voyage more than 24 hours | 24 hours prior to arrival |
| Bulk Cargo | Voyage less than 24 hours | Time of Sailing |

---

1. The editorial content for this article is based on U.S. Customs and Border Protection material (www.cbp.gov).

| Cargo Declaration Data (CBP Form 1302) Including FROB* | | |
|---|---|---|
| Type of Cargo | Qualifier | Time of Receipt by CBP in AMS |
| Break Bulk Cargo (exempt) | Voyage more than 24 hours | 24 hours prior to arrival |
| Break Bulk Cargo (exempt) | Voyage less than 24 hours | Time of Sailing |

*FROB = Foreign Remaining On Board Cargo
The 24-hour period prior to loading begins from CBP receipt of information. The information is transmitted to CBP and must pass system edits and validations with a receipt message back to the transmitter to be considered received.

## Effective Dates
The "Final Rule" became effective January 5, 2004. However, within the Final Rule there were various implementation dates for automated transmissions for each mode of transportation. Carriers and/or automated NVOCCs are required to submit an electronic cargo declaration to CBP for all vessels loading on or after March 4, 2004. Any vessel that began its voyage on or after March 4, 2004 must comply with the specified reporting timeframe. Those vessels that were between foreign ports of call on March 4, 2004 were not required to comply with the electronic requirement for that voyage. The implemention dates were as follows:

| Inbound | Implementation Date |
|---|---|
| Air | Beginning August 13, 2004 (See below) |
| Rail | Beginning July 12, 2004 (See below) |
| Truck | Beginning November 15, 2004 (See below) |
| Vessel | Voyages Commencing March 4, 2004 or later |

### Air AMS Implementation Dates (69FR10151)
The dates when air carriers were required to comply varied depending on the air carrier's port of entry in the U.S. Airports in the named states were required to automate data transmissions by the listed dates.
**August 13, 2004**
Connecticut, Delaware, District of Columbia, Florida, Georgia, Maine, Maryland, Massachusetts, New Hampshire, New Jersey, New York, North Carolina, Pennsylvania, Puerto Rico, Rhode Island, South Carolina, Vermont, Virginia and West Virginia
**October 13, 2004**
Alabama, Arkansas, Illinois, Indiana, Iowa, Kansas, Kentucky, Louisiana, Michigan, Minnesota, Mississippi, Missouri, Nebraska, New Mexico, Ohio, Oklahoma, South Dakota, Tennessee, Texas and Wisconsin
**December 13, 2004**
Alaska, Arizona, California, Colorado, Hawaii, Idaho, Montana, Nevada, North Dakota, Oregon, Utah and Washington
### Rail AMS Implementation Dates (69FR19207)
The dates when rail carriers were required to comply varied depending on the inbound rail cargo's port of entry in the U.S. Listed are the implementation dates, CBP Ports, corresponding port codes and field office locations in parentheses.
**July 12, 2004 (First Implementation)**
Buffalo, NY (0901, Buffalo); Detroit, MI (3801, Detroit); Richford, VT (0203, Boston); Ft. Covington/Trout River, NY

(0715, Buffalo); Norton, VT (0211, Boston); Highgate Springs, VT (0212, Boston); Champlain-Rouses Point, NY (0712, Buffalo); Brownsville, TX (2301, Laredo); Eagle Pass, TX (2303, Laredo); Laredo, TX (2304, Laredo); El Paso, TX (2402, El Paso); Calexico, CA (2503, San Diego); Nogales, AZ (2604, Tucson); Blaine, WA (3004, Seattle/Tacoma); Sumas, WA (3009, Seattle/Tacoma); Eastport, ID (3302, Seattle/Tacoma); Sweetgrass, MT (3310, Seattle/Tacoma); Noyes, MN (3402, Seattle/Tacoma); Portal, ND (3403, Seattle/Tacoma); Frontier/Boundary, WA (3015,Seattle/Tacoma); Laurier, WA (3016, Seattle/ Tacoma); International Falls, MN (3604, Chicago); Port Huron, MI (3802, Detroit); Sault Ste. Marie, MI (3803, Detroit)
**August 10, 2004 (Second Implementation)**
Jackman, ME (0104, Boston); Van Buren, ME (0108, Boston); Vanceboro, ME (0105, Boston); Calais, ME (0115, Boston)
**September 9, 2004 (Third Implementation)**
Tecate, CA (2505, San Diego); Otay Mesa, CA (2506, San Diego); Presidio, TX (2403, El Paso)
### Truck Implementation Dates
The dates when truck carriers were required to comply vary depending on the inbound truck's port of entry in the U.S. Listed are the implementation dates, CBP Ports and corresponding port code locations in parentheses.
**November 15, 2004**
Buffalo, NY (0901; Alexandria Bay, NY (0708; Ogdensburg, NY (0701; Massena, NY (0704; Detroit, MI (3801; Port Huron, MI (3802; Sault Ste. Marie, MI (3803; Algonac, MI (3814; Blaine, WA (3004; Sumas, WA (3009; Lynden, WA (3023; Oroville, WA (3019; Frontier, WA (3020; Laurier, WA (3016; Point Roberts, WA (3017; Danville, WA (3012; Ferry, WA (3013; Metaline Falls, WA (3025; Laredo, TX (2304; Eagle Pass, TX (2303; Brownsville, TX (2301; Progresso, TX (2309; Del Rio, TX (2302; Hidalgo/Pharr, TX (2305; Roma, TX (2310; Rio Grande City, TX (2307; El Paso, TX (2402; Presidio, TX (2403; Fabens, TX (2404; Columbus, NM (2406; Santa Teresa, NM (2408; Douglas, AZ (2601; Lukeville, AZ (2602; Naco, AZ (2603; Nogales, AZ (2604; Sasabe, AZ (2606; San Luis, AZ (2608; Tecate, CA (2505; Calexico, CA (2507; Otay Mesa, CA (2506)
**December 15, 2004**
Champlain, NY (0712), Trout River, NY (0715), Pembina, ND (3401), Noyes, MN (3402), Portal, ND (3403), Neche, ND (3404), St. John, ND (3405), Northgate, ND (3406), Walhalla, ND (3407), Hannah, ND (3408), Sarles, ND (3409), Ambrose, ND (3410), Antler, ND (3413), Sherwood, ND (3414), Hansboro, ND (3415), Maida, ND (3416), Fortuna, ND (3417), Westhope, ND (3419), Noonan, ND (3420), Carbury, ND (3421), Dunseith, ND (3422), Warroad, MN (3423), Baudette, MN (3424), Pine Creek, MN (3425), Roseau, MN (3426), International Falls, MN (3604), Grand Portage, MN (3613), Richford, VT (0203), Derby Line, VT (0209), Norton, VT (0211), Beecher Falls, VT (0206), Highgate Springs, VT (0212), Houlton, ME (0106), Bridgewater, ME (0127), Fort Fairfield, ME (0107), Limestone, ME (0118), Van Buren, ME (0108), Madawaska, ME (0109), Fort Kent, ME (0110), Calais, ME (0115), Vanceboro, ME (0105), Eastport/Lubec, ME (0103), Jackman, ME (0104)
**January 14, 2004**
Eastport, ID (3302), Porthill, ID (3308), Sweetgrass, MT (3310), Raymond, MT (3301), Turner, MT (3306), Scobey, MT (3309), Whitetail, MT (3312), Piegan, MT (3316), Opheim, MT (3317), Roosville, MT (3318), Morgan, MT (3319), Whitlash, MT (3321), Del Bonita, MT (3320), Alcan, AK (3104), Skagway, AK (3103), Dalton Cache, AK (3106)
### Vessels
Effective July 6, 2004 vessels required to make entry in accordance with Customs regulations at 19 CFR, Part 4 and

SECURITY

scheduled to arrive at anchor or at a dock in any harbor within the Customs territory of the U.S. must comply with the Trade Act Regulations. There are no exceptions or waivers to the automation requirement for electronic transmission of cargo declaration data mandated by the Trade Act. The Port Director will deny permission to unlade cargo to vessel carriers that continue to arrive and present paper Inward Cargo Declarations (CBP Form 1302) to CBP in violation of the Trade Act Regulations. However, passenger vessels will be allowed to disembark passengers.

### Bulk and Break Bulk Vessels
As of April 2, 2004, the CBP started enforcement actions against carriers operating bulk and break bulk vessels that failed to comply with the Required Advance Electronic Presentation of Cargo Information. The enforcement actions include denial of preliminary entry, issuance of penalties at each port of arrival and denial of unlading.
The CBP was aware of several bulk and break bulk carriers who because they were foreign entities, were unable to secure the required Activity Code 3 International Carriers bond by the original automation deadline of March 4, 2004, and allowed a period of informed compliance which ended on April 2, 2004.

### Passenger Vessels
All passenger vessels that began a voyage on or after April 2, 2004 must transmit cargo declaration data electronically to CBP utilizing Sea AMS. CBP commenced enforcement actions on that date. The enforcement actions include denial of preliminary entry and issuance of penalties at each port of arrival.

### The Authorized Transmitting Party
Generally, an authorized transmitting party is an entity approved by CBP to transmit cargo declaration data via the Automated Manifest System (AMS). However, authorized transmitting parties can include:
- An NVOCC approved by CBP to transmit cargo declaration data via the Vessel Automated Manifest System.
- An Automated Broker Interface (ABI) filer (importer or Customs broker as identified by its ABI filer code).
- A Container Freight Station/deconsolidator as identified by its FIRMS code.
- An Express Consignment Carrier Facility as identified by its FIRMS code.
- An importer or broker.

## Automated Manifest System (AMS)
All sea, air, and rail carriers are required to be Automated Manifest System (AMS) participants. Sea Carriers per 19 CFR 4.7(b)(2), Air Carriers per 19 CFR (Code of Federal Regulations) 122.48a(a), Rail Carriers per 19 CFR 123.91. NVOCCs are not required to automate, but may choose to become automated. The time frame given for NVOCCs to submit paper cargo declarations directly to CBP expired on February 2, 2003.
There are several options for this segment of the trade to provide information in an automated format to CBP. These options are:
- Utilize a service provider,
- Utilize a port authority,
- Establish a direct interface with CBP, or
- Submit paper cargo declarations to the carrier for input into AMS for inclusion on the non-automated carriers cargo declaration.
It should be noted that a direct interface with CBP requires a period of lead-time and therefore, companies may want to use one of the other options until their direct interface is completed.
Those companies electing to establish a direct interface must develop all the necessary records required by the module. In

addition, those users electing to develop a direct interface or purchase a vendor's software package must successfully complete a four-step test phase.
Automated NVOCCs are afforded the same AMS features as an automated carrier, such as auto arrival of the vessel, electronic request for permit to transfers (PTT), Second Notify Party designation and participation in the Paperless Master In-bond Program (AMS/MIB).

### Vessel Agents
The carrier may designate a vessel agent to enter data on behalf of the carrier; however, the carrier is responsible for the content and timeliness of the data. The information may be transmitted directly to CBP or through a participating AMS service center or port authority.

### Third-party AMS Service Providers
A listing of third-party service providers for Sea can be found under the heading of Sea AMS Data Processing Services on the following CBP web site:
www.cbp.gov/ImageCache/cgov/content/import/operations_5fsupport/ams/sea_5fvendor_2edoc/v7/sea_5fvendor.doc
This document is in two parts: The first is a list of service centers, port authorities, and software vendors that presently have the capability to provide carriers and NVOCCs with an interface to CBP. The second is the Sea AMS Respondent Checklist that interested parties must complete. This one-page document should be completed and faxed to: (703) 650-3538. A CBP client representative will then be assigned to work with the company.

### Responsibility for Inaccurate Data
The party that provides cargo declaration information to CBP is responsible for ensuring that the information is accurate.
If a shipment is examined by CBP, either in the United States or at a foreign port, and the manifest description of the contents is, in CBP opinion, inaccurate, the carrier can be held liable for penalties. Authorized transmitting parties can be held liable for liquidated damages. As a result, carriers should establish good business relationships with shippers to ensure that accurate information is provided.
CBP will initially use informed compliance with the carriers, but if repeated violations occur CBP may assess penalties or claims for liquidated damages.
The final rule indicates that in addition to penalties applicable under other provisions of law, carriers may be liable for civil penalties.

### Paperless Master In-bond (AMS/MIB) Program
To participate in the CBP Paperless Master In-bond Program, the carrier or the authorized transmitting party must acquire a CBP Activity Code 2 - Custodial Bond. The authorized transmitting party will then prepare on their letterhead a request to participate in the program identifying their assigned Internal Revenue Service employer identification number (IRS#) and what in-bond entry types they would like to be designated to transmit.
They may elect:
- Immediate Transportation (IT- entry type 61),
- Transportation and Exportation (T&E - entry type 62),
- Immediate Exportation (IE - entry type 63)
- or all three.
The letter should be provided to their CBP Client Representative for action. The IRS# will be validated against a bond table existing in the ACS (Automated Commercial System) and if valid, a "V#" (Validation Number) will be assigned to the carrier or NVOCC. The carrier or NVOCC will then create a control number using the "V#" and the in-bond movement will be tracked in AMS. The party initiating the paperless master in-bond move will then be responsible for the arrival/export of the movement in the system.

### Public Lists of AMS Participants

CBP has posted a list of AMS approved carriers who have obtained an International Carrier Bond on the CBP web site at: http://www.cbp.gov/xp/cgov/import/carriers/ams_ports/. This document is continuously changing and cannot be considered 100 percent accurate.

### Automated Manifest System Outline

The CBP has an established process for NVOCCs and Carriers in order to automate with CBP.

Participants in the Automated Manifest System (AMS) are required to have a Standard Carrier Alpha Code (SCAC) issued by the National Motor Freight Traffic Association, located in Alexandria, VA. If they do not have a SCAC, information can be obtained from the web site: www.nmfta.org/ scac2.htm or the association can be called at (703) 838-1810. Once you have received the confirmation letter for your SCAC code from the National Motor Freight Traffic Association, send or fax a copy of the letter to:

> Mr. Charles Bennett, Branch Chief
> CBP SCAC Processing
> Bureau of Customs and Border Protection
> 7681 Boston Blvd.
> Beauregard 1st Fl Wing A
> Springfield, VA 22153
> Fax: (703) 650-3650
> E-mail: AMS.SCAC@dhs.gov

AMS participants are also required to have a type 3 CBP International Carriers Bond and a type 2 Custodial Bond if business practices involve creating in-bond shipments. Initial bond requirements were set at $50,000. However, Port Directors may increase the bond amount at their discretion. If you do not have an International Carriers Bond or a Custodial Bond, contact a surety company from a list of Treasury approved surety companies that are listed at: www.fms.treas.gov/ c570/index.html/ to obtain a bond.

Such bonds require that foreign entities have a CBP assigned number. Request for CBP Assigned numbers must be made on CF 5106 "Importer ID Input record"; the form can be found on the CBP web site: www.cbp.gov. Completed forms should be sent to the Entry Branch of the local port for input into ACS. Upon receipt of a completed CF 5106, CBP will assign an "Importer Number" to a foreign-based entity. This CF 5106 can be completed by the foreign entity and submitted to CBP, there is also a $50 processing fee (for type 2 Custodial Bonds only) associated with this transaction. A copy of the form, with the CBP-assigned number indicated in block 2D, will be returned to the applicant. This CBP-assigned number will serve as the identifying number for the foreign entity on the bond application.

Once these procedures are complete there are three basic ways for an NVOCC to participate in AMS:

1. Through a service center/port authority:
   A service center/port authority can transmit the NVOCC's data to CBP. The NVOCC's data remain confidential from the operating carrier. This is the fastest way to start AMS participation.

2. Purchase a software and communications package from a software vendor:
   The software vendor will set up required interface software. The NVOCC will have to be certified in AMS prior to submitting actual manifest data.

3. Program their own software interface:
   This process requires a full AMS certification test be completed prior to submitting actual manifest data.

Interested participants in the Sea Automated Manifest System (AMS) Program are required to submit a written letter of intention on company letterhead and include a point of contact, name, title, phone number, e-mail address and office location. In addition, identify your interest in Sea AMS (i.e., becoming a Sea AMS carrier, service center, software vendor, NVOCC, etc.). This letter can be mailed or faxed to the following location:

> U.S. Customs and Border Protection
> Office of Information and Technology
> Director, Client Representative Branch
> Bureau of Customs and Border Protection
> 7681 Boston Blvd.
> Attention: Beauregard, Room A-31
> Springfield, VA 22153
> (703) 650-3500

## Confidentiality of Data

Once a completed manifest is filed with the CBP it becomes public information. This can present a problem to importers and consignees who feel that public knowledge of their shippers and/or suppliers can damage their commercial activities. Importers and consignees, however, may request confidential treatment of their name and address contained in inward manifests, including identifying marks and numbers. In addition, an importer or consignee may request confidential treatment of the name and address of the shipper or shippers to such importer or consignee by using the following procedures:

An importer or consignee, or authorized employee, attorney or official of the importer or consignee, must submit a certification claiming confidential treatment of its name and address, including marks and numbers which reveal the name and address of the importer or consignee. An importer or consignee may also file a certification requesting confidentiality for all its shippers.

There is no prescribed format for a certification. However, the certification should include the importer's or consignee's Internal Revenue Service Employer Number, if available. There is no requirement to provide sufficient facts to support the conclusion that the disclosure of the names and addresses would likely cause substantial harm to the competitive position of the importer or consignee.

The certification must be submitted to:

> Disclosure Law Officer
> Headquarters
> U.S. Customs and Border Protection
> 1300 Pennsylvania Ave., NW
> Washington, DC 20229

Each initial certification will be valid for a period of two years from the date of receipt. Renewal certifications should be submitted to the Disclosure Law Officer at least 60 days prior to the expiration of the current certification. Information so certified, may be copied, but not published, by the press during the effective period of the certification. An importer or consignee shall be given written notification by Customs of receipt of its certification of confidentiality.

To ensure that requested information is deleted from public disclosure, the importer or consignee should ensure that the company's name and shipper's name is identified to Customs in all known variations that may be used on shipping documentation such as bills of lading, purchase orders and manifests. The CBP's computer searches for the exact spelling that is included on the request for confidentiality, and any variations of the company/commercial party name not specified in the confidentiality request may not be deleted from the public disclosures.

Presently, it takes between 1 to 5 days from the time of receipt of a request to the time the request is processed and placed into the system. Protection is effective once the information is placed into the system, and the requestor will be notified that this has been done. CBP processes requests on a daily basis.

SECURITY

# General Issues

## C-TPAT Partners
The CBP expects that its partners in C-TPAT (Customs-Trade Partnership Against Terrorism) will provide the required information under this rule as a regular part of their security-related procedures. Accurate and timely cargo declarations are critical to the delivery of the cargo release benefits that are part of C-TPAT participation. While C-TPAT participants will not be excluded from the advance reporting requirements, their participation in the program will be taken into account during the targeting process. Furthermore, C-TPAT participation by a carrier or a NVOCC will be a mitigating factor in determining penalties and liquidated damages.

## Canada/Mexico Shipments
The Final Rule does not apply to cargo that is shipped to Canada or Mexico and subsequently trucked or sent by rail into the U.S., if the vessel does not call on a U.S. port. CBP has targeting personnel stationed at seaports in Canada and is in close cooperation with Canadian Customs authorities. If either Customs administration suspects that goods are being routed in an attempt to evade scrutiny, those goods will be treated as high risk and be subject to cargo examination. For vessels that are departing Canada or Mexico with cargo destined for the United States, the 24-hour rule does apply.

## Containers at Dock
In response to concerns from the trade that containers will have to be delivered to a carrier several days before lading, CBP has said that it wants the information on the cargo delivered earlier, not the container.

For CBP purposes, the cargo information can be transmitted to CBP prior to the physical arrival of the container itself at the dock.

## Empty Containers
Cargo declaration information for bills of lading consisting solely of empty containers must be received by CBP in the AMS 24 hours prior to the arrival of the vessel for voyages 24 hours in duration or more. For voyages less than 24 hours in duration, the cargo declaration information must be received by CBP in AMS at the time of sailing.

For truck carriers, with the exception of FAST (Free And Secure Trade) participants, CBP will not require any advance notification if the shipment consists solely of empty articles (pallets, tanks, cores, containers and the like) that have been designated as instruments of international traffic (IITs). However, if the IITs are commingled with other commercial cargo, CBP will require the requisite arrival notification for such commercial cargo via the authorized CBP-approved electronic data interchange system; and any empty IITs carried aboard the conveyance must be identified as such and listed on the carrier's cargo declaration.

## Carrier
CBP views the carrier as the entity that controls the vessel, which includes:
- Determining the ports of call
- Controlling the loading and discharging cargo
- Knowledge of cargo information
- Issuing bills of lading
- The entity that has typically provided the CF 1302 cargo declaration or the cargo information to prepare the CF 1302 to the vessel agent.

In the event that the parties to a contract cannot determine who is the carrier, a request for a CBP ruling may be made in accordance with Part 177 of the CBP regulations (19 CFR, Part 177). Information on this procedure can be found on the CBP Web site at:
http://www.cbp.gov/xp/cgov/toolbox/legal/Rulings/ruling_letters.xml

Once a carrier has obtained a continuous bond it is valid for all vessels controlled by the bonded entity. CBP regulations covering bonds are published at 19 CFR, Part 113. An Activity Code 3 International Carrier single transaction bond is only valid for one entrance and one clearance for one transaction (e.g., one voyage) at one port.

## Foreign Remaining On Board Cargo (FROB)
"FROB" cargo is cargo that is loaded in a foreign port and is to be unloaded in another foreign port with an intervening vessel stop in one or more ports in the United States. CBP considers FROB cargo a security concern because although the cargo does not have a final destination in the U.S., the cargo is transiting the U.S.

All of the data elements required under the regulations must be provided for FROB cargo. CBP recognizes that for FROB cargo, the actual shipper, consignee and notify party may not be associated with an address in the United States. Therefore, CBP does not require a U.S. address on these data elements.

If a shipper changes the cargo destination from FROB to a U.S. port after the vessel has sailed, it can be handled through a manifest correction. Manifest corrections are handled as a manifest discrepancy. Since the cargo was FROB and falls under the 24-hour requirement, information would have already been received 24 hours before lading. However, the shipment is subject to screening and examination due to the change in information.

## Record Keeping
CBP regulations impose a five-year statutory record keeping requirement for carriers and NVOCCs.

## Perishables
For purposes of the 24-hour rule, the term "perishable merchandise" is defined as merchandise that: is organic and produced for human consumption, that is not frozen, is subject to spoilage, and requires controlled temperature during transportation. Examples include fruits, vegetables, meat and fish products.

Since many perishable commodities (e.g., bananas, pineapples) are harvested and loaded within the 24-hour time window before vessel loading, information (such as final seal number, precise quantity, and container number) will be preliminary 24 hours before vessel loading.

The majority of the data elements, however, should be known. The only unknown data elements would be the exact weight and quantity. To address weight and quantity concerns, CBP has concluded that in the case of perishable merchandise, the carrier or NVOCC must provide CBP with a good faith estimate of the quantity and weight 24 hours before loading. CBP will allow a discrepancy tolerance of plus or minus 5 percent; if the good faith estimate is within this range, CBP will not require the manifest to be amended. With respect to other matters, CBP fully expects that the industry can adapt their business practice to designate a specific container and seal that will be used on a specific bill of lading and provide that information 24 hours prior to lading. Since much of the perishable industry operates utilizing containers, CBP will not authorize a break-bulk exemption for the perishable commodities community as a whole, although perishables that are not containerized and otherwise meet the definition of break bulk may seek an exemption. As for overbooking, this is a practice that CBP has worked very hard over the years to eliminate, and it would be extremely difficult for both the industry and CBP to maintain proper documentation of overbooked cargo. Accordingly, CBP will not permit overbooking for perishables. CBP does not agree with reducing the 24-hour reporting requirement, as other mechanisms exist for addressing concerns regarding perishables.

### Missed Voyages

If information on a container has been transmitted 24 hours prior to lading on the vessel in compliance with the rules, and the 24 hours have expired without the carrier receiving a "do not load" message from CBP, but for some reason the container misses the sailing of the vessel, the container is allowed to sail on the next scheduled voyage without requiring a new 24-hour period, provided that:

- The original bill of lading is deleted from the original vessel.
- The bill of lading is input on the second vessel manifest without any changes to the bill information with the exception of the changes required to the transportation/voyage data.
- The next scheduled voyage sails within 24 hours of the previous departure time. If this is not the case, a new 24-hour time frame will be required prior to loading on the second vessel.

In all cases, the cargo declaration must be amended to reflect the deletions and additions of the bills of lading that were deleted or added to a voyage.

## Non-Compliant Cargo Targets

### "No-Load" Orders

The 24-hour rule gives CBP officers time to analyze the container content information and identify potential terrorist threats before the U.S.-bound container is loaded at the foreign seaport, not after it arrives in a U.S. port.

On May 4, 2003 CBP began to enforce the 24-Hour Rule by issuing "No Load" orders. A "No-Load" directive means that CBP has instructed the ocean shipping line not to load a container at a foreign port for delivery to the U.S. Selected non-compliant cargo targets are referred to the National Targeting Center (NTC) for coordination of the issuance of the "Do Not Load" message to the carrier or NVOCC.

Non-compliant cargo targets include those where the contents of a cargo container were not adequately identified. For example, the use of such vague cargo descriptions as "Freight-All-Kinds," "Said-To-Contain," or "General Merchandise," are no longer acceptable.

The major goal of this initiative is to require that the valid description be input by the carrier or NVOCC in the cargo description field, including marks and numbers.

### Monetary Penalties

Commencing on May 4, 2003, CBP ports were authorized to issue monetary penalties for egregious violations of timeliness. Seaports will be responsible for the review and enforce the timeliness of cargo declaration submissions. The selection of targets will be coordinated through the NTC. The issuance of penalties will be coordinated and approved through CBP Headquarters.

On May 15, 2003, CBP ports were authorized to issue monetary penalties for Foreign Remaining On Board (FROB) cargo that has an invalid cargo description and that has been loaded on board the vessel without providing CBP a 24-hour time frame to place a "Do Not Load" message on the cargo. Carriers and NVOCC's may be subject to penalties and liquidated damages per each vessel arrival for violation of manifest requirements. On behalf of carriers, masters of vessels will be assessed penalties per vessel arrival in accordance with 19 USC 1436 (penalties of $5,000 for the first violation and $10,000 for any subsequent violation attributable to the master). NVOCCs will incur claims for liquidated damages of $5,000 per vessel arrival in accordance with 19 CFR 113.64(c) and 19 CFR 4.7(b) and/or 19 CFR 4.7a(c). If there are multiple automated NVOCCs in violation of the FROB requirements on a vessel arrival, each automated NVOCC may be assessed liquidated damages.

### Consignee Name Violations

On May 15, 2003, seaports started to take enforcement action on egregious consignee name and address violations leading to issuance of Headquarters-approved "Do Not Load" messages. Egregious consignee errors include fields left blank; the use of "To Order" and "To Order of Shipper" without corresponding information in the consignee field (e.g., a bank's name and address); and notify party field or consignee name with no address, incomplete address (only city and state) or an invalid address.

These selected non-compliant cargo targets will be referred to the NTC for coordination and approval prior to the issuance of the "Do Not Load" message to the automated carrier or NVOCC. When selecting non-compliant cargo, CBP realizes that Foreign Remaining On Board cargo and some in-bond movements will not have a U.S. or standardized addresses.

## Consolidators

Consolidators are in the business of consolidating cargo for one consignee from multiple vendors, as opposed to NVOCCs who consolidate cargo for many shippers to many consignees. CBP has authorized NVOCCs to participate in Sea AMS, but not consolidators.

**Issue #1 "Shipper" Definition**

Since, CBP has not yet defined "Shipper," and consolidators were not addressed in the 24-hour Final Rule, in the interim, CBP will accept a consolidator's complete name and address in the "shipper field". The consolidator's name and/or address should not appear in the consignee field.

**Issue #2 Who is the Shipper?**

Suppose the following:

A "US Customer", places an order with "Foreign Vendor" located in England. "Foreign Vendor" takes the order and advises that they will produce and ship the goods from their "Factory" located in Italy. The "Factory" produces the goods, and advises "Foreign Vendor" that they are ready for shipment. "Foreign Vendor" prepares shipping instructions and selects a local England NVOCC to move the goods directly from "Factory" in Italy, to Customer in the US. The terms of shipment are under a Line of Credit, between the "Foreign Vendor" and "U.S. Customer".

Who should be shown as the Shipper on the Master Bill of Lading if no House bill is involved? If a House Bill is involved, the Master Bill of Lading will reflect the "Foreign NVOCC" as shipper to their "US NVOCC" office as the consignee. The House Bill will reflect the actual "US Customer" as consignee. Should "Foreign Vendor" or "Factory" be shown as the shipper on the House Bill?

Answer: The shipper should be, either "Foreign Vendor" or the "Factory".

Although, CBP would like to have the most detailed information on the shipper available, for targeting purposes, CBP will accept either party as the shipper until CBP can clearly identify the term "shipper" to the trade. Also, the consignee will not be the "U.S. NVOCC" office, it should be the actual "US Customer".

**Issue #3 Multiple Vendor Consolidations**

Imagine that a "U.S. Customer" advises their NVOCC that they are making several purchases from three Vendors, and want the NVOCC to collect the goods and ship them under one House Bill.

The "U.S. NVOCC" relays the various vendors' information to their "Foreign NVOCC" office for cargo collection. The "Foreign NVOCC" picks up all the goods from three different vendors and prepares a House Bill of Lading. Since there will be three different vendors, who should be shown as the shipper(s)?

**SECURITY**

Each shipment that has different shipper and consignee information must be identified on its own bill of lading. For example:

- 1st bill of lading - 1st vendor or factory is the shipper - U.S. customer is the consignee
- 2nd bill of lading - 2nd vendor or factory is the shipper - U.S. customer is the consignee
- 3rd bill of lading - 3rd vendor or factory is the shipper - U.S. customer is the consignee

Each shipment will be identified in AMS under their own NVOCC bill of lading but, in most cases, listed in the same container.

### Issue #4 Multiple Shippers

CBP will not allow for multiple shippers or multiple consignees on one bill of lading. For every shipper/consignee relationship a separate bill of lading must be created.

Issue #5 In Care of Party

The CBP will accept the name of the in care of party to be referred to in the shipper and/or consignee field, along with the actual shipper and/or consignee name and complete address. An example of this would be "Consolidator X on behalf of shipper A, with the complete address of the shipper A".

## Break Bulk Cargo Exemptions

Carriers of break bulk cargo may apply for an exemption from the 24-hour rule filing requirements. Exemption requests can be mailed to:

Customs and Border Protection
Border Targeting and Analysis, Room 5.5-B
1300 Pennsylvania Avenue, NW
Washington, D.C. 20229

The CBP prefers that requests for information, exemptions and amendments be sent by e-mail to:

E-mail (preferred): 24hour.exemptions@dhs.gov
Tel: (866) 324-9169
Fax: (703) 621-7780

Make sure that all e-mails and phone calls clearly reference "24 Hour Exemptions" and the CBP Exemption Application number, if assigned.

Generally, exemption processing takes approximately two to three weeks for a complete review.

The following information should be supplied in order to be considered for an exemption (per 19 CFR 4.7(b)(4)(ii)(A)): The carrier's IRS number; the source, identity and means of the packaging or bundling of the commodities being shipped; the ports of call both foreign and domestic; the number of vessels the carrier uses to transport break bulk cargo, along with the names of the vessels and their International Maritime Organization (IMO) numbers; and the list of the carrier's importers and shippers, identifying any who are members of C-TPAT (Customs-Trade Partnership Against Terrorism). CBP reserves the right to request any additional information it deems necessary and appropriate to ensure adequate compliance with 19CFR 4.7(b)(4) and to perform necessary national security risk analysis.

In general, all exempt carriers will receive a notice for one of the following decisions:

- a full exemption (initial research complete, no expiration date)
- an extension of their current exemption (further research required or more information necessary and temporary exemption extended)
- a denial (decision and appeals process will be explained to carrier)

NOTE: Any cargo stowed in containers, including containers referred to as "ship's convenience," will be considered general cargo. No such containerized cargo will be exempt from the manifesting reporting requirements. For example,

palletized boxes of bananas (not loose or loaded directly into a hold) stowed in shipping containers will be treated the same as all containerized cargo requiring information to be submitted 24 hours prior to loading.

### Bulk Cargo

For the purposes of the 24-hour advanced manifest rule only, the following definition will be used for bulk cargo: "Homogenous cargo that is stowed loose in the hold and is not enclosed in any container such as a box, bale, bag, cask, or the like. Such cargo is also described as bulk freight. Specifically, bulk cargo is composed of either: (A) free flowing articles such as oil, grain, coal, ore, and the like which can be pumped or run through a chute or handled by dumping; or (B) uniform cargo that stows as solidly as bulk cargo and requires mechanical handling for lading and discharging."

Customs and Border Protection (CBP), Border Targeting and Analysis (BTA) has determined that the following list of commodities and commodity types can be classified as bulk cargo. To be classified as bulk, this cargo may not be containerized and must be easily identifiable as laden on the vessel. Any bundling of the following commodities must only be for the purposes of securing the cargo. This list may be changed and updated as deemed appropriate by CBP.

- Coils of steel and other metals
- Rails of steel and other metals
- Wire rods of steel and other metals (may be coiled or flat)
- Ingots of metal (precious or otherwise)
- Round bars of steel or other metal
- Deformed Bars/Rebars (of metal)
- Plates (of metal)
- Billets (of metal)
- Slabs (of metal)
- Pipes (of metal)
- Beams (of metal)
- Tubes/Tubing (of metal)
- Angles, shapes and sections (of metal)
- Sheets (of metal)
- Expanded metal
- Flat bars (of metal)
- Strand wire (of metal)
- Sawn Timber/Lumber as a commodity (not as packaging material)
- Paperboard/Fiberboard/Plywood as a commodity (not as packaging material)
- Paper products as commodity (wood pulp, newsprint and paper rolls and not as packaging material)
- Certain perishable goods, not in boxes, bags or containerized, and not frozen, but laden and stowed in a way similar to other types of bulk cargo (includes seafood and produce).
- Blooms (similar to "billets and of metal)
- Anodes/Cathodes, in sheets only (may be corrugated)

### Break Bulk Cargo

Break bulk cargo is defined as cargo that is not containerized and that cannot be classified as "bulk" cargo under the above definition. For example, new and used vehicles will be classified as break bulk cargo. Although uniform in nature, vehicles have identifying marks (such as a Vehicle Identification Number or VIN). One necessary aspect of bulk cargo is fungibility. The presence of a VIN removes that component from the shipment of new or used vehicles.

It is important to note that the difference between bulk and break bulk is based not only on the type of cargo, but also on the way in which the cargo is stowed or loaded. For example, bananas stowed loosely in a hold (not in boxes or containers) will be considered bulk. Palletized boxes of bananas loaded directly into a hold (but not loose or containerized) will be considered break bulk.

## Data Elements
## (Form 3171)

The manner in which data elements are reported to CBP is very important and requires conscious consideration on the part of both the carrier and the shipper. Reviewing every data element is beyond the scope of this work, but listed below are several data elements and a discussion of the types of issues that must be addressed.

### Data Element – Cargo Description

CBP regulations require a "precise description and weight of the cargo or, for a sealed container, the shipper's declared description and weight of the cargo." The cargo's 6-digit tariff number may also be provided for those with the skill to provide it correctly. If there is doubt about the accuracy of a 6-digit tariff number, which can sometimes be difficult to ascertain, the AMS transmission should only include the precise narrative description. If the cargo description is left blank, AMS will reject the transmission.

The party that provides the cargo declaration information to CBP is responsible for ensuring that the information is accurate. A precise narrative description is a description that is precise enough for CBP to be able to identify the shapes, physical characteristics, and likely packaging of the manifested cargo so that CBP can identify any anomalies in the cargo when a container is run through imaging equipment. The description must also be precise enough to identify any goods, which may emit radiation. How specific that information must be depends on the nature of the commodity. For example, "electronics" is not a precise description, but "CD players" or "computer monitors" would be.

CBP will continue to work with the trade to refine what descriptions are acceptable. CBP will continue to notify carriers and authorized transmitting parties when more difficult commodities are not adequately described. However, cargo descriptions are one of the most important elements to assist CBP in precise targeting, and it is in the trade's interest to become precise and compliant as quickly as possible. Not only will this avoid eventual enforcement action, but it may also avoid container "Do Not Load" messages (vessel only) and other "holds" due to CBP not having enough information to know what is in an individual shipment.

IN NO CASE are the following descriptions acceptable: blank description; freight all kinds (FAK); said to contain (STC) with or without other description; general merchandise; "26 pallets"; various retail merchandise; consolidated cargo; or other similarly vague descriptions.

The following table is intended as a guide to acceptable and not acceptable cargo descriptions. The examples are illustrative, not exhaustive. Phrases or words in parenthesis are meant as examples.

| CARGO DESCRIPTIONS | |
| --- | --- |
| **Not Acceptable** | **Acceptable** |
| Apparel<br>Wearing Apparel<br>Ladies' Apparel<br>Men's Apparel | Clothing<br>Shoes<br>Footwear<br>Jewelry (may include watches) |
| Appliances | Kitchen Appliances<br>Industrial Appliances<br>Heat Pump |
| Auto parts<br>Parts | New Taproots<br>Used Taproots |
| Caps | Baseball Caps<br>Blasting Caps<br>Bottle Caps<br>Hub Caps |

| CARGO DESCRIPTIONS | |
| --- | --- |
| **Not Acceptable** | **Acceptable** |
| Chemicals, hazardous<br>Chemicals, non-hazardous | Actual Chemical Name (not brand name)<br>Or U.N. HAZMAT Code Identifier # |
| Electronic Goods<br>Electronics | Computers<br>Consumer Electronics<br>Telephones<br>Electronic Toys (can include Gameboys, Game Cubes, Dancing Elmo Doll etc.)<br>Personal/Household Electronics (i.e. PDAs, VCRs, TVs) |
| Equipment | Industrial Equipment,<br>Oil Well Equipment<br>Automotive Equipment,<br>Poultry Equipment etc. |
| Flooring | Wood Flooring<br>Plastic Flooring<br>Carpet<br>Ceramic Tile<br>Marble Flooring |
| Foodstuffs | Orange<br>Fish<br>Packaged Rice<br>Packaged Grain<br>Bulk Grain |
| Iron | Iron Pipes<br>Steel Pipe |
| Steel | Iron Building Material<br>Steel Building Material |
| Leather Articles | Saddles<br>Leather Handbags<br>Leather Jackets<br>Shoes |
| Machinery | Metal Working Machinery<br>Cigarette Making Machinery |
| Machines | Sewing Machines<br>Printing Machines |
| Pipes | Plastic Pipes<br>PVC Pipes<br>Steel Pipes<br>Copper Pipes |
| Plastic Goods | Plastic Kitchenwares<br>Plastic Housewares<br>Industrial Plastics<br>Toys<br>New/Used Auto Parts |
| Polyurethane | Polyurethane Threads<br>Polyurethane Medical Gloves |
| | Personal Effects<br>Household Goods |
| Rubber Articles | Rubber Hoses<br>Tires<br>Toys<br>Rubber Conveyor Belts |
| Rods | Welding Rods<br>Rebar<br>Aluminum Rods<br>Reactor Rods |
| Scrap | Plastic Scrap<br>Aluminum Scrap<br>Iron Scrap |

SECURITY

| CARGO DESCRIPTIONS | |
| --- | --- |
| **Not Acceptable** | **Acceptable** |
| STC (Said to Contain) General Cargo FAK (Freight All Kinds) "No Description" | |
| Tiles | Ceramic Tiles Marble Tiles |
| Tools | Hand Tools Power Tools Industrial Tools |
| Wires | Electric Wires Auto Harness Coiled Wire (Industrial) |

### Data Element – Shipper's Name and Address

CBP requires that the name and address of the actual shipper be used in this data element. Identifying the shipper as a carrier, bank or importer does not provide the CBP with useful information and doing so will invite closer scrutiny and increase the likelihood that the shipment will be examined.

Also, while freight forwarders may contract with carriers under FMC (Federal Maritime Commission) service contracts as "agents for" various shippers, this too will invite closer scrutiny and increase the likelihood that the shipment will be examined.

### Data Element – Consignee and To Order Bills

The regulations require the complete name and address of the consignee (owner). Importers should confer with the foreign shipper to review such information for accuracy.

For "to order" bills of lading, where there is no consignee, this data element should include the name of the cargo "owner or the owner's representative."

CBP recognizes that for business and financial reasons "to order" must be placed in the consignee field. Therefore, CBP has decided that "to order" without corresponding information will be acceptable in the consignee field. However, when "to order" is used in the consignee field the first notify field must contain the owner or owner's representative with the U.S. name and address.

CBP recognizes that for Foreign Remaining On Board (FROB) cargo the actual consignee will not be located in the United States. Therefore, in such cases where the bill of lading is "to order" and FROB cargo, the owner or owner's representative name and foreign address must be listed in the first notify field.

### Data Element – Seals

Proper reporting includes listing the "seal numbers for all seals affixed to containers." There are, however, a number of issues regarding seals.

### No Seal, Broken or Damaged Seal

Technically, there is no requirement in law that a shipper loading a container must seal the container. Nor can a vessel carrier necessarily confirm who affixed the seal when the container is stuffed. Only the shipper is in a position to do that. The carrier, however, can check the seal number when it receives the container.

What should a carrier do if it receives a container from a shipper without a seal or discovers that the original seal has been broken or damaged?

This issue raises implications for C-TPAT (Customs-Trade Partnership Against Terrorism) carrier participants as well as non-C-TPAT carriers.

With regard to C-TPAT carriers, as stipulated in the Agreement to Voluntarily Participate in C-TPAT, sea carriers are expected to "ensure high security seals or locks are affixed on all loaded containers".

Concern has been expressed that carriers, as the recipients of most loaded containers, are often not in a position to ensure the secure sealing of those containers. While that may be true, the sealing of containers is an essential element of a secure supply chain and remains a critical part of a carrier's commitment to C-TPAT.

Furthermore, the C-TPAT agreement for sea carriers reads, "The Carrier agrees to develop and implement, within a framework consistent with the listed recommendations, a verifiable, documented program to enhance security procedures throughout its supply-chain process. Where the Carrier does not exercise control of a production facility, distribution entity, or process in the supply chain, the Carrier agrees to communicate the attached recommendations/guidelines to those entities."

Even though a carrier may not "exercise control" over the sealing of containers, carriers that join C-TPAT are expected to promote effective security measures throughout the entire supply chain. That must include doing whatever a carrier can to ensure the sealing of all loaded containers and may require that the carrier work or negotiate with shippers, forwarders, and/or others to arrange for that sealing.

These steps could include applying a high-security seal, requiring a shipper to verify the contents and add a seal, or refusing to lade the container. In addition, for those containers that are not sealed or the seal has been broken, a C-TPAT carrier should consider the container a vulnerability and work with the responsible parties (shippers/forwarders) to address that vulnerability for future shipments.

Therefore, if the carrier receives a container where the seal has been tampered with or the seal number does not match the shipping documents, the carrier should notify CBP. This notification should happen as soon as the discrepancy is noted. If the discovery of the discrepancy is noted after receipt of the transmission of the bill of lading the carrier should notify CBP.

The lack of a seal or a damaged seal on a container will pose a level of risk. Several options for addressing this risk are available to both C-TPAT and non-C-TPAT carriers and their trading partners. The first option, listed below, represents the highest level of diligence and, therefore, poses the lowest risk from a targeting standpoint. In the event that a container is delivered to a carrier facility without a seal, the carrier can undertake any of the following options:

- The carrier could examine and verify the contents of the container and place a new seal on the container.
- The carrier could request that the shipper verify the contents of the container and place a seal on the container.
- The carrier could seal the container without verifying the contents. (Not recommended!)
- The carrier could refuse to load the container.
- The carrier could accept the container, but transmit information in AMS, which would indicate the status of the seal (no seal, tampered, or broken).

CBP will provide the capability in AMS to allow carriers/authorized transmitting parties to transmit information in the seal data field that indicates no seal, tampered seal or broken seal.

### Data Element – Port

The filing carrier must indicate: "The first foreign port where the carrier takes possession of the cargo destined to the United States".

For example, a carrier contracts to move a container from Berlin to Chicago under a through transportation contract. Carrier picks up the container in Berlin, trucks it to Hamburg. The carrier loads it aboard the vessel in Hamburg, sails to Southhampton, and then New York. In this case, "the last foreign port before the vessel departs for the US" is Southhampton, "the first foreign port where the carrier takes possession of the cargo destined to the United States"- is Berlin and "the foreign port where the cargo is laden on board"- is Hamburg.

## SUMMARY OF RULE BY TRANSPORTATION MODE

| Mode | In/Out | Data System | Transmittal Timeframe (Final Ruling) | Responsible Parties | Length of transition period after publication of final rule |
|------|--------|-------------|--------------------------------------|---------------------|------------------------------------------------------------|
| AIR & COURIER | In | Air AMS | a) 4 hours before "wheels up", or<br>b) By "wheels up" from certain nearby areas prior to arrival in U.S. | a) Air carriers<br>b) Importer or its broker<br>c) Freight forwarder<br>d) Express consignment facility<br>e) Other air carriers | 90 days. However, CBP could delay the implementation at a given port until the necessary training has been provided to CBP personnel at that port. Also, CBP could delay the effective date if any essential programming changes to the approved data interchange system were not in place. |
|  | Out | AES | 2 hours prior to departure from U.S. | Exporter | Current AES exporter reporting requirements will be employed on an interim basis, until the AES Commodity Redesign Project is developed pursuant to Census regulations due to be issued in 2004. |
| RAIL | In | Rail AMS | 2 hours prior to arrival in U.S. | Rail carrier | 90 days after rail AMS is operational at port. |
|  | Out | AES | 2 hours prior to arrival at the border | Exporter | Current AES exporter reporting requirements will be employed on an interim basis, until the AES Commodity Redesign Project is developed pursuant to Census regulations due to be issued in 2004. |
| VESSEL | In | Vessel AMS | 24 hours prior to lading at foreign port | a) Vessel carriers<br>b) NVOCCs | Parties to be automated on vessel AMS within 90 days at all ports where their vessels arrive. |
|  | Out | AES | 24 hours prior to departure from U.S. port where cargo is laden | Exporter | Current AES exporter reporting requirements will be employed on an interim basis, until the AES Commodity Redesign Project is developed pursuant to Census regulations due to be issued in 2004. |
| TRUCK | In | FAST, PAPS, BRASS, or CAFES | FAST: 30 minutes before arrival<br>Non-FAST: 1 hour prior to arrival in U.S. | a) Truck carriers<br>b) Importer<br>c) Customs broker | 90 days from the date CBP has officially notified affected carriers by Federal Register publication that an approved data interchange is in place and fully operational. |
|  | Out | AES | 1 hour prior to border crossing | Exporter | Current AES exporter reporting requirements will be employed on an interim basis, until the AES Commodity Redesign Project is developed pursuant to Census regulations due to be issued in 2004. |

SECURITY

# Key Words in 8 Languages

| English | German | French | Spanish |
|---|---|---|---|
| aboard | an Bord | à bord | a bordo |
| accept | annehmen | accepter | aceptar |
| acceptable | annehmbar | acceptable | aceptable, admisible, de calidad suficiente |
| acceptance | Annahme, Empfang | acceptation | aceptación |
| acceptance, by | durch Akzeptleistung, Akzeptierung | par acceptation | mediante aceptación |
| accident | Unfall | accident | accidente |
| account | Konto, Rechnung | compte | cuenta |
| account number | Kontonummer | numéro de compte | número de cuenta |
| accounts payable | Verbindlichkeiten | comptes fournisseurs | cuentas de proveedores |
| accounts receivable | Forderungen | compte clients | cuentas a clientes |
| acknowledgement | Bestätigung | reconnaissance | reconocimiento |
| acknowledgement of receipt | Empfangsbestätigung, Empfangsanzeige | accusé de réception, reçu | acuse de recibo |
| Act of God | höhere Gewalt | force majeure | fuerza mayor, caso fortuito (sobre el valor) |
| ad valorem | ad valorem | ad valorem | ad valorem |
| ad valorem duty | Wertzoll | droits de douane proportionnels | derecho aduanero "ad valorem" |
| addendum | Nachtrag, Anhang | avenant, clause additionne | cláusula adicional |
| address | Anschrift, Adresse | adresse | dirección, domicilio |
| adjustment | Anpassung, Berichtigung | ajustement | reajuste, corrección |
| admission temporaire/ temporary admission (ATA) | vorübergehende Einfuhr | admission temporaire (ATA) | admisión temporal |
| admitted | zugestanden, anerkannt | agréé | a cuerdo |
| advance payment | Vorauszahlung, Anzahlung | paiement anticipé | pago por adelantado |
| advice | Anzeige | avis, notification | aviso, notificación |
| advice note | Versandanzeige | note de crédit | aviso de abono bancario |
| advice of fate | Benachrichtigung (über den Stand der Angelegenheit) | avis de destin | aviso de resultados de gestión |
| advice, credit | Gutschriftanzeige | avis de crédit | aviso de crédito |
| advice, debit | Belastungsanzeige | avis de débit | aviso de débito |
| against all risks | gegen alle Gefahren | tous risques | a todo riesgo |
| agency | Agentur | agence | agencia |
| agent | Agent | agent | agente |
| agent, commissioned | Kommissionär | commissionnaire | comisionista |
| agent, forwarding | Spediteur | transitaire | transitario, agente expedidor |
| agent, purchasing | Einkaufsagent | courtier | agente de compras |

# Key Words in 8 Languages

| Italian | Portuguese (Br) | Japanese | Chinese |
|---|---|---|---|
| a bordo | a bordo | 乗船（する） | 上船（车、飞机） |
| accettare | aceitar | 受け取る | 接受，承兑 |
| accettabile | aceitável, admissível | 受け入れられる | 可接受的，可承兑的 |
| mediante accettazione | aceitação | 引き受け | 承兑，认付 |
| mediante accettazione | por, mediante a aceitação | 承諾する | 接受，接收 |
| infortunio, sinistro | acidente | 事故 | 突发事件，事故 |
| conto | conta | 顧客，口座 | 漳 ，栈 |
| numero del conto | número de(a) conta | 客先番号 | 蘸 |
| debiti verso fornitori, conto fornitori | conta(s) a pagar | 未払勘定 | 应付湛 |
| conto clienti, crediti da clienti | conta(s) a receber | 受取勘定 | 应收湛 |
| riconoscimento | confirmação | 承諾 | 承认，确认 |
| accusa, di ricevuta, avviso di ricevimento | confirmação, notificação de recebimento | 領収書 | 回执，收悉 |
| causa di forza maggiore | caso fortuito | 不可抗力 | 不可抗拒力，天灾 |
| ad valorem | ad valorem | 従価の | 按值，从价帐 |
| dazio ad valorem | direitos aduaneiros ad valorem | 従価税 | 从价课税 |
| appendice | adendo, anexo | 付録 | 附约 |
| indirizzo | endereço | 住所 | 地址 |
| aggiustamento | acomodação, liquidação, retificação | 照瞬瞬 {停 | 调 |
| temporanea importazione | admissão temporária (ATA) | 仮輸入許可 | 临时许可进口 / 货物暂准通关证制度 (ATA) |
| autorizzato, concordato | admitido, aceito | 輸入許可済み | 承认 |
| pagamento anticipato | pagamento antecipado | 前払い金 | 预付款项 |
| avviso | aviso | 通知 | 通知，通知书 |
| avviso, lettera di avviso, notifica | aviso de recebimento | 通知書 | 通告单，通知书 |
| avviso d'esito | notificação bancária sobre status de cobrança pendente | | 出险事故通知，通知托收结果 |
| avviso de credito | aviso de crédito | 入金通知 | 贷记报单 |
| avviso di debito | aviso de débito | 借記通知 | 借记报单 |
| contro tutti I rischi | contra todos os riscos | 全危険負担 | 综合险 |
| agenzia | agência, órgão | 代理店 | 代理 |
| agente | agente | 代理人 | 代理人，代理商 |
| commissionario | agente comissionado | 委託販売人 | 代理佣金 |
| spedizioniere | agente transitário, de transporte | 運送業 | 运送代理商，货运代理 |
| agente degli acquisti | agente de compras | 購買担当 | 采购代理商 |

KEY WORDS

| English | German | French | Spanish |
|---|---|---|---|
| **agreement** | Vereinbarung, Vertrag, Abkommen | accord, convention | acuerdo, convenio |
| **air** | Luft | aérien | aéreo |
| **air cargo** | Luftfracht | cargo aérien | carga aérea |
| **air freight** | Luftfrachtkosten | fret aérien | flete aéreo |
| **air mail** | Luftpost | envoyer par avion | correo aéreo |
| **air waybill (AWB)** | Luftfrachtbrief | lettre de transport aérien (LTA) | conocimiento (de transporte) aéreo, guía aérea |
| **airport-to-airport** | Verlade- bis - Bestimmungsflughafen | aéroport à aéroport | de aeropuerto a aeropuerto |
| **all** | alles | tous | todo |
| **all risks** | alle Risiken | tous risques | a todo riesgo |
| **all risks insurance policy** | Gesamtversicherungspolice | police asssurance tous risques | póliza de seguro a todo riesgo |
| **allowance** | Zuschuss Beihilfe, Unterstüfzung | indemnité, allocation | asignación, subsidio, subvención |
| **amend, to** | ändern | amender | modificar, enmendar |
| **amendment** | Anderung | amendement, modification | modificación, enmienda |
| **amount** | Betrag, Summe | montant, somme | montante, cantidad |
| **annual** | jährlich | annuel | anual |
| **antidumping** | Antidumping | anti-dumping | antidúmping |
| **antidumping duty** | Antidumpingzoll | taxe anti-dumping | tasa de antidúmping |
| **apologize** | um Entschuldigung bitten | présenter ses excuses | disculparse, excusarse, pedir disculpas |
| **apology** | Entschuldigung | excuse | disculpa |
| **applicant** | Antragssteller | demandeur, candidat | solicitante |
| **application** | Antrag | dossier de candidature, bulletin de demande | solicitud |
| **application for a credit** | Kreditantrag | demande de crédit | solicitud de un crédito |
| **arbitration** | Schlichtung, Schiedsgerichtsbarkeit | arbitrage | arbitraje |
| **arbitration agreement** | Schiedsvertrag | accord d'arbitrage | acuerdo de arbitraje |
| **arbitration clause** | Schieds(gerichts)klausel | clause d'arbitrage | cláusula arbitral |
| **arrangement** | Abmachung, Vergleich | accord, arrangment | arreglo, medida, disposiciones |
| **arrival** | Ankunft | arrivée | llegada |
| **arrival date** | Ankunftsdatum | date d'arrivée | fecha de llegada |
| **arrival notice** | Ankunftsbestätigung | bon d'arrivée | aviso de llegada de mercancías |
| **as is** | Abbedingen der Haftung für einen bestimmten Zweck | en l'état | tal cual, en el estado que está |
| **ASAP (as soon as possible)** | möglichst schnell | dès que possible | lo antes posible, tan pronto como sea posible |
| **assessment** | Veranlagung, Festsetzung, Schätzung | évaluation, estimation, appréciation | evaluación, estimación, apreciación |

| Italian | Portuguese (Br) | Japanese | Chinese |
|---|---|---|---|
| accordo, contratto | acordo, contrato | 契約 | 协议 |
| aereo | ar, aéreo | 飛行機；空気 | 航空 |
| carico aereo | carga aérea | 空輸貨物 | 航空货物 |
| trasporto aereo, merci trasportate via aerea | frete aéreo | 航空貨物 | 航空运费 |
| posta aerea | via aérea | 航空郵便物 | 航空邮件 |
| lettera di trasporto aereo | conhecimento de embarque aéreo (AWB) | 航空貨物運送状 | 航空货运单 (AWB) |
| da un aeroporto a un altro aeroporto | de aeroporto a aeroporto | 空港から空港まで | 机场对机场 |
| tutto | tudo | 全部 / 全体 / 全て | 所有，全部 |
| tutti i rischi | todos os riscos | オールリスク | 综合险保险 |
| polizza di assicurazione cotro tutti i rischi | apólice de seguro contra todos os riscos | オールリスク保険 | 综合险保险单 |
| indennità, assegnazione | abatimento, benefício, concessão, pensão | 支給額；許容額 | 津贴，减价，补贴 |
| modificare | aditar, alterar | 改める | 改貶睕拚 |
| modifica, rettifica | alteração, modificação | 改 | 修改，订盏 |
| ammontare, mentante | valor, quantia, soma | 金額 / 額 | 量 |
| annuale, annuo | anual | 年次 / 年間 | 年鉴 |
| antidumping | antidumping | ダンピング防止 | 反倾销 |
| dazio doganale antidumping | imposto contra o dumping | ダンピング防止関税 | 反倾销税 |
| chiedere scusa | desculpar-se, pedir desculpas | 謝る / 詫び | 道歉 |
| scusa | desculpas | 詫び | 道歉 |
| richiedente | candidato, requerente, solicitante | 申込 | 申请人 |
| domanda | pedido, solicitação, requerimento | 申込書 | 申请单 |
| domanda di credito | solicitação de crédito | 掛売勘定を申し込む | 信用证申请 |
| arbitrato | arbitragem | 仲裁 | 仲裁 |
| compromesso arbitrale | acordo de arbitragem | 仲裁契約 | 仲裁协议 |
| clausola compromissoria | cláusula arbitral, de arbitragem | 仲裁条項 | 仲裁条款 |
| accordo, misura, disposizione | acordo, contrato | 手配、準備；配列、配置 | 安排 |
| arrivo | chegada | 着荷 | 到达 |
| data d'arrivo | data de chegada | 到着日 | 到达日期 |
| avviso di ricevimento | aviso de chegada | 着荷通知 | 到货通知，到港通知 |
| nello stato in cui trovasi | como em, tal qual | 現状のままで | 按货样，按现状 |
| il più presto possibile | assim que possível, o mais rápido possível | 早急に / 至急 | 尽快 |
| accertamento, valutazione | avaliação, determinação, verificação | 評価 | 评估 |

| English | German | French | Spanish |
|---|---|---|---|
| **assessment of charges** | Kostenvoranschlag | évaluation des frais | valoración de cargos, valoración de gastos |
| **assessment of loss** | Verlustermittlung, Aktivposten, Aktiva | évaluation des pertes | valoración de pérdidas |
| **assets** | Vermögenswerte | actifs, avoirs, biens | activos |
| **assign, to** | abtreten | céder | asignar, ceder, trasladar, traspasar |
| **assignee** | Zessionar | cessionnaire | apoderado, cesionario, sucesor |
| **assignment** | Zession, Abtretung, Auftrag, Aufgabe | cession | asignación, cesión, traspaso, atribución |
| **assignor** | Zedent | cédant | asignante, cedente, cesionista |
| **ATA carnet** | | carnet ATA | Tarjeta de admisión temporal |
| **attachment** | Beschlagnahme | saisie | incautación, embargo |
| **attorney** | Rechtsanwalt | avocat | abogado, letrado, representante, abogado |
| **attorney in fact (power of attorney)** | Vollmacht | pouvoir de représentation | poder notarial |
| **availability** | Verfügbarkeit | disponibilité | disponibilidad |
| **available** | benutzbar, verfügbar | disponible, utilisable, réalisable | disponible, utilizable |
| **available by** | benutzbar durch | utilisable par | utilizable mediante..., |
| **average** | Havarie | avaries | avería, pérdida |
| **average, general** | grosse Havarie | avarie commune, grosse avarie | avería común, gruesa |
| **average, particular** | besondere Havarie | avarie particulière | avería particular |
| **award (a contract), to** | (einen) Zuschlag erteilen | adjuger un marché | adjudicar un contrato |
| **back order** | unerledigter Auftrag | commande en souffrance | pedido pendiente, pedido atrasado |
| **backdated** | rückdatieren | antidaté | con efectos retroactivos |
| **balance due** | Restschuld, geschuldeter Betrag | solde du | saldo debido |
| **balance on current account** | Leistungsbilanz, Bilanz der laufenden Posten | balance des paiements courants | balanza o saldo de cuenta corriente |
| **balance, credit** | Habensaldo, Kreditsaldo | solde créditeur | saldo acreedor |
| **balance, debit** | Sollsaldo, Passivsaldo | solde débiteur | saldo deudor, débito |
| **bank** | Bank | banque | banco |
| **bank charges** | Bankgebühren | commissions, frais divers de banque | gastos bancarios diversos, comisiones |
| **bank confirmation** | Bankbestätigung | confirmation bancaire | confirmación bancaria |
| **bank draft** | Banktratte | traite bancaire | efecto bancario, instrumento |
| **bank transfer** | Banküberweisung | virement bancaire | transferencia bancaria |

KEY WORDS

| Italian | Portuguese (Br) | Japanese | Chinese |
|---|---|---|---|
| valutazione delle spese | avaliação, determinação das despesas | 評価された費用 | 费用的评估 |
| valutazione di un sinistro | avaliação, determinação do(s) prejuízo(s) | 損害査定額 | 损失的评估 |
| attività | ativo, patrimônio global | 資産 | 资产 |
| cedere, trasferire | ceder, transferir, trasladar | 割当てる／指定する | 分配，指定，转让 |
| cessionario | cessionário, sucessor, procurador | 譲受人 | 代理人，受让人 |
| trasferimento, cessione (es. atto di cessione) | cessão, transferência, traslado | 譲渡 | 产权转让 |
| cedente | cedente, nomeador | 譲渡人 | 让与人 |
| carnet doganale | carnet ATA | ATA　カルネ | 官方证明信件 |
| pignoramento, sequestro | anexo | 添付 | 官方证明信件 |
| procuratore | advogado, procurador, representante legal | 弁護士 | 律师，代理人 |
| procura notarile | procurador (poder judicial) | 委任状 | 代理人，私人律师 |
| disponibilità | disponibilidade | 有用性 | 可用性，有效性 |
| disponibile, utilzzabile | disponível | 有効／利用可能／使用可能 | 可用的，有效的 |
| utilizzabile mediante | disponível por | ～で入手可能な | 通过…加以利用，由…提供 |
| avaria | avarias, danos | 平均 | 海损 |
| avaria comune/generale | avarias grossas, comuns | 共同海損 | 共同海损 |
| avaria particolare | avaria(s) simples, particular(es) | 単独海損 | 单独海损 |
| aggiudicare un contratto | adjudicar (um contrato) | （人）に栅必摘铯护 | 裁决（合同）给… |
| ordine arretrato | pedido pendente, em atraso | バックオーダー／入荷待ち | 延期交货 |
| retrodatare | antedatado, retroativo | 前の日付にする | 追溯到过去某日期 |
| saldo dovuto | saldo devedor, saldo a pagar | 不足額 | 结欠金额 |
| saldo di unconto corrente | saldo da conta corrente | 経常収支尻 | 经常项目收支 |
| saldo creditore | saldo credor | 貸方残高 | 贷方余额 |
| saldo debitore | saldo devedor | 借方残高 | 借方余额 |
| banca | banco | 銀行 | 银行 |
| commissioni bancarie | encargos, tarifas bancários(as) | 銀行手数料 | 银行手续费 |
| conferma bancaria | confirmação bancária | 銀行の承 | 银行确认 |
| stima giornaliera del credito bancario | saque bancário, letra de câmbio | 銀行手形 | 银行汇票 |
| bonifico bancario | transferência bancária | 銀行辙z | 银行转眨瞒瞒谢瞒 |

| English | German | French | Spanish |
|---|---|---|---|
| **bank wire** | Clearingnetz | virement télégraphique | transferencia bancaria |
| **bank, accepting** | akzeptierende Bank | banque acceptante | banco aceptador, banco aceptante |
| **bank, buyer's** | Käuferbank | banque d'acheteur | banco del comprador |
| **bank, confirming** | bestätigende Bank | banque confirmatrice | banco confirmador |
| **bank, paying** | zahlende Bank | banque chargée du réglement | banco pagador |
| **bank, presenting** | vorlegende Bank | banque présentatrice | banco presentador |
| **bank, seller's** | Verkäuferbank | banque vendeuse | banco del vendedor |
| **banker** | Bankier | banquier | banquero, banco |
| **bargain, a** | Gelegenheitskauf, Ausverkauf | soldes, occasions | rebajas |
| **bargain, to** | handeln | marchander, négocier | regatear |
| **barter** | Tauschgeschäft, Tausch (Warenaustausch) | troc, échange | trueque, compensación |
| **bay** | Bucht | baie | bahía |
| **bearer, to** | (zum) Inhaber | au porteur | al portador |
| **beneficiary** | Begünstigter | bénéficiaire | beneficiario |
| **bid** | Gebot, Angebot | offre, enchère | puja, oferta |
| **bid, to** | bieten, anbieten | faire une offre | hacer una oferta, pujar |
| **bidder** | Anbieter, Bieter | offrant, enchérisseur | postor |
| **bill** | Bescheinigung, Wechsel, Rechnung | effet, traite, billet | factura, giro, letra, efecto de comercio |
| **bill for charges** | Rechnung | états des frais | cuenta de gastos |
| **bill for collection** | Inkassowechsel | effet à l'encaissement | efecto al cobro |
| **bill of entry** | Zollerklärung | déclaration en douane | declaración de aduanas hecha por importador |
| **bill of exchange** | Wechsel | lettre de change | letra de cambio |
| **bill of lading** | Seefrachtbrief, Konnossement | connaissement, nantissement | conocimiento de embarque |
| **bill of lading, air** | Luftfrachtbrief | connaissement aérien | conocimiento de embarque aéreo |
| **bill of lading, claused** | Konnossement mit Vorbehalt | connaissement clausé | conocimiento con cláusula adicional |
| **bill of lading, clean** | reines Konnossement | connaissement net | conocimiento limpio |
| **bill of lading, clean onboard** | reines Bordkonnossement | connaissement net à bord | conocimiento a bordo limpio |
| **bill of lading, combined** | Sammelkonnossement | connaissement de transport combiné | conocimiento de embarque combinado |
| **bill of lading, multimodal** | kombiniertes Konnossement | connaissement multimodal | conocimiento de embarque multimoda |
| **bill of lading, negotiable** | Orderkonnossement | connaissement négociable | conocimiento de embarque negociable |
| **bill of lading, non-negotiable** | nicht übertragbares Konnossement | connaissement intransmissible | conocimiento no negociable |

KEY WORDS

| Italian | Portuguese (Br) | Japanese | Chinese |
|---|---|---|---|
| bonifico telegrafico | transferência bancária | 電信送金 | 银行电报 |
| banca accettante | banco aceitante (de carta de crédito) | 引受銀行 | 承兑银行 |
| banca del compratore | banco do comprador | 買い手銀行 | 买方银行 |
| banca confermante | banco confirmador | 確浙y行 | 保兑银行 |
| banca pagante | banco pagador | 支払銀行 | 付找瞒 |
| banca presentatrice | banco apresentante | 提示銀行 | 兑换银行 |
| banca del venditore | banco do vendedor | 売り手銀行 | 卖方银行 |
| banchiere | banqueiro, bancário | 銀行業 | 银行家 |
| affare, svendita | acordo, pechincha | 安売り | 交易 |
| contrattare, negoziare, trattare sul prezzo | negociar, regatear | 交渉する | 讲价，谈判 |
| baratto | permutar, trocar | 物々交換 | 物物交换 |
| baia | baía | 入江 | 海湾 |
| al portatore | ao portador | 持参人払い | 持票人 |
| beneficiario (dir.), ordinatario (banc.) | beneficiário(a) | 受益 | 受益人 |
| offerta, bando d'appalto | oferta, concorrência | 入札 | 投标 |
| fare un'offerta | oferecer, leiloar | 入札する | 出价 |
| offerente, concorrente | lançador, licitante | 入札 | 出价人，投标人 |
| conto, titolo, cambiale | fatura, nota, conta, título bancário | 涨甡 | 盏亻瞒本 |
| conto delle spese | nota de débito | 料金表 | 费用的盏 |
| titolo di incasso | letra para cobrança | 取立手形 | 托收票据 |
| bolletta d'entrata doganale | declaração de entrada de mercadorias | 税関申告書 | 报关单 |
| cambiale, tratta | letra de câmbio | 為替手形 | 汇票 |
| polizza di carico (P/C) | conhecimento de embarque | 船荷証券 | 提货单 |
| polizza di carico aereo | conhecimento de embarque aéreo | 航空貨物受取証 | 航空提货单 |
| polizza di carico sporca | conhecimento de embarque clausulado | 条項付き船荷証券 | 附条款提单，附条件提单 |
| polizza di carico netta | conhecimento de embarque limpo | 無故沾瞒稍^券 | 清洁提单 |
| polizza di carico pulita a bordo | conhecimento de embarque limpo a bordo | 無故沾瞒eみ船荷証券 | 随车清洁提单 |
| polizza di carico combinata | conhecimento de embarque combinado | 複合運送証券 | 联运提单 |
| polizza di carico multimodale | conhecimento de embarque multimodal, B/L multimodal | 複合船荷証券 | 多种方式联运提单 |
| polizza di carico negoziabile | conhecimento de embarque negociável, B/L negociável | 譲渡可能船荷証券 | 流通提单，可转让提单 |
| polizza di carico non negoziabile | conhecimento de embarque não negociável B/L não negociável | 非流通船荷証券 | 不流通提单，不可转让提单 |

KEY WORDS

| English | German | French | Spanish |
|---|---|---|---|
| bill of lading, ocean | Bordkonnossement | connaissement maritime | conocimiento de embarque marítimo, conocimiento de embarque a la orden |
| bill of lading, onboard | An-Bord-Konnossement | connaissement à bord | conocimiento a bordo |
| bill of lading, received | Übernahme-Konnossement | connaissement reçu à quai | conocimiento recibido en muelle |
| bill of lading, received for shipment | Konnossement 'empfangen zur Vershiffung' | connaissement reçu pour embarquement | conocimiento recibido para embarque |
| bill of lading, straight | Orderkonnossement | connaissement nominatif | conocimiento nominativo |
| bill of lading, through | Durch(fracht)konnossement | connaissement direct | conocimiento directo |
| bill of parcels | | liste de colis expédiés | listado de la mercancía |
| bill of sale | Kassenbon | acte de vente | factura, comprobante o documento de venta |
| bill, outstanding | nicht beglichene Rechnung, offene Rechnung | facture en souffrance, non réglée | factura pendiente |
| bill-to party | Rechnungsempfänger | facture à la partie | parte a facturar |
| binder | Versicherungsschein | engagement | póliza de seguros provisional, nota de cobertura |
| bond | Obligation, Garantie, Verpflichtungsschein | obligation, engagement, contrat | obligación, caución, contrato |
| bond, bearer | Inhaberschuldver-schreibung | obligation au porteur | obligación al portador |
| bond, under | unter Zollverschluss | sous régime de douane | bajo régimen de aduana, sometido a despacho aduanero |
| bonded (goods in bond) | unter Zolllagerschluss | marchandises sous douane | mercancias en almacén aduanero |
| bonded stores | Zolllager | magasin sous douane | provisiones en depósito |
| bonded terminal | | terminal sous douane | terminal en depósito |
| bonded warehouse | Zolllager | entrepôt sous douane | almacén general de depósito, depósito aduanero |
| book (an order), to | Auftrag erteilen | enregistrer (une commande) | contabilizar (un pedido) |
| booking | buchen | retenir (le fret) | reserva, inscripción |
| breach of contract | Vertragsverletzung, Vertragsbruch | rupture de contrat | ruptura de contrato |
| break bulk | Verteilung des Sammelguts | dégroupage | traccionamiento de carga |
| break bulk cargo | Sammelgut | marchandises diverses | carga fraccionada |
| breakage | Bruch | casse | destrozo, ruptura |
| bribe | Bestechungsgeld | pot-de-vin | soborno |
| broker | Makler | courtier | broker, agente de bolsa, corredor, comisionista |

KEY WORDS

| Italian | Portuguese (Br) | Japanese | Chinese |
|---|---|---|---|
| polizza di carico per trasporto oceanico | conhecimento de embarque marítimo | 船荷証券 | 船货提单 |
| polizza di caricoper merce a bordo | conhecimento de embarque a bordo | 船積み船荷証券 | 随车携带提单 |
| polizza di carico 'ricevuto per imbarco' | conhecimento de embarque recebido | 受取船荷証券 | 收到提单 |
| polizza di carico ricevuto per l'imbarco | conhecimento de embarque acreditador de recepção de mercadorias para sua carga | 受取船荷証券 | 待装船运提单 |
| polizza di carico nominativa | conhecimento de embarque nominativo | 記名式船荷証券 | 记名提单 |
| polizza di carico diretta | conhecimento de embarque corrido | 通し船荷証券 | 全程提单 |
| bolla di consegna | lista de mercadorias | 貨物証券 | 装运明细单，发票 |
| atto di vendita | nota, comprovante de venda de venda | 売買証書 | 卖据，所有权转移证书 |
| titolo insoluto | título, fatura a receber | 未払い手形 | 未尝票据 |
| fatturare | título nominal | 涨鬓瞒透断 | 接受票据方 |
| polizza d'assicurazione provvisoria | contrato provisório de seguro, contrato provisório | 仮保険証 | 临时合同，临时保险单 |
| titolo, obbligazione, garanzia | título, garantia | 債券 | 杖 |
| obbligazione al portatore | portador de ação | 無記名債券 | 不记名杖 |
| in custodia doganale | (mercadorias) em garantia, em depósito (temporariamente) | 保税中 | 保兑，未完税扣存关 |
| merce depositata non sdoganata | produtos retidos, armazenados na alfândega (até pagamento de impostos) | 保税倉庫留置の商品 | 以杖瞒鞅Ｖさ？ 存入保税仓库的 |
| provviste di bordo | armazéns alfandegados | 保税船舶用品 | 保税仓库 |
| terminale doganale autorizzata | terminal alfandegado | 保税ターミナル | 保税码头 |
| magazzino doganale | depósito alfandegado | 保税倉庫 | 保税仓库 |
| contabilizzare | contabilizar, registrar (um pedido) | 注文する | 预订，登记 |
| prenotazione | reserva | 貨物運送引受け | 预订 |
| inadempienza, inadempimento contrattuale | violação de contrato | 違約する | 违约，违反合同 |
| frazionamento di carico alla rinfusa | fragmentar, descarregar | 船荷を下ろす | 开始卸货；零担 |
| carico alla rinfusa da frazionare | carga fracionada, fragmentada | 船荷を下ろす | 零碎装卸货物，普通货物 |
| rottura e/o danni | indenização, desconto por danos | 破損 | 破损 |
| tangente, bustarella | subornar | 贈賄 | 贿赂 |
| mediatore, intermediario, sensale | corretor | 仲介業 | 经纪人 |

KEY WORDS

| English | German | French | Spanish |
|---------|--------|--------|---------|
| **broker, customs** | Zollspediteur | commissionnaire en douane, agent | agente de aduana |
| **broker, insurance** | Versicherungsmakler | courtier d'assurance | corredor de seguro |
| **budget** | Haushalt, Etat, Budget | budget | presupuesto preventivo |
| **bulk cargo** | Massengut | cargaison de vrac | carga (mento) a granel |
| **bulk transport** | Massengut-Transport | transport en vraq | transporte a granel |
| **bunker adjustment factor (BAF)** | Zuschlag für Bunkerung | surtaxe de soutage | factor de ajuste por combustible |
| **business** | Geschäftswelt, Wirtschaft | affaires, business | negocio, empresa |
| **business entity** | Geschäftsentität | entité commerciale | entidad comercial |
| **business name** | Firma, Gegenstand der Gesellschaft | raison sociale | razón social |
| **business opportunity** | Marktlücke | créneau commercial | oportunidad comercial, de negocio |
| **business plan** | Geschäftsplan | projet d'entreprise | planes económicos, comerciales |
| **business trip** | Geschäftsreise | voyage d'affaires | viaje de negocios |
| **buy** | kaufen | acheter | comprar |
| **buyer** | Käufer | acheteur | comprador |
| **cancel, to** | rückgängig machen, für ungültig erklären | annuler, résilier | cancelar, anular, rescindir |
| **capital** | Kapital | capital, capitaux | capital |
| **cargo** | Fracht, Ladung | cargaison | carga, cargamento |
| **cargo insurance** | Frachtversicherung, Ladungsversicherung | assurance faculté | seguro de carga |
| **cargo, break bulk** | Sammelgut | marchandises diverses | carga fraccionada |
| **cargo, general** | Stückgut | marchandises générales | carga mixta, mercancías varias |
| **cargo, unitized** | unitizierte Ladung | cargaison sous forme d'unité de charge | cargamento unitarizado (bajo forma de unidad de carga) |
| **carnet** | Carnet | carnet | carné |
| **carnet/ATA Carnet** | Carnet für vorübergehende Einfuhr | carnet ATA | carné ATA |
| **carriage** | Fracht Porto | port, transport | portes, transporte |
| **carrier** | Frachtführer | transporteur | transportador, porteador |
| **carrier, common** | Frachtführer (gewerbsmässiger) | transporteur général | transportador general |
| **cartage** | Fuhrlohn | camionnage | empresa de transporte por carretera, transportista |
| **cash** | Bargeld | espèces, numéraire, liquide | numerario, efectivo, liquido, caja |
| **cash against documents (CAD)** | Zahlung gegen Dokumente | comptant contre document | pago contra documentos |

**K E Y W O R D S**

| Italian | Portuguese (Br) | Japanese | Chinese |
|---|---|---|---|
| spedizioniere doganale | despachante aduaneiro | 税関貨物取扱人 | 报关经纪人 |
| mediatore di assicurazione | corretor de seguros | 保険仲介人 | 保险经纪人 |
| previsione, bilancio | orçamento | 予算 | 预算 |
| carico alla rinfusa | carga a granel | 散荷 | 散装货 |
| trasporto alla rinfusa | transporte a granel | 船荷運送 | 散装运输，张瞔耸 |
| coefficiente di adeguamento per il bunker | fator de ajuste de combustível | バンカー照麄S数 | 燃油调找蛋 |
| affari, commercio | negócio(s), empresa, assunto, profissão | ビジネス / 仕事 / 取引 | 商业 |
| entità aziendale | entidade comercial | 企業実体 | 企业单位，营业单位 |
| nome dell'azienda, ragione sociale | nome comercial, razão social | 商号 | 企业名称，商号 |
| possibilità di realizzare un affare | oportunidade comercial | ビジネスチヤンス / 商機 | 商业机会，商机 |
| programma di gestione aziendale | plano econômico, comercial | 経営計画 | 商务计划 |
| viaggio per affari | viagem de negócios | 出張 | 商务旅行 |
| comprare, acquistare | comprar | 買う | 购买 |
| compratore | comprador | 購入 | 购买眨瞔晒涸 |
| annullare, risolvere, rescindere | cancelar | 取り消す | 取消 |
| capitale | capital | 資本 | 资本 |
| carico | carga | 積み荷 | 货物 |
| assicurazione del carico | seguro da carga, mercadoria | 積荷保険 | 货物保险 |
| carico alla rinfusa da frazionare | carga fracionada, fragmentada | 積荷を下ろす | 零担货物货物 |
| carico di merci varie | carga mista | 一般貨物 | 普通货物 |
| carico unitizzato | carga unificada | ユニタイズド貨物 | 成套货物 |
| carnet | carnê | 無関税許可書 | 官方证明信件 |
| carnet ATA | carnê / carnê ATA | カルネ | 官方证明信件 /ATA Carnet |
| trasporto, porto | transporte, frete, transporte | 運賃 | 运费，搬运费 |
| vettore, trasportatore | transportador, transportadora | キャリヤー | 运载工 |
| vettore generico/ordinario | transportador(a) público(a) | 一般通信事業 | 承运商 |
| spese di trasporto a mezzo carri | transporte intermunicipal rodoviário (em reboques ou caminhões) | 荷車運送 | 货车运输 |
| contante, pronta cassa | dinheiro (em espécie), ativo disponível | 現金 | 现金 |
| pagamento contro documenti | pagamento contra apresentação de documento | 書類引換現金払い | 凭单据付现 |

KEY WORDS

| English | German | French | Spanish |
|---|---|---|---|
| **cash terms** | Barzahlung | condition au comptant | condiciones de pago al contado |
| **cash with order (CWO)** | Zahlung bei Auftragserteilung | comptant à la commande | pagado a la orden |
| **certificate** | Zeugnis, Zertifikat | certificat | certificado |
| **certificate of inspection** | Inspektionszertifikat | certificat d'inspection | certificado de inspección |
| **certificate of insurance** | Versicherungszertifikat | certificat d'assurance | certificado de seguro |
| **certificate of origin** | Ursprungszeugnis | certificat d'origine | certificado de origen |
| **certificate, health** | Gesundheits-bescheinigung | certificat sanitaire, certificat de santé | certificado de sanidad |
| **certification** | Beglaubigung | attestation | certificación, atestación |
| **CFR Cost and Freight (named port of destination)** | CFR Kosten und Fracht (... benannter Bestimmungshafen) | CFR cout et fret (... port de destination convenu) | CFR coste y flete (...puerto de destino convenido) |
| **charge card** | Debetkarte | carte de crédit | tarjeta de débito |
| **charge(s)** | Kosten, Gebühren, Fracht | frais, prix, droits, redevances | gasto(s), precio, derecho |
| **chargeable weight** | Taxgewicht | poids taxé | peso imputable |
| **charges collect (cc)** | unfrei, unfrankiert | frais dus | gastos por cobrar |
| **charges prepaid** | franko | frais payés | gastos pagados |
| **check** | Scheck | chèque | cheque |
| **check, certified** | bestätigter Scheck | chèque certifié | cheque conformado |
| **CIF Cost, Insurance and Freight (...named port of destination)** | CIF Kosten, Versicherung und Fracht (...benannter Bestimmungshafen) | CIF coût, assurance et frêt (...porte de destination convenu) | CIF coste, seguro y flete (...puerto de destino convenido) |
| **CIP Carriage and Insurance Paid To (...named place of destination)** | CIP Frachtfrei versichert (...Benannter Bestimmungsort) | CIP port payé, assurance comprise (...lieu de destination convenu) | CIP transporte y seguro pagados hasta (...lugar de destino) |
| **claim** | Forderung, Anspruch, Reklamation | demande, créance, réclamation | reclamación, demanda |
| **claim, insurance** | Versicherungsanspruch | réclamation | reclamación de seguro |
| **claim, submission of a** | Anmeldung eines Anspruchs, Inanspruchnahme (der Garantie) | présentation d'une demande | presentación de una reclamación |
| **class or kind (of merchandise)** | Warenkategorie | classe ou type (de marchandise) | clase o tipo (de mercancías) |
| **classification** | Klassizierung | nomenclature | clasificación |
| **classify, to** | klassifizieren | déterminer l'espèce tarifaire | clasificar |
| **clause(s)** | Klausel, Bestimmung, Bedingung | clause, stipulation, disposition, article | cláusula, artículo, pacto, disposición |
| **clause, contract** | Vertragbestimmung | clause d'un contrat | cláusula de un contrato |
| **clause, standard** | Standardklausel | clause type | cláusula tipo |
| **claused** | unrein | avec réserve | con reservas |
| **clean** | vorbehaltlos, uneingeschränkt | net | limpio, neto |

K
E
Y
W
O
R
D
S

| Italian | Portuguese (Br) | Japanese | Chinese |
|---|---|---|---|
| condizioni per pagamento in contanti | condições de pagamento a vista | 現金支払条件 | 现金术语 |
| pagamento all'ordine | pagamento contra o pedido | 現金注文 | 定货付现，认购即付 |
| certificato | certificado | 証明書 | 证明书 |
| certificato d'ispezione | certificado de inspeção | 検査証明書 | 检验证书 |
| certificato di assicurazione | certificado de seguro | 保険証明書 | 保险证书 |
| certificato d'origine | certificado de origem | 原産地証明書 | 原产地证明书 |
| certificato di sana costituzione, certificato medico | certificado de saúde | 健康証明書 | 健康证书 |
| certificazione | certificação | 証明 | 举证，证明 |
| CFR costo e nolo (... porto di destinazione convenuto) | CFR custo e frete pagos até¶ (... porto de destino) | CFR 運賃込 （... 指定仕向港） | CFR 成本加运费 （... 指定目的港口） |
| carta di addebito | cartão de débito | クレジットカード | 信用卡，签湛 |
| spese, onere, addebito | encargo(s), despesa(s), gasto(s) | 料金 | 费用 |
| peso addebitabile | peso cobrável | 账翱赡茎示 | 收费重量 |
| spese assegnate/da incassare | encargos, despesas a cobrar | 運賃着払い | 费用收集 |
| spese prepagate | despesas pagas, encargos pagos | 前納の料金 | 预付费用 |
| assegno bancario | cheque | 小切手 | 支票 |
| assegno bancario a copertura garantita | cheque visado | 支払保証小切手 | 保付支票 |
| CIF costo, assicurazione e nolo (...porto di destinazione convenuto) | CIF - custo, seguro e frete pagos até (... porto de destino) | CIF 運賃保険料込 （... 指定仕向港） | CIF 成本、保险费加运费 （... 指定目的港） |
| CIP trasporto e assicurazione pagati fino a (...luogo di destinazione convenuto) | CIP transporte e seguro pagos, incluídos até (... local de destino) | CIP 輸送費保険料込 （... 指定仕向地） | CIP 运费、保险费，付至 （... 目的地名） |
| domanda, reclamo | reclamação, reivindicação, demanda | 涨蟥工 | 索赔 |
| dichiarazione di sinistro | reivindicação de indenização por sinistro | 保険金涨 | 保险索赔 |
| presentazione di una domanda | instauração de uma ação de reclamação ou demanda | 涨蟥工 | 要求索赔 |
| classe, categoria | classe ou tipo (de mercadoria(s)) | 種類 | 或罩掷郸 lass ( 商品的 ) |
| classificazione | classificação | 分類 | 分类类别 |
| classificare | classificar | 分類する | 分类 |
| clausola | cláusula(s) | 条項 | 条款 |
| clausola contrattuale | cláusula contratual | 契約条項 | 合同条款 |
| clausola tipo | cláusula normal, padrão | 基準条項 | 标准条款 |
| Sporco, con riserva | clausulado(a), com reservas | 条項付き | 条款 |
| senza riserve, netto | limpo(a) | 無故 | 清洁 |

| English | German | French | Spanish |
|---|---|---|---|
| cleared, customs | zollabgefertigt, verzollt | dédouané | despachado de aduanas |
| clearance, customs | Zollabfertigung | dédouanement | despacho de aduanas |
| client | Kunde | client | cliente |
| close a sale | einen Verkauf abschließen | conclure une vente | cerrar un trato de venta |
| collect on delivery (COD) | Barzahlung bei Lieferung | paiement à la livraison | pago contra reembolso |
| collection order | Inkassoauftrag | ordre d'encaissement | orden de cobro |
| collection, documentary | dokumentäres Inkasso | encaissement documentaire | cobro documentario |
| combined transport (CT) | kombinierter Transport | transport combiné (TC) | transporte combinado (TC) |
| commercial invoice | Handelsrechnung | facture commerciale | factura comercial |
| commercial sample | Warenmuster | échantillion | muestra comercial |
| commission, sales | Verkaufsprovision | commission sur vente | comisión sobre ventas |
| commodity | Ware, Handelsware, Rohstoff | produit, marchandise, denrée | mercancía, producto |
| company | Gesellschaft, Firma, Unternehmen | société, compagnie, entreprise | compañía, empresa, sociedad |
| company, insurance | Versicherungs-gesellschaft | compagnie d'assurances | compañía de seguros, compañía aseguradora |
| compensation | Ausgleich | rémunération | compensación |
| complaint | Klage, Beschwerde, Reklamation | réclamation, litige | reclamación, litigio |
| comply, to | entsprechen, entsprochen | satisfaire, satisfait à | satisfacer, satisfecho cumplir, cumplido con |
| compromise | Kompromiss | compromis | compromiso |
| computer | Computer | ordinateur | ordenador, computadora |
| confirm, to | bestätigen | confirmer | confirmar, declarar, afirmar, ratificar |
| confirmed | bestätigt | confirmé | confirmado |
| congratulations | Glückwunsch | félicitations | felicitaciones |
| consign, to | in Konsignation geben, abschicken | expédier | consignar, remitir, enviar |
| consignee | Empfänger | destinataire, consignataire | consignatario, destinatario |
| consignment | Sendung, Warensendung | expédition, envoi | expedición, envío |
| consignor | Absender | expéditeur, consignateur | expedidor, consignador, remitente |
| consolidate goods, to | (eine) Sammelladung zusammenstellen | grouper des marchandises | agrupar o consolidar mercancias |
| consolidation | Sammelladung | groupage | agrupamiento |
| consolidator | Sammelladungs-spediteur | groupeur | agrupador, consolidador |
| consular invoice | Konsularfaktura | facture consulaire | factura consular |
| container | Container | conteneur | contenedor |

| Italian | Portuguese (Br) | Japanese | Chinese |
|---|---|---|---|
| sdoganato | desembaraçao na alfândega | 税関を通過 | 进行结关 |
| sdoganamento | desembaraço aduaneiro | 通関手続き | 结关 |
| cliente | cliente | クライアント | 顾客 |
| concludere un affare | fechar uma venda | 取引を成立させる | 关闭销售 |
| da pagare alla consegna, contrassegno | entrega contra reembolso | 代金引換払い | 货到收款 |
| ordine d'incassos | ordem de cobrança | 手形取立指図書 | 托收委托书 |
| incasso documentario | cobrança documentária | 荷為替手形取り立て | 单据托收 |
| trasporto combinato (TC) | transporte combinado (TC) | 複合輸送 | 联运 |
| fattura commerciale | fatura comercial | 商業送り状 | 商业发票 |
| campione commerciale | amostra comercial | 商品サンプル | 商品试样 |
| provvigione sulle vendite | comissão de venda | 売上手数料 | 回扣 |
| derrata, materia prima, merce | artigo, bem, produto | 商品 | 日用品 |
| compagnia, società, impresa | companhia, empresa, sociedade | 会社 | 公司 |
| compagnia di assicurazione | companhia de seguros, seguradora | 保険会社 | 保险公司 |
| rimunerazione | compensação | 報酬 | 补偿 |
| reclamo, protesta, querela | reclamação, queixa | 訴状 | 抱怨 |
| soddisfare, adempiere | ater-se a, cumprir, obedecer | 応じる | 顺从 |
| compromesso | concessão mútua, compromisso | 譲歩する | 妥协 |
| computer, calcolatore, elaboratore | computador | コンピュータ | 计算机 |
| confermare | confirmar | 確柵工 | 确认 |
| confermato | confirmado | 確諟gみの | 保兑；证实的 |
| congratulazioni, complimenti | congratulações, cumprimento | おめでとう | 祝贺 |
| consegnare | consignar | 委託する | 托运 |
| destinatario, consegnatario | consignatário | 荷受人 | 受货人 |
| spedizione, invi | carregamento, consignação | 出荷 | 托付 |
| mittente, speditore | consignador | 荷送人 | 发货人 |
| consolidare le merci | consolidar | 連結する | 集中 |
| consolidamento | consolidação | 連結 | 集中 |
| consolidatore, operatore di groupage | consolidador | 統合綻碚 | 并装业眍? 混载业 |
| fattura consolare | fatura consular | 領事送り状 | 领事发票 |
| contenitore | contêiner | コンテナ | 集装箱 |

| English | German | French | Spanish |
|---|---|---|---|
| **container load** | Container-Fracht | lot de marchandises suffisant pour remplir un conteneur | carga del contenedor |
| **container ship** | Container-Schiff | navire porte-conteneurs | buque de contenedores |
| **container, air freight** | Luftfracht-Container | conteneur pour fret aérien | contenedor para carga aérea |
| **container, ocean freight** | Seefracht-Container | conteneur pour fret maritime | contenedor para transporte marítimo |
| **containerization** | Verfrachtung in einen Container | mise en conteneurs | transporte en contenedores |
| **contents** | Inhalt | contenu | contenido |
| **contract** | Vertrag | contrat | contrato, acuerdo |
| **contract of carriage** | Frachtführervertrag | contrat de transport | contrato de transporte |
| **contract term** | Vertragsbedingung | durée d'un contrat | duración del contrato |
| **contract terms** | Vertragsbedingungen | clause d'un contrat | cláusulas de un contrato |
| **contract, draft** | Vertragsentwurf | projet de contrat | precontrato |
| **contract, sales** | Kaufvertrag | contrat de vente | contrato de compraventa |
| **copy(ies)** | Kopie | exemplaire, copie | copia(s) |
| **copyright** | Urheberrecht, Verlagsrecht | droit d'auteur, droits de reproduction | derechos de reproducción/ autor |
| **cost(s)** | Kosten | coût, frais | gasto(s), costo(s) |
| **costs, total** | Gesamtkosten | coût total | gastos totales |
| **counteroffer** | Gegenangebot | contre-offre | contraoferta |
| **country of destination** | Bestimmungsland | pays destinataire | país de destino |
| **country of origin** | Ursprungsland | pays d'origine | país de origen |
| **courier** | Kurier | transporteur | mensajero |
| **courier service** | Kurierdienst | messagerie express | servicio de mensajería |
| **coverage** | Deckung | couverture, portée, protection | cobertura, alcance, garantía, protección |
| **CPT Carriage Paid To (...named place of destination)** | CPT Frachtfrei (...Benannter Bestimmungsort) | CPT port payé jusqu'à (...lieu de destination convenu) | CPT transporte pagado hasta (...lugar de destino convenido) |
| **credit** | Kredit | crédit | crédito |
| **credit application** | Akkreditiver öffnungsauftrag | demande d'ouverture de crédit | solicitud de apertura de crédito |
| **credit card** | Kreditkarte | carte de crédit | tarjeta de crédito |
| **credit card expiration date** | Kreditkarte-Verfalldatum | date limite d'une carte de crédit | fecha de caducidad de la tarjeta de crédito |
| **credit card number** | Kreditkartennummer | numéro de carte de crédit | número de la tarjeta de crédito |
| **credit, acceptance** | Akzeptkredit | acceptation de crédit | crédito de aceptación |
| **credit, advise of** | Kreditavis | note de crédit | notificación de disponibilidad de crédito |
| **credit, amendment of the** | Kreditänderung | amendemant de crédit | modificación del crédito |

KEY WORDS

| Italian | Portuguese (Br) | Japanese | Chinese |
|---|---|---|---|
| carico del container | carga para a capacidade do contêiner | コンテナロード | 集装箱装载 |
| nave portacontainer | navio para transporte de contêineres | コンテナ船 | 集装箱货船 |
| container per il trasporto aereo | contêiner de carga aérea | 航空貨物コンテナ | 空运集装箱 |
| Container per trasporto marittimo | contêiner de carga marítima | 海上運賃コンテナ | 海运集装箱 |
| spedizione e trasporto in container | conteinerização | コンテナ輸送 | 货柜运输 |
| contenuto | conteúdo | コンテンツ／内容 | 内容 |
| contratto | contrato | 契約 | 合同 |
| contratto di trasporto | contrato de transporte | 運送契約 | 运费合同 |
| durata del contratto | prazo do contrato | 契約期間 | 合同术语 |
| clausole (condizioni) del contratto | termos do contrato | 契約条件 | 合同术语 |
| bozza di contratto | minuta de contrato | 契約案 | 合同草案 |
| contratto di vendita | contrato de venda(s) | 販売契約 | 销售合同 |
| copia(e), esemplare | cópia(s), via(s) | コピー | 复制 |
| diritti d'autore | direitos autorais, direitos de reprodução | 著作権 | 版权 |
| costo(i) | custo(s), despesa(s) | コスト | 成本 |
| costi totali | custo(s), despesa(s) total(is) | 総費用 | 总成本 |
| controfferta | contra-oferta | 逆提案 | 还盘 |
| paese di destinazione | país de destino | 出向国 | 目的国 |
| paese d'origine | país de origem | 原産国 | 生产国 |
| corriere | emissário, mensageiro, courier | 配達する | 送急件的人 |
| servizio di corriere | serviço de emissário, de courier | 国際张浔 | 送急件服务 |
| copertura | cobertura | 担保（保険） | 保险总额 |
| CPT trasporto pagato a (...luogo di destinazione convenuto) | CPT transporte pago até (... local de destino) | 輸送費込（... 指定仕向地） | 运费，支付到目的地的（... 地名） |
| credito | crédito | 信用 | 贷方 |
| richiesta di apertura di credito | solicitação de crédito | 借入申込書 | 贷款申请 |
| carta di credito | cartão de crédito | クレジットカード | 信用卡 |
| data di scadenza della carta di credito | data de validade do cartão de crédito | クレジットカード有効期限 | 信用卡有效期 |
| numero della carta di credito | número do cartão de crédito | クレジットカード番号 | 信用卡号 |
| credito di accettazione | aceitação de crédito | 引受条件付き信用 | 承兑信贷 |
| nota di credito | assessoria de crédito | 入金通知 | 贷方建议 |
| revisione del credito | aditamento, ajuste de crédito | 信用状の変更 | 贷款修 |

KEYWORDS

| English | German | French | Spanish |
|---|---|---|---|
| **credit, confirmed irrevocable** | bestätigtes unwiderrufliches Akkreditiv | crédit confirmé irrévocable | crédito irrevocable confirmado |
| **credit, date of** | Akkreditivdatum | date de crédit | fecha del crédito |
| **credit, documentary (letter of)** | Dokumentenakkreditiv | lettre de crédit documentaire | carta de crédito documentario |
| **credit, irrevocable** | unwiderrufliches Akkreditiv | crédit irrévocable | crédito irrevocable |
| **currency adjustment factor / charge (CAF or CAC)** | Währungszuschlag | surcharge monétaire | recargo por ajustes cambiarios |
| **currency of payment** | Zahlungswährung | monnaie de paiement | moneda de pago |
| **customer** | Kunde | client | cliente |
| **customs bond** | Zollkaution | marchandises en entrepôt sous douane | fianza aduanera |
| **customs broker** | Zollspediteur | commissionnaire ou agent en douane | agente o corredor de aduanas |
| **customs clearance** | Zollabfertigung | formalités douanières, dédouanement | trámite aduanero, despacho aduanal |
| **customs declaration** | Zollerklärung | déclaration en douane | declaración aduanera |
| **customs entry** | Zollanmeldung | déclaration en douane | declaración o entrada de aduana |
| **DAF Delivered at Frontier (...named place)** | DAF geliefert Grenze (...genannter Bestimmungsort) | DAF rendu frontière (...lieu convenu) | DAF entreda en frontera (...lugar convenido) |
| **damage** | Schaden | dommage | daño, perjuicio, siniestro |
| **damage to goods** | Warenbeschädigung | dommage aux marchandises | daños de las mercancías |
| **damages, to claim** | Schadenersatzverlangen | réclamer une indemnité | reclamar una indemnización |
| **data** | Daten, Information | donnée, information | datos, información |
| **date** | Datum, Zeitangabe | date | fecha |
| **date of arrival** | Ankunftsdatum | date d'arrivée | fecha de llegada |
| **date of issuance** | Ausstellungsdatum | date d'émission | fecha de emisión |
| **date of shipment** | Verschiffungsdatum | date d'embarquement | fecha de embarque |
| **date, acceptance** | Annahmedatum | date d'acceptation | fecha de aceptación |
| **date, expiry** | Verfalldatum | date de validité | fecha de vencimiento |
| **DDP Delivered Duty Paid (named place of destination)** | DDP geliefert verzollt (... genannter Bestimmungsort) | DDP rendu droits acquittés (... lieu de destination convenu) | DDP entregada derechos pagados (... lugar de destino convenido) |
| **DDU Delivered Duty Unpaid (named place of destination)** | DDP geliefert unverzollt (... genannter Bestimmungsort) | DDP rendu droits non acquittés (... lieu de destination convenu) | DDU entregada derechos no pagados (... lugar de destino convenido) |
| **debit** | Belastung | débit | débito |
| **debt** | Schuld | dette | deuda, oblagación |
| **decision** | Entscheidung | décision | decisión |
| **decision maker** | Entscheidender | décideur | responsable de decidir |

**KEY WORDS**

| Italian | Portuguese (Br) | Japanese | Chinese |
|---|---|---|---|
| credito confermato irrevocabile | crédito irrevogável confirmado | 確杖∠瞕荒芐庞 | 不可取消贷款 |
| data del credito | data do crédito | 信用状開始日 | 贷款日期 |
| lettera di credito documentario | crédito documentário (carta de) | 荷為替信用状 | 信用记录（文件） |
| credito irrevocabile | crédito irrevogável | 取引不能信用状 | 不能可消贷款 |
| coefficiente di adeguamento monetario | fator de ajuste de moeda | 通貨照瞕 | 币值调找蛋 |
| valuta di pagamento | moeda de pagamento | 支払通貨 | 支付货币 |
| cliente | cliente | 取引先 | 消费 |
| vincolo doganale | cauções alfandegárias | 関税支払保証書 | 进口税合同 |
| spedizioniere doganale | despachante aduaneiro | 税関貨物取扱人 | 报关行 |
| formalità doganali, sdoganamento | desembaraço aduaneiro, alfandegário | 通関手続き | 海关放行 |
| dichiarazione doganale | declaração aduaneira, alfandegária | 税関申告 | 海关申报单 |
| dichiarazione in dogana | declaração aduaneira de entrada de mercadorias (feita pelo importador) | 通関申告 | 海关登记 |
| DAF reso frontiera (...luogo convenuto) | DAF entrega na fronteira (... local) | DAF 国境渡し条件 | DAF 边界交货（...指定地点） |
| danno | avaria, dano, prejuízo, sinistro | 損害 | 损害 |
| danno alla merce | avaria nos produtos, nas mercadorias | 貨物の損害 | 对商品的损害 |
| richiedere un risarcimento | reclamar danos e prejuízos | 損害賠償金を要求する | 赔偿金索赔 |
| dati | dados | データ | 数据 |
| data | data | 日付 | 日期 |
| data d'arrivo | data de chegada | 納期を柵焙悉 | 到达日期 |
| data di emissione | data de emissão | 発行日 | 发出日期 |
| data d'imbarco | data de embarque | 出荷予定日 | 装运日期 |
| data di accettazione | data de aceitação | 承諾 | 承诺日期 |
| data di scadenza | data de validade | 有効期限 | 期满日 |
| DDP reso sdoganato (... luogo di destinazione convenuto) | DDP com entrega e impostos pagos até (... local de destino) | DDP 関税込持込渡 (.. 指定仕向地) | DDP 完税后交货（..指定目的地） |
| DDP reso non sdoganato (... luogo di destinazione convenuto) | DDU com entrega e impostos a pagar em (... local de destino) | DDU 関税抜き持込渡 (... 指定仕向地) | DDU 完税前交货（..指定目的地） |
| addebito | débito | 借方 | 借方 |
| debito | divida consolidada | 借金 | 瘴 |
| decisione | decisão | 決定 | 决定 |
| decisore | tomador de decisões | 意思決定 | 决策人 |

KEYWORDS

| English | German | French | Spanish |
|---|---|---|---|
| declaration | Erklärung | déclaration en douane | declaración |
| declared value | Verzollungswert | valeur déclarée | valor declarado |
| declared value for carriage | Deklarationswert für Fracht | valeur déclarée pour transport | valor declarado para el transportista |
| declared value for customs | Verzollungswert | valeur déclarée en douane | valor declarado en aduanas |
| delay | Verzögerung, Verzug | retard | demora, retraso |
| delayed | verzögerte | retardé | retrasado |
| delivered | geliefert | (de)livré | entregado |
| delivery | Aus Lieferung, Übergabe | livraison, délivrance, émise | entrega |
| delivery date | Liefertermin | date de livraison | fecha de entrega |
| demand for payment | Mahnbescheid, Zahlungsaufforderung | mise en demeure | intimación de pago, requerimiento de pago |
| demurrage (charges) | Überliegegeld | (indemnités de) surestaries | (gastos de) sobreestadías, demoras |
| departure date | Abfahrtsdatum | date de départ | fecha de salida |
| deposit | Einlage, Guthaben | dépôt | depósito |
| depot | Lager | entrepôt | bodega, almacén, depósito para distribución, almacén central |
| DEQ Delivered Ex Quay (...named port of destination) | DEQ geliefert ab Kai (...genannter Bestimmungshafen) | DEQ rendu à quai (...port de destination convenu) | DEQ entregada en muelle (...puerto de destino convenido) |
| DES Delivered Ex Ship (...named port of destination) | DES geliefert ab Schiff (...genannter Bestimmungshafen) | DES rendu ex ship (...port de destination convenu) | DES entregada sobre buque (...puerto de destino convenido) |
| destination | Bestimmungsort, Lieferort | lieu de livraison, destination | (lugar de) destino, destinación |
| disclosure | Offenlegung, Enthüllung, Aufdeckung | divulagation, donner communication | divulgación, revelación |
| discount (on goods) | Preisnachlass, Diskont | rabais, escompte | descuento (sobre la mercancía) |
| discrepancies | Abweichungen | irrégularités | discrepancias |
| dispatch (goods) | Ware versenden | expédier | envío, despacho |
| dispute | widerlegen | dirrérend, litige | conflicto, litigio, controversia, diferencia |
| document | Dokument | document | documento |
| document, combined transport | Dokument des kombinierten Transports | document de transport combiné | documento de transporte combinado |
| document, negotiable | übertragbares Dokument | document négociable | documento negociable |
| Document, Single Administrative (SAD) | Einheitspapier | Document Administratif Unique | documento único aduanero |
| documentary credit | Dokumentenakkreditiv | crédit documentaire | crédito documentario |
| documentation | Dokumentation | documentation | documentación |
| documents against acceptance (D/A) | Dokumente gegen Akzept | (remise des) document contre acceptation | (entrega de) documentos contra aceptación |

| Italian | Portuguese (Br) | Japanese | Chinese |
|---|---|---|---|
| dichiarazione | declaração | 積出申告 | 申报单 |
| valore dichiarato | valor declarado | 公示価格 | 申报价格 |
| valore dichiarato del porto | valor declarado para transporte | 輸送用公示価格 | 申报价格以确定运费 |
| valore dichiarato per la dogana | valor declarado na alfândega | 公示価格 | 向海关申报价格 |
| ritardo | atraso | 遅れる | 延迟 |
| ritardato, rinviato, differito | atrasado | 遅延した | 延时的 |
| consegnato | entregue | 配達費込みの | 运费包括在内的 |
| consegna | entrega | 配達 | 交货 |
| data di consegna | data de entrega | 配送日 | 交货日期 |
| intimazione di pagamento | demanda, solicitação de pagamento | 支払涨 | 付款要求 |
| controstallìe (indennità) | sobrestada, demurrage | 滞船料 | 逾期费 |
| data di partenza | data de partida | 搭乗日 | 开船日期 |
| deposito, versamento | depósito | 預金 | 保证金 |
| deposit, magazzino, parco di deposito, stazione merci | depósito | デポー | 仓库 |
| DEQ reso banchina (...porto di destinazione convenuto) | DEQ entrega no cais (... porto de destino) | DEQ 埠頭持込渡 （... 指定仕向港） | DEQ 目的港码头交货 （.. 指定目的港） |
| DES reso exship (...porto di destinazione convenuto) | DES entrega no navio em (... porto de destino) | DES 本船持込渡 （... 指定仕向港） | DES 目的港船上交货 （... 指定目的港口） |
| destinazione | destino | 宛て先 | 目的地 |
| informazione, rivelazione divulgazione (es. del bilancio) | revelação, descoberta | 公開 | 透漏 |
| sconto (sul prezzo delle merci) | desconto, dedução | 割引 | 湛 |
| discrepanze, divergenze | discrepâncias | 過不足 | 偏差 |
| spedire (merci) | despachar, enviar (produtos) | 発送する | 发送（商品） |
| controversia, lite, vertenza | disputa, litígio | 照 | 章 |
| documento | documento | ドキュメント | 文件 |
| documento di trasporto combinàto | documento de transporte combinado | 複合運送証券 | 联合运输文件 |
| documento negoziabile | documento, título negociável | 譲渡可能書類 | 可谈判文件 |
| documento unico amministrativo | Documento Aduaneiro Único | 単回投与書類 | 单一管理文件 (SAD) |
| credito documentario | crédito documentário | 荷為替信用状 | 贷款文件 |
| documentazione | documentação | ドキュメンテイション | 文件 |
| documenti contro accettazione | entrega de documentos contra aceitação | 引渡書類渡し | 承兑交单托收 |

| English | German | French | Spanish |
|---|---|---|---|
| documents against payment (D/P) | Dokumente gegen Zahlung | (remise des) document contre paiement | (entrega de) documentos contra pago |
| draft | Tratte, Wechsel | traite | giro, letra |
| draft at tenor | Datowechsel | traite à échéance | letra a vencimiento, giro |
| draft, (30) days sight | (30) Tage Nachsichttratte | traite à (30) jours de vue | giro, letra a (30) días vista |
| draft, claused | unreine Tratte | effet avec réserve | letra con reservas |
| draft, clean | reine Tratte | effet sans réserve | letra limpia |
| draft, sight | Sichttratte | traite à vue | giro, letra a vista |
| draft, usance | Usancetratte | traite à échéance | letra de cambio con vencimiento común |
| drawee | Bezogener | tiré | girado, librador |
| drawer | Aussteller | tireur | girador, librador |
| due | fällig, (das) Geschuldete | dû, exigible, échu | exigible, dado, derechos |
| due, past | überfällig | en souffrance | vencido y no pagado |
| duties, import | Einfuhrabgaben, Importzölle | droits d'entrée | derechos de entrada |
| duty | Zoll, Steure, Pflicht, Obliegenheit, Abgabe, Zölle | droit(s) de douane | derecho(s) de aduana, derecho, impuesto derechos, impuestos |
| duty free | zollfrei | exempt de droits (de douane) | libre de impuestos (aduaneros) |
| electronic funds transfer (EFT) | elektronischer Zahlungsverkehr | transfert électronique de fonds (TEF) | transferencia electrónica de fondos |
| e-mail | E-Mail | messagerie électronique | correo electrónico, e-mail |
| endorsement | Ubertragung, Indossierung | endossement, avenant | endorso, póliza |
| endorser | Indossant | endosseur | endosante |
| entry | Eingang | déclaration en douane | entrada, admisión |
| entry documents | Zollantrag | documents de déclaration en douane | documentos de admisión |
| entry for consumption | Zollantrag auf Abfertigung zum freien Verkehr | entrée pour consommation | admisión para consumo |
| estimate | Schätzung | estimation | estimación, previsión, presupuesto |
| estimated date of arrival | voraussichtlicher Abfahrtstermin | date d'arrivée prévue | fecha de llegada estimada |
| estimated date of departure | voraussichtlicher Ankunftstermin | date de départ prévue | fecha de salida estimada |
| exchange rate | Wechselkurs | taux de change | tipo de cambio |
| expense(s) | Koste(n), Spese(n) | frais | gasto(s) |
| expiry date | Verfalltag, Ablauftermin | date d'éxpiration, de péremption | fecha de vencimiento |
| export | Ausfuhr, Export | exportation | exportación |
| export charges | Ausfuhrkosten | frais d'exportation | gastos de exportación |
| export declaration | Ausfuhrerklärung | déclaration d'export | declaración de exportación |
| export license | Ausfuhrerlaubnis | licence d'exportation | licencia/permiso de exportación |

| Italian | Portuguese (Br) | Japanese | Chinese |
|---|---|---|---|
| documenti contro pagamento | documentos contra pagamento | 代金引換書類渡し | 付款交单托收 |
| tratta | saque | ドラフト | 汇票 |
| tratta a scadenza | título pagável de acordo com seus próprios termos | 手形の支払期間 | 汇票期限副本 |
| tratta a (30) giorni vista | título pagável a (30) dias da apresentação | (30)日の参着為替 | (30)天汇票 |
| tratta sporca, con riserva | letra de câmbio clasulada | 条件付き手形 | 汇票条款 |
| tratta libera | letra de câmbio sem garantia | 普通為替 | 光本汇票 |
| tratta a vista | letra de câmbio a vista | 参着為替 | 可见汇票 |
| tratta a tempo vista | título pagável em prazo estabelecido pelo, costume local | 手形支払猶予期間 | 票据期限 |
| trassato | sacado | 手形名宛人 | 付款人 |
| traente (di un assegno) | sacador | 粘鎜 | 发票人 |
| scaduto, esigibile | a vencer | デュー | 应付款 |
| in sofferenza | vencido e não pago | 不渡り | 过去应付款 |
| diritti d'importazione | imposto de importação | 輸入税 | 进口关税 |
| dazio, diritto, i doganale (i) | imposto | 関税 | 关税 |
| esente da diritti (doganali) | livre de impostos | 無税 | 免税 |
| trasferimento elettronico di fondi | transferência eletrônica de fundos | 電子資金取引 | 电子资金过户 |
| posta elettronica | e-mail | 電子メール | 电子邮件 |
| girata, clausola | endosso | 裏書き | 背书 |
| girante | endossante | 譲渡人 | 背书人 |
| dichiarazione | entrada | 通関手続き | 报关 |
| documenti di dichiarazione | documentos de entrada | 記入文書 | 报关文件 |
| bolletta doganale per merci da consumo | admissão, entrada para consumo | 輸入申告書 | 消费品报关手续 |
| stima, stima, previsione (es. previsioni di spesa) | estimativa, orçamento | 予測 | 评估 |
| data prevista di arrivo | data prevista de chegada | 到着予定日 | 预计到岸日期 |
| data prevista di partenza | data prevista de partida | 出発予定日 | 预计开船日期 |
| corso del combio, rata di cambio | taxa de câmbio | 為替レート | 汇率 |
| spese | despesa(s) | 費用 | 支出 |
| data di scadenza | data de vencimento | 満了日 | 期满日 |
| esportazione | exportação | 輸出 | 出口 |
| spese d'esportazione | taxas de exportação | 輸出手数料 | 出口费用 |
| dichiarazione d'esportazione | declaração de exportação | 輸出申告 | 出口申报单 |
| licenza d'espotazione | licença de exportação | 輸出承 | 出口许可 |

KEY WORDS

| English | German | French | Spanish |
|---|---|---|---|
| export permit | Ausfuhrlizenz, Exportlizenz | permis d'exportation | permiso/licencia de exportación |
| exporter | Exporteur | exportateur | exportador |
| FAS Free Alongside Ship (named port of shipment) | FAS frei Langsseite Schiff (... benannter Verschiffungshafen) | FAS franco le long du navire (... port d'embarquement convenu) | FAS libre al costado del buque (... puerto de carga convenido) |
| fax | Telefax | télécopie | fax, facsímil |
| FCA Free Carrier (...named place) | FCA frei Frachtführer (...benannter Ort) | FCA franco transporteur (...lieu convenu) | FCA franco transportista (...lugar convenido) |
| fee(s) | Gebühr, Taxe(n) | droit, taxe | derechos, impuesto, tasa(s), tarifas |
| final payment | Endzahlung | paiement final | pago final, último plazo, último pago |
| fine | Geldstrafe | amende | multa |
| firm commitment | feste Zusage | engagement ferme | compromiso en firme |
| FOB Free On Board (named port of ship-ment) | FOB frei an Bord (... benannter Verschiffungshafen) | FOB Franco bord (port d'embarquement convenu) | FOB franco a bordo (... puerto de embarque convenido) |
| force majeure | höhere Gewalt | force majeure | fuerza mayor |
| foreign exchange | Devisen | devises | cambio exterior |
| foreign exchange rate | Devisenkurs | taux de change | tipo de cambio de divisas |
| foreign trade zone | Außenhandelszone | zone franche | zona franca |
| forwarder | Spediteur | transporteur, chargeur, expéditeur | transportista, embarcador, expedidor de carga |
| forwarding instructions | Versandinstruktionen | instructions d'expédition | instrucciones de expedición |
| fragile | zerbrechlich | fragile | frágil |
| freight | Fracht | fret | flete |
| freight all kinds (FAK) | Fracht (für Güter) aller Art | fret pour tous genres (de marchandises) | carga de toda clase |
| freight bill | Frachtbrief | état du tarif de transport | carta de porte, albarán, nota de expedición, nota del flete |
| freight charges | Frachtkosten | tarif du transport marchandise | gastos de transporte |
| freight collect | unfrei | fret payable à l'arrivée | portes debidos |
| freight forwarder | Spediteur | expéditeur, transporteur | transportista, expedidor de carga |
| freight prepaid | Fracht im voraus bezahlt | frét payé | flete prepagado, flete pagado en origen |
| freight rate | Frachtrate | taux de fret | tasa de flete, cuota de flete |
| full container load (FCL) | Voll-Containerladung | conteneur complet | (carga por) contenedor completo |
| full set | voller Satz | jeu de documents complet | juego completo |
| full truckload | komplette Wagenladung | wagon complet | carga plena del camión |

**KEY WORDS**

| Italian | Portuguese (Br) | Japanese | Chinese |
|---|---|---|---|
| permesso d'esportazione | permissão de exportação | 輸出許可書 | 出口许可 |
| esportatore | exportador | 輸出業 | 出口商 |
| FAS franco lungo bordo (... porto di imbarco convenuto) | FAS Livre ao Lado do Navio (... porto de embarque) | FAS船側渡し | FAS 船边交货 (.. 指定装运港) |
| fax | fax | ファックス | 传 |
| FCA franco vettore (...luogo convenuto) | FCA livre no transportador (... local) | FCA運送人渡し | FCA 货交承运人 (... 指定地点) |
| onorario, diritti | taxa, pagamento, taxa de entrada, salário, honorários | 料金 | 费用 |
| ultimo pagamento | pagamento final | 最終払い | 最终付款 |
| multa (es. pagare una multa) | multa | ファイン | 罚金 |
| impegno fermo | compromisso firme | 確約 | 公司承担义务 |
| FOB franco a bordo (... porto di imbarco convenuto) | FOB Livre a Bordo (... porto de embarque) | FOB本船渡し | FOB 装运港船上交货 (... 指定装运港) |
| forza maggiore | força maior | 不可抗力 | 不可抗力 |
| cambio estero | câmbio exterior | 外為 | 外币兑换 |
| cambio | taxa de câmbio exterior | 外国為替相場 | 汇率 |
| punto franco, zona franca, zona di libero scambio | zona de comércio exterior | 外国貿易地域 | 对外贸易地区 |
| spedizioniere | despachante | 運送業 | 代运人 |
| istruzioni per la spedizione | instruções de despacho | 運送指図書 | 货物发送细则 |
| fragile, delicato | frágil | 虚弱な | 易碎的 |
| nolo | frete | 運送貨物 | 运费 |
| nolo per ogni tipo (di merci) | fretes de todo o tipo (FAK) | 品目無差別で | 所有种类运费 (FAK) |
| certificato di imbarco | nota de frete | 運賃勘定 | 运费单 |
| spese di trasporto | despesas de frete | 運送料 | 货运收费 |
| nolo assegnato, spese a carico del destinatario | frete a pagar | 荷受人払い運賃 | 运费向收货人索取 |
| spedizioniere | despachante aduaneiro | 運送会社 | 运输代理人 |
| nolo prepagato | frete pré-pago | 運賃前払い | 预付运费 |
| rata di nolo | taxa de frete | 運賃率 | 货运价格 |
| contenitore a carico completo | carga total do container | フルコンテナ?ロード | 集装箱障浠跷 ? FCL) |
| set completo, tutti | conjunto completo (de documentos) | フルセット | 全套 |
| carico completo di camion | carga total do caminhão | トラック1台分の積荷 | 货车满载 |

KEY WORDS

| English | German | French | Spanish |
|---|---|---|---|
| general average (g/a) | grosse Havarie | avarie commune | avería común, gruesa |
| general cargo | Stückgut | marchandises générales, marchandises diverses | carga mixta, mercancías varias |
| global business | globales Geschäft | affaires globales | negocios a nivel mundial |
| global market | globaler Markt | marché global | mercado mundial, mercado global |
| good faith | guter Glaube | bonne foi | buena fe |
| goods | Waren, Güter | marchandises, produits, biens | mercancías, productos, bienes |
| goods, dutiable | verzollbare Güter | biens soumis à droit de douane | mercancías sujetas a impuestos |
| guarantee | Garantie, Sicherheit, Bürgschaft | garantie | garantía, aval |
| guarantee, to | garantieren | garantir | garantizar, avalar |
| handling charges | Ladekosten | frais de mautention | gastos por gestión/ tramitación |
| hazardous goods | gefährliche Güter | produits dangereux | bienes peligrosos |
| hazardous materials | Gefahrstoffe | matériel dangereux | materiales peligrosos |
| house air waybill (HAWB) | Hausluftfrachtbrief (des Spediteurs) | émise par transitaire | guía aérea emitida por un expedidor de carga |
| import | Import | importation | importación |
| import authority | Importstelle | autorités d'importation | autoridades de importación |
| import declaration | Importerklärung | déclaration d'importation | declaración de importación |
| import duty | Importzölle, Einfuhrzölle | droits d'entrée à l'importation | aranceles |
| import license | Importlizenz, Einfuhrlizenz | licence d'importation | licencia/permiso de importación |
| import quota(s) | Einfuhrquoten | contingent d'importation | cuota de importación |
| import, to | importieren, einführen | importer | importar |
| importer | Importeur | importateur | importador |
| in bond | unter Zollverschluss | en entrepôt sous douane | en garantía |
| in bond shipment | Sendung unter Zollverschluss | expédition en entrepôt sous douane | en depósito, en admisión temporal |
| information | Information | informations | informaciones |
| inspection | Inspektion | contrôle | inspección |
| inspection service | Kontrollservice | servoce de contrôle | servicio de inspecciones |
| inspection, agricultural | Landwirtschafts-überprüfung | contrôle agricole | inspección agrícola |
| inspection, customs | Zollkontrolle | contrôle douanier | inspección aduanera |
| instruction(s) | Anweisung(en) | instruction(s) | instrucción(es) |
| instrument, negotiable | übertragbares Wertpapier | document négociable | documento negociable |
| insurance | Versicherung | assurance | seguro |
| insurance agent | Versicherungsagent | courtier | agente de seguros |
| insurance certificate | Versicherungszertifikat | certificat d'assurance | certificado de seguro |

K
E
Y

W
O
R
D
S

| Italian | Portuguese (Br) | Japanese | Chinese |
|---|---|---|---|
| avaria comune/generale | média geral | 共同海損 | 一般平均值 |
| carico di merci varie | carga geral | 一般貨物 | 一般的货物 |
| affari globali | empresa, negócios internacional(s), global(is), mundial(is) | 世界ビジネス | 全球商业 |
| mercato globale | mercado global | 世界市場 | 全球市场 |
| buona fede | boa fé | 誡gな | 粘 |
| merce, prodotti, beni | produtos | 貨物 | 商品 |
| merci soggete a dazio | produtos taxáveis | 账捌纺 | 应纳关税的商品 |
| garanzia | garantia | 保証 | 保证 |
| garantire, fornire garanzia | garantir | 保証する | 保证 |
| spese di movimentazione, costi di trasporto interno | custo de manuseio, tratamento | 手数料 | 装卸费 |
| merce pericolose | produtos perigosos | 危険貨物 | 危险品 |
| materiali pericolosi | materiais perigosos | 危険物 | 危险材料 |
| lettera di trasporto aereo emessa da un consolidatore | conhecimento de embarque de frete aéreo consolidado | 混載業瞻k行の航空貨物運送状 | 空运分提单 (HAWB) |
| importazione | importar | 輸入 | 进口 |
| autorità per l'importazione | autoridade de importação | 輸入権限 | 进口当局 |
| dichiarazione d'importazione | declaração de importação | 輸入申告 | 进口申报单 |
| dazio d'importazione | imposto de importação | 輸入税 | 进口税 |
| licensa d'importazione | licença de importação | 輸入許可書／輸入承諾 | 进口许可 |
| quota d'importazione | quotas de importação | 輸入割当て | 进口限额 |
| importare | importar | 輸入先 | 进口到 |
| importatore | importador | 輸入業 | 进口商 |
| soggetto a vincolo doganale, in deposito doganale | em garantia | 倉庫渡し | 关毡A糁 |
| spedizione franco deposito doganale | carga de importação ou exportação já desembaraçada | 保税出荷 | 关毡A舫龌 |
| informazioni | informações | 情報 | 信息 |
| ispezione, esame, verifica | inspeção | 検査 | 检验 |
| servizio d'ispezione | serviço de inspeção | 検査サービス | 检验程序 |
| ispezione agricola | inspeção agrícola | 農業検査 | 农业检验 |
| controllo doganale | inspeção aduaneira | 税関検査 | 海关检验 |
| istruzione(i), disposizione(i), avvertenza(e), direttiva(e) | instruções | 指示 | 指令 |
| effetto negoziabile | instrumento negociável | 譲渡可能証券 | 可转让的仪器 |
| assicurazione | seguro | 保険 | 保险 |
| agente di assicurazione | agente de seguro | 保険代理店 | 保险代理 |
| certificato di assicurazione | certificado de seguro | 保険証明書 | 保险凭证 |

KEY WORDS

| English | German | French | Spanish |
|---|---|---|---|
| **insurance claim** | Anspruch auf Versicherungsleistung | sinistre | reclamación, demanda de seguro |
| **insurance policy** | Versicherungspolice | police d'assurance | póliza de seguros |
| **insurance, all risk** | Versicherung gegen alle Risiken | assurance tous risques | seguro a todo riesgo |
| **insurance, cargo** | Frachtversicherung, Ladungsversicherung | assurance faculté | seguro de carga |
| **insurance, war risk** | Kriegsgefahrversicherung | assurance de guerre | seguro de riesgo de guerra |
| **insured** | versichert | assuré | asegurado |
| **insured value** | versicherter Wert | valeur assurée | valor asegurado |
| **insurer** | Versicherer | assureur | asegurador, aseguradora |
| **intermodal** | kombiniert | intermodal | combinado |
| **intermodal transport** | intermodaler Transport | transport intermodal | transporte intermodal |
| **inventory** | Liste, Inventurliste, Lagerbestand | stock, inventaire | inventario |
| **invoice** | Rechnung | facture | factura |
| **invoice number** | Rechnungsnummer | numéro de facture | número de factura |
| **invoice, commercial** | Handelsrechnung | facture commerciale | factura comercial |
| **invoice, consular** | Konsularfaktura | facture consulaire | factura consular |
| **invoice, proforma** | Pro-Forma-Rechnung | facture pro forma | factura pro forma |
| **invoice, signed** | unterschriebene Rechnung | facture visée | factura firmada |
| **issuance** | Ausgabe | émission | emisión |
| **issuance date** | Ausgabedatum | date d'émission | fecha de emisión |
| **joint venture** | Joint-Venture | entreprise commune | joint venture, empresa conjunta |
| **label(s)** | Etikett(en) | étiquette | etiqueta(s) |
| **label, to** | etikettieren | étiqueter | etiquetar |
| **late** | spät | en retard | tarde |
| **law** | Gesetz, Recht, Gesetzgebung | loi, législation, droit | ley, leyes, legislación, derecho |
| **law suit** | Verfahren, Prozess | procès juridique | pleito, litigio |
| **legal entity** | Rechtspersönlichkeit | personne morale | entidad jurídica |
| **less thancontainer load (LCL)** | Teil-Containerladung | charge incompléte du conteneur | menos de contenedor completo |
| **less than truck load (LTL)** | LkW-Stückgut | camion incomplet | menos de camión completo |
| **letter** | Brief, Schreiben | lettre, requête | carta, petición |
| **letter of credit** | Akkreditiv, Kreditbrief | lettre de crédit | carta de crédito |
| **liability** | Verbindlichkeit, Haftung, Verantwortung | responsabilité, obligation, passif | responsabilidad, pasivo, obligación |
| **license** | Bewilligung, Erlaubnis | licence | licencia, permiso, autorización |

KEY WORDS

| Italian | Portuguese (Br) | Japanese | Chinese |
|---|---|---|---|
| richiesta di risarcimento | reclamação de seguro | 保険金涨 | 保险索赔 |
| polizza di assicurazione | apólice de seguro | 保険契約 | 保险詹 |
| assicurazione contro tutti I rischi | seguro contra todos os riscos | オールリスク保険 | 保全险 |
| assicurazione merci/facoltà | seguro de carga | 貨物保険 | 货物保险 |
| assicurazione contro il rischio della guerra | seguro contra risco de guerra | 戦蕃瞻Ｐｊ | 照瞻 |
| assicurato, sottoscrittore | segurado | 保険付きの | 保户 |
| valore assicurato | valor segurado | 保険価額 | 保险价值 |
| assicuratore, persona che assicura | companhia de seguro | 保険加入 | 承保人 |
| intermodale | intermodal | 複合 | 联合运输的 |
| trasporto intermodale | transporte intermodal | 複合輸送 | 联合运输 |
| inventario, rimanenze di magazzino | estoque | 在庫 | 存货 |
| fattura | fatura | インボイス | 发票 |
| numero della fattura | número da fatura | 送り状番号 | 发票号码 |
| fattura commerciale | fatura comercial | 商業送り状 | 商业发票 |
| fattura consolare | fatura consular | 領事送り状 | 领事签证的发票 |
| fattura pro forma | fatura pro forma | 見積送り状 | 形式发票 |
| fattura firmata | fatura assinada | 署名インボイス | 签署发票 |
| emissione | emissão | 発行 | 发行 |
| data di emissione | data de emissão | 発行日付 | 发行日期 |
| joint venture | empreendimento conjunto | 共同事業 | 合资企业 |
| etichetta(e) (es. etichetta del prezzo) | rótulo(s) | ラベル | 标号 |
| etichettare, contrassegnare (es. carico contrassegnato) | rotular | 名付ける | 标签贴于… |
| tardo (es. a ora tarda), avanzato, inoltrato | tarde, atrasado | 遅い | 迟到 |
| legge(i), diritto | lei, Direito | 法律 | 法律 |
| causa, azione legale, processo civile, querela | ação judicial | 告訴 | （律）诉讼 |
| persona giuridica | pessoa jurídica (entidade com personalidade jurídica) | 合法的な組織 | 法人实体 |
| carico incompleto del contenitore (di groupage) | menos que a carga do contêiner | 貨物（LCL） | 少于集装箱装载 (LCL) |
| camion a carico parziale | menos que a carga do caminhão | 貨物 (LTL) | 少于卡车装载 (LTL) |
| lettera | carta, letra | レター | 信件 |
| lettera di credito | carta de crédito | 銀行信用状 | 信用证 |
| responsabilità, impegni (finanziari) | obrigação, responsabilidade legal | 責任保険 | 责任 |
| licenza | licença | ライセンス | 许可证 |

| English | German | French | Spanish |
|---|---|---|---|
| **licensee** | Lizenznehmer, Lizenzinhaber, Konzessionsinhaber | concessionnaire | concesionario, licenciatario |
| **licensor** | Lizenzgeber, Konzessionsgeber | concédant | cedente, otorgante, licenciador |
| **load, to** | laden | charger | cargar |
| **logistics** | Logistik | logistique | logística |
| **logistics, integrated** | vernetzte Logistik | logistique intégrée | logística integrada |
| **loss, constructive total** | konstruktiver Totalverlust | perte censée etre totale | pérdida estimada ser total |
| **mandatory** | zwingend, obligatorisch | impératif, obligatoire | inderogable, imperativo, obligatorio |
| **manifest, cargo** | Frachtliste, Ladungsverzeichnis | manifeste de bord | manifiesto, guia de carga |
| **market** | Markt | marché | mercado |
| **market, domestic** | Binnenmarkt | marché intérieur | mercado nacional |
| **market, foreign** | Auslandsmarkt | marché extérieur, marché international | mercado internacional, exterior |
| **marks** | Marken | marques | marcas |
| **measurement(s)** | Abmessung(en) | mesure | medida(s) |
| **merchandise** | Ware, Güter | marchandise | mercancía, mercadería |
| **minimum price** | Mindestpreis | prix minimal | precio mínimo |
| **money** | Geld, Münze, Geldmittel, Kapital | argent, numéraire, monnaie légale | dinero, liquido, moneda legal |
| **multimodal** | multimodaler, kombiniert | multimodal | combinado/a, multimodal |
| **multimodal transport** | multimodaler Transport | transport multimodal | transporte multimodal |
| **name** | Name | nom | nombre |
| **negligence** | Fahrlässigkeit, Nachlässigkeit | omission, négligence | omisión, negligencia |
| **negotiable** | negozierbar | négociable | negociable |
| **negotiable instrument** | übertragbares Wertpapier | document négociable | documento negociable |
| **negotiated price** | verhandelter Preis | prix négocié | precio negociado |
| **net** | Netto | net | neto |
| **net amount due** | fälliger Nettobetrag | montant échu net | importe neto debido |
| **net price** | Nettopreis | prix net | precio neto |
| **never** | nie | jamais | nunca |
| **next month** | nächster Monat | le mois prochain | el mes siguiente, el próximo mes |
| **next week** | nächste Woche | la semaine prochaine | la semana que viene, la próxima semana |
| **next year** | nächstes Jahr | l'année prochaine | el año que viene |
| **no** | nein | non | no |
| **nondisclosure agreement (NDA)** | Geheimhaltungsvsertrag | accord de non révélation | acuerdo/pacto/convenio de confidencialidad/buena fe |
| **non negotiable** | nicht negozierbar | non-négociable | no negociable |

| Italian | Portuguese (Br) | Japanese | Chinese |
|---|---|---|---|
| concessionario, licenziatario | licenciado | ライセンシー | 领有许可证 |
| chi concede o emette licenze | licenciante | 実施許諾 | 认可证颁发 |
| caricare (es. caricare una nave di merci) | carregar | 積む | 装载于 ... |
| logistica | logística | ロジスティックス | 后勤 |
| logistica integrata | logística integrada | 集中兵 | 后勤综合 |
| perdita totale equivalente | perda total implícita | 準全損 | 拟定全损 |
| imperativa, obbligatorio | obrigatório | 必須の | 强制性 |
| manifesto di carico | manifesto de carga | 積荷目録 | 货物舱单 |
| mercato | mercado | マーケット | 市场 |
| mercato interno | mercado doméstico | 国内市場 | 国内市场 |
| mercato estero | mercado exterior | 海外市場 | 国外市场 |
| segnalazioni | marcas | マーク寸法 | 标记 |
| misura(e) | medida(s) | 寸法 | 测量 |
| merce | mercadoria(s) | 商業化する | 商品 |
| prezzo minimo | preço mínimo | 最低価格 | 最低价格 |
| denaro, moneta, capitale | dinheiro | 金額 | 金额 |
| multimodale | multimodal | 多モードの | 多方式 |
| trasporto multimodale | transporte multimodal | 複合一貫輸送 | 多式联运 |
| nome | nome | 名前 | 名称 |
| negligenza, colpa | negligência | 無頓着 | 疏忽 |
| negoziabile | negociável | 交渉できる | 可通过谈判解决 |
| effetto negoziabile | instrumento negociável | 流通証券 | 可流通票据 |
| prezzo negoziato | preço negociado | 交渉価格 | 仪付价格 |
| netto | líquido | ネット | 净价 |
| importo netto dovuto | valor líquido devido | 瘴吨瞒B金 | 应付净总值 |
| prezzo netto | preço líquido | 諄 | 纯价格 |
| mai | nunca | 以前に〜したことがない | 决不 |
| il mese prossimo | no próximo mês | 来月 | 下个月 |
| la settimana prossima | na próxima semana | 来週 | 下星期 |
| anno prossimo | no próximo ano | 来年 | 明年 |
| No | não | なし | 没有 |
| accordo di segreto industriale | acordo de confidencialidade | 機密保持契約 | 保密协议 (NDA) |
| non negoziabile | não negociável | 交渉のできない | 不可协商的 |

**KEYWORDS**

| English | German | French | Spanish |
|---|---|---|---|
| notice | Notiz, Nachricht, Benachrichtigung | avis | aviso, anuncio |
| notification | Mitteilung, Bekanntmachung, Notifizierung | avis, déclaration, notification | notificación, declaracion |
| null and void | null und nichtig, rechtsunwirksam | nul et non avenu | nulo y sin valor, nulo de pleno derecho |
| ocean | Ozean | océan | mar |
| ocean bill of lading | Bordkonnossement | connaissement maritime | conocimiento de embarque a la orden |
| offer | Angebot | offre | oferta |
| on time | rechtzeitig | à l'heure | a tiempo, puntual |
| open account | offene Rechnung, Kontokorrent | compte courant | cuenta abierta |
| open policy | laufende Versicherung | police ouverte | póliza abierta |
| opportunity | Gelegenheit | occasion | oportunidad |
| order | Auftrag, Bestellung, Order | commande, ordre | pedido, orden |
| order, to | bestellen | commander | ordenar, pedir |
| order, to cancel an | einen Auftrag stornieren | annuler une commande | cancelar un pedido |
| order, to place an | einen Auftrag erteilen | passer une commande | entregar un pedido |
| original documents | Originaldokumente | original d'un document | documentos originales |
| overcharge | Überlastung, Überladung | surcharge | recargo |
| packing | Verpackung, Packmaterial | emballage | embalaje, envase, empaquetado |
| packing cost | Verpackungskosten | frais d'emballage | gastos de embalaje |
| packing list | Packliste | liste de colisage | lista de empaquetado |
| packing materials | Verpackungsmaterialien | matériel d'emballage | materiales de embalaje |
| packing, export | Exportverpackung | emballage pour l'exportation | embalaje para exportaciones |
| partial delivery | Teillieferung | livraison partielle | entrega parcial |
| particular average | besondere Havarie | avaries particulières | avería particular |
| partner | Partner, Teilhaber | associé, partenaire | asociado |
| partnership | Partnerschaft, Personengesellschaft | partenariat, société de personnes | asociado, sasociación |
| past due | überfällig | en souffrance | vencido y no pagado |
| pay at sight, to | bei Sicht zahlen | payer à vue | pagar a la vista |
| pay at tenor, to | zahlen | payer à échéance | pagar a vencimiento |
| pay in advance, to | vorauszahlen | payer à l'avance | pagar con anticipación |
| pay in installments, to | in Raten zahlen an | payer à tempérament | pagar a plazos |
| pay, to | zahlen, bezahlen | payer | pagar |
| payee | Wechselnehmer, Begünstigter | bénéficiare, preneur d'un effet | beneficiario, tomador de una letra |
| payer | Zahler | payeur | pagador |
| payment | Zahlung | paiement, versement | pago |
| payment at sight | Zahlung bei Sicht | paiement à vue | pago a la vista |

| Italian | Portuguese (Br) | Japanese | Chinese |
|---|---|---|---|
| avviso, notifica, avvertenza | aviso, advertência | 通告 | 通告 |
| notificazione, comunicazione | notificação | 通告 | 通告 |
| nullo, nullo e non valido, privo di valore legale | nulo e anulado | 無効 | 无效的 |
| oceano | oceano | オーシャン | 海洋 |
| polizza di carico oceanico | conhecimento de embarque marítimo | 船荷証券 | 海运提单 |
| offerta | oferta | 勧める | 提案，出价 |
| puntualmente, in orario | na hora | 時間とおりに | 准时 |
| conto aperto | conta aberta, sem restrições | オープン勘定 | 未清结的漳? 往来栈 |
| polizza aperta | apólice aberta | 予定保険 | 开放詹 |
| opportunità, occasione | oportunidade | 機会 | 机会，时机 |
| ordine, mandato, ordinazione | pedido, ordem | 命令 | 订购 |
| ordinare, commissionare | pedir, solicitar, fazer pedido | 注文する | 订购于… |
| cancellare, annullare un' ordine | cancelar um pedido | 注文の取り消し | 取消订购 |
| passare un ordine | colocar, fazer um pedido | 注文する | 订货 |
| documenti in originale | documentos originais | 原始文書 | 原始文件 |
| sovraccarico, sovrapprezzo | preço excessivo, sobretaxa | 値段を高く涨 | 滥开（漳浚 |
| imballaggio, confezione | empacotamento, embalagem, fechamento | 梱包 | 包装 |
| spese di imballaggio | custo de embalagem | 包装費 | 包装成本 |
| distinta colli, lista di imballaggio | lista de embalagem | パッキングリスト | 包装单 |
| materiali da imballaggio | materiais de embalagem | 梱包材 | 包装材料 |
| imballaggio destinato all'esportazione | embalagem para exportação | 輸出包装 | 出口包装 |
| consegna parziale | entrega parcial | 分割出荷 | 分期交货 |
| avaria particolare | perda ou avaria particular | 分損担保 | 单独海损 |
| partner, socio | sócio, parceiro | パートナー | 合作 |
| associazione, società (di persone) | sociedade | パートナーシップ | 合作关系 |
| scaduto, in sofferenza | vencido | 期日経過 | 赊欠的金额 |
| pagare a vista | pagar contra apresentação | 一覧払い | 见票即付于… |
| pagare ad una scadenza | efetuar pagamento conforme indicado no documento | テナーで払う | 限期付款于… |
| pagare anticipatamente | pagar antecipadamente | 先払い | 预先支付于… |
| pagare a rate | pagar a prestação | 月賦で払う | 分期支付于… |
| pagare | pagar | 支払う | 支付于… |
| beneficiario, creditore | recebedor | 払受人 | 收款人 |
| pagatore, soggetto pagante | pagador | 支払人 | 付款人 |
| pagamento, versamento | pagamento | 支払い | 付款 |
| pagamento a vista | pagamento a vista | 一覧払い | 见票即付于… |

KEY WORDS

| English | German | French | Spanish |
|---|---|---|---|
| payment in advance | vorauszahlbar | paiement à l'avance | pago anticipado |
| phytosanitary inspection certificate | phytosanitäre zertifikate | certificat de contrôle phztosanitaire | certificado de inspección fitosanitaria |
| point of origin | Ursprungsort | point d'origine | punto de origen |
| policy, insurance | Versicherungspolice | police d'assurance | póliza de seguro |
| port | Hafen | port | puerto |
| port facilities | Hafenanlage | installations portuaires | instalaciones del puerto |
| port of departure | Abgangshafen | port de départ | puerto de salida |
| port of destination | Bestimmungshafen | port de destination | puerto de destino |
| port of entry | Eingangshafen | port d'arrivée | puerto de entrada |
| power of attorney | Vollmacht | procuration écrite | poder para pleitos |
| prepaid charges | franko | frais payés | gastos pagados |
| price | Preis, Kurs | prix | precio |
| price adjustment | Abschöpfung | ajustement des prix | ajuste del precio |
| price schedule | Preisliste | tarif | lista de precios |
| price, fixed selling | festgelegter Verkaufspreis | prix imposé | precio fijado |
| price, offered | Preisangebot | prix offert | precio ofrecido |
| principal | Auftraggeber, Lieferant, Hauptperson | cédant, donneur d'ordrel | principal, ordenante, concedente |
| problem | Problem | problème | problema, dificultad |
| product | Produkt | produit | producto |
| profit(s) | Gewinn(e) | bénéfices, profit | beneficio, ganancia, utilidad |
| proof of receipt | Empfangsbeweis | récépissé | comprobante de recepción |
| proposal | Angebot | proposition | propuesta |
| protest | Protest, Einspruch | protêt, rapport, procès-verbal | protesta, rechazo, reporte, proceso verbal |
| prototype | Prototyp | prototype | prototipo |
| purchase | Kauf, Ankauf, Einkauf | achat | compra |
| purchase order | Bestellung | commande d'achat | pedido de compra, orden de compra |
| purchaser | Einkäufer | acheteur | comprador |
| quality, acceptable | akzeptable Qualität | qualité acceptable | calidad aceptable |
| quality, good | gute Qualität | bonne qualité | buena calidad |
| quality, poor | schlechte Qualität | mauvaise qualité | poca calidad |
| quota | Quote | contingent | cuota |
| quote | Zitat | citation | cita |
| rail car | Wagon | wagon de chemin de fer | vehículo ferroviario |
| rail waybill | Bahnfrachtbrief | lettre de voiture ferroviaire | resguardo de transporte por tren |
| rate | Kurs, Tarif, Zinssatz | taux, cours, tarif | tasa, tarifa, indice |
| rate, duty | Zollsatz | taxe douanière | tasa de derechos |
| receipt | Quittung | reçu, récépissé | recibo, resguardo, talón |

| Italian | Portuguese (Br) | Japanese | Chinese |
|---|---|---|---|
| pagamento anticipato | pagamento antecipado | 前払い | 预付 |
| certificato d'ispezione fitosanitaria | certificado de inspeção fitossanitária | 植物衛生の検査証明書 | 植物检疫证书 |
| punto di origine | ponto de origem | 原産地 | 起源地 |
| polizza di assicurazione | apólice de seguro | 保険証券 | 保险詹 |
| porto | porto | ポート | 港口 |
| attrezzature portuali | instalações portuárias | 港湾施設 | 港口设施 |
| porto di partenza | porto de saída | 出帆港 | 离港处 |
| porto di destinazione | porto de destino | 仕向港 | 到港点 |
| porto d'entrata | porto de entrada | 輸入港 | 港口入口处 |
| procura | procuração, poder | 委任権 | 委托权 |
| spese prepagate | despesas prépagas | 前納料 | 预先付讫的费用 |
| prezzo | preço | 価格 | 价格 |
| riallineamento dei prezzi | ajuste de preço | 価格照 | 调占鄂 |
| lista dei prezzi | lista de preços | 価格表 | 价格计划表 |
| prezzo imposto | preço fixo | 固定価格 | 固定的价格 |
| prezzo offerto | preço oferecido | 売り出し価格 | 提供的价格 |
| ordinante, concedente | principal | 主役 | 负责人 |
| problema, difficoltà | problema | 問題 | 问题 |
| prodotto | produto | 製品 | 产品 |
| profitto, guadagno, utile | lucro(s) | 利益 | 利润 |
| prova di ricevimento | comprovação recebimento | 領収証明書 | 收据证明 |
| porposta | proposta | 提案 | 提议 |
| protesta, riserva, protesto | protesto | 主張する | 抗议 |
| prototipo | protótipo | プロトタイプ | 原型 |
| acquisto | compra | 購入する | 购买 |
| ordine d'acquisto | ordem de compra | 注文書 | 购买定单 |
| acquirente, compratore | comprador | 購入 | 买方 |
| qualità accettabile | qualidade aceitável | 合格品質 | 可接受质量 |
| buona qualità | boa qualidade | 良質 | 优质 |
| qualità scadente | má qualidade | 質が悪い | 劣质 |
| contingente doganale | cota | クォータ | 限额 |
| quotazione | cotação, cotação de preço | 引用 | 报价 |
| carrozza, vagone ferroviario | carro, veículo ferroviário | 軌道車 | 机动轨道车 |
| polizza di carico ferroviario | conhecimento de embarque ferroviário | 鉄道建設法案 | 铁路运货单 |
| tasso, tariffa, tassa | preço, taxa, valor, alíquota | レート | 比率 |
| aliquota doganale | alíquota de imposto, taxa alfandegária | 通関料 | 税率 |
| ricevuta, ricevimento | recibo, comprovante | 領収書 | 收据 |

KEY WORDS

| English | German | French | Spanish |
|---|---|---|---|
| regulation(s), customs | Vorschriften, Regeln (Zollordnung) | réglements (des douanes) | reglamento aduanero |
| reject | ablehnen | rejeter | rechazar |
| remittance | Überweisung | versement | remesa, giro |
| representative | Vertreter | représentant | representante |
| request for bid | Ausschreibung | demande d'offre | petición de oferta |
| request for proposal (RFP) | Aufforderung zur Angebotsabgabe | demande d'offre (RFP) | petición de propuestas (RFP) |
| request for quotation (RFQ) | Aufforderung zur Angebotsabgabe | demande de cotation | petición de presupuesto |
| requirements | Bedingungen | conditions, exigences | requisitos |
| return, to (send back) | zurückgeben, zurücksenden | renvoyer, retourner | retornar, devolver |
| revenue(s) | Einkommen | revenu, rapport, recettes | ingresos, reporte |
| review, to | überprüfen | réviser | revisar, controlar, examinar |
| right | Recht, Anspruch | droit | derecho, privilegio |
| risk | Risiko | risque | riesgo |
| road waybill | Straßenfrachtbrief | feuille de voiture | conocimiento de embarque terrestre |
| route | Weg, Strecke | itinéraire, route | itinerario, ruta |
| rule(s) | Regel, Vorschrift, Norm, Bestimmung | règle, norme, principe | regla, norma, principio, artículo |
| sale | Verkäuf, Umsatz | vente, chiffre d'affaires | venta, compraventa |
| sample(s) with no commercial value | Muster ohne Wert | échantillon sans valeur commerciale | muestra(s) sin valor comercial |
| schedule | Fahrplan, Zeitplan | horaire, programme | horario, programa |
| sea | Meer | mer | mar |
| sea waybill | Seefrachtbrief | permis de navigation | conocimiento de embarque marítimo |
| seizure, customs | Pfändung, Zollbeschlagnahme | saisie douanière | embargo, confiscación en aduanas |
| sell | verkaufen | vendre | vender |
| seller | Verkäufer | vendeur | vendedor |
| ship | Schiff | navire | buque |
| ship, to | absenden, verschiffen | expédier | despachar, enviar |
| shipment | Sendung, Verschiffung | expédition, embarquement | expedición, despacho, embarque |
| shipper | Befrachter, Verlader, Absender | expéditeur, chargeur | expedidor, remitente, cargador, embarcador |
| shipper's letter of instruction | Anweisungen des Befrachters | lettre d'instruction pour le chargement | carta de instrucciones del expedidor/embarcador |
| shipping company | Rederei | compagnie maritime | empresa naviera o marítima |

**KEY WORDS**

| Italian | Portuguese (Br) | Japanese | Chinese |
|---|---|---|---|
| regolamento doganale | regulamentações alfandegárias | 関税規則 | 进口税规 |
| rifiutare | recusar, rejeitar | 拒否 | 拒绝 |
| rimessa | pagamento, transferência de dinheiro | 送金 | 汇款额 |
| rappresentante | representante | 代理人 | 代表 |
| sollecitare l'offerta | pedidos de ofertas ou lances | 入札要求 | 投标要求 |
| sollecitazione di proposta (RFP) | requisição formal de proposta (RFP) | 提案要求 | 提议要求 （RFP) |
| sollecitazione di quotazione | requisição formal de cotação | 見積依頼書 | 报价要求 (RFQ) |
| condizioni, requisiti | requisitos, necessidades | 要求 | 需求，必要条件 |
| rispedire, rimandare, restituire | devolver | 戻る | （退还）利润 |
| entrata(e), reddito(i) | receita(s) | 収益 | 收入 |
| rassegnare | revisar, estudar, examinar, pesquisar, rever | 再検討する | 回顾 |
| diritto | direito, correto, privilégio | 権利 | 权力 |
| rischio | risco | 危険 | 风险 |
| lettera di trasporto stradale | conhecimento de carga rodoviária | 道貨物運送状 | 公路运货单 |
| itinerario, percorso | rota | 輸送 | 路线 |
| regola, norma | regra | ルール | 规则 |
| vendita | liquidação, promoção, venda | セール | 销售 |
| campione(i) senza valore commerciale | amostra(s) sem valor comercial | 商品価値のない標本 | 毫无商业价值的样品 |
| programma, orario, calendario | programação, horário, planejamento, anexo | スケジュール | 时间表，进度表 |
| mare | mar | 海 | 海洋 |
| lettera di trasporto via mare | conhecimento de embarque marítimo | 海貨物運送状 | 海运单 |
| sequestro doganale, confisca | confisco, apreensão alfandegário(a) | 関税の差し押さえ | 海关没收 |
| vendire | vender | 販売 | 出售 |
| venditore | vendedor | 売り方 | 卖主 |
| nave | navio, nau | シップ | 船 |
| spedire, inviare | despachar, enviar | 乗船する | 装运 |
| spedizione, invio, imbarco | carga, carregamento | 出荷 | 装船，出货 |
| speditore, caricatore | expedidor, despachante, transportador | 荷送人 | 托运人，. 装货？　货主 |
| dichiarazione dello speditore | carta de instruções do expedidor | 荷送人信用指図書 | 托运人信函通知书 |
| compagnia di navigazione, società di navigazione | companhia navieira | 船会社 | 航运公司 |

K
E
Y

W
O
R
D
S

| English | German | French | Spanish |
|---|---|---|---|
| **shipping line** | Reederei, Schifffahrtsgesellschaft | compagnie de navigation | compañia naviera, línea marítima |
| **shortage** | Fehlmenge, Manko | manquant | menoscabo, faltante, escasez |
| **signature** | Unterschrift | signature | firma, rúbrica |
| **sold** | verkauft | vendu | vendido |
| **specifications** | Lastenheft, Vorgaben | cahier des charges, spécifications | especificaciones, pliego de condiciones |
| **statement** | Erklärung, Ausführung, Kontoauszug | déclaration, constat, décompte, état | declaración, constancia, extracto de cuenta, estado |
| **storage** | Lagerung | stockage, entreposage | almacenamiento, almacenaje, depósito |
| **storage charges** | Lagerkosten | frais de stockage | gastos de depósito/ almacenaje |
| **store, to** | aufbewahren, lagern | stocker | almacenar, depositar |
| **stow, to** | verstauen | arrimer | arrumar, estibar, almacenar |
| **supplier** | Lieferant, Hersteller | fournisseur | proveedor, abastecedor |
| **surcharge** | Zuschlag, Aufgeld | surtaxe, surcharge | recargo, sobretasa |
| **tariff** | Tarif, Preis | tarif | tarifa, arancel |
| **tariff schedule** | Tariftabelle | barème des tarifes, liste tarifaire | indice de tarifa, arancel |
| **tax** | Steuer, Abgabe | impôt, taxe | impuesto |
| **tax, value added (VAT)** | Mehrwertsteuer | taxe à valeur ajoutée (TVA) | impuesto sobre el valor añadido (IVA) |
| **telephone** | Telefon | téléphone | teléfono |
| **terms and conditions** | Bedingungen | conditions | condiciones |
| **terms of a contract** | Vertragsbedingungen | clauses d'un contrat | cláusulas de un contrato |
| **terms of payment** | Zahlungsbedingungen | conditions de paiement | condiciones de pago |
| **thank you** | Danke | merci | gracias |
| **third-party** | Dritter | tiers | terceros |
| **today** | heute | aujourd'hui | hoy |
| **tomorrow** | morgen | demain | mañana |
| **total cost** | Gesamtkosten | coût total | gasto/coste total |
| **trade barrier** | Handelshemmnis | barrière douanière | arancel aduanero |
| **trailer** | Anhänger | remorque | (carro de) remolque, trailer |
| **transaction** | Transaktion, Geschäft | opération, transaction | transacción, operación, negocio |
| **transaction value** | Verkehrswert | valeur de transaction | valor de la transacción |
| **transport** | Transport | transport | transporte |
| **transport documents** | Beförderungspapiere | documents de transport | documentos de transporte |
| **transport, air** | Lufttransport | transport aérien | transporte aéreo |
| **transport, ocean** | Transport per Schiff | transport maritime | transporte marítimo, transporte transoceánico |
| **transport, rail** | Transport per Bahn | transport ferroviaire | transporte ferroviario |

**K
E
Y

W
O
R
D
S**

| **Italian** | **Portuguese (Br)** | **Japanese** | **Chinese** |
|---|---|---|---|
| compagnia di navigazione, linea marittima | linha de transporte marítimo | 船会社 | 航运线 |
| mancante, insufficienza, ammanco | falta, deficiência | 不足 | 不足，缺乏 |
| firma | assinatura | 署名 | 签名 |
| venduto | vendido | 特定関税金利 | 特别税率 |
| specificazioni, capitolato | especificações | 仕様書 | 说明书，规格 |
| dichiarazione, prospetto | declaração, demonstração, demonstrativo | 決算報告 | 陈述，声明 |
| magazzinaggio, stoccaggio | armazenamento | 保管 | 存储 |
| spese di magazzinaggio | custo de armazenamento | 倉敷料 | 存储费用 |
| immagazzinare, stoccare | armazenar | 保管する | 存储 |
| stivare, mettere nella stiva | armazenar | 積み込む | 装载 |
| fornitore | fornecedor | 供給 | 供给眨瞒瞒 |
| sovrimposta, sovrattassa | acréscimo, sobretaxa | 割り増し料金 | 额外费 |
| tariffa | tarifa | 関税 | 关税 |
| tabella della tariffa | pauta aduaneira | 関税表 | 关税时间表 |
| imposta, tassa | taxa, imposto | 税金 | 税收 |
| imposta sul valore aggiunto (IVA) | imposto acrescentado ao valor (IAV) | 付加価値税 | 增值税（VAT） |
| telefono | telefone | 電話 | 电话 |
| termini e condizioni | termos e condições | 諸条件 | 条款与条件 |
| clausole contrattuali | termos de um contrato | 契約条件 | 合同条款 |
| condizioni di pagamento | condições, termos de pagamento | 支払条件 | 付款条款 |
| grazie | obrigado(a) | ありがとうございます | 谢谢你 |
| terzo | terceiro | 第三 | 第三方 |
| oggi | hoje | 今日 | 今天 |
| domani | amanhã | 明日 | 明天 |
| costo totale | custo total | 総原価計算 | 总成本 |
| barriera agli scambi | barreira comercial | 貿易砥 | 贸易壁垒 |
| rimorchio | reboque, trailer | トレーラ | 拖车 |
| transazione, operazione commerciale | transação | 取引 | 交易，处理 |
| valore della transazione | valor da transação | 取引額 | 交易价值 |
| trasporto | transporte | 輸送 | 运输 |
| documenti di trasporto | documentos de transporte | 運送書類 | 运输单据 |
| trasporto aereo | transporte aéreo | 航空輸送 | 航空运输 |
| trasporto oceanico | transporte marítimo | 海上輸送 | 海洋运输 |
| trasporti ferroviari | transporte ferroviário | 鉄道輸送 | 轨道运输 |

**KEYWORDS**

| English | German | French | Spanish |
|---|---|---|---|
| **transport, road** | Transport per LkW | transport routier | transporte por carretera |
| **transportation** | Transport | transport | transporte |
| **under deck** | unter Deck | sous pont | bajo cubierta |
| **unit** | Einheit | unité | unidad |
| **unit cost** | Stückkosten | cout unitaire | coste unitario |
| **unit load** | Ladungseinheit | unité de charge, charge unitaire | unidad de carga, carga unitaria |
| **unit price** | Stückpreis | prix unitaire | precio unitario |
| **valid** | gültig | valable | válido, vigente |
| **valuation** | Bewertung | évaluation | tasación, valoración |
| **value** | Wert, Valuta | valeur | valor |
| **vessel** | Schiff, Dampger | navire, bateau | buque, nave, barco |
| **vessel, container** | Container-Schiff | navire porte- conteneurs | buque transportador de contenedores |
| **vessel, ocean** | Frachtschiff | navire de haute mer | buque de navegación oceánica, buque |
| **visa** | Aufenthaltserlaubnis | visa | visado |
| **visa, consular** | Aufenthaltserlaubnis | consulaire | visado consular |
| **volume** | Volumen | volume | volumen |
| **warehouse** | Lagerhaus | entrepôt, dépôt | almacén, depósito |
| **warehouse charges** | Lagerkosten | frais de magasinage | gastos de depósito |
| **warehouse, bonded** | Zollager | entrepôt en douane | almacén aduanero, depósito de aduana |
| **warranty** | Garantie, Zusicherung | garantie, autorisation | garantía, autorización |
| **waybill** | Frachtbrief | lettre de voiture, feuille de voiture | carta de porte, guia de carga |
| **weight, gross** | Bruttogewicht | poids brut | peso bruto |
| **weight, net** | Nettogewicht | poids net | peso neto |
| **with average** | mit Havarie | avec avaries | con avería |
| **with particular average (WPA)** | mit besonderer Havarie | avec avarie particulière | con avería particular |
| **yes** | ja | oui | sí |

**KEYWORDS**

| Italian | Portuguese (Br) | Japanese | Chinese |
|---|---|---|---|
| trasporto stradale | transporte rodoviário | 道路輸送 | 道路运输 |
| trasporto | transporte | 輸送 | 运输 |
| sotto ponte | sob o deque | 甲板下 | 在甲板下 |
| unità | unidade | 一団 | 单元 |
| costo unitario | custo unitário | 単位原価 | 单位成本 |
| unità di carico, carico unitario | unidade de carga | 航空貨物コンテナー | 单元装载设备 (ULD) |
| prezzo unitario | preço unitário | 単価 | 单价 |
| valido, valevole | válido, vigente | 有効 | 有效的 |
| valutazione | avaliação | 評価額 | 估价 |
| valore, valuta | valor | 値；価値 | 价值 |
| nave | navio, embarcação | 船舶 | 船舶 |
| nave portacontainer | navio para (transporte de) contêineres | コンテナ船 | 集装箱船 |
| nave di lungo corso, nave di linea transoceanica | navio | 外航船 | 远洋船舶 |
| visto | visto | 査証 / ビザ | 签证 |
| visto consolare | visto consular, do consulado | 領事査証 | 领事签证 |
| volume | volume | 容積 / 体積 | 体积 |
| magazzino, deposito | depósito, armazém | 倉庫 | 仓库 |
| spese di immagazzinaggio | custos de armazenagem | 倉庫料 | 仓库费 |
| deposito/magazzino doganale | armazém alfandegado | 保税倉庫 | 有担保的仓库 |
| garanzia, autorizzazione | garantia | 保証 | 保证，担保，授权 |
| lettera di vettura, bollettino di spedizione | conhecimento de embarque | ウエービル | 运货单 |
| peso lordo | peso bruto | 総重量 | 毛重 |
| peso netto | peso líquido | 瘴吨元 | 净重 |
| avaria inclusa | com avaria(s) | 海損担保 | 平均 |
| avaria particolare inclusa | com avaria(s) particular(es) | 単独海損担保 | 单独海损 |
| sì | sim | はい | 是 |

KEY WORDS

# Quotations

*We rail at trade, but the historian of the world will see that it was the principle of liberty; that it settled America, and destroyed feudalism, and made peace and keeps peace; that it will abolish slavery.*

Ralph Waldo Emerson
American Poet, Essayist (1803-1882)

*Trade is the natural enemy of all violent passions. Trade loves moderation, delights in compromise, and is most careful to avoid anger. It is patient, supple, and insinuating, only resorting to extreme measures in cases of absolute necessity. Trade makes men independent of one another and gives them a high idea of their personal importance: it leads them to want to manage their own affairs and teaches them to succeed therein. Hence it makes them inclined to liberty but disinclined to revolution.*

Alexis de Tocqueville
French Philosopher (1805-1859)

*Free trade consists simply in letting people buy and sell as they want to buy and sell. Protective tariffs are as much applications of force as are blockading squadrons, and their objective is the same to prevent trade. The difference between the two is that blockading squadrons are a means whereby nations seek to prevent their enemies from trading; protective tariffs are a means whereby nations attempt to prevent their own people from trading.*

Henry George
*Protection or Free Trade*, US Social Philosopher, 1886

*Free trade, one of the greatest blessings which a government can confer on a people, is in almost every country unpopular.*

Thomas Babington
Lord Macaulay, British (1800-1859)

*If I had my life to live over again, I would elect to be a trader of goods rather than a student of science. I think barter is a noble thing.*

Albert Einstein
Swiss-German-US physicist (1879-1955)

*[O]ur present civilization rests on the basis of an international exchange of commodities. Every nation of the world has felt the evil effects of recent efforts to erect trade barriers of every known kind. Every individual citizen has suffered from them. It is no accident that the nations which have carried this process farthest are those which proclaim most loudly that they require war as an instrument of their policy. ... It is no accident that, because of these suicidal policies and the suffering attending them, many of their people have come to believe with despair that the price of war seems less than the price of peace.*

President Franklin D. Roosevelt
President (Democrat) USA, 1936

*When goods don't cross borders, armies do.*

Cordell Hull
Secretary of State (Roosevelt Administration) USA

*We merely want to live in peace with all the world, to trade with them, to commune with them, to learn from their culture as they may learn from ours, so that the product of our toil may be used for our schools and our roads and our churches and not for guns and planes and tanks and ships of war.*

Dwight D. Eisenhower
President (Republican) USA

*From the point of view of international law, the World Trade Organization is perhaps the most advanced of our international institutions because it has binding judicial power. The NGOs [non-governmental organizations] that protested in Seattle did have a valid point about the WTO: its rules pay no attention whatsoever to important issues like the protection of the environment or labor standards. But the solution to this problem is not to destroy the WTO but to establish similarly binding rules regarding these issues.*

George Soros
President and Chairman of Soros Fund Management

*People want to raise their children in a world without fear and without war. They want to have some of the good things over and above bare subsistence that make life worth living. They want to work at some craft, trade, or profession that gives them satisfaction and a sense of worth. Their common interests cross all borders.*

*There are no great limits to growth because there are no limits of human intelligence, imagination, and wonder.*

Ronald Reagan
President (Republican) USA, 1984

*The key insight of Adam Smith's Wealth of Nations is misleadingly simple: if an exchange between two parties is voluntary, it will not take place unless both believe they will benefit from it. Most economic fallacies derive from the neglect of this simple insight, from the tendency to assume that there is a fixed pie, that one party can gain only at the expense of another.*

Milton and Rose Friedman
US Economists
*Free to Choose*, 1980

*The evidence is overwhelmingly persuasive that the massive increase in world competition—a consequence of broadening trade flows—has fostered markedly higher standards of living for almost all countries who have participated in cross-border trade. I include most especially the United States.*

Alan Greenspan
Chairman of the U.S. Federal Reserve Board of Governors, 1987-2006. Speech: Boston, Massachusetts, June 2, 1999

*Underlying most arguments against the free market is a lack of belief in freedom itself.*

Milton Friedman
US Economist
1976 Nobel Prize, Economics

*We do not need to be afraid to trade with the rest of the world. ... There will always be new jobs being created and some going away. But [more open trade] will promote peace; it will promote freedom; it will promote stability; it will raise the level of living standards in other parts of the world even as it maintains America as the world's most prosperous nation.*

Bill Clinton
President (Democrat) USA, 1997

*The case for trade is not just monetary, but moral. Economic freedom creates habits of liberty. And habits of liberty create expectations of democracy.*

George W. Bush
President (Republican) USA, 1999

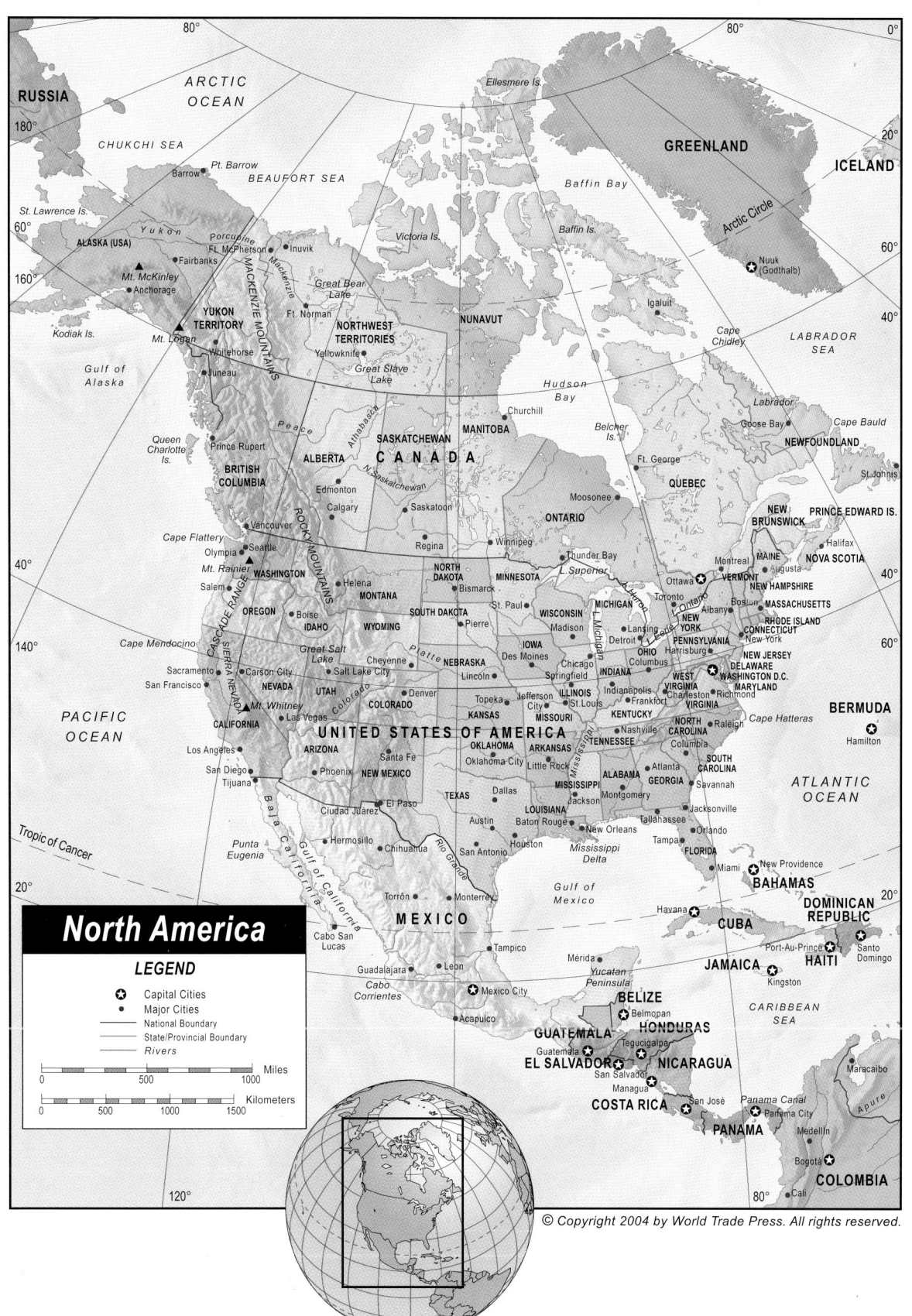

# North America

## LEGEND

⊛ Capital Cities
• Major Cities
── National Boundary
── State/Provincial Boundary
── Rivers

Miles
0    500    1000

Kilometers
0    500    1000    1500

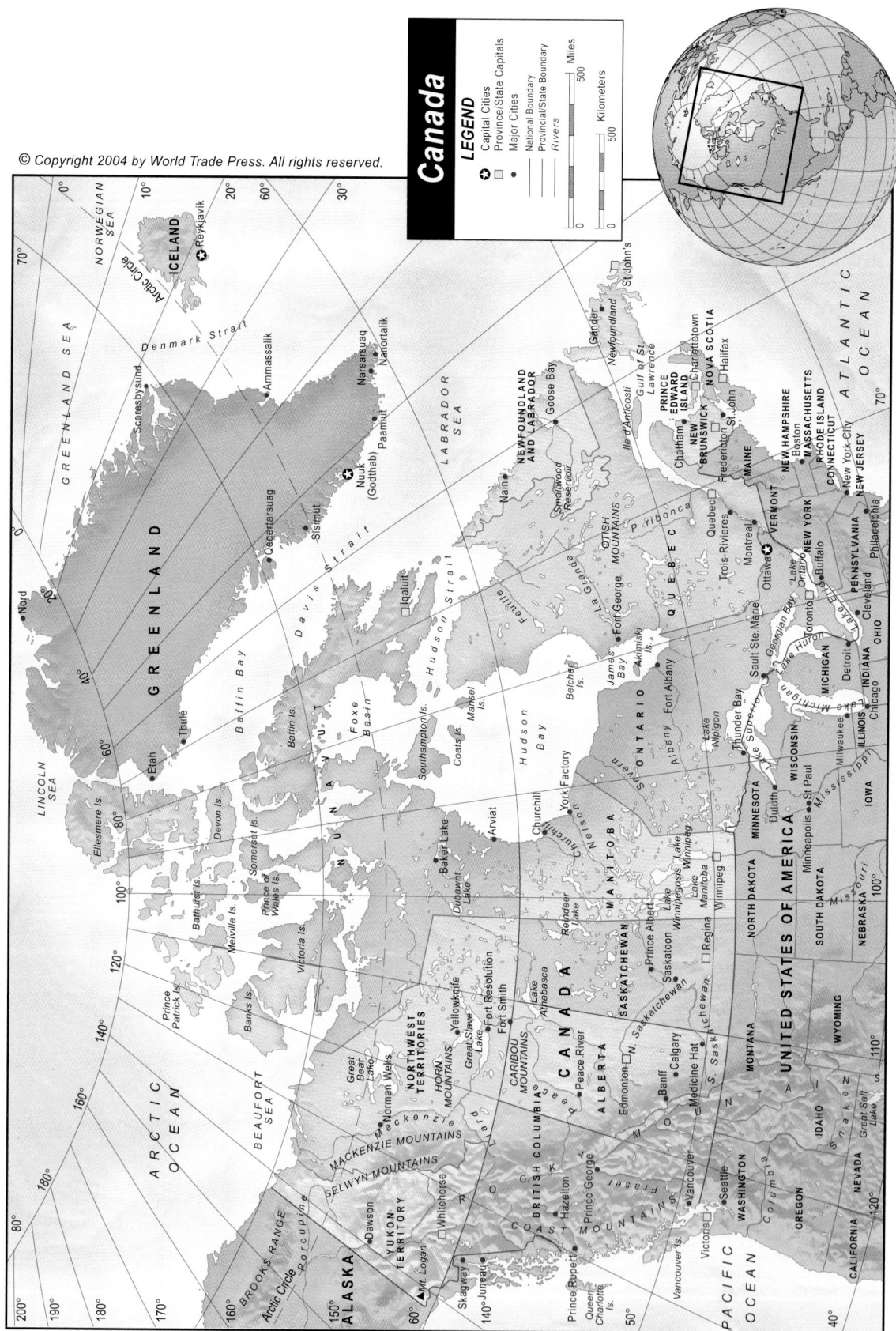

# Canada

**LEGEND**

- ✪ Capital Cities
- ▣ Province/State Capitals
- ▪ Major Cities
- — National Boundary
- — Provincial/State Boundary
- Rivers

Miles
0 — 500

Kilometers
0 — 500

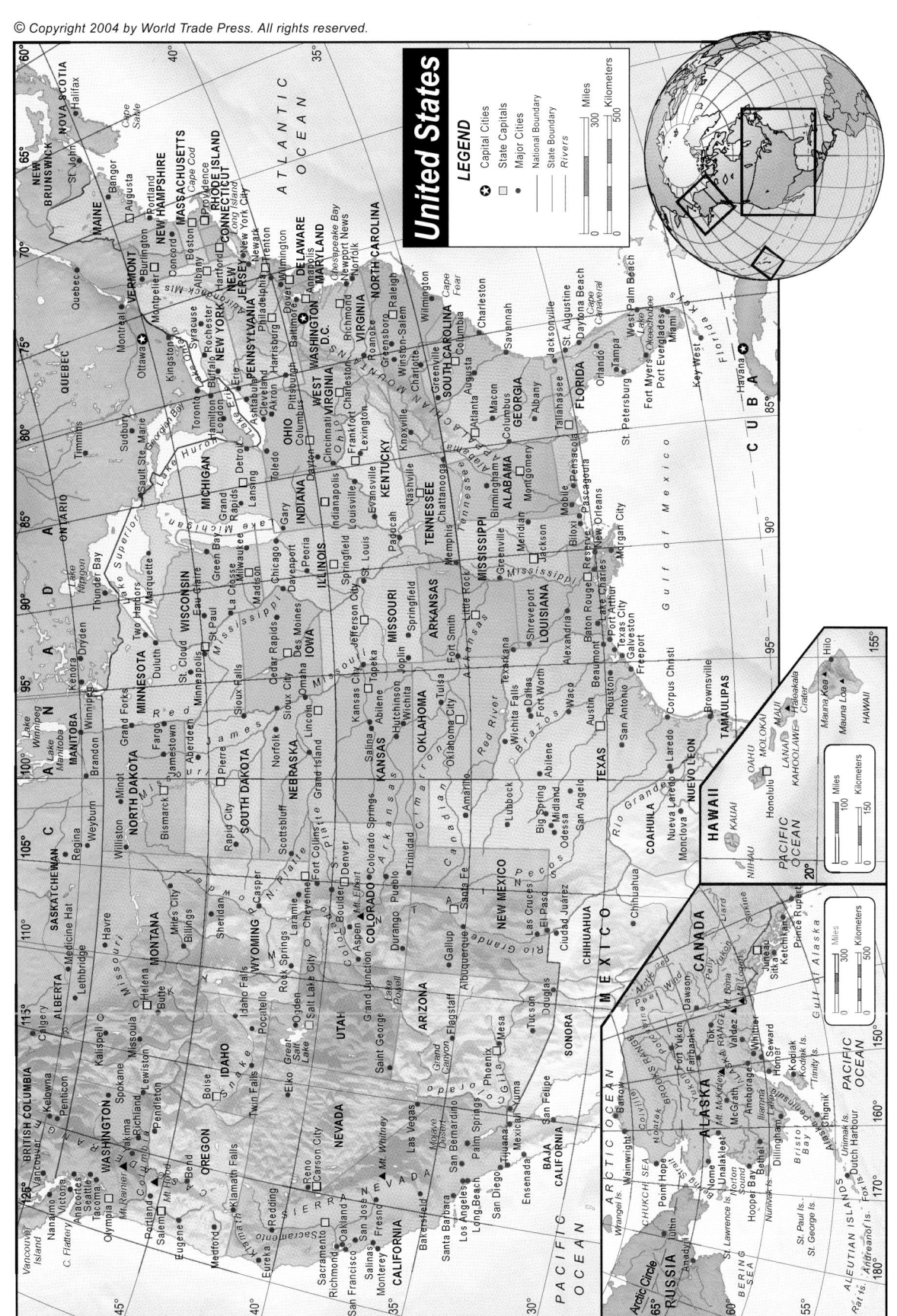

## United States

### LEGEND

| | |
|---|---|
| ⊛ | Capital Cities |
| ▢ | State Capitals |
| • | Major Cities |
| — | National Boundary |
| — | State Boundary |
| — | Rivers |

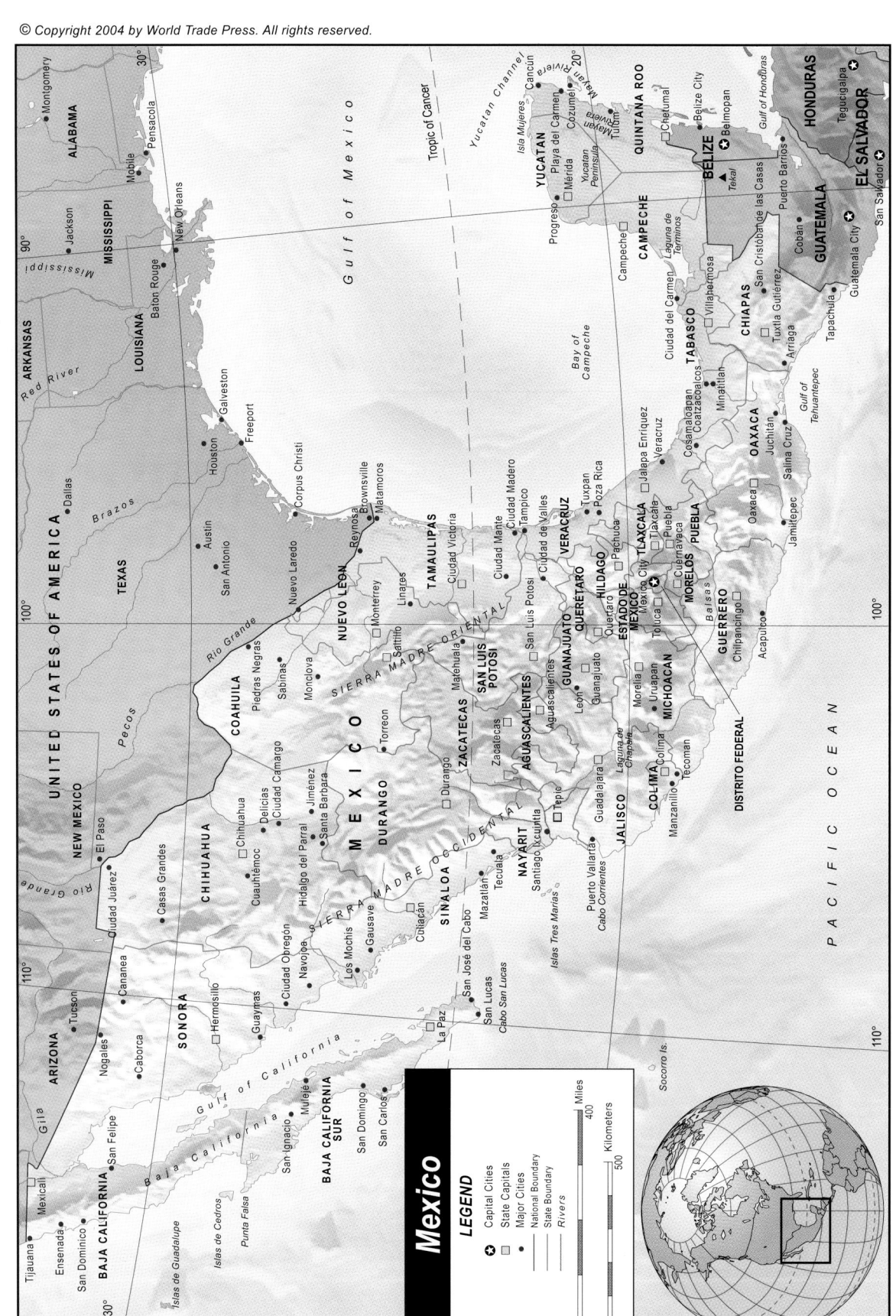

## Mexico

### LEGEND

- ✪ Capital Cities
- ◻ State Capitals
- • Major Cities
- — National Boundary
- — State Boundary
- ～ Rivers

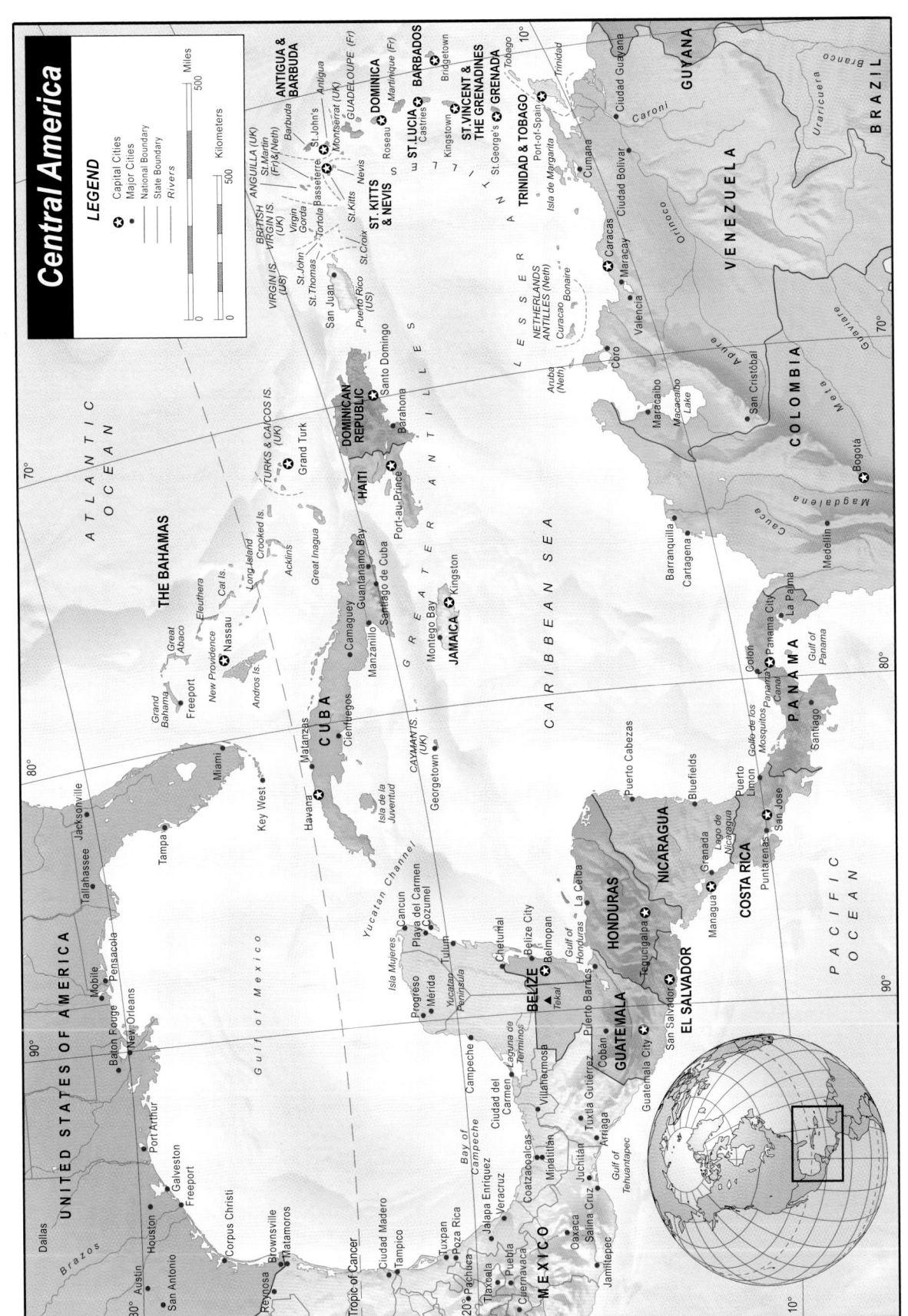

## Central America

### LEGEND

- ⊛ Capital Cities
- • Major Cities
- National Boundary
- State Boundary
- Rivers

Miles
0   500

Kilometers
0   500

South America

LEGEND
✪ Capital Cities
• Major Cities
— National Boundary
— Rivers

Miles
0   500   1000

Kilometers
0   500   1000   1500

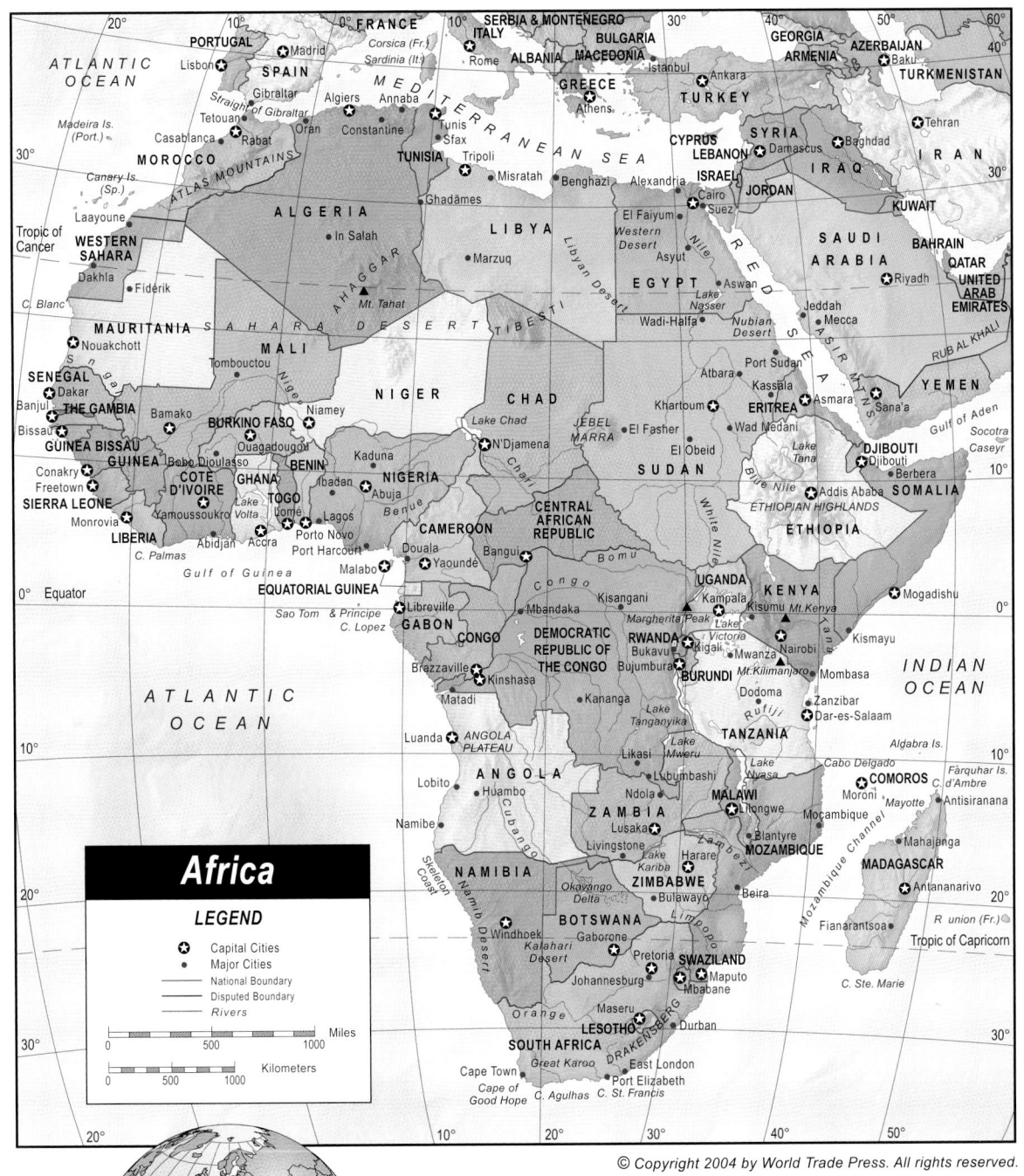

# Africa

## LEGEND

✪ Capital Cities
• Major Cities
— National Boundary
— Disputed Boundary
— Rivers

Miles
0   500   1000

Kilometers
0   500   1000

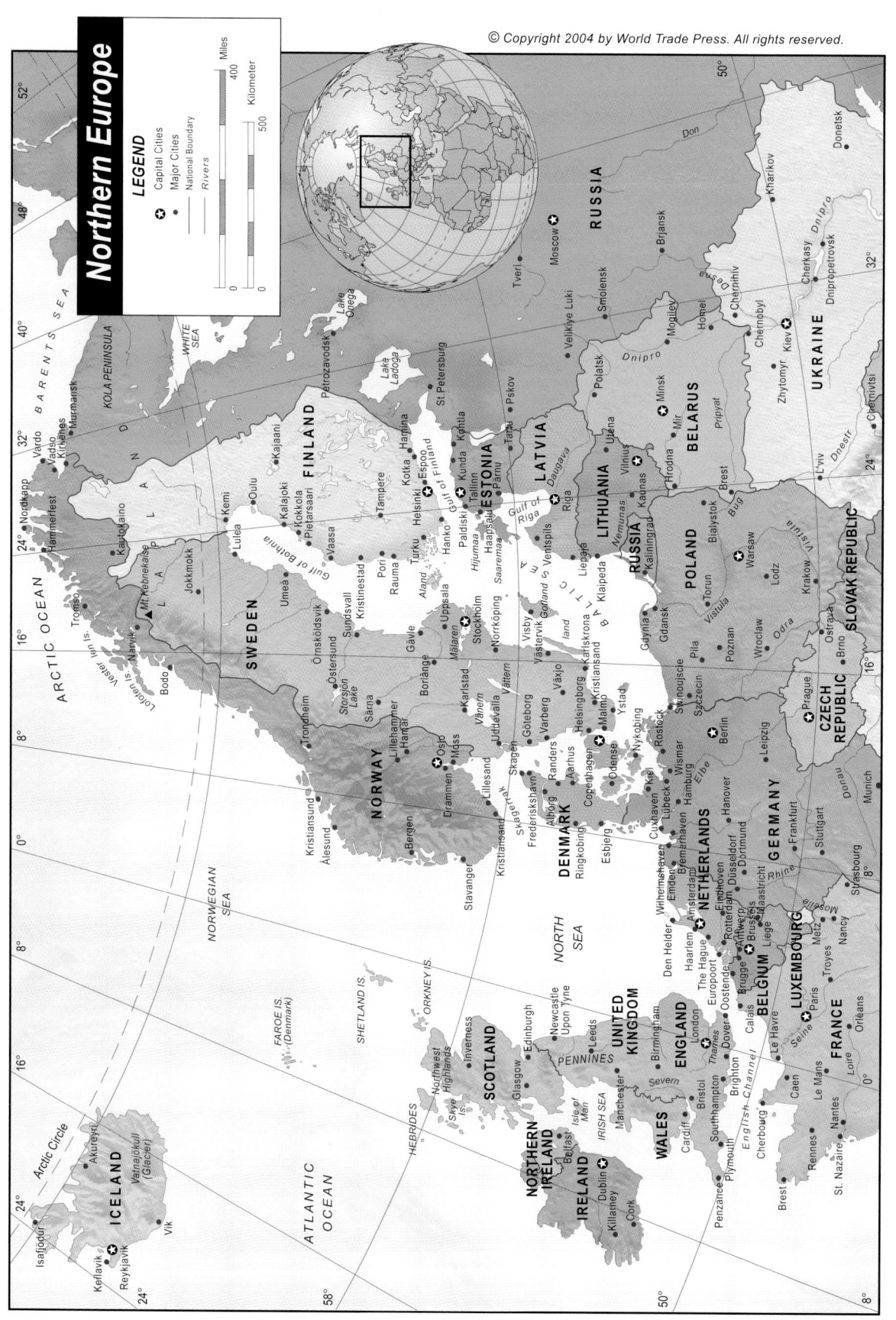

# Northern Europe

**LEGEND**

- ✪ Capital Cities
- • Major Cities
- — National Boundary
- ~ Rivers

Miles
400
Kilometer
500

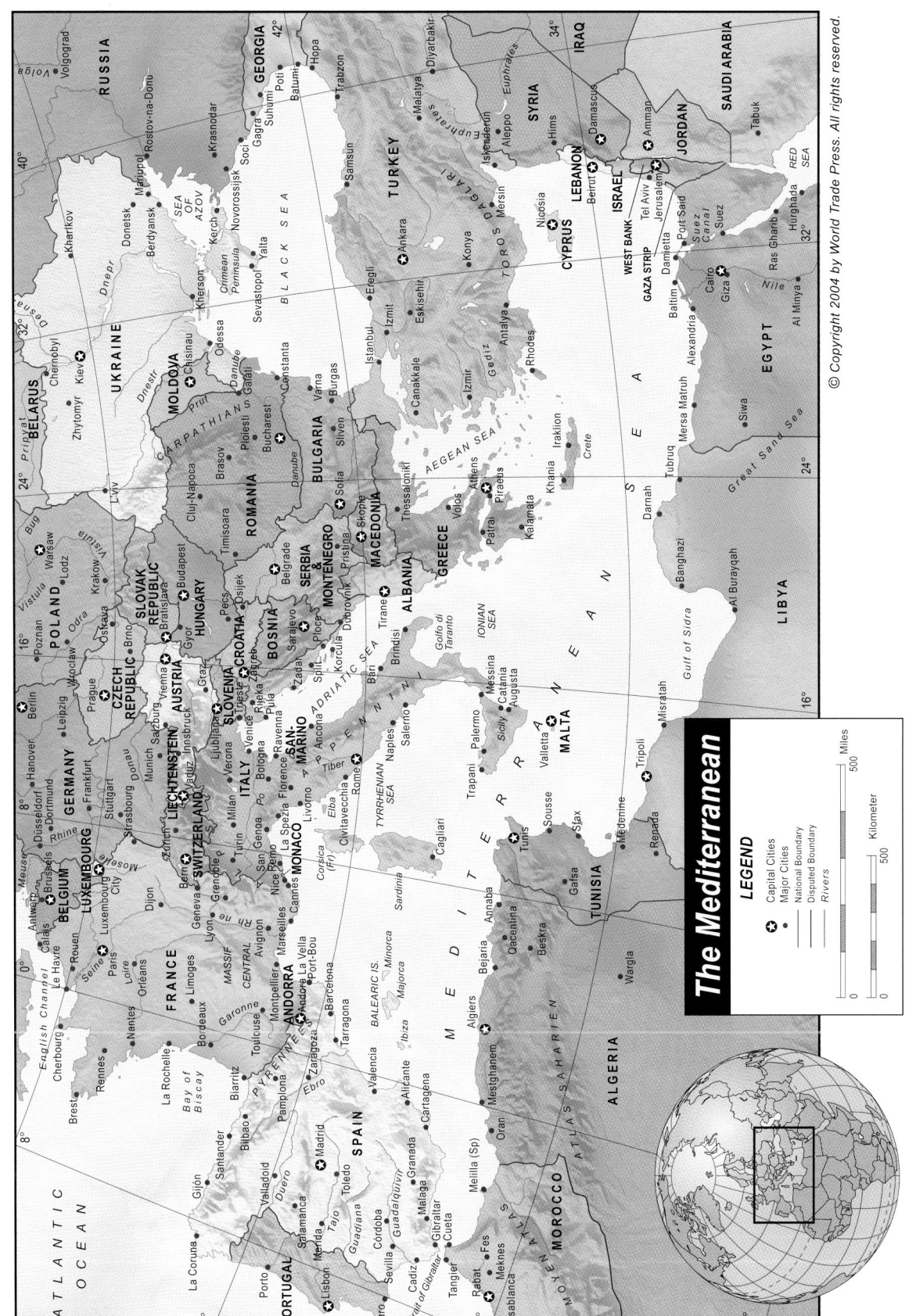

The Mediterranean

LEGEND
- ✪ Capital Cities
- • Major Cities
- National Boundary
- Disputed Boundary
- Rivers

Miles
0    500

Kilometer
0    500

714

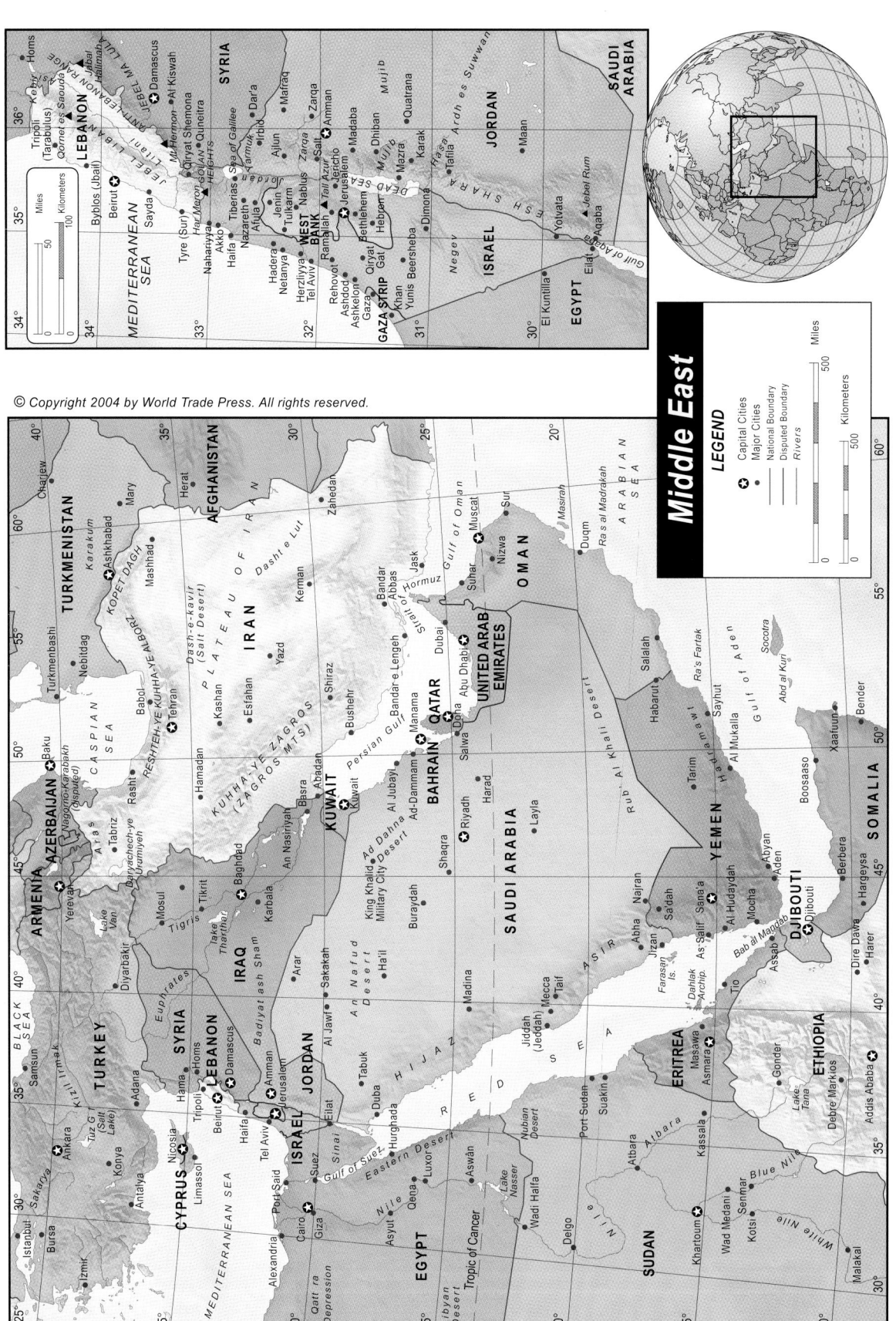

© Copyright 2004 by World Trade Press. All rights reserved.

715

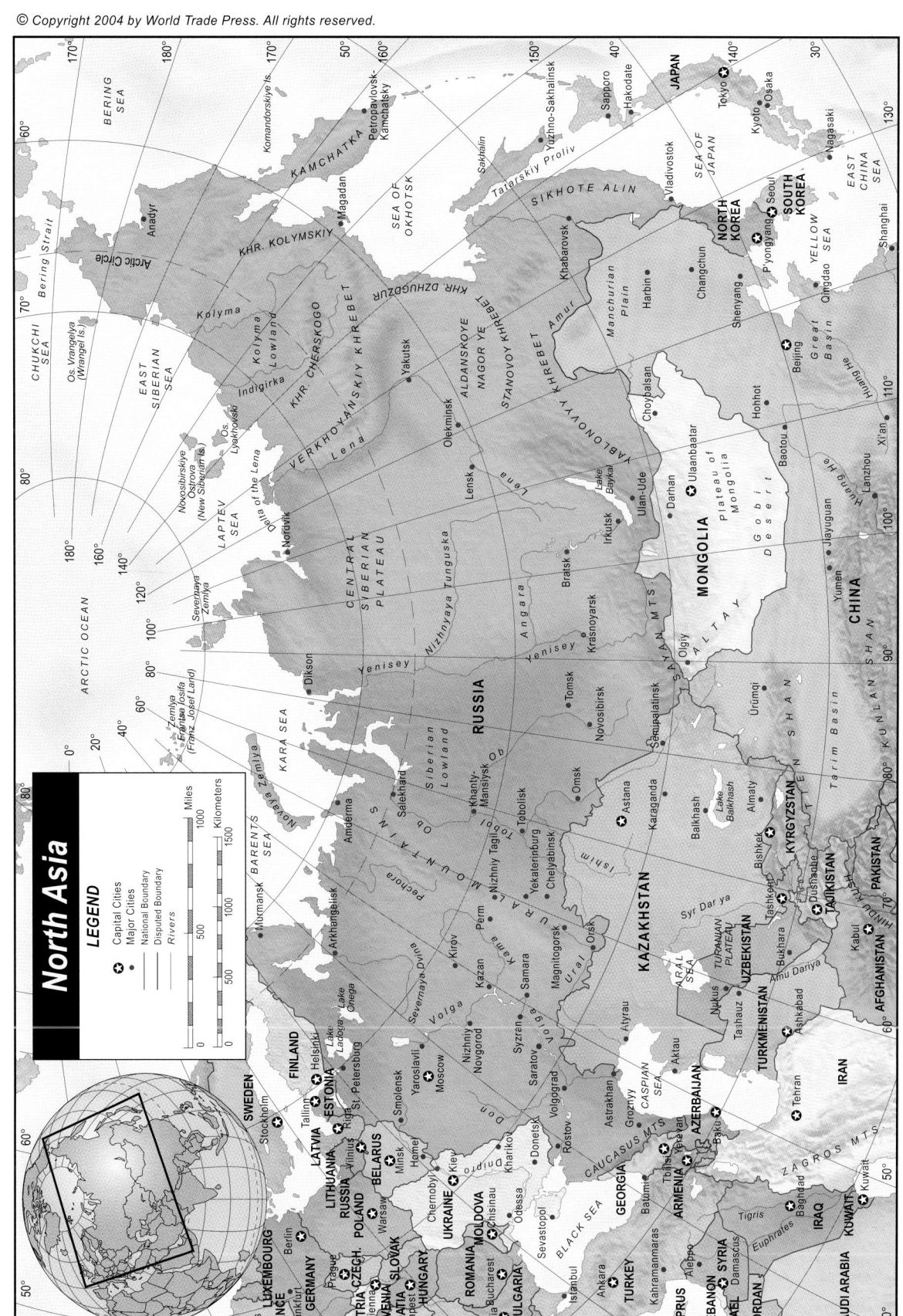

RUSSIA
CHINA
NORTH KOREA
SOUTH KOREA
JAPAN
SEA OF JAPAN
YELLOW SEA
Korea Bay
Cheju haehyop
Korea Strait



China / Korea
LEGEND
Capital Cities
Major Cities
National Boundary
Rivers
Miles
Kilometers
MONGOLIA
C H I N A
NORTH KOREA
SOUTH KOREA
YELLOW SEA
EAST CHINA SEA
SOUTH CHINA SEA
TAIWAN
PHILIPPINES
VIETNAM
LAOS
THAILAND
MYANMAR
INDIA

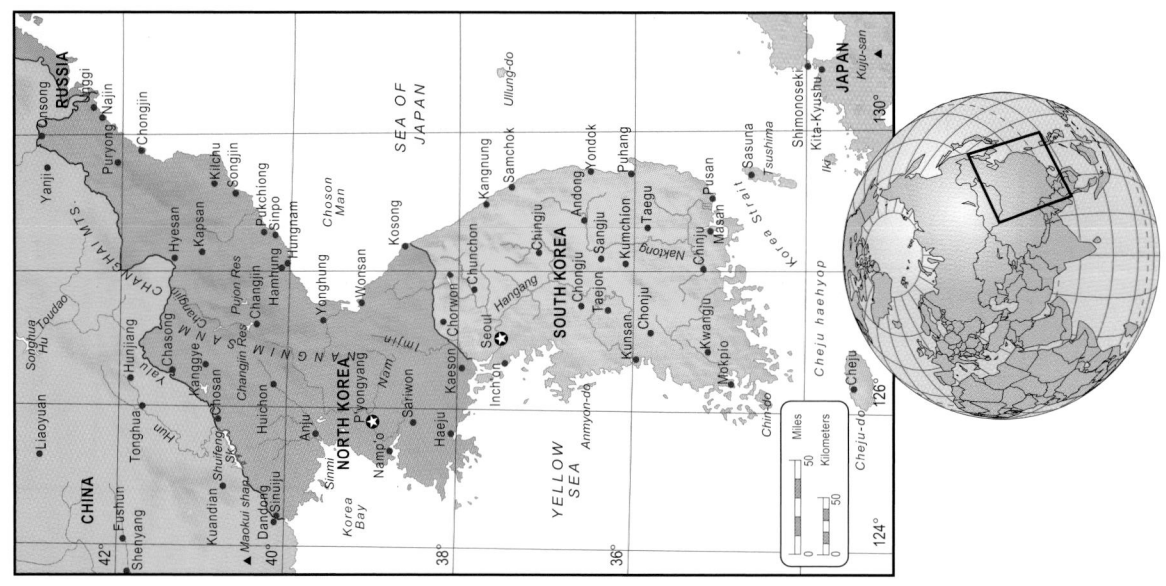

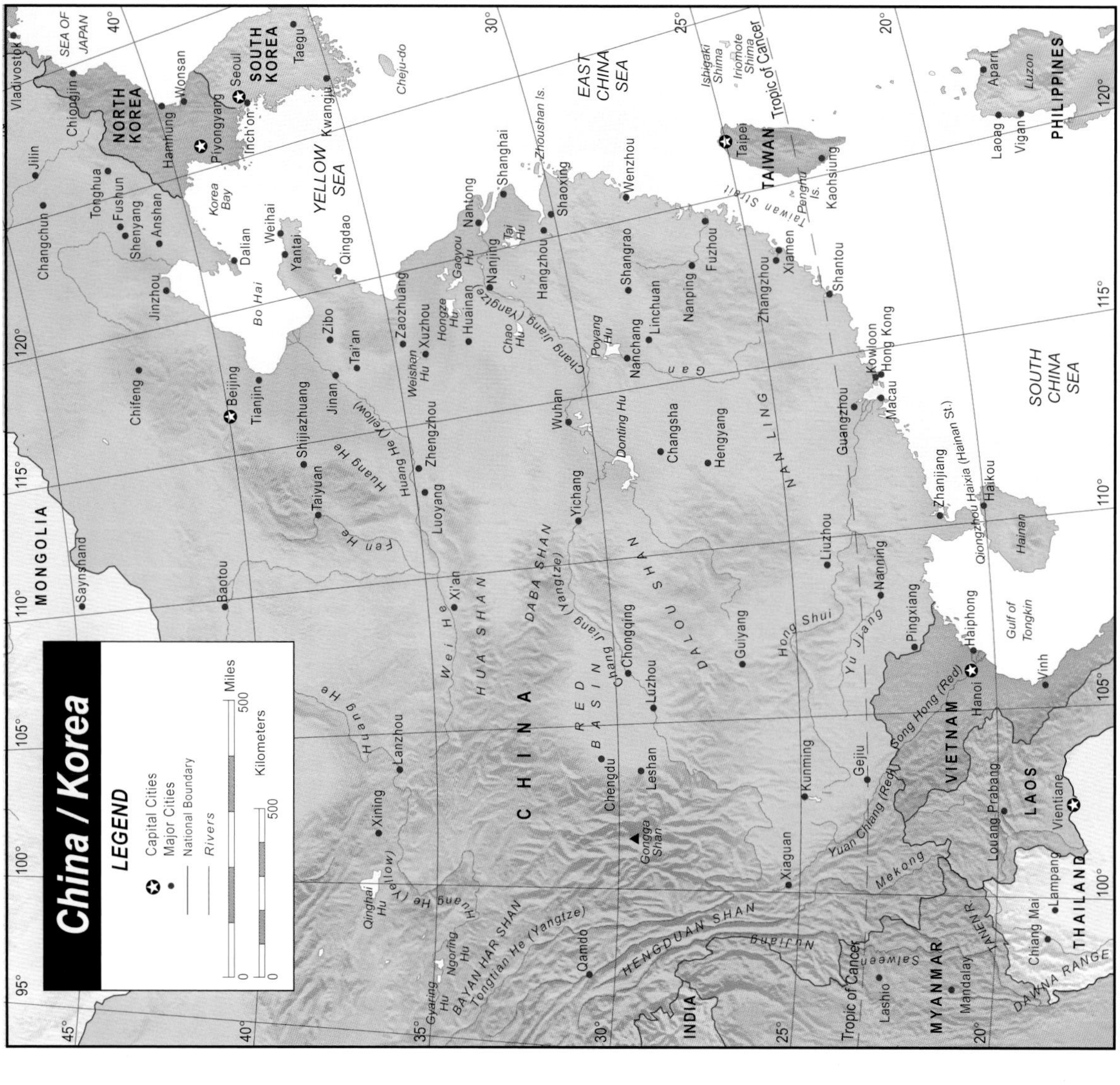

717

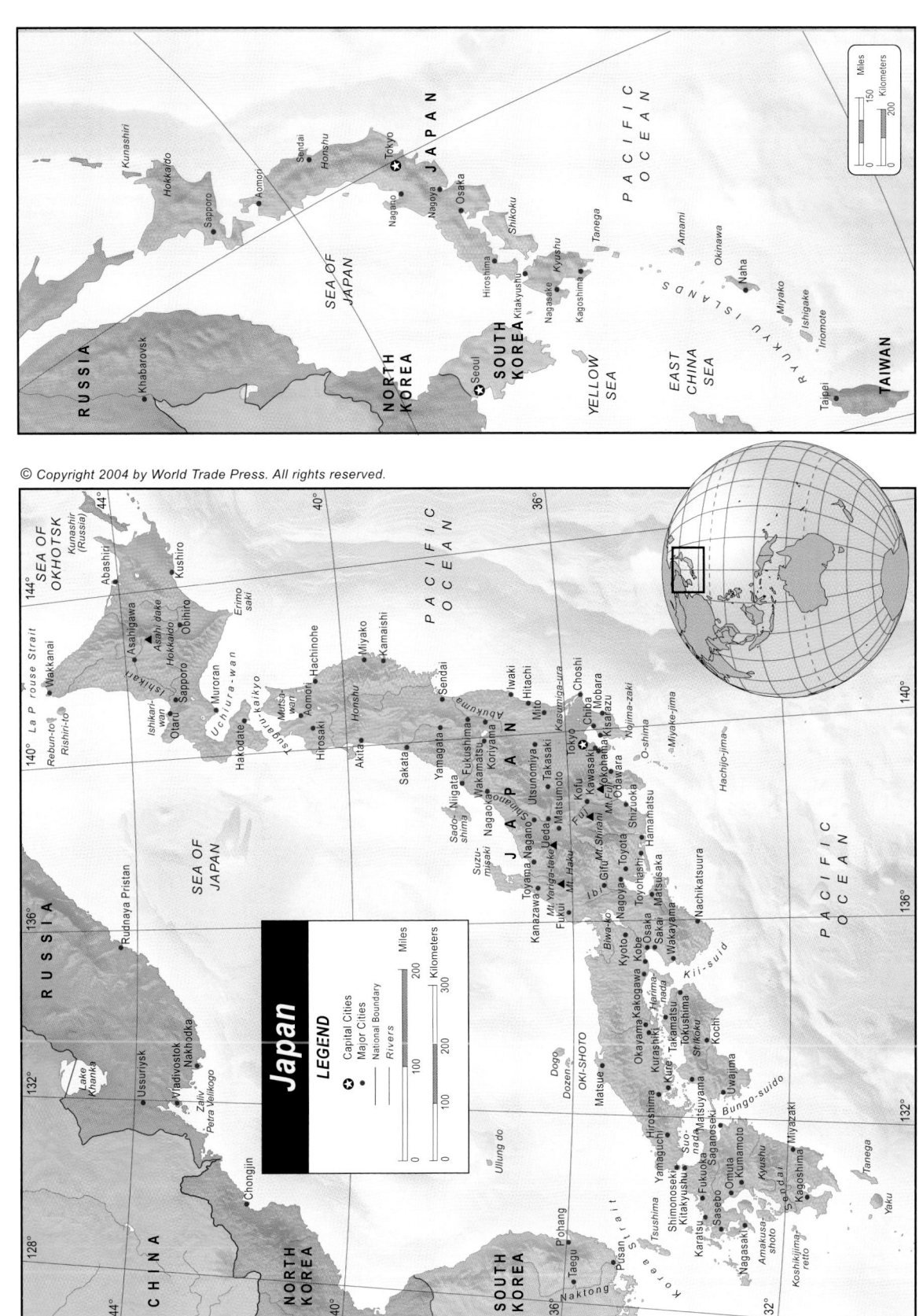

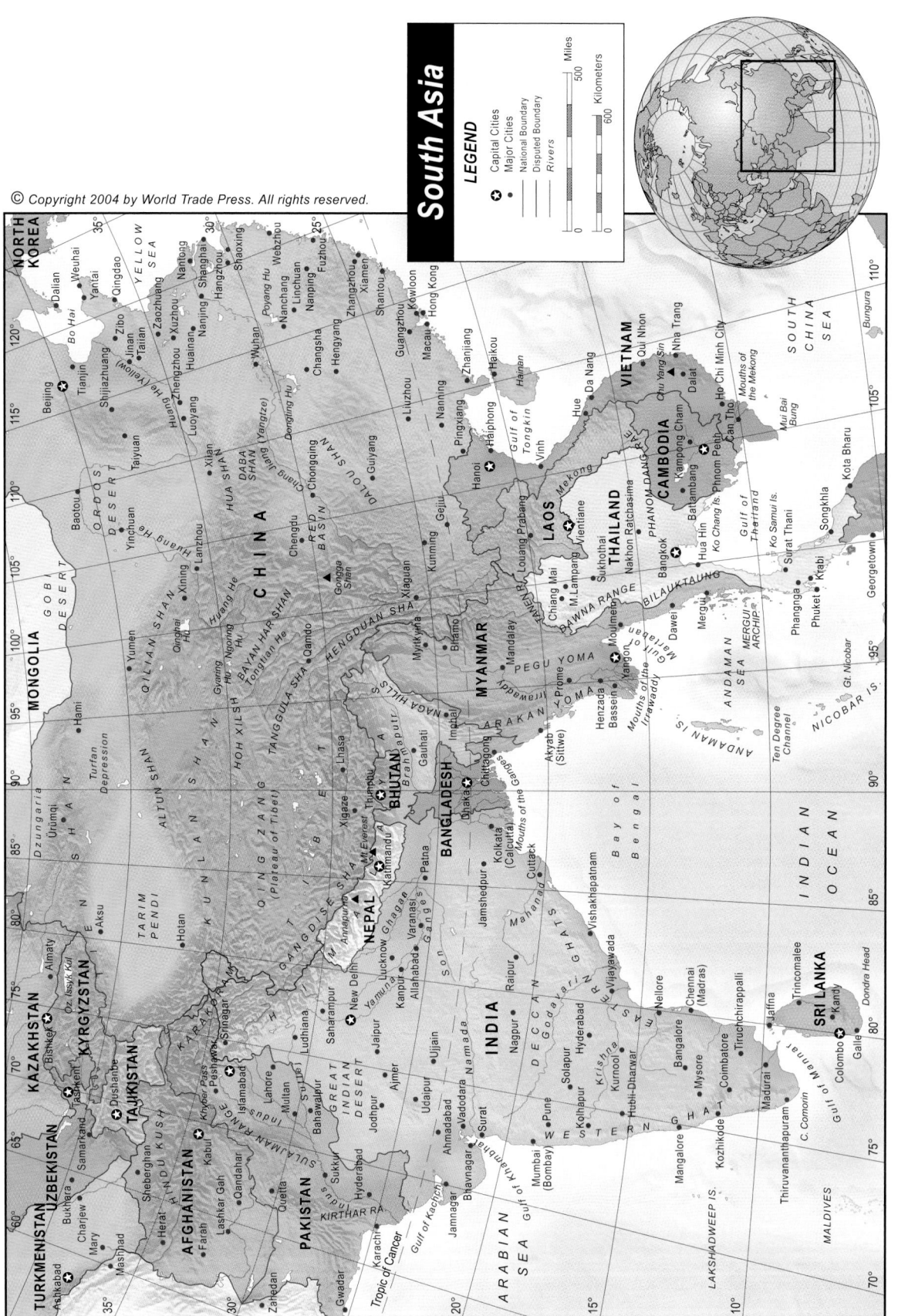

## South Asia

**LEGEND**

- ✪ Capital Cities
- • Major Cities
- National Boundary
- Disputed Boundary
- Rivers

Miles
500
0

Kilometers
600
0

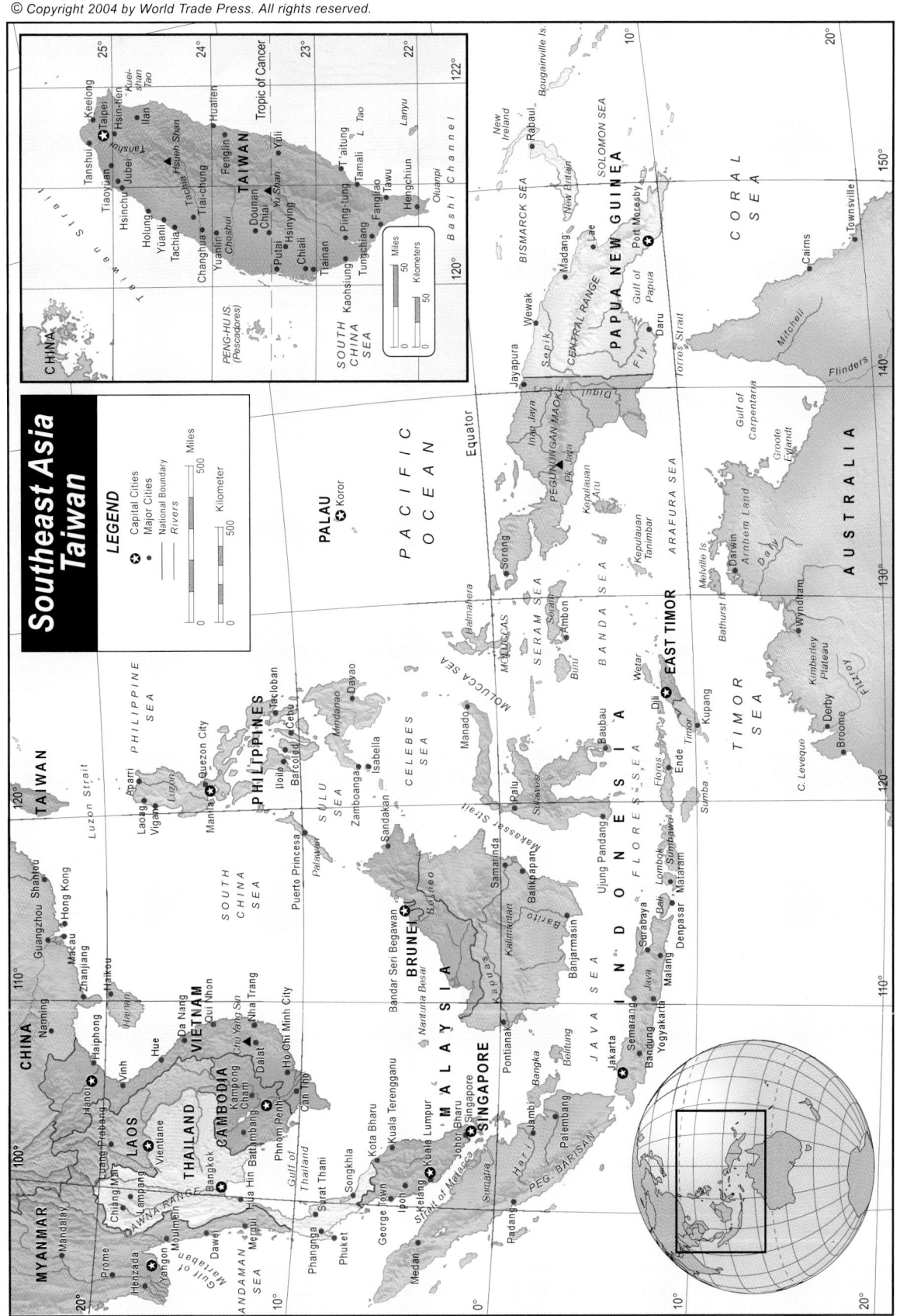

# Southeast Asia
## Taiwan

**LEGEND**

⭐ Capital Cities
● Major Cities
— National Boundary
— Rivers

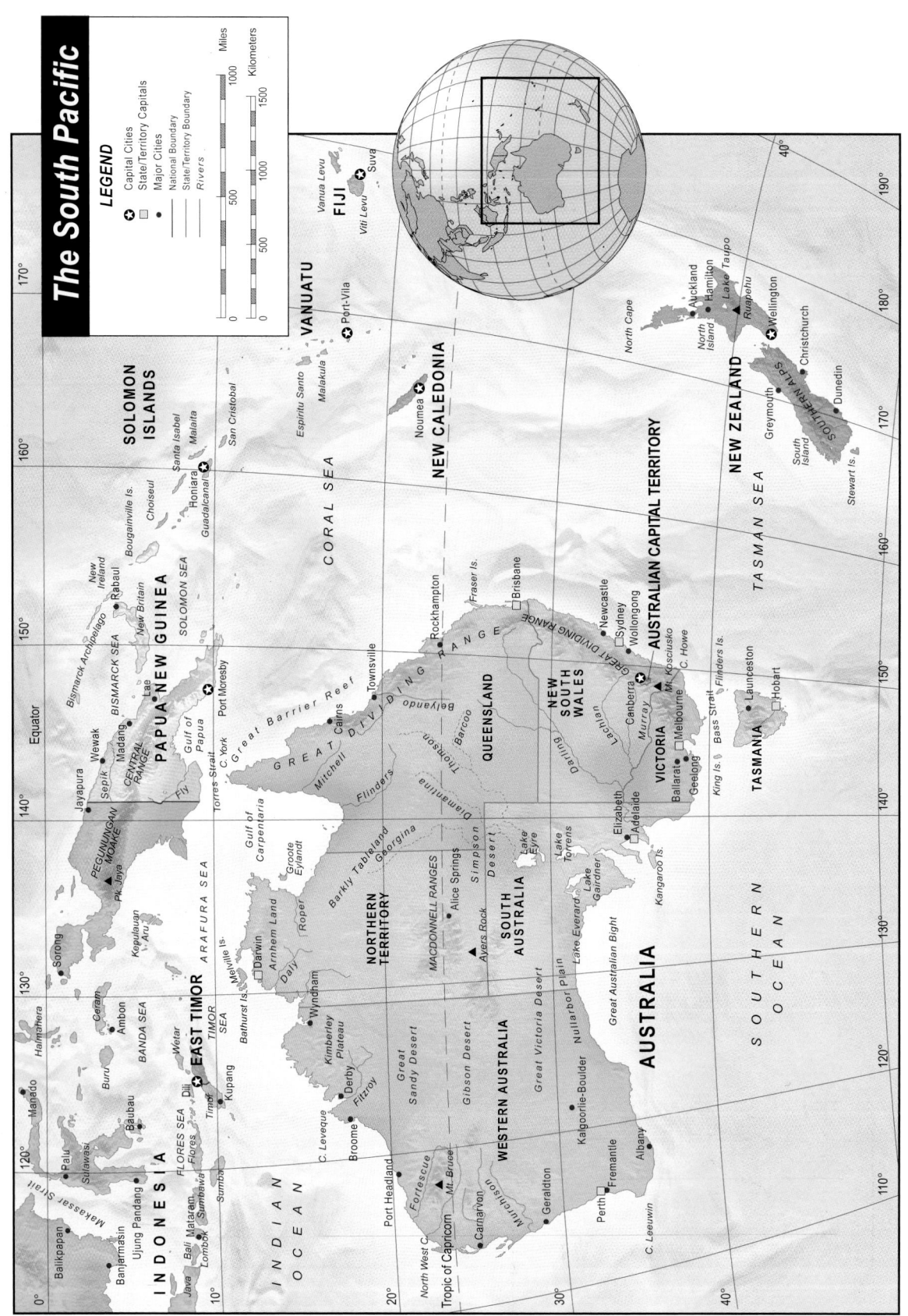

## The South Pacific

LEGEND

⊛ Capital Cities
□ State/Territory Capitals
• Major Cities
—— National Boundary
—— State/Territory Boundary
—— Rivers

Miles
Kilometers

FIJI
Vanua Levu
Viti Levu
Suva

VANUATU
Espiritu Santo
Malakula
Port-Vila

NEW CALEDONIA
Noumea

SOLOMON ISLANDS
Bougainville Is.
Choiseul
Santa Isabel
San Cristobal
Honiara
Guadalcanal
Malaita
SOLOMON SEA

PAPUA NEW GUINEA
New Ireland
New Britain
Rabaul
Bismarck Archipelago
BISMARCK SEA
Madang
Wewak
Sepik
Lae
CENTRAL RANGE
Gulf of Papua
Port Moresby
Fly
PEGUNUNGAN MAOKE
Pk. Jaya
Jayapura
Sorong

NEW ZEALAND
North Cape
North Island
Auckland
Hamilton
Lake Taupo
Ruapehu
Wellington
Greymouth
SOUTHERN ALPS
South Island
Christchurch
Dunedin
Stewart Is.

TASMAN SEA

CORAL SEA

Great Barrier Reef
Fraser Is.
Rockhampton
Brisbane
Townsville
Cairns
C. York
Torres Strait
Gulf of Carpentaria
Groote Eylandt
Arnhem Land

GREAT DIVIDING RANGE
Belyando
Barcoo
Thomson
Mitchell
Flinders
Diamantina
Georgina

QUEENSLAND

NEW SOUTH WALES
Newcastle
Sydney
Wollongong
Canberra
AUSTRALIAN CAPITAL TERRITORY
Darling
Lachlan
Murray
Mt. Kosciusko
C. Howe

VICTORIA
Melbourne
Ballarat
Geelong
Murrumbidgee

Elizabeth
Adelaide
Lake Eyre
Lake Torrens
Lake Gairdner
Lake Everard
Kangaroo Is.
King Is.
Bass Strait
Flinders Is.

TASMANIA
Launceston
Hobart

SOUTH AUSTRALIA
Simpson Desert
Alice Springs
MACDONNELL RANGES
Barkly Tableland
NORTHERN TERRITORY
Daly
Roper
Wyndham
Melville Is.
Bathurst Is.
Darwin
TIMOR SEA

WESTERN AUSTRALIA
Great Sandy Desert
Gibson Desert
Great Victoria Desert
Nullarbor Plain
Great Australian Bight
Kimberley Plateau
Derby
Fitzroy
Broome
C. Leveque
Port Headland
North West C.
Fortescue
Mt. Bruce
Carnarvon
Gascoyne
Murchison
Geraldton
Kalgoorlie-Boulder
Perth
Fremantle
Albany
C. Leeuwin

AUSTRALIA

SOUTHERN OCEAN

INDIAN OCEAN

Tropic of Capricorn

ARAFURA SEA

EAST TIMOR
Dili
Kupang
Timor
Flores
Wetar
Sumba
Sumbawa
Lombok
Bali
Bali Mataram

BANDA SEA
Ceram
Ambon
Buru
Halmahera
Manado
Palu
Sulawesi
Ujung Pandang
Balikpapan
Banjarmasin
Baubau
Java

FLORES SEA

INDONESIA

Makassar Strait

Kepulauan Aru

Equator

© Copyright 2004 by World Trade Press. All rights reserved.